The Vital Records of Hudson New Hampshire

1734–1985

by
Gerald Q. Nash
Sandra J. Martinson
Roland A. Marchand

HERITAGE BOOKS
2009

HERITAGE BOOKS
AN IMPRINT OF HERITAGE BOOKS, INC.

Books, CDs, and more—Worldwide

For our listing of thousands of titles see our website at
www.HeritageBooks.com

Published 2009 by
HERITAGE BOOKS, INC.
Publishing Division
100 Railroad Ave. #104
Westminster, Maryland 21157

Copyright © 1997 Gerald Q. Nash

Other Heritage Books by Gerald Q. Nash,
Sandra J. Martinson, and Roland A. Marchand:

The Vital Birth Records of Nashua, New Hampshire, 1887–1935
The Vital Death Records of Nashua, New Hampshire, 1887–1935
The Vital Records of Hudson, New Hampshire, 1734–1985
CD: *The Vital Marriage Records of Nashua, New Hampshire, 1887–1935*

All rights reserved. No part of this book may be reproduced or transmitted in any form or by any means, electronic or mechanical, including photocopying, recording or by any information storage and retrieval system without written permission from the author, except for the inclusion of brief quotations in a review.

International Standard Book Numbers
Paperbound: 978-0-7884-0799-4
Clothbound: 978-0-7884-8281-6

DEDICATION

This book is dedicated to all Genealogists wherever they may be, and further to The American-Canadian Genealogical Society of 4 Elm Street, Manchester, New Hampshire, which has been designated to receive all royalties from the publication of this book.

                              Gerald Q. Nash
                              Sandra J. Martinson
                              Roland A. Marchand

TABLE OF CONTENTS

Dedication..iii

Introduction...vii

History..ix

Births..1

Marriages...245

Deaths...492

INTRODUCTION

This book contains a transcript of the births, marriages and deaths of Hudson, NH (formerly Nottingham West) for 252 years from 1734 to 1985. The information was taken from three sources as follows:
   (1) 1739 to 1885 came from microfilm of the Annual Ledgers of the Town Clerk, Hudson, NH.
   (2) 1886 to June 30, 1985 came from the published Annual Town Reports of Hudson, NH.
   (3) Kimball Webster's private records which cover 1734 to 1876 were given to the Town of Hudson, NH for the public's use. Kimball Webster was a Civil Engineer who gathered much information on Hudson and genealogy of its residents. A good portion of his material of Birth, Marriage and Death Records cannot be found in any other record. The sources of Kimball Webster's records were taken from old town records (some now lost), individual family records and from old cemetery headstones (some no longer in existence).

The data contained here was transcribed verbatim, except for a few obvious errors which were corrected. The information was sorted and all exact duplications were eliminated. Those duplicates that had some conflicting information were left in, with you as the user to determine which of the information is correct. All the above sources are on microfilm or in yearly town reports in the Town of Hudson Public Library.

HUDSON BIRTH RECORDS

The Birth Records have the child's name listed first, then the child's sex and date of birth, followed by, where known, the child's birth position in family and the parent's name and their place of birth in ( ).

HUDSON MARRIAGE RECORDS

The Marriage Records have both the male, maiden female names listed in one continuous record followed by date and place of marriage. Where known, the parents names and place of birth in ( ) are indented and under the marriage listing. The groom's parents are listed on first indented line and bride's parents are listed on second indented line.

HUDSON DEATH RECORDS

The Death Records list the deceased's name, followed by, where known, the age at death with first number being years, second number being months and third number being days, then the date of death, the place of death and, if known, the parents names and place of birth in ( ).

Hudson History

Before Hudson

The English made the earliest permanent settlement in New England in Plymouth, Mass. in 1620. Later, a few families settled in Gloucester and Salem. Between 1632 and 1645 a number of families made farms near the mouth of the Merrimack River in Newbury and Salisbury. The families of these people moved north along the river to Haverhill. These families were granted, or purchased land in Dunstable. The town of Dunstable, MA was incorporated in 1673. It included the town of Hudson and many other Southern New Hampshire towns. The first settlement in Hudson was around 1672. The first recorded grant of land was made in 1661 to Joseph Hills. Three of his grandchildren were perhaps the first settlers in Hudson. The settlers petitioned to have a separate town due to the hardship of attending worship services in Dunstable, the hardship being that there was no bridge in place to cross the Merrimack River.

Nottingham

The town of Nottingham which included the present town of Hudson as well as parts of Tyngsboro, Pelham, and Litchfield, was incorporated Jan 4th, 1733. The first town meeting was held at the home of Ensign John Snow on May 1, 1733. The first meeting house was built on what is now called Musquash Road in 1734. In 1746 a meeting house was built near what is called Blodgett cemetery at the junction of Pelham Road and Lowell Road.

Nottingham West

Since there was a town called Nottingham in the eastern part of New Hampshire before the town was divided, the general court on July 5th, 1846 chartered the new town of Nottingham West, having the same boundary lines as the present town of Hudson.

A Town Called Hudson

The town was renamed Hudson in 1830. The first school houses were built around 1806. No records were kept until 1847 when 346 pupils attended for a total cost of $433.

Indians were a problem to the early residents. Many residents had fled in fear of the Indians. Hudson's most famous Indian fighter was Zaccheus Lovewell. A house called a garrison was located in each settlement and was built especially strong to withstand attacks.

The first bridge built across the Merrimack was a wooden structure built in 1827. It was also a toll bridge. There were also several ferries. The first post office was established in 1818 at the home of the postmaster, Reuben Greeley.

HUDSON,NH BIRTHS

ABATE,Allison M   Sex:F   18 Feb 1976 Louis G Abate & Linda A Luba
ABBERTON,Michael K   Sex:M   17 Mar 1969 David L Abberton & Cecile M LaPierre
ABBOT,Samuel S   Sex:M   23 May 1788 Hudson, NH Benjamin Abbot & Anne
ABBOT,Sarah   Sex:F   27 Jul 1786 Hudson, NH Benjamin Abbot & Anne
ABBOTT,Aaron G   Sex:M   19 Apr 1968 George H Abbott & Barbara M Tomashefsk
ABBOTT,Alan M   Sex:M   28 Jun 1978 Gerald R Abbott & Dolores Avila
ABBOTT,Ann L   Sex:F   26 Aug 1958 William E Abbott & Jean C Switser
ABBOTT,Betty J   Sex:F   (Child #5) 16 Oct 1945 Kenneth T Abbott (Hudson, NH)
   & Hilda M English (Barring, ME)
ABBOTT,Clayton   Sex:M   (Child #4) 15 Jul 1906 George H Abbott(Litchfield,NH)
   & Mary N Webster (Hudson, NH)
ABBOTT,David G   Sex:M   24 Aug 1971 George H Abbott & Barbara M Tomashefsk
ABBOTT,Delia Maria   Sex:F   04 Aug 1862 Hudson, NH Herman Abbott & Elvira
ABBOTT,Donna M   Sex:F   22 May 1957 William H Abbott, Jr & Pauline R Pelkey
ABBOTT,Gail W   Sex:F   18 Aug 1952 William H Abbott & Pauline R Pelkey
ABBOTT,George Herman   Sex:M   (Child #1) 14 Nov 1933 Roland W Abbott (Hudson,
   NH) & Hazel A Packard (Wakefield, MA)
ABBOTT,Gerald R   Sex:M   16 Jul 1953 William H Abbott & Pauline R Pelkey
ABBOTT,James H   Sex:M   04 Nov 1951 William H Abbott & Pauline R Pelkey
ABBOTT,John Kenneth   Sex:M   (Child #3) 11 Jun 1938 Kenneth T Abbott (Hudson,
   NH) & Hilda M English (Baring, ME)
ABBOTT,Jonathan C   Sex:M   18 Oct 1966 James C Abbott & Linda L Morrill
ABBOTT,Keith A   Sex:M   28 Jul 1967 John K Abbott & Priscilla J Quigley
ABBOTT,Kenneth Sex:M (Child #3) 26 May 1904 George H Abbott (Litchfield, NH)
   & Mary N Webster (Hudson, NH)
ABBOTT,Kenneth J   Sex:M   13 May 1966 John K Abbott & Priscilla J Quigley
ABBOTT,Kimball W   Sex:M   23 Feb 1970 John K Abbott & Priscilla J Quigley
ABBOTT,Marjorie   Sex:F   (Child #2) 18 Jan 1900 Geo H Abbott (Litchfield, NH)
   & Mary Webster (Hudson, NH)
ABBOTT,Marjorie   Sex:F   (Child #2) 17 Aug 1936 Kenneth Abbott (Hudson, NH)
   & Hilda M English (Baring, ME)
ABBOTT,Mary Frances   Sex:F   12 Jun 1974 John K Abbott & Priscilla Quigley
ABBOTT,Mary Jane   Sex:F   (Child #1) 23 Aug 1935 Clayton B Abbott (Hudson, NH)
   & Helen M Tandy (Melrose, MA)
ABBOTT,Michael A   Sex:M   13 Jul 1958 William H Abbott, Jr & Pauline R Pelkey
ABBOTT,Nancy Jean   Sex:F   (Child #1) 04 Jan 1935 Kenneth T Abbott (Hudson,
   NH) & Hilda English (Baring, ME)
ABBOTT,Nathan J   Sex:M   10 Oct 1963 James C Abbott & Linda L Morrill
ABBOTT,Paula M   Sex:F   27 Jun 1955 William H Abbott & Pauline R Pelkey
ABBOTT,Richard W   Sex:M   04 Jul 1964 William E Abbott & Jean C Switser
ABBOTT,Robert W   Sex:M   (Child #6) 16 Oct 1945 Kenneth T Abbott (Hudson, NH)
   & Hilda M English (Barring, ME)
ABBOTT,Roland C   Sex:M   12 Feb 1962 William E Abbott & Jean C Switser
ABBOTT,Roland Webster   Sex:M   (Child #1) 13 Sep 1897 George H Abbott
   (Litchfield, NH) & Mary N Webster (Hudson, NH)
ABBOTT,Samuel Smith   Sex:M   23 May 1788 Hudson, NH Benjamin Abbott & Anna
ABBOTT,Sarah   Sex:F   27 Jul 1786 Hudson, NH Benjamin Abbott & Anna
ABBOTT,Shannon Christi Sex:F 10 Apr 1981 Michael A Abbott & Laura L Guerrette
ABBOTT,Timothy F   Sex:M   17 Apr 1965 Thomas W Abbott & Barbara A Donahue
ABBOTT,William C   Sex:M   24 Nov 1950 William H Abbott & Pauline R Pelkey
ABBOTT,William Everett   Sex:M   (Child #2) 29 Dec 1934 Roland W Abbott
   (Hudson, NH) & Hazel A Packard (Wakefield, MA)
ABBOTT,[Unknown]   Sex:M   (Child #2) 15 Mar 1941 Roland W Abbott (Hudson, NH)
   & Hazel A Packard (Wakefield, MA)
ABODEELY,Eric Michael   Sex:M   05 Nov 1982 Ned M Abodeely & Marian L Laliberte
ABREU,Sabrina Ann   Sex:F   05 Jul 1978 Dennis P Abreu & Melinda J Marques
ABUCEWICZ,Walter S   Sex:M   06 Jun 1965 Stanley W Abucewicz & Theresa St Jean
ACKERMAN,Edna Blanche   Sex:F   (Child #2) 17 Jan 1902 Wm G Ackerman (Hill, NH)
   & Mary E Hamlett (Hudson, NH)
ACKERMAN,Maurice W   Sex:M   (Child #2) 01 Jul 1905 Wm G Ackerman (Hill, NH)

HUDSON,NH BIRTHS

  & Mary E Hamlett (Hudson, NH)
ACKERMAN,Pamela L   Sex:F   29 Apr 1949 Thomas R Ackerman & Drinette A Dionne
ACKERMAN,[Unknown]   Sex:M (Child #1) 20 Aug 1892 W D Ackerman (Alexandria, NH) & Mary P Osgood (Boston, MA)
ACKERMAN,[Unknown]   Sex:F (Child #1) 04 Nov 1900 Wm G Ackerman (Hill, NH)
  & Mary E Hamlet (Hudson, NH)
ACKLEY,Stephen F   Sex:M   (Child #2) 22 Jan 1944 Harry F Ackley (Nashua, NH)
  & Dorothy P Hujsak (Merrimack, NH)
ADAMS,Benjamin S   Sex:M   (Child #4) 24 Apr 1944 Arthur W Adams (Wilton, ME)
  & Thelma A Hiscock (Dixfield, ME)
ADAMS,Demetra A   Sex:F 01 Jun 1967 Nicholas Adams & Georgianna E Manos
ADAMS,Dennis G   Sex:M   (Child #1) 17 Nov 1940 George L Adams (Dixfield, ME)
  & Sophie M Jerry (Northfield, VT)
ADAMS,Ernest D   Sex:M   17 Jun 1947 Arthur L Adams (Wilton, ME)
  & Thelma A Hiscock (Dixfield, ME)
ADAMS,Jessica Lynne Sex:F 02 Aug 1984 Carleton H Adams Jr & Dawna A Faulkner
ADAMS,Linda M   Sex:F   (Child #4) 16 May 1944 George L Adams (E Dixfield, ME)
  & Sophia M Jerry (E Roxbury, VT)
ADAMS,Spencer Gerald Sex:M 06 Aug 1982 Kenneth G Adams & Cynthia L Farrington
ADAMS,Steven P   Sex:M   15 Mar 1954 Paul Adams & Mildred E Farrington
ADAMS,Timothy G   Sex:M   01 Feb 1977 Kenneth G Adams & Catherine Ann Shanah
ADAMS,Veronica A   Sex:F   25 Jun 1964 Carl H Adams & Rita A Cook
ADAMS,Warren W   Sex:M   (Child #2) 20 Jan 1942 George L Adams (Wilton, ME)
  & Sophia M Jerry (E Roxbury, VT)
ADAMS,[Unknown]   Sex:M   (Child #1) 23 Jul 1937 George L Adams (Wilton, ME)
  & Sophia Jerry (E Roxbury, VT)
ADAMYK,Keith J   Sex:M   12 Jan 1962 Alec E Adamyk & Dorothy F Marcotte
ADKINS,John Jay II   Sex:M   20 Apr 1959 Bernis Adkins & Ruth Mellen
ADKINS,Nancy B   Sex:F   12 Dec 1961 Bernis Adkins & Ruth J Mellen
ADRENDT,Richard W   Sex:M   (Child #1) 12 Feb 1941 Wallace C Adrendt (Iowa)
  & Madeline M Gallant (Lincoln, NH)
AFONSO,David Pires Sex:M 21 Apr 1984 Manuel A Afonso & Maria Pires-Dafonte
AGATI,Andrew James   Sex:M   29 Mar 1985 Salvatore P Agati & Wendy Joy Emanuel
AHEARN,Brian Lake Sex:M 18 Jan 1983 Brian Edward Ahearn & Michelle G Munday
AHEARN,Danielle Kelly Sex:F 25 Nov 1979 George S Ahearn & Helen Louise Barton
AHEARN,Meridith M   Sex:F   01 Jan 1979 Brian E Ahearn & Michelle G Munday
AHEARN,Scott George   Sex:M   05 Jun 1982 George S Ahearn & Helen Louise Barton
AHERN,Douglas C   Sex:M   07 May 1971 Richard C Ahern & Cheryl C Healy
AHERN,Kenneth R   Sex:M   20 Feb 1974 Richard C Ahern & Cheryl C Healy
AHRENDT,Jane C   Sex:F   (Child #2) 24 Feb 1945 Wallace C Ahrendt (Dubuque, IA)
  & Madeline M Gallant (Lincoln, NH)
AHRENS,Tracie A   Sex:F   18 Aug 1966 Thomas C Ahrens, Jr & Catherine E Ensor
AKEY,Kenneth E Jr   Sex:M   09 Feb 1961 Kenneth E Akey & Joanne A Cegelis
ALBEE,Brenda J   Sex:F   12 Sep 1957 Royce K Albee & Priscilla Plasse
ALBEE,Craig S   Sex:M   (Child #2) 23 Jun 1946 George W Albee (Lewiston, ME)
  & Elizabeth E Smith (Hudson, NH)
ALBEE,David S   Sex:M   25 Sep 1958 Royce K Albee & Priscilla Plasse
ALBEE,Richard J   Sex:M   31 May 1961 Royce K Albee & Priscilla Plasse
ALBERT,Courtney Ann   Sex:F   01 Sep 1981 Harold Alvin Albert & Ann Marie Morse
ALBERT,Davey   Sex:M   02 Nov 1955 Richard G Albert & Mildred M Trail
ALBERT,George R Jr   Sex:M   18 Apr 1953 Richard G Albert & Mildred M Trail
ALBERT,Jennifer H   Sex:F   06 Jul 1968 James D Albert & Ann M Stevens
ALBERT,Mary A   Sex:F   25 Mar 1951 Richard G Albert & Mildred M Troil
ALBERT,Nancy K   Sex:F   04 May 1958 Richard G Albert & Mildred M Trail
ALDRICH,Janet L   Sex:F   19 May 1962 Donald E Aldrich & Mildred H Rice
ALDRICH,Maxann   Sex:F   24 Oct 1984 Glenn E Aldrich & Sheri Gayle Kurman
ALEXA,Bradley Edward Sex:M 10 May 1985 Bruce E Alexa & Barbara Jean Boulard
ALEXANDER,Dwight Calvin   Sex:M   (Child #3) 25 Jul 1924 Earl J Alexander
  (Greenfield, NH) & Lena H Hill (Nashua, NH)
ALEXANDER,Joy Lynn   Sex:F   15 Jul 1977 Joe H Alexander & Judith D Viselman

HUDSON,NH BIRTHS

ALEXANDER,Leonard Earle   Sex:M   (Child #6) 06 Jun 1934 Earl J Alexander (Greenfield, NH) & Lena Hill (Nashua, NH)
ALFONSIN,Stephanie J   Sex:F   01 May 1972 William C Alfonsin & Susan A Fialka
ALFSEN,Elizabeth F   Sex:F   13 May 1967 David P Alfsen Sr & Sandra F King
ALLAIRE,Antonio   Sex:M   (Child #3) 29 Apr 1939 Antonio Allaire (Hudson, NH) & Julieanne Raymond (Canada)
ALLAIRE,Jason K   Sex:M   02 Feb 1979 John T Allaire & Donna M Stairs
ALLAIRE,Michelle Ryan Sex:F 12 May 1983 Ronald Mark Allaire & Kathleen McGranahan
ALLARD,James N   Sex:M   09 Dec 1973 Donald R Allard & Janet Ann Gauvin
ALLARD,Julie Ann   Sex:F   13 Mar 1977 Donald R Allard & Janet Ann Gauvin
ALLARD,Mark D   Sex:M   03 Nov 1975 Rene N Allard & Eleanore I Magner
ALLARD,Patrick M   Sex:M   30 Apr 1974 Rene M Allard & Eleanor I Magner
ALLARD,Tracy A   Sex:F   01 Nov 1964 Lee J Allard & Candace C Bates
ALLARD,Troy W III   Sex:M   22 Jun 1979 Troy W Allard Jr & Elizabeth A Kerrick
ALLEN,Douglas W   Sex:M   25 Jul 1951 Prescott H Allen & Julia S Janas
ALLEN,George W   Sex:M   05 Dec 1960 Richard T Allen & Barbara J Talbot
ALLEN,Georgeana Pearl   Sex:F   (Child #13) 16 Jan 1922 George A Allen (Colchester, VT) & Phoebe Mason (Milton, VT)
ALLEN,Gloria Joyce Sex:F   (Child #15) 17 Jun 1924 George Allen (Milton, VT) & Phoebe Mason (Milton, VT)
ALLEN,John E   Sex:M   (Child #1) 29 Nov 1892 Phineas D Allen (Boston, MA) & Mary A Boyd (Calais, ME)
ALLEN,John E   Sex:M   24 Nov 1892 Hudson, NH Phineas Allen & Mary A Boyd
ALLEN,Joyce Beverley   Sex:F   (Child #4) 29 May 1937 Lylam N Allen (Prescott, MA) & Enola Clifford (Oakham, MA)
ALLEN,Karena M   Sex:F   06 Mar 1977 Frank G Allen Jr & Lynne Marie Weeks
ALLEN,Lavina Beverly Sex:F   (Child #19) 16 May 1928 George A Allen (Colchester, VT) & Phoebe Mason (Milton, VT)
ALLEN,Marjorie Alma   Sex:F   (Child #20) 31 Jan 1930 George Allen (Colchester, Vt) & Phoebe Mason (Milton, VT)
ALLEN,Mary Ruby   Sex:F   (Child #14) 06 Mar 1923 George A Allen (Colchester, VT) & Phoebe Mason (Milton, VT)
ALLEN,Monique   Sex:F   07 Mar 1968 Harold L Allen & Marcelle T Doyon
ALLEN,Robert Deering   Sex:M   (Child #17) 27 Feb 1926 George A Allen (Vermont) & Phoebe Mason (Vermont)
ALLEN,Wilma   Sex:F   (Child #12) 28 Nov 1919 George Allen (Colchester, VT) & Phoebe Mason (Milton, VT)
ALLEY,[Unknown]   Sex:F   06 May 1937 Samuel B Alley (Nahant, MA) & Enid M McDonald (Isle of Man)
ALLGROVE,Daniel A   Sex:M   26 Oct 1966 Ernest A Allgrove & Beverly J Martin
ALLISON,Brian R   Sex:M   08 Oct 1970 David F Allison & Diane T Deschamps
ALLISON,Charles J   Sex: 12 Mar 1973 Charles J Allison & Jacqueline A Larouch
ALLISON,Charles S   Sex:M   (Child #6) 28 Jan 1946 Simon R Allison (Nashua, NH) & Gloria M Bonnette (Mt Pleasant, MA)
ALLISON,David W   Sex:M   07 Sep 1948 Simon R Allison (Nashua, NH) & Gloria M Bonnette (Mt Pleasant, MA)
ALLISON,Debra L   Sex:F   02 Jan 1969 David F Allison & Diane T Deschamps
ALLISON,Gary J   Sex:M   30 May 1962 Simon R Allison, Jr & Claire I Casey
ALLISON,Jaime Melissa   Sex:F   13 Mar 1983 John M Allison & Patricia A Dailey
ALLISON,James Matthew   Sex:M   07 Jul 1979 John M Allison & Patricia A Dailey
ALLISON,Jeffrey M   Sex:M   23 Sep 1975 John M Allison & Patricia Ann Dailey
ALLISON,John M   Sex:M   12 Apr 1950 Simon R Allison & Gloria M Bonnette
ALLISON,Margaret F   Sex:F   (Child #5) 06 May 1944 Simon R Allison (Nashua, NH) & Gloria M Bonnette (Mt Pleasant, MA)
ALLISON,Michael R   Sex:M   24 Feb 1961 Simon R Allison & Claire I Casey
ALLISON,Paula A   Sex:F   18 Mar 1971 Charles J Allison & Jacqueline A Larouch
ALLISON,Shirly A M   Sex:F   (Child #2) 18 Aug 1939 Simon R Allison (Nashua, NH) & Gloria M Bonnette (Mt Pleasant,MA)
ALLISON,[Unknown]   Sex:F   (Child #1) 29 May 1938 Simon R Allison (Nashua, NH)

HUDSON, NH BIRTHS

& Gloria M Bonnette (Mt Pleasant,MA)
ALUKONIS,Florence H   Sex:F   20 Jul 1951 Vito S Alukonis & Harriet F Cooke
ALUKONIS,Stanley   Sex:M   (Child #3) 06 Mar 1918 Stevens Alukonis (Russia)
   & M Patckkonski (Russia)
AMADON,Christopher L   Sex:M 04 Feb 1971 Leslie J Amadon Jr & Nancy E Billings
AMADON,Kimberly E   Sex: 17 May 1973 Leslie J Amadon Jr & Nancy E Billings
AMATO,Janessa A   Sex:F   24 Aug 1973 Philip D Amato & Susan M Reddy
AMBURG,James R   Sex: 10 Apr 1973 Robert C Amburg & Eileen M Cannon
AMBURG,Michael J   Sex:M   13 Feb 1965 Robert C Amburg & Eileen M Cannon
AMBURG,Robert J   Sex:M   27 Jan 1964 Robert C Amburg & Eileen M Cannon
AMES,Douglas Seeley   Sex:M 11 Jul 1978 Lauris Charles Ames & Mary Jane Seeley
AMLAW,Karolyn B   Sex:F   24 Mar 1976 William D Amlaw & Sandra B Shanahan
AMORELLI,Elizabeth G Sex:F   24 May 1979 Michael Amorelli & Kathleen E Johnson
AMORELLI,Tracy Anne   Sex:F   25 May 1976 Michael Amorelli & Kathleen E Johnson
ANAIR,Linda J Sex:F (Child #4) 26 Jul 1945 Leonard A Anair (St Johnsbury, VT)
   & Geraldine L Rock (Keeseville, NY)
ANCTIL,Crystal Ann   Sex:F   07 Mar 1977 Denis J Anctil & Denise Ann LaBelle
ANCTIL,Elaine C   Sex:F   (Child #5) 28 Oct 1940 Emile E Anctil (Nashua, NH)
   & Thelma LaPlante (Antrim, NH)
ANCTIL,Joseph Leo Roger Sex:M (Child #13) 10 Jun 1929 Gerard Anctil(Canada)
   & Florilda Deschamp (Canada)
ANDERSON,Elaine R   Sex:F   (Child #2) 02 Mar 1940 Stanley E Anderson
   & Ruth L Wyman (Boston, MA)
ANDERSON,John M Jr   Sex: 05 Jun 1973 John M Anderson & Marie T Allmaras
ANDERSON,Laura M   Sex:F   03 Dec 1970 John M Anderson & Marie T Allmaras
ANDERSON,Mary E   Sex:F   22 Mar 1948 Carl R Anderson (Kansas City)
   & Emily Willett (Hudson, NH)
ANDERSON,Steven C   Sex:M   16 Oct 1958 Frederick M Anderson & Maria I Flores
ANDERSON,Theodore R   Sex:M   19 Dec 1969 Richard A Anderson & Kay M Rivers
ANDERSON,Vikki Leigh   Sex:F   11 Nov 1983 Roy E Anderson Jr & Cheryl L Lemire
ANDREW,Alice Mabel   Sex:F   (Child #3) 20 Nov 1914 Arnold Andrew (England)
   & Carrie Connell (Hudson, NH)
ANDREW,Charles R   Sex:M   (Child #4) 21 May 1906 Arnold Andrew (England)
   & Carrie L Connell (Hudson, NH)
ANDREW,Patricia   Sex:F   (Child #5) 22 Mar 1938 Robert Andrew (Hudson, NH)
   & Violetta Andrew (Nashua, NH)
ANDREW,Priscilla   Sex:F   (Child #4) 22 Mar 1938 Robert Andrew (Hudson, NH)
   & Violetta Andrew (Nashua, NH)
ANDREW,Robert Allen Jr Sex:M (Child #2) 28 Apr 1934 Robert A Andrew
   (Hudson, NH) & Violetta Doherty (Nashua, NH)
ANDREW,Ruth   Sex:F   (Child #1) 01 Aug 1911 Allen Andrew (Lancashire, England)
   & Amy Webster (Lowell, MA)
ANDREW,Vivian L   Sex:F   (Child #1) 05 Jul 1903 Walter E Andrew (England)
   & Ida Groves (Hudson, NH)
ANDREWS,Allen   Sex:M   23 Jul 1796 Hudson, NH Thomas Andrews & Hannah
ANDREWS,Allen B   Sex:M   (Child #2) 18 Oct 1889 Arthur S Andrews (Hudson, NH)
   & Linnie F Butler (Pelham, NH)
ANDREWS,Beatrice   Sex:F   (Child #2) 02 Jul 1913 Allan Andrews (England)
   & Ainice Webster (Lowell, MA)
ANDREWS,Chester   Sex:M   (Child #1) 13 Sep 1888 William A Andrews (Hudson, NH)
   & Willetta Annis (Londonderry, NH)
ANDREWS,Christopher T   Sex:M   25 Nov 1968 Harold G Andrews & Jill Goldsmith
ANDREWS,Dorothy L   Sex:F   (Child #1) 14 Nov 1915 Hudson, NH Allen B Andrews
   (Hudson, NH) & Josie Gowing (Hudson, NH)
ANDREWS,Dustin   Sex:M   31 Dec 1797 Hudson, NH Thomas Andrews & Hannah
ANDREWS,Fanny   Sex:F   10 Apr 1814 Hudson, NH Thomas Andrews & Prisca
ANDREWS,Flora Ivaneth   Sex:F   Jul 1866 Hudson, NH Rufus D Andrews & Almira
ANDREWS,Flora J   Sex:F   Jul 1866 Hudson, NH Rufus D Andrews & Alvira
ANDREWS,Gilman   Sex:M   26 Dec 1806 Hudson, NH Thomas Andrews & Prisca
ANDREWS,Hannah   Sex:F   03 Jan 1780 Hudson, NH Levi Andrews & Bridget

HUDSON,NH BIRTHS

ANDREWS,Hannah   Sex:F   14 Jan 1810 Hudson, NH Thomas Andrews & Prisca
ANDREWS,Helen A   Sex:F   (Child #3) 23 Oct 1895 Wm A Andrews (Hudson, NH)
   & Williette Annis (Londonderry, NH)
ANDREWS,Howard A   Sex:M   (Child #1) 08 Feb 1883 Hudson, NH Arthur S Andrews
   (Hudson, NH) & Linie F Butler (Hudson, NH)
ANDREWS,James   Sex:M   12 Oct 1768 Hudson, NH Levi Andrews & Bridget
ANDREWS,Joel   Sex:M   03 Sep 1764 Hudson, NH Levi Andrews & Bridget
ANDREWS,Joel   Sex:M   30 Sep 1764 Hudson, NH Levi Andrews & Briget
ANDREWS,John   Sex:M   07 Nov 1819 Hudson, NH Nathan Andrews & Abigail Jones
ANDREWS,Letice   Sex:F   20 Aug 1762 Hudson, NH Levi Andrews & Bridget
ANDREWS,Lettice   Sex:F   20 Aug 1762 Hudson, NH Levi Andrews & Briget
ANDREWS,Levi   Sex:M   02 Oct 1766 Hudson, NH Levi Andrews & Bridget
ANDREWS,Levi   Sex:M   30 Mar 1795 Hudson, NH Thomas Andrews & Hannah
ANDREWS,Lucinda   Sex:F   01 Jul 1792 Hudson, NH Thomas Andrews & Hannah
ANDREWS,Maria Sophia   Sex:F 28 Aug 1871 Hudson, NH George G Andrews & Anabel
ANDREWS,Nathan   Sex:M   21 Mar 1794 Hudson, NH Thomas Andrews & Hannah
ANDREWS,Nathan   Sex:M   24 Mar 1794 Hudson, NH Thomas Andrews & Hannah
ANDREWS,Robert   Sex:M   21 Mar 1805 Hudson, NH Thomas Andrews & Prisca
ANDREWS,Stephen E   Sex:M   26 May 1967 Harold G Andrews & Jill Goldsmith
ANDREWS,Thomas   Sex:M   02 May 1771 Hudson, NH Levi Andrews & Bridget
ANDREWS,Virginia Natalie   Sex:F (Child #1) 05 Sep 1911 Howard A Andrews
   (Hudson, NH) & Ina L Brown (Hudson, NH)
ANDREWS,[Unknown]   Sex: 09 Feb 1864 Hudson, NH Rufus D Andrews & Almira
ANDREWS,[Unknown]   Sex:M   07 Feb 1864 Hudson, NH Rufus Andrews & Alvira
ANGER,David P   Sex:M   13 Jan 1955 Paul H Anger & Jeannette D Bonville
ANGER,Jonathan Mark   Sex:M   04 Nov 1983 Mark John Anger & Mariane A Fauteux
ANGER,Joseph M   Sex:M   10 Jun 1959 Paul H Anger & Jeannette D Bonville
ANGER,Robert Paul   Sex:M   22 Jul 1978 David Paul Anger & Carla Ann Levesque
ANGER,Shawn R   Sex: 21 Dec 1972 Paul H Anger & Donna L Levesque
ANNALARO,Dianne M   Sex:F   19 Jan 1949 Charles P Annalaro & Pauline M Coles
ANNIS,Elizabeth   Sex:F   05 Aug 1871 Hudson, NH Parker P Annis & Roxanna
ANNIS,Ema E   Sex:F   Hudson, NH William P Annis & Drusett
ANNIS,Emma E   Sex:F   18 Aug 1879 Hudson, NH William P Annis & Drusett S
ANNIS,Howard N   Sex:M   05 Sep 1874 Hudson, NH Joseph Annis & Jane
ANNIS,Katie Brooke   Sex:F   12 Dec 1980 Glenn A Annis & Jennifer Marie Retza
ANNIS,Linda   Sex:F   20 Jan 1951 Harold J Annis & Madeline F Harwood
ANNIS,Nellie J   Sex:F   17 Jun 1866 Hudson, NH Parker B Annis & Reform
ANNIS,Nellie Jane   Sex:F   19 Jan 1866 Hudson, NH Parker B Annis & Reform W
ANNIS,Seth R   Sex:M   19 Mar 1977 Glenn A Annis & Jennifer M Retza
ANNIS,William Carlton   Sex:M   (Child #3) 01 Sep 1926 Andrew J Annis
   (Plattsburgh, NY) & Marion Moody (Ogunquit, ME)
ANNIS,[Unknown]   Sex:F   (Child #3) 29 Jan 1906 Everett P Annis (Hudson, NH)
   & Katherine McArthur (St John, N B)
ANNIS,[Unknown]   Sex:F   30 Sep 1874 Hudson, NH William Annis & Lucretia
ANNIS,[Unknown]   Sex:F 03 Apr 1877 Hudson, NH William P Annis (Londonderry,NH)
   & Drusett (Manchester, NH)
ANNIS,[Unknown] Sex:M 31 Aug 1881 Hudson, NH William P Annis (Londonderry,NH)
   & Tursetta Stearns (Bangor, ME)
ANTONI,Brandon J   Sex:M   09 Mar 1978 William Antoni & Jacqueline M Kiolbas
ANTONI,Douglas T   Sex:M   20 Jan 1980 William Antoni & Jacqueline M Kiolbas
ANTOSCA,Kerri Ann   Sex:F   30 Jan 1985 Albert J Antosca & Anne M Browning
APPLER,Douglas R   Sex:M   13 Oct 1977 David V Appler & Phyllis Ann Kline
APRIL,Kyle Charles Sex:M 28 Aug 1984 Charles H April Jr & Loretta Jean Bolduc
APRIL,Laurie A   Sex:F   25 Sep 1964 Norman R April & Norma N Martin
APRIL,Ryan Joseph   Sex:M   12 Oct 1981 Charles H April & Loretta Jean Bolduc
ARAKELIAN,Jason M   Sex:M   24 Apr 1970 Arthur Arakelian & Marian A Tahmizian
ARAKELIAN,Richard A   Sex:M   16 May 1968 Arthur Arakelian & Marian A Tahmizian
ARCHAMBAULT,Justin Aric Sex:M 14 May 1985 Richard G Archambault
   & Debra J Baker
ARCHAMBEAULT,William R   Sex:M   24 Jun 1954 Joseph L Archambeault

HUDSON,NH BIRTHS

& Lorraine R D'Amour
ARCHIBALD,Charles W Sex:M (Child #2) 01 Mar 1915 Hudson, NH Charles E
  Archibald (Maine) & Martha Young (Londonderry, NH)
ARDAGNA,David Michael Sex:M 19 Apr 1982 Paul Ardagna & Jean Marie Sawtelle
ARDAGNA,Paul V Sex:M 30 Jan 1978 Paul J Ardagna Jr & Jean Marie Sawtelle
AREL,Leon R Jr Sex:M 11 May 1969 Leon R Arel & Marie Marcotte
AREY,Kevin L Sex:M 26 Mar 1971 Henry L Arey Jr & Florence E McIsaac
ARMSTRONG,Ada E Sex:F 24 Feb 1878 Hudson, NH Oscar O Armstrong (Windham, NH)
  & Nellie A Titcomb (Londonderry, NH)
ARMSTRONG,Alice K Sex:F 07 Jul 1881 Hudson, NH Oscar O Armstrong (Windham,
  NH) & Nellie J Titcomb (Londonderry, NH)
ARMSTRONG,Clifford George Sex:M (Child #1) 18 Nov 1917 George Armstrong
  (Hudson, NH) & Hattie Greene (Billerica, MA)
ARMSTRONG,Fred Hildreth Sex:M 21 May 1869 Hudson, NH Oscar O Armstrong
  & Hattie J
ARMSTRONG,Geo C Sex:M 07 Jun 1886 Oscar O Armstrong & Nellie J
ARMSTRONG,James S Sex:M (Child #4) 11 Feb 1883 Hudson, NH Oscar O Armstrong
  (Windham, NH) & Nellie J Titcomb (Londonderry, NH)
ARMSTRONG,John O Sex:M (Child #6) 13 Aug 1888 Oscar O Armstrong (Windham,
  NH) & Nellie E Titcomb (Londonderry, NH)
ARMSTRONG,Ola Bell Sex:F 29 Jul 1879 Hudson, NH Oscar O Armstrong
  (Windham, NH) & Nellie J Titcomb (Londonderry, NH)
ARNOLD,Roger M Sex:M 27 Feb 1971 Denis A Arnold & Lise M Veilleux
ARNOLD,Sharon M Sex:F 30 Sep 1963 Roger M Arnold & Dolores A Smith
ARPIN,Arthur Sex:M (Child #6) 12 Feb 1920 Pierre Arpin (Burlington, VT)
  & Georgiana Provencal (Concord, NH)
ARPIN,Ernest Peter Sex:M (Child #2) 07 Jul 1938 Peter Arpin (Burlington, VT)
  & Ann Marie Levesque (St Louis, Canada)
ARPIN,Florence Sex:F (Child #10) 30 Nov 1920 Pierre Arpin (Burlington, VT)
  & Georgianna Provencal (Concord, NH)
ARPIN,Jeanne Sex:F (Child #10) 05 Jun 1922 Pierre Arpin (Burlington, VT)
  & Georgianna Provencal (Concord, NH)
ARPIN,Leo Sex:M (Child #10) 20 Mar 1927 Pierre Arpin (Burlington, VT)
  & Georgianna Provencal (Concord, NH)
ARPIN,Robert Sex:M (Child #9) 30 Nov 1920 Pierre Arpin (Burlington, VT)
  & Georgianna Provencal (Concord, NH)
ARRIS,Michelle K Sex:F 16 Oct 1975 George A Arris & Barbara L Savage
ARRIS,Scott T Sex:M 13 Sep 1968 George A Arris & Barbara L Savage
ARSENEAULT,James Alan Sex:M 21 Nov 1980 James R Arseneault & Dianna L Penno
ARSENEAUX,Paul D Sex:M 14 Mar 1977 Paul J Arseneaux & Debra Marie Peters
ARSHALIAN,Richard N Sex:M 12 Oct 1975 Paul R Arshalian & Janet M Waters
ASHE,Harry B Sex:M (Child #2) 11 Mar 1940 Harry B Ashe (Bloomfield, NY)
  & Katherine Averill (Manchester, NH)
ASIMACOGSOULOS,[Unknown] Sex:M (Child #5) 16 Jul 1938 Rodis Asimacogsoulos
  (Greece) & Zoitsa Tsakonas (Greece)
ASKHAM,Westley A Sex:M (Child #2) 04 Sep 1940 Frank Askham (Nashua, NH)
  & Armandine Leclair (Canada)
ASSELIN,Alan A Sex:M 04 Oct 1953 Roger E Asselin & Gertrude D Dube
ASSELIN,Alecia A Sex:F 21 Dec 1957 Roger E Asselin & Gertrude D Dube
ATKOCHAITIS,Stanley T Sex:M 17 Jun 1961 Stanley B Atkochaiti & Ala Krutulis
ATWOOD,Daniel Sex:M 25 Jul 1816 Hudson, NH John Atwood & Sarah
ATWOOD,David Sex:M 27 Jan 1808 Hudson, NH John Atwood & Sarah
ATWOOD,Elizabeth Sex:F 18 Jan 1798 Hudson, NH John Atwood & Elizabeth
ATWOOD,Elizebeth Sex:F 18 Jan 1798 Hudson, NH John Atwood & Elizebeth
ATWOOD,John Sex:M 03 Oct 1790 Hudson, NH John Atwood & Elizabeth
ATWOOD,John Sex:M 03 Oct 1795 Hudson, NH John Atwood & Elizebeth
ATWOOD,Marc Joseph Sex:M 13 Jul 1979 Jonathan P Atwood & Dianne M Hachey
ATWOOD,Rachel Sex:F 28 Aug 1805 Hudson, NH John Atwood & Sarah
ATWOOD,Salley Sex:F 27 Jun 1790 Hudson, NH John Atwood & Elizebeth
ATWOOD,Sally Sex:F 07 Jan 1799 Hudson, NH John Atwood & Elizabeth

HUDSON,NH BIRTHS

ATWOOD,Simeon H Sex:M 26 Jul 1789 Hudson, NH Jacob Atwood & Rebeccah
ATWOOD,Simeon Hills Sex:M 26 Jul 1789 Hudson, NH Jacob Atwood & Rebecca
ATWOOD,William Sex:M 22 May 1792 Hudson, NH   & Ruth Atwood
ATWOOD,William Sex:M 15 Aug 1810 Hudson, NH John Atwood & Sarah
ATWOOD,William Sex:M 27 May 1792 Hudson, NH   & Ruth Atwood
AUBCEWICZ,Stanley W Sex:M (Child #2) 15 Oct 1940 Alexander Abucewicz
   (Walpole, MA) & Monica Barkowski (Nashua, NH)
AUDET,Matthew E Sex: 05 Feb 1973 Donald R Audet & Patricia A Fox
AUDET,Thomas P Sex:M 05 Feb 1974 Real J Audet & Claire T Maynard
AUDETTE,Diana E Sex:F 24 Jul 1957 Wilfred J Audette & Janice C Santwire
AUDETTE,Katherine Leigh Sex:F 17 Mar 1978 Paul J Audette & Linda Carroll
AUDETTE,Lauren C Sex:F 25 May 1975 Paul J Audette & Linda Carroll
AUDETTE,Michael T Sex:M 19 Oct 1959 Wilfred J Audette & Janice C Sautwire
AUDETTE,Nancy A Sex:F 24 Nov 1953 Wilfred J Audette & Janice C Santwire
AUSTIN,Alice M Sex:F 08 Feb 1878 Hudson, NH William O Austin (Charlestown,MA)
   & Rachel W Osgood (Hudson, NH)
AUSTIN,Richard A Sex:M 16 Aug 1956 Richard H Austin & Carol J White
AVERY,James Sex:M (Child #5) 21 Nov 1931 Edward H Avery (Saugus, MA)
   & Lola Chapman (Charlestown, MA)
AXTMAN,Lynn Sex:F 31 Mar 1982 Stephen F Axtman & Katherine A Johnson
AYER,Abigail Sex:F 29 Nov 1772 Hudson, NH Simon Ayer & Abigail
AYER,Douglas Wilton Sex:M (Child #2) 30 May 1916 Hudson, NH Willis E Ayer
   (Claremont, NH) & Myrtle Sawyer (Thetford, VT)
AYER,Hannah Sex:F 21 Dec 1644 Hudson, NH John Ayer &
AYER,Kevin T Sex:M 02 Dec 1962 Harold M Ayer & Colette A Bell
AYER,William Sex:M 25 Sep 1770 Hudson, NH Simon Ayer & Abigail
AYERS,Deborah J Sex:F 02 Jun 1975 Donald F Ayers Jr & Joan M Fullam
BACHELDER,Molle Sex:F 20 Jul 1769 Hudson, NH Reuben Bachelder & Mary
BACON,Ola May Sex:F   06 Oct 1894 John L Bacon (Hardwick, MA)
   & Edith I Reynolds (Orange, MA)
BADEAU,Kim M Sex:F 28 Jul 1959 Roger O Badeau & Lorraine R Donovan
BAGGS,Susan L Sex:F 14 May 1961 James W Baggs & Mildred E Athey
BAGLEY,Gregory J Sex:M 17 Jan 1970 John J Bagley & Florence A Kanavos
BAILEY,Benjamin Patrick Sex:M 25 May 1984 B Richard Bailey
   & Patricia A Leclerc
BAILEY,Chadd Parkhurst Sex:M 20 Jun 1981 Thomas C Bailey & Roseann Morin
BAILEY,Eliphalet Sex:M 07 Sep 1756 Hudson, NH Timothy Bailey & Sarah
BAILEY,Elizabeth Sex:F 07 Sep 1756 Hudson, NH Timothy Bailey & Sarah
BAILEY,M Lorraine Marj Sex:F (Child #2) 04 Feb 1936 Clifford Bailey
   (Milford, NH) & Florette Marquis (Nashua, NH)
BAILEY,Oliver Sex:M 01 Sep 1763 Hudson, NH Timothy Bailey & Sarah
BAILEY,Rachel Marie Sex:F 22 May 1981 B Richard Bailey
   & Patricia Ann Leclerc
BAILEY,Sarah Sex:F 30 May 1754 Hudson, NH Timothy Bailey & Sarah
BAILEY,[Unknown] Sex:F 31 Aug 1936 Clyde M Bailey (New Hampshire)
   & Violet Ford (Merrimack, NH)
BAILLARGEON,Beulah M Sex:F 10 Mar 1965 David V Baillargeon & Lila A Pond
BAILY,Oliver Sex:M 01 Sep 1763 Hudson, NH Timothy Baily & Sarah
BAILY,Sarah Sex:F 20 May 1754 Hudson, NH Timothy Baily & Sarah
BAKAIAN,Bruce K Sex:M 07 Sep 1951 Dickram M Bakaian & Shirley A Whitney
BAKAIAN,Keith A Sex:M 24 Jul 1948 Dickran M Bakaian (Boston, MA)
   & Shirley A Whitney (Warren, NH)
BAKAIAN,Scott M Sex:M 08 Apr 1958 Dickran M Bakaian & Shirley A Whitney
BAKAIAN,Shaun P Sex:M 26 Jan 1968 Keith A Bakaian & Colleen E O'Neil
BAKER,Constance J Sex:F (Child #3) 27 Aug 1943 Wallace G Baker (Hudson, NH)
   & H Beatrice Smith (Worcester, MA)
BAKER,Diane Carol Sex:F (Child #1) 22 May 1934 Reuben Baker (Hudson, NH)
   & Frances Maloney (Schenectady, NY)
BAKER,Edie Ella Sex:F 14 Sep 1853 Hudson, NH John H Baker & Louisa U Webster
BAKER,Frank Perkins Sex:M (Child #3) 05 Jan 1898 Oswald P Baker (Derry, NH)

HUDSON,NH BIRTHS

  && Letitia M Church (Nova Scotia)
BAKER,Fred Palmer   Sex:M   (Child #2) 05 Jan 1898 Oswald P Baker (Derry, NH)
  && Letitia M Church (Nova Scotia)
BAKER,Helen R   Sex:F   (Child #7) 18 Apr 1907 Oswald P Baker (Derry, NH)
  && Letitia N Church (Nova Scotia)
BAKER,Joanne Elizabeth Sex:F (Child #2) 15 Mar 1937 William H Baker
  (Nashua, NH) & Mildred Kelley (Sandown, NH)
BAKER,John Earl   Sex:M   (Child #1) 25 Feb 1901 Hudson, NH William W Baker
  (Hudson, NH) & Sarah R Oldall (Montreal, Canada)
BAKER,John Julian Sex:M 21 Aug 1856 Hudson, NH John H Baker&Louisa U Webster
BAKER,Joseph Charles   Sex:M   24 Dec 1894 Charles O Baker (Hooksett, NH)
  & Rose Norman (Canada)
BAKER,Marie   Sex:F   (Child #1) 09 Dec 1917 Joseph Baker (Canada)
  & Dora Barrette (New Hampshire)
BAKER,Nettie Howes Sex:F 03 Dec 1859 Hudson, NH John H Baker&Louisa U Webster
BAKER,Russell J   Sex:M   17 Dec 1973 John S Baker & Anne Stoltz
BAKER,Sidney F   Sex:M   (Child #2) 25 May 1905 Wm W Baker (Hudson, NH)
  & Sarah Oldall (Montreal, Canada)
BAKER,Susan J   Sex:F   05 Sep 1952 John R Baker & Lois M Olson
BAKER,Wallace Grant   Sex:M   (Child #3) 08 Feb 1907 Wm W Baker (Hudson, NH)
  & Sarah L Oldall (Montreal, Canada)
BAKER,William   Sex:M   21 Sep 1865 Hudson, NH John L Baker & Louisa
BAKER,William E   Sex:M   24 Nov 1958 George H Baker & Drina L Worthley
BAKER,William Wallace   Sex:M   (Child #2) 31 Aug 1933 Wallace G Baker (Hudson,
  NH) & Beatrice Smith (Worcester, MA)
BAKER,William Wallace Sex:M 21 Sep 1865 Hudson, NH John H Baker
  & Louisa U Webster
BAKER,[Unknown]   Sex:M   (Child #1) 20 Apr 1896 Oswald P Baker (Derry, NH)
  & Letitia M Church (Nova Scotia)
BAKER,[Unknown]   Sex:F   (Child #4) 07 Jul 1901 Hudson, NH Oswald P Baker
  (Derry, NH) & Letitia H Church (Nova Scotia)
BAKER,[Unknown]   Sex:F   (Child #5) 03 Jan 1903 Oswald Baker (Derry, NH))
  & Letitia Church (Nova Scotia)
BAKER,[Unknown]   Sex:F   (Child #6) 14 Oct 1904 Oswald P Baker (Derry, NH)
  & Letitia Church (Nova Scotia)
BAKER,[Unknown]   Sex:F   (Child #8) 15 Nov 1908 Oswald P Baker (Derry, NH)
  & Nettie M Church (Nova Scotia)
BALDWIN,Ana   Sex:F   08 Mar 1731 Hudson, NH John Baldwin & Sarah
BALDWIN,Anna   Sex:F   08 Mar 1731 John Baldwin & Sarah
BALDWIN,Daniel   Sex:M   11 Aug 1733 Hudson, NH John Baldwin & Sarah
BALDWIN,Daniel   Sex:M   11 Aug 1735 Hudson, NH John Baldwin & Sarah
BALDWIN,Hannah   Sex:F   25 Dec 1744 Hudson, NH Henry Baldwin & Abigail
BALDWIN,John   Sex:M   21 Sep 1745 Hudson, NH John Baldwin & Sarah
BALDWIN,Levi   Sex:M   31 Jan 1741 Hudson, NH John Baldwin & Sarah
BALDWIN,Lewis   Sex:M   21 Jan 1741 Hudson, NH John Baldwin & Sarah
BALDWIN,Mary   Sex:F   22 Dec 1743 Hudson, NH Henry Baldwin & Abigail
BALDWIN,Sarah   Sex:F   22 Oct 1728 John Baldwin & Sarah
BALDWIN,Simeon   Sex:M   16 Jun 1738 Hudson, NH John Baldwin & Sarah
BALDWIN,Susanna   Sex:F   08 Mar 1733 John Baldwin & Sarah
BALDWIN,[Unknown]   Sex:F   25 Dec 1745 Hudson, NH Henry Baldwin & Abigail
BALINKEIRCIUS,Alfred Sex:M (Child #11) 09 Jun 1923 Wm Balinkeircius (Russia)
  & Eva Rutkwicz (Russia)
BALL,Elizabeth S   Sex:F   04 Mar 1953 John D Ball & Eleanor R Potter
BALSER,Troy D   Sex:M   02 Nov 1970 John F Balser & Lana J Martin
BANCROFT,Earl R   Sex:M   06 Jun 1949 Lewis E Bancroft & Dorothy E Young
BANCROFT,Patricia A   Sex:F   31 May 1947 Louis E Bancroft (Hollis, NH)
  & Dorothy Young (Penacook, NH)
BANKS,Gertrude C   Sex:F   17 Jun 1870 Hudson, NH Josiah H Banks & Eliza A
BARABE,Marie Jeanne Y   Sex:F   (Child #8) 24 Sep 1904 George Barabe (Canada)
  & Anna Lacroix (Canada)

HUDSON,NH BIRTHS

BARBER,Tracy Elizabeth Sex:F 08 Oct 1983 William J Barber&Patricia A O'Neill
BARBER,William J III Sex:M 20 Jan 1978 William J Barber Jr
   & Patricia Anne O'Neil
BARCHARD,Brooke Alexandra Sex:F 20 Nov 1980 Lawrence W Barchard
   & Laura V Peters
BARDSLEY,Gerald S Sex:M 24 Sep 1951 James H Bardsley & Thelma L Bancroft
BARDSLEY,Katie Rebecca Sex:F 09 Apr 1984 James H Bardsley III
   & Nancy Ann Manning
BARDSLEY,Richard A Sex:M (Child #4) 21 Sep 1946 James H Bardsley (New
   Bedford, MA) & Thelma L Bancroft (Londonderry, NH)
BARDZIK,Stanley J Jr Sex:M 24 Dec 1951 Stanley J Bardzik & Helen R Johnson
BARFOOT,Timothy D Sex:M 12 Jun 1968 David H Barfoot & Deborah M Jerge
BARITEAU,Andrea J Sex:F 23 May 1965 Caleb N Bariteau & Sheila M Widener
BARITEAU,Brenda A Sex:F 19 Sep 1963 Caleb N Bariteau & Sheila M Widener
BARKER,Edith Mary Sex:F (Child #3) 31 Oct 1900 Eugene S Barker (Antrim, NH)
   & Jennie M Ellis (Nashua, NH)
BARKER,Elizabeth Sex:F (Child #2) 05 Mar 1918 Walter L Barker (Nashua, NH)
   & Edith Marsh (Winchester, MA)
BARKER,Ruby L Sex:F (Child #4) 12 Dec 1903 Clarence C Parker (Hudson, NH)
   & Hattie L Robinson (Hudson, NH)
BARKER,Sarah Sex:F 19 Feb 1775 Hudson, NH Thomas Barker & Hannah
BARLOW,Leo R Sex:M 05 Jan 1957 Leo Barlow & Cecile Belanger
BARNARD,Carla Sex:F 30 Jul 1874 Hudson, NH David Barnard & Eliza
BARNARD,Lina M Sex:F 19 Dec 1880 Hudson, NH David Barnard (Ireland)
   & Eliza Connell (Tyngsborough, MA)
BARNES,Bernadette R Sex:F 26 Jul 1975 Richard J Barnes & Regina A Rodsheaver
BARNES,Charles A Sex:M 11 Feb 1958 Charles W Barnes & Ruby E Curtis
BARNES,Deborah A Sex:F 24 Jan 1966 Stephen D Barnes & Paula L April
BARNES,Doreen E Sex:F 03 Jun 1969 Cleyon D Barnes & Patricia A Fowler
BARNES,Edna Sex:F 28 Nov 1796 Hudson, NH
BARNES,Elizabeth A Sex:F 01 Mar 1967 Cleyon D Barnes & Patricia A Fowler
BARNES,Rebecca Lynn Sex:F 20 Sep 1975 Gary L Barnes & Sandra J Kearns
BARNETT,[Unknown] Sex:F 04 Sep 1871 Hudson, NH James V Barnett & Mary L
BARNETTE,Brian K Sex:M 15 Jan 1970 William O Barnette & Jean M Williamson
BARNETTE,Craig A Sex:M 01 Jan 1972 William O Barnette & Jean M Williamson
BARNETTE,[Unknown] Sex:F (Child #1) 24 Oct 1912 Frank Barnette (W Marlboro)
   & Delia Jacques (Lowell, MA)
BARON,Brandon Edward Sex:M 01 Feb 1981 Bryan Lloyd Baron & Karen Ann Little
BARON,Nicole M Sex:F 12 Dec 1971 Hector R Baron & Judith M Redhead
BARR,Melanie S Sex:F (Child #3) 23 Feb 1946 Otis D Barr (Nova Scotia)
   & Julia E Terris (Nashua, NH)
BARR,Richard O Sex:M 02 Jun 1956 Otis D Barr & Julia E Terris
BARR,Suzanne J Sex:F 09 Feb 1949 Otis D Barr & Julia A Terris
BARR,Wendy R Sex:F 31 Jan 1959 Otis D Barr & Julia E Terris
BARREIRO,Grant Michael Sex:M 29 Jan 1984 Mark A Barreiro & Linda Ann Specht
BARRET,Abel Sex:M 03 Apr 1777 Hudson, NH Isaac Barret & Susanna
BARRET,Daniel Sex:M 25 Aug 1768 Hudson, NH Simon Barret & Mary
BARRET,Daniel Sex:M 29 Dec 1788 Hudson, NH Thomas Barret & Abigail
BARRET,Hannah Sex:F 03 May 1759 Hudson, NH James Barret & Rebeckah
BARRET,Isaac Sex:M 20 Dec 1780 Hudson, NH Isaac Barret & Susannah
BARRET,James Sex:M 17 Dec 1749 Hudson, NH James Barret & Mary
BARRET,Lydia Sex:F 21 Dec 1746 Hudson, NH Moses Barret & Hannah
BARRET,Marcy Sex:F 16 Jan 1778 Hudson, NH Simon Barret & Mary
BARRET,Mollie Sex:F 20 Apr 1755 Hudson, NH James Barret & Rebeckah
BARRET,Rachel Sex:F 03 Mar 1787 Hudson, NH Thomas Barret & Abigail
BARRET,Sarah Sex:F 20 Apr 1763 Hudson, NH James Barret & Rebeckah
BARRET,Susannah Sex:F 20 Feb 1779 Hudson, NH Isaac Barret & Susannah
BARRET,Thomas Sex:M 06 Apr 1761 Hudson, NH James Barret & Rebeckah
BARRET,William M Sex:F 08 May 1783 Hudson, NH Isaac Barret & Susannah
BARRETT,Abel Sex:M 03 Apr 1777 Hudson, NH Isaac Barrett & Susanna Page

HUDSON,NH BIRTHS

BARRETT,Aphia   Sex:F   05 Jun 1787 Hudson, NH James Barrett & Phebe
BARRETT,Apphia Sex: 05 Jan 1787 Hudson, NH James Barrett & Phebe
BARRETT,Charlene M Sex:F   14 May 1963 Laurence E Barrett & Gloria M Black
BARRETT,Daniel Sex:M 24 Aug 1768 Hudson, NH Simeon Barrett & Mary
BARRETT,Daniel Sex:M 29 Dec 1788 Hudson, NH Thomas Barrett & Abigail Parker
BARRETT,Debbie T Sex:F   26 Jul 1961 David F Barrett & Freda E Sumerlin
BARRETT,Eunice Evelyn   Sex:F   (Child #1) 13 Sep 1907 Leonard V Barrett
    (Nashua, NH) & Carrie E Raulsin (Lebanon, ME)
BARRETT,Florence Louise   Sex:F   (Child #5) 27 Mar 1939 Leslie J Barrett
    (Bowdoin, ME) & Florence R Chadwick (Bowdoinham, ME)
BARRETT,Frank L   Sex:F   11 Oct 1876 Hudson, NH Charles Barrett & T W Smith
BARRETT,Hannah   Sex:F   03 May 1759 Hudson, NH James Barrett & Rebecca
BARRETT,Isaac   Sex:M 12 Apr 1753 Hudson, NH Moses Barrett & Hannah Proctor
BARRETT,Isaac   Sex:M 09 May 1758 Hudson, NH Moses Barrett & Hannah Proctor
BARRETT,Isaac   Sex:M 30 Dec 1780 Hudson, NH Isaac Barrett & Susanna Page
BARRETT,Jacob   Sex:M 17 Dec 1749 Hudson, NH James Barrett & Mary
BARRETT,Jacob   Sex:M 22 Jul 1789 Hudson, NH James Barrett & Phebe
BARRETT,James   Sex:M 04 May 1757 Hudson, NH James Barrett & Rebecca
BARRETT,John A Sex:M   15 Jul 1878 Hudson, NH Alverado Barrett (Hudson, NH)
    & Anna M (Pembrook)
BARRETT,Joseph J Sex:M   07 May 1872 Hudson, NH James Barrett & Viletta
BARRETT,Kittie M Sex:F   27 Jun 1963 John C Barrett & Catherine S Farringt
BARRETT,Laurie A Sex: 14 Jul 1972 Thomas M Barrett Jr & Margaret A Roehrig
BARRETT,Leon Oscar   Sex:M   (Child #1) 08 Jul 1923 Wm E Barrett (Nashua, NH)
    & Merilda Mignault (Canada)
BARRETT,Leroy G   Sex:M   (Child #6) 20 Nov 1940 Leslie J Barrett (Bowdoin, ME)
    & Florence Chadwick (Bowdoinham, ME)
BARRETT,Linda C   Sex:F   13 Nov 1959 Gerald F Barrett & Dorothy I Ford
BARRETT,Lucille Olive   Sex:F   (Child #1) 24 Mar 1921 Alfred Barrett (Nashua,
    NH) & Helen Moriarty (Nashua, NH)
BARRETT,Lydia   Sex:F   21 Dec 1746 Hudson, NH Moses Barrett & Hannah Proctor
BARRETT,Marlene E   Sex:F   14 May 1963 Laurence E Barrett & Gloria M Black
BARRETT,Mary   Sex:F   (Child #3) 07 Aug 1918 Joseph Barrett (Canada)
    & Georgianna Lavoie (Boston, MA)
BARRETT,Mary   Sex:F   16 Jan 1778 Hudson, NH Simeon Barrett & Mary
BARRETT,Michael H   Sex:M   26 Jul 1962 James H Barrett & Marie T Watts
BARRETT,Molly   Sex:F   20 Apr 1755 Hudson, NH James Barrett & Rebecca
BARRETT,Moses   Sex:M   08 Jul 1751 Hudson, NH Moses Barrett & Hannah Proctor
BARRETT,Noah   Sex:M   28 Jun 1772 Hudson, NH Moses Barrett & Rhoda
BARRETT,Rachel   Sex:F   03 Mar 1787 Hudson, NH Thomas Barrett & Abigail Parker
BARRETT,Ralph L Sex:M (Child #10) 17 Nov 1946 Leslie J Barrett (Bowdoin, ME)
    & Florence R Chadwick (Bowdoinham, ME)
BARRETT,Raymond L Sex:M (Child #8) 20 Nov 1943 Leslie J Barrett (Bowdoin, ME)
    & Florence R Chadwick (Bowdoinham, ME)
BARRETT,Rhoda   Sex:F   06 Mar 1775 Hudson, NH Moses Barrett & Rhoda
BARRETT,Salley   Sex:F   29 Sep 1784 Hudson, NH James Barrett & Phebe
BARRETT,Sally   Sex:F   08 Jun 1781 Hudson, NH Moses Barrett & Rhoda
BARRETT,Sally   Sex:F   29 Sep 1784 Hudson, NH James Barrett & Phebe
BARRETT,Sarah   Sex:F   20 Apr 1763 Hudson, NH James Barrett & Rebecca
BARRETT,Sarah   Sex:F   21 Feb 1767 Hudson, NH Simeon Barrett & Mary
BARRETT,Sharon M   Sex:F   24 Apr 1964 James H Barrett & Marie T Watts
BARRETT,Simeon   Sex:M   Jul 1745 Hudson, NH Moses Barrett & Hannah Proctor
BARRETT,Susanna   Sex:F   20 Feb 1779 Hudson, NH Isaac Barrett & Susanna Page
BARRETT,Thomas   Sex:M   06 Apr 1761 Hudson, NH James Barrett & Rebecca
BARRETT,William   Sex:M   08 May 1783 Hudson, NH Isaac Barrett & Susanna Page
BARRETTE,Georgianna Adeline   Sex:F (Child #2) 18 May 1914 Joseph Barrette
    (Canada) & Georgianna Lavoie (Massachusetts)
BARRETTE,Jos Arthur A   Sex:M   (Child #7) 22 Nov 1907 Alfred Barrette (Canada)
    & Edevidge Bautin (Canada)
BARRETTE,Joseph Victor Sex:M   (Child #1) 01 Feb 1913 Joseph Barrette (Canada)

HUDSON,NH BIRTHS

   & Georgianna Lavoie (Canada)
BARRETTE,Mary Eva   Sex:F   (Child #4) 29 Aug 1920 Joseph Barrette (Hudson, NH)
   & Eugenia Lavoie (Boston, MA)
BARRIAULT,Alan R   Sex:M   17 Jul 1955 Raymond T Barriault & Florence MJ Cote
BARRIAULT,James R   Sex:M   15 Nov 1975 Gary E Barriault & Judith E Cunningham
BARRIAULT,Keith A   Sex:M   29 Jun 1974 Alan R Barriault & Caren E Lamper
BARRIAULT,Leo P   Sex:M   05 Oct 1950 Raymond T Barriault & Florence M J Cote
BARRITT,Mary J   Sex:F   04 Aug 1872 Hudson, NH Charles Barritt & Achsa
BARRON,Edwin Ellsworth   Sex:M   04 Jul 1862 Hudson, NH Alden Barron & Laura E
BARRON,Ervin Elsworth   Sex:M   04 Jul 1862 Hudson, NH Alden Barron & Lora E
BARROT,Isaac   Sex:M   12 Apr 1753 Hudson, NH Moses Barrot & Hannah
BARROT,Joel   Sex:M   09 May 1758 Hudson, NH Moses Barrot & Hannah
BARROT,Moses   Sex:M   08 Jul 1751 Hudson, NH Moses Barrot & Hannah
BARROT,Noah   Sex:M   28 Jun 1772 Hudson, NH Moses Barrot & Rhoda
BARROT,Rhoda   Sex:F   06 Mar 1775 Hudson, NH Moses Barrot & Rhoda
BARROT,Salley   Sex:F   08 Jun 1781 Hudson, NH Moses Barrot & Rhoda
BARROT,Sarah   Sex:F   21 Feb 1767 Hudson, NH Simeon Barrot & Mary
BARROWS,Walter   Sex:M   (Child #5) 02 Jun 1918 F W Barrows (Middleboro, MA)
   & Ethel Smith (Middleboro, MA)
BARSORIAN,Celisa A   Sex:F   24 Jun 1971 John B Barsorian & Claire V Arevian
BARSTOW,John Tisdale   Sex:M   (Child #1) 08 Oct 1911 Henry C Barstow (Sharon,MA)
   & Bessie G Tisdale (Norwell, MA)
BARTER,Sherry M   Sex:F   12 Aug 1973 William H Barter & Elaine S Sargent
BARTLETT,Clyde   Sex:M   03 Jan 1882 Hudson, NH Wm P Bartlett (Plymouth, MA)
   & Emily F Stevens (Springfield, NH)
BARTLETT,Jacqueline Mae   Sex:F   (Child #2) 13 Jul 1936 John E Bartlett
   (Providence, RI) & Mary Carr (Hillsborough, NH)
BARTLETT,Janet M   Sex:F   06 Aug 1953 Howard E Bartlett & Ada M Walton
BARTLETT,John E   Sex:M   13 May 1948 Thurland A Bartlett (Buxton, MA)
   & Alice M Melinkewich (Walpole, MA)
BARTLETT,Randall C   Sex:M   09 Apr 1968 Arthur H Bartlett & Pamela T Barr
BARTLOW,Jennifer L   Sex:F   18 Oct 1974 Raymond C Bartlow & Anne F Baugher
BARTOLUCCI,Valerie M   Sex:F   03 Mar 1969 Vincent N Bartolucci
   & Edna M Watters
BARTOLUCCI,Vincent N Jr   Sex:M   09 Aug 1966 Vincent N Bartolucci
   & Edna M Watters
BARTON,Helen L   Sex:F   24 Feb 1952 Alfred W Barton & Rita V Lemay
BARTON,Victor A   Sex:M   17 Feb 1950 Alfred W Barton & Rita V Lemay
BASHA,Danielle Marie   Sex:F   16 Feb 1984 Sidney P Basha & Louise R St Pierre
BASHARA,Amy Beth   Sex:F   23 Mar 1977 Thomas F Bashara & Karen May Beckwith
BASHARA,Brian Thomas   Sex:M   06 Nov 1980 Thomas F Bashara & Karen May Beckwith
BASIL,Sarah Dawn   Sex:F   03 Aug 1982 Henry A Basil Jr & Cheryl Ann Place
BASS,Tracy L   Sex:F   13 Oct 1962 William E Bass & Sandi D VanGeffen
BASSETT,Almeda Irene   Sex:F   (Child #3) 27 Apr 1901 Hudson, NH Joseph E Bassett
   (Groton, MA) & Katie Mulhair (Louisville, NY)
BASSETT,Obeline B   Sex:F   (Child #1) 27 Feb 1892 Joseph C Bassett (Groton, MA)
   & Katie A Mulhair (Louisville, NY)
BASSETT,Oberline R   Sex:M   27 Feb 1872 Hudson, NH Joseph C Bassett
   & Katie E Mulhair
BASTILLE,Kristin E   Sex:F 10 Nov 1982 Davie A Bastille & Marie Suzanne Bedard
BATCHELDER,Allen H   Sex:M   27 Oct 1863 Hudson, NH William A Batchelder
   & Nira Cummings
BATCHELDER,Angie R   Sex:F   18 Jan 1851 Hudson, NH William A Batchelder
   & Nira Cummings
BATCHELDER,Charles Henry   Sex:M   26 Mar 1870 Hudson, NH Mark Batchelder
   & Lydia
BATCHELDER,Charles R   Sex:M   (Child #4) 31 Mar 1920 Lester W Batchelder
   (Greenville, NH) & Carrie G Keysar (Colebrook, NH)
BATCHELDER,Cynthia L   Sex:F   09 Sep 1960 William L Batchelder
   & Phyllis E Ferguson

HUDSON,NH BIRTHS

BATCHELDER,Ethan   Sex:M   13 Jul 1862 Hudson, NH Mark Batchelder & Lydia
BATCHELDER,Etherine Ellsworth   Sex:M   13 Jul 1862 Hudson, NH Mark Batchelder
  & Lydia Steele
BATCHELDER,George A   Sex:M   26 Aug 1842 Hudson, NH William A Batchelder
  & Belinda Cummings
BATCHELDER,Henry A   Sex:M   27 Oct 1863 Hudson, NH William Batchelder & Anna
BATCHELDER,Hubert C   Sex:M   22 Dec 1865 Hudson, NH Mark Batchelder
  & Lydia Steele
BATCHELDER,Julia   Sex:F   25 Mar 1849 Hudson, NH William A Batchelder
  & Nira Cummings
BATCHELDER,Lucinda   Sex:F   07 Dec 1845 Hudson, NH William A Batchelder
  & Nira Cummings
BATCHELDER,Marcie E   Sex:F   21 Nov 1893 C H Batchelder (Hudson, NH)
  & Martha A Lund (Hollis, NH)
BATCHELDER,Mehitable   Sex:F   21 Sep 1771 Hudson, NH Reuben Batchelder
  & Mary
BATCHELDER,Mehittable   Sex:F   21 Sep 1771 Hudson, NH Reuben Batchelder
  & Mary Carlton
BATCHELDER,Molly   Sex:F   29 Jul 1769 Hudson, NH Reuben Batchelder
  & Mary Carlton
BATCHELDER,Reuben   Sex:M   26 Nov 1767 Hudson, NH Reuben Batchelder
  & Mary Carlton
BATCHELDER,Robert L   Sex:M   22 Dec 1865 Hudson, NH Mark Batchelder & Lydia
BATCHELDER,Walter R   Sex:M   01 Feb 1854 Hudson, NH William A Batchelder
  & Nira Cummings
BATEMAN,Cindy J   Sex:F   26 Jun 1957 Richard S Bateman & Dorothy A Walsh
BATHALON,Jeannette L   Sex:F   (Child #2) 26 Oct 1944 Robert J Bathalon
  (S Durham, Canada) & Alfreda C Ledoux (Putnam, CT)
BATURA,Mary   Sex:F   (Child #6) 18 Jul 1924 Balesta Batura (Poland)
  & Katarina Sankooki (Poland)
BATURA,Sonjie G   Sex:F   25 Jul 1948 Stanley Batura (Hudson, NH)
  & Vivian I Grimard (Derry, NH)
BATURA,Sophie   Sex:F   (Child #8) 23 Sep 1928 Boleslaw Batura (Poland)
  & Katherine Sankowska (Lithuania)
BAUBLIS,Kimberly D   Sex:F   23 Nov 1962 Edward L Baublis & Dorothy F Judkins
BAUBLIS,Lisa A   Sex:F   12 Apr 1961 Edward L Baublis & Dorothy F Judkins
BAUSHA,Anthony E   Sex:M   16 Sep 1969 Bennie W Bausha & Jeanne L Hall
BAUSHA,Kim M   Sex:F   05 Oct 1961 William F Bausha & Judith A Sudsbury
BAUSHA,Matthew R   Sex:M   10 Feb 1976 Robert B Bausha & Susan C Travers
BAUSHA,Michael R   Sex: 11 Jun 1973 Robert R Bausha & Susan C Travers
BAYBUTT,Sharon L   Sex:F   19 Nov 1966 James S Baybutt & Karen E Ahola
BAYBUTT,Stephen M   Sex:M   11 Dec 1968 James S Baybutt & Karen E Ahola
BEAL,Eugence C II   Sex:M   08 Dec 1963 William C Beal & Pauline B Duckworth
BEAL,James H   Sex:M   07 Nov 1949 Eugene C Beal & Grace E Moulton
BEALAND,Candace Lee   Sex:F   31 Aug 1983 Christopher L Bealan & Alice D Mercier
BEAN,Andrew Thomas   Sex:M   09 Dec 1983 Thomas Roy Bean & Charlene M Bourgeaul
BEAN,Kevin W   Sex:M   23 Jun 1960 Robert L Bean & Betty L Lilley
BEAN,Paulette F   Sex:F   18 Aug 1952 Jerry A Bean & Millicent F Reed
BEAN,[Unknown]   Sex:M   12 Dec 1865 Hudson, NH Jonas M Bean & Nancy M
BEARD,Billie-Jo   Sex:F   23 Sep 1974 Wayne C Beard & Linda A Farrow
BEARD,James A   Sex:M   (Child #1) 13 Nov 1940 Ralph E Beard (Merrimack, NH)
  & Rita K McNulty (Leominster, MA)
BEARD,James E   Sex:M   18 Jun 1965 Wayne C Beard & Diane R Stickney
BEAUCHENE,Rita Clara   Sex:F   (Child #4) 29 Jan 1923 Alfred Beauchene
  (Lewiston, ME) & Clara Desmarais (Hudson, NH)
BEAUCHESNE,David G   Sex:M   23 Sep 1952 Gerard J Beauchesne & Jean M McManus
BEAUCHESNE,Jenni Lee Sex:F 19 Dec 1981 Michael D Beauchesne & Denise D Hebert
BEAUCHESNE,Marie L   Sex:F   23 Sep 1952 Gerard J Beauchesne & Jean M McManus
BEAUCHESNE,Sherri Lynn   Sex:F   10 Oct 1984 Michael D Beauchesne
  & Denise Dianne Hebert

HUDSON,NH BIRTHS

BEAUDETTE,John David Sex:M 24 Oct 1983 Louis D Beaudette & Kristine A Holmes
BEAUDETTE,Leigh K   Sex:F   28 Apr 1977 Louis D Beaudette & Kristine A Holmes
BEAUDETTE,Marc Louis Sex:M 24 Oct 1983 Louis D Beaudette & Kristine A Holmes
BEAUDETTE,Michael H Sex:M 27 Feb 1980 Louis D Beaudette & Kristine A Holmes
BEAUDIN,Roger A J   Sex:M   30 Oct 1956 Arthur O Beaudin & Juliette A Gagnon
BEAUDRY,Deanne C Sex:F   02 May 1977 David F Beaudry & Claire Marie Bedard
BEAUDRY,Jennifer Lee Sex:F   25 Oct 1983 Daniel A Beaudry & Debra J DeCola
BEAUDRY,Justin Daniel   Sex:M   13 Jul 1981 Daniel A Beaudry & Debra J DeCola
BEAULIEU,Chelsie Marie Sex:F 07 Jul 1984 Donald J Beaulieu & Susan Marie Goss
BEAULIEU,Lawrence P   Sex:M   15 Feb 1960 Alfred A Beaulieu & Janet E Kopka
BEAULIEU,Lee A   Sex:M   07 May 1961 Alfred A Beaulieu & Janet E Kopka
BEAUREGARD,Barbara A   Sex:F   11 Apr 1966 Richard O Beauregard
  & Dorothy M Barton
BEAUREGARD,Ernest R   Sex:M   (Child #2) 09 Sep 1940 Victor R Beauregard
  (Nashua, NH) & Antoinette Alukash (Nashua, NH)
BEAUREGARD,Mark A   Sex:M   30 Nov 1977 Arnold J Beauregard & Joanne M Leach
BEAUREGARD,Nine L   Sex:F   22 Jul 1974 Arnold H Beauregard & Joanne M Leach
BEAUREGARD,Renee J Sex:F   05 Sep 1969 Richard O Beauregard & Dorothy M Barton
BEAUREGARD,Sandra L Sex:F   07 Mar 1967 Raymond F Beauregard & Brenda D McLeod
BEAUREGARD,Tammy J   Sex:F   10 May 1968 Arnold H Beauregard & Joanne M Leach
BEAUREGARD,Victor Sex:M (Child #1) 09 Apr 1933 Victor Beauregard (Nashua, NH)
  & Antoinette Laukash (Nashua, NH)
BEAUREGARD, [Unknown] Sex:F 06 Mar 1975 Richard O Beauregard&Dorothy M Barton
BECHARD,Deborah L   Sex:F   05 Feb 1968 Henry A Bechard Jr & Nancye L Hapner
BECHARD,John S   Sex:M   08 Jul 1964 Henry A Bechard, Jr & Nancye L Hapner
BECHARD,Matthew D   Sex:M   08 Jun 1977 Leon R Bechard & Kathleen G Desrosier
BECHARD,Michelle D   Sex:F   27 Dec 1967 Rodney D Bechard & Sandra G Lemery
BECKER,David C   Sex: 05 Jul 1972 Charles J Becker & Elaine R Driscoll
BECKHAM,Daniel S   Sex:M   24 Sep 1968 Joseph R Beckham & Ruth E Hammond
BECKHARDT,Rachel S   Sex:F   06 Feb 1980 Steven R Beckhardt & Eileen C Schanier
BEDARD,Madeleine B   Sex:F   15 Apr 1958 Albert E Bedard & Marthe H Schelling
BEDARD,Marie S   Sex:F   24 Jun 1960 Albert E Bedard & Marthe H Schelling
BEDARD,Monique Aurise   Sex:F   17 Mar 1982 Brian E Bedard & Janet I Tgibides
BEDARD,William J   Sex:M   27 Aug 1963 Albert Bedard & Marthe H Schelling
BEDNAR,Suzanne   Sex:F   25 Feb 1954 John M Bednar & Agnes P Greene
BEEBE,Mary Jane   Sex:F   02 Jul 1871 Hudson, NH Willard H Beebe & Emma L
BEEBE,Sarah Sex:F   20 Oct 1879 Hudson, NH Willard H Beebe
  & Emma L Richardson
BEECY,Michael J   Sex:M   03 Jun 1967 William Beecy & Susanne J Field
BEECY,William Jr   Sex:M   10 Jul 1966 William Beecy & Susanne J Field
BEEDE,Walter Bruce   Sex:M   19 Sep 1979 Bruce Alan Beede & Jean Marie Schlagle
BEGIN,Daniel J   Sex:M   22 Jun 1968 Roland O Begin & Carmen M Bernier
BEGIN,Kenneth M   Sex:M   04 Jan 1967 Roland O Begin & Carmen M Bernier
BELAND,Gloria Madeline Sex:F (Child #6) 06 Oct 1932 Nashua, NH Rosario Beland
  (Nashua, NH) & Evangeline Anctil (Nashua, NH)
BELAND,Irene Alice   Sex:F   (Child #3) 04 Apr 1921 Rosario Beland (NH)
  & Evangeline Anctil (New Hampshire)
BELAND,Roger Phillip   Sex:M   (Child #7) 17 Oct 1935 Rosario Beland (Nashua,
  NH) & Evangeline Anctil (Nashua, NH)
BELANGER,Brett R   Sex:M   25 Nov 1975 Normand R Belanger & Linda M Jean
BELANGER,Brian P   Sex:M   16 Jun 1974 Normand H Belanger & Anne Theresa Tombor
BELANGER,Dena Eve   Sex:F   24 Dec 1982 Dennis R Belanger & Judith S Baker
BELANGER,Donna L   Sex:F   31 Aug 1966 Roger G Belanger & Patricia A Desrocher
BELANGER,Jason Wayne   Sex:M   08 Aug 1980 Wayne G Belanger & Lenora L Libby
BELANGER,Jeremy G   Sex:M   11 May 1971 Dennis A Belanger & Lorrette M Boilard
BELANGER,Kevin S   Sex:M   23 Sep 1964 George R Belanger & Kathleen M Colburn
BELANGER,Lorraine Evelyn   Sex:F   (Child #9) 22 Mar 1931 George Belanger
  (Nashua, NH) & Eva Gauvin (Sutton, MA)
BELANGER,Marianne Y   Sex:F   (Child #4) 24 Dec 1920 Adelard Belanger (Canada)
  & Rosanna Boucher (Canada)

HUDSON,NH BIRTHS

BELANGER,Mark R   Sex:M   29 Aug 1970 Roger G Belanger & Patricia A Desrocher
BELANGER,Renee B   Sex:F   28 Apr 1979 Dennis R Belanger & Judith S Baker
BELANGER,Richard J   Sex:M   30 Nov 1970 Normand R Belanger & Linda M Jean
BELANGER,Steven R   Sex:M   08 Jan 1970 Normand R Belanger & Linda A Jean
BELDEN,Tiffany Rachel Sex:F 27 Sep 1984 Eric Henry Belden
   & Antonette Zaccagnini
BELHUMEUR,Ronald C   Sex:M   28 Sep 1947 Clement E Belhumeur (Nashua, NH)
   & Palmyre R Pelletier (Nashua, NH)
BELKUS,Jessica A   Sex: 29 Aug 1972 Paul R Belkus & Jeanne A McCartin
BELL,Sandra A   Sex:F   27 Sep 1950 Basil T Bell & Barbara A Manley
BELLAND,Lillian Jeanette   Sex:F   (Child #4) 18 Sep 1922 Rosario Belland
   (Nashua, NH) & Evangeline Anctil (Nashua, NH)
BELLEAU,Lorna R   Sex:F   19 Feb 1952 Edward O Belleau & Barbara L Post
BELLEFEUILLE,Debra D Sex:F 19 Feb 1958 Raymond G Bellefeuil&Theresa R Nadeau
BELLEVICH,Bernita   Sex:F   13 Jun 1908 Max Bellevich &
BELMORE,Christopher R Sex:M 20 Feb 1976 Robert A Belmore & Marlene C Baribeau
BENEDETTO,David Alan   Sex:M   23 Feb 1984   Jeffrey A Benedetto & Janet Sue Law
BENJAMIN,James Earl   Sex:M   (Child #1) 01 Jul 1925 James E Benjamin (Nova
   Scotia) & Lena Sterre (Manchester, NH)
BENNER,Blair S   Sex:F   (Child #1) 17 May 1945 Perl S Benner (Augusta, ME)
   & Shirley M Jaquith (Boston, MA)
BENNER,Dana S   Sex:M   29 Jun 1960 Perl S Benner & Shirley M Jaquith
BENNER,Gordon D   Sex:M   01 Dec 1950 Perl S Benner & Shirley Jaquith
BENNER,Leslie E   Sex:F   24 Jan 1948 Perl S Benner (Augusta, ME)
   & Shirley M Jaquith (Boston, MA)
BENNER,Susan   Sex:F   29 Jun 1952 Perl S Benner & Shirley Jaquith
BENNETT,Dennis A Jr Sex:M 30 Dec 1974 Dennis A Bennett Sr & Helen BA Anderson
BENNETT,Frank Sex:M 12 May 1857 Hudson, NH Joseph Bennett & Clarissa A Wilson
BENNETT,Michael S   Sex:M   26 Jan 1962 Raymond Bennett & Mary E Boyle
BENNETT,Tina C   Sex:F   10 Jul 1968 Floyd A Bennett & Nancy K Chase
BENNETT,[Unknown]   Sex:F   22 Apr 1964 Raymond Bennett & Mary E Boyle
BENNOCHE,Joseph Eddie   Sex:M   (Child #6) 04 Jul 1907 Amedee Bennoche
   (Massachusetts) & Lucie Bontin (Canada)
BENOIT,Vicki L   Sex:F   18 Aug 1966 Richard A Benoit & Viola M Dorr
BENSON,Barbara Ilona Sex:F 14 Dec 1984 Thomas R Benson & Ilona Barbara Jaeger
BENSON,Carol A   Sex:F   19 Apr 1949 George T Benson, Jr & Lois E Littlefield
BENSON,George T   Sex:M   (Child #4) 10 Dec 1920 George T Benson (Valley Falls,
   RI) & N Ida Steele (Hudson, NH)
BENSON,George T 4th   Sex:M   (Child #1) 17 Jan 1946 George T Benson,3rd
   (Hudson, NH) & Lois E Littlefield (Boston, MA)
BENSON,James D   Sex:M   14 Jul 1959 George T Benson, Jr & Lois E Littlefield
BENSON,John B   Sex:M   (Child #5) 25 Aug 1922 George T Benson (Providence, RI)
   & Ida N Steele (Hudson, NH)
BENSON,Peter C   Sex:M   17 Apr 1966 Ronald W Benson & Judith A Joy
BENSON,Susan J   Sex:F   23 Jan 1953 George T Benson, Jr & Lois E Littlefield
BENTLEY,Charles D   Sex:M   21 Jan 1970 David C Bentley & Barbara L Dover
BERARD,Pauline Elaine   Sex:F   (Child #1) 19 Nov 1935 Edgar Berard (Auburn,
   MA) & Lorette Theriault (Nashua, NH)
BERARD,Ruth Hazel   Sex:F   (Child #2) 17 Dec 1913 Louis Berard (Vermont)
   & Daisy Johnson (Vermont)
BERBAUM,Darlene F   Sex:F   27 Jul 1950 Louis J Berbaum & Emma L Troop
BERGER,Philip Roman Sex:M   04 Feb 1982 Andre Rockey Berger & Lynn Rae Susalka
BERGERON,Andre J P O   Sex:M   (Child #1) 12 Aug 1940 Omer Bergeron (Canada)
   & Laurette Dionne (Canada)
BERGERON,Brenda A   Sex:F   31 May 1954 Joseph P Bergeron & Ruth A Miller
BERGERON,Catherine E   Sex:F   21 Jun 1963 Robert P Bergeron & Ann T Hansberry
BERGERON,Christine Renee Sex:F 02 Sep 1984 Paul R Bergeron&Shirley A Gilbert
BERGERON,Eleanor May   Sex:F   (Child #1) 06 Apr 1935 Wilfred Bergeron (Lowell,
   MA) & Mary Rogers (Nashua, NH)
BERGERON,George Arthur Sex:M(Child #2) 09 Apr 1941 Leo A Bergeron (Nashua,NH)

HUDSON,NH BIRTHS

   & Janice T Durivage (Hudson, NH)
BERGERON,Jessica Dawn Sex:F 28 Jan 1982 Paul R Bergeron & Shirley Ann Gilbert
BERGERON,John G Sex:M 20 Sep 1966 Robert P Bergeron & Ann T Hansberry
BERGERON,Linda L Sex:F 27 Apr 1970 Emilien Bergeron & Cecile M Gaillardetz
BERGERON,Martin J Sex:M 19 May 1958 Robert P Bergeron & Ann T Hansberry
BERGERON,Mary A Sex:F 25 Apr 1960 Robert P Bergeron & Ann T Hansberry
BERGERON,Philip E Sex:M 15 Jan 1965 Robert P Bergeron & Ann T Hansberry
BERGERON,Richard Allen Sex:M (Child #5) 07 Jan 1937 Raymond C Bergeron
   (Winooski, VT) & Grace Monette (Derry, NH)
BERNARD,Anne M Sex:F 15 Dec 1960 Leo N Bernard & Olive H Glover
BERNARD,Beatrice Lillienne Sex:F(Child #2) 16 Apr 1917 Oscar Bernard (Canada)
   & Alice Marquis (New Hampshire)
BERNARD,Beth E Sex:F 26 Apr 1958 Leo N Bernard & Olive H Glover
BERNARD,Billie Clare Sex:F 16 May 1983 George R Bernard Jr&Cathy G Whitehurst
BERNARD,Irene R Sex:F 21 Feb 1949 Laureat R Bernard & Rita A Deshainais
BERNARD,James J Sex:M 20 Jun 1962 George R Bernard & Lucille M Fortier
BERNARD,Jesse Steven Sex:M 19 Mar 1985 George R Bernard & Cathy G Whiteburst
BERNARD,Larry W Sex:M 28 Sep 1959 Paul L Bernard & Roxy P Anderson
BERNARD,Leo C Sex:M 07 Mar 1968 Roger L Bernard & Theresa G Raymond
BERNARD,Lizzie E Sex:F 09 Dec 1870 Hudson, NH David Bernard & Eliza
BERNARD,Marc L Sex:M 09 Mar 1957 Leo N Bernard & Olive H Glover
BERNARD,Mari N G Sex:F 24 Jan 1969 Clermont A Bernard & Gisele C Mathieu
BERNASCONI,Jay Russell Sex:M 17 Feb 1976 Fidele J Bernasconi&Priscilla G Dorr
BERNASCONI,Jon Philip Sex:M 17 Feb 1976 Fidele J Bernasconi&Priscilla G Dorr
BERNAT,Debora E Sex:F 16 Aug 1976 Paul T Bernat & Carmen E Fox
BERNEBURG,Peter K Sex:M 12 May 1969 Philip L Berneburg & Barbara C Taylor
BERNECHE,Joseph Sex:M (Child #7) 07 Jan 1909 Amedee Berneche (MA)
   & Lucie Boutin (Canada)
BERNECHE,Marie Sex:F (Child #4) 09 Feb 1902 Amedes Berneche (New Hampshire)
   & Lucie Boutin (New Hampshire)
BERNIER,Jill E Sex:F 26 Mar 1968 Gerald L Bernier & Carole A Hussey
BERNIER,Lawrence A Sex:M 15 Apr 1953 Emile J Bernier & Gertrude A Labrie
BERNIER,Raymond Louis Sex:M (Child #2) 28 Jan 1941 Emile Bernier (Canada)
   & Gertrude A Labrie (Salem, MA)
BERNIER,[Unknown] Sex:F (Child #4) 06 Oct 1942 Emile J Bernier (Canada)
   & Gertrude A Labrie (Salem, MA)
BERROT,James Sex:M 04 May 1757 Hudson, NH James Berrot & Rebecah
BERRY,Andrew J Sex:M 03 Dec 1840 Hudson, NH Edward F Berry & Joanna Wilson
BERRY,Charles Sex:M 16 Jun 1870 Hudson, NH John W Berry & Edna L
BERRY,Herbert M Sex:M 16 Oct 1872 Hudson, NH John W Berry & Edna S
BERRY,Jennifer L Sex: 16 Dec 1972 Kenneth E Berry & Janice L Nutting
BERRY,Leslie A Sex:F 25 Mar 1962 Frederick C Berry & Mary-Louise Spear
BERRY,Mathew James Sex:M 01 Oct 1981 Norman H Berry & Cheryl Kay Ota
BERRY,Nellie H Sex:F 29 Feb 1868 Hudson, NH John W Berry & Edna S Putnam
BERRY,Nellie H Sex:F 29 Jun 1868 Hudson, NH John W Berry & S Edna
BERRY,Sarah E Sex:F 10 Jul 1864 Hudson, NH John W Berry & Edna S Putnam
BERRY,Sarah S Sex:F 10 Jul 1864 Hudson, NH John W Berry & Esther L
BERRY,Sharon A Sex:F 29 Nov 1954 Robert E Berry & Margaret E MacKenzie
BERTRAM,Dorianne Sex:F 26 Feb 1968 Charles L Bertram & Estelle M Sardelis
BERTSCH,Jason S Sex:M 16 Apr 1971 Theodore F Bertsch & Geraldine Burke
BERUBE,Constance R Sex:F 08 Mar 1949 John C Berube & Lorraine O LeBlanc
BERUBE,Jacqueline P Sex:F 12 Dec 1963 John C Berube & Lorraine O LeBlanc
BERUBE,Jeanne N Sex:F 08 Mar 1951 Norman E Berube & Mary E Simon
BERUBE,Joanne L Sex:F 06 Feb 1950 John C Berube & Lorraine O LeBlanc
BESSETTE,Tammy M Sex:F 11 Mar 1959 Roger J Bessette & Carol A Anderson
BESTON,Dorothy Sex:F (Child #4) 06 Feb 1919 James E Beston (Nashua, NH)
   & Lorilla Annis (Londonderry, NH)
BETTES,Matthew Stockwell Sex:M 30 Jan 1984 Richard S Bettes III
   & Denise S Paquette
BETTEYS,Hannah Sex:F 15 Apr 1773 Hudson, NH Robert Betteys & Hannah

HUDSON,NH BIRTHS

BETTYS,Hannah   Sex:F   15 Apr 1773 Hudson, NH Robert Bettys & Hannah
BETTYS,Sarah   Sex:F   07 Oct 1770 Hudson, NH Robert Bettys & Hannah
BEZA,[Unknown]   Sex:M   (Child #2) 07 Apr 1935 Sam Beza (Greece)
   & Vasila Paleoseliti (Greece)
BIBBER,Earl Vaughn   Sex:M   (Child #1) 18 Jul 1913 Grey L Bibber (Auburn, ME)
   & Nellie M Vaughn (Foxcroft, ME)
BIBBER,[Unknown]   Sex:M   (Child #2) 08 Sep 1914 Guy Sturgis Bibber (Auburn,
   ME) & Nellie M Vaughn (Foxcroft, ME)
BICKFORD,Martin Wallace   Sex:M   (Child #1) 14 Jul 1898 Waldo E Bickford
   (Conway, NH) & Em F Thompson (Londonderry, NH)
BICKFORD,Marvel Arthur   Sex:F   (Child #1) 12 Aug 1896 Frank P Bickford
   (Canada) & Abbie Jewett (North Carolina)
BICKFORD,Mary E   Sex:F   (Child #1) 08 Jul 1896 G K Bickford (Conway, NH)
   & Marian E Jewett (Conway, NH)
BICKFORD,Roger K   Sex:M   03 Jun 1952 Chester W Bickford & Judith Mannel
BICKFORD,Sandra C   Sex:F   09 Feb 1954 Chester W Bickford & Judy Laskorn
BICKNELL,Jeffrey E   Sex:M   13 May 1960 Elbert I Bicknell & Brenda E Truelove
BICKNELL,Robin J   Sex:F   01 May 1957 Robert C Bicknell & Millicent D Belanger
BIELAWA,Megan Marie   Sex:F   31 Aug 1982 Robert J Bielawa & Kathleen M Scully
BIG'NACHE,Joseph N   Sex:M   (Child #8) 25 Jun 1912 Napoleon Big'nache (Canada)
   & Alida Doucette (Canada)
BIGLER,Carol M   Sex:F   30 Dec 1949 Ralph B Bigler & Sylvia H Gould
BIGLER,Louis J   Sex:M   14 Aug 1948 Ralph B Bigler (Potwen, KS)
   & Sylvia H Gould (Swanton, VT)
BILLINGS,Cheryl L   Sex:F   09 Jan 1967 Barry A Billings & Charlene J Winterer
BILLINGS,Lisa Ann   Sex:F   02 Aug 1973 David G Billings & Carol M Hill
BILLINGSLEY,Kelly Lynn   Sex:F   19 Jan 1981 Farris W Billingsley&Cleo E Ratliff
BILLS,Christine M   Sex: 23 Dec 1972 Galen W Bills & Carol A Pelletier
BILLS,Cynthia L   Sex:F   17 May 1974 Galen W Bills & Carol A Pelletier
BILLS,Galen W   Sex:M   (Child #1) 27 Dec 1942 Wallace A Bills (Nashua, NH)
   & Lillian B LaRoss (Warren, VT)
BILLS,Melissa   Sex:F   (Child #3) 18 May 1944 Wallace A Bills (Nashua, NH)
   & Lillian B LaRose (Warren, VT)
BILODEAU,Candace S   Sex:F   08 Oct 1962 Robert L Bilodeau & Ella M Demanche
BILODEAU,Jeremy Roger   Sex:M   16 Nov 1978 Lucien R Bilodeau
   & Suzanne Y Desjardins
BILODEAU,Roberta L   Sex:F   25 Dec 1959 Robert I Bilodeau & Ella M Demanche
BINKS,Patricia Leslye   Sex:F   (Child #1) 13 Jun 1938 Leslie D Binks (Ipswich,
   England) & Gloria Lillian Smith (Hudson, NH)
BINKS,Sheryl L   Sex:F   20 May 1947 Leslie D Binks (Ipswich, England)
   & Gloria L Smith (Hudson, NH)
BIRCHALL,Elliot Wm   Sex:M   (Child #2) 17 Sep 1913 Wm Birchall (Manchester,
   NH) & Grace A Rush (Manchester, NH)
BIRCHALL,Heather April   Sex:F 25 Jan 1984 Russell M Birchall&Veronica A Taylor
BIRD,Alan M   Sex:M   27 Nov 1966 Ronald J Bird & Nancy E Stark
BIRD,Brandon Douglas   Sex:M   02 Dec 1979 Lawrence I Bird & Cecile I Marquis
BIRD,James L   Sex:M   10 Jul 1974 Lawrence I Bird & Cecile I Marquis
BIRD,Karen L   Sex:F   31 Jan 1961 Ronald J Bird & Nancy E Stark
BIRR,Charles B J Jr   Sex:M   20 Feb 1974 Charles A Birr & Mary Ann Kramer
BISBING,Elizabeth Ann   Sex:F   13 Jun 1983 Eddy J Bisbing & Pamela L Burroughs
BISBING,Jonathan David   Sex:M   27 Sep 1981 Eddy J Bisbing & Pamela L Burroughs
BISHOP,Angela M   Sex: 16 Dec 1972 Larry M Bishop & Lenora L Libby
BISHOP,Cynthia L   Sex:F   22 Feb 1975 Thomas F Bishop & Barbara C Zimmermann
BISHOP,Keith A   Sex:M   18 Apr 1967 David G Bishop & Diana L Coburn
BISHOP,Kelly J   Sex:F   23 Oct 1968 David G Bishop & Diana L Coburn
BISHOP,Margaret A   Sex:F   14 Nov 1964 John N Bishop & Shari P Arruda
BISHOP,Thomas William   Sex:M 15 Jun 1984 Thomas F Bishop & Barbara C Zimmerman
BISKADUROS,Leonard S   Sex:M 26 Oct 1963 Manuel Biskaduros&Evelyn R Farrington
BISKADUROS,Matthew A   Sex:M 10 Jan 1966 Manuel Biskaduros&Evelyn R Farrington
BISKADUROS,Melanie A   Sex:F 19 Apr 1968 Manuel Biskaduros&Evelyn R Farrington

HUDSON,NH BIRTHS

BISKADUROS,Nicholas G Sex:M 07 Jul 1974 Manuel Biskaduros&Evelyn R Farrington
BISON,Joseph G   Sex:M   11 Nov 1965 Joseph R Bison & Lorraine M Dean
BISON,Paulette M Sex:F 29 Oct 1966 Joseph R Bison & Lorraine M Dean
BISSON,Brian M   Sex:M 28 Feb 1980 Richard Bisson & Martha L Bergeron
BISSON,Paula G   Sex:F   12 Nov 1968 Joseph R Bisson & Lorraine M Dean
BISSON,Shelley Rae Sex:F 27 Oct 1978 Richard Bisson & Martha L Bergeron
BISSON,Steven R Sex:M 10 Dec 1975 Richard Bisson & Martha L Bergeron
BITGOOD,Robert C Sex: 20 Jul 1972 Robert F Bitgood & Beth E Coon
BIXBY, [Unknown] Sex:M   05 Feb 1893 Ile Bixby (NH) & Mary Christy (Scotland)
BIZIER,James M Jr Sex:M   11 Jul 1971 James M Bizier Sr & Barbara A Poston
BJORK,Stephen P   Sex:M   09 Aug 1968 Paul H Bjork & Kathryn D Ward
BLACK,Nicole Sex:F   18 Nov 1981 Christopher A Black & Nancy Louise Nason
BLACKLEDGE,Jeff J   Sex:M   28 Apr 1957 David J Blackledge & Nancy M Weirich
BLACKLEDGE,Jon J Sex:M   04 Oct 1960 David J Blackledge & Nancy M Weirich
BLACKMAR,Madlyn L   Sex:F   25 Oct 1957 Richard G Blackmar & Grace M Croke
BLAIR,Frederick D Jr Sex:M 29 Apr 1975 Frederick D Blais Sr
   & Christine E Rollins
BLAIR,Kelly J   Sex:F   09 Jul 1969 Robert M Blair & Cynthia R McDonald
BLAIR,Marie A Clara Sex:F (Child #2) 28 Oct 1916 Hudson, NH Phillipe S Blair
   (Canada) & Fedilise Paradis (Wilton, NH)
BLAIS,Andrea Danielle Sex:F 30 Jul 1980 Steven M Blais Sr & Tammy Lynn Dolan
BLAIS,Janna Marie Sex:F 19 Feb 1982 Steven Mark Blais Sr & Tammy Lynn Dolan
BLAIS,Lauri A   Sex:F   18 Jan 1970 Ronald P Blais & Sandra F Lussier
BLAIS,Linda S M   Sex:F 29 Sep 1949 Roland J Blais & Roberta W Harris
BLAIS,Lisa J   Sex:F   08 Jun 1975 Remi Blais & Christine D Loubier
BLAIS,Raymond V   Sex:M   03 Nov 1968 Ronald P Blais & Sandra F Lussier
BLAIS,Stephen W R Jr   Sex:M 10 Nov 1971 Stephen W R Blais & Susan E Whiting
BLAIS,Steven Mark Jr Sex:M   10 Jul 1978 Steven M Blais Sr & Tammy Lynn Dolan
BLAIS,Susan L Sex:F   09 Apr 1955 Roger R Blais & Eleanor M Lathe
BLAIS,Timothy Lathe Sex:M   12 Jul 1979 Steven Mark Blais & Tammy Lynn Dolan
BLAISDELL,Lisa A   Sex:F   02 Sep 1969 Kent M Blaisdell & Catherine B Carney
BLAKE,Beda Amanda   Sex:F (Child #2) 29 Jul 1907 Lyman Blake (Hudson, NH)
   & Nellie M Corey (Newburyport, MA)
BLAKE,Margery L Sex:F   16 Dec 1962 Franklin H Blake & Winona M Witham
BLAKE, [Unknown] Sex:M   14 Feb 1879 Hudson, NH Rosnell Blake (Concord, MA)
   & Mary (Groton, MA)
BLAKELEY,William J Jr Sex:M 05 Jan 1952 William J Blakeley & Mildred A Hebert
BLAKELY,Edward A   Sex:M   14 Oct 1954 William J Blakely & Mildred A Hebert
BLANCE,George C III   Sex:M   03 Feb 1967 George C Blance Jr & Alberta L Pike
BLANCHARD,Amy Ruth   Sex:F   22 Dec 1978 Glenn R Blanchard & Sandra Ann Malette
BLANCHARD,Joel   Sex:M 31 Jul 1767 Hudson, NH & Ruth Blanchard
BLANCHARD,Kevin P   Sex:M 22 Aug 1961 Kenneth P Blanchard & Patricia A Kalil
BLANCHARD,Lee A   Sex:F   18 Jan 1963 Charles L Blanchard & Lois F Reynolds
BLANCHARD,Mark C   Sex:M   28 May 1966 Charles L Blanchard & Lois F Reynolds
BLANCHARD,Michelle A Sex:F 03 Nov 1967 Kenneth P Blanchard & Patricia A Kalil
BLANCHARD,Robert B Sex:M 19 Apr 1960 Sheldon G Blanchard & Beverly F Campbell
BLANCHARD,Susan J   Sex:F   30 Jun 1959 Kenneth P Blanchard & Patricia A Kalil
BLANCHARD,Tod M   Sex:M   03 Jan 1964 Kenneth P Blanchard & Patricia A Kalil
BLANCHARD, [Unknown]   Sex: 31 Mar 1872 Hudson, NH Silas M Blanchard & Elnora
BLANCHETTE,Donald R Sex:M   23 May 1953 Roland J Blanchette & Ann K Cherkes
BLANEY,James E   Sex:M   01 Dec 1958 James O Blaney & Joan McLauchlan
BLANEY,Patricia E   Sex:F   20 Nov 1959 James O Blaney & Joan McLauchlan
BLEAU,Kelly A   Sex:F   08 Jul 1966 Ronald G Bleau & Claudia J Scott
BLEAU,Timothy S   Sex:M   11 Aug 1967 Ronald G Bleau & Claudia J Scott
BLIER,Paul A A   Sex:M   11 Jun 1964 Donald G Blier & Josette M Jeannotte
BLODGET,Abigail   Sex:F 25 Jun 1763 Hudson, NH Joseph Blodget & Dorcas
BLODGET,Asa Sex:M 19 Jan 1755 Hudson, NH Jeremiah Blodget & Miriam
BLODGET,Benaiah   Sex: 03 Mar 1765 Hudson, NH Jeremiah Blodget & Miriam
BLODGET,Dorcas Sex:F   11 Dec 1757 Hudson, NH Joseph Blodget & Dorcas
BLODGET,Hannah   Sex:F 24 Sep 1757 Hudson, NH Jeremiah Blodget & Miriam

HUDSON,NH BIRTHS

```
BLODGET,Isaac     Sex:M  02 May 1762 Hudson, NH Jeremiah Blodget & Miriam
BLODGET,James     Sex:M  15 Dec 1756 Hudson, NH James Blodget & Sarah
BLODGET,Jeremiah  Sex:M  07 May 1751 Hudson, NH Jeremiah Blodget & Miriam
BLODGET,Jerimiah  Sex:M  13 May 1759 Hudson, NH James Blodget & Sarah
BLODGET,Jonathan  Sex:M  29 Jan 1750 Hudson, NH Jonathan Blodget & Sarah
BLODGET,Judah     Sex:M  25 Jun 1763 Hudson, NH Joseph Blodget & Dorcas
BLODGET,Lucy      Sex:F  20 Nov 1775 Hudson, NH Jeremiah Blodget & Lucy
BLODGET,Miriam    Sex:F  15 Feb 1758 Hudson, NH Jonathan Blodget & Hannah
BLODGET,Phinehas  Sex:M  09 Oct 1761 Hudson, NH Joseph Blodget & Dorcas
BLODGET,Rachel    Sex:F  24 Aug 1764 Hudson, NH Jonathan Blodget & Elizabeth
BLODGET,Rebeckah  Sex:F  05 Jan 1754 Hudson, NH Jonathan Blodget & Sarah
BLODGET,Salla     Sex:F  28 Jul 1783 Hudson, NH Phineheas Blodget & Martha
BLODGET,Sarah     Sex:F  16 May 1760 Hudson, NH Jeremiah Blodget & Miriam
BLODGET,Sarah     Sex:F  23 Nov 1754 Hudson, NH James Blodget & Sarah
BLODGETT,Abial    Sex:   20 Feb 1762 Hudson, NH James Blodgett & Sarah
BLODGETT,Abiel    Sex:M  20 Feb 1762 Hudson, NH James Blodgett & Sarah
BLODGETT,Abigail  Sex:F  25 Jun 1763 Hudson, NH Joseph Blodgett&Dorcas Wheeler
BLODGETT,Abner    Sex:M  05 Dec 1802 Hudson, NH Ashael Blodgett & Lois Pollard
BLODGETT,Alfred   Sex:M  21 May 1801 Hudson, NH Jabez Blodgett & Rachel
BLODGETT,Alfred   Sex:M  02 May 1801 Hudson, NH Jabez Blodgett & Rachel
BLODGETT,Asa      Sex:M  22 Aug 1774 Hudson, NH Jonathan Blodgett & Elizabeth
BLODGETT,Asa      Sex:M  02 Aug 1774 Hudson, NH Jonathan Blodgett & Elizebeth
BLODGETT,Asabel   Sex:M  15 Jul 1784 Hudson, NH Asabel Blodgett & Catherine
BLODGETT,Asahael  Sex:M  19 Jun 1755 Hudson, NH Jeremiah Blodgett
    & Miriam Provender
BLODGETT,Ashael   Sex:M  15 May 1784 Hudson, NH Ashael Blodgett
    & Catherine Pollard
BLODGETT,Austin   Sex:M  14 Jun 1861 Hudson, NH Austin Blodgett & Susan
BLODGETT,Austin J Sex:M  14 Jan 1861 Hudson, NH Austin Blodgett & Susan Davis
BLODGETT,Beniah Blodgett Sex:  26 Mar 1801 Hudson, NH Lemuel Colburn
    & Miriam
BLODGETT,Berniah  Sex:   Apr 1804 Hudson, NH Ashael Blodgett & Lois Pollard
BLODGETT,Betsey   Sex:F  14 May 1810 Hudson, NH Ashael Blodgett & Lois Pollard
BLODGETT,Caleb    Sex:M  13 Dec 1793 Hudson, NH Ashael Blodgett
    & Catherine Pollard
BLODGETT,Caleb    Sex:M  30 Dec 1793 Hudson, NH Asabel Blodgett & Catherine
BLODGETT,Cara A   Sex:F  08 Jul 1860 Hudson, NH Warren Blodgett & Elizabeth
BLODGETT,Catherine Sex:F 24 Nov 1782 Hudson, NH Ashael Blodgett
    & Catherine Pollard
BLODGETT,Charles  Sex:M  29 Mar 1808 Hudson, NH Nehemiah Blodgett & Sally
BLODGETT,Clarissa Sex:F  09 May 1798 Hudson, NH Jabez Blodgett & Rachel
BLODGETT,Cora A Sex:F 08 Jul 1860 Hudson, NH Warren Blodgett
    & Elizabeth B Webster
BLODGETT,Daniel C Sex:M  21 Apr 1816 Hudson, NH Jaby Blodgett Jr & Hannah
BLODGETT,Daniel Colburn Sex:M 21 Apr 1816 Hudson, NH Jabez Blodgett Jr&Hannah
BLODGETT,Dolley   Sex:F  04 Jan 1777 Hudson, NH Jonathan Blodgett & Elizebeth
BLODGETT,Dorcas Sex:F 11 Dec 1757 Hudson, NH Joseph Blodgett & Dorcas Wheeler
BLODGETT,Dorothy  Sex:F  18 Feb 1724 Joseph Blodgett & Dorothy Perham
BLODGETT,Ebenezer Sex:M  03 Jan 1720 Joseph Blodgett & Dorothy Perham
BLODGETT,Ebenezer Sex:M  29 Jan 1753 Hudson, NH Jeremiah Blodgett
    & Miriam Provender
BLODGETT,Ebenezer Sex:M  14 Jan 1786 Hudson, NH Ashael Blodgett
    & Catherine Pollard
BLODGETT,Elias    Sex:M  09 Aug 1807 Hudson, NH Asahael Blodgett Jr & Polly
BLODGETT,Elizabeth Sex:F 11 Oct 1789 Hudson, NH Joseph Blodgett&Hannah Davis
BLODGETT,Elizebeth  Sex:F  11 Oct 1789 Hudson, NH Joseph Blodgett & Hannah
BLODGETT,Fanny    Sex:F  07 Feb 1795 Hudson, NH Jabez Blodgett & Rachel
BLODGETT,Fanny    Sex:F  07 Jan 1795 Hudson, NH Jaby Blodgett & Rachel
BLODGETT,Frederic Sex:M  08 Apr 1806 Hudson, NH Jabez Blodgett & Rachel
BLODGETT,Frederick Sex:M 03 Apr 1806 Hudson, NH Jabez Blodgett & Rachel
```

HUDSON,NH BIRTHS

BLODGETT,Hannah   Sex:F   11 Aug 1759 Hudson, NH Jonathan Blodgett & Hannah
BLODGETT,Hannah   Sex:F   24 Sep 1757 Hudson, NH Jeremiah Blodgett
    & Miriam Provender
BLODGETT,Hannah   Sex:F   15 Aug 1787 Hudson, NH Joseph Blodgett & Hannah Davis
BLODGETT,Hannah Jane   Sex:F   24 Feb 1859 Hudson, NH Warren Blodgett
    & Elizabeth B Webster
BLODGETT,Harry D Sex:M 26 Nov 1863 Hudson, NH Augustus G Blodgett
    & Lucy E Chase
BLODGETT,Henry C   Sex:M   26 Nov 1863 Hudson, NH Augustus F Blodgett & Lucy E
BLODGETT,Hiram   Sex:M   08 May 1806 Hudson, NH Nehemiah Blodgett & Sally
BLODGETT,Isaac   Sex:M   02 May 1762 Hudson, NH Jeremiah Blodgett
    & Miriam Provender
BLODGETT,Isaac   Sex:M   12 Aug 1787 Hudson, NH Ashael Blodgett
    & Catherine Pollard
BLODGETT,Jabeth   Sex:M   04 Jan 1767 Hudson, NH Jonahan Blodgett & Elizabeth
BLODGETT,Jabeth   Sex:M   10 Apr 1791 Hudson, NH Jabeth Blodgett & Rachel
BLODGETT,Jabey   Sex: 04 Jan 1767 Hudson, NH Jonathan Blodgett & Elizabeth
BLODGETT,Jabez   Sex:M   10 Apr 1791 Hudson, NH Jabez Blodgett & Rachel
BLODGETT,Jacob   Sex:M   09 Jan 1781 Hudson, NH Jonathan Blodgett & Elizabeth
BLODGETT,James   Sex:M   17 Feb 1734 Joseph Blodgett & Dorothy Perham
BLODGETT,James   Sex:M   15 Dec 1756 Hudson, NH James Blodgett & Sarah
BLODGETT,Jeremiah   Sex:M   20 Jul 1721 Joseph Blodgett & Dorothy Perham
BLODGETT,Jeremiah   Sex:M   09 May 1751 Hudson, NH Jeremiah Blodgett
    & Miriam Provender
BLODGETT,Jeremiah   Sex:M   09 Mar 1806 Hudson, NH Ashael Blodgett
    & Lois Pollard
BLODGETT,Joanna   Sex:F   25 Jul 1793 Hudson, NH Jabez Blodgett & Rachel
BLODGETT,Joanna   Sex:F   28 Jul 1793 Hudson, NH Jaby Blodgett & Rachel
BLODGETT,Jonathan   Sex:M   05 Dec 1730 Joseph Blodgett & Dorothy Perham
BLODGETT,Jonathan   Sex:M   23 Jun 1751 Hudson, NH Jonathan Blodgett & Sarah
BLODGETT,Joseph   Sex:M   09 Feb 1719 Joseph Blodgett & Dorothy Perham
BLODGETT,Joseph   Sex:M   10 Feb 1760 Hudson, NH Joseph Blodgett
    & Dorcas Wheeler
BLODGETT,Joseph   Sex:M   31 Mar 1786 Hudson, NH Joseph Blodgett & Hannah Davis
BLODGETT,Joseph S   Sex:M   30 Sep 1813 Hudson, NH Joseph Blodgett & Sarah
BLODGETT,Joseph Spalding   Sex:M   30 Sep 1813 Hudson, NH Joseph Blodgett
    & Sarah Spalding
BLODGETT,Judah   Sex:M   25 Jun 1763 Hudson, NH Joseph Blodgett
    & Dorcas Wheeler
BLODGETT,Laura P Sex:F 10 Oct 1861 Hudson, NH Augustus G Blodgett
    & Lucy E Chase
BLODGETT,Lauren   Sex:F   10 Oct 1861 Hudson, NH Augustus Blodgett & Lucy
BLODGETT,Lois   Sex:F   17 Feb 1792 Hudson, NH Ashael Blodgett
    & Catherine Pollard
BLODGETT,Louis   Sex:F   17 Feb 1792 Hudson, NH Asabel Blodgett & Catherine
BLODGETT,Lucinda Sex:F   18 Nov 1800 Hudson, NH Ashael Blodgett & Lois Pollard
BLODGETT,Lucy   Sex:F   20 Nov 1775 Hudson, NH Jeremiah Blodgett Jr & Lucy
BLODGETT,Miriam   Sex:F   15 Feb 1758 Hudson, NH Jonathan Blodgett & Hannah
BLODGETT,Nabbey   Sex:F   10 Nov 1789 Hudson, NH Jabeth Blodgett & Rachel
BLODGETT,Nabby Winn   Sex: 10 Nov 1789 Hudson, NH Jabez Blodgett & Rachel
BLODGETT,Nathan   Sex:M   22 Feb 1800 Hudson, NH Jabez Blodgett & Rachel
BLODGETT,Nehemiah Sex:M   13 Sep 1782 Hudson, NH Jonathan Blodgett & Elizabeth
BLODGETT,Nehemiah Sex:M   19 Sep 1782 Hudson, NH Jonathan Blodgett & Elizebeth
BLODGETT,Peniah   Sex: 03 Mar 1765 Hudson, NH Jeremiah Blodgett
    & Miriam Provencher
BLODGETT,Persis   Sex: 31 May 1803 Hudson, NH Jabez Blodgett & Rachel
BLODGETT,Phineas Wheeler   Sex:M   09 Oct 1761 Hudson, NH Joseph Blodgett
    & Dorcas Wheeler
BLODGETT,Polly Sex: 20 Dec 1781 Hudson, NH Phineas Blodgett & Martha Hamblett
BLODGETT,Rachel   Sex:F   24 Aug 1764 Hudson, NH Jonathan Blodgett & Elizabeth

HUDSON, NH BIRTHS

BLODGETT,Rachel   Sex:F   26 Aug 1788 Hudson, NH Jabez Blodgett & Rachel
BLODGETT,Rebecca   Sex:F   03 Feb 1728 Joseph Blodgett & Dorothy Perham
BLODGETT,Rebecca   Sex:F   03 Jan 1754 Hudson, NH Jonathan Blodgett & Sarah
BLODGETT,Rufus   Sex:M   12 Nov 1798 Hudson, NH Ashael Blodgett & Lois Pollard
BLODGETT,Salley   Sex:F   30 Sep 1805 Hudson, NH Jabez Blodgett & Rachel
BLODGETT,Sally   Sex:F   04 Jan 1777 Hudson, NH Jonathan Blodgett & Elizabeth
BLODGETT,Sally Sex:F 28 Jul 1783 Hudson, NH Phineas Blodgett
  & Martha Hamblett
BLODGETT,Sally   Sex:F   30 Sep 1805 Hudson, NH Jabez Blodgett & Rachel
BLODGETT,Sarah   Sex:F   16 May 1760 Hudson, NH Jeremiah Blodgett
  & Miriam Provencher
BLODGETT,Sarah   Sex:F   23 Nov 1754 Hudson, NH James Blodgett & Sarah
BLODGETT,Sarah   Sex:F   02 Dec 1771 Hudson, NH Joseph Blodgett & Sarah Cross
BLODGETT,Sarah   Sex:F   25 Oct 1791 Hudson, NH Joseph Blodgett & Hannah Davis
BLODGETT,Sarah L   Sex:F   25 Sep 1815 Hudson, NH Joseph Blodgett & Sarah
BLODGETT,Sarah Louisa Sex:F 25 Sep 1815 Hudson, NH Joseph Blodgett
  & Sarah Spalding
BLODGETT,Sibbel   Sex:F   13 Nov 1789 Hudson, NH Asabel Blodgett & Catherine
BLODGETT,Sophia   Sex:F   18 Feb 1797 Hudson, NH Jabez Blodgett & Rachel
BLODGETT,Susan   Sex:F   29 Apr 1812 Hudson, NH Jabez Blodgett & Rachel
BLODGETT,Sybel   Sex:F   13 Nov 1789 Hudson, NH Ashael Blodgett
  & Catherine Pollard
BLODGETT,Warren   Sex:M   25 Dec 1809 Hudson, NH Jabez Blodgett & Rachel
BLODGETT,William   Sex:M   03 Aug 1807 Hudson, NH Jabez Blodgett & Rachel
BLODGETT,Zerysia   Sex: 13 May 1759 Hudson, NH James Blodgett & Sarah
BLOGGIT,James   Sex:M   17 Feb 1834 Hudson, NH Joseph Bloggit & Dorrity
BLOOD,Charles F Jr Sex:M 20 Oct 1958 Charles F Blood & Barbara L Freeman
BLOOMBERG,Sarah Beth Sex:F 25 Nov 1984 Neil R Bloomberg & Patricia Ann Tarney
BLOW,Ronald Seward Sex:M (Child #1) 11 Jun 1941 Seward J Blow (New York)
  & Theresa J Gagne (Hudson, NH)
BOETTE,Mark Robert   Sex:M 05 Dec 1978 Jonathan B Boette & Ingrid N Peiser
BOGGIA,John Anthony III Sex:M 28 Nov 1979 John A Boggia & Maryann Swiderski
BOILARD,Alan H   Sex:M   26 Dec 1962 Gerald R Boilard & Patricia A Loraine
BOILARD,Brenda L   Sex:F   18 Jun 1958 Richard G Boilard & Jacqueline E Tessier
BOILARD,Cathleen E Sex:F 29 May 1956 Gerald R Boilard & Patricia A Loraine
BOILARD,Corey Dearborn Sex:M 12 Jul 1978 Jamie O Boilard & Anne C Dearborn
BOILARD,Erryn Ashley   Sex:F 03 Jan 1983 Michael R Boilard & Norma Lee Rock
BOILARD,Jamie O   Sex:M   27 Feb 1959 Oswald D Boilard & Margaret E Seaver
BOILARD,John R   Sex:M   27 Feb 1959 Oswald D Boilard & Margaret E Seaver
BOILARD,Kerri M   Sex:F   31 Mar 1978 Michael R Boilard & Norma Lee Rock
BOILARD,Leonard C Sex:M   30 Jan 1963 Oswald D Boilard & Margaret E Seaver
BOILARD,Leonard F Sex:M   (Child #7) 22 Dec 1944 Oswald Boilard (Nashua, NH)
  & Adrienne Marquis (Nashua, NH)
BOILARD,Mark L   Sex:M   19 Aug 1962 Richard G Boilard & Jacqueline E Tessier
BOILARD,Nathalie J Sex:F (Child #6) 07 Oct 1942 Oswald Boilard (Nashua, NH)
  & Adrienne Marquis (Nashua, NH)
BOILARD,Richard G Jr Sex:M 14 Sep 1959 Richard G Boilard
  & Jacqueline E Tessier
BOILARD,Stephen D   Sex:M 22 Jul 1960 Oswald D Boilard & Margaret E Seaver
BOILARD,Tara C   Sex: 04 May 1973 Michael R Boilard & Norma L Rock
BOILARD,Teresa L   Sex:F   01 Apr 1958 Gerald R Boilard & Patricia A Loraine
BOISJOLY,Elissa Sue Sex:F 31 Aug 1980 Richard T Boisjoly & Karen J Dureault
BOISVERT,Daniel R Sex:M   13 Feb 1971 Ronald R Boisvert & Pauline R St Cyr
BOISVERT,David R   Sex:M   13 May 1969 Ronald R Boisvert & Pauline R St Cyr
BOISVERT,Tammy L   Sex:F   07 Aug 1966 Raymond E Boisvert & Clara B Trimble
BOIVIN,Leslie M   Sex:F   07 May 1969 Richard J Boivin & Carmen E Parra
BOKOUSKY,David Lee Jr   Sex:M 06 Apr 1978 David L Bokousky & Patricia A Rock
BOLA,Charles A   Sex:M   (Child #5) 11 Jun 1897 Charles Albert Bola (New York)
  & Ellen Couture (Canada)
BOLDUC,Darlene   Sex:F   20 Sep 1964 Lionel R Bolduc & Maureen C O'Brien

HUDSON,NH BIRTHS

BOLDUC,Lisa M   Sex:F   29 Mar 1966 Raymond W Bolduc & Eva R Kierstead
BOLDUC,Robert   Sex:M   21 May 1968 Lionel R Bolduc & Maureen C O'Brien
BOLDUC,Steve C   Sex:M   04 Nov 1974 Camil L Bolduc & Pauline L Gremier
BOLES,Lydia B   Sex:F   13 Jan 1886 Gilbert E Boles & Lizzie J
BOLTON,Daniel J Sex:M   24 May 1961 Nicholas J Bolton & Cornelia A Cronin
BOMAN,Calvin   Sex:M   03 Apr 1825 Hudson, NH John Boman & Lydia
BOMAN,Hiram   Sex:M   25 Jul 1818 Hudson, NH John Boman & Lydia
BOMAN,John   Sex:M   29 Mar 1837 Hudson, NH John Boman & Lydia
BOMAN,Lucy C   Sex:F   18 Apr 1823 Hudson, NH John Boman & Lydia
BOMAN,Sarah   Sex:F   21 Jul 1827 Hudson, NH John Boman & Lydia
BONA,Lindsey Kate   Sex:F 04 Jun 1984 Steven W Bona & Barbara Mae Anthony
BONA,Staci M   Sex:F   28 Apr 1980 Steven W Bona & Barbara M Anthony
BOND,Rocky R   Sex:M   27 Apr 1957 Rufus J Bond & Pearl E Smith
BONNETTE,Dennis A   Sex:M   15 Feb 1950 David F Bonnette & Leah E Savage
BONNETTE,Kimberly S Sex:F   04 Jan 1976 Allen P Bonnette & Linda J Kempton
BONNETTE,Marie M A   Sex:F   (Child #4) 27 May 1902 Frank Bonnette (Canada)
    & Rose Archambault (Canada)
BONNETTE,Patricia A Sex:F 19 Mar 1952 Philip H Bonnette & Jeannette R Landry
BONOLLO,Joseph L   Sex:M   17 Jun 1969 Leo E Bonollo & Deborah J Carlson
BONOLLO,Michael J Sex:M   30 Jul 1967 Lee E Bonollo & Deborah J Carlson
BOOLBA,Charles P W Sex:M   22 Apr 1963 Peter M Boolba & Jane E Ness
BOONE,Kristen A   Sex:F   07 Jan 1967 Daniel A Boone & Priscilla C Woodbury
BOOSKA,Mark E   Sex:M   02 Jul 1959 Emery P Booska & Margaret T Hartnett
BOOSKA,Mary A   Sex:F   21 Aug 1960 Emery P Booska & Margaret T Hartnett
BOOSKA,Paul M   Sex:M   15 Jul 1963 Emery P Booska & Margaret T Hartnett
BORAK,Gary P   Sex:M   (Child #1) 05 Aug 1944 Alphonse P Borak (Nashua, NH)
    & Phyllis E Robinson (Londonderry, NH)
BORBEAU,Paul J O   Sex:M   (Child #1) 22 Nov 1946 Oscar J Borbeau (Canada)
    & Laurianne A Fleury (Nashua, NH)
BORDEAU,Leslie L   Sex:F   29 Nov 1958 Wallace W Bordeau & Bette A Bellisle
BORDEN,Wayne E   Sex:M   23 Jul 1954 Edward R Borden & Phyllis J Beach
BORGHI,Anthony R   Sex:M   06 Apr 1947 Raymond Borghi (Nashua, NH)
    & Beatrice A Calawa (Nashua, NH)
BORNEMAN,Dorothy L Sex:F   (Child #1) 09 Jan 1943 Ernest T Borneman
    (Townsend, MA) & Ann D Markarian (Watertown, MA)
BORNEMAN,Frank P   Sex:M   01 Jun 1968 James W Borneman & Louise E Dobens
BORNSTEIN,Lise   Sex:F   29 Jul 1952 Joseph Bornstein & Clara L Ferguson
BORUNDON,Marguerite Alice Sex:F (Child #1) 10 May 1914 George Borundon
    (Massachusetts) & Yvonne Gagnon (New Hampshire)
BOSKA,Alan D   Sex:M L 20 Jul 1947 Aleck Boska (Hudson, NH)
    & Jeanne C Gagnon (Nashua, NH)
BOSKA,Elaine   Sex:F   09 Jul 1950 Charles R Boska & Dorothy J Ford
BOSKA,Gary   Sex:M   02 Oct 1951 Charles R Boska & Dorothy J Ford
BOSKA,Genice   Sex:F   (Child #1) 09 May 1920 John Boska (Russia)
    & Veronica Glatnik (Russia)
BOSKA,John S   Sex:M   22 Feb 1971 Stanley J Boska & Judith F Fisk
BOSKA,Kathleen H   Sex:F   31 Mar 1955 Frank Boska & Marie-Blanche Gagnon
BOSKA,Scott K   Sex:M   24 May 1957 Frank Boska & Marie-Blanche Gagnon
BOSKA,Stanley   Sex:M   (Child #2) 16 Mar 1927 John Boska (Russia)
    & Veronica Zlotnik (Russia)
BOSKA,Stephanie A Sex:F   02 Jun 1967 Stanley J Boska & Judith F Fisk
BOSKA,William N   Sex:M   22 Mar 1951 Aleck Boska & Jeanne K Gagnon
BOSLEY,Adam Arthur Sex:M   21 Aug 1984 Arthur Bruce Bosley & Anne Sheldon
BOSSE,Lionel   Sex:M   (Child #3) 16 Mar 1924 Hector Bosse (Nashua, NH)
    & Julia Jackson (Nashua, NH)
BOSSIE,Daniel A   Sex:M   16 Feb 1960 Roland A Bossie, Jr & Irene E Garside
BOSSIE,Frederick R Sex:M   04 Jan 1958 Roland A Bossie, Jr & Irene E Garside
BOSSIE,JoAnn   Sex:F   10 Dec 1958 Roland A Bossie, Jr & Irene F Garside
BOSSIE,John A   Sex:M   04 Jan 1958 Roland A Bossie, Jr & Irene E Garside
BOSSIE,Rhonda L   Sex:F   29 Mar 1957 Roland A Bossie, Jr & Irene E Garside

HUDSON,NH BIRTHS

BOSTOCK,Randall M   Sex:M   06 Nov 1964 Gordon Bostock & Martha L Gravelle
BOTELHO,Matthew B   Sex:M   30 Dec 1976 David B Botelho & Christine S Raposa
BOTHWICK,Harold M III Sex:M 06 May 1979 Harold M Bothwick Jr
  & Cynthia A Hardy
BOTHWICK,Kevin A   Sex:M   15 Feb 1968 Harold M Bothwick & Helen A Kirwan
BOTT,Erik R   Sex:M   16 Sep 1976 Raymond J Bott Jr & Sharon E Forestall
BOUCHARD,Kathleen A   Sex:F   18 Jun 1966 Richard J Bouchard & Laura I Brady
BOUCHARD,Richard J Jr   Sex:M   16 May 1965 Richard J Bouchard & Laura I Brady
BOUCHER,Adam P   Sex:M   23 Sep 1974 Thomas A Boucher & Anne M Devlin
BOUCHER,Alexandrina   Sex:F   (Child #7) 12 Nov 1919 Antoine Boucher (Canada)
  & Alexandrina LeClair (Winchendon, MA)
BOUCHER,Bruce A   Sex:M   22 May 1955 Roland P Boucher & Lucille H Stevens
BOUCHER,Christopher J   Sex:M   18 Mar 1979 Lucien A Boucher & Nancy Lee Wilson
BOUCHER,Daniel B   Sex:M   01 Feb 1950 Gerard J Boucher & Rose A Bouvier
BOUCHER,Daniel R   Sex:M   17 May 1965 Lionel R Boucher & Dorothy A Polak
BOUCHER,David R   Sex:M   14 Jan 1949 Romeo A Boucher & Lillian Ledger
BOUCHER,Dawna M   Sex:F   15 May 1972 Robert R Boucher & Marie A St Jacques
BOUCHER,Deanna M   Sex:F   26 Dec 1963 Gerald M Boucher & Kathleen E O'Sulliva
BOUCHER,Deborah A   Sex:F   14 Sep 1957 Roland P Boucher & Lucille H Stevens
BOUCHER,Denise L   Sex:F   26 Feb 1971 Joseph A Boucher & Sherry L Fairfield
BOUCHER,Dennis E   Sex:M   20 Mar 1950 Roger L Boucher & Esther B Daneault
BOUCHER,Diane L   Sex:F   03 Feb 1953 Roger L Boucher & Esther B Daneault
BOUCHER,Eric Andrew   Sex:M   28 Aug 1981 Andrew G Boucher & Louise Ann Barnaby
BOUCHER,Eric P   Sex:M   30 Jun 1962 Lionel R Boucher & Dorothy A Polak
BOUCHER,Gerald M   Sex:M   12 Apr 1955 Roger L Boucher & Esther B Daneault
BOUCHER,Gerald M II   Sex:M   13 Mar 1965 Gerald M Boucher
  & Kathleen E O'Sullivan
BOUCHER,Geraldine G   Sex:F   (Child #2) 07 Dec 1938 Gerard Joseph Boucher
  (Nashua, NH) & Rose Alma Bouvier (Ste Theod, Canada)
BOUCHER,Glen A   Sex:M   21 May 1969 Henri P Boucher & Joanne M Radziwill
BOUCHER,James A   Sex:M   13 Sep 1965 Gerald Boucher & Jean R Gagnon
BOUCHER,Jason S   Sex:M   04 Oct 1973 Robert R Boucher & Marie A St Jacques
BOUCHER,Jeremiah Lee   Sex:M   30 May 1981 Dana Lee Boucher & Nita Gay Tallent
BOUCHER,Jessica Lynn   Sex:F   31 Jul 1979 Gerald A Boucher & Donna M Blaney
BOUCHER,Joseph   Sex:M   (Child #2) 06 Jul 1946 Roger L Boucher (Nashua, NH)
  & Esther B Daneault (Allenstown, NH)
BOUCHER,Joseph Gerald   Sex:M   (Child #3) 15 Dec 1928 Armand Boucher (Canada)
  & Marie Anne Charest (Canada)
BOUCHER,Laurie A   Sex:F   11 Jul 1967 Stephen R Boucher & Claire R Chasse
BOUCHER,Lionel D   Sex:M   12 Apr 1961 Lionel R Boucher & Dorothy A Polak
BOUCHER,Lisa A   Sex:F   06 Sep 1961 Gerald Boucher & Jean R Gagnon
BOUCHER,Lisa Jeanne   Sex:F   08 Mar 1983 Andrew G Boucher & Louise Ann Barnaby
BOUCHER,M C Rachael   Sex:F   (Child #7) 11 Mar 1938 Armand Boucher (Canada)
  & Marie Anne Charest (Canada)
BOUCHER,Marie Annette Floren   Sex:F   (Child #6) 29 Jul 1935 Armand Boucher
  (Canada) & Marie Anna Charest (Canada)
BOUCHER,Marie Jeanette Fleur   Sex:F   (Child #5) 29 Jul 1935 Armand Boucher
  (Canada) & Marie Anna Charest (Canada)
BOUCHER,Mary E   Sex:F   (Child #2) 31 May 1944 Joseph M Boucher (Mon Ctr, VT)
  & Goldie G Ward (Sheldon, VT)
BOUCHER,Matthew R   Sex:M   16 Jul 1974 Normand A Boucher & Susan M Caron
BOUCHER,Michael D   Sex:M   23 Nov 1956 Gerald Boucher & Jean R Gagnon
BOUCHER,Michael D   Sex:M   16 Nov 1965 Norman R Boucher & Nancy A Dery
BOUCHER,Michael Gerald Sex:M   03 Jun 1984 Gerald M Boucher & Kathleen J Tocci
BOUCHER,Michael S   Sex:M   21 Mar 1966 Stephen R Boucher & Claire R Chasse
BOUCHER,Michele L   Sex:F   27 Dec 1957 Ronald P Boucher & Betty M Cudworth
BOUCHER,Michelle K   Sex:F   09 Aug 1976 Normand A Boucher & Susan Maria Caron
BOUCHER,Nanette S   Sex:F   16 Jul 1956 Lionel R Boucher & Dorothy A Polak
BOUCHER,Nola D   Sex:F   (Child #5) 21 May 1944 Richard A Boucher (Freemont,
  NH) & Claudia R Parker (Hudson, NH)

HUDSON,NH BIRTHS

BOUCHER,Paul R   Sex:M   (Child #1) 11 Feb 1945 Roger L Boucher (Nashua, NH)
  & Esther B Daneault (Allenstown, MA)
BOUCHER,Paul Robert   Sex:M   (Child #9) 22 Jun 1924 Antoine Boucher (Canada)
  & Alex Leclair (Washington, DC)
BOUCHER,Rachel Annette   Sex:F   (Child #5) 25 Jun 1928 Arthur Boucher (Canada)
  & Eva Tremblay (Nashua, NH)
BOUCHER,Robert A   Sex:M   30 Oct 1962 Roger M Boucher & Virginia L Duncklee
BOUCHER,Robert Lionel   Sex:M   (Child #4) 09 Feb 1931 Armand Boucher (Canada)
  & Marie Anna Charest (Canada)
BOUCHER,Scott D   Sex:M   07 Dec 1967 Norman R Boucher & Nancy A Dery
BOUCHER,Scott R   Sex:M   11 Mar 1969 Thomas A Boucher & Anne M Devlin
BOUCHER,Stephanie L   Sex:F   01 Apr 1978 Dennis E Boucher & Dianna R Thornton
BOUCHER,Stephen C   Sex:M   28 Aug 1957 Roger M Boucher & Virginia L Duncklee
BOUCHER,Stephen R   Sex:M   (Child #3) 07 Nov 1940 Richard A Boucher (Freemont,
  NH) & Claudia E Parker (Hudson, NH)
BOUCHER,Susan E   Sex:F   11 Feb 1963 Wilfred H Boucher & Marjorie M Miller
BOUCHER,Todd T   Sex:M   04 Jul 1965 Thomas A Boucher & Anne M Devlin
BOUCHER,Wilfred Howard   Sex:M   (Child #2) 23 May 1934 Richard Boucher
  (Freemont, NH) & Claudia Parker (Hudson, NH)
BOUCHER, [Unknown]   Sex:F   (Child #8) 27 Nov 1921 Antoine Boucher (Canada)
  & Alexandena Leclaire (Washington, D C)
BOUDREAU,Denise M   Sex:F   21 Jun 1971 Norman R Boudreau & Carol A Ducharme
BOUFFARD,Cynthia A   Sex:F   28 Apr 1966 Ronald N Bouffard & Marianne V Cook
BOUFFARD,Marie L   Sex:F   22 Mar 1969 George E Bouffard Jr & Gloria A LaChance
BOUFFARD,Michael R   Sex:M   07 Nov 1960 Paul E Bouffard & Claire L Dube
BOUFFARD,Monique G   Sex:F   26 Apr 1965 George E Bouffard,Jr & Gloria A LaChance
BOULANGER,Allison B   Sex:F   05 Jan 1970 William G Boulanger & Lizbeth P Caron
BOULANGER,Kenneth Albert   Sex:M   (Child #3) 28 Mar 1937 Joseph Boulanger
  (Salem, MA) & Mildred B Parker (Nottingham, NH)
BOULANGER,Wesley Parker   Sex:M   (Child #2) 03 Dec 1934 Joseph Boulanger
  (Salem, MA) & Mildred Parker (Nottingham, NH)
BOULARD,Jessica Sue   Sex:F   29 Jun 1979 Kevin J Boulard & Diane C Maynard
BOULAY,Beth Ann M   Sex:F   27 Feb 1967 Edmond A Boulay & Pauline J Gosler
BOULAY,Nancy L   Sex:F   14 Sep 1970 Edmond A Boulay & Pauline J Gosler
BOULAY,Scott G   Sex:M   17 Mar 1969 Edmond A Boulay & Pauline J Gosler
BOULETTE,Richard W   Sex:M   11 May 1968 Richard E Boulette & Linda L Alexander
BOULETTE,Wilbert O   Sex:M   05 Mar 1970 David O Boulette & Anne F Boutilier
BOULEY,Brya L   Sex:F   23 Dec 1974 Kevin R Bouley & Barbara A Curran
BOULEY,Carol L   Sex:F   25 Mar 1959 Glenn E Bouley & Leanne I Mercier
BOULEY,Eva L   Sex:F   15 Sep 1953 William R Bouley & Eva L Ramsey
BOULEY,Glenn J   Sex:M   29 Dec 1960 Glenn E Bouley & Leanne I Mercier
BOULEY,Jason R   Sex:M   05 Dec 1968 Stephen A Bouley & Theresa A Dube
BOULEY,Jerome Gregory   Sex:M   (Child #1) 23 Mar 1933   & Irene E Bouley
  (Nashua, NH)
BOULEY,John R Jr   Sex:M   06 Aug 1958 John R Bouley & Marion A Shepherd
BOULEY,Kevin R   Sex:M   10 Mar 1955 Philip R Bouley & Marguerita L Sagrue
BOULEY,Lucille G   Sex:F   (Child #1) 26 May 1940 Emile Bouley (Nashua, NH)
  & Yvonne Pelletier (Nashua, NH)
BOULEY,M Rose Jennette   Sex:F   (Child #2) 07 Apr 1934   & Irene Bouley
  (Nashua, NH)
BOULEY,Maureen E   Sex:F   05 Jan 1961 Philip R Bouley & Marguerita L Sagrue
BOULEY,Patricia A   Sex:F   04 Mar 1958 Glenn E Bouley & Leanne I Mercier
BOULEY,Paul A   Sex:M   12 Mar 1960 John R Bouley, Sr & Marion A Shepherd
BOULEY,Rachel Elizabeth   Sex:F   20 Mar 1985 Dennis R Bouley
  & Angela Beth Elliott
BOULEY,Renee Tatum   Sex:F   26 May 1983 Dennis R Bouley & Angela Beth Elliott
BOULEY,Richard A   Sex:M   02 Jan 1954 Raymond Bouley & Priscilla Kapiski
BOULEY,Richard E   Sex:M   31 May 1972 Richard A Bouley & Nancy J Campbell
BOULEY,Robin L   Sex:F   16 Jan 1962 John R Bouley, Sr & Marion A Shepherd
BOULEY,Sarah M   Sex:F   03 Jun 1977 David E Bouley & Michele E Wilmot

HUDSON,NH BIRTHS

BOULEY,Shirley A   Sex:F   09 Apr 1948 Raymond R Bouley (Nashua, NH)
  & Priscilla Kapisky (Nashua, NH)
BOULEY,Stephen A   Sex:M   (Child #4) 06 Sep 1945 Raymond R Bouley (Nashua, NH)
  & Priscilla C Kapisky (Nashua, NH)
BOULEY,Susan M   Sex:F   16 Dec 1962 Glenn E Bouley & Leanne I Mercier
BOULEY,Thomas P Jr   Sex:M   26 Jan 1970 Thomas P Bouley & Joan T Daniels
BOULEY,Virginia Carol   Sex:F   (Child #3) 02 Nov 1941 Raymond R Bouley
  (Nashua, NH) & Priscilla Kajesky (Nashua, NH)
BOULEY,William R Jr   Sex:M   14 Mar 1955 William R Bouley & Eva L Ramsey
BOURASSA,George Lewis   Sex:M   (Child #2) 02 Apr 1899 Thomas Bourassa (Canada)
  & Jane Pranes (Canada)
BOURASSA,Melissa Renee Sex:F 28 Jul 1979 Roger E Bourassa & Ellen Mary Verley
BOURASSA,Michele S   Sex:F   27 Dec 1955 Robert A Bourassa & Marie L Rousseau
BOURASSA,Nicholas Raymond   Sex:M   10 Jan 1981 Roger E Bourassa Sr
  & Ellen Mary Verley
BOURBEAU,James R   Sex:M   02 Jan 1961 Robert E Bourbeau & Elaine B Carr
BOURDEAU,Kristine Ann   Sex:F   26 Feb 1980 Ronald D Bourdeau & Joyce H Sojka
BOURDON,Arthur Louis   Sex:M   (Child #4) 31 Dec 1921 George Bourdon
  (Massachusetts) & Eva Gagnon (New Hampshire)
BOURDON,Brian J   Sex:M   10 Sep 1969 James A Bourdon & Linda D Lavallee
BOURDON,Charles   Sex:M   (Child #2) 16 Apr 1919 Charles Bourdon
  (Massachusetts) & Roseanna Gagnon (New Hampshire)
BOURDON,Dianne J   Sex:F   (Child #2) 12 Oct 1943 James R Bourdon (Medford, MA)
  & Claire A Richard (St Arsene, Canada)
BOURDON,James A   Sex:M   19 Oct 1948 Arthur L Bourdon (Litchfield, NH)
  & Mildred L Law (Hooksett, NH)
BOURDON,Jeannette C   Sex:F   (Child #1) 03 Dec 1921 Charles Bourdon
  (Massachusetts) & Rose Gagnon (New Hampshire)
BOURDON,John E   Sex:M   17 Sep 1968 James A Bourdon & Linda D Lavallee
BOURDON,Jos G L   Sex:M   (Child #2) 03 Mar 1916 Hudson, NH George Bourdon
  (Winchester, MA) & Ivonne Gagnon (Nashua, NH)
BOURDON,Judith M   Sex:F   (Child #2) 05 Mar 1946 Arthur L Bourdon (Litchfield,
  NH) & Mildred L Law (Hooksett, NH)
BOURDON,Louis Edward   Sex:M   (Child #8) 22 Jan 1934 Charles Bourdon (Woburn,
  MA) & Rose Gagnon (Nashua, NH)
BOURDON,Marie Agathe Rita   Sex:F   (Child #5) 31 Jan 1924 Charles Bourdon
  (Massachusetts) & Rose Anna Gagnon (New Hampshire)
BOURDON,Robert   Sex:M   (Child #3) 24 Sep 1919 George Bourdon (Massachusetts)
  & Yvonne Gagnon (New Hampshire)
BOURGAULT,Bryan Thomas   Sex:M   16 May 1983 Thomas P Bourgault
  & Linda M Sunderland
BOURGEOIS,Justin Michael Sex:M 14 May 1985 Roland J Bourgeois
  & Sandra L Lawruk
BOURGEOIS,Wanda G   Sex:F   22 Nov 1953 John B Bourgeois, Jr & Barbara M Holt
BOUTHILLIER,Christine A Sex:F 31 Jan 1970 Roger G Bouthillier
  & Donna M Lavery
BOUTHILLIER,Mark R   Sex:M   20 Mar 1968 Roger G Bouthillier & Donna M Lavery
BOUTILIER,Bruce E   Sex:M   18 Jun 1965 Gaylord Boutilier & Lois Rudderow
BOUTILIER,Jean L   Sex:F   09 Jun 1956 Gordon W Boutilier & Frances M Sylvester
BOUTILIER,Joanne L   Sex:F   23 Oct 1953 Gordon W Boutilier
  & Frances M Sylvester
BOUTIN,Irene S   Sex:F   14 Nov 1953 Jean B Boutin & Mary A Gill
BOUTIN,James L   Sex:M   17 Nov 1954 Jean B Boutin & Mary A Gill
BOUTIN,Kimberly M   Sex:F   08 Jun 1974 Girard J Boutin & Bonnie Sue Bell
BOUTIN,Rose E   Sex:F   26 Nov 1952 Jean B Boutin & Mary A Gill
BOUTWELL,Daniel J   Sex:M   19 Mar 1961 Richard A Boutwell & Janice B Silveira
BOUTWELL,Douglas A   Sex:M   14 Nov 1962 Richard A Boutwell & Janice Silveira
BOUVIER,Elizabeth E   Sex:F   29 Jan 1968 Robert N Bouvier & Ellen M Lotti
BOWDEN,Dale M   Sex:M   20 Mar 1963 Donald F Bowden, Jr & Janet M Meuse
BOWDEN,Leonard A   Sex:M   03 Dec 1961 Donald F Bowden, Jr & Janet M Meuse

HUDSON,NH BIRTHS

BOWDEN,Sherry L   Sex:F   18 Oct 1964 Donald F Bowden, Jr & Janet M Meuse
BOWEN,Charles W   Sex:M   24 Jan 1965 Richard A Bowen & Ruth-Anne M Quaglia
BOWEN,Keith D   Sex: 06 Apr 1973 Thomas H Bowen & Diane L Boucher
BOWEN,William D   Sex:M   07 Nov 1966 Richard A Bowen & Ruth A Quaglia
BOWERSOX,Brian Patrick Sex:M 12 Mar 1982 George L Bowersox & Jean Anne Madden
BOWERSOX,Kaitlyn Elizabeth Sex:F 03 Apr 1985 George L Bowersox
   & Jean Anne Madden
BOWERSOX,Kevin G   Sex:M   23 Jun 1980 George L Bowersox Jr & Jean Anne Madden
BOWLBY,Christopher P   Sex:M   29 Feb 1976 Richard A Bowlby & Louise E Brodeur
BOWMAN,Alfred   Sex:M   25 Nov 1814 Hudson, NH John Bowman & Lydia
BOWMAN,Calvin   Sex:M   23 Apr 1825 Hudson, NH John Bowman & Lydia
BOWMAN,Hiram   Sex:M   25 Jul 1818 Hudson, NH John Bowman & Lydia
BOWMAN,John   Sex:M   29 Mar 1837 Hudson, NH John Bowman & Lydia
BOWMAN,Joyce Lillian   Sex:F   (Child #1) 14 Aug 1941 Francis A Bowman
   (Winthrop, MA) & Christine Baines (Manchester, NH)
BOWMAN,Lucy Cole   Sex:F   18 Mar 1823 Hudson, NH John Bowman & Lydia
BOWMAN,Sarah   Sex:F   21 Jul 1827 Hudson, NH John Bowman & Lydia
BOYD,Belinda M   Sex:F   15 May 1965 John M Boyd & Marie Walsh
BOYER,Amy L   Sex:F   13 Mar 1976 Kenneth R Boyer & Donna Marie McIntyre
BOYER,Dennis G   Sex:M   01 Sep 1951 Joseph J Boyer & Bertha M Mooney
BOYER,Edgar Jr   Sex:M   (Child #1) 27 May 1927 Edgar Boyer (Nashua, NH)
   & Mildred Nutting (Waterville, ME)
BOYER,George   Sex:M   (Child #11) 27 Nov 1938 Joseph Edward Boyer (Hudson, NH)
   & Albina Fournier (Taftville, CT)
BOYER,Karl J   Sex:M   30 Oct 1960 Donald R Boyer & Mona J Beach
BOYER,Leeann M   Sex: 15 Aug 1972 Donald A Boyer & Nancy L Daigle
BOYER,Mary J L   Sex:F   (Child #10) 27 Jan 1940 Joseph E Boyer (Hudson, NH)
   & Albina Fournier (Taftville, CT)
BOYER,Matthew D   Sex:M   30 Jul 1975 Donald A Boyer & Nancy L Daigle
BOYER,Melissa A   Sex:F   04 Mar 1975 Norman C Boyer & Rosemarie J Cloutier
BOYER,Robert Roger   Sex:M   (Child #10) 29 Sep 1937 Joseph Edouard Boyer (USA)
   & Albina Fournier (Canada)
BOYER,Sherry H   Sex:F   (Child #1) 28 Aug 1945 Albert C Boyer (Manchester, NH)
   & Lucille L Boucher (Lewiston, ME)
BOYER,Todd Alan   Sex:M   29 Nov 1976 Norman C Boyer & Rosemarie J Cloutier
BOYER,Tracy A   Sex:F   20 May 1972 Norman C Boyer & Rosemarie J Cloutier
BOYLE,Kevin A   Sex:M   22 May 1967 David P Boyle & Joyce B Allen
BOYLE,Mena R   Sex:F   21 Feb 1954 Frederick P Boyle & Lelia L Finch
BOYNTON,Lenora   Sex:F   (Child #8) 23 Jun 1892 Frank E Boynton (Milford, NH)
   & Josephine LaDue (New York, NY)
BOYNTON,Leonora Sex:F 23 Jun 1892 Hudson, NH Frank E Boynton&Josephine LaDue
BOYSON,Gladice F   Sex:F   (Child #1) 28 Jul 1892 Fred C Boyson (Vermont)
   & Blanche Getchell (Lewiston, ME)
BOYSON,Gladys F Sex:F   28 Jul 1892 Hudson, NH Fred C Boyson & Blanch Getchell
BRACANI,Melissa Ann   Sex:F   19 Sep 1979 Michael A Bracani & Mary Ann Preeper
BRACAULT,Mary Doris Sex:F(Child #3) 29 Nov 1932 Grasmere, NH Francis Bracault
   (Manchester, NH) & Adele Archambeault (Canada)
BRACCIO,Kendra Lee   Sex:F   13 Aug 1973 Kenneth J Braccio & Nancy Lee Gravelle
BRACCIO,Vincent F   Sex:M   16 Oct 1974 Kenneth J Braccio & Nancy L Gravelle
BRACKETT,Eleanor Alice   Sex:F   (Child #1) 19 Jul 1907 Albert F Brackett
   (Cincinnati, OH) & Alice M Chase (Roxbury, MA)
BRACKETT,Jill S   Sex:F   17 Apr 1965 Edwin W Brackett & Janis Ramsay
BRACKETT,Mark O   Sex:M   26 Feb 1962 Edwin W Brackett & Janis Ramsay
BRACKETT,Scott E   Sex:M   21 Jul 1967 Edwin W Brackett & Janis Ramsay
BRADBURY,Abner   Sex:M   Mar 1770 Hudson, NH Sanders Bradbury & Sarah
BRADBURY,Abner   Sex:M   04 Mar 1770 Hudson, NH Sanders Bradbury & Sarah
BRADBURY,Betsey   Sex:F   25 Feb 1773 Hudson, NH Sanders Bradbury & Sarah
BRADBURY,Betsy   Sex:F   25 Feb 1773 Hudson, NH Sanders Bradbury & Sarah
BRADBURY,Ephraim   Sex:M   18 Feb 1748 Hudson, NH Roland Bradbury & Mary
BRADBURY,Ephraim   Sex:M   18 Feb 1747 Hudson, NH Roland Bradbury & Mary

HUDSON,NH BIRTHS

```
BRADBURY,Gail A   Sex:F   26 Jun 1971 Henry A Bradbury & Gayle M Lyon
BRADBURY,Jacob    Sex:M   09 Jun 1778 Hudson, NH Sanders Bradbury & Sarah
BRADBURY,Jacob    Sex:M   09 Jun 1775 Hudson, NH Sanders Bradbury & Sarah
BRADBURY,James    Sex:M   1768 Hudson, NH Sanders Bradbury & Sarah
BRADBURY,James    Sex:M   20 Apr 1768 Hudson, NH Sanders Bradbury & Sarah
BRADBURY,Joseph   Sex:M   05 Dec 1778 Hudson, NH Sanders Bradbury & Sarah
BRADBURY,Molle    Sex:F   30 Jan 1771 Hudson, NH Sanders Bradbury & Sarah
BRADBURY,Molly    Sex:F   30 Jan 1771 Hudson, NH Sanders Bradbury & Sarah
BRADBURY,William  Sex:M   06 Dec 1776 Hudson, NH Sanders Bradbury & Sarah
BRADLEY,Allen F   Sex:M   (Child #1) 01 Sep 1946 Chester J Bradley (Hudson, NH)
   & Gladys Miller (E Falmouth, MA)
BRADLEY,Alphy     Sex:    01 Jan 1788 Hudson, NH Jonathan Bradley & Hannah
BRADLEY,Aphia     Sex:    01 Jan 1788 Hudson, NH Jonathan Bradley & Hannah
BRADLEY,Chester J Sex:M   (Child #7) 31 May 1908 Allen F Bradley (New York)
   & Clara E Dennison (Cutler, ME)
BRADLEY,Elizabeth Sex:F   15 Apr 1777 Hudson, NH Jonathan Bradley & Hannah
BRADLEY,Ellen V   Sex:F   26 Jun 1952 Chester J Bradley & Gladys M Miller
BRADLEY,Hannah M  Sex:F   20 Jun 1782 Hudson, NH Jonathan Bradley & Hannah
BRADLEY,Hannah Moody Sex:F 20 Jun 1782 Hudson, NH Jonathan Bradley & Hannah
BRADLEY,Hazel V   Sex:F   (Child #6) 14 Jan 1904 Allen F Bradley (New York)
   & Clara E Dennison (Cutler, ME)
BRADLEY,Jonathan  Sex:M   02 Mar 1785 Hudson, NH Jonathan Bradley & Hannah
BRADLEY,Joseph    Sex:M   19 Feb 1786 Hudson, NH Joseph Bradley & Mary
BRADLEY,Leslie D  Sex:M   11 Jan 1948 Chester J Bradley (Hudson, NH)
   & Gladys E Miller (E Falmouth, MA)
BRADLEY,Marjorie L Sex:F  (Child #1) 05 Feb 1946 Norman E Bradley
   (Topsfield, MA) & Helen C Hemmelgarn (New Weston, OH)
BRADLEY,Normand E Jr Sex:M 10 Jan 1953 Normand E Bradley & Helen C Hemmelgarn
BRADLEY,Patricia J Sex:F  17 Dec 1947 Norman E Bradley (Topsfield, MA)
   & Helena C Hemmelgarn (New Weston, OH)
BRADLEY,Saley     Sex:F   16 Sep 1788 Hudson, NH Joseph Bradley & Mary
BRADLEY,Salley    Sex:F   11 Jan 1780 Hudson, NH Jonathan Bradley & Hannah
BRADLEY,Sally     Sex:F   11 Jan 1780 Hudson, NH Jonathan Bradley & Hannah
BRADLEY,Sally     Sex:F   16 Sep 1788 Hudson, NH Joseph Bradley & Mary
BRADY,Aimee Beth  Sex:F   23 Feb 1984 Stephen Earl Brady & Patricia Giguere
BRADY,Deborah L   Sex:F   02 Nov 1958 Robert H Brady & Phyllis A Malonson
BRADY,Robert H Jr Sex:M   30 Nov 1959 Robert H Brady & Phyllis A Malonson
BRAFFITT,Marlene L Sex:F  27 Sep 1966 Peter R Braffitt & Paulette M Howe
BRALEY,Elaine R   Sex:F   09 Apr 1964 George M Braley, Jr & Beverly J Ellison
BRANZETTI,Nicholas Charles  Sex:M  24 Oct 1980 Joseph O Branzetti
   & Pauline Napolitano
BRAUGH,Mary E     Sex:F   (Child #1) 07 Jul 1887 Charles Braugh (Canada)
   & Mary E Butler (Ireland)
BREEN,Cynthia R   Sex:F   19 Sep 1975 Barry W Breen & Louise L St Jean
BREITBART,Mark A  Sex:M   05 Oct 1962 John T Breitbart & Janine A Carson
BRESNAHAM,Madeline Sex:F  (Child #5) 12 Jul 1923 John J Bresnaham (Vermont)
   & Zilda Laironel (New York)
BRESNAHAN,Michael C Sex:M    19 Oct 1947 Joseph H Bresnahan (Roxbury, MA)
   & Rolande A Tardif (Nashua, NH)
BRETON,Marisa Renee Sex:F  06 Jan 1981 Raymond J Breton & Denise G M Soucy
BRETTELL,Charles H Sex:M  24 Feb 1950 Herbert S Brettell
   & Helen E Steckewiecz
BRETTELL,Cynthia J Sex:F   27 Apr 1948 Herbert S Brettell (Canada)
   & Helen E Steckiewicz (E Mansfield, MA)
BREWER,Karl E     Sex:    01 Jul 1972 Timothy M Brewer & Susan C Roberts
BREWER,Keith John Sex:M   02 Jul 1981 John Arthur Brewer & Claire L Ledoux
BREWER,Lisa A     Sex:F   26 May 1975 John A Brewer & Claire L Ledoux
BREZINSKI,Chandra Sex:F   21 Feb 1956 James J Brezinski & Cynthia G Foster
BRIAND,Adelard Reni Sex:M (Child #5) 06 May 1923 Etienne Briand (Canada)
   & Ludwicki Savoie (Canada)
```

HUDSON,NH BIRTHS

BRIAND,Alfred D Sex:M   24 Oct 1948 Joseph R Briand, Sr (Lawrence, MA)
  & Esther Young (Merrimack, NH)
BRIAND,Brenda L Sex:F 21 Mar 1951 Maurice L Briand & Arlene V Campbell
BRIAND,Bridget L Sex:F 02 Jan 1971 Raymond P Briand & Doreen M Gallant
BRIAND,Bruce A Sex:M 11 May 1954 George R Briand & Joanne V Lemire
BRIAND,Bruce L Sex:M 19 May 1955 Raymond O Briand & Phyllis E Hopwood
BRIAND,Carol A Sex:F 17 Sep 1956 George R Briand & Joanne V Lemire
BRIAND,Conrad Normand Sex:M (Child #6) 18 May 1923 Auguste Briand (Canada)
  & Leonie Pelletier (Canada)
BRIAND,David Michael Sex:M 24 Sep 1978 Raymond W Briand & Kathlyne McManus
BRIAND,Donald B Sex:M 20 Feb 1949 Maurice L Briand & Arlene V Campbell
BRIAND,Donald D Sex:M 18 Mar 1960 David K Briand & Claudette T Peno
BRIAND,Donna L Sex:F 11 Jul 1963 David K Briand & Claudette T Peno
BRIAND,Douglas A Sex:M 22 Apr 1975 John M Briand & Linda A Paine
BRIAND,Earl G Sex:M 31 Jan 1951 Rene A Briand & Madeline F Harwood
BRIAND,Esther L Sex:F (Child #2) 03 Jun 1940 Joseph R Briand (Lawrence, MA)
  & Esther L Young (Merrimack, NH)
BRIAND,Eva Dorothy Sex:F (Child #6) 31 May 1924 Auguste Briand (Canada)
  & Leonie Pelletier (Canada)
BRIAND,George P Jr Sex:M 31 Jan 1967 George P Briand & Mary Jane B LaFlamme
BRIAND,J A Dollar Sex:M (Child #4) 31 Dec 1920 Auguste Briand (Canada)
  & Leonie Pelletier (Canada)
BRIAND,Jarred P Sex:M 04 Apr 1979 Michael G Briand & Linda S Valcourt
BRIAND,Jason J Sex:M 26 Jul 1975 Gene R Briand & Rita I Bosse
BRIAND,Jason M Sex:M 26 Oct 1975 Michael G Briand & Linda Valcourt
BRIAND,Jean Evelyn Sex:F (Child #1) 28 Jul 1936 Ernest Briand (Lawrence, MA)
  & Violet LaFleur (Nashua, NH)
BRIAND,Jennifer Ann Sex:F 10 May 1982 James Thomas Briand & June M Johnson
BRIAND,John M Sex:M 04 Dec 1947 Ernest E Briand (Lawrence, MA)
  & Violet A La Fleur (Nashua, NH)
BRIAND,Jos Geo Paul Sex:M (Child #9) 17 Jul 1934 Etienne Briand (Canada)
  & Lodowiska Savoy (Canada)
BRIAND,Judith G Sex:F (Child #1) 22 Aug 1946 Maurice L Briand (Nashua, NH)
  & Arlene V Campbell (Nashua, NH)
BRIAND,Keith J Sex:M 17 Jun 1966 Raymond O Briand & Diane L Doran
BRIAND,Kelly J Sex:F 04 Dec 1970 Raymond O Briand & Diane L Doran
BRIAND,Kevin J Sex:M 04 Aug 1967 Raymond O Briand & Diane L Doran
BRIAND,Kevin S Sex:M 11 May 1960 Maurice L Briand & Arlene V Campbell
BRIAND,Kimberly D Sex:F 28 Jul 1969 Earl G Briand & Linda D Munday
BRIAND,Kurt J Sex:M 04 Jul 1973 Raymond O Briand & Diane L Doran
BRIAND,Larry D Sex:M 07 Nov 1955 Maurice L Briand & Arlene V Campbell
BRIAND,Leo Edouard Sex:M (Child #9) 20 Nov 1932 Nashua, NH Auguste Briand
  (Canada) & Leonie Pelletier (Canada)
BRIAND,Marie T R Sex:F (Child #4) 25 Nov 1921 Etienne Briand (Canada)
  & Lodoiska Lavoie (Canada)
BRIAND,Mary Edna Sex:F (Child #8) 08 Nov 1930 Etienne Briand (Canada)
  & Lodioiska Savoy (Canada)
BRIAND,Maurice L Sex:M (Child #5) 07 Jun 1922 Auguste Briand (Canada)
  & Leonie Pelletier (Canada)
BRIAND,Merrilee G Sex:F 12 Oct 1957 Edmond O Briand & Janet R Rollins
BRIAND,Oscar Raymond Sex:M (Child #7) 22 Aug 1929 Etienne Briand (Canada)
  & Lodaiska Sovaie (Canada)
BRIAND,Paula J Sex:F 30 Mar 1964 George P Briand & Mary Jane B LaFlamme
BRIAND,Raymond P Sex:M 23 Jul 1950 Joseph R Briand & Esther L Young
BRIAND,Raymond W Sex:M 21 Jul 1953 Raymond O Briand & Phyllis E Hopwood
BRIAND,Sabrina S Sex:F 17 Oct 1971 Alfred D Briand & Diane C Bosse
BRIAND,Sandra E Sex:F 24 Dec 1952 Joseph R Briand & Esther L Young
BRIAND,Tammy L Sex:F 12 Mar 1961 David K Briand & Claudette T Peno
BRIAND,Virginia L Sex:F 23 Aug 1948 Rene A Briand (Hudson, NH)
  & Alice L Quint (Nashua, NH)

HUDSON,NH BIRTHS

BRICAULT,M Clara Irene   Sex:F   (Child #4) 05 Nov 1937 Francis Bricault
   (Manchester, NH) & Adele Archambault (Canada)
BRICKER,Brian Paul   Sex:M   12 Nov 1981 Paul James Bricker & Kathleen E Gray
BRIEDIS,Grace   Sex:F   (Child #1) 15 Nov 1938 & Mildred A Briedis (Nashua, NH)
BRIER,Donald W   Sex:M   25 Dec 1971 Rudolph D Brier & Charlotte B Poor
BRIERE,Donna M   Sex:F   25 May 1965 Leonard J Briere & Beverly Hill
BRIGGS,Alicia Leigh   Sex:F   02 Aug 1981 Richard Andre Briggs & Jan Schoepflin
BRIGGS,Kimberly K   Sex:F   07 Sep 1977 Kenneth R Briggs & Donna Hutson
BRIGGS,Kyle Jason   Sex:M   20 Sep 1978 Kenneth R Briggs & Donna Hutson
BRIGGS,Sherri Anne   Sex:F   22 Aug 1975 Robert F Briggs & Candace L Batchelder
BRIGGS,Stacy E   Sex:F   22 May 1979 Richard A Briggs & Jan L Schoepflin
BRIGHAM,Jennifer Anya   Sex:F   06 Oct 1980 Ricky J Brigham & Deborah Lee Story
BRIGHAM,Travis Michael   Sex:M   26 Apr 1983 George W Brigham Jr
   & Carlene D Jackson
BRITTON,Allan Winslow   Sex:M   (Child #2) 29 Jul 1912 Joseph Britton(Amadale,
   VA) & Bertha Campbell (Riverside, N S)
BRITTON,Warren Otis   Sex:M   (Child #3) 10 Sep 1914 Joseph A Britton (Virginia)
   & Bertha A Campbell (Nova Scotia)
BROCK,Deborah J   Sex:F   21 Oct 1975 William K Brock & Jeanne C Lizotte
BROCK,William R   Sex:M   25 Apr 1972 William K Brock & Jeanne C Lizotte
BRODEAU,Elaine Constance   Sex:F   (Child #1) 11 Mar 1941 Paul L Brodeau
   (Milford, NH) & Cecilla Jette (Nashua, NH)
BRODEAU,Oberline Rita   Sex:F   (Child #2) 12 Jun 1941 Victor C Brodeau
   (Nashua, NH) & Rose O Noel (Nashua, NH)
BRODEUR,Brenda L   Sex:F   24 Apr 1966 Norman P Brodeur & Katherine E Wilmot
BRODEUR,Donna L   Sex:F   04 Sep 1954 Roger G Brodeur & Bernadette T Landry
BRODEUR,Gary P   Sex:M   07 May 1952 Roger G Brodeur & Bernadette T Landry
BRODEUR,Janet L   Sex:F   21 Jan 1957 Roger G Brodeur & Bernadette T Landry
BRODEUR,Kathleen E   Sex:F   23 Mar 1965 Norman P Brodeur & Katherine E Wilmot
BRODEUR,Linda A   Sex:F   10 Jun 1953 Roger G Brodeur & Bernadette T Landry
BRODEUR,Madeleine E   Sex:F   18 Apr 1954 Gerard L Brodeur & Hazel L Beebie
BRODEUR,Rose M   Sex:F   04 Sep 1968 Norman P Brodeur & Katherine E Wilmot
BROOK,Heather J   Sex:F   28 Dec 1976 Mark Geo Brook III & Sharon E Regan
BROOK,Robynne E   Sex: 25 Aug 1972 Mark G Brook III & Sharon E Regan
BROOKS,Debra J   Sex:F   16 Aug 1963 David A Brooks & Pearl M Smith
BROOKS,Eva B   Sex:F   (Child #2) 27 Jun 1887 Wm C Brooks (Amherst, N S)
   & Augusta Grant (Holmsville, N B)
BROOKS,Kathleen A   Sex:F   15 Nov 1969 Roland E Brooks & Carolyn A Moody
BROOKS,Kristy A   Sex: 19 Aug 1972 David A Brooks & Pearl M Smith
BROPHY,June M   Sex:F   16 Jul 1963 Robert A Brophy & Arlene N Johnson
BROSSARD,Doris E   Sex:F   10 Jul 1948 Frederick D Brossard (Nashua, NH)
   & Doris Prince (Southbridge, MA)
BROTHERS,Donald E   Sex:M   (Child #1) 12 Aug 1940 Ervin L Brothers(E Barre, VT)
   & Marion E Scott (Websterville, VT
BROTHERS,Malvina Marie   Sex:F   (Child #2)14 Jul 1941 Erwin Brothers(Barre, VT)
   & Marion Scott (Barre, VT)
BROTHERS,Sandra M   Sex:F   (Child #3) 15 Dec 1944 Erwin L Brothers(E Barre, VT)
   & Marion E Scott (Websterville, VT)
BROUGH,David Kerry   Sex:M   01 May 1977 Richard D Brough & Patricia Ann Dufour
BROUSSEAU,Gerald L   Sex:M   01 Nov 1961 Joseph C Brousseau & Therese O Michaud
BROUSSEAU,Judi I O   Sex:F   12 Jul 1956 Joseph C Brousseau & Therese O Michaud
BROWN,Amasa   Sex: 04 Mar 1805 Hudson, NH Robinson Brown & Elizabeth
BROWN,Amasy   Sex: 04 Mar 1805 Hudson, NH Robinson Brown & Elizebeth
BROWN,Benjamin   Sex:M   14 Dec 1865 Hudson, NH James M Brown & Nancy
BROWN,Betsey   Sex:F   14 Dec 1782 Hudson, NH Samuel Brown & Bridget
BROWN,Betsy   Sex:F   14 Dec 1782 Hudson, NH Samuel Brown & Bridget
BROWN,Bruce A   Sex:M   24 Oct 1958 Duane F Brown & Joan L Morse
BROWN,Carl A   Sex:M   22 Sep 1963 Russell E Brown, Jr & Jeanne P Aiken
BROWN,Carol L   Sex:F   10 Jan 1967 Henry A Brown & Kathleen A Dwyer
BROWN,Christina Dawn   Sex:F   29 Jun 1982 Ernest Harvey Brown & Susan K Foster

HUDSON, NH BIRTHS

BROWN,Corey Lynn Sex:F   12 Aug 1978 Peter Alan Brown & Suzanne A Mousseau
BROWN,Corinna J   Sex:F   15 Jun 1971 Danny C Brown & Kathleen A Audet
BROWN,Corinne E   Sex:F   (Child #3) 04 Oct 1921 Charles D Brown (Nashua, NH)
  & Lillian V Dichard (Nashua, NH)
BROWN,Daniel P Sex:M   02 Feb 1969 George H Brown & Annie L Cram
BROWN,Darkis L   Sex: 08 Oct 1782 Hudson, NH Samuel Brown & Sarah
BROWN,Darlene A Sex:F   12 Jan 1968 Richard N Brown & Colean B Corson
BROWN,Diane Jeanine Sex:F   (Child #2) 12 Jun 1937 Herbert Milton Brown
  (Keene, NH) & Charlene Steele (Hudson, NH)
BROWN,Donna L   Sex:F   28 Sep 1967 Leon F Brown & Barbara E Dapolito
BROWN,Dorcas Lane   Sex:F   08 Oct 1782 Hudson, NH Samuel Brown & Sarah Gould
BROWN,Elizabeth   Sex:F   15 Apr 1793 Hudson, NH Robinson Brown & Elizabeth
BROWN,Elizebeth   Sex:F   15 Apr 1793 Hudson, NH Robinson Brown & Elizebeth
BROWN,Emily Caitlin   Sex:F   22 Apr 1981 David Paul Brown & Christina R Coyne
BROWN,Everett N   Sex:M   04 Oct 1966 William W Brown & Judith A Yeaton
BROWN,Harriet   Sex:F   (Child #7) 11 Jun 1919 William Brown (E Princeton, MA)
  & Harriet Holbrook (Worcester, MA)
BROWN,Herberta Mildred Sex:F   (Child #2) 10 Aug 1928 Arthur F Brown (Nashua,
  NH) & Mildred C Smith (Nashua, NH)
BROWN,Holly A   Sex:F   03 Aug 1965 Charles H Brown & Patricia A Mizoras
BROWN,Ina L   Sex:F   (Child #2) 06 Oct 1889 Henry C Brown (Delton, WI)
  & Clara J Bryant (Irasburg, VT)
BROWN,Ivan Wallace   Sex:M   (Child #11) 01 Aug 1929 Harry G Brown(St John, NB)
  & Nina Mann (Edinborough, Scotland)
BROWN,James   Sex:M   26 Jun 1780 Hudson, NH Samuel Brown & Bridget
BROWN,James K   Sex:M   23 Sep 1961 Russell E Brown, Jr & Jeanne P Aiken
BROWN,Jamie Suzanne   Sex:F   03 Aug 1984 Peter Alan Brown & Suzanne A Mousseau
BROWN,Jeffrey S   Sex:M   24 Jul 1958 Milton H Brown & Joan C Willey
BROWN,Jodi A   Sex:F   12 Jun 1975 Glenn A Brown & Judith A Elliott
BROWN,John   Sex:M   24 Nov 1780 Hudson, NH Samuel Brown & Sarah Gould
BROWN,Jonathan Parker Sex:M 03 Aug 1984 Peter Alan Brown & Suzanne A Mousseau
BROWN,Jonathan William Sex:M 31 Oct 1981 Steven J Brown & Anita Louise Waldo
BROWN,Joseph   Sex:M   18 Sep 1769 Hudson, NH Samuel Brown & Mary
BROWN,Joseph   Sex:M   20 Mar 1791 Hudson, NH Robinson Brown & Elizabeth
BROWN,Karen L   Sex:F   05 Nov 1956 Rollin E Brown & Lorraine A Tremblay
BROWN,Katharine   Sex:F   (Child #6) 29 Apr 1895 Ambrose A Brown (Nashua, NH)
  & Carrie L Wheeler (Nashua, NH)
BROWN,Kathie L   Sex:F   03 Jun 1970 Danny C Brown & Kathleen A Audet
BROWN,Kelley Anne   Sex:F   29 Feb 1980 Peter A Brown & Suzanne A Mousseau
BROWN,Kenneth A   Sex:M   05 Oct 1976 Glenn A Brown & Judith A Elliott
BROWN,Kenneth J   Sex:M   12 Sep 1965 Thomas P Brown & Jeanne E L'Heureux
BROWN,Kevin D   Sex:M   25 Nov 1958 Carroll F Brown & Anita L Linscott
BROWN,Laurie B   Sex:F   28 Aug 1966 Charles H Brown & Patricia A Mizoras
BROWN,Lori A   Sex:F   28 Sep 1967 Glenn A Brown & Judith A Elliott
BROWN,Matthew H   Sex:M   16 Jan 1963 Walter A Brown & Judith E Cunningham
BROWN,Michael A   Sex: 13 Jun 1973 Carleton H Brown & Joanne S Hartson
BROWN,Milton H Jr   Sex:M   23 May 1957 Milton H Brown & Joan C Willey
BROWN,Milton Harvey   Sex:M   (Child #1) 18 Mar 1933 Herbert Brown (Keene, NH)
  & Charlene Steele (Hudson, NH)
BROWN,Myrtle M   Sex:F   (Child #5) 18 Mar 1943 Henry E Brown (Bowdoinham, ME)
  & Lillian R Pinkham (Brunswick, ME)
BROWN,Nancy J   Sex:F   20 Dec 1957 Larry C Brown & Jean M Pike
BROWN,Nathan   Sex:M   08 Aug 1795 Hudson, NH Robinson Brown & Elizabeth
BROWN,Raymond Columbus   Sex:M   (Child #6) 12 Oct 1916 Hudson, NH William
  Brown (Princeton, MA) & Harriet Holbrook (Worcester, MA)
BROWN,Rena J   Sex:F   18 Dec 1967 Thomas P Brown & Jeanne E L'Heureux
BROWN,Richard A   Sex:M   (Child #1) 14 Oct 1940 Elgin Brown (Hudson, NH)
  & Lauretta Lamire (Nashua, NH)
BROWN,Rollin L   Sex:M   03 Jun 1958 Rollin E Brown & Lorraine A Tremblay
BROWN,Russell E III   Sex:M   23 Aug 1959 Russell E Brown, Jr & Jeanne P Aiken

HUDSON,NH BIRTHS

BROWN,Samantha C   Sex:F   26 Mar 1979 David P Brown & Christine R Coyne
BROWN,Sarah   Sex:F   19 Feb 1779 Hudson, NH Samuel Brown & Sarah Gould
BROWN,Sarah   Sex:F   19 Feb 1776 Hudson, NH Samuel Brown & Sarah
BROWN,Shirley R   Sex:F   10 Nov 1968 Charles H Brown & Patricia A Mizoras
BROWN,Susan L   Sex:F   06 Nov 1957 George H Brown & Annie L Cram
BROWN,Thomas G   Sex:M   12 Dec 1959 George H Brown & Annie L Cram
BROWN,William Algin   Sex:M   (Child #5) 07 Jul 1913 William M Brown
   (Princeton, MA) & Hariet Holbrook (Worcester, MA)
BROWN, [Unknown]   Sex: 11 Oct 1901 Hudson, NH Wm Brown (Texas)
   & Blanche Heath (Tyngsboro, MA)
BROWNE,Jennifer L   Sex:F   04 Nov 1975 Merrill L Browne Jr & Susan J Detro
BROWNING,Jessica Marie Sex:F   24 Apr 1981 Dennis G Browning & Karen M Searles
BRUCE,Clarence E   Sex:M   (Child #2) 10 Jun 1890 Elias A Bruce (Nova Scotia)
   & Addie Farmer (Nashua, NH)
BRUCE,Denise M   Sex:F   02 Jul 1968 Raymond A Bruce & Bernadean D Wright
BRUCE,Edith H   Sex:F   02 Feb 1894 Elias A Bruce (Nova Scotia)
   & Addie B Farmer (Nashua, NH)
BRUCE,Marcia Helen   Sex:F   (Child #6) 20 Sep 1904 Elias A Bruce (Nova Scotia)
   & Addie B Farmer (Nashua, NH)
BRUCE,Margery Viola   Sex:F   (Child #2) 20 Nov 1924 Walter Bruce (Hudson, NH)
   & Anna Hessler (Nashville, TN)
BRUCE,Susie Elsie   Sex:F   (Child #5) 02 Dec 1900 Elias A Bruce (Nova Scotia)
   & Addie B Farmer (Nashua, NH)
BRUCE,Walter Joseph   Sex:M   (Child #4) 15 Jun 1896 Elias A Bruce(Nova Scotia)
   & Addie B Farmer (Nashua, NH)
BRUEN,Amy Beth   Sex:F   06 Nov 1983 Timothy Casey Bruen & Erin Maria Cassel
BRUEN,Meghan Whitney Sex:F 31 May 1981 Timothy C Bruen & Erin Maria Cassel
BRUNT,Marjorie L   Sex:F   (Child #2) 07 May 1944 Arthur Brunt (Boston, MA)
   & Muriel M Canfield (Nashua, NH)
BRYAND,Heidi Anne   Sex:F   15 Jul 1975 Ronald J Bryand & Janet L Schaaf
BRYANT,George W   Sex:M   27 Jul 1874 Hudson, NH Phineus Bryant &
BRYANT,Ronald D Jr   Sex:M   23 Aug 1965 Ronald D Bryant & Susan M Benway
BUBAR,Scott M   Sex:M   01 Jul 1975 Clyde F Bubar & Elaine Brickey
BUCK,Alexander Edgett Sex:M   28 Mar 1985 Bruce Edgett Buck & Patricia A Davis
BUCK,Chelsea Averill   Sex:F   13 Jun 1983 Bruce Edgett Buck & Patricia A Davis
BUCK,Kathryn M   Sex:F   18 Nov 1970 Robert J Buck & Karen L Hurst
BUCKLEY,Dawn M   Sex:F   09 Jan 1966 Robert G Buckley & Barbara J Hopkins
BUCKLEY,Rita M   Sex:F   13 Jul 1966 Dennis J Buckley & Marie J Quinn
BUJNOWSKI,David   Sex:M   17 Aug 1964 Walter R Bujnowski & Phyllis M Lowe
BUJNOWSKI,Gwen Elizabeth Sex:F 30 Nov 1982 Kevin J Bujnowski
   & Teresa L Boilard
BUJNOWSKI,Joshua Richard   Sex:M   19 Mar 1984 Walter R Bujnowski
   & Judith Rita Gagne
BUJNOWSKI,Justin J Sex:M 22 Nov 1982 Richard Bujnowski Sr & Debra M O'Donnell
BUJNOWSKI,Kristen Lee Sex:F 12 Nov 1979 Walter R BujnowskiJr & Judith R Gagne
BUJNOWSKI,Lisa M   Sex:F   24 Jun 1961 Walter R Bujnowski & Phyllis M Lowe
BUJNOWSKI,Richard Jr Sex:M 22 Nov 1982 Richard Bujnowski Sr
   & Debra M O'Donnell
BUJNOWSKI,Scott Alan   Sex:M   24 Jan 1985 Kevin J Bujnowski & Teresa L Boilard
BUKOFSKE,David Alan Sex:M 02 Feb 1983 Alan David Bukofske & Cheryl Ann Rhyner
BULKLEY,Lynn A   Sex:F   28 Jun 1967 Edward E Bulkley & Helen M Carroll
BULKLEY,Paige E   Sex:F   16 May 1970 Edward E Bulkley & Helen M Carroll
BULLARD,Jeffrey B   Sex:M   08 Mar 1958 John O Bullard, Jr & Patricia L Binks
BULLIS,John   Sex:M   11 Mar 1878 Hudson, NH John L Bullis (Peru NY)
   & Josephine (Peru, NY)
BURANT,Paul F   Sex:M   09 Jun 1965 Frederick T Burant & Patricia A Roarke
BURBANK,Betsey Sex:F 04 Dec 1790 Hudson, NH Jonathan Burbank
   & Elizabeth Cummings
BURBANK,Betsy   Sex:F   04 Dec 1790 Hudson, NH Jonathan Burbank & Elizabeth
BURBANK,Cummings   Sex:M   25 May 1805 Hudson, NH Jonathan Burbank

HUDSON,NH BIRTHS

   & Elizabeth Cummings
BURBANK,Daniel   Sex:M   02 May 1794 Hudson, NH Jonathan Burbank & Elizebeth
BURBANK,David Sex:M 02 May 1794 Hudson, NH Jonathan Burbank
   & Elizabeth Cummings
BURBANK,Ebenezer   Sex:M   11 Mar 1751 Hudson, NH Samuel Burbank & Eunice Hardy
BURBANK,Ebenezer   Sex:M   11 Mar 1750 Hudson, NH Samuel Burbank & Eunice
BURBANK,Frederick F   Sex:M   15 Feb 1861 Hudson, NH Horace J Burbank & Lydia
BURBANK,Frederick F P   Sex:M   15 Feb 1861 Hudson, NH Henry Burbank & Lydia
BURBANK,Hannah   Sex:F   11 Mar 1757 Hudson, NH Samuel Burbank & Eunice Hardy
BURBANK,Hannah   Sex:F   18 Sep 1798 Hudson, NH Jonathan Burbank
   & Elizabeth Cummings
BURBANK,John   Sex:M   08 Aug 1800 Hudson, NH Jonathan Burbank
   & Elizabeth Cummings
BURBANK,Jonathan   Sex:M   03 Mar 1759 Hudson, NH Samuel Burbank & Eunice Hardy
BURBANK,Jonathan   Sex:M   16 Sep 1796 Hudson, NH Jonathan Burbank
   & Elizabeth Cummings
BURBANK,Lydia   Sex:F   04 Feb 1745 Hudson, NH Samuel Burbank & Eunice Hardy
BURBANK,Lydia   Sex:F   21 Oct 1785 Hudson, NH Samuel Burbank & Molly Farmer
BURBANK,Lydia   Sex:F   04 Feb 1744 Hudson, NH Samuel Burbank & Eunice
BURBANK,Samuel   Sex:M   04 Feb 1749 Hudson, NH Samuel Burbank & Eunice Hardy
BURBANK,Samuel   Sex:M   09 Jul 1792 Hudson, NH Jonathan Burbank
   & Elizabeth Cummings
BURBANK,Samuel   Sex:M   04 Feb 1746 Hudson, NH Samuel Burbank & Eunice
BURBINE,Paula M   Sex:F   26 Dec 1964 Robert F Burbine & Grace R Brisson
BURDEN,Barbara J Sex:F 26 Jan 1960 William A Burden, Jr & Dorothy J Bushnell
BURDEN,David E   Sex:M   15 Feb 1961 William A Burden, Jr & Dorothy J Bushnell
BUREN,Benjamin D   Sex:M   03 Sep 1967 Charles D Buren & Mary K Neff
BUREN,Nicole K   Sex:F   25 Mar 1969 Charles D Buren & Mary K Neff
BURGESS,David G   Sex:M   09 Feb 1966 Ralph G Burgess & Elizabeth C Burton
BURGESS,Jonathan E   Sex:M   29 Nov 1968 Ralph G Burgess & Elizabeth C Burton
BURGESS,Justin M   Sex:M   18 Mar 1979 Ricky N Burgess & Estelle R Lavoie
BURGESS,Marilyn J   Sex:F   08 Mar 1955 Arthur E Burgess & Irene M McCarthy
BURGESS,Ruth E   Sex:F   03 Oct 1960 Ralph G Burgess & Elizabeth C Burton
BURGESS,Shannon S   Sex:F   19 Mar 1972 Peter J Burgess & Sharon E Post
BURGESS,Sharon J   Sex:F   27 Apr 1949 Arthur E Burgess & Irene M McCarthy
BURGESS,Shelley D   Sex:F   24 Feb 1969 Peter J Burgess & Sharon E Post
BURGESS,Stacie L   Sex:F   09 Mar 1967 Peter J Burgess & Sharon E Post
BURGESS,Terence A   Sex:M   05 Aug 1951 Arthur E Burgess & Irene M McCarthy
BURKE,Frances E   Sex:F   20 Sep 1967 LeRoy S Burke & Mary G McCarthy
BURKE,Susan J   Sex:F   23 May 1969 Leroy S Burke & Mary G McCarthy
BURNELL,David E   Sex:M   19 Aug 1953 Walter A Burnell & Ruth A Foster
BURNELL,Heather Lee Sex:F 09 Jul 1982 David Earl Burnell & Karen L Kierstead
BURNHAM,April L   Sex:F   13 May 1975 Oliver W Burnham Jr & Barbara A Schurman
BURNHAM,Nellie M   Sex:F   28 Apr 1870 Hudson, NH W Burnham & Acsah Ford
BURNS,Abigail Elliot Sex:F 18 Feb 1819 Hudson, NH David Burns & Eliza Childs
BURNS,Alice Veronica Sex:F   (Child #3) 17 Jul 1913 Charles J Burns (Concord)
   & Mary Ame Taylor (Bolton, England)
BURNS,Ann   Sex:F   05 Aug 1741 Hudson, NH George Burns & Martha
BURNS,Anne L   Sex:F   30 Sep 1947 Richard M Burns (Whitefield, NH)
   & Elizabeth H Buxton (Hudson, NH)
BURNS,Charles Freeman Sex:M   (Child #2) 01 Dec 1911 Charles J Burns (NH)
   & Mary Taylor (England)
BURNS,Daniel George Parker   Sex:M   12 Nov 1853 Hudson, NH George H Parker
   & Nora A
BURNS,Daniel Merrill Sex:M 19 Apr 1821 Hudson, NH David Burns & Eliza Childs
BURNS,David   Sex:M   11 Jul 1751 Hudson, NH George Burns & Martha
BURNS,David   Sex:M   14 Sep 1787 Hudson, NH William Burns & Abigail
BURNS,David   Sex:M   04 Jul 1751 Hudson, NH George Burns & Martha
BURNS,David Warren   Sex:M   08 Feb 1813 Hudson, NH David Burns & Eliza Childs
BURNS,Deanna L   Sex:F   16 Jan 1975 David H Burns & JoAnn A Tate

HUDSON,NH BIRTHS

BURNS,Eliza Ann   Sex:F   05 Aug 1811 Hudson, NH David Burns & Eliza Childs
BURNS,Elizabeth   Sex:F   08 Jul 1739 Hudson, NH George Burns & Martha
BURNS,Elizabeth   Sex:F   08 Oct 1771 Hudson, NH George Burns Jr & Anna Adams
BURNS,Frederick   Sex:M   23 Feb 1817 Hudson, NH David Burns & Eliza Childs
BURNS,George   Sex:M   05 Feb 1743 Hudson, NH George Burns & Martha
BURNS,Harriet Newell Sex:F 01 May 1824 Hudson, NH David Burns & Eliza Childs
BURNS,James   Sex:M   18 Mar 1780 Hudson, NH William Burns & Margaret Gibson
BURNS,James   Sex:M   28 Mar 1780 Hudson, NH William Burns & Margaret
BURNS,James   Sex:M   23 May 1805 Hudson, NH & Rebecker Underwood
BURNS,James   Sex:M   17 Aug 1859 Hudson, NH George H Burns &
BURNS,James E   Sex:M   17 Aug 1859 Hudson, NH George H Parker & Nora A
BURNS,Jay S   Sex:M   13 May 1952 Robert B Burns, Jr & Helen E Wadsworth
BURNS,Jeffrey M   Sex:M   16 May 1977 Dennis M Burns & Madeleine L Heroux
BURNS,John   Sex:M   08 Jul 1737 Hudson, NH George Burns & Martha
BURNS,John B   Sex:M   24 May 1950 Richard M Burns & Elizabeth H Buxton
BURNS,John William   Sex:M   19 Aug 1856 Hudson, NH George H Parker & Nora A
BURNS,Keith R   Sex: 07 Nov 1972 Allan L Burns & Denise A Heroux
BURNS,Latish   Sex:F   02 Mar 1754 Hudson, NH George Burns & Martha
BURNS,Latitia   Sex:F   01 Oct 1774 Hudson, NH William Burns & Margaret Gibson
BURNS,Lattish   Sex:F   02 Mar 1754 Hudson, NH George Burns & Martha
BURNS,Lettece   Sex:F   01 Oct 1774 Hudson, NH William Burns & Margerett
BURNS,Lois Irene   Sex:F   (Child #8) 23 Sep 1921 John C Burns (St Paul, MN)
    & Nida Schnider (Bedford, NH)
BURNS,Lydia Childs   Sex:F   01 Mar 1815 Hudson, NH David Burns & Eliza Childs
BURNS,Margaret   Sex:F   21 Dec 1772 Hudson, NH William Burns & Margaret Gibson
BURNS,Margerett   Sex:F   21 Dec 1772 Hudson, NH William Burns & Margerett
BURNS,Martha   Sex:F   29 Nov 174 Hudson, NH George Burns & Martha
BURNS,Mary   Sex:F   12 Feb 1756 Hudson, NH George Burns & Martha
BURNS,Melissa Ann   Sex:F   17 Aug 1981 Randall Kent Burns & Denise E Beaupre
BURNS,Michael D   Sex: 21 Oct 1972 David H Burns & JoAnn A Tate
BURNS,Nancy Judson   Sex:F   01 May 1824 Hudson, NH David Burns & Eliza Childs
BURNS,Nancy P   Sex:F   10 Jun 1948 John C Burns, Jr (Nashua, NH)
    & Marilyn P Gordon (Raymond, NH)
BURNS,Robert   Sex:M   29 Jan 1749 Hudson, NH George Burns & Martha
BURNS,Robert   Sex:M   29 Jan 1748 Hudson, NH George Burns & Martha
BURNS,Robert J   Sex:M   25 May 1978 Randall K Burns & Denise E Beaupre
BURNS,Samuel   Sex:M   05 Dec 1773 Hudson, NH George Burns Jr & Anna Adams
BURNS,Samuel   Sex:M   05 Dec 1775 Hudson, NH George Burns & Anne
BURNS,Sarah   Sex:F   05 Mar 1762 Hudson, NH George Burns & Martha
BURNS,Sarah   Sex:F   05 Apr 1776 Hudson, NH George Burns Jr & Anna Adams
BURNS,William   Sex:M   29 Oct 1744 Hudson, NH George Burns & Martha
BURNS, 3RD,Robert B   Sex:M   08 Nov 1948 Robert B Burns, Jr (Nashua, NH)
    & Helen E Wadsworth (W Campton, NH)
BURPEE,Dorothy F   Sex:F   (Child #1) 29 Dec 1912 Charles S Burpee (E Jaffrey,
    NH) & Maude S Fay (Peterborough, NH)
BURRIS,Timothy A   Sex:M   05 Jun 1976 James A Burris & Deborah Kay Swales
BURROUGHS,Martha   Sex:F   29 Mar 1759 Hudson, NH Joseph Burroughs & Martha
BURROUGHS,Sarah   Sex:F   04 Apr 1761 Hudson, NH Joseph Burroughs & Martha
BURTON,Allysia Laura Sex:F 06 Apr 1985 David Kevin Burton & Mary Anne Welcome
BURTON,Ashley Marie   Sex:F   15 Mar 1985 Brent Ward Burton & Jan Marie Riley
BURTON,Cheryl L   Sex:F   11 Sep 1964 Clifford J Burton & Barbara L Hammond
BURTON,Clifford J   Sex:M   (Child #9) 06 Feb 1943 Ervin J Burton (Pelham, NH)
    & Mary L Prince (Nashua, NH)
BURTON,Jenna Lynn   Sex:F   05 Jul 1982 Paul Kenneth Burton & Joanne L Potter
BURTON,Justin Charles   Sex:M   23 Sep 1984 David A Burton & Linda S St Hilaire
BURTON,Kelly R   Sex:F   08 Apr 1969 Paul F Burton & Myrtie M Marshall
BURTON,Lisa M   Sex:F   15 Oct 1965 Earl C Burton & Melba A Bardas
BURTON,Marion Mabel   Sex:F   (Child #4) 22 Sep 1927 Ervin J Burton (Pelham, NH)
    & Mary L Prince (Nashua, NH)
BURTON,Marjorie E   Sex:F   (Child #9) 12 Mar 1940 Ervin J Burton (Pelham, NH)

HUDSON,NH BIRTHS

& Mary L Prince (Nashua, NH)
BURTON,Melina Ann Sex:F 25 May 1983 Albert August Burton & Michelle C Gagnon
BURTON,Michael K Sex:M 31 May 1958 Earl C Burton & Melba A Bardas
BURTON,Paul K Sex:M 17 Sep 1956 Paul F Burton & Myrtle M Marshall
BURTON,Wallace E Sex:M (Child #1) 21 Jul 1942 Charles E Burton (Pelham, NH)
  & Mary M Scripter (Hague, NY)
BURTON,William P Sex:M (Child #1) 19 Apr 1946 Kenneth E Burton (Nashua, NH)
  & Margaret M Pelletier (Nashua, NH)
BURTSELL,Kellie J Sex:F 29 Jun 1964 Theodore W Burtsell & Marilyn M DeWitt
BURTT,Morris Earl Sex:M (Child #1) 28 Aug 1901 Hudson, NH Wm H Burtt
  (Pelham, NH) & Annie C Lyness (Belfast)
BUSH,Rodney L Sex:M (Child #1) 22 Nov 1946 Harold L Bush(Dover-Foxcroft, ME)
  & Virginia A Jenks (Hudson, NH)
BUSWELL,Laura K Sex:F 28 Aug 1973 Albert A Buswell & Leslie R Wolcott
BUSWELL,Sara D Sex:F 18 May 1972 A Andrew Buswell & Leslie Wolcott
BUTEAU,Daniele Sex:F 24 Nov 1967 Paul Buteau & Huguette P Brochu
BUTLER,Abigail Sex:F 25 Sep 1742 Hudson, NH Joseph Butler & Abagail
BUTLER,Abigail Sex:F 21 Sep 1742 Hudson, NH Joseph Butler & Abigail
BUTLER,Arthur W Sex:M (Child #1) 12 Jul 1896 Albert S Butler (Pelham, NH)
  & Martha E Farnum (Hudson, NH)
BUTLER,Belinda Frances Sex:F 29 Jun 1857 Hudson, NH Henry Butler
  & Belinda Smith
BUTLER,Benjamin Sex:M 01 Feb 1740 Hudson, NH Samuel Butler & Mary
BUTLER,Benjamin Sex:M 04 Feb 1740 Hudson, NH Samuel Butler & Mary
BUTLER,Betty Sex:F 08 Feb 1802 Hudson, NH Jesse Butler & Mehitable
BUTLER,Caleb Sex:M 25 Jul 1741 Hudson, NH Samuel Butler & Mary
BUTLER,Charles Henry Sex:M 28 Dec 1861 Hudson, NH Henry Butler
  & Belinda Smith
BUTLER,David Sex:M 07 Dec 1743 Hudson, NH John Butler & Mary
BUTLER,Deborah Sex:F 04 Sep 1744 Hudson, NH Samuel Butler & Mary
BUTLER,Elizabeth Sex:F 12 Apr 1748 Hudson, NH John Butler & Mary
BUTLER,Emma Maria Sex:F 29 Aug 1859 Hudson, NH Henry Butler
  & Belinda Smith
BUTLER,George F Sex:M 31 Jul 1874 Hudson, NH Moses Butler & Susan
BUTLER,Hannah Sex:F 23 Apr 1793 Hudson, NH Jesse Butler & Mehitable
BUTLER,Henry Sex:M 17 May 1868 Hudson, NH Moses Butler & Susan
BUTLER,James Sex:M 13 Aug 1804 Hudson, NH Jesse Butler & Mehitable
BUTLER,Jesse Sex:M 24 Jul 1794 Hudson, NH Jesse Butler & Mehitable
BUTLER,Jesse Sex:M 24 Jul 1795 Hudson, NH Jesse Butler & Mehitable
BUTLER,John Sex:M 29 Dec 1739 Hudson, NH John Butler & Mary
BUTLER,John Sex:M 29 Dec 1738 Hudson, NH John Butler & Mary
BUTLER,Jonathan Sex:M 11 Jun 1746 Hudson, NH John Butler & Mary
BUTLER,Jonathan Sex:M 11 Jan 1745 Hudson, NH John Butler & Mary
BUTLER,Levi Sex:M 29 Apr 1821 Hudson, NH Levi Butler & Betsey
BUTLER,Levis Sex:M 04 Feb 1784 Hudson, NH Gideon Butler & Molly
BUTLER,Louis Sex:M 04 Feb 1784 Hudson, NH Gideon Butler & Molley
BUTLER,Martina Sex:F 18 Dec 1866 Hudson, NH Henry Butler & Belinda
BUTLER,Mary Sex:F 01 Feb 1737 Hudson, NH Samuel Butler & Mary
BUTLER,Mary Sex:F 22 Mar 1737 Hudson, NH John Butler & Mary
BUTLER,Mehetable Sex:F 05 Sep 1799 Hudson, NH Jesse Butler & Mehitable
BUTLER,Mehitable Sex:F 05 Sep 1799 Hudson, NH Jesse Butler & Mehitable
BUTLER,Melissa S Sex:F 25 Apr 1975 Roger S Butler & Susan Peters
BUTLER,Nathan Sex:M 06 Mar 1741 Hudson, NH John Butler & Mary
BUTLER,Nathaniel Sex:M 06 Mar 1741 Hudson, NH John Butler & Mary
BUTLER,Nellie Martinah Sex:F 13 Dec 1866 Hudson, NH Henry Butler
  & Belinda Smith
BUTLER,Richard Sex:M 04 Aug 1797 Hudson, NH Jesse Butler & Mehitable
BUTLER,Rosey Sex: 18 Dec 1806 Hudson, NH Jesse Butler & Mehitabel
BUTLER,Roxa Sex:F 12 Dec 1806 Hudson, NH Jesse Butler & Mehitable
BUTLER,Samuel Sex:M 20 Jun 1743 Hudson, NH Samuel Butler & Mary

HUDSON,NH BIRTHS

BUTLER,Sarah W   Sex:F   12 Apr 1754 Hudson, NH John Butler & Sarah
BUTLER,Sarah Wyman   Sex:F   12 Apr 1754 Hudson, NH John Butler & Wyman
BUTLER,William   Sex:M   24 Jan 1810 Hudson, NH Jesse Butler & Mehitable
BUTLER,[Unknown]   Sex:M   25 Jul 1741 Hudson, NH Samuel Butler & Mary
BUTRICK,George H Sex:M 10 Jun 1879 Hudson, NH Clifton E Butrick
  & Lottie Colburn
BUTTRICK,Abel   Sex:M   15 Jul 1786 Hudson, NH Abel Buttrick & Abia Colburn
BUTTRICK,Abia   Sex:F   10 Apr 1779 Hudson, NH Abel Buttrick & Abia Colburn
BUTTRICK,Betsey   Sex:F   03 Aug 1783 Hudson, NH Abel Buttrick & Abia Colburn
BUTTRICK,Clara A   Sex:F   18 Dec 1870 Hudson, NH Clifton E Buttrick & Marietta
BUTTRICK,Danford   Sex:M   16 Feb 1789 Hudson, NH Abel Buttrick & Abia Colburn
BUTTRICK,Ernest Clifton   Sex:M   12 Sep 1869 Hudson, NH Clifton E Buttrick
  & Marietta
BUTTRICK,George H   Sex:M   10 Jun 1879 Hudson, NH Clifton E Buttrick
  (Wentworth, NH) & Lottie Colburn
BUTTRICK,Grace Sex:F   19 Feb 1878 Hudson, NH Clifton E Buttrick (Wentworth,
  NH) & Charlotte Colburn (Dracut, MA)
BUTTRICK,Hannah   Sex:F   18 Aug 1796 Hudson, NH Abel Buttrick & Abia Colburn
BUTTRICK,Leander C   Sex:F   13 May 1886 Clifton E Buttrick & Ella F
BUTTRICK,Roger   Sex:M   16 Nov 1794 Hudson, NH Abel Buttrick & Abia Colburn
BUTTRICK,Sarah M   Sex:F   18 Dec 1870 Hudson, NH Clifton E Buttrick & Marietta
BUTTRICK,William   Sex:M   05 May 1775 Hudson, NH Abel Buttrick & Abia Colburn
BUTTRICK,[Unknown]   Sex:M   (Child #2) 20 Sep 1897 C E Buttrick (NH)
  & Ella F Boyington (Augusta, ME)
BUXTON,Deborah M   Sex:F 18 Feb 1955 Robert C Buxton & Lorraine O Brunelle
BUXTON,Elizabeth H   Sex:F   (Child #1) 17 Feb 1920 Paul W Buxton (Nashua, NH)
  & Hazel E Reynolds (Nashua, NH)
BUXTON,Jeanne A I Sex:F   (Child #2) 23 May 1946 Madison J Buxton (Manchester,
  NH) & Marie T Brochu (Somersworth, NH)
BUXTON,Mary Louise   Sex:F   08 Jan 1958 Robert C Buxton & Lorraine O Brunelle
BUXTON,Michael P   Sex:M   26 Jun 1950 Robert C Buxton & Lorraine O Brunelle
BUXTON,Robert N   Sex:M   02 Feb 1972 Michael P Buxton & Susan M Beaudry
BUXTON,Timothy F   Sex:M   30 Aug 1962 Robert C Buxton & Lorraine O Brunelle
BUZZELL,Amy Genevieve Sex:F 23 Oct 1982 Gary M Buzzell & Deborah June Ashton
BUZZELL,Kristina-Marie Kelly   Sex:F   16 Dec 1984 Freeman E BuzzellIII
  & Tina Marie Burrows
BUZZELL,Terry L   Sex:F   18 Jan 1956 Donald E Buzzell & Roxie A Real
BUZZELL,Trevor Ashton Sex:M 28 Feb 1984 Gary M Buzzell & Deborah June Ashton
BYRON,Amy Lynn   Sex:F   03 Jan 1981 Frank A Byron & Patricia A Nixon
BYRON,Belynda L   Sex:F   21 Apr 1970 George R Byron Jr & Bertha L Soliwocki
BYRON,Erik Thomas   Sex:M   22 Jun 1977 George R Byron & Bertha L Soliwocki
BYRON,Justine Marie Sex:F   10 Aug 1973 George R Byron Jr & Bertha L Soliwocki
BYRON,Megan Leigh   Sex:F   26 Mar 1982 Frank Arnold Byron & Patricia Ann Nixon
BYRON,Michael Carlton   Sex:M   13 Mar 1984 Frank Arnold Byron
  & Patricia Ann Nixon
CABRAL,Erica   Sex:F   27 Jun 1977 Ernest E Cabral & Christine Cody
CADDELL,Daniel R   Sex: 30 Aug 1972 Joseph N Caddell & Lynne M Myers
CADDELL,Heather L   Sex:F   17 Mar 1977 Joseph M Caddell & Lynne Marie Myers
CADY,Elizabeth A   Sex:F   29 Oct 1950 Gerald R Cady & Blanche R Hebert
CADY,Eric James   Sex:M   12 Mar 1983 Timothy John Cady & Ann G Nickerson
CADY,Gerald Arthur   Sex:M   (Child #1) 15 Jul 1933 Arthur H Cady (Nashua, NH)
  & Jennie A Poulousky (Nashua, NH)
CADY,James A   Sex:M   28 Mar 1966 Leon J Cady & Victoria M Champagne
CADY,Jean Ann   Sex:F   (Child #2) 15 Aug 1934 Arthur Cady (Nashua, NH)
  & Jennie Powlowsky (Nashua, NH)
CADY,Kathleen S   Sex:F   08 Jun 1949 Gerald R Cady & Blanche R Hebert
CADY,Leon J Jr   Sex:M   22 Feb 1965 Leon J Cady, Sr & Victoria M Champagne
CADY,Michael W   Sex:M   30 Dec 1952 Gerald R Cady & Blanche R Hebert
CADY,Patricia A   Sex:F   14 Oct 1952 George A Cady & Barbara Burnham
CADY,Patrick T   Sex:M   16 Jun 1956 Gerald R Cady & Blanche R Hebert

HUDSON, NH BIRTHS

```
CADY,Paul Gregory   Sex:M   12 Mar 1983 Timothy John Cady & Ann G Nickerson
CADY,Steven F   Sex:M   05 May 1948 George A Cady, Jr (Nashua, NH)
   & Barbara Burnham (Nashua, NH)
CADY,Tamara A   Sex:F   12 Jan 1964 Leon J Cady & Victoria M Champagne
CADY,Timothy J   Sex:M   22 Mar 1956 George A Cady & Barbara Burnham
CAINE,Melissa F   Sex:F   17 Feb 1975 Roger R Caine & Claudette R Bureau
CALAWA,Jill   Sex:F   06 Nov 1954 Leon C Calawa & Rosalyn E Wilson
CALDWELL,Alexander   Sex:M   06 Feb 1748 Hudson, NH John Caldwell & Isabel
CALDWELL,Alexander   Sex:M   29 May 1778 Hudson, NH John Caldwell & Margaret
CALDWELL,Alexander   Sex:M   04 Apr 1783 Hudson, NH Samuel Caldwell & Susanna
CALDWELL,Almira   Sex:F   16 Aug 1809 Hudson, NH Alexander Caldwell & Hannah
CALDWELL,Alysenia   Sex:F   16 Aug 1809 Hudson, NH Alexander Caldwell & Hannah
CALDWELL,Anna   Sex:F   17 Apr 1789 Hudson, NH Joseph Caldwell & Sarah
CALDWELL,Anna   Sex:F   08 Feb 1753 Hudson, NH John Caldwell & Isebel
CALDWELL,Annie   Sex:F   08 Feb 1753 Hudson, NH John Caldwell & Isabel
CALDWELL,Arthur N   Sex:M   29 Jun 1872 Hudson, NH Nathan Caldwell & Clarisa A
CALDWELL,Asa   Sex:M   06 Mar 1787 Hudson, NH Joseph Caldwell & Sarah
CALDWELL,Batsa   Sex:   27 Apr 1787 Hudson, NH James Caldwell & Christine
CALDWELL,Betsey   Sex:F   22 Apr 1787 Hudson, NH James Caldwell & Christin
CALDWELL,Betsey   Sex:F   23 May 1792 Hudson, NH Samuel Caldwell & Susanna
CALDWELL,Betsy   Sex:F   23 May 1792 Hudson, NH Samuel Caldwell & Susanna
CALDWELL,Clarissa   Sex:F   24 May 1795 Hudson, NH Joseph Caldwell & Sarah
CALDWELL,Clarissa   Sex:F   29 May 1795 Hudson, NH Joseph Caldwell & Sarah
CALDWELL,David   Sex:M   28 Nov 1767 Hudson, NH John Caldwell & Letitia
CALDWELL,Dorcas   Sex:F   16 Jul 1816 Hudson, NH Alexander Caldwell & Hannah
CALDWELL,Dorcas S   Sex:F   16 Jan 1816 Hudson, NH Alexander Caldwell & Hannah
CALDWELL,Elizabeth   Sex:F   18 Mar 1764 Hudson, NH John Caldwell & Letitia
CALDWELL,Elizabeth   Sex:F   21 Feb 1797 Hudson, NH Joseph Caldwell & Sarah
CALDWELL,Elizabeth   Sex:F   25 Aug 1818 Hudson, NH Caldwell &
CALDWELL,Elizebeth   Sex:F   21 Feb 1797 Hudson, NH Joseph Caldwell & Sarah
CALDWELL,George   Sex:M   14 Mar 1814 Hudson, NH Alexander Caldwell & Hannah
CALDWELL,George E   Sex:M   06 Jun 1846 Hudson, NH Caldwell &
CALDWELL,Hamler   Sex:   28 Feb 1812 Hudson, NH Alexander Caldwell & Hannah
CALDWELL,Hamlin   Sex:M   28 Feb 1812 Hudson, NH Alexander Caldwell & Hannah
CALDWELL,Hannah   Sex:F   31 Mar 1785 Hudson, NH James Caldwell & Christin
CALDWELL,Hannah   Sex:F   09 Sep 1781 Hudson, NH Samuel Caldwell & Susanna
CALDWELL,Hannah   Sex:F   07 Sep 1787 Hudson, NH Samuel Caldwell & Susanna
CALDWELL,Henry M   Sex:M   08 Aug 1853 Hudson, NH Caldwell &
CALDWELL,Isabel   Sex:F   02 Jan 1737 Hudson, NH John Caldwell & Isabel
CALDWELL,Isabel   Sex:F   01 Feb 1785 Hudson, NH Joseph Caldwell & Sarah
CALDWELL,Isabela   Sex:F   05 Aug 1783 Hudson, NH John Caldwell & Lettice
CALDWELL,Isabilla   Sex:F   05 Aug 1783 Hudson, NH John Caldwell & Letitia
CALDWELL,Isebel   Sex:F   03 Jan 1737 Hudson, NH John Caldwell & Isebel
CALDWELL,James   Sex:M   06 Oct 1745 Hudson, NH John Caldwell & Isabel
CALDWELL,James   Sex:M   11 Oct 1783 Hudson, NH James Caldwell & Christin
CALDWELL,Jane   Sex:F   10 Mar 17 Hudson, NH John Caldwell & Isabel
CALDWELL,Jennet   Sex:F   11 Dec 1779 Hudson, NH Samuel Caldwell & Susanna
CALDWELL,Jennett   Sex:F   11 Apr 1781 Hudson, NH James Caldwell & Jenett
CALDWELL,Jennett   Sex:F   11 Dec 1779 Hudson, NH Samuel Caldwell & Susanna
CALDWELL,Jennie E   Sex:F   17 Jan 1852 Hudson, NH Caldwell &
CALDWELL,John   Sex:M   15 Apr 1740 Hudson, NH John Caldwell & Isabel
CALDWELL,John   Sex:M   15 Feb 1766 Hudson, NH John Caldwell & Letitia
CALDWELL,John   Sex:M   12 May 1773 Hudson, NH James Caldwell & Jenett
CALDWELL,John   Sex:M   09 Oct 1781 Hudson, NH Samuel Caldwell & Susanna
CALDWELL,John   Sex:M   01 Oct 1781 Hudson, NH Samuel Caldwell & Susanna
CALDWELL,Joseph   Sex:M   30 Mar 1756 Hudson, NH John Caldwell & Isabel
CALDWELL,Joseph   Sex:M   01 May 1772 Hudson, NH John Caldwell & Margaret
CALDWELL,Joseph III   Sex:M   24 Aug 1825 Hudson, NH Caldwell &
CALDWELL,Louisa A   Sex:F   18 Nov 1823 Hudson, NH Caldwell &
CALDWELL,Margaret   Sex:F   24 Nov 1769 Hudson, NH John Caldwell & Margaret
```

HUDSON,NH BIRTHS

CALDWELL,Margaret Sex:F 02 Nov 1769 Hudson, NH John Caldwell & Margaret
CALDWELL,Martha Sex:F 30 Oct 1771 Hudson, NH James Caldwell & Jenett
CALDWELL,Mary Sex:F 12 Jun 1814 Hudson, NH Caldwell &
CALDWELL,Meredith Lindsey Sex:F 21 Oct 1979 Robert Earl Caldwell
  & Susan P De Loach
CALDWELL,Olive Sex:F 17 Nov 1780 Hudson, NH John Caldwell & Margaret
CALDWELL,Rachael Sex:F 27 May 1816 Hudson, NH Caldwell &
CALDWELL,Rebecca Sex:F 08 May 1779 Hudson, NH James Caldwell & Jenett
CALDWELL,Robert Sex:M 15 Mar 1774 Hudson, NH John Caldwell & Margaret
CALDWELL,Robert Sex:M 13 Jul 1792 Hudson, NH James Caldwell & Christin
CALDWELL,Robert D Sex:M 02 Oct 1820 Hudson, NH Caldwell &
CALDWELL,Salla Sex:F 02 Oct 1793 Hudson, NH Joseph Caldwell & Sarah
CALDWELL,Sally Sex:F 02 Oct 1792 Hudson, NH Joseph Caldwell & Sarah
CALDWELL,Samuel Sex:M 29 Jul 1750 Hudson, NH John Caldwell & Isabel
CALDWELL,Samuel Sex:M 09 Apr 1776 Hudson, NH John Caldwell & Margaret
CALDWELL,Samuel Sex:M 19 Aug 1789 Hudson, NH James Caldwell & Christin
CALDWELL,Samuel Sex:M 19 Apr 1776 Hudson, NH John Caldwell & Margaret
CALDWELL,Sarah Sex:F 05 Oct 1762 Hudson, NH John Caldwell & Letitia
CALDWELL,Sarah Sex:F 05 Dec 1762 Hudson, NH John Caldwell & Lettice
CALDWELL,Sophia Sex:F 14 Mar 1802 Hudson, NH Joseph Caldwell & Sarah
CALDWELL,William C Sex:M 19 Feb 1783 Hudson, NH Joseph Caldwell & Sarah
CALDWELL,William, Jr Sex:M 17 Oct 1812 Hudson, NH Caldwell &
CALKIN,Dana R Sex:M 22 Jun 1951 Thomas B Calkin & Joan E Robinson
CALL,Floyd R Sex:M 24 Oct 1973 Daron L Call & Toni J Pendzimas
CALLAHAN,Matthew M Sex:M 22 Jun 1978 Michael P Callahan & Ann Marie Croteau
CALLAHAN,Patrick J Sex:M 27 Aug 1960 John P Callahan & Josephine E Seminato
CALLAHAN,Wm Brennard Sex:M (Child #6) 24 Feb 1934 Robert Callahan (Malden,
  MA) & Marguerite Chandler (Marshfield, MA)
CALLAHAN,[Unknown] Sex:M (Child #3) 01 Jul 1915 Hudson, NH William Callahan
  (Lawrence, MA) & Katherine McGravey (Pennsylvania)
CALLIS,Jennifer G Sex:F 01 Mar 1961 Ewell W Callis & Lois S Lip
CALVINO,Jessica Rae Sex:F 10 Apr 1981 Gary A Calvino & Robin Lee Mason
CALZINI,Robert E Sex:M 14 Sep 1970 Lawrence J Calzini & Margaret E Yeo
CAMERON,Debby C Sex:F 27 Jul 1968 Raymond R Cameron & Clara J Prehemo
CAMILLERI,Erin Anthony Sex:F 06 Aug 1984 Mark A Camilleri & Susan E Beaulieu
CAMIRAND,Cheryl L Sex:F 09 Mar 1969 William P Camirand & Veronica R Widener
CAMIRAND,William P Jr Sex:M 26 Nov 1966 William P Camirand
  & Veronica R Widener
CAMIRE,Steven Ronald Sex:M 17 May 1982 Ronald Joseph Camire & Justine F Cote
CAMMETT,Linda S Sex:F 12 Feb 1966 Samuel S Cammett & Norma E West
CAMPBELL,Armon J Sex:M 19 Dec 1877 Hudson, NH Bradford Campbell (Bedford,
  NH) & Harriet L (Danvers, MA)
CAMPBELL,Bettey Sex:F Jan 1780 Hudson, NH & Anne Smith
CAMPBELL,Betty Sex:F Jan 1780 Hudson, NH & Anna Smith
CAMPBELL,Candia A Sex:F 28 Feb 1955 Robert O Campbell & Alice I Gordon
CAMPBELL,Catherine M Sex:F 23 Mar 1970 Robert O Campbell & Alice I Gordon
CAMPBELL,Clarance F Sex:M (Child #7) 18 Aug 1882 Hudson, NH Bradford
  Campbell (Bedford, NH) & Hattie E Putnam (Danvers, MA)
CAMPBELL,Crystal L Sex:F 16 Jan 1954 Robert O Campbell & Alice I Gordon
CAMPBELL,Everett C Sex:M (Child #9) 27 Jul 1908 Charles E Campbell (Nova
  Scotia) & Annie Knight (Hyde Park, MA)
CAMPBELL,Gertrude M Sex:F (Child #2) 25 Aug 1904 Orman S Campbell (Hudson,
  NH) & Hattie L Mortlock (Nova Scotia)
CAMPBELL,Harlan Hobson Sex:M (Child #1) 16 May 1898 Waldo B Campbell
  (Nashua, NH) & Mabel E Quimby (Springfield)
CAMPBELL,Jane K Sex:F 26 Aug 1948 Arnold C Campbell (Nashua, NH)
  & Olive J Haskins (Nashua, NH)
CAMPBELL,Janice A Sex:F 31 Mar 1951 Bennie L Campbell & Marion A Pelkey
CAMPBELL,Jessica Ann Sex:F 03 Oct 1984 Charles A Campbell & Karen Ann Miller
CAMPBELL,John Alma Sex:M 14 Oct 1866 Hudson, NH Bradford Campbell

HUDSON,NH BIRTHS

& Harriet E Putnam
CAMPBELL,John F   Sex:M   14 Oct 1866 Hudson, NH Bradford Campbell & Harriet E
CAMPBELL,Judy K   Sex:F   (Child #5) 09 Jul 1946 Oscar J Campbell (Nashua, NH)
  & Mary K Atherton (Nova Scotia)
CAMPBELL,Marion A   Sex:F   (Child #3) 15 Mar 1912 Orman Campbell (Hudson, NH)
  & Hattie Mortlock (Truro, N S)
CAMPBELL,Mary E   Sex:F   08 Aug 1956 Bennie L Campbell & Marion A Pelkey
CAMPBELL,Nancy J   Sex:F   02 Apr 1952 Bennie L Campbell & Marion A Pelkey
CAMPBELL,Nelly Fiore   Sex:F   13 Dec 1874 Hudson, NH   & Francie Campbell
CAMPBELL,Oscar   Sex:M   28 Sep 1902 Orman S Campbell (Hudson, NH)
  & Hattie L Mortlock (Nova Scotia)
CAMPBELL,Oscar P   Sex: 15 Feb 1973 Robert O Campbell & Alice I Gordon
CAMPBELL,Perley James   Sex:M   30 Jul 1880 Hudson, NH Bradford Campbell
  (Bedford, NH) & Hattie E Putnam (Danvers, MA)
CAMPBELL,Robert O Jr   Sex:M   19 Nov 1952 Robert O Campbell & Alice I Gordon
CAMPBELL,Robert Oscar   Sex:M   (Child #4) 23 Dec 1928 Oscar P Campbell
  (Hudson, NH) & Louise M Jennette (Nashua, NH)
CAMPBELL,Ruby M   Sex:F   (Child #6) 15 Feb 1905 Chas E Campbell (Nova Scotia)
  & Annie M Knight (Hyde Park, MA)
CAMPBELL,Ruth M   Sex:F   (Child #7) 15 Feb 1905 Chas E Campbell (Nova Scotia)
  & Annie M Knight (Hyde Park, MA)
CAMPBELL,Sandra L Sex:F   (Child #1) 23 Oct 1946 Bennie L Campbell (Richmond,
  VA) & Marion A Pelkey (Nashua, NH)
CAMPBELL,Suzanne A   Sex:F   07 Feb 1949 Bennie L Campbell & Marion A Pelky
CAMPBELL,Theresa   Sex:F   05 Nov 1957 Bennie L Campbell & Marion A Pelkey
CAMPBELL,Virginia   Sex:F   26 Apr 1912 Charles Campbell (Nova Scotia)
  & Annie Knight (Hyde Park, MA)
CAMPBELL,[Unknown]   Sex:F   (Child #4) 12 Nov 1915 Hudson, NH Orman S Campbell
  (Hudson, NH) & Hattie Mortlock
CAMPOLIETO,John A II Sex:M 04 Jul 1966 John A Campolieto&Shirley A Plynkofsky
CANTARA,Jamey Shawn   Sex:M   04 Sep 1978 Norman Leo Cantara & Dolly K Dillavou
CANTARA,John Edmund Sex:M   (Child #1) 09 Feb 1935 Jerome Cantara (Nashua, NH)
  & Grace Young (Everett, MA)
CANTARA,Kathryn R   Sex:F   19 Jan 1969 John E Cantara & Jacqueline R A Roger
CANTARA,Kenneth M   Sex:M   24 Jul 1958 John E Cantara & Jacqueline R Rogers
CANTARA,Margaret R   Sex:F   21 Apr 1974 John E Cantara & Jacqueline R Rogers
CANTARA,Maria J   Sex:F   18 Nov 1967 John E Cantara & Jacqueline R Rogers
CANTARA,Peter A   Sex:M   08 Nov 1962 John E Cantara & Jacqueline R A Roger
CANTARA,Ryan James Sex:M   04 Aug 1983 Kenneth M Cantara & Lynn Marie Routhier
CANTARA,Thomas A   Sex:M   25 Aug 1965 John E Cantara & Jacqueline R A Roger
CANTELLI,Tara Lyn   Sex:F   17 Jun 1983 Paul R Cantelli & Karen Louise Ricker
CAPISTA,David A   Sex:M   03 Jul 1952 Albert H Capista & Eleanor A Graziano
CAPOZZO,Christopher   Sex:M   18 Dec 1978 Joseph J Capozzo & Jane Marie Stanley
CAPOZZO,Michelle   Sex:F   25 May 1981 Joseph J Capozzo & Jane Marie Stanley
CARBONE,John P   Sex:M   30 May 1979 Robert J Carbone & Peggy Ann Sackel
CARBONE,Kerry L   Sex:F   12 Sep 1959 Robert J Carbone & Dorothy M Saffomilla
CARD,John   Sex:M   02 Jan 1977 John F Card & Barbara J Felton
CARDIN,Brady A   Sex:M   15 Jul 1970 John C Cardin & Nancy L Kennedy
CARDIN,Julia Laing   Sex:F   11 Nov 1984 Gregory Paul Cardin & Katherine E Laing
CARDIN,Steven S   Sex:M   17 Nov 1954 Clifford J Cardin & Lucille R Denoncourt
CARDIN,William T   Sex:M   11 Dec 1966 Clifford J Cardin & Lucille R Denancourt
CARDINAL,Paul R S Sex:M 24 Jul 1982 Paul E Cardinal & Linda Khachadoorian
CAREY,Brian Patrick   Sex:M   06 Aug 1984 Patrick Leo Carey & Diane Marie Carey
CARIGNAN,Michael D P   Sex:M   08 Nov 1971 Dennis H Carignan & Ann T DiRubbo
CARKIN,Geo Benj Frank   Sex:M   (Child #7) 05 Jan 1934 Albert N Carkin
  (Dunstable, MA) & Sarah Nutting (Lowell, MA)
CARKIN,John   Sex:M   18 Dec 1735 Hudson, NH John Carkin & Esther
CARLEN,Ann M   Sex: 24 Mar 1973 James E Carlen Jr & Joan M Lima
CARLEN,Daniel T   Sex:M   11 Sep 1969 James E Carlen & Joan M Lima
CARLEN,Tracy A   Sex:F   18 Sep 1969 John M Carlen & Dorothy A Turgeon

HUDSON,NH BIRTHS

CARLONE,Christy Ann Sex:F 28 Jul 1981 Nicholas J Carlone & Carol Ann Sobinski
CARLSON,Dael D   Sex:M   14 Sep 1974 David R Carlson & Maureen A Thompson
CARLSON,Elana R   Sex:F   27 Apr 1961 Ernest L Carlson & Mildred M Heatwole
CARLSON,Scott R   Sex:M   15 Oct 1966 Robert H Carlson & Betty L Ellis
CARLSON,Timothy A   Sex:M   25 Feb 1968 Robert H Carlson & Betty L Ellis
CARLSTROM,Kimberly J   Sex:F   14 Oct 1970 Hurst D Carlstrom & Kathleen Jones
CARLSTROM,Lisa L   Sex:F   05 May 1969 Hurst D Carlstrom & Kathleen Jones
CARLTON,Jacob Paul   Sex:M   29 Mar 1983 Frank P Carlton Jr & Mary Grace Branco
CARLTON,[Unknown]   Sex:M   17 Jun 1741 Hudson, NH Jeremiah Carlton & Eunice
CARON,Christopher S   Sex:M   12 Jul 1975 A Roland Caron & Linda D Ackley
CARON,David S   Sex:M   01 Sep 1965 Gerard L Caron & Johanna L Anderson
CARON,Drew C   Sex:M   21 Oct 1968 Emery J Caron & Valerie A Kingston
CARON,Edward Robert   Sex:M   30 Apr 1982 Edward Francis Caron & Diana Wright
CARON,Gregory   Sex:M   08 Apr 1960 Ralph F Caron & Doris M Gould
CARON,Holly A   Sex:F   10 Dec 1971 Richard F Caron & Judith A Bracy
CARON,Jeffrey D   Sex:M   31 Oct 1961 Gregory P Caron & Nancy A Ford
CARON,John P   Sex:M   10 Feb 1947 Paul E Caron (Nashua, NH)
  & Eva F Houle (E Hampton, MA)
CARON,Kirsten Wright   Sex:F   15 Aug 1979 Edward F Caron & Diana Wright
CARON,Linda A   Sex:F   14 Jul 1947 Wilfred J Caron (Nashua, NH)
  & Mina G Gagnon (Portland, ME)
CARON,Michele F   Sex:F   09 Feb 1976 John P Caron & Lorraine S Akita
CARON,Pamela A   Sex:F   25 Jul 1965 Reginald G E Caron & Jeannette P Boucher
CARON,Rosalee M   Sex:F   23 Nov 1954 Paul E Caron & Eva F Houle
CARON,Scott J   Sex:M   18 Jun 1978 Albert P Caron & Linda D Ackley
CARON,Shelby Jean   Sex:F   13 Sep 1976 Timothy J Caron & Monna Lou Stone
CARON,Theresa L   Sex:F   29 May 1958 Paul E Caron & Eva F Houle
CARON,Theresa Marie   Sex:F   17 Feb 1982 Gerald Dollard Caron & Gayle P Gagnon
CARON,Timothy P   Sex:M   27 Jan 1964 Gregory P Caron & Nancy A Ford
CARON,[Unknown]   Sex:M   (Child #1) 11 Jul 1905 & Florida Caron (Canada)
CARON,[Unknown]   Sex:F   22 Jun 1980 Gerald D Caron & Gayle P Gagnon
CARPENITO,Philip L Sex:M 01 Apr 1956 Phillip A Carpenito
  & Gloria D Archambault
CARPENTER,Jeffrey A Sex:M   15 Jan 1979 James H Carpenter & Deborah E Williams
CARPENTER,Rebecca Lynn Sex:F 02 Apr 1981 James Hall Carpenter
  & Deborah E Williams
CARR,Carl P   Sex:M   26 Nov 1961 Philip M Carr, Jr & Joyce M Clogston
CARR,Dorothy M   Sex:F   31 Jul 1969 Joseph I Carr Jr & Janet L Bunnell
CARR,Erik M   Sex:M   22 Jun 1963 Philip M Carr & Joyce M Clogston
CARR,Ernest George   Sex:M   (Child #3) 30 Jul 1927 Alfred M Carr (Chester, NH)
  & Bessie W Wentworth (Plaistow, NH)
CARR,Susan E   Sex:F   12 Nov 1953 Robert G Carr & Ruth Dawson
CARRIER,Lisa C   Sex:F   24 Mar 1971 Benoit P Carrier & Francoise M Blondeau
CARROLL,Cindy L   Sex:F   31 Jan 1967 Roy Carroll & Sylvia M Rioux
CARROLL,David Wheeler   Sex:M   (Child #3) 07 Jan 1920 Mark D Carroll
  (Plattsburgh, NY) & Esther Peterson (Nashua, NH)
CARROLL,John Walter   Sex:M   (Child #1) 24 Apr 1935 Mark D Carroll, Jr
  (Litchfield, NH) & Elsie Tanarovicz (Nashua, NH)
CARROLL,Jon   Sex:M   (Child #4) 27 Mar 1943 John E Carroll (Litchfield, NH)
  & Lauretta A Shepard (Nashua, NH)
CARROLL,Lisa J   Sex:F   19 Sep 1965 Roy Carroll & Sylvia M Rioux
CARROLL,Lisa Marie   Sex:F   27 Dec 1978 Charles W Carroll & Janice Lee Wright
CARROLL,Lorie J   Sex:F   12 Nov 1964 Jon Carroll & Judith E Farrington
CARROLL,Raymond E   Sex:M   (Child #2) 03 Nov 1942 David W Carroll (Hudson, NH)
  & Virginia M Robinson (Nashua, NH)
CARROLL,Roy   Sex:M   (Child #2) 05 Jun 1940 John Carroll (Litchfield, NH)
  & Lauretta Shepard (Nashua, NH)
CARROLL,Susan   Sex:F   19 Apr 1949 John E Carroll & Lauretta A Shepard
CARROLL,Tracy L   Sex:F   04 Nov 1966 John Carroll & Judith E Farrington
CARRUBBA,James E   Sex:M   26 Jan 1963 Joseph Carrubba & Marguerite R Moore

HUDSON,NH BIRTHS

CARRUBBA,Nicole K   Sex:F   17 Jan 1970 Joseph A Carrubba & Margaret R Moore
CARSON,Laurie M   Sex:F   19 Nov 1956 Kenneth E Carson & Frances M Potter
CARSON,Scot M   Sex:M   25 Apr 1974 James L Carson & Laurel V Blanchette
CARTER,Carolyn A   Sex:F   12 Jan 1947 Merrill L Carter (Stowe, VT)
   & Eva M Martin (Canada)
CARTER,Cheryl A   Sex:F   29 Dec 1956 Chester R Carter & Ramona L Edwards
CARTER,Christine Rose   Sex:F   30 Aug 1979 Richard H Carter & Rose Lee Durwin
CARTER,Craig J   Sex:M   05 Nov 1967 William E Carter & Gloria R Leclerc
CARTER,Douglas C   Sex:M   18 Feb 1963 Ray C Carter, Sr & Dolores J Jalbert
CARTER,Glen W   Sex:M   14 Mar 1965 William E Carter & Gloria R Leclerc
CARTER,Graig W   Sex:M   18 Mar 1975 Richard H Carter & Rose L Durwin
CARTER,James L   Sex:M   01 Sep 1955 Merrill L Carter & Eva M Martin
CARTER,Jane Louise   Sex:F   (Child #3) 10 Apr 1941 Merrill L Carter (Vermont)
   & Eva M Martin (Canada)
CARTER,Jason Philip Sex:M 21 Oct 1981 Leonard J Carter & Robin Brenda Quigley
CARTER,Joy S   Sex:F   08 Oct 1960 Ray C Carter & Dolores J Jalbert
CARTER,Leonard J Jr   Sex:M   01 Apr 1978 Leonard J Carter & Robin B Quigley
CARTER,Matthew E   Sex:M   18 Feb 1963 Ray C Carter, Sr & Dolores J Jalbert
CARTER,Nancy M   Sex:F   (Child #3) 16 Nov 1943 Merrill Carter (Vermont)
   & Eva M Martin (Canada)
CARTER,Neal D   Sex:M   16 Feb 1965 Ray C Carter & Dolores J Jalbert
CARTER,Ray C Jr   Sex:M   03 Mar 1962 Ray C Carter, Sr & Dolores J Jalbert
CARTER,Richard H   Sex:M   17 Sep 1953 Merrill L Carter & Eva M Martin
CARTER,Richard H Jr   Sex:M   08 Aug 1971 Richard H Carter & Rose L Durwin
CARTER,Robert Sayles   Sex:M   (Child #3) 29 Nov 1936 Clyde R Carter
   (N Haverhill, NH) & Minnie Esty (Hudson, NH)
CARTIER,Derek A   Sex: 27 Dec 1972 Michael J Cartier & Audrey A Thibodeau
CARTOOF,Beverly   Sex:F   03 Jul 1956 David Cartoof & Dorothy M Phillips
CARTY,Anna Brigid   Sex:F   07 Nov 1982 Thomas J Carty, III & Susan Jankowski
CASALE,Barbara J   Sex:F   03 Aug 1965 Vincent J Casale & Carlotta A Randall
CASALE,Sandra J   Sex:F   18 Jan 1970 Vincent J Casale & Carlotta A Randall
CASANOVA,John A   Sex:M   08 Mar 1971 Ronald A Casanova & Janet M Bell
CASAVANT,Jeanine Diane Sex:F 28 May 1985 Gerard J Casavant & Diane P Labonte
CASAVANT,Sarah Marie   Sex:F   18 May 1981 Gerard J Casavant & Diane P Labonte
CASE,Hamlin S   Sex:M   08 Sep 1877 Hudson, NH George F Case (Boston, MA)
   & Mary T Sanford (Nashua, NH)
CASELEY,Christopher M   Sex:M   06 Feb 1970 Clifford D Caseley & Maureen Berry
CASELEY,Scott R   Sex:M   21 Aug 1975 Clifford D Caseley & Maureen Berry
CASEY,Cynthia L   Sex:F   18 May 1962 Raymond J Casey & Claire D Letourneau
CASEY,Meghan Ruth   Sex:F   20 May 1985 John Andrew Casey & Diane R Thompson
CASEY,Michael H   Sex:M   19 Oct 1963 Raymond J Casey & Claire D Letourneau
CASEY,Pamela J   Sex:F   03 Dec 1967 Peter W Casey & Brenda E Goodwin
CASEY,Steven E   Sex:M   19 Nov 1958 Raymond J Casey & Claire D Letourneau
CASPER,Peter   Sex:M   (Child #1) 27 Sep 1936 Peter Casper (Nashua, NH)
   & Anna Petkevich (Dracut, MA)
CASSALIA,David B   Sex:M   08 Jun 1977 David L Cassalia & Coleen Sue Sullivan
CASSANERIO,Jo-Ann   Sex:F   23 Aug 1954 John Cassanerio & Louise A Crowley
CASSARINO,Jennifer L   Sex:F   07 Dec 1974 James Cassarino & Gail A Dwire
CASSAVAUGH,Marissa Dawn Sex:F 24 Mar 1982 David A Cassavaugh & Laura S Yates
CASSAVAUGH,Michael David Sex:M 11 Feb 1981 David A Cassavaugh & Laura S Yates
CASSAVAUGH,Richard D   Sex:M   09 Nov 1964 Alfred M Cassavaugh
   & Carmen M P Choiniere
CASSIDY,Amanda E   Sex:F   08 Mar 1976 Richard A Cassidy & Judith D Maine
CASSIDY,Matthew R   Sex:M   04 Mar 1974 Richard A Cassidy & Judith D Maine
CASSOTIS,Nicholas E Sex:M 04 Jan 1975 Emmanuel N Cassotis & Judith A Hagerman
CASSOTIS,Rebecca Marie Sex:F 14 Jul 1978 Emanuel N Cassotis
   & Judith Ann Hagerman
CATANZARO,Michael J   Sex:M   17 Jun 1975 John J Catanzaro & Maryann Makowiec
CATE,Jessica Michelle   Sex:F   23 Nov 1980 Stephen M Cate & Janet P Demanche
CATE,Stephanie Lee   Sex:F   24 Apr 1983 Stephen M Cate & Janet P Demanche

HUDSON,NH BIRTHS

CATES,Elizabeth Anna Sex:F 08 Nov 1983 Robert Normand Cates & Barbara E Brown
CATLAND,Jeremy N   Sex:M   10 Mar 1972 Jay W Catland & Judith Dunbar
CATLAND,Jonathan S Sex:F 07 Mar 1964 Jay W Catland & Judith E Dunbar
CATLIN,Everett N   Sex:M   09 May 1974 Erith A Catlin & Viterose E Reed
CATTON,Alford   Sex:M   17 Jun 1741 Hudson, NH Jeremiah Catton & Eunice
CAVANAUGH,Lyn M   Sex:F   29 May 1964 John F Cavanaugh & Mary J Perkins
CAVANAUGH,Maria C Sex:F 10 Oct 1970 William M Cavanaugh & Aree Visuthiwong
CENTER,Colleen A   Sex:F   01 May 1967 Henderson C Center & Jean T Belanger
CENTER,Karen M   Sex:F   27 Feb 1965 Henderson C Center & Jean T Belanger
CHAFIN,Heather J   Sex:F   24 Jul 1969 Robert L Chafin & Jeanne L Yoh
CHALIFOUX,Laura V Sex:F (Child #1) 01 May 1940 Levi J Chalifoux (Tupper
   Lake, NY) & Mildred E Shunaman (Leominster, MA)
CHALIFOUX,Margery C Sex:F (Child #2) 12 Aug 1945 Levi J Chalifoux (Tupper
   Lake, NY) & Mildred E Shunaman (Leominster, MA)
CHAMARD,Fernande   Sex:F   (Child #7) 01 Sep 1925 Eustache Chamard (Canada)
   & Lumina Guilmain (Canada)
CHAMARD,M Theresa I Sex:F (Child #9) 29 Jan 1927 Eustache Chamard (Canada)
   & Lumina Guilmain (Canada)
CHAMARD,Rolande   Sex:F   (Child #8) 01 Sep 1925 Eustache Chamard (Canada)
   & Lumina Guilmain (Canada)
CHAMART,Gertrude J Sex:F (Child #5) 17 May 1922 Eustache Chamart (Canada)
   & Lumina Guilmain (Canada)
CHAMART,Therese Rita Sex:F (Child #6) 29 Apr 1924 Eustache Chamart (Canada)
   & Lumina Grielmain (Canada)
CHAMAST,Blanche Eva Sex:F (Child #3) 26 Jul 1917 Eustache Chamast (Canada)
   & Leunina Goilmain (Canada)
CHAMBERLAND,Eric G Sex:M 18 Apr 1978 Guy J Chamberland & Jacqueline Landry
CHAMBERS,Jessica Jean Sex:F 24 Jan 1980 Gary W Chambers & Patricia I McHugh
CHAMPAGNE,Danny A Sex:M 25 Oct 1976 Gilles A Champagne & Jacqueline J Gagnon
CHAMPIGNY,Gloria J   Sex:F   21 Jul 1947 Calix Champigny (Tyngsboro, MA)
   & Emmabell J Osmer (Nashua, NH)
CHAMPIGNY,Janet B Sex:F   25 Nov 1948 Calix Champigny (Tyngsboro, MA)
   & Emmabelle Osmer (Nashua, NH)
CHAMPIGNY,Judith A Sex:F 07 May 1952 Calix Champigny & Emmabelle J Osmer
CHAMPIGNY,Kathy J Sex:F 15 Feb 1954 Calix Champigny & Emmabell J Osmer
CHAMPIGNY,Michael J Sex:M (Child #1) 16 Oct 1944 Calix Champigny
   (Tyngsboro, MA) & Emmabelle J Osmer (Nashua, NH)
CHAMPIGNY,Patricia L Sex:F (Child #2) 29 Oct 1945 Calix Champigny
   (Tyngsboro, MA) & Emmabell J Osmer (Nashua, NH)
CHAMPIGNY,Robert E Sex:M (Child #1) 15 Oct 1944 Ernest C Champigny
   (Tyngsboro, MA) & Charlotte I Burns (Merrimack, NH)
CHAPDELAINE,Robert AJ II Sex:M 23 Jan 1972 Robert A J Chapdelai & Ruth C Dery
CHAPLICK,Barbara A Sex:F   11 Aug 1947 Adolph M Chaplick (Nashua, NH)
   & Anne P Zapnicke (Lowell, MA)
CHAPLIN,Daniel Tenney Sex:M 20 Apr 1822 Hudson, NH Samuel Chaplin & Elizabeth
CHAPLIN,David T Sex:M 20 Apr 1822 Hudson, NH Samuel Chaplin &
CHAPLIN,Helen Elizabeth   Sex:F   (Child #10) 06 Jul 1930 James W Chaplin
   (Brighton, ME) & Mary David (Standish, NY)
CHAPLIN,Samuel   Sex:M   07 Nov 1810 Hudson, NH Samuel Chaplin & Elizabeth
CHAPMAN,Adaline E   Sex:F   18 Sep 1892 Hudson, NH Frank M Chapman & Lefebvre
CHAPMAN,Adeline E Sex:F   (Child #2) 18 Sep 1892 Frank M Chapman (Newmarket,
   NH) & Lefebere (Nashua, NH)
CHAPMAN,Angela K   Sex:F   12 Dec 1969 James A Chapman & Jacqueline R Fillion
CHAPMAN,Chad K   Sex: 04 May 1973 Kenneth V Chapman & Jeanne Carson
CHAPMAN,Daisy C Sex:F (Child #6) 09 Jun 1901 Hudson, NH Frank M Chapman
   (New Market) & Mederise Lefebvre (Nashua, NH)
CHAPMAN,Dawn L   Sex:F   01 May 1975 James A Chapman & Jacqueline R Fillion
CHAPMAN,Frank H Jr Sex:M 23 May 1963 Frank H Chapman, Sr & Audry F Chapman
CHAPMAN,Frank W   Sex:M   (Child #1) 01 Oct 1891 Frank Chapman (Newmarket, NH)
   & Lefebvre (Nashua, NH)

HUDSON,NH BIRTHS

CHAPMAN,Guy I H   Sex:M   (Child #5) 28 Apr 1899 Frank M Chapman (New Market)
  & Mederise Lefabvre (Nashua, NH)
CHAPMAN,John P W   Sex:M   (Child #7) 19 Jul 1908 Frank M Chapman (Newmarket,
  NH) & Mederise Lefebvre (Nashua, NH)
CHAPMAN,Kevin P   Sex: 06 May 1973 James A Chapman & Jacqueline R Fillion
CHAPMAN,Michele A   Sex:F   18 Aug 1952 John P Chapman & Elizabeth Christian
CHAPUT,Amanda Anne Sex:F 05 Mar 1983 Raymond L Chaput & Martha Joyce Lemieux
CHAPUT,Laurie A   Sex:F   03 Jul 1956 Ralph C Chaput & Patricia M Powers
CHAPUT,Patty S   Sex:F   15 May 1960 Ralph C Chaput & Patricia M Powers
CHAPUT,Peter J   Sex:M   03 Aug 1958 Ralph C Chaput & Mary P Powers
CHAPUT,[Unknown]   Sex:M   01 Dec 1962 Ralph Chaput & Patricia Powers
CHARBONNEAU,Alida I   Sex:F   21 Jan 1963 Claude M Charboneau & Rhona M Shay
CHARBONNEAU,Claudia M   Sex:F   21 May 1954 Claude M Charbonneau & Rhona M Shay
CHARBONNEAU,Diane A Sex:F 10 Oct 1957 Marcel L Charbonneau
  & Virginia E Perkins
CHARBONNEAU,Mark Y   Sex:M   29 Nov 1957 Claude M Charbonneau & Rhona M Shay
CHARBONNEAU,Pauline   Sex:F   (Child #15) 15 Jul 1930 Joseph Charbonneau
  (Canada) & Alice Veilleux (Canada)
CHARBONNEAU,Rhona M   Sex:F   03 Nov 1958 Claude M Charbonneau & Rhona M Shay
CHARBONNEAU,Richard H   Sex:M   26 Aug 1955 Claude M Charbonneau & Rhona M Shay
CHAREST,Diane G   Sex:M   07 Dec 1950 Alphonse J Charest & Clara F Bouley
CHAREST,Nancy L   Sex:F   18 Oct 1965 Robert T Charest & Marian C Sawyer
CHAREST,Stephen Charles   Sex:M   28 Sep 1978 Robert D Charest Sr
  & Pauline T Compagna
CHARETTE,Bonny M   Sex:F   02 Feb 1960 Norman Charette & Jeanine B Chamberlan
CHARETTE,Eric S   Sex:M   12 Aug 1970 John R Charette & Aline M Chamberland
CHARETTE,James J Jr   Sex:M   24 Apr 1968 James J Charette Sr & Barbara F Byrd
CHARETTE,John C   Sex:M   04 Jun 1969 James J Charette Sr & Barbara F Byrd
CHARLAND,Joey A M   Sex:M   13 Nov 1975 Normand G Charland & Liliane G Poulin
CHARLAND,Michele L   Sex:F   07 May 1968 Normand G Charland & Liliane G Poulin
CHARLAND,Michelle A   Sex:F   11 Apr 1968 Onil G Charland & Lorraine E Poulin
CHARLAND,Randy F   Sex: 05 Aug 1972 Normand G Charland & Lilliane G Poulin
CHARLAND,Richard M   Sex:M   31 Jul 1966 Normand G Charland & Liliane G Poulin
CHARPENTIER,Richard J Sex:M 19 May 1949 Charles R Charpenti & Helen E Froton
CHARRON,Keith A   Sex:M   05 Jun 1971 Maurice G Charron & Elizabeth A Desbiens
CHARRON,Kenneth J   Sex:M   (Child #1) 20 Jul 1943 Joseph H Charron (Ayer, MA)
  & Doris E Owens (Peabody, MA)
CHARRON,Phyllis E   Sex:F   (Child #2) 14 Apr 1946 Joseph H Charron (Ayer, MA)
  & Doris E Ovens (Peabody, MA)
CHARWIN,Dora   Sex:F   (Child #2) 24 Apr 1930 Napoleon Charwin (Massachusetts)
  & Antoinette Foisie (Nashua, NH)
CHASE,Abigail   Sex:F   26 Sep 1732 Hudson, NH Ezekiel Chase & Priscilla
CHASE,Abigail   Sex:F   01 Jun 1742 Hudson, NH Roger Chase & Abigail Morrison
CHASE,Alice P Sex:F   11 Apr 1863 Hudson, NH William F Chase & Sarah F Greeley
CHASE,Allice B   Sex:F   04 Apr 1863 Hudson, NH William F Chase & Sarah
CHASE,Amos   Sex:M   19 Jul 1787 Hudson, NH Micajah Chase & Elizabeth
CHASE,Amos   Sex:M   01 Jul 1787 Hudson, NH Micajah Chase & Elizebeth
CHASE,Ann Martha Rhodes   Sex:F   05 Aug 1835 John Chase & Martha L Rhodes
CHASE,Anna   Sex:F   06 Nov 1760 Hudson, NH Henry Chase & Rebecca
CHASE,Anne   Sex:M   06 Nov 1760 Hudson, NH Henry Chase & Rebecca
CHASE,Arthur E   Sex:M   02 Aug 1893 Bertram F Chase (Montpelier, VT)
  & Mary J Dobson (England)
CHASE,Benjamin   Sex:M   17 Aug 1765 Hudson, NH Joshua Chase & Mary Hadley
CHASE,Benjamin   Sex:M   29 Dec 1791 Hudson, NH Benjamin Chase & Dolly
CHASE,Benjamin Durant   Sex:M   13 Apr 1769 Hudson, NH Moses Chase
  & Elizabeth Hamblett
CHASE,Benjamin F   Sex:M   29 Dec 1807 Hudson, NH Jacob Chase & Rebecca
CHASE,Benjamin Franklin   Sex:M   29 Dec 1807 Hudson, NH Jacob Chase & Rebecca
CHASE,Betsey   Sex:F   24 Oct 1794 Hudson, NH Benjamin Chase & Dolly
CHASE,Bettey   Sex:F   26 Oct 1794 Hudson, NH Benjamin Chase & Dorothy

HUDSON,NH BIRTHS

```
CHASE,Betty    Sex:F  25 Jun 1770 Hudson, NH Joshua Chase & Mary Hadley
CHASE,Charles    Sex:M  11 Nov 1810 Hudson, NH Jacob Chase & Rebecca
CHASE,Charles H  Sex:M  03 Aug 1867 Hudson, NH Samuel Chase & Harriet E
CHASE,Daniel   Sex:M  12 Aug 1770 Hudson, NH Stephen Chase Jr & Phebe Chandler
CHASE,Daniel   Sex:M  14 Aug 1777 Hudson, NH Stephen Chase & Hannah
CHASE,Daniel   Sex:M  16 Nov 1788 Hudson, NH Benjamin Chase & Dolley
CHASE,David    Sex:M  14 Aug 1777 Hudson, NH Stephen Chase Jr & Hannah Blodgett
CHASE,David    Sex:M  16 Nov 1778 Hudson, NH Benjamin Chase & Dolly
CHASE,David    Sex:M  12 Aug 1770 Hudson, NH Stephen Chase & Phebe
CHASE,DeWitt   Sex:M  24 Feb 1867 Hudson, NH Gilman F Chase & Mary E
CHASE,Dorothea   Sex:F  05 Apr 1793 Hudson, NH Benjamin Chase & Dorothy
CHASE,Dorothie   Sex:F  05 Apr 1793 Hudson, NH Benjamin Chase & Dolly
CHASE,Elizabeth  Sex:F  06 Jun 1757 Hudson, NH James Chase & Abigail
CHASE,Elizabeth Sex:F 30 Mar 1763 Hudson, NH Moses Chase & Elizabeth Hamblett
CHASE,Elizabeth  Sex:F  06 May 1791 Hudson, NH John Chase & Elizabeth Gibson
CHASE,Elizebeth  Sex:F  06 Dec 1791 Hudson, NH John Chase & Elizebeth
CHASE,Ellen Maria  Sex:F  01 Jan 1849 Hudson, NH John Chase & Martha L Rhodes
CHASE,Enoch    Sex:M  18 Aug 1769 Hudson, NH Henry Chase & Rebecca
CHASE,Enoch    Sex:M  04 Jul 1753 Hudson, NH Stephen Chase & Catherine
CHASE,Ephraim Chandler   Sex:M  28 Aug 1758 Hudson, NH Stephen Chase Jr
   & Phebe Chandler
CHASE,Ezekiel   Sex:M  28 Aug 1730 Hudson, NH Ezekiel Chase & Priscilla
CHASE,Ezekiel   Sex:M  24 May 1727 Hudson, NH Roger Chase & Abigail Morrison
CHASE,Ezekiel   Sex:M  05 May 1768 Hudson, NH Stephen Chase Jr
   & Phebe Chandler
CHASE,Hannah Sex:F  13 Mar 1779 Hudson, NH Stephen Chase Jr & Hannah Blodgett
CHASE,Harold B Sex:F 29 Aug 1894 BF Chase(Vermont) & Mary J Dobson (England)
CHASE,Harriet Eliza Sex:F 02 Apr 1851 Hudson, NH John Chase & Martha L Rhodes
CHASE,Henry    Sex:M  14 Jul 1749 Hudson, NH Henry Chase & Rebecca
CHASE,Jabez Nelson   Sex:M  11 Jul 1833 John Chase & Martha L Rhodes
CHASE,Jacob    Sex:M  30 Nov 1778 Hudson, NH Joshua Chase & Mary Hadley
CHASE,James    Sex:M  25 Dec 1735 Hudson, NH Nathaniel Chase & Sarah
CHASE,James    Sex:M  21 Dec 1735 Hudson, NH Nathaniel Chase & Sarah
CHASE,Jeremiah Sex:M 13 May 1781 Hudson, NH Stephen Chase Jr
   & Hannah Blodgett
CHASE,John    Sex:M  28 Jan 1761 Hudson, NH Stephen Chase Jr & Phebe Chandler
CHASE,John    Sex:M  17 May 1783 Hudson, NH John Chase & Priscilla
CHASE,John    Sex:M  14 Mar 1789 Hudson, NH John Chase & Elizabeth Gibson
CHASE,Joshua   Sex:M  16 Oct 1776 Hudson, NH Joshua Chase & Mary Hadley
CHASE,Kajia    Sex:   11 Jun 1772 Hudson, NH Joshua Chase & Mary
CHASE,Kezia    Sex:   11 Jun 1772 Hudson, NH Joshua Chase & Mary Hadley
CHASE,Lydia    Sex:F  07 May 1789 Hudson, NH Joshua Chase & Mary Hadley
CHASE,Martha   Sex:F  16 Mar 1745 Hudson, NH Ezekiel Chase & Priscilla
CHASE,Martha   Sex:F  16 Mar 1744 Hudson, NH Ezekiel Chase & Priscilla
CHASE,Mary    Sex:F  20 Mar 1748 Hudson, NH Roger Chase & Abigail Morrison
CHASE,Mary    Sex:F  02 May 1774 Hudson, NH Joshua Chase & Mary Hadley
CHASE,Mary    Sex:F  20 Mar 1747 Hudson, NH Roger Chase & Abigail
CHASE,Mary Ann Childs   Sex:F  11 Aug 1828 John Chase & Martha L Rhodes
CHASE,Mary Isabella   Sex:F  14 Jan 1816 Hudson, NH Jacob Chase & Rebecca
CHASE,Mary T   Sex:F  14 Jan 1810 Hudson, NH Jacob Chase & Rebecca
CHASE,Mathew   Sex:M  20 Oct 1739 Hudson, NH Roger Chase & Abigail
CHASE,Matthew   Sex:M  20 Oct 1739 Hudson, NH Roger Chase & Abigail Morrison
CHASE,Micaiah   Sex:M  28 Aug 1758 Hudson, NH Stephen Chase & Phebe
CHASE,Micajah  Sex:M  28 Aug 1758 Hudson, NH Stephen Chase Jr & Phebe Chandler
CHASE,Mollie   Sex:F  13 Apr 1756 Hudson, NH Henry Chase & Rebeckah
CHASE,Molly    Sex:F  13 Apr 1756 Hudson, NH Henry Chase & Rebecca
CHASE,Moses    Sex:M  10 Sep 1760 Hudson, NH Moses Chase & Elizabeth Hamblett
CHASE,Moses    Sex:M  12 Oct 1775 Hudson, NH Henry Chase & Mary
CHASE,Nancy    Sex:F  27 Dec 1843 Hudson, NH John Chase & Martha L Rhodes
CHASE,Nathaniel   Sex:M  27 Mar 1736 Hudson, NH Ezekiel Chase & Priscilla
```

HUDSON,NH BIRTHS

```
CHASE,Phebe    Sex:F   04 Sep 1771 Hudson, NH Henry Chase & Rebecca
CHASE,Phebe    Sex:F   31 May 1763 Hudson, NH Stephen Chase Jr & Phebe Chandler
CHASE,Phebe    Sex:F   25 Apr 1783 Hudson, NH Joshua Chase & Mary Hadley
CHASE,Pheobe   Sex:F   10 May 1786 Hudson, NH John Chase & Elizabeth Gibson
CHASE,Pheby    Sex:F   25 Apr 1783 Hudson, NH Joshua Chase & Mary
CHASE,Pheby    Sex:F   10 May 1786 Hudson, NH John Chase & Elizabeth
CHASE,Poley    Sex:F   11 Jul 1790 Hudson, NH Benjamin Chase & Poley
CHASE,Polly    Sex:F   11 Jul 1790 Hudson, NH Benjamin Chase & Dolly
CHASE,Priscilla  Sex:F  28 Sep 1749 Hudson, NH Ezekiel Chase & Priscilla
CHASE,Rebecca  Sex:F   25 Sep 1751 Hudson, NH Henry Chase & Rebecca
CHASE,Rebecca Nichols Sex:F 21 Feb 1838 Hudson, NH John Chase
   & Martha L Rhodes
CHASE,Rebeckah  Sex:F  25 Sep 175  Hudson, NH Henry Chase & Rebeckah
CHASE,Ruth     Sex:F   25 Mar 1787 Hudson, NH Joshua Chase & Mary Hadley
CHASE,Ruth Rhodes  Sex:F  09 Mar 1842 Hudson, NH John Chase & Martha L Rhodes
CHASE,Samuel   Sex:M   15 Mar 1785 Hudson, NH Joshua Chase & Mary Hadley
CHASE,Sarah    Sex:F   14 Mar 1739 Hudson, NH Ezekiel Chase & Priscilla
CHASE,Sarah    Sex:F   19 Apr 1758 Hudson, NH Henry Chase & Rebecca
CHASE,Sarah    Sex:F   30 Apr 1765 Hudson, NH Stephen Chase Jr & Phebe Chandler
CHASE,Sarah    Sex:F   17 Feb 1781 Hudson, NH Joshua Chase & Mary Hadley
CHASE,Sarah    Sex:F   19 Apr 1756 Hudson, NH Henry Chase & Rebecca
CHASE,Sarah    Sex:F   14 Mar 1738 Hudson, NH Ezekiel Chase & Priscilla
CHASE,Sarah Ellen  Sex:F  27 May 1845 Hudson, NH John Chase & Martha L Rhodes
CHASE,Sarah Maria George  Sex:F  04 Jun 1831 John Chase & Martha L Rhodes
CHASE,Stephen  Sex:M   01 May 1735 Hudson, NH Roger Chase & Abigail
CHASE,Solomon  Sex:M   12 Jun 1797 Hudson, NH John Chase & Elizabeth Gibson
CHASE,Stephen  Sex:M   21 Apr 1755 Hudson, NH Stephen Chase & Catherine
CHASE,Stevens  Sex:M   01 May 1735 Hudson, NH Roger Chase & Abigail Morrison
CHASE,Susanna  Sex:F   28 Mar 1766 Hudson, NH Henry Chase & Rebecca
CHASE,Susannah Sex:F   28 Mar 1766 Hudson, NH Henry Chase & Heberkiah
CHASE,William D  Sex:M  31 Mar 1821 Hudson, NH Jacob Chase & Rebecca
CHASE,Wm Franklin Hadley  Sex:M  24 Apr 1840 Hudson, NH John Chase
   & Martha L Rhodes
CHASE,[Unknown]  Sex:M     1862 Hudson, NH Gilman F Chase & Mary E
CHASE,[Unknown]  Sex:M  Mar 1862 Hudson, NH Gilman F Chase & Mary J
CHASSE,Paul M III  Sex:M  15 Mar 1976 Paul M Chasse Jr & Patricia Ann Poliquin
CHAUVIN,Reta   Sex:F  (Child #9) 27 Jan 1915 Hudson, NH Hyacinth Chauvin
   (N Grovesdale, CT) & Emma Michaud (Canada)
CHENEY,Brian E  Sex:M  01 Aug 1957 Norman W Cheney & Theresa A Dube
CHENEY,Charles E  Sex:M  (Child #3) 19 Nov 1942 Charles C Cheney (Antrim, NH)
   & Jennie M Goodwin (Greenfield, NH)
CHENEY,William R Sex:M 12 Mar 1984 Robert A Cheney & Shirley A Senneville
CHERKES,Janice L Sex:F  (Child #7) 04 Mar 1932 Hudson, NH Julian Cherkes
   (Poland) & Anna Lamopowicz (Poland)
CHERKES,Lillian  Sex:F  (Child #6) 26 Jan 1928 Julian Cherkes (Russia)
   & Anna Tarnysowich (Russia)
CHESBROUGH,[Unknown]  Sex:M  (Child #4) 22 Nov 1912 Walter Chesbrough
   (Albion, NY) & Bertha Manning (Manchester, NH)
CHESNULEVICH,Alan R  Sex:M  17 Sep 1956 Harry J Chesnulevich & Dorothy Poff
CHESNULEVICH,David R Sex:M  13 Dec 1960 Harry J Chesnulevich & Dorothy B Poff
CHESNULEVICH,Eric J  Sex:M  07 Jan 1970 Harry J Chesnulevich & Dorothy B Poff
CHESNULEVICH,John K  Sex:M  10 Dec 1954 Harry J Chesnulevich & Dorothy B Poff
CHICKERING,Allen S  Sex:M  21 Jun 1972 William O Chickering & Rebecca J Guay
CHILCOAT,Gary A  Sex:M  27 Mar 1956 Jack W Chilcoat & Catherine Wisnosky
CHILTON,James E  Sex:M  06 Mar 1965 William D Chilton & Katherine C Hart
CHOUINARD,Jonathan C  Sex:M  28 Jan 1970 Bertrand A Chouinard
   & Shirley A Galipeau
CHOUINARD,Jonathan Philip  Sex:M  08 Aug 1981 Philip A Chouinard
   & Susan Frances Ford
CHRIST,Stephen Thomas Sex:M 06 Aug 1984 Robert T Christ & Susan Elaine Helm
```

HUDSON,NH BIRTHS

CHRISTIANSEN,Athena Marie Sex:F 06 Jul 1979 Gary A Christiansen
   & Jean T Frenette
CHRISTIANSEN,Erica Lyn Sex:F 04 Sep 1979 Kevin L Christiansen
   & Michelle E Small
CHRISTIANSEN,Hans H Sex:M 24 Sep 1967 Keith A Christiansen & Carol A Rock
CHRISTIANSEN,Kristi Sue Sex:F 25 May 1981 Kevin L Christiansen
   & Michele E Small
CHRISTIANSEN,Laurie A Sex:F 24 Mar 1980 Bruce J Christiansen & Donna M Tate
CHRISTIANSEN,[Unknown] Sex:F 12 Jul 1978 Bruce J Christiansen & Donna M Tate
CHRISTINO,Glen T Sex:M 29 Oct 1969 Theodore T Christino & Joy A Fagan
CHRISTO,Jeffrey P Sex:M 18 Oct 1965 Harry Christo & Gloria Sakey
CHRISTOPHER,David B Sex:M 08 Apr 1947 Geo A Christopher (Londonderry, NH)
   & Anne Kapisky (Hudson, NH)
CHRISTOPHER,Dorothy A Sex:F 06 Dec 1954 George A Christopher & Anne Kapisky
CHRISTOPHER,Dorothy Emily Sex:F (Child #2) 11 Jun 1902 Bernard Christopher
   (Nova Scotia) & Dorothy Ring (Amesbury, MA)
CHRISTOPHER,Francis B Sex:M (Child #3) 19 Oct 1903 Bernard Christopher
   (Nova Scotia) & Dorothy Ring (Amesbury, MA)
CHRISTOPHER,Scott A Sex:M 02 Mar 1970 David B Christopher & Elaine M Scott
CHRZANOWSKI,A F Jr Sex:M (Child #2) 16 Jun 1943 A F Chrzanowski (New
   Britain, CT) & Genevieve S Polak (Nashua, NH)
CHRZANOWSKI,Carol A Sex:F (Child #3) 16 Jan 1946 Anthony F Chrzanows
   (New Britain, CT) & Genevieve Polak (Nashua, NH)
CHURCH,Carl E Sex:M (Child #1) 21 Sep 1906 Hosmer C Church (Boston, MA)
   & Jessie M Barnard (Peterborough, NH)
CHZANOWSKI,Michael Anthony Sex:M (Child #1) 01 Oct 1941 Anthony Chzanowski
   (New Britain, CT) & Genevieve Polak (Nashua, NH)
CIAMPA,Deanna B Sex:F 23 Aug 1969 Robert A Ciampa & Orella M Flynn
CINQ-MARS,Donald R Sex:M 18 May 1972 Roland D Cinq-Mars & Mary Ann Raybold
CISSON,Mary A Sex:F 24 Oct 1959 William A Cisson & Wanda L Stage
CLARK,Ansel D Sex:M L 25 Apr 1881 Hudson, NH George M Clark (Nashua, NH)
   & Helen C Holt (Weston, Vt)
CLARK,Bertha Irene Sex:F   20 Feb 1879 Hudson, NH George M Clark (Nashua,
   NH) & Helen (Wester VT)
CLARK,Beth E Sex:F 01 Apr 1956 Kenneth G Clark & Delnette A Crosby
CLARK,Edward P Sex:M 27 Aug 1960 Richard L Clark & Roseanna B Moreau
CLARK,Frederick E Sex:M (Child #1) 27 Mar 1944 Frederick A Clark (Nashua,
   NH) & Charlotte B Oakley (Foracre, OK)
CLARK,Gail K Sex:F 01 Nov 1955 John P Clark & Patricia E Atkinson
CLARK,Gale L Sex:F 25 Sep 1957 Richard L Clark & Roseanna B Moreau
CLARK,Glenn R Sex:M 06 Apr 1951 Robert W Clark & Helen B Kashulines
CLARK,Jane M Sex:F 18 Mar 1958 Kenneth G Clark & Delnette A Crosby
CLARK,John P Sex:M 20 May 1949 Richard M Clark & Ruth Preston
CLARK,John P Sex:M 24 Mar 1961 Kenneth G Clark & Delnette A Crosby
CLARK,Joyce L Sex:F 02 Dec 1947 Frederick A Clark (Nashua, NH)
   & Charlotte B Oakley (4 Acre, OK)
CLARK,Karen L Sex:F 10 Sep 1952 Frederick A Clark & Charlotte B Oakley
CLARK,Karen T Sex:F 08 Dec 1953 Richard L Clark & Roseanna B Moreau
CLARK,Kelly A Sex:F 04 Apr 1960 Robert W Clark & Helen B Kashulines
CLARK,Linda C Sex:F (Child #2) 24 Mar 1946 Frederick A Clark (Nashua, NH)
   & Charlotte B Oakley (Fouracre, OK)
CLARK,Margaret L Sex:F 02 May 1954 John P Clark & Patricia Atkinson
CLARK,Muriel Ruby Sex:F (Child #9) 19 Aug 1936 Willis Clark (Barnett, VT)
   & Arlene Carter (Danville, VT)
CLARK,Patricia L Sex:F (Child #1) 01 Apr 1944 Robert B Clark (Venice
   Center, NY) & Shirley M Crompton (Nashua, NH)
CLARK,Paul M Sex:M 03 Nov 1966 Richard L Clark & Roseanna B Moreau
CLARK,Peter K Sex:M 06 Jun 1953 Robert W Clark & Helen B Kashulines
CLARK,Richard L Jr Sex:M 13 Nov 1958 Richard L Clark, Sr
   & Roseanna B Moreau

HUDSON,NH BIRTHS

CLARK,Ruth Esther   Sex:F   (Child #8) 12 Sep 1934 Wallace T Clark (Barnett,
    VT) & Arline G Carter (Danville, VT)
CLARK,Sharon A   Sex:F   10 Sep 1952 Frederick A Clark & Charlotte B Oakley
CLARK,Sheryl A   Sex:F   27 Jul 1955 Richard L Clark & Roseanna B Moreau
CLARK,Steven L   Sex:M   26 Jan 1963 Richard L Clark & Roseanne Moreau
CLARK,Susan J   Sex:F   20 May 1959 Roger L Clark & Carolyn L Neuman
CLARK,William K   Sex:M   18 Jan 1972 William A Clark & Anne R Boulanger
CLARK,[Unknown]   Sex:F   (Child #6) 05 Aug 1933 Wallace T Clark (Barnet, VT)
    & Arline G Carter (Danville, VT)
CLARKE,Andrew D   Sex:M   06 Jan 1971 Gerald M Clarke & Diane Harvey
CLARKE,Aric L   Sex:M   30 Jun 1975 Donald W Clarke & Cynthia E Smith
CLARKE,Autumn-Rose   Sex:F   11 Oct 1977 Brian M Clarke & Doris M DiFonzo
CLARKE,Deborah A   Sex:F   20 Dec 1964 John D Clarke & Lucille G Pepin
CLARKE,Michael H   Sex:M   08 Oct 1969 Kenneth E Clarke & Linda M Coburn
CLARKE,Richard L   Sex:M   21 Feb 1966 Kenneth E Clarke & Linda M Coburn
CLARKE,Thomas Albert   Sex:M   17 Jun 1984 Thomas Clarke & Danuta Bielawski
CLARKE,Troy B   Sex:M   16 Nov 1977 Donald W Clarke & Cynthia E Smith
CLAVEAU,Linda A   Sex:F   27 Aug 1947 Albert D Claveau (Salem, MA)
    & Evelyn M Mayhew (Montgomery, VT)
CLAVEAU,Pauline   Sex:F   (Child #5) 06 Sep 1940 Peter Claveau (Canada)
    & Hilda L Nason (Bloomfield, VT)
CLAXTON,Maxene   Sex:F   (Child #4) 21 Nov 1937 Fay Claxton (Marion, IL)
    & Edna Pulley (Marion, IL)
CLAXTON,Rosalie Louise   Sex:F   (Child #3) 13 Sep 1933 Jay Claxton (Marion,
    IL) & Eleanor Pulley (Marion, IL)
CLAY,Henry A   Sex:M   02 Mar 1878 Hudson, NH Samuel A Clay & Mary L Reix
CLAY,Ruth S   Sex:F   07 Sep 1855 Hudson, NH Samuel J Clay & Mary Ann Webster
CLAY,Samuel A   Sex:M   03 May 1854 Hudson, NH Samuel J Clay & Mary Ann Webster
CLAY,William H Sex:M   10 Jan 1851 Hudson, NH Samuel J Clay & Mary Ann Webster
CLEGG,Tammy L   Sex:F   26 Jun 1976 David A Clegg & Sheila Ann Marchant
CLEMENT,   Sex:F   27 Jul 1806 Hudson, NH Clement, Jr &
CLEMENT,Addie W   Sex:F   (Child #1) 04 May 1882 Hudson, NH Elmer D Clement
    (Hudson, NH) & Emily S Wilcox (E Boston, MA)
CLEMENT,Christopher J   Sex:M   29 Feb 1976 John T Clement & Laura M Pointer
CLEMENT,Clara A   Sex:F   29 Jul 1860 Hudson, NH David Clement Jr & Maria H
CLEMENT,Dorcas   Sex:F   (Child #8) 19 Mar 1905 Elmer D Clement (Hudson, NH)
    & Emily Wilcox (E Boston, MA)
CLEMENT,Edward   Sex:M   (Child #7) 28 Feb 1903 Elmer Clement (Hudson, NH)
    & Emily Wilcox (E Boston, MA)
CLEMENT,Harry E   Sex:M   (Child #2) 07 Jan 1887 Elmer D Clement (Hudson, NH)
    & Emily Wilcox (E Boston, MA)
CLEMENT,Jonathan A   Sex:M   30 Aug 1963 Maurice R Clement & Patricia L Binks
CLEMENT,Kevin A   Sex:M   10 Sep 1960 David A Clement & Shirley E Norcross
CLEMENT,Nettie J   Sex:F   (Child #4) 24 Apr 1890 Elmer D Clement (Hudson, NH)
    & Emily E Wilcox (E Boston, MA)
CLEMENT,Otis D   Sex:M   (Child #5) 25 Jan 1895 Elmer D Clement (Hudson, NH)
    & Emily Wilcox (E Boston, MA)
CLEMENT,[Unknown]   Sex:F   (Child #6) 22 Aug 1897 Elmer D Clement (Hudson, NH)
    & Emily E Wilcox (E. Boston, MA)
CLEMENTS,Mark Roy   Sex:M   09 Feb 1985 Edward L Clements & Nancy L Carlson
CLERMONT,Thomas Michael   Sex:M   23 Oct 1979 Philip A Clermont
    & Cynthia Lee Sexton
CLEVELAND,Penney L   Sex:F   13 Sep 1970 Richard W Cleveland & Winifred E Hines
CLEVELAND,Wendy J   Sex:F   13 Apr 1966 Richard W Cleveland & Winifred E Hines
CLEWS,Patricia M   Sex:F   17 Mar 1958 Frank J Clews & Anna M Lawless
CLIFFORD,Alice   Sex:F   11 Feb 1893 Patrick Clifford (Ireland)
    & Mary A Downey (Nashua, NH)
CLIFFORD,Augustus   Sex:M   (Child #8) 08 Apr 1905 Patrick Clifford (Ireland)
    & Mary A Downey (Ireland)
CLIFFORD,Joey M   Sex:M   26 Jan 1963 Thomas H Clifford & Louise A Marciano

HUDSON,NH BIRTHS

CLIFFORD,Margaret   Sex:F   (Child #6) 10 Dec 1900 Patrick Clifford (Ireland)
  & Mary A Downey (Nashua, NH)
CLIFFORD,Mark S   Sex:M   24 Feb 1965 Thoms H Clifford, Jr & Louise A Marciano
CLIFFORD,Mary   Sex:F   18 Aug 1894 Patrick Clifford (Ireland)
  & Mary Downey (Nashua, NH)
CLIFFORD,Richard S Sex:M 23 Mar 1969 Thomas H Clifford Jr & Louise A Marciano
CLIFFORD,Timothy   Sex:M   (Child #5) 14 Nov 1897 Patrick Clifford (Ireland)
  & Mary A Downey (Nashua, NH)
CLIFFORD,[Unknown]   Sex:M   (Child #7) 12 Nov 1902 Patrick Clifford (Ireland)
  & Mary Downey (Nashua, NH)
CLOSSER,Carissa B   Sex:F   02 Jan 1971 James A Closser & Mary J Plumer
CLOUGH,Chester M   Sex:M   21 Mar 1966 Donald E Clough & Rita I Demers
CLOUGH,Joseph L   Sex:M   16 Aug 1969 Joseph L Clough & Maureen L Mullen
CLOUGH,Kathryn H   Sex:F   10 Aug 1970 Joseph L Clough & Maureen L Mullen
CLOUGH,Nathaniel   Sex:M   16 Apr 1860 Hudson, NH Thomas Clough & Mary
CLOUGH,Nathaniel W   Sex:M   16 Apr 1860 Hudson, NH Thomas Clough & Mary
CLOUGH,Noah Darrah   Sex:M   03 Mar 1785 Londonderry   & Nancy Clough
CLOUTHIER,Joseph Roger   Sex:M   (Child #10) 23 May 1940 Henry Clouthier
  (Lowell, MA) & Blanche Paquin (Canada)
CLOUTIER,Catherine Ann Sex:F 22 May 1979 Roland J Cloutier & Carol A Dunstan
CLOUTIER,Claudette Yolande   Sex:F   (Child #5) 14 Apr 1941 Joseph Cloutier
  (Canada) & Ella Levesque (Vermont)
CLOUTIER,David E   Sex:M   18 Feb 1969 Norman C Cloutier & Susan C Auguin
CLOUTIER,Derek J   Sex:M   28 Sep 1966 Norman C Cloutier & Susan C Arguin
CLOUTIER,Diane E   Sex:F   26 Jun 1965 Norman R Cloutier & Simonne M Dupont
CLOUTIER,Heather Ann Sex:F 05 Jul 1982 Daniel E Cloutier & Linda Ann Paradis
CLOUTIER,Heather Marie   Sex:F   02 Nov 1983 Michael D Cloutier & Gail T Rodier
CLOUTIER,Jana L   Sex:F   15 Jun 1965 Ronald D Cloutier & Joyce E Smith
CLOUTIER,Jay S   Sex:M   07 Apr 1963 Ronald D Cloutier & Joyce E Smith
CLOUTIER,Jill Lauren   Sex:F   08 Jan 1982 Gerald K Cloutier & Susan L Mitchell
CLOUTIER,Joshua Ryan   Sex:M   26 May 1977 Ronald D Cloutier & Joyce E Smith
CLOUTIER,Patrick J Sex:M 18 Mar 1965 Richard M Cloutier & Micheline M Mougel
CLOUTIER,Ronald E   Sex: 19 Feb 1973 Norman E Cloutier & Louise L Roy
CLOUTIER,Ronald R   Sex:M   17 Jun 1948 Donald J Cloutier (Lowell, MA)
  & June A Tate (Milford, NH)
CLOUTIER,Rosemarie J   Sex:F   24 Nov 1949 Donald Cloutier & June A Tate
CLUFF,Danie Edgar Sex:M 13 Oct 1854 Hudson, NH Daniel P Cluff
  & Lucy A Webster
CLUFF,Flora Louise   Sex:F   22 Jun 1862 Hudson, NH Daniel P Cluff
  & Lucy A Webster
CLUFF,Fred E   Sex:M   24 Oct 1856 Hudson, NH Daniel P Cluff & Lucy A Webster
CLUFF,Howard Milton   Sex:M   30 Nov 1860 Hudson, NH Daniel P Cluff
  & Lucy A Webster
CLUFF,Lucy Annie   Sex:F   09 Mar 1865 Hudson, NH Daniel P Cluff
  & Lucy A Webster
CLUFF,Milon O   Sex:M   31 Aug 1851 Hudson, NH Daniel P Cluff & Lucy A Webster
CLYDE,Esther Jane   Sex:F   (Child #5) 04 Mar 1914 George W Clyde (Dracut, MA)
  & Anna Bertha Wells (Concord)
CLYDE,Margaret E   Sex:F   (Child #2) 09 Apr 1906 George W Clyde (Hudson, NH)
  & A Bertha Wells (Concord, NH)
CLYDE,Morris Gilmore Sex:M   (Child #4) 03 Dec 1911 George W Clyde (Dracut,
  MA) & Anna B Wells (Concord, NH)
CLYDE,Priscilla E   Sex:F   (Child #3) 01 Nov 1907 Geo W Clyde (Hudson, NH)
  & A Bertha Wells (Concord, NH)
CLYDE,Wilson W   Sex:M   (Child #1) 09 Mar 1903 Geo W Clyde (Hudson, NH)
  & A Bertha Wells (Concord, NH)
COAKLEY,Brian M   Sex:M   08 Sep 1975 Laurence F Coakley & Alice M Perkins
COAKLEY,Daniel F   Sex:M   10 Jul 1974 Laurence F Coakley & Alice M Perkins
COBB,Jennifer   Sex: 23 Oct 1972 James L Cobb & Susan Carroll
COBURN,Bruce A Jr   Sex:M   18 Feb 1968 Bruce A Coburn & Linda M Gagnon

HUDSON,NH BIRTHS

COBURN,Kathi A   Sex:F   25 Sep 1964 Bernard W Coburn, Sr & Pauline M Garfield
COBURN,Michael A   Sex:M   24 Aug 1961 Bernard W Coburn & Pauline M Garfield
COBURN,Sandra L   Sex:F   01 Oct 1960 Dexter I Coburn & Norma J Proctor
COBURN,Vickie M   Sex:F   23 Feb 1965 Bruce A Coburn & Linda M Gagnon
COCHRAN IV,Arthur W   Sex:M   31 Jan 1970 Arthur W Cochran III & Wanda A Swift
COFFEY,Christopher J   Sex:M   17 Jun 1971 John J Coffey & Marilyn A Richo
COLBURN,Brenda A   Sex:F   21 Jun 1968 Francis A Colburn & Mary E O'Neill
COLBURN,Donna B   Sex:F   25 Dec 1970 Francis A Colburn & Mary E O'Neill
COLBURN,Edith   Sex:F   25 Jan 1872 Hudson, NH Henry F Colburn
    & M Frances Gould
COLBURN,Edith Frances   Sex:F   25 Jan 1872 Hudson, NH Henry L Colburn
    & Mary F
COLBURN,Edward   Sex:M   14 Sep 1705 Dunstable Thomas Colburn & Mary
COLBURN,Edward   Sex:M   14 Dec 1706 Dunstable Thomas Colburn & Mary
COLBURN,Elijah   Sex:M   08 Sep 1795 Hudson, NH Zaccheus Colburn & Rachel Hills
COLBURN,Elizabeth   Sex:F   24 Sep 1700 Dunstable Thomas Colburn & Mary
COLBURN,Elizabeth   Sex:F   10 Apr 1789 Hudson, NH Isaac Colburn & Lydia Davis
COLBURN,Elizebeth   Sex:F   10 Jun 1789 Hudson, NH Isaac Colburn & Lydia
COLBURN,Emma B   Sex:F   29 Dec 1867 Hudson, NH Henry F Colburn
    & M Frances Gould
COLBURN,Heather A   Sex:F   05 Aug 1975 Paul A Colburn & Roselyn A Moore
COLBURN,Isaac   Sex:M   25 Jan 1763 Hudson, NH Thomas Colburn & Mary
COLBURN,Isaac   Sex:M   11 Dec 1798 Hudson, NH Isaac Colburn & Lydia Davis
COLBURN,James   Sex:M   30 Apr 1783 Hudson, NH Daniel Colburn & Sally
COLBURN,Jeremiah   Sex:M   03 Dec 1731 Hudson, NH Jeremiah Colburn & Sarah
COLBURN,Lena   Sex:F   11 Sep 1870 Hudson, NH Henry F Colburn & M Frances Gould
COLBURN,Luce   Sex:F   20 Oct 1737 Hudson, NH Jeremiah Colburn & Sarah
COLBURN,Lucy   Sex:F   14 Feb 1735 Hudson, NH Oliver Colburn & Lucy
COLBURN,Lucy   Sex:F   20 Oct 1737 Hudson, NH Jeremiah Colburn & Sarah
COLBURN,Lydia   Sex:F   16 Aug 1787 Hudson, NH Isaac Colburn & Lydia Davis
COLBURN,Lydia Maria   Sex:F   01 Jul 1843 Hudson, NH Paul Colburn & Maria E
COLBURN,Mariane   Sex:F   26 Feb 1789 Hudson, NH Zacaheus Colburn & Rachel
COLBURN,Martha R   Sex:F   (Child #4) 22 Jan 1913 Alfred L Colburn (Lowell, MA)
    & Lulah Gee (Cornish Flat, NH)
COLBURN,Mary   Sex:F   03 May 1786 Hudson, NH Isaac Colburn & Lydia Davis
COLBURN,Miriam   Sex:F   26 Feb 1789 Hudson, NH Zaccheus Colburn & Rachel Hills
COLBURN,Molley   Sex:F   21 Dec 1793 Hudson, NH Zacheus Colburn & Rachel
COLBURN,Molly   Sex:F   21 Oct 1793 Hudson, NH Zaccheus Colburn & Rachel Hills
COLBURN,Paul   Sex:M   22 Jan 1796 Hudson, NH Isaac Colburn & Lydia Davis
COLBURN,Paul   Sex:M   27 Jan 1796 Hudson, NH Isaac Colburn & Lydia
COLBURN,Periah   Sex: 26 Mar 1801 Hudson, NH Lemuel Colburn & Miriam
COLBURN,Rachel   Sex:F   18 Sep 1721 Dunstable Thomas Colburn & Mary
COLBURN,Sarah   Sex:F   20 Oct 1737 Hudson, NH Jeremiah Colburn & Sarah
COLBURN,Sarah   Sex:F   25 Feb 1773 Hudson, NH Thomas Colburn & Ruth
COLBURN,Sarah   Sex:F   20 Aug 1794 Hudson, NH Isaac Colburn & Lydia Davis
COLBURN,Sarah   Sex:F   24 Aug 1794 Hudson, NH Isaac Colburn & Lydia
COLBURN,Thomas   Sex:M   28 Apr 1702 Dunstable Thomas Colburn & Mary
COLBURN,Thomas   Sex:M   12 Nov 1761 Hudson, NH Thomas Colburn & Mary
COLBURN,Thomas   Sex:M   27 Feb 1792 Hudson, NH Zaccheus Colburn & Rachel Hills
COLBURN,Thomas   Sex:M   12 Nov 1759 Hudson, NH Thomas Colburn & Mary
COLBURN,Titus   Sex:M   02 Apr 1742 Hudson, NH A Negro
COLBURN,Willard   Sex:M   30 Mar 1799 Hudson, NH Lemuel Colburn & Miriam
COLBURN,Zaccheus   Sex:M 05 Jan 1801 Hudson, NH Zaccheus Colburn & Rachel Hills
COLBURN,Zacheus   Sex:M   16 Feb 1765 Hudson, NH Thomas Colburn & Mary
COLBURN,Zacheus   Sex:M   05 Jan 1800 Hudson, NH Zacheus Colburn & Rachel
COLBURN,[Unknown]   Sex: Hudson, NH Henry T Colburn & M Frances
COLBY,Alice Blanche   Sex:F   (Child #6) 27 Mar 1911 John Colby (Franklin, NH)
    & Ida Eayers (Merrimack, NH)
COLBY,Helen Louise   Sex:F   (Child #5) 28 Dec 1909 John Colby (Franklin, NH)
    & Ida Eayrs (Merrimack, NH)

HUDSON,NH BIRTHS

COLBY,Sally Margarite   Sex:F   (Child #7) 15 Apr 1912 John Colby (Franklin, NH) & Ida Eayrs (Merrimack, NH)
COLBY,Sarah Ann   Sex:F   25 Apr 1981 Colin S Colby Jr & Pauline Y St Laurent
COLDIRON,Carmen A   Sex:F   05 Jan 1959 James Coldiron & Maria A Adan
COLE,Cheryl L   Sex:F   15 Aug 1950 Raymond E Cole & Margaret E Cook
COLE,Clarinda   Sex:F   (Child #2) 28 Jan 1943 Russell Cole, Jr. (Nashua, NH) & Selma E Gatz (Hudson, NH)
COLE,Cynthia G   Sex:F   06 Mar 1972 Donald W Cole & Patricia M Spellenbe
COLE,Donald W   Sex:M   18 Feb 1980 Donald W Cole & Patricia M Spellenbe
COLE,Frederick G   Sex:M   (Child #3) 24 Jul 1882 Hudson, NH Charles B Cole (New Brunswick) & Lizzie J Green (Lowell, MA)
COLE,Kevin A   Sex:M   26 Aug 1968 William C Cole & Suzanne J Aldrich
COLE,Paul R   Sex:M   16 Sep 1951 Raymond E Cole & Margaret E Cook
COLE,Percival E   Sex:M   22 Jan 1872 Hudson, NH William Cole & Jennie
COLE,Theresa A   Sex:F   03 Mar 1968 Donald W Cole & Patricia M Spellenbe
COLE,Tracy E   Sex:F   22 Mar 1971 James E Cole & Diane J Gower
COLEMAN,Donald F   Sex:M   17 Mar 1957 George F Coleman & Mary O Wheeler
COLES,Donna L   Sex:F   24 Mar 1950 John T Coles & Claire E Gould
COLES,Susan D   Sex:F L 17 Dec 1947 John T Coles (Cornish, NH) & Claire E Gould (Swanton, VT)
COLLARD,Joseph   Sex:M   (Child #1) 17 Oct 1930 Leo Collard (Canada) & Liliane Gendron (Nashua, NH)
COLLARD,Lauretta M L   Sex:F   (Child #5) 07 May 1941 Leonidas Collard (Canada) & Lillian Gendron (Nashua, NH)
COLLARD,Leo Eugene   Sex:M   (Child #2) 16 Nov 1932 Hudson, NH Leo Collard (Canada) & Liliane Gendron (Nashua, NH)
COLLARD,Marcel J   Sex:M   11 Apr 1951 Leonidas J Collard & Lillian Y Gendron
COLLARD,Maurice J J   Sex:M   15 Jul 1948 Leonidas Collard (Canada) & Lillian Y Gendron (Nashua, NH)
COLLINS,Aaron Michael   Sex:M   05 Dec 1982 David M Collins & Nancy Ann Dichard
COLLINS,Ashley Elizabeth Sex:F 29 Sep 1983 Robert T Collins & Barbara ADurkin
COLLINS,Brooks Ann   Sex:F   29 Sep 1983 Robert T Collins & Barbara Ann Durkin
COLLINS,Kathleen M   Sex:F   26 Aug 1976 Glen W Collins & Bonita D Chesley
COLLINS,Patricia L   Sex:F   22 Dec 1964 Michael J Collins & Florence A Bois
COLLINS,Robert W   Sex:M   18 Jun 1975 Robert C Collins & Margaret A Miniscalc
COLLINS,Stephen   Sex:M   30 Jun 1971 Peter R Collins & Jane Flavell
COLLINS,Tasha Alexis   Sex:F   24 Apr 1981 Frank G Collins & Sherry L Hemingway
COLLINS,[Unknown]   Sex:F   12 Mar 1976 Roland J Collins & Donna Marie Wrigley
COLOMBE,Diane S   Sex:F   15 Aug 1963 Walter L Colombe & Mary G Foster
COLVILLE,James Allen   Sex:M   (Child #1) 22 May 1902 John Allen Colville (Peterborough, NH) & Ester Isabelle Howe (Nashua, NH)
COMBS,Augusta   Sex:M   14 Apr 1823 Hudson, NH Simeon Combs & Hannah
COMBS,Jane   Sex:F   23 Sep 1814 Hudson, NH James Combs & Jane
COMPTON,Krystyn Lee   Sex:F   14 May 1981 Roy R Compton Jr & Lois Ann Wesson
CONATY,James G   Sex:M   07 Jul 1965 Albert S Conaty & Jane Steele
CONATY,Leonard J   Sex:M   27 Jan 1969 Albert S Conaty & Jane Steele
CONDO,Toby B   Sex:M   23 May 1971 Maurice A Condo & Janis M Bossie
CONLIN,Ann J   Sex:F   03 Feb 1966 James E Conlin & Marguerite E Granger
CONLIN,Eric J   Sex:M   20 Jan 1963 James E Conlin & Marguerite E Granger
CONLIN,Kevin M   Sex:M   31 Jul 1964 James E Conlin & Marguerite E Granger
CONLIN,Thomas E   Sex:M   24 Dec 1968 James E Conlin & Marguerite E Granger
CONLIN,William S   Sex:M   01 Jun 1967 James E Conlin & Marguerite E Granger
CONLON,Kimberly S   Sex:F   04 Nov 1970 Paul W Conlon & Georgette M LaHair
CONNELL,Carrie L   Sex:F   (Child #2) 24 May 1882 Hudson, NH Robert T Connell (Hudson, NH) & Lizze M Marshall (Hudson, NH)
CONNELL,Clarence J   Sex:M   24 Mar 1881 Hudson, NH James E Connell (Hudson, NH) & Sarah McEmbry (Lemons NB)
CONNELL,Clarence P   Sex:M   06 Aug 1877 Hudson, NH Philip J Connell (Hudson, NH) & Hannah E Hardy (Hudson, NH)
CONNELL,Clarence Philip   Sex:M   06 Aug 1877 Hudson, NH Philip J Connell

HUDSON,NH BIRTHS

& Hannah E Hardy
CONNELL,Daisy Evelyn Sex:F   (Child #3) 22 Jul 1907 Frank A Connell (Hudson, NH) & May Watts (Moores, NY)
CONNELL,Edna Pearl Sex:F (Child #3) 27 May 1928 Otis R Connell (Hudson, NH) & Lucy Longard (Nova Scotia)
CONNELL,Elizabeth Sex:F   (Child #3) 20 Sep 1919 Orrin Connell (Hudson, NH) & Clarabelle Hare (Burke, NY)
CONNELL,Ethel   Sex:F   (Child #4) 15 May 1890 Robert T Connell (Hudson, NH) & Lizzie Marshall (Hudson, NH)
CONNELL,Frank A Sex:M   27 Nov 1878 Hudson, NH Philip J Connell (Hudson, NH) & Hanna E (Hudson, NH)
CONNELL,Frank Aaron   Sex:M   27 Nov 1878 Hudson, NH Philip J Connell & Hannah E Hardy
CONNELL,Frank H   Sex:M   (Child #2) 07 Apr 1905 Frank Connell (Hudson, NH) & Mary Watts (New York)
CONNELL,Frederick R   Sex:M   (Child #1) 10 Jul 1906 Otis R Connell (Hudson, NH) & Lucy R Longard (Tantallon, N S)
CONNELL,Grace H   Sex:F   (Child #3) 21 Jun 1915 Hudson, NH Harry Connell (Hudson, NH) & Vera Coffin (Anderson, ME)
CONNELL,Harry Julius   Sex:M   21 Aug 1880 Hudson, NH Philip J Connell & Hannah E Hardy
CONNELL,Henry J   Sex:M   21 Aug 1880 Hudson, NH Philip J Connell (Hudson, NH) & Hannah E Hardy (Hudson, NH)
CONNELL,Ida May   Sex:F   13 Mar 1886 Hudson, NH Philip H Connell & Hattie M
CONNELL,Ila May   Sex:F   13 Mar 1886 Phillip H Connell & Hattie M
CONNELL,Jason P   Sex:M   21 Apr 1878 Hudson, NH Philip H Connell (Ireland) & Hattie M (Cornish, VT)
CONNELL,Mabel A   Sex:F   29 Dec 1884 Hudson, NH Robert T Connell (Hudson, NH) & Lizzie M Marshall (Hudson, NH)
CONNELL,Madaline A   Sex:F   (Child #1) 16 Jun 1912 Harry Connell (Hudson, NH) & Vera Coffin (Addition, NY)
CONNELL,Maude   Sex:F   (Child #2) 15 Feb 1883 Hudson, NH James E Connell (Hudson, NH) & Sadie McInerny (New Brunswick)
CONNELL,Maurice R   Sex:M   12 Oct 1953 Maurice W Connell & Doris E Richard
CONNELL,Nellie E   Sex:F   22 Jun 1874 Hudson, NH Philip Connell & Hattie
CONNELL,Noyse Hardy   Sex:M   (Child #2) 09 Feb 1914 Harry Connell (Hudson, NH) & Vera D Coffin (Anderson, ME)
CONNELL,Orrin Hardy   Sex:M   12 Oct 1873 Hudson, NH Philip J Connell & Hannah E Hardy
CONNELL,Otis R   Sex:M   14 Jul 1880 Hudson, NH Robert T Connell (Hudson, NH) & Lizzie M Marshall (Hudson, NH)
CONNELL,Philip Clarence   Sex:M   (Child #1) 18 Nov 1902 Frank A Connell (Hudson, NH) & Mary Watts (New York)
CONNELL,Phillip John   Sex:M   (Child #4) 25 Oct 1909 Frank A Connell (Hudson, NH) & Mary E Watts (Moores, NY)
CONNELL,Raymond   Sex:M   (Child #5) 24 Mar 1888 James E Connell (Hudson, NH) & Sarah McEnery (St John, N B)
CONNELL,Roberta L   Sex:F   26 May 1948 Noyes H Connell (Hudson, NH) & Margaret G Christie (Lowell, MA)
CONNELL,Sadie Rena   Sex:F   11 Apr 1886 James E Connell & Sadie
CONNELL,[Unknown]   Sex:M   12 Oct 1874 Hudson, NH Philip Connell & Lenore
CONNELL,[Unknown]   Sex:M   (Child #3) 07 Jan 1885 Hudson, NH James E Connell (Hudson, NH) & Sadie McInerny (New Brunswick)
CONNOR,Bradford James Sex:M 04 Jan 1984 William J Connor & Michele M Beaulieu
CONNOR,John M   Sex: 11 May 1973 Francis J Connor & Margo M Felton
CONNORS,Barbara L   Sex:F   (Child #1) 10 Aug 1942 Walter J Connors (Lowell, MA) & Mary G Chisholm (Nashua, NH)
CONNORS,Leon W   Sex:M   24 Aug 1949 Walter J Connors & Mildred E McCoy
CONNORS,Lisa M   Sex:F   22 Feb 1975 Ronald A Connors & Donna M Silva
CONRAD,Deborah L   Sex:F   15 Nov 1977 Peter F Conrad & Janet Ann Strafella

HUDSON,NH BIRTHS

CONRAD,Gregory M   Sex:M   09 Jun 1975 Peter F Conrad & Janet A Strafella
CONRAD,Jennifer L   Sex:F   11 Apr 1972 Joseph F Conrad & Nancy L Gagnon
CONRAD,Jillian Ann   Sex:F   19 Apr 1981 Peter F Conrad & Janet Ann Strafella
CONRAD,Joseph F III   Sex:M   27 Jun 1975 Joseph F Conrad Jr & Nancy L Gagnon
CONRAD,Karen Sue   Sex:F   11 Jul 1983 Peter F Conrad & Janet Ann Strafella
CONREY,Martha W   Sex:F   28 Jun 1858 Hudson, NH William P Conrey & Elizabeth
CONREY,[Unknown]   Sex:M   (Child #2) 18 Jun 1885 Hudson, NH Irving B Conrey
  (Nashua, NH) & Nellie A (Brookline, NH)
CONSIGNEY,Doris B   Sex:F   (Child #1) 19 Aug 1921 Jean B Consigney (New
  Hampshire) & Agnes Gaudette (New Hampshire)
CONSIGNY,Barry W   Sex:M   25 Mar 1947 William H Consigny (Hudson, NH)
  & Norma M Billings (Nashua, NH)
CONSIGNY,Wm Henry   Sex:M   (Child #2) 28 Mar 1923 Jean B Consigney (Nashua, NH)
  & Agnes E Gaudette (Nashua, NH)
CONSTANT,Adrian J   Sex:M   (Child #7) 02 Jul 1942 Leo E Constant (Nashua, NH)
  & Jeannette Vignola (Hudson, NH)
CONSTANT,Albert Joseph   Sex:M   (Child #5) 22 Nov 1938 Leo Ernest Constant
  (Nashua, NH) & Jeanette RDM Vignola (Hudson, NH)
CONSTANT,Dale R   Sex:M   22 Feb 1961 Robert L Constant & Rose M Porter
CONSTANT,Darlene A   Sex:F   03 Mar 1960 Robert L Constant & Rose M Porter
CONSTANT,Doris M   Sex:F   (Child #10) 19 Jul 1946 Leo E Constant (Nashua, NH)
  & Jeanette M Vignola (Hudson, NH)
CONSTANT,Paul L J   Sex:M   29 Nov 1949 Leo E Constant & Jeannette Vignola
CONSTANT,Regina   Sex:F   (Child #9) 24 Apr 1945 Leo E Constant (Nashua, NH)
  & Jeannette Vignola (Hudson, NH)
CONSTANT,Rita M J   Sex:F   01 Apr 1944 Leo E Constant (Nashua, NH)
  & Jeanette Vignola (Hudson, NH)
CONSTANT,Theresa   Sex:F   04 May 1941 Leo Constant (Nashua, NH)
  & Janet Vignola (Hudson, NH)
CONSTANT,[Unknown]   Sex:M   (Child #3) 27 Feb 1938 Leo Ernest Constant
  (Nashua, NH) & Jeannette Vignola (Hudson, NH)
CONSTANT,[Unknown]   Sex:M   07 Dec 1947 Leo E Constant (Nashua, NH)
  & Jeannette M Vignola (Hudson, NH)
CONSTANTIAN,John Andrew   Sex:M   01 Aug 1980 Mark B Constantian
  & Judy Ann Tompkins
CONTI,James Scott   Sex:M   22 Mar 1985 Allen James Conti & Janice Louise Merry
CONVERSE,Tracy M   Sex:F   02 Apr 1980 Harry W Converse Jr & Pamela J Cutter
COOK,Christopher J   Sex:M   07 May 1969 James E Cook & Elizabeth M Martin
COOK,Diane S   Sex:F   13 Dec 1950 Leon A Cook & Mary V Raudonis
COOK,Jennifer Lynn   Sex:F   11 Jan 1982 Irving Edwards Cook & Nancy Lee Roy
COOK,Laura A   Sex:F   17 Jun 1970 James E Cook & Elizabeth M Martin
COOK,Linda M Sex:F   03 Jul 1947 Leon A Cook (Westbrook, ME)
  & Mary V Raudonis (Nashua, NH)
COOK,Nancy M   Sex:F   03 Jul 1947 Leon A Cook (Westbrook, ME)
  & Mary V Raudonis (Nashua, NH)
COOKE,Cynthia A   Sex:F   29 Jan 1947 Hersey F Cooke (Lockport, N S)
  & Lucy J Burnham (Wilton, NH)
COOKE,Florence Harriet   Sex:F   (Child #1) 25 Aug 1927 Hersey Cooke (Canada)
  & Lucy Burnham (New Hampshire)
COOKE,Hershey Frederick   Sex:M   (Child #3) 14 Jan 1941 Hershey F Cooke (Nova
  Scotia) & Lucy J Burnham (Wilton, NH)
COOKE,Marlene Marie   Sex:F   (Child #2) 27 Sep 1937 Hector Roger Cooke (Nova
  Scotia) & Marion Dane (Hudson, NH)
COOLBETH,Ellen L   Sex:F   26 Oct 1964 John R Coolbeth & Ellen L Daniels
COOLEY,Barbara A   Sex:F   23 Jul 1960 Boyd E Cooley & Janet M Connor
COOLEY,Carolyn R   Sex:F   21 Jul 1964 Boyd E Cooley & Janet M Connor
COOLEY,Kevin B   Sex:M   07 Jul 1959 Boyd E Cooley & Janet M Connor
COOLIDGE,Geraldine M   Sex:F   (Child #2) 19 Oct 1946 Harold B Coolidge Jr
  (Concord, NH) & Virginia G Dunn (Franklin, NH)
COOLIDGE,Richard D   Sex:M   (Child #1) 18 Oct 1943 Harold B Coolidge Jr

HUDSON,NH BIRTHS

(Concord, MA) & Virginia G Dunn (Franklin, NH)
COOMBS,Cladis Sex:F (Child #2) 05 Feb 1897 Charles B Coombs (Brandon, ME)
  & Maud E Austin (Peterborough, NH)
COOMBS,Fred Melvin Sex:M (Child #1) 31 Oct 1925 Charles B Coombs
  (Bowdoinham, ME) & Mildred L Theall (Everett, MA)
COON,Diane M Sex:F 21 Jan 1963 David S Coon & Maureen K Burke
COOPER,Claudia E Sex:F 08 Mar 1969 Johnny H Cooper & Edith F Neubarth
COOPER,Frank W Sex:M 28 Jul 1961 Johnny H Cooper & Edith F Neubarth
COOPER,Lindsey Ann Sex:F 17 Oct 1976 Robert J Cooper & Nancy Jackson
COOPER,Stephen J Sex:M 07 Dec 1962 Johnny H Cooper & Edith F Neubarth
COOPER,[Unknown] Sex:F 01 May 1975 Robert J Cooper & Nancy Jackson
COPELAND,Jennifer A Sex:F 09 Oct 1971 Peter A Copeland & Marie A Pepin
COPPIN,Linsdey Marie Sex:F 27 Nov 1984 Paul James Coppin & Nancy Jean O'Neill
CORBETT,Randall W Sex:M 21 Mar 1965 Gerald W Corbett & Paula A Henderson
CORBIN,Gerald F Sex:M L 28 Sep 1947 Frank A Corbin (Canada)
  & Cecile R Lamount (Canada)
CORBIT,Dean J Sex:M 14 Oct 1957 Cardin L Corbit & Shirley M Morrissette
CORBIT,Kevin J Sex:M 13 Jul 1955 Cardin L Corbit & Shirley M Morissette
CORBIT,Michael A Sex:M 07 Feb 1959 Cardin L Corbit & Shirley M Morrissette
CORBIT,Teresa A Sex:F 31 Mar 1963 Cardin L Corbit & Shirley M Morrissette
CORDIMA,Daniel S Sex:M 14 Jun 1975 Sebastian M Cordima & Grace A Miller
CORDIMA,Michael S Sex:M 05 Nov 1976 Sebastian M Cordima & Grace A Miller
COREY,Betsey Sex:F 24 May 1812 Hudson, NH Samuel Corey & Betsey
COREY,Polly Sex:F 08 Apr 1805 Hudson, NH Samuel Corey & Sally
COREY,Reuben Sex:M 11 May 1808 Hudson, NH Samuel Corey & Betsey
COREY,William F III Sex:M 23 Apr 1971 William F Corey Jr & Vera M Belida
CORKUM,Kenneth R Sex:M 30 Sep 1963 Raymond E Corkum & JoAnne B Bonin
CORLIS,James A Sex:M 22 Jul 1878 Hudson, NH James N Corlis (Hudson, NH)
  & Hattie E (Moultonborough)
CORLISS,Daniel P Sex:M 19 Apr 1804 Hudson, NH Jonathan Corliss & Sally
CORLISS,George E Sex:M 21 Dec 1868 Hudson, NH George Smith & Christina
CORLISS,Hattie M Sex:F 19 Feb 1875 Hudson, NH J N Corliss & H E
CORLISS,James Sex:M 07 Dec 1802 Hudson, NH Jonathan Corliss & Sally
CORLISS,Jonathan Sex:M 26 May 1780 Hudson, NH James Corliss & Sarah
CORLISS,Levi W Sex:M 14 Aug 1873 Hudson, NH James N Corliss & Hattie E
CORLISS,Moses F Sex:M 24 Jun 1881 Hudson, NH James N Corliss (Hudson, NH)
  & Bunker
CORLISS,Walter Sex:M 05 Mar 1871 Hudson, NH James N Corliss & Harriet E
CORMAN,Erin Elizabeth Sex:F 08 Jul 1981 Philip J Corman & Marie E Cafarchio
CORNISH,Monika L Sex:F 17 Apr 1955 Kenneth G Cornish & Elfriede M Richter
COROSA,Daniel Michael Sex:M 27 Oct 1981 Michael P Corosa & RoseAnn Mihelis
COROSA,Joanne M Sex:F 30 May 1949 Charles V Corosa & Etiennette A Cote
COROSA,Michael P Sex:M 03 Mar 1952 Vito P Corosa & Sophie J Wolczok
CORRIVEAU,Adam Michael Sex:M 27 Aug 1980 Dennis A Corriveau
  & Louise R Belanger
CORRIVEAU,Debbra E Sex:F 28 Dec 1962 Paul P Corriveau & Elaine L Ducharme
CORRIVEAU,Dennis A Sex:M 15 Jul 1955 Normand E Corriveau & Martha C Haggett
CORRIVEAU,Janine Aimee Sex:F 22 Apr 1978 Richard G Corriveau
  & Denise Quarella
CORRIVEAU,Kenneth M Sex:M 29 Jun 1951 Normand E Corriveau & Martha C Haggett
CORRIVEAU,Maureen Ashley Sex:F 11 Dec 1982 Richard G Corriveau
  & Denise Quarella
CORRIVEAU,Nathan Allan Sex:M 25 Sep 1978 Dennis A Corriveau
  & Louise R Belanger
CORSON,Jamie M Sex:M 19 Oct 1973 Melvin R Corson & Penny Lou Coburn
CORSON,Kelly R Sex:F 25 Oct 1977 Robert F Corson & Linda N Richardson
CORSON,Laura A Sex:F 23 Jul 1968 Melvin R Corson & Penny L Coburn
CORSON,Laurie A Sex:F 12 Dec 1963 Lynn A Corson & Mary L Gowing
CORSON,Shelley L Sex:F 01 Sep 1971 Melvin R Corson & Penny L Coburn
CORTESE,Charlene E Sex:F 02 May 1972 Robert R Cortese & Jane R Whittaker

HUDSON,NH BIRTHS

CORY,Betsy   Sex:F   24 May 1812 Hudson, NH Samuel Cory & Betsy
CORY,Carole S   Sex:F   14 Sep 1970 Donald B Cory & M Gayle Fitzgerald
CORY,Polley   Sex:F   08 Apr 1805 Hudson, NH Samuel Cory & Salley
CORY,Reuben   Sex:M   11 May 1808 Hudson, NH Samuel Cory & Betsy
COSSETTE,David J   Sex:M   05 Nov 1958 Paul N Cossette & Jeanne G Wiggins
COSSETTE,James W   Sex:M   17 Nov 1966 Paul N Cossette & Jeanne G Wiggins
COSSETTE,Thomas P   Sex:M   12 Jan 1975 Thomas L Cossette & Gayle H Latour
COSSETTE,Timothy M   Sex:M   07 Jul 1965 Paul N Cossette & Jeanne G Wiggins
COSTELLO,Barrie L   Sex:F   27 Nov 1960 William B Costello
   & Genevieve L Morrissette
COSTELLO,Bryan P Sex:M 25 Nov 1957 William B Costello & Genevieve L Morrisse
COSTELLO,Carolyn Ann Sex:F 03 Apr 1981 Robert J Costello & Barbara Ann Nelson
COSTELLO,Robert C   Sex:M   02 Sep 1965 Robert R Costello & Gladys R Maguire
COTE,Allen Robert   Sex:M   26 Jan 1984 Steven John Cote & Elizabeth A Delyani
COTE,Brian J   Sex:M   09 Mar 1967 Ernest J Cote & Joan M McQuinn
COTE,Christine A   Sex:F   28 Dec 1970 Robert F Cote & Sherry A Bridges
COTE,Christopher   Sex:M   28 Nov 1969 Ernest J Cote & Joan M McQuinn
COTE,Debora M   Sex:F   19 Apr 1961 Roger L Cote & Phyllis E Hopwood
COTE,Eric S   Sex:M   01 Oct 1974 Laurent F Cote Jr & Barbara J Cracraft
COTE,James A   Sex: 21 Jun 1973 Alfred P Cote & Jeannette A Landry
COTE,Jason S   Sex: 21 Jun 1973 Alfred P Cote & Jeannette A Landry
COTE,Jennifer A   Sex: 08 Jul 1972 Robert L Cote & Nan C Whitehead
COTE,Joey D   Sex:M   26 Feb 1971 Kenneth S Cote & Betty A Mellon
COTE,Karen M   Sex:F   09 Apr 1964 Ernest J Cote, Jr & Joan M McQuinn
COTE,Kathryn M   Sex:F   07 Feb 1960 Alfred P Cote & Jeannette A Landry
COTE,Kenneth M   Sex:M   23 Dec 1969 Alfred P Cote & Jeannette A Landry
COTE,Lisa F   Sex:F   24 Jun 1967 Alfred P Cote & Jeannette A Landry
COTE,Martha E   Sex:F   25 Sep 1967 Robert L Cote & Nan C Whitehead
COTE,Pamela C   Sex:F   01 Oct 1969 Robert E Cote & Pauline G Pare
COTE,Rebecca L   Sex:F   23 Aug 1969 Robert L Cote & NanCarol Whitehead
COTE,Steven J   Sex:M   21 Dec 1960 Alfred P Cote & Jeannette A Landry
COULTER,Anne Marie Sex:F   28 Dec 1983 Timothy M Coulter & Barbara Ann Prieto
COURNOYER,Kimberly A Sex:F 08 Nov 1960 Frederick F Cournoye & Sandra A Brown
COURNOYER,Kristin Michelle Sex:F 17 Jan 1985 Paul W Cournoyer & Mary M Quirk
COUROUNIS,Chris   Sex:M   13 Jun 1968 William Courounis & Mabel G Landry
COURTEMANCHE,April Ann Sex:F 11 Feb 1983 William E Courtemanc
   & Sharon Ann Mattison
COURTEMANCHE,Cindy G Sex:F 02 Jul 1957 Albert M Courtemanche& Elaine M Martin
COURTEMANCHE,Estel M   Sex:F   24 Jan 1979 Donald R Courtemanche
   & Linda D Andersen
COURTEMANCHE,Mazie C   Sex:F   23 Dec 1977 Donald R Courtemanche
   & Linda D Anderson
COURTEMANCHE,Natalie Muriel   Sex:F   18 Jan 1982 Donald R Courtemanche
   & Linda D Andersen
COURTEMARCHE,Jos R   Sex:M   (Child #1) 10 Sep 1922   & Lucille Depont
   (New Hampshire)
COURVILLE,Adam Ross   Sex:M   14 Oct 1978 Richard G Courville & Gail Ann Barlow
COURVILLE,Michael R   Sex:M   15 Apr 1976 Richard G Courville & Gail A Barlow
COURVILLE,Ryan G   Sex: 10 Sep 1972 Richard G Courville & Gail Ann Barlow
COUTU,Bryan J   Sex:M   20 Dec 1962 Roger J Coutu & Constance A Lemire
COUTU,Daniel J   Sex:M   14 Aug 1965 Roger J Coutu & Constance A Lemire
COUTU,Denise A   Sex:F   28 Dec 1963 Roger J Coutu & Constance A Lemire
COUTU,Nancy J   Sex:F   29 Mar 1967 Roger J Coutu & Constance A Lemire
COUTURE,Cathy L   Sex:F   20 Nov 1970 Bertrand H Couture & Paulette C Turcotte
COUTURE,Christine E   Sex:F   02 Mar 1967 Roger C Couture & Denise A Robert
COUTURE,Gerald R   Sex:M   02 Apr 1965 Roger C Couture & Denise A Robert
COUTURE,Jacqueline L   Sex:F   26 Feb 1964 Roger C Couture & Denise A Robert
COUTURIER,Brian J   Sex:M   19 Nov 1967 Emile H Couturier & Priscilla C Royer
COUTURIER,Joshua James   Sex:M   17 Oct 1979 Dennis F Couturier
   & Jean L Swinerton

HUDSON,NH BIRTHS

COUTURIER,Noreen B   Sex:F   12 Apr 1978 Dennis F Couturier & Jean L Swinerton
COVERT,Mark J   Sex:M   08 Nov 1965 Robert J Covert & Mary A Jameson
COVEY,Dawn L   Sex:F   21 Sep 1967 Harold R Covey & Patricia L LaFlamme
COVEY,Ernest V   Sex:M   (Child #1) 28 Sep 1944 Charles A Covey (Nashua, NH)
   & Sophie Makarawicz (Nashua, NH)
COWGILL,Eleane May   Sex:F   19 May 1936 Wilfred Cowgill (England)
   & Mable Ford (S Merrimack, NH)
COWGILL,Ruth Helen   Sex:F   (Child #4) 28 Jan 1939 Wilfred Cowgill (England)
   & Mabel Ford (S Merrimack, NH)
COWGILL,[Unknown]   Sex:F   13 Sep 1934 Wilfred Cowgill (England)
   & Mabel Ina Ford (S Merrimack, NH)
COX,Brenda L   Sex:F   13 Nov 1957 Gilbert W Cox & Hazel M Smith
COX,Jeffrey E   Sex:M   22 Feb 1972 Jan E Cox & Madlyn M Hill
COX,Mark L   Sex:M   22 May 1958 Lloyd D Cox & Nancy E Morley
COY,Michael D   Sex:M   17 Feb 1980 Gregory R Coy & Susan Carmichael
CRABTREE,Allen Frederick   Sex:M   (Child #3) 18 Feb 1941 Allen F Crabtree
   (Orange, NH) & Dorothea A Shay (Cambridge, MA)
CRANDALL,Cheryl L   Sex:F   19 Nov 1970 Richard J Crandall & Diane M Jasinski
CRANDALL,Melissa A   Sex:F   08 May 1969 Richard J Crandall & Diane M Jasinski
CRAWFORD,Aaron S   Sex:M   27 Aug 1974 Adrian S Crawford & June A St Amand
CRAWFORD,Daniel   Sex: 03 Nov 1972 James R Crawford & Elaine D Chamberlain
CRAWFORD,Jeffrey R   Sex:M   01 Jul 1966 James R Crawford
   & Elaine D Chamberlain
CRAWFORD,Stephen A   Sex:M   02 Jul 1976 Adrien S Crawford & June Anne St Amand
CRAYTON,Colleen J   Sex: 06 May 1973 Ronald R Crayton & Joy A Kuhnen
CREELEY,Meghan E   Sex:F   18 Jan 1979 Ronald F Creeley & M Diane Blanchette
CRENNER,Anabelle   Sex:F   12 Oct 1862 Hudson, NH Samuel Z Crenner & Anna Pease
CRENNER,Annabelle   Sex:F   12 Oct 1862 Hudson, NH Samuel F Crenner & Susan
CRENNER,Samuel P   Sex:M   Hudson, NH Samuel Crenner &
CRENNER,Sarah R P   Sex:F   1861 Hudson, NH Samuel Z Crenner & Anna Pease
CRETE,David A   Sex:M   01 Jan 1965 Adrien E Crete & Theresa A Biron
CRETE,Richard R   Sex:M   06 Oct 1963 Adrian E Crete & Theresa A Biroux
CRIPPS,Kyle M   Sex:M   25 Sep 1969 George W Cripps Jr & Patricia L Smith
CRISMAN,Kyle John   Sex:M   04 Apr 1984 Erik Crisman & Kathleen L Flynn
CROCHETIERE,Karen A   Sex:F   09 May 1950 Norman P Crochetiere & Gladys R McGee
CROCHETIERE,Norman P   Sex:M   13 Nov 1948 Norman P Crochetiere (Cheshire, CT)
   & Gladys R McGee (Lowell, MA)
CROCKER,Lindsay Anne   Sex:F   02 Apr 1978 Thomas G Crocker & Lenore Noce
CROCKETT,Beth L   Sex:F   08 Jun 1949 David R Crockett & Dorothy G Jasper
CROCKETT,Julianne   Sex:F   22 Mar 1953 David R Crockett & Dorothy G Jasper
CROCKETT,Thomas P   Sex:M   09 Jan 1947 David R Crockett (New London, NH)
   & Dorothy G Jasper (Nashua, NH)
CROFT,Laura M   Sex:F   26 Jun 1862 Hudson, NH Levi Croft & Mary J
CROMBIE,Karen E   Sex:F   10 Oct 1968 Peter A Crombie Jr & Patricia A Devlin
CROMPTON,Barbara W   Sex:F   (Child #1) 04 Dec 1912 Harry Crompton (Nashua, NH)
   & Helen Marshall (Hudson, NH)
CROOKER,Erin M   Sex:F   17 Jan 1968 Walter T Crooker & Noreen L Turner
CROOKER,Kerry A   Sex:F   17 Jun 1963 Walter T Crooker & Noreen L Turner
CROOKER,Kevin B   Sex:M   28 Nov 1964 Walter T Crooker & Noreen L Turner
CROOKER,Sean P   Sex:M   17 Jun 1969 Walter T Crooker & Noreen L Turner
CROP,Robert A   Sex:M   14 Jul 1866 Hudson, NH Hiram Crop & Barack
CROP,[Unknown]   Sex:M   07 Mar 1864 Hudson, NH Levi E Crop & Mary J
CROPLEY,Matthew C   Sex: 16 Aug 1972 Nelson E Cropley & Eleanora C Knudsen
CROPLEY,Peter A   Sex: 16 Aug 1972 Nelson E Cropley & Eleanora C Knudsen
CROSBIE,Denise   Sex:F   02 May 1961 William J Crosbie,Jr & Clara E Mercier
CROSBY,Bradford W   Sex:M   05 Nov 1954 Norman J Crosby & Muriel E Winslow
CROSBY,Dorothy A   Sex:F   29 Nov 1957 Stanley M Crosby & Caroline H Morin
CROSBY,Marsha L   Sex:F   (Child #2) 13 Aug 1946 Norman J Crosby (Nashua, NH)
   & Muriel E Winslow (Nashua, NH)
CROSBY,Richard F   Sex:M   (Child #1) 22 Oct 1942 Norman J Crosby (Nashua, NH)

HUDSON, NH BIRTHS

& Muriel E Winslow (Nashua, NH)
CROSBY, Sandra J   Sex:F   13 Oct 1950 Richard F Crosby & Marjorie J Irvine
CROSS, Arthur H   Sex:M   12 Oct 1873 Hudson, NH Levi E Cross & Mary J
CROSS, Birney A   Sex:M   (Child #2) 12 Jul 1903 Andrew W Cross (Swanton, VT)
  & Effie Currier (Coventry, VT)
CROSS, Everett A   Sex:M   (Child #2) 13 Aug 1882 Hudson, NH Adison S Cross
  (Hudson, NH) & Hattie J Marshall (Hudson, NH)
CROSS, Frank M   Sex:M   01 Aug 1877 Hudson, NH Adison S Cross (Hudson, NH)
  & Hattie Marshall (Hudson, NH)
CROSS, Hubert A   Sex:M   14 Jul 1866 Hudson, NH Hiram Cross & Barack C
CROSS, J P F   Sex: 10 Mar 1799 Hudson, NH Peter Cross & Sarah
CROSS, Jabez Pond Fisher Sex: 10 Mar 1799 Hudson, NH Peter Cross Jr
  & Sarah Barrett
CROSS, John   Sex:M   09 Oct 1735 Hudson, NH Nathan Cross & Mary
CROSS, John   Sex:M   12 Sep 1782 Hudson, NH Samuel Cross & Elizabeth Cummings
CROSS, Joseph   Sex:M   17 Feb 1759 Hudson, NH Peter Cross & Sarah
CROSS, Lary A   Sex:M   01 Jan 1947 Albert R Cross (Andover, MA)
  & Barbara T Tracey (Milan, NH)
CROSS, Laura M   Sex:F   26 Jan 1862 Hudson, NH Levi E Cross & Mary Jane
CROSS, Lucy W   Sex:F   26 Oct 1796 Hudson, NH Peter Cross & Sarah
CROSS, Lucy Wright Sex:F 22 Oct 1796 Hudson, NH Peter Cross Jr & Sarah Barrett
CROSS, Lynda   Sex:F   24 Jul 1794 Hudson, NH Peter Cross Jr & Sarah Barrett
CROSS, Lynda   Sex:F   24 Jul 1793 Hudson, NH Peter Cross Jr & Sarah
CROSS, N Irwin   Sex:M   10 Aug 1894 Arden C Cross (Hudson, NH)
  & Mary Willoughby (Hollis, NH)
CROSS, Nancy   Sex:F   06 Aug 1803 Hudson, NH Peter Cross Jr & Sarah Barrett
CROSS, Nathan   Sex:M   Hudson, NH Nathan Cross & Mary
CROSS, Nathan   Sex:M   11 Mar 1772 Hudson, NH Peter Cross & Sarah
CROSS, Peter   Sex:M   28 Sep 1729 Dunstable Nathan Cross & Sarah
CROSS, Peter   Sex:M   12 Mar 1766 Hudson, NH Peter Cross & Sarah
CROSS, Rachel   Sex:F   15 Aug 1768 Hudson, NH Peter Cross & Sarah
CROSS, Ruth Vivian Sex:F   (Child #2) 02 May 1898 Arden C Cross (Hudson, NH)
  & Mary E Willoughby (Hollis, NH)
CROSS, Sarah   Sex:F   26 Jun 1731 Dunstable Nathan Cross & Sarah
CROSS, Sarah   Sex:F   20 Aug 1763 Hudson, NH Peter Cross & Sarah
CROSS, Sarah   Sex:F   13 Mar 1790 Hudson, NH Peter Cross Jr & Sarah Barrett
CROSS, Thomas   Sex:M   21 Mar 1761 Hudson, NH Peter Cross & Sarah
CROSS, Thomas   Sex:M   02 Mar 1761 Hudson, NH Peter Cross & Sarah
CROSS, Wilder   Sex: 19 Dec 1805 Hudson, NH Peter Cross Jr & Sarah Barrett
CROSS, [Unknown]   Sex: 07 Mar 1864 Hudson, NH Levi E Cross & Mary Jane
CROSSCUP, William H   Sex:M   (Child #2) 02 Oct 1946 Arthur L Crosscup (Lowell,
  MA) & Phyllis A Sudsbury (Woburn, MA)
CROTEAU, Alexi F   Sex:M   19 May 1976 Fernand A Croteau & Collette G Grenier
CROTEAU, Sonia B   Sex:F   28 Jun 1972 Jean-Guy C Croteau & Diane C Lamothe
CROTEAU, Stephene J   Sex:M   31 Oct 1970 Jean C Croteau & Diane J LaMothe
CROTEAU, Valerie C   Sex:F   02 Jun 1974 Fernand A Croteau & Collette G Grenier
CROWLEY, Anne   Sex:F   22 Aug 1966 William J Crowley & Marion E Owen
CROWLEY, Jeffrey D   Sex:M   21 Sep 1970 Daniel J Crowley & Gail J Davis
CROWLEY, Nicholas Burke   Sex:M   27 Jul 1978 Edmond J Crowley & Teresa A Burke
CROWLEY, Taylor Michelle   Sex:F   24 Mar 1984 Edmond J Crowley & Teresa A Burke
CUDMORE, Shirley   Sex:F   26 Jan 1961 Thomas C Cudmore & Barbara M Bradley
CUDWORTH, Arthur I   Sex:M   (Child #4) 14 Apr 1895 A I Cudworth (Peterborough,
  NH) & Emma Perry (N Bangor, NY)
CUDWORTH, Ernest Sex:M   (Child #3) 24 Aug 1892 Alden J Cudworth (Peterborough,
  NH) & Emma Perry (N Bangor, NY)
CUDWORTH, Hildred C   Sex:M   (Child #2) 09 Apr 1891 A J Cudworth (Peterborough,
  NH) & Emma Perry (N Bangor, NY)
CUDWORTH, Irene Mary Perry   Sex:F   (Child #5) 15 Feb 1900 A J Cudworth
  (Peterborough, NH) & Emma Perry (Bangor, NY)
CUDWORTH, Melvin E   Sex:M   (Child #1) 30 Jun 1889 Alden J Cudworth

HUDSON,NH BIRTHS

(Peterborough, NH) & Emma Perry (Bangor, NY)
CUFF,Jennifer M   Sex:F   28 May 1969 Richard W Cuff & Eileen V Drake
CUFF,Veronica D   Sex:F   21 Mar 1974 Richard W Cuff & Eileen V Drake
CUMMING,Cynthia M   Sex:F   08 Aug 1971 James A Cumming & Janet E Gabriel
CUMMING,Virginia A   Sex:F   28 Feb 1970 James A Cumming & Janet E Gabriel
CUMMINGS,Abraham   Sex:M   09 Sep 1759 Hudson, NH Eleazer Cummings Jr & Martha
CUMMINGS,Abraham   Sex:M   01 Jun 1734 Hudson, NH Ebenezer Cummings & Rachel
CUMMINGS,Albine C   Sex:M   27 Aug 1855 Hudson, NH Hiram Cummings & Abby Clark
CUMMINGS,Alden E   Sex:M   03 Mar 1857 Hudson, NH John Cummings &
CUMMINGS,Alden Edson Sex:M   03 Mar 1857 Hudson, NH John Cummings
& Emeline Kemp
CUMMINGS,Alfred   Sex:M   24 May 1804 Hudson, NH Eleazer Cummings & Sarah Hale
CUMMINGS,Allen   Sex:M   Boston Thomas Cummings & Hannah Webster
CUMMINGS,Amos   Sex:M   11 Sep 1766 Hudson, NH John H Cummings & Sarah
CUMMINGS,Angelina Whilmeen   Sex:F   01 Jul 1836 Nashua, NH Alfred Cummingss
& Martha C Barns
CUMMINGS,Anna Florence   Sex:F   21 May 1878 Hudson, NH James M Cummings
& Nellie Burke
CUMMINGS,Anna M   Sex:F   06 Sep 1857 Hudson, NH Hiram Cummings & Abby Clark
CUMMINGS,Belinda   Sex:F   03 Feb 1820 NH   Willard Cummings & Nancy Smith
CUMMINGS,Benjamin   Sex:M   15 Jan 1764 Hudson, NH John H Cummings & Sarah
CUMMINGS,Benjamin   Sex:M   15 Jun 1764 Hudson, NH John H Cummings & Sarah
CUMMINGS,Bertha E   Sex:F   12 Mar 1875 Hudson, NH Willis P Cummings
& Hattie D Lawrence
CUMMINGS,Betsey   Sex:F   02 Jul 1798 Hudson, NH Eleazer Cummings & Sarah Hale
CUMMINGS,Betsy   Sex:F   19 Apr 1796 Hudson, NH Daniel Cumings & Phebe
CUMMINGS,Betsy   Sex:F   02 Jul 1798 Hudson, NH Ebenezer Cummings & Sarah
CUMMINGS,Betty   Sex:F   06 Feb 1772 Hudson, NH Ephraim Cummings Jr
& Betsey B Merrill
CUMMINGS,Betty   Sex:F   19 Apr 1796 Hudson, NH David Cummings Jr & Phebe Wyman
CUMMINGS,Calvin   Sex:M   New Hampshire Thomas Cummings & Hannah Webster
CUMMINGS,Caroline Nevins   Sex:F   Windham Thomas Cummings & Hannah Webster
CUMMINGS,Charles   Sex:M   04 Jun 1804 Hudson, NH Moody Cummings & Lucy
CUMMINGS,Charles E   Sex:M   19 Nov 1862 Hudson, NH Hiram Cummings & Abby Clark
CUMMINGS,Clarissa   Sex:F Willard Cummings & Nancy Smith
CUMMINGS,Daniel   Sex:M   27 Jan 1766 Hudson, NH Ebenezer Cummings & Sarah
CUMMINGS,Daniel   Sex:M   03 Apr 1806 Hudson, NH John Cummings & Molly
CUMMINGS,Daniel   Sex:M   20 May 1730 Hudson, NH Ephraim Cummings & Elizabeth
CUMMINGS,Daniel   Sex:M   14 Feb 1805 Hudson, NH Daniel Cumings & Phebe
CUMMINGS,David   Sex:M   20 May 1738 Hudson, NH Ephraim Cummings
& Elizabeth Butler
CUMMINGS,David   Sex:M   14 Feb 1804 Hudson, NH David Cummings Jr & Phebe Wyman
CUMMINGS,David   Sex:M David Cummings & Elizabeth Butterfield
CUMMINGS,Deliah Sex:F   06 Jun 1802 Hudson, NH David Cummings Jr & Phebe Wyman
CUMMINGS,Delila   Sex:F   06 Jan 1802 Hudson, NH Daniel Cumings & Phebe
CUMMINGS,Ebenezer   Sex:M   18 Oct 1768 Hudson, NH Ebenezer Cummings & Sarah
CUMMINGS,Ebenezer   Sex:M   07 Dec 1801 Hudson, NH John Cummings & Molly
CUMMINGS,Ebenezer   Sex:M   17 Dec 1801 Hudson, NH John Cummings & Polle
CUMMINGS,Eleazer   Sex:M   19 Oct 1701 Dunstable Nathaniel Cummings &
CUMMINGS,Eleazer   Sex:M   16 Jun 1765 Hudson, NH Eleazer Cummings
& Phebe Richardson
CUMMINGS,Eleazer   Sex:M   15 Dec 1730 Hudson, NH Eleazer Cummings Jr & Rachel
CUMMINGS,Elizabeth   Sex:F   26 Oct 1740 Hudson, NH Ephraim Cummings
& Elizabeth Butler
CUMMINGS,Elizabeth   Sex:F   26 Mar Hudson, NH Ebenezer Cummings & Sarah
CUMMINGS,Elizabeth   Sex:F   1765 David Cummings & Elizabeth Butterfield
CUMMINGS,Elizabeth   Sex:F   01 Oct 1736 Dunstable
CUMMINGS,Elizabeth   Sex:F   26 Mar 17 Hudson, NH Ebenezer Cummings & Sarah
CUMMINGS,Ellen E   Sex:F   1842 Nashua, NH Enoch Cummings & Louisa C McAlpine
CUMMINGS,Enoch   Sex:M   19 Oct 1753 Hudson, NH Ebenezer Cummings & Sarah

HUDSON,NH BIRTHS

CUMMINGS,Enoch   Sex:M   12 May 1803 Hudson, NH John Cummings & Molly
CUMMINGS,Enoch   Sex:M   19 May 1816 NH Willard Cummings & Nancy Smith
CUMMINGS,Ephraim   Sex:M   09 Apr 1743 Hudson, NH Ephraim Cummings
    & Elizabeth Butler
CUMMINGS,Ethel M   Sex:F   (Child #2) 02 May 1888 Aldon E Cummings (Hudson, NH)
    & Nellie Stevens (Nashua, NH)
CUMMINGS,Francis M   Sex: Windham Thomas Cummings & Hannah Webster
CUMMINGS,Frank A   Sex:M   06 Mar 1851 Hudson, NH Nathan Cummings
    & Elizabeth Conant
CUMMINGS,Freddie H Sex:M   11 Aug 1878 Hudson, NH Willis P Cummings (Lowell,
    MA) & Hattie D (Merrimack, NH)
CUMMINGS,Freddy L   Sex:M   11 Apr 1878 Hudson, NH Willis P Cummings
    & Hattie D Lawrence
CUMMINGS,George   Sex:M   Hudson, NH Reuben Cummings & Rhoda Hills
CUMMINGS,George Clinton   Sex:M   20 Jul 1835 Hudson, NH John Cummings
    & Sophia Lawrence
CUMMINGS,George W   Sex:M   Windham Thomas Cummings & Hannah Webster
CUMMINGS,Hannah   Sex:F   04 Aug 1794 Hudson, NH Eleazer Cummings & Sarah Hale
CUMMINGS,Hannah   Sex:F   29 Apr 1745 Hudson, NH Ephraim Cummings
    & Elizabeth Butler
CUMMINGS,Hannah   Sex:F   David Cummings & Elizabeth Butterfield
CUMMINGS,Hannah   Sex:F   29 Apr 1741 Hudson, NH Ephraim Cummings & Elizabeth
CUMMINGS,Hannah W   Sex:F   1818 NH Thomas Cummings & Hannah Webster
CUMMINGS,Helen A   Sex:F   05 Oct 1852 Hudson, NH Hiram Cummings & Abby Clark
CUMMINGS,Hiram   Sex:M   28 Sep 1821 NH Willard Cummings & Nancy Smith
CUMMINGS,Israel   Sex:M   23 Aug 1762 Hudson, NH Eleazer Cummings Jr
    & Hannah Whitney
CUMMINGS,Israel W   Sex:M   23 Aug 17 Hudson, NH Eleazer Cummings & Hannah
CUMMINGS,James   Sex:M   09 Dec 1784 Hudson, NH Ebenezer Cummings & Sarah
CUMMINGS,James Sex:M 12 May 1767 Hudson, NH Peter Cummings & Sarah Richardson
CUMMINGS,James M   Sex:M   03 Oct 1857 Hudson, NH Nathan Cummings
    & Elizabeth Conant
CUMMINGS,Jane Sophia   Sex:F   22 Dec 1856 Hudson, NH John Cummings
    & Sophia Lawrence
CUMMINGS,Joanna   Sex:F   26 Nov 1806 Hudson, NH Samuel Cummings & Joanna
CUMMINGS,Johanna   Sex:F   26 Nov 1806 Hudson, NH Samuel Cummings & Johanna
CUMMINGS,John   Sex:M   14 Jan 1698 Dunstable Nathaniel Cummings &
CUMMINGS,John   Sex:M   18 Feb 1806 Hudson, NH Eleazer Cummings & Sarah Hale
CUMMINGS,John   Sex:M   21 Apr 1771 Hudson, NH Ebenezer Cummings & Sarah
CUMMINGS,John   Sex:M   10 Jul 1796 Hudson, NH John Cummings & Molly
CUMMINGS,Joseph   Sex:M   26 May 1704 Dunstable Nathaniel Cummings &
CUMMINGS,Joseph   Sex:M   15 Oct 1742 Hudson, NH William Cummings & Sarah
CUMMINGS,Leander Hale   Sex:M   18 Jan 1846 Hudson, NH John Cummings
    & Emeline Kemp
CUMMINGS,Lila   Sex:F   1816 Pelham Thomas Cummings & Hannah Webster
CUMMINGS,Louisa   Sex:F Willard Cummings & Nancy Smith
CUMMINGS,Lucinda   Sex:F   21 Aug 1797 Hudson, NH David Cummings Jr
    & Phebe Wyman
CUMMINGS,Lucinda   Sex:F   21 Apr 1797 Hudson, NH Daniel Cumings & Phebe
CUMMINGS,Lucy   Sex:F   1824 NH Thomas Cummings & Hannah Webster
CUMMINGS,Mary   Sex:F   18 Sep 1884 Hudson, NH James M Cummings (Hudson, NH)
    & Nellie M Burke (Stoddard, NH)
CUMMINGS,Mary Frances   Sex:F   12 Apr 1840 Hudson, NH John Cummings
    & Sophia Lawrence
CUMMINGS,Moody   Sex:M   10 Oct 1777 Hudson, NH Ebenezer Cummings & Sarah
CUMMINGS,Moody   Sex:M   13 Oct 1777 Hudson, NH Ebenezer Cummings & Sarah
CUMMINGS,Nathan   Sex:M   04 Feb 1818 NH Willard Cummings & Nancy Smith
CUMMINGS,Nathaniel   Sex:M   08 Sep 1699 Dunstable Nathaniel Cummings &
CUMMINGS,Nathaniel   Sex:M   26 Jun 1770 Hudson, NH Ephraim Cummings Jr
    & Betsey B Merrill

HUDSON,NH BIRTHS

CUMMINGS,Nehemiah   Sex:M   17 Jul 1756 Hudson, NH Ebenezer Cummings & Sarah
CUMMINGS,Nehemiah   Sex:M   11 Oct 1798 Hudson, NH John Cummings & Molly
CUMMINGS,Nellie   Sex:F   1854 Hudson, NH Reuben Cummings & Rhoda Hills
CUMMINGS,Nina   Sex:F   22 Nov 1824 Willard Cummings & Nancy Smith
CUMMINGS,Peter   Sex:M   08 Dec 1733 Hudson, NH Ephraim Cummings
  & Elizabeth Butler
CUMMINGS,Peter Sex:M 18 Feb 1766 Hudson, NH Peter Cummings & Sarah Richardson
CUMMINGS,Phebe   Sex:F   08 Jul 1768 Hudson, NH Eleazer Cummings
  & Phebe Richardson
CUMMINGS,Phebe   Sex:F   16 Oct 1799 Hudson, NH David Cummings Jr & Phebe Wyman
CUMMINGS,Polly   Sex:F   01 Sep 1792 Hudson, NH Eleazer Cummings & Sarah Hale
CUMMINGS,Priscilla   Sex:F   07 Jul 1747 Hudson, NH Ephraim Cummings
  & Elizabeth Butler
CUMMINGS,Rachel   Sex:F   29 Apr 1757 Hudson, NH Eleazer Cummings Jr & Martha
CUMMINGS,Rachel   Sex:F David Cummings & Elizabeth Butterfield
CUMMINGS,Rebecca   Sex:F   17 Mar 1740 Hudson, NH William Cummings & Sarah
CUMMINGS,Reuben   Sex:M   04 Jul 1830 Willard Cummings & Nancy Smith
CUMMINGS,Robert M   Sex:M   22 Feb 1802 Hudson, NH Moody Cummings & Lucy
CUMMINGS,Robert Means   Sex:M   22 Feb 1802 Hudson, NH Moody Cummings & Lucy
CUMMINGS,Rowena M Sex:F   28 Sep 1842 Lowell Alfred Cummingss & Martha C Barns
CUMMINGS,Sarah   Sex:F   1823 Thomas Cummings & Hannah Webster
CUMMINGS,Samuel   Sex:M   18 Dec 1753 Hudson, NH Eleazer Cummings Jr & Martha
CUMMINGS,Samuel   Sex:M   24 Feb 1779 Hudson, NH Ebenezer Cummings & Sarah
CUMMINGS,Samuel   Sex:M   06 Apr 1781 Hudson, NH Ebenezer Cummings & Sarah
CUMMINGS,Samuel   Sex:M   07 Jul 1805 Hudson, NH Samuel Cummings & Joanna
CUMMINGS,Sarah   Sex:F   03 Oct 1786 Hudson, NH Eleazer Cummings & Sarah Hale
CUMMINGS,Sarah   Sex:F   12 May 1736 Hudson, NH Ephraim Cummings
  & Elizabeth Butler
CUMMINGS,Sarah   Sex:F   23 Feb 1765 Hudson, NH Peter Cummings
  & Sarah Richardson
CUMMINGS,Sarah   Sex:F   02 Nov 1793 Hudson, NH John Cummings & Molly
CUMMINGS,Sarah   Sex:F David Cummings & Elizabeth Butterfield
CUMMINGS,Sarah Ann Graves   Sex:F   03 Mar 1839 Lowell Alfred Cummingss
  & Martha C Barns
CUMMINGS,Sarah Hale   Sex:F   Lowell Thomas Cummings & Hannah Webster
CUMMINGS,Thaddeus   Sex:M   17 May 1745 Hudson, NH William Cummings & Sarah
CUMMINGS,Thadeus   Sex:M   17 May 1745 Hudson, NH William Cummings & Sarah
CUMMINGS,Thomas   Sex:M   20 Sep 1788 Hudson, NH Eleazer Cummings & Sarah Hale
CUMMINGS,Willard   Sex:M   21 Jul 1790 Hudson, NH Eleazer Cummings & Sarah Hale
CUMMINGS,William   Sex:M   18 Feb 1759 Hudson, NH Ebenezer Cummings & Sarah
CUMMINGS,William   Sex:M   07 Aug 1793 Hudson, NH John Cummings & Molly
CUMMINGS,William   Sex:M   10 Feb 1759 Hudson, NH Ebenezer Cummings & Sarah
CUMMINGS,William   Sex:M   07 Aug 1792 Hudson, NH John Cummings & Molley
CUMMINGS,William   Sex:M   21 Jul 1790 Hudson, NH Ebenezer Cummings & Sarah
CUMMINGS,Willis P   Sex:M   27 Jan 1850 Lowell Hiram Cummings & Abby Clark
CUMMINGS,[Unknown]   Sex:F   29 Jul 1832 Hudson, NH John Cummings
  & Sophia Lawrence
CUMMINGS,[Unknown]   Sex:M   08 Aug 1833 Hudson, NH John Cummings
  & Sophia Lawrence
CUMMINGS,[Unknown]   Sex:M   04 Jul 1843 Hudson, NH John Cummings
  & Sophia Lawrence
CUMMINGS,[Unknown]   Sex: 07 Oct 1876 Hudson, NH James M Cummings
  & Nellie Burke
CUMMINGS,[Unknown]   Sex:M   25 Jun 1875 Hudson, NH Henry J Cummings & Ellen
CUNHA,Keith R   Sex: 02 Feb 1973 Daniel A Cunha & Agnes V Arel
CUNNINGHAM,Carol M   Sex:F   (Child #3) 03 Apr 1943 H E Cunningham (Nashua, NH)
  & Helen Miller (Braintree, MA)
CUNNINGHAM,Marion A Sex:F   (Child #4) 03 Apr 1943 H E Cunningham (Nashua, NH)
  & Helen Miller (Braintree, MA)
CUNNINGHAM,[Unknown]   Sex:F   (Child #1) 08 Jul 1940 Horace Cunningham

HUDSON,NH BIRTHS

(Nashua, NH) & Gladys E Miller (E Falmouth, MA)
CURRAN,Donna M   Sex:F   16 May 1961 John J Curran & Ethel G Hanson
CURRAN,Jason E   Sex:M   16 Jul 1975 Edward J Curran & Debra L Levesque
CURRAN,Keith W   Sex:M   19 Aug 1963 Edward A Curran & Barbara L Sullivan
CURRAN,Nancy J   Sex:F   31 Oct 1966 Edward A Curran & Barbara L Sullivan
CURRAN,Shelley M   Sex:F   05 Jul 1959 John J Curran & Ethel G Hanson
CURRAN,Thomas F   Sex:M   16 Mar 1964 John J Curran & Ethel G Hanson
CURRAN,Tracey M   Sex:F   25 Sep 1965 John J Curran & Ethel G Hanson
CURRIE,Jennifer R   Sex:F   09 Sep 1969 Bernard D Currie & Renee J Showalter
CURRIE,Richard W   Sex:M   17 Jun 1952 Stephen D Currie & Carolyn B Roundy
CURTIS,Bryan S   Sex:M   04 Aug 1967 Carl G Curtis & Sheila M Howland
CURTIS,Carla Christina   Sex:F   20 Aug 1980 Carl G Curtis & Sheila Mae Howland
CURTIS,Patricia L   Sex:F   30 Oct 1971 Donald A Curtis & Helen C McCready
CURTIS,Russell G   Sex:M   23 Apr 1969 Carl G Curtis & Sheila M Howland
CUSICK,Ashley Broderick   Sex:F   22 Aug 1983 James M Cusick & Gail M Broderick
CUTHBERTSON,Andrew R Sex:M   10 Sep 1969 Ray C Cuthbertson & Patricia M Grillo
CUTHBERTSON,Debra A   Sex:F   12 Sep 1961 David E Cuthbertson & Marlene E Shaw
CUTHBERTSON,Gail E   Sex:F   15 Apr 1963 David E Cuthbertson & Marlene E Shaw
CUTHBERTSON,James L   Sex:M   21 Sep 1967 Lee A Cuthbertson & Jessie A McGee
CUTHBERTSON,Michael R Sex:M 23 Nov 1970 Ray C Cuthbertson & Patricia M Grillo
CUTLER,Betsey   Sex:F   07 Dec 1807 Hudson, NH James Cutler & Sarah Abbott
CUTLER,Charles   Sex:M   12 Apr 1811 Hudson, NH James Cutler & Sarah Abbott
CUTLER,Charlotte S   Sex:F   19 Jan 1815 Hudson, NH James Cutler & Sarah Abbott
CUTLER,Elizabeth Sex:F   26 Nov 1771 Hudson, NH Richard Cutler & Keziah Pierce
CUTLER,Hannah   Sex:F   16 Jan 1754 Hudson, NH Richard Cutler & Keziah Pierce
CUTLER,James   Sex:M   13 Sep 1805 Hudson, NH James Cutler & Sarah Abbott
CUTLER,Jane A   Sex:F   27 Jan 1810 Hudson, NH James Cutler & Sarah Abbott
CUTLER,John   Sex:M   14 Apr 1767 Hudson, NH Richard Cutler & Keziah Pierce
CUTLER,Keziah   Sex:F   10 Nov 1751 Hudson, NH Richard Cutler & Keziah Pierce
CUTLER,Lucy   Sex:F   19 Jun 1765 Hudson, NH Richard Cutler & Keziah Pierce
CUTLER,Mary Ann   Sex:F   01 May 1813 Hudson, NH James Cutler & Sarah Abbott
CUTLER,Rhoda   Sex:F   04 Dec 1762 Hudson, NH Richard Cutler & Keziah Pierce
CUTLER,Richard   Sex:M   26 Mar 1756 Hudson, NH Richard Cutler & Keziah Pierce
CUTLER,Ruhannah   Sex:F   06 Mar 1750 Hudson, NH Richard Cutler & Keziah Pierce
CUTLER,Sarah   Sex:F   12 Dec 1803 Hudson, NH James Cutler & Sarah Abbott
CUTLER,Seltz   Sex: 14 Apr 1758 Hudson, NH Richard Cutler & Keziah Pierce
CUTLER,Susanna   Sex:F   14 Oct 1760 Hudson, NH Richard Cutler & Keziah Pierce
CUTLER,Thomas   Sex:M   29 May 1748 Hudson, NH Richard Cutler & Keziah Pierce
CUTTER,Betsy C   Sex:F   29 Dec 1874 Hudson, NH James Cutter & Caroline
CUTTER,Elizabeth   Sex:F   26 Nov 1771 Hudson, NH Richard Cutler & Lydia
CUTTER,Peter A   Sex:M   19 Jul 1960 Robert E J Cutter & Virginia E Pike
CYRULIK,Michael E Sex:M 02 Dec 1977 Edward J Cyrulik & Jeannette Ann Wjotow
CZARNIONKA,J P Jr   Sex:M   (Child #1) 07 Oct 1943 Joseph P Czarnionka
  (E Pepperell, MA) & Marion A Jankauskas (Nashua, NH)
CZOHARA,Cami C   Sex: 25 Jan 1973 Edmund G Czohara & Mary A Panek
CZOHARA,Cari Lynne   Sex:F   02 Jul 1975 Edmund G Czohara & Mary Ann Panek
D'AMBROISE,Joseph M   Sex:M   09 Jul 1965 Robert L D'Ambroise & Donna A Leddy
D'AMOUR,James W II   Sex:M   16 Feb 1974 James W D'Amour & Diane L Poulin
D'AMOUR,Joanne S   Sex:F   16 Mar 1970 James W D'Amour & Diane L Poulin
D'AMOUR,Marie G J   Sex:F   (Child #1) 04 Oct 1940 Andre D'Amour (Canada)
  & Alice Theriault (Canada)
D'AMOUR,[Unknown]   Sex:F   (Child #2) 17 Dec 1936 Paul Emmett D'Amour
  (Plattsburgh, NY) & Lillian Ruby Nichols (Nashua, NH)
DADANT,Laura K   Sex:F   01 May 1968 Andrew R Dadant & Jane C Farrell
DAGESSE,Jimmy H   Sex:M   12 Aug 1973 Reginald B Dagesse & Diane S Gelinas
DAGESSE,Johnny F   Sex:M   05 Mar 1971 Reginald B Dagesse & Diane S Gelineau
DAGESSE,Reginald J   Sex:M   04 Aug 1974 Reginald B Dagesse & Diane S Gelinas
DAHLMANN,Brian J   Sex:M   06 Jul 1976 Heinz R Dahlmann & Linda Ann Biniewicz
DAIGLE,Bruce R   Sex:M   04 Jul 1954 Robert N Daigle & Jeanne M Pelletier
DAIGLE,Douglas R   Sex:M   20 Jun 1954 Roy L Daigle & Phyllis C Cox

HUDSON,NH BIRTHS

DAIGLE,Ellen M   Sex:F   25 Feb 1966 Roger J Daigle & Sharon L Masters
DAIGLE,Julie   Sex:F   21 Aug 1975 Renald G Daigle & Madeleine C LaFlamme
DAIGLE,Linda T   Sex:F   06 Apr 1971 Renald G Daigle & Madeleine C Laflame
DAIGLE,Lisa A   Sex:F   12 Dec 1970 Jean L Daigle Jr & Carol T Rapaglia
DAILEY,Erin Chasse Sex:F 30 Sep 1979 Albert Harold Dailey & Louise F R Chasse
DAKIN,Ebenezer   Sex:M   06 Feb 1772 Hudson, NH Levi Dakin & Sarah
DAKIN,Ebenezer   Sex:M   06 Jan 1772 Hudson, NH Levi Dakin & Sarah
DAKIN,Joseph   Sex:M   20 Apr 1774 Hudson, NH Levi Dakin & Sarah
DAKIN,Joseph   Sex:M   25 Apr 1774 Hudson, NH Levi Dakin & Sarah
DAKIN,Priscilla   Sex:F   13 Jan 1764 Hudson, NH Justus Darkin & Sarah
DAKIN,Salle   Sex:F   20 Oct 1760 Hudson, NH Justin Dakin & Sarah
DAKIN,Sally   Sex:F   20 Oct 1760 Hudson, NH Justus Darkin & Sarah
DAKIN,Sarah   Sex:F   20 Nov 1776 Hudson, NH Levi Dakin & Sarah
DAKIN,Sarah   Sex:F   25 Nov 1776 Hudson, NH Levi Dakin & Sarah
DAKIN,Susanna   Sex:F   11 Feb 1770 Hudson, NH Levi Dakin & Sarah
DALESSIO,Ellen M   Sex:F   19 Jun 1966 Gerald J Dalessio & Ellen M Marcil
DALESSIO,Gary J   Sex:M   09 Aug 1967 Gerald J Dalessio & Ellen M Marcil
DALESSIO,John J Jr   Sex:M   13 Sep 1966 John J Dalessio & Irene F Doucette
DALY,Jacob Daniel R   Sex:M   09 Apr 1984 Daniel T Daly & Sandra L MacIntosh
DALZELL,Celeste A Sex:F 31 Jul 1956 William F Dalzell & Antoinette C Kashuli
DAME,John R   Sex:M   01 Jun 1957 Robert D Dame & Irene M Barbour
DAME,Meredith Lois   Sex:F   16 Jul 1977 Richard L Dame & Mary L Howe
DAME,Robert L   Sex: 05 Jan 1973 Richard L Dame & Mary L Howe
DAME,Rodney L   Sex:M   21 Nov 1974 Richard L Dame & Mary L Howe
DAME,Roger L   Sex:M   09 Mar 1976 Richard L Dame & Mary L Howe
DAMELAWICZ,Anthony   Sex:M   (Child #4) 30 Oct 1925 Joseph Damelawicz (Poland)
   & Mary Kaliowska (Poland)
DAMERY,Robert L   Sex:M   27 Oct 1949 Thomas C Damery & Evangeline Corbett
DAMON,Linda K   Sex:F   (Child #1) 25 Nov 1946 Earle A Damon (Nashua, NH)
   & Norma E Wiggin (Nashua, NH)
DAMON,Martha A   Sex:F   08 Jan 1949 Earl A Damon & Norma E Wiggin
DANBOISE,Jenna Lyn Sex:F 05 Aug 1973 Reginald P Danboise & Bonnie Rae Kaufman
DANE,Eleana Charlene   Sex:F   (Child #2) 11 Oct 1923 Richard C Dane (Nashua,
   NH) & Madeline V Campbell (Nashua, NH)
DANE,Kelly J   Sex:F   25 Mar 1971 Stephen W Dane & Jean W Dumais
DANE,Phyllis Natalie   Sex:F   (Child #9) 16 Jun 1926 Richard C Dane (Nashua,
   NH) & Madeline V Campbell (Nashua, NH)
DANES,Marion Alice Eayrs   Sex:F   (Child #1) 20 Feb 1909 James Danes (Greece)
   & Nellie Eayrs (Hudson, NH)
DANIELS,Carl W   Sex:M   26 Apr 1949 Howard R Daniels & Andrea L Savage
DANIELS,Deborah R   Sex:F   31 Jul 1952 Howard R Daniels & Andrea L Savage
DANIELS,Drake H   Sex:M   19 Mar 1951 Howard R Daniels & Andrea L Savage
DANIELS,Ellen L   Sex:F   05 Feb 1947 Howard R Daniels (New Brunswick)
   & Andrea L Savage (Nashua, NH)
DANIELS,Frederick Irvin   Sex:M   (Child #3) 07 Jun 1898 Frederick H Daniels
   (London, England) & Annie M Wheeler (Nashua, NH)
DANIELS,Howard A Jr   Sex:M   05 Jan 1951 Howard A Daniels & Gertrude A Marsh
DANIELS,Loraine W   Sex:F   (Child #2) 05 May 1903 Chas A Daniels (England)
   & Annie W Sheldon (Stoddard)
DANIELS,Lucy Ella   Sex:F   (Child #4) 18 Dec 1899 Frederick H Daniels (London)
   & Annie M Wheeler (Nashua, NH)
DANIELS,Paul H   Sex:M   06 Jul 1952 Rudolph E Daniels & Rose M Cowgill
DANIELS,Raymond Harris   Sex:M   (Child #1) 11 Feb 1901 Hudson, NH
   Charles A Daniels (England) & Anne W Sheldon (Stoddard)
DANIELS,Rhianna M   Sex:F   24 May 1976 Raymond D Daniels & Catherine D Lemay
DANIELS,Robert C   Sex:M   29 Jan 1953 Howard A Daniels & Gertrude A Marsh
DANIELS,Shannon P   Sex:F   07 Apr 1980 James E Daniels & Carol Ann Peters
DANNA,Laurel E   Sex:F   05 Sep 1960 Charles P Danna & Ellen I Edwards
DANNA,Maria T   Sex:F   28 Jul 1959 Charles P Danna & Ellen I Edwards
DANNAT,Jeffrey Robert Sex:M 22 Mar 1985 Kenneth R Dannat & Anne M Beauchesne

HUDSON,NH BIRTHS

DANNEWITZ,Chad   Sex:M   24 Sep 1973 Mickey L Dannewitz & Linda R Nutting
DAOUST,Deborah A   Sex:F   01 Jun 1956 Eugene J Daoust & Eleanor F Walker
DAOUST,Donna M   Sex:F   30 Aug 1958 Eugene J Daoust & Eleanor F Walker
DARLING,[Unknown]   Sex:M   (Child #1) 31 Jul 1908 Frank H Darling
   & Florence L Merrill (Dedham, MA)
DARREN,Noah   Sex:M   03 Mar 1785 Hudson, NH   & Nancy Clough
DARRIGO,Peter III   Sex:M   13 Dec 1980 Peter Darrigo Jr & Deborah Ann Timony
DAVALA,Melinda A   Sex:F   14 Apr 1971 James A Davala & Pamela R Albert
DAVEY,[Unknown]   Sex:M   (Child #3) 02 Feb 1932 Hudson, NH James P Davey
   (Oakland, CA) & Maude E Snow (Boston, MA)
DAVID,Christopher Paul Sex:M 30 Oct 1979 Robert A David & Donna M Danforth
DAVIDSON,Gordon B   Sex: 20 Dec 1972 Charles D Davidson & Leslie E Benner
DAVIDSON,Kathleen P   Sex:F   21 Jun 1976 William N Davidson & Paula Elwood
DAVIDSON,Laura Nicole   Sex:F   04 Jul 1982 Charles D Davidson & Elaine L Viens
DAVIES,Bruce H   Sex:M   21 Jul 1952 Raymond H Davies & Barbara A Moore
DAVIES,Deborah A   Sex:F   27 Oct 1964 Harry C Davies, Jr & Nancy A Rafuse
DAVIS,Achsah   Sex:M   25 Sep 1817 Hudson, NH Daniel Taylor Davis
   & Susannah Robinson
DAVIS,Altha   Sex:F   12 Jun 1774 Hudson, NH Asa Davis & Elizabeth
DAVIS,Amos   Sex:M   08 Jun 1769 Hudson, NH Nathaniel Davis & Martha
DAVIS,Amos   Sex:M   24 Sep 1803 Hudson, NH Amos Davis & Esther Kelley
DAVIS,Annie Belle   Sex:F   16 Nov 1902 Henry C Davis (Hudson, NH)
   & Grace Heath (Danvers, MA)
DAVIS,Asa   Sex: 27 Feb 1737 Amesbury
DAVIS,Athia   Sex:F   12 Jun 1774 Hudson, NH Asa Davis & Elizabeth Cummings
DAVIS,Bernice V   Sex:F   (Child #2) 13 Sep 1913 Henry C Davis (Hudson, NH)
   & Grace Heath (Danvers, MA)
DAVIS,Brenda L   Sex:F   (Child #1) 08 Nov 1945 Edward A Davis (Detroit, MI)
   & Sylvia J Brown (Newport, NH)
DAVIS,Daniel T   Sex:M   05 Dec 1776 Hudson, NH Asa Davis & Elizabeth
DAVIS,Daniel Taylor   Sex:M   05 Dec 1776 Hudson, NH Asa Davis
   & Elizabeth Cummings
DAVIS,David   Sex:M   30 Jun 1767 Hudson, NH Nathaniel Davis & Martha
DAVIS,Deborah E   Sex:F   24 Jan 1952 Austin E Davis & Barbara P Otis
DAVIS,Elizabeth   Sex:F   04 Feb 1762 Hudson, NH Asa Davis & Elizabeth Cummings
DAVIS,Elizabeth   Sex:F   10 Feb 1767 Hudson, NH Asa Davis & Elizabeth Cummings
DAVIS,Ephraim   Sex:M   27 Aug 1766 Hudson, NH Abraham Davis & Abiah
DAVIS,Eunice   Sex:F   20 Jun 1796 Hudson, NH Amos Davis & Esther Kelley
DAVIS,Florence May   Sex:F   16 Nov 1902 Henry C Davis (Hudson, NH)
   & Grace Heath (Danvers, MA)
DAVIS,George Wilbur   Sex:M   25 May 1876 Hudson, NH George W Davis & Abbie
DAVIS,Hannah   Sex:F   1756 Hudson, NH Nathaniel Davis & Martha
DAVIS,Hannah   Sex:F   21 Dec 1805 Hudson, NH Daniel Taylor Davis
   & Susannah Robinson
DAVIS,Harry H   Sex:M   Dec 1878 Hudson, NH George H Davis (Hudson, NH)
   & Addie E (Hudson, NH)
DAVIS,Henry Chester   Sex:M   29 Jun 1871 Hudson, NH George H Davis & Abbie E
DAVIS,Jacob   Sex:M   19 Mar 1765 Hudson, NH Asa Davis & Elizabeth Cummings
DAVIS,Jacob   Sex:M   27 Feb 1807 Hudson, NH Daniel Taylor Davis
   & Susannah Robinson
DAVIS,Jacob   Sex:M   14 Mar 1765 Hudson, NH Asa Davis & Elizabeth
DAVIS,James M   Sex:M   24 Oct 1808 Hudson, NH Daniel Davis & Susanna
DAVIS,James Madison   Sex:M   24 Oct 1808 Hudson, NH Daniel Taylor Davis
   & Susannah Robinson
DAVIS,Jeanette M   Sex:F   03 Nov 1955 Austin E Davis & Barbara P Otis
DAVIS,John   Sex:M   27 Mar 1771 Hudson, NH Nathaniel Davis & Martha
DAVIS,Joseph C   Sex:M   23 Jul 1824 Hudson, NH Joseph Davis & Aphia
DAVIS,Joseph Converse   Sex:M   23 Jul 1824 Hudson, NH Joseph Davis & Aphia
DAVIS,Joseph W   Sex:M   01 May 1957 Henry C Davis & Mae E Saunders
DAVIS,Linda M   Sex:F   20 Nov 1951 Whitney W Davis & Sylvia N Eaton

HUDSON,NH BIRTHS

DAVIS,Lou Ann   Sex:F   31 Jan 1953 Austin E Davis & Barbara P Otis
DAVIS,Louisa   Sex:F   28 Jul 1810 Hudson, NH Daniel Taylor Davis
  & Susannah Robinson
DAVIS,Lydia   Sex:F   24 Feb 1763 Hudson, NH Asa Davis & Elizabeth Cummings
DAVIS,Lydia   Sex:F   21 Feb 1763 Hudson, NH Asa Davis & Elizabeth
DAVIS,Marguerite Louise   Sex:F   (Child #1) 05 Jul 1904 G Wilbur Davis
  (Hudson, NH) & Lucy P Fuller (Jefferson City, MO)
DAVIS,Martha   Sex:F   20 Sep 1775 Hudson, NH Nathaniel Davis & Martha
DAVIS,Martha   Sex:F   24 Apr 1793 Hudson, NH Amos Davis & Esther Kelley
DAVIS,Mary   Sex:F   21 Sep 1769 Hudson, NH Asa Davis & Elizabeth Cummings
DAVIS,Nathaniel   Sex:M   07 Dec 1763 Hudson, NH Nathaniel Davis & Martha
DAVIS,Olive   Sex:F   12 Mar 1779 Hudson, NH Asa Davis & Elizabeth Cummings
DAVIS,Robert   Sex:M   11 May 1954 Henry Davis & May E Saunders
DAVIS,Ruth   Sex:F   31 Jul 1761 Hudson, NH Nathaniel Davis & Martha
DAVIS,Ruth   Sex:F   13 Jul 1761 Hudson, NH Nathaniel Davis & Martha
DAVIS,Samuel   Sex:M   21 Dec 1757 Hudson, NH Nathaniel Davis & Martha
DAVIS,Sarah   Sex:F   08 Apr 175 Hudson, NH Nathaniel Davis & Martha
DAVIS,Sarah   Sex:F   08 Aug 1799 Hudson, NH Amos Davis & Esther Kelley
DAVIS,Sarah   Sex:F   08 Apr 1759 Hudson, NH Nathaniel Davis & Martha
DAVIS,Sebel   Sex:F   17 Feb 1772 Hudson, NH Asa Davis & Elisebeth
DAVIS,Simeon R   Sex:M   03 Mar 1812 Hudson, NH Daniel T Davis & Susanna
DAVIS,Simeon Robinson   Sex:M   03 Mar 1812 Hudson, NH Daniel Taylor Davis
  & Susannah Robinson
DAVIS,Suzanne   Sex:F   04 Jun 1966 William A Davis & June M Silva
DAVIS,Sybel   Sex:F   17 Feb 1772 Hudson, NH Asa Davis & Elizabeth Cummings
DAVIS,Thomas   Sex:M   08 Apr 1733 Hudson, NH Jabez Davis & Ruth
DAVIS,Timothy C   Sex:M   06 Dec 1976 Robert D Davis Jr & Marguerite M Ricard
DAVIS,Virginia J   Sex:F   24 Dec 1951 Donald C Davis & Phyllis J Alexander
DAVIS,[Unknown]   Sex:F   (Child #4) 17 Jun 1888 George H Davis (Hudson, NH)
  & Abbie E Batchelder (Hudson, NH)
DAWALGA,Mark H   Sex:M   02 Feb 1962 Henry C Dawalga & Dorothy M Lussier
DAY,Erica Jean   Sex:F   07 Jan 1979 James R Day & Muriel A Brooks
DEAN,Aaron Owens   Sex:M   25 Sep 1984 Gerald Ozwald Dean & Debra Ann Cross
DEAN,Brian R   Sex:F   23 Oct 1968 Charles W Dean & Lorraine N Vaillancourt
DEAN,Carrie L   Sex:F   28 Jun 1974 Charles W Dean & Lorraine N Vaillancourt
DEAN,Claude R Jr   Sex:M   15 Oct 1960 Claude R Dean & Helen J Thompson
DEAN,Daniel S   Sex:M   10 Oct 1965 Robert C Dean & Jean N Blais
DEAN,Debra E   Sex:F   16 Jan 1967 Charles W Dean & Lorraine N Vaillancourt
DEAN,Donna J   Sex:F   06 Apr 1959 Claude R Dean & Helen J Thompson
DEAN,Harry   Sex:M   04 Mar 1947 Robert J Dean (Nashua, NH)
  & Elizabeth J Meredit (St Charles, VA)
DEAN,James C   Sex:M   27 Jan 1970 Robert C Dean & Jean N Blais
DEAN,Scott W   Sex:M   31 May 1965 Charles W Dean & Lorraine N Vaillancourt
DEAN,Shannon E   Sex:F   01 Apr 1978 Gilbert J Dean & Cecile N Gagnon
DEAN,Timothy James   Sex:M   06 Dec 1981 James Gerard Dean & Patricia Anne Dube
DEANE,Cassandra A   Sex:F   07 Nov 1970 Orman O Deane & Helen I Perry
DEARBORN,Anne C   Sex:F   20 May 1958 Grant W Dearborn & Joan M Kalil
DEARBORN,Candace A   Sex:F   29 Apr 1952 Grant W Dearborn & Joan M Kalil
DEARBORN,Chas Gregory   Sex:M   04 Jul 1934 Wayne Rodmn Dearborn (Melrose, MA)
  & Anne Margaret Carroll (Gloucester, MA)
DEARBORN,Dana E   Sex:M   26 Jan 1955 Charles G Dearborn & Geraldine H McLavey
DEARBORN,Gerald Anthony   Sex:M   (Child #3) 18 Apr 1936 Wayne R Dearborn
  (Woburn, MA) & Anne Carroll (Gloucester, MA)
DEARBORN,Karen M   Sex:F   09 Mar 1954 Grant W Dearborn & Joan M Kalil
DEARBORN,Lynn F   Sex:F   02 May 1960 Charles G Dearborn & Geraldine H McClavey
DEARBORN,Pamela J   Sex:F   03 Mar 1966 Gerald A Dearborn & Clarice R Boucher
DEARBORN,Rhonda J   Sex:F   19 May 1959 Gerald A Dearborn & Clarice R Boucher
DEARBORN,Tracey J   Sex:F   11 Aug 1956 Grant W Dearborn & Joan M Kalil
DeCATO,Ginger L   Sex:F   22 Jan 1962 Willard L DeCato & Cynthia L Clifford
DECATO,Jodi E   Sex: 31 Dec 1972 Joseph E Decato & Rachel M Ashline

HUDSON,NH BIRTHS

DECKER,Christopher Daniel   Sex:M   11 Jun 1981 David William Decker
   & Mary Ellen Morin
DEERING,John R   Sex:M   26 Apr 1966 Robert E Deering & Diane J Simard
DEERY,Matthew J   Sex: 11 Apr 1973 Roland J Deery Jr & Sandra J Nadeau
DELBOVE,Christina Marie Sex:F 08 Jul 1978 David G Delbove & Nancy Jean Sparks
DELBOVE,Lindsey Sue   Sex:F   02 Jul 1981 David J DelBove & Nancy Jean Sparks
DELISLE,Raymond G Jr Sex:M 17 Sep 1966 Raymond G Delisle & Beatrice B Lavigne
DELONG,Dustie Marie   Sex:F   13 Feb 1982 Craig O Delong & Anita Louise Scott
DELONG,Garrett Craig   Sex:M   23 Jan 1981 Craig O Delong & Anita Louise Scott
DeLUCA,Amy Christine   Sex:F   25 Mar 1976 Dennis M DeLuca Sr & Cheryl R Bowman
DEMAKIS,Demetra E   Sex:F   20 Aug 1967 James A Demakis & Veronica E Rand
DEMANCHE,Ella M   Sex:F   (Child #3) 15 Mar 1940 Hector J Demanche (Nashua, NH)
   & Elvina Jerou (N Conway, NH)
DEMANCHE,Jon M   Sex:M   11 Mar 1971 Roland H Demanche & Melissa Bills
DEMANCHE,Judith A   Sex:F   01 Jun 1949 Hector J Demanche & Elvina Gerow
DEMANCHE,Lillian V   Sex:F   25 Feb 1948 Henry A Demanche (Nashua, NH)
   & Irene M Baxter (St John, N B)
DEMANCHE,Matthew R   Sex:M   02 Jun 1967 Roland H Demanche & Melissa Bills
DEMARETT,Heather Ann   Sex:F   09 Aug 1977 Raymond E Demarett & Nancy J Germon
DEMELO,Christopher C   Sex:M   21 Jun 1977 Carlos Demelo & Colette Guignard
DEMERS,Chris   Sex:M   08 Jul 1967 Leo P Demers, Jr & Penny Sullivan
DEMERS,John Andrew   Sex:M   09 Nov 1980 Robert James Demers
   & Kathleen G McKeating
DEMMONS,Shawn E   Sex:M   18 Jan 1968 Gerald J Demmons & Jean Sheppard
DENAULT,Pamela A   Sex:F   (Child #3) 21 Oct 1945 Gilbert M Denault
   (Whittingham, VT) & Agnes P Boska (Nashua, NH)
DENNISON,[Unknown]   Sex:M   05 Mar 1873 Hudson, NH John Dennison & Addie E
DEPONT,Donald N   Sex:M   23 Apr 1958 Normand M Depont & Pauline C Paradise
DeROSA,Beth E   Sex: 04 Aug 1972 Richard L DeRosa & Diane M Paquette
DeROSA,Christine P   Sex:F   03 Feb 1971 Richard L DeRosa & Diane M Paquette
DeROSA,Stephen R   Sex:M   06 Feb 1969 Richard L DeRosa & Diane M Paquette
DERY,David P   Sex:M   30 Jan 1961 David P Dery & Carol E Klee
DERY,Deborah K   Sex:F   22 Apr 1965 David P Dery & Karola E Klee
DERY,Kevin M   Sex:M   18 Apr 1962 David P Dery & Carol E Klee
DERY,Kurt J   Sex:M   14 Sep 1970 David P Dery & Karola E Klee
DERY,Nancy Ann   Sex:F   (Child #1) 14 Feb 1937 Albert Dery (Manchester, NH)
   & Lillian Oliver (Nashua, NH)
DERY,Nancy J   Sex:F   29 Mar 1964 David P Dery & Karola E Klee
DERY,William David   Sex:M   (Child #2) 25 Jun 1938 Albert Dery (Manchester,
   NH) & Lillian Olivier (Nashua, NH)
DeSALVO,Rita A   Sex:F   27 Feb 1965 Anthony R DeSalvo & Eileen M Hirst
DESAU,Frank   Sex:M   (Child #3) 09 Apr 1919 Frank Desau (Champlain, NY)
   & Lena Coon (Plattsburg, NY)
DESAW,Lillian Marie   Sex:F   (Child #4) 06 Dec 1921 Frank Desaw (Champlain,
   NY) & Lena Loon (Plattsburg, NY)
DESBIENS,Andrea   Sex:F   25 Jul 1955 Joseph B Desbiens & Beatrice M Warren
DESBIENS,Karen A   Sex:F   16 Jul 1957 Joseph B Desbiens & Beatrice M Warren
DESBIENS,Leslie V   Sex:F   02 Nov 1961 Joseph B Desbiens & Beatrice M Warren
DESBIENS,Mark S   Sex:M   25 Mar 1959 Joseph B Desbiens & Beatrice M Warren
DESBIENS,Peter M   Sex:M   28 Oct 1952 Joseph B Desbiens & Beatrice M Warren
DESCHENES,Jon Paul   Sex:M   20 Aug 1984 Marc R Deschenes & Marilyn R L'Heureux
DESCHENES,Kathleen M Sex: 05 Aug 1972 Albert A Deschenes&Pauline A Rosborough
DESCLOS,David R   Sex:M   07 Nov 1962 Timothy R Desclos & Joan C Lavoie
DESCLOS,Marie Patricia   Sex:F   (Child #4) 19 Mar 1936 Wilfred G Desclos
   (Newmarket, NH) & Lucienne Milliard (Canada)
DESELL,David P   Sex:M   07 Jul 1957 Louis F Desell & Theresa C Pelletier
DESHARNAIS,Marjorie E   Sex:F   22 Jun 1965 William Desharnais & Mary E Reil
DESJARDINS,Ashley Theresa   Sex:F   10 May 1985 Bruce E Desjardins
   & Wendy L Blanchette
DESJARDINS,Bruce E Sex:M 10 Jun 1958 Raymond A Desjardins & Theresa M Simard

HUDSON,NH BIRTHS

DESJARDINS,Gail A   Sex:F   17 Feb 1960 Raymond A Desjardins & Theresa M Simard
DESJARDINS,Joseph Paul   Sex:M   03 Nov 1981 Paul C Desjardins & Nicole Landry
DESJARDINS,Melissa Nicole   Sex:F   13 Jul 1983 Paul C Desjardins IV
   & Nicole Landry
DESJARDINS,Ricky J   Sex:M   (Child #1) 05 Feb 1946 Jean A Desjardins (Nashua,
   NH) & Rita D Bosley (E Jaffrey, NH)
DESMARAIS,Amedee   Sex:M   (Child #3) 15 Jul 1930 Roland Desmarais (Manchester,
   NH) & Victoire Lussier (Canada)
DESMARAIS,Cynthia E Sex:F 21 May 1961 Amedee B Desmarais
   & Constance O Belanger
DESMARAIS,Keith A Sex:M   09 Sep 1975 Ronald R Desmarais & Deborah Ann Boucher
DESMARAIS,Leona   Sex:F   (Child #5) 16 Aug 1935 Roland A Desmarais
   (Manchester, NH) & Victoria Lucier (Canada)
DESMARAIS,Lucien   Sex:M   (Child #4) 15 Jul 1930 Roland Desmarais (Manchester,
   NH) & Victoire Lussier (Canada)
DESMARAIS,M A Claire Sex:F (Child #1) 01 Jul 1931 Albert Desmarais (Nashua,
   NH) & Lucille Theriault (Nashua, NH)
DESMARAIS,Patrick   Sex:M   (Child #5) 17 Mar 1919 Joseph Desmarais (Nashua,
   NH) & Rose Semard (Canada)
DESMARAIS,[Unknown]   Sex:F   (Child #2) 06 Apr 1914 Joseph Desmarais (Nashua,
   NH) & Rose Samerd (Canada)
DESMARAIS,[Unknown] Sex:F   (Child #3) 11 Jan 1916 Hudson, NH Joseph Desmarais
   (Nashua, NH) & Rose Larnerd (Canada)
DESMARAIS,[Unknown]   Sex:M   (Child #4) 15 Sep 1917 Joseph Desmarais (Nashua,
   NH) & Rose Simard (Canada)
DESMOND,Constance   Sex:F   08 Oct 1963 Lawrence G Desmond & Helen Viclan
DESPRES,Cherie A   Sex:F   07 Mar 1976 Alfred S Despres Jr & Marian K Schrader
DESROCHERS,Robert E II Sex:M 22 Apr 1968 Robert E Desrochers & Laura A Wiggin
DesROCHES,Dale M   Sex:M   19 Feb 1963 Gerald R DesRoches & Mary C Ballard
DesROCHES,Kerrie A   Sex:F   28 Jul 1959 Gerald R DesRoches & Mary C Ballard
DESROSIERS,Kathleen G Sex:F 24 Mar 1953 Albert L Desrosiers & Simone G StJean
DESROSIERS,Leslie Ann   Sex:F   10 Oct 1983 Gerald J Desrosiers & Ann K Kinnen
DESROSIERS,Matthew A Sex:M 12 Jun 1978 George M Desrosiers & Debra J Breault
DESROSIERS,Nicole F   Sex:F   15 Jan 1965 Norman L Desrosiers & Claire C Largy
DESROSIERS,Robert A   Sex:M   23 Aug 1948 Albert L Desrosiers (Nashua, NH)
   & Simone St Jean (Nashua, NH)
DEV,Laura Lee   Sex:F   03 Feb 1984 Roger Hanuman Dev & Satya Surya Hooker
DEVANEY,Kevin Tighe   Sex:M   04 Jul 1981 Robert C Devaney & Elizabeth J Martin
DeWAELE,Audrey Eleanor   Sex:F   04 Aug 1982 Timothy F DeWaele
   & Elizabeth A Graham
DEWITZ,Andrea Lynn   Sex:F   05 Aug 1984 Eric Wayne Dewitz & Darlene Ann Bishop
DEWYNGAERT,Samuel Broch Sex:M 20 Sep 1983 Ronald D Dewyngaert
   & Marion O Garneau
DEWYNGAERT,Timothy Garneau   Sex:M   20 Apr 1981 Ronald D Dewyngaert
   & Marion O Garneau
DICHARD,Diana Loraine   Sex:F   (Child #4) 17 Mar 1938 George Julius Dichard
   (Merrimack, NH) & Loraine R Boucher (Nashua, NH)
DICHARD,Donald Henry Sex:M   (Child #2) 16 Oct 1931 Edward Dichard (Merrimack,
   NH) & Christine Rogers (Nashua, NH)
DICHARD,Jacqueline G   Sex:F   (Child #2) 27 Sep 1934 Geo Julius Dichard
   (Merrimack, NH) & Lorraine R Boucher (Nashua, NH)
DICHARD,John Richard   Sex:M   (Child #3) 21 Jan 1937 George Julius Dichard
   (Merrimack, NH) & Lorraine R Boucher (Nashua, NH)
DICHARD,Robert   Sex:M   (Child #4) 08 Apr 1936 Albert Dichard (Merrimack, NH)
   & Beatrice Davis (Central Falls, RI)
DICHARD,Steven F   Sex:M   23 Feb 1951 Edward A Dichard, Jr & Rita C Berube
DiCLEMENTE,Andrea J   Sex:F   31 Aug 1962 John J DiClemente & Rita M Siciliano
DiCLEMENTE,Michael J   Sex:M   16 Jul 1963 John J DiClemente & Rita M Siciliano
DIENER,Erik Roger Sex:M   06 Sep 1978 Roger Barry Diener & Doreen J Cunningham
DIENER,Jeffrey Scott Sex:M 11 Sep 1980 Roger Barry Diener&Doreen J Cunningham

HUDSON,NH BIRTHS

DIETRICH,Janet M   Sex:F   20 Oct 1973 Arthur J Dietrich & Elaine C Lawson
DIGGINS,Amanda J   Sex:F   08 Jul 1969 Gary D Diggins & Diana J Minot
DIGGINS,Timothy P   Sex:M   25 Feb 1961 Donald P Diggins & Charlene A Pray
DILLEY,Jennie L   Sex:F   15 Sep 1963 Richard L Dilley & Ann-Marie Pizzutiell
DILLON,Jeffrey M   Sex:M   18 Oct 1977 James P Dillon Sr & Margaret M Dolan
DIMOND,John W   Sex:M   17 Feb 1949 James S Dimond & Rita B Messier
DIMOND,Rodney A   Sex:M   05 Jan 1948 James S Dimond, Sr (New London, NH)
  & Rita B Messier (Nashua, NH)
DINGEE,Renee L   Sex:F   06 Jun 1971 Robert L Dingee & Rosanne J Snow
DINSMORE,Bertha L   Sex:F   29 Jun 1871 Hudson, NH Oscar Dinsmore & Ellen
DINSMORE,Gladys I   Sex:F   07 Aug 1893 F W Dinsmore (Glendon, ME)
  & Jeanette Douglas (N S)
DION,Bertha Lorraine   Sex:F   (Child #6) 14 Oct 1916 Hudson, NH J B Dion
  (Winooski Falls, VT) & Dora Gauthier (Nashua, NH)
DION,Christine M   Sex:F   25 Apr 1968 Ernest E Dion & Constance F Albert
DION,David C   Sex:M   15 Jun 1951 Maurice E Dion & Yvette B Bibeau
DION,Denise E   Sex:F   25 Jan 1959 Maurice E Dion & Yvette B Bibeau
DION,Donna L   Sex:F   04 Feb 1967 Donald F Dion & Lucille Y Ledoux
DION,Gerald Albert   Sex:M   (Child #7) 05 Aug 1917 John B Dion (Burlington,
  VT) & Dora Gauthier (Nashua, NH)
DION,Henry G   Sex:M   01 Apr 1953 Sylvio H Dion & Georgette J Raymond
DION,Justin William Sex:M 24 Oct 1983 Joseph C Dion Jr & Kristin W Wordsworth
DION,Mary A   Sex:F   09 Feb 1953 Maurice E Dion & Yvette B Bibeau
DION,Rebecca Ann Sex:F   19 Mar 1985 Joseph C C Dion Jr & Kristin K Wordsworth
DIONNE,Corey A   Sex:M   25 Dec 1974 Gerard A Dionne & Karen R Guerette
DIONNE,Duane M   Sex:M   28 Nov 1968 Richard D Dionne & Jacqueline L Ricard
DIONNE,Jason D   Sex:M   24 Mar 1967 Roland A Dionne & Elaine L Swabowicz
DIONNE,Kathleen M Sex:F   08 Mar 1960 Richard D Dionne & Jacqueline L Ricard
DIONNE,Kenneth R   Sex:M   25 Oct 1965 Uldege E Dionne & Marie Y Vincent
DIONNE,Lisa A   Sex:F   24 Apr 1964 C Nelson Dionne & Sally A Plumer
DIONNE,Michael J   Sex:M   07 Oct 1962 Gerard N Dionne & Sally A Plumer
DIONNE,Peter M   Sex:M   15 Oct 1973 Roland A Dionne & Elaine L Swabowicz
DIONNE,Renee Jean   Sex:F   25 Nov 1981 Andrew S Dionne & Bella Rose Fortin
DIONNE,Scott R   Sex:M   30 Aug 1962 Richard D Dionne & Jacqueline L Ricard
DIONNE,[Unknown]   Sex:M   02 Jan 1966 Richard R Dionne & Patricia L Champigny
DiPAOLA,Janet L   Sex:F   25 Apr 1971 Frank S DiPaola & Francine M Milla
DISLA,Carlos Ramon Jr Sex:M   31 May 1985 Carolos R Disla Sr & Arlene F Kearns
DOBROWOLSKI,Nina   Sex:F   10 Dec 1955 Charles Dobrowolski & Patricia A Murray
DOCKHAM,Susan M   Sex:F   11 Dec 1965 Edward P Dockham & Therese A LeHoullier
DODDS,Stefani Mae   Sex:F   11 Aug 1984 Stephen G Dodds & Claudia M Charbonneau
DODT,Jessica Lynn   Sex:F   14 Feb 1980 Frederick C Dodt & Linda L Podewitz
DOHERTY,Lester Albert   Sex:M   (Child #2) 22 Jun 1938 Henry Austin Doherty
  (Nashua, NH) & Sarah Ophelia Lewis (Boston, MA)
DOHERTY,Lillian A   Sex:F   20 Oct 1950 John E Doherty & Margaret K Small
DOHERTY,Linda M   Sex:F   16 Mar 1948 John E Doherty (Nashua, NH)
  & Margaret K Small (Wilton, NH)
DOHERTY,Lorraine A   Sex:F   04 Jan 1949 John E Doherty & Margaret C Small
DOHLMAN,Kristen A   Sex:F   18 Sep 1974 Heinz R Dohlman & Linda A Biniewicz
DOIRON,Joseph R II   Sex:M   07 Dec 1961 Joseph A Doiron & Alice O Lovely
DOLAN,Loretta Ann   Sex:F   (Child #3) 19 Mar 1925 Fred Dolan (Worcester, MA)
  & Mamie Meehan (Ireland)
DOLAN,Michael L   Sex:M   22 Jun 1956 Charles E Dolan & Patricia C Martin
DOLAN,Valerie Jean   Sex:F   24 Oct 1977 Arthur F Dolan & Gail E Field
DOLL,Andrea Lynn   Sex:F   10 Feb 1983 Darrel John Doll & Thea Evangelista
DOLLET,Petra Maria   Sex:F   04 Nov 1978 Georg Michael Dollet & Gabriele B Eder
DOLLOFF,Benjamin W   Sex:M   Hudson, NH Samuel Dolloff & Polly Webster
DOLLOFF,Charles W   Sex:M   Hudson, NH Samuel Dolloff & Polly Webster
DOLLOFF,Edwin   Sex:M   Hudson, NH Samuel Dolloff & Polly Webster
DOLLOFF,Elmira A   Sex:M   Hudson, NH Samuel Dolloff & Polly Webster
DOLLOFF,George   Sex:M   Hudson, NH Samuel Dolloff & Polly Webster

HUDSON,NH BIRTHS

DOLLOFF,Levi Sex:M   Hudson, NH Samuel Dolloff & Polly Webster
DONAGHY,Jeffery Scott   Sex:M 31 Mar 1981 Robert C Donaghy Jr
   & Sandra Ann Sullivan
DONAH,Edgar J Sex:M   18 Dec 1950 Edgar J Donah & Nellie E Klimas
DONAH,Janet L Sex:F 04 Aug 1974 Edgar Joseph Donah & Mary C Duval
DONALLY,James H Sex:M   (Child #4) 30 Mar 1908 John Donally (Hudson, NH)
   & Dolly A Cornock (Lowell, MA)
DONNELLY,Edward D Sex:M 16 Apr 1869 Hudson, NH Eugene Donnelly & Johanna
DONNELLY,Eugene Sex:M 20 Aug 1875 Hudson, NH Owen Donnelly & Jane
DONNELLY,Jason G Sex:M 22 Mar 1975 Gregg N Donnelly & Daneen G Joziatis
DONNELLY,Mary Sex:F 16 Oct 1871 Hudson, NH Owen Donnelly & Johanna
DONNELLY,Phyllis Eugenia Sex:F (Child #2) 07 Aug 1923 Eugene E Donnelly
   (Hudson, NH) & Lillian M Lambert (Nashua, NH)
DONOVAN,Kari A Sex:F 07 Aug 1968 George H Donovan Jr & Donna M Flynn
DONOVAN,Kathleen A Sex:F 16 Jan 1961 Harvey C Donovan & Bertha M Gero
DONOVON,Leigh Janelle Sex:F 16 Jun 1982 Richard J Donovon
   & Patricia A Janelle
DOODY,David R Sex:M 09 Dec 1963 Kenneth D Doody & Elsie L Wheeler
DOOLEY,Arthur M Sex:M (Child #1) 02 Aug 1911 Geo N Dooley (Londonderry, NH)
   & Ella W Hadley (Lancaster, MA)
DOOLEY,Elaine D Sex:F   02 Nov 1948 Horace J Dooley, Jr (Londonderry, NH)
   & Donna Smith (Nashua, NH)
DOOLEY,Ella Jane Sex:F (Child #3) 19 May 1916 Hudson, NH George N Dooley
   (Londonderry, NH) & Ella W Hadley (Lancaster, MA)
DOOLEY,George H Sex:M (Child #4) 21 Oct 1919 George Dooley (Londonderry,
   NH) & Ella Hadley (Lancaster, MA)
DOOLEY,Phillip G Sex:M (Child #5) 12 Nov 1921 George N Dooley (Londonderry,
   NH) & Ella W Hadley (Lancaster, MA)
DOOLEY, [Unknown] Sex:M (Child #2) 28 Aug 1913 George N Dooley (Londonderry,
   NH) & Ella W Hadley (Lancaster, MA)
DOPP,Christopher James Sex:M 14 Mar 1985 James Howard Dopp & Nancy M Talbott
DOPP,Sarah Amanda Sex:F 01 May 1983 James Howard Dopp & Nancy Marie Talbott
DORE,Christie A Sex:F 09 Feb 1971 Richard M Dore & Sharon J Jarest
DORE,Laurie J Sex: 15 Dec 1972 Richard M Dore & Sharon J Jarest
DORE,Michael Alan Sex:M 27 May 1976 Richard M Dore & Sharon Jean Dore
DOSTIE,Richard C J Sex:M 16 Jul 1949 Robert Dostie & Cecile M Corneau
DOSTIE,Robert J Sex:M   07 Aug 1947 Robert Dostie (Methode, Canada)
   & Cecile Corneau (St Edwige, Canada)
DOTY,Floyd Dearborn Sex:M (Child #2) 15 Jul 1910 Orman Doty (Vermontville,
   NY) & Theresa Kennesknecht (Westland, NY)
DOUCET,Denis F Sex:M (Child #4) 01 Nov 1943 Frank Doucet (New Brunswick,
   Canada) & Emily Landry (New Brunswick, Canada)
DOUCET,Irene J Sex:F (Child #2) 06 Jul 1942 Germain E Doucet (St Fel'ite,
   Canada) & Gabrielle Lachance (Nashua, NH)
DOUCET,Marie T G Sex:F (Child #2) 16 May 1940 Germain E Doucet (Canada)
   & Gabrielle Lachance (Nashua, NH)
DOUCETTE,Kenneth W Sex:M 05 Dec 1959 Raymond H Doucette & Pauline B Gauthier
DOUCETTE,Michael G Sex:M 23 Apr 1957 Raymond H Doucette & Pauline B Gauthier
DOUCETTE,Paula A Sex:F 06 Jan 1971 Raymond L Doucette & Patricia A Forrence
DOUCETTE,Raymond L Sex:M 24 Mar 1953 Raymond H Doucette & Pauline B Gauthier
DOUCETTE,Stephanie M Sex:F   17 Feb 1974 Maurice J Doucette & Sandra L Davis
DOUVILLE,Cara C Sex:F 02 Jul 1973 Gary J Douville & Linda M Sirois
DOUVILLE,Lea M Sex:F 22 Nov 1974 Gary J Douville & Linda M Sirois
DOUVILLE,Ryan Courtney Sex:F 12 Jul 1984 Raymond H Douville&Theresa L Battey
DOW,Alicia Lauren Sex:F 13 Jul 1981 Michael Philip Dow & Anna Ludia Bruno
DOW,Donald A Sex:M 28 Mar 1963 Joseph L Dow & Marjorie L Staples
DOW,Harold Earl Sex:M (Child #1) 18 Jan 1928 Earl Dow (Wentworth, NY)
   & Margaret Noyes (Graham, NY)
DOW,Jessica Laura Sex:F 30 Jul 1980 Robert Stanley Dow & Sara E Brown
DOW,Joyce Sex:F (Child #4) 31 Jan 1942 Earl C Dow (Wentworth, NH)

HUDSON,NH BIRTHS

   & Margaret Noyes (Groton, NH)
DOW,Kelly Anne   Sex:F   09 May 1979 Michael P Dow & Anna L Bruno
DOW,Lisa M   Sex:F   05 Jul 1966 Darrell F Dow & Bonnie E LaPointe
DOW,Peter L   Sex:M   07 Apr 1962 Joseph L F Dow & Marjorie L Staples
DOW,[Unknown]   Sex:M   07 Nov 1984 Michael Philip Dow & Anna Lucia Bruno
DOW-JONES,Scott Dennis   Sex:M   25 Nov 1982 Harold E Dow Jr & Dawn Marie Jones
DOWLING,Patricia A   Sex:F   19 Apr 1948 Raymond E Dowling (Nashua, NH)
   & Rose M Ives (El Paso, TX)
DOWNS,Lauri A   Sex:F   01 Oct 1967 Harry L Downs & Lucille A Bisson
DOYLE,Kevin J   Sex:M   31 Dec 1964 Sherman P Doyle & Priscilla M Rogers
DOYLE,Leah R   Sex:F   17 Dec 1971 Daniel T Doyle & Julie Oldfield
DOYLE,Roscoe C   Sex:M   (Child #2) 06 Jul 1892 Samuel W Doyle (Canada)
   & Nellie H Smith (New Hampshire)
DRAKE,Dorothy   Sex:F   31 May 1892 Hudson, NH Charles E Drake & Susan E Gay
DRAKE,Dorothy J   Sex:F   (Child #2) 31 May 1892 Charles E Drake (Tyngsboro,
MA) & Susan E Gay (Litchfield, NH)
DREGAN,Richard Norman   Sex:M   (Child #2) 20 Dec 1932 Grasmere, NH
Kastanter J Dregan (Nashua, NH) & Alice Nevitt (Taunton, MA)
DREVOJAN,William S Sex:M   22 Oct 1975 Raymond Drevojan & Sally Jane Gallagher
DREW,Christina M   Sex:F   02 Apr 1967 Paul A Drew & Dolores S Van Ness
DREW,Melissa M   Sex:F   22 Jun 1970 Paul A Drew & Dolores S Van Ness
DROUIN,Heidi E   Sex:F   30 Dec 1973 Donald R Drouin & Betty Jean Moody
DROUIN,Paula E   Sex:F   17 Jun 1980 Raymond J Drouin & Shirley L Bilodeau
DROWN,Carol A   Sex:F   (Child #1) 27 Dec 1942 Alton L Drown (Ellenburg, NY)
   & Frances S Winn (Hudson, NH)
DROWN,Norma J   Sex:F   01 Sep 1952 Alton L Drown & Frances S Winn
DRUBA,Adrian Thomas Sex:M   10 Oct 1979 Arthur J Druba Jr & Jane H Stickland
DUBE,Angela I   Sex:F   28 Aug 1970 Charles I Dube & Irene C Jasmin
DUBE,Ann M   Sex:F   18 Mar 1953 Norman A Dube & Doris J Tremblay
DUBE,Brandon Scott Sex:M 23 Mar 1984 Steven William Dube & Michelle M Scott
DUBE,Brian R   Sex:M   23 Apr 1958 Roland N Dube & Joanne M Drapeau
DUBE,Bryan D   Sex:M   04 May 1968 Claude Dube & Muriel A Pare
DUBE,Carol J   Sex:F   (Child #1) 27 Feb 1944 Edward J Dube (Nashua, NH)
   & Beatrice E Beaulieu (Nashua, NH)
DUBE,Cassandra Andrea Sex:F   18 Dec 1982 Thomas Edward Dube & Marion E Tierno
DUBE,Daniel Dennis   Sex:M   03 Mar 1982 Dennis Allen Dube & Linda Baker Morin
DUBE,Dennis R   Sex:M   03 Mar 1949 Norman A Dube & Doris J Tremblay
DUBE,Diane I   Sex:F   27 Mar 1960 Daniel T Dube & Sara A Reynolds
DUBE,Douglas J   Sex:M   28 Aug 1969 Charles I Dube & Irene C Jasmin
DUBE,George   Sex:M   (Child #2) 18 May 1924 Albert Dube (Nashua, NH)
   & Alice Lasonde (Canada)
DUBE,Joseph N A   Sex:M   (Child #3) 27 Nov 1920 Arthur Dube (Nashua, NH)
   & Bertha Monier (Nashua, NH)
DUBE,Joseph Raoul G   Sex:M   (Child #4) 07 Jun 1922 Arthur Dube (Nashua, NH)
   & Bertha Monier (Nashua, NH)
DUBE,Joshua P   Sex:M   13 Apr 1978 Dennis A Dube & Linda B Morin
DUBE,Katie Ann   Sex:F   14 Aug 1980 Joseph A Dube III & Paula Ann Laine
DUBE,Maria A   Sex:F   18 Dec 1965 Daniel T Dube & Sara A Reynolds
DUBE,Marie Julia Bertha   Sex:F   (Child #5) 20 Aug 1923 Arthur Dube (Nashua,
NH) & Bertha Morier (Nashua, NH)
DUBE,Marie Lorette   Sex:F   (Child #2) 08 Dec 1934 Albert Dube (Nashua, NH)
   & Clara Aubut (Nashua, NH)
DUBE,Michael D   Sex:M   14 Jul 1968 Charles I Dube & Irene C Jasmin
DUBE,Paul A   Sex:M   (Child #5) 14 Jan 1942 Albert Dube (Ile Verte, Quebec)
   & Lydia Morin (Graniteville, VT)
DUBE,Steven W   Sex:M   22 Apr 1961 Robert P Dube & Rose M Roberts
DUBE,Susanne M   Sex:F   16 May 1970 Daniel T Dube & Sara A Reynolds
DUBE,Tanya Patricia   Sex:F   15 Oct 1984 Thomas Edward Dube & Marion E Tierno
DUBE,Thomas E   Sex:M   28 Nov 1958 Daniel T Dube & Sara A Reynolds
DUBOIS,Andrew Monroe   Sex:M   19 Oct 1984 Dale Rodney Dubois & Kellie P Monroe

HUDSON,NH BIRTHS

DUBOIS,Clifton J   Sex:M   20 Aug 1973 Earl J Dubois & Rosemary E Frenette
DUBOIS,Donna M   Sex:F   19 Aug 1947 Arthur J Dubois (Worcester, MA)
   & Rita R Brooks (Bangor, ME)
DUBOIS,Kevin J   Sex:M   22 Aug 1967 Joseph H Dubois & Joan Bowie
DUBORD,Sandra K   Sex:F   19 Apr 1979 Marcel P Dubord & Ginette C Doyon
DUBOWIK,Adam Daniel   Sex:M   05 Jun 1981 Daniel A Dubowik & Judith A McDonough
DUBOWIK,Anthony Paul Sex:M 04 Jul 1980 Paul Peter Dubowik & Therese M Theroux
DUBOWIK,Audrey   Sex:F   08 Aug 1984 Daniel A Dubowik & Judith A McDonough
DUBOWIK,Daniel A   Sex:M   13 Jul 1957 Peter Dubowik & Rita T Atkins
DUBOWIK,Danielle Mary Sex:F 20 Apr 1983 Daniel A Dubowik & Judith A McDonough
DUBOWIK,Paul P   Sex:M   23 Oct 1955 Peter Dubowik & Rita T Atkins
DUBOWIK,Rosemary E   Sex:F   30 Jan 1954 Peter Dubowik & Rita T Atkins
DUBOWIK,Timothy Alan Sex:M 21 May 1982 Paul Peter Dubowik & Therese M Theroux
DUBUC,Russell J   Sex:M   07 Nov 1955 Wilfred A Dubuc & Ruth L Blood
DUBUC,Stephen J   Sex:M   12 Mar 1954 Wilfred A Dubuc & Ruth L Blood
DUCA,Kristen M   Sex:F   15 Feb 1969 William H Duca & Sharon A Harding
DUCHARME,Arther D   Sex:M   (Child #4) 28 Jun 1940 Leo Ducharme (Canada)
   & Laura Houle (Nashua, NH)
DUCHARME,Edw Roland   Sex:M   (Child #4) 07 Jul 1936 Leo Ducharme (Canada)
   & Laura Houle (Nashua, NH)
DUCHARME,Gloria Y   Sex:F   19 Mar 1963 Henry W Ducharme & Gertrude F Lemay
DUCHARME,Hector E Sex:M (Child #6) 12 Jul 1943 Walter F Ducharme (Lowell, MA)
   & Eva Frenette (Quebec, Canada)
DUCHARME,Joan C   Sex:F   (Child #7) 06 Feb 1946 Walter F Ducharme (Lowell, MA)
   & Eva Frennette (Canada)
DUCHARME,Kurt C   Sex:M   07 Sep 1965 Robert F Ducharme & Gayle C Hadlock
DUCHARME,Lean Laura Sex:F (Child #1) 28 Jun 1928 Walter F Ducharme(Lowell,MA)
   & Eva Frenette (Canada)
DUCHARME,Leo Roger   Sex:M   (Child #2) 11 Aug 1934 Leo Ducharme (Canada)
   & Helen Blais (Canada)
DUCHARME,Leona   Sex:F   (Child #4) 04 Jul 1938 Leo Ducharme (Canada)
   & Laura Houle (Nashua, NH)
DUCHARME,Margie S   Sex:F   04 Sep 1964 Robert F Ducharme & Gayle C Hadlock
DUCHARME,Pamela A   Sex:F   21 Oct 1965 Thomas A Ducharme & Patricia A Dumont
DUCHARME,Pauline L   Sex:F   (Child #9) 17 May 1943 Leo Ducharme (Canada)
   & Laura Houle (Nashua, NH)
DUCHARME,Richard A   Sex:M   29 Apr 1948 Leo Ducharme (Canada)
   & Laura H Houle (Nashua, NH)
DUCHARME,Robert A Jr   Sex:M   23 Mar 1964 Robert A Ducharme & Annette J Judd
DUCHARME,Stephen S   Sex:M   04 Feb 1962 Robert A Ducharme & Annette J Judd
DUCHARME,Sylvia Eva   Sex:F   (Child #5) 22 Sep 1939 Walter F Ducharme (Lowell,
   MA) & Eva Frenette (Canada)
DUCHARME,Tammy P   Sex:F   06 Aug 1976 Robert E Ducharme & Linda May Little
DUCHARME,Therese   Sex:F   (Child #1) 27 Sep 1933 Leo Ducharme (Canada)
   & Helen Blais (Canada)
DUCHARME,Timothy M   Sex:M   10 Aug 1973 Robert E Ducharme & Linda May Little
DUCHARME,Walter J   Sex:M   (Child #2) 03 Sep 1929 Walter Ducharme (Lowell, MA)
   & Eva Frenette (Canada)
DUCHESNEAU,Shirley I Sex:M 29 Nov 1950 Maurice Duchesneau&Constance R Malette
DUCLOS,Thomas J   Sex:M   11 Nov 1949 Arthur A Duclos & Marguerite Cadorette
DUCLOS,Wendy L   Sex:F   24 Sep 1959 Armand E Duclos & Jo-Ann Briand
DUFAULT,Christina M   Sex:F   22 Dec 1967 Robert L Dufault & Susan M Holt
DUFAULT,Mary E   Sex:F   (Child #1) 22 Jun 1908 Oliver Dufault (Marlboro, MA)
   & Annie Coates (Newport, NH)
DUFOUR,Maura Leslie   Sex:F   04 Aug 1983 Robert Paul Dufour & Laurie C Trudeau
DUFOUR,Nicholas Adam   Sex:M   10 Dec 1983 Kevin R Dufour & Donna Marie DeCola
DUFRESNE,Amy Lee   Sex:F   16 Jun 1977 Kevin R Dufresne & Cheryl Ann Gosselin
DUGAN,Kevin D   Sex:M   25 Dec 1957 William J Dugan & Priscilla M Menard
DUGAN,[Unknown]   Sex:M   (Child #8) 24 Feb 1920 John Dugan (Russia)
   & Mary Grigas (Russia)

HUDSON,NH BIRTHS

DUGUAY,Diane M   Sex:F   07 May 1963 Wilfred J Duguay & Dorothy E Grenon
DUHAMEL,Bryan S Sex:M   14 Dec 1959 Maurice P Duhamel & Claire R Fournier
DUKE,Robert L   Sex:M (Child #2) 05 Sep 1946 Forrest R Duke (Groton, MA)
  & Margaret A Gallant (Berlin, NH)
DULEY,Jodi L   Sex:F   28 Jul 1971 Howard C Duley & Evelyn Phillips
DUMAINE,Christopher T Sex:M 17 Jun 1980 Thomas M Dumaine & Denise P Bourbeau
DUMAINE,Jessica L Sex:F   14 May 1975 Thomas M Dumaine & Denise P Bourbeau
DUMAIS,Amy L   Sex:F   19 Jan 1967 Louis P Dumais & Carol A Lee
DUMAIS,Brian A   Sex:M   12 Feb 1965 Louis P Dumais & Carol A Lee
DUMAIS,Cheryl A Sex:F   15 Jul 1969 Joseph C Dumais & Patricia A Cope
DUMAIS,Debora A Sex:F   07 Feb 1957 Lucien R Dumais & Violet L Frenette
DUMAIS,Deborah J Sex:F   05 Nov 1964 Albert R Dumais & Jean H Bedore
DUMAIS,Jean W   Sex:F (Child #1) 14 Dec 1944 Joseph A Dumais (Nashua, NH)
  & Winifred M LaCross (Lowell, MA)
DUMAIS,Karen A   Sex:F   30 Jul 1965 Joseph C Dumais & Patricia A Cope
DUMAIS,Kent R   Sex:M   21 Sep 1964 Lucien R Dumais & Violet L Frenette
DUMAIS,Lisa J   Sex:F   11 Aug 1966 Albert R Dumais & Jean H Bedore
DUMAIS,Lynn M   Sex:F   16 Feb 1974 Joseph C Dumais & Patricia A Cope
DUMAIS,Marie Noela T   Sex:F (Child #3) 25 Dec 1939 Alphonse E Dumais
  (Canada) & Irene J Paradis (Nashua, NH)
DUMAIS,Michael R Sex:M   24 Dec 1958 Lucien R Dumais & Violet L Frenette
DUMAIS,Richard A Sex:M   16 Apr 1970 Albert R Dumais & Jean H Bedore
DUMAIS,Susan I   Sex:F   22 Feb 1949 Lucien R Dumais & Violet L Frenette
DUMAS,Deborah J Sex:F   11 Mar 1949 Richard S Dumas & Ellen L Soper
DUMAS,Dennis L   Sex:M   09 Apr 1960 Lawrence M Dumas & Bernadette Labrie
DUMAS,Kenneth J Sex: 06 Mar 1973 Dennis O Dumas & Mary E Holmes
DUMAS,Pamela A   Sex:F   01 Apr 1955 Lawrence M Dumas & Bernadette ML Labrie
DUMONT,Cheryl A Sex:F   21 Jan 1961 Raymond E Dumont & Loretta P Ayotte
DUMONT,Daniel G Jr Sex:M 02 Mar 1974 Daniel G Dumont Sr & Virginia L Hannigan
DUMONT,David F   Sex:M   21 Apr 1951 Leo A Dumont & Theresa Michaud
DUMONT,Denise M Sex:F   11 Apr 1963 Robert T Dumont & Lucille M Ledoux
DUMONT,Joseph B Sex:M   21 May 1976 Daniel G Dumont & Virginia L Hannigan
DUMONT,Leo A III Sex:M   29 Apr 1975 Leo A Dumont Jr & Elizabeth L Georges
DUMONT,Linda M   Sex:F   07 Sep 1959 Raymond E Dumont & Loretta P Ayotte
DUMONT,Nicholas Joseph Sex:M   14 Jan 1981 Daniel L Dumont
  & Rhonda R Courtemanche
DUMONT,Shane R   Sex:M   25 Oct 1970 Normand A Dumont & Roberta R DeVeau
DUMONT,Steven Michael Sex:M 28 Sep 1979 Harry Arthur Dumont & Ann Marie Byrne
DUMONT,Theresa P Sex:F   10 Sep 1959 Robert T Dumont & Lucille M Ledoux
DUMONT,Tina M   Sex:F   24 Sep 1966 Joseph R Dumont & Lee A Posey
DUMOUCHEL,Wm A   Sex:M   27 May 1947 Albert E Dumouchel (Worcester, MA)
  & Lillian I Guevin (Manchester, NH)
DUN,Aaron J   Sex:M   03 Aug 1971 Angus Dun III & Laurel D Browstein
DUNCKLEE,Cheryl A Sex:F   22 Oct 1956 Charles F Duncklee & Mary T Soucy
DUNCKLEE,Gerald Reed   Sex:M (Child #3) 18 Aug 1914 Merton L Duncklee
  (Grafton) & Clara L Harvey (Nashua, NH)
DUNKLEE,Barbara A Sex:F   04 Nov 1949 Herbert H Dunklee & Helen A Trumbull
DUNKLEE,Cynthia J Sex:F   27 Sep 1953 Herbert H Dunklee & Helen A Trumbull
DUNKLEE,Herbert W Sex:M (Child #8) 09 May 1945 Herbert H Dunklee (Nashua,
  NH) & Helen A Trumbull (Nashua, NH)
DUNKLEE,Marjorie T Sex:F   19 Sep 1952 Herbert H Dunklee & Helen A Trumbull
DUNKLEE,Patricia L Sex:F   29 May 1947 Herbert H Dunklee (Nashua, NH)
  & Helen A Trumbull (Nashua, NH)
DUNKLEE,Sally A Sex:F   31 May 1956 Herbert H Dunklee & Helen A Trumbull
DUNKLEE,Sylvia J Sex:F   22 Nov 1948 Herbert H Dunklee (Nashua, NH)
  & Helen A Trumbull (Nashua, NH)
DUNKLEE,Virginia M Sex:F (Child #7) 23 Jan 1944 Herbert H Dunklee (Nashua,
  NH) & Helen Trumbull (Nashua, NH)
DUNKLEE,Willard D Sex:M (Child #9) 10 Jun 1946 Herbert H Dunklee (Nashua, NH)
  & Helen Trumbull (Nashua, NH)

HUDSON,NH BIRTHS

DUNLAP,Betty J   Sex:F   08 Sep 1964 Fred M Dunlap & Margaret J Smolski
DUNLAP,Michael T   Sex:M   11 Nov 1962 Fred M Dunlap & Margaret J Smolski
DUNT,Calvin Robert   Sex:M   (Child #3) 08 Jun 1926 Herman A Dunt (Pike, NH)
   & Zelma Lereier (Biddeford, ME)
DUPLEASE,Denise G   Sex:F   26 Mar 1953 Julien G Duplease & Rita R Duclos
DUPLEASE,Richard E   Sex:M   28 Aug 1956 Julien G Duplease & Rita R Duclos
DUPLEASE,Ronald G   Sex:M   06 Jan 1950 Julien G Duplease & Rita R A Duclos
DUPONT,Angela Renee   Sex:F   13 Oct 1981 Dennis David Dupont & Michele L Jarry
DUPONT,Anthony W   Sex:M   19 Apr 1974 Benoit Y Dupont & Paula C Lyfert
DUPONT,Darlene A   Sex:F   (Child #3) 10 Jul 1944 Louis H Dupont (Nashua, NH)
   & Marguerite D Turcot (Canada)
DUPONT,Debra A   Sex:F   21 Nov 1959 George C Dupont & Victoria J Paquette
DUPONT,Donna L   Sex:F   12 Jul 1967 George C Dupont & Victoria J Paquette
DUPONT,Dorothy A   Sex:F   05 Jan 1966 George C Dupont & Victoria T Paquette
DUPONT,George C Jr   Sex:M   17 Dec 1962 George C Dupont & Victoria J Paquette
DUPONT,Lisa M   Sex:F   31 May 1964 George C Dupont & Victoria M Paquette
DUPONT,Marguerite L   Sex:F   (Child #4) 21 Oct 1945 Louis H Dupont (Nashua,
   NH) & Marguerit D Turcott (E Brockton, CA)
DUPONT,Scott Michael   Sex:M   19 Aug 1980 Dennis David Dupont & Michele L Jarry
DUPRAS,Edwin M   Sex:M   04 Feb 1980 Gilbert E Dupras & Cynthia Ann Munday
DUPRAS,Florence   Sex:F   (Child #2) 27 Jun 1912 Henry Dupras (U S A)
   & Elina Belanger (Canada)
DUPRAS,Joseph George Albert   Sex:M   (Child #5) 18 Mar 1917 Henry Dupras
   (Lowell, MA) & Celina Bellanger (Canada)
DUPUIS,Deborah A   Sex:F   20 Dec 1953 Raymond W Dupuis & Sylvia L Cote
DUPUIS,Frederick W Jr   Sex:M   01 Jan 1970 Frederick W Dupuis&Elaine M Balukonis
DUPUIS,James M   Sex:M   18 Jul 1966 Robert R Dupuis & Dorothy M Harmon
DUQUETTE,Claire L   Sex:F   13 Aug 1950 Raymond A Duquette & Loretta A Gagnon
DUQUETTE,Dennis M   Sex:M   20 Feb 1971 Robert H Duquette & Yvette M A Bergeron
DUQUETTE,Peter A   Sex:M   07 Oct 1958 Raymond E Duquette & Loretta A Gagnon
DUQUETTE,Robert R   Sex:M   09 Jul 1951 Raymond E Duquette & Loretta A Gagnon
DUQUETTE,Sally A   Sex:F   17 Feb 1953 Raymond E Duquette & Laurette A Gagnon
DURAND,Brian Kenneth   Sex:M   24 Jul 1979 Robert K Durand & Donna Marie Landry
DURAND,Daniel R   Sex:M   25 May 1962 Paul T Durand & Jeanine N Levesque
DURAND,Edmond P   Sex:M   29 Jan 1963 Normand E Durand & Lillian M Blair
DURAND,Jessica Marie   Sex:F   13 Jun 1983 Robert K Durand & Donna Marie Landry
DURAND,Laurette M   Sex:F   28 Oct 1952 Normand E Durand & Lilian M Blais
DURAND,Mark E   Sex:M   17 Dec 1970 Edward A Durand & Janet L Martin
DURAND,Michael M   Sex:M   26 Jun 1969 Paul T Durand & JoAnn R Paquette
DURAND,Phillip A   Sex:M   27 Sep 1954 Norman E Durand & Lillian M Blais
DURAND,Rachel D   Sex:F   22 Jun 1957 Normand E Durand & Lillian M Blais
DURAND,Raymond   Sex:M   01 Sep 1958 Normand E Durand & Lillian M Blais
DURAND,Robert N   Sex:M   26 Jul 1949 Normand E Durand & Lillian M Blais
DURANT,Benjamin   Sex:M   29 May 1776 Hudson, NH Samuel Durant & Rachel
DURANT,George Otis   Sex:M   (Child #6) 06 Apr 1899 Geo Otis Durant (Hudson,
   NH) & Mary E Anthony (Troy, NY)
DURANT,Laura J   Sex:F   15 Dec 1872 Hudson, NH George W Durant & Georgianna
DURANT,Leroy O   Sex:M   12 Jan 1871 Hudson, NH George W Durant & Eliza A
DURANT,Mary C   Sex:F   17 Dec 1874 Hudson, NH George Durant & Georgianna
DURANT,Milo L   Sex:M   28 Apr 1868 Hudson, NH George W Durant & Anna
DURANT,Nathan   Sex:M   02 Jul 1774 Hudson, NH Samuel Durant & Rachel
DURGIN,Frank   Sex:M   22 Oct 1871 Hudson, NH James A Durgin & Emily
DURGIN,Fred B   Sex:M   19 Aug 1873 Hudson, NH James A Durgin & Emily
DURGIN,Hiram P   Sex:M   26 Feb 1877 Hudson, NH James A Durgin (Portsmouth)
   & Emily Bullis (Peru, NY)
DURGIN,Lenora Bell   Sex:F   02 Oct 1869 Hudson, NH James A Durgin & Emily S
DURIVAGE,Ellsworth   Sex:M   (Child #1) 20 Feb 1903 Geo E Durivage (Lowell, VT)
   & Halga Harwood (Canada)
DURIVAGE,Gertrude M   Sex:F   (Child #2) 17 May 1906 Frank H Durivage (Lowell,
   VT) & Bertha G Thorne (Hudson, NH)

DURIVAGE,Janice Thea   Sex:F   (Child #2) 03 Jul 1909 George E Durivage
   (Lowell, VT) & Hulga Harwood (Canada)
DURIVAGE,Margaret Ann   Sex:F   (Child #1) 24 Nov 1937 Floyd Durivage (Hudson,
   NH) & Yvonne Lemay (Plymouth, NH)
DURIVAGE,Mildred Eunice   Sex:F   (Child #1) 20 Apr 1904 Frank H Durivage
   (Lowell, VT) & Bertha G Thorne (Hudson, NH)
DURIVAGE,Nancy May   Sex:F   (Child #2) 28 Jan 1939 Floyd Durivage (Hudson, NH)
   & Yvonne Lemay (Plymouth, NH)
DURIVAGE,Robert N   Sex:M   (Child #7) 26 Jan 1944 Floyd C Durivage (Hudson,
   NH) & Yvonne Lemay (Plymouth, NH)
DURIVAGE,[Unknown]   Sex:M   (Child #3) 08 May 1908 Frank H Durivage (Lowell,
   VT) & Bertha G Thorne (Hudson, NH)
DURIVAGE,[Unknown]   Sex:M   (Child #4) 23 Jan 1917 Frank Durivage (Lowell, VT)
   & Bertha G Thorn (Hudson, NH)
DUROCHER,Maurice H   Sex:M   05 Feb 1947 Hervey J Durocher (St David, Canada)
   & Marie I Pare (St Francois, Canada)
DURWIN,Constance M Sex:F 12 Sep 1956 William F Durwin & Constance M Kitchener
DURWIN,Sara S   Sex:F   24 Mar 1954 William F Durwin & Constance M Kitchener
DUSSAULT,Tina M   Sex:F   09 Jan 1966 Richard E Dussault & Mary T Carbonneau
DUSSEAULT,Gerard E Jr Sex:M 02 Aug 1957 Gerard E Dusseault & Arlene L Torrey
DUSSEAULT,Marion E   Sex:F   03 Jul 1947 Gerard E Dusseault (Nashua, NH)
   & Arlene L Torrey (Pepperell, MA)
DUSSEAULT,Marlene L   Sex:F 26 Nov 1952 Gerard E Dusseault & Arlene L Torrey
DUSSEAULT,Tammy L   Sex:F   24 Mar 1962 Gerard E Dusseault & Arlene L Torrey
DUSTIN,Dusty E   Sex:M   07 Jan 1974 Donald K Dustin & Linda Lee Venne
DUSTIN,Ethenen   Sex:M   (Child #2) 26 Jun 1882 Hudson, NH Washington F Dustin
   (Antrim, NH) & Alfaretta Batchelder (Hudson, NH)
DUSTIN,[Unknown]   Sex:M   (Child #3) 04 Feb 1888 W F Dustin (Antrim, NH)
   & Alfaretta Batchelder (Hudson, NH)
DUTTON,Amy S   Sex:F   15 Feb 1969 Ruel W Dutton & Anastasia Paraskevak
DUTTON,Asa   Sex:M   29 Nov 1748 Hudson, NH Josiah Dutton & Sarah
DUTTON,Asa   Sex:M   27 Nov 1748 Hudson, NH Josiah Dutton & Sarah
DUTTON,Benjamin   Sex:M   27 Jun 1746 Hudson, NH Josiah Dutton & Sarah
DUTTON,Beth E   Sex:F   14 May 1965 Ruel W Dutton & Anastasia Paraskevak
DUTTON,Christine M   Sex:F   12 Mar 1965 Leon A Dutton & Janice A Tomolonis
DUTTON,Cynthia M   Sex:F   25 Mar 1957 Elwin W Dutton & Shirley M Brown
DUTTON,Edelbert   Sex:M   10 Dec 1867 Hudson, NH John E Dutton & Sarah E Winn
DUTTON,Edelbert L   Sex:M   10 Dec 1867 Hudson, NH John G Dutton & Elizabeth
DUTTON,Ephraim   Sex:M   14 Oct 1766 Hudson, NH Josiah Dutton & Sarah
DUTTON,Ezra   Sex:M   30 Aug 1755 Hudson, NH Josiah Dutton & Sarah
DUTTON,Jacob   Sex:M   08 Aug 1751 Hudson, NH Josiah Dutton & Sarah
DUTTON,Lowella   Sex:F   06 Dec 1863 Hudson, NH John E Dutton & Sarah E Winn
DUTTON,Luella   Sex:F   06 Dec 1863 Hudson, NH John E Dutton & Sarah
DUTTON,Lydia   Sex:F   06 Oct 1763 Hudson, NH Josiah Dutton & Sarah
DUTTON,Mary   Sex:F   30 Sep 1753 Hudson, NH Josiah Dutton & Sarah
DUTTON,Pamela A   Sex:F   22 Sep 1961 James A Dutton & Jeanne B Pepin
DUTTON,Rachel   Sex:F   09 Sep 1757 Hudson, NH Josiah Dutton & Sarah
DUTTON,Sarah   Sex:F   18 Apr 1744 Hudson, NH Josiah Dutton & Sarah
DUTTON,Timothy A   Sex:M   10 Dec 1959 James A Dutton & Jeanne B Pepin
DUTTON,Timothy D   Sex:M   24 Apr 1961 Elwin W Dutton & Shirley M Brown
DUTTON,William   Sex:M   23 May 1760 Hudson, NH Josiah Dutton & Sarah
DUTY,Charlotte   Sex:F   25 Aug 1795 Hudson, NH Andrew W Duty & Mary
DUTY,Isaac D   Sex:M   08 Aug 1797 Hudson, NH Andrew W Duty & Mary
DUTY,Sally Plumer   Sex:F   11 Mar 1783 Hudson, NH   & Elizabeth Duty
DUVAL,Christopher Joseph Sex:M 11 Aug 1983 Norbert J Duval&Patricia A Notter
DUVAL,Claude   Sex:M   19 Jul 1965 Andre Duval & Therese C Dionne
DUVAL,Jeffrey M   Sex:M   29 Mar 1980 Danny M Duval & Deborah Wilshire
DUVAL,Marie Claudette A   Sex:F   28 Feb 1967 Andre Duval & Therese C Dionne
DUVAL,Robert Paul   Sex:M   19 Jul 1978 Norbert Duval & Patricia Ann Notter
DUVALL,Benjamin C   Sex:M   21 Aug 1970 Scott E Duvall & JoAnn E LaForge

HUDSON,NH BIRTHS

DUVALL,Marcia G   Sex:F   (Child #1) 19 Jul 1946 Arthur H Duvall (Worcester,
   MA) & Eva B Lucier (Bellows Falls, VT)
DWIRE,Deanna L   Sex:F   13 Aug 1971 Earl A Dwire & Deborah H Thompson
DWIRE,Gail A   Sex:F   23 Aug 1957 Earl H Dwire & Lucille I Richards
DWIRE,Jason Anthony Sex:M 17 Apr 1984 Gerald A Dwire & Nancy Rita Beaulieu
DWIRE,Terri L   Sex: 09 Sep 1972 Earl A Dwire & Deborah H Thompson
DWYER,Robert Joseph Sex:M 24 Nov 1978 David John Dwyer & Patricia J McDonald
DWYER,Stacy L   Sex:F   11 Apr 1972 Kenneth W Dwyer & Terry M Saucier
DYER,Arthur W   Sex:M   (Child #2) 28 Apr 1946 William D Dyer (Boston, MA)
   & Constance Dodd (Milton, MA)
DYER,Mark G   Sex:M   08 Apr 1958 Victor E Dyer & Pauline L Truchon
DYMENT,Henry E   Sex:M   04 Oct 1900 Eli Dyment (P E Island)
   & Susan Poole (P E Island)
EACHUS,Robert Thomas   Sex:M   08 Sep 1981 Robert I Eachus & Ashley Deas
EAGLE,Stephen Paul   Sex:M   17 Dec 1979 Gary Stephen Eagle & Holly Ann Powell
EAGLES,Nellie M   Sex:F   26 Jun 1893 Edward F Eagles (Nashua, NH)
   & Augusta Ford (Hudson, NH)
EARLEY,Karen J   Sex:F   14 Oct 1964 William J Earley & Nancy P Torrey
EARLEY,Raybon J   Sex:M   07 Mar 1966 William J Earley & Nancy P Torrey
EASTMAN,Ichabod   Sex:M   07 Mar 1792 Hudson, NH Ichabod Eastman & Mary
EASTMAN,James   Sex:M   13 Jun 1788 Hudson, NH Ichabod Eastman & Mary
EASTMAN,James   Sex:M   13 Jun 1788 Hudson, NH Jehabonah Eastman & Molly
EASTMAN,Jeney   Sex:F   22 Aug 1783 Hudson, NH Jehabonah Eastman & Molly
EASTMAN,Jenny   Sex:F   22 Aug 1783 Hudson, NH Ichabod Eastman & Mary
EASTMAN,Johabonah   Sex:M   17 Mar 1792 Hudson, NH Johabonah Eastman & Molly
EASTMAN,Joseph   Sex:M   05 Nov 1777 Hudson, NH Nicholas Eastman & Olive
EASTMAN,Joseph B   Sex:M   12 Mar 1780 Hudson, NH Nicholas Eastman & Olive
EASTMAN,Joseph Barnes   Sex:M   12 Mar 1780 Hudson, NH Nicholas Eastman & Olive
EASTMAN,Mollie   Sex:F   20 Nov 1774 Hudson, NH Ichabod Eastman & Mary
EASTMAN,Molly   Sex:F   20 Nov 1774 Hudson, NH Ichabod Eastman & Mary
EASTMAN,Nabby   Sex: 20 Nov 1777 Hudson, NH Ichabod Eastman & Mary
EASTMAN,Rachel   Sex:F   25 May 1781 Hudson, NH Ichabod Eastman & Mary
EASTMAN,Rachel   Sex:F   06 May 1776 Hudson, NH Nicholas Eastman & Olive
EASTMAN,Sally   Sex:F   02 Jun 1779 Hudson, NH Ichabod Eastman & Mary
EASTMAN,William   Sex:M   06 Dec 1785 Hudson, NH Ichabod Eastman & Mary
EATON,Albert Clifford   Sex:M   (Child #4) 03 Apr 1923 Albert H Eaton
   (N Reading, MA) & Eva R Smith (Hudson, NH)
EATON,Barbara A   Sex:F   06 Nov 1950 Albert C Eaton & Mary R Lefebvre
EATON,Carroll B   Sex:M   (Child #3) 03 Jun 1926 Perry L Eaton (Westfield, IN)
   & Mabel E Caverly (Franklin, NH)
EATON,Clara Eliza   Sex:F   (Child #1) 15 Aug 1901 Hudson, NH Walter D Eaton
   (Hudson, NH) & Bertha Smith (Wakefield, MA)
EATON,Doris Elizabeth   Sex:F   (Child #2) 19 Feb 1907 Walter D Eaton (Hudson,
   NH) & Bertha M Smith (Wakefield, MA)
EATON,Edson W   Sex:M   14 Dec 1868 Hudson, NH Alfred Eaton & Harriet Smith
EATON,Elizabeth E   Sex:F   27 Sep 1967 Richard V Eaton & Robbie E Broadway
EATON,Erwin W   Sex:M   14 Dec 1868 Hudson, NH Alfred Eaton & Harriet S
EATON,Marion E   Sex:F   (Child #3) 09 Jul 1921 Albert H Eaton (N Reading, MA)
   & Eva R Smith (Hudson, NH)
EATON,Sharon L   Sex:F   27 Mar 1952 Albert C Eaton & Mary Rose Lefebvre
EAYRS,Cora B   Sex:F   (Child #3) 12 May 1889 Edward F Eayrs (Nashua, NH)
   & Charlotte A Ford (Hudson, NH)
EBERLE,Ernest C Jr   Sex:M   20 Nov 1962 Ernest C Eberle & Joyce A Brooks
EBNER,Brian Donald   Sex:M   26 Aug 1984 Emanuel C Ebner Jr & Donna Rose Dupuis
ECONOMOU,Amanda D   Sex:F   28 Mar 1980 John N Economou & Maria C Alexion
EDWARDS,Carla R   Sex:F   07 Dec 1962 Carl R Edwards & Gloria M Thebodeau
EDWARDS,Carol A   Sex:F   10 Mar 1957 Ira A Edwards & Pauline H Knox
EDWARDS,Joan H   Sex:F   01 Mar 1960 Ira A Edwards & Pauline H Knox
EDWARDS,Laine E   Sex:M   04 Apr 1967 Lee E Edwards & Nancy A Mason
EDWARDS,Lee E Jr   Sex:M   13 May 1957 Lee E Edwards & Nancy A Mason

HUDSON,NH BIRTHS

EDWARDS,Lon E   Sex:M   06 Oct 1960 Lee E Edwards & Nancy A Mason
EDWARDS,Pearl M   Sex:F   (Child #4) 26 Feb 1906 Arthur P Edwards (New Brunswick) & Lucy Eayrs (Hudson, NH)
EGERIS,Joseph C   Sex:M   (Child #2) 10 May 1946 Joseph C Egeris (Lithuania) & Constance Murauckos (Rumford, ME)
EHRLICH,Amy M   Sex:F   23 Jul 1975 Rick A Ehrlich & Sandra L Banks
EINSIDLER-MOORE,Emily   Sex:F   30 Oct 1981 Bruce W Einsidler & Betty Ann Moore
ELAM,Amanda Joy   Sex:F   21 Oct 1983 Terrell Lynn Elam & Robyn D Peaslee
ELDRIDGE,Kristy Lynn   Sex:F   05 Dec 1978 Robert P Eldridge & Diane H Belanger
ELDRIDGE,Thelma E   Sex:F   (Child #1) 19 Mar 1905 Arthur W Eldridge (Fellowship, NJ) & Helen L Rounseville (Lowell, MA)
ELDRIDGE,Vivian A   Sex:F   (Child #2) 31 Aug 1906 Arthur W Eldridge (New Jersey) & Helen L Rounsavelle (Lowell, MA)
ELIACOPOULOS,Lisa   Sex:F   03 Oct 1966 Harry Eliacopoulos & Mary A Manikas
ELKINS,Amy Dawn   Sex:F   17 Jan 1977 Michael D Elkins & Barbara Ann Starratt
ELLIOT,Brian E   Sex:M   19 Feb 1964 Elmer O Elliot & Rosezetta C Orser
ELLIOTT,Joseph A   Sex:M   02 Mar 1961 Wilfred A Elliott & Bernice A Pike
ELLIOTT,Kevin D   Sex:M   04 Mar 1953 George E Elliott & Theresa M Canton
ELLIOTT,Leesa R   Sex:F   06 Jun 1965 Elmer O Elliott & Rosezetta C Orser
ELLIOTT,Linda Y   Sex:F   08 Feb 1958 Frank H Elliott & Theresa I St Laurent
ELLIOTT,Michael F   Sex:M   06 Oct 1956 Frank H Elliott & Theresa I St Laurent
ELLIOTT,Robert A   Sex:M   12 Sep 1956 Wilfred A Elliott & Bernice A Pike
ELLIOTT,Sandra A   Sex:F   25 Jun 1958 Wilfred A Elliott & Bernice A Pike
ELLIOTT,Sharon A   Sex:F   22 Nov 1955 George E Elliott & Theresa M Canton
ELLIOTT,Steven M   Sex:M   28 May 1954 George E Elliott & Theresa M Canton
ELLIOTT,Susan A   Sex:F   16 Apr 1954 Wilfred A Elliott & Bernice A Pike
ELLIOTT,Terri A   Sex:F   16 Mar 1964 Wilfred A Elliott & Bernice A Pike
ELLIOTT,Wendy L   Sex:F   01 Jul 1957 George E Elliott & Theresa M Canton
ELLIOTT,William A   Sex:M   10 Feb 1952 Wilfred A Elliott & Bernice A Pike
ELLIS,Brian M   Sex:M   29 Nov 1966 William L Ellis & Francine T Saulnier
ELLIS,Everett W   Sex:M   (Child #2) 09 Aug 1944 Clifton F Ellis (Londonderry, NH) & Alice M Fuller (Nashua, NH)
ELLIS,Herbert Palmer   Sex:M   (Child #7) 18 Oct 1932 Hudson, NH John W Ellis (Haverhill, MA) & Irene Henry (Saco, ME)
ELLIS,Jeanne Elizabeth   Sex:F   (Child #6) 13 Sep 1931 John W Ellis (Haverhill, MA) & Irene Henri (Saco, ME)
ELLIS,Michael L   Sex:M   07 Oct 1959 Herbert P Ellis & Patricia A Courtemanche
ELLIS,Paul Vernard   Sex:M   (Child #3) 26 Jan 1937 John Wm Ellis (Haverhill, MA) & Irene M Henri (Saco, ME)
ELLIS,Richard Willard   Sex:M   (Child #5) 22 Jun 1930 John W Ellis (MA) & Irene M Henri (Saco, ME)
ELWOOD,Sharon A   Sex:F   22 Jan 1954 Quentin D Elwood & Lorraine R Clark
EMERSON,Benjamin H   Sex:M   14 Apr 1759 Hudson, NH Timothy Emerson & Hannah
EMERSON,Benjamin Harnden   Sex:M   14 Apr 1759 Hudson, NH Timothy Emerson & Hannah
EMERSON,Bruce M   Sex:M   08 Mar 1947 Stirling P Emerson & Janice E Martin (Nashua, NH)
EMERSON,Elizabeth   Sex:F   05 Apr 1765 Hudson, NH Thomas Emerson & Judith
EMERSON,Elizabeth   Sex:F   06 Dec 1762 Hudson, NH Thomas Emerson & Judith
EMERSON,Elizabeth   Sex:F   15 Apr 1765 Hudson, NH Thomas Emerson & Judith
EMERSON,Esther   Sex:F   24 Dec 1744 Hudson, NH Timothy Emerson & Hannah
EMERSON,Hannah   Sex:F   28 Jan 1743 Hudson, NH Timothy Emerson & Hannah
EMERSON,Jonathan   Sex:M   14 Jun 1750 Hudson, NH Timothy Emerson & Hannah
EMERSON,Mary   Sex:F   28 Mar 1755 Hudson, NH Timothy Emerson & Hannah
EMERSON,Moses   Sex:M   09 Jan 1768 Hudson, NH Thomas Emerson & Judith
EMERSON,Moses   Sex:M   05 Nov 1761 Hudson, NH Timothy Emerson & Hannah
EMERSON,Moses   Sex:M   07 Jan 1763 Hudson, NH Thomas Emerson & Judith
EMERSON,Nathan D   Sex:M   07 May 1975 David R Emerson & Loretta E Clark
EMERSON,Ruth   Sex:F   23 Sep 1746 Hudson, NH Timothy Emerson & Hannah
EMERSON,Sarah   Sex:F   06 Dec 1762 Hudson, NH Thomas Emerson & Judith

HUDSON,NH BIRTHS

EMERSON,Sarah   Sex:F   21 Apr 1752 Hudson, NH Timothy Emerson & Hannah
EMERSON,Sarah   Sex:M   20 Apr 1752 Hudson, NH Timothy Emerson & Hannah
EMERSON,Sibbel   Sex:F   07 Mar 1774 Hudson, NH Jonathan Emerson & Sibbel
EMERSON,Sybil   Sex:F   07 Mar 1774 Hudson, NH Jonathan Emerson & Sybil
EMERSON,Thomas   Sex:M   01 Apr 1741 Hudson, NH Timothy Emerson & Hannah
EMERSON,Thomas   Sex:M   21 Apr 1741 Hudson, NH Timothy Emerson & Hannah
EMERSON,Timothy Sex:M   09 May 1748 Hudson, NH Timothy Emerson & Hannah
EMERSON,Wallen R   Sex:M   (Child #1) 20 Apr 1940 Russell W Emerson
   (Manchester, NH) & Janice Shepard (Joliet, IL)
EMERY,Heidi M   Sex:F   01 Dec 1956 John C Emery & Rita L Lemire
EMMETT,Steven D   Sex:M   06 Jul 1970 David S Emmett & Eleanor S Stevens
ENGLISH,Jerry A   Sex:M   19 Apr 1953 Donald L English & Olivette J Thebodeau
ENMAN,Carol F   Sex:F   19 Nov 1975 Douglas H Enman & Frances I Hodges
ENMAN,Paul D   Sex:M   26 Jul 1971 Douglas H Enman & Frances J Hodges
ERB,David A   Sex:M   28 Feb 1949 Leslie H Erb & Margaret J Neilly
ERICKSON,Corinne M   Sex:F   21 Dec 1982 Matthew A Erickson
   & Jeannette E M Labrie
ERICKSON,Nathan Andrew   Sex:M   03 Aug 1981 Matthew A Erickson
   & Jeannette E M Labrie
ERICKSON,Niles Joseph Sex:M 05 Jun 1984 Matthew A Erickson
   & Jeannette E M Labrie
ESTES,Karen A   Sex:F   25 Mar 1966 Blynn L Estes Sr & Elaine L Bickford
ESTEY,Della L   Sex:F   (Child #4) 07 Jul 1905 Aaron P Estey (Derry, NH)
   & Annie Frost (Petersham, MA)
ESTEY,Eva G   Sex:F   (Child #3) 01 Sep 1891 Aaron P Estey (Derry, NH)
   & Mary E Ackerman (Farmington, NH)
ESTEY,Gilbert Arnold Sex:M   (Child #5) 28 Apr 1926 Arnold R Estey (Windham,
   NH) & Lottie Williams (S Vernon, VT)
ESTEY,Jennie Eloise Sex:F   (Child #3) 29 Apr 1902 Aaron P Estey (Derry, NH)
   & Annie Frost (Petersham, MA)
ESTEY,Karen J   Sex:F   08 Jul 1969 William J Estey & Betty J Abbott
ESTEY,Lynne A   Sex:F   02 Jul 1970 William J Estey & Betty J Abbott
ESTEY,Nancy A   Sex: 06 Jun 1973 William J Estey & Betty J Abbott
ESTEY,[Unknown]   Sex:F   (Child #2) 18 Dec 1889 Aaron P Estey (Derry, NH)
   & Mary E (Farmington, NH)
ESTEY,[Unknown] Sex:M Jan 1894 Aaron P Estey (Derry, NH) & Mary Ackerman
   (Farmington, NH)
ESTY,Barbara Ida   Sex:F   (Child #3) 21 Apr 1927 Ralph Esty (Hudson, NH)
   & Vera Bagley (Burlington, VT)
ESTY,Eva G   Sex:F   01 Sep 1891 Hudson, NH Aaron P Esty & Mary E Ackerman
ESTY,Florence C   Sex:F   (Child #1) 03 Jan 1899 Aaron Esty (Derry, NH)
   & Annie F Frost (Petersham, MA)
ESTY,Phillip Edward   Sex:M   (Child #6) 25 Sep 1913 Aaron P Esty (Derry, NH)
   & Anna F Frost (Peterborough, NH)
EVANGELOUS,Meghann Rose Sex:F 05 Feb 1984 Anthony F Evangelous&JoAnne K Lund
EVANS,Robert   Sex:M   05 Jul 1741 Hudson, NH Robert Evans & Delia
EVERETT,Cylina Rae Sex:F 16 Mar 1985 Harry R Everett Jr & Robin Marie Pelkey
EVICCI,Wilfred H   Sex:M   28 Apr 1961 Arthur L Evicci & Eleanor J Peterson
FABICH,Beth A   Sex:F   22 Nov 1968 George Fabich & Shirlien R Collentro
FADDEN,Wendy J   Sex:F   14 Oct 1959 Richard G Fadden & Ellen C Richardson
FAGAN,Keith R   Sex:M   26 Jun 1966 Ronald E Fagan & Mary E Simms
FAGAN,Theresa L   Sex:F   07 Jun 1966 John J Fagan & Bessie L Deblois
FAIRBANKS,Lucy A   Sex:F   25 Apr 1863 Hudson, NH Charles Fairbanks & Mary
FAIRBANKS,Lucy Ann Sex:F 25 Apr 1863 Hudson, NH Charles Fairbanks & Mary A
FAIRFIELD,Alan E   Sex:M   20 Nov 1963 Alan F Fairfield & Suzanne R Largy
FAIRFIELD,Angela F   Sex:F   02 Sep 1970 Alan F Fairfield & Suzanne R Largy
FAIRFIELD,Sherry L   Sex:F   03 Mar 1947 Francis E Fairfield (Wilton, NH)
   & Florence L Guay (St Lambert, Canada)
FAIRFIELD,Tammy L   Sex:F   06 Jan 1965 Alan F Fairfield & Suzanne R Largy
FAIRFIELD,Thomas J   Sex:M   25 Jan 1969 Alan F Fairfield & Suzanne R Largy

HUDSON,NH BIRTHS

FALLON,Amy L   Sex:F   17 Aug 1962 John W Fallon & Kathleen W Miller
FALLON,Jennifer Marie Sex:F 29 Nov 1973 Steven E Fallon
   & Marguerite A Constant
FARAR,Danielle   Sex:F   30 Sep 1981 Milton Vern Farar & Lynette Herlin
FARAR,John Earl   Sex:M   12 Feb 1978 Milton V Farar & Lynette Herlin
FARLAND,Daniel A   Sex:M   31 Mar 1948 Albert W Farland (Nashua, NH)
   & Olivette I Fleury (Nashua, NH)
FARLAND,Dianne E   Sex:F   07 Apr 1969 Daniel A Farland & Patricia H MacDougal
FARLAND,Donald A   Sex: 08 Feb 1973 Daniel A Farland & Patricia H MacDougal
FARLAND,Elizabeth A   Sex:F   (Child #2) 20 Apr 1920 Joseph E Farland
   (St Antonio, P Q) & Laurietta Gokey (West Chazy, NY)
FARLAND,Ethel Louise   Sex:F   (Child #3) 17 Jan 1922 Joseph E Farland
   (St Antonio, Quebec) & Loretta Gokey (W Chazy, NY)
FARLAND,Irene Edna   Sex:F   (Child #5) 12 Mar 1925 Joseph Farland (Canada)
   & Loretta Gokey (W Chazy, NY)
FARLAND,Katrina A   Sex:F   30 Jun 1978 Roland A Farland & Sandra F Penkofski
FARLAND,Kendra Alissa Sex:F 23 Sep 1979 Norman R Farland & Simonne S Chenard
FARLAND,Pearl Beatrice   Sex:F   (Child #4) 15 Feb 1923 Joseph E Farland
   (Canada) & Loretta Gokey (W Chazy, NY)
FARLAND,Robert Emile   Sex:M   (Child #6) 18 Apr 1935 Joseph Farland (Canada)
   & Lauretta Gokey (United States)
FARLEY,Bruce A   Sex:M   27 May 1948 Arthur Farley (Manchester, NH)
   & Evelyn E Hanscom (Lewiston, ME)
FARMER,Brian B   Sex:M   (Child #2) 12 Jul 1946 Charles B Farmer (Manchester,
   NH) & Lucille V Gamache (Nashua, NH)
FARMER,Bruce D   Sex:M   (Child #1) 01 Jun 1944 Charles B Farmer (Manchester,
   NH) & Lucille V Gamache (Nashua, NH)
FARMER,Joshua William L   Sex:M   05 Sep 1785 Hudson, NH James Farmer & Martha
FARMER,Julius W L   Sex:M   05 Sep 1788 Hudson, NH James Farmer & Martha
FARMER,Moley W   Sex:F   08 Dec 1786 Hudson, NH James Farmer & Martha
FARMER,Molly Winn   Sex:F   08 Dec 1786 Hudson, NH James Farmer & Martha
FARMER,Nancy S   Sex:F   08 Jan 1788 Hudson, NH James Farmer & Martha
FARMER,William B   Sex:M   26 May 1970 Brian B Farmer & Gloria D Harris
FARNHAM,Mattie   Sex:F   1868 Hudson, NH John D Farnham & Mary M
FARNHAM,[Unknown]   Sex: 1867 Hudson, NH John D Farnham & Mary M Steele
FARNSWORTH,Lucy Reed   Sex:F   (Child #2) 15 Jul 1911 Milton E Farnsworth
   (Beddington, ME) & Agnes Russell (Grand Falls, NB)
FARR,Timothy Scott Jr Sex:M 24 Oct 1979 Timothy S Farr Sr & Michele M Crosbie
FARRIN,John A   Sex:M   19 Apr 1974 Albert U Farrin & Jean Marie Pierro
FARRINGTON,Debra L   Sex:F   23 Dec 1960 Laurence M Farringto & Mary E Campbell
FARRINGTON,Emily Jane Sex:F 11 Dec 1977 Guy I Farrington & Patricia A Batura
FARRINGTON,Mary N   Sex:F   23 Mar 1964 Stanley M Farrington & Ruth V Bouley
FARRINGTON,Paul A   Sex:M   26 Sep 1968 Guy I Farrington & Patricia A Batura
FARRINGTON,Thomas A   Sex:M   29 May 1961 Milton S Farrington & Eleanor C Dodge
FAUCHER,Robert E Jr   Sex:M   30 Nov 1957 Robert E Faucher & Anna M Daub
FAULKNER,Douglas L   Sex:M   22 Apr 1968 Robert J Faulkner Jr & Sheryl L Binks
FAUVEL,Amy Melinda   Sex:F 14 Jul 1983 Jean-Paul G Fauvel & Darlene Anne Giles
FAUVEL,Keith G   Sex:M   25 Mar 1980 Gerard R Fauvel & Linda G Weston
FAY,Rebecca A   Sex:F   17 Oct 1968 Norman S Fay & Carol A Kalley
FEBONIO,Scott C   Sex:M   18 Jan 1972 Donald L Febonio & Sally A Kelly
FECTEAU,Andre M   Sex:M   02 Jan 1964 Richard C Fecteau & Laurel R Salley
FELLOWS,Gregory P   Sex:M   07 Mar 1964 Robert A Fellows & Virginia C Brown
FELLOWS,Karen D   Sex:F   23 Dec 1968 Robert A Fellows & Virginia C Brown
FELTMATE,Colleen M   Sex:F   25 Nov 1965 Douglas R Feltmate & Janice M Just
FELTON,Melissa A   Sex:F   16 Aug 1968 Robert A Felton & Jean A Marshall
FEMIA,Amity K   Sex:F   10 Oct 1974 Rocco M Femia & Margaret A Melnick
FEMIA,William R   Sex:M   04 Mar 1972 Rocco M Femia & Margaret A Melnick
FENNELL,Patrick Francis   Sex:M   23 Oct 1979 Thomas J Fennell Jr
   & Donna Frances Boris
FERGUSON,Mary   Sex:F   17 Nov 1860 Hudson, NH Thomas Ferguson & Elizabeth

HUDSON, NH BIRTHS

FERGUSON, Mary Elizabeth Sex:F 17 Nov 1860 Hudson, NH Thomas Ferguson & Elizabeth
FERNS, Kathryn Mary Sex:F 15 Nov 1982 Laurence J Ferns & Shirley Ann Maciejko
FERNS, Michael Laurence Sex:M 04 Jun 1984 Laurence J Ferns&Shirley A Maciejko
FERRYALL, Loula Olena Sex:F (Child #4) 04 Jan 1911 Fred Ferryall (Nashua, NH) & Angelina Salvail (Greenfield, NH)
FESITTE, Carrie Sex:F (Child #3) 19 Jan 1896 Manson Fesitte (New York) & Carrie Pronto (New York)
FESSENDEN, Dana M Sex:F 07 Oct 1970 Donald E Fessenden & Judith A Heelen
FIELD, Elizabeth M Sex:F 01 Mar 1970 Joseph J Field, Jr & Cynthia M Roy
FIELD, Randall P Sex:M 08 Nov 1959 Charles H Field & Jean Taylor
FIELD, Rebecca J Sex:F 23 May 1964 Joseph J Field, Jr & Cynthia M Roy
FIELD, Robert A Sex:M 10 May 1967 Elwood F Field & Vivian F Woodard
FIELD, Scott H Sex:M 12 Apr 1958 Charles H Field & Jean T Taylor
FIFIELD, Pauline Luellen Sex:F (Child #2) 26 Nov 1909 Pliny E Fifield (Moores, NY) & Mina Waldron (Rye Beach, NH)
FIGUEIREDO, Christine Marques Sex:F 25 Apr 1985 James C Figueiredo & Maria I Marques
FINDLEY, Merrill E Sex:F 20 Mar 1893 Wm N Findley (Canada) & Grace E Smith (NH)
FINLAY, Gregory W Sex:M 29 Nov 1967 Joseph G Finlay & Alice M Curran
FINLAY, Sheila A Sex:F 12 Oct 1963 Joseph G Finlay & Alice M Curran
FINNEGAN, Amy Lynn Sex:F 10 Mar 1978 Paul F Finnegan & Bonnie Lynn Leonard
FINNEGAN, Paul James Sex:M 26 Mar 1982 Paul F Finnegan & Bonnie Lynn Leonard
FINNERAL, Elizabeth A Sex:F 03 May 1963 Anthony J Finneral&Ferrelyn M Dillard
FINNERAL, Mark J Sex:M 30 Jan 1962 Anthony J Finneral & Ferrelyn M Dillard
FIORE, Michael John Sex:M 25 Jun 1983 John Dominick Fiore & Carol Anne McGowan
FIORE, Steven William Sex:M 22 Mar 1985 John D Fiore & Carol Anne McGowan
FISCHER, Brian J Sex:M 14 Mar 1966 Donald S Fischer & Beverly A Christian
FISCHER, Kristen S Sex:F 16 May 1967 Donald S Fischer & Beverly A Christian
FISH, Irving L Sex:M (Child #2) 28 Sep 1906 Burton K Fish (Canada) & Annie Robinson (Hudson, NH)
FISH, Ruby E Sex:F (Child #3) 01 Nov 1908 Burton K Fish (Canada) & Annie Robinson (Hudson, NH)
FISH, Vena Persis Sex:F (Child #1) 21 Oct 1902 Burton K Fish (Canada) & Anna L Robinson (Hudson, NH)
FISHBAUGH, Melissa J Sex:F 24 Sep 1974 John H Fishbaugh & Marilyn L Daulton
FISHBAUGH, Sharon D Sex:F 25 Mar 1971 John H Fishbaugh & Marilyn L Daulton
FISHER, Anna Charlotte Sex:F (Child #6) 08 Oct 1914 George Fisher (Pennsylvania) & Agnes Meehan (New York)
FISHER, Hildreth Amela Sex:F (Child #3) 11 Jun 1909 Oliver A Fisher (Lyndonville, NH) & Lulah A Gee (Cornish Flat, NH)
FISHOW, Samantha Linzie Sex:F 30 Jan 1985 Alan Douglas Fishow & Tina V Thormin
FISKE, Cindy L Sex:F 31 Jan 1967 Wayne S Fiske & Maureen F Gedney
FISKE, Wayne Stanton Sex:M (Child #1) 06 Sep 1938 Theodore Calvin Fisk (Lexington, MA) & Margaret M MacDonald (Moncton, NB)
FITZGERALD, Amanda Jane Sex:F 13 Aug 1980 William B Fitzgerald & Jane M Reeves
FITZGERALD, Ann L Sex:F 18 Aug 1967 Herbert P Fitzgerald & Elaine T Eagan
FITZPATRICK, Stacey Ann Sex:F 15 Nov 1979 James L Fitzpatrick & Elizabeth M Gallo
FITZSIMMONS, [Unknown] Sex:F 17 Nov 1981 Paul P Fitzsimmons & Carolyn May
FLAGG, Alton Leroy Sex:M 07 Apr 1856 Lawrence, MA Bailey K Flagg & Elmira Webster
FLAGG, Clara Frances Sex:F 16 Mar 1841 Methuen, MA Samuel C Flagg & Sarah A Webster
FLAGG, George Washington Sex:M 04 Jul 1848 Lowell, MA Bailey K Flagg & Elmira Webster
FLAGG, Henry Haskell Sex:M 02 Jan 1843 Methuen, MA Samuel C Flagg & Sarah A Webster
FLAGG, Lester Samuel Sex:M 29 Apr 1866 Palmyra, MI Bailey K Flagg

HUDSON,NH BIRTHS

  & Elmira Webster
FLAGG,Lizzie Anna   Sex:F   07 Jan 1861 Lawrence, MA Bailey K Flagg
  & Elmira Webster
FLAGG,Nellie Elmira   Sex:F   07 Dec 1875 Keene George W Flagg & Mary F Lake
FLAGG,Pearl Ellsworth   Sex:F   10 Oct 1873 Methuen, MA William Bailey Flagg
  & Minerva A Powers
FLAGG,William Bailey   Sex:M   29 Nov 1851 Lawrence, MA Bailey K Flagg
  & Elmira Webster
FLAHIVE,Donna M   Sex:F   08 Nov 1959 John D Flahive & Juanita R Pelkey
FLAHIVE,Mark T   Sex:M   08 May 1962 John D Flahive & Juanita Pelkey
FLAHIVE,Wendy R   Sex:F   08 May 1962 John D Flahive & Juanita Pelkey
FLANAGAN,William C Sex:M   14 Apr 1968 Francis K Flanagan & Rita F Szczypinski
FLANDERS,James M   Sex:M   21 Feb 1962 Alfred E Flanders & Rita R Boisvert
FLANDERS,Lisa E   Sex:F   11 May 1963 Alfred E Flanders & Rita R Boisvert
FLANDERS,Thomas J   Sex:M   19 Mar 1979 Gary Lee Flanders & Linda L Dube
FLANDERS,[Unknown]   Sex:M   (Child #1) 17 Jul 1906 Homer W Flanders (Canada)
  & Louise L Aderson (Canada)
FLECHTNER,Laurie A   Sex:F   08 Nov 1962 Charles W Flechtner & Diane F Harvell
FLECHTNER,Rebecca A   Sex:F   30 Dec 1964 Charles W Flechtner & Diane F Harvell
FLETCHER,Arline Nattie   Sex:F   (Child #4) 20 May 1925 George Fletcher
  (Nashua, NH) & Alice Powers (Lawrence, MA)
FLETCHER,Edmund   Sex:M   18 Aug 1862 Hudson, NH   & Mary Fletcher
FLETCHER,Edmund Fletcher Sex:M 18 Aug 1862 Hudson, NH & Mary Augusta Fletche
FLETCHER,Elijah   Sex:M   07 Sep 1736 Hudson, NH Robert Fletcher & Sarah
FLETCHER,Gideon   Sex:M   17 Nov 1737 Hudson, NH Daniel Fletcher & Rachel
FLETCHER,Gilman   Sex:M   18 Sep 1801 Boxford James Fletcher & Hannah Hills
FLETCHER,Jacob   Sex:M   13 May 1733 Hudson, NH Robert Fletcher & Sarah
FLETCHER,Judson   Sex:M   13 Nov 1734 Hudson, NH Daniel Fletcher & Rachel
FLETCHER,Olive   Sex:F   07 Sep 1741 Hudson, NH Robert Fletcher & Sarah
FLETCHER,Olliver   Sex:M   07 Sep 1741 Hudson, NH Robert Fletcher & Sarah
FLETCHER,Rebecca   Sex:F   20 Nov 1738 Hudson, NH Robert Fletcher & Sarah
FLETCHER,Rebeckah   Sex:F   20 Nov 1738 Hudson, NH Robert Fletcher & Sarah
FLETCHER,Samuel   Sex:M   03 Jul 1736 Hudson, NH Daniel Fletcher & Rachel
FLEURY,Scott V   Sex:M   15 Oct 1971 Theodore A Fleury & Linda S Poysa
FLEWELLING,Robert G   Sex:M   (Child #2) 28 May 1943 Russell S Flewelling
  (Groton, MA) & Eunice E Porter (Revere, MA)
FLEWELLING,Russell R   Sex:M   27 Sep 1968 David P Flewelling
  & Carol A Whittemore
FLEWELLING,Thomas S   Sex:M   01 Jan 1971 David P Flewelling
  & Carol A Whittemore
FLOOD,Gillian Cordene Sex:F   18 May 1983 Clifford J Flood & Kathleen A Forino
FLOOD,Janessa Jaye   Sex:F   10 Feb 1985 Clifford J Flood & Kathleen A Forino
FLORA,Shane M   Sex:M   08 Mar 1974 Ronald W Flora & Vicki-Lu Lavoie
FLOYD,Amy Suzanne Sex:F 31 Mar 1981 Michael J Floyd & Suzanne Marie Martin
FLOYD,Nina Michelle Sex:F 16 Aug 1983 Michael J Floyd & Suzanne Marie Martin
FLOYD,Ronald P   Sex:M   24 Oct 1970 Roger F Floyd & Sandra L Tucker
FLOYD,Shirley M   Sex:F   12 Jun 1972 Roger F Floyd & Sandra L Tucker
FLUET,Lorri L   Sex:F   01 Mar 1960 Romeo E Fluet & Carol E Belanger
FLYNN,Debra A   Sex: 07 Dec 1972 Thomas V Flynn & Marie A De Petrillo
FLYNN,John J   Sex:M   24 Oct 1969 Thomas V Flynn & Marie A De Petrillo
FLYNN,Michael D   Sex:M   11 Jun 1966 Thomas V Flynn & Marie A De Petrillo
FLYNN,Steven Edward   Sex:M   30 Mar 1985 Robert Paul Flynn & Linda Jean Landry
FLYNN,Susan M   Sex:F   28 Dec 1970 Thomas V Flynn & Marie A DePetrillo
FODEN,Joseph N   Sex: 26 Nov 1972 Vincent T Foden & Alicia J Bozahara
FODEN,Thomas V   Sex:M   21 Nov 1973 Vincent Thomas Foden & Alicia J Bozahara
FOGG,Sean E   Sex:M   19 May 1968 James H Fogg & Judith A Murray
FOGG,Stephen P   Sex:M   06 May 1969 James H Fogg & Judith A Murray
FOLEY,Brian Francis Sex:M 10 Sep 1981 John Charles Foley & Linda Louise Pilat
FOLEY,David A   Sex:M   02 Jan 1949 William F Foley & Phyllis Gallup
FOLEY,David E   Sex:M   01 Sep 1967 William F Foley & Doris P Chamberlain

HUDSON,NH BIRTHS

```
FOLEY,Karen M    Sex:F   25 May 1972 William F Foley & Doris P Chamberlain
FOLLANSBEE,Matthew L    Sex:M   24 Jun 1976 Bernard L Follansbee
    & Elizabeth Anne Symon
FOLTZ,Karen L    Sex:F   24 Jan 1952 William H Foltz & Odette N Dumais
FONG,Jonathan Chin   Sex:M   21 Sep 1978 George C Fong & Patricia A Winterson
FONG,Peter Pei-Yin   Sex:M   24 Feb 1974 David S Fong & Helen S Yin
FONG,Scott Chin   Sex:M   17 Feb 1976 George C Fong & Patricia A Winterson
FONTAINE,Wayne J   Sex:M   24 Jul 1949 Julien J Fontaine & Theresa R Briand
FOOTE,Abby V   Sex:F   15 May 1846 Hudson, NH Thomas Foote & Caroline Fosdick
FOOTE,Elias L   Sex:M   21 Dec 1843 Hudson, NH Thomas Foote & Caroline Fosdick
FOOTE,George H   Sex:M   04 Sep 1842 Hudson, NH Thomas Foote & Caroline Fosdick
FOOTE,George H   Sex:M   21 Feb 1854 Hudson, NH Thomas Foote & Caroline Fosdick
FOOTE,George H O Sex:M 21 Feb 1854 Hudson, NH Thomas Foote & Caroline Fosdick
FOOTE,Leander Scott Sex:M 06 Dec 1848 Hudson, NH Thomas Foote
    & Caroline Fosdick
FOOTE,Lorenzo S Sex:M   06 Dec 1848 Hudson, NH Thomas Foote & Caroline Fosdick
FOOTE,Lydia C   Sex:F   13 Feb 1851 Hudson, NH Thomas Foote & Caroline Fosdick
FOOTE,Lydia E   Sex:F   13 Feb 1851 Hudson, NH Thomas Foote & Caroline Fosdick
FOOTE,Thomas    Sex:M   06 Oct 1815 Hudson, NH
FORBES,Tyrone Irving   Sex:M   (Child #1) 04 Oct 1941 Theodore Forbes
    (Clarksville, VT) & Edna Broderick (Hudson, NH)
FORCIER,Theresa M   Sex:F   02 Dec 1950 Leonard L Forcier
    & Jeanne d'Arc Provencher
FORD,Arthur C    Sex:M   16 Jul 1862 Hudson, NH James C Ford & Abbie J
FORD,Barbara E   Sex:F   18 Dec 1955 Fred H Ford & Frances T Hamel
FORD,Bradley Harold   Sex:M   (Child #2) 23 Mar 1938 Fred Hardy Ford
    (S Merrimack, NH) & Marie Bronard (Bradley Point, NY)
FORD,Caleb S    Sex:M   19 Dec 1775 Hudson, NH James Ford & Sarah
FORD,Caleb S    Sex:M   27 Jan 1808 Hudson, NH Caleb Ford & Mary
FORD,Caleb Swan   Sex:M   19 Dec 1775 Hudson, NH James Ford & Sarah
FORD,Caleb Swan   Sex:M   27 Jan 1808 Hudson, NH Caleb S Ford & Mary
FORD,Calfin    Sex:M   05 Jul 1821 Hudson, NH Caleb S Ford & Mary
FORD,Calvin    Sex:M   05 Jul 1821 Hudson, NH Caleb S Ford & Mary
FORD,Dianne C   Sex:F   09 Apr 1959 Fred H Ford, Jr & Frances T Hamel
FORD,Donna A    Sex:F   09 Apr 1959 Fred H Ford, Jr & Frances T Hamel
FORD,Ebenezer   Sex:M   24 Nov 1777 Hudson, NH James Ford & Sarah
FORD,Elisha    Sex:M   07 Nov 1769 Hudson, NH James Ford & Sarah
FORD,Elisha    Sex:M   07 Nov 1767 Hudson, NH James Ford & Sarah
FORD,Elizabeth   Sex:F   23 Feb 1783 Hudson, NH James Ford & Sarah
FORD,Elizabeth   Sex:F   23 Feb 1782 Hudson, NH James Ford & Sarah
FORD,Frank    Sex:M   08 May 1874 Hudson, NH   & Charlotte Ford
FORD,Harriet    Sex:F   29 Jun 1865 Hudson, NH James C Ford & Abbie J
FORD,Harriet P   Sex:F   29 Jun 1865 Hudson, NH James C Ford & Abbie J
FORD,James    Sex:M   23 May 1799 Hudson, NH Timothy Ford & Mehitable
FORD,James K    Sex:M   09 Mar 1960 Bradley H Ford & Mary C Hunnewell
FORD,Jefferson   Sex:M   20 Jun 1803 Hudson, NH   & Judith Perry
FORD,John    Sex:M   24 Jan 1774 Hudson, NH James Ford & Sarah
FORD,John Henry   Sex:M   20 Jun 1871 Hudson, NH James C Ford & Abbie Jane
FORD,Joyce A    Sex:F   09 Mar 1955 Howard B Ford, Jr & Madeline V Stitham
FORD,Lydia    Sex:F   21 Aug 1767 Hudson, NH James Ford & Sarah
FORD,Mary    Sex:F   09 Apr 1765 Hudson, NH James Ford & Sarah
FORD,Mary C    Sex:F   09 Sep 1810 Hudson, NH Caleb Ford & Mary
FORD,Mary Colburn    Sex:F   09 Sep 1810 Hudson, NH Caleb S Ford & Mary
FORD,Mercy    Sex:F   11 Jan 1817 Hudson, NH Caleb S Ford & Mary
FORD,Nancy    Sex:F   09 Aug 1811 Hudson, NH Caleb S Ford & Mary
FORD,Nancy    Sex:F   09 Aug 1812 Hudson, NH Caleb S Ford & Mary
FORD,Parker    Sex:M   14 Dec 1814 Hudson, NH Caleb S Ford & Mary
FORD,Sarah    Sex:F   14 Dec 1814 Hudson, NH Caleb S Ford & Mary
FORD,Susan P    Sex:F   29 Jul 1824 Hudson, NH Caleb S Ford & Dorcas
FORD,Susan Perham    Sex:F   29 Jul 1824 Hudson, NH Caleb S Ford & Dorcas
```

HUDSON,NH BIRTHS

```
FORD,Susanna    Sex:F   18 Jan 1780 Hudson, NH James Ford & Sarah
FORD,Susanna    Sex:F   18 Jan 1781 Hudson, NH James Ford & Sarah
FORD,Timothy    Sex:M   31 Dec 1771 Hudson, NH James Ford & Sarah
FORD,[Unknown]  Sex:M   (Child #3) 14 Dec 1942 Fred H Ford (Merrimack, NH)
   & Mary D Brossard (Bra'ey P'd, NY)
FORENCE,Anna Arlene Sex:F  (Child #6) 21 Nov 1917 George Forence (New York)
   & Anna Obin (New York)
FORENCE,Della Helena Sex:F  (Child #5) 30 Apr 1925 William Forence (New York)
   & Eva Provencal (Exeter, NH)
FORENCE,Dorothy  Sex:F   (Child #4) 30 Apr 1925 William Forence (New York)
   & Eva Provencal (Exeter, NH)
FOREST,Herbert   Sex:M   (Child #3) 17 Oct 1918 Lewis Forest (Provincetown, MA)
   & Carrie Melvin (Merrimack, NH)
FOREST,James D   Sex:M   18 Jul 1970 David A Forest & Lorraine C Lachance
FOREST,Julie A   Sex:F   01 May 1967 John F Forest & Jean M Starr
FORGIONE,Valerie A Sex:F  21 Aug 1969 Albert E Forgione Jr & Linda S Lavigne
FORMALARIE,Erin Hannah Sex:F 15 Oct 1983 Craig T Formalarie & Janet E Crowley
FORRENCE,Allison Sex:F   18 Nov 1966 George L Forrence & Florence E Hollabaug
FORRENCE,Bruce   Sex:M   10 Jan 1959 George L Forrence & Florence E Hollabaug
FORRENCE,Carolyn E Sex:F 26 Dec 1954 George L Forrence & Florence E Hollabaug
FORRENCE,George R Sex:M  12 Aug 1957 George L Forrence & Florence E Hollabaug
FORRENCE,James R  Sex:M   19 Jun 1964 John A Forrence & Ruth L Kenyon
FORRENCE,Jess P   Sex:M   02 Jul 1956 John A Forrence & Ruth L Kenyon
FORRENCE,Jess Paul Jr  Sex:M  12 Aug 1984 Jess Paul Forrence Sr
   & Susan Marie Daniels
FORRENCE,John A   Sex:M   (Child #2) 31 Jul 1933 George Forrence, Jr (Nashua,
   NH) & Lillian Palmer (Nashua, NH)
FORRENCE,John A Jr  Sex:M  10 Apr 1963 John A Forrence & Ruth I Kenyon
FORRENCE,Lee      Sex:M   03 Aug 1963 George L Forrence & Florence E Hollabaug
FORRENCE,Lillian Shirley  Sex:F  (Child #3) 24 Nov 1936 George A Forrence
   (Nashua, NH) & Lillian Palmer (Nashua, NH)
FORRENCE,Patricia A  Sex:F  26 Jan 1952 George A Forrence & Lilliam V Palmer
FORRENCE,Timothy R  Sex:M  17 Nov 1977 Kenneth H Forrence & Diana Marie Gagnon
FORRENCE,Wayne A   Sex:M  07 Jul 1961 George L Forrence & Florence E Hollabaug
FORREST,Cynthia M  Sex:F  26 Apr 1949 Kenneth D Forrest & Christine M Carter
FORREST,Kenneth D Jr  Sex:M  (Child #2) 30 Aug 1946 Kenneth D Forrest
   (Southborough, MA) & Christine M Carter (Nashua, NH)
FORREST,Norman S   Sex:M   25 Jul 1947 Kenneth D Forrest (Southboro, MA)
   & Christine M Carter (Nashua, NH)
FORSHAW,Kelly B    Sex:F   07 Sep 1963 Edward G Forshaw & Irene D Kane
FORTIER,Adam David Sex:M  27 Jan 1985 Davie Hubert Fortier & Gail Marie Gould
FORTIER,Miguel S   Sex:M   05 Sep 1973 Raynald L Fortier & Normande L Boutin
FORTIER,Sonia N    Sex:F   04 Feb 1972 Raynald L Fortier & Normande L Boutin
FORTIN,Erin Marie  Sex:F   07 Jun 1979 Roger E Fortin & Mary J McCarthy
FORTNEY,Gerald Roy Sex:M   (Child #5) 06 Nov 1924 Otis Fortney (Kentucky)
   & Violet Lucier (Biddeford, ME)
FORTNEY,Theodore   Sex:M   (Child #6) 07 Mar 1928 Otis Fortney (Kentucky)
   & Violet Lucier (Maine)
FOSDICK,Caroline   Sex:F   20 May 1816 Hudson, NH
FOSS,Deborah J     Sex:F   22 Jan 1972 Robert E Foss & Helen R Wills
FOSS,Sharon M      Sex:F   08 Sep 1964 Robert E Foss & Helen R Wills
FOSTER,Charles Edward  Sex:M  (Child #5) 16 Mar 1937 George L Foster
   (Lyndeboro, NH) & Lilia Currier (W Lynn, MA)
FOSTER,Debora A    Sex:F   04 May 1957 Ralph N Foster & Barbara A Lilley
FOSTER,Emily       Sex:F   25 Aug 1813 Hudson, NH John Foster & Lucy
FOSTER,Emily       Sex:F   25 Sep 1813 Hudson, NH John Foster & Lucy
FOSTER,George      Sex:M   23 Sep 1821 Hudson, NH John Foster & Lucy
FOSTER,John        Sex:M   30 Dec 1817 Hudson, NH John Foster & Lucy
FOSTER,John H      Sex:M   07 Dec 1811 Hudson, NH John Foster & Lucy
FOSTER,John Hastings  Sex:M  11 Dec 1811 Hudson, NH John Foster & Lucy
```

HUDSON,NH BIRTHS

FOUNDAS,Constantine   Sex:M   (Child #1) 19 Jul 1935 Constantine Foundas
   (Greece) & Euphemia Panagoulis (Nashua, NH)
FOURNIER,John E L   Sex:M   12 Apr 1964 Joseph F Fournier & Judith M Gleason
FOURNIER,Richard L   Sex:M   13 Aug 1970 Robert H Fournier & Donna M Braccio
FOURNIER,Stacey Lynn   Sex:F   26 Aug 1979 Robert H Fournier & Donna M Braccio
FOURNIER,Steven E   Sex:M   05 Oct 1966 Richard R Fournier & Nancy E Brooks
FOWLER,Caleb Mark   Sex:M   01 Jul 1982 Mark Lionel Fowler & Laurie Alene Frink
FOWLER,Cynthia L   Sex:F   19 Mar 1962 Carl D Fowler & Winnifred R Pottle
FOX,Jamie S   Sex:M   11 May 1969 Bryan S Fox & Claudette P Tourigny
FOX,Livnie Eunice   Sex:F   (Child #1) 14 Jun 1900 John Irving Fox (Maine)
   & Annie Smith (Hudson Center, NH)
FRADETTE,Kathleen Mary   Sex:F   30 Jun 1982 Brian R Fradette & Carol Ann Baker
FRANCEY,Elizabeth A   Sex:F   23 Apr 1968 Ronald W Francey & Carol A MacPherson
FRANCEY,Julie S   Sex:F   11 Mar 1972 Ronald W Francey & Carol A McPherson
FRANCIS,Sarah   Sex:F   15 Nov 1770 Hudson, NH Richard Francis & Hannah
FRANCO,David R   Sex:M   16 Sep 1969 Leonard J Franco & Josephine A Abbondan
FRANCOEUR,Anthony J   Sex:M   21 Aug 1968 Rene J Francoeur & Suzanne A Cote
FRANCOEUR,Brian R   Sex:M   19 Nov 1970 Robert H Francoeur & Carol A Gagnon
FRANCOEUR,Constance R Sex:F 24 Apr 1951 Robert R Francoeur & Theresa Y Rodier
FRANCOEUR,Daniel L   Sex:M   07 Dec 1970 Leo R Francoeur & Suzanne R Forrence
FRANCOEUR,Gary R   Sex:M   14 Jun 1957 Robert W Francoeur & Rachel A Boucher
FRANCOEUR,Gary R   Sex:M   27 Jan 1965 Robert R Francoeur & Theresa Y Rodier
FRANCOEUR,James R   Sex:M   04 Jan 1960 Robert W Francoeur & Rachel A Boucher
FRANCOEUR,Laurel L   Sex:F   22 Oct 1969 Leo R Francoeur & Suzanne R Forrence
FRANCOEUR,Leo D   Sex:M   24 Oct 1959 Robert R Francoeur & Theresa Y Rodier
FRANCOEUR,Lynn A   Sex:F   26 Jun 1955 Robert W Francoeur & Rachel A Boucher
FRANCOEUR,Malissa A   Sex:F   27 Sep 1969 Rene J Francoeur & Suzanne A Cote
FRANCOEUR,Meghan R   Sex:F   15 Jun 1976 Leo R Francoeur & Suzanne R Forrence
FRANCOEUR,Nancy A   Sex:F   11 Jan 1964 Rene J Francoeur & Suzanne A Cote
FRANCOEUR,Robert H   Sex:M 24 Apr 1947 Robert R Francoeur (Nashua, NH)
   & Theresa Y Rodier (Nashua, NH)
FRANCOEUR,Robert H Jr   Sex:M   31 Mar 1969 Robert H Francoeur & Carol A Gagnon
FRANCOEUR,Roger L   Sex:M   18 Feb 1958 Robert R Francoeur & Theresa Y Rodier
FRANGUS,Stacey   Sex:F   25 Oct 1975 Vasilias P Frangus & Xenia Papagiotas
FRANK,Robert K   Sex:M   (Child #2) 04 Oct 1933 Robert Frank (Nashua, NH)
   & Beulah Griffin (Stanford, CT)
FRANK,Suzanne M   Sex: 21 Dec 1972 Morris B Frank & Donna L Huber
FRASER,Brian H   Sex:M   08 Apr 1955 Henry A Fraser & Gloria T Gaudette
FRASER,Denise J   Sex:F   18 Oct 1965 Robert A Fraser & Helen B Smith
FRASER,Kelly R   Sex:M   04 Feb 1958 Henry A Fraser & Gloria T Gaudette
FRASER,Leslie A   Sex:F   03 Oct 1953 Henry A Fraser & Gloria T Gaudette
FRASER,Megan Teresa   Sex:F   03 Apr 1982 Fred Daniel Fraser & Jo-Ann Smith
FRASER,Rachel   Sex:F   02 Feb 1984 Alan Joseph Fraser & Ramona Lynn Harney
FRASER,Ryan A   Sex:M   25 May 1980 Peter E Fraser & Susan M Klimas
FRASER,Shannon Lee   Sex:F   12 Feb 1978 Peter E Fraser & Susan M Klimas
FRASER,Timothy J   Sex: 10 Jul 1972 Henry A Fraser & Gloria T Gaudette
FRAWLEY,Daniel J   Sex:M   23 May 1958 John P Frawley & Georgia Kesmetis
FRAZEE,[Unknown]   Sex:M   (Child #3) 07 May 1899 Burton Frazee (St Johns, N B)
   & Lexie Church (Nova Scotia)
FRAZIER,John P   Sex:M   12 Feb 1961 Philip F Frazier & Mary J Brady
FRAZIER,Sheila J   Sex:F   02 Mar 1962 Philip F Frazier & Mary J Brady
FREDETTE,Tammy L   Sex:F   29 Sep 1970 Claude E Fredette & Shirley A Martin
FREEMAN,Adam James   Sex:M   23 Jun 1982 Daniel R Freeman & Denise Marie Louf
FREEMAN,Amanda Jean Sex:F 23 Jun 1983 Daniel R Freeman & Denise Marie Loug
FREEMAN,Andrew Joseph Sex:M 22 Feb 1984 Harold J Freeman
   & Deborah A Francoeur
FREEMAN,Candice A   Sex:F   08 Apr 1963 Lloyd A Freeman & Barbara R Webster
FREEMAN,Christopher T Sex:M 26 Jul 1961 Raymond L Freeman & Theresa D Murphy
FREEMAN,Colin R   Sex:M   17 Aug 1963 Raymond L Freeman & Theresa D Murphy
FREEMAN,Harlan E   Sex:M   29 Oct 1965 Louis J Freeman & Carol A Boss

HUDSON,NH BIRTHS

FREEMAN,Jennifer Ann Sex:F 04 Oct 1977 Raymond L Freeman Jr & Sara Sue Durwin
FREEMAN,Joseph S Sex:M 06 Oct 1960 Raymond L Freeman & Theresa D Murphy
FREEMAN,Laurie Beth Sex:F 26 Aug 1980 David Nelson Freeman
  & Patricia A DellaCroc
FREEMAN,Lindsay Marie Sex:F 04 Apr 1984 David Nelson Freeman
  & Patricia A DellaCroc
FREEMAN,Matthew Raymond Sex:M 17 Dec 1981 John Michael Freeman
  & Veronica Dale Long
FREEMAN,Scott M Sex:M 17 Sep 1973 Raymond L Freeman & Sara Sue Durwin
FREITAS,Barbara A Sex:F 09 Oct 1962 Donald J Freitas & Patricia L Josey
FREITAS,Lisa A Sex:F 25 Nov 1964 Donald J Freitas & Patricia L Josey
FRENCH,Abigail Sex:F 25 Mar 1761 Hudson, NH Samuel French & Sarah
FRENCH,Beman Sex:M 06 Sep 1775 Hudson, NH Samuel French & Sarah
FRENCH,Benjamin Sex:M 06 Sep 1775 Hudson, NH Samuel French & Sarah
FRENCH,Betty Sex:F 19 Sep 1763 Hudson, NH Samuel French & Sarah
FRENCH,Brian K Sex:M 05 May 1975 George R French & Jane A Pizzelli
FRENCH,Deborah A Sex:F 02 Jan 1950 Maurice R French & Theodora P Puckett
FRENCH,Harold Gordon Sex:M (Child #3) 28 Jul 1899 Menzell S French
  (Templeton, MA) & Jennie P Stevens (Nashua, NH)
FRENCH,Isaac Sex:M 26 May 1734 Hudson, NH Joseph French & Bridget
FRENCH,Isaac Sex:M 26 Oct 1765 Hudson, NH Samuel French & Sarah
FRENCH,Joseph Houston Jr Sex:M 13 Oct 1983 Joseph H French Sr&Constance Hyde
FRENCH,Laurahannah Sex:F 16 Mar 1773 Hudson, NH Samuel French & Sarah
FRENCH,Lorenah Sex:F 16 Mar 1773 Hudson, NH Samuel French & Sarah
FRENCH,Meghan Renae Sex:F 19 Feb 1982 Joseph H French & Constance Hyde
FRENCH,Olive Sex:F 20 Mar 1757 Hudson, NH Samuel French & Sarah
FRENCH,Olive Sex:F 07 Mar 1757 Hudson, NH Samuel French & Sarah
FRENCH,Patricia Pearl Sex:F (Child #3) 05 Nov 1932 Nashua, NH
  Harold G French (Hudson, NH) & Maude Sargent (Leominster, MA)
FRENCH,Peter D Sex:M 05 Jun 1964 Joseph W French, Jr & Elizabeth A Little
FRENCH,Rebecca Sex:F 08 Dec 1768 Hudson, NH Samuel French & Sarah
FRENCH,Rebeckah Sex:F 08 Dec 1768 Hudson, NH Samuel French & Sarah
FRENCH,Richard A Sex:M 16 Dec 1949 Gordon L French & Elizabeth C Haug
FRENCH,Samantha E Sex:F 03 Oct 1977 John L French Jr & Patricia R Tomarelli
FRENCH,Samuel Sex:M 09 Mar 1759 Hudson, NH Samuel French & Sarah
FRENCH,Sarah Sex:F 03 Nov 1754 Hudson, NH Samuel French & Sarah
FRENCH,Sarah Sex:F 03 Nov 1764 Hudson, NH Samuel French & Sarah
FRENCH,Susan B Sex:F 02 Jan 1952 Maurice R French & Theodora P Puckett
FRENCH,[Unknown] Sex:F 11 Jun 1976 Robert E French & Julie Turcotte
FRENETTE,Dana A Sex:M 01 Oct 1961 Lionel G Frenette & Helen E Morrell
FRENETTE,Denise D M Sex:F 14 May 1957 Eugene J Frenette & Rita T Nadeau
FRENETTE,Dennis S Sex:M 18 Aug 1965 Lionel G Frenette & Helen E Morrell
FRENETTE,Donna L Sex:F 26 Sep 1957 Lionel G Frenette & Helen E Morrell
FRENETTE,Edith Joanne Sex:F (Child #1) 16 Jun 1937 Harvey J Frenette
  (Lowell, MA) & May Chaplin (Pepperell, MA)
FRENETTE,Henry E Sex:M 13 Jul 1958 Eugene J Frenette & Rita T Nadeau
FRENETTE,J Arthur Roger Sex:M (Child #12) 12 Sep 1930 George Frenette
  (Canada) & Laura Roy (Lowell, MA)
FRENETTE,Jean T Sex:F 14 May 1949 Robert W Frenette & Gertrude G Castonguay
FRENETTE,John L Sex:M 20 Jun 1948 Lionel G Frenette (Hudson, NH)
  & Helen E Morrell (Brighton, MA)
FRENETTE,Kimberly L Sex:F 18 Jun 1968 Roger A Frenette & Peggy L Vignola
FRENETTE,Patricia H Sex:F 07 Oct 1958 Robert W Frenette
  & Gertrude G Castonguay
FRENETTE,Ricky P Sex:M 14 Aug 1961 Roger A Frenette & Peggy L Vignola
FRENETTE,Robert W Jr Sex:M 29 Oct 1950 Robert W Frenette
  & Gertrude G Castonguay
FRENETTE,Roger E Sex:M 06 Apr 1956 Eugene T Frenette & Rita T Nadeau
FRENETTE,Rosemary E Sex:F (Child #1) 21 Dec 1946 Lionel G Frenette (Hudson,
  NH) & Helen E Morrell (Brighton, MA)

HUDSON,NH BIRTHS

FRENETTE,William R Sex:M 18 Aug 1956 Robert W Frenette
 & Gertrude G Castonguay
FRENETTE,[Unknown]   Sex:F   23 Apr 1952 Eugene J Frenette & Rita T Nadeau
FRENETTE,[Unknown]   Sex:F   28 Jan 1954 Eugene J Frenette & Rita T Nadeau
FRENETTE,[Unknown]   Sex:F   02 Mar 1955 Eugene J Frenette & Rita T Nadeau
FRIEND,Michael J   Sex: 23 Jan 1973 Charles E Friend & Agusta R Wood
FRITZ,Kimberly A   Sex:F   09 Feb 1972 Samuel A Fritz & Patricia A Pulaski
FRIZZELL,Rebecca A   Sex:F   07 Mar 1951 George S Frizzell & Mary E Simon
FROST,Ai J   Sex:M   25 Mar 1969 Ai J Frost & Catherine F Wallace
FROST,Amanda Marie   Sex:F   01 Jan 1978 Richard F Frost & Barbara Ann Mendes
FROST,Benjamin   Sex:M   01 Jan 1745 Hudson, NH Benjamin Frost & Miriam
FROST,Benjamin   Sex:M   01 Jan 1744 Hudson, NH Benjamin Frost & Miriam
FROST,Michael S   Sex:M   31 Aug 1973 Ai J Frost & Catherine F Wallace
FROST,Miriam   Sex:F   18 Nov 1748 Hudson, NH Benjamin Frost & Miriam
FROST,Rebecca   Sex:F   02 Aug 1746 Hudson, NH Benjamin Frost & Miriam
FROST,Rebecca   Sex:F   07 Aug 1746 Hudson, NH Benjamin Frost & Miriam
FROST,Rebeckah   Sex:F   02 Aug 1746 Hudson, NH Benjamin Frost & Miriam
FROST,Richard H Sex:M   (Child #1) 28 Jun 1945 Charles H Frost (Haverhill, MA)
 & Alice M Martin (Hudson, NH)
FROST,Robert C   Sex:M   (Child #2) 15 Nov 1946 Charles H Frost (Haverhill, MA)
 & Alice M Martin (Hudson, NH)
FROST,[Unknown]   Sex:F   18 Aug 1974 James C Frost & Susan M Levesque
FRYE,Erik Michael   Sex:M   15 Oct 1984 Scott George Frye & Judith E Johnston
FUCCI,Megan Elizabeth   Sex:F   13 Sep 1976 Anthony E Fucci & Jane E Soucy
FULLER,Abbie T   Sex:F   29 Mar 1878 Hudson, NH Lovery Fuller (Hudson, NH)
 & Caroline S Trull (Tewksbury, MA)
FULLER,Alison J   Sex:F   11 Sep 1977 Frederick J Fuller & Sharen J Burgess
FULLER,Arthur E   Sex:M   (Child #7) 10 Aug 1895 Albert A Fuller (Hudson, NH)
 & Mary C Fuller (Danvers, MA)
FULLER,Barbara Anne   Sex:F   (Child #2) 18 Feb 1938 Walter Willis Fuller
 (Nashua, NH) & Annette C LeClaire (Nashua, NH)
FULLER,Barbara L   Sex: 21 Dec 1972 Roger J Fuller & Elaine M Anctil
FULLER,Beatrice Norma   Sex:F   (Child #6) 10 Sep 1915 Hudson, NH
 Joseph A Fuller (Hudson, NH) & Nettie Mortlock (Keene, NH)
FULLER,Carol J   Sex:F   (Child #4) 16 Dec 1942 George A Fuller, Sr
 (Hudson, NH) & Virginia M Mitchell (Derry, NH)
FULLER,Donald Mitchell   Sex:M   (Child #3) 31 Jan 1941 George A Fuller
 (Hudson, NH) & Virginia M Mitchell (Derry, NH)
FULLER,Earnest E   Sex:M   (Child #9) 10 Oct 1899 Albert A Fuller (Hudson, NH)
 & Mary C Fuller (Danvers, MA)
FULLER,Ernest A   Sex:M   (Child #3) 21 Dec 1940 Walter N Fuller (Nashua, NH)
 & Anette Leclerce (Nashua, NH)
FULLER,Frederick J   Sex:M   07 Feb 1948 William E Fuller (Hudson, NH)
 & June A King (Nashua, NH)
FULLER,George Albert Sex:M   (Child #4) 02 Jun 1912 Joseph A Fuller (Hudson,
 NH) & Nettie Mortlock (Keene, NH)
FULLER,George Albert   Sex:M   (Child #1) 06 Mar 1936 George A Fuller (Hudson,
 NH) & Virginia Mitchell (Derry, NH)
FULLER,George R   Sex:M   Oct 1878 Hudson, NH Willis Fuller (Hudson, NH)
 & Adelia (New York)
FULLER,Georgia   Sex:F   31 Jan 1962 George A Fuller, Jr & Joyce Carroll
FULLER,Gordon A Jr   Sex:M   15 May 1965 Gordon A Fuller, Sr & Nancy V Grace
FULLER,Gordon Arthur   Sex:M   (Child #3) 17 May 1938 George Albert Fuller
 (Hudson, NH) & Virginia May Mitchel (Derry, NH)
FULLER,Harold P   Sex:M   (Child #5) 07 Nov 1913 Joseph A Fuller (Hudson, NH)
 & Nettie A Mortlock (Keene, NH)
FULLER,Harold Putnam   Sex:M   (Child #1) 07 Sep 1938 Harold Putnam Fuller
 (Nashua, NH) & Irene E Chalifoux (Berlin, NH)
FULLER,Hellen C Sex:F 02 Dec 1873 Hudson, NH Lorenzo Fuller & Carrie S
FULLER,James J   Sex:M   20 Mar 1965 Joseph W Fuller & Margaret M Mooney

HUDSON,NH BIRTHS

FULLER,Jason   Sex:M   30 Jan 1871 Hudson, NH Lorenzo Fuller & Carrie L
FULLER,Jeffrey D   Sex:M   25 Sep 1961 Joseph W Fuller & Margaret M Mooney
FULLER,Jesse Trull Sex:M 02 Jan 1880 Hudson, NH Lorenzo Fuller
    & Carrie S Trull
FULLER,Jesse Trull   Sex:M   02 Jan 1879 Hudson, NH Lorenzo Fuller
    (Hudson, NH) & Carrie S Trull (Tewksbury, MA)
FULLER,John Joseph   Sex:M   (Child #2) 05 Feb 1941 Harold P Fuller
    (Hudson, NH) & Irene Chalifoux (Berlin, NH)
FULLER,Joseph A   Sex:M   (Child #3) 22 Oct 1888 Albert A Fuller (Hudson, NH)
    & Mary C Fuller (Danvers, MA)
FULLER,Joseph Wallace Sex:M   (Child #3) 28 May 1911 Joseph A Fuller
    (Hudson, NH) & Nettie A Mortlock (Keene, NH)
FULLER,Kelly J   Sex:F   24 Feb 1961 Gordon A Fuller & Nancy V Grace
FULLER,Laurie L   Sex: 26 Feb 1973 Frederick J Fuller & Sharen J Burgess
FULLER,Leonard A   Sex:M   22 Jun 1957 Leonard A Fuller & Bette M Milliard
FULLER,Lucy F   Sex:F   13 Nov 1891 Hudson, NH Albert A Fuller & Mary C Fuller
FULLER,Lucy P   Sex:F   (Child #5) 13 Nov 1891 Albert A Fuller (Hudson, NH)
    & Mary C Fuller (Danvers, MA)
FULLER,Lynn A   Sex:F   16 Oct 1959 Joseph W Fuller & Margaret M Mooney
FULLER,Melissa J Sex:F   21 May 1878 Hudson, NH Charles H Fuller (Hudson, NH)
    & Mary A (Vermont)
FULLER,Michael   Sex:M   01 Mar 1961 George A Fuller, Jr & Joyce Carroll
FULLER,Mildred May Sex:F   (Child #6) 17 Aug 1890 Albert A Fuller (Hudson, NH)
    & Mary C Fuller (Danvers, MA)
FULLER,Nellie B   Sex:F   16 Oct 1863 Hudson, NH Joseph Fuller & Belinda
FULLER,Nellie P   Sex:F   16 Oct 1863 Hudson, NH Joseph Fuller & Belinda Steele
FULLER,Patricia M   Sex:F   03 Apr 1951 Walter W Fuller & Annette C LeClaire
FULLER,Sheila A   Sex:F   21 Apr 1963 Joseph W Fuller & Margaret M Mooney
FULLER,Susan J   Sex:F   21 May 1951 William E Fuller & June A King
FULLER,Tamblyn L   Sex:F   06 Mar 1959 Gordon A Fuller & Nancy V Grace
FULLER,Virginia M   Sex:F   03 Jun 1963 Gordon A Fuller & Nancy V Grace
FULLER,William D   Sex:M   10 Jul 1948 William J Fuller (Harrison, AR)
    & June H Lampron (Nashua, NH)
FULLER,William Ernest   Sex:M   (Child #7) 19 Oct 1917 Joseph Fuller
    (Hudson, NH) & Nettie Mortlock (Keene, NH)
FULLER,Willis L   Sex:M   07 Feb 1893 Albert A Fuller (Hudson, NH)
    & Mary C Fuller (Danvers, MA)
FULLER,[Unknown]   Sex:M   (Child #8) 07 Jan 1898 Albert A Fuller (Hudson, NH)
    & Mary C Fuller (Danvers, MA)
FULLER,[Unknown]   Sex: 29 Jul 1886 Hudson, NH Albert A Fuller
    & Mary C Fuller
FURBER,Amy June   Sex:F   02 Nov 1977 Joseph T Furber & Susan J Fuller
FURBER,Katherine Diane Sex:F 04 Dec 1979 Joseph T Furber & Susan Joyce Fuller
FUSCUS,George A Jr   Sex:M   25 Dec 1948 George A Fuscus, Sr (Brownsville, PA)
    & Marjorie P Hurd (Nashua, NH)
FUSSELL,Marcelline Marie Sex:F 31 Aug 1980 Dennis P Fussell & Judith A McVey
GAGE,Charles   Sex:M   20 Jul 1816 Hudson, NH Daniel Gage & Betsey
GAGE,Clara J M   Sex:F   03 Nov 1870 Hudson, NH Daniel Gage & Mary L
GAGE,Clarifea J M Sex:F 03 Nov 1870 Hudson, NH Daniel Gage & Marietta L Marsh
GAGE,Edmond   Sex:M   26 Dec 1818 Hudson, NH Daniel Gage & Betsey
GAGE,Edward   Sex:M   26 Dec 1818 Hudson, NH Daniel Gage & Betsey
GAGE,Edwin L   Sex:M   21 Mar 1873 Hudson, NH Daniel Gage & Marietta
GAGE,Edwin Stanton Sex:M 24 Mar 1873 Hudson, NH Daniel Gage
    & Marietta L Marsh
GAGE,Joanna   Sex:F   20 Jun 1744 Hudson, NH Thomas Gage & Phebe
GAGE,John   Sex:M   16 Dec 1738 Hudson, NH Thomas Gage & Phebe
GAGE,Mary E   Sex:F   01 Jul 1878 Hudson, NH Daniel Gage (Hudson, NH)
    & Mary L (Hudson NH)
GAGE,Mary Ella   Sex:F   01 Jul 1878 Hudson, NH Daniel Gage & Marietta L Marsh
GAGE,Mary L   Sex:F   10 Jun 1869 Hudson, NH Daniel Gage & Marietta L Marsh

HUDSON,NH BIRTHS

GAGE,Mary L   Sex:F   10 Jan 1869 Hudson, NH Daniel Gage & Mary L
GAGE,Phebe   Sex:F   18 Oct 1741 Hudson, NH Thomas Gage & Phebe
GAGE,Phebe   Sex:F   13 Oct 1741 Hudson, NH Thomas Gage & Phebe
GAGE,William D   Sex:M   26 Nov 1866 Hudson, NH Daniel Gage & Marietta
GAGE,Willis D   Sex:M   26 Nov 1866 Hudson, NH Daniel Gage & Marietta L Marsh
GAGNE,Christopher R   Sex:M   25 May 1971 Richard Gagne & Rita J Boucher
GAGNE,Diane V   Sex:F   25 Apr 1967 Jean N Gagne & Pierrette T Rodrigue
GAGNE,Edward B   Sex:M   09 Jun 1954 Raymond A Gagne & Leona M Byrnes
GAGNE,Eric R   Sex:M   17 Oct 1967 Richard Gagne & Rita J Boucher
GAGNE,Francine M   Sex:F   22 Jul 1965 Paul L Gagne & Bibiane R Roussel
GAGNE,Henri   Sex:M   (Child #3) 22 Jun 1921 Alfred Gagne (Canada)
    & Roseanna Arpin (Canada)
GAGNE,Jane Kristin   Sex:F   14 Jun 1983 Stephen R Gagne & Patricia Ann Potter
GAGNE,Joshua   Sex:M   24 Dec 1978 Terrence B Gagne & Maureen Lyons
GAGNE,Lauretta M   Sex:F   14 Aug 1948 Eli Gagne (Canada) & Yvonne Faucher
    (Lawrence, MA)
GAGNE,Mary Rita   Sex:F   (Child #2) 07 Aug 1929 Louis Gagne (Providence, RI)
    & Ida Meunier (Nashua, NH)
GAGNE,Ryan   Sex:M   05 Oct 1981 Terrence Blake Gagne & Maureen Lyons
GAGNE,Sandra A   Sex:F   15 Feb 1969 Jean N Gagne & Pierrette T Rodrique
GAGNE,Stephen R   Sex:M   29 Jul 1953 Robert J Gagne & Norma F Greenleaf
GAGNE,Timothy W   Sex:M   10 Jun 1957 Robert J Gagne & Norma F Greenleaf
GAGNE,[Unknown]   Sex:F   (Child #2) 01 Mar 1919 Alfred Gagne (Canada)
    & Rose Arpin (Canada)
GAGNI,Dorothy Visian Sex:F   (Child #1) 26 Jan 1924 Louis Gagni (Providence,
    RI) & Ida Manier (Nashua, NH)
GAGNON,Adam James   Sex:M   12 May 1985 John A S Gagnon Sr & Tammy F Lacasse
GAGNON,Alfred Maurice   Sex:M   (Child #7) 04 Jun 1923 Louis J Gagnon (Canada)
    & Lydia Boulanger (Canada)
GAGNON,Brenda R   Sex:F   (Child #2) 26 Feb 1945 Eli E Gagnon (Hudson, NH)
    & Ruby E Kinville (Hudson, NH)
GAGNON,Brian R   Sex: 06 Jan 1973 Raymond R Gagnon & Brenda L Fogg
GAGNON,Carol A   Sex:F   (Child #2) 31 Oct 1946 Victor A Gagnon (Hudson, NH)
    & Rita M Osmer (Nashua, NH)
GAGNON,Carol J   Sex:F   (Child #4) 22 Dec 1944 Leo J Gagnon (Nashua, NH)
    & Marjorie Forrence (Nashua, NH)
GAGNON,Christina A   Sex:F   01 Mar 1961 David P Gagnon & Theresa M Maksymik
GAGNON,Christopher J   Sex:M   22 Aug 1977 Jean L Gagnon & Theresa M Neault
GAGNON,Christopher M   Sex:M   06 Oct 1971 David J Gagnon & Linda S Jean
GAGNON,Christopher W   Sex:M   30 Oct 1975 Richard W Gagnon & Linda L Given
GAGNON,Claire Germaine   Sex:F   (Child #1) 21 Aug 1933 Arthur M Gagnon
    (Nashua, NH) & Mathilde Brodeur (Hooksett, NH)
GAGNON,Daniel G   Sex:M   27 Feb 1958 David P Gagnon & Theresa M Maksymik
GAGNON,David J   Sex:M   04 Dec 1962 Ernest R Gagnon & Phyllis M Warren
GAGNON,David J   Sex:M   14 Sep 1965 Robert Gagnon & Madeleine J Dumais
GAGNON,David Philip Sex:M   (Child #1) 16 Jun 1936 Andre Gagnon (Nashua, NH)
    & Esther Haslan (Lowell, MA)
GAGNON,Diane L   Sex:F   04 Dec 1960 Roland T Gagnon & Beverly A Dalton
GAGNON,Donna M   Sex:F   05 May 1967 Joseph A Gagnon & Anne M Cyr
GAGNON,Emile   Sex:M   (Child #5) 22 May 1919 Louis Gagnon (Canada)
    & Lydia Boulanger (Canada)
GAGNON,Ernest R   Sex:M   (Child #14) 13 Dec 1921 Eugene Gagnon (Canada)
    & Clara Sinis (Canada)
GAGNON,Ernest R Jr   Sex:M   17 Jul 1955 Ernest R Gagnon & Phyllis M Warren
GAGNON,Eva Rose   Sex:F   (Child #3) 17 Nov 1916 Hudson, NH Louis Gagnon
    (Canada) & Lydia Boulanger (Canada)
GAGNON,George Arthur Roger   Sex:M   (Child #15) 06 Dec 1923 Eugene Gagnon
    (Canada) & Clara Sirois (Canada)
GAGNON,Gertrude R   Sex:F   16 Jan 1952 George W Gagnon & Louise C Dube
GAGNON,Gloria R   Sex:F   12 Mar 1953 George W Gagnon & Louise C Dube

HUDSON,NH BIRTHS

GAGNON,Guadalupe   Sex:M   07 Oct 1959 George N Gagnon & Cecilia Saucedo
GAGNON,Henri N   Sex:M   (Child #6) 14 Jul 1920 Louis Gagnon (Canada)
   & Lydia Boulanger (Canada)
GAGNON,J Art Michael Sex:M   (Child #3) 26 Jan 1936 Arthur Gagnon (Nashua, NH)
   & Mathilda Brodeur (Hooksett, NH)
GAGNON,J B Albert   Sex:M   (Child #9) 20 Jun 1918 Joseph Gagnon (Canada)
   & Maria Goss (Canada)
GAGNON,Jean E   Sex:F   26 Nov 1965 Roland T Gagnon & Beverly A Dalton
GAGNON,Jennifer M   Sex:F   05 Nov 1967 David P Gagnon & Theresa M Maksymik
GAGNON,John A S Jr   Sex:M   30 Nov 1982 John A S Gagnon Sr & Tammy F Lacasse
GAGNON,John R   Sex:M   17 Sep 1957 Rene O Gagnon & Simone Camden
GAGNON,John R   Sex:M   20 May 1974 Richard E Gagnon & Diana Lynn Burdick
GAGNON,Joseph A   Sex:M   (Child #5) 22 Oct 1905 Eugene Gagnon (Canada)
   & Clara Sirois (Canada)
GAGNON,Joseph Alfred   Sex:M   (Child #3) 20 May 1907 Joseph Gagnon (Canada)
   & Maria Case (Canada)
GAGNON,Joseph Arthur   Sex:M   (Child #1) Apr 1904 Joseph Gagnon (Canada)
   & Maria Ross (Canada)
GAGNON,Joseph C   Sex:M   (Child #4) 05 Oct 1903 Eugene Gagnon (Canada)
   & Clara Sciois (Canada)
GAGNON,Joseph Francois Sex:M 09 Apr 1982 Ronald F Gagnon & Donna Marie Reitan
GAGNON,Joseph Henri   Sex:M   (Child #6) 26 Oct 1914 Joseph Gagnon (Canada)
   & Maria Ross (Canada)
GAGNON,Karen L   Sex:F   02 Apr 1963 David P Gagnon & Theresa M Maksymik
GAGNON,Leo Gerard   Sex:M   (Child #4) 06 Oct 1920 George Gagnon (Canada)
   & Celanira Ricard (Canada)
GAGNON,Leo J Jr   Sex:M   07 Nov 1947 Leo J Gagnon (Nashua, NH)
   & Marjorie A Forrence (Nashua, NH)
GAGNON,Lisa M   Sex:F   28 Dec 1959 David P Gagnon & Theresa M Maksymik
GAGNON,Loretta   Sex:F   (Child #4) 17 Jan 1918 Louis Gagnon (Canada)
   & Lydia Boulanger (Canada)
GAGNON,Louise Shirley Sex:F   (Child #6) 15 Mar 1929 Henry Gagnon (Nashua, NH)
   & Irene Trombley (Haverhill, MA)
GAGNON,M Silian   Sex:F   (Child #10) 24 Nov 1918 Eugene Gagnon (Canada)
   & Clara Sirois (Canada)
GAGNON,Marie Alice   Sex:F   (Child #8) 02 Dec 1909 Eugene Gagnon (Canada)
   & Clara Sirois (Canada)
GAGNON,Marie Bertha   Sex:F   (Child #8) 26 Feb 1917 Joseph Gagnon (Canada)
   & Marie Goss (Canada)
GAGNON,Marie Frances   Sex:F   (Child #12) 07 May 1917 Eugene Gagnon (Canada)
   & Clara Sirois (Canada)
GAGNON,Marie Ida F   Sex:F   (Child #11) 03 Mar 1915 Hudson, NH Eugene Gagnon
   (Canada) & Clara Sirois (Canada)
GAGNON,Mary Agnes   Sex:F   (Child #1) 31 Oct 1918 William Gagnon (Canada)
   & Jephirine Malhon (Nashua, NH)
GAGNON,Matthew P   Sex:M   28 Feb 1966 David P Gagnon & Theresa M Maksymik
GAGNON,Matthew Steven   Sex:M   31 May 1982 Steven A Gagnon & Theresa C Proulx
GAGNON,Maureen D   Sex:F   09 Jun 1966 Henry J Gagnon & Claire P Bisson
GAGNON,Michele L   Sex:F   28 Aug 1967 Leo J Gagnon & Lorraine G Viens
GAGNON,Michelle L   Sex:F   25 Apr 1968 Richard E Gagnon & Geraldine M Coolidge
GAGNON,Nancy J   Sex:F   17 May 1971 Clermont W Gagnon & Rejeanne L Labbe
GAGNON,Richard E   Sex:M   (Child #1) 08 Mar 1943 Eli E Gagnon (Hudson, NH)
   & Ruby Kinville (Hudson, NH)
GAGNON,Richard W Jr   Sex:M   20 Dec 1976 Richard W Gagnon Sr & Linda Lee Given
GAGNON,Rita Lucienne   Sex:F   (Child #8) 05 Sep 1925 Louis Gagnon (Canada)
   & Lydia Boulanger (Canada)
GAGNON,Sarah Risa   Sex:F   24 Jan 1978 Paul A Gagnon & Priscilla E Levesque
GAGNON,William H   Sex:M   (Child #7) 16 Oct 1915 Hudson, NH Joseph Gagnon
   (Maine) & Maria Ross (Canada)
GAGNON,[Unknown]   Sex:F   (Child #15) 15 Jul 1901 Hudson, NH Louis Gagnon

HUDSON,NH BIRTHS

   (Canada) & Cassie Fournier (Canada)
GAGNON,[Unknown]   Sex:F   (Child #10) 28 Dec 1919 Joseph Gagnon (Canada)
   & Maria Ross (Canada)
GAGNON,[Unknown]   Sex:M   (Child #11) 03 Jan 1924 Joseph Gagnon (Canada)
   & Maria Ross (Canada)
GAGNON,[Unknown]   Sex:F   28 Mar 1938 William Gagnon (Hudson, NH)
   & Irene Boyle (Lowell, MA)
GALIPEAU,Douglas C   Sex:M   12 Aug 1969 Peter J Galipeau & Mary T Zolkos
GALIPEAU,Jean R   Sex:F   11 Aug 1962 Paul R Galipeau & Theresa G Gamache
GALIPEAU,Michelle M   Sex:F   22 Feb 1971 Peter J Galipeau & Mary T Zolkos
GALIPEAU,Paula A   Sex:F   18 Feb 1967 Paul R Galipeau & Theresa G Gamache
GALIPEAU,Peter J   Sex:M   17 Mar 1949 Paul R Galipeau & Mabel A Miner
GALIPEAU,Sandra L   Sex:F   10 Mar 1956 Paul R Galipeau & Theresa G Gamache
GALIPEAU,Thomas P   Sex:M   16 May 1959 Paul R Galipeau & Theresa G Gamache
GALIPEAULT,James Julius   Sex:M   31 Jan 1981 Richard J Galipeault
   & Nancy L Grigas
GALIPEAULT,Jeremie Rosaire   Sex:M   09 Dec 1983 Richard J Galipeault
   & Nancy Laura Grigas
GALIPEAULT,Lorrie A   Sex:F   19 Feb 1968 Richard J Galipeault & Nancy L Grigas
GALIPEAULT,Richard J Jr   Sex:M   25 Jun 1971 Richard J Galipeault
   & Nancy L Grigas
GALIPEAULT,Shellie A   Sex:F   12 Feb 1969 Richard J Galipeault & Nancy L Grigas
GALIPEAULT,William R   Sex:M   05 Mar 1967 Richard J Galipeault & Nancy L Grigas
GALIPEAULT,[Unknown]   Sex:F   22 Jun 1977 Richard J Galipeault & Nancy L Grigas
GALLAGHER,David A   Sex:M   26 Jan 1950 John J Gallagher & Yvonne B Perusse
GALLAGHER,Debra J   Sex:F   26 Feb 1958 James T Gallagher & Theresa I Cote
GALLAGHER,Richard J   Sex:M   04 Nov 1961 James T Gallagher & Theresa I Cote
GALLAGHER,Robin J   Sex:F   06 Jul 1964 James T Gallagher & Theresa I Cote
GALLAGHER,Scott D   Sex:M   02 Mar 1959 James T Gallagher & Theresa I Cote
GALLANT,Craig L   Sex:M   18 Aug 1969 Gerald J Gallant Jr & Judith L Doherty
GALLANT,Jennifer L   Sex:F   13 Sep 1974 Jean-Claude Gallant & Rena A Alexander
GALLANT,Mary P   Sex:F   23 Feb 1965 Thomas A Gallant & Flora L Candela
GALLOP,Jennifer Lee   Sex:F   14 Jul 1984 Michael J Gallop & Deborah Ann North
GALUSHA,Kristin Charlene   Sex:F   14 Dec 1982 Wayne F Galusha
   & Erin C Davidson
GAMACHE,Ellen M   Sex:F   18 Jul 1950 Alfred W Gamache & Marcella O Girard
GAMACHE,George D   Sex:M   18 Feb 1959 Edward G Gamache & Monique R Lajeunesse
GAMACHE,Jean F   Sex:F   (Child #3) 11 Sep 1945 Gerard T Gamache (Nashua, NH)
   & Virginia F Allison (Nashua, NH)
GAMACHE,Jerry T   Sex:M   (Child #4) 11 Sep 1945 Gerard T Gamache (Nashua, NH)
   & Virginia F Allison (Nashua, NH)
GAMACHE,Kathy A   Sex:F   20 Jul 1967 Donald R Gamache & Claire Beaulieu
GAMACHE,Robert G   Sex:M   (Child #2) 24 Nov 1940 Gerard T Gamache (Nashua, NH)
   & Virginia F Allison (Nashua, NH)
GAMACHE,Sharon D   Sex:F   16 Jun 1977 William B Marks & Donna Marie Gamache
GAMACHE,Susan L   Sex:F   11 Nov 1948 Gerard F Gamache (Nashua, NH)
   & Virginia Allison (Nashua, NH)
GAMACHE,Virginia Sandra   Sex:F   (Child #1) 25 Sep 1937 Gerard Gamache
   (Nashua, NH) & Virginia Allison (Nashua, NH)
GARCEAU,Heidi L   Sex:F   20 Jun 1963 Grenville G Garceau & Joann M Bleakley
GARD,Amy   Sex:F   17 Dec 1970 James T Gard & Michelle J Chateaune
GARDNER,Brian D   Sex:M   24 Apr 1968 Paul F Gardner Jr & Carol J Emerson
GARDNER,Darcy C   Sex:F   28 Feb 1967 Ronald C Gardner & Charlotte V Cooke
GARDNER,Todd C   Sex:M   09 Jun 1968 Ronald C Gardner & Charlotte V Cooke
GARDNER,Tracy L   Sex:F   29 Mar 1970 William H Gardner & Karin J Berg
GARFIELD,George   Sex:M   17 Nov 1877 Boston, MA George Garfield (Springfield,
   MA) &   (Bath, ME)
GARLAND,Sandra H   Sex:F   17 Oct 1952 Albert F Garland & Helen G Swist
GARRITY,Michael A   Sex:M   18 Apr 1963 Danis D Garrity & Carolyn A Russell
GARRON,Cathy L   Sex:F   03 Feb 1960 Alfred M Garron & Shirley A Temple

85

HUDSON,NH BIRTHS

GARROW,Carrie E   Sex:F   09 Sep 1969 Cecil M Garrow & Barbara J Dence
GARSIDE,Alan R   Sex:M   13 Nov 1947 Frederick N Garside (Dover, NH)
  & Madelene C Hackett (Pepperell, MA)
GARSIDE,Alan R Jr   Sex:M   10 Jun 1972 Alan R Garside Sr & Linda G Bowman
GARSIDE,David W Sex:M   (Child #6) 05 Mar 1945 Frederick N Garside (Dover, NH)
  & Madeline C Hackett (Pepperell, MA)
GARSIDE,Kimberly M   Sex:F   11 Feb 1976 Alan R Garside & Linda G Bowman
GARSIDE,Patricia J Sex:F   11 Dec 1961 Frederick J Garside & Cynthia A Widener
GARSIDE,Philip M   Sex:M   19 Nov 1963 Frederick J Garside & Cynthia A Widener
GARSIDE,Stephen C   Sex:M   05 Feb 1965 Frederick J Garside & Cynthia A Widener
GASKA,Eric G   Sex:M   09 Jul 1974 Bruce H Gaska & Denise M Lowe
GATCHELL,James B Jr   Sex:M   26 Nov 1967 James B Gatchell & Kathleen Shea
GATES,Beverly Joyce   Sex:F   (Child #3) 16 Apr 1936 Joseph E Gates (Nashua,
  NH) & Lillian Haselton (Chelmsford, MA)
GATES,Charles Martin   Sex:M   (Child #2) 26 Jul 1933 Joseph E Gates (Nashua,
  NH) & Lillian M Haselton (Chelmsford, MA)
GATES,[Unknown]   Sex:F   (Child #4) 15 Jul 1933 Wallace E Gates (Nashua, NH)
  & Velma Jeannotte (Nashua, NH)
GATTA,Kerry Ann   Sex:F   22 Nov 1977 Edward J Gatta & Zena F Glassman
GATTA,Sherry Lee   Sex:F   22 Nov 1977 Edward J Gatta & Zena F Glassman
GATZKE,Robin E   Sex:F   12 Mar 1968 Ronald D Gatzke & Linda J Morman
GAUDET,Stephen A   Sex:M   07 Feb 1958 George L Gaudet & Helen J Bundy
GAUDETTE,Alexis E   Sex:F   19 Dec 1977 Ronald R Gaudette & Linda G Russell
GAUDETTE,Michelle L   Sex:F   15 Jun 1971 Robert J Gaudette & Jane T Sheffer
GAUDETTE,Pamela M   Sex:F   15 Nov 1956 Roland R Gaudette & Lucille I Landry
GAUDETTE,Randall S   Sex:M   07 Dec 1974 Raymond P Gaudette & Linda M LaBrecque
GAUDETTE,Raymond P   Sex:M   08 Jul 1951 Roland R Gaudette & Lucille I Landry
GAUDETTE,Robert H   Sex:M   (Child #3) 11 May 1932 Hudson, NH
  William A Gaudette (Lowell, MA) & Carrie Labombarde (Nashua, NH)
GAUDETTE,Roger P   Sex:M   07 Aug 1949 Roland R Gaudette & Lucille I Landry
GAUDETTE,Ronald R   Sex:M   25 Apr 1947 Roland R Gaudette (Nashua, NH)
  & Lucille I Landry (Hudson, NH)
GAUDREAU,Christopher J   Sex:M   10 Jul 1977 James M Gaudreau & Mary Ann Berube
GAUDREAU,Stephen D   Sex:M   29 Nov 1967 Eugene L Gaudreau & Sheryl L Young
GAUTHIER,David M   Sex:M   09 May 1968 Normand D Gauthier & Jacqueline D Berube
GAUTHIER,Jason S   Sex:M   28 Oct 1971 Normand D Gauthier & Jacqueline D Berube
GAUTHIER,Lee N   Sex:M   14 Jan 1963 Raymond Gauthier & Judith Scott
GAUTHIER,Lisa J   Sex:F   18 Sep 1975 Gerard L Gauthier & Ellenor Fournier
GAUTHIER,Michael J R Sex:M 22 Dec 1968 Richard JR Gauthier & Claire A Tessier
GAUTHIER,Peter A   Sex:M   01 Mar 1965 Gerald O Gauthier & Gloria Y Gaudette
GAUTHIER,Richard J R Sex:M 30 Apr 1963 Richard JR Gauthier & Claire A Tessier
GAUTHIER,Russell Eugene Sex:M   (Child #2) 17 Apr 1934 Joseph E Gauthier
  (Rumford, ME) & May F Tibbetts (Milford, MA)
GAUVREAU,Matthew B   Sex: 07 May 1973 Paul F Gauvreau & Amy L Torcomian
GAVELL,Jessica E   Sex:F   30 Apr 1976 James F Gavell & Sandra M Waters
GEER,Amy L   Sex:F   08 Nov 1974 Bruce M Geer & Patricia A Clark
GEER,Shannon B   Sex:F   02 Apr 1979 Bruce M Geer & Patricia Ann Clark
GELINAS,Allen D   Sex:M   14 Jan 1964 Maurice R Gelinas,Jr & Rachel R Desmarais
GELINAS,Kristina A   Sex:F   28 Apr 1972 Maurice R Gelinas Jr
  & Rachel R M Desmarais
GENDRON,Arthur D   Sex:M   23 Nov 1955 Romeo A Gendron & Adeline J Desrosiers
GENDRON,Brian Michael Sex:M   20 May 1983 Robert J Gendron & Cynthia L Herling
GENDRON,Cheryl A   Sex:F   11 Mar 1966 Raymond V Gendron & Mary A Provencal
GENDRON,David M   Sex:M   07 Mar 1964 Raymond V Gendron & Mary A Provencal
GENDRON,Diane E   Sex:F   05 Apr 1947 Henry A Gendron (Nashua, NH)
  & Germ M Coutourier (Montreal, Canada)
GENDRON,Gail R   Sex:F   (Child #1) 30 Apr 1946 Roland A Gendron (Nashua, NH)
  & Theresa A Poirier (Nashua, NH)
GENDRON,Gary H   Sex:M   (Child #5) 09 Sep 1944 Henry Gendron (Dracut, MA)
  & Margaret A Noyes (Groton, NH)

HUDSON,NH BIRTHS

GENDRON,Gary H Jr Sex:M 07 Aug 1970 Gary H Gendron & Margaret E Kierstead
GENDRON,Jeffrey C Sex:M 03 Sep 1969 Raymond V Gendron & Mary A Provencal
GENDRON,Linda M Sex:F 14 Oct 1962 Raymond V Gendron & Mary Ann M Provencal
GENDRON,Marie Cecile Sex:F (Child #5) 27 Jul 1921 Joseph P Gendron (Canada)
   & Alma Paul (New Hampshire)
GENDRON,Michael P Sex:M 06 Feb 1957 Raymond A Gendron & Diane J Brown
GENDRON,Pamela J Sex:F 28 Feb 1952 Adrian A Gendron & Lillian M Signor
GENDRON,Rachel H Sex:F 22 Oct 1961 Raymond V Gendron & Mary A Provencal
GENDRON,Raymond Sex:M (Child #8) 09 Oct 1929 Joseph P Gendron (Canada)
   & Elma Paul (Nashua, NH)
GENEST,Aaron R Sex:M 14 Jun 1974 Robert R Genest & Linda A Levesque
GENEST,Joseph Henri Sex:M (Child #4) 04 Oct 1899 Arthur Genest (Canada)
   & Dina Gauthier (Canada)
GENEST,Martin R Sex:M 30 Oct 1975 Robert R Genest & Linda A Levesque
GENEST,Mary Sex:F (Child #9) 12 Jun 1900 Ernest T Genest (Canada)
   & Alvina Poisson (Canada)
GENEST,Oscar Joseph Sex:M (Child #10) 27 Apr 1901 Hudson, NH Ernest Genest
   (Canada) & Alvina Poisson (Canada)
GEORGE,Louis H Sex:M (Child #1) 07 Aug 1943 Louis S George (Penacook, NH)
   & Arlene R Heath (Boscowen, NH)
GERMAIN,Edward A Sex:M 12 Aug 1970 Renaud C Germain & Diana S Berube
GERMAIN,Lance J Sex: 11 Apr 1973 Joseph W Germain & Vickie M Richey
GERMAIN,Richard Robert Sex:M 05 Mar 1985 Ronald R Germain & Sheryl Ann Faria
GERMAIN,Roy B Sex:M 26 Dec 1965 Renaud C Germain & Diane S Berube
GERMAIN,Suzanne M Sex:F 14 Mar 1969 Renaud C Germain & Diana S Berube
GEROW,Angelina Collette Sex:F (Child #4) 11 Jan 1936 Bernice Gerow
   (Vermont) & Collette Laplante (Connecticut)
GEROW,Theresa Alvira Sex:F (Child #5) 05 Jan 1937 Bernice Gerow (Vermont)
   & Collette Laplant (New Britain, CT)
GEROW,William J Jr Sex:M 29 Nov 1963 William J Gerow & Brenda L Harriman
GERRIER,Clifford B Sex:M 25 Jun 1970 Edward R Gerrier & Nancy L Cote
GERRIOR,Peter E Sex:M 12 Sep 1962 Joseph D Gerrior & Neila M Morrison
GERRY,Amanda G Sex:F 25 Oct 1977 Edward M Gerry & Diane C Silvia
GERRY,David L Sex:M 22 Oct 1975 Edward M Gerry & Diane C Silvia
GERVAIS,Douglas John Sex:M 17 Oct 1983 Daniel A Gervais & Sandra E Roberts
GESTER,Bernice H Sex:F (Child #5) 08 Aug 1905 Albert Gester (Westphalia)
   & Frederica Napp (Westphalia)
GETTINGS,Andrew M Sex:M 20 Jun 1964 George L Gettings,Jr & Anne M Day
GETTINGS,Myles J Sex:M 19 Jul 1965 George L Gettings Jr & Anne M Day
GETTY,Albert M Sex: 11 Jul 1972 Albert R Getty & Therese A Alves
GETZ,Philip Arno Sex:M (Child #1) 16 Feb 1907 Ernest Arno Getz (Germany)
   & Ida Hunter (Tyngsboro, MA)
GIANNOTTI,Christina Sex:F 18 Oct 1976 Charles J Giannotti & Guadalupe A Gomez
GIBBS,Annie J Sex:F (Child #7) 05 Sep 1943 Perry N Gibbs (Sheldon, VT)
   & Florence D Kent (Chateaugay, NY)
GIBBS,Peter E Sex:M (Child #6) 21 Dec 1940 Perry N Gibbs (Sheldon, VT)
   & Florence D Kent (Chateaugay, NY)
GIBSON,Archabald Sex:M 09 Mar 1783 Hudson, NH William Gibson & Mary
GIBSON,Archibald Sex:M 09 Mar 1783 Hudson, NH William Gibson & Mary
GIBSON,Barnabas Sex:M Mar 1739 Hudson, NH James Gibson & Elizabeth
GIBSON,Barnabus Sex:M Mar 1739 Hudson, NH James Gibson & Elizabeth
GIBSON,Butterfield Sex: 17 Apr 1805 Hudson, NH James Gibson & Dorcas
GIBSON,Calvin Sex:M 24 Nov 1800 Hudson, NH John Gibson & Lucy
GIBSON,Dana W Sex:M 01 Oct 1957 Paul B Gibson, Jr & Nancy J Abbott
GIBSON,David G Sex:M 09 Feb 1966 Lawrence G Gibson & Elaine A Michaud
GIBSON,David W Sex:M 15 Mar 1959 Paul B Gibson, Jr & Nancy J Abbott
GIBSON,Dorcas Sex:F 01 Apr 1816 Hudson, NH James Gibson & Dorcas
GIBSON,Elizabeth Sex:F 08 Dec 1780 Hudson, NH William Gibson & Mary
GIBSON,Erik Whitney Sex:M 19 Oct 1981 David W Gibson & Tami Marie Wigmore
GIBSON,Glenn L Sex:M 12 Feb 1964 Paul B Gibson, Jr & Nancy J Abbott

HUDSON, NH BIRTHS

GIBSON, James   Sex:M   Jul 1741 Hudson, NH James Gibson & Elizabeth
GIBSON, James   Sex:M   10 Jun 1811 Hudson, NH James Gibson & Dorcas
GIBSON, James   Sex:M   Jul 1745 Hudson, NH James Gibson & Elizabeth
GIBSON, James M   Sex:M   25 Apr 1949 James E Gibson, Jr & Helen V Ruiter
GIBSON, John   Sex:M   16 Sep 1795 Hudson, NH John Gibson & Lucy
GIBSON, Kathleen D Sex:F   20 Jan 1953 James E Gibson, Jr & Helen V Ruiter
GIBSON, Kathy J   Sex:F   18 Mar 1960 Paul B Gibson, Jr & Nancy J Abbott
GIBSON, Laurie A   Sex:F   18 Oct 1977 Robert E Gibson & Nancy J Rugoletti
GIBSON, Linda D   Sex:F   22 Apr 1947 James E Gibson, Jr (Rochester, NH)
   & Helen V Ruiter (Nashua, NH)
GIBSON, Lorrie J   Sex:F   18 Dec 1973 Lawrence G Gibson & Elaine A Michaud
GIBSON, Luanne M   Sex:F   26 Nov 1954 James E Gibson, Jr & Helen V Ruiter
GIBSON, Lucy   Sex:F   07 Jun 1799 Hudson, NH John Gibson & Lucy
GIBSON, Luther   Sex:M   07 Jun 1797 Hudson, NH John Gibson & Lucy
GIBSON, Mary   Sex:F   10 Nov 1787 Hudson, NH William Gibson & Mary
GIBSON, Patricia A Sex:F   26 May 1951 James E Gibson & Helen V Ruiter
GIBSON, Richard J Sex:M   09 Feb 1966 Lawrence G Gibson & Elaine A Michaud
GIBSON, Romand   Sex:M   12 Jun 1786 Hudson, NH William Gibson & Mary
GIBSON, Samuel   Sex:M   12 Dec 1793 Hudson, NH John Gibson & Lucy
GIBSON, Sarah   Sex:F   08 Jan 1809 Hudson, NH James Gibson & Dorcas
GIBSON, Sarah   Sex:F   26 Sep 1767 Pelham, NH
GIBSON, Sarah   Sex:F   26 Dec 1806 Hudson, NH James Gibson & Dorcas
GIBSON, Sarah   Sex:F   08 Jun 1809 Hudson, NH James Gibson & Dorcas
GIBSON, Stephen A Sex:M   25 Feb 1970 Lawrence G Gibson & Elaine A Michaud
GIBSON, Thomas Darley Sex:M   12 Jun 1791 Pepperell, MA John Gibson & Lucy
GIDEON, Beth   Sex:F   17 Nov 1962 Victor C Gideon & Ruth A Munroe
GILBERT, Dale A   Sex: 12 Nov 1972 David C Gilbert & Sandra A Murphy
GILBERT, Jesse   Sex:F   (Child #1) 15 May 1909 Charles B Gilbert (Windham, NH)
   & Edna M Jones (Moncton, N B)
GILBERT, John   Sex:M   (Child #4) 28 Jan 1928 Louis Gilbert (Vermont)
   & Albina Aubutin (New Hampshire)
GILBERT, Lorraine Eveline   Sex:F   (Child #3) 05 Aug 1927 Frank O Gilbert
   (Proctor, VT) & Florida Coll (Suncook, NH)
GILBERT, Phillip E Sex:M   24 Nov 1956 Edward P Gilbert & Isabelle H Crooker
GILBERT, Teresa C Sex:F   07 Aug 1961 George B Gilbert & Mary F Kierce
GILBERT, [Unknown] Sex:F   (Child #2) 10 Sep 1910 Charles Gilbert (Windham, NH)
   & Edna M Jones (Moncton, N B)
GILBERT, [Unknown] Sex:F   (Child #2) 7 Oct 1882 Hudson, NH George P Gilbert
   (Hanover, NH) & Sarah A Rowell (Malone, NY)
GILCREAST, Brandon Ralph   Sex:M   02 Feb 1981 Ralph L Gilcreast
   & Patricia L Reynolds
GILCREAST, Cheryle H   Sex:F   (Child #5) 09 Jul 1945 Francis G Gilcreast
   (Derry, NH) & Bertha P Newman (Nashua, NH)
GILCREAST, Francis W Jr   Sex:M   06 Sep 1969 Francis W Gilcreast
   & Alice P Carson
GILCREAST, Gloria Ann   Sex:F   (Child #1) 22 Jan 1942 Francis G Gilcreast
   (Hudson, NH) & Bertha P Newman (Nashua, NH)
GILCREAST, Jennifer R   Sex:F   06 Feb 1975 Ralph L Gilcreast
   & Patricia L Reynolds
GILCREAST, John A Sex:M   (Child #5) 30 Apr 1944 Francis G Gilcreast
   (Derry, NH) & Bertha P Newman (Hudson, NH)
GILCREAST, Judith E   Sex:F   (Child #2) 17 Jan 1943 Francis G Gilcreast
   (Derry, NH) & Bertha Newman (Nashua, NH)
GILCREAST, MaryLou Ann Sex:F 11 Nov 1975 Robert F Gilcreast & Mary Ann Stanley
GILCREAST, Ralph L Sex:M   04 Oct 1949 Francis G Gilcreast & Bertha P Newman
GILCREAST, Robert F Sex:M   05 Aug 1953 Francis G Gilcreast & Bertha P Newman
GILCREAST, Sandra L Sex:F   (Child #6) 21 Aug 1946 Francis G Gilcreast
   (Derry, NH) & Bertha P Newman (Nashua, NH)
GILCREAST, Steven R Sex:M   26 Apr 1955 Francis G Gilcreast & Bertha P Newman
GILCREAST, Steven R Jr Sex: 15 Jun 1973 Steven R Gilcreast & Deborah A Dionne

HUDSON, NH BIRTHS

GILDAY, Jonathan T   Sex:M   23 Nov 1971   John P Gilday & Karen D Cook
GILE, Brenda B   Sex:F   06 Jun 1962   George D Gile & Jacqueline A Legendr
GILE, Daniel J   Sex:M   29 Aug 1958   George D Gile & Jacqueline A Legendr
GILE, David   Sex:M   20 Nov 1960   George D Gile & Jacqueline A Legendr
GILE, Sarah Marie   Sex:F   28 Mar 1981   Stephen Joseph Gile & Debra May Perry
GILE, Susan C   Sex:F   16 Nov 1966   George D Gile & Jacqueline A Legendr
GILES, Harold William   Sex:M   (Child #4)   17 Feb 1917   William G Giles
    (Lime Mountain) & Bertha Nealy (Lowell, MA)
GILLETTE, Cheryl A   Sex:F   (Child #2)   25 Jul 1946   Charles W Gillette
    (Chatahutia, GA) & Iva A Marshall (Hudson, NH)
GILLETTE, Paul D   Sex:M   06 Mar 1956   Charles W Gillette & Iva A Marshall
GILLIS, Thomas J Jr   Sex:M   18 Dec 1966   Thomas J Gillis & Jeanine L Boucher
GILMAN, Jeffrey L   Sex:M   26 Feb 1968   Richard L Gilman & Judith A Guilford
GILMAN, Jennifer P   Sex:F   12 Feb 1980   Kenneth B Gilman & AnnMarie Dube
GILMAN, Keith E B   Sex:M   22 Apr 1977   Kenneth B Gilman II & AnnMarie Dube
GILMAN, Matthew N   Sex:M   26 Oct 1970   Peter H Gilman & Lorraine M Nason
GILPATRICK, Lesa S   Sex:F   14 Jun 1956   Lindy L Gilpatrick & Thelma Hopkins
GILSON, Calvin   Sex:M   24 Nov 1800   Hudson, NH   John Gilson & Lucey
GILSON, John   Sex:M   16 Sep 1795   Nottingham   John Gilson & Lucey
GILSON, Lucy   Sex:F   07 Jun 1799   Hudson, NH   John Gilson & Lucey
GILSON, Luther   Sex:M   07 Jun 1797   Hudson, NH   John Gilson & Lucey
GILSON, Samuel   Sex:M   12 Dec 1793   Nottingham   John Gilson & Lucey
GILSON, Thomas D   Sex:M   12 Jan 1791   Pepperell, MA   John Gilson & Lucey
GIMIAN, Todd Allan   Sex:M   22 Feb 1982   Allan D Gimian & Karen Lee Jones
GINGRAS, Bruce R   Sex:M   27 Nov 1966   Raymond L Gingras & Georgette B Durand
GINGRAS, Christopher A   Sex:M   16 Mar 1968   Raymond L Gingras
    & Georgette B Durand
GINGRAS, Keith R   Sex:M   20 Jan 1971   Raymond L Gingras & Georgette B Durand
GINGRAS, Peter J   Sex:M   25 Mar 1972   Donald W Gingras & Carol A Thistle
GINGRAS, Richard W   Sex:M   (Child #3)   06 Oct 1940   Omer O Gingras (Peabody, MA)
    & Irene Beauchesne (Lawrence, MA)
GIRARD, Douglass Marvin   Sex:M   27 Dec 1979   Paul Joseph Girard & Anita V Bernard
GIROUARD, Eugene   Sex:M   (Child #8)   15 Aug 1897   Joseph Girouard (Canada)
    & Marie Conturier (Canada)
GIROUARD, Joseph A   Sex:M   (Child #14)   20 Nov 1905   Joseph Girouard (Canada)
    & Marie Couturier (Canada)
GIROUARD, Marie   Sex:F   (Child #15)   08 Aug 1907   Joseph Girouard (MA)
    & Marie Couturier (Canada)
GIROUARD, Marie Bernadetta   Sex:F   (Child #16)   22 May 1911   Joseph Girouard
    (Massachusetts) & Marie Coutuier (Canada)
GIROUARD, Marie C   Sex:F   (Child #13)   23 Aug 1903   Joseph Girouard (Canada)
    & Mari Couturier (Canada)
GIROUARD, Marie E C   Sex:F   (Child #11)   13 May 1902   Joseph Girouard (Canada)
    & Marie Coutourier (Canada)
GIROUARD, Marie Rose Anna   Sex:F   (Child #12)   13 May 1902   Joseph Girouard
    (Canada) & Marie Coutourier (Canada)
GIROUARD, Mary D A   Sex:F   (Child #10)   25 Nov 1900   Joseph Girouard (MA)
    & Marie Couturier (Canada)
GIROUX, Eric G   Sex:M   22 Jun 1971   Guy H Giroux & Madeleine Y Poulin
GIZA, Lydia   Sex:M   17 Jan 1985   Ludwik S Giza & Martha Elaine Green
GLASS, Katherine E   Sex:F   21 Dec 1966   Charles D D Glass Jr & Linda D Clarke
GLASSER, Nancy L   Sex:F   27 Jun 1947   James C Glasser (Marion Ctr, PA)
    & Dorothy L Moore (Indianapolis, IN)
GLASTETTER, Ann Elizabeth   Sex:F   13 Oct 1978   Albert F Glastetter
    & Antonina F Salamon
GLASTETTER, Jason A   Sex:M   20 Jun 1980   Albert F Glastetter
    & Antonina F Salamon
GLASTETTER, Marilyn G   Sex:F   14 Aug 1976   Albert F Glastetter
    & Antonina F Salamon
GLASZ, Garry P   Sex:M   26 Jun 1956   Nicholas L Glasz & Elizabeth W Jung

HUDSON,NH BIRTHS

GLENDAY,Charles A Jr Sex:M   04 Oct 1951 Charles A Glenday & Edith M Hurk
GLENECK,Sara Ann Sex:F 06 Jul 1982 James Arthur Gleneck & Karen Ann Couronis
GLENN,Marie E   Sex:F   31 Jul 1965 James K Glenn, Jr & Mary H Ryan
GLENN,Robin V   Sex:F   25 Jul 1977 Michael A Glenn & Gail D McCarthy
GLISPIN,Richard A Sex:M   (Child #1) 24 Aug 1940 James E Glispin (Lowell, MA)
  & Stella Zinkawich (Nashua, NH)
GLISPIN,Virginia E   Sex:F   18 Dec 1948 James E Glispin (Lowell, MA)
  & Stella N Zinkawich (Nashua, NH)
GLOUDEMANS,Zachary Richard   Sex:M   08 Dec 1984 Joseph R Gloudemans
  & Lucinda J Shepard
GLOVER,Benjamin Sex:M 11 Dec 1786 Hudson, NH Robert Glover Jr & Lydia Hadley
GLOVER,David   Sex:M   07 Feb 1778 Hudson, NH Robert Glover Jr & Lydia Hadley
GLOVER,David E   Sex:M   (Child #4) 22 Nov 1908 Charles Glover (Nashua, NH)
  & Carrie Stanton (St John, N B)
GLOVER,Elizabeth   Sex:F   15 Aug 1747 Hudson, NH Robert Glover & Jane
GLOVER,Elizabeth Sex:F 08 Jun 1774 Hudson, NH Robert Glover Jr & Lydia Hadley
GLOVER,Jane   Sex:F   08 Oct 1751 Hudson, NH Robert Glover & Jane
GLOVER,John   Sex:M   09 Jul 1741 Hudson, NH Robert Glover & Jane
GLOVER,Lydia   Sex:F   29 Jul 1779 Hudson, NH Robert Glover Jr & Lydia Hadley
GLOVER,Mollie   Sex:F   12 Jun 1776 Hudson, NH Robert Glover & Lydia
GLOVER,Molly   Sex:F   12 Jun 1777 Hudson, NH Robert Glover Jr & Lydia Hadley
GLOVER,Naomi   Sex:F   03 Apr 1770 Hudson, NH Robert Glover Jr & Lydia Hadley
GLOVER,Nellie   Sex:F   19 Oct 1781 Hudson, NH Robert Glover Jr & Lydia Hadley
GLOVER,Olive   Sex:F   17 Oct 1784 Hudson, NH Robert Glover Jr & Lydia Hadley
GLOVER,Olive   Sex:F   07 Oct 1784 Hudson, NH Robert Glover & Lydia
GLOVER,Rachel   Sex:F   13 Sep 1791 Hudson, NH Robert Glover Jr & Lydia Hadley
GLOVER,Richard   Sex:M   13 Sep 1791 Hudson, NH Robert Glover & Lydia
GLOVER,Robert   Sex:M   04 Oct 1743 Hudson, NH Robert Glover & Jane
GLOVER,Robert   Sex:M   12 Jun 1777 Hudson, NH Robert Glover Jr & Lydia Hadley
GLOVER,Robert   Sex:M   12 Jun 1776 Hudson, NH Robert Glover & Lydia
GLOVER,Sally   Sex:F   19 Oct 1781 Hudson, NH Robert Glover & Lydia
GLOVER,Seth   Sex:M   26 Mar 1789 Hudson, NH Robert Glover Jr & Lydia Hadley
GOBEIL,Claudette J   Sex:F   08 Mar 1966 Claude H Gobeil & Doris E Brossard
GOBEIL,Diane D   Sex:F   17 Jul 1968 Claude J Gobeil & Doris E Brossard
GOBEIL,Michelle N   Sex:F   17 Jan 1970 Claude J Gobeil & Doris E Brossard
GODBOUT,Bruce Edmond   Sex:M   (Child #4) 10 Oct 1939 Florant J Godbout
  (Haverhill, MA) & Thelma T Hubbard (Haverhill, MA)
GODBOUT,Margaret Louise   Sex:F   (Child #3) 25 Aug 1935 Florant Godbout
  (Haverhill, MA) & Thelma Hubbard (Haverhill, MA)
GODBOUT,Richard P   Sex:M   (Child #1) 05 Nov 1946 George H Godbout (Unknown)
  & B M Boissonnault (Canada)
GODBOUT,Susan Y   Sex:F   12 Nov 1947 George H Godbout (Salem, MA)
  & B M Boissonault (Canada)
GOETZ,Selena Evelyn   Sex:F   (Child #2) 26 Oct 1912 Arno Goetz (Germany)
  & Ida Hunter (Tyngsboro, MA)
GOLDSMITH,Jessica Lynn Sex:F 17 Sep 1984 Jon E Goldsmith & Sharon A Lewellen
GOLDTHWAITE,Danagel E Sex:F 05 Feb 1976 David B Goldthwaite & Andrea L Duffy
GOLEMBESKI,Elizabeth J   Sex:F   09 Apr 1979 Thomas J Golembeski
  & Katherine A Dooley
GOLEMBESKI,Karen M Sex:F 25 Mar 1976 Thomas J Golembeski & Katherine A Dooley
GOLEN,Jennifer L   Sex: 30 Aug 1972 Francis A Golen & Carol A Gentle
GOLETSKI,Mary   Sex:F   (Child #1) 09 May 1922 Joseph Goletski (Russia)
  & Mary Kasper (Nashua, NH)
GOODHUE,Jane Sex:F   06 Jan 1948 Edmond L Goodhue (Lowell, MA)
  & Stella R Vaslock (Nashua, NH)
GOODRICH,Lisa Marie   Sex:F   17 Nov 1973 David O Goodrich & Marie P Cote
GOODSPEED,Fred A   Sex:M   24 Jun 1878 Hudson, NH Namar Goodspeed (Wentworth)
  & Luella (Dudswell, PQ)
GOODWIN,Betty J   Sex:F   (Child #2) 05 Apr 1946 Frdrk T Goodwin, Jr (Salem,
  MA) & Marie C Theriault (Lowell, MA)

HUDSON,NH BIRTHS

GOODWIN,Betty L   Sex:F   (Child #3) 17 Dec 1944 Harold E Goodwin (Nashua, NH)
  & Dorothy E Holbrook (Nashua, NH)
GOODWIN,Carl D   Sex:M   19 Feb 1953 Frederick T Goodwin & Claire M Therriault
GOODWIN,David R   Sex:M   03 Dec 1954 Francis N Goodwin & Pearl M Williams
GOODWIN,Eric E   Sex:M   26 Jan 1965 Lawrence O Goodwin & Carole A Chacos
GOODWIN,Francis Nielson   Sex:M   (Child #4) 06 Oct 1923 Frederick T Goodwin
  (Massachusetts) & Anniemae Nielson (Massachusetts)
GOODWIN,Jimmy L   Sex:M   05 Jan 1966 Paul W Goodwin & Doris J Constant
GOODWIN,Mary F   Sex:F   28 Feb 1968 Francis N Goodwin & Muriel A Reid
GOODWIN,Matthew J   Sex:M   04 Mar 1969 Allan F Goodwin & Constance J Baker
GOODWIN,Paul W Jr   Sex:M   10 Oct 1964 Paul W Goodwin, Sr & Doris J Constant
GOODWIN,Tammy E   Sex:F   13 Aug 1966 Lawrence O Goodwin & Carole A Chacos
GOODWIN,[Unknown]   Sex: 07 Mar 1863 Hudson, NH Alpheus Goodwin & Lydia
GORDON,Douglas L   Sex:M   01 Mar 1966 Lloyd F Gordon & Martha L Lavertu
GORDON,Jeannette E   Sex:F   07 Dec 1976 John J Gordon & Cynthia A Rock
GORDON,Judith A   Sex:F   21 Oct 1968 Lloyd F Gordon & Martha L Lavertu
GORDON,Kevin   Sex:M   30 Dec 1970 Ralph E Gordon & Suzanne A Bray
GORDON,Sandra L   Sex:F   19 Aug 1969 Lloyd F Gordon & Martha L Lavertu
GORDON,Sean   Sex:M   20 Oct 1968 Ralph E Gordon & Suzanne A Bray
GORDON,Susan L   Sex:F   13 Feb 1963 Lloyd F Gordon & Martha L Lavertu
GORTON,Shirley M   Sex:F   11 Feb 1950 Robert R Gorton & Cecile M Dumont
GORVEATT,Joshua William   Sex:M   21 Dec 1978 Floyd W Gorveatt
  & Antoinette Abbouzzes
GOSCIMINSKI,Kristen Anne   Sex:F   10 Jan 1985 Edmund A Gosciminski
  & Jeanne Marie Cote
GOSS,Charlotte M   Sex:F   30 Oct 1954 Charles R Goss & Mary A Baio
GOSS,Thomas P   Sex:M   12 Oct 1963 Russell E Goss & Lillian P Kenny
GOSSELIN,Amy E   Sex:F   22 Apr 1971 Richard H Gosselin & Constance M Turner
GOSSELIN,Dennis G   Sex:M   11 Jan 1965 Gaston A Gosselin & Raymonde Y Dubard
GOSSELIN,Lynn C M   Sex:F   02 Dec 1968 Leon J Gosselin & Helene R Roy
GOSSELIN,Michael S   Sex:M   19 Jul 1964 Richard A Gosselin & Jeannette M Dionne
GOSSELIN,Robert R   Sex:M   09 Apr 1969 Roland R Gosselin & Frances C Morency
GOSSELIN,Steven M   Sex:M   25 Oct 1965 Richard A Gosselin & Jeannette M Dionne
GOSSELIN,Tanya Jean   Sex:F   17 Nov 1983 Louis D Gosselin & Donna Jean Heath
GOSSELIN,Tiffany Ann   Sex:F   10 Jan 1982 David J Gosselin & Cheryl Ann Gannon
GOSSELIN,[Unknown]   Sex:F   08 Dec 1950 Odilon T Gosselin & Claire J Durette
GOTHAM,Matthew David   Sex:M   11 Oct 1983 Edward W Gotham & Rita A Flannery
GOTT,Arlene M   Sex:F   30 Mar 1970 Kenneth M Gott & Patricia A Craig
GOTT,Kenneth M II   Sex:M   19 Feb 1971 Kenneth M Gott & Patricia A Craig
GOUDREAU,Nicole Renee   Sex:F   13 Jan 1984 John L Goudreau & Anne Marie Goulette
GOULD,Adam Hamilton   Sex:M   22 Jul 1979 George A Gould & Sandra Lee Dunn
GOULD,Alfred   Sex:M   27 Aug 1813 Hudson, NH Asa Gould & Mary Cummings
GOULD,Anna   Sex:F   23 Feb 1783 Hudson, NH Jonathan Gould & Anna Chase
GOULD,Asa   Sex:M   13 Jun 1774 Hudson, NH Joseph Gould Jr & Sarah Seavey
GOULD,Chester E   Sex:M   08 Oct 1955 Chester E Gould & Ethel M Perry
GOULD,Clara Ellen   Sex:F   22 Nov 1849 Hudson, NH David Gould & Mary Cummings
GOULD,Clarissa   Sex:F   05 Apr 1809 Hudson, NH Asa Gould & Mary Cummings
GOULD,Daniel   Sex:M   12 Nov 1789 Hudson, NH Isaac Gould & Abigail
GOULD,Davis Cunningham   Sex:M   08 Sep 1805 Hudson, NH Asa Gould & Mary Cummings
GOULD,Elijah   Sex:M   26 Nov 1759 Hudson, NH Joseph Gould & Mary Piper
GOULD,Elizabeth   Sex:F   25 Mar 1752 Hudson, NH Samuel Gould & Elizabeth
GOULD,Emma C   Sex:F   22 Oct 1852 Hudson, NH David Gould & Mary Cummings
GOULD,Eric J   Sex: 04 Oct 1972 Dale R Gould Sr & Constance J Fogg
GOULD,Hannah   Sex:F   15 Jun 1789 Hudson, NH Jonathan Gould & Anna Chase
GOULD,Hannah   Sex:F   15 Jan 1789 Hudson, NH Jonathan Gould & Anna
GOULD,Isaac   Sex:M   27 Sep 1791 Hudson, NH Isaac Gould & Abigail
GOULD,John   Sex:M   03 Mar 1753 Hudson, NH Joseph Gould & Mary Piper
GOULD,John   Sex:M   20 Sep 1757 Hudson, NH Joseph Gould & Mary Piper
GOULD,Jonathan   Sex:M   27 Dec 1761 Hudson, NH Joseph Gould & Mary Piper
GOULD,Jonathan   Sex:M   18 Jan 1793 Hudson, NH Jonathan Gould & Anna Chase

GOULD,Joseph   Sex:M   23 Feb 1749 Hudson, NH Joseph Gould & Mary Piper
GOULD,Joseph   Sex:M   02 Aug 1781 Hudson, NH Elijah Gould & Sarah Ingalls
GOULD,Joseph   Sex:M   28 Sep 1794 Hudson, NH Jonathan Gould & Anna Chase
GOULD,Joseph   Sex:M   23 Feb 1748 Hudson, NH Joseph Gould & Mary
GOULD,Laura Jane   Sex:F   27 Jul 1842 Hudson, NH David Gould & Mary Cummings
GOULD,Lysander Sex:M   29 Aug 1798 Hudson, NH Jonathan Gould & Anna Chase
GOULD,Lysmeda   Sex: 29 aug 1798 Hudson, NH Jonathan Gould & Anna
GOULD,Maria Asenath Sex:F 05 Feb 1856 Hudson, NH David Gould & Mary Cummings
GOULD,Mary   Sex:F   02 Aug 1755 Hudson, NH Joseph Gould & Mary Piper
GOULD,Mary   Sex:F   22 Mar 1802 Hudson, NH Asa Gould & Mary Cummings
GOULD,Mary Frances   Sex:F   14 Jun 1840 Hudson, NH David Gould & Mary Cummings
GOULD,Molley   Sex:F   05 Apr 1775 Hudson, NH   & Sarah Gould
GOULD,Molly   Sex:F   05 Apr 1775 Hudson, NH   & Sarah Gould
GOULD,Polly   Sex:F   1785 Hudson, NH Jonathan Gould & Anna Chase
GOULD,Rebecca   Sex:F   01 May 1787 Hudson, NH Jonathan Gould & Anna Chase
GOULD,Rebekah   Sex:F   01 May 1787 Hudson, NH Jonathan Gould & Anna
GOULD,Sarah   Sex:F   12 Jan 1751 Hudson, NH Joseph Gould & Mary Piper
GOULD,Sarah   Sex:F   06 Dec 1790 Hudson, NH Jonathan Gould & Anna Chase
GOULD,Sarah   Sex:F   12 Jan 1750 Hudson, NH Joseph Gould & Mary
GOULD,Sarah Angeline Sex:F 27 Sep 1844 Hudson, NH David Gould & Mary Cummings
GOULD,Steven P   Sex:M   03 Dec 1974 George A Gould & Sandra L Dunn
GOULET,Billy   Sex: 20 Sep 1972 John T Goulet & Wendy Peters
GOULET,Bonnie   Sex:F   26 Nov 1973 John T Goulet & Wendy Peters
GOULET,Richard L Jr Sex:M   04 Sep 1975 Richard L Goulet & Judith Ann Akey
GOURLEY,Cheryl A   Sex:F   05 Mar 1970 William D Gourley & Elaine M Steinbacher
GOURLEY,Michele M Sex:F 05 Mar 1970 William D Gourley & Elaine M Steinbacher
GOVE,Charles F   Sex:M   (Child #3) 24 Aug 1943 Lester E Gove (Sunapee, NH)
   & Ethel M Forbes (Nashua, NH)
GOVE,Charles F Jr   Sex:M   17 Sep 1970 Charles F Gove & Susan G Nichols
GOVE,Megan Elizabeth   Sex:F   18 Jun 1984 Lester Paul Gove & June Diane Heino
GOWDY,Mary E   Sex:F   11 Jan 1966 Donald H Gowdy & Berthe R Maurice
GOWING,Carrie E   Sex:F   13 Mar 1886 Hudson, NH George L Gowing & Ida E
GOWING,Deborah L   Sex:F   09 Jan 1969 Frederick L GowingJr & Winifred L Nadeau
GOWING,Edwin E   Sex:M   (Child #1) 05 Apr 1882 Hudson, NH Sidney P Gowing
   (Hudson, NH) & Clementine Fuller (Dracut, MA)
GOWING,Edwin Harold Sex:M (Child #1) 13 Apr 1909 Edwin E Gowing (Hudson, NH)
   & Josephine Donally (Hudson, NH)
GOWING,Eva E   Sex:F   (Child #4) 07 Oct 1888 Sidney P Gowing (Hudson, NH)
   & Clementine Fuller (Dracut, MA)
GOWING,Frederick L Sex:M (Child #3) 03 Apr 1921 Edward E Gowing (Hudson, NH)
   & Josephine A Donally (Hudson, NH)
GOWING,Frederick L Jr Sex:M   (Child #3) 11 Mar 1944 Frederick L Gowing
   (Hudson, NH) & Bertha M Hardy (Durham, NH)
GOWING,Jacqueline A Sex:F 16 Feb 1967 Frederick L GowingJr
   & Winifred L Nadeau
GOWING,Mary E   Sex:F   (Child #2) 15 May 1910 Elwin E Gowing (Hudson, NH)
   & Josephine Donnelly (Hudson, NH)
GOWING,Mary L   Sex:F   06 Oct 1884 Hudson, NH George T Gowing (Hudson, NH)
   & Ida E Seavy (Pelham, NH)
GOWING,Mary Louise   Sex:F   (Child #1) 06 Jan 1941 Frederick L Gowing (Hudson,
   NH) & Bertha M Hardy (Durham, NH)
GOWING,Perley F   Sex:M   11 Aug 1894 Sidney P Gowing (Hudson, NH)
   & Clementine Fuller (Dracut, MA)
GOWING,Susan A   Sex:F   (Child #4) 21 Nov 1945 Frederick L Gowing (Hudson, NH)
   & Bertha M Hardy (Durham, NH)
GOWING,Willie Sex:M 11 Apr 1886 Hudson, NH Sidney P Gowing&Clementine Fuller
GOWING,Willie J   Sex:M   11 Apr 1886 Sidney P Gowing & Clementine
GOYAIT,Diane J   Sex:F   25 May 1955 Hector C Goyait & Irene T Nadeau
GOYETTE,Michael P   Sex:M   28 Mar 1971 Peter R Goyette Jr & Theresa B Coutu
GOYETTE,Michelle L   Sex:F   23 Jan 1969 Peter R Goyette, Jr & Theresa B Coutu

HUDSON,NH BIRTHS

GRACE,Matthew B   Sex:M   17 Aug 1976 William A Grace & Susan Berman
GRACE,Melanie A   Sex: 03 Dec 1972 John D Grace Jr & Sandra M Nadeau
GRACE,Michael J   Sex:M   03 May 1974 John D Grace Jr & Sandra M Nadeau
GRAHAM,Arthur Newton   Sex:M   (Child #3) 04 Jun 1933 Arthur G Graham (Windham,
    NH) & Pauline Chamberlan (Nashua, NH)
GRAHAM,John R   Sex:M   23 Dec 1798 Hudson, NH Samuel Graham & Nabby
GRAHAM,John Robinson Sex:M 23 Dec 1798 Hudson, NH Samuel Scott Graham & Nabby
GRAICHEN,Joseph D   Sex:M   10 Jan 1971 John C Graichen & Janice C Tuniewicz
GRAINER,Joanne   Sex:F   26 Apr 1957 Donald K Grainger & Agnes M McDermott
GRAINGER,Donna M   Sex:F   01 Jan 1956 Donald K Grainger & Agnes M McDermott
GRAINGER,Linda J   Sex:F   30 Jun 1963 Donald K Grainger & Agnes M McDermott
GRAINGER,Marilyn J   Sex:F   08 Dec 1959 Donald K Grainger & Agnes M McDermott
GRAINGER,Michael J   Sex:M   06 Aug 1954 Donald K Grainger & Agnes M McDermott
GRAINGER,Stephanie Jo Sex:F 23 Oct 1984 Michael J Grainger & Lynn A Francoeur
GRANGER,Brian M   Sex:M   29 Oct 1973 Gary M Granger & Lorna R Belleau
GRANGER,Dennis M   Sex: 15 Aug 1972 Gary M Granger & Lorna R Belleau
GRANGER,Scott M   Sex:M   09 May 1977 Gary M Granger & Lorna Rae Belleau
GRANT,Carolann R   Sex:F   24 May 1968 Donald E Grant & Barbara A Morton
GRANT,Donald E   Sex:M   20 Nov 1954 Donald E Grant & Barbara A Morton
GRANT,Douglas E   Sex:M   01 Oct 1970 Donald E Grant & Barbara A Morton
GRANT,Gary S   Sex:M   13 Apr 1957 Donald E Grant & Barbara A Morton
GRANT,Jodi L   Sex:F   27 Jan 1971 John A Grant & Noreen J Leonard
GRANT,Ryan A   Sex:M   07 Jun 1972 John A Grant & Noreen J Leonard
GRANT,Shannon L   Sex:F   22 Aug 1971 William E Grant & Martha J Taylor
GRANT,William Roger   Sex:M   (Child #1) 23 Jul 1935 William Grant (Nashua, NH)
    & Doris Martin (Moors, NY)
GRAUSLYS,Anthony P   Sex:M   08 Mar 1967 Charles P Grauslys & Julia M Virbalas
GRAVEL,Leslie A   Sex:F   23 May 1969 George A Gravel & Olive H Corriveau
GRAVELLE,Gene R K   Sex:M   31 Jul 1967 Gene R J Gravelle & Lucille R Trudeau
GRAVELLE,Joan   Sex:F (Child #3) 27 Dec 1945 Sylvio T Gravelle (Nashua, NH)
    & Cecila M Lavoie (Nashua, NH)
GRAVELLE,Justine J   Sex:F   24 Oct 1969 Gene R A Gravelle & Lucille R Trudeau
GRAVELLE,Lucy S   Sex:F   (Child #2) 07 Apr 1945 William A Gravelle (Lowell,
    MA) & Jeanne L Tubinas (Hudson, NH)
GRAVELLE,Nadine C   Sex:F   05 Aug 1966 Gene R Gravelle & Lucille R Trudeau
GRAVELLE,Raymond G   Sex:M   25 Sep 1968 Gene R Gravelle & Lucille R Trudeau
GRAVELLE,[Unknown]   Sex:F   19 Sep 1971 Gene R Gravelle & Lucille R Trudeau
GRAVELLINE,Marie Rita   Sex:F (Child #7) 12 Jul 1924 Joseph Gravelline
    (Canada) & Rose Corriveau (Canada)
GRAVES,Arthur M   Sex:M   (Child #4) 22 Oct 1889 Newell Graves (Champlain, NY)
    & Alvina LaForce (Plattsburg, NY)
GRAVES,Brian C   Sex:M   11 Jul 1968 Clark D Graves & Ellen R Goyette
GRAVES,Craig D   Sex:M   13 Jun 1962 David W Graves & Judith M Kauppi
GRAVES,Eric L   Sex:M   06 Mar 1970 Melvin R Graves & Marie-Claire Cheneba
GRAVES,Jane A   Sex:F   03 Mar 1893 Newell Graves (Champlain, NY)
    & Alonica LaForce (Plattsburg, NY)
GRAVES,Lillian Agnes   Sex:F (Child #10) 07 Apr 1896 Newell Graves
    (Champlain, NY) & Alvina LaForce (Plattsburg, NY)
GRAVES,Mary B   Sex:F (Child #5) 27 Apr 1891 Newell Graves (Champlain, NY)
    & Alvina LaForce (Plattsburg, NY)
GRAVES,Mary P   Sex:F   27 Apr 1891 Hudson, NH Newell Graves & Alvinia La Favre
GRAVES,Michael F   Sex:M   27 Sep 1964 Clark D Graves & Ellen R Goyette
GRAVES,Robert L Jr   Sex:M   23 May 1974 Robert L Graves Sr & Dorothy J Wheeler
GRAVES,Stephen A   Sex:M   16 Oct 1966 Clark D Graves & Ellen R Goyette
GRAY,Henry   Sex:M   27 May 1783 Hudson, NH Joseph Gray & Susan
GRAY,Joseph   Sex:M   09 Feb 1788 Hudson, NH Joseph Gray & Lucy
GRAY,Leon E Jr   Sex:M   (Child #1) 15 Jul 1945 Leon E Gray (Memphis, TN)
    & Mary A Virbalas (Lithuania)
GRAY,Lovona R   Sex:F   (Child #2) 09 Aug 1945 Edwin H Gray (Baltimore, MD)
    & Florence E Hall (Boston, MA)

HUDSON,NH BIRTHS

GRAY,Lucy   Sex:F   05 Feb 1785 Hudson, NH Joseph Gray & Lucy
GREATCHUS,Jo Ann   Sex:F   19 Jan 1951 Leo D Greatchus & Josephine M Greatch
GREATCHUS,Matthew E W Sex: 13 Mar 1973 Michael L Greatchu & Donna P Paquette
GREELE,Bridget   Sex:F   03 Feb 1764 Hudson, NH Ezekiel Greele & Esther
GREELE,Gilbert   Sex:M   30 Jan 1752 Hudson, NH Ezekiel Greele & Esther
GREELE,Mary   Sex:F   15 Oct 1760 Hudson, NH Samuel Greele & Abigail
GREELE,Rachel   Sex:F   17 Jan 1761 Hudson, NH Jonathan Greele & Ruth
GREELE,Rose   Sex:F   17 Jun 1757 Hudson, NH A negro girl &
GREELE,Sarah   Sex:F   09 Apr 1761 Hudson, NH Ezekiel Greele & Esther
GREELEY,Abigail   Sex:F   10 Apr 1750 Hudson, NH Samuel Greeley Jr & Abigail
GREELEY,Adeline Amanda   Sex:F   20 Apr 1830 Hudson, NH Seneca Greeley
   & Priscilla Fields
GREELEY,Adoniram Judson   Sex:M   10 Sep 1818 Hudson, NH Reuben Greeley
   & Joanna C Merrill
GREELEY,Alfred   Sex:M   17 Apr 1788 Hudson, NH Joseph Greeley & Sarah Greeley
GREELEY,Alfred   Sex:M   15 May 1821 Hudson, NH Seneca Greeley & Priscilla
GREELEY,Alfred Henry   Sex:M   15 May 1821 Hudson, NH Seneca Greeley
   & Priscilla Fields
GREELEY,Andrew   Sex:M   1620
GREELEY,Andrew, Jr Sex:M 10 Dec 1646 Hudson, NH Andrew Greeley&Mary Goldmyre
GREELEY,Arthur   Sex:M   (Child #2) 30 Mar 1883 Hudson, NH James C Greeley
   (Hudson, NH) & Ida B Twiss (Londonderry, NH)
GREELEY,Benjamin   Sex:M   22 Apr 1756 Hudson, NH Ezekiel Greeley & Esther
GREELEY,Benjamin   Sex:M   06 Jan 1779 Hudson, NH Zacheus Greeley & Esther
GREELEY,Benjamin Sex:M 09 Dec 1654 Hudson, NH Andrew Greeley & Mary Goldmyre
GREELEY,Benjamin Sex:M 28 Feb 1700 Hudson, NH Joseph Greeley & Martha Wilford
GREELEY,Benjamin   Sex:M   16 Jan 1779 Hudson, NH Zacheus Greeley & Esther
GREELEY,Bridget   Sex:F   03 Feb 1764 Hudson, NH Ezekiel Greeley & Esther
GREELEY,Bridget   Sex:F   01 Jul 1777 Hudson, NH Zacheus Greeley & Esther
GREELEY,Bridgett   Sex:F   01 Jul 1777 Hudson, NH Zacheus Greeley & Esther
GREELEY,Carl L   Sex:M   06 Oct 1951 Earle V Greeley & Beth A Legallee
GREELEY,Clara B   Sex:F   17 Apr 1878 Hudson, NH Jameson Greeley (Hudson, NH)
   & Christina A (Hudson, NH)
GREELEY,Clarissa   Sex:F   03 Nov 1808 Hudson, NH Moses Greeley & Mary Derby
GREELEY,Daniel   Sex:M   19 Nov 1789 Hudson, NH Zacheus Greeley & Esther
GREELEY,Daniel W Sex:M 12 Oct 1821 Hudson, NH Reuben Greeley&Joanna C Merrill
GREELEY,David   Sex:M   19 Nov 1789 Hudson, NH Zacheus Greeley & Esther
GREELEY,Dustin   Sex:M   04 May 1793 Hudson, NH Zacheus Greeley & Esther
GREELEY,Edith M   Sex:F   (Child #2) 07 Nov 1885 Hudson, NH Samuel A Greeley
   (Hudson, NH) & Suzanna C Richardson (Hudson, NH)
GREELEY,Elbridge J   Sex:M   15 Nov 1815 Hudson, NH Moses Greeley & Hannah
GREELEY,Elbridge Jackson   Sex:M   15 Nov 1815 Hudson, NH Moses Greeley
   & Mary Derby
GREELEY,Elbridge Osgood   Sex:M   26 Apr 1841 Hudson, NH Seneca Greeley
   & Priscilla Fields
GREELEY,Elizabeth Priscilla   Sex:F   29 Aug 1819 Hudson, NH Seneca Greeley
   & Priscilla Fields
GREELEY,Elizabeth P   Sex:F   29 Aug 1819 Hudson, NH Seneca Greeley & Priscilla
GREELEY,Emily Frances   Sex:F   07 Feb 1837 Hudson, NH Seneca Greeley
   & Priscilla Fields
GREELEY,Emily H Sex:F   07 Jan 18 Hudson, NH Seneca Greeley & Priscilla Fields
GREELEY,Ervin Seneca   Sex:M   30 May 1832 Hudson, NH Seneca Greeley
   & Priscilla Fields
GREELEY,Esther   Sex:F   17 Feb 1750 Hudson, NH Ezekiel Greeley & Esther
GREELEY,Esther   Sex:F   28 Jun 1780 Hudson, NH Zacheus Greeley & Esther
GREELEY,Ezekiel   Sex:M   20 Jan 1786 Hudson, NH Joseph Greeley & Sarah Greeley
GREELEY,Ezekiel Sex:M 21 Oct 1725 Hudson, NH Benjamin Greeley & Ruth Whittier
GREELEY,Ezekiel   Sex:M   20 Jun 1786 Hudson, NH Joseph Greeley & Sarah
GREELEY,Fanny   Sex:F   14 Feb 1790 Hudson, NH Joseph Greeley & Sarah Greeley
GREELEY,Frances Victoria   Sex:F   04 Feb 1839 Hudson, NH Reuben Greeley

HUDSON,NH BIRTHS

  & Joanna C Merrill
GREELEY,Franklin Marston Sex:M 07 Jan 1835 Hudson, NH Seneca Greeley
  & Priscilla Fields
GREELEY,Fred C Sex:M 28 May 1881 Hudson, NH James C Greeley (Hudson, NH)
  & Ida B Smith (Londonderry, NH)
GREELEY,Gilbert Sex:M 30 Jan 1752 Hudson, NH Ezekiel Greeley & Esther
GREELEY,Gilbert Sex:M 10 Nov 1791 Hudson, NH Zacheus Greeley & Esther
GREELEY,Hannah Sex:F 22 Nov 1736 Hudson, NH Samuel Greeley & Rachel
GREELEY,Hannah Sex:F 27 Aug 1747 Hudson, NH Samuel Greeley Jr & Abigail
GREELEY,Hannah Sex:F 01 Oct 1768 Hudson, NH Ezekiel Greeley & Esther
GREELEY,Hannah Sex:F 07 Nov 1795 Hudson, NH Moses Greeley & Mary Derby
GREELEY,Hannah Sex:F 19 Jul 1806 Hudson, NH Moses Greeley & Mary Derby
GREELEY,Harriet Sex:F 04 Mar 1790 Hudson, NH Moses Greeley & Hannah Greeley
GREELEY,Henry Clay Sex:M 15 Oct 1830 Hudson, NH Reuben Greeley
  & Joanna C Merrill
GREELEY,Isaac Sex:M 22 Mar 1787 Hudson, NH Zacheus Greeley & Esther
GREELEY,John Sex:M 26 Apr 1759 Hudson, NH Jonathan Greeley & Ruth
GREELEY,John Sex:M 11 Dec 1783 Hudson, NH Zacheus Greeley & Esther
GREELEY,John T Sex:M 03 Apr 1825 Hudson, NH Reuben Greeley
  & Joanna C Merrill
GREELEY,John Thomas Sex:M 27 Aug 1828 Hudson, NH Reuben Greeley
  & Joanna C Merrill
GREELEY,Jonathan Sex:M 26 Feb 1732 Hudson, NH Samuel Greeley & Rachel
GREELEY,Jonathan Sex:M 25 Apr 1756 Hudson, NH Jonathan Greeley & Ruth
GREELEY,Joseph Sex:M 09 Sep 1756 Hudson, NH Samuel Greeley Jr & Abigail
GREELEY,Joseph Sex:M 22 Dec 1747 Hudson, NH Ezekiel Greeley & Esther
GREELEY,Joseph Sex:M 19 Aug 1750 Hudson, NH Moses Greeley & Mehittable
GREELEY,Joseph Sex:M 03 May 1784 Hudson, NH Joseph Greeley & Sarah Greeley
GREELEY,Joseph Sex:M 07 Jul 1797 Hudson, NH Moses Greeley & Mary Derby
GREELEY,Joseph Sex:M 05 Feb 1652 Hudson, NH Andrew Greeley & Mary Goldmyre
GREELEY,Joseph Sex:M 17 Feb 1697 Hudson, NH Joseph Greeley & Martha Wilford
GREELEY,Joseph Sex:M 18 Feb 1730 Hudson, NH Benjamin Greeley & Ruth Whittier
GREELEY,Joseph S Sex:M (Child #1) 02 Jan 1883 Hudson, NH Samuel A Greeley
  (Hudson, NH) & Susanna C Richardson (Hudson, NH)
GREELEY,Leonard Sex:M 27 Sep 1794 Hudson, NH Zacheus Greeley & Esther
GREELEY,Lewis C Sex:M 01 Jan 1874 Hudson, NH James Greeley & Ella
GREELEY,Lucey Sex:F 27 Apr 1774 Hudson, NH Ezekiel Greeley & Esther
GREELEY,Lucy Sex:F 27 Apr 1774 Hudson, NH Ezekiel Greeley & Esther
GREELEY,Lucy Sex:F 13 Feb 1781 Hudson, NH Joseph Greeley & Sarah Greeley
GREELEY,Lucy Sex:F 03 Sep 1785 Hudson, NH Zacheus Greeley & Esther
GREELEY,Lydia Sex:F 14 Mar 1794 Hudson, NH Wilder Greeley & Lydia
GREELEY,Martha Sex:F 26 Sep 1726 Hudson, NH Samuel Greeley & Rachel
GREELEY,Mary Sex:F 01 Mar 1734 Hudson, NH Samuel Greeley & Rachel
GREELEY,Mary Sex:F 15 Oct 1760 Hudson, NH Samuel Greeley Jr & Abigail
GREELEY,Mary Sex:F 07 Jan 1758 Hudson, NH Ezekiel Greeley & Esther
GREELEY,Mary Sex:F 14 Oct 1757 Hudson, NH Jonathan Greeley & Ruth
GREELEY,Mary Sex:F 01 Apr 1801 Hudson, NH Moses Greeley & Mary Derby
GREELEY,Mary Sex:F 16 Jul 1649 Hudson, NH Andrew Greeley & Mary Goldmyre
GREELEY,Mary Sex:F 17 Nov 1714 Hudson, NH Joseph Greeley & Martha Wilford
GREELEY,Mary H Sex:F 28 Dec 1865 Hudson, NH Edward Dana Greeley &
GREELEY,Mary Hannah Sex:F 31 Oct 1832 Hudson, NH Reuben Greeley
  & Joanna C Merrill
GREELEY,May R Sex:F 28 Dec 1865 Hudson, NH Edward Greeley & Dana
GREELEY,Mehitable Sex:F 01 Oct 1724 Hudson, NH Samuel Greeley & Rachel
GREELEY,Miriam Sex:F 08 Oct 1722 Hudson, NH Samuel Greeley & Rachel
GREELEY,Moody Sex:M 07 Oct 1793 Hudson, NH Wilder Greeley & Lydia
GREELEY,Moses Sex:M 1702 Hudson, NH Joseph Greeley & Martha Wilford
GREELEY,Moses Sex:M 31 Mar 1711 Hudson, NH Joseph Greeley & Martha Wilford
GREELEY,Moses Sex:M 1723 Hudson, NH Benjamin Greeley & Ruth Whittier
GREELEY,Moses Sex:M 18 Dec 1802 Hudson, NH Moses Greeley & Hannah

HUDSON,NH BIRTHS

GREELEY,Moses R   Sex:M   07 Sep 1823 Hudson, NH Reuben Greeley
   & Joanna C Merrill
GREELEY,Moses R   Sex:M   13 Aug 1826 Hudson, NH Reuben Greeley
   & Joanna C Merrill
GREELEY,Moses T D   Sex:M   18 Dec 1802 Hudson, NH Moses Greeley & Mary Derby
GREELEY,Nancy Holland Sex:F 13 Nov 1780 Hudson, NH Samuel Greeley&Olive Read
GREELEY,Nathaniel   Sex:M   14 Mar 1739 Hudson, NH Samuel Greeley & Rachel
GREELEY,Nathaniel   Sex:M   28 Oct 1744 Hudson, NH Samuel Greeley Jr & Abigail
GREELEY,Noah   Sex:M   26 May 1766 Hudson, NH Ezekiel Greeley & Esther
GREELEY,Parker   Sex:M   13 Sep 1796 Hudson, NH Zacheus Greeley & Esther
GREELEY,Philip   Sex:M   21 Sep 1644 Hudson, NH Andrew Greeley & Mary Goldmyre
GREELEY,Polly   Sex:F   29 Sep 1799 Hudson, NH Zacheus Greeley & Esther
GREELEY,Rachel   Sex:F   15 Oct 1729 Hudson, NH Samuel Greeley & Rachel
GREELEY,Rachel   Sex:F   17 Jan 176 Hudson, NH Jonathan Greeley & Ruth
GREELEY,Reuben   Sex:M   08 Jul 1794 Hudson, NH Moses Greeley & Mary Derby
GREELEY,Reuben   Sex:M   18 Jul 1794 Hudson, NH Moses Greeley & Hannah
GREELEY,Salley   Sex:F   30 Jul 1782 Hudson, NH Joseph Greeley & Sarah
GREELEY,Sally   Sex:F   30 Jul 1782 Hudson, NH Joseph Greeley & Sarah Greeley
GREELEY,Samuel   Sex:M   10 May 1721 Hudson, NH Samuel Greeley & Rachel
GREELEY,Samuel   Sex:M   29 Sep 1752 Hudson, NH Samuel Greeley Jr & Abigail
GREELEY,Samuel   Sex:M   04 Jun 1799 Hudson, NH Joseph Greeley & Sarah Greeley
GREELEY,Samuel   Sex:M   22 Dec 1695 Hudson, NH Joseph Greeley & Martha Wilford
GREELEY,Samuel Field   Sex:M   16 Nov 1825 Hudson, NH Seneca Greeley
   & Priscilla Fields
GREELEY,Sarah   Sex:F   09 Apr 1761 Hudson, NH Ezekiel Greeley & Esther
GREELEY,Sarah   Sex:F   25 May 1799 Hudson, NH Wilder Greeley & Lydia
GREELEY,Sarah   Sex:F   25 May 1797 Hudson, NH Wilder Greeley & Lydia
GREELEY,Sarah Ann Elizabeth   Sex:F   25 Jan 1836 Hudson, NH Reuben Greeley
   & Joanna C Merrill
GREELEY,Sarah P   Sex:F   12 Jan 1824 Hudson, NH Seneca Greeley & Priscilla
GREELEY,Sarah Pollard   Sex:F   12 Jan 1824 Hudson, NH Seneca Greeley
   & Priscilla Fields
GREELEY,Seneca   Sex: 29 May 1794 Hudson, NH Joseph Greeley & Sarah Greeley
GREELEY,Senece   Sex:M   29 May 1794 Hudson, NH Joseph Greeley & Sarah
GREELEY,Sophia   Sex:F   15 Feb 1788 Hudson, NH Moses Greeley & Hannah Greeley
GREELEY,Stephen D   Sex:M   10 Sep 1810 Hudson, NH Moses Greeley & Mary Derby
GEELEY,Susan W   Sex:F   21 Dec 1819 Hudson, NH Reuben Greeley
   & Joanna C Merrill
GREELEY,Susanna   Sex:F   19 Apr 1748 Hudson, NH Moses Greeley & Mehittable
GREELEY,Wilder   Sex:M   19 Feb 1771 Hudson, NH Ezekiel Greeley & Esther
GREELEY,Wilford   Sex:M   29 Jan 1659 Hudson, NH Andrew Greeley & Mary Goldmyre
GREELEY,William Sex:M   11 Apr 1704 Hudson, NH Joseph Greeley & Martha Wilford
GREELEY,William Cary   Sex:M   01 Oct 1834 Hudson, NH Reuben Greeley
   & Joanna C Merrill
GREELEY,Zaccheus   Sex:M   27 Nov 1753 Hudson, NH Ezekiel Greeley & Esther
GREELEY,Zacheus   Sex:M   23 Mar 1782 Hudson, NH Zacheus Greeley & Esther
GREELEY,[Unknown]   Sex:M   (Child #4) 01 Sep 1890 James C Greeley (Hudson, NH)
   & Ida Twiss (Londonderry, NH)
GREEN,Jeffrey   Sex:M   05 Feb 1968 Cecil Green Jr & Victoria G Rich
GREENWOOD,Jake Wallace Sex:M 18 Jan 1983 Gary W Greenwood & Carol Ann Pointer
GREENWOOD,Katherine Jeannette   Sex:F   11 Aug 1981 Charles L Greenwood
   & Nancy Ruth Cates
GREENWOOD,Leonard A   Sex:M   06 Nov 1964 Lester S Greenwood & Rita P Spaulding
GREENWOOD,Lester M   Sex:M   16 Sep 1963 Lester S Greenwood & Rita P Spaulding
GREGOIRE,Heather J   Sex:F   19 May 1970 Paul E Gregoire & Jean A Cady
GREGOIRE,Lauren   Sex:F   02 Feb 1981 Paul Curtis Gregoire & Jeri-Ann Pelletier
GREGOIRE,Paula K   Sex:F   27 Jun 1967 Paul E Gregoire & Jean A Cady
GRELE,Abigail   Sex:F   10 Apr 1750 Hudson, NH Samuel Grele & Abigail
GRELE,Benjamin   Sex:M   22 Apr 1756 Hudson, NH Ezekiel Grele & Esther
GRELE,Esther   Sex:F   17 Feb 1749 Hudson, NH Ezekiel Grele & Esther

HUDSON, NH BIRTHS

GRELE, Hannah   Sex:F   22 Aug 1747 Hudson, NH Samuel Grele & Abigail
GRELE, Hannah   Sex:F   27 Nov 1736 Hudson, NH Samuel Grele & Rachel
GRELE, John   Sex:M   26 Apr 1759 Hudson, NH Jonathan Grele & Ruth
GRELE, Jonathan   Sex:M   25 Apr 1776 Hudson, NH Jonathan Grele & Ruth
GRELE, Jonathan   Sex:M   26 Feb 1731 Hudson, NH Samuel Grele & Rachel
GRELE, Joseph   Sex:M   19 Aug 1750 Hudson, NH Moses Grele & Mehitabel
GRELE, Joseph   Sex:M   09 Sep 1756 Hudson, NH Samuel Grele & Abigail
GRELE, Joseph   Sex:M   22 Dec 1747 Hudson, NH Ezekiel Grele & Esther
GRELE, Martha   Sex:F   26 Sep 1726 Hudson, NH Samuel Grele & Rachel
GRELE, Mary   Sex:F   14 Oct 1757 Hudson, NH Jonathan Grele & Ruth
GRELE, Mary   Sex:F   01 Mar 1733 Hudson, NH Samuel Grele & Rachel
GRELE, Mehitable   Sex:F   01 Oct 1724 Hudson, NH Samuel Grele & Rachel
GRELE, Miriam   Sex:F   08 Oct 1722 Hudson, NH Samuel Grele & Rachel
GRELE, Nathaniel   Sex:M   28 Oct 1744 Hudson, NH Samuel Grele & Abigail
GRELE, Nathaniel   Sex:M   14 Mar 1738 Hudson, NH Samuel Grele & Rachel
GRELE, Rachel   Sex:F   15 Oct 1729 Hudson, NH Samuel Grele & Rachel
GRELE, Samuel   Sex:M   29 Sep 1752 Hudson, NH Samuel Grele & Abigail
GRELE, Samuel   Sex:M   10 May 1721 Hudson, NH Samuel Grele & Rachel
GRELE, Susanna   Sex:F   19 Apr 1748 Hudson, NH Moses Grele & Mehitabel
GRELE, Zacheus   Sex:M   27 Nov 1753 Hudson, NH Ezekiel Grele & Esther
GRENIER, Joseph A Henry   Sex:M   (Child #1) 29 Aug 1904 Adelard Grenier
   (Canada) & Marie A Theriault (Canada)
GRENNAN, Damon G   Sex:M   22 Nov 1966 Joseph W Grennan & Eleanor M Dunn
GRENON, [Unknown]   Sex:F   (Child #2) 20 May 1946 Joseph E Grenon (Manchester,
   NH) & Albertine Cossette (Nashua, NH
GRIFFIN, Gardner F   Sex:M   (Child #3) 02 Aug 1905 John E Griffin (Hudson, NH)
   & Rebecca E Cargill (Charlestown, MA)
GRIFFIN, Jennifer Anne   Sex:F   20 Jul 1984 Robert E Griffin Sr
   & Harriet Ursula Page
GRIFFIN, John Rufus   Sex:M   (Child #1) 07 Jan 1896 John E Griffin (Hudson, NH)
   & Rebecca Cargill
GRIFFIN, Linn A   Sex:F   15 May 1860 Hudson, NH Rufus Griffin &
GRIFFIN, Lorena T   Sex:F   15 May 1860 Hudson, NH Rufus K Griffin &
GRIFFIN, Robert Emmett Jr   Sex:M   20 Jul 1984 Robert E Griffin Sr
   & Harriet Ursula Page
GRIFFIN, Sally   Sex:F   24 Mar 1792 Hudson, NH   & Rachel Griffin
GRIFFUS, Jenny L   Sex:F   26 Oct 1977 John W Griffus & Kathleen Michaud
GRIFFUS, Jeremy John   Sex:M 22 Dec 1981 John William Griffus & Kathleen Michaud
GRIFFUS, Kelly Karen   Sex:F   03 Jan 1976 John W Griffus & Kathleen Michaud
GRIGAS, Barbara J   Sex:F   14 Mar 1965 Joseph Grigas & Barbara E Berry
GRIGAS, Gerard F   Sex:M   14 May 1950 Frank J Grigas & Jeannette M St Laurent
GRIGAS, Joseph W   Sex:M   24 Feb 1961 Joseph Grigas & Barbara E Berry
GRIGAS, [Unknown]   Sex:F   01 Feb 1940 Albert P Grigas (Maynard, MA)
   & Elaine A Bouley (Nashua, NH)
GRIMES, Dolly   Sex:F   28 Feb 1802 Hudson, NH Samuel Grimes & Nabby
GRIMES, James M   Sex:M   17 Nov 1800 Hudson, NH Samuel Grimes & Nabby
GRIMES, James Merrill   Sex:M   17 Nov 1800 Hudson, NH Samuel Grimes & Nabby
GRIMES, Rachel M   Sex:F   08 Dec 1804 Hudson, NH Samuel Grimes & Salla
GRIMES, Rachel Marshall   Sex:F   08 Sep 1804 Hudson, NH Samuel Grimes & Nabby
GRIMES, Sally   Sex:F   28 Feb 1803 Hudson, NH Samuel Grimes & Nabbe
GRINSTEIN-CAMAC, Eliana Petrina   Sex:F   22 Oct 1983 David Grinstein
   & Christina E Camacho
GRISSO, Virginia A   Sex:F   07 Apr 1949 Wayne E Grisso & Norma Niedermeyer
GRISSON, Daniel R   Sex:M   08 Sep 1959 Allen G Grisson & Marie-Claire Pelleti
GRISWOLD, Gail A   Sex:F   30 Aug 1955 Robert F Griswold & Laura A Ciarla
GROCHOWSKI, John   Sex:M   (Child #7) 24 Jun 1926 Frank Grochowski (Poland)
   & Nellie Pytka (Poland)
GROCHOWSKI, Sophia   Sex:F   28 Jan 1924 Frank Grochowski (Poland)
   & Auglon Majkaptka (Poland)
GROHESKY, Annie   Sex:F   (Child #4) 08 Jan 1922 Frank Grohesky (Poland)

HUDSON,NH BIRTHS

& Mary Pelcosky (Austria)
GROHOSKY,Anne M   Sex:F   14 Aug 1960 Edward G Grohosky & Claudette A Cote
GROHOSKY,Lydia N Sex:F (Child #3) 26 Apr 1942 George C Grohosky (Nashua, NH)
  & Julia Sazinsky (Nashua, NH)
GROHOSKY,Sheila M   Sex:F   11 May 1969 Victor J Grohosky & Patricia M Frost
GROHOSKY,Steven E   Sex:M   03 Oct 1961 Edward G Grohosky & Claudette A Cote
GROHOSKY,Victor H   Sex:M   14 Jun 1968 Victor J Grohosky & Patricia M Frost
GROLEAU,Michael P   Sex:M   06 Sep 1974 Paul R Groleau & Mary E Cancro
GRONDIN,Allison R   Sex:F   26 Mar 1962 George E Grondin & Ruth E Clermont
GRONDIN,Jerome P   Sex:M   11 Jan 1979 Jacques Y Grondin & Francine M Marchand
GRONDIN,Tracy L   Sex:F   21 Sep 1963 George E Grondin & Ruth E Clermont
GROSSMAN,Jessica Samantha   Sex:F   08 Nov 1979 Charles R Grossman
  & Juliana Brozman
GROVES,Brian Patrick   Sex:M   17 Nov 1981 Robert John Groves
  & Patricia A McLlarky
GROVES,Catherine   Sex:F   13 Mar 1873 Hudson, NH Robert Groves & Elizebeth
GROVES,Ida E   Sex:F   04 Jul 1877 Hudson, NH Robert Groves (Ireland)
  & Elizebeth E (Ireland)
GROVES,James W   Sex:M   02 May 1950 E Stuart Groves & Doris E Clogston
GROVES,Jo-Ann   Sex:F   09 Nov 1953 John S Groves & Phyllis Buxton
GROVES,John S Jr   Sex:M   (Child #1) 24 Nov 1942 John S Groves (Nashua, NH)
  & Phyllis Buxton (Nashua, NH)
GROVES,Judith A   Sex:F   07 Feb 1960 E Stuart Groves & Sheila M Sullivan
GROVES,Katherine Ann   Sex:F   23 Nov 1984 Robert John Groves
  & Patricia A McLlarky
GROVES,Lindsay Rae   Sex:F   21 Feb 1985 Michael W Groves & Sally Ann Stultz
GROVES,Margarett   Sex:F   1864 Hudson, NH Robert Groves &
GROVES,Margarite A   Sex:F   186 Hudson, NH Robert Groves & Elizabeth
GROVES,Reuben S   Sex:M   28 Jul 1893 John C Groves (Lowell, MA)
  & S M Spaulding (Nashua, NH)
GROVES,Richard S   Sex:M   (Child #2) 29 Mar 1946 John S Groves (Nashua, NH)
  & Phyllis Buxton (Nashua, NH)
GROVES,Robert George   Sex:M   03 Oct 1871 Hudson, NH Robert Groves & Elizabeth
GROVES,Robert J   Sex:M   20 Jan 1954 E Stuart Groves & Doris E Clogston
GROVES,Shannon P   Sex:F   08 Dec 1976 James W Groves & Ann Mary Pinard
GROVES,Steven P   Sex:M   02 Oct 1947 John S Groves (Nashua, NH)
  & Phyllis Buxton (Nashua, NH)
GROVES,Stuart L   Sex:M   02 Nov 1947 E Stuart Groves (Nashua, NH)
  & Doris E Clogston (Dracut, MA)
GROVES,Thomas S   Sex:M   29 Apr 1956 E Stuart Groves & Doris E Clogston
GROVES,William H   Sex:M   09 Dec 1866 Hudson, NH Robert Groves & Elizabeth
GROVES,William Henry   Sex:M   09 Dec 1866 Hudson, NH Robert Groves & Elizabeth
GROVES,[Unknown]   Sex:M   (Child #1) 18 Oct 1905 Wm H Groves (Hudson, NH)
  & Minnie Ola Farwell (Newport, VT)
GROVES,[Unknown]   Sex:F   (Child #2) 19 Dec 1907 William H Groves (Hudson, NH)
  & Minnie O Farrell (Newport, VT)
GRUENFELDER,Nancy L   Sex: 28 Sep 1972 James A Gruenfelder
  & Margarite K Regewitz
GRUIZINGA,Paula E   Sex:F   24 Sep 1976 John R Gruizinga & Peggy Ann Morford
GRYGIEL,Jeffrey A   Sex:M   07 Sep 1962 Henry Grygiel & Judith Munson
GRYGIEL,Wendy L   Sex:F   06 Sep 1964 Henry G Grygiel & Judith E Munson
GUARINO,Gerald J Jr   Sex:M   14 Apr 1962 Gerald J Guarino, Sr & Susan L Ford
GUAY,Betty A   Sex:F   20 Feb 1956 Harry A Guay & Amy A Smith
GUAY,Harry R   Sex:M   13 Sep 1950 Harry A Guay & Amy Jacobs
GUAY,Joyce B   Sex:F   (Child #6) 01 Jan 1945 Harry A Guay (Nashua, NH)
  & Amy Jacobs (Nashua, NH)
GUAY,Robert M   Sex:M   08 Feb 1962 Smith S Guay & Lorraine J Doucet
GUAY,Shawn K   Sex:M   04 Jul 1964 Smith S Guay & Lorraine J Doucet
GUAY,Shirley A   Sex:F   14 Jan 1947 Harry A Guay (Nashua, NH)
  & Amy Jacobs (Nashua, NH)

HUDSON,NH BIRTHS

GUAY,Steven R   Sex: 12 Jun 1973 Raymond A Guay Jr & Sandra L Kinville
GUERETTE,Corene E   Sex:F 22 Oct 1967 Richard R Guerette & Paula J Doyle
GUERETTE,Jason J   Sex:M 17 Jan 1977 Ronald D Guerette & Priscilla G Desroche
GUERETTE,Karen A   Sex:F 24 Mar 1972 Leo B Guerette & Norma L Bois
GUERETTE,Samuel L   Sex:M 02 Jul 1976 Leo B Guerette & Norma L Bois
GUERETTE,Therese D   Sex: 05 Sep 1972 Arthur G Guerette & Anita J Asselin
GUERRA,Ann M   Sex:F 21 Jun 1969 Richard J Guerra & Clara J Tiernan
GUERRA,James R   Sex:M 08 Sep 1964 Richard J Guerra & Clara J Tiernan
GUERRA,Joseph F   Sex:M 22 Oct 1965 Richard J Guerra & Clara J Tiernan
GUERRETTE,Michael M Sex:M 28 Jul 1968 Maurice L Guerrette & Sandra L Leonard
GUERRETTE,Susan H   Sex:F 19 Dec 1970 Maurice L Guerrette & Sandra L Leonard
GUERTIN,Mary R L   Sex:F (Child #8) 19 Aug 1913 John B H Guertin (Nashua, NH)
  & Angelina Dueque (Ireland)
GUERTIN,Maurice P A Sex:M (Child #9) 01 May 1915 Hudson, NH John B Guertin
  (Nashua, NH) & Angeline Burque (Nashua, NH)
GUIDICE,Anthony Alan Sex:M 05 Mar 1983   Alan J Guidice & Rosemary A Mancuso
GUILL,James T   Sex:M 24 Aug 1965 Charles F Guill Jr & Jeannette D Jacques
GUILL,John C   Sex:M 27 May 1961 Charles F Guill & Jeannette D Jacques
GUILL,Patricia A Sex:F 26 May 1958 Charles F Guill, Jr & Jeannette D Jacques
GUILLEMETTE,Laura Ann Sex:F 06 Nov 1984 Kenneth L Guillemett
  & Cheryl Ann Landry
GUILLOU,Daniel R   Sex:M   09 Feb 1975 Robert A Guillou & Brenda Jill Lord
GUILLOU,Lisa Jean   Sex:F 24 Mar 1974 Francis J Guillou & Susan Ann Notter
GUILMAIN,Brenda S   Sex:F 03 Sep 1975 Richard P Guilmain & Elaine M Fillion
GUILMAIN,Deberah E   Sex:F 12 Aug 1971 Richard P Guilmain & Elaine M Fillion
GUILMAIN,Jeffrey R   Sex: 03 Dec 1972 Richard P Guilmain & Elaine M Fillion
GUIMOND,Denise A   Sex:F 15 Jan 1966 Alfred P Guimond & Denise D Desclos
GUIMOND,Michael A   Sex:M 25 Aug 1962 David A Guimond & Gabrielle H Guill
GUIRTIN,George Adelarde Sex:M (Child #7) 11 Aug 1911 John Guirtin (Nashua,
  NH) & Angeline Burque (Nashua, NH)
GULLAGE,Thomas S   Sex:M   (Child #2) 19 Jun 1944 Thomas A Gullage
  (Newfoundland) & Faith E Johnson (Hooksett, NH)
GUNNING,Ryen William Sex:M 16 Oct 1983 Steven P Gunning & Debra Jean Wright
GURLEY,Charles A   Sex:M 08 Dec 1962 Johnny A Gurley & Elaine L Paige
GURLEY,Johnny A Jr   Sex:M   13 Aug 1958 Johnny A Gurley & Elaine L Paige
GUTHRIE,Margaret J   Sex:F 27 Jun 1959 Thomas Guthrie & Elaine M Papatolica
GUYETTE,Joyce B   Sex:F 08 Mar 1949 Charles E Guyette & Catherine Brooks
GUYETTE,Margaret A   Sex:F 17 Feb 1950 Charles E Guyette & Catherine N Brooks
HAAS,Benjamin E   Sex:M 08 Jan 1978 Roger E Haas & Meribeth Ann Ratzel
HABETS,David M Jr   Sex:M 18 Jan 1962 David M Hebets, Sr & Gloria J Donovan
HACK,Sargent Page   Sex:M 28 Feb 1769 Hudson, NH   & Elizabeth Hack
HACKETT,Craig L   Sex:M 24 Nov 1971 Robert M Hackett & Elizabeth M Herr
HACKETT,Emily Hazel   Sex:F 23 Jun 1976 Robert R Hackett & Helen L Salls
HACKETT,Kevin M   Sex:M 15 Feb 1961 Robert M Hackett & Elizabeth M Herr
HACKETT,Sharon C   Sex:F 18 May 1965 Robert M Hackett & Elizabeth M Herr
HADLEY,Aaron C   Sex:M 24 Oct 1773 Hudson, NH Stephen Hadley & Anne
HADLEY,Aaron Colby   Sex:M 24 Oct 1773 Hudson, NH Stephen Hadley & Anna
HADLEY,Abijah   Sex:M 15 Feb 1794 Hudson, NH Abijah Hadley & Nabby
HADLEY,Anna   Sex:F 12 Oct 1787 Hudson, NH Stephen Hadley & Anna
HADLEY,Annah   Sex:F 12 Oct 1787 Hudson, NH Stephen Hadley & Annah
HADLEY,Ebenezer   Sex:M 03 Feb 1783 Hudson, NH Eliphalet Hadley Jr & Ruth
HADLEY,Elijah   Sex:M 15 Feb 1795 Hudson, NH Abyah Hadley & Nabbey
HADLEY,Elizabeth Sex:F 08 Jul 1771 Hudson, NH Nehemiah Hadley&Hannah Emerson
HADLEY,Elizabeth   Sex:F 29 Sep 1783 Hudson, NH Moses Hadley & Rebecca
HADLEY,Esther   Sex:F 21 Oct 1781 Hudson, NH Moses Hadley & Rebecca
HADLEY,Esther   Sex:F 21 Oct 1782 Hudson, NH Moses Hadley & Rebecah
HADLEY,Hannah   Sex:F 29 Jan 1765 Hudson, NH Nehemiah Hadley & Hannah Emerson
HADLEY,Hannah   Sex:F 29 Jun 1765 Hudson, NH Nehemiah Hadley & Hannah
HADLEY,Isaac   Sex:M 15 Mar 1790 Hudson, NH Moses Hadley & Rebecca
HADLEY,Isabel   Sex:F 24 Aug 1781 Hudson, NH   & Rachel Merrill

HUDSON,NH BIRTHS

HADLEY,Isabel Merrill   Sex:F   24 Aug 1781 Hudson, NH   & Rachel M Peabody
HADLEY,Joyce   Sex:F   12 Apr 1791 Hudson, NH Eliphalet Hadley Jr & Ruth
HADLEY,Lydia   Sex:F   12 Aug 1794 Hudson, NH Stephen Hadley & Anna
HADLEY,Lydia   Sex:F   24 Dec 1776 Hudson, NH Moses Hadley & Rebecca
HADLEY,Lydia   Sex:F   02 Dec 1776 Hudson, NH Moses Hadley & Rebeccah
HADLEY,Maria A   Sex:F   28 Jun 1799 Hudson, NH Moses Hadley & Rebeccah
HADLEY,Maria Antoinette   Sex:F   28 Jun 1799 Hudson, NH Moses Hadley & Rebecca
HADLEY,Moses   Sex:M   26 Apr 1773 Hudson, NH Nehemiah Hadley & Hannah Emerson
HADLEY,Moses   Sex:M   02 May 1778 Hudson, NH Moses Hadley & Rebecca
HADLEY,Moses   Sex:M   20 Jul 1787 Hudson, NH Moses Hadley & Rebecca
HADLEY,Nehemiah Sex:M 05 Jul 1767 Hudson, NH Nehemiah Hadley & Hannah Emerson
HADLEY,Nehemiah   Sex:M   09 May 1792 Hudson, NH Stephen Hadley & Anna
HADLEY,Parrot   Sex: 28 Jul 1763 Hudson, NH Nehemiah Hadley & Hannah Emerson
HADLEY,Polley   Sex:F   14 Mar 1790 Hudson, NH Stephen Hadley & Annah
HADLEY,Polly   Sex:F   14 Mar 1790 Hudson, NH Stephen Hadley & Anna
HADLEY,Rebecca   Sex:F   25 Feb 1780 Hudson, NH Moses Hadley & Rebecca
HADLEY,Rebecca   Sex:F   22 Jul 1792 Hudson, NH Moses Hadley & Rebecca
HADLEY,Rebeccah   Sex:F   25 Feb 1780 Hudson, NH Moses Hadley & Rebeccah
HADLEY,Rebekeh   Sex:F   22 Jul 1792 Hudson, NH Moses Hadley & Rebekeh
HADLEY,Samuel   Sex:M   18 May 1769 Hudson, NH Nehemiah Hadley & Hannah Emerson
HADLEY,Samuel M   Sex:M   06 May 1820 Hudson, NH Seth Hadley & Sally Blodgett
HADLEY,Samuel P   Sex:M   04 Aug 1794 Hudson, NH Moses Hadley & Rebecka
HADLEY,Samuel Page   Sex:M   04 Aug 1794 Hudson, NH Moses Hadley & Rebecca
HADLEY,Samuel S   Sex:M   12 Nov 1781 Hudson, NH Stephen Hadley & Anna
HADLEY,Samuel Smith   Sex:M   10 Nov 1781 Hudson, NH Stephen Hadley & Anna
HADLEY,Sarah   Sex:F   10 Apr 1776 Hudson, NH Stephen Hadley & Anna
HADLEY,Sarah   Sex:F   26 Sep 1782 Hudson, NH Stephen Hadley & Anna
HADLEY,Sarah   Sex:F   17 Jun 1779 Hudson, NH Eliphalet Hadley Jr & Ruth
HADLEY,Sarah   Sex:F   21 Aug 1818 Hudson, NH Seth Hadley & Sally Blodgett
HADLEY,Seth   Sex:M   25 Feb 1788 Hudson, NH Eliphalet Hadley Jr & Ruth
HADLEY,Seth D   Sex:M   27 Mar 1816 Hudson, NH Seth Hadley & Sarah
HADLEY,Seth Davis   Sex:M   27 Mar 1816 Hudson, NH Seth Hadley & Sally Blodgett
HADLEY,Stephen   Sex:M   16 May 1778 Hudson, NH Stephen Hadley & Anna
HADLEY,Stephen   Sex:M   10 Aug 1778 Hudson, NH Stephen Hadley & Annah
HADLEY,Timothy   Sex:M   12 Mar 1785 Hudson, NH Stephen Hadley & Anna
HADLEY,Timothy   Sex:M   12 Mar 1788 Hudson, NH Stephen Hadley & Annah
HADLEY,Tyler Kelley   Sex:M   29 Apr 1800 Hudson, NH   & Sarah Hadley
HADLEY,William   Sex:M   06 Oct 1785 Hudson, NH Moses Hadley & Rebecca
HADLOCK,Karen B   Sex:F   22 Jun 1979 Kenneth E Hadlock Sr & Susan Anne Stuart
HADLOCK,Laurel L   Sex:F   14 Apr 1969 Glendie S Hadlock & Bertina J Taylor
HAERINCK,Amie Marie   Sex:F   09 Sep 1979 Dennis P Haerinck & Rachel A Gagnon
HAERINCK,Catherine J Sex:F 11 Aug 1964 Joseph R Haerinck
 & Maria M Caltagirone
HAERINCK,Christine M   Sex:F   28 Jun 1978 Donald C Haerinck & Donna M Curran
HAERINCK,Dennis D   Sex:M   17 Jun 1977 Dennis P Haerinck & Rachel A Gagnon
HAERINCK,Dwaine H   Sex:M   20 Nov 1965 Theophile C Haerinck & Stella T Rivard
HAGERT,Judith L   Sex:F   (Child #2) 30 Mar 1945 Edward J Hagert (Baltimore,
 MD) & Emily M Givans (Salisbury, MD)
HAGGERTY,Neil S   Sex:M   09 Sep 1967 Russell O Haggerty & Bridget N O'Flaherty
HAGGETT,Albert B Sex:M   (Child #1) 27 Nov 1945 Albert B Haggett (Concord, NH)
 & Dorothy I Ford (Nashua, NH)
HAGGETT,David A   Sex:M   22 Apr 1958 Raymond A Haggett & Marie E Farley
HAGGETT,Douglas P   Sex:M   17 Aug 1959 Raymond A Haggett & Marie E Farley
HAGGETT,Raymond A Jr   Sex:M   29 Sep 1954 Raymond A Haggett & Marie E Farley
HAIGHT,Debbie L   Sex:F   27 Jul 1963 Clarence W Haight & Frances A Wright
HAIGHT,Randall W   Sex:M   07 Feb 1961 Clarence W Haight,Jr & Frances A Wright
HAIGIS,Brendan Patrick Sex:M   20 Mar 1983 Erwin G Haigis & Christine McNamara
HAIGLER,Brian Richard Sex:M   08 Jul 1981 Richard G Haigler & Louise D LeBoeuf
HAIGLER,David R   Sex:M   01 Sep 1955 George F Haigler & Dora Y Lefebvre
HAIGLER,John L   Sex:M   20 May 1952 George F Haigler & Dora Y Lefebvre

HUDSON, NH BIRTHS

HAIGLER, Michael J   Sex:M   13 Nov 1964 George F Haigler & Dora Y Lefebvre
HAIGLER, Richard G   Sex:M   09 Jan 1954 George F Haigler & Dora Y Lefebvre
HAINES, Elizabeth M Sex:F   07 Dec 1976 Arthur A Haines Jr & Sheila M Forestell
HAINES, Matrina A   Sex:F   16 Dec 1974 Arthur A Haines Jr & Mary S Forestell
HAITHWAITE, David P Sex:M   03 Nov 1959 James Haithwaite, Jr & Dorothy M Paige
HAKKARAINEN, Paul R Jr Sex:M 21 Jan 1978 Paul R Hakkarainen & Donna M Godfrey
HALE, Abner   Sex:M   09 Dec 1786 Hudson, NH Thomas Hale & Sarah
HALE, Deborah A   Sex:F   05 Apr 1969 Robert D Hale & Sandra L Clairmont
HALE, Hannah   Sex:F   Hudson, NH Henry Hale & Mary Bartlett
HALE, Hannah   Sex:F   11 Aug 1799 Hudson, NH Zacheus Hale & Polly Chase
HALE, Henry   Sex:M   21 May 1740 Hudson, NH Henry Hale & Mary Bartlett
HALE, John   Sex:M   Mar 1730 Hudson, NH Henry Hale & Mary Bartlett
HALE, John   Sex:M   25 Jun 1762 Hudson, NH John Hale & Sarah H Severance
HALE, John   Sex:M   25 Jun 17 Hudson, NH John Hale & Sarah
HALE, Lewis   Sex:M   11 Apr 1788 Hudson, NH John Hale Jr & Hannah
HALE, Lydia   Sex:F   13 Mar 1789 Hudson, NH Thomas Hale & Sarah
HALE, Margaret   Sex:F   Hudson, NH Henry Hale & Mary Bartlett
HALE, Mary   Sex:F   Hudson, NH Henry Hale & Mary Bartlett
HALE, Molley   Sex:F   30 aug 1784 Hudson, NH Thomas Hale & Sarah
HALE, Molly   Sex:F   30 Aug 1784 Hudson, NH Thomas Hale & Sarah
HALE, Moody   Sex:M   17 Sep 1771 Hudson, NH John Hale & Sarah H Severance
HALE, Nathaniel   Sex:M   20 Apr 1767 Hudson, NH John Hale & Sarah H Severance
HALE, Polley   Sex:F   22 Dec 1797 Hudson, NH Zacheus Hale & Polley
HALE, Polly   Sex:F   22 Dec 1797 Hudson, NH Zacheus Hale & Polly Chase
HALE, Richard   Sex:M   10 Sep 1749 Hudson, NH Henry Hale & Mary Bartlett
HALE, Sarah   Sex:F   Mar 1732 Hudson, NH Henry Hale & Mary Bartlett
HALE, Sarah   Sex:F   20 Apr 1767 Hudson, NH John Hale & Sarah H Severance
HALE, Sarah   Sex:F   06 Mar 1790 Hudson, NH John Hale Jr & Hannah
HALE, Sewell   Sex:M   13 Dec 1791 Hudson, NH Thomas Hale & Sarah
HALE, Thomas   Sex:M   1743 Hudson, NH Henry Hale & Mary Bartlett
HALE, Thomas   Sex:M   18 Sep 1764 Hudson, NH John Hale & Sarah H Severance
HALETKY, Edward L   Sex:M   29 Apr 1966 Gerald E Haletky & Ann W Bryan
HALETKY, Eileen L   Sex:F   15 Aug 1969 Gerald E Haletky & Ann W Bryan
HALEY, Colin C   Sex:M   12 Oct 1971 John A Haley & Barbara J Barno
HALEY, Ryan D   Sex:M   13 Feb 1975 John A Haley & Barbara J Barno
HALL, Christopher C   Sex:M   04 Oct 1964 Charles E Hall & Linda P Knapp
HALL, Christopher R   Sex:M   31 May 1976 Robert R Hall & Tristen H Leavis
HALL, Erin Elizabeth   Sex:F   23 Mar 1978 Robert R Hall & Tristen H Leavis
HALL, Gregory Richard Sex:M 19 Nov 1979 Robert R Hall & Tristen Helen Leavis
HALL, Ida Carter Sex:F 25 Sep 1875 Hudson, NH Charles Hall & Clara F Flagg
HALL, James Francis Sex:M 09 Dec 1983 Terry Maurice Hall & Patricia A Kingston
HALL, John   Sex:M   26 Feb 1779 Hudson, NH John Hall & Alice
HALL, Patricia A   Sex:F   07 Apr 1961 Gilbert M Hall & Norine P Gosselin
HALL, Randy A   Sex:M   03 Sep 1968 Gilbert M Hall & Norine P Gosselin
HALL, Thomas   Sex:M   02 Feb 1780 Hudson, NH John Hall & Alice
HALL, Thomas   Sex:M   21 Feb 1780 Hudson, NH John Hall & Alice
HALLIBURTON, Kimberly L Sex:F 02 Sep 1966 Dennis L Halliburton&Sharon K Jordan
HALLOWELL, Patrick A Sex:M 09 Feb 1977 Dale M Hallowel & Victoria Sue Wing
HALVERSON, Richard R   Sex:M   24 May 1964 Richard G Halverson
  & MaryEllen Wigglesworth
HAMBLEN, Stephen J   Sex:M   05 Oct 1956 John B Hamblen & Mary P Everson
HAMBLET, Addie M   Sex:F   20 Oct 1865 Hudson, NH Alvin Hamblet & Almira
HAMBLET, Asa   Sex:M   11 Oct 1758 Hudson, NH Hezekiah Hamblet & Mehitable
HAMBLET, Betsey M   Sex:F   25 Nov 1814 Hudson, NH Joseph Hamblet & Hannah
HAMBLET, Betty   Sex:F   23 Jan 1775 Hudson, NH Thomas Hamblet & Elizabeth
HAMBLET, Eli   Sex:M   12 May 1810 Hudson, NH Thomas Hamblet & Tamra
HAMBLET, Elizabeth   Sex:F   17 May 1761 Hudson, NH Hezekiah Hamblet & Mehitabel
HAMBLET, Fanne Greeley   Sex:F   10 Jan 1795 Hudson, NH Samuel Hamblet & Naomi
HAMBLET, Friend M   Sex:F   22 Mar 1787 Hudson, NH Thomas Hamblet & Elizabeth
HAMBLET, Hannah A   Sex:M   14 Jan 1824 Hudson, NH Joseph Hamblet & Hannah

HUDSON, NH BIRTHS

HAMBLET,Hejekiah Sex:M 22 Jun 1756 Hudson, NH Hejekiah Hamblet & Mehitable
HAMBLET,Jonathan Sex:M 05 Feb 1753 Hudson, NH Hajekiah Hamblet & Mehitable
HAMBLET,Joseph Sex:M 30 Aug 1795 Hudson, NH Thomas Hamblet & Elizebeth
HAMBLET,Josiah E Sex:M 06 Dec 1820 Hudson, NH Joseph Hamblet & Hannah
HAMBLET,Martha Sex:F 28 Aug 1762 Hudson, NH Thomas Hamblet & Elizabeth
HAMBLET,Mary E Sex:F 27 Jan 1867 Hudson, NH Alvan D Hamblet & Almira
HAMBLET,Mehitable Sex:F 16 Oct 1746 Hudson, NH Hajekiah Hamblet & Mehitable
HAMBLET,Molle Sex:F 23 Apr 1750 Hudson, NH Hajekiah Hamblet & Mehitable
HAMBLET,Nellie Lucinda Sex:F 22 Feb 1870 Hudson, NH Daniel Hamblet & Sarah E
HAMBLET,Olive Sex:M 28 Feb 1766 Hudson, NH Hajekiah Hamblet & Mehitable
HAMBLET,Philip Sex:M 02 Jun 1785 Hudson, NH Thomas Hamblet & Elizabeth
HAMBLET,Samuel Sex:M 23 Jul 1763 Hudson, NH Hajekiah Hamblet & Mehitable
HAMBLET,Thomas Sex:M 21 Jun 1780 Hudson, NH Thomas Hamblet & Elizabeth
HAMBLET,William Sex:M 26 Jun 1748 Hudson, NH Hajekiah Hamblet & Mehitable
HAMBLETT,Addie M Sex:F 20 Oct 1865 Hudson, NH Alvin Hamblett & Almira
HAMBLETT,Alvin Sex:M   Hudson, NH Thomas Hamblett & Farna Gibson
HAMBLETT,Arvilla Sex: 28 Aug 1852 Hudson, NH Eli Hamblett & Rebecca Butler
HAMBLETT,Asa Sex:M 11 Oct 1758 Hudson, NH Hezekiah Hamblett
 & Mehitable Greeley
HAMBLETT,Bertha M Sex:F 15 Jun 1872 Hudson, NH Alvin Hamblett & Almira
HAMBLETT,Betsey Maria Sex:F 25 Nov 1814 Hudson, NH Josiah Hamblett
 & Hannah Buttrick
HAMBLETT,Betty Sex:F 23 Jan 1775 Hudson, NH Thomas Hamblett & Elizabeth
HAMBLETT,Bruce L Sex:M   21 Sep 1947 Leonard L Hamblett (Hudson, NH)
 & Lorraine G Plantier (Manchester, NH)
HAMBLETT,David A Sex:M 29 Dec 1958 David H Hamblett & Beatrice E Harvey
HAMBLETT,Diane B Sex:F 04 Mar 1951 David H Hamblett & Zara Zottu
HAMBLETT,Dorcas Sex:F   Hudson, NH Thomas Hamblett & Farna Gibson
HAMBLETT,Doris Arline Sex:F (Child #5) 23 May 1927 Aaron L Hamblett
 (Nashua, NH) & Margaret Munroe (Nashua, NH)
HAMBLETT,Drusilla Sex:F   Hudson, NH Thomas Hamblett & Farna Gibson
HAMBLETT,Ed Sex:M   Hudson, NH Alvin Hamblett & Almira
HAMBLETT,Eli Sex:M 12 May 1810 Hudson, NH Thomas Hamblett & Farna Gibson
HAMBLETT,Elizabeth Sex:F 17 May 176 Hudson, NH Hezekiah Hamblett
 & Mehitable Greeley
HAMBLETT,Elizabeth Sex:F 13 Mar 1738 Hudson, NH Joseph Hamblett
 & Susanna Durant
HAMBLETT,Elizabeth Sex:F 12 Mar 1738 Hudson, NH Joseph Hamblett & Susanna
HAMBLETT,Fanny Greeley Sex:F 10 Jan 1795 Hudson, NH Samuel Hamblett & Naomi
HAMBLETT,Friend Moody Sex: 22 Mar 1787 Hudson, NH Thomas Hamblett & Elizabeth
HAMBLETT,Gilbert Sex:M   Hudson, NH Thomas Hamblett & Farna Gibson
HAMBLETT,Grace L Sex:F 04 Jul 1875 Hudson, NH Horace Hamblett &
HAMBLETT,Hannah Augusta Sex:F 14 Jan 1821 Hudson, NH Josiah Hamblett
 & Hannah Buttrick
HAMBLETT,Hezekiah Sex:M 22 Jun 1756 Hudson, NH Hezekiah Hamblett
 & Mehitable Greeley
HAMBLETT,Janice N Sex:F 05 Jun 1951 Leonard L Hamblett & Marie V Plantier
HAMBLETT,John Sex:M 14 Aug 1745 Hudson, NH Joseph Hamblett & Susanna Durant
HAMBLETT,John D Sex:M 18 Apr 1777 Hudson, NH Thomas Hamblett & Elizabeth
HAMBLETT,John Durant Sex:M 08 Apr 1777 Hudson, NH Thomas Hamblett & Elizabeth
HAMBLETT,Jonathan Sex:M 05 Feb 1753 Hudson, NH Hezekiah Hamblett
 & Mehitable Greeley
HAMBLETT,Joseph Sex:M 05 Apr 1743 Hudson, NH Joseph Hamblett & Susanna Durant
HAMBLETT,Joseph Sex:M 30 Aug 1795 Hudson, NH Thomas Hamblett & Elizabeth
HAMBLETT,Joseph Sex:M   Hudson, NH Thomas Hamblett & Farna Gibson
HAMBLETT,Josiah E Sex:M 06 Dec 1819 Hudson, NH Josiah Hamblett
 & Hannah Buttrick
HAMBLETT,Joyce E Sex:F 02 Jan 1955 David H Hamblett & Beatrice E Harvey
HAMBLETT,Leonard Luther Sex:M (Child #4) 15 Dec 1923 Aaron L Hamblett
 (Manchester, NH) & Margaret Munroe (Nashua, NH)

HUDSON,NH BIRTHS

HAMBLETT,Leonard P   Sex:M   18 Oct 1948 Leonard L Hamblett (Hudson, NH)
  & Lorraine Plantier (Manchester, NH)
HAMBLETT,Lina M Sex:F   03 May 1880 Hudson, NH Wilber D Hamblett (Pelham, NH)
  & Sarah J Coburn (Dracut, MA)
HAMBLETT,Martha   Sex:F   08 Aug 1762 Hudson, NH Thomas Hamblett & Martha
HAMBLETT,Mary Ellen   Sex:F   27 Jan 1867 Hudson, NH Alvin Hamblett & Almira
HAMBLETT,Mehitable   Sex:F   16 Oct 1746 Hudson, NH Hezekiah Hamblett
  & Mehitable Greeley
HAMBLETT,Miriam   Sex:F   03 Feb 1745 Hudson, NH Hezekiah Hamblett
  & Mehitable Greeley
HAMBLETT,Miriam   Sex:F   06 Feb 1744 Hudson, NH Hejekiah Hamblett & Mehitabel
HAMBLETT,Molly   Sex:F   23 Apr 1750 Hudson, NH Hezekiah Hamblett
  & Mehitable Greeley
HAMBLETT,Olive   Sex:F   28 Feb 1766 Hudson, NH Hezekiah Hamblett
  & Mehitable Greeley
HAMBLETT,Philip   Sex:M   02 Jun 1783 Hudson, NH Thomas Hamblett & Elizabeth
HAMBLETT,Rebecca Souvina   Sex:F   20 Aug 1845 Hudson, NH Eli Hamblett
  & Rebecca Butler
HAMBLETT,Reuben Sex:M 11 Oct 1732 Hudson, NH Joseph Hamblett & Susanna Durant
HAMBLETT,Reuben P   Sex:M   11 Nov 1824 Hudson, NH Josiah Hamblett
  & Hannah Buttrick
HAMBLETT,Richard J   Sex:M   29 Jun 1952 Leonard L Hamblett & Lorraine Plantier
HAMBLETT,Samuel   Sex:M   23 Jul 1763 Hudson, NH Hezekiah Hamblett
  & Mehitable Greeley
HAMBLETT,Sarah   Sex:F   19 Jun 1790 Hudson, NH Thomas Hamblett & Elizabeth
HAMBLETT,Sarah Ann   Sex:F   24 Oct 1826 Hudson, NH Josiah Hamblett
  & Hannah Buttrick
HAMBLETT,Sharon L   Sex:F   17 Feb 1953 David H Hamblett & Beatrice E Harvey
HAMBLETT,Susanah   Sex:F   13 May 1736 Hudson, NH Joseph Hamblett & Susanah
HAMBLETT,Susanna   Sex:F 13 May 1736 Hudson, NH Joseph Hamblett
  & Susanna Durant
HAMBLETT,Thomas Sex:M 01 Dec 1740 Hudson, NH Joseph Hamblett & Susanna Durant
HAMBLETT,Thomas   Sex:M   21 Jun 1780 Hudson, NH Thomas Hamblett & Elizabeth
HAMBLETT,William   Sex:M   26 Jun 1748 Hudson, NH Hezekiah Hamblett
  & Mehitable Greeley
HAMBLETT,Willis   Sex:M   Hudson, NH Alvin Hamblett & Almira
HAMBLETT,[Unknown]   Sex:M   28 Jun 1767 Hudson, NH Thomas Hamblett & Martha
HAMEL,Jeffrey John Sex:M 03 Nov 1980 John Wilfred Hamel & Janet Lee Severance
HAMELL,William W   Sex:M   28 Feb 1863 Hudson, NH John Hamell & Charlotte
HAMILTON,Edith Bell   Sex:F   (Child #1) 06 Oct 1902 L C Hamilton (Dedham, MA)
  & Ida Durrant (Londonderry, NH)
HAMILTON,Erin K   Sex:F   01 Nov 1962 James D Hamilton & Florence R Vickery
HAMILTON,Ira Devine Sex:M   (Child #5) 27 Mar 1911 Leonard Hamilton (Dedham,
  MA) & Ida Durant (Londonderry, NH)
HAMILTON,Kerri E   Sex:F   02 Jul 1967 James D Hamilton & Florence R Vickery
HAMILTON,Michael S   Sex:M   18 Feb 1969 Paul D Hamilton & Beverly A Fortier
HAMILTON,Vicki L   Sex:F   08 Jan 1964 James D Hamilton & Florence R Vickery
HAMILTON,[Unknown]   Sex:M   (Child #4) 09 Oct 1909 Leonard C Hamilton
  (Dedham, MA) & Ida M Durant (Londonderry, NH)
HAMLET,Mabel M   Sex:F   10 May 1870 Hudson, NH Horace L Hamlet & Lavinia L
HAMLET,[Unknown]   Sex:M   28 Jan 1874 Hudson, NH Horace Hamlet & Lavinia D
HAMLIN,Harold   Sex:M   (Child #8) 18 Jan 1904 Willard Hamlin (New York)
  & Marie L Gauthier (Canada)
HAMLIN,[Unknown]   Sex:M   (Child #3) 18 Sep 1899 Frank Hamlin (Middlesex, VT)
  & Anna G Fitts (Dunbarton)
HAMM,Carlton A   Sex:M   07 Mar 1966 Carlton E Hamm & Lucy M Novello
HAMMAR,Elizabeth Ann Sex:F 22 Oct 1976 Michael F Hammar & Cynthia Jean Peters
HAMMAR,Jamie L L   Sex:F   18 Nov 1965 John A Hammar & Geraldine G Boucher
HAMMAR,Marcella A   Sex:F   10 May 1958 John A Hammar & Geraldine G Boucher
HAMMAR,Mary C   Sex:F   07 Aug 1964 John A Hammar & Geraldine G Boucher

HUDSON, NH BIRTHS

HAMMILL, William W   Sex:M   28 Feb 1863 Hudson, NH John Hammill & Charlotte
HAMMOND, Benj Walker   Sex:M   (Child #1) 08 Jun 1934 Claude E Hammond
  (Schenectady, NY) & Louise Walker (Sanford, ME)
HAMMOND, David Aldero Sex:M   (Child #8) 13 Jun 1931 Lewis Hammond (Freeport,
  ME) & Gladys Blood (Whitman, MA)
HAMMOND, David G   Sex:M   (Child #1) 05 Dec 1942 Leon G Hammond (Worcester, MA)
  & Gertrude B Harris (Wilmington, MA)
HAMMOND, Don Gordon Sex:M   (Child #7) 11 Apr 1926 Lewis F Hammond (Freeport,
  ME) & Gladys F Blood (Whitman, MA)
HAMMOND, Verne Alton   Sex:M   (Child #2) 15 Oct 1909 Harvey L Hammond (Boston,
  MA) & Ina Martin (Hudson, NH)
HAMMOND, Victoria E C   Sex:F   30 Mar 1985 Rodney Hammond & Judith B Fielden
HAMSON, David Bartlett Sex:M 26 Aug 1984 Donald B Hamson & Kathleen Mary Shea
HANEKE, Joseph W Jr   Sex:M   06 Apr 1964 Joseph W Haneke & Jacqueline K Olsson
HANEKE, Pamela K   Sex:F   09 Feb 1963 Joseph W Haneke & Jacqueline Olsson
HANNAFORD, Carole Anne   Sex:F   (Child #1) 06 Jan 1938 Winthrop H Hannaford
  (S Portland, ME) & Anne Eliz Harwood (Hudson, NH)
HANNAH, Jeffrey P   Sex:M   28 Jul 1963 Frederick A Hannah & Karen A Caron
HANNAH, Pamela E   Sex:F   04 Aug 1965 Frederick A Hannah & Karen A Caron
HANSCOM, Charles Herbert   Sex:M   (Child #4) 18 Apr 1904 Charles H Hanscom
  (Somersworth, NH) & Effie Ann Smith (Albany, NY
HANSCOM, Dorothy Francis   Sex:F   (Child #6) 10 Jul 1909 Charles H Hanscom
  (Somersworth, NH) & Effie M Smith (Albany, NH)
HANSCOM, Ella M   Sex:F   (Child #1) 16 Sep 1898 Chas H Hanscom (Somersworth)
  & Effie M Smith (Albany, NH)
HANSCOM, Lewis G   Sex:M   (Child #5) 02 Jun 1906 Charles H Hanscom
  (Somersworth, NH) & Effie M Smith (Albany, NH)
HANSCOMB, Delia May   Sex:F   17 Aug 1874 Hudson, NH John Hanscomb & Matice
HANSCOMB, Nettie Everline   Sex:F   (Child #2) 11 Mar 1900 Charles H Hanscomb
  (Somersworth, NH) & Effie M Smith (Albany, NH)
HANSON, Richard Martin   Sex:M   (Child #1) 14 Dec 1917 Maurice Hanson (Canada)
  & Evanline Lesesione (Nashua, NH)
HARDY, Abigail   Sex:F   14 Nov 1764 Hudson, NH Nathaniel Hardy & Esther
HARDY, Abigail   Sex:F   10 Mar 1780 Hudson, NH Richard Hardy & Lydia
HARDY, Anna   Sex:F   25 Mar 1745 Hudson, NH Jonathan Hardy & Sarah
HARDY, Asa   Sex:M   15 Sep 1780 Hudson, NH Jonathan Hardy & Frances
HARDY, Benjamin   Sex:M   12 Jul 1799 Hudson, NH Jonathan Hardy & Frances
HARDY, Bethiah   Sex:F   01 Oct 1762 Hudson, NH Nathaniel Hardy & Esther
HARDY, Betsey   Sex:F   09 Sep 1776 Hudson, NH Jonathan Hardy & Frances
HARDY, Betty   Sex:F   04 Jan 1790 Hudson, NH Jonathan Hardy & Frances
HARDY, Betty   Sex:F   09 Sep 1776 Hudson, NH Jonathan Hardy & Frances
HARDY, Carl A   Sex:M   08 Aug 1970 Donald A Hardy & Cecile J Blais
HARDY, Charles   Sex:M   (Child #11) 05 Oct 1934 Robert Hardy (W Boylston, MA)
  & Bertha Moore (Lee, NH)
HARDY, Clara Augusta   Sex:F   Hudson, NH Paul Hardy & Mary Kendall
HARDY, Cynthia A   Sex:F   02 Dec 1953 John R Hardy & Elaine O Esty
HARDY, Daniel Merrill   Sex:M   09 May 1820 Hudson, NH Zachariah Hardy
  & Hannah Hadlock
HARDY, David M   Sex:M   09 May 1820 Hudson, NH Zachariah Hardy & Hannah
HARDY, Donald A   Sex:M   23 Jun 1947 Robert E Hardy (Durham, NH)
  & Ruth A Campbell (Nashua, NH)
HARDY, Dorcas   Sex:F   06 Sep 1816 Hudson, NH Zachariah Hardy & Hannah Hadlock
HARDY, Elise D   Sex:F   14 Mar 1975 Donald A Hardy & Cecile J Blais
HARDY, Eric C   Sex:M   12 Feb 1968 Charles H Hardy & Margery L Bailey
HARDY, Esther   Sex:F   14 Apr 1767 Hudson, NH Nathaniel Hardy & Esther
HARDY, Esther   Sex:F   06 Sep 1780 Hudson, NH Daniel Hardy & Esther
HARDY, Esther   Sex:F   20 Oct 1792 Hudson, NH Jonathan Hardy & Frances
HARDY, Fred B Jr   Sex:M   18 Feb 1961 Fred B Hardy, Sr & Frances H Morton
HARDY, Hannah   Sex:F   16 Apr 1772 Hudson, NH Nathaniel Hardy & Esther
HARDY, Hannah   Sex:F   10 Oct 1777 Hudson, NH Richard Hardy & Lydia

HUDSON, NH BIRTHS

HARDY, Hannah Sex:F 19 Dec 1810 Hudson, NH Zachariah Hardy & Hannah Hadlock
HARDY, Hannah Elizabeth Sex:F 07 Aug 1838 Hudson, NH Paul Hardy & Mary Gould
HARDY, Isaac Sex:M 23 May 1784 Hudson, NH Isaac Hardy & Lydia
HARDY, John Sex:M 05 Mar 1743 Hudson, NH Jonathan Hardy & Sarah
HARDY, John Sex:M 17 Aug 1778 Hudson, NH Jonathan Hardy & Frances
HARDY, John Sex:M 11 Aug 1806 Hudson, NH Zacariah Hardy & Hannah
HARDY, John P Sex:M 03 Mar 1791 Hudson, NH Richard Hardy & Lydia
HARDY, John Peters Sex:M 03 Mar 1791 Hudson, NH Richard Hardy & Lydia
HARDY, John Pollard Sex:M 11 Aug 1806 Hudson, NH Zachariah Hardy
 & Hannah Hadlock
HARDY, Jonathan Sex:M 03 Oct 1795 Hudson, NH Jonathan Hardy & Frances
HARDY, Joseph Sex:M 06 May 1775 Hudson, NH Daniel Hardy & Esther
HARDY, Joyce Ethel Sex:F (Child #2) 29 Oct 1934 Russell Hardy (Nashua, NH)
 & Birdena Wheelock (Ft Kent, ME)
HARDY, Judith E Sex:F 12 Mar 1955 John R Hardy & Elaine O Esty
HARDY, Judith Mae Sex:F (Child #1) 29 Oct 1934 Russell Hardy (Nashua, NH)
 & Birdena Wheelock (Ft Kent, ME)
HARDY, Lavina Sex:F 21 Aug 1798 Hudson, NH Zachariah Hardy & Hannah Hadlock
HARDY, Levine Sex:M 21 Aug 1798 Hudson, NH Zacariah Hardy & Hannah
HARDY, Loren R Sex:M (Child #1) 18 May 1942 Robert E Hardy (Durham, NH)
 & Ruth A Campbell (Nashua, NH)
HARDY, Lydia Sex:F 17 Jun 1787 Hudson, NH Isaac Hardy & Lydia
HARDY, Mary Sex:F 18 Apr 1780 Hudson, NHM Isaac Hardy & Lydia
HARDY, Mary Adaline Sex:F 19 Jul 1829 Hudson, NH Paul Hardy & Mary Gould
HARDY, Mary J Sex:F 17 Jan 1819 Hudson, NH Zachariah Hardy & Hannah
HARDY, Mary Jane Sex:F 17 Jan 1819 Hudson, NH Zachariah Hardy & Hannah Hadlock
HARDY, Michael A Sex:M 02 Feb 1958 Charles H Hardy & Margery L Bailey
HARDY, Molly Sex:F 22 Aug 1786 Hudson, NH Jonathan Hardy & Frances
HARDY, Nathaniel Sex:M 13 Mar 1812 Hudson, NH Zachariah Hardy & Hannah Hadlock
HARDY, Parskel E Sex:M 28 Sep 1801 Hudson, NH Zacariah Hardy & Hannah
HARDY, Paskel E Sex: 28 Sep 1801 Hudson, NH Zachariah Hardy & Hannah Hadlock
HARDY, Paul Otis Sex:M 1836 Hudson, NH Paul Hardy & Mary Gould
HARDY, Phebe Sex:F 12 Mar 1782 Hudson, NH Isaac Hardy & Lydia
HARDY, Reuben Sex:M 02 May 1779 Hudson, NH Daniel Hardy & Esther
HARDY, Reuben Sex:M 21 Oct 1780 Hudson, NH Moody Hardy & Hannah Wicom
HARDY, Ruben Sex:M 02 May 1779 Hudson, NH Daniel Hardy & Esther
HARDY, Sarah Sex:F 06 Oct 1772 Hudson, NH Daniel Hardy & Esther
HARDY, Sarah Sex:F 08 Feb 1788 Hudson, NH Richard Hardy & Lydia
HARDY, Sarah Sex:F 09 Oct 1783 Hudson, NH Jonathan Hardy & Frances
HARDY, Sarah Sex:F 04 May 1814 Hudson, NH Zachariah Hardy & Hannah Hadlock
HARDY, Stephen A Sex:M 04 Sep 1965 Fred B Hardy & Frances H Morton
HARDY, Susan Martine Sex:F   Hudson, NH Paul Hardy & Mary Kendall
HARDY, Susanna Sex:F 17 Jul 1777 Hudson, NH Daniel Hardy & Esther
HARDY, Thomas Sex:M 19 Aug 1782 Hudson, NH Richard Hardy & Lydia
HARDY, Thomas W Sex:M 19 Mar 1779 Hudson, NH Moody Hardy & Hannah
HARDY, Thomas Wicom Sex:M 29 Mar 1779 Hudson, NH Moody Hardy & Hannah Wicom
HARDY, Tim J Sex:M 18 Oct 1959 John R Hardy & Elaine O Estey
HARDY, Tom R Sex:M 11 Jul 1958 John R Hardy & Elaine O Esty
HARDY, William Sex:M 08 Jun 1785 Hudson, NH Richard Hardy & Lydia
HARDY, Zacariah H Sex:M 21 Aug 1805 Hudson, NH Zachariah Hardy & Hannah
HARDY, Zachariah Sex:M 12 Oct 1769 Hudson, NH Nathaniel Hardy & Esther
HARDY, Zachariah K Sex:M 21 Aug 1805 Hudson, NH Zachariah Hardy&Hannah Hadlock
HARITAS, Christina J Sex:F 12 Jul 1968 William D Haritas & Beverly A Nolet
HARITAS, Michael D Sex:M 08 Jun 1965 William D Haritas & Beverly A Nolet
HARITAS, Sherri L Sex:F 29 Jul 1971 William D Haritas & Beverly A Nolet
HARMON, Brian E Sex:M 19 Jun 1968 Roland F Harmon Jr & Jeanie Dufton
HARMON, Michael John Sex:M 13 Nov 1983 Carl Dana Harmon & Marlene Dawn Mason
HARRIGAN, Karen J Sex:F 15 Apr 1970 John D Harrigan II & Belinda J Ramirez
HARRIMAN, Dennis W Sex:M 04 Feb 1954 Wallace B Harriman & Diana G Sutcliffe
HARRINGTON, Frank N Sex:M 26 Jan 1972 Rodney E Harrington & Clara J Thornton

HUDSON,NH BIRTHS

HARRIS,Albert Henry Sex:M   27 Oct 1842 Hudson, NH Albert Harris
  & Sarah F Williamson
HARRIS,Amy R Sex:F   16 Nov 1962 Douglas A Harris & Ruth M Stockbridge
HARRIS,Brooke Taylor Sex:F 05 Feb 1983 Robert C Harris & Kathleen Mary Burke
HARRIS,Charles Austin Sex:M   23 Jan 1847 Hudson, NH Albert Harris
  & Sarah F Williamson
HARRIS,David A Sex:M   21 Jan 1966 Douglas A Harris & Ruth M Stockbridge
HARRIS,Donald Sex:M (Child #1) 19 Oct 1919 Fred Harris (Littleton, NH)
  & Cora Smith (S Royalton, VT)
HARRIS,Edward Page Sex:M   11 Jun 1834 Hudson, NH Albert Harris
  & Sarah F Williamson
HARRIS,Hannah Catherine Sex:F   17 Apr 1836 Hudson, NH Albert Harris
  & Sarah F Williamson
HARRIS,Harriet Amanda Sex:F   22 Oct 1844 Hudson, NH Albert Harris
  & Sarah F Williamson
HARRIS,Heidi E Sex:F   19 Mar 1960 Douglas A Harris & Ruth M Stockbridge
HARRIS,Jennifer Parker Sex:F 27 Apr 1984 John T Harris & Lisa Parker Reece
HARRIS,Kristine L Sex:F   13 Oct 1951 Leo Harris & Mary K Fitzpatrick
HARRIS,Lydia Frances Sex:F   06 Aug 1840 Hudson, NH Albert Harris
  & Sarah F Williamson
HARRIS,Myron Winslow Sex:M   09 Jul 1838 Hudson, NH Albert Harris
  & Sarah F Williamson
HARRIS,Noreen A Sex:F   17 Dec 1953 Leo Harris & Mary K Fitzpatrick
HARRIS,Phillip D Sex:M   06 Nov 1961 Douglas A Harris & Ruth M Stockbridge
HARRIS,Viola Sex:F   Aug 1870 Hudson, NH Henry A Harris & Dora
HARROLD,Timothy P Sex:M   01 Dec 1961 James D Harrold & Nancy R Rich
HARRON,Derek R Sex:M   07 Dec 1974 Ralph T Harron Sr & Laura L Coll
HARRON,Kelly Ann Sex:F   17 Aug 1977 Ralph R Harron Sr & Laura Lee Coll
HART,Amanda Leigh Sex:F   12 Feb 1982 Dana Tracy Hart & Diane Susan McLean
HARTT,Thomas Douglas Jr Sex:M   09 Sep 1983 Thomas D Hartt Sr
  & Anne Stanisiawscwk
HARTWELL,Lee A Sex:F   18 Nov 1968 Wayne B Hartwell & Betty J Jessee
HARTZ,Carrie Michelle Sex:F 12 Nov 1982 Claude Edwin Hartz & Maureen Griffin
HARTZ,Melanie Maureen Sex:F 17 Oct 1980 Claude Edwin Hartz & Maureen Griffin
HARVEY,Harold Davis Sex:M (Child #9) 04 Sep 1901 Hudson, NH John F Harvey
  (Freedom) & Maud Parmenter (Nashua, NH)
HARVEY,Jamie L Sex:F   13 Sep 1967 James A Harvey & Lorraine J Corgin
HARVEY,Jeffrey E Sex:M   01 Feb 1955 Harlan R Harvey & Lois M McCormack
HARVEY,Marion P Sex:F (Child #6) 11 Dec 1891 John F Harvey (Freedom, NH)
  & Maude Parmenter (Nashua, NH)
HARVEY,Steven E Sex:M   30 Jan 1961 Robert E Harvey & Sandra M Kezar
HARWOOD,Anna E Sex:F (Child #2) 29 Sep 1915 Hudson, NH Wm H Harwood
  (Nashua, NH) & Katherine MacDonald (Prince Edward Is
HARWOOD,Annie Sex:F (Child #1) 02 Nov 1933 Guy Harwood (Hudson, NH)
  & Annie Alukonis (Nashua, NH)
HARWOOD,Bruce J Sex:M   09 Dec 1947 James C Harwood (Hudson, NH)
  & Myrtle M Wells (Nashua, NH)
HARWOOD,Cornelius J Sex:M (Child #7) 02 Jun 1926 Guy Cornelius Harwood
  (Nashua, NH) & Mary A MacDonald (P E Island,
HARWOOD,Donald J Sex:M   11 Jan 1947 John W Harwood (Hudson, NH)
  & Charlotte E Bagley (Nashua, NH)
HARWOOD,Francis A Sex:M (Child #2) 07 Nov 1915 Hudson, NH Harold J Harwood
  (Canada) & Selina Anderson (Canada)
HARWOOD,Gail Frances Sex:F (Child #6) 23 Mar 193 Guy Cornelius Harwood
  (Nashua, NH) & Agnes Mary MacDonald (Canada)
HARWOOD,Gail P Sex:F   16 Feb 1951 John W Harwood & Charlotte E Bagley
HARWOOD,Judith Virginia Sex:F (Child #1) 03 Jan 1938 Guy Harwood (Hudson,
  NH) & Anne Helen Alukonis (Nashua, NH)
HARWOOD,Margaret L Sex:F (Child #1) 25 Feb 1906 Harold Harwood (Canada)
  & Lena Anderson (Canada)

HUDSON,NH BIRTHS

HARWOOD,Paula S   Sex:F   02 Nov 1948 Robert J Harwood (Nashua, NH)
 & Pauline D Berube (Nashua, NH)
HARWOOD,Phyllis Harmona   Sex:F   (Child #1) 09 Jul 1914 Ralph W Harwood
 (Hudson, NH) & Estella M Downing (Groveton)
HARWOOD, [Unknown] Sex:M   (Child #1) 14 Aug 1913 William H Harwood (Nashua,
 NH) & Katherine Macdonald (Prince Edward Island)
HARWOOD, [Unknown]   Sex:F   (Child #2) 03 May 1917 Ralph Harwood (Hudson, NH)
 & Stella Downing (Groveton)
HASELTINE,David   Sex:M   08 Nov 1795 Hudson, NH Nathaniel Haseltine & Rachel
HASELTINE,Dora E Sex:F   (Child #2) 07 Jan 1895   W C Haseltine (W Townsend,
 MA) & B M Hamblett (Hudson, NH)
HASELTINE,Hannah Page   Sex:F   01 Feb 1802 Hudson, NH Nathaniel Haseltine
 & Rachel
HASELTINE,Luther   Sex:M   24 Jul 1797 Hudson, NH Nathaniel Haseltine & Rachel
HASELTINE,Nathaniel   Sex:M   17 Aug 1762 Hudson, NH Nathaniel Haseltine
 & Elizabeth Cummings
HASELTINE,Polly   Sex:F   19 Aug 1799 Hudson, NH Nathaniel Haseltine & Rachel
HASELTINE,Solomon   Sex:M   13 Apr 1761 Hudson, NH Nathaniel Haseltine
 & Elizabeth Cummings
HASELTON,Allice May   Sex:F   27 Dec 1864 Hudson, NH George W Haselton &
HASELTON,Arthur   Sex:M   22 Apr 1863 Hudson, NH George W Haselton & Lora
HASELTON,David   Sex:M   08 Nov 1795 Hudson, NH Nathaniel Haselton & Rachel
HASELTON,Ellen M   Sex:F   (Child #3) 17 Nov 1905 Wm C Haselton (W Townsend,
 MA) & Bertha M Hamlett (Hudson, NH)
HASELTON,Hannah   Sex:F   01 Feb 1802 Hudson, NH Nathaniel Haselton & Rachel
HASELTON,Luther   Sex:M   24 Jul 1797 Hudson, NH Nathaniel Haselton & Rachel
HASELTON,Polle   Sex:F   19 Aug 1799 Hudson, NH Nathaniel Haselton & Rachel
HASELTON,Wallace S F   Sex:M   10 Jan 1893 Wm C Haselton (W Townsend, MA)
 & B M Hambert (Hudson, NH)
HASSEY,Beth A   Sex:F   13 Jun 1972 William A Hassey & Margaret A Choquette
HASSEY,Jennifer Marian Sex:F 08 May 1984 William B Hassey
 & Margaret A Choquette
HASTINGS,James H   Sex:M   01 Feb 1951 Henry J Hastings & Ruth Bemis
HATCH,Cindy L   Sex:F   13 Feb 1959 James H Hatch & Jessie E Field
HATCH,Karyl J   Sex:F   28 Jun 1962 Warren E Hatch & Barbara A Emerson
HATCH,Mark W   Sex:M   24 Aug 1958 Warren E Hatch & Barbara A Emerson
HATHAWAY,Neil J   Sex:M   07 Nov 1974 Kenneth J Hathaway & Laura A Cook
HAUG,James   Sex:M   03 Dec 1948 Charles L Haug (Nashua, NH)
 & Doris M Lynch (Beacon, NY)
HAUSBERGER,Martin S   Sex:M   05 Jun 1974 Gert T Hausberger & Evelyn M Crump
HAUSBERGER,Stefan P   Sex:M   25 Apr 1972 Gert T Hausberger & Evelyn M Crump
HAWTHORNE,John M   Sex:M   01 Jul 1949 Bruce C Hawthorne & Verna M Kahofer
HAWTHORNE,Marjorie E   Sex:F   22 May 1951 Bruce Hawthorne & Verna M Kahofer
HAWTHORNE,Stephanie Noel Sex:F 10 Feb 1984 John M Hawthorne & Ann Dee Boarman
HAWXWELL,Michael W Sex:M 22 Feb 1977 Donald R Hawxwell & Barbara Jane Eastbur
HAYDEN,Paul T   Sex:M   15 Mar 1963 George P Hayden & Muriel J Rowell
HAYES,John R   Sex:M   12 Jun 1951 John R Hayes & Gertrude K Uglum
HAYES,John R Jr   Sex:M   11 Oct 1968 John R Hayes Sr & Catherine A McCallum
HAYES,Kathryn A   Sex:F   20 Apr 1966 John Hayes & Julie McDonough
HAYES,Kimberlie M   Sex:F   29 Jan 1980 James W Hayes & Sandra D Smith
HAYES,Philip C   Sex:M   12 Jun 1951 John R Hayes & Gertrude K Uglum
HAYES,Sean M   Sex:M   21 May 1967 Calvin T Hayes & Jane L Carter
HAYES,Stephen J   Sex:M   04 Oct 1962 Robert W Hayes & Patricia G Porter
HAYFORD,Lindsey Megan   Sex:F   17 Mar 1983 Ronald A Hayford & Maureen E Hart
HAYMANN,Donald E   Sex:M   16 Jun 1971 Perry M Haymann & Barbara A Adshade
HAYMANN,Heidi Anne   Sex:F   24 Jun 1978 Perry I Haymann & Diane Jean Wieczhalek
HAYMANN,Holly Ann   Sex:F   12 Feb 1981 Perry I Haymann & Diane J Wieczhalek
HAYMANN,Leslie A   Sex:F   09 Oct 1965 Perry M Haymann & Barbara A Adshade
HAYNES,Jill   Sex:F   06 Mar 1951 George E Haynes & Alice B Stearns
HAZELTINE,Nathaniel   Sex:M   17 Aug 1762 Hudson, NH Nathaniel Hazeltine

HUDSON,NH BIRTHS

& Elizabeth
HAZELTON,Merton L Sex:M (Child #1) 11 Oct 1892 Arthur W Hazelton (Hudson, NH) & Mary E McCoy (Hudson, NH)
HAZELTON,Page Smith Sex:M (Child #2) 07 May 1896 Arthur W Hazelton (Hudson, NH) & Mary E McCoy (Hudson, NH)
HAZZARD,Bertha W Sex:F 05 Mar 1877 Hudson, NH George W Hazzard (Norwich, VT) & Mary E (Charlestown, MA)
HAZZARD,Herbert N Sex:M 05 Mar 1878 Hudson, NH George W Hazzard (Norwich, VT) & Mary E (Charlestown, MA)
HEAD,Mary Frances Sex:F (Child #1) 18 Jan 1935 William Head (Watertown, MA) & Martha Haddad (Berlin, NH)
HEALD,Dawn Kristin Sex: 13 Aug 1972 Norman E Heald & Joyce L Bowman
HEATH,Courtney Beth Sex:F 06 Sep 1978 Jeffrey J Heath & Rebecca A Mitchell
HEATH,Nathaniel Sex:M 12 Aug 1791 Hudson, NH Richard Heath & Ruth
HEATH,Nathaniel Davis Sex:M 12 Aug 1791 Hudson, NH Richard Heath & Ruth
HEBERT,Christopher B Sex:M 30 Nov 1966 James W Hebert & Dorothy M Trahan
HEBERT,Sherri L Sex:F 01 Jan 1968 James W Hebert & Dorothy M Trahan
HEDLER,Elizabeth E Sex:F 13 Mar 1972 Robert A Hedler & Patricia E Phillips
HEFFERNAN,Adam C Sex:M 26 Feb 1974 Edmund T Heffernan & Sharon L Buccuzzo
HEFFERNAN,Beth L Sex:F 12 Jan 1970 Edmund T Heffernan & Sharon L Buccuzzo
HEIL,Julie A Sex:F 21 Nov 1967 George E Heil & Gail Phillips
HEINECKE,Heidi R Sex: 05 Feb 1973 Edwin R Heinecke & Bette-Jean Woodland
HELIE,James C Sex:M 25 Apr 1968 Richard L Helie & Doris E Richards
HELIE,Michael S Sex:M 20 Nov 1970 Richard L Helie & Doris E Richards
HEMEON,Albert P Sex:M 28 Nov 1977 Gordon A Hemeon & Wanda D Braley
HEMEON,Gordon A Jr Sex:M 05 Aug 1955 Gordon A Hemeon & Katherine T Briand
HENDERSON,James F 3rd Sex:M 25 Feb 1950 James F Henderson,Jr & Corona S Kashulines
HENDERSON,Justin J Sex:M 04 Apr 1976 John H Henderson Jr & Carol L Rioux
HENDERSON,Maryann F Sex:F 28 Jan 1970 James F HendersonIII & Gail E Boutilier
HENEY,George F Jr Sex:M 06 Sep 1966 George F Heney & Elaine M Poulios
HENNESSEY,Amy R Sex:F 06 Apr 1979 Robert M Hennessey & Phyllis T Gauthier
HENNESSEY,Shane Philippe Sex:M 03 Mar 1982 Robert M Hennessey & Phyllis T Gauthier
HENNESSEY,Shawn Michael Sex:M 11 Jan 1977 Robert M Hennessey Jr & Phyllis Therese Gauthier
HERALD,[Unknown] Sex:F 27 Nov 1973 William C Herald & Patsy K Rhodes
HERBERT,David Greeley Sex:M (Child #1) 29 Mar 1934 William S Herbert (Pelham, NH) & Georgia Greeley (Londonderry, NH
HERBERT,Gerald C Sex:M (Child #2) 06 Sep 1946 Edmond F Herbert (Norwich, CT) & Virginia A Williams (Lynn, MA)
HERBERT,Kay L Sex:F 11 Apr 1950 Paul K Herbert & Nada M Tibbetts
HERBERT,Meaghan Eileen Sex:F 27 Jul 1980 James H Herbert Jr & Judith E Dandrea
HERMAN,Anthony Joseph Sex:M 05 Jan 1983 Barry Lee Herman Jr & Elisabeth Faye Nutt
HERNDON,David Horner Sex:M 29 Jun 1983 Frederick W Herndon & Kathleen M O'Hara
HERNDON,Maryelle Sex:F 26 Jul 1981 Frederick W Herndon & Kathleen O'Hara
HEROUX,Daniel P Sex:M 18 Jan 1958 Paul J Heroux & Cecile F Lemay
HEROUX,Janet C Sex:F 02 Apr 1956 Paul J Heroux & Cecile F Lemay
HEROUX,Susan M Sex:F 01 Jun 1961 Nelson E Heroux & Norma H Millett
HERRICK,Ian Francis Sex:M 15 Nov 1983 David Lee Herrick & Johanna E Morrison
HERRICK,Tristan McKenzie Sex:M 21 Nov 1981 David Leo Herrick & Johanna E Morrison
HESELTON,Alice May Sex:F 27 Dec 1764 Hudson, NH George W Heselton & Lora A Poor
HESELTON,Arthur Sex:M 22 Apr 1863 Hudson, NH George W Heselton & Lora A Poor
HESELTON,Merton L Sex:M 11 Oct 1892 Hudson, NH Arthur W Heselton & Mary E McCoy

HUDSON,NH BIRTHS

HESS,Jennifer L   Sex:F   14 Jul 1969 Frank E Hess & Carol A Reeves
HICKOX,Thomas S   Sex:M   07 Dec 1864 Hudson, NH Frederick F Hickox & Frances
HICOX,Thomas S   Sex:M   07 Dec 1864 Hudson, NH Frederick Hicox & Francis
HIER,Andrew G   Sex:M   28 May 1974 George B Hier Jr & Suzanne C Nadeau
HIER,Michael J   Sex:M   02 Oct 1975 George B Hier Jr & Suzanne C Nadeau
HIGGINS,Anthony E   Sex:M   12 Oct 1977 Charles E Higgins & Marsh Jean Harding
HIGGINS,Herbert W   Sex:M   (Child #3) 17 Sep 1943 Joseph R Higgins
    (Presque Isle, ME) & Barbara C Miner (Antrim, NH)
HIGGINS,Peter L   Sex:M   11 Mar 1974 Lawrence Higgins & Susan M Blanchette
HIGHAM,Steven F   Sex:M   09 Nov 1965 Frank Higham & Mary H Beamish
HIGSON,Elizabeth   Sex:F   (Child #3) 24 Aug 1899 William H Higson (Fall River,
    MA) & Harriet A Tomlinson (England)
HIGSON,Ellen Mary   Sex:F   (Child #4) 11 Sep 1901 Hudson, NH Wm H Higson
    (Fall River, MA) & Harriet Tomlinson (England)
HIGSON,John Thomas   Sex:M   (Child #2) 30 Nov 1897 Wm H Higson (Fall River,
    MA) & Harriet Tomlinson (England)
HILBERT,Bion Matthew   Sex:M   08 Feb 1984 Bruce B Hilbert & Susan Hagen Miller
HILFIKER,Jeffrey S   Sex:M   23 May 1975 Ronald C Hilfiker & Kathryn E Whiteside
HILFIKER,Kerry Anne   Sex:F   05 Feb 1974 Ronald C Hilfiker & Kathryn E Whiteside
HILL,Alice M   Sex:F   04 Sep 1877 Hudson, NH Alonzo Hill (Litchfield, NH)
    & Jennie Hodgman (Lyndeboro, NH)
HILL,Arthur   Sex:M   (Child #2) 17 May 1882 Hudson, NH Osgood Hill (Hudson,
    NH) & Calista Campbell (Bedford)
HILL,Calvin Wingate   Sex:M   18 Sep 1869 Hudson, NH Clifton M Hill & Emma S
HILL,David M   Sex:M   (Child #1) 21 Apr 1945 Richard M Hill (Nashua, NH)
    & Mary E Mahoney (Manchester, NH)
HILL,David S   Sex:M   (Child #1) 21 Apr 1942 Stafford S Hill (Augusta, GA)
    & Edna F Lyon (Nashua, NH)
HILL,Emma Frances   Sex:F   08 Feb 1872 Hudson, NH Alonzo Hill & Jennie
HILL,George E   Sex:M   06 Oct 1836 Hudson, NH Oliver Hill & Rebecca
HILL,George Walter   Sex:M   18 Mar 1881 Hudson, NH Alonzo Hill (Litchfield,
    NH) & Jennie Hodgman (Lyndeboro, NH)
HILL,Grace Blanche   Sex:F   07 Jan 1884 Hudson, NH Alonzo Hill (Litchfield,
    NH) & Jennie S Hodgeman (Lyndeboro, NH)
HILL,Harland S   Sex:M   (Child #2) 27 Sep 1891 Orlando G Hill (Hudson, NH)
    & Nettie L Young (Hudson, NH)
HILL,Helen M   Sex:F   06 Oct 1881 Hudson, NH Franklin A Hill (Hudson, NH)
    & Luella E Campbell (Windham, NH)
HILL,Justin E   Sex:M   28 Jan 1844 Hudson, NH Warren Hill & Mary Chase
HILL,Mary E   Sex:F   25 May 1878 Hudson, NH Charles W Hill (Lowell, MA)
    & Mary A (Brookline, NH)
HILL,Orlando Greenleaf   Sex:M   02 Oct 1890 Hudson, NH Orlando G Hill
    & Nellie L Young
HILL,Sylvia A   Sex:F   06 Jul 1966 Robert W Hill & Nancy L Thompson
HILL,[Unknown]   Sex:M   (Child #2) 1925 James A Hill (England)
    & Carrie McCall (North Carolina)
HILL,[Unknown]   Sex: 04 Dec 1972 John R Hill & Aldine C Abron
HILL,[Unknown]   Sex:F   23 Mar 1870 Hudson, NH Justin E Hill & S Carrie B
HILL,[Unknown]   Sex: 07 Oct 1871 Hudson, NH Justin E Hill & Carrie L
HILL,[Unknown]   Sex:M   15 Mar 1873 Hudson, NH Clifton N Hill & Emma S
HILL,[Unknown]   Sex: 09 May 1873 Hudson, NH Osgood Hill & Cohita
HILL,[Unknown]   Sex: 26 Jan 1874 Hudson, NH Justin Hill & Carrie L
HILL,[Unknown]   Sex:F   29 Jan 1875 Hudson, NH Osgood Hill & Calista
HILL,[Unknown]   Sex:M   (Child #4) 04 Nov 1882 Hudson, NH Clifton M Hill
    (Manchester, NH) & Emma S Cross (Boston, MA)
HILLMAN,Meredith Louise   Sex:F   19 Nov 1984 George J Hillman Jr
    & Janice L Elliott
HILLS,Abagail   Sex:F   05 Sep 1725 Hudson, NH James Hills & Abigail
HILLS,Abigail   Sex:F   20 Aug 1770 Hudson, NH Oliver Hills & Abigail
HILLS,Abigail   Sex:F   30 Mar 1775 Hudson, NH Jeremiah Hills & Hannah Moody

HUDSON,NH BIRTHS

```
HILLS,Abner      Sex:M     Hudson, NH Nathaniel Hills & Sarah
HILLS,Abraham    Sex:M     Hudson, NH Nathaniel Hills & Sarah
HILLS,Alden      Sex:M     10 Sep 1807 Hudson, NH Elijah Hills Jr & Elizabeth Tarbox
HILLS,Amos       Sex:M     05 Sep 1787 Hudson, NH Thomas Hills & Ruth
HILLS,Amos       Sex:M     05 Sep 1781 Hudson, NH Thomas Hills & Ruth
HILLS,Andrews    Sex:M     29 Sep 1821 Hudson, NH Philip Hills Jr &
HILLS,Ann        Sex:F     Hudson, NH Nathaniel Hills & Sarah
HILLS,Benjamin   Sex:M     02 Sep 1823 Hudson, NH Philip Hills Jr &
HILLS,Betsey     Sex:F     20 Aug 1817 Hudson, NH Philip Hills Jr &
HILLS,Carol J    Sex:F     05 Jun 1958 Donald E Hills & Jean J Smith
HILLS,Charles    Sex:M     17 Jan 1816 Hudson, NH Philip Hills Jr &
HILLS,David      Sex:M     15 Jul 1770 Hudson, NH Jeremiah Hills & Hannah Moody
HILLS,David      Sex:M     01 Mar 1801 Hudson, NH David Hills & Mehittabel Robinson
HILLS,David      Sex:M     27 Dec 1810 Hudson, NH William Hills & Rachel
HILLS,Ebenezer   Sex:M     25 Dec 1767 Hudson, NH Oliver Hills & Abigail
HILLS,Ebenezer   Sex:M     20 Feb 1727 Dunstable, MA Henry Hills & Abigail
HILLS,Edna       Sex:F     03 Aug 1736 Hudson, NH James Hills & Abigail
HILLS,Edwin      Sex:M     10 Jul 1818 Hudson, NH Elijah Hills & Betsey
HILLS,Edwin      Sex:M     10 Apr 1818 Hudson, NH Elijah Hills & Betsey
HILLS,Elijah     Sex:M     15 Mar 1738 Hudson, NH James Hills & Abigail
HILLS,Elijah     Sex:M     14 Dec 1778 Hudson, NH Elijah Hills & Miriam
HILLS,Elijah     Sex:M     14 Dec 1779 Hudson, NH Elijah Hills & Miriam
HILLS,Elijah     Sex:M     30 May 1809 Hudson, NH  Elijah Hills & Elizebeth
HILLS,Eliphalet  Sex:M     Hudson, NH Nathaniel Hills & Sarah
HILLS,Eliza      Sex:F     30 May 1809 Hudson, NH Elijah Hills Jr & Elizabeth Tarbox
HILLS,Elva       Sex:M     18 Nov 1807 Hudson, NH James Hills & Abigail
HILLS,Enoch      Sex:M     15 Oct 1776 Hudson, NH Jeremiah Hills & Hannah Moody
HILLS,Enoch      Sex:M     15 Oct 1766 Hudson, NH Jeremiah Hills & Hannah
HILLS,Esther     Sex:F     08 Oct 1754 Hudson, NH Ezekiel Hills & Hannah
HILLS,Esther     Sex:F     28 Sep 1819 Hudson, NH Philip Hills Jr &
HILLS,Florence M Sex:F     17 Oct 1871 Hudson, NH Alfred M Hills & Mary A
HILLS,George Washington    Sex:M     26 Apr 1810 Hudson, NH Samuel Hills
  & Rhoda Bowers
HILLS,Gilbert    Sex:M     Nov 1805 Hudson, NH William Hills & Rachel
HILLS,Granville  Sex:M     26 Jan 1809 Hudson, NH William Hills & Rachel
HILLS,Granville  Sex:M     06 Jan 1809 Hudson, NH William Hills & Rachel
HILLS,Hannah     Sex:F     25 Sep 1731 Hudson, NH James Hills & Abigail
HILLS,Hannah     Sex:F     Mar 1752 Hudson, NH Oliver Hills & Abigail
HILLS,Hannah     Sex:F     10 Apr 1769 Hudson, NH Elijah Hills & Miriam
HILLS,Hannah     Sex:F     Hudson, NH Jeremiah Hills & Hannah Davidson
HILLS,Hannah     Sex:F     14 Mar 1788 Hudson, NH Thomas Hills & Ruth
HILLS,Hannah     Sex:F     01 Nov 1798 Hudson, NH James Hills & Nabby Hills
HILLS,Hannah     Sex:F     08 Mar 1752 Hudson, NH Oliver Hills & Abigail
HILLS,Hannah     Sex:F     13 Apr 1767 Hudson, NH Elijah Hills & Miriam
HILLS,Henry      Sex:M     25 Jan 1789 Hudson, NH William Hills & Sarah
HILLS,Henry      Sex:M     Dunstable, MA Henry Hills & Abigail
HILLS,Isaac      Sex:M     18 May 1775 Hudson, NH Oliver Hills & Abigail
HILLS,Isaac      Sex:M     15 Oct 1782 Hudson, NH Thomas Hills & Ruth
HILLS,James      Sex:M     10 Aug 1728 Hudson, NH James Hills & Abigail
HILLS,James      Sex:M     08 Nov 1763 Hudson, NH Elijah Hills & Miriam
HILLS,James      Sex:M     03 Aug 1768 Hudson, NH Jeremiah Hills & Hannah Moody
HILLS,James      Sex:M     16 Jul 1800 Hudson, NH James Hills & Nabby
HILLS,James Davidson   Sex:M     Hudson, NH Jeremiah Hills & Hannah Davidson
HILLS,Jeremiah   Sex:M     01 Mar 1727 Hudson, NH James Hills & Abigail
HILLS,Jeremiah   Sex:M     08 Feb 1773 Hudson, NH Jeremiah Hills & Hannah Moody
HILLS,Jeremiah   Sex:M     Hudson, NH Jeremiah Hills & Hannah Davidson
HILLS,Jeremiah Sex:M 23    1798 Hudson, NH David Hills & Mehittabel Robinson
HILLS,John       Sex:M     03 Oct 1779 Hudson, NH Jeremiah Hills & Hannah Moody
HILLS,John       Sex:M     Hudson, NH Jeremiah Hills & Hannah Davidson
HILLS,Jonathan   Sex:M     15 Feb 1729 Dunstable, MA Henry Hills & Abigail
```

HUDSON,NH BIRTHS

HILLS,Joseph   Sex:M   31 Mar 1767 Hudson, NH Elijah Hills & Miriam
HILLS,Kimball Sex:M 30 Aug 1803 Hudson, NH Elijah Hills Jr & Elizabeth Tarbox
HILLS,Leonard B   Sex:M   01 Nov 1948 James L Hills (Marlboro, MA)
   & Ellen B Annable (Pittsburgh, PA)
HILLS,Lottie M   Sex:F   15 Apr 1958 Walter E Hills & Arlene V Estey
HILLS,Lyman W   Sex:M   14 Mar 1894 Orlando G Hills (Hudson, NH)
   & Nettie L Young (Hudson, NH)
HILLS,Margaret   Sex:F   Hudson, NH Jeremiah Hills & Hannah Davidson
HILLS,Mary V   Sex:F   (Child #2) 23 Aug 1895 Dr A K Hills (Hudson, NH)
   & Ida V Creulzborg (Philadelphia, PA)
HILLS,Mehitabel   Sex:F   20 Jul 1749 Hudson, NH Ezekiel Hills & Hannah
HILLS,Mehitable   Sex:F   20 Jul 1749 Hudson, NH Ezekiel Hills & Hannah
HILLS,Mollie   Sex:F   18 Apr 1758 Hudson, NH Oliver Hills & Abigail
HILLS,Molly   Sex:F   18 Apr 1758 Hudson, NH Oliver Hills & Abigail
HILLS,Molly   Sex:F   18 Oct 1771 Hudson, NH Elijah Hills & Miriam
HILLS,Moses   Sex:M   02 Oct 1781 Hudson, NH Jeremiah Hills & Hannah Moody
HILLS,Nancy   Sex:F   03 May 1807 Hudson, NH William Hills & Rachel
HILLS,Nathaniel   Sex:M   Hudson, NH Jeremiah Hills & Hannah Davidson
HILLS,Nathaniel   Sex:M   18 Feb 1788 Hudson, NH Samuel Hills & Sarah
HILLS,Nathaniel   Sex:M   03 Mar 1799 Hudson, NH Samuel Hills & Rhoda Bowers
HILLS,Olive   Sex:F   03 May 1776 Hudson, NH Elijah Hills & Miriam
HILLS,Oliver   Sex:M   23 Oct 1772 Hudson, NH Oliver Hills & Abigail
HILLS,Oliver   Sex:M   Hudson, NH Nathaniel Hills & Sarah
HILLS,Orlando Greenleaf   Sex:M   (Child #1) 02 Oct 1890 Orlando G Hills
   (Hudson, NH) & Nettie L Young (Hudson, NH)
HILLS,Parker Sex:M   07 Oct 1801 Hudson, NH Elijah Hills Jr & Elizabeth Tarbox
HILLS,Philip   Sex:M   02 Mar 1754 Hudson, NH Oliver Hills & Abigail
HILLS,Philip   Sex:M   11 Sep 1825 Hudson, NH Philip Hills Jr &
HILLS,Rachel   Sex:F   06 Apr 1756 Hudson, NH Oliver Hills & Abigail
HILLS,Rachel   Sex:F   15 Apr 1765 Hudson, NH Elijah Hills & Miriam
HILLS,Reis   Sex:M   Hudson, NH Jeremiah Hills & Hannah Davidson
HILLS,Reuben   Sex:M   07 Jun 1764 Hudson, NH Oliver Hills & Abigail
HILLS,Reuben   Sex:M   07 Jun 1766 Hudson, NH Oliver Hills & Abigail
HILLS,Robert D   Sex:M   14 Oct 1956 Walter E Hills & Arlene V Estey
HILLS,Robert D   Sex:M   19 Dec 1813 Hudson, NH William Hills & Rachel
HILLS,Robert Douglass   Sex:M   19 Dec 1813 Hudson, NH William Hills & Rachel
HILLS,Russell   Sex:M   06 Apr 1801 Hudson, NH Samuel Hills & Rhoda Bowers
HILLS,Ruth   Sex:F   20 Mar 1793 Hudson, NH Thomas Hills & Ruth
HILLS,Salley   Sex:F   02 Nov 1789 Hudson, NH Thomas Hills & Ruth
HILLS,Sally   Sex:F   02 Nov 1789 Hudson, NH Thomas Hills & Ruth
HILLS,Samuel   Sex:M   06 Feb 1769 Hudson, NH Nathaniel Hills & Susanna
HILLS,Samuel   Sex:M   Hudson, NH Nathaniel Hills & Sarah
HILLS,Sarah   Sex:F   02 Jul 1735 Hudson, NH James Hills & Abigail
HILLS,Sarah   Sex:F   10 Feb 1766 Hudson, NH Oliver Hills & Abigail
HILLS,Sarah   Sex:F   13 Apr 1774 Hudson, NH Elijah Hills & Miriam
HILLS,Sarah   Sex:F   Hudson, NH Nathaniel Hills & Sarah
HILLS,Silas   Sex:M   Hudson, NH Jeremiah Hills & Hannah Davidson
HILLS,Sumner M   Sex:M   11 Oct 1875 Hudson, NH Clifton Hills & Emma
HILLS,Susanna   Sex:F   25 May 1750 Hudson, NH Oliver Hills & Abigail
HILLS,Susanna   Sex:F   17 Jun 1797 Hudson, NH Samuel Hills & Rhoda Bowers
HILLS,Sylvia   Sex:F   (Child #4) 13 Jun 1897 Orlando G Hills (Hudson, NH)
   & Nettie Lee Young (Hudson, NH)
HILLS,Thadeus   Sex:M   Hudson, NH Nathaniel Hills & Sarah
HILLS,Thomas   Sex:M   30 Mar 1751 Hudson, NH Ezekiel Hills & Hannah
HILLS,Thomas   Sex:M   20 Jul 1784 Hudson, NH Thomas Hills & Ruth
HILLS,Thomas   Sex:M   16 Jul 1800 Hudson, NH James Hills & Nabby Hills
HILLS,Thomas   Sex:M   30 Mar 1750 Hudson, NH Ezekiel Hills & Hannah
HILLS,Thomas   Sex:M   05 Mar 1805 Hudson, NH Elijah Hills & Elizebeth
HILLS,Thoms   Sex:M   05 Mar 1805 Hudson, NH Elijah Hills Jr & Elizabeth Tarbox
HILLS,Timothy S   Sex:M   05 May 1784 Hudson, NH William Hills & Sarah

HUDSON,NH BIRTHS

HILLS,Timothy Smith   Sex:M   23 Aug 1784 Hudson, NH William Hills & Sarah
HILLS,Wanda A   Sex:F   04 Sep 1959 Walter E Hills & Arlene V Estey
HILLS,Warren Sex:M   14 Jan 1811 Hudson, NH Elijah Hills Jr & Elizabeth Tarbox
HILLS,William   Sex:M   23 May 1730 Hudson, NH James Hills & Abigail
HILLS,William   Sex:M   14 Jul 1777 Hudson, NH Jeremiah Hills & Hannah Moody
HILLS,William   Sex:M   02 Dec 1786 Hudson, NH William Hills & Sarah
HILLS,William   Sex:M   20 Jan 1817 Hudson, NH William Hills & Rachel
HILLS,William   Sex:M   02 Oct 1789 Hudson, NH William Hills & Sarah
HILLS,[Unknown]   Sex:F   (Child #1) 16 Feb 1914 Harley S Hills (Hudson, NH)
    & Gladys A Snow (Boston, MA)
HILS,David   Sex:M   01 Mar 1801 Hudson, NH Daniel Hills & Mehatible
HILTON,Andrew Scott   Sex:M   02 Feb 1977 George L Hilton III
    & Wilhelmina R Miller
HINTON,Cassandra L   Sex:F   28 Sep 1966 James A Hinton & Cynthia A Murray
HIRKO,Andrew M   Sex:M   10 Jan 1980 Michael A Hirko & Patricia L Russell
HIRKO,Lyndsey Patricia Sex:F 21 Nov 1982 Michael A Hirko & Patricia L Russell
HIRTH,Gary   Sex:M   22 Jan 1964 Bernard P Hirth & Dorothy E Demanche
HIRTH,Margaret Mary   Sex:F   30 Jan 1981 Thomas J Hirth & Margaret M Tupper
HIRTH,Martha Ann   Sex:F   06 Aug 1978 Thomas Jerome Hirth & Margaret M Tupper
HIRTH,Mary E   Sex:F   25 Jan 1972 Thomas J Hirth & Margaret M Tupper
HIRTH,Matthew   Sex:M   04 Jan 1980 Thomas J Hirth & Margaret M Tupper
HIRTH,Ruth Ellen   Sex:F   19 Feb 1977 Thomas J Hirth & Margaret M Tupper
HOAG,Charles E   Sex:M   (Child #3) 14 Sep 1903 David W Hoag (Hudson, NH)
    & Nellie M Sherman (Belmont)
HOAG,Sharon A   Sex:F   19 Oct 1950 Ronald E Hoag & Elizabeth E Dube
HOCKE,Abigail Moody   Sex:F   05 May 1793 Hudson, NH Hocke & Sarah
HODGE,Christopher Daniel   Sex:M   07 Nov 1978 Daniel Hodge & Diana C Scrivener
HODGE,Kevin   Sex:M   03 Mar 1953 Frederick D Hodge & Edith M Young
HODGE,Mark   Sex:M   15 Jan 1958 Frederick D Hodge & Edith M Young
HODGMAN,Dennis W   Sex:M   27 Oct 1964 Robert M Hodgman & Sandra L Lampron
HODGMAN,Fredie L   Sex:M   15 Dec 1874 Hudson, NH John Hodgman & Mary
HODGMAN,Marlene C   Sex:F   08 Oct 1966 Robert M Hodgman & Sandra L Lampron
HODGSON,Joseph Phillip Jr   Sex:M   22 Jun 1984 Joseph P Hodgson
    & Susan E Nickerson
HOEPNER,Matthew Todd   Sex:M   14 Dec 1980 John M Hoepner & Gail Ellen Gifford
HOFFMAN,Sarah Jane   Sex:F   13 Jun 1871 Hudson, NH George Hoffman & Fannie
HOFFMAN,Willie James   Sex:M   06 Jul 1869 Hudson, NH George Hoffman & Fannie
HOFFMAN,[Unknown]   Sex:M   14 Feb 1867 Hudson, NH George Hoffman & Fanny
HOGAN,Eileen B   Sex:F   02 May 1966 Shawn B Hogan & Suzanne F Taylor
HOGAN,Jennifer Marie   Sex:F   02 Feb 1978 Daniel P Hogan & Christine E Rollins
HOGAN,Sean Ryan   Sex:M   23 Sep 1984 Timothy James Hogan & Susan Smith Samson
HOGAN,Shannon P   Sex:M   30 Oct 1970 Shawn B Hogan & Suzanne F Taylor
HOLBROOK,David Frederick   Sex:M   (Child #2) 30 Nov 1931 Clarence Holbrook
    (Massachusetts) & Elizabeth Dalcourt (Massachus
HOLBROOK,Dorothy E   Sex:F   (Child #3) 07 Mar 1915 Hudson, NH Elmer H Holbrook
    (New Hampshire) & Minnie Obin (New York)
HOLBROOK,Edna   Sex:F   (Child #11) 08 Aug 1918 Elmer Holbrook (Penacook)
    & Emelia Obin (Plattsburgh, NY)
HOLBROOK,William Earl   Sex:M   (Child #4) 09 Aug 1937 Elmer A Holbrook
    (Nashua, NH) & Marion L Riley (Worcester, MA)
HOLDEN,Cynthia M   Sex: 21 Jan 1973 Wilfred L Holden & Diane M Bowlison
HOLDEN,Jake Thomas   Sex:M   18 Oct 1984 Daniel G Holden & Paula Amy Bardsley
HOLEVAS,Athena C   Sex:F   28 Aug 1973 Antone S Holevas & Elizabeth B Clark
HOLEVAS,Peter A   Sex:M   12 Apr 1978 Antone S Holevas & Elizabeth B Clark
HOLMES,Amanda Beth   Sex:F   26 Jan 1981 Stephen C Holmes & Karen J McCrady
HOLMES,Charles F Sex:M   18 May 1853 Hudson, NH Luke Holmes & Catherine Butler
HOLMES,Craig Jeffrey   Sex:M   18 Jul 1978 Stephen C Holmes & Karen J McCrady
HOLMES,David P   Sex:M   22 Sep 1960 James W Holmes & Gertrude E Simpson
HOLMES,George L   Sex:M   18 Oct 1851 Hudson, NH Luke Holmes & Catherine Butler
HOLMES,James E   Sex:M   18 Apr 1959 James W Holmes & Gertrude E Simpson

HUDSON,NH BIRTHS

HOLMES,James E Sex:M 25 May 1855 Hudson, NH Luke Holmes & Catherine Butler
HOLMES,Jane A Sex:F (Child #2) 17 Nov 1888 George L Holmes (Hudson, NH)
    & Maria A J Butler (Ireland)
HOLMES,Levi J Sex:M 18 Oct 1851 Hudson, NH Luke Holmes & Catherine Butler
HOLMES,[Unknown] Sex: 13 Sep 1886 Geo L Holmes & Maria A J
HOLMSTEDT,Eric M Sex:M 27 Dec 1976 Richard A Holmstedt & Diane Mary Whan
HOLMSTEDT,Stacy W Sex:F 10 Jun 1975 Richard A Holmstedt & Diane M Whan
HOLT,Amanda Leigh Sex:F 13 Jul 1983 Frank Alpheus Holt & Deborah Dawn Freund
HOLT,Amy Marie Sex:F 31 May 1977 Charles K Holt & Doris E Trafford
HOLT,Amy Virginia Sex:F 30 Jun 1981 Brian Alvin Holt & Dale Lois L'Heureux
HOLT,Bernice R Sex:F (Child #7) 28 Jan 1943 Harvey F Holt (Nashua, NH)
    & Gladys B King (Nashua, NH)
HOLT,Charles S Sex:M 26 Feb 1953 Charles W Holt, Jr & Gertrude E Merrill
HOLT,Cynthia L Sex:F (Child #8) 15 Jul 1944 Harvey Holt (Nashua, NH)
    & Gladys King (Nashua, NH)
HOLT,Dexter S Jr Sex:M (Child #1) 27 Aug 1942 Dexter S Holt (Temple, NH)
    & Edna M Gallagher (Nashua, NH)
HOLT,Donald P Sex:M (Child #4) 21 Nov 1940 Harvey F Holt (Nashua, NH)
    & Gladys King (Nashua, NH)
HOLT,George Sex:M (Child #2) 28 Sep 1919 William Holt (Massachusetts)
    & Florence Dube (Canada)
HOLT,Harold Arthur Sex:M (Child #5) 11 Dec 1935 Harvey Holt (Nashua, NH)
    & Gladys King (Nashua, NH)
HOLT,Heidi L Sex:F 14 Dec 1974 Charles K Holt & Doris E Trafford
HOLT,Joseph Sex:M (Child #7) 20 Feb 1938 Harvey Holt (Nashua, NH)
    & Gladys King (Nashua, NH)
HOLT,Kimberly Ann Sex:F 19 Jul 1979 Brian Alvin Holt & Dale Lois L'Heureux
HOLT,Kristina Lynn Sex:F 19 Jul 1978 Richard Seth Holt & Elizabeth J Alton
HOLT,Richard S II Sex:M 06 Dec 1976 Richard S Holt & Elizabeth J Alton
HOLTON,Charlotte J Sex:F (Child #2) 27 Jan 1906 Lewis M Holton (Northboro,
    MA) & Blanche F Buckham (Tyngsboro, MA)
HOLTON,Jessie M Sex:F (Child #1) 09 Jul 1903 Lewis M Holton (Northboro, MA)
    & Blanche F Buckham (Tyngsboro, MA)
HOLTON,Louise I Sex:F (Child #6) 03 Apr 1915 Hudson, NH Louis M Holton
    (Tyngsboro, MA) & Blanche Buckham (Northboro, MA)
HOLTON,Patricia A Sex: 26 Mar 1973 Roy E Holton & JoAnne E Kennedy
HOLTON,Roy L Sex:M (Child #3) 12 Jul 1908 Lewis M Holton (Northboro, MA)
    & Blanche M F Buckham (Tyngsboro, MA)
HOLTON,Sherry Lee Sex:F 18 Aug 1976 Bruce W Holton & Theresa R Landry
HOLTON,[Unknown] Sex:M (Child #4) 02 Jun 1910 Lewis M Holton (Northboro, MA)
    & Blanche Buckham (Tyngsboro, MA)
HOLTON,[Unknown] Sex:M (Child #5) 02 Jun 1913 Louis M Holton (Northboro, MA)
    & Blanche Buckham (Tyngsboro, MA)
HOOK,John Sex:M (Child #7) 07 Apr 1927 James Hook (Russia)
    & Victoria Gerdos (Russia)
HOOK,[Unknown] Sex:M (Child #4) 18 Dec 1920 James Hook (Russia)
    & Victoria Gerdon (Russia)
HOOK,[Unknown] Sex:F (Child #3) 12 Oct 1922 Walery Hook (Russia)
    & Antonina Wolan (Russia)
HOOK,[Unknown] Sex:M (Child #5) 10 May 1923 James Hook (Russia)
    & Victoria Gerdos (Russia)
HOOKE,Abigail Moody Sex:F 05 May 1793 Hudson, NH Farnton Hooke & Sarah
HOOPER,James A Sex:M 07 Jul 1970 Paul R Hooper & Dorothy A Bowen
HOOSON,Jennifer E Sex:F 20 Oct 1965 Robert W Hooson & Judith E Simmons
HOPKINS,Edith L Sex:F (Child #3) 20 Nov 1892 C H Hopkins (Trenton, ME)
    & Ida Webster (Hudson, NH)
HOPKINS,Emma J Sex:F 10 Jun 1864 Hudson, NH Charles H Hopkins & Susan
HOPKINS,Heather M Sex:F 01 Apr 1969 Richard G Hopkins & Carolyn K Phelps
HOPKINS,Marc R Sex:M 26 Dec 1967 Richard G Hopkins & Carolyn K Phelps
HOPKINS,Robert A Jr Sex:M 09 Nov 1967 Robert A Hopkins & Barbara J Ralston

HUDSON,NH BIRTHS

HOPKINS,[Unknown]   Sex:F   28 Dec 1894 Chas H Hopkins (Trenton, MN)
  & Ida S Webster (Hudson, NH)
HOPKINSON,Thomas R   Sex:M   11 Oct 1970 Richard L Hopkinson & Deborah L Hunt
HORN,Denise O   Sex:F   19 Apr 1968 Richard A Horn & Mary V Lockard
HORN,Jeffrey A   Sex:M   19 Apr 1968 Richard A Horn & Mary V Lockard
HORN,Marlene   Sex:F   01 Apr 1967 Richard A Horn & Mary V Lockard
HORNE,Debra S   Sex:F   16 May 1955 Lawrence E Horne & Vivian E Dunn
HORNE,Michael R   Sex:M   27 Mar 1954 Lawrence E Horne & Vivian E Dunn
HORNE,Richard A   Sex:M   (Child #2) 01 Apr 1945 Alan N Horne (Cambridge, MA)
  & Eadwega I Lemanski (Westfield, MA)
HORTA,Ramona Marie   Sex:F   (Child #5) 20 Nov 1941 Ramon Horta (Boston, MA)
  & Marie Pearson (Greenfield, MA)
HOSLEY,Leon Edson   Sex:M   11 Feb 1869 Hudson, NH Harlan P Hosley
  & Mary F Cummings
HOSLEY,Luna Estelle   Sex:F   21 Oct 1861 Hudson, NH Harlan P Hosley
  & Mary F Cummings
HOSLEY,[Unknown]   Sex:F   11 Feb 1869 Hudson, NH Harlan P Hosley
  & Mary F Cummings
HOULE,Albert   Sex:M   17 Nov 1894 Amede Houle (Canada)
  & Sarah Norman (Canada)
HOULE,Amedee J Jr   Sex:M   10 Sep 1965 Amedee J Houle & Flora M Kierstead
HOULE,Andrea L   Sex:F   18 Dec 1974 Andrew H Houle Jr & Phyllis M Dumont
HOULE,Darren C   Sex:M   07 Feb 1967 Larry W Houle & Gloria C Poliquin
HOULE,Jacques R Jr   Sex:M   30 May 1968 Jacques R Houle & Marie I Dumont
HOULE,Joseph A   Sex:M   04 Nov 1893 Ameda Houle (Canada) & Sarah Normon
  (Canada)
HOUSE,Lee A   Sex:F   27 Jan 1958 Philip R House & Arlene A Peterson
HOUSE,Peter K   Sex:M   11 Apr 1960 Philip R House & Arlene Peterson
HOUSE,Philip R   Sex:M   (Child #4) 14 Sep 1933 Frederic R House (Parish, NY)
  & Helen M Wallace (Hanover, NH)
HOUSE,Robin L   Sex:F   24 Jun 1956 Philip R House & Arlene A Peterson
HOUSEMAN,Rae E   Sex:F   27 Jul 1973 Ronald D Houseman & Rose M Giallanza
HOUSEMAN,Randal C   Sex:M   14 Jul 1969 Ronald D Houseman & Rose M Giallanza
HOVIOUS,Christopher Neil   Sex:M   01 May 1984 Neil O Hovious & Janet Lee Smith
HOVLING,Carl P   Sex:M   06 Jan 1965 Ronald C Hovling & Susanne Clement
HOVLING,Hans Kurt   Sex:M   31 Aug 1973 Ronald C Hovling & Susanne Clement
HOVLING,John E   Sex:M   25 Apr 1969 Ronald C Hovling & Susanne Clement
HOVLING,Linda L   Sex:F   19 Dec 1967 Ronald C Hovling & Susanne Clement
HOWARD,   Sex:M   20 Jun 1861 Hudson, NH Charles Howard & Abby
HOWARD,Barbara J   Sex:F   24 Mar 1955 Frank Howard & Barbara A Rock
HOWARD,Debra J   Sex:F   05 Nov 1955 Donald R Howard & Christine M Carter
HOWARD,Donna L   Sex:F   03 Aug 1951 Frank Howard & Barbara A Howard
HOWARD,Ernest H   Sex:M   31 May 1950 Leland E Howard & Lydia M Woodward
HOWARD,Frank C   Sex:M   01 Apr 1954 Frank Howard & Barbara A Rock
HOWARD,Gary W   Sex:M   09 Oct 1952 Frank Howard & Barbara A Rock
HOWARD,Jennifer   Sex:F   26 Jan 1985 S David Howard & Joyce E Howard
HOWARD,Jennifer L   Sex: 24 Sep 1972 Ernest H Howard & Suzanne Bouley
HOWARD,Jonathan Lee   Sex:M   05 Apr 1977 Ernest H Howard & Suzanne L Bouley
HOWARD,Philip R   Sex: 14 May 1973 Wendall F Howard & Kay E Barton
HOWARD,Robert Elwin   Sex:M   (Child #2) 26 Jan 1935 Joseph E Howard (Piermont,
  NH) & Ruby Shreves (Rochester, MO)
HOWARD,[Unknown]   Sex:M   (Child #3) 09 Nov 1936 Joseph E Howard (Piermont,
  NH) & Ruby Shreves (Rochester, MO)
HOWARD,[Unknown]   Sex:M   20 Jun 1861 Hudson, NH Charles Howard & Abby Jane
HOWARTH,Wilfred L A   Sex:M   (Child #5) 01 Apr 1908 Thomas E Howarth (England)
  & Jane Ellen Holt (England)
HOWE,Alice Sophia   Sex:F   (Child #4) 16 Apr 1916 Hudson, NH Andrew E Howe
  (Nashua, NH) & Elizabeth Koch (Turners Falls, MA)
HOWE,Amy Marie   Sex:F   19 Dec 1976 James P Howe & Mona Gail Paquin
HOWE,Derek A   Sex:M   15 Dec 1973 Kenneth L Howe Sr & Sue Anne Locke

HUDSON,NH BIRTHS

HOWE,James W   Sex:M   12 Jan 1967 Kenneth L Howe & Sue A Locke
HOWE,Jonathan D Sex:M   26 Jun 1979 David L Howe & Jane E Portigue
HOWE,Karen M   Sex:F   18 May 1969 David L Howe & Jane E Portique
HOWE,Kelley Ann   Sex:F   06 Sep 1978 David Charles Howe & Mary Ann Dion
HOWE,Megan Jean   Sex:F   09 Feb 1985 Charles L Howe & Dianne Eva Bisson
HOWE,Patricia J   Sex:F   27 May 1972 James P Howe & Mona G Paquin
HOWE,Priscilla Barbara   Sex:F   (Child #4) 24 Jun 1930 Everett W Howe
   (Ipswich, MA) & Margarite T Callahan (Nashua, NH)
HOWE,Stephen D   Sex:M   29 Apr 1970 David L Howe & Jane E Portigue
HOWELL,Warren B   Sex:M   03 Sep 1964 Warren B Howell & Brenda A LaFlamme
HUBBARD,[Unknown]   Sex:F   (Child #1) 07 May 1901 Hudson, NH Wm E Hubbard
   (Littleton) & Flora B Walker (Webster)
HUBNER,Richard A   Sex:M   21 Jun 1969 John P Hubner & Lynda M Ege
HUBNER,Robert J   Sex:M   04 Aug 1970 John P Hubner & Lynda M Ege
HUDON,Christopher D   Sex:M   15 Jun 1974 Roland W Hudon & Loretta J Beaulieu
HUDON,Stephen M   Sex:M   14 Oct 1970 Roland W Hudon & Loretta J Beaulieu
HUDSON,Christopher R Sex:M   18 Apr 1968 Marshall R HudsonIII & Janice M Pulpi
HUDSON,Karen L   Sex:F   08 Aug 1964 Larry C Hudson & Mary J Lavarnway
HUE,James   Sex:M   07 Aug 1740 Hudson, NH John Hue & Ane
HUEY,Ann   Sex:F   10 May 1713 Hudson, NH Henry Huey & Agnes
HUEY,Ann   Sex:F   15 May 1773 Hudson, NH Henry Huey & Agnas
HUEY,Anna   Sex:F   07 Aug 1740 Hudson, NH John Huey & Anna
HUEY,James   Sex:M   May 1769 Hudson, NH Henry Huey & Agnes
HUEY,Jennie   Sex:F   18 Mar 1765 Hudson, NH Henry Huey & Agnas
HUEY,Jenny   Sex:F   18 Mar 1765 Hudson, NH Henry Huey & Agnes
HUEY,John   Sex:M   10 Feb 1767 Hudson, NH Henry Huey & Agnes
HUEY,Mary   Sex:F   15 May 1771 Hudson, NH Henry Huey & Agnes
HUEY,Samuel   Sex:M   16 Nov 1778 Hudson, NH Henry Huey & Agnes
HUFF,Melissa S   Sex:F   14 Mar 1970 Stephen G Huff & Susan J Carter
HUGAR,Julianne M   Sex:F   13 Sep 1971 Anthony L Hugar & Sandra G Hochard
HUGHES,Adam James   Sex:M   02 Oct 1978 Bruce Archie Hughes & Ruth N Bonhomme
HUGHES,David M   Sex:M   26 Nov 1969 Thomas H Hughes & Pauline M Sweet
HUGHES,Randall E   Sex:M   03 Oct 1970 Samuel E Hughes & Debra A Teixeira
HUGHES,Russell L   Sex:M   16 Oct 1971 Samuel E Hughes & Debra A Teixeira
HUGHES,Tiffany N   Sex: 14 May 1973 Fred S Hughes & Bettina R Craige
HUJSAK,Richard S   Sex:M   02 Jul 1947 Alexander F Hujsak (Merrimack, NH)
   & Annis P Wilson (Nashua, NH)
HUJSAK,William C   Sex:M   17 Mar 1949 Alexander F Hujsak & Annis P Wilson
HULL,Jennifer Brooke Sex:F 19 Sep 1982 Gregory A Hull & Susan J McLaughlin
HULL,Ryan Alton   Sex:M   16 Apr 1981 Gregory Allen Hull & Susan J McLaughlin
HUME,Allyson J   Sex:F   03 Jun 1970 Alex M Hume & Joan L Wilson
HUNNEWELL,Ralph Edward   Sex:M   (Child #2) 28 Mar 1925 Ralph E Hunnewell
   (Watertown, MA) & Josephine Flanagan (Lowell, MA)
HUNNEWELL,Richard W   Sex:M   30 Nov 1967 Albert J Hunnewell & Anne F Briggs
HUNT,[Unknown]   Sex:F   (Child #3) 09 Jan 1916 Hudson, NH John H Hunt
   (Salem, NH) & Lucy D Ball (Kingston, NH)
HUNTER,Andrew H Sex:M   (Child #4) 16 Jan 1903 Frank A Hunter (Rockbottom, MA)
   & Anez Beal (Harrisville)
HUNTER,Elizabeth M   Sex:F   01 Nov 1954 Robert R Hunter & Joan B Lilley
HUNTER,Kenneth M Sex:M   (Child #5) 18 Dec 1906 Frank A Hunter (Rockbottom,
   MA) & Amy Beal (Harrisville, NH)
HUNTER,Melanie J   Sex:F   03 Sep 1957 Harry B Hunter & June V Noonan
HUNTER,Ryan Russell Sex:M   03 Mar 1984 Hannibal R Hunter Jr & Susan Ann Boyer
HUNTER,Susan L   Sex:F   17 Jun 1966 Donald M Hunter & Alice E Littlefield
HUOT,Jeffrey D   Sex:M   07 Nov 1968 Raymond L Huot & Louise C St Onge
HURD,Chester   Sex:M   (Child #3) 15 Mar 1936 George Hurd (Nashua, NH)
   & Mary McLeon (Nova Scotia)
HURD,George G   Sex:M   17 Feb 1970 Chester E Hurd & Joyce M Giderian
HURD,Hollis M   Sex:F   29 Nov 1966 Chester E Hurd & Patricia B Desmarais
HURD,Horace Robert Sex:M   (Child #1) 13 Jul 1935 Horace Hurd (Manchester, NH)

HUDSON,NH BIRTHS

  & Doris Green (Nashua, NH)
HURD,Phyllis A   Sex:F   (Child #4) 12 Nov 1943 George E Hurd (Nashua, NH)
  & Mary A McLean (Nova Scotia)
HURD,Stacey D   Sex:F   06 May 1968 Chester E Hurd & Joyce M Giderian
HURDER,Derek J   Sex:M   09 Mar 1977 Dennis F Hurder & Gail E Martin
HURDER,Robyn Courtney   Sex:F   01 Jan 1982 Dennis F Hurder & Gail Ethel Martin
HURLEY,Eileen J   Sex:F   09 Aug 1971 David J Hurley & Eileen J Connell
HURLEY,Meghan Ann Sex:F 13 Oct 1980 John M Hurley & Mary Elizabeth Espie
HURLEY,Shawn Michael   Sex:M   23 Dec 1982 John M Hurley & Mary Elizabeth Espie
HURSHMAN,Melissa Ann   Sex:F   23 Apr 1985 William J Hurshman & Angela F Kisich
HURWITZ,Justin William Sex:M 18 Nov 1980 Bruce A Hurwitz & Karen Sue McEwen
HUSEIN,Raj Amery   Sex:M   23 Nov 1976 Firoz M Husein & Diane Clark
HUSTON,Abigail   Sex:F   12 Mar 1744 Hudson, NH Samuel Huston & Sarah
HUSTON,Devin   Sex:M   20 Oct 1983 Roland E Huston Jr & Colleen Ann O'Meara
HUSTON,Mary   Sex:F   31 Jan 1741 Hudson, NH Samuel Huston & Sarah
HUSTON,Mary   Sex:F   31 Jan 1740 Hudson, NH Samuel Huston & Sarah
HUSTON,Samuel   Sex:M   18 Feb 1745 Hudson, NH Samuel Huston & Sarah
HUTCHINS,Albert Sex:M 16 Feb 1869 Hudson, NH Monza G Hutchins
  & Nancy J Fuller
HUTCHINS,Edna R   Sex:F   24 Jul 1872 Hudson, NH Alonzo G Hutchins & Nancy J
HUTCHINS,Joseph F   Sex:M   01 Jun 1875 Hudson, NH A G Hutchins & Nancy
HUTCHINS,[Unknown] Sex:M   15 Jan 1871 Hudson, NH Alonzo G Hutchins & Nancy J
ILLG,Daniel Laurence   Sex:M   20 Jul 1984 David James Illg & Laura Hean DeWitt
ILLG,David James II   Sex:M   20 Apr 1983 David James Illg & Laura Jean De Witt
INGALLS,Julie   Sex:F   (Child #1) 27 Feb 1941 Elston P Ingalls (Bar Mills, ME)
  & Paulette L Roussin (Biddeford, ME)
INGERSOLL,Aaron F   Sex: 05 Jan 1973 James H Ingersoll & Janet M Mullins
INGRAM,Elizabeth A   Sex:F   10 Dec 1961 William C Ingram & Judith A Dobens
INGRAM,Timothy P   Sex:M   24 Jul 1965 William C Ingram & Judith A Dobens
INGRAM,William M   Sex:M   09 Sep 1960 William C Ingram & Judith A Dobens
INKEL,Susannah   Sex:F   03 Nov 1977 John P Inkel & Virginia J Davis
IRVING,Richard D   Sex:M   22 Jan 1966 Richard G Irving & Audrey J Witmor
IRWIN,Michelle Dorogea   Sex:F   01 Aug 1979 Kevin Francis Irwin
  & Katherine A Polkey
ISABELLE,Keith R   Sex:M   10 Jan 1972 Roger L Isabelle & Frances Harmon
IVES,Aaron C   Sex:M   17 Apr 1970 Charles M Ives & Linda J Sprague
IVES,Barbara A   Sex:F   06 Feb 1950 Merrill M Ives, Jr & Thelma E McCoy
IVES,Brenda L   Sex:F   18 Jan 1955 Howard F Ives & Shirley A Foster
IVES,Cynthia J   Sex:F   03 Feb 1952 Earl L Ives & Jane I Bouley
IVES,Earl L Jr   Sex:M   16 Mar 1950 Earl L Ives & June I Bouley
IVES,Eric Sven   Sex:M   21 Apr 1977 Howard W Ives & Lora Lee Hetzer
IVES,Gayle E   Sex:F   09 Mar 1951 Howard F Ives & Shirley A Foster
IVES,Howard W   Sex:M   22 Nov 1956 Charles W Ives & Mabel G Landry
IVES,James M   Sex:M   21 Oct 1948 Merrill M Ives, Jr (Nashua, NH)
  & Thelma McCoy (Hudson, NH)
IVES,Jennifer L   Sex:F   14 Mar 1974 James M Ives & Suzanne L Burner
IVES,Michael J   Sex:M   23 Sep 1977 James M Ives & Suzanne L Burner
IVES,Ruth Esther   Sex:F   (Child #7) 06 Feb 1934 Merrill M Ives (Chazy, NY)
  & Bessie Burnice (Chazy, NY)
IVES,[Unknown]   Sex:F   28 Jan 1953 Earl L Ives & June I Bouley
IVON,Robert   Sex:M   (Child #3) 21 Aug 1919 Arthur Ivon (Canada)
  & Rosanna Desmarais (Nashua, NH)
JACKSON,Don Juan Sex:M   (Child #6) 14 Aug 1934 Elmer Jackson (Manchester, NH)
  & Ora Rioux (Canada)
JACKSON,Jeffrey W   Sex:M   19 Mar 1968 James H Jackson & Judith A Surprenant
JACKSON,Michael E   Sex:M   06 May 1953 Ovila W Jackson & Patricia R Lamper
JACKSON,Nathan W   Sex:M   20 Aug 1976 Wayne C Jackson & Patricia Ann Gruizin
JACOBS,Michael Douglas Jr   Sex:M   20 Dec 1984 Michael D Jacobs Sr
  & Laurie Lee Brown
JACQUES,Alfred W   Sex:M   30 Jan 1956 Alfred A Jacques, Jr & Dolores E Graham

HUDSON,NH BIRTHS

JACQUES,Allen D   Sex:M   21 Dec 1958 Alfred A Jacques & Dolores E Graham
JACQUES,Cheryl A   Sex:F   16 Jul 1966 Paul E Jacques & Carmel F Arpin
JACQUES,Craig P   Sex:M   09 Aug 1974 Paul E Jacques & Carmel F Arpin
JACQUES,Denise L M Sex:F   (Child #1) 02 Apr 1927 Alfred A Jacques (Lowell,
   MA) & Yvonne Rodier (Nashua, NH)
JACQUES,Eric P   Sex:M   20 Aug 1960 Alfred A Jacques & Dolores E Graham
JACQUES,Karen S   Sex:F   16 Oct 1970 Alfred A Jacques & Dolores E Graham
JACQUES,Lori A   Sex:F   09 Sep 1963 Alfred A Jacques & Dolores E Graham
JACQUES,Paul Ernest Sex:M   (Child #3) 07 Sep 1934 Alfred Jacques (Lowell, MA)
   & Yvonne Rodier (Nashua, NH)
JAKUTIS,Ann M   Sex:F   08 Mar 1956 Edward B Jakutis & Lucille M Dumont
JALBERT,Ann Marie Sex:F   21 Dec 1978 John Raymond Jalbert & Linda J Pawelczyk
JALBERT,Beatrice Rachel   Sex:F   (Child #5) 09 Jul 1936 Eugene Jalbert
   (Nashua, NH) & Rose Boucher (Nashua, NH)
JALBERT,Carole Y   Sex:F   22 Jun 1960 George E Jalbert & Gertrude A Levesque
JALBERT,John H   Sex:M   16 May 1954 Walter L Jalbert & Joan M Raymond
JALBERT,Joseph R R   Sex:M   26 Dec 1947 Eugene A Jalbert (Lowell, MA)
   & Rose D Boucher (Nashua, NH)
JALBERT,Mary A   Sex:F   23 Jan 1948 George E Jalbert (Lowell, MA)
   & Gertrude A Levesque (Hudson, NH)
JALBERT,Norman P Jr   Sex:M   02 May 1969 Norman P Jalbert & Linda M Porter
JALBERT,Sally A   Sex:F   24 Jun 1958 Walter L Jalbert & Joan M Raymond
JALBERT,Sarah Marie Sex:F   14 Apr 1982 John Henry Jalbert & Linda Mary Winter
JALBERT,Theresa Adra Sex:F   (Child #3) 10 Dec 1932 Hudson, NH Eugene Jalbert
   (Lowell, MA) & Rose Boucher (Nashua, NH)
JAMBARD,Suzanne C   Sex:F   23 Sep 1960 Norman C Jambard & Pauline Berthiaume
JAMESON,Clarence Theodore   Sex:M   (Child #2) 19 Nov 1917 Edwin Jameson
   (Hooksett, NH) & Marion Knights (Merrimack, NH)
JAMESON,Daniel G   Sex:M   07 Sep 1947 Clarence T Jameson (Hudson, NH)
   & Dorothy L Todd (Nashua, NH)
JAMESON,Mildred   Sex:F   (Child #3) 18 Oct 1919 Edwin Jameson (Bow, NH)
   & Marion Knights (Merrimack, NH)
JANKAUSKAS,Edward   Sex:M   (Child #3) 05 Oct 1936 Joseph Jankauskas
   (Lithuania) & Marion Waisivilous (Lithuania)
JANKAUSKAS,Edward T Jr Sex:M 03 Sep 1958 Edward T Jankauskas
   & Elaine A Boilard
JANKAUSKAS,Jason P   Sex:M   14 May 1969 Joseph J Jankauskas & Alice G Galipeau
JANKAUSKAS,Joseph Jr   Sex:M   (Child #2) 24 Feb 1930 Joseph Jankauskas
   (Lithuania) & Marion Vaisivilute (Lithuania)
JANKAUSKAS,Karen E   Sex:F   24 Nov 1957 Joseph J Jankauskas & Alice G Galipeau
JANKAUSKAS,Steven J Sex:M   17 Dec 1959 Joseph J Jankauskas & Alice G Galipeau
JANKAUSKAS,Susan A   Sex:F   06 Oct 1955 Joseph J Jankauskas & Alice G Galipeau
JANKAUSKAS,Tracey J   Sex:F   29 Feb 1964 Edward T Jankauskas
   & Elaine A Boilard
JANKOUSKAS,Kimberly A Sex:F 26 Apr 1961 Edward T Jankouskas
   & Elaine A Boilard
JAQUITH,Anna   Sex:F   12 Aug 1867 Hudson, NH George D Jaquith & Sarah J Fox
JAQUITH,Anna   Sex:F   15 Aug 1867 Hudson, NH George D Jaquith & Sarah J
JARRET,Thomas George II   Sex:M   05 Nov 1984 Thomas George Jarret
   & Denise C Provencher
JARRY,Jonathan M   Sex:M   29 Mar 1978 Albert H Jarry & Patricia M Gallo
JARRY,Nathan R   Sex:M   05 Feb 1980 Michael R Jarry & Donna M Landry
JARRY,Sarah Kathleen Sex:F 18 Dec 1978 Michael R Jarry & Donna Marie Landry
JARVIS,Michael E   Sex:M   10 Dec 1969 Elton L Jarvis Jr & Patricia A Knechtel
JASPER,Bruce R   Sex:M   10 Apr 1947 Robert A Jasper (Nashua, NH)
   & Una B Hayes (Farmington, NH)
JASPER,Gregg H   Sex:M   12 Jan 1953 Robert A Jasper & Una B Hayes
JASPER,James A   Sex:M   07 Jul 1951 Robert A Jasper & Una B Hayes
JASPER,Maria A   Sex:F   11 Feb 1962 Robert A Jasper & Reita A Newton
JASPER,Shawn N   Sex:M   23 Jan 1959 Robert A Jasper & Reita A Newton

HUDSON,NH BIRTHS

JASPER,Susan U   Sex:F   09 Mar 1949 Robert A Jasper & Una B Hayes
JATKEWICZ,Paul P   Sex:M   (Child #5) 28 Jun 1930 Walter Jatkewicz (Poland)
   & Stela Junszewski (Poland)
JATKWICZ,Morgan C   Sex:M   18 Nov 1966 Frank Jatkwicz & Grace-Marie Brunelle
JATKWICZ,Stafana   Sex:F   (Child #3) 14 Feb 1926 Walter Jatkwicz (Russia)
   & Stafana Janusefska (Russia)
JATKWICZ,Stephen   Sex:M   (Child #2) 12 Dec 1923 Walter Jatkwicz (Russia)
   & Stephona Janusewski (Russia)
JEAN,Elizabeth M   Sex:F   20 Mar 1963 Ronald A Jean & Irene A Tiernan
JEAN,Jesse Allen   Sex:M   13 Aug 1978 Leonard Allen Jean & Nicole F St Amour
JEAN,Juliette   Sex:F   (Child #1) 05 Dec 1907 Thomas Jean (Canada)
   & Julie Jean (Nashua, NH)
JEAN,Karen Elise Sex:F 16 Feb 1983 Peter Michael Jean & Denise Claire Albert
JEAN,Linda M   Sex:F   12 Jun 1948 Raymond R Jean (Nashua, NH)
   & Emilienne M Cote (Westford, MA)
JEAN,Mark A   Sex:M   08 Jan 1962 Norman M Jean & Rita C Kashulines
JEAN,Norman M   Sex:M   19 Jan 1953 Norman M Jean & Rita C Kashulines
JEAN,Robert A   Sex:M   (Child #1) 10 Oct 1945 Amedee A Jean (Nashua, NH)
   & Louise B St Laurent (Manchester, NH)
JEAN,Romio   Sex:M   (Child #2) 05 Dec 1907 Thomas Jean (Canada) & Julie Jean
   (Nashua, NH)
JEAN,Shayla Rose   Sex:F   01 Jun 1978 Ernest V Jean & Joanne I Gilmartin
JEAN,Tracy Nicole   Sex:F   23 Apr 1981 Leonard Allen Jean & Nicole F St Amour
JEANNOTTE,Elaine Florence   Sex:F   (Child #2) 29 Jan 1935 Valmore Bapt
   Jeannotte (Nashua, NH) & Bernice Viola Davis (Hudson, NH)
JEFFERSON,Colleen A   Sex:F   27 Oct 1971 Eaton F Jefferson & Patricia A Alton
JEFFERY,Katrina Lynn   Sex:F   24 Mar 1983 Scott T Jeffery & Rhonda Ann Harwood
JEFFREY,Erik Scott Sex:M 01 Nov 1984 Scott T Jeffrey & Rhonda Ann Harwood
JELLEY,Bonnie M   Sex:F   03 Feb 1958 Leonard J Jelley & Edith L LaFlamme
JELLISON,Edwin Forest Sex:M 20 Oct 1869 Hudson, NH Hiram P Jellison
   & Lillie N
JENKINS,Jeremy Wayne   Sex:M   24 Jan 1984 Lawrence J Jenkins
   & MaryAnn Julia McHugh
JENKINS,John Thomas   Sex:M   22 Oct 1982 Jack Jay Jenkins & Susan Jean Lawhead
JENKINS,Joshua Donald   Sex:M   03 Apr 1982 Lawrence J JenkinsJr
   & Mary Ann J McHugh
JENKINS,Turney B   Sex:F   07 Dec 1966 Richard G Jenkins & Theresa L McKinney
JENKS,Joanne K   Sex:F   17 Oct 1958 Kenneth D Jenks & Andrea M Gagnon
JENKS,Scott E   Sex:M   17 May 1960 Kenneth D Jenks & Andrea M Gagnon
JENKS,Sean P   Sex:M   10 Nov 1971 Andrew B Jenks & Mary R Foss
JENNESS,Jeffrey L   Sex:M   21 May 1978 Wayne B Jenness & Irene E Doucette
JENNINGS,Timothy W   Sex:M   28 Apr 1965 Peter M Jennings & Virginia M Hemenway
JENSEN,William Bert   Sex:M   05 Feb 1985 Francis B Jensen & Denise G Duplease
JETTE,Andrea Rose   Sex:F   10 Sep 1981 Andre Roland Jette & Alice Neves
JETTE,Ann M   Sex:F   23 Jun 1963 Louis W Jette & Frances J Brown
JETTE,Arthur G   Sex:M   02 Apr 1951 Norman E Jette & Madeline L Cartier
JETTE,Cecile J   Sex:F   12 Nov 1965 Louis W Jette & Frances J Brown
JETTE,Craig R   Sex:M   16 Feb 1961 Louis W Jette & Frances J Brown
JETTE,Gerard E   Sex:M   15 Jun 1954 Edmond L Jette & Rose M Boissonneault
JETTE,Jennifer Ann   Sex:F   14 Nov 1975 Louis W Jette & Frances J Brown
JETTE,Jos Ed Luc Art   Sex:M   (Child #1) 23 May 1934 Edmund Jette (Nashua, NH)
   & Rose Boissonneault (Nashua, NH)
JETTE,Jos Errick Roger   Sex:M   (Child #4) 15 Jan 1938 Edmond Louis Jette
   (Nashua, NH) & Marie R Boissonneault (Nashua, NH)
JETTE,Joseph Henry   Sex:M (Child #1) 29 Jun 1935 Edmond Jette (Nashua, NH)
   & Rose Boissonneault (Nashua, NH)
JETTE,Joseph R A   Sex:M   09 Jan 1951 Edmond L Jette & Rose M Boissoneault
JETTE,Linda M   Sex:F   19 May 1957 Normand E Jette & Madeleine L Cartier
JETTE,Lorraine M   Sex:F   (Child #6) 30 May 1946 Edmond L Jette (Nashua, NH)
   & Rose M Boissonneault (Nashua, NH)

HUDSON,NH BIRTHS

JETTE,Marie Gert Ther Sex:F (Child #4) 14 May 1925 Adelbert Jette (Nashua, NH) & Cecile Marquis (Manchester, NH)
JETTE,Marie M Sex:F (Child #4) 27 Jan 1942 Edmond L Jette (Nashua, NH) & Rose M Boissonneault (Nashua, NH)
JETTE,Marie Rita Adria Sex:F (Child #3) 18 Aug 1923 Adalbert Jette (Nashua, NH) & Cecile Marquis (Manchester, NH)
JETTE,Maurice Andre J Sex:M (Child #2) 04 Jun 1922 Adalbert Jette (Nashua, NH) & Cecile Marquis (Manchester, NH)
JETTE,Michelle B Sex:F 23 Feb 1958 Edmond L Jette & Rose M Boissonneault
JETTE,Rene A Sex:M 15 Jun 1954 Edmond L Jette & Rose M Boissonneault
JETTE,Robert A Sex:M 10 Apr 1952 Norman E Jette & Madeline L Cartier
JETTE,Rose Marie Pauline Sex:F (Child #3) 25 Jun 1936 Edmund Jette (Nashua, NH) & Rose Boissonneault (Nashua, NH)
JETTE,Tricia Renee Sex:F 19 Jul 1982 Rene Adrien Jette & Sheila Ann Keenan
JEWELL,Frederick M Sex:M (Child #2) 26 Oct 1902 Albert P Jewell (Nashua, NH) & Bertha S Marshall (Hudson, NH)
JEWELL,Gothard G Sex:M (Child #3) 28 Dec 1907 Albert P Jewell (Nashua, NH) & Bertha S Marshall (Hudson, NH)
JEWELL,Hazel May Sex:F (Child #1) 27 Sep 1900 Albert P Jewell (Nashua, NH) & Bertha S Marshall (Hudson, NH)
JEWELL,Helen Christina Sex:F (Child #2) 30 May 1932 Hudson, NH Gothard Jewell (Nashua, NH) & Gladys Camble (Howland, ME)
JEWETT,Leonard M Jr Sex:M 30 Aug 1977 Leonard M Jewett & Catherine E Grigas
JEZIERSKI,Francis M Sex:M 27 Sep 1948 Frank Jezierski (Pittsburg, MA) & Alice Leary (Haverhill, MA)
JEZIERSKI,Philip E Sex:M 14 Oct 1950 Frank Jezierski & Alice E Leary
JIMERSON,Paul H Sex:M 13 Feb 1954 Norman C Jimerson & Melva J Brooks
JODOIN,Lisa M Sex:F 15 Sep 1962 Norman R Jodoin & Roberta C Belhumeur
JODOIN,Richard A Jr Sex:M 10 Dec 1970 Richard A Jodoin & Susan G Martin
JOHNSON,Aaron Michael Sex:M 28 Nov 1983 Robert N Johnson & Mary Ann Spellman
JOHNSON,Abigail Sex:F 22 Jan 1762 Hudson, NH Moses Johnson & Anna
JOHNSON,Alonzo Sex:M 12 Feb 1828 Hudson, NH Dolivar Johnson & Louisa Underwood
JOHNSON,Andrew Vincent Sex:M 19 Jul 1983 David A Johnson & Debra J Locicero
JOHNSON,Anna Sex:F 15 Jul 1758 Hudson, NH Moses Johnson & Anna
JOHNSON,Anna Sex:F 25 Jul 1755 Hudson, NH Moses Johnson & Anne
JOHNSON,Bertie Sex:F Dec 1881 Hudson, NH Moses Johnson & Abbie
JOHNSON,Bette Bradstreet Sex:F 21 Feb 1766 Hudson, NH Moses Johnson & Anna
JOHNSON,Betty Bradstreet Sex:F 21 Feb 1766 Hudson, NH Moses Johnson & Anna
JOHNSON,Charles Harold Sex:M (Child #1) 07 Oct 1935 Charles H Johnson (Portsmouth, NH) & Almeda Bassett (Hudson, NH)
JOHNSON,Christopher N Sex:M 19 Nov 1971 Lawrence N Johnson & Mona R Lajoie
JOHNSON,Clinton W Sex:M 17 May 1976 David A Johnson & Nancy Ann Elie
JOHNSON,David P Sex:M 19 Sep 1955 Paul O Johnson & Annette F Boucher
JOHNSON,Donald A Sex:M 09 Oct 1966 Charles H Johnson & Carolyn A Donnelly
JOHNSON,Donna M Sex:F 25 May 1960 Charles H Johnson & Carolyn A Donnelly
JOHNSON,Edmund Luke Sex:M (Child #1) 30 Dec 1933 John A Johnson (New Brunswick) & Edith V Kelly (New Brunswick)
JOHNSON,Gary W Sex:M 02 Jul 1964 Carl H Johnson & Nancy E Spears
JOHNSON,George Lewis Sex:M 08 Jan 1879 Hudson, NH James U Johnson & Mary Valentine
JOHNSON,Hannah Sex:F 23 Dec 1778 Hudson, NH Moses Johnson & Anna
JOHNSON,Heather Cooke-Corey Sex:F 03 Sep 1978 Herbert L Jordan & Cynthia Anna Cooke
JOHNSON,Heather J Sex:F 24 Jun 1971 Gregory E Johnson & Joan L Boyer
JOHNSON,Jacob M Sex:M 10 Jan 1768 Hudson, NH Moses Johnson & Anna
JOHNSON,Jacob Moody Sex:M 10 Jun 1768 Hudson, NH Moses Johnson & Anna
JOHNSON,James E Sex:M 15 Feb 1962 Charles H Johnson,Jr & Carolyn A Donnelly
JOHNSON,James Underwood Sex:M 28 Aug 1831 Hudson, NH Dolivar Johnson & Louisa Underwood

HUDSON,NH BIRTHS

```
JOHNSON,Jason R   Sex:M   31 Dec 1975 Willard W Johnson Jr & Martha J Gottsche
JOHNSON,Joseph    Sex:M   29 Feb 1760 Hudson, NH Moses Johnson & Anna
JOHNSON,Karen     Sex:F   (Child #1) 27 Aug 1941 Dexter Johnson (Nashua, NH)
    & Annabelle Spence (Nashua, NH)
JOHNSON,Karen B   Sex:F   19 Jan 1954 Robert L Johnson & Elizabeth E Worth
JOHNSON,Karin E   Sex:F   17 Jul 1968 John C Johnson & Deborah E Calder
JOHNSON,Karl E K  Sex:M   18 Jul 1966 Richard P Johnson & Phebe A Bloomberg
JOHNSON,Kenneth L Sex:M   18 Aug 1956 Erlon K Johnson & Mary A Southard
JOHNSON,Kristina M  Sex:F   30 Mar 1972 Raymond M Johnson & Rhae C Cote
JOHNSON,Leonard H Sex:M   11 Sep 1812 Hudson, NH Kimball Johnson & Mary
JOHNSON,Leonard Haseltine  Sex:M   12 Sep 1812 Hudson, NH Kimball Johnson
    & Mary Merrill
JOHNSON,Linda G   Sex:F   18 Nov 1948 Gale W Johnson (Derry, NH)
    & Patricia Perry (Manchester, NH)
JOHNSON,Lynne A   Sex:F   08 Feb 1963 Carlton A Johnson & Christine A Curran
JOHNSON,Mark T    Sex:M   22 Dec 1957 Paul O Johnson & Annette F Boucher
JOHNSON,Molle     Sex:F   17 Oct 1776 Hudson, NH Moses Johnson & Anne
JOHNSON,Molly     Sex:F   17 Oct 1776 Hudson, NH Moses Johnson & Anna
JOHNSON,Moses     Sex:M   17 Dec 1769 Hudson, NH Moses Johnson & Anna
JOHNSON,Pamela J  Sex:F   02 Feb 1950 Gale N Johnson & Patricia M Perry
JOHNSON,Paula A   Sex:F   23 Aug 1956 Paul O Johnson & Annette F Boucher
JOHNSON,Robert L Jr  Sex:M   06 Oct 1949 Robert L Johnson & Elizabeth E Worth
JOHNSON,Robin L   Sex:F   27 Jan 1964 Gale W Johnson & Patricia M Perry
JOHNSON,Ruth M    Sex:F   04 Dec 1771 Hudson, NH Moses Johnson & Anna
JOHNSON,Ruth Moody  Sex:F   04 Dec 1771 Hudson, NH Moses Johnson & Anna
JOHNSON,Ruth Simira  Sex:F   05 May 1860 Hudson, NH Thomas Johnson
    & Ruth Simira Webster
JOHNSON,Sarah     Sex:F   17 Mar 1764 Hudson, NH Moses Johnson & Anna
JOHNSON,Sarah Anne  Sex:F   28 Jun 1981 Ralph G Johnson & Monique C Dionne
JOHNSON,Stacy Lyn  Sex:F   17 May 1976 David A Johnson & Nancy Ann Elie
JOHNSON,Suzanne M Sex:F   01 Sep 1959 Paul O Johnson & Annette F Boucher
JOHNSON,Thomas    Sex:M   29 Nov 1856 Hudson, NH Thomas Johnson & Ruth S Webster
JOHNSON,Walter Elroy  Sex:M   09 Aug 1874 Hudson, NH James U Johnson
    & Mary Valentine
JOHNSON,William   Sex:M   07 Feb 1774 Hudson, NH Moses Johnson & Anna
JOHNSON,William   Sex:M   07 Jul 1794 Hudson, NH Moses Johnson Jr & Molly
JOHNSTON,Juliane  Sex:F   15 Jul 1948 Thomas W Johnston (Newark, NJ)
    & Patricia M Gregoire (Wilton, NH)
JOHNSTON,Laura Lynn  Sex:F   06 Apr 1984 Mark C Johnston & Cheryl Anne Gosse
JOKI,Jill H       Sex:F   18 Jan 1964 Herbert W Joki & Dorothy M Austin
JOLES,Mona Lisa S Sex:F   01 Aug 1965 Marvin J Joles & Susan A Campbell
JOLLY,Elizabeth A Sex:F   (Child #1) 11 Jul 1946 Raymond L Jolly (Boston, MA)
    & Ruth M Wilcox (Nashua, NH)
JONES,Barbara A   Sex:F   27 May 1954 Clarence W Jones & Alice M Hemingway
JONES,Bessie E    Sex:F   (Child #1) 07 Sep 1891 Joshua W Jones (Danbury, NH)
    & Kate A Morrison (Canada)
JONES,Cynthia C   Sex:F   14 Jan 1957 Clarence W Jones & Alice M Hemingway
JONES,Daniel C    Sex:M   18 Sep 1967 Kenneth A Jones & Shirley A Ducheneau
JONES,Daniel Ian  Sex:M   10 Feb 1984 James Joseph Jones & Annette Huxford
JONES,Darrell Guy Jr Sex:M   28 Jul 1980 Darrell Guy Jones Sr & Beth Ann Bogan
JONES,Deborah L   Sex:F   22 Oct 1953 Herman W Jones & Frances V Sager
JONES,Henry C     Sex:M   22 Sep 1866 Hudson, NH Alden Jones & Louisa A
JONES,Henry Clinton  Sex:M   22 Sep 1866 Hudson, NH Alden M Jones & Susan A
JONES,Pamela K    Sex:F   11 Nov 1958 Clarence W Jones & Alice M Hemingway
JONES,Scott M     Sex:M   28 Nov 1965 Kenneth A Jones & Shirley A Ducheneau
JORDAN,Craig L    Sex:M   28 Nov 1973 Lester J Jordan & Gayle A Broadbent
JORDAN,Joyce L    Sex:F   17 Mar 1965 Ralph L Jordan & Edith L Adams
JORDAN,Matthew Joseph Sex:M   16 Mar 1984 Joseph L Jordan & Mary Theresa Spahn
JORDAN,Wesley W   Sex:M   09 Dec 1961 Herbert L Jordan & Esther H Dubois
JOSEF,Anne        Sex:F   (Child #4) 28 Sep 1934 John Wm Josef (Germany) & Anna King
```

HUDSON, NH BIRTHS

(Nashua, NH)
JOSEF,Carolyn Sex:F (Child #5) 12 Jan 1941 John W Josef (Nashua, NH)
  & Ann M King (Albania)
JOSEF,Raymond King Sex:M (Child #3) 28 Dec 1933 John Josef (Germany)
  & Anna King (Nashua, NH)
JOSEF,Richard M Sex:M 03 Jul 1967 Raymond K Josef & Helen F Villemure
JOSEF,Thomas E Sex:M 22 Aug 1964 Raymond K Josef & Helen F Villemare
JOY,Arthur L Sex:M 03 Feb 1864 Hudson, NH Lionel F Joy & May E
JOY,Laura J Sex:F (Child #2) 01 Mar 1895 Arthur L Joy (Hudson, NH)
  & Lucy A Ingalls (Nashua, NH)
JOY,Lester Arthur Sex:M (Child #3) 31 Mar 1901 Hudson, NH A L Joy (Hudson,
  NH) & Lucy A Ingalls (Nashua, NH)
JOY,Marion I Sex:F 20 May 1893 Arthur L Joy (Hudson, NH) & Lucy A Ingalls
  (Nashua, NH)
JOY,[Unknown] Sex: 03 Feb 1861 Hudson, NH Lemuel T Joy & Mary E Hadley
JOY,[Unknown] Sex:M 22 May 1869 Hudson, NH Lemuel G Joy & Mary E
JOYAL,Bryan Joseph Sex:M 15 Mar 1983 Rene Philip Joyal & Diane Marie Gagnon
JOYAL,Christine Rachel Sex:F 23 Dec 1980 Rene P Joyal & Diane Marie Gagnon
JOYCE,Arease N Sex:F (Child #8) 18 Feb 1940 James H Joyce (Tilton, NH)
  & Ida U Quint (Haverhill, NH)
JOYCE,David A Sex:M 02 Oct 1958 Constant J Joyce & Mary H Schoolcraft
JOYCE,George Howard Sex:M (Child #4) 13 Jan 1930 James H Joyce (Tilton, NH)
  & Velma I Quint (Woodsville, NH)
JOYCE,Gerald R Sex:M 18 Jul 1948 Constant C Joyce (Clinton, MA)
  & Mary H Schoolcraft (Nashua, NH)
JOYCE,Glenwood John Sex:M (Child #9) 13 Apr 1937 James H Joyce (Tilton, NH)
  & Velma Quint (Haverhill, NH)
JOYCE,Mabel Erdine Sex:F (Child #5) 21 Aug 1931 James H Joyce (Tilton, NH)
  & Velma I Quint (Haverhill, NH)
JOYCE,Pearl Lorraine Sex:F (Child #7) 03 May 1934 James H Joyce (Tilton, NH)
  & Ida Quint (Woodsville, NH)
JOYCE,Richard A Sex:M 30 Aug 1951 Constant C Joyce & Mary H Schoolcraft
JOYCE,Robert Henry Sex:M (Child #6) 01 Dec 1932 Grasmere, NH James H Joyce
  (Tilton, NH) & Velma I Quint (Woodsville, NH)
JUBERT,William R Sex:M 21 Mar 1947 Russell J Jubert (Nashua, NH)
  & Cecile L Ledoux (Nashua, NH)
JUBERT,[Unknown] Sex:M 01 Jul 1948 Russell Jubert (Nashua, NH)
  & Cecile Ledoux (Nashua, NH)
JUDKINS,Laura J Sex:F 01 Oct 1966 William R Judkins & Sylvia J Cramer
JULIEN,April Marie Sex:F 30 Apr 1982 Kenneth G Julien & Lisa Mary Giroux
JURDAK,Mellissa Beth Sex:F 25 Jun 1976 George E Jurdak & Kathryn E Rowe
JUREK,Jill M Sex:F 07 Jun 1969 Ronald A Jurek & Judith A Hayes
KABLIK,Erian K Sex:M 11 Oct 1968 Kenneth J Kablik & Pamela K Sherwin
KABLIK,Jeffrey J Sex:M 19 Sep 1969 Kenneth J Kablik & Pamela K Sherwin
KACMARCIK,Martha A Sex:F 04 Feb 1965 William Kacmarcik & Frances Niedziela
KACMARCIK,Mary E Sex:F 30 Sep 1960 William F Kacmarcik & Frances Niedziela
KACMARCIK,[Unknown] Sex:M 02 Oct 1961 William F Kacmarcik & Frances Niedziela
KAETZ,Charles Jeffrey Sex:M 18 Dec 1980 Charles C Kaetz & Susan Marie Dever
KAETZ,Timothy Christopher Sex:M 01 Jul 1983 Charles C Kaetz & Susan M Dever
KALIL,Charles D Sex:M 22 Jul 1963 Charles W Kalil & Brenda V Bossie
KALIL,Lisa J Sex:F 28 Jun 1960 Charles W Kalil & Brenda V Bossie
KALIL,Lynn J Sex:F 28 Jun 1960 Charles W Kalil & Brenda V Bossie
KAMENSKI,David Joseph Sex:M 18 Nov 1980 Robert S Kamenski
  & Kathleen L Simpson
KANAVOS,Christine Sex:F 01 Jun 1966 Nicholas C Kanavos & Joyce D Jackson
KANAVOS,Kathleen D Sex:F 12 Jun 1968 Nicholas C Kanavos & Joyce D Jackson
KANAVOS,Matthew N Sex:M 20 Jul 1971 Nicholas C Kanavos & Joyce D Jackson
KANAVOS,Stephanie L Sex:F 11 Jun 1969 John T Kanavos & Barbara L Cappi
KANAVOS,[Unknown] Sex:M 28 May 1971 John T Kanavos & Barbara L Cappi
KANE,Karen N Sex:F 29 May 1954 John T Kane & Barbara J Risley

HUDSON, NH BIRTHS

KANE, Susan J   Sex:F   08 Dec 1960 John T Kane & Barbara J Risley
KARRFALT, Carl B   Sex:M   11 Oct 1963 Carl A Karrfalt & Esther M Bradshaw
KARUZIS, Helen A   Sex:F   (Child #8) 07 Mar 1924 Michael Karuzis (Lithuania)
  & Antonette Stausick (Lithuania)
KASHULINES, Donna L   Sex:F   01 Nov 1952 Robert Kashulines & Shirley I Dumas
KASHULINES, Gary W   Sex:M   28 Sep 1965 Richard J Kashulines
  & Katherine M Flanders
KASHULINES, Peter E Sex:M 22 Nov 1964 Arthur J Kashulines & Martha A Spaulding
KASHULINES, Peter Thomas   Sex:M   (Child #7) 31 Aug 1935 Albert Kashulines
  (Nashua, NH) & Celestine Girouard (Nashua, NH)
KASPER, Joseph Peter   Sex:M   (Child #2) 21 Sep 1937 Peter Kasper (Nashua, NH)
  & Anna Petkevich (Lowell, MA)
KASTEN, Sybil-Lee   Sex:F   01 Apr 1964 Elliott A Kasten & Maxine V Stafford
KATSIREBAS, Jeffrey T Sex:M   07 Aug 1973 John T Katsirebas Sr & Janis E Dumont
KATSIREBAS, John T Jr Sex:M   24 Apr 1971 John T Katsirebas Sr & Janis E Dumont
KAULBACK, Clarence   Sex:M   12 Jul 1879 Hudson, NH William Kaulback & Emma E
KAVEHRAD, Amir Ahmad   Sex:M   13 Nov 1981 Mohsen Kavehrad & Susan Alice Carney
KAY, James Douglas   Sex:M   28 Sep 1982 Douglas James Kay & Patricia E Farrar
KAYE, May E   Sex:F   (Child #6) 17 Nov 1892 Andrea Kaye (Scotland)
  & Mary Hutchinson (N B)
KAYRAS, Alice   Sex:F   (Child #7) 28 Feb 1926 Anthony Kayras (Russia)
  & Frances Alukonis (Russia)
KAYRAS, Florence   Sex:F   (Child #8) 19 Jun 1928 Anthony Kayras (Russia)
  & Frances Alkornis (Russia)
KAYRAS, [Unknown]   Sex:F   (Child #6) 29 Jan 1924 Anthony Kayras (Russia)
  & Frances Alukonis (Russia)
KAYROS, Barbara I   Sex:F   (Child #2) 15 Apr 1946 Stanley Kayros (Nashua, NH)
  & May H Aparowske (Manchester, NH)
KAYROS, Gloria H   Sex:F   (Child #1) 14 Jul 1942 Stanley Kayros (Nashua, NH)
  & Hedwig Ogorowski (Manchester, NH)
KAYROS, Peter A   Sex:M   15 May 1948 Stanley Kayros (Nashua, NH)
  & Hedwig M Oparowski (Manchester, NH)
KAYROS, Theresa M   Sex:F   02 Sep 1959 Stanley Kayros & May H Oparowske
KAZLAUSKAS, Frank S Sex:M   28 Sep 1953 Stanley Kazlauskas & Elaine E Pelletier
KAZLOUSKAS, Stanley L   Sex:M   13 Feb 1947 Stanley Kazlouskas (Nashua, NH)
  & Elaine E Pelletier (Nashua, NH)
KEACH, Stanley J Jr   Sex:M   (Child #2) 30 Jun 1944 Stanley J Keach (New
  Britain, CT) & Lola B Rawson (Worcester, MA)
KEACH, Susan J   Sex:F   (Child #1) 01 Mar 1942 Stanley J Keach (New Britain,
  CT) & Lola B Rawson (Worcester, MA)
KEANE, Caitlin Elizabeth Sex:F 09 Aug 1984 Brian O Keane & Theresa Ann Meehan
KEANE, Jennifer L   Sex: 23 Feb 1973 Paul A Keane & Frances M Binette
KEARNS, Arlene F   Sex:F   04 Nov 1963 Frederick F Kearns & Mildred K James
KEARNS, Kellie R   Sex: 04 Jun 1973 Paul J Kearns & Carol G Arel
KEEGAN, Briana Lynn   Sex:F   05 Apr 1985 Michael F Keegan & Donna L VanBuskirk
KEEGAN, Sean Geoffrey   Sex:M   21 Nov 1984 Charles E Keegan & Sandra J Chadwick
KEENAN, Ann M   Sex:F   01 Nov 1963 Paul C Keenan & Laurette A Langelier
KEENAN, Brian M   Sex:M   22 Oct 1960 Paul C Keenan & Laurette A Langelier
KEENAN, Carolyn A   Sex:F   12 May 1969 Paul D Keenan & Beverly J Hickey
KEENAN, Charles P   Sex:M   06 Apr 1959 Paul C Keenan & Laurette A Langelier
KEENAN, Maureen E   Sex:F   19 Apr 1958 Paul C Keenan & Laurette A Langelier
KEENE, Kevin R   Sex:M   09 Mar 1955 Robert D Keene & Juliette L Parent
KEENEY, Norwood H III   Sex:M   28 Nov 1958 Norwood H Keeney, Jr
  & Phyllis R Mottram
KEESER, Jayme Ann Sex:F   10 Nov 1976 Robert W Keeser Jr & Carol Ann Laviolette
KEHE, Lauren Marie   Sex:F   24 May 1985 James William Kehe & Patricia M Warner
KELLER, Justin T   Sex:M   27 Jun 1979 Thomas G Keller & Denise T Paquette
KELLEY, Donald A   Sex:M   30 Jan 1965 David R Kelley & Barbara L Colcord
KELLEY, Douglas E   Sex:M   03 Jun 1953 Almon H Kelley & Helen Albers
KELLEY, Elizabeth   Sex:F   23 Aug 1768 Hudson, NH Joseph Kelley & Sarah

HUDSON,NH BIRTHS

KELLEY,Elizebeth   Sex:F   23 Aug 1768 Hudson, NH Joseph Kelley & Sarah
KELLEY,George Willie   Sex:M   03 Mar 1862 Hudson, NH William Kelley
  & Dorcas Clement
KELLEY,John R   Sex:M   04 Oct 1947 Frank E Kelley (Nashua, NH)
  & Adrienne C Richard (Nashua, NH)
KELLEY,Joseph   Sex:M   04 May 1778 Hudson, NH Joseph Kelley & Sarah
KELLEY,Kathleen M   Sex:F   06 Dec 1949 Frank E Kelley & Adrienne C Richard
KELLEY,Keith W   Sex:M   31 Dec 1969 William J Kelley Jr & Cheryl N Houle
KELLEY,Lisa M   Sex: 07 Oct 1972 Richard A Kelley & Deborah L Thornton
KELLEY,Margaret   Sex:F   11 Jul 1770 Hudson, NH Joseph Kelley & Sarah
KELLEY,Margeret   Sex:F   11 Jul 1770 Hudson, NH Joseph Kelley & Sarah
KELLEY,Mary Ann   Sex:F   08 Dec 1950 Frank E Kelley & Adrienne C Richard
KELLEY,Paula E   Sex:F   09 Dec 1947 Almon H Kelley (Dorchester, MA)
  & Helen Albers (Andover, MA)
KELLEY,Ralph A   Sex:M   13 Jan 1952 Almon H Kelley & Helen Albers
KELLEY,Richard G   Sex:M   02 Nov 1954 Frank E Kelley & Adrienne C Richard
KELLEY,Sarah   Sex:F   21 Oct 1775 Hudson, NH Joseph Kelley & Sarah
KELLEY,Steven W   Sex:M   01 Jul 1961 David R Kelley & Barbara L Colcord
KELLEY,Susan F   Sex:F   26 Nov 1951 Frank E Kelley & Adrienne C Richard
KELLEY,Tyler   Sex:M   21 Apr 1800 Hudson, NH & Sarah Hadley
KELLEY,Willian N E   Sex:M   (Child #10) 14 Apr 1913 Walter E Kelley (Sandown,
  NH) & Nellie Riley (Ireland)
KELLEY,Wiseman   Sex:M   10 Sep 1780 Hudson, NH Joseph Kelley & Sarah
KELLEY,[Unknown] Sex:F 01 Sep 1865 Hudson, NH William Kelley & Dorcas Clement
KELLEY,[Unknown]   Sex: 03 Mar 1862 Hudson, NH William Kelley & Dorcas
KELLOGG,Julie A   Sex:F   04 Jul 1971 Charles B Kellogg Jr & Carole J Manter
KELLOWAY,Jeffrey Ryan Sex:M 13 Jul 1981 Joel K Kelloway & Betty Ann Zimmerman
KELLY,Candice Lee   Sex:F   28 Sep 1978 Colin Patrick Kelly & Debra Ann Goulet
KELLY,Eric James   Sex:M   29 Jan 1984 James Francis Kelly & Diane Sophie DeRoo
KELLY,Patricia S   Sex:F   15 Mar 1966 Paul T Kelly & Marion S Whittemore
KELLY,Sharon S   Sex:F   03 Mar 1965 Paul T Kelly & Marion S Whittemore
KEMP,Emeline M   Sex:F   07 Apr 1817 Hudson, NH Timothy Kemp & Sarah Brown
KEMPTON,Calvin A Jr   Sex:M   22 May 1964 Calvin A Kempton & Florence P Mears
KEMPTON,Charles C   Sex:M   04 Jul 1953 Calvin A Kempton & Florence P Mears
KEMPTON,Katherine A   Sex:F   27 Jan 1952 Calvin A Kempton & Florence P Mears
KEMPTON,Lora L   Sex:F   16 Apr 1959 Calvin A Kempton & Florence P Mears
KENDALL,Joan A   Sex:F   02 Apr 1952 Allan M Kendall & Florence I Newey
KENDRICK,David   Sex:M   17 Feb 1819 Billerica, MA David Kendrick & Clarissa
KENDRICK,David   Sex:M   19 Feb 1819 Hudson, NH David Kendrick & Clarissa
KENDRICK,Elbridge   Sex:M   16 Nov 1817 Hudson, NH David Kendrick & Clarissa
KENDRICK,Sarah   Sex:F   04 May 1820 Hudson, NH David Kendrick & Clarissa
KENICK,Tanya D   Sex:F   18 Jun 1975 Earl R Kenick & Luce M LaPlante
KENISTON,Albert Leroy   Sex:M   (Child #8) 31 Jan 1924 Charles F Keniston
  (Massachusetts) & Mary L Gowing (New Hampshire)
KENISTON,Earl F   Sex:M   (Child #5) 09 Aug 1919 Charles Keniston (Lowell, MA)
  & Mary Gowing (Hudson, NH)
KENISTON,Ethel Lillian   Sex:F   (Child #3) 04 Sep 1916 Hudson, NH Charles F
  Keniston (Lowell, MA) & Mary L Gowing (Hudson, NH)
KENISTON,Evelyn Louise   Sex:F   (Child #2) 04 Sep 1916 Hudson, NH Charles F
  Keniston (Lowell, MA) & Mary L Gowing (Hudson, NH)
KENISTON,Leslie H   Sex:M   (Child #1) 11 Nov 1915 Hudson, NH Charles F
  Keniston (Lowell, MA) & Mary L Gowing (Hudson, NH)
KENISTON,Maxwell   Sex:M   (Child #7) 18 JUl 1922 Chas F Keniston (Lowell, MA)
  & Mary L Gowing (Hudson, NH)
KENISTON,Myrtle Evelyn   Sex:F   (Child #9) 28 Sep 1926 Charles F Keniston
  (Lowell, MA) & Mary L Gowing (Hudson, NH)
KENISTON,Violet   Sex:F   (Child #4) 16 Jun 1918 Charles Keniston (Lowell, MA)
  & Mary Gowing (Hudson, NH)
KENNA,Catherine D   Sex:F   15 Apr 1955 Paul J Kenna & Mary D Fredette
KENNEDY,Allen B   Sex:M   30 Apr 1948 Frank L Kennedy (Canada)

HUDSON,NH BIRTHS

   & Elizabeth M Bishop (Nashua, NH)
KENNEDY,April Elizabeth Sex:F 13 Aug 1981 Leonard P Kennedy Sr
   & Susan Mary Bryand
KENNEDY,Carol A   Sex:F   22 Dec 1957 Frank L Kennedy, Jr & Mary E Gaffney
KENNEDY,Chad Allen Sex:M 03 May 1980 Leonard P Kennedy Sr & Susan M Bryand
KENNEDY,Daniel J   Sex:M   19 Jun 1971 Frank L Kennedy Jr & Mary E Gaffney
KENNEDY,Dianne L   Sex:F   22 Feb 1959 Frank L Kennedy, Jr & Mary E Gaffney
KENNEDY,Elizabeth Sex:F 21 Nov 1960 Walter E Kennedy & Gertrude A Martin
KENNEDY,Gordon D   Sex:M   (Child #8) 14 Feb 1946 Frank Kennedy (Canada)
   & Elizabeth M Bishop (Nashua, NH)
KENNEDY,Jacqueline R Sex:F 15 Mar 1964 Walter E Kennedy & Gertrude A Martin
KENNEDY,Joanne E   Sex:F   17 Oct 1950 Frank L Kennedy & Elizabeth M Bishop
KENNEDY,John James   Sex:M   29 Apr 1983 John J Kennedy Jr & Beverly Helfrich
KENNEDY,Joseph Michael Sex:M 17 Dec 1984 John J Kennedy Jr & Beverly Helfrich
KENNEDY,Julie A   Sex:F   27 Jun 1972 Frank L Kennedy Jr & Mary E Gaffney
KENNEDY,Kathleen M   Sex:F   12 Dec 1955 Frank L Kennedy & Mary E Gaffney
KENNEDY,Kimberly L Sex: 05 Oct 1972 Allen B Kennedy Sr & Louelle A Mansfield
KENNEDY,Leonard P   Sex:M   02 Dec 1953 Frank L Kennedy & Elizabeth M Bishop
KENNEDY,Leonard P Jr Sex:M 03 Apr 1977 Leonard P Kennedy Sr & Susan M Bryand
KENNEDY,Lottie B   Sex:F   29 Apr 1874 Hudson, NH Daniel Kennedy & Frances
KENNEDY,Mary E   Sex:F   30 Jun 1960 Frank L Kennedy, Jr & Mary E Gaffney
KENNEDY,Matthew Aaron Sex:M 10 Jun 1983 Teddy S Kennedy & Nona Vivian Ahearn
KENNEDY,Paul L   Sex:M   26 Jun 1968 Gordon D Kennedy & Suzette M Deschenes
KENNEDY,Randy W   Sex:M   28 Nov 1959 Walter E Kennedy & Gertrude A Martin
KENNEDY,Richard L Jr Sex:M (Child #2) 23 Nov 1946 Richard L Kennedy
   (Erie, PA) & Ellen L Bazinet (Nashua, NH)
KENNEDY,Roger D Jr   Sex:M   29 Jun 1970 Roger D Kennedy & Nancy K Hamlett
KENNEDY,Sandra L   Sex:F   24 Sep 1947 Richard L Kennedy (Erie, PA)
   & Ellen L Bazinet (Nashua, NH)
KENNEDY,[Unknown]   Sex:F   09 Dec 1962 Walter E Kennedy & Gertrude A Martin
KENNERSON,Joseph Corey Sex:M 15 Oct 1982 William C Kennerson & Wanda Jo Houle
KENNEVILLE,Francis   Sex:M   (Child #5) 26 Apr 1920 Gilbert Kenneville
   (Douglas, NY) & Emma Charbouneau (Plattsburg, NY)
KENNEY,Amos   Sex:M   14 Jan 1765 Hudson, NH Amos Kenney & Hannah
KENNEY,Carol A   Sex:F   30 Aug 1955 Richard G Kenney & Priscilla A Hammel
KENNEY,Donald G   Sex:M   06 Aug 1953 Richard G Kenney & Phyllis B Fish
KENNEY,Elizabeth   Sex:F   09 Mar 1768 Hudson, NH Amos Kenney & Thankful
KENNEY,Elizabeth   Sex:F   30 Mar 1767 Hudson, NH Stephen Kenney & Sarah
KENNEY,Elizabeth   Sex:F   11 Mar 1770 Hudson, NH Stephen Kenney & Sarah
KENNEY,Jessica Lynn Sex:F 09 Sep 1982 Gary R Kenney & Roberta Ann Hunter
KENNEY,Molle   Sex:F   14 Nov 175 Hudson, NH Amos Kenney & Hannah
KENNEY,Molly   Sex:F   14 Nov 175 Hudson, NH Amos Kenney & Hannah
KENNEY,Phebe   Sex:F   14 Oct 1738 Hudson, NH Thomas Kenney & Phebe
KENNEY,Samuel   Sex:M   09 Sep 1768 Hudson, NH Stephen Kenney & Sarah
KENNEY,Samuel   Sex:M   21 Feb 1760 Hudson, NH Amos Kenney & Hannah
KENNEY,Sarah   Sex:F   16 Sep 1740 Hudson, NH Thomas Kenney & Phebe
KENNEY,Sarah   Sex:F   25 Jan 175 Hudson, NH Amos Kenney & Hannah
KENNEY,Sarah   Sex:F   24 Nov 1771 Hudson, NH Stephen Kenney & Sarah
KENNEY,Sarah   Sex:F   31 Jan 1751 Hudson, NH Amos Kenney & Hannah
KENNEY,Sarah   Sex:F   21 Nov 1771 Hudson, NH Stephen Kenney & Sarah
KENNEY,Stephen   Sex:M   03 May 1845 Hudson, NH Thomas Kenney & Phebe
KENNEY,Stephen   Sex:M   06 Feb 1775 Hudson, NH Stephen Kenney & Sarah
KENNEY,Stephen   Sex:M   03 May 1745 Hudson, NH Thomas Kenney & Phebe
KENNEY,Thomas   Sex:M   10 Jul 1736 Hudson, NH Thomas Kenney & Phebe
KENNEY,Thomas   Sex:M   04 Mar 1757 Hudson, NH Amos Kenney & Hannah
KENNEY,Thomas   Sex:M   04 May 1754 Hudson, NH Amos Kenney & Hannah
KENNISON,Mary   Sex:F   14 Jul 1968 Harold Kennison & Anne C Rufo
KENT,Frank C   Sex:M   06 Jun 1950 James C Kent & Jane Clarke
KENTRA,David G   Sex:M   09 Nov 1964 Anthony C Kentra & Shirley A Baker
KENVILLE,Doris Viola   Sex:F   (Child #8) 18 Jan 1927 Gilbert Kenville

HUDSON,NH BIRTHS

(New York) & Emma Charbonneau (Plattsburgh, NY)
KENYON,Colleen Erin   Sex:F   23 Jul 1975 James J Kenyon & Karla D Bignell
KENYON,Dawn A   Sex:F   29 Aug 1973 James J Kenyon & Karla D Bignell
KEROUAC,Michael R   Sex:M   26 Apr 1953 Roger J Kerouac & Leona G Murphy
KERR,Mary Elizabeth   Sex:F   (Child #2) 22 Mar 1900 John L Kerr (Ireland)
   & Mabel Parker (Hudson, NH)
KERSEY,Alyssa J   Sex:F   14 Apr 1965 Ronald J Kersey & Elaine L Morin
KERSEY,Audrey L   Sex:F   13 Jul 1968 Ronald J Kersey & Elaine L Morin
KETCHAM,Lisa J   Sex:F   09 Jul 1971 Richard A Ketcham & Marie L John
KETCHEN,Jillian Leigh   Sex:F   20 Jun 1984 David B Ketchen & Dana S Canney
KEUENHOFF,Walter J Jr   Sex:M   30 Jul 1958 Walter J Keuenhoff & Jeanne Miller
KEUNENHOFF,Joseph H   Sex:M   19 Oct 1954 Walter J Keuenhoff & Jeanne Miller
KIDD,Darlene A   Sex:F   30 Apr 1974 Daryl L Kidd & Sharon E Wright
KIDDER,Cynthia G   Sex:F   12 Apr 1963 Arthur D Kidder & Martha J Gottsche
KIDDER,Eleazer   Sex:M   24 Apr 1758 Hudson, NH Noah Kidder & Eunice
KIDDER,Hannah   Sex:F   24 May 1765 Hudson, NH Benjamin Kidder & Lois
KIDDER,Hannah   Sex:F   15 Jun 1762 Hudson, NH Benjamin Kidder & Lois
KIDDER,John   Sex:M   06 Jan 1777 Hudson, NH Stephen Kenney & Sarah
KIDDER,Reuben   Sex:M   05 Jan 1760 Hudson, NH Noah Kidder & Eunice
KIDDER,Samson   Sex:F   24 May 1765 Hudson, NH Benjamin Kidder & Lois
KIENIA,Douglas E   Sex:M   08 Feb 1958 Edward Kienia & Irene E Barton
KIENIA,Wendy D   Sex:F   29 Oct 1950 George W Kienia & Marion I Ellis
KIERSTEAD,Arthur J   Sex:M   28 Sep 1958 Gerald T Kierstead & Muriel A Cummings
KIERSTEAD,Christopher T   Sex:M   29 Aug 1959 Thomas M Kierstead
   & Rita L Charpentier
KIERSTEAD,Gregg Matthew Sex:M 24 Sep 1982 Brent T Kierstead & Denise J Landry
KIERSTEAD,Thomas B   Sex:M   23 Jan 1979 Brian K Kierstead & Linda Ann Tate
KILLINGSWORTH,Shawn Philip   Sex:M   23 Oct 1981 William R Killingsworth
   & Joan E Kazlouskas
KIMBALL,Eliza B   Sex:F   17 Jul 1862 Hudson, NH Kimball Webster & Alice
KIMBALL,Kathryn   Sex:F   (Child #3) 03 Nov 1945 Rowe W Kimball (Dunstable, MA)
   & Helen L Thompson (Hudson, NH)
KIMBALL,Laura M   Sex:F   11 May 1968 Daniel P Kimball & Rena A Alexander
KIMBALL,Maida Barbara   Sex:F   (Child #1) 25 Sep 1921 Samuel L R Kimball
   (Nashua, NH) & Pearl A McGee (Manitoba, Canada
KIMBALL,Marjorie L   Sex:F   (Child #2) 08 Mar 1940 Rowe W Kimball (Dunstable,
   MA) & Helen L Thompson (Hudson, NH)
KIMBALL,Richard Wilson   Sex:M   (Child #1) 14 Aug 1938 Rowe Wilson Kimball
   (Dunstable, MA) & Helen L Thompson (Hudson, N
KIMBALL,Ryan Matthew   Sex:M   29 Jul 1984 Ronald C Kimball & Kathleen Ryan
KIMBALL,Samuel Raymond   Sex:M   (Child #2) 04 Feb 1924 Samuel R L Kimball (NH)
   & Pearl A McGee (Canada)
KIMBALL,Theodore S   Sex:M   (Child #5) 01 May 1903 John R Kimball (Wilton, NH)
   & Delora Tarbell (Wilton, NH)
KIMBALL,Wilbur L   Sex:M   (Child #3) 16 Nov 1911 Elmer A Kimball (Peabody, MA)
   & Grace Goodridge (Peabody, MA)
KING,Charles S   Sex:M   04 Apr 1949 Sanford E King & Geraldine Parshley
KING,Dennis M   Sex:M   06 Jul 1965 Richard D King & Diane L Vignola
KING,Walter E   Sex:M   22 Jan 1948 Sanford E King (Nashua, NH)
   & Geraldine Parshley (Derry, NH)
KINGSLEY,Edgar L   Sex:M   09 Jul 1969 Edward L Kingsley & Cynthia M Noakes
KINGSLEY,Jonathan Michael Sex:M 07 Mar 1983 Michael R Kingsley & Lynda M Clay
KINGSLEY,Leonard E   Sex:M   05 Apr 1961 Edgar W Kingsley & Evelyn M Signor
KINGSLEY,Louise M   Sex:F   07 Jun 1970 Edward L Kinglsey & Cynthia M Noakes
KINGSTON,Kaesy C   Sex:F   20 Dec 1965 Neil A Kingston & Patricia L Evans
KINGSTON,Kelly L   Sex:F   20 Dec 1965 Neil A Kingston & Patricia L Evans
KINGSTON,Timothy B   Sex:M   26 Sep 1964 Neil A Kingston & Patricia L Evans
KINIRLIE,[Unknown]   Sex:M   (Child #15) 21 Feb 1921 Antoine J Kinirlie
   (Douglas, NY) & Rose Dufrey (Chesterfield, NY)
KINNEY,John   Sex:M   06 Jan 1777 Hudson, NH Stephen Kinney & Sarah

HUDSON,NH BIRTHS

KINVILLE,Adam P   Sex:M   10 Mar 1972 Paul W Kinville & Janice A Campbell
KINVILLE,Apryl M   Sex:F   28 Apr 1970 Paul W Kinville & Janice A Campbell
KINVILLE,Edward   Sex:M   (Child #1) 05 Jul 1930 Edward Kinville (Vermont) & Ruth Idella Nichols (New Hampshire)
KINVILLE,Joyce E   Sex:F   22 Nov 1956 Francis G Kinville & Ruth G Dionne
KINVILLE,Paul W   Sex:M   27 Jun 1950 Francis G Kinville & Ruth G Dionne
KINVILLE,Richard E   Sex:M   01 Mar 1967 Gene H Kinville & Norma J Wheeler
KINVILLE,Robert Harold   Sex:M   (Child #11) 04 Jul 1929 George A Kinville (Douglas, NY) & Emma Charbonneau (Plattsburgh,
KINVILLE,Ruby Helen   Sex:F   (Child #7) 28 Aug 1924 Gilbert Kinville (New York) & Emma Charbonneau (New York)
KINVILLE,Sandra L   Sex:F   30 Jan 1954 Francis G Kinville & Ruth G Dion
KINVILLE,[Unknown]   Sex:F   (Child #2) 18 Feb 1922 Gilbert A Kinville (Douglas, NY) & Emma Charbonneau (Plattsburgh, NY)
KIPNES,Ethan R   Sex:M   25 Nov 1976 Jack L Kipnes & Linda Walkley
KIPNES,Jessica Jane Sex:F   23 Oct 1980 Jack L Kipnes & Linda Barry Walkley
KIRKPATRICK,Jonathan W   Sex:M   18 Oct 1973 William R Kirkpatrick & Jane M Barka
KIRKPATRICK,Matthew T   Sex:M   29 Jul 1974 Gerald G Kirkpatrick & Doreen M McGary
KIRKPATRICK,Philip R   Sex:M   30 Mar 1947 Philip W Kirkpatrick (Nashua, NH) & Cecile R Gagnon
KIRKPATRICK,Sean M Sex:M   29 Mar 1974 Bruce W Kirkpatrick & Joanne I Fontaine
KITCHENER,Judith H   Sex:F   08 Jul 1948 George H Kitchener (Nashua, NH) & Virginia I Dicey (Bristol, NH)
KITCHENER,Pamela A   Sex:F   (Child #1) 01 Nov 1943 George H Kitchener (Nashua, NH) & Virginia I Dicey (Bristol, NH)
KITTREDGE,Colleen Ann   Sex:F   14 Feb 1980 John C Kittredge & Patricia M Smith
KITTREDGE,Daniel Allen Sex:M   21 Jan 1984 John C Kittredge & Patricia M Smith
KIZER,Chester Benson   Sex:M   (Child #4) 05 Jul 1913 Ira D Kizer (Nova Scotia) & Eveline Cotter (Nova Scotia)
KLATSKY,Adam P   Sex:M   16 Feb 1979 Allen J Klatsky & Hinda Medoff
KLEEMAN,Heather Renee Sex:F   02 Sep 1983 Matthew M Kleeman & Ellen B Volk
KLEEMAN,Ryan Harrison   Sex:M   11 Jul 1980 Matthew M Kleeman & Ellen B Volk
KLEIN,Anna Joan   Sex:F   31 Dec 1980 Stephen Jay Klein & Leslie Jean Hansen
KLEINER,Daniel Wallace Sex:M   09 Dec 1978 Kenneth F Kleiner & Mary L Griswold
KLEINER,Randall L   Sex:M   07 Jun 1952 Leo Kleiner & Dorothy M Peacock
KLEINOTAS,Heather I   Sex:F   16 Dec 1973 Allen J Kleinotas & Carol A Griffin
KLEINOTAS,Jeffrey A Sex:M   10 Mar 1978 Allen J Kleinotas & Carole Ann Griffin
KLEMENT,John W   Sex:M   26 Jul 1962 John A Klement & Edna A Abucewucz
KLIMAS,Holly Ann   Sex:F   03 Jan 1983 Kenneth A Klimas & Brenda Ann Rodgers
KLIMAS,Kenneth A   Sex:M   13 Sep 1952 Andrew A Klimas & Isabelle U Skuzinski
KLOSE,Sheryl L   Sex:F   12 Jul 1963 Fred W Klose & Joanne Gustafson
KLOSE,Steven F   Sex:M   24 Mar 1967 Frederick W Klose & Joanne Gustafson
KNIGHT,Eric M   Sex:M   02 Dec 1959 Richard D Knight & Doris M Albro
KNIGHT,Lorraine L   Sex:F   (Child #2) 22 Mar 1921 George C Knight (Hollis, NH) & Eva Richard (Nashua, NH)
KNIGHTS,Carolyn Frances   Sex:F   (Child #1) 19 Aug 1941 Francis R Knights (Hudson, NH) & Mildred M Martin (Nashua, NH)
KNIGHTS,Horace Leonard   Sex:M   (Child #3) 09 Oct 1927 George C Knights, Jr (Hollis, NH) & Eva R Richards (Nashua, NH)
KNIGHTS,Jeffrey P   Sex:M   08 May 1957 Horace L Knights & Marion L Grant
KNIGHTS,Joshua M   Sex:M   20 Jun 1974 Gerard P Knights & Glenna D Cleveland
KNIGHTS,Orilla Sex:F   (Child #2) 09 Nov 1924 Luther L Knights (Merrimack, NH) & Victoria Boucher (Freemont, NH)
KNIGHTS,[Unknown]   Sex:M   (Child #1) 10 May 1919 George Knights (Hudson, NH) & Eva Richards (Nashua, NH)
KNIGHTS,[Unknown]   Sex:F   (Child #1) 27 Oct 1923 Luther Knights (Merrimack, NH) & Victoria Boucher (Freemont, NH)
KNOLL,Jeffrey E   Sex:M   21 Sep 1968 Robert J Knoll & Donna L Hayes

HUDSON,NH BIRTHS

KNOPE,Micah Scott Sex:M   23 May 1985 Kenton W Knope & Suzanne E Smith
KOBZIK,Stephen Philip Sex:M   13 Oct 1980 Jay Anthony Kobzik & Debra Lynn Main
KOCH,Anthony R Jr Sex:M   16 Sep 1967 Anthony R Koch & Linda J Bendotti
KOCH,Wendy-Ann Sex:F   25 Aug 1970 Anthony R Koch Sr & Linda J Bendotti
KOCHAKIAN,Rose Sex:F (Child #5) 22 Oct 1904 Stephen Kochakian (Armenia)
  & Badashan Kosaian (Armenia)
KOCHAKIAN,[Unknown]   Sex:M   (Child #4) 13 Feb 1906 Stephen Kochakian
  (Armenia) & Badashan Koaian (Armenia)
KOCHAKIAN,[Unknown]   Sex:M   (Child #5) 26 Jun 1907 Stephen Kochakian
  (Armenia) & Bedashian Kosaian (Armenia)
KOLLEY,Kathleen M Sex:F   05 May 1966 Joseph M Kolley & Mary E Larson
KONECNY,Leilani Jean Sex:F   09 Jun 1982 Benes M Konecny & Patricia E Smith
KONECNY,Tobin Milan Sex:M   06 Jul 1978 Benes M Konecny & Patricia E Smith
KONOTCHICK,Karin J Sex:F   09 Apr 1969 John A Konotchick & Susan M Stevens
KONOTCHICK,Kristi A Sex:F   11 Mar 1967 John A Konochick & Susan M Stevens
KONTOR,Alishia J Sex: 08 May 1973 Attila J Kontor & Judith D Palm
KONTOR,Kristina L Sex:F   22 Oct 1974 Attila J J Kontor & Judith D Palm
KOPACZ,Michael Merrill Sex:M   29 Jul 1983 Mitchell W Kopacz & Barbara Merrill
KOPACZ IV,Mitchell Walter Sex:M 13 Jan 1982 Mitchell W Kopacz III
  & Barbara Merrill
KOPCKO,Mary Sex:F (Child #5) 26 Dec 1922 Albert Kopcko (Poland)
  & Mary Mackofcki (Poland)
KOPENITS,Melissa Erin Sex:F 21 Oct 1983 Michael S Kopenits
  & Christine M Cuddy
KOPICKO,Annie Sex:F (Child #4) 23 Jul 1920 Albert Kopicko (Russia, Poland)
  & Mary Metkofski (Russia, Poland)
KOPISKI,Stephanie L Sex:F   16 Dec 1962 Stephen Kopiski & Lois M Hochard
KOPISKI,Stephen A Sex:M   19 Jun 1964 Stephen Kopiski & Lois M Hochard
KOPKA,Diane Sex:F   04 Feb 1959 Joseph J Kopka & Shirley A Poulin
KOPKA,Gail V Sex:F   17 May 1955 Edmund J Kopka & Elizabeth Hagerty
KOPKA,Gary J Sex:M   30 Aug 1952 Edmund J Kopka & Elizabeth Hagerty
KOPKA,Joyce A Sex:F   31 Jan 1958 Edmund J Kopka & Elizabeth Hagerty
KOPKA,Stacey Leigh Sex:F   29 Mar 1984 Kenneth J Kopka & June Helen Nazaka
KOPSKA,Mary Sex:F (Child #5) 05 Jan 1928 Albert Kopska (Poland)
  & Mary Macjokko (Poland)
KOUTSOTASEOS,[Unknown]   Sex:M   (Child #4) 13 Jan 1920 George Koutsotaseos
  (Greece) & Nellie Kourthanos (Greece)
KOUTSOTASIOS,[Unknown]   Sex:F (Child #3) 24 Oct 1917 George Koutsotasios
  (Greece) & Ellen Karthanan (Greece)
KOZICK,Jessica Ryan Sex:F   17 Sep 1983 Theodore C Kozick & Patricia Flis
KRAJEWSKI,Chad Scott Sex:M   01 Jan 1980 Theodore Krajewski & Sandra M Rhodes
KRAJEWSKI,Theodore A Sex:M   26 Jan 1976 Theodore Krajewski & Sandra M Rhodes
KRAMER,Ann-Marie Sex:F   01 Mar 1965 Roger L Kramer & Carmen C Chalifoux
KRAMER,Kim T M Sex:F   08 Apr 1967 Roger L Kramer & Carmen C Chalifour
KRAUSS,Kendra M Sex:F   17 May 1979 Peter R Krauss & Dorene L LeBlanc
KRAVITZ,Jason A Sex:M   31 Aug 1977 Robert A Kravitz & Lois E Brown
KRAVITZ,Kristen I Sex:F   28 Sep 1977 James A Kravitz & Bernice C Cohen
KREBS,Jeremy Russell Sex:M   12 Oct 1978 Michael John Krebs
  & Patricia A Kessler
KREBS,Timothy Michael Sex:M   27 Feb 1981 Michael John Krebs
  & Patricia A Kessler
KREMER,Kaitlin Elizabeth Sex:F   05 Dec 1984 Dan Jefferey Kramer
  & Francine E Stetzler
KREWSKI,Elaine F Sex:F   02 Oct 1953 Walter W Krewski & Mary A Kasper
KRIEBEL,Timothy G Sex:M   22 Jul 1977 James G Kreibel & Sally A Stannard
KRISTOFF,Lorraine C Sex:F (Child #1) 22 Apr 1946 Carl J Kristoff
  (Manchester, CT) & Leona Lavoie (Hudson, NH)
KRISTOPOWICZ,Adam Sex:M (Child #6) 21 Jun 1921 Frank Kristopowicz (Poland)
  & Fannie Weitrill (Poland)
KRIVICICH,Erica E Sex:F   24 Jan 1971 Robert F Krivicich & Carol L Poreda

HUDSON,NH BIRTHS

KRIVICICH,Robert E   Sex:M   20 Jun 1965 Robert F E Krivicich & Carol L Poreda
KRIVICICH,Ronda E   Sex:F   01 Apr 1968 Robert F Krivicich & Carol L Poreda
KRUPA,Jason Lee   Sex:M   07 Jan 1979 Kevin J Krupa & Pamela A Oikle
KRYSKOW,Adam Patrick   Sex:M   13 May 1985 Joseph M Kryskow & Pamela J Robbins
KRYSKOW,Arianne Beth   Sex:F   19 Nov 1973 Joseph M Kryskow & Pamela J Robbins
KRYSKOW,Mark Alan Robin   Sex:M   11 Mar 1983 Joseph M Kryskow Jr
  & Pamela J Robbins
KRYSTAPOVICZ,Branislow   Sex:M   (Child #5) 23 Feb 1920 Frank Krystapovicz
  (Poland) & Genice Wytrowal (Poland)
KRYSTAPOWICZ,[Unknown]   Sex:M   (Child #7) 27 Dec 1922 Frank Krystapowicz
  (Russia) & Fannie Vydfol
KUCIJ,Corryn Cecile   Sex:F   19 Oct 1978 Richard S Kucij & Kim Louise Simard
KUCIJ,Jillian Rose   Sex:F   06 Mar 1983 Richard Stevan Kucij & Kim Louise Simard
KULINGOSKI,Cara Jean   Sex:F   07 Apr 1977 Philip M Kulingoski
  & Jennice M Galipeau
KULINGOSKI,Charnel H   Sex:F   26 Dec 1967 Bernard R Kulingoski & Elaine B Smith
KULINGOSKI,Doreen A   Sex:F   05 Jun 1965 Bernard R Kulingoski & Elaine B Smith
KUPCHUNAS,Edward S   Sex:M   (Child #1) 15 Mar 1942 Stanley B Kupchunas
  (Nashua, NH) & Anna D Chess (Nashua, NH)
KUPCHUNAS,Frank B   Sex:M   (Child #2) 07 Oct 1946 Frank B Kupchunas (Nashua,
  NH) & Alice N Sakovich (Nashua, NH)
KUPCHUNAS,Kara F   Sex:F   10 Apr 1978 Frank B Kupchunas Jr & Kathleen C Andruskev
KUPCHUNAS,Kristen   Sex:F   10 Nov 1980 Frank B Kupchunas & Kathleen C Andruskev
KUPCHUNAS,Mary A   Sex:F   (Child #1) 01 Dec 1942 Frank B Kupchunas (Nashua, NH)
  & Alice N Sackovich (Nashua, NH)
KUPCHUNAS,Richard P   Sex:M   13 Jun 1949 Stanley B Kupchunas & Anna D Chess
KUPCHUNAS,Thomas R   Sex:M   22 Sep 1947 Stanley B Kupchunas (Nashua, NH)
  & Anna D Chess (Nashua, NH)
KUS,Daniel   Sex:M   30 Sep 1969 Crawford M Kus & Beth E Libby
KUSHNER,David A   Sex:M   20 Jun 1979 Jeffrey A Kushner & Melodee A Walker
KUSHNER,Jeremy Austin   Sex:M 22 Mar 1983 Jeffrey A Kushner
  & Melodee Ann Walker
KUSHNER,Philip Adam   Sex:M   22 Mar 1983 Jeffrey A Kushner & Melodee Ann Walker
KUSHNER,Tiffany Ajoy Walker   Sex:F   11 Feb 1981 Jeffrey A Kushner
  & Melodee Ann Walker
L'ETOILE,Daniel C   Sex:M   22 Sep 1970 Claude C L'Etoile & Nicole R Poulin
LA VOIE,Frederick C   Sex:M   06 Dec 1947 Edmond A La Voie (Nashua, NH)
  & Amy F Hammond (Nashua, NH)
LaBARRE,Audrey Elizabeth   Sex:F   04 Oct 1978 George Henry LaBarre
  & Linda Jean Kata
LABATTE,Christine Lee   Sex:F   21 May 1974 Wayne P Labatte & Kathy Lee Edwards
LABAUGH,Elizabeth F   Sex:F   01 Jun 1963 Kenneth D Labaugh & Suzy Groseclose
LABBE,Brian N   Sex:M   27 Oct 1974 Norman J Labbe & Loretta T Berube
LABEDNICK,Tammy A   Sex:F   03 May 1969 Dennis E Labednick & Jean G Griffin
LABEDNICK,Tina M   Sex:F   07 Apr 1971 Dennis E Labednick & Jean G Griffin
LaBLOND,Clarence   Sex:M   (Child #2) 04 Sep 1903 Exias LaBlond (Canada)
  & Mary L Wibber (Newfoundland)
LaBLOND,Ethel   Sex:F   18 Jun 1902 George LaBlond (Canada) & Louise Webber
  (Newfoundland)
LABOMBARD,Victoria Ella   Sex:F   (Child #1) 08 Feb 1924 Joseph E Labombard
  (W Chazy, NY) & Regina M Morton (Nashua, NH)
LABOMBARDE,Bernadette I   Sex:F   (Child #8) 02 Apr 1933 J E Labombarde
  (W Chazy, NY) & Regina Morton (Nashua, NH)
LaBONTE,Ann M   Sex:F   05 Jan 1966 Robert J LaBonte & Dorothy A Wallace
LABONTE,Jason M   Sex:M   18 Jan 1979 William J Labonte & Jeanne M Gagnon
LABONTE,Matthew T   Sex:M   08 May 1965 Roland C Labonte & Vivian E Guilmette
LaBONTE,Melissa T   Sex:F   25 Sep 1966 Roland C Labonte & Vivian E Guilmette
LaBONTE,Richard F   Sex:M   04 Oct 1962 Robert J LaBonte & Dorothy A Wallace
LABONTE,Russell L   Sex:M   19 Dec 1982 William J Labonte & Jeanne Marie Gagnon
LABONVILLE,Eric D   Sex:M   04 Sep 1968 Peter J Labonville & Annie J Gibbs

HUDSON,NH BIRTHS

LaBOUNTY,Jeffery S Sex:M 30 Oct 1962 Clayton E LeBounty & Barbara L Fortier
LaBRECQUE,Frederick James Sex:M 21 Jul 1980 Raymond D LaBrecque
  & Jeanine E Therriault
LaBRECQUE,Lori Lynne Sex:F 16 May 1982 Raymond D LaBrecque
  & Jeanine E Therriault
LaBRECQUE,Stephen G Sex:M 23 Mar 1970 Gary W LaBrecque & Judith A Malboeuf
LABRIE,Adrien A Jr Sex:M 02 Feb 1949 Adrien A Labrie & Theresa Y Nantel
LABRIE,Francoise A A Sex:F (Child #1) 03 Jul 1946 Philippe Labrie
  (St Lazare, Canada) & Simone M Blondel (Havre, Fr
LABRIE,Jacqueline L Sex:F   02 Apr 1948 Adrian A Labrie (Manchester, NH)
  & Theresa Y Nantel (Hudson, NH)
LACASSE,David Roger II Sex:M 31 Dec 1971 David R Lacasse & Patricia A Dillon
LACASSE,Deborah L Sex:F 11 Jan 1955 Adrien J LaCasse & Lorraine M Little
LACASSE,Joseph F Sex:M 26 Apr 1966 George R Lacasse & Frances A Henderson
LACASSE,Shirley E Sex:F   24 Dec 1947 Conrad R Lacasse (Nashua, NH)
  & Elizabeth E Johnson (Epping, NH)
LACASSE,Steve R Sex:M 18 Feb 1972 Roger P Lacasse & Florianne R Poulin
LACASSE,Tammy F Sex:F 29 Aug 1964 George R Lacasse & Frances A Henderson
LACHANCE,Barbara Sex:F (Child #2) 27 Dec 1943 Joseph P Lachance (Nashua, NH)
  & Marie A Levesque (Nashua, NH)
LaCHANCE,David J   Sex:M   14 Aug 1951 Leopold A LaChance & Betty L Terry
LACHANCE,Joan P Sex:F 16 Feb 1947 Leopold A Lachance (Nashua, NH)
  & Betty L Terry (Courtland, AL)
LaCHANCE,Louis L Sex:M 15 Mar 1972 William R LaChance & Lucille Y Bouley
LACHANCE,Marie Gloria Ann Sex:F (Child #1) 24 Sep 1941 Henri P P Lachance
  (Nashua, NH) & Marie A J Levesque (Nashua, NH)
LACHANCE,Martha A Sex:F 09 Sep 1950 Henry P Lachance & Antoinette J Levesque
LaCHANCE,Matthew David Sex:M 21 Jun 1981 Ralph David LaChance
  & Vicki Lynn Genett
LaCHANCE,Michael William Sex:M 21 Jun 1981 Ralph David LaChance
  & Vicki Lynn Genett
LACHANCE,Peter A Sex:M 03 Jun 1949 Henry P Lachance & Antoinette J Levesque
LACHANCE,Raymond J Jr Sex:M 11 Jun 1969 Raymond J Lachance
  & Patricia R Quigley
LACHANCE,Roland H Sex:M (Child #3) 12 Jan 1945 Henry P Lachance (Nashua, NH)
  & Antoinette J Levesque (Nashua, NH)
LACKIE,Lois C Sex:F 03 Jun 1970 Donald C Lackie & Phyllis A Hurd
LACKIE,Mary V Sex:F 15 Jan 1968 Donald C Lackie & Phyllis A Hurd
LACOSHUS,Frank A III   Sex:M 15 Feb 1971 Frank A Lacoshus Jr
  & Patricia A Matyjasik
LACOY,Tara Lynn Sex:F 06 Feb 1981 Robert Ernest Lacoy & Tamblynne Oliveira
LACROIX,Matthew Paul Sex:M 31 Jul 1980 Michel P Lacroix & Louise I Cloutier
LACROIX,Nicole L Sex:F 04 Apr 1979 Michel P Lacroix & Louise I Cloutier
LADAS,Christopher J Sex:M 20 Sep 1977 George L Ladas & Gloria E Roberge
LADAS,Kathryn A Sex:F 13 Jul 1970 George L Ladas & Gloria E Roberge
LADOW,Samantha J Sex:F 23 Jun 1968 Thomas V Ladow & Pauline J Angell
LADUE,Irving S Sex:M 25 Dec 1952 Norman P Ladue & Adeline G Little
LaDUKE,Amy Jennifer Sex:F 06 Dec 1973 Maurice R LaDuke Jr & Anita L Dube
LaDUKE,Carrie Ann Sex:F 30 Apr 1976 Maurice R LaDuke Jr & Anita L Dube
LAFLAMME,Bonnie A Sex:F 07 Mar 1968 Robert E Laflamme & Florence L Rowell
LaFLAMME,Brenda A Sex:F (Child #4) 19 Feb 1945 Ernest B LaFlamme (Nashua,
  NH) & Doris M Young (Nashua, NH)
LAFLAMME,Doris Nelda Sex:F (Child #6) 27 Nov 1925 George Laflamme (Nashua,
  NH) & Emma LaForest (Nashua, NH)
LaFLAMME,Ernest J Sex:M (Child #1) 03 Mar 1940 Ernest J LaFlamme (Nashua,
  NH) & Doris M Young (Nashua, NH)
LaFLAMME,Ernest R Sex:M 16 Feb 1957 Ernest B LaFlamme & Doris M Young
LAFLAMME,Frances Sex:F (Child #2) 07 May 1935 Francis Laflamme (Canada)
  & Rose Lavoie (Barre, VT)
LAFLAMME,Marion Sex:F (Child #1) 07 May 1935 Francis Laflamme (Canada)

HUDSON,NH BIRTHS

& Rose Lavoie (Barre, VT)
LaFLAMME,Patricia L Sex:F (Child #3) 12 Aug 1942 Ernest B LaFlamme (Nashua, NH) & Doris M Young (Nashua, NH)
LaFLAMME,Robin L Sex:F 21 Nov 1955 Ernest B LaFlamme & Doris M Young
LAFLAMME,Sheila E M Sex:F (Child #3) 28 Oct 1938 Francis Laflamme (Toronto, Canada) & Rose Lavoie (Granville, VT)
LAFLEUR,Benjamin Alden Sex:M 19 Sep 1984 Robert T Lafleur & Patricia A Schueller
LaFLEUR,Richard A Sex:M 20 Sep 1962 Arthur J LaFleur, Jr & Sandra M Classon
LaFLEUR,Robert T Sex:M 08 Aug 1951 Raymond G LaFleur & Lillian T Boisvert
LAFLEUR,Thomas R Sex:M 12 Feb 1955 Raymond G Lafleur & Lillian T Boisvert
LAFLOTTE,Duane L Sex:M 23 Jul 1977 David L Laflotte & Roberta Ann Shattuck
LAFLOTTE,Jarrod D Sex:M 23 Jul 1977 David L Laflotte & Roberta Ann Shattuck
LAFOND,Jay A Sex:M 16 Jan 1969 Roger D Lafond & Muriel T A Thomson
LAFOND,Norman Elie Jr Sex:M 06 Oct 1976 Norman E Lafond Sr & Francine J Simoneau
LaFONTAINE,Karen A Sex:F 08 Nov 1963 Robert N LaFontaine & Barbara A Martin
LaFONTAINE,Lisa A Sex:F 03 Mar 1965 Robert N LaFontaine & Barbara A Martin
LaFOREST,Neal B Sex:M 17 Apr 1961 Gerard J LaForest & June E LaFontaine
LAFOREST,Raymond A Jr Sex:M 10 Dec 1975 Raymond A Laforest Sr & Janice I Raby
LAFOREST,Victoria Lee Sex:F 15 Mar 1974 Raymond A Laforest & Janice Raby
LaFOREST,Wayne D Sex:M 31 Aug 1966 Gerard J LaForest & June E LaFontaine
LaFOREST,[Unknown] Sex:M 31 Aug 1959 Gerard J LaForest & June E LaFontaine
LAGALLEE,Frances Phoebe Sex:F (Child #3) 15 Mar 1934 Howard S Lagallee (Somerville, MA) & Phoebe Tyler (Contoocook, NH
LAGASSE,Holly A Sex:F 21 Dec 1964 Armand C Lagasse & Muriel Tessier
LAGASSE,Janet N Sex:F 11 Nov 1961 Armand C Lagasse & Muriel L Tessier
LAGASSE,Mary Pauline Sex:F (Child #2) 29 Apr 1935 Euclid Lagasse (Canada) & Malvina Boyer (Nashua, NH)
LAINE,Daniel A Sex:M 28 Nov 1961 Aldeo O Laine & Pauline J Cote
LAINE,David A Sex:M 12 Feb 1958 Aldeo O Laine & Pauline J Cote
LAINE,Dennis L Sex:M 19 Oct 1963 Lionel A Laine & Claudette L Dumais
LAINE,Donna A Sex:F 25 Jun 1960 Aldeo O Laine & Pauline J Cote
LAINE,Nancy A Sex:F 29 Apr 1970 Gabriel M Laine & Aline L Labrecque
LAINE,Paul A Sex:M 31 Jan 1956 Aldeo O Laine & Pauline J Cote
LAINE,Paula A Sex:F 03 Mar 1957 Aldeo O Laine & Pauline J Cote
LAINE,Peter A Sex:M 28 Jan 1966 Aldeo O Laine & Pauline J Cote
LAINE,Philip A Sex:M 20 Mar 1963 Aldeo O Laine & Pauline J Cote
LAINE,Susan C Sex:F 17 Nov 1966 Lionel A Laine & Claudette L Dumais
LAINE,Sylvia C Sex:F 16 Nov 1966 Gabriel M Laine & Aline L Labrecque
LAINEY,Cindy L Sex:F 04 Dec 1970 Lewis L Lainey & Lona J Cray
LAJEUNESSE,M E Sex:F 31 Jul 1947 Harold Lajeunesse (Lowell, MA) & Catherin R Kinch (N Chelmsford, MA)
LAJOIE,Allen D Sex:M 20 Nov 1960 Normand J Lajoie & Jeannette R Daneault
LaJOIE,Danielle R Sex: 10 Oct 1972 Richard G LaJoie & Gloria A Boyster
LAJOIE,Elizabeth Ann Sex:F (Child #8) 09 Jun 1937 George Lajoie (Nashua, NH) & Ernestine Lapointe (Springfield, MA)
LAJOIE,[Unknown] Sex:M (Child #9) 14 May 1938 George Lajoie (Nashua, NH) & Theodine Lapointe (Springfield, MA)
LALIBERTE,Elizabeth Sex:F 21 Jan 1972 Richard L Laliberte & Kathleen E Smith
LALIBERTE,Matthew Richard Sex:M 04 May 1982 Richard L Laliberte & Kathleen E Smith
LALIME,Sharlee Anne Sex:F 03 Mar 1980 Harold W Lalime & Sandra L Frink
LALMONT,Raymond David Sex:M (Child #2) 18 May 1941 Charles Lalmond (Lowell, MA) & Lottie Whittle (Nashua, NH)
LALUMIERE,Michael W Sex:M 06 Mar 1957 William O Lalumiere & Janice N Carlton
LALUMIERE,Ronni L Sex:F 13 Dec 1955 William O Lalumiere & Janice N Carlton
LAMARRE,Jason E Sex: 27 Jul 1972 Raymond G Lamarre & Franicianna L Lambert
LAMARRE,Raymond G II Sex:M 23 May 1970 Raymond G Lamarre

HUDSON,NH BIRTHS

& Francianna L Lambert
LAMB,Deborah M   Sex:F   06 Mar 1955 Reginald E Lamb & Eleanor M Parker
LAMB,Judith C   Sex:F   13 Aug 1971 Lowell C Lamb & Gail S Drury
LAMB,Rhiannon G   Sex:F   23 May 1979 William S Lamb & Patricia Ann Burton
LAMBERT,Blair Ashley Sex:F 27 Mar 1985 Robert Henry Lambert & Lori E Whitten
LAMBERT,Bob Earl   Sex:M   (Child #5) 17 Mar 1922 J E Lambert (Nashua, NH)
  & May Harvey (Enfield, NH)
LAMBERT,Donna L   Sex:F   21 Oct 1959 Raymond R Lambert & Gloria M Beland
LAMBERT,Jason M   Sex:M   31 Dec 1974 Robert R Lambert & Jeanne M Lafleur
LAMBERT,Joseph   Sex:M   (Child #4) 21 Aug 1903 Anthoine Lambert (Canada)
  & Marie L Caron (Canada)
LAMBERT,Joseph Romeo   Sex:M   (Child #5) 19 Mar 1934 Alfred Lambert (Canada)
  & Rose A Raymond (Canada)
LAMBERT,Keith Richard Fieldi   Sex:M   01 Oct 1981 Richard M Lambert
  & Laurie Ann Chaput
LAMBERT,Marc A   Sex:M   15 Jul 1968 Richard H Lambert & Carla A Neuffer
LAMBERT,Marie Alice   Sex:F   (Child #5) 19 Dec 1904 Anthoine Lambert (Canada)
  & Marie Louise Caron (Canada)
LAMBERT,Marie Blanche   Sex:F   (Child #9) 21 Mar 1917 Antoine Lambert (Canada)
  & Marie Caron (Canada)
LAMBERT,Marie R A   Sex:F   (Child #6) 11 Jun 1906 Anthoine Lambert (Canada)
  & Marie L Caron (Canada)
LAMBERT,Richard R   Sex:M   15 Aug 1956 Raymond R Lambert & Gloria M Beland
LAMBERT,Robert H   Sex:M   12 Feb 1955 William M Lambert & Alice M Dionne
LAMBERT,Roger R   Sex:M   18 Sep 1957 Raymond R Lambert & Gloria M Beland
LAMBERT,Rosalie   Sex:F   (Child #6) 29 Jan 1935 Alfred Lambert (Canada)
  & Rosanna Raymond (Canada)
LAMBERT,Todd C   Sex:M   17 Jun 1977 Robert R Lambert & Jeanne M Lafleur
LAMEIRAS,Jason A   Sex:M   14 Jan 1971 Alan M Lameiras & Cheryl-Ann E Donovan
LAMOTHE,Jeffrey Stephen Sex:M   01 Dec 1978 William E Lamothe & Diane Erma Dow
LAMOTHE,John Christian   Sex:M   07 Dec 1979 James Emile Lamothe
  & Constance D Pelletier
LAMOTHE,Joseph Louis Aime   Sex:M   (Child #2) 03 Apr 1917 Theophile Lamothe
  (Connecticut) & Albertine Harnois (Canada)
LAMOTHE,Rose   Sex:F   (Child #3) 07 Jun 1918 Theophile Lamothe (Connecticut)
  & Albertine Arnois (Canada)
LAMOUNTAIN,Jason Robert   Sex:M   27 May 1985 Robert L Lamountain
  & Debbie L Lovering
LAMOUNTAIN,Shawn Adam   Sex:M   08 Nov 1979 Robert L Lamountain
  & Debbie L Lovering
LAMOUREUX,Nancy A   Sex:F   31 May 1969 Alfred L Lamoureux & Carolyn A Watson
LAMOUREUX,Steven A   Sex:M   04 Aug 1966 Alfred L Lamoureux & Carolyn A Watson
LAMPRON,Edward Oliver Sex:M   (Child #2) 21 Oct 1931 Wilfred E Lampron
  (Nashua, NH) & Hildreth Fisher (Hudson, NH)
LAMSON,Wesley A Jr   Sex:M   30 Jul 1959 Wesley A Lamson & Pauline E Stickney
LAMY,Brian D   Sex:M   07 Feb 1967 Robert A Lamy & Pauline F Beaulac
LANDRY,Ada May   Sex:F   17 Nov 1871 Hudson, NH Ezekiel Landry & Anna
LANDRY,Albert   Sex:M   (Child #2) 19 Sep 1920 Joseph Landry (Canada)
  & Bernadette Belanger (Canada)
LANDRY,Alphonse   Sex:M   (Child #9) 01 Feb 1934 Joseph Landry (Canada)
  & Bernadette Belanger (Canada)
LANDRY,Annette T   Sex:F   30 Jul 1953 Normand G Landry & Rachel T Denis
LANDRY,Cheryl A   Sex:F   27 Mar 1960 Leonard F Landry & Gertrude A Sullivan
LANDRY,Christiann C   Sex:F   04 Oct 1961 Alphonse E Landry & Catherine A Pritz
LANDRY,Christine Natalie Sex:F 24 Jan 1984 Douglas D Landry
  & Deborah Joan Dobens
LANDRY,Daniel R   Sex:M   08 Jan 1969 Raymond A Landry & Clarice Petrain
LANDRY,David E   Sex:M   15 Jun 1947 Romeo W Landry (Nashua, NH)
  & Vita Y Pariseau (Nashua, NH)
LANDRY,Deborah A   Sex:F   09 Mar 1959 Donald A Landry & Eleanor M Cowgill

HUDSON,NH BIRTHS

LANDRY,Dennis   Sex:M   (Child #5) 30 Nov 1946 Thomas M Landry (Nashua, NH)
 & Irene G Livernois (Derry, NH)
LANDRY,Donald Denis   Sex:M   (Child #2) 12 Oct 1937 Denis Landry (Canada)
 & Nellie Beaudette (Canada)
LANDRY,Donald L   Sex:M   28 Mar 1947 Albert A Landry (Nashua, NH)
 & Dorothy F Gaudette (Nashua, NH)
LANDRY,Donna M   Sex:F   09 Mar 1959 Donald A Landry & Eleanor M Cowgill
LANDRY,Eric J   Sex:M   08 Sep 1966 George L Landry & Carol A Hamel
LANDRY,Gerard D   Sex:M   20 Mar 1966 Normand L Landry & Marlene E Dow
LANDRY,Gerard N   Sex:M   24 Dec 1953 Normand L Landry & Marlene E Dow
LANDRY,Gerard R   Sex:M   10 Jul 1957 Raymond A Landry & Clarice Petrain
LANDRY,Germain Norm   Sex:M   (Child #6) 03 Nov 1927 Joseph Landry (Canada)
 & Bernadette Belanger (Canada)
LANDRY,Jacqueline A   Sex:F   28 Aug 1957 Alphonse E Landry & Catherine A Pritz
LANDRY,James A   Sex:M   16 Mar 1958 Normand G Landry & Rachel T Denis
LANDRY,Jeremiah J   Sex:M   15 Mar 1979 Paul M Landry & Arlene E Bourgeois
LANDRY,Joan   Sex:F   (Child #6) 05 Apr 1945 Jewell E Landry (Haynesville, ME)
 & Laura M Gingras (Peabody, MA)
LANDRY,Karen Marie Sex:F   09 Jul 1981 Christopher S Landry & Nancy A Thompson
LANDRY,Kevin Scott Sex:M 07 Apr 1983 Christopher S Landry & Nancy A Thompson
LANDRY,Lillie M   Sex:F   12 Jul 1873 Hudson, NH Ezekiel M Landry & Annie M
LANDRY,Lisa A   Sex:F   28 Aug 1965 George L Landry & Carol A Hamel
LANDRY,Lucile Irene   Sex:F   (Child #4) 19 Sep 1924 Joseph Landry (Canada)
 & Bernadette Belanger (Canada)
LANDRY,M Ange Ida   Sex:F   (Child #3) 26 Apr 1922 Joseph Landry (Canada)
 & Bernadette Belanger (Canada)
LANDRY,M T Bernadette   Sex:F   (Child #7) 14 Oct 1929 Joseph Landry
 (St Bruno, P Q) & Bernadette Belanger (S Antoinette
LANDRY,Melanie J   Sex:F   21 Sep 1968 Donald L Landry & Cathleen J Noyes
LANDRY,Michael A   Sex:M   11 Dec 1961 Raymond A Landry & Clarice Petrain
LANDRY,Neil R   Sex:M   (Child #7) 28 Jul 1945 Thomas M Landry (Nashua, NH)
 & Irene G Livernois (Derry, NH)
LANDRY,Paul   Sex:M   (Child #1) 27 Mar 1918 Joseph Landry (Canada)
 & Bernadette Belanger (Canada)
LANDRY,Paul A   Sex:M   27 Mar 1954 Albert A Landry & Dorothy F Gaudette
LANDRY,Raymond Armand   Sex:M   (Child #8) 17 Jul 1931 Joseph Landry (Canada)
 & Bernadette Belanger (Canada)
LANDRY,Raymond G   Sex:M   15 Jan 1965 Raymond A Landry & Clarice Petrain
LANDRY,Raymond T   Sex:M   (Child #5) 18 Mar 1940 Jewell E Landry (Haynesville,
 ME) & Laura M Gingras (Peabody, MA)
LANDRY,Richard A   Sex:M   20 May 1963 Raymond A Landry & Clarice Petrain
LANDRY,Rita Jeannette   Sex:F   (Child #7) 18 Jun 1926 Joseph Landry (Canada)
 & Bernadette Belanger (Canada)
LANDRY,Robert George   Sex:M   (Child #2) 25 Jul 1933 Albert Landry (Nashua,
 NH) & Eva Lizotte (Canada)
LANDRY,Robert P   Sex:M   09 May 1959 Raymond A Landry & Clarice Petrain
LANDRY,Ronald J   Sex:M   11 Oct 1949 Jewell E Landry & Laura M Gingras
LANDRY,Steven C   Sex:M   04 Jun 1958 Alphonse E Landry & Catherine A Pritz
LANDRY,Tara A   Sex:F   28 Jun 1972 George L Landry & Carol A Hamel
LANDRY,Thomas P   Sex:M   21 May 1974 Daniel R Landry & Carol Ann Hamblett
LANDRY,Virginia Jay Sex:F   (Child #3) 22 Apr 1941 Thomas M Landry (Nashua,
 NH) & Irene Livernois (Derry, NH)
LANDRY,Yvette L   Sex:F   08 Aug 1961 Albert A Landry & Dorothy F Gaudette
LANDRY,[Unknown]   Sex:M   22 Sep 1947 Jewell E Landry (Haynesville, ME)
 & Laura M Gingras (Peabody, MA)
LANDRY,[Unknown]   Sex:M   12 May 1975 Roger J Landry & Sandra J Meier
LANG,Diana B   Sex:F   27 Apr 1970 Elliot A Lang & Joan M Scarlott
LANGEVIN,David T   Sex:M   13 Nov 1966 Frank J Langevin & Sandra A Snape
LANGEVIN,Kenneth S   Sex:M   18 Jul 1964 Frank J Langevin & Sandra A Snape
LANGGUTH,Andrew D   Sex:M   12 Mar 1980 Alfred Langguth & Adele L Motz

HUDSON,NH BIRTHS

LANGGUTH,Dana Katherine Sex:F 06 Apr 1984 Alfred Langguth & Adele LMotz
LANGLAIS,David Peter Sex:M 06 Jan 1981 Peter P Langlais & Donna Marie Bois
LANGLAIS,Joseph William Sex:M 31 Aug 1979 Peter P Langlais & Donna Marie Bois
LANGLAIS,Robert Charles Sex:M 19 Mar 1983 Peter P Langlais & Donna Marie Bois
LANGTHORNE,Karen M Sex:F 06 Apr 1947 Morton J Langthorne (Nova Scotia)
 & Edith I Lindbohm (Cochituate,
LANNAN,Katie Lynn Sex:F 21 Aug 1980 Richard G Lannan & Brenda Jayne Brooks
LANTAGNE,Nicholas G Sex:M 25 Jun 1980 Martin J Lantagne & Jean F Miron
LANZILLO,Gregory Peter Sex:M 15 Aug 1978 Peter G Lanzillo & Donna Kay Gilbert
LANZILLO,Julia Dawn Sex:F 27 Feb 1980 Peter G Lanzillo & Donna K Gilbert
LAPIN,Carol A Sex:F 03 Mar 1963 Frank J Lapin & Angeline M Larocque
LAPIN,Lisa A Sex:F 13 Apr 1961 Frank J Lapin & Angeline M Larocque
LAPIN,Mary A Sex:F 20 Sep 1965 Frank J Lapin & Angeline M Larocque
LAPLANTE,David Conrad Sex:M (Child #2) 22 Sep 1923 David Laplante (Canada)
 & Elizabeth Dilling (Germany)
LAPLANTE,Deborah A Sex:F 21 Dec 1971 Patrick H Laplante & Joane M Martin
LAPOINTE,Albert Gerard Sex:M (Child #3) 07 Jul 1927 Leo Lapointe (Nashua,
 NH) & Stella Irene Jacques (Lowell, MA)
LaPORTA,Mark E Sex:M 17 May 1957 Edward P LaPorta & Gladys J Berard
LAPORTE,Christine J Sex:F 28 Nov 1966 Arthur Laporte & Christine I Cotner
LaPORTE,Craig R Sex:M 30 Dec 1975 Gary R LaPorte & Denise C Ducharme
LaPORTE,Jeffrey S Sex:M 05 Mar 1978 Gary R LaPorte & Denise C Ducharme
LAQUERRE,Alb Raymond Sex:M (Child #4) 03 Oct 1925 Jean Bapt Laquerre
 (New Hampshire) & Victoria Ouellette (Nashua, NH)
LAQUERRE,James R Sex:M 20 Nov 1958 Roger A Laquerre & Rachel C Dumas
LAQUERRE,Lauren Elisabeth Sex:F 03 Jan 1983 Richard A Laquerre
 & LuAnn Marie Bausha
LAQUERRE,Mary C Sex:F (Child #1) 17 Feb 1918 Arthur Laquerre (Canada)
 & Alma Charpentier (Canada)
LAQUERRE,Pauline Geneva Sex:F (Child #1) 07 Apr 1924 Arthur Laquerre
 (Canada) & Odelie Roy (Canada)
LAQUERRE,Robert J Sex:M 25 Apr 1961 Roger A Laquerre & Rachel C Dumas
LAQUERRE,Susan A Sex:F 17 Jul 1953 Norman V Laquerre & Fleurette Y Boudreau
LARKIN,James Charles Sex:M 20 Jan 1983 Charles F Larkin & Shelley Mary Curran
LARLEE,Jennifer K Sex:F 09 Oct 1967 David A Larlee & Marilyn J Towne
LARLEE,Melinda B Sex:F 02 Oct 1969 David A Larlee & Marilyn J Towne
LARMOUTH,Kimberly Ann Sex:F 29 Apr 1982 Robert S Larmouth & Janice S Zawatski
LARMOUTH,Ryan Stanton Sex:M 21 Mar 1985 Robert S Larmouth & Janice S Zawatski
LARO,Paul B Sex:M 01 Aug 1964 Jon E Laro & Gloria A Lachance
LaROCHE,Chris M Sex:M 12 Nov 1967 Armand E LaRoche & Aline C Lussier
LaROCHE,Kimberly A Sex:F 07 Jul 1970 Armand E LaRoche & Aline C Lussier
LAROCHELLE,Keith R Sex:M 02 Jul 1973 Louis M Larochelle & Diane M Marsolais
LAROCHELLE,Marc I Sex:M 22 Oct 1969 Louis M Larochelle & Diane M M Marsolais
LaROCQUE,Jane Martha Sex:F 25 Nov 1980 George R LaRocque Jr & Paula L Smith
LaROCQUE,Joanne M Sex:F 03 Jul 1968 George R LaRocque & Margaret M Cavanaugh
LAROCQUE,Katy Sex:F 07 Mar 1979 George R Larocque Jr & Paula L Smith
LAROCQUE,Robert Michael Sex:M 19 Jun 1982 George R LaRocque & Paula L Smith
LAROSE,Amanda Renee Sex:F 03 Dec 1983 Robert Nestor Larose & Barbara Ann Ives
LaROSE,Michelle A Sex: 09 Feb 1973 John E LaRose & Nancy A Gheodore
LAROUCHE,Joseph P Sex:M 14 Jan 1972 Maurice R Larouche & Charlotte E Carlton
LARRABEE,Gary L Sex:M 06 Jul 1964 Allan C Larrabee & Janet N Paquette
LaSALLE,Jennifer Elizabeth Sex:F 12 Jul 1981 Richard A LaSalle
 & Mary Beth Fantetti
LASTOWKA,Cheryl A Sex:F 07 Dec 1959 John F Lastowka & Evelyn A Breen
LASTOWKA,John F Jr Sex:M (Child #1) 07 Dec 1942 John F Lastowka (Denver, CO)
 & Evelyn A Breen (Nashua, NH)
LATOUR,Bonnie L Sex:F 20 Nov 1968 George C Latour Jr & Sandra L Davis
LATOUR,Deanna J Sex:F 18 Feb 1962 Joseph E Latour & Janet A Smith
LATOUR,Kevin S Sex:M 04 Jul 1965 Donald Latour & Carol M J Lavallee
LATOUR,Vincent Sex:M 08 Sep 1964 Joseph E Latour & Janet A Smith

HUDSON,NH BIRTHS

LATULIPPE,Marc L   Sex:M   19 Mar 1972 Leo R Latulippe & Claire M Paradise
LATULIPPE,Michael A   Sex:M   15 May 1965 Leo R Latulippe & Claire M Paradise
LATVIS,Brian E   Sex:M   21 Nov 1955 Stanley Latvis & Lucille Y Gora
LAUKAHS,Peter   Sex:M   (Child #10) 26 Dec 1926 James Laukahs (Lithuania)
  & Antoinette Lelonpiri (Lithuania)
LAURENDEAU,Suzette L   Sex:F   11 Apr 1964 Leon G Laurendeau & Emily A Stafford
LAVALLE,Annette   Sex:F   (Child #2) 13 Nov 1938 Severain Lavalle (Nashua, NH)
  & Anna Levesque (Nashua, NH)
LAVALLEE,Bonnie L   Sex:F 29 Jul 1962 William R Lavallee & Lucille J Brisebois
LAVALLEE,Brenda L   Sex:F 01 Dec 1957 William R Lavallee & Lucille J Brisebois
LAVALLEE,Carol M J   Sex:F   (Child #7) 26 Dec 1942 Joseph E Lavallee
  (Manchester, NH) & Eva A Boucher (Nashua, NH)
LAVALLEE,Deborah L   Sex:F   25 Oct 1956 Raymond S Lavallee & Jean D Lavoie
LAVALLEE,Doreen G Sex:F   04 Feb 1971 William R Lavallee & Lucille J Brisebois
LAVALLEE,Glenn D   Sex:M   22 May 1961 William R Lavallee & Lucille J Brisebois
LAVALLEE,Kim L   Sex:F   06 Nov 1966 William R Lavallee & Lucille J Brisebois
LAVALLEE,Linda D   Sex:F   01 Jun 1949 Raymond S Lavallee & Jean D Lavoie
LAVALLEE,Mark A   Sex:M   08 Mar 1955 William R Lavallee & Lucille J Brisebois
LAVALLEE,Maurice T   Sex:M   (Child #6) 04 Nov 1937 Ernest Lavallee
  (Manchester, NH) & Eva Boucher (Nashua, NH)
LAVALLEE,Randy E   Sex:M   28 Jan 1960 Roland W Lavallee & Lucille J Brisbois
LAVALLEE,Ricky B   Sex:M 26 Dec 1958 William R Lavallee & Lucille J Brisebois
LAVALLEE,Rodney S J   Sex:M   19 Dec 1963 William R Lavallee Sr
  & Lucille J Brisbois
LAVALLEE,Roger David   Sex:M   (Child #5) 17 Feb 1933 Joseph E Lavallee
  (Manchester, NH) & Eva Boucher (Nashua, NH)
LAVALLEE,Sheryl L   Sex:F   23 Jan 1955 Raymond S Lavallee & Jean D Lavoie
LAVALLEE,Todd M   Sex:M   11 Nov 1967 William R Lavallee & Lucille J Brisebois
LAVALLEE,William Roland   Sex:M   (Child #4) 22 Apr 1931 Joseph E Lavallee
  (Manchester, NH) & Eva Boucher (Nashua, NH)
LaVALLEY,Donald A   Sex:M   30 Jan 1960 Arthur E LaValley & Sharley E Blodgett
LAVALLEY,Thomas A   Sex:M   24 Jan 1961 Charles E Lavalley & Elaine E Addis
LAVARNWAY,Jared M   Sex:M   04 Jun 1975 Roger O Lavarnway & Jewel C Page
LAVARNWAY,Jason D   Sex:M   07 Sep 1977 Roger O Lavarnway & Jewell C Page
LAVARNWAY,Joyce G   Sex:F   22 Jan 1958 Leo J Lavarnway & Gertrude G Leclerc
LAVARNWAY,Renee Danielle   Sex:F   06 May 1982 Roger O Lavarnway
  & Jewel Cynthia Page
LaVERGNE,Joey R   Sex:M   04 Sep 1953 Jean R LaVergne & Juliette L Barriault
LAVERY,Lorraine Mary   Sex:F   (Child #1) 27 Apr 1937 Alfred Lavery
  (Winchendon, MA) & Evelyn Provencal (Nashua, NH)
LAVIN,John   Sex:M   15 Oct 1898 Joseph Lavin (Manchester, NH)
  & Kate O Lanlins
LAVOIE,Dylan Steven Sex:M   28 Oct 1983 George T Lavoie & Kathleen S Sienkiewi
LaVOIE,Gary E   Sex:M   29 Apr 1959 Jon L LaVoie & Nancy T Moreau
LAVOIE,Janet L   Sex:F   11 May 1951 Leonard D Lavoie & Beatrice E Ives
LAVOIE,Jason J   Sex:M   15 Mar 1968 John P Lavoie & Elaine T Fontaine
LAVOIE,Jennifer M   Sex:F   13 Oct 1970 Albert E Lavoie & Marianne C Larouche
LAVOIE,Joel L   Sex: 08 Mar 1973 Richard A Lavoie & Linda J Howe
LAVOIE,John P Jr   Sex:M   02 Apr 1958 John P Lavoie, Sr & Elaine T Fontaine
LAVOIE,Jon Lance   Sex:M   (Child #2) 25 May 1938 Edmund Lavoie (Nashua, NH)
  & Amy Hammond (Nashua, NH)
LAVOIE,Kallie   Sex:F   20 Jan 1982 Gary E Lavoie & Debra Lee Levesque
LAVOIE,Katie Marie   Sex:F   01 Sep 1980 Leonard Leo Lavoie & Paula Marie Foisy
LAVOIE,Laurie   Sex: 10 Jul 1972 Donald P Lavoie & Patricia K Monroe
LAVOIE,Laurie J   Sex:F   17 Sep 1971 George E Lavoie & Alice A Dube
LAVOIE,Leah Elizabeth   Sex:F   06 Feb 1981 George Thomas Lavoie
  & Kathleen S Siehiewic
LAVOIE,Leona Therese   Sex:F   (Child #9) 10 Apr 1927 Albert J Lavoie (Maine)
  & Marie Anne Thibodeau (Canada)
LAVOIE,Lisa M   Sex:F   08 Oct 1960 George E Lavoie & Alice A Dube

HUDSON,NH BIRTHS

LAVOIE,Mark D   Sex:M   22 Nov 1954 Armand H Lavoie & Lena A Berube
LAVOIE,Mary B   Sex:F   14 Sep 1974 Ronald P Lavoie & Patricia K Monroe
LAVOIE,Matthew S   Sex:M   06 Nov 1970 Richard A Lavoie & Linda J Howe
LAVOIE,Meghan L   Sex:F   24 Jul 1977 Richard A Lavoie & Linda J Howe
LAVOIE,Michael P   Sex:M   27 Jun 1975 Eugene L Lavoie & Beverly E Wood
LAVOIE,Neal P   Sex:M   04 Dec 1964 George E Lavoie & Alice A Dube
LAVOIE,Oscar Raymond   Sex:M   (Child #6) 25 Oct 1925 Albert J Lavoie (Maine)
   & Marie A Thibodeau (Canada)
LAVOIE,Paul A   Sex:M   19 Jul 1951 Alfred J Lavoie & Isabelle Gendron
LAVOIE,Philip M   Sex:M   (Child #3) 01 Feb 1943 Augustin N Lavoie (Augusta,
   ME) & Doris P Clough (Lowell, MA)
LAVOIE,Richard A   Sex:M   (Child #2) 03 Apr 1940 Augustin N Lavoie (Augusta,
   ME) & Doris B Clough (Lowell, MA)
LAVOIE,Sara Alayne Sex:F 28 Jan 1983 Paul Lucius Lavoie & Jacqueline L Gilman
LAVOIE,Shayne R   Sex:M   13 Mar 1969 Richard A Lavoie & Linda J Howe
LAVOIE,Steven W   Sex:M   02 Feb 1970 Robert L Lavoie & Pamela A Morse
LAVOIE,William T   Sex:M   05 Oct 1952 Norman A Lavoie & Ethel Houle
LAW,Alan Jacob   Sex:M   11 Oct 1981 James Joseph Law & Tamara Lee Cobb
LAW,Earlene Ann   Sex:F   (Child #3) 03 Oct 1936 Earl Law (Wentworth, NH)
   & Margaret Noyes (Groton, NH)
LAW,James J   Sex:M   11 Nov 1959 Robert O Law & Rita Y Plourde
LAW,Janet M   Sex:F   22 Mar 1958 Robert O Law & Rita Y Plourde
LAW,Jo Anne   Sex:F   01 May 1956 Robert O Law & Rita Y Plourde
LAWLESS,Andrew Michael Sex:M 18 Oct 1984 James W Lawless & Anne L Gelinas
LAWRENCE,Eleazer   Sex:M   09 Jun 1738 Hudson, NH David Lawrence & Sarah
LAWRENCE,Mary Rose   Sex:F   04 May 1984 Edward S Lawrence & Karlene May Ahern
LAWRENCE,Sarah   Sex:F   31 Jan 1739 Hudson, NH David Lawrence & Sarah
LEACH,Andrew S   Sex:M   04 Aug 1975 Leonard K Leach & Frances E Franklin
LEACH,Barbara Ann   Sex:F   09 Mar 1978 Leonard K Leach & Frances E Franklin
LEACH,Daniel R   Sex:M   15 Dec 1963 Leonard K Leach & Frances E Franklin
LEACH,Debra A   Sex:F   19 Jan 1955 Clesson W Leach & Beverly A Poliquin
LEACH,Gerald A   Sex:M   06 Dec 1957 Leonard K Leach & Frances E Franklin
LEACH,James D   Sex:M   15 Jul 1965 Leonard K Leach & Frances E Franklin
LEACH,Jeffrey David   Sex:M   02 Feb 1978 Joseph F Leach & Karen Ruth Murphy
LEACH,Lynda L   Sex:F   17 Sep 1958 Clesson W Leach & Beverly A Poliquin
LEACH,Mark E   Sex:M   16 May 1959 Leonard K Leach & Frances E Franklin
LEACH,Michael E   Sex:M   18 Feb 1956 Clesson W Leach & Beverly A Poliquin
LEACH,Nathan Michael Sex:M 05 Apr 1984 Michael E Leach & Patrice R Beaulac
LEACH,Neil Patrick Sex:M 05 Apr 1984 Michael Ernest Leach & Patrice R Beaulac
LEACH,Ruth-Ann   Sex:F   10 Jul 1964 Clesson W Leach & Beverly A Poliquin
LEACH,Timothy P   Sex:M   03 May 1960 Leonard K Leach & Frances E Franklin
LEACH,Tracy W   Sex:F   10 Jul 1964 Clesson W Leach & Beverly A Poliquin
LEAOR,Bonnie R   Sex:F   27 Dec 1961 Edward G Leaor & Darlene A LaPan
LEAOR,Carl E   Sex:M   18 Aug 1964 Edward G Leaor & Darlene A LaPan
LEAOR,Edward G Jr   Sex:M   13 Dec 1957 Edward G Leaor & Darlene A LaPan
LEAOR,Edward Girouard   Sex:M   (Child #4) 17 Sep 1936 Carl Leaor
   (New Hampshire) & Lillian Martin (Massachusetts)
LEAOR,Jason S   Sex:M   15 Feb 1970 Maurice R Leaor & Judith J Levesque
LEAOR,Joseph Carl   Sex:M   (Child #2) 21 Jul 1933 Carl Leaor (Meredith, NH)
   & Lillian Martin (New Bedford, MA)
LEAOR,Linda A   Sex:F   27 Jan 1959 Edward G Leaor & Darlene A LaPan
LEAOR,M Theresa Aileen   Sex:F   (Child #3) 14 Dec 1934 Carl Leaor
   (Meredith, NH) & Lillian Martin (New Bedford, MA)
LEAOR,Timothy M   Sex:M   09 Jul 1967 Maurice R Leaor & Judith J Levesque
LEAOR,Walter Robert   Sex:M   (Child #1) 31 Oct 1933 Walter Leaor (USA)
   & Rose Larouche (Nashua, NH)
LEAOR,[Unknown]   Sex:M   (Child #4) 18 Aug 1940 Carl E Leaor (Meredith, NH)
   & Lillian A Martin (New Bedford, MA)
LEAZOTT,Harold   Sex:M   (Child #11) 21 Sep 1905 James F Leazott (Chazy, NY)
   & Linda S Clark (Peterborough, NH)

HUDSON,NH BIRTHS

LEAZOTT,Hattie M   Sex:F   03 Aug 1877 Hudson, NH Deneat Leazott (Canada)
 & Mary (Canada)
LEAZOTT,Raemona   Sex:F   (Child #1) 16 Jun 1913 Joseph E Leazott (Nashua, NH)
 & Agnes B Tierney (Nashua, NH)
LEAZOTTE,Sophronia A   Sex:F   (Child #7) 30 Nov 1896 James T Leazotte
 (Altoona, NY) & Linda S Clark (Peterborough, NH)
LeBARON,Dennis E   Sex:M   07 Feb 1951 Everett T LeBaron & Leatrice T Fellett
LeBARON,Scott M   Sex:M   07 Jan 1956 Everett T LeBaron & Leatrice T Follett
LeBARRON,Kenneth R   Sex:M   18 Dec 1953 Everett T LeBarron & Sylvia L Cote
LeBLANC,Amber L   Sex:F   05 Sep 1961 Joseph H LeBlanc & Carolyn F Knights
LeBLANC,Candice K   Sex:F   22 Nov 1963 Joseph H LeBlanc & Carolyn F Knights
LeBLANC,Craig D   Sex:M   26 Aug 1971 Paul R LeBlanc & Kathleen A Rafferty
LeBLANC,Curtis D   Sex:M   26 Aug 1971 Paul R LeBlanc & Kathleen A Rafferty
LeBLANC,Jason Victor Sex:M 22 Dec 1980 Normand A LeBlanc & Janet Maxine Perry
LeBLANC,Jill E   Sex:F   02 May 1979 Philip A LeBlanc & Jane A Cheverie
LeBLANC,Joseph Wayne Sex:M 08 Jun 1982 Philip A LeBlanc & Jane A Cheverie
LeBLANC,Loretta A   Sex:F   22 Apr 1959 Leopold LeBlanc & Edith S Parker
LEBLANC,M Claire G   Sex:F   (Child #5) 28 Apr 1927 Jean Baptiste Leblan
 (St David, P Q) & M Anne R Bellavance (Remou
LeBLANC,Pearl T   Sex:F   11 Mar 1957 Leopold LeBlanc & Edith S Parker
LeBLANC,Roy L   Sex:M   13 May 1956 Leonard J LeBlanc & Annette E Sherwood
LeBLANC,Sharon I   Sex:F   20 Jan 1967 Paul N LeBlanc & Paulette A Proulx
LeBLANC,William H   Sex:M   02 May 1954 Arthur W LeBlanc & Arlene M Hanson
LeBLANC,[Unknown]   Sex:F   10 Feb 1955 Leonard J LeBlanc & Annette E Sherwood
LeBOEUF,Anne M   Sex:F   30 May 1959 Gerard L LeBoeuf & Lorette E Bruneau
LeBOEUF,Claire C M   Sex:F   (Child #2) 03 Nov 1942 Eugene J LeBoeuf
 (Tupper Lake, NY) & Anna M Bibeau (St Eugene, Ca
LeBOEUF,Eva H   Sex:F   (Child #11) 07 Feb 1903 Archie LeBoeuf (Canada)
 & Lumine Poisson (Canada)
LeBOEUF,Isabelle C   Sex:F   (Child #12) 19 May 1905 Archie LeBoeuf (Canada)
 & Lumina Poisson (Canada)
LEBOEUF,J Raymond Alf   Sex:M   (Child #1) 26 Jul 1938 Eugene Leboeuf
 (Tup Lake, NY) & Anna Marie Bibeau (St Eugene, Can
LEBOEUF,Louise D   Sex:F   07 Jul 1956 Gerard L Leboeuf & Lorette E Bruneau
LECLAIR,Jos Ed Maurice   Sex:M   (Child #4) 04 May 1925 Antoine Leclair
 (Canada) & Dorilla Laroche (Canada)
LECLAIR,Karen J   Sex:F   10 Aug 1966 Albert W Leclair & Beverly A Rossi
LECLAIR,Leo Ronald   Sex:M   (Child #8) 03 Sep 1934 Antonio Leclair (Canada)
 & Dorila Laroche (Canada)
LECLERC,Anthony R   Sex:M   20 Oct 1957 Amedee R Leclerc & Pauline M Smith
LECLERC,Brian D   Sex:M   09 Mar 1963 Oscar S Leclerc & Betty C Cass
LECLERC,Gerald J   Sex:M   11 Aug 1960 Amedee R Leclerc & Pauline M Smith
LECLERC,Jennifer Lyn   Sex:F   11 Mar 1982 Anthony R Leclerc & Debra Jo Hirsch
LECLERC,Paula S   Sex:F   12 Apr 1968 Leo R Leclerc & Ruth E Doland
LECLERC,Sally J   Sex:F   26 Mar 1966 Leo R LeClerc & Ruth E Doland
LeCLERC,Scott A   Sex:M   06 Dec 1960 Leo R LeClerc & Ruth E Doland
LEDDY,Norene E   Sex:F   27 Apr 1972 John E Leddy & Helen N Cotter
LEDOUX,Aaron P   Sex:M   10 Jan 1980 Paul N Ledoux & Debra T Kliss
LEDOUX,Christopher James Sex:M 30 Oct 1982 James D Ledoux & Becky A Hartt
LEDOUX,Diane L   Sex:F   25 Aug 1948 Norbert B Ledoux (Nashua, NH)
 & Henriette L Jeannot (Nashua, NH)
LEDOUX,Gregory M   Sex:M   14 Jun 1974 Norman W Ledoux & Jacqueline B Pelleti
LEDOUX,Jennifer R   Sex:F   06 Jul 1971 Andre E Ledoux & Beverly R Despres
LEDOUX,Jeremy A   Sex:M   30 Jul 1975 Andre E Ledoux & Beverly R Despres
LEDOUX,Judith A   Sex:F   08 Jan 1952 Norbert B Ledoux & Henriette L Jeannot
LEDOUX,Kevin John   Sex:M   04 May 1977 Andre E Ledoux & Beverly Ruth Despres
LEDOUX,Lucille Margaret   Sex:F   (Child #5) 01 Jul 1937 Gregory Ledoux
 (St Albans, VT) & Mary Masson (Canada)
LEDOUX,Mark A   Sex:M   19 Sep 1964 Armand W Ledoux & Jeannine S Migneault
LEDOUX,Michael R   Sex:M   04 Nov 1969 Ralph A Ledoux & Elizabeth A Hunnewel

HUDSON,NH BIRTHS

LEDOUX,Michele J   Sex:F   03 Dec 1969 Norman W Ledoux & Jacqueline B Pelleti
LEDOUX,Michelle J   Sex:F   04 Oct 1967 Armand W Ledoux & Jeannine S Migneault
LEDOUX,Neil P   Sex:M   11 Mar 1952 Leo J Ledoux & Frances A Owens
LEDOUX,Noah John   Sex:M   13 Oct 1975 Daniel J Ledoux & Paula M Jacques
LEDOUX,Randall R   Sex:M   14 Jul 1967 Ralph A Ledoux & Elizabeth A Hunnewel
LEDOUX,Rhonda Lynn   Sex:F   04 Nov 1976 Alan D Ledoux & Brenda L Bardas
LEDOUX,Stephen G   Sex:M   24 Jul 1958 Norbert B Ledoux & Henriette L Jeannott
LEE,Allen D   Sex:M   24 Dec 1947 Fred L Lee (Woodstock, VT) & Ruth O Hills
   (Windsor, VT)
LEE,Derek Michael Sex:M 27 Aug 1984 Michael Shane Lee & Ellen Marie Gauthier
LEE,Fred R   Sex:M   (Child #2) 09 Feb 1946 Fred L Lee (Woodstock, NH)
   & Ruth O Hills (Windsor, VT)
LEE,Jesse R   Sex:M   15 Aug 1967 Richard F Lee & Paula M Alger
LEE,John T   Sex:M   14 Sep 1965 Lawrence T Lee & Constance J Labbe
LEE,Joseph   Sex:M   (Child #1) 02 Aug 1922 Adelard Lee (Canada)
   & Delia Lecompte (Canada)
LEE,Karen A   Sex:F   20 Jan 1965 Fred R Lee & Paula M Alger
LEE,Rose Deleina G   Sex:F   (Child #3) 13 Sep 1926 Joseph Lee (Canada)
   & Maria Lemay (Canada)
LEE,Sharon A   Sex:F   22 Aug 1949 Fred L Lee & Ruth O Hills
LEEDBERG,Troy T   Sex:M   21 Jul 1973 Melvin E Leedberg Sr & Gail F Pilato
LEFEBVRE,Andrea M   Sex:F   19 Dec 1963 Robert N Lefebvre & Germaine Y Guilbert
LEFEBVRE,Anita Gloria   Sex:F   (Child #2) 01 Aug 1934 Geo Theodore Lefebvre
   (Tilton, NH) & Clara Lillian Martin (Manchester, NH)
LEFEBVRE,Dennis R   Sex:M   07 Mar 1962 Robert N Lefebvre & Germaine Guilbert
LEFEBVRE,Frank A Sex:M   (Child #4) 05 Jan 1943 George T Lefebvre (Tilton, NH)
   & Clara L Martin (Manchester, NH)
LEFEBVRE,John Roger   Sex:M   (Child #3) 28 Jul 1938 Geo Theodore Lefebvre
   Tilton, NH) & Clara Lillian Martin (Manchester, NH)
LEFEBVRE,Jos Raymond   Sex:M   (Child #5) 06 Dec 1935 Joseph Lefebvre
   (Brookline, MA) & Mary Labombard (W Chazy, NY)
LEFEBVRE,Karen L   Sex:F   07 Mar 1960 Robert J Lefebvre & Elizabeth A DeGrenie
LEFEBVRE,Keith Roland   Sex:M   03 Aug 1978 Donald W LeFebvre & Susan B Beland
LEFEBVRE,Leonard Allen   Sex:M   05 Feb 1941 George T Lefebvre (Tilton, NH)
   & Clara L Martin (Manchester, NH)
LEFEBVRE,Marie-Rose   Sex:F   22 Jul 1960 Robert A Lefebvre & Patricia E Roy
LEFEBVRE,Mary-Beth   Sex:F   01 Dec 1973 Robert R Lefebvre & Margaret R Marquis
LEFEBVRE,Raymond M   Sex:M   27 Jul 1961 Raymond L Lefebvre & Marie Russell
LEFEBVRE,Robert Joseph   Sex:M   (Child #5) 07 Jun 1937 Joseph Henry Lefebvre
   (Brookline, NH) & Mary Labombard (W Chazy, NY)
LEFEBVRE,Robert R   Sex:M   17 Apr 1948 Ernest E Lefebvre (Nashua, NH)
   & Yvonne M Rioux (Nashua, NH)
LEFBVRE,William E   Sex:M   (Child #1) 18 Sep 1946 Edmond E Lefebvre
   (Nashua, NH) & Magdalene M Shelley (Mullin, SC)
LEFEBVRE,[Unknown] Sex:M   (Child #7) 11 Dec 1944 George T Lefebvre
   (Tilton, NH) & Clara L Martin (Manchester, NH)
LEFEVRE,Gloria   Sex:F   (Child #2) 23 Jan 1940 Charles Lefevre (Nashua, NH)
   & Florence Barrett (Hudson, NH)
LEGASSE,Claire Doris I   Sex:F   (Child #1) 05 Nov 1933 Euclide Legasse
   (Canada) & Melvina C Boyer (Nashua, NH)
LeGROU,Shirley Parker   Sex:F   29 May 1934 Edward LeGrou (Michigan)
   & Kathleen Ray (Canada)
LEIGH,Sharyl P   Sex:F   10 Apr 1961 Robert E Leigh & Carol A Morse
LEIGH,Tammy A   Sex:F   23 Jun 1959 Robert F Leigh & Carol A Morse
LEIGHTON,Linda A   Sex:F   (Child #1) 22 Dec 1946 Roger K Leighton (Nashua, NH)
   & Nellie V McAdoo (Nashua, NH)
LEIGHTON,Robert H Jr   Sex:M   24 May 1965 Robert H Leighton Sr
   & Carolyn J Beaudet
LEKAS,Christopher Daniel Sex:M 19 Jan 1985 Andreas A Lekas & Alicia D Wiley
LELAND,Buffy   Sex:F   03 Oct 1969 Bramwell P Leland & Wendeline Hodge

HUDSON,NH BIRTHS

LEMAIRE,David W   Sex:M   27 Aug 1967 Willard R Lemaire & Linda B Thoren
LEMAY,Christopher Roger Sex:M 05 Jul 1984 Peter J Lemay & Lynda Ann Lacroix
LEMAY,Debra A   Sex:F   05 Nov 1956 Marcel R Lemay & Gloria M Diggins
LEMAY,Gerard E Jr   Sex:M   01 Mar 1958 Gerard E Lemay & Patricia A Reilly
LEMAY,James M   Sex:M   01 May 1960 Gerard E Lemay & Patricia A Reilly
LEMAY,Jeanne Louise   Sex:F   (Child #7) 11 Aug 1934 Omer Lemay (Canada)
  & Yvonne Dionne (Canada)
LEMAY,Marcel   Sex:M   (Child #5) 21 Feb 1931 J Omer Lemary (Canada)
  & Yvonne Dionne (Canada)
LEMAY,Marie Gert F   Sex:F   (Child #6) 29 Oct 1932 Nashua, NH Omer Lemay
  (Canada) & Yvonne Dionne (Canada)
LEMAY,Simonne Carmen   Sex:F   (Child #8) 25 Oct 1939 Omer Lemay (Canada)
  & Yvonne D Lemay (Canada)
LEMAY,Victor A   Sex:M   27 Oct 1961 Marcel R Lemay & Gloria M Diggins
LEMERY,Linda L   Sex:F   01 Aug 1947 Raymond V Lemery (Nashua, NH)
  & Lurena Donah (Nashua, NH)
LEMERY,Roland J Jr   Sex:M   18 Sep 1964 Roland J Lemery & Shirley R Plante
LEMIEUX,Jason A   Sex:M   15 Jun 1970 Robert G Lemieux & Deanna A Holt
LEMIEUX,Shirley A   Sex:F   02 Apr 1967 Joseph T Lemieux & Elizabeth M Sirois
LEMIEUX,Thomas A   Sex:M   15 Jan 1966 Joseph T Lemieux & Marie E Sirois
LEMIRE,Christin A   Sex:F   28 Jun 1970 R Paul Lemire & Diane N Moreau
LEMIRE,Debora A   Sex:F   21 Mar 1956 William A Lemire & Maria T Bravos
LEMIRE,Elaine R   Sex:F   22 Jul 1952 George H Lemire & Lorraine P Moreau
LEMIRE,Steven Christopher   Sex:M   27 Apr 1983 Albert A Lemire Jr
  & Ann Elizabeth Blaser
LEMIRE,William Alfred   Sex:M   (Child #2) 26 May 1934 Alfred Lemire
  (Nashua, NH) & Thelma Fifield (Nashua, NH)
LEMMO,Jason Christopher R   Sex:M 16 Dec 1983 Donald J Lemmo & Suzanne D Allen
LEMOINE,Ethan A   Sex: 14 Aug 1972 Alan E Lemoine & Janice E Kuchinski
LENEHAN,Mary   Sex:F   15 Jan 1873 Hudson, NH John Lenehan & Mary
LENTZ,Amanda Sara   Sex:F   03 Sep 1982 Scott Lewis Lentz & Jeanne M Lafleur
LEONARD,Christopher A   Sex: 18 Aug 1972 Edward A Leonard & Louise A Cota
LEONARD,Samantha Lee   Sex:F   03 May 1985 Mark A Leonard & Sharon Ann Griffin
LEONE,Dean C   Sex:M   22 May 1961 Burton S Leone & Dolores D Dandley
LePAGE,Adam James   Sex:M   21 May 1977 James N Lepage & Debra Lee Maschmeier
LePAGE,Aimee Elizabeth Sex:F 09 Sep 1980 James N LePage& Deborah L Maschmeier
LESCARD,David B   Sex:M   21 Mar 1979 Albert J Lescard & Frances R Lemire
LESLIE,Eleanor S   Sex:F   (Child #1) 08 Oct 1906 Eugene W Leslie (Hudson, NH)
  & Lettie V Shepard (W Boylston, MA)
LESLIE,Eugene W   Sex:M   (Child #1) 13 Apr 1882 Hudson, NH Charles C Leslie
  (Warner, NH) & Eliza B Webster (Hudson, NH)
LESLIE,Eugene William   Sex:M   10 Apr 1882 Hudson, NH Charls C Leslie
  & Eliza P Webster
LESLIE,Gordon Charles Sex:M   (Child #2) 27 May 1911 Eugene W Leslie (Hudson,
  NH) & Lette V Shepard (W Boylston, MA)
LESNIAK,Felicia A   Sex:F   13 Oct 1962 Joseph V Lesniak & Mary L McKone
LESNIAK,Steven J   Sex:M   20 Apr 1964 Joseph V Lesniak & Mary L McKone
LESSARD,Christina L   Sex:F   16 Jun 1976 Paul P Lessard & Joanne M Vezina
LESSARD,Christopher David   Sex:M   05 Feb 1985 Daniel E Lessard
  & Cynthia A Lefebvre
LESSARD,Derek R   Sex:M   01 May 1979 Dennis R Lessard & Donna Marie Chaisson
LESSARD,Justin Matthew   Sex:M   03 May 1981 Dennis R Lessard
  & Donna Marie Chaisson
LESSARD,Robert A Jr   Sex:M   06 Jun 1978 Robert A Lessard Jr
  & Suzanne T G Fontaine
LETELLIER,Richard E Jr   Sex:M   03 Dec 1967 Richard E Letellier
  & Jeanne Y Gagnon
LETOURNEAU,Mark J   Sex:M   08 Jun 1962 Joseph C Letourneau & Lucille M Fortin
LETOURNEAU,Michael J Sex:M 08 Jun 1962 Joseph C Letourneau & Lucille M Fortin
LETOURNEAUX,Norman P Sex:M   21 Mar 1971 Norman W Letourneaux & Pauline M Dube

HUDSON,NH BIRTHS

LETTY,Pamela A   Sex:F   09 Mar 1967 Ronald J Letty & Henriette Grenier
LEVASSEUR,Emily Ann   Sex:F   13 Aug 1979 Paul A Levasseur & Priscilla A Hevey
LEVASSEUR,Jo Ann M   Sex:F   20 Mar 1970 Paul L Levasseur & Theresa M Neault
LEVASSEUR,Nancy M   Sex:F   06 May 1967 Paul L Levasseur & Theresa M Neault
LEVASSEUR,Sandra R   Sex:F   10 Jan 1966 Paul L Levasseur & Theresa M Neault
LEVESQUE,Alice G   Sex:M   (Child #3) 20 Oct 1922 Etienne Levesque (Canada) & Cleance Belanger (Canada)
LEVESQUE,Andrew J   Sex:M   08 Oct 1970 Jean A Levesque & Antoinette D Briand
LEVESQUE,Angela Marie Sex:F   07 Mar 1983 Ronald G Levesque & Andrea J Roberge
LEVESQUE,Bertha Theresa Sex:F   (Child #8) 16 Mar 1930 Etienne Levesque (Canada) & Cleance Belanger (Canada)
LEVESQUE,Brian J   Sex:M   13 May 1972 Richard B Levesque & Shirley A Fournier
LEVESQUE,Carla A   Sex:F   22 Nov 1957 Robert A Levesque & Rachel E Michaud
LEVESQUE,Carole A   Sex:F   29 Nov 1960 Lionel E Levesque & Phyllis M Dumont
LEVESQUE,Charlene A   Sex:F   20 Mar 1968 Norman A Levesque & Judith A Duggan
LEVESQUE,Claudia R   Sex:F   19 Mar 1951 Alcide S Levesque & Leona T Lavoie
LEVESQUE,Debra L   Sex:F   26 Jun 1960 Ernest R Levesque & Esther Mitchell
LEVESQUE,Dennis P   Sex:M   14 Dec 1954 Robert A Levesque & Rachel E Michaud
LEVESQUE,Diane L   Sex:F   19 Aug 1949 Maurice J Levesque & Gloria A Gaudreau
LEVESQUE,Dolores L   Sex:F   30 Sep 1951 Raymond J Levesque & Lucille B Guay
LEVESQUE,Douglas R   Sex:M   05 Dec 1968 Paul R Levesque & Marlene J Johnson
LEVESQUE,Elaine Y   Sex:F   07 Jul 1956 Henry A Levesque & Therese F Moreau
LEVESQUE,Emile   Sex:M   (Child #5) 29 Jan 1925 Etienne Levesque (Canada) & Cleance Belanger (Canada)
LEVESQUE,James J   Sex:M   15 Jul 1969 Rene E Levesque & Sheila J Zedalis
LEVESQUE,James M   Sex:M   08 Mar 1970 Romeo J Levesque & Rita I Roy
LEVESQUE,Janine T   Sex:F   21 May 1955 Maurice J Levesque & Gloria A Gaudreau
LEVESQUE,Jeanne M   Sex:F   (Child #8) 24 Jun 1940 Sylvio Levesque (Nashua, NH) & Viola Lambert (Berwick, ME)
LEVESQUE,Jeffrey R Sex:M   30 Jan 1970 Richard B Levesque & Shirley A Fournier
LEVESQUE,Joan L   Sex:F   (Child #1) 23 Apr 1943 Robert P Levesque (Hudson, NH) & Olivette E Delude (Nashua, NH)
LEVESQUE,Jonathan P   Sex:M   12 Jan 1978 William R Levesque & Gail L Shipley
LEVESQUE,Joshua S   Sex:M   15 Dec 1976 William R Levesque & Gail L Shipley
LEVESQUE,Julie A   Sex:F   24 Aug 1963 Norbert E Levesque & Elaine J Gagne
LEVESQUE,Kathy M   Sex:F   18 Dec 1974 Gerard A Levesque & Maria T Mossotti
LEVESQUE,Kristal D   Sex:F   22 May 1976 Richard A Levesque & Ida M Wood
LEVESQUE,Laurie L   Sex:F   05 Jun 1968 Jean A Levesque & Antoinette D Briand
LEVESQUE,Leo R   Sex:M   (Child #9) 18 Feb 1942 Joseph Levesque (Norwich, CT) & Bernadette Levesque (Nashua, NH)
LEVESQUE,Linda L   Sex:F   24 Jun 1955 Archie Levesque & Maxine M Ketch
LEVESQUE,Lionel Eugene   Sex:M   (Child #7) 06 Jul 1928 Etienne Levesque (Canada) & Cleance Belanger (Canada)
LEVESQUE,Louise J   Sex:F   10 Aug 1951 Maurice J Levesque & Gloria A Gaudreau
LEVESQUE,Lynn A   Sex:F   03 May 1967 Romeo J Levesque & Rita I Roy
LEVESQUE,Michael G   Sex:M   13 Feb 1959 Gilbert A Levesque & Martha L Pond
LEVESQUE,Michael N   Sex:M   23 Oct 1964 Norbert E Levesque & Elaine J Gagne
LEVESQUE,Michael T Sex:M   21 Sep 1967 Lionel E Levesque Sr & Phyllis M Dumont
LEVESQUE,Normand R Sex:M   22 Oct 1959 Lionel E Levesque,Sr & Phyllis M Dumont
LEVESQUE,Patricia N   Sex:F   17 Aug 1954 Henry A Levesque & Therese F Moreau
LEVESQUE,Priscilla E   Sex:F   (Child #1) 21 Jan 1944 Alphonse J Levesque (Nashua, NH) & Georgianna C Tessie (Nashua, NH)
LEVESQUE,Rita Cherese   Sex:F   (Child #6) 12 Mar 1926 Etienne Levesque (Canada) & Cleance Belanger (Canada)
LEVESQUE,Robert J Jr Sex:M   23 Mar 1971 Robert J Levesque & Adrienne Letendre
LEVESQUE,Robert P Jr Sex:M   14 Mar 1959 Robert P Levesque & Olivette E Delude
LEVESQUE,Roland   Sex:M   (Child #4) 23 Sep 1923 Etienne Levesque (Canada) & Cleance Belanger (Canada)
LEVESQUE,Scott E   Sex:M   18 May 1958 Edward J Levesque & Cecile B Bastille
LEWIS,Esther   Sex:F   09 Dec 1894 Harvey G Lewis (Hudson, NH) & Nellie Condon

HUDSON,NH BIRTHS

(Canada)
LEWIS,Harry G Sex:M 01 Dec 1852 Hudson, NH William F Lewis & Lydia
LEWIS,Harvey G Sex:M 01 Dec 1852 Hudson, NH William F Lewis & Lucy
LEWIS,Heather C Sex:F 07 Jun 1962 Lloyd A Lewis & Lois A Dawes
LEWIS,Katherine F Sex:F 27 Jun 1968 Lloyd A Lewis & Lois A Dawes
LEWIS,Linda M Sex:F 15 Dec 1957 Lloyd A Lewis & Lois A Dawes
LEWIS,Lyman D Sex:M 01 Jun 1959 Lloyd A Lewis & Lois A Dawes
LEWIS,Michael J Sex:M 04 Aug 1962 Earl W Lewis & Gloria G Lefebvre
LEWONIS,Tammi J Sex:F 13 Jun 1975 Steven A Lewonis & Judith A Lavallee
LEYLAND,Lillie Sex:F 23 Apr 1903 Geo C Leyland (England)
  & Elizabeth Costello (Boston, MA)
LIAKOS,Andrew Arthur Sex:M 11 Aug 1982 Arthur Liakos & Leslie Ann Martin
LIBBY,Kathleen E Sex:F 22 Apr 1954 Chester A Libby & Helen M Farrington
LIBBY,Peggy J Sex:F 14 Apr 1957 Chester A Libby & Helen M Farrington
LIGHT,Corrine Elizabeth Sex:F 19 Feb 1983 Rogert J Light & Cindy Marie Lemire
LIGHT,David N Sex:M 03 Apr 1954 Andrew J Light & Yvonne Labrie
LIGHT,Doreen R Sex:F 14 Jun 1957 Andrew J Light & Yvonne A Labrie
LIGHT,Sandra M Sex:F 27 May 1955 Andrew J Light & Yvonne A Labrie
LIGHT,Simonne D Sex:F 22 Jun 1956 Andrew J Light & Yvonne A Labrie
LILLEY,Barbara Ann Sex:F (Child #3) 11 Nov 1938 William Henry Lilley
  (Providence, RI) & Mary Manchester (Wesport, ME)
LILLEY,Betty Lou Sex:F (Child #4) 19 Dec 1939 William H Lilley (Providence,
  RI) & Mary Manchester (Westport, ME)
LILLEY,Bing G Sex:M (Child #5) 27 Oct 1942 William H Lilley (Providence, RI)
  & Mary E Manchester (Westport, ME)
LILLEY,Leonard J Sex:M 16 Aug 1969 William R Lilley & Linda S Dixon
LILLEY,Lillian S Sex:F (Child #6) 07 Jul 1944 William H Lilley (Providence,
  RI) & Mary E Manchester (Westport, ME)
LILLIBRIDGE,Rose M Sex:F (Child #1) 27 May 1906 Jesse T Lillibridge
  (E Greenwich, RI) & Lillian B Stacy (Revere, MA)
LIMMER,Bryn Elizabeth Sex:F 31 Aug 1979 John Steven Limmer & Juliet M Gessman
LINCK,Alexander Richard Sex:M 03 Jun 1983 Richard E Linck & Gail Anita Lang
LINDAHL,Allen R Sex:M 15 Nov 1958 Roland E Lindahl & May N Ekstrand
LINDAHL,Arthur C Sex:M 22 May 1961 Roland E Lindahl & May N Ekstrand
LINDQUIST,Andrew P Sex:M (Child #2) 21 Nov 1944 Theodore A Lindquist
  (Hopkinton, NH) & Mary A Climas (Nashua, NH)
LINDQUIST,Andrew Richard Sex:M 08 Nov 1978 Richard J Lindquist
  & Susanne G Levesque
LINDQUIST,Janice Sex:F 29 Nov 1974 Andrew P Lindquist & Carol A Guzdowski
LINDQUIST,Jeffrey Sex:M 21 Aug 1959 William F Lindquist & Lorraine G Hinton
LINDQUIST,Jennifer Marie Sex:F 31 Oct 1976 Richard J Lindquist
  & Susanne G Levesque
LINDQUIST,John C Sex:M (Child #1) 11 Jul 1940 Theodore Lindquist
  (Hopkinton, NH) & Mary Klinas (Nashua, NH)
LINDQUIST,Richard J Sex:M 25 May 1949 Theodore A Lindquist & Mary A Klimas
LINDQUIST,Theodore John Sex:M 31 Oct 1978 John C Lindquist & Donna Lee Tilton
LINDSAY,Peter J Sex:M 25 Jul 1957 Anthony C Lindsay & Nellie Grigas
LINDSEY,Michael J Sex:M 09 May 1974 Gerald W Lindsey & Catherine M Curran
LINEHAN,George L Sex:M 12 Jul 1881 Hudson, NH John Linehan (Ireland)
  & Mary Clancy (Ireland)
LINEHAN,John P Sex:M 03 Mar 1878 Hudson, NH John Linehan (Ireland)
  & Mary Clancey (Ireland)
LINEHAN,Peace Sex:F 20 May 1875 Hudson, NH John Linehan & Mary
LIPTAK,Glenn T Sex:M 27 Jun 1961 Gordon C Liptak & Joyce E Fieldstad
LISTER,Jeffrey G Sex:M 08 Nov 1973 Raymond R Lister & Sherry E Dowd
LITMAN,Elaine L Sex:F 31 May 1974 Abraham Litman & Edith L Duran
LITMAN,Kenneth R Sex:M 29 Mar 1972 Abraham Litman & Edith L Duran
LITTLE,Harry R Sex:M 03 Nov 1949 Robert H Little & Jeannette E Emmond
LITTLEFIELD,Heather A Sex:F 27 Feb 1969 Dana M Littlefield
  & Elizabeth A Malone

HUDSON,NH BIRTHS

LITTLEFIELD,Scott D Sex:M 26 Mar 1971 Dana M Littlefield & Elizabeth A Malone
LIVINGSTON,Laura Ann Sex:F 14 Jan 1854 Hudson, NH Benjamin Livingston&Lucy C
LIVINGSTON,Lizzie Maria Sex:F 22 Mar 1858 Hudson, NH Benjamin Livingston
  & Lucy C
LIVINGSTON,Lucy Jane Sex:F 02 Sep 1852 Hudson, NH Benjamin Livingston
  & Lucy C
LIZOTTE,Christopher R Sex:M 07 Jun 1983 Leo Arnold Lizotte & Nancy Bellia
LOCHHEAD,Jay G Sex:M 22 Sep 1963 William R Lochhead & Nancy J Hobbs
LOCHHEAD,Susan J Sex:F 15 Jan 1966 William R Lochhead & Nancy J Hobbs
LOCKE,Kristen A Sex:F 22 Nov 1970 Daniel D Locke & Marcia L Westgate
LOCKE,Shirley Mae Sex:F (Child #3) 06 Feb 1942 John Locke (Charlestown, MA)
  & Olive Chamberlain (Gardner, ME)
LOCKMAN,Jennifer A Sex:F 05 Sep 1970 Richard A Lockman & Geri A Carter
LOCKMAN,Jesse M Sex:M 05 Sep 1970 Richard A Lockman & Geri A Carter
LODER,Jason Sex:M 18 Dec 1976 John K Loder Jr & Elizabeth H Bavuso
LODER,Kristie Sex:F 10 Mar 1975 John K Loder & Elizabeth H Bavuso
LOFGREN,James T III Sex:M 10 Dec 1964 James T Lofgren, Jr & Belle M Yerus
LOFREDDO,Marie A Sex:F (Child #1) 18 Sep 1942 Ferdinand Lafreddo
  (Lawrence, MA) & Dorella Gingras (Pelham, NH)
LOGAN,Helen Anita Sex:F (Child #3) 27 May 1936 Douglas Logan, Jr (Glasgow,
  Scotland) & Lois Eudora Bradley (Nas
LOIGNON,Tracy-Jean Sex:F 26 Nov 1968 Donald A Loignon & Marie E Lanthier
LOISEL,Edward A Sex:M 26 Sep 1964 Ernest E Loisel & Ruby I Hill
LOMBARDI,Richard F Sex:M 21 Jul 1967 Robert F Lombardi & Ruth J DeMaula
LONES,Diane T Sex:F 07 Sep 1960 Richard P Lones & Pauline E Fortier
LONES,Donald R Sex:M 07 Jul 1957 Richard P Lones & Pauline E Fortier
LONES,Donna M Sex:F 23 Oct 1958 Richard P Lones & Pauline E Fortier
LONG,Muriel Ivy Sex:F 04 Jan 1921 Asmond Long (Bradford, England)
  & Pearl Irene Simpson (Aspen, CO)
LONGFELLOW,George David Sex:M 13 Sep 1978 James F Longfellow
  & Geraldine M Coolidge
LONGFELLOW,James F IV Sex: 20 Jul 1972 James F Longfellow
  & Geraldine M Coolidge
LONGFELLOW,Kathleen Virginia Sex:F 13 Sep 1978 James F Longfellow
  & Geraldine M Coolidge
LOOMIS,Jeremy Lester Sex:M 08 May 1977 James Lester Loomis & Anne Y Granger
LORAINE,Katherine C Sex:F 03 Oct 1958 Robert E Loraine & Evelyn C Berube
LORAINE,Michael H Sex:M 12 Jul 1951 Donald E Loraine & Laurine M Rodier
LORAINE,Miriam H Sex:F 21 Mar 1957 Robert E Loraine & Evelyn C Berube
LORANGER,Brian S Sex:M 14 Oct 1970 Roland C Loranger & Diane G Nadeau
LORANGER,Mark D Sex:M 14 Sep 1968 Roland C Loranger & Diane G Nadeau
LORANGER,Ramona L Sex:F 15 Jul 1954 Raymond A Loranger & Lorraine Y Bernard
LORANGER,Raymond A Jr Sex:M 05 Sep 1955 Raymond A Loranger&Lorraine Y Bernard
LORMAN,Richard M Sex:M 24 Nov 1965 Wayne H Lorman & Lois A Mann
LORRAINE,[Unknown] Sex:F (Child #5) 15 Nov 1933 Henry Lorraine (Nashua, NH)
  & Gertrude Pelletier (Nashua, NH)
LOSIER,Joan Sex:F (Child #2) 16 Feb 1933 Joseph Losier (Canada)
  & Alice Landry (Canada)
LOUBIER,Marie L J Sex:F 19 Jun 1964 Normand Loubier & Jeannine Doyon
LOUBIER,Steeve Sex:M 23 May 1965 Normand Loubier & Jeannine Doyon
LOUGEE,Arline E Sex:F (Child #1) 06 May 1918 Bert Lougee (Piermont)
  & Jessie M Lake (Manchester, NH)
LOUGEE,Bert L Sex:M (Child #2) 06 May 1918 Bert Lougee (Piermont)
  & Jessie M Lake (Manchester, NH)
LOVEJOY,Gail A Sex:F (Child #3) 03 May 1942 Robert J Lovejoy (Woburn, MA)
  & Eileen (Sherbrook, Canada)
LOVEJOY,Jeffrey R Sex:M 03 Mar 1968 Robert Lovejoy & Michele F LaVoie
LOVERING,Robert R Sex:M 02 Jan 1959 William W Lovering & Judith L Taylor
LOVERING,William A Sex:M 10 Dec 1962 William W Lovering & Judith L Taylor
LOVEWELL,Esther Sex:F 10 Nov 1728 Hudson, NH Zacheus Lovewell & Esther

HUDSON,NH BIRTHS

```
LOVEWELL,Hannah    Sex:F   16 Feb 1747  Hudson, NH  Zacheus Lovewell & Esther
LOVEWELL,Lucy      Sex:F   12 Jan 1730  Hudson, NH  Zacheus Lovewell & Esther
LOVEWELL,Mary      Sex:F   20 May 1732  Hudson, NH  Zacheus Lovewell & Esther
LOVEWELL,Noah      Sex:M   01 Apr 1742  Hudson, NH  Zacheus Lovewell & Esther
LOVEWELL,Sarah     Sex:F   25 Oct 1744  Hudson, NH  Zacheus Lovewell & Esther
LOVEWELL,Sarah     Sex:F   24 Oct 1744  Hudson, NH  Zaccheus Lovewell & Esther
LOVEWELL,Zaccheus  Sex:M   16 Dec 1735  Hudson, NH  Zaccheus Lovewell & Esther
LOVEWELL,Zacheus   Sex:M   16 Dec 1730  Hudson, NH  Zacheus Lovewell & Esther
LOWE,Robert D      Sex:M   18 Dec 1954  Robert D Lowe & Joan M LaMontagne
LOWEL,Febe         Sex:F   28 Oct 1746  Hudson, NH  Joseph Lowel & Martha
LOWEL,Hannah       Sex:F   30 Sep 17    Hudson, NH  Moses Lowel & Sarah
LOWEL,Hannah       Sex:F   20 Aug 1756  Hudson, NH  Joseph Lowel & Martha
LOWEL,Hannah       Sex:F   23 Oct 1768  Hudson, NH  Stephen Lowel & Lydia
LOWEL,Jacob        Sex:M   14 May 1762  Hudson, NH  Joseph Lowel & Martha
LOWEL,Jacob        Sex:M   07 Apr 1762  Hudson, NH  Moses Lowel & Sarah
LOWEL,John M       Sex:M   06 Aug 17    Hudson, NH  Stephen Lowel &
LOWEL,Joseph       Sex:M   20 Dec 1748  Hudson, NH  Joseph Lowel & Martha
LOWEL,Molle        Sex:F   19 Jul 1760  Hudson, NH  Stephen Lowel & Lydia
LOWEL,Molle        Sex:F   30 Dec 1750  Hudson, NH  Joseph Lowel & Martha
LOWEL,Moses        Sex:M   25 Aug 1764  Hudson, NH  Moses Lowel & Sarah
LOWEL,Ruth         Sex:F   02 Jul 1758  Hudson, NH  Stephen Lowel & Lydia
LOWEL,Samuel       Sex:M   11 Oct 1754  Hudson, NH  Moses Lowel & Sarah
LOWEL,Stephen      Sex:M   28 Feb 1756  Hudson, NH  Stephen Lowel & Lydia
LOWEL,Suse         Sex:F   17 Jan 1760  Hudson, NH  Joseph Lowel & Martha
LOWEL,Suse         Sex:F   05 Sep 1767  Hudson, NH  Stephen Lowel & Lydia
LOWEL,Timothy      Sex:M   21 Feb 1754  Hudson, NH  Joseph Lowel & Marthy
LOWELL,Abraham     Sex:M   1774 Mason   Moses Lowell & Sarah Bradbury
LOWELL,Hannah      Sex:F   30 Sep 1760  Hudson, NH  Moses Lowell & Sarah Bradbury
LOWELL,Hannah      Sex:F   20 Aug 1756  Hudson, NH  Joseph Lowell & Martha Bradbury
LOWELL,Hannah      Sex:F   23 Oct 1768  Hudson, NH  Stephen Lowell & Lydia
LOWELL,Hannah      Sex:F   16 Feb 1746  Hudson, NH  Zaccheus Lowell & Esther
LOWELL,Jacob       Sex:M   07 Apr 1762  Hudson, NH  Moses Lowell & Sarah Bradbury
LOWELL,Jacob       Sex:M   14 May 1762  Hudson, NH  Joseph Lowell & Martha Bradbury
LOWELL,Jemima      Sex:F   07 Feb 1757  Hudson, NH  Moses Lowell & Sarah Bradbury
LOWELL,John Messer Sex:M   06 Aug 1762  Hudson, NH  Stephen Lowell & Lydia
LOWELL,Joseph      Sex:M   20 Dec 1748  Hudson, NH  Joseph Lowell & Martha Bradbury
LOWELL,Molly       Sex:F   30 Dec 1750  Hudson, NH  Joseph Lowell & Martha Bradbury
LOWELL,Molly       Sex:F   19 Jul 1760  Hudson, NH  Stephen Lowell & Lydia
LOWELL,Moses       Sex:M   1726         Hudson, NH  Moses Lowell & Sarah Bradbury
LOWELL,Moses       Sex:M   25 Aug 1764  Hudson, NH  Moses Lowell & Sarah Bradbury
LOWELL,Phebe       Sex:F   28 Oct 1746  Hudson, NH  Joseph Lowell & Martha Bradbury
LOWELL,Roland      Sex:M   1767 Mason   Moses Lowell & Sarah Bradbury
LOWELL,Ruth        Sex:F   02 Jul 1758  Hudson, NH  Stephen Lowell & Lydia
LOWELL,Samuel      Sex:M   11 Oct 1754  Hudson, NH  Moses Lowell & Sarah Bradbury
LOWELL,Sarah       Sex:F   1770 Mason   Moses Lowell & Sarah Bradbury
LOWELL,Stephen     Sex:M   28 Feb 1756  Hudson, NH  Stephen Lowell & Lydia
LOWELL,Susey       Sex:F   17 Jan 1760  Hudson, NH  Joseph Lowell & Martha Bradbury
LOWELL,Susy        Sex:F   05 Sep 1767  Hudson, NH  Stephen Lowell & Lydia
LOWELL,Timothy     Sex:M   21 Feb 1754  Hudson, NH  Joseph Lowell & Martha Bradbury
LOYKO,Christopher R  Sex:M 20 Nov 1975  Raymond P Loyko & Donna M Burl
LUBY,Karen E       Sex:F   25 Feb 1964  Warren C Luby & Patricia A Sawyer
LUCAS,Robert R     Sex:M   10 Aug 1960  Ronald N Lucas & Pauline A Pariseau
LUCIEN,Frances     Sex:F   (Child #1) 18 Feb 1935  Joseph Lucien (Nashua, NH)
   & Marie Burke (Lowell, MA)
LUCIER,Jennie A    Sex:F   22 Sep 1874  Hudson, NH  Hector Lucier & Julia
LUDLOW,Kimberly A  Sex:F   16 Mar 1971  James H Ludlow Jr & Joyce A Bothwick
LUND,David         Sex:M                Hudson, NH  Jonathan Lund Jr & Priscilla Cummings
LUND,Elizabeth     Sex:F                Hudson, NH  Jonathan Lund Jr & Priscilla Cummings
LUND,Ephraim       Sex:M                Hudson, NH  Jonathan Lund Jr & Priscilla Cummings
LUND,Hannah        Sex:F                Hudson, NH  Jonathan Lund Jr & Priscilla Cummings
```

HUDSON,NH BIRTHS

LUND,Homer   Sex:M   22 Sep 1875 Hudson, NH Samuel Lund & Mary
LUND,Jonathan   Sex:M   Hudson, NH Jonathan Lund Jr & Priscilla Cummings
LUND,Mary   Sex:F   Hudson, NH Jonathan Lund Jr & Priscilla Cummings
LUND,Oliver   Sex:M   Hudson, NH Jonathan Lund Jr & Priscilla Cummings
LUND,Priscilla   Sex:F   Hudson, NH Jonathan Lund Jr & Priscilla Cummings
LUND,Samuel   Sex:M   Hudson, NH Jonathan Lund Jr & Priscilla Cummings
LUSSIER,[Unknown]   Sex:M   22 Oct 1963 William Lussier & Eileen A Sullivan
LUSZCZ,Matthew T   Sex:M   21 Mar 1979 Joseph M Luszcz & Diane G Lavoie
LUSZCZ,Nathan Alexander   Sex:M 21 Oct 1982 Joseph M Luszcz & Diane G Lavoie
LUTHI,Edith T   Sex:F   05 Jun 1954 Oscar Luthi & Trudy Leuenberger
LUZ,Robert Adam   Sex:M   14 May 1981 Robert Thomas Luz & Susan Carol Jolliff
LYNCH,Charles William   Sex:M 02 Dec 1982 Terrence M Lynch
   & Catherine Ann Hearne
LYON,Anita E   Sex:F   (Child #4) 30 Apr 1943 Richard S Lyon (Dracut, MA)
   & Naomi A Rollins (Nashua, NH)
LYON,Carl W   Sex:M   (Child #3) 16 Jul 1940 Richard Lyon (Dracut, MA)
   & Naomi Rollins (Nashua, NH)
LYON,John George   Sex:M 06 Apr 1984 Glen George Lyon & Monica M Manson
LYON,Raymond Ernest Sex:M   (Child #1) 08 Jul 1938 Richard S Lyon (Dracut, MA)
   & Naomi Anita Rollins (Nashua, NH)
LYONS,Pamela A   Sex:F   08 Nov 1971 Daniel D Lyons & Evelyn M Smith
LYONS,Steven D   Sex:M   22 Sep 1967 Daniel D Lyons & Evelyn M Smith
LYTWYN,Kenneth Ryan Sex:M 17 Oct 1979 Kenneth D Lytwyn & Michelle D McDonnoug
MacARTHUR,Emily Robin   Sex:F   23 Nov 1984 Scott W MacArthur
   & Laura A Workenthiens
MacARTHUR,Trace A   Sex:F   13 Jul 1964 Donald J MacArthur & Mary B MacArthur
MacCANN,Carolyn E   Sex:F   24 Aug 1953 John D MacCann & Anna Tokanel
MacCANN,Deborah A   Sex:F   22 Jun 1957 John D MacCann & Anna Tokanel
MacCANN,Douglas B   Sex:M   03 Dec 1954 John D MacCann & Anna Tokanel
MacCANN,George S   Sex:M   12 Jul 1971 John D MacCann & Anna Tokanel
MacCANN,Steven W   Sex:M   03 May 1957 Donald J MacCann & Jacquelene E Bresnah
MacDONALD,George P   Sex:M   14 Sep 1966 Charles J MacDonald
   & Loretta M Summerfold
MacDONALD,Scott J   Sex:M: 13 Feb 1968 James A MacDonald & Apryl P Dame
MacDONALD,Stacey T   Sex: 11 Jul 1972 James A MacDonald & Apryl P Dame
MacDOUGALL,Alan S   Sex:M   18 Sep 1959 Larry G MacDougall & Irene E Gendron
MacDOUGALL,Judith L   Sex:F   (Child #2) 13 Dec 1944 Donald W MacDougall
   (Londonderry, NH) & Erdine Mabry (Nashua, NH)
MacDOUGALL,Tammy A   Sex:F   23 May 1965 Larry G MacDougall & Irene E Gendron
MacEACHERN,Kim I   Sex:F   04 Apr 1957 Earl F MacEachern & Eunice P Keller
MacEACHERN,Shawne   Sex:F   27 Jun 1961 Earl F MacEachern & Eunice P Keller
MacGRATH,Adam John Sex:M   12 Aug 1984 Gary Wayne MacGrath & Theresa M Bourque
MacGRATH,Gary W   Sex:M   21 Feb 1956 John D MacGrath & Helen S MacEachern
MacGRATH,Kenneth L   Sex:M   30 Sep 1957 John D MacGrath & Helen S MacEachern
MacGRATH,Matthew Joseph Sex:M 19 Feb 1983 Gary W MacGrath & Theresa M Bourque
MACIE,Sandra L   Sex:F   02 Mar 1967 Alexander R Macie & Judith I Rowe
MACIE,Susan J   Sex:F   27 Mar 1965 Alexander R Macie & Judith I Rowe
MacINTIRE,Leanne L   Sex:F   20 Apr 1954 Raymond J MacIntire & Lois A Lilja
MacINTOSH,Kenneth J Jr Sex:M 27 Sep 1977 Kenneth J MacIntosh
   & Barbara J Paulk
MacINTOSH,Matthew C   Sex:M   18 Apr 1978 John D MacIntosh & Michelle Popovich
MacINTOSH,Timothy Cletus   Sex:M 02 Jan 1981 Kenneth J MacIntosh
   & Barbara J Paulk
MACK,Brenda L   Sex:F   02 Oct 1964 James T Mack & Bertha M McBride
MacKAY,David S   Sex:M   21 Aug 1947 Frederick MacKay (Earltown, N S)
   & Doris A Peters (Nashua, NH)
MacKAY,Evelyn Dorothy   Sex:F   (Child #1) 12 Sep 1926 Howard P MacKay
   (New York) & Minnie Josphn Vanier (Vermont)
MacKAY,Mary E   Sex:F   (Child #1) 09 Oct 1943 Frederick MacKay (Nova Scotia)
   & Doris A Peters (Nashua, NH)

HUDSON,NH BIRTHS

MacKAY,Sharon L   Sex:F   12 Jul 1961 John F MacKay & Nancy E Glidden
MacKENZIE,Jane E   Sex:F   (Child #1) 16 Dec 1946 Richard W MacKenzie
   (Roslindale, MA) & Helene Phippard (Nashua, NH)
MacLEOD,Ian B   Sex: 30 Aug 1972 Robert A MacLeod & Nancy T Jaquith
MacLEOD,Patrick D   Sex:M   12 Apr 1968 Douglas A MacLeod & Patricia I Gagnon
MacMILLAN,Charles T   Sex:M   08 Jul 1967 James A MacMillan
   & Jacqueline M McKelve
MacNEIL,Cynthia Rose   Sex:F   10 May 1982 Vincent MacNeil & Susan E Lynch
MACOMBER,Naomi A   Sex:F   09 Jun 1969 Walter J Macomber & Anne H Dusart
MACOMBER,Nicole A   Sex:F   13 Aug 1973 Walter J Macomber & Anne H Dusart
MACRI,Stephen Vincent Sex:M 16 Mar 1981 Dennis Earle Macri & Heather Hollidge
MacRITCHIE,Wallace S   Sex:M   16 Sep 1952 Harold D MacRitchie & Patrycia Reid
MacSWEENEY,Darlene M Sex:F 12 Nov 1968 Philip J MacSweeney & Joan M Denninger
MacSWEENEY,John W   Sex:M   30 Mar 1967 Philip J MacSweeney & Joan M Denninger
MacVICAR,David P   Sex:M   19 Dec 1968 Philip A MacVicar & Susan V Knox
MADER,Lee A   Sex:F   15 Aug 1970 Richard T Mader & Marilyn G Miller
MADORE,Richard MacKay   Sex:M   12 Jun 1982 Richard J Madore & Deborah D MacKay
MAGEE,William F   Sex:M   19 Jul 1971 William B Magee & Dorothy A Carlin
MAGNIN,Alan R   Sex:M   03 Jul 1952 Russell J Magnin & Mildred H Poliquin
MAGNIN,Cheryle D   Sex:F   (Child #3) 11 Oct 1946 Henry F Magnin (Westfield,
   VT) & Iona N Warburton (Nashua, NH)
MAGNIN,Judith Ann   Sex:F   (Child #1) 07 Aug 1941 Henry F Magnin (Vermont)
   & Iona Waburton (Nashua, NH)
MAGNIN,Kathleen G   Sex:F   (Child #2) 19 Jul 1945 Henry F Magnin (Westfield,
   VT) & Iona M Warburton (Nashua, NH)
MAGNIN,William H   Sex:M   06 Sep 1947 Henry F Magnin (Westfield, VT)
   & Iona N Warburton (Nashua, NH)
MAGRATH,Adrian G   Sex:M   15 Aug 1951 Adrian G Magrath & Hedwidge L Todd
MAGRESE,Mary Hazel Schoolcraft   Sex:F (Child #1) 03 Aug 1924 Joseph Magrese
   (Boston, MA) & Mary O Schoolcraft (Manchester, NH)
MAGUIRE,[Unknown] Sex:F 22 Sep 1971 John F Maguire III & Judith M Fitzgerald
MAHAR,Charles H   Sex:M   08 Jul 1971 Harold W Mahar Jr & Claudette Labonte
MAHER,Melody Anne   Sex:F   07 Jul 1982 Michael T Maher & Julie Ann Messer
MAHMOT,Maxine   Sex:F   (Child #3) 22 May 1936 Riza Mahmot (Turkey)
   & Helen Hurd (Manchester, NH)
MAHONEY,Carol L   Sex:F   (Child #7) 06 Mar 1944 Timothy M Mahoney
   (Charlestown, MA) & Goldie J Balcom (Mansfield,
MAHONEY,[Unknown] Sex:M (Child #8) 24 Mar 1945 Timothy M Mahoney (Nashua,
   NH) & Goldie J Balcom (Mansfield, MA)
MAILLOUX,Sandy L   Sex:F   21 Jan 1969 Conrad C Mailloux & Sharon A Grainger
MAIN,Corey R   Sex:M   14 Jul 1974 Larry E Main & Theresa C Arel
MAJOR,Martha   Sex:F   22 Jul 1949 Jack R Major & Mary E Williams
MAJOR,Monica   Sex:F   19 Aug 1958 Jack R Major & Mary E Williams
MAJOR,Patricia A   Sex:F   19 Feb 1954 James H Major & Alice A Lowe
MAKARAWICZ,Kristi   Sex:F   14 Sep 1971 William P Makarawicz
   & Marjorie I Duquette
MAKEPEACE,[Unknown]   Sex:F   (Child #4) 28 Apr 1910 Fred A Makepeace (Nashua,
   NH) & Gertrude M Grave (Florence, MA)
MAKINEN,Ronald J   Sex:M   06 Mar 1960 Oscar J Makinen & Irene C Daigneault
MAKOWIEC,Michael T   Sex:M   25 Jun 1971 Walter J Makowiec & Sandra McQuesten
MAKOWIEC,Veronica   Sex:F   29 Jul 1965 Walter J Makowiec & Sandra McQuesten
MALAY,Lucy   Sex:F   (Child #1) 07 Sep 1932 Nashua, NH John H Malay (Nashua,
   NH) & Lucy Lucien (Nashua, NH)
MALCOLM,James M   Sex:M   28 Sep 1968 Neil W Malcolm & Eleanor A Poulin
MALCOLM,Scott N   Sex:M   13 Jan 1967 Neil W Malcolm & Eleanor A Poulin
MALENFANT,Armand V   Sex:M   13 Jul 1947 Armand V Malenfant (Canada)
   & Irene E Bouley (Nashua, NH)
MALENFANT,Lisa M   Sex:F   06 Jun 1970 Armand V Malenfant & Barbara A Eaton
MALENFANT,Michael A   Sex:M   24 Jul 1952 Armand Malenfant & Irene E Bouley
MALETTE,Brian T   Sex:M   22 Nov 1955 Norman R Malette & Shirley M Belanger

HUDSON,NH BIRTHS

MALETTE,Deborah I   Sex:F   21 Mar 1950 Oscar L Malette & Elaine D Reardon
MALETTE,Jason Michael   Sex:M   19 Apr 1985 Scott M Malette
    & Susan T Laurencille
MALETTE,Victoria Lena   Sex:F   (Child #4) 21 Dec 1938 Raymond Royal Malett
    (Nashua, NH) & Mary Julia Andrews (Minsk, Ru
MALETTE,Wendy E   Sex:F   26 Mar 1953 Oscar L Mallette & Elaine D Reardon
MALHOIT,Lewis Alfred   Sex:M   07 Jan 1879 Hudson, NH Joseph Malhoit (Canada)
    & Mary Ann
MALHOIT,Mary L   Sex:F   10 Jul 1881 Hudson, NH Joseph Malhoit (Canada)
    & Mary Ann (Canada)
MALIK,Sean Anthony   Sex:M   23 Feb 1981 Robert John Malik & Hannah M Parker
MALINOWSKI,Phillip J Sex: 29 May 1973 Walter J Malinowski
    & Jeannette S Fleischman
MALINOWSKI,Walter S   Sex:M   16 Jul 1971 Walter J Malinowski
    & Jeanette S Fleischman
MALONIS,George C   Sex:M   17 Apr 1958 Christo C Malonis & Mary V Tomou
MALOUIN,Desiree M   Sex:F   18 Nov 1958 Leon F Malouin, Jr & Lena L Ducharme
MALOUIN,Victoria M   Sex:F   28 Jun 1979 Richard E Malouin & Mae Ellen M Faria
MALPASS,Melanie R   Sex:F   20 Mar 1963 Harvey W Malpass & Ethel R Woodman
MALTBY,Travis John   Sex:M   26 May 1983 John Lester Maltby & Pamela Sue Sohre
MANCE,Katherine J   Sex:F   28 Apr 1979 Robert E Mance & Karla M Miller
MANN,Christopher J   Sex:M   22 Aug 1971 Larry B Mann & Jovita B McDonald
MANN,Karen G   Sex:F   09 Aug 1949 Loring W Mann & Joyce Clemons
MANSFIELD,Alfred Byron   Sex:M   (Child #4) 10 Jul 1917 Walter Mansfield
    (Windsor, VT) & Lavina Jeanotte (Nashua, NH)
MANSFIELD,Joane L   Sex:F   29 Sep 1974 John A Mansfield Jr & Diane L Howard
MANSFIELD,Sally E   Sex:F   01 Oct 1952 Alfred B Mansfield & Lucille S Richard
MANSFIELD,Susan L   Sex:F   14 Dec 1947 Alfred B Mansfield (Hudson, NH)
    & Lucille S Richard (Nashua, NH)
MANSON,Courtney Rose   Sex:F   20 aug 1980 Robert M Manson & Karen Ann Flanagan
MANTEL,Gerard   Sex:M   (Child #4) 06 Nov 1932 Hudson, NH Ernest Mantel
    (Canada) & Lydia Denault (Nashua, NH)
MANTEL,Jos Francois Paul   Sex:M   (Child #3) 21 Feb 1931 Ernest Mantel
    (Canada) & Lydia Denault (Nashua, NH)
MARCELLINO,Elizabeth Ann   Sex:F   07 Oct 1983 Gary S Marcellino
    & Kathy Lou Krieger
MARCELLINO,Jessica Lou   Sex:F   07 Oct 1983 Gary S Marcellino
    & Kathy Lou Krieger
MARCHAND,Corey Sex:M 11 Jan 1985 Pierre D Marchand & Diane Marie Guthro
MARCHAND,Steven   Sex:M   11 Jan 1985 Pierre D Marchand & Diane Marie Guthro
MARCHI,Daniel R   Sex:M   24 Apr 1959 Richard E Marchi & Janet E Temple
MARCHI,Kathie M   Sex:F   20 Oct 1970 Henry A Marchi Jr & MaryAnn De Pascale
MARCHI,Sarah L   Sex:F   18 Feb 1975 Henry A Marchi Jr & Mary Ann DePascale
MARCLEY,Dallas A   Sex:F   (Child #2) 24 Apr 1921 Frank Marcley (Italy)
    & Helen R Kinirlie (Douglas, NY)
MARCOTTE,Lynn Marie Sex:F 30 Sep 1983 Raymond V Marcotte & Gayle Marie Taylor
MARCUM,Jesse Cohen   Sex:M 23 Sep 1981 Alan Thomas Marcum & Elaine M Lariviere
MARCUM,Jill   Sex:F   04 Jun 1974 Russell L Marcum & Marie A Barrett
MARCUM,Johanna   Sex:F   06 Apr 1981 Russell L Marcum & Marie A Barrett
MARCUM,Luke Aaron   Sex:M   19 Nov 1983 Alan Thomas Marcum & Elaine M Lariviere
MARCUM,Matthew   Sex:M   31 Oct 1976 Russell L Marcum & Marie A Barrett
MARDEN,Mary E   Sex:F   02 Jul 1968 Mark A Marden & Jacqueline B Hanson
MARDEN,Timothy J   Sex:M   14 Sep 1965 Mark A Marden & Jacqueline B Hanson
MARIANI,Christian M   Sex: 18 Oct 1972 Robert J Mariani & Joann M Miller
MARINACCIO,Eric Charles Sex:M 22 Aug 1979 Charles J Marinaccio&Gail M Coward
MARINO,Dawn M   Sex:F   29 Jan 1967 John C Marino & Virginia L Lebel
MARION,Christopher Denis   Sex:M   15 Feb 1984 Denis Pierre Marion
    & Patricia Ann Gerlak
MARKS,Vincent Alexander   Sex:M   12 Feb 1983 Bernard John Marks
    & Kathy Ellen Upton

HUDSON,NH BIRTHS

MARQUIS,David P   Sex:M   27 May 1970 Roland L Marquis & Suzanne S Morin
MARQUIS,Holly Jean   Sex:F   30 Oct 1978 Roland Leo Marquis & Suzanne S Morin
MARQUIS,Jessica Lynn   Sex:F   26 Jun 1981 Arno Marquis & Vicky Arlene Trow
MARQUIS,Laura Joy   Sex:F   18 Nov 1977 Roland Leo Marquis & Suzanne S Morin
MARQUIS,Lynn Elaine   Sex:F   18 Nov 1977 Roland Leo Marquis & Suzanne S Morin
MARQUIS,Michele L   Sex:F   06 Apr 1970 Robert R Marquis & Helen D Guerette
MARQUIS,Paula A   Sex:F   25 Jan 1968 Paul R Marquis & Sylvia A Beland
MARQUIS,William A   Sex:M   05 Feb 1967 Paul R Marquis & Sylvia A Beland
MARR,Geoffrey D   Sex:M   24 Sep 1967 James R Marr & Margaret L Hill
MARR,James R Jr   Sex:M   13 Jan 1965 James R Marr & Margaret L Hill
MARR,Mary F   Sex:F   19 Feb 1948 Vernett E Marr (New York, NY)
   & Rita L Gauthier (Nashua, NH)
MARR,Michael P   Sex:M   05 Feb 1966 J Robert Marr & Margaret L Hill
MARRION,Elizabeth A   Sex:F   18 Nov 1963 James N Marrion & Constance M Feinen
MARRION,Jennifer K   Sex:F   08 Mar 1966 James N Marrion & Constance M Feinen
MARSCHKE,Lori A   Sex:F   05 Oct 1974 James E Marschke & Judy M Becker
MARSH,Abel   Sex:M   26 Apr 1769 Hudson, NH Samuel Marsh & Abigail Merrill
MARSH,Abigail   Sex:F   10 Mar 1763 Hudson, NH Samuel Marsh & Abigail Merrill
MARSH,Abigail Ann Sex:F   23 Apr 1827 Hudson, NH Thomas Marsh & Abigail Putnam
MARSH,Adaline W Sex:F 20 Feb 1830 Hudson, NH Fitch Poole Marsh & Mary J Emory
MARSH,Benjamin Clement Sex:M 16 Aug 1820 Hudson, NH Samuel Marsh&Mary Clement
MARSH,Betsey   Sex:F   18 Dec 1806 Hudson, NH Jonathan Marsh & Betsey
MARSH,Brian James Sex:M 28 Jun 1982 William J Marsh & Agnes Stephanie Rood
MARSH,Calvin Goodspeed   Sex:M   14 Oct 1829 Hudson, NH Hiram Marsh
   & Olivia Goodspeed
MARSH,Clarence   Sex:M   10 Oct 1866 Hudson, NH Otis R Marsh
   & Lizzie Persis Stiles
MARSH,Clarion Josephine   Sex:F   12 Aug 1844 Hudson, NH Hiram Marsh
   & Olivia Goodspeed
MARSH,Clarissa   Sex:F   Oct 1866 Hudson, NH   Marsh & Lizzie
MARSH,Daniel   Sex:M   23 Sep 1827 Hudson, NH Thomas Marsh & Rebecca Marsh
MARSH,Daniel Merrill Sex:M 02 Apr 1823 Hudson, NH Samuel Marsh & Mary Clement
MARSH,Daniel Webster Sex:M 15 Aug 1838 Hudson, NH Enoch S Marsh
   & Martha Whittier
MARSH,David   Sex:M   28 Nov 1754 Hudson, NH Thomas Marsh & Anna Greeley
MARSH,Ebenezer   Sex:M   13 Jan 1767 Hudson, NH Samuel Marsh & Abigail Merrill
MARSH,Ebenezer   Sex:M   06 May 1796 Hudson, NH Ebenezer Marsh & Susanna Chase
MARSH,Ebenezer   Sex:M   17 Jan 1767 Hudson, NH Samuel Marsh & Abigail
MARSH,Ebenezer Grosvenor   Sex:M   03 Jun 1827 Hudson, NH Ebenezer Marsh
   & Pauline C Grosvenor
MARSH,Eliza J   Sex:F   11 Sep 1811 Hudson, NH Thomas Marsh & Rebecca
MARSH,Eliza Jane   Sex:F   11 Sep 1811 Hudson, NH Thomas Marsh & Rebecca Marsh
MARSH,Elizabeth   Sex:F   England George Marsh & Elizabeth
MARSH,Elizabeth Olivia   Sex:F   27 Jan 1833 Hudson, NH Hiram Marsh
   & Olivia Goodspeed
MARSH,Enoch Newton   Sex:M   27 Feb 1841 Hudson, NH Enoch S Marsh
   & Martha Whittier
MARSH,Enoch Sawyer   Sex:M   01 Nov 1796 Hudson, NH Jonathan Marsh & Betsey
MARSH,Esther   Sex:F   16 Aug 1786 Hudson, NH John Marsh & Esther
MARSH,Fitch Poole   Sex:M   01 Nov 1794 Hudson, NH Samuel Marsh
   & Abigail Merrill
MARSH,Frank Woodbury   Sex:M   Oct 1848 Hudson, NH Thomas Marsh
   & Sarah Woodbury
MARSH,George O   Sex:M   23 Sep 1833 Hudson, NH Ebenezer Marsh
   & Pauline C Grosvenor
MARSH,Gilman   Sex:M   03 Oct 1826 Hudson, NH Enoch S Marsh & Martha Whittier
MARSH,H Stanley   Sex:M   11 Aug 1875 Hudson, NH W H Marsh & Lizzie S
MARSH,Hannah   Sex:F   23 Aug 1744 Hudson, NH James Marsh & Hannah
MARSH,Hannah   Sex:F   22 Jan 1757 Hudson, NH Thomas Marsh & Anna Greeley
MARSH,Hannah   Sex:F   20 Apr 1764 Hudson, NH Samuel Marsh & Abigail Merrill

HUDSON,NH BIRTHS

MARSH,Hannah   Sex:F   23 Mar 1805 Hudson, NH Ebenezer Marsh & Susanna Chase
MARSH,Hannah   Sex:F   02 Jan 1757 Hudson, NH Thomas Marsh & Anne
MARSH,Hannah Francis   Sex:F   23 Mar 1847 Hudson, NH Hiram Marsh
  & Olivia Goodspeed
MARSH,Harriet Abby   Sex:F   03 Dec 1833 Hudson, NH Enoch S Marsh
  & Martha Whittier
MARSH,Hiram   Sex:M   09 Nov 1800 Hudson, NH Jonathan Marsh & Betsey
MARSH,Isaac   Sex:M   03 Aug 1776 Hudson, NH Samuel Marsh & Abigail Merrill
MARSH,Isaac   Sex:M   25 Mar 1800 Hudson, NH Ebenezer Marsh & Susanna Chase
MARSH,Jacob   Sex:M   17 Apr 1747 Hudson, NH Onesphomus Marsh & Lydia
MARSH,James   Sex:M   22 Apr 1790 Hudson, NH John Marsh & Esther
MARSH,James Bartlett   Sex:M   05 Jan 1829 Hudson, NH Samuel Marsh
  & Mary Clement
MARSH,John   Sex:M   10 Dec 1746 Hudson, NH James Marsh & Hannah
MARSH,John   Sex:M   21 Nov 1767 Hudson, NH Thomas Marsh & Anna Greeley
MARSH,John   Sex:M   14 Dec 1753 Hudson, NH Samuel Marsh & Abigail Merrill
MARSH,John   Sex:M   17 Jun 1757 Hudson, NH Samuel Marsh & Abigail Merrill
MARSH,John   Sex:M   1784 Hudson, NH John Marsh & Esther
MARSH,John   Sex:M   19 Aug 1693 Haverhill, MA John Marsh &
MARSH,John   Sex:M   04 Mar 1725 Hudson, NH John Marsh & Sarah Severance
MARSH,John   Sex:M   19 Jun 1757 Hudson, NH Samuel Marsh & Abigail
MARSH,John Fenimore   Sex:M   01 Feb 1828 Hudson, NH Fitch Poole Marsh
  & Mary J Emory
MARSH,Jonathan   Sex:M   27 Jan 1752 Hudson, NH Thomas Marsh & Anna Greeley
MARSH,Jonathan   Sex:M   02 Mar 1759 Hudson, NH Thomas Marsh & Anna Greeley
MARSH,Joseph   Sex:M   01 Aug 1749 Hudson, NH Thomas Marsh & Anna Greeley
MARSH,Leonard   Sex:M   02 Feb 1837 Hudson, NH Fitch Poole Marsh & Mary J Emory
MARSH,Louisa Maria   Sex:F   15 Aug 1827 Hudson, NH Enoch S Marsh
  & Martha Whittier
MARSH,Lucinda   Sex:F   28 Jun 1809 Hudson, NH Jonathan Marsh & Betsey
MARSH,Lydia   Sex:F   14 Jun 1750 Hudson, NH Onesphomus Marsh & Lydia
MARSH,Lydia   Sex:F   29 Sep 1755 Hudson, NH Samuel Marsh & Abigail Merrill
MARSH,Lydia   Sex:F   02 Oct 1721 Hudson, NH John Marsh & Sarah Severance
MARSH,Lydia   Sex:F   29 Sep 1756 Hudson, NH Samuel Marsh & Abigail
MARSH,Marietta Lund   Sex:F   10 Jun 1840 Hudson, NH Hiram Marsh
  & Olivia Goodspeed
MARSH,Martha Frances   Sex:F   20 Apr 1836 Hudson, NH Enoch S Marsh
  & Martha Whittier
MARSH,Mary   Sex:F   29 Aug 1752 Hudson, NH Onesphomus Marsh & Lydia
MARSH,Mary   Sex:F   31 Aug 184 Hudson, NH Fitch Poole Marsh & Mary J Emory
MARSH,Mary   Sex:F   England George Marsh & Elizabeth
MARSH,Mary Ann   Sex:F   31 Jan 1821 Hudson, NH Thomas Marsh & Rebecca Marsh
MARSH,Mary Elizabeth   Sex:F   21 Mar 1825 Hudson, NH Thomas Marsh
  & Abigail Putnam
MARSH,Mary Orne   Sex:F   08 Aug 1830 Hudson, NH Ebenezer Marsh
  & Pauline C Grosvenor
MARSH,Maryann   Sex:F   31 Jan 1821 Hudson, NH Thomas Marsh & Rebecca
MARSH,Mehitabel   Sex:F   1745 Hudson, NH Thomas Marsh & Anna Greeley
MARSH,Mehitabel   Sex:F   11 Sep 1793 Hudson, NH Jonathan Marsh & Betsey
MARSH,Mehitabel   Sex:F   31 Mar 1728 Hudson, NH John Marsh & Sarah Severance
MARSH,Molley   Sex:F   09 Aug 176 Hudson, NH Thomas Marsh & Anne
MARSH,Molly   Sex:F   09 Aug 1761 Hudson, NH Thomas Marsh & Anna Greeley
MARSH,Moses   Sex:M   1747 Hudson, NH Thomas Marsh & Anna Greeley
MARSH,Moses   Sex:M   03 Mar 1774 Hudson, NH Samuel Marsh & Abigail
MARSH,Moses Merrill   Sex:M   03 Mar 1774 Hudson, NH Samuel Marsh
  & Abigail Merrill
MARSH,Nancy   Sex:F   22 Apr 1808 Hudson, NH Ebenezer Marsh & Susanna Chase
MARSH,Nancy Whittier   Sex:F   03 May 1829 Hudson, NH Enoch S Marsh
  & Martha Whittier
MARSH,Nathaniel   Sex:M   20 Aug 1791 Hudson, NH Jonathan Marsh & Betsey

HUDSON,NH BIRTHS

```
MARSH,Nathaniel Peabody   Sex:M  20 Aug 1790 Hudson, NH Jonathan Marsh & Betty
MARSH,Onesephonus   Sex:M   1630 England George Marsh & Elizabeth
MARSH,Otis Robinson   Sex:M   25 Sep 1831 Hudson, NH Enoch S Marsh
    & Martha Whittier
MARSH,Patty  Sex:F   12 May 1788 Hudson, NH Ebenezer Marsh & Susanna Chase
MARSH,Phebe  Sex:F   05 Oct 1801 Hudson, NH Ebenezer Marsh & Susanna Chase
MARSH,Polly  Sex:F   22 May 1788 Hudson, NH Ebenezer Marsh & Susanna
MARSH,Rebecca   Sex:F   08 Apr 1794 Hudson, NH Ebenezer Marsh & Susanna Chase
MARSH,Rebecca Helen Sex:F 17 May 1832 Hudson, NH Thomas Marsh
    & Sarah Woodbury
MARSH,Rebeckah   Sex:F   08 Apr 1794 Hudson, NH Ebenezer Marsh & Susannah
MARSH,Reuben   Sex:M   07 Oct 1798 Hudson, NH Jonathan Marsh & Betsey
MARSH,Ruth   Sex:F   26 Mar 1751 Hudson, NH John Marsh & Martha Rolfe
MARSH,Ruth   Sex:F   20 Mar 1750 Hudson, NH John Marsh & Martha
MARSH,Samuel   Sex:M   14 Feb 1745 Hudson, NH Onesphomus Marsh & Lydia
MARSH,Samuel   Sex:M   01 Nov 1759 Hudson, NH Samuel Marsh & Abigail Merrill
MARSH,Samuel   Sex:M   22 Sep 1790 Hudson, NH Ebenezer Marsh & Susanna Chase
MARSH,Samuel   Sex:M   08 Mar 1815 Hudson, NH Thomas Marsh & Rebecca Marsh
MARSH,Samuel   Sex:M   18 Jan 1733 Hudson, NH John Marsh & Sarah Severance
MARSH,Samuel   Sex:M   27 Feb 1745 Hudson, NH Onesephemus Marsh & Libby
MARSH,Samuel   Sex:M   14 Feb 1744 Hudson, NH Onesephorus Marsh & Lydia
MARSH,Sarah   Sex:F   1769 Hudson, NH Onesphomus Marsh &
MARSH,Sarah   Sex:F   22 Nov 1764 Hudson, NH Thomas Marsh & Anna Greeley
MARSH,Sarah   Sex:F   13 Aug 1761 Hudson, NH Samuel Marsh & Abigail Merrill
MARSH,Sarah   Sex:F   29 Apr 1804 Hudson, NH Jonathan Marsh & Betsey
MARSH,Sarah   Sex:F   10 Apr 1798 Hudson, NH Ebenezer Marsh & Susanna Chase
MARSH,Sarah   Sex:F   18 Aug 1761 Hudson, NH Samuel Marsh & Abigail
MARSH,Sarah Louise   Sex:F   04 Aug 1837 Hudson, NH Hiram Marsh
    & Olivia Goodspeed
MARSH,Stanley E   Sex:M   05 Aug 1870 Hudson, NH Otis R Marsh & Lizzie P
MARSH,Stanley Elmer   Sex:M   05 Aug 1870 Hudson, NH Otis R Marsh
    & Lizzie Persis Stiles
MARSH,Submit   Sex:F   07 Mar 1749 Hudson, NH James Marsh & Hannah
MARSH,Submit   Sex:F   02 Mar 1748 Hudson, NH James Marsh & Hannah
MARSH,Susanah   Sex:F   01 Jul 1792 Hudson, NH Ebenezer Marsh & Sarah
MARSH,Susanna   Sex:F   01 Jul 1792 Hudson, NH Ebenezer Marsh & Susanna Chase
MARSH,Thomas   Sex:M   20 Sep 1786 Hudson, NH Jonathan Marsh & Betsey
MARSH,Thomas   Sex:M   06 May 1796 Hudson, NH Ebenezer Marsh & Susanna Chase
MARSH,Thomas   Sex:M   1618 England George Marsh & Elizabeth
MARSH,Thomas   Sex:M   14 Dec 1719 Hudson, NH John Marsh & Sarah Severance
MARSH,Thomas Franklin   Sex:M   10 Dec 1828 Hudson, NH Thomas Marsh
    & Abigail Putnam
MARSH,Twins   Sex:MF   24 May 1831 Hudson, NH Hiram Marsh & Olivia Goodspeed
MARSH,Walter Hiram   Sex:M   06 Dec 1852 Hudson, NH Hiram Marsh
    & Olivia Goodspeed
MARSH,William   Sex:M   27 Jun 1771 Hudson, NH Samuel Marsh & Abigail Merrill
MARSH,William   Sex:M   28 May 1803 Hudson, NH Ebenezer Marsh & Susanna Chase
MARSH,[Unknown]   Sex:M   19 Oct 1788 Hudson, NH Jonathan Marsh & Betsey
MARSH,[Unknown]   Sex:M   17 Sep 1825 Hudson, NH Enoch S Marsh & Martha Whittier
MARSH,Fitch P   Sex:M   01 Nov 1794 Hudson, NH Samuel Marsh & Sarah
MARSHALL,Abigail   Sex:F   19 Jun 1750 Hudson, NH Daniel Marshall & Rachel
MARSHALL,Abigail   Sex:F   23 Aug 1791 Hudson, NH Henry F Marshall
    & Abigail Pollard
MARSHALL,Abigail   Sex:F   02 Dec 1814 Hudson, NH Nathan Marshall & Mehitabel
MARSHALL,Abigail   Sex:F   02 Mar 176 Hudson, NH Daniel Marshall & Rachel
MARSHALL,Abigail   Sex:F   24 Dec 1814 Hudson, NH Nathan Marshall & Mehitabel
MARSHALL,Abigail Parker Sex:F  02 Mar 176 Hudson, NH Daniel Marshall & Rachel
MARSHALL,Alfred   Sex:M   23 Jan 1813 Hudson, NH Nathan Marshall & Mehitabel
MARSHALL,Alfred   Sex:M   25 Jan 1813 Hudson, NH Nathan Marshall & Mehitabel
MARSHALL,Arthur L   Sex:M   11 Dec 1958 Lewis R Marshall & Elsie O Goodwin
```

HUDSON,NH BIRTHS

MARSHALL,Benjamin Sex:M   24 Apr 1789 Hudson, NH Henry F Marshall
& Abigail Pollard
MARSHALL,Benjamin Sex:M   24 Aug 1789 Hudson, NH Henry Marshall & Abigail
MARSHALL,Bertha Sex:F   25 Nov 1880 Hudson, NH George W Marshall Jr
(Hudson, NH) & Ann Elizabeth Osgood (Hudson,
MARSHALL,Betsey Sex:F   29 Sep 1797 Hudson, NH Elijah Marshall & Mary
MARSHALL,Betsey Sex:F   29 Sep 1799 Hudson, NH Elijah Marshall & Mary
MARSHALL,Betty Sex:F   01 Feb 1758 Hudson, NH John Marshall & Deborah
MARSHALL,Dana C Sex:M   (Child #1) 27 Dec 1889 Dana S Marshall (Hudson, NH)
& Martha Griffin (E Boston, MA)
MARSHALL,Dana L Sex:M   Jun 1863 Hudson, NH George W Marshall &
MARSHALL,Dana S Sex:M 07 Jan 1863 Hudson, NH George W Marshall
& Miranda Hadley
MARSHALL,Daniel Sex:M   01 Jun 1768 Hudson, NH Daniel Marshall & Rachel
MARSHALL,Daniel A Sex:M   22 Oct 1797 Hudson, NH John Marshall & Betty
MARSHALL,David Sex:M   26 May 1854 Hudson, NH Daniel Marshall & Rachel
MARSHALL,David Sex:M   29 Jun 1866 Hudson, NH John P Marshall & Ellen
MARSHALL,David Sex:M   26 May 1754 Hudson, NH Daniel Marshall & Rachel
MARSHALL,David A Sex:M (Child #1) 03 Oct 1892 David O Marshall (Hudson, NH)
& Gertrude H Smith (Haverhill, MA)
MARSHALL,David A   Sex:M   22 Oct 1797 Hudson, NH John Marshall & Betty
MARSHALL,Deborah Sex:F   03 Dec 1759 Hudson, NH John Marshall & Deborah
MARSHALL,Dustin Sex:M   18 Feb 1789 Hudson, NH Samuel Marshall & Lydia
MARSHALL,Edith M Sex:F (Child #1) 20 May 1892 Eugene J Marshall (Hudson, NH)
& Lenora Robinson (Hudson, NH)
MARSHALL,Edith M Sex:F   20 May 1872 Hudson, NH Eugene J Marshall
& Leonora Robinson
MARSHALL,Edward G Sex:M (Child #1) 27 Apr 1902 Geo N Marshall (Hudson, NH)
& Cora A Marshall (Saranac, NY)
MARSHALL,Elijah Sex:M   14 Aug 1788 Hudson, NH Elijah Marshall & Mary
MARSHALL,Elizabeth Sex:F   23 Jan 1851 Hudson, NH George W Marshall
& Miranda Hadley
MARSHALL,Elizabeth E Sex:F   23 Jun 1851 Hudson, NH George W Marshall
& Harriet
MARSHALL,Eugene Sex:M   27 Jul 1872 Hudson, NH George W Marshall & Marinda
MARSHALL,Fannie Sex:F   06 Mar 1781 Hudson, NH Nathaniel Marshall & Hannah
MARSHALL,Fanny Sex:F 06 Mar 1781 Hudson, NH Nathaniel Marshall & Hannah Marsh
MARSHALL,Farwell Sex:M   30 Aug 1787 Hudson, NH Henry F Marshall
& Abigail Pollard
MARSHALL,Frank Eugene Sex:M (Child #2) 01 Jun 1907 Frank E Marshall
(Annapolis, N S) & Flora Walker (Webster, MA)
MARSHALL,George Sex:M   05 Oct 1802 Hudson, NH Henry F Marshall
& Abigail Pollard
MARSHALL,George M Sex:M   15 Aug 1971 Richard E Marshall & Beverly J Lacasse
MARSHALL,George W Sex:M   28 Nov 1857 Hudson, NH George W Marshall
& Miranda Hadley
MARSHALL,Hannah Sex:F   13 Dec 1747 Hudson, NH John Marshall & Deborah
MARSHALL,Hannah Sex:F   08 Jun 1763 Hudson, NH Daniel Marshall & Rachel
MARSHALL,Hannah Sex:F   04 Oct 1774 Hudson, NH John Marshall & Susanna
MARSHALL,Hannah Sex:F 20 Jan 1783 Hudson, NH Nathaniel Marshall
& Hannah Marsh
MARSHALL,Hannah Sex:F   16 Dec 1781 Hudson, NH John Marshall Jr & Sarah
MARSHALL,Hannah Sex:F   24 Mar 1807 Hudson, NH William Marshall & Polly
MARSHALL,Harland H Sex:M (Child #4) 01 Jun 1920 Dana C Marshall (Hudson, NH)
& Myrtle M Hill (Raymond, NH)
MARSHALL,Harriet J Sex:F   24 Jun 1852 Hudson, NH George W Marshall
& Miranda Hadley
MARSHALL,Helen E Sex:F (Child #2) 22 Jun 1895 Eugene I Marshall (Hudson, NH)
& Leona Robinson (Hudson, NH)
MARSHALL,Henry Sex:M 27 Nov 1781 Hudson, NH Henry F Marshall

HUDSON,NH BIRTHS

  & Abigail Pollard
MARSHALL,Henry Sex:M 25 Dec 1796 Hudson, NH Henry F Marshall
  & Abigail Pollard
MARSHALL,Henry Sex:M 25 Dec 1795 Hudson, NH Henry Marshall & Abigail
MARSHALL,Herbert W Sex:M 23 Apr 1870 Hudson, NH George W Marshall & Marinda
MARSHALL,Isaac Sex:M 26 Jan 1771 Hudson, NH Daniel Marshall & Rachel
MARSHALL,Iver Sex:F (Child #3) 23 Sep 1918 Dana Marshall (Hudson, NH)
  & Myrtle Hill (Raymond, NH)
MARSHALL,James Sex:M 16 Oct 1800 Hudson, NH Elijah Marshall & Mary
MARSHALL,Jemima Sex:F 29 May 1786 Hudson, NH Elijah Marshall & Mary
MARSHALL,John Sex:M 25 Nov 1753 Hudson, NH John Marshall & Deborah
MARSHALL,John Sex:M 04 Aug 1756 Hudson, NH Daniel Marshall & Rachel
MARSHALL,John Sex:M 28 Oct 1776 Hudson, NH John Marshall & Susanna
MARSHALL,John Sex:M 27 Mar 1784 Hudson, NH John Marshall & Susanna
MARSHALL,John Sex:M 27 Aug 1787 Hudson, NH John Marshall & Susanna
MARSHALL,John Sex:M 06 Apr 1791 Hudson, NH Elijah Marshall & Mary
MARSHALL,John Sex:M 29 Mar 1784 Hudson, NH John Marshall & Susannah
MARSHALL,Lois Sex:F 01 Jun 1751 Hudson, NH John Marshall & Deborah
MARSHALL,Lois Sex:F 03 Dec 1766 Hudson, NH John Marshall & Deborah
MARSHALL,Lois Sex:F 30 Dec 1766 Hudson, NH John Marshall & Deborah
MARSHALL,Lot Sex:M 06 Nov 1764 Hudson, NH John Marshall & Deborah
MARSHALL,Martha M Sex:F (Child #2) 23 Jul 1915 Hudson, NH Dana C Marshall
  (Hudson, NH) & Myrtle M Hill (Raymond, NH)
MARSHALL,Mary Sex:F 05 Aug 1805 Hudson, NH William Marshall & Polly
MARSHALL,Matilda Sex:F 02 May 1866 Hudson, NH Benjamin Marshall & Louisa
MARSHALL,Minnie W Sex:F Feb 1878 Hudson, NH William H Marshall (Hudson, NH)
  & Clora Barube (Canada)
MARSHALL,Nathan Sex:M 25 Apr 1785 Hudson, NH Henry F Marshall
  & Abigail Pollard
MARSHALL,Nathan Sex:M 23 Dec 1819 Hudson, NH Nathan Marshall & Mehitabel
MARSHALL,Nathan Jr Sex:M 23 Dec 1819 Hudson, NH Nathan Marshall & Mehitabel
MARSHALL,Nathaniel Sex:M 25 Apr 1785 Hudson, NH Henry Marshall & Abigail
MARSHALL,Parker Sex:M 18 Jun 1787 Hudson, NH Samuel Marshall & Lydia
MARSHALL,Parker Sex:M 18 Jun 1789 Hudson, NH Samuel Marshall & Lydia
MARSHALL,Paul H Sex:M 23 Jun 1966 Marden W Marshall & Katherine E Torr
MARSHALL,Peter J Sex:M 23 Jun 1966 Marden W Marshall & Katherine E Torr
MARSHALL,Philip Sex:M 02 Aug 1799 Hudson, NH Benjamin L Marshall & Hannah
MARSHALL,Polley Sex:F 25 Apr 1795 Hudson, NH Elijah Marshall & Mary
MARSHALL,Polly Sex:F 15 Apr 1795 Hudson, NH Elijah Marshall & Mary
MARSHALL,Rachel Sex:F 30 Dec 1817 Hudson, NH Nathan Marshall & Mehitabel
MARSHALL,Rachel R Sex:F 11 Dec 1768 Hudson, NH Daniel Marshall & Rachel
MARSHALL,Rachel Robinson Sex:F 11 Dec 1758 Hudson, NH Daniel Marshall
  & Rachel
MARSHALL,Ryan P Sex:M 26 Mar 1977 Patrick G Marshall & Jane Ellen Zurbrick
MARSHALL,Sampson Sex:M 03 Apr 1786 Hudson, NH Nathaniel Marshall & Hannah
MARSHALL,Samson Sex:M 03 Apr 1786 Hudson, NH Nathaniel Marshall&Hannah Marsh
MARSHALL,Samuel Sex:M 26 Mar 1752 Hudson, NH Daniel Marshall & Rachel
MARSHALL,Samuel Sex:M 11 Apr 1785 Hudson, NH John Marshall & Susanna
MARSHALL,Samuel Sex:M 20 Apr 1783 Hudson, NH Henry F Marshall
  & Abigail Pollard
MARSHALL,Samuel Sex:M 16 Apr 1785 Hudson, NH John Marshall & Susanna
MARSHALL,Samuel Sex:M 30 Apr 1783 Hudson, NH Henry Marshall & Abigail
MARSHALL,Sarah Sex:F 05 Sep 1765 Hudson, NH Daniel Marshall & Rachel
MARSHALL,Sarah Sex:F 21 Jun 1788 Hudson, NH Nathaniel Marshall & Hannah Marsh
MARSHALL,Silas Sex:M 22 Nov 1798 Hudson, NH Henry F Marshall&Abigail Pollard
MARSHALL,Stacey Jean Sex:F 22 Jun 1976 Richard E Marshall & Beverly J Lacasse
MARSHALL,Stephen C Sex:M 08 Jul 1789 Hudson, NH John Marshall & Susanna
MARSHALL,Stephen Chase Sex:M 08 Jul 1789 Hudson, NH John Marshall & Susanna
MARSHALL,Susanna Sex:F 01 Jun 1779 Hudson, NH John Marshall & Susanna
MARSHALL,Thomas Sex:M 12 Dec 1781 Hudson, NH Elijah Marshall & Mary

HUDSON,NH BIRTHS

MARSHALL,Vena Maude Sex:F   (Child #5) 02 Feb 1923 Dana C Marshall
  (Hudson, NH) & Myrtle M Hill (Raymond, NH)
MARSHALL,William   Sex:M   06 Apr 1781 Hudson, NH John Marshall & Susanna
MARSHALL,William A Sex:M 08 Sep 1856 Hudson, NH George W Marshall & Harriet
MARSHALL,William E Sex:M 26 Mar 1804 Hudson, NH William Marshall & Polley
MARSHALL,William Emerson   Sex:M 26 Mar 1804 Hudson, NH William Marshall
  & Polly
MARSHALL,William H   Sex:M   08 Sep 1856 Hudson, NH George W Marshall
  & Miranda Hadley
MARSHALL,[Unknown] Sex:F (Child #3) 06 Dec 1897 Eugene Marshall (Hudson, NH)
  & Leona Robinson (Hudson, NH)
MARSHALL,[Unknown]   Sex:F   20 Oct 1865 Hudson, NH George W Marshall
  & Miranda Hadley
MARSHALL,[Unknown]   Sex:F   02 Oct 1865 Hudson, NH George W Marshall & Marinda
MARSOLAIS,Brian P Sex:M   14 Oct 1964 Paul R Marsolais & Claire A Provencher
MARSTON,Andrew Raymond Sex:M 19 Aug 1983 Donald A Marston & Laurie M Judkins
MARSTON,Timothy Alex   Sex:M   15 Aug 1981 Kenneth J Marston & Julie Ann Ross
MARTEL,Ernest   Sex:M   (Child #1) 18 Mar 1925 Ernest Martel (Canada)
  & Donalda Deneault (Canada)
MARTELL,Jennifer S   Sex:F   18 Sep 1970 David R Martell & Daphny B Murray
MARTIN,Aaron Lindsay   Sex:F 06 Nov 1980 Steven W Martin & Gail Marie DeHaas
MARTIN,Alice Mary   Sex:F   (Child #2) 17 Sep 1920 Moise Martin (Canada)
  & Maria Pelletier (France)
MARTIN,Alma Jeannette   Sex:F   (Child #6) 12 Feb 1926 Moise Martin (Canada)
  & Maria Pelletier (France)
MARTIN,Almon E   Sex:M   (Child #2) 10 Nov 1895 Ezra A Martin (Chapman, CT)
  & Minnie E Tobin (Worcester, MA)
MARTIN,Amy E   Sex:F 07 Apr 1970 Joseph R Martin & Muriel J Scurrah
MARTIN,Carol L   Sex:F   10 May 1965 Harrison Martin & Eva C Diehl
MARTIN,Darlene R   Sex:F   18 Feb 1958 Harry J Martin & Ruth A Estey
MARTIN,David A   Sex:M   14 Sep 1960 Alfred B Martin & Dorothy M McDonald
MARTIN,David E   Sex:M   07 Feb 1947 Fred E Martin (New Bedford, MA)
  & Edith M Flint (Berkley, MA)
MARTIN,Devin Uriah   Sex:M 06 Dec 1982 Brian Ross Martin & Mary E Gruenfelder
MARTIN,Dolores M   Sex:F   05 Oct 1954 Harry J Martin & Ruth A Estey
MARTIN,Donald J   Sex:M   (Child #1) 18 Mar 1942 Joseph Martin (Sanford, ME)
  & Marcella Bernier (St Fran, Canada)
MARTIN,Edna E   Sex:F   06 Feb 1874 Hudson, NH Elisha A Martin & Susie S
MARTIN,George   Sex:M   (Child #3) 15 Dec 1921 Moise Martin (Canada)
  & Marie Pelletier (France)
MARTIN,Gerard R   Sex:M   (Child #10) 21 Jul 1942 Donat Martin (Canada)
  & Alice Payeur (Canada)
MARTIN,Henry A   Sex:M   18 May 1877 Hudson, NH Ezra A Martin (Eastford, Ct)
  & Margaret J Clyde (Dracut, MA)
MARTIN,Howard E   Sex:M   (Child #2) 20 Jan 1905 Kimball W Martin (Hudson, NH)
  & Bertha Cunningham (St John, N B)
MARTIN,Ina Viola   Sex:F   27 Sep 1881 Hudson, NH Horace A Martin
  (Eastford, CT) & Lizzie J Webster (Hudson, NH)
MARTIN,Jamie D   Sex:M   23 Aug 1960 Ronald K Martin & Eva J Coston
MARTIN,Joseph E   Sex:M   (Child #2) 25 Nov 1944 Harry J Martin (Nashua, NH)
  & Ruth A Estey (Londonderry, NH)
MARTIN,Joseph R Jr   Sex:M   29 Mar 1967 Joseph R Martin & Muriel J Scurrah
MARTIN,Juliana E   Sex:F   20 Apr 1878 Hudson, NH Elisha A Martin
  (Chaplin, CT) & Susie E (Woodstock, CT)
MARTIN,Kelly J   Sex:F   20 May 1963 Ronald K Martin & Eva J Coston
MARTIN,Kimball W   Sex:M   (Child #1) 10 Mar 1903 Kimball Martin (Hudson, NH)
  & Bertha Cunningham (St John, N B)
MARTIN,Kimball W   Sex:M   04 Sep 1877 Hudson, NH Martin (Eastford, CT)
  & (Hudson, NH)
MARTIN,Kimball Webster   Sex:M 24 Sep 1877 Hudson, NH Horace A Martin

& Lizzie J Webster
MARTIN,Kristal Renee Sex:F 11 Feb 1982 Clarence R Martin Jr & Sheila A Ellis
MARTIN,Leonard A Sex:M 24 Jan 1947 Harry J Martin (Nashua, NH)
  & Ruth A Estey (Londonderry, NH)
MARTIN,Leroy C Sex:M (Child #2) 29 Sep 1943 Hugh R Martin (Hartford, CT)
  & Lorraine L Knights (Hudson, NH)
MARTIN,Lisa R Sex:F 10 Dec 1969 Raymond E Martin & Annette C Wyman
MARTIN,Lora M Sex:F (Child #5) 13 May 1923 Moise Martin (Canada)
  & Maria Pelletier (France)
MARTIN,Marie G Sex:F (Child #2) 03 Mar 1943 Joseph Martin (Sanford, ME)
  & Marcella A Bernier (St Francois, Ca
MARTIN,Noreen J Sex:F 22 Sep 1949 Harry J Martin & Ruth A Estey
MARTIN,Olive M Sex:F (Child #3) 25 Dec 1889 Ezra A Martin (Chaplin, CT)
  & Minnie E Toben (Worcester, MA)
MARTIN,Patricia S Sex:F 10 Oct 1952 Harry J Martin & Ruth A Estey
MARTIN,Paul Franklin Sex:M 04 Jul 1894 John T Martin (Albert Mines, N B)
  & Jennie C Winn (Hudson, NH)
MARTIN,Remon Sex:M (Child #4) 15 Dec 1921 Moise Martin (Canada)
  & Marie Pelletier (France)
MARTIN,Ruth M Sex:F (Child #3) 30 Apr 1898 Ezra A Martin (Chaplin, CT)
  & Minnie E Tobin (Worcester, MA)
MARTIN,Shannon J Sex:F 07 Nov 1970 Leonard A Martin & Cynthia J Cote
MARTIN,Shirley A Sex:F 11 Nov 1948 Harry J Martin (Nashua, NH)
  & Ruth A Estey (Londonderry, NH)
MARTIN,Stephen J Sex:M 18 Dec 1968 Joseph R Martin & Muriel J Scurrah
MARTIN,Stephen Joshua Sex:M 19 Nov 1981 Brian Ross Martin
  & Mary E Gruenfelder
MARTIN,Tammy L Sex:F 24 Oct 1961 Alfred B Martin & Dorothy A McDonald
MARTIN,Thomas William Sex:M 22 Sep 1984 Davis Simon Martin & Claire L St Cyr
MARTIN,Veldawna D Sex:F 24 Oct 1961 Ronald K Martin & Eva J Coston
MARTIN,Victoria Sex:F 21 Jun 1958 Leonard H Martin & Mary H Rodela
MARTIN,[Unknown] Sex:M 15 Dec 1876 Hudson, NH Horace Martin & Lizzie
MARTINEAU,Ronnie P Sex:M 18 Aug 1957 Joseph E Martineau & Mildred E George
MARTINELLI,Angela Marie Sex:F 31 Aug 1979 Frank Martinelli & Sandra N Gagnon
MARTINSON,John W Sex:M 23 Nov 1969 William H Martinson & Sandra J Nutting
MARZILLI,Theodore V Sex:M 03 Jan 1966 Bernard V Marzilli & Mary A Coppolelli
MASON,Alexander Porter Sex:M (Child #3) 18 Sep 1924 Emery Mason (Milton, VT)
  & Winnie Mitchell (Westford, VT)
MASON,Andrea Jennifer Sex:F 16 Dec 1982 Brian L Mason & Beverly Ann Stanley
MASON,Brenda L Sex:F 30 Apr 1965 Peter C Mason & Linda A Harris
MASON,Caroline M Sex:F 10 Dec 1973 Kenneth R Mason & Ann M Brush
MASON,David M Sex:M 22 May 1966 Daniel W Mason & Suzanne B Brown
MASON,Douglas A Sex:M 14 Sep 1964 Theodore A Mason & Rita P Collins
MASON,George J Jr Sex:M 07 Feb 1968 George J Mason & Georgette L Frost
MASON,Gilberta Avis Sex:F (Child #3) 09 Jul 1941 Leonard F Mason
  (Conway, NH) & Dorothy Fox (Nashua, NH)
MASON,Heather Grace Sex:F 18 Sep 1982 Kenneth Peter Mason & Ruth-Ellen Kobb
MASON,Kathleen M Sex:F 08 Feb 1966 George J Mason & Georgette L Frost
MASON,Otis James Sex:M (Child #2) 16 Jan 1910 Pearley Mason (Milan, NH)
  & Fannie E Moore (Berwick, ME)
MASON,Rhonda Pamela Sex:F 12 Jul 1980 Brian L Mason & Beverly Ann Stanley
MASON,Scott R Sex:M 06 Aug 1971 Kenneth R Mason & Ann M Brush
MASON,Shelly Sloan Sex:F 04 Mar 1984 Manfred Mason & Sloan Spence
MASON,Stanley R Sex:M 08 Feb 1970 George J Mason & Georgette L Frost
MASSEY,Craig Adelard Sex:M 17 Oct 1980 Robert L Massey & Doris G Vaillancourt
MASSEY,Melissa M Sex:F 08 Mar 1976 Robert L Massey & Doris G Vaillancourt
MASSEY,Shawn M Sex:M 24 Jun 1976 Gregory J Massey & Maria G Estrela
MASSOOD,Christos F Sex:M 31 Aug 1968 Arthur F Massood & Theresa B Hackett
MASSOOD,Paula J Sex:F 14 Jun 1965 Arthur F Massood & Theresa B Hackett
MASTERSON,Chris R Sex:M 22 Dec 1954 Chris R Masterson & Irene M Auclair

HUDSON,NH BIRTHS

MASTERSON,James P Jr   Sex:M   02 Nov 1971 James P Masterson & Jeanne L Poulin
MASTERSON,John Warren   Sex:M   10 Mar 1981 John M Masterson & Kathy M McDowell
MASTERSON,Julie A   Sex: 07 Oct 1972 Chris R Masterson & Darlene T Twiss
MASTERSON,Laurence E   Sex:M   24 Jul 1947 Earl T Masterson (W Lebanon, NH)
   & Shirley M Sharkey (Lebanon, NH)
MASTIC,Mary M   Sex:F   (Child #10) 09 Jan 1898 Herbert E Mastic (New York)
   & Mary Manning (New York)
MATHER,Marc Allan Sex:M 17 Jan 1981 Allan Normn Mather & Georgianna M Trefeth
MATHEWS,Evelyn Flora Sex:F   (Child #2) 03 Aug 1911 Hudson, NH John Mathews
   (Ireland) & Florence Trufant (Nashua, NH)
MATHEWS,[Unknown]   Sex:F   (Child #4) 11 Nov 1915 Hudson, NH John Mathews
   (Belfast, Ireland) & Florence Trufant (Nashua, NH)
MATHIEU,Bernyse S   Sex:F   03 Jun 1972 Guy R Mathieu & Laureanne M B Lessar
MATHIEU,Christine   Sex:F   25 Apr 1976 Jules Mathieu & Lorraine C Grondin
MATHIEU,Dave   Sex:M   23 Aug 1973 Jules Mathieu & Lorraine C Grondin
MATHIEU,Vicki L   Sex:F   11 Mar 1975 Guy R Mathieu & Laureanne M B Lessard
MATTHEWS,Francis A   Sex:M   (Child #3) 27 Dec 1913 John Matthews (Ireland)
   & Florance Trufant (Nashua, NH)
MATTHEWS,Hazel Hildreth   Sex:F   (Child #1) 22 Jul 1933   & Hazel Matthews
   (Hudson, NH)
MATTICE,Melvin W   Sex:M   09 Apr 1951 Lendall R Mattice & Eleanor M Austin
MAUGHAN,Erin D   Sex: 19 Dec 1972 Harold E Maughan & Dorothy E Long
MAUGHAN,Kenna D   Sex:F   26 Sep 1974 Harold E Maughan & Dorothy E Long
MAXFIELD,Earl F   Sex:M   (Child #3) 18 Dec 1908 H S Maxfield (New York)
   & Millie Doty (New York)
MAXFIELD,James E   Sex:M   18 Apr 1963 William E Maxfield & Eleanor R Gowing
MAXFIELD,Janet E   Sex:F   26 Aug 1964 William E Maxfield & Eleanor R Gowing
MAXWELL,Meghan Heather Sex:F   18 Jun 1983 Bruce E Maxwell & Heather Jean Cook
MAYBERRY,Craig S   Sex:M   05 Feb 1968 Donald K Mayberry & Cynthia J Young
MAYHEW,Arthur P Jr   Sex:M   06 Jul 1964 Arthur P Mayhew & Rita C Gallant
MAYNARD,Bethany L   Sex:F   23 Jun 1980 Glenn S Maynard & Linda Ann Althin
MAYNARD,Diane Y   Sex:F   18 Nov 1960 Donald R Maynard & Lucille Y Levesque
MAYNARD,Jeffrey R   Sex:M   07 Apr 1970 Ronald F Maynard & Carol M Berube
MAYNARD,Jillian Kate   Sex:F   18 Jan 1985 Glenn S Maynard & Linda Ann Althin
MAYNARD,Jonathan Weddle   Sex:M   09 Nov 1980 Steven L Maynard & Joan C Weddle
MAYNARD,Kevin J   Sex:M   30 Jan 1978 Glenn S Maynard & Linda Ann Althin
MAYNARD,Paula M   Sex:F   01 Jul 1966 Henry P Maynard Sr & Nancy A Noble
MAYNARD,Peter J   Sex:M   19 Mar 1965 Henry P Maynard & Nancy A Noble
MAYNARD,Tina L   Sex:F   23 Apr 1969 Ronald F Maynard & Carol M Berube
MAYNARD,Tracy L   Sex:F   23 Apr 1969 Ronald F Maynard & Carol M Berube
MAYO,Vivian A   Sex:F   06 May 1959 Leo E Mayo & Eileen Brislen
MAYO,[Unknown]   Sex:F   21 Jul 1955 Maurice G Mayo & Doris T Vander-Heyde
MAYS,Patrick   Sex:M   07 Aug 1964 Frederick L May, Jr & Judith A Curran
MAZE,David Z   Sex:M   10 Mar 1978 Steven Maze & Eva Maria Chlebowska
MAZE,Gabriel Alexander   Sex:M   25 Jun 1981 Steven Maze & Eva Maria Chiebowska
MAZEIKA,Frances V   Sex:F   (Child #1) 02 Jan 1940 Edward Mazeika (Poland)
   & Stella Mazeika (Nashua, NH)
MAZZARO,Christine M   Sex:F   20 May 1967 John R Mazzaro & Donna M Mitchell
McADOO,Allena Hazel   Sex:F   (Child #8) 04 Jul 1933 George McAdoo (Nashua, NH)
   & Pauline Lucier (Nashua, NH)
McADOO,Korleen Beatrice Sex:F   (Child #9) 12 Sep 1934 George McAdoo
   (Nashua, NH) & Pauline Lucier (Nashua, NH)
McAFEE,Kelli Lynn   Sex:F   25 Feb 1980 Scott B McAfee & Valerie L Leclerc
McAFEE,Violet R   Sex:F   09 Feb 1903 Chas A McAfee (Bedford, NH)
   & Susie Drucker (Pembroke, NH)
McAFEE,Willie E   Sex:M   20 Jul 1893 Chas A McAfee (Bedford, NH)
   & Lucy E Drecker (Pembroke, NH)
McALISTER,Diane L   Sex:F   07 Mar 1957 Franklyn H McAlister & Gladys I Chaput
McALISTER,James E   Sex:M   (Child #2) 30 Jul 1943 Franklyn H McAlister
   (Enfield, NH) & Clara E Duffine (Nashua, NH)

HUDSON,NH BIRTHS

McALISTER,Victoria M   Sex:F   (Child #2) 23 Mar 1942 Franklin McAlister
   (Enfield, NH) & Clara Duffine (Nashua, NH)
McALLISTER,Angela Beth Sex:F 15 Jul 1975 Donald F McAllister
   & Sheryl E Boutwell
McALLISTER,Kathleen M Sex:F 05 Feb 1971 Raymond R McAllister
   & Arlene F Knight
McALLISTER,Kelly M   Sex: 03 Oct 1972 Raymond R McAllister & Arlene F Knight
McALLISTER,[Unknown]   Sex:F 27 Sep 1966 Franklyn H McAlister & Gladys I Chaput
McANDREW,Daniel B   Sex:M   21 Jun 1974 Bryan D McAndrew & Anne L Higgins
McANISTAN,Joseph S Jr   Sex:M   20 Dec 1976 Joseph S McAnistan Sr
   & Kathleen M Kennedy
McARDLE,Thomas A   Sex:M   15 Sep 1968 Bernard F McArdle & Phyllis N Linton
McBRIDE,Hope A   Sex:F   27 May 1952 George E McBride & Sandra H Kierstead
McCANN,Amanda Joy   Sex:F   27 Jan 1974 Arthur T McCann & Margaret J Arnold
McCANN,Arthur T II   Sex:M   10 May 1971 Arthur T McCann & Margaret J Arnold
McCANN,Dorothy Elizabeth   Sex:F   (Child #1) 12 Jun 1904 George W McCann
   (Lowell, MA) & Alice Richardson (Sussex, N B)
McCANN,Jill M   Sex:F   (Child #2) 22 Jul 1946 Thomas R McCann (Nashua, NH)
   & Pauline M Clark (Cooper, ME)
McCANN,Marion Alice   Sex:F   (Child #2) 04 Jul 1911 Geo W McCann (Lowell, MA)
   & Alice Robinson (Sussex, N B)
McCANN,Pamela   Sex:F   20 Apr 1970 John A McCann & Christine J Dalton
McCARTHY,Anna   Sex:F   (Child #5) 13 Apr 1913 James McCarthy (Massachusetts)
   & Anna Mehan (Ireland)
McCARTHY,Cathlin   Sex:F   08 Sep 1976 Peter McCarthy & Bonnie Malburne
McCARTHY,Dorothy   Sex:F   (Child #4) 20 Mar 1912 James McCarthy (Salem, MA)
   & Annie Meehan (Ireland)
McCARTHY,Elizabeth Sex:F   (Child #7)10 May 1918 James McCarthy (MA)
   & Annie Meehan (Ireland)
McCARTHY,Elizabeth   Sex:F   06 Jan 1983 Peter McCarthy & Bonnie Malburne
McCARTHY,Gail D   Sex:F   14 Feb 1951 Robert J McCarthy & Virginia F Hayes
McCARTHY,Helen L   Sex:F   (Child #6) 22 Aug 1915 Hudson, NH James J McCarthy
   (Salem, MA) & Annie Meehan (Ireland)
McCARTHY,Herbert E Sex:M   06 Oct 1964 Herbert O McCarthy & Gloria L Ouellette
McCARTHY,Karen K   Sex:F   26 May 1967 Dennis J McCarthy & Jacqueline P Townsen
McCARTHY,Katelin Ashley   Sex:F   01 Jul 1984 Philip K McCarthy
   & Catherine J McMahon
McCARTHY,Laura   Sex:F   22 Apr 1981 Peter McCarthy & Bonnie Malburne
McCARTHY,Lisa M   Sex:F   25 May 1966 Donald J McCarthy & Irene G Labrecque
McCARTHY,Paul   Sex:M   02 Feb 1979 Peter McCarthy & Bonnie Malburne
McCARTHY,Shane   Sex:M   20 Apr 1969 Peter McCarthy & Bonnie Malburne
McCLELLAN,Cody Roland   Sex:M   28 Mar 1985 Wayne W McClellan
   & Judith Ann Guilbert
McCLELLAN,Wayne William Jr   Sex:M   30 Oct 1980 Wayne W McClellan
   & Judith Ann Guilbert
McCOLLOR,James A   Sex:M   26 Jun 1962 Donald G McCollor & Alma R Stamps
McCOLLOR,Patrick T   Sex:M   30 Jan 1964 Donald G McCollor & Alma R Stamps
McCONNELL,Jennifer A   Sex:F   06 Feb 1967 Robert A McConnell
   & Alise H Cokelette
McCORMACK,Matthew David Sex:M 13 Nov 1979 David J McCormack & Sharon E Buhl
McCOY,Arus H   Sex:M   09 Aug 1838 Hudson, NH Daniel G McCoy & H N
McCOY,Barbara Amy   Sex:F   (Child #12) 06 Jun 1931 Daniel McCoy (Hudson, NH)
   & Bessie Rivers (Montgomery, VT)
McCOY,Brian Dana   Sex:M   25 Nov 1981 Norman Craig McCoy & Janet Ann Dubois
McCOY,Clifford Ams   Sex:M   (Child #6) 04 Apr 1915 Hudson, NH Daniel G McCoy
   (Hudson, NH) & Bessie Rivers (Montgomery, VT)
McCOY,Daniel G   Sex:M   22 Mar 1881 Hudson, NH James McCoy (Boston, MA)
   & Emma C Richards (Manchester, NH)
McCOY,Diana W   Sex:F   08 Apr 1950 Ernest E McCoy & Mildred M Wheeler
McCOY,Elgin Leon   Sex:M   15 Dec 1885 Hudson, NH James McCoy (Boston, MA)

HUDSON,NH BIRTHS

& Emily C Richards (Manchester, NH)
McCOY,Ella Alice   Sex:F   (Child #2) 08 Feb 1908 Daniel McCoy (Hudson, NH)
  & Belle Rivers (Montgomery, VT)
McCOY,Ernest E   Sex:M   (Child #3) 02 May 1919 Elgin McCoy (Hudson, NH)
  & Flora Weston (Massachusetts)
McCOY,George Henry   Sex:M   31 Jan 1870 Hudson, NH George S McCoy & Ella A
McCOY,George S   Sex:M   26 Dec 1840 Hudson, NH Daniel G McCoy & H N
McCOY,Gertrude May   Sex:F   (Child #2) 09 Jul 1917 Elgin McCoy (Hudson, NH)
  & Flora Weston (New Hampshire)
McCOY,Harold Richard   Sex:M   (Child #1) 09 Jun 1938   & Mildred Emily McCoy
  (Hudson, NH)
McCOY,Henry H   Sex:M   26 Dec 1840 Hudson, NH Daniel G McCoy & H N
McCOY,Herbert Wyatt   Sex:M   29 Nov 1873 Hudson, NH James McCoy & Emma C
McCOY,Herman R   Sex:M   25 Dec 1878 Hudson, NH James McCoy (Hudson, NH)
  & Emma L (Manchester, NH)
McCOY,Holly Diane   Sex:F   05 Dec 1977 Dana W McCoy & Lillian Ann Doherty
McCOY,James Otis   Sex:M   20 Aug 1869 Hudson, NH James McCoy & Emma E
McCOY,Kristi L   Sex:F   24 Jun 1975 Dana W McCoy & Lillian A Doherty
McCOY,Madeline Helen   Sex:F   (Child #6) 10 May 1926 Daniel McCoy
  (New Hampshire) & Bessie Rivers (Vermont)
McCOY,Mary Emma   Sex:F   04 Jun 1871 Hudson, NH James V McCoy & Emma C
McCOY,Mildred   Sex:F   (Child #1) 15 May 1918 Hermon McCoy (Hudson, NH)
  & Ethel Woodward (Nashua, NH)
McCOY,Nancy J   Sex:F   05 Sep 1951 Ernest E McCoy & Mildred M Wheeler
McCOY,Norman C   Sex:M   10 Jan 1955 Ernest E Mc Coy & Mildred M Wheeler
McCOY,Otis M   Sex:M   27 Oct 1839 Hudson, NH Daniel G McCoy & H N
McCOY,Ralph Evans   Sex:M   (Child #10) 27 Jan 1929 Daniel McCoy (Hudson, NH)
  & Bessie Rivers (Montgomery, VT)
McCOY,Richard Walter   Sex:M   (Child #10) 05 Mar 1924 Dan G McCoy (Hudson, NH)
  & Bessie L Rivers (Vermont)
McCOY,Robert D   Sex:M   (Child #2) 31 Oct 1921 Harmon R McCoy (Hudson, NH)
  & Ethel A Woodard (Nashua, NH)
McCOY,Ryan T   Sex:M   18 Sep 1971 Thomas E McCoy & Nancy J Lappen
McCOY,Sylvia M   Sex:F   (Child #1) 16 Nov 1906 Daniel G McCoy (Hudson, NH)
  & Bessie L Rivers (Belvidere Jct, VT)
McCOY,Terence Donato Sex:M 11 Jan 1981 Lyle E McCoy Sr & Margaret E Fischetti
McCOY,Thelma E   Sex:F   (Child #3) 07 Feb 1925 Hermon R McCoy (Hudson, NH)
  & Ethel A Woodward (Nashua, NH)
McCOY,Thomas E   Sex:M   31 May 1948 Ernest E McCoy (Hudson, NH)
  & Mildred M Wheeler (Nashua, NH)
McCOY,[Unknown]   Sex:M   (Child #5) 14 Jul 1913 Daniel G McCoy (Hudson, NH)
  & Bessie L Rivers (Montgomery, VT)
McCRADY,Daniel M   Sex:M   04 Mar 1961 Donald B McCrady & Dorothy D Hamilton
McCRADY,Douglas B   Sex:M   24 Nov 1958 Donald B McCrady & Dorothy D Hamilton
McCRADY,Laura B   Sex:F   26 Sep 1969 Donald R McCrady & Elizabeth R Peterson
McCRADY,Tara Rose   Sex:F   15 Dec 1981 Donald R McCrady & Denise Mary Lowe
McCRADY,Todd J   Sex:M   06 Jun 1978 Douglas B McCrady & Lucinda M Jackson
McCUE,Kevin S   Sex:M   19 Sep 1967 Howard K McCue & Erma J Higgins
McCULLOUGH,Gregory A   Sex:M   08 May 1971 Joseph P McCullough
  & Jeannette M Folven
McCULLOUGH,Troy A   Sex:M   04 Sep 1965 Emerson E McCullough & Rosalie F Dunn
McDERMOTT,Kate Avery   Sex:F   22 Mar 1983 John J McDermott Jr & Janice D Breed
McDONALD,Edna Gladys   Sex:F   (Child #2) 07 Mar 1926 Ray A McDonald
  (Greenwood, MA) & Edna Burtt (Amherst, NH)
McDOUGALL,Sharon D   Sex:F   15 Jan 1963 Larry G MacDougall & Irene E Gendron
McELWAIN,Louise R   Sex:F   08 May 1953 William H McElwain & Mary Redfield
McEVOY,Lee A   Sex:F   24 Jan 1964 Raymond A McEvoy & Donna K Hanson
McEVOY,Lynne A   Sex:F   07 Nov 1961 Raymond A McEvoy & Donna K Hanson
McFADDEN,Laura A   Sex:F   03 Jun 1977 William C McFadden & Dorothy Ann Silva
McFADDEN,Robert E   Sex:M   27 Jul 1974 William C McFadden & Dorothy A Silva

HUDSON,NH BIRTHS

McFADDEN,William C III   Sex: 04 Jul 1972 Wm C McFadden Jr & Dorothy A Silva
McGANDY,Peter M   Sex:M   25 Jul 1967 Douglas P McGandy & Ann M Roy
McGEE,Jessie A   Sex:F   02 Dec 1950 Thomas M McGee & Anna L Lemay
McGEE,Kimberly M   Sex:F   30 Jun 1969 Howard L McGee & Eleanor D Belanger
McGEE,Kristen D   Sex:F   30 Nov 1971 Howard L McGee & Eleanor D Belanger
McGEE,Lauria F   Sex:F   06 Jan 1958 Thomas M McGee & Anna L Lemay
McGEE,Michael R   Sex:M   14 Feb 1953 Thomas M McGee & Anna L Lemay
McGEE,Nicole L   Sex:F   22 Jan 1979 Michael R McGee & Yvonne L Kingman
McGEE,Robert M   Sex:M   30 Oct 1949 Thomas M McGee & Anna L Lemay
McGEE,Robin A   Sex:F   04 Mar 1962 Thomas M McGee & Anna L Lemay
McGONAGLE,Arthur J III   Sex:M   24 May 1967 Arthur J McGonagle Jr
  & Roselinda D Serrago
McGONAGLE,Kathryn Elizabeth   Sex:F   26 Mar 1985 Edward F McGonagle
  & Mary Beth Brown
McGOVERN,David A   Sex:M   31 May 1959 Philip J McGovern & Jacquelyn E Cole
McGOWAN,[Unknown]   Sex:M   31 Dec 1969 James A McGowan & Ellen A Genova
McGRAIL,Eric J   Sex:M   09 Jun 1972 Thomas B McGrail & Melanie J Pratt
McGRANAGHAN,Patrick Michael   Sex:M   03 May 1985 Peter R McGranaghan
  & Kelly Leigh Tower
McGRATH,Kyle D   Sex:M   20 Mar 1979 Christie P McGrath & Gloria R Lemire
McGRATH,Matthew Joseph   Sex:M   19 Feb 1983 Gary Wayne McGrath
  & Theresa M Bourque
McGRATH,Robert D   Sex:M   26 Jan 1955 John D McGrath & Helen S MacEachern
McGRAW,Daniel Lee   Sex:M   20 Jan 1979 Michael R McGraw & Debbie Lee Rogers
McGRAW,Ellen A   Sex:F   17 Sep 1956 E Richard McGraw & Esther B Ruiter
McGRAW,Georgia L   Sex:F   09 Oct 1959 Richard E McGraw & Esther B Ruiter
McGRAW,Kathy A   Sex:F   09 Mar 1954 Joseph G McGraw & Stella M Brideau
McGRAW,Michael R   Sex:M   03 Jun 1958 Richard E McGraw & Esther B Ruiter
McGUINESS,Erin R   Sex:F   22 Mar 1966 Donald J McGuiness & Joyce M Swomia
McGUIRE,John A   Sex:M   11 Nov 1966 Harold I McGuire & Frances A DePerry
McGUIRE,Shaun T   Sex:M   08 Feb 1979 Kevin T McGuire & Vivian L Freeman
McHUGH,Tracey-Ann   Sex:F   07 May 1967 Donald E McHugh & Jeannette T Fortin
McKEATING,Kevin III   Sex:M   28 Jun 1972 Kevin McKeating Jr & Remedios Teneal
McKENNA,Jennifer Ann   Sex:F   20 Apr 1974 Paul D McKenna & Claudette L Gagnon
McKENNEY,Allen R   Sex:M   18 Jan 1958 Henry P McKenney & Gloria E Bouley
McKENNEY,Candace A   Sex:F   12 Aug 1952 Henry P McKenney & Gloria E Bouley
McKENNEY,Spring H   Sex:F   24 Mar 1969 Henry P McKenney & Gloria E Bouley
McKEY,Andrew J   Sex:M   30 Jul 1976 George F Mackey & Sandra Ann Joyce
McKINELY,Shawn D   Sex:M   27 Dec 1969 Philip S McKinely & Mary W Aylsworth
McKINLEY,Beverly Ann   Sex:F   (Child #2) 18 Jul 1938 Lawrence P McKinley
  (Warren, NH) & Simonne L Pelletier (Nashua, NH)
McKINLEY,Daren G   Sex:M   03 Jan 1966 Philip S McKinley & Mary S Alysworth
McKINLEY,Steven P   Sex:M   07 Apr 1966 Ronald R McKinley & Jolterry A Dubuc
McLAIN,Daniel S   Sex:M   12 Nov 1966 Scott B McLain & Raelene L Wood
McLAUGHLIN,Diane J   Sex:F   16 Jun 1961 Thomas J McLaughlin
  & Christine R Times
McLAUGHLIN,Elaine F   Sex:F   02 Oct 1955 Thomas J McLaughlin
  & Christine R Times
McLAUGHLIN,Mandie Lee Sex:F   22 Jul 1979 John R McLaughlin & Adele M Tailleur
McLAUGHLIN,Pamela J   Sex:F   01 Aug 1967 John R McLaughlin & Faye A McCarthy
McLAUGHLIN,Paul R Jr Sex:M 21 Jan 1953 Paul R McLaughlin & Barbara Montgomery
McLAUGHLIN,Sandra J   Sex:F   15 Dec 1957 Thomas J McLaughlin & Christine Times
McLAUGHLIN,Timothy Isadore   Sex:M   22 Feb 1983 John R McLaughlin
  & Adele Marie Tailleur
McLAUGHLIN,Wendy A   Sex:F   12 Jun 1962 Allan W McLaughlin & Lauretta J Porter
McLEAN,Gary L   Sex:M   17 Jun 1966 Cecil E McLean & Sylvia L Richards
McLEAN,Judy L   Sex:F   07 Oct 1961 Cecil E McLean & Sylvia L Richards
McLEAN,Linda J   Sex:F   16 Apr 1956 Cecil E McLean & Sylvia L Richards
McMAHON,Joshua Marc   Sex:M   25 Mar 1985 Shane P McMahon & Manon F Fauteux
McMANUS,Cheryl L   Sex:F   16 Aug 1965 Daniel D McManus Jr & Doris M Wills

HUDSON,NH BIRTHS

McMANUS,Daniel P   Sex:M   20 Mar 1964 Clayton F McManus & Mary Tokanel
McMANUS,Lisa J   Sex:F   16 Nov 1966 Daniel D McManus & Doris M Wills
McMANUS,Nancy J   Sex:F   18 Jul 1960 Clayton F McManus & Mary Tokanel
McMANUS,Shannon Lee   Sex:F   10 Apr 1981 Frederick W McManus & Linda Hardy
McMULLEN,Maureen C   Sex:F   (Child #1) 14 Nov 1942 William A McMullen
   (Brooklyn, NY) & Floretta P Clausen (Brooklyn,
McNABB,Alyssa Doran   Sex:F   05 Sep 1984 Francis J McNabb & Barbara Santuccio
McNALLY,Carolyn   Sex:F   25 Feb 1962 James McNally & Claire T Korvas
McNAMARA,Melissa Ann   Sex:F   08 Dec 1975 Robert P McNamara & Lorraine Massa
McNEIL,Brenda J   Sex:F   30 Jan 1964 Daniel O McNeil & Virginia I Ouellette
McNEIL,Jaclyn Rose   Sex:F   09 Apr 1984 Donald F McNeil & Jeanne G Ferguson
McNEIL,James P   Sex:M   31 Aug 1949 Arthur J McNeil & Madeline P Gardner
McNEIL,Lisa Louise   Sex:F   25 Jun 1977 James P McNeil & Sandra Lee Graves
McNEIL,Margaret A   Sex:F   25 May 1953 Arthur J McNeil & Madeleine P Gardener
McNEIL,Robert Daniel   Sex:M   12 Jul 1981 Donald F McNeil & Jeanne G Ferguson
McNEIL,Shawn P   Sex:M   11 May 1980 James P McNeil & Sandra Lee Graves
McNEILL,Daniel John Sex:M   26 Aug 1978 John Daniel McNeill & Mary Ellen Lacoy
McPHERSON,Lori J   Sex:F   08 Mar 1962 Charles N McPherson & Minnie F Collins
McPHERSON,Matthew John Sex:M   14 Oct 1982 John J McPherson & Laurie J Phaneuf
McQUESTEN,Benjamin Sex:M 22 Mar 1836 Hudson, NH John McQuesten & Edna Barnes
McQUESTEN,Charles   Sex:M   09 Jan 1832 Hudson, NH John McQuesten & Edna Barnes
McQUESTEN,Charles D   Sex:M   (Child #3) 06 Dec 1889 Chas D McQuesten (Hudson,
   NH) & Eunice Wright (Nashua, NH)
McQUESTEN,George   Sex:M   15 Apr 1828 Hudson, NH John McQuesten & Edna Barnes
McQUESTEN,John   Sex:M   19 Dec 1790 Hudson, NH   &
McQUESTEN,John   Sex:M   04 Oct 1819 Hudson, NH John McQuesten & Edna Barnes
McQUESTEN,John   Sex:M   02 Jan 1834 Hudson, NH John McQuesten & Edna Barnes
McQUESTEN,Joseph   Sex:M   01 Aug 1821 Hudson, NH John McQuesten & Edna Barnes
McQUESTEN,Lucinda   Sex:F   28 Jun 1826 Hudson, NH John McQuesten & Edna Barnes
McQUESTEN,Mary Jane Sex:F 30 Apr 1823 Hudson, NH John McQuesten & Edna Barnes
McQUESTEN,Robert   Sex:M   28 Mar 1830 Hudson, NH John McQuesten & Edna Barnes
McQUESTEN,Sally   Sex:F   03 Apr 1825 Hudson, NH John McQuesten & Edna Barnes
McQUESTEN,Sarah Jane Sex:F 28 Sep 1838 Hudson, NH John McQuesten & EdnaBarnes
McSWAIN,Richard F Sex:M   (Child #3) 28 Jan 1946 Alfred J McSwain
   (Norwood, MA) & Elizabeth F Wilson (Falmouth, MA
McVICKER,Eric Scott   Sex:M   19 Dec 1973 Scott W McVicker & Adeline M Clymo
McWHA,Meghan Elizabeth Sex:F 09 Apr 1983 Robert J McWha & Dolores Ann Franco
McWHA,Shawn Robert   Sex:M   28 Jul 1981 Robert John McWha & Delores Ann Franco
MEAD,Dawn M   Sex:F   26 Aug 1965 Donald F Mead & Judith E Nutting
MEAD,Hazle   Sex:F   (Child #6) 19 Oct 1895 C H Mead (New York) & Carrie Marvin
   (New York)
MEAD,Mari-Lee   Sex:F   23 May 1967 Donald F Mead & Judith E Nutting
MEADER,Glen J   Sex:M   07 Dec 1962 Dwight V Meader & Lois Makechnie
MEADER,Jocelyn L   Sex:F   14 May 1959 Dwight V Meader & Lois Makechnie
MEARS,Philip J R   Sex:M   12 Feb 1971 Robert F Mears & Sharon L Russo
MEDBERY,Penny L   Sex:F   25 Apr 1969 Dale S Medbery & Donna M Reagan
MEDINA,Geoffrey Robert Sex:M   21 Jan 1982 Robert W Medina & Kathryn L Kopriva
MEEHAN,Robin E   Sex:F   09 Apr 1959 Earl N Meehan & Beverly M Cleary
MEIER,Charles R   Sex:M   03 May 1951 Ralph A Meier & Ann J Lisio
MEIER,Heidi L   Sex:F   11 Apr 1969 Robert G Meier & Nancy L Wardwell
MEIER,Ralph R   Sex:M   28 Sep 1949 Ralph A Meier & Ann J Lisio
MEIER,Susan G   Sex:F   22 Sep 1965 Robert G Meier & Nancy L Wardwell
MEIR,Sandra J   Sex:F   20 Nov 1953 Ralph A Meir & Ann G Lisio
MELANCON,Patricia A   Sex:F   (Child #1) 27 Sep 1945 Maynard S Melancon
   (Lowell, MA) & Olive C Brown (Newport, NH)
MELANSON,Brian Dana   Sex:M   26 Nov 1984 Richard D Melanson & Donna Anne Laine
MELLEN,Ester   Sex:F   (Child #3) 28 Aug 1940 Judah H Mellen (Lowell, MA)
   & Charlotte L McKeen (New York, NY)
MELVILLE,Justin C   Sex:M   28 Feb 1972 Terrence C Melville & Claire M Danereau
MELVIN,Ella May Sex:F 09 Sep 1862 Hudson, NH William Melvin & Betsey Hamblett

HUDSON,NH BIRTHS

MELVIN,Etta May   Sex:F   02 Sep 1862 Hudson, NH William Melvin & Betsy
MELVIN,Jerome A Sex:M 20 Apr 1866 Hudson, NH Tolford D Melvin
  & Julia C Hopkins
MELVIN,Laura W   Sex:F   (Child #1) 25 May 1884 Hudson, NH Tolford J Melvin Jr
  (Hudson, NH) & Ida S Webster (Hudson, NH)
MELVIN,Michael F   Sex:M   04 Feb 1953 Thomas F Melvin & Ruth L King
MELVIN,Mildred Catherine   Sex:F   (Child #1) 26 Jul 1917 Albert Melvin
  (Lewiston, ME) & Pauline Porter (Nashua, NH)
MELVIN,Scott H   Sex:M   23 May 1950 Thomas F Melvin & Ruth L King
MELVIN,Taulford   Sex:M   28 Jul 1861 Hudson, NH Taulford Melvin & Julia
MELVIN,Tolford Sex:M 28 Jul 1861 Hudson, NH Tolford D Melvin
  & Julia C Hopkins
MELVIN,[Unknown]   Sex: 09 Aug 1886 Tolford Melvin, Jr & Ida S
MELVIN,[Unknown]   Sex:F   (Child #1) 09 Sep 1895 Jerome A Melvin (Hudson, NH)
  & Sarah M Buttrick (Hudson, NH)
MENARD,Brian R   Sex:M   09 Mar 1972 Gabriel R Menard Jr & Virginia C Bouley
MENARD,John W   Sex:M   (Child #1) 08 Aug 1946 Raymond G Menard (Brunswick, ME)
  & Eunice M Roy (Nashua, NH)
MENDES,Michael Anthony Jr   Sex:M   22 Sep 1980 Michael A Mendes Sr
  & Frances Elsie Hall
MENKO,Andries D   Sex:M   28 Jan 1978 Russell H Menko & Susan B Wood
MERCER,Danielle Denise   Sex:F   03 May 1984 Warner Paul Mercer
  & Jacqueline L Couture
MERCER,Jonathan Edward Sex:M   11 Aug 1982 Edward D Mercer & Karen Ann Trainor
MERCHANT,Christopher Dean Sex:M 13 Aug 1981 William J Merchant
  & Darlene B Piper
MERCHANT,David C   Sex:M   23 Dec 1969 David T Merchant & Kathleen A Moran
MERCHANT,Nicole Lynn   Sex:F   30 Aug 1978 William J Merchant & Darlene P Piper
MERCIER,Marc L   Sex:M   03 Oct 1975 Gerald M Mercier & Ginette M Harvey
MERCIER,Martha P   Sex:F   03 Aug 1952 Alfred J Mercier & Lillian C Trombly
MEREWETHER,Michelle J Sex:F   29 May 1967 Carle H Merewether & Jerry L Francis
MERRIFIELD,John A   Sex:M   04 Feb 1970 Richard C Merrifield & Merilyn E Latour
MERRIFIELD,Michael J   Sex:M   25 Mar 1972 Curtis J Merrifield
  & Shirley A McDermott
MERRIFIELD,Shelly S Sex:F 22 Sep 1966 Richard C Merrifield & Marilyn E Latour
MERRIFIELD,Susan M   Sex:F   30 Aug 1961 Curtis J Merrifield & Paula J Bozek
MERRILL,Abel   Sex:M   23 Dec 1747 Hudson, NH Nathaniel Merrill & Elizabeth
MERRILL,Abigail Marsh   Sex:F   08 Mar 1771 Hudson, NH Samuel Merrill & Ruth
MERRILL,Abijah Marsh   Sex:M   08 Mar 1771 Hudson, NH Samuel Merrill & Ruth
MERRILL,Anna Gertrude   Sex:F   04 May 1858 Hudson, NH James P Merrill
  & Persis A Winn
MERRILL,Annie G   Sex:F   04 May 1858 Hudson, NH James B Merrill & Persis
MERRILL,Asa   Sex:M   07 Nov 1781 Hudson, NH Nathaniel F Merrill & Olive Lund
MERRILL,Asa S   Sex:M   11 Oct 1814 Hudson, NH Isaac Merrill & Susan
MERRILL,Asa Swan   Sex:M   11 Oct 1814 Hudson, NH Isaac Merrill Jr & Susanna
MERRILL,Barbara A   Sex:F   20 Apr 1965 Bruce K Merrill & Helen F Basil
MERRILL,Benjamin   Sex:M   13 Apr 1756 Hudson, NH Nathaniel Merrill & Elizabeth
MERRILL,Benjamin Sex:M24 Jan 1768 Hudson, NH Nathaniel F Merrill & Olive Lund
MERRILL,Benjamin   Sex:M   17 Jun 1821 Hudson, NH Benjamin Merrill & Sarah
MERRILL,Benjamin A   Sex:M   17 Jun 1821 Hudson, NH Benjamin Merrill & Sarah
MERRILL,Bertha S   Sex:F   07 Apr 1876 Hudson, NH George Merrill & Anna
MERRILL,Betsey   Sex:F   17 Apr 1768 Hollis, NH Daniel Merrill & Mary Hale
MERRILL,Betty   Sex:F   17 Apr 1768 Hudson, NH Daniel Merrill & Mary
MERRILL,Betty B   Sex:F   16 Mar 1768 Hudson, NH Nathaniel Merrill & Mary
MERRILL,Betty Bradstreet   Sex:F   06 Sep 1741 Hudson, NH Nathaniel Merrill
  & Elizabeth
MERRILL,Betty Bradstreet   Sex:F   16 Mar 1768 Hudson, NH Nathaniel Merrill Jr
  & Mary
MERRILL,Bonita L   Sex:F   06 Aug 1949 Harold F Merrill & Edna M Hills
MERRILL,Brenda L   Sex:F   14 Nov 1950 Harold F Miller & Edna M Hills

HUDSON,NH BIRTHS

MERRILL,Bruce K Jr   Sex:M   10 Jun 1962 Bruce K Merrill & Helen F Basil
MERRILL,Christopher D   Sex:M   25 May 1961 Donald A Merrill & Faith D Dadmun
MERRILL,Dana H   Sex:M   09 Jul 1948 Ernest L Merrill (Milford, NH)
   & Doris E Teachant (Grand Rapids, MI)
MERRILL,Daniel   Sex:M   31 Mar 1761 Hollis, NH Daniel Merrill & Mary Hale
MERRILL,Daniel   Sex:M   13 Mar 1761 Hudson, NH Daniel Merrill & Mary
MERRILL,Daniel B   Sex:M   10 Mar 1958 Bruce K Merrill & Helen F Basil
MERRILL,Daniel Tyler   Sex:M   31 Mar 1828 Hudson, NH John Merrill & Sarah
MERRILL,Donald K   Sex:M   (Child #3) 02 Aug 1903 Jas E Merrill (Hudson, NH)
   & Sarah E Marble (Nashua, NH)
MERRILL,Dorothy   Sex:F   10 Feb 1749 Hudson, NH Nathaniel Merrill & Elizabeth
MERRILL,Ebenezer B   Sex:M   07 Aug 1822 Hudson, NH Benjamin Merrill & Sarah
MERRILL,Ebenezer Burbank   Sex:M   07 Aug 1822 Hudson, NH Benjamin Merrill
   & Sarah
MERRILL,Electa   Sex: 13 Sep 1812 Hudson, NH Isaac Merrill Jr & Susanna
MERRILL,Electa   Sex:F   14 Sep 1814 Hudson, NH Isaac Merrill & Susan
MERRILL,Elizabeth H   Sex:F   07 May 1796 Hudson, NH Henry Merrill
   & Barshaba Winn
MERRILL,Elizabeth H   Sex:F   07 May 1796 Hudson, NH Henry Merrill & Barsheba
MERRILL,Esther   Sex:F   14 Apr 1767 Hudson, NH Nathaniel Merrill Jr & Mary
MERRILL,Ethel G   Sex:F   (Child #2) 16 Sep 1892 Jas E Merrill (Hudson, NH)
   & Etta S Marble (Nashua, NH)
MERRILL,Ezekiel   Sex:M   19 Oct 1770 Hudson, NH Nathaniel Merrill Jr & Mary
MERRILL,Frank G Sex:M 23 Apr 1863 Hudson, NH Benjamin A Merrill & Mary J Winn
MERRILL,Fred R   Sex:M   (Child #4) 21 Jun 1904 George A Merrill (Hudson, NH)
   & Emma B Winn (Hudson, NH)
MERRILL,George A Sex:M 26 Jul 1862 Hudson, NH James P Merrill & Persis A Winn
MERRILL,Hannah   Sex:F   26 May 1747 Hudson, NH Daniel Merrill & Tamisin
MERRILL,Hannah   Sex:F   20 May 1747 Hudson, NH Daniel Merrill & Tamisen
MERRILL,Harriet   Sex:F   13 Sep 1810 Hudson, NH Isaac Merrill Jr & Susanna
MERRILL,Harriet   Sex:F   01 Jul 1816 Hudson, NH Daniel Merrill & Susanna
MERRILL,Harriet R   Sex:F   01 Jul 1816 Hudson, NH Daniel Merrill & Susanna
MERRILL,Henry   Sex:M   17 Jul 1763 Hollis, NH Daniel Merrill & Mary Hale
MERRILL,Henry Hale Sex:M 09 Feb 1793 Hudson, NH Henry Merrill & Barshaba Winn
MERRILL,Irena   Sex:F   07 Dec 1818 Hudson, NH John Merrill & Sarah
MERRILL,Isaac   Sex:M   20 Aug 1754 Hudson, NH Samuel Merrill & Susanna
MERRILL,Isaac   Sex:M   16 Mar 1781 Hudson, NH Isaac Merrill & Olive Merrill
MERRILL,Isaac   Sex:M   15 Mar 1781 Hudson, NH Isaac Merrill & Olive
MERRILL,James B   Sex:M   06 May 1824 Hudson, NH Benjamin Merrill & Sarah
MERRILL,James C   Sex:M   27 Jul 1860 Hudson, NH James B Merrill & Persis
MERRILL,James E   Sex:M   27 Jul 1860 Hudson, NH James B Merrill & Persis
MERRILL,James Everett   Sex:M   27 Jul 1860 Hudson, NH James P Merrill
   & Persis A Winn
MERRILL,James P   Sex:M   06 May 1824 Hudson, NH Benjamin Merrill & Sarah
MERRILL,John   Sex:M   26 Oct 1745 Hudson, NH Nathaniel Merrill & Elizabeth
MERRILL,John   Sex:M   17 May 1783 Hudson, NH Isaac Merrill & Olive Merrill
MERRILL,Judith A   Sex:F   09 Aug 1956 Maurice D Merrill & Gertrude A Colburn
MERRILL,Karl E   Sex:M   (Child #1) 02 Jul 1889 James E Merrill (Hudson, NH)
   & Etta S Marble (Nashua, NH)
MERRILL,Laurie A   Sex:F   19 May 1960 Richard D Merrill & Celina M Gaulin
MERRILL,Leventhey   Sex: 28 Aug 1806 Hudson, NH Henry Merrill & Barsheba
MERRILL,Lucinda   Sex:F   28 Aug 1806 Hudson, NH Henry Merrill & Barshaba Winn
MERRILL,Lucy   Sex:F   19 Jun 1823 Hudson, NH Isaac Merrill Jr & Susanna
MERRILL,Lydia   Sex:F   04 Apr 1780 Hudson, NH Abel Merrill & Ruth
MERRILL,Margaret   Sex:F   15 Nov 1756 Hollis, NH Daniel Merrill & Mary Hale
MERRILL,Marjorie   Sex:F   (Child #2) 30 Sep 1900 Geo A Merrill (Hudson, NH)
   & Emma B Winn (Hudson, NH)
MERRILL,Mary   Sex:F   28 Aug 1743 Hudson, NH Nathaniel Merrill & Elizabeth
MERRILL,Mary   Sex:F   07 Dec 1765 Hollis, NH Daniel Merrill & Mary Hale
MERRILL,Mary   Sex:F   04 Sep 1765 Hudson, NH Nathaniel Merrill Jr & Mary

HUDSON, NH BIRTHS

MERRILL,Mary   Sex:F   14 Oct 1790 Hudson, NH Henry Merrill & Barshaba Winn
MERRILL,Mary   Sex:F   04 Sep 1765 Hudson, NH Nathaniel Merrill Jr & Mary
MERRILL,Mary A Sex:F   30 Jul 1853 Hudson, NH Ebenezer P Merrill & Letitia
MERRILL,Mary A Sex: 30 Jul 1855 Hudson, NH Ebenezer Merrill & Lettice
MERRILL,Mary E Sex:F   19 Apr 1960 Bruce K Merrill & Helen F Basil
MERRILL,Maurice C Sex:M (Child #3) 05 Jun 1902 George A Merrill (Hudson, NH)
    & E B Winn (Hudson, NH)
MERRILL,Moses   Sex:M   24 Dec 1752 Hudson, NH Daniel Merrill & Tamisin
MERRILL,Natalie Sex:F   (Child #5) 22 Aug 1907 Geo A Merrill (Hudson, NH)
    & E D Winn (Hudson, NH)
MERRILL,Nathaniel Sex:M 25 Sep 1739 Hudson, NH Nathaniel Merrill & Elizabeth
MERRILL,Olive   Sex:F   04 Dec 1751 Hudson, NH Nathaniel Merrill & Elizabeth
MERRILL,Olive   Sex:F   05 Dec 1769 Hudson, NH Nathaniel F Merrill & Olive Lund
MERRILL,Olive   Sex:F   01 Jan 1788 Hudson, NH Isaac Merrill & Olive Merrill
MERRILL,Oliver Sex:M   23 May 1779 Hudson, NH Nathaniel F Merrill & Olive Lund
MERRILL,Ollive Sex:F   05 Dec 1769 Hudson, NH Nathaniel Merrill & Ollive
MERRILL,Rachel Sex:F   27 Apr 1756 Hudson, NH Samuel Merrill Jr
    & Rebecca Blodgett
MERRILL,Rachel Sex:F   18 Jun 1826 Hudson, NH Isaac Merrill Jr & Susanna
MERRILL,Rachel Sex:F   31 Jan 1821 Hudson, NH John Merrill & Sarah
MERRILL,Rachel G Sex:F   31 Jan 1821 Hudson, NH John Merrill & Sarah
MERRILL,Rebecca Sex:F   24 Nov 1751 Hudson, NH Samuel Merrill Jr
    & Rebecca Blodgett
MERRILL,Rebecca Sex:F   01 Jul 1816 Hudson, NH Daniel Merrill & Susanna
MERRILL,Rosamond Heaton Sex:F (Child #1) 13 Apr 1917 Karl E Merrill
    (Hudson, NH) & Josie Jeanotte (Nashua, NH)
MERRILL,Ruth   Sex:F   13 Apr 1756 Hudson, NH Nathaniel Merrill & Elizabeth
MERRILL,Ruth   Sex:F   20 Mar 1745 Hudson, NH Daniel Merrill & Tamisin
MERRILL,Ruth   Sex:F   07 Dec 1765 Hollis, NH Daniel Merrill & Mary Hale
MERRILL,Ruth   Sex:F   16 Mar 1754 Hudson, NH Samuel Merrill Jr
    & Rebecca Blodgett
MERRILL,Ruth   Sex:F   26 Jul 1772 Hudson, NH Abel Merrill & Ruth
MERRILL,Ruth   Sex:F   20 Mar 1746 Hudson, NH Daniel Merrill & Tamisen
MERRILL,Samuel Sex:M   01 Jan 1759 Hollis, NH Daniel Merrill & Mary Hale
MERRILL,Samuel Sex:M   30 Jul 1779 Hudson, NH Isaac Merrill & Olive Merrill
MERRILL,Samuel Sex:M   02 Oct 1820 Hudson, NH Isaac Merrill Jr & Susanna
MERRILL,Samuel B Sex:M   05 Aug 1799 Hudson, NH Henry Merrill & Barsheba
MERRILL,Sarah   Sex:F   31 Oct 1753 Hudson, NH Nathaniel Merrill & Elizabeth
MERRILL,Sarah   Sex:F   23 Jan 1755 Hudson, NH Daniel Merrill & Tamisin
MERRILL,Sarah   Sex:F   26 Apr 1776 Hudson, NH Abel Merrill & Ruth
MERRILL,Sarah   Sex:F   16 Apr 1776 Hudson, NH Abel Merrill & Ruth
MERRILL,Sarah B Sex:F   13 Jan 1863 Hudson, NH William F Merrill & Lucy
MERRILL,Sarah Butler Sex:F 05 Aug 1799 Hudson, NH Henry Merrill
    & Barshaba Winn
MERRILL,Sarah E Sex:F   25 Nov 1811 Hudson, NH John Merrill & Sarah
MERRILL,Sarah Emeline Sex:F 25 Nov 1811 Hudson, NH John Merrill & Sarah
MERRILL,Sarah P Sex:F   13 Jan 1863 Hudson, NH William T Merrill & Lucy A Byam
MERRILL,Stacey A Sex:F   12 Nov 1969 David Merrill & Susan P Young
MERRILL,Stephen C Sex:M 02 May 1814 Hudson, NH John Merrill & Sarah
MERRILL,Stephen Currier Sex:M 02 May 1814 Hudson, NH John Merrill & Sarah
MERRILL,Susan J Sex:F   03 Oct 1950 Maurice D Merrill & Gertrude A Colburn
MERRILL,Susanna Sex:F   28 Aug 1785 Hudson, NH Isaac Merrill & Olive Merrill
MERRILL,Susanna S Sex:F 27 Jan 1817 Hudson, NH Isaac Merrill Jr & Susanna
MERRILL,Susannah Sex:F   28 Aug 1785 Hudson, NH Isaac Merrill & Olive
MERRILL,Tabatha Sex:F   12 Sep 1779 Hudson, NH Abel Merrill & Ruth
MERRILL,Tabitha Sex:F   29 Nov 1749 Hudson, NH Samuel Merrill Jr
    & Rebecca Blodgett
MERRILL,Tabitha Sex:F   12 Sep 1779 Hudson, NH Abel Merrill & Ruth
MERRILL,Tamesin Sex:F   12 Jun 1758 Hudson, NH Samuel Merrill & Rebeckah
MERRILL,Tamisin Sex:F   12 Jan 1758 Hudson, NH Samuel Merrill Jr

HUDSON,NH BIRTHS

& Rebecca Blodgett
MERRILL,Thomas Sex:M 05 May 1763 Hudson, NH Nathaniel Merrill Jr & Mary
MERRILL,Tina Sex:F 07 Dec 1818 Hudson, NH John Merrill & Sarah
MERRILL,William Talbot Sex:M 19 Jan 1826 Hudson, NH Benjamin Merrill
  & Sarah
MERRILL,Winn Sex:M (Child #1) 28 Jun 1895 Geo A Merrill (Hudson, NH)
  & Emma B Winn (Hudson, NH)
MESSER,Charles J Sex:M 11 Oct 1806 Hudson, NH Dudley Messer & Phebe
MESSER,Charles Johnson Sex:M 11 Oct 1806 Hudson, NH Dudley Messer & Phebe
MESSER,Susanna Sex:F 17 Apr 1767 Hudson, NH Stephen Messer & Anna
MESSIER,Diane G Sex:M 18 Dec 1950 Arthur F Messier & Gertrude M McCoy
MESSIER,Donald Erenst Sex:M (Child #1) 23 Mar 1941 Arthur Messier
  (Stoneham, MA) & Gertrude McCoy (Hudson, NH)
MESSIER,Douglas A Sex:M (Child #2) 08 Mar 1942 Arthur F Messier (Stoneham,
  MA) & Gertrude M McCoy (Hudson, NH)
MESSIER,Kelley L L Sex:F 21 Jan 1958 Paul F Messier & Shirley B Lawrence
MESSIER,Kevin W Sex:M 15 Mar 1960 Paul F Messier & Shirley B Lawrence
MESSIER,Russell F Sex:M (Child #3) 30 Jul 1944 Arthur F Messier (Stoneham,
  MA) & Gertrude M McCoy (Hudson, NH)
MESSNIER,Joseph Sex:M (Child #11) 10 Sep 1918 Joseph Messnier (Canada)
  & Josephine Dionne (Canada)
METRANO,Jason R Sex:M 29 Sep 1974 Richard R Metrano & Carmelle P McKeating
METTA,Kimberly Gail Sex:F 27 Apr 1985 Richard N Metta & Lynn C Paquette
METZER,William Joseph Patri Sex:M 23 Sep 1983 William Frank Metzer
  & Michelle McGandy
MEYER,Christian J Jr Sex:M 12 Nov 1970 Christian J Meyer & Christine E Dowd
MICHAUD,Amy D Sex: 26 Mar 1973 Henry P Michaud Sr & Constance M Roussel
MICHAUD,Bertha Sex:F 14 Sep 1955 Victor J Michaud & Edna S Pavlow
MICHAUD,Brian Sex:M 09 May 1963 Roland G Michaud & Barbara Carroll
MICHAUD,Craig E Sex:M 03 Jul 1976 Russell F Michaud & Melanie Sue Day
MICHAUD,Darren G Sex:M 15 Jul 1973 Alfred P Michaud & Florence E Tanguay
MICHAUD,Jennifer A Sex:F 12 Dec 1970 Ronald E Michaud & Lucille V April
MICHAUD,Joseph A R Sex:M (Child #5) 02 Jun 1915 Hudson, NH Elvi Michaud
  (Canada) & Leopoldine Cote (Canada)
MICHAUD,Keith G Sex:M 10 Dec 1974 Alfred P Michaud & Florence E Tanguay
MICHAUD,Kevin Sex:M 06 Mar 1968 Roland G Michaud & Barbara Carroll
MICHAUD,Kris P Sex:M 02 May 1979 Paul R Michaud & Nancy Lee Patnaude
MICHAUD,Pamela R Sex:F 13 Mar 1966 Ronald E Michaud & Lucille V April
MICHAUD,Paul J Sex:M 12 Jan 1972 Henry P Michaud & Constance M Roussel
MICHAUD,Tamye Sex:F 28 Jul 1958 Roland G Michaud & Barbara Carroll
MIDDLETON,Herbert A Sex:M 28 Jun 1979 Robert J Middleton & Stella M Sampson
MIGNEAULT,Mary Sex:F (Child #4) 12 Apr 1924 Monci Migneault (Canada)
  & Helen Kaivelle (Douglas, NY)
MIGNEAULT,Maurice A Sex:M (Child #4) 15 May 1926 Maurice Migneault (Canada)
  & Helen Kinville (New York)
MILANO,Larissa Anne Sex:F 15 Oct 1983 Alfred L Milano Jr & Kathleen Ann Kenny
MILES,Douglas J Sex:M 01 Mar 1975 John T Miles & Linda J Elliott
MILEWSKI,Kristen Marie Sex:F 04 May 1982 Stephen M Milewski & Susan Ann Bell
MILEWSKI,Sarah Jean Sex:F 24 Apr 1985 Stephen M Milewski & Susan Ann Bell
MILLER,Adrienne N Sex:F 08 Mar 1978 Phillip J Miller & Beverly M Noel
MILLER,Arthur A J Sex:M (Child #2) 17 Feb 1940 Joseph W Miller (Canada)
  & Yvonne L Miller (Manchester, NH)
MILLER,Arthur D Sex:M 10 Mar 1962 Ronald L Miller & Betty A Frost
MILLER,Bonnie L Sex:F (Child #1) 03 Nov 1946 Perley S Miller (Wayland, MA)
  & Leona M Burge (Pleasant Hill, IL)
MILLER,Cynthia M Sex:F 29 Mar 1963 Linwood T Miller & Katherine E Mohr
MILLER,Eric Leonard Sex:M 17 Dec 1983 Ernest A Miller & Janice Lynn Merrill
MILLER,Jennifer Donna Sex:F 03 May 1982 Ernest A Miller & Janice Lynn Merrill
MILLER,Jennifer E Sex: 26 Sep 1972 Scott H Miller & Lois Ann Rouillard
MILLER,Joseph W Sex:M 24 Jan 1952 Joseph W Miller & Yvonne L Provencher

HUDSON, NH BIRTHS

MILLER, Judson W   Sex:M   18 Sep 1969 Hughey M Miller & Constance A Baker
MILLER, Karen   Sex:F   15 Aug 1956 LeRoy C Miller & Carol P Haug
MILLER, Karen A   Sex:F   20 Dec 1960 Robert A Miller & Sylvia E Cote
MILLER, Kathryn Y   Sex:F   24 Apr 1950 Joseph W Miller & Yvonne L Provencher
MILLER, Laura E   Sex:F   06 Jan 1965 Robert J Miller & Nancy E Landry
MILLER, Linda   Sex:F   06 Apr 1955 LeRoy C Miller & Carol P Haug
MILLER, Linda A   Sex:F   08 Aug 1956 Robert J Miller & Sylvia E Cote
MILLER, Linda M   Sex:F   26 Aug 1954 George W Miller, Jr & Pauline C Gosselin
MILLER, Linwood Travis   Sex:M   (Child #2) 15 Oct 1938 Harry Lee Miller
  (Canterbury, NH) & Marion G Travis (Manchester,
MILLER, Marie J T   Sex:F   (Child #3) 23 Nov 1944 Joseph W Miller (St Francis,
  Canada) & Yvonne L Provencher (Manch
MILLER, Mark S   Sex:M   27 Aug 1952 LeRoy C Miller & Carol P Haug
MILLER, Mary E   Sex:F   02 Feb 1961 Paul A Miller & Doris M St Pierre
MILLER, Nichole M   Sex:F   21 Feb 1976 Phillip J Miller & Beverly M Noel
MILLER, Robert S   Sex:M   23 Feb 1963 Robert J Miller & Nancy E Landry
MILLER, Steven S   Sex:M   14 Jul 1967 Paul A Miller & Doris M St Pierre
MILLER, [Unknown]   Sex:F   17 Mar 1984 Gerald A Miller & Nancy A Glover
MILLETT, Diane E   Sex:F   23 Mar 1948 Everett L Millett (Hudson, NH)
  & Josephine L Annarel (Somerville, MA)
MILLETT, Everett L   Sex:M   (Child #3) 12 May 1915 Hudson, NH Eugene G Millett
  (Washington, NH) & Pearl M Griswold (Nashua, NH)
MILLETT, Joan E   Sex:F   (Child #2) 16 Nov 1943 Everett L Millett (Hudson, NH)
  & Ina E Campbell (Hudson, NH)
MILLETTE, Alice Dora   Sex:F   (Child #4) 27 Mar 1917 Eugene Millette
  (Washington, NH) & Pearl Griswold (Nashua, NH)
MILLETTE, Jeffrey L   Sex:M   14 Mar 1968 Lee J Millette & Joan L Mitton
MILLETTE, Leslie Eugene   Sex:M   (Child #2) 22 May 1912 Eugene Millette
  (Washington, NH) & Pearl Griswold (Nashua, NH)
MILLETTE, Michael L   Sex:M   27 May 1964 Lee J Millette & Joan L Mitton
MILLETTE, Steven L   Sex:M   05 May 1966 Lee J Millette & Joan L Milton
MINASIAN, Alexander Scott   Sex:M   11 Jul 1984 Richard P Minasian
  & Florence A Boucher
MINER, Alan P   Sex:M   28 Jul 1956 Peter J Miner & Edith I Grace
MINER, Richard William   Sex:M   (Child #1) 20 Feb 1935 William Miner (Troy, NH)
  & Olivette Richard (Nashua, NH)
MINOT, Benjamin N   Sex:M   14 Aug 1961 H Parker Minot & J Patricia Stubbins
MINOT, Judith A V   Sex:F   10 Oct 1958 Herbert P Minot & Jacynth P Stubbins
MIRICK, Joseph   Sex:M   05 Mar 1812 Hudson, NH Joseph Mirick & Bridget
MISEK, Carl A   Sex:M   16 Apr 1965 Victor A Misek & Susan Woodbury
MISEK, Stevan A   Sex:M   17 Dec 1958 Victor A Misek & Susan Woodbury
MISEK, William F   Sex:M   19 Dec 1962 Victor A Misek & Susan Woodbury
MITCHEL, Agnes   Sex:F   05 Apr 1734 Hudson, NH John Mitchel & Jane
MITCHEL, Elizabeth   Sex:F   05 Jun 1745 Hudson, NH John Mitchel & Jane
MITCHEL, John   Sex:M   16 May 1741 Hudson, NH John Mitchel & Jane
MITCHEL, Mary   Sex:F   13 Feb 1735 Hudson, NH John Mitchel & Jane
MITCHEL, William   Sex:M   25 Sep 1744 Hudson, NH John Mitchel & Jane
MITCHELL, Christopher Michael   Sex:M   21 Oct 1978 Steven M Mitchell
  & Teresa A Arsenault
MITCHELL, Donna M   Sex:F   07 Mar 1956 Peter R Mitchell & Yvonne E Lajoie
MITCHELL, Elizabeth   Sex:F   03 Aug 1961 Donald E Mitchell & Judith A McCormack
MITCHELL, Elizabeth   Sex:F   05 Jun 1745 Hudson, NH John Mitchell & Jane
MITCHELL, John   Sex:M   (Child #1) 08 Apr 1927 Mike Mitchell (Nashua, NH)
  & Pearl D'Armour (Plattsburgh, NY)
MITCHELL, John   Sex:M   06 Mar 1741 Hudson, NH John Mitchell & Jane
MITCHELL, Kate Elizabeth   Sex:F   09 Mar 1981 James F Mitchell
  & Frances M Levesque
MITCHELL, Laurie A Sex:F   29 Jun 1959 Ludovic E Mitchell & Winnifred L Kimball
MITCHELL, Leanne   Sex:F   17 Jul 1963 Donald E Mitchell & Judith A McCormack
MITCHELL, Lisa D   Sex:F   15 Sep 1967 Ludovic Mitchell & Winnifred L Kimball

HUDSON,NH BIRTHS

```
MITCHELL,Mary    Sex:F   13 Feb 1735 Hudson, NH John Mitchell & Jane
MITCHELL,Matthew J   Sex:M   12 Jun 1978 James F Mitchell & Frances M Levesque
MITCHELL,Michael G   Sex:M    26 Oct 1948 Alfred R Mitchell (Pennsylvania)
  & Alice M Barrett (Tarrytown, NY)
MITCHELL,Nicole Erin Sex:F  16 Apr 1982 Ricky Allen Mitchell & Janet Marie Law
MITCHELL,Patricia J   Sex:F   11 Nov 1966 William P Mitchell & Anne M Cookman
MITCHELL,Randy W    Sex:M   27 Mar 1956 Ludovic Mitchell & Winnifred L Kimball
MITCHELL,Ricky A    Sex:M   08 Dec 1957 Ludovic E Mitchell & Winifred L Kimball
MITCHELL,Ronny S    Sex:M   01 Mar 1964 Larry Mitchell & Winnifred L Kimball
MITCHELL,Roy Earl    Sex:M   (Child #2) 08 Apr 1914 Rolleus K Mitchell (Acworth)
  & Gertrude Banks (Boston, MA)
MITCHELL,Sharon L   Sex:F   27 Sep 1969 George Mitchell & Donna A Turcotte
MITCHELL,Susan   Sex:F   16 Oct 1957 Peter R Mitchell & Yvonne E Lajoie
MITCHELL,Wendy L   Sex:F   12 May 1966 Peter R Mitchell & Yvonne E Lajoie
MITCHELL,William   Sex:M   25 Sep 1744 Hudson, NH John Mitchell & Jane
MITCHELL,[Unknown]   Sex:   05 Apr 1734 Hudson, NH John Mitchell & Jane
MITE,Kirk D   Sex:M   11 Mar 1967 John E Mite & Linda A Farrow
MITTON,Larry M   Sex:   01 May 1973 Vernon P Mitton & Yvette M Paquette
MIZO,Ann   Sex:F   (Child #3) 28 Nov 1942 Earl C Mizo (Nashua, NH)
  & Mary E Powlosky (Nashua, NH)
MIZO,Guy M   Sex:M   30 Aug 1955 Earl C Mizo & Mary E Powlosky
MIZO,[Unknown]   Sex:M   (Child #3) 30 Sep 1943 Earl C Mizo (Nashua, NH)
  & Mary E Powlowsky (Nashua, NH)
MOFFITT,Laura L   Sex:F   24 Feb 1968 Waldo P Moffitt & Linda D Clarke
MOLINARI,Julie   Sex:F   03 Nov 1977 Richard Molinari & Holly D Harwood
MOLKENTINE,John W Sex:M   16 Jan 1968 Warren W Molkentine & Evelyn R Ackerman
MOLKENTINE,Laurie A Sex:F 24 Sep 1965 Warren W Molkentine & Evelyn R Ackerman
MOLKENTINE,Wayne T Sex:M   29 Oct 1964 Warren W Molkentine & Evelyn R Ackerman
MONAHAN,Heather E   Sex:F   16 May 1968 Leo M Monahan Jr & Florence A Atherley
MONAHAN,Kathleen M   Sex:F   09 Aug 1969 Leo M Monahan & Florence A Atherley
MONCADA,Amber Lee   Sex:F   31 Aug 1980 Robert T Moncada & Roberta V Piontek
MONCADA,Erica Jean   Sex:F   01 Jul 1979 Robert T Moncada & Roberta V Piontek
MONDOUX,Gregory R   Sex:M   25 Feb 1967 Roland J Mondoux & Lucille E Eldridge
MONTANARI,Matthew D   Sex:M   13 Mar 1978 David A Montanari & Alice J Bray
MONTENARO,Richard   Sex:M   14 Dec 1973 Paul J Montenaro & Joanne M McCullough
MONTENERO,Jill   Sex:   03 Jul 1972 Paul J Montenero & Joanne M McCullough
MONTENERO,Julie   Sex:F   09 Mar 1976 Paul J Montenero & Joanne M McCullough
MONTENERO,Russell   Sex:M   09 Mar 1976 Paul J Montenero & Joanne M McCullough
MOODY,Angela M   Sex:F   24 Jan 1980 Stephen M Moody & Lisa J McCarthy
MOODY,Stephen M   Sex:M   09 Oct 1961 Maurice M Moody & Alice V Kirwan
MOODY,Todd Evan   Sex:M   25 Mar 1976 Robert H Moody & Nancy A Audette
MOODY,Travis J   Sex:M   15 Jun 1978 Robert H Moody & Nancy Ann Audette
MOODY,[Unknown]   Sex:   Feb 1865 Hudson, NH Jeremiah B Moody &
MOODY,[Unknown]   Sex:F   Feb 1864 Hudson, NH Jeremiah B Moody &
MOONEY,Anna Katherine   Sex:F   28 Jan 1985 Edward L Mooney Jr & Mary J Gorman
MOONEY,Arlene M   Sex:F   03 Jun 1957 James A Mooney & Bertha A LaMountain
MOONEY,James P   Sex:M   18 Dec 1968 James L Mooney & Sandra A Lambert
MOORE,Adam Mark   Sex:M   07 Aug 1980 Andrew Mason Moore & Diane Louise Goulet
MOORE,Alison Debra   Sex:F   31 Dec 1978 Andrew M Moore & Diane L Goulet
MOORE,Betty A   Sex:F   09 Feb 1953 Harold L Moore & Vivian S Ladner
MOORE,Brenda A   Sex:F   31 Mar 1948 Harold L Moore (Nashua, NH)
  & Vivian S Ledoux (Canada)
MOORE,Brian P   Sex:M   17 Feb 1969 Stephen B Moore & Roberta L Griffin
MOORE,Brian T   Sex:M   03 Jul 1973 Bernard E Moore & Sarsha M Dodge
MOORE,Edwin   Sex:M   (Child #3) 06 Jun 1898 Stephen J Moore (Nova Scotia)
  & Edith Boynton (Brownfield, ME)
MOORE,Edwin Roby   Sex:M   (Child #1) 28 Jun 1917 Earl B Moore (Hudson, NH)
  & Vesta Harris (Nashua, NH)
MOORE,Gordon M   Sex:M   22 Jul 1957 Gordon A Moore & Patricia A Patnaude
MOORE,Heather Rae   Sex:F   11 Jan 1985 Thomas J Moore III & Glenda Rae Nelson
```

HUDSON, NH BIRTHS

MOORE,Hildy Jane Sex:F (Child #2) 11 Feb 1941 Edwin R Moore (Hudson, NH)
  & Doris D MacInnis (Canada)
MOORE,Janice G Sex:F 05 Feb 1959 Gordon A Moore & Patricia A Patenaude
MOORE,Justin C Sex:M 20 Nov 1977 Kenneth F Moore & Karen Ann Collins
MOORE,Kenneth F Sex:M 13 Feb 1950 Kenneth M Moore & Henrietta A Cayer
MOORE,Lawrence E III Sex:M 25 Nov 1969 Lawrence E Moore Jr & Lucille B Smith
MOORE,Marlene A Sex:F 21 Jun 1953 Kenneth M Moore & Henrietta A Cayer
MOORE,Michelle A Sex:F 21 Dec 1971 Lawrence E Moore Jr & Lucille B Smith
MOORE,Michelle Renate Sex:F 29 Dec 1978 William Moore & Ursula Hugelschaffne
MOORE,Robert E Sex:M (Child #2) 13 Jan 1919 Earle Moore (Hudson, NH)
  & Vesta Harris (Nashua, NH)
MOORE,Steven Paul Sex:M 29 May 1984 Paul Steven Moore & Maureen Murray
MOORE,Travis McKay Sex:M 19 Oct 1980 Kenneth Frank Moore & Karen Ann Collins
MOORE,William V Sex:M 03 Apr 1976 William Moore & Ursula Hugelschaffne
MOORE,[Unknown] Sex:M (Child #2) 22 Jun 1896 Steven Moore (Nova Scotia)
  & Edith Boynton (Bromfield, ME)
MOQUIN,Heidi J Sex:F 15 Jan 1967 Ronald L Moquin & Diana R Lones
MORAN,Katherine Jean Sex:F 27 Mar 1985 John J Moran Jr & Donna Jean Kowalski
MORAN,Kathryn J Sex:F 25 Feb 1971 John W Moran & Mary E Cast
MORAN,Margaret E Sex:F 06 Nov 1966 John W Moran & Mary E Cast
MORAN,Michael S Sex:M 02 Oct 1975 James P Moran Sr & Ruth L Gray
MORAN,Patricia E Sex:F 24 Jun 1968 John W Moran & Mary E Cast
MORAN,Richard Greeley Sex:M (Child #1) 16 Apr 1908 James Moran (Nashua, NH)
  & Marion Greeley (Hudson, NH)
MOREAU,Beatrice A Sex:F 18 Apr 1953 Edward E Moreau & Clara M Stebbins
MOREAU,Deborah N Sex:F 06 Apr 1955 Norbert Moreau & Violet O Begnoche
MOREAU,Diane L Sex:F 10 Apr 1959 Norman N Moreau & Shirley A Wiggin
MOREAU,Katherine A Sex:F 29 Apr 1952 Edward E Moreau & Clara M Stebbins
MOREAU,Lois A Sex:F 28 May 1955 Normand N Moreau & Shirley A Wiggin
MOREAU,Normand R Sex:M 19 Feb 1957 Normand N Moreau & Shirley A Wiggin
MOREAU,Patricia A Sex:F 28 Jul 1955 Joseph N R Moreau & Ruth J Tiernan
MOREAU,Pauline J Sex:F 10 May 1955 Edward E Moreau & Clara M Stebbins
MOREAU,Ronald E Sex:M (Child #6) 30 Oct 1944 Norbert J Moreau (St Louis,
  Canada) & Violet O Begnoche (Nashua, NH)
MORELAND,Amos D Sex:M 01 Apr 1799 Hudson, NH William Moreland & Elizebeth
MORELAND,Amos Davis Sex:M 01 Apr 1799 Hudson, NH William Moreland
  & Elizabeth Kenney
MORELAND,Cyrus Sex:M 01 Aug 1804 Hudson, NH William Moreland
  & Elizabeth Kenney
MORELAND,Hannah Sex:F 11 Jan 1807 Hudson, NH William Moreland
  & Elizabeth Kenney
MORELAND,Hannah Sex:F 11 Jun 1807 Hudson, NH William Moreland & Elizebeth
MORELAND,James Sex:M 04 May 1795 Hudson, NH William Moreland
  & Elizabeth Kenney
MORELAND,Phebe Sex:F 24 May 1801 Hudson, NH William Moreland
  & Elizabeth Kenney
MORELAND,Salley Sex:F 09 Dec 1797 Hudson, NH William Moreland & Elizebeth
MORELAND,Sally Sex:F 09 Dec 1797 Hudson, NH William Moreland
  & Elizabeth Kenney
MORELAND,Sybil Sex:F 06 Dec 1802 Hudson, NH William Moreland
  & Elizabeth Kenney
MORELAND,Thomas Sex:M 12 Oct 1808 Hudson, NH William Moreland
  & Elizabeth Kenney
MORELL,[Unknown] Sex:F 07 Apr 1873 Hudson, NH George Morell & Anne
MORENCY,Andrew K Sex:M 24 Apr 1974 Robert H Morency Jr & Sandra E Tate
MORENCY,Brian C Sex:M 30 May 1977 Raymond G Morency & Maureen N Dustin
MORENCY,Karen M Sex:F 20 Mar 1972 Raymond G Morency & Maureen N Dustin
MORENCY,Sheila D Sex:F 20 Nov 1974 Raymond G Morency & Maureen N Dustin
MOREY,Eileen E Sex:F (Child #2) 22 Apr 1946 Ernest R Morey (Hudson, NH)
  & Rose A Levesque (Nashua, NH)

HUDSON,NH BIRTHS

MOREY,Ernest   Sex:M   (Child #7) 16 May 1906 Henry Morey (Hudson, NH)
  & Addie L Conery (Canada)
MOREY,Marie Lucille   Sex:F   21 Sep 1941 Noel E Morey (Londonderry, NH)
  & Marie Levesque (Canada)
MORGAN,Brandy Marie   Sex:F   28 Sep 1984 Eric Allen Morgan & Gail Ann Glines
MORGAN,Julie Ann   Sex:F   09 Sep 1980 Harold S Morgan & Catherine A Scott
MORGAN,Michelle S   Sex:F   26 Feb 1977 Harold S Morgan & Catherine Ann Scott
MORGAN,Shane L   Sex:M   01 Nov 1973 Larry L Morgan & Linda A Bell
MORIN,Anna Priscilla   Sex:F   (Child #5) 16 Jul 1924 Joseph Morin (Canada)
  & Josephine Hanson (Canada)
MORIN,Bridget Y   Sex:F   13 May 1966 Raymond R Morin & Diana R Gagnon
MORIN,Christopher R   Sex:M   12 Oct 1968 Raymond R Morin & Diana R Gagnon
MORIN,Diane L   Sex:F   22 Oct 1958 Fernand J Morin & Irene B Labrecque
MORIN,Duane B   Sex:M   07 Mar 1954 Romeo H Morin & Barbara A Baker
MORIN,Francis Alfred   Sex:M   (Child #2) 07 Mar 1920 Joseph Morin (Canada)
  & Josephine Hanson (Canada)
MORIN,Gloria   Sex:F   (Child #4) 05 Dec 1922 Joseph E Morin (Canada)
  & Josephine Hanson (Canada)
MORIN,Harold Leon   Sex:M   (Child #6) 10 Dec 1928 Joseph Morin (Canada)
  & Josephine Hanson (Canada)
MORIN,Heather Ann   Sex:F   29 Aug 1973 Leo J Morin & Wanda Lee Gould
MORIN,Jos Norris   Sex:M   (Child #6) 15 Mar 1926 Joseph Morin (Canada)
  & Josephine Hanson (Canada)
MORIN,Judith D   Sex:F   31 Mar 1953 Fernand Morin & Helen O Brown
MORIN,Laura Jane B   Sex:F   29 Sep 1962 Romeo H Morin & Barbara A Baker
MORIN,Linda B   Sex:F   31 Jul 1955 Romeo H Morin & Barbara A Baker
MORIN,Maurice B   Sex:M   23 Feb 1957 Romeo H Morin & Barbara A Baker
MORIN,Michael B   Sex:M   01 Feb 1952 Romeo H Morin & Barbara A Baker
MORIN,Nancy Jean   Sex:F   (Child #8) 14 Jan 1935 Joseph Morin (Canada)
  & Josephine Hanson (Canada)
MORIN,Richard E   Sex:M   (Child #1) 27 Jun 1943 Roger A Morin (Nashua, NH)
  & Rita M Hill (Nashua, NH)
MORISSETTE,Jacqueline M   Sex:F   (Child #2) 13 Aug 1938 Leo Morissette
  (Nashua, NH) & Rose May Gagnon (Hudson, NH)
MORRILL,Francis Gerard   Sex:M   (Child #1) 18 Sep 1932 Hudson, NH
  Francis G Morrill (Quincy, MA) & Ardis Hayes (Boston, MA)
MORRILL,Heather   Sex: 28 Jan 1973 Lee E Morrill & Mary Ann Jalbert
MORRILL,Leslie Holt   Sex:M   (Child #3) 10 Feb 1934 Arthur E Morrill
  (Merrimack, NH) & Leona M Stone (S Ashburn, MA)
MORRILL,Pamela J   Sex:F   (Child #1) 01 Jan 1945 Arthur E Morrill (Nashua, NH)
  & Muriel Hunnewell (Nashua, NH)
MORRILL,[Unknown]   Sex:M   09 Nov 1878 Hudson, NH George J Morrill
  (North Berwick, ME) & Anna A
MORRIS,Eileen M   Sex:F   18 Dec 1971 Robert J Morris & Nora C Lynch
MORRIS,Jason Stuart   Sex:M   15 Jan 1981 Stuart J Morris & Tracey J Campbell
MORRIS,Jeremy   Sex:M   15 May 1983 Stuart J Morris & Tracey Jean Campbell
MORRISON,Aaron James Sex:M 14 Aug 1983 Stephen H Morrison & Brenda Ann Walker
MORRISON,Allen R   Sex:M   25 Feb 1964 Richard A Morrison & Nancy J Weaver
MORRISON,Gregory A   Sex:M   17 Aug 1968 Bruce A Morrison & Mary Ann Felch
MORRISON,Hary A   Sex:M   21 May 1875 Hudson, NH Augustus Morrison & Nellie
MORRISON,Jeffrey S   Sex:M   08 Jun 1975 Stephen F Morrison & Lee-Ann M Roy
MORRISON,Joan Dorothy   Sex:F   (Child #6) 07 Sep 1930 Frause R Morrison
  (Warner, NH) & Elizabeth Lamb (England)
MORRISON,Leanne   Sex:F   22 Mar 1982 Stephen H Morrison & Brenda Ann Walker
MORRISON,Lydia   Sex:F   26 Jun 1861 Hudson, NH Charles Morrison & Abby Floyd
MORRISON,Lydia A   Sex:F   Hudson, NH Charles Morrison & Abby
MORRISON,Meghan Ann Sex:F   23 Dec 1984 Stephen H Morrison & Brenda Ann Walker
MORRISON,Neil A   Sex:M   30 Apr 1962 Richard A Morrison & Nancy J Weaver
MORRISON,Valerie J   Sex:F   11 Jun 1961 Donald A Morrison & Priscilla Rand
MORRISON,[Unknown] Sex:F 04 Oct 1872 Hudson, NH Augustus R Morrison & Nellie

HUDSON,NH BIRTHS

MORROW,Sara Colleen   Sex:F   31 Aug 1982 Douglas Lee Morrow & Janice E Leonard
MORSE,Asa H   Sex:M   30 Aug 1785 Hudson, NH Benjamin Morse & Mary
MORSE,Asa Hildreth   Sex:M   30 Aug 1785 Hudson, NH Benjamin Morse & Mary
MORSE,Brian D   Sex:M   14 Aug 1966 John M Morse & Jacqueline A Constan
MORSE,James M   Sex:M   04 Mar 1789 Hudson, NH Benjamin Morse & Mary
MORSE,James Merrill   Sex:M   04 Mar 1789 Hudson, NH Benjamin Morse & Mary
MORSE,Lillian D   Sex:F   (Child #1) 28 Jan 1897 & Daisy Ida Eayrs (Hudson, NH)
MORSE,Nathaniel M   Sex:M   13 Sep 1791 Hudson, NH Benjamin Morse & Mary
MORSE,Nathaniel Merrill   Sex:M   13 Sep 1791 Hudson, NH Benjamin Morse & Mary
MORSE,Samantha A   Sex:F   29 Oct 1973 Raymond G Morse & Joan C Gravelle
MORSE,Sean P   Sex:M   27 Dec 1969 Raymond F Morse Jr & Joan M Gravelle
MORTIMER,Scott A   Sex:M   07 Feb 1971 Thomas J Mortimer & Mary J Chiarenza
MORTLOCK,Beverly Loretta   Sex:F   (Child #2) 28 Sep 1933 Harry W Mortlock
   (Hudson, NH) & Jeanette Landry (Nashua, NH)
MORTLOCK,Harry William   Sex:M   (Child #6) 26 Dec 1901 Hudson, NH
   George Mortlock (England) & Louisa J Brown (Nashua, NH)
MORTLOCK,Mabel Aldusta   Sex:F   (Child #5) 04 Feb 1899 Geo A Mortlock (London)
   & Louisa J Brown (Nashua, NH)
MORTON,Susan D   Sex:F   16 Jan 1950 Frank G Morton & Hazel Betson
MOSER,Matthew S   Sex:M   07 Oct 1975 George P Moser & Barbara A Baker
MOSHER,Vance A   Sex:M   25 Feb 1964 John A Mosher & Roberta A Levesque
MOULTON,Beatrice Marg   Sex:F   (Child #2) 24 Jan 1933 William Moulton (Nashua,
   NH) & Helen Fairfield (Nashua, NH)
MOULTON,Cindy M   Sex:F   07 Feb 1965 Robert O Moulton & Doris J Taylor
MOUMBLOW,Lewis A   Sex:M   18 Sep 1886 Lewis Moumblow & Rosa
MOUSSEAU,Jason L   Sex:M   28 Feb 1975 George L Mousseau & B Elizabeth Soukas
MOUSSEAU,Nicolle J   Sex:F   23 Aug 1973 George J Mousseau & B Elizabeth Soukas
MOUSSEAU,Philip George   Sex:M   17 Apr 1976 George L Mousseau & Bessie E Soukas
MULCAHEY,Mary K   Sex:F   29 Dec 1977 John F Mulcahey & Susan A Elliott
MULLER,Casey L   Sex:M   05 Jan 1967 Thomas A Muller & Stella L Curry
MULLER,Thomas V   Sex:M   04 Aug 1968 Thomas A Muller & Stella L Curry
MULLIN,Sean Patrick   Sex:M   18 Jun 1983 Lawrence P Mullin Jr
   & Madeleine E Brodeur
MULRONEY,Donald G Jr   Sex:M   02 Mar 1965 Donald G Mulroney,Sr & Mercy E Gerrior
MUNDAY,Michelle G   Sex:F   16 Nov 1959 Lake M Munday & Florette D St Jean
MUNICHIELLO,Edward R   Sex:M   30 Apr 1967 Albert J Munichiello
   & Elaine M Loughran
MUNICHIELLO,Gina E   Sex:F   26 Jul 1970 Albert J Munichiello
   & Elaine M Loughran
MUNRO,Ryan Daniel   Sex:M   03 Jun 1983 Donald A Munro & Laurie Ann Wright
MUNROE,James N   Sex: 05 Oct 1972 Thomas W Munroe & Joyce A Watts
MUNROE,Jo-Ann   Sex:F   24 Jul 1967 Thomas W Munroe & Joyce A Watts
MUNROE,Wendy A   Sex:F   20 Aug 1963 Warren T Munroe & Ruth E Wiezel
MUNSON,April S   Sex:F   02 May 1948 Earl W Munson (Nashua, NH)
   & Alice E Clark (Beverly, MA)
MUNSON,Earl W Jr   Sex:M   04 Apr 1951 Earl W Munson & Alice E Clark
MUNSON,Kenneth Lane   Sex:M   (Child #2) 17 Feb 1941 Willis Munson (Champlain,
   NY) & Clara Gerow (Woodstock, VT)
MUNSON,Lynn A   Sex:F   07 Jun 1961 Earl W Munson & Alice E Clark
MUNSON,Marilyn A   Sex:F   14 Jul 1953 Earl W Munson & Alice E Clark
MURPHY,Dane Montana   Sex:M   11 Jan 1983 William B Murphy & Gisele A Langlois
MURPHY,Edward JamesIII   Sex:M   19 Jan 1985 Edward J MurphyII
   & Gretchen S O'Dell
MURPHY,Erin Eir   Sex:F   06 Dec 1979 Terence M Murphy & Nancy Woodward
MURPHY,John L   Sex:M   06 Nov 1967 Lawrence R Murphy & Patricia R Gunderson
MURPHY,Kimberly A   Sex:F   13 Feb 1971 Michael J Murphy & Linda M Yetman
MURPHY,Richard T Jr   Sex:M   03 Nov 1960 Richard T Murphy, Sr & Sandra G Kerouac
MURPHY,Shanna Lee   Sex:F   22 Sep 1982 Terence M Murphy & Nancy Woodward
MURRAY,Christopher J   Sex:M   13 Jun 1967 Eugene F Murray & Ann V Feerick
MURRAY,David C   Sex: 01 May 1973 James M Murray & Nina Crafts

HUDSON,NH BIRTHS

MURRAY,Jonathan A   Sex: 01 May 1973 James M Murray & Nina Crafts
MURRAY,Julie B   Sex:F   01 Sep 1971 Barry D Murray & Barbara M A Lister
MURRAY,Pamela Anne Sex:F   17 Jun 1982 Stephen V Murray & Janice M Morrissette
MUSGRAVE,Linda E   Sex:F   23 Jan 1952 Charles R Musgrave & Ruth M Minor
MUSGRAVE,Linda E   Sex:F   23 Jan 1958 Charles R Musgrave & Ruth M Miner
MUSKIEWICZ,Kristina M   Sex:F   29 Jul 1977 Jack P Muskiewicz & Marion R Schulz
MUSKIEWICZ,Stephen C   Sex:M   30 Dec 1973 Jack P Muskiewicz & Marion R Schulz
MUZZEY,Harland A Jr   Sex:M   (Child #3) 30 Jan 1936 Harland A Muzzey
   (W Somerville, MA) & Betsy Hawes (Lebanon, NH)
MUZZEY,Marion Louise   Sex:F   (Child #2) 19 Sep 1934 Harland A Muzzey
   (W Somerville, MA) & Betsy L Howes (Lebanon, NH)
MYERS,Laura Kristine   Sex:F   27 Dec 1984 Steven H Myers & Kathleen E Jones
MYERS,Michael J   Sex:M   09 Jun 1976 James F Myers & Sandra J Munafo
MYNAHAN,Karen   Sex:F   21 Aug 1978 John E Mynahan & Joan N Seaboyer
MYNAHAN,Karlene   Sex:F   21 Aug 1978 John E Mynahan & Joan N Seaboyer
MYRICK,Amy Beth   Sex:F   27 Mar 1984 Brian Jay Myrick & Robin Mary Stowell
MYRICK,Pamela A   Sex:F   04 Sep 1973 Paul B Myrick & Barbara J Grace
NADEAU,Cheryl A   Sex:F   26 Sep 1958 Fernand R Nadeau & Sandra V Gamache
NADEAU,Claudette M   Sex:F   23 Dec 1956 Wilfred J Nadeau & Helen E Gagnon
NADEAU,Craig F   Sex:M   11 Nov 1957 Fernand R Nadeau & Sandra V Gamache
NADEAU,David A   Sex:M   02 Jul 1961 Gerard E Nadeau & Marguerite J Desjard
NADEAU,Elizabeth A   Sex:F   28 Jan 1967 Emery A Nadeau & Shirley A Craig
NADEAU,Emery A Jr   Sex:M   15 Aug 1963 Emery A Nadeau, Sr & Shirley A Craig
NADEAU,Garrett Alan   Sex:M   02 Mar 1980 Denis G Nadeau & Susan M Carrozzo
NADEAU,Jennelle Kathryn Sex:F28 Jul 1982 Mark L Nadeau & Kathryn A Pignatella
NADEAU,Joseph Rudolph   Sex:M   (Child #3) 01 Jul 1931 Paul Nadeau (Canada)
   & Lydia Lennilery (Canada)
NADEAU,Kathleen   Sex:F   09 Nov 1952 Joseph A Nadeau & Gloria M Carr
NADEAU,Kelly Elizabeth   Sex:F   11 Apr 1982 Denis G Nadeau & Susan M Carrozzo
NADEAU,Linda M   Sex:F   02 Jun 1955 Joseph P Nadeau & Gloria M Carr
NADEAU,Lori A   Sex:F   23 Mar 1962 Emery A Nadeau & Shirley A Craig
NADEAU,Marcia L   Sex:F   22 Oct 1969 Leon E Nadeau & Marilyn M Boyce
NADEAU,Marion I   Sex:F   (Child #2) 24 Apr 1943 Emery H Nadeau (Ft Kent, ME)
   & Marion Lambert (Hudson, NH)
NADEAU,Mark L   Sex:M   31 Oct 1955 Gerard E Nadeau & Marguerite J Desjard
NADEAU,Michelle K   Sex:F   17 Nov 1970 David P Nadeau & Katherine A Provenca
NADEAU,Sandra J   Sex:F   (Child #1) 09 Oct 1946 Arthur J Nadeau (Nashua, NH)
   & Lillian L Russell (Lowell, MA)
NADEAU,Vanessa Ann Sex:F 05 Aug 1978 Robert Leo Nadeau & Demetria A Siemanowi
NADEAU,William R   Sex:M   24 Jun 1963 Gerard E Nadeau & Marguerite J Desjard
NADO,Louise Ella   Sex:F   (Child #4) 27 Dec 1920 Archie L Nado (S Norwich, ME)
   & Elizabeth Boska (Winchester, NH)
NADREAU,Donald A   Sex:M   30 Mar 1958 Armand T Nadreau & Rita L Lavallee
NADREAU,Ronald J   Sex:M   30 Mar 1958 Armand T Nadreau & Rita L Lavallee
NADREAU,Sandra G   Sex:F   07 Feb 1957 Armand T Nadreau & Rita L Lavallee
NAGLE,Mark Edward   Sex:M   11 Nov 1984 Edward G Nagle & Kathleen Mary Taylor
NANTEL,Danielle A   Sex:F   06 Apr 1965 Gerard J Nantel & Janice A D'Amour
NANTEL,Donna L   Sex:F   16 Sep 1967 Gerard J Nantel & Janice A D'Amour
NANTEL,Norman G   Sex:M   01 Jul 1958 Gerard J Nantel & Janice A D'Amour
NARO,Carol A   Sex:F   12 May 1960 Henry L Naro & Nancy I Labednick
NARO,David H   Sex:M   06 Jun 1963 Henry L Naro & Nancy I Labednick
NARO,James E   Sex:M   02 Jul 1956 Robert H Naro & Joan T Champagne
NARO,Joseph Levi Henry   Sex:M   (Child #8) 26 Sep 1935 Henry Naro (Sciota, NY)
   & Angelina Gendron (Canada)
NARO,Karen L   Sex:F   20 Jan 1962 Henry L Naro, Jr & Nancy I Labednick
NARO,Kevin J   Sex:M   07 Feb 1961 Robert H Naro & Joan T Champagne
NARO,Marie Jeannette R   Sex:F   (Child #9) 31 May 1937 Henry Naro (Sciota, NY)
   & Angeline Gendron (Canada)
NARO,Michael A   Sex:M   30 Jul 1954 Albert A Naro & Martha J Torrey
NARO,Richard J   Sex:M   02 Jun 1964 Henry L Naro, Jr & Nancy I Labednick

HUDSON,NH BIRTHS

NARO,Sharon J   Sex:F   24 Dec 1959 Robert H Naro & Joan T Champagne
NARO,Susan L   Sex:F   08 Nov 1957 Robert H Naro & Joan T Champagne
NARO,Timothy M   Sex:M   10 Jun 1955 Robert H Naro & Joan T Champagne
NASH,Debra A   Sex:F   16 Jul 1952 Gerald Q Nash & Lucille P LaFontaine
NASH,Jeffrey L   Sex:M   04 Sep 1959 Gerald Q Nash & Lucille P LaFontaine
NASH,Kimberly M   Sex:F   17 Dec 1966 Stewart A Nash, Jr & Joan D Mannering
NASH,Mark A   Sex:M   20 Nov 1953 Gerald Q Nash & Lucille P LaFontaine
NASH,Priscilla L   Sex:F   16 Jul 1955 Gerald Q Nash & Lucille P LaFontaine
NASH,Rebecca J   Sex:F   19 Oct 1961 Gerald Q Nash & Lucille P LaFontaine
NASON,Diane E   Sex:F   11 Jul 1964 Richard C Nason & Shirley A Grant
NASON,Nancy L   Sex:F   15 Mar 1958 Richard C Nason & Shirley A Grant
NAUGLER,Joanna B   Sex:F   31 Aug 1969 John R Naugler & Jo-Anne T Ciampi
NEGRICH,Joshua D   Sex:M   04 Oct 1976 George Negrich Jr & Marilyn R Hinkle
NELSON,Charles E   Sex:M   07 Aug 1959 Asher R Nelson & Marjorie L Nelson
NELSON,Holly Ann   Sex:F   22 Dec 1978 Gregory A Nelson & Lee Ann Perry
NELSON,Meredith Lynn Sex:F   19 Nov 1984 Ronald James Nelson & Ann Maria Learn
NESKEY,Joanne L   Sex:F   27 Aug 1952 Anthony S Neskey & Evelyn M Hutchinson
NESKEY,June L   Sex:F   06 Nov 1956 Anthony S Neskey & Evelyn M Hutchinson
NETTO,Jonathan R   Sex:M   03 Apr 1979 Richard N Netto & Sandra E Henderson
NETTO,Richard A   Sex:M   02 Aug 1975 Richard N Netto & Sandra E Henderson
NEUMANN,Melissa   Sex:F   28 May 1980 William C Neumann & Elfriede H Knura
NEUMANN,Sonia   Sex:F   17 May 1978 William C Neumann & Heidi Knura
NEVENS,Laura J   Sex:F   05 May 1962 Mervin R Nevens & Pearl S Roy
NEVINS,Betsey   Sex:F   03 Apr 1800 Hudson, NH James Nevins & Betse
NEVINS,Betsey   Sex:F   03 Apr 1800 Hudson, NH James Nevins & Betsey Johnson
NEVINS,Sally H   Sex:F   18 Nov 1802 Hudson, NH James Nevins & Betse
NEVINS,Sally Hardy Sex:F 18 Nov 1802 Hudson, NH James Nevins & Betsey Johnson
NEWCOMB,Benjamin F Sex:M 21 Nov 1865 Hudson, NH Benjamin A Newcomb & Eliza J
NEWCOMB,Eliza A   Sex:F   12 Nov 1863 Hudson, NH Benjamin Newcomb & Eliza
NEWCOMB,Eliza Ann   Sex:F 12 Nov 1863 Hudson, NH Benjamin A Newcomb & Eliza J
NEWCOMB,Hannah Jane Sex:F11 Jan 1862 Hudson, NH Benjamin A Newcomb & Eliza J
NEWCOMB,Hannah Jane Sex:F   11 Jun 1862 Hudson, NH B Newcomb & Eliza
NEWCOMBE,Leanne E   Sex:F   12 Jun 1958 William A Newcombe & Nancy E Knowles
NEWELL,Cynthia L   Sex:F   27 Nov 1965 Millard H Newell & Cecilia T Parks
NEWELL,Eric W   Sex:M   03 Feb 1968 Millard H Newell & Cecilia T Parks
NEWMAN,Tyrone D   Sex:M   01 Jun 1969 William E Newman & Hoszel Cooley
NEWTON,Sophia Noelle Sex:F   10 Oct 1984 Philip T Newton & Tamara N Carter
NGOON,Kara Leigh   Sex:F   15 May 1983 Kenneth Wong Ngoon & Maryann Crowley
NICHOLS,Alan J   Sex:M   24 Nov 1958 Horace A Nichols & Bertha Richards
NICHOLS,Annie Bell Sex:F   08 Nov 1881 Hudson, NH Joseph E Nichols (Nashua, NH) & Leona A Griffin (Hudson, NH)
NICHOLS,Chester Leroy   Sex:M   (Child #3) 21 Sep 1885 Hudson, NH
   Joseph E Nichols (Nashua, NH) & Liona A Griffin (Hudson, NH)
NICHOLS,Dana A   Sex:M   11 Mar 1966 Ramon E Nichols & Shirley A York
NICHOLS,Eugene   Sex:M   (Child #1) 17 Jun 1889 George F Nichols (Hudson, NH) & Maggie E Fellen (Nashua, NH)
NICHOLS,Eugene   Sex:M   07 Jun 1889 Hudson, NH George F Nichols
   & Maggie E Follen
NICHOLS,Florence Edith   Sex:F   (Child #1) 21 Mar 1901 Hudson, NH Wm E Nichols (New York) & Florence A Joslin (Lyndeboro, NH)
NICHOLS,Frank B   Sex:M   (Child #5) 20 Oct 1890 Joseph E Nichols (Hollis, NH) & Liona A Griffin (Hudson, NH)
NICHOLS,Glenn J   Sex:M   31 May 1965 Horace A Nichols Sr & Bertha A Richards
NICHOLS,Horace Armand   Sex:M   (Child #9) 25 Jul 1928 Arthur E Nichols (Nashua, NH) & Etta B York (Fremont, NH)
NICHOLS,Jeffrey Lester Sex:M 25 Dec 1982 James M Nichols & Helen M Orleans
NICHOLS,John W   Sex:M   11 Jan 1869 Hudson, NH Ensign J Nichols & Viletta
NICHOLS,Kevin C   Sex:M   13 Aug 1961 Norman C Nichols & Georgia E Sutton
NICHOLS,Kevin M   Sex: 14 Jun 1973 Bruce R Nichols Sr & Cecile Y Durand
NICHOLS,Lori E   Sex:F   08 Jun 1963 Horace A Nichols & Bertha A Richards

HUDSON,NH BIRTHS

NICHOLS,Lydia   Sex:F   186 Hudson, NH Ensign J Nichols & Viletta
NICHOLS,Lydia   Sex:F   1864 Hudson, NH Zacheus E Nichols & Violett
NICHOLS,Martin R   Sex:M   08 Jul 1963 Norman C Nichols & Georgia E Sutton
NICHOLS,Philip S   Sex:M   03 Nov 1963 Ramon E Nichols & Shirley A York
NICHOLS,Raymond A   Sex:M   25 Jun 1951 Horace A Nichols & Bertha A Richards
NICHOLS,Roberta A   Sex:F   25 Sep 1953 Horace A Nichols & Bertha A Richardson
NICHOLS,Susan G   Sex:F   25 Apr 1949 Horace A Nichols & Bertha A Richards
NICHOLS,Tabitha Lee Sex:F 26 Mar 1982 Philip S Nichols & Pamela Jean Fournier
NICHOLS,Walter E   Sex:M   (Child #2) 20 Jan 1883 Hudson, NH Joseph E Nichols
    (Nashua, NH) & Liona A Griffin (Hudson, NH)
NICHOLS,[Unknown]   Sex:F   (Child #1) 27 Jan 1913 Gilman S Nichols (Bradford)
    & Mary Robinson (Nova Scotia)
NICHOLS,[Unknown]   Sex:F   (Child #2) 25 Sep 1915 Hudson, NH Gilman S Nichols
    (Bradford, NH) & M Blanche Robinson (Nova Scotia
NICHOLSON,Kelly Lee Sex:F 25 Aug 1973 Woodford P Nicholson
    & Estelle F Heppell
NICHOLSON,Scott W   Sex:M   17 Aug 1971 Wayne S Nicholson & June M Beliveau
NICKERSON,Daniel J Sex:M 23 Sep 1962 Raymond L Nickerson & Cornelia A Donovan
NICKERSON,Gertrude Willoby   Sex:F   (Child #3) 18 May 1904 Harry Nickerson
    (Wilton, NH) & Nellie Hardy (Milford, NH)
NIHAN,Lawrence D III   Sex:M   18 Feb 1958 Lawrence D Nihan, Jr & Laura H Hodge
NIHAN,Theresa A M   Sex:F   27 Aug 1960 Lawrence D Nihan & Laura H Hodge
NIQUETTE,Leonard R   Sex:M   (Child #1) 08 Aug 1943 Leo P Niquette (Canada)
    & Lucienne A Bissonet (Nashua, NH)
NIQUETTE,Marylee A   Sex:F   02 Feb 1964 Leonard R Niquette & Mary R Guyette
NIQUETTE,Pauline A   Sex:F   30 Jun 1955 Leo P Niquette & Lucienne A Bisson
NITA,Donna   Sex:F   25 Mar 1970 Albert A Nita & Ramona M Kulas
NIXON,Aaron Richard   Sex:M   18 Jun 1982 Richard A Nixon & Linda T Pelletier
NIXON,David R   Sex:M   09 Mar 1962 Henry L Nixon & Doris V Andrew
NOEL,Alfred L   Sex:M   (Child #1) 04 Dec 1944 Alfred E Noel (Nashua, NH)
    & Barbara L Nichols (Nashua, NH)
NOEL,Germaine L   Sex:F   (Child #6) 18 Jan 1920 Pierre Noel (Canada)
    & Marie Pelletier (Canada)
NOEL,Jessica Lyn   Sex:F   04 Oct 1978 Arthur Jean Noel & Linda Anne Bouley
NOEL,Jonathan Wallace   Sex:M   05 Oct 1978 John Richardson Noel
    & Patricia O Arthur
NOEL,Judith A   Sex:F   04 Sep 1948 Alfred E Noel (Nashua, NH)
    & Barbara L Nichols (Nashua, NH)
NOEL,Justin E   Sex:M   07 Apr 1980 John R Noel & Patricia O Arthur
NOEL,Michael P   Sex:M   21 Jul 1977 Paul C Noel & Sharon M Jeanson
NOEL,[Unknown]   Sex:M   09 Mar 1954 Leon P Noel & Alice Wright
NOLIN,Irene Leona   Sex:F   24 Mar 1938 Walter L Nolin (Dracut, MA)
    & Gertrude B Cote (Lowell, MA)
NOLIN,Kelley L   Sex:F   13 Jul 1966 Maurice D Nolin & Rolande M Dumoulin
NOLIN,Lee E   Sex:M   02 Dec 1967 Maurice D Nolin & Rolande M Dumoulin
NOLIN,Lisa M   Sex:F   27 Jan 1968 Leo E Nolin & Linda R Judkins
NORMAN,Ethel M   Sex:F   (Child #15) 22 May 1891 Louis Norman (Canada)
    & Elfon Aschambeau (Holyoke, MA)
NORMAN,Eugenie   Sex:F   26 May 1894 Louis Norman (Canada)
    & Alp'e Archambie (New York)
NORMAN,Rose Agnes   Sex:F   (Child #1) 15 Aug 1897 John Norman (Canada)
    & Angelina Goulette (Canada)
NORMAN,[Unknown]   Sex:F   (Child #2) 02 Feb 1899 John Norman (Canada)
    & Angelina Goulette (Canada)
NORMAND,Charles Noel   Sex:M   (Child #7) 25 Jan 1901 Hudson, NH Paul Normand
    (Canada) & Josephine Dusnoulin (Vermont)
NORMAND,Joseph Albert   Sex:M   (Child #4) 23 Jun 1902 John Normand (Canada)
    & Angelina Goulet (Canada)
NORMAND,Mari Cecelia   Sex:F   (Child #3) 12 Aug 1900 John Normand (Canada)
    & Angelina Boutelle (Canada)

HUDSON,NH BIRTHS

NORMAND,Marie Hina Isabelle Sex:F (Child #9) 11 Feb 1904 Paul Normand
  (Canada) & Josephine Dusnoulin (Vermont)
NORMAND,Monique R Sex:F   13 Dec 1968 Raymond P Normand & Donna L Martin
NORMANDIN,Christine Genevieve Sex:F 20 Feb 1982 David J Normandin
  & Sandra Ann Greenleaf
NORMANDIN,Joseph Jean Sex:M 30 Jul 1984 Kenneth R Normandin & Marie P Bibard
NORMANDIN,Michael R Sex:M 26 Oct 1974 Robert A Normandin & Patricia M Mills
NORMANDIN,Michele A Sex:F 11 Dec 1971 Robert A Normandin & Patricia M Mills
NORMON,George A G Sex:M   23 Sep 1893 Louis P Normon (Canada)
  & Josephine Miller (S Village, VT)
NORWAL,Harold Paul   Sex:M (Child #4) 24 Jan 1899 Paul Norwal (Canada)
  & Mary J Miller (Montpelier, VT)
NOTTER,Donna M Sex:F   08 Oct 1962 William J Notter & Gloria M Staudt
NOURY,Peter D Sex:M   06 Nov 1969 Richard R Noury & Claire D Desfosses
NOURY,Thomas A Sex:M   16 Jan 1971 Richard R Noury & Claire D Desfosses
NOVAK,Nina A Sex:F   11 Dec 1949 James I Novak & Jean E Rolinge
NOVAK,Tanya Sex:F   (Child #1) 16 Dec 1946 James I Novak (Nashua, NH)
  & Jean E Roling (Dotham, AL)
NOYES,Cathleen J Sex:F   23 May 1950 Harrison H Noyes & Lorraine T Jalbert
NOYES,Clyde L Sex:M   31 Aug 1974 Wayne L Noyes & Susan L Truell
NOYES,Flora Sex:F   (Child #1) 16 Aug 1916 Hudson, NH Joel Noyes
  (Connecticut) & Anna Morris (Hartford, CT)
NOYES,Roland Modglin Sex:M (Child #8) 25 Nov 1932 Nashua, NH Harry H Noyes
  (Lowell, MA) & Lola Stevens (Rumney, NH)
NOYES,Timothy J Sex:M 21 Sep 1964 Harrison H Noyes, Sr & Lorraine T Jalbert
NUTE,Alan J Sex:M   05 May 1962 James A Nute & Mary A Kupchunas
NUTE,Barbara A Sex:F   10 Apr 1971 Leonard W Nute & Gail E Monroe
NUTE,Deborah A Sex:F   15 Jul 1971 James A Nute & Mary A Kupchunas
NUTE,Frank Leonard   Sex:M (Child #1) 22 Jan 1914 Frank W Nute (Nashua, NH)
  & Etta Marshall (Hudson, NH)
NUTE,Leonard K Sex:M (Child #4) 12 Dec 1946 Frank L Nute (Hudson, NH)
  & Melba C King (Nashua, NH)
NUTE,Pamela J Sex:F   03 May 1965 James A Nute & Mary A Kupchunas
NUTE,William C Sex:M 28 Jul 1954 Marshall A Nute & Theresa R Ackerman
NUTTING,Amber Rose Sex:F 26 Aug 1975 Charles R Nutting & Cynthia R Campbell
NUTTING,Gloria Simonds Sex:F (Child #2) 19 Sep 1899 Will Nutting
  (Bridgewater, MA) & Mytie Downs (Milton)
NUTTING,Judith E Sex:F (Child #1) 13 Mar 1943 Frank A Nutting, Jr (Nashua,
  NH) & Rosamond H Merrill (Hudson, NH)
NUTTING,Lawrence H Sex:M 24 Aug 1957 Herbert H Nutting & Ruth A Stoughton
NUTTING,Linda R Sex:F (Child #2) 29 Apr 1945 Frank A Nutting (Nashua, NH)
  & Rosamond H Merrill (Hudson, NH)
NUTTING,Nancy E Sex:F   10 Sep 1947 Frank A Nutting (Nashua, NH)
  & Rosamond H Merrill (Hudson, NH)
NUTTING,Shawn R Sex:M 11 Jun 1970 Charles R Nutting & Cynthia R Campbell
O'BRIEN,Colleen M L Sex:F (Child #2) 20 Nov 1940 William O'Brien (Nashua,
  NH) & Leona Beaudette (Nashua, NH)
O'BRIEN,[Unknown] Sex:M (Child #2) 24 Sep 1920 George E O'Brien (Lowell,
  MA) & Mary E Abbertan (Lowell, MA)
O'BRYANT,Brian Earl Sex:M 18 Feb 1977 Michael W O'Bryant & Cynthia D Santoro
O'CONNELL,Kathleen M Sex:F 09 Jun 1965 Daniel K O'Connell & Geraldine E Wiley
O'CONNELL,Michael C Sex:M 07 Mar 1975 J Dennis O'Connell & Avis A Concannon
O'CONNOR,Daniel   Sex:M 26 Mar 1866 Hudson, NH John O'Connor & Lucy Clement
O'CONNOR,Daniel O Sex:M 26 Mar 1865 Hudson, NH John O O'Connor & Lucy
O'CONNOR,Erin Marie Sex:F 20 Jul 1979 Cornelius D O'Connor & Teresa L Hamelin
O'CONNOR,Michael Sean Sex:M 06 Jul 1984 John E O'Connor Jr & Cheryl Ann Lewis
O'DEA,Kathrine A Sex:F   25 Sep 1953 Thomas F O'Dea & Bernice Kerpluk
O'DELL,Kelley P Sex:F   03 Feb 1970 George L O'Dell & Harriet M Smith
O'DONAGHUE,Shawn Patrick Sex:M 08 Dec 1981 Charles J O'Donaghue
  & Barbara J Higham

HUDSON,NH BIRTHS

O'DONAGHUE,Timothy Charles   Sex:M   08 Dec 1981 Charles J O'Donaghue
   & Barbara J Higham
O'DONNELL,Timothy Stephen   Sex:M   09 Aug 1983 Thomas J O'Donnell
   & Gail E Lantagne
O'DOWD,Thomas T   Sex:M   12 Jun 1976 Thomas M O'Dowd & Rita M Tousignant
O'HARA,David K   Sex:M   21 Jun 1969 William P O'Hara & Mary A Driscoll
O'KEEFE,Rebecca Eaton Sex:F 25 Sep 1979 Edmond L O'Keefe & Linda Louise Koloc
O'KEEFE,Sarah Elizabeth   Sex:F   28 Apr 1982 Edmond L O'Keefe Jr
   & Linda Louise Koloc
O'LEARY,Megan Kathleen Sex:F   15 Jan 1984 Robert G O'Leary & Laura Y Ferreira
O'LOUGHLIN,Jamie J   Sex:M   03 Feb 1969 William J O'Loughlin
   & Carol A Laliberte
O'LOUGHLIN,Jeralyn G   Sex:F   12 Oct 1970 William J O'Loughlin
   & Carol A Laliberte
O'LOUGHLIN,Kara A Sex:F   31 Jul 1967 William J O'Loughlin & Carol A Laliberte
O'LOUGHLIN,Matthew P   Sex:M 15 Dec 1960 Thomas J O'Loughlin & Jeanne A Demers
O'LOUGHLIN,Thomas J   Sex:M   03 Jun 1958 Thomas J O'Loughlin & Jeanne A Demers
O'MEARA,Brian T   Sex:M   12 Apr 1966 Richard H O'Meara & Shirley A Benoit
O'MEARA,Marc C   Sex:M   14 Sep 1969 Richard H O'Meara & Shirley A Benoit
O'NEAL,James W   Sex:M   06 Apr 1956 Walter W O'Neal, Jr & Marjorie Hardy
O'NEAL,Nancy J   Sex:F   17 Jan 1955 Walter W O'Neal, Jr & Marjorie S Hardy
O'NEIL,Howard P   Sex:M   23 May 1948 Paul H O'Neil (Beverly, MA)
   & Ruth E Martin (Nashua, NH)
O'NEIL,Kathleen Ann   Sex:F   04 Apr 1984 Michael P O'Neil & Maureen A Malette
O'NEIL,Kevin B   Sex:M   06 Apr 1968 Owen B O'Neil & Carole-Ann Roberts
O'NEILL,Brian Stephen Sex:M 28 Apr 1984 Stephen J O'Neill & Mary D Francis
O'NEILL,Susan M   Sex:F   06 Apr 1957 Francis C O'Neill & Matilda Stawasz
OAK,Pandora J   Sex:F   06 Feb 1965 Norman E Oak & Earline L McKechnie
OBEN,Philip E   Sex:M   (Child #1) 31 Oct 1906 Charles F Oben (Beverly, MA)
   & Edith M Phillips (Lynn, MA)
OBER,Mahlon Escott   Sex:M   (Child #3) 16 Oct 1914 Charles F Ober (Beverly,
   MA) & Edith M Phillips (Lynn, MA)
OBER,Phillis E   Sex:F   (Child #2) 04 Feb 1908 Charles F Ober (Beverly, MA)
   & Edith M Phillips (Lynn, MA)
ODEKERK,William P   Sex:M   02 Jan 1893 Wm W Odekerk (Danville, VT)
   & Alice Davis (Concord, NH)
OEHLERT,David J   Sex:M   04 Sep 1970 John T Oehlert & Patricia A Barron
OGRABISZ,Alison Marie   Sex:F   15 Aug 1980 Lucian B Ograbisz & Donna M Hackett
OHMAN,Taren Leigh   Sex:F 19 Oct 1979 Timothy Alan Ohman & Brooks A Greenfield
OIKLE,Therese M   Sex:F   01 Feb 1964 Ronald F Oikle & Harriet J Sandelin
OLDFORD,Susan Ann   Sex:F   29 Jul 1979 William T Oldford & Judy Ann Brown
OLDFORD,Valerie K   Sex:F   18 Oct 1977 William T Oldford & Judy Ann Brown
OLEAD,Ernest W   Sex:M   (Child #1) 17 Jan 1909 William J Olead (Sciota, NY)
   & Ida M Santerre (Ayer Jct, MA)
OLENA,Virginia V   Sex:F   12 Apr 1947 Arthur R Olena (Nashua, NH)
   & V V LaFontaine (Nashua, NH)
OLGA,Matthew M   Sex:M   07 Feb 1965 Michael M Olga & Elizabeth B Detroia
OLIVER,Diane E   Sex:F   (Child #1) 11 Oct 1940 Carl D Oliver (Orange, MA)
   & Miriam Golden (Manchester, NH)
OLIVER,Donna M   Sex:F   07 Apr 1947 George K Oliver (Nashua, NH)
   & Katherine M Harwood (Nashua, NH)
OLIVER,Michele A   Sex:F   29 Sep 1956 Ernest A Oliver & Mary A Hall
OLSON,Richard E Jr   Sex:M   18 Jun 1965 Richard E Olson, Sr & Nancy L Lindsey
OLSZEWSKI,James M Sex:M 04 Jun 1978 William J Olszewski & Cynthia A Samowski
OLSZEWSKI,William J Sex:M 23 Oct 1976 William J Olszewski&Cynthia A Samowski
ONDERDONK,Jillian K   Sex:F   04 Aug 1977 Adrian D Onderdonk & Susan Jane Marrs
ORMSBY,Kevin M   Sex:M   07 Jul 1969 Jay L Ormsby & Kathleen A Murphy
OROWITZ,Joanne L   Sex:F   01 Oct 1966 Alfred H Orowitz & Maureen Nickles
OSBORN,Carol   Sex:F   (Child #3) 02 Jun 1915 Hudson, NH John H Osborn (Canada)
   & Evangeline Donovan (Arlington, MA)

HUDSON,NH BIRTHS

OSBORN,George Francis   Sex:M   (Child #1) 04 Oct 1911 John A D Osborn
  (Sherbrook, Canada) & Eva Donovan (Arlington, MA)
OSBORN,Paul Wilds   Sex:M   (Child #2) 27 Dec 1913 John Osborn (Sherbrook,
  Canada) & Eva Donovan (Arlington, MA)
OSBORNE, [Unknown]   Sex:F   19 Jun 1934 Norman Osborne (New Hampshire)
  & Edna Henderson (New Brunswick)
OSMER,Frank J   Sex:M   (Child #3) 08 Nov 1925 Frank J Osmer (Bridgewater, VT)
  & Olivene C Marvis (Canada)
OSMER,Karen J   Sex:F   03 Jan 1953 Frank J Osmer, Jr & Louise M Farley
OSMER,Kelly D   Sex:M   17 Mar 1956 Frank J Osmer, Jr & Louise M Farley
OSMER,Stephen R   Sex:M   27 Oct 1950 Frank J Osmer, Jr & Louise M Farley
OSTREICHER,Arica Beth   Sex:F   10 Sep 1979 Kim John Ostreicher & Ellen Dorner
OSTREICHER,Justen Kim   Sex:M   31 Oct 1982 Kim John Ostreicher & Ellen Dorner
OTIS,Naomi R   Sex:F   11 Apr 1980 David C Otis & Debra Ann Hughes
OTIS,Scott E   Sex: 24 Mar 1973 Lloyd E Otis Jr & Dorothy A Boyer
OTTMAN,Bradley A   Sex:M   16 Jan 1953 Herbert W Ottman & Rachel A Haskell
OTTMAN,Douglas P   Sex:M   15 Mar 1954 Herbert W Ottman & Rachel A Haskell
OTTMAN,Paul L   Sex:M   10 Dec 1957 Herbert W Ottman & Rachel A Haskell
OTTMAN,Timothy F   Sex:M   06 Jan 1956 Herbert W Ottman & Rachel A Haskell
OUELLET,Stephanie G   Sex:F   05 Mar 1976 Omer J Ouellet & Marie C Beaulieu
OUELLETT,Mary Eileen   Sex:F   (Child #2) 07 Feb 1929 Alfred P Ouellett
  (Nashua, NH) & Gertrude M Dudzisk (Poland)
OUELLETT,Robert John   Sex:M   (Child #1) 21 May 1927 Alfred Ouellett (Nashua,
  NH) & Gertrude Dudzick (Poland)
OUELLETTE,Elaine P Sex:F 27 Jan 1950 Auguste R Ouellette & Pauline G Laquerre
OUELLETTE,Jennifer Lee   Sex:F   21 Mar 1985 Daniel P Ouellette
  & Sandra A McAlpine
OUELLETTE,Jeremiah Lionel Sex:M 04 Sep 1982 Philip E Ouellette
  & Alecia Ann Asselin
OUELLETTE,Katie Ann   Sex:F   12 Jan 1981 Donald H Ouellette
  & Deborah A Rondeau
OUELLETTE,Melissa Ann Sex:F 28 Jan 1982 Paul R Ouellette & Louise I Plamondon
OUELLETTE,Nancy A   Sex:F   30 Dec 1952 Richard P Ouellette & Theresa A Chenell
OUELLETTE,Nathaniel Jon Sex:M 18 Jul 1977 John M Ouellette & Cheryl S Hetzer
OUELLETTE,Nicole Marie   Sex:F   12 Jul 1983 Daniel P Ouellette
  & Sandra Ann McAlpine
OUELLETTE,Paula Marie Sex:F 29 Jan 1981 Grant E Ouellette & Patricia L Mayer
OUELLETTE,Roland E   Sex:M   07 Jul 1948 Auguste R Ouellette (Dracut, MA)
  & Pauline G Laquerre (Hudson, NH)
OUILLETTE,Noreen C D   Sex:F   (Child #1) 10 Apr 1933   & Yvette Ouillette
  (Oldtown, ME)
OUIMET,Noemi A   Sex: 05 Jun 1973 Douglas P Ouimet & Sheila A Murphy
OVASKA,Ruth E   Sex:F   04 Jun 1949 Otis G Ovaska & Elizabeth S Field
OWENS,James Michael   Sex:M   24 Aug 1980 David James Owens & Rosemarie L Hart
PACIELLO,Shane Michael   Sex:M   02 Nov 1982 Michael G Paciello & Kim A West
PACKOR,Mary E   Sex:F   (Child #1) 07 Dec 1942 Edward J Packor (Nashua, NH)
  & Ruth A Reynolds (Nashua, NH)
PACZAN,Holly Joelle   Sex:F   26 Jan 1981 Michael W Paczan & Linda J Jakubowski
PAGE,Abraham   Sex:M   23 Jan 1761 Hudson, NH Samuel Page & Sarah Cummings
PAGE,Aurelia Spalding   Sex:F   11 Sep 1848 Hudson, NH William Page & Phebe G
PAGE,Benjamin   Sex:M   08 Sep 1766 Hudson, NH Samuel Page & Sarah Cummings
PAGE,David S   Sex:M   30 Apr 1962 James Page & Beverly M Thomas
PAGE,Dustin James   Sex:M   10 Sep 1982 Steven Peter Page & Janice Ann McKean
PAGE,Elizabeth   Sex:F   29 Oct Hudson, NH Samuel Page & Sarah Cummings
PAGE,Elizabeth   Sex:F   29 Oct 17 Hudson, NH Samuel Page & Sarah
PAGE,Ephraim   Sex:M   24 Feb 1765 Hudson, NH Samuel Page & Sarah Cummings
PAGE,Esther   Sex:F   02 Nov 1751 Hudson, NH Samuel Page & Esther
PAGE,Hannah   Sex:F   10 Aug 1755 Hudson, NH Samuel Page & Esther
PAGE,Hannah   Sex:F   10 Aug 1758 Hudson, NH Samuel Page & Esther
PAGE,James   Sex:M   25 Apr 1773 Hudson, NH Samuel Page & Sarah Cummings

HUDSON,NH BIRTHS

PAGE,Molle   Sex:F   06 Apr 1769 Hudson, NH Samuel Page & Sarah
PAGE,Molly   Sex:F   06 Apr 1769 Hudson, NH Samuel Page & Sarah Cummings
PAGE,Rebecca Sex:F   17 Aug 1753 Hudson, NH Samuel Page & Esther
PAGE,Rebeckah   Sex:F   17 Aug 1753 Hudson, NH Samuel Page & Esther
PAGE,Samuel   Sex:M   10 Jun 1771 Hudson, NH Samuel Page & Sarah Cummings
PAGE,Sarah   Sex:F   10 Jul 1759 Hudson, NH Samuel Page & Sarah Cummings
PAGE,Susan Elizabeth   Sex:F   11 Dec 1844 Hudson, NH William Page & Phebe G
PAIGE,Elaine Lovilla   Sex:F   (Child #1) 20 Mar 1933 George Sidney Paige
   (Nashua, NH) & Helen Burns (Nashua, NH)
PAINE,John   Sex:M   08 Dec 1873 Hudson, NH Peter Paine & Bridget
PALADINO,Anthony J Jr   Sex:M   11 Jul 1956 Anthony J Paladino
   & Rita Y Lamoureux
PALEVICIUS,Anthony J   Sex:M   05 Aug 1971 Alphonse F Palevicius
   & Elaine C Morency
PALEVICIUS,Laura A   Sex:F   29 May 1967 Alphonse F Palevicius
   & Elaine C Morency
PALEVICIUS,Lynn M Sex:F   13 Dec 1968 Alphonse F Palevicius & Elaine C Morency
PALEVICIUS,Sharon E   Sex: 26 Oct 1972 Alphonse F Paleviciu & Elaine C Morency
PALMER,Carol Rina Sex:F   02 Jun 1984 James Sidney Palmer & Rinette M Bouchard
PALMER,Charles W Jr   Sex:M   05 Jan 1963 Charles W Palmer & Joanne R Almeida
PALMER,Cheryl L   Sex:F   12 Nov 1964 Charles W Palmer & Joanne A Almeida
PALMER,Danielle Rinette   Sex:F   15 Jul 1980 James Palmer & Rinette M Bouchard
PALMER,Frank   Sex:M   01 Dec 1863 Hudson, NH Sidney H Palmer & Mary E Greeley
PALMER,John E   Sex:M   01 Jul 1959 George R Palmer & Edna M Hull
PALMER,Joyce E   Sex:F   27 May 1957 George R Palmer & Edna M Hull
PALMER,Krystal Jade   Sex:F   23 Nov 1984 Ralph C Palmer Jr & Lauri L Bourgeois
PALMER,Nicholas Ian   Sex:M   28 Jan 1985 Ian David Palmer & Georgia Lynn Snell
PALMER,Sarah   Sex:F   02 Mar 1744 Hudson, NH Benjamin Palmer & Martha
PALMERI,Jonathan Nicholas   Sex:M   04 Nov 1984 Mario N Palmeri & Laurie Heald
PANAGEOTES,[Unknown]   Sex:M   30 Mar 1955 Alexander K Panageot & Nancy Howard
PANAGOULAS,Charles Jr   Sex:M   (Child #4) 05 Aug 1945 Charles Panagoulas
   (Greece) & Rita Koufopoulas (Beverly, MA)
PANAGOULIAS,[Unknown]   Sex:M   (Child #4) 22 Oct 1942 Charles E Panagoulis
   (Greece) & Rita Kofopoulos (Beverly, MA)
PANAGOULIS,Christine   Sex:F   24 Oct 1947 Charles E Panagoulis (Greece)
   & Rita Koufopoulos (Beverly, MA)
PANAGOULIS,[Unknown]   Sex:M   (Child #2) 25 Oct 1936 Chas Ernest Panagou
   (Greece) & Rita Koufopoulis (Beverly, MA)
PAPPAL,Adrienne Lee Sex:F 01 Sep 1979 Samuel John Pappal & Patricia A Carbone
PAPPAL,Sherilyn Rose Sex:F 22 Jun 1984 Samuel J Pappal & Patricia A Carbone
PAPPALARDO,Kala Lynn Sex:F 03 Nov 1984 Joseph A Pappalardo
   & Cheryl Ann Rodgers
PAPPALARDO,Kara Mia   Sex:F   03 Nov 1984 Joseph A Pappalardo
   & Cheryl Ann Rodgers
PAPPALARDO,Kyle J Sex:M   24 Dec 1982 Joseph A Pappalardo & Cheryl Ann Rodgers
PAPPAS,Nicole C   Sex:F   07 May 1972 John N Pappas & Rosemarie B Lebel
PAQUETTE,Anne M   Sex:F   20 Mar 1959 Donald Paquette & Therese Vallerand
PAQUETTE,Deborah A Sex:F   03 Aug 1963 Donald E Paquette & Therese I Vallerand
PAQUETTE,Denise T   Sex:F   06 Dec 1961 Donald E Paquette & Therese I Vallerand
PAQUETTE,Georgianna E   Sex:F   (Child #3) 09 Nov 1931 Joseph F Paquette
   (Nashua, NH) & Elma Lefebvre (Nashua, NH)
PAQUETTE,James D   Sex:M   26 Dec 1975 Gerard A Paquette & Diane E Couturier
PAQUETTE,Joseph E   Sex:M   19 Aug 1967 Donald E Paquette & Therese I Vallerand
PAQUETTE,Linda J Sex:F   (Child #1) 16 Aug 1944 Albert J Paquette (Nashua, NH)
   & Rita C Bourgault (Nashua, NH)
PAQUETTE,Maurice G Sex:M   20 Aug 1973 Gerard A Paquette & Diane E Couturier
PAQUETTE,Steven L   Sex:M   09 Apr 1951 Joseph L Paquette & Adeline Nichols
PAQUIN,Allen Michael   Sex:M   18 Oct 1981 Real A Paquin & Marlene M Levesque
PAQUIN,Dennis James   Sex:M   18 May 1985 Real A Paquin & Marlene M Levesque
PAQUIN,Edward L   Sex:M   16 Jan 1966 Charles E Paquin & Ann N Flynn

HUDSON,NH BIRTHS

PAQUIN,Holly Ann Sex:F 18 May 1983 Jeffrey A Paquin Jr & Connie Gail Lavoie
PAQUIN,Jeffrey Gilbert Sex:M 08 Nov 1983 Real A Paquin & Marlena M Levesque
PAQUIN,Steven A Sex:M 21 Jan 1968 Charles E Paquin & Ann N Flynn
PARADIAS,Theresa Jean Sex:F (Child #1) 03 Mar 1931 Favius Paradais (Canada)
  & Beatrice St Laurier (Massachusetts)
PARADIS,Matthew D Sex:M 11 Feb 1975 Paul M Paradis & Patricia A Langelier
PARADISE,Alice M Sex:F 14 Dec 1971 Ernest O Paradise & Dolores C Maynard
PARADISE,Bryan Maurice Sex:M 19 Oct 1983 Maurice A Paradise
  & Pauline L Marquis
PARADISE,Claire M Sex:F (Child #1) 23 Aug 1943 Conrad J Paradise (Nashua,
  NH) & Clarice A (Nashua, NH)
PARADISE,Jason M Sex:M 15 Nov 1970 Normand J Paradise & Candace A Dearborn
PARADISE,Joseph E O Sex:M (Child #3) 31 Aug 1942 Joseph A L Paradise
  (Nashua, NH) & Mary B Bernard (Hudson, NH)
PARADISE,Joshua G Sex: 26 May 1973 Normand J Paradise & Candace A Dearborn
PARADISE,Lisa M Sex:F 05 Dec 1970 Ernest O Paradise & Dolores C Maynard
PARADISE,Normand J Jr Sex:M 26 Jan 1976 Normand J Paradise Sr
  & Candice A Dearborn
PARADISE,Roger E Sex:M 28 Oct 1973 Ernest O Paradise & Dolores C Maynard
PARDEE,Jennifer A Sex:F 24 Nov 1973 Jay J Pardee & Jean Ann Schell
PARDEE,Jocelyn Ann Sex:F 06 Nov 1979 Jay James Pardee & Jean Ann Schell
PARE,Christine A Sex:F 21 Mar 1969 Julien Pare & Helen Boulet
PARE,Daniel Sex:M 01 Jul 1962 Arthur L Pare & Collette E Marquis
PARE,Lisa A Sex:F 06 Nov 1964 Arthur L Pare & Collette E Marquis
PARE,Marie C A Sex:F 19 Dec 1970 Julien Pare & Marie E Boulet
PARENT,Aaron William Marc Sex:M 03 Apr 1981 Marc Robert Parent
  & Cathy A Groenendal
PARENT,Amanda Lynn Sex:F 09 Dec 1981 Richard David Parent & Darlene Braccio
PARENT,Angela Beth Sex:F 06 Jun 1982 Michael S Parent & Carol Ann Ladue
PARENT,Christine Sex:F 01 Sep 1978 Kenneth A Parent & Pamela Sue Boyle
PARENT,Dawn M Sex:F 29 Jun 1971 Donald P Parent & Mayre F Benoit
PARENT,Mandy Sex:F 23 Mar 1975 Donald P Parent & Mayre F Benoit
PARENT,Sean Kenneth Sex:M 13 Apr 1976 Kenneth A Parent & Pamela Sue Boyle
PARENT,Tricia A Sex:F 10 Apr 1972 Chester R Parent & Judith M Snyder
PAREY,Judith Sex:F 25 Apr 1780 Hudson, NH Joseph Parey & Olive
PARILLO,Allison Britt Sex:F 15 Oct 1982 Kevin Frank Parillo
  & Patricia J Visokay
PARISEAU,Claire Germaine Sex:F (Child #2) 20 Jan 1930 Eugene Pariseau
  (Holyoke, MA) & Germaine Leclerc (Canada)
PARISEAU,Pauline Alice Sex:F (Child #3) 06 Jan 1936 Eugene Pariseau
  (Holyoke, MA) & Germaine Leclerc (Canada)
PARKER,Brenda M Sex:F (Child #2) 01 Jul 1946 Philip A Parker (Ft Fairfield,
  ME) & Orise M Mitchell (Hooksett, NH)
PARKER,Charles C Sex:M (Child #3) 04 Jun 1901 Hudson, NH Clarence C Parker
  (Hudson, NH) & Hattie L Robinson (Hudson, NH)
PARKER,Evelyne Elizabeth Sex:F (Child #4) 01 Sep 1907 Phineas A Parker
  (Pepperell, MA) & Lillian M Dekocher (Malone, NY)
PARKER,George H Sex:M 29 Oct 1879 Hudson, NH Charles Parker
  & Lydia Batchelder (Hudson, NH)
PARKER,George Henry Sex:M (Child #2) 03 Feb 1912 George H Parker (Hudson,
  NH) & Edith Snow (Boston, MA)
PARKER,Gerald R Sex:M 25 Sep 1965 Raymond E Parker & June Brickett
PARKER,Hope W Sex:F (Child #1) 12 May 1890 Charles S Parker (Moores, NY)
  & Jennie C Winn (Hudson, NH)
PARKER,John Sex:M (Child #1) 01 Apr 1907 Gerry F Parker (Hudson, NH)
  & Georgia Boynton (Bromfield, MA)
PARKER,Karen J Sex:F 22 Mar 1952 Philip A Parker & Orise M Mitchell
PARKER,Kathleen A Sex:F 19 Feb 1958 Raymond E Parker & June Brickett
PARKER,Lillie Ernestine Sex:F (Child #2) 28 Aug 1898 Clarence C Parker
  (Hudson, NH) & Hat L Robinson (Hudson, NH)

HUDSON,NH BIRTHS

PARKER,Linda E   Sex:F   20 Apr 1947 Alden S Parker (Ft Fairfield, ME)
  & Marion A Post (Westfield, ME)
PARKER,Lydia J   Sex:F   28 Jul 1877 Hudson, NH Charles C Parker (Warrin)
  & Lydia L Batchelder (Hudson, NH)
PARKER,Mabel C   Sex:F   22 Aug 1867 Hudson, NH Emery Parker & Clara K
PARKER,Madeline E   Sex:F   (Child #3) 07 Apr 1905 Phineas A Parker (Pepperell,
  MA) & Lillian M Derochia (Malone, NY)
PARKER,Marilyn Hattie   Sex:F   (Child #1) 31 Jan 1936 Charles C Parker
  (Hudson, NH) & Ruth Blood (Nashua, NH)
PARKER,Ralph Edwin   Sex:M   (Child #1) 07 Apr 1936 John E Parker (Nashua, NH)
  & Grace Connell (Hudson, NH)
PARKER,Rodney S   Sex:M   02 Oct 1960 Raymond E Parker & June Brickett
PARKER,Sara Lyn   Sex:F   29 Jan 1974 Philip J Parker & Sheila Ann Nutting
PARKER,Steven W   Sex:M   10 May 1952 Winston C Parker & Dorothy L Murphy
PARKER,Vicki L   Sex:F   05 Jun 1964 David N Parker & Sandra L Stillings
PARKER,Wendy A   Sex:F   01 Nov 1969 Philip J Parker & Sheila A Nutting
PARKER,William   Sex:M   25 Aug 1795 Hudson, NH Farwell Parker & Olive
PARKER, [Unknown]   Sex:F   (Child #1) 03 Jul 1910 Geo H Parker (Hudson, NH)
  & Edith F Snow (Boston, MA)
PARKER, [Unknown]   Sex:M   21 Feb 1871 Hudson, NH Emery Parker & Clarisa H
PARKHURST,Brandi R   Sex:F   21 Nov 1975 Michael P Parkhurst
  & Darlene E Charette
PARKHURST,Matthew S   Sex:M   09 Feb 1967 Charles F Parkhurst & Mary I Page
PARKHURST,Michelle P   Sex:F   24 Nov 1971 Michael P Parkhurst
  & Darlene E Charette
PARKINSON,Herbert J   Sex:M   (Child #2) 13 Mar 1887 John Parkinson (Ireland)
  & Amelia Groves (Ireland)
PARKS,Dean A Jr   Sex:M   16 Mar 1965 Dean A Parks, Sr & Patricia A Comeau
PARKS,Karen A   Sex:F   23 Oct 1971 Dean A Parks & Patricia A Comeau
PARKS,Michele A   Sex:F   09 Apr 1969 Dean A Parks & Patricia A Comeau
PAROLOSKI,Peter   Sex:M   (Child #7) 16 Dec 1921 Anthony Paroloski (Russia)
  & Nadja Belchico (Russia)
PARONTO,Keith P   Sex:M   02 Mar 1964 Kenneth W Paronto & Kathleen M Walsh
PARONTO,Kerry A   Sex:M   22 Feb 1970 Kenneth W Paronto & Kathleen M Walsh
PARR,Michael W   Sex:M   15 Aug 1953 Albert M Parr & Pauline R Fish
PARSONS,Donald E   Sex:M   10 Jun 1949 Elliot W Parsons & Bernice M Nichols
PARSONS,Elliot D   Sex:M   12 Feb 1947 Elliot W Parsons (Gloucester, MA)
  & Bernice M Nichols (Nashua, NH)
PASKALI,James A   Sex:M   01 Aug 1961 Louis Paskali & Doris L Lambert
PASKO,Michael Joseph   Sex:M   30 Apr 1982 Gerald V Pasko & Michelle J Anglum
PASKO,Patricia Ann   Sex:F   06 Oct 1980 Gerald V Pasko & Michelle J Anglum
PATCH,Arthur G   Sex:M   22 Jan 1882 Hudson, NH O S Patch (Hollis, NH)
  & Fannie J Cory (Boston, MA)
PATE,Andrea Louise   Sex:F   02 Jan 1982 Jerry Wayne Pate & Susan C Staples
PATENAUDE,Amanda Marion   Sex:F   26 Mar 1981 Michael J Patenaude
  & Susan R Thibault
PATENAUDE,John Abel   Sex:M   29 Nov 1976 John L Patenaude & Suzanne M Smith
PATENAUDE,Sarah Lynn   Sex:F   23 Jun 1978 John L Patenaude & Suzanne M Smith
PATENAUDE,Theresa Jean   Sex:F   11 Dec 1981 John L Patenaude & Suzanne M Smith
PATIENT,Tina C   Sex:F   04 Jun 1971 Andre R Patient & Therese F Vandal
PATRIQUIN,Kenneth W   Sex:M   03 Jun 1954 Lawrence W Patriquin & Louise M Clarke
PATTEN,Amy L   Sex:F   02 Mar 1969 Raymond E Patten & Elaine A Duplease
PATTEN,Betsey   Sex:F   29 Jan 1802 Hudson, NH Cochran Patten & Martha
PATTEN,Betty   Sex:F   29 Jan 1802 Hudson, NH Cochran Patten & Martha
PATTEN,Cochran   Sex:M   21 Aug 1804 Hudson, NH Cochran Patten & Martha
PATTEN,Cochran   Sex:M   21 Apr 1804 Hudson, NH Cochran Patten & Martha
PATTEN,Cynthia A   Sex:F   11 Jul 1962 Allen F Patten & Gloria A Gilcreast
PATTEN,Dawn Marie   Sex:F   11 Mar 1978 Roger E Patten & Denise G Duplease
PATTEN,Ella Mabel   Sex:F   (Child #9) 10 Feb 1939 Clarence E Patten
  (Alexandria, NH) & Nellie A Nutting (Kennebunk,

HUDSON,NH BIRTHS

PATTEN,Gloria Hope Sex:F (Child #7) 29 Jan 1932 Hudson, NH Clarence E Patten
  (Alexandria, NH) & Nettie A Nutting (Kennebunk, ME)
PATTEN,Hugh   Sex:M   26 Aug 1793 Hudson, NH Cochran Patten & Martha
PATTEN,Hugh Smith   Sex:M   26 Aug 1793 Hudson, NH Cochran Patten & Martha
PATTEN,Jean   Sex: 20 Apr 1799 Hudson, NH Cochran Patten & Martha
PATTEN,Jenessa M   Sex:F   17 Sep 1975 Michael A Patten & Mary J Kuchinski
PATTEN,Jennifer E   Sex:F   07 Mar 1968 Raymond E Patten & Elaine A Duplease
PATTEN,Joanna   Sex:F   20 Apr 1799 Hudson, NH Cochran Patten & Martha
PATTEN,John   Sex:M   14 Jun 1791 Hudson, NH Cochran Patten & Martha
PATTEN,John P   Sex: 15 Feb 1973 Roger E Patten & Denise G Duplease
PATTEN,Lisa M   Sex:F   25 Apr 1971 Raymond E Patten & Elaine A Duplease
PATTEN,Mark S   Sex:M   06 Jan 1966 Victor R Patten & May J Henderson
PATTEN,Nabby   Sex:F   26 Jul 1788 Hudson, NH Cochran Patten & Martha
PATTEN,Nabey   Sex: 26 Jul 1788 Hudson, NH Cochran Patten & Martha
PATTEN,Raymond Arthur   Sex:M   (Child #8) 31 Dec 1934 Clarence E Patten
  (Alexandria, NH) & Nettie A Nutting (Kennebunk, ME)
PATTEN,Richard E   Sex:M   24 Jan 1961 Harold A Patten & Dorothy I Creighton
PATTEN,Robert C   Sex:M   02 Aug 1796 Hudson, NH Cochran Patten & Martha
PATTEN,Robert Cochran   Sex:M   02 Aug 1796 Hudson, NH Cochran Patten & Martha
PATTEN,Samuel C   Sex:M   25 Jan 1809 Hudson, NH Cochran Patten & Martha
PATTEN,Samuel Cochran   Sex:M   25 Jan 1809 Hudson, NH Cochran Patten & Martha
PATTEN,Shannon Marie Sex:F 21 Sep 1981 Robin L Patten & Diane Marie Paradise
PATTEN,Tammey A   Sex:F   30 Aug 1959 Harold A Patten & Dorothy I Creighton
PATTERSON,Benjamin J   Sex: 11 Dec 1972 James E Patterson & Christine E Reid
PATTERSON,John T III   Sex:M   28 Oct 1966 John T Patterson Jr
  & Brenda M Zagorites
PAUK,Christina L   Sex:F   22 May 1967 Richard E Pauk & Sandra L Landry
PAUL,George Walter   Sex:M   (Child #3) 14 May 1933 Amedee J Paul (Nashua, NH)
  & Ruth Rochelle (Concord, NH)
PAUL,Jenna Ruth   Sex:F   19 Dec 1984 Brian James Paul & Ruth Ellen Anderson
PAUL,Marissa W   Sex:F   27 Apr 1958 George W Paul & Mary E Stephens
PAUL,Mark S   Sex:M   29 Mar 1957 George W Paul & Mary E Stephens
PAULHUS,Colleen   Sex:F   11 Feb 1977 Raymond G Paulhus & Pauline J Richard
PAULHUS,Jenifer   Sex:F   06 Oct 1978 Raymond G Paulhus & Pauline J Richard
PAVLOSKY,Brandy Marie Sex:F 24 Oct 1976 John Pavlosky Jr & Marie P R Boucher
PAVLOSKY,Dawna L   Sex:F   16 Dec 1974 John Pavlosky Jr & Marie Phyllis R Bouc
PAVLOSKY,Jacki A   Sex:F   03 Nov 1966 John Pavlosky, Jr & Rena P Boucher
PAYETTE,Tabatha A   Sex:F   17 Mar 1971 Marshall G Payette & Wendy J Bell
PEABODY,Isabel   Sex:F   09 May 1784 Hudson, NH   & Rachel Merrill
PEABODY,Jennifer Lynn Sex:F 08 Apr 1984 Richard A Peabody II & Carol A Beaucher
PEABODY,John   Sex:M   02 Feb 1787 Hudson, NH David Peabody Jr & Eunice
PEABODY,Moody   Sex:M   12 May 1789 Hudson, NH David Peabody Jr & Eunice
PEACH,Ernest C   Sex:M   14 Oct 1886 William Peach & Dora B
PEARCE,James   Sex:M   30 May 1792 Hudson, NH Joshua Pearce & Sally
PEARCE,John   Sex:M   22 Apr 1785 Hudson, NH Joshua Pearce & Sally
PEARCE,Joseph   Sex:M   04 Dec 1794 Hudson, NH Joshua Pearce & Sally
PEARCE,Joshua   Sex:M   09 Jul 1787 Hudson, NH Joshua Pearce & Sally
PEARCE,Robert   Sex:M   05 Oct 1790 Hudson, NH Daniel Pearce & Hannah
PEARL,Cheryl J   Sex:F   16 Nov 1950 Harold R Pearl & Ina G Kierstead
PEARL,Holly A   Sex:F   23 May 1954 Harold R Pearl & Ina G Kierstead
PECK,Meritt Augustus   Sex:M   (Child #2) 06 Jan 1907 George I Peck
  (North Adams, MA) & Edith M Greeley (Hudson, NH)
PEEL,[Unknown]   Sex:F   06 Jun 1978 Chris C Peel & Donna Jean Misch
PELKEY,Anthony V   Sex:M   27 Aug 1948 Raymond A Pelkey (Nashua, NH)
  & Trinidad Benavidez (Santa Fe, NM)
PELKEY,Dean M   Sex:M   14 Aug 1951 Raymond A Pelkey & Trinidad Benavides
PELKEY,Doreen L   Sex:F   26 May 1955 Raymond A Pelkey & Trinidad Benavediz
PELKEY,Linda I   Sex:F   08 Mar 1950 Raymond A Pelkey & Trinidad Benavidez
PELKEY,Robert R   Sex:M   (Child #1) 31 Aug 1946 Raymond A Pelkey (Nashua, NH)
  & Trinidad Penavides (Sante Fe, NM)

HUDSON,NH BIRTHS

PELLERIN,Michael R H   Sex:M   04 Oct 1974 Roger J Pellerin & Linda J Bausemer
PELLERIN,Scott R   Sex:M   23 Dec 1969 Roger J Pellerin & Linda J Bausemer
PELLETIER,Amanda A   Sex:F   (Child #3) 22 Mar 1908 Lewis Pelletier (Canada)
   & Marie L Roy (Canada)
PELLETIER,Arlene R   Sex:F   18 Dec 1952 Lawrence J Pelletier & Rita M Soucy
PELLETIER,Cheryl A Sex:F   01 Feb 1968 Normand L Pelletier & Theresa P Lussier
PELLETIER,Christopher R Sex:M 24 Feb 1970 Roland H Pelletier&Sharrel L Daigle
PELLETIER,Corinne T   Sex:F   (Child #6) 09 Jul 1944 Lawrence J Pelletier (Van
   Buren, ME) & Rita M Soucy (Van Buren, ME)
PELLETIER,Daniel L   Sex:M   07 May 1957 Lawrence J Pelletier & Rita M Soucy
PELLETIER,David L   Sex:M   14 Mar 1954 Lawrence J Pelletier & Rita M Soucy
PELLETIER,Dennis L   Sex:M   22 Jun 1949 Lawrence J Pelletier & Rita M Soucy
PELLETIER,Gerard L   Sex:M   04 Dec 1958 Lawrence J Pelletier & Rita M Soucy
PELLETIER,Gregory Robert   Sex:M   08 Jan 1981 Robert R Pelletier
   & Paula L Levesque
PELLETIER,Jacqueline A Sex:F   23 Apr 1958 Raymond A Pelletier & Rita L Gagnon
PELLETIER,James L   Sex:M   20 Feb 1963 Lawrence J Pelletier & Rita M Soucy
PELLETIER,Jason Andrew Sex:M   08 Jan 1984 Paul N Pelletier & Sandra M Peaslee
PELLETIER,Jason H   Sex:M   12 Apr 1980 Normand R Pelletier & JoAnne Efthymiou
PELLETIER,Jennifer R   Sex:F   21 Sep 1976 Raymond H Pelletier & Claire T Neveu
PELLETIER,Jessica Rose   Sex:F   16 Nov 1976 Maurice H Pelletier
   & Linda Marie McDonald
PELLETIER,Karen Marie Sex:F 02 Jul 1980 Maurice H Pelletier
   & Linda M McDonald
PELLETIER,Keith R   Sex:M   11 May 1974 Richard R Pelletier & Patricia A Vacca
PELLETIER,Leslie G A   Sex:F   05 Mar 1958 George H Pelletier & Betty R Blaney
PELLETIER,Linda T   Sex:F   02 Sep 1954 Roland E Pelletier & Aurore C Soucy
PELLETIER,Louis P Sex:M   10 Oct 1953 Marcel L Pelletier & Marguerite C Ledoux
PELLETIER,Maureen C   Sex:F   13 Jan 1966 Victor J Pelletier & Kathleen Walsh
PELLETIER,Maurice H Sex:M 22 Mar 1949 Marcel L Pelletier&Marguerite C Ledoux
PELLETIER,Milynda-Jo   Sex:F   18 Oct 1968 Michael R Pelletier & Judith M Gay
PELLETIER,Nicole Lynne Sex:F 25 May 1976 Roland H Pelletier&Sharrel L Daigle
PELLETIER,Norman P   Sex:M   (Child #6) 04 Sep 1945 Lawrence J Pelletier (Van
   Buren, ME) & Rita M Soucy (Van Buren, ME)
PELLETIER,Pamela A   Sex:F   25 Feb 1964 Rudolph N Pelletier
   & Lucille R Vaillancourt
PELLETIER,Paul L   Sex:M   18 May 1947 Lawrence J Pelletier (Van Buren, ME)
   & Rita M Soucy (Van Buren, ME)
PELLETIER,Pauline J   Sex:F   05 Jun 1948 Lawrence J Pelletier (Van Buren, ME)
   & Rita M Soucy (Van Buren, ME)
PELLETIER,Raymond L   Sex:M   31 Jul 1960 Lawrence J Pelletier & Rita M Soucy
PELLETIER,Rebecca Anne Sex:F 08 Jan 1981 Robert R Pelletier&Paula L Levesque
PELLETIER,Richard L   Sex:M   15 Oct 1951 Lawrence J Pelletier & Rita M Soucy
PELLETIER,Robert N   Sex:M   (Child #4) 23 Jul 1946 Roland E Pelletier
   (Karaboe, ME) & Aurora C Soucy (Van Buren, ME)
PELLETIER,Ronald L   Sex:M   08 Jul 1955 Lawrence J Pelletier & Rita M Soucy
PELLETIER,Sandra A   Sex:F   07 Aug 1947 Roland E Pelletier (Van Buren, ME)
   & Aurore C Soucy (Van Buren, ME)
PELLETIER,Scott L   Sex: 18 Nov 1972 Leo O Pelletier & Laura A Spencer
PELLETIER,Scott R   Sex:M   15 Jun 1975 Richard R Pelletier & Rachel E B Lebrun
PELLETIER,Shane N   Sex:M   05 Apr 1974 Normand R Pelletier & Nadine E Daigle
PELLETIER,Shawn J   Sex:M   12 Feb 1969 Victor J Pelletier & Kathleen T Walsh
PELLETIER,Shawna N   Sex:F   03 May 1977 Normand R Pelletier & Nadine E Daigle
PELLETIER,Susan L   Sex:F   25 Jun 1962 Roland E Pelletier & Aurore C Soucy
PELLETIER,Suzanne R   Sex:F   16 Dec 1948 Raymond A Pelletier (Nashua, NH)
   & Rita L Gagnon (Nashua, NH)
PELLETIER,Tammy J   Sex:F   26 Mar 1971 Thomas F Pelletier & Joan V Bedore
PELLETIER,Tammy Jo   Sex:F   04 Nov 1975 Paul L Pelletier Sr & Elaine T Weeks
PELLETIER,Theresa Jeanette   Sex:F   (Child #2) 23 Jul 1928 Telesphore
   Pelletier (Canada) & Irene Savoie (Canada)

HUDSON,NH BIRTHS

PELLETIER,Thomas P Jr   Sex:M   27 Nov 1967 Thomas P Pelletier & Joan V Bedore
PELLETIER,Travis W   Sex:M   17 Feb 1974 Roland H Pelletier & Sharrel L Daigle
PELT,Max Jr   Sex:M   15 Dec 1947 Max Pelt (Norway) & Annette H Jackson
  (Nashua, NH)
PEMBERTON,Abel   Sex:M   22 Jun 1774 Hudson, NH James Pemberton & Rachel
PEMBERTON,John   Sex:M   06 Sep 1782 Hudson, NH James Pemberton & Rachel
PEMBERTON,Rachel   Sex:F   14 Nov 1771 Hudson, NH James Pemberton & Rachel
PEMBERTON,William   Sex:M   09 Mar 1780 Hudson, NH James Pemberton & Rachel
PENO,Steven G   Sex:M   01 Jun 1967 Normand C Peno & Lucy M Dallaire
PEPIN,Arthur P   Sex:M   24 Jun 1965 Raymond O Pepin & Dorothy M Jalbert
PEPIN,Briand K   Sex:M   30 Mar 1978 John F Pepin & Laura Anne Cloutier
PEPIN,Deborah M   Sex:F   14 Oct 1962 Raymond O Pepin & Dorothy M Jalbert
PEPIN,Diane L   Sex:F   12 May 1965 Richard L Pepin & Priscilla F Tremblay
PEPIN,John A   Sex:M   12 Dec 1974 John F Pepin & Laura A Cloutier
PEPIN,Katherine A   Sex:F   11 Jul 1964 Raymond O Pepin & Dorothy M Jalbert
PERHAM,Hannah   Sex:F   01 Jul 1743 Hudson, NH John Perham & Hannah
PERKINS,Alicia E   Sex:F   21 Jul 1973 Richard W Perkins Jr & Elaine D Tefts
PERKINS,Annie Madeline   Sex:F   (Child #2) 10 Jul 1917 John H Perkins
  (Cambridge, MA) & Marion H Sanders (Nashua, NH)
PERKINS,Dorothy Gertrude   Sex:F   (Child #5) 11 Nov 1911 Osborn Murray Perkins
  (Providence, RI) & Gertrude Osborn (Sherbrook)
PERKINS,Jennifer A   Sex:F   25 Aug 1970 Richard W Perkins Jr & Elaine D Tefts
PERKINS,Karl Linden   Sex:M   (Child #11) 04 Mar 1933 Fred Perkins (Claremont,
  NH) & Ethel Cobbett (Wilton, NH)
PERKINS,Laura Beth   Sex:F   16 Aug 1979 Richard W Perkins Jr & Elaine Tefts
PERKINS,Shirley Hayden   Sex:F   (Child #2) 04 Oct 1922 Herbert S Perkins
  (Conway, NH) & May E Sherburn (Canaan, NH)
PERREAULT,Paul J   Sex:M   (Child #1) 07 Jun 1946 Joseph O Perreault
  (Rollinsford, NH) & Ruth Morning (Lowell, MA)
PERRON,Jason Robert   Sex:M   09 Feb 1978 Robert N Perron & Sharon J Neal
PERRON,Kelcey Anne   Sex:F   21 Dec 1978 Daniel R Perron & Candice B Jutras
PERRON,Mildred D   Sex:F   (Child #3) 22 Apr 1940 Wilfred J Perron (Chelsea,
  MA) & Dorothy D Foster (Boston, MA)
PERRY,David M   Sex:M   17 Apr 1962 Bruce L Perry & Rita G Labrecque
PERRY,Fiore   Sex: 29 Dec 1774 Hudson, NH Ebenezer Perry & Dolly
PERRY,Isaac   Sex:M   29 Dec 1774 Hudson, NH Ebenezer Perry & Dolly
PERRY,Jefferson Ford   Sex:M   20 Jun 1804 Hudson, NH & Judith Perry
PERRY,Judith   Sex:F   25 Apr 1780 Hudson, NH Joseph Perry & Olive
PERRY,Robin M   Sex:F   22 Jun 1964 Bruce L Perry & Rita G Labrecque
PERRY,Stephen W   Sex: 17 Apr 1973 William A Perry & Myrna J Bahnsen
PETERS,Brooke Anna   Sex:F   29 Oct 1981 Scott Peters & Patricia Ann Burns
PETERS,Charles E   Sex:M   22 Dec 1961 Larry D Peters & Erma E Foster
PETERS,Cheryl A   Sex:F   15 Dec 1959 Larry D Peters & Erma E Foster
PETERS,Dale M   Sex:M   27 Aug 1943 Harry C Peters (W W'am, NH) & Pearl L Otis
  (Winchendon, MA)
PETERS,Gary D   Sex:M   21 Mar 1975 Richard P Peters Sr & Elaine T Lessard
PETERS,Mandy Holloman   Sex:F   24 Jun 1981 Armand J R Peters & Teresa S Holloman
PETERS,Michael G   Sex:M   17 Mar 1980 George H Peters & Paula M Marsolais
PETERS,Michael I   Sex:M   28 Aug 1967 Ronald J Peters & Patricia G Scurrah
PETERS,Michelle T   Sex:F   02 Jun 1979 Armand J R Peters & Teresa S Holloman
PETERS,Travis Scott   Sex:M   19 Mar 1979 Scott A Peters & Patricia Ann Burns
PETERS, 3RD,George H   Sex:M   (Child #4) 10 Oct 1944 Harry C Peters (Windham,
  NH) & Pearl L Otis (Winchendon, MA)
PETERSEN,Sally A   Sex:F   13 Jan 1949 Martin H Petersen & Albina R Laukosh
PETERSON,Brian Andrew Sex:M 28 Oct 1984 Richard K Peterson & Nancy A Holland
PETERSON,David Martin   Sex:M   02 Feb 1981 John L Peterson III
  & Melody A Greenleaf
PETERSON,Karen Patricia   Sex:F   19 Apr 1984 Karl Anton Peterson
  & Patricia L Roberts
PETERSON,Kathleen Elizabeth   Sex:F   21 Nov 1981 Karl A Peterson III

HUDSON,NH BIRTHS

& Patricia L Roberts
PETERSON,William M Sex:M   13 May 1979 John L Peterson III
  & Melody A Greenleaf
PETHIC,Bruce W Sex:M   26 Oct 1950 Willis E Pethic & Nancy E Cooke
PETHIC,Everett L Sex:M (Child #2) 20 May 1944 Everett L Pethic (W Lebanon,
  NH) & Helen B Morris (Rumney, NH)
PETNER,Emily Ann Sex:F   24 Aug 1979 Steven Paul Petner & Jane E Harrison
PETRAIN,Alan D Sex:M   31 Oct 1951 Raymond A Petrain & Gloria J Johnson
PETRAIN,Davie E Sex:M   22 Jun 1976 Ovila D Petrain & Diane Y Vaillancourt
PETRAIN,Emily Donna Sex:F   03 Mar 1981 Ovila D Petrain & Diane Y Vaillancourt
PETRAIN,Gina M Sex:F   21 Feb 1970 Albert W Petrain & Joan Z Russell
PETRAIN,Shane C Sex: 03 Sep 1972 Albert W Petrain & Joan Z Russell
PETRAIN,Shawn M Sex:M   03 May 1971 Albert W Petrain & Joan Z Russell
PETRILLO,William R III Sex:M   20 Oct 1961 William R Petrillo Jr
  & Delia E Therrien
PETRIN,Jason Maurice Sex:M 29 Aug 1982 Marc Francis Petrin & Karen A Hamilton
PETRITZ,Scott Michael Sex:M 15 Mar 1982 George L Petritz & Deborah Ann Prieve
PETRO,Timothy B Sex:M   21 Apr 1969 Bruce P Petro & Donna R Pierce
PETROULES,Catherine A Sex:F   31 Oct 1970 Peter R Petroules & Dorothy R Gagne
PETROULES,Doris J Sex:F   11 Apr 1969 Peter R Petroules & Dorothy R Gagne
PETROULES,Lauretta M Sex:F   25 Aug 1967 Peter R Petroules & Dorothy R Gagne
PETROULES,Peter J Sex:M   06 Mar 1965 Peter R Petroules & Dorothy R Gagne
PETRUNO,Edward Michael Sex:M   12 Nov 1980 Gary L Petruno & Elizabeth C Uhl
PETTE,Clayton H Jr Sex:M   (Child #3) 02 Nov 1942 Clayton H Petts
  (Southbridge, MA) & Edna M Thompsend (Hurlock, MD)
PETTINATO,Matthew Joseph II Sex:M   18 May 1984 Matthew P Pettinato
  & Denise M Charlone
PEVERILL,Keith M Sex:M   22 Feb 1975 Robert G Peverill & Michael-Ellen Kepler
PEVERLY,Janet M Sex:F   20 Mar 1972 David E Peverly & Patricia A Shea
PHANEUF,Caitlin Brienna Sex:F 06 Jul 1979 Marc Jean Phaneuf & Michel Fleming
PHELPS,Andrew Wesley Sex:M 11 Feb 1982 David Roger Phelps & Rhonda L Hackett
PHELPS,Meredith Helen Sex:F   01 Sep 1983 David R Phelps & Rhonda Lee Hackett
PHILBRICK,Eleanor Sex:F   (Child #4) 28 Sep 1932 Nashua, NH Edward C Philbrick
  (Springfield, NH) & Gertrude E Messer (Sunapee
PHILBRICK,Hazel M Sex:F   12 Jun 1915 Hudson, NH Clayton O Philbrick
  (Sutton, VT) & Maude A Richards (New Boston,
PHILBRICK,James L Sex:M   15 Apr 1953 Walter J Philbrick & Arlene V Hall
PHILBRICK,Pamela G Sex:F   (Child #1) 10 Oct 1946 Wesley A Philbrick
  (New Hampshire) & Barbara H Russell (Nashua, N
PHILBROOK,Christine D Sex:F 27 Oct 1966 Richard P Philbrook&Phyllis M Powers
PHILBROOK,Dawn Marie Sex:F 21 May 1978 Donald P Philbrook&Katherine T Hemeon
PHILBROOK,Deborah J Sex:F   06 Jan 1955 Arthur C Philbrook & Nellie E Lefebvre
PHILBROOK,Donald P Jr Sex:M 06 Oct 1976 Donald P Philbrook&Katherine T Hemeon
PHILBROOK,Lynne M Sex:F   25 Feb 1965 Richard P Philbrook & Phyllis M Powers
PHILBROOK,Peter Thomas Sex:M 06 Oct 1979 Thomas W Philbrook & Judy J Larose
PHILBROOK,Ronald G Sex:M   12 Sep 1953 Arthur C Philbrook & Nellie E Lefebvre
PHILBROOK,Sue E Sex:F   19 Feb 1968 Ralph E Philbrook & Carol M Crocker
PHILIPS,Charles S Sex:M   (Child #2) 25 Sep 1899 H D Philips (Ayer Jct, MA)
  & L E Wright (Brookline)
PHILIPS,Lilian E Sex:F   03 Apr 1877 Hudson, NH John Philips (England)
  & Emma (England)
PHILLIPS,Beebe Pamelia Sex:F   04 Jun 1849 Jellasore Jeremiah Phillips
  & Hannah W Cummings
PHILLIPS,Emily Louise Sex:F   24 Dec 1850 Jellasore Jeremiah Phillips
  & Hannah W Cummings
HILLIPS,Grace M Sex:F   27 Nov 1894 James A Phillips (New Brunswick)
  & Blance Blodgett (Stratford)
PHILLIPS,Hannah Carrie Sex:F   19 Sep 1843 Jellasore Jeremiah Phillips
  & Hannah W Cummings
PHILLIPS,Hattie Preston Sex:F   11 Mar 1848 Jellasore Jeremiah Phillips

HUDSON,NH BIRTHS

& Hannah W Cummings
PHILLIPS,Henrietta D   Sex:F   15 Aug 1878 Hudson, NH John Phillips
   (Kingsbridge, England) & Emma
PHILLIPS,Ida Orissa   Sex:F   24 Jul 1856 Whitestone NY Jeremiah Phillips
   & Hannah W Cummings
PHILLIPS,Jay William   Sex:M   13 Jan 1983 Jay W Phillips & Carrie N Latour
PHILLIPS,Jeremiah   Sex:M   24 Dec 1846 Jellasore Jeremiah Phillips
   & Hannah W Cummings
PHILLIPS,Joshua Kane   Sex:M   13 Nov 1982 Craig R Phillips & Charlene P Harris
PHILLIPS,Julia Emma   Sex:F   05 Jun 1845 Jellasore Jeremiah Phillips
   & Hannah W Cummings
PHILLIPS,Lucy Marilla   Sex:F   06 Sep 1854 New Hampton NH Jeremiah Phillips
   & Hannah W Cummings
PHILLIPS,Mary Anne   Sex:F   20 Feb 1842 Jellasore Jeremiah Phillips
   & Hannah W Cummings
PHILLIPS,Mildred E   Sex:F   (Child #3) 18 Nov 1903 H D Phillips (Ayer, MA)
   & L H Wright (Brookline)
PHILLIPS,Nellie Maria   Sex:F   15 Jun 1852 Jellasore Jeremiah Phillips
   & Hannah W Cummings
PHILLIPS,Ruth   Sex:F   (Child #4) 12 Apr 1908 H D Phillips (Hudson, NH)
   & L E Wright (Brookline, NH)
PHILLIPS,Ryan Jay   Sex:M   02 Apr 1984 Jay Warren Phillips
   & Carrie Nadine Latour
PHILLIPS,William A   Sex:M   24 Aug 1956 William E Phillips & Martha I Pinkham
PHILLIPS,William Carey   Sex:M   26 Mar 1861 Prairie City Jeremiah Phillips
   & Hannah W Cummings
PHINNEY,Sue   Sex:F   24 Nov 1954 Gerald R Phinney & Laura E Tuohy
PIASECZNY,Deborah A Sex:F 09 Sep 1968 Isadore J Piaseczny & Theresa M Brunelle
PIASECZNY,Steven R Sex:M 05 Dec 1966 Isadore J Piaseczny & Theresa M Brunelle
PIATEK,Sandra J   Sex:F   (Child #2) 23 Jul 1946 Lewis Piatek (Providence, RI)
   & Ruth M Nelson (Manchester, NH)
PICARD,Barbara M   Sex:F   (Child #1) 10 Nov 1944 Roland N Picard (Nashua, NH)
   & Susie E Dutton (Dorchester, MA)
PIDGEON,Katherine E   Sex:F   01 Oct 1969 Donald A Pidgeon & Martha E Peabody
PIED,Aaron David Sex:M 11 Jul 1978 Paul Phillippe Pied & Carol Mae Hjermenrud
PIED,Karen D   Sex:F   21 Jan 1974 Paul P Pied & Carol Mae Hiermehrud
PIEIKONIS,Julia   Sex:F   (Child #6) 19 Sep 1925 John Pieikonis (Lithuania)
   & Victoria Wilerynska (Lithuania)
PIERCE,Alia Ann   Sex:F   20 Dec 1973 Gerald R Pierce & Gwendolyn W Barklow
PIERCE,Beverly Ann Sex:F   (Child #3) 11 Jul 1934 Theodore Pierce (Nashua, NH)
   & Emma Martin (Manchester, NH)
PIERCE,Cummings P   Sex:M   Hudson, NH Nathan Pierce & Phebe Cummings
PIERCE,Daniel   Sex:M   31 May 1788 Hudson, NH Daniel Pierce & Hannah
PIERCE,Daniel   Sex:M   Hudson, NH Nathan Pierce & Phebe Cummings
PIERCE,Frank Ronald   Sex:M   (Child #4) 03 Apr 1937 Theodore Wood Pierce
   (Nashua, NH) & Emma Martin (Manchester, NH)
PIERCE,George L   Sex:M   (Child #5) 20 Jan 1940 Theodore W Pierce (Nashua, NH)
   & Emma E Martin (Manchester, NH)
PIERCE,James   Sex:M   11 Sep 1768 Hudson, NH Joshua Pierce & Esther Richardson
PIERCE,James   Sex:M   30 May 1792 Hudson, NH Joshua Pierce & Sally
PIERCE,John   Sex:M   22 Apr 1785 Hudson, NH Joshua Pierce & Sally
PIERCE,Joseph   Sex:M   04 Dec 1794 Hudson, NH Joshua Pierce & Sally
PIERCE,Joshua   Sex:M   09 Jul 1787 Hudson, NH Joshua Pierce & Sally
PIERCE,L'Tanya J   Sex:F   12 May 1972 Gerald R Pierce & Gwendolyn W Barklow
PIERCE,Lauri A   Sex:F   27 Jan 1962 Michael E Pierce & Jacqueline M Lachari
PIERCE,LeighAnn   Sex:F   07 Jan 1984 Paul Roger Pierce & Deidre Ann Leger
PIERCE,Mary   Sex:F   Hudson, NH Nathan Pierce & Phebe Cummings
PIERCE,Nathan   Sex:M   1763 Hudson, NH Joshua Pierce & Esther Richardson
PIERCE,Nathan, Jr Sex:M   Hudson, NH Nathan Pierce & Phebe Cummings
PIERCE,Renee L   Sex:F   27 Aug 1976 Gerald R Pierce & Gwendolyn W Barklow

HUDSON,NH BIRTHS

PIERCE,Robert   Sex:M   05 Oct 1790 Hudson, NH Daniel Pierce & Hannah
PIERCE,Samuel   Sex:M   25 Mar 1784 Hudson, NH Daniel Pierce & Hannah
PIERCE,Sarah   Sex:F   12 Mar 1786 Hudson, NH Daniel Pierce & Hannah
PIERCE,Sarah   Sex:F   12 Mar 1784 Hudson, NH Daniel Pierce & Hannah
PIERCE,Stephen C Sex:M   Hudson, NH Nathan Pierce & Phebe Cummings
PIERCE,Susan   Sex:F   Hudson, NH Nathan Pierce & Phebe Cummings
PIERSON,Laura L Sex:F   25 Aug 1962 Roland L Pierson & Frances M Yeomans
PIETROWSKI,Amy K Sex:F   25 Apr 1974 Richard J Pietrowski & Margaret A Cartier
PIJOAN,Lisa A   Sex:F   11 Apr 1966 Peter J Pijoan & Emma L Elliott
PIJOAN,Michael A Sex:M   15 Apr 1961 Peter J Pijoan & Emma L Elliott
PIJOAN,Timothy E Sex:M   12 Feb 1963 Peter J Pijoan & Emma L Elliott
PIKE,Amos   Sex:M   28 Jun 1798 Hudson, NH Thomas Pike & Ruth
PIKE,Anna   Sex:F   28 Jun 1798 Hudson, NH Thomas Pike & Ruth
PIKE,Arline M   Sex:F   (Child #1) 06 Jun 1918 Leon Pike (Whitingham, VT)
  & Cora Melvin (Merrimack, NH)
PIKE,David R   Sex:M   (Child #4) 31 Jan 1944 Amos J Pike (Halifax, VT)
  & Violet B Leard (Nashua, NH)
PIKE,Eben   Sex:M   27 Jul 1796 Hudson, NH Thomas Pike & Ruth
PIKE,Eber   Sex:M   27 Jul 1796 Hudson, NH Thomas Pike & Ruth
PIKE,Justice   Sex:M   24 Aug 1792 Hudson, NH Thomas Pike & Ruth
PIKE,Justus Sex:M   24 Aug 1792 Hudson, NH Thomas Pike & Ruth
PIKE,Mahalie   Sex:F   23 May 1803 Hudson, NH Thomas Pike & Ruth
PIKE,Natalia   Sex:F   23 May 1803 Hudson, NH Thomas Pike & Ruth
PIKE,Rebecca   Sex:F   11 Jan 1794 Hudson, NH Thomas Pike & Ruth
PIKE,Rebecca   Sex:F   11 Jun 1794 Hudson, NH Thomas Pike & Ruth
PIKE,Sally Sex:F   28 Jun 1801 Hudson, NH Thomas Pike & Ruth
PIKE,Sally Sex:F   23 Jun 1801 Hudson, NH Thoms Pike & Ruth
PIKE,Timothy W   Sex:M   03 Dec 1965 Reginald D Pike & Leslie A Lizotte
PIKE,Virginia Elizabeth Sex:F   (Child #3) 20 May 1941 Amos J Pike (Nashua,
  NH) & Violet B Leard (Nashua, NH)
PIKE,Wesley C Jr Sex:M   29 Sep 1950 Wesley C Pike & Helen K Kane
PILANT,Adam Samuel Sex:M   26 Sep 1984 Lawrence M Pilant & Stephanie E Samson
PINARD,Matthew Norman   Sex:M   11 Feb 1985 Norman J Pinard & Dolores P Atencio
PINARD,Michelle Aurore Sex:F   14 Nov 1983 Norman J Pinard & Dolores P Atencio
PINET,Kathleen E Sex:F   15 Aug 1948 Alfred G Pinet (Canada) & Helen G Hardy
  (Durham, NH)
PINKHAM,Janice L Sex:F   (Child #1) 19 May 1940 Winton L Pinkham (Nashua, NH)
  & Eleanor B Dumbrack (Smithtown, NH
PINKHAM,Lorelei N   Sex:F   01 Jan 1954 Frederick G Pinkham & Gertrude Dagne
PIPPIN,Jennifer Eliz Olson   Sex:F   13 Jul 1982 Richard C Pippin
  & Linea Diane Olson
PITARYS,Nicholas A Jr Sex:M 27 Feb 1970 Nicholas A Pitarys
  & Patricia Robertson
PIZZIFERRI,Lisa M   Sex:F   17 Apr 1962 Frank C Pizziferri & Shirley M Robinson
PLAMANDON,Peter A   Sex:M   (Child #3) 16 Dec 1945 Joseph E Plamandon (Sanford,
  ME) & Mary E Miller (Auburndale, MA)
PLAMONDON,Alison Rhea Sex:F 04 May 1981 Robert A Plamondon & Donna C Renshaw
PLAMONDON,Anne G Sex:F   27 Feb 1963 Ronald R Plamondon & Joyce E Malcolm
PLAMONDON,Gail R Sex:F   26 Mar 1966 Ronald R Plamondon & Joyce E Malcolm
PLAMONDON,Gerard J   Sex:M   29 May 1960 Ronald R Plamondon & Joyce E Malcolm
PLAMONDON,Kathryn Ann Sex:F 18 Mar 1982 Peter A Plamondon & Judith Ann Ledoux
PLAMONDON,Kevin Norbert Sex:M   26 Aug 1979 Peter A Plamondon
  & Judith Ann Ledoux
PLAMONDON,Kyle K Sex:M   18 Dec 1973 Kenneth R Plamondon & Claire C Farland
PLAMONDON,Lisa J Sex:F   28 Feb 1970 Robert W Plamondon & Constance I Levesque
PLAMONDON,Mark J Sex:M   24 Mar 1959 Ronald R Plamondon & Joyce E Malcolm
PLAMONDON,Paula K   Sex:F   27 Jun 1979 Paul Plamondon & Kathleen E Widener
PLAMONDON,Roger J   Sex:M   (Child #1) 14 Jan 1943 Joseph E Plamondon (Sanford,
  ME) & Mary E Miller (Auburndale, MA)
PLAMONDON,Ronald J   Sex:M   29 Nov 1966 Roger J Plamondon & Faye Winstanley

HUDSON,NH BIRTHS

PLAMONDON,Sarah Elizabeth   Sex:F   03 Dec 1980 Paul P Plamondon
    & Kathleen E Widener
PLAMONDON,Susan M Sex:F 22 Apr 1963 Robert W Plamondon & Constance I Levesque
PLAMONDON,William A Sex:M   06 Apr 1971 Roger J Plamondon & Faye Winstanley
PLANTE,Christine Sylvie   Sex:F   25 Nov 1982 Mario R Plante & Denyse P Blais
PLANTE,Jennie M   Sex:F   05 Jun 1974 Mario R Plante & Denise P Blais
PLANTE,Melissa Sue   Sex:F   09 Mar 1982 Kevin Wayne Plante & Karen Ann Anctil
PLANTE,Miguel M   Sex:M   18 Jul 1975 Claude L Plante & Helene S Nadeau
PLANTE,Robert Wayne   Sex:M 18 Dec 1983 Kevin Wayne Plante & Karen Ann Anctil
PLANTE,Roberta A   Sex:F   29 Apr 1965 Robert O Plante & Betty L Lilley
PLANTE,Vicki S   Sex:F   05 Dec 1967 Robert O Plante Jr & Betty L Lilley
PLANTIER,Eugene G Jr   Sex:M   (Child #1) 29 Apr 1943 Eugene G Plantier
    (Manchester, NH) & Merilda M Knights (Hudson, NH)
PLANTIER,Kathleen R   Sex:F   23 May 1953 Paul E Plantier & Oralie K Knight
PLANTIER,Peter A   Sex:M   16 Apr 1955 Paul E Plantier & Oralie K Knights
PLATT,Kathleen A   Sex:F   24 Jul 1971 James E Platt & Margaret L Curtin
PLAZA,Aaron M   Sex:M   28 Mar 1971 Nathaniel M Plaza & Carol E Niedbala
PLAZA,David J   Sex:M   05 Mar 1966 Nathaniel M Plaza & Carol E Niedbala
PLOURDE,Leo Robert   Sex:M   (Child #4) 10 May 1933 Horace Plourde (Nashua, NH)
    & Blanche Caron (Brodrick, ME)
PLUMLEY,James S   Sex:M   02 Jun 1966 Harold A Plumley & Anne P MacKenney
PLUMLEY,Jennifer L   Sex:F   14 Sep 1970 Harold A Plumley & Anne P MacKenney
PLUMLEY,Rebecca A   Sex:F   18 Aug 1967 Harold A Plumley & Anne P MacKenney
PLUMLEY,Timothy E   Sex:M   05 Aug 1969 Harold A Plumley & Anne P MacKenney
PLUMMER,April R   Sex:F   26 Aug 1974 Alexander J Plummer & Mary C Sullivan
PLUMMER,Dale R   Sex:M   07 Nov 1969 Donald R Plummer & Rose M De Cunto
PLUMMER,James R   Sex:M   17 Jul 1968 Richard B Plummer & Linda H Berry
PLUMMER,Jennifer L   Sex:F   23 Nov 1970 Richard B Plummer & Linda H Berry
PLUMMER,Salley   Sex:F   11 Mar 1783 Hudson, NH   & Elizebeth Duty
PLYBON,Wesley James Sex:M 29 Jan 1982 Harry Wesely Plybon & Deborah J Everett
PLYNKOFSKY,Cynthia M   Sex:F   25 Jul 1947 Adam P Plynkofsky (New York, NY)
    & Midlred B Johnson (Hudson, NH)
PLYNKOFSKY,Patricia L   Sex:F   (Child #1) 17 Jul 1944 Adam P Plynkofsky
    (New York, NY) & Mildred B Jameson (Hudson, NH)
PLYNKOFSKY,Shirley A   Sex:F   (Child #2) 25 Sep 1945 Adam P Plynkofsky
    (New York, NY) & Mildred B Jameson (Hudson, NH)
POFF,George W   Sex:M   23 Jun 1866 Hudson, NH Edward Poff & Jane
POFF,Jane   Sex:F   1863 Hudson, NH Francis Poff &
POFF,Margaret F   Sex:F   06 Apr 1868 Hudson, NH Francis Poff & Mary Jane
POFF,Margaritt A   Sex:F   06 Apr 1868 Hudson, NH Francis Poff & Mary Jane
POFF,Robert   Sex:M   09 Nov 1862 Hudson, NH Francis Poff & Mary Jane
POINTER,Darlene   Sex:F   01 Jun 1970 Richard M Pointer & Dona M Trafford
POINTER,Kathleen Ann   Sex:F   17 Sep 1979 Richard M Pointer
    & Kathleen A DeCarlos
POINTER,Laura M   Sex:F   14 Jun 1957 William G Pointer & Mary K Hufnagle
POINTER,Richard M   Sex:M   20 Apr 1951 William G Pointer & Mary K Hufnagle
POIRIER,Laura   Sex:F   24 May 1982 Daniel W Poirier & Janet Lee Robinson
POISSON,Jason Paul   Sex:M   30 Oct 1979 Paul J Poisson & Suzanne M St Gelais
POISSON,Michael Andrew Sex:M 07 Jul 1982 Paul J Poisson & Suzanne M St Gelais
POLAK,Celia   Sex:F   (Child #2) 08 Sep 1946 Andrew J Polak (I Orchard, MA)
    & Stella Tomaski (Manchester, NH)
POLAK,Dora   Sex:F   (Child #10) 23 Feb 1936 Simon Polak (Poland)
    & Theodora Pasek (Poland)
POLAK,Joseph Richard   Sex:M   (Child #9) 27 Aug 1931 Simon Polak (Poland)
    & Theodora Pasek (Poland)
POLAK,Phyllis   Sex:F   (Child #6) 01 Apr 1924 Simon Polak (Poland)
    & Feodozia Pasek (Poland)
POLAK,Robert   Sex:M   (Child #7) 20 Jul 1927 Simon Polak (Poland)
    & Theodose Pasek (Poland)
POLANEC,Christopher Brian   Sex:M   09 Mar 1981 Gary Keith Polanec

HUDSON,NH BIRTHS

   & Frances E Yearick
POLANEC,Laura Elizabeth   Sex:F   20 Mar 1984 Gary Keith Polanec
   & Frances E Yeareck
POLIQUIN,Beatrice E Sex:F 13 Jul 1958 Alfred C Poliquin, Jr
   & Beatrice E Lambert
POLIQUIN,Tanya L   Sex:F   27 Sep 1973 Gerard L Poliquin & Donna L Martin
POLKEY,Cheryl Ann   Sex:F   28 Jun 1978 Edward S Polkey & Juanita M Prosper
POLKEY,Deborah Chereyle   Sex:F   23 Nov 1979 Edward S Polkey
   & Juanita M Prosper
POLLARD,Abel   Sex:M   04 Feb 1773 Hudson, NH Ebenezer Pollard & Abigail
POLLARD,Abigail   Sex:F   18 Oct 1778 Hudson, NH John Pollard & Elizabeth
POLLARD,Abigail   Sex:F   14 Feb 1759 Hudson, NH Ebenezer Pollard & Abigail
POLLARD,Abigail W   Sex:F   26 Jul 1771 Hudson, NH Amos Pollard & Miriam
POLLARD,Abigail W   Sex:F   14 Nov 1798 Hudson, NH Abel Pollard & Abigail
POLLARD,Abigail Whitney   Sex:F   26 Jul 1771 Hudson, NH Amos Pollard & Miriam
POLLARD,Abigail Winn Sex:F 14 Nov 1798 Hudson, NH Abel Pollard
   & Abigail Hills
POLLARD,Adaline   Sex:F   22 Mar 1811 Hudson, NH Joseph Pollard & Betsey
POLLARD,Adeline   Sex:F   22 Mar 1811 Hudson, NH Joseph Pollard & Betsey
POLLARD,Alpheus   Sex:M   06 Jul 1806 Hudson, NH Joseph Pollard & Betsey
POLLARD,Amanda   Sex:F   27 Oct 1813 Hudson, NH Joseph Pollard & Betsey
POLLARD,Amos   Sex:M   02 Mar 1737 Hudson, NH Thomas Pollard & Mary
POLLARD,Asa   Sex:M   15 Aug 1769 Hudson, NH Samuel Pollard & Lydia
POLLARD,Asa D   Sex:M   05 Oct 1805 Hudson, NH Asa Pollard & Susanna
POLLARD,Asa Davis   Sex:M   05 Oct 1805 Hudson, NH Asa Pollard & Susanna
POLLARD,Barbara   Sex:F   06 Dec 1695 Thomas Pollard & Mary Farmer
POLLARD,Benjamin   Sex:M   18 Aug 1715 Thomas Pollard & Mary Farmer
POLLARD,Betty   Sex:F   16 Oct 1773 Hudson, NH Samuel Pollard & Lydia
POLLARD,Betty   Sex:F   17 Jun 1787 Hudson, NH John Pollard & Sarah Gould
POLLARD,Bettye   Sex:F   17 Jun 1787 Hudson, NH John Pollard & Sarah
POLLARD,Calvin   Sex:M   09 Jul 1804 Hudson, NH Abel Pollard & Abigail Hills
POLLARD,Charlott   Sex:F   27 Jun 1799 Hudson, NH Asa Pollard & Susanna
POLLARD,Charlotte   Sex:F   27 Jun 1799 Hudson, NH Asa Pollard & Susanna
POLLARD,Cummings   Sex:M   10 Nov 1767 Hudson, NH Samuel Pollard & Lydia
POLLARD,Daniel   Sex:M   05 Mar 1771 Hudson, NH Samuel Pollard & Lydia
POLLARD,Daniel   Sex:M   04 Nov 1793 Hudson, NH Asa Pollard & Susanna
POLLARD,Daniel   Sex:M   22 Aug 1762 Hudson, NH Amos Pollard & Miriam
POLLARD,Daniel   Sex:M   11 Oct 1792 Hudson, NH John Pollard & Sarah
POLLARD,Daveod   Sex:M   20 Nov 1767 Hudson, NH Amos Pollard & Miriam
POLLARD,David   Sex:M   22 Aug 1762 Hudson, NH Amos Pollard & Miriam
POLLARD,David   Sex:M   11 Oct 1792 Hudson, NH John Pollard & Sarah Gould
POLLARD,Delmer W   Sex:M   09 Jun 1963 Billy R Pollard & Lucy G Butler
POLLARD,Doratha   Sex:F   12 Oct 1803 Hudson, NH Ebenezer Pollard
   & Doratha Blodgett
POLLARD,Dorcas   Sex:F   12 Jan 1735 Hudson, NH Thomas Pollard & Mary
POLLARD,Dorcas   Sex:F   20 Nov 1767 Hudson, NH Amos Pollard & Miriam
POLLARD,Dorkis   Sex:F   12 Jan 1734 Hudson, NH Thomas Pollard & Mary
POLLARD,Dorothy   Sex:F   12 Oct 1803 Hudson, NH Ebenezer Pollard & Dorothy
POLLARD,Ebenezer   Sex:M   04 Dec 1728 Dunstable MA Thomas Pollard & Mary
POLLARD,Ebenezer   Sex:M   10 Jun 1765 Hudson, NH Ebenezer Pollard & Abigail
POLLARD,Ebenezer   Sex:M   01 Jul 1800 Hudson, NH Ebenezer Pollard
   & Doratha Blodgett
POLLARD,Edward   Sex:M   04 Nov 1694 Thomas Pollard & Mary Farmer
POLLARD,Electa   Sex: 29 Oct 1801 Hudson, NH Asa Pollard & Susanna
POLLARD,Electa   Sex: 03 Jul 1803 Hudson, NH Asa Pollard & Susanna
POLLARD,Electa   Sex:F   14 Nov 1809 Hudson, NH Ebenezer Pollard
   & Doratha Blodgett
POLLARD,Electa   Sex:F   14 Nov 1804 Hudson, NH Ebenezer Pollard & Dorothy
POLLARD,Elesta   Sex: 24 Oct 1801 Hudson, NH Asa Pollard & Susanna
POLLARD,Elesta   Sex: 03 Jul 1803 Hudson, NH Asa Pollard & Susanna

HUDSON, NH BIRTHS

```
POLLARD,Elizabeth  Sex:F  19 Sep 1754 Hudson, NH John Pollard & Elizabeth
POLLARD,Elizabeth  Sex:F  05 Mar 1713 Thomas Pollard & Mary Farmer
POLLARD,Forest A  Sex:M  28 Dec 1872 Hudson, NH Joseph Pollard & Emily
POLLARD,Granvil  Sex:M  28 Dec 1813 Hudson, NH Ebenezer Pollard & Dorothy
POLLARD,Granville  Sex:M  28 Dec 1813 Hudson, NH Ebenezer Pollard
   & Doratha Blodgett
POLLARD,Hannah  Sex:F  24 May 1797 Hudson, NH Abel Pollard & Abigail
POLLARD,Hannah Dow Sex:F  24 May 1797 Hudson, NH Abel Pollard & Abigail Hills
POLLARD,Irena  Sex:F  31 Jan 1808 Hudson, NH Joseph Pollard & Betsey
POLLARD,Irene  Sex:F  31 Jan 1808 Hudson, NH Joseph Pollard & Betsey
POLLARD,Isaac  Sex:M  19 Aug 1745 Hudson, NH Joseph Pollard & Ann Hills
POLLARD,Isaac  Sex:M  19 Aug 1748 Hudson, NH Joseph Pollard & Anne
POLLARD,James  Sex:M  01 Nov 1763 Hudson, NH John Pollard & Elizabeth
POLLARD,James  Sex:M  05 Oct 1708 Thomas Pollard & Mary Farmer
POLLARD,Joel  Sex:M  15 May 1749 John Pollard & Sarah Dean
POLLARD,John  Sex:M  20 Sep 1727 Dunstable MA Thomas Pollard & Mary
POLLARD,John  Sex:M  20 Nov 1752 Hudson, NH John Pollard & Elizabeth
POLLARD,John  Sex:M  19 Jan 1779 Hudson, NH John Pollard & Sarah Gould
POLLARD,John  Sex:M  01 Sep 1699 Thomas Pollard & Mary Farmer
POLLARD,John  Sex:M  24 Jun 1729 John Pollard & Mary Stearns
POLLARD,Joseph  Sex:M  04 Mar 1737 Hudson, NH Joseph Pollard & Ann Hills
POLLARD,Joseph  Sex:M  19 Apr 1781 Hudson, NH John Pollard & Sarah Gould
POLLARD,Joseph  Sex:M  03 May 1702 Thomas Pollard & Mary Farmer
POLLARD,Joseph B Sex:M  13 May 1878 Hudson, NH Joseph L Pollard (Hudson, NH)
   & Emily (Bath)
POLLARD,Karen M  Sex:F  25 Aug 1956 James P Pollard & Ruth M Naylor
POLLARD,Katharine  Sex:F  12 Jun 1761 Hudson, NH Ebenezer Pollard & Abigail
POLLARD,Katherine  Sex:F  12 Jun 1761 Hudson, NH Ebenezer Pollard & Abigail
POLLARD,Lois  Sex:F  18 Aug 1770 Hudson, NH Ebenezer Pollard & Abigail
POLLARD,Lorjee  Sex:F  27 Jan 1817 Hudson, NH Joseph Pollard & Betsey
POLLARD,Louisa  Sex:F  27 Jan 1817 Hudson, NH Joseph Pollard & Betsey
POLLARD,Lucinda  Sex:F  20 Apr 1792 Hudson, NH Asa Pollard & Susanna
POLLARD,Lydia  Sex:F  13 Jun 1775 Hudson, NH Samuel Pollard & Lydia
POLLARD,Mary  Sex:F  06 May 1777 Hudson, NH Amos Pollard & Miriam
POLLARD,Mary  Sex:F  20 Aug 1693 Thomas Pollard & Mary Farmer
POLLARD,Mary  Sex:F  16 May 1777 Hudson, NH Amos Pollard & Marian
POLLARD,Mehitable  Sex:F  24 Jun 1765 Hudson, NH Amos Pollard & Miriam
POLLARD,Mehittabel  Sex:F  24 Jun 1765 Hudson, NH Amos Pollard & Miriam
POLLARD,Molly  Sex:F  10 Jun 1741 Hudson, NH Thomas Pollard & Mary
POLLARD,Moses  Sex:M  22 Oct 1769 Hudson, NH Amos Pollard & Miriam
POLLARD,Nancy  Sex:F  28 Jul 1802 Hudson, NH Abel Pollard & Abigail Hills
POLLARD,Nathan  Sex:M  06 Jun 1775 Hudson, NH Ebenezer Pollard & Abigail
POLLARD,Nathaniel  Sex:M  18 Oct 1706 Thomas Pollard & Mary Farmer
POLLARD,Oliver  Sex:M  14 Dec 1788 Hudson, NH John Pollard & Sarah Gould
POLLARD,Oliver  Sex:M  23 Jul 1703 Thomas Pollard & Mary Farmer
POLLARD,Preston  Sex:M  19 Sep 1797 Hudson, NH Asa Pollard & Susanna
POLLARD,Rachel  Sex:F  26 Mar 1739 Hudson, NH Thomas Pollard & Mary
POLLARD,Rachel  Sex:F  03 Sep 1767 Hudson, NH Ebenezer Pollard & Abigail
POLLARD,Rhoda  Sex:F  14 Nov 1763 Hudson, NH Amos Pollard & Miriam
POLLARD,Richard K  Sex:M  09 Mar 1964 Bobby G Pollard & Elaine E Pickering
POLLARD,Salley  Sex:F  06 Nov 1784 Hudson, NH John Pollard & Sarah
POLLARD,Sally  Sex:F  06 Nov 1784 Hudson, NH John Pollard & Sarah Gould
POLLARD,Samuel  Sex:M  10 Jul 1743 Hudson, NH Thomas Pollard & Mary
POLLARD,Samuel  Sex:M  14 Oct 1777 Hudson, NH Samuel Pollard & Lydia
POLLARD,Sarah  Sex:F  05 May 1749 Hudson, NH Joseph Pollard & Ann Hills
POLLARD,Sarah  Sex:F  27 Sep 1806 Hudson, NH Ebenezer Pollard
   & Doratha Blodgett
POLLARD,Sarah  Sex:F  16 Feb 1700 Thomas Pollard & Mary Farmer
POLLARD,Sarah  Sex:F  21 Dec 1704 Thomas Pollard & Mary Farmer
POLLARD,Sarah  Sex:F  06 May 1749 Hudson, NH Joseph Pollard & Anne
```

HUDSON, NH BIRTHS

POLLARD,Sarah   Sex:F   27 Sep 1807 Hudson, NH Ebenezer Pollard & Dorothy
POLLARD,Sarah F Sex:F   17 Apr 1793 Hudson, NH Thomas Pollard & Olive
POLLARD,Sarah Fletcher   Sex:F   17 Apr 1793 Hudson, NH Thomas Pollard & Olive
POLLARD,Sibel   Sex:F   23 Mar 1783 Hudson, NH Samuel Pollard & Lydia
POLLARD,Solomon Sex:M   18 May 1847 Hudson, NH Joseph Pollard & Ann Hills
POLLARD,Solomon Sex:M   18 May 1747 Hudson, NH Joseph Pollard & Anne
POLLARD,Susanna Sex:F   10 Jul 1763 Hudson, NH Ebenezer Pollard & Abigail
POLLARD,Susanna Sex:F   13 Jul 1800 Hudson, NH Abel Pollard & Abigail Hills
POLLARD,Sybil   Sex:F   23 Mar 1783 Hudson, NH Samuel Pollard & Lydia
POLLARD,Sybil   Sex:F   19 Jan 1796 Hudson, NH Asa Pollard & Susanna
POLLARD,Thomas   Sex:M   17 Sep 1732 Dunstable MA Thomas Pollard & Mary
POLLARD,Thomas   Sex:M   14 Oct 1758 Hudson, NH John Pollard & Elizabeth
POLLARD,Thomas   Sex:M   01 Oct 1789 Hudson, NH Thomas Pollard & Olive
POLLARD,Thomas   Sex:M   16 Feb 1696 Thomas Pollard & Mary Farmer
POLLARD,Timothy Sex:M   24 Aug 1745 Hudson, NH Thomas Pollard & Mary
POLLARD,Vernetia Sex:F   (Child #1) 30 Jul 1902 Raymond Pollard (Hudson, NH)
 & Cora May Cooper (Lowell, MA)
POLLARD,Walter   Sex:M   28 Dec 1709 Thomas Pollard & Mary Farmer
POLLARD,William Sex:M   03 Aug 1698 Thomas Pollard & Mary Farmer
POMEROY,Linda S Sex:F   06 Jul 1961 Robert E Pomeroy & Joan T Carline
POMEROY,Teresa A Sex:F   06 May 1960 Robert E Pomeroy & Joan T Carline
PONTBRIAND,Linda D Sex:F   01 Jul 1965 Maurice E Pontbriand & Denise C Duval
PONTBRIAND,Robert M Sex:M   26 Aug 1968 Maurice E Pontbriand & Denise C Duval
POOLE,David J   Sex:M   28 Sep 1965 Richard R Poole & Joyce J Duston
POOLE,Joseph R   Sex:M   29 May 1963 Richard R Poole & Joyce J Duston
POON,Selena O   Sex: 01 Feb 1973 Kam N Poon & Hong K Ong
POPE,Trevor A   Sex: 31 Jan 1973 Glenn A Pope & Joyce A Eriberg
POPER,Sean Jason Sex:M   22 Nov 1979 Harry F Poper & Carol I Williamson
POPER,Stacie L   Sex:F   04 Apr 1972 Harry F Poper II & Jean C Brisebois
POPP,Ryan Joseph Sex:M   17 Sep 1982 Douglas Carl Popp & Maureen May Fader
PORTER,Beverley J   Sex:F   (Child #5) 29 May 1945 Edward W Porter (Stoughton,
 MA) & Silvia Smith (Amherst, NH)
PORTER,Debra L   Sex:F   03 Nov 1956 Edward W Porter & Silvia E Smith
PORTER,George A Sex:M   (Child #2) 08 Nov 1942 Edward W Porter (Stoughton,
 MA) & Silvia U Smith (Amherst, NH)
PORTER,Irene R   Sex:F   16 Aug 1952 Edward W Porter & Sylvia V Smith
PORTER,Jennie   Sex:F   21 Jun 1983 Lawrence B PorterIII & Kellie Mary Winn
PORTER,John R   Sex:M   08 May 1954 Edward W Porter & Sylvia V Smith
PORTER,Linda M   Sex:F   (Child #4) 21 May 1944 Edward W Porter (Stoughton, MA)
 & Sylvia V Smith (Amherst, NH)
PORTER,Mary E   Sex:F   (Child #1) 16 Apr 1884 Hudson, NH Charles A Porter
 (Woburn, MA) & Jennie S Heald (Greenville, NH)
PORTER,Nancy E   Sex:F   07 Dec 1947 Edward W Porter (Stoughton, MA)
 & Sylvia V Smith (Amherst, NH)
PORTER,Patricia A   Sex:F   24 May 1970 Edward W Porter Jr & Carol A Dobens
PORTER,Robert L Sex:M   16 Sep 1950 Edward W Porter & Sylvia V Smith
PORTER,Sandra J Sex:F   11 Jul 1949 Edward W Porter & Sylvia V Smith
PORTER,Sheryl A Sex:F   08 Oct 1959 Edward W Porter & Sylvia V Smith
PORTER,Walther H Sex:M   (Child #6) 22 Jul 1946 Edward W Potter (Stoughton,
 MA) & Sylvia V Smith (Amherst, NH)
PORTER, [Unknown]   Sex:F   (Child #2) 15 Oct 1885 Hudson, NH Charles A Porter
 (Woburn, MA) & Jennie S Heald (Mason Village, NH
PORUSTA,Amy Kristin Sex:F   29 Jul 1979 David M Porusta & Catherine Linda Roy
PORUSTA,Eric M   Sex:M   02 Mar 1971 David M Porusta & Catherine L Roy
POST,Ramzy S   Sex:M   04 Nov 1968 Gary F Post & Jacqueline D Wagner
POST,Sharon E   Sex:F   (Child #1) 15 Sep 1946 Marillo E Post (Westfield, ME)
 & Doris I Moore (Nashua, NH)
POTTER,Jeffrey R Sex:M   26 Oct 1968 Robert W Potter & Jane M Gallien
POTTER,Kristen Amy Sex:F   04 Aug 1976 James H Potter & Cynthia M Caples
POTTER,Michael R Sex:M   19 Apr 1978 James H Potter & Cynthia M Caples

HUDSON,NH BIRTHS

POTTER,Neil V   Sex:M   (Child #5) 26 Aug 1946 Floyd S Potter (Wolcott, VT)
  & Esther D Johnson (Manchester, NH)
POTTER,Richard L   Sex:M   (Child #4) 07 Apr 1944 Floyd S Potter (Wilcott, VT)
  & Esther D Johnson (Manchester, NH)
POTTER,Robert W   Sex:M   (Child #3) 03 Feb 1942 Floyd S Potter (Wilcott, VT)
  & Esther Johnson (Manchester, NH)
POTVIN,David M   Sex:M   09 Oct 1973 Thomas F Potvin & Lesley S Philbrick
POTZNER,Jeffrey S   Sex:M   06 Mar 1968 Joseph J Potzner & Angeline M Duprey
POULIN,Bernice A   Sex:F   28 Jun 1966 Leonard R Poulin & Jacqueline Vaillanco
POULIN,Brian Joseph   Sex:M   30 Oct 1978 Robert Joseph Poulin & Joann White
POULIN,Elaine A   Sex:F   12 Oct 1969 Leonard R Poulin & Jacqueline Vaillanco
POULIN,Howard C III Sex:M   10 Apr 1970 Howard C Poulin Jr & Roberta A Elliott
POULIN,Jeffrey R   Sex:M   01 Feb 1958 Robert J Poulin & Evelyn P Stevens
POULIN,Steven Michael   Sex:M   31 Dec 1983 Michael V Poulin
  & Judith A Pickering
POWELL,Jacqueline C   Sex:F   01 Feb 1965 John E Powell & Caroline O Harsagi
POWELL,Joanne E   Sex:F   11 Nov 1968 John E Powell Jr & Caroline O Harsagi
POWERS,David A   Sex:M   30 Apr 1966 John H Powers & Marie Y Byrnes
POWLOWSKY,Anthony J Jr Sex:M   18 Feb 1958 Anthony J Powlowsky & Ann L Lavoie
POWLOWSKY,Jeffrey R   Sex:M   25 Nov 1962 Peter M Powlowsky & Aline M Maurice
POWLOWSKY,Kathryn L   Sex:F   28 Feb 1952 Anthony J Powlowsky & Ann L Lavoie
POWLOWSKY,Michael A   Sex:M   06 Jul 1960 Anthony J Powlowsky & Ann L Lavoie
POWLOWSKY,Nancy A   Sex:F   30 Jan 1954 Peter M Powlowsky & Aline M Maurice
POWLOWSKY,Patricia A   Sex:F   24 Oct 1950 Anthony J Powlowsky & Anna L Lavoie
POWLOWSKY,Peter M   Sex:M   17 Oct 1957 Peter M Powlowsky & Aline M Maurice
POWLOWSKY,Richard A   Sex:M   13 Dec 1961 Peter M Powlowsky & Aline M Maurice
PRAGER,Matthew L   Sex:M   10 Sep 1976 Jay M Prager & Sharon A Blumenkrant
PRATT,Charles A   Sex:M   (Child #4) 10 Oct 1921 George A Pratt (Boston, MA)
  & Lillian M Wade (Brockton, MA)
PRATT,Dorothy May   Sex:F   (Child #3) 09 Jul 1914 George Pratt (Maine)
  & Lillienne May Wade (Massachusetts)
PRATT,Eric William Sex:M 26 Jan 1983 Richard W PrattJr & Catharine A Levesque
PRATT,George A   Sex:M   (Child #3) 29 May 1919 George Pratt (Lewiston, ME)
  & Lillian Wade (Brockton, MA)
PRATT,Leslie S   Sex:M   23 Sep 1948 Dana C Pratt (Rutland, VT)
  & Priscilla Luty (Pittsburgh, PA)
PRATT,Lynda P   Sex:F   08 Apr 1948 Charles A Pratt (Hudson, NH)
  & Theresa R Briand (Hudson, NH)
PRATT,Mabel Edna   Sex:F   (Child #2) 06 Sep 1916 Hudson, NH George A Pratt
  (Lewiston, ME) & Lillian Wade (Brockton, MA)
PRATT,Shari Lynn Sex:F   12 Apr 1979 Richard W Pratt Jr & Catharine A Levesque
PRATT,Sylvia A   Sex:F   26 Jun 1949 Charles A Pratt & Theresa R Briand
PRATTE,Barry J   Sex:M   04 Feb 1962 Gaston G Pratte & Simone M A Ouellette
PRATTE,Holly J   Sex:F   24 Dec 1964 Gaston G Pratte & Simone M A Ouellette
PRATTE,Kenneth L   Sex:M   31 Mar 1969 Gaston G Pratte & Simone M Ouellette
PRATTE,Marcel N   Sex:M   14 Nov 1965 Alphonse I Pratte & Laurence V Roy
PREBLE,Christopher C   Sex:M   19 Aug 1973 Paul C Preble & Rosemarie Brzozowski
PREBLE,Kori L   Sex:F   07 Nov 1971 Paul C Preble & Rosemarie Brzozowski
PRICE,Jeffrey J   Sex:M   17 May 1968 Julius L Price & Alice J Pyne
PRICE,Matthew H   Sex:M   15 Feb 1968 Robert S Price & Dorothy J Baynes
PRIOR,Edward A   Sex:M   10 Mar 1952 Perley W Prior & Madaline A Uhl
PRIOR,Susan A   Sex:F   10 Jan 1951 Perley W Prior & Madaline A Uhl
PRIVE,Eric Matthew   Sex:M   21 Dec 1978 James Joseph Prive & Donna L Pruneau
PROCTOR,Sarah E   Sex:F   06 Dec 1973 Jeffrey C Proctor & Marilyn L Cameron
PROKO,Jameson Peter   Sex:M   29 May 1983 James Richard Proko
  & Nila Jean Belowski
PROKO,Margaret A   Sex:F   04 Nov 1958 Peter B Proko & June M Theriault
PROKO,Marian K   Sex:F   04 Nov 1958 Peter B Proko & June M Theriault
PROSKOW,Christine   Sex:F   03 Mar 1967 William A Proskow & Janet L Eilenberg
PROULX,Cathy L   Sex:F   23 Jan 1961 Julien L Proulx & Lorraine F Poliquin

HUDSON,NH BIRTHS

PROULX,Cynthia K   Sex:F   01 Oct 1958 Paul F Proulx & Betty J Jackson
PROULX,Gary P   Sex:M   02 Sep 1961 Paul F Proulx & Betty J Jackson
PROULX,Rodney A   Sex:M   08 Apr 1965 Paul F Proulx & Betty J Jackson
PROULX,Therese C   Sex:F   13 Feb 1957 Julien L Proulx & Lorraine T Poliquin
PROVENCAL,Alfred E   Sex:M   (Child #3) 10 Mar 1931 George Jos Provencal
  (Sherbrook, P Q) & Mary Blanche Lusignan (Nashua, NH)
PROVENCAL,Carl J   Sex:M   15 Apr 1953 Clement H Provencal & Rita L Belanger
PROVENCAL,Donald R   Sex:M   23 Feb 1954 Robert R Provencal & Doris B Ledoux
PROVENCAL,George R   Sex:M   06 Mar 1960 Ernest A Provencal & Marie-Anne E Roy
PROVENCAL,Gregory G   Sex:M   14 May 1950 Robert R Provencal & Doris B Ledoux
PROVENCAL,Howard Elzear   Sex:M   (Child #1) 12 Mar 1926 Eugene Provencal
  (Providence, RI) & Alice Fontaine (Claremont, NH)
PROVENCAL,Joyce Doreen   Sex:F   (Child #2) 09 Sep 1934 Eugene Provencal
  (Providence, RI) & Alice Fontain (Claremont, NH)
PROVENCAL,Leo Wilfred   Sex:M   (Child #2) 02 Oct 1923 George J Provencal
  (Sherbrook, P Q) & Mary Blance Lusignan (Nashu
PROVENCAL,Linda C   Sex:F   13 Mar 1962 Clement H Provencal & Rita L Belanger
PROVENCAL,Noah Jon   Sex:M   30 Dec 1977 Donald R Provencal & Sally E Bisbing
PROVENCAL,Rene J   Sex:M   21 Aug 1953 Ernest A Provencal & Janice N Carlton
PROVENCAL,Roger W   Sex:M   28 Sep 1951 Ernest A Provencal & Janice N Carlton
PROVENCAL,Toby J   Sex:M   12 Jul 1976 Donald R Provencal & Sally E Bisbing
PROVENCHER,David R   Sex:M   16 Apr 1959 Amede R Provencher & Yolande M Ouellet
PROVENCHER,Shana S   Sex:F   28 Dec 1968 Claude A Provencher & Shirley J Walser
PROVOST,Keith F   Sex:M   09 Jan 1967 Edward R Provost & Beatrice L Miron
PROVOST,Keven J   Sex:M   09 Jan 1967 Edward R Provost & Beatrice L Miron
PROVOST,Stephen R   Sex:M   24 Jan 1966 Edward R Provost & Beatrice L Miron
PRUNIER,Sherri Marie   Sex:F   10 Jul 1983 David Allan Prunier & Rosemary Costa
PURCELL,William Joseph Sex:M 31 Dec 1984 William M Purcell & Nancy M Currie
PURINGTON,Brenda L Sex:F   15 Jun 1963 Ronald G Purington & Jacquine E Norbert
PURINGTON,Gary A   Sex:M   11 Jan 1961 Ronald G Purrington & Jacquine E Nobert
PURINGTON,Jonathan Gary   Sex:M   06 Dec 1980 Gary A Purington & Dawn L Parent
PUTNAM,Flora E   Sex:F   25 Jul 1864 Hudson, NH Moses A Putnam & Lizzie
PUTNAM,Flora Ednah   Sex:F   25 Jul 1864 Hudson, NH Moses A S Putnam & Lizzie
PUTNAM,Florence Etta Sex:F 28 Oct 1869 Hudson, NH Moses A Putnam
  & Elizebeth H
PUTNAM,Grace M   Sex:F   (Child #6) 21 Mar 1908 Walter H Putnam (Massachusetts)
  & Carrie Page (Vermont)
PYNN,Branden R   Sex:M   23 Jul 1975 Barry G Pynn & Cynthia M Plynkofsky
QIERNON,Leo Richard   Sex:M   (Child #2) 21 Nov 1930 Charles W Qiernon
  (Nashua, NH) & Yvonne E Parent (Nashua, NH)
QUEEN,Francis X Jr   Sex:M   24 Dec 1974 Francis X Queen Sr & Joanne M Crowley
QUEEN,John F   Sex:M   22 Mar 1818 Hudson, NH John Queen & Sarah
QUEEN,John Franklin   Sex:M   22 Mar 1813 Hudson, NH John Queen & Sarah Pollard
QUEEN,Joseph G   Sex:M   01 Apr 1815 Dunstable John Queen & Sarah
QUEEN,Joseph Granville Sex:M 01 Apr 1815 Hudson, NH John Queen & Sarah Pollard
QUEEN,Sarah   Sex:F   31 Dec 1808 Hudson, NH John Queen & Sarah Pollard
QUEEN,Sophia   Sex:F   12 Feb 1811 Hudson, NH John Queen & Sarah Pollard
QUIGLEY,Charles M   Sex:M   27 Nov 1947 John A Quigley (Portland, ME)
  & Victoria L Grinnell (Bath, ME)
QUIGLEY,Colleen A   Sex:F   22 Jul 1961 John P Quigley & Jeanne H Morin
QUIGLEY,Herbert N   Sex:M   08 Jun 1962 William L Quigley & Sandra A Test
QUIGLEY,John P Jr   Sex:M   27 Jan 1960 John P Quigley & Jeanne H Morin
QUIGLEY,Kathryn N   Sex:F   03 Nov 1968 John P Quigley & Jeanne H Morin
QUIGLEY,Kellie J   Sex:F   13 Jul 1963 John P Quigley & Jeanne H Morin
QUIGLEY,Marie F   Sex:F   22 Feb 1960 William F Quigley & Carolyn E Jordan
QUIGLEY,Michael F Jr Sex:M   20 Jul 1973 Michael F Quigley Sr & Kathleen M Guz
QUIGLEY,Rachel A   Sex:F   05 Aug 1953 John A Quigley & Victoria L Grinnell
QUIGLEY,Richard G   Sex:M   (Child #6) 08 Jun 1946 John A Quigley
  (Portland, ME) & Victoria L Grinnell (Bath, ME)
QUIGLEY,Ruth E   Sex:F   30 May 1956 John A Quigley & Victoria L Grinnell

HUDSON, NH BIRTHS

QUIGLEY, Sarah A E   Sex:F   14 Jul 1949 John A Quigley & Victoria L Grinnell
QUIGLEY, Timothy S   Sex:M   31 Jan 1965 Philip A Quigley & Faith C Baldwin
QUINLAN, Kenith Cane   Sex:M   10 Dec 1984 Michael P Quinlan & Gail M Follansbee
QUINN, Jennifer M   Sex:F   16 Dec 1967 Robert H Quinn & Marjorie A Huntley
QUINN, Jessica Ann   Sex:F   22 Dec 1976 Timothy Quinn & Mary Ann Rondeau
QUINN, Megan Ashley   Sex:F   06 Mar 1985 William Paul Quinn
  & Madeleine A Whittier
QUINTAL, Marcia M B   Sex:F   14 Jun 1968 Richard R Quintal & Betty A McKinnon
QUINTAL, Richard R Jr Sex:M   11 Jun 1970 Richard R Quintal & Betty-Ann McKinnon
QUIRION, Brian Real Sex:M   15 Jun 1978 Paulin Andre Quirion & Diane Anna Audet
QUIRION, Corey Pierre Sex:M 31 Jul 1984 Rock J Quirion & Barbara J O'Leary
RABY, Eugene R   Sex:M   13 Mar 1954 Eugene R Raby & Helen C Palanski
RABY, Linda A   Sex:F   21 Dec 1951 Normand R Raby & Pauline G Hebert
RABY, Michelle T   Sex:F   07 Sep 1962 Maurice G Raby & Gloria M J Marquis
RABY, Sandra A   Sex:F   16 Dec 1949 Normand R Raby & Pauline G Hebert
RABY, Steven M   Sex:M   06 Dec 1952 Normand R Raby & Pauline G Hebert
RACHES, Gary S   Sex:M   23 Apr 1978 Stephen W Raches & Patricia Mills
RACKLIFF, Jolene Ann   Sex:F   26 Sep 1981 Joseph W Rackliff & Tammy Ann Leigh
RACKLIFF, Larry L   Sex:M   16 Aug 1969 Carl E Rackliff & Donna L Gehrlein
RAFFERTY, Carol E   Sex:F   16 Jun 1952 Lenard A Rafferty & Lillian J Beland
RAFFERTY, Charles H   Sex:M   (Child #1) 25 Jul 1946 Lenard A Rafferty
  (Hudson, NH) & Lillian J Beland (Hudson, NH)
RAFFERTY, Daniel F   Sex:M   10 Jul 1948 Daniel J Rafferty Jr (Nashua, NH)
  & Barbara Young (Nashua, NH)
RAFFERTY, Daniel J   Sex:M   (Child #1) 13 Jan 1922 Daniel J Rafferty
  (Ticonderoga, NY) & Lena B Reynolds (Manchester, NH)
RAFFERTY, Ian C   Sex:M   02 Aug 1974 Gary D Rafferty & Linda E Musgrave
RAFFERTY, Kathleen A   Sex:F   12 Mar 1950 Leonard A Rafferty & Lillian J Beland
RAFFERTY, Leonard Alfred   Sex:M   (Child #2) 27 Jun 1923 Daniel J Rafferty
  (Crown Point, NY) & Helena B Reynolds (Manchestester, NH)
RAFFERTY, Paul L   Sex:M   22 Jan 1949 Leonard A Rafferty & Lillian J Beland
RAFFERTY, Shawn Michael   Sex:M   19 Jan 1982 Gary D Rafferty & Linda E Musgrave
RAICHE, Brian William   Sex:M   19 Aug 1984 Michael W Raiche & Caren E Lamper
RAMASKA, Kerri Lee   Sex:F   31 Aug 1978 Peter J Ramaska Jr
  & Pamela Gail Williams
RAMSAY, Keith A   Sex:M   28 Oct 1968 Carlton A Ramsay & Janice C Parker
RAMSDELL, Christopher Michael   Sex:M   18 Oct 1980 Clifford L Ramsdell
  & Andrea Marie Wald
RAMSEY, Brad C   Sex:M   26 Aug 1974 Harry C Ramsey & Alma J Faulkner
RAMSEY, Keith B   Sex:M   04 Sep 1969 Harry C Ramsey & Alma J Faulkner
RAMSEY, Lynne I   Sex:F   21 Jan 1971 William P Ramsey & June C Robertson
RANCOURE, Peter A   Sex:M   (Child #1) 30 Jun 1906 Henry Rancoure (Maine)
  & Mary Southerland (Soctland, England)
RANCOURT, Heidi J   Sex:F   25 Jun 1968 Robert N Rancourt & Gloria E Lizotte
RANCOURT, Lisa M   Sex:F   29 Aug 1963 Robert N Rancourt & Gloria E Lizotte
RANCOURT, Marco S   Sex:M   15 Sep 1964 Claude C Rancourt & Lisette A Veilleux
RANDALL, Forest Stanley   Sex:M   (Child #2) 04 Jul 1911 Harold M Randall
  (Chester, VT) & Edythe L Hopkins (Hudson, NH)
RANDALL, James F Jr   Sex:M   (Child #1) 13 Jun 1944 James F Randall
  (Brownington, VT) & Edith E Johnson (Hooksett, NH)
RANDALL, Justin Pete Sex:M   07 Jun 1982 Stephen F Randall & Carla J Beauregard
RANDALL, Sara F   Sex:F   (Child #2) 30 Nov 1946 James F Randall (Brownington,
  VT) & Edith E Johnson (Hooksett, NH)
RANDALL, Walter Anderson   Sex:M   (Child #4) 15 Jul 1914 Harold M Randall
  (Chester, VT) & Edith L Hopkins (Hudson, NH)
RANDALL, [Unknown]   Sex:M   (Child #5) 02 Oct 1915 Hudson, NH Harold M Randall
  (Chester, VT) & Edith L Hopkins (Hudson, NH)
RANKIN, Kennan Rhyne   Sex:F   04 Apr 1985 John Rhyne Rankin & Maureen Ann Dumas
RANNEY, William F   Sex:M   22 Nov 1977 William F Ranney & Carolyn Ann Moody
RATTE, Craig   Sex:M   09 Mar 1968 Alphonse C Ratte & Vilma Morath

HUDSON,NH BIRTHS

RATTE,Denise   Sex:F   05 Apr 1966 Alphonse C Ratte & Vilma Morath
RATTE,Ellen   Sex:F   (Child #2) 30 Nov 1900 Peter Ratte (Canada)
   & Nellie Holden (Lowell, MA)
RATTE,Mary N   Sex:F   (Child #1) 31 Dec 1899 Peter Ratte (Canada)
   & Nellie Holden (Lowell, MA)
RATTE,Ralph Gilbert   Sex:M   (Child #1) 24 Sep 1907 Peter T Ratte (Canada)
   & Nellie D Holden (Lowell, MA)
RATTIN,Isaac P   Sex:M   21 Jun 1979 Michael R Rattin & Susanne L Schultz
RAU,Shane A   Sex:M   06 Jan 1966 Alan R Rau & Muriel E McLaughlin
RAUDONIS,Matthew R Sex:M 04 Mar 1978 Christopher A Raudon
   & Karen E Hulslander
RAUDONIS, [Unknown] Sex:F 11 Apr 1957 Alphonse J Raudonis & Sophie Raucykevich
RAUSER,Christine Elaine Sex:F 14 May 1982 Peter A Rauser & Elaine A Drugas
RAUSER,Kendra N   Sex:F   10 Aug 1976 Peter A Rauser & Elaine A Drugas
RAY,Barbara J   Sex:F   20 Sep 1957 Charles T Ray & Cynthia A Hilton
RAY,Charlene A   Sex:F   11 Oct 1956 Charles T Ray & Cynthia A Hilton
RAY,Delbert   Sex:M   (Child #1) 05 Jul 1943 Delbert Ray (Canada)
   & Gretchen Bowden (Stowe, MA)
RAY,Elsie Ada   Sex:F   (Child #1) 12 Oct 1912 Frank Ray (Hudson, MA)
   & Sarah McLaren (Sandown, NH)
RAY,Teresa L   Sex:F   09 Oct 1971 John R Ray & Elnyr L Moore
RAYMOND,Christopher S   Sex:M   15 Jun 1975 Robert W Raymond & Sally A Higgins
RAYMOND,Marilyn A   Sex:F   (Child #3) 23 Apr 1940 Ernest M Raymond (Barre, VT)
   & Florence M Bernier (Manchester, NH)
RAYMOND,Scott Joseph Sex:M   07 Dec 1978 Richard D Raymond & Carol Joan Gagnon
RAYNO,Amy R   Sex:F   04 Nov 1971 Arlo T Rayno & Judith A DeToro
RAYNO,Arlo T II   Sex:M   23 Jun 1968 Arlo T Rayno & Judith A DeToro
RAYNO,Heidi J   Sex:F   02 Dec 1964 Arlo T Rayno & Judith A DeToro
RAYNO,Rita M   Sex:F   10 Apr 1965 Merrill E Rayno & Sylvia I Lavarnway
REA,Jason F   Sex:M   09 May 1984 Frank Rea & Jacqueline E Prager
READ,Wayne A   Sex:M   23 Jan 1952 Lewis F Read & Lucille I Poney
REALEAU,[Unknown]   Sex:M   (Child #4) 10 May 1906 John Realeau (Salem, MA)
   & Josephine Duchesnean (Switzerland)
RECARD,[Unknown]   Sex:M   (Child #3) 02 Apr 1899 Leo L Recard (Fairfax, VT)
   & Grace Pettengell (Acworth)
RECKIS,Robert P   Sex:M   20 Mar 1979 Ralph P Reckis Jr & Joanne E Fowden
RECORD,[Unknown]   Sex:F   (Child #2) 22 Jun 1897 Leo L Record (Fairfax, VT)
   & Grace Pettengill (Acworth)
REDMAN,Benjamin Haynes Sex:M 19 Oct 1981 John B Redman & Janice Van Fleet
REDMAN,Sarah Anne   Sex:F   05 Sep 1979 John B Redman Jr & Janice Van Fleet
REED,Bernadette M   Sex:F   (Child #5) 31 Aug 1944 Ellsworth Reed (Northfield,
   VT) & Alice Jerry (Northfield, VT)
REED,Carrie Alyn   Sex:F   31 Jan 1978 Carl Bradley Reed & Carlene McKinley
REED,Dorothy Lucile   Sex:F   (Child #5) 10 Apr 1909 George Dustin Reed
   (Nashua, NH) & Eudora Mott (Sandy Hill, NY)
REED,Jennifer L   Sex:F   28 Jul 1969 Everett L Reed & Mandy C Kimball
REED,Kimberly D   Sex:F   07 Feb 1974 Dennis B Reed & Brenda L Merrill
REED,Mark J   Sex:M   18 Sep 1963 Joseph E Reed & Frieda Stenzel
REED,Roy T   Sex:M   22 Nov 1961 Richard A Reed & Elizabeth E Taylor
REED,Sonja E   Sex:F   15 May 1971 Everett L Reed Jr & Mandy C Kimball
REED,Steven J   Sex:M   18 Aug 1973 Everett L Reed Jr & Mandy C Kimball
REGAN,Michael David   Sex:M   14 Jul 1981 John Edward Regan & Debra Ann Silva
REILLY,David William   Sex:M   04 Sep 1979 Daniel P Reilly Sr & Lucille M Ihle
REILLY,Heather   Sex:F   16 Dec 1969 Richard R Reilly & Phyllis A McQuesten
REILLY,James M   Sex:M   03 Dec 1976 Daniel P Reilly & Lucille Maria Ihle
REILLY,Kathlyn H   Sex:F   10 Aug 1958 Raymond P Reilly & Ramona M Willette
REILLY,Robin   Sex:F   15 Nov 1961 Richard R Reilly & Phyllis A McQuesten
REITAN,Debra J   Sex:F   01 Dec 1963 David A Reitan & Alberta C Paton
REITAN,Kathryn A   Sex:F   19 Mar 1960 David A Reitan & Alberta C Paton
RELATION,Judith L   Sex:F   (Child #1) 18 Jun 1940 William H Relation (Nashua,

HUDSON,NH BIRTHS

NH) & Edith L Aldrich (Ruxbury, NY)
REMEIS,Valerie A   Sex:F   (Child #2) 07 Aug 1942 Walter Remeis (E Cambridge,
   MA) & Anne Casper (S Boston, MA)
RENAUD,Jeannette   Sex:F   (Child #2) 04 Aug 1926 Henry Renaud (Nashua, NH)
   & Regina Prevost (Lowell, MA)
RENAUD,Miranda J   Sex:F   02 May 1975 Paul E Renaud & Sandra A Kelley
RENZULLO,James L   Sex:M   26 Jun 1977 Andrew Renzullo & Faith E Hadsell
REVELS,Harry R   Sex:M   27 Aug 1957 Richard E Revels & Carol A Stenstream
REYNA,Randi Lee   Sex:F   25 Feb 1980 Anselmo M Reyna & Jerri Lynn O'Neil
REYNOLDS,Cory L   Sex:F   28 Sep 1974 George W Reynolds Jr & Donna M Kelley
REYNOLDS,David A Jr   Sex:M   25 Apr 1978 David A Reynolds Sr
   & Catherine May McIlve
REYNOLDS,David Michael Sex:M 24 Feb 1982 David M Cardos & Sharon A Reynolds
REYNOLDS,Edward F Jr   Sex:M   (Child #3) 09 Aug 1921 Edward F Reynolds
   (Bedford, NH) & Mary Burnham (Limrick, Ireland)
REYNOLDS,Joan Gertrude   Sex:F   (Child #1) 18 Jul 1938 George Reynolds (Epsom,
   NH) & Viola Willard (New Ipswich, NH)
REYNOLDS,Kimberly M   Sex:F   03 Mar 1972 George W Reynolds & Donna M Kelley
REYNOLDS,Lois F   Sex:F   (Child #2) 15 Mar 1940 George Reynolds (Epsom, NH)
   & Viola Willard (New Ipswich, NH)
REYNOLDS,Mildred E   Sex:F   (Child #4) 13 Apr 1899 Wm B Reynolds
   (Massachusetts) & Clara L Bailey (Nashua, NH)
REYNOLDS,Pamela E   Sex:F   05 Mar 1967 George W Reynolds Jr & Donna M Kelley
REYNOLDS,Patricia L   Sex:F   19 Jan 1954 George W Reynolds & Violet M Willard
REYNOLDS,Susan A   Sex:F   17 Aug 1949 Edward J Reynolds & Mary F Cole
REYNOLDS,William G   Sex:M   24 Feb 1970 George W Reynolds & Donna M Kelley
REYNOLDS,William Ray Sex:M 01 Jul 1980 David A Reynolds Sr
   & Catherine M McIlveen
REZK,Alisha Marie   Sex:F   10 Jul 1980 Peter Deeb Rezk & Joyce Lee Benoit
REZK,Michael A   Sex:M   01 Jul 1964 Ferris A Rezk & Jewell K Swift
RHEAUME,Barbara J   Sex:F   29 Mar 1965 Robert E Rheaume & Maureen F Smith
RHEAUME,Gloria J   Sex:F   20 Aug 1948 David R Rheaume (Nashua, NH)
   & Jeannette M Beaulieu (Nashua, NH)
RHEAUME,James P   Sex:M   (Child #4) 01 Apr 1945 David R Rheaume (Nashua, NH)
   & Jeannette M Beaulie (Nashua, NH)
RHEAUME,Marie R M   Sex:F   (Child #12) 19 May 1925 Joseph Rheaume (Quebec)
   & Rosalie Pelletier (Canada)
RHEAUME,Richard A   Sex:M   14 Jun 1971 Charles F Rheaume & Karen A Burton
RHEAUME,Richard D   Sex:M   (Child #3) 24 Nov 1943 David R Rheaume (Nashua, NH)
   & Jeannette Beaulieu (Nashua, NH)
RHYNER,Gordon B   Sex:M   23 Aug 1971 Gordon J Rhyner & Nancy C Marschke
RHYNER,Marc G   Sex: 28 May 1973 Gordon J Rhyner & Nancy C Marschke
RICARD,Audrey J   Sex:F   10 Nov 1970 Carl A Ricard & Mona C Boudreau
RICARD,Brian S   Sex: 03 Feb 1973 Paul R Ricard & Linda V Lemire
RICARD,David M   Sex:M   02 Jan 1975 Paul R Ricard & Linda V Lemire
RICARD,Laura G   Sex:F   16 Aug 1968 Carl A Ricard & Mona C Boudreau
RICARD,Ralph M   Sex:M   03 Nov 1953 Herve C Ricard & Theresa A Ducharme
RICARD,Raymond A   Sex:M   26 Feb 1957 Herve C Ricard & Therese A Ducharme
RICARD,Raymond Alan Jr   Sex:M   27 Apr 1983 Raymond A Ricard Sr
   & Denise A Robichaud
RICARD,Renee Marie Sex:F 05 Jan 1985 Raymond A Ricard Sr & Denise A Robicheau
RICARD,Robert C   Sex:M   18 Nov 1960 Herve C Ricard & Therese A Ducharme
RICARD,Ronald J   Sex:M   27 Dec 1965 Herve C Ricard & Therese A Ducharme
RICARD,Susan T   Sex:F   01 Aug 1958 Herve C Ricard & Therese A Ducharme
RICCARDI,Melissa   Sex:F   01 Nov 1984 Richard J Riccardi & Gail Chambers
RICCIO,Anthony R III   Sex:M   07 Jun 1978 Anthony R Riccio II
   & Debora Mae Vayens
RICE,Stephanie Lynn   Sex:F   16 Jul 1978 Joseph Matthew Rice
   & Martha Lynn Brown
RICH,Allen W   Sex:M   23 Apr 1966 William A Rich & Julia C Maddox

HUDSON, NH BIRTHS

RICH, Merilynn   Sex:F   (Child #1) 11 Nov 1938 Leon Reginald Rich (Haverhill, MA) & Olivette Lillian Cot (Nashua, NH)
RICH, Michael J   Sex:M   09 Dec 1964 Lester R Rich, Jr & Linda A Flanders
RICHARD, Brian K   Sex:M   11 Jan 1961 Joseph R E Richard & Eleanor B M Russell
RICHARD, Cindy A   Sex:F   15 Apr 1958 Joseph R Richard & Eleanor B Russell
RICHARD, Conrad Edgar   Sex:M   (Child #8) 13 Apr 1920 Alphonse Richard (Canada) & Marie L'ami (Centralville, MI)
RICHARD, Dana J   Sex:M   18 Dec 1959 Joseph R E Richard & Eleanor B Russell
RICHARD, Deborah L   Sex:F   22 Sep 1969 Michael G Richard & Sandra S Wallace
RICHARD, Denise M   Sex:F   08 Jan 1962 Joseph R E Richard & Eleanor B M Russell
RICHARD, Gary J   Sex:M   11 Apr 1964 Joseph R E Richard & Eleanor B M Russell
RICHARD, Joseph   Sex:M   (Child #6) 10 Dec 1915 Hudson, NH Alphonse Richard (Canada) & Mary Lamie (Canada)
RICHARD, Lorette R   Sex:F   (Child #9) 05 May 1921 Alphonse Richard (Canada) & Marie Lami (Centreville, MI)
RICHARD, Marie Isabelle   Sex:F   (Child #7) 21 Nov 1916 Hudson, NH Alphonse Richard (Canada) & Marie Lounie (Cedar, MI)
RICHARD, Michael G   Sex:M   (Child #3) 07 Nov 1943 Paul A Richard (Nashua, NH) & Esther J Clyde (Hudson, NH)
RICHARD, Paula M   Sex:F   24 Jan 1968 Michael G Richard & Sandra S Wallace
RICHARD, Raymond M   Sex:M   (Child #1) 16 Mar 1921 Albert Richard (Nashua, NH) & Yvonne Leclere (Canada)
RICHARD, Rosanna   Sex:F   (Child #10) 05 Feb 1922 Alphonse Richard (Canada) & Mary Lamy (Centralville, MI)
RICHARD, Sara Louise   Sex:F   09 Sep 1978 Arthur M Richard & Ruth Elaine Drown
RICHARD, [Unknown]   Sex:M   (Child #1) 10 Mar 1940 George E Richard (Nashua, NH) & Jean R Trazer (Manchester, NH)
RICHARDS, Bonnie M   Sex:F   02 Mar 1961 Charles A Richards & Gloria A Gagnon
RICHARDS, Brenda J   Sex:F   09 Oct 1964 Charles A Richards & Gloria A Gagnon
RICHARDS, John D   Sex:M   29 Aug 1968 Charles A Richards & Gloria A Gagnon
RICHARDS, Raymond Paul   Sex:M   (Child #1) 05 Feb 1934 Albert P Richards (Nashua, NH) & Esther Clyde (Hudson, NH)
RICHARDS, Robert Noe   Sex:M   (Child #2) 11 Nov 1937 Paul Richards (Nashua, NH) & Esther Clyde (Hudson, NH)
RICHARDSON, Anna   Sex:F   21 Nov 1801 Hudson, NH Samuel Richardson & Anna
RICHARDSON, Betsey   Sex:F   13 Nov 1802 Hudson, NH Asa Richardson & Lydia Mirick
RICHARDSON, Bette   Sex:F   13 Nov 1802 Hudson, NH Asa Richardson & Lydia
RICHARDSON, David   Sex:M   05 Aug 1763 Hudson, NH Zebediah Richardson & Rebecca
RICHARDSON, Ebenezer   Sex:M   04 Feb 1734 Hudson, NH Ebenezer Richardson & Ruth
RICHARDSON, Ebenezer   Sex:M   04 Feb 1733 Hudson, NH Ebenezer Richardson & Ruth
RICHARDSON, Elijah   Sex:M   13 Dec 1742 Hudson, NH Hugh Richardson & Jane
RICHARDSON, Hannah   Sex:F   03 Dec 1792 Hudson, NH Samuel Richardson & Anna
RICHARDSON, Henry   Sex:M   03 Nov 1738 Hudson, NH Thomas Richardson & Margaret
RICHARDSON, Honey   Sex:F   08 Jul 1739 Hudson, NH Amos Richardson & Sarah
RICHARDSON, Hugh   Sex:M   23 Jun 1737 Hudson, NH Hugh Richardson & Jane
RICHARDSON, Hugh   Sex:M   23 Jan 1736 Hudson, NH Hugh Richardson & Jane
RICHARDSON, James   Sex:M   10 May 1732 Hudson, NH Hugh Richardson & Jane
RICHARDSON, Jonas   Sex:M   04 Aug 1736 Hudson, NH Ebenezer Richardson & Ruth
RICHARDSON, Jonathan Harlow Jr   Sex:M   01 Jun 1983 Jonathan H Richardson & Judith M Mirocha
RICHARDSON, Kent T   Sex:M   23 May 1970 Thomas F Richardson & Janet Brown
RICHARDSON, Lattish   Sex:F   16 Jul 1740 Hudson, NH Thomas Richardson & Margaret
RICHARDSON, Letitia   Sex:F   16 Jul 1740 Hudson, NH Thomas Richardson & Margaret
RICHARDSON, Mary   Sex:F   08 Jul 1739 Hudson, NH Amos Richardson & Sarah
RICHARDSON, Michael S   Sex:M   19 Oct 1957 Robert B Richardson & Mary E Taylor
RICHARDSON, Phebe   Sex:F   19 Jan 1728 Litchfield Josiah Richardson & Phebe
RICHARDSON, Robert   Sex:M   19 Apr 1737 Hudson, NH Thomas Richardson & Margaret
RICHARDSON, Sarah   Sex:F   09 Feb 1798 Hudson, NH Samuel Richardson & Anna
RICHARDSON, Sarah   Sex:F   02 Feb 1798 Hudson, NH Samuel Richardson & Anna
RICHARDSON, Shane T   Sex: 10 Mar 1973 Thomas F Richardson & Janet Brown

HUDSON,NH BIRTHS

RICHARDSON,Sophia M   Sex:F   15 Jan 1801 Hudson, NH Asa Richardson & Lydia
RICHARDSON,Sophronia Merrill   Sex: 15 Jan 1801 Hudson, NH Asa Richardson
  & Lydia Mirick
RICHARDSON,Stephen   Sex:M   26 Oct 1738 Hudson, NH Hugh Richardson & Jane
RICHARDSON,Susanna   Sex:F   12 Nov 1756 Hudson, NH Seth Richardson & Sarah
RICHARDSON,Thomas   Sex:M   23 Aug 1740 Hudson, NH Hugh Richardson & Jane
RICHARDSON,Willis Sex:M   03 Jan 1805 Hudson, NH Asa Richardson & Lydia Mirick
RICHARDSON, [Unknown]   Sex:M   12 Jun 1741 Hudson, NH Amos Richardson & Sarah
RICHEY,Eleanor   Sex:F   1804 Hudson, NH James Richey & Abigail
RICHEY,Elenor   Sex:F   1804 Hudson, NH James Richey & Abigail
RICHEY,Elizabeth   Sex:F   10 Jul 1795 Hudson, NH James Richey & Abigail
RICHEY,Elizebeth   Sex:F   10 Jul 1795 Hudson, NH James Richey & Abigail
RICHEY,Hannah H   Sex:F   02 Apr 1791 Hudson, NH James Richey & Abigail
RICHEY,James   Sex:M   19 May 1793 Hudson, NH James Richey & Abigail
RICHEY,James   Sex:M   19 May 1798 Hudson, NH James Richey & Abigail
RICHEY,John   Sex:M   20 Nov 1808 Hudson, NH James Richey & Abigail
RICHEY,Martha B   Sex:F   19 Mar 1802 Hudson, NH James Richey & Abigail
RICHEY,Martha P   Sex:F   19 Mar 1802 Hudson, NH James Richey & Abigail
RICHEY,Mary C   Sex:F   19 Mar 1802 Hudson, NH James Richey & Abigail
RICHEY,Samuel E   Sex:M   19 Mar 1800 Hudson, NH James Richey & Abigail
RICHEY,Samuel S   Sex:M   19 Mar 1800 Hudson, NH James Richey & Abigail
RICHEY,Sarah S   Sex:F   12 Aug 1788 Hudson, NH James Richey & Abigail
RICHEY,Sarah S   Sex:F   20 Aug 1788 Hudson, NH James Richey & Abigail
RICHEY,Susanna   Sex:F   20 Nov 1797 Hudson, NH James Richey & Abigail
RIENDEAU,Linda D   Sex:F   07 Jun 1972 Jean M Riendeau & Rose M Lemire
RIENDEAU,Richard R   Sex:M   09 Jul 1974 Jean M Riendeau & Rose M Lemire
RIESE,Timothy J   Sex:M   02 Sep 1974 William Riese III & Marcia J Roberts
RIESENBERG,Elizabeth E Sex:F 10 Apr 1960 John J Riesenberg & Gloria P Cleary
RIESENBERG,Maria A   Sex:F   13 Mar 1964 John J Riesenberg & Gloria P Cleary
RILEY,Harry B   Sex:M   10 Jan 1958 Joseph J Riley & Patricia M Duclos
RILEY,Kerry A   Sex:F   06 Aug 1954 William T Riley & Dolores A Smith
RILEY,Laurie J   Sex:F   14 Jul 1959 William T Riley & Dolores A Smith
RILEY,Mary Kathleen   Sex:F   14 Apr 1983 William M Riley & Nancy Louise Babin
RILEY,Wendy L   Sex:F   07 Jul 1971 William T Riley Jr & Rhonda L Flora
RILEY,William T III   Sex: 05 Jan 1973 William T Riley Jr & Rhonda L Flora
RILEY,[Unknown]   Sex:M   14 Nov 1942 Walter Riley (Tyngsboro, MA)
  & Madelyn Welch (Lowell, MA)
RIOUX,April L   Sex:F   22 May 1974 Dennis W Rioux & Elaine T Parent
RIOUX,Jeffrey M   Sex: 13 Sep 1972 Edmund G Rioux & Linda S Walker
RIOUX,Mark L   Sex:M   15 May 1970 Ronald J Rioux & Jane A Mackey
RIOUX,Michelle L   Sex:F   11 Dec 1974 Edmund G Rioux Jr & Linda S Walker
RIPLEY,Albert Warren Sex:M Sep 1857 Hudson, NH Dustin Ripley & Melvina Palmer
RIPLEY,Alfred Cummings   Sex:M   16 Sep 1834 Hudson, NH Spencer Ripley
  & Mary Cummings
RIPLEY,Daniel   Sex:M   10 Feb 1823 Hudson, NH Spencer Ripley & Mary Cummings
RIPLEY,Dustin Sex:M   15 Oct 1819 Litchfield NH Spencer Ripley & Mary Cummings
RIPLEY,Edwin   Sex:M   09 Jan 1832 Hudson, NH Spencer Ripley & Mary Cummings
RIPLEY,Elizabeth Cummings   Sex:F   30 Sep 1824 Hudson, NH Spencer Ripley
  & Mary Cummings
RIPLEY,Elvira A   Sex: 1851 Hudson, NH Dustin Ripley & Melvina Palmer
RIPLEY,Eugene A   Sex:M   Apr 1849 Hudson, NH Dustin Ripley & Melvina Palmer
RIPLEY,Hannah S   Sex:F   04 Aug 1838 Hudson, NH Spencer Ripley & Mary Cummings
RIPLEY,Mary Ann Sex:F 30 Mar 1821 Litchfield NH Spencer Ripley & Mary Cummings
RIPLEY,Nathaniel Hale   Sex:M   28 May 1829 Hudson, NH Spencer Ripley
  & Mary Cummings
RIPLEY,Sarah Jane Sex:F 10 Nov 1826 Hudson, NH Spencer Ripley & Mary Cummings
RIVARD,Aime L Jr   Sex:M   03 Jul 1968 Aime L Rivard & Lucille A Scanlon
RIVARD,Kimberly B   Sex:F   03 Jul 1968 Aime L Rivard & Lucille A Scanlon
RIVARD,Richard N   Sex:M   (Child #11) 10 Jun 1946 Aime H Rivard (Nashua, NH)
  & Irene M Prince (Southbridge, MA)

HUDSON,NH BIRTHS

RIVARD,Roy P   Sex:M   (Child #10) 10 Jun 1946 Aime H Rivard (Nashua, NH)
  & Irene M Prince (Southbridge, MA)
RIVARD,Walter W   Sex:M   22 Mar 1948 Aime H Rivard (Nashua, NH)
  & Irene M Prince (Southbridge, MA)
RIVARD,[Unknown]   Sex:M   (Child #10) 06 Jul 1944 Aime J Rivard (Nashua, NH)
  & Irene M Prince (Southbridge, MA)
ROARKE,Ellen   Sex:F   (Child #2) 18 Nov 1904 John Roarke (Ireland)
  & Mary Considine (Ireland)
ROBADEAU,Roger W   Sex:M   (Child #2) 28 Jan 1922 Roger J Robadeau (Wilton, NH)
  & Luella M Scribner (Portland, ME)
ROBARGE,Joseph E   Sex:M   (Child #5) 14 Sep 1915 Hudson, NH Joseph F Robarge
  (Lowell, MA) & Marie R Labell (Nashua, NH)
ROBARGE,Stacey Peter Lentz Sex:M 31 Jan 1985 Peter R Robarge
  & Patricia A Lentz
ROBBINS,Franklin E Jr   Sex:M   11 Jan 1952 Franklin E Robbins & Emma L Troop
ROBBINS,Idell Henrietta   Sex:F   (Child #4) 31 Jul 1923 Carl E Robbins
  (Dunstable, MA) & Maude Fairhother (Westminster, VT)
ROBBINS,Michael A   Sex:M   26 Jul 1956 Frank E Robbins & Emma L Troop
ROBBINS,Sarah W   Sex:F   12 Aug 1958 Claude N Robbins & Patricia A Walker
ROBBINS,Willie E   Sex:M   10 Oct 1861 Hudson, NH David G Robbins & Amanda W
ROBBINS,[Unknown]   Sex:F   (Child #3) 15 Jun 1931 & Vera Wilson (Sandown, NH)
ROBBS,Cindy A   Sex:F   11 May 1970 Thomas E Robbs & Susan R Bearse
ROBEDEAU,Joseph M   Sex:M   03 May 1977 Michael L Robedeau & Diane Marie Drouin
ROBEDEAU,Tricia   Sex:F   06 Oct 1973 Michael L Robedeau & Diane M Drouin
ROBERGE,Leo Romeo   Sex:M   (Child #4) 06 Apr 1928 Adelard Roberge
  (Amoskeag, NH) & Eva Lupien (Newburyport, MA)
ROBERT,Barry J   Sex:M   12 Jul 1971 Jean G Robert & Sueallen Burleigh
ROBERT,David G   Sex:M   01 Jul 1971 Gerald A Robert & Susanne R Trepanier
ROBERT,Lisa Natalie   Sex:F   20 Jul 1976 Jean Guy Robert & Anna Elsie Pinette
ROBERT,Richard James Jr   Sex:M   10 Nov 1981 Richard J Robert Sr
  & Judy May Van Ness
ROBERTS,Alice Marion   Sex:F   30 Mar 1872 Hudson, NH Timothy Roberts
  & Clara F Webster
ROBERTS,Beth L   Sex:F   19 Feb 1969 Harry A Roberts & Carol R Covell
ROBERTS,Carl M   Sex:M   14 Apr 1971 Carl E Roberts & Marguerite E Anctil
ROBERTS,Catherine A Sex:F 23 Jun 1959 Joseph A Roberts & Catherine A Enwright
ROBERTS,Hugh E   Sex:M   28 Oct 1956 William L Roberts & Nancy J Spann
ROBERTS,Jennifer J Sex:F 02 Nov 1969 Joseph A Roberts Jr & Gloria J Champigny
ROBERTS,Jeremy D   Sex:M   25 Nov 1977 Mark Roberts & Kathleen R Beyer
ROBERTS,Jonathan F   Sex:M   18 Jan 1977 Joseph A Roberts & Gloria J Champigny
ROBERTS,Joseph AIII Sex:M 28 Jan 1975 Joseph A RobertsJr & Gloria J Champigny
ROBERTS,Kevin Marc   Sex:M   15 Oct 1975 Carl E Roberts & Marguerite E Anctil
ROBERTS,Marjorie E   Sex:F   30 Oct 1955 William L Roberts & Nancy J Spann
ROBERTS,Philip   Sex:M   08 Jun 1961 Joseph A Roberts & Catherine A Enwright
ROBERTS,Richard D   Sex:M   30 Sep 1969 Carl E Roberts & Marguerite E Anctil
ROBERTS,Susan D   Sex:F   11 Mar 1972 Carl E Roberts & Marguerite E Anctil
ROBERTSON,Owen D   Sex:M   30 Jun 1960 Edward J Robertson & Deborah A Siart
ROBERTSON,Paul S   Sex:M   22 Sep 1971 Thomas A Robertson & Mary A Casey
ROBIC,Tammy L   Sex:F   31 Jan 1959 Everett W Robic & Cynthia J Rollins
ROBIE,James E   Sex:M   30 Apr 1963 Everett W Robie & Cynthia J Rollins
ROBIE,Kenneth A   Sex:M   30 Jun 1967 Everett W Robie & Cynthia J Rollins
ROBINSON,Abigail   Sex:F   14 Aug 1779 Hudson, NH John Robinson & Rachel
ROBINSON,Alan P   Sex:M   27 Jan 1964 Prentice I Robinson & Donna L Ball
ROBINSON,Caren T   Sex:F   22 Apr 1965 Prentice I Robinson & Donna L Ball
ROBINSON,Carolyn Esther   Sex:F   08 Feb 1985 Michael L Robinson
  & Laura E Reeves
ROBINSON,Charlotte E Sex:F   (Child #1) 16 Apr 1888 Frank P Robinson (Hudson,
  NH) & Alecia A Young (Hudson, NH)
ROBINSON,Denis O   Sex:M   20 Jul 1966 Prentice I Robinson & Donna L Ball
ROBINSON,Ethel A   Sex:F   (Child #4) 24 Jul 1885 Hudson, NH Henry C Robinson

HUDSON,NH BIRTHS

(Hudson, NH) & Mary A Merrill (Nashua, NH)
ROBINSON,Grace F   Sex:F   (Child #5) 25 Oct 1889 H C Robinson (Hudson, NH)
  & Mary A Merrill (Nashua, NH)
ROBINSON,Hattie Louisa   Sex:F   14 Apr 1871 Hudson, NH Alphonso Robinson
  & Louisa A
ROBINSON,J Almer   Sex:M   28 Dec 1863 Hudson, NH Alphonzo Robinson
  & Louisa
ROBINSON,James C Sex:M   15 Apr 1881 Hudson, NH Henry C Robinson (Hudson, NH)
  & Mary A Merrill (Nashua, NH)
ROBINSON,Jody E   Sex:F   14 Dec 1956 Joseph C Robinson & Dorice M Demarais
ROBINSON,John Abner   Sex:M   28 Dec 1863 Hudson, NH Alphonsio Robinson
  & Louisa A Heselton
ROBINSON,John C   Sex:M   15 Mar 1977 John B Robinson & Mary E Beauregard
ROBINSON,John J   Sex:M   17 Jun 1952 Joseph C Robinson & Nancy B Lello
ROBINSON,Joseph C Jr Sex:M 27 Jan 1955 Joseph C Robinson, Sr
  & Dorice M Demarais
ROBINSON,Kevin J   Sex:M   21 Apr 1967 John B Robinson & Mary E Beauregard
ROBINSON,Laurie J   Sex:F   14 May 1971 John B Robinson & Mary E Beauregard
ROBINSON,Leona M   Sex:F   13 Oct 1874 Hudson, NH Henry Robinson & Addie
ROBINSON,Luther C   Sex:M   Feb 1867 Hudson, NH Alphonzo Robinson & Louisa
ROBINSON,Luther Clarence   Sex:M   Feb 1867 Hudson, NH Alphonsio Robinson
  & Louisa A Heselton
ROBINSON,Marjorie Lillian   Sex:F   (Child #7) 06 Jul 1928 Roger Robinson
  (Boston, MA) & Bertha Rowell (Salem, NH)
ROBINSON,Marylyn Leona Sex:F   (Child #9) 30 Mar 1933 Roger Robinson (Boston,
  MA) & Bertha Rowell (Salem, NH)
ROBINSON,Nettie Louisa   Sex:F   (Child #2) 24 Oct 1890 Frank P Robinson
  (Hudson, NH) & Alicia A Young (Hudson, NH)
ROBINSON,Sandra A Sex:F   (Child #2) 31 Oct 1944 Roger L Robinson (Hudson, NH)
  & Dorothy Bresnahan (Nashua, NH)
ROBINSON,Stephen M   Sex:M   10 Jan 1966 Benjamin P Robinson & Joan M Facteau
ROBINSON,Susan E   Sex:F   20 Apr 1967 Benjamin P Robinson & Joan M Facteau
ROBINSON,Thelma Evelyn   Sex:F   (Child #8) 12 Mar 1930 Roger L Robinson
  (Boston, MA) & Bertha V Rowell (Salem, NH)
ROBINSON,W E E   Sex:F   Hudson, NH   &
ROBINSON,[Unknown]   Sex:F   15 Nov 1872 Hudson, NH Henry C Robinson & Mary A
ROCHAKIAN,Leron   Sex:M   (Child #3) 25 Apr 1903 Stephen Rochakian (Armenia)
  & Badashan Kosaian (Armenia)
ROCHUSSEN,Alan G   Sex:M   08 Apr 1962 George A Rochussen & Jeanne D Provencal
ROCK,Barbara Ann   Sex:F   (Child #4) 04 Dec 1932 Hudson, NH Clarence Rock
  (Malone, NY) & Yvonne Coursy (Nashua, NH)
ROCK,Cheryl A   Sex:F   16 Oct 1958 Willard E Rock & Lorraine B Gagnon
ROCK,Leona M   Sex:F   25 Apr 1960 Leonard J Rock & Lorraine G Kirwan
ROCK,Marie Rose Anna Sex:F   (Child #6) 14 Jan 1936 Clarence Rock (Malone, NY)
  & Yvonne Coursey (Nashua, NH)
ROCKWELL,Amy E   Sex:F   08 Sep 1970 Albert L Rockwell Jr & Mari-Lee Seavey
ROCKWELL,Jennifer L Sex:F   09 Aug 1964 Albert L Rockwell,Jr & Mari-Lee Seavey
ROCKWELL,Kristen M   Sex:F   20 Jun 1966 Albert L Rockwell Jr & Mari-Lee Seavey
ROCKWELL,Stacey L   Sex:F   06 Dec 1967 Albert L Rockwell & Mari-Lee Seavey
ROCKY,[Unknown]   Sex:M   11 Jan 1874 Hudson, NH Joseph Rocky & Georgia
ROCQUE,Jennifer K   Sex:F   22 Sep 1975 Roger B Rocque & Donna L King
RODGERS,Angela D   Sex:F   21 Feb 1978 Dana A Rodgers & Beverly J Griffin
RODGERS,Barry J   Sex:M   15 Dec 1964 Kenneth J Rodgers & Patricia A Diggins
RODGERS,Bonnie F   Sex:F   05 Aug 1961 Kenneth J Rodgers & Patricia A Diggins
RODGERS,Brenda A   Sex:F   12 May 1960 Kenneth J Rodgers & Patricia A Diggins
RODGERS,Brett A   Sex: 10 Jul 1972 Kenneth J Rodgers & Patricia A Diggins
RODGERS,Brian K   Sex:M   16 Feb 1959 Kenneth J Rodgers & Patricia A Diggins
RODGERS,Dana A   Sex:M   17 Mar 1958 George P Rodgers & Barbara M Haight
RODGERS,Gary J   Sex:M   23 Jul 1957 Alvin H Rodgers & Mary E Reilly
RODGERS,Jeffrey Michael   Sex:M   06 May 1982 Gary James Rodgers

HUDSON,NH BIRTHS

& Robin Ann Scott
RODGERS,Joseph Duane Sex:M (Child #4) 29 Jan 1939 George H Rodgers (Nashua,
   NH) & Ella Landry (Canada)
RODGERS,Katie Elizabeth Sex:F 19 Nov 1984 Gary James Rodgers
   & Robin Ann Scott
RODGERS,Keith A Sex:M 07 Feb 1961 Alvin H Rodgers & Mary E Reilly
RODGERS,Kenneth James Sex:M (Child #3) 08 May 1935 George H Rodgers
   (Nashua, NH) & Ella Landry (Canada)
RODGERS,Lee A Sex:F 27 Jul 1960 George P Rodgers & Barbara M Haight
RODGERS,Linda A Sex:F 15 Jul 1968 Alvin H Rodgers & Betty A Morse
RODGERS,Lisa A Sex:F 12 Oct 1958 Alvin H Rodgers & Mary E Reilly
RODGERS,Mark R Sex:M 05 Jun 1963 Ronald F Rodgers & Patricia L Vaillanco
RODGERS,Nessa M Sex:F 16 Dec 1975 Michael H Rodgers & Diana C Duchesneau
RODGERS,Pamela J Sex:F 21 Feb 1965 Alvin H Rodgers & Betty A Morse
RODGERS,Ronald F Sex:M (Child #5) 26 Feb 1942 George H Rodgers (Nashua, NH)
   & Mary E Landry (Canada)
RODGERS,Todd A Sex:M 06 Oct 1964 George P Rodgers & Barbara M Haight
RODIER,Curtis A Sex:M 06 Mar 1953 Roland J Rodier & Helen D Quint
RODIER,Gale T Sex:F 22 Dec 1954 Hormidas D Rodier & Marie-Ange Bosse
RODIER,Jaime Lynn Sex:F 12 Jan 1977 Ronald W Rodier & Madeleine A Maltais
RODIER,Joseph Henri Sex:M (Child #7) 06 Mar 1937 Henri Rodier (Nashua, NH)
   & Rosanna Deschamps (Nashua, NH)
RODIER,Mary Sex:F (Child #3) 07 Sep 1917 John Rodier (Biddeford, ME)
   & Omerine Gagnon (Canada)
RODIER,Michel Robert Sex:M 26 Nov 1978 Ronald W Rodier & Madeleine M A Maltai
RODIER,Ronald W Sex:M 08 Mar 1948 Hormidas D Rodier (Nashua, NH)
   & Marie A Bosse (Manchester, NH)
RODONIS,Joseph A Jr Sex:M 18 Apr 1966 Joseph A Rodonis & Marilyn F MacDougall
RODONIS,Steven G Sex:M 07 Dec 1970 William J Rodonis Jr & Linda M Adams
ROEMER,Meghan Marie Sex:F 05 Apr 1984 Randolp L Roemer & Kimberly A Severance
ROGERS,Darrel H Sex:M 25 May 1965 James W Rogers & Thea A Bennett
ROGERS,David F Sex:M (Child #1) 19 Nov 1946 George A Rogers, Jr
   (Pittsfield, NH) & Natalie L Burnham (Nashua, NH)
ROGERS,Deborah A Sex:F 14 Jan 1948 George A Rogers, Jr (Pittsfield, NH)
   & Natalie L Burnham (Nashua, NH)
ROGERS,Geoffrey M Sex:M 21 Mar 1978 William H Rogers Jr & Joan M O'Brien
ROGERS,Jason C Sex:M 19 Feb 1962 George A Rogers, Jr & Natalie L Burnham
ROGERS,Jeffrey A Sex:M 21 Aug 1954 George A Rogers, Jr & Natalie L Burnham
ROGERS,Jonathan M Sex:M 25 May 1964 George A Rogers, Jr & Natalie L Burnham
ROGERS,Kirk Sex:M 03 Mar 1971 Thomas E Rogers & Darlene M Biberg
ROLEAU,Fay Vernay Sex:M 14 Jan 1902 John Roleau (Salem, MA) & Mary Andrezz
   (Switzerland)
ROLEAU,[Unknown] Sex:F (Child #3) 13 Oct 1903 John Roleau (Salem, MA)
   & Mary S Anderzz (Switzerland)
ROLEAU,[Unknown] Sex:F (Child #6) 15 Jun 1908 John Roleau (Salem, MA)
   & Marie Anderezz (Switzerland)
ROLFE,Clarissa Ann Sex:F 05 Sep 1853 Hudson, NH Stephen Rolfe & Caroline A
ROLLINS,Jacquelyn P Sex:F 22 Apr 1952 Irvine A Rollins & Ruth F Ford
ROLLINS,Leona G Sex:F 09 Aug 1950 Irvine A Rollins, Jr & Ruth F Ford
ROLLINS,Richard P Sex:M 22 Feb 1959 Gerald M Rollins & Estelle M Desmarais
ROLLINS,Roberta L Sex:F 16 Oct 1956 Irvine A Rollins & Ruth F Ford
ROLLINS,Susan J Sex:F 01 Jan 1948 Irvine A Rollins (Nashua, NH)
   & Ruth F Ford (Nashua, NH)
ROLLINS,Wesley I Sex:M 04 Jul 1960 Irvine A Rollins, Jr & Ruth F Ford
ROLO,Warren Atherton Sex:F (Child #1) 29 Dec 1922 Arthur C E Rolo (Nashua,
   NH) & Susan A Byrnes (S Boston, MA)
ROMANCZUK,Theodore Sex:M (Child #4) 04 Jun 1919 Louis Romanczuk (Ukrania)
   & Marie Kranouski (Austria)
ROMANO,Vincent L Sex:M (Child #1) 31 Jul 1946 Louis V Romano (W Lebanon, NH)
   & Jeannette B Desjard (Bradley, ME)

HUDSON,NH BIRTHS

ROMANOWSKI,Wtadystaw Stanistaw Sex:M (Child #2) 03 Jul 1914
  Antoni Romanowski (Russie) & Franciszka Grus (Austria)
ROOD,William Roger Jr Sex:M 24 Mar 1984 William Roger Rood & Sandra C Powell
ROOME,Jeffrey L Sex:M 17 Aug 1968 Theodore F Roome Jr & Catherine R McGonagle
ROONEY,Christine Meredith Sex:F 17 May 1982 Steven A Rooney & Martha J Price
ROONEY,Pamela Jeanne Sex:F 06 Oct 1980 Steven A Rooney & Martha Jeanne Price
ROPER,Lindsay Amelia Sex:F 16 May 1984 Stephen A Roper & Kelly K Sheedy
ROSAMOND,Julie A Sex:F 24 Feb 1967 John D Rosamond Jr & Jennifer A Owen
ROSE,Jessie Lametta Sex:F (Child #1) 25 Nov 1898 Bertram J Rose (Stockholm,
  NY) & Mary H Chestnut (Studholm, N B)
ROSEN,Heather B Sex: 15 Nov 1972 Lawrence J Rosen & Suzanne M Gilbride
ROSEN,Joshua John Sex:M 26 Nov 1978 Lawrence J Rosen & Suzanne M Gilbride
ROSMUS,Torrey A Sex:F 10 Jun 1967 Charles T Rosmus & Estella F Torrey
ROSS,Amanda Lea Sex:F 10 Jun 1974 James P Ross & Donna M Lea
ROSS,Jodi Lynn Sex:F 14 Mar 1982 Denis Albert Ross & Jill C MacDonald
ROSSI,Shawn P Sex:M 19 Mar 1970 Alfred F Rossi & Christina M Dumond
ROUILLARD,Peter F Sex:M 09 Apr 1968 Gary W Rouillard & Roxanne Fletcher
ROUILLARD,Scott A Sex:M 03 Sep 1969 Gary W Rouillard & Roxanne Fletcher
ROUILLE,Debra L Sex:F 16 Jul 1968 Henry F Rouille & Linda M Craig
ROUILLE,Robert F Sex:M 26 Jun 1969 Henry F Rouille & Linda M Craig
ROULEAU,Matthew Gerald Sex:M 06 Aug 1982 Raymond L Rouleau
  & Anne Marie P Bohan
ROULEAU,Stephen Raymond Sex:M 21 Sep 1978 Raymond L Rouleau
  & Anne Marie P Brohan
ROUNTREE,James J M Sex:M 07 Dec 1976 Bruce N Rountree & Janet L Doyle
ROUSSEAU,Erica Jeanne Sex:F 25 May 1984 Michael D Rousseau
  & Karen C Adamaitis
ROUSSEAU,James Joseph Jr Sex:M 18 Aug 1978 James J Rousseau Sr
  & Alfreda M P LeBlanc
ROUSSEAU,Karen M Sex:F 27 Jul 1966 James J Rousseau & Alfreda P LeBlanc
ROUSSEAU,Rebecca Ann Sex:F 01 Nov 1975 James J Rousseau & Alfreda M LeBlanc
ROUSSEL,Andrea J Sex:F 22 Aug 1968 Normand C Roussel & Vivianne E Beaudry
ROUSSEL,Jeanne A Sex:F 17 Jul 1967 Normand C Roussel & Vivianne E Beaudry
ROUSSEL,Luc O Sex:M 04 Nov 1965 Normand C Roussel & Vivianne E Beaudry
ROUSSEL,Michele L Sex:F 08 Oct 1971 Ronald A Roussel & Winifred E Reed
ROUSSIN,Christopher Michael Sex:M 09 Dec 1981 Richard J Roussin Sr
  & Monique L LaForest
ROWAN,Mary A Sex:F (Child #1) 22 Sep 1889 Thomas Rowan (Ireland)
  & Anna Burchall (Ireland)
ROWE,Adam Wallem Sex:M 10 Jun 1982 Michael Alan Rowe & Marjorie G Wallem
ROWE,Amber Elizabeth Sex:F 03 May 1984 Michael Alan Rowe & Marjorie G Wallem
ROWELL,Albert E H Sex:M 18 Jan 1962 Harold E Rowell & Yolande E Carrier
ROWELL,Barbara M Sex:F 15 Jun 1956 Clifton H Rowell & Mary E Keenan
ROWELL,Betty Edna Sex:F (Child #3) 10 Oct 1936 Clarence Rowell (Hudson, NH)
  & Elsie Gerow (Paris, ME)
ROWELL,Charles Clarence Sex:M (Child #4) 16 May 1938 Clarence E Rowell
  (Hudson, NH) & Elsie Mildred Gerow (Paris, ME)
ROWELL,Clarence E Sex:M (Child #9) 28 Aug 1910 Clarence Rowell (Lowell, MA)
  & May Wilson (Windham, NH)
ROWELL,Earl Clifton Sex:M (Child #3) 27 Apr 1933 Edwin E Rowell (Salem, NH)
  & Winnibel Merrill (W Buxton, ME)
ROWELL,Eugene W Sex:M 25 May 1971 Harold E Rowell & Yolande E Carrier
ROWELL,Florence R Sex:F (Child #8) 24 Oct 1943 Clarence E Rowell(Hudson, NH)
  & Elsie M Gerow (Paris, ME)
ROWELL,Forest A Jr Sex:M 12 Feb 1970 Forest A Rowell & Gail L Bell
ROWELL,George J Sex:M 12 Mar 1972 Charles C Rowell & Donna L Porter
ROWELL,Harold E Jr Sex:M 04 Oct 1964 Harold E Rowell, Sr & Yolande E Carrier
ROWELL,Harold Eugene Sex:M (Child #5) 03 Dec 1939 Clarence E Rowell
  (Hudson, NH) & Elsie M Gerow (Paris, ME)
ROWELL,Milton Frank Sex:M (Child #4) 16 Aug 1937 Edwin Rowell (Salem, NH)

HUDSON,NH BIRTHS

& Winnibel Merrill (W Buxton, ME)
ROWELL,Raymond P   Sex:M   07 Feb 1968 Harold E Rowell & Yolande E Carrier
ROWELL,Richard G   Sex:M   13 Jan 1951 Clarence E Rowell & Madaline A Uhl
ROWELL,Richard R   Sex:M   12 Sep 1966 Harold E Rowell & Yolande E Carrier
ROWELL,Russell R   Sex:M   19 Aug 1949 Clarence E Rowell & Elsie M Gerow
ROWELL,Susan C   Sex:F   23 Feb 1954 Clarence E Rowell & Elsie M Gerow
ROWELL,Theresa E   Sex:F   25 May 1974 Harold E Rowell Sr & Yolande E Carrier
ROWELL,William R   Sex:M   31 Jul 1948 Clarence E Rowell (Hudson, NH)
   & Elsie Gerow (Paris, ME)
ROWLETT,Brooks H   Sex:M   18 May 1980 Ira A Rowlett & Dawn K Hardy
ROWMAN,Jay T   Sex:M   22 Nov 1965 Philip J Rowman & Margaret H Burleigh
ROWMAN,Philip J Jr   Sex:M   10 Feb 1961 Philip J Rowman & Patricia A Douglas
ROY,Charles E J II   Sex:M   15 Jul 1966 Richard D Roy & Deborah G King
ROY,Christopher R   Sex:M   27 Jan 1970 Richard D Roy & Deborah G King
ROY,Garry R   Sex:M   16 Nov 1954 Gerard A Roy & Lesley N Loring
ROY,Gerard Lionel   Sex:M   (Child #4) 05 Jan 1932 Hudson, NH Theopli Roy
   (Canada) & Alonie Poulin (Canada)
ROY,Jacqueline Diane Sex:F   09 Oct 1981 Michael Walter Roy & Denise Ann Viens
ROY,Jeffrey Richard Sex:M 30 Jul 1984 Richard Arthur Roy & Jane I Fitzpatrick
ROY,Jimmy R   Sex:M   26 Apr 1969 Joseph R Roy & Claire Y Ruel
ROY,Joanne G   Sex:F   (Child #4) 21 Jul 1943 Leo S Roy (Canada)
   & Lauretta L Levesque (Nashua, NH)
ROY,Lawrence   Sex:M   (Child #12) 02 Mar 1934 Theophile Roy (Canada)
   & Alvine Poulin (Canada)
ROY,M Lebane Georgette   Sex:F   19 Jun 1929 Theophile Roy (Canada)
   & Aldine Poulin (Canada)
ROY,Marguerite   Sex:F   (Child #13) 03 Jan 1936 Theophile Roy (Canada)
   & Alvine Poulin (Canada)
ROY,Michael James   Sex:M 30 Jan 1982 Richard Arthur Roy & Jane I Fitzpatrick
ROY,Paul Joseph   Sex:M   06 Jul 1980 Paul Richard Roy & Marsha Ann Antoon
ROY,Richard A   Sex:M   27 Nov 1948 Arthur A Roy (Nashua, NH) & Helen G Hunt
   (Lebanon, NH)
ROY,Richard A   Sex:M   26 May 1961 Robert L Roy & Elaine P Berard
ROY,Richard R   Sex:M   03 May 1950 Joachim J Roy & Bertha Laliberte
ROY,Robert R   Sex:M   13 Oct 1948 Joachim Roy (Canada) & Bertha Laliberte
   (Suncook, NH)
RUCKMAN,Leanna D   Sex:F   13 Dec 1966 Donald S Ruckman & Alice C Matheny
RUEHRWEIN,Robert Mitchell   Sex:M   31 Aug 1984 Kevin R Ruehrwein
   & Catherine L Fraser
RUITER,Joan B   Sex:F   02 Nov 1957 Miles L Ruiter & Jane Cuthbertson
RUITER,Keith D   Sex:M   31 May 1963 Miles L Ruiter & Jane Cuthbertson
RUITER,Mark A   Sex:M   20 Dec 1961 Miles L Ruiter & Jane Cuthbertson
RUITER,Miles L   Sex:M   11 Aug 1956 Miles L Ruiter & Jane Cuthbertson
RUITER,Miles Leon Sex:M   (Child #7) 21 Feb 1933 Miles L Ruiter (Manchester,
   NH) & Helen V Sweeney (Manchester, NH)
RUSOL,Brenda J   Sex:F   30 Aug 1948 Joseph Rusol (Redbank, NJ)
   & Dorothy G Wood (Nashua, NH)
RUSSELL,Ann Helen Sex:F   (Child #1) 17 Sep 1941 Raymond T Russell(Hudson, NH)
   & Eva R Gingras (Peabody, MA)
RUSSELL,Brett A   Sex:M   11 Feb 1979 William A Russell & Dale Jane O'Brien
RUSSELL,Brian D   Sex:M   05 Mar 1975 Donald L Russell & Mary P Howes
RUSSELL,Carolyn E   Sex:F   09 Jun 1949 Raymond T Russell & Eva R Gingras
RUSSELL,Christopher P   Sex: 05 Apr 1973 Michael W Russell & Penny E Adams
RUSSELL,Kristi Jane Sex:F 20 Feb 1977 William A Russell Sr & Dale J O'Brien
RUSSELL,Marguerite E   Sex:F   (Child #1) 10 May 1908 Harry U Russell
   (Townsend, MA) & Helen A Center (Chelmsford, MA)
RUSSELL,Mark John Arthur   Sex:M   09 Jul 1983 Harold A Russell
   & Deborah Ann Moguin
RUSSELL,Michael W   Sex:M   04 Mar 1951 William Russell & Zara Zottu
RUSSELL,Nicholas Charles   Sex:M   29 Aug 1983 Toby Richard Russell

HUDSON,NH BIRTHS

& Lorrie A Wieczhalek
RUSSELL,Raymond Sex:M (Child #5) 16 Nov 1913 Herbert C Russell (W Medford, MA) & Etta E Osgood (Canada)
RUSSELL,Richard R Sex:M (Child #3) 26 Oct 1945 Raymond T Russell (Hudson, NH) & Eva R Gingras (Peabody, MA)
RUSSELL,Sylvia R Sex:F (Child #2) 23 Oct 1943 Raymond T Russell (Hudson, NH) & Eva R Gingras (Peabody, MA)
RUSSELL,William Harry Sex:M (Child #1) 15 Jun 1916 Hudson, NH Harry Russell (Mason, NH) & Annie Norton (Nova Scotia)
RUSSELL,[Unknown] Sex:F (Child #1) 05 Aug 1914 Clifford W Russell (Windham, NH) & Bertha S Sortelle (Lancaster,
RUSSO,Kerri Jean Sex:F 11 Feb 1983 Kenneth James Russo & Mary F Areseneaux
RUSSO,Nicole Marie Sex:F 08 Apr 1985 Kenneth James Russo & Mary F Arseneaux
RUSTON,Jesse David Sex:M 28 Jul 1981 Robert H Ruston Sr & Elaine Marie DeWitt
RUSTON,Joseph F Sex:M 03 Apr 1974 William F Ruston & Pauline R Richard
RUSTON,Nicholas J Sex:M 26 May 1978 Robert H Ruston Sr & Elaine Marie DeWitt
RUSTON,Robert H Jr Sex:M 05 May 1976 Robert R Ruston Sr & Elaine M DeWitt
RUTHERFORD,Bryana Lee Sex:F 22 Jan 1985 John A Rutherford & Brenda Lee Potter
RYAN,Elizabeth A Sex:F 09 May 1959 James L Ryan & Barbara A Lones
RYAN,Kelly A Sex:F 19 Dec 1968 Thomas M Ryan & Linda A Farrow
RYAN,Lisa A Sex:F 27 May 1958 Donald M Ryan & Eleanora Cagnina
RYAN,Thomas J Sex: 30 May 1973 Thomas J Ryan & Lorraine H Fellrath
RYAN,[Unknown] Sex:F (Child #2) 25 Dec 1914 Frank N Ryan (Nashua, NH) & Dora E Haselton (Hudson, NH)
RYAN,[Unknown] Sex:F (Child #3) 17 Aug 1916 Hudson, NH Frank Ryan (Nashua, NH) & Dora Haselton (Hudson, NH)
SABOL,Shalin Daisy Sex:F 13 Jan 1981 Frank E Sabol & Cathy Rene Traverse
SABOL,Tristin L Sex:F 23 Feb 1980 Frank E Sabol & Cathy Rene Traverse
SAFFORD,Cynthia J Sex:F 11 Aug 1952 Elmer K Safford & Mary B Spencer
SAGE,Eva M Sex:F 21 Jun 1960 Walter C Sage & Carmelle D Theriault
SAGE,Wynne F Sex:F 03 Aug 1957 Walter C Sage & Carmelle D Theriault
SAHAGIAN,Samuel Sex:M (Child #6) 08 Mar 1904 Avedis Sahagian (Armenia) & Ovsana Sarkisian (Armenia)
SAHAGIAN,[Unknown] Sex:M 22 May 1905 Aredis Sahagian (Armenia) & Oresan Tersorsian (Armenia)
SAIN,Elizabeth L Sex:F 13 Jul 1960 George T Sain & Elizabeth L Buttrey
SAKELLAR,Matthew Thomas Sex:M 10 Nov 1978 Jeffrey T Sakellar & Charlene L LaRocque
SALEK,Joan Sex:F (Child #8) 23 Nov 1931 Frank Salek (Lowell, MA) & Mary Cavanaugh (Lowell, MA)
SALESKY,Eric J Sex:M 16 Jun 1974 James P Salesky & Joanne L Boutilier
SALESKY,James P Sex:M 23 Feb 1951 Edward W Salesky & Constance A McInnis
SALESKY,[Unknown] Sex:F 22 Mar 1953 Edward Salesky & Constance McInnis
SALISBURY,Beverly Ann Sex:F (Child #5) 21 Jan 1938 Wm Putnam Salisbury (Putnam, CT) & Arline May Sears (Nashua, NH)
SALVAIL,Betty J Sex:F 21 Sep 1949 Clarence T Salvail & Emma I Martin
SALVAIL,Clarence P Sex:M 11 May 1947 Clarence T Salvail (Manchester, NH) & Emma I Martin (Manchester, NH)
SALVAIL,Ronald Sex:M (Child #3) 24 Aug 1934 Harry Salvail (Nashua, NH) & Sylvia Bellavance (Nashua, NH)
SALVUCCI,Julia Sex:F 24 Mar 1978 Germano Salvucci & Paula Mazzola
SAMALE,Marcus Walter Sex:M 25 Feb 1983 Marcus A Samale & Mary Cecilia Conuel
SANBORN,Eric A Sex:M 24 Sep 1968 Wilson A Sanborn & Jean E Jacobs
SANBORN,Fred E Sex:M 13 Mar 1883 Hudson, NH Fred Sanborn (Concord, NH) & Jennie H (Haverhill, NH)
SANBORN,Marilyn Sex:F (Child #1) 09 Nov 1938 Austin Wing Sanborn (Cranston, RI) & Roselle Eliz Morris (Nashua,
SANDERS,Gladis Eliza Sex:F 13 May 1898 Abraham L Sanders (Vermont) & Em M Bernard (Hudson, NH)
SANDERS,Gordon G Sex:M (Child #7) 23 Apr 1940 Theodore P Sanders

HUDSON,NH BIRTHS

(Pepperell, MA) & Ella N Rowell (Salem, NH)
SANDERS,Leola B Sex:F (Child #4) 13 Aug 1905 Abraham L Sanders (Washington, VT) & Emma M Bernard (Hudson, NH)
SANDERS,Mabel Linda Sex:F   03 Nov 1893 George O Sanders (Hudson, NH) & L P Thomas (Hudson, NH)
SANDERS,Robert Louis Sex:M (Child #1) 30 Jul 1910 Louis H Sanders (Nashua, NH) & Mary Conlon (Lynn, MA)
SANDERS,Viola B Sex:F (Child #5) 13 Aug 1905 Abraham L Sanders (Washington, VT) & Emma M Bernard (Hudson, NH)
SANFORD,John H Sex:M   25 Jan 1878 Hudson, NH Wilmot P Sanford (Nashua, NH) Bell (Illinois)
SANFORD, [Unknown] Sex:M May 1874 Hudson, NH George Sanford & Mary
SANGELEER,Carl A Sex:M 01 Sep 1970 Kenneth J Sangeleer & Beverly J Smith
SANTERRE,Marcella F Sex:F (Child #2) 31 Mar 1936 Arthur Santerre (Nashua, NH) & Cecile Beaulieu (Canada)
SARACENO,Justin C Sex:M 02 Jul 1977 Charles M Saraceno & Diane Johnson
SARACENO, [Unknown] Sex:M 24 Aug 1978 Charles M Saraceno & Diane Johnson
SARGENT,Abel Sex:M 27 Nov 1765 Hudson, NH Reuben Sargent & Lydia
SARGENT,Frances Sex:F 04 Apr 1875 Hudson, NH William F Sargent & Bridget Cutter
SARGENT,Henry William Sex:M 15 Jan 1771 Hudson, NH Reuben Sargent & Lydia
SARGENT,Henry William Sex:M 15 Jan 1770 Hudson, NH Reuben Sargent & Lydia
SARGENT,Karen Billie Sex:F 02 Jul 1976 William E Sargent & Cheryl Ann Beede
SARGENT,Kristi A Sex: 09 May 1973 William E Sargent & Cheryl A Beede
SARGENT,Lydia Sex:F 06 Nov 1773 Hudson, NH Reuben Sargent & Lydia
SARGENT,Page Sex:M 02 Feb 1769 Hudson, NH   & Elisebeth
SARGENT,Reuben Sex:M 28 Mar 1768 Hudson, NH Reuben Sargent & Lydia
SARGENT, [Unknown] Sex:M (Child #1) 21 Apr 1908 Harley M Sargent (Canada) & Alice S Deaette (Canada)
SARGENT, [Unknown] Sex:M (Child #1) 25 Jan 1913 Frank N Sargent (Nashua, NH) & Dora E Haselton (Hudson, NH)
SARNO,Anthony Joseph Sex:M 21 Mar 1984 Anthony John Sarno & Doreen Anne Dunn
SAUNDERS,Janet A Sex:F 06 Sep 1950 William R Saunders & Bette J Brodrib
SAUNDERS,Miles M Sex:M 28 Sep 1961 Arthur L Saunders,Jr & Sylvia F Moulton
SAUNDERS,Richard Wilbur Sex:M (Child #5) 15 Mar 1934 Theodore Saunders (Pepperell, MA) & Ella Rowell (Salem, NH)
SAVAGE,Darlene Sex:F 04 Dec 1958 Edward E Savage & Barbara E Jacobs
SAVAGE,Lorraine Sex:F 09 Dec 1964 Edward E Savage & Barbara E Jacobs
SAVICKAS,James V Sex:M 24 Aug 1958 Vytautas P Savickas & Bertha B Stoncius
SAVIKI,William Joseph Sex:M (Child #1) 18 Feb 1935 William J Saviki (Poland) & Mary Grohosky (Nashua, NH)
SAWYER,Ann M Sex:F 08 Jan 1969 Roger D Sawyer & Linda L Mountain
SAWYER,Blaine R Sex:M 06 Feb 1968 Irving H Sawyer & Leona M Demmons
SAWYER,Matthew Ryan Sex:M 14 Apr 1982 Dana Ray Sawyer & Linda Sherry Norman
SAWYER,Michael A Sex:M 25 Aug 1976 Lawrence A Sawyer & Linda M Kennery
SAWYER,Roger D Sex:M (Child #4) 27 Jun 1943 Ovila R Sawyer (Lowell, MA) & Cecile C Perrin (Lowell, MA)
SAWYER,Scott R Sex:M 24 Jun 1978 Dana R Sawyer & Linda S Norman
SAYRE,Benjamin G Sex:M 05 Jan 1977 Robert A Sayre & Mary E Cannan
SCALES,Deborah Sex:F 07 Feb 1951 Leslie E Scales & Marjorie T Kierstead
SCANLON,Jennifer J Sex:F 23 Mar 1969 Kevin H Scanlon & Annie K Patton
SCARBOROUGH,Jason M Sex:M 30 Dec 1974 William E Scarboroug & Joan E Brousseau
SCENNA,Ian Alexander Sex:F 03 May 1981 Leslie Scenna & Susan E Koppenhofer
SCHAEFFER,Brian Alan Sex:M 28 Feb 1985 William A Schaeffer & Faith A Coutermarsh
SCHARCH,Frank E Sex:M 12 Mar 1969 Donald P Scharch & Lucille Y Bouley
SCHEIBNER,Bethany Anne Sex:F 20 May 1980 Walter J Scheibner & Mary E Clark
SCHEIBNER,Meredith Joy Sex:F 09 Dec 1982 Walter J Scheibner & Mary Elisabeth Clark
SCHIAPPA,Christopher James Sex:M 22 Aug 1982 John Schiappa Jr & Susan Flynn

HUDSON,NH BIRTHS

SCHIAPPA,John III   Sex:M   10 Jul 1980 John Schiappa Jr & Susan Flynn
SCHIBANOFF,Justin Andrew   Sex:M   03 Feb 1982 Harry A Schibanoff
  & Judith A Kingsbury
SCHINDLER,Nancy G   Sex:F   19 Oct 1947 Walter R Schindler (Londonderry, NH)
  & Lillian E Winn (Nashua, NH)
SCHLOSSER,Alfred   Sex:M   30 May 1965 Bent Schlosser & Ulla-Britt Branstrom
SCHLOSSER,Ann K   Sex:F   15 Feb 1971 William A Schlosser & Patricia A Walter
SCHLOSSER,Matthew A Sex:M 26 May 1969 William A Schlosser & Patricia A Walter
SCHNEIDER,June Genevieve   Sex:F   (Child #6) 01 Jun 1924 Leon J Schneider
  (Burlington, VT) & Ruby Pearl Holbrook (Nashua, NH)
SCHNEPEL,Frederick W Jr Sex:M 18 Nov 1973 Frederick G Schnepel&Melody L Bent
SCHNEPEL,Randy John   Sex:M   30 Mar 1976 Frederick W Schnepel & Melody L Bent
SCHOEN,Kristina L   Sex:F   10 Jan 1980 Steven R Schoen & Dona J Haythorn
SCHOOLCRAFT,Winnie Etta   Sex:F   15 Jul 1869 Hudson, NH David M Schoolcraft
  & Georgianna S
SCHREITERER,Patty A Sex:F 27 Aug 1951 Robert F Schreiterer&Gloria R Campbell
SCHROEDER,Gerard E   Sex:M   20 Dec 1964 Donald A Schroeder & Ann M Ibach
SCHUMAN,Earle R   Sex:M   (Child #4) 04 Oct 1903 W G Schuman (Nova Scotia)
  & Grace Walker (Hudson, NH)
SCHUMAN,Gerry H Sex:M   (Child #3) 11 Jan 1902 Wenford H Schuman (Nova Scotia)
  & Grace Walker (Hudson, NH)
SCHUMAN,Lila May   Sex:F   (Child #2) 04 Oct 1899 Wenford Schuman (Nova Scotia)
  & Grace M Walker (Hudson, NH)
SCHUMAN,Winnie Frances   Sex:F   (Child #1) 23 Feb 1898 Wenford Schuman
  (Nova Scotia) & Grace Walker (Hudson, NH)
SCIRE,Catherine   Sex:F   17 Sep 1981 Robert Charles Scire & Jacqueline Errico
SCIRE,Robert Michael Sex:M 12 May 1983 Robert Charles Scire
  & Jacqueline Errico
SCLAR,Andrew G   Sex:M   24 Nov 1967 Stanley D Sclar & Maxine Rosenfeld
SCLAR,Jeremy M   Sex:M   21 Aug 1966 Stanley D Sclar & Maxine Rosenfeld
SCOTT,Claudia J   Sex:F   (Child #1) 18 Feb 1945 Woodrow F Scott (Websterville,
  VT) & Ida M Landry (Hudson, NH)
SCOTT,Elaine M   Sex:F   (Child #2) 22 Oct 1946 Woodrow F Scott (Barre, VT)
  & Ida M Landry (Hudson, NH)
SCOTT,Gilbert G   Sex:M   23 May 1958 Richard J Scott & Gloria G Martin
SCOTT,Jason D   Sex:M   06 Jan 1974 Murray D Scott & Dixy Lee Evans
SCOTT,Richard J Jr   Sex:M   17 Sep 1956 Richard J Scott & Gloria G Martin
SCOTT,Robin A   Sex:F   11 Nov 1961 Woodrow F Scott & Ida M Landry
SCOTT,Susan L   Sex:F   20 Aug 1950 Woodrow F Scott & Ida M Landry
SEABURY,Stacy A   Sex:F   29 Jul 1968 J Bradford Seabury & Ann M McNally
SEACE,Cathleen R   Sex:F   11 Feb 1971 Clayton R Seace & Colette M Gosselin
SEACE,Christopher R Sex:M 29 May 1969 Clayton R Seace Jr & Colette M Gosselin
SEACE,Daryl L   Sex:F   17 Sep 1970 Meredith B Seace & Dania L Bernard
SEALS,Elnathan   Sex:M   08 Jan 1815 Hudson, NH Elnathan Seals & Lydia
SEAMAN,Daniel A   Sex:M   22 Apr 1965 William R Seaman & Joann Gove
SEAMAN,Kathleen   Sex:F   07 Oct 1954 William R Seaman & Joann Gove
SEAMAN,Lisa   Sex:F   13 Apr 1960 William R Seaman & Joann Gove
SEAMAN,Robin   Sex:F   03 Nov 1957 William R Seaman & Joann Gove
SEARLES,Beatrice Helen   Sex:F   (Child #2) 16 Oct 1929 Edwin A Searles
  (Pelham, NH) & Beatrice May Patnaud (Derry, NH)
SEARLES,Blanche Beatrice   Sex:F   (Child #2) 30 Sep 1930 Edwin A Searles
  (Pelham, NH) & Beatrice May Patnaud (Derry, NH)
SEARLES,Cynthia A   Sex:F   01 Nov 1962 Emery A Searles & Vera E Chipman
SEARLES,Daniel   Sex:M   17 Jul 1715 Billerica MA Samuel Searles & Sarah
SEARLES,Daniel B   Sex:M   21 Oct 1779 Hudson, NH Thomas Searles & Lucy
SEARLES,David Bixby   Sex:M   21 Oct 1779 Hudson, NH Thomas Searles & Jenny
SEARLES,Elihia   Sex: 28 Sep 1759 Hudson, NH Jonathan Searles & Thankful
SEARLES,Eliker   Sex: 28 Sep 1759 Hudson, NH Jonathan Searles & Thankful
SEARLES,Elnathan   Sex:M   26 Mar 1763 Hudson, NH Jonathan Searles & Thankful
SEARLES,Elnathan   Sex:M   08 Jan 1815 Hudson, NH Elnathan Searles & Lydia

HUDSON,NH BIRTHS

SEARLES,Jacob   Sex:M   15 Apr 1757 Hudson, NH Jonathan Searles & Thankful
SEARLES,Jonathan   Sex:M   21 Sep 1720 Billerica MA Samuel Searles & Sarah
SEARLES,Jonathan   Sex:M   11 Apr 1752 Hudson, NH Jonathan Searles & Thankful
SEARLES,Jonathan   Sex:M   25 Sep 1720 Hudson, NH   &
SEARLES,Lydia   Sex:F   01 Jul 1765 Hudson, NH Jonathan Searles & Thankful
SEARLES,Lydia   Sex:F   12 Aug 1781 Hudson, NH Thomas Searles & Jenny
SEARLES,Samuel   Sex:M   01 Mar 1707 Billerica MA Samuel Searles & Sarah
SEARLES,Thankful   Sex:F   23 May 1750 Hudson, NH Jonathan Searles & Thankful
SEARLES,Thankfull   Sex:F   23 May 1750 Hudson, NH Jonathan Searles & Thankful
SEARLES,Thomas   Sex:M   28 Aug 1754 Hudson, NH Jonathan Searles & Thankful
SEARLES,Thomas   Sex:M   28 Aug 1758 Hudson, NH Jonathan Searles & Thankful
SEAVERANCE,Ann   Sex:F   14 Nov 1752 Hudson, NH Joseph Seaverance & Sarah
SEAVERANCE,Anna   Sex:F   14 Nov 1752 Hudson, NH Joseph Seaverance
   & Sarah Hills
SEAVERANCE,Caleb   Sex:M   15 May 1755 Hudson, NH Joseph Seaverance
   & Sarah Hills
SEAVERANCE,Joseph   Sex:M   12 Sep 1750 Hudson, NH Joseph Seaverance
   & Sarah Hills
SEAVERANCE,Joshua Sex:M 22 Dec 1757 Hudson, NH Joseph Seaverance
   & Sarah Hills
SEAVERANCE,Washington   Sex:M   08 Aug 1779 Hudson, NH & Elizabeth Crampton
SEAVEY,George H   Sex:M   (Child #1) 25 Sep 1891 Jos A Seavey (Pelham, NH)
   & Annie M Stewart (New Brunswick)
SEAVEY,Hannah   Sex:F   10 Nov 1784 Hudson, NH James Seavey & Elizabeth Davis
SEAVEY,Sibbel   Sex:F   06 Dec 1786 Hudson, NH James Seavey & Elizabeth
SEAVEY,Sybil   Sex:F   06 Dec 1786 Hudson, NH James Seavey & Elizabeth Davis
SEBOR,Mary L   Sex: 06 Dec 1972 Warren R Sebor & Mildred E Hoffman
SEDDON,William L   Sex:M   01 Jun 1970 Kenneth L Seddon & Linda L Bourdreau
SELFRIDGE,Aaron Micah   Sex:M   28 Sep 1975 Richard J Selfridge
   & Joanne E Deschenes
SELFRIDGE,Derek A   Sex: 12 Jul 1972 Richard J Selfridge & Joanne E Deschenes
SEMPLE,Victoria Lynn   Sex:F   13 Mar 1984 Alan R Semple & Suzanne Marie Crete
SENECAL,Gary P   Sex:M   06 Dec 1958 Louis M Senecal & Eleanor M Paige
SENECAL,Sandra D   Sex:F   27 Apr 1957 Louis M Senecal & Eleanor M Paige
SENNERVILLE,Lionel A   Sex:M   (Child #2) 10 Mar 1940 Amedee Sennerville
   (Suncook, NH) & Florida LeBlanc (Nashua, NH)
SENTER,Charles A   Sex:M   08 Jan 1863 Hudson, NH Thomas Senter & Roxanna
SENTER,James C   Sex:M   14 Dec 1963 James P Senter & Joyce A McGuire
SENTER,Jodi A   Sex:F   13 Dec 1961 James P Senter & Joyce A McGuire
SENTER,Melbourne E   Sex:M   08 Aug 1866 Hudson, NH George E Senter & Helen J
SENTER,William E   Sex:M   08 Aug 1866 Hudson, NH George E Senter & Louisa
SENTER,[Unknown]   Sex:F   22 May Hudson, NH John L Senter & S
SEUSS,Ellen   Sex:F   (Child #2) 20 Sep 1938 James Seuss (Clinton, MA)
   & Angela Despotopulos (Leominster, MA)
SEVERANCE,Joseph   Sex:M   23 Feb 1749 Hudson, NH   &
SEVERANCE,Joshua   Sex:M   22 Dec 1757 Hudson, NH Joseph Severance & Sarah
SEVERANCE,Ross William   Sex:M   08 Feb 1985 Timothy W Severance
   & Carolyn Dee Caissie
SEVERANCE,Todd L   Sex:M   16 Nov 1971 William L Severance & Helen L Mushrow
SEVIGNY,Michael R   Sex:M   15 Jan 1954 Andrew M Sevigny & Lorraine C Champoux
SEVIGNY,Paul A   Sex:M   (Child #2) 26 Aug 1943 Andre M Sevigny (Manchester,
   NH) & Lorraine C Champoux (St Johnsbury, VT)
SEYMOUR,Diane M   Sex:F   15 Oct 1962 Richard S Seymour & Annette Ouellette
SEYMOUR,Raymond W III Sex:M   13 Apr 1966 Raymond W Seymour Jr & Lynda A Allen
SEYMOUR,Steven N   Sex:M   23 Jul 1959 Richard S Seymour & Annette Ouellette
SEYMOUR,Sue A   Sex:F   01 Apr 1958 Richard S Seymour & Annette Ouellette
SHANAHAN,Benjamin Michael   Sex:M   10 Jan 1984 Michael D Shanahan
   & Nancy L Chrisicos
SHAPIRO,Mark W   Sex:M   15 Aug 1959 Alfred R Shapiro & Pauline R Michaud
SHARKEY,Kaitlyn Anne Sex:F 31 Dec 1984 Clifford J Sharkey & Janet Marie Plaia

HUDSON,NH BIRTHS

SHAUGHNESSY,James F IV   Sex:M   12 Jan 1970 James F Shaughnessy
   & Margaret A Guyette
SHAW,Emma E   Sex:F   25 Jun 1868 Hudson, NH James H Shaw & Ellen E Cummings
SHAW,Emma L   Sex:F   05 Jan 1868 Hudson, NH J Henry Shaw & Ellen E
SHAW,Hernon O   Sex:M   25 Jun 1875 Hudson, NH J H Shaw & Nellie
SHAW,John Taylor   Sex:M   23 May 1981 John Shaw & Janet Mary Dasey
SHAW,Nina L   Sex:F   09 Feb 1947 Kenneth L Shaw (Manchester, NH) & Alice Rook
   (Quincy, MA)
SHAW,Percy R   Sex:M   28 Jun 1963 Richard O Shaw & Arlene F Gagnon
SHAW,[Unknown]   Sex:M   04 Oct 1909 Frank O Shaw (Lowell, MA)
   & Grace H Blodgett (Lowell, MA)
SHEA,Anabel Susie   Sex:F   17 Nov 1873 Hudson, NH John Shea & Smith
SHEA,Christine M   Sex:F   24 Nov 1971 Edward P Shea Sr & Elizabeth A Clasby
SHEA,Donald Eugene   Sex:M   (Child #3) 02 Mar 1920 Daniel Shea (New Bedford,
   MA) & Margueritte Willette (Manchester, NH)
SHEA,Kevin J   Sex:M   04 Dec 1956 James D Shea & Eleanore R Seaman
SHEA,Terence M   Sex:M   30 Mar 1959 James D Shea & Eleanor R Seaman
SHEA,William J   Sex:M   12 Nov 1968 Edward P Shea & Elizabeth A Clasby
SHEEHAN,Cristin Ann   Sex:F   08 Oct 1982 Donald Sheehan & Ann Louise Meier
SHEFFIELD,Brent J   Sex:M   02 May 1975 William J Sheffield & Marcia E Huff
SHEPARD,Alfred H   Sex:M   12 Feb 1878 Hudson, NH Richard Shepard
   & Hannah S Ripley
SHEPARD,Edwin K   Sex:M   14 Jul 1871 Hudson, NH Richard Shepard
   & Hannah S Ripley
SHEPARD,Hope   Sex:F   08 Nov 1965 William M Shepard & Margaret H Cast
SHEPARD,Jennifer L   Sex:F   16 Aug 1971 William M Shepard & Margaret H Cast
SHEPARD,Larissa Maye   Sex:F   15 Dec 1982 James T Shepard III & Lisa Y Gourley
SHEPARD,Lisabeth A   Sex:F   07 Jul 1961 William M Shepard & Margaret H Cast
SHEPARD,Lizzie D   Sex:F   08 Aug 1869 Hudson, NH Richard Shepard
   & Hannah S Ripley
SHEPARD,Robert M   Sex:M   17 Feb 1958 Donald C Shepard & Rita A Nazer
SHEPARD,Tara Marie   Sex:F   07 Feb 1981 Frederick E Shepard & Lynne Marie Bates
SHEPARD,Wanda   Sex:F   (Child #1) 02 Jul 1918 Basil Shepard (Hudson, NH)
   & Ethel Merrill (Hudson, NH)
SHEPARD,William Merrill   Sex:M   (Child #6) 09 Mar 1935 Basil Shepard (Hudson,
   NH) & Ethel Merrill (Hudson, NH)
SHEPARD,Willie R   Sex:M   16 Feb 1875 Hudson, NH Richard Shepard
   & Hannah S Ripley
SHEPARDSON,David J   Sex:M   17 May 1970 David P Shepardson & Claire M MacDonald
SHEPHERD,Arthur H   Sex:M   (Child #4) 22 May 1912 Alfred Shepherd (Litchfield,
   NH) & Ada Armstrong (Hudson, NH)
SHEPHERD,Basil   Sex:M   (Child #3) 02 Jan 1896 Chas A Shepherd (Maine)
   & Addie C Doyle (Massachusetts)
SHEPHERD,Brian A   Sex:M   28 Aug 1965 Arthur H Shepherd Jr & Reta M Garside
SHEPHERD,Jeffrey S   Sex:M   03 Nov 1961 Arthur H Shepherd,Jr & Reta M Garside
SHEPHERD,Jodi A   Sex:F   29 Sep 1970 Arthur H Shepherd & Reta M Garside
SHEPHERD,LuAnn N   Sex:F   11 Feb 1956 Arthur H Shepherd & Beatrice N Fuller
SHEPHERD,Miriam Anna   Sex:F   (Child #2) 06 Nov 1926 Herbert A Shepherd
   (Massachusetts) & Mary E Perkins (Ossipee, NH)
SHEPHERD,Randy A   Sex:M   27 Feb 1964 Arthur H Shepherd,Jr & Reta M Garside
SHEPHERD,Robert W   Sex:M   (Child #2) 09 Aug 1943 Arthur H Shepherd (Hudson,
   NH) & Beatrice N Fuller (Hudson, NH)
SHEPHERD,[Unknown]   Sex:M   (Child #5) 19 Feb 1915 Hudson, NH Alfred H Shepherd
   (Litchfield, NH) & Ada E Armstrong (Hudson, NH)
SHEPPARD,[Unknown]   Sex:M   23 May 1963 Norman Sheppard & Sandra Tatosian
SHERMAN,Rebecca B   Sex:F   13 Aug 1977 Paul H Sherman & Diane J Leveille
SHERMAN,Scott F   Sex:M   27 Jul 1973 Paul H Sherman & Diane J Leveille
SHIEBLER,Daniel J   Sex:M   13 Jan 1970 Edward D Shiebler & Diana E Bardsley
SHIEBLER,Judith E   Sex:F   15 Jul 1957 Edward D Shiebler & Diana E Bardsley
SHIEBLER,Russell E   Sex:M   29 Jun 1958 Edward D Shiebler & Diana E Bardsley

HUDSON,NH BIRTHS

SHIEBLER,Susan E   Sex:F   08 Feb 1960 Edward D Shiebler & Diana E Bardsley
SHORT,Ethel F   Sex:F   (Child #9) 16 Oct 1891 George Short (Nashua, NH)
  & Roseanne Gerow (Hodgden, ME)
SHORT,Hattie E   Sex:F   27 Aug 1893 George Short (Nashua, NH) & Rose Gerow
  (Hodgden, ME)
SHORT,Percy Harrington Sex:M   (Child #7) 18 Feb 1890 George Short (Nashua,
  NH) & Roseann Gerow (Hodgden, ME)
SHORT,Percy Morrison Sex:M18 Feb 1890 Hudson, NH George Short & Rosanne Gerow
SHUMAN,Russell Owen   Sex:M   14 Nov 1983 Raymond Lewis Shuman & Donna M McGee
SHUMSKY,Kim E   Sex:F   01 Jul 1956 Sigismond Shumsky & Dorothy L Robinson
SHUMSKY,Linda L   Sex:F   (Child #2) 17 Aug 1946 Sigismund Shumsky (Nashua, NH)
  & Dorothy L Robinson (Nashua, NH)
SHUMSKY,Michael   Sex:M   13 Jun 1949 Sigisimond Shumsky & Dorothy L Robinson
SHUMSKY,Steven J   Sex:M   22 Dec 1959 Sigismond Shumsky & Dorothy L Robinson
SHUMSKY,William   Sex:M   (Child #1) 11 Jan 1943 Sigismund Shumsky (Nashua, NH)
  & Dorothy L Robinson (Nashua, NH)
SHUNAMAN,Amy Ruth   Sex:F   08 Nov 1915 Hudson, NH Charles G Shunaman
  (Nova Scotia) & Jessie M Logan (Nova Scotia)
SHUNAMAN,Charles L   Sex:M   07 Jan 1955 Leslie J Shunaman & Edna L Eugley
SHUNAMAN,Frances L   Sex:F   26 Oct 1953 Leslie J Shunaman & Edna L Eugley
SHUNAMAN,Ruth E   Sex:F   17 Sep 1950 Leslie J Shunaman & Edna L Eugley
SHUNEMAN,Leslie J Sex:M   (Child #2) 30 Nov 1913 Chas G Shuneman (E Passage,
  N S) & Jessie Logan (Nova Scotia)
SIBLEY,Erin Louise Sex:F   12 Jun 1982 Leslie Ray Sibley & Jennifer L Washburn
SIBLEY,Leisha Elaine Sex:F 10 Nov 1980 Leslie Ray Sibley & Jennifer L Washburn
SIDERIS,Darla F   Sex:F   12 Oct 1967 Nicholas C Sideris & Faith D Thomas
SIDERIS,Jason D   Sex:M   11 Jan 1969 Nicholas Sideris & Faith D Thomas
SIDILEAU,Janice L   Sex:F   09 Nov 1961 Roger W Sidileau & Joan P Mahan
SIDILEAU,Richard R   Sex:M   25 Apr 1964 Roger W Sidileau & Joan P Mahan
SIENKIEWICZ,Kathleen A   Sex:F   18 Dec 1953 Joseph Sienkiewicz & Sylvia L Cote
SIENKIEWICZ,Steven M   Sex:M   09 Jun 1958 Joseph Sienkiewicz & Sylvia L Cote
SILVA,David Jr   Sex:M   27 Feb 1948 David Silva (Canaan, NH)
  & Irene D Barrett (Holyoke, MA)
SILVA,Linda L   Sex:F   04 Apr 1968 John A Silva & Dorothy L Morton
SILVA,Todd C   Sex:M   11 Feb 1967 Robert J Silva & Gail Carson
SILVER,Burton W   Sex:M   Hudson, NH George W Silver & Hannah J Webster
SILVER,Daniel   Sex:M   Hudson, NH George W Silver & Hannah J Webster
SILVER,Edgar C   Sex:M   Hudson, NH George W Silver & Hannah J Webster
SILVER,John P   Sex:M   Hudson, NH George W Silver & Hannah J Webster
SIMARD,Aldea M   Sex:F   30 Mar 1950 Roland J Simard & Lillian J Pinard
SIMARD,Dorothy L   Sex:F   16 Jun 1951 Alphonse J Simard & Rhea A Dionne
SIMARD,Eugene E   Sex:M   (Child #1) 04 Jun 1940 Alphonse Simard (Canada)
  & Rhea Dionne (Nashua, NH)
SIMARD,Gerard B   Sex:M   (Child #3) 27 Sep 1946 Alphonse J Simard (Canada)
  & Rhea A Dionne (Nashua, NH)
SIMARD,Jennifer K   Sex: 30 Apr 1973 Gerard B Simard & Katherine J Bates
SIMARD,Michael P   Sex:M   05 Dec 1966 Eugene E Simard & Patricia F Morse
SIMARD,Philip A   Sex:M   11 Oct 1965 Ronald E Simard & Jeanne D Poney
SIMARD,Raymond D   Sex:M   12 Aug 1947 Roland J Simard (Canada)
  & Lillian J Pinard (Nashua, NH)
SIMARD,Roland A   Sex:M   12 Apr 1964 Ronald E Simard & Jeanne D Poney
SIMARD,Ronald G   Sex:M   (Child #2) 16 Feb 1943 Alphonse J Simard
  (St Francois, Canada) & Rhea A Dionne (Nashua, NH)
SIMARD,Thomas J   Sex:M   04 Feb 1974 Eugene E Simard & Patricia F Morse
SIMMONS,Linita E   Sex:F   27 Sep 1962 Lucious M Simmons & Gail P Allard
SIMONDS,Benjamin   Sex:M   16 Nov 1761 Hudson, NH Daniel Simonds & Martha
SIMONDS,Daniel   Sex:M   20 May 1753 Hudson, NH Daniel Simonds & Martha
SIMONDS,Eliphalet   Sex:M   20 Jun 1765 Hudson, NH Daniel Simonds & Martha
SIMONDS,Eliphalet   Sex:M   20 Jan 1765 Hudson, NH Daniel Simonds & Martha
SIMONDS,Joseph   Sex:M   19 Sep 1757 Hudson, NH Daniel Simonds & Martha

HUDSON,NH BIRTHS

SIMONDS,Martha Sex:F 23 Nov 1755 Hudson, NH Daniel Simonds & Martha
SIMONDS,Martha Sex:F 23 Nov 1756 Hudson, NH Daniel Simonds & Martha
SIMONDS,Rebecca Sex:F 18 Mar 1751 Hudson, NH Daniel Simonds & Martha
SIMONDS,Rebecca Sex:F 18 Mar 1750 Hudson, NH Daniel Simonds & Martha
SIMONDS,Susanna Sex:F 13 Dec 1759 Hudson, NH Daniel Simonds & Martha
SIMPSON,Deanna C Sex:F 17 Dec 1973 Emory L Simpson & Frances E Corbett
SIMPSON,Edward G Sex:M (Child #2) 08 Jun 1908 Edward G Simpson (Cambridge,
    MA) & Edith L Brintnall (Mansfield, NH)
SIMPSON,Edward Jr Sex:M (Child #2) 31 May 1943 Edward Simpson (Pelham, NH)
    & Cora B Smith (Hudson, NH)
SIMPSON,Herbert Sex:M (Child #4) 31 May 1945 Edward Simpson (Pelham, NH)
    & Cora B Smith (Hudson, NH)
SIMPSON,John J Sex: 14 Jul 1972 Emory L Simpson Jr & Frances E Corbett
SIMPSON,Joyce R Sex:F (Child #1) 20 Apr 1940 Edward Simpson (Pelham, NH)
    & Cora B Smith (Hudson, NH)
SIMPSON,Myrtle Louise Sex:F   01 May 1896 Alfred L Simpson (Methuen, MA)
    & Abbie L Nichols (Dracut, MA)
SIMPSON,Nellis S Sex:F 11 Jun 1875 Hudson, NH Isaac W Hale &
SIMPSON,[Unknown] Sex:M (Child #3) 30 Aug 1910 Edward Simpson
    (Cambridge, MA) & Edith Brautnall (Mansfield, MA)
SIMS,Tracy D Sex:F 20 Apr 1969 Richard J Sims & Sally Plouf
SIROIS,Andrew D Sex:M 21 Apr 1961 Donald H Sirois & Gladys F Carr
SIROIS,Anne J Sex:F (Child #2) 29 Jul 1945 Ralph Sirois (Caribou, ME)
    & Jennie Bankowski (Nashua, NH)
SIROIS,James A Sex:M 15 Nov 1965 Donald H Sirois & Gladys F Carr
SIROIS,Jane D Sex:F 19 Apr 1954 Leonce A Sirois & Beatrice I Charron
SIROIS,Lisa A Sex:F 07 Jun 1963 Donald H Sirois & Gladys F Carr
SIROIS,Mark E Sex:M 04 May 1970 Donald H Sirois & Gladys F Carr
SIROIS,Mark J Sex:M 11 Oct 1973 Richard J Sirois & Carol A Simpson
SIROIS,Norman A Sex:M 20 Nov 1954 Ralph Sirois & Jennie M Bankowski
SIROIS,Raymond A Sex:M 16 Apr 1956 Leonce A Sirois & Beatrice I Charron
SIROIS,Richard N Sex:M 31 Dec 1966 Donald H Sirois & Gladys F Carr
SIROIS,Robert C Sex:M 04 May 1970 Donald H Sirois & Gladys F Carr
SIROIS,Ryan Richard Sex:M 26 Sep 1979 J Richard Sirois & Elaine H Edington
SIRVYDAS,John D Sex:M 11 Dec 1964 John A Sirvydas & Marion M Stevenson
SIRVYDAS,Kristine A Sex:F 16 Nov 1966 John A Sirvydas & Marion C Stevenson
SITEMAN,Michael T Sex:M 01 Aug 1970 Thomas J Siteman & Patricia A Winterson
SITEMAN,Thomas J Jr Sex:M 13 Apr 1968 Thomas J Siteman Sr
    & Patricia A Winterson
SIVES,Draper J Sex:M   23 Feb 1948 John W Sives (Manchester, NH)
    & Rae Parmenter (Derry, NH)
SKELTON,Heidi Sex:F 28 Jan 1980 Clifford L Skelton & Judith T McCullough
SKLUITAS,Bertha Sex:F (Child #1) 29 Aug 1946 Anthony J Skluitas (Worcester,
    MA) & Bertha Akstin (Nashua, NH)
SKORKO,Frank B Sex: 08 Aug 1972 John E Skorko & Elaine G Skeats
SLADE,Elvis Aaron Presley Sex:M 01 Oct 1978 Danny K Slade & Pamela G Townsend
SLADE,Tammy L Sex:F 20 Aug 1971 Danny K Slade & Diane C Wolczok
SLATE,Clarance Sex:M   26 May 1881 Hudson, NH Clarance A Slate (Londonderry,
    NH) & Annie P Pendergast (Newmarket, NH)
SLATE,Phylis Laura Sex:F (Child #1) 19 Sep 1914 Clarence Slate, Jr
    (Hudson, NH) & Leah Ramsdell (Nashua, NH)
SLATER,Melissa Sex:F 17 Sep 1971 Joseph F Slater & Donna E Fielding
SLATTERY,Jameson P Sex:M 27 Jan 1979 Kevin T Slattery & Diane M Fraser
SLATTERY,Jaron Thomas Sex:M 01 Nov 1980 Kevin T Slattery & Diane Marie Fraser
SLATUNAS,Shawn M Sex:M 24 Jul 1974 William J Slatunas & Suzanne N Vadney
SLATUNAS,Timothy J Sex:M 01 Apr 1976 William J Slatunas & Suzanne N Vadney
SLOCUM,Frederick D Jr Sex:M (Child #2) 10 Jul 1946 Frederick D Slocum
    (Winthrop, MA) & Mildred E Reich (Manchester,
SLOCUM,Ramona Sex:M 09 Dec 1950 Frederick D Slocum & Mildred E Reich
SLOCUM,William S Sex:M   25 Jul 1947 Frederick D Slocum (Boston, MA)

HUDSON,NH BIRTHS

& Mildred E Reich (Manchester, NH)
SMALL,Dustin Edward Sex:M 14 Oct 1983 Francis Edward Small
& Valeria Ann Cranston
SMALL,Holly A Sex:F 27 Aug 1956 Francis E Small & Arlene C Kashulines
SMALL,Kevin F Sex:M 27 Aug 1956 Francis E Small & Arlene C Kashulines
SMART,Gregory W Sex:M 04 Sep 1965 William J Smart & Judith A Belliveau
SMART,Jason Jeffrey Sex:M 29 Jul 1981 Jeffrey Albert Smart
& Michelle M Hodgkins
SMILIKIS,James M Sex:M 03 May 1977 Michael J Smilikis & Joann Marie Faucher
SMILIKIS,Jennifer J Sex: 30 Oct 1972 Michael J Smilikis & JoAnn M Faucher
SMILIKIS,Michael J Sex:M (Child #3) 01 May 1945 Alphonse P Smilikis
(Nashua, NH) & Amelia E Balukevich (Nashua, NH)
SMILIKIS,Michelle Lorraine Sex:F 15 Apr 1981 Michael J Smilikis
& JoAnn Marie Faucher
SMILIKIS,William J Sex:M (Child #2) 29 Sep 1943 Alphonse P Smilikis
(Nashua, NH) & Amelia E Balukevich (Nashua, NH)
SMITH,Aidan L Sex: 10 Jun 1973 Peter N Smith & Susan E Shinn
SMITH,Albert E Sex:M (Child #1) 11 Aug 1891 Marcell H Smith (Charlestown,
MA) & Mary E Eaton (Kanawha, KS)
SMITH,Alfred A Jr Sex:M 15 Mar 1969 Alfred A Smith & Catherine M Redhead
SMITH,Alice G Sex:F 08 Feb 1861 Hudson, NH Norris Smith & Mary F Greeley
SMITH,Allice G Sex:F 08 Feb 1861 Hudson, NH Norris Smith & Mary F
SMITH,Amanda K Sex:F 29 Jun 1969 Clayton A Smith & Joanne Cloutier
SMITH,Angela M Sex:F 28 Feb 1979 David M Smith & Gwendolyn R Dean
SMITH,Ann Sex:F 13 Apr 1762 Hudson, NH Samuel Smith & Jenett
SMITH,Ann B Sex:F 14 Nov 1952 Leonard A Smith & Claire F Richard
SMITH,Aurentz F Sex: 05 Jan 1857 Hudson, NH Andrew J Smith & Abbie E Davis
SMITH,Barbara Sex:F 23 May 1766 Hudson, NH Samuel Smith & Jenett
SMITH,Barbara Ann Sex:F (Child #9) 13 Dec 1932 Nashua, NH Herbert D Smith
(Hudson, NH) & Blanche Greeley (Londonderry, NH)
SMITH,Benjamin Sex:M 04 Oct 1810 Hudson, NH Huey Smith & Lois
SMITH,Betsey Sex:F 12 May 1806 Hudson, NH James Smith & Mary Lawrence
SMITH,Betsey Sex:F 25 Aug 1792 Hudson, NH Samuel Smith & Elizabeth
SMITH,Bette Sex:F 12 May 1806 Hudson, NH James Smith & Mary
SMITH,Bette J Sex:F 21 Nov 1956 Harold D Smith & Hazel V Wilmot
SMITH,Bonny D Sex:F 17 Dec 1956 Kenneth R Smith & Lenita J Packard
SMITH,Brenda C Sex:F 08 Oct 1953 Harrison E Smith & Ellie B Clark
SMITH,Byron Butler Sex:M (Child #1) 27 Nov 1910 Arthur W Smith (Hudson, NH)
& May L Snow (Boston, MA)
SMITH,Catherine Sex:F 05 Aug 1796 Hudson, NH Mansfield Smith & Molly
SMITH,Charles Sex:M 30 Oct 1811 Hudson, NH James Smith & Mary Lawrence
SMITH,Charles Morgan Sex:M (Child #4) 11 Oct 1941 Ellsworth M Smith
(Middleton, MA) & Olga L Weeks (Warren, NH)
SMITH,Charles W Sex:M 21 Feb 1866 Hudson, NH Obediah F Smith &
SMITH,Chester R Sex:M 23 Sep 1970 Frank R Smith & Sharon L Pearl
SMITH,Christopher E Sex:M 06 Jul 1971 Walter H Smith Jr & Joan A Denbow
SMITH,Christopher J Sex:M 26 Jul 1968 James T Smith & Marjorie L Grover
SMITH,Christopher J Sex:M 22 Apr 1972 Kenneth W Smith & Donna M Crotty
SMITH,Clarence Leon Sex:M 06 Jan 1894 Edgar Smith (Hudson, NH)
& Addie A Austin (Haverhill, MA)
SMITH,Clarissa Sex:F 14 Aug 1808 Hudson, NH James Smith & Mary Lawrence
SMITH,Clayton Sex:M (Child #3) 07 Aug 1918 Arthur Smith (Nashua, NH)
& Ethelyn Batchelder (Haverhill, MA)
SMITH,Cora Blanche Sex:F (Child #2) 24 May 1917 Herbert D Smith (Hudson,
NH) & Blanche Greeley (Londonderry, NH)
SMITH,Cory R Sex:M 03 Sep 1977 Robert W Smith & Patricia Homan
SMITH,Craig R Sex:M 27 Nov 1948 Leonard A Smith (Manchester, NH)
& Claire F Richard (Nashua, NH)
SMITH,Curtis R Sex:M (Child #1) 24 Jun 1946 Robert C Smith (Nashua, NH)
& Martha E Smith (Hudson, NH)

HUDSON,NH BIRTHS

SMITH,Dana H   Sex:M   10 May 1954 Harold D Smith & Hazel V Wilmot
SMITH,Dana L   Sex:M   12 Mar 1955 John K Smith & Marjorie A Carter
SMITH,Daniel   Sex:M   09 Jul 1795 Hudson, NH John Smith & Martha
SMITH,Danielle M   Sex:F   21 Nov 1965 Daniel H Smith & Bonita J Manley
SMITH,Danielle Melissa Sex:F 06 Dec 1982 David M Smith & Catherine Ann Picard
SMITH,David Benjamin Sex:M 16 Mar 1981 Gerald Duane Smith & Lucy Jean Mantsch
SMITH,David Matthew Sex:M 19 Jul 1984 David M Smith & Catherine Ann Picard
SMITH,David W   Sex: 20 Apr 1973 Warren F Smith & Elizabeth Slowik
SMITH,Deborah A   Sex:F   08 Jul 1947 Clayton E Smith (Hudson, NH)
    & Victoria Ladner (P E Island)
SMITH,Deborah L   Sex:F   03 Jul 1951 Richard P Smith & Edith M Chaplin
SMITH,Deering Greeley   Sex:M   (Child #1) 05 Jun 1896 Henry O Smith (Hudson,
    NH) & Marcia A Deering (Waterboro, ME)
SMITH,Donald R Jr   Sex:M   28 Jun 1958 Donald R Smith & Helen S Forsten
SMITH,Dorothy   Sex:F   (Child #4) 09 Sep 1902 Marcell H. Smith (Boston, MA)
    & Mary Eaton (Kansas)
SMITH,Dustin H   Sex:M   (Child #3) 05 Sep 1943 Henry E Smith (Hudson, NH)
    & Mary Kayros (Nashua, NH)
SMITH,Dylan Nicholas Henry   Sex:M   31 Jan 1984 Thomas Elmer Smith
    & Katherine Vassilakos
SMITH,Edmund G   Sex:M   Oct 1857 Hudson, NH David O Smith & Mary H Greeley
SMITH,Edna T   Sex:F   (Child #1) 04 Sep 1915 Hudson, NH Herbert D Smith
    (Hudson Centre, NH) & Blanche Greeley (Londonderry, NH)
SMITH,Eileen Bernadette   Sex:F   (Child #10) 23 Oct 1934 Harry Smith (Grand
    Rapids, WI) & Cecile Beauregard (Canada)
SMITH,Elizabeth Ella   Sex:F   (Child #3) 11 Nov 1914 Elmer F Smith (Hudson,
    NH) & Ethel M Connell (Hudson, NH)
SMITH,Elizabeth H   Sex:F   04 Feb 1771 Hudson, NH Timothy Smith & Lydia
SMITH,Elizabeth Haseltine Sex:F 04 Feb 1772 Hudson, NH Timothy Smith & Lydia
SMITH,Ella E   Sex:F   (Child #2) 22 Oct 1885 Hudson, NH Henry F Smith (Hudson,
    NH) & Elvira T Chamberlain (Nashua, NH)
SMITH,Eric B   Sex:M   26 Dec 1949 Harold D Smith & Hazel V Wilmot
SMITH,Ethel F   Sex:F   09 Aug 1875 Hudson, NH Watson Smith & Lucy
SMITH,Eva Roxanna   Sex:F   (Child #2) 29 Nov 1897 Perley Smith (Hudson, NH)
    & Lizzie J Rollins (Nashua, NH)
SMITH,Evelyn M   Sex:F   (Child #4) 17 Sep 1946 Gardner I Smith (Hudson, NH)
    & Ruth A Henry (Nashua, NH)
SMITH,Fanny   Sex:F   26 Apr 1813 Hudson, NH James Smith & Mary Lawrence
SMITH,Flora E   Sex:F   30 Nov 1881 Hudson, NH Edgar Smith (Hudson, NH)
    & Addie A (Haverhill, MA)
SMITH,Frank E   Sex:M   21 Jan 1949 Harold D Smith & Hazel Wilmot
SMITH,Frank H   Sex:M   (Child #2) 24 Sep 1940 Henry E Smith (Hudson, NH)
    & Mary Kayros (Nashua, NH)
SMITH,Frank Herbert Sex:M (Child #5) 11 Apr 1924 Herbert D Smith (Hudson,
    NH) & Blanche Greeley (Londonderry, NH)
SMITH,Fred Ray   Sex:M   (Child #2) 18 Jun 1928 Fred Ray Smith (Orange, NJ)
    & Freda Lillian Bailey (Morrisville, NJ)
SMITH,Gary P   Sex:M   09 Dec 1963 Joseph M Smith & Margaret M Haley
SMITH,Gasbery   Sex:M   23 May 1760 Hudson, NH Samuel Smith & Jennet
SMITH,Gloria Lillian   Sex:F   (Child #4) 04 Jan 1920 Elmer Smith (Hudson, NH)
    & Ethel Connell (Hudson, NH)
SMITH,Gordon Henry Sex:M   (Child #2) 08 Mar 1941 Gardner J Smith (Hudson, NH)
    & Ruth A Henry (Nashua, NH)
SMITH,Gretchen E   Sex:F   02 Sep 1977 Thomas J Smith & Carol L Brattain
SMITH,Hannah   Sex:F   09 Aug 1781 Hudson, NH Samuel Smith & Jenett
SMITH,Hannah   Sex:F   15 Aug 1782 Hudson, NH Page Smith & Lydia
SMITH,Hannah   Sex:F   27 Apr 1787 Hudson, NH Thomas Smith & Sarah
SMITH,Heidi A   Sex:F   24 May 1960 Harold D Smith & Hazel V Wilmot
SMITH,Heidi Lynn   Sex:F   14 Aug 1984 Gerald Duane Smith & Lucy Jean Mantsch
SMITH,Helen   Sex:F   (Child #3) 04 Dec 1918 Herbert Smith (Hudson, NH)

HUDSON,NH BIRTHS

   & Blanche Greeley (Londonderry, NH)
SMITH,Henry   Sex:M   29 May 1760 Hudson, NH Samuel Smith & Jenett
SMITH,Henry   Sex:M   17 Jan 1779 Hudson, NH Samuel Smith & Jenett
SMITH,Henry Elmer Sex:M (Child #1) 23 Apr 1911 E F Smith (Hudson, NH)
   & Ethel Mary Connell (Hudson, NH)
SMITH,Henry O   Sex:M   18 Dec 1864 Hudson, NH David O Smith & Mary H Greeley
SMITH,Henry O   Sex:M   24 Dec 1864 Hudson, NH David O Smith & Mary H
SMITH,Henry P W Sex:M 24 Apr 1867 Hudson, NH Obadiah F Smith & Philena Wason
SMITH,Henry W W Sex:M 24 Apr 1867 Hudson, NH Obediah F Smith & Philena
SMITH,Herbert L   Sex:M   Jan 1862 Hudson, NH David O Smith & Mary H Greeley
SMITH,Holly S   Sex:F   17 Dec 1969 Paul R Smith & Dawn M Leonard
SMITH,Hugh   Sex:M   17 Oct 1781 Hudson, NH Thomas Smith & Sarah
SMITH,Hurbert   Sex:M   Hudson, NH David Smith & Mary A
SMITH,Ivan Robinson Sex:M (Child #3) 22 Jul 1897 Marcell H Smith
   (Boston, MA) & Mary E Eaton (Kanwaka, KS)
SMITH,James   Sex:M   14 Jun 1784 Hudson, NH Thomas Smith & Sarah
SMITH,James   Sex:M   07 Oct 1802 Hudson, NH James Smith & Mary Lawrence
SMITH,James W Jr   Sex:M   30 Jul 1956 James W Smith & Georgette Briand
SMITH,Jamie Leigh   Sex:F   22 Dec 1984 Michael J Smith & Jayne M Matthewman
SMITH,Janet Athalie   Sex:F   (Child #1) 07 Sep 1938 Gardner Isaac Smith
   (Hudson, NH) & Ruth Athalie Henry (Nashua, NH)
SMITH,Jason W   Sex:M   09 Mar 1970 James F Smith & Brenda D Severance
SMITH,Jeffrey Curtis Sex:M 03 May 1977 Curtis Robert Smith & Deborah A French
SMITH,Jeffrey L   Sex:M   13 Feb 1959 John K Smith & Marjorie A Carter
SMITH,Jenette   Sex:F   10 Apr 1772 Hudson, NH Samuel Smith & Jenett
SMITH,Jennett   Sex:F   10 Apr 1772 Hudson, NH Samuel Smith & Jennet
SMITH,Jennifer L   Sex:F   24 Mar 1969 Harrison E Smith & Arline M Mason
SMITH,Jennifer Lee   Sex:F   13 Jul 1978 Scott Dustin Smith & Darlene E Davis
SMITH,Jennifer M Sex:F 25 Jun 1979 R Wayne Smith & Patricia H Homan
SMITH,Jeremiah   Sex:M   29 Apr 1780 Hudson, NH Page Smith & Lydia
SMITH,Jeremy J   Sex:M   12 Sep 1977 James W Smith Jr & Julia C Potter
SMITH,Jeremy P   Sex:M   06 Dec 1970 Larry Smith & Lucy A Hutton
SMITH,Jesse   Sex:M   24 Oct 1794 Hudson, NH Samuel Smith & Elizabeth
SMITH,Jesse   Sex:M   25 Oct 1794 Hudson, NH Samuel Smith & Elizebeth
SMITH,Jesse Davidson   Sex:M   27 Feb 1803 Hudson, NH Mansfield Smith & Molly
SMITH,John   Sex:M   03 Jul 1768 Hudson, NH Samuel Smith & Jenett
SMITH,John   Sex:M   12 May 1806 Hudson, NH James Smith & Mary Lawrence
SMITH,John B   Sex:M   12 apr 1795 Hudson, NH William Smith & Sarah
SMITH,John Bodwell   Sex:M   12 Apr 1795 Hudson, NH William Smith & Sarah
SMITH,John Haseltine   Sex:M   03 Jan 1776 Hudson, NH Page Smith & Lydia
SMITH,John Kilton   Sex:M   (Child #6) 11 May 1926 Albert E Smith (Hudson, NH)
   & Florence H Small (Stockton, ME)
SMITH,Jon Guy Jr   Sex:M   31 Jul 1979 Jon Guy Smith & Lisa Pearl Levesque
SMITH,Jonathan E   Sex:M   23 Jul 1977 Michael P Smith & Elizabeth A Carton
SMITH,Jonathan P   Sex:M   27 Dec 1952 Robert C Smith & Martha E Smith
SMITH,Joseph   Sex:M   08 Feb 1778 Hudson, NH Timothy Smith & Lydia
SMITH,Joseph B   Sex:M   07 Jun 1808 Hudson, NH Henry Smith & Louisa
SMITH,Joseph Butler   Sex:M   07 Jun 1808 Hudson, NH Huey Smith & Lois
SMITH,Joseph R   Sex:M   04 Oct 1977 Ray M Smith & Dianne S Jarvis
SMITH,Joyce E   Sex:F   (Child #2) 19 May 1940 Raymond F Smith (Manchester, NH)
   & Virginia Billingsby (Burlington,
SMITH,Kathleen E   Sex:F   22 Oct 1948 Robert C Smith (Nashua, NH)
   & Martha Smith (Hudson, NH)
SMITH,Kathy J   Sex:F   03 Jul 1951 Harold D Smith & Hazel V Wilmot
SMITH,Kevin G   Sex:M   27 Aug 1962 Gordon H Smith & Natalie J Ballard
SMITH,Kittridge A II Sex:M 14 Nov 1969 Kittridge A Smith & Catherine M Quinton
SMITH,Laura L   Sex:F   05 Aug 1952 Richard H Smith & Theresa L Morin
SMITH,Linnie A   Sex:F   09 Apr 1853 Hudson, NH Andrew J Smith & Abbie E Davis
SMITH,Lucas Adam   Sex:M   06 Feb 1980 Neil P Smith & Linda M Dornier
SMITH,Lydia   Sex:F   30 Apr 1774 Hudson, NH Timothy Smith & Lydia

HUDSON,NH BIRTHS

SMITH,Mansfield   Sex:M   30 Apr 1770 Hudson, NH Samuel Smith & Jenett
SMITH,Marc A   Sex:M   12 Apr 1959 Harold D Smith & Hazel V Wilmot
SMITH,Marcy   Sex:F   23 Aug 1784 Hudson, NH Samuel Smith & Marcy
SMITH,Margo A   Sex:F   26 Jun 1951 Glen S Smith & Beverly C Gale
SMITH,Marion C   Sex:F   (Child #1) 26 Apr 1906 Fred E Smith (Massachusetts)
  & Mary Sigel (New York)
SMITH,Marjorie Joyce   Sex:F   (Child #10) 04 Aug 1935 Herbert D Smith
  (Hudson, NH) & Blanche Greeley (Londonderry, NH)
SMITH,Mark D   Sex:M   23 Dec 1949 Glen S Smith & Beverly C Gale
SMITH,Mark H   Sex:M   07 Jun 1972 James T Smith & Marjorie L Grover
SMITH,Marsha Jane   Sex:F   14 Mar 1980 Thomas E Smith & Katherine Vassilakos
SMITH,Martha   Sex:F   25 Apr 1772 Hudson, NH Thomas Smith & Sarah
SMITH,Martha Elizabeth   Sex:F   (Child #5) 30 Nov 1924 Albert E Smith
  (Hudson, NH) & Florence Small (Stockton, ME)
SMITH,Martha R   Sex:F   Jul 1859 Hudson, NH David O Smith & Mary H Greeley
SMITH,Mary   Sex:F   23 Aug 1784 Hudson, NH Samuel Smith & Mary
SMITH,Mary   Sex:F   25 Feb 1817 Hudson, NH Huey Smith & Lois
SMITH,Matthew T   Sex:M   04 Jul 1970 Clayton A Smith & Joanne Cloutier
SMITH,Mehitabel   Sex:F   02 Feb 1778 Hudson, NH Page Smith & Lydia
SMITH,Mehitable   Sex:F   02 Feb 1778 Hudson, NH Page Smith & Lydia
SMITH,Melissa R   Sex:F   09 Mar 1975 Dana H Smith & Cynthia H Marquis
SMITH,Michael J   Sex:M   20 Jun 1957 John K Smith & Marjorie A Carter
SMITH,Minnie E   Sex:F   05 Jun 1856 Hudson, NH David O Smith & Mary H Greeley
SMITH,Nancy Jane   Sex:F   (Child #1) 11 Feb 1937 Henry E Smith (Hudson, NH)
  & Mary Kayros (Nashua, NH)
SMITH,Neal Onslow   Sex:M   (Child #4) 13 Nov 1901 Hudson, NH Perley B Smith
  (Hudson, NH) & Lizzie J Robbins (Nashua, NH)
SMITH,Newton Parker Sex:M   (Child #1) 16 Jan 1907 Herburt N Smith (Pelham,
  NH) & Lillie J Parker (Hudson, NH)
SMITH,Orin Newton Sex:M   (Child #3) 30 Jun 1899 Perley B Smith (Hudson, NH)
  & Lizzie J Robbins (Nashua, NH)
SMITH,Page   Sex:F   12 May 1779 Hudson, NH Thomas Smith & Sarah
SMITH,Parker   Sex:M   19 Apr 1804 Hudson, NH James Smith & Mary Lawrence
SMITH,Patricia A   Sex:F   23 Aug 1955 Harrison E Smith & Effie D Clark
SMITH,Patricia M   Sex:F   28 Feb 1957 Walter W Smith & Rita M Cote
SMITH,Paul R Jr   Sex:M   29 May 1971 Paul R Smith Sr & Dawn M Leonard
SMITH,Paula L   Sex:F   06 Jan 1955 Robert C Smith & Martha E Smith
SMITH,Peggy   Sex:F   12 May 1779 Hudson, NH Thomas Smith & Sarah
SMITH,Perley Butler   Sex:M   29 Aug 1871 Hudson, NH Isaac N Smith & Roxanna
SMITH,Phillis Helene   Sex:F   (Child #3) 15 Sep 1931 Harry Edward Smith (NH)
  & Mary Rosodofsky (MA)
SMITH,Polley   Sex:F   19 Feb 1800 Hudson, NH James Smith & Mary
SMITH,Polly   Sex:F   22 Dec 1793 Hudson, NH Mansfield Smith & Molly
SMITH,Polly   Sex:F   19 Feb 1800 Hudson, NH James Smith & Mary Lawrence
SMITH,Rebecca Jean   Sex:F   03 Jun 1976 Michael P Smith & Elizabeth Ann Carton
SMITH,Reed Montgomery III Sex:M 29 Apr 1985 Reed M Smith I&Theresa Y Noiseux
SMITH,Rhoda   Sex:F   02 Mar 1797 Hudson, NH James Smith & Mary Lawrence
SMITH,Robert   Sex:M   05 Mar 1799 Hudson, NH Mansfield Smith & Molly
SMITH,Robert Connell   Sex:M   (Child #2) 16 Nov 1912 Elmer Smith (Hudson, NH)
  & Ethel Connell (Hudson, NH)
SMITH,Roberta M   Sex:F   01 Oct 1955 Walter W Smith & Rita M Cote
SMITH,Ross George IV   Sex:M   18 Jun 1984 Ross George Smith III
  & Mary Ann VonDette
SMITH,Ruth E   Sex:F   (Child #1) 06 Nov 1895 Perley B Smith (Hudson, NH)
  & Lizzie J Robbins (Nashua, NH)
SMITH,Ruth Ethel   Sex:F   (Child #4) 17 Jan 1922 Herbert D Smith (Hudson, NH)
  & Blanche Greeley (Londonderry, NH)
SMITH,Samuel   Sex:M   02 Apr 1764 Hudson, NH Samuel Smith & Jenett
SMITH,Samuel   Sex:M   01 Apr 1764 Hudson, NH Samuel Smith & Jennet
SMITH,Samuel G   Sex:M   11 Dec 1767 Hudson, NH Thomas Smith & Sarah

HUDSON, NH BIRTHS

SMITH, Sandra D   Sex:F   (Child #1) 17 Jan 1945 Gordon L Smith (Manchester, NH)
& Marion D Dansevich (Nashua, NH)
SMITH, Sara   Sex:F   18 Mar 1798 Hudson, NH James Smith & Mary
SMITH, Sarah   Sex:F   22 Oct 1980 Richard Albert Smith & Beverly Diane Norton
SMITH, Sarah   Sex:F   03 Dec 1776 Hudson, NH Thomas Smith & Sarah
SMITH, Sarah   Sex:F   18 Mar 1798 Hudson, NH James Smith & Mary Lawrence
SMITH, Sarah E   Sex:F   02 Apr 1980 Ray M Smith & Dianne S Jarvis
SMITH, Sarah Frances   Sex:F   12 Feb 1981 Ross George Smith III
& Mary Ann VonDette
SMITH, Sarah Isabel   Sex:F   21 Jan 1874 Hudson, NH Fred F Smith & Sarah A
SMITH, Scott D   Sex:M   09 Dec 1957 Harold D Smith & Hazel V Wilmot
SMITH, Scott D   Sex:M   24 Jul 1962 John K Smith & Marjorie A Carter
SMITH, Shane M   Sex:M   10 Dec 1971 John W Smith & Jeanne A LaBounty
SMITH, Shannon   Sex:F   28 Jan 1984 Reed M Smith & Theresa Y Noiseux
SMITH, Sharon Lee   Sex:F   21 Jun 1976 Thomas E Smith & Katherine Vassilakos
SMITH, Sheri A   Sex:F   22 Mar 1961 Clyde F Smith & Mary J Garrison
SMITH, Sophia   Sex:F   26 Apr 1810 Hudson, NH James Smith & Mary Lawrence
SMITH, Sullivan   Sex:M   31 May 1814 Hudson, NH Huey Smith & Lois
SMITH, Terence J   Sex:M   28 Jul 1955 Harold D Smith & Hazel V Wilmot
SMITH, Thomas   Sex:M   01 Oct 1774 Hudson, NH Thomas Smith & Sarah
SMITH, Thomas E   Sex:M   28 Sep 1953 Henry E Smith & Mary Kayros
SMITH, Timothy   Sex:M   02 Oct 1952 Henry E Smith & Mary K Kayros
SMITH, Timothy C   Sex:M   04 Feb 1969 Warren F Smith & Elizabeth Slowik
SMITH, Toby L   Sex:M   11 Jan 1974 Clayton A Smith & Joanne Cloutier
SMITH, Trevor Merrick   Sex:M   24 Apr 1981 David M Smith & Gwendolyn Ruth Dean
SMITH, Trishia E   Sex:F   03 Nov 1975 Terence J Smith & Theresa H Smith
SMITH, Victor Haskell   Sex:M   18 Mar 1893 Marcell H Smith (Boston, MA)
& Mary E Eaton (Kanwaka, KS)
SMITH, Virginia L   Sex:F   (Child #2) 07 Feb 1943 Robert E Smith (Geneva, WI)
& Crystal A Coburn (Keene, NH)
SMITH, Wayne D   Sex:M   05 Nov 1970 Milton F Smith & Marian R Hind
SMITH, Zachary Paul   Sex:M   24 Sep 1984 Neil Patrick Smith & Linda Marie Dornier
SMITH, [Unknown]   Sex:M   (Child #5) 30 Sep 1887 James A Smith (Nashua, NH)
& Emma Cummings (Plaistow, NH)
SMITH, [Unknown]   Sex:M   (Child #2) 19 Nov 1908 Fred E Smith (Haverhill, MA)
& Addie L Conery (Constable, NY)
SMITH, [Unknown]   Sex:M   (Child #2) 20 Dec 1912 Arthur Smith (Hudson, NH)
& Mary Snow (Boston, MA)
SMITH, [Unknown]   Sex:M   (Child #3) 30 Nov 1914 Arthur W Smith (Hudson, NH)
& May L Snow (Boston, MA)
SMITH, [Unknown]   Sex:M   (Child #4) 19 Nov 1917 Arthur Smith (Hudson, NH)
& May Snow (Boston, MA)
SMITH, [Unknown]   Sex:F   23 May 1956 Gardner I Smith & Ruth A Henry
SMITH, [Unknown]   Sex:F   26 Oct 1977 G Terance Smith Sr & Theresa E Smith
SMITH, [Unknown]   Sex:M   12 Mar 1869 Hudson, NH Isaac Smith & Roxanna Butler
SMITHER, Michele Marie   Sex:F   01 Apr 1976 Terry H Smithers & Gale W Sparks
SMITHERS, Richard W   Sex:M   01 Oct 1971 Terry H Smithers & Gale W Sparks
SNAY, Justin P   Sex:M   08 Mar 1976 Joseph P Snay & Judith A Merrill
SNELL, Dana V S   Sex:M   01 Aug 1959 Dana W Snell & Shirley M Nolette
SNELL, Georgia L   Sex:F   21 Jul 1958 Dana W Snell & Shirley M Nolette
SNELL, Jay A   Sex:M   19 Jul 1962 Dana W Snell & Shirley M Nolette
SNETSINGER, Richard N   Sex:M   31 Oct 1958 Richard J Snetsinger & Nancy C Latour
SNOW, Alice J   Sex:F   (Child #4) 21 Feb 1943 Henry G Snow (Hudson, NH)
& Andrea J Birch (St John, N B)
SNOW, Benjamin   Sex:M   15 Dec 1754 Hudson, NH Henry Snow & Miriam
SNOW, Bridget   Sex:F   29 Jul 1719 Dunstable MA Joseph Snow & Bridget
SNOW, Donn H   Sex:M   18 Jan 1953 Henry G Snow & Andrea J Birch
SNOW, Edward J   Sex:M   21 Dec 1953 Harry W Snow & Estelle V Porier
SNOW, Henry   Sex:M   17 Nov 1725 Dunstable MA Joseph Snow & Bridget
SNOW, Henry   Sex:M   17 Apr 1757 Hudson, NH Henry Snow & Miriam

HUDSON,NH BIRTHS

SNOW,Henry G   Sex:M   (Child #6) 27 Oct 1908 Royal G Snow (Milton, MA)
  & Adelle E Walker (Boston, MA)
SNOW,John   Sex:M   11 Jan 1723 Dunstable MA Joseph Snow & Bridget
SNOW,Joseph   Sex:M   12 Apr 1739 Hudson, NH Jonathan Snow & Sarah
SNOW,Joseph   Sex:M   19 Mar 1721 Dunstable MA Joseph Snow & Bridget
SNOW,Joyce Marie   Sex:F   (Child #3) 18 Jan 1939 Henry G Snow (Hudson, NH)
  & Andrea Birch (Canada)
SNOW,Kenneth Lawrence   Sex:M   (Child #1) 11 Sep 1934 Roy E Snow (Nashua, NH)
  & Mae Strait (Lanett, AL)
SNOW,Mary   Sex:F   1737 Hudson, NH Jonathan Snow & Sarah
SNOW,Mary   Sex:F   Nov 1737 Hudson, NH Jonathan Snow & Sarah
SNOW,Miriam   Sex:F   16 Aug 1761 Hudson, NH Henry Snow & Miriam
SNOW,Nehemiah   Sex:M   04 Apr 1759 Hudson, NH Henry Snow & Miriam
SNOW,Philip   Sex:M   06 Sep 1735 Hudson, NH Jonathan Snow & Sarah
SNOW,Robert   Sex:M   11 Jan 1764 Hudson, NH Henry Snow & Miriam
SNYDER,Barbara   Sex:F   (Child #4) 14 Mar 1921 Leon J Snyder (Burlington, VT)
  & Ruby P Holbrook (Nashua, NH)
SNYDER,Darcy J   Sex:F   26 Jul 1974 Leon J Snyder III & Nancy J Pacheco
SNYDER,Lillie Sylvia   Sex:F   (Child #1) 08 Apr 1917 Leon J Snyder
  (Burlington, VT) & Ruby P Holbrook (Nashua, NH)
SNYDER,Louise Viola Sex:F   (Child #5) 26 May 1922 Leon J Snyder (Burlington,
  VT) & Ruby P Holbrook (Nashua, NH)
SNYDER,Rubie   Sex:F   (Child #2) 30 May 1918 Leon Snyder (Burlington, VT)
  & Pearl Holbrook (Nashua, NH)
SNYDER,Thomas J   Sex: 23 Aug 1972 Leon J Snyder III & Nancy J Pacheco
SOJKA,Alan A   Sex:M   30 Apr 1965 John F Sojka & Anne L Palanski
SOJKA,Brian M   Sex:M   12 Mar 1963 John F Sojka & Anne L Palanski
SOJKA,Eric C   Sex:M   30 Jul 1950 Chester W Sojka & Mary V Bogusz
SOJKA,Joyce H   Sex:F   25 Nov 1948 Chester W Sojka (Derby, CT)
  & Mary V Bogusz (Hudson, NH)
SOJKA,Kathryn M   Sex:F   (Child #1) 11 Oct 1945 Chester W Sojka (Derby, CT)
  & Mary V Bogusz (Hudson, NH)
SOJKA,Steven J   Sex:M   27 Jan 1959 John F Sojka & Ann L Palanski
SORENSON,Lynn M   Sex:F   30 May 1969 Maurice A Sorenson & Cynthia E Ronta
SOUCY,Armand Lucien   Sex:M   (Child #8) 30 Mar 1922 Auguste Soucy (Canada)
  & Rose Anna Hudon (Canada)
SOUCY,Daniel Mark   Sex:M   15 Jul 1981 Robert H Soucy Sr & Anne M Chapdelaine
SOUCY,Gerard L   Sex:M   (Child #4) 01 Feb 1916 Hudson, NH Auguste Soucy
  (Canada) & Rosanna Hudon (Canada)
SOUCY,Gregory Brian   Sex:M   19 Jun 1984 Brian Arthur Soucy & Sherry Ann Basch
SOUCY,Jennifer L   Sex:F   03 Jan 1975 Gerard R Soucy & Janice E Huhtala
SOUCY,Matthew Robert   Sex:M   17 Sep 1984 Gerald Soucy & Carol Maude Dumont
SOUCY,Patricia A   Sex:F   (Child #1) 10 Jan 1945 Armand L Soucy (Hudson, NH)
  & Mary F Viens (Nashua, NH)
SOUCY,Paul Emile   Sex:M   (Child #7) 26 Feb 1921 Auguste Soucy (Canada)
  & Rosanna Hudon (Canada)
SOUCY,Peter L   Sex:M   (Child #3) 15 Apr 1946 Roger Soucy (Nashua, NH)
  & Jeanette La Rose (Canada)
SOUCY,Robert J   Sex:M   30 Jun 1964 Andrew J Soucy & Josephine M Pelletier
SOUCY,Timothy A   Sex:M   04 Feb 1967 Gerald A Soucy & Roberta I Hartwell
SOUCY,Wayne A   Sex:M   03 Jul 1965 Gerald A Soucy & Roberta I Hartwell
SOUSA,Alan T   Sex:M   04 Sep 1965 John P Sousa & Patricia A McAweeney
SOUSA,Manuel Dias Jr   Sex:M   26 Jul 1976 Manuel D Sousa Sr & Kathleen M Hamel
SOUSA,Scott P   Sex:M   27 Jan 1968 John P Sousa & Patricia A McAweeney
SOUTHWICK,Eric S   Sex:M   28 Jun 1964 Richard R Southwick & Joan A Blackbrough
SOUTHWICK,Raymond B Sex:M 06 May 1962 Richard R Southwick&Jean A Blakebrough
SPACEK,Allyson Lynne Sex:F 19 Jul 1976 Robert E Spacek & Barbara B Vonderhors
SPACEK,[Unknown]   Sex:M   28 Oct 1979 Robert E Spacek & Barbara B Vonderhors
SPALDING,Albert   Sex:M   29 Nov 1867 Hudson, NH Jacob F Spalding & Delia
SPALDING,Alfred   Sex:M   22 Aug 1797 Hudson, NH Reuben Spalding & Susan Pierce

HUDSON, NH BIRTHS

SPALDING,Betty   Sex:F   18 Nov 17 Hudson, NH Levi Spalding & Anna
SPALDING,Charles W Sex:M   03 Oct 1835 Hudson, NH Willard Spalding
   & Sally Marsh
SPALDING,Dean H   Sex:M   28 Sep 1950 Donald H Spalding & Dorothy M Johnson
SPALDING,Dustin   Sex:M   27 Jul 1795 Hudson, NH Reuben Spalding & Susan Pierce
SPALDING,Ebenezer Sex:M   27 Mar 1750 Hudson, NH Stephen Spalding & Martha
SPALDING,Edward   Sex:M   17 Oct 1736 Hudson, NH Phineas Spalding & Mary
SPALDING,Edward   Sex:M   19 Nov 1764 Hudson, NH Levi Spalding & Anna
SPALDING,Elizabeth Sex:F   26 Nov 1741 Hudson, NH Edward Spalding & Elizabeth
SPALDING,Emeline F Sex:F   23 Aug 1830 Hudson, NH Willard Spalding
   & Sally Marsh
SPALDING,Ephraim Sex:M   27 Sep 1866 Hudson, NH Jacob F Spalding & Delia
SPALDING,Ephraim Sex:M   24 Sep 1866 Hudson, NH Jacob F Spalding &
SPALDING,Esther   Sex:F   11 Aug 1747 Hudson, NH Edward Spalding & Elizabeth
SPALDING,Esther   Sex:F   07 Jul 1770 Hudson, NH Levi Spalding & Anna
SPALDING,Esther   Sex:F   29 Jul 1755 Hudson, NH Reuben Spalding & Sarah
SPALDING,Esther P Sex:F   29 Jul 1817 Hudson, NH Willard Spalding
   & Sally Marsh
SPALDING,Esther Richardson Sex:F 20 Feb 1789 Hudson, NH Reuben Spalding
   & Susan Pierce
SPALDING,George   Sex:M   14 Sep 1766 Hudson, NH Levi Spalding & Anna
SPALDING,Hannah   Sex:F   19 Sep 1808 Hudson, NH Reuben Spalding
   & Hannah Barrett
SPALDING,Harold M Sex:M   (Child #2) 20 Jul 1889 Chas L Spalding (Nashua, NH)
   & Sarah B Merrill (Hudson, NH)
SPALDING,Helen C Sex:F   10 Jan 1887 Hudson, NH Charles L Spalding
   & Sarah P Merrill
SPALDING,Joseph Farley Sex:M 02 Nov 1760 Hudson, NH Stephen Spalding & Martha
SPALDING,Joshua Pierce Sex:M 15 Apr 1787 Hudson, NH Reuben Spalding
   & Susan Pierce
SPALDING,Levi   Sex:M   23 Oct 1737 Hudson, NH Edward Spalding & Elizabeth
SPALDING,Lizzie M Sex:F   20 Jun 1870 Hudson, NH Jacob F Spalding & Delia
SPALDING,Lucinda M Sex:F   01 Aug 1825 Hudson, NH Willard Spalding
   & Sally Marsh
SPALDING,Lucy   Sex:F   27 Jun 1744 Hudson, NH Edward Spalding & Elizabeth
SPALDING,Lydia   Sex:F   19 Dec 1743 Hudson, NH Phineas Spalding & Mary
SPALDING,Martha   Sex:F   03 Aug 1755 Hudson, NH Stephen Spalding & Martha
SPALDING,Martha   Sex:F   06 Apr 1768 Hudson, NH Levi Spalding & Anna
SPALDING,Molly   Sex:F   03 Feb 1748 Hudson, NH Stephen Spalding & Martha
SPALDING,Nathaniel Sex:M   18 May 1869 Hudson, NH Stephen Spalding & Martha
SPALDING,Olive   Sex:F   08 Apr 17 Hudson, NH Levi Spalding & Anna
SPALDING,Patricia J Sex:F 14 Apr 1947 Donald H Spalding (Hudson, NH)
   & Dorothy M Johnson (Pittsfield, NH)
SPALDING,Phebe   Sex:F   22 Jul 1828 Hudson, NH Willard Spalding & Sally Marsh
SPALDING,Phineas Sex:M   27 Apr 1745 Hudson, NH Phineas Spalding & Mary
SPALDING,Rachel   Sex:F   16 Apr 1758 Hudson, NH Stephen Spalding & Martha
SPALDING,Rachel   Sex:F   29 Apr 1771 Hudson, NH Stephen Spalding & Martha
SPALDING,Reuben   Sex:M   06 Sep 1761 Hudson, NH Reuben Spalding & Sarah
SPALDING,Reuben   Sex:M   02 Mar 1781 Hudson, NH Reuben Spalding & Susan Pierce
SPALDING,Reuben   Sex:M   01 Jul 1811 Hudson, NH Reuben Spalding
   & Hannah Barrett
SPALDING,Rhoda   Sex:F   09 May 1757 Hudson, NH Reuben Spalding & Sarah
SPALDING,Samuel   Sex:M   27 Mar 1763 Hudson, NH Stephen Spalding & Martha
SPALDING,Sarah   Sex:F   09 Aug 1740 Hudson, NH Phineas Spalding & Mary
SPALDING,Sarah   Sex:F   06 Apr 1754 Hudson, NH Edward Spalding & Elizabeth
SPALDING,Sarah A Sex:F   29 Dec 1818 Hudson, NH Willard Spalding
   & Sally Marsh
SPALDING,Sarah C Sex:F   31 Jan 1785 Hudson, NH Reuben Spalding & Susannah
SPALDING,Sarah Chandler Sex:F 30 Jun 1785 Hudson, NH Reuben Spalding
   & Susan Pierce

HUDSON,NH BIRTHS

SPALDING,Sewell   Sex:M   03 Apr 1791 Hudson, NH Reuben Spalding & Susan Pierce
SPALDING,Stephen   Sex:M   28 Oct 1766 Hudson, NH Stephen Spalding & Martha
SPALDING,Susan   Sex:F   23 Dec 1806 Hudson, NH Reuben Spalding
& Hannah Barrett
SPALDING,Susan   Sex:F   10 Sep 1821 Hudson, NH Willard Spalding & Sally Marsh
SPALDING,Susanna Sex:F   20 May 1783 Hudson, NH Reuben Spalding & Susan Pierce
SPALDING,Susannah   Sex:F   20 May 1783 Hudson, NH Reuben Spalding & Susannah
SPALDING,Thankful   Sex:F   16 Aug 1752 Hudson, NH Stephen Spalding & Martha
SPALDING,Willard Sex:M   10 Mar 1793 Hudson, NH Reuben Spalding & Susan Pierce
SPALDING,Willard Sex:M   19 Aug 1823 Hudson, NH Willard Spalding & Sally Marsh
SPALDING,[Unknown]   Sex:M   05 Nov 1737 Hudson, NH Phineas Spalding & Mary
SPAULDING,Betty   Sex:F   18 Nov 17 Hudson, NH Levi Spaulding & Anne
SPAULDING,Colleen Nicole   Sex:F   01 Jan 1982 Maurice A Spaulding
& Robin J Giguere
SPAULDING,Daniel   Sex:M   05 Nov 1737 Hudson, NH Phinehas Spaulding & Mary
SPAULDING,Dustin   Sex:M   27 Jul 1795 Hudson, NH Reuben Spaulding & Susanna
SPAULDING,Ebenezer   Sex:M   27 Mar 1750 Hudson, NH Stephen Spaulding & Martha
SPAULDING,Edward   Sex:M   17 Oct 1736 Hudson, NH Phineas Spaulding & Mary
SPAULDING,Edward   Sex:M   19 Nov 1764 Hudson, NH Levi Spaulding & Anne
SPAULDING,Elizabeth Sex:F 26 Nov 1741 Hudson, NH Edward Spaulding & Elizabeth
SPAULDING,Esther   Sex:F   11 Aug 1747 Hudson, NH Edward Spaulding & Elizabeth
SPAULDING,Esther   Sex:F   29 Jul 1755 Hudson, NH Reuben Spaulding & Sarah
SPAULDING,Esther   Sex:F   07 Jul 1770 Hudson, NH Levi Spaulding & Anne
SPAULDING,Esther R   Sex:F   20 Feb 1789 Hudson, NH Reuben Spaulding & Susanna
SPAULDING,George   Sex:M   14 Sep 1766 Hudson, NH Levi Spaulding & Anne
SPAULDING,Hannah   Sex:F   19 Sep 1808 Hudson, NH Reuben Spaulding & Hannah
SPAULDING,Hattie Louisa Sex:F   14 Apr 1874 Hudson, NH Jacob Spaulding & Delia
SPAULDING,Helen C Sex:F   (Child #1) 10 Jan 1887 Chas L Spaulding (Nashua, NH)
& Sarah B Merrill (Hudson, NH)
SPAULDING,Jessica Lynn   Sex:F   06 Jul 1982 Robert F Spaulding
& Barbara J Sherwood
SPAULDING,Joan Louise Greeley Sex:F   (Child #1) 13 Nov 1930 William Spaulding
& Francis Greeley (Lebanon, NH)
SPAULDING,Joseph F   Sex:M   02 Nov 1760 Hudson, NH Stephen Sapulding & Martha
SPAULDING,Joshua R   Sex:M   15 Apr 1787 Hudson, NH Reuben Spaulding & Susanna
SPAULDING,Leon E   Sex:M   28 Nov 1954 Albert M Spaulding & Theresa R Tessier
SPAULDING,Lucy   Sex:F   27 Jun 1744 Hudson, NH Edward Spaulding & Elizabeth
SPAULDING,Lydia   Sex:F   19 Dec 1743 Hudson, NH Phinehas Spaulding & Mary
SPAULDING,Martha   Sex:F   03 Aug 1755 Hudson, NH Stephen Spaulding & Martha
SPAULDING,Martha   Sex:F   06 Apr 1768 Hudson, NH Levi Spaulding & Anne
SPAULDING,Martha Ann Sex:F   (Child #1) 29 Jun 1937 Ned Spaulding (Hudson,
NH) & Ruth Ekstrom (Nashua, NH)
SPAULDING,Maurice A Sex:M   01 Oct 1953 Albert M Spaulding & Theresa R Tessier
SPAULDING,Maurice E Sex:M   28 Jan 1952 Albert M Spaulding & Theresa R Tessier
SPAULDING,Molle   Sex:F   03 Feb 1748 Hudson, NH Stephen Spaulding & Martha
SPAULDING,Molle   Sex:F   03 Feb 1747 Hudson, NH Stephen Spaulding & Martha
SPAULDING,Nathaniel   Sex:M   18 May 1769 Hudson, NH Stephen Sapulding & Martha
SPAULDING,Ned   Sex:M   (Child #2) 26 May 1910 Edward Spaulding (Hudson, NH)
& Anna E Sanders (Washington, VT)
SPAULDING,Ollive   Sex:F   08 Apr 17 Hudson, NH Levi Spaulding &
SPAULDING,Phinehas   Sex:M   27 Apr 1745 Hudson, NH Phinehas Spaulding & Mary
SPAULDING,Rachel   Sex:F   16 Apr 1758 Hudson, NH Stephen Spaulding & Martha
SPAULDING,Rachel   Sex:F   29 Apr 1771 Hudson, NH Stephen Sapulding & Martha
SPAULDING,Reuben   Sex:M   06 Sep 1761 Hudson, NH Reuben Spaulding & Sarah
SPAULDING,Reuben   Sex:M   01 Jul 1811 Hudson, NH Reuben Spaulding & Hannah
SPAULDING,Rhoda   Sex:F   09 Mar 1757 Hudson, NH Reuben Spaulding & Sarah
SPAULDING,Robert F   Sex:M   30 Dec 1959 Albert M Spaulding & Theresa R Tessier
SPAULDING,Samuel   Sex:M   27 Mar 1763 Hudson, NH Stephen Sapulding & Martha
SPAULDING,Sarah   Sex:F   09 Aug 1740 Hudson, NH Phinehas Spaulding & Mary
SPAULDING,Sarah   Sex:F   06 Apr 1754 Hudson, NH Edward Spaulding & Elizabeth

HUDSON,NH BIRTHS

SPAULDING,Sewel   Sex:M   03 Apr 1791 Hudson, NH Reuben Spaulding & Susanna
SPAULDING,Shawn Leon Sex:M   25 Sep 1981 Leon Earl Spaulding & Arlene M Mooney
SPAULDING,Stephen   Sex:M   28 Oct 1766 Hudson, NH Stephen Sapulding & Martha
SPAULDING,Susan   Sex:F   23 Dec 1806 Hudson, NH Reuben Spaulding & Hannah
SPAULDING,Thankful   Sex:F   16 Aug 1752 Hudson, NH Stephen Spaulding & Martha
SPAULDING,Willard   Sex:M   18 Mar 1793 Hudson, NH Reuben Spaulding & Susanna
SPAULDING,[Unknown]   Sex:F   (Child #1) 07 Jul 1904 Edw A Spaulding (Hudson, NH) & Annie E Sanders (Washington, VT)
SPAULDING,[Unknown]   Sex:F   (Child #2) 22 Feb 1917 William Spaulding (Freemont) & Cora Buzzell (Haverhill, MA)
SPAULDING,[Unknown]   Sex: Hudson, NH   & Sarah Ford
SPEAR,Daniel J   Sex:M   22 Sep 1947 Joseph Spear (Bridgeport, O) & Wanda C Legarsky (Nashua, NH)
SPEAR,Mark A   Sex:M   26 Feb 1971 Daniel J Spear & Betty D Morin
SPEAR,Steven P   Sex:M   14 Aug 1951 Joseph Spear & Wanda C Legarsky
SPECK,Brenda G   Sex:F   12 Sep 1954 William J Speck & Verna R Presby
SPENCE,Shannon E   Sex:F   18 May 1978 John H Spence & Jane Marie Ouellette
SPENCER,Kelly A   Sex:F   04 Feb 1967 Robert F Spencer & Karen M Truax
SPERBERG,[Unknown]   Sex:F   06 Feb 1975 David J Sperberg & Linda J Goffe
SPINNEY,James S   Sex:M   17 Aug 1963 Willard D Spinney & June L Albrewczynski
SPOONER,Kelly A   Sex:F   31 Jul 1973 Gary M Spooner & Johanne J Cheverton
SPRAGUE,April L   Sex:F   08 Mar 1966 Frank G Sprague & Annie L Small
SPRAGUE,Barbara Carlton   Sex:F   (Child #1) 17 Nov 1937 Stanley Sprague (Amityville, NY) & Charlotte Benson (Hudson, NH)
SPRAGUE,Debra L   Sex:F   25 Feb 1972 George R Sprague Jr & Kathleen M West
SPRAGUE,Frederick W Sex:M   (Child #2) 15 Jan 1915 Hudson, NH Harris O Sprague (Grand Lake Stream) & Mary Fagga (Burlington, VT)
SPRAGUE,George R III Sex:M   17 Feb 1975 George R Sprague Jr & Kathleen M West
SPRAGUE,Lyn A   Sex:F   12 Oct 1956 Frank G Sprague & Annie L Small
SPRAGUE,Ronald F   Sex:M   25 Aug 1969 Frank G Sprague & Lillian A Small
SPRAKE,Charles   Sex:M   11 Dec 1808 Hudson, NH Samuel Sprake Jr & Lucy
SPRAKE,Hannah   Sex:F   10 Apr 1799 Hudson, NH Samuel Sprake & Anna
SPRAKE,Lucy   Sex:F   08 Aug 1807 Hudson, NH Samuel Sprake Jr & Lucy
SPRAKE,Lucy   Sex:F   08 Nov 1807 Hudson, NH Samuel Sprake & Lucy
SPRAKE,Samuel   Sex:M   07 Sep 1803 Hudson, NH Samuel Sprake Jr & Lucy
SPRAKE,Sarah Barret   Sex:F   03 Feb 1813 Hudson, NH Samuel Sprake & Lucy
SPRAKE,Sarah Barrett   Sex:F   03 Feb 1813 Hudson, NH Samuel Sprake Jr & Lucy
SPRAKE,Susanna   Sex:F   18 Apr 1811 Hudson, NH Samuel Sprake Jr & Lucy
SPRAKE,Thomas   Sex:M   19 Apr 1797 Hudson, NH Samuel Sprake & Anna
SPRINGER,Stefanie Ann Sex:F 07 Jun 1981 Edward C Springer & Patricia A Chase
SPRINGFIELD,Allen R   Sex:M   (Child #2) 26 Sep 1944 Joseph M Springfield (Portland, ME) & Jairetta E Main (Nashua, NH)
SPROUT,Stephanie Allison Sex:F 13 Jun 1984 Dennis L Sprout & Joan L Finfrock
SPURLIN,Jason E   Sex:M   26 May 1975 Edward R Spurlin & Dawn L Yalenezian
ST PIERRE,Doria   Sex:F   (Child #4) 03 Mar 1936 Joseph St. Pierre (Canada) & Cora Pepin (Nashua, NH)
ST AMAND,Donna M   Sex:F   14 Jun 1951 Camille E St Amand & Celia I Jackson
ST AMAND,June A   Sex:F   13 Mar 1947 Camille E St Amand (St Eugene, Canada) & Celia I Jackson (Derry, NH)
ST AMAND,Kevin N   Sex:M   04 Oct 1973 Alfred J St Amand & Kathleen M Gilcreast
ST AMAND,Marcia C   Sex:F   13 Nov 1954 Camille E St Amand & Celia I Jackson
ST ARMAND,Kathleen I   Sex:F   26 Jun 1948 Camille E St Armand (Canada) & Celia I Jackson (Derry, NH)
ST CYR,Heather L   Sex:F   20 Apr 1979 William P St Cyr & Gayle E Ives
ST GEORGE,Christopher H Sex:M 16 Jun 1967 Henry T St George & Frances T Hamel
ST GEORGE,Jeffrey A Sex:M 31 Dec 1973 Lucien R St George & Darlene E Wardwell
ST GEORGE,Paul F   Sex:M   01 Apr 1969 Henry T St George & Frances T Hamel
ST HILAIRE,David G   Sex:M   27 Jan 1976 George A St Hilaire & Judith R Tanguay
ST JAMES,Spencer Sinclair   Sex:M   04 Jul 1984 Christopher C St James & Jacinthe E Levesque

HUDSON,NH BIRTHS

ST JEAN,Dennis H   Sex:M   07 Jul 1951 Harvey A St Jean & Constance R Niquette
ST JEAN,Elissa D   Sex:F   09 Sep 1968 Raymond L St Jean & Diane C Baker
ST JEAN,Michael R   Sex:M   14 Oct 1956 Raymond L St Jean & Diane C Baker
ST JOHN,Dale S   Sex:M   30 Apr 1968 Dale C St John & Deborah E Bean
ST LAURENT,Adelard R   Sex:M   (Child #2) 22 May 1922 Adelard St Laurent
   (Canada) & Yvonne Ricard (Greenville, NH)
ST LAURENT,Andrew A   Sex:M   16 Jun 1951 Roger J St Laurent & Pearl T Bernier
ST LAURENT,Christine A   Sex: 24 Jul 1972 Roger J St Laurent & Nancy J Roy
ST LAURENT,Deborah A   Sex:F   20 Mar 1954 Robert L St Laurent & Rita Gosselin
ST LAURENT,Donna M   Sex:F   09 Jun 1968 Roger J St Laurent & Pearl T Bernier
ST LAURENT,Gary M Jr   Sex:M   28 Aug 1970 Gary M St Laurent & Dorothy E Beane
ST LAURENT,Jos Chs G   Sex:M   (Child #5) 04 Aug 1933 Adelard St Laurent
   (Canada) & Yvonne Ricard (Greenville, NH)
ST LAURENT,Laura M   Sex:F   12 Oct 1947 Roger J St Laurent (Nashua, NH)
   & Pearl T Bernier (Nashua, NH)
ST LAURENT,Michelle R   Sex:F   21 Jul 1968 Gary M St Laurent & Dorothy E Beane
ST LAURENT,Pauline Y   Sex:F   11 Feb 1963 Roger J St Laurent & Pearl T Bernier
ST LAURENT,Roger J   Sex:M   05 May 1949 Roger J St Laurent & Pearl T Bernier
ST LAURENT,Steven P   Sex:M   15 Oct 1976 Andre A St Laurent & Kathleen E Glenn
ST LOUIS,Diane M   Sex:F   03 Jul 1969 Roland P St Louis & Joan A M Ouellet
ST MARTIN,James F Sex:M   (Child #1) 27 Mar 1946 James J St Martin (Nashua,
   NH) & Ruth M Reynolds (Checotah, OK)
ST ONGE,William B   Sex:M   22 Aug 1948 Bernard C St Onge (Nashua, NH)
   & Doris Y St Jean (Nashua, NH)
ST PIERRE,Ronald   Sex:M   (Child #3) 14 Apr 1932 Hudson, NH Joseph St Pierre
   (Canada) & Cora St Pierre (New Hampshire)
STACKHOUSE,Teresa D   Sex:F   18 Feb 1976 Richard J Stackhouse & Nancy T Rodio
STAGNER,Lisa A   Sex:F   02 Jul 1965 Joseph H Stagner Jr & Sandra L Morse
STALKER,[Unknown]   Sex:F   (Child #4) 17 Dec 1907 William D Stalker (Canada)
   & Annie C McMavine (Canada)
STALKER,[Unknown]   Sex:F   (Child #4) 13 Jan 1910 Wm D Stalker (Brompton Gor,
   P Q) & Annie K McMorine (Flodden, P Q)
STAMM,Elizabeth Anne   Sex:F   05 Feb 1984 Karl Albert Stamm & Carol B Schuman
STANCHFIELD,James   Sex:M   11 Jul 1737 Hudson, NH John Stanchfield & Elizabeth
STANCHFIELD,James   Sex:M   11 Jun 1737 Hudson, NH John Stanchfield & Elizabeth
STANCOMB,Andrew Keith   Sex:M   (Child #5) 19 Sep 1936 Wm Andrew Stancomb
   (Dunstable, MA) & Inez Towne (Yorkshire, England)
STANCOMBE,James W   Sex:M   14 Oct 1948 William E Stancombe (Nashua, NH)
   & Marie I Fulton (Nashua, NH)
STANLEY,Cynthia J   Sex:F   01 Mar 1969 Carl T Stanley & Donna J Shaw
STANLEY,Kim A   Sex:F   28 Mar 1967 Carl T Stanley & Donna J Shaw
STANLEY,Richard A   Sex:M   19 Oct 1961 Warren F Stanley & Florence T Utka
STANLEY,Roseann A   Sex:F   11 Oct 1957 Warren F Stanley & Florence T Utka
STANTON,E Thomas M   Sex:M   28 Nov 1973 John J Stanton Jr & Patricia M Coccoro
STARK,Andrea M   Sex:F   11 Aug 1961 H Andrew Stark & Dawna C Cetrangolo
STARK,Fannie A   Sex:F   05 Nov 1881 Hudson, NH William H Stark (Manchester,
   NH) & Emma L Smith (Hudson, NH)
STARK,Kim L   Sex:F   25 Aug 1962 Henry A Stark & Dawna C Cetrangolo
STARRATT,Linda M   Sex:F   15 Jul 1949 Kenneth M Starratt & Dorothy M Daley
STAVRO,Daniel W   Sex:M   30 Apr 1977 Philip N Stavro & Nancy Ann Lewis
STAVRO,Kevin Philip Sex:M   14 Aug 1978 Philip Norman Stavro & Nancy Ann Lewis
STAVRO,Michael Andrew Sex:M 20 Mar 1985 Philip Norman Stavro&Nancy Ann Lewis
STEARNS,Martha   Sex:F   13 Jan 1863 Hudson, NH Ephraim Stearns & Mary J
STEARNS,Martha J   Sex:F   13 Jan 1863 Hudson, NH Ephraim Stearns & Mary J
STEARNS,Walter D   Sex:M   (Child #5) 16 Feb 1902 Willie D Stearns (Lowell, MA)
   & Louise V Stark (Chazy, NY)
STEARNS,Willie   Sex:M   Jun 1865 Hudson, NH Ephraim Stearns & Mary J
STECK,Heather L   Sex:F   04 Jun 1970 David J Steck & Audrey L Magoon
STECKEVICZ,Edwin M   Sex:M   25 May 1953 Edwin F Steckevicz & Josephine F Moran
STECKEVICZ,Joan Eleanor   Sex:F   (Child #5) 12 Sep 1934 Alphonse Steckevicz

HUDSON,NH BIRTHS

(Poland) & Eleanor Wolensevicz (Poland)
STECKEVICZ,Mary Jo Sex:F 22 Feb 1951 Edwin F Steckevicz & Josephine F Moran
STEELE,Alice Maritta Sex:F 18 Nov 1869 Hudson, NH Samuel A Steele & Mary A
STEELE,Charlene Elizabeth Sex:F (Child #1) 14 Sep 1909 Fred G Steele
 (Goshen, NH) & Addie B Moody (Lancaster, NH)
STEELE,Charles Sex:M 25 Oct 1860 Hudson, NH Charles Steele & Martha Boyd
STEELE,Charles Boyd Sex:M (Child #1) 07 Jun 1915 Hudson, NH Charles L Steele
 (Hudson, NH) & Mina A Boyd (Rockland, N S)
STEELE,Curtis A Sex:M 28 Feb 1964 Ralph L Steele & Marilyn R Brown
STEELE,Cynthia R Sex:F 22 May 1965 Ralph L Steele & Marilyn R Brown
STEELE,Daniel Sex:M 04 Apr 1799 Hudson, NH William Steele
 & Polly Mary Barrett
STEELE,Everett Sex:M (Child #5) 25 Feb 1912 George S Steele (Hudson, NH)
 & Edith Colburn (Hudson, NH)
STEELE,Florence E Sex:F Aug 1864 Hudson, NH Silas L Steele & Elizabeth
STEELE,George L Sex:M 01 Jan 1866 Hudson, NH Silas F Steele & Eliza
STEELE,George S Sex:M 01 Jan 1866 Hudson, NH Silas L Steele & Elizabeth
STEELE,Hannah Sex:F 04 Sep 1786 Hudson, NH William Steele
 & Polly Mary Barrett
STEELE,Harold George Sex:M (Child #2) 03 Jun 1901 Hudson, NH George Steele
 (Hudson, NH) & Edith Coburn (Hudson, NH)
STEELE,Helen Sex:F (Child #5) 06 Jan 1910 George S Steele (Hudson, NH)
 & Edith F Colburn (Hudson, NH)
STEELE,Ida Sex:F (Child #2) 09 Jan 1885 Hudson, NH Charles A Steele
 (Hudson, NH) & Lottie A Reynolds (Windham, NH)
STEELE,James Sex:M 25 May 1784 Hudson, NH William Steele & Polly Mary Barrett
STEELE,Jane Sex:F (Child #2) 15 May 1944 Moody G Steele (Hudson, NH)
 & Elnora Gilbert (Nashua, NH)
STEELE,John Sex:M 07 Mar 1743 Hudson, NH William Steele & Janett Mullican
STEELE,Joseph Sex:M 1750 Hudson, NH William Steele & Janett Mullican
STEELE,Marion B Sex:F (Child #1) 30 May 1942 Moody G Steele (Hudson, NH)
 & Elnora Gilbert (Nashua, NH)
STEELE,Mary Sex:F 08 Sep 1738 Hudson, NH William Steele & Janett Mullican
STEELE,Minot A Sex:M 19 Nov 1867 Hudson, NH Samuel A Steele & Mary A Buttrick
STEELE,Minot A Sex:M 17 Nov 1867 Hudson, NH Alpheus Steele & Mary A
STEELE,Moody Gilbert Sex:M (Child #2) 16 Jan 1911 Fred G Steele (Goshen, NH)
 & Addie B Moody (Lancaster, NH)
STEELE,Moses Sex:M 13 Jun 1796 Hudson, NH William Steele
 & Polly Mary Barrett
STEELE,Moses Sex:M 1748 Hudson, NH William Steele & Janett Mullican
STEELE,Osgood Sex:M 18 Apr 1782 Hudson, NH William Steele
 & Polly Mary Barrett
STEELE,Peggy Sex:F 11 Jun 1794 Hudson, NH William Steele
 & Polly Mary Barrett
STEELE,Polley Sex:F 25 Sep 1791 Hudson, NH William Steele & Polley
STEELE,Polly Sex:F 25 Sep 1791 Hudson, NH William Steele
 & Polly Mary Barrett
STEELE,Ralph Harland Sex:M (Child #4) 18 Mar 1904 George S Steele (Hudson,
 NH) & Edith F Colburn (Hudson, NH)
STEELE,Ralph L Sex:M (Child #2) 06 Feb 1942 Ralph Steele (Hudson, NH)
 & Lenia Karstosk (Nashua, NH)
STEELE,Rhoda Sex:F 26 Jan 1778 Hudson, NH William Steele
 & Polly Mary Barrett
STEELE,Ruth M Sex:F 11 Aug 1902 George S Steele (Hudson, NH)
 & Edith F Colburn (Hudson, NH)
STEELE,Samuel Sex:M 02 Apr 1740 Hudson, NH William Steele & Janett Mullican
STEELE,Sylvia Sex:F (Child #3) 13 Dec 1946 Moody G Steele (Hudson, NH)
 & Elnora Gilbert (Nashua, NH)
STEELE,William Sex:M 28 Feb 1780 Hudson, NH William Steele
 & Polly Mary Barrett

HUDSON,NH BIRTHS

STEELE,William Sex:M   1747 Hudson, NH William Steele & Janett Mullican
STEELE,[Unknown] Sex:M   (Child #3) 18 Jun 1888 Charles A Steele (Hudson, NH)
 & Charlott A Reynolds (Windham, NH)
STEELE,[Unknown] Sex:F   (Child #4) 04 Nov 1890 Charles A Steele (Hudson, NH)
 & Lottie Reynolds (Windham, NH)
STEELE,[Unknown] Sex:M   12 Nov 1894 Chas A Steele (Hudson, NH)
 & Lottie Reynolds (Windham, NH)
STEELE,[Unknown] Sex:M   (Child #2) 03 Nov 1917 Charles L Steele (Hudson, NH)
 & Mina A Boyd (Rockland, N S)
STEELE,[Unknown] Sex:F   (Child #5) 01 Dec 1923 Charles L Steele (Hudson, NH)
 & Mina A Boyd (Nova Scotia)
STEELE,[Unknown] Sex:M   (Child #1) 06 Feb 1942 Ralph Steele (Hudson, NH)
 & Lenia Karstosk (Nashua, NH)
STEELE,[Unknown] Sex: 12 Mar 1864 Hudson, NH James H Steele & Elizabeth
STEELE,[Unknown] Sex:F   1745 Hudson, NH William Steele & Janett Mullican
STEFANIK,Brenda M Sex:F   12 Feb 1968 Michael J Stefanik & Dorothy J Serwa
STEFANIK,Debra M Sex:F   15 Aug 1969 Michael J Stefanik & Dorothy Serwa
STEPHEN,Jacob Francis Sex:M   09 Mar 1981 Joseph F Stephen
 & Jocelyne M Desrosier
STEPHENS,Jason Sex:M   01 Mar 1978 Joseph F Stephens & Jocelyn M Desrosiers
STERBA,Christina Rachel Sex:F   04 Nov 1978 Robert F Sterba & Janet E Brun
STETSON,Shawn Joseph Sex:M 15 Jul 1983 Donald Paul Stetson & Marianne DeVitto
STEVENS,Benjamin W Sex:M   04 Jun 1824 Lyman NH John Stevens & Nancy Webster
STEVENS,Charles W Sex:M   Lisbon, NH Richard K Stevens & Hannah G Richardson
STEVENS,Cheryl L Sex:F   26 Sep 1964 Ronald C Stevens & Wilma A Reardon
STEVENS,Clark E Sex:M   Lisbon, NH Richard K Stevens & Hannah G Richardson
STEVENS,David Sex:M   12 Dec 1814 Haverhill, MA John Stevens & Nancy Webster
STEVENS,Eben Sex:M   New Hampton NH John Stevens & Nancy Webster
STEVENS,Eliza Sex:F   12 Jan 1812 Haverhill, MA John Stevens & Nancy Webster
STEVENS,Evelyn Priscilla Sex:F   (Child #8) 22 Jan 1938 Geo Loveren Stevens
 (Woodsville, NH) & Marion A Knights (Merrimack, NH)
STEVENS,George Lester Sex:M   (Child #7) 08 Nov 1935 George L Stevens
 (Woodsville, NH) & Marion Adelia Knight (Merrimack, NH)
STEVENS,John Sex:M   05 Apr 1783 Plaistow, NH   &
STEVENS,Michael G Sex:M   12 Jan 1957 William H Stevens & Emma E Gagnon
STEVENS,Nancy Sex:F   18 Mar 1817 Meredith NH John Stevens & Nancy Webster
STEVENS,Nathaniel Sex:M   New Hampton NH John Stevens & Nancy Webster
STEVENS,Richard K Sex:M   11 Jun 1827 Lyman NH John Stevens & Nancy Webster
STEVENS,William H Sex:M   (Child #6) 23 Dec 1933 George L Stevens
 (Woodsville, NH) & Marion Adelia Knight (Merrimack, NH)
STEWART,Albert A Sex:M   26 Jul 1872 Hudson, NH Robert L Stewart & Augusta
STEWART,Ian Andrew Sex:M   30 Sep 1982 Charles T Stewart & Barbara Ellen Ford
STEWART,Mary Sex:F   11 Nov 1811 Hudson, NH Francis Stewart & Abigail
STEWART,Rex Allen Sex:M   01 Sep 1984 Rex Allen Stewart & Jeanne Marie Rinker
STICKNEY,Charles Sex:M   Hudson, NH Gilman Stickney & Sarah Webster
STICKNEY,Earl H Sex:M   (Child #1) 20 Jun 1889 Walter A Stickney
 (Massachusetts) & Minnie S Randall (Vermont)
STICKNEY,Frank Sex:M   Hudson, NH Gilman Stickney & Sarah Webster
STICKNEY,Fred Alexander Sex:M   (Child #4) 12 Apr 1931 Elmer Stickney
 (Nashua, NH) & Margaret Sullivan (Denver, CO)
STICKNEY,James Franklin Sex:M   (Child #6) 01 Jan 1934 Elmer James Stickney
 (Nashua, NH) & Margaret Sullivan (Denver, CO)
STICKNEY,Phillip E Sex:M 16 Feb 1955 Phillip J Stickney & Patricia A Connell
STICKNEY,Shirley L Sex:F   (Child #5) 24 Jun 1932 Hudson, NH E J Stickney
 (Nashua, NH) & Mary Sullivan (Denver, CO)
STIFF,April P Sex:F   03 Jun 1966 Cramer J Stiff & Fernande J Moses
STILES,Kimberly Ann Sex:F 17 Feb 1983 Herbert R Stiles & Patricia Ann Camidge
STILES,Rebecca Marie Sex:F 23 Dec 1981 Herbert R Stiles&Patricia Ann Comidge
STILLMAN,Madison Sex:M   22 Oct 1808 Hudson, NH Elijah Stillman & Judy
STINCHFIELD,Brian A Sex:M   (Child #2) 15 Apr 1946 Richard D Stinchfield

HUDSON,NH BIRTHS

(Skowhegan, ME) & Constance Blaisdall (Longbr
STINCHFIELD,Corina Ann   Sex:F   17 Jun 1976 James Owen Stinchfie
  & Brenda Faye Jarrell
STINCHFIELD,Cynthia D   Sex:F   30 Jun 1978 James O Stinchfield
  & Brenda Faye Jarrell
STINCHFIELD,Duane M Sex:M   16 May 1948 Richard D Stinchfield (Skowhegan, ME)
  & Constance H Blaisdell (Long
STINCHFIELD,James S   Sex:M   10 Nov 1949 Richard D Stinchfield
  & Constance H Blaisdell
STITT,Alan K   Sex:M   26 Nov 1954 John W Stitt & Muriel E Grogan
STONE,Corina M   Sex:F   19 Mar 1980 Michael W Stone & Elaine C Bouley
STONE,David A   Sex:M   31 Dec 1953 Charles L Stone & Geneva Jeannott
STONE,James S   Sex:M   29 Dec 1952 Charles L Stone & Geneva G Jenott
STONE,Judith A   Sex:F   26 Sep 1948 Wilfred W Stone (Francestown, NH)
  & Barbara Butler (E Jaffrey, NH)
STONE,Kathleen A   Sex:F   01 Aug 1947 Wilfred W Stone (Francestown, NH)
  & Barbara Butler (E Jaffrey, NH)
STONE,Michael W   Sex:M   25 Jul 1958 Ernest G Stone & Mona J Atkinson
STONE,Nancy J   Sex:F   15 May 1957 Ernest G Stone & Mona J Atkinson
STONE,Nathan Lawrence Sex:M 02 Sep 1981 Lawrence L Stone & Cynthia May Dutton
STONE,Richard Ernest Sex:M 25 May 1983 Michael Wayne Stone & Elaine C Bouley
STOUT,Cindy L   Sex:F   23 Apr 1958 John A Stout & Helen M Moore
STOWELL,Joseph F Sex:M 27 Oct 1971 Joseph F Stowell Jr & Jacquelyn A McLarnan
STRAPP,Richard L   Sex:M   07 Aug 1969 Lawrence A Strapp & Carol A Krenzer
STRATTON,Jeffrey Ian Sex:M 19 Jul 1980 Mark D Stratton & Gloria Jean Boucher
STRAW,Sean Andrew   Sex:M   23 May 1985 Eldred V Straw & Carol Ann Andrews
STRAWBRIDGE,Catherine Ann   Sex:F   15 Jan 1974 Paul F Strawbridge
  & Doreen M Wilcher
STRAWBRIDGE,Paul J Sex:M 14 May 1976 Paul F Strawbridge&Doreen Marie Wilcher
STRICKLAND,Abner III   Sex:M   02 Oct 1781 Hudson, NH John Strickland & Betty
STRICKLAND,Abner Stone   Sex:M   02 Oct 1781 Hudson, NH John Strickland & Betty
STRICKLAND,John   Sex:M   19 Jul 1774 Hudson, NH John Strickland & Betty
STRICKLAND,Lucinda   Sex:F   07 Nov 1778 Hudson, NH John Strickland & Betty
STRICKLAND,Lucretia   Sex:F   22 Dec 1776 Hudson, NH John Strickland & Betty
STRICKLAND,Stephen F   Sex:M   10 Aug 1953 Frank F Strickland & Muriel M Allard
STRICKLAND,Tabitha   Sex:F   22 Mar 1783 Hudson, NH John Strickland & Betty
STRONG,Elizabeth A   Sex:F   31 Aug 1968 William J Strong & Barbara Richards
STUART,Mary   Sex:F   11 Nov 1811 Hudson, NH Francis Stuart & Abigail
STUCLIFFE,Elizabeth Anne   Sex:F   10 Jun 1983 Michael A Sutcliffe
  & Sara E Macomber
STULTZ,Nancy A   Sex:F   24 Sep 1954 Kenneth D Stultz & Gloria A Holt
STULTZ,Scottie Lee Sex:M 16 Nov 1982 Clayton A Stultz Jr & Pamela J Tessier
STUPKA,Dennis Edward Sex:M 24 Jun 1982 Robert E Stupka & Freida Joanne Mello
STURTEVANT,Michael Robert   Sex:M   01 Jun 1983 Robert A Sturtevant
  & Sharon B Whitcomb
STURTEVANT,Sheri A   Sex:F   11 Feb 1968 Donald H Sturtevant & Ruth J Mellen
STURTEVANT,Timothy William   Sex:M   10 Oct 1984 Robert A Sturtevant
  & Sharon B Whitcomb
STYGLES,Rebecca H   Sex:F   16 Jan 1966 Durwood G Stygles & Deanna S Liberty
STYS,James K   Sex:M   16 Jun 1965 Kenneth T Stys & Mary E Handley
STYS,Karen E   Sex:F   16 Jun 1965 Kenneth T Stys & Mary E Handley
SUDSBURY,John B   Sex:M   31 Jan 1971 Robert E Sudsbury & Jean C Simonds
SUDSBURY,Noreen D   Sex:F   22 May 1963 Robert E Sudsbury & Jean C Simonds
SUDSBURY,Robert L   Sex:M   05 Jan 1965 Robert E Sudsbury & Jean C Simonds
SULIVAN,Nancy   Sex:F   23 Aug 1878 Hudson, NH John Sulivan (Ireland)
  & Jane (Ireland)
SULLIVAN,Blanche Sex:F   18 Jan 1881 Derry, NH Dennis Sullivan (Lewiston, ME)
  & Laura E (Crompton Fls, Canada)
SULLIVAN,Carlie Ann Sex:F 27 Oct 1983 Joseph A Sullivan & Colleen Ann Quigley
SULLIVAN,Cheryl A   Sex:F   10 Jun 1963 Leroy G Sullivan & Marlyn J Post

HUDSON,NH BIRTHS

SULLIVAN,Christin E Sex:F 31 Aug 1975 Herbert A Sullivan & Karen Jane Bruni
SULLIVAN,Cornelius Sex:M 06 Sep 1875 Hudson, NH John Sullivan & Jane
SULLIVAN,Craig S Sex:M 20 Aug 1959 John E Sullivan & Jean A Cady
SULLIVAN,Daniel Sex:M 15 Apr 1868 Hudson, NH John Sullivan & Ellen
SULLIVAN,David P Sex:M 14 Jul 1955 William J Sullivan & Lorice K Mansour
SULLIVAN,Erinn E Sex:F 23 Jun 1974 Herbert A Sullivan & Karen Jane Bruni
SULLIVAN,Ernest Richard Sex:M 24 Mar 1981 Ernest R Sullivan
  & Michelle A Perreault
SULLIVAN,Jane L Sex:F 01 Sep 1870 Hudson, NH John W Sullivan & Jane L
SULLIVAN,Jennie Sex:F 13 Jan 1872 Hudson, NH John Sullivan & Jane
SULLIVAN,John Sex:M 09 Jun 1869 Hudson, NH Bartholemew Sullivan & Mary
SULLIVAN,John Everett Sex:M (Child #5) 26 Sep 1932 Nashua, NH William J
  Sullivan (Nashua, NH) & Mildred Jean (Nashua, NH)
SULLIVAN,Kevin F Sex:M 27 Jun 1961 Paul W Sullivan & Cathleen E Shortell
SULLIVAN,Lizzie Sex:F 20 Mar 1872 Hudson, NH Bartholemew Sullivan & Mary
SULLIVAN,Lynn A Sex:F 25 Jan 1955 John E Sullivan & Jean A Cady
SULLIVAN,Maria Elena Sex:F 13 Apr 1985 John G Sullivan & Carmen M Torrente
SULLIVAN,Matthew Sex:M 12 Oct 1873 Hudson, NH John Sullivan & Jane
SULLIVAN,Michael J Sex:M 22 May 1962 Leroy G Sullivan & Marlyn J Post
SULLIVAN,Thomas C Sex:M 11 Apr 1963 William J Sullivan & Lorice K Mansour
SULLIVAN,Tracey L Sex:F 14 Jun 1972 John F Sullivan Jr & Carol R Fredette
SULLIVAN,William D Sex:M 16 Jan 1972 Charles B Sullivan & Constance R Tyrrell
SUSI,David E Sex:M 12 Dec 1964 Michael W Susi & Jodell M Schroyer
SUSI,Jeffrey S Sex:M 04 Oct 1963 Michael W Susi & Jodell M Schroyer
SUSI,Kevin W Sex:M 08 Aug 1961 Michael W Susi & Madeline J Schrayer
SUTCLIFFE,Gregory George Sex:M 27 Jul 1978 Michale A Sutcliffe
  & Sara E Macomber
SUTHERLAND,David A Sex:M 14 Feb 1972 David C Sutherland & Dorothy E Civetti
SUYKERBUYK,Monique Liliane Sex:F 18 Mar 1983 Guy Paul Suykerbuyk
  & Margaret Anne Carter
SUYKERBUYK,Phillip Paul Sex:M 08 Apr 1984 Guy P Suykerbuyk
  & Margaret Ann Carter
SWAN,Susanna Sex:F 27 Jan 1817 Hudson, NH Isaac Swan & Susanna
SWAN,William C Jr Sex:M 08 Aug 1962 William C Swan & Helen F Wing
SWANBURG,Heidi A Sex:F 02 Jun 1968 Donald A Swanburg & Jacqueline N Fellows
SWEENEY,Matthew Robert Sex:M 06 Apr 1983 Robert L Sweeney & Laura C Burke
SWENSEN,Leif Hunter Sex:M 10 Jun 1981 Donald F Swensen & Mary Dorothy Miller
SWERINGEN,Amanda Jean Sex:F 30 Apr 1983 Thomas B Sweringen&Patricia S Todaro
SYMONDS,Carl J Sex:M 18 Feb 1958 George A Symonds & Ruth P Wharton
SYOPA,Sadensy Wladyslaw Sex:M   10 Mar 1912 Stanislaw Syopa (Galicya,
  Austria) & Honorata Raymian (Galicya, Austria)
SZAFRAN,Jamie Lynn Sex:F 26 Apr 1981 Paul John Szafran Jr & Lorraine Hoffman
SZOPER,Henryk Sex:M (Child #4) 29 May 1913 Stanishaus Szoper (Austria)
  & Honrata Rzymian (Austria)
SZUGDA,Bethanie S Sex:F 11 Dec 1973 Chester F Szugda & Judith A Keeler
SZUGDA,David E Sex: 26 Jun 1973 Leonard W Szugda & Gail A Minnick
SZUGDA,Janet E Sex:F 17 Jun 1966 Leonard W Szugda & Gail A Minnick
SZUGDA,John L Sex:M 23 Oct 1971 Leonard W Szugda & Gail A Minnick
SZUGDA,Sharon A Sex:F 08 Mar 1971 Chester F Szugda & Judith A Keeler
TABER,Kirsten G Sex:F 05 Apr 1980 Carl W Traber & Gizella H Tar
TAFE,Matthew B Sex:M 03 Mar 1965 Bradley E Tafe & Barbara J Turcotte
TAGLIAFERRO,Julie L Sex: 18 Feb 1973 James C Tagliaferro & Joyce Y Sheffer
TAGLIAFERRO,Todd A Sex:M 07 Dec 1974 James C Tagliaferro & Joyce Y Sheffer
TALBOT,Jennifer C Sex:F 01 Nov 1970 Arthur J Talbot & Edwina B Blackburn
TALBOT,Pamela A Sex:F 21 Oct 1967 Arthur J Talbot & Edwina B Blackburn
TALBOT,William K Sex:M 17 Jun 1799 Hudson, NH   &
TALTY,Sarah Elizabeth Sex:F 30 Sep 1984 Christopher F Talty
  & Debra D Bellefeuille
TANDY,Eben Forbes Sex:M 11 mar 1873 Hudson, NH Ezekiel Tandy & Annie
TANDY,Lillie M Sex:F 12 Jul 1874 Hudson, NH Ezekiel Tandy & Annie Jane

HUDSON,NH BIRTHS

TANGUAY,Christine E   Sex:F   23 Apr 1969 Richard G Tanguay & Faye Ferguson
TANGUAY,Debra A   Sex:F   13 Jan 1970 Charles A Tanguay & Aldea R Boisvert
TANGUAY,Linda A   Sex:F   31 Oct 1962 Robert J Tanguay & Constance R Desclos
TANGUAY,Marie J   Sex:F   31 Oct 1968 Robert J Tanguay & Constance R Desclos
TANGUAY,Robert J Jr Sex:M   28 Nov 1966 Robert J Tanguay & Constance R Desclos
TARBAL,Molley   Sex:F   18 Apr 1771 Hudson, NH Daniel Tarbal & Ester
TARBELL,Anna   Sex:F   26 May 1810 Hudson, NH David Tarbell Jr & Anna
TARBELL,Betsey   Sex:F   29 Jan 1801 Hudson, NH Jesse Tarbell & Avis
TARBELL,David   Sex:M   14 Oct 1767 Hudson, NH David Tarbell & Hannah
TARBELL,Esther   Sex:F   12 Apr 1773 Hudson, NH David Tarbell & Esther
TARBELL,Jesse   Sex:M   16 Nov 1778 Hudson, NH David Tarbell & Esther
TARBELL,John   Sex:M   19 Jul 1785 Hudson, NH David Tarbell & Esther
TARBELL,Lucinda   Sex:F   31 Jan 1805 Hudson, NH David Tarbell Jr & Anna
TARBELL,Molly   Sex:F   18 Apr 1771 Hudson, NH David Tarbell & Esther
TARBELL,Rhoda   Sex:F   14 May 1775 Hudson, NH David Tarbell & Esther
TARBELL,Sally   Sex:F   09 Jul 1803 Hudson, NH Jesse Tarbell & Avis
TARBELL,Samuel   Sex:M   21 Jul 1788 Hudson, NH David Tarbell & Esther
TARBELL,William   Sex:M   04 Mar 1782 Hudson, NH David Tarbell & Esther
TARBLE,Betsey   Sex:F   29 Jan 1801 Hudson, NH Jesse Tarble & Avis
TARBLE,Ester   Sex:F   12 Apr 1775 Hudson, NH Daniel Tarble & Ester
TARBLE,Jesse   Sex:M   16 Nov 1778 Hudson, NH Daniel Tarble & Ester
TARBLE,John   Sex:M   19 Jul 1785 Hudson, NH Daniel Tarble & Ester
TARBLE,Lucinda   Sex:F   31 Jan 1806 Hudson, NH Daniel Tarble & Anna
TARBLE,Nancy   Sex:F   26 May 1810 Hudson, NH Daniel Tarble & Anna
TARBLE,Rhoda   Sex:F   17 May 1775 Hudson, NH Daniel Tarble & Ester
TARBLE,Salley T   Sex:F   09 Jul 1803 Hudson, NH Jesse Tarble & Avis
TARBLE,Samuel   Sex:M   21 Jul 1788 Hudson, NH Daniel Tarble & Ester
TARBLE,William   Sex:M   24 Mar 1782 Hudson, NH Daniel Tarble & Ester
TARBOX,Aaron   Sex:M   05 Feb 1770 Hudson, NH Henry Tarbox & Sarah
TARBOX,Betty   Sex:F   26 Jan 1782 Hudson, NH Henry Tarbox & Sarah
TARBOX,Betty   Sex:F   26 Jun 1782 Hudson, NH Henry Tarbox & Sarah
TARBOX,Deborah   Sex:F   03 Jan 1768 Hudson, NH Henry Tarbox & Sarah
TARBOX,Hannah   Sex:F   06 Apr 1775 Hudson, NH Henry Tarbox & Sarah
TARBOX,Lydia   Sex:F   14 Jun 1785 Hudson, NH Henry Tarbox & Sarah
TARBOX,Rhoda   Sex:F   19 Dec 1772 Hudson, NH Henry Tarbox & Sarah
TARBOX,Roda   Sex:F   19 Dec 1772 Hudson, NH Henry Tarbox & Sarah
TARBOX,Sarah   Sex:F   14 Jul 1777 Hudson, NH Henry Tarbox & Sarah
TARBOX,Sarah   Sex:F   21 Jul 1780 Hudson, NH Henry Tarbox & Sarah
TARBOX,Submit   Sex:F   04 Jun 1788 Hudson, NH Henry Tarbox & Sarah
TARDIF,Michelle T   Sex:F   08 Nov 1965 Paul A Tardif & Arline M Lemaire
TARLSON,Nellie   Sex:F   (Child #3) 28 Mar 1929 Anthony Tarlson (Russia) & Helen (Russia)
TARTACHNY,David A   Sex:M   17 Nov 1958 Paul Tartachny & Dorothy Morrison
TATE,Amy L   Sex:F   23 Mar 1972 Michael F Tate & Linda A McLaughlin
TATE,Caroline D   Sex:F   02 Jun 1977 Richard W Tate & Joan C Ducharme
TATE,Christine L   Sex: 10 Oct 1972 Richard W Tate & Joan C Ducharme
TATE,David A   Sex:M   08 Sep 1948 Robert A Tate (Milford, NH) & Priscilla Lynch (Manchester, NH)
TATE,David A Jr   Sex: 24 Mar 1973 David A Tate Sr & Rosemary A Pacheco
TATE,Donna M   Sex:F   22 Jun 1949 Rupert E Tate & Alice E Bullard
TATE,Geraldine J Sex:F   (Child #2) 19 Aug 1944 Rupert E Tate, Jr (Milford, NH) & Alice E Bouley (Nashua, NH)
TATE,Gordon B Jr   Sex:M   12 Apr 1952 Gordon B Tate & Dorothy L Beaubien
TATE,Jeffrey A   Sex:M   14 Oct 1969 Robert A Tate Jr & Diane L Ledoux
TATE,Joan A   Sex:F   12 Oct 1947 Rupert E Tate (Milford, NH) & Alice E Bouley (Hudson, NH)
TATE,Jonathan M   Sex:M   18 May 1974 David A Tate & Rosemary A Pacheco
TATE,Kimberly A   Sex:F   24 Mar 1971 Robert A Tate Jr & Diane L Ledoux
TATE,Linda A   Sex:F   09 Nov 1959 Gordon B Tate & Dorothy L Beaubien
TATE,Michael A   Sex:M   23 Jun 1976 David A Tate Sr & Rosemary A Pacheco

HUDSON,NH BIRTHS

TATE,Michael J   Sex:M   19 Jun 1964 Michael F Tate & Linda A McLaughlin
TATE,Nancy L   Sex:F   22 May 1952 Rupert E Tate & Olive E Bouley
TATE,Norman P   Sex:M   10 Oct 1957 Gordon B Tate & Dorothy L Beaubien
TATE,Patrick M   Sex:M   27 Jun 1975 Richard W Tate & Joan C Ducharme
TATE,Richard J   Sex:M   24 Nov 1973 Richard W Tate & Joan C Ducharme
TATE,Richard W   Sex:M   16 Feb 1948 William W Tate (Milford, NH)
  & Catherine M Ruiter (Manchester, NH)
TATE,Robert A Jr   Sex:M   09 Jun 1947 Robert A Tate, Sr (Milford, NH)
  & Priscilla M Lynch (Litchfield, NH)
TATE,Rodney B   Sex:M   09 Mar 1953 Gordon B Tate & Dorothy L Beaubien
TATE,Roger A   Sex:M   29 Jul 1954 Gordon B Tate & Dorothy L Beaubien
TATE,Sandra E   Sex:F   (Child #1) 14 Oct 1942 Rupert E Tate, Jr (Milford, NH)
  & Alice E Bouley (Nashua, NH)
TATE,Stephanie J   Sex:F   03 Nov 1968 Richard W Tate & Joan C Ducharme
TATE,Steven W   Sex:M   04 Nov 1955 Gordon B Tate & Dorothy L Beaubien
TATE,Wesley W   Sex:M   09 May 1972 William M Tate & Jacquelene L Allard
TATEM,Jessica Vann   Sex:F   23 May 1985 James Martin Tatem & Julie A Lankhorst
TATRO,Jenny Jeanne   Sex:F   11 Aug 1976 Charles E Tatro & Brenda Ann Kierstead
TAYLOR,David G   Sex:M   20 Apr 1967 David R Taylor & Sandra J Christian
TAYLOR,Elizabeth   Sex:F   01 Oct 1753 Hudson, NH William Taylor & Sarah
TAYLOR,Elmer J II   Sex:M   22 Jul 1963 Elmer J Taylor & Mary J Caron
TAYLOR,Jane   Sex:F   11 Jan 1847 Hudson, NH Thomas Taylor & Susan
TAYLOR,Jason A   Sex:M   08 Jun 1975 Laurence P Taylor & Kathryn L Powlowsky
TAYLOR,Jill B   Sex:F   27 Oct 1969 Winslow A Taylor & Patricia B Gelinas
TAYLOR,Joseph   Sex:M   18 Nov 1758 Hudson, NH William Taylor & Sarah
TAYLOR,Karen Beth   Sex:F   04 Aug 1977 Laurence P Taylor & Kathryn L Powlowsky
TAYLOR,Melina May   Sex:F   20 May 1982 Mark Andrew Taylor & Karen M St Laurent
TAYLOR,Molle   Sex:F   26 Jul 1745 Hudson, NH William Taylor & Sarah
TAYLOR,Molly   Sex:F   26 Jul 1745 Hudson, NH William Taylor & Sarah
TAYLOR,Rebecca   Sex:F   27 Mar 1769 Hudson, NH William Taylor & Sarah
TAYLOR,Rebeckah   Sex:F   27 Mar 1769 Hudson, NH William Taylor & Sarah
TAYLOR,Samuel   Sex:M   02 Oct 1761 Hudson, NH William Taylor & Sarah
TAYLOR,Samuel   Sex:M   03 Oct 1761 Hudson, NH William Taylor & Sarah
TAYLOR,Sandra A   Sex:F   27 Jan 1948 Richard D Taylor (Nashua, NH)
  & Alice L Brown (Jamaica Plain, MA)
TAYLOR,Sarah   Sex:F   18 Oct 1766 Hudson, NH William Taylor & Sarah
TAYLOR,Scott Michael Sex:M 26 Apr 1984 Glenn D Taylor & Celeste Marie Aubin
TAYLOR,Simeon   Sex:M   30 Nov 1755 Hudson, NH William Taylor & Sarah
TAYLOR,Theresa E   Sex:F   30 Jun 1965 Stanley E Taylor & Evalee Phillips
TAYLOR,Thomas   Sex:M   08 Apr 1751 Hudson, NH William Taylor & Sarah
TAYLOR,Thomas   Sex:M   17 Feb 1764 Hudson, NH William Taylor & Sarah
TAYLOR,William   Sex:M   10 Aug 1851 Hudson, NH Thomas Taylor & Susan
TAYLOR,William   Sex:M   30 Jan 1748 Hudson, NH William Taylor & Sarah
TAYNOR,James M   Sex:M   23 Feb 1976 Kenneth L Taynor & Rachel R Delisle
TEDESCHI,Jessica A Sex:F   29 Oct 1968 Lamberto E Tedeschi & Louise A Beaudoin
TEICHMAN,Wm A Jr   Sex:F   10 Dec 1950 William A Teichman & Ethel M Noyes
TEICHMANN,Holly Ann Sex:F 01 Jan 1979 William A Teichmann & Sandra L Goodwin
TEICHMANN,Michele L Sex:F 05 Apr 1975 William A Teichmann & Sandra L Goodwin
TEMPLE,Allyn Lee   Sex:M   (Child #6) 06 Sep 1938 Joseph Francis Temple
  (Nashua, NH) & Algenia Lee Burrill (Col Vall
TEMPLE,John Albert   Sex:M   (Child #4) 13 Aug 1935 Joseph Temple (Nashua, NH)
  & Algenia Burrill (Nashua, NH)
TEMPLE,Jos Francis Jr   Sex:M   (Child #5) 25 Feb 1937 Joseph Francis Temple
  (Nashua, NH) & Algenia Burrill (Col Valley,
TEMPLETON,[Unknown]   Sex: Oct 1864 Hudson, NH Ira Templeton &
TENNEY,Bally   Sex: 08 Nov 1786 Hudson, NH Edmund Tenney & Sarah
TENNEY,Betty   Sex:F   08 Nov 1786 Hudson, NH Edman Tenney & Sarah
TENNEY,Charles Carroll   Sex:M   01 Jan 1833 Hudson, NH Noyes Tenney
  & Olivia Butler
TENNEY,Daniel   Sex:M   19 Jan 1789 Hudson, NH Edman Tenney & Sarah

HUDSON, NH BIRTHS

TENNEY,Daniel   Sex:M   15 Jun 1795 Hudson, NH Paul Tenney & Sarah Gibson
TENNEY,Daniel   Sex:M   19 Jun 1789 Hudson, NH Edmund Tenney & Sarah
TENNEY,Daniel Gibson   Sex:M 02 May 1790 Hudson, NH Jonathan Tenney & Martha
TENNEY,Elizabeth   Sex:F   22 Mar 1786 Hudson, NH Jonathan Tenney & Martha
TENNEY,Franklin   Sex:M   17 Jan 1808 Hudson, NH Paul Tenney & Sarah Gibson
TENNEY,George Clinton   Sex:M   24 Oct 1830 Hudson, NH Noyes Tenney
  & Olivia Butler
TENNEY,James   Sex:M   25 Jun 1798 Hudson, NH Paul Tenney & Sarah Gibson
TENNEY,Kimball   Sex:M   18 Apr 1793 Hudson, NH Paul Tenney & Sarah Gibson
TENNEY,Martha   Sex:F   23 Jul 1788 Hudson, NH Jonathan Tenney & Martha
TENNEY,Mary   Sex:F   27 Dec 1792 Hudson, NH Jonathan Tenney & Martha
TENNEY,Mary B   Sex:F   02 Feb 1835 Hudson, NH Noyes Tenney & Olivia Butler
TENNEY,Noyes   Sex:M   26 Sep 1791 Hudson, NH Paul Tenney & Sarah Gibson
TENNEY,Olivia Butler   Sex:F   18 Dec 1823 Hudson, NH Noyes Tenney
  & Olivia Butler
TENNEY,Paul   Sex:M   11 Apr 1763 Rowley, MA   &
TENNEY,Paul   Sex:M   01 Mar 1802 Hudson, NH Paul Tenney & Sarah Gibson
TENNEY,Robert   Sex:M   17 Sep 1784 Hudson, NH Jonathan Tenney & Martha
TENNEY,Silas   Sex:M   04 Sep 1805 Hudson, NH Paul Tenney & Sarah Gibson
TENNY,Daniel   Sex:M   15 Jun 1795 Hudson, NH Paul Tenny & Sarah
TENNY,Kimball   Sex:M   18 Apr 1793 Hudson, NH Paul Tenny & Sarah
TENNY,Noyes   Sex:M   26 Sep 1791 Hudson, NH Paul Tenny & Sarah
TENTERIS,Tracie L   Sex:F   10 Aug 1971 Robert Tenteris & Loretta M Dugdale
TERRILL,Robinson J   Sex:M   08 Aug 1961 Rogert P Terrill & Norma L Bardsley
TERWILLIGER,Kevin James   Sex:M   21 Aug 1984 Daniel J Terwilliger
  & Roberta M McCaughern
TERWILLIGER,Lisa Ann   Sex:F   31 May 1981 Daniel J Terwilliger
  & Roberta M McCaughern
TERWILLIGER,Mark D   Sex:M   15 May 1979 Daniel J Terwilliger
  & Roberta M McCaughern
TESSIER,David R   Sex:M   04 Sep 1955 Henry A Tessier & Rose R Ducas
TESSIER,Delaine N   Sex:F   17 Feb 1948 Norman L Tessier (Nashua, NH)
  & Olive T Ouelette (Nashua, NH)
TESSIER,Denis L   Sex:M   16 Oct 1950 Albert L Tessier & Jeannette Marquis
TESSIER,Donald J   Sex:M   21 Apr 1968 Donald R Tessier & Mildred M York
TESSIER,Donald Roger Sex:M   (Child #3) 15 Nov 1941 Albert Tessier (Hudson,
  NH) & Jeannette Marquis (Lowell, MA)
TESSIER,Doris L   Sex:F   11 Jun 1947 Albert L Tessier (Hudson, NH)
  & Jeannette C Marquis (Lowell, MA)
TESSIER,Henry R   Sex:M   03 Dec 1957 Henry R Tessier & Rose R Ducas
TESSIER,Henry R III   Sex:M   08 Oct 1975 Henry R Tessier Jr & Teresa M Gioe
TESSIER,Jamie Lee   Sex:F   29 Jan 1983 David R Tessier & Carlene Ann Viera
TESSIER,Marie Tarace R   Sex:F   (Child #5) 16 Jun 1926 Eugene Tessier (Canada)
  & Dorella Tessier (Canada)
TESSIER,Nicole P   Sex:F   29 Dec 1975 Roland W Tessier & Sandra L Raymond
TESSIER,Norman K   Sex:M   30 Mar 1956 Norman L Tessier & Olive T Ouelette
TESSIER,Raymond J   Sex:M   22 Apr 1950 Henry R Tessier & Rose R Ducas
TESSIER,Robin J   Sex:F   17 Jun 1964 Donald R Tessier & Mildred M York
TESSIER,Scott T   Sex:M   05 Oct 1965 Paul Albert Tessier & Rita V Larouche
TESSIER,Todd M   Sex:M   20 Apr 1979 Conrad H Tessier & Margaret M Curran
TESSIER,Travis James Sex:M   06 Dec 1984 Conrad H Tessier & Margaret M Curran
TEST,Lori P   Sex:F   10 Sep 1967 Thomas J Test & Lucy A Hester
TETREAU,Matthew Paul   Sex:M   09 Jul 1984 Albert Paul Tetreau
  & Cynthia R Avedisian
TETREAULT,Richard C   Sex:M   16 Nov 1957 Emery J Tetreault & Rita A Brady
THEBERGE,Neil E   Sex:M   15 Jan 1968 Roland E Theberge & Joan M Mallon
THEBODEAU,C C Jr   Sex:M   20 Mar 1947 C C Thebodeau, Sr (Richford, VT)
  & Margaret H Fecteau (Sweetsburg)
THEBODEAU,Donna L Sex:F   19 May 1952 Carlton C Thebodeau & Margaret H Fecteau
THEBODEAU,Paula M   Sex:F   21 Feb 1971 Raymond P Thebodeau & Dorothy A Lacasse

HUDSON,NH BIRTHS

THEBODEAU,Raymond P Jr Sex:M 04 Jun 1960 Raymond P Thebodeau & Donna L Yeaton
THEBODEAU,Robert D Sex:M 22 Apr 1953 Calrton C Thebodeau & Margaret H Fecteau
THEODORE,Gretchen Renee Sex:F 30 Sep 1980 Robert B Theodore & Karen Ann Quinn
THERIAULT,Shaun D Sex:M 15 Jan 1971 David R Theriault & Yvette M Demers
THEROUX,Michelle L Sex:F 17 Jul 1970 Robert G Theroux & Janet M Jones
THEROUX,Robert R Sex:M 05 Aug 1947 Romeo H Theroux (Nashua, NH)
 & Lucille M Provencher (Manchester, NH)
THERRIAULT,David L Sex:M 02 Nov 1956 Roland L Therriault & Jean H Ackerman
THERRIAULT,Diane M Sex:F 16 Jan 1958 Roland L Therriault & Jean H Ackerman
THIBEAULT,Derek J Sex:M 08 Aug 1971 Dennis L Thibeault & Louise A Vallee
THIBEAULT,Doreen A Sex:F 18 Feb 1956 Alfred A Thibeault & Anita M Bergeron
THIBEAULT,Jennifer J Sex:F 25 Mar 1969 Leonard E Thibault & Sandra M Leach
THIBEAULT,Leon V Sex:M 05 Jul 1956 Roland H Thibeault & Laurette T Simard
THIBEAULT,Maureen E Sex:F 19 Apr 1957 Albert A Thibeault & Anita M Bergeron
THIBODEAU,Melvina B Sex:F 16 Mar 1959 Robert R Thibodeau
 & Mildred F McCormack
THIBODEAU,Teagan Leigh Sex:F 23 Mar 1985 James P Thibodeau
 & Elizabeth W Schaeffer
THIEVIERGE,Pauline M Sex:F (Child #1) 02 Jun 1940 Paul Thievierge (Canada)
 & Theresa Cote (Canada)
THIRSTON,Esther Sex:F 17 Jan 1742 Hudson, NH James Thirston & Mary
THIRSTON,Hannah Sex:F 15 Feb 174 Hudson, NH James Thirston & Mary
THIRSTON,Hannah Sex:F 15 Feb 1741 Hudson, NH James Thirston & Mary
THIRSTON,Mary Sex:F 03 Dec 1736 Hudson, NH James Thirston & Mary
THIRSTON,Stephen Sex:M 24 Apr 1738 Hudson, NH James Thirston & Mary
THOMAS,Baylen D Sex:M 17 Sep 1971 Ray T Thomas & Gayle I Salter
THOMAS,Elmer E Sex:M 16 Dec 1867 Hudson, NH William H Thomas & Josephine
THOMAS,Frank Albert Sex:M (Child #5) 01 Jun 1916 Hudson, NH Frank A Thomas
 (Browneville, ME) & Ida A Sawyer (Hillsboro, NH)
THOMAS,Gary A Sex:M 01 May 1963 Arthur D Thomas & Bernice L Cote
THOMAS,Hazel May Sex:F (Child #1) 08 Sep 1896 Pearl T Thomas (Hudson, NH)
 & Winifred M Wells (Montpelier, VT)
THOMAS,Helen Sex:F (Child #2) 12 Feb 1899 Pearl T Thomas (Hudson, NH)
 & Winifred M Wells (Albany, VT)
THOMAS,Lani C Sex:F 15 Jul 1976 Arthur D Thomas & Sonjie G Batura
THOMAS,Laura Maile Sex:F 01 Jul 1978 Arthur D Thomas & Sonjie G Batura
THOMAS,Sherrie A Sex:F 17 Feb 1965 Arthur D Thomas & Bernice L Cote
THOMAS,Willie Sex:M 11 Jun 1865 Hudson, NH William H Thomas & Josephine
THOMAS,Yvonne D Sex:F 21 Sep 1967 Edmund K Thomas & Angela M Hammond
THOMAS,[Unknown] Sex:F (Child #3) 15 Jun 1900 Pearl Thomas (Hudson, NH)
 & Winnefred Wells (Vermont)
THOMAS,[Unknown] Sex: 15 Nov 1866 Hudson, NH Tyler Thomas & Eliza A Sprake
THOMPSON,Benjamin Sex:M 01 Dec 1725 Hudson, NH Hugh Thompson & Jane
THOMPSON,Blanch M Sex:F 23 Jan 1874 Hudson, NH John M Thompson
 & Elizabeth O Marsh
THOMPSON,Brandi L Sex:F 20 Jan 1971 Wayne L Thompson & Claire L Letendre
THOMPSON,Christopher Mark Sex:M 05 Oct 1979 Stephen M Thompson
 & Pamela Dayle Pow
THOMPSON,Clara Belle Sex:F 30 Dec 1859 Hudson, NH John M Thompson
 & Elizabeth O Marsh
THOMPSON,Edna Elaine Sex:F (Child #2) 28 Aug 1933 George Thompson
 & Frances Clark (LaRue, OH)
THOMPSON,Fred Sex:M 10 Aug 1865 Hudson, NH John M Thompson & Elizabeth O
THOMPSON,Fred Wilbert Sex:M 10 Apr 1865 Hudson, NH John M Thompson
 & Elizabeth O Marsh
THOMPSON,Grace M Sex:F 23 Jan 1874 Hudson, NH John M Thompson & Lizzie
THOMPSON,Helen Louise Sex:F (Child #5) 01 Dec 1917 George Thompson
 (Londonderry, NH) & Henrietta Small (Stoelm Sprin
THOMPSON,Jennifer L Sex:F 04 Feb 1971 John C Thompson & Mary L Messery
THOMPSON,Jenny Lind Sex:F 19 Jul 1863 Hudson, NH John M Thompson

HUDSON,NH BIRTHS

& Elizabeth O Marsh
THOMPSON,John C Sex:M (Child #4) 29 Oct 1943 Robert M Thompson (Hudson, NH)
    & Georgia B Greeley (Londonderry, NH)
THOMPSON,John Clemence Sex:M 01 May 1856 Hudson, NH John M Thompson
    & Elizabeth O Marsh
THOMPSON,John Willis Sex:M 23 Sep 1853 Hudson, NH John M Thompson
    & Elizabeth O Marsh
THOMPSON,Lilian Sex:F 24 Jul 1867 Hudson, NH John M Thompson & Elizabeth O
THOMPSON,Lillian A Sex:F 24 Jul 1867 Hudson, NH John M Thompson
    & Elizabeth O Marsh
THOMPSON,Lucie Greeley Sex:F 08 Sep 1870 Hudson, NH John M Thompson
    & Elizabeth O Marsh
THOMPSON,Lucy A G Sex:F 08 Sep 1870 Hudson, NH John M Thompson
    & Elizabeth M
THOMPSON,Michelle Marie Sex:F 02 Aug 1982 Richard R Thompson
    & Rose Marie Straughan
THOMPSON,Nellie May Sex:F 25 May 1858 Hudson, NH John M Thompson
    & Elizabeth O Marsh
THOMPSON,Robert Martin Sex:M (Child #2) 15 Jun 1938 Robert Martin Thompson
    (Hudson, NH) & Georgia Belle Greele (Londonderry, NH)
THOMPSON,Scott A Sex:M 05 Feb 1969 Randall D Thompson & Victoria V Vurpillat
THOMPSON,Wayne L Sex:M (Child #3) 12 Feb 1940 Robert M Thompson (Hudson, NH)
    & Georgia B Greeley (Londonderry, NH)
THOMPSON,Willie Herbert Sex:M 23 Jun 1861 Hudson, NH John M Thompson
    & Elizabeth O Marsh
THOMPSON,[Unknown] Sex:F 16 Feb 1871 Hudson, NH W C B Thompson & Eliza A
THORN,Albert Sex:M (Child #3) 10 May 1885 Hudson, NH Charles E Thorn
    (Brownfield, ME) & Eliza E Estey (Windham, NH)
THORN,Herbert Sex:M (Child #4) 10 May 1885 Hudson, NH Charles E Thorn
    (Brownfield, ME) & Eliza E Estey (Windham, NH)
THORN,Sandra C Sex:F 04 May 1971 Paul D Thorn & Donna I Hodgkins
THORNE,Janice M Sex:F 14 May 1959 Harold E Thorne & Marilyn J Strout
THORP,John Sex:M 17 May 1783 Hudson, NH John Thorp & Priscilla
THUNBERG,Debra C Sex:F 02 Oct 1961 Jon C Thunberg & Mary E White
THURSTON,Sean G Sex:M 04 Nov 1974 Ronald F Thurston Sr & Joanne G Hill
THYLIN,Robin M Sex:F 08 Jan 1958 Robert S Thylin & Jeannette E Rich
TIBBETTS,Kathleen M Sex:F 18 Jun 1962 George E Tibbetts & Sandra J Pobuda
TIERNAN,Crystal Lynn Sex:F 05 Jun 1980 Gregory C Tiernan & Cheryl Ann Rhyner
TIERNAN,Neil Patrick Sex:M 29 Aug 1980 Thomas G Tiernan & Margo Leigh Ruckman
TIERNEY,Corri Anne Sex:F 02 Oct 1977 Daniel F Tierney & Margaret Ann Smith
TIERNEY,Melissa Ann Sex:F 17 Apr 1983 Brian F Tierney & Michelle Peloquin
TIERNEY,Scott J Sex:M 12 Aug 1967 James E Tierney & Carole A MacMillan
TILDSLEY,Judith A Sex:F 21 Apr 1961 Sidney A Tildsley & Margaret A Fitzgerald
TINNEY,David G Sex:M 02 May 1790 Hudson, NH Jonathan Tinney & Martha
TINNEY,Elizebeth Sex:F 27 Mar 1786 Hudson, NH Jonathan Tinney & Martha
TINNEY,Franklin Sex:M 17 Jan 1808 Hudson, NH Paul Tinney & Sarah
TINNEY,Martha Sex:F 23 Jul 1788 Hudson, NH Jonathan Tinney & Martha
TINNEY,Mary Sex:F 27 Dec 1792 Hudson, NH Jonathan Tinney & Martha
TINNEY,Paul Sex:M 01 Mar 1802 Hudson, NH Paul Tinney & Sarah
TINNEY,Robert Sex:M 17 Sep 1784 Hudson, NH Jonathan Tinney & Martha
TINNEY,Silas Sex:M 04 Sep 1805 Hudson, NH Paul Tinney & Sarah
TITCOMB,Albert O Sex:M 16 Sep 1870 Hudson, NH Albert G Titcomb & Ella S
TITCOMB,Albert Oliver Sex:M 27 Jul 1846 Hudson, NH Simeon C Titcomb
    & Sally H Webster
TITCOMB,Charles Kimball Sex:M 09 Apr 1850 Hudson, NH Simeon C Titcomb
    & Sally H Webster
TITCOMB,Frank Ferdinand Sex:M 12 Oct 1852 Hudson, NH Simeon C Titcomb
    & Sally H Webster
TITCOMB,Nellie Jane Sex:F 13 May 1855 Hudson, NH Simeon C Titcomb
    & Sally H Webster

HUDSON,NH BIRTHS

TITUS,Alfred Joseph   Sex:M   26 Mar 1864 Hudson, NH Orlando E Titus
    & Rowena M Cummings
TITUS,Alphonse Elmer   Sex:M   22 Jun 1875 Hudson, NH Orlando E Titus
    & Rowena M Cummings
TITUS,Arthur Orlando   Sex:M   30 Jan 1870 Hudson, NH Orlando E Titus
    & Rowena M Cummings
TITUS,Martha Almira   Sex:F   22 Jul 1865 Hudson, NH Orlando E Titus
    & Rowena M Cummings
TOBIAS,Michael J   Sex:M   22 Feb 1980 Martin B Tobias & Agatha M Moya
TOEPFER,Leslie A   Sex:F   04 Nov 1967 Robert W Toepfer & Sherry K Edwards
TOMBARELLO,Amber Winn   Sex:F   09 Oct 1981 James A Tombarello & Janet V Lysik
TOMILSON,James R   Sex:M   08 Mar 1967 Gordon D Tomilson & Cynthia E Johnston
TOMILSON,Katherine A Sex:F 08 May 1968 Gordon D Tomilson & Cynthia E Johnston
TONKS,Brian G   Sex:M   24 Jan 1960 Gerald D Tonks & Roberta J Locke
TONNESON,Sean P   Sex:M   02 Oct 1971 Robert E Tonneson & Helen M Gould
TOOM,Allison M   Sex:F   16 Mar 1977 Paul Toom & Regina P Michaud
TOOMEY,Katie Sue   Sex:F   25 Jul 1979 Ronald James Toomey & Susan Paula Burton
TOOMEY,Lisa Beth   Sex:F   23 Oct 1973 Ronald J Toomey & Susan P Burton
TORMEY,Margaret K   Sex:F   22 Jun 1968 Joseph H Tormey Jr & Linda M Bullard
TORMEY,Michael I   Sex:M   22 May 1966 Joseph H Tormey Jr & Linda M Bullard
TORMEY,Peter H   Sex:M   17 Jul 1964 Joseph H Tormey, Jr & Linda M Bullard
TORRES,[Unknown]   Sex:M   05 Aug 1982 John Richard Torres & Zoe Ann MacDonald
TORREY,Carol A   Sex:F   01 Jul 1950 Lester W Torrey & Estella F Powell
TORREY,Christopher T   Sex:M   12 Dec 1970 David R Torrey & Joyce E Besco
TORREY,Diane G   Sex:F   31 Jul 1953 Lester W Torrey & Estella F Powell
TORREY,Estella F   Sex:F   13 Jan 1947 Lester W Torrey (Pepperell, MA)
    & Estella F Powell (Nashua, NH)
TOWER,Amanda S   Sex:F   11 Oct 1965 John H Tower & Nora K Pierce
TOWER,Michelle L   Sex:F   12 Jan 1968 John H Tower & Nora K Pierce
TOWERS,Christopher John Sex:M   15 Sep 1983 Arthur W Towers & Deborah Heighton
TOWERS,Scott M   Sex:M   26 May 1974 Arthur W Towers & Deborah Heighton
TOWLE,Karen L   Sex:F   04 Sep 1960 Carroll R Towle & Nancy L Nelson
TOWNSEND,Penny E   Sex:F   04 Aug 1965 Harold A Townsend & Mary A Cirillo
TRAINER,Jennifer Laura   Sex:F   20 Nov 1981 John Kennedy Trainer
    & Justine Star Stinson
TRAYER,Jared T   Sex:M   23 Mar 1978 Thomas S Trayer & Denise Ellis
TREMBALY,Jessica Barrett Sex:F 12 Nov 1979 William H Tremblay
    & Nancy Lee Barrett
TREMBLAY,Amy J   Sex:F   13 Jun 1975 Robert R Tremblay & Joan B Perry
TREMBLAY,Carmen M   Sex:F   16 Nov 1955 Robert A Tremblay & Laurette J Berube
TREMBLAY,Eric P   Sex:M   27 Sep 1959 Robert A Tremblay & Laurette J Berube
TREMBLAY,Guy J   Sex:M   08 Dec 1964 Jean-Guy Tremblay & Jeannine M Routhier
TREMBLAY,Keli L   Sex:F   30 Jun 1967 Robert R Tremblay & Joan B Perry
TREMBLAY,Kenneth J   Sex:M   09 Feb 1962 Robert A Tremblay & Laurette J Berube
TREMBLAY,Marc   Sex:M   01 Aug 1967 Jean R Tremblay & Lucille J Lavigne
TRETTEL,Christine M   Sex:F   27 Mar 1967 James L Trettel Jr & Maureen M Grady
TRIPPLETON,Stephanie L   Sex:F   07 Aug 1957 Simeon Trippleton, Jr
    & Vivian A Martin
TROMBLEY,Kristi G   Sex: 24 Sep 1972 Ronald R Trombley & Diane H Fulton
TROMBLEY,Sandra J   Sex:F   16 Sep 1952 Jesse W Trombley & Doris M Levesque
TROMBLEY,Stephanie Lynn   Sex:F   24 Aug 1978 Ronald R Trombley
    & Diane Hope Fulton
TROMBLY,Fred Napoleon Sex:M   (Child #2) 30 Jan 1933 Fred Trombly (Nashua, NH)
    & Christine Mattison (Canada)
TROMBLY,James Norman Sex:M   (Child #3) 01 Aug 1934 Fred Trombly (Nashua, NH)
    & Christine Matherson (Nova Scotia)
TROMBLY,Leona Emma May Sex:F   (Child #4) 01 Aug 1935 Fred Trombly (Nashua,
    NH) & Christina Matheson (Canada)
TROMBLY,Sandra Mae   Sex:F   (Child #2) 02 Aug 1938 Ellsworth Trombly (Sciota,
    NY) & Viola Jennie Polak (Fulton, NY)

HUDSON,NH BIRTHS

TROUP,James Robert   Sex:M   02 Jul 1981 Robert M Troup & Joan F Sweeney
TROW,Arthur A   Sex:M   22 Apr 1863 Hudson, NH George W Trow &
TROW,David R   Sex:M   (Child #3) 14 May 1946 Stuart A Trow (Mont Vernon, NH)
   & Ruth Warren (Boston, MA)
TROW,George W   Sex:M   28 Jun 1868 Hudson, NH George W Trow & Permilla
TROW,Stuart A   Sex:M   (Child #1) 07 Jun 1942 Stuart A Trow (Mont Vernon, NH)
   & Ruth Warren (Boston, MA)
TROW,Walter R   Sex:M   (Child #2) 19 Nov 1943 Stuart A Trow (Mont Vernon, NH)
   & Ruth Warren (Boston, MA)
TROW,[Unknown]   Sex: 22 Apr 1863 Hudson, NH George W Trow & Permilla
TRUDEAU,Albert H   Sex:M   (Child #2) 03 Oct 1943 Edgar A Trudeau (Nashua, NH)
   & Lilianne H Levesque (Nashua, NH)
TRUDEAU,Linda E   Sex:F   20 Oct 1959 Edgar A Trudeau & Lillian H Levesque
TRUDEAU,Lucille R   Sex:F   (Child #3) 26 Oct 1944 Edgar A Trudeau (Nashua, NH)
   & Lilianne H Levesque (Nashua, NH)
TRUDEAU,Mary J   Sex:F   19 Mar 1950 Edgar A Trudeau & Lilianne H Levesque
TRUDEAU,Nancy A   Sex:F   10 May 1952 Edgar A Trudeau & Lillian H Levesque
TRUDEAU,Pauline M   Sex:F   28 Jan 1947 Edgar A Trudeau (Nashua, NH)
   & Lilianne H Levesque (Nashua, NH)
TRUDEL,Karen M   Sex:F   18 May 1972 Richard L Trudel & Anne-Marie Beland
TRUFANT,Alice R   Sex:F   (Child #6) 12 Jan 1912 John M Trufant (Harpswell, ME)
   & Flora Turner (Levant, ME)
TRUFANT,Kenneth Chase Sex:M   (Child #1) 20 Dec 1914 Frank A Trufant (Nashua,
   NH) & Marion Ethel Chase (Nashua, NH)
TRUFONT,[Unknown] Sex:F   (Child #5) 27 Nov 1899 John N Trufont (Harpswell,
   ME) & Flora Turner (Leavant, ME)
TUBINAS,Jenny   Sex:F   (Child #7) 20 Feb 1917 John Tubinas (Russia)
   & Mary Gregas (Russia)
TUCCI,Anthony A   Sex:M   10 Sep 1977 Ralph J Tucci & Gail Ann Smith
TUCCI,Daniel J   Sex:M   24 Sep 1962 Reginald E Tucci, Jr & Laura M Willard
TUCCI,Theresa M   Sex:F   23 Jun 1975 Ralph J Tucci & Gail A Smith
TUCKER,Cheryl C   Sex:F   18 Nov 1969 Norman H Tucker & Teresa Marie Walsh
TUCKER,Mark A   Sex:M   03 Nov 1960 Carl C Tucker & Helen M Labombarde
TUCKFIELD,Matthew Addams Sex:M   21 Mar 1985 Melvyn E Tuckfield
   & Heather A Welch
TUCKFIELD,Tara A   Sex:F   25 Jun 1980 Melvyn E Tuckfield & Heather A Welch
TUEFFERD,Max D   Sex:M   13 Nov 1971 Francois Tuefferd & Helen McDougall
TUEFFERD,Nanook A   Sex:M   10 Jul 1969 Francois Tuefferd & Helen McDougall
TUITE,Emma E   Sex:F   (Child #1) 09 Mar 1916 Hudson, NH Augustin Tuite
   (Massachusetts) & Ida Bourdon (Massachusetts)
TURCOGEORGE,John E   Sex:M   29 Jul 1970 Nicholas Turcogeorge
   & Lorraine M Swanson
TURCOGEORGE,Joy   Sex:F   16 Feb 1965 Nicholas Turcogeorge & Lorraine M Swanson
TURCOTT,Daniel S   Sex:M   24 Aug 1961 Valere R Turcott & Jennie J Dombrosky
TURCOTT,Denise G   Sex:F   17 Aug 1961 Robert V Turcott & Faith L Kierstead
TURCOTT,Ricky D   Sex:M   27 Jun 1951 Valere Turcott & Jean Dombrowsky
TURCOTT,Scott D   Sex:M   20 Feb 1960 Robert V Turcott & Faith L Kierstead
TURCOTTE,Jean-Paul N Sex:M   17 Feb 1977 Jean-Paul Turcotte & Ginette Duquette
TURCOTTE,Joan E   Sex:F   14 Feb 1969 Pamphile G Turcotte & Louise M Nadeau
TURCOTTE,Shane R   Sex:M   13 Feb 1975 Robert G Turcotte & Kathleen M Kulesza
TURILLI,John W   Sex:M   23 Apr 1953 Raymond Turilli & Marilyn D Cote
TURLO,Jeffrey A   Sex:M   08 Dec 1958 Louis J Turlo & Kathryn M Morse
TURMEL,Debra J   Sex:F   30 Jul 1963 Richard O Turmel & Jean E Cote
TURMEL,Golanda   Sex:F   (Child #12) 04 Jul 1935 David Turmel (Central Falls,
   RI) & Octavia Rodier (Nashua, NH)
TURMEL,James C   Sex:M   05 Mar 1967 Robert L Turmel & Janice L Cherkes
TURMEL,Joseph Girouard   Sex:M   (Child #1) 21 Jun 1931 David Turmel (Rhode
   Island) & Octavia Rodier (Nashua, NH)
TURMEL,Paula M   Sex:F   24 Sep 1966 Richard O Turmel & Jeanne E Cote
TURMEL,Richard O   Sex:M   (Child #12) 30 Aug 1940 David Turmel (Central Falls,

HUDSON,NH BIRTHS

RI) & Octavia Rodier (Nashua, NH)
TURMEL,Sheryl A   Sex:F   05 Mar 1967 Robert L Turmel & Janice L Cherkes
TURMEL,Theodore E Sex:M   (Child #15) 15 Oct 1944 David Turmel (Central Falls, RI) & Octavia Rodier (Nashua, NH)
TURNELLE,Robert Louis   Sex:M   (Child #11) 28 May 1933 David Turnelle (Rhode Island) & Octavia Rodier (Nashua, NH)
TURNER,Cheryl E   Sex:F   14 May 1947 Robert D Turner (Nashua, NH) & Norma N Martin (Nashua, NH)
TURNER,Daniel   Sex:M   16 Oct 1948 Joseph B Turner (Mexico) & Pauline F Heddeman (Manchester, NH)
TURNER,George Francis   Sex:M   (Child #1) 18 Feb 1913 Chester D Turner (Rockland, MA) & Nellie Montgomery (Nashua, NH)
TURNER,Hayley Jayne Sex:F 14 Sep 1983 William M Turner & Jayne Carol Nelson
TURNER,Judith A   Sex:F   (Child #2) 10 Jan 1946 Joseph B Turner (Quadalajoia, M) & Pauline F Heddeman (Manchester, NH)
TURNER,William R   Sex:M   21 Apr 1969 William R Turner & Gloria A Ross
TUTTLE,Deanne M   Sex:F   17 Dec 1958 Everett A Tuttle & Dolores K Dodge
TWARDOSKY,Bonnie L   Sex:F   07 Jan 1964 William T Twardosky & Doris A Noel
TWARDOSKY,Jason A   Sex: 11 Jun 1973 Ronald K Twardosky & Geraldine J Tate
TWARDOSKY,Pamela J   Sex:F   06 Dec 1965 William T Twardosky & Doris A Noel
TWARDOSKY,Ronald K Jr Sex:M 17 Jul 1970 Ronald K Twardosky & Geraldine J Tate
TWARDOSKY,Steven W   Sex:M   25 Feb 1949 Peter T Twardosky & Cora M Cox
TWARDOSKY,William J   Sex:M   20 Oct 1962 William T Twardosky & Doris A Noel
TWISS,Howard Alfred Sex:M   (Child #2) 24 Jan 1922 Walter F Twiss (Boston, MA) & Ethel M Wheeler (Nashua, NH)
TWITCHELL,Ariana Julia Sunshin   Sex:F   18 Dec 1978 Allan L Twitchell & Jane Mary Fournier
TWITCHELL,Benjamin J   Sex:M   21 Aug 1976 Allan L Twitchell & Jane Fournier
TWOMBLY,Kathleen   Sex:F   15 Sep 1948 Robert J Twombly (Laconia, NH) & Rita Denoncour (Franklin, NH)
TWOMBLY,Renee Michelle Sex:F 19 Oct 1984 James M Twombly & Nancy L MacKenzie
TYLER,Colleen   Sex:F   17 Mar 1966 Richard J Tyler & Joan V St Pierre
TYLER,Heather G   Sex:F   28 Dec 1975 David T Tyler & Marilyn L Harrington
TYLER,Kimberly P   Sex:F   11 Feb 1974 David T Tyler & Marilyn L Harrington
TYLER,Lisa P   Sex:F   17 Mar 1967 Gerald J Tyler & Carol B Allison
TYLER,Paul E   Sex:M   05 Feb 1961 Gerald J Tyler & Carol A Allison
UHL,Jon Michael   Sex:M   06 Oct 1980 Mervin Edward Uhl & Barbara Jane Nobles
ULERY,James P   Sex:M   19 Aug 1974 Jordan G Ulery & Janice E Lesieur
ULERY,Jonathan D   Sex:M   11 Mar 1978 Jordon G Ulery & Janice E Lesieur
UNDERWOOD,Dustin Sex:M 20 Apr 1807 Hudson, NH Jeptha Underwood & Sarah Cummings
UNDERWOOD,James Sex:M 14 Aug 1788 Hudson, NH Phineas Underwood & Rebecca Dunn
UNDERWOOD,James   Sex:M   01 May 1790 Hudson, NH Phinehas Underwood & Rebecah
UNDERWOOD,James Burns   Sex:M   23 May 1805 Hudson, NH   & Rebecca Underwood
UNDERWOOD,Jeptha Sex:M 14 Feb 1784 Hudson, NH Phineas Underwood&Rebecca Dunn
UNDERWOOD,John W   Sex:M   18 Apr 1786 Hudson, NH Phinheas Underwood & Rebeccah
UNDERWOOD,John Winslow   Sex:M   28 Apr 1786 Hudson, NH Phineas Underwood & Rebecca Dunn
UNDERWOOD,Jonas Sex:M 01 May 1790 Hudson, NH Phineas Underwood & Rebecca Dunn
UNDERWOOD,Jonas   Sex:M   14 Aug 1788 Hudson, NH Phinheas Underwood & Rebeccah
UNDERWOOD,Louisa Sex:F 06 Oct 1805 Hudson, NH Jeptha Underwood&Sarah Cummings
UNDERWOOD,Louise   Sex:F   06 Oct 1805 Hudson, NH Jeptha Underwood & Sarah
UNDERWOOD,Mary Elizabeth   Sex:F   27 Sep 1827 Hudson, NH John W Underwood &
UNDERWOOD,Sherilyn A Sex:F 28 Nov 1950 Robert C Underwood & Genevieve F Fifty
UPHAM,Pauline Yvonne   Sex:F   (Child #9) 02 Nov 1930 Henry J Upham (Goffstown, NH) & Alberta M Dionne (Fraserville, CA)
UPTON,Jonathan R   Sex:M   14 Oct 1808 Hudson, NH Jonathan Upton &
UPTON,Jonathan Russell   Sex:M   14 Oct 1808 Hudson, NH Jonathan D Upton &
UPTON,Mary   Sex:F   16 May 1810 Hudson, NH Jonathan D Upton &
USOVICZ,Ann M   Sex:F   (Child #2) 17 Feb 1945 Peter Usovicz (Brockton, MA)

HUDSON, NH BIRTHS

& Maude E Miller (Nobscot, MA)
USOVICZ,Peter M Sex:M   18 Aug 1947 Peter Usovicz (Brockton, MA)
& Maude E Miller (Nobscott, MA)
UTO,Andrea L Sex:F 27 Mar 1980 Anthony R Uto & Kathleen M Ducharme
UTO,Jessica Ann Sex:F 05 Nov 1982 Anthony Richard Uto & Kathleen M Ducharme
VACHON,Ricky Jean Sex:M 28 Apr 1976 Jean-Paul Vachon & Solange M Laflamme
VACHON,Sandy V Sex:F 16 Nov 1973 Jean-Paul Vachon & Solange M Laflamme
VADNEY,Adam Daniel Sex:M 29 Dec 1983 Daniel R Vadney & France M Fauteux
VADNEY,Brian W Sex:M 19 Mar 1961 Raymond L Vadney & Marie M Simard
VADNEY,Bruce D Sex:M 02 Dec 1963 Raymond L Vadney & Marie M Simard
VADNEY,Karen L Sex:F 01 Sep 1977 Daniel R Vadney & Frances M Fauteux
VADNEY,Tina M Sex:F 26 Jan 1966 Raymond L Vadney & Marie M Simard
VAIL,Keith R Sex:M 13 May 1978 Raymond J Vail & Eleanor Ann Perry
VAILLANCOURT,Brian Joseph Sex:M 18 Mar 1985 Dennis R Vaillancourt
& Kathleen N Godin
VAILLANCOURT,David R Sex:M 30 Sep 1967 Ronald H Vaillancourt
& Beverly L Lefebvre
VAILLANCOURT,Gerard L Sex:M 27 Jul 1948 Adiren F Vaillancourt (Nashua, NH)
& Loretta P Marcoux (Nashua, NH)
VAILLANCOURT,Lucien S Jr Sex:M 04 May 1959 Lucien S Vaillancourt
& Yolande L Turmel
VAILLANCOURT,Melissa Ann Sex:F 10 Sep 1979 Arthur L Vaillancourt
& Margaret A Buslovich
VAILLANCOURT,Patricia A Sex:F (Child #3) 19 Sep 1944 Lucien S Vaillancourt
(Nashua, NH) & Lillian B Malette (Fall River, MA)
VAILLANCOURT,Rene A Sex:M 18 Jun 1975 Michael A Vaillancourt & Diane R Dube
VAILLANCOURT,Scott L Sex:M 09 Jul 1969 Lionel J Vaillancourt & Nancy A Swift
VAILLANCOURT,William D Sex:M 03 Dec 1977 Dennis R Vaillancourt
& Kathleen N Godin
VALCOURT,Brenda F Sex:F 13 Apr 1965 Leon E Valcourt & Irene E Garside
VALCOURT,Glenn A Sex:M 10 Mar 1962 Leon E Valcourt & Lorraine N Vaillancourt
VALCOURT,Nadine A Sex:F 18 Feb 1964 Donat A Valcourt & Beverly A McKinley
VALLERAND,Anthony J Sex:M 06 Sep 1962 Leo R Vallerand & Rose-Alma G Thibault
VALLERAND,Paul R Sex:M 31 Jul 1964 Leo R Vallerand & Rose A Thibeault
VALLIERE,David R Sex:M 06 Jun 1952 Robert A Valliere & Dorothy A Richardson
VAN DINTER,G L Sex:F (Child #1) 21 Aug 1942 Robert A Van Dinter (Little
Chute, WI) & Juliette Camp (Lowell, MA)
VAN EPPS,Amy E Sex:F 17 Sep 1966 Robert F Van Epps & Geraldine K Tauber
VAN ROSE,Glennis A Sex:F 11 Sep 1953 Joseph P Van Rose & Charlotte N Young
VANAGS,Alan K Sex:M 25 Apr 1966 Gunars Vanags & Lucille G Hunninghac
VanBUSKIRK,Bennett I Sex:M (Child #2) 05 Oct 1915 Hudson, NH G B VanBuskirk
(Algona,Iowa) & Irva Basham (Arcadia, KS)
VANDER HEYDEN,Gerald L Sex:M 15 Feb 1961 Leon J VanderHeyden
& Laura T Poisson
VANDERBECK,Jason Michael Sex:M 27 Dec 1978 Richard A Vanderbeck
& Cheryl Ann Lampron
VANDERBECK,Joshua J Sex:M 24 Jan 1972 Kenneth J Vanderbeck & Leota F Wilmot
VANDERBECK,Trudi J Sex:F 15 Oct 1966 Kenneth J Vanderbeck & Leota F Wilmot
VANDERPOOL,Thomas James Sex:M 04 Feb 1983 Gordon D Vanderpool&Sandra A Argie
VANDERVOET,Dirk L Sex:M (Child #2) 03 Feb 1921 Dirk VanderVoet (Holland)
& Martha A Jones (Lawrence, MA)
VANIER,Andrea M Sex:F 01 Nov 1976 Morris R Vanier & Kathleen H Boska
VANIER,Clarence George Sex:M (Child #2) 23 Feb 1927 Alfred L Vanier
(Suncook, NH) & Irene G Mercier (Newport, VT)
VANIER,Philip Steven Sex:M 01 Feb 1982 Morris R Vanier & Kethleen Heidi Boska
VANIER,Wallace Alfred Sex:M (Child #1) 02 Jan 1926 Alfred Z Vanier
(Pembroke, NH) & Irene G Mercier (Newport, VT)
VARNEY,Eric J Sex:M 27 Aug 1969 Robert D Varney & Colleen M L O'Brien
VARNEY,James R Sex:M 02 Mar 1960 Charles E Varney & Rita H Charles
VARNEY,Laurie A Sex:F 21 Aug 1962 Charles E Varney & Rita H Charles

HUDSON,NH BIRTHS

VARNEY,Scott T   Sex:M   19 Jun 1978 Steven A Varney & Kathleen A Griffin
VARNEY,Steven W   Sex:M   20 Jul 1964 Robert D Varney & Colleen M O'Brien
VASKELIONIS,Keith III   Sex:M   04 Dec 1980 Keith Vaskelionis Jr
  & Janice Marie Drouin
VASKELIONIS,Sarah Anne   Sex:F   21 Apr 1982 Keith Vaskelionis Jr
  & Janice Marie Drouin
VAYENS,Arthur Dominic Datu Sex:M 01 Jun 1984 Arthur Vayens Jr & Velda V Datu
VAZZANA,Lawrence Sex:M   (Child #1) 21 Jan 1942 Nichols L Vazzana (Hudson, NH)
  & Helen T Smith (Nashua, NH)
VEILLEUX,Kelly E   Sex:F   01 Apr 1977 Yvan Leo Veilleux & Judith Ann Demanche
VENNE,Maureen R   Sex:F   26 Mar 1971 Charles M Venne & Janet G Bean
VERRETTE,Julia L   Sex:F   04 Oct 1966 David A Verrette & Claire M Routhier
VICKERY,Cherie L   Sex:F   06 Mar 1963 William R Vickery & Leontine Burelle
VICKERY,Edward A   Sex:M   11 Nov 1964 William R Vickery & Leontine Burelle
VIENS,Denise A   Sex:F   09 Jan 1952 Maurice N Viens & Evelyn E Drobek
VIENS,Irene C   Sex:F   12 Nov 1949 Gerard L Viens & Medora M Lefebvre
VIENS,Leonard R   Sex:M   19 Jul 1951 Gerard L Viens & Medora Lefebvre
VIENS,Louise M   Sex:F   03 Oct 1957 Gerard L Viens & Medora M Lefebvre
VIENS,Normand P   Sex:M   12 Jul 1952 Gerard L Viens & Medora Lefebvre
VIENS,Robert M   Sex:M   24 Sep 1949 Maurice N Viens & Evelyn E Drobak
VIENS,Roger G   Sex:M   10 Feb 1966 Leo G Viens & Priscilla R Comeau
VIGEANT,Gregory E   Sex:M   24 Jun 1967 Roland G Vigeant & Christine E Baron
VIGNEAULA,George   Sex:M   10 Feb 1914 Joseph Vigneaula (Canada)
  & Elmina Normand (Lowell, MA)
VIGNEAULT,M Simone G   Sex:F   (Child #2) 22 Feb 1936 Rodolphe Vigneault
  (Lowell, MA) & Olivette Dion (Canada)
VIGNOLA,Alan M   Sex:M   05 Oct 1953 Paul A Vignola & Rose M Bauer
VIGNOLA,Anna Lucile   Sex:F   (Child #6) 14 Jan 1925 Joseph Vignola (Canada)
  & Amelia Normand (Lowell, MA)
VIGNOLA,Arthur David   Sex:M   10 May 1921 Joseph Vignola (Canada)
  & Elmira Normand (Lowell, MA)
VIGNOLA,Brian J   Sex:M   24 Oct 1951 Paul A Vignola & Rose M Bauer
VIGNOLA,Carol A   Sex:F   (Child #1) 05 Sep 1942 Victor D Vignola (Hudson, NH)
  & Mary E Tierney (Lowell, MA)
VIGNOLA,Donna M   Sex:F   11 Oct 1949 Arthur V Vignola & Mary E Tierney
VIGNOLA,Jeannette R M   Sex:F   (Child #2) 25 Jan 1912 Joseph Vignola
  (St Auacler, Canada) & Elmira Normand (Lowell, MA)
VIGNOLA,Karen L   Sex:F   08 Aug 1966 Paul A Vignola & Rose M Bauer
VIGNOLA,Michael Ruane Sex:M 12 Sep 1983 Alan M Vignola & Mary Lynette Ruane
VIGNOLA,Patricia Carol Sex:F   (Child #2) 23 Feb 1938 Paul Vignola (Hudson,
  NH) & Dorothy E Chaplin (Groton, MA)
VIGNOLA,Paul   Sex:M   16 Mar 1919 Joseph Vignola (Canada) & Elmiria Nismand
  (Lowell, MA)
VIGNOLA,Paul A III   Sex:M   07 Nov 1970 Paul A Vignola Jr & June L Davis
VIGNOLA,Paul Armedus   Sex:M   (Child #4) 29 Aug 1941 Paul A Vignola (Hudson,
  NH) & Dorothy E Chapman (Groton, MA)
VIGNOLA,Paulette S   Sex:F   (Child #6) 06 Jan 1945 Paul Vignola (Hudson, NH)
  & Dorothy Chaplin (Groton, MA)
VIGNOLA,Peggy Lucille   Sex:F   (Child #3) 15 Jun 1939 Paul Vignola (Hudson,
  NH) & Dorothy E Chapman (Groton, MA)
VIGNOLA,Philip E   Sex:M   16 Sep 1943 Paul A Vignola (Hudson, NH)
  & Dorothy E Chaplin (Groton, MA)
VIGNOLA,Robin M   Sex:F   25 Sep 1962 Paul A Vignola & Rose M Bauer
VIK,Paul Gustav III Sex:M 02 Apr 1982 Paul Gustav Vik Jr & Jacinta A Fusco
VILLAR,Melissa K   Sex: 10 May 1973 Raul Villar & Maureen Canfield
VINECOMBE,Christopher Ryan   Sex:M   24 Feb 1984 Westerley L Vinecomb
  & Rita Marie Diamond
VISOCCHI,Derek Alfred Sex:M 07 Dec 1981 David R Visocchi & Patricia Ann Muise
VOKES,Elizabeth A   Sex:F   08 Dec 1968 Robert R Vokes & Judith A Moraski
VOKES,Mary A   Sex:F   30 Apr 1966 Robert R Vokes & Judith A Moraski

HUDSON,NH BIRTHS

VOKES,Robert R Jr Sex:M   31 Mar 1965 Robert R Vokes, Sr & Judith A Moraski
VYDFOL,Fred A Sex:M   30 Jun 1940 Albert Vydfol (Poland) & Franciska Sczbak
   (Poland)
VYDFOL,Henry Sex:M   (Child #9) 09 Jul 1926 Albert Vydfol (Poland)
   & Francis Szozebak (Poland)
VYDFOL,[Unknown] Sex:F   (Child #6) 21 Dec 1919 Albert Vydfol (Austria)
   & Frances Szczebak (Austria)
WADE,Donna L Sex:F   05 Nov 1953 Charles F Wade & Emily P Fissette
WAISWILOS,Anthony A Sex:M   (Child #2) 07 Jan 1933 Anthony A Waiswilos
   (Lithuania) & Ruth Brockelbank (Newburyport, MA)
WALANGEWICZ,Charles Sex:M   (Child #4) 24 May 1927 Michael Walangewicz
   (Russia) & Mary Kierute (Russia)
WALCH,Kelley E Sex:F   26 Nov 1968 Myron D Walch & Jacqueline L Dubois
WALCH,Kim M Sex:F   26 Nov 1968 Myron D Walch & Jacqueline L Dubois
WALCH,Roy H Sex:M   (Child #5) 22 May 1892 Clarence E Walch (Lowell, MA)
   & Delia Hutchinson (Milford, NH)
WALKER,Florance Sex:F   13 Feb 1876 Hudson, NH Isham Walker & Margaret
WALKER,Gracia Sex:F   25 Aug 1878 Hudson, NH James G Walker (New York City)
   & Mary E (Newburg)
WALKER,Sarah Anne Sex:F   (Child #4) 28 Feb 1931 Reginald Guy Walker
   (Ossipee, NH) & Edrie Gouin (Wolfeboro, NH)
WALKER,Tammy L Sex:F   30 Aug 1968 John R Walker & Constance L Smith
WALKER,Thomas R Jr Sex:M   02 Jun 1967 Thomas R Walker & Brenda D Mitton
WALKER,Tina M Sex:F   06 Sep 1966 John R Walker & Constance L Smith
WALLACE,Abbey E Sex:F   27 Oct 1960 Bruce E Wallace & Joyce L Pfeifer
WALLACE,Edgar C Jr Sex:M   11 Jan 1949 Edgar C Wallace & Elizabeth Fuller
WALLACE,Katherine M Sex:F   27 Oct 1975 Thomas J Wallace & Carol D Dick
WALLACE,Kristen A Sex:F   11 Jul 1974 Thomas J Wallace & Carol D Dick
WALLACE,Lucas Perry Sex:M   06 May 1982 Gregg Perry Wallace & Ev Lynn Carey
WALLACE,Patricia L Sex:F   16 Nov 1965 Richard E Wallace & Marie E Munroe
WALLACE,William A Sex:M   11 Apr 1866 Hudson, NH Joseph W Wallace & Linda A
WALLACE,William H Sex:M   11 Apr 1866 Hudson, NH Joseph Wallace & Linda
WALLEN,Janice Sex:F   12 Jun 1947 Michael Wallen (Nashua, NH) & Mary Puez
   (Lowell, MA)
WALSER,Joyce H Sex:F   10 Nov 1967 John D Walser, Jr & Rosalie K Andrews
WALSH,Kathryn Hollis Sex:F   12 Jul 1979 Kevin Michael Walsh
   & Linda Jean Whitehead
WALSH,Matthew Ryan Sex:M   26 Jun 1977 Kevin M Walsh & Linda Jean Whitehead
WALSH,Patrick John Sex:M   15 Mar 1981 James Thomas Walsh & Mary Jane Pisani
WALSH,Patrick L Sex:M   02 Apr 1978 Edward M Walsh & Joanne E Marshall
WALTERS,Aaron C Sex:M   06 Apr 1977 William C Walters & Rosalie G Lopez
WALTERS,Adina M Sex:F   28 Jul 1970 Harry S Walters & Betty E Clough
WALTERS,Jean E Sex:F   13 Dec 1967 Harry S Walters & Betty E Clough
WALTERS,Katherine E Sex: 26 Sep 1972 Harry S Walters & Betty E Clough
WAMBOLDT,Joel Philip Sex:M 27 Feb 1985 James P Wamboldt & Jeanne Anne Roussel
WARBURTON,Angelina Sex:F   (Child #1) 12 Dec 1905 Wm Warburton (England)
   & Minnie Hanson (Nashua, NH)
WARD,Anthony D Sex:M   27 Oct 1968 David R Ward & Nina M Mattei
WARD,Clifton David Sex:M   05 Feb 1981 Paul Raymond Ward & Susan May Roby
WARD,Gina M Sex:F   23 Nov 1966 David R Ward & Nina M Mattei
WARDWELL,Dona Sex:F   30 Jan 1954 Philip H Wardwell & Claudine M Nadeau
WARDWELL,Dora Sex:F   30 Jan 1954 Philip H Wardwell & Claudine M Nadeau
WARDWELL,Kimberly J Sex: 01 Mar 1973 Thurlow E Wardwell & Laurette J Nadeau
WAREING,Kimberly Ann Sex:F   14 May 1979 Richard A Wareing & Kathy Ann Packard
WARNER,Donald Edward Jr Sex:M   09 Apr 1983 Donald E Warner Sr & Nancy E Shute
WARNER,Jennifer Leigh Sex:F   22 Nov 1980 Donald E Warner & Nancy E Shute
WARREN,Donald S Sex:M   19 Apr 1966 Donald H Warren & Arlene N Johnson
WARREN,Irene Ruth Sex:F   (Child #5) 14 Aug 1915 Hudson, NH
     Oscar G Warren (Derry, NH) & Ida L Proctor (Wrentham, MA)
WARREN,Marilyn Lois Sex:F   (Child #4) 15 Jan 1914 Oscar G Warren (Derry, NH)

HUDSON,NH BIRTHS

   & Ida L Proctor (Wrentham, MA)
WARREN,Michael H Sex:M   (Child #1) 20 Nov 1946 Forrest H Warren (Derry, NH)
   & Joyce E Beckham (Plant City, FL)
WARREN,Patricia A   Sex:F   15 Mar 1948 Forrest H Warren (Derry, NH)
   & Joyce E Beckham (Plant City, FL)
WASON,Alinda   Sex:F   10 Nov 1804 Hudson, NH James Wason & Mary Anderson
WASON,Anna   Sex:F   19 Oct 1739 Hudson, NH James Wason & Hannah
WASON,Elizabeth   Sex:F   26 Nov 1740 Hudson, NH James Wason & Hannah
WASON,George   Sex:M   24 Aug 1818 Hudson, NH Thomas P Wason & Mary Colburn
WASON,Hannah   Sex:F   24 Mar 1778 Hudson, NH Samuel Wason & Margaret
WASON,Hannah   Sex:F   17 Apr 1788 Hudson, NH Thomas Wason & Mary
WASON,Hannah   Sex:F   19 Oct 1739 Hudson, NH James Wason & Hannah
WASON,Henda   Sex: 10 Nov 1804 Hudson, NH James Wason & Mary
WASON,Isabel   Sex:F   11 Jan 1742 Hudson, NH James Wason & Hannah
WASON,James   Sex:M   22 Sep 1737 Hudson, NH James Wason & Hannah
WASON,James   Sex:M   04 Oct 1781 Hudson, NH Samuel Wason & Margaret
WASON,James   Sex:M   11 Nov 1773 Hudson, NH Thomas Wason & Mary
WASON,James   Sex:M   29 Jan 1779 Hudson, NH Thomas Wason & Mary
WASON,James   Sex:M   29 Jun 1779 Hudson, NH Thomas Wason & Mary
WASON,Jane   Sex:F   05 Jul 1776 Hudson, NH Samuel Wason & Margaret
WASON,Jane   Sex:F   05 Jun 1776 Hudson, NH Samuel Wason & Margaret
WASON,Mary   Sex:F   06 Oct 1775 Hudson, NH Thomas Wason & Mary
WASON,Mary   Sex:F   19 Dec 1814 Hudson, NH Thomas P Wason & Mary Colburn
WASON,Milton   Sex:M   17 Jan 1817 Hudson, NH Thomas P Wason & Mary Colburn
WASON,Moses   Sex:M   09 Nov 1771 Hudson, NH Samuel Wason & Margaret
WASON,Rachel   Sex:F   05 Jun 1813 Hudson, NH Thomas P Wason & Mary Colburn
WASON,Reuben   Sex:M   02 May 1770 Hudson, NH Samuel Wason & Margaret
WASON,Robert   Sex:M   14 Mar 1812 Hudson, NH James Wason & Mary Anderson
WASON,Robert   Sex:M   14 Jun 1781 Hudson, NH Thomas Wason & Mary
WASON,S Anderson   Sex:M   25 Apr 1806 Hudson, NH James Wason & Mary
WASON,Samuel Anderson Sex:M 25 Apr 1806 Hudson, NH James Wason
   & Mary Anderson
WASON,Sarah   Sex:F   11 Jan 1742 Hudson, NH James Wason & Hannah
WASON,Sarah   Sex:F   24 Mar 1778 Hudson, NH Samuel Wason & Margaret
WASON,Thomas   Sex:M   03 Mar 1808 Hudson, NH James Wason & Mary Anderson
WASON,Thomas B   Sex:M   02 Nov 1785 Hudson, NH Thomas Wason & Mary
WASON,Thomas Boyd   Sex:M   02 Nov 1785 Hudson, NH Thomas Wason & Mary
WASON,William   Sex:M   19 Jun 1810 Hudson, NH James Wason & Mary Anderson
WATERMAN,Jill A   Sex:F   24 Apr 1960 Theodore V Waterman & Martha A Trudeau
WATERMAN,Lynne A   Sex:F   21 Sep 1961 Theodore V Waterman & Martha A Trudeau
WATERMAN,Michael D   Sex:M   06 Sep 1975 James G Waterman & Margaret M Lund
WATERMAN,Theodore V Jr Sex:M 11 Jun 1963 Theodore V Waterman&Martha A Trudeau
WATERMAN,Timothy J   Sex:M   26 Jul 1966 Theodore V Waterman & Martha A Trudeau
WATERS,Jamie Kathleen Sex:F 21 Jun 1983 John Joseph Waters & Rose Anne Grande
WATERS,Joshua John   Sex:M   26 Sep 1981 John Joseph Waters & Rose Anne Grande
WATKINS,Christy A   Sex:F   11 May 1966 Randolph Watkins & Sandra L Robinson
WATKINS,Pamela L   Sex:F   06 Feb 1966 Howard G Watkins & Margaret J Fairfield
WATKINS,Sherri L   Sex:F   10 Mar 1968 Randolph Watkins & Sandra L Robinson
WATKINS,Traci   Sex:F   17 Mar 1971 James Watkins & Amanda R Howard
WATROUSE,Christopher L   Sex: 04 Jul 1972 Curtis M Watrouse
   & Germaine A Laquerre
WATROUSE,Kevin C   Sex:M   23 Jul 1970 Curtis M Watrouse & Germaine A Laquerre
WATSON,Amanda S   Sex:F   22 Oct 1977 Richard A Watson & Priscille Anne Marsh
WATSON,Elbert E   Sex:M   03 Jun 1957 Elbert B Watson & Shelby J Hayes
WATSON,Seth M   Sex:M   08 Feb 1974 Richard A Watson & Priscilla A Marshall
WATTS,Alice P   Sex:F   (Child #7) 23 Feb 1918 William H Watts (Moores, NY)
   & Ida Weston (Wilton, NH)
WATTS,Ethel May   Sex:F   (Child #3) 20 Feb 1902 Robert G Watts (Moores, NY)
   & Anna C Walker (Ellenburg, NY)
WATTS,Gale R   Sex:F   24 Feb 1959 Ralph N Watts & Thelma I Fay

HUDSON,NH BIRTHS

WATTS,Linda J   Sex:F   06 Jun 1951 Ralph N Watts & Thelma I Fay
WATTS,Ralph Edward Sex:M (Child #4) 22 Feb 1912 William H Watts (Moores, NY)
   & Ida Weston (Wilton, NH)
WATTS,Ruth Ina   Sex:F   (Child #6) 21 Feb 1917 William H Watts (Moore, NY)
   & Ida Weston (Wilton, NH)
WATTS,Wayne Stanley   Sex:M   (Child #5) 10 Jul 1938 John Parker Watts
   (Londonderry, NH) & Arvilla C Stevens (Deerfield, NH)
WATTS,Wesley Herbert   Sex:M   (Child #5) 27 Jan 1915 Hudson, NH Wm H Watts
   (Movars, NY) & Ida Weston (Milton, NH)
WATTS,William H   Sex:M   (Child #3) 06 Jun 1910 Wm H Watts (Moores, NY)
   & Ida J Weston (Wilton, NH)
WEAVER,Joseph Lee   Sex:M   05 Aug 1982 Joseph D Weaver & Susan F Boucher
WEBB,Sandra L   Sex:F   23 Apr 1944 Ralph Webb (Dracut, MA) & Amelia Ballas
   (Lowell, MA)
WEBB,[Unknown]   Sex:M   28 Feb 1970 Brian K Webb & Nancy J Hamblet
WEBSTER,Aaron C   Sex:M   Isaac Webster & Wealthy Chase
WEBSTER,Abigail Sex:F 27 May 1676 Haverhill, MA Stephen Webster & Hannah Ayer
WEBSTER,Adele G   Sex:F   17 May 1880 Hudson, NH Nathan P Webster (Pelham, NH)
   & Josephine E Rollins (Sanbornton,
WEBSTER,Adella Georgette   Sex:F   17 May 1880 Hudson, NH Nathan P Webster
   & Josephine E Rollins
WEBSTER,Alice Edna   Sex:F   02 May 1872 Hingham, MA Charles O Webster
   & Densie L Peasley
WEBSTER,Amos D   Sex:M   Moses Webster & Mary Dolloff
WEBSTER,Asa   Sex:M   11 May 1789 Hudson, NH Ebenezer Webster
   & Elizabeth Bradford
WEBSTER,Belinda P   Sex:F   23 Mar 1825 Meredith Isaac Webster & Sibbel Kelly
WEBSTER,Benjamin   Sex:M   07 Oct 1793 Hudson, NH Ebenezer Webster
   & Elizabeth Bradford
WEBSTER,Betsey   Sex:F   01 Apr 1796 Hudson, NH Ebenezer Webster
   & Elizabeth Bradford
WEBSTER,Betsey   Sex:F   23 Mar 1827 Meredith Isaac Webster & Sibbel Kelly
WEBSTER,Brinton M   Sex: 06 Oct 1864 Hudson, NH Nathan P Webster
   & Susan M Morrison
WEBSTER,Carl C Jr   Sex:M   26 Dec 1964 Carl C Webster & Carol J Fuller
WEBSTER,Carrie E   Sex:F   08 Jun 1860 Hudson, NH John Webster & Luella A Piper
WEBSTER,Charles   Sex:M   Hudson, NH George M Webster & Sarah Clatur
WEBSTER,Charles A   Sex:M   Hudson, NH Eben W Webster & Ellen Wentworth
WEBSTER,Charles Otis   Sex:M   17 Aug 1829 Methuen, MA Benjamin Webster
   & Submitte Kittredge
WEBSTER,Charles W   Sex:M   Hudson, NH George M Webster & Sarah Clatur
WEBSTER,Clara Francis   Sex:F   18 Jan 1851 Hudson, NH Simon G Webster
   & Maria Dolloff
WEBSTER,Daniel Hazen   Sex:M   05 Apr 1821 Hudson, NH Simon B Webster
   & Relief Johnson
WEBSTER,Dean A   Sex:M   02 Jul 1975 Carl C Webster Sr & Cynthia A DiFiore
WEBSTER,Eben Woodbury   Sex:M   1843 Hudson, NH John P Webster & Sarah Woodbury
WEBSTER,Ebenezer   Sex:M   20 Sep 1711 Haverhill, MA Stephen Webster & Mary
   (Wid Cook)
WEBSTER,Ebenezer   Sex:M   01 Feb 1744 Haverhill, MA Ebenezer Webster
   & Mehittabel Kimball
WEBSTER,Ebenezer   Sex:M   07 Mar 1773 Haverhill, MA Ebenezer Webster &
WEBSTER,Edwin H   Sex:M   26 Jun 1867 Hudson, NH Mark H Webster
   & Melissa Pettingil
WEBSTER,Eleazer Cummings   Sex:M   18 Aug 1821 Pelham, NH John Webster
   & Hannah Cummings
WEBSTER,Eliza Ball   Sex:F   14 Jul 1862 Hudson, NH Kimball Webster
   & Abiah Cutter
WEBSTER,Elizabeth Bradford   Sex:F   30 Nov 1815 Pelham, NH John Webster
   & Hannah Cummings

HUDSON,NH BIRTHS

WEBSTER,Ella   Sex:F Moses Webster & Mary Dolloff
WEBSTER,Ella Frances   Sex:F   19 Aug 1859 Hudson, NH Kimball Webster
  & Abiah Cutter
WEBSTER,Elmira   Sex:M   02 Mar 1826 Methuen, MA Benjamin Webster
  & Submitte Kittredge
WEBSTER,Eric J   Sex:M   02 Jul 1975 Carl C Webster Sr & Cynthia A DiFiore
WEBSTER,Frank   Sex:M Moses Webster & Mary Dolloff
WEBSTER,Frank Harvey   Sex:M   Hudson, NH George M Webster & Sarah Clatur
WEBSTER,Frank Kenniston   Sex:M   22 Feb 1858 Hudson, NH John C Webster
  & Hannah C Kenniston
WEBSTER,Frank Woodbury   Sex:M   13 Mar 1867 Methuen MA George K Webster
  & Emily A Woodbury
WEBSTER,Freddie H   Sex:M   07 Jun 1863 Hudson, NH Lyman Webster & Sarah
WEBSTER,Freddy H   Sex:M   07 Jan 1863 Hudson, NH Lyman Webster & Sarah N
WEBSTER,Freddy Sanford   Sex:M   01 Jul 1876 Methuen MA Charles O Webster
  & Densie L Peasley
WEBSTER,George Gilman   Sex:M   26 Apr 1857 Hudson, NH Simon G Webster
  & Maria Dolloff
WEBSTER,George H   Sex:M Moses Webster & Mary Dolloff
WEBSTER,George Kittredge   Sex:M   09 May 1843 Methuen, MA Benjamin Webster
  & Submitte Kittredge
WEBSTER,George M   Sex:M Isaac Webster & Wealthy Chase
WEBSTER,George M   Sex:M   29 May 1831 Hudson, NH Mark H Webster
  & Sarah L Palmer
WEBSTER,George Orin   Sex:M   Hudson, NH George M Webster & Sarah Clatur
WEBSTER,George Roberts   Sex:M   Hudson, NH John Webster & Emily Roberts
WEBSTER,George Walton   Sex:M   31 Aug 1864 Hudson, NH Willard H Webster
  & Addie M Walton
WEBSTER,Hannah Sex:F   10 May 1666 Haverhill, MA Stephen Webster & Hannah Ayer
WEBSTER,Hannah Jane   Sex:F   24 Feb 1831 Pelham, NH John Webster
  & Hannah Cummings
WEBSTER,Hannah Jane   Sex:F   25 Jun 1836 Hudson, NH John P Webster
  & Sarah Woodbury
WEBSTER,Henry Kimball   Sex:M   12 May 1845 Hudson, NH Moses Webster
  & Lydia M Baker
WEBSTER,Henry Nelson   Sex:M   Hudson, NH Mark H Webster & Melissa Pettingil
WEBSTER,Ida L   Sex:F   10 Jul 1860 Hudson, NH Willard Webster & Lydia
WEBSTER,Ida May Sex:F   Hudson, NH Charles O Webster & Lauretta Hamblett
WEBSTER,Ida S   Sex:F   18 Jul 1860 Hudson, NH Willard H Webster
  & Sophia C Foster
WEBSTER,Isaac   Sex:M   20 Mar 1740 Haverhill, MA Ebenezer Webster
  & Mehittabel Kimball
WEBSTER,Isaac   Sex:M   17 Dec 1786 Hudson, NH Ebenezer Webster
  & Elizabeth Bradford
WEBSTER,Isaac   Sex:M   16 Apr 1817 Meredith Isaac Webster & Sibbel Kelly
WEBSTER,James   Sex:M   26 Jun 1861 Hudson, NH Kimball Webster & Abiah Cutter
WEBSTER,Jesse   Sex:M   Hudson, NH Ebenezer Webster & Polly Poor
WEBSTER,John   Sex:M   15 Mar 1668 Haverhill, MA Stephen Webster & Hannah Ayer
WEBSTER,John   Sex:M   12 Nov 1703 Haverhill, MA Stephen Webster & Mary
  (Wid Cook)
WEBSTER,John   Sex:M   28 Oct 1758 Haverhill, MA Ebenezer Webster
  & Mehittabel Kimball
WEBSTER,John   Sex:M   25 Dec 1791 Hudson, NH Ebenezer Webster
  & Elizabeth Bradford
WEBSTER,John   Sex:M   13 Aug 1830 Meredith Isaac Webster & Sibbel Kelly
WEBSTER,John   Sex:M   20 Feb 1829 Hudson, NH Mark H Webster & Sarah L Palmer
WEBSTER,John   Sex:M   Hudson, NH John Webster & Emily Roberts
WEBSTER,John B   Sex:M   Hudson, NH Eben W Webster & Ellen Wentworth
WEBSTER,John Baldwin   Sex:M   29 Nov 1805 Hudson, NH Ebenezer Webster
  & Mary Harris

HUDSON,NH BIRTHS

WEBSTER,John Cummings Sex:M 14 Feb 1833 Pelham, NH John Webster
  & Hannah Cummings
WEBSTER,John Johnson Sex:M 15 Sep 1812 Hudson, NH Simon B Webster
  & Relief Johnson
WEBSTER,Jonathan Sex:M 06 Jul 1747 Haverhill, MA Ebenezer Webster
  & Mehittabel Kimball
WEBSTER,Julia A Sex:F 1867 Hudson, NH Kimball Webster & Alice
WEBSTER,Julia Anna Sex:F 26 Oct 1867 Hudson, NH Kimball Webster
  & Abiah Cutter
WEBSTER,Kimball Sex:M 02 Nov 1828 Pelham, NH John Webster & Hannah Cummings
WEBSTER,Kimball Sex:M 20 Jun 1862 Hudson, NH Kimball Webster &
WEBSTER,Kimball C Sex:M 26 Jun 1861 Hudson, NH Kimball Webster
  & Abiah Cutter
WEBSTER,Latina Sex: 26 Jul 1865 Hudson, NH Kimball Webster & Kim
WEBSTER,Latina Ray Sex:M 26 Jul 1865 Hudson, NH Kimball Webster
  & Abiah Cutter
WEBSTER,Laura Augusta Sex:F Feb 1847 Hudson, NH Simon G Webster
  & Relief Jones
WEBSTER,Lillian C Sex:F 04 Oct 1869 Hudson, NH Mark H Webster
  & Melissa Pettingil
WEBSTER,Lizzie Jane Sex:F 11 Jan 1858 Hudson, NH Kimball Webster
  & Abiah Cutter
WEBSTER,Louisa Baker Sex:F 15 Apr 1849 Hudson, NH Mark H Webster
  & Sally Baker
WEBSTER,Louisa Underwood Sex:F 31 Jan 1824 Pelham, NH John Webster
  & Hannah Cummings
WEBSTER,Lucy Ann Sex:F 28 Feb 1826 Pelham, NH John Webster & Hannah Cummings
WEBSTER,Lucy Ellen Sex:F 08 Oct 1848 Hudson, NH Moses Webster & Lydia M Baker
WEBSTER,Lydia Sex:F 08 Jan 1737 Haverhill, MA Ebenezer Webster
  & Mehittabel Kimball
WEBSTER,Lydia Sex:F Hudson, NH Ebenezer Webster & Polly Poor
WEBSTER,Lydia Frances Sex:F 09 Jan 1856 Hudson, NH Mark H Webster
  & Sally Baker
WEBSTER,Lynne C Sex:F 24 Jan 1948 George H Webster, Jr (Nashua, NH)
  & Ruth E Corey (Nashua, NH)
WEBSTER,Mark H Sex:M 16 May 1844 Hudson, NH Mark H Webster & Sally Baker
WEBSTER,Mark H Sex:M Hudson, NH George M Webster & Sarah Clatur
WEBSTER,Mark Harris Sex:M 10 Nov 1803 Hudson, NH Ebenezer Webster
  & Mary Harris
WEBSTER,Martha Sex:F Moses Webster & Mary Dolloff
WEBSTER,Mary Sex:F 21 Apr 1670 Haverhill, MA Stephen Webster & Hannah Ayer
WEBSTER,Mary Sex:F 03 Aug 1713 Haverhill, MA Stephen Webster & Mary
  (Wid Cook)
WEBSTER,Mary Sex:F 20 Nov 1742 Haverhill, MA Ebenezer Webster
  & Mehittabel Kimball
WEBSTER,Mary Sex:F Hudson, NH Ebenezer Webster & Polly Poor
WEBSTER,Mary Ann Sex:F 26 Aug 1829 Hudson, NH Simon B Webster
  & Relief Johnson
WEBSTER,Mary Estelle Sex:F Hudson, NH George M Webster & Sarah Clatur
WEBSTER,Mary Louisa Sex:F 26 Jun 1851 Hudson, NH Mark H Webster
  & Sally Baker
WEBSTER,Mary Lucretia Sex:F 07 Jun 1846 Hudson, NH Mark H Webster
  & Sally Baker
WEBSTER,Mary Newton Sex:F 09 Aug 1869 Hudson, NH Kimball Webster
  & Abiah Cutter
WEBSTER,Melville Trevett Sex:M 06 May 1866 Hudson, NH Willard H Webster
  & Addie M Walton
WEBSTER,Milton Edward Sex:M 18 Apr 1839 Pelham, NH John Webster
  & Hannah Cummings
WEBSTER,Minnie Louisa Sex:F 21 Feb 1869 Hudson, NH Willard H Webster

HUDSON,NH BIRTHS

& Addie M Walton
WEBSTER,Mittie Grace   Sex:F   10 Mar 1869 Winchendon MA Charles O Webster
& Densie L Peasley
WEBSTER,Moses   Sex:M   17 Nov 1817 John Webster & Hannah Cummings
WEBSTER,Moses   Sex:M   23 May 1754 Haverhill, MA Ebenezer Webster
& Mehittabel Kimball
WEBSTER,Moses   Sex:M   09 Oct 1782 Hudson, NH Ebenezer Webster
& Elizabeth Bradford
WEBSTER,Moses   Sex:M   28 Dec 1814 Meredith Isaac Webster & Sibbel Kelly
WEBSTER,Moses G   Sex:M   Moses Webster & Mary Dolloff
WEBSTER,Moses R Sex:M   24 Apr 1879 Hudson, NH Nathaniel P Webster (Pelham, NH) & Josie E Rollins
WEBSTER,Moses Rollins   Sex:M   24 Apr 1879 Hudson, NH Nathan P Webster
& Josephine E Rollins
WEBSTER,Nancy   Sex:F   28 Jan 1780 Pelham, NH   &
WEBSTER,Nancy   Sex:F   17 Jan 1781 Hudson, NH Ebenezer Webster
& Elizabeth Bradford
WEBSTER,Nathan Sex:M   14 Nov 1674 Haverhill, MA Stephen Webster & Hannah Ayer
WEBSTER,Nathan Pierce   Sex:M   19 May 1835 Pelham, NH John Webster
& Hannah Cummings
WEBSTER,Nelson   Sex:M   15 Mar 1839 Hudson, NH Mark H Webster & Sally Baker
WEBSTER,Orrin Prescott   Sex:M   10 Apr 1843 Amherst, NH John Webster
& Hannah Cummings
WEBSTER,Phebe   Sex:F   14 Mar 1819 Meredith Isaac Webster & Sibbel Kelly
WEBSTER,Polly H   Sex:F   01 Sep 1812 Salem, NH Isaac Webster & Sibbel Kelly
WEBSTER,Rebecca   Sex:F   13 Jul 1774 Haverhill, MA Ebenezer Webster &
WEBSTER,Rebecca   Sex:F   17 Sep 1778 Hudson, NH Ebenezer Webster
& Elizabeth Bradford
WEBSTER,Rebecca   Sex:F   23 Mar 1827 Meredith Isaac Webster & Sibbel Kelly
WEBSTER,Relief Maria   Sex:F   08 Aug 1814 Hudson, NH Simon B Webster
& Relief Johnson
WEBSTER,Ruth Simira Sex:F 06 Apr 1823 Hudson, NH Simon B Webster
& Relief Johnson
WEBSTER,Sally Hale Sex:F   25 Aug 1819 Meredith John Webster & Hannah Cummings
WEBSTER,Samuel   Sex:M   15 Dec 1701 Haverhill, MA Stephen Webster & Mary
(Wid Cook)
WEBSTER,Samuel Kelly Sex:M   01 Mar 1823 Meredith Isaac Webster & Sibbel Kelly
WEBSTER,Sarah   Sex:F   07 Sep 1771 Haverhill, MA Ebenezer Webster &
WEBSTER,Sarah   Sex:F   Hudson, NH Ebenezer Webster & Polly Poor
WEBSTER,Sarah Ann   Sex:F   13 Sep 1817 Pelham, NH Benjamin Webster
& Submitte Kittredge
WEBSTER,Sarah Jane Sex:F   07 Nov 1837 Hudson, NH Mark H Webster & Sally Baker
WEBSTER,Sarah Jane   Sex:F   Hudson, NH John Webster & Emily Roberts
WEBSTER,Sibbel   Sex:F   01 Jun 1821 Meredith Isaac Webster & Sibbel Kelly
WEBSTER,Simon Bradford   Sex:M   16 Apr 1784 Hudson, NH Ebenezer Webster
& Elizabeth Bradford
WEBSTER,Simon Gilman   Sex:M   22 May 1819 Hudson, NH Simon B Webster
& Relief Johnson
WEBSTER,Stephen   Sex:M   01 Jan 1672 Haverhill, MA Stephen Webster
& Hannah Ayer
WEBSTER,Stephen   Sex:M   02 Jan 1706 Haverhill, MA Stephen Webster & Mary
(Wid Cook)
WEBSTER,Stephen   Sex:M   23 Jun 1750 Haverhill, MA Ebenezer Webster
& Mehittabel Kimball
WEBSTER,Susan J Sex:F 24 Oct 1834 Hudson, NH Simon B Webster & Relief Johnson
WEBSTER,Wendy   Sex:F   30 Sep 1968 Carl C Webster & Carol J Fuller
WEBSTER,Willard Holbrook   Sex:M   22 Mar 1837 Pelham, NH John Webster
& Hannah Cummings
WEBSTER,William   Sex:M   17 Mar 1709 Haverhill, MA Stephen Webster & Mary
(Wid Cook)

HUDSON,NH BIRTHS

WEBSTER,Winfield Wallace Sex:M Hudson, NH Mark H Webster & Melissa Pettingil
WEBSTER,[Unknown] Sex:M 10 Jun 1876 Hudson, NH Kimball Webster & Abiah Cutter
WEBSTER,[Unknown]   Sex:F 21 Feb 1869 Hudson, NH William H Webster & Addie
WEBSTER,[Unknown] Sex:M   28 Feb 1875 Hudson, NH Nathan Webster & Josephine
WEBSTER,[Unknown] Sex:M   13 Apr 1877 Hudson, NH Nathan P Webster (Pelham,
   NH) & Josephine E Rollins
WEGHORST,Heidi Ann Sex:F 05 Aug 1984 George W Weghorst & Susan B Jones
WEISMAN,Lu-Ann Sex:F 14 Sep 1953 Harry Weisman & Hazel L Matthews
WELCH,Dorothy Elizabeth Sex:F (Child #1) 10 Jul 1937 Ralph Welch (Bethel,
   VT) & Elizabeth Blair (N Reading, MA)
WELCH,Jeanne L Sex:F 10 Feb 1959 Richard F Welch, Jr & Nancy L Mercer
WELCH,Laura Elizabeth Sex:F 31 May 1984 Richard R Welch & Cindi Lu Sims
WELCH,Mabel Frances Sex:F 21 Oct 1881 Nashua, NH Frank A Welch
   & Ella Frances Webster
WELCH,Richard Kenneth Sex:M (Child #2) 26 Aug 1938 Ralph Bernard Welch
   (Bethel, VT) & Elizabeth A Blair (N Reading, MA)
WELCH,Roy H Sex:M 22 May 1892 Hudson, NH Clarence E Welch & Delia Hutchinson
WELCH,Samantha A Sex:F 21 Nov 1971 Kenneth D Welch & Sylvia R Champagne
WELDON,John E Sex:M 19 Jul 1964 John B Weldon & Geraldine C Hill
WELLS,Matthew A Sex:M 12 Jun 1979 Allen B Wells & Marie E MacDonald
WELLS,Maxine Grace Sex:F (Child #1) 18 Sep 1912 Edward Wells (W Lebanon)
   & Lula Wright (Lowell, MA)
WENTWORTH,Daniel G Sex:M (Child #5) 04 Apr 1882 Hudson, NH Nathaniel
   Wentworth (Brighton, MA) & Edwina Greeley (Hudson, NH)
WENTWORTH,Edwin Sex:M   26 Dec 1878 Hudson, NH Nathaniel Wentworth
   (Brighton, MA) & Edwina M (Hudson, NH)
WENTWORTH,James G Sex:M 11 May 1873 Hudson, NH Nathaniel Wentworth
   & Edvinia
WENTWORTH,Kate Shapleigh Sex:F 16 Sep 1871 Hudson, NH Nathaniel Wentworth
WENTWORTH,Minnie E Sex:F (Child #6) 14 Apr 1885 Hudson, NH Nathaniel
   Wentworth (Brighton, MA) & Edwina M Greeley (Hudson, NH
WENTWORTH,Vicki A Sex:F 03 Mar 1972 Albert E Wentworth & Christine L Kergis
WENZEL,Peter J Sex:M 13 May 1962 Carl E Wenzel & Sandra J Lannan
WERTZ,Susan A Sex:F 06 Apr 1970 Jacob B Wertz & Barbara A Bettencourt
WERZANSKI,Bruce A Sex:M 26 Sep 1967 Walter J Werzanski & Constance J Bourassa
WEST,Christopher Munro Sex:M 20 Aug 1980 Terry Lee West & Juliet Mable Munro
WEST,James O Sex:M 20 Nov 1967 Robert W West & Edna M Murray
WEST,Robert W Jr Sex:M 16 Sep 1964 Robert W West & Edna M Murray
WESTBROOK,Jeffrey B Sex:M 30 Nov 1969 Benjamin E Westbrook & Garnette R Smith
WESTBROOK,Kim F Sex:F 20 Jun 1962 LeRoy J Westbrook & Faith C Temple
WESTBROOK,Scott Sex:M 09 Nov 1960 LeRoy J Westbrook & Faith C Temple
WESTGATE,Barbara Frances Sex:F 31 May 1984 John B Westgate
   & Betsey Wasson Scheid
WESTON,Charles E Sex:M (Child #1) 19 Mar 1883 Hudson, NH Edward E Weston
   (Nashua, NH) & Christiana E Weston (Lyndeboro, NH
WESTON,Esther A A Sex:F 29 Oct 1893 Jesse E Weston (Nashua, NH)
   & A Willoughby (Omaha, Neb)
WESTON,Franklin W Sex:M (Child #1) 02 Sep 1892 Jesse S Weston (Nashua, NH)
   & A Willoughby (Omaha, Neb)
WHALEN,Dennis Michael Jr Sex:M 15 Nov 1983 Dennis M Whalen Sr&Judith A Nixon
WHALIN,Eliot Alden Sex:M (Child #1) 22 Sep 1941 Myron E Whalin
   (Francestown, NH) & Mildred Rogers (New London, CT
WHARFF,Kelley A Sex:F 01 May 1974 Conray P Wharff Jr & Vivian A Kelley
WHARTON,Erin E Sex:F 16 Apr 1972 Richard C Wharton Jr & Leslie A Bell
WHEELER,Jeffrey S Sex:M 29 May 1970 James R Wheeler & Shirley A Straub
WHEELER,Kelly A Sex:F 19 Jul 1968 James R Wheeler & Shirley A Straub
WHEELER,Norma J Sex:F 06 Apr 1947 Richard J Wheeler (Nashua, NH)
   & Eleanor R Boyer (Ilion, NY)
WHIDDEN,Annie B Sex:F   24 Jun 1881 Hudson, NH John C Whidden (Loudon, NH)
   & Mary J Adams (Derry, NH)

HUDSON,NH BIRTHS

WHITCOMB,Lucy   Sex:F   23 Feb 1802 Merrimack NH Paul Whitcomb & Sally
WHITE,Amanda Courtney Sex:F 08 Jan 1983 William Robert White & Sharon M Russo
WHITE,Anna   Sex:F   16 Dec 1803 Hudson, NH Mark White & Anna
WHITE,Anne   Sex:F   18 Dec 1803 Hudson, NH Mark White & Anne
WHITE,Bertha Anabel   Sex:F   19 Feb 1879 Hudson, NH Charles White
  & Marcia Grant
WHITE,Bertha Ann   Sex:F   19 Feb 1880 Hudson, NH Charles White & Marcia Grant
WHITE,Bonnie R   Sex:F   23 Jun 1978 William M White & Katherine H Marttila
WHITE,Brian D   Sex:M   13 Oct 1959 Ernest H White & Elizabeth Holt
WHITE,Chad R   Sex:M   01 Sep 1976 Arthur W White & Judith A Blaisdell
WHITE,Clarissa   Sex:F   13 Feb 1802 Hudson, NH Mark White & Anna
WHITE,George F   Sex:M   11 Nov 1876 Hudson, NH Charles White & Marcia Grant
WHITE,Jennifer F   Sex:F   04 May 1976 Richard A White & Judith M Fitzgibbon
WHITE,John D   Sex:M   07 Dec 1966 Allan G White & Joy R Andrews
WHITE,Joyce H   Sex:F   26 May 1958 Ernest H White & Elizabeth Holt
WHITE,Lawrence D   Sex:M   16 Aug 1955 Ernest H White & Elizabeth Holt
WHITE,Lucien   Sex:M L 27 Sep 1884 Hudson, NH Charles White (Haverhill, NH)
  & Marcia Grant (Pownell, ME)
WHITE,Richard F   Sex:M   (Child #1) 04 Jun 1943 Donald E White (Goffstown, NH)
  & Sarah P Mullen (Manchester, NH)
WHITFIELD,Jesse H   Sex:M   (Child #4) 01 Aug 1890 Elias E Whitfield
  (Francestown, NH) & Rosella Cota (Canada)
WHITMORE,Tim   Sex:M   01 Jan 1964 Philip Whitmore & Irene Rossignol
WHITNEY,Charles A   Sex:M   27 Sep 1976 William R Whitney & Susan J Whittemore
WHITNEY,Darryl Campbell Sex:M 25 Apr 1981 James Leigh Whitney
  & Kathryn I Newman
WHITNEY,Eleanor Myrtle   Sex:F   (Child #9) 14 Feb 1939 Earl H Whitney
  (Lancaster, NH) & Cora E Flanders (Warren, NH)
WHITNEY,Gail F   Sex:F   12 Nov 1974 William R Whitney & Susan J Whittemore
WHITNEY,Jason E   Sex:M   18 Dec 1973 Earle L Whitney Jr & Katherine A Moreau
WHITNEY,Joan Susie   Sex:F   (Child #9) 12 Feb 1938 Earl Harry Whitney
  (Lancaster, NH) & Cora Ellen Flanders (Warren,
WHITNEY,Karen R   Sex:F   14 Oct 1968 Earle L Whitney & Rosette T Lavoie
WHITNEY,Kevin W   Sex:M   08 Mar 1965 Earle L Whitney & Rosette T Lavoie
WHITNEY,Lee K   Sex:M   01 Aug 1961 Earle L Whitney & Rosette T Lavoie
WHITNEY,Michael L   Sex:M   01 May 1979 James L Whitney & Kathryn I Newman
WHITNEY,Parker O   Sex:M   (Child #4) 17 Feb 1905 James A Whitney (Maine)
  & Harriet Ingham (England)
WHITNEY,Richard P   Sex:M   02 Jun 1953 Earle L Whitney & Rosette T Lavoie
WHITNEY,Shaun Eric   Sex:M   02 Sep 1979 William R Whitney & Susan J Whittemore
WHITNEY,Sonya I   Sex:F   10 Jun 1963 Earle L Whitney & Rosette T Lavoie
WHITNEY,Steven F   Sex:M   04 Apr 1976 Richard P Whitney & Martha E Fox
WHITNEY,[Unknown]   Sex:F   (Child #10) 09 Dec 1940 Earl H Whitney (Lancaster,
  NH) & Cora E Flanders (Warren, NH)
WHITTEMORE,Benjamin Sex:M   16 Mar 1752 Hudson, NH Benjamin Whittemore & Sarah
WHITTEMORE,Benjamin Sex:M   06 Mar 1752 Hudson, NH Benjamin Whittemore & Sarah
WHITTEMORE,Brian James Sex:M 18 Sep 1982 James R Whittemore
  & Doreen Fern Tallant
WHITTEMORE,Carol A Sex:F   (Child #1) 09 Apr 1942 Roy L Whittemore (Nashua,
  NH) & Annamay Doherty (Nashua, NH)
WHITTEMORE,Collins Sex:M 07 Jun 1767 Hudson, NH Amos Whittemore & Mary Taylor
WHITTEMORE,Daniel W   Sex:M   01 Apr 1952 Wesley A Whittemore & Wanda S Slosek
WHITTEMORE,Esther   Sex:F   18 May 1766 Hudson, NH Benjamin Whittemore & Sarah
WHITTEMORE,Gail K   Sex:F   27 Oct 1949 Charles R Whittemore & Wanda F Kayros
WHITTEMORE,Hannah   Sex:F   09 Apr 1756 Hudson, NH Benjamin Whittemore & Sarah
WHITTEMORE,Hannah   Sex:F   29 Apr 1756 Hudson, NH Benjamin Whittemore & Sarah
WHITTEMORE,Phebe   Sex:F   18 Aug 1763 Hudson, NH Benjamin Whittemore & Sarah
WHITTEMORE,Ross G   Sex:M   (Child #2) 14 Dec 1946 Chester M Whittemore
  (Nashua, NH) & Frances L Berg (Quincy, MA)
WHITTEMORE,Sarah   Sex:F   09 Aug 1748 Hudson, NH Jacob Whittemore & Sarah

HUDSON,NH BIRTHS

WHITTEMORE,Sarah   Sex:F   18 Jun 1754 Hudson, NH Benjamin Whittemore & Sarah
WHITTEMORE,Susan J   Sex:F   18 Nov 1948 Chas R Whittemore (Hudson, NH)
   & Wanda F Kayros (Hudson, NH)
WHITTENBURG,Juliana C Sex:F 27 Jul 1964 James V Whittenburg&Marion C Simmons
WHITTENBURG,Karl E   Sex:M   02 Aug 1966 James V Whittenburg & Marion C Simmons
WHITTIER,Ellen   Sex:F   Hudson, NH Harris Whittier & Mary Webster
WHITTIER,Jane E   Sex:F   Hudson, NH Harris Whittier & Mary Webster
WHITTIER,Julia A   Sex:F   Hudson, NH Harris Whittier & Mary Webster
WHITTIER,Mary C   Sex:F   Hudson, NH Harris Whittier & Mary Webster
WHITTLE,Lydia   Sex:F   14 Aug 1782 Hudson, NH John Whittle & Lydia
WHITTLE,Margaret   Sex:F   23 May 1787 Hudson, NH John Whittle & Lydia
WHITTLE,Molley   Sex:F   23 Feb 1785 Hudson, NH John Whittle & Lydia
WHITTLE,Molly   Sex:F   23 Feb 1785 Hudson, NH John Whittle & Lydia
WICOM,William   Sex:M   18 Jul 1782 Hudson, NH Thomas Wicom & Abby
WIDERMAN,Fawn Rae Sex:F 30 Mar 1983 John K Widerman III & Jody Lynn Greenough
WIEDMER,Adam Dylan   Sex:M   14 Sep 1984 David A Wiedmer & Amy Christine Smock
WIGGIN,[Unknown]   Sex:M   04 Mar 1871 Hudson, NH Andrew C Wiggin & Addie E
WIHLBORG,Steven J   Sex:M   19 Jan 1962 Edward Wihlborg & Florence A Bishop
WILCOX,Elmer E   Sex:M   (Child #7) 07 May 1882 Hudson, NH Wm S Wilcox
   (England) & Eliza Hughes (England)
WILCOX,Jeffrey Allen Sex:M 09 Nov 1984 John G Wilcox & Joyce Ann Forrence
WILCOX,John C   Sex:M   07 Mar 1979 John G Wilcox & Joyce Ann Forrence
WILCOX,William G   Sex:M   1881 Hudson, NH William S Wilcox (England)
   & Eliza (England)
WILDER,Milan R   Sex:M   23 Feb 1893 Frank R Wilder (Maine) & Minnie King
   (Maine)
WILKINS,Jennifer Elizabeth   Sex:F   19 Sep 1981 Frank W Wilkins III
   & Debora Mary Burt
WILKINS,Michael Christopher Sex:M 17 May 1984 Frank W Wilkins & Debora M Burt
WILKINSON,Zachery Alexander   Sex:M   19 Oct 1984 Brian C Wilkinson
   & Patricia Ann Nichols
WILKOSKY,William E   Sex:M   (Child #2) 09 May 1942 John Wilkosky (Nashua, NH)
   & Helen C Moore (Lynn, MA)
WILLETT,Emily E   Sex:F   (Child #1) 02 Nov 1906 Alfred Willett (Canada)
   & Buda M Collins (Warren, MA)
WILLETTE,[Unknown]   Sex:M   (Child #5) 19 Nov 1916 Hudson, NH Alfred Willette
   (Canada) & Bresda Collins (Warren, MA)
WILLEY,[Unknown]   Sex:M   (Child #3) 21 Jan 1885 Hudson, NH Albert Willey
   (Lisbon, NH) & Eliza (Richford, VT)
WILLIAMS,Amanda Lynn Sex:F   29 Dec 1984 Scott D Williams & Carol Lynn Nichols
WILLIAMS,Christine Lee Sex:F 05 Jun 1978 Mark E Williams & Marguerite J Chac
WILLIAMS,Danielle K Sex:F   27 Mar 1977 Matthew D Williams & Dianne K Sorenson
WILLIAMS,David S   Sex:M   25 Jul 1967 Kent D Williams & June C Eiserman
WILLIAMS,Eugene G   Sex:M   (Child #2) 23 Oct 1944 Melvin L Williams (Benesett,
   PA) & Phyllis H Williams (Mayburg, P
WILLIAMS,Frederick K II   Sex:M   20 Feb 1963 Kent D Williams & June C Eiserman
WILLIAMS,Gordon Edmund   Sex:M   (Child #1) 08 Nov 1935 Edmund H Williams
   (Taunton, MA) & Doris Smith (Nashua, NH)
WILLIAMS,Jean M   Sex:F   03 Jan 1967 Jeremiah J Williams & Dorothy A O'Connor
WILLIAMS,Justin Troy   Sex:M   24 Apr 1983 S David Williams & Carol L Nichols
WILLIAMS,Kristine Michelle Sex:F 12 Jul 1983 James C Williams
   & Merideth L Mount
WILLIAMS,Lee B Sex:M   (Child #4) 03 Mar 1946 Melvin L Williams (Benezette,
   PA) & Phyllis H MacMartin (Mayburg,
WILLIAMS,Leonard F Sex: 02 Jun 1973 Leonard C Williams & Barbara A McDonough
WILLIAMS,Rodger L   Sex:M   (Child #2) 16 Apr 1943 Melvin L Williams
   (Benezette, PA) & Phyllis H MacMartin (Mayburgh
WILLIAMS,Scott E   Sex:M   26 Jul 1969 Michael H Williams & Bonnie J Truax
WILLIAMSON,Keith R Sex:M 19 Jul 1971 Richard G Williamson & Julie E Thibodeau
WILLIAMSON,Robin J   Sex:F   25 Nov 1960 Richard G Williamson

HUDSON,NH BIRTHS

   & Juliette E Thibodeau
WILLIAMSON,Scott D   Sex:M   27 Dec 1964 Richard G Williamson
   & Juliette E Thibodeau
WILLIAMSON,Stephen A   Sex:M   27 Dec 1964 Richard G Williamson
   & Juliette E Thibodeau
WILLOUGHBY,Mary F   Sex:F   06 Jun 1865 Hudson, NH Edwin Willoughby & Eliza
WILLOUGHBY,Mary F   Sex:F   06 Jun 1868 Hudson, NH Edwin Willoughby & Eliza
WILMOT,Barbara A Sex:F   (Child #8) 09 Sep 1944 Herbert L Wilmot (Concord, NH)
   & Rita M Guyette (W Chazy, NY)
WILMOT,Carol A   Sex:F   18 Jan 1948 Herbert L Wilmot (Concord, NH)
   & Rita M Guyette (W Chazy, NY)
WILMOT,Harold L   Sex:M   25 Jan 1947 Herbert L Wilmot (Concord, NH)
   & Rita M Guyette (New York)
WILMOT,Herbert P   Sex:M   (Child #7) 20 Nov 1942 Herbert L Wilmot (Concord,
   NH) & Rita M Guyette (W Chazy, NY)
WILMOT,Marcin A   Sex:F   17 May 1940 Herbert Wilmot (Concord, NH)
   & Rita Guyette (W Chazy, NY)
WILSON,Alice Gertrude   Sex:F   17 Sep 1851 Hudson, NH Franklin Wilson
   & Clarissa Gould
WILSON,Arthur R   Sex:M   20 Jul 1877 Hudson, NH James F Wilson & Sarah Reiley
WILSON,Benjamin   Sex:M   30 Aug 1780 Hudson, NH Joseph Wilson & Abigail
WILSON,Benjamin   Sex:M   10 Aug 1780 Hudson, NH Joseph Wilson & Abigail
WILSON,Clarissa   Sex:F   11 Oct 1795 Hudson, NH Joseph Butler Wilson & Phebe
WILSON,Clarissa Adaline   Sex:F   10 Jan 1836 Hudson, NH Franklin Wilson
   & Clarissa Gould
WILSON,Clarissa Edna   Sex:F   01 Dec 1879 Hudson, NH George H Wilson
   & Susan Griffin
WILSON,David   Sex:M   30 Mar 1771 Hudson, NH Joseph Wilson & Abigail
WILSON,Frank A   Sex:M   23 Dec 1871 Hudson, NH James F Wilson & Sarah Reiley
WILSON,Franklin   Sex:M   08 Aug 1806 Hudson, NH James Wilson &
WILSON,George Henry   Sex:M   26 Jul 1847 Hudson, NH Franklin Wilson
   & Clarissa Gould
WILSON,Hildah   Sex:F   03 Oct 1775 Hudson, NH Joseph Wilson & Abigail
WILSON,Huldah   Sex:F   03 Oct 1775 Hudson, NH Joseph Wilson & Abigail
WILSON,James Franklin   Sex:M   08 Oct 1837 Hudson, NH Franklin Wilson
   & Clarissa Gould
WILSON,Jennifer   Sex:F   30 Apr 1971 Richard J Wilson & Linda M Jones
WILSON,Joanna   Sex:F   22 Jun 1802 Hudson, NH Joseph Wilson & Phebe
WILSON,Joseph B   Sex:M   22 Apr 1790 Hudson, NH Joseph Wilson & Phebe
WILSON,Joseph Butler Sex:M 22 Apr 1790 Hudson, NH Joseph Butler Wilson
   & Phebe
WILSON,Judith   Sex:F   20 Apr 1957 Frank E Wilson & Constance A Haug
WILSON,Julianna   Sex:F   22 Jun 1802 Hudson, NH Joseph Butler Wilson & Phebe
WILSON,Justin M   Sex:M   04 Jan 1977 Donald W Wilson & Kathy D McCrady
WILSON,Kenneth Oliver Sex:M   (Child #3) 25 Jun 1914 Frank A Wilson (Hudson,
   NH) & Nettie Colby (Nashua, NH)
WILSON,Kimberly E   Sex:F   03 Jul 1965 Henry C Wilson Jr & Sonja E Davidson
WILSON,Lucinda   Sex:F   26 Aug 1793 Hudson, NH Joseph Butler Wilson & Phebe
WILSON,Lusenda   Sex:F   26 Aug 1793 Hudson, NH Joseph Wilson & Phebe
WILSON,Mary Lucinda   Sex:F   15 Mar 1845 Hudson, NH Franklin Wilson
   & Clarissa Gould
WILSON,Matilda   Sex:F   16 Apr 1800 Hudson, NH Joseph Butler Wilson & Phebe
WILSON,Mattie Augusta   Sex:F   23 Dec 1876 Hudson, NH George H Wilson
   & Susan Griffin
WILSON,Melissa Marie Sex:F 03 Oct 1980 Michael B Wilson & Lisa Marie Wollen
WILSON,Metilda   Sex:F   16 Apr 1800 Hudson, NH Joseph Wilson & Phebe
WILSON,Michelle Lynn   Sex:F   01 Oct 1983 Steven H Wilson & Jeanne M Dugan
WILSON,Mollie   Sex:F   07 Mar 1773 Hudson, NH Joseph Wilson & Abigail
WILSON,Molly   Sex:F   07 Mar 1773 Hudson, NH Joseph Wilson & Abigail
WILSON,Phebe   Sex:F   15 Dec 1785 Hudson, NH Joseph Butler Wilson & Phebe

HUDSON,NH BIRTHS

WILSON,Phebe Sex:F   11 Dec 1786 Hudson, NH Joseph Wilson & Phebe
WILSON,Rebecca L   Sex: 14 Nov 1972 Malcolm A Wilson & Sheila P Pierce
WILSON,Ruth Geneva   Sex:F   (Child #6) 24 Aug 1897 John W Wilson (Andover)
  & Carrie B Cheney (Wilmot)
WILSON,Sarah   Sex:F   30 May 1787 Hudson, NH Joseph Butler Wilson & Phebe
WILSON,Sarah Nicole   Sex:F   30 Jun 1984 Michael B Wilson & Lisa Marie Wollen
WILSON,Seneca   Sex: 25 Dec 1797 Hudson, NH Joseph Butler Wilson & Phebe
WILSON,Stephanie B   Sex:F   28 Jul 1976 Richard B Wilson & Janice M Shapiro
WILSON,Timothy   Sex:M   30 Jun 1959 Frank E Wilson & Constance A Haug
WILSON,William W   Sex:M   27 Feb 1790 Hudson, NH Joseph B Wilson & Phebe
WILSON,William Wyman   Sex:M   27 Feb 1791 Hudson, NH Joseph Butler Wilson
  & Phebe
WILSON,[Unknown]   Sex:M   23 Dec 1871 Hudson, NH J F V Wilson & Sarah H
WILSON,[Unknown]   Sex: S 13 Jun 1873 Hudson, NH Nathan P Wilson & Josie E
WINANS,Charles H   Sex:M   04 Aug 1878 Hudson, NH Wm L Winans (Manchester)
  & Martha A (South Danvers)
WINCH,Sarah E   Sex:F   18 Feb 1974 Carroll E Winch & Barbara L Mahan
WINDT,Sheila M   Sex:F   11 Feb 1962 Robert J Windt & Jean F Malonson
WINKLER,Kirk R   Sex:M   07 Sep 1956 George R Winkler & Lois A Grant
WINN,Abiah   Sex:M   27 Feb 1760 Hudson, NH Benjamin Winn & Judith
WINN,Abiathar   Sex:M   04 Jan 1746 Hudson, NH Joseph Winn & Elizabeth
WINN,Abiathar   Sex:M   10 Oct 1777 Hudson, NH Abiathar Winn & Abigail
WINN,Abiather   Sex:M   04 Jan 1746 Hudson, NH Joseph Winn & Elizabeth
WINN,Abiather   Sex:M   10 Oct 1777 Hudson, NH Abiather Winn & Abigail
WINN,Abigail   Sex:F   06 Aug 1769 Hudson, NH Abiathar Winn & Abigail
WINN,Abigail   Sex:F   27 Feb 1760 Hudson, NH Benjamin Winn & Judith
WINN,Alvah   Sex:M   1796 Hudson, NH Nathan Winn & Elizabeth Kelley
WINN,Arianna   Sex:F   12 Nov 1834 Hudson, NH William Winn & Persis G Moore
WINN,Barshaba   Sex:F   08 Apr Hudson, NH Benjamin Winn & Judith
WINN,Benjamin   Sex:M   14 Mar 1749 Hudson, NH Benjamin Winn & Judith
WINN,Benjamin   Sex:M   11 Apr 1752 Hudson, NH Benjamin Winn & Judith
WINN,Benjamin   Sex:M   06 Dec 1775 Hudson, NH Abiathar Winn & Abigail
WINN,Benjamin   Sex:M   14 Mar 1748 Hudson, NH Benjamin Winn & Judith
WINN,Bertha Alice   Sex:F   24 Apr 1894 Elmer C Winn (Hudson, NH)
  & Ella A Barker (Windham, NH)
WINN,Bethsheba   Sex:F   08 Apr 17 Hudson, NH Benjamin Winn &
WINN,Betty   Sex:F   11 Sep 1781 Hudson, NH Abiathar Winn & Abigail
WINN,Catherine   Sex:F   13 Apr 1733 Hudson, NH Joseph Winn & Elizabeth
WINN,Charles B   Sex:M   1807 Hudson, NH Nathan Winn & Elizabeth Kelley
WINN,Cora M   Sex:F   (Child #1) 18 Jun 1887 Elmer C Winn (Hudson, NH)
  & Ella A Barker (Windham, NH)
WINN,Cyrus   Sex:M   15 Dec 1793 Hudson, NH Joseph Winn Jr & Sarah Chase
WINN,Eliza Maria   Sex:F   30 Nov 1830 Hudson, NH William Winn & Persis G Moore
WINN,Elizabeth   Sex:F   06 Sep 1787 Hudson, NH Nathan Winn & Elizabeth Kelley
WINN,Elizebeth   Sex:F   04 Sep 1787 Hudson, NH Nathan Winn & Elizebeth
WINN,Ella A   Sex:F   23 Mar 1858 Hudson, NH Joseph G Winn & Louisa P
WINN,Eva Grace   Sex:F   15 Jul 1895 Elmer C Winn (Hudson, NH)
  & Ella A Barker (Windham, NH)
WINN,Franklin Moore   Sex:M   14 Mar 1839 Hudson, NH William Winn
  & Persis G Moore
WINN,Fred E   Sex:M   14 Dec 1864 Hudson, NH William F Winn & Lucy M Richardson
WINN,Fred E   Sex:M   14 Dec 1863 Hudson, NH William F Winn & Lucy
WINN,Hatiker   Sex: 21 Jan 1801 Hudson, NH Nathaniel Winn & Bettey
WINN,Irvin Richardson   Sex:M   (Child #2) 05 Jun 1904 Leon E Winn (Hudson, NH)
  & Alice Mortlock (Nova Scotia)
WINN,Isaac   Sex:M   20 May 1803 Hudson, NH Joseph Winn Jr & Sarah Chase
WINN,John   Sex:M   03 Apr 1800 Hudson, NH Joseph Winn Jr & Sarah Chase
WINN,Joseph   Sex:M   16 Apr 1760 Hudson, NH Joseph Winn Jr & Mary French
WINN,Joseph   Sex:M   22 Jun 1786 Hudson, NH Joseph Winn Jr & Sarah Chase
WINN,Joseph   Sex:M   16 Apr 1768 Hudson, NH Joseph Winn & Mary

HUDSON,NH BIRTHS

WINN,Joseph N G   Sex:M   12 Sep 1861 Hudson, NH Joseph G Winn & Louisa P
WINN,Katherine   Sex:F   11 Apr 1733 Hudson, NH Joseph Winn & Elizabeth
WINN,Kellie   Sex:F   18 Nov 1959 Edward P Winn & Norma Ducharme
WINN,Levi E   Sex:M   19 May 1874 Hudson, NH William Winn & Lucy
WINN,Lidia   Sex:F   21 Jun 1735 Hudson, NH Josiah Winn & Lidia
WINN,Lucene   Sex:F   22 Apr 1792 Hudson, NH Nathan Winn & Elizabeth Kelley
WINN,Lydia   Sex:F   21 Jun 1735 Hudson, NH Josiah Winn & Lydia
WINN,Mary F   Sex:F   28 Feb 1810 Hudson, NH Joseph Winn & Page
WINN,Mary French   Sex:F   28 Feb 1810 Hudson, NH Joseph Winn & Margaret Burns
WINN,Micajah   Sex:M   24 Oct 1735 Hudson, NH Joseph Winn & Elizabeth
WINN,Micajah   Sex:M   01 May 1772 Hudson, NH Abiathar Winn & Abigail
WINN,Nathan   Sex:M   15 Oct 1738 Hudson, NH Joseph Winn & Elizabeth
WINN,Nathan   Sex:M   05 Oct 1764 Hudson, NH Nathan Winn & Ruth Hadley
WINN,Nathan   Sex:M   13 May 1790 Hudson, NH Nathan Winn & Elizabeth Kelley
WINN,Nathan   Sex:M   15 Oct 1730 Hudson, NH Joseph Winn & Elizabeth
WINN,Nehemiah   Sex:M   23 Aug 1754 Hudson, NH Benjamin Winn & Judith
WINN,Olive   Sex:F   31 Oct 1757 Hudson, NH Benjamin Winn & Judith
WINN,Olive   Sex:F   21 Oct 1757 Hudson, NH Benjamin Winn & Judith
WINN,Paul T   Sex:M   01 Aug 1805 Hudson, NH Joseph Winn & Sarah
WINN,Paul Tenney   Sex:M   01 Aug 1805 Hudson, NH Joseph Winn Jr & Sarah Chase
WINN,Persis Ann   Sex:F   10 Jun 1832 Hudson, NH William Winn & Persis G Moore
WINN,Phebe Ellen   Sex:F   02 Jan 1837 Hudson, NH William Winn & Persis G Moore
WINN,Reuben   Sex:M   25 Aug 1779 Hudson, NH Abiathar Winn & Abigail
WINN,Sarah   Sex:F   07 Apr 1789 Hudson, NH Joseph Winn Jr & Sarah Chase
WINN,Sarah   Sex:F   27 Apr 1774 Hudson, NH Abiathar Winn & Abigail
WINN,Sarah   Sex:F   02 Feb 1805 Hudson, NH Nathan Winn & Elizabeth Kelley
WINN,Sarah   Sex:F   21 Feb 1805 Hudson, NH Nathan Winn & Elizebeth
WINN,Slatira   Sex: 21 Jan 1801 Hudson, NH Nathan Winn & Elizabeth Kelley
WINN,Susanna   Sex:F   10 Sep 1741 Hudson, NH Joseph Winn & Elizabeth
WINN,Susanna   Sex:F   01 Oct 1770 Hudson, NH Abiathar Winn & Abigail
WINN,Susanna   Sex:F   02 Aug 1803 Hudson, NH Nathan Winn & Elizabeth Kelley
WINN,Susanna   Sex:F   21 Apr 1792 Hudson, NH Nathan Winn & Betty
WINN,Wijeman   Sex: 06 Sep 1794 Hudson, NH Nathaniel Winn & Betty
WINN,William   Sex:M   19 Nov 1797 Hudson, NH Joseph Winn Jr & Sarah Chase
WINN,Wizeman C   Sex:M   Hudson, NH Nathan Winn & Elizabeth Kelley
WINN,Wizeman H   Sex:M   06 Sep 1794 Hudson, NH Nathan Winn & Elizabeth Kelley
WINN,[Unknown]   Sex:F   (Child #2) 18 Feb 1919 Frank Winn (Pelham, NH)
  & Effie Wyeth (Nashua, NH)
WINN,[Unknown]   Sex:F   (Child #3) 03 Oct 1922 Frank A Winn (Pelham, NH)
  & Effie M Wyeth (Nashua, NH)
WINSLOW,Brianna L   Sex: 11 Jun 1973 Kenneth E Winslow & Donnajean Bishop
WINSLOW,Debra L   Sex:F   06 Dec 1954 Gerald R Winslow & Elizabeth A Hamel
WINSLOW,Nancy A   Sex:F   02 Sep 1957 Gerald R Winslow & Elizabeth A Hamel
WINSLOW,Scott J   Sex:M   27 Oct 1961 Gerald R Winslow & Elizabeth A Hamel
WINTERS,Brian Michael Sex:M 05 Apr 1982 William R Winters Jr
  & Laura Marie Metrano
WINTERS,Louise Mary Sex:F   (Child #2) 15 Feb 1915 Hudson, NH Alfred H Winters
  (Haverhill, MA) & Laura Comeau (Nova Scotia)
WINTLE,Steeve M   Sex:M   26 Dec 1973 Amos R Wintle & Claudette R Drouin
WISE,Andrew W   Sex:M   10 Dec 1976 William H Wise & Janyce V Flurkey
WISEMAN,Caryn Ann   Sex:F   01 Apr 1978 George H Wiseman & Patricia S Benjamin
WISEMAN,Lindsay S   Sex:F   07 Mar 1980 George H Wiseman & Patricia S Benjamin
WITHERS,Gregory S   Sex: 26 Mar 1973 Stephen L Withers & Susan Antonick
WITHERS,Scott A   Sex:M   18 Jun 1970 Stephen L Withers & Susan Antonick
WOJTASZEK,Heather Marie   Sex:F   24 Sep 1984 Ronald V Wojtaszek
  & Deborah Ann Landry
WOJTASZEK,Sarah Michelle   Sex:F   23 May 1983 Ronald V Wojtaszek
  & Deborah Ann Landry
WOLANGEURE,[Unknown]   Sex:M   (Child #3) 21 May 1924 Michael Wolangeure
  (Russia) & Mary Kempte (Russia)

HUDSON,NH BIRTHS

WOLANGEWIC,[Unknown] Sex:M (Child #2) 18 Oct 1922 Michael Wolangewic
  (Russia) & Mary Kemte (Russia)
WOLCZOK,Diane K Sex:F 08 Oct 1951 John S Wolczok & Lucille A Bentley
WOLCZOK,John S Jr Sex:M 19 Oct 1953 John S Wolczok & Lucille A Bentley
WOLLEN,Deborah G Sex:F 01 Aug 1957 Joseph Wollen & Jennie D Ferus
WOLLEN,John Frederick Sex:M 08 Sep 1983 John M Wollen & Doris May Carkin
WOLLEN,Karen A Sex:F 10 Apr 1962 Joseph Wollen & Jennie D Ferus
WOLLEN,Richard J Sex:M 09 Jul 1948 John Wollen (Hudson, NH)
  & Irene Leclerc (Nashua, NH)
WOMBLE,Nicole B Sex:F 17 Sep 1977 William J Womble & Debra L Stanistreet
WOMBLE,[Unknown] Sex:M 12 Nov 1981 William John Womble & Debra L Stanistreet
WONKKA,Alyssa J Sex: 29 Jan 1973 John E Wonkka & Joan E Clark
WONKKA,Erin E Sex:F 03 Feb 1969 John E Wonkka & Joan E Clark
WOOD,Bigelow Jr Sex:M 13 Mar 1970 Bigelow Wood & Sandra A Lang
WOOD,Cynthia M Sex:F 19 Feb 1957 Allison C Wood & Shirley M Coldwell
WOOD,Ella Sex:F 29 Jul 1852 Hudson, NH Charles Wood & Louisa Cummings
WOOD,Emma Sex:F 29 Oct 1853 Hudson, NH Charles Wood & Louisa Cummings
WOOD,James F Sex:M 22 Aug 1968 William F Wood & Margaret F Donovan
WOOD,Jason A Sex:M 18 Sep 1969 Robert L Wood & Linda L Morrill
WOOD,Kristin A Sex:F 19 Feb 1953 James A Wood & Constance A Arne
WOOD,Licia A Sex:F 26 Sep 1955 James A Wood & Constance A Arne
WOOD,Nellie Jane Sex:F (Child #1) 05 Dec 1885 Hudson, NH Joseph E Wood
  (Chelmsford, MA) & Martha L J Durant (Hudson, NH)
WOOD,Sandra J Sex:F 29 Feb 1972 Robert L Wood Sr & Linda A Morrill
WOOD,Tamara L Sex:F 26 Sep 1967 John C Wood & Karen L Gott
WOODBRIDGE,Fred A Sex:M 06 Dec 1867 Hudson, NH Albert W Woodbridge
  & Abby J
WOODBRIDGE,Fred Albert Sex:M 06 Dec 1867 Hudson, NH Albert W Woodbridge
  & Abbie J
WOODBURY,Ida May Sex:F (Child #9) 05 May 1899 Edgar Woodbury & Eva Wheeler
  (Nashua, NH)
WOODBURY,Willie Elliott Sex:M (Child #7) 23 Sep 1896 Edgar C Woodbury
  (Hudson, NH) & Eva Wheeler (Nashua, NH)
WOODMAN,Christopher S Sex:M 08 Jan 1974 Robert E Woodman & Marcella B Soucie
WOODMAN,Elizabeth A Sex:F 16 Jan 1967 Eldon T Woodman & Janice L McCrellis
WOODMAN,Rebecca D Sex: 23 Feb 1973 Robert E Woodman & Marcella B Soucie
WOODRUFF,Robert W Sex:M 26 Apr 1957 Daniel M Woodruff & Maryann Marshall
WOODRUFF,Wendy A Sex:F 30 May 1967 Daniel M Woodruff & Ann Marshall
WOODS,Shawn M Sex:M 12 Nov 1973 Maurice E Woods & Annie L Brown
WOODWARD,Arthur J Sex:M (Child #8) 25 Mar 1898 Edgar C Woodward
  (Londonderry, NH) & Eva Wheeler (Nashua, NH)
WOODWARD,Dolly Sex:F (Child #3) 17 Jan 1883 Hudson, NH George P Woodward
  (Nashua, NH) & Eldora F Leonard (Piermont, NH)
WOOLDRIDGE,Michael Edward Sex:M 23 Jun 1983 Daniel E Wooldridge
  & Brenda J MacFarlane
WOOLEY,David D Sex:M 23 Oct 1963 David V Wooley & Marie N Farrington
WOOLLEY,Deborah K Sex:F 12 Apr 1955 Milton E Woolley & Reby A Ladner
WORSTER,Hannah Sex:F 30 Sep 1755 Hudson, NH Benjamin Worster & Hannah
WORTH,Johnna Autumn Sex:F 21 Nov 1984 William Arthur Worth
  & Ronna Carol Langlois
WORTHLEY,George Edwin Sex:M 08 Aug 1874 Hudson, NH Edwin Worthley & Lottie
WOSTER,Hannah Sex:F 30 Sep 1755 Hudson, NH Benjamin Woster & Hannah
WRIGHT,Benjamin David Sex:M 11 Nov 1980 Wayne Alden Wright
  & Lorraine A Hanrahan
WRIGHT,Jayne L Sex:F 16 Aug 1962 Charles M Wright & Janet L Paul
WRIGHT,JoEllen J Sex:F 05 Jul 1956 Charles M Wright & Janet L Paul
WRIGHT,Kristin Elizabeth Sex:F 17 Nov 1980 Phillip C Wright & Susan E Ayles
WRIGHT,Maribeth J Sex:F 13 Jun 1952 Charles M Wright & Janet L Paul
WRIGHT,Melissa Sue Sex:F 16 Nov 1978 Philip C Wright & Susan E Ayles
WRIGHT,Ruth A Sex:F 30 Sep 1950 Charles M Wright & Janet L Paul

HUDSON,NH BIRTHS

```
WRIGHT,Tammy Marie   Sex:F   08 Jun 1978 Wayne A Wright & Lorraine A Hanrahan
WRIGHT,Walter   Sex:M   (Child #3) 13 Aug 1920 John E Wright (England)
    & Elizabeth McLeod (Lowell, MA)
WRIGHT,[Unknown]   Sex:M   17 Sep 1875 Hudson, NH Ephraim Wright & E S
WRINKLES,Taddy R   Sex:M   19 Jul 1963 Randolph E Wrinkles & Linda M Roy
WU,Victoria Szu-Hua   Sex:F   24 Jul 1973 Alan Chung-Wei Wu & San-Ty Gu
WULF,Brenda A   Sex:F   30 Jul 1957 John F Wulf & Joan S Whitney
WULF,Brian A   Sex:M   30 Jul 1957 John F Wulf & Joan S Whitney
WUNSCHEL,Mark R   Sex:M   21 Feb 1979 David H Wunschel & Nancy J Chase
WYATT,Christy A   Sex:F   08 May 1948 Richard L Wyatt (Minneapolis, MN)
    & Rena P Rosedoff (Nashua, NH)
WYATT,Deborah L   Sex:F   02 May 1956 Richard L Wyatt & Rena P Rosedoff
WYATT,Richard L Jr   Sex:M   21 Mar 1951 Richard L Wyatt & Rena P Rosedoff
WYKA,Lyndsay Nicole   Sex:F   07 Feb 1984 Gary Edward Wyka & Paula Mary Arnold
WYMAN,Abigail   Sex:F   29 Apr 1758 Hudson, NH Seth Wyman & Abigail
WYMAN,Amos N   Sex:M   26 Sep 1793 Hudson, NH Amos Wyman & Molly
WYMAN,Amos Nelson   Sex:M   26 Sep 1793 Hudson, NH Amos Wyman & Molly
WYMAN,Betsey   Sex:F   21 Jul 1798 Pelham, NH Ezra Wyman & Hannah
WYMAN,Betsy   Sex:F   21 Jul 1798 Hudson, NH Ezra Wyman & Hannah
WYMAN,Cary Douglas   Sex:M   (Child #1) 24 Aug 1941 Clair E Wyman (Manchester,
    NH) & Harriette Crosley (Beverly, MA)
WYMAN,Charles   Sex:M   22 Sep 1809 Hudson, NH Ezra Wyman & Hannah
WYMAN,Daniel   Sex:M   06 Feb 1754 Hudson, NH Seth Wyman & Abigail
WYMAN,Daniel   Sex:M   28 Aug 1807 Hudson, NH Seth Wyman & Betsey
WYMAN,Daniel   Sex:M   04 Feb 1796 Pelham, NH Ezra Wyman & Hannah
WYMAN,David   Sex:M   28 Aug 1807 Hudson, NH Seth Wyman & Betsey
WYMAN,Dorcas   Sex:F   19 Sep 1764 Hudson, NH Seth Wyman & Abigail
WYMAN,Dorcas   Sex:F   14 Apr 1810 Hudson, NH Seth Wyman & Betsey
WYMAN,Ebenezer   Sex:M   15 Mar 1794 Pelham, NH Ezra Wyman & Hannah
WYMAN,Elbridge   Sex:M   03 Dec 1802 Pelham, NH Ezra Wyman & Hannah
WYMAN,Ezra   Sex:M   10 Nov 1762 Hudson, NH Seth Wyman & Abigail
WYMAN,Fanney   Sex:F   10 Dec 1808 Hudson, NH Seth Wyman & Betsey
WYMAN,Fanny   Sex:F   10 Dec 1808 Hudson, NH Seth Wyman & Betsey
WYMAN,Hannah   Sex:F   11 Aug 1756 Hudson, NH Seth Wyman & Abigail
WYMAN,Hannah   Sex:F   09 Mar 1806 Hudson, NH Ezra Wyman & Hannah
WYMAN,Hannah   Sex:F   11 Aug 1776 Hudson, NH Seth Wyman & Abigail
WYMAN,Holly L   Sex:F   08 Apr 1964 Donald R Wyman & Rosalie S Allison
WYMAN,Ira   Sex:M   10 Mar 1801 Hudson, NH Isaac Wyman & Sarah
WYMAN,Isaac   Sex:M   13 Jun 1798 Hudson, NH Isaac Wyman & Sarah
WYMAN,Isaac   Sex:M   10 Mar 1801 Hudson, NH Isaac Wyman & Sarah
WYMAN,Jeffrey P   Sex:M   15 May 1961 Donald R Wyman & Rosalie S Allison
WYMAN,Joseph   Sex:M   25 Oct 1795 Hudson, NH Isaac Wyman & Sarah
WYMAN,Leonard   Sex:M   06 Dec 1800 Pelham, NH Ezra Wyman & Hannah
WYMAN,Liva   Sex:F   29 Aug 1812 Hudson, NH Ezra Wyman & Hannah
WYMAN,Mark S   Sex:M   11 Feb 1960 Donald R Wyman & Rosalie S Allison
WYMAN,Nancy   Sex:F   21 Jul 1792 Pelham, NH Ezra Wyman & Hannah
WYMAN,Nancy   Sex:F   02 Jul 1792 Hudson, NH Ezra Wyman & Hannah
WYMAN,Randall J   Sex:M   29 Apr 1969 Donald R Wyman & Rosalie S Allison
WYMAN,Relief   Sex:F   25 Jun 1761 Hudson, NH Seth Wyman & Abigail
WYMAN,Salley   Sex:F   21 Feb 1805 Hudson, NH Seth Wyman & Betsey
WYMAN,Sally   Sex:F   21 Feb 1805 Hudson, NH Seth Wyman & Betsey
WYMAN,Sarah   Sex:F   29 Jun 1758 Hudson, NH Simon Wyman & Thankful
WYMAN,Sarah   Sex:F   29 Jun 1768 Hudson, NH Simon Wyman & Thankful
WYMAN,Seth   Sex:M   20 Sep 1770 Hudson, NH Seth Wyman & Abigail
WYMAN,Susanna   Sex:F   24 Oct 1811 Hudson, NH Seth Wyman & Betsey
WYMAN,Thomas   Sex:M   04 Sep 1774 Hudson, NH Seth Wyman & Abigail
WYMAN,Thomas   Sex:M   15 Sep 1790 Pelham, NH Ezra Wyman & Hannah
WYNOTT,Christina Marie   Sex:F   05 May 1983 Scott L Wynott & Sheryl Ann Bosse
WYNOTT,Dennis W   Sex:M   18 Apr 1953 Raymond W Wynott & Joan E Rowell
WYNOTT,Kevin R   Sex:M   27 Jan 1959 Raymond W Wynott & Joan E Rowell
```

HUDSON,NH BIRTHS

WYNOTT,Scott L   Sex:M   14 May 1960 Lawrence R Wynott,Jr & Nancy L Tibbetts
WYNOTT,Shawn M   Sex:M   27 Jul 1962 Raymond W Wynott & Joan Rowell
YANUSZEWSKI,C Jr Sex:M   (Child #2) 10 May 1943 Kasjanty Yanuszewski (Nashua,
    NH) & Cecile Levesque (Nashua, NH)
YARMO,Jacqueline E   Sex:F   09 Sep 1966 John S Yarmo & Jacqueline L Malhoit
YARMO,John C   Sex:M   03 May 1962 John S Yarmo & Jacqueline L Malhoit
YEATON,Eileen M   Sex:F   19 Oct 1959 Harold F Yeaton & Betty A Green
YEATON,Elizabeth M   Sex:F   30 Mar 1962 Harold F Yeaton & Elizabeth A Green
YETTON,Effie Grace Sex:F   (Child #2) 28 Nov 1914 Ralph N Yetton (Houlton, ME)
    & Flora M Ramney (Nashua, NH)
YOHN,Tamela R   Sex: 06 Dec 1972 Richard W Yohn & Carolyn J Shoop
YOHN,Tara R   Sex: 06 Dec 1972 Richard W Yohn & Carolyn J Shoop
YOKOFF,Heidi A   Sex:F   03 Jan 1975 John A Yokoff & Nancy A Hellmann
YOKOFF,Sonya G   Sex:F   30 May 1976 John A Yokoff & Nancy A Hellmann
YON,Davie Allen   Sex:M   16 Aug 1965 Richard P Yon & Elizabeth A Lehman
YORK,Amy B   Sex: 09 Jan 1973 Roland W York & Gail C Morse
YORK,Anna H   Sex:F   (Child #2) 24 Nov 1943 Andrew J York (Nashua, NH)
    & Christine M Carter (Nashua, NH)
YORK,Barry C   Sex:M   05 Jun 1962 Roland W York & Gail C Morse
YORK,Bernise E   Sex:F   (Child #1) 28 Nov 1903 Fred F York (Durham, NH)
    & Ola Armstrong (Hudson, NH)
YORK,Craig R   Sex:M   31 Jul 1965 Roland W York & Gail C Morse
YORK,Daryl E   Sex:M   26 Feb 1967 Roland W York & Gail C Morse
YORK,Douglass Ryan Sex:M   12 Sep 1983 Barry C York & Karen Louise Lemery
YORK,Pamela L   Sex:F   16 Aug 1963 Roland W York & Gail C Morse
YORK,Richard M III   Sex:M   25 Mar 1969 Richard M York Jr & Theresa A Tupper
YORK,Theresa Helen   Sex:F   (Child #9) 18 Dec 1932 Hudson, NH Jesse York
    (Freemont, NH) & Harriet Dudley (Hollis, NH)
YORK,Toni A   Sex:F   13 Mar 1972 Jesse L York & Barbara A Hill
YORK,William R   Sex:M   30 Jun 1948 Jesse A York, Jr (Nashua, NH)
    & Elizabeth M Sweeney (Nashua, NH)
YORK,Willie A   Sex:M   08 Jun 1872 Hudson, NH David York & Flora
YOUNG,Benjamin A   Sex:M   06 Feb 1868 Hudson, NH Amos Young & Hattie E
YOUNG,Blanche H   Sex:F   (Child #1) 02 Nov 1908 Walter H Young (Lowell, MA)
    & Ida W Lambert (Newport, MA)
YOUNG,Cindy M   Sex:F   07 Jun 1963 Willard N Young & Eleanor F Kane
YOUNG,Debora J   Sex:F   16 Jan 1964 Donald C Young & Elaine C Smith
YOUNG,Edward C   Sex:M   (Child #2) 11 Mar 1945 Kenneth E Young (Merrimack, NH)
    & Alice B LaFlamme (Nashua, NH)
YOUNG,Jane R   Sex:F   12 Sep 1956 Kenneth E Young & Alice B LaFlamme
YOUNG,Kimberly M   Sex:F   25 Jun 1970 Leavitt L Young & Mary C Mulcahey
YOUNG,Loretta S   Sex:F   22 Oct 1958 Kenneth E Young & Alice B LaFlamme
YOUNG,Lucile Edna   Sex:F   (Child #4) 18 Jul 1925 George C Young (Auburn, ME)
    & Estella M Porter (Patten, ME)
YOUNG,Milton   Sex:M   07 Feb 1869 Hudson, NH Israel W Young & Elizabeth Moss
YOUNG,Milton   Sex:M   04 Feb 1869 Hudson, NH Israel W Young & Elisabeth
YOUNG,Norman Colby Sex:M   (Child #3) 25 Mar 1924 George C Young (Auburn, ME)
    & Stella M Porter (Patten, ME)
YOUNG,Peter Austin   Sex:M   02 Feb 1978 Gregg A Young & Gail Anne Peterson
YOUNG,Sheryl L   Sex:F   13 Aug 1949 Kenneth E Young & Alice B Laflamme
YU,Jennifer Alice Sex:F   19 Aug 1982 Robert Hsi-Chi Yu & Janet Alice Metcalf
ZABIEREK,Mary   Sex:F   (Child #2) 13 Aug 1919 Stanley Zabierek (Poland)
    & Wladysiana Kurzana (Poland)
ZABIEREK,Stanley   Sex:M   (Child #1) 31 Jul 1914 Stanley Zabierek (Russia)
    & Wladyslawa Kurzana (Russia)
ZACCAGNINI,Terri L   Sex:F   20 Aug 1971 John F Zaccagnini & Katherine M Carr
ZALANSKAS,Kevin R II   Sex:M   09 Jun 1967 Kevin R Zalanskas & Alleyne M Rush
ZANDBOD,Amanda   Sex:F   30 May 1985 Morteza Zandbod & Elizabeth B Moore
ZANI,Paul A   Sex:M   11 Jan 1968 Leo A Zano Jr & Betty B Burks
ZEDALIS,Adolph Joseph   Sex:M   (Child #1) 27 Sep 1941 Adolph J Zedalis

HUDSON,NH BIRTHS

(Nashua, NH) & Anna M Hurd (Nashua, NH)
ZELONIS,Charles M   Sex:M   17 Feb 1948 Vincent J Zelonis (Lowell, MA)
   & Mary E Wisneski (Chelsea, MA)
ZELONIS,Daniel   Sex:M   (Child #2) 28 Oct 1946 Vincent J Zelonis (Lowell, MA)
   & Mary E Wisneski (Chelsea, MA)
ZELONIS,Erica Lynn   Sex:F   29 Mar 1976 William J Zelonis & Susan D Joyal
ZELONIS,Laurie A   Sex:F   15 Feb 1961 Vincent J Zelonis & Mary E Wisneski
ZELONIS,Marian E   Sex:F   27 May 1955 Vincent J Zelonis & Mary E Wisneski
ZELONIS,Mark E   Sex:M   11 Dec 1949 Vincent J Zelonis & Mary E Wisneski
ZELONIS,Peter Joseph Sex:M   17 Jul 1978 William J Zelonis & Susan Diane Joyle
ZELONIS,William J   Sex:M   29 Dec 1951 Vincent J Zelonis & Mary E Wisneski
ZENOR,Christine M   Sex:F   10 Jul 1965 Donald P Zenor & Shirley M Webb
ZERBINOS,Kathryn L   Sex:F   25 Jul 1949 Nicholas Zerbinos & Rachel P Laflamme
ZIDEK,Robert J   Sex:M   01 May 1974 Joseph A Zidek & Maureen L Rock
ZIDEK,Steven J   Sex:M   10 Aug 1971 Joseph A Zidek & Maureen L Rock
ZIMMERMAN,Adam David   Sex:M   30 Aug 1979 David A Zimmerman & Sandra Lee Petok
ZINK,Charles W   Sex:M   (Child #1) 30 Jan 1926 Ernest Zink (Dorchester, MA)
   & Priscilla R Blood (Nashua, NH)
ZINS,Mark P   Sex:M   12 Feb 1962 Eugene P Zins & Jeannine R Gagne
ZINTEL,Deborah L   Sex:F   22 Jan 1952 Bruce R Zintel & Eunice A Cox
ZOES,George   Sex:M   (Child #1) 22 Jan 1931 Dionysios Zoes (Greece)
   & Eva Gagnon (Nashua, NH)
ZURAKOWSKI,Pamela Elizabeth   Sex:F   04 Jun 1983 Robert E Zurakowski
   & Joyce Irene Parsons
ZWOLENIK,Jackie E   Sex:M   03 Sep 1958 Charles Zwolenik & Melzia M Adams
ZWOLENIK,Jacquelyn S   Sex:F   03 Sep 1958 Charles Zwolenik & Melzia M Adams
[A NEGRO],Enod   Sex:M   17 Nov 1768 Hudson, NH Sisco & Dinah
[UNKNOWN],[Unknown]   Sex:M   29 Jul 1861 Hudson, NH James & Emily
[UNKNOWN],[Unknown]   Sex:F   Oct 1866 Hudson, NH John A & Jemima
[UNKNOWN],[Unknown]   Sex:M   14 Feb 1867 Hudson, NH George & Fanny

HUDSON, NH MARRIAGES

ABBEY, Steven C and Emily Anne CARVER, 22 May 1971 Nashua, NH
ABBOTT, Betty J and William J ESTEY, 24 Sep 1966 Hudson, NH
ABBOTT, Carol A and John C BRADDOCK, 19 Apr 1969 Hudson, NH
ABBOTT, Clayton B and Helen M TANDY, 08 Jun 1935 Amherst, NH
ABBOTT, Gail W and Ralph F OWENS, 26 Sep 1970 Hudson, NH
ABBOTT, George H and Mary N WEBSTER, 13 Aug 1896 Hudson, NH
  Herman Abbott & Elvira Bancroft
  Kimball Webster(Hudson, NH) & Abiah C Cutter (Pelham, NH)
ABBOTT, Gerald R and Dolores AVILA, 03 Dec 1977 Hudson, NH
ABBOTT, Hannah D and William H MELLEN, 29 Oct 1892 Hudson, NH
  Geo H Abbott & Rose Abbott
  Hugh Mellen(Nova Scotia) & Emma Hutchinson (N Reading, MA)
ABBOTT, Jacob and Melinda LEWIS, 04 Feb 1863
ABBOTT, James C and Linda L MORRILL, 23 Nov 1962 Antrim, NH
ABBOTT, James H and Susan B VASSILAKOS, 05 Feb 1970 Nashua, NH
ABBOTT, James K and Ellen ADRION, 06 Dec 1856
ABBOTT, John K and Priscilla QUIGLEY, 24 Jul 1965 Hudson, NH
ABBOTT, Linda L and Robert L WOOD, 03 Aug 1968 Hudson, NH
ABBOTT, Marjorie and Paul B DEQUOY, 10 Nov 1956 Hudson, NH
ABBOTT, Marjorie and Otis Nelson GOVE, 30 Jun 1927 Hudson, NH
ABBOTT, Mary-Jane and Wilfred L HOLDEN, 26 Feb 1957 Hudson, NH
ABBOTT, Nancy J and Paul B Jr GIBSON, 20 Aug 1955 Hudson, NH
ABBOTT, Paula M and David P ANGER, 01 Jun 1973 Hudson, NH
ABBOTT, Pauline R and Stephen L TRZOS, 22 Jan 1971 Hudson, NH
ABBOTT, Sarah and William E ROBINSON, 30 Nov 1846
ABBOTT, Thomas W and Barbara A DONAHUE, 04 Jul 1964 Hudson, NH
ABBOTT, William E and Jean C SWITSER, 06 Feb 1957 Hudson, NH
ABRAMVITZ, Jonas and Marion DELINSKY, 11 Sep 1938 Hudson, NH
ABUCEWICZ, Edna A and John A KLEMENT, 23 Jul 1960 Nashua, NH
ACKERMAN, Horace H and Carrie E McKUSICK, 12 Oct 1897 Hudson, NH
  Wm H Ackerman & Henrietta Lane
  F C McKusick & Viola Corson
ACKERMAN, Maurice Wm and Florence J BUTMAN, 06 Jun 1937 Fairlee, VT
ACKERMAN, Thomas R and Drinette A DIONNE, 07 Apr 1947 Nashua, NH
ACKERMAN, William G and Lanora P TUCKER, 27 Aug 1914 Nashua, NH
  William Ackerman & Henrietta Lane
  Samuel Porter & Elenora Brothers
ACKERMAN, Willis D and Mary P F OSGOOD, 02 May 1891 Hudson, NH
  Wm H Ackerman (Alexandria) & Henrietta Lane (Lee)
  Anson A Osgood(Lyndeboro, NH) & Hannah M Parker (Boston, MA)
ACKERMAN, Willis Z and Mary OSGOOD, 02 Mar 1891
ADAIR, Marie D and John Henry McCOMB, 24 Apr 1982 Hudson, NH
ADAMS, Alice R and Willard I TRUMBULL, 06 Sep 1926 Manchester, NH
ADAMS, Angeline P and Eben A THATCHER, 30 Jun 1903 Plymouth, MA
  Prescott Adams & Addie P Hills
  Frank Thatcher & Eleanor Knowles
ADAMS, Anna and George Jr BURNS, 01 Nov 1770
ADAMS, Augusta M and Albert N FLINN, 07 Oct 1869 Hudson, NH
ADAMS, Augusta M and Albert N WINN, Hudson, NH
ADAMS, Carl H and Rita A KNIGHT, 04 Jan 1964 Windham, NH
ADAMS, Carleton H Jr & Dawna Anne FAULKNER, 26 Jun 1982 Nashua, NH
ADAMS, Charles W and Elaine HORNE, 27 Oct 1984 W Ossipee, NH
ADAMS, Daniel N and Sarah A DAVIS, 19 Aug 1857
ADAMS, Elmer H and Lorraine R MORAN, 16 Oct 1948 Nashua, NH
ADAMS, George G and Alice H HOWES, 25 Nov 1927 Nashua, NH
ADAMS, George L and Marguerite CONEGRATTE, 02 Jan 1923 Nashua, NH
ADAMS, Hannah and Granville HILL, 29 Jun 1858
ADAMS, Janice L and John A MELLEN, 31 Jan 1970 Keene, NH
ADAMS, Marvin C and Glenna M BILLINGS, 01 May 1948 Hudson, NH
ADAMS, Neal J and Elizabeth KEMPENEERS, 29 Sep 1984 Nashua, NH

HUDSON, NH MARRIAGES

ADAMS, Penny E and Michael W RUSSELL, 14 Oct 1972 Hudson, NH
ADAMS, Percy L and Dora M BEEDE, 04 May 1972 Hudson, NH
ADAMS, Phyllis T and Harold N GIBSON, 17 Jan 1942 Nashua, NH
ADAMS, Prescott and Adaliza HILLS, 26 Jan 1871
ADAMS, Prescott A and Addie P HILLS, 26 Jan 1870 Hudson, NH
ADAMS, Theophalin and Margaret J SHARPE, 16 Jan 1866
ADAMS, Vergil L and Claire L DESCLOS, 09 May 1953 Hudson, NH
ADAMS, William and Abigail HARDY, 05 May 1785
ADKINS, Bernis and Ruth J MELLEN, 03 Aug 1957 Hudson, NH
ADKINS, Paul B and Cheryl A LAPLANTE, 10 Jun 1974 Hudson, NH
ADKINS, Ruth J and Donald H STURTEVANT, 01 Oct 1966 Hudson, NH
ADRION, Ellen and James K ABBOTT, 06 Dec 1856
AGRELLA, John F and Carol A SPARKS, 25 Nov 1966 Nashua, NH
AHEARN, Brian E and Michelle G MUNDAY, 25 Jun 1978 Hudson, NH
AHEARN, George S and Helen L BARTON, 22 Oct 1978 Hudson, NH
AHEARN, Gregory M and Claire G GAGNON, 18 Sep 1971 Nashua, NH
AHEARN, Nona V and Teddy S KENNEDY, 18 May 1981 Hudson, NH
AHEARN, Nona V and Michael W RUSSELL, 19 Sep 1976 Nashua, NH
AHIGIAN, Karyn A and Patrick M BYRNE, 27 May 1978 Hudson, NH
AHLERS, Lisa Ann and William A LEMIRE, 26 Jan 1980 Hudson, NH
AHRENDT, Jane C and James L III BATTS, 17 Aug 1968 Hudson, NH
AHRENDT, Richard W and Jacqueline HAYNES, 20 Aug 1966 Hudson, NH
AIJALA, Helmi and Zaven A TARPINIAN, 04 Mar 1950 Hudson, NH
AKERS, Jasper D and Katherine STUDLEY, 01 Mar 1932 Nashua, NH
AKSTEN, Victor and Helen I MORAN, 05 Sep 1942 Milford, NH
AKSTIN, Bertha and Anthony J SKLINTAS, 01 Dec 1945 Nashua, NH
ALAVAREZ, Luisa M and Gregori M RODRIGUEZ, 18 Nov 1967 Nashua, NH
ALBANO, Louis S and Marion J BUTTERS, 17 May 1942 Hudson, NH
ALBEE, George W and Elizabeth SMITH, 22 Feb 1938 Hudson, NH
ALBERT, David Lee and LuAnn C FAUCHER, 02 Feb 1974 Hudson, NH
ALBERTA, Esther P and Arthur E SIPOLA, 15 Jun 1946 Hudson, NH
ALBERTINI, Bernice M and Robert S ROBINSON, 17 Jan 1948 Hudson, NH
ALBERTINI, Ralph P and Elsie V GROSSO, 12 Apr 1947 Hudson, NH
ALBERTSON, Pamela J and Stephen R HARTWELL, 29 May 1981 Hudson, NH
ALDRICH, Donald E and Mildred H RICE, 28 Sep 1957 Hudson, NH
ALDRICH, Glenn E and Sheri G KURMAN, 11 Dec 1983 Salem, NH
ALDRICH, Rachel E and Robert M SMITH, 06 Jun 1949 Hudson, NH
ALEJANDRO, Robert J and Deborah K BLAKE, 01 Dec 1967 Hudson, NH
ALESSANDRO, C R and Charles J RUSSO, 04 Oct 1947 Hudson, NH
ALEXANDER, Albert I and Sophia JANULEWIC, 30 Dec 1928 Hudson, NH
ALEXANDER, Bonnie F and David B CHESTERLEY, 09 Jun 1972 Hudson, NH
ALEXANDER, Caroline H and Edwin H PROCTOR, 09 Jan 1949 Hudson, NH
ALEXANDER, Dwight C and Wanda S SUSALKA, 23 Nov 1947 Hudson, NH
ALEXANDER, Earline C and Lawrence L DRAPER, 07 Jun 1942 Nashua, NH
ALEXANDER, George F and Doris A LAFRANCE, 05 Feb 1949 Hudson, NH
ALEXANDER, Irving C and Joan G REYNOLDS, 14 Jun 1958 Hudson, NH
ALEXANDER, Lawrence W Jr & Margaret L POULIOT, 14 Feb 1979 Nashua,NH
ALEXANDER, Nathaniel and Ella J ROACH, 16 Jun 1866
ALEXANDER, Robert D and Bonnie F GRANT, 14 Dec 1968 Hudson, NH
ALEXANDER, Willis and Sarah J DANE, 02 Jun 1873 Hudson, NH
ALEXKNOVITCH, Catharine & Dennis P BOUCHER, 08 Jun 1974 Hudson, NH
ALEXKNOVITCH, Susan M and Allen N STRAUB, 25 May 1984 Hudson, NH
ALGER, Georgina and Arnold W TOZER, 24 Jun 1949 Hudson, NH
ALIE, Gary J and Cindy S GREER, 30 Aug 1982 Hudson, NH
ALIMANDI, Genense and Jerry CAPOZZOLE, 15 May 1937 Nashua, NH
ALLARD, Denise G and Conrad H TESSIER, 25 Apr 1969 Nashua, NH
ALLARD, Garry E and Donna L PURINTON, 10 Sep 1966 Nashua, NH
ALLARD, George N and Ellen M HASELTON, 22 Jun 1946 Hudson, NH
ALLARD, Joan V and Derrick B FIGUEROA, 09 Dec 1972 Nashua, NH
ALLARD, Paul A and Carol Ann ENGLISH, 24 Aug 1973 Merrimack, NH

HUDSON,NH MARRIAGES

ALLARD, Rebel L and Theresa M CRAM, 26 Apr 1985 Hudson, NH
ALLARD, Troy W Jr and Elizabeth SMITH, 18 Jun 1978 Nashua, NH
ALLEN, Carolyn A and Paul A MOISAN, 28 Aug 1971 Nashua, NH
ALLEN, Charles W and Brenda L COX, 08 Mar 1975 Hudson, NH
ALLEN, Claire and Angelo LEFTER, 02 Aug 1941 Hudson, NH
ALLEN, Deborah A and Joseph S SIENKIEWICZ, 20 Nov 1970 Nashua, NH
ALLEN, Emma Jane and Albert YOUNG, 12 Nov 1871 Hudson, NH
ALLEN, Ernest F and Beverly HAYWARD, 19 Jun 1948 Hudson, NH
ALLEN, Frances R and Frank L Jr IRVINE, 03 Oct 1959 New London, CT
ALLEN, Franklin H and Alice A CORY, 29 May 1873 Nashua, NH
ALLEN, Jennie H and Dwight CROSS, 01 Apr 1923 Hudson, NH
ALLEN, Judith N and John R HODSDON, 20 Feb 1960 Tuftonboro, NH
ALLEN, Marie M and Melbourne AMOS, 29 Jan 1949 Hudson, NH
ALLEN, Mark W and Donna M SIRVYDAS, 31 Mar 1984 Nashua, NH
ALLEN, Mary E and Albert HUTCHINSON, 24 Nov 1868 Hudson, NH
ALLEN, Melvin C and Evelyn TAYLOR, 06 Sep 1941 Hudson, NH
ALLEN, Michael and Gail WESCOTT, 14 Feb 1975 Londonderry, NH
ALLEN, Robert D and Edith LILLIE, 02 Apr 1910 Hudson, NH
   Robert D Allen & Belda Kimball
   Albert Lillie & Lydia Sherman
ALLEN, Steven C and Sandra J PIATEK, 21 Jan 1966 Hudson, NH
ALLEN, Steven E and Loretta F BEAN, 23 Apr 1939 Nashua, NH
ALLEN, Steven M and Lynn C GEORGE, 27 May 1974 Hudson, NH
ALLEN, Susan A and Donald R Jr WINSLOW, 14 Mar 1985 Manchester, NH
ALLESON, Joseph and Sophie SABANSKI, 30 May 1929 Manchester, NH
ALLEY, David H and Gertrude R GAGNON, 11 Aug 1973 Hudson, NH
ALLGROVE, Virginia J and Elmer R McLAVEY, 19 Jun 1943 Hudson, NH
ALLISON, Carol A and Gerald T TYLER, 05 Sep 1960 Nashua, NH
ALLISON, Charles W and Lena PERRON, 07 Apr 1945 Nashua, NH
ALLISON, David F and Diane T DESCHAMPS, 28 Jun 1968 Nashua, NH
ALLISON, Janice E and Kenneth E BERRY, 10 May 1969 Nashua, NH
ALLISON, John M and Patricia A DAILEY, 11 Nov 1972 Nashua, NH
ALLISON, Margaret F and Ross E Jr KIERSTEAD, 01 Feb 1963 Nashua, NH
ALLISON, Robert J and Cynthia L BROOKES, 24 Jun 1984 Hudson, NH
ALLISON, Rosalie S and Donald R WYMAN, 01 Aug 1959 Hudson, NH
ALLISON, Simon R Jr and Claire I CASEY, 20 Aug 1960 Hudson, NH
ALLISON, Simon R and Gloria M BONNETTE, 14 Nov 1937 Dracut, MA
ALLISON, William J III and Muriel D SZABO, 12 Feb 1966 Hudson, NH
ALMEIDA, Joanne R and Charles W PALMER, 05 Aug 1961 Hudson, NH
ALMEIDA, Kevin J and Mary A SARNO, 12 Dec 1982 Hudson, NH
ALMEIDA, Rita D and Lawrence R ROGERS, 04 Nov 1967 Nashua, NH
ALTOMARE, Antoinette and Leo M BOFFOLI, 12 Nov 1948 Hudson, NH
ALUKONIS, Amelia A and Wesley E Jr BOLES, 24 Jun 1944 Nashua, NH
ALUKONIS, Annie and Guy HARWOOD, 03 Sep 1933 Dunstable, MA
ALUKONIS, John J and Theresa L MICHAUD, 06 Nov 1954 Nashua, NH
ALUKONIS, Michael H and Jacqueline SPRAGUE, 30 Jan 1982 Nashua, NH
ALUKONIS, Nancy V and Charles WOLLEN, 03 Feb 1951 Nashua, NH
ALUKONIS, Stanley and Sophie BATURA, 20 Dec 1950 Hudson, NH
ALUKONIS, Vito S and Harriet F COOKE, 01 Jul 1950 Hudson, NH
ALUKONIS, William A and Alice E CHERNES, 20 Feb 1943 Nashua, NH
ALVAREZ, Louis and Margaret L HARDY, 10 Oct 1953 Nashua, NH
AMADEN, Arlene C and Joseph A KING, 15 May 1936 Nashua, NH
AMARAL, Robert L and JoAnn A LARGY, 02 Jan 1982 Litchfield, NH
AMATO, Philip D and Susan M REDDY, 14 Apr 1973 Nashua, NH
AMBAR, Eugenia P and Jose E R PIMENTAL, 05 Jul 1984 Hudson, NH
AMBROSE, David J and Elaine M SIMARANO, 18 Jan 1969 Hudson, NH
AMES, Linda M and Alan F LOCICERO, 10 Apr 1971 Pelham, NH
AMES, Seth N and Nancy W BOSQUET, 23 Nov 1979 Hollis, NH
AMOS, Melbourne and Marie M ALLEN, 29 Jan 1949 Hudson, NH
AMOUR, Emma D and Gilburt KUIVILLE, 16 Aug 1919 Nashua, NH

HUDSON, NH MARRIAGES

AMSDEN, Dorothy L and James F MOORE, 11 Aug 1962 Alton, NH
ANAGNOST, William & Antonia PANAGOULIS, 11 Sep 1948 Manchester, NH
ANASTAS, Georgianna and William J SKEAHAN, 04 Oct 1952 Hudson, NH
ANASTASOFF, Robert G and Brenda J SOUCY, 09 Aug 1980 Hudson, NH
ANCTIL, Albert and Evelyn GUAY, 08 Sep 1945 Hudson, NH
ANCTIL, Albert R and Elaine A PARADISE, 05 Feb 1982 Nashua, NH
ANCTIL, Denis J and Denise Ann LABELLE, 07 Dec 1974 Nashua, NH
ANCTIL, Diane J and David P EDELSTEIN, 22 Nov 1970 Nashua, NH
ANCTIL, Elaine M and Roger J FULLER, 08 May 1971 Nashua, NH
ANCTIL, Karen Ann and Kevin Wayn PLANTE, 13 Jun 1981 Nashua, NH
ANCTIL, Lucille A and Robert L DENIS, 04 Jul 1942 Nashua, NH
ANCTIL, Marguerite and Carl E ROBERTS, 30 May 1968 Nashua, NH
ANCTIL, Sylvio and Claire ARCHAMBAULT, 23 Jun 1945 Nashua, NH
ANDERSEN, Carol A and Roger J BESSETTE, 23 Aug 1958 Hudson, NH
ANDERSON, Alfred J and Bertha M GOWING, 01 May 1960 Hudson, NH
ANDERSON, Carl H and Olivette B ESPOSITO, 18 May 1984 Nashua, NH
ANDERSON, Chris M and Linda A KULA, 28 Aug 1982 Manchester, NH
ANDERSON, Dawn E and James C MacDONALD, 04 Sep 1983 Windham, NH
ANDERSON, Elizabeth and Pedro B PEREZ, 23 Dec 1983 Hudson, NH
ANDERSON, George H and Mary F BENSON, 10 Oct 1896 Hudson, NH
  John Anderson (Melrose, MA) & Abbie Munro (Boston, MA)
  C E Benson & Helen Eames (Henry, ME)
ANDERSON, Ivar and June EASTWOOD, 25 Oct 1940 Hudson, NH
ANDERSON, Jeffrey P and Brenda A BARITEAU, 27 Jul 1983 Hudson, NH
ANDERSON, Marion E and George E CAVANAUGH, 27 Jul 1949 Hudson, NH
ANDERSON, Mary E and Bruce R JASPER, 28 Jun 1968 Nashua, NH
ANDERSON, Olinda L and Homer W FLANDERS, 08 Jul 1905 Hudson, NH
  Charles Anderson
  Charles A Flanders & Annie Welch
ANDERSON, Richard O and Geraldine O'NEIL, 22 Feb 1934 Hudson, NH
ANDERSON, Ruth E and William F ROGERS, 02 Jun 1937 Hudson, NH
ANDERSON, Susan A and Raymond H BONENFANT, 20 Jun 1964 Nashua, NH
ANDERSON, Theodore A and Pearl May SOWER, 13 Jun 1907 Hudson, NH
  Ole Anderson & Tenker Oleson
  Harvey Lower & Mary Vintener
ANDRE, Janine A H and Robert S SCHWARTZ, 06 Sep 1963 Hudson, NH
ANDREW, Alice M and Charles R WHITTEMORE, 28 Nov 1935 Nashua, NH
ANDREW, Arnold and Carrie E CONNELL, 24 May 1901 Nashua, NH
  Robert Andrew (England) & Emma Thorn (England)
  Robert T Connell(Hudson, NH) & Mary E Marshall (Hudson, NH)
ANDREW, Doris V and Henry L NIXON, 07 Jul 1951 Hudson, NH
ANDREW, Robert A and Violet DORHERTY, 29 Jan 1921 Hudson, NH
ANDREW, Robert A and Dorothy B BELAND, 26 Apr 1969 Hudson, NH
ANDREW, Robert A and Marion R DINGLE, 07 Apr 1973 Hudson, NH
ANDREW, Walter and Ida Esther GROVES, 22 Oct 1902 Hudson, NH
  Robert Andrew & Emma Thorns
  Robert Groves & Elizabeth Boyle
ANDREWS, Abigail and John CHASE, 04 Dec 1854
ANDREWS, Allen and Asenath HILLS, 30 Mar 1824
ANDREWS, Allen B and Josephine GOWING, 01 Sep 1914 Hudson, NH
  Arthur S Andrews & Linnie F Butler
  Sidney P Gowing & Clemintine Fuller
ANDREWS, Arthur S and Linnie F BUTLER, 20 Apr 1882 Hudson, NH
  Robert A Andrews (Hudson, NH) & Mary M Keniston (Andover, NH)
  Henry Butler(Pelham, NH) & Belinda Smith (Hudson, NH)
ANDREWS, Chester A and Ada L BRITTON, 01 Jun 1915 Nashua, NH
  William A Andrews (Hudson, NH) & Willette Annis (Londonderry, NH)
  Arthur W Britton(W Milan, NH) & Tilea L Chadwick (Norwich, VT)
ANDREWS, Deena J and David A LEVESQUE, 30 Apr 1983 Hudson, NH
ANDREWS, Donna A and John R DUDLEY, 07 Nov 1981 Nashua, NH

HUDSON, NH MARRIAGES

ANDREWS, Elizabeth and Charles ANNABLE, 11 Jul 1919 Hudson, NH
ANDREWS, Helen A and Harrison E SMALL, 16 Oct 1917 Hudson, NH
ANDREWS, Herb and Jane C KINLEY, 26 Sep 1966 Hudson, NH
ANDREWS, Howard A and Ina L BROWN, 12 May 1908 Nashua, NH
   Arthur S Andrews & Linnie F Butler
   Henry C Brown & Clara L Bryant
ANDREWS, John and Lucy A FARWELL, 16 Sep 1851
ANDREWS, Mary Jane and Harvard P SMITH, 28 Jan 1864
ANDREWS, Mary Jane and Howard P SMITH, 28 Jan 1864
ANDREWS, Nathan and Abigail JONES, 27 May 1819
ANDREWS, Olga Marsh and Henry Lee PAINE, 22 May 1938 Nashua, NH
ANDREWS, Robert A and Mary M KENISTON, 12 May 1853
ANDREWS, Robert A and Mary E CHASE, 17 Apr 1879 Nashua, NH
   Allen Andrews (Hudson, NH) & Asinath Hills (Litchfield)
   Moody Chase(Hudson, NH) & Submit Marshall (Hudson, NH)
ANDREWS, Rufus D and Almira SMITH, 13 Nov 1853
ANDREWS, Sarah and Stephen C MARSHALL, 12 Apr 1814
ANDREWS, Virginia A and Horace L EMMONS, 11 Apr 1975 Hudson, NH
ANDREWS, William A and Williette ANNIS, 23 Dec 1885 Nashua, NH
   Robert A Andrews (Hudson, NH) & Mary M Keniston (Andover, NH)
   Geo W Annis(Londonderry, NH) & Alvira French (Litchfield, NH)
ANDREWS, William L III & Karen L BRIGGS, 16 May 1980 Harrisville,NH
ANDRIKOWICH, Denitry and Annie LULA, 21 Oct 1932 Nashua, NH
ANGELO, Rita M and Valdamas VERSECKES, 04 May 1946 Hudson, NH
ANGER, David P and Paula M ABBOTT, 01 Jun 1973 Hudson, NH
ANGER, David P and Carla A LEVESQUE, 15 Oct 1977 Hudson, NH
ANGER, Mark J and Mariane A FAUTEUX, 30 Jul 1977 Nashua, NH
ANGER, Paul H E and Jeannette BONVILLE, 24 Jul 1954 Hudson, NH
ANGER, Paul H E and Donna L LEVESQUE, 16 Apr 1971 Hudson, NH
ANGER, Paula M and Donald R DROUIN, 26 May 1984 Hudson, NH
ANGLUIN, Robert J and Alice M FRAZA, 22 Jun 1957 Hudson, NH
ANGWIN, Nancy A and Raymond P RICHARD, 22 Jun 1957 Concord, NH
ANNABLE, Charles and Elizabeth ANDREWS, 11 Jul 1919 Hudson, NH
ANNABLE, Ellen M and James L HILLS, 21 Jun 1947 Hudson, NH
ANNABLE, Shirley J and Leonard A BIRON, 05 Jun 1954 Nashua, NH
ANNABLE, Thelma I and Berkley E SWINERTON, 23 Mar 1974 Hudson, NH
ANNALORO, Dianne M and Charles V DEMOSS, 02 Jul 1966 Nashua, NH
ANNIS, Eliza Jane and William P ANNIS, 17 Feb 1862
ANNIS, Emma E and Enoch E CHASE, 11 Jun 1873 Hudson, NH
ANNIS, Everett P and Cathine M McARTHUR, 24 Apr 1900 Hudson, NH
   N P Annis & Drusetta Stearns
   William McArthur & Mary Canick
ANNIS, Frank and Marion D LYNN, 14 Oct 1940 Lowell, MA
ANNIS, Frank J and Angra S GLOVER, 15 Mar 1876 Hudson, NH
ANNIS, Fred A and Lellie R WATKINS, 24 Jan 1901 Hudson, NH
   Wm P Annis (Londonderry, NH) & Drusetta S Stearns (Lincolnville)
   John O Clark(Hopkinton) & Arvilla J Runnells (Deering)
ANNIS, Harold J and Madeline HARWOOD, 24 May 1944 Dracut, MA
ANNIS, Joseph F and Jenny TAYLOR, 15 Feb 1871 Hudson, NH
ANNIS, Joseph F and Sarah A GOULD, 15 Mar 1876
ANNIS, Ruth and Roland VENNE, 15 Nov 1941 Dracut, MA
ANNIS, Susan and Gary L STETZLER, 27 Aug 1977 Nashua, NH
ANNIS, William C and Evelyn F HARTSHORN, 04 Sep 1954 Milford, NH
ANNIS, William C and Barbara J YORK, 29 Jan 1966 Warner, NH
ANNIS, William P and Eliza Jane ANNIS, 17 Feb 1862
ANNIS, Williette and William A ANDREWS, 23 Dec 1885 Nashua, NH
   Geo W Annis (Londonderry, NH) & Alvira French (Litchfield, NH)
   Robert A Andrews(Hudson, NH) & Mary M Keniston (Andover, NH)
ANNON, John W Jr and Shirley A JOHNSON, 06 May 1950 Hudson, NH
ANTHONY, Philip and Barbara A FITZPATRICK, 26 Aug 1950 Hudson, NH

HUDSON, NH MARRIAGES

ANTON, Ronald P and Claire M DIONNE, 20 Feb 1971 Nashua, NH
APRIL, Charles H and Loretta Jean BOLDUC, 21 Jul 1978 Hudson, NH
APRIL, Norman R and Norma N TURNER, 05 Aug 1950 Hudson, NH
ARBETTER, Joseph D and Anna SILVERSTEIN, 28 Sep 1927 Nashua, NH
ARBOUR, Bernice J and Leopold LAVOIE, 28 Jun 1969 Nashua, NH
ARCHAMBAULT, Claire and Sylvio ANCTIL, 23 Jun 1945 Nashua, NH
ARCHAMBAULT, Edith M and Ronald MacDONALD, 26 Feb 1955 Hudson, NH
ARCHAMBAULT, Joseph D A and Marie R MORIN, 27 Jul 1960 Hudson, NH
ARCHAMBAULT, Judith C & Peter A SEDLEWICZ, 02 Sep 1966 Manchester,NH
ARCHAMBAULT, Richard G and Debra J BAKER, 04 Sep 1983 Nashua, NH
ARCHAMBAULT, William P and Joann MARQUIS, 06 Feb 1977 Nashua, NH
ARCHAMBEAULT, David A & Marilyn S MORGAN, 30 Jun 1973 Merrimack, NH
ARCHAMBEAULT, Joseph L & Lorranie R D'AMOUR, 21 Jan 1950 Nashua, NH
ARCHAMBEAULT, Richard P and Jean M LUCIANO, 22 May 1981 Nashua, NH
AREL, Barbara M and Donald R LAREAU, 24 Sep 1966 Hudson, NH
AREL, Carol G and Paul J KEARNS, 26 Jun 1971 Nashua, NH
AREL, Diane M and Donald A ROBERT, 14 Jul 1973 Hudson, NH
AREL, Leon R and Marie J MARCOTTE, 06 Jan 1968 Hudson, NH
AREL, Lorraine M and Thomas P GALIPEAU, 06 Jan 1978 Hudson, NH
AREL, Theresa C and Larry E MAIN, 01 Jun 1968 Hudson, NH
AREY, Theresa A and Kenneth R GROFF, 01 May 1982 Nashua, NH
ARGUIN, Barbara E and Joseph GRIGAS, 12 Jun 1954 Nashua, NH
ARMOUR, Robert J and Barbara F BURNS, 08 May 1937 Nashua, NH
ARMS, William H and Susan E BALLOU, 24 Jan 1929 Hudson, NH
ARMSTRONG, Alice K and Charles C CANNEY, 21 Apr 1920 Hudson, NH
ARMSTRONG, Clifford G and Anna A FORRENCE, 25 Feb 1941 Nashua, NH
ARMSTRONG, Donald J and Michelle R GROFF, 27 Oct 1984 Hudson, NH
ARMSTRONG, Elizabeth and Antonio C MOSQUEDA, 14 May 1948 Hudson, NH
ARMSTRONG, Hattie J and Addison L CROP, 16 Oct 1876 Hudson, NH
ARMSTRONG, Oscar O and Hattie J MARSHALL, 14 Nov 1868 Hudson, NH
ARMSTRONG, Oscar O and Nellie J TITCOMB, 14 Mar 1877 Hudson, NH
ARNOLD, Catherine and Kevin M McARTHUR, 13 Apr 1985 Hudson, NH
ARNOLD, Delores A and Leo J BASTILLE, 03 Nov 1978 Hudson, NH
ARNOLD, Delores A and Carroll R FAVRE, 20 Jun 1969 Hudson, NH
ARNOLD, Gary W and Bessie TSOTSIS, 19 Aug 1972 Manchester, NH
ARNOLD, Preston T and Betty A HALEN, 18 Nov 1978 Hudson, NH
ARNOLD, Roger M and Delores A RILEY, 06 Dec 1962 Hudson, NH
ARPIN, Carmel F and Paul E JACQUES, 04 May 1957 Hudson, NH
ARPIN, Dennis C and Kelly A DOWLING, 29 May 1976 Hudson, NH
ARPIN, Peter and Marie Anna LEVESQUE, 20 Oct 1934 Nashua, NH
ARRAGG, Lillian N and Clair A CARLSON, 02 Apr 1949 Hudson, NH
ARREDONDO, Paula K & Kenneth A GREENSPAN, 27 Apr 1985 Manchester,NH
ARRIS, Barbara L and Donald P P GADILAUSKAS, 26 Aug 1982 Nashua, NH
ARRUDA, Lorraine M and John F SILVA, 08 Jan 1949 Hudson, NH
ARSENAULT, Donna J and William J MUNROE, 05 Feb 1982 Hudson, NH
ARSENAULT, James R and Dianna L PENNO, 06 Jun 1980 Nashua, NH
ARSENAULT, Jane E and Mark A PIDHORODECKY, 20 Jul 1969 Nashua, NH
ARSENAULT, Lawrence P and Diane T TANGUAY, 29 Sep 1973 Hudson, NH
ARSENAULT, Leo H and Yoland M C LEVESQUE, 30 Jul 1949 Hudson, NH
ARSENAULT, Lynn A and Kelvin F RHODES, 06 Feb 1977 Hudson, NH
ARSENEAULT, William M and Pamela L HOVEY, 14 Jul 1984 Nashua, NH
ARVISAIS, Esther I and Harvey MEUNIER, 18 Dec 1948 Hudson, NH
ASHFORD, Karen B and James M IVES, 06 Apr 1985 Hudson, NH
ASHFORD, Shirley E and Ronald E RIVARD, 02 May 1959 Hudson, NH
ASPREY, Raymond W and Dawn F WILSON, 04 Oct 1980 Hudson, NH
ASSELIN, Alan A and Carrie R COLBY, 06 Sep 1974 Manchester, NH
ASSELIN, Alecia Ann and Phillip E OUELLETTE, 07 Nov 1981 Hudson, NH
ASSELIN, Anita J and Arthur G GUERETTE, 26 Apr 1968 Nashua, NH
ASSELIN, Roger E and Gertrude D DUBE, 27 Nov 1952 Hudson, NH
ATHERTON, George C and Martha K RIPLEY, 30 Jun 1865

HUDSON, NH MARRIAGES

ATKINS, Grace M and Wallace W ROWELL, 14 Jun 1936 Hudson, NH
ATKINS, Rita and Peter DUBOWIK, 28 Jun 1952 Nashua, NH
ATKINSON, A Jack and Lucille M BERNARD, 11 Jan 1974 Hudson, NH
ATKINSON, Arlene M and Paul R MARQUIS, 11 Sep 1982 Merrimack, NH
ATKINSON, Mona J and Ernest G STONE, 13 Jul 1956 Canterbury, NH
ATWOOD, Abijah and Betsy SMITH, 30 Dec 1819
ATWOOD, Edward S and Pamela C PERRY, 22 Aug 1950 Hudson, NH
ATWOOD, Salley and John R HAMBLET, 09 May 1824
ATWOOD, Sally and John HAMBLETT, 09 May 1824
ATWOOD, William and Electa HAYWOOD, 03 Mar 1843
AUBERTIN, Scott J and Anne M LEBOEUF, 31 Jul 1982 Hudson, NH
AUBUT, Joseph A and Marie B GIROUARD, 07 Nov 1932 Nashua, NH
AUDET, Joseph D and Marie A CONSIGNY, 11 Apr 1921 Nashua, NH
AUDET, Kerin E and James E BELLISLE, 11 Jul 1981 Hudson, NH
AUDET, Real J and Claire T MAYNARD, 22 Jun 1963 Nashua, NH
AUDETTE, Daniel N and Deborah J WILKINSON, 22 Sep 1979 Raymond, NH
AUDETTE, Estella B and Howard F SWAIN, 06 Aug 1960 Hudson, NH
AUDETTE, Nancy Ann and Robert H MOODY, 01 Jun 1973 Hudson, NH
AUDETTE, Paul J and Linda CARROLL, 06 Jul 1973 Hudson, NH
AUGER, Beverly J and Paul D McKENNA, 28 Jul 1981 Londonderry, NH
AURELIO, Concetta J and Pasquale CORSARO, 21 Jan 1950 Hudson, NH
AUSTIN, Andrew M and Theresa L TETRAULT, 12 Feb 1983 Hudson, NH
AUSTIN, Harold L and Henrietta MORTON, 03 Nov 1946 Hudson, NH
AUSTIN, Harold R and Marion L JOLICOEUR, 23 Aug 1948 Hudson, NH
AUSTIN, Hazel J and Olin John COCHRAN, 18 Jul 1975 Hudson, NH
AUSTIN, Jewell A and James W Jr WIGGIN, 24 Nov 1955 Hudson, NH
AUSTIN, Malinda and Jasper M LEWIS, 17 Apr 1853
AUSTIN, Mary and David CLOW, 28 Aug 1783
AUSTIN, Raymond E and Lillian M FORTIER, 11 Sep 1948 Hudson, NH
AUTTELET, Lorraine I and Romeo J LEDOUX, 02 Dec 1967 Hudson, NH
AVEDISIAN, Cynthia R and Albert P TETREAU, 09 Aug 1981 Salem, NH
AVERILL, Myra and Harvey H ROBINSON, 08 May 1871 Hudson, NH
AVERY, Frank E and Florence E PUTNAM, 27 Aug 1889 Hudson, NH
   J M Avery (Londonderry, NH) & Julia A Upton (Dunstable, MA)
   M A S Putnam(Danvers, MA) & Lizzie Cross (Litchfield, NH)
AVILA, Dolores and Gerald R ABBOTT, 03 Dec 1977 Hudson, NH
AXTELL, Brian A and Pamela S RAND, 15 Oct 1983 Londonderry, NH
AXTMAN, Bruce P and Antonette ZACCAGNINI, 21 Mar 1981 Hudson, NH
AXTMAN, Stephen F and Katherine JOHNSON, 30 Jun 1979 Hudson, NH
AYER, Constance and Howard E BARTLETT, 18 Feb 1965 Nashua, NH
AYER, Hannah and Stephen WEBSTER, 24 Mar 1663
AYER, William E Jr and Ruth B MAXFIELD, 14 May 1960 Nashua, NH
AYLWARD, Thomas R and Maureen A CLARK, 01 Sep 1979 Salem, NH
AZEVEDO, Virginia R & Walter L III STOWELL, 25 Apr 1982 Hudson, NH
BABCOCK, Vera P and Albert E WESTON, 10 Oct 1936 Hudson, NH
BABIN, Virginia M and Lawrence H SEGGELIN, 01 Jun 1934 Nashua, NH
BABINEAU, Laura A and Richard W STANDISH, 02 Sep 1983 Hudson, NH
BACHE, Janet L and Robert E GARDNER, 06 Feb 1958 Hudson, NH
BACON, Geniene A and Jeffery P MAYO, 30 Mar 1985 Hudson, NH
BADGER, Nellie E and George A PERHAM, 22 Dec 1908 Hudson, NH
   Lovejoy & Ellen R Hardy
   William M Perham & Susan H Clark
BAENDALE, Doris H and Richard H DILL, 28 Dec 1947 Hudson, NH
BAGLEY, Charlotte and John W HARWOOD, 28 Nov 1946 Nashua, NH
BAGLEY, Gerald W and Charlotte BUTTRICK, 06 Apr 1918 Nashua, NH
BAGLEY, Thelma and Armand P LAMONTAGNE, 22 Oct 1937 Nashua, NH
BAGLEY, Vera M and Ralph A ESTY, 24 Jun 1922 Hudson, NH
BAHAM, Amos N and Gloria S SINGLETARY, 03 Jan 1956 Hudson, NH
BAILEY, Albon H and Alcinda WASON, 01 Sep 1864
BAILEY, Austin and Martha J WALKER, 05 Sep 1860

HUDSON,NH MARRIAGES

BAILEY, B Richard and Patricia A LECLERC, 01 Sep 1979 Hudson, NH
BAILEY, Barbara E and Gordon C LESLIE, 01 May 1933 Nashua, NH
BAILEY, Charles A and Elizabeth COLBURN, 02 Sep 1847
BAILEY, Clyde M and Violet F MILLER, 29 Nov 1934 Hudson, NH
BAILEY, Doris E and Archie KING, 17 Nov 1944 Hudson, NH
BAILEY, Dorothy A and Phillip E Jr SMALLEY, 01 Jun 1985 Nashua, NH
BAILEY, Herbert A and Maybelle LOVELAND, 16 Jul 1910 Nashua, NH
  Mason T Bailey & Emma J Porter
  Orville Loveland & Jennie Harding
BAILEY, Herbert R and Annie R LONG, 08 Apr 1879 Hudson, NH
  Samuel N Bailey (West Wilton) & Adaline Winn (Dunstable, MA)
  Samuel Long(Ireland) & Margaret Lockhart (Ireland)
BAILEY, June A and Raymond E PETTS, 25 Jun 1949 Nashua, NH
BAILEY, Margery L and Charles H HARDY, 25 Sep 1954 Nashua, NH
BAILEY, Marion E and Joseph L PORTER, 09 Feb 1946 Hudson, NH
BAILEY, Thomas C and Roseann MORIN, 26 Jun 1976 Hudson, NH
BAILEY, William H and Rosa NEWMAN, 09 Feb 1881 Hudson, NH
  Benjamin Bailey & Sarah Chase
  Samuel Newman & Julia
BAKAIAN, Bruce K and Linda Anne CARPENTIER, 24 Nov 1973 Pelham, NH
BAKAIAN, Keith A and Colleen E O'NEIL, 07 Jul 1967 Hudson, NH
BAKER, Bryan S and Dale L HOLT, 21 Jun 1985 Nashua, NH
BAKER, Calvin E and Phyllis A LACKIE, 14 Sep 1974 Hudson, NH
BAKER, Constance and Allan F GOODWIN, 01 Sep 1962 Hudson, NH
BAKER, Debra J and Richard G ARCHAMBAULT, 04 Sep 1983 Nashua, NH
BAKER, Donald R and Sharon YATES, 29 May 1976 Hudson, NH
BAKER, Edward J and Edith S DENNETT, 30 Dec 1945 Hudson, NH
BAKER, Etta I and Scott W McGLORY, 05 Apr 1902 Hudson, NH
  Henry J Squires & Mary Nash
  R L McGlory & Julia Nutter
BAKER, Janice G and George E LENZ, 19 Nov 1957 Hudson, NH
BAKER, Jean F and Joseph K POLLOCK, 24 Apr 1954 Hudson, NH
BAKER, Joan E and Douglas A HARRIS, 28 Aug 1976 Nashua, NH
BAKER, John E and Vera R TIERNEY, 05 Nov 1927 Nashua, NH
BAKER, John H and Louisa U WEBSTER, 09 Dec 1846
BAKER, John R and Lois M OLSON, 23 Dec 1950 Marlboro, NH
BAKER, Joseph A and Dora BARRETT, 15 Sep 1917 Nashua, NH
BAKER, Leslie L and Rita R BERGERON, 25 Feb 1954 Durham, NH
BAKER, Lucius T and Fanny SHECTE, 28 Nov 1861
BAKER, Lucy and William McINTIRE, 22 May 1893 Hudson, NH
  E Baker (New York) & Josephine Fagto (New York)
  John McIntire(Canada) & Marion Wells (Canada)
BAKER, Lydia M and Moses WEBSTER, 16 Dec 1841
BAKER, Mary J and Ernest G ESTY, 02 Jun 1926 Hudson, NH
BAKER, Oswald P and Letitia M CHURCH, 27 Mar 1895 Boston, MA
  Elijah Baker & Juliaette Baker
  Reuben Church & Mary O
BAKER, Reuben J and Frances A MALONEY, 04 Jun 1928 Hudson, NH
BAKER, Robert Lee Jr & Corinne A VAILLANCOURT, 15 Sep 1984 Hudson,NH
BAKER, Sally and Mark H WEBSTER, 29 Jan 1837
BAKER, Sarah E and Richard E GRAY, 15 Jul 1934 Hudson, NH
BAKER, Shirley A and Anthony C KENTRA, 12 Apr 1947 Nashua, NH
BAKER, Sidney F & Frances M SLAVIN, 18 Jun 1928 Dunstable, MA
BAKER, Thomas L and Kristina A BRACKENBUSCH, 28 Aug 1982 Hudson, NH
BAKER, Wallace G and Helen Beatrice SMITH, 22 Jul 1928 Hudson, NH
BAKER, William W and Norma M EDMUNDS, 22 Sep 1956 Nashua, NH
BALDWIN,   and William CROSS, 03 Jan 1858
BALDWIN, Anstris B and Egbert O WOOD, 25 Dec 1867
BALDWIN, Anstris P and Egbert O WOOD, 25 Dec 1867
BALDWIN, Henry and Abigail BUTLER, 26 May 1743

HUDSON,NH MARRIAGES

BALDWIN, John F and Eliza A LUND, 27 May 1856
BALDWIN, Lizzie J and Charles H TOWLE, 20 Aug 1871
BALDWIN, Rosalina and Merton L Jr DUNCKLEE, 25 May 1974 Hudson, NH
BALDWIN, Violet and Vern Y STEEVES, 19 Feb 1931 Nashua, NH
BALICKI, Wanda R and James W WILSON, 01 Aug 1935 Hudson, NH
BALL, Ella E and Nathan O MARSHALL, 09 Sep 1869 Hudson, NH
BALL, Terrance C and Noreen D LORDAN, 02 Jul 1966 N Stratford, NH
BALLEW, Esther E and Romeo RANDAZZO, 31 Dec 1949 Nashua, NH
BALLOU, Susan E and William H ARMS, 24 Jan 1929 Hudson, NH
BALLUM, John N Jr and Patrice C McCLUSKEY, 07 Oct 1949 Hudson, NH
BALSAMO, Mario and Carol-Ann CARDOZA, 27 May 1983 Hudson, NH
BALSER, John F and Linda Lou ROY, 21 Jul 1972 Nashua, NH
BALSER, Marcia E and Stanley E Jr PULLEN, 03 Feb 1974 Hudson, NH
BALUTS, George G and Cortena TSVOULEA, 07 Sep 1921 Manchester, NH
BAMFORTH, Paul E and Ann G HANSEN, 07 Feb 1950 Hudson, NH
BANAKOS, Charles N and Terri L MORRISON, 22 Jun 1975 Hudson, NH
BANCROFT, Elizabeth and Joseph BUTTERFIELD, 03 Mar 1785
BANCROFT, Frank C and Olive N DERBY, 11 Nov 1865
BANCROFT, Fred W and Sarah GUIOTT, 18 Sep 1880 Hudson, NH
BANCROFT, J Kendall and Callie E YOUNG, 03 Jun 1939 Hudson, NH
BANEY, Timothy H and Susan M LABBE, 02 Dec 1978 Hudson, NH
BANKS, Archie E and Ethel M ELSON, 05 Aug 1935 Hudson, NH
BANKS, David G and R Lynn DESCHENAUX, 24 Apr 1976 Hudson, NH
BANKS, Quentin H and Ruth A HASKELL, 31 Dec 1935 Nashua, NH
BANNON, Carl J and Frances L WOODMAN, 17 Jun 1972 Claremont, NH
BARANOWSKA, Helen B and Leon E BELAND, 02 Aug 1950 Hudson, NH
BARBARITO, Nicholas J and Mary A MARGESON, 12 Apr 1974 Hudson, NH
BARBER, Lena May and Everett W MUNN, 12 Feb 1933 Hudson, NH
BARBOUR, Irene M and Robert D DAME, 27 Nov 1952 Nashua, NH
BARBOUR, Paul F and Barbara E HEYDWEILLER, 10 May 1974 Hudson, NH
BARBOUR, Sally J and Mark A SCHOFIELD, 30 Jun 1984 Nashua, NH
BARCLAY, Marlene R and Joseph M CASILLO, 31 Jul 1976 Hudson, NH
BARDAS, Melba A and Earl C BURTON, 11 Feb 1956 Hudson, NH
BARDSLEY, Diana E and Edward D SHIEBLER, 10 Sep 1955 Nashua, NH
BARDSLEY, Harold J and Mildred A BENNETT, 27 Jul 1946 Hudson, NH
BARDSLEY, James H III and Nancy A MANNING, 26 Nov 1983 Nashua, NH
BARDSLEY, Norma L and Roger P TERRILL, 15 Oct 1960 Hudson, NH
BARDSLEY, Richard A and Monique J POULIN, 23 Nov 1974 Hudson, NH
BARGER, Mark W and Pauline QUINNO, 11 Nov 1984 Nashua, NH
BARINGER, Candace S and Richard Ch WHARTON, 04 Jul 1981 Nashua, NH
BARITEAU, Brenda A and Jeffrey P ANDERSON, 27 Jul 1983 Hudson, NH
BARITEAU, Lois M and Dennis P BROWN, 23 Jan 1965 Nashua, NH
BARKER, Angeline and Charles K BARKER, 04 Apr 1861
BARKER, Carl E and Margaret E BAXTER, 22 Nov 1913 Hudson, NH
  E J Barker & Lizzie Wheeler
  Robert Snodgrass & Mary A Noble
BARKER, Charles K and Angeline BARKER, 04 Apr 1861
BARKER, Ella A and Elmer C WINN, 16 Sep 1885 N Chelmsford, MA
  James Barker(Windham, NH) & Agnes L Park(Windham, NH)
  ·Paul T Winn(Hudson, NH) & Fanny B Parkhurst(Wilton, NH)
BARKER, Lucius T and Fannie STEELE, 28 Nov 1861
BARKER, Myrtle D and Joseph C DEBRAVA, 17 Jan 1981 Nashua, NH
BARKER, Walter Lor and Edith Eliz MARSH, 11 Jun 1914 Hudson, NH
  Allen F Barker & Emma J Dunklee
  Walter H Marsh & Addie E Mason
BARLOW, Claire T and Roger W PELLAND, 02 Jun 1956 Hudson, NH
BARNARD, James and Abigail MARSHALL, 14 Mar 1816
BARNARD, Jessie M and Hosmer C CHURCH, 19 Apr 1905 Hudson, NH
  Homer C Barnard & Addie E Taylor
  Edward A Church & Harriet Corbin

HUDSON,NH MARRIAGES

BARNARD, Lena M and James O McCOY, 20 Jun 1943 Nashua, NH
BARNARD, Robert R and Deborah E BOLTON, 08 Sep 1979 Hudson, NH
BARNES, Angeline W and John H GILE, 14 Oct 1836
BARNES, Charles E and Susan A DUCHARME, 02 Aug 1975 Hudson, NH
BARNES, Charles W and Emma M MORSE, 29 Jun 1872 Hudson, NH
BARNES, Cleyon D and Linda M MUNROE, 28 Nov 1970 Hudson, NH
BARNES, Dana E and Mary Jane TRUDEAU, 28 Jun 1980 Hudson, NH
BARNES, Herbert B and Enez L KNAPP, 13 Jan 1875 Hudson, NH
BARNES, Jane and Robert GLOVER, 29 Oct 1741
BARNES, Linda M and Donald R BISTANY, 29 Jun 1974 Nashua, NH
BARNES, Nancy J and James R CAMPBELL, 28
BARNES, Reuben and Emily F WINN, 22 Jan 1854
BARNES, Robert E & Barbara A VANDER-HEYDEN, 06 Sep 1977 Hudson, NH
BARNES, Roy L and Joan P LACHANCE, 03 May 1969 Hudson, NH
BARNES, Sarah and Gideon PUTNAM, 19 Sep 1799
BARNES, Sarah and Samuel SPRAKE, 17 Oct 1830
BARNES, Vernon L and Denise M DUBE, 12 May 1973 Derry, NH
BARNES, William S and Lona J LAINEY, 14 May 1977 Nashua, NH
BARNET, James and Sally WASON, 02 Mar 1800
BARNETT, Robert W and Sophie A STANAVICH, 25 Oct 1947 Hudson, NH
BARNEY, Richard E and Lucille BONNER, 28 Sep 1938 Hudson, NH
BARNS, Francis and Lizzie HILDRETH, 13 Oct 1859
BARNS, Herbert B and Eva L KNAPP, 13 Jun 1875 Hudson, NH
BARNS, Marrietta and David E TAINTER, 15 Sep 1876 Nashua, NH
BARNS, Martha C and Alfred CUMMINGS, 24 Feb 1833
BARR, Melanie S and Glenn N JOZIATIS, 18 Feb 1967 Hudson, NH
BARREIRO, Mark A and Linda A WOLFSON, 12 Feb 1983 Hudson, NH
BARRESE, Marie A and David L HORKEY, 07 Dec 1973 Hudson, NH
BARRET, Margaret A and Edward GOURDEAU, 21 Feb 1928 Manchester, NH
BARRET, William E and Marie A I MIGNEAULT, 29 Jun 1922 Nashua, NH
BARRETT, and Dustin RIPLEY,
BARRETT, Alfred J and Helen MORIARTY, 14 Apr 1920 Nashua, NH
BARRETT, Alice M and Alfred R MITCHELL, 01 Nov 1947 Nashua, NH
BARRETT, Charles E and Achsah FORD, 21 Oct 1871 Hudson, NH
BARRETT, Charles W and Charlotte NELSON, 11 Nov 1852
BARRETT, Coburn and Betsey MARSHALL, 18 May 1817
BARRETT, Dora and Joseph A BAKER, 15 Sep 1917 Nashua, NH
BARRETT, Dorothy I and Thomas C WILLIAMSON, 07 Aug 1965 Hudson, NH
BARRETT, Dr Dustin and Hannah CHADWICK, 08 Jun 1826
BARRETT, Florence L and Roger E SMITH, 11 Jun 1960 Claremont, NH
BARRETT, Gerald F and Louise A HAYES, 01 Jul 1983 Londonderry, NH
BARRETT, Hannah and James WHITTLE, 19 Jan 1797
BARRETT, Helen R and Charles B CAMPBELL, 30 Jul 1955 Nashua, NH
BARRETT, James and Sally WASON, 08 Mar 1800
BARRETT, Jayne M and Elmer J TAYLOR, 04 Feb 1984 Nashua, NH
BARRETT, Julia A and Amos H McCOY, 16 Oct 1862
BARRETT, Kenneth F and Lillian C FARRINGTON, 15 May 1982 Hudson, NH
BARRETT, Leslie M and Burt T WELLS, 19 Jul 1955 Milton, NH
BARRETT, Lilla E and Charles DYER, 31 Mar 1900 Hudson, NH
   Almado Barrett & Annie M Hartford
   Charles Dyer & Zoe Grace
BARRETT, Lilla E and Herbert W MARSHALL, 19 Nov 1891 Nashua, NH
   Alverado Barrett (Hudson, NH) & Anna Hartford (Allenstown, NH)
   Geo W Marshall(Sharon) & Miranda Hadley (Hudson, NH)
BARRETT, Lilla E and Robert W MARSHALL, 19 Nov 1891
BARRETT, Lottie S and Albert LOVEJOY, 29 Apr 1872 Hudson, NH
BARRETT, Marie Avis and Russell L MARCUM, 29 Jul 1972 Nashua, NH
BARRETT, Moses and Nancy WYMAN, 21 Feb 1811
BARRETT, Richard A and Carol A POINTER, 28 Mar 1969 Hudson, NH
BARRETT, Ronald G and Vivianne Y NEPVEU, 19 Apr 1969 Nashua, NH

HUDSON,NH MARRIAGES

BARRETT, Roxie J and Henry SWEET, 10 May 1873 Hudson, NH
BARRETT, Susanna and William MARSH, 15 Feb 1797
BARRIAULT, Alan R and Caren E LAMPER, 31 Mar 1974 Hudson, NH
BARRIAULT, Gary E and Judith E BROWN, 18 Jun 1971 Hollis, NH
BARRIAULT, Leo P and Dianne T CARON, 11 Mar 1972 Hudson, NH
BARRIAULT, Raymond J and Florence M COTE, 01 Sep 1947 Nashua, NH
BARRIEAU, Robert J and Ruth E QUIGLEY, 19 Aug 1978 Sanbornton, NH
BARRIS, Hannah J and William B LEWIS, 28 Aug 1862
BARRISO, Hannah J and William P LEWIS, 22 Aug 1862
BARRON, Alden H and Laura G DUDLEY, 16 Jun 1856
BARRON, Lydia and Samuel GOULD, 26 Nov 1782
BARRON, Martha C and Charles T WHITE, 23 Apr 1850
BARROSO, Henry A and Frances E JULIAN, 19 Apr 1969 Nashua, NH
BARROWS, George and Edna HARDEY, 28 Mar 1782
BARRY, Francis B and Madeline A JEANNOTTE, 17 Sep 1966 Hudson, NH
BARRY, Gertrude C and John S BRENNAN, 09 Sep 1937 Hudson, NH
BARRY, John E and Eula F KREWSKI, 03 Feb 1951 Hudson, NH
BARRY, Nettie L and Chester A WORDEN, 05 Jan 1927 Hudson, NH
BARTER, William H and Elaine S SARGENT, 06 Oct 1972 Nashua, NH
BARTHOLEMEW, Noyes N and Doris Mari WHYMAN, 22 Aug 1937 Hudson, NH
BARTLETT, Alice M and Horace G DURANT, 15 Feb 1958 Hudson, NH
BARTLETT, Arthur H and Pamela T GANNON, 06 Mar 1965 Hudson, NH
BARTLETT, Edna M E and William J PYE, 25 Jan 1934 Nashua, NH
BARTLETT, Frank V and Susie A GERRY, 28 Jul 1910 Hudson, NH
   Wm A Bartlett & Rebecca Valentine
   Elbridge W Gerry & Margaret Connors
BARTLETT, Howard E and Constance AYER, 18 Feb 1965 Nashua, NH
BARTLETT, Robert D and Mary M MASTERS, 11 Oct 1969 Derry, NH
BARTLETT, Robert J and Diane GREEN, 12 Aug 1977 Windham, NH
BARTLETT, Ruth A and Charles A BRAY, 1878
   Morill C Bartlett & Ann O
   L Bray(Deerisle, ME) & Mary E Bray
BARTLETT, Wilhemina and Neville A BOOTH, 16 Jun 1938 Hudson, NH
BARTON, Donald G and Dorothy T SMITH, 06 Sep 1929 Hudson Ctr, NH
BARTON, Helen L and George S AHEARN, 22 Oct 1978 Hudson, NH
BARTON, Jeanne S and Paul A III MOISAN, 21 Dec 1980 Hudson, NH
BARTON, Victor A and Margaret E GRAHAM, 09 Apr 1972 Nashua, NH
BARTOSZWICZ, Veronica and Ernest A DUMONT, 06 May 1937 Hudson, NH
BARVO, Burton and Sandra F SOLOMON, 14 Oct 1950 Hudson, NH
BASANISI, Harry and Florence G HODGKINS, 31 Aug 1924 Hudson, NH
BASCOM, Daniel P and Kimber Lea PELTON, 14 Aug 1976 Rochester, NH
BASHALANY, Patricia M & Jude D CHARPENTIER, 26 Jun 1981 Bristol, NH
BASKIN, Sophie R and Nathan BREDTHOLTZ, 28 Aug 1938 Nashua, NH
BASLEY, Mary E and Oliver B WELLS, 17 Jan 1874 Hudson, NH
BASNAR, Frances E and Joseph E MARTINEAU, 18 Aug 1956 Hudson, NH
BASSETT, Almeda I and Charles H JOHNSON, 08 Jun 1929 Rochester, NH
BASSETT, Joseph and Katie MULHAIR, 12 Aug 1890 Nashua, NH
   Charles H Bassett (Bangor, ME) & Almeda Pomroy (Bangor, ME)
   Michale Mulhair(Ireland) & Bridget McGlynn (Ireland)
BASSETT, O B and F MONTGOMERY, 27 Jun 1916 Lee, NH
   Joseph Bassett (Hudson, NH) & Katie Mulhair (New York)
   Francis Montgomery(Belfast, Ireland) & Ellen Ellis (Ireland)
BASTILLE, Alfred E and Marie L BRIAND, 16 Jan 1971 Hudson, NH
BASTILLE, Alfred E & Marguerite EASTMAN, 27 Apr 1974 Litchfield, NH
BASTILLE, Cecile Y and Donald N SIMARD, 18 Jun 1955 Nashua, NH
BASTILLE, David A and Maire S BEDARD, 21 Nov 1980 Hudson, NH
BASTILLE, Donna M and Steven R PREST, 25 Feb 1978 Hudson, NH
BASTILLE, Leo J and Delores A ARNOLD, 03 Nov 1978 Hudson, NH
BASTILLE, Ronald L and Ann E SAYERS, 23 Jun 1984 Hudson, NH
BATCH, Samuel A and Elsie M SQUIRES, 10 Jan 1876 Nashua, NH

HUDSON, NH MARRIAGES

BATCHELDER, Abbie E and George H DAVIS, 25 Nov 1868
BATCHELDER, Alfaretta and Washington DUSTIN, 08 Feb 1876 Hudson, NH
BATCHELDER, Angie R and Henry L DAVIS, 01 Oct 1872
BATCHELDER, Candace L and Robert F BRIGGS, 27 Jun 1970 Hudson, NH
BATCHELDER, Carria A and Harlan GREGG, 08 Nov 1878 Hudson, NH
  Mark Batchelder & Susan (Hudson, NH)
  Daniel Gregg(New Boston) & H Augusta
BATCHELDER, Chas H and Martha E LUND, 29 Mar 1890 Hudson, NH
  Mark Batchelder (Hill, NH) & Lydia Steele (Hudson, NH)
  Francis Lund(Hollis, NH) & Marcie E Whitaker (Nashua, NH)
BATCHELDER, Cynthia L and Jeffrey L SMITH, 03 Mar 1979 Hudson, NH
BATCHELDER, Herbert L and Lydia J DEXTER, 26 Mar 1887 Haverhill, MA
  Mark Batchelder (Grantham, NH) & Lydia L Steele (Hudson, NH)
  Byron H Dexter(Lisbon, NH) & Jeanette Stickney (Lisbon, NH)
BATCHELDER, Joseph & Bertha CHESBROUGH, 14 Jun 1919 Brattleboro, VT
BATCHELDER, Julia and James F WATSON, 20 May 1875
BATCHELDER, June V and S Wilder BROWN, 21 Feb 1952 Nashua, NH
BATCHELDER, Lucinda F and Sylvester TINKER, 30 Dec 1867
BATCHELDER, Mark and Johanna STEELE, 17 Mar 1842
BATCHELDER, Mark and Lydia STEELE, 13 Dec 1849
BATCHELDER, Mary A and Charles M HOLMES, 25 Nov 1847
BATCHELDER, Reuben and Hannah D JOHNSON, 05 Apr 1896 Hudson, NH
  Jonathan Batchelder (Andover) (Andover)
  John Carter(Concord) & Margaret Dow (Concord,)
BATCHELDER, Reuben and Mary CARLTON, 06 Nov 1766
BATCHELDER, William A and Nira CUMMINGS, 23 Jan 1844
BATCHELDER, William N and Belinda CUMMINGS, Hudson, NH
BATCHELDOR, Abby E and George W DAVIS, 26 Nov 1868 Hudson, NH
BATES, Betty Jane and Gordon R GREEN, 05 May 1965 Hudson, NH
BATES, Maria L and Anthony J VERRILLI, 30 May 1982 Hudson, NH
BATTEY, Theresa L and Raymond H DOUVILLE, 20 Oct 1979 Hudson, NH
BATTLES, Francis J Jr and Joan E PIERCE, 17 Jan 1948 Hudson, NH
BATTS, James L III and Jane C AHRENDT, 17 Aug 1968 Hudson, NH
BATURA, Jennie and Stanley GAWEL, 14 Oct 1944 Nashua, NH
BATURA, Joseph J and Jane V KARCZEWSKI, 07 May 1949 Nashua, NH
BATURA, Michael and Mary SADAUSKIEVE, 11 Feb 1925 Nashua, NH
BATURA, Patricia A and Guy I FARRINGTON, 29 Apr 1967 Hudson, NH
BATURA, Sophie and Stanley ALUKONIS, 20 Dec 1950 Hudson, NH
BATURA, Stanley and Vivian I ROBINSON, 16 Aug 1947 Hudson, NH
BATURA, Stanley and Mary S LATULIPPE, 04 Feb 1963 Hudson, NH
BAUCHMAN, Lloyd D and Judith E SHIEBLER, 05 May 1979 Hudson, NH
BAUER, Barbara E and Robert N CATES, 27 Feb 1982 Hudson, NH
BAUSHA, LuAnn M and Richard A LAQUERRE, 08 Oct 1977 Hudson, NH
BAXTER, Doreen M and Harry DEMANCHE, 03 Dec 1942 Hudson, NH
BAXTER, John E and Esther H GENDRON, 19 May 1941 Nashua, NH
BAXTER, Lillian V and John E MARTIN, 12 Jul 1939 Hudson, NH
BAXTER, Margaret E and Carl E BARKER, 22 Nov 1913 Hudson, NH
  Robert Snodgrass & Mary A Noble
  E J Barker & Lizzie Wheeler
BAYLIS, Thomas J and Kathleen M LAFOREST, 08 Jun 1974 Auburn, NH
BAZINET, Michelle M and Roger R GUIMOND, 17 Nov 1973 Hudson, NH
BEACH, Margaret H and Philip J ROWMAN, 20 Feb 1965 Amherst, NH
BEACHMONT, T R and Annie F BLAKE, 08 Jul 1900 Nashua, NH
  Daniel Beachmont & Margaret (Walsh)
  Roswell Blake
BEADEN, Ellen and Richard GROHOSKY, 24 Jun 1967 Nashua, NH
BEALS, Emma J and Richard BRUCE, 31 Oct 1889 Hudson, NH
  Wm J Beals (Larnstown) & Tracy McGregor (Tremont, N S)
  Henry Bruce(Brooklyn, N S) & Lydia Gustave (Brookfield)
BEALS, Warren E and Lillian S HAYES, 19 Jul 1964 Hudson, NH

HUDSON,NH MARRIAGES

BEAN, Betty L and Robert O Jr PLANTE, 25 Jun 1962 Nashua, NH
BEAN, Harley A and Loretta I STEEVES, 26 Apr 1977 Pelham, NH
BEAN, Loretta F and Steven E ALLEN, 23 Apr 1939 Nashua, NH
BEAN, Robert L and Betty L LILLEY, 05 Sep 1959 Hudson, NH
BEAN, Robert L and Edith M BRIAND, 26 Aug 1963 Hudson, NH
BEAR, Eliza J and Henry M CALDWELL, 23 Nov 1878 Hudson, NH
   Addison M Blankin (Iresburg, VT) & Harriet M (Hudson, NH)
   William Caldwell(Hudson, NH) & Jane (Cape Cod, MA)
BEARD, Wayne C and Linda A RYAN, 12 Sep 1970 Hudson, NH
BEASON, Stephen R and Patricia A STIGLIANI, 06 Aug 1983 Hudson, NH
BEATON, Frederick and Ruth A CONNOLLY, 06 Mar 1948 Hudson, NH
BEATTY, Helen M and Kirk A JONES, 10 Sep 1984 Bedford, NH
BEAUBIEN, Dorothy L and Gordon B TATE, 29 Apr 1950 Hudson, NH
BEAUCAGE, Donald R & Patricia A STAPANOWICH, 25 Mar 1967 Hudson, NH
BEAUCHEMIN, Gerogette and Rene DUVAL, 12 Nov 1938 Manchester, NH
BEAUCHENE, Alfred H and Clara DEMASRAIS, 24 Jun 1913 Nashua, NH
   Joseph Beauchene & Artencen Bolduc
   Joseph Demasrais & Mary Puague
BEAUCHESNE, Michael D and Denise D HEBERT, 20 May 1978 Hudson, NH
BEAUDIN, Florence E and George E RICHARD, 24 Dec 1945 Nashua, NH
BEAUDOIN, Joseph A and Lea R BERTHOLD, 08 Jul 1950 Hudson, NH
BEAUDRY, Daniel A and Debra J DeCOLA, 29 May 1981 Hudson, NH
BEAUDRY, Dennis and Cheryl J POSTON, 13 Apr 1974 Hudson, NH
BEAUDRY, Gene S and Doris M MONACO, 25 Mar 1977 Nashua, NH
BEAUDRY, Michael N and Claudette NADEAU, 14 May 1975 Hudson, NH
BEAUDRY, Mylene J and Bryan M GRIGAS, 30 Dec 1978 Hudson, NH
BEAUDRY, Robert J and Barbara J BUXTON, 09 May 1953 Lebanon, NH
BEAUDRY, Robert J and Michelle GUTHRO, 20 Oct 1979 Hudson, NH
BEAUDRY, Susan M and Michael P BUXTON, 14 May 1971 Nashua, NH
BEAULAC, Patrice R and Michael E LEACH, 06 Sep 1980 Rindge, NH
BEAULE, Rene G and Carolyn M JACQUES, 03 Sep 1959 Manchester, NH
BEAULIEU, Anne M and Robert W SHADLE, 29 Nov 1982 Hudson, NH
BEAULIEU, Dennis L and Emily M LESSARD, 08 Jun 1974 Hudson, NH
BEAULIEU, Keith M and Christine GAGNON, 07 Jun 1985 Nashua, NH
BEAULIEU, Leah A and Michael C VALERAS, 23 Jun 1979 Nashua, NH
BEAULIEU, Lorraine C and Thomas REAGAN, 04 Apr 1952 Hudson, NH
BEAULIEU, Michel J and Michelle A LAVALLEE, 18 Sep 1982 Nashua, NH
BEAULIEU, Nancy R and Gerald A DWIRE, 30 Mar 1979 Hudson, NH
BEAULIEU, Robert L and Sandra J CROSBY, 03 Jun 1972 Hudson, NH
BEAULIEU, Sandra Ann and David M McKINLEY, 04 Jun 1977 Nashua, NH
BEAULIEU, Shirley A and Paul G OUELLETTE, 19 Jan 1979 Hudson, NH
BEAUMIER, Dorothy C and Gilbert J GENDRON, 30 Jul 1950 Hudson, NH
BEAUMONT, Lynne S and Robert A PALLERIA, 15 Jul 1978 Nashua, NH
BEAUMONT, William F and Rose A ROCK, 14 Mar 1954 Nashua, NH
BEAUMONT, William F and Eleanor N CASAVANT, 20 Sep 1969 Nashua, NH
BEAUREGARD, Brenda D & Samuel J Jr CHAPMAN, 05 Nov 1983 Hudson, NH
BEAUREGARD, Carla J and Stephen F RANDALL, 20 Jun 1981 Nashua, NH
BEAUREGARD, Marie C and Rosario N CARISTIA, 15 Nov 1942 Hudson, NH
BEAUREGARDE, Paul G and Josephine WILLIAMS, 23 Nov 1984 Hudson, NH
BECHARD, Daniel C and Betty J BEECHAM, 18 Sep 1965 Hudson, NH
BECHARD, Jeannette and Robert C McCARTHY, 11 Sep 1971 Nashua, NH
BECHARD, Laura O and Conrad A DUCAS, 14 Jun 1969 Hudson, NH
BECHARD, Lea A and Roland L JEAN, 21 Oct 1944 Nashua, NH
BECHARD, Leon R and Kathleen G DESROSIERS, 04 Sep 1972 Hudson, NH
BECHARD, Mona J and Philippe H BOUTHILLIER, 12 Nov 1966 Hudson, NH
BECHARD, Philip R and Tracy A ROBERTS, 07 Nov 1981 Nashua, NH
BECHARD, Rodney D and Sandra G LEMERY, 27 Nov 1965 Nashua, NH
BECKER, Jerome and Donna M LITTLE, 14 May 1983 Hudson, NH
BECKHAM, Carol J and Wayne M PAQUETTE, 06 Nov 1970 Nashua, NH
BEDARD, Edwin C and Pauline L SIMARD, 04 Nov 1961 Hudson, NH

HUDSON, NH MARRIAGES

BEDARD, Irene F and Raymond L PHANEUF, 31 Jan 1946 Hudson, NH
BEDARD, John M and Debra A LEACH, 06 Aug 1983 Nashua, NH
BEDARD, Maire S and David A BASTILLE, 21 Nov 1980 Hudson, NH
BEDFORD, Frederick and Elaine R WILDMAN, 14 May 1945 Nashua, NH
BEDORE, Jean H and Albert R DUMAIS, 21 Sep 1963 Hudson, NH
BEDORE, Joan V and Thomas P PELLETIER, 29 Jul 1967 Hudson, NH
BEEBE, Willard H and Emma L RICHARDSON, 14 Mar 1871
BEEBIE, Hillard F and Gabrielle BRAULT, 15 Nov 1952 Nashua, NH
BEECHAM, Betty J and Daniel C BECHARD, 18 Sep 1965 Hudson, NH
BEEDE, Bruce A and Jean M SCHLAGLE, 17 Jun 1978 Hudson, NH
BEEDE, Bruce Alan and Kim Irene MITCHELL, 08 Sep 1973 Nashua, NH
BEEDE, Cheryl A and William E SARGENT, 20 May 1972 Hudson, NH
BEEDE, Dora M and Percy L ADAMS, 04 May 1972 Hudson, NH
BEIRN, Alice C and George J LEEWITZ, 03 Mar 1923 Portsmouth, NH
BELAND, Dorothy B and Robert A ANDREW, 26 Apr 1969 Hudson, NH
BELAND, Gloria M and Raymond R LAMBERT, 08 Oct 1955 Hudson, NH
BELAND, Irene A and Leslie B SMITH, 27 Jun 1942 Nashua, NH
BELAND, Leon E and Helen B BARANOWSKA, 02 Aug 1950 Hudson, NH
BELAND, Lillian and Leonard RAFFERTY, 25 Mar 1944 Nashua, NH
BELAND, Lorraine M and Robert L CHATTLEY, 07 Apr 1962 Hudson, NH
BELAND, Lucille M and Oscar L DUBE, 17 Jun 1944 Amherst, NH
BELAND, Peter J and Dorothy R BUSWELL, 10 Jul 1959 Hudson, NH
BELAND, Ruth B E and Robert L GIROUARD, 06 Jun 1953 Nashua, NH
BELAND, Yvonne L and Charles G ST LAURENT, 30 Jun 1962 Hudson, NH
BELANGER, Adelard R and Agnes M COMI, 17 Feb 1962 Brookline, NH
BELANGER, Bernadette and Joseph LANDRY, 11 Jun 1917 Nashua, NH
BELANGER, Carolina and Charles V ST MARTIN, 08 May 1924 Nashua, NH
BELANGER, Denise C & Michael C BILODEAU, 11 Feb 1978 Merrimack, NH
BELANGER, Edward J and Elizabeth McCARTHY, 17 Feb 1984 Rye, NH
BELANGER, George R and Kathleen M COLBURN, 16 May 1964 Nashua, NH
BELANGER, Kathleen M and John L FRENETTE, 27 Jun 1981 Hudson, NH
BELANGER, Lilla E and Cleaborn R KIMBERLIN, 20 Jul 1946 Nashua, NH
BELANGER, Linda A and George T SAMUEL, 29 Sep 1982 Nashua, NH
BELANGER, Lorrette M and Richard R CYR, 22 Mar 1975 Nashua, NH
BELANGER, Martha Ann and Ralph H HORTON, 28 Oct 1972 Nashua, NH
BELANGER, Nancy L and Edmund A SHOLKOFF, 18 Sep 1983 Hudson, NH
BELANGER, Polly and Winfield L BELANGER, 18 May 1979 Nashua, NH
BELANGER, Sandra L and Steven M BERRY, 01 May 1982 Nashua, NH
BELANGER, Sedulie and Elie CORNIELLIER, 21 Apr 1913 Nashua, NH
  Joseph Belanger & Flornie Broux
  Charles Corniellier & Emilie Turcelle
BELANGER, Thomas J and Regina GIROUARD, 05 Aug 1927 Nashua, NH
BELANGER, Winfield L and Polly BERNASCONI, 18 May 1962 Nashua, NH
BELANGER, Winfield L and Polly BELANGER, 18 May 1979 Nashua, NH
BELANGER, Yvonne A and Leopold E LEVESQUE, 20 Sep 1947 Nashua, NH
BELDEN, Cecile M and George T BENSON, 16 Feb 1974 Litchfield, NH
BELDEN, Ronald R and Dorothea M COURTEMANCHE, 17 Aug 1968 Derry, NH
BELENGER, Audrey A and George R HICKS, 22 Aug 1949 Hudson, NH
BELHUMEUR, Richard M and Debora A LACOY, 21 Oct 1978 Hudson, NH
BELIVEAU, June M and Scott W NICHOLSON, 06 Feb 1971 Nashua, NH
BELKNAP, Charlotte and David L HOAG, 22 Sep 1860
BELKNAP, Charlotte and David C HOAGG, 29 Dec 1860
BELKNAP, Esther P and James P HOWE, 12 Jul 1869 Hudson, NH
BELL, Aaron C and Clara J MARSH, 02 Oct 1861
BELL, Harold O and Jeannette GRANT, 14 May 1915 Nashua, NH
  Claude A Bell (Lowell, MA) & Edith M Thissell (Lowell, MA)
  Eugene Grant(Irasburg, VT) & Laura L Durivage (Lowell, VT)
BELL, Jeannette and Raymond W BOURGEOIS, 13 Mar 1948 Hudson, NH
BELL, John P and Aphrodite KUTRUBES, 12 Dec 1936 Hudson, NH
BELL, Michael B and Patricia A INGRAM, 08 Jun 1973 Hollis, NH

HUDSON,NH MARRIAGES

BELL, Samuel M and Mercy M RICHARDSON, 13 Jan 1861
BELLAVANCE, Louis M and Patricia A GOSSELIN, 27 Dec 1952 Nashua, NH
BELLAVANCE, Thomas L and Marcia E HUFF, 22 Feb 1969 Hollis, NH
BELLEAU, Barbara L and Charles E BUKER, 14 Dec 1955 Hudson, NH
BELLEFEUILLE, Aurelle V & Arthur H BURNHAM, 09 Dec 1942 Manchester,NH
BELLEFEUILLE, Bonnie A & Raymond L GINGRAS, 16 Jan 1981 Manchester,NH
BELLEFEUILLE, Debra D and Christopher TALTY, 21 Oct 1978 Hudson, NH
BELLEFEUILLE, Denise B & Adrian J Jr PELCHAT, 16 Aug 1969 Hudson,NH
BELLEFEUILLE, Pamela M & Maurice H DUROCHER, 23 Aug 1972 Hudson, NH
BELLEFEUILLE, Raymond G & Theresa R NADEAU, 18 Sep 1948 Nashua, NH
BELLERIVE, Rodney R & Elizabeth NASUTOWICZ, 04 Mar 1967 Hudson, NH
BELLEVANCE, Edward J and Renay L BRYANT, 13 Dec 1975 Hudson, NH
BELLISLE, James E and Kerin E AUDET, 11 Jul 1981 Hudson, NH
BELLOFATTO, Lillian D and Anthony CARAMANIS, 15 Sep 1973 Nashua, NH
BELLROSE, Janice C and Leonard A JACKSON, 02 Mar 1973 Nashua, NH
BELLROSE, Victor T and Janice C HIRTH, 08 Dec 1953 Hudson, NH
BELMONT, Charles K and Mary G NORTON, 14 Apr 1945 Hudson, NH
BELMORE, Denise D and Richard M SIMMONS, 24 Nov 1984 Hudson, NH
BEMIS, Emily and Joseph F POLLARD, 22 Nov 1869
BENJAMIN, Cyrus and Eva M REGGIO, 19 Jul 1919 Hudson, NH
BENN, Ernest E and Vivian L GREENE, 03 Jul 1938 Hudson, NH
BENN, Olive E and Raymond E PICHETTE, 25 Apr 1942 Hudson, NH
BENNER, Leslie E and Charles D DAVIDSON, 05 Aug 1966 Hudson, NH
BENNER, Susan A and Charles D SPAULDING, 23 Jul 1971 Hudson, NH
BENNERT, Alfred R and Eleanor J HOWARD, 19 Oct 1929 Nashua, NH
BENNETT, Beatrice and Raymond GUAY, 16 Sep 1944 Nashua, NH
BENNETT, Bernice D and Stephen M CHESS, 25 Apr 1981 Hudson, NH
BENNETT, Joseph and Clarissa A WILSON, 02 Nov 1854
BENNETT, Joseph S and Clara A WILSON, 31 Oct 1854
BENNETT, Mary L and Zephirin A PELLETIER, 24 Jun 1950 Hudson, NH
BENNETT, Merton C and Alberta TERRY, 15 Jun 1910 Hudson, NH
   Edward N Bennett & Jennie F Perry
   Charles A Terry & Lucy M Cushing
BENNETT, Mildred A and Harold J BARDSLEY, 27 Jul 1946 Hudson, NH
BENNETT, Phoebe and George W POLLARD, 17 Dec 1914 Lawrence, MA
   Hiram Bennett
   John F Pollard & Janette Macartney
BENNETT, Raymond and Shirley N RUSSELL, 19 Aug 1967 Pelham, NH
BENNETT, Robert W and Elaine N O'CONNOR, 19 Feb 1955 Hudson, NH
BENNETT, Thomas W and Norma L MARCIL, 22 Aug 1974 Nashua, NH
BENNETT, Vinal E and Isabel D MARDEN, 19 Feb 1938 Nashua, NH
BENNETT, Walter A Jr&Pauline M WHEELER, 29 Oct 1960 Harrisville,NH
BENOIT, Joyce L and Ralph H BERUBE, 24 Aug 1968 Nashua, NH
BENOIT, Leon R and June E LAFOREST, 26 Dec 1960 Derry, NH
BENOIT, Richard A and Theresa J MILLER, 27 Jul 1963 Hudson, NH
BENSON, Barbara J and Richard O NIEMI, 15 Jun 1963 Concord, MA
BENSON, Charlotte and Stanley R SPRAGUE, 08 Aug 1932 Merrimack, NH
BENSON, George T and Ida N STEELE, 12 Jul 1909 Nashua, NH
   Walter E Benson & Laura F Caldwell
   Charles A Steele & Lottie A Reynolds
BENSON, George T and Cecile M BELDEN, 16 Feb 1974 Litchfield, NH
BENSON, George T Jr and Lois E LITTLEFIELD, 04 Nov 1944 Nashua, NH
BENSON, Laura and Arthur A TROW, 26 Jun 1912 Londonderry, NH
   Levi Cadwell & Abbie Bullard
   George W Trow & Permelia Shattuck
BENSON, Mary F and George H ANDERSON, 10 Oct 1896 Hudson, NH
   C E Benson & Helen Eames (Henry, ME)
   John Anderson(Melrose, MA) & Abbie Munro (Boston, MA)
BENT, Clarence F and Ruth E SUDSBURY, 13 Jun 1936 Hudson, NH
BENT, Hatford O and Ruth M ORMES, 15 Dec 1925 Hudson, NH

HUDSON, NH MARRIAGES

BENT, Marjorie M and Peter P CARFARO, 03 Jul 1937 Hudson, NH
BENT, Mildred F & Harold B CORNELL, 04 Aug 1927 Melvin Village, NH
BENTLEY, George W and June O CLOUGH, 16 Aug 1937 Hudson, NH
BERANGER, Rita B and Paul J RAAB, 18 Oct 1941 Hudson, NH
BERARD, Donald A and Margaret M MAHONEY, 07 May 1949 Nashua, NH
BERARD, Edgar R and Lorette M THERIAULT, 01 Dec 1934 Nashua, NH
BERARD, Elaine P and Robert L ROY, 20 Nov 1954 Hudson, NH
BERARD, George H and Irene C SIMARD, 05 Aug 1950 Nashua, NH
BERARD, Gloria E and Gerard J GOGUEN, 05 May 1956 Hudson, NH
BERARD, Leon and Clarice MARQUIS, 03 Sep 1923 Nashua, NH
BERARDI, John J and Gertrude A MITCHESS, 26 Jun 1954 Hudson, NH
BERBAUM, Emma L and Frank E ROBBINS, 12 Jan 1951 S Lyndeboro, NH
BERG, Bonnie D and Yvon A RAYMOND, 08 Feb 1969 Nashua, NH
BERG, Stephen D and Judy M MILLER, 16 Jan 1971 Hudson, NH
BERGER, Andre R and Lynn Rae GURNEY, 09 Jan 1982 Nashua, NH
BERGERON, Alice M and Arthur J OUELLET, 09 May 1959 Nashua, NH
BERGERON, Constance and Anthony LEONE, 19 Mar 1949 Hudson, NH
BERGERON, Dean J and Patricia A BOULE, 07 Jul 1973 Londonderry, NH
BERGERON, Eleanor M and Roger A MARTIN, 22 Nov 1956 Hudson, NH
BERGERON, Janet M and Wayne R GELINAS, 29 Apr 1978 Pelham, NH
BERGERON, Leo A and Janice T DURIVAGE, 04 Sep 1937 Hudson, NH
BERGERON, Pierre C and Susan J ROLLINS, 15 Apr 1967 Hollis, NH
BERGERON, Raymond C and Grace F MONETTE, 30 Sep 1929 Nashua, NH
BERGERON, Rita P and Donald R FOISIE, 13 Sep 1952 Nashua, NH
BERGERON, Rita R and Leslie L BAKER, 25 Feb 1954 Durham, NH
BERGERON, Theresa M and Michael P GUERRETTE, 04 Sep 1977 Pelham, NH
BERGERON, Wilfred and Mary Ellen ROGERS, 16 May 1926 Nashua, NH
BERKOWITZ, Leopold and Selma BILLOW, 14 Aug 1937 Hudson, NH
BERNAICHE, Edward and Irene NEVEN, 26 Dec 1932 Nashua, NH
BERNARD, Barbara C and Robert A BURTON, 25 Apr 1945 Nashua, NH
BERNARD, Beatrice and Armand PARADIS, 29 Jun 1936 Nashua, NH
BERNARD, Clarice and Conrad PARADIS, 25 Oct 1934 Nashua, NH
BERNARD, Dania L and Meredith B SEACE, 10 Feb 1967 Hudson, NH
BERNARD, Edmond J P and Lydia COTE, 12 Apr 1930 Hudson, NH
BERNARD, Emma and Abraham L SANDERS, 12 Apr 1896 Hudson, NH
   Daria Bernard & Eliza Connell (Tyngsboro, MA)
   Thomas Sanders(Whitefield, VT) & Mary Connell
BERNARD, Gail M and Ronald P MORGAN, 21 Apr 1972 Hudson, NH
BERNARD, George R and Barbara L KELLEY, 29 May 1971 Hudson, NH
BERNARD, Grace M and Donald J STRESSENGER, 10 Feb 1940 Hudson, NH
BERNARD, John L and Robin L LAFLAMME, 14 Dec 1974 Hudson, NH
BERNARD, Kathleen S and George DELLECHIAIE, 12 Mar 1977 Hudson, NH
BERNARD, Linda E and Robert M SHEPARD, 15 Aug 1981 Nashua, NH
BERNARD, Lucille M and A Jack ATKINSON, 11 Jan 1974 Hudson, NH
BERNARD, Margaret L and Glenn Robert CLARK, 04 Aug 1973 Hudson, NH
BERNARD, Pauline R and Arthur J LUCIANO, 08 May 1971 Hudson, NH
BERNARD, Priscilla and Frederick CORCORAN, 13 Jun 1981 Hudson, NH
BERNARD, Roxy P and Frederick BOURQUE, 20 Apr 1968 Windham, NH
BERNARD, Theresa A and Henry L GAGNON, 24 Nov 1945 Nashua, NH
BERNASCONI, Polly and Winfield L BELANGER, 18 May 1962 Nashua, NH
BERNIER, Anne M and Robert E JACKSON, 19 May 1962 Hudson, NH
BERNIER, Gerald L and Carole A HUSSEY, 17 Jun 1967 Wilton, NH
BERNIER, Jean M and Dana L McGUIRE, 10 Mar 1973 Nashua, NH
BERNIER, John R and Ann Marie BRAHANEY, 28 Apr 1984 Nashua, NH
BERNIER, Pauline L and Richard D LEVESQUE, 09 May 1964 Hudson, NH
BERNIER, Pearl T and Roger J ST LAURENT, 01 Feb 1947 Nashua, NH
BERNIER, Raymond L and Jacqueline FROST, 25 Aug 1958 Hudson, NH
BERNIER, Richard A and Rita L HOVATTER, 23 Apr 1976 Derry, NH
BERNIER, Robert E and Sandra J DESROCHERS, 20 Aug 1981 Nashua, NH
BERNTSEN, Frances M and John G LELACHEUR, 22 Feb 1985 Nashua, NH

HUDSON, NH MARRIAGES

BERRY, Beatrice and Edward J McMULLEN, 04 May 1946 Hudson, NH
BERRY, Bonnie L and Douglas C WISEMAN, 08 Oct 1960 Hudson, NH
BERRY, Bradford T and Linda A PETRAIN, 28 Dec 1979 Hartford, VT
BERRY, David R and Marie A SEGUIN, 01 Jun 1974 Hudson, NH
BERRY, Kenneth E and Janice E ALLISON, 10 May 1969 Nashua, NH
BERRY, Steven M and Sandra L BELANGER, 01 May 1982 Nashua, NH
BERTHIAUME, Rita L and Maurice G PARADISE, 20 Jul 1946 Nashua, NH
BERTHIAUME, Theresa J and Ronald G SIMARD, 25 Jul 1975 Hudson, NH
BERTHOLD, Lea R and Joseph A BEAUDOIN, 08 Jul 1950 Hudson, NH
BERTHOLDT, William A and Carol Ann NARO, 19 Mar 1983 Hudson, NH
BERTHOLDT, William F and Paula J MERRIFIELD, 30 Jul 1971 Gilford, NH
BERTRAND, Deborah S and Paul T McNALLY, 19 Feb 1972 Nashua, NH
BERTRAND, James M and Sandra A SEAMAN, 05 Sep 1975 Hudson, NH
BERUBE, Carol M and Ronald F MAYNARD, 08 Feb 1964 Nashua, NH
BERUBE, Chas Eugene and Laurette I JETTE, 04 Jun 1923 Nashua, NH
BERUBE, Constance and Nickie A PECK, 24 Jan 1970 Hudson, NH
BERUBE, Dennis N and Theresa M FARLEY, 14 Jul 1974 Hudson, NH
BERUBE, Doreen L R and Joseph E HAFEMAN, 14 Jun 1980 Hudson, NH
BERUBE, Edward R and Janet Flor MALETTE, 20 Aug 1938 Nashua, NH
BERUBE, Elsie G and Herbert L DEARBORN, 11 Jul 1974 Nashua, NH
BERUBE, Ernest C and Juliette A DROUIN, 08 Apr 1949 Hudson, NH
BERUBE, Evelyn C and Robert E LORAINE, 23 May 1953 Nashua, NH
BERUBE, Gisele G and Paul E LEVESQUE, 25 Nov 1944 Nashua, NH
BERUBE, Gloria and W H MARSHALL, 21 Aug 1876 Nashua, NH
BERUBE, Jacqueline and Scott D CANTELLA, 24 Sep 1983 Hudson, NH
BERUBE, Jeanne N and Bruce N VIGNOLA, 08 Dec 1972 Hudson, NH
BERUBE, Joanne L and Barry M PECK, 07 Nov 1970 Hudson, NH
BERUBE, Laurette J and Robert A TREMBLAY, 15 Nov 1947 Nashua, NH
BERUBE, Lena A and Armand H LAVOIE, 30 Jun 1951 Nashua, NH
BERUBE, Pauline D and Joseph R HARWOOD, 31 Oct 1944 Nashua, NH
BERUBE, Pauline Y and Thomas P MULHERN, 21 Sep 1968 Hudson, NH
BERUBE, Ralph H and Joyce L BENOIT, 24 Aug 1968 Nashua, NH
BERUBE, Sandra T and Robert G BOUTILIER, 06 Nov 1965 Nashua, NH
BESCO, Margaret L and Emerise E DEMERS, 16 Jun 1956 Hudson, NH
BESSETTE, Clemence F and Gilles J COTE, 07 Aug 1971 Manchester, NH
BESSETTE, Roger J and Carol A ANDERSEN, 23 Aug 1958 Hudson, NH
BESSEY, George H and Harriet R PERDUE, 28 Mar 1948 Hudson, NH
BETE, Barbara and Clarence J LAMOY, 05 Jul 1935 Nashua, NH
BETTENCOURT, Christine and Brian E CLARKE, 27 Dec 1980 Hudson, NH
BETTENCOURT, Harold F and Muriel B BOISVERT, 24 Feb 1948 Hudson, NH
BETTY, Janie P and Roger R SIMONEAU, 30 Aug 1969 Hudson, NH
BEYER, Dennis R and Robin P LaFOREST, 25 Aug 1972 Nashua, NH
BEYER, Kathleen R and Mark ROBERTS, 12 Oct 1968 Hudson, NH
BEYER, Linda B and Randall O HEBERT, 21 Jan 1974 Nashua, NH
BEYER, Linda B and Jonathan Paul SMITH, 02 Jul 1978 Hudson, NH
BEYER, Michael P and Linda M LANGELIER, 30 Jan 1972 Hudson, NH
BEYER, Robin P and Dana V S SNELL, 19 Mar 1984 Hudson, NH
BEZA, Angell G and Jacqueline BOWEN, 08 Jul 1956 Hanover, NH
BEZA, Sotiri and Vasila PALEOSELITI, 10 Jun 1928 Hudson, NH
BIAVA, Stacey Ann and David L OIKLE, 20 Apr 1985 Hudson, NH
BIBEAU, Anna and Eugene LEBOEUF, 27 Jun 1936 Nashua, NH
BIBEAU, Celeste C and Thomas M DIAMANTINI, 03 Nov 1979 Hudson, NH
BIBEAU, Roland J and Jeannette LEVESQUE, 30 Jun 1945 Nashua, NH
BIBEAU, Solange D and Romeo E PELLETIER, 13 May 1950 Hudson, NH
BICKFORD, Frank P and Abby S JEWETT, 25 Mar 1894 Londonderry, NH
  C D Bickford (Ossipee, NH) & Hattie A Pitman (Bartlett, NH)
  O D Jewett(Sweden, ME) & Sarah J Eastman (Conway)
BICKFORD, Geo K and Marion A JEWETT, 03 Mar 1895 Hudson, NH
  Edwin D Bickford (Ossipee) & Hattie Pitman (Bartlett)
  O J Jewett & Sarah Eastman (Conway)

HUDSON,NH MARRIAGES

BICKFORD, Lane E and Mary A JOHNSON, 17 Sep 1977 Hudson, NH
BIELAWSKI, Danuta and Thomas CLARKE, 20 Feb 1982 Nashua, NH
BIELSKI, Henry J and Joyce M DOONAN, 11 Jan 1965 Hudson, NH
BIENSTOCK, Isadore and Helen GOLDEN, 11 Dec 1935 Hudson, NH
BIERMAN, Vickie J and Robert D DIONNE, 12 Oct 1982 Hudson, NH
BIGELOW, Stephen C and Rita K KINERSON, 15 Jul 1972 Hudson, NH
BIGLEY, Jeffrey J and Jaine E PETRINO, 29 Aug 1981 Hudson, NH
BIGWOOD, Lorraine O and Herschel W COX, 03 Aug 1946 Nashua, NH
BILANGER, Charles and Rose NORMAN, 17 Jul 1894 Hudson, NH
   Arthemin Dube & Auguste Bilanger
   Lewis Norman(Canada) & A Archambeault (Mass)
BILBOW, Herbert A and Lillian M GIROUARD, 09 Feb 1942 Nashua, NH
BILLINGS, Glenna M and Marvin C ADAMS, 01 May 1948 Hudson, NH
BILLINGS, Norma M and William H CONSIGNY, 30 May 1942 Hudson, NH
BILLINGSLEY, Virginia P and Raymond F SMITH, 16 Dec 1934 Nashua, NH
BILLOW, Selma and Leopold BERKOWITZ, 14 Aug 1937 Hudson, NH
BILLS, Galen W and Carol A PELLETIER, 01 Jul 1967 Londonderry, NH
BILLS, Melissa and Roland H DEMANCHE, 15 May 1965 Nashua, NH
BILODEAU, Ella M and William E GOSSELIN, 14 Jun 1970 Nashua, NH
BILODEAU, Michael C & Denise C BELANGER, 11 Feb 1978 Merrimack, NH
BILODEAU, Oscar and Ethel M HUNTER, 31 Dec 1915 Hudson, NH
   Joseph Bilodeau (Canada) & Mary (Canada)
   Frank A Hunter(Rockbottom, MA) & Amy A Beal (Harrisville, NH)
BILODEAU, Oscar and Mildred HUNTER, 09 Feb 1925 Hudson, NH
BILODEAU, Paul R and Donna E PATENAUDE, 04 Jul 1959 Hudson, NH
BILODEAU, Robert L and Ella M DEMANCHE, 18 May 1970 Hudson, NH
BILODEAU, Robert L and Margaret A BRYANT, 07 Jul 1969 Nashua, NH
BILODEAU, Shirley and Bertrand DUMAIS, 31 Aug 1957 Hudson, NH
BILODEAU, Shirley L and Raymond J DROUIN, 17 Jun 1977 Milford, NH
BINGHAM, Dorothy M and John W GILMAN, 12 Jun 1924 Hudson, NH
BINKS, Leslie D and Gloria L SMITH, 22 Nov 1937 Hudson, NH
BINKS, Patricia L and John O Jr BULLARD, 08 Jun 1957 Nashua, NH
BINKS, Sheryl L and Robert J Jr FAULKNER, 23 Sep 1967 Hudson, NH
BIRCH, David P and Yvette D TANEY, 04 Dec 1976 Hudson, NH
BIRCHALL, Mary E and Edward B DONNELLY, 31 Mar 1913 Nashua, NH
   John W Birchall & Ellen Scanlon
   Eugene Donnelly & Joanna Buckley
BIRCHALL, Maxine V and Frederick WILLETTE, 05 Mar 1955 Wilton, NH
BIRD, Elsie E and Edgar H GABRIEL, 19 Nov 1941 Epping, NH
BIRD, Karen L and Bryan R SOUTHWICK, 04 Sep 1982 Hudson, NH
BIRD, Sandra E and Robert A LITTLE, 28 Apr 1979 Hudson, NH
BIRON, Kathleen P and Jon CARROLL, 24 Aug 1967 Hudson, NH
BIRON, Leonard A and Shirley J ANNABLE, 05 Jun 1954 Nashua, NH
BISBING, Eddy J and Pamela L BURROUGHS, 02 Aug 1980 Hudson, NH
BISBING, Marion R and Richard A STEVENS, 12 Feb 1966 Derry, NH
BISBING, Patricia L & William R Jr ROBERTS, 15 Jun 1985 Hudson, NH
BISBING, Sally E and Donald R PROVENCAL, 02 Aug 1975 Hudson, NH
BISCHOFF, Raymond C and Viola E WHEELOCK, 06 Oct 1938 Nashua, NH
BISE, Terrie L and John L HAIGLER, 12 Jul 1975 Nashua, NH
BISHOP, Carol A and Pedro P PAGAN, 02 Aug 1969 Hudson, NH
BISHOP, David G and Diana L COBURN, 02 Jul 1966 Hudson, NH
BISHOP, Denise G and Raymond R Jr GAGNON, 15 Jul 1967 Hudson, NH
BISHOP, Juanita P and Alfred J PRINCE, 26 Nov 1947 Nashua, NH
BISHOP, Larry M and Lenora L LIBBY, 16 Oct 1971 Hudson, NH
BISHOP, Viola A and Harry F MORSE, 24 Jun 1930 Hudson, NH
BISHOP, Walter E and Annie G HAGERTY, 25 Dec 1911 Hudson, NH
   George Bishop & Phebe Hall
   Daniel Hagerty & Delia Foley
BISHOP, Wesley B and Mary J LEAOR, 30 Jun 1951 Hudson, NH
BISKADUROS, Manuel and Evelyn R FARRINGTON, 18 Jun 1955 Nashua, NH

HUDSON, NH MARRIAGES

BISKADUROS, Mary and Roger A DESJARDINS, 20 Sep 1952 Nashua, NH
BISSON, J Conrad and Therese F DUMAS, 22 Nov 1945 Nashua, NH
BISSONETTE, Odelie and Arthur P LAQUENE, 02 Apr 1923 Nashua, NH
BISSONNETT, Elizabeth and Jesse PARKES, 31 Jul 1948 Hudson, NH
BISSONNETTE, Anita and Gordon L HASTINGS, 03 Jul 1948 Hudson, NH
BISSONNETTE, Teresa L and David J MARYANSKI, 20 Jun 1981 Nashua, NH
BISSONNETTE, Theodore & Beatrice CHEVRETTE, 15 Apr 1939 Nashua, NH
BISTANY, Donald R and Linda M BARNES, 29 Jun 1974 Nashua, NH
BIXBY, Chas H and Lizzie M EMERY, 06 Jun 1876 Hudson, NH
BLACK, Mavis M and Herbert W DUNKLEE, 01 Apr 1967 Wilton, NH
BLACK, Nancy J and Glen D ELLIOTT, 24 Aug 1974 Nashua, NH
BLACK, Thomas G and Elizabeth MORSE, 14 May 1983 Hudson, NH
BLACKBURN, Robert Lee and Sheila F BURKE, 15 Sep 1973 Hudson, NH
BLACKETT, Rita M and Elmer M MacKINNON, 01 Jul 1950 Hudson, NH
BLACKSTONE, Mari L and William D WOOD, 23 Jan 1973 Nashua, NH
BLAIS, Cecile J and Donald A HARDY, 21 Feb 1970 Manchester, NH
BLAIS, Charles and Linda M FREEMAN, 13 Oct 1984 Nashua, NH
BLAIS, Christine and Daniel P HOGAN, 16 Jul 1977 Nashua, NH
BLAIS, Helen and Leo DUCHARME, 22 Mar 1933 Nashua, NH
BLAIS, James R and Geraldine WILSON, 08 May 1952 Hudson, NH
BLAIS, Jean N and Robert C DEAN, 26 May 1962 Hudson, NH
BLAIS, Lucien L and Muriel D ROBERGE, 22 Nov 1973 Berlin, NH
BLAIS, Norman K and Pauline M LECLERC, 07 Mar 1980 Londonderry, NH
BLAIS, Pauline L and Michael K BURTON, 25 Oct 1980 Nashua, NH
BLAIS, Roland and Roberta HARRIS, 28 Apr 1947 Nashua, NH
BLAIS, Stephen W and Susan E WHITING, 09 Dec 1967 Hudson, NH
BLAISDELL, Laura E and Pearl T THOMAS, 10 Sep 1902 Conway, NH
   James Blaisdell & Laura Deering
   Tyler Thomas & Elizabeth A Sprake
BLAISDELL, Sophia G and James John WEBSTER, 12 Feb 1833
BLAKE, Annie F and T R BEACHMONT, 08 Jul 1900 Nashua, NH
   Roswell Blake
   Daniel Beachmont & Margaret (Walsh)
BLAKE, Carroll F and Terry Ann MASON, 19 Jul 1975 Conway, NH
BLAKE, Deborah K and Robert J ALEJANDRO, 01 Dec 1967 Hudson, NH
BLAKE, Frank W and Amanda M WATSON, 31 Aug 1893 Hudson, NH
   Joseph H Blake (Alexandria) & Elizabeth Barrett (Charlestown, MA)
BLAKE, Margaret E and Robert S ROBINSON, 04 Oct 1941 Hudson, NH
BLAKE, Winston L and Rosamond URQUHART, 01 Jan 1940 Lowell, MA
BLAKELY, William J and Mildred A HEBERT, 12 Aug 1950 Nashua, NH
BLANCHARD, Charles L and Lois F REYNOLDS, 03 Feb 1962 Hudson, NH
BLANCHARD, Edward B & Wilhelmena I ROBBINS, 21 Aug 1889 Nashua, NH
   Silas M Blanchard(Windham, NH) & Elener I Bickford(Barnstead, NH)
   George W Robbins(Groton, MA) & Alice M Hall (Derry, NH)
BLANCHARD, Elton E and Clara L NEWTON, 08 Jul 1956 Sandown, NH
BLANCHARD, Florence J and L Don LEET, 02 Jul 1956 Hudson, NH
BLANCHARD, Glenn R and Sandra A MALETTE, 14 May 1971 Manchester, NH
BLANCHARD, Harriet and Advastus LEW, 29 Jun 1815
BLANCHARD, Harriet and Adrastus LOW, 29 Jun 1815
BLANCHARD, Henry W and Ada KIDDER, 28 Nov 1900 Cambridge, MA
   S M Blanchard & Eleanor J Bickford
   Daniel Kidder & Emeline F Hardy
BLANCHARD, Jossie M and Joseph E NICHOLS, 10 Aug 1901 Hudson, NH
   Charles Marvell (Milford, NH) & May Duscoll (Boston, MA)
   L F Nichols(Nashua, NH) & Nettie A Austin (Hollis, NH)
BLANCHARD, Kenneth P and Patricia A KALIL, 16 Aug 1958 Hudson, NH
BLANCHARD, Lucy and Andrew WILKINS, 29 Sep 1779
BLANCHARD, Pauline L and Henry D TOLLES, 06 Jun 1924 Hudson, NH
BLANCHARD, Peter and Dianna COBURN, 26 Jan 1823
BLANCHARD, Rita and Albert LEMERY, 12 Aug 1947 Nashua, NH

HUDSON,NH MARRIAGES

BLANCHARD, Shelley L and Dean J PIPER, 29 Nov 1975 Contoocook, NH
BLANCHARD, Susan Joan and Ricky James SMART, 15 Jul 1978 Hudson, NH
BLANCHARD, Vauhn S and Zoa E CLARKE, 18 Nov 1911 Nashua, NH
   Fred S Seavey & Marie L Halfman
   Theodore L Clarke & Jessie F Erskine
BLANCHETTE, Arthur P and Jo-Ann DUCLOS, 01 Jun 1963 Hudson, NH
BLANCHETTE, Arthur P and Theresa J BURGESS, 07 Dec 1968 Nashua, NH
BLANCHETTE, JoAnn and John I GOODNESS, 09 Nov 1968 Hudson, NH
BLANCHETTE, Kenneth J and Marie B ROSS, 24 Nov 1984 Hudson, NH
BLANCHETTE, Lorraine P & Joseph L LEVESQUE, 14 Jan 1950 Nashua, NH
BLANCHETTE, Roland J and Ann T CHERKES, 31 May 1952 Nashua, NH
BLANCHETTE, Wendy L and Bruce E DESJARDINS, 22 Apr 1978 Hudson, NH
BLANEY, Donna Marie and Gerald A BOUCHER, 03 Mar 1979 Hudson, NH
BLEASE, Dorothy M and Walter A KENNEDY, 23 Sep 1933 Hudson, NH
BLEAU, Annette C and John E SYRENE, 05 May 1956 Nashua, NH
BLEAU, Kenneth N and Nancy A DeMONTIGNY, 09 Sep 1961 Hudson, NH
BLEAU, Ronald G and Claudia J SCOTT, 01 May 1965 Hudson, NH
BLIER, Donald G and Josette L JEANNOTTE, 05 Jan 1952 Nashua, NH
BLINN, Ruth and Gustave J ERICSON, 29 May 1948 Hudson, NH
BLISS, Mialma and Joseph DAVIS, 15 Dec 1842
BLIZZARD, Allan G and Marilyn A DELANEY, 21 Oct 1949 Hudson, NH
BLODGETT, Abigail and Ephraim CHASE, 02 May 1816
BLODGETT, Abigail and Samuel GREELEY, 27 May 1744
BLODGETT, Asahal and Elizabeth POLLARD, 13 Dec 1781
BLODGETT, Asahel and Lois POLLARD, 11 Oct 1798
BLODGETT, Augustus F and Lucy E CHASE, 29 Dec 1860
BLODGETT, Austin and Susan DAVIS, 03 Jan 1847
BLODGETT, Bertha L and Daniel E CANTARA, 22 Oct 1914 Manchester, NH
   Harry B Blodgett & Eliza Summerville
   Daniel Cantara & Olivine Lemery
BLODGETT, Dorothy and Ebenezer POLLARD, 21 Feb 1799
BLODGETT, Elizabeth and John CHENEY, 12 Aug 1777
BLODGETT, Ella F and George W SILVER, 19 May 1877 Hudson, NH
   Warren Blodgett & Balinda Barrett (Hudson, NH)
   Daniel Silver(Hudson, NH)
BLODGETT, Elmer H and Hannah L CLYDE, 07 Sep 1876 Hudson, NH
BLODGETT, Fannie and Samuel STEELE, 21 Sep 1815
BLODGETT, Fanny and Samuel STEELE, 21 Sep 1815
BLODGETT, Fred C and Lizzie F FULLER, 30 Nov 1898 Hudson, NH
   Aug F Blodgett & Lucy Ellen Chaw
   Willis L Fuller & Adelia C Yettaw
BLODGETT, Hannah and Barrude BROWN, 06 Jun 1780
BLODGETT, Hannah and Benzilla BROWN, 06 Jun 1780
BLODGETT, Hannah and John BURNHAM, 11 Mar 1810
BLODGETT, Hannah and Stephen Jr CHASE, 31 Oct 1776
BLODGETT, Hannah and Stephen Jr CHASE, 31 Oct 1770
BLODGETT, Harry D and Eliza J SOMERVILL, 01 May 1889 Waitsfield, VT
   Augus F Blodgett (Dorchester, MA) & Lucy E Chase (Hudson, NH)
   John Somervill(Waitsfield, VT) & Ann Hoffman (Ireland)
BLODGETT, Horatio N and Anna W CLARK, 26 Mar 1864
BLODGETT, Joseph and Hannah DAVIS, 05 May 1785
BLODGETT, Laura B and C E CUMMINGS, 30 Sep 1896 Haverhill, MA
   A F Blodgett (Hudson, NH)
   Hiram Cummings(Hudson, NH)
BLODGETT, Phineas and Martha HAMBLETT, 27 Sep 1781
BLODGETT, Sally and Seth HADLEY, 25 Dec 1814
BLODGETT, Sally and Joseph McKEAN, 01 Apr 1812
BLODGETT, Sophia and James DOIL, 22 Feb 1819
BLODGETT, Sophia and James DOYLE, 22 Feb 1819
BLODGETT, Warren and Elizabeth WEBSTER, 18 May 1858

HUDSON,NH MARRIAGES

BLODGETT, William and Clarissa BOWLES, 12 Sep 1844
BLOOD, Arthur V Jr and Philomena BORTAS, 11 Sep 1943 Hudson, NH
BLOOD, Colburn and Aba CLARK, 23 Aug 1854
BLOOD, Philomene and Harvey W TREMBLAY, 14 Sep 1969 Hudson, NH
BLOOD, Priscilla and Ernest ZINK, 23 Dec 1925 Nashua, NH
BLOOD, Ruth E and Charles C PARKER, 09 Apr 1933 Hollis, NH
BLOOD, Wilber L & Ida Alice PHILLIPS, 28 Jun 1930 Arlington, MA
BLOOM, Claus A A and Ada L JOHNSON, 07 Aug 1948 Hudson, NH
BLOOMBERG, Phebe Ann and Richard P JOHNSON, 21 Jul 1965 Hudson, NH
BLOW, Georgianna and Arthur FOURNIER, 23 Apr 1938 Nashua, NH
BLOW, Luvia and Henry J ROBINSON, 30 Jun 1934 Nashua, NH
BLOW, Seward and Theresa J GAGNE, 10 Aug 1940 Nashua, NH
BLOW, Theresa S and Julien J FONTAINE, 16 Nov 1946 Nashua, NH
BLUNDEN, Raymond E and Mary E PALMIERI, 11 Jun 1966 Hudson, NH
BLUNT, Vivianne S and Dana A HOAG, 07 Oct 1980 Nashua, NH
BLUSDAYS, Nathaniel and Sophia C HODGDON, 13 Feb 1860
BLYE, Erma A and James C BOWMAN, 29 Jun 1944 Hudson, NH
BOARDMAN, Calvin and Susan J WEBSTER,
BOARDMAN, John and Lydia SMITH, 16 Oct 1814
BOCCHINO, Charles J and Patricia C DESIMONE, 02 Jun 1962 Hudson, NH
BOCH, Victor A and Margaret MORRISSEY, 07 Jun 1947 Hudson, NH
BOCK, Mary A and Fred S GUGGENHEIMER, 30 Oct 1948 Hudson, NH
BODAMAS, Theophilas and Margaret SHARP, 16 Jan 1866
BODEN, A A and Susie E MELLIS, 22 Nov 1898 Hudson, NH
  Henry J Boden & Mary J Drumm
  George F Mellis & Mary B Adams
BODGE, Charlotte and Alden W WHITNEY, 02 Sep 1939 Hudson, NH
BODMAN, Margaret and Byrd S FINE, 26 Jun 1948 Hudson, NH
BODWELL, Frank W and Annie S BRIDGES, 16 May 1888 Hudson, NH
  Amos C Bodwell (Salem, NH) & Sarah J Bodwell (Derry, NH)
  Jackson Bridges(Marion, ME) & Mary Card (Lubic, ME)
BOFFOLI, Leo M and Antoinette ALTOMARE, 12 Nov 1948 Hudson, NH
BOGAN, Beth Ann and Darrell G JONES, 24 Feb 1980 Hudson, NH
BOGATY, John H and Cecylia T POLAK, 23 Nov 1968 Nashua, NH
BOGDZVICH, Helen C and Alphonse B KUPCHUN, 22 Dec 1942 Nashua, NH
BOGGS, Sally and David CALDWELL, 20 Sep 1810
BOGUSZ, Mary V and Chester W SOJKA, 30 Dec 1944 Nashua, NH
BOILARD, Cathleen E and Brian D FESSENDEN, 29 Apr 1978 Hudson, NH
BOILARD, Constance and James E PICARD, 23 Oct 1954 Hudson, NH
BOILARD, Elaine A and Edward T JANKAUSKAS, 15 Oct 1955 Hudson, NH
BOILARD, Gerald R and Patricia A LORAINE, 02 Jul 1955 Hudson, NH
BOILARD, Jamie O and Anne C DEARBORN, 05 Jun 1977 Hudson, NH
BOILARD, Nathalie J and Gordon H SMITH, 13 May 1961 Nashua, NH
BOILARD, Oswald D and Margaret E SEAVER, 20 Aug 1955 Keene, NH
BOILARD, Richard G and Jacqueline TESSIER, 22 Jun 1957 Hudson, NH
BOILARD, Richard G and Joyce R FISHER, 02 Nov 1963 Exeter, NH
BOILARD, Richard G and Bernice R HOLT, 08 May 1967 Nashua, NH
BOILARD, Teresa L and Kevin J BUJNOWSKI, 20 Oct 1979 Hudson, NH
BOIS, Jean R and Rita T LEVESQUE, 17 Aug 1946 Nashua, NH
BOIS, Norma L and Leo B GUERETTE, 11 Jul 1969 Nashua, NH
BOIS, Pearl and Edward C MASKEWICZ, 20 Dec 1952 Hudson, NH
BOISCLAIR, Gloria D and Michael J SULLIVAN, 22 Jul 1967 Nashua, NH
BOISKO, John and Veronica YLOTRUK, 21 May 1919 Nashua, NH
BOISSONNAULT, Bernadette & George H GODBOUT, 31 Oct 1945 Nashua, NH
BOISSONNAULT, Charles J & Elaine Y ROUSSEL, 30 Nov 1974 Hudson, NH
BOISSONNEAULT, Charles J&Susan C WELDON, 06 Oct 1984 Chichester, NH
BOISVERT, Alan R and Carolyn F LEBLANC, 19 Aug 1968 Manchester, NH
BOISVERT, Donald E and Trudy A CARON, 11 Jul 1981 Hudson, NH
BOISVERT, Muriel B and Harold F BETTENCOURT, 24 Feb 1948 Hudson, NH
BOISVERT, Ralph P and Cheryl A RODGERS, 30 Jun 1973 Hudson, NH

HUDSON,NH MARRIAGES

BOISVERT, Raymond J and Kathleen J CASEY, 01 Sep 1973 Hudson, NH
BOISVERT, Shirley T and William F NEAULT, 02 Jun 1985 Pelham, NH
BOKOUSKY, Brenda and Rene C GUERTIN, 26 Mar 1966 Milford, NH
BOLAND, David R and Marie F DOW, 22 Apr 1967 Hudson, NH
BOLAND, Eric N and G H SHAFNER, 24 Jun 1916 Hudson, NH
 Elisha S Boland (Canada) & Esther Nichols (Newburyport, MA)
 Ernest Shafner(Nova Scotia) & Belle J Thompson (Hudson, NH)
BOLDUC, Loretta J and Charles H APRIL, 21 Jul 1978 Hudson, NH
BOLDUC, Phoebe A and Tommy W CRAIS, 23 Sep 1967 Hudson, NH
BOLES, Barbara A and Robert H CONSIGNY, 05 Apr 1947 Hudson, NH
BOLES, Gilbert E and Lizzie J ESTY, 16 May 1883 Windham, NH
 Alphonse Boles (Methuen, MA) & Mary A Peabody (Pelham, NH)
 Richard Esty & Clara Nichols
BOLES, Wesley E Jr and Amelia A ALUKONIS, 24 Jun 1944 Nashua, NH
BOLGER, Winifred E and Joseph T RUSSO, 10 Aug 1947 Hudson, NH
BOLIS, Marion R and George C JOSLIN, 04 Sep 1948 Nashua, NH
BOLIVER, Willis A and Anne M FRIZELLE, 14 Dec 1946 Hudson, NH
BOLLIVER, Aubrey W and Mabel F PUTNEY, 07 Sep 1927 Hudson, NH
BOLSTER, Norman E and Karina FOSTER, 21 Sep 1936 Hudson, NH
BOLTON, Deborah E and Robert R BARNARD, 08 Sep 1979 Hudson, NH
BOLTON, Kathleen A and Jonathan P WARD, 27 May 1978 Hudson, NH
BOMENGEN, Judith E and John H WOHLWEND, 27 Jun 1980 Nashua, NH
BONACCORSI, Joseph F Jr and Pamela J HOLROYD, 04 Aug 1979 Salem, NH
BOND, Cynthia J and Stephen A LITTLEFIELD, 17 Jul 1982 Hudson, NH
BONDURA, Sandra H and George E McBRIDE, 09 Dec 1950 Hudson, NH
BONENFANT, Raymond H and Susan A ANDERSON, 20 Jun 1964 Nashua, NH
BONESKI, Marie E and Thomas J FRIETSCH, 17 Jan 1948 Hudson, NH
BONHOMME, Cosmo R and Lucy M GENTILE, 15 Dec 1973 Hudson, NH
BONHOMME, Ruth N and Bruce A HUGHES, 10 Mar 1973 Nashua, NH
BONICA, Shirley A and Carroll J STEVENS, 05 Feb 1964 Hudson, NH
BONNEAU, Fabiana and Dedier TRUDEL, 21 Dec 1929 Nashua, NH
BONNER, Lucille and Richard E BARNEY, 28 Sep 1938 Hudson, NH
BONNER, Sandra L and George C Jr LATOUR, 01 Jun 1963 Hudson, NH
BONNETTE, Alice T and George D SPEARS, 03 Sep 1960 Hudson, NH
BONNETTE, Allen P and Linda J KEMPTON, 08 Jun 1968 Hudson, NH
BONNETTE, Cecile and Harold S CARTER, 07 Jun 1941 Nashua, NH
BONNETTE, Denise A and Gerard J BROUSSEAU, 11 Apr 1969 Nashua, NH
BONNETTE, Dennis A and Colette S CLOUTIER, 17 Feb 1968 Hudson, NH
BONNETTE, Francois and Lucier P MORELLE, 27 Nov 1924 Nashua, NH
BONNETTE, Gloria Mar and Simon Rich ALLISON, 14 Nov 1937 Dracut, MA
BONNETTE, Patricia A and Terry W DURHAMMER, 13 Aug 1969 Hudson, NH
BONNETTE, Philip H and Jeannette LANDRY, 31 May 1947 Nashua, NH
BONNETTE, Raoul A and Alma M JACQUES, 25 Aug 1919 Nashua, NH
BONNETTE, Stephen J and Joan Ellen SCHEER, 28 Aug 1976 Nashua, NH
BONOLLO, Leo E and Deborah J CARLSON, 23 Oct 1965 Nashua, NH
BONVILLE, Jeannette and Paul H E ANGER, 24 Jul 1954 Hudson, NH
BOOLBA, Jane E and Robert J McVICAR, 02 Apr 1983 Northwood, NH
BOOSKA, Emery P and Margaret T HARTNETT, 28 Jun 1958 Hudson, NH
BOOTH, Benjamin J and Melvina MARCHENONIS, 02 Jul 1938 Nashua, NH
BOOTH, Neville A and Wilhemina BARTLETT, 16 Jun 1938 Hudson, NH
BORDEN, Esther A and George D VADNEY, 07 Apr 1979 Hudson, NH
BORDEN, Florence M and Bernard L OLIVER, 31 Dec 1949 Hudson, NH
BORDEN, Gay N and Joseph N WINKLER, 10 Nov 1967 Nashua, NH
BORGMAN, Gary M and Susan M TROTTER, 21 Jan 1984 Hudson, NH
BORNEMAN, Arthur B and Ethel M SHEPHERD, 03 Apr 1929 Nashua, NH
BORTAS, Philomena and Arthur V Jr BLOOD, 11 Sep 1943 Hudson, NH
BORTHWICK, Raymond P and Katherine HEALY, 06 Nov 1948 Hudson, NH
BOSKA, Aleck and Jeanne A ROY, 02 Sep 1943 Nashua, NH
BOSKA, Pamela E and Richard W SZOPA, 21 Oct 1983 Canterbury, NH
BOSKA, Veronica and Lawrence GABRIEL, 03 Sep 1938 Nashua, NH

HUDSON, NH MARRIAGES

BOSLEY, Olida B and Romeo LAMBERT, 02 Oct 1954 Hudson, NH
BOSLEY, Rita D and Jean A DESJARDINS, 11 Nov 1944 Nashua, NH
BOSQUET, Nancy W and Seth N AMES, 23 Nov 1979 Hollis, NH
BOSSE, Diane C and Alfred D BRIAND, 21 Dec 1968 Hudson, NH
BOSSE, Marie A and Hormidas D RODIER, 09 Aug 1947 Nashua, NH
BOSSE, Rita I and Gene R BRIAND, 21 Jun 1969 Nashua, NH
BOSSE, Roland A and Alice L PAQUET, 18 Jul 1954 Dublin, NH
BOSSIE, Brenda V and Charles W KALIL, 25 Jul 1959 Nashua, NH
BOSSIE, Janice M and Morris CONDO, 26 Jun 1970 Nashua, NH
BOTHWICK, David S and Crystal L BROOK, 04 Sep 1970 Hudson, NH
BOTHWICK, Harold M Jr and Cynthia Ann HARDY, 02 Jul 1972 Hudson, NH
BOTHWICK, Walter J and Linda L CASE, 04 May 1974 Nashua, NH
BOUCHARD, Roger E & Madeline M SZERLOG, 28 May 1974 Manchester, NH
BOUCHARD, Suzanne T and Michael W SULLIVAN, 01 Feb 1981 Nashua, NH
BOUCHER, Alphonse M and Gloria M RODRIGUEZ, 12 Dec 1944 Nashua, NH
BOUCHER, Annette F and Paul O JOHNSON, 21 Aug 1954 Hudson, NH
BOUCHER, Clarice R and Gerald A DEARBORN, 01 Jun 1957 Hudson, NH
BOUCHER, Dana L and Nita G TALLENT, 25 Apr 1980 Hudson, NH
BOUCHER, Deborah A and Ronald R DESMARAIS, 22 Mar 1975 Hudson, NH
BOUCHER, Dennis E and Dianna T GRAHAM, 20 Aug 1977 Nashua, NH
BOUCHER, Dennis P & Catharine ALEXKNOVITCH, 08 Jun 1974 Hudson, NH
BOUCHER, Diane L and Thomas H BOWEN, 14 Oct 1972 Hudson, NH
BOUCHER, Edgar E and Doris B MOREAU, 09 Jun 1972 Hudson, NH
BOUCHER, Edward G and Gloria R LECLERC, 05 Nov 1955 Hudson, NH
BOUCHER, Florence A and Albert J MILLARD, 20 Nov 1969 Nashua, NH
BOUCHER, George J Jr and Cheryl A THEBODEAU, 16 May 1981 Hudson, NH
BOUCHER, Gerald and Jean R GAGNON, 25 Oct 1952 Nashua, NH
BOUCHER, Gerald A and Donna Marie BLANEY, 03 Mar 1979 Hudson, NH
BOUCHER, Geraldine and John A HAMMAR, 10 Aug 1957 Hudson, NH
BOUCHER, Gerard A and Teresa M MEEHAN, 15 Jun 1946 Nashua, NH
BOUCHER, Gloria J and Mark D STRATTON, 27 Sep 1974 Pelham, NH
BOUCHER, Gloria L and William E CARTER, 19 Oct 1963 Hudson, NH
BOUCHER, Jeannette and Richard S MARVELL, 23 Aug 1958 Hudson, NH
BOUCHER, Joseph A and Sherry L FAIRFIELD, 21 Aug 1965 Hudson, NH
BOUCHER, Joseph L and Lucille N JOHNSON, 25 Jun 1949 Hudson, NH
BOUCHER, Joseph R L and Esther B DANEAULT, 04 Jul 1942 Nashua, NH
BOUCHER, Judith A and Edward J GIFFORD, 29 Jun 1970 Nashua, NH
BOUCHER, Juliette F and Robert F SPENCER, 02 Dec 1939 Nashua, NH
BOUCHER, Lionel R and Dorothy A POLAK, 08 Oct 1955 Nashua, NH
BOUCHER, Lisa A and Edward W RILEY, 11 Aug 1984 Hudson, NH
BOUCHER, Lucille I and Andrew T KINVILLE, 28 Apr 1944 Nashua, NH
BOUCHER, Lucille L and Albert C BOYER, 05 Aug 1944 Nashua, NH
BOUCHER, Nadine R and Alan J LAMBERT, 16 Jun 1984 Hudson, NH
BOUCHER, Nanette S and David M CONSTANT, 01 Jun 1979 Hudson, NH
BOUCHER, Nelson and Herbine ST JACQUES, 13 Nov 1933 Nashua, NH
BOUCHER, Norman N and Laura DUBE, 24 Apr 1928 Nashua, NH
BOUCHER, Norman R and Nancy A DERY, 18 Jun 1955 Hudson, NH
BOUCHER, Norman R and Janice C KICZA, 14 Aug 1970 Seabrook, NH
BOUCHER, Norman R and Reina I VIENS, 27 Jun 1975 Hudson, NH
BOUCHER, Normand A and Donna L LOGAN, 07 Apr 1984 Nashua, NH
BOUCHER, Patricia E and Edward V Jr YOUNG, 05 Sep 1955 Nashua, NH
BOUCHER, Rachel A and Robert W FRANCOEUR, 22 Sep 1951 Hudson, NH
BOUCHER, Rheal J and Evelyn R LANDRY, 28 May 1955 Hudson, NH
BOUCHER, Richard A and Claudia E PARKER, 28 Jun 1930 Hudson, NH
BOUCHER, Rita and Charles E FORRENCE, 14 Jun 1941 Nashua, NH
BOUCHER, Robert A and Lori A NADEAU, 29 Sep 1984 Hudson, NH
BOUCHER, Roger M and Virginia L DUNCKLEE, 27 Aug 1949 Nashua, NH
BOUCHER, Roland P and Lucille H STEVENS, 13 Nov 1954 Hudson, NH
BOUCHER, Ronald P and Betty M CUDWORTH, 21 Nov 1953 Hollis, NH
BOUCHER, Rose and Eugene JALBERT, 23 Nov 1929 Nashua, NH

HUDSON, NH MARRIAGES

BOUCHER, Stephen C and Wanita R LAMON, 30 Apr 1983 Hudson, NH
BOUCHER, Stephen R and Claire R CHASSE, 11 Aug 1961 Lincoln, NH
BOUCHER, Susan F and Joseph D WEAVER, 05 Sep 1981 Londonderry, NH
BOUCHER, Theresa A and Roland G Jr HANSON, 01 Jun 1946 Nashua, NH
BOUCHER, Victoria M and Luther L KNIGHTS, 25 Jan 1923 Hudson, NH
BOUCHEY, Dorothy L and Tauno S MAKI, 05 Jan 1949 Hudson, NH
BOUDLE, Elaine M and John G POULIN, 02 Feb 1963 Lancaster, NH
BOUDREAU, Charles R and Rita E COMTOIS, 12 Oct 1984 Hudson, NH
BOUDREAU, Wayne P and Sandra M ZIRPOLO, 18 May 1985 Derry, NH
BOUDREAULT, Marcel J and Lillian S LILLEY, 06 Jul 1963 Hudson, NH
BOUDROT, Edward J and Mary V ORPIK, 17 Jul 1948 Hudson, NH
BOUFFARD, Arthur A and Claudette THIBAULT, 08 Jun 1968 Nashua, NH
BOUFFARD, David P and Sylvie M PLANTE, 29 Oct 1983 Hudson, NH
BOUFFARD, Paul E and Claire L DUBE, 31 Aug 1957 Hudson, NH
BOUFFARD, Ronald N and Mary V COOK, 07 Oct 1961 Nashua, NH
BOULANGER, Florence T and Arthur C DANIELS, 11 Oct 1947 Dover, NH
BOULANGER, Geraldine and Harry W BOWL, 20 Jun 1979 Nashua, NH
BOULANGER, Jean-Paul and Rita A STYNES, 30 May 1970 Nashua, NH
BOULANGER, Joseph R and Edith THOLANDER, 06 Jun 1953 Durham, NH
BOULANGER, Kenneth A and Virginia L CURRIER, 01 Apr 1966 Hudson, NH
BOULANGER, Leonard M & Judith A DESLAURIERS, 25 Sep 1971 Hudson, NH
BOULANGER, Virginia L and Leon R NADEAU, 09 Jul 1983 Hudson, NH
BOULANGER, Vivian Y and John K CLEMENT, 13 Aug 1966 Hudson, NH
BOULANGER, William G and Lizbeth P CARON, 17 Aug 1968 Hudson, NH
BOULARD, Deborah L and Gerald L PELLETIER, 06 Sep 1980 Hudson, NH
BOULAY, Donat and Florida ROBERGE, 09 May 1922 Manchester, NH
BOULDRY, Howard E and Alma C MARGESON, 26 Nov 1935 Nashua, NH
BOULE, Patricia A and Dean J BERGERON, 07 Jul 1973 Londonderry, NH
BOULE, Sharon Ann and Michael Ja MILLER, 17 Dec 1984 Nashua, NH
BOULERISSE, Betty A and Joseph R MILLER, 13 Nov 1965 Nashua, NH
BOULEY, Alice E and Rupert E TATE, 07 Jun 1941 Nashua, NH
BOULEY, Ann M and Steven A GRIFFIN, 10 Sep 1977 Hudson, NH
BOULEY, David E and Michele E WILMOT, 17 May 1975 Nashua, NH
BOULEY, David E and Teresa M DABILIS, 08 Jul 1982 Nashua, NH
BOULEY, Dennis R and Holly A SMALL, 13 Sep 1975 Hudson, NH
BOULEY, Dennis R and Angela B ELLIOTT, 17 Oct 1981 Nashua, NH
BOULEY, Elaine C and Michael W STONE, 17 Jun 1978 Hudson, NH
BOULEY, Eleanor J and Donald R MAIN, 29 Nov 1943 Nashua, NH
BOULEY, Emile and Yvonne PELLETIER, 04 Jul 1935 Nashua, NH
BOULEY, Fern N and William P BRIAND, 04 Jul 1961 Hudson, NH
BOULEY, Glenn E and Leanne I MERCIER, 24 Aug 1957 Hudson, NH
BOULEY, Glenn E and Veronica E DEMAKIS, 05 Jan 1972 Hudson, NH
BOULEY, Glenn J and Patricia L PERRY, 24 Jul 1982 Brookline, NH
BOULEY, Gloria E and Henry P McKENNEY, 13 Jan 1949 Nashua, NH
BOULEY, Irene E and Armand MALENFANT, 28 Aug 1946 Nashua, NH
BOULEY, John R and Marion A SHEPHERD, 10 Sep 1957 Hudson, NH
BOULEY, John R Jr and Cindy L MARTIN, 14 Feb 1981 Nashua, NH
BOULEY, June and Earl L IVES, 06 Nov 1949 Hudson, NH
BOULEY, Kevin R and Barbara A CURRAN, 15 Sep 1973 Hudson, NH
BOULEY, Linda A and Arthur J NOEL, 14 Apr 1971 Hudson, NH
BOULEY, Lorna M and Ronald N NADEAU, 16 Jul 1966 Hudson, NH
BOULEY, Louise M and Robert O Jr CAMPBELL, 28 Jul 1973 Hudson, NH
BOULEY, Lucille Y and Donald P SCHARCH, 22 Aug 1959 Hudson, NH
BOULEY, Marjorie J and Bernard MENDES, 01 May 1948 Hudson, NH
BOULEY, Raymond P and Marie F JEANNOTTE, 29 Dec 1956 Hudson, NH
BOULEY, Raynold A and Linda Jane HOLM, 14 Sep 1972 Nashua, NH
BOULEY, Richard A and Priscilla LAVALLEE, 23 Apr 1949 Nashua, NH
BOULEY, Richard A and Nancy J CAMPBELL, 10 Jul 1971 Hudson, NH
BOULEY, Ruth V and Stanley M FARRINGTON, 16 Sep 1961 Nashua, NH
BOULEY, Shirley A and Larry A CARLSON, 01 Oct 1965 Hudson, NH

HUDSON,NH MARRIAGES

BOULEY, Stephen A and Theresa A DUBE, 11 Sep 1965 Hudson, NH
BOULEY, Suzanne L and Ernest H HOWARD, 13 Sep 1969 Hudson, NH
BOULEY, Thomas P and Joan T DANIELS, 24 May 1969 Hudson, NH
BOULEY, Virginia C and Gabriel R Jr MENARD, 03 Dec 1960 Hudson, NH
BOULTZ, Roberta C and Arthur E CHRISTIAN, 06 Jul 1935 Hudson, NH
BOURASSA, Emery R and Germaine C BREAULT, 26 Apr 1928 Nashua, NH
BOURASSA, Mary Ellen and Michael SHUMSKY, 22 Aug 1981 Brookline, NH
BOURASSA, Nancy B and Barry C LAUGHTON, 08 Nov 1980 Atkinson, NH
BOURASSA, Roger R and Ronalyn D BRAZA, 18 Mar 1983 Hudson, NH
BOURBEAU, Paul O and Laura M ST LAURENT, 24 Sep 1966 Hudson, NH
BOURDEAU, Ronald D and Joyce H LEMIRE, 26 May 1979 Hudson, NH
BOURDON, C H and Rose A GAGNON, 09 Oct 1916 Nashua, NH
   Adolph Bourdon (Canada) & Zoe Demerse (Canada)
   Louis Gagnon(Canada) & Sesari Fournier (Canada)
BOURDON, James A and Linda D LAVALLEE, 24 Feb 1968 Hudson, NH
BOURDON, Margaret and Emile TRUDEAU, 05 Jul 1937 Nashua, NH
BOURGAULT, Rita C and Albert J PAQUETTE, 04 Jul 1943 Nashua, NH
BOURGAULT, Wilfred N and Martha L FORSMAN, 08 Feb 1946 Nashua, NH
BOURGEOIS, Arlene E and Paul M LANDRY, 30 Apr 1960 Hudson, NH
BOURGEOIS, John B Jr and Barbara M HOLT, 26 Sep 1952 Hudson, NH
BOURGEOIS, Lauri L and Ralph C Jr PALMER, 29 May 1982 Nashua, NH
BOURGEOIS, Margaret M and Arthur D GIGUERE, 07 Sep 1973 Nashua, NH
BOURGEOIS, Paula J and Richard E MARSHALL, 17 Oct 1981 Hudson, NH
BOURGEOIS, Raymond W and Jeannette BELL, 13 Mar 1948 Hudson, NH
BOURGEOIS, Roland J A & Francine M GRONDIN, 29 Jun 1985 Nashua, NH
BOURGEOIS, Roland J and Sandra Lee LAWRUK, 26 Jan 1985 Nashua, NH
BOURQUE, Frederick and Roxy P BERNARD, 20 Apr 1968 Windham, NH
BOURQUE, M Donalda and Joseph J LUCHUN, 30 Dec 1933 Salem, NH
BOURQUE, Pauline R and Alan A MORGAN, 12 Aug 1978 Merrimack, NH
BOURQUE, Roxy P and Reginald L ROUX, 19 Nov 1970 Nashua, NH
BOURQUE, Theresa M and Gary W MacGRATH, 28 May 1982 Nashua, NH
BOURQUE, Wilfred R and Constance CHAPUT, 16 Apr 1983 Nashua, NH
BOURRET, David A and Michele D ROY, 25 Jan 1985 Pelham, NH
BOURSO, Fred and Adeline J BOYER, 30 Aug 1919 Nashua, NH
BOUTHILLIER, Philippe H and Mona J BECHARD, 12 Nov 1966 Hudson, NH
BOUTILIER, Gail E and James F III HENDERSON, 15 Aug 1969 Hudson, NH
BOUTILIER, Jean L and Richard H Jr PETERSON, 11 Aug 1973 Hudson, NH
BOUTILIER, Linda F and Peter L HANSEN, 11 Feb 1971 Nashua, NH
BOUTILIER, Robert G and Sandra T BERUBE, 06 Nov 1965 Nashua, NH
BOUTILLIER, Joanne L and James P SALESKY, 06 Nov 1971 Hudson, NH
BOUTIN, Gary J and Kathleen M LAVALLEE, 28 Nov 1983 Litchfield, NH
BOUTIN, Jean B and Mary A GILL, 05 Aug 1950 Nashua, NH
BOUTSELIS, James J and Rachel M DAIGLE, 01 Sep 1949 Hudson, NH
BOVYN, Albert A III and Flora A REED, 14 Apr 1979 Auburn, NH
BOWDEN, Dexter T and Rosamond L BRIGGS, 05 Aug 1940 Hudson, NH
BOWDEN, Donald F and Ann B WRIGHT, 12 Nov 1977 Hudson, NH
BOWDEN, Leonard A and Louann M THEBODEAU, 28 Jul 1984 Plaistow, NH
BOWDEN, Sherry L and Michael E SANBORN, 17 Sep 1983 Hudson, NH
BOWEN, Jacqueline and Angell G BEZA, 08 Jul 1956 Hanover, NH
BOWEN, Richard A and Barbara A HARVEY, 14 May 1975 Nashua, NH
BOWEN, Susie Walch and Willis PERHAM, 12 Sep 1910 Hudson, NH
   James E Walch & Susan M Beaman
   Oliver Perham & Rebecca B Clark
BOWEN, Thomas H and Diane L BOUCHER, 14 Oct 1972 Hudson, NH
BOWERS, Rhoda and Samuel Jr HILLS, 02 Jun 1796
BOWL, Harry W and Geraldine BOULANGER, 01 Jun 1979 Nashua, NH
BOWL, Harry W and Florence L MANSUR, 10 Oct 1980 Hudson, NH
BOWLES, Alice V and James B WHIPPLE, 27 Aug 1882 Hudson, NH
   William Bowles & Mary Greenleaf (Calais, ME)
   John Whipple(New Boston, NH) & Philantha Reed (Berry, VT)

HUDSON, NH MARRIAGES

BOWLES, Clarissa and William BLODGETT, 12 Sep 1844
BOWMAN, Cheryl R and Dennis M DELUCA, 31 May 1974 Nashua, NH
BOWMAN, James C and Erma A BLYE, 29 Jun 1944 Hudson, NH
BOWMAN, Linda G and Alan R GARSIDE, 12 Oct 1968 Nashua, NH
BOWMAN, Michael R and Janice L FORTNAM, 10 Nov 1984 Nashua, NH
BOWRING, Allison F and George C Jr WYMAN, 14 Feb 1983 Hudson, NH
BOWSER, Lorraine B and Edward J MURPHY, 25 Dec 1949 Hudson, NH
BOYD, Charlotte and Nathan PLUMMER, 10 Apr 1846
BOYD, Mina A and Charles L STEELE, 25 Nov 1913 Newton Ctre, MA
  Hirma J Boyd & Sarah L Jameson
  Charles A Steele & Lottie A Reynolds
BOYD, Thomas and Sarah A CHASE, 24 Aug 1854
BOYDEN, Edmund A and Ruth T LAPHAM, 04 Aug 1934 Effingham Fls, NH
BOYER, Adeline J and Fred BOURSO, 30 Aug 1919 Nashua, NH
BOYER, Albert C and Lucille L BOUCHER, 05 Aug 1944 Nashua, NH
BOYER, Albert E and Dorothy M LEMAY, 27 Nov 1952 Nashua, NH
BOYER, Alfred F and Rose A GILMAN, 17 Jul 1943 Nashua, NH
BOYER, Dorothy A and Lloyd E OTIS, 31 Jul 1965 Hudson, NH
BOYER, Eleanor R and Richard J WHEELER, 12 May 1945 Hudson, NH
BOYER, George and Therese Y POULIN, 28 Jun 1958 Nashua, NH
BOYER, Ivon and Joan E PARTRIDGE, 28 Oct 1960 Nashua, NH
BOYER, Janet M and Robert A BRIAND, 16 Apr 1983 Hudson, NH
BOYER, Joan L and Gregory E JOHNSON, 06 Jan 1962 Hudson, NH
BOYER, Joseph J and Eva E KINVILLE, 16 Feb 1920 Nashua, NH
BOYER, Lucienne A and Edward J LAROSE, 11 Feb 1956 Hudson, NH
BOYER, Norman C and Rosemarie CLOUTIER, 17 Oct 1971 Hudson, NH
BOYER, Roger R and Marion L THOMPSON, 31 Oct 1959 Hudson, NH
BOYER, Shirley A and Chester A COULOMBE, 03 Sep 1955 Nashua, NH
BOYINGTON, Ellen F and Clifton E BUTTRICK, 14 Aug 1880 Augusta, ME
  John W Boyington(Dresden, ME) & Militiah S Glidden(Jefferson, ME)
  Ephraem Buttrick(Pelham, NH) & Sarah Cutter (Nashua, NH)
BOYKO, Dennis M and Nancy A PATRIDGE, 22 Aug 1981 Bedford, NH
BOYLE, Leo A and Vivian J MALAQUIAS, 05 Jan 1948 Hudson, NH
BOYLE, Leo J and Norma J MITCHELL, 01 Nov 1947 Hudson, NH
BOYLE, Marion A and Robert J TAYLOR, 21 Aug 1937 Hudson, NH
BOYNTON, Georgie and Gerry F PARKER, 10 Nov 1904 Hudson, NH
  John E Boynton & Frances Haskell
  John Parker & Eldora M Dodge
BOYNTON, Janice E and Clayton P OGILVIE, 08 Oct 1971 Hudson, NH
BOYSTER, Gloria A and Ronald J LAJOIE, 12 Sep 1969 Hudson, NH
BRACCIO, Darlene A and Richard D PARENT, 21 Sep 1974 Hudson, NH
BRACCIO, Donna M and Robert H FOURNIER, 13 May 1967 Hudson, NH
BRACCIO, Kenneth J and Nancy L GRAVELLE, 16 Feb 1963 Hudson, NH
BRACHETTI, Emma M and Robert S DRAKE, 15 Apr 1945 Hudson, NH
BRACKENBUSCH, Kristina A and Thomas L BAKER, 28 Aug 1982 Hudson, NH
BRACY, Judith A and Richard F CARON, 21 Sep 1968 Hudson, NH
BRADBURY, Carrie S and Justin E HILL, 05 Jul 1868
BRADBURY, Henry A and Gayle M LYON, 17 Apr 1971 Nashua, NH
BRADBURY, Nathaniel and Carmela J COLARUSSO, 17 Dec 1949 Hudson, NH
BRADDOCK, John C and Carol A ABBOTT, 19 Apr 1969 Hudson, NH
BRADFORD, Brenda L and Clifford M LANDRY, 09 Sep 1978 Hudson, NH
BRADFORD, Robert S and Edith I LINDBOHM, 19 Sep 1937 Nashua, NH
BRADLEE, Herbert G and Celena W DEAN, 28 Jul 1939 Hudson, NH
BRADLEY, Bessie V and Roland W HARDY, 05 Dec 1925 Hudson, NH
BRADLEY, Chester J and Gladys CUNNINGHAM, 25 Nov 1945 Hudson, NH
BRADLEY, Daniel L and Paula A DUBE, 05 May 1984 Hudson, NH
BRADLEY, Frederick and Elizabeth SULLIVAN, 18 Jun 1918 Nashua, NH
BRADLEY, Frederick and Lucille M LANGLOIS, 10 Feb 1947 Hudson, NH
BRADLEY, George W and Maria C COLBURN, 15 Nov 1870 Hudson, NH
BRADLEY, Hazel D and William H MARTIN, 22 Jun 1917 Hudson, NH

HUDSON,NH MARRIAGES

BRADLEY, Helen F and James Murray WHITNEY, 29 Sep 1923 Hudson, NH
BRADLEY, Margaret E and Stanley A JOHNSON, 03 Jul 1950 Hudson, NH
BRADLEY, Maurice A and Dora McLELLAN, 28 Jun 1930 Nashua, NH
BRADLEY, Patricia J and Robert D GALLAGHER, 08 Apr 1967 Hudson, NH
BRADLEY, Roger E and Mary A O'CONNOR, 08 Aug 1969 Jaffrey, NH
BRADLEY, Zoe M and Alfred P NELSON, 26 Oct 1916 Hudson, NH
   Allen Bradley (Plattsburgh, NY) & Clara Dennison (Cutler, ME)
   Myron H Nelson(Dorchester, NH) & Lillian Applefee (Dover, NH)
BRADT, Henry and Betsey WYMAN, 28 Jun 1826
BRADY, John F and Geraldine BUCKINGHAM, 19 Mar 1949 Hudson, NH
BRADY, Stephen E and Patricia GIGUERE, 10 Oct 1981 Hudson, NH
BRAGINTON, Peter R and Helen M ROSS, 30 Jul 1971 Exeter, NH
BRAHANEY, Ann Marie and John R BERNIER, 28 Apr 1984 Nashua, NH
BRALEY, Myrna A and Fernand J PREVOST, 15 Jun 1957 Hebron, NH
BRALEY, Robert N and LeReine G LEWIS, 01 Jun 1963 Hudson, NH
BRANEY, Robert E and Aile C FRYKBERG, 11 Nov 1948 Hudson, NH
BRANN, William J and Brenda Jea RODERICK, 29 Sep 1984 Nashua, NH
BRAUGH, Charles and Mary E BUTLER, 23 Sep 1887 Nashua, NH
   Samuel Braugh (Canada) & Duchess (Canada)
BRAULT, Gabrielle and Hillard F BEEBIE, 15 Nov 1952 Nashua, NH
BRAULT, Laurent S and Rita E LEBOEUF, 01 Oct 1946 Nashua, NH
BRAUNFELD, Frank J and Marjorie FRENCH, 09 Nov 1940 Hudson, NH
BRAY, Charles A and Ruth A BARTLETT, 1878
   L Bray (Deerisle, ME) & Mary E Bray
   Morill C Bartlett & Ann O
BRAZA, Ronalyn D and Roger R BOURASSA, 18 Mar 1983 Hudson, NH
BREAULT, Debra Joy and Maurice G DESROSIERS, 23 Jun 1973 Hudson, NH
BREAULT, Germaine C and Emery R BOURASSA, 26 Apr 1928 Nashua, NH
BREAULT, Jacqulyn A and Robert L Jr CHASSE, 26 Jun 1982 Hudson, NH
BREAULT, JoAnn M and Michael William DIONNE, 25 Aug 1978 Hudson, NH
BREAULT, Richard N and Joyce M GRIECE, 01 Nov 1973 Hudson, NH
BRECK, Rose M and Ronald O LECLAIR, 25 Sep 1981 Hudson, NH
BREDTHOLTZ, Nathan and Sophie Rac BASKIN, 28 Aug 1938 Nashua, NH
BREED, Abbie F and Frank B SHATTUCK, 24 Nov 1880 Hudson, NH
BREED, Alice V and Ernest W LYON, 17 Dec 1960 Nashua, NH
BREED, Harold E and Alice V FORD, 08 Jun 1925 Nashua, NH
BREEN, John M and Lillian E TRUFANT, 05 Oct 1920 Nashua, NH
BREEN, John M Jr and Shirley M DUNCKLEE, 11 Oct 1947 Nashua, NH
BREEN, Michael D and Deborah A FANCOVIC, 18 Aug 1972 Hudson, NH
BREEN, Paul G and Brenda B SIMPSON, 17 Jun 1961 Nashua, NH
BREEN, Thomas J and Catherine PAUL, 11 Sep 1937 Hudson, NH
BRENNAN, Cameron J and John D CASSIDY, 15 Sep 1984 Hudson, NH
BRENNAN, Catherine and William DAREY, 27 May 1919 Hudson, NH
BRENNAN, Donald R and Edith C BROWN, 25 May 1967 Nashua, NH
BRENNAN, John S and Gertrude C BARRY, 09 Sep 1937 Hudson, NH
BRENNAN, Lillian M and James M FITZGERALD, 26 Aug 1932 Nashua, NH
BRESCIA, Rose Marie and Roy E Jr MILLIKEN, 24 Jun 1953 Nashua, NH
BRESNAHAN, Jacqueline and Donald J MacCANN, 15 Jun 1956 Pelham, NH
BRESNAHAN, John T and Josephine ZEDALIS, 16 Jan 1928 Nashua, NH
BRESNAHAN, Joseph H and Rolande A TARDIF, 13 Nov 1946 Salem, NH
BRESNEHAN, Lawrence and Sylvis TURGEAN, 07 Nov 1936 Milford, NH
BRETON, Carole A and Stephen R OSMER, 10 Jun 1972 Hudson, NH
BRETON, Nelson R and Cynthia I RAYMOND, 23 Oct 1983 Hudson, NH
BRETTELL, Herbert S&Helen E STECKIEWICZ, 11 Oct 1947 Manchester, NH
BRETTELL, Kathleen I and Donald W KELLEY, 26 Jul 1943 Hampton, NH
BREWER, Linda S and Thomas E Jr REED, 29 Nov 1982 Hudson, NH
BREWER, Shirley A and George J GALLOWAY, 28 Apr 1965 Nashua, NH
BRIANAS, Penelope S and Mark A BRUNELLE, 24 Apr 1982 Hudson, NH
BRIAND, Abraham J and Dorothy I WILLIAMSON, 13 Oct 1984 Hudson, NH
BRIAND, Alfred D and Diane C BOSSE, 21 Dec 1968 Nashua, NH

HUDSON,NH MARRIAGES

BRIAND, Brenda L and Walter E KING, 29 Jul 1972 Hudson, NH
BRIAND, Bruce L and Andrea VOLIANITES, 04 Mar 1979 Pelham, NH
BRIAND, Carol A and Martin C SHEIL, 17 Jun 1978 Hudson, NH
BRIAND, David K and Claudette PENO, 05 Sep 1959 Hudson, NH
BRIAND, David K and Deborah E WORSTER, 11 Feb 1978 Hudson, NH
BRIAND, Donald B and Betty A DOOLEY, 31 Jan 1969 Hudson, NH
BRIAND, Donald B and Lorraine M JETTE, 11 Aug 1973 Hudson, NH
BRIAND, Doris I and Forest D FOSTER, 12 Jul 1952 Hudson, NH
BRIAND, Earl G and Linda D MUNDAY, 08 Feb 1969 Hudson, NH
BRIAND, Earl G and Peggy J LIBBY, 18 Sep 1976 Nashua, NH
BRIAND, Edith M and Robert L BEAN, 26 Aug 1963 Hudson, NH
BRIAND, Edmond O and Janet R ROLLINS, 01 Apr 1955 Nashua, NH
BRIAND, Ernest A and Shirley A SMITH, 27 Aug 1955 Hudson, NH
BRIAND, Ernest A and Fern N BRIAND, 08 Apr 1967 Hudson, NH
BRIAND, Ernest E and Claudette MARKS, 28 Jun 1980 Hudson, NH
BRIAND, Fern N and Ernest A BRIAND, 08 Apr 1967 Hudson, NH
BRIAND, Gene R and Rita I BOSSE, 21 Jun 1969 Nashua, NH
BRIAND, George P and Mary J LAFLAMME, 24 Dec 1954 Nashua, NH
BRIAND, George P and Linda A RICARD, 27 Jun 1970 Hudson, NH
BRIAND, Janet R and Gerard J LAFERRIERE, 15 May 1982 Hudson, NH
BRIAND, Jo Ann R and Armand E DUCLOS, 19 Mar 1959 Hudson, NH
BRIAND, John M and Judith A RACKLIFF, 10 Jan 1967 Hudson, NH
BRIAND, John M and Linda Ann PAINE, 29 Jul 1972 Hudson, NH
BRIAND, Joseph R Jr and Donna L THEBODEAU, 31 Oct 1968 Nashua, NH
BRIAND, Judith G and John H MOODY, 31 Jul 1965 Hudson, NH
BRIAND, Larry D and Michele F CHARTIER, 17 Nov 1978 Hudson, NH
BRIAND, Lorraine E and Robert C LEVESQUE, 18 Aug 1951 Hudson, NH
BRIAND, Marie L and Alfred E BASTILLE, 16 Jan 1971 Hudson, NH
BRIAND, Michael G and Linda S VALCOURT, 19 Apr 1975 Litchfield, NH
BRIAND, Paul R and Linda M DOHERTY, 28 Jun 1969 Nashua, NH
BRIAND, Paula J and Steven G POOLE, 15 Mar 1980 Nashua, NH
BRIAND, Phyllis E and Roger L COTE, 06 Apr 1959 Nashua, NH
BRIAND, Raymond O and Diane L DORAN, 16 Oct 1965 Hudson, NH
BRIAND, Raymond P and Doreen M GALLANT, 11 Jun 1970 Hudson, NH
BRIAND, Rita and Charles A PRATT, 18 Apr 1942 Nashua, NH
BRIAND, Robert A and Janet M BOYER, 16 Apr 1983 Hudson, NH
BRIAND, Sandra E and David A COURTEMANCHE, 01 Sep 1972 Hudson, NH
BRIAND, Sylvia J and Norman A DUQUETTE, 27 Sep 1958 Durham, NH
BRIAND, William P and Fern N BOULEY, 04 Jul 1961 Hudson, NH
BRIAND, William P and Dolores C WHITAKER, 09 Aug 1968 Nashua, NH
BRICAULT, Irene C and Alfred J ST ARMAND, 19 Feb 1955 Nashua, NH
BRICKETT, June and Raymond E PARKER, 16 Oct 1955 Hampstead, NH
BRIDGES, Annie S and Frank W BODWELL, 16 May 1888 Hudson, NH
   Jackson Bridges (Marion, ME) & Mary Card (Lubic, ME)
   Amos C Bodwell(Salem, NH) & Sarah J Bodwell (Derry, NH)
BRIDGES, Raymond T and Rose A MARTINEAU, 14 Oct 1961 Hudson, NH
BRIDGES, Sherry A and Robert F COTE, 18 Jun 1966 Hampstead, NH
BRIEN, Michael J and Barbara S ST LAURENT, 20 Aug 1982 Hudson, NH
BRIENZA, Lena R and Walter VENTURA, 14 May 1943 Hudson, NH
BRIENZI, Daniel A and Freida R OBELSKY, 24 Jan 1931 Nashua, NH
BRIER, Elaine M and Pirley E II WISEMAN, 12 Sep 1970 Portsmouth, NH
BRIER, Manuel Ant and Denise Rit PERRON, 06 Jul 1974 Nashua, NH
BRIERE, Leo P and Marlene C MILLER, 09 Aug 1952 Hudson, NH
BRIERE, Marlene C and Edward O LAMPRON, 09 Sep 1955 Hudson, NH
BRIGGS, John E and Thelma A WORTHINGTON, 22 Jan 1950 Hudson, NH
BRIGGS, Karen L & William L III ANDREWS, 16 May 1980 Harrisville,NH
BRIGGS, Robert F and Candace L BATCHELDER, 27 Jun 1970 Hudson, NH
BRIGGS, Rosamond L and Dexter T BOWDEN, 05 Aug 1940 Hudson, NH
BRIGHAM, Barbara J and Roderick W TURNER, 26 Mar 1983 Nashua, NH
BRIGHAM, George W Jr and Andria D SPICER, 06 Apr 1970 Hudson, NH

HUDSON,NH MARRIAGES

BRIGHAM, George W Jr and Faye E LUCIER, 23 Jul 1977 New Boston, NH
BRIGHAM, Ricky James and Deborah Lee STORY, 19 Aug 1978 Hudson, NH
BRIGHT, Ellen F and Charles WHEELER, 07 Sep 1862
BRINER, Byron O Jr and Susan L CROSBY, 24 Aug 1968 Hudson, NH
BRINKER, Love S and William R NELSON, 16 Dec 1967 Nashua, NH
BRINTNALL, Benjamin and Dorothy F HOMER, 14 Jun 1947 Hudson, NH
BRISCOE, Jean W and Thomas C III BUCHANAN, 23 Jul 1949 Hudson, NH
BRISEBOIS, Irene E and Roland M DION, 21 Jun 1968 Allenstown, NH
BRISEBOIS, Lucille J and William R LAVALLEE, 30 Dec 1952 Nashua, NH
BRITH, Karen F and Thomas A Jr DALY, 23 Mar 1972 Hudson, NH
BRITO, James M and Barbara J DIAS, 10 Mar 1985 Hudson, NH
BRITTON, Ada L and Chester A ANDREWS, 01 Jun 1915 Nashua, NH
   Arthur W Britton (W Milan, NH) & Tilea L Chadwick (Norwich, VT)
   William A Andrews(Hudson, NH) & Willette Annis (Londonderry, NH)
BROADBENT, Alfred J and Arlene A MARTELL, 30 Sep 1949 Hudson, NH
BROADBENT, Gayle A and Lester J JORDAN, 28 Feb 1970 Pelham, NH
BROCK, George M and Blanche M THOMPSON, 08 Sep 1897 Hudson, NH
   William S Brock & Helen F Johnson
   John M Thompson & Elizabeth Marsh
BROCK, Linda A and Ronald G GILCREAST, 16 Oct 1971 Concord, NH
BRODERICK, Flora and Ernest E PERKINS, 12 Sep 1940 Nashua, NH
BRODEUR, Camille and Oberline NOEL, 30 May 1933 Nashua, NH
BRODEUR, Elaine C and Robert S LANGELIER, 25 Aug 1962 Hudson, NH
BRODEUR, Hormidas E and Bertha DUVAL, 20 Jun 1921 Nashua, NH
BRODEUR, Katherine and LaMar CALDWELL, 19 Nov 1983 Nashua, NH
BRODEUR, Robert C and Phyllis A TRUDEAU, 11 Jun 1960 Nashua, NH
BRODEUR, Roger G and Bernadette LANDRY, 23 Jun 1951 Hudson, NH
BRODSKY, Stephen R and Claudia A HENRY, 19 Dec 1981 Hudson, NH
BROGGI, Allen and Carolyn V CARSON, 12 Jan 1980 Amherst, NH
BROGIE, Paul J and Catherine CONLON, 04 Sep 1933 Nashua, NH
BROMLEY, Dennis R and Jacqueline DALESSIO, 28 Jul 1979 Hudson, NH
BRONSON, Deborah J and Walter E LANCESTER, 06 Sep 1975 Hudson, NH
BROOK, Crystal L and David S BOTHWICK, 04 Sep 1970 Hudson, NH
BROOK, Stephen P and Elaine T ROBBINS, 15 May 1970 Nashua, NH
BROOKES, Cynthia L and Robert J ALLISON, 24 Jun 1984 Hudson, NH
BROOKS, Antoinette and Norman J RICARD, 16 Aug 1969 Hudson, NH
BROOKS, Carolyn A and Robert W RANNEY, 01 Aug 1975 Hudson, NH
BROOKS, Catherine and Charles E GUYETTE, 02 Apr 1941 Nashua, NH
BROOKS, Debra J and James T ROUSSELL, 14 Nov 1981 Pelham, NH
BROOKS, Earl T and Dorothy E WEEKS, 09 Jul 1932 Manchester, NH
BROOKS, Helen M and Oscar W PARKER, 19 Feb 1950 Hollis, NH
BROOKS, Leland V and Carolyn A CARTER, 15 Jan 1966 Hudson, NH
BROOKS, Nancy R and Charles L McQUESTEN, 16 Apr 1967 Nashua, NH
BROOKS, Olive and George ROHAN, 07 Feb 1947 Hudson, NH
BROOKS, Raymond C Jr and Rita M LAVARNWAY, 07 Jan 1946 Nashua, NH
BROOKS, Roland E and Carolyn A MOODY, 20 Nov 1965 Hudson, NH
BROUGH, Richard D and Patricia A DUFOUR, 13 Nov 1976 Litchfield, NH
BROUILLARD, Diane M and William E MORSE, 21 Sep 1984 Hudson, NH
BROUILLET, Marie E and Raymond A Jr RICE, 26 Feb 1968 Nashua, NH
BROUILLETTE, Richard and Marilyn D McNEIL, 03 May 1947 Hudson, NH
BROUSSEAU, Anthony P and Virginia A MANNING, 26 Nov 1982 Hudson, NH
BROUSSEAU, Danielle P and Carl D RAPSIS, 28 Oct 1978 Hudson, NH
BROUSSEAU, Gerard J and Denise A BONNETTE, 11 Apr 1969 Nashua, NH
BROWN, Albert N and Marguerite E RUSSELL, 06 Nov 1926 Hudson, NH
BROWN, Arthur F and Virginia LEVESQUE, 25 Oct 1947 Hudson, NH
BROWN, Arthur F and Mildred Smith RUSSELL, 05 Jul 1928 Worcester,MA
BROWN, Ashton W and Mary J PEARSON, 27 Sep 1922 Hudson, NH
BROWN, Barbara and Frank PEDATO, 23 Jun 1949 Hudson, NH
BROWN, Barrude and Hannah BLODGETT, 06 Jun 1780
BROWN, Beatrice M and Walter T TAYLOR, 01 Apr 1950 Hudson, NH

HUDSON, NH MARRIAGES

BROWN, Benzilla and Hannah BLODGETT, 06 Jun 1780
BROWN, Betsey and Peter DOFF, 18 Apr 1866
BROWN, Betsey and Peter POFF, 08 Apr 1866 Lowell, MA
BROWN, Carlton H and Joanne S HARTSON, 12 Aug 1972 Nashua, NH
BROWN, Carlton H and Pauline A NIQUETTE, 04 Jun 1983 Hudson, NH
BROWN, Charles D & Lillian V DICCHARD, 01 Feb 1917 Bellows Fls, VT
BROWN, Charles E and Martha S PAPPAS, 10 Dec 1977 Pelham, NH
BROWN, Charles E and Therese M OIKLE, 30 Apr 1982 Nashua, NH
BROWN, Cynthia L and Stephen W McINTOSH, 06 Nov 1982 Hudson, NH
BROWN, Daniel T and Lynn A CLEMENT, 16 Aug 1980 Hudson, NH
BROWN, David W and Jeanne R MORIN, 08 Nov 1958 Hudson, NH
BROWN, Deanna J and Lester K RHEAUME, 11 Aug 1973 Bristol, NH
BROWN, Deborah An and Daniel L PELLETIER, 06 Aug 1977 Pelham, NH
BROWN, Dennis P and Lois M BARITEAU, 23 Jan 1965 Nashua, NH
BROWN, Diane J and Raymond A GENDRON, 01 Oct 1955 Nashua, NH
BROWN, Douglas E and Betty L DOHERTY, 28 Apr 1957 Hudson, NH
BROWN, Douglas H and Shirley A CROTEAU, 24 Jul 1965 Marlborough, NH
BROWN, Edith C and Donald R BRENNAN, 25 May 1967 Nashua, NH
BROWN, Elizabeth and James V KEMP, 20 Nov 1822
BROWN, Elizabeth and John MANOLAKIS, 14 Mar 1948 Hudson, NH
BROWN, Frances J and Louis W JETTE, 03 Mar 1958 Hudson, NH
BROWN, Francis K and Denise CROSBIE, 22 Apr 1980 Milford, NH
BROWN, Harold L and Marie E DEAN, 23 Aug 1965 Hudson, NH
BROWN, Harry W and Pearl B OLIVER, 20 Jul 1941 Hudson, NH
BROWN, Harry W and Alice Evelyn FRENCH, 17 Mar 1928 Hudson, NH
BROWN, Helen O and Fernand MORIN, 17 Jul 1948 Hudson, NH
BROWN, Herbert M and Charlene E STEELE, 15 Jun 1932 Nashua, NH
BROWN, Ina L and Howard A ANDREWS, 12 May 1908 Nashua, NH
  Henry C Brown & Clara L Bryant
  Arthur S Andrews & Linnie F Butler
BROWN, James J and Jayne E MITCHELL, 30 Sep 1982 Londonderry, NH
BROWN, James J and Jayne E MITCHELL, 04 Jun 1983 Hudson, NH
BROWN, Jeannette and Richard A GAGNON, 10 Oct 1981 Hudson, NH
BROWN, Jessie G and Herbert A PHELAN, 27 May 1922 Hudson, NH
BROWN, Joan L and Donald J REED, 17 Jul 1971 Hollis, NH
BROWN, Joann A and James J LARGY, 01 Apr 1967 Nashua, NH
BROWN, Joseph and Abigail Underwd ESTERBROOK, 01 Jan 1800
BROWN, Judith E and Gary E BARRIAULT, 18 Jun 1971 Hollis, NH
BROWN, June V and Harry B HUNTER, 17 Oct 1956 Nashua, NH
BROWN, Kathleen A and Kenneth F PETERSON, 15 May 1976 Hudson, NH
BROWN, Leon E and Blanche H YOUNG, 30 Aug 1930 Hudson, NH
BROWN, Lois M and Robert H BUTLER, 19 Feb 1977 Hudson, NH
BROWN, Marjorie E and William J Jr SAWICKI, 14 Feb 1976 Nashua, NH
BROWN, Patricia A and David L STAPANOWICH, 28 Sep 1963 Hudson, NH
BROWN, Perry M and Virginia M BUTCHER, 08 Jun 1946 Hudson, NH
BROWN, Raymond C and Evelyn M LEVESQUE, 01 Mar 1946 Nashua, NH
BROWN, Richard E and Marlene M COOKE, 18 May 1963 Nashua, NH
BROWN, Robert Lee and Janice F CARTER, 22 May 1976 Nashua, NH
BROWN, Rollin E and Lorraine A TREMBLAY, 21 Jan 1956 Hollis, NH
BROWN, Rosalie M and John E McQUAID, 25 Sep 1983 Nashua, NH
BROWN, S Wilder and June V BATCHELDER, 21 Feb 1952 Nashua, NH
BROWN, Samuel and Sarah GOULD, 20 Apr 1778
BROWN, Samuel and Sarah Gould GREELEY, 20 Apr 1778
BROWN, Sarah N and Lyman O WEBSTER, 07 Sep 1851
BROWN, Simon and Lydia CALDWELL, Jul 1817
BROWN, Sullivan W and Vernita POLLARD, 14 Jun 1924 Nashua, NH
BROWN, Turner K and Claire A TANGUAY, 31 Aug 1957 Hudson, NH
BROWN, Vernon S and Lilla L WILSHIRE, 15 Jun 1921 Hudson, NH
BROWN, Virginia and Michael J KAROS, 20 Jan 1968 Hudson, NH
BROWN, Walter A and Judith E CUNNINGHAM, 07 Apr 1962 Hudson, NH

HUDSON, NH MARRIAGES

BRUCE, Edith H and Francis P HENNESSY, 16 Dec 1914 Hudson, NH
  Elias A Bruce & Addie B Farmer
  John F Hennessy & Margaret A King
BRUCE, Richard and Emma J BEALS, 31 Oct 1889 Hudson, NH
  Henry Bruce (Brooklyn, N S) & Lydia Gustave (Brookfield)
  Wm J Beals(Larnstown) & Tracy McGregor (Tremont, N S)
BRUCE, Walter J and Anna HASSLER, 23 Feb 1924 Nashua, NH
BRUDO, Alexander and Lucy BULTER, 18 May 1891
BRUDZISZ, Ronald K and JoAnne LAW, 12 Jan 1974 Nashua, NH
BRUN, Alice L and Roland L SALOIS, 04 May 1976 Nashua, NH
BRUNEAU, Lorette E and Gerard L LEBOEUF, 11 Jun 1955 Nashua, NH
BRUNELLE, Ernestine and Joseph F COTE, 15 Oct 1949 Nashua, NH
BRUNELLE, Grace M and Frank JATKWICZ, 29 May 1965 Nashua, NH
BRUNELLE, Lorraine O and Robert C BUXTON, 26 Sep 1949 Nashua, NH
BRUNELLE, Marie F and Charles W SNYDER, 12 Jun 1948 Hudson, NH
BRUNELLE, Mark A and Penelope S BRIANAS, 24 Apr 1982 Hudson, NH
BRUNELLE, Maurice E and Norma I McANESPIE, 15 Jul 1966 Hudson, NH
BRUNELLE, Roland J B and Isabel R DOYLE, 28 Sep 1938 Nashua, NH
BRUNESFIELD, Katherine & Walter G RICH, 11 Apr 1911 Manchester, NH
  Patrick Brunsfield & Nora Flinn
  F A Rich & Nellie Caverling
BRUNT, Arthur and Muriel CANFIELD, 06 Jun 1927 Hudson, NH
BRUNT, Arthur R and Marjorie E MINER, 06 Mar 1954 Nashua, NH
BRUNT, Marjorie L and Richard A GLISPIN, 29 Mar 1974 Hudson, NH
BRUSSARD, Donald J and Georgia FULLER, 15 Sep 1984 Nashua, NH
BRYAND, David J and Patricia A DROLET, 30 Jun 1973 Nashua, NH
BRYAND, Francois J and Carol A KENNEDY, 11 Feb 1977 Nashua, NH
BRYAND, Ronald J and Janet S LOYD, 03 Mar 1973 Nashua, NH
BRYAND, Susan M and Leonard P KENNEDY, 02 Jul 1976 Hudson, NH
BRYANT, James H Jr and Loris V CRABB, 30 Sep 1946 Hudson, NH
BRYANT, Jean I and Paul T DION, 02 Jun 1948 Hudson, NH
BRYANT, Malcolm K and Joyce F REYNOLDS, 23 May 1964 Nashua, NH
BRYANT, Margaret A and Robert L BILODEAU, 07 Jul 1969 Nashua, NH
BRYANT, Renay L and Edward J BELLEVANCE, 13 Dec 1975 Hudson, NH
BRYANT, William E and Marjorie A BURNHAM, 27 May 1951 Hudson, NH
BRYAR, Winton S and Marjorie McKAY, 02 Feb 1934 Nashua, NH
BRYDER, Phyllis J and John FAIA, 25 Sep 1937 Hudson, NH
BUCHANAN, D M Jr and Catherine MORAN, 28 Aug 1948 Nashua, NH
BUCHANAN, Kenneth M and Barbara S CRAVEN, 26 Oct 1947 Hudson, NH
BUCHANAN, Thomas C III and Jean W BRISCOE, 23 Jul 1949 Hudson, NH
BUCK, Jennie M and John W CONNELL, 01 Apr 1866
BUCKAWICKI, Helen G & Ralph J Jr WHITTAKER, 02 May 1982 Hudson, NH
BUCKERIE, Joseph S and Claire A GREGORY, 31 Dec 1941 Hudson, NH
BUCKINGHAM, Geraldine and John F BRADY, 19 Mar 1949 Hudson, NH
BUCKMINSTER, Harriet E and J Parker SMITH, 27 Oct 1853
BUDER, Darthy A and Steven F CADY, 27 Nov 1971 Nashua, NH
BUDRO, Albert N and Joyce B GUYETTE, 26 Aug 1972 Hudson, NH
BUDRO, Alex and Lucy BUTLER, 18 May 1891 Hudson, NH
  David Budro (Chazy, NY) & Clara Ferryall (Scotia, NY)
BUFFUM, Vernon M and Geraldine WEBSTER, 13 Aug 1955 Hudson, NH
BUHRMEISTER, Gary L and Judy E COLL, 16 Jul 1966 Hudson, NH
BUJINOWSKI, Richard and Shari L ESTABROOK, 28 Oct 1972 Hudson, NH
BUJNOWSKI, Kevin J and Teresa L BOILARD, 20 Oct 1979 Hudson, NH
BUJNOWSKI, Richard and Debra M NICHOLS, 20 Nov 1982 Nashua, NH
BUJOLD, Michele S and Robert N Jr HANSEN, 20 Feb 1970 Hudson, NH
BUKER, Charles E and Barbara L BELLEAU, 14 Dec 1955 Hudson, NH
BUKLEREWICZ, Julian J and Pamela A JORDAN, 24 Jun 1978 Rindge, NH
BUKOFSKE, Alan David and Cheryl Ann RHYNER, 29 Aug 1981 Nashua, NH
BULDINI, Irene M and Henry W PARKINSON, 17 Aug 1940 Hudson, NH
BULENS, Collette and Gary G WOODS, 09 Feb 1980 Hudson, NH

HUDSON, NH MARRIAGES

BULGER, Shirley R and Manuel J PLOCKETT, 27 Jul 1946 Hudson, NH
BULLARD, Doreen Ann and Allen Dona LAJOIE, 18 Jul 1981 Hudson, NH
BULLARD, John O Jr and Patricia L BINKS, 08 Jun 1957 Nashua, NH
BULLARD, Patricia L and Maurice R CLEMENT, 01 Sep 1962 Hudson, NH
BULLOCK, Barbara and Charles Jr KLATT, 11 Nov 1942 Hudson, NH
BULPETT, Helen and George M FLECHTNER, 31 Dec 1942 Hudson, NH
BULTER, Lucy and Alexander BRUDO, 18 May 1891
BULTER, Mary and Reuben MELVIN, 20 Oct 1846
BULZOMI, Margharita and Milburn B WHITLOW, 01 Feb 1950 Hudson, NH
BUNDY, Ellen D and Gerry WALKER, 04 Jun 1890 Hudson, NH
   Amasa T Bundy (Walpole, MA) & Ellen F Worcester (Groton, MA)
   James G Walker(New York) & Sarah Bragdon (New York)
BUNKER, Cheryle A and Donald A HASTINGS, 26 Aug 1972 Derry, NH
BUNKER, Hattie E and James N CASLIP, 01 Dec 1869 Hudson, NH
BUNKER, Hattie E and James N CORLISS, 30 Nov 1869
BUNKER, James S and Ellen A FOSS, 29 Nov 1879 Hudson, NH
  Levi H Bunker (Moultonboro, NH) & Harriet T (Andover, NH)
  Alonzo H Foss(Rochester, NH) & Rebecca (Rochester, NH)
BUNTIN, Henry C and Rita M MASON, 05 Feb 1949 Hudson, NH
BURBANK, Frank A III and Susan J COLBY, 05 Aug 1967 Claremont, NH
BURBANK, Hannah and John PETTENGAIL, 16 Nov 1784
BURBANK, Hannah and John REDINGAIL, 16 Nov 1784
BURBANK, Jonathan and Lucinda WILSON, 28 Nov 1822
BURBANK, Jonathan and Ann GOODSPEED, 05 Apr 1855
BURBANK, Jonathan and Lucinda WILSON, 28 Nov 1823
BURBANK, Lucinda A and Horace SPRAGUE, 18 Apr 1847
BURBANK, Lydia and Joseph JOHNSON, 10 Sep 1807
BURBANK, Samuel Jr and Molly FARMER, 23 Jun 1785
BURBINE, Lynne-Ann and Kevin John TRASK, 08 Jun 1985 Hudson, NH
BURCH, Horace and Mary S DAIL, 11 Nov 1852
BURDEN, David E and Diane STRATOTI, 22 Jun 1985 Nashua, NH
BURELLE, Beatrice and Aurele J MICHAUD, 22 Jun 1935 Nashua, NH
BURELLE, Jacqueline and Lloyd A FREEMAN, 04 Aug 1973 Hudson, NH
BURELLE, Leontine and William R VICKERY, 23 Dec 1961 Nashua, NH
BURGESON, Sandra A and Joseph E Jr CHRISTY, 10 Dec 1960 Milford, NH
BURGESS, Deborah Lee and Robert E DAVIS, 26 May 1979 Salem, NH
BURGESS, Diana V and Girard J TURMEL, 12 Jan 1957 Hudson, NH
BURGESS, Elisabeth and Alejandro HERNANDEZ, 17 Dec 1983 Salem, NH
BURGESS, Gertrude M and Nathaniel CARMEN, 02 Jul 1955 Hudson, NH
BURGESS, Patricia A and Richard C NUCCI, 09 Nov 1974 Hudson, NH
BURGESS, Peter and Sharon E POST, 02 Oct 1965 Hudson, NH
BURGESS, Sharen J and Frederick FULLER, 27 Jun 1970 Hudson, NH
BURGESS, Terence A and Patricia A TANGUAY, 14 Aug 1971 Nashua, NH
BURGESS, Theresa J and Arthur P BLANCHETTE, 07 Dec 1968 Nashua, NH
BURGIN, Eliza and Adelbert WHITE, 30 Mar 1860
BURK, Jeffrey R and Rosemary E DUBOWIK, 18 Jun 1971 Nashua, NH
BURKE, David W and Linda L RAMSAY, 14 Feb 1964 Hudson, NH
BURKE, Jane M and Lawrence A CONLEY, 16 Jul 1983 Salem, NH
BURKE, Jeffrey H and Linda T DIONNE, 19 May 1979 Pelham, NH
BURKE, Joseph K and Gloria G GAGNE, 15 Apr 1950 Hudson, NH
BURKE, Laura C and Robert L SWEENEY, 28 Apr 1981 Hudson, NH
BURKE, Marie J and Philip R CINCOTTA, 16 Dec 1949 Hudson, NH
BURKE, Nellie and James M CUMMINGS, 28 Mar 1876
BURKE, Sheila F and Robert Lee BLACKBURN, 15 Sep 1973 Hudson, NH
BURKE, Teresa A and Edmund J CROWLEY, 31 Mar 1978 Hudson, NH
BURKE, Teresa L and Francis H MILLARD, 02 Dec 1949 Hudson, NH
BURKETT, Francis W and Alice J RAMSDELL, 25 Jun 1971 Nashua, NH
BURNELL, David E and Karen L KIERSTEAD, 30 Aug 1975 Hudson, NH
BURNER, Helen B and Arthur W SOLES, 24 Apr 1974 Nashua, NH
BURNER, Maurice R and Gail L BYRON, 25 May 1973 Nashua, NH

HUDSON, NH MARRIAGES

BURNER, Suzanne L and James M IVES, 30 Jul 1971 Nashua, NH
BURNETT, James F and Georganna TOWNE, 12 Jun 1889 Nashua, NH
   James Burnett (Lowell, MA) & Mary L McDonald (Annapolis, NS)
      & Lydia E Towne (Nashua, NH)
BURNETT, Jerry C and Sheila R HUGHES, 25 Sep 1977 Hudson, NH
BURNEY, Katherine and Terrance R SHARP, 19 Aug 1982 Nashua, NH
BURNHAM, Arthur H&Aurelle V BELLEFEUILLE, 09 Dec 1942 Manchester,NH
BURNHAM, Barbara and George A Jr CADY, 16 Mar 1947 Hudson, NH
BURNHAM, Gertrude M and George A GREELEY, 16 May 1935 Salem, NH
BURNHAM, Hannah J and Albert O TOWNS, 31 Oct 1881 Hudson, NH
  Amory Burnham (Hudson, NH) & Martha C Fowler
  C J Towns(Londonderry, NH) & Clara H Brewster
BURNHAM, John and Hannah BLODGETT, 11 Mar 1810
BURNHAM, Lucy J and Hersey F COOKE, 08 Oct 1926 S Lyndeboro, NH
BURNHAM, Marjorie A and William E BRYANT, 27 May 1951 Hudson, NH
BURNHAM, Martha and Walter F FORTIER, 02 Apr 1949 Epping, NH
BURNHAM, Mary L and George W DUTTON, 02 Jan 1882 Acworth, NH
  Omer B Burnham (Antrim, NH) & Mary M Gould (Greenfield, NH)
  John E Dutton(Hudson, NH) & Sarah E Winn (Hudson, NH)
BURNHAM, Natalie M and George A ROGERS, 09 Dec 1945 Hudson, NH
BURNS, Abigail and Justice DAKIN, 12 Jan 1803
BURNS, Allan L and Denise A HEROUX, 12 Mar 1971 Hudson, NH
BURNS, Anne L and Robert W JOHNSON, 16 Aug 1969 Hudson, NH
BURNS, Barbara F and Robert J ARMOUR, 08 May 1937 Nashua, NH
BURNS, Catherine and Anthony C VIGLONE, 12 Dec 1934 Hudson, NH
BURNS, Charlotte and Ernest CHAMPAGNY, 03 Sep 1938 Nashua, NH
BURNS, Daniel H and Lydia C MARCH, 21 Nov 1850
BURNS, Daniel M and Emily M CLEMENTS, 02 Apr 1857
BURNS, Dennis M and Madeleine HEROUX, 26 Jun 1970 Hudson, NH
BURNS, Florence M and Robert T MATTHEWS, 29 Jun 1935 Nashua, NH
BURNS, Francis L Jr and Linda J POWERS, 31 Dec 1982 Hudson, NH
BURNS, George Jr and Anna ADAMS, 01 Nov 1770
BURNS, Helen B and George S PAIGE, 26 Aug 1932 Nashua, NH
BURNS, James and Lydia CHASE, 13 Jun 1809
BURNS, Jane and Robert GLOVER, 29 Oct 1741
BURNS, John C Jr and Marilyn P GORDON, 21 Mar 1945 Derry, NH
BURNS, John J and Jennie V COFFEY, 06 Sep 1911 Hudson, NH
  John J Burns & Abbie Henderson
  John Coffey & Bridget Shea
BURNS, Lorinda P and George ROLFE, 23 Apr 1862
BURNS, Lucinda P and George ROLF, 03 Apr 1861
BURNS, Luke and Livia HILLS, 01 Nov 1842
BURNS, Mary and Nathaniel SEAVEY, 27 Sep 1781
BURNS, Mary and Nathaniel [UNKNOWN], 27 Sep 1781
BURNS, Nora and Vinton E STEVENS, 28 Jan 1947 Hudson, NH
BURNS, Peggy and Joseph WINN, 17 Dec 1808
BURNS, Peggy and Joseph Jr WINN, 17 Dec 1808
BURNS, Richard M and Elizabeth BUXTON, 24 Nov 1942 Hudson, NH
BURNS, Robert D and Louise A PHENEUF, 14 Feb 1976 Manchester, NH
BURNS, Sarah and Gideon PUTNAM, 19 Sep 1799
BURON, June P and Leroy A HAWKINS, 25 Sep 1948 Hudson, NH
BURPEE, Dora C and Paul L THIBODEAU, 18 Nov 1950 Hudson, NH
BURPEE, Henry Jr and Gabrielle PLANTE, 08 Oct 1938 Nashua, NH
BURR, Geoffrey A and Susan T RICARD, 30 Sep 1977 Hudson, NH
BURR, Howard R and Mary C THIEBAULT, 01 Nov 1948 Hudson, NH
BURR, Myron F and Lorna D WHITNEY, 18 Sep 1931 Hudson, NH
BURRILL, Helen G and William J O'DONNELL, 21 Apr 1943 Hudson, NH
BURRILL, Josephine and Arthur C HALL, 03 Jul 1915 Nashua, NH
  Frank Burrill (England) & Mary Whiting (England)
  William H Hall(England) & Elizabeth Blowen (England)

HUDSON, NH MARRIAGES

BURROUGHS, Horace N and Martha A MOREY, 05 Feb 1868
BURROUGHS, Pamela L and Eddy J BISBING, 02 Aug 1980 Hudson, NH
BURROWS, George and Esther HARDY, 28 Mar 1782
BURROWS, Horace N and Martha A MARCY, 05 Feb 1868
BURSIEL, Thomas and Mary Ann RIPLEY, 24 Feb 1858
BURTON, Albert A and Michelle C GAGNON, 28 Aug 1981 Hudson, NH
BURTON, Ann Marie and Gerard J PLAMONDON, 23 May 1981 Hudson, NH
BURTON, Bernice E and Henry L PARENT, 09 Jun 1950 Hudson, NH
BURTON, Cheryl Lyn and Thomas Edm NADEAU, 09 Jun 1984 Hudson, NH
BURTON, Clifford J and Barbara L HAMMOND, 30 Mar 1963 Hudson, NH
BURTON, David A and Linda S ST HILAIRE, 03 Mar 1984 Nashua, NH
BURTON, David K and Mary-Anne WELCOME, 05 Oct 1984 Hudson, NH
BURTON, Earl C and Melba A BARDAS, 11 Feb 1956 Hudson, NH
BURTON, Ernest H and Nancy L FITZGERALD, 22 Jan 1955 Hudson, NH
BURTON, Ervin J and Mary A FAHEY, 11 Nov 1966 Nashua, NH
BURTON, Herbert and Elaine D LACHAPELLE, 28 May 1955 Manchester, NH
BURTON, Kenneth E and Margaret M PELLETIER, 04 Sep 1944 Nashua, NH
BURTON, Leonard R and Ingrid E FRANZEN, 03 Jun 1961 Nashua, NH
BURTON, Lisa M and Glenn D SHULTZ, 14 Apr 1985 Hudson, NH
BURTON, Marion M and Roland A ST LAURENT, 23 Aug 1947 Nashua, NH
BURTON, Michael K and Pauline L BLAIS, 25 Oct 1980 Nashua, NH
BURTON, Patricia A and William S LAMB, 22 Apr 1978 Hudson, NH
BURTON, Paul F and Myrtie E HANSON, 03 Jul 1950 Hudson, NH
BURTON, Paul K and JoAnne L POTTER, 26 May 1978 Hudson, NH
BURTON, Richard A and Elaine L MIGNEAULT, 10 Oct 1971 Nashua, NH
BURTON, Robert A and Barbara C BERNARD, 25 Apr 1945 Nashua, NH
BURTT, W H and Annie C LYNESS, 06 Dec 1899 Hudson, NH
  Crandal Burtt & Isabell Carter
  William Lyness & May Gordon
BURZIEL, Eliza and Nathaniel FIFIELD, 23 Sep 1856
BUSH, Charles W III and Marsha K PATTERSON, 09 Sep 1967 Nashua, NH
BUSHEE, Carl T and Joan S WULF, 16 Dec 1983 Milford, NH
BUSHEY, Claude W and Gloria M SLATTERY, 22 Jan 1950 Hudson, NH
BUSSIERE, Madelyn L and Lafayette MORENCY, 14 Oct 1960 Hudson, NH
BUSWELL, A Andrew and Leslie R WOLCOTT, 20 Aug 1966 Claremont, NH
BUSWELL, Chas E and Abbie S MITCHELL, 13 Aug 1875 Nashua, NH
BUSWELL, Dorothy R and Peter J BELAND, 10 Jul 1959 Hudson, NH
BUSWELL, Horace and Mary E MITCHELL, 29 Aug 1869 Hudson, NH
BUTCHER, Virginia M and Perry M BROWN, 08 Jun 1946 Hudson, NH
BUTEAU, Suzanne M and Christophe DONOVAN, 16 Aug 1981 Nashua, NH
BUTLER, Abigail and Henry BALDWIN, 26 May 1743
BUTLER, Albert S and Martha E FARNUM, 24 Nov 1892 Hudson, NH
  Jas M Butler (Pelham, NH) & Sarah J Steele (Hudson, NH)
  John Farnum & Mary Steele (Hudson, NH)
BUTLER, Donna L and F Stanley SMITH, 29 Aug 1975 Nashua, NH
BUTLER, Ernest and Marguerite GRIMES, 25 May 1933 Hudson, NH
BUTLER, Hannah and Joseph BUTLER, 05 Mar 1812
BUTLER, Henry and Belinda SMITH, 24 Apr 1856
BUTLER, James M and Sarah J STEELE, 02 Oct 1862
BUTLER, Joseph and Hannah BUTLER, 05 Mar 1812
BUTLER, Lewis and Betsey MERRILL, 06 Mar 1816
BUTLER, Linnie F and Arthur S ANDREWS, 20 Apr 1882 Hudson, NH
  Henry Butler (Pelham, NH) & Belinda Smith (Hudson, NH)
  Robert A Andrews(Hudson, NH) & Mary M Keniston (Andover, NH)
BUTLER, Lucy and Alex BUDRO, 18 May 1891 Hudson, NH
  David Budro(Chazy, NY) & Clara Ferryall (Scotia, NY)
BUTLER, Maria A J and George L HOLMES, 24 Oct 1885 Hudson, NH
  William Butler (Ireland) & Mary A Brady (Ireland)
  Luke Holmes(Canada) & Catherine Butler (Hudson, NH)
BUTLER, Mary E and Charles BRAUGH, 23 Sep 1887 Nashua, NH

HUDSON, NH MARRIAGES

Samuel Braugh(Canada) & Duchess (Canada)
BUTLER, Robert H and Lois M BROWN, 19 Feb 1977 Hudson, NH
BUTLER, Roger S and Susan PETERS, 14 Dec 1974 Hudson, NH
BUTLER, Roxanna and Isaac N SMITH, 06 Apr 1863
BUTLER, Ruth N and John M PHILLIPS, 30 Dec 1950 Hudson, NH
BUTLER, Susan E and George A SMITH, 27 Feb 1883 Pelham, NH
  James Caldwell (Hudson, NH) & Susan E Senter
  Edwin Smith(Hudson, NH) & Sybil Wilson (Dracut, MA)
BUTLER, Thomas and Eleanor GILLINGHAM, 08 Apr 1851
BUTMAN, Florence J and Maurice Wm ACKERMAN, 06 Jun 1937 Fairlee, VT
BUTMAN, William L and Geraldine THOMSON, 24 Aug 1969 Nashua, NH
BUTRICK, Caldwell and Ann L HALL, 27 Jul 1865
BUTTER, James M and Sarah J STEELE, 20 Oct 1862
BUTTERFIELD, Asa and Abiah COLBURN, 23 Mar 1784
BUTTERFIELD, Joseph and Elizabeth RICHARDS, 15 Dec 1741
BUTTERFIELD, Joseph and Elizabeth BANCROFT, 03 Mar 1785
BUTTERFIELD, MaryJPiper and David CLEMENT, 21 Feb 1870
BUTTERFIELD, Rufus and Jane CAMPBELL, 20 May 1866
BUTTERFIELD, Rufus and June CAMPBELL, 17 May 1860
BUTTERICK, Asa and Lydia SEARLES, 15 Mar 1810
BUTTERICK, Hannah and Josiah HAMBLET, 10 May 1818
BUTTERICK, Maria and Thomas CALDWELL, 05 Sep 1844
BUTTERICK, Sally and John B ROBINSON, 24 Apr 1850
BUTTERS, Idore M and Susan I GAMACHE, 19 Apr 1969 Hudson, NH
BUTTERS, Marion J and Louis S ALBANO, 17 May 1942 Hudson, NH
BUTTERWORTH, Kevin E and Deborah J MATTHIAS, 26 Sep 1981 Hudson, NH
BUTTRESS, Jennie M and Phillip J CONNELL, 03 Jul 1911 Nashua, NH
  William Buttress & Annie McCullough
  Tobias Connell & Mary Hoffman
BUTTRICK, Abel and Anna HADLEY, 30 May 1819
BUTTRICK, Asa and Lydia SEARLES, 15 Mar 1810
BUTTRICK, Caldwell and Ellen R LOVEJOY, 25 Apr 1899 Hudson, NH
  Samuel Buttrick & Margaret Caldwell
  Eli Hardy & Eunice B Williams
BUTTRICK, Caldwell and Ann L HALL, 27 Jul 1865
BUTTRICK, Charlotte and Gerald W BAGLEY, 06 Apr 1918 Nashua, NH
BUTTRICK, Clifton E and Charlotte COLBURN, 18 Jun 1874 Hudson, NH
BUTTRICK, Clifton E and Ellen F BOYINGTON, 14 Aug 1880 Augusta, ME
  Ephraem Buttrick (Pelham, NH) & Sarah Cutter (Nashua, NH)
  John W Boyington(Dresden, ME) & Militiah S Glidden(Jefferson, ME)
BUTTRICK, Ephrium and Sally NELSON, 22 Nov 1842
BUTTRICK, Hannah and Josiah HAMBLETT, 10 May 1818
BUTTRICK, Leander C&Charlotte ROBINSON, 31 Jul 1910 Londonderry, NH
  Clifton E Buttrick & Ella F Boynton
  Frank R Robinson & Alecia A Young
BUTTRICK, Mabel S and Jerome A MELVIN, 24 Dec 1891 Hudson, NH
  Clifton E Buttrick (Wentworth) & Marietta Haselton (Hudson, NH)
  Tolford D Melvin(Hudson, NH) & Julia G (Hopkins)
BUTTRICK, Mary A and Samuel A STEELE, 30 Sep 1862
BUTTRICK, Roger and Elizabeth HALE, 12 Jan 1815
BUTTRICK, Sally and John P ROBINSON, 24 Apr 1850
BUXTON, Barbara J and Robert J BEAUDRY, 09 May 1953 Lebanon, NH
BUXTON, Deborah M and William Al SCIACCA, 29 Jun 1974 Hudson, NH
BUXTON, Elizabeth and Richard M BURNS, 24 Nov 1942 Hudson, NH
BUXTON, Harvey E and Lydia F CURRIER, 16 Sep 1868
BUXTON, James W and Susan W FOLLETT, 24 Nov 1866
BUXTON, Mary Ann and Ronald MacDONALD, 06 Apr 1942 Manchester, NH
BUXTON, Mary Louise and Shawn P McGUINNESS, 12 Aug 1978 Hudson, NH
BUXTON, Michael P and Susan M BEAUDRY, 14 May 1971 Nashua, NH
BUXTON, Paul W and Hazel E REYNOLDS, 17 Aug 1918 Nashua, NH

HUDSON, NH MARRIAGES

BUXTON, Phyllis and John S GROVES, 22 Feb 1942 Hudson, NH
BUXTON, Robert C and Lorraine O BRUNELLE, 26 Sep 1949 Nashua, NH
BUZAREWICZ, Stella A and John F TAMERLEVICH, 24 Jul 1942 Nashua, NH
BUZZELL, Doris C and Leo M GAGNON, 12 Oct 1943 Nashua, NH
BYAM, Lucy A and William T MERRILL, 28 Apr 1856
BYRNE, Louise R and Sarkis SALIAN, 25 Jun 1938 Hudson, NH
BYRNE, Patrick M and Karyn A AHIGIAN, 27 May 1978 Hudson, NH
BYRNES, Gladys M and Waldo I POWELL, 11 Sep 1929 Nashua, NH
BYRON, Frank A and Patricia A NIXON, 11 Sep 1976 Hudson, NH
BYRON, Gail L and Maurice R BURNER, 25 May 1973 Nashua, NH
CABANA, Henry F and Sylvia A PRATT, 26 Jun 1981 Nashua, NH
CABRAL, Sandra A and Donald C SHEPARD, 03 Oct 1982 Nashua, NH
CACCIA, Robert P and Laura E WOLFE, 22 Apr 1978 Salem, NH
CADAVID, Maria E and Roberto A RODGERS, 25 Sep 1982 Hudson, NH
CADIGAN, Dorothea P and Robert P O'BRIEN, 05 Oct 1946 Hudson, NH
CADORETTE, William C & Mae Ellen MALOUIN, 01 Nov 1984 Merrimack, NH
CADY, Edward M and Ida EAYERS, 30 May 1899 Hudson, NH
   Joseph Cady & Elmira Lernay
   E F Eayers & Augusta Ford
CADY, George A Jr and Barbara BURNHAM, 16 Mar 1947 Hudson, NH
CADY, Jean A and John E SULLIVAN, 31 Jul 1954 Hudson, NH
CADY, Katherine and Robert E HIGH, 20 Aug 1960 Merrimack, NH
CADY, Leon J and Victoria M CHAMPAGNE, 03 Aug 1963 Hudson, NH
CADY, Patricia A and Matthew R CLARK, 15 Feb 1975 Hudson, NH
CADY, Steven F and Darthy A BUDER, 27 Nov 1971 Nashua, NH
CADY, Timothy J and Ann G NICKERSON, 10 Jun 1978 Pelham, NH
CAGE, Donna J and Owen G WATSON, 05 Dec 1983 Nashua, NH
CAHILL, Paul B and Bernice J HARWOOD, 15 Aug 1925 Nashua, NH
CAHILL, William R and Karen M CAZA, 24 May 1985 Hudson, NH
CAHOON, Clarence E and Blanche M FRENCH, 14 Oct 1928 Nashua, NH
CAHOON, David and Mary F CAREY, 04 Jul 1935 Hudson, NH
CAIN, Lucille and Vinet I CURDY, 28 Dec 1950 Hudson, NH
CALAWA, Daniel R and Ann V CRESTA, 31 Jul 1982 Hudson, NH
CALAWA, Jill and Richard H CHARBONNEAU, 30 Aug 1978 Litchfield, NH
CALDEIRA, Mary S and Anthony RODRICK, 24 Aug 1968 Nashua, NH
CALDER, William G and Hilda W REEVES, 20 Jun 1942 Hudson, NH
CALDWELL, Ardello and Rufus E WINN, 25 Dec 1877 Hudson, NH
   Thomas Caldwell (Litchfield, NH) & Maria Buttrick (Pelham, NH)
   John Winn(Hudson, NH) & Annah Patch (Groton, MA)
CALDWELL, David and Sally BOGGS, 20 Sep 1810
CALDWELL, Dustin and Elizabeth DAVIS, 12 Apr 1849
CALDWELL, Henry M and Eliza J BEAR, 23 Nov 1878 Hudson, NH
   William Caldwell (Hudson, NH) & Jane (Cape Cod, MA)
   Addison M Blankin(Iresburg, VT) & Harriet M (Hudson, NH)
CALDWELL, James and Susan CONANT, 13 Oct 1822
CALDWELL, LaMar and Katherine BRODEUR, 19 Nov 1983 Nashua, NH
CALDWELL, Lydia and Simon BROWN, Jul 1817
CALDWELL, Rachel and John KNOWLES, 24 Mar 1876
CALDWELL, Rachel and John KNOWLES, 24 Mar 1816
CALDWELL, Sally L and David J ELLIS, 28 Mar 1980 Hudson, NH
CALDWELL, Solomon O and Lydia D GOSS, 23 Nov 1862
CALDWELL, Susan and Dana SMITH, 12 Oct 1829
CALDWELL, Thomas and Maria BUTTERICK, 05 Sep 1844
CALDWELL, William and Jane MARSHALL, 28 Apr 1842
CALHOUN, Edwin A and Hazel E WELLS, 18 Oct 1949 Hudson, NH
CALISH, Leroy V and Dolores E MITCHELL, 08 Jan 1949 Hudson, NH
CALL, Joseph and Hannah CARLTON, 22 Aug 1780
CALLAHAN, Francis J and Edith L PLUMMER, 04 Oct 1941 Hudson, NH
CALLAHAN, Justin J and Marion R PIERCE, 28 Jun 1938 Hudson, NH
CALLAHAN, Patricia A and Donald R SELVIS, 18 Oct 1952 Nashua, NH

HUDSON, NH MARRIAGES

CALLISON, Malcolm W and Priscilla ENNIS, 03 Oct 1970 Nashua, NH
CALOGERRO, Sylvia J and Francis M SULLIVAN, 27 Sep 1947 Hudson, NH
CALZINI, Lisa A and Kenneth J YORK, 16 Jun 1984 Nashua, NH
CAMARA, Maria L and Ja A SNELL, 19 Jul 1980 Pelham, NH
CAMERON, Alfred J Jr and Helga M MADSEN, 23 Oct 1948 Hudson, NH
CAMERON, Donald O and Hilda P GODSOE, 18 Jan 1947 Hudson, NH
CAMMARATA, Bernard and Dolores M ZIMMERMAN, 29 Apr 1971 Nashua, NH
CAMMARATA, Rocco and Caroline J MALAGUTI, 17 May 1936 Hudson, NH
CAMP, Josephine and Charles A MORTON, 28 Apr 1942 Hudson, NH
CAMPAS, Albert P and Ruth A DODSON, 26 Jan 1946 Hudson, NH
CAMPBELL, Albert A and Lucinda P CLEMENT, 08 Jul 1866
CAMPBELL, Andrew A and Sophronia SEAVEY, 05 Nov 1859
CAMPBELL, Barbara J and Neil E MILLER, 11 Nov 1950 Hudson, NH
CAMPBELL, Bradford and Hattie L PUTNAM, 04 Jan 1866
CAMPBELL, Calesta J and Osgood HILL, 20 Feb 1870 Hudson, NH
CAMPBELL, Calisha J and Osgood HILL, 20 Feb 1870
CAMPBELL, Charles A and Karen A MILLER, 08 Oct 1982 Amherst, NH
CAMPBELL, Charles B and Helen R BARRETT, 30 Jul 1955 Nashua, NH
CAMPBELL, Clarence T and Ella B WHITCHER, 25 Oct 1902 Hudson, NH
   Bradford Campbell & Hattie Putnam
   Bert Whitcher & Mary
CAMPBELL, Cynthia R and Charles R NUTTING, 21 Jun 1969 Hudson, NH
CAMPBELL, David M and Donna G STONE, 15 Aug 1976 Hudson, NH
CAMPBELL, Dorothy S and Richard H HARDY, 06 May 1945 Hudson, NH
CAMPBELL, Genevieve and Walter S NESMITH, 28 Jun 1951 Nashua, NH
CAMPBELL, Gertrude M and Arthur TRUFANT, 27 Jun 1923 Hudson, NH
CAMPBELL, Gloria R and Robert R SCHREITERER, 06 Jun 1948 Nashua, NH
CAMPBELL, Harold W and Bertha G GAGNON, 17 Sep 1934 Brattleboro, VT
CAMPBELL, Ina E and Everett L MILLETT, 21 Aug 1936 Nashua, NH
CAMPBELL, James R and Nancy J BARNES, 28
CAMPBELL, Jane and Rufus BUTTERFIELD, 20 May 1866
CAMPBELL, Janice A and Paul W KINVILLE, 09 Aug 1969 Hudson, NH
CAMPBELL, June and Rufus BUTTERFIELD, 17 May 1860
CAMPBELL, Lucinda P and Smith P DAVIDSON, 13 Sep 1870 Hudson, NH
CAMPBELL, Madeleine and Richard C DANE, 06 Oct 1920 Nashua, NH
CAMPBELL, Mary E & Laurence M FARRINGTON, 28 Nov 1959 Litchfield, NH
CAMPBELL, Mary E and Kevin Paul PENO, 20 Apr 1974 Hudson, NH
CAMPBELL, Mary Eliza and Barden D PAQUETTE, 07 Nov 1981 Nashua, NH
CAMPBELL, Maud and Even McDONALD, 08 Apr 1901 Londonderry, NH
   Lyman Campbell (Nova Scotia) & Mary A Ross (Nova Scotia)
   John McDonald(Nova Scotia) & Maggie McIntoch (Nova Scotia)
CAMPBELL, Myrtle M and Donald T MURHEAD, 16 Oct 1948 Hudson, NH
CAMPBELL, Nancy J and Richard A BOULEY, 10 Jul 1971 Hudson, NH
CAMPBELL, Orman S and Hattie L MORTLOCK, 27 Jun 1900 Nashua, NH
   Bradford Campbell & Hattie E Putnam
   Geo A Mortlock & Eliza Hawes
CAMPBELL, Oscar P and Louise C JENENETTE, 27 May 1923 Hudson, NH
CAMPBELL, Pearl and Lizzie M McAFEE, 27 Jun 1906 Nashua, NH
   Bradford Campbell & Hattie E Putnam
   Charles F McAfee & Susie Dunken
CAMPBELL, Robert O Jr and Louise M BOULEY, 28 Jul 1973 Hudson, NH
CAMPBELL, Ross W and Cynthia DURAND, 11 Jun 1981 Nashua, NH
CAMPBELL, Ruth and Robert E HARDY, 28 Sep 1940 Hudson, NH
CAMPBELL, Sandra L and Donald E Jr COMIRE, 02 Nov 1970 Hudson, NH
CAMPBELL, Thomas R Jr & Marilyn G HARTWELL, 25 Oct 1952 Nashua, NH
CAMPBELL, Velma O and Jonathan D MacINTYRE, 31 Aug 1925 Hudson, NH
CAMPIONE, Irene R and Nicholas ZANNINI, 01 Oct 1941 Nashua, NH
CANAVAN, Esther R and John D Jr DUGAN, 09 Sep 1921 Nashua, NH
CANFIELD, Barbara R and William P Jr YUILL, 20 Jul 1935 Hudson, NH
CANFIELD, George M Jr and Patti J O'NEILL, 29 May 1971 Nashua, NH

HUDSON, NH MARRIAGES

CANFIELD, Muriel and Arthur BRUNT, 06 Jun 1927 Hudson, NH
CANNEY, Charles C and Alice K ARMSTRONG, 21 Apr 1920 Hudson, NH
CANNEY, Dana S and David B KETCHEN, 06 Aug 1983 Hudson, NH
CANNON, Pamela R and Richard D GRAY, 25 May 1975 Nashua, NH
CANTARA, Daniel E and Bertha L BLODGETT, 22 Oct 1914 Manchester, NH
  Daniel Cantara & Olivine Lemery
  Harry B Blodgett & Eliza Summerville
CANTARA, Kenneth M and Lynn M ROUTHIER, 30 Jun 1980 Nashua, NH
CANTELLA, Scott D and Jacqueline BERUBE, 24 Sep 1983 Hudson, NH
CANTIN, Alex and Alice LANDRY, 09 Apr 1938 Nashua, NH
CANTIN, Joseph W and Denise L SILVERIA, 23 Nov 1973 Hudson, NH
CANTY, George W and Helen M STACKNIS, 19 Jun 1937 Nashua, NH
CAPOZZOLE, Jerry and Genense ALIMANDI, 15 May 1937 Nashua, NH
CAPRIO, Vito A and Jacqueline TAYLOR, 04 Jul 1959 Nashua, NH
CARACOTSIOS, Dino and Jane KUS, 05 Mar 1948 Hudson, NH
CARAMANIS, Anthony and Lillian D BELLOFATTO, 15 Sep 1973 Nashua, NH
CARD, Edward Jam and Sandra Jo DROWN, 26 Jul 1980 Hudson, NH
CARD, John F and Connie DURWIN, 07 Jun 1980 Hudson, NH
CARDIN, John C and Donna L KOPKA, 16 Feb 1985 Nashua, NH
CARDINAL, Elizabeth and Walter T CROOKER, 13 Dec 1981 Nashua, NH
CARDINAL, Katherine and Emile E HEBERT, 30 Aug 1973 Hudson, NH
CARDINAL, Katherine and David Emil NADEAU, 04 May 1975 Derry, NH
CARDOZA, Carol-Ann and Mario BALSAMO, 27 May 1983 Hudson, NH
CAREY, Craig M and Jacqueline SMITH, 04 Apr 1983 Nashua, NH
CAREY, Ev Lynn and Gregg P WALLACE, 17 Nov 1981 Nashua, NH
CAREY, Mary F and David CAHOON, 04 Jul 1935 Hudson, NH
CAREY, Richard P and Tracey L FILLEBROWN, 16 Jun 1985 Nashua, NH
CARFARO, Peter P and Marjorie M BENT, 03 Jul 1937 Hudson, NH
CARIE, Jennie M and Willard O WINN, 01 Jan 1866
CARIGNAN, Irene J and Walter J MORNEAU, 24 Apr 1945 Manchester, NH
CARISTIA, Rosario N and Marie C BEAUREGARD, 15 Nov 1942 Hudson, NH
CARLE, Alan W and Gail M JACQUE, 27 Dec 1984 Hudson, NH
CARLE, Charles I and Ruth E FORD, 08 Dec 1969 Nashua, NH
CARLE, R Bradley and Ruth E PITCHER, 09 May 1935 Hudson, NH
CARLETON, Florence and Ralph A ESTY, 21 May 1917 Nashua, NH
CARLETON, George F and Jane E DAVIS, 16 May 1976 Nashua, NH
CARLETON, Janice N and Ernest A PROVENCAL, 30 Aug 1950 Nashua, NH
CARLSON, Antoinette and Henry A ESSEX, 20 Mar 1982 Hudson, NH
CARLSON, Betty L and Spencer H NOEL, 06 Apr 1985 Hudson, NH
CARLSON, Clair A and Lillian N ARRAGG, 02 Apr 1949 Hudson, NH
CARLSON, Deborah J and Leo E BONOLLO, 23 Oct 1965 Nashua, NH
CARLSON, Esther M and Edward KIENIA, 30 Jul 1952 Merrimack, NH
CARLSON, Fred O and Ludmilla L STR'GSTEIN, 10 Jun 1950 Hudson, NH
CARLSON, George A and Mary E GALLAGHER, 03 Jan 1949 Nashua, NH
CARLSON, Larry A and Shirley A BOULEY, 01 Oct 1965 Hudson, NH
CARLSON, Robert H and Betty L ELLIS, 05 Jun 1965 Hudson, NH
CARLSTROM, Christophe and Deanna J HULL, 11 Jul 1981 Nashua, NH
CARLTON, Donald E and Isabella A GOFF, 15 May 1949 Hudson, NH
CARLTON, Hannah and Joseph CALL, 22 Aug 1780
CARLTON, Hannah and Joseph HALL, 22 Apr 1780
CARLTON, Jeremiah and Emma TAYLOR, 20 Jun 1740
CARLTON, Mary and Reuben BATCHELDER, 06 Nov 1766
CARMAN, Josephine L and Redmond L MARTIN, 18 Apr 1911 Hudson, NH
  J H Carman
  Joseph J Martin & Martha Clulland
CARMEN, Nathaniel and Gertrude M BURGESS, 02 Jul 1955 Hudson, NH
CARMICHAEL, Quentin L and Alice E JOHNSON, 07 Sep 1938 Nashua, NH
CARNES, James and Wilhemina OSGOOD, 09 Sep 1869
CARNES, James and Willemene OSGOOD, 04 Apr 1869
CARNEY, Thelma and Dennis C CROSS, 22 Jan 1944 Hudson, NH

HUDSON,NH MARRIAGES

CARON, Brian S and Ruth M SCHULZ, 04 Jul 1983 Nashua, NH
CARON, Denise R and Stephen L OTIS, 30 May 1981 Hudson, NH
CARON, Diane L and Robert G HARDING, 16 Apr 1979 Nashua, NH
CARON, Dianne T and Leo P BARRIAULT, 11 Mar 1972 Hudson, NH
CARON, Dwight H and JoEllen J WRIGHT, 14 Sep 1974 Merrimack, NH
CARON, Jeannette and Louis V ROMANO, 03 Sep 1945 Hanover, NH
CARON, Joseph E and Cecile T CHOMARD, 15 May 1943 Nashua, NH
CARON, Karen A and Frederick HANNAH, 30 Jun 1962 Hudson, NH
CARON, Leo R and Eveline A SMITH, 28 Jul 1967 Nashua, NH
CARON, Lizbeth P and William G BOULANGER, 17 Aug 1968 Hudson, NH
CARON, Michael H and Linda J ROBINSON, 09 Apr 1983 Hudson, NH
CARON, Nancy C and Mitchell DANE, 03 Jun 1967 Nashua, NH
CARON, Nancy L and Richard J SIROIS, 09 Nov 1979 Nashua, NH
CARON, Olivette M and Paul JETTE, 25 Apr 1935 Nashua, NH
CARON, Patricia A and Edward G Jr GAMACHE, 24 Jun 1972 Hudson, NH
CARON, Raya and Armand DESAUTELS, 17 Feb 1930 Nashua, NH
CARON, Regnet R and Mona P DELUDE, 31 Jan 1959 Nashua, NH
CARON, Reina I and Antoine I VIENS, 26 Nov 1949 Nashua, NH
CARON, Richard E and Tamye MICHAUD, 02 Jul 1977 Hudson, NH
CARON, Richard F and Judith A BRACY, 21 Sep 1968 Hudson, NH
CARON, Robin A and Rene W Jr COLL, 06 Oct 1972 Nashua, NH
CARON, Ronald J and Pauline I GALLOW, 17 Jan 1975 Hudson, NH
CARON, Therese L and Robert B COCKERLINE, 20 Nov 1976 Nashua, NH
CARON, Trudy A and Donald E BOISVERT, 11 Jul 1981 Hudson, NH
CARPENTER, Myrtle M and Orin SMITH, 19 Jan 1924 Hudson, NH
CARPENTIER, Linda Anne and Bruce K BAKAIAN, 24 Nov 1973 Pelham, NH
CARPENTIERE, Pamela L & Richard L Jr FRUCI, 01 Jun 1985 Concord, NH
CARR, Hannah and William G KENNISTON, 19 Jun 1853
CARRAHER, Alexandria and William J TOLLE, 01 Aug 1981 Hudson, NH
CARRIER, Paul Z and Diane S COOK, 14 Dec 1968 Hudson, NH
CARRIGAN, Lucille C and Charles P STANTON, 07 Feb 1943 Nashua, NH
CARRIGAN, Marguerite and Josiah C CLOUGH, 12 Oct 1935 Milford, NH
CARROLL, Allison W and Thelma E IVES, 23 Nov 1972 Nashua, NH
CARROLL, Barbara and Roland G MICHAUD, 05 Oct 1957 Hudson, NH
CARROLL, Bruce A and Joyce P McCUTCHEON, 25 Nov 1971 Nashua, NH
CARROLL, Bruce A and Rosemary A MONACO, 19 May 1979 Hudson, NH
CARROLL, David W and Maryann MAKOWIEC, 14 Jun 1958 Manchester, NH
CARROLL, Jill A and George S SMITH, 30 Jun 1984 Hudson, NH
CARROLL, John E and Lauretta A SHEPARD, 14 Sep 1936 Nashua, NH
CARROLL, Jon and Judith E FARRINGTON, 11 Jan 1964 Hudson, NH
CARROLL, Jon and Kathleen P BIRON, 24 Aug 1967 Hudson, NH
CARROLL, Linda and Paul J AUDETTE, 06 Jul 1973 Hudson, NH
CARROLL, Madeline D and John C HUGHES, 23 Jul 1942 Hudson, NH
CARROLL, Margaret J and Robert A LEVESQUE, 17 Apr 1957 Hudson, NH
CARROLL, Mark D and Esther J PETERSON, 28 Aug 1912 Hudson, NH
  Frank N Carroll & Anna Dunbar
  Gustave Peterson & Bessie Anderson
CARROLL, Maryann and John J CATANZARO, 04 Sep 1970 Nashua, NH
CARROLL, Raymond E and Linda S TAYLOR, 14 Jun 1969 Nashua, NH
CARROLL, Richard P and Lillian R WARLEY, 27 Jan 1961 Pelham, NH
CARROLL, Roy and Sylvia M RIOUX, 15 Jul 1961 Nashua, NH
CARROLL, Susan and James L COBB, 04 Jun 1970 Hudson, NH
CARROZZO, Susan M and Denis G NADEAU, 07 Jun 1975 Plaistow, NH
CARSON, Carolyn V and Allen BROGGI, 12 Jan 1980 Amherst, NH
CARSON, Jeanne and Kenneth V CHAPMAN, 14 Feb 1970 Nashua, NH
CARTER, Albion J Jr and Cathy L WATTS, 15 Feb 1969 Hudson, NH
CARTER, Amanda and Albert H SIMPSON, 25 Aug 1975 Hudson, NH
CARTER, Carolyn A and Leland V BROOKS, 15 Jan 1966 Hudson, NH
CARTER, Cecile B and Harold S CARTER, 02 Oct 1950 Hudson, NH
CARTER, Dorothy M and Harry J TUFTS, 23 Apr 1949 Hudson, NH

HUDSON,NH MARRIAGES

CARTER, Harold S and Cecile BONNETTE, 07 Jun 1941 Nashua, NH
CARTER, Harold S and Cecile B CARTER, 02 Oct 1950 Hudson, NH
CARTER, Harold S and Barbara A SPENCE, 03 Jul 1959 Nashua, NH
CARTER, Janice F and Robert Lee BROWN, 22 May 1976 Nashua, NH
CARTER, Leonard J and Eva M DANIELEVITCH, 23 Apr 1945 Nashua, NH
CARTER, Leonard J and Robin B QUIGLEY, 21 Oct 1977 Hudson, NH
CARTER, Margaret A and Guy P SUYKERBUYK, 31 Jul 1982 Derry, NH
CARTER, Marjorie A and John K SMITH, 07 Jul 1951 Hudson, NH
CARTER, Merrill L and Gladys M MITCHELL, 22 Jan 1966 Hudson, NH
CARTER, Nicholas M and Linda A HOULE, 08 Jun 1968 Nashua, NH
CARTER, Ray C and Dolores J JALBERT, 24 Oct 1959 Nashua, NH
CARTER, Richard H and Rose Lee DURWIN, 09 Jan 1971 Hudson, NH
CARTER, Susan J and Stephen G HUFF, 03 Sep 1969 Nashua, NH
CARTER, William E and Gloria L BOUCHER, 19 Oct 1963 Hudson, NH
CARTIER, Madeline L and Normand E JETTE, 01 Jul 1950 Exeter, NH
CARUSO, Anthony and Pearl COUGHLIN, 05 Aug 1941 Hudson, NH
CARVER, Emily Anne and Steven C ABBEY, 22 May 1971 Nashua, NH
CARVILLE, Berchman T and Grace M PLOURDE, 21 Dec 1954 Hudson, NH
CARVILLE, Roy J and Rose T SHEA, 01 Dec 1970 Nashua, NH
CASALE, Deborah A and Steven E DOLBEC, 06 May 1983 Hudson, NH
CASALE, Kathleen M and John M SNYDER, 21 Nov 1980 Hudson, NH
CASARANO, Karen L and Joseph A RIBEIRO, 20 Apr 1985 Hudson, NH
CASAVANT, Eleanor N and William F BEAUMONT, 20 Sep 1969 Nashua, NH
CASCIANO, Camillo and Jennie RUSSO, 13 Jun 1938 Hudson, NH
CASE, George F and Mary T LAMFORD, 02 Sep 1873 Hudson, NH
CASE, Linda L and Walter J BOTHWICK, 04 May 1974 Nashua, NH
CASE, Pauline J and Richard A TURCOTTE, 25 Jun 1960 Hudson, NH
CASEY, Carol L and Leo W SOUCY, 08 May 1971 Hudson, NH
CASEY, Claire I and Simon R Jr ALLISON, 20 Aug 1960 Hudson, NH
CASEY, Helen and Chas Louis LAVIOLETTE, 19 Aug 1938 Nashua, NH
CASEY, Kathleen J and Raymond J BOISVERT, 01 Sep 1973 Hudson, NH
CASEY, Peter W and Kathleen R McCAULEY, 03 Dec 1977 Hudson, NH
CASHMAN, Ruth L and Fred M GREIM, 15 Jan 1937 Nashua, NH
CASILLO, Joseph M and Marlene R BARCLAY, 31 Jul 1976 Hudson, NH
CASLIP, James N and Hattie E BUNKER, 01 Dec 1869 Hudson, NH
CASPARRO, Rita M A and Brian W SHIPLEY, 09 Jul 1977 Rindge, NH
CASPER, Peter Jose and Anna PETKEVICH, 26 Oct 1935 Lowell, MA
CASSALIA, David L and Coleen Sue SULLIVAN, 01 Sep 1972 Nashua, NH
CASSALIA, Dennis J & Patricia G TINGLOF, 09 Oct 1982 Merrimack, NH
CASSALIA, Donald F and Marie L MICHAUD, 19 Aug 1984 Manchester, NH
CASSARINO, James and Gail Ann DWIRE, 14 Sep 1974 Nashua, NH
CASSAVAUGH, David A and Laura S YATES, 05 Aug 1978 Hudson, NH
CASSIDY, Clifford V and Ethel M CUMMINGS, 26 Jun 1912 Hudson, NH
   John J Cassidy & Mary Mead
   Alden E Cummings & Nellie C Stevens
CASSIDY, George T and Eva J COLUMB, 19 May 1937 Hudson, NH
CASSIDY, John D and Cameron J BRENNAN, 15 Sep 1984 Hudson, NH
CASSIDY, John M and Patricia A DESCHENES, 03 Sep 1983 Nashua, NH
CASSISTA, Robert F and Virginia D FARLEY, 20 Jun 1956 Nashua, NH
CAST, Mary E and John W MORAN, 12 Sep 1964 Hudson, NH
CASTLE, Chris and Cleopatra VOTSOTIS, 17 Aug 1948 Hudson, NH
CASTONGUAY, Germain E and Louis P GAUVIN, 03 Dec 1949 Hudson, NH
CASTONGUAY, Gertrude and Robert W FRENETTE, 07 Apr 1945 Nashua, NH
CATANUSO, Linda J and Barry J YUHAS, 12 Jun 1970 Nashua, NH
CATANZARO, John J and Maryann CARROLL, 04 Sep 1970 Nashua, NH
CATE, Annie L and Arthur A WILSON, 05 Jun 1906 Hudson, NH
   Byron H Cate & Anna Taylor
   James F Wilson & Sarah H Riley
CATES, Diane D and Joseph A FARIZ, 14 Jul 1984 Manchester, NH
CATES, Robert N and Barbara E BAUER, 27 Feb 1982 Hudson, NH

HUDSON,NH MARRIAGES

CATLAND, Jay W and Barbara J McGIRT, 14 Aug 1981 Hollis, NH
CATLETT, Karin S and Carl R PETERSON, 10 Jun 1977 Londonderry, NH
CATON, Louisa and Benjamin A DAVIS, 09 Aug 1880 Hudson, NH
   William Caton (England) & Mary Nagle (England)
   Benjamin A Davis & Sarah W Gilson
CAULEY, Thomas P and Patricia M YOUNG, 07 Jan 1984 Hudson, NH
CAVANAUGH, George E and Marion E ANDERSON, 27 Jul 1949 Hudson, NH
CAVENEY, Margaret G and Kevin E DESAUTELS, 23 Jun 1979 Nashua, NH
CAYFORD, Michael J and Donna L GOLDEN, 30 Dec 1977 Hudson, NH
CAZA, Karen M and William R CAHILL, 24 May 1985 Hudson, NH
CENSULLO, Joseph P and Mildred L KELLEY, 13 Apr 1948 Hudson, NH
CENTER, Hellen A and Harry U RUSSELL, 09 Oct 1907 Hudson, NH
   Warren Center & Carrie E Howe
   Herbert E Russell & Octava E Elliott
CHABOT, Rose M and Robert R SHARP, 27 Oct 1937 Hudson, NH
CHACOS, David R and Cynthia Lo SUMRALL, 02 Aug 1980 Merrimack, NH
CHADBURN, Eldon J and M Irene NADEAU, 31 Dec 1966 Hudson, NH
CHADWICK, Hannah and Dr Dustin BARRETT, 08 Jun 1826
CHAFIN, Earl and Mary Ann McGOVERN, 15 Mar 1980 Nashua, NH
CHAGNON, Brit A and Joan L McAULIFFE, 05 Oct 1979 Hudson, NH
CHAGNON, Charles E and Susan J SANFORD, 31 Jul 1982 Nashua, NH
CHAGNON, Michael J and Juanita E HARVEY, 22 Jul 1950 Hudson, NH
CHAISSON, Yvonne R and Edward J DESMOND, 28 Sep 1947 Hudson, NH
CHALIFOUX, Beulah L and Royal L STROMBECK, 17 Oct 1936 Nashua, NH
CHALIFOUX, Levi J and Mildred SHUNAMAN, 23 Jan 1939 Hudson, NH
CHALIFOUX, Margery C and Walter P Jr COOMBS, 01 Feb 1969 Hudson, NH
   CHAMBERLAIN, Doris P and William F FOLEY, 23 Oct 1965 Hudson, NH
CHAMBERLAIN, Elvira T and Henry F SMITH, 03 Jan 1882 Hudson, NH
   Caleb Chamberlain & Maria Robbins
   Dustin B Smith(Hudson, NH) & Sarah J Watts (Peterboro, NH)
CHAMBERLAIN, Hannah and Frederick RUNNELS, 20 Aug 1817
CHAMBERLAND, Aline M and John R CHARETTE, 17 Jun 1961 Nashua, NH
CHAMBERS, Gary W and Patricia I McHUGH, 28 Aug 1976 Hudson, NH
CHAMPAGNE, Joan T and Robert H NARO, 03 Jul 1953 Hudson, NH
CHAMPAGNE, Victoria M and Leon J CADY, 03 Aug 1963 Hudson, NH
CHAMPAGNY, Ernest and Charlotte BURNS, 03 Sep 1938 Nashua, NH
CHAMPIGNY, Gloria J and Joseph A Jr ROBERTS, 29 Jun 1968 Hudson, NH
CHAMPIGNY, Judith A and Steven J ZELONIS, 20 Sep 1974 Nashua, NH
CHAMPIGNY, Kathy J and Richard J NIQUETTE, 18 Aug 1972 Hudson, NH
CHAMPIGNY, Michael J and Elizabeth FARLEY, 20 Jun 1964 Meriden, CT
CHAMPIGNY, Patricia and Richard DIONNE, 10 Sep 1962 Nashua, NH
CHANDLER, Phebe and Stephen CHASE, 24 Nov 1757
CHANDRONNAIT, Tina M and Allen R COCKERLINE, 26 Jan 1974 Hudson, NH
CHAPERON, Mark R and Catherine THEODORE, 01 Apr 1981 Nashua, NH
CHAPLICK, John M and Ruby E GAGNON, 06 Feb 1950 Hudson, NH
CHAPLIN, Edith M and Richard P SMITH, 24 Jun 1949 Rindge, NH
CHAPLIN, Ruth and Cecil Jr TIBBETTS, 30 Jul 1938 Hudson, NH
CHAPLIN, Ruth H and Peter J DYS, 07 Dec 1946 Hudson, NH
CHAPMAN, Audrey F and Frank H CHAPMAN, 02 Sep 1961 Merrimack, NH
CHAPMAN, David M and Mary L CORSON, 02 Aug 1969 Hudson, NH
CHAPMAN, Dorothy A and Albert J HUNNEWELL, 30 Dec 1981 Hudson, NH
CHAPMAN, Frank H and Audrey F CHAPMAN, 02 Sep 1961 Merrimack, NH
CHAPMAN, Hubert G and Margaret I GALLAGHER, 30 May 1927 Nashua, NH
CHAPMAN, James A and Jacqueline FILLION, 22 Jun 1968 Berlin, NH
CHAPMAN, Kenneth V and Jeanne CARSON, 14 Feb 1970 Nashua, NH
CHAPMAN, Laura A and George F STEWART, 18 Oct 1876 Hudson, NH
CHAPMAN, Marie J and John J MANTENUTO, 12 May 1937 Hudson, NH
CHAPMAN, Philip S and Marie J NOVICK, 29 Aug 1931 Nashua, NH
CHAPMAN, Samuel J Jr & Brenda D BEAUREGARD, 05 Nov 1983 Hudson, NH
CHAPONIS, Charles Jr and Ella MARKERICH, 12 Feb 1938 Nashua, NH

HUDSON,NH MARRIAGES

CHAPPAS, John and Mary GOSHGARIAN, 24 Jan 1948 Hudson, NH
CHAPPELLE, Grace and David O MCKEE, 07 Feb 1935 Hudson, NH
CHAPPELLE, Inez W and Millard F TATE, 28 Sep 1934 Hudson, NH
CHAPUT, Constance and Wilfred R BOURQUE, 16 Apr 1983 Nashua, NH
CHAPUT, Gladys I and Franklyn H McALISTER, 29 Nov 1952 Hudson, NH
CHAPUT, Laurie A and Richard M LAMBERT, 24 Apr 1981 Hudson, NH
CHAPUT, Martha J and Daniel G JAMESON, 18 Jan 1975 Nashua, NH
CHARBONNEAU, Claudia M and Stephen G DODDS, 10 Mar 1979 Amherst, NH
CHARBONNEAU, Cynthia A and Kevin R SULLIVAN, 27 Dec 1981 Hudson, NH
CHARBONNEAU, Mark Y & Donna J YOUNGHUSBAND, 25 Jul 1980 Hudson, NH
CHARBONNEAU, Regina E and Antoine J LECLERC, 26 Apr 1952 Nashua, NH
CHARBONNEAU, Richard H and Jill CALAWA, 30 Aug 1978 Litchfield, NH
CHAREST, Albert O and Brenda R GAGNON, 28 Dec 1963 Hudson, NH
CHAREST, Carol A and Gerard L LEMAY, 19 Jun 1970 Manchester, NH
CHAREST, Diane G and Mark J FLAHERTY, 27 Feb 1971 Hudson, NH
CHAREST, Leon J and Lorraine P MAGNIN, 31 Jul 1943 Nashua, NH
CHAREST, Lorinda J and Francis NATURALE, 07 May 1977 Hudson, NH
CHAREST, Pauline C and Duane C Jr GORDON, 09 Jul 1960 Hudson, NH
CHARETTE, Bernice C and James Jr MANIKAS, 17 Apr 1977 Hudson, NH
CHARETTE, Darlene E and Michael P PARKHURST, 22 May 1971 Hudson, NH
CHARETTE, John R and Aline M CHAMBERLAND, 17 Jun 1961 Nashua, NH
CHARETTE, John R and Linda S LEE, 01 Jun 1974 Hudson, NH
CHARPENTIER, Albert J and Eva V WHITE, 26 Oct 1935 Nashua, NH
CHARPENTIER, Alma and Arthur P LAQUERRE, 29 Jan 1917 Nashua, NH
CHARPENTIER, Elaine and Victor LAQUERRE, 30 Dec 1918 Nashua, NH
CHARPENTIER, Jude D & Patricia M BASHALANY, 26 Jun 1981 Bristol, NH
CHARPENTIER, Rita L and Thomas M KIERSTEAD, 30 Oct 1954 Nashua, NH
CHARRON, Doris E and Raymond E PETTS, 06 May 1967 Hudson, NH
CHARRON, Phyliss E and Roger J PELLERIN, 30 Mar 1967 Nashua, NH
CHARRON, Suzanne M and Emile J TETU, 16 Jun 1962 Hudson, NH
CHARTIER, Michele F and Larry D BRIAND, 17 Nov 1978 Hudson, NH
CHARTRAIN, Edith I and Patrick F QUIRK, 12 Jul 1947 Hudson, NH
CHARTRAIN, Norma F and Mark J DUNLEA, 21 Sep 1975 Nashua, NH
CHASE, Amos B and Sarah CROSS, 11 Apr 1820
CHASE, Anna and Jonathan GOULD, 26 Nov 1782
CHASE, Arthur W Jr and Betty E ORSER, 30 Nov 1945 Hudson, NH
CHASE, Bertram F and Mary J DOBSON, 10 Aug 1892 Hudson, NH
 Edmund H Chase & Listine E Guptel
 Thomas Dobson(England) & Nancy Reiley (England)
CHASE, Carl C and Mary Louis GRENON, 20 Jul 1974 Concord, NH
CHASE, Charles A and Anna H WELLMAN, 16 Jun 1841
CHASE, Charles H and Hattie E THOMPSON, 09 Aug 1899 Nashua, NH
 Samuel Chase & Harriet E Brown
 M V R Thompson & Eliza E Heath
CHASE, Charles H and Rose A LENAHAN, 18 Jul 1867
CHASE, Cornelia C and William C MARSHALL, 24 Dec 1866
CHASE, Edgar P and S Chastina CROSS, 16 Nov 1854
CHASE, Enoch E and Emma E ANNIS, 11 Jun 1873 Hudson, NH
CHASE, Ephraim and Abigail BLODGETT, 02 May 1816
CHASE, Helena H and Otis Norcr LEWIS, 26 Jan 1918 Hudson, NH
CHASE, Howard T and Marion A JAMESON, 10 May 1925 Hudson, NH
CHASE, John and Elizabeth GIBSON, 16 Feb 1786
CHASE, John and Abigail ANDREWS, 04 Dec 1854
CHASE, John and Lois UNDERWOOD, 27 Jun 1864
CHASE, John and Priscilla DAHLEN, Sep 1782
CHASE, John E and Frances LAKEMAN, 30 Dec 1876 Hudson, NH
CHASE, Joshua and Mary HADLEY, 22 Nov 1763
CHASE, Lucy E and Augustus F BLODGETT, 29 Dec 1860
CHASE, Lydia and James BURNS, 13 Jun 1809
CHASE, Marion A and Theodore GINGRAS, 05 Mar 1927 Hudson, NH

HUDSON,NH MARRIAGES

CHASE, Marion E and Frank A TRUFANT, 01 Oct 1913 Hudson, NH
  DeWitt C Chase & Mabel A Nutt
  John M Trufant & Flora E Turner
CHASE, Martha E and J Preble PIERCE, 24 Oct 1854
CHASE, Mary and Samson FRENCH, 18 Oct 1739
CHASE, Mary E and Robert A ANDREWS, 17 Apr 1879 Nashua, NH
  Moody Chase (Hudson, NH) & Submit Marshall (Hudson, NH)
  Allen Andrews(Hudson, NH) & Asinath Hills (Litchfield)
CHASE, Mary Isabe and David Cumm GOULD, 25 Apr 1837
  Jacob Chase
CHASE, Moses and Elizabeth HAMBLETT, 01 Mar 1759
CHASE, Polly and Zachius HALE, 05 Oct 1797
CHASE, Rebecca F and Horace SPRAGUE, 14 Oct 1856
CHASE, Russell A and Elizabeth MUNROE, 03 Jul 1938 Hudson, NH
CHASE, Ruth and James HALE, 18 Apr 1809
CHASE, Samuel and Harriet E HADLEY, 12 Nov 1862
CHASE, Sarah and Joseph Jr WINN, 23 Mar 1786
CHASE, Sarah A and Thomas BOYD, 24 Aug 1854
CHASE, Stephen and Phebe CHANDLER, 24 Nov 1757
CHASE, Stephen Jr and Hannah BLODGETT, 31 Oct 1776
CHASE, Stephen Jr and Hannah BLODGETT, 31 Oct 1770
CHASE, Walter B and Annie F CROSS, 19 Aug 1873 Hudson, NH
CHASE, William F and Sarah F GREELEY, 30 Sep 1862
CHASSE, Claire R and Stephen R BOUCHER, 11 Aug 1961 Lincoln, NH
CHASSE, Paul M and Theresa B NADEAU, 28 Jun 1947 Nashua, NH
CHASSE, Robert L Jr and Jacqulyn A BREAULT, 26 Jun 1982 Hudson, NH
CHATEAUNEUF, Roger B and Judith E KNOWLES, 08 May 1965 Hudson, NH
CHATMAS, Jay C III and Carmen M TREMBLAY, 24 Jul 1981 Hudson, NH
CHATTLEY, Robert L and Lorraine M BELAND, 07 Apr 1962 Hudson, NH
CHAVES, Michael M and Lillian L HEBERT, 22 Nov 1950 Hudson, NH
CHEN, Szu Cheng and Li-Hsi HO, 28 Dec 1980 Nashua, NH
CHENARD, Cathy A and Michael K ST AMANT, 31 Mar 1984 Nashua, NH
CHENARD, Cecile and Raymond DESBOISBRIAND, 02 Jul 1938 Nashua, NH
CHENARD, Kim D and Daniel James II MURPHY, 18 Jul 1981 Hudson, NH
CHENELLE, Marilyn M & Richard R Sr WATTS, 11 May 1985 Merrimack,NH
CHENETTE, Emma P and Marcius L GATES, 28 Dec 1914 Nashua, NH
  Louis Chenette & Melvina Morin
  Charles E Gates & Martena Durant
CHENEVERT, Jeannine C and William F NEVILLE, 06 Oct 1984 Hudson, NH
CHENEVERT, Rita T and Thomas S KLISS, 29 Jan 1974 Salem, NH
CHENEY, John and Elizabeth BLODGETT, 12 Aug 1777
CHENEY, Joseph M and Marguerite POULIN, 17 Sep 1946 Nashua, NH
CHENEY, Robert A and Shirley A SENNEVILLE, 29 May 1982 Hudson, NH
CHERKES, Ann T and Roland J BLANCHETTE, 31 May 1952 Nashua, NH
CHERKES, Janice L and Robert L TURMEL, 27 Apr 1957 Nashua, NH
CHERNES, Alice E and William A ALUKONIS, 20 Feb 1943 Nashua, NH
CHESBROUGH, Bertha & Joseph BATCHELDER, 14 Jun 1919 Brattleboro, VT
CHESNULEVICH, Alan R and Susan A WRIGHT, 21 May 1983 Hudson, NH
CHESNULEVICH, Harry J and Dorothy B POFF, 05 Sep 1953 Nashua, NH
CHESNULEVICH, Ralph O&Annette M LAMBERT, 17 Jul 1954 Manchester, NH
CHESS, Anna and Stanley KUPCHUNAS, 05 Sep 1936 Nashua, NH
CHESS, Frank G and Gloria KONDRAT, 18 Aug 1945 Nashua, NH
CHESS, Stephen M and Brenda A LAPORTE, 17 Jun 1972 Hudson, NH
CHESS, Stephen M and Bernice D BENNETT, 25 Apr 1981 Hudson, NH
CHESTERLEY, David B and Bonnie F ALEXANDER, 09 Jun 1972 Hudson, NH
CHESTNUT, Mary H and Bertram J ROSE, 05 Oct 1897 Hudson, NH
  Robert Chestnut & Susan Chestnut
  D P Rose & Laura Kingsbury
CHEVALIER, Denise J and Kevin G HOWES, 19 May 1979 Nashua, NH
CHEVRETTE, Beatrice & Theodore BISSONNETTE, 15 Apr 1939 Nashua, NH

HUDSON,NH MARRIAGES

CHIARELLA, Elena and Gilbert TITELBAUM, 15 Nov 1947 Hudson, NH
CHIASSON, Paul W and Margaret M REGAN, 08 Oct 1977 Hudson, NH
CHISHOLM, Jeannette and Manuel LEVISON, 06 Aug 1942 Hudson, NH
CHODAKOWSKI, Jeannie A & Albert L Jr LAMBERT, 23 Dec 1972 Pelham,NH
CHOINIERE, Jacalyn A and William L SLAIBY, 31 Oct 1981 Hudson, NH
CHOMARD, Antonia and Alfred COUTURIER, 11 Jun 1938 Nashua, NH
CHOMARD, Cecile T and Joseph E CARON, 15 May 1943 Nashua, NH
CHOQUETTE, Treffie and Anna SINVENIE, 21 Feb 1921 Nashua, NH
CHOUINARD, Daniel G and Lori J LETOURNEAU, 13 Sep 1980 Hudson, NH
CHOUINARD, Philip A and Susan F FORD, 14 May 1977 Hudson, NH
CHRISICOS, Nancy L and Michael D SHANAHAN, 24 Jul 1981 Nashua, NH
CHRISTENSEN, Christian and Ada M WINSLOW, 09 Aug 1921 Derry, NH
CHRISTENSEN, Mark W and Holly M GEISINGER, 23 Jun 1984 Hudson, NH
CHRISTIAN, Arthur E and Roberta C BOULTZ, 06 Jul 1935 Hudson, NH
CHRISTIAN, Evelyn C and Frank D Jr LEARD, 07 Jul 1951 Nashua, NH
CHRISTIAN, Sandra J and David R TAYLOR, 18 Sep 1965 Nashua, NH
CHRISTIANSEN, Barbara M and John W Jr REED, 25 Apr 1970 Nashua, NH
CHRISTIANSEN, Bruce J and Donna M TATE, 18 Jul 1971 Hudson, NH
CHRISTIANSEN, Cheryl L & Russell E SHIEBLER, 20 Feb 1982 Hudson, NH
CHRISTIANSEN, Gary A and Jean T FRENETTE, 21 Sep 1968 Hudson, NH
CHRISTIANSEN, Henry A & Laurie J NELSON, 26 Jan 1953 Manchester, NH
CHRISTIANSEN, Keith A and Carol A ROCK, 16 May 1964 Hudson, NH
CHRISTIANSEN, Kevin L and Sandra L JETTE, 01 Jun 1985 Nashua, NH
CHRISTOPHER, David B and Elaine M SCOTT, 23 Sep 1967 Hudson, NH
CHRISTOPHER, David B and Carol A HART, 01 Apr 1983 Hollis, NH
CHRISTOPHER, Dorothea C and Lyman C HARDING, 07 Jul 1934 Hudson, NH
CHRISTOPHER, Dorothy A & Ignacio T GONZALEZ, 26 May 1979 Hudson, NH
CHRISTOPHER, Esther W and Arthur N GRAY, 12 Aug 1933 Hudson, NH
CHRISTOPHER, George A and Annie KAPISKY, 30 Aug 1942 Rye, NH
CHRISTY, Joseph E Jr and Sandra A BURGESON, 10 Dec 1960 Milford, NH
CHUBADA, Rita and Charles A WORMWOOD, 08 Aug 1936 Hudson, NH
CHURCH, Hosmer C and Jessie M BARNARD, 19 Apr 1905 Hudson, NH
   Edward A Church & Harriet Corbin
   Homer C Barnard & Addie E Taylor
CHURCH, Katherine and Leon F HOPWOOD, 30 Dec 1944 N Haverhill, NH
CHURCH, Letitia M and Oswald P BAKER, 27 Mar 1895 Boston, MA
   Reuben Church & Mary O
   Elijah Baker & Juliaette Baker
CHUTE, Phyllis E and Arnold O MAURITSON, 15 Aug 1954 Hudson, NH
CHZANOWSKI, A F and Jennie S POLAK, 12 Oct 1940 Nashua, NH
CIBELLO, Isabel C and Daniel F LYONS, 17 Jun 1950 Hudson, NH
CILLEY, Warner W and Laura M HUMPHREYS, 11 Jan 1928 Goffstown, NH
CINCOLA, Sue I and Ross M HILLSON, 30 Apr 1934 Hudson, NH
CINCOTTA, Philip R and Marie J BURKE, 16 Dec 1949 Hudson, NH
CINQ-MARS, Roland D and Mary Ann RAYBOLD, 06 Nov 1971 Nashua, NH
CLAFLIN, Charles E and Helen S HAKALA, 01 Jul 1936 Hudson, NH
CLANCY, Mary A and John O DONOHUE, 07 Feb 1880 West Newbury, MA
   J B Clancy (Ireland) & Mary Leander (Ireland)
   Timothy Donohue(Ireland) & Ellen Sweeney (Ireland)
CLARENBACH, Sara J and Michael P SICILIANO, 05 Jul 1963 Hudson, NH
CLARK, Aba and Colburn BLOOD, 23 Aug 1854
CLARK, Alexander and Donna S CUMMINGS, 20 Jul 1968 Nashua, NH
CLARK, Alice E and Earl W MUNSON, 28 Jun 1947 Hudson, NH
CLARK, Anna W and Horatio N BLODGETT, 26 Mar 1864
CLARK, Arline G and Wallace T CLARK, 22 Dec 1932 Nashua, NH
CLARK, Debbie M and Brian R COTE, 24 Apr 1971 Hudson, NH
CLARK, Edward Paul and Dawn Marie STRANGE, 27 Mar 1982 Hudson, NH
CLARK, Elbridge M and Ruth T PETTINGILL, 30 Nov 1831
CLARK, Gale L and Arthur J DOIRON, 02 Nov 1974 Hudson, NH
CLARK, George H Jr and Lucille G DIGGINS, 04 Oct 1947 Nashua, NH

HUDSON,NH MARRIAGES

CLARK, Glenn Robert and Margaret L BERNARD, 04 Aug 1973 Hudson, NH
CLARK, Hilda J and John E WHARTON, 01 Dec 1960 Merrimack, NH
CLARK, John D and Eliza STEVENS, Oct 1840
   John Stevens & Nancy Webster
CLARK, Josephine and Lowell TUTTLE, 15 Jan 1894 Nashua, NH
   Silas M Clark (Hillsborough, NH) & Caroline Sargent (Stone, MA)
   Francis Tuttle, Jr(Acton, MA) & Lucy Sargent (Stone, MA)
CLARK, Karen T and Dennis Romeo DUBE, 22 Sep 1973 Hudson, NH
CLARK, Lawrence N and Alice R LASSITER, 22 Aug 1931 Hudson, NH
CLARK, Lewis F and Virginia B CURTIS, 19 Oct 1934 Hudson, NH
CLARK, Mabel C and James GREENHALGE, 14 Nov 1954 Nashua, NH
CLARK, Marjory A and Dwight P MARZOLF, 19 Dec 1981 Pelham, NH
CLARK, Mark D and Molly UZZLE, 15 Mar 1985 Merrimack, NH
CLARK, Mary E and Lennart C GUSTAFSON, 01 Nov 1940 Hudson, NH
CLARK, Matthew R and Patricia A CADY, 15 Feb 1975 Hudson, NH
CLARK, Maureen A and Thomas R AYLWARD, 01 Sep 1979 Salem, NH
CLARK, Mercy F and Frank L SMITH, 16 Aug 1866
CLARK, Nathaniel and Joanna P PODGE, 26 Apr 1832
CLARK, Raymond W and Jeannette DURANT, 09 Apr 1972 Nashua, NH
CLARK, Regina L and Kenneth N TESSIER, 26 Sep 1981 Hudson, NH
CLARK, Richard L and Roseanna B MOREAU, 14 Feb 1953 Hudson, NH
CLARK, Richard L Jr and Cathy A ST AMANT, 26 Aug 1978 Hudson, NH
CLARK, Robert W and Helen B KASHULINES, 20 May 1950 Hudson, NH
CLARK, Robert W and Rita DOYLE, 26 Jul 1975 Hudson, NH
CLARK, Shirley L and Melvin R TROTT, 28 Oct 1950 Hudson, NH
CLARK, Stella L and Paul A DERY, 26 Jul 1980 Nashua, NH
CLARK, Wallace T and Arline G CLARK, 22 Dec 1932 Nashua, NH
CLARK, Washburn and Ella A McCOY, 29 Jan 1874 Hudson, NH
CLARK, William T and Harriet M WINN, 13 Dec 1851
CLARKE, Amanda M and Walter S VRABLIC, 31 Dec 1982 Hudson, NH
CLARKE, Blakely L and Hazel MORTON, 02 Jul 1954 Hampton, NH
CLARKE, Brian E and Christine BETTENCOURT, 27 Dec 1980 Hudson, NH
CLARKE, Frances M and Daniel A Jr MacINNIS, 12 Nov 1944 Hudson, NH
CLARKE, Karen L and Roger L FRANCOEUR, 22 Oct 1977 Hudson, NH
CLARKE, Thomas and Danuta BIELAWSKI, 20 Feb 1982 Nashua, NH
CLARKE, Zoa E and Vauhn S BLANCHARD, 18 Nov 1911 Nashua, NH
   Theodore L Clarke & Jessie F Erskine
   Fred S Seavey & Marie L Halfman
CLARKSON, Terry L and Priscilla WILSON, 01 Jul 1972 Nashua, NH
CLATUR, Sarah and George M WEBSTER, 1855
CLAUSON, Ruth May G and E Harold NORDLING, 23 Nov 1933 Nashua, NH
CLAVEAU, Imelda and Louis E GAGNON, 18 Oct 1920 Nashua, NH
CLAVEAU, Jeanne M and Russell R MARCOUX, 15 Jul 1967 Nashua, NH
CLAVEAU, Judith A and Laurent G LEVESQUE, 09 Aug 1969 Hudson, NH
CLAVEAU, Lawrence J and Diane S FOREST, 21 Apr 1973 Hudson, NH
CLAXTON, Odell M and Archie L TOWNSEND, 05 Jan 1946 Hudson, NH
CLAY, Samuel A and Mary L REIX, 20 Apr 1877
   Samuel J Clay
CLAY, Samuel J and Mary Ann WEBSTER, 18 Dec 1849
CLAYDON, Norma and Albert MANCINE, 05 Jul 1941 Hudson, NH
CLEAVELAND, Chong-Cha and Robert J TREITEL, 30 Sep 1982 Nashua, NH
CLEGG, David A and Sheila A O'KEEFE, 16 Nov 1973 Salem, NH
CLEGG, Edward F and Rita M COWGILL, 29 Jul 1967 Hudson, NH
CLEGG, Patricia A and Brian C WILKINSON, 01 May 1982 Nashua, NH
CLEGG, Robert E Jr and Priscilla NASH, 24 May 1974 Nashua, NH
CLEM, Mary and Sampson FRENCH, 18 Oct 1739
CLEMENT, Aravinta and George G SARGENT, 07 Mar 1858
CLEMENT, Arthur E and Jane L JOHNSON, 30 Dec 1942 Nashua, NH
CLEMENT, David and Mary A HOLMAN, 18 Sep 1867 West Roxbury, MA
CLEMENT, David and MaryJPiper BUTTERFIELD, 21 Feb 1870

HUDSON, NH MARRIAGES

CLEMENT, David and Dorcas WILSON, 29 Nov 1821
CLEMENT, David and Mary R HOLTON, 18 Sep 1867
CLEMENT, David and Mary R PIPER, 23 Feb 1870 Hudson, NH
CLEMENT, Dorcas A and William KELLEY, 29 Dec 1869
CLEMENT, Edward W and Ruby Georgia JAQUITH, 08 Jun 1924 Hudson, NH
CLEMENT, Elmer D and Emily E WILCOX, 05 Oct 1881 Hudson, NH
  David Clement, Jr (Hudson, NH) & Mariah Hall (Pelham, NH)
  William Wilcox(England) & Eliza Hewes (England)
CLEMENT, John K and Vivian Y BOULANGER, 13 Aug 1966 Hudson, NH
CLEMENT, John T and Laura M POINTER, 26 Oct 1975 Hudson, NH
CLEMENT, Lucinda P and Albert A CAMPBELL, 08 Jul 1866
CLEMENT, Lucy E and John O'CONNOR, 21 Mar 1865
CLEMENT, Lynn A and Daniel T BROWN, 16 Aug 1980 Hudson, NH
CLEMENT, Maurice R and Patricia L BULLARD, 01 Sep 1962 Hudson, NH
CLEMENT, May and Allan F LINSCOTT, 05 Mar 1901 Lowell, MA
  Elmer Clement
  Frank G Linscott & Mary J Parker
CLEMENT, Nancy J and Llewellyn WHITNEY, 05 Apr 1952 Nashua, NH
CLEMENT, Phyllis E and Harold D HARVEY, 28 Sep 1927 Nashua, NH
CLEMENT, Rachel P and David M GOULD, 04 Sep 1856
CLEMENT, Susanne and Ronald C HOVLING, 30 Nov 1963 Hudson, NH
CLEMENTS, Blanche F and Arthur E FULLER, 24 Jun 1939 Nashua, NH
CLEMENTS, Emily M and Daniel M BURNS, 02 Apr 1857
CLEMONS, Frederick and Shirley A KENTRA, 22 Jun 1973 Merrimack, NH
CLEVELAND, Amy E and Robert P SEARLES, 14 Jan 1967 Pelham, NH
CLEVELAND, Caroline M and Delma B DELANEY, 21 Aug 1947 Hudson, NH
CLEVELAND, Glenna D and Gerard P KNIGHTS, 30 Aug 1969 Hudson, NH
CLIFFORD, Harold M Jr and Greta A PORTER, 05 Feb 1943 Nashua, NH
CLIFFORD, Joseph M and Jodie Mari HUGHEY, 11 Jun 1983 Hudson, NH
CLINE, Leo and Ida PECKER, 19 Apr 1934 Hudson, NH
CLOHESY, Francis M and Frances A ELLIS, 25 Nov 1959 Hudson, NH
CLOUGH, Chester and Nancy STEVENS, Oct 1849
  John Stevens & Nancy Webster
CLOUGH, Doris P and Augustin N LAVOIE, 09 Jul 1938 Lowell, MA
CLOUGH, Joseph L and Patricia A ROWMAN, 23 May 1964 Nashua, NH
CLOUGH, Josiah C and Marguerite CARRIGAN, 12 Oct 1935 Milford, NH
CLOUGH, June O and George W BENTLEY, 16 Aug 1937 Hudson, NH
CLOUGH, Zoe E and P Michael FIMBEL, 06 Jul 1980 Gilford, NH
CLOUTIER, Colette S and Dennis A BONNETTE, 17 Feb 1968 Hudson, NH
CLOUTIER, Constance and Clifford A TROMBLEY, 28 Nov 1959 Hudson, NH
CLOUTIER, Daniel E and Linda A PARADIS, 24 Apr 1982 Nashua, NH
CLOUTIER, Donald J and June A TATE, 06 Sep 1947 Nashua, NH
CLOUTIER, Gerald K and Susan Lynn MITCHELL, 02 Jun 1979 Hudson, NH
CLOUTIER, Jacqueline and Normand A LAPLANTE, 28 May 1960 Nashua, NH
CLOUTIER, Joanne and Clayton A SMITH, 12 Jun 1965 Keene, NH
CLOUTIER, Kenneth E and Lorraine B CLOUTIER, 18 Dec 1954 Nashua, NH
CLOUTIER, Laura A and John F PEPIN, 24 Apr 1971 Hudson, NH
CLOUTIER, Lionel C Sr and Kathleen A MILLER, 10 Nov 1978 Hudson, NH
CLOUTIER, Lisa M J and Clinton M Jr WEAVER, 21 Aug 1982 Hudson, NH
CLOUTIER, Lorraine B and Kenneth E CLOUTIER, 18 Dec 1954 Nashua, NH
CLOUTIER, Louise I and Michel P LACROIX, 27 Jun 1970 Hudson, NH
CLOUTIER, Maurice R and Sheila A TULLIS, 04 Nov 1967 Nashua, NH
CLOUTIER, Michael D and Gail T HYSETTE, 13 Oct 1979 Nashua, NH
CLOUTIER, Raymond J and Julienne F MOREAU, 25 Apr 1946 Nashua, NH
CLOUTIER, Richard O and Jacqueline PROULX, 11 Nov 1972 Hudson, NH
CLOUTIER, Robert H and Patricia A SWEENEY, 15 Apr 1961 Nashua, NH
CLOUTIER, Robert W and Terri L MARDEN, 01 Aug 1964 Nashua, NH
CLOUTIER, Roger R and Deborah M FRASER, 07 May 1977 Hudson, NH
CLOUTIER, Roland J and Irene A PLANTE, 26 Jan 1946 Nashua, NH
CLOUTIER, Ronald D and Joyce E SMITH, 25 Mar 1961 Hudson, NH

HUDSON,NH MARRIAGES

CLOUTIER, Ronald R and Paula E RICHARD, 15 Jun 1968 Nashua, NH
CLOUTIER, Rosemarie and Norman C BOYER, 17 Oct 1971 Hudson, NH
CLOW, David and Mary AUSTIN, 28 Aug 1783
CLUFF, Daniel P and Lucy Ann WEBSTER, 29 Dec 1849
CLUFF, Hannah and John T KIMBALL, 27 Dec 1920 Hudson, NH
CLYDE, Esther J and Albert P RICHARD, 29 Apr 1933 Hudson, NH
CLYDE, George W and Anna Berth WELLS, 19 Feb 1902 Manchester, NH
   Samuel W Clyde & Hannah J Boles
   Martin Wells & Ella I Colby
CLYDE, Hannah L and Elmer H BLODGETT, 07 Sep 1876 Hudson, NH
CLYDE, Maggie J and Ezra A MARTIN, 21 Feb 1877 Hudson, NH
CLYDE, Priscilla and Clayton A READ, 04 Jun 1932 Hudson, NH
CLYDE, Wilson W and Veronique ST FRANCOIS, 11 Nov 1930 Keene, NH
COATE, David A and Roberta P MILLINA, 05 Sep 1981 Nashua, NH
COATES, Ralph W and Doris E EATON, 16 Jun 1932 Hudson, NH
COATS, Annie and Oliver DUFAULT, 19 Jul 1905 Nashua, NH
   James G Coats & Hannah McAndrews
   John B Dufault & Josephine Palady
COBB, Freeman and Dorothy V DUKE, 05 Dec 1925 Hudson, NH
COBB, James L and Susan CARROLL, 04 Jun 1970 Hudson, NH
COBB, Ruth and John R HAMBLETT, 25 Feb 1863
COBB, Tamara L and James J LAW, 22 Dec 1978 Nashua, NH
COBLEIGH, Gerald R and Patricia I VIVIER, 23 Jan 1982 Hudson, NH
COBLEIGH, Merlin I and Dorothy M HAYWARD, 25 Nov 1960 Merrimack, NH
COBURN, Diana L and David G BISHOP, 02 Jul 1966 Hudson, NH
COBURN, Dianna and Peter BLANCHARD, 26 Jan 1823
COBURN, James Mars and Mary Lucin WILSON, 04 Sep 1869
COBURN, Mary Ann and Hezekiah LOWLIN, 27 Aug 1846
COBURN, Norma J and Robert G KASHULINES, 21 Feb 1970 Nashua, NH
COCCHIARO, Alexander and Angela T COCCHIARO, 30 Dec 1961 Hudson, NH
COCCHIARO, Alexander and Jeanne B GONTHIER, 22 Apr 1967 Hudson, NH
COCCHIARO, Angela T and Alexander COCCHIARO, 30 Dec 1961 Hudson, NH
COCHRAN, John and Rebecca EAYRES, 07 Jan 1800
COCHRAN, Olin John and Hazel J AUSTIN, 18 Jul 1975 Hudson, NH
COCKERLINE, Allen R and Tina M CHANDRONNAIT, 26 Jan 1974 Hudson, NH
COCKERLINE, Robert B and Therese L CARON, 20 Nov 1976 Nashua, NH
COE, Carolyn and Michael Allan HARDY, 14 Nov 1978 Hudson, NH
COE, Cynthia A and Richard C MEISCHEID, 14 Mar 1981 Hudson, NH
COFFEY, Jennie V and John J BURNS, 06 Sep 1911 Hudson, NH
   John Coffey & Bridget Shea
   John J Burns & Abbie Henderson
COFFILL, Steven P and Denise G WELLS, 23 May 1982 Hudson, NH
COFFIN, Eileen L and Robert W HOITT, 03 Aug 1935 Hudson, NH
COFFIN, Vera B and Harry J CONNELL, 16 Jun 1909 Hudson, NH
   Holmes W Coffin & Ida D Fish
   Philip J Connell & Hannah E Hardy
COHEN, Adele F and Sidney K RABINOVITZ, 21 Apr 1934 Hudson, NH
COHEN, Diana B and Nathan I FREEDMAN, 20 Jun 1935 Hudson, NH
COHEN, Leonard and Esther ENGELL, 07 May 1938 Hudson, NH
COHN, Curtis H and Carolyn G DAVIS, 30 Mar 1981 Nashua, NH
COLARUSSO, Carmela J and Nathaniel BRADBURY, 17 Dec 1949 Hudson, NH
COLBATH, Paulette D and David F JOKI, 26 Aug 1984 Nashua, NH
COLBURN, Abiah and Asa BUTTERFIELD, 23 Mar 1784
COLBURN, Abiel Jr and Sarah MINOT, 23 Mar 1797
COLBURN, Agnes B and Thomas A COLBURN, 24 Dec 1948 Hudson, NH
COLBURN, Asa and Susanna LAWRENCE, 20 Oct 1785
COLBURN, Bruce A and Linda M GAGNON, 19 Oct 1963 Hudson, NH
COLBURN, Charlotte and Clifton E BUTTRICK, 18 Jun 1874 Hudson, NH
COLBURN, Clara and William CROSS, 20 May 1875 Hudson, NH
COLBURN, Cynthia L and Michael J McCLURE, 24 Apr 1982 Hudson, NH

HUDSON,NH MARRIAGES

COLBURN, Daniel and Sally DAKIN, 24 May 1782
COLBURN, Daniel A&Henrietta LIVINGSTON, 24 Dec 1891 Londonderry, NH
   Newton Colburn (Dracut, MA) & Sarah J Richardson (Dracut, MA)
   Henry L C Newton(Marlboro, NH) & Mary W Moulton (Holderness, NH)
COLBURN, David and Sally DAHLEN, 25 May 1782
COLBURN, Edith F and George S STEELE, 05 Oct 1893 Nashua, NH
   Henry T Colburn (Hudson, NH) & Fanny F Gould (Tyngsboro, MA)
   Silas T Steele(Hudson, NH) & Elizabeth McDonald (New York)
COLBURN, Elizabeth and Charles A BAILEY, 02 Sep 1847
COLBURN, Elizabeth and William GOULD, 25 May 1785
COLBURN, Gertrude A and Maurice D MERRILL, 12 Oct 1945 Hudson, NH
COLBURN, Henry F and M Frances GOULD, 12 Jun 1865
COLBURN, Isaac and Lydia DAVIS, 04 Aug 1785
COLBURN, Isaac and Eldesta POLLARD, 28 Dec 1826
COLBURN, Kathleen M and George R BELANGER, 16 May 1964 Nashua, NH
COLBURN, Lydia and Thomas HARRIS, 01 Oct 1829
COLBURN, Lynn M and Richard E GENDRON, 06 Feb 1976 Hudson, NH
COLBURN, Maria C and George W BRADLEY, 15 Nov 1870 Hudson, NH
COLBURN, Mary J and Granville SMITH, 24 Dec 1874 Hudson, NH
COLBURN, Mehittabel and Stephen S FIFIELD, 23 Nov 1870
COLBURN, Miriam and Daniel T POLLARD, 26 Jun 1817
COLBURN, Patte and Jedediah HARDY, 22 Dec 1800
COLBURN, Pattie and Jedidiah HARVEY, 22 Dec 1800
COLBURN, Paul A and Roselyn Am MOORE, 09 Jun 1973 Hudson, NH
COLBURN, Rebecca and John MERRILL, 26 Feb 1818
COLBURN, Simeon and Abigail RUSSELL, 27 Sep 1781
COLBURN, Susan J and Michael J LAROCQUE, 22 Aug 1981 Hudson, NH
COLBURN, Tammy J and David R Jr LANOUE, 18 May 1985 Hudson, NH
COLBURN, Thomas A and Agnes B COLBURN, 24 Dec 1948 Hudson, NH
COLBURN, Tracy W and Jill R LIS, 11 Jun 1983 Hudson, NH
COLBURN, Zaccheus and Rachel HILLS, 29 Apr 1788
COLBY, Abram and Lucy CUMMINGS, 16 Aug 1855
COLBY, Carrie R and Alan A ASSELIN, 06 Sep 1974 Manchester, NH
COLBY, Colin S and Pauline Y ST LAURENT, 15 Nov 1980 Hudson, NH
COLBY, Edward W and Ruth E THOMPSON, 30 Aug 1938 Hudson, NH
COLBY, Nettie O and Frank A WILSON, 21 Jun 1905 Nashua, NH
   Luke B Colby & Annie O Cate
   James F Wilson & Sarah H Riley
COLBY, Susan J and Frank A III BURBANK, 05 Aug 1967 Claremont, NH
COLBY, Thomas S and Priscilla ROBINSON, 11 Sep 1976 Manchester, NH
COLE, Colleen M and Ronald F MAYNARD, 18 Mar 1978 Nashua, NH
COLE, Frank W and Gladys E SANDERS, 08 Dec 1919 Nashua, NH
COLE, Kathleen A and Richard M POINTER, 01 Oct 1976 Nashua, NH
COLE, Paul F and Janet M COTE, 20 Aug 1983 Hudson, NH
COLE, Robert A and Joan L LEVESQUE, 17 Nov 1962 Hudson, NH
COLE, Russell Jr and Selma E GATZ, 17 Oct 1936 Hudson, NH
COLEMAN, Robert N and Patricia M LINNELL, 29 Mar 1947 Nashua, NH
COLL, Deborah K and James W Jr SMITH, 29 Feb 1980 Hudson, NH
COLL, Judy E and Gary L BUHRMEISTER, 16 Jul 1966 Hudson, NH
COLL, Laura Lee and Ralph T HARRON, 15 Jul 1972 Hudson, NH
COLL, Rene W Jr and Robin A CARON, 06 Oct 1972 Nashua, NH
COLLEY, Linda L and Thomas M ESTEE, 05 Dec 1970 Hudson, NH
COLLIER, James and Ida MARTELLE, 05 Mar 1905 Hudson, NH
   Joseph Collier & Emeline Duprey
   Azale Martelle & Olive Hill
COLLINS, James P and Sylvie Line PELLETIER, 09 May 1981 Nashua, NH
COLLINS, Jennie and William H JEWETT, 09 Apr 1869
COLLINS, Jennie and George MITCHELL, 31 Dec 1869 Hudson, NH
COLLINS, Kenneth A and Susan Lisa RICH, 03 Feb 1979 Hudson, NH
COLLINS, Marjorie R and Herbert A MILLETT, 30 Jul 1944 Nashua, NH

HUDSON,NH MARRIAGES

COLLINS, Mark W and Gail A DUPLEASE, 04 Feb 1983 Nashua, NH
COLLINS, Robert T and Barbara A DURKIN, 09 May 1982 Hudson, NH
COLLINS, Robin R and Ronald N LUSSIER, 08 May 1982 Hudson, NH
COLLINS, Ruth and John HAMBLET, 25 Feb 1863
COLLINS, Sandra M and Paul N PELLETIER, 07 Aug 1983 Hudson, NH
COLLINS, William J and Florence F LACROIX, 22 May 1932 Hudson, NH
COLLISHAW, Cynthia A and Raymond M FLUETTE, 16 Aug 1980 Hudson, NH
COLOMBE, Mary G and Walter L Jr COLOMBE, 26 Sep 1964 Hudson, NH
COLOMBE, Norman A and Sheila I PHILBROOK, 08 Oct 1965 Hudson, NH
COLOMBE, Walter L Jr and Mary G COLOMBE, 26 Sep 1964 Hudson, NH
COLOMBO, Rose A and Harold W DULEY, 26 Sep 1937 Hudson, NH
COLON, Luc and Edeline MARCELIN, 03 Mar 1976 Hudson, NH
COLSON, Brenton R and Helene A RANKINS, 29 Jan 1977 Merrimack, NH
COLT, Lester R and Agnes C HEBERT, 02 Feb 1947 Hudson, NH
COLUMB, Eva J and George T CASSIDY, 19 May 1937 Hudson, NH
COMAN, Raye A and Frederick J TIERNEY, 28 Jan 1978 Nashua, NH
COMEAU, Jean C and Lawrence M Jr HORTON, 20 Oct 1932 Nashua, NH
COMEAU, Marie Emma A and Berton K FISH, 07 Jul 1927 Keene, NH
COMER, Dale Ann and Henry R ZUKOWSKI, 04 Sep 1982 Hudson, NH
COMI, Agnes M and Adelard R BELANGER, 17 Feb 1962 Brookline, NH
COMIRE, Donald E Jr and Sandra L CAMPBELL, 02 Nov 1970 Hudson, NH
COMTOIS, Rita E and Charles R BOUDREAU, 12 Oct 1984 Hudson, NH
CONANT, Ada S and James W B SMITH, 25 Feb 1905 Hudson, NH
   Sam Simpson & Sabina Tibbetts
   John Smith & Mary Ball
CONANT, Elizabeth and Nathan CUMMINGS, 21 Feb 1850
CONANT, Susan and James CALDWELL, 13 Oct 1822
CONANT, Susan M and James E MARSHALL, 08 Feb 1893 Hudson, NH
   James Ridgeway (N S) & Jane Hewitt (N S)
   Alfred Marshall(Hudson, NH) & Lynia M Hamblet (Hudson, NH)
CONATY, Gary L and Betty L KAROS, 09 May 1959 Hudson, NH
CONCANNON, Eleanor H and Joseph P GRAZIO, 01 Jun 1974 Hudson, NH
CONDO, Morris and Janice M BOSSIE, 26 Jun 1970 Nashua, NH
CONDON, Dorothy M and William T JACQUES, 26 Aug 1950 Hudson, NH
CONDON, Nellie and Harvey G LEWIS, 17 Jul 1889 Lowell, MA
   James Condon & Johanna Howard
   Wm F Lewis & Lucy F Boynton (Pepperell, MA)
CONE, Judith A and Robert N FROMENT, 26 Jun 1981 Hudson, NH
CONEENY, Alice M and Joseph L LEGERE, 01 Jul 1950 Hudson, NH
CONEGRATTE, Marguerite and George L ADAMS, 02 Jan 1923 Nashua, NH
CONERY, Addie L and Fred E SMITH, 16 Nov 1904 Nashua, NH
   S A Conery & Sarah E Hollister
   Nelson Smith & Caroline M Lee
CONLEY, Lawrence A and Jane M BURKE, 16 Jul 1983 Salem, NH
CONLEY, Lillian W and Philip J CONNELL, 26 Dec 1940 Bangor, ME
CONLON, Catherine and Paul J BROGIE, 04 Sep 1933 Nashua, NH
CONNELL, Carrie E and Arnold ANDREW, 24 May 1901 Nashua, NH
   Robert T Connell (Hudson, NH) & Mary E Marshall (Hudson, NH)
   Robert Andrew(England) & Emma Thorn (England)
CONNELL, Dennis and Anna NUNES, 30 Jun 1942 Hudson, NH
CONNELL, Eliza and Edward POFF, 31 Aug 1854 Lowell, MA
CONNELL, Ethel M and Elmer F SMITH, 07 Sep 1910 Londonderry, NH
   Robert T Connell & Mary E Marshall
   Henry F Smith & Elmira Chamberlain
CONNELL, Frank A and Mary E WATTS, 12 Jun 1901 Hudson, NH
   Philip J Connell (Hudson, NH) & Hannah E Hardy (Hudson, NH)
   Lorenzo Watts(Chazy, NY) & Alvira Parks (Moores, NY)
CONNELL, Frederick and Ella Alice McCOY, 03 May 1931 Chelmsford, MA
CONNELL, Grace H and John E PARKER, 10 Nov 1934 Hudson, NH
CONNELL, Harry J and Vera B COFFIN, 16 Jun 1909 Hudson, NH

HUDSON,NH MARRIAGES

Philip J Connell & Hannah E Hardy
Holmes W Coffin & Ida D Fish
CONNELL, John W and Jennie M BUCK, 01 Apr 1866
CONNELL, Mabel F and Daniel G WENTWORTH, 03 Jun 1903 Nashua, NH
　Robert T Connell & Lizzie Marshall
　Nathaniel Wentworth & Martha E Greeley
CONNELL, Madeline A & Frederick O'BRIEN, 24 Dec 1930 Harrington, ME
CONNELL, Mary Jane and David C FORD, 11 Jan 1865
CONNELL, Otis R and Lucy M LONGARD, 23 Nov 1904 Nashua, NH
　Robert T Connell & Lizzie Marshall
　Stephen Longard & Margaret Coory
CONNELL, Philip and Margaret WILLIAMSTON, 20 Nov 1864
CONNELL, Philip J and Lillian W CONLEY, 26 Dec 1940 Bangor, ME
CONNELL, Philip J and Deborah A HAMILTON, 06 Oct 1973 Merrimack, NH
CONNELL, Philip J and Hannah E HARDY, 21 May 1873
CONNELL, Philip J and Hannah E HARDY, 20 May 1873 Lowell, MA
CONNELL, Philip Jr and Hattie M FARWELL, 01 Apr 1866
CONNELL, Phillip J and Jennie M BUTTRESS, 03 Jul 1911 Nashua, NH
　Tobias Connell & Mary Hoffman
　William Buttress & Annie McCullough
CONNELL, Robert T and Mary E MARSHALL, 06 Dec 1879 Pelham, NH
　Tobias Connell (Ireland) & Mary (Ireland)
　Henry Marshall & Mary E
CONNELL, Thomas H and Edwina J PECK, 11 Mar 1873 Dracut, MA
CONNER, James H and Helen DOYLE, 19 Jun 1938 Hudson, NH
CONNER, Lucy E and Ephraim SNELL, 09 Sep 1869 Hudson, NH
CONNER, Muriel and Ralph B NELSON, 04 Jul 1872 Hudson, NH
CONNOLLY, Ruth A and Frederick BEATON, 06 Mar 1948 Hudson, NH
CONNORS, Walter J and Mildred E McCOY, 25 Sep 1948 Hudson, NH
CONOMICK, Lillian I and Earl L HUTCHINSON, 24 Mar 1935 Hudson, NH
CONOPKA, Charles and Pearl HASSEY, 16 Nov 1938 Nashua, NH
CONRAD, Cynthia F and Richard M PELLETIER, 21 Jun 1969 Hudson, NH
CONRAD, Joseph F Jr and Nancy L GAGNON, 17 Jun 1967 Hudson, NH
CONRAD, Pearl I and Carl C TARBOX, 22 Dec 1934 Hudson, NH
CONRAN, Thomas W and Deborah L RICHARDS, 24 Aug 1974 Hudson, NH
CONREY, Margaret H and Bert L LOUGEE, 11 Apr 1942 Hudson, NH
CONSIDINE, Bridget MJ and William SWEENEY, 11 Oct 1891 Hudson, NH
　Jonas Considine (Ireland) (Ireland)
　Edward Sweeney & Almira Martin
CONSIGNY, Doris B and Anthony S STAWSKI, 27 Apr 1943 Hudson, NH
CONSIGNY, Marie A and Joseph D AUDET, 11 Apr 1921 Nashua, NH
CONSIGNY, Robert H and Barbara A BOLES, 05 Apr 1947 Hudson, NH
CONSIGNY, William H and Norma M BILLINGS, 30 May 1942 Hudson, NH
CONSTANT, Adrien J and Mary E VIGNOLA, 05 Jul 1952 Hudson, NH
CONSTANT, David M and Nanette S BOUCHER, 01 Jun 1979 Hudson, NH
CONSTANT, Doris J and Paul W GOODWIN, 21 Dec 1963 Hudson, NH
CONSTANT, Regina I M and Chester C DEMERITT, 24 Nov 1962 Nashua, NH
CONSTANT, Rita and Richard J RANKIN, 05 Feb 1966 Hudson, NH
CONSTANT, Robert L and Rose M PORTER, 20 Jul 1957 Hudson, NH
CONSTANTINEAU, Donna J and Daniel J MURPHY, 09 Jul 1983 Salem, NH
CONSTANTINO, Donald A and Judith M MUELLER, 22 Jun 1985 Hudson, NH
CONVERSE, Eben and Betsey A HILL, 30 Dec 1866
CONVERSE, Eben and Betsey A HILL, 13 Dec 1866
CONWAY, Alicia J and Vincent T Jr FODEN, 02 Oct 1971 Manchester, NH
COOK, Charles E and Nellie M ELLIOT, 28 May 1868 Hudson, NH
COOK, Cynthia M and Derrick F SOUZA, 26 Nov 1983 Hudson, NH
COOK, Diane S and Paul Z CARRIER, 14 Dec 1968 Hudson, NH
COOK, Dora A and Thomas J FORD, 24 Oct 1907 Nashua, NH
　Frank S Avery & Adeline Wood
　Timothy S Ford & Sarah Fuller

HUDSON, NH MARRIAGES

COOK, Irving E and Nancy L ROY, 23 Aug 1981 Hudson, NH
COOK, Leon A Jr and Lynda E TRAVIS, 24 Nov 1966 Exeter, NH
COOK, Linda M and Richard E Jr GILMARTIN, 05 Oct 1963 Hudson, NH
COOK, Lois E and Andrew A LANDRY, 09 Sep 1967 Hudson, NH
COOK, Mary V and Ronald N BOUFFARD, 07 Oct 1961 Nashua, NH
COOK, Nepherbeth and Jn PRATT, 29 Jun 1779
COOKE, Charlotte and Ronald C GARDNER, 26 Nov 1964 Hudson, NH
COOKE, Harold Edmond and Theresa O GIROUARD, 26 Nov 1925 Nashua, NH
COOKE, Harriet F and Vito S ALUKONIS, 01 Jul 1950 Hudson, NH
COOKE, Hector R and Marion DANE, 24 Aug 1930 Milford, NH
COOKE, Hersey E and Diane M SPAULDING, 26 Dec 1962 Nashua, NH
COOKE, Hersey F and Lucy J BURNHAM, 08 Oct 1926 S Lyndeboro, NH
COOKE, Marlene M and Richard E BROWN, 18 May 1963 Nashua, NH
COOKE, Nancy E and Willis E PETHIC, 02 Jul 1949 Hudson, NH
COOKMAN, Anne M and William P MITCHELL, 24 Dec 1961 Hudson, NH
COOKMAN, Elizabeth and James A GELESZINSKI, 04 May 1968 Nashua, NH
COOKMAN, Peter H and Linda I HALL, 15 Nov 1967 Hudson, NH
COOKSON, Leah and Frank M DEMONT, 02 Sep 1938 Hudson, NH
COOLBETH, Kathrine and Henry G POWERS, 20 Oct 1964 Hudson, NH
COOLBROTH, Frederick & Jeaneen M SESTA, 01 Dec 1979 Manchester, NH
COOLBROTH, Larry D and Patricia A TELLIER, 11 Sep 1971 Hollis, NH
COOLBROTH, Sarsha M and Bernard E MOORE, 10 Dec 1971 Hudson, NH
COOLEY, Barbara A and Peter J FRAPPIER, 29 May 1982 Litchfield, NH
COOLEY, Boyd E and Elsie R SMITH, 19 Jun 1971 Milford, NH
COOLIDGE, Abby Ann and James RICHARDSON, 30 Nov 1871 Hudson, NH
COOLIDGE, Harold B and Virginia C DUNN, 16 Sep 1942 Nashua, NH
COOLIDGE, Virginia G and John E PARKER, 21 Jun 1968 Moultonboro, NH
COOMAS, Kathleen and Bobby D ROSE, 05 Aug 1950 Hudson, NH
COOMBS, Walter P Jr and Margery C CHALIFOUX, 01 Feb 1969 Hudson, NH
COOPER, Audrey B and Edward W NOYES, 17 Jan 1948 Hudson, NH
COOPER, Carol R and Joel M DROZNICK, 19 Jul 1975 Hudson, NH
COOPER, Catherine and Kenneth N LODDING, 01 Oct 1983 Hudson, NH
COOPER, James F and Diane J DUQUETTE, 11 Apr 1975 Nashua, NH
COOPER, Patricia A and David B MILLER, 07 May 1977 Nashua, NH
COOPER, Theresa J and Kenneth W WATSON, 22 Jun 1974 Nashua, NH
COPELAND, Andrea K and Richard P TURCOTTE, 21 May 1977 Nashua, NH
COPP, Patricia D and Dennis L EKMAN, 14 Apr 1984 Hudson, NH
COPPI, Agnes L and Lewis C GILPATRICK, 08 Jul 1939 Hudson, NH
CORBETT, Muriel Elizabet and Joseph LYDEN, 22 Jul 1978 Hudson, NH
CORBETT, Walter and Lorraine NICHOLS, 04 May 1941 Hudson, NH
CORBETT, William and Florence DEWOLFE, 13 Sep 1950 Hudson, NH
CORBIN, Gerald F and Sandra J LILLEY, 08 Jul 1967 Hudson, NH
CORBIT, Cardin L and Shirley M MORISSETTE, 02 Oct 1954 Hudson, NH
CORBITT, Cynthia J and Daniel R QUIGLEY, 16 May 1981 Salem, NH
CORBY, Wm J and Mary Hazel MacELROY, 17 Dec 1922 Hudson, NH
CORCORAN, Frederick and Priscilla BERNARD, 13 Jun 1981 Hudson, NH
CORCORAN, Lawrence R and Denise M LAVOIE, 25 Jun 1976 Nashua, NH
CORDEAU, Eleanor M and Charles J PELRINE, 28 Mar 1949 Hudson, NH
CORDESCO, Mary F and Maurice D FORTIER, 17 Nov 1946 Hudson, NH
COREIA, Joseph B and Myrtle O HELME, 27 Mar 1937 Nashua, NH
CORLIS, Chastina A and Jameson GREELEY, 23 Mar 1875 Hudson, NH
CORLISS, Austin D and Alice F SIMONDS, 21 Mar 1888 Hudson, NH
   James Corliss (Hudson, NH) & Sarah Hamlett (Hudson, NH)
   Amos F Churchill(Solon, ME) & Eleanor Chase (Solon, ME)
CORLISS, James N and Hattie N BUNKER, 30 Nov 1869
CORLISS, Sarah A and Frederick SMITH, 19 Oct 1865
CORMIER, Jeanne L and Gary T McCULLOUGH, 25 Jan 1974 Nashua, NH
CORMIER, Joseph A Jr and Eleanor M SILVA, 29 Dec 1984 Nashua, NH
CORMIER, Lorraine G and Earle H WILLIAMS, 03 Jun 1967 Hudson, NH
CORMIER, Lucille I and James T WILLIAMS, 04 May 1975 Hudson, NH

HUDSON, NH MARRIAGES

CORMIER, Mark P and Betsy McGREGOR, 31 Mar 1984 Goffstown, NH
CORMIER, Raymond R and Janice M LELAND, 16 Dec 1961 Nashua, NH
CORNELL, Harold B & Mildred F BENT, 04 Aug 1927 Melvin Village, NH
CORNELL, Ruth and Gordon C MacPHAIL, 17 Nov 1945 Hudson, NH
CORNETTA, Francis and Mary INGERSON, 05 Aug 1941 Hudson, NH
CORNIELLIER, Elie and Sedulie BELANGER, 21 Apr 1913 Nashua, NH
    Charles Corniellier & Emilie Turcelle
    Joseph Belanger & Flornie Broux
CORONIS, Lucille B and Lawrence E Jr MOORE, 02 Nov 1968 Hudson, NH
COROSA, Charles V and Etienette COTE, 02 Sep 1946 Nashua, NH
COROSA, Joanne M and Roger R GAUDETTE, 22 Jun 1973 Hudson, NH
COROSA, Michael P and Rose-Ann MIHELIS, 01 Jun 1974 Hudson, NH
COROSA, Vito P and Sophie WOLCZOK, 11 Sep 1943 Nashua, NH
CORRIVEAU, Paul P and Elaine L DUCHARME, 17 Feb 1962 Hudson, NH
CORSARO, Pasquale and Concetta J AURELIO, 21 Jan 1950 Hudson, NH
CORSON, Lynn A and Mary L GOWING, 14 Jul 1962 Hudson, NH
CORSON, Mary L and David M CHAPMAN, 02 Aug 1969 Hudson, NH
CORSON, Robert F and Linda N PRIEST, 19 Jun 1977 Hudson, NH
CORTAGENA, Eric E and Marguerita RAMIREZ, 16 Jul 1981 Hudson, NH
CORTELL, Donald E and Lillian L PALMER, 26 Feb 1950 Hudson, NH
CORTI, Anacleto and Olive P DREWETT, 26 Jun 1921 Hudson, NH
CORY, Alice A and Franklin H ALLEN, 29 May 1873 Nashua, NH
COSSE, Cheryl A and Mark C JOHNSTON, 10 Jul 1983 Nashua, NH
COSSETTE, David J and Denise D DUDASH, 18 Sep 1982 Merrimack, NH
COSSETTE, Paul N and Arlene L HAWKINS, 27 Jun 1974 Sandown, NH
COSSETTE, Paul N Jr and Linda M MERRILL, 25 Jun 1976 Hudson, NH
COSSETTE, Thomas L and Gayle H LATOUR, 17 Aug 1974 Hudson, NH
COSTA, Judith E and Scott G FRYE, 07 Jul 1984 Hudson, NH
COSTA, Rosemary and David A PRUNIER, 21 Aug 1982 Windham, NH
COSTELLO, Gertrude and William H FREEMAN, 16 Aug 1934 Hudson, NH
COSTELLO, Marion M and Joseph A DOYLE, 13 Mar 1937 Hudson, NH
COTE, Alfred P and Jeannette LANDRY, 26 Sep 1959 Hudson, NH
COTE, Brian R and Debbie M CLARK, 24 Apr 1971 Hudson, NH
COTE, Claire E and Howard B NADEAU, 25 Nov 1954 Hudson, NH
COTE, Claudette and Edward G GROHOSKY, 21 Nov 1953 Hudson, NH
COTE, Conrad C and Theresa M PELLETIER, 03 Jul 1946 Nashua, NH
COTE, Cynthia J and Leonard A MARTIN, 11 Oct 1969 Nashua, NH
COTE, Denise S and Randal S ELLIS, 01 May 1970 Hudson, NH
COTE, Emilienne and Raymond R JEAN, 17 Jan 1942 Nashua, NH
COTE, Etienette and Charles V COROSA, 02 Sep 1946 Nashua, NH
COTE, Florence M and Raymond J BARRIAULT, 01 Sep 1947 Nashua, NH
COTE, Gaetan R and Patricia A COURTEMANCHE, 23 Jul 1977 Hollis, NH
COTE, Gerald R and Carol Ann O'LOUGHLIN, 30 Mar 1973 Litchfield, NH
COTE, Gilles J and Clemence F BESSETTE, 07 Aug 1971 Manchester, NH
COTE, Gloria P and David O GOODRICH, 26 Nov 1964 Hudson, NH
COTE, Jacqueline and Donald R SAVARD, 02 Jul 1955 Hudson, NH
COTE, Janet M and Paul F COLE, 20 Aug 1983 Hudson, NH
COTE, Jeanne B and Theodore B MARSHALL, 26 Feb 1977 Nashua, NH
COTE, Jeanne E and Richard O TURMEL, 31 Oct 1959 Nashua, NH
COTE, Joanne D and Maurice G PAQUETTE, 23 Nov 1968 Hudson, NH
COTE, Joseph F and Ernestine BRUNELLE, 15 Oct 1949 Nashua, NH
COTE, Linda Ann and David N GRIFFIN, 21 Mar 1975 Hudson, NH
COTE, Lydia and Edmond J P BERNARD, 12 Apr 1930 Hudson, NH
COTE, Norman J and Cecile L NOLET, 04 Nov 1983 Nashua, NH
COTE, Norman T and Donna B SMITH, 12 May 1962 Nashua, NH
COTE, Olivette and Leon R RICH, 28 Aug 1937 Nashua, NH
COTE, Paul N and Anne R GAFFNEY, 05 Dec 1961 Hudson, NH
COTE, Pauline J and Aldeo O LAINE, 25 Nov 1954 Hudson, NH
COTE, Phebe and Peter T RATTE, 19 Jul 1925 Merrimack, NH
COTE, Pierrette and Karlton E POTTER, 25 Oct 1969 Hudson, NH

HUDSON, NH MARRIAGES

COTE, Robert F and Sherry A BRIDGES, 18 Jun 1966 Hampstead, NH
COTE, Roger L and Phyllis E BRIAND, 06 Apr 1959 Nashua, NH
COTE, Roger P and Sandra M USOVICZ, 27 Jan 1962 Nashua, NH
COTE, Rose S and Yvan D COTE, 18 Sep 1976 Hudson, NH
COTE, Steven J and Elizabeth DELYANI, 29 Oct 1983 Nashua, NH
COTE, Sylvia E and Robert A MILLER, 25 Jun 1955 Hudson, NH
COTE, Tammy C and Peter E GIZA, 20 Mar 1982 Hollis, NH
COTE, Theodore E and Kelly A DOWLING, 20 Feb 1982 Nashua, NH
COTE, Yvan D and Rose S COTE, 18 Sep 1976 Hudson, NH
COTNOIR, Sylvie L and Mark E LAPORTA, 19 Sep 1981 Manchester, NH
COTTING, Margaret A and Bernard E QUINN, 05 Nov 1948 Hudson, NH
COUGHLIN, Charles W and Edna M LILJEHOLM, 24 Oct 1942 Hudson, NH
COUGHLIN, Pearl and Anthony CARUSO, 05 Aug 1941 Hudson, NH
COUGHLIN, Roger J and Imogene SODERBERY, 21 Oct 1888 Fishkill, NY
   Michael Coughlin (Boston, MA) & Ann (Boston, MA)
   Robert Soderbery(New York) & Mary Walker (New York)
COUGHLIN, Roger J and SADERBERRY, 24 Oct 1888
COUGLE, Janetta K and Kenneth J MOHLER, 07 Apr 1979 Hudson, NH
COULIS, Thomas A and Miriam L STOVER, 11 Mar 1933 Hudson, NH
COULOMBE, Chester A and Shirley A BOYER, 03 Sep 1955 Nashua, NH
COULOMBE, Claudia L and Jeffrey A ROGERS, 28 Sep 1974 Hudson, NH
COURCY, Claire and Alfred V THERRIEN, 15 Jul 1942 Nashua, NH
COURCY, Patrick J and Ursula M SZCZECHURA, 01 Jun 1957 Nashua, NH
COURET, Virginia K and Oscar E PETERSON, 12 Jun 1982 Nashua, NH
COURNOYER, Paul W and Mary Marci QUIRK, 04 Jun 1983 Manchester, NH
COUROUNIS, William and Mabel G IVES, 20 Jan 1967 Nashua, NH
COURTEMANCHE, Cindy G and Gerard F GRIGAS, 13 Oct 1979 Hudson, NH
COURTEMANCHE, David A and Sandra E BRIAND, 01 Sep 1972 Hudson, NH
COURTEMANCHE, Dorothea M and Ronald R BELDEN, 17 Aug 1968 Derry, NH
COURTEMANCHE, Henry A and Barbara W KIMBALL, 14 Aug 1946 Hudson, NH
COURTEMANCHE, Jane A & Roger P GREGOIRE, 02 Aug 1969 Manchester, NH
COURTEMANCHE, Patricia A and Gaetan R COTE, 23 Jul 1977 Hollis, NH
COURTEMANCHE, Rhonda R and Daniel L DUMONT, 21 Feb 1975 Nashua, NH
COURTEMANCHE, Robert L and Claudette LABRIE, 14 Jun 1958 Nashua, NH
COURTEMANCHE, William E & Sharon A MATTISON, 05 Dec 1981 Nashua, NH
COURTNEY, Michael W and Lisa K SMITH, 28 Oct 1979 Hudson, NH
COUTERMARSH, Marie A&James PEWN III DRISCOLL, 27 Jun 1981 Hudson,NH
COUTIER, Mark A and Janet E MOORE, 01 Oct 1983 Nashua, NH
COUTU, Leo Chas and Lucille M THEROUX, 19 Nov 1976 Hudson, NH
COUTU, Rudolph R and Aline M POWLOWSKY, 29 Aug 1981 Hudson, NH
COUTURE, Jacqueline & Warner P MERCER, 18 Jun 1983 New Ipswich, NH
COUTURE, Philip J and Helen YOUNGMAN, 19 Jul 1948 Hudson, NH
COUTURIER, Alfred and Antonia CHOMARD, 11 Jun 1938 Nashua, NH
COUTURIER, Dennis F and Jean L SWINERTON, 21 Nov 1973 Pelham, NH
COUTURIER, Philip and Kathleen M GUIGNARD, 21 Jan 1985 Nashua, NH
COVERT, Robert J and Mary A JAMESON, 06 Apr 1963 Hudson, NH
COVEY, Barbara J and Thomas F HAMILTON, 25 Jun 1983 Hudson, NH
COVEY, Fernanade and Royal A FRASER, 30 Jun 1956 Hudson, NH
COVEY, Gretchen A and James A MASON, 16 Jan 1965 Hudson, NH
COVEY, Harold R and Patricia L LAFLAMME, 17 Nov 1962 Hudson, NH
COVEY, Louisa D and Horace J HAMBLETT, 30 Apr 1862
COVEY, Lyle and Helen REED, 25 Aug 1934 Nashua, NH
COVEY, Wm W and Emma A ROCKWELL, 21 Jun 1922 Hudson, NH
COWAN, Anne L and Clifford A LEVI, 08 May 1967 Nashua, NH
COWGILL, Eleanor M and Donald A LANDRY, 04 Jul 1958 Nashua, NH
COWGILL, Rita M and Edward F CLEGG, 29 Jul 1967 Hudson, NH
COWGILL, Wilfred and Mabel I FORD, 21 Feb 1929 Hudson, NH
COWLES, Doris G and Raymond H GAGNON, 19 Jul 1941 Hudson, NH
COX, Brenda L and Charles W ALLEN, 08 Mar 1975 Hudson, NH
COX, Edward F and Constance SCALERA, 18 Oct 1948 Hudson, NH

HUDSON,NH MARRIAGES

COX, Eunice A and Bruce R ZINTEL, 01 Jan 1949 Merrimack, NH
COX, Herschel W and Lorraine O BIGWOOD, 03 Aug 1946 Nashua, NH
COX, Linda S and Gary T LEE, 21 Oct 1967 Hudson, NH
COX, Lloyd D and Nancy E MORLEY, 01 Jul 1957 Merrimack, NH
COX, Wilma J and James B SMURDA, 25 May 1957 Hudson, NH
COYNE, William J and Elizabeth SMITH, 11 Oct 1947 Hudson, NH
CRABB, Loris V and James H Jr BRYANT, 30 Sep 1946 Hudson, NH
CRACROFT, Barbara A and Clement DEROSA, 21 Jul 1949 Hudson, NH
CRAIG, Charles R and Mary E MAJOR, 01 Jun 1872 Hudson, NH
CRAIGEN, William S and Ruth A FOWLE, 08 Oct 1949 Hudson, NH
CRAIGLE, Frances A and Charles DEXTER, 05 Jan 1946 Hudson, NH
CRAIK, Elaine M and Phillip A DURAND, 24 May 1975 Hudson, NH
CRAIN, Lydia G and Reuben P SMITH, 18 Dec 1849
CRAIS, Tommy W and Phoebe A BOLDUC, 23 Sep 1967 Hudson, NH
CRAM, Theresa M and Rebel L ALLARD, 26 Apr 1985 Hudson, NH
CRAMTON, Verna J and Raymond Sargent HARRIS, 03 Jun 1928 Hudson, NH
CRANMER, Ronald E and Joanne M GARMORY, 28 Dec 1963 Hudson, NH
CRANSTON, Valerie and Francis E Jr SMALL, 09 May 1981 Nashua, NH
CRAVEN, Barbara S and Kenneth M BUCHANAN, 26 Oct 1947 Hudson, NH
CRAWFORD, Daniel T and Annette M GILE, 18 Jul 1981 Hudson, NH
CRAWFORD, June A and John C LATVIS, 22 Feb 1941 Nashua, NH
CRAWFORD, Nathan C and Sandra H LEVESQUE, 23 May 1970 Milford, NH
CREAMER, Francis E and Dorothy M WHITMORE, 04 Jun 1940 Hudson, NH
CRENNER, Doris Laighton and Lee Guy SIMONDS, 24 Jun 1920 Hudson, NH
CRENNER, Eva L and William H STOODLY, 23 Dec 1871 Charlestown, MA
CRESSY, Alice C and Herbert W LOCKE, 11 Oct 1914 Hudson, NH
   Charles H Locke & Ellen C Russell
CRESSY, Laura J and Willis C TUFTS, 17 Apr 1912 Hudson, NH
   John G Cressy & Alice M Seavey
   Joseph W Tufts & Mary S Rowell
CRESTA, Ann V and Daniel R CALAWA, 31 Jul 1982 Hudson, NH
CRESTA, Joan Marie and Michael W WALKER, 03 Aug 1974 Hudson, NH
CRETE, Robert S and Laurie A ZELONIS, 05 Sep 1981 Hudson, NH
CRETE, Suzanne M and Alan R III SEMPLE, 01 Oct 1980 Hudson, NH
CRIPPS, Colleen A and Steven A LAVOIE, 23 Aug 1980 Hudson, NH
CRISMAN, Erik and Deborah A LENT, 23 Aug 1975 Hudson, NH
CROCKETT, Alvah G and Eva LIPSON, 11 Sep 1937 Hudson, NH
CROCKETT, Julianne and K Michael SCARKS, 01 Jun 1974 Hudson, NH
CROCKETT, Lloyd E and Anella SHUMAN, 15 May 1945 Hudson, NH
CROFT, Barbara R and Thomas D TERRY, 23 Mar 1949 Hudson, NH
CROMPTON, Harriet J and Dudley D HARDY, 21 Jun 1947 Hudson, NH
CROMPTON, Helen E and Bertele E FORD, 29 May 1919 Hudson, NH
CRONIN, Susan I and Bart G ROUSSEAU, 04 Sep 1971 Deerfield, NH
CROOKER, Walter T and Elizabeth CARDINAL, 13 Dec 1981 Nashua, NH
CROOKS, Brenda G and Robert F MUNROE, 11 Dec 1976 Nashua, NH
CROOKS, David B and Brenda G McCRADY, 20 Nov 1971 Hudson, NH
CROP, Addison L and Hattie J ARMSTRONG, 16 Oct 1876 Hudson, NH
CROP, Leni K and Tillie WELLS, 23 Feb 1875 Nashua, NH
CROSBIE, Denise and Francis K BROWN, 22 Apr 1980 Milford, NH
CROSBY, Louise C and Barton M McQUAID, 06 Jan 1934 Hudson, NH
CROSBY, Marsha L and Richard N McAFEE, 26 Sep 1970 Nashua, NH
CROSBY, Norman J and Muriel E WINSLOW, 20 Sep 1941 Nashua, NH
CROSBY, Richard F and Eldene M GAGNON, 21 Dec 1963 Nashua, NH
CROSBY, Sandra J and Robert L BEAULIEU, 03 Jun 1972 Hudson, NH
CROSBY, Susan L and Byron O Jr BRINER, 24 Aug 1968 Hudson, NH
CROSS, Annie F and Walter B CHASE, 19 Aug 1873 Hudson, NH
CROSS, Arden C and Mary E WILLOUGHBY, 13 Jun 1893 Nashua, NH
   Hiram Cross (Litchfield, NH) & Sarah E Savage (Greenfield, NH)
   Nathan Willoughby & Elizabeth Marshall
CROSS, David E and Lynn Marie DOZOIS, 22 Jun 1985 Hudson, NH

HUDSON, NH MARRIAGES

CROSS, Debra A and Gerald Oswald DEAN, 03 Mar 1984 Hudson, NH
CROSS, Dennis C and Thelma CARNEY, 22 Jan 1944 Hudson, NH
CROSS, Dwight and Jennie H ALLEN, 01 Apr 1923 Hudson, NH
CROSS, Edward L and Mary J MILLER, 05 Oct 1851
CROSS, Elizabeth and Moses A S PUTNAM, 17 Apr 1861
CROSS, Frances and Frederick HICKCOX, 28 Nov 1850
CROSS, Frances J and Frederick HICOX, 28 Nov 1850
CROSS, Hannah and Aaron P WOODWARD, 04 May 1847
CROSS, Herbert A and Nellie E SMITH, 28 Apr 1887 Hudson, NH
   Hiram Cross (Hudson, NH) & Sarah E Savage (Greenfield, NH)
   Daniel B Smith(Hudson, NH) & Hannah Smith (Hudson, NH)
CROSS, Hiram and Sarah E SAWYER, 12 Dec 1847
CROSS, Nancy and Foster TOWNES, 28 Dec 1826
CROSS, Ronald and Eleanor SALVATERRA, 31 May 1947 Hudson, NH
CROSS, Ruth V and Percy W INNESS, 28 Aug 1920 Nashua, NH
CROSS, S Chastina and Edgar P CHASE, 16 Nov 1854
CROSS, Samuel and Elizabeth CUMMINGS, 21 Mar 1782
CROSS, Samuel and Sarah LAWRENCE, 04 Mar 1779
CROSS, Sarah and Amos B CHASE, 11 Apr 1820
CROSS, Thomas and Sarah PEMBERTON, 10 Feb 1785
CROSS, William and BALDWIN, 03 Jan 1858
CROSS, William and M Jennie CURRIER, 30 Apr 1864
CROSS, William and Clara COLBURN, 20 May 1875 Hudson, NH
CROSS, William L and Bettie WADE, 31 Aug 1872 Hudson, NH
CROSSAYS, Arthur L and Phyllis A SUDSBURY, 15 Apr 1939 Hudson, NH
CROTEAU, Brian D and Mary J PHILLIPS, 10 Sep 1983 Nashua, NH
CROTEAU, Edward J Jr and Georgette LAPRISE, 16 Jun 1956 Hudson, NH
CROTEAU, Jean-Guy C and Diane G LAMOTHE, 15 Feb 1969 Nashua, NH
CROTEAU, Leopold J and Shirley M LAPOINTE, 15 Feb 1984 Hudson, NH
CROTEAU, Shirley A and Douglas H BROWN, 24 Jul 1965 Marlborough, NH
CROTTY, Phyllis M and Curtis W HOUSTON, 25 Sep 1944 Hudson, NH
CROUTEAU, Russell P and Diane T PAQUETTE, 11 Sep 1976 Hudson, NH
CROWELL, James M and M Jennie STEELE, 18 May 1882 Hudson, NH
   Henry C Crowell (Windham, NH) & Mary A Watts (Londonderry, NH)
   Chas Steele(Hudson, NH) & Martha A Boyd (Londonderry, NH)
CROWLEY, Charles T and Virginia A HEUSS, 30 Sep 1950 Hudson, NH
CROWLEY, Edmund J and Teresa A BURKE, 31 Mar 1978 Hudson, NH
CROWLEY, James E Jr and Wava M WHITING, 04 Nov 1978 Hudson, NH
CROWLEY, Julia A and Joseph E DONDREA, 21 Jun 1923 Nashua, NH
CRUTCHFIELD, Linda B and Jack L KIPNES, 14 Apr 1973 Manchester, NH
CRYMBLE, Hazel M and William J DOWNS, 09 Nov 1929 Nashua, NH
CUDMORE, Sheldon K and Linda M WITTHUN, 12 Jun 1968 Nashua, NH
CUDWORTH, Alden J and Emma PERRY, 28 Oct 1884 Manchester, NH
   John Cudworth (Peterboro, NH) & Sarah Spalding (Haverhill, NH)
   David E Perry(Bangor, NY) & Mary Bell
CUDWORTH, Betty M and Ronald P BOUCHER, 21 Nov 1953 Hollis, NH
CUMMINGS, Alfred and Martha C BARNS, 24 Feb 1833
CUMMINGS, Arthur L and Shirley B LAWRENCE, 24 Dec 1949 Nashua, NH
CUMMINGS, Belinda and William N BATCHELDER, Hudson, NH
CUMMINGS, Bertha E and Frederick NOKES, 12 Mar 1900 Cambridge, MA
   W P Cummings & Hattie D Lawrence
   William Nokes & Hannah Rouse
CUMMINGS, C E and Laura B BLODGETT, 30 Sep 1896 Haverhill, MA
   Hiram Cummings (Hudson, NH)
   A F Blodgett(Hudson, NH)
CUMMINGS, Chester E and Alice WROBLEWSKI, 24 Nov 1943 Hudson, NH
CUMMINGS, Clarissa and Henry Jr SMITH, 19 Feb 1847
CUMMINGS, David Jr and Phebe WYMAN, 24 Dec 1793
CUMMINGS, Donna S and Alexander CLARK, 20 Jul 1968 Nashua, NH
CUMMINGS, Eleazer and Mary VARNUM, 28 Jul 1734

HUDSON, NH MARRIAGES

CUMMINGS, Eleazer and Phebe RICHARDSON, 12 Jul 1764
CUMMINGS, Eleazer and Sarah HALE, 19 Apr 1786
CUMMINGS, Eleazer Jr and Hannah WHITNEY, 26 Nov 1761
CUMMINGS, Eleazer Jr and Hannah WHITNEY, 26 Nov 1763
CUMMINGS, Elizabeth and Samuel CROSS, 21 Mar 1782
CUMMINGS, Ellen E and James H SHAW, 02 May 1865
CUMMINGS, Enoch and Louisa C McALPINE,
CUMMINGS, Ephraim Jr and Betty Brad MERRILL, 08 Sep 1768
CUMMINGS, Ethel M and Clifford V CASSIDY, 26 Jun 1912 Hudson, NH
    Alden E Cummings & Nellie C Stevens
    John J Cassidy & Mary Mead
CUMMINGS, Frank A and Elizabeth MARSHALL, 28 Mar 1878 Hudson, NH
    Nathan Cummings (Hudson, NH)
    G W Marshall & Marinda Hadley (Hudson, NH)
CUMMINGS, Hannah and John WEBSTER, 22 Aug 1815
CUMMINGS, Hannah W and Jeremiah PHILIPS, 12 Feb 1841
    Thomas Cummings
CUMMINGS, James M and Nellie BURKE, 28 Mar 1876
CUMMINGS, John and Sophia LAWRENCE, 01 Aug 1831
CUMMINGS, John and Emeline M KEMP, 08 Aug 1844
CUMMINGS, Louisa and Charles WOOD, 23 Apr 1851
CUMMINGS, Lucy and Abram COLBY, 16 Aug 1855
CUMMINGS, Mary and Spencer RIPLEY, 31 Dec 1818
CUMMINGS, Mary Franc and Harlan P HORSLEY, 27 Jan 1861
CUMMINGS, Molley and Asa GOULD, 03 Jun 1801
CUMMINGS, Nathan and Elizabeth CONANT, 21 Feb 1850
CUMMINGS, Nira and William A BATCHELDER, 23 Jan 1844
CUMMINGS, Peter and Sarah RICHARDSON, 22 Nov 1763
CUMMINGS, Reuben and Rhoda HILLS,
CUMMINGS, Rowena M and Orlanda E TITUS, 05 Feb 1863
CUMMINGS, Sarah and Jeptha UNDERWOOD, 05 Aug 1805
CUMMINGS, Shirley B and Paul F MESSIER, 22 Jun 1957 Dracut, MA
CUMMINGS, Thankful and Joseph WILSON, 09 Apr 1805
CUMMINGS, Thomas and Hannah WEBSTER, Nov 1815
CUMMINGS, Willard and Nancy SMITH, 07 Dec 1815
CUMMINGS, Willis P and Hattie D LAWRENCE, 20 Mar 1873
CUMMINGS, Willis P and Frankie M DREW, 11 Nov 1885 Gilford, NH
    Hiram Cummings (Hudson, NH) & Abby Clark (Lyndeboro, NH)
    David Clement, Jr(Hudson, NH) & Hannah M Hall (Nashua, NH)
CUMMINS, Susan E and Vincent MCNEIL, 20 Oct 1979 Londonderry, NH
CUMMINS, Walter B and Marie E GREEN, 09 Jul 1983 Hudson, NH
CUNHA, Ronald V and Diane L LAROSE, 28 Jun 1969 Nashua, NH
CUNNINGHAM, Bertha and Kimball W MARTIN, 04 Sep 1901 Nashua, NH
    James Cunningham(St Johns, NB)&Elizabeth Patterson(St Johns, NB)
    Horace A Martin(Eastford, CT) & Lizzie J Webster (Hudson, NH)
CUNNINGHAM, Brian and Sylvia A PRATT, 28 Jul 1970 Nashua, NH
CUNNINGHAM, Elizabeth and Gary D REDISKE, 09 May 1982 Hudson, NH
CUNNINGHAM, Gladys and Chester J BRADLEY, 25 Nov 1945 Hudson, NH
CUNNINGHAM, Judith E and Walter A BROWN, 07 Apr 1962 Hudson, NH
CUNNINGHAM, Marion A and John D HENDRICKSON, 21 Jul 1962 Hudson, NH
CUNNINGHAM, William S and Barbara A SMITH, 29 Jul 1961 Hudson, NH
CURDY, Vinet I and Lucille CAIN, 28 Dec 1950 Hudson, NH
CURRAN, Barbara A and Kevin R BOULEY, 15 Sep 1973 Hudson, NH
CURRAN, Catherine and Gerald W LINDSEY, 04 Sep 1971 Nashua, NH
CURRAN, Donna M and Donald C HAERINCK, 06 May 1978 Hudson, NH
CURRAN, Edward J and Debra L LEVESQUE, 19 Dec 1974 Nashua, NH
CURRAN, John J and Ethel G HANSON, 01 Jul 1950 Hudson, NH
CURRAN, John J and Sandra L ROUSSEAU, 20 Mar 1976 Hudson, NH
CURRAN, Linda C and Raymond J TESSIER, 29 Jul 1972 Hudson, NH
CURRAN, Margaret M and Conrad H TESSIER, 12 Aug 1978 Hudson, NH

HUDSON, NH MARRIAGES

CURRAN, Mary M and Walter F PICKARD, 28 Jun 1934 Nashua, NH
CURRAN, Shelley M and Charles F LARKIN, 20 Oct 1979 Hudson, NH
CURRAN, Stephen W and Christina MORLEY, 20 Dec 1984 Hudson, NH
CURREN, Robert W and Joyce V McCARTHY, 15 Oct 1966 Hudson, NH
CURRIE, John H Jr and Caroline DAIOGIELLA, 20 Dec 1935 Nashua, NH
CURRIE, Margaret E and Walter A SUTHERLAND, 25 Oct 1935 Hudson, NH
CURRIE, Nancy M and William M PURCELL, 24 Jun 1983 Nashua, NH
CURRIER, Addie Lucr and John C WEBSTER, 19 Mar 1865
CURRIER, Bernice and Richard C JENNINGS, 18 Feb 1941 Nashua, NH
CURRIER, Gertrude A and Wayne S PETERS, 05 Jul 1917 Cambridge, MA
CURRIER, Juanita M and Edward S POLKEY, 27 Aug 1977 Nashua, NH
CURRIER, Lydia F and Harvey E BUXTON, 16 Sep 1868
CURRIER, M Jennie and William CROSS, 30 Apr 1864
CURRIER, Rosa E and George A SMITH, 24 Oct 1881 Hudson, NH
  D S Currier & Clarise T Russ
  Chas H Smith & Mary Wells
CURRIER, Virginia L and Kenneth A BOULANGER, 01 Apr 1966 Hudson, NH
CURTIS, Mary I and Edwin C ELDREDGE, 22 Dec 1948 Hudson, NH
CURTIS, Virginia and Alois W Jr KRAUSE, 13 Jun 1942 Hudson, NH
CURTIS, Virginia B and Lewis F CLARK, 19 Oct 1934 Hudson, NH
CUSHING, Shirley A and Alfred A MARTIN, 28 Jun 1952 Hudson, NH
CUSSON, Harry M and Doris V GAGNON, 14 Mar 1947 Hudson, NH
CUTHBERTSON, Debra A and Bruce B HANKS, 18 Jun 1983 Hudson, NH
CUTHBERTSON, Jessie A & Darron A STEPHENS, 10 Dec 1983 Atkinson, NH
CUTHBERTSON, Sue and Normand L GUILBERT, 10 Jun 1967 Nashua, NH
CUTLER, Adelbert C and Eleanor S LESLIE, 22 Jun 1929 Hudson, NH
CUTLER, Elizabeth and Hugh SMITH, 26 Jan 1853
CUTLER, Frederick and Clara August HARDY, 01 Jan 1868
CUTLER, Richard and Ruth MERRILL, 06 Apr 1789
CUTLER, Roxanna and Thomas SENTER, 15 Jul 1851
CUTLIFFE, Verna and Howard W SEACE, 22 Dec 1946 Hudson, NH
CUTTELL, Wilson F and Alice J KUGIMA, 26 Jun 1948 Hudson, NH
CUTTER, Abiah and Kimball WEBSTER, 29 Jan 1857
CUTTER, Fred L and Winifred E KIMBALL, 24 Jun 1960 Hudson, NH
CUTTER, Frederick and Susan Martha HARDY, 12 Oct 1872
CUTTER, Janice M and Bruce S LATVIS, 06 Dec 1969 Nashua, NH
CUTTER, Richard and Ruth MERRILL, 06 Apr 1789
CUTTER, Ruth and Aaron HAMBLET, 07 Jul 1796
CUTTER, Ruth and Aaron HAMBLETT, 07 Jul 1796
  Barrett Hadley
CUTTER, Sarah and Francis STEWART, 27 Jan 1820
CUTTING, Frank W and Helen E MORRELL, 12 Feb 1944 Hudson, NH
CUTULLE, Anthony J and Theodora C HOOPER, 16 Aug 1947 Hudson, NH
CYR, Diane T and Louis R Jr MILARDO, 17 Jul 1976 Nashua, NH
CYR, Donald W and Joanne L NESKEY, 26 Oct 1974 Hudson, NH
CYR, Nicole D and Peter M LIND, 10 Sep 1977 Salem, NH
CYR, Richard R and Lorrette M BELANGER, 22 Mar 1975 Nashua, NH
D'AGOSTINO, Gary P and Janice L JODICE, 12 Jun 1982 Nashua, NH
D'AMBROISE, Lynn A and Kenneth B NYE, 28 Sep 1980 Hudson, NH
D'AMBROISE, Robert D and Denise G POLIQUIN, 17 Oct 1982 Nashua, NH
D'AMOUR, Janice A and Gerard G NANTEL, 23 Jun 1956 Nashua, NH
D'AMOUR, Lorranie R & Joseph L ARCHAMBEAULT, 21 Jan 1950 Nashua, NH
D'ANJOU, Alphonse T and Pearl R QUIGLEY, 03 Jul 1971 Hudson, NH
DABBS, Kenneth I and Mildred M JONES, 27 Feb 1981 Nashua, NH
DABILIS, Teresa M and David E BOULEY, 08 Jul 1982 Nashua, NH
DAGGETT, Lucille L and Charles A NOWAK, 04 Jan 1975 Rochester, NH
DAHLEN, Priscilla and John CHASE, Sep 1782
DAHLEN, Sally and David COLBURN, 25 May 1782
DAIGLE, Nadine E and Norman R PELLETIER, 28 May 1966 Hudson, NH
DAIGLE, Rachel M and James J BOUTSELIS, 01 Sep 1949 Hudson, NH

HUDSON,NH MARRIAGES

DAIGLE, Robert L and Olive B MICHAUD, 27 Jun 1981 Hudson, NH
DAIGLE, Roy L and Phyllis C KIENIA, 19 Jan 1952 Pembroke, NH
DAIGLE, Sharrel L & Roland H PELLETIER, 08 Feb 1970 Manchester, NH
DAIGLE, Susan E and Kevin R RICHARDSON, 16 Dec 1978 Nashua, NH
DAIL, Mary S and Horace BURCH, 11 Nov 1852
DAILEY, Patricia A and John M ALLISON, 11 Nov 1972 Nashua, NH
DAILY, Frances M and Bernard L SLINEY, 08 Nov 1969 Nashua, NH
DAIOGIELLA, Caroline and John H Jr CURRIE, 20 Dec 1935 Nashua, NH
DAKIN, Justice and Abigail BURNS, 12 Jan 1803
DAKIN, Sally and Daniel COLBURN, 24 May 1782
DALE, Barbara E and David Bens NEWELL, 04 Aug 1981 Hudson, NH
DALESSIO, Deborah R and Richard G GAGNON, 24 Nov 1973 Hudson, NH
DALESSIO, Jacqueline and Dennis R BROMLEY, 28 Jul 1979 Hudson, NH
DALESSIO, John J and Geraldine TIKKANEN, 21 Oct 1983 Hudson, NH
DALEY, Peter J and Phyllis SHOKAL, 11 May 1946 Nashua, NH
DALTON, Beverly A and Roland T GAGNON, 29 Sep 1956 Hudson, NH
DALTON, Edward F and Eunice R STOUGHTON, 28 Sep 1957 Hudson, NH
DALY, Daniel T and Sandra L MacINTOSH, 27 Aug 1983 Hudson, NH
DALY, Thomas A Jr and Karen F BRITH, 23 Mar 1972 Hudson, NH
DALY, William R and Eleanor M SUTTON, 23 Dec 1950 Hudson, NH
DAME, Robert D and Irene M BARBOUR, 27 Nov 1952 Nashua, NH
DAMERY, Leda-Marie and Ernest G Jr NICHOLS, 29 Jun 1953 Hudson, NH
DAMON, Clara F and Charles HALL, 30 Sep 1868
DAMON, Milton and Clara Fran FLAGG, 05 Feb 1862
DANAHY, Paul A and Emily A LABAIRE, 24 Oct 1975 Hudson, NH
DANDA, Angeline and Ralph A SIANO, 06 Sep 1936 Hudson, NH
DANDELEY, Francenia and S A FLANDERS, 23 Jul 1877 Hudson, NH
  W H Dandeley
  Daniel Flanders
DANDLEY, Herbert W and Josephine M O'NEIL, 20 Dec 1921 Nashua, NH
DANDLEY, Isaiah and Lucy T SMITH, 22 Sep 1844
DANE, Clarence B and Bernice F LINTOTT, 21 May 1924 Nashua, NH
DANE, Eleanor C and Franklyn H McALISTER, 26 Jun 1977 Nashua, NH
DANE, Marion and Hector R COOKE, 24 Aug 1930 Milford, NH
DANE, Mitchell and Nancy C CARON, 03 Jun 1967 Nashua, NH
DANE, Phyllis N and Robert A READ, 03 Jul 1948 Nashua, NH
DANE, Richard C and Madeleine CAMPBELL, 06 Oct 1920 Nashua, NH
DANE, Sarah J and Willis ALEXANDER, 02 Jun 1873 Hudson, NH
DANE, Stephen W and Jean W DUMAIS, 09 Oct 1965 Merrimack, NH
DANEAULT, Andre J and Pauline L SIMARD, 16 Nov 1963 Manchester, NH
DANEAULT, Esther B and Joseph R L BOUCHER, 04 Jul 1942 Nashua, NH
DANEAULT, Jeanette R and Normand J LAJOIE, 29 Jun 1946 Nashua, NH
DANIELEVITCH, Eva M and Leonard J CARTER, 23 Apr 1945 Nashua, NH
DANIELL, Eugene S III and Kathryn J HOLT, 10 Aug 1968 Hudson, NH
DANIELS, Arthur C and Florence T BOULANGER, 11 Oct 1947 Dover, NH
DANIELS, Charles A and Anna M SHELDON, 15 Sep 1897 Hudson, NH
  John Daniels & Sarah Harris
  David P Sheldon & Mary A Knight
DANIELS, Helen P and Michael A OUELLETTE, 06 Jun 1973 Windham, NH
DANIELS, Howard R and Andrea L SAVAGE, 23 Mar 1946 Nashua, NH
DANIELS, James E and Carol A PETERS, 20 Oct 1979 Nashua, NH
DANIELS, Joan T and Thomas P BOULEY, 24 May 1969 Hudson, NH
DANIELS, Joseph J and Eva C MOFFA, 02 Sep 1950 Hudson, NH
DANIELS, Mary L and Alton E GAY, 18 Jun 1906 Hudson, NH
  Ezra Daniels & Nettie Tatro
  Elbridge Gay & Lydia M Abbott
DANIELS, Raymond D and Catherine LEMAY, 05 Apr 1975 Hudson, NH
DANIELS, Rosella A and Charles H Jr HOOD, 17 Jul 1942 Nashua, NH
DANIELS, Susan M and Jess P FORRENCE, 05 Jun 1976 Nashua, NH
DANNER, Irene and Joseph LAMEY, 03 Apr 1948 Hudson, NH

HUDSON,NH MARRIAGES

DANNEWITZ, Mickey L and Linda R NUTTING, 25 Nov 1967 Hudson, NH
DANSEVICH, Marion and Gordon L SMITH, 29 Aug 1936 Nashua, NH
DANZIG, Diana P and Louis P DUPONT, 01 Mar 1979 Nashua, NH
DAREY, William and Catherine BRENNAN, 27 May 1919 Hudson, NH
DARLING, Charles E and Anita DUBE, 29 Nov 1941 Nashua, NH
DATU, Velda V and Arthur Jr VAYENS, 12 Jun 1983 Hudson, NH
DAUDELIN, Frances A and Joseph M DOWNES, 06 Jul 1938 Hudson, NH
DAUDELIN, John R Jr and Kim P WELCH, 10 May 1970 Hudson, NH
DAUPHINAIS, Harvey E and Mary L DRUKE, 22 Dec 1972 Hudson, NH
DAUPHINEE, Bernard F and Evelyn T SAVAGE, 18 May 1949 Hudson, NH
DAVENPORT, Persis R D and Thomas MARSH, 26 Dec 1858
DAVEY, Mary Ann and Joel Stanley HUGHES, 24 May 1981 Hudson, NH
DAVIDSON, Charles D and Leslie E BENNER, 05 Aug 1966 Hudson, NH
DAVIDSON, Charles D and Elaine L VIENS, 02 May 1981 Hudson, NH
DAVIDSON, Dorothy M & Michael J McNICHOLAS, 19 Feb 1949 Hudson, NH
DAVIDSON, Erin C and Wayne F GALUSHA, 29 Aug 1981 Hudson, NH
DAVIDSON, Hannah J and Ambrose RICHARDSON, 21 Oct 1869 Hudson, NH
DAVIDSON, Harold A and Grace E FRYE, 07 Jul 1940 Hudson, NH
DAVIDSON, Ruth May and Arthur E YOUNG, 23 Sep 1936 Hudson, NH
DAVIDSON, Smith P and Lucinda P CAMPBELL, 13 Sep 1870 Hudson, NH
DAVIDSON, Sonja E and Henry C Jr WILSON, 03 Sep 1960 Nashua, NH
DAVIDSON, William N and Eileen M MARCHAND, 28 Nov 1981 Hudson, NH
DAVIES, George V and Patricia M HOY, 16 Sep 1949 Hudson, NH
DAVIES, Muriel H and William E MACNEIL, 22 Sep 1938 Nashua, NH
DAVIS, Alfred J and Barbara M ROWELL, 22 Oct 1955 Hudson, NH
DAVIS, Alfred S and Mary L STEELE, 15 Jun 1866
DAVIS, Amos Jr and Hannah SMITH, 24 Nov 1825
DAVIS, Austin E and Barbara P ELLIS, 28 Sep 1951 Windham, NH
DAVIS, Benjamin A and Louisa CATON, 09 Aug 1880 Hudson, NH
   Benjamin A Davis & Sarah W Gilson
   William Caton(England) & Mary Nagle (England)
DAVIS, Bernice V and Valmore J JEANNOTTE, 27 May 1933 Nashua, NH
DAVIS, Beverly J and Kelly D OSMER, 10 Jun 1978 Hudson, NH
DAVIS, Carolyn G and Curtis H COHN, 30 Mar 1981 Nashua, NH
DAVIS, Clayton and Marie A ROBBINS, 28 May 1965 Nashua, NH
DAVIS, Clifford M and Marion E RICH, 31 Dec 1955 Hudson, NH
DAVIS, Darlene E and Scott D SMITH, 29 Jun 1978 Nashua, NH
DAVIS, Dudley and Mary WOOD, 11 Aug 1785
DAVIS, Edgar A and Sarah L HARRIS, 19 Nov 1867
DAVIS, Edwin C and Margaret W MONROE, 29 May 1934 Hudson, NH
DAVIS, Elizabeth and Dustin CALDWELL, 12 Apr 1849
DAVIS, Elizabeth and James SEAVEY, 03 Jun 1784
DAVIS, Emma A and Samuel P SMITH, 05 Dec 1855
DAVIS, Francis J and Albina L LAFLEUR, 27 Sep 1947 Hudson, NH
DAVIS, Fred E and Thelma L DAVIS, 13 Dec 1971 Bennington, NH
DAVIS, George H and Abbie E BATCHELDER, 25 Nov 1868
DAVIS, George W and Lucy P FULLER, 13 Apr 1904 Nashua, NH
   George H Davis & A E Batchelder
   Nehemiah Fuller & Maria Fuller
DAVIS, George W and Abby E BATCHELDOR, 26 Nov 1868 Hudson, NH
DAVIS, Hadley and Mary WOOD, 11 Aug 1785
DAVIS, Hannah and Joseph BLODGETT, 05 May 1785
DAVIS, Hannah and John MOSS, 15 Feb 1810
DAVIS, Henry A and May E SAUNDER, 16 Jan 1943 Nashua, NH
DAVIS, Henry C and Gracie M HEATH, 26 Nov 1901 Hudson, NH
   George H Davis (Hudson, NH) & Abby Batchelder (Hudson, NH)
   T P Heath(Sheffield, VT) & F B Philbrick (Charlestown, VT)
DAVIS, Henry L and Angie R BATCHELDER, 01 Oct 1872
DAVIS, Ida G and Richard C DICKEY, 20 Jul 1872 Hudson, NH
DAVIS, Jane E and George F CARLETON, 16 May 1976 Nashua, NH

HUDSON,NH MARRIAGES

DAVIS, John H and May TAYLOR, 11 Aug 1915 Nashua, NH
   George W Davis (England) & Mary A Wilson (England)
   Sidney T Oldall(England) & Elizabeth Brown (Nova Scotia)
DAVIS, Joseph and Mialma BLISS, 15 Dec 1842
DAVIS, Lydia and Isaac COLBURN, 04 Aug 1785
DAVIS, Maureen W and Richard F USSERY, 18 Mar 1970 Nashua, NH
DAVIS, Mildred and Percy GOWING, 11 Nov 1919 Nashua, NH
DAVIS, Robert E and Deborah Lee BURGESS, 26 May 1979 Salem, NH
DAVIS, Sandra J and James R LAWLOR, 29 Aug 1964 Lisbon, NH
DAVIS, Sarah A and Daniel N ADAMS, 19 Aug 1857
DAVIS, Solomon A and Dorothy POLLARD, 22 Dec 1852
DAVIS, Susan and Austin BLODGETT, 03 Jan 1847
DAVIS, Susan R and Orrin P WEBSTER, 10 Apr 1865
DAVIS, Thelma L and Fred E DAVIS, 13 Dec 1971 Bennington, NH
DAVIS, Vinton Ear and Frances G ROGERS, 26 Sep 1938 Hudson, NH
DAVISON, Marion L and Malcolm E GRAHAM, 15 Sep 1962 Nashua, NH
DAW, Harry M and Maureen A SULLIVAN, 24 Sep 1960 Hudson, NH
DAWALGA, Christine and Michael A ROY, 26 Jan 1973 Hudson, NH
DAWALGA, Henry C and Dorothy M LUSSIER, 04 Jul 1958 Hudson, NH
DAWSON, Francis C III and Evan SYMONDS, 07 Sep 1971 Hudson, NH
DAWSON, Hattie M and James C THORNING, 24 Aug 1885 Nashua, NH
   Frederick Dawson (England) & Maria Cook (England)
   Frederick Thorning(Mass) & Hannah Currier (Wilmington, MA)
DAY, Dorothy M and Ernest W LITTLEHALE, 01 Jul 1950 Hudson, NH
DAY, Lafayette and Cynthia U HOWE, 26 Oct 1854
DE'COSTE, Linda G and Arthur D GENDRON, 30 Jul 1982 Nashua, NH
DEAN, Celena W and Herbert G BRADLEE, 28 Jul 1939 Hudson, NH
DEAN, Charles W and Lucille E LAFLAMME, 20 Nov 1954 Hudson, NH
DEAN, Dorothy and Charles MARQUIS, 27 May 1935 Nashua, NH
DEAN, Gerald Oswald and Debra A CROSS, 03 Mar 1984 Hudson, NH
DEAN, Marie E and Harold L BROWN, 23 Aug 1965 Hudson, NH
DEAN, Robert C and Jean N BLAIS, 26 May 1962 Hudson, NH
DEAN, Solomon and Polly PARKER, 25 Feb 1796
DEARBORN, Anne C and Jamie O BOILARD, 05 Jun 1977 Hudson, NH
DEARBORN, Candace A and Normand J PARADISE, 02 May 1970 Hudson, NH
DEARBORN, Charles G and Geraldine McLAVEY, 01 Aug 1953 Hudson, NH
DEARBORN, Gerald A and Clarice R BOUCHER, 01 Jun 1957 Hudson, NH
DEARBORN, Grant W and Joan M KALIL, 23 Jun 1951 Hudson, NH
DEARBORN, Herbert L and Elsie G BERUBE, 11 Jul 1974 Nashua, NH
DEARBORN, Tracey J and Thomas D HARTT, 19 Oct 1974 Hudson, NH
DEARBORN, Wayne R and Antoinette DUBE, 18 Jun 1966 Nashua, NH
DEARING, Marcia A and Henry O SMITH, 04 Sep 1889 Waterboro, ME
   Isaac N Dearing (Waterboro, ME) & Almira Guptill (Limerick, ME)
   David O Smith(Hudson, NH) & Mary H Greeley (Hudson, NH)
DEARVILLE, Alice M and Raymond W A HIMMER, 21 Sep 1927 Hudson, NH
DEARVILLE, Edith and Richard HOH, 17 May 1927 Hudson, NH
DEAU, Alice M and Harvey A Jr SCRANTON, 24 Aug 1946 Hudson, NH
DEBRAVA, Joseph C and Myrtle D BARKER, 17 Jan 1981 Nashua, NH
DECAMP, Ernest B and Dorothy KENISTON, 11 Nov 1941 Penacook, NH
DECAROLIS, Joanne M and Randall L KLEINER, 08 Jun 1974 Pelham, NH
DECICCO, Angelo and Sandra S STENGER, 09 Oct 1977 Amherst, NH
DECOLA, Debra J and Daniel A BEAUDRY, 29 May 1981 Hudson, NH
DECOLEAU, Elias E and Cora J LAQUERRE, 29 Jun 1946 Nashua, NH
DECOSTA, Blanche E and John G VARGAN, 22 Feb 1938 Hudson, NH
DECOSTA, Manuel and Ruth HUBBARD, 21 Feb 1948 Hudson, NH
DECOSTE, Mary and Edgar LEBLANC, 19 Apr 1934 Hudson, NH
DECOTEAU, Armand A and Lilyan M DIONNE, 07 Oct 1946 Nashua, NH
DECOTEAU, Armand A Jr and Evelyn R TROMBLEY, 30 May 1964 Nashua, NH
DECOTEAU, Henry J Jr and Eileen M MITCHELL, 18 Sep 1971 Nashua, NH
DECOTY, Ralph and Edith W MOORE, 14 Jun 1920 Hudson, NH

HUDSON, NH MARRIAGES

DEE, Carole L and Robert P MURPHY, 03 Oct 1980 Hudson, NH
DEEGAN, Mary A and Leo PIRANI, 20 Sep 1947 Hudson, NH
DEERING, Marcia A and Henry O SMITH, 04 Sep 1899
DEERY, Roland J Jr and Sandra J NADEAU, 26 Apr 1969 Nashua, NH
DEEVAR, Isobel and Edward G SNOW, 21 Dec 1947 Hudson, NH
DEFELICE, Joseph T and Joanne D GOFFREDO, 07 Oct 1950 Hudson, NH
DEFOREST, Julia and Arthur L HAYWARD, 31 Dec 1903 Hudson, NH
   Wm Deforest
   Leon Hayward & Lenore White
DEFRONZO, Nicholas and Mabel E PRATT, 01 Sep 1946 Nashua, NH
DEGULIS, Joseph M and Janice L TURNER, 18 Dec 1971 Nashua, NH
DELANEY, Catherine and Gary L MEADOR, 17 Sep 1983 Nashua, NH
DELANEY, Delma B and Caroline M CLEVELAND, 21 Aug 1947 Hudson, NH
DELANEY, Marilyn A and Allan G BLIZZARD, 21 Oct 1949 Hudson, NH
DELEANHO, Jessie L and Samuel PINTO, 01 Sep 1937 Nashua, NH
DELESCLUSE, Madeline I and Patrick B NAGLE, 20 Oct 1972 Hudson, NH
DELINSKY, Marion and Jonas ABRAMVITZ, 11 Sep 1938 Hudson, NH
DELISLE, Rachel R and Kenneth L TAYNOR, 10 Jul 1975 Nashua, NH
DELLECHIAIE, George and Kathleen S BERNARD, 12 Mar 1977 Hudson, NH
DELOGE, Philip A and Evelyn A LEWIS, 22 Jun 1985 Nashua, NH
DELONG, Craig O and Anita L SCOTT, 06 Aug 1977 Hudson, NH
DELONG, Robert C and Joyce A SYLVESTER, 04 Mar 1933 Hudson, NH
DELTUFO, Rita M and Emil S KAZAKA, 24 Dec 1949 Hudson, NH
DELUCA, Dennis M and Cheryl R BOWMAN, 31 May 1974 Nashua, NH
DELUCA, Vincent and Ida E SMITH, 14 Jan 1950 Hudson, NH
DELUDE, Gail B and James A KENTRA, 06 Jun 1981 Nashua, NH
DELUDE, Joyce A and Stanley E WAISWILOS, 27 Nov 1965 Hudson, NH
DELUDE, Mona P and Regnet R CARON, 31 Jan 1959 Nashua, NH
DELYANI, Angela and Paul A WHITE, 14 Jun 1980 Nashua, NH
DELYANI, Elizabeth and Steven J COTE, 29 Oct 1983 Nashua, NH
DEMAKIS, Veronica E and Glenn E BOULEY, 05 Jan 1972 Hudson, NH
DEMANCHE, Dorothy E and Bernard P HIRTH, 30 Jan 1960 Hudson, NH
DEMANCHE, Edward J and Lucille ROWELL, 15 Aug 1959 Hudson, NH
DEMANCHE, Ella M and Robert L BILODEAU, 18 May 1957 Hudson, NH
DEMANCHE, Harry and Doreen M BAXTER, 03 Dec 1942 Hudson, NH
DEMANCHE, Hector J and Gemma M LAGASSE, 10 Jan 1966 Nashua, NH
DEMANCHE, Jennie G and Leo J DIONNE, 03 Jan 1953 Hudson, NH
DEMANCHE, Judith A and Yvan VEILLEUX, 12 Jun 1967 Hudson, NH
DEMANCHE, Lillian V and Richard H FROST, 17 Aug 1980 Hudson, NH
DEMANCHE, Rita and Roger L ST LAURENT, 26 Sep 1953 Nashua, NH
DEMANCHE, Roland H and Melissa BILLS, 15 May 1965 Nashua, NH
DEMARAIS, Theresa M and Lionel W NADEAU, 16 May 1968 Hudson, NH
DEMARCO, Joseph P Jr and Lila R JENSEN, 16 Oct 1948 Hudson, NH
DEMARIA, Ethel P and Joseph C SCHIAVI, 09 Oct 1955 Hudson, NH
DEMASRAIS, Clara and Alfred H BEAUCHENE, 24 Jun 1913 Nashua, NH
   Joseph Demasrais & Mary Puague
   Joseph Beauchene & Artencen Bolduc
DEMERITT, Chester C and Regina I M CONSTANT, 24 Nov 1962 Nashua, NH
DEMERS, Emerise E and Margaret L BESCO, 16 Jun 1956 Hudson, NH
DEMERS, Joyce E and David R TORREY, 16 Jul 1960 Hudson, NH
DEMERS, Luc A and Valerie J LAROUCHE, 22 Aug 1981 Hudson, NH
DEMERS, Paul D and Denise L MARTINEZ, 14 May 1982 Hudson, NH
DEMERS, Roland J and Sophie JOHNSON, 09 Oct 1982 Hudson, NH
DEMMING, Ella L and Moses B FORD, 12 Sep 1877 Cornish, NH
   D P Demming (West Fairlee)
   Timothy S Ford(Hudson, NH) & Sarah Fuller (Hudson, NH)
DEMONE, Fenwick W and Melency E HIGGINS, 20 Mar 1943 Hudson, NH
DEMONT, Frank M and Leah COOKSON, 02 Sep 1938 Hudson, NH
DeMONTIGNY, Nancy A and Kenneth N BLEAU, 09 Sep 1961 Hudson, NH
DEMOSS, Charles V and Dianne M ANNALORO, 02 Jul 1966 Nashua, NH

HUDSON,NH MARRIAGES

DEMOURA, Robert A and Deborah A EATON, 19 Jun 1982 Pelham, NH
DEMPSEY, James J and Helen V McNEIL, 11 Jun 1949 Hudson, NH
DEMRLY, Charles E and Flora G JONES, 31 Mar 1877 Nashua, NH
DENEAULT, Shirley G and Louis P GUERTIN, 01 Jul 1983 Hudson, NH
DENESKA, Louise P and John F WEBER, 25 Sep 1948 Hudson, NH
DENICOLA, Adelaide M and Bentham A WALLACE, 27 Feb 1976 Hudson, NH
DENIS, Natalie L and Ralph R LECLAIRE, 13 Nov 1954 Nashua, NH
DENIS, Rachel T and Norman G LANDRY, 24 Apr 1948 Nashua, NH
DENIS, Robert L and Lucille A ANCTIL, 04 Jul 1942 Nashua, NH
DENNE, Maurice and Dorothy ROLFE, 28 Nov 1940 Lowell, MA
DENNETT, Edith S and Edward J BAKER, 30 Dec 1945 Hudson, NH
DENNIS, Wilna G and Blanche T GUILBEAULT, 02 Aug 1950 Hudson, NH
DENNO, George and Mary MANDIGO, 30 May 1908 Hudson, NH
   Simeon Denno & Olive Duchane
   Lewis Oben & Mary Latuee
DENSMORE, Cordelia and John G WRIGHT, 04 Apr 1869
DENTON, Ellen and Benjamin F SPRAGUE, 24 Nov 1860
DEPERRY, Kenneth S and Brenda L THIBODEAU, 04 May 1974 Hudson, NH
DEPONTBRIAND, Judith A and John E Jr MARTIN, 04 Oct 1975 Hudson, NH
DEQUOY, Bruce E and Carol A DICKEY, 24 Jul 1945 Nashua, NH
DEQUOY, Paul B and Marjorie ABBOTT, 10 Nov 1956 Hudson, NH
DERBY, George W and Marion L GURNEY, 26 Oct 1949 Nashua, NH
DERBY, Lynda M and Donald J LABONTE, 09 Apr 1983 Mont Vernon, NH
DERBY, Olive N and Frank C BANCROFT, 11 Nov 1865
DERBY, Polly and Moses GREELEY, 20 Mar 1794
DERNOGA, James W and Mary M PETRONI, 27 Jul 1984 Hudson, NH
DEROCHE, Norma M and John SINCLAIR, 16 Apr 1949 Hudson, NH
DEROSA, Clement and Barbara A CRACROFT, 21 Jul 1949 Hudson, NH
DEROSIER, Adeline J and Romeo A GENDRON, 27 Dec 1952 Nashua, NH
DEROSIER, Cyrus L and Elena C LIMOLI, 17 Jun 1950 Hudson, NH
DEROSIER, Dana M and Linda G LAFRANCE, 26 Nov 1982 Hudson, NH
DERY, David P and Karola E KLEE, 20 Aug 1960 Hudson, NH
DERY, Nancy A and Norman R BOUCHER, 18 Jun 1955 Hudson, NH
DERY, Paul A and Stella L CLARK, 26 Jul 1980 Nashua, NH
DESAUTELS, Armand and Raya CARON, 17 Feb 1930 Nashua, NH
DESAUTELS, Kevin E and Margaret G CAVENEY, 23 Jun 1979 Nashua, NH
DESAUTELS, Virginia G & Paul E ST FRANCOIS, 24 Jan 1962 Hudson, NH
DESBIENS, Corinne E and Paul T LAFRANCE, 17 Jul 1954 Nashua, NH
DESBOISBRIAND, Dorilda I & Robert J PAQUETTE, 04 Aug 1939 Hudson,NH
DESBOISBRIAND, Raymond and Cecile CHENARD, 02 Jul 1938 Nashua, NH
DESBOISBRIAND, Roger P and Betty A PIATEK, 13 Aug 1955 Hudson, NH
DESCHAMPS, Diane T and David F ALLISON, 28 Jun 1968 Nashua, NH
DESCHENAUX, R Lynn and David G BANKS, 24 Apr 1976 Hudson, NH
DESCHENES, Anne M and Jose L ESCALANTE, 21 May 1983 Hudson, NH
DESCHENES, Brenda Lee and John Paul JOSEF, 20 Jan 1973 Hudson, NH
DESCHENES, Daniel P & Catherine ZACCAGNINI, 30 Aug 1980 Hudson, NH
DESCHENES, Lois M and Andre R JETTE, 09 Jun 1972 Nashua, NH
DESCHENES, Lucien R and Christine GOUDREAU, 28 Apr 1984 Hudson, NH
DESCHENES, Marc R & Marilyn R L'HEUREUX, 17 Sep 1983 Manchester, NH
DESCHENES, Patricia A and John M CASSIDY, 03 Sep 1983 Nashua, NH
DESCHENES, Suzette M and Gordon D KENNEDY, 16 Apr 1966 Nashua, NH
DESCLOS, Claire L and Vergil L ADAMS, 09 May 1953 Hudson, NH
DESCLOS, Diane J and Marcel G LAVOIE, 21 Apr 1979 Hudson, NH
DESCLOS, Henry E and Joan E RODIER, 22 Jul 1970 Nashua, NH
DESCLOS, Susan C and Jon F MANN, 04 Aug 1984 Hudson, NH
DESCOTEAUX, Louise M and Bruce C LANDRY, 04 Nov 1967 Nashua, NH
DESCOUTEAUX, Michel R & Pauline J PELLETIER, 28 Jan 1967 Hudson, NH
DESFOSSES, Charles H and Cynthia D NEVILLE, 30 Aug 1974 Nashua, NH
DESFOSSES, Cynthia P & George H III PETERSEN, 20 Aug 1983 Hudson,NH
DESIATA, Mary and Lorenzo DIANA, 16 Mar 1946 Hudson, NH

HUDSON,NH MARRIAGES

DESILVIO, JoAnn and Peter J SKEFFINGTON, 08 Nov 1975 Nashua, NH
DESIMONE, Frank and Marguerite HALLSON, 19 Oct 1932 Hudson, NH
DESIMONE, Pasquale and M Jean PALMER, 18 Jul 1964 Hudson, NH
DESIMONE, Patricia C and Charles J BOCCHINO, 02 Jun 1962 Hudson, NH
DESJARDINS, Alice R and Dana S THOMPSON, 27 Aug 1937 Nashua, NH
DESJARDINS, Bruce E and Wendy L BLANCHETTE, 22 Apr 1978 Hudson, NH
DESJARDINS, Jean A and Rita D BOSLEY, 11 Nov 1944 Nashua, NH
DESJARDINS, Linda M and Thomas P Jr GAFFNEY, 11 Jun 1971 Nashua, NH
DESJARDINS, Louise E & Lawrence R SALLINGER, 15 Feb 1969 Nashua, NH
DESJARDINS, Neil F and Linda J WATTS, 25 Jul 1969 Hudson, NH
DESJARDINS, Paul C and Nicole LANDRY, 23 May 1981 Nashua, NH
DESJARDINS, Raymond A and Theresa M SIMARD, 01 Oct 1949 Nashua, NH
DESJARDINS, Roger A and Mary BISKADUROS, 20 Sep 1952 Nashua, NH
DESJARDINS, Roland A and Cecile B GAMACHE, 07 Jul 1956 Hudson, NH
DESLAURIER, Armand J Jr & Barbara A FULLER, 11 Apr 1959 Hudson, NH
DESLAURIERS, Donald G Jr & Nancy M LAVALLEE, 10 Aug 1973 Nashua, NH
DESLAURIERS, Judith A & Leonard M BOULANGER, 25 Sep 1971 Hudson, NH
DESMARAIS, Dennis R and Barbara A GAMUSO, 18 Dec 1977 N Salem, NH
DESMARAIS, Gerard A and Marilyn J KLAUS, 27 Dec 1980 Nashua, NH
DESMARAIS, Kenneth E & Ruth Ann HOLDEN, 12 Mar 1978 Manchester, NH
DESMARAIS, Mark R and Pamela Ann WINN, 14 Jun 1975 Hudson, NH
DESMARAIS, Patricia B and Chester E HURD, 01 Sep 1962 Nashua, NH
DESMARAIS, Ronald R and Deborah A BOUCHER, 22 Mar 1975 Hudson, NH
DESMARAIS, Suezann R and Paul W RICHARDSON, 28 Dec 1970 Hudson, NH
DESMOND, Edward J and Yvonne R CHAISSON, 28 Sep 1947 Hudson, NH
DESROCHERS, Sandra J and Robert E BERNIER, 20 Aug 1981 Nashua, NH
DESROCHES, Kerrie Ann and Peter M MAGNIN, 06 Oct 1979 Hudson, NH
DESROCHES, Tony J and Linda C ZIMMERMAN, 07 May 1977 Hudson, NH
DESROSIERS, Albert L and Simone G ST JEAN, 22 Jun 1946 Nashua, NH
DESROSIERS, Brenda J and Chester D KENNEDY, 07 Nov 1975 Hudson, NH
DESROSIERS, Gerald J Jr and Ann A KINNEEN, 26 Mar 1983 Hudson, NH
DESROSIERS, Juliette and Robert E FRENCH, 30 Aug 1974 Hollis, NH
DESROSIERS, Kathleen G and Leon R BECHARD, 04 Sep 1972 Hudson, NH
DESROSIERS, Maurice G and Debra Joy BREAULT, 23 Jun 1973 Hudson, NH
DESROSIERS, Monique M & Raymond P THEBODEAU, 24 May 1985 Nashua, NH
DESSERT, Roberta M and George J DRAPER, 22 Jul 1950 Hudson, NH
DESTEFANO, Richard E and Peggy D TATRO, 21 Aug 1982 Nashua, NH
DETORO, Hazel V and Harold D SMITH, 22 Feb 1948 Hudson, NH
DETORO, Judith A and Arlo T RAYNO, 07 Mar 1964 Hudson, NH
DEVENS, Diana L and Richard D SCHOFIELD, 08 Jun 1985 Temple, NH
DEVLIN, Margaret and Alfred DUVAL, 27 Feb 1922 Nashua, NH
DEWAELE, Timothy F and Elizabeth GRAHAM, 30 Apr 1982 Hudson, NH
DEWITT, Elaine M and Robert H RUSTON, 20 Apr 1974 Hudson, NH
DEWITT, Lorraine W and David S HARDY, 15 Apr 1977 Nashua, NH
DEWITT, Lorraine W and James L RABY, 27 Nov 1975 Hudson, NH
DEWOLFE, Florence and William CORBETT, 13 Sep 1950 Hudson, NH
DEWOLFE, Harriet and Albert J HILDRETH, 05 Nov 1854
DEWOLFE, William and Kittie SOMERS, 21 Jul 1917 Nashua, NH
DEXTER, Arnold C and Mary Ann FORTUNE, 22 Jun 1957 Hudson, NH
DEXTER, Charles and Frances A CRAIGLE, 05 Jan 1946 Hudson, NH
DEXTER, Deborah S and Paul F SNELL, 19 Nov 1971 Pelham, NH
DEXTER, Lydia J and Herbert L BATCHELDER, 26 Mar 1887 Haverhill, MA
    Byron H Dexter (Lisbon, NH) & Jeanette Stickney (Lisbon, NH)
    Mark Batchelder(Grantham, NH) & Lydia L Steele (Hudson, NH)
DEYETT, Karen M and Edward R Jr PENDLETON, 11 Jun 1983 Windham, NH
DeYOUNG, Simon Jr and Geraldine FISHER, 07 Jan 1945 Hudson, NH
DIAMANTINI, Thomas M and Celeste C BIBEAU, 03 Nov 1979 Hudson, NH
DIANA, Lorenzo and Mary DESIATA, 16 Mar 1946 Hudson, NH
DIAS, Barbara J and James M BRITO, 10 Mar 1985 Hudson, NH
DIAZ, William J and Sylvia A PRATT, 29 Oct 1966 Hudson, NH

HUDSON,NH MARRIAGES

DICCHARD, Lillian V & Charles D BROWN, 01 Feb 1917 Bellows Falls,VT
DICHARD, Paul F and Priscilla RABY, 26 Aug 1950 Hudson, NH
DICK, Myron and Ethel PARROTTE, 31 May 1947 Hudson, NH
DICKERMAN, Josephine and Anson OSGOOD, 10 Aug 1905 Hudson, NH
    Jonathan B Foss & Hannah Coombs
    Robert B Osgood & Susanne Senter
DICKEY, Carol A and Bruce E DEQUOY, 24 Jul 1945 Nashua, NH
DICKEY, Richard C and Ida G DAVIS, 20 Jul 1872 Hudson, NH
DICKEY, Steven C and Donna-Mari RONDEAU, 12 Jul 1975 Hudson, NH
DICKINSON, Harold L and Paula KALDIS, 14 Feb 1972 Nashua, NH
DIDONATO, Ellena and Fred F RICELLI, 03 Sep 1950 Hudson, NH
DIETTE, Bertha J and George GEORGOPOULOS, 03 Sep 1948 Hudson, NH
DIFONZO, Doris M and Conrad G LABRIE, 07 May 1977 Hudson, NH
DIGGINS, Daniel P and Carol I WILLIAMSON, 31 Jul 1971 Nashua, NH
DIGGINS, Gary D and Diana J MINOT, 28 Dec 1968 Nashua, NH
DIGGINS, Gary D and Joan Ann KENNEY, 17 Aug 1974 Merrimack, NH
DIGGINS, Gloria M and Marcel R LEMAY, 12 Aug 1950 Nashua, NH
DIGGINS, Lucille G and George H Jr CLARK, 04 Oct 1947 Nashua, NH
DIGGINS, Mary M and Peter M USOVICZ, 16 Feb 1968 Nashua, NH
DIGGINS, Patricia A and Kenneth J RODGERS, 22 Sep 1956 Nashua, NH
DILL, Richard H and Doris H BAENDALE, 28 Dec 1947 Hudson, NH
DILLAIRE, Paul R and Phyllis M WEBSTER, 15 Jan 1949 Hudson, NH
DILWORTH, Deborah An and John Lee HAYES, 15 Sep 1974 Litchfield, NH
DINGLE, Marion R and Robert A ANDREW, 07 Apr 1973 Hudson, NH
DION, David C and Sue SBAT, 06 Jan 1976 Derry, NH
DION, Denise E and Marcel LAMONTAGNE, 15 Jun 1979 Merrimack, NH
DION, Donald F and Lucille Y LEDOUX, 22 Jan 1966 Nashua, NH
DION, Jeanne J and Albert DUMOUCHEL, 30 Jul 1956 Hudson, NH
DION, Mary A and Clarence D McELROY, 20 Oct 1928 Nashua, NH
DION, Mary Ann and David C HOWE, 15 Apr 1972 Hudson, NH
DION, Paul F and Beverly J PORTER, 26 Nov 1966 Nashua, NH
DION, Paul T and Jean I BRYANT, 02 Jun 1948 Hudson, NH
DION, Raymond F and Vivian L LAVARNWAY, 07 May 1966 Nashua, NH
DION, Richard N and Judith C ROY, 11 Mar 1967 Hudson, NH
DION, Robert D and Irene R PORTER, 05 Jun 1971 Nashua, NH
DION, Roger J and Jeannette SURPRENANT, 21 Jan 1967 Pelham, NH
DION, Roland M and Irene E BRISEBOIS, 21 Jun 1968 Allenstown, NH
DION, Sylvio H and Georgette RAYMOND, 21 May 1949 Nashua, NH
DION, Wayne C and BarbaraAnn HOWARD, 23 Apr 1966 Hudson, NH
DIONNE, Claire F and Robert E KENNEY, 04 Sep 1964 Hudson, NH
DIONNE, Claire M and Ronald P ANTON, 20 Feb 1971 Nashua, NH
DIONNE, Daniel A and Erma E PETERS, 23 Nov 1962 Hudson, NH
DIONNE, Doris and Maurice H RODIER, 27 Apr 1957 Nashua, NH
DIONNE, Drinette A and Thomas R ACKERMAN, 07 Apr 1947 Nashua, NH
DIONNE, Elaine J and Ronald G SIMARD, 21 Mar 1964 Nashua, NH
DIONNE, Ida E and Bernard G LEDOUX, 27 Apr 1946 Nashua, NH
DIONNE, Jeannette and Richard A GOSSELIN, 08 Apr 1961 Nashua, NH
DIONNE, Kathleen M and Francis K REGAN, 10 Sep 1983 Hudson, NH
DIONNE, Kim M and Neil B LaFOREST, 23 Sep 1983 Nashua, NH
DIONNE, Leo J and Jennie G DEMANCHE, 03 Jan 1953 Hudson, NH
DIONNE, Leon A and Gloria M STEARNS, 30 Aug 1972 Manchester, NH
DIONNE, Lilyan M and Armand A DECOTEAU, 07 Oct 1946 Nashua, NH
DIONNE, Linda T and Jeffrey H BURKE, 19 May 1979 Pelham, NH
DIONNE, Michael W and JoAnn M BREAULT, 25 Aug 1978 Hudson, NH
DIONNE, Pierre L and Stasia B GRZESIK, 07 Aug 1982 Nashua, NH
DIONNE, Richard and Patricia CHAMPIGNY, 10 Sep 1962 Nashua, NH
DIONNE, Richard A and Louise G FARIOLE, 07 Sep 1980 Nashua, NH
DIONNE, Robert D and Vickie J BIERMAN, 12 Oct 1982 Hudson, NH
DIONNE, Robert M and Lisa A MacQUEEN, 06 Oct 1984 Hudson, NH
DIONNE, Ruth G and Francis G KINVILLE, 30 Jun 1945 Nashua, NH

HUDSON, NH MARRIAGES

DIONNE, Wayne L and Vikki L WULF, 18 Jun 1977 Hudson, NH
DIPIETRO, Elizabeth and Mark J HETZER, 29 Nov 1980 Hudson, NH
DIRUSSO, Raymond and Catherine LANE, 10 Apr 1937 Hudson, NH
DISTEFANO, Robert A and Mary J STACK, 05 Jul 1969 Salem, NH
DITSON, Elizabeth and Nathaniel INGALLS, Jun 1783
DITSON, Thankful and Silas GOULD, 29 Jun 1779
DITSON, Thankful and Silas GREELEY, 29 Jun 1779
DIVIDO, Christine and Vincent L INGALLS, 14 Dec 1984 Nashua, NH
DIXON, Ann E and Anthony M LANZA, 19 Dec 1981 Hudson, NH
DIXON, Richard R and Ann M FRASER, 11 Oct 1980 Hudson, NH
DMITRUK, Stephen G and Evelyn M HOWARD, 25 Oct 1973 Hudson, NH
DOBENS, Deborah J and Douglas D LANDRY, 03 Oct 1982 Hudson, NH
DOBENS, Vivian L and Jerry T GAMACHE, 27 Sep 1968 Nashua, NH
DOBROWOLSKI, Theodore J & Sylvia A MAHAR, 23 Sep 1961 Manchester,NH
DOBSON, Frances C and Harold L SIMMONS, 30 Nov 1933 Nashua, NH
DOBSON, Mary J and Bertram F CHASE, 10 Aug 1892 Hudson, NH
  Thomas Dobson (England) & Nancy Reiley (England)
  Edmund H Chase & Listine E Guptel
DOCKHAM, Edward P and Sylvia A THURLOW, 08 Jul 1972 Merrimack, NH
DODDS, Stephen G and Claudia M CHARBONNEAU, 10 Mar 1979 Amherst, NH
DODGE, Carl V and Beatrice MONETTE, 29 Apr 1936 Nashua, NH
DODGE, Cora M and Eben A WOODBURY, 24 Feb 1917 Nashua, NH
DODGE, John F and Katie F PEASE, 15 Dec 1864
DODGE, Marjorie E and Russell L STODDARD, 23 May 1951 Hudson, NH
DODSON, Ruth A and Albert P CAMPAS, 26 Jan 1946 Hudson, NH
DOERR, Michael E and Terri W REED, 22 Jun 1975 Nashua, NH
DOFF, Peter and Betsey BROWN, 18 Apr 1866
DOHERTY, Anna May and Roy L WHITTEMORE, 22 Feb 1940 Hudson, NH
DOHERTY, Betty L and Douglas E BROWN, 28 Apr 1957 Hudson, NH
DOHERTY, John E and Margaret K SMALL, 26 Apr 1947 Hollis, NH
DOHERTY, Lillian A and Dana W McCOY, 20 May 1972 Hudson, NH
DOHERTY, Linda M and Paul R BRIAND, 28 Jun 1969 Nashua, NH
DOHERTY, Steven M and Carol Ann EDWARDS, 10 Mar 1974 Hudson, NH
DOHERTY, William C and Clarabelle RICARD, 12 May 1934 Nashua, NH
DOIL, James and Sophia BLODGETT, 22 Feb 1819
DOIRON, Arthur J and Gale L CLARK, 02 Nov 1974 Hudson, NH
DOLAN, Arthur F and Gail E STONE, 22 Nov 1975 Litchfield, NH
DOLAN, Gail M and Stephen G RICHARDSON, 14 Jun 1980 Hudson, NH
DOLAN, Mary C and Ralph E RAPSON, 02 Sep 1949 Hudson, NH
DOLAND, Ruth E and Leo R LECLERC, 04 Jun 1955 Hudson, NH
DOLBEC, Steven E and Deborah A CASALE, 06 May 1983 Hudson, NH
DOLLOFF, Lawrence S and Jane E ZWICKER, 07 Apr 1945 Hudson, NH
DOLLOFF, Maria and Simon G WEBSTER, 18 Dec 1849
DOLLOFF, Peter Jr and Laura E POTTER, 30 Apr 1983 Hudson, NH
DOMENICI, Margaret J and Gordon B ERSKINE, 07 Apr 1973 Nashua, NH
DOMIJAN, Gregory J and Judith A JAKAITIS, 13 Jan 1968 Hudson, NH
DONAH, Edgar J Jr and Mary Clair DUVAL, 16 Feb 1974 Hudson, NH
DONAHUE, Barbara A and Thomas W ABBOTT, 04 Jul 1964 Hudson, NH
DONAHUE, James F and Helen B SARGENT, 15 Jul 1934 Hudson, NH
DONAHUE, John R and Lola V WASHBURN, 07 Jul 1950 Hudson, NH
DONALDSON, John W and Barbara A McDOUGALL, 10 Aug 1963 Hudson, NH
DONDREA, Joseph E and Julia A CROWLEY, 21 Jun 1923 Nashua, NH
DONNELLY, Carolyn A & Charles H Jr JOHNSON, 13 Sep 1958 Nashua, NH
DONNELLY, Cynthia M and William S LAMB, 26 Oct 1974 Nashua, NH
DONNELLY, Daneen G and Jerald E WHEELER, 29 Jan 1983 Hudson, NH
DONNELLY, E Emmett and Lillian M LAMBERT, 01 Nov 1921 Nashua, NH
DONNELLY, Edward B and Mary E BIRCHALL, 31 Mar 1913 Nashua, NH
  Eugene Donnelly & Joanna Buckley
  John W Birchall & Ellen Scanlon
DONNELLY, Frank Will Jr and Susan A LACOUNT, 28 Oct 1978 Hudson, NH

HUDSON,NH MARRIAGES

DONNELLY, Josephine and Edward E GOWING, 06 Oct 1908 Nashua, NH
    Eugene Donelly
    Sidney P Gowing & Clemintine Fuller
DONNELLY, Steven J and Barbara An MERCIER, 10 Oct 1981 Hudson, NH
DONOHUE, John O and Mary A CLANCY, 07 Feb 1880 West Newbury, MA
    Timothy Donohue (Ireland) & Ellen Sweeney (Ireland)
    J B Clancy(Ireland) & Mary Leander (Ireland)
DONOVAN, Christophe and Suzanne M BUTEAU, 16 Aug 1981 Nashua, NH
DONOVAN, Eileen T and Jay P GAGNON, 31 Jul 1982 Hudson, NH
DONOVAN, John M and Betty L EMERY, 31 Dec 1941 Hudson, NH
DONOVAN, Kimberly A and John J Jr PATRONICK, 05 Jun 1982 Hudson, NH
DONOVAN, Shirley A and Elwin R MARSH, 30 Mar 1970 Hudson, NH
DOOLEY, Alice V and Leonard R GRAVELLE, 09 Oct 1948 Nashua, NH
DOOLEY, Arthur M and Ruth M OTIS, 09 Mar 1935 Hudson, NH
DOOLEY, Betty A and Donald B BRIAND, 31 Jan 1969 Hudson, NH
DOONAN, Joyce M and Henry J BIELSKI, 11 Jan 1965 Hudson, NH
DORAN, Diane L and Raymond O BRIAND, 16 Oct 1965 Nashua, NH
DORAN, Marilyn H and Patrick J HOGAN, 15 Jan 1949 Hudson, NH
DOREY, Maude A F and Carl E ROBBINS, 16 Jun 1923 Tyngsboro, MA
DORHERTY, Violet and Robert A ANDREW, 29 Jan 1921 Nashua, NH
DORR, George G and Annie L JAQUITH, 31 Dec 1914 Nashua, NH
    Sylvester H Dorr & Celia H Austin
    George D Jaquith & Sarah J Fox
DORRIS, Virginia M and Elliott C WILLIAMS, 20 May 1950 Hudson, NH
DORRISON, Mary E and Newton C MARTIN, 17 Sep 1873 Fitchburg, MA
DORT, Rebecca and Alfred GREELEY, 15 Jan 1850
DORTY, Anne and Charles RICE, 25 Jun 1879 Hudson, NH
    James Dorty (Ireland) & Ellen (Ireland)
    Michael Rice(Ireland) & Martha (England)
DORVAL, Grace A and Ronald LEDGISTER, 18 Sep 1981 Brentwood, NH
DOSS, Willburr C Jr and Clara G LAMBERT, 16 Nov 1970 Hudson, NH
DOTY, Mary and Ezekiel RICHARDSON, 19 Sep 1805
DOTY, Nancy and Charles MILES, 01 Feb 1887 Hudson, NH
    Samuel Shrier (Germany) & Eliza Cota (Canada)
    William Miles(Maine) & Hannah Scates (Berwick, ME)
DOUCET, Germain and Gabriel LaCHANCE, 29 Aug 1936 Nashua, NH
DOUCET, Jeanne I and Norman J SERVANT, 18 Oct 1958 Hudson, NH
DOUCET, Lorraine J and Smith S GUAY, 09 Aug 1960 Nashua, NH
DOUCET, Norman C and Sheila M HYAM, 04 Aug 1984 Hudson, NH
DOUCET, Theresa G and Kenneth L MUNSON, 04 Feb 1961 Hudson, NH
DOUCETTE, Debra P and Alex J TAYLOR, 01 May 1971 Nashua, NH
DOUCETTE, Ernest T and Carol A TWARDOSKY, 27 Jun 1964 Merrimack, NH
DOUCETTE, Maurice J and Sandra L LATOUR, 15 Sep 1973 Nashua, NH
DOUCETTE, Patricia A and Roland G HAMEL, 14 May 1977 Hudson, NH
DOUCETTE, Raymond L and Patricia A FORRENCE, 04 Aug 1970 Nashua, NH
DOUCETTE, Thomas R and Barbara J LAVALETTE, 31 Dec 1967 Hudson, NH
DOUGHTY, Donald S and Louise H HAMMOND, 09 Oct 1943 Nashua, NH
DOUGLAS, Patricia A and Philip J ROWMAN, 05 Dec 1959 Hudson, NH
DOUGLASS, David and Horsly Evans, 1741
DOUGLASS, Robert and Rachel MERRILL, 22 Nov 1810
DOURIS, Nicholas and Sally A RUDOLPH, 02 Feb 1964 Hudson, NH
DOUVILLE, Gary J and Linda M SIROIS, 08 Nov 1969 Hudson, NH
DOUVILLE, Raymond H and Theresa L BATTEY, 20 Oct 1979 Hudson, NH
DOUVILLE, Roger J and Kathleen S O'DONNELL, 07 Sep 1979 Nashua, NH
DOUZANIS, Arthur J and Margaret E LEMERISE, 01 Feb 1964 Hudson, NH
DOVE, Francis T and Patricia M SAVOY, 01 Jul 1950 Hudson, NH
DOW, Andrea E and Dennis P GREENWOOD, 19 Jul 1981 Pelham, NH
DOW, Earlene A and Norman E STONE, 30 Jul 1955 Nashua, NH
DOW, Elbridge and Anna D ROBINSON, 24 Jun 1830
DOW, Harold E and Therese N VALCOURT, 03 Sep 1945 Nashua, NH

HUDSON,NH MARRIAGES

DOW, Leonard A and Janet C HEROUX, 05 Jul 1975 Hudson, NH
DOW, Lori A and Brian W VADNEY, 21 Jun 1980 Nashua, NH
DOW, Marie F and David R BOLAND, 22 Apr 1967 Hudson, NH
DOW, Marlene E and Normand L LANDRY, 26 Apr 1952 Nashua, NH
DOW, Sandra Lee and Dennis And LEONARD, 18 Jan 1975 Nashua, NH
DOW, Victor L and Barbara L PERKINS, 26 Sep 1962 Hudson, NH
DOWD, Barbara L and Richard SHAUGHNESSY, 26 Jan 1976 Hudson, NH
DOWELL, Grace D and Nishan P MAIKASIAN, 16 Feb 1935 Manchester, NH
DOWLING, Kelly A and Dennis C ARPIN, 29 May 1976 Hudson, NH
DOWLING, Kelly A and Theodore E COTE, 20 Feb 1982 Nashua, NH
DOWLING, Sharon M and Frederick OTTE, 14 May 1983 Nashua, NH
DOWNES, Joseph M and Frances A DAUDELIN, 06 Jul 1938 Hudson, NH
DOWNING, Estelle M and Ralph W HARWOOD, 10 Sep 1912 Hudson, NH
  William Downing & Roehil Main
  Walter J Harwood & Thea Hanson
DOWNING, Stephen D & Constance MORIARTY, 02 Sep 1968 Merrimack, NH
DOWNS, William J and Hazel M CRYMBLE, 09 Nov 1929 Nashua, NH
DOYLE, Arthur H and Anabel J FALLON, 03 Jan 1937 Hudson, NH
DOYLE, Evelyn S and Wilbur F HAGER, 19 Dec 1948 Hudson, NH
DOYLE, Helen and James H CONNER, 19 Jun 1938 Hudson, NH
DOYLE, Helen E and John T MURPHY, 06 Jul 1973 Nashua, NH
DOYLE, Isabel R and Roland J B BRUNELLE, 28 Sep 1938 Nashua, NH
DOYLE, James and Sophia BLODGETT, 22 Feb 1819
DOYLE, Joseph A and Marion M COSTELLO, 13 Mar 1937 Hudson, NH
DOYLE, Karen M and Gordon E GARVIN, 09 Apr 1983 Hudson, NH
DOYLE, Rita and Robert W CLARK, 26 Jul 1975 Hudson, NH
DOYLE, Thomas E and Gloria F EDDINGER, 09 Sep 1950 Hudson, NH
DOYON, Lorraine J and Bobby C REED, 02 Mar 1956 Hudson, NH
DOZOIS, Lynn Marie and David E CROSS, 22 Jun 1985 Hudson, NH
DRAKE, Bettylou and Maurice M Jr MOODY, 17 Oct 1970 Hudson, NH
DRAKE, Charles E and Susan E GAY, 20 Sep 1882 Tyngsboro, MA
  Charles L Drake & Lydinna
  Elbridge E Gay & Lydia M
DRAKE, Nancy J and Kevin M O'CONNELL, 24 Sep 1983 Nashua, NH
DRAKE, Robert S and Emma M BRACHETTI, 15 Apr 1945 Hudson, NH
DRAPER, George J and Roberta M DESSERT, 22 Jul 1950 Hudson, NH
DRAPER, Lawrence L and Earline C ALEXANDER, 07 Jun 1942 Nashua, NH
DREVOJAN, Raymond and Sally J R GALLAGHER, 01 Feb 1971 Nashua, NH
DREW, Frankie M and Willis P CUMMINGS, 11 Nov 1885 Gilford, NH
  David Clement, Jr (Hudson, NH) & Hannah M Hall (Nashua, NH)
  Hiram Cummings(Hudson, NH) & Abby Clark (Lyndeboro, NH)
DREWETT, Olive P and Anacleto CORTI, 26 Jun 1921 Hudson, NH
DRISCOLL, Catherine and John H ROBINSON, 29 Aug 1935 Hudson, NH
DRISCOLL, Charles F and Lila E NATES, 05 Feb 1949 Hudson, NH
DRISCOLL, James PEWN III&Marie A COUTERMARSH, 27 Jun 1981 Hudson,NH
DROLET, Myrtle E and Kenneth N WRIGHT, 23 Nov 1933 Nashua, NH
DROLET, Patricia A and David J BRYAND, 30 Jun 1973 Nashua, NH
DROLLETT, Lois E and George J WHITE, 28 Mar 1932 Nashua, NH
DROUIN, Albert J and Elizabeth HAMBLETT, 09 Apr 1960 Manchester, NH
DROUIN, Bernice E and Anthony J RIZZITANO, 11 Nov 1971 Nashua, NH
DROUIN, Betty-Jean and Roderick A THIBODEAU, 05 Mar 1975 Nashua, NH
DROUIN, Dennis R and Patricia A POWLOWSKY, 26 Jul 1975 Hudson, NH
DROUIN, Donald R and Paula M ANGER, 26 May 1984 Hudson, NH
DROUIN, Gilbert and Brenda L LAVALLEE, 19 Nov 1983 Londonderry, NH
DROUIN, Juliette A and Ernest C BERUBE, 08 Apr 1949 Hudson, NH
DROUIN, Raymond J and Shirley L BILODEAU, 17 Jun 1977 Milford, NH
DROUIN, Robert J and Grace M HANSON, 22 Aug 1953 Hudson, NH
DROWN, Alton L and Frances S WINN, 04 Apr 1942 Hudson, NH
DROWN, Sandra Jo and Edward Jam CARD, 26 Jul 1980 Hudson, NH
DROZNICK, Joel M and Carol R COOPER, 19 Jul 1975 Hudson, NH

HUDSON,NH MARRIAGES

DRUCKMAN, Michael M and Patricia A SMITH, 08 Jan 1977 Hudson, NH
DRUKE, Mary L and Harvey E DAUPHINAIS, 22 Dec 1972 Hudson, NH
DUBAY, Mark L and Michelle S LEE, 22 Sep 1984 Hudson, NH
DUBE, Adolph and Helen KEENAN, 12 Feb 1938 Nashua, NH
DUBE, Alice A and George E LAVOIE, 12 Jan 1957 Hudson, NH
DUBE, Anita and Charles E DARLING, 29 Nov 1941 Nashua, NH
DUBE, Ann Marie and Kenneth B II GILMAN, 14 Jun 1975 Hudson, NH
DUBE, Antoinette and Wayne R DEARBORN, 18 Jun 1966 Nashua, NH
DUBE, Claire L and Paul E BOUFFARD, 31 Aug 1957 Hudson, NH
DUBE, Daniel T and Sara A REYNOLDS, 25 Jun 1955 Hudson, NH
DUBE, Denise M and Vernon L BARNES, 12 May 1973 Derry, NH
DUBE, Dennis A and Linda B MORIN, 18 Sep 1976 Hudson, NH
DUBE, Dennis Romeo and Karen T CLARK, 22 Sep 1973 Hudson, NH
DUBE, Donna D and Donald E Jr SMITH, 09 Sep 1984 Nashua, NH
DUBE, Gary Robert and Elizabeth STICKNEY, 05 Feb 1982 Nashua, NH
DUBE, Gertrude D and Roger E ASSELIN, 27 Nov 1952 Hudson, NH
DUBE, John G and Jennifer J MILLER, 20 Oct 1984 Nashua, NH
DUBE, Joseph A III and Paula A LAINE, 06 Oct 1979 Hudson, NH
DUBE, Joyce A and Daniel R NIQUETTE, 03 Mar 1973 Manchester, NH
DUBE, Julia B and Romeo R GENDRON, 07 Jun 1947 Nashua, NH
DUBE, Laura and Norman N BOUCHER, 24 Apr 1928 Nashua, NH
DUBE, Normand A and Doris J TEMBLEY, 05 May 1945 Nashua, NH
DUBE, Normand T and Joyce E GIGUERE, 06 Oct 1973 Nashua, NH
DUBE, Oscar L and Lucille M BELAND, 17 Jun 1944 Amherst, NH
DUBE, Paula A and Daniel L BRADLEY, 05 May 1984 Hudson, NH
DUBE, Pauline M and Norman W LETOURNEAUX, 24 Jun 1967 Nashua, NH
DUBE, Ronald R and Joyce A KAROS, 30 May 1963 Hudson, NH
DUBE, Steven W and Michelle M SCOTT, 16 Oct 1982 Hudson, NH
DUBE, Theresa A and Stephen A BOULEY, 11 Sep 1965 Hudson, NH
DUBE, Theresa Y and Rene L GENDRON, 20 May 1950 Hudson, NH
DUBOIS, Albert J and Marilyn L NAGY, 14 Jun 1974 Hudson, NH
DUBOIS, Alma and Louis LEBOEUF, 01 Oct 1919 Nashua, NH
DUBOIS, Dale R and Kellie P MONROE, 07 Aug 1982 Hudson, NH
DUBOIS, Earl J and Rosemary E FRENETTE, 09 Feb 1968 Hudson, NH
DUBOIS, Janet A and Norman C McCOY, 16 Aug 1975 Hudson, NH
DUBOIS, Marion and Charles B SMITH, 29 Jul 1927 Nashua, NH
DUBOIS, Romeo N and Marion M JOHNSON, 17 Jan 1914 Nashua, NH
    Oliver Dubois & Octavia Lanceau
    James Johnson & Lizzie Wallace
DUBOIS, Susan Lynn and Andrew J HARMON, 07 Jan 1983 Hudson, NH
DUBORD, Raynald A & Ginette L LAURENDEAU, 21 Aug 1965 Manchester,NH
DUBOWIK, Paul P and Therese M THEROUX, 09 Oct 1976 Nashua, NH
DUBOWIK, Peter and Rita ATKINS, 28 Jun 1952 Nashua, NH
DUBOWIK, Rosemary E and Jeffrey R BURK, 18 Jun 1971 Nashua, NH
DUBUC, Maurice H and Frances B LUCIEN, 03 Jul 1940 Nashua, NH
DUBUC, Wilfred A and Mary Lou METIVIER, 31 Dec 1974 Nashua, NH
DUCAS, Conrad A and Laura O BECHARD, 14 Jun 1969 Hudson, NH
DUCAS, Florence L and Ernest R Sr THOMAS, 31 Dec 1953 Hudson, NH
DUCAS, Rose R and Henry A TESSIER, 12 Nov 1945 Nashua, NH
DUCHARME, Arthur D and Nancy E PORTER, 02 Dec 1967 Hudson, NH
DUCHARME, Denise D and Dana J HARTNETT, 24 Oct 1981 Hudson, NH
DUCHARME, Diane L and John R RICHARDSON, 13 Apr 1973 Hudson, NH
DUCHARME, Dorothy S and Vernon A LYON, 28 Nov 1957 Hudson, NH
DUCHARME, Elaine L and Paul P CORRIVEAU, 17 Feb 1962 Hudson, NH
DUCHARME, Florence and Megrdich SARKISIAN, 27 Nov 1947 Nashua, NH
DUCHARME, Hector E and Lucille N SOMERVILLE, 12 Sep 1971 Nashua, NH
DUCHARME, Henry W and Gertrude F LEMAY, 28 Jun 1952 Hudson, NH
DUCHARME, Lena and Leon F Jr MALOUIN, 28 Jun 1952 Hudson, NH
DUCHARME, Leo and Helen BLAIS, 22 Mar 1933 Nashua, NH
DUCHARME, Pauline L and James E McALISTER, 02 Dec 1961 Nashua, NH

HUDSON,NH MARRIAGES

DUCHARME, Rachel D and Walter R GREEN, 29 Jul 1969 Hudson, NH
DUCHARME, Robert E and Linda M LITTLE, 28 Oct 1967 Hudson, NH
DUCHARME, Susan A and Charles E BARNES, 02 Aug 1975 Hudson, NH
DUCHARME, Sylvia E and Roland L GUERETTE, 19 May 1978 Hudson, NH
DUCHARME, Theresa A and Herve C RICARD, 01 Sep 1952 Hudson, NH
DUCHARME, Thomas A & Patricia A DUMONT, 02 Oct 1964 New Ipswich, NH
DUCHARME, Walter F and Eva FRENNETTE, 17 Nov 1927 Bristol, NH
DUCHESNEAU, Diane C and Michael H RODGERS, 13 Nov 1971 Nashua, NH
DUCHESNEAU, Maurice R and Constance MALETTE, 07 Apr 1951 Hudson, NH
DUCLOS, Armand E and Jo Ann R BRIAND, 19 Mar 1959 Hudson, NH
DUCLOS, Armand E and Vivian A GUERRETTE, 02 Jan 1965 Hudson, NH
DUCLOS, Jo-Ann and Arthur P BLANCHETTE, 01 Jun 1963 Hudson, NH
DUDASH, Denise D and David J COSSETTE, 18 Sep 1982 Merrimack, NH
DUDEVOIR, Jean A and Robert J HEVEY, 01 Nov 1980 Pelham, NH
DUDLEY, Eva M and Arthur L EMERSON, 08 Jun 1870 Hudson, NH
DUDLEY, John R and Donna A ANDREWS, 07 Nov 1981 Nashua, NH
DUDLEY, Laura G and Alden H BARRON, 16 Jun 1856
DUDLEY, Ralph and Joyce B TAYLOR, 05 Apr 1980 Nashua, NH
DUDLEY, Ralph E and Bertha M VIOLETTE, 15 May 1965 Hudson, NH
DUDLEY, Roberta M and Richard D HARTT, 23 Oct 1971 Nashua, NH
DUDLEY, Sandra E and Kenneth I WALTER, 08 Jul 1972 Mont Vernon, NH
DUFAULT, Oliver and Annie COATS, 19 Jul 1905 Nashua, NH
   John B Dufault & Josephine Palady
   James G Coats & Hannah McAndrews
DUFAULT, Robert L and Susan M HOLT, 04 Feb 1967 Hudson, NH
DUFF, Charlotte and Maurice E FITZGERALD, 11 Oct 1969 Nashua, NH
DUFF, Norman J A and Lucy A ROLLINS, 26 Mar 1960 Nashua, NH
DUFFINE, Clara E and Franklyn H McALLISTER, 04 Nov 1938 Hudson, NH
DUFFY, Edward T and Rose V POIRIER, 08 Sep 1962 Hudson, NH
DUFFY, Nancy C and Andrew D SIROIS, 11 May 1985 Hudson, NH
DUFOE, Earl R and Pauline B GODIN, 30 May 1957 Hudson, NH
DUFOUR, Arthur and Marjorie T SCALES, 29 Aug 1959 Hudson, NH
DUFOUR, Gail E and Morris C LUTHER, 09 Dec 1972 Nashua, NH
DUFOUR, Patricia A and Richard D BROUGH, 13 Nov 1976 Litchfield, NH
DUGAN, Bonnie L and Philip C LAURIEN, 11 Apr 1985 Nashua, NH
DUGAN, Jeanne M and Steven H WILSON, 17 Apr 1982 Merrimack, NH
DUGAN, John D Jr and Esther R CANAVAN, 09 Sep 1921 Nashua, NH
DUGAN, Marie E and James T Jr GALLAGHER, 30 Jun 1971 Nashua, NH
DUGGAN, Judith A and Norman A LEVESQUE, 20 May 1967 Manchester, NH
DUGLESS, Daniel and Horsley EVENS, 29 Oct 1741
DUGUAY, Wilfred J and Dorothy E RICARD, 21 Aug 1959 Hudson, NH
DUHAMEL, Richard J and Laura N GERRARD, 29 Jul 1967 Derry, NH
DUKE, Charles R and Anna F HILL, 18 Aug 1962 Hudson, NH
DUKE, Dorothy V and Freeman COBB, 05 Dec 1925 Hudson, NH
DUKE, Helen M and Albert A GOODROW, 19 Jun 1920 Nashua, NH
DUKETTE, George F and Phyllis E PRITCHARD, 20 Nov 1954 Hudson, NH
DULEY, Harold W and Rose A COLOMBO, 26 Sep 1937 Hudson, NH
DULEY, Howard C and Evalee TAYLOR, 26 Jul 1970 Hudson, NH
DULUDE, Olivette E and Robert P LEVESQUE, 27 Nov 1941 Nashua, NH
DUMAIS, Albert R and Jean H BEDORE, 21 Sep 1963 Hudson, NH
DUMAIS, Alphonse and Irene PARADIS, 19 Apr 1934 Nashua, NH
DUMAIS, Anita C and George R FRECHETTE, 21 Jul 1972 Hudson, NH
DUMAIS, Bertrand and Shirley BILODEAU, 31 Aug 1957 Hudson, NH
DUMAIS, Claudette and Lionel A LAINE, 13 Oct 1962 Hudson, NH
DUMAIS, Donald O and Paula Jean ROWELL, 02 Aug 1980 Nashua, NH
DUMAIS, Elizabeth and Clarence A LaPORTE, 22 Feb 1964 Claremont, NH
DUMAIS, Jean W and Stephen W DANE, 09 Oct 1965 Merrimack, NH
DUMAIS, Jeannette and Jon M GLINES, 14 Oct 1967 Hudson, NH
DUMAIS, Lucien R and Violet L FRENETTE, 03 Apr 1948 Nashua, NH
DUMAIS, Marie V and Joseph R TESSIER, 26 Oct 1944 Nashua, NH

HUDSON,NH MARRIAGES

DUMAIS, Noella T and Louis J MICHAUD, 06 May 1961 Hudson, NH
DUMAIS, Susan I and Dennis F LAMPHEAR, 22 Jan 1969 Nashua, NH
DUMAS, Rachel C and Roger A LAQUERRE, 16 Sep 1950 Hudson, NH
DUMAS, Ruby E and Benjamin W PALMER, 02 Jul 1927 Hudson, NH
DUMAS, Therese F and J Conrad BISSON, 22 Nov 1945 Nashua, NH
DUMOND, Jean F and Eugene S FARNAM, 12 May 1979 Hudson, NH
DUMONT, Alfred F and Bertha LEBOEUF, 03 Jul 1918 Nashua, NH
DUMONT, Claire T and Raymond G ELLIS, 21 May 1949 Nashua, NH
DUMONT, Daniel L and Rhonda R COURTEMANCHE, 21 Feb 1975 Nashua, NH
DUMONT, Debra A and Randy K RHODES, 19 Feb 1977 Hudson, NH
DUMONT, Ernest A and Veronica BARTOSZWICZ, 06 May 1937 Hudson, NH
DUMONT, Lea and Theophile LECLERC, 10 Jan 1917 Nashua, NH
DUMONT, Margaret M and Karl P LIEBERWIRTH, 28 Apr 1984 Hudson, NH
DUMONT, Patricia A & Thomas A DUCHARME, 02 Oct 1964 New Ipswich, NH
DUMONT, Phyllis M and Lionel E LEVESQUE, 30 May 1953 Nashua, NH
DUMONT, Robert T and Lucille M LEDOUX, 06 Sep 1958 Hudson, NH
DUMOUCHEL, Albert and Jeanne J DION, 30 Jul 1956 Hudson, NH
DUNBAR, Zenas and Laura C LEONARD, 29 Dec 1847
DUNCKLEE, Gerald R and Anita O PELLETIER, 24 Sep 1938 Nashua, NH
DUNCKLEE, Irving L and Maxine G WELLS, 18 Jun 1932 Hudson, NH
DUNCKLEE, Merton L and Clara L HARVEY, 06 Oct 1908 Nashua, NH
    Charles E Duncklee & Flora J Jones
    J Frank Harvey & Maud Parmenter
DUNCKLEE, Merton L Jr and Rosalina BALDWIN, 25 May 1974 Hudson, NH
DUNCKLEE, Richard H and Orise D MORAN, 12 Feb 1944 Milford, NH
DUNCKLEE, Richard H and Christine GAGNON, 30 Jun 1956 Windham, NH
DUNCKLEE, Shirley M and John M Jr BREEN, 11 Oct 1947 Nashua, NH
DUNCKLEE, Virginia L and Roger M BOUCHER, 27 Aug 1949 Nashua, NH
DUNHAM, Alice M and Eric E IVERSON, 21 Aug 1976 Manchester, NH
DUNKLEE, Cheryl A and John S WOLCZOK, 13 May 1978 Nashua, NH
DUNKLEE, Herbert W and Mavis M BLACK, 01 Apr 1967 Wilton, NH
DUNKLEE, Marguerite and Stanley H FOGG, 25 Oct 1957 Hudson, NH
DUNKLEE, Virginia M and Philip A PENNELL, 18 Apr 1964 Hudson, NH
DUNKLEE, Walter C and Marguerite SMITH, 24 Jul 1945 Hudson, NH
DUNLEA, Mark J and Norma F CHARTRAIN, 21 Sep 1975 Nashua, NH
DUNN, John P and Bonnie L MacRAE, 21 Jun 1969 Hudson, NH
DUNN, Ruth A and Ralph A NICKERSON, 03 Dec 1904 Hudson, NH
    John H Dunn & Mary A Trickett
    Joseph Nickerson & Rose Dexter
DUNN, Virginia C and Harold B COOLIDGE, 16 Sep 1942 Nashua, NH
DUNN, William I and Barbara E PARKER, 04 Nov 1933 Hudson, NH
DUNNE, Dorothy G and Clarence E MACOMBER, 18 Nov 1940 Hudson, NH
DUNSKY, Peter P and Inez H MERCIER, 12 Sep 1947 Hudson, NH
DUPIUS, Raymond W and Jeanne E ELLIS, 21 Mar 1953 Hudson, NH
DUPLEASE, Denise G and Roger E PATTEN, 31 May 1971 Hudson, NH
DUPLEASE, Elaine A and Raymond E PATTEN, 04 Jul 1966 Nashua, NH
DUPLEASE, Gail A and Mark W COLLINS, 04 Feb 1983 Nashua, NH
DUPLEASE, Richard E and Gail A LINDVALL, 24 Nov 1973 Hudson, NH
DUPLEASE, Ronald G and Dianne L GAMACHE, 15 Jul 1967 Hudson, NH
DUPLEASE, Ronald G and Ernestine WATTS, 12 Oct 1973 Nashua, NH
DUPLESSIS, Deborah and Mark A FECTEAU, 15 Mar 1985 Hudson, NH
DUPLESSIS, Regina L and Ernest R LAFLAMME, 03 Jul 1982 Hudson, NH
DUPONT, Alma D and Napoleon GENDRON, 06 Aug 1937 Hudson, NH
DUPONT, Cecile D and Ralph T LONES, 24 Jul 1954 Nashua, NH
DUPONT, George C and Victoria T PAQUETTE, 25 Apr 1959 Hudson, NH
DUPONT, Louis P and Diana P DANZIG, 01 Mar 1979 Nashua, NH
DUPONT, Marguerite and William J Jr MULHERN, 14 May 1966 Hudson, NH
DUPRES, Emery L and M Cecile TOUSIGNANT, 04 Oct 1935 Hudson, NH
DUPREY, Ann S and John J Jr STEVENS, 09 Mar 1974 Nashua, NH
DUPUIS, Donna R and Emanuel C Jr EBNER, 24 May 1980 Nashua, NH

HUDSON, NH MARRIAGES

DUQUETTE, Claire L and Dennis W FULLER, 09 May 1970 Hudson, NH
DUQUETTE, Diane J and James F COOPER, 11 Apr 1975 Nashua, NH
DUQUETTE, Norman A and Sylvia J BRIAND, 27 Sep 1958 Durham, NH
DUQUETTE, Raymond E and Lorette A GAGNON, 04 Nov 1942 Nashua, NH
DUQUETTE, Robert R and Nancy A POWLOWSKY, 04 Oct 1975 Hudson, NH
DUQUETTE, Sally A and Robert N DURAND, 30 Jun 1973 Hudson, NH
DURAND, Cynthia and Ross W CAMPBELL, 11 Jun 1981 Nashua, NH
DURAND, Doris E and Gerard F GRIGAS, 05 Dec 1970 Nashua, NH
DURAND, Edmond P and Joyce M LANDRY, 09 Jul 1983 Hudson, NH
DURAND, Edward J and Clarina GAGNE, 07 Jul 1950 Hudson, NH
DURAND, Laurette M and Kevin M HICKS, 29 Nov 1969 Nashua, NH
DURAND, Paul T and JoAnn R PAQUETTE, 01 Jun 1968 Nashua, NH
DURAND, Phillip A and Elaine M CRAIK, 24 May 1975 Hudson, NH
DURAND, Robert K and Donna M LANDRY, 20 May 1978 Nashua, NH
DURAND, Robert N and Sally A DUQUETTE, 30 Jun 1973 Hudson, NH
DURANT, Cheryl L and Russell T REID, 20 Sep 1969 Rochester, NH
DURANT, George O and Ella M LUND, 26 May 1898 Hudson, NH
  George W Durant
  William Anthony
DURANT, George O and Edith HENNESEY, 30 Apr 1938 Hudson, NH
DURANT, Horace G and Alice M BARTLETT, 15 Feb 1958 Hudson, NH
DURANT, Jeannette and Raymond W CLARK, 09 Apr 1972 Nashua, NH
DURANT, Joel P and Jessie A TOLMAN, 15 Jul 1912 Hudson, NH
  George W Durant & Georgianna Lunol
  Alexander Walker & Annie M Baker
DURANT, Martha L J and Joseph E WOOD, 09 Mar 1885 Nashua, NH
  George W Durant & Anna Lund
  George S Wood(Chelmsford, MA) & Susan Pierce
DURANT, Milo A and Sadie Bell WILSON, 05 Feb 1889 Derry, NH
  George W Durant & Anna Lund (Hollis, NH)
DURHAM, Debra D and Patrick F HEUVELINE, 17 Dec 1983 Litchfield, NH
DURHAM, Lynn A and Larry C HILEMAN, 20 Oct 1979 Litchfield, NH
DURHAMMER, Terry W and Patricia A BONNETTE, 13 Aug 1969 Hudson, NH
DURIRAGE, George E and Halga M HARWOOD, 25 Sep 1901 Hudson, NH
  Ranson M Durirage(St Albans, VT) & Janette Goodridge(Fletcher,VT)
  W J Harwood(England) & Thea Hanson (Norway)
DURIVAGE, Ellsworth H and Priscilla B ELLIS, 25 Sep 1926 Nashua, NH
DURIVAGE, Frank H and Bertha G THORNE, 27 May 1903 Hudson, NH
  Ransom Durivage & Genett Goodrich
  Chas E Thorne & Eliza Esty
DURIVAGE, Janice T and Leo A BERGERON, 04 Sep 1937 Hudson, NH
DURIVAGE, Mildred and Gordon R POOLE, 11 Oct 1924 Hudson, NH
DURKEE, Eleanor G and Russell A GRANTON, 05 May 1924 Hudson, NH
DURKIN, Barbara A and Robert T COLLINS, 09 May 1982 Hudson, NH
DUROCHER, Maurice H & Pamela M BELLEFEUILLE, 23 Aug 1972 Hudson, NH
DUROCHER, Yolande F and Alan E MARSHALL, 29 Dec 1949 Nashua, NH
DURWIN, Connie and John F CARD, 07 Jun 1980 Hudson, NH
DURWIN, Cynthia H and Richard B MITCHELL, 18 Nov 1970 Nashua, NH
DURWIN, Rose Lee and Richard H CARTER, 09 Jan 1971 Hudson, NH
DURWIN, Sara S and Raymond L Jr FREEMAN, 29 May 1971 Hudson, NH
DURWIN, William F and Constance KITCHENER, 28 Feb 1946 Nashua, NH
DUSSEAULT, Patricia A and John E GRAFTON, 25 Aug 1962 Hudson, NH
DUSSEAULT, Tammy L and Marc A SMITH, 20 Jun 1981 Hudson, NH
DUSTIN, Washington and Alfaretta BATCHELDER, 08 Feb 1876 Hudson, NH
DUSTON, John and Sarah PARKER, 06 Apr 1743
DUTTON, Dorothy M and Frank J TAVERNA, 18 Mar 1972 Nashua, NH
DUTTON, George W and Mary L BURNHAM, 02 Jan 1882 Acworth, NH
  John E Dutton (Hudson, NH) & Sarah E Winn (Hudson, NH)
  Omer B Burnham(Antrim, NH) & Mary M Gould (Greenfield, NH)
DUTTON, John and Susanna HADLEY, 23 Apr 1815

HUDSON, NH MARRIAGES

DUTTON, John and Joyce HADLEY, 02 May 1816
DUTTON, Josiah and Sarah PARKER, 06 Apr 1743
DUVAL, Alfred and Margaret DEVLIN, 27 Feb 1922 Nashua, NH
DUVAL, Bertha and Hormidas E BRODEUR, 20 Jun 1921 Nashua, NH
DUVAL, Debra Ann and Robert L PORTER, 25 Aug 1973 Nashua, NH
DUVAL, Lea D and Frank E SMITH, 14 Aug 1970 Hudson, NH
DUVAL, Mary C and Edgar J Jr DONAH, 16 Feb 1974 Hudson, NH
DUVAL, Norbert and Patricia A NOTTER, 22 May 1976 Hudson, NH
DUVAL, Rene and Gerogette BEAUCHEMIN, 12 Nov 1938 Manchester, NH
DUVALL, Marcia G and Thomas P GILCHRIST, 07 Sep 1968 Hudson, NH
DWIRE, Dennis H and Paula J LATOUR, 15 May 1971 Hudson, NH
DWIRE, Earl A and Deborah H THOMPSON, 19 Jun 1971 Hudson, NH
DWIRE, Gail Ann and James CASSARINO, 14 Sep 1974 Nashua, NH
DWIRE, Gerald A and Nancy R BEAULIEU, 30 Mar 1979 Hudson, NH
DWYER, Helen M and James M NICHOLS, 26 Jun 1981 Nashua, NH
DWYER, Janice E and Eric L SUNDQUIST, 08 Aug 1982 Hudson, NH
DYER, Charles and Lilla E BARRETT, 31 Mar 1900 Hudson, NH
   Charles Dyer & Zoe Grace
   Almado Barrett & Annie M Hartford
DYS, Peter J and Ruth H CHAPLIN, 07 Dec 1946 Hudson, NH
EAGLES, Marion I and Raymond L WATTS, 03 Sep 1932 Hudson, NH
EARLEY, William J and Nancy P PARADISE, 19 May 1963 Hollis, NH
EASTMAN, Estelle A and Richard J MARLEY, 08 Apr 1967 Litchfield, NH
EASTMAN, Mahlon P and Rachel R RODIER, 30 Aug 1954 Hudson, NH
EASTMAN, Marguerite & Alfred E BASTILLE, 27 Apr 1974 Litchfield, NH
EASTMAN, Samuel and Sarah LINCH, 16 Nov 1798
EASTON, Walter D and Bertha M SMITH, 01 Aug 1900 Lyme, CT
   Alfred Eaton & Harriet T Smith
   Wm H Smith & Eliza M Tuck
EASTWOOD, June and Ivar ANDERSON, 25 Oct 1940 Hudson, NH
EASTY, Lot and Mary F WINN, 30 Mar 1832
EATON, Albert C and Mary R G LEFEBVRE, 27 Oct 1945 Hudson, NH
EATON, Alice M and Edwin C WIGHTMAN, 15 Feb 1948 Hudson, NH
EATON, Arthur P and Melody L HAISMAN, 27 Jan 1968 Hudson, NH
EATON, Barbara A and Armand V Jr MALENFANT, 07 Jun 1969 Nashua, NH
EATON, Deborah A and Robert A DEMOURA, 19 Jun 1982 Pelham, NH
EATON, Doris E and Ralph W COATES, 16 Jun 1932 Hudson, NH
EATON, Doris E and Kent O McLEAN, 14 Apr 1939 Hudson, NH
EATON, Elaine H and Richard Joseph SIROIS, 08 Jul 1978 Nashua, NH
EATON, Isaac and Harriet KIDDER, 02 May 1850
EATON, Jeffrey A and Janet A GALLANT, 21 Aug 1981 Hudson, NH
EATON, Martina and Willis P SMITH, 01 Jan 1873 Hudson, NH
EATON, Mary E and Marcell H SMITH, 06 Sep 1890 Wakefield, MA
   Noah M Eaton (Wakefield, MA) & Eliza R Walton (Wakefield, MA)
   Wm H Smith(Guilford, ME) & Eliza M Tuck (Salem, MA)
EATON, Sarah and Benjamin MERRILL, 25 Jul 1820
EATON, Walter D and Edith F PARKER, 12 Oct 1932 Hudson, NH
EATON, William J and Janet E SCRIBNER, 19 Mar 1971 Hudson, NH
EATON, Willie W and Sylvia J HUFF, 23 Mar 1884 Hudson, NH
   Alfred Eaton & Harriet Smith (Hudson, NH)
   Samuel Huff & Sarah
EAVES, Jacqueline and John A TIERNEY, 17 Dec 1945 Nashua, NH
EAYERS, Ida and Edward M CADY, 30 May 1899 Hudson, NH
   E F Eayers & Augusta Ford
   Joseph Cady & Elmira Lernay
EAYRES, James and Susannah SENTER, 25 Jan 1798
EAYRES, Rebecca and John COCHRAN, 07 Jan 1800
EAYRES, Rebecca and John HACKMAN, 07 Jan 1800
EAYRS, Cora and Orrin P MOODY, 06 Feb 1915 Hudson, NH
   Edward Eayrs (Nashua, NH) & Augusta Ford (Hudson, NH)

HUDSON, NH MARRIAGES

Alexander Moody(London, NH) & Betsy Wilson (London, NH)
EBNER, Emanuel C Jr and Donna R DUPUIS, 24 May 1980 Nashua, NH
ECK, Carl O and Dorothy L RINGDAHL, 14 Sep 1940 Hudson, NH
ECKHARDT, Ronna L and Tim J HARDY, 20 May 1983 Exeter, NH
ECKLUND, William R and Virginia P TURMEL, 21 Nov 1959 Hudson, NH
EDDINGER, Gloria F and Thomas E DOYLE, 09 Sep 1950 Hudson, NH
EDDINGS, Harold and Vicki L LAVOIE, 16 Nov 1984 Nashua, NH
EDDY, Marcia E and John O LILLY, 03 Sep 1900 Nashua, NH
   P Eddy & Mary Wheeler
   O F Lilly & Mary J Shaw
EDELMAN, Peter S and Geraldine WALLACE, 14 Feb 1970 Nashua, NH
EDELSTEIN, David P and Diane J ANCTIL, 22 Nov 1970 Nashua, NH
EDELSTEIN, Eve V and John R SARRIS, 27 Aug 1975 Dublin, NH
EDGAR, Ruth A and Andrew A MURPHY, 13 Feb 1934 Nashua, NH
EDMONDS, Richard R Jr & Elaine M McCAFFERY, 22 Jun 1985 Hudson, NH
EDMUNDS, Norma M and William W BAKER, 22 Sep 1956 Nashua, NH
EDMUNDS, Sandra L & William J III GREENE, 19 Dec 1981 Litchfield, NH
EDWARDS, Carl R and Gloria M THEBODEAU, 21 Sep 1956 Nashua, NH
EDWARDS, Carl R and Jean M FOREST, 09 Feb 1968 Hudson, NH
EDWARDS, Carol Ann and Steven M DOHERTY, 10 Mar 1974 Hudson, NH
EDWARDS, Ira A and Pauline H KNOX, 22 Jun 1956 Keene, NH
EDWARDS, Lee E and Nancy A MASON, 23 Mar 1956 Nashua, NH
EDWARDS, Sandra Eve and James Paul PAGE, 23 Aug 1980 Hudson, NH
EDWARDS, Thelma E and Peter PAMAGOULIS, 07 Jun 1928 Dunstable, MA
EGHTESADI, Khosrow and Farahnaz FARNIA, 10 Jun 1984 Nashua, NH
EGLE, Carrie and Bartolo FIORETTE, 15 Jul 1917 Hudson, NH
EGLEY, William and Ada L SPRAGUE, 30 Sep 1919 Nashua, NH
EINSIDLER, Bruce W and Betty Ann MOORE, 24 Aug 1974 Windham, NH
EKMAN, Dennis L and Patricia D COPP, 14 Apr 1984 Hudson, NH
ELAM, Terrell L and Robyn D PEASLEE, 14 Jun 1980 Litchfield, NH
ELDER, Robert D and Cheryl L KILLAM, 10 Jun 1978 Hampstead, NH
ELDRED, Phyllis I and Lawrence A HOJABOOM, 06 Oct 1962 Hudson, NH
ELDREDGE, Edwin C and Mary I CURTIS, 22 Dec 1948 Hudson, NH
ELDRIDGE, Arthur M and Louisa A NASON, 17 Oct 1952 Hudson, NH
ELDRIDGE, Arthur W and Helen L ROUNSEVILLE, 24 Sep 1903 Hudson, NH
   A F Eldridge & Anna Britton
   John Rounseville & Cora B Clifford
ELDRIDGE, Rosilla and Wm H SMITH, 12 Jun 1873 Hudson, NH
ELIA, James W and Wendy L WILLIAMS, 16 Aug 1980 Nashua, NH
ELKE, Allan John and Katherine RYAN, 08 Apr 1984 Hudson, NH
ELKIND, Bernice and Benjamin J TAYLOR, 26 Sep 1938 Nashua, NH
ELLIOT, Nellie M and Charles E COOK, 28 May 1868 Hudson, NH
ELLIOT, Roy E and Michele A MURELLI, 05 Sep 1981 Hudson, NH
ELLIOTT, Angela B and Dennis R BOULEY, 17 Oct 1981 Nashua, NH
ELLIOTT, Frank H and Theresa I ST LAURENT, 28 May 1955 Hudson, NH
ELLIOTT, Glen D and Nancy J BLACK, 24 Aug 1974 Nashua, NH
ELLIOTT, Jean L and Maurice A LOCKE, 09 Dec 1944 Nashua, NH
ELLIOTT, Kenneth C and Winetta T HILL, 23 Oct 1969 Salem, NH
ELLIOTT, Linda Y and J Edward NEWCOMB, 19 May 1979 Hudson, NH
ELLIOTT, Michael F and Theta R SWINGLER, 30 Aug 1975 Hudson, NH
ELLIOTT, Richard S and Darcy Ann LANGDON, 15 Jan 1983 Pelham, NH
ELLIOTT, Robert A and Robin T PRATT, 02 Sep 1977 Hudson, NH
ELLIOTT, Robert A and Agnes S MARSH, 14 Jul 1984 Nashua, NH
ELLIOTT, Robert E and Joanne F HALE, 13 Oct 1978 Hudson, NH
ELLIOTT, Thomas and Jennie E ESTY, 01 Aug 1951 Hudson, NH
ELLIOTT, Wilfred A and Bernice A PIKE, 01 Nov 1947 Merimack, NH
ELLIOTT, William A and Carmelle L GAGNON, 27 Oct 1979 Nashua, NH
ELLIS, Arthur E and Priscilla MOOREHEAD, 24 Jul 1971 Nashua, NH
ELLIS, Barbara P and Austin E DAVIS, 28 Sep 1951 Windham, NH
ELLIS, Betty L and Robert H CARLSON, 05 Jun 1965 Hudson, NH

HUDSON,NH MARRIAGES

ELLIS, Cora Esthe and Walter T HARWOOD, 21 Jun 1913 Hudson, NH
   Robert Ellis & Hannah A Payne
   Walter J Harwood & Thea Hanson
ELLIS, David J and Sally L CALDWELL, 28 Mar 1980 Hudson, NH
ELLIS, Everett W and Jacqueline LABRIE, 19 Apr 1968 Nashua, NH
ELLIS, Frances A and Francis M CLOHESY, 25 Nov 1959 Hudson, NH
ELLIS, James E and Sandra M HARVEY, 03 Jul 1964 Hudson, NH
ELLIS, Jeanne E and Raymond W DUPIUS, 21 Mar 1953 Hudson, NH
ELLIS, Lorraine B and Ashok K KHURANA, 02 Jun 1979 Nashua, NH
ELLIS, Mary O and George L GAMACHE, 25 Jun 1960 Hudson, NH
ELLIS, Muriel E and Herbert F Jr HATCH, 08 Sep 1938 Hudson, NH
ELLIS, Paul V and Sandra L JAMESON, 07 Jul 1962 Hudson, NH
ELLIS, Priscilla B and Ellsworth H DURIVAGE, 25 Sep 1926 Nashua, NH
ELLIS, Randal S and Denise S COTE, 01 May 1970 Hudson, NH
ELLIS, Raymond G and Claire T DUMONT, 21 May 1949 Nashua, NH
ELLIS, Richard W and Beverly A TETLER, 11 Oct 1952 Hudson, NH
ELLIS, Robert S and L B MacDOWELL, 05 Sep 1947 Nashua, NH
ELLIS, Warren F and Janet D PALMER, 07 Nov 1969 Dover, NH
ELLIS, Willard T and Barbara P OTIS, 24 Dec 1944 Hudson, NH
ELLISON, Daisy M and Lewis A REYNOLDS, 07 Jun 1967 Hudson, NH
ELLSTROM, Robert J and Bonnie J LACASSE, 17 Nov 1984 Hudson, NH
ELSON, Edith Caro and Paul C LAXTON, 09 Sep 1938 Hudson, NH
ELSON, Ethel M and Archie E BANKS, 05 Aug 1935 Hudson, NH
ELWOOD, Sharon A and Ralph R MEIER, 19 Jun 1976 Londonderry, NH
EMERSON, Arthur L and Eva M DUDLEY, 08 Jun 1870 Hudson, NH
EMERSON, Asenath and John P WEBSTER, 10 Sep 1818
EMERSON, Dierdra L and David L PAGE, 02 Sep 1984 Nashua, NH
EMERSON, Hannah and Nehemiah HADLEY, 12 Apr 1762
EMERSON, Hannah and Nehemiah HADLEY, 12 Aug 1762
EMERSON, Jacob P and Cordelia A HASELTON, 08 May 1861
EMERSON, Moses W and Harriet N HILL, 04 Sep 1883 Hudson, NH
   Kimball Emerson (Haverhill, MA) & Sarah Webster (Salem, NH)
   David Burns(Hudson, NH) & Eliza Childs (Salem, MA)
EMERSON, Samuel and Sarah LINCH, 16 Nov 1798
EMERSON, Sterling P and Janice E MARTIN, 02 Feb 1946 Nashua, NH
EMERSON, Susan and Jonathan HARDY, 10 Sep 1818
EMERSON, Susan and Jonathan HARVEY, 10 Sep 1818
EMERSON, William E III and Julia A GRAUSLYS, 11 Nov 1978 Nashua, NH
EMERY, Betty L and John M DONOVAN, 31 Dec 1941 Hudson, NH
EMERY, Elizabeth and Benjamin B SPALDING, 30 Oct 1850
EMERY, Elizabeth and Benj Brook SPAULDING, 30 Oct 1850
EMERY, Lizzie M and Chas H BIXBY, 06 Jun 1876 Hudson, NH
EMMETT, David S and Eleanor S STEVENS, 03 Oct 1969 Hudson, NH
EMMONS, Horace L and Virginia A ANDREWS, 11 Apr 1975 Hudson, NH
EMPEY, Barbara R and Charles W Jr JOHNSON, 21 May 1966 Hudson, NH
ENGELL, Esther and Leonard COHEN, 07 May 1938 Hudson, NH
ENGER, Ralph D and Eileen F SMITH, 12 Jul 1947 Windham, NH
ENGLISH, Carol A and Paul Arthur ALLARD, 24 Aug 1973 Merrimack, NH
ENGLISH, Grace M and Fred OLDFIELD, 09 Nov 1946 Hudson, NH
ENGLISH, Timothy D and Paula J OUELLETTE, 29 Sep 1972 Hudson, NH
ENGSTROM, Gunnar and Isabelle OBORNE, 17 Dec 1941 Manchester, NH
ENNIS, Priscilla and Malcolm W CALLISON, 03 Oct 1970 Nashua, NH
ENO, Celeste M and Donald D NELSON, 23 Oct 1982 Hudson, NH
ENO, Michelle A and Stephen WEBSTER, 26 Sep 1981 Hudson, NH
EPSTEIN, William and Hilda WENERIP, 15 Dec 1928 Hudson, NH
ERALI, Marcellino and Regina C HENRY, 11 May 1985 Hudson, NH
ERB, Christine and Richard M SMALL, 15 Jun 1973 Nashua, NH
ERB, Katherine and Dennis W WELCH, 31 Mar 1976 Nashua, NH
ERICSON, Gustave J and Ruth BLINN, 29 May 1948 Hudson, NH
ERNEST, William A and Katherine KEARNS, 30 Jun 1917 Nashua, NH

HUDSON, NH MARRIAGES

ERSKINE, Gordon B and Margaret J DOMENICI, 07 Apr 1973 Nashua, NH
ERWIN, Richard H Jr and Margaret MARSTON, 26 Apr 1931 Dunstable, MA
ESCALANTE, Jose L and Anne M DESCHENES, 21 May 1983 Hudson, NH
ESCOBAR, George H and Jacqueline JOYCE, 29 Oct 1972 Hudson, NH
ESIELIONIS, Caroline & Michael WOLANGEWICZ, 17 Sep 1944 Hudson, NH
ESKELAND, David S and Janis LEAVITT, 29 Aug 1981 Hudson, NH
ESKELAND, Eric R and Debra T TURMEL, 24 Aug 1979 Nashua, NH
ESPOSITO, Olivette B and Carl H ANDERSON, 18 May 1984 Nashua, NH
ESSEX, Henry A and Antoinette CARLSON, 20 Mar 1982 Hudson, NH
ESTABROOK, Shari L and Richard BUJINOWSKI, 28 Oct 1972 Hudson, NH
ESTEE, Lucille F and James B GILL, 16 May 1970 Hudson, NH
ESTEE, Thomas M and Linda L COLLEY, 05 Dec 1970 Hudson, NH
ESTERBROOK, Abigail Underwd and Joseph BROWN, 01 Jan 1800
ESTEY, Aaron P and Anna F FROST, 23 Mar 1897 Hudson, NH
   Edward P Estey & Lydia C Hemphill
   Samuel J Frost & Caroline Pingree
ESTEY, Barbara E and Earl W Sr THOMAS, 06 Jan 1968 Hudson, NH
ESTEY, William J and Betty J ABBOTT, 24 Sep 1966 Hudson, NH
ESTY, Elaine O and John R HARDY, 09 Nov 1952 Nashua, NH
ESTY, Ernest G and Mary J BAKER, 02 Jun 1926 Hudson, NH
ESTY, Florence and Arthur HAZELTON, 28 Mar 1918 Hudson, NH
ESTY, Jennie E and Thomas ELLIOTT, 01 Aug 1951 Hudson, NH
ESTY, Lizzie J and Gilbert E BOLES, 16 May 1883 Windham, NH
   Richard Esty & Clara Nichols
   Alphonse Boles(Methuen, MA) & Mary A Peabody (Pelham, NH)
ESTY, Philip E and Mary T GRAHAM, 04 Nov 1938 Hudson, NH
ESTY, Ralph A and Florence CARLETON, 21 May 1917 Nashua, NH
ESTY, Ralph A and Vera M BAGLEY, 24 Jun 1922 Hudson, NH
EVANICO, Anne M and Donald B McKINNON, 16 Oct 1982 Gorham, NH
EVANS, Alma and George NEE, 13 Dec 1934 Hudson, NH
EVANS, Charles R and Victoria M McALLISTER, 27 Jul 1957 Nashua, NH
EVANS, Horsly and David DOUGLASS, 1741
EVANS, JoAnne M and Gordon G GAUDREAU, 27 Sep 1984 Nashua, NH
EVANS, Robert and Emily SPAULDING, 16 Aug 1937 Nashua, NH
EVENS, Horsley and Daniel DUGLESS, 29 Oct 1741
EVERETT, Harry R Jr and Robin Mari PELKEY, 01 Sep 1984 Nashua, NH
EVIRS, Eva D and Eugene J SMITH, 20 Nov 1946 Hudson, NH
EWENS, Rose M and Earle M GATCOMB, 20 Sep 1952 Belmont, NH
FADER, Mark R and Linda J GRAINGER, 08 Jun 1985 Hudson, NH
FAGAN, Lois H and James W STRAWBRIDGE, 22 Nov 1967 Hudson, NH
FAGNANT, Leo R and Virginia H SNOW, 07 Jun 1958 Hudson, NH
FAHEY, Mary A and Ervin J BURTON, 11 Nov 1966 Nashua, NH
FAIA, John and Phyllis J BRYDER, 25 Sep 1937 Hudson, NH
FAIN, Samuel and Lavania H KENNER, 12 Aug 1950 Hudson, NH
FAIRBANKS, Katherine&Herbert N SHEPHERD, 15 Jul 1961 Manchester, NH
FAIRBANKS, Mary A and Pitman N TREPEN, 11 Oct 1868 Hudson, NH
FAIRFIELD, Alan F and Suzanne R LARGY, 11 Nov 1961 Nashua, NH
FAIRFIELD, Benjamin and Nora M MASON, 11 Jan 1896 Hudson, NH
   Henry W Fairfield & Salvina Leach (New Boston, NH)
   W H Ackerman(Charlotte, NC) & Henrietta C Lane (Lee)
FAIRFIELD, Sherry L and Joseph A BOUCHER, 21 Aug 1965 Hudson, NH
FAIRFIELD, William and Hannah PEARSONS, 01 Jan 1826
FALARDEAU, Deborah A & Donald S Jr RUCKMAN, 11 Nov 1983 Hudson, NH
FALCOS, Sophie and Dimitrios VAZAKAS, 31 Dec 1981 Hudson, NH
FALES, David S and Judith M HAYES, 01 Jul 1961 Nashua, NH
FALL, Lester Alonzo and Eva R Ober SMITH, 29 Jul 1924 Billerica, MA
FALLON, Anabel J and Arthur H DOYLE, 03 Jan 1937 Hudson, NH
FALZARONE, Madeleine and Louis C TRACEY, 18 Jan 1937 Hudson, NH
FANCOVIC, Deborah A and Michael D BREEN, 18 Aug 1972 Hudson, NH
FANEZ, Florence L and Webster D HARLEY, 17 Sep 1965 Hudson, NH

HUDSON,NH MARRIAGES

FANNING, Hope and Albert H NUTTALL, 31 Aug 1940 Hudson, NH
FARIA, MaeEllen M and Richard E MALOUIN, 20 Jan 1979 Hudson, NH
FARIA, Raymond F and Beatrice J STEVENS, 08 Jan 1972 Hudson, NH
FARIA, Stephen E and Tangie F WYANT, 16 Mar 1974 Hudson, NH
FARIOLE, Louise G and Richard A DIONNE, 07 Sep 1980 Nashua, NH
FARIZ, Joseph A and Diane D CATES, 14 Jul 1984 Manchester, NH
FARLAND, Albert W and Olivette I FLEURY, 07 Jun 1947 Nashua, NH
FARLAND, Betty A and Raymond A NOLIN, 12 Dec 1964 Hudson, NH
FARLAND, Daniel A and Patricia H MacDOUGALL, 22 Jun 1968 Hudson, NH
FARLAND, Joseph E and Eva M FORENCE, 02 Dec 1950 Nashua, NH
FARLAND, Mary Ella and Maynard P NASON, 12 Apr 1935 Dracut, MA
FARLAND, Susan B and William B ST ONGE, 26 Sep 1969 Nashua, NH
FARLEY, Arthur and Alice V JORDAN, 28 Jun 1953 Hudson, NH
FARLEY, Benjamin and Mary HAMBLETT, 12 Nov 1816
FARLEY, Elizabeth and Michael J CHAMPIGNY, 20 Jun 1964 Meriden, CT
FARLEY, George C and Gerogiana SEVERANCE, 29 Dec 1879 Hudson, NH
   James Farley (Hollis, NH) & Lucinda Cadwell (Hollis, NH)
   Hezekiah Severance & Sarah J
FARLEY, Louise M and Frank J Jr OSMER, 08 Sep 1946 Nashua, NH
FARLEY, Marie E and Raymond A HAGGETT, 08 Jul 1951 Hudson, NH
FARLEY, Parker and Clarissa PIKE, 20 Oct 1842
FARLEY, Theresa M and Dennis N BERUBE, 14 Jul 1974 Hudson, NH
FARLEY, Virginia D and Robert F CASSISTA, 20 Jun 1956 Nashua, NH
FARMER, Charles B and Lucille V GAMACHE, 25 Nov 1937 Dracut, MA
FARMER, Joseph and Francis P WINN, 06 Jun 1871
FARMER, Lillian M and Eugene W PUDSEY, 20 Jun 1948 Hudson, NH
FARMER, Lucille V & Archibald Jr WILLIAMSON, 21 Apr 1951 Hudson, NH
FARMER, Molly and Samuel Jr BURBANK, 23 Jun 1785
FARMER, Moses and Hanna MARSHALL, 23 Mar 1823
FARNAM, Eugene S and Jean F DUMOND, 12 May 1979 Hudson, NH
FARNHAM, John D and Mary M STEELE, 12 Oct 1866
FARNIA, Farahnaz and Khosrow EGHTESADI, 10 Jun 1984 Nashua, NH
FARNUM, Cortes Ear and Marion Jen WALCH, 27 Sep 1909 Hudson, NH
   Frank N Farnum & Anna F Curey
   Clarence E Walch & Delia E Hutchins
FARNUM, Henry J and Myrtle L MORAN, 18 Sep 1948 Hudson, NH
FARNUM, John D and Mary M SLEETE, 14 Oct 1866
FARNUM, Martha E and Albert S BUTLER, 24 Nov 1892 Hudson, NH
   John Farnum & Mary Steele (Hudson, NH)
   Jas M Butler(Pelham, NH) & Sarah J Steele (Hudson, NH)
FARNUM, Mary M and Charles W SPAULDING, 30 Nov 1882 Hudson, NH
   Charles Steele (Hudson, NH) & Martha Boyd (Londonderry, NH)
   William Spaulding(Hudson, NH) & Sally Marsh (Hudson, NH)
FARRAR, Bert W and Susan E FARROW, 20 Sep 1968 Nashua, NH
FARREIRA, James and Louise QUINN, 15 Dec 1934 Hudson, NH
FARRELL, Christophe and Linda W KIRSCH, 18 Sep 1982 Hudson, NH
FARRINGTON, Evelyn R and Manuel BISKADUROS, 18 Jun 1955 Nashua, NH
FARRINGTON, Guy I and Patricia A BATURA, 29 Apr 1967 Hudson, NH
FARRINGTON, Judith E and Jon CARROLL, 11 Jan 1964 Hudson, NH
FARRINGTON, Laurence M & Mary E CAMPBELL, 28 Nov 1959 Litchfield,NH
FARRINGTON, Lillian C and Kenneth F BARRETT, 15 May 1982 Hudson, NH
FARRINGTON, Martha J and Benjamin NUTTING, 20 Mar 1842
FARRINGTON, Mary E and Robert L WHITE, 18 Aug 1962 Hudson, NH
FARRINGTON, Richard P and Linda J HOOD, 20 Apr 1985 Nashua, NH
FARRINGTON, Stanley M and Ruth V BOULEY, 16 Sep 1961 Nashua, NH
FARRINGTON, Walter L and Dona Mae POINTER, 11 Nov 1977 Hudson, NH
FARRIS, George S and Ann A KINNEEN, 25 Aug 1978 Nashua, NH
FARRIS, George S Jr and Marcela KAUFMAN, 24 Dec 1981 Hudson, NH
FARRIS, John D and Ann E KLEINFELDER, 02 Nov 1946 Hudson, NH
FARROW, Carol A and Kenneth A JONES, 09 Oct 1983 Hudson, NH

HUDSON, NH MARRIAGES

FARROW, Ronald E and Kristen G VALLANCOURT, 26 Dec 1965 Nashua, NH
FARROW, Susan E and Bert W FARRAR, 20 Sep 1968 Nashua, NH
FARWELL, Hattie M and Philip Jr CONNELL, 01 Apr 1866
FARWELL, Lottie A and Wm I MITCHELL, 13 Aug 1875 Nashua, NH
FARWELL, Lucy A and John ANDREWS, 16 Sep 1851
FARWELL, Mary and Elnathan SEARLES, 17 Mar 1814
FARWELL, Mary and Daniel WYMAN, 10 May 1826
FAUCHER, Dean F and Karen L HUDSON, 23 Jul 1983 Merrimack, NH
FAUCHER, JoAnn M and Michael J SMILIKIS, 28 Apr 1972 Hudson, NH
FAUCHER, LuAnn C and David Lee ALBERT, 02 Feb 1974 Hudson, NH
FAUCHER, Rita L and Wayne H ROYCE, 21 Oct 1967 Hudson, NH
FAUCHER, Robert F and Melaine R SMITH, 15 Feb 1975 Hudson, NH
FAUCHER, Yolande M and Roland J LEVESQUE, 17 May 1941 Nashua, NH
FAULKNER, Dawna Anne & Carleton H Jr ADAMS, 26 Jun 1982 Nashua, NH
FAULKNER, Robert J Jr and Sheryl L BINKS, 23 Sep 1967 Hudson, NH
FAULKNER, William J and Robin SEAMAN, 30 Aug 1978 Gilmanton, NH
FAUTEUX, France M and Daniel R VADNEY, 24 Jul 1976 Nashua, NH
FAUTEUX, Manon F and Shane P McMAHON, 29 Aug 1981 Hudson, NH
FAUTEUX, Mariane A and Mark J ANGER, 30 Jul 1977 Nashua, NH
FAUVEL, Jean-Paul and Darlene A GILES, 04 Oct 1980 Nashua, NH
FAVRE, Carroll R and Delores A ARNOLD, 20 Jun 1969 Nashua, NH
FAWCETT, John J and Gloria R McGRATH, 23 Oct 1982 Hudson, NH
FAY, Sally M and Clayton P TRACY, 15 Feb 1969 New Ipswich, NH
FAY, Sarah J and Rufus E WINN, 29 Dec 1903 Hudson, NH
    Peter Carlin & Eliza Clark
    John Winn & Anna Patch
FEARON, Walter R and Gertrude E MARR, 09 Sep 1936 Hudson, NH
FEBONIO, Laurie Ann and Howard W IVES, 30 Aug 1981 Hudson, NH
FEBONIO, Steven M and Denise A NORTON, 28 Aug 1982 Nashua, NH
FECTEAU, Mark A and Deborah DUPLESSIS, 15 Mar 1985 Hudson, NH
FEDESHEN, Jill M and John V FOLEY, 21 Jun 1985 Hudson, NH
FEINSTEIN, Bernard E and Lillian HERZBERG, 29 Nov 1923 Nashua, NH
FELLOWS, John David and Valerie R LAMBERT, 30 Jun 1973 Nashua, NH
FELTON, Robert A and Jean A MARSHALL, 30 Jun 1957 Milford, NH
FEMIA, Joseph E and Dorothy A MAHONEY, 05 Apr 1947 Hudson, NH
FENGILL, Beatrice I and Matthew G McCOMISH, 30 Sep 1944 Hudson, NH
FENTON, Diane P and William W JORDAN, 17 Oct 1981 Nashua, NH
FENTON, Jolene S and Leo Earl NOLIN, 06 Jul 1973 Nashua, NH
FENTON, William W and Robin L LILLIE, 25 Aug 1979 Nashua, NH
FERBERT, John R Jr and Ellen M STANULONIS, 27 Dec 1967 Hudson, NH
FERBERT, Kathleen L and Royal E III MILLER, 07 Jun 1969 Hudson, NH
FERGUSON, Jonathan and Janna WARSON, 23 Oct 1800
FERMOYLE, James E and Diane M GAYNOR, 28 Jul 1966 Nashua, NH
FEROLITO, John F and Jean TARTAGLIA, 13 May 1941 Hudson, NH
FERRARA, Paul M and Annette I LAROUCHE, 21 Jun 1980 Hudson, NH
FERREIRA, Anthony J and Brenda L TAYLOR, 23 Sep 1978 Nashua, NH
FERREIRA, Manuel M and Sandra HODGE, 17 Aug 1974 Manchester, NH
FERREURA, Nancy M and William E PERCH, 04 Oct 1976 Pelham, NH
FERRIERA, Cora and Edward R GUIDO, 17 May 1947 Hudson, NH
FERRIS, Louise C and Edward A SAMIA, 27 Mar 1935 Hudson, NH
FERRYALL, Zoula O and Harold C ROWELL, 18 Sep 1923 Nashua, NH
FESSENDEN, Brian D and Cathleen E BOILARD, 29 Apr 1978 Hudson, NH
FESTA, Mary and Joseph MICARI, 28 Oct 1950 Hudson, NH
FIELD, Dorothy M and Merton W HARWOOD, 01 Sep 1938 Hudson, NH
FIELD, R E and Levi C McPHERSON, 29 Apr 1849
FIELD, Rebecca J and Philip M GARSIDE, 07 May 1983 Hudson, NH
FIFIELD, Bernard G and E Louise McQUADE, 09 Sep 1978 Litchfield, NH
FIFIELD, Nathaniel and Eliza BURZIEL, 23 Sep 1856
FIFIELD, Stephen S and Mehittabel COLBURN, 23 Nov 1870
FIGUEROA, Derrick B and Joan V ALLARD, 09 Dec 1972 Nashua, NH

HUDSON,NH MARRIAGES

FILIPEK, Stanley and Amy HEARN, 06 Dec 1947 Hudson, NH
FILLEBROWN, Tracey L and Richard P CAREY, 16 Jun 1985 Nashua, NH
FILLION, Jacqueline and James A CHAPMAN, 22 Jun 1968 Berlin, NH
FIMBEL, P Michael and Zoe E CLOUGH, 06 Jul 1980 Gilford, NH
FINDLEY, Robert A and Joyce M NADEAU, 11 Nov 1977 Hudson, NH
FINE, Byrd S and Margaret BODMAN, 26 Jun 1948 Hudson, NH
FINN, Donna J and Ralph C MANNO, 06 Aug 1978 Moultonboro, NH
FINNEGAN, Janice R and Raymond E Jr VERLEY, 12 Sep 1981 Hudson, NH
FINNEGAN, Mary V and Thomas J KENNEDY, 21 Nov 1914 Nashua, NH
  Miles Finnegan & Sarah Maguire
  Thomas Kenndey & Isabella Binns
FIORETTE, Bartolo and Carrie EGLE, 15 Jul 1917 Hudson, NH
FISH, Berton K and Marie Emma A COMEAU, 07 Jul 1927 Keene, NH
FISH, Ruby E and Ernest J PELLETIER, 18 Aug 1934 Manchester, NH
FISH, Vena P and Basil T MALONEY, 21 Jun 1924 Hudson, NH
FISHER, George A and Virginia A PEASLEE, 18 Jun 1949 Hudson, NH
FISHER, Geraldine and Simon Jr DeYOUNG, 07 Jan 1945 Hudson, NH
FISHER, Joyce R and Richard G BOILARD, 02 Nov 1963 Exeter, NH
FISHER, Sylvia A and Richard P JONES, 28 Nov 1975 Nashua, NH
FISKE, Theodore E&Margaret M MacDONALD, 12 Jul 1934 Manchester, NH
FISKE, Wayne S and Maureen F GEDNEY, 23 Jul 1960 Derry, NH
FITZGERALD, Donna M and Albert J LAMBERT, 23 Jul 1972 Pelham, NH
FITZGERALD, James A and Hester D GRANT, 30 Dec 1950 Hudson, NH
FITZGERALD, James M and Lillian M BRENNAN, 26 Aug 1932 Nashua, NH
FITZGERALD, Maurice E and Charlotte DUFF, 11 Oct 1969 Nashua, NH
FITZGERALD, Nancy L and Ernest H BURTON, 22 Jan 1955 Hudson, NH
FITZGERALD, Thomas R and Betsy ROBBINS, 01 Apr 1979 Hudson, NH
FITZGERALD, Timothy S and Kay Lois HERBERT, 21 Oct 1972 Nashua, NH
FITZPATRICK, Barbara A and Philip ANTHONY, 26 Aug 1950 Hudson, NH
FLAGG, Bailey Kim and Elmira WEBSTER, 28 Nov 1847
  Benjamin Webster
FLAGG, Clara Fran and Milton DAMON, 05 Feb 1862
FLAGG, Ellen M and Hosea C KNOWLTON, 07 May 1870 Hudson, NH
FLAGG, George W and Mary Franc LAKE, 18 Mar 1874
FLAGG, Samuel C and Sarah Ann WEBSTER, 29 Nov 1839
  Benjamin Webster
FLAGG, William and Minerva A POWERS, 04 Jul 1872
  George W Flagg
FLAHERTY, Mark J and Diane G CHAREST, 27 Feb 1971 Hudson, NH
FLAHIVE, John D and Juanita R PELKEY, 31 Jan 1958 Hudson, NH
FLANAGAN, Josephine and Ralph E HUNNEWELL, 14 Apr 1923 Nashua, NH
FLANAGAN, Karen A and Robert M MANSON, 02 Sep 1978 N Hampton, NH
FLANDERS, Annie L and Edward G MARSHALL, 09 Jun 1923 Hudson, NH
FLANDERS, Douglas W Jr and Catherine HARTT, 15 Apr 1978 Hudson, NH
FLANDERS, Homer W and Olinda L ANDERSON, 08 Jul 1905 Hudson, NH
  Charles A Flanders & Annie Welch
  Charles Anderson
FLANDERS, Jeanne M and Jeffrey B KLEIN, 01 Apr 1967 Hudson, NH
FLANDERS, Katherine and Richard J KASHULINES, 07 Dec 1959 Derry, NH
FLANDERS, Laura Lee and Mark Leo RAVENELLE, 26 Jul 1980 Nashua, NH
FLANDERS, Ronald A and Jeannette NARO, 27 Oct 1956 Hudson, NH
FLANDERS, S A and Francenia DANDELEY, 23 Jul 1877 Hudson, NH
  Daniel Flanders
  W H Dandeley
FLANNERY, John P and Theresa M PANARELLI, 01 Oct 1973 Hudson, NH
FLECHTNER, Charles W and Diane F HARVELL, 03 Dec 1960 Nashua, NH
FLECHTNER, George M and Helen BULPETT, 31 Dec 1942 Hudson, NH
FLEMING, William J and Florence M GILCHRIST, 24 Jul 1933 Hudson, NH
FLEMMING, Alfred P and Sylvia HILLS, 13 Jul 1941 Nashua, NH
FLETCHER, Elijah and Hannah P HASELTON, 05 Dec 1843

HUDSON, NH MARRIAGES

FLETCHER, George W and Alice POWERS, 09 Feb 1924 Nashua, NH
FLETCHER, Gilman and Hannah HILLS, 10 May 1826
FLETCHER, Guy C and Seena M MORIN, 12 May 1928 Nashua, NH
FLETCHER, John P and Electa B GRIFFIN, 25 Oct 1861
FLETCHER, John W and M Addie TAYLOR, 01 Sep 1864
FLETCHER, M Augusta and William JENKINS, 17 Feb 1866
FLETCHER, Marcy and Theodore MERRILL, 13 Nov 1783
FLETCHER, Mary and Theodore MERRILL, 13 Nov 1783
FLETCHER, Roxanne and Gary W ROUILLARD, 11 Aug 1967 Nashua, NH
FLETCHER, Rufus M and Mary A ROGERS, 06 Jun 1864
FLETCHER, Rufus M and Mary A ROGERS, 06 Jun 1867
FLETCHER, Sarah L and Joseph C MILLETT, 25 Oct 1861
FLEURY, Olivette I and Albert W FARLAND, 07 Jun 1947 Nashua, NH
FLEWELLING, David P and Carol A WHITTEMORE, 22 Aug 1964 Hudson, NH
FLEWELLING, Robert G and Judith A KENTRA, 01 Aug 1969 Hudson, NH
FLIGG, Bruce E and Margo E MacCONNELL, 30 Jun 1984 Hudson, NH
FLINN, Albert N and Augusta M ADAMS, 07 Oct 1869 Hudson, NH
FLOOD, Clifford J and Kathleen MILLER, 06 Nov 1982 Hudson, NH
FLORA, Ronald W and Vicki-Lu V LAVOIE, 21 Jul 1973 Hudson, NH
FLORE, John D and Carol A McGOWAN, 07 Aug 1982 Hudson, NH
FLOYD, Abbie A and Charles H MORRISON, 30 Jul 1858
FLOYD, Cheryl A and Robert H SHALLOW, 18 May 1973 Nashua, NH
FLOYD, Roger F and Lucille V POWER, 23 Feb 1985 Hudson, NH
FLUET, George and Clara GAGNON, 09 Jun 1924 Nashua, NH
FLUET, Lorraine M and George J JEANNOTTE, 11 Nov 1965 Nashua, NH
FLUETTE, Raymond M and Cynthia A COLLISHAW, 16 Aug 1980 Hudson, NH
FLYNN, Dorothy M and Frederick HATCH, 26 Apr 1970 Nashua, NH
FLYNN, Edward H and Rachel M PHILBROOK, 09 May 1951 Hudson, NH
FLYNN, John David and Deborah K McLAIN, 15 Aug 1981 Hudson, NH
FLYNN, Robert P and Linda J LANDRY, 18 Jul 1982 Hudson, NH
FODEN, Vincent T Jr and Alicia J CONWAY, 02 Oct 1971 Manchester, NH
FOGG, Brenda Lee and Raymond R GAGNON, 23 Dec 1972 Nashua, NH
FOGG, James H and Judith A MURRAY, 15 Dec 1967 Nashua, NH
FOGG, Philip W Jr and Prudence A WEST, 15 Dec 1967 Nashua, NH
FOGG, Stanley H and Marguerite DUNKLEE, 25 Oct 1957 Hudson, NH
FOGG, Walter S and Annie L SWASEY, 15 Jan 1900 Hudson, NH
   W W Fogg & Susan E Lord
   W B Swasey & Fanny Ayre
FOISIE, Donald R and Rita P BERGERON, 13 Sep 1952 Nashua, NH
FOISIE, Dorothy K and William E HASKELL, 02 Jul 1949 Nashua, NH
FOISY, Jodi J and Richard H HOLT, 05 Jun 1982 Nashua, NH
FOLEY, David A and Kathleen A TREMBLAY, 28 Feb 1970 Nashua, NH
FOLEY, John V and Jill M FEDESHEN, 21 Jun 1985 Hudson, NH
FOLEY, Margaret E and Albert G PROSSER, 08 Jul 1950 Hudson, NH
FOLEY, Paul H and Ruth L LINDSAY, 05 Feb 1949 Hudson, NH
FOLEY, Sharon A and Charles E WORGIOTIS, 26 Nov 1983 Hudson, NH
FOLEY, Thomas J and Ellen J PEARSON, 04 Sep 1939 Manchester, NH
FOLEY, Thomas P and Lisa SEAMAN, 18 Feb 1980 Derry, NH
FOLEY, William F and Doris P CHAMBERLAIN, 23 Oct 1965 Hudson, NH
FOLEY, William G and Gloria J MIELE, 26 Sep 1981 Hudson, NH
FOLGER, Franklin G and Elizabeth NICHOLS, 01 Dec 1934 Hudson, NH
FOLLANSBEE, Bernard L Jr & Elizabeth JOLLY, 06 Dec 1974 Seabrook, NH
FOLLETT, Caroline E and Frederick STEELE, 07 May 1856
FOLLETT, Susan W and James W BUXTON, 24 Nov 1866
FOLTZ, Timothy G and Maureen T RUSH, 04 Nov 1978 Hudson, NH
FONTAIN, John A and Angie M WATSON, 09 Apr 1894 Londonderry, NH
   Joseph Fontain & Loraine Turong (Prov Quebec)
   Richard S Lund(Conway) & Mary G Maxwell (Madison)
FONTAINE, Herbert A and Stacia YARMOLOVICH, 28 Jun 1947 Nashua, NH
FONTAINE, Joanne I and Bruce W KIRKPATRICK, 24 Jul 1970 Nashua, NH

HUDSON, NH MARRIAGES

FONTAINE, Julien J and Theresa S BLOW, 16 Nov 1946 Nashua, NH
FONTAINE, Ronald J and Doris L TESSIER, 17 Sep 1966 Hudson, NH
FOOTE, Debra A and Carl J PROVENCAL, 04 Aug 1984 Manchester, NH
FOOTE, Thomas and Caroline FOSDICK, 20 May 1841 Nashua, NH
FORBES, Donald R Jr&Sandra A ROUTHIER, 23 Apr 1977 Londonderry, NH
FORBES, E E and Ada OGDON, 01 Jul 1876 Hudson, NH
FORBES, Martha B and John P QUIGLEY, 29 Sep 1979 Londonderry, NH
FORBES, Stephanie and Leonard E KINGSLEY, 25 Jul 1981 Nashua, NH
FORCIER, Theresa M and Mark E ST AMAND, 04 Jul 1969 Hudson, NH
FORD, Achsah and Charles E BARRETT, 21 Oct 1871 Hudson, NH
FORD, Alice V and Harold E BREED, 08 Jun 1925 Nashua, NH
FORD, Barbara E and Charles T STEWART, 20 Aug 1983 Hudson, NH
FORD, Barbara W and Philip V KIMBALL, 06 Jun 1936 Hudson, NH
FORD, Bertele E and Helen E CROMPTON, 29 May 1919 Hudson, NH
FORD, Betsey and John Jr POLLARD, 05 Feb 1801
FORD, Bradley H and Mary C HUNNEWELL, 20 Jul 1957 Hudson, NH
FORD, Caleb S and Dorcas GIBSON, 20 Nov 1823
FORD, David C and Mary WILLETT, 31 Mar 1890 Hudson, NH
  Timothy S Ford (W Fairlee, VT) & Sarah G Fuller (Hudson, NH)
  Louis Willett(Quebec, P Q) & Hattie Mashiel (Quebec, P Q)
FORD, David C and Mary Jane CONNELL, 11 Jan 1865
FORD, Diane C and Alfred E SHAPIRO, 15 Sep 1979 Hudson, NH
FORD, Dorothy I and Alberto B HAGGETT, 07 Dec 1943 Nashua, NH
FORD, Eleanor D and Delvin T GREENLEAF, 27 Nov 1970 Claremont, NH
FORD, Elwyn E and Barbara J PETERS, 17 Apr 1942 Hudson, NH
FORD, Jessee L and Harold F GRAY, 05 Jun 1942 Hudson, NH
FORD, John and Elizabeth GLOVER, 07 Nov 1799
FORD, John E and Pauline NICHOLS, 08 Apr 1922 Hudson, NH
FORD, L Jennie and Joseph L RICHARDSON, 09 May 1871
FORD, Lizzie F B and Charles H SLATE, 23 Aug 1882 Hudson, NH
  Timothy S Ford (Hudson, NH) & Sarah G Fuller (Hudson, NH)
  Lyman J Slate(Mass) & Abby B (Candia)
FORD, Mabel I and Wilfred COWGILL, 21 Feb 1929 Hudson, NH
FORD, Mehittabel and Jeremiah VARNUM, 05 Mar 1822
FORD, Moses B and Lizzie PELKEY, 16 Oct 1888 Hudson, NH
  Timothy S Ford (W Fairlee, VT) & Sarah G Fuller (Hudson, NH)
  Herbert Pelkey(Houlton, ME) & Virginia Mashiel (Madawaskee, ME)
FORD, Moses B and Ella L DEMMING, 12 Sep 1877 Cornish, NH
  Timothy S Ford (Hudson, NH) & Sarah Fuller (Hudson, NH)
  D P Demming(West Fairlee)
FORD, Nellie G and Amedee J RECORD, 24 Jun 1920 Nashua, NH
FORD, Robert and Jemima MARSHALL, 11 Jul 1809
FORD, Ronald E and Willhelmen ROBILLARD, 05 Feb 1972 Nashua, NH
FORD, Ruth E and Charles I CARLE, 08 Dec 1969 Nashua, NH
FORD, Sarah and Joseph JOHNSON, 04 Mar 1784
FORD, Sarah E and Daniel W HAMBLETT, 17 Apr 1869
FORD, Susan F and Philip A CHOUINARD, 14 May 1977 Hudson, NH
FORD, Susanna and Charles PERHAM, 07 May 1811
FORD, Thomas J and Dora A COOK, 24 Oct 1907 Nashua, NH
  Timothy S Ford & Sarah Fuller
  Frank S Avery & Adeline Wood
FORD, Timothy and Mehitable ROWELL, 27 Dec 1796
FORDHAM, Juliann and Donald NEWMAN, 03 Apr 1982 Hudson, NH
FORENCE, Eva M and Joseph E FARLAND, 02 Dec 1950 Nashua, NH
FOREST, Diane S and Lawrence J CLAVEAU, 21 Apr 1973 Hudson, NH
FOREST, Jean M and Carl R EDWARDS, 09 Feb 1968 Hudson, NH
FORGET, Alice and Raymond C THERIAULT, 14 Oct 1936 Nashua, NH
FORKEY, Steven A and Sheryl A McKINNON, 01 Jul 1983 Hudson, NH
FORRENCE, Anna A and Clifford G ARMSTRONG, 25 Feb 1941 Nashua, NH
FORRENCE, Carolyn E and Leo W LAMBERT, 08 Oct 1977 Hudson, NH

HUDSON, NH MARRIAGES

FORRENCE, Charles E and Rita BOUCHER, 14 Jun 1941 Nashua, NH
FORRENCE, Drusilla M and Harry C Jr PETERS, 29 Aug 1969 Nashua, NH
FORRENCE, Earl and Loretta LEVESQUE, 20 Aug 1938 Nashua, NH
FORRENCE, Florence E and Ronald L STICKNEY, 22 Sep 1984 Hudson, NH
FORRENCE, George A Jr and Lillian PALMER, 14 Feb 1931 Dunstable, MA
FORRENCE, James R and Lori Ann KELLY, 09 Apr 1983 Hudson, NH
FORRENCE, Jess P and Susan M DANIELS, 05 Jun 1976 Nashua, NH
FORRENCE, John A and Ruth L KENYON, 16 May 1954 Hudson, NH
FORRENCE, Joyce A and John G WILCOX, 19 Sep 1976 Hudson, NH
FORRENCE, Lillian S and Henri R SENNEVILLE, 23 Nov 1957 Hudson, NH
FORRENCE, Patricia A and Raymond L DOUCETTE, 04 Aug 1970 Nashua, NH
FORRENCE, Ruth L and Norman J SERVANT, 15 Nov 1974 Nashua, NH
FORRENCE, Wayne A and Laurie A TOWER, 01 Oct 1983 Nashua, NH
FORSAITH, James S and Linda M GLADKI, 05 Apr 1981 Wilmot Flat, NH
FORSAITH, Jon A and Patricia L HILL, 27 Nov 1982 Hudson, NH
FORSMAN, Martha L and Wilfred N BOURGAULT, 08 Feb 1946 Nashua, NH
FORSMAN, Rose-Mari and Robert Jr WADLEGGER, 25 Oct 1969 Keene, NH
FORTIER, Anne C and Richard M LACROIX, 01 Jun 1985 Hudson, NH
FORTIER, David H and Gail M GOULD, 07 Mar 1972 Merrimack, NH
FORTIER, Lillian M and Raymond E AUSTIN, 11 Sep 1948 Hudson, NH
FORTIER, Linda A and Stephen F Jr STOFANAK, 01 Aug 1981 Hudson, NH
FORTIER, Maurice D and Mary F CORDESCO, 17 Nov 1946 Hudson, NH
FORTIER, Pauline E and Richard P LONES, 04 Jun 1955 Nashua, NH
FORTIER, Richard D and Mary G PETRONI, 16 Oct 1982 Nashua, NH
FORTIER, Robert E Jr and Lisa M SILVERIA, 18 May 1985 Manchester,NH
FORTIER, Sandra M and Allen D GELINAS, 25 Feb 1984 Hudson, NH
FORTIER, Walter F and Martha BURNHAM, 02 Apr 1949 Epping, NH
FORTIN, Alice and Euclide GAUDETTE, 06 Sep 1920 Nashua, NH
FORTIN, Ronald Rog and Maureen Ka PHILLIPS, 19 Jul 1980 Nashua, NH
FORTIN, Ruth E and Waldo E JOHNSON, 20 Oct 1962 Derry, NH
FORTNAM, Janice L and Michael R BOWMAN, 10 Nov 1984 Nashua, NH
FORTUNE, Mary Ann and Arnold C DEXTER, 22 Jun 1957 Hudson, NH
FOSDICK, Caroline and Thomas FOOTE, 20 May 1841 Nashua, NH
FOSDICK, Caroline and Thomas KOPKA, 20 May 1841
FOSS, Ellen A and James S BUNKER, 29 Nov 1879 Hudson, NH
  Alonzo H Foss (Rochester, NH) & Rebecca (Rochester, NH)
  Levi H Bunker(Moultonboro, NH) & Harriet T (Andover, NH)
FOSS, George W and Olive H JOHNSON, 03 Jul 1937 Nashua, NH
FOSTER, Abigail and Samuel SMITH, 01 Apr 1824
FOSTER, Charles E and Marie E LAVOIE, 23 Mar 1957 Hudson, NH
FOSTER, Donald J and Phyllis M REYNOLDS, 01 Nov 1961 Nashua, NH
FOSTER, Donnette C and Winfred V MANSFIELD, 05 Dec 1949 Chester, NH
FOSTER, Dorothy M and George E LONG, 13 Jul 1947 Hudson, NH
FOSTER, Erma E and Larry D PETERS, 08 Jan 1958 Hudson, NH
FOSTER, Forest D and Doris I BRIAND, 12 Jul 1952 Hudson, NH
FOSTER, Harriet J and John F GOSS, 20 Dec 1842
FOSTER, Karina and Norman E BOLSTER, 21 Sep 1936 Hudson, NH
FOSTER, Laurent R and Geraldine MILLER, 03 Mar 1956 Nashua, NH
FOSTER, Mable L and Victor H SMITH, 29 Aug 1917 Claremont, NH
FOSTER, Mehitable and Sargent PERHAM, 29 Jan 1824
FOSTER, Mehittabel and Sargent PERHAM, 29 Jan 1824
FOSTER, Moody and Hannah PAGE, 17 Mar 1830
FOSTER, Ralph N and Barbara A LILLEY, 11 Nov 1956 Hudson, NH
FOSTER, Sherwood L and Victoria SIMPSON, 28 Aug 1920 Nashua, NH
FOSTER, Shirley A and Howard F IVES, 26 Aug 1950 Hudson, NH
FOSTER, Sophia C and William H WEBSTER, 09 Jun 1859
FOUNDAS, Constine and Euphemia PANAGOULIS, 02 Dec 1934 Nashua, NH
FOURNIER, Arthur and Georgianna BLOW, 23 Apr 1938 Nashua, NH
FOURNIER, Donald J and Anita H HENDRICKSON, 13 Sep 1969 Nashua, NH
FOURNIER, Edwin L & Maryanne F MALOUIN, 03 May 1985 Manchester, NH

HUDSON, NH MARRIAGES

FOURNIER, Francis H and Carmela M MOFFA, 15 Jun 1946 Hudson, NH
FOURNIER, Jane M and Allan L TWITCHELL, 30 Dec 1972 Nashua, NH
FOURNIER, Keith R and Joanna R PEPAU, 10 Sep 1983 Northumberland
FOURNIER, Mitchell R and Theresa E TAYLOR, 26 May 1984 Hudson, NH
FOURNIER, Pamela J and Philip S NICHOLS, 14 Nov 1981 Hudson, NH
FOURNIER, Patricia G and Arthur C FRANZ, 21 Jul 1984 Hudson, NH
FOURNIER, Rachel T and John C GUILL, 15 Oct 1983 Hudson, NH
FOURNIER, Robert H and Donna M BRACCIO, 13 May 1967 Hudson, NH
FOURNIER, Ronald R and Sandra L GALIPEAU, 21 Jun 1975 Hudson, NH
FOURNIER, Ronald R and Sandra M SMART, 04 Apr 1980 Hudson, NH
FOWLE, Alan A and Linda A JOHNSON, 27 Oct 1984 Greenland, NH
FOWLE, Ruth A and William S CRAIGEN, 08 Oct 1949 Hudson, NH
FOWLER, Carol A and Richard A HOWE, 29 Jun 1974 Nashua, NH
FOWLER, Leighton C and Eva R INSLEY, 22 Jan 1910 Hudson, NH
   Edward Fowler & Catherine Harris
   Caleb T Insley & Annie M Thompson
FOWLES, Jackson G & Catherine VAILLANCOURT, 19 May 1979 Hudson, NH
FOX, Anna M and Frank D ORDWAY, 01 Oct 1861
FOX, Irving J and Annie I SMITH, 16 Nov 1898 Manchester, NH
   Calvin C Fox & Emme N French
   Andrew J Smith & Abby A Davis
FOX, Leighton D and Barbara L SMALL, 11 Jul 1963 Hudson, NH
FOX, Martha E and Richard P WHITNEY, 19 Oct 1973 Merrimack, NH
FOX, Sarah J and George D JAQUITH, 12 Nov 1866
FRANCIONE, A Susan and Francis S PIPER, 03 Mar 1950 Hudson, NH
FRANCIS, Vernon E and Beverly J SAWYER, 11 Jul 1981 Hudson, NH
FRANCO, Delores Ann and Robert John McWHA, 27 Feb 1981 Nashua, NH
FRANCOEUR, Constance and Leonard J POIRIER, 26 Jun 1971 Nashua, NH
FRANCOEUR, Gary R and Beatrice F KOESTER, 22 Oct 1983 Hudson, NH
FRANCOEUR, Leo D and Diane M SOUCY, 14 Feb 1982 Hudson, NH
FRANCOEUR, Lynn Ann and Michael J GRAINGER, 08 Oct 1977 Hudson, NH
FRANCOEUR, Robert H and Carol A GAGNON, 05 Oct 1968 Hudson, NH
FRANCOEUR, Robert H and Eva Anne RICKER, 12 Aug 1972 Pittsburgh, NH
FRANCOEUR, Robert W and Rachel A BOUCHER, 22 Sep 1951 Hudson, NH
FRANCOEUR, Roger L and Karen L CLARKE, 22 Oct 1977 Hudson, NH
FRANK, Patricia A and Donald E HURD, 07 Apr 1962 Nashua, NH
FRANKLIN, Frances E and Leonard K LEACH, 15 Oct 1955 Hudson, NH
FRANKLIN, Jesse W and Thelma T TUBINIS, 29 Jun 1940 Nashua, NH
FRANZ, Arthur C and Patricia G FOURNIER, 21 Jul 1984 Hudson, NH
FRANZEN, Ingrid E and Leonard R BURTON, 03 Jun 1961 Nashua, NH
FRANZEN, Virginia L and Philip S HARWOOD, 23 Sep 1933 Hudson, NH
FRAPPIER, Peter J and Charlene M GAUTHIER, 07 May 1978 Hudson, NH
FRAPPIER, Peter J and Barbara A COOLEY, 29 May 1982 Litchfield, NH
FRASER, Alan J and Ramona L HARNEY, 24 Nov 1979 Hudson, NH
FRASER, Ann M and Richard R DIXON, 11 Oct 1980 Hudson, NH
FRASER, Brian H and Deborah A JOHNSON, 31 Jan 1976 Hudson, NH
FRASER, Deborah M and Roger R CLOUTIER, 07 May 1977 Hudson, NH
FRASER, Fred Daniel and Jo-Ann SMITH, 08 Jul 1978 Goffstown, NH
FRASER, Henry A and Gloria T GAUDETTE, 10 May 1952 Nashua, NH
FRASER, Kelly R and Jody L ILLG, 11 Oct 1980 Hudson, NH
FRASER, Marguerite and Maurice T LAVALLEE, 11 May 1957 Nashua, NH
FRASER, Mark R and Sheila M IRWIN, 05 May 1984 Hudson, NH
FRASER, Peter E and Susan M KLIMAS, 28 Aug 1976 Hudson, NH
FRASER, Renie J and Ruth I VENNE, 25 Jun 1955 Hudson, NH
FRASER, Royal A and Fernanade COVEY, 30 Jun 1956 Hudson, NH
FRAWLEY, John P and Georgia KESMETIS, 30 Jun 1957 Nashua, NH
FRAZA, Alice M and Robert J ANGLUIN, 22 Jun 1957 Hudson, NH
FRAZER, Charles E and Etta A MALONEY, 03 Jul 1920 Hudson, NH
FRECHETTE, Etta and T SUCLEANTOPOLOS, 06 Jul 1940 Hudson, NH
FRECHETTE, George R and Anita C DUMAIS, 21 Jul 1972 Hudson, NH

HUDSON, NH MARRIAGES

FREDERICK, Barry L and Carol A JOHNSON, 28 Aug 1982 Hudson, NH
FREDETTE, Claude E and Shirley A MARTIN, 12 May 1967 Hudson, NH
FREDETTE, Debra A & Ernest R Jr GAGNON, 17 Aug 1974 Londonderry, NH
FREDETTE, Shirley A and Harvey O JODOIN, 27 Oct 1972 Hudson, NH
FREEDMAN, Herbert D and Ruth L SULKIN, 21 Nov 1937 Hudson, NH
FREEDMAN, Nathan I and Diana B COHEN, 20 Jun 1935 Hudson, NH
FREEMAN, Charles W and Joan L POTTER, 08 May 1972 Nashua, NH
FREEMAN, John F and Maraget E SNOW, 19 Dec 1936 Nashua, NH
FREEMAN, Linda M and Charles BLAIS, 13 Oct 1984 Nashua, NH
FREEMAN, Lloyd A and Jacqueline BURELLE, 04 Aug 1973 Hudson, NH
FREEMAN, Raymond L Jr and Sara S DURWIN, 29 May 1971 Hudson, NH
FREEMAN, William H and Gertrude COSTELLO, 16 Aug 1934 Hudson, NH
FREILICH, John D and Pamela M GAUDETTE, 02 Aug 1980 Hudson, NH
FRENCH, Alan D and Christine MARIREA, 13 May 1983 Nashua, NH
FRENCH, Alice B and Arthur S WESTNEAT, 06 Jul 1920 Hudson, NH
FRENCH, Alice Evelyn & Harry William BROWN, 17 Mar 1928 Hudson, NH
FRENCH, Blanche M and Clarence E CAHOON, 14 Oct 1928 Nashua, NH
FRENCH, Cornelia E and Clarence B WADLEIGH, 20 Jun 1922 Hudson, NH
FRENCH, Deborah A and Curtis R SMITH, 23 Oct 1971 Nashua, NH
FRENCH, Edward P and Servia P KITTREDGE, 11 Oct 1954
FRENCH, Gordon L and Elizabeth HAUG, 01 May 1948 Nashua, NH
FRENCH, Joseph Q and Harriet S SMITH, 17 Feb 1842
FRENCH, Lucius P and Amanda KENDALL, 18 Feb 1871 Hudson, NH
FRENCH, Marjorie and Frank J BRAUNFELD, 09 Nov 1940 Hudson, NH
FRENCH, Mary and Joseph Jr WINN, 05 May 1757
FRENCH, Mary K and Frederick HATCH, 21 Jul 1972 Merrimack, NH
FRENCH, Maurice R and Theodora P PUCKETT, 31 May 1947 Nashua, NH
FRENCH, Patricia P and Avard D ROGERS, 12 Jul 1958 Hudson, NH
FRENCH, Robert E and Juliette DESROSIERS, 30 Aug 1974 Hollis, NH
FRENCH, Sampson and Mary CLEM, 18 Oct 1739
FRENCH, Samson and Mary CHASE, 18 Oct 1739
FRENCH, Susan B and Ronald A VIENS, 07 Sep 1974 Nashua, NH
FRENETTE, Eugene J and Rita T NADEAU, 14 Feb 1947 Nashua, NH
FRENETTE, Jean T and Gary A CHRISTIANSEN, 21 Sep 1968 Hudson, NH
FRENETTE, John L and Kathleen M BELANGER, 27 Jun 1981 Hudson, NH
FRENETTE, Robert W and Gertrude CASTONGUAY, 07 Apr 1945 Nashua, NH
FRENETTE, Roger A and Peggy L VIGNOLA, 15 Jun 1959 Hudson, NH
FRENETTE, Rosemary E and Earl J DUBOIS, 09 Feb 1968 Hudson, NH
FRENETTE, Violet L and Lucien R DUMAIS, 03 Apr 1948 Nashua, NH
FRENNETTE, Eva and Walter F DUCHARME, 17 Nov 1927 Bristol, NH
FRIEL, Philip J III and Ellen C ZAHOS, 25 Oct 1980 Nashua, NH
FRIES, Peter C and Florence M RAPOZA, 11 Dec 1948 Hudson, NH
FRIETSCH, Thomas J and Marie E BONESKI, 17 Jan 1948 Hudson, NH
FRIZELLE, Anne M and Willis A BOLIVER, 14 Dec 1946 Hudson, NH
FROIO, Concetta and John H IODICE, 13 Mar 1937 Nashua, NH
FROMENT, Robert N and Judith A CONE, 26 Jun 1981 Hudson, NH
FROST, Anna F and Aaron P ESTEY, 23 Mar 1897 Hudson, NH
   Samuel J Frost & Caroline Pingree
   Edward P Estey & Lydia C Hemphill
FROST, Benjamin and Miriam RUSS, 21 Nov 1743
FROST, Benjamin and Miriam RUSS, 21 Dec 1743
FROST, Charlene R and Daniel R MACK, 02 Jun 1984 Nashua, NH
FROST, Charlotte and George TAYLOR, 08 May 1859
FROST, Jacqueline and Raymond L BERNIER, 25 Aug 1958 Hudson, NH
FROST, James C and Suzanne M LEVESQUE, 06 Jan 1973 Hudson, NH
FROST, Patricia M and Victor J GROHOSKY, 22 Apr 1967 Hudson, NH
FROST, Richard H and Lillian V DEMANCHE, 17 Aug 1980 Hudson, NH
FROST, Sarah L and William HUNT, 23 Jan 1858
FROTTON, Jessie E and Walter PALLEMANS, 12 Oct 1925 Tilton, NH
FRUCI, Richard L Jr & Pamela L CARPENTIERE, 01 Jun 1985 Concord, NH

HUDSON,NH MARRIAGES

FRYE, Ethlyn M and Edward I RITSON, 21 Oct 1961 Pittsfield, NH
FRYE, Grace E and Harold A DAVIDSON, 07 Jul 1940 Hudson, NH
FRYE, Impi I and Alfred J PERANI, 09 Oct 1949 Hudson, NH
FRYE, Scott G and Judith E COSTA, 07 Jul 1984 Hudson, NH
FRYKBERG, Aile C and Robert E BRANEY, 11 Nov 1948 Hudson, NH
FU, Linda H M and Fred M WOLFENBERGER, 29 Dec 1971 Hudson, NH
FUCCI, Anthony E and Jane E SOUCY, 24 Jun 1972 Hudson, NH
FULLER, Albert A and Mary C FULLER, 18 Oct 1882 Peabody, MA
  Joseph Fuller (Hudson, NH) & Belinda Steele (Hudson, NH)
  Joseph Fuller(Hudson, NH) & Mary Glass
FULLER, Arthur E and Helen J RUSSELL, 30 Aug 1931 Milford, NH
FULLER, Arthur E and Blanche F CLEMENTS, 24 Jun 1939 Nashua, NH
FULLER, Barbara A & Armand J Jr DESLAURIER, 11 Apr 1959 Hudson, NH
FULLER, Beatrice N and Arthur H SHEPHERD, 10 Sep 1934 Hudson, NH
FULLER, Carol J and Richard R LEVESQUE, 13 Oct 1961 Hudson, NH
FULLER, Charles H and Mary M SANBORN, 09 Oct 1877 Hudson, NH
  Joseph Fuller (Hudson, NH) & Balinda Steele (Hudson, NH)
  James Sanborn
FULLER, Clementine and Sidney P GOWING, 21 Jun 1881 Nashua, NH
  Rodney Fuller (Hudson, NH) & Martha Farwell (Westford, MA)
  Samuel Gowing(Hudson, NH) & Sarah Penham (Tyngsboro, MA)
FULLER, Dennis W and Claire L DUQUETTE, 09 May 1970 Hudson, NH
FULLER, Donald M and Faye A McLAUGHLIN, 23 Jun 1969 Hudson, NH
FULLER, Frederick and Sharen J BURGESS, 27 Jun 1970 Hudson, NH
FULLER, George B and Helen A KELSO, 14 Feb 1877 Hudson, NH
FULLER, Georgia and Donald J BRUSSARD, 15 Sep 1984 Nashua, NH
FULLER, Gordon A and Nancy V GRACE, 28 Jun 1958 Hudson, NH
FULLER, Ida Alice and James Angus PHILLIPS, 25 Aug 1924 Hudson, NH
FULLER, James R and Lillian E GARNETT, 15 Jan 1949 Hudson, NH
FULLER, Joseph and Melissa W MOON, 18 Dec 1894 Hudson, NH
  Daniel Fuller & Ruth Goodale
FULLER, Joseph and Belinda STEELE, 23 Dec 1841
FULLER, Joseph W and Margaret M MOONEY, 20 Jul 1957 Manchester, NH
FULLER, Lizzie F and Fred C BLODGETT, 30 Nov 1898 Hudson, NH
  Willis L Fuller & Adelia C Yettaw
  Aug F Blodgett & Lucy Ellen Chaw
FULLER, Lucy P and George W DAVIS, 13 Apr 1904 Nashua, NH
  Nehemiah Fuller & Maria Fuller
  George H Davis & A E Batchelder
FULLER, Martha J and Luther READ, 23 Mar 1865
FULLER, Martha J and Luther REED, 03 Mar 1865
FULLER, Mary C and Albert A FULLER, 18 Oct 1882 Peabody, MA
  Joseph Fuller (Hudson, NH) & Mary Glass
  Joseph Fuller(Hudson, NH) & Belinda Steele (Hudson, NH)
FULLER, Michael and Virginia C KEANE, 13 Aug 1983 Hudson, NH
FULLER, Nancy J and Henry G HUTCHINS, 22 Jan 1868
FULLER, Patricia M and Edgar A Jr GAGNON, 07 Aug 1971 Hudson, NH
FULLER, Roger J and Elaine M ANCTIL, 08 May 1971 Nashua, NH
FULLER, Ruth G and Ralph G SOMES, 20 Feb 1964 Hudson, NH
FULLER, Susan J and Joseph T FURBER, 16 Oct 1976 Hudson, NH
FULLER, Tamblyn L and Andrew GOSLING, 09 Feb 1985 Warner, NH
FULLER, Walter W and Annette LECLERE, 25 Aug 1930 Nashua, NH
FULLER, William E and June A KING, 20 Jul 1940 Hudson, NH
FULLER, Willis L and Adelia YETTAW, 19 Jan 1876 Hudson, NH
FURBER, Joseph T and Susan J FULLER, 16 Oct 1976 Hudson, NH
FURMAN, Neal M and Mary F JUTRAS, 20 Sep 1980 Hudson, NH
GABRIEL, Edgar H and Elsie E BIRD, 19 Nov 1941 Epping, NH
GABRIEL, Lawrence and Veronica BOSKA, 03 Sep 1938 Nashua, NH
GADILAUSKAS, Donald P P and Barbara L ARRIS, 26 Aug 1982 Nashua, NH
GADOWRY, Jeanette and Alexander PERIGNY, 25 Jul 1941 Salem, NH

HUDSON, NH MARRIAGES

GAFFNEY, Anne R and Paul N COTE, 05 Dec 1961 Hudson, NH
GAFFNEY, Jeannie K and John GUGLIELMI, 12 Feb 1949 Hudson, NH
GAFFNEY, Thomas P Jr and Linda M DESJARDINS, 11 Jun 1971 Nashua, NH
GAFFORD, Vincent D and Florence M WORTH, 16 Feb 1952 Hudson, NH
GAGE, Abel and Anna M JOHNSON, 06 Dec 1826
GAGE, Daniel and Marietta L MARSH, 07 Dec 1865
GAGE, Frye and Sarah TENNEY, 24 Oct 1816
GAGE, George G and Theresa E PEASE, 13 Dec 1864
GAGE, Sheila A and Robert E LAFLAMME, 22 Oct 1958 Manchester, NH
GAGNE, Antoine and Laurette RIVARD, 09 Nov 1925 Nashua, NH
GAGNE, Blanche H and Allen P NICKERSON, 05 Feb 1936 Hudson, NH
GAGNE, Clarina and Edward J DURAND, 07 Jul 1950 Hudson, NH
GAGNE, Gloria G and Joseph K BURKE, 15 Apr 1950 Hudson, NH
GAGNE, Henry J and Marguerite JETTE, 02 Mar 1946 Nashua, NH
GAGNE, Ovide J and Eva B KASHULINES, 30 May 1941 Nashua, NH
GAGNE, Raymond R and Leda M GUERETTE, 12 Apr 1947 Nashua, NH
GAGNE, Robert J and Norma F GREENLEAF, 28 Dec 1946 Nashua, NH
GAGNE, Stephen R and Patricia A POTTER, 10 Aug 1980 Hudson, NH
GAGNE, Theresa J and Seward BLOW, 10 Aug 1940 Nashua, NH
GAGNON, Adrian D and Rachel LORRAINE, 28 Nov 1935 Nashua, NH
GAGNON, Alexander and Betty M HAYES, 08 Feb 1960 Hudson, NH
GAGNON, Allen L and Mary Jane GLINES, 21 Sep 1968 Nashua, NH
GAGNON, Arlene T and Donald C MacINTYRE, 01 May 1954 Hudson, NH
GAGNON, Arthur J and Isabel M MORRILL, 27 Feb 1933 Nashua, NH
GAGNON, Arthur M and Nancy M PLANTE, 04 Feb 1961 Nashua, NH
GAGNON, Audrey J and Patrick W GODIN, 07 Jul 1973 Hudson, NH
GAGNON, Barbara A and Thomas O PELKEY, 05 Sep 1959 Hudson, NH
GAGNON, Bertha G and Harold W CAMPBELL, 17 Sep 1934 Brattleboro, VT
GAGNON, Brenda R and Albert O CHAREST, 28 Dec 1963 Hudson, NH
GAGNON, Carmelle L and William A ELLIOTT, 27 Oct 1979 Nashua, NH
GAGNON, Carol A and Robert H FRANCOEUR, 05 Oct 1968 Hudson, NH
GAGNON, Carol J and Richard D RAYMOND, 18 Apr 1964 Hudson, NH
GAGNON, Cheryl A and Paul A Jr MARTIN, 07 Jan 1972 Nashua, NH
GAGNON, Christine and Keith M BEAULIEU, 07 Jun 1985 Nashua, NH
GAGNON, Christine and Richard H DUNCKLEE, 30 Jun 1956 Windham, NH
GAGNON, Claire G and Gregory M AHEARN, 18 Sep 1971 Nashua, NH
GAGNON, Clara and George FLUET, 09 Jun 1924 Nashua, NH
GAGNON, Diane L and James A MACK, 15 Oct 1977 Hudson, NH
GAGNON, Diane M and Rene P JOYAL, 15 Oct 1977 Hudson, NH
GAGNON, Donald E and Frances E HAMILTON, 20 Jan 1932 Hudson, NH
GAGNON, Donna R and Carl J PROVENCAL, 14 Aug 1971 Nashua, NH
GAGNON, Doris V and Harry M CUSSON, 14 Mar 1947 Hudson, NH
GAGNON, Edgar A Jr and Patricia M FULLER, 07 Aug 1971 Hudson, NH
GAGNON, Eldene M and Richard F CROSBY, 21 Dec 1963 Nashua, NH
GAGNON, Emile and Doris V KINVILLE, 22 Apr 1944 Nashua, NH
GAGNON, Emma E and William H STEVENS, 21 May 1955 Hudson, NH
GAGNON, Ernest R Jr & Debra A FREDETTE, 17 Aug 1974 Londonderry, NH
GAGNON, Eva R and John P SUZEDELYS, 12 Jun 1948 Nashua, NH
GAGNON, Geraldine & James F LONGFELLOW, 04 Feb 1972 Moultonboro, NH
GAGNON, Gerard L and Adrie L WHITING, 30 Jun 1956 Nashua, NH
GAGNON, Gertrude R and David H ALLEY, 11 Aug 1973 Hudson, NH
GAGNON, Gloria T and Edward H TRIPPLETON, 04 Jul 1973 Nashua, NH
GAGNON, Henry L and Theresa A BERNARD, 24 Nov 1945 Nashua, NH
GAGNON, Jamie L and David J PLUMLEY, 09 Jan 1983 Hudson, NH
GAGNON, Jay P and Eileen T DONOVAN, 31 Jul 1982 Hudson, NH
GAGNON, Jean R and Gerald BOUCHER, 25 Oct 1952 Nashua, NH
GAGNON, John A S and Tammy F LACASSE, 25 Apr 1981 Nashua, NH
GAGNON, Joseph C and Heidi V KENNA, 11 Oct 1980 Hudson, NH
GAGNON, Judith A and Thomas W McNEIL, 15 Jan 1971 Nashua, NH
GAGNON, Leo J Jr and Lorraine G VIENS, 21 May 1966 Hudson, NH

HUDSON, NH MARRIAGES

GAGNON, Leo J Jr and Maureen An MURPHY, 02 Jun 1973 Merrimack, NH
GAGNON, Leo M and Doris C BUZZELL, 12 Oct 1943 Nashua, NH
GAGNON, Linda M and Bruce A COLBURN, 19 Oct 1963 Hudson, NH
GAGNON, Lorette and Robert L NICHOLS, 26 Oct 1946 Nashua, NH
GAGNON, Lorette A and Raymond E DUQUETTE, 04 Nov 1942 Nashua, NH
GAGNON, Louis E and Imelda CLAVEAU, 18 Oct 1920 Nashua, NH
GAGNON, Maria T and James E RILEY, 23 Sep 1972 Nashua, NH
GAGNON, Mark T and Doreen A LANDRY, 30 Apr 1983 Hudson, NH
GAGNON, Mary Delima V & Napoleon L PELLETIER, 02 Feb 1920 Nashua, NH
GAGNON, Michelle C and Albert A BURTON, 28 Aug 1981 Hudson, NH
GAGNON, Nancy L and Joseph F Jr CONRAD, 17 Jun 1967 Hudson, NH
GAGNON, Norma J and Edward P NIQUETTE, 03 Jun 1978 Nashua, NH
GAGNON, Patricia A and Mario A JEANNOTTE, 12 Nov 1966 Nashua, NH
GAGNON, Pauline D and Donald L Jr WHITE, 16 Feb 1979 Hudson, NH
GAGNON, Raymond H and Doris G COWLES, 19 Jul 1941 Hudson, NH
GAGNON, Raymond R and Brenda Lee FOGG, 23 Dec 1972 Nashua, NH
GAGNON, Raymond R Jr and Denise G BISHOP, 15 Jul 1967 Hudson, NH
GAGNON, Richard A and Jeannette BROWN, 10 Oct 1981 Hudson, NH
GAGNON, Richard F and Claire D LAGACE, 08 Oct 1960 Hudson, NH
GAGNON, Richard G and Deborah R DALESSIO, 24 Nov 1973 Hudson, NH
GAGNON, Richard G and Beverly D MacPHEE, 22 Oct 1983 Hudson, NH
GAGNON, Richard R and Margaret M SULLIVAN, 28 Aug 1971 Hudson, NH
GAGNON, Rita L and Richard L TOUSSAINT, 08 Feb 1947 Nashua, NH
GAGNON, Robert P and Kathryn A REITAN, 24 Sep 1983 Hudson, NH
GAGNON, Roland T and Beverly A DALTON, 29 Sep 1956 Nashua, NH
GAGNON, Ronald F and Donna M REITAN, 06 May 1978 Hudson, NH
GAGNON, Rose A and C H BOURDON, 09 Oct 1916 Nashua, NH
  Louis Gagnon (Canada) & Sesari Fournier (Canada)
  Adolph Bourdon(Canada) & Zoe Demerse (Canada)
GAGNON, Ruby E and John M CHAPLICK, 06 Feb 1950 Hudson, NH
GAGNON, Sandra G and Richard Al JOYCE, 10 Oct 1980 Nashua, NH
GAGNON, Sharon A and Donald P LAVOIE, 19 Jan 1980 Nashua, NH
GAGNON, Stephen L and Florina S SHERMAN, 07 Aug 1954 Hudson, NH
GAGNON, Susan and David J LOUGEE, 20 Jun 1969 Hudson, NH
GAGNON, Theresa H and Paul J A LEVESQUE, 26 May 1973 Hudson, NH
GAGNON, Theresa M and Steven P MAHONEY, 15 Feb 1980 Nashua, NH
GAGNON, Victor A and Rita M R OSMER, 03 Jan 1944 Hudson, NH
GAGNON, Victor L and Anita Y NARO, 31 Aug 1946 Nashua, NH
GAGUE, Leah and Euserbe TEBERAGE, 17 Jul 1915 Nashua, NH
  Jules Gague (Canada) & Berube (Canada)
  Peter Teberage(Canada) & Julia Alair (Canada)
GALE, Barbara E and Michael KIENIA, 15 Nov 1963 Salem, NH
GALE, Lucille E and Herbert E McCARTHY, 18 Jul 1964 Salem, NH
GALECKI, Stacia and Adolph A SADAUSKAS, 03 May 1947 Nashua, NH
GALECKI, Stanley and Wladyslowa SZOT, 17 Jan 1942 Manchester, NH
GALESKY, Joseph and Anna WYSKIEL, 28 Jun 1930 Manchester, NH
GALIPEAU, Alice G and Joseph J JANKAUSKAS, 26 Jun 1954 Hudson, NH
GALIPEAU, Jean R and Richard A TAYLOR, 18 Sep 1981 Hudson, NH
GALIPEAU, Jennice M & Philip M Jr KULINGOSKI, 16 Oct 1976 Nashua, NH
GALIPEAU, Nola and Victor NOLETTE, 27 Jul 1940 Nashua, NH
GALIPEAU, Paul R and Theresa G GAMACHE, 02 Jan 1954 Hudson, NH
GALIPEAU, Paula A and Sylvain J GELE, 19 Nov 1983 Litchfield, NH
GALIPEAU, Peter J and Mary T ZOLKOS, 22 Mar 1969 Pelham, NH
GALIPEAU, Peter J and Catherine GAMBLE, 28 Jun 1975 Salem, NH
GALIPEAU, Sandra L and Ronald R FOURNIER, 21 Jun 1975 Hudson, NH
GALIPEAU, Sandra L and Robert A LAJOIE, 06 Sep 1980 Hudson, NH
GALIPEAU, Theresa G and Charles R MALONE, 27 Oct 1972 Nashua, NH
GALIPEAU, Thomas P and Lorraine M AREL, 06 Jan 1978 Hudson, NH
GALIPEAULT, Jeannette and Franklin R TORREY, 27 Nov 1952 Nashua, NH
GALLAGHER, Edna M and Dexter S HOLT, 29 May 1937 Fitchburg, MA

HUDSON,NH MARRIAGES

GALLAGHER, James T Jr and Marie E DUGAN, 30 Jun 1971 Nashua, NH
GALLAGHER, Janet R and Gerard L ROY, 01 Oct 1955 Hudson, NH
GALLAGHER, John T and Marion Nas WHITHAM, 23 Jun 1934 Nashua, NH
GALLAGHER, Jos P and Annie O'BRIEN, 30 Nov 1910 Hudson, NH
  Jos A Gallagher & Margaret Brodie
  John O'Brien & Margaret Tannerhill
GALLAGHER, Margaret I and Hubert G CHAPMAN, 30 May 1927 Nashua, NH
GALLAGHER, Mary E and George A CARLSON, 03 Jan 1949 Nashua, NH
GALLAGHER, Robert D and Patricia J BRADLEY, 08 Apr 1967 Hudson, NH
GALLAGHER, Sally J R and Raymond DREVOJAN, 01 Feb 1971 Nashua, NH
GALLANT, Doreen M and Raymond P BRIAND, 11 Jun 1970 Hudson, NH
GALLANT, Janet A and Jeffrey A EATON, 21 Aug 1981 Hudson, NH
GALLANT, Jean Claude and Rena Ann KIMBALL, 31 Aug 1973 Hudson, NH
GALLANT, Pamela A and John F WANDERS, 07 Jun 1975 Hudson, NH
GALLOW, Pauline I and Ronald J CARON, 17 Jan 1975 Hudson, NH
GALLOWAY, George J and Shirley A BREWER, 28 Apr 1965 Nashua, NH
GALUSHA, Wayne F and Erin C DAVIDSON, 29 Aug 1981 Hudson, NH
GALVIN, Alva and Patricia TAFFE, 18 Apr 1941 Hudson, NH
GALVIN, Clara A and John J SULLIVAN, 04 Feb 1956 Hudson, NH
GALVIN, Eleanor E and Walter H HICKEY, 12 Oct 1908 Nashua, NH
  Dennis F Galvin & Joanna Grimes
  Walter H Hickey & Elizabeth M Campbell
GALVIN, Lillian D and Edward T LAROCQUE, 11 Apr 1950 Hudson, NH
GAMACHE, Alfred W and Marcella O GIRARD, 23 Oct 1948 Hudson, NH
GAMACHE, Cecile B and Roland A DESJARDINS, 07 Jul 1956 Hudson, NH
GAMACHE, David A and Barbara A KAMIENIECKI, 20 Apr 1968 Hudson, NH
GAMACHE, Dianne L and Ronald G DUPLEASE, 15 Jul 1967 Hudson, NH
GAMACHE, Edward G and Lois A JACKSON, 13 Dec 1947 Nashua, NH
GAMACHE, Edward G and Monique R LAJEUNESSE, 01 Nov 1952 Nashua, NH
GAMACHE, Edward G Jr and Patricia A CARON, 24 Jun 1972 Hudson, NH
GAMACHE, George L and Mary O ELLIS, 25 Jun 1960 Hudson, NH
GAMACHE, Janet E and David P REID, 10 Sep 1971 Nashua, NH
GAMACHE, Jean F and Henry C MIGNEAULT, 11 Sep 1965 Hudson, NH
GAMACHE, Jerry T and Vivian L DOBENS, 27 Sep 1968 Nashua, NH
GAMACHE, Leo A and Lorraine B LANDRY, 28 May 1948 Nashua, NH
GAMACHE, Lucette and Raymond A LEFEBVRE, 24 Aug 1963 Hudson, NH
GAMACHE, Lucille V and Charles B FARMER, 25 Nov 1937 Dracut, MA
GAMACHE, Mary F and Ernest R LEVEILLE, 07 Apr 1947 Nashua, NH
GAMACHE, Robert A and Simonne C LEMAY, 09 Jul 1960 Hudson, NH
GAMACHE, Roland L and Cecile E LEVESQUE, 06 May 1944 Nashua, NH
GAMACHE, Sandra V and Ferdnand R NADEAU, 25 Aug 1956 Hudson, NH
GAMACHE, Susan I and Idore M BUTTERS, 19 Apr 1969 Hudson, NH
GAMACHE, Theresa G and Paul R GALIPEAU, 02 Jan 1954 Hudson, NH
GAMBLE, Catherine and Peter J GALIPEAU, 28 Jun 1975 Salem, NH
GAMBLE, Ernest A and Leona M JAMESON, 22 Sep 1945 Hudson, NH
GAMMELL, John A and Louisa A HIGGINS, 05 Dec 1883 Hudson, NH
  Warren E Gammell (Boston, MA) & Elmirea A Bonous
  Sparrow Higgins(W Boylston,MA) & Juliett A Pierce(Providence, RI)
GAMUSO, Barbara A and Dennis R DESMARAIS, 18 Dec 1977 N Salem, NH
GANNON, Cheryl Ann and David John GOSSELIN, 19 Sep 1981 Hudson, NH
GANNON, Pamela T and Arthur H BARTLETT, 06 Mar 1965 Hudson, NH
GARABEDIAN, Martin and Linda K LEVI, 19 Mar 1982 Hudson, NH
GARANT, Carol P and Albert H TRUDEAU, 20 Aug 1966 Nashua, NH
GARD, Shirley A and Curtis J MERRIFIELD, 30 Apr 1970 Candia, NH
GARDNER, Ned and Phyllis A TROISI, 23 Jun 1984 Nashua, NH
GARDNER, Robert E and Janet L BACHE, 06 Feb 1958 Hudson, NH
GARDNER, Ronald C and Shirley J KENYON, 29 Oct 1952 Hudson, NH
GARDNER, Ronald C and Charlotte COOKE, 26 Nov 1964 Hudson, NH
GARDNER, Shirley J and Harold H VANVLIET, 26 May 1966 Nashua, NH
GARLAND, Helen P and John H MORSE, 18 Jul 1983 Hudson, NH

HUDSON,NH MARRIAGES

GARLAND, Leith L and Sharon L PHINNEY, 29 Dec 1984 Nashua, NH
GARLAND, Sydney A and Cynthia O WILSON, 27 Oct 1868
GARMORY, Joanne M and Ronald E CRANMER, 28 Dec 1963 Hudson, NH
GARNET, Fletcher A and Idris A HUTCHINSON, 01 Sep 1940 Hudson, NH
GARNETT, Lillian E and James R FULLER, 15 Jan 1949 Hudson, NH
GARON, Cecile L and Frank KAYROS, 06 Jul 1963 Nashua, NH
GARRIGAN, David P and Mary G WALLACE, 22 May 1946 Nashua, NH
GARRITY, Carolyn A and William F KERNDL, 20 Apr 1974 Nashua, NH
GARRITY, Mary P and John H SHINKWIN, 07 Aug 1948 Hudson, NH
GARSIDE, Alan R and Linda G BOWMAN, 12 Oct 1968 Nashua, NH
GARSIDE, David W and Doreen A GODDARD, 24 Apr 1965 Hudson, NH
GARSIDE, David W and Christine WENTWORTH, 03 Jul 1972 Hudson, NH
GARSIDE, Gene A and Carol F GRACE, 05 Jul 1961 Hudson, NH
GARSIDE, Joan M and Eugene W OTIS, 10 Nov 1956 Hudson, NH
GARSIDE, Lisa M and Douglas G WILHELMI, 17 Oct 1981 Hudson, NH
GARSIDE, Philip M and Rebecca J FIELD, 07 May 1983 Hudson, NH
GARSIDE, Reta M and Arthur H Jr SHEPHERD, 29 Jul 1960 Nashua, NH
GARSIDE, Sheryll Ann and Alan Peter GEORGE, 21 Sep 1980 Salem, NH
GARSIDE, Stephan C and Christine WHITAKER, 27 Apr 1985 Hudson, NH
GARVEY, John M Jr and Mary A MURPHY, 14 Oct 1950 Hudson, NH
GARVIN, Gordon E and Karen M DOYLE, 09 Apr 1983 Hudson, NH
GASKA, Denise M and Donald R McCRADY, 04 Jul 1980 Nashua, NH
GATCOMB, Earle M and Rose M EWENS, 20 Sep 1952 Belmont, NH
GATES, Beverly J and Don J JACKSON, 16 Apr 1955 Hudson, NH
GATES, David E and Laurie A PACKER, 24 Dec 1972 Mont Vernon, NH
GATES, Joseph E and Lillian M HASELTON, 20 Jul 1929 Hudson, NH
GATES, Marcius L and Emma P CHENETTE, 28 Dec 1914 Nashua, NH
  Charles E Gates & Martena Durant
  Louis Chenette & Melvina Morin
GATZ, Philip Arno and Ruth Ann LINSCOTT, 16 Nov 1929 E Milton, MA
GATZ, Selma E and Russell Jr COLE, 17 Oct 1936 Hudson, NH
GAUDET, Joyce E and Carl R RIPALDI, 13 Nov 1983 Hudson, NH
GAUDETTE, Dorothy F and Albert J LANDRY, 27 Apr 1946 Nashua, NH
GAUDETTE, Euclide and Alice FORTIN, 06 Sep 1920 Nashua, NH
GAUDETTE, Gloria T and Henry A FRASER, 10 May 1952 Nashua, NH
GAUDETTE, Jean and Joseph MODINI, 07 Dec 1933 Hudson, NH
GAUDETTE, Pamela M and John D FREILICH, 02 Aug 1980 Hudson, NH
GAUDETTE, Paul E and M Irene NADEAU, 17 Oct 1971 Nashua, NH
GAUDETTE, Raymond P and Linda M LABRECQUE, 09 Nov 1968 Hudson, NH
GAUDETTE, Rita L and Paul R SANTERRE, 12 Sep 1942 Nashua, NH
GAUDETTE, Roger R and Joanne M COROSA, 22 Jun 1973 Hudson, NH
GAUDETTE, Roland R and Lucille I LANDRY, 18 May 1946 Nashua, NH
GAUDETTE, Ronald R and Linda G RUSSELL, 11 Jan 1974 Hudson, NH
GAUDETTE, William and Carrie A LABOMBARD, 20 Jul 1929 Hudson, NH
GAUDREAU, Eugene L Jr and Sheryl L YOUNG, 22 Jul 1967 Hudson, NH
GAUDREAU, Gordon G and JoAnne M EVANS, 27 Sep 1984 Nashua, NH
GAULIN, Karen R and William W WISNOSKY, 17 Dec 1971 Nashua, NH
GAULIN, Ludger H and Dorothy A RATTE, 26 Dec 1969 Hudson, NH
GAULIN, Robert W and Karen R LAWRENCE, 24 Apr 1965 Hudson, NH
GAUTHIER, Charlene M and Peter J FRAPPIER, 07 May 1978 Hudson, NH
GAUTHIER, Daniel J and Mary A MacCLELLAN, 14 Feb 1948 Hudson, NH
GAUTHIER, Ellen M and Michael S LEE, 10 Aug 1980 Hudson, NH
GAUTHIER, Norman D Jr and Diane M McQUAID, 19 Feb 1982 Hudson, NH
GAUTHIER, Rosaire R Jr & Catherine ROBERTS, 27 Dec 1975 Nashua, NH
GAUTHIER, Russell E and Fleurette MORIN, 24 Nov 1956 Nashua, NH
GAUVIN, Louis P and Germain E CASTONGUAY, 03 Dec 1949 Hudson, NH
GAUVREAU, Paul F and Amy L TORCOMIAN, 26 Nov 1972 Hudson, NH
GAWEL, Stanley and Jennie BATURA, 14 Oct 1944 Nashua, NH
GAWTHORP, Floyd L and Donna M OLIVER, 23 Dec 1968 Hudson, NH
GAY, Alton E and Mary L DANIELS, 18 Jun 1906 Hudson, NH

HUDSON,NH MARRIAGES

   Elbridge Gay & Lydia M Abbott
   Ezra Daniels & Nettie Tatro
GAY, Ethel A and Benjamin PEASLEE, 15 Jun 1919 Hudson, NH
GAY, George G and Thirza PEASE, 13 Dec 1864
GAY, Judith M and Michael R PELLETIER, 19 Feb 1966 Nashua, NH
GAY, Pamela M and Dennis L PELLETIER, 31 Jul 1971 Nashua, NH
GAY, Susan E and Charles E DRAKE, 20 Sep 1882 Tyngsboro, MA
   Elbridge E Gay & Lydia M
   Charles L Drake & Lydinna
GAYNOR, Diane M and James E FERMOYLE, 28 Jul 1966 Nashua, NH
GEDNEY, Maureen F and Wayne S FISKE, 23 Jul 1960 Derry, NH
GEEHAN, Martin E and Dianne L ROBERT, 16 Sep 1967 Hudson, NH
GEER, David G and Judith A HOLT, 14 Apr 1969 Nashua, NH
GEHL, Janalee L and Richard A GILMAN, 03 Jun 1972 Hudson, NH
GEHRLEIN, Thomas L and Mary E LEARY, 03 Apr 1971 Hudson, NH
GEIGER, Gregory R and Suzanne C TESSIER, 26 Aug 1972 Hudson, NH
GEISINGER, Gregory J and Maureen T RILEY, 14 Dec 1984 Nashua, NH
GEISINGER, Holly M and Mark W CHRISTENSEN, 23 Jun 1984 Hudson, NH
GELE, Sylvain J and Paula A GALIPEAU, 19 Nov 1983 Litchfield, NH
GELESZINSKI, James A and Elizabeth COOKMAN, 04 May 1968 Nashua, NH
GELINAS, Allen D and Sandra M FORTIER, 25 Feb 1984 Hudson, NH
GELINAS, Wayne R and Janet M BERGERON, 29 Apr 1978 Pelham, NH
GEMIGNANI, John Jr and Leslie G SOLARI, 07 Jul 1984 Merrimack, NH
GENDRON, Annette J and Richard A LAVOIE, 30 May 1969 Nashua, NH
GENDRON, Annette L and Wilfred F SYRENE, 08 Oct 1960 Hudson, NH
GENDRON, Arthur D and Linda G DE'COSTE, 30 Jul 1982 Nashua, NH
GENDRON, Esther H and John E BAXTER, 19 May 1941 Nashua, NH
GENDRON, Gary H and Natalie D MERRILL, 28 Apr 1973 Hudson, NH
GENDRON, Gilbert J and Dorothy C BEAUMIER, 30 Jul 1950 Nashua, NH
GENDRON, Irene E and Larry G MacDOUGALL, 29 Jun 1957 Nashua, NH
GENDRON, James D and Susan L RODGERS, 19 Sep 1970 Hudson, NH
GENDRON, Linda M and Christophe MASSUCCI, 15 Sep 1984 Hudson, NH
GENDRON, Lorraine A and Alfred A LAWRENCE, 08 Sep 1951 Hudson, NH
GENDRON, Napoleon and Alma D DUPONT, 06 Aug 1937 Hudson, NH
GENDRON, Raymond A and Diane J BROWN, 01 Oct 1955 Nashua, NH
GENDRON, Rene L and Theresa Y DUBE, 20 May 1950 Hudson, NH
GENDRON, Richard E and Lynn M COLBURN, 06 Feb 1976 Hudson, NH
GENDRON, Roland A and Theresa A POIRIER, 20 Oct 1945 Hudson, NH
GENDRON, Romeo A and Adeline J DEROSIER, 27 Dec 1952 Nashua, NH
GENDRON, Romeo R and Julia B DUBE, 07 Jun 1947 Nashua, NH
GENDRON, Wayne B and Robin E STAHL, 11 Sep 1976 Meredith, NH
GENEST, Linda A and Peter D STERITI, 20 Aug 1982 Hudson, NH
GENEST, Paul W and Constance McWILLIAMS, 27 Dec 1980 Hudson, NH
GENEST, Robert R and Veronica J RUSSELL, 23 Nov 1981 Litchfield, NH
GENEST, Sylvia A and Paul E LEHNERT, 19 Aug 1973 Hudson, NH
GENOVA, Ellen L and John H MARTIN, 28 Mar 1969 Nashua, NH
GENTILE, Lucy M and Cosmo R BONHOMME, 15 Dec 1973 Hudson, NH
GEOBOSKY, Sophie J and Vincent B NELSON, 08 Apr 1945 Nashua, NH
GEORGE, Alan Peter and Sheryll Ann GARSIDE, 21 Sep 1980 Salem, NH
GEORGE, Lynn C and Steven M ALLEN, 27 May 1974 Hudson, NH
GEORGES, Josephine and Robert L MILLER, 07 Nov 1974 Nashua, NH
GEORGOPOULOS, George and Bertha J DIETTE, 03 Sep 1948 Hudson, NH
GERMAIN, Irene L and Ernest P LIPORTO, 13 Jun 1965 Dracut, MA
GERRARD, Laura N and Richard J DUHAMEL, 29 Jul 1967 Derry, NH
GERRISH, Hattie M and George L REED, 14 Nov 1908 Hudson, NH
   H Scales & Hattie Allen
   Fred H Reed & Seline Libberty
GERRY, Susie A and Frank V BARTLETT, 28 Jul 1910 Hudson, NH
   Elbridge W Gerry & Margaret Connors
   Wm A Bartlett & Rebecca Valentine

HUDSON,NH MARRIAGES

GERVAIS, Linda M and Robert L MORSE, 18 Aug 1981 Bartlett, NH
GETCHELL, Naomi C and Mario A JEANNOTTE, 26 Aug 1979 Nashua, NH
GETT, Dorothy F and Harold W HADLOCK, 06 Apr 1946 Hudson, NH
GETTY, Albert R and Therese A SULLIVAN, 10 Jan 1970 Hudson, NH
GIAMMARCO, Wendy J and Steven SILVA, 13 Aug 1975 Hudson, NH
GIAMPIETRO, Thomas L Jr & Elizabeth PRETTI, 17 Jul 1982 Hudson, NH
GIBB, Matthew D and Pamela J HICKS, 26 Jun 1982 Wolfeboro, NH
GIBSON, David W and Tami WIGMORE, 04 Apr 1981 Hudson, NH
GIBSON, Dorcas and Caleb S FORD, 20 Nov 1823
GIBSON, Elizabeth and John CHASE, 16 Feb 1786
GIBSON, Harold N and Phyllis T ADAMS, 17 Jan 1942 Nashua, NH
GIBSON, James E Jr and Helen V RUITER, 15 Nov 1946 Nashua, NH
GIBSON, Kathy J and Mark H HINRICHS, 16 Aug 1980 Hudson, NH
GIBSON, Paul B Jr and Nancy J ABBOTT, 20 Aug 1955 Hudson, NH
GIBSON, Stephen W and Eva C WHITING, 28 Aug 1881 Hudson, NH
  John A Gibson (Sulebury, VT) & Mary S Davis (Dunston, VT)
  Edwiche C Woodbury(Cavendish, VT) & Chestina Baker (Lyme, NH)
GIDEON, Victor C and Ruthann MUNROE, 31 Mar 1962 Hudson, NH
GIDLEY, Cheryl A and John J TRANT, 10 Aug 1981 Hudson, NH
GIESEKE, Clarence Jr and Betty I SIMPSON, 03 Feb 1945 Nashua, NH
GIFFORD, Charlene D and Philip E VIGNOLA, 15 Oct 1966 Nashua, NH
GIFFORD, Edward J and Judith A BOUCHER, 29 Jun 1970 Nashua, NH
GIGNAC, Pauline M and Jos M MARYNOWSKI, 10 Jun 1949 Hudson, NH
GIGUERE, Arthur D and Margaret M BOURGEOIS, 07 Sep 1973 Nashua, NH
GIGUERE, Joyce E and Normand T DUBE, 06 Oct 1973 Nashua, NH
GIGUERE, Kathy J and Tyler A WAISANEN, 30 Jun 1984 Nashua, NH
GIGUERE, Patricia and Stephen E BRADY, 10 Oct 1981 Hudson, NH
GIGUERE, Robert O and Ann-Marie PORCARO, 05 Feb 1965 Hudson, NH
GIGUERE, Robin J and Maurice A SPAULDING, 26 Aug 1978 Hudson, NH
GILBERT, Charles H and Eliza A GOULD, 06 Sep 1870 Hudson, NH
GILBERT, Charles L and Donna L MARSHALL, 29 Aug 1970 Hollis, NH
GILBERT, David C and Sandra A MURPHY, 20 Jun 1970 Nashua, NH
GILBERT, Elnora and Moody G STEELE, 21 Jun 1941 Nashua, NH
GILBERT, Fred and Emma F SAVARY, 05 Dec 1936 Hudson, NH
GILBERT, Jessie S and John WENTWORTH, 21 Sep 1904 Hudson, NH
  George P Gilbert & Sarah A Rowell
  Nathaniel Wentworth & Martha E Greeley
GILBERT, Judith A and David E LANDRY, 22 Aug 1970 Littleton, MA
GILBERT, Maureen and James E Jr HOLT, 14 Jun 1975 Pelham, NH
GILBERT, Robin W & Matthew D SHEVENELL, 08 Jun 1985 Hampton Fls, NH
GILBERT, Stanley R and Barbara D SAWYER, 26 Jun 1976 Hudson, NH
GILBLAIR, Richard N and June M JOHNSON, 31 Aug 1978 Hudson, NH
GILBRIDE, William J and Rosemary E WALSH, 19 Aug 1950 Hudson, NH
GILCHRIST, Florence M and William J FLEMING, 24 Jul 1933 Hudson, NH
GILCHRIST, Thomas P and Marcia G DUVALL, 07 Sep 1968 Hudson, NH
GILCREASE, Warren J and Mary McDERMOTT, 29 Sep 1924 Nashua, NH
GILCREAST, Gloria A and John J MANNING, 17 Aug 1963 Hudson, NH
GILCREAST, Ralph L and Patricia L REYNOLDS, 16 Jun 1973 Hudson, NH
GILCREAST, Robert F and Mary-Ann STANLEY, 28 Sep 1974 Nashua, NH
GILCREAST, Ronald G and Linda A BROCK, 16 Oct 1971 Concord, NH
GILE, Annette M and Daniel T CRAWFORD, 18 Jul 1981 Hudson, NH
GILE, John H and Angeline W BARNES, 14 Oct 1836
GILE, Stephen J and Debra M JORDAN, 25 Mar 1978 Hudson, NH
GILES, Darlene A and Jean-Paul FAUVEL, 04 Oct 1980 Nashua, NH
GILKES, Mildred M and Charles F SCOTT, 16 Dec 1935 Hudson, NH
GILL, James B and Lucille F ESTEE, 16 May 1970 Hudson, NH
GILL, Mary A and Jean B BOUTIN, 05 Aug 1950 Nashua, NH
GILLESPIE, Mary A and Herbert J HALLEY, 16 Mar 1942 Hudson, NH
GILLIAM, Barbara A and Clarence D ROCK, 05 May 1962 Hudson, NH
GILLINGHAM, Eleanor and Thomas BUTLER, 08 Apr 1851

HUDSON,NH MARRIAGES

GILLIS, Anna and Ralph NEGRI, 06 Nov 1938 Hudson, NH
GILLIS, William T and Martha E GLOOR, 24 Nov 1949 Windham, NH
GILLOOLY, Robert L and Debra J LEBLANC, 16 Jul 1977 Hudson, NH
GILMAN, Charles E & Frances H LITTLEFIELD, 22 Feb 1932 Enfield, NH
GILMAN, Dorothy M and Robert G KASHULINES, 15 Apr 1983 Hudson, NH
GILMAN, John W and Dorothy M BINGHAM, 12 Jun 1924 Hudson, NH
GILMAN, Kenneth B II and Ann Marie DUBE, 14 Jun 1975 Hudson, NH
GILMAN, Richard A and Janalee L GEHL, 03 Jun 1972 Hudson, NH
GILMAN, Rose A and Alfred F BOYER, 17 Jul 1943 Nashua, NH
GILMAN, Susan J and Leland C LEPORE, 16 Apr 1983 Hudson, NH
GILMARTIN, Richard E Jr and Linda M COOK, 05 Oct 1963 Hudson, NH
GILMORE, Anna M and Alexander GULLILAND, 14 Aug 1859
GILPATRICK, Lewis C and Agnes J COPPI, 08 Jul 1939 Hudson, NH
GILSON, Allen R and Doreen WINSTANLEY, 31 Aug 1968 Nashua, NH
GINGRAS, Dorella A and Ferdinand LOFFREDO, 14 Feb 1942 Salem, NH
GINGRAS, Eva and Raymond T RUSSELL, 10 Oct 1937 Nashua, NH
GINGRAS, Marguerite and Randy R SEYMOUR, 12 May 1984 Manchester, NH
GINGRAS, Raymond L&Bonnie A BELLEFEUILLE, 16 Jan 1981 Manchester,NH
GINGRAS, Raymond L and Margaret M HOWE, 23 Jul 1982 Nashua, NH
GINGRAS, Theodore and Marion A CHASE, 05 Mar 1927 Hudson, NH
GINGRASS, MA Knight and George L STEVENS, 29 Oct 1932 Dunstable, MA
GINNETTY, John L and Barbara A O'HALLORAN, 31 May 1981 Hudson, NH
GIOE, Teresa M and Robert G HAMPTON, 28 May 1983 Hudson, NH
GIOE, Teresa M and Henry R TESSIER, 12 Apr 1975 Nashua, NH
GIRARD, Doris F and Edgar L TURMEL, 27 Sep 1952 Nashua, NH
GIRARD, Lylona D and Eugene M WHALEN, 16 Aug 1941 Hudson, NH
GIRARD, Marcella O and Alfred W GAMACHE, 23 Oct 1948 Nashua, NH
GIROUARD, Blanche and Frank PELLETIER, 25 Nov 1915 Nashua, NH
    Joseph Girouard (Canada) & Calestine Courterie (Canada)
    Frank Pelletier(Canada) & Marguerite Peno (Canada)
GIROUARD, Celistin and Albert J KASHULINES, 01 Jun 1925 Nashua, NH
GIROUARD, Eugene and Nettie THERIAN, 21 Jan 1919 Nashua, NH
GIROUARD, Exilia and John H PERRAULT, 09 Aug 1897 Hudson, NH
    Joseph Girouard & Armini Macy
    Lewis Perrault & Ellen Kelly
GIROUARD, Lillian M and Herbert A BILBOW, 09 Feb 1942 Nashua, NH
GIROUARD, Marie and Francis V GUERTIN, 26 Jun 1928 Nashua, NH
GIROUARD, Marie B and Joseph A AUBUT, 07 Nov 1932 Nashua, NH
GIROUARD, Marion and Valmore GRANDMAISON, 01 Jun 1925 Nashua, NH
GIROUARD, Regina and Thomas J BELANGER, 05 Aug 1927 Nashua, NH
GIROUARD, Robert L and Ruth B E BELAND, 06 Jun 1953 Nashua, NH
GIROUARD, Theresa O and Harold Edmond COOKE, 26 Nov 1925 Nashua, NH
GISH, Charles F and Carolyn LEGARSKY, 26 Nov 1966 Nashua, NH
GIZA, Peter E and Tammy C COTE, 20 Mar 1982 Hollis, NH
GLADKI, Linda M and James S FORSAITH, 05 Apr 1981 Wilmot Flat, NH
GLEASON, Alfred C and Annie E ROGERS, 11 Sep 1913 Hudson, NH
    William H Gleason & Augusta Brooks
    Charles O Rogers & Lizzie
GLEASON, Karen A and John J POISSON, 14 Apr 1985 Hudson, NH
GLEASON, Thomas R and Wanda N PERLAK, 20 Dec 1949 Hudson, NH
GLENN, Kathleen E and Andre A ST LAURENT, 04 Mar 1972 Hudson, NH
GLENN, Michael A and Gail D McCARTHY, 17 Oct 1970 Hudson, NH
GLIDDEN, Charlotte and Simeon ROBINSON, 14 Dec 1848
GLIDDEN, Edmund F and Jane H LAFLAMME, 16 Sep 1977 Nashua, NH
GLIDDEN, Linda A and Bruce A ROCKWELL, 11 Jun 1982 Hudson, NH
GLINES, Gail A and Brian A WULF, 27 Sep 1974 Litchfield, NH
GLINES, Jon M and Jeannette DUMAIS, 14 Oct 1967 Hudson, NH
GLINES, Mary Jane and Allen L GAGNON, 21 Sep 1968 Nashua, NH
GLISPIN, James E and Stella N ZINKAWICH, 15 Jun 1935 Nashua, NH
GLISPIN, Richard A and Marjorie L BRUNT, 29 Mar 1974 Hudson, NH

HUDSON, NH MARRIAGES

GLISPIN, Virginia E and John D HOVEY, 30 May 1970 Nashua, NH
GLOOR, Martha E and William T GILLIS, 24 Nov 1949 Windham, NH
GLOVER, Angra S and Frank J ANNIS, 15 Mar 1876 Hudson, NH
GLOVER, Elizabeth and John FORD, 07 Nov 1799
GLOVER, Margaret and Ralph McQUESTEN, 29 Apr 1824
GLOVER, Neil R and Michelle B JETTE, 30 Jun 1979 Hudson, NH
GLOVER, Rhoda and Simon McQUESTEN, 23 Oct 1825
GLOVER, Robert and Jane BARNES, 29 Oct 1741
GLOVER, Robert and Jane BURNS, 29 Oct 1741
GLYNN, Virginia M and Norman E LINSON, 04 Mar 1974 Hudson, NH
GOBEIL, Micheline and Ronald G SIMARD, 27 Feb 1970 Nashua, NH
GODBOUT, George H & Bernadette BOISSONNAULT, 31 Oct 1945 Nashua, NH
GODDARD, Doreen A and David W GARSIDE, 24 Apr 1965 Hudson, NH
GODDARD, Francis W and Gloria A OLIARI, 17 Feb 1949 Hudson, NH
GODDARD, Richard J and Wendy D KIENIA, 13 Oct 1973 Chester, NH
GODFREY, Donna M and Paul R HAKKARAINEN, 25 Jun 1977 Hudson, NH
GODFREY, James P and Joan C KASHULINES, 26 Sep 1959 Hudson, NH
GODIN, David A and Susan L POULIN, 24 Jun 1972 Nashua, NH
GODIN, Kathleen N and Dennis R VAILLANCOURT, 13 Sep 1975 Hudson, NH
GODIN, Patrick W and Audrey J GAGNON, 07 Jul 1973 Hudson, NH
GODIN, Pauline B and Earl R DUFOE, 30 May 1957 Hudson, NH
GODSOE, Hilda P and Donald O CAMERON, 18 Jan 1947 Hudson, NH
GOFF, Isabella A and Donald E CARLTON, 15 May 1949 Hudson, NH
GOFFREDO, Joanne D and Joseph T DEFELICE, 07 Oct 1950 Hudson, NH
GOGUEN, Gerard J and Gloria E BERARD, 05 May 1956 Hudson, NH
GOING, Marion E and Lester E VOSE, 11 Oct 1940 Hudson, NH
GOLDEN, Donna L and Michael J CAYFORD, 30 Dec 1977 Hudson, NH
GOLDEN, Helen and Isadore BIENSTOCK, 11 Dec 1935 Hudson, NH
GOLDOFF, Sylvia and Max KAPLAN, 06 Apr 1939 Salem, NH
GOLDSMITH, Jabez and Lucinda POLLARD, 30 Jun 1814
GONSALVES, John E Jr and Joan B RUITER, 03 Jun 1978 Hudson, NH
GONSALVES, Leslie F and Maureen J HIGGINS, 16 Aug 1975 Hudson, NH
GONSALVES, Patricia A & Norbert B Jr LEDOUX, 30 Nov 1974 Pelham, NH
GONSALVES, Ruth V and John J WHITE, 04 Nov 1950 Hudson, NH
GONTHIER, Jeanne B and Alexander COCCHIARO, 22 Apr 1967 Hudson, NH
GONTHIER, Susan M and Rodney A PROULX, 08 Jun 1985 Hudson, NH
GONZALEZ, Ignacio T & Dorothy A CHRISTOPHER, 26 May 1979 Hudson, NH
GOODMAN, Harry and Rosamond MUSIKER, 30 Jun 1940 Hudson, NH
GOODNESS, John I and JoAnn BLANCHETTE, 09 Nov 1968 Hudson, NH
GOODRICH, David O and Gloria P COTE, 26 Nov 1964 Hudson, NH
GOODROW, Albert A and Helen M DUKE, 19 Jun 1920 Nashua, NH
GOODROW, Mary and Robert C MARBLE, 29 Mar 1919 Pelham, NH
GOODRUM, Stacey L and Ricky W JETTE, 18 Aug 1984 Nashua, NH
GOODSPEED, Ann and Jonathan BURBANK, 05 Apr 1855, Hudson, NH
GOODSPEED, John and Esther HADLEY, 05 Jun 1800
GOODSPEED, Olivia and Hiram MARSH, 27 Nov 1828
GOODWIN, Allan F and Constance BAKER, 01 Sep 1962 Hudson, NH
GOODWIN, David R and Joyce E KINVILLE, 16 Aug 1975 Hudson, NH
GOODWIN, Elizabeth and Samuel W WALKER, 11 Jul 1866
GOODWIN, Elsie and Lewis R MARSHALL, 12 Jun 1940 Hudson, NH
GOODWIN, Frances A and Ralph H STEELE, 12 Jul 1926 Hudson, NH
GOODWIN, Francis N and Myra WILLIAMS, 07 Dec 1947 Hudson, NH
GOODWIN, Fred T Jr and M Claire THERIAULT, 27 Feb 1943 Hudson, NH
GOODWIN, Gail C and Lester H TOWNSEND, 24 Jun 1967 Hudson, NH
GOODWIN, Paul W and Doris J CONSTANT, 21 Dec 1963 Hudson, NH
GOODWIN, Penney B and James O KATSOHIS, 22 Jun 1980 Nashua, NH
GOODWIN, Philip and Peggy KELLEY, 25 Feb 1796
GOODWIN, Ruth J and Robert E MORRILL, 06 Sep 1941 Hudson, NH
GOODWIN, Sandra L & William A Jr TEICHMANN, 08 Jul 1972 Hudson, NH
GOODWIN, Sarah J and Charles SMITH, 11 Mar 1869 Hudson, NH

HUDSON, NH MARRIAGES

GORA, Russell E and Brenda A MOORE, 03 Oct 1970 Hudson, NH
GORANSON, Alva M and Senard B PARENT, 21 Dec 1940 Hudson, NH
GORDON, Duane C Jr and Pauline C CHAREST, 09 Jul 1960 Hudson, NH
GORDON, Hymen and Helen L LETTS, 05 Jun 1935 Hudson, NH
GORDON, Katherine and Eugene J SCHUMAKER, 25 Jun 1949 Hudson, NH
GORDON, Marilyn P and John C Jr BURNS, 21 Mar 1945 Derry, NH
GORDON, Mark S and Kathleen A ROY, 25 May 1985 Nashua, NH
GORDON, Pamela J and Augustus II JACOME, 24 Jan 1981 Nashua, NH
GORNE, Jeffrey L and Kathleen A MONROE, 07 Oct 1979 Hudson, NH
GOSBEE, Richard K and Jacquelyn ROLLINS, 30 Jul 1977 Nashua, NH
GOSHGARIAN, Mary and John CHAPPAS, 24 Jan 1948 Hudson, NH
GOSLING, Andrew and Tamblyn L FULLER, 09 Feb 1985 Warner, NH
GOSS, Henry G and Martha R SENTER, 26 Mar 1826
GOSS, John F and Harriet Ja FOSTER, 20 Dec 1842
GOSS, Lydia D and Solomon O CALDWELL, 23 Nov 1862
GOSS, Rachel and Everett KENDALL, 23 Oct 1851
GOSSELIN, Barbara G and Sidney L WYER, 25 Jun 1971 Hudson, NH
GOSSELIN, David John and Cheryl Ann GANNON, 19 Sep 1981 Hudson, NH
GOSSELIN, James G and Linda D JENNEX, 05 May 1984 Nashua, NH
GOSSELIN, Patricia A and Louis M BELLAVANCE, 27 Dec 1952 Nashua, NH
GOSSELIN, Richard A and Jeannette DIONNE, 08 Apr 1961 Nashua, NH
GOSSELIN, William E and Ella M BILODEAU, 14 Jun 1970 Nashua, NH
GOTT, Jean C and Emil NEUMULLER, 18 Jun 1982 Hudson, NH
GOTT, Karen L and John C WOOD, 02 Nov 1963 Hudson, NH
GOU, Suh J and Glenn A VOGEL, 29 Dec 1979 Salem, NH
GOUDEY, Francis R and Valerie F WEST, 01 Dec 1934 Nashua, NH
GOUDREAU, Christine and Lucien R DESCHENES, 28 Apr 1984 Hudson, NH
GOUDREAU, John L and Anne M GOULETTE, 04 Sep 1981 Hudson, NH
GOULD, Althea W and Joseph WINN, 04 Jun 1839
GOULD, Anna and Ethan WILLOUGHBY, 23 Jun 1805
GOULD, Asa and Molley CUMMINGS, 03 Jun 1801
GOULD, Clarissa and Franklin WILSON, 07 Feb 1833
GOULD, David C and Mary I CHASE, 25 Apr 1837
  Jacob Chase
GOULD, David M and Rachel P CLEMENT, 04 Sep 1856
GOULD, Elijah and Sarah INGALLS, 30 Nov 1780
GOULD, Eliza A and Charles H GILBERT, 06 Sep 1870 Hudson, NH
GOULD, Elizabeth and Benjamin MOODY, 13 Sep 1781
GOULD, Gail M and David H FORTIER, 07 Mar 1972 Merrimack, NH
GOULD, George and Delia LANDRY, 08 Sep 1924 Nashua, NH
GOULD, Jonathan and Anna CHASE, 26 Nov 1782
GOULD, Kathy A and Brian L YEATON, 05 Nov 1970 Nashua, NH
GOULD, M Frances and Henry F COLBURN, 12 Jun 1865
GOULD, Maria A and James Otis TITCOMB, 21 Jul 1880
GOULD, Mary and Paul HARDY, 17 Apr 1826
GOULD, Robert W and Mary E SKAPINSKY, 14 Jan 1977 Hudson, NH
GOULD, Samuel and Lydia BARRON, 26 Nov 1782
GOULD, Sandra L and Jean A LEVESQUE, 24 Jun 1983 Hudson, NH
GOULD, Sarah and Samuel BROWN, 20 Apr 1778
GOULD, Sarah and John POLLARD, 20 Apr 1778
GOULD, Sarah Ange and Joseph Fra ANNIS, 15 Mar 1876
GOULD, Silas and Thankful DITSON, 29 Jun 1779
GOULD, William and Elizabeth COLBURN, 25 May 1785
GOULDSMITH, Jaby and Lucinda POLLARD, 30 Jun 1814
GOULET, Charles O and Lynne G HIGH, 13 Nov 1965 Hudson, NH
GOULET, Debra Ann and Colin D KELLY, 23 Feb 1973 Nashua, NH
GOULET, Janet M and Brian A PAQUETTE, 19 May 1984 Nashua, NH
GOULET, John T and Wendy PETERS, 11 Feb 1972 Pelham, NH
GOULETTE, Anne M and John L GOUDREAU, 04 Sep 1981 Hudson, NH
GOUR, Wilbur L and Doris W SELLERS, 12 Oct 1950 Hudson, NH

HUDSON,NH MARRIAGES

GOURDEAU, Edward and Margaret E BARRET, 21 Feb 1928 Manchester, NH
GOVE, Charles F and Susan G NICHOLS, 12 Oct 1968 Hudson, NH
GOVE, Joann and William R SEAMAN, 24 Jun 1950 Milford, NH
GOVE, Lester E and Margaret H JONES, 15 Oct 1966 Manchester, NH
GOVE, Lester F and Rita M OUELLETTE, 28 Jun 1948 Nashua, NH
GOVE, Otis Nelson and Marjorie ABBOTT, 30 Jun 1927 Hudson, NH
GOVE, Susan G and Douglas L HALLAHAN, 30 Jul 1982 Hudson, NH
GOWING, Bertha M and Alfred J ANDERSON, 01 May 1960 Hudson, NH
GOWING, Clarissa and Joshua GOWING, 25 Nov 1830
GOWING, Edward E and Josephine DONNELLY, 06 Oct 1908 Nashua, NH
  Sidney P Gowing & Clemintine Fuller
  Eugene Donelly
GOWING, Eleanor R and William E MAXFIELD, 26 May 1962 Hudson, NH
GOWING, Eva E and Alfred H McAFEE, 03 Mar 1921 Hudson, NH
GOWING, Frederick and Bertha M HARDY, 25 Aug 1940 Hudson, NH
GOWING, Frederick Jr and Winifred L NADEAU, 11 Apr 1964 Hudson, NH
GOWING, George T and Ida E SEAVEY, 01 Jan 1884 Pelham, NH
  Thomas Gowing (Wilmington, MA) & Harriet Greeley (Pelham, NH)
  Augustus Seavey(Pelham, NH) & Louisa A Swan (N Andover, MA)
GOWING, Josephine and Allen B ANDREWS, 01 Sep 1914 Hudson, NH
  Sidney P Gowing & Clemintine Fuller
  Arthur S Andrews & Linnie F Butler
GOWING, Joshua and Clarissa GOWING, 25 Nov 1830
GOWING, Marion I and Arlo P JOHNSON, 01 Nov 1968 Derry, NH
GOWING, Mary I and Charles F KENISTON, 08 Aug 1914 Hudson, NH
  George T Gowing & Ida E Seavey
  George Keniston & Ida M Borton
GOWING, Mary L and Lynn A CORSON, 14 Jul 1962 Hudson, NH
GOWING, Percy and Mildred DAVIS, 11 Nov 1919 Nashua, NH
GOWING, Sidney P and Clementine FULLER, 21 Jun 1881 Nashua, NH
  Samuel Gowing (Hudson, NH) & Sarah Penham (Tyngsboro, MA)
  Rodney Fuller(Hudson, NH) & Martha Farwell (Westford, MA)
GRABOSKI, Mary Jane and David S QUIMBY, 21 May 1983 Hudson, NH
GRACE, Barbara J and Paul B MYRICK, 15 Jul 1961 Nashua, NH
GRACE, Carol F and Gene A GARSIDE, 05 Jul 1961 Hudson, NH
GRACE, John D Jr and Sandra M NADEAU, 21 Feb 1970 Nashua, NH
GRACE, Nancy V and Gordon A FULLER, 28 Jun 1958 Hudson, NH
GRACEY, Joseph A and Yvette L LANDRY, 30 Aug 1984 Nashua, NH
GRAF, Janet E and Christopher SIEG, 02 Oct 1983 Manchester, NH
GRAFTON, John E and Patricia A DUSSEAULT, 25 Aug 1962 Hudson, NH
GRAHAM, Dianna T and Dennis E BOUCHER, 20 Aug 1977 Nashua, NH
GRAHAM, Dolores E and Alfred A Jr JACQUES, 14 Jun 1952 Hudson, NH
GRAHAM, Donna D and Kevin D KEANE, 20 Apr 1968 Manchester, NH
GRAHAM, Elizabeth and Timothy F DEWAELE, 30 Apr 1982 Hudson, NH
GRAHAM, Malcolm E and Marion L DAVISON, 15 Sep 1962 Nashua, NH
GRAHAM, Margaret E and Victor A BARTON, 09 Apr 1972 Nashua, NH
GRAHAM, Mary T and Philip E ESTY, 04 Nov 1938 Hudson, NH
GRAINGER, Donna M and James F Jr LAURA, 14 Mar 1975 Hudson, NH
GRAINGER, Joanne and Douglas S HARRIS, 15 Apr 1978 Hudson, NH
GRAINGER, Linda J and Mark R FADER, 08 Jun 1985 Hudson, NH
GRAINGER, Michael J and Lynn Ann FRANCOEUR, 08 Oct 1977 Hudson, NH
GRAINGER, Sharon A and Conrad C MAILLOUX, 04 Jul 1967 Hudson, NH
GRANDMAISON, Valmore and Marion GIROUARD, 01 Jun 1925 Nashua, NH
GRANDONE, Louise F and Paul A LAUF, 03 Aug 1935 Hudson, NH
GRANGER, George E and Ernestine THOMAS, 17 Oct 1939 Hudson, NH
GRANT, Bonnie F and Robert D ALEXANDER, 14 Dec 1968 Hudson, NH
GRANT, Charles C and Salome V SENTER, 19 Jan 1843
GRANT, Coreen and Robert J LEFEBVRE, 22 Nov 1980 Nashua, NH
GRANT, Donald E II and Joy K WHITNEY, 11 Jun 1977 Hudson, NH
GRANT, Gladys and Fred A Jr MARTIN, 02 Jun 1950 Hudson, NH

HUDSON, NH MARRIAGES

GRANT, Hannah A and Abner MASON, 07 Mar 1849
GRANT, Hester D and James A FITZGERALD, 30 Dec 1950 Hudson, NH
GRANT, Jeannette and Harold O BELL, 14 May 1915 Nashua, NH
   Eugene Grant (Irasburg, VT) & Laura L Durivage (Lowell, VT)
   Claude A Bell(Lowell, MA) & Edith M Thissell (Lowell, MA)
GRANT, John H and Annie M SMITH, 01 Aug 1880 Londonderry, NH
   Lynzey W Grant (Berwick, ME) & Martha G Farnham (Rumford, ME)
   Norris Smith(Hudson, NH) & Francis M Greeley (Hudson, NH)
GRANT, Julia A and Edwin RIPLEY, 20 Nov 1858
GRANT, Laura M and Alfred F STONE, 21 Mar 1969 Hudson, NH
GRANT, Lillian G and Arthur E NICHOLS, 10 Dec 1943 Nashua, NH
GRANT, Lorraine J and James A HARVEY, 01 Jun 1967 Hudson, NH
GRANT, Marion L and Horace L KNIGHTS, 22 Nov 1947 Nashua, NH
GRANT, Marita M and Robert L SEGG, 04 Apr 1942 Hudson, NH
GRANT, Russell R and Ruth NICHOLSON, 12 Feb 1938 Milford, NH
GRANT, S Lizzie and Henry A MERRILL, 15 Dec 1869
GRANT, S Lizzie and Henry A MERRILL, 01 Jan 1870 Lowell, MA
GRANT, Shirley A and Richard C NASOU, 21 Jun 1957 Nashua, NH
GRANT, Susan J and David A NADEAU, 13 Nov 1982 Hudson, NH
GRANT, William J and Doris L MARTIN, 05 Feb 1930 Winchester, MA
GRANTON, Russell A and Eleanor G DURKEE, 05 May 1924 Hudson, NH
GRASSETT, Gail M and Frank E GRAVINA, 29 Sep 1974 Hudson, NH
GRAUSLYS, Julia A and William E III EMERSON, 11 Nov 1978 Nashua, NH
GRAVEL, Claire E and Theodore E TURMEL, 12 Jul 1968 Nashua, NH
GRAVELLE, Gene R and Lucille R TRUDEAU, 12 Feb 1966 Hudson, NH
GRAVELLE, Joan M and Raymond G MORSE, 19 Apr 1969 Hudson, NH
GRAVELLE, Leonard R and Alice V DOOLEY, 09 Oct 1948 Nashua, NH
GRAVELLE, Nancy L and Kenneth J BRACCIO, 16 Feb 1963 Hudson, NH
GRAVELLE, Sylvio and Cecile LAVOIE, 07 Jun 1941 Nashua, NH
GRAVES, Clark D Jr and Ann-Marie SOBEL, 22 Aug 1981 Hudson, NH
GRAVES, Corinne A and Thomas L TETRAULT, 16 May 1976 Hudson, NH
GRAVES, James W and Dorothy HARVEY, 30 Jul 1949 Hudson, NH
GRAVES, Kevin C and Debra L MORIN, 08 Nov 1980 Nashua, NH
GRAVINA, Frank E and Gail M GRASSETT, 29 Sep 1974 Hudson, NH
GRAY, Arthur N and Esther W CHRISTOPHER, 12 Aug 1933 Hudson, NH
GRAY, David R III and Candace J HANSON, 24 Aug 1974 Hudson, NH
GRAY, Harold F and Jessee L FORD, 05 Jun 1942 Hudson, NH
GRAY, Ida F and Charles A STEELE, 12 Jun 1888 Nashua, NH
   Charles A Gray (Nashua, NH) & Sarah A P Angier (Amherst, NH)
   Silas T Steele(Hudson, NH) & Elizabeth McDonald (Scotland)
GRAY, Richard D and Pamela R CANNON, 25 May 1975 Nashua, NH
GRAY, Richard E and Sarah E BAKER, 15 Jul 1934 Hudson, NH
GRAY, Roger E and Linda A STEPHENS, 14 Mar 1970 Hudson, NH
GRAY, Sandra E and Michael H POWLOWSKI, 29 Jul 1972 Pelham, NH
GRAYDEN, David A and Sandra J McLAUGHLIN, 18 Dec 1982 Nashua, NH
GRAZIO, Joseph P and Eleanor H CONCANNON, 01 Jun 1974 Hudson, NH
GREATCHUS, Jo Ann and Thomas S PAVELKA, 05 Jul 1969 Hudson, NH
GREATCHUS, Leo D and Josephine PUTIS, 07 Jan 1943 Nashua, NH
GREAVES, Roy A and Debra A WALSH, 19 Sep 1982 Hudson, NH
GREELEY, Alfred and Lucy SENTER, 29 Mar 1842
GREELEY, Alfred and Rebecca DORT, 15 Jan 1850
GREELEY, Blanche M and Herbert D SMITH, 13 Nov 1912 Londonderry, NH
   Charles Greeley & Phebe Clinch
   Henry F Smith & Elona Chamberlain
GREELEY, Earl V and Beth A LEGALLEE, 08 Feb 1947 Hudson, NH
GREELEY, Edwina and Nathaniel Jr WENTWORTH, 09 May 1870 Hudson, NH
GREELEY, Frederick and Beverly RAMSEY, 03 Oct 1936 Nashua, NH
GREELEY, George A and Gertrude M BURNHAM, 16 May 1935 Salem, NH
GREELEY, James M and Nancy W MARSH, 10 Sep 1850
GREELEY, Jameson and Chastina A CORLIS, 23 Mar 1875 Hudson, NH

HUDSON,NH MARRIAGES

GREELEY, John and Polly NICHOLS, 08 Jun 1829
GREELEY, John T and Electa P GRIFFIN, 25 Oct 1861
GREELEY, Joseph and Sarah GREELEY, 07 Mar 1780
GREELEY, Joseph and Charlotte POLLARD, 17 Dec 1818
GREELEY, L Augustus and Lizzie E GREELEY, 13 Sep 1864
GREELEY, Lizzie E and L Augustus GREELEY, 13 Sep 1864
GREELEY, Mary and David MERRILL, 12 Oct 1824
GREELEY, Mary A and Horace WOODS, 09 Jan 1853
GREELEY, Mary E and Sidney H PALMER, 17 May 1862
GREELEY, Mary E and Sidney H PALMER, 14 May 1862
GREELEY, Mary H and David O SMITH, 30 Aug 1855
GREELEY, Meheteble and Hezekiah HAMBLETT, 26 Apr 1744
GREELEY, Mehittabel and Hezekiah HAMBLETT, 26 Apr 1744
GREELEY, Moses and Polly DERBY, 20 Mar 1794
GREELEY, Reuben and Joanna C MERRILL, 27 Nov 1817
GREELEY, Samuel and Abigail BLODGETT, 27 May 1744
GREELEY, Samuel and Olive READ, 08 Nov 1779
GREELEY, Samuel A and Susan C RICHARDSON, 15 Mar 1879 Tyngsboro, MA
  Samuel Greeley (Hudson, NH) & Mary Ann (Hudson, NH)
  Elijah Richardson(Hudson, NH) & Sarah (Hudson, NH)
GREELEY, Sarah and Joseph GREELEY, 07 Mar 1780
GREELEY, Sarah and Daniel HAYDEN, 11 Dec 1800
GREELEY, Sarah and Jon POLLARD, 20 Apr 1778
GREELEY, Sarah F and William F CHASE, 30 Sep 1862
GREELEY, Sarah Gould and Samuel BROWN, 20 Apr 1778
GREELEY, Silas and Thankful DITSON, 29 Jun 1779
GREELEY, Susan M and G P SMITH, 07 Dec 1847
GREEN, Diane and Robert J BARTLETT, 12 Aug 1977 Windham, NH
GREEN, Gordon R and Betty Jane BATES, 05 May 1965 Hudson, NH
GREEN, Marie E and Walter B CUMMINS, 09 Jul 1983 Hudson, NH
GREEN, Marie E and Edward O MacDONALD, 06 Sep 1952 Windham, NH
GREEN, Mildred J and Giovanni J SCIABA, 10 Jul 1938 Hudson, NH
GREEN, Susannah and Eliphelet HADLEY, 08 Mar 1798
GREEN, Walter R and Rachel D DUCHARME, 29 Jul 1969 Hudson, NH
GREEN, Wayne and Sherry SMYTHE, 27 Dec 1982 Nashua, NH
GREEN, William E and Ada E TAYLOR, 14 Jul 1908 Hudson, NH
  Henry Green & Ida Henchrig
  W L Taylor & Ada A Leusotte
GREENE, Agnes M and Willard N ROCK, 10 Sep 1945 Hudson, NH
GREENE, Frank and Constance JOHNSTON, 02 Mar 1918 Hudson, NH
GREENE, Vivian L and Ernest E BENN, 03 Jul 1938 Hudson, NH
GREENE, William J III & Sandra L EDMUNDS, 19 Dec 1981 Litchfield,NH
GREENHALGE, James and Mabel C CLARK, 14 Nov 1954 Nashua, NH
GREENLAW, David P and Donna M MITCHELL, 24 May 1980 Hudson, NH
GREENLEAF, Delvin T and Eleanor D FORD, 27 Nov 1970 Claremont, NH
GREENLEAF, Melody A and John L III PETERSON, 05 Aug 1978 Hudson, NH
GREENLEAF, Norma F and Robert J GAGNE, 28 Dec 1946 Nashua, NH
GREENSPAN, Kenneth A & Paula M ARREDONDO, 27 Apr 1985 Manchester,NH
GREENWOOD, Cheryl L and William H McKENNEY, 20 Nov 1969 Dover, NH
GREENWOOD, Dennis P and Andrea E DOW, 19 Jul 1981 Pelham, NH
GREENWOOD, Gary and Carol POINTER, 24 Dec 1977 Hudson, NH
GREENWOOD, Lester S and Rita P TESSIER, 26 Feb 1963 Nashua, NH
GREER, Cindy S and Gary J ALIE, 30 Aug 1982 Hudson, NH
GREGG, Daniel and Elizabeth JONES, 15 Jun 1878 Hudson, NH
  Joseph Gregg & Jenny
  Nathan Philbrick & Ester T
GREGG, Harlan and Carria A BATCHELDER, 08 Nov 1878 Hudson, NH
  Daniel Gregg (New Boston) & H Augusta
  Mark Batchelder & Susan (Hudson, NH)
GREGOIRE, Eugene C III and Donna M KNIGHT, 01 Sep 1979 Nashua, NH

HUDSON, NH MARRIAGES

GREGOIRE, Roger P & Jane A COURTEMANCHE, 02 Aug 1969 Manchester, NH
GREGORY, Alfred W and Mary R MORIN, 30 Jul 1955 Hudson, NH
GREGORY, Alfred W and Rachel M RIOUX, 23 Jun 1962 Nashua, NH
GREGORY, Claire A and Joseph S BUCKERIE, 31 Dec 1941 Hudson, NH
GREIM, Fred M and Ruth L CASHMAN, 15 Jan 1937 Nashua, NH
GRENIER, Brigitte M and Donald W SCHLAGLE, 02 Aug 1980 Hudson, NH
GRENIER, Carol S and Paul R LEMAY, 05 Jun 1982 Hudson, NH
GRENIER, Carol S and Jay M RICARD, 13 May 1978 Hudson, NH
GRENIER, Elizabeth and Paul LECLERC, 04 Jul 1936 Nashua, NH
GRENON, Dorothy E and Normand J RICARD, 03 Jul 1954 Hudson, NH
GRENON, Mary Louis and Carl C CHASE, 20 Jul 1974 Concord, NH
GREYWACZ, Briggs and JoAnne B McINTOSH, 17 Feb 1979 Hudson, NH
GRIECE, Joyce M and Richard N BREAULT, 01 Nov 1973 Hudson, NH
GRIFFIN, Beverly J and Dana A RODGERS, 26 Nov 1977 Hudson, NH
GRIFFIN, Clarissa H and Elbridge WYMAN, 07 Apr 1829
GRIFFIN, Cynthia E and William C YUKNEWICZ, 14 Dec 1968 Nashua, NH
GRIFFIN, David N and Linda Ann COTE, 21 Mar 1975 Hudson, NH
GRIFFIN, Electa B and John P FLETCHER, 25 Oct 1861
GRIFFIN, Electa P and John T GREELEY, 25 Oct 1861
GRIFFIN, Florence H and Herbert B SIMPSON, 03 Aug 1973 Nashua, NH
GRIFFIN, Jean G and Dennis E LABEDNICK, 29 Jun 1968 Nashua, NH
GRIFFIN, John E and Maggie NICHOLS, 07 Jun 1890 Londonderry, NH
   Rufus K Griffin (Manchester, NH) & Susan Merriam (Nashua, NH)
   Thomas Fallon(Ireland) & Mary McLeon (Ireland)
GRIFFIN, Kathleen A and Steven Arm VARNEY, 21 Jul 1973 Hudson, NH
GRIFFIN, Kenneth Jr and Margaret M LANDRY, 30 Dec 1978 Milford, NH
GRIFFIN, Kenneth Jr and Lorraine C NEAULT, 10 Oct 1981 Pelham, NH
GRIFFIN, Steven A and Ann M BOULEY, 10 Sep 1977 Hudson, NH
GRIGAS, Bryan M and Mylene J BEAUDRY, 30 Dec 1978 Hudson, NH
GRIGAS, Catherine and Joseph A LEGENDRE, 01 Aug 1964 Nashua, NH
GRIGAS, Frank J and Jeannette ST LAURENT, 30 Jul 1949 Nashua, NH
GRIGAS, Gerard F and Doris E DURAND, 05 Dec 1970 Nashua, NH
GRIGAS, Gerard F and Cindy G COURTEMANCHE, 13 Oct 1979 Hudson, NH
GRIGAS, Joseph and Barbara E ARGUIN, 12 Jun 1954 Nashua, NH
GRIGAS, Joseph W and Barbara H TAYLOR, 26 Jun 1982 Salem, NH
GRIGAS, Yvonne L and Robert A OUELLETTE, 02 Sep 1967 Hudson, NH
GRIGGS, Constance and Alden C ROBINSON, 28 Aug 1976 Nashua, NH
GRILLO, Paul W and Lucy E REGAN, 28 Oct 1984 Nashua, NH
GRIMES, Marguerite and Ernest BUTLER, 25 May 1933 Hudson, NH
GRISH, Elaine M and John A LANDRY, 02 Jul 1983 Nashua, NH
GROFF, Kenneth R and Theresa A AREY, 01 May 1982 Nashua, NH
GROFF, Michelle R and Donald J ARMSTRONG, 27 Oct 1984 Hudson, NH
GROHOSKY, Anne M and Timothy P MARSHALL, 12 Apr 1980 Nashua, NH
GROHOSKY, Edward G and Claudette COTE, 21 Nov 1953 Hudson, NH
GROHOSKY, John and Rita E MOQUIN, 28 May 1971 Nashua, NH
GROHOSKY, Lydia N and Donald S KUCHINSKI, 08 May 1965 Hudson, NH
GROHOSKY, Lydia N and Phillip C SNYDER, 30 Dec 1978 Nashua, NH
GROHOSKY, Richard and Ellen BEADEN, 24 Jun 1967 Nashua, NH
GROHOSKY, Victor J and Patricia M FROST, 22 Apr 1967 Hudson, NH
GROHOSKY, Victor W and Mary E LILLEY, 23 Jan 1948 Hudson, NH
GRONDIN, Francine M & Roland J A BOURGEOIS, 29 Jun 1985 Nashua, NH
GROSS, Nancy E and John D SALESKY, 16 Feb 1978 Lincoln, NH
GROSSO, Elsie V and Ralph P ALBERTINI, 12 Apr 1947 Hudson, NH
GROSSO, Wendy B and Robert Bur Jr PACKARD, 29 Dec 1984 Hudson, NH
GROVER, Arthur B and Jennie L THOMPSON, 25 Dec 1893 Hudson, NH
   A H Grover (Berwick, ME) & E K Stoddard (Hingham, MA)
   John M Thompson(Bridgewater) & Elizabeth Marsh (Hudson, NH)
GROVER, Jane T and Edwin G MORRISON, 26 Jun 1912 Hudson, NH
   John M Thompson & Elizabeth M Marsh
   Byron K Morrison & Hannah Munsey

HUDSON, NH MARRIAGES

GROVER, John C and Sarah M SPALDING, 23 Jun 1892
GROVER, TerryAnn and Richard W JEAN, 09 Mar 1985 Hollis, NH
GROVES, Elizabeth and Palmer C THOMPSON, 05 Dec 1933 Lowell, MA
GROVES, Ida Esther and Walter ANDREW, 22 Oct 1902 Hudson, NH
   Robert Groves & Elizabeth Boyle
   Robert Andrew & Emma Thorns
GROVES, James W and Ann M PINARD, 04 Jul 1975 Hudson, NH
GROVES, John C and Sarah M SPALDING, 23 Jun 1892 Hudson, NH
   Robert Groves (Ireland) & Lizzie Boyle (Ireland)
   Reuben Spaulding(Hudson, NH) & Sarah Laton (Nashua, NH)
GROVES, John S and Phyllis BUXTON, 22 Feb 1942 Hudson, NH
GROVES, Robert J and Patricia A McLLARKY, 08 Aug 1975 Pelham, NH
GROVES, Rueben and Mary Eunic POTTER, 24 Jun 1918 Hudson, NH
GROVES, William H and Minnie Ola MEAD, 22 Oct 1902 Hudson, NH
   Robert Groves & Elizabeth Boyle
   J B Farwell & H E J Chesley
GRUENFELDER, Mary-Eliza and Brian R MARTIN, 01 Jul 1981 Hudson, NH
GRUND, Allan J and Sharon M McGUINNESS, 23 Aug 1969 Hudson, NH
GRYGIEL, Ernest G and Sophie VYDFOL, 01 Feb 1947 Nashua, NH
GRZESIK, Stasia B and Pierre L DIONNE, 07 Aug 1982 Nashua, NH
GUAY, Evelyn and Albert ANCTIL, 08 Sep 1945 Hudson, NH
GUAY, Lucille B and Raymond J LEVESQUE, 14 Jun 1947 Nashua, NH
GUAY, Raymond and Beatrice BENNETT, 16 Sep 1944 Nashua, NH
GUAY, Raymond A Jr and Sandra L KINVILLE, 18 Nov 1972 Hudson, NH
GUAY, Smith S and Lorraine J DOUCET, 09 Aug 1960 Nashua, NH
GUELI, Charles M and Helen M VESEY, 01 May 1934 Hudson, NH
GUERETTE, Arthur G and Anita J ASSELIN, 26 Apr 1968 Nashua, NH
GUERETTE, Leda M and Raymond R GAGNE, 12 Apr 1947 Nashua, NH
GUERETTE, Leo B and Norma L BOIS, 11 Jul 1969 Nashua, NH
GUERETTE, Roland L and Sylvia E DUCHARME, 19 May 1978 Hudson, NH
GUERRETTE, Auguste N and Emelienne MONIER, 18 Oct 1958 Hudson, NH
GUERRETTE, Edgar G and Vivian A TRIPPLETON, 27 May 1959 Hudson, NH
GUERRETTE, Edgar G and Doreen B MARTIN, 21 Dec 1968 Hudson, NH
GUERRETTE, Michael P and Theresa M BERGERON, 04 Sep 1977 Pelham, NH
GUERRETTE, Vivian A and Armand E DUCLOS, 02 Jan 1965 Hudson, NH
GUERTIN, Francis V and Marie A GIROUARD, 26 Jun 1928 Nashua, NH
GUERTIN, Louis P and Shirley G DENEAULT, 01 Jul 1983 Hudson, NH
GUERTIN, Rene C and Brenda BOKOUSKY, 26 Mar 1966 Milford, NH
GUGGENHEIMER, Fred S and Mary A BOCK, 30 Oct 1948 Hudson, NH
GUGLIELMI, John and Jeannie K GAFFNEY, 12 Feb 1949 Hudson, NH
GUIDO, Edward R and Cora FERRIERA, 17 May 1947 Hudson, NH
GUIGNARD, Kathleen M and Philip COUTURIER, 21 Jan 1985 Nashua, NH
GUILBEAULT, Blanche T and Wilna G DENNIS, 02 Aug 1950 Hudson, NH
GUILBERT, Judith A & Wayne W McCLELLAN, 26 Apr 1980 Londonderry, NH
GUILBERT, Lionel and Lucienne PAGE, 30 May 1940 Nashua, NH
GUILBERT, Normand L and Sue CUTHBERTSON, 10 Jun 1967 Nashua, NH
GUILL, John C and Rachel T FOURNIER, 15 Oct 1983 Hudson, NH
GUILL, Michelle M and John W RUDOLPH, 18 Jun 1983 Goffstown, NH
GUILL, Patricia A and David A LAINE, 20 Jun 1981 Nashua, NH
GUILLEMETTE, Victor F and Theresa F RICARD, 10 Feb 1968 Nashua, NH
GUILLOU, Anne M and Ronald L PELLETIER, 02 Sep 1978 Hudson, NH
GUILMETTE, Vivian E and Roland C LABONTE, 18 Jul 1964 Hudson, NH
GUIMOND, Roger R and Michelle M BAZINET, 17 Nov 1973 Hudson, NH
GUINAN, Linda J and Kenneth A LAINE, 22 Feb 1969 Hudson, NH
GUIOTT, Sarah and Fred W BANCROFT, 18 Sep 1880 Hudson, NH
GUIRGUIS, Maher A and Deborah J MONK, 21 May 1983 Nashua, NH
GULLILAND, Alexander and Anna M GILMORE, 14 Aug 1859
GUMBRAVICK, Annie and Philip T LAMOY, 15 Sep 1924 Nashua, NH
GUMBRIS, William J and Helen H WHITING, 10 Oct 1942 Hudson, NH
GUNDERSEN, Gertrude R and J Roy SMITH, 29 Aug 1934 Nashua, NH

HUDSON,NH MARRIAGES

GURLEY, Johnny A and Elaine L PAIGE, 27 Apr 1957 Nashua, NH
GURNEY, Lynn Rae and Andre R BERGER, 09 Jan 1982 Nashua, NH
GURNEY, Marion L and George W DERBY, 26 Oct 1949 Hudson, NH
GURSKA, Felix P and Alice M WHITTEMORE, 28 Jun 1952 Hudson, NH
GURSKA, Felix Peter and Georgette MASON, 15 May 1981 Nashua, NH
GUSTAFSON, Lennart C and Mary E CLARK, 01 Nov 1940 Hudson, NH
GUTHREAU, William H and Elizabeth VISCO, 13 Sep 1947 Nashua, NH
GUTHRO, Diane M and Pierre D MARCHAND, 15 Sep 1979 Hudson, NH
GUTHRO, Donna J and Alan J NICHOLS, 02 Dec 1977 Nashua, NH
GUTHRO, Mark W and Mary Lou PLANTE, 09 Jun 1979 Hudson, NH
GUTHRO, Michelle and Robert J BEAUDRY, 20 Oct 1979 Hudson, NH
GUTIERREZ, Dave and Dianne HUNTER, 09 Oct 1982 Hudson, NH
GUTOWSKI, David T and Robin SIMARD, 20 Oct 1978 Hudson, NH
GUYETTE, Charles E and Catherine BROOKS, 02 Apr 1941 Nashua, NH
GUYETTE, Joyce B and Albert N BUDRO, 26 Aug 1972 Hudson, NH
GUYETTE, Margaret A&James F III SHAUGHNESSY, 29 Mar 1969 Nashua, NH
GUYETTE, Mary R and Leonard R NIQUETTE, 13 Jan 1962 Hudson, NH
GUYETTE, Rita M and Herbert L WILMOT, 27 Apr 1935 Nashua, NH
GUZDOWSKI, Carol A and Andrew P LINDQUIST, 09 May 1970 Pelham, NH
H'T'ISON, Marguerite & George J Jr OUELLETTE, 29 Sep 1950 Hudson,NH
HACHEY, Denise M and Robert A MOORE, 15 Apr 1972 Hudson, NH
HACKETT, Kevin M and Karen A QUIGLEY, 26 Aug 1983 Hudson, NH
HACKMAN, John and Rebecca EAYRES, 07 Jan 1800
HADDAD, Minnie and Robert W RUSSELL, 04 Nov 1934 Hudson, NH
HADLEY, Anna and Abel BUTTRICK, 30 May 1819
HADLEY, Catherine and Joseph LEICESTER, 08 Aug 1826
HADLEY, Dorothy and Abraham PAGE, 04 Dec 1784
HADLEY, Eliphelet and Susannah GREEN, 08 Mar 1798
HADLEY, Elizabeth and Wiseman KELLEY, 05 Mar 1801
HADLEY, Elizabeth and Morse SMITH, 15 Oct 1843
HADLEY, Esther and John GOODSPEED, 05 Jun 1800
HADLEY, Harriet E and Samuel CHASE, 12 Nov 1862
HADLEY, Joyce and John DUTTON, 02 May 1816
HADLEY, Lydia and Charles WHITTEMORE, 28 Oct 1813
HADLEY, Mary and Joshua CHASE, 22 Nov 1763
HADLEY, Mary and William HILLS, 28 Jun 1808
HADLEY, Mary and William W HILLS, 28 Jan 1808
HADLEY, Mary and Lemuel T JOY, 27 Oct 1849
HADLEY, Nehemiah and Hannah EMERSON, 12 Apr 1762
HADLEY, Nehemiah and Hannah EMERSON, 12 Aug 1762
HADLEY, Rebecca and Charles H NEWCOMB, 23 May 1859
HADLEY, Ruth and Nathan WINN, 18 Mar 1762
HADLEY, Seth and Sally BLODGETT, 25 Dec 1814
HADLEY, Susanna and John DUTTON, 23 Apr 1815
HADLOCK, Hannah and Zachariah HARDY, 27 Dec 1796
HADLOCK, Harold W and Dorothy F GETT, 06 Apr 1946 Hudson, NH
HADRYCH, Edwin A and Charlotte NAPSEY, 16 Dec 1970 Hudson, NH
HAERINCK, David R and Krystal L MUNROE, 11 Aug 1984 Nashua, NH
HAERINCK, Donald C and Donna M CURRAN, 06 May 1978 Hudson, NH
HAERINCK, Dwaine H and Christina JOHNSON, 25 Feb 1984 Hudson, NH
HAES, Donald L Jr and Barbara A PARKER, 28 Jul 1984 Hudson, NH
HAFEMAN, Joseph E and Doreen L R BERUBE, 14 Jun 1980 Hudson, NH
HAGER, Wilbur F and Evelyn S DOYLE, 19 Dec 1948 Hudson, NH
HAGERTY, Annie G and Walter E BISHOP, 25 Dec 1911 Hudson, NH
   Daniel Hagerty & Delia Foley
   George Bishop & Phebe Hall
HAGGETT, Alberto B and Dorothy I FORD, 07 Dec 1943 Nashua, NH
HAGGETT, Bernice M and Elliot W PARSONS, 03 Aug 1946 Hudson, NH
HAGGETT, Edward B Jr and Bernice NICHOLS, 19 Nov 1944 Hudson, NH
HAGGETT, Raymond A and Marie E FARLEY, 08 Jul 1951 Hudson, NH

HUDSON,NH MARRIAGES

HAIGHT, Barbara and George P RODGERS, 03 Jul 1948 Nashua, NH
HAIGHT, Clarence W and Mary E HOPWOOD, 19 Sep 1925 Hudson, NH
HAIGHT, Clarence W Jr & Frances A SPAULDING, 28 Jun 1959 Hudson,NH
HAIGHT, Sandra L and Paul G McKINNEY, 06 Nov 1982 Nashua, NH
HAIGLER, Charles P and Pamela A SENNEVILLE, 14 Apr 1978 Hudson, NH
HAIGLER, George F and Dora Y LEFEBVRE, 30 Apr 1949 Nashua, NH
HAIGLER, John L and Terrie L BISE, 12 Jul 1975 Nashua, NH
HAIGLER, Richard G and Louise D LEBOEUF, 24 May 1975 Hudson, NH
HAINES, Agnes M and Floyd E PENDLEY, 27 Jul 1946 Hudson, NH
HAINES, Sheila M and M Dean WILLIAMS, 15 Oct 1982 Hudson, NH
HAISMAN, Melody L and Arthur P EATON, 27 Jan 1968 Hudson, NH
HAITHWAITE, Dorothy M and Philip A STONE, 22 Apr 1962 Nashua, NH
HAKALA, Helen S and Charles E CLAFLIN, 01 Jul 1936 Hudson, NH
HAKKARAINEN, Paul R and Donna M GODFREY, 25 Jun 1977 Hudson, NH
HALE, Charles A and Annjene THOMAS, 24 Feb 1872
HALE, Elizabeth and Roger BUTTRICK, 12 Jan 1815
HALE, Frederick and Barbara T SANDALL, 02 Dec 1978 Litchfield, NH
HALE, James and Ruth CHASE, 18 Apr 1809
HALE, Joanne F and Robert E ELLIOTT, 13 Oct 1978 Hudson, NH
HALE, Rita M and William J STREIT, 22 Mar 1978 Hudson, NH
HALE, Sarah and Eleazer CUMMINGS, 19 Apr 1786
HALE, Zachius and Polly CHASE, 05 Oct 1797
HALEN, Betty A and Preston T ARNOLD, 18 Nov 1978 Hudson, NH
HALEY, Catherine and Rosario NOVELLO, 19 Jul 1941 Nashua, NH
HALEY, Frank I and Ida M HALLER, 15 Jun 1929 Hudson, NH
HALGREN, Robert Swa and Harriet Jo OIKLE, 25 Apr 1981 Nashua, NH
HALL, Amand J and Albert S THOMAS, 06 Oct 1878 Hudson, NH
  John Hall (Orford, NH)
  Augustus W Thomas(Middleboro, MA) & Sarah C (Middleboro, MA)
HALL, Ann L and Caldwell BUTRICK, 27 Jul 1865
HALL, Ann L and Caldwell BUTTRICK, 27 Jul 1865
HALL, Arthur C and Josephine BURRILL, 03 Jul 1915 Nashua, NH
  William H Hall (England) & Elizabeth Blowen (England)
  Frank Burrill(England) & Mary Whiting (England)
HALL, Charles and Clara F DAMON, 30 Sep 1868
HALL, Eva and Edgar L SILVER, 1875
  George W Silver
HALL, Frances E and Michael A MENDES, 12 Oct 1980 Hudson, NH
HALL, Joseph and Hannah CARLTON, 22 Apr 1780
HALL, Kenneth and Rena TRUFANT, 25 Dec 1919 Hudson, NH
HALL, Leopold and Ruth Ann HOLT, 21 Sep 1981 Brentwood, NH
HALL, Linda I and Peter H COOKMAN, 15 Nov 1967 Hudson, NH
HALL, Smith and Minnie J LYNESS, 28 Nov 1900 Hudson, NH
  Wm T Hall & Rachael McDonald
  Wm Lyness & Mary Gordon
HALLAHAN, Douglas L and Susan G GOVE, 30 Jul 1982 Hudson, NH
HALLER, Ida M and Frank I HALEY, 15 Jun 1929 Hudson, NH
HALLEY, Herbert J and Mary A GILLESPIE, 16 Mar 1942 Hudson, NH
HALLEY, Stanley M and Ellen J JUZOKONIS, 12 Apr 1942 Hudson, NH
HALLSON, Marguerite and Frank DESIMONE, 19 Oct 1932 Hudson, NH
HAMBLET, Aaron and Ruth CUTTER, 07 Jul 1796
HAMBLET, Betty and Henry Colb OSGOOD, 08 Jun 1797
HAMBLET, Horace G and Lavina C HOVEY, 30 Apr 1862
HAMBLET, John and Ruth COLLINS, 25 Feb 1863
HAMBLET, John R and Salley ATWOOD, 09 May 1824
HAMBLET, Joseph M and Mary J HOLMES, 04 Oct 1869 Hudson, NH
HAMBLET, Josiah and Hannah BUTTERICK, 10 May 1818
HAMBLET, Mehetible and Daniel HOWE, 04 Apr 1788
HAMBLETT, A Luther and Lillian E LECLERC, 17 Jul 1967 Hudson, NH
HAMBLETT, Aaron and Ruth CUTTER, 07 Jul 1796

HUDSON,NH MARRIAGES

Barrett Hadley
HAMBLETT, Aaron L and Dorothy M WRIGHT, 08 Jun 1957 Hudson, NH
HAMBLETT, Anna and Samuel RICHARDSON, 12 Oct 1826
HAMBLETT, Bertha M and William C HASELTON, 02 Apr 1890 Hudson, NH
  Alvin Hamblett (Hudson, NH) & Almira F McKean (Merrimack, NH)
  David Haselton(Hudson, NH) & Harriet F Wood (Leominster, MA)
HAMBLETT, Carol A and Daniel R LANDRY, 06 Sep 1969 Hudson, NH
HAMBLETT, Daniel W and Sarah E FORD, 17 Apr 1869
HAMBLETT, David A and Maragaret PROVOST, 28 Apr 1979 Nashua, NH
HAMBLETT, David H and Beatrice E HARVEY, 25 Dec 1948 Nashua, NH
HAMBLETT, Edith C and Everett M HAMBLETT, 04 Jan 1972 Hudson, NH
HAMBLETT, Elizabeth and Moses CHASE, 01 Mar 1759
HAMBLETT, Elizabeth and Albert J DROUIN, 09 Apr 1960 Manchester, NH
HAMBLETT, Everett M and Edith C HATCH, 10 Aug 1967 Hudson, NH
HAMBLETT, Everett M and Edith C HAMBLETT, 04 Jan 1972 Hudson, NH
HAMBLETT, Everett M and Rachel L WHITE, 05 Feb 1973 Hudson, NH
HAMBLETT, Everett M and Ruth Elizabeth SMITH, 24 Feb 1922 Hudson,NH
HAMBLETT, Hezekiah and Mehittabel GREELEY, 26 Apr 1744
HAMBLETT, Hezekiah and Meheteble GREELEY, 26 Apr 1744
HAMBLETT, Horace J and Louisa D COVEY, 30 Apr 1862
HAMBLETT, John and Sally ATWOOD, 09 May 1824
HAMBLETT, John and Pathenia ROBINSON, 17 May 1832
HAMBLETT, John R and Ruth COBB, 25 Feb 1863
HAMBLETT, Jonathan and Elizabeth RICHARDSON, 13 Dec 1781
HAMBLETT, Joseph and Lucy M THAYER, 21 Apr 1846
HAMBLETT, Josiah and Hannah BUTTRICK, 10 May 1818
HAMBLETT, Laurette and Charles Ot WEBSTER, 17 Apr 1856
Benjamin Webster
HAMBLETT, Leonard L and Lorraine T PLANTIER, 11 Oct 1946 Nashua, NH
HAMBLETT, Lydia M and Alonzo N WINN, 17 Mar 1846
HAMBLETT, Martha and Phineas BLODGETT, 27 Sep 1781
HAMBLETT, Mary and Benjamin FARLEY, 12 Nov 1816
HAMBLETT, Mary S and Deering G SMITH, 02 Jul 1921 Nashua, NH
HAMBLETT, Mehittable and Daniel HOWE, 04 Apr 1771
HAMBLETT, Ruth G and Foster F SHEPARD, 17 Mar 1940 Hudson, NH
HAMEL, Carol A and George L LANDRY, 20 Jun 1959 Nashua, NH
HAMEL, Elizabeth and Gerald R WINSLOW, 23 May 1953 Nashua, NH
HAMEL, James and Jeanne A ROUSSELLE, 16 Aug 1941 Nashua, NH
HAMEL, Joseph J and Marie C HARBOUR, 23 Dec 1933 Laconia, NH
HAMEL, Roland G and Patricia A DOUCETTE, 14 May 1977 Hudson, NH
HAMELIN, Alfred R and Gloria J PINET, 23 Aug 1958 Hudson, NH
HAMELIN, Rita G and Ludovic MITCHELL, 10 Apr 1948 Nashua, NH
HAMELIN, Theresa G and James F PALADINO, 26 Jan 1957 Hudson, NH
HAMILTON, Deborah A and Philip J CONNELL, 06 Oct 1973 Merrimack, NH
HAMILTON, Frances E and Donald E GAGNON, 20 Jan 1932 Hudson, NH
HAMILTON, Linda M and Andrew G ZUORSKI, 02 Sep 1983 Nashua, NH
HAMILTON, Thomas F and Barbara J COVEY, 25 Jun 1983 Hudson, NH
HAMMAR, John A and Geraldine BOUCHER, 10 Aug 1957 Hudson, NH
HAMMAR, Michael F and Cynthia J PETERS, 08 Sep 1973 Hudson, NH
HAMMEL, Priscilla and Richard G KENNEY, 16 Dec 1964 Tilton, NH
HAMMOND, Amy and Edmond LAVOIE, 01 Dec 1934 Nashua, NH
HAMMOND, Barbara L and Clifford J BURTON, 30 Mar 1963 Hudson, NH
HAMMOND, Claude E & Louise C WALKER, 06 Aug 1933 Old Orchard Bch,ME
HAMMOND, Leon C and Gertrude B HARRIS, 21 Mar 1936 Nashua, NH
HAMMOND, Louise H and Donald S DOUGHTY, 09 Oct 1943 Nashua, NH
HAMMOND, Nancy L and Terence J HEDGES, 15 Mar 1959 Hudson, NH
HAMMOND, Robert L and Lilla May WATSON, 07 Feb 1940 Hudson, NH
HAMMOND, Susan and Jacob HOBBS, 04 Jun 1860
HAMPSON, Valerie A and Michael C JESSON, 26 May 1972 Derry, NH
HAMPTON, Robert G and Teresa M GIOE, 28 May 1983 Hudson, NH

HUDSON,NH MARRIAGES

HANCOCK, Stanton A Jr and Mary Alice OTIS, 06 Oct 1962 Hollis, NH
HAND, Dianna and Stephen P MOLLOY, 20 Jun 1980 Hudson, NH
HANDLEY, William F and Rolande G NADEAU, 29 Dec 1947 Nashua, NH
HANDY, Phyllis and George F MILLER, 11 Aug 1938 Hudson, NH
HANKS, Bruce B and Debra A CUTHBERTSON, 18 Jun 1983 Hudson, NH
HANLON, Arthur R Jr and Pamela J JOHNSON, 17 Jun 1972 Pelham, NH
HANNAH, Frederick and Karen A CARON, 30 Jun 1962 Hudson, NH
HANNIGAN, George E and Carol B TURGEON, 22 Feb 1971 Nashua, NH
HANNIGAN, John L and Bernadette REGAN, 22 Oct 1931 Nashua, NH
HANSBERRY, David M and Sheila A KEENAN, 16 Aug 1975 Hudson, NH
HANSCOMB, Chas W and Mary E HAYES, 18 Oct 1900 Strafford Cr
  L G Hanscomb & Nancy Thomas
  C R Foss
HANSEN, Ann G and Paul E BAMFORTH, 07 Feb 1950 Hudson, NH
HANSEN, Jennie G and Robert A RICHARDSON, 23 Nov 1931 Merrimack, NH
HANSEN, Peter L and Linda F BOUTILIER, 11 Feb 1971 Nashua, NH
HANSEN, Robert N Jr and Michele S BUJOLD, 20 Feb 1970 Hudson, NH
HANSON, Candace J and David R III GRAY, 24 Aug 1974 Hudson, NH
HANSON, Charles S and Dorothy L ROUILLARD, 21 Oct 1966 Hudson, NH
HANSON, Donald E and Judith E POORE, 26 May 1984 Hudson, NH
HANSON, Ethel G and John J CURRAN, 01 Jul 1950 Hudson, NH
HANSON, Grace M and Robert J DROUIN, 22 Aug 1953 Hudson, NH
HANSON, Lila H and Charles G LEDOUX, 12 Jul 1943 Nashua, NH
HANSON, Linda M and Scott K HERBERT, 14 Jun 1969 Nashua, NH
HANSON, Myrtie E and Paul F BURTON, 03 Jul 1950 Hudson, NH
HANSON, Roland G Jr and Theresa A BOUCHER, 01 Jun 1946 Nashua, NH
HARALDSTAD, Ruth S and Walter F NALLY, 21 Jan 1949 Hudson, NH
HARBOUR, Marie C and Joseph J HAMEL, 23 Dec 1933 Laconia, NH
HARDEY, Edna and George BARROWS, 28 Mar 1782
HARDIMAN, Stephen B and Linda J SLAIBY, 27 Nov 1982 Hudson, NH
HARDING, Lyman C and Dorothea C CHRISTOPHER, 07 Jul 1934 Hudson, NH
HARDING, Robert G and Diane L CARON, 16 Apr 1979 Nashua, NH
HARDMAN, John F and Eva F MONETTE, 22 Jun 1929 Nashua, NH
HARDMAN, Marion Post and Victor R VIGNEAULT, 09 Sep 1978 Nashua, NH
HARDY, Abigail and William ADAMS, 05 May 1785
HARDY, Abigail and William McADAMS, 05 May 1785
HARDY, Bertha M and Frederick GOWING, 25 Aug 1940 Hudson, NH
HARDY, Bessie V and Roger L ROBINSON, 28 Dec 1957 Hudson, NH
HARDY, Charles H and Margery L BAILEY, 25 Sep 1954 Nashua, NH
HARDY, Clara August and Frederick CUTLER, 01 Jan 1868
HARDY, Cynthia Ann and Harold M Jr BOTHWICK, 02 Jul 1972 Hudson, NH
HARDY, Cynthia-Ruth and David G THOMPSON, 19 Nov 1954 Nashua, NH
HARDY, David and Zoe MARSHALL, 31 Mar 1859
HARDY, David S and Lorraine W DEWITT, 15 Apr 1977 Nashua, NH
HARDY, Dawn K and Ira A ROWLETT, 23 Sep 1979 Hudson, NH
HARDY, Donald A and Cecile J BLAIS, 21 Feb 1970 Manchester, NH
HARDY, Dudley D and Harriet J CROMPTON, 21 Jun 1947 Hudson, NH
HARDY, Elizabeth and William KELLEY, 05 Mar 1801
HARDY, Esther and George BURROWS, 28 Mar 1782
HARDY, Fred B and Frances H MORTON, 26 Jun 1954 Hudson, NH
HARDY, Gladys C and Sylvanus Herber SAGER, 25 Mar 1925 Hudson, NH
HARDY, Hannah E and Philip J CONNELL, 21 May 1873
HARDY, Hannah E and Philip J CONNELL, 20 May 1873 Lowell, MA
HARDY, Helen G and Alfred G PINET, 06 Sep 1946 Hudson, NH
HARDY, Jedediah and Patte COLBURN, 22 Dec 1800
HARDY, John and Nancy MARSHALL, 31 Oct 1850
HARDY, John R and Elaine O ESTY, 09 Nov 1952 Nashua, NH
HARDY, Jonathan and Susan EMERSON, 10 Sep 1818
HARDY, Margaret L and Louis ALVAREZ, 10 Oct 1953 Nashua, NH
HARDY, Michael Allan and Carolyn COE, 14 Nov 1978 Hudson, NH

HUDSON, NH MARRIAGES

HARDY, Moody and Hannah WICOM, 21 Jan 1779
HARDY, Moody and Hannah WASON, 21 Jan 1779
HARDY, Paul and Mary P KENDALL, 25 Jan 1844
HARDY, Paul and Mary GOULD, 17 Apr 1826
HARDY, Richard H and Dorothy S CAMPBELL, 06 May 1945 Hudson, NH
HARDY, Robert E and Ruth CAMPBELL, 28 Sep 1940 Hudson, NH
HARDY, Roland W and Bessie V BRADLEY, 05 Dec 1925 Hudson, NH
HARDY, Susan Martha and Frederick CUTTER, 12 Oct 1872
HARDY, Tim J and Ronna L ECKHARDT, 20 May 1983 Exeter, NH
HARDY, William and Mary A SENTER, 19 May 1846
HARDY, Zachariah and Hannah HADLOCK, 27 Dec 1796
HARDY, Zachariah and Abigail WEBSTER, 14 Nov 1822
HARLEY, Webster D and Florence L FANEZ, 17 Sep 1965 Hudson, NH
HARMON, Andrew J and Susan Lynn DUBOIS, 07 Jan 1983 Hudson, NH
HARMON, Carl D and Marlene D MASON, 12 Jan 1980 Pelham, NH
HARMON, John J Jr and Louise A WHITNEY, 07 Mar 1934 Nashua, NH
HARNETT, Robert O and Joan A M ST LOUIS, 18 Oct 1980 Hudson, NH
HARNEY, Ramona L and Alan J FRASER, 24 Nov 1979 Hudson, NH
HARPER, Sarah and John WEBSTER, 17 Nov 1865
HARRAR, Earl L Jr and Mildred M JAHUKE, 05 Jan 1944 Hudson, NH
HARRINGTON, Mary M and Louis S TREMBLAY, 24 Jun 1971 Hudson, NH
HARRIS, Albert and Amanda STEWART, 28 Nov 1854
HARRIS, Catherine and Donald M LARSON, 09 Feb 1950 Hudson, NH
HARRIS, Debra Lee and Stephen Roger PHANEUF, 23 Sep 1978 Nashua, NH
HARRIS, Douglas A and Joan E BAKER, 28 Aug 1976 Nashua, NH
HARRIS, Douglas S and Joanne GRAINGER, 15 Apr 1978 Hudson, NH
HARRIS, Ebenezer and Rebecca HILLS, 03 Jan 1782
HARRIS, Eleanor S and Mario A JEANNOTTE, 05 Sep 1981 Manchester, NH
HARRIS, Frances G and William C HOLLEY, 30 Oct 1948 Hudson, NH
HARRIS, Gertrude B and Leon C HAMMOND, 21 Mar 1936 Nashua, NH
HARRIS, John H and Marjorie A WYMAN, 15 Oct 1925 Hudson, NH
HARRIS, Mary and Abiather WINN, 08 Apr 1824
HARRIS, Raymond Sargent and Verna J CRAMTON, 03 Jun 1928 Hudson, NH
HARRIS, Roberta and Roland BLAIS, 28 Apr 1947 Nashua, NH
HARRIS, Sarah L and Edgar A DAVIS, 19 Nov 1867
HARRIS, Sharon A and Timothy A WOODMAN, 10 Apr 1970 Nashua, NH
HARRIS, Susan D and Charles M IVES, 09 Mar 1974 Hudson, NH
HARRIS, Thomas and Lydia COLBURN, 01 Oct 1829
HARRIS, Vesta I and Earle B MOORE, 08 Jul 1916 Hudson, NH
   Robert Harris (Nova Scotia) & Elizabeth McKay (Nova Scotia)
   Stephen Moore(Nova Scotia) & Edith Boynton (Bromfield, ME)
HARRISON, Doris C and Paul A WHEELER, 09 Oct 1959 Nashua, NH
HARROLD, James D and Nancy RICH, 10 Jan 1953 Hudson, NH
HARRON, Kathleen M and Allan J QUIGLEY, 26 Feb 1972 Hudson, NH
HARRON, Ralph T and Laura Lee COLL, 15 Jul 1972 Hudson, NH
HARROP, Grace B and Herbert L JOYCE, 16 Jul 1938 Hudson, NH
HART, Carol A and David B CHRISTOPHER, 01 Apr 1983 Hollis, NH
HART, Jacob C and Shirley A RAISIG, 12 Oct 1938 Nashua, NH
HART, Kim and Richard J QUINN, 01 Jan 1981 Hudson, NH
HART, Theresa D and Joseph G PARADISE, 28 Feb 1959 Merrimack, NH
HARTEL, Bruce D and Virginia G LARSON, 27 Nov 1976 Nashua, NH
HARTIGAN, Michael J and Rose E HOBBS, 21 Apr 1932 Nashua, NH
HARTLEN, Casianna and Wayne M PARADIS, 15 Feb 1975 Hudson, NH
HARTLEY, Lynne M and Guido M MARDONES, 19 Jan 1980 Hudson, NH
HARTNETT, Dana J and Denise D DUCHARME, 24 Oct 1981 Hudson, NH
HARTNETT, Margaret T and Emery P BOOSKA, 28 Jun 1958 Hudson, NH
HARTSHORN, Evelyn F and William C ANNIS, 04 Sep 1954 Milford, NH
HARTSHORN, James and Mary KNIGHT, 14 Nov 1819
HARTSHORN, James and Mary NIGHTS, 14 Nov 1819
HARTSON, Joanne S and Carlton H BROWN, 12 Aug 1972 Nashua, NH

HUDSON,NH MARRIAGES

HARTT, Becky A and James D LEDOUX, 08 May 1982 Hudson, NH
HARTT, Catherine and Douglas W Jr FLANDERS, 15 Apr 1978 Hudson, NH
HARTT, Richard D and Roberta M DUDLEY, 23 Oct 1971 Nashua, NH
HARTT, Thomas D and Tracey J DEARBORN, 19 Oct 1974 Hudson, NH
HARTWELL, Marilyn G & Thomas R Jr CAMPBELL, 25 Oct 1952 Nashua, NH
HARTWELL, Stephen R and Pamela J ALBERTSON, 29 May 1981 Hudson, NH
HARVELL, Diane F and Charles W FLECHTNER, 03 Dec 1960 Nashua, NH
HARVEY, Barbara A and Richard A BOWEN, 14 May 1975 Nashua, NH
HARVEY, Beatrice E and David H HAMBLETT, 25 Dec 1948 Nashua, NH
HARVEY, Charles W and Jean MEADY, 19 Aug 1941 Nashua, NH
HARVEY, Clara L and Merton L DUNCKLEE, 06 Oct 1908 Nashua, NH
   J Frank Harvey & Maud Parmenter
   Charles E Duncklee & Flora J Jones
HARVEY, Dorothy and James W GRAVES, 30 Jul 1949 Hudson, NH
HARVEY, Edna Frances and George Hadley HILL, 11 Oct 1910 Hudson, NH
   Charles H Harvey & Celia M Fellows
   George H Hill & Mary Morris
HARVEY, Ethel M and Milton D READ, 29 Dec 1942 Nashua, NH
HARVEY, Harold D and Phyllis E CLEMENT, 28 Sep 1927 Nashua, NH
HARVEY, James A and Lorraine J GRANT, 01 Jun 1967 Hudson, NH
HARVEY, Jedidiah and Pattie COLBURN, 22 Dec 1800
HARVEY, Jonathan and Susan EMERSON, 10 Sep 1818
HARVEY, Juanita E and Michael J CHAGNON, 22 Jul 1950 Hudson, NH
HARVEY, Leonard N and Patricia A KOPKA, 14 Jan 1967 Hudson, NH
HARVEY, Sandra M and James E ELLIS, 03 Jul 1964 Hudson, NH
HARWOOD, Anne D and John H ZELONIS, 07 Nov 1948 Hudson, NH
HARWOOD, Bernice J and Paul B CAHILL, 15 Aug 1925 Nashua, NH
HARWOOD, Elaine B and Charles H SEAMANS, 28 Oct 1937 Nashua, NH
HARWOOD, Grace H and Leland E HOWARD, 06 Apr 1921 Nashua, NH
HARWOOD, Gretchen K and John P LAUZIERE, 01 Dec 1979 Hudson, NH
HARWOOD, Guy and Annie ALUKONIS, 03 Sep 1933 Dunstable, MA
HARWOOD, Halga M and George E DURIRAGE, 25 Sep 1901 Hudson, NH
   W J Harwood (England) & Thea Hanson (Norway)
   Ranson M Durirage(St Albans,VT) & Janette Goodridge(Fletcher, VT)
HARWOOD, Holly Dawn and Richard MOLINARI, 29 Apr 1974 Nashua, NH
HARWOOD, James E and Ruth C HUDON, 01 Dec 1962 Nashua, NH
HARWOOD, John W and Charlotte BAGLEY, 28 Nov 1946 Nashua, NH
HARWOOD, Joseph R and Pauline D BERUBE, 31 Oct 1944 Nashua, NH
HARWOOD, Katherine and George K OLIVER, 21 Aug 1946 Hudson, NH
HARWOOD, Louise M and Nelson E PERKINS, 19 Sep 1914 Portsmouth, NH
   Henry Harwood & Mary Brennan
   Jeremiah Perkins & Dora Hilton
HARWOOD, Madeline and Harold J ANNIS, 24 May 1944 Dracut, MA
HARWOOD, Maude Harmon J & John Moyse PRISKE, 21 Jun 1911 Hudson, NH
   Walter J Harwood & Theo Hanson
   John Priske & Lylie Pascoe
HARWOOD, Merton W and Dorothy M FIELD, 01 Sep 1938 Hudson, NH
HARWOOD, Philip S and Virginia L FRANZEN, 23 Sep 1933 Hudson, NH
HARWOOD, Ralph W and Estelle M DOWNING, 10 Sep 1912 Hudson, NH
   Walter J Harwood & Thea Hanson
   William Downing & Roehil Main
HARWOOD, Sarah and Mark H WEBSTER, 11 Nov 1835
HARWOOD, Sarah Louise and Frederick ROLLS, 16 Aug 1927 Hudson, NH
HARWOOD, Walter T and Cora Esthe ELLIS, 21 Jun 1913 Hudson, NH
   Walter J Harwood & Thea Hanson
   Robert Ellis & Hannah A Payne
HASELTINE, John and Molly LADD, 06 Nov 1794
HASELTINE, Phineas and Clarissa WILSON, 17 Dec 1818
HASELTON, Arthur W and Mary E McCOY, 30 Dec 1891 Hudson, NH
   Geo W Haselton (Hudson, NH) & Lora Poor (Montpelier, VT)

HUDSON, NH MARRIAGES

Jas McCoy(Boston, MA) & Emma C Richards
HASELTON, Cordelia A and Jacob P EMERSON, 08 May 1861
HASELTON, David and H Francena WARD, 28 Nov 1861
HASELTON, David and H Francena WOOD, 28 Nov 1861
HASELTON, Ellen M and George N ALLARD, 22 Jun 1946 Hudson, NH
HASELTON, George W and Lora A POOR, 18 Feb 1862
HASELTON, George W and M Frances PAGE, 25 May 1860
HASELTON, George W and Laura A POOR, 14 Jun 1862
HASELTON, Hannah P and Elijah FLETCHER, 05 Dec 1843
HASELTON, Lillian M and Joseph E GATES, 20 Jul 1929 Hudson, NH
HASELTON, Louisa A and Alphonse ROBINSON, 23 Dec 1862
HASELTON, Luther and Polly L SMITH, 11 Apr 1826
HASELTON, Phineas and Clarissa WILSON, 07 Dec 1818
HASELTON, Sarah W and E Wesley HILL, 12 Oct 1864
HASELTON, William C and Bertha M HAMBLETT, 02 Apr 1890 Hudson, NH
    David Haselton (Hudson, NH) & Harriet F Wood (Leominster, MA)
    Alvin Hamblett(Hudson, NH) & Almira F McKean (Merrimack, NH)
HASKELL, Melvin B and Cecelia NESTOR, 14 Aug 1948 Hudson, NH
HASKELL, Ruth A and Quentin H BANKS, 31 Dec 1935 Nashua, NH
HASKELL, William E and Dorothy K FOISIE, 02 Jul 1949 Nashua, NH
HASKINS, Basil K and Marion R POLLOCK, 25 Oct 1933 Hudson, NH
HASSEY, Pearl and Charles CONOPKA, 16 Nov 1938 Nashua, NH
HASSLER, Anna and Walter J BRUCE, 23 Feb 1924 Nashua, NH
HASTINGS, Donald A and Cheryle A BUNKER, 26 Aug 1972 Derry, NH
HASTINGS, Gordon L and Anita BISSONNETTE, 03 Jul 1948 Hudson, NH
HASTINGS, Susan M and George E HILL, 21 Oct 1874 Hudson, NH
HATCH, Edith C and Everett M HAMBLETT, 10 Aug 1967 Hudson, NH
HATCH, Frederick and Dorothy M FLYNN, 26 Apr 1970 Nashua, NH
HATCH, Frederick and Mary K FRENCH, 21 Jul 1972 Merrimack, NH
HATCH, Herbert F Jr and Muriel E ELLIS, 08 Sep 1938 Hudson, NH
HATCH, Joseph B and Jean E OPSAHL, 04 Jul 1938 Hudson, NH
HATFIELD, Christine and Bruce D TURNQUIST, 21 Apr 1979 Hudson, NH
HAUAR, Earl L Jr and Barbara MILLIGAN, 14 Oct 1946 Hudson, NH
HAUG, Elizabeth and Gordon L FRENCH, 01 May 1948 Nashua, NH
HAUSWIRTH, Albert J Jr and Diane M KILGORE, 18 Sep 1948 Hudson, NH
HAVEY, Ann Marie and Donald J LeBLANC, 01 May 1982 Londonderry, NH
HAWES, C Arthur and Edith May STEWART, 15 Jun 1934 Hudson, NH
HAWES, Carol O and Leonard G LaFOREST, 16 Oct 1968 Hudson, NH
HAWKINS, Arlene L and Paul N COSSETTE, 27 Jun 1974 Sandown, NH
HAWKINS, Earleen M & Charles H SALISBURY, 16 Nov 1935 Brookline, NH
HAWKINS, Leroy A and June P BURON, 25 Sep 1948 Hudson, NH
HAWKINS, Lillian J and Glen J STRUBINGER, 12 May 1954 Nashua, NH
HAWTHWORTH, Sara C C and George W KUHN, 15 Oct 1846
HAYDEN, Daniel and Sarah GREELEY, 11 Dec 1800
HAYDEN, William V Jr and Ruth JOHNSON, 31 Jul 1937 Nashua, NH
HAYEK, Charles F Jr and Nancy J SMITH, 21 Jun 1958 Pelham, NH
HAYES, Alice M and Ronald D JEAN, 24 Oct 1970 Nashua, NH
HAYES, Betty M and Alexander GAGNON, 08 Feb 1960 Hudson, NH
HAYES, Calvin T and Jane L VAYENS, 13 Oct 1962 Hudson, NH
HAYES, Charles F and Ida B MORIN, 05 Aug 1950 Hudson, NH
HAYES, Douglas J and Dennise L MORRIS, 31 Oct 1981 Nashua, NH
HAYES, Evelyn L and Vernon E MacROBERTS, 22 Feb 1969 Nashua, NH
HAYES, James W and Sandra D SMITH, 17 May 1967 Hudson, NH
HAYES, John Lee and Deborah An DILWORTH, 15 Sep 1974 Litchfield, NH
HAYES, Judith A and Ronald A JUREK, 01 Aug 1964 Hudson, NH
HAYES, Judith M and David S FALES, 01 Jul 1961 Nashua, NH
HAYES, Lillian S and Warren E BEALS, 19 Jul 1964 Hudson, NH
HAYES, Linda M and Richard L PELLETIER, 05 Jun 1971 Hudson, NH
HAYES, Louise A and Gerald F BARRETT, 01 Jul 1983 Londonderry, NH
HAYES, Mary E and Chas W HANSCOMB, 18 Oct 1900 Strafford Cr

HUDSON,NH MARRIAGES

 C R Foss
 L G Hanscomb & Nancy Thomas
HAYES, Una B and Robert A JASPER, 05 Feb 1944 Nashua, NH
HAYMANN, Perry I and Diane J WIECZHALEK, 16 Oct 1976 Hudson, NH
HAYNES, Jacqueline and Richard W AHRENDT, 20 Aug 1966 Hudson, NH
HAYNES, Walter N and Lori M QUINN, 18 Feb 1978 Hudson, NH
HAYWARD, Adele and Herbert SHOLENBERGER, 06 Jul 1974 Manchester, NH
HAYWARD, Arthur L and Julia DEFOREST, 31 Dec 1903 Hudson, NH
 Leon Hayward & Lenore White
 Wm Deforest
HAYWARD, Beverly and Ernest F ALLEN, 19 Jun 1948 Hudson, NH
HAYWARD, Dorothy M and Merlin I COBLEIGH, 25 Nov 1960 Merrimack, NH
HAYWARD, Roger H and Mary Jane HOWELL, 23 Sep 1961 Hudson, NH
HAYWOOD, Electa and William ATWOOD, 03 Mar 1843
HAZELDINE, Pauline F and Henry L SCHOFIELD, 12 Nov 1949 Hudson, NH
HAZELTON, Arthur and Florence ESTY, 28 Mar 1918 Hudson, NH
HAZELTON, Dora E and Frank N SARGENT, 10 Jul 1912 Londonderry, NH
 William Hazelton & Bertha Hamblet
 Nathiel Sargent & Ellen Potter
HEALEY, Karen L and John E SETTLE, 03 Jul 1976 Nashua, NH
HEALY, Katherine and Raymond P BORTHWICK, 06 Nov 1948 Hudson, NH
HEANEY, Patricia B and Vernon S RIVET, 28 Aug 1950 Hudson, NH
HEARN, Amy and Stanley FILIPEK, 06 Dec 1947 Hudson, NH
HEATH, Gracie M and Henry C DAVIS, 26 Nov 1901 Hudson, NH
 T P Heath (Sheffield, VT) & F B Philbrick (Charlestown, VT)
 George H Davis(Hudson, NH) & Abby Batchelder (Hudson, NH)
HEATH, Jeffrey J and Rebecca A MITCHELL, 11 Jun 1978 Hudson, NH
HEBB, Winston P and Janet E TINKER, 04 Jul 1941 Nashua, NH
HEBERT, Agnes C and Lester R COLT, 02 Feb 1947 Hudson, NH
HEBERT, Denise D and Michael D BEAUCHESNE, 20 May 1978 Hudson, NH
HEBERT, Emile E and Katherine CARDINAL, 30 Aug 1973 Hudson, NH
HEBERT, Gail M and Raymond G HILTON, 01 Apr 1967 Nashua, NH
HEBERT, Irene A and Everett M SNOW, 12 May 1930 Hudson, NH
HEBERT, Lillian L and Michael M CHAVES, 22 Nov 1950 Hudson, NH
HEBERT, Michael W and Suzanne E TELLIER, 14 May 1983 Hudson, NH
HEBERT, Mildred A and William J BLAKELY, 12 Aug 1950 Nashua, NH
HEBERT, Pauline G and Normand R RABY, 12 Oct 1946 Nashua, NH
HEBERT, Peter W and Teresa M MARQUIS, 20 Aug 1976 Nashua, NH
HEBERT, Randall O and Linda B BEYER, 21 Jan 1974 Nashua, NH
HEBERT, Raymond and Sylvia SUND, 04 Oct 1947 Hudson, NH
HEBERT, Yolande P and Lester E OSMER, 23 Jun 1951 Nashua, NH
HEDGES, Terence J and Nancy L HAMMOND, 15 Mar 1959 Hudson, NH
HEIGHTON, Harold and Louise WETHERELL, 04 Oct 1947 Hudson, NH
HELIE, Richard L and Doris E RICHARDS, 03 Jul 1951 Hudson, NH
HELINSKI, Richard R and Brenda M MOSKOWITZ, 06 Aug 1981 Hudson, NH
HELME, Myrtle O and Joseph B COREIA, 27 Mar 1937 Nashua, NH
HEMEON, Betty J and Frederick SMITH, 09 Jun 1955 Nashua, NH
HEMEON, Katherine and Walter TAYLOR, 31 Oct 1964 Hudson, NH
HEMPEL, Carl W and Ida M INGLESTON, 17 Oct 1927 Hudson, NH
HENDERSON, Edna L and Norman G OSBORN, 03 Jul 1930 Hudson, NH
HENDERSON, Elizabeth and Thomas M LEE, 29 Dec 1984 Hudson, NH
HENDERSON, James F III and Gail E BOUTILIER, 15 Aug 1969 Hudson, NH
HENDERSON, James L and Sharon L KEYSER, 13 Apr 1968 Franklin, NH
HENDRICKS, Margaret M and Kenneth B SMITH, 21 Aug 1943 Hudson, NH
HENDRICKSON, Anita H and Donald J FOURNIER, 13 Sep 1969 Nashua, NH
HENDRICKSON, John D and Marion A CUNNINGHAM, 21 Jul 1962 Hudson, NH
HENKEL, Isabelle H and Harry B JONES, 21 May 1938 Hudson, NH
HENNESEY, Edith and George O DURANT, 30 Apr 1938 Hudson, NH
HENNESSY, Francis P and Edith H BRUCE, 16 Dec 1914 Hudson, NH
 John F Hennessy & Margaret A King

HUDSON, NH MARRIAGES

Elias A Bruce & Addie B Farmer
HENRY, Claudia A and Stephen R BRODSKY, 19 Dec 1981 Hudson, NH
HENRY, Lillian R and Edward V YOUNG, 29 Dec 1970 Hudson, NH
HENRY, Regina C and Marcellino ERALI, 11 May 1985 Hudson, NH
HENRY, Ruth Athal and Gardner SMITH, 11 Jun 1937 Nashua, NH
HENRY, Warren E and Rosemarie LAVOIE, 30 Jun 1951 Hudson, NH
HENSHAW, R Annette and Albert W NICHOLS, 17 Mar 1934 Nashua, NH
HERBERT, Georgia B and Robert M THOMPSON, 12 Dec 1937 Nashua, NH
HERBERT, Kay Lois and Timothy S FITZGERALD, 21 Oct 1972 Nashua, NH
HERBERT, Scott K and Linda M HANSON, 14 Jun 1969 Nashua, NH
HERNANDEZ, Alejandro and Elisabeth BURGESS, 17 Dec 1983 Salem, NH
HEROUX, Cecile F and Girard J RILEY, 01 Nov 1975 Hudson, NH
HEROUX, Daniel Paul and Susan Paul WELLS, 18 Jul 1980 Nashua, NH
HEROUX, Denise A and Allan L BURNS, 12 Mar 1971 Hudson, NH
HEROUX, Janet C and Leonard A DOW, 05 Jul 1975 Hudson, NH
HEROUX, Madeleine and Dennis M BURNS, 26 Jun 1970 Hudson, NH
HEROUX, Nelson E and Norma H MILLETT, 10 Sep 1960 Nashua, NH
HEROUX, Paul J and Cecile F LEMAY, 07 Aug 1948 Nashua, NH
HERRICK, James D and Louisa ROBINSON, 17 May 1848
HERRICK, Norma G and George M H Jr PIKE, 03 Oct 1943 Nashua, NH
HERRIN, Deborah A and David F LINDQUIST, 10 Aug 1982 Hudson, NH
HERRING, Alan J and Tinamarie ROCHEVILLE, 15 Sep 1979 Hudson, NH
HERSHEY, Lillian and Raymond J SCAMPORINO, 26 Dec 1942 Hudson, NH
HERZBERG, Lillian and Bernard E FEINSTEIN, 29 Nov 1923 Nashua, NH
HETZER, Cheryl S and John M OUELLETTE, 22 Jun 1974 Hudson, NH
HETZER, Lora L and Howard W IVES, 05 Feb 1977 Hudson, NH
HETZER, Lora L and James A WOODWARD, 04 Jun 1983 Hudson, NH
HETZER, Mark J and Elizabeth DIPIETRO, 29 Nov 1980 Hudson, NH
HEUSS, Virginia A and Charles T CROWLEY, 30 Sep 1950 Hudson, NH
HEUVELINE, Patrick F and Debra D DURHAM, 17 Dec 1983 Litchfield, NH
HEVEY, Robert J and Jean A DUDEVOIR, 01 Nov 1980 Pelham, NH
HEWITT, Paul Anson and Nellie M THOMPSON, 28 Apr 1892 Hudson, NH
   Wm Hewett (St John, N B) & Frances Wright (St John, N B)
   John M Thompson(Bridgewater) & Elizabeth Marsh (Hudson, NH)
HEYDWEILLER, Barbara E and Paul F BARBOUR, 10 May 1974 Hudson, NH
HICKCOX, Frederick and Frances CROSS, 28 Nov 1850
HICKEY, Aloysia E and Richard Sr POOLE, 15 Oct 1983 Deerfield, NH
HICKEY, Walter H and Eleanor E GALVIN, 12 Oct 1908 Nashua, NH
   Walter H Hickey & Elizabeth M Campbell
   Dennis F Galvin & Joanna Grimes
HICKS, George R and Audrey A BELENGER, 22 Aug 1949 Hudson, NH
HICKS, Kevin M and Laurette M DURAND, 29 Nov 1969 Nashua, NH
HICKS, Pamela J and Matthew D GIBB, 26 Jun 1982 Wolfeboro, NH
HICKS, Patricia B and Paul F SMITH, 26 Jul 1975 Nashua, NH
HICOX, Frederick and Frances J CROSS, 28 Nov 1850
HIDDEN, George and Mary J McQUESTEN, 10 Nov 1861
HIER, George B and Suzanne C NADEAU, 30 Jun 1973 Hudson, NH
HIGGINS, Louisa A and John A GAMMELL, 05 Dec 1883 Hudson, NH
   Sparrow Higgins(W Boylston,MA) & Juliett A Pierce(Providence, RI)
   Warren E Gammell(Boston, MA) & Elmirea A Bonous
HIGGINS, Maureen J and Leslie F GONSALVES, 16 Aug 1975 Hudson, NH
HIGGINS, Melency E and Fenwick W DEMONE, 20 Mar 1943 Hudson, NH
HIGH, Lynne G and Charles O GOULET, 13 Nov 1965 Hudson, NH
HIGH, Robert E and Katherine CADY, 20 Aug 1960 Merrimack, NH
HIGTON, Ernest and Helen L McCRADY, 08 Sep 1979 Nashua, NH
HILBARD, Helen and Herbert W HOPKINS, 24 Jan 1942 Hudson, NH
HILDRETH, Albert J and Harriet DEWOLFE, 05 Nov 1854
HILDRETH, Lizzie and Francis BARNS, 13 Oct 1859
HILEMAN, Larry C and Lynn A DURHAM, 20 Oct 1979 Litchfield, NH
HILL, Anna F and Charles R DUKE, 18 Aug 1962 Hudson, NH

HUDSON,NH MARRIAGES

HILL, Artemas and Sophia LOUGEE, 28 Apr 1867
HILL, Artemus and Sophia LOUGER, 28 Apr 1867
HILL, Betsey A and Eben CONVERSE, 30 Dec 1866
HILL, Betsey A and Eben CONVERSE, 13 Dec 1866
HILL, E Wesley and Sarah W HASELTON, 12 Oct 1864
HILL, George E and Susan M HASTINGS, 21 Oct 1874 Hudson, NH
HILL, George Hadley and Edna Frances HARVEY, 11 Oct 1910 Hudson, NH
   George H Hill & Mary Morris
   Charles H Harvey & Celia M Fellows
HILL, Gordon S and Bridget L STACK, 27 Aug 1948 Hudson, NH
HILL, Granville and Hannah ADAMS, 29 Jun 1858
HILL, Harriet N and Moses W EMERSON, 04 Sep 1883 Hudson, NH
   David Burns (Hudson, NH) & Eliza Childs (Salem, MA)
   Kimball Emerson(Haverhill, MA) & Sarah Webster (Salem, NH)
HILL, Justin E and Carrie S BRADBURY, 05 Jul 1868
HILL, Marie D and Ronald W JACOBSEN, 10 Jul 1965 Hudson, NH
HILL, Mary F and Elias A PERKINS, 29 Oct 1863
HILL, Mary T F and Elias A PERKINS, 29 Oct 1864
HILL, Myrtle M and Dana C MARSHALL, 18 Sep 1913 Hudson, NH
   David B Hill & Abbie A Batchelder
   Dana S Marshall & Martha A Griffin
HILL, Osgood and Calisha J CAMPBELL, 20 Feb 1870
HILL, Osgood and Calesta J CAMPBELL, 20 Feb 1870 Hudson, NH
HILL, Patricia L and Jon A FORSAITH, 27 Nov 1982 Hudson, NH
HILL, Rebecca N and Elijah TINKER, 12 Oct 1864
HILL, Rita M and Roger A MORIN, 19 Aug 1942 Nashua, NH
HILL, Roger S and Elsie M WILLS, 11 Mar 1917 Hudson, NH
HILL, Stafford S and Edna F LYON, 09 May 1931 Hudson, NH
HILL, Winetta T and Kenneth C ELLIOTT, 23 Oct 1969 Salem, NH
HILLI, Karl A and Mary A RIHINOMA, 13 Apr 1941 Hudson, NH
HILLS, Abigail and James HILLS, 27 Feb 1787
HILLS, Abigail and Abel POLLARD, 28 Jun 1796
HILLS, Adaliza and Prescott ADAMS, 26 Jan 1871
HILLS, Addie P and Prescott A ADAMS, 26 Jan 1870 Hudson, NH
HILLS, Alfred M and Mary A UNDERWOOD, 08 Mar 1865
HILLS, Alphonse and Mary A UNDERWOOD, 28 Mar 1865
HILLS, Asenath and Allen ANDREWS, 30 Mar 1824
HILLS, David and Mehitable ROBINSON, 08 Sep 1796
HILLS, Edna and Philip HILLS, 26 Sep 1778
HILLS, Edna and Philip HILLS, 24 Sep 1778
HILLS, Edna M and Harold F MERRILL, 05 Sep 1948 Londonderry, NH
HILLS, Elijah and Betsey TARBOX, 12 Mar 1801
HILLS, Eliza and Dana SARGENT, 31 Dec 1829
HILLS, Hannah and Gilman FLETCHER, 10 May 1826
HILLS, Harland S and Gladys I SNOW, 12 Jul 1913 Litchfield, NH
   Orlando G Hills & Nettie L Young
   Royal G Snow & Addie E Walker
HILLS, James and Abigail HILLS, 27 Feb 1787
HILLS, James L and Ellen M ANNABLE, 21 Jun 1947 Hudson, NH
HILLS, Livia and Luke BURNS, 01 Nov 1842
HILLS, Marjorie E and Winthrop H PACKARD, 27 May 1948 Hudson, NH
HILLS, Orlando G and Nettie L YOUNG, 17 Jun 1889 Hudson, NH
   Silas Hills (Windham, NH) & Roxanna Farnham (Londonderry, NH)
   Israel W Young(Manchester, NH) & Elizabeth S Morse (Methuen, MA)
HILLS, Orlando G and Nettie L YOUNG, 17 Jun 1887
HILLS, Orlando G Jr and Julia A SHERMAN, 15 Oct 1945 Hudson, NH
HILLS, Paul W and Margaret LATTI, 06 Jun 1981 Nashua, NH
HILLS, Philip and Edna HILLS, 26 Sep 1778
HILLS, Philip and Edna HILLS, 24 Sep 1778
HILLS, Rachel and Zaccheus COLBURN, 29 Apr 1788

HUDSON, NH MARRIAGES

HILLS, Rebecca and Ebenezer HARRIS, 03 Jan 1782
HILLS, Rhoda and Reuben CUMMINGS,
HILLS, Sally and Paul TENNEY, 02 Dec 1819
HILLS, Samuel Jr and Rhoda BOWERS, 02 Jun 1796
HILLS, Sarah and Joseph Jr WINN, 08 Feb 1753
HILLS, Sarah J and William H SHAPLEY, 27 Sep 1852
HILLS, Sylvia and Alfred P FLEMMING, 13 Jul 1941 Nashua, NH
HILLS, William and Mary HADLEY, 28 Jun 1808
HILLS, William W and Mary HADLEY, 28 Jan 1808
HILLSON, Ross M and Sue I CINCOLA, 30 Apr 1934 Hudson, NH
HILLYARD, Wayne A & Julie Anne MAILHOT, 02 Jun 1984 Londonderry, NH
HILTON, Jean E and Ralph A KELLEY, 11 Aug 1957 Hudson, NH
HILTON, Raymond G and Gail M HEBERT, 01 Apr 1967 Nashua, NH
HILTON, Susan J and Daniel R SHEA, 05 Aug 1977 Hudson, NH
HIMMER, Raymond W A and Alice M DEARVILLE, 21 Sep 1927 Hudson, NH
HINCHMAN, Richard M and Phyllis W PEACOCK, 03 Oct 1936 Hudson, NH
HINDS, Gertrude I and Wilbur L WALLS, 18 Mar 1949 Hudson, NH
HINES, John F Jr and Jane M NAGLE, 25 Mar 1949 Hudson, NH
HINES, Nicholas and Marlene A MOORE, 18 Aug 1979 Hudson, NH
HINRICHS, Mark H and Kathy J GIBSON, 16 Aug 1980 Hudson, NH
HINTON, Donald A and Harriet L MAGNIN, 08 Aug 1953 Hudson, NH
HIRSCH, Debra J and Anthony R LECLERC, 12 May 1979 Hudson, NH
HIRTH, Bernard P and Dorothy E DEMANCHE, 30 Jan 1960 Hudson, NH
HIRTH, Janice C and Victor T BELLROSE, 08 Dec 1953 Hudson, NH
HIRTH, Thomas J and Margaret M TUPPER, 27 Feb 1965 Hudson, NH
HIRTLE, Lois M and Joseph E RACY, 16 Jun 1979 Nashua, NH
HO, Cynthia T and Hai HUANG, 04 Oct 1983 Nashua, NH
HO, Li-Hsi and Szu Cheng CHEN, 28 Dec 1980 Nashua, NH
HOAG, Dana A and Vivianne S BLUNT, 07 Oct 1980 Nashua, NH
HOAG, David L and Charlotte BELKNAP, 22 Sep 1860
HOAG, Edith Blan and Chas E Jr NICHOLS, 02 Jun 1898 Nashua, NH
  David T Hoag & Charlotte Belknap
  Charles E Nichols & Kate C Frye
HOAG, Kenneth E and Sherri M WOOD, 07 Nov 1981 Merrimack, NH
HOAGG, David C and Charlotte BELKNAP, 29 Dec 1860
HOBBS, Jacob and Susan HAMMOND, 04 Jun 1860
HOBBS, Marilyn J and Bruce E WESSON, 09 Jun 1973 Candia, NH
HOBBS, Mary and Phinehas NICHOLS, 22 Feb 1822
HOBBS, Nancy and Phineas NICHOLS, 22 Feb 1823
HOBBS, Rose E and Michael J HARTIGAN, 21 Apr 1932 Nashua, NH
HODGDON, Sophia C and Nathaniel BLUSDAYS, 13 Feb 1860
HODGE, Daniel and Diane C SCRIVENER, 31 May 1975 Nashua, NH
HODGE, Sandra and Manuel M FERREIRA, 17 Aug 1974 Manchester, NH
HODGE, Wendeline and Branwell P LELAND, 18 Jan 1969 Hudson, NH
HODGKINS, Florence G and Harry BASANISI, 31 Aug 1924 Hudson, NH
HODGKINS, Linda and Mark E PARDY, 16 May 1981 Hudson, NH
HODGKINS, Michelle M and Jeffrey A SMART, 09 Jun 1979 Hudson, NH
HODGKINS, Pearl I and Joseph E TETREAULT, 04 Nov 1922 Hudson, NH
HODGMAN, John S and Mary E NICHOLS, 08 Mar 1873 Hudson, NH
HODGMAN, Robert M and Sandra L LAMPRON, 10 Nov 1962 Wilton, NH
HODGMAN, Wayne P and Rebecca E WELCH, 12 Aug 1978 Hudson, NH
HODSDON, John R and Judith N ALLEN, 20 Feb 1960 Tuftonboro, NH
HODSDON, Judith and Vincent M IZZI, 01 Jun 1985 Hudson, NH
HOFFMAN, Katie Ann and George W KELLEY, 29 Jul 1885 Lowell, MA
  Philip Hoffman (Ireland) & AnnPoff (Ireland)
  William Kelley & Dorcus Clement (Hudson, NH)
HOGAN, Daniel P and Christine BLAIS, 16 Jul 1977 Nashua, NH
HOGAN, Michael W and Paula T RICHARDS, 13 Oct 1973 Hudson, NH
HOGAN, Patrick J and Marilyn H DORAN, 15 Jan 1949 Hudson, NH
HOGAN, Pauline C and Friend L SKINNER, 22 Jul 1950 Hudson, NH

HUDSON, NH MARRIAGES

HOGAN, Shawn B and Suzanne F TAYLOR, 01 Apr 1964 Nashua, NH
HOGARTY, Joan M and Howard LEVINE, 20 Sep 1973 Hudson, NH
HOH, Richard and Edith DEARVILLE, 17 May 1927 Hudson, NH
HOITT, Robert W and Eileen L COFFIN, 03 Aug 1935 Hudson, NH
HOJABOOM, Lawrence A and Phyllis I ELDRED, 06 Oct 1962 Hudson, NH
HOLDEN, Debra Anne and Russell P SAUCIER, 20 Nov 1982 Hudson, NH
HOLDEN, Elizabeth and Edward MILNE, 18 Aug 1941 Hudson, NH
HOLDEN, Ruth A & Kenneth E DESMARAIS, 12 Mar 1978 Manchester, NH
HOLDEN, Wilfred L and Mary-Jane ABBOTT, 26 Feb 1957 Hudson, NH
HOLDEN, Wilfred L and Diane M POWLISON, 22 Apr 1972 Burand, MI
HOLLAND, Marjorie G and Clarence L SWEENEY, 09 Aug 1947 Hudson, NH
HOLLEY, William C and Frances G HARRIS, 30 Oct 1948 Hudson, NH
HOLM, Kenneth and Helen SMITH, 14 Feb 1944 Hudson, NH
HOLM, Linda Jane and Raynold A BOULEY, 14 Sep 1972 Nashua, NH
HOLM, Marjorie M and John E MALPIEDI, 28 Aug 1970 Laconia, NH
HOLM, Mary Lou and James R SEVIGNY, 04 Aug 1972 Windham, NH
HOLMAN, Mary A and David CLEMENT, 18 Sep 1867 West Roxbury, MA
HOLMES, Agnes J and Herbert E MOORE, 22 Jun 1907 Hudson, NH
  George I Holmes & Maria A J Butler
  John Moore & Annie L Littlefield
HOLMES, Blanche D and Basil N PERKINS, 05 Oct 1912 Lunenburg, MA
  Elmer Holmes & Abbie Merrill
  Sumner Perkins & Annie Hayden
HOLMES, Charles M and Mary A BATCHELDER, 25 Nov 1847
HOLMES, George L and Malissa A WHEELER, 22 Nov 1881 Hollis, NH
  Luke Holmes (Canada) & Catherine Butler (Hudson, NH)
  Theodore Wheeler
HOLMES, George L and Maria A J BUTLER, 24 Oct 1885 Hudson, NH
  Luke Holmes (Canada) & Catherine Butler (Hudson, NH)
  William Butler(Ireland) & Mary A Brady (Ireland)
HOLMES, L Frances and Russell H KITTREDGE, 24 Dec 1857
HOLMES, Marjean and Steven G WORKMAN, 29 Mar 1985 New Ipswich, NH
HOLMES, Mary J and Joseph M HAMBLET, 04 Oct 1869 Hudson, NH
HOLMES, Stephen C and Karen J McCRADY, 12 Mar 1977 Nashua, NH
HOLMES, Victoria M and Charles E PETERSON, 25 May 1911 Nashua, NH
  Victor Holm & Marie Somnersum
  Nelse P Peterson & Sarah Johnson
HOLROYD, Pamela J and Joseph F Jr BONACCORSI, 04 Aug 1979 Salem, NH
HOLT, Barbara M and John B Jr BOURGEOIS, 26 Sep 1952 Hudson, NH
HOLT, Bernice R and Richard G BOILARD, 08 May 1967 Nashua, NH
HOLT, Charles K and Doris E TRAFFORD, 27 May 1972 Hudson, NH
HOLT, Charles W and G Elaine MERRILL, 12 May 1942 Hudson, NH
HOLT, D Augustus and Nellie C WOODWARD, 25 Apr 1858
HOLT, Dale L and Bryan S BAKER, 21 Jun 1985 Nashua, NH
HOLT, Dexter S and Edna M GALLAGHER, 29 May 1937 Fitchburg, MA
HOLT, Gladys A and Robert L HOOD, 29 Jun 1910 Hudson, NH
  Bert J Holt & Dora Mott
  Samuel Hood & Margaret Hayes
HOLT, Gloria A and Kenneth D STULTZ, 04 Mar 1950 Hudson, NH
HOLT, James E Jr and Maureen GILBERT, 14 Jun 1975 Pelham, NH
HOLT, Judith A and David G GEER, 14 Apr 1969 Nashua, NH
HOLT, Kathryn J and Eugene S III DANIELL, 10 Aug 1968 Hudson, NH
HOLT, Ralph L and Jeannette MALENFANT, 12 Sep 1953 Hudson, NH
HOLT, Ralph L and Catherine HUNINK, 02 Sep 1976 Nashua, NH
HOLT, Richard H and Jodi J FOISY, 05 Jun 1982 Nashua, NH
HOLT, Ruth Ann and Leopold HALL, 21 Sep 1981 Brentwood, NH
HOLT, Susan M and Robert L DUFAULT, 04 Feb 1967 Hudson, NH
HOLT, Thomas C and Mita MITRA, 26 Jun 1983 Hudson, NH
HOLTON, Bruce W and Theresa R LANDRY, 29 Jun 1974 Litchfield, NH
HOLTON, John H and Dorothy E SMITH, 17 Sep 1938 Londonderry, NH

HUDSON,NH MARRIAGES

HOLTON, Marion E and Luther E STANHOPE, 31 Aug 1940 Hudson, NH
HOLTON, Mary R and David CLEMENT, 18 Sep 1867
HOLTON, Roy E and JoAnne E KENNEDY, 22 Nov 1969 Hudson, NH
HOMER, Dorothy F and Benjamin BRINTNALL, 14 Jun 1947 Hudson, NH
HONEYWELL, Roy J and Annabell MORGAN, 19 Apr 1922 Hudson, NH
HOOD, Charles H Jr and Rosella A DANIELS, 17 Jul 1942 Nashua, NH
HOOD, Linda J and Richard P FARRINGTON, 20 Apr 1985 Nashua, NH
HOOD, Robert L and Gladys A HOLT, 29 Jun 1910 Hudson, NH
   Samuel Hood & Margaret Hayes
   Bert J Holt & Dora Mott
HOOKER, Francis C and Clara V KAY, 16 Apr 1949 Hudson, NH
HOOKS, Cora E and Alexander PROWKER, 30 Sep 1961 Hudson, NH
HOOPER, Cora M and Raymond J POLLARD, 21 Mar 1900 Lowell, MA
   Charles F Cooper & Leah Barnard
   Joseph F Pollard & Emily Bemas
HOOPER, Theodora C and Anthony J CUTULLE, 16 Aug 1947 Hudson, NH
HOOPER, Thomas J and Wilhelmina HUTCHINS, 24 Apr 1934 Hudson, NH
HOPE, Boyd C Jr and Louise I LUNDBERG, 04 Jul 1947 Hudson, NH
HOPKINS, Charles E and Carlene M HUMPHREY, 29 Dec 1948 Hudson, NH
HOPKINS, Charles H and Susan TAYLOR, 09 Oct 1860
HOPKINS, Edith L and Harold M RANDOLL, 26 Jun 1909 Nashua, NH
   Charles H Hopkins & Ida S Webster
   Martin Randoll & Ida M Dary
HOPKINS, Herbert W and Helen HILBARD, 24 Jan 1942 Hudson, NH
HOPWOOD, Leon F and Katherine CHURCH, 30 Dec 1944 N Haverhill, NH
HOPWOOD, Mary E and Clarence W HAIGHT, 19 Sep 1925 Hudson, NH
HORKEY, David L and Marie A BARRESE, 07 Dec 1973 Hudson, NH
HORNE, Elaine and Charles W ADAMS, 27 Oct 1984 W Ossipee, NH
HORNE, Martha D and George E STEVENS, 30 Dec 1927 Hudson, NH
HORNIG, Herman E and Dorothy G TOLON, 21 Aug 1934 Hudson, NH
HORR, Anna L and William V TUFTS, 14 Oct 1939 Nashua, NH
HORSLEY, Harlan P and Mary Franc CUMMINGS, 27 Jan 1861
HORSTKOTTE, Rosemary G and Alan B URQUHART, 17 Jun 1984 Hudson, NH
HORTON, Lawrence M Jr and Jean C COMEAU, 20 Oct 1932 Nashua, NH
HORTON, Ralph H and Martha Ann BELANGER, 28 Oct 1972 Nashua, NH
HORTON, Viola and Walter L NICHOLS, 17 Sep 1937 Dunstable, MA
HOUDESHELL, Patricia S and Francis K PERRY, 22 Aug 1980 Hampton, NH
HOULE, Amedee J Jr and Flora M KIERSTEAD, 25 May 1957 Hudson, NH
HOULE, Andrew M and Phyllis M LEVESQUE, 18 May 1974 Allenstown, NH
HOULE, Cheryl N and William J KELLEY, 28 Oct 1967 Hudson, NH
HOULE, Douglas M and Belinda L McCOY, 26 May 1984 Hudson, NH
HOULE, Elaine L and Robert A LINSCOTT, 25 Jun 1983 Hudson, NH
HOULE, Georgianna and John J NONNAN, 06 May 1895 Nashua, NH
   Jestin Houle
   Lewis Nonnan & Mary Shambeau
HOULE, Linda A and Nicholas M CARTER, 08 Jun 1968 Nashua, NH
HOULE, Nelson B and Marcelle A ROBICHAUD, 20 Sep 1957 Hudson, NH
HOULE, Stewart C and Lucille R LESSARD, 11 Jul 1970 Nashua, NH
HOULE, Walter P Jr and Delaine N TESSIER, 24 Aug 1968 Hudson, NH
HOULEY, Margaret L and Frank G RANNEY, 21 Nov 1927 Nashua, NH
HOULEY, William R and Josephine KULESZ, 01 Dec 1945 Nashua, NH
HOUSE, Philip R and Arlene PETERSON, 24 Sep 1955 Hudson, NH
HOUSTON, Curtis W and Phyllis M CROTTY, 25 Sep 1944 Hudson, NH
HOUSTON, Gerald and Esther SHEPHERD, 27 Oct 1926 Hudson, NH
HOVATTER, Rita L and Richard A BERNIER, 23 Apr 1976 Derry, NH
HOVEY, John D and Virginia E GLISPIN, 30 May 1970 Nashua, NH
HOVEY, Lavina C and Horace G HAMBLET, 30 Apr 1862
HOVEY, Pamela L and William M ARSENEAULT, 14 Jul 1984 Nashua, NH
HOVIOUS, Neil O and Janet L SMITH, 16 Apr 1983 Nashua, NH
HOVLING, Ronald C and Susanne CLEMENT, 30 Nov 1963 Hudson, NH

HUDSON,NH MARRIAGES

HOWARD, BarbaraAnn and Wayne C DION, 23 Apr 1966 Hudson, NH
HOWARD, Charles A and Josephine NEWCOMBE, 09 Jul 1949 Hudson, NH
HOWARD, Charles L and Abby J RICE, 01 Aug 1859
HOWARD, Eleanor J and Alfred R BENNERT, 19 Oct 1929 Nashua, NH
HOWARD, Elizabeth and Alfred KARGAARD, 26 Mar 1942 Hudson, NH
HOWARD, Ernest H and Suzanne L BOULEY, 13 Sep 1969 Hudson, NH
HOWARD, Evelyn M and Stephen G DMITRUK, 25 Oct 1973 Hudson, NH
HOWARD, Leland E and Grace H HARWOOD, 06 Apr 1921 Nashua, NH
HOWARD, Leland E and Lydia M THOMPSON, 11 May 1940 Swanzey, NH
HOWARD, Sarah and Samuel LEWIS, 04 Mar 1779
HOWE, Andrew E and Mary E PELLETIER, 18 Sep 1924 Hudson, NH
HOWE, Charles L and Francine L WOOD, 11 Mar 1967 Nashua, NH
HOWE, Cynthia and Hugh SMITH, 10 Nov 1842
HOWE, Cynthia U and Lafayette DAY, 26 Oct 1854
HOWE, Daniel and Mehittable HAMBLETT, 04 Apr 1771
HOWE, Daniel and Mehetible HAMBLET, 04 Apr 1788
HOWE, David C and Mary Ann DION, 15 Apr 1972 Hudson, NH
HOWE, David L and Jane E PORTIGUE, 18 May 1968 Hudson, NH
HOWE, Gary and Cynthia J McGEE, 19 Feb 1966 Hudson, NH
HOWE, Harriet E and James F SANBORN, 28 Apr 1856
HOWE, Harry E and Judith C PENNO, 08 Sep 1984 Hudson, NH
HOWE, James P and Esther P BELKNAP, 12 Jul 1869 Hudson, NH
HOWE, Kenneth L and Sue A LOCKE, 27 Nov 1965 Hudson, NH
HOWE, Margaret M and Raymond L GINGRAS, 23 Jul 1982 Nashua, NH
HOWE, Paul E and Deborah E WALKER, 29 May 1971 Hudson, NH
HOWE, Phyllis E and Allen I MERCHANT, 14 May 1966 Hudson, NH
HOWE, Rhoda L and Theodore F LAMBERT, 15 Jun 1963 Nashua, NH
HOWE, Richard A and Carol A FOWLER, 29 Jun 1974 Nashua, NH
HOWE, Robert L and Jean E LAWRENCE, 29 Jun 1963 Hudson, NH
HOWE, Stephen M and Barbara A McGUIRE, 05 Sep 1970 Nashua, NH
HOWELL, Mary Jane and Roger H HAYWARD, 23 Sep 1961 Hudson, NH
HOWELL, Warren B and Brenda A LAFLAMME, 31 Aug 1963 Hudson, NH
HOWES, Alice H and George G ADAMS, 25 Nov 1927 Nashua, NH
HOWES, Donald H and Maitland M TRACEY, 01 Jun 1929 Nashua, NH
HOWES, Kevin G and Denise J CHEVALIER, 19 May 1979 Nashua, NH
HOWLAND, Dana P and Carol A SMITH, 18 Apr 1970 Hudson, NH
HOY, Patricia M and George V DAVIES, 16 Sep 1949 Hudson, NH
HOYME, Maxine K and Matthew E SEKELLA, 21 Aug 1980 Nashua, NH
HOYT, David R and Pamela M THORNTON, 28 Jan 1970 Hudson, NH
HOYT, Deborah and Jonathan E SHAFER, 24 Oct 1981 Nashua, NH
HOYT, Jeffrey A and Cindy S SEBOR, 18 Aug 1984 Hudson, NH
HOYT, Stephen R and Bonnie L JOHNSON, 29 Jan 1972 Nashua, NH
HUANG, Hai and Cynthia T HO, 04 Oct 1983 Nashua, NH
HUARD, William J Jr and Vivian R LACASSE, 08 Nov 1969 Nashua, NH
HUBBARD, Flora W and Frank E MARSHALL, 21 Aug 1906 Hudson, NH
   L E Walker & Maria Nearch
   William S Marshall & Mary E Libbey
HUBBARD, James and Phebe WALKER, 13 Dec 1818
HUBBARD, Ruth and Manuel DECOSTA, 21 Feb 1948 Hudson, NH
HUDACEK, Terry Lee and Robert B MERRILL, 28 Oct 1972 Hudson, NH
HUDON, Donald R and Lorraine M WILLIAMS, 03 May 1980 Hudson, NH
HUDON, Ruth C and James E HARWOOD, 01 Dec 1962 Nashua, NH
HUDSON, Charles W&Denise E LIVINGSTON, 08 Oct 1978 Londonderry, NH
HUDSON, Emily A and William MONTGOMERY, 15 Aug 1917 Barrington
HUDSON, Isaac C and Flora E SHATTUCK, 27 Dec 1879 Hudson, NH
   Silas P Hudson & Eliza A Lemery
   Alfred Shattuck(Mont Vernon, NH) & Rosa Holden
HUDSON, Julian L and Lena M JOSSELYN, 11 Jun 1934 Hudson, NH
HUDSON, Karen L and Dean F FAUCHER, 23 Jul 1983 Merrimack, NH
HUDSON, Kenneth J and Judy Ann KORPETER, 22 Jan 1966 Hudson, NH

HUDSON,NH MARRIAGES

HUDSON, Thomas D and Kellie J QUIGLEY, 01 Jul 1983 Hudson, NH
HUFF, Marcia E and Thomas L BELLAVANCE, 22 Feb 1969 Hollis, NH
HUFF, Marcia E and David A SARASIN, 21 Jan 1967 Nashua, NH
HUFF, Marcia E and William J SHEFFIELD, 26 Aug 1972 Nashua, NH
HUFF, Stephen G and Susan J CARTER, 03 Sep 1969 Nashua, NH
HUFF, Sylvia J and Willie W EATON, 23 Mar 1884 Hudson, NH
  Samuel Huff & Sarah
  Alfred Eaton & Harriet Smith (Hudson, NH)
HUGHES, Bruce A and Ruth N BONHOMME, 10 Mar 1973 Nashua, NH
HUGHES, Debra Anne and David C OTIS, 19 Nov 1976 Windham, NH
HUGHES, Fred S and Marie Y ST LAURENT, 05 Oct 1963 Nashua, NH
HUGHES, Gary A and Eleanor L JACKSON, 19 Oct 1968 Nashua, NH
HUGHES, Irene and Harvey E SCHOFIELD, 23 Jul 1938 Hudson, NH
HUGHES, James Frank and Irma MUELLER, 16 Apr 1929 Hudson, NH
HUGHES, Joel Stanley and Mary Ann DAVEY, 24 May 1981 Hudson, NH
HUGHES, John C and Madeline D CARROLL, 23 Jul 1942 Hudson, NH
HUGHES, Sharon Lee and Roland R ROY, 04 Feb 1967 Nashua, NH
HUGHES, Sheila R and Jerry C BURNETT, 25 Sep 1977 Hudson, NH
HUGHEY, Jodie Mari and Joseph M CLIFFORD, 11 Jun 1983 Hudson, NH
HUGHY, Ruth C and Henry KAUFHOLD, 19 Feb 1983 Concord, NH
HULL, Deanna J and Christophe CARLSTROM, 11 Jul 1981 Nashua, NH
HULL, Gregory A and Susan J WALLACE, 30 Aug 1980 Nashua, NH
HULS, Raymond W and Gloria J RICHARDSON, 19 May 1945 Hudson, NH
HULSE, Arthur Jr and Doris M LAVOIE, 08 Nov 1969 Hudson, NH
HUME, Douglas M and Cynthia A KENNEDY, 11 Jul 1981 Hudson, NH
HUMPHREY, Carlene M and Charles E HOPKINS, 29 Dec 1948 Hudson, NH
HUMPHREY, Margaret A and Oscar A ITZKOWITZ, 07 Jul 1956 Hudson, NH
HUMPHREYS, Laura M and Warner W CILLEY, 11 Jan 1928 Goffstown, NH
HUMPTON, Joseph B and Melissa D KRUEGER, 16 Oct 1982 Nashua, NH
HUNINK, Catherine and Ralph L HOLT, 02 Sep 1976 Nashua, NH
HUNNEWELL, Albert J and Dorothy A CHAPMAN, 30 Dec 1981 Hudson, NH
HUNNEWELL, Elizabeth and Ralph A Jr LEDOUX, 29 Sep 1962 Nashua, NH
HUNNEWELL, Josephine and Robert C LYNCH, 18 Jul 1946 Hudson, NH
HUNNEWELL, Mary C and Bradley H FORD, 20 Jul 1957 Hudson, NH
HUNNEWELL, Ralph E and Josephine FLANAGAN, 14 Apr 1923 Nashua, NH
HUNT, Bertha M and Ernest E WILLIAMS, 12 Jun 1909 Nashua, NH
  Riley Smith & Mary Berry
  John F Williams & Maria Tate
HUNT, David W and Kathryn M MASTERSON, 16 Nov 1968 Hudson, NH
HUNT, Stanley L and Harriet H PORTMORE, 13 Feb 1937 Nashua, NH
HUNT, William and Sarah L FROST, 23 Jan 1858
HUNT, William C Jr and Helen E MILLS, 10 Aug 1935 Hudson, NH
HUNTER, Dianne and Dave GUTIERREZ, 09 Oct 1982 Hudson, NH
HUNTER, Ethel M and Oscar BILODEAU, 31 Dec 1915 Hudson, NH
  Frank A Hunter (Rockbottom, MA) & Amy A Beal (Harrisville, NH)
  Joseph Bilodeau(Canada) & Mary (Canada)
HUNTER, Harry B and June V BROWN, 17 Oct 1956 Nashua, NH
HUNTER, Marshall O and Effie D WOOD, 13 Aug 1906 Hudson, NH
  Henry Hunter & Julia F Gurney
  Wentworth Wood & Ada M Anderson
HUNTER, Mildred and Oscar BILODEAU, 09 Feb 1925 Hudson, NH
HUNTER, Robert R and Joan B LILLEY, 05 Apr 1953 Hudson, NH
HUNTER, Violet E and Frederick TAYLOR, 25 Dec 1936 Hudson, NH
HUNTING, Irene and Andrew J SMITH, 27 May 1857
HUNTLEY, Ella G and Alfred L MOORE, 24 Feb 1875 Hudson, NH
HUOT, Donald R and Patricia A NADEAU, 02 Jul 1976 Hudson, NH
HURD, Anna M and Adolph J ZEDALIS, 02 Dec 1939 Nashua, NH
HURD, Chester E and Patricia B DESMARAIS, 01 Sep 1962 Nashua, NH
HURD, Donald E and Patricia A FRANK, 07 Apr 1962 Nashua, NH
HURLBERT, Jack and Joyce R TULEJA, 24 Jun 1967 Hudson, NH

HUDSON, NH MARRIAGES

HURTEAU, Clement E and Anne M LENNON, 17 Jun 1950 Hudson, NH
HUSSEY, Carole A and Gerald L BERNIER, 17 Jun 1967 Wilton, NH
HUSSEY, Deborah L and Brian K RAY, 18 May 1985 Hudson, NH
HUSSEY, Doris I and Elwin R MOSS, 23 Dec 1961 Hudson, NH
HUTCHINS, Henry G and Nancy J FULLER, 22 Jan 1868
HUTCHINS, Pat and John F SPALDING, 13 Jan 1946 Durham, NH
HUTCHINS, Wilhelmina and Thomas J HOOPER, 24 Apr 1934 Hudson, NH
HUTCHINSON, Albert and Mary E ALLEN, 24 Nov 1868 Hudson, NH
HUTCHINSON, Bartlett M & Priscilla THOMSON, 04 Jun 1967 Nashua, NH
HUTCHINSON, Earl L and Lillian I CONOMICK, 24 Mar 1935 Hudson, NH
HUTCHINSON, Idris A and Fletcher A GARNET, 01 Sep 1940 Hudson, NH
HUTTON, Lucy A and Larry SMITH, 07 Jun 1969 Stratham, NH
HUTTON, Nancy E and John P SEAGER, 01 Jul 1971 Hudson, NH
HYAM, Sheila M and Norman C DOUCET, 04 Aug 1984 Hudson, NH
HYDE, Forrest F and Blanche R MOREAU, 26 May 1946 Nashua, NH
HYDE, Janet and Harry L ROTE, 17 Dec 1947 Hudson, NH
HYSETTE, Gail T and Michael D CLOUTIER, 13 Oct 1979 Nashua, NH
ILLG, Jody L and Kelly R FRASER, 11 Oct 1980 Hudson, NH
INFERRERA, Stella J and Arthur P SAMPSON, 17 Jul 1948 Hudson, NH
INGALLS, Alice and Thomas POLLARD, 14 Dec 1785
INGALLS, Kenneth J and Katherine SPAULDING, 10 Oct 1981 Nashua, NH
INGALLS, Lucy A and Arthur L JOY, 14 Oct 1891 Nashua, NH
  John H Ingalls (Chelmsford, MA) & Nancy M Blood (Dunstable, MA)
  Lemuel T Joy(Quincy, MA) & Mary E Hadley (Nashua, NH)
INGALLS, Mary S and Samuel H STEVENS, 17 Mar 1863
INGALLS, Nathaniel and Elizabeth DITSON, Jun 1783
INGALLS, Sarah and Elijah GOULD, 30 Nov 1780
INGALLS, Vincent L and Christine DIVIDO, 14 Dec 1984 Nashua, NH
INGERNI, Angelo and Dorothy A SULLIVAN, 28 Jun 1947 Hudson, NH
INGEROWKSI, Mary L and Robert A NEVEUX, 11 Mar 1972 Hudson, NH
INGERSOLL, Sandra J and Dennis J LEITH, 07 Jul 1984 Nashua, NH
INGERSON, Mary and Francis CORNETTA, 05 Aug 1941 Hudson, NH
INGLESTON, Ida M and Carl W HEMPEL, 17 Oct 1927 Hudson, NH
INGRAM, Catherine and Roger S SIROIS, 09 Oct 1971 Nashua, NH
INGRAM, Kimberly A and Scott E LEVESQUE, 16 Apr 1983 Nashua, NH
INGRAM, Patricia A and Michael B BELL, 08 Jun 1973 Hollis, NH
INGRAM, Walter E and Lucille I PARADISE, 21 Aug 1981 Hudson, NH
INNESS, Percy W and Ruth V CROSS, 28 Aug 1920 Nashua, NH
INSLEY, Eva R and Leighton C FOWLER, 22 Jan 1910 Hudson, NH
  Caleb T Insley & Annie M Thompson
  Edward Fowler & Catherine Harris
IODICE, John H and Concetta FROIO, 13 Mar 1937 Nashua, NH
IRELAND, Allan J and June I LAMONT, 15 Oct 1942 Hudson, NH
IRVINE, Frank L Jr and Frances R ALLEN, 03 Oct 1959 New London, CT
IRWIN, Cathy A and Mark R PEARSON, 19 Jun 1976 Hudson, NH
IRWIN, Kevin F and Katherine POLKEY, 06 Oct 1975 Raymond, NH
IRWIN, Sheila M and Mark R FRASER, 05 May 1984 Hudson, NH
ITZKOWITZ, Oscar A and Margaret A HUMPHREY, 07 Jul 1956 Hudson, NH
IVALIS, George and Shirley I KASHULINES, 20 Dec 1970 Nashua, NH
IVERSON, Eric E and Alice M DUNHAM, 21 Aug 1976 Manchester, NH
IVES, Beatrice and Leonard D LAVOIE, 28 Feb 1946 Hudson, NH
IVES, Brenda L and Robert L PROCTOR, 15 Aug 1976 Hudson, NH
IVES, Charles M and Gail S MacGRATH, 13 Oct 1971 Nashua, NH
IVES, Charles M and Susan D HARRIS, 09 Mar 1974 Hudson, NH
IVES, Charles W and Mabel G LANDRY, 30 Jul 1955 Hudson, NH
IVES, Earl L and June BOULEY, 06 Nov 1949 Hudson, NH
IVES, Gayle E and William P ST CYR, 16 Jun 1973 Hudson, NH
IVES, Howard F and Shirley A FOSTER, 26 Aug 1950 Hudson, NH
IVES, Howard W and Lora L HETZER, 05 Feb 1977 Hudson, NH
IVES, Howard W and Laurie Ann FEBONIO, 30 Aug 1981 Hudson, NH

HUDSON, NH MARRIAGES

IVES, James M and Suzanne L BURNER, 30 Jul 1971 Nashua, NH
IVES, James M and Karen B ASHFORD, 06 Apr 1985 Hudson, NH
IVES, Kenneth T and Heidi J RAYNO, 02 Mar 1985 Hudson, NH
IVES, Mabel G and William COUROUNIS, 20 Jan 1967 Nashua, NH
IVES, Merrill M Jr and Thelma E McCOY, 14 Jul 1944 Hudson, NH
IVES, Thelma E and Allison W CARROLL, 23 Nov 1972 Nashua, NH
IZZI, Vincent M and Judith HODSDON, 01 Jun 1985 Hudson, NH
JACKSON, Don J and Beverly J GATES, 16 Apr 1955 Hudson, NH
JACKSON, Eleanor L and Gary A HUGHES, 19 Oct 1968 Nashua, NH
JACKSON, Leonard A and Rose A ROCK, 06 Sep 1958 Hudson, NH
JACKSON, Leonard A and Janice C BELLROSE, 02 Mar 1973 Nashua, NH
JACKSON, Lois A and Edward G GAMACHE, 13 Dec 1947 Nashua, NH
JACKSON, Lucinda M and Douglas B McCRADY, 19 May 1978 Nashua, NH
JACKSON, Robert E and Anne M BERNIER, 19 May 1962 Hudson, NH
JACOBS, Della and Frank LAMBERT, 05 Dec 1896 Nashua, NH
JACOBS, Jeannette and Waslaw M LOUKIEWICZ, 08 Aug 1946 Hudson, NH
JACOBS, John T and Dolores T WAGNER, 31 Mar 1947 Hudson, NH
JACOBS, Smith S and Minnie S SULLIVAN, 14 Apr 1900 Hudson, NH
   Lorenzo Jacobs & Amelia Brown
   John Mulkey & Katherine Dundon
JACOBSEN, Franklyn E and Lucy PAPASODORO, 31 Dec 1949 Hudson, NH
JACOBSEN, Ronald W and Marie D HILL, 10 Jul 1965 Hudson, NH
JACOBSON, Louise C and Steven KUSLEIKA, 02 Apr 1949 Hudson, NH
JACOME, Augustus II and Pamela Jo GORDON, 24 Jan 1981 Nashua, NH
JACQUE, Gail M and Alan W CARLE, 27 Dec 1984 Hudson, NH
JACQUES, Alfred A and Yvonne I RODIED, 27 Oct 1924 Nashua, NH
JACQUES, Alfred A Jr and Dolores E GRAHAM, 14 Jun 1952 Hudson, NH
JACQUES, Alma M and Raoul A BONNETTE, 25 Aug 1919 Nashua, NH
JACQUES, Carolyn M and Rene G BEAULE, 03 Sep 1959 Manchester, NH
JACQUES, EllaMarie and Joseph Art JODOIN, 02 Jun 1913 Nashua, NH
   Napoleon Jacques & Angelina Bonsiquest
   Alfred Jodoin & Julie Carbonneau
JACQUES, Eva and Armand PAUL, 18 Nov 1920 Nashua, NH
JACQUES, Laurette M and Albert F RODIER, 17 Sep 1955 Hudson, NH
JACQUES, Paul E and Carmel F ARPIN, 04 May 1957 Hudson, NH
JACQUES, Paula M and Daniel J LEDOUX, 14 Jun 1975 Hudson, NH
JACQUES, William T and Dorothy M CONDON, 26 Aug 1950 Hudson, NH
JAHUKE, Mildred M and Earl L Jr HARRAR, 05 Jan 1944 Hudson, NH
JAKAITIS, Judith A and Gregory J DOMIJAN, 13 Jan 1968 Hudson, NH
JALBERT, Dolores J and Ray C CARTER, 24 Oct 1959 Nashua, NH
JALBERT, Eugene and Rose BOUCHER, 23 Nov 1929 Nashua, NH
JALBERT, Frank E and Jeanne E LEVESQUE, 11 Sep 1965 Nashua, NH
JALBERT, George E and Gertrude A LEVESQUE, 12 Oct 1946 Nashua, NH
JALBERT, John R and Linda J POWELCZYK, 29 May 1978 Hudson, NH
JALBERT, Norman P and Linda M PORTER, 05 Oct 1968 Hudson, NH
JAMES, Alexandra and Aemil J STATTA, 18 Aug 1950 Hudson, NH
JAMES, Alfred S and Sandra M WING, 17 Sep 1982 Merrimack, NH
JAMESON, Charles R and Angelina M STEWART, 20 Sep 1975 Hudson, NH
JAMESON, Clarence T and Lena M RICARD, 09 Sep 1944 Hudson, NH
JAMESON, Clarence T and Dorothy TODD, 12 Oct 1946 Hudson, NH
JAMESON, Daniel G and Martha J CHAPUT, 18 Jan 1975 Nashua, NH
JAMESON, Leona M and Ernest A GAMBLE, 22 Sep 1945 Hudson, NH
JAMESON, Marion A and Howard T CHASE, 10 May 1925 Hudson, NH
JAMESON, Mary A and Robert J COVERT, 06 Apr 1963 Hudson, NH
JAMESON, Mildred B and Adam P PLYNKOFSKY, 24 Jan 1942 Hudson, NH
JAMESON, Sandra L and Paul V ELLIS, 07 Jul 1962 Hudson, NH
JAMROS, Adam M and Ruth M POWERS, 24 Nov 1945 Nashua, NH
JANKAUSKAS, Edward T and Elaine A BOILARD, 15 Oct 1955 Hudson, NH
JANKAUSKAS, Joseph J and Alice G GALIPEAU, 26 Jun 1954 Hudson, NH
JANSKY, Mildred and James F MOORE, 08 Aug 1950 Hudson, NH

HUDSON,NH MARRIAGES

JANULEWIC, Sophia and Albert I ALEXANDER, 30 Dec 1928 Hudson, NH
JAQUITH, Annie L and George G DORR, 31 Dec 1914 Nashua, NH
  George D Jaquith & Sarah J Fox
  Sylvester H Dorr & Celia H Austin
JAQUITH, George D and Sarah J FOX, 12 Nov 1866
JAQUITH, Ruby Georgia and Edward W CLEMENT, 08 Jun 1924 Hudson, NH
JARDIN, Marion and Raymond R ROWE, 15 Dec 1947 Hudson, NH
JARRY, Constance and Norman PELLETIER, 27 Apr 1985 Nashua, NH
JARRY, Lisa A and Richard A POWERS, 01 Jun 1985 Hudson, NH
JARRY, Michael R and Donna M SPAULDING, 03 Sep 1977 Nashua, NH
JARVIS, Lillian C and Russell C STACKHOUSE, 16 Mar 1974 Hudson, NH
JASINSKI, Sandra M and Mark D LEAVITT, 08 Oct 1977 Hudson, NH
JASKOLKA, Jacqueline&Richard E LECOMPTE, 29 Jun 1974 W Hartford, CT
JASPER, Bruce R and Mary E ANDERSON, 28 Jun 1968 Nashua, NH
JASPER, Forrest W and Arlene E LOUGEE, 07 Jul 1939 Hudson, NH
JASPER, Joseph A and Barbara A TURRELL, 16 Sep 1947 Hudson, NH
JASPER, Robert A and Una B HAYES, 05 Feb 1944 Nashua, NH
JASPER, Robert A and Reita A NEWTON, 15 Mar 1958 Epping, NH
JATKWICZ, Frank and Grace M BRUNELLE, 29 May 1965 Nashua, NH
JAUNBRAL, Janis C and John L UMSTEADT, 21 Apr 1985 Nashua, NH
JAWORSKY, Eva N and Eugene NORRIS, 21 Nov 1942 Hudson, NH
JEAN, Alice M and Eugene C SMITH, 03 Aug 1974 Hudson, NH
JEAN, Donald T and Cynthia G OLENA, 31 Dec 1964 Salem, NH
JEAN, Jeanne T and Robert L MAYNARD, 16 Jan 1968 Hudson, NH
JEAN, Norman and Rita C KASHULINES, 31 Jul 1948 Nashua, NH
JEAN, Raymond R and Emilienne COTE, 17 Jan 1942 Nashua, NH
JEAN, Richard W and TerryAnn GROVER, 09 Mar 1985 Hollis, NH
JEAN, Roland L and Lea A BECHARD, 21 Oct 1944 Nashua, NH
JEAN, Ronald D and Alice M HAYES, 24 Oct 1970 Nashua, NH
JEANNOTTE, George J and Lorraine M FLUET, 11 Nov 1965 Nashua, NH
JEANNOTTE, Henrietta and Norbert B LEDOUX, 18 Jan 1947 Nashua, NH
JEANNOTTE, J M and Karl E MERRILL, 21 Jun 1916 Nashua, NH
  Cornelius Jeannotte(Bellows Fls, VT) & Rosamond Heaton(Lyme, NH)
  James E Merrill(Hudson, NH) & Etta S Marble (Nashua, NH)
JEANNOTTE, Joseph J and Yvonne TALBOT, 07 Nov 1925 Hudson, NH
JEANNOTTE, Josette L and Donald G BLIER, 05 Jan 1952 Hudson, NH
JEANNOTTE, Madeline A and Francis B BARRY, 17 Sep 1966 Hudson, NH
JEANNOTTE, Marie F and Raymond P BOULEY, 29 Dec 1956 Nashua, NH
JEANNOTTE, Mario A and Patricia A GAGNON, 12 Nov 1966 Nashua, NH
JEANNOTTE, Mario A and Naomi C GETCHELL, 26 Aug 1979 Nashua, NH
JEANNOTTE, Mario A and Eleanor S HARRIS, 05 Sep 1981 Manchester, NH
JEANNOTTE, Theodore G Jr & Mary E PLAMONDON, 21 Aug 1965 Hudson, NH
JEANNOTTE, Valmore J and Bernice V DAVIS, 27 May 1933 Nashua, NH
JEFFERY, Linda A and Timothy W UPHAM, 21 May 1983 Hudson, NH
JEFTS, Mary and Nathaniel RIPLEY, 20 Apr 1854
JELLEY, Leonard R and Edith L LAFLAMME, 14 Jul 1956 Hudson, NH
JELLEY, Pamela M and Mark C LOULAKIS, 11 Jun 1983 Hudson, NH
JENENETTE, Louise C and Oscar P CAMPBELL, 27 May 1923 Hudson, NH
JENKINS, Cathy Lynn and Richard A LASALLE, 19 Feb 1977 Nashua, NH
JENKINS, Christine and Howard J RANDALL, 11 Sep 1969 Concord, NH
JENKINS, Janice M and Frank S KAZLOUSKAS, 26 May 1979 Hudson, NH
JENKINS, Lawrence J and Mary Ann J McHUGH, 16 May 1981 Hudson, NH
JENKINS, William and M Augusta FLETCHER, 17 Feb 1866
JENKS, Patience and Thomas NEWAL, 19 Jul 1785
JENKS, Patience and Thomas NEWEL, 19 Jul 1785
JENKS, Phyllis and Normand A PELLETIER, 26 Jun 1948 Nashua, NH
JENNEX, Linda D and James G GOSSELIN, 05 May 1984 Nashua, NH
JENNEY, David L and Mary-Ellen PACKOR, 13 Jun 1964 Hudson, NH
JENNEY, Dorothy and Nelson Les McINTIRE, 04 Dec 1933 Hudson, NH
JENNINGS, Bertha N and Milton YOUNG, 29 Apr 1895 Hudson, NH

HUDSON, NH MARRIAGES

Jennings & Abbie Nichols
Israel W Young & E S Morse (Methuen, MA)
JENNINGS, John W and Ann P MEDINA, 22 Jan 1949 Hudson, NH
JENNINGS, Richard C and Bernice CURRIER, 18 Feb 1941 Nashua, NH
JENSEN, Francis B and Denise G PATTEN, 17 Mar 1984 Hudson, NH
JENSEN, Lila R and Joseph P Jr DEMARCO, 16 Oct 1948 Hudson, NH
JERARD, Alice V and Eugene L PROVENCAL, 20 Dec 1924 Claremont, NH
JERRY, Linda M and Roland E LAFLEUR, 05 Sep 1981 Salem, NH
JERSZYK, William David and Catherine Mary ROBB, 15 Jul 1978 Rye, NH
JESSIMAN, George and Clarissa KENDRICK, 28 Dec 1851
JESSON, Michael C and Valerie A HAMPSON, 26 May 1972 Derry, NH
JESSOP, John F Jr and Lisa M LAVOIE, 06 Nov 1982 Hudson, NH
JETTE, Adelbert and Cecile MARQUIS, 05 Jul 1920 Manchester, NH
JETTE, Andre R and Lois M DESCHENES, 09 Jun 1972 Nashua, NH
JETTE, Andre R and Alice N LUSSIER, 26 Oct 1979 Hudson, NH
JETTE, Craig Roland & Sandra Louise MARQUIS, 15 May 1981 Nashua, NH
JETTE, Laurette I and Chas Eugene BERUBE, 04 Jun 1923 Nashua, NH
JETTE, Lorraine M and Donald B BRIAND, 11 Aug 1973 Hudson, NH
JETTE, Louis W and Frances J BROWN, 03 Mar 1958 Hudson, NH
JETTE, Madeleine and Ronald R THERRIEN, 24 Nov 1960 Hudson, NH
JETTE, Marguerite and Henry J GAGNE, 02 Mar 1946 Nashua, NH
JETTE, Michelle B and Neil R GLOVER, 30 Jun 1979 Hudson, NH
JETTE, Normand E and Madeline L CARTIER, 01 Jul 1950 Exeter, NH
JETTE, Paul and Olivette M CARON, 25 Apr 1935 Nashua, NH
JETTE, Rene A and Sheila Ann KEENAN, 13 Sep 1980 Hudson, NH
JETTE, Ricky W and Stacey L GOODRUM, 18 Aug 1984 Nashua, NH
JETTE, Roger E and Julie L VAILLANCOURT, 07 Jan 1961 Nashua, NH
JETTE, Sandra L and Kevin L CHRISTIANSEN, 01 Jun 1985 Nashua, NH
JEWELL, Albert P and Bertha S MARSHALL, 15 Mar 1900 Lowell, MA
  W A Jewell & Christina Schurer
  Geo W Marshall & Annie E Osgood
JEWELL, Donald E and Laura M SMITH, 20 Oct 1959 Concord, NH
JEWETT, Abby S and Frank P BICKFORD, 25 Mar 1894 Londonderry, NH
  O D Jewett (Sweden, ME) & Sarah J Eastman (Conway)
  C D Bickford(Ossipee, NH) & Hattie A Pitman (Bartlett, NH)
JEWETT, Leonard M and Catherine LEGENDRE, 28 May 1977 Nashua, NH
JEWETT, Marion A and Geo K BICKFORD, 03 Mar 1895 Hudson, NH
  O J Jewett & Sarah Eastman (Conway)
  Edwin D Bickford(Ossipee) & Hattie Pitman (Bartlett)
JEWETT, William H and Jennie COLLINS, 09 Apr 1869
JOBIN, Stephen P and LuAnn N SHEPHERD, 12 Jul 1980 Nashua, NH
JODICE, Janice L and Gary P D'AGOSTINO, 12 Jun 1982 Nashua, NH
JODOIN, Harvey O and Shirley A FREDETTE, 27 Oct 1972 Hudson, NH
JODOIN, Joseph Art and EllaMarie JACQUES, 02 Jun 1913 Nashua, NH
  Alfred Jodoin & Julie Carbonneau
  Napoleon Jacques & Angelina Bonsiquest
JODOIN, Richard A and Susan G MARTIN, 13 Jan 1970 Nashua, NH
JOHNSON, Aaron H and Janis T RESNICK, 20 Nov 1959 Nashua, NH
JOHNSON, Ada L and Claus A A BLOOM, 07 Aug 1948 Hudson, NH
JOHNSON, Alice E and Quentin L CARMICHAEL, 07 Sep 1938 Nashua, NH
JOHNSON, Alonzo and Sarah SINCLAIR, 1850
JOHNSON, Ann and David E LAVALLEE, 26 Oct 1962 Hudson, NH
JOHNSON, Anna M and Abel GAGE, 06 Dec 1826
JOHNSON, Arlene N and George F SYRENE, 04 Jun 1957 Nashua, NH
JOHNSON, Arlo P and Marion I GOWING, 01 Nov 1968 Derry, NH
JOHNSON, Augusta M and George C KIMBALL, 15 Feb 1864
JOHNSON, Augustus and Frances N WOODS, 26 Aug 1859
JOHNSON, Betsey and James NEVENS, 06 Jun 1799
JOHNSON, Betty and James NEVENS, 06 Jun 1799
JOHNSON, Bonnie L and Stephen R HOYT, 29 Jan 1972 Nashua, NH

HUDSON,NH MARRIAGES

JOHNSON, Bonnie Lee and Roger R SWEATT, 06 Oct 1962 Nashua, NH
JOHNSON, Caleb and Susanna MARSH, 06 Apr 1826
JOHNSON, Carol A and Barry L FREDERICK, 28 Aug 1982 Hudson, NH
JOHNSON, Charles H and Almeda I BASSETT, 08 Jun 1929 Rochester, NH
JOHNSON, Charles H Jr & Carolyn A DONNELLY, 13 Sep 1958 Nashua, NH
JOHNSON, Charles L and Pauline Y ST LAURENT, 21 Jun 1980 Hudson, NH
JOHNSON, Charles W Jr and Barbara R EMPEY, 21 May 1966 Hudson, NH
JOHNSON, Christina and Dwaine H HAERINCK, 25 Feb 1984 Hudson, NH
JOHNSON, Clifton H and Glenna G TROAST, 04 Sep 1971 Hudson, NH
JOHNSON, Deborah A and Brian H FRASER, 31 Jan 1976 Hudson, NH
JOHNSON, Doliver and Louisa UNDERWOOD, Mar 1827
JOHNSON, Dorothy M and Donald H SPALDING, 11 Apr 1943 Nashua, NH
JOHNSON, Edward E and Dolores T MITCHELL, 03 Jun 1950 Hudson, NH
JOHNSON, Gloria J and Raymond A PETRAIN, 20 Feb 1953 Hudson, NH
JOHNSON, Gregory E and Joan L BOYER, 06 Jan 1962 Hudson, NH
JOHNSON, Hannah D and Reuben BATCHELDER, 05 Apr 1896 Hudson, NH
  John Carter (Concord) & Margaret Dow (Concord,)
  Jonathan Batchelder(Andover) (Andover)
JOHNSON, Hazen O and Ada V OUELLETTE, 18 Nov 1967 Nashua, NH
JOHNSON, Hazen O and Jeannette NOEL, 05 Oct 1974 Nashua, NH
JOHNSON, Herb M Jr and Dorothy J McCANN, 14 Jan 1950 Hudson, NH
JOHNSON, James Unde and Mary VALENTINE, 03 Jun 1863
JOHNSON, Jane L and Arthur E CLEMENT, 30 Dec 1942 Nashua, NH
JOHNSON, Joseph and Sarah FORD, 04 Mar 1784
JOHNSON, Joseph and Lydia BURBANK, 10 Sep 1807
JOHNSON, June M and Richard N GILBLAIR, 31 Aug 1978 Hudson, NH
JOHNSON, Katherine and Stephen F AXTMAN, 30 Jun 1979 Hudson, NH
JOHNSON, Kenneth J and Carole H LAPIERRE, 14 Jun 1947 Hudson, NH
JOHNSON, Linda A and Alan A FOWLE, 27 Oct 1984 Greenland, NH
JOHNSON, Linda G and Charles M ZELONIS, 03 May 1969 Hudson, NH
JOHNSON, Louise J and Alton B SNELL, 09 Nov 1940 Hudson, NH
JOHNSON, Lucille N and Joseph L BOUCHER, 25 Jun 1949 Hudson, NH
JOHNSON, Lynne A and Gary J ROBINSON, 27 May 1984 Hudson, NH
JOHNSON, Marion M and Romeo N DUBOIS, 17 Jan 1914 Nashua, NH
  James Johnson & Lizzie Wallace
  Oliver Dubois & Octavia Lanceau
JOHNSON, Mary A and Lane E BICKFORD, 17 Sep 1977 Hudson, NH
JOHNSON, Olive H and George H FOSS, 03 Jul 1937 Nashua, NH
JOHNSON, Olive R and William A SPENCER, 01 Nov 1947 Hudson, NH
JOHNSON, Pamela J and Arthur R Jr HANLON, 17 Jun 1972 Pelham, NH
JOHNSON, Paul O and Annette F BOUCHER, 21 Aug 1954 Hudson, NH
JOHNSON, Pauline Y&Maurice G PELLITIER, 02 Jul 1983 Londonderry, NH
JOHNSON, Polly and Zebulon PARKER, 18 Mar 1812
JOHNSON, Relief and Simon Brad WEBSTER, 23 Nov 1811
JOHNSON, Richard P and Phebe Ann BLOOMBERG, 21 Jul 1965 Hudson, NH
JOHNSON, Robert N and Mary A SPELLMAN, 30 May 1981 Hudson, NH
JOHNSON, Robert W and Anne L BURNS, 16 Aug 1969 Hudson, NH
JOHNSON, Roberta L and Forrest H SPINNEY, 18 Jun 1931 Nashua, NH
JOHNSON, Roger S and Lois A MacDONALD, 23 Oct 1971 Hudson, NH
JOHNSON, Ruth and William V Jr HAYDEN, 31 Jul 1937 Nashua, NH
JOHNSON, Ruth Moody and Joseph VARNUM, 21 Feb 1800
JOHNSON, Ruth Moody and Joseph VARNUM, 20 Feb 1800
JOHNSON, Shirley A and John W Jr ANNON, 06 May 1950 Hudson, NH
JOHNSON, Sophie and Roland J DEMERS, 09 Oct 1982 Hudson, NH
JOHNSON, Stanley A and Margaret E BRADLEY, 03 Jul 1950 Hudson, NH
JOHNSON, Thomas and Ruth Simer WEBSTER, 23 Feb 1843
JOHNSON, Vera and Edwin A ROWLINGS, 26 Jun 1948 Hudson, NH
JOHNSON, Waldo E and Ruth E FORTIN, 20 Oct 1962 Derry, NH
JOHNSON, Walter W and Rita M VERRIER, 13 Jan 1949 Hudson, NH
JOHNSON, William A Jr and Joy E REYNOLDS, 23 Jul 1981 Durham, NH

HUDSON,NH MARRIAGES

JOHNSTON, Constance and Frank GREENE, 02 Mar 1918 Hudson, NH
JOHNSTON, James W and Barbara L NOEL, 30 Aug 1963 Hudson, NH
JOHNSTON, Mark C and Cheryl A COSSE, 10 Jul 1983 Nashua, NH
JOHNSTON, Walter E and Marjorie J POLLARD, 11 Apr 1964 Hudson, NH
JOKI, David F and Paulette D COLBATH, 26 Aug 1984 Nashua, NH
JOLICOEUR, Marion L and Harold R AUSTIN, 23 Aug 1948 Hudson, NH
JOLIN, Deborah A and Bruce M RICE, 30 Jan 1982 Hudson, NH
JOLLY, Elizabeth & Bernard L Jr FOLLANSBEE, 06 Dec 1974 Seabrook,NH
JONES, Abigail and Nathan ANDREWS, 27 May 1819
JONES, Benjamin K and Elizabeth WOODWARD, 29 Mar 1859
JONES, Charles E and Patricia A YOUNG, 02 Dec 1950 Hudson, NH
JONES, Cynthia C and Jack V Jr WILLIAMS, 21 Aug 1982 Nashua, NH
JONES, Cynthia J and Walter R WOODS, 08 Aug 1969 Merrimack, NH
JONES, Darrell G and Beth Ann BOGAN, 24 Feb 1980 Hudson, NH
JONES, David Mich and Susan Mari WARRINER, 22 Nov 1980 Hudson, NH
JONES, Elizabeth and Daniel GREGG, 15 Jun 1878 Hudson, NH
   Nathan Philbrick & Ester T
   Joseph Gregg & Jenny
JONES, Flora G and Charles E DEMRLY, 31 Mar 1877 Nashua, NH
JONES, Harry B and Isabelle H HENKEL, 21 May 1938 Hudson, NH
JONES, James T and Hattie T MARSH, 03 May 1864
JONES, John L and Mary E LOWE, 17 Jan 1948 Hudson, NH
JONES, Kenneth A and Carol A FARROW, 09 Oct 1983 Hudson, NH
JONES, Kimberly A and Kenneth E Jr UPTON, 30 Jun 1984 Nashua, NH
JONES, Kirk A and Helen M BEATTY, 10 Sep 1984 Bedford, NH
JONES, Linda E and George E MARQUIS, 31 Aug 1968 Nashua, NH
JONES, Linda M and Richard J WILSON, 25 Jan 1969 Hudson, NH
JONES, Margaret H and Lester E GOVE, 15 Oct 1966 Manchester, NH
JONES, Martha M and William K JONES, 10 Apr 1856
JONES, Mary and Diamond TWISS, 10 Jul 1817
JONES, Michael P and Jacqueline A MOBSBY, 21 Oct 1978 Hudson, NH
JONES, Mildred M and Kenneth I DABBS, 27 Feb 1981 Nashua, NH
JONES, Pamela K and James J SZROM, 10 Jan 1982 Nashua, NH
JONES, Relief and Simon Gilm WEBSTER, 16 Dec 1841
JONES, Richard P and Sylvia A FISHER, 28 Nov 1975 Nashua, NH
JONES, Ruth and Edward M VARA, 26 Jun 1939 Hudson, NH
JONES, Susan B and George W WEGHORST, 17 Jun 1978 Hudson, NH
JONES, William K and Martha M JONES, 10 Apr 1856
JONES, William R and Frances H SENTER, 02 May 1855
JONES, William R and Georgiana SENTER, 09 Apr 1874 Hudson, NH
JORDAN, Alice V and Arthur FARLEY, 28 Jun 1953 Hudson, NH
JORDAN, Debra M and Stephen J GILE, 25 Mar 1978 Hudson, NH
JORDAN, Joseph L and Mary T SPAHN, 05 Dec 1975 Hudson, NH
JORDAN, June A and David E WOOD, 16 Aug 1969 Hudson, NH
JORDAN, Lester J and Gayle A BROADBENT, 28 Feb 1970 Pelham, NH
JORDAN, Pamela A and Julian J BUKLEREWICZ, 24 Jun 1978 Rindge, NH
JORDAN, William W and Diane P FENTON, 17 Oct 1981 Nashua, NH
JOSE, Frederick and Emily A RICHARDSON, 11 Mar 1858
JOSEF, Carolyn and Frederick POLLARD, 06 Nov 1965 Nashua, NH
JOSEF, John Paul and Brenda Lee DESCHENES, 20 Jan 1973 Hudson, NH
JOSEF, Raymond K and Helene F VILLEMURE, 29 Sep 1956 Manchester, NH
JOSEPH, Nellie R and Alphonse L MAURO, 16 Oct 1937 Hudson, NH
JOSLIN, George C and Marion R BOLIS, 04 Sep 1948 Nashua, NH
JOSSELYN, Lena M and Julian L HUDSON, 11 Jun 1934 Hudson, NH
JOY, Arthur L and Lucy A INGALLS, 14 Oct 1891 Nashua, NH
   Lemuel T Joy (Quincy, MA) & Mary E Hadley (Nashua, NH)
   John H Ingalls(Chelmsford, MA) & Nancy M Blood (Dunstable, MA)
JOY, Lemuel T and Mary HADLEY, 27 Oct 1849
JOY, Lester A and Gertrude E TARBELL, 16 Aug 1924 S Lyndeboro, NH
JOY, Marion E and Philip M STULTZ, 22 Jun 1946 Nashua, NH

HUDSON, NH MARRIAGES

JOY, Noah T and Martha A SPALDING, 06 Feb 1852
JOYAL, Mark P and Linda A LEFAVE, 11 Jun 1983 Hudson, NH
JOYAL, Michael S and Maria D LINO, 05 Dec 1981 Nashua, NH
JOYAL, Rene P and Diane M GAGNON, 15 Oct 1977 Hudson, NH
JOYAL, Susan D and William J ZELONIS, 20 Apr 1974 Hudson, NH
JOYCE, Constant J and Mary H SCHOOLCRAFT, 30 Aug 1947 Nashua, NH
JOYCE, Herbert L and Grace B HARROP, 16 Jul 1938 Hudson, NH
JOYCE, Jacqueline and George H ESCOBAR, 29 Oct 1972 Hudson, NH
JOYCE, Richard A and Sandra G GAGNON, 10 Oct 1980 Nashua, NH
JOZAITIS, William D and Brenda J ZINN, 31 Aug 1962 Pittsfield, NH
JOZIATIS, Glenn N and Melanie S BARR, 18 Feb 1967 Hudson, NH
JUDKINS, Darlene E and Robert S VEINOT, 14 Jun 1975 Hudson, NH
JUDKINS, Kelly J and Michael S TRIPPLETON, 11 Sep 1976 Nashua, NH
JUDKINS, Laurie M and Donald A MARSTON, 26 Apr 1980 Nashua, NH
JUDKINS, Linda R and Leo E NOLIN, 02 Oct 1966 Milford, NH
JUDKINS, Raymond H and Evelyn C LORAINE, 18 Feb 1984 Hudson, NH
JULIAN, Frances E and Henry A BARROSO, 19 Apr 1969 Nashua, NH
JUNKINS, Leone and Walter O KALLIO, 02 Sep 1944 Hudson, NH
JUREK, Ronald A and Judith A HAYES, 01 Aug 1964 Hudson, NH
JURKOWSKI, Jennifer L and William J MILLER, 27 Oct 1979 Hudson, NH
JUSTASON, Steven R and Doreen KENNISON, 16 May 1981 Hudson, NH
JUTRAS, Candice B and Daniel R PERRON, 24 Jul 1971 Hudson, NH
JUTRAS, Mary F and Neal M FURMAN, 20 Sep 1980 Hudson, NH
JUZOKONIS, Ellen J and Stanley M HALLEY, 12 Apr 1942 Hudson, NH
KABLIK, Kenneth J and Donna Ann PARKER, 08 Jan 1977 Nashua, NH
KADE, Fred C and Margaret McGUIRE, 28 Mar 1919 Nashua, NH
KAEFER, Margery A and William J Jr SLATUNAS, 04 Aug 1980 Nashua, NH
KAGEN, Kathryn Le and Bruce A PROVENCAL, 01 Jul 1972 Nashua, NH
KAHN, Sarah and Benjamin MERRILL, 20 Jul 1820
KALDIS, Paula and Harold L DICKINSON, 14 Feb 1972 Nashua, NH
KALIL, Charles W and Brenda V BOSSIE, 25 Jul 1959 Nashua, NH
KALIL, Joan M and Grant W DEARBORN, 23 Jun 1951 Hudson, NH
KALIL, Lynn J and Daniel L SCOTT, 28 Oct 1978 Hudson, NH
KALIL, Patricia A and Kenneth P BLANCHARD, 16 Aug 1958 Hudson, NH
KALLIO, Walter O and Leone JUNKINS, 02 Sep 1944 Hudson, NH
KAMIENIECKI, Barbara A and David A GAMACHE, 20 Apr 1968 Hudson, NH
KANE, Lois A and George PORTER, 23 Jul 1962 Dracut, MA
KANTARGIS, Cynthia R and Robert R MOREAU, 07 Dec 1957 Nashua, NH
KAPIKSY, John P and Nancy J SMITH, 19 Feb 1970 Dunbarton, NH
KAPISKY, Annie and George A CHRISTOPHER, 30 Aug 1942 Rye, NH
KAPISKY, John E and Agnes S WALKAWICZ, 04 Sep 1937 Nashua, NH
KAPLAN, Max and Sylvia GOLDOFF, 06 Apr 1939 Salem, NH
KARCZEWSKI, Jane V and Joseph J BATURA, 07 May 1949 Nashua, NH
KAREM, Laureen and Julian D OSORIO, 22 Jan 1985 Nashua, NH
KARGAARD, Alfred and Elizabeth HOWARD, 26 Mar 1942 Hudson, NH
KARLONAS, Judith M and Thomas D QUINT, 06 Dec 1965 Hudson, NH
KAROS, Betty L and Gary L CONATY, 09 May 1959 Hudson, NH
KAROS, Joseph S and Vera B OGINSKY, 27 Nov 1944 Nashua, NH
KAROS, Joyce A and Ronald R DUBE, 30 May 1963 Hudson, NH
KAROS, Michael J and Virginia BROWN, 20 Jan 1968 Hudson, NH
KARSTOK, Helen R and Ralph H STEELE, 16 Sep 1938 Hudson, NH
KASHULINES, Albert J and Celistin GIROUARD, 01 Jun 1925 Nashua, NH
KASHULINES, Arlene C and Robert J RICHARDS, 21 Oct 1950 Hudson, NH
KASHULINES, Arthur J Jr & Eileen U WATKINS, 09 Sep 1950 Nashua, NH
KASHULINES, Arthur J Jr & Martha A SPAULDING, 03 Jan 1963 Hudson,NH
KASHULINES, Eva B and Ovide J GAGNE, 30 May 1941 Nashua, NH
KASHULINES, Francis A Jr&Sandra C LATULIPPE, 19 Jun 1965 Hudson, NH
KASHULINES, Helen and Ernest LEBLANC, 16 Sep 1919 Nashua, NH
KASHULINES, Helen B and Robert W CLARK, 20 May 1950 Hudson, NH
KASHULINES, Joan C and James P GODFREY, 26 Sep 1959 Hudson, NH

HUDSON, NH MARRIAGES

KASHULINES, Joseph and Blanche E MENARD, 18 Aug 1919 Nashua, NH
KASHULINES, Richard J and Rachel I PINETTE, 01 Sep 1956 Nashua, NH
KASHULINES, Richard J and Katherine FLANDERS, 07 Dec 1959 Derry, NH
KASHULINES, Rita C and Norman JEAN, 31 Jul 1948 Nashua, NH
KASHULINES, Robert G and Norma J COBURN, 21 Feb 1970 Nashua, NH
KASHULINES, Robert G and Dorothy M GILMAN, 15 Apr 1983 Hudson, NH
KASHULINES, Shirley I and George IVALIS, 20 Dec 1970 Nashua, NH
KASPER, Donald A and Cheryl J PARKHURST, 09 Mar 1968 Nashua, NH
KASPER, M Antoine and Albert J SUKIS, 14 Feb 1955 Nashua, NH
KASPER, Martin and Mary R WISNIEWSKI, 15 Aug 1942 Nashua, NH
KATSOHIS, James O and Penney B GOODWIN, 22 Jun 1980 Nashua, NH
KAUFHOLD, Hans and Roberta MUTTI, 30 Jun 1956 Proctor, VT
KAUFHOLD, Henry and Ruth C HUGHY, 19 Feb 1983 Concord, NH
KAUFHOLD, Werner and Nancy PARKER, 27 Dec 1958 Proctor, VT
KAUFMAN, Marcela and George S Jr FARRIS, 24 Dec 1981 Hudson, NH
KAUFMANN, Bessie and Fredrick S POLAK, 13 Nov 1943 Hudson, NH
KAY, Clara V and Francis C HOOKER, 16 Apr 1949 Hudson, NH
KAYROS, Frank and Cecile L GARON, 06 Jul 1963 Nashua, NH
KAYROS, Mary F and Henry E SMITH, 13 May 1933 Hudson, NH
KAYROS, Peter A and Kathleen M MEHRON, 30 Aug 1974 Nashua, NH
KAYROS, Stanley and Hedwig OPAROWSKI, 17 May 1941 Manchester, NH
KAYROS, Wanda F and Charles R WHITTEMORE, 29 Nov 1947 Nashua, NH
KAZAKA, Emil S and Rita M DELTUFO, 24 Dec 1949 Hudson, NH
KAZLOUSKAS, Frank S and Janice M JENKINS, 26 May 1979 Hudson, NH
KAZLOUSKAS, Joan E & William KILLINGSWORTH, 18 Jan 1981 Hudson, NH
KAZLOUSKAS, Stanley and Elaine E PELLETIER, 10 May 1946 Nashua, NH
KEANE, Kevin D and Donna D GRAHAM, 20 Apr 1968 Manchester, NH
KEANE, Virginia C and Michael FULLER, 13 Aug 1983 Hudson, NH
KEARNS, Bill G and Stephanie WILSHERE, 02 Oct 1982 Hudson, NH
KEARNS, Ellen M and Paul A LANDRY, 31 Jul 1983 Nashua, NH
KEARNS, Jean Elizabeth & James E SAYTANDIES, 09 Sep 1978 Hollis, NH
KEARNS, John F Jr and Betty C WALTERS, 27 Oct 1984 Hudson, NH
KEARNS, Katherine and William A ERNEST, 30 Jun 1917 Nashua, NH
KEARNS, Katherine and John F Jr MORAN, 19 Nov 1978 Pelham, NH
KEARNS, Paul J and Carol G AREL, 26 Jun 1971 Nashua, NH
KEARNS, Stephen F and Theresa R LAROUCHE, 16 Dec 1972 Hudson, NH
KEELER, Judith A and Chester F SZUGDA, 18 Apr 1969 Keene, NH
KEEN, Anne M and Russell C Jr LAWSON, 22 Jul 1979 Hudson, NH
KEENAN, Carol Loui and James F POWERS, 31 Jul 1982 Hudson, NH
KEENAN, Helen and Adolph DUBE, 12 Feb 1938 Nashua, NH
KEENAN, Mary E and Clifton H ROWELL, 17 Sep 1955 Nashua, NH
KEENAN, Maureen E & Thaddeus S RANDALL, 28 Jul 1984 Manchester, NH
KEENAN, Sheila A and David M HANSBERRY, 16 Aug 1975 Hudson, NH
KEENAN, Sheila Ann and Rene A JETTE, 13 Sep 1980 Hudson, NH
KELLEHER, Jamie M and Barry N SCHMIDT, 30 Mar 1984 Nashua, NH
KELLER, Caroline D and Rex A ROBERTS, 21 Jun 1969 Hudson, NH
KELLER, Thomas G and Denise T PAQUETTE, 06 Apr 1979 Hudson, NH
KELLERBERG, Clara V and John KREWSKI, 20 Jul 1951 Hudson, NH
KELLEY, Almon H and Mary E VARNEY, 28 May 1955 Nashua, NH
KELLEY, Barbara L and George R BERNARD, 29 May 1971 Hudson, NH
KELLEY, Carol A and Robert B MAKINEN, 27 Sep 1969 Hudson, NH
KELLEY, Cheryl M and Ronald E SHEPHERD, 15 Apr 1977 Hudson, NH
KELLEY, Cheryl N and Steven H PACKHURST, 13 Nov 1971 Nashua, NH
KELLEY, David R Jr and Mildred A WHEELER, 20 Jun 1970 Nashua, NH
KELLEY, Donald W and Kathleen I BRETTELL, 26 Jul 1943 Hampton, NH
KELLEY, Donna M and George W Jr REYNOLDS, 06 Aug 1966 Nashua, NH
KELLEY, Elizabeth and Nathan WINN, 23 Nov 1786
KELLEY, Frank E and Adrienne C RICHARD, 22 Jun 1946 Nashua, NH
KELLEY, Frank J and Patricia A TARRANT, 13 Apr 1985 Hudson, NH
KELLEY, George W and Katie Ann HOFFMAN, 29 Jul 1885 Lowell, MA

HUDSON,NH MARRIAGES

William Kelley & Dorcus Clement (Hudson, NH)
Philip Hoffman(Ireland) & AnnPoff (Ireland)
KELLEY, Kathleen M and Roland H SWEET, 10 Nov 1970 Nashua, NH
KELLEY, Laura J and William A PALUMBO, 04 Jul 1982 Hudson, NH
KELLEY, Louisa and Daniel Haz WEBSTER, 13 Jan 1847
KELLEY, Margaret V and Jesse MARTIN, 04 Nov 1948 Hudson, NH
KELLEY, Michael D and June L KIERSTEAD, 09 Apr 1983 Nashua, NH
KELLEY, Mildred L and Joseph P CENSULLO, 13 Apr 1948 Hudson, NH
KELLEY, Peggy and Philip GOODWIN, 25 Feb 1796
KELLEY, Ralph A and Jean E HILTON, 11 Aug 1957 Hudson, NH
KELLEY, Richard A and Deborah L THORNTON, 14 Aug 1971 Hudson, NH
KELLEY, Sandra A and Paul E RENAUD, 22 Jun 1974 Hudson, NH
KELLEY, Theresa A and Frederick STACEY, 18 Feb 1950 Hudson, NH
KELLEY, William and Elizabeth HARDY, 05 Mar 1801
KELLEY, William and Dorcas A CLEMENT, 29 Dec 1869
KELLEY, William J and Cheryl N HOULE, 28 Oct 1967 Hudson, NH
KELLEY, William P and Domenica M MALTESE, 12 Aug 1950 Hudson, NH
KELLEY, Wiseman and Elizabeth HADLEY, 05 Mar 1801
KELLY, Colin D and Debra Ann GOULET, 23 Feb 1973 Nashua, NH
KELLY, Dennis M & Evelina J LALIBERTE, 30 Jun 1984 Moultonboro, NH
KELLY, Kevin W and Susan L MANSFIELD, 12 Sep 1970 Hudson, NH
KELLY, Lori Ann and James R FORRENCE, 09 Apr 1983 Hudson, NH
KELLY, Sibbel and Isaac WEBSTER, 1812
KELSEA, Jennie B & Clifford W STRUTHERS, 11 Jan 1941 Goffstown, NH
KELSO, Helen A and George B FULLER, 14 Feb 1877 Hudson, NH
KEMP, Emeline M and John CUMMINGS, 08 Aug 1844
KEMP, James V and Elizabeth BROWN, 20 Nov 1822
KEMPENEERS, Elizabeth and Neal J ADAMS, 29 Sep 1984 Nashua, NH
KEMPTON, Charles C and Lynn A ST AMAND, 23 Nov 1974 Hudson, NH
KEMPTON, Katherine and Robert E SPAULDING, 09 Oct 1971 Hudson, NH
KEMPTON, Linda J and Allen P BONNETTE, 08 Jun 1968 Hudson, NH
KENDALL, Alfred P and Hattie A MARSH, 17 Apr 1865
KENDALL, Allan M and Dorothy L KLEINER, 29 Oct 1966 Nashua, NH
KENDALL, Amanda and Lucius P FRENCH, 18 Feb 1871 Hudson, NH
KENDALL, Barbara R and Howard H KINGLSEY, 27 Aug 1949 Hudson, NH
KENDALL, Everett and Rachel GOSS, 23 Oct 1851
KENDALL, Guy F and Pamela A SMITH, 24 Aug 1966 Hudson, NH
KENDALL, Mary P and Paul HARDY, 25 Jan 1844
KENDALL, Peter W & Christine KOULETSIS, 07 Jul 1973 Manchester, NH
KENDRICK, Clarissa and George JESSIMAN, 28 Dec 1851
KENEFINK, Grace A and George J WALWOOD, 13 Aug 1940 Hudson, NH
KENISTON, Charles F and Mary I GOWING, 08 Aug 1914 Hudson, NH
  George Keniston & Ida M Borton
  George T Gowing & Ida E Seavey
KENISTON, Charles F & Julia A QUACKENBUSH, 24 Aug 1938 Penacook, NH
KENISTON, Dorothy and Ernest B DECAMP, 11 Nov 1941 Penacook, NH
KENISTON, Mary M and Robert A ANDREWS, 12 May 1853
KENNA, Heidi V and Joseph C GAGNON, 11 Oct 1980 Hudson, NH
KENNEDY, Allen B and Louella A MANSFIELD, 23 Nov 1965 Hudson, NH
KENNEDY, Carol A and Francois J BRYAND, 11 Feb 1977 Nashua, NH
KENNEDY, Chester D and Brenda J DESROSIERS, 07 Nov 1975 Hudson, NH
KENNEDY, Cynthia A and Douglas M HUME, 11 Jul 1981 Hudson, NH
KENNEDY, David I and Ethel D SHUTZER, 15 Jun 1931 Nashua, NH
KENNEDY, Gordon D and Suzette M DESCHENES, 16 Apr 1966 Nashua, NH
KENNEDY, JoAnne E and Roy E HOLTON, 22 Nov 1969 Hudson, NH
KENNEDY, Leonard P and Susan M BRYAND, 02 Jul 1976 Hudson, NH
KENNEDY, Mary E and Michael J VIOLETTE, 15 Jun 1985 Hudson, NH
KENNEDY, Richard W and Gloria J ROBY, 16 Dec 1967 Nashua, NH
KENNEDY, Teddy S and Nona V AHEARN, 18 May 1981 Hudson, NH
KENNEDY, Thomas J and Mary V FINNEGAN, 21 Nov 1914 Nashua, NH

HUDSON, NH MARRIAGES

   Thomas Kenndey & Isabella Binns
   Miles Finnegan & Sarah Maguire
KENNEDY, Walter A and Dorothy M BLEASE, 23 Sep 1933 Hudson, NH
KENNEDY, Walter E and Gertrude A MARTIN, 19 Dec 1955 Hudson, NH
KENNEDY, Walter E and Beverly G NICHOLS, 04 Jul 1966 Nashua, NH
KENNEDY, Walter E and Phyllis J KIMBALL, 20 Aug 1983 Hudson, NH
KENNER, Lavania H and Samuel FAIN, 12 Aug 1950 Hudson, NH
KENNEY, Joan Ann and Gary D DIGGINS, 17 Aug 1974 Merrimack, NH
KENNEY, Richard G and Priscilla HAMMEL, 16 Dec 1964 Tilton, NH
KENNEY, Robert E and Claire F DIONNE, 04 Sep 1964 Hudson, NH
KENNEY, Ruth I and Herman K SMITH, 13 May 1955 Hudson, NH
KENNISON, Doreen and Steven R JUSTASON, 16 May 1981 Hudson, NH
KENNISTON, Hannah C and John E WEBSTER, 13 Nov 1856
KENNISTON, William G and Hannah CARR, 19 Jun 1853
KENNON, Therese M and Roger B MALONSON, 06 Apr 1965 Hudson, NH
KENNY, Elizabeth and William MORELAND, 31 Aug 1797
KENT, Edi-Lu and Stephen W WARTELLA, 14 Aug 1982 Nashua, NH
KENTRA, Anthony C and Shirley A BAKER, 12 Apr 1947 Nashua, NH
KENTRA, James A and Gail B DELUDE, 06 Jun 1981 Nashua, NH
KENTRA, Judith A and Robert G FLEWELLING, 01 Aug 1969 Hudson, NH
KENTRA, Judith A and Paul D MacDONALD, 20 May 1972 Hudson, NH
KENTRA, Shirley A and Frederick CLEMONS, 22 Jun 1973 Merrimack, NH
KENYON, Ruth L and John A FORRENCE, 16 May 1954 Hudson, NH
KENYON, Shirley J and Ronald C GARDNER, 29 Oct 1952 Hudson, NH
KERNDL, William F and Carolyn A GARRITY, 20 Apr 1974 Nashua, NH
KEROUAC, Charlotte and Scott E MARCHAND, 19 Jan 1979 Nashua, NH
KEROUAC, Jeffrey M and Barbara Jean ROCK, 03 Sep 1976 Nashua, NH
KESMETIS, Georgia and John P FRAWLEY, 30 Jun 1957 Nashua, NH
KESSLER, Patricia A and Michael J KREBS, 06 Sep 1975 Rindge, NH
KETCHEN, David B and Dana S CANNEY, 06 Aug 1983 Hudson, NH
KEUENHOFF, Jeanne P & Maurice K II KIMBALL, 26 Aug 1967 Hudson, NH
KEUENHOFF, Joseph H and Nancy J O'NEAL, 30 Mar 1974 Nashua, NH
KEUENHOFF, Walter J Jr and Mary K LAVALLEY, 06 Jun 1981 Hudson, NH
KEUENOFF, Joseph H and Cheryl S OUELLETTE, 11 Jul 1981 Hudson, NH
KEYSER, Sharon L and James L HENDERSON, 13 Apr 1968 Franklin, NH
KEZAR, Benjamin and Yvonne A MARTIN, 15 Jun 1936 Newport, NH
KHURANA, Ashok K and Lorraine B ELLIS, 02 Jun 1979 Nashua, NH
KICZA, Janice C and Norman R BOUCHER, 14 Aug 1970 Seabrook, NH
KIDD, Daryl L and Sharon E WRIGHT, 06 Apr 1974 Hollis, NH
KIDDER, Ada and Henry W BLANCHARD, 28 Nov 1900 Cambridge, MA
   Daniel Kidder & Emeline F Hardy
   S M Blanchard & Eleanor J Bickford
KIDDER, Benjamin H and Caroline P PIERCE, 13 May 1847
KIDDER, Benjamin H and Martha C MARSHALL, 24 Apr 1849
KIDDER, Frank E and Abbie A WOODBURN, 04 Apr 1881 Hudson, NH
   Benjamin Kidder (Boston, MA) & Martha C Marshall (Sharon, NH)
   John Woodburn(Londonderry, NH) & L A Truell (Nashua, NH)
KIDDER, George and Mary J McQUESTEN, 10 Nov 1861
KIDDER, Harriet and Isaac EATON, 02 May 1850
KIENIA, Edward and Esther M CARLSON, 30 Jul 1952 Merrimack, NH
KIENIA, Michael and Barbara E GALE, 15 Nov 1963 Salem, NH
KIENIA, Phyllis C and Roy L DAIGLE, 19 Jan 1952 Pembroke, NH
KIENIA, Wendy D and Richard J GODDARD, 13 Oct 1973 Chester, NH
KIERSTEAD, Brent T and Denise J LANDRY, 04 Dec 1976 Hudson, NH
KIERSTEAD, Brian K and Linda A TATE, 31 Aug 1978 Nashua, NH
KIERSTEAD, Faith L and Robert V TURCOTT, 21 Aug 1959 Hudson, NH
KIERSTEAD, Flora M and Amedee J Jr HOULE, 25 May 1957 Nashua, NH
KIERSTEAD, Ina G and Harold R PEARL, 12 Aug 1950 Hudson, NH
KIERSTEAD, June L and Michael D KELLEY, 09 Apr 1983 Nashua, NH
KIERSTEAD, Karen L and David E BURNELL, 30 Aug 1975 Hudson, NH

HUDSON,NH MARRIAGES

KIERSTEAD, Ross E Jr and Margaret F ALLISON, 01 Feb 1963 Nashua, NH
KIERSTEAD, Thomas M and Rita L CHARPENTIER, 30 Oct 1954 Nashua, NH
KIJOWSKI, Charlotte & Francis J PREVOST, 11 Feb 1961 Manchester, NH
KILDERRY, Elizabeth and Otis A NEWHALL, 11 Apr 1920 Hudson, NH
KILDUFF, Kathleen M and Bruce A MORTON, 30 Oct 1983 Hudson, NH
KILDUFF, Thomas P and Kimberly A TARDIE, 22 Jun 1985 Hudson, NH
KILGORE, Damon M and Effie MONROE, 22 Aug 1929 Nashua, NH
KILGORE, Diane M and Albert J Jr HAUSWIRTH, 18 Sep 1948 Hudson, NH
KILLAM, Cheryl L and Robert D ELDER, 10 Jun 1978 Hampstead, NH
KILLINGSWORTH, William & Joan E KAZLOUSKAS, 18 Jan 1981 Hudson, NH
KILPECK, Nora R and Frank J KOWALCZYK, 20 Sep 1947 Hudson, NH
KIMBALL, Annie I and Clarence E PECKHAM, 19 Feb 1907 Hudson, NH
  John R Kimball (Delora Tarbell)
  Stepehn C Peckham & Grace I Eldridge
KIMBALL, Barbara W and Henry A COURTEMANCHE, 14 Aug 1946 Hudson, NH
KIMBALL, George C and Augusta M JOHNSON, 15 Feb 1864
KIMBALL, John T and Ethel A ROBINSON, 09 Jun 1905 Hudson, NH
  John R Kimball & Delora Tarbell
  Henry C Robinson & Mary A Merrill
KIMBALL, John T and Hannah CLUFF, 27 Dec 1920 Hudson, NH
KIMBALL, Joseph H and Marion SARGENT, 28 Sep 1908 Hudson, NH
  Salon Kimball & Fannie Hoyt
  Charles H Sargent & Esther H Tenny
KIMBALL, Maurice K II & Jeanne P KEUENHOFF, 26 Aug 1967 Hudson, NH
KIMBALL, Philip V and Barbara W FORD, 06 Jun 1936 Hudson, NH
KIMBALL, Phyllis J and Walter E KENNEDY, 20 Aug 1983 Hudson, NH
KIMBALL, Ray A and Isabelle H STULTZ, 04 Mar 1944 Hudson, NH
KIMBALL, Rena Ann and Jean Claude GALLANT, 31 Aug 1973 Hudson, NH
KIMBALL, Rowe W and Helen L THOMPSON, 20 Oct 1937 Hudson, NH
KIMBALL, Samuel L and Pearl A McGEE, 06 Feb 1918 Hudson, NH
KIMBALL, Winifred E and Fred L CUTTER, 24 Jun 1960 Hudson, NH
KIMBALL, Winnifred and Ludovic L MITCHELL, 03 Sep 1955 Hudson, NH
KIMBERLIN, Cleaborn R and Lilla E BELANGER, 20 Jul 1946 Nashua, NH
KINERSON, Rita K and Stephen C BIGELOW, 15 Jul 1972 Hudson, NH
KING, Archie and Doris E BAILEY, 17 Nov 1944 Hudson, NH
KING, Claudya and James W McDERMOT, 04 Oct 1975 Salem, NH
KING, Edward H and Phyllis E VAYENS, 28 Jun 1980 Hudson, NH
KING, Gordon D and Mary D KING, 26 Oct 1974 Hudson, NH
KING, Joseph A and Arlene C AMADEN, 15 May 1936 Nashua, NH
KING, June A and William E FULLER, 20 Jul 1940 Hudson, NH
KING, Mary D and Gordon D KING, 26 Oct 1974 Hudson, NH
KING, Maude Lucinda and Elbridge G MORSE, 30 Nov 1910 Hudson, NH
  Wallace E King & Ada Brooks
  Warren G Morse & Belle Evans
KING, Melba C and Frank L NUTE, 04 Jul 1934 Hudson, NH
KING, Ruth L and Thomas F MELVIN, 22 Sep 1944 Hartford, CT
KING, Sanford E and Geraldine PARSHLEY, 07 Dec 1946 Hudson, NH
KING, Walter E and Brenda L BRIAND, 29 Jul 1972 Hudson, NH
KINGLSEY, Howard H and Barbara R KENDALL, 27 Aug 1949 Hudson, NH
KINGSLEY, Edward L and Cynthia M NOAKES, 24 Feb 1968 Milford, NH
KINGSLEY, Leonard E and Stephanie FORBES, 25 Jul 1981 Nashua, NH
KINGSLEY, Timothy J and Donna M SUMRALL, 24 Sep 1978 Hudson, NH
KINLEY, Jane C and Herb ANDREWS, 26 Sep 1966 Hudson, NH
KINNEEN, Ann A and Gerald J Jr DESROSIERS, 26 Mar 1983 Hudson, NH
KINNEEN, Ann A and George S FARRIS, 25 Aug 1978 Nashua, NH
KINVILLE, Andrew T and Lucille I BOUCHER, 28 Apr 1944 Nashua, NH
KINVILLE, Dallas E and Frank P LITZENBERGER, 19 Nov 1945 Hudson, NH
KINVILLE, Doris V and Emile GAGNON, 22 Apr 1944 Nashua, NH
KINVILLE, Edward R and Ruth A NICHOLS, 16 Nov 1929 Hudson, NH
KINVILLE, Eva E and Joseph J BOYER, 16 Feb 1920 Nashua, NH

HUDSON,NH MARRIAGES

KINVILLE, Francis G and Rita T NORMANDIE, 29 Nov 1942 Dracut, MA
KINVILLE, Francis G and Ruth G DIONNE, 30 Jun 1945 Nashua, NH
KINVILLE, Gene H and Norma J WHEELER, 17 Jul 1965 Nashua, NH
KINVILLE, Joyce E and David R GOODWIN, 16 Aug 1975 Hudson, NH
KINVILLE, Paul W and Janice A CAMPBELL, 09 Aug 1969 Hudson, NH
KINVILLE, Sandra J and Ronald J PERUSSE, 09 Mar 1976 Hudson, NH
KINVILLE, Sandra L and Raymond A Jr GUAY, 18 Nov 1972 Hudson, NH
KIPNES, Jack L and Linda B CRUTCHFIELD, 14 Apr 1973 Manchester, NH
KIRKPATRICK, Bruce W and Joanne I FONTAINE, 24 Jul 1970 Nashua, NH
KIRKPATRICK, Gerald G & Doreen M McGARY, 15 Feb 1974 Litchfield, NH
KIRPALANI, Mohan S and Averil A MAYNARD, 26 Mar 1948 Hudson, NH
KIRSCH, Linda W and Christophe FARRELL, 18 Sep 1982 Hudson, NH
KITCHENER, Constance and William F DURWIN, 28 Feb 1946 Nashua, NH
KITTREDGE, Russell H and L Frances HOLMES, 24 Dec 1857
KITTREDGE, Servia P and Edward P FRENCH, 11 Oct 1954
KITTREDGE, Submitte and Benjamin WEBSTER, 1816
    Jonathan Kittredge
KLATT, Charles Jr and Barbara BULLOCK, 11 Nov 1942 Hudson, NH
KLATT, Laurie A and Marc E SWANSON, 20 Oct 1984 Hudson, NH
KLAUS, Marilyn J and Gerard A DESMARAIS, 27 Dec 1980 Nashua, NH
KLEE, Karola E and David P DERY, 20 Aug 1960 Hudson, NH
KLEIN, Jeffrey B and Jeanne M FLANDERS, 01 Apr 1967 Hudson, NH
KLEIN, Stephen J and Leslie J MILLER, 14 Jun 1979 Nashua, NH
KLEINER, Dorothy L and Allan M KENDALL, 29 Oct 1966 Nashua, NH
KLEINER, Randall L and Joanne M DECAROLIS, 08 Jun 1974 Pelham, NH
KLEINER, Richard L and Paula E TIPPING, 04 Feb 1967 Nashua, NH
KLEINER, Ronald L and Jane Marie MERCHANT, 24 Aug 1974 Nashua, NH
KLEINFELDER, Ann E and John D FARRIS, 02 Nov 1946 Hudson, NH
KLEMENT, John A and Edna A ABUCEWICZ, 23 Jul 1960 Nashua, NH
KLIMAS, Kenneth A and Brenda A RODGERS, 20 Jun 1981 Hudson, NH
KLIMAS, Mary and Theodore A LINDQUIST, 25 Jun 1938 Nashua, NH
KLIMAS, Susan M and Peter E FRASER, 28 Aug 1976 Hudson, NH
KLISS, Thomas S and Rita T CHENEVERT, 29 Jan 1974 Salem, NH
KLUCK, Mary T and Alex C ROSS, 19 Jun 1982 Hudson, NH
KNAPP, Enez L and Herbert B BARNES, 13 Jan 1875 Hudson, NH
KNAPP, Eva L and Herbert B BARNS, 13 Jun 1875 Hudson, NH
KNAPP, Sarah and Benjamin WOOD, 27 Aug 1871 Hudson, NH
KNEPPER, Carol L and Joseph M Jr PUFFER, 24 Oct 1981 Nashua, NH
KNIGHT, Diane E and Scott D TOWLE, 14 Jul 1984 Nashua, NH
KNIGHT, Donna M and Eugene C III GREGOIRE, 01 Sep 1979 Nashua, NH
KNIGHT, George C and Eva R RICHARD, 11 Jul 1918 Hudson, NH
KNIGHT, Mary and James HARTSHORN, 14 Nov 1819
KNIGHT, Rita A and Carl H ADAMS, 04 Jan 1964 Windham, NH
KNIGHTS, Carolyn F and Joseph R LEBLANC, 11 Nov 1960 Hudson, NH
KNIGHTS, Elaine T and Paul L PELLETIER, 14 Feb 1975 Hudson, NH
KNIGHTS, Francis and Mildred MARTIN, 17 Aug 1940 Dracut, MA
KNIGHTS, Gerard P and Glenna D CLEVELAND, 30 Aug 1969 Hudson, NH
KNIGHTS, Horace L and Marion L GRANT, 22 Nov 1947 Nashua, NH
KNIGHTS, Luther L and Victoria M BOUCHER, 25 Jan 1923 Hudson, NH
KNIGHTS, Merilda M and Eugene G PLANTIER, 02 Mar 1942 Hudson, NH
KNOWLES, John and Rachel CALDWELL, 24 Mar 1876
KNOWLES, John and Rachel CALDWELL, 24 Mar 1816
KNOWLES, Judith E and Roger B CHATEAUNEUF, 08 May 1965 Hudson, NH
KNOWLES, Wendy L and Charles L MOBILIA, 09 Jun 1985 Nashua, NH
KNOWLTON, Hosea C and Ellen M FLAGG, 07 May 1870 Hudson, NH
KNOWLTON, Joseph and Nancy E UPTON, 26 Nov 1877 Hudson, NH
    Asa Knowlton (Shirley, MA) & Ina Spaffoni (Sharon, VT)
KNOX, Gilbert A and Karen L WOOD, 08 Oct 1983 Hudson, NH
KNOX, Pauline H and Ira A EDWARDS, 22 Jun 1956 Keene, NH
KNUDSEN, Lloyd H and Marie E SULLIVAN, 22 May 1948 Hudson, NH

HUDSON,NH MARRIAGES

KOBISKY, Maureen E & James Basil STEPHENS, 13 Oct 1973 Windham, NH
KOCH, Ronald W and Irene J LEVESQUE, 30 May 1964 Hudson, NH
KOCHAKIAN, Barbel and Ogapan SEMONIAN, 08 Sep 1906 Boston, MA
  C Kochakian & V Wolfician
  Simon Semonian & H Duredepain
KOCHAKIAN, Dan and Highgory MELBRIDIAN, 30 Jun 1906 Hudson, NH
  C Kochakian & V Molfaian
  Aikel Nallridian & Anna Lakacian
KOCJARSKI, Amelia M and Thaddeus WROBLOWSKI, 22 Jan 1947 Hudson, NH
KOESTER, Beatrice F and Gary R FRANCOEUR, 22 Oct 1983 Hudson, NH
KOFFINK, June C and Justin H WHITE, 25 Dec 1950 Hudson, NH
KOGLER, Thomas A and Carlene M LAWRENCE, 24 Jun 1983 Hudson, NH
KONDRAT, Gloria and Frank G CHESS, 18 Aug 1945 Nashua, NH
KOPACZ, Mitchell W and Barbara MERRILL, 08 Jun 1981 Hudson, NH
KOPISKI, Stephen and Lois M STRAUB, 21 Oct 1961 Hudson, NH
KOPKA, Donna L and John C CARDIN, 16 Feb 1985 Nashua, NH
KOPKA, Joseph J Jr and Shirley A POULIN, 05 Feb 1955 Hudson, NH
KOPKA, Kenneth J and June H NAZAKA, 10 May 1980 Nashua, NH
KOPKA, Patricia A and Leonard N HARVEY, 14 Jan 1967 Hudson, NH
KOPKA, Thomas and Caroline FOSDICK, 20 May 1841
KOPPENHOFER, Susan E and Leslie SCENNA, 18 Dec 1980 Hudson, NH
KORPETER, Judy Ann and Kenneth J HUDSON, 22 Jan 1966 Hudson, NH
KOSSIVAS, John and Anne McEALHERN, 02 Aug 1938 Hudson, NH
KOSTYK, Walter J and Pamela L PELLETIER, 05 Mar 1971 Nashua, NH
KOTOPOULIS, Madeline and Ardres SOULEOTIS, 18 May 1942 Hudson, NH
KOULETSIS, Christine & Peter W KENDALL, 07 Jul 1973 Manchester, NH
KOWALCZYK, Frank J and Nora R KILPECK, 20 Sep 1947 Hudson, NH
KOZIOL, John W and Estelle F NICHOLSON, 02 Sep 1984 Hudson, NH
KOZLOVSKI, Albert D and Pamela D LANKHORST, 03 May 1975 Hudson, NH
KOZLOVSKI, Gail B and Ernest D III ROSS, 06 Jun 1981 Hudson, NH
KOZUSZEK, Helen G and Bernard F Jr MELANSON, 19 May 1984 Nashua, NH
KRAEMER, Sean M and Marion L YOUNG, 07 Aug 1982 Hudson, NH
KRAMER, Dan J and Francine E STETZLER, 30 Jun 1984 Nashua, NH
KRAMER, Francina and Marcel THAU, 27 Jul 1943 Hudson, NH
KRAUCHUK, Walter and Hilda E PLATHNER, 29 Jan 1949 Hudson, NH
KRAUSE, Alois W Jr and Virginia CURTIS, 13 Jun 1942 Hudson, NH
KREBS, Michael J and Patricia A KESSLER, 06 Sep 1975 Rindge, NH
KREKORIAN, Dorothy and Andrew A LEIGHTON, 04 Sep 1948 Hudson, NH
KREWSKI, Eula F and John E BARRY, 03 Feb 1951 Hudson, NH
KREWSKI, John and Clara V KELLERBERG, 20 Jul 1951 Hudson, NH
KRISTOFF, Leona T and Alcide S LEVESQUE, 24 Dec 1947 Hudson, NH
KRUEGER, Melissa D and Joseph B HUMPTON, 16 Oct 1982 Nashua, NH
KRUPA, Kevin J and Pamela A OIKLE, 08 Feb 1977 Nashua, NH
KRZYZEK, Raymond A and Cathy T KULCH, 15 Jan 1983 Pelham, NH
KUCHINSKI, Donald S and Lydia N GROHOSKY, 08 May 1965 Hudson, NH
KUCHINSKI, Mary Jane and Michael A PATTEN, 15 Mar 1975 Nashua, NH
KUCIJ, Richard S and Kim L SIMARD, 12 May 1978 Hudson, NH
KUGIMA, Alice J and Wilson F CUTTELL, 26 Jun 1948 Hudson, NH
KUHN, George W and Sara C C HAWTHWORTH, 15 Oct 1846
KUIVILLE, Gilburt and Emma D AMOUR, 16 Aug 1919 Nashua, NH
KULA, Linda A and Chris M ANDERSON, 28 Aug 1982 Manchester, NH
KULCH, Cathy T and Raymond A KRZYZEK, 15 Jan 1983 Pelham, NH
KULESZ, Josephine and William R HOULEY, 01 Dec 1945 Nashua, NH
KULESZA, Stanley O and Cynthia V McLAVEY, 16 Aug 1969 Hudson, NH
KULINGOSKI, Philip M Jr & Jennice M GALIPEAU, 16 Oct 1976 Nashua,NH
KUNGULUS, George D and Claire TETREAULT, 26 Nov 1965 Hudson, NH
KUNIGENAS, John V and Helen A LAVICK, 05 Nov 1946 Hudson, NH
KUPCHUN, Alphonse B and Helen C BOGDZVICH, 22 Dec 1942 Nashua, NH
KUPCHUN, Helen C and George W Jr TETLER, 20 Aug 1949 Nashua, NH
KUPCHUNAS, Frank and Alice SAKOVICH, 20 Jun 1936 Nashua, NH

HUDSON, NH MARRIAGES

KUPCHUNAS, Mary A and James A NUTE, 16 Sep 1961 Nashua, NH
KUPCHUNAS, Stanley and Anna CHESS, 05 Sep 1936 Nashua, NH
KURMAN, Sheri G and Glenn E ALDRICH, 11 Dec 1983 Salem, NH
KURTA, Stephanie and Chester J STECKEVICZ, 09 May 1946 Nashua, NH
KUS, Jane and Dino CARACOTSIOS, 05 Mar 1948 Hudson, NH
KUSLEIKA, Steven and Louise C JACOBSON, 02 Apr 1949 Hudson, NH
KUTRUBES, Aphrodite and John P BELL, 12 Dec 1936 Hudson, NH
KVEDAR, Cyprian P Jr and Georgia E NUTE, 01 Jul 1961 Hudson, NH
L'HEUREUX, Marilyn R & Marc R DESCHENES, 17 Sep 1983 Manchester, NH
LABAIRE, Emily A and Paul A DANAHY, 24 Oct 1975 Hudson, NH
LABARRE, Raymond P and Linda J WILSON, 29 May 1982 Hudson, NH
LABBE, Susan M and Timothy H BANEY, 02 Dec 1978 Hudson, NH
LABEDNICK, Dennis E and Jean G GRIFFIN, 29 Jun 1968 Nashua, NH
LABEDNICK, Nancy I and Henry L Jr NARO, 16 May 1959 Nashua, NH
LABELLE, Denise Ann and Denis J ANCTIL, 07 Dec 1974 Nashua, NH
LABOMBARD, Carrie A and William GAUDETTE, 20 Jul 1929 Hudson, NH
LABOMBARD, Mary Eliza and Joseph LEFEBVRE, 06 Sep 1924 Hudson, NH
LABOMBARDE, Elie and Yvonne C LEBOEUF, 08 Sep 1943 Nashua, NH
LABONTE, Donald J and Lynda M DERBY, 09 Apr 1983 Mont Vernon, NH
LABONTE, Roland C and Vivian E GUILMETTE, 18 Jul 1964 Hudson, NH
LABOUNTY, Pearl R and Mervin R NEVENS, 26 Nov 1959 Rye, NH
LABRANCHE, Jeanine A and Robert L PELLETIER, 31 Aug 1963 Nashua, NH
LABRECQUE, Linda M and Raymond P GAUDETTE, 09 Nov 1968 Hudson, NH
LABRECQUE, Raymond D & Jeanine E THERRIAULT, 03 May 1974 Nashua, NH
LABRIE, Adrien A and Theresa NANTEL, 07 Jun 1947 Nashua, NH
LABRIE, Celeste M and Robert Jos Jr SCHMITT, 11 Nov 1978 Nashua, NH
LABRIE, Claudette and Robert L COURTEMANCHE, 14 Jun 1958 Nashua, NH
LABRIE, Conrad G and Doris M DIFONZO, 07 May 1977 Hudson, NH
LABRIE, Jacqueline and Everett W ELLIS, 19 Apr 1968 Nashua, NH
LABRIE, Josephine and Val VERSECKES, 03 Jul 1948 Hudson, NH
LABRIE, Romeo R Jr and Kathleen E LIBBY, 04 Mar 1972 Nashua, NH
LABRIE, Yvonne A and Andrew J LIGHT, 09 Sep 1950 Nashua, NH
LACASSE, Barbara R and Raymond J LACHANCE, 06 Oct 1979 Hudson, NH
LACASSE, Bonnie J and Robert J ELLSTROM, 17 Nov 1984 Hudson, NH
LACASSE, Elizabeth and Edward E MOREAU, 28 Jun 1969 Hudson, NH
LACASSE, Frances A and Robert R RODRIGUES, 27 Aug 1971 Hudson, NH
LACASSE, Tammy F and John A S GAGNON, 25 Apr 1981 Nashua, NH
LACASSE, Vivian R and William J Jr HUARD, 08 Nov 1969 Nashua, NH
LaCHANCE, Gabriel and Germain DOUCET, 29 Aug 1936 Nashua, NH
LACHANCE, Gabrielle and Raymond A OUELLET, 02 Jun 1956 Nashua, NH
LACHANCE, Gerard R and Sandra R SANBORN, 09 Sep 1978 Hudson, NH
LACHANCE, Gloria A and Jon E LARO, 04 Sep 1961 Hudson, NH
LACHANCE, Henry and Antoinette LEVESQUE, 10 Aug 1940 Nashua, NH
LACHANCE, Joan P and Roy L BARNES, 03 May 1969 Hudson, NH
LACHANCE, Maurice E and Joan S VIGNEAULT, 23 Nov 1967 Nashua, NH
LACHANCE, Peter A and Judith A NOEL, 15 Jun 1968 Hudson, NH
LACHANCE, Raymond J and Patricia R QUIGLEY, 07 Jul 1967 Nashua, NH
LACHANCE, Raymond J and Barbara R LACASSE, 06 Oct 1979 Hudson, NH
LACHANCE, William R and Lucille Y SCHARCH, 31 Jul 1971 Hudson, NH
LACHAPELLE, Elaine D and Herbert BURTON, 28 May 1955 Manchester, NH
LACHAPELLE, June O and Michael W NOLET, 20 Nov 1976 Hudson, NH
LACKIE, Phyllis A and Calvin E BAKER, 14 Sep 1974 Hudson, NH
LACOSHUS, Frank M and Patricia A MATYJASIK, 20 Sep 1970 Hudson, NH
LACOUNT, Albert J Jr and Doreen Rhea LIGHT, 17 Nov 1973 Hudson, NH
LACOUNT, Susan Ann and Frank W Jr DONNELLY, 28 Oct 1978 Hudson, NH
LACOY, Debora A and Richard M BELHUMEUR, 21 Oct 1978 Hudson, NH
LACOY, Mary E and John D McNEILL, 25 Apr 1978 Nashua, NH
LACROIX, Florence F and William J COLLINS, 22 May 1932 Hudson, NH
LACROIX, Michel P and Louise I CLOUTIER, 27 Jun 1970 Hudson, NH
LACROIX, Richard M and Anne C FORTIER, 01 Jun 1985 Hudson, NH

HUDSON, NH MARRIAGES

LADD, Kierscey C and Norma E LESIEUR, 02 Jun 1946 Hudson, NH
LADD, Molly and John HASELTINE, 06 Nov 1794
LADD, Rebecca W and William H WADLEIGH, 10 Mar 1859
LADNER, Reby A and Milton E WOOLEY, 02 Aug 1952 Hudson, NH
LADNER, Victoria and Clayton E SMITH, 31 Aug 1941 Hudson, NH
LADNER, Vivian S and Harold L MOORE, 20 Jun 1942 Hudson, NH
LADUE, Kenneth W and Theresa A YORK, 16 Sep 1971 Nashua, NH
LADUKE, Florence C and Winthrop L MARINEL, 25 Nov 1950 Hudson, NH
LAFERRIERE, Gerard J and Janet R BRIAND, 15 May 1982 Hudson, NH
LAFLAMME, Brenda A and Warren B HOWELL, 31 Aug 1963 Hudson, NH
LAFLAMME, Daniel B and Jane H LAFLAMME, 30 May 1975 Nashua, NH
LAFLAMME, Daniel B and Priscilla SMITH, 10 Sep 1977 Nashua, NH
LAFLAMME, Edith L and Leonard R JELLEY, 14 Jul 1956 Hudson, NH
LAFLAMME, Ernest and Doris YOUNG, 03 Apr 1937 Nashua, NH
LAFLAMME, Ernest R and Regina L DUPLESSIS, 03 Jul 1982 Hudson, NH
LAFLAMME, Francis and Rose LAVOIE, 30 Jun 1934 Nashua, NH
LAFLAMME, Jane H and Edmund F GLIDDEN, 16 Sep 1977 Nashua, NH
LAFLAMME, Jane H and Daniel B LAFLAMME, 30 May 1975 Nashua, NH
LAFLAMME, Lucille E and Charles W DEAN, 20 Nov 1954 Hudson, NH
LAFLAMME, Mary J and George P BRIAND, 24 Dec 1954 Nashua, NH
LAFLAMME, Patricia L and Harold R COVEY, 17 Nov 1962 Hudson, NH
LAFLAMME, Reuben J and Lorette H RIOUX, 04 May 1946 Nashua, NH
LAFLAMME, Robert E and Sheila A GAGE, 22 Oct 1958 Manchester, NH
LAFLAMME, Robin L and John L BERNARD, 14 Dec 1974 Hudson, NH
LAFLEUR, Albina L and Francis J DAVIS, 27 Sep 1947 Hudson, NH
LAFLEUR, Gerald R and Brenda L LEMIRE, 27 Jun 1970 Hudson, NH
LAFLEUR, Jeanne M and Robert R LAMBERT, 20 Apr 1968 Hudson, NH
LAFLEUR, Roland E and Linda M JERRY, 05 Sep 1981 Salem, NH
LAFLEUR, Thomas R and Sandra J WITCOMB, 10 Jun 1978 Durham, NH
LAFLOTTE, Irene J and Richard D MAJOR, 20 Jun 1964 Nashua, NH
LAFOND, Irene M and Alfred O LAFRENIERE, 09 Sep 1950 Manchester, NH
LAFORD, Richard J and Elaine A SILK, 19 Sep 1981 Nashua, NH
LAFOREST, Donald W and Sandra A WEDICK, 21 Dec 1963 Hudson, NH
LAFOREST, June E and Albert P ST AMANT, 05 Nov 1969 Nashua, NH
LAFOREST, June E and Leon R BENOIT, 26 Dec 1960 Derry, NH
LAFOREST, Kathleen M and Thomas J BAYLIS, 08 Jun 1974 Auburn, NH
LAFOREST, Leonard G and Carol O HAWES, 16 Oct 1968 Hudson, NH
LAFOREST, Neil B and Kim M DIONNE, 23 Sep 1983 Nashua, NH
LAFOREST, Raymond A and Janice I RABY, 24 Nov 1966 Hudson, NH
LAFOREST, Robin P and Dennis R BEYER, 25 Aug 1972 Hudson, NH
LAFOREST, Yvonne P and Normand R LEVESQUE, 25 Apr 1970 Nashua, NH
LAFRANCE, Doris A and George F ALEXANDER, 05 Feb 1949 Hudson, NH
LAFRANCE, Gerard J and Lillian A RICARD, 31 Jul 1943 Nashua, NH
LAFRANCE, Linda G and Dana M DEROSIER, 26 Nov 1982 Hudson, NH
LAFRANCE, Lucille A and Henry J ROBINSON, 15 Dec 1945 Hudson, NH
LAFRANCE, Paul T and Corinne E DESBIENS, 17 Jul 1954 Nashua, NH
LAFRENIERE, Alfred O and Irene M LAFOND, 09 Sep 1950 Manchester, NH
LAGACE, Claire D and Richard F GAGNON, 08 Oct 1960 Hudson, NH
LAGASSE, Alphonse J and Jeanette L McLEOD, 06 Jul 1946 Hudson, NH
LAGASSE, Armand C and Muriel L TESSIER, 22 Nov 1956 Hudson, NH
LAGASSE, Debra J and Stephen A TIRRELL, 02 May 1981 Hudson, NH
LAGASSE, Gemma M and Hector J DEMANCHE, 10 Jan 1966 Nashua, NH
LAGASSE, Henry E and Nancy A MOREY, 28 Nov 1957 Hudson, NH
LAGASSE, Leon V Jr and Lucy A TWARDOSKY, 18 Jan 1964 Hudson, NH
LAHAN, Ann F and Paul P STARTA, 23 Oct 1947 Hudson, NH
LAINE, Aldeo O and Pauline J COTE, 25 Nov 1954 Hudson, NH
LAINE, David A and Patricia A GUILL, 20 Jun 1981 Nashua, NH
LAINE, Donna A and Richard D MELANSON, 21 May 1983 Hudson, NH
LAINE, Kenneth A and Linda J GUINAN, 22 Feb 1969 Hudson, NH
LAINE, Lionel A and Claudette DUMAIS, 13 Oct 1962 Hudson, NH

HUDSON,NH MARRIAGES

LAINE, Paul A and Jacqueline PELLETIER, 01 Sep 1979 Hudson, NH
LAINE, Paula A and Joseph A III DUBE, 06 Oct 1979 Hudson, NH
LAINEY, Lona J and William S BARNES, 14 May 1977 Nashua, NH
LAJEUNESSE, Marie A and Raymond ROBBINS, 05 May 1945 Nashua, NH
LAJEUNESSE, Monique R and Edward G GAMACHE, 01 Nov 1952 Nashua, NH
LAJOIE, Allen Dona and Doreen Ann BULLARD, 18 Jul 1981 Hudson, NH
LAJOIE, Celine C and Jeffrey M LAW, 19 Jun 1976 Pelham, NH
LAJOIE, Edward R and Vicki L PARKHURST, 22 Nov 1975 Hudson, NH
LAJOIE, Normand J and Jeanette R DANEAULT, 29 Jun 1946 Nashua, NH
LAJOIE, Robert A and Sandra L GALIPEAU, 06 Sep 1980 Hudson, NH
LAJOIE, Ronald J and Gloria A BOYSTER, 12 Sep 1969 Hudson, NH
LAJOIE, Yvonne E and Peter R MITCHELL, 20 Jun 1953 Nashua, NH
LAKE, Mary Franc and George W FLAGG, 18 Mar 1874
LAKEMAN, Frances and John E CHASE, 30 Dec 1876 Hudson, NH
LALIBERTE, Evelina J & Dennis M KELLY, 30 Jun 1984 Moultonboro, NH
LALIBERTE, Gerald R and Laura J TAYLOR, 28 Aug 1965 Nashua, NH
LALIBERTE, Marie J and Alfred P RICHARD, 30 Aug 1947 Nashua, NH
LALIBERTE, Richard L and Kathleen E SMITH, 27 Dec 1969 Hudson, NH
LALLY, James J and Mary PALANGI, 03 Jul 1948 Hudson, NH
LALUMIERE, William O and Janice N PROVENCAL, 31 Jan 1954 Hollis, NH
LAMB, Josephine and Charles J RODONIS, 10 Nov 1956 Nashua, NH
LAMB, William S and Cynthia M DONNELLY, 26 Oct 1974 Nashua, NH
LAMB, William S and Patricia A BURTON, 22 Apr 1978 Hudson, NH
LAMBERT, Alan J and Nadine R BOUCHER, 16 Jun 1984 Hudson, NH
LAMBERT, Albert and Madeline R ORLANDO, 01 Oct 1949 Hudson, NH
LAMBERT, Albert J and Donna M FITZGERALD, 23 Jul 1972 Pelham, NH
LAMBERT, Albert L Jr & Jeannie A CHODAKOWSKI, 23 Dec 1972 Pelham,NH
LAMBERT, Annette M&Ralph O CHESNULEVICH, 17 Jul 1954 Manchester, NH
LAMBERT, Aurore and Joseph LAPOINTE, 29 May 1937 Nashua, NH
LAMBERT, Christine and Joseph F MILOT, 15 Jan 1983 Hudson, NH
LAMBERT, Clara G and Willburr C Jr DOSS, 16 Nov 1970 Hudson, NH
LAMBERT, Clara N and Edmond VIGNEAULT, 07 Nov 1915 Hudson, NH
   Albert Langelier (Holbrook, MA) & Phebe Ouilette (Canada)
   Petrus Vigneault(Canada) & Elenard Gaudette (Canada)
LAMBERT, Dennis M and Alyce M NOAKES, 12 Jul 1969 Hudson, NH
LAMBERT, Frank and Della JACOBS, 05 Dec 1896 Nashua, NH
LAMBERT, Ida W and Walter H YOUNG, 30 Sep 1907 Hudson, NH
   Edwin Lambert & Lizzie P Aubin
   Martin J Young & Flora E Thompson
LAMBERT, Irene N and Philip L ROY, 23 Jun 1934 Nashua, NH
LAMBERT, Jeanne M and Scott L LENTZ, 14 Feb 1982 Hudson, NH
LAMBERT, Joseph E & Olive M Harvey SMITH, 07 Apr 1928 Chelmsford,MA
LAMBERT, Judith G and Leonard G OUELLETTE, 10 Aug 1968 Hudson, NH
LAMBERT, Leo W and Carolyn E FORRENCE, 08 Oct 1977 Hudson, NH
LAMBERT, Lillian M and E Emmett DONNELLY, 01 Nov 1921 Nashua, NH
LAMBERT, Marion and Emery NADEAU, 06 Oct 1934 Nashua, NH
LAMBERT, Raymond R and Gloria M BELAND, 08 Oct 1955 Hudson, NH
LAMBERT, Richard H and Carla A NEUFFER, 29 Jan 1966 Hudson, NH
LAMBERT, Richard M and Laurie A CHAPUT, 24 Apr 1981 Hudson, NH
LAMBERT, Robert H and Lori E WHITTEN, 27 Jul 1974 Hudson, NH
LAMBERT, Robert R and Jeanne M LAFLEUR, 20 Apr 1968 Hudson, NH
LAMBERT, Romeo and Olida B BOSLEY, 02 Oct 1954 Hudson, NH
LAMBERT, Theodore F and Rhoda L HOWE, 15 Jun 1963 Nashua, NH
LAMBERT, Valerie R and John David FELLOWS, 30 Jun 1973 Nashua, NH
LAMBERT, Walter O and Arline M WILSON, 17 Jul 1946 Hudson, NH
LAMEY, Joseph and Irene DANNER, 03 Apr 1948 Hudson, NH
LAMFORD, Mary T and George F CASE, 02 Sep 1873 Hudson, NH
LAMON, Wanita R and Stephen C BOUCHER, 30 Apr 1983 Hudson, NH
LAMONT, June I and Allan J IRELAND, 15 Oct 1942 Hudson, NH
LAMONTAGNE, Armand P and Thelma BAGLEY, 22 Oct 1937 Nashua, NH

HUDSON, NH MARRIAGES

LAMONTAGNE, Marcel and Denise E DION, 15 Jun 1979 Merrimack, NH
LAMONTAGNE, Richard M and Linda A ROBERT, 27 Aug 1971 Hudson, NH
LAMOTHE, Diane G and Jean-Guy C CROTEAU, 15 Feb 1969 Nashua, NH
LAMOTHE, Roland J and Sandra L MERRILL, 05 Sep 1970 Nashua, NH
LAMOUREUX, Robert P&Marlea M LAUTENSCHLAGER, 08 Jun 1985 Hudson, NH
LAMOY, Betty A and Roger C LANDRY, 04 May 1963 Hudson, NH
LAMOY, Clarence J and Barbara BETE, 05 Jul 1935 Nashua, NH
LAMOY, Philip T and Annie GUMBRAVICK, 15 Sep 1924 Nashua, NH
LAMPER, Caren E and Alan R BARRIAULT, 31 Mar 1974 Hudson, NH
LAMPER, Roberta L and George H PETERS, 13 Feb 1965 Hudson, NH
LAMPHEAR, Dennis F and Susan I DUMAIS, 22 Jan 1969 Nashua, NH
LAMPRON, Barbara A and James L RYAN, 11 Oct 1958 Hudson, NH
LAMPRON, Edward O and Barbara A LONES, 19 Jul 1952 Hudson, NH
LAMPRON, Edward O and Marlene C BRIERE, 09 Sep 1955 Hudson, NH
LAMPRON, Gary P and Jeannine D VINCENT, 11 Apr 1973 Manchester, NH
LAMPRON, Sandra L and Robert M HODGMAN, 10 Nov 1962 Wilton, NH
LAMSON, John and Jane WOODBURY, 31 Oct 1860
LAMSON, John O and June WOODBURY, 31 Oct 1860
LAMSON, Joseph O and Winnebel MERRILL, 24 Aug 1922 Salem Depot, NH
LAMSON, Winnebel and Edwin E ROWELL, 06 Aug 1931 Hudson, NH
LANCESTER, Walter E and Deborah J BRONSON, 06 Sep 1975 Hudson, NH
LANDOLT, Raymond W and Cynthia C SOUCY, 29 Jul 1979 Nashua, NH
LANDREY, Joseph and Esther McQUESTEN, 05 Jul 1880 Hudson, NH
LANDRY, Albert J and Dorothy F GAUDETTE, 27 Apr 1946 Nashua, NH
LANDRY, Alice and Alex CANTIN, 09 Apr 1938 Nashua, NH
LANDRY, Alphonse E and Catherine PRITZ, 10 Nov 1956 Hudson, NH
LANDRY, Alvine and Peter SOUCI, 30 May 1916 Nashua, NH
   Joseph Landry (Canada) & Aglae Gogne (Canada)
   Andrew Souci(Canada) & Emilia Arsenault (Maine)
LANDRY, Andrew A and Lois E COOK, 09 Sep 1967 Hudson, NH
LANDRY, Annette T and Robert H LESSARD, 14 Aug 1971 Hudson, NH
LANDRY, Barbara J and John M McILVEEN, 14 Apr 1984 Hudson, NH
LANDRY, Bernadette and Roger G BRODEUR, 23 Jun 1951 Hudson, NH
LANDRY, Bruce C and Louise M DESCOTEAUX, 04 Nov 1967 Nashua, NH
LANDRY, Clifford M and Brenda L BRADFORD, 09 Sep 1978 Hudson, NH
LANDRY, Daniel R and Carol A HAMBLETT, 06 Sep 1969 Hudson, NH
LANDRY, David E and Judith A GILBERT, 22 Aug 1970 Littleton, MA
LANDRY, Delia and George GOULD, 08 Sep 1924 Nashua, NH
LANDRY, Denise J and Brent T KIERSTEAD, 04 Dec 1976 Hudson, NH
LANDRY, Dennis P and Suzanne R PELLETIER, 27 Sep 1969 Hudson, NH
LANDRY, Donald A and Eleanor M COWGILL, 04 Jul 1958 Nashua, NH
LANDRY, Donald L and Cathleen J NOYES, 07 Oct 1967 Hudson, NH
LANDRY, Donna M and Robert K DURAND, 20 May 1978 Nashua, NH
LANDRY, Donna M and Leon E SPAULDING, 24 Jul 1971 Nashua, NH
LANDRY, Doreen A and Mark T GAGNON, 30 Apr 1983 Hudson, NH
LANDRY, Douglas D and Deborah J DOBENS, 03 Oct 1982 Hudson, NH
LANDRY, Edward L and Irene D WILMOT, 11 Apr 1969 Nashua, NH
LANDRY, Estelle I and Harry Jr PENDLETON, 17 Jun 1967 Hudson, NH
LANDRY, Evelyn R and Rheal J BOUCHER, 28 May 1955 Hudson, NH
LANDRY, George A and Alma MANSFIELD, 30 Jun 1934 Nashua, NH
LANDRY, George L and Carol A HAMEL, 20 Jun 1959 Nashua, NH
LANDRY, Germia M and Joseph P LEGASSE, 24 Aug 1940 Nashua, NH
LANDRY, Henry J and Bernice I VASHER, 06 Mar 1965 Nashua, NH
LANDRY, Ida M and Woodrow F SCOTT, 20 May 1943 Nashua, NH
LANDRY, Jeannette and Philip H BONNETTE, 31 May 1947 Nashua, NH
LANDRY, Jeannette and Alfred P COTE, 26 Sep 1959 Hudson, NH
LANDRY, Joann and Charles J MICHIE, 27 Jan 1967 Nashua, NH
LANDRY, John A and Elaine M GRISH, 02 Jul 1983 Nashua, NH
LANDRY, Joseph and Bernadette BELANGER, 11 Jun 1917 Nashua, NH
LANDRY, Joyce M and Edmond P DURAND, 09 Jul 1983 Hudson, NH

HUDSON, NH MARRIAGES

LANDRY, Judith M and Raymond L TURCOTTE, 04 Oct 1975 Hudson, NH
LANDRY, Linda J and Robert P FLYNN, 18 Jul 1982 Hudson, NH
LANDRY, Lisa E and Ralph M RICARD, 23 Jan 1981 Hudson, NH
LANDRY, Lorraine B and Leo A GAMACHE, 28 May 1948 Nashua, NH
LANDRY, Lucille I and Roland R GAUDETTE, 18 May 1946 Nashua, NH
LANDRY, Mabel G and Charles W IVES, 30 Jul 1955 Hudson, NH
LANDRY, Margaret M and Kenneth Jr GRIFFIN, 30 Dec 1978 Milford, NH
LANDRY, Nancy E and Robert J MILLER, 17 Jul 1960 Nashua, NH
LANDRY, Nicole and Paul C DESJARDINS, 23 May 1981 Nashua, NH
LANDRY, Norman A and Lorraine P ROBINSON, 12 Oct 1963 Nashua, NH
LANDRY, Norman G and Rachel T DENIS, 24 Apr 1948 Nashua, NH
LANDRY, Normand L and Marlene E DOW, 26 Apr 1952 Nashua, NH
LANDRY, Paul and Estelle I MICHAUD, 12 Jun 1943 Nashua, NH
LANDRY, Paul A and Catherine PELLETIER, 25 Sep 1976 Hudson, NH
LANDRY, Paul A and Ellen M KEARNS, 31 Jul 1983 Nashua, NH
LANDRY, Paul M and Arlene E BOURGEOIS, 30 Apr 1960 Hudson, NH
LANDRY, Phelomene L and Joseph E LECLERE, 19 Apr 1926 Nashua, NH
LANDRY, Raymond A and Clarice PETRAIN, 02 Jun 1956 Nashua, NH
LANDRY, Robert P and Carole J OUELLET, 19 May 1984 Hudson, NH
LANDRY, Roger C and Betty A LAMOY, 04 May 1963 Hudson, NH
LANDRY, Romeo W and Vita Y PARISEAU, 21 Sep 1946 Nashua, NH
LANDRY, Theresa R and Bruce W HOLTON, 29 Jun 1974 Litchfield, NH
LANDRY, Yvette L and Joseph A GRACEY, 30 Aug 1984 Nashua, NH
LANE, Anne Marie and Paul A SEVIGNY, 09 Aug 1980 Hudson, NH
LANE, Catherine and Raymond DIRUSSO, 10 Apr 1937 Hudson, NH
LANE, Charlotte and Raymond W OLENA, 29 Jun 1964 Manchester, NH
LANE, Edna and Lawrence QUINN, 05 Sep 1925 Nashua, NH
LANE, Marion B and Archie M TAGG, 07 Oct 1935 Hudson, NH
LANFEAR, Robert H and Helen L STARK, 25 Apr 1950 Hudson, NH
LANGDON, Darcy Ann and Richard S ELLIOTT, 15 Jan 1983 Pelham, NH
LANGEIN, Yvonne and Joseph Z VANIER, 13 Jun 1925 Hudson, NH
LANGELIER, Linda M and Michael P BEYER, 30 Jan 1972 Hudson, NH
LANGELIER, Philip R and Mae R OUELLETTE, 14 Feb 1953 Nashua, NH
LANGELIER, Robert S and Elaine C BRODEUR, 25 Aug 1962 Hudson, NH
LANGFORD, Virginia W and Herbert W SHAW, 04 Jul 1981 Hudson, NH
LANGLOIS, Kathy A and Donald A SMITH, 21 May 1982 Windham, NH
LANGLOIS, Lucille M and Frederick BRADLEY, 10 Feb 1947 Hudson, NH
LANGLOIS, Lucille P and Walter J SURPRENANT, 26 Jul 1981 Hudson, NH
LANGLOIS, Ronna C and William A WORTH, 01 Jan 1984 Hudson, NH
LANGLOIS, Ulfrand and Isabelle SPEAR, 25 Jun 1932 Hudson, NH
LANKHORST, Julie A and James M TATEM, 25 Jun 1983 Hudson, NH
LANKHORST, Pamela D and Albert D KOZLOVSKI, 03 May 1975 Hudson, NH
LANOIE, Cynthia A and Steve A PROVINS, 25 Jun 1977 Hudson, NH
LANOUE, David R Jr and Tammy J COLBURN, 18 May 1985 Hudson, NH
LANPHEAR, Susan I and Joseph L SOUTHWICK, 20 Aug 1977 Hudson, NH
LANPHER, Omar P and Cindy M TACEWICZ, 22 Nov 1984 Nashua, NH
LANTAGNE, Barbara A and Steve M SPONGBERG, 21 Aug 1949 Hudson, NH
LANZA, Anthony M and Ann E DIXON, 19 Dec 1981 Hudson, NH
LAPAN, Darlene A and Edward G LEAOR, 14 Jul 1956 Hudson, NH
LAPHAM, Gary P and June M WALSH, 03 Aug 1968 Hudson, NH
LAPHAM, Ruth T and Edmund A BOYDEN, 04 Aug 1934 Effingham Fls, NH
LAPIERRE, Carole H and Kenneth J JOHNSON, 14 Jun 1947 Hudson, NH
LAPLANTE, Cheryl A and Paul B ADKINS, 10 Jun 1974 Hudson, NH
LAPLANTE, Normand A and Jacqueline CLOUTIER, 28 May 1960 Nashua, NH
LAPOINTE, Jeannette and Joseph A PHILIBERT, 02 Aug 1958 Hudson, NH
LAPOINTE, Joseph and Aurore LAMBERT, 29 May 1937 Nashua, NH
LAPOINTE, Shirley M and Leopold J CROTEAU, 15 Feb 1984 Hudson, NH
LAPORTA, Mark E and Sylvie L COTNOIR, 19 Sep 1981 Manchester, NH
LAPORTE, Brenda A and Stephen M CHESS, 17 Jun 1972 Hudson, NH
LAPORTE, Clarence A and Elizabeth DUMAIS, 22 Feb 1964 Claremont, NH

HUDSON, NH MARRIAGES

LAPPEN, Nancy J and Thomas E McCOY, 13 Jun 1970 Pelham, NH
LAPRISE, Georgette and Edward J Jr CROTEAU, 16 Jun 1956 Hudson, NH
LAQUENE, Arthur P and Odelie BISSONETTE, 02 Apr 1923 Nashua, NH
LAQUERRE, Arthur P and Alma CHARPENTIER, 29 Jan 1917 Nashua, NH
LAQUERRE, Cora J and Elias E DECOLEAU, 29 Jun 1946 Nashua, NH
LAQUERRE, Gedeon and Rose ROUSSEAU, 12 Jan 1920 Nashua, NH
LAQUERRE, Germaine A and Curtis M WATROUSE, 13 Jun 1970 Nashua, NH
LAQUERRE, Karen L and Donald A STEPNEY, 11 Sep 1976 Hudson, NH
LAQUERRE, Linda A and Stephen J TOBIN, 27 Aug 1977 Hudson, NH
LAQUERRE, Pauline G and August R OUELLETTE, 29 Sep 1947 Nashua, NH
LAQUERRE, Richard A and LuAnn M. BAUSHA, 08 Oct 1977 Hudson, NH
LAQUERRE, Roger A and Rachel C DUMAS, 16 Sep 1950 Nashua, NH
LAQUERRE, Victor and Elaine CHARPENTIER, 30 Dec 1918 Nashua, NH
LAREAU, Donald R and Barbara M AREL, 24 Sep 1966 Hudson, NH
LARGY, James J and Joann A BROWN, 01 Apr 1967 Nashua, NH
LARGY, JoAnn A and Robert L AMARAL, 02 Jan 1982 Litchfield, NH
LARGY, Suzanne R and Alan F FAIRFIELD, 11 Nov 1961 Nashua, NH
LARKIN, Charles F and Shelley M CURRAN, 20 Oct 1979 Hudson, NH
LARO, Gloria A and Philip C WARREN, 18 Jun 1983 Hudson, NH
LARO, Jon E and Gloria A LACHANCE, 04 Sep 1961 Hudson, NH
LAROCHE, Constance and Richard T PLANTIER, 11 May 1953 Nashua, NH
LAROCHE, Dorilla and Antoine LECLERC, 25 Aug 1919 Nashua, NH
LAROCHE, Shawn E and Christine MICHAUD, 14 Aug 1982 Hudson, NH
LAROCQUE, Charlene L and Jeffrey T SAKELLAR, 23 Nov 1974 Hudson, NH
LAROCQUE, Edward T and Lillian D GALVIN, 11 Apr 1950 Hudson, NH
LAROCQUE, George R Jr and Paula L SMITH, 04 Sep 1976 Hudson, NH
LAROCQUE, Mary Ellen&Walter F Jr SZUKSTA, 03 Nov 1984 Hudson, NH
LAROCQUE, Michael J and Susan J COLBURN, 22 Aug 1981 Hudson, NH
LAROSE, Diane L and Ronald V CUNHA, 28 Jun 1969 Nashua, NH
LAROSE, Edward J and Lucienne A BOYER, 11 Feb 1956 Hudson, NH
LAROSE, John S and Shirley L RIVARD, 15 Oct 1983 Nashua, NH
LAROSE, Judy J and Thomas W PHILBROOK, 19 Dec 1976 Hudson, NH
LAROSE, Monique A and Mark J NIEMASZYK, 29 Jun 1985 Hudson, NH
LAROSE, Paul P and Kim E SHUMSKY, 19 Apr 1975 Hudson, NH
LAROUCHE, Annette I and Paul M FERRARA, 21 Jun 1980 Hudson, NH
LAROUCHE, Craig A and Debra J REITAN, 05 May 1984 Nashua, NH
LAROUCHE, Marianne C and Albert E LAVOIE, 29 Nov 1969 Hudson, NH
LAROUCHE, Maurice R Jr & Deborah J MERRILL, 25 Sep 1971 Hudson, NH
LAROUCHE, Rita V and Paul A TESSIER, 25 Apr 1959 Hudson, NH
LAROUCHE, Rose A Y and Walter H LEAOR, 04 Apr 1933 Nashua, NH
LAROUCHE, Theresa R and Stephen F KEARNS, 16 Dec 1972 Hudson, NH
LAROUCHE, Valerie J and Luc A DEMERS, 22 Aug 1981 Hudson, NH
LARSON, Donald M and Catherine HARRIS, 09 Feb 1950 Hudson, NH
LARSON, Virginia G and Bruce D HARTEL, 27 Nov 1976 Nashua, NH
LASALLE, Beatrice A and Leo W PROVENCAL, 19 Feb 1944 Nashua, NH
LASALLE, Richard A and Cathy Lynn JENKINS, 19 Feb 1977 Nashua, NH
LASSITER, Alice R and Lawrence N CLARK, 22 Aug 1931 Hudson, NH
LASSITER, Roy W and Leslie B WOODS, 23 Dec 1983 Nashua, NH
LASTOWKA, Cheryl L and Michael D THEBODEAU, 23 Apr 1977 Hudson, NH
LATHAM, Johney M and Janet M POULIN, 20 Mar 1971 Hudson, NH
LATIMER, Dianne E and Wheeler E ZALANSKAS, 24 Apr 1981 Nashua, NH
LATOUR, Donald and Carol M LAVALLEE, 17 Oct 1959 Hudson, NH
LATOUR, Eleanore T and Harvey L READ, 15 Jul 1961 Hudson, NH
LATOUR, Gayle H and Thomas L COSSETTE, 17 Aug 1974 Hudson, NH
LATOUR, George C Jr and Sandra L BONNER, 01 Jun 1963 Hudson, NH
LATOUR, Joseph E and Janet A SMITH, 04 Oct 1957 Hudson, NH
LATOUR, Paula J and Dennis H DWIRE, 15 May 1971 Hudson, NH
LATOUR, Richard J and April S MUNSON, 27 Nov 1970 Nashua, NH
LATOUR, Roland E and Cecile A THIBODEAU, 20 Jun 1946 Salem, NH
LATOUR, Sandra L and Maurice J DOUCETTE, 15 Sep 1973 Nashua, NH

HUDSON,NH MARRIAGES

LATTI, Margaret and Paul W HILLS, 06 Jun 1981 Nashua, NH
LATULIPPE, Alfred and Alberta C TESSIER, 24 Nov 1938 Nashua, NH
LATULIPPE, Carollee and Leonard G MERCIER, 01 May 1976 Nashua, NH
LATULIPPE, Leo R and Claire M PARADISE, 25 Apr 1964 Hudson, NH
LATULIPPE, Mary S and Stanley BATURA, 04 Feb 1963 Hudson, NH
LATULIPPE, Sandra C&Francis A Jr KASHULINES, 19 Jun 1965 Hudson, NH
LATVIS, Bruce S and Janice M CUTTER, 06 Dec 1969 Nashua, NH
LATVIS, John C and June M CRAWFORD, 22 Feb 1941 Nashua, NH
LAUF, Paul A and Louise F GRANDONE, 03 Aug 1935 Hudson, NH
LAUGHTON, Barry Char and Nancy B BOURASSA, 08 Nov 1980 Atkinson, NH
LAUKASH, Albina R and Martin Y PETERSON, 11 Jul 1936 Nashua, NH
LAURA, James F Jr and Donna M GRAINGER, 14 Mar 1975 Hudson, NH
LAURENCE, William W and Evelyn PENNEY, 30 Jul 1930 Hudson, NH
LAURENDEAU, Ginette L&Raynald A DUBORD, 21 Aug 1965 Manchester, NH
LAURIEN, Philip C and Bonnie L DUGAN, 11 Apr 1985 Nashua, NH
LAUSIER, Betty A and John A LINDSAY, 26 Aug 1967 Hudson, NH
LAUTENSCHLAGER, Marlea M&Robert P LAMOUREUX, 08 Jun 1985 Hudson, NH
LAUZIERE, John P and Gretchen K HARWOOD, 01 Dec 1979 Nashua, NH
LAVALETTE, Barbara J and Thomas R DOUCETTE, 31 Dec 1967 Hudson, NH
LAVALLEE, Brenda L and Gilbert DROUIN, 19 Nov 1983 Londonderry, NH
LAVALLEE, Carol M and Donald LATOUR, 17 Oct 1959 Hudson, NH
LAVALLEE, Celeste S and Francis P SECOR, 15 Feb 1942 Hudson, NH
LAVALLEE, David E and Ann JOHNSON, 26 Oct 1962 Hudson, NH
LAVALLEE, Deborah L and John R MAKER, 03 May 1975 Hudson, NH
LAVALLEE, Kathleen M and Gary J BOUTIN, 28 Nov 1983 Litchfield, NH
LAVALLEE, Linda D and James A BOURDON, 24 Feb 1968 Hudson, NH
LAVALLEE, Lisa A and Douglas P SOUCY, 19 Jan 1985 Nashua, NH
LAVALLEE, Maurice T and Marguerite FRASER, 11 May 1957 Nashua, NH
LAVALLEE, Michelle A and Michel J BEAULIEU, 18 Sep 1982 Nashua, NH
LAVALLEE, Nancy M & Donald G Jr DESLAURIERS, 10 Aug 1973 Nashua, NH
LAVALLEE, Priscilla and Richard A BOULEY, 23 Apr 1949 Nashua, NH
LAVALLEE, Raymond S and Jeanne D LAVOIE, 03 Jul 1948 Nashua, NH
LAVALLEE, Rita L and Armand T NADREAU, 28 Aug 1954 Nashua, NH
LAVALLEE, William R and Lucille J BRISEBOIS, 30 Dec 1952 Nashua, NH
LAVALLEY, Mary K and Walter J Jr KEUENHOFF, 06 Jun 1981 Hudson, NH
LAVALLEY, Victoria E and Frank A SILVA, 18 Mar 1977 Hudson, NH
LAVANWAY, Leo and Gertrude G LECLERC, 23 Jun 1945 Nashua, NH
LAVARNWAY, Rita M and Raymond C Jr BROOKS, 07 Jan 1946 Nashua, NH
LAVARNWAY, Roger O and Jewel C PAGE, 08 Jun 1974 Nashua, NH
LAVARNWAY, Vivian L and Raymond F DION, 07 May 1966 Nashua, NH
LAVICK, Helen A and John V KUNIGENAS, 05 Nov 1946 Hudson, NH
LAVIOLETTE, Arthur J Jr and Pauline M WHITE, 14 Aug 1937 Nashua, NH
LAVIOLETTE, Chas Louis and Helen CASEY, 19 Aug 1938 Nashua, NH
LAVOIE, Albert E and Marianne C LAROUCHE, 29 Nov 1969 Hudson, NH
LAVOIE, Andre L and Pauline O ROY, 05 Jun 1950 Hudson, NH
LAVOIE, Ann L and Anthony J POWLOWSKY, 26 Jun 1948 Hudson, NH
LAVOIE, Arlene Edna and Theodore P PRICKETT, 21 Feb 1928 Nashua, NH
LAVOIE, Armand H and Lena A BERUBE, 30 Jun 1951 Nashua, NH
LAVOIE, Augustin N and Doris P CLOUGH, 09 Jul 1938 Lowell, MA
LAVOIE, Cecile and Sylvio GRAVELLE, 07 Jun 1941 Nashua, NH
LAVOIE, Connie G and Jeffrey A PAQUIN, 29 Nov 1980 Hudson, NH
LAVOIE, Denise M and Lawrence R CORCORAN, 25 Jun 1976 Nashua, NH
LAVOIE, Diane J and Michael J McCOY, 08 Jan 1984 Hudson, NH
LAVOIE, Donald A and Susan L SCOTT, 17 Feb 1973 Hudson, NH
LAVOIE, Donald P and Carol A OBAN, 23 Feb 1963 Nashua, NH
LAVOIE, Donald P and Sharon A GAGNON, 19 Jan 1980 Nashua, NH
LAVOIE, Doris M and Arthur Jr HULSE, 08 Nov 1969 Hudson, NH
LAVOIE, Edmond and Amy HAMMOND, 01 Dec 1934 Nashua, NH
LAVOIE, Gary E and Debra L LEVESQUE, 15 Sep 1979 Hudson, NH
LAVOIE, George E and Alice A DUBE, 12 Jan 1957 Hudson, NH

HUDSON, NH MARRIAGES

LAVOIE, Gerard W and Marie-Therese PARE, 05 Oct 1953 Nashua, NH
LAVOIE, Jeanne D and Raymond S LAVALLEE, 03 Jul 1948 Nashua, NH
LAVOIE, John P and Elizabeth SCHINDLER, 05 Jun 1982 Hudson, NH
LAVOIE, Jon L and Nancy T MORGAN, 27 Apr 1957 Hudson, NH
LAVOIE, Joseph A L and Mari G ROY, 21 Aug 1942 Nashua, NH
LAVOIE, Juliette S and Charles A SMITH, 28 Apr 1973 Nashua, NH
LAVOIE, Leonard D and Beatrice IVES, 28 Feb 1946 Hudson, NH
LAVOIE, Leopold and Bernice J ARBOUR, 28 Jun 1969 Nashua, NH
LAVOIE, Linda Ann and Kenneth W II PENDERS, 01 Jun 1985 Hudson, NH
LAVOIE, Lisa M and John F Jr JESSOP, 06 Nov 1982 Hudson, NH
LAVOIE, Marcel G and Diane J DESCLOS, 21 Apr 1979 Hudson, NH
LAVOIE, Marcel G and Lisa M PERRON, 04 May 1985 Nashua, NH
LAVOIE, Marie E and Charles E FOSTER, 23 Mar 1957 Hudson, NH
LAVOIE, Marion and Sylvio SOUCY, 14 Sep 1925 Nashua, NH
LAVOIE, Michele F and Robert LOVEJOY, 31 Oct 1964 Hudson, NH
LAVOIE, Paul L and Debra-Jean ROSS, 19 Jul 1969 Hudson, NH
LAVOIE, Paul L and Jacqueline McLAUGHLIN, 31 Jul 1982 Hudson, NH
LAVOIE, Philip M and Debra L NEFF, 09 Oct 1982 Hudson, NH
LAVOIE, Richard A and Annette J GENDRON, 30 May 1969 Nashua, NH
LAVOIE, Rita G and Albert A NARO, 28 May 1944 Manchester, NH
LAVOIE, Rose and Francis LAFLAMME, 30 Jun 1934 Nashua, NH
LAVOIE, Rosemarie and Warren E HENRY, 30 Jun 1951 Hudson, NH
LAVOIE, Rosemarie and Stephen L TRZOS, 15 Aug 1953 Hudson, NH
LAVOIE, Steven A and Colleen A CRIPPS, 23 Aug 1980 Hudson, NH
LAVOIE, Vicki L and Harold EDDINGS, 16 Nov 1984 Nashua, NH
LAVOIE, Vicki-Lu V and Ronald W FLORA, 21 Jul 1973 Hudson, NH
LAW, James J and Tamara L COBB, 22 Dec 1978 Nashua, NH
LAW, Janet and Ricky A MITCHELL, 01 Jan 1980 Hudson, NH
LAW, Jeffrey M and Celine C LAJOIE, 19 Jun 1976 Pelham, NH
LAW, JoAnne and Ronald K BRUDZISZ, 12 Jan 1974 Nashua, NH
LAW, John M and Denise B TREMBLAY, 15 Jan 1972 Nashua, NH
LAWLER, Richard S and Arline M THIBODEAU, 22 Sep 1979 Hudson, NH
LAWLOR, James R and Sandra J DAVIS, 29 Aug 1964 Lisbon, NH
LAWRENCE, Alfred A and Lorraine A GENDRON, 08 Sep 1951 Hudson, NH
LAWRENCE, Carlene M and Thomas A KOGLER, 24 Jun 1983 Hudson, NH
LAWRENCE, Hattie D and Willis P CUMMINGS, 20 Mar 1873
LAWRENCE, Irene S and John P LAWRENCE, 05 Jul 1968 Hudson, NH
LAWRENCE, Jean E and Robert L HOWE, 29 Jun 1963 Hudson, NH
LAWRENCE, John P and Irene S LAWRENCE, 05 Jul 1968 Hudson, NH
LAWRENCE, John P and Helen M ZALANSKAS, 27 Jul 1984 Hudson, NH
LAWRENCE, Karen R and Robert W GAULIN, 24 Apr 1965 Hudson, NH
LAWRENCE, Mary and James SMITH, 19 Jul 1796
LAWRENCE, Sarah and Samuel CROSS, 04 Mar 1779
LAWRENCE, Shirley B and Arthur L CUMMINGS, 24 Dec 1949 Nashua, NH
LAWRENCE, Sophia and John CUMMINGS, 01 Aug 1831
LAWRENCE, Susanna and Asa COLBURN, 20 Oct 1785
LAWRUK, Sandra Lee and Roland Jos BOURGEOIS, 26 Jan 1985 Nashua, NH
LAWSON, Arthur C and Madaline E MIXTER, 07 May 1936 Hudson, NH
LAWSON, Robert B and Patricia M THOMPSON, 23 Sep 1978 Hudson, NH
LAWSON, Russell C Jr and Anne M KEEN, 22 Jul 1979 Hudson, NH
LAWTON, Thomas C and Linda I PELKEY, 22 Jul 1967 Hudson, NH
LAXTON, Paul C and Edith Caro ELSON, 09 Sep 1938 Hudson, NH
LEACH, Clarence and Emma D LINDSAY, 27 Jun 1931 Hudson, NH
LEACH, Clesson W and Beverly A POLIQUIN, 11 Sep 1948 Hudson, NH
LEACH, Debra A and John M BEDARD, 06 Aug 1983 Nashua, NH
LEACH, Leonard K and Frances E FRANKLIN, 15 Oct 1955 Hudson, NH
LEACH, Michael E and Patrice R BEAULAC, 06 Sep 1980 Rindge, NH
LEACH, Richard C and Emily Y USSERY, 06 Nov 1965 Hudson, NH
LEAKEAS, Louis R and Frances M WYMAN, 02 Jun 1962 Hudson, NH
LEAOR, Bonnie R and Eric P MYERS, 10 Oct 1981 Hudson, NH

HUDSON,NH MARRIAGES

LEAOR, Carl E and Liliane B MARTIN, 18 Jun 1928 Nashua, NH
LEAOR, Edward G and Darlene A LAPAN, 14 Jul 1956 Hudson, NH
LEAOR, Linda A and Allen R McKENNEY, 02 Sep 1978 Hudson, NH
LEAOR, Mary J and Wesley B BISHOP, 30 Jun 1951 Hudson, NH
LEAOR, Maurice R and Judith J LEVESQUE, 26 Sep 1964 Hudson, NH
LEAOR, Walter H and Rose A Y LAROUCHE, 04 Apr 1933 Nashua, NH
LEAR, Benjamin C and Lucy A TOWNE, 19 Sep 1849
LEARD, Frank D Jr and Evelyn C CHRISTIAN, 07 Jul 1951 Nashua, NH
LEARY, Catherine and Larry W TOWNSEND, 16 Aug 1975 Litchfield, NH
LEARY, Helen M and Thomas F QUIMBY, 09 Feb 1910 Hudson, NH
   J A Leary & N F Campbell
   Benjamin F Quimby & Ella Hawkes
LEARY, Mary E and Thomas L GEHRLEIN, 03 Apr 1971 Hudson, NH
LEAVITT, Gail Ann and Joseph D VAILLANCOURT, 04 Jul 1982 Hudson, NH
LEAVITT, Janis and David S ESKELAND, 29 Aug 1981 Hudson, NH
LEAVITT, Joni and James WOVORIS, 22 Mar 1980 Hudson, NH
LEAVITT, Mark D and Sandra M JASINSKI, 08 Oct 1977 Hudson, NH
LEAZOTT, Addie E and Willie S TAYLOR, 25 Dec 1876 Hudson, NH
LEBEL, Christine and Ronald A III NENNI, 29 Oct 1982 Hudson, NH
LEBEL, Lucy M and Martin R PETERSEN, 29 Jun 1963 Nashua, NH
LEBLANC, Carolyn F and Alan R BOISVERT, 19 Aug 1968 Manchester, NH
LEBLANC, Debra J and Robert L GILLOOLY, 16 Jul 1977 Hudson, NH
LEBLANC, Donald J and Ann Marie HAVEY, 01 May 1982 Londonderry, NH
LEBLANC, Donna JoAn and Richard J MILOSH, 19 May 1979 Hudson, NH
LEBLANC, Doris M and Anthony C MORGADO, 10 Jun 1950 Hudson, NH
LEBLANC, Edgar and Mary DECOSTE, 19 Apr 1934 Hudson, NH
LEBLANC, Elizabeth and Arthur E NAGEL, 27 Dec 1939 Hudson, NH
LEBLANC, Ernest and Helen KASHULINES, 16 Sep 1919 Nashua, NH
LEBLANC, Gayle A and Leon R NADEAU, 18 Sep 1971 Hudson, NH
LEBLANC, Gloria R and Christie P McGRATH, 30 Jan 1977 Hudson, NH
LEBLANC, Janice H and James F MOODY, 02 Dec 1967 Nashua, NH
LEBLANC, Joseph R and Carolyn F KNIGHTS, 11 Nov 1960 Hudson, NH
LEBLANC, Leo A and Merciale M LOUGEE, 09 Oct 1965 Hudson, NH
LEBLANC, Lionel A Jr and Claire L LESSARD, 23 Sep 1967 Nashua, NH
LEBLANC, Lorraine L and Robert B ROY, 31 Oct 1974 Nashua, NH
LEBLANC, Paul N and Paulette A PROULX, 27 Dec 1965 Hudson, NH
LEBLANC, Paul R and Kathleen A RAFFERTY, 17 May 1971 Nashua, NH
LEBLANC, William H and Alice M PERRY, 30 Dec 1973 Nashua, NH
LEBOEUF, Anne M and Scott J AUBERTIN, 31 Jul 1982 Hudson, NH
LEBOEUF, Bertha and Alfred F DUMONT, 03 Jul 1918 Nashua, NH
LEBOEUF, Eugene and Anna BIBEAU, 27 Jun 1936 Nashua, NH
LEBOEUF, Gerard L and Lorette E BRUNEAU, 11 Jun 1955 Nashua, NH
LEBOEUF, Imelda T and Robert E SMITH, 23 Sep 1950 Hudson, NH
LEBOEUF, Louis and Alma DUBOIS, 01 Oct 1919 Nashua, NH
LEBOEUF, Louise D and Richard G HAIGLER, 24 May 1975 Hudson, NH
LEBOEUF, Rita E and Laurent S BRAULT, 01 Oct 1946 Nashua, NH
LEBOEUF, Yvonne C and Elie LABOMBARDE, 08 Sep 1943 Nashua, NH
LEBOWITZ, Nathan and Rebecca R MEZIKOFSKY, 26 Jul 1933 Nashua, NH
LEBRUN, Edward J and Marie O'MALLEY, 21 Aug 1982 Derry, NH
LECLAIR, Paul E and Ethelyn M MORGAN, 04 May 1946 Nashua, NH
LECLAIR, Ronald O and Erlyan O TATRO, 06 May 1972 Hudson, NH
LECLAIR, Ronald O and Rose M BRECK, 25 Sep 1981 Hudson, NH
LECLAIRE, Ralph R and Natalie L DENIS, 13 Nov 1954 Nashua, NH
LECLER, Donna M and Richard A PEARCE, 01 May 1976 Hudson, NH
LECLERC, Amedee R and Pauline M SMITH, 02 Feb 1952 Nashua, NH
LECLERC, Anthony R and Debra J HIRSCH, 12 May 1979 Hudson, NH
LECLERC, Antoine and Dorilla LAROCHE, 25 Aug 1919 Nashua, NH
LECLERC, Antoine J and Regina E CHARBONNEAU, 26 Apr 1952 Nashua, NH
LECLERC, Ernest E and Sandra D SHAW, 08 Jan 1966 Nashua, NH
LECLERC, Gertrude G and Leo LAVANWAY, 23 Jun 1945 Nashua, NH

HUDSON,NH MARRIAGES

```
LECLERC, Gloria R and Edward G BOUCHER, 05 Nov 1955 Hudson, NH
LECLERC, Henry A and Beatrice D UPHAM, 05 Oct 1946 Nashua, NH
LECLERC, Jeannette and James F PATTON, 13 Aug 1974 Hudson, NH
LECLERC, Juliette M and Claude LOZEAU, 11 May 1946 Nashua, NH
LECLERC, Leo R and Ruth E DOLAND, 04 Jun 1955 Hudson, NH
LECLERC, Lillian E and A Luther HAMBLETT, 17 Jul 1967 Hudson, NH
LECLERC, Patricia A and B Richard BAILEY, 01 Sep 1979 Hudson, NH
LECLERC, Paul and Elizabeth GRENIER, 04 Jul 1936 Nashua, NH
LECLERC, Pauline M and Norman K BLAIS, 07 Mar 1980 Londonderry, NH
LECLERC, Theophile and Lea DUMONT, 10 Jan 1917 Nashua, NH
LECLERE, Annette and Walter W FULLER, 25 Aug 1930 Nashua, NH
LECLERE, Germaine and Eugene PARISEAU, 06 Sep 1926 Nashua, NH
LECLERE, Joseph E and Phelomene L LANDRY, 19 Apr 1926 Nashua, NH
LECOMPTE, Richard E&Jacqueline JASKOLKA, 29 Jun 1974 W Hartford, CT
LECUYER, Pauline P and Francis B MULDOON, 26 Feb 1945 Hudson, NH
LEDGISTER, Ronald and Grace A DORVAL, 18 Sep 1981 Brentwood, NH
LEDOUX, Armand W and Jeanine S MIGNEAULT, 11 Apr 1953 Nashua, NH
LEDOUX, Beatrice M and Benjamin F STEWART, 10 Oct 1942 Nashua, NH
LEDOUX, Bernard G and Ida E DIONNE, 27 Apr 1946 Nashua, NH
LEDOUX, Charles G and Lila H HANSON, 12 Jul 1943 Nashua, NH
LEDOUX, Daniel J and Paula M. JACQUES, 14 Jun 1975 Hudson, NH
LEDOUX, Diane L and Robert A Jr TATE, 16 Sep 1967 Hudson, NH
LEDOUX, Doris and Robert R PROVENCAL, 30 May 1945 Nashua, NH
LEDOUX, James D and Becky A HARTT, 08 May 1982 Hudson, NH
LEDOUX, Judith A and Peter A PLAMONDON, 28 Jul 1973 Hudson, NH
LEDOUX, Lucille M and Robert T DUMONT, 06 Sep 1958 Hudson, NH
LEDOUX, Lucille Y and Donald F DION, 22 Jan 1966 Nashua, NH
LEDOUX, Norbert B and Henrietta JEANNOTTE, 18 Jan 1947 Nashua, NH
LEDOUX, Norbert B Jr & Patricia A GONSALVES, 30 Nov 1974 Pelham, NH
LEDOUX, Ralph A Jr and Elizabeth HUNNEWELL, 29 Sep 1962 Nashua, NH
LEDOUX, Romeo J and Lorraine I AUTTELET, 02 Dec 1967 Hudson, NH
LEE, Caroline M and Nelson SMITH, 21 Dec 1861
LEE, Gary T and Linda S COX, 21 Oct 1967 Hudson, NH
LEE, Linda S and John R CHARETTE, 01 Jun 1974 Hudson, NH
LEE, Michael S and Ellen M GAUTHIER, 10 Aug 1980 Hudson, NH
LEE, Michelle S and Mark L DUBAY, 22 Sep 1984 Hudson, NH
LEE, Sharmon and Steven J MOES, 31 Jul 1982 Hudson, NH
LEE, Thomas M and Elizabeth HENDERSON, 29 Dec 1984 Hudson, NH
LEES, Mildred and Francis A STOESSEL, 30 Sep 1923 Nashua, NH
LEET, L Don and Florence J BLANCHARD, 02 Jul 1956 Hudson, NH
LEEWITZ, George J and Alice C BEIRN, 03 Mar 1923 Portsmouth, NH
LEFABVRE, William Jr & Sharon E STONE, 29 Aug 1975 Londonderry, NH
LEFAVE, Linda A and Mark P JOYAL, 11 Jun 1983 Hudson, NH
LEFAVOR, Robert G Jr and Barbara I NICKEL, 30 Mar 1980 Nashua, NH
LEFEBURE, Alma and Joseph A PAQUETTE, 01 Oct 1923 Nashua, NH
LEFEBVRE, Charles J Jr and Florence J LEMAY, 27 Aug 1960 Nashua, NH
LEFEBVRE, Cynthia A and Daniel E LESSARD, 04 Sep 1981 Nashua, NH
LEFEBVRE, Dora Y and George F HAIGLER, 30 Apr 1949 Nashua, NH
LEFEBVRE, George T and Clara L MARTIN, 02 Jul 1932 Nashua, NH
LEFEBVRE, Gloria G and Earl W LEWIS, 06 Feb 1960 Hudson, NH
LEFEBVRE, Joseph and Mary Eliza LABOMBARD, 06 Sep 1924 Hudson, NH
LEFEBVRE, Lorraine M and David A RODD, 21 Aug 1965 Hudson, NH
LEFEBVRE, Mary R G and Albert C EATON, 27 Oct 1945 Hudson, NH
LEFEBVRE, Medora and Gerard L VIENS, 18 May 1946 Allenstown, NH
LEFEBVRE, Raymond A and Lucette GAMACHE, 24 Aug 1963 Hudson, NH
LEFEBVRE, Raymond L and Marie RUSSELL, 20 Sep 1958 Hudson, NH
LEFEBVRE, Robert A and Patricia E ROY, 19 Sep 1959 Hudson, NH
LEFEBVRE, Robert J and Coreen GRANT, 22 Nov 1980 Nashua, NH
LEFEBVRE, Roland S and Clarie E NADEAU, 12 Sep 1960 Nashua, NH
LEFTER, Angelo and Claire ALLEN, 02 Aug 1941 Hudson, NH
```

HUDSON,NH MARRIAGES

LEGALLEE, Beth A and Earl V GREELEY, 08 Feb 1947 Hudson, NH
LEGALLEE, Howard and Phoebe TYLER, 02 Jul 1919 Barrington
LEGARSKY, Carolyn and Charles F GISH, 26 Nov 1966 Nashua, NH
LEGARSKY, Wanda C and Joseph SPEAR, 28 Nov 1940 Nashua, NH
LEGASSE, Ellen L and Richard D TAYLOR, 01 Apr 1970 Nashua, NH
LEGASSE, Joseph P and Germia M LANDRY, 24 Aug 1940 Nashua, NH
LEGENDRE, Catherine and Leonard M JEWETT, 28 May 1977 Nashua, NH
LEGENDRE, Joseph A and Catherine GRIGAS, 01 Aug 1964 Nashua, NH
LEGERE, Joseph L and Alice M CONEENY, 01 Jul 1950 Hudson, NH
LEHNERT, Paul E and Sylvia A GENEST, 19 Aug 1973 Hudson, NH
LEHTO, Uno A and Dorothy E MacNICHOLS, 29 Apr 1950 Hudson, NH
LEICESTER, Joseph and Catherine HADLEY, 08 Aug 1826
LEIGH, Robert E and Carol A MORSE, 01 Jul 1958 Hudson, NH
LEIGH, Sharyl P and James E McCRUM, 27 Feb 1983 Hudson, NH
LEIGH, Tammy A and Joseph W RACKLIFF, 16 Jul 1976 Hudson, NH
LEIGHTON, Andrew A and Dorothy KREKORIAN, 04 Sep 1948 Hudson, NH
LEIGHTON, Roger K and Nellie V McADOO, 21 Jun 1941 Nashua, NH
LEITH, Dennis J and Sandra J INGERSOLL, 07 Jul 1984 Nashua, NH
LELACHEUR, John G and Frances M BERNTSEN, 22 Feb 1985 Nashua, NH
LELAND, Branwell P and Wendeline HODGE, 18 Jan 1969 Hudson, NH
LELAND, Janice M and Raymond R CORMIER, 16 Dec 1961 Nashua, NH
LEMAY, Catherine and Raymond D DANIELS, 05 Apr 1975 Hudson, NH
LEMAY, Cecile F and Paul J HEROUX, 07 Aug 1948 Nashua, NH
LEMAY, Dorothy M and Albert E BOYER, 27 Nov 1952 Nashua, NH
LEMAY, Florence J and Charles J Jr LEFEBVRE, 27 Aug 1960 Nashua, NH
LEMAY, Gerard E and Patricia A REILLY, 07 Jun 1952 Hudson, NH
LEMAY, Gerard L and Carol A CHAREST, 19 Jun 1970 Manchester, NH
LEMAY, Gertrude F and Henry W DUCHARME, 28 Jun 1952 Hudson, NH
LEMAY, Gloria M and Edward T SAVAGE, 20 Dec 1974 Hudson, NH
LEMAY, Louise H and Raymond G MARQUIS, 30 May 1955 Hudson, NH
LEMAY, Marcel R and Gloria M DIGGINS, 12 Aug 1950 Nashua, NH
LEMAY, Paul R and Carol S GRENIER, 05 Jun 1982 Hudson, NH
LEMAY, Simonne C and Robert A GAMACHE, 09 Jul 1960 Hudson, NH
LEMELIN, Helene and Raymond SMITH, 11 Mar 1944 Hudson, NH
LEMERISE, Jean L and Donald M OUELLETTE, 22 Dec 1956 Hudson, NH
LEMERISE, Joan J and Peter G SCONTSAS, 21 Feb 1956 Hudson, NH
LEMERISE, Margaret E and Arthur J DOUZANIS, 01 Feb 1964 Hudson, NH
LEMERISE, Raymond G and Constance TANGUAY, 30 May 1955 Nashua, NH
LEMERY, Albert and Rita BLANCHARD, 12 Aug 1947 Nashua, NH
LEMERY, Georgette and Paul A LESSARD, 25 Apr 1969 Nashua, NH
LEMERY, Linda L and Terry W ROBINSON, 14 Jun 1969 Hudson, NH
LEMERY, Sandra G and Rodney D BECHARD, 27 Nov 1965 Nashua, NH
LEMIEUX, Mary P and Romeo P POLIQUIN, 07 Feb 1958 Hudson, NH
LEMIEUX, Thomas R Jr & Gail Jean SZEMKOWICZ, 26 Nov 1984 Hudson, NH
LEMIRE, Brenda L and Gerald R LAFLEUR, 27 Jun 1970 Hudson, NH
LEMIRE, Cindy M and Roger Joseph LIGHT, 09 Aug 1980 Nashua, NH
LEMIRE, Elaine R and Thomas P TORREY, 03 Jun 1972 Hudson, NH
LEMIRE, Joyce H and Ronald D BOURDEAU, 26 May 1979 Hudson, NH
LEMIRE, Linda V and Paul R RICARD, 06 Apr 1968 Hudson, NH
LEMIRE, Vivian A and Simeon Jr TRIPPLETON, 19 Nov 1955 Hudson, NH
LEMIRE, William A and Lisa Ann AHLERS, 26 Jan 1980 Hudson, NH
LEMIUEX, Mary P and Charles E LLOYD, 21 Jan 1956 Hudson, NH
LENAHAN, Rose A and Charles H CHASE, 18 Jul 1867
LENNON, Anne M and Clement E HURTEAU, 17 Jun 1950 Hudson, NH
LENT, Deborah A and Erik CRISMAN, 23 Aug 1975 Hudson, NH
LENTSCH, Alfred S and Sharen Ann NICHOLSON, 27 Jan 1973 Nashua, NH
LENTZ, Scott L and Jeanne M LAMBERT, 14 Feb 1982 Hudson, NH
LENZ, George E and Janice G BAKER, 19 Nov 1957 Hudson, NH
LENZI, Lawrence and Gloria J LOMBARDI, 15 May 1946 Hudson, NH
LEONARD, Dennis And and Sandra Lee DOW, 18 Jan 1975 Nashua, NH

HUDSON,NH MARRIAGES

LEONARD, Laura C and Zenas DUNBAR, 29 Dec 1847
LEONARD, Orrin and Ann LUCE, 10 Aug 1849
LEONARD, William E and Louisa D MILES, 20 Sep 1846
LEONE, Anthony and Constance BERGERON, 19 Mar 1949 Hudson, NH
LEONE, Carmel M and Mary A ROSSI, 25 Sep 1948 Hudson, NH
LEPORE, Leland C and Susan J GILMAN, 16 Apr 1983 Hudson, NH
LESIEUR, Norma E and Kierscey C LADD, 02 Jun 1946 Hudson, NH
LESLIE, Charles C and Eliza Ball WEBSTER, 16 Dec 1880
LESLIE, Charles C and Eliza B WEBSTER, 16 Dec 1880 Londonderry, NH
   William H Leslie (Cornish, NH) & Betsy McAlpine (Hopkinton, NH)
   Kimball Webster(Pelham, NH) & Abiah Cutter (Pelham, NH)
LESLIE, Eleanor S and Adelbert C CUTLER, 22 Jun 1929 Hudson, NH
LESLIE, Eugene W and Lettie V SHEPARD, 14 Sep 1905 Hudson, NH
   Charles C Leslie & Eliza B Leslie
   Charles A Shepard & Addie C Doyle
LESLIE, Frank B and Alida R STEWART, 01 Nov 1924 Hudson, NH
LESLIE, Gordon C and Barbara E BAILEY, 01 May 1933 Nashua, NH
LESSARD, Claire L and Lionel A Jr LEBLANC, 23 Sep 1967 Nashua, NH
LESSARD, Daniel E and Cynthia A LEFEBVRE, 04 Sep 1981 Nashua, NH
LESSARD, Emily M and Dennis L BEAULIEU, 08 Jun 1974 Hudson, NH
LESSARD, Lucille R and Stewart C HOULE, 11 Jul 1970 Nashua, NH
LESSARD, Paul A and Georgette LEMERY, 25 Apr 1969 Nashua, NH
LESSARD, Robert H and Annette T LANDRY, 14 Aug 1971 Hudson, NH
LETENDRE, Claire L and Wayne L THOMPSON, 18 Nov 1961 Nashua, NH
LETOURNEAU, Glenn B and Anne L POULIOT, 26 Sep 1981 Merrimack, NH
LETOURNEAU, Lori J and Daniel G CHOUINARD, 13 Sep 1980 Hudson, NH
LETOURNEAUX, Norman W and Pauline M DUBE, 24 Jun 1967 Nashua, NH
LETTS, Helen L and Hymen GORDON, 05 Jun 1935 Hudson, NH
LEVASSEUR, Joseph R and Linda A POST, 11 Jun 1977 Londonderry, NH
LEVASSEUR, Rita Y and James A STEELE, 21 Jun 1975 Nashua, NH
LEVEILLE, Ernest R and Mary F GAMACHE, 07 Apr 1947 Nashua, NH
LEVESQUE, Alcide S and Leona T KRISTOFF, 24 Dec 1947 Hudson, NH
LEVESQUE, Antoinette and Henry LACHANCE, 10 Aug 1940 Nashua, NH
LEVESQUE, Carla A and David P ANGER, 15 Oct 1977 Hudson, NH
LEVESQUE, Cathy Loui and Stephen W NOEL, 26 Jul 1980 Litchfield, NH
LEVESQUE, Cecile E and Roland L GAMACHE, 06 May 1944 Nashua, NH
LEVESQUE, Cecile G and Clement J RIVARD, 19 Apr 1947 Nashua, NH
LEVESQUE, Claudia Ro and Dean Micha PELKEY, 03 Feb 1973 Hudson, NH
LEVESQUE, David A and Deena J ANDREWS, 30 Apr 1983 Hudson, NH
LEVESQUE, Debra L and Edward J CURRAN, 19 Dec 1974 Nashua, NH
LEVESQUE, Debra L and Gary E LAVOIE, 15 Sep 1979 Hudson, NH
LEVESQUE, Donna C and Paul H E ANGER, 16 Apr 1971 Hudson, NH
LEVESQUE, Donna Lee and Louis P PELLETIER, 05 Jun 1982 Nashua, NH
LEVESQUE, Ernest R and Lorraine M MERRILL, 31 May 1947 Nashua, NH
LEVESQUE, Ernest R and Esther MITCHELL, 11 Aug 1956 Hudson, NH
LEVESQUE, Evelyn M and Raymond C BROWN, 01 Mar 1946 Nashua, NH
LEVESQUE, Gertrude A and George E JALBERT, 12 Oct 1946 Nashua, NH
LEVESQUE, Henrietta and Edgar A TRUDEAU, 30 Aug 1941 Nashua, NH
LEVESQUE, Irene J and Ronald W KOCH, 30 May 1964 Hudson, NH
LEVESQUE, Jean A and Sandra L GOULD, 24 Jun 1983 Hudson, NH
LEVESQUE, Jeanne E and Frank E JALBERT, 11 Sep 1965 Nashua, NH
LEVESQUE, Jeannette and Roland J BIBEAU, 30 Jun 1945 Nashua, NH
LEVESQUE, Joan L and Robert A COLE, 17 Nov 1962 Hudson, NH
LEVESQUE, Joseph L & Lorraine P BLANCHETTE, 14 Jan 1950 Nashua, NH
LEVESQUE, Judith J and Maurice R LEAOR, 26 Sep 1964 Hudson, NH
LEVESQUE, Laurent G and Judith A CLAVEAU, 09 Aug 1969 Hudson, NH
LEVESQUE, Leopold E and Yvonne A BELANGER, 20 Sep 1947 Nashua, NH
LEVESQUE, Lionel E and Phyllis M DUMONT, 30 May 1953 Nashua, NH
LEVESQUE, Loretta and Earl FORRENCE, 20 Aug 1938 Nashua, NH
LEVESQUE, Marian J and Larry E TIBBETTS, 01 Jun 1974 Hudson, NH

HUDSON,NH MARRIAGES

LEVESQUE, Marianne and Joseph R TALBOT, 04 Aug 1934 Nashua, NH
LEVESQUE, Marie Anna and Peter ARPIN, 20 Oct 1934 Nashua, NH
LEVESQUE, Marie C and Kastanty YANUSZEWSKI, 20 Sep 1941 Nashua, NH
LEVESQUE, Marie L and Joseph H POMERLEAU, 17 Nov 1934 Nashua, NH
LEVESQUE, Marlene M and Real A PAQUIN, 05 Sep 1970 Hudson, NH
LEVESQUE, Mildred F and Robert R THIBODEAU, 15 Mar 1958 Hudson, NH
LEVESQUE, Nancy L and Paul R MICHAUD, 04 Apr 1980 Manchester, NH
LEVESQUE, Norman A and Judith A DUGGAN, 20 May 1967 Manchester, NH
LEVESQUE, Normand R and Yvonne P LaFOREST, 25 Apr 1970 Nashua, NH
LEVESQUE, Patricia J and Neil A MORRISON, 11 Jun 1983 Hudson, NH
LEVESQUE, Paul E and Gisele G BERUBE, 25 Nov 1944 Nashua, NH
LEVESQUE, Paul J A and Theresa H GAGNON, 26 May 1973 Hudson, NH
LEVESQUE, Phyllis M and Andrew H HOULE, 18 May 1974 Allenstown, NH
LEVESQUE, Raymond J and Lucille B GUAY, 14 Jun 1947 Nashua, NH
LEVESQUE, Richard D and Pauline L BERNIER, 09 May 1964 Hudson, NH
LEVESQUE, Richard R and Carol J FULLER, 13 Oct 1961 Hudson, NH
LEVESQUE, Rita T and Jean R BOIS, 17 Aug 1946 Nashua, NH
LEVESQUE, Robert A and Margaret J CARROLL, 17 Apr 1957 Hudson, NH
LEVESQUE, Robert C and Lorraine E BRIAND, 18 Aug 1951 Hudson, NH
LEVESQUE, Robert P and Olivette E DULUDE, 27 Nov 1941 Nashua, NH
LEVESQUE, Roland J and Yolande M FAUCHER, 17 May 1941 Nashua, NH
LEVESQUE, Roland J and Grace M ROY, 23 Jun 1948 Hudson, NH
LEVESQUE, Romeo J and Rita I ROY, 15 Jun 1963 Hudson, NH
LEVESQUE, Ronald L and Mildred F McCORMACK, 03 Apr 1954 Hudson, NH
LEVESQUE, Rosanna and Ernest R MOREY, 30 Apr 1934 Nashua, NH
LEVESQUE, Sandra H and Nathan C CRAWFORD, 23 May 1970 Milford, NH
LEVESQUE, Scott E and Kimberly A INGRAM, 16 Apr 1983 Nashua, NH
LEVESQUE, Susanne G and Richard J LINDQUIST, 17 Feb 1973 Hudson, NH
LEVESQUE, Suzanne M and James C FROST, 06 Jan 1973 Hudson, NH
LEVESQUE, Virginia and Arthur F BROWN, 25 Oct 1947 Hudson, NH
LEVESQUE, Yoland M C and Leo H ARSENAULT, 30 Jul 1949 Hudson, NH
LEVI, Clifford A and Anne L COWAN, 08 May 1967 Nashua, NH
LEVI, Linda K and Martin GARABEDIAN, 19 Mar 1982 Hudson, NH
LEVINE, Howard and Joan M HOGARTY, 20 Sep 1973 Hudson, NH
LEVISON, Manuel and Jeannette CHISHOLM, 06 Aug 1942 Hudson, NH
LEW, Advastus and Harriet BLANCHARD, 29 Jun 1815
LEWIS, Earl W and Gloria G LEFEBVRE, 06 Feb 1960 Hudson, NH
LEWIS, Edna M and Joseph W McKENZIE, 09 Apr 1947 Hudson, NH
LEWIS, Evelyn A and Philip A DELOGE, 22 Jun 1985 Nashua, NH
LEWIS, Guilford A and Lydia Fran WEBSTER, 15 Apr 1877
LEWIS, Harvey G and Nellie CONDON, 17 Jul 1889 Lowell, MA
  Wm F Lewis & Lucy F Boynton (Pepperell, MA)
  James Condon & Johanna Howard
LEWIS, Jasper M and Malinda AUSTIN, 17 Apr 1853
LEWIS, LeReine G and Robert N BRALEY, 01 Jun 1963 Hudson, NH
LEWIS, Melinda and Jacob ABBOTT, 04 Feb 1863
LEWIS, Otis Norcr and Helena H CHASE, 26 Jan 1918 Hudson, NH
LEWIS, Samuel and Sarah HOWARD, 04 Mar 1779
LEWIS, Sarah A and Matthew W SCHACHTER, 02 Dec 1967 Concord, NH
LEWIS, William B and Hannah J BARRIS, 28 Aug 1862
LEWIS, William P and Hannah J BARRISO, 22 Aug 1862
LEWISTON, Robert and Phebe F SPAULDING, 05 Apr 1864
LIBBY, Clifford H and Edith L PERRY, 25 Apr 1912 Hudson, NH
  Henry R Libby & Mary C Libby
  Lewis E Perry & Sarah L Lawrence
LIBBY, Kathleen E and Romeo R Jr LABRIE, 04 Mar 1972 Nashua, NH
LIBBY, Lenora L and Larry M BISHOP, 16 Oct 1971 Hudson, NH
LIBBY, Peggy J and Earl G BRIAND, 18 Sep 1976 Nashua, NH
LIBBY, Peggy Jean and Ron K RYAN, 14 Apr 1984 Hollis, NH
LICCIARDONE, Emily and Donald WISELL, 12 Jul 1941 Nashua, NH

HUDSON, NH MARRIAGES

LIEBERWIRTH, Karl P and Margaret M DUMONT, 28 Apr 1984 Hudson, NH
LIGHT, Andrew J and Yvonne A LABRIE, 09 Sep 1950 Nashua, NH
LIGHT, Doreen Rhea and Albert J Jr LACOUNT, 17 Nov 1973 Hudson, NH
LIGHT, Roger Joseph and Cindy M LEMIRE, 09 Aug 1980 Nashua, NH
LILJEHOLM, Edna M and Charles W COUGHLIN, 24 Oct 1942 Hudson, NH
LILLEY, Barbara A and Ralph N FOSTER, 11 Nov 1956 Hudson, NH
LILLEY, Betty L and Robert L BEAN, 05 Sep 1959 Hudson, NH
LILLEY, Joan B and Robert R HUNTER, 05 Apr 1953 Hudson, NH
LILLEY, Lillian S and Marcel J BOUDREAULT, 06 Jul 1963 Hudson, NH
LILLEY, Mary E and Victor W GROHOSKY, 23 Jan 1948 Hudson, NH
LILLEY, Sandra J and Gerald F CORBIN, 08 Jul 1967 Hudson, NH
LILLEY, William C and Joyce M RICHARDSON, 19 Apr 1981 Nashua, NH
LILLIE, Edith and Robert D ALLEN, 02 Apr 1910 Hudson, NH
  Albert Lillie & Lydia Sherman
  Robert D Allen & Belda Kimball
LILLIE, Robin L and William W FENTON, 25 Aug 1979 Nashua, NH
LILLY, John O and Marcia E EDDY, 03 Sep 1900 Nashua, NH
  O F Lilly & Mary J Shaw
  P Eddy & Mary Wheeler
LIMOLI, Elena C and Cyrus L DEROSIER, 17 Jun 1950 Hudson, NH
LINCH, Sarah and Samuel EASTMAN, 16 Nov 1798
LINCH, Sarah and Samuel EMERSON, 16 Nov 1798
LINCOLN, Susan M and Richard J SELFRIDGE, 23 Mar 1985 Hudson, NH
LIND, Peter M and Nicole D CYR, 10 Sep 1977 Salem, NH
LINDAHL, Arne J and Doris E SMEAD, 15 Aug 1937 Hudson, NH
LINDBOHM, Edith I and Robert S BRADFORD, 19 Sep 1937 Nashua, NH
LINDQUIST, Andrew P and Carol A GUZDOWSKI, 09 May 1970 Pelham, NH
LINDQUIST, David F and Deborah A HERRIN, 10 Aug 1982 Hudson, NH
LINDQUIST, John C and Donna L TILTON, 01 Jul 1972 Hudson, NH
LINDQUIST, Richard J and Susanne G LEVESQUE, 17 Feb 1973 Hudson, NH
LINDQUIST, Theodore A and Mary KLIMAS, 25 Jun 1938 Nashua, NH
LINDSAY, Emma D and Clarence LEACH, 27 Jun 1931 Hudson, NH
LINDSAY, John A and Betty A LAUSIER, 26 Aug 1967 Hudson, NH
LINDSAY, Margaret and Jeremiah MILLETT, 06 Jun 1856
LINDSAY, Peter J and Patricia A LUND, 20 Oct 1984 Nashua, NH
LINDSAY, Ruth L and Paul H FOLEY, 05 Feb 1949 Hudson, NH
LINDSEY, Gerald W and Catherine CURRAN, 04 Sep 1971 Nashua, NH
LINDVALL, Gail A and Richard E DUPLEASE, 24 Nov 1973 Hudson, NH
LINEHAN, Dennis V Jr and Eileen F PYNE, 30 Jul 1955 Hudson, NH
LING, Brenda J and Raymond R PROULX, 01 Jul 1970 Londonderry, NH
LINNELL, Patricia M and Robert N COLEMAN, 29 Mar 1947 Nashua, NH
LINNEMANN, Kathryn L and David C MORES, 20 Feb 1977 Hudson, NH
LINO, Maria D and Michael S JOYAL, 05 Dec 1981 Nashua, NH
LINSCOTT, Allan F and May CLEMENT, 05 Mar 1901 Lowell, MA
  Frank G Linscott & Mary J Parker
  Elmer Clement
LINSCOTT, Edna F and Robert E MOORE, 05 May 1939 New Boston, NH
LINSCOTT, Robert A and Elaine L HOULE, 25 Jun 1983 Hudson, NH
LINSCOTT, Ruth Ann and Philip Arno GATZ, 16 Nov 1929 E Milton, MA
LINSON, Norman E and Virginia M GLYNN, 04 Mar 1974 Hudson, NH
LINTNER, Nancy C and James W NOEL, 10 Jul 1965 Hudson, NH
LINTOTT, Bernice F and Clarence B DANE, 21 May 1924 Nashua, NH
LIPORTO, Ernest P and Irene L GERMAIN, 13 Jun 1965 Dracut, MA
LIPSON, Eva and Alvah G CROCKETT, 11 Sep 1937 Hudson, NH
LIS, Jill R and Tracy W COLBURN, 11 Jun 1983 Hudson, NH
LISLE, Olive and Safford SWEATT, 03 Nov 1941 Hudson, NH
LISTER, Susan E and Peter J SMILIKIS, 08 Oct 1960 Concord, NH
LITALIEN, Donald J and Fay L THOMAS, 16 Jun 1951 Hudson, NH
LITALIEN, Linda A and Michael D WHITAKER, 19 Oct 1968 Nashua, NH
LITCHFIELD, Dorothy A&Douglas M MacARTHUR, 14 May 1983 Merrimack, NH

HUDSON,NH MARRIAGES

LITTELL, Susan A and Horace A Jr NICHOLS, 15 Dec 1973 Nashua, NH
LITTLE, Donna M and Jerome BECKER, 14 May 1983 Hudson, NH
LITTLE, Linda M and Robert E DUCHARME, 28 Oct 1967 Hudson, NH
LITTLE, Robert A and Sandra E BIRD, 28 Apr 1979 Hudson, NH
LITTLEFIELD, Frances H & Charles E GILMAN, 22 Feb 1932 Enfield, NH
LITTLEFIELD, Lois E and George T Jr BENSON, 04 Nov 1944 Nashua, NH
LITTLEFIELD, Lorraine G & William C SALTZER, 07 Nov 1976 Hudson, NH
LITTLEFIELD, Roy E Jr & Mary A PRESTIPINO, 09 Jun 1951 Milford, NH
LITTLEFIELD, Stephen A and Cynthia J BOND, 17 Jul 1982 Hudson, NH
LITTLEHALE, Abraham and Rebecca REED, 24 Feb 1785
LITTLEHALE, Ernest W and Dorothy M DAY, 01 Jul 1950 Hudson, NH
LITTLEHALE, Ezra and Lydia RICHARDSON, 04 Apr 1777
LITTLEHALE, Ezra and Lidia RICHARDSON, 04 Sep 1777
LITZENBERGER, Frank P and Dallas E KINVILLE, 19 Nov 1945 Hudson, NH
LIVINGSTON, Denise E&Charles W HUDSON, 08 Oct 1978 Londonderry, NH
LIVINGSTON, George and Mary Ann SULLIVAN, Aug 1869 Hudson, NH
LIVINGSTON, Henrietta&Daniel A COLBURN, 24 Dec 1891 Londonderry, NH
   Henry L C Newton (Marlboro, NH) & Mary W Moulton (Holderness, NH)
   Newton Colburn(Dracut, MA) & Sarah J Richardson (Dracut, MA)
LIVINGSTON, Herbert and Adelaide C VALEQUET, 18 Oct 1903 Nashua, NH
   Samuel Livingston & Henrietta Newton
   Manson B Patten & Nellie M Pemson
LIZOTTE, Alma A and Allen B MORGAN, 24 Jun 1950 Nashua, NH
LLOYD, Charles E and Mary P LEMIEUX, 21 Jan 1956 Hudson, NH
LOCICERO, Alan F and Linda M AMES, 10 Apr 1971 Pelham, NH
LOCKE, Calvin W Jr and Patti L PAGE, 27 Oct 1973 Nashua, NH
LOCKE, Gerard F and Carolyn E RUSSELL, 13 Nov 1971 Hudson, NH
LOCKE, Herbert W and Alice C CRESSY, 11 Oct 1914 Hudson, NH
   Charles H Locke & Ellen C Russell
LOCKE, Karen J and Edward H SUTHERLAND, 26 Jan 1963 Hudson, NH
LOCKE, Maurice A and Jean L ELLIOTT, 09 Dec 1944 Nashua, NH
LOCKE, Robert A and Beatrice K MUNSON, 09 Oct 1965 Nashua, NH
LOCKE, Sue A and Kenneth L HOWE, 27 Nov 1965 Hudson, NH
LOCKLEAR, Newberry and Barbara A WILLOCK, 04 Jul 1947 Hudson, NH
LOCKWOOD, Louis P and Lucille T PROVINS, 24 Mar 1973 Nashua, NH
LODDING, Kenneth N and Catherine COOPER, 01 Oct 1983 Hudson, NH
LOFFREDO, Ferdinand and Dorella A GINGRAS, 14 Feb 1942 Salem, NH
LOGAN, Donna L and Normand A BOUCHER, 07 Apr 1984 Nashua, NH
LOGHMANI, Mehrdad and Susan Jean MESSENGER, 11 Jun 1982 Nashua, NH
LOMBARDI, Gloria J and Lawrence LENZI, 15 May 1946 Hudson, NH
LONES, Barbara A and Edward O LAMPRON, 19 Jul 1952 Hudson, NH
LONES, Diana R and Ronald L MOQUIN, 05 May 1962 Hudson, NH
LONES, Linas B and Beatrice A MOREAU, 07 Jan 1972 Hudson, NH
LONES, Ralph T and Cecile D DUPONT, 24 Jul 1954 Nashua, NH
LONES, Richard P and Pauline E FORTIER, 04 Jun 1955 Nashua, NH
LONG, Annie R and Herbert R BAILEY, 08 Apr 1879 Nashua, NH
   Samuel Long (Ireland) & Margaret Lockhart (Ireland)
   Samuel N Bailey(West Wilton) & Adaline Winn (Dunstable, MA)
LONG, Dorothy M and George E LONG, 11 May 1957 Nashua, NH
LONG, George E and Dorothy M FOSTER, 13 Jul 1947 Hudson, NH
LONG, George E and Dorothy M LONG, 11 May 1957 Nashua, NH
LONG, John T and Bettina NOTO, 08 Jul 1977 Londonderry, NH
LONGARD, Lucy M and Otis R CONNELL, 23 Nov 1904 Nashua, NH
   Stephen Longard & Margaret Coory
   Robert T Connell & Lizzie Marshall
LONGFELLOW, James F & Geraldine GAGNON, 04 Feb 1972 Moultonboro, NH
LONGMIRE, Robert and Theresa L MARTINANGELO, 31 Mar 1979 Hudson, NH
LONGUA, William C and Marguerite WASSON, 29 Jan 1972 Nashua, NH
LONSBERRY, Susan D&Francis G Jr WILSON, 02 Apr 1971 Manchester, NH
LOOK, Rose D and Harold O MOARATTY, 30 Sep 1950 Hudson, NH

HUDSON,NH MARRIAGES

LOPES, Manuel J and Beverly A STEWART, 09 Dec 1976 Pelham, NH
LORAINE, Donald E and Rosemarie ROCKWOOD, 20 Aug 1955 Nashua, NH
LORAINE, Evelyn C and Raymond H JUDKINS, 18 Feb 1984 Hudson, NH
LORAINE, Henry and Gertrude PELLETIER, 19 May 1924 Nashua, NH
LORAINE, Patricia A and Gerald R BOILARD, 02 Jul 1955 Hudson, NH
LORAINE, Robert E and Evelyn C BERUBE, 23 May 1953 Nashua, NH
LORDAN, Noreen D and Terrance C BALL, 02 Jul 1966 N Stratford, NH
LORENTO, Samuel A and Bonnie M RICHARDS, 28 Apr 1984 Nashua, NH
LORING, Fay E and Herbert T PICKARD, 14 Nov 1942 Hudson, NH
LORING, Lesley N and Gerard A ROY, 20 Feb 1954 Hudson, NH
LORRAINE, Rachel and Adrian D GAGNON, 28 Nov 1935 Nashua, NH
LOUGEE, Arlene E and Forrest W JASPER, 07 Jul 1939 Hudson, NH
LOUGEE, Bert L and Margaret H CONREY, 11 Apr 1942 Hudson, NH
LOUGEE, David J and Susan GAGNON, 20 Jun 1969 Hudson, NH
LOUGEE, Francis E and Violet VENNE, 04 Feb 1939 Lowell, MA
LOUGEE, Jessie M and Judson A WHEELER, 01 Dec 1936 Ayer, MA
LOUGEE, Merciale M and Leo A LEBLANC, 09 Oct 1965 Hudson, NH
LOUGEE, Sophia and Artemas HILL, 28 Apr 1867
LOUGER, Sophia and Artemus HILL, 28 Apr 1867
LOUGHLIN, James J and Leona K SIMPSON, 30 Sep 1946 Hudson, NH
LOUIS, Sarah M and John E NELSON, 03 Dec 1934 Hudson, NH
LOUKIEWICZ, Waslaw M and Jeannette JACOBS, 08 Aug 1946 Hudson, NH
LOULAKIS, Mark C and Pamela M JELLEY, 11 Jun 1983 Hudson, NH
LOUPRETTE, Maude and Byron B SMITH, 15 Nov 1935 Hudson, NH
LOVEJOY, Albert and Lottie S BARRETT, 29 Apr 1872 Hudson, NH
LOVEJOY, Anna P and George N McGILVARY, 17 Dec 1859
LOVEJOY, Carl P and J Jeannet MERRY, 14 Jun 1947 Nashua, NH
LOVEJOY, Elizabeth and Francis SEARLES, 16 Apr 1864
LOVEJOY, Elizabeth and Francis SENTER, 16 Apr 1864
LOVEJOY, Ellen R and Caldwell BUTTRICK, 25 Apr 1899 Hudson, NH
  Eli Hardy & Eunice B Williams
  Samuel Buttrick & Margaret Caldwell
LOVEJOY, Frances and J H SMITH, 16 Apr 1864
LOVEJOY, Maria J and Alonzo D NEFF, 08 Apr 1873 Hudson, NH
LOVEJOY, Robert and Michele F LAVOIE, 31 Oct 1964 Hudson, NH
LOVELAND, Maybelle and Herbert A BAILEY, 16 Jul 1910 Nashua, NH
  Orville Loveland & Jennie Harding
  Mason T Bailey & Emma J Porter
LOVELL, Linnian A and Charles E OVERY, 16 May 1942 Nashua, NH
LOVELY, Charles and Diana ROUSSELL, 29 Sep 1933 Nashua, NH
LOVERING, Nancy J and William A SWALLOW, 14 Jan 1873 Hudson, NH
LOW, Adrastus and Harriet BLANCHARD, 29 Jun 1815
LOWE, Brian E and Gail M PITTS, 24 Jan 1975 Hudson, NH
LOWE, Edwin T and Virginia D LYON, 29 Sep 1951 Hudson, NH
LOWE, Frederick and Estelle M RICHARDS, 07 Oct 1949 Hudson, NH
LOWE, Mary E and John L JONES, 17 Jan 1948 Hudson, NH
LOWE, Robert D and Maryann J SWIDERSKA, 21 Jul 1955 Nashua, NH
LOWLIN, Hezekiah and Mary Ann COBURN, 27 Aug 1846
LOWTHER, Henry E Jr and Therese M WILSON, 03 Jul 1983 Nashua, NH
LOYD, Janet S and Ronald J BRYANT, 03 Mar 1973 Nashua, NH
LOZEAU, Claude and Juliette M LECLERC, 11 May 1946 Nashua, NH
LUCAS, Ronald N and Pauline A PARISEAU, 20 Jun 1959 Hudson, NH
LUCE, Ann and Orrin LEONARD, 10 Aug 1849
LUCHUN, Joseph J and M Donalda BOURQUE, 30 Dec 1933 Salem, NH
LUCIANO, Arthur J and Pauline R BERNARD, 08 May 1971 Hudson, NH
LUCIANO, Jean M and Richard P ARCHAMBEAULT, 22 May 1981 Nashua, NH
LUCIEN, Frances B and Maurice H DUBUC, 03 Jul 1940 Nashua, NH
LUCIER, Alice and William McNTYRE, 30 Jan 1901 Nashua, NH
  Lucier (Canada) & Mrs Ledaux (Canada)
  John McNtyre(Canada) & Maryann Welch (Canada)

HUDSON,NH MARRIAGES

LUCIER, Faye E and George W Jr BRIGHAM, 23 Jul 1977 New Boston, NH
LUDLAM, Marguerite and Raymond C MOREAU, 16 Aug 1971 Nashua, NH
LUFKIN, Walter E and Rebecca C ROSS, 16 Sep 1972 Hampton, NH
LUGIN, Albert John and Olive Lest THOMAS, 14 Jan 1939 Hudson, NH
LULA, Annie and Denitry ANDRIKOWICH, 21 Oct 1932 Nashua, NH
LUND, Eliza A and John F BALDWIN, 27 May 1856
LUND, Ella M and George O DURANT, 26 May 1898 Hudson, NH
   William Anthony
   George W Durant
LUND, Henry F and Helen M WELLS, 29 Mar 1893 Nashua, NH
   Francis Lund (Hollis, NH) & Marcia E Whiteker (Deering, NH)
   George E Wells(Albany, VT) & Sarah Doying (Albany, VT)
LUND, Martha E and Chas H BATCHELDER, 29 Mar 1890 Hudson, NH
   Francis Lund (Hollis, NH) & Marcie E Whitaker (Nashua, NH)
   Mark Batchelder(Hill, NH) & Lydia Steele (Hudson, NH)
LUND, Olive and Nathaniel MERRILL, 25 Feb 1767
LUND, Olive and Nathaniel MERRILL, 25 Feb 1761
LUND, Patricia A and Peter J LINDSAY, 20 Oct 1984 Nashua, NH
LUND, Winthrop E and Isabelle E OTIS, 21 Sep 1936 Hudson, NH
LUNDBERG, Louise I and Boyd C Jr HOPE, 04 Jul 1947 Hudson, NH
LUONGE, Ronald K and Diane L NOBLE, 10 Apr 1976 Londonderry, NH
LUONGO, Anthony J and Mary C ROBITO, 15 Nov 1948 Hudson, NH
LUPIEN, Sheila A and Steven D YOUNG, 21 Jul 1984 Durham, NH
LUSIGNAN, Blanche and Joseph A PROVENCAL, 03 Nov 1915 Nashua, NH
   Henri Lusignan (E Dublin, MA) & Clista Dupray (Sciotia, NY)
   Pradent Provencal(Canada) & Delma Gane (Canada)
LUSIGNAN, Raymond E and Pauline D VIGNOLA, 08 Jun 1957 Hudson, NH
LUSSIER, Alice N and Andre R JETTE, 26 Oct 1979 Hudson, NH
LUSSIER, Dorothy M and Henry C DAWALGA, 04 Jul 1958 Hudson, NH
LUSSIER, Ronald N and Robin R COLLINS, 08 May 1982 Hudson, NH
LUTHER, Morris C and Gail E DUFOUR, 09 Dec 1972 Nashua, NH
LUZ, Diane S and Eugene F LUZ, 16 Mar 1976 Hudson, NH
LUZ, Eugene F and Diane S STARK, 05 Jul 1975 Hudson, NH
LUZ, Eugene F and Diane S LUZ, 16 Mar 1976 Hudson, NH
LYDEN, Joseph and Muriel Elizabet CORBETT, 22 Jul 1978 Hudson, NH
LYNAH, Thomas H and Bernice D MORIN, 28 Jan 1950 Hudson, NH
LYNCH, Henry K and Nellie SULLIVAN, 13 Jun 1869 Hudson, NH
LYNCH, Robert C and Josephine HUNNEWELL, 18 Jul 1946 Hudson, NH
LYNESS, Annie C and W H BURTT, 06 Dec 1899 Hudson, NH
   William Lyness & May Gordon
   Crandal Burtt & Isabell Carter
LYNESS, Minnie J and Smith HALL, 28 Nov 1900 Hudson, NH
   Wm Lyness & Mary Gordon
   Wm T Hall & Rachael McDonald
LYNN, Marion D and Frank ANNIS, 14 Oct 1940 Lowell, MA
LYON, Bernard R and Louise TENNERINI, 28 Mar 1948 Hudson, NH
LYON, Edna F and Stafford S HILL, 09 May 1931 Hudson, NH
LYON, Ernest W and Alice V BREED, 17 Dec 1960 Nashua, NH
LYON, Gayle M and Henry A BRADBURY, 17 Apr 1971 Nashua, NH
LYON, Glenn G and Monica M MANSON, 26 Aug 1983 Hudson, NH
LYON, Vernon A and Dorothy S DUCHARME, 28 Nov 1957 Hudson, NH
LYON, Virginia D and Edwin T LOWE, 29 Sep 1951 Hudson, NH
LYONS, Daniel D and Evelyn M SMITH, 29 May 1965 Hudson, NH
LYONS, Daniel F and Isabel C CIBELLO, 17 Jun 1950 Hudson, NH
MACARTHUR, Douglas M&Dorothy A LITCHFIELD, 14 May 1983 Merrimack,NH
MACCANN, Carolyn E & Dennis J RAFFERTY, 15 Apr 1978 Litchfield, NH
MACCANN, Donald J and Jacqueline BRESNAHAN, 15 Jun 1956 Pelham, NH
MACCAUSLAND, Grace and Lloyd SNOW, 13 Mar 1938 Nashua, NH
MACCLELLAN, Mary A and Daniel J GAUTHIER, 14 Feb 1948 Hudson, NH
MACCONNELL, Margo E and Bruce E FLIGG, 30 Jun 1984 Hudson, NH

HUDSON,NH MARRIAGES

MACCOY, Hannah and Snow MARSHALL, 14 Mar 1799
MACDONALD, Dorothy C and Thomas F WHILDEGG, 22 Oct 1938 Nashua, NH
MACDONALD, Edward O and Marie E GREEN, 06 Sep 1952 Windham, NH
MACDONALD, Florence and Fred W SCOTT, 26 Oct 1929 Nashua, NH
MACDONALD, James C and Dawn E ANDERSON, 04 Sep 1983 Windham, NH
MACDONALD, Joseph T and Elizabeth SEYER, 04 May 1974 Nashua, NH
MACDONALD, Lois A and Roger S JOHNSON, 23 Oct 1971 Hudson, NH
MACDONALD, Margaret M&Theodore E FISKE, 12 Jul 1934 Manchester, NH
MACDONALD, Marie E and Allen B WELLS, 08 Apr 1978 Hudson, NH
MACDONALD, Mary C and Randall D THOMPSON, 18 Jun 1978 Nashua, NH
MACDONALD, Paul D and Judith A KENTRA, 20 May 1972 Hudson, NH
MACDONALD, Ronald and Mary Ann BUXTON, 06 Apr 1942 Manchester, NH
MACDONALD, Ronald and Edith M ARCHAMBAULT, 26 Feb 1955 Hudson, NH
MACDONALD, Virginia R&Geo D Jr MacDOWELL, 26 May 1956 Manchester,NH
MACDONALD, Zoe A and John R TORRES, 22 Oct 1977 Hudson, NH
MACDOUGALL, Larry G and Irene E GENDRON, 29 Jun 1957 Nashua, NH
MACDOUGALL, Martha and Minton A WINSLOW, 29 May 1958 Hudson, NH
MACDOUGALL, Patricia H and Daniel A FARLAND, 22 Jun 1968 Hudson, NH
MACDOWELL, Geo D Jr&Virginia R MacDONALD, 26 May 1956 Manchester,NH
MACDOWELL, L B and Robert S ELLIS, 05 Sep 1947 Nashua, NH
MACELROY, Mary Hazel and Wm J CORBY, 17 Dec 1922 Hudson, NH
MACGRATH, Gail S and Charles M IVES, 13 Oct 1971 Nashua, NH
MACGRATH, Gail S and Rene PAQUIN, 23 Jun 1973 Nashua, NH
MACGRATH, Gary W and Theresa M BOURQUE, 28 May 1982 Nashua, NH
MACHIA, Conrad A and Sally A WENTWORTH, 17 Aug 1968 Derry, NH
MACIE, Alexander and Judith I ROWE, 20 Jun 1959 Nashua, NH
MACINNIS, Agnes D and Edwin R MOORE, 20 Aug 1937 Boston, MA
MACINNIS, Daniel A Jr and Frances M CLARKE, 12 Nov 1944 Hudson, NH
MACINTOSH, Sandra L and Daniel T DALY, 27 Aug 1983 Hudson, NH
MACINTYRE, Donald C and Arlene T GAGNON, 01 May 1954 Hudson, NH
MACINTYRE, Jonathan D and Velma O CAMPBELL, 31 Aug 1925 Hudson, NH
MACIVER, Kenneth A and Iris M PAQUET, 21 Jun 1957 Lakeport, NH
MACK, Daniel R and Charlene R FROST, 02 Jun 1984 Nashua, NH
MACK, James A and Diane L GAGNON, 15 Oct 1977 Hudson, NH
MACKAY, Pamela J and Anthony H SKOVIRA, 13 Jun 1964 Nashua, NH
MACKENZIE, Lois and Joseph H POWERS, 17 Jul 1932 Nashua, NH
MACKENZIE, Nancy L and James M TWOMBLY, 07 Nov 1981 Nashua, NH
MACKEY, Howard P and Minnie J VANIER, 25 Feb 1922 Hudson, NH
MACKINNON, Diane T and Robert M WEILD, 23 Jun 1984 Nashua, NH
MACKINNON, Elmer M and Rita M BLACKETT, 01 Jul 1950 Hudson, NH
MACKINON, Isabel C and Wilhelm E MacRAE, 07 Aug 1937 Hollis, NH
MACLATCHEY, Gordon F and Leona P SUDSBURY, 11 Nov 1941 Nashua, NH
MACLATCHY, Christine and Carl E SWOYER, 06 Feb 1982 Nashua, NH
MACLENNAN, Edward R and Jane M SCHINDLER, 23 Jan 1971 Hudson, NH
MACLEOD, Donald D and June WENTWORTH, 06 Apr 1942 Milford, NH
MACLEOD, Georgena M and Robert H THOMPSON, 30 Dec 1941 Hudson, NH
MACLEOD, Marjorie M and Francis E TERRIN, 16 Apr 1944 Hudson, NH
MACMILLAN, Richard J & Josephine WORCESTER, 30 Jul 1967 Nashua, NH
MACNEIL, William E and Muriel H DAVIES, 22 Sep 1938 Nashua, NH
MACNICHOLS, Dorothy E and Uno A LEHTO, 29 Apr 1950 Hudson, NH
MACOMBER, Clarence E and Dorothy G DUNNE, 18 Nov 1940 Hudson, NH
MACOMBER, Colleen L & Joseph M Jr ZACCARDO, 17 Mar 1982 Nashua, NH
MACOMBER, Nancy and Raymond A NOLIN, 03 Jul 1971 Warner, NH
MACPHAIL, Gordon C and Ruth CORNELL, 17 Nov 1945 Hudson, NH
MACPHEE, Beverly D and Richard G GAGNON, 22 Oct 1983 Hudson, NH
MACQUEEN, Joanne and Dennis L ZALUSKY, 29 May 1982 Hudson, NH
MACQUEEN, Lisa A and Robert M DIONNE, 06 Oct 1984 Hudson, NH
MACRAE, Bonnie L and John P DUNN, 21 Jun 1969 Hudson, NH
MACRAE, Wilhelm E and Isabel C MACKINON, 07 Aug 1937 Hollis, NH
MACROBERTS, Vernon E and Evelyn L HAYES, 22 Feb 1969 Nashua, NH

HUDSON,NH MARRIAGES

MADDEN, Melanie S and James D POITRAS, 28 May 1983 Nashua, NH
MADDY, John W and Irene MARTELLUCCI, 11 Mar 1944 Hudson, NH
MADSEN, Helga M and Alfred J Jr CAMERON, 23 Oct 1948 Hudson, NH
MAEDA, Mari and Norman Jr WHITAKER, 17 Dec 1983 Hudson, NH
MAGNIN, Harriet L and Donald A HINTON, 08 Aug 1953 Hudson, NH
MAGNIN, Lorraine P and Leon J CHAREST, 31 Jul 1943 Nashua, NH
MAGNIN, Peter M and Kerrie Ann DESROCHES, 06 Oct 1979 Hudson, NH
MAGNIN, Russell J and Mildred H POLIQUIN, 23 Dec 1950 Hudson, NH
MAGRATH, Adrian G and Hedwidge L TODD, 30 Nov 1946 Nashua, NH
MAGUDER, Valeria T and John F E O'NEIL, 03 Sep 1942 Hudson, NH
MAGUE, David R and Elizabeth STOUT, 23 May 1981 Hudson, NH
MAGUIRE, Peter and Rose MURPHY, 22 Oct 1910 Hudson, NH
   Patrick Maguire & Catherine Riley
   John Murphy & Catherine Henry
MAHAR, Sylvia A&Theodore J DOBROWOLSKI, 23 Sep 1961 Manchester, NH
MAHER, Michael T and Julie A MESSER, 01 May 1975 Hollis, NH
MAHFUZ, Alec A and Rachel M WHITTEMORE, 23 Sep 1972 Wilmot Flat, NH
MAHONEY, Dorothy A and Joseph E FEMIA, 05 Apr 1947 Hudson, NH
MAHONEY, Isabel Woods and Leon E WINN, 13 Jan 1927 Hudson, NH
MAHONEY, Margaret M and Donald A BERARD, 07 May 1949 Nashua, NH
MAHONEY, Maureen R and Glenn A WRIGHT, 24 Jul 1981 Hudson, NH
MAHONEY, Steven P and Theresa M GAGNON, 15 Feb 1980 Nashua, NH
MAIKASIAN, Nishan P & Grace Dean DOWELL, 16 Feb 1935 Manchester, NH
MAILHOT, Julie A and Wayne A HILLYARD, 02 Jun 1984 Londonderry, NH
MAILLOUX, Alice and Victor PARADIS, 23 Aug 1928 Nashua, NH
MAILLOUX, Conrad C and Sharon A GRAINGER, 04 Jul 1967 Hudson, NH
MAIN, Donald R and Eleanor J BOULEY, 29 Nov 1943 Nashua, NH
MAIN, Larry E and Theresa C AREL, 01 Jun 1968 Hudson, NH
MAINE, William G and Michelle J PAGLIUCA, 16 May 1981 Hudson, NH
MAIOCCHI, James R and Jeanne M ZIMMERMAN, 10 Jul 1971 Hudson, NH
MAJOR, Martha and Joseph G Jr SHEA, 23 Aug 1969 Nashua, NH
MAJOR, Mary E and Charles R CRAIG, 01 Jun 1872 Hudson, NH
MAJOR, Richard D and Irene J LAFLOTTE, 20 Jun 1964 Nashua, NH
MAKER, John R and Deborah L LAVALLEE, 03 May 1975 Hudson, NH
MAKI, Naomi M and Robert I STONE, 11 Mar 1966 New Ipswich, NH
MAKI, Tauno S and Dorothy L BOUCHEY, 05 Jan 1949 Hudson, NH
MAKINEN, Robert B and Carol A KELLEY, 27 Sep 1969 Hudson, NH
MAKOWIEC, Maryann and David W CARROLL, 14 Jun 1958 Manchester, NH
MALAGUTI, Caroline J and Rocco CAMMARATA, 17 May 1936 Hudson, NH
MALAQUIAS, Vivian J and Leo A BOYLE, 05 Jan 1948 Hudson, NH
MALCOLM, Jessie K and Martin J O'NEIL, 11 Nov 1940 Hudson, NH
MALENFANT, Armand and Irene E BOULEY, 28 Aug 1946 Nashua, NH
MALENFANT, Armand V Jr and Barbara A EATON, 07 Jun 1969 Nashua, NH
MALENFANT, Jeannette and Ralph L HOLT, 12 Sep 1953 Hudson, NH
MALETTE, Constance and Maurice R DUCHESNEAU, 07 Apr 1951 Hudson, NH
MALETTE, Janet Flor and Edward R BERUBE, 20 Aug 1938 Nashua, NH
MALETTE, Lillian and Lucien VAILLANCOURT, 24 Nov 1938 Nashua, NH
MALETTE, Oscar L and Elaine D REARDON, 14 Sep 1944 Nashua, NH
MALETTE, Sandra A and Glenn R BLANCHARD, 14 May 1971 Manchester, NH
MALIAR, Michael and Milagros MILLAR, 10 Jan 1981 Hudson, NH
MALONE, Charles R and Theresa G GALIPEAU, 27 Oct 1972 Nashua, NH
MALONEY, Basil T and Vena P FISH, 21 Jun 1924 Hudson, NH
MALONEY, Etta A and Charles E FRAZER, 03 Jul 1920 Hudson, NH
MALONEY, Frances A and Reuben James BAKER, 04 Jun 1928 Hudson, NH
MALONIS, Christo C and Mary V TOMOU, 23 Sep 1956 Nashua, NH
MALONSON, Roger B and Therese M KENNON, 06 Apr 1965 Hudson, NH
MALOUIN, Leon F Jr and Lena DUCHARME, 28 Jun 1952 Hudson, NH
MALOUIN, Mae Ellen & William C CADORETTE, 01 Nov 1984 Merrimack, NH
MALOUIN, Maryanne F & Edwin L FOURNIER, 03 May 1985 Manchester, NH
MALOUIN, Richard E and MaeEllen M FARIA, 20 Jan 1979 Hudson, NH

HUDSON,NH MARRIAGES

MALPIEDI, John E and Marjorie M HOLM, 28 Aug 1970 Laconia, NH
MALTBY, Francis D and Norma C VIGDOR, 15 Apr 1947 Hudson, NH
MALTESE, Domenica M and William P KELLEY, 12 Aug 1950 Hudson, NH
MANAHAN, Dorothea and Chester W NORTON, 24 Dec 1941 Hudson, NH
MANCINE, Albert and Norma CLAYDON, 05 Jul 1941 Hudson, NH
MANCINI, Michael J & Crystine A SUMNER, 22 Apr 1978 Litchfield, NH
MANDERSON, Blanche J and George J MAROTTA, 24 Jun 1945 Hudson, NH
MANDIGO, Mary and George DENNO, 30 May 1908 Hudson, NH
   Lewis Oben & Mary Latuee
   Simeon Denno & Olive Duchane
MANGAN, Kerry M and Sharon Ann WELDON, 21 Oct 1972 Hudson, NH
MANIKAS, James Jr and Bernice C CHARETTE, 17 Apr 1977 Hudson, NH
MANIOU, Leon Josep and Hazeldel PEARULT, 31 Dec 1933 Nashua, NH
MANN, Jon F and Susan C DESCLOS, 04 Aug 1984 Hudson, NH
MANNARINI, Rose M and Eric B SMITH, 02 Oct 1970 Derry, NH
MANNING, Arther A and Alice M WELCH, 21 Sep 1941 Hudson, NH
MANNING, Frances A and James WOOD, 11 Mar 1862
MANNING, James D and Emma J MITCHELL, 23 Sep 1876 Hudson, NH
MANNING, John J and Gloria A GILCREAST, 17 Aug 1963 Hudson, NH
MANNING, Nancy A and James H III BARDSLEY, 26 Nov 1983 Nashua, NH
MANNING, Natt Head and Ethel B RICH, 15 Apr 1935 Concord, MA
MANNING, Richard J and Mary E OLHA, 22 May 1983 Hudson, NH
MANNING, Virginia A and Anthony P BROUSSEAU, 26 Nov 1982 Hudson, NH
MANNIX, Albert J III & Patrice A POTTER, 04 Sep 1982 Manchester, NH
MANNO, Ralph C and Donna J FINN, 06 Aug 1978 Moultonboro, NH
MANOLAKIS, John and Elizabeth BROWN, 14 Mar 1948 Hudson, NH
MANOLI, Salvatore and Claudia E SMITH, 03 Jul 1980 Hudson, NH
MANSFIELD, Alfred B and Lucille S RICHARD, 10 Aug 1946 Hudson, NH
MANSFIELD, Alma A and George A LANDRY, 30 Jun 1934 Nashua, NH
MANSFIELD, Louella A and Allen B KENNEDY, 23 Nov 1965 Hudson, NH
MANSFIELD, Sally E and Michael L PAGE, 02 Sep 1978 Hudson, NH
MANSFIELD, Susan L and Kevin W KELLY, 12 Sep 1970 Hudson, NH
MANSFIELD, Winfred V and Donnette C FOSTER, 05 Dec 1949 Chester, NH
MANSON, Marilyn M and Manuel L MAYORAL, 12 Jan 1974 Hudson, NH
MANSON, Monica M and Glenn G LYON, 26 Aug 1983 Hudson, NH
MANSON, Robert M and Karen A FLANAGAN, 02 Sep 1978 N Hampton, NH
MANSUR, Florence L and Harry W BOWL, 10 Oct 1980 Hudson, NH
MANSUR, Kenneth and Hazel ROCKWELL, 09 Jun 1928 Nashua, NH
MANSUR, Linda L and Anthony V PELKEY, 01 Jul 1968 Hudson, NH
MANTENUTO, John J and Marie J CHAPMAN, 12 May 1937 Hudson, NH
MANTENUTO, Marie and John F OAKES, 07 Feb 1942 Hudson, NH
MANZONI, Peter L and Patricia C MARCOTTE, 26 Apr 1974 Hudson, NH
MARBLE, Etta S and James E MERRILL, 05 Sep 1888 Nashua, NH
   Eben Marble (Poland, ME) & Sarah G Jewett (Pepperell, MA)
   James B Merrill(Hudson, NH) & Persis A Winn (Hudson, NH)
MARBLE, Robert C and Mary GOODROW, 29 Mar 1919 Pelham, NH
MARCELIN, Edeline and Luc COLON, 03 Mar 1976 Hudson, NH
MARCELLO, Robert and Cindy Loui QUIGLEY, 24 Dec 1981 Hudson, NH
MARCH, Lydia C and Daniel H BURNS, 21 Nov 1850
MARCH, Samuel and Sybel MORELAND, 27 Sep 1842
MARCH, Sarah and William A NICHOLS, 25 Dec 1851
MARCHAND, Eileen M and William N DAVIDSON, 28 Nov 1981 Hudson, NH
MARCHAND, Pierre D and Diane M GUTHRO, 15 Sep 1979 Hudson, NH
MARCHAND, Scott E and Charlotte KEROUAC, 19 Jan 1979 Nashua, NH
MARCHENONIS, Melvina and Benjamin J BOOTH, 02 Jul 1938 Nashua, NH
MARCHESE, William and Marthe G WHITE, 30 Jun 1984 Nashua, NH
MARCIL, Norma L and Thomas W BENNETT, 22 Aug 1974 Nashua, NH
MARCLEY, Helen R and Morris MIGNEAULT, 11 Jun 1923 Nashua, NH
MARCOTTE, Cecile D and Joseph E RAMOS, 03 Dec 1950 Hudson, NH
MARCOTTE, Marie J and Leon R AREL, 06 Jan 1968 Hudson, NH

HUDSON,NH MARRIAGES

MARCOTTE, Patricia C and Peter L MANZONI, 26 Apr 1974 Hudson, NH
MARCOUX, Russell R and Jeanne M CLAVEAU, 15 Jul 1967 Nashua, NH
MARCUM, Russell L and Marie Avis BARRETT, 29 Jul 1972 Nashua, NH
MARCY, Martha A and Horace N BURROWS, 05 Feb 1868
MARDEN, Calvin C and Helen A PEARSONS, 02 Jun 1865
MARDEN, Calvin C and Kelly PEARSONS, 12 Jun 1865
MARDEN, Edward P & Patricia L OUIMETTE, 10 Jan 1981 Somersworth, NH
MARDEN, Isabel D and Vinal E BENNETT, 19 Feb 1938 Nashua, NH
MARDEN, John N and Hattie E STEEL, 01 Sep 1868 Hudson, NH
MARDEN, Lois A and James E TAYLOR, 01 Aug 1982 Nashua, NH
MARDEN, Terri L and Robert W CLOUTIER, 01 Aug 1964 Nashua, NH
MARDONES, Guido M and Lynne M HARTLEY, 19 Jan 1980 Hudson, NH
MARGESON, Alma C and Howard E BOULDRY, 26 Nov 1935 Nashua, NH
MARGESON, Mary A and Nicholas J BARBARITO, 12 Apr 1974 Hudson, NH
MARIA, Alice T and John W RAND, 01 Apr 1950 Hudson, NH
MARINEL, Winthrop L and Florence C LADUKE, 25 Nov 1950 Hudson, NH
MARINELLO, Natale R and Joan T VAYO, 03 Jul 1950 Hudson, NH
MARION, Edith and John McCORMACK, 07 Jan 1934 Nashua, NH
MARIREA, Christine and Alan D FRENCH, 13 May 1983 Nashua, NH
MARKERICH, Ella and Charles Jr CHAPONIS, 12 Feb 1938 Nashua, NH
MARKS, Bernard J and Kathy E UPTON, 09 Jan 1982 Nashua, NH
MARKS, Claudette and Ernest E BRIAND, 28 Jun 1980 Hudson, NH
MARLEY, Richard J and Estelle A EASTMAN, 08 Apr 1967 Litchfield, NH
MARLIN, John and Abigail B SMITH, 14 Sep 1826
MAROTTA, George J and Blanche J MANDERSON, 24 Jun 1945 Hudson, NH
MARQUIS, Alice M and Francis F MOREY, 11 Oct 1945 Nashua, NH
MARQUIS, Cecile and Adelbert JETTE, 05 Jul 1920 Manchester, NH
MARQUIS, Charles and Dorothy DEAN, 27 May 1935 Nashua, NH
MARQUIS, Clarice and Leon BERARD, 03 Sep 1923 Nashua, NH
MARQUIS, Cynthia H and Dana H SMITH, 07 Sep 1974 Hudson, NH
MARQUIS, David P and Sandra A SPINNEY, 02 Oct 1971 Hudson, NH
MARQUIS, George E and Linda E JONES, 31 Aug 1968 Nashua, NH
MARQUIS, Gloria M and Maruice G RABY, 12 Aug 1950 Nashua, NH
MARQUIS, Jeannette and Albert TESSIER, 08 May 1937 Lowell, MA
MARQUIS, Joann and William P ARCHAMBAULT, 06 Feb 1977 Nashua, NH
MARQUIS, Paul R and Arlene M ATKINSON, 11 Sep 1982 Merrimack, NH
MARQUIS, Raymond G and Louise H LEMAY, 30 May 1955 Hudson, NH
MARQUIS, Romeo A and Lucille A SILLANPAA, 15 Aug 1947 Nashua, NH
MARQUIS, Sandra L and Craig Roland JETTE, 15 May 1981 Nashua, NH
MARQUIS, Teresa M and Peter W HEBERT, 20 Aug 1976 Nashua, NH
MARQUIS, Theotice and Octave NADEAU, 02 Sep 1933 Nashua, NH
MARR, Gertrude E and Walter R FEARON, 09 Sep 1936 Hudson, NH
MARRIOTT, Lenora M and Ronald E PELLETIER, 03 Sep 1966 Hudson, NH
MARSDEN, Henry and Eleanor F MORAN, 07 Jun 1947 Hudson, NH
MARSH, Abbie A and Joseph K WHEELER, 22 Nov 1849
MARSH, Agnes S and Robert A ELLIOTT, 14 Jul 1984 Nashua, NH
MARSH, Clara J and Aaron C BELL, 02 Oct 1861
MARSH, Daniel and Sophia C TUFTS, 23 Sep 1849
MARSH, Edith Eliz and Walter Lor BARKER, 11 Jun 1914 Hudson, NH
  Walter H Marsh & Addie E Mason
  Allen F Barker & Emma J Dunklee
MARSH, Eliza H and Edwin WILLOUGHBY, 30 May 1868
MARSH, Eliza H and Edwin WILLOUGHBY, 13 May 1868
MARSH, Elizabeth and John M THOMPSON, 05 Oct 1852
MARSH, Elwin R and Shirley A DONOVAN, 30 Mar 1970 Hudson, NH
MARSH, Fannie H and Fred E WHITFORD, 09 Jun 1869 Hudson, NH
MARSH, Frank W and Maggie REILEY, Jan 1861
MARSH, Hattie A and Alfred P KENDALL, 17 Apr 1865
MARSH, Hattie T and James T JONES, 03 May 1864
MARSH, Hiram and Olivia GOODSPEED, 27 Nov 1828

HUDSON,NH MARRIAGES

MARSH, John F and Harriet L WARREN, 22 Jan 1849
MARSH, Marietta L and Daniel GAGE, 07 Dec 1865
MARSH, Marion and Francis L O'BRYAN, 17 Jun 1902 Nashua, NH
  Walter H Marsh & Lizzie S Wilder
  Lafayette O'Bryan & Betty
MARSH, Nancy W and James M GREELEY, 10 Sep 1850
MARSH, Sally and Willard SPALDING, 24 Apr 1817
MARSH, Sarah L and Moses P RICHARDSON, 16 Nov 1865
MARSH, Susanna and Caleb JOHNSON, 06 Apr 1826
MARSH, Thomas and Eunice K SARGENT, 02 Jul 1830
MARSH, Thomas and Persis R D DAVENPORT, 26 Dec 1858
MARSH, William and Susanna BARRETT, 15 Feb 1797
MARSH, William J and Agnes Step ROOD, 23 Jan 1982 Nashua, NH
MARSHALL, Abigail and James BARNARD, 14 Mar 1816
MARSHALL, Alan E and Yolande F DUROCHER, 29 Dec 1949 Nashua, NH
MARSHALL, Arthur L and Cheryl P PALMER, 13 Jun 1981 Hudson, NH
MARSHALL, Bertha S and Albert P JEWELL, 15 Mar 1900 Lowell, MA
  Geo W Marshall & Annie E Osgood
  W A Jewell & Christina Schurer
MARSHALL, Betsey and Coburn BARRETT, 18 May 1817
MARSHALL, Betsey and Oliver SPRAKE, 14 Mar 1820
MARSHALL, Dana C and Myrtle Mau HILL, 18 Sep 1913 Hudson, NH
  Dana S Marshall & Martha A Griffin
  David B Hill & Abbie A Batchelder
MARSHALL, David O and Henrietta SMITH, 23 Dec 1885 Hudson, NH
  John B Marshall (Hudson, NH) & Ellen A Senter (Hudson, NH)
  Norris Smith(Hudson, NH) & Fannie M Greeley (Hudson, NH)
MARSHALL, Donna L and Charles L GILBERT, 29 Aug 1970 Hollis, NH
MARSHALL, Edith M and Frank W NUTE, 29 May 1912 Hudson, NH
  Eugene J Marshall & Leona Robinson
  Frank W Nute & Etta M Gordon
MARSHALL, Edward G and Annie L FLANDERS, 09 Jun 1923 Hudson, NH
MARSHALL, Elizabeth and Frank A CUMMINGS, 28 Mar 1878 Hudson, NH
  G W Marshall & Marinda Hadley (Hudson, NH)
  Nathan Cummings(Hudson, NH)
MARSHALL, Ethel M and Robert S WHITNEY, 21 Aug 1976 Nashua, NH
MARSHALL, Eva G M and Frank C SMITH, 09 Feb 1943 Hudson, NH
MARSHALL, Frank E and Flora W HUBBARD, 21 Aug 1906 Hudson, NH
  William S Marshall & Mary E Libbey
  L E Walker & Maria Nearch
MARSHALL, Fred R and Louisa W WHEELER, 25 May 1886 Hudson, NH
MARSHALL, Fred R and Louisa WHEELER, 25 May 1886 Hudson, NH
  John B Marshall (Hudson, NH) & Ellen A Senter (Hudson, NH)
  Frank C Wheeler & Louisa Gorham
MARSHALL, George W and Josephine MARSHALL, 22 Apr 1908 Nashua, NH
  Josiah Marshall & Mary Clark
  Patrick Holland & Margaret Mead
MARSHALL, George W Jr and Ania E OSGOOD, 16 Jun 1878 Tyngsboro, MA
  George W Marshall (Sharon, NH) & Miranda (Hudson, NH)
  Josiah Osgood(Milford, NH) & Willminia (Hooksett)
MARSHALL, Hanna and Moses FARMER, 23 Mar 1823
MARSHALL, Harold H and Eva G MORRILL, 26 Jun 1922 Hudson, NH
MARSHALL, Hattie J and Oscar O ARMSTRONG, 14 Nov 1868 Hudson, NH
MARSHALL, Henry and Abigail POLLARD, 04 Sep 1781
MARSHALL, Herbert W and Lilla E BARRETT, 19 Nov 1891 Nashua, NH
  Geo W Marshall (Sharon) & Miranda Hadley (Hudson, NH)
  Alverado Barrett(Hudson, NH) & Anna Hartford (Allenstown, NH)
MARSHALL, James E and Sarah J MULLIGAN, 16 Nov 1889 Lowell, MA
  Alfred Marshall (Hudson, NH) & Lydia M Hamblett (Hudson, NH)
  John B Thibodeau(Madanosko, PQ) & Mary Dupont

HUDSON,NH MARRIAGES

MARSHALL, James E and Susan M CONANT, 08 Feb 1893 Hudson, NH
   Alfred Marshall (Hudson, NH) & Lynia M Hamblet (Hudson, NH)
   James Ridgeway(N S) & Jane Hewitt (N S)
MARSHALL, Jane and William CALDWELL, 28 Apr 1842
MARSHALL, Jean A and Robert A FELTON, 30 Jun 1957 Milford, NH
MARSHALL, Jemima and Robert FORD, 11 Jul 1809
MARSHALL, JoAnn S and John W WORTH, 05 Dec 1953 Hudson, NH
MARSHALL, Josephine and George W MARSHALL, 22 Apr 1908 Nashua, NH
   Patrick Holland & Margaret Mead
   Josiah Marshall & Mary Clark
MARSHALL, Lewis R and Elsie GOODWIN, 12 Jun 1940 Hudson, NH
MARSHALL, Louis J and Marion L WHITE, 28 Jun 1941 Milford, NH
MARSHALL, Martha C and Benjamin H KIDDER, 24 Apr 1849
MARSHALL, Mary E and Robert T CONNELL, 06 Dec 1879 Pelham, NH
   Henry Marshall & Mary E
   Tobias Connell(Ireland) & Mary (Ireland)
MARSHALL, Muriel E and Peter N PLUMMER, 27 Oct 1962 Hudson, NH
MARSHALL, Nancy and John HARDY, 31 Oct 1850
MARSHALL, Nathan O and Ella E BALL, 09 Sep 1869 Hudson, NH
MARSHALL, Nettie and Sherman J SWALLOW, 05 Feb 1923 Nashua, NH
MARSHALL, Polly and James McCOY, 17 Mar 1814
MARSHALL, Priscilla and Richard A WATSON, 25 Apr 1970 Nashua, NH
MARSHALL, Rebecca and Daniel STEELE, 18 Nov 1819
MARSHALL, Richard E and Patricia A MAYO, 29 Aug 1964 Nashua, NH
MARSHALL, Richard E and Paula J BOURGEOIS, 17 Oct 1981 Hudson, NH
MARSHALL, Robert W and Lilla E BARRETT, 19 Nov 1891
MARSHALL, Snow and Hannah MacCOY, 14 Mar 1799
MARSHALL, Stephen C and Sarah ANDREWS, 12 Apr 1814
MARSHALL, Theodore B and Jeanne B COTE, 26 Feb 1977 Nashua, NH
MARSHALL, Timothy P and Anne M GROHOSKY, 12 Apr 1980 Nashua, NH
MARSHALL, Vera M and Hudson L WILSON, 17 Jan 1953 Chester, NH
MARSHALL, Virginia and Richard P SMITH, 16 Sep 1942 Hudson, NH
MARSHALL, W H and Gloria BERUBE, 21 Aug 1876 Nashua, NH
MARSHALL, William C and Cornelia C CHASE, 24 Dec 1866
MARSHALL, Zoe and David HARDY, 31 Mar 1859
MARSTON, Donald A and Laurie M JUDKINS, 26 Apr 1980 Nashua, NH
MARSTON, Margaret and Richard H Jr ERWIN, 26 Apr 1931 Dunstable, MA
MARTEIN, Carol H and James PAGE, 23 Feb 1974 Hudson, NH
MARTEIN, Cynthia S and Joseph M UNDERCOFLER, 25 May 1980 Hudson, NH
MARTEL, Leonard W and Coleen A MITCHELL, 04 Feb 1972 Hudson, NH
MARTELL, Arlene A and Alfred J BROADBENT, 30 Sep 1949 Hudson, NH
MARTELLE, Ida and James COLLIER, 05 Mar 1905 Hudson, NH
   Azale Martelle & Olive Hill
   Joseph Collier & Emeline Duprey
MARTELLUCCI, Irene and John W MADDY, 11 Mar 1944 Hudson, NH
MARTIN, Alfred A and Shirley A CUSHING, 28 Jun 1952 Hudson, NH
MARTIN, Almira M and Daniel SHERMAN, 25 May 1880 Hudson, NH
   Daniel Eageton (Munson, MA) & Mindwell Fane (Brookfield, MA)
   Telphnah Sherman(Pomfort, CT) & Betsey Allton (Tompson, CT)
MARTIN, Brian R and Mary-Eliza GRUENFELDER, 01 Jul 1981 Hudson, NH
MARTIN, Charlene R and Gannon RATLIFF, 23 Feb 1965 Nashua, NH
MARTIN, Cindy L and John R Jr BOULEY, 14 Feb 1981 Nashua, NH
MARTIN, Clara L and George T LEFEBVRE, 02 Jul 1932 Nashua, NH
MARTIN, Daniel A and Mabel A TOWNES, 18 Feb 1894 Londonderry, NH
   Wm H Martin (Canada) & Pennock
   Silas Townes & Robinson
MARTIN, Dolores M and Charles D III SMITH, 27 May 1972 Nashua, NH
MARTIN, Donna L and Raymond P NORMAND, 02 Jul 1966 Hudson, NH
MARTIN, Doreen B and Edgar G GUERRETTE, 21 Dec 1968 Hudson, NH
MARTIN, Doris L & William Joseph GRANT, 05 Feb 1930 Winchester, MA

HUDSON,NH MARRIAGES

MARTIN, Ezra A and Sadie B TRACY, 24 Jun 1903 Nashua, NH
  Elisha Martin & Almira M Egerton
  James Wilson & Sarah B Wheeler
MARTIN, Ezra A and Maggie J CLYDE, 21 Feb 1877 Hudson, NH
MARTIN, Francis J and Mary A ROBERTSON, 29 Jan 1977 Litchfield, NH
MARTIN, Fred A Jr and Gladys GRANT, 02 Jun 1950 Hudson, NH
MARTIN, Gertrude A and Walter E KENNEDY, 19 Dec 1955 Hudson, NH
MARTIN, Grace and George C SHAW, 08 Sep 1908 Hudson, NH
  Ezra A Martin & Maggie J Clyde
  Frank C Shaw & Mabel L Tyler
MARTIN, Horace A and Lizzie Jan WEBSTER, 18 Jun 1875
MARTIN, Horace J and Lizzie WEBSTER, 17 Jun 1876 Hudson, NH
MARTIN, Ida M and James W Jr McGUIRE, 01 Aug 1951 Hudson, NH
MARTIN, Janice E and Sterling P EMERSON, 02 Feb 1946 Nashua, NH
MARTIN, Jennie A and Waldo P WALTON, 19 Feb 1877 Hudson, NH
MARTIN, Jesse and Margaret V KELLEY, 04 Nov 1948 Hudson, NH
MARTIN, John E and Lillian V BAXTER, 12 Jul 1939 Hudson, NH
MARTIN, John E Jr and Judith A DEPONTBRIAND, 04 Oct 1975 Hudson, NH
MARTIN, John H and Ellen L GENOVA, 28 Mar 1969 Nashua, NH
MARTIN, John T and Jennie C WINN, 30 Sep 1891 Hudson, NH
  Silas W Martin (Amy, N B) & Prudence Sage (P E Island)
  William F Winn(Hudson, NH) & Lucy Richardson (Woburn, MA)
MARTIN, Joseph R and Muriel J SCURRAH, 20 Nov 1965 Hudson, NH
MARTIN, Kimball W and Bertha CUNNINGHAM, 04 Sep 1901 Nashua, NH
  Horace A Martin (Eastford, CT) & Lizzie J Webster (Hudson, NH)
  James Cunningham(St Johns, NB)& Elizabeth Patterson(St Johns, NB)
MARTIN, Laura M and George A WEST, 30 May 1942 Hudson, NH
MARTIN, Lee M and Donald W TRIPPLETON, 12 Apr 1958 Hudson, NH
MARTIN, Leonard A and Cynthia J COTE, 11 Oct 1969 Nashua, NH
MARTIN, Liliane B and Carl E LEAOR, 18 Jun 1928 Nashua, NH
MARTIN, Mildred and Francis KNIGHTS, 17 Aug 1940 Dracut, MA
MARTIN, Moise and Marie R PELLETIER, 22 Sep 1921 Nashua, NH
MARTIN, Newton C and Mary E DORRISON, 17 Sep 1873 Fitchburg, MA
MARTIN, Noreen A and William A MOLIS, 04 Oct 1969 Nashua, NH
MARTIN, Paul A Jr and Cheryl A GAGNON, 07 Jan 1972 Nashua, NH
MARTIN, Raymond J and Grace D VILLEMAIRE, 31 Dec 1957 Derry, NH
MARTIN, Redmond Lester & Josephine L CARMAN, 18 Apr 1911 Hudson, NH
  Joseph J Martin & Martha Clulland
  J H Carman
MARTIN, Roger A and Eleanor M BERGERON, 22 Nov 1956 Hudson, NH
MARTIN, Shirley A and Claude E FREDETTE, 12 May 1967 Hudson, NH
MARTIN, Simon and Claire L PERAULT, 04 Jun 1982 Nashua, NH
MARTIN, Susan G and Richard A JODOIN, 13 Jan 1970 Nashua, NH
MARTIN, Thomas G and Edith L VENO, 14 Oct 1950 Hudson, NH
MARTIN, Wilfred J and Edith I MINER, 05 May 1962 Hudson, NH
MARTIN, William H and Hazel D BRADLEY, 22 Jun 1917 Hudson, NH
MARTIN, Yvonne and Lionel THERIAULT, 22 Jun 1935 Nashua, NH
MARTIN, Yvonne A and Benjamin KEZAR, 15 Jun 1936 Newport, NH
MARTINANGELO, Theresa L and Robert LONGMIRE, 31 Mar 1979 Hudson, NH
MARTINEAU, Joseph E and Frances E BASNAR, 18 Aug 1956 Hudson, NH
MARTINEAU, Lois J and Charles M QUIGLEY, 17 Dec 1971 Hudson, NH
MARTINEAU, Rose A and Raymond T BRIDGES, 14 Oct 1961 Hudson, NH
MARTINEZ, Denise L and Paul D DEMERS, 14 May 1982 Hudson, NH
MARTINSON, Sandra J and William H MARTINSON, 09 Sep 1966 Nashua, NH
MARTINSON, William H and Sandra J MARTINSON, 09 Sep 1966 Nashua, NH
MARTYN, Lois H and Francis P SNAY, 20 Feb 1965 Nashua, NH
MARVELL, Richard S and Jeannette BOUCHER, 23 Aug 1958 Hudson, NH
MARVELLI, Edmund M and Barbara A SWORD, 24 Dec 1949 Hudson, NH
MARYANSKI, David John & Teresa L BISSONNETTE, 20 Jun 1981 Nashua,NH
MARYNOWSKI, Jos M and Pauline M GIGNAC, 10 Jun 1949 Hudson, NH

HUDSON,NH MARRIAGES

MARZOLF, Dwight P and Marjory A CLARK, 19 Dec 1981 Pelham, NH
MASKEWICZ, Edward C and Pearl BOIS, 20 Dec 1952 Hudson, NH
MASLANKA, Robert R and Irene M MROZEK, 04 Jul 1963 Hudson, NH
MASON, Abner and Hannah A GRANT, 07 Mar 1849
MASON, Arline M and William D III SHINN, 06 Nov 1954 Hudson, NH
MASON, Brian L and Beverly A STANLEY, 27 Jun 1975 Nashua, NH
MASON, Debra Jean and Albert J ST AUBIN, 21 Dec 1980 Hudson, NH
MASON, Georgette and Felix Peter GURSKA, 15 May 1981 Nashua, NH
MASON, James A and Gretchen A COVEY, 16 Jan 1965 Hudson, NH
MASON, Kathleen M and John F Jr ZACCAGNINI, 06 Nov 1982 Nashua, NH
MASON, Marlene D and Carl D HARMON, 12 Jan 1980 Pelham, NH
MASON, Nancy A and Lee E EDWARDS, 23 Mar 1956 Nashua, NH
MASON, Nora M and Benjamin FAIRFIELD, 11 Jan 1896 Hudson, NH
   W H Ackerman (Charlotte, NC) & Henrietta C Lane (Lee)
   Henry W Fairfield & Salvina Leach (New Boston, NH)
MASON, Patricia Jean & Raymond Edward SMITH, 26 Aug 1978 Hudson, NH
MASON, Rita M and Henry C BUNTIN, 05 Feb 1949 Hudson, NH
MASON, Terry Ann and Carroll F BLAKE, 19 Jul 1975 Conway, NH
MASSE, Leanne M and William C WELDON, 23 Jul 1971 Pelham, NH
MASSEY, Robert L and Doris G VAILLANCOURT, 04 Feb 1967 Nashua, NH
MASSUCCI, Christophe and Linda M GENDRON, 15 Sep 1984 Hudson, NH
MASTEN, Walter J and Dorothy C MITE, 05 Feb 1972 Merrimack, NH
MASTERS, Mary M and Robert D BARTLETT, 11 Oct 1969 Derry, NH
MASTERSON, Chris and Darlene TWISS, 25 Mar 1972 Pelham, NH
MASTERSON, Clyde H and Diane L VIENS, 03 Jul 1970 Bennington, NH
MASTERSON, Frances M and Keith H WITTEMAN, 15 Jun 1974 Hudson, NH
MASTERSON, James P and Jeanne L POULIN, 17 Apr 1971 Nashua, NH
MASTERSON, Kathryn M and David W HUNT, 16 Nov 1968 Hudson, NH
MASTROFINE, Brian E and Roberta Le POTZNER, 28 May 1983 Hudson, NH
MATAROZZO, James A & Nancy P TURCOTTE, 25 Aug 1973 Hampton Fls, NH
MATHER-LEES, Joanna C and Donald J ROUSSEL, 23 Dec 1983 Nashua, NH
MATHERSON, Reginald & Harriet V ZMITROWICZ, 19 Mar 1949 Nashua, NH
MATHEWS, Charles E and Mabella L NORRIS, 02 Dec 1936 Nashua, NH
MATHEWS, John and Florence M TRUFENT, 18 Oct 1909 Nashua, NH
   John Mathews & Isabella Hayes
   John M Trufent & Flora Turner
MATKOWSKY, Albert S & Lorraine D [UNKNOWN], 25 Aug 1979 Nashua, NH
MATTHEWS, Duncan C and J Estelle MELVIN, 10 Nov 1896 Hudson, NH
   William Matthews & Amy Hoyt (N Brunswick)
   T D Melvin & Julia Hopkins (W Trenton, ME)
MATTHEWS, Hildreth H and Clayton A STULTZ, 17 Nov 1956 Hudson, NH
MATTHEWS, Robert T and Florence M BURNS, 29 Jun 1935 Nashua, NH
MATTHEWS, Sheryl A and Girard A McKINNON, 31 Aug 1979 Hudson, NH
MATTHIAS, Deborah J and Kevin E BUTTERWORTH, 26 Sep 1981 Hudson, NH
MATTISON, Sharon A & William E COURTEMANCHE, 05 Dec 1981 Nashua, NH
MATYJASIK, Patricia A and Frank M LACOSHUS, 20 Sep 1970 Hudson, NH
MAURER, Margo A and John H Jr RUBLEE, 29 Jun 1963 Hudson, NH
MAURICE, Aline M and Peter POWLOWSKY, 11 Apr 1953 Nashua, NH
MAURITSON, Arnold O and Phyllis E CHUTE, 15 Aug 1954 Hudson, NH
MAURO, Alphonse L and Nellie R JOSEPH, 16 Oct 1937 Hudson, NH
MAXFIELD, Donna S and David K RICHARD, 15 Jul 1983 Nashua, NH
MAXFIELD, Doris E and Donald G WILLIAMS, 27 Jun 1970 Hudson, NH
MAXFIELD, Dorothy H and Edward C SHEPHERD, 02 May 1969 Hudson, NH
MAXFIELD, Ruth B and William E Jr AYER, 14 May 1960 Nashua, NH
MAXFIELD, William E and Eleanor R GOWING, 26 May 1962 Hudson, NH
MAYES, Clyde and Agnes McHUGH, 02 Sep 1942 Hudson, NH
MAYNARD, Anjanette M&Gerald LeRoy RUSH, 24 Dec 1982 Londonderry, NH
MAYNARD, Averil A and Mohan S KIRPALANI, 26 Mar 1948 Hudson, NH
MAYNARD, Claire T and Real J AUDET, 22 Jun 1963 Nashua, NH
MAYNARD, Dolores C and Ernest O PARADISE, 12 Nov 1960 Nashua, NH

HUDSON, NH MARRIAGES

MAYNARD, Felix J and Hedwidge M NADEAU, 06 Jun 1932 Nashua, NH
MAYNARD, Robert L and Jeanne T JEAN, 16 Jan 1968 Hudson, NH
MAYNARD, Ronald F and Carol M BERUBE, 08 Feb 1964 Nashua, NH
MAYNARD, Ronald F and Colleen M COLE, 18 Mar 1978 Nashua, NH
MAYO, Jeffery P and Geniene A BACON, 30 Mar 1985 Hudson, NH
MAYO, Patricia A and Richard E MARSHALL, 29 Aug 1964 Nashua, NH
MAYORAL, Manuel L and Marilyn M MANSON, 12 Jan 1974 Hudson, NH
MCADAMS, William and Abigail HARDY, 05 May 1785
MCADOO, Nellie V and Roger K LEIGHTON, 21 Jun 1941 Nashua, NH
MCAFEE, Alfred H and Eva E GOWING, 03 Mar 1921 Hudson, NH
MCAFEE, Carl A and Nellie M WESTON, 26 Apr 1916 Nashua, NH
  Charles A McAfee (Bedford, NH) & Susie Druker (Pembroke, NH)
  Alvah K Weston(Portland, ME) & Emma Healey (Chester, NH)
MCAFEE, Lizzie M and Pearl CAMPBELL, 27 Jun 1906 Nashua, NH
  Charles F McAfee & Susie Dunken
  Bradford Campbell & Hattie E Putnam
MCAFEE, Richard N and Marsha L CROSBY, 26 Sep 1970 Nashua, NH
MCALISTER, Franklyn H and Gladys I CHAPUT, 29 Nov 1952 Hudson, NH
MCALISTER, Franklyn H and Eleanor C DANE, 26 Jun 1977 Nashua, NH
MCALISTER, James E and Pauline L DUCHARME, 02 Dec 1961 Nashua, NH
MCALLISTER, Franklyn H and Clara E DUFFINE, 04 Nov 1938 Hudson, NH
MCALLISTER, Victoria M and Charles R EVANS, 27 Jul 1957 Nashua, NH
MCALMAN, Dorothy I and Robert A MUNROE, 13 Apr 1957 Nashua, NH
MCALPINE, Louisa C and Enoch CUMMINGS,
MCANESPIE, Norma I and Maurice E BRUNELLE, 15 Jul 1966 Hudson, NH
MCARTHUR, Cathine M and Everett P ANNIS, 24 Apr 1900 Hudson, NH
  William McArthur & Mary Canick
  N P Annis & Drusetta Stearns
MCARTHUR, Eugene M and Linda I SAVAGE, 08 Aug 1964 Hudson, NH
MCARTHUR, Kevin M and Catherine ARNOLD, 13 Apr 1985 Hudson, NH
MCAULIFFE, Joan L and Brit A CHAGNON, 05 Oct 1979 Hudson, NH
MCBRIDE, George E and Sandra H BONDURA, 09 Dec 1950 Hudson, NH
MCCABE, Gladys and William C WALLACE, 06 Dec 1941 Hudson, NH
MCCAFFERY, Elaine M & Richard R Jr EDMONDS, 22 Jun 1985 Hudson, NH
MCCAFFREY, James W and Irenie E SCANNELL, 20 Nov 1937 Hudson, NH
MCCALL, John W and Marjorie C THOMAS, 19 Oct 1947 Hudson, NH
MCCALLUM, Leonard F and Joann A SAJDAK, 25 May 1947 Lowell, MA
MCCAMMOND, Margaret R and Robert C ROGERS, 16 Jun 1946 Hudson, NH
MCCANN, Dorothy J and Herb M Jr JOHNSON, 14 Jan 1950 Hudson, NH
MCCANN, Mary and Richard R RHEAULT, 30 Jul 1977 Nashua, NH
MCCARTHY, Dennis J & Jacqueline TOWNSEND, 26 Nov 1966 Plaistow, NH
MCCARTHY, Elizabeth and Edward J BELANGER, 17 Feb 1984 Rye, NH
MCCARTHY, Faye A and John R McLAUGHLIN, 25 Sep 1965 Nashua, NH
MCCARTHY, Gail D and Michael A GLENN, 17 Oct 1970 Hudson, NH
MCCARTHY, Herbert E and Lucille E GALE, 18 Jul 1964 Salem, NH
MCCARTHY, Herbert O and Gloria L OUELLETTE, 12 Jul 1963 Hudson, NH
MCCARTHY, Joyce V and Robert W CURREN, 15 Oct 1966 Hudson, NH
MCCARTHY, Lisa J and Stephen M MOODY, 27 Oct 1979 Hudson, NH
MCCARTHY, Robert C and Jeannette BECHARD, 11 Sep 1971 Nashua, NH
MCCARTY, John A and Rita L SMITH, 04 Apr 1971 Hudson, NH
MCCARTY, Lillian G and William J McCORMICK, 24 Nov 1932 Hudson, NH
MCCAUGNEY, Andrew S and Emma A STECKEWICZ, 05 Aug 1940 Nashua, NH
MCCAULEY, Kathleen R and Peter W CASEY, 03 Dec 1977 Hudson, NH
MCCLELLAN, Wayne W & Judith A GUILBERT, 26 Apr 1980 Londonderry, NH
MCCLELLAND, Dorothy M and Raymond V ORANGE, 26 Aug 1950 Hudson, NH
MCCLURE, Anna-Maria and Roland A POOLE, 03 Jan 1981 Hudson, NH
MCCLURE, Michael J and Cynthia L COLBURN, 24 Apr 1982 Hudson, NH
MCCLUSKEY, Patrice C and John N Jr BALLUM, 07 Oct 1949 Hudson, NH
MCCOMB, John Henry and Marie D ADAIR, 24 Apr 1982 Hudson, NH
MCCOMISH, Matthew G and Beatrice I FENGILL, 30 Sep 1944 Hudson, NH

HUDSON,NH MARRIAGES

MCCORMACK, John and Edith MARION, 07 Jan 1934 Nashua, NH
MCCORMACK, Mildred F and Ronald L LEVESQUE, 03 Apr 1954 Hudson, NH
MCCORMICK, William J and Lillian G McCARTY, 24 Nov 1932 Hudson, NH
MCCOY, Amos H and Julia A BARRETT, 16 Oct 1862
MCCOY, Belinda L and Douglas M HOULE, 26 May 1984 Hudson, NH
MCCOY, Clifford and Jessie RELATION, 07 Apr 1937 Billerica, MA
MCCOY, Dana W and Lillian A DOHERTY, 20 May 1972 Hudson, NH
MCCOY, Ella A and Washburn CLARK, 29 Jan 1874 Hudson, NH
MCCOY, Ella Alice and Frederick CONNELL, 03 May 1931 Chelmsford, MA
MCCOY, Ernest E and Mildred M WHEELER, 30 Apr 1946 Hudson, NH
MCCOY, Gertrude M and Arthur F MESSIER, 27 Jul 1940 Nashua, NH
MCCOY, H R and E A WOODWARD, 04 Oct 1916 Nashua, NH
   James McCoy (Boston, MA) & Emma Richards (Manchester, NH)
   Frank A Woodward(Warner, NH) & Carrie Fellows (Newbury, NH)
MCCOY, James and Eliza STREETER, 26 Aug 1867
MCCOY, James and Polly MARSHALL, 17 Mar 1814
MCCOY, James and Eliza A STREETER, 26 Aug 1867
MCCOY, James and Emma C RICHARDS, 22 Dec 1868 Hudson, NH
MCCOY, James II and Emma C RICHARDS, 22 Dec 1868
MCCOY, James O and Jennie C SMITH, 16 Aug 1897 Hudson, NH
   James McCoy
   George L Smith & Clara O Stevens
MCCOY, James O and Lena M BARNARD, 20 Jun 1943 Nashua, NH
MCCOY, Mary E and Arthur W HASELTON, 30 Dec 1891 Hudson, NH
   Jas McCoy (Boston, MA) & Emma C Richards
   Geo W Haselton(Hudson, NH) & Lora Poor (Montpelier, VT)
MCCOY, Michael J and Diane J LAVOIE, 08 Jan 1984 Hudson, NH
MCCOY, Mildred E and Walter J CONNORS, 25 Sep 1948 Hudson, NH
MCCOY, Norman C and Janet A DUBOIS, 16 Aug 1975 Hudson, NH
MCCOY, Polly and James MELVIN, 24 Mar 1801
MCCOY, Thelma E and Merrill M Jr IVES, 14 Jul 1944 Hudson, NH
MCCOY, Thomas E and Nancy J LAPPEN, 13 Jun 1970 Pelham, NH
MCCRADY, Brenda G and David B CROOKS, 20 Nov 1971 Hudson, NH
MCCRADY, Donald R and Denise M GASKA, 04 Jul 1980 Nashua, NH
MCCRADY, Douglas B and Lucinda M JACKSON, 19 May 1978 Nashua, NH
MCCRADY, Helen L and Ernest HIGTON, 08 Sep 1979 Nashua, NH
MCCRADY, Karen J and Stephen C HOLMES, 12 Mar 1977 Nashua, NH
MCCRADY, Kathy D and Donald W WILSON, 28 Jul 1973 Nashua, NH
MCCRUM, James E and Sharyl P LEIGH, 27 Feb 1983 Hudson, NH
MCCULLOUGH, Gary T and Jeanne L CORMIER, 25 Jan 1974 Nashua, NH
MCCULLOUGH, Mildred L and Harold M WELLS, 16 Sep 1929 Hudson, NH
MCCUTCHEON, Joyce P and Bruce A CARROLL, 25 Nov 1971 Nashua, NH
MCDERMOT, James W and Claudya KING, 04 Oct 1975 Salem, NH
MCDERMOTT, Mary and Warren J GILCREASE, 29 Sep 1924 Nashua, NH
MCDONALD, Alice and Henry PARSLOE, 19 Mar 1930 Hudson, NH
MCDONALD, Annie J and Ralph S TRUFANT, 18 Oct 1920 Nashua, NH
MCDONALD, Carolyn and William A SCHUPE, 31 Oct 1947 Hudson, NH
MCDONALD, Even and Maud CAMPBELL, 08 Apr 1901 Londonderry, NH
   John McDonald (Nova Scotia) & Maggie McIntoch (Nova Scotia)
   Lyman Campbell(Nova Scotia) & Mary A Ross (Nova Scotia)
MCDONALD, Jacqueline and William M TATE, 19 Sep 1971 Nashua, NH
MCDONALD, Joseph D and Leslie A SIMARD, 06 Apr 1974 Hudson, NH
MCDONALD, Timothy J Jr&Geraldine MESSENGER, 18 Aug 1979 Londonderry
MCDOUGALL, Barbara A and John W DONALDSON, 10 Aug 1963 Hudson, NH
MCEALHERN, Anne and John KOSSIVAS, 02 Aug 1938 Hudson, NH
MCELROY, Clarence D and Mary A DION, 20 Oct 1928 Nashua, NH
MCEWEN, Henry D and Ina L PACKARD, 07 Aug 1938 Hudson, NH
MCFADDEN, William C Jr and Dorothy A SILVA, 10 Aug 1963 Hudson, NH
MCGAFFIHAN, Margaret and Thomas D SHORT, 07 Mar 1937 Hudson, NH
MCGANDY, Michelle and William F METZGER, 02 Apr 1982 Hudson, NH

HUDSON, NH MARRIAGES

MCGANN, Henry and Nellie SARGENT, 16 Jun 1917 Hudson, NH
MCGARY, Doreen M & Gerald G KIRKPATRICK, 15 Feb 1974 Litchfield, NH
MCGEE, Cynthia J and Gary HOWE, 19 Feb 1966 Hudson, NH
MCGEE, Lauria F and Gilles RAYMOND, 04 Jul 1981 Hudson, NH
MCGEE, Pearl A and Samuel L KIMBALL, 06 Feb 1918 Hudson, NH
MCGILLIVRAY, Georgina T and Robert W ROY, 05 Jan 1946 Hudson, NH
MCGILLIVRAY, John A and Lillian F SMITH, 11 Feb 1972 Hudson, NH
MCGILVARY, George N and Anna P LOVEJOY, 17 Dec 1859
MCGIRT, Barbara J and Jay W CATLAND, 14 Aug 1981 Hollis, NH
MCGLORY, Scott W and Etta I BAKER, 05 Apr 1902 Hudson, NH
   R L McGlory & Julia Nutter
   Henry J Squires & Mary Nash
MCGONIGLE, E Natalie and Wayne F STANLEY, 02 Oct 1982 Hudson, NH
MCGOVERN, Mary Ann and Earl CHAFIN, 15 Mar 1980 Nashua, NH
MCGOWAN, Carol A and John D FLORE, 07 Aug 1982 Hudson, NH
MCGRANAGHAN, Peter & Kelly Leigh TOWER, 30 Nov 1984 Londonderry, NH
MCGRATH, Christie P and Gloria R LEBLANC, 30 Jan 1977 Hudson, NH
MCGRATH, Elaine F and Leonard R NIQUETTE, 03 Jul 1965 Hudson, NH
MCGRATH, Gloria R and John J FAWCETT, 23 Oct 1982 Hudson, NH
MCGRAW, Alden D and Diane THERIAULT, 15 May 1982 Brookline, NH
MCGRAW, Ellen A and William D NOLEN, 15 Oct 1977 Hudson, NH
MCGRAW, Michael R and Gail K SPARKS, 21 Jul 1984 Hudson, NH
MCGRAW, Richard E and Esther B RUITER, 03 Sep 1955 Hudson, NH
MCGREGOR, Betsy and Mark P CORMIER, 31 Mar 1984 Goffstown, NH
MCGUINNESS, Sharon M and Allan J GRUND, 23 Aug 1969 Hudson, NH
MCGUINNESS, Shawn P and Mary Louise BUXTON, 12 Aug 1978 Hudson, NH
MCGUINNESS, Theresa B and Michael F O'NEIL, 23 Jun 1984 Hudson, NH
MCGUIRE, Barbara A and Stephen M HOWE, 05 Sep 1970 Nashua, NH
MCGUIRE, Betty L and Michael C WALKER, 20 Jun 1981 Hudson, NH
MCGUIRE, Dana L and Jean M BERNIER, 10 Mar 1973 Nashua, NH
MCGUIRE, Dorothy A and Joseph A McKINNON, 22 Jul 1949 Hudson, NH
MCGUIRE, James W and Madeline N STEFFENS, 19 Jul 1976 Hudson, NH
MCGUIRE, James W Jr and Ida M MARTIN, 01 Aug 1951 Hudson, NH
MCGUIRE, Margaret and Fred C KADE, 28 Mar 1919 Nashua, NH
MCHUGH, Agnes and Clyde MAYES, 02 Sep 1942 Hudson, NH
MCHUGH, Debra A and James A NORMANDIN, 20 Oct 1984 Wilton, NH
MCHUGH, Jean and William J PUTNAM, 31 Oct 1930 Nashua, NH
MCHUGH, Mary Ann J and Lawrence J JENKINS, 16 May 1981 Hudson, NH
MCHUGH, Patricia I and Gary W CHAMBERS, 28 Aug 1976 Hudson, NH
MCILVEEN, Catherine and David A REYNOLDS, 03 Sep 1977 Hudson, NH
MCILVEEN, Donna M and James S STONE, 30 Jun 1973 Hudson, NH
MCILVEEN, John M and Barbara J LANDRY, 14 Apr 1984 Hudson, NH
MCINTIRE, Nelson Les and Dorothy JENNEY, 04 Dec 1933 Hudson, NH
MCINTIRE, William and Lucy BAKER, 22 May 1893 Hudson, NH
   John McIntire (Canada) & Marion Wells (Canada)
   E Baker(New York) & Josephine Fagto (New York)
MCINTOSH, JoAnne B and Briggs GREYWACZ, 17 Feb 1979 Hudson, NH
MCINTOSH, Leonard A and Cecile B RODIER, 12 Jun 1943 Nashua, NH
MCINTOSH, Stephen W and Cynthia L BROWN, 06 Nov 1982 Hudson, NH
MCKAY, Christine and Edmund A ORDZIE, 24 Jun 1972 Pelham, NH
MCKAY, Marjorie and Winton S BRYAR, 02 Feb 1934 Nashua, NH
MCKEAN, Joseph and Sally BLODGETT, 01 Apr 1812
MCKEATING, Carmel P and Richard R METRANO, 28 Jul 1974 Hudson, NH
MCKEE, Carol C and Francis TOTTE, 16 Mar 1962 Hudson, NH
MCKEE, David O and Grace CHAPPELLE, 07 Feb 1935 Hudson, NH
MCKENNA, Paul D and Beverly J AUGER, 28 Jul 1981 Londonderry, NH
MCKENNEY, Allen R and Linda A LEAOR, 02 Sep 1978 Hudson, NH
MCKENNEY, Henry P and Gloria E BOULEY, 13 Jan 1949 Nashua, NH
MCKENNEY, William H and Cheryl L GREENWOOD, 20 Nov 1969 Dover, NH
MCKENZIE, Joseph W and Edna M LEWIS, 09 Apr 1947 Hudson, NH

HUDSON,NH MARRIAGES

MCKINLEY, David M and Sandra Ann BEAULIEU, 04 Jun 1977 Nashua, NH
MCKINNEY, Lora E and Nicholas G PANAGOULIS, 04 Oct 1952 Hudson, NH
MCKINNEY, Paul G and Sandra L HAIGHT, 06 Nov 1982 Nashua, NH
MCKINNON, Donald B and Anne M EVANICO, 16 Oct 1982 Gorham, NH
MCKINNON, Girard A and Sheryl A MATTHEWS, 31 Aug 1979 Hudson, NH
MCKINNON, Joseph A and Dorothy A McGUIRE, 22 Jul 1949 Hudson, NH
MCKINNON, Mary T and Gary M MENDES, 06 Sep 1980 Pelham, NH
MCKINNON, Sheryl A and Steven A FORKEY, 01 Jul 1983 Hudson, NH
MCKUSICK, Carrie E and Horace H ACKERMAN, 12 Oct 1897 Hudson, NH
   F C McKusick & Viola Corson
   Wm H Ackerman & Henrietta Lane
MCLAIN, Deborah K and John David FLYNN, 15 Aug 1981 Hudson, NH
MCLAREN, Edward J and Marie R OLIVIERA, 02 Jan 1949 Hudson, NH
MCLAREN, James W and Dorothy R SIROIS, 19 May 1961 Nashua, NH
MCLAUGHLIN, Faye A and Donald M FULLER, 23 Jun 1969 Hudson, NH
MCLAUGHLIN, Jacqueline and Paul L LAVOIE, 31 Jul 1982 Hudson, NH
MCLAUGHLIN, John R and Faye A McCARTHY, 25 Sep 1965 Nashua, NH
MCLAUGHLIN, John R and Adele M TAILLEUR, 20 Feb 1983 Hudson, NH
MCLAUGHLIN, Paul R and Barbara MONTGOMERY, 10 Sep 1949 Nashua, NH
MCLAUGHLIN, Sandra J and David A GRAYDEN, 18 Dec 1982 Nashua, NH
MCLAVEY, Bruce R and Sandra L POWELL, 20 Nov 1971 Nashua, NH
MCLAVEY, Cynthia V and Stanley O KULESZA, 16 Aug 1969 Hudson, NH
MCLAVEY, Elmer R and Virginia J ALLGROVE, 19 Jun 1943 Hudson, NH
MCLAVEY, Geraldine and Charles G DEARBORN, 01 Aug 1953 Hudson, NH
MCLAVEY, Virginia L and Harland D TAYLOR, 24 Jun 1956 Hudson, NH
MCLEAN, Kent O and Doris E EATON, 14 Apr 1939 Hudson, NH
MCLELLAN, Dora and Maurice A BRADLEY, 28 Jun 1930 Nashua, NH
MCLEOD, Brian N and Cheryl L ROTH, 04 Jun 1983 Litchfield, NH
MCLEOD, Jeanette L and Alphonse J LAGASSE, 06 Jul 1946 Hudson, NH
MCLLACKY, Kathleen A and Jonathan P SMITH, 27 Dec 1974 Hudson, NH
MCLLARKY, Patricia A and Robert J GROVES, 08 Aug 1975 Pelham, NH
MCMAHON, Shane P and Manon F FAUTEUX, 29 Aug 1981 Hudson, NH
MCMANUS, Margaret I & Daniel W SULLIVAN, 16 Nov 1963 Merrimack, NH
MCMANUS, Paul F and Mary E WIEGMANN, 08 Jul 1976 Nashua, NH
MCMASTER, Catherine and John J McPARTLEN, 04 Sep 1948 Hudson, NH
MCMULLEN, Edward J and Beatrice BERRY, 04 May 1946 Hudson, NH
MCNALLY, Paul T and Deborah S BERTRAND, 19 Feb 1972 Nashua, NH
MCNEIL, David A and Margaret J REGAN, 26 Nov 1971 Nashua, NH
MCNEIL, Frank E and Sharon L PLANK, 30 Jun 1973 Nashua, NH
MCNEIL, Helen V and James J DEMPSEY, 11 Jun 1949 Hudson, NH
MCNEIL, Marilyn D and Richard BROUILLETTE, 03 May 1947 Hudson, NH
MCNEIL, Thomas W and Judith A GAGNON, 15 Jan 1971 Nashua, NH
MCNEIL, Vincent and Susan E CUMMINS, 20 Oct 1979 Londonderry, NH
MCNEILL, Eileen F and Michael O'CONNELL, 01 Nov 1975 Nashua, NH
MCNEILL, John D and Mary E LACOY, 25 Apr 1978 Nashua, NH
MCNICHOLAS, Michael J & Dorothy M DAVIDSON, 19 Feb 1949 Hudson, NH
MCNTYRE, William and Alice LUCIER, 30 Jan 1901 Nashua, NH
   John McNtyre (Canada) & Maryann Welch (Canada)
   Lucier(Canada) & Mrs Ledaux (Canada)
MCPARTLEN, John J and Catherine McMASTER, 04 Sep 1948 Hudson, NH
MCPHERSON, John J and Laurie J PHANEUF, 17 Nov 1979 Hudson, NH
MCPHERSON, Levi C and R E FIELD, 29 Apr 1849
MCQUADE, E Louise and Bernard G FIFIELD, 09 Sep 1978 Litchfield, NH
MCQUAID, Barton M and Louise C CROSBY, 06 Jan 1934 Hudson, NH
MCQUAID, Diane M and Norman D Jr GAUTHIER, 19 Feb 1982 Hudson, NH
MCQUAID, John E and Rosalie M BROWN, 25 Sep 1983 Nashua, NH
MCQUESTEN, Charles L and Nancy R BROOKS, 16 Apr 1967 Nashua, NH
MCQUESTEN, Daniel and Eunice R WRIGHT, 07 Jun 1882 Hudson, NH
   Simon McQuesten (Hudson, NH) & Rhoda Glover (Hudson, NH)
   Lorenzo Wright(Maine) & Nancy Robbins (Nashua, NH)

HUDSON,NH MARRIAGES

MCQUESTEN, Esther and Joseph LANDREY, 05 Jul 1880 Hudson, NH
MCQUESTEN, Fred P and Linda D SMITH, 17 Oct 1981 Nashua, NH
MCQUESTEN, Mary J and George HIDDEN, 10 Nov 1861
MCQUESTEN, Mary J and George KIDDER, 10 Nov 1861
MCQUESTEN, Phyllis A & Richard R REILLY, 27 Jun 1959 Litchfield, NH
MCQUESTEN, Ralph and Margaret GLOVER, 29 Apr 1824
MCQUESTEN, Robert and Almira S PRATT, 16 Jul 1854
MCQUESTEN, Simon and Rhoda GLOVER, 23 Oct 1825
MCQUESTEN, Susanna and John H MERRILL, 02 Jul 1835
MCTIGUE, Francis and Marguerite PERRY, 26 Dec 1935 Hudson, NH
MCVICAR, Robert J and Jane E BOOLBA, 02 Apr 1983 Northwood, NH
MCVICCAR, Loraine A and Horace C REED, 17 Oct 1941 Nashua, NH
MCWHA, Robert John and Delores Ann FRANCO, 27 Feb 1981 Nashua, NH
MCWILLIAMS, Constance and Paul W GENEST, 27 Dec 1980 Hudson, NH
MCWILLIAMS, Pansy E and Walter N SMITH, 14 Sep 1928 Nashua, NH
MEAD, Harry J and Doris E WHITE, 24 Nov 1923 Manchester, NH
MEAD, Minnie Ola and William H GROVES, 22 Oct 1902 Hudson, NH
   J B Farwell & H E J Chesley
   Robert Groves & Elizabeth Boyle
MEADOR, Gary L and Catherine DELANEY, 17 Sep 1983 Nashua, NH
MEADOWS, David J and Jane D SIROIS, 08 Feb 1975 Hudson, NH
MEADY, Jean and Charles W HARVEY, 19 Aug 1941 Nashua, NH
MEARS, Sharon L and Roland F Jr TIEBOR, 02 Apr 1971 Nashua, NH
MECKLEY, Thomas A and Meredith S MELHADO, 25 Nov 1977 Hudson, NH
MEDEIROS, Alva F and Hedrick P SHERMAK, 22 Feb 1948 Hudson, NH
MEDINA, Ann P and John W JENNINGS, 22 Jan 1949 Hudson, NH
MEEDEN, Ronald V and Mary A THOMAS, 27 Sep 1980 Hudson, NH
MEEHAN, Teresa M and Gerard A BOUCHER, 15 Jun 1946 Nashua, NH
MEHRON, Kathleen M and Peter A KAYROS, 30 Aug 1974 Nashua, NH
MEIER, Ralph R and Sharon A ELWOOD, 19 Jun 1976 Londonderry, NH
MEIER, Robert G and Nancy L WARDWELL, 14 Mar 1964 Hudson, NH
MEISCHEID, Richard Charles & Cynthia A COE, 14 Mar 1981 Hudson, NH
MELANSON, Bernard F Jr and Helen G KOZUSZEK, 19 May 1984 Nashua, NH
MELANSON, Nancy L and Richard E OLSON, 17 Apr 1965 Seabrook, NH
MELANSON, Richard D and Donna A LAINE, 21 May 1983 Hudson, NH
MELBRIDIAN, Highgory and Dan KOCHAKIAN, 30 Jun 1906 Hudson, NH
   Aikel Nallridian & Anna Lakacian
   C Kochakian & V Molfaian
MELDREM, JoAnn R and Alan M III SUTHERLAND, 04 Apr 1981 Hudson, NH
MELENDY, Pearl and Clifford S WOODS, 25 Dec 1916 Hudson, NH
   Charles Melendy (Brookline, NH) & Eva Hutchinson (Milford, NH)
   John V Woods(Hollis, NH) & Eliza Clifford (Colebrook, NH)
MELHADO, Meredith S and Thomas A MECKLEY, 25 Nov 1977 Hudson, NH
MELLEN, John A and Janice L ADAMS, 31 Jan 1970 Keene, NH
MELLEN, Ruth J and Bernis ADKINS, 03 Aug 1957 Hudson, NH
MELLEN, William H and Hannah D ABBOTT, 29 Oct 1892 Hudson, NH
   Hugh Mellen (Nova Scotia) & Emma Hutchinson (N Reading, MA)
   Geo H Abbott & Rose Abbott
MELLIS, Susie E and A A BODEN, 22 Nov 1898 Hudson, NH
   George F Mellis & Mary B Adams
   Henry J Boden & Mary J Drumm
MELOFSKY, Karyn E and Antonios TOUPLIKIOTIS, 28 Apr 1976 Hudson, NH
MELTON, Grace N and Bruce SNAVELY, 02 Jun 1978 Litchfield, NH
MELVIN, Hazel B and Guy H WOO S, 27 Mar 1918 Nashua, NH
MELVIN, J Estelle and Duncan C MATTHEWS, 10 Nov 1896 Hudson, NH
   T D Melvin & Julia Hopkins (W Trenton, ME)
   William Matthews & Amy Hoyt (N Brunswick)
MELVIN, James and Polly McCOY, 24 Mar 1801
MELVIN, Jerome A and Mabel S BUTTRICK, 24 Dec 1891 Hudson, NH
   Tolford D Melvin (Hudson, NH) & Julia G (Hopkins)

HUDSON,NH MARRIAGES

    Clifton E Buttrick(Wentworth) & Marietta Haselton (Hudson, NH)
MELVIN, John and Betsey SMITH, 20 Apr 1797
MELVIN, John and Betty SMITH, 20 Apr 1797
MELVIN, Philip and Janna SMITH, 16 Nov 1797
MELVIN, Reuben and Mary BULTER, 20 Oct 1846
MELVIN, Thomas F and Ruth L KING, 22 Sep 1944 Hartford, CT
MENARD, Blanche E and Joseph KASHULINES, 18 Aug 1919 Nashua, NH
MENARD, Frank R and Carol A SUMRALL, 06 May 1978 Hudson, NH
MENARD, Gabriel R Jr and Virginia C BOULEY, 03 Dec 1960 Hudson, NH
MENDES, Bernard and Marjorie J BOULEY, 01 May 1948 Hudson, NH
MENDES, Gary M and Mary T McKINNON, 06 Sep 1980 Pelham, NH
MENDES, Michael A and Frances E HALL, 12 Oct 1980 Hudson, NH
MENTER, Alen S and Ida M TAYLOR, 20 Jan 1876 Hudson, NH
MERCER, Warner P & Jacqueline COUTURE, 18 Jun 1983 New Ipswich, NH
MERCHANT, Allen I and Phyllis E HOWE, 14 May 1966 Hudson, NH
MERCHANT, Jane Marie and Ronald L KLEINER, 24 Aug 1974 Nashua, NH
MERCHANT, Robert and Elaine A MURPHY, 14 Dec 1957 Hudson, NH
MERCHANT, William J and Darlene B PIPER, 04 Sep 1976 Nashua, NH
MERCIER, Barbara An and Steven J DONNELLY, 10 Oct 1981 Hudson, NH
MERCIER, Inez H and Peter P DUNSKY, 12 Sep 1947 Hudson, NH
MERCIER, Irene I and Alfred Z VANIER, 29 Jan 1925 Hudson, NH
MERCIER, Leanne I and Glenn E BOULEY, 24 Aug 1957 Hudson, NH
MERCIER, Leonard G and Carollee LATULIPPE, 01 May 1976 Nashua, NH
MERCIER, Martha P and William E WUNDERLICH, 29 Aug 1970 Hudson, NH
MERCIER, Normand A and Ann L OUELLETTE, 05 Sep 1970 Nashua, NH
MERILL, Ethel G and Basil W SHEPHERD, 05 Dec 1917 Barrington
MERRIFIELD, Curtis J and Shirley A GARD, 30 Apr 1970 Candia, NH
MERRIFIELD, Paula J & William F BERTHOLDT, 30 Jul 1971 Gilford, NH
MERRILL, Amos and Mehitabel SMITH, 25 Dec 1800
MERRILL, Amos and Mehitible SMITH, 25 Dec 1800
MERRILL, Arthur E & Leona M STONE, 23 Jan 1932 Peterborough, NH
MERRILL, Barbara and Mitchell W KOPACZ, 08 Jun 1981 Hudson, NH
MERRILL, Benjamin and Sarah KAHN, 20 Jul 1820
MERRILL, Benjamin and Sarah EATON, 25 Jul 1820
MERRILL, Benjamin A and Mary J WINN, 23 Nov 1843
MERRILL, Betsey and Lewis BUTLER, 06 Mar 1816
MERRILL, Betty Brad and Ephraim Jr CUMMINGS, 08 Sep 1768
MERRILL, Bonita L and Samuel F MILNE, 14 Aug 1971 Amherst, NH
MERRILL, Brenda L and Dennis B REED, 10 Apr 1971 Hudson, NH
MERRILL, Bruce K and Helen F NEVILLE, 04 May 1957 Ctr Barnstead, NH
MERRILL, David and Susan P YOUNG, 28 Mar 1969 Salem, NH
MERRILL, David and Mary GREELEY, 12 Oct 1824
MERRILL, Deborah J & Maurice R Jr LAROUCHE, 25 Sep 1971 Hudson, NH
MERRILL, Denice M and Alan C ROBERTS, 01 Jul 1972 Hudson, NH
MERRILL, G Elaine and Charles W Jr HOLT, 12 May 1942 Hudson, NH
MERRILL, George A and Emma B WINN, 02 Oct 1890 Hudson, NH
    James B Merrill (Hudson, NH) & Persis A Winn (Hudson, NH)
    William F Winn(Hudson, NH) & Lucy Richardson (Wilmington)
MERRILL, Harold F and Edna M HILLS, 05 Sep 1948 Londonderry, NH
MERRILL, Hattie J and Daniel ROHER, 06 Sep 1855
MERRILL, Henry A and S Lizzie GRANT, 15 Dec 1869
MERRILL, Henry A and S Lizzie GRANT, 01 Jan 1870 Lowell, MA
MERRILL, Isaac and Olive MERRILL, 25 Feb 1779
MERRILL, James E and Etta S MARBLE, 05 Sep 1888 Nashua, NH
    James B Merrill (Hudson, NH) & Persis A Winn (Hudson, NH)
    Eben Marble(Poland, ME) & Sarah G Jewett (Pepperell, MA)
MERRILL, James P and Persis A WINN, 21 Jan 1857
MERRILL, Joanna C and Reuben GREELEY, 27 Nov 1817
MERRILL, John and Rebecca COLBURN, 26 Feb 1818
MERRILL, John H and Susanna McQUESTEN, 02 Jul 1835

HUDSON, NH MARRIAGES

MERRILL, John S and Claire T PICARD, 03 Sep 1966 Hudson, NH
MERRILL, Judith A and Joseph P SNAY, 18 Jan 1975 Nashua, NH
MERRILL, Karl E and J M JEANNOTTE, 21 Jun 1916 Nashua, NH
  James E Merrill (Hudson, NH) & Etta S Marble (Nashua, NH)
  Cornelius Jeannotte(Bellows Falls, VT) & Rosamond Heaton (Lyme, NH)
MERRILL, Leona M and Edwin E ROWELL, 06 Sep 1938 Lowell, MA
MERRILL, Linda M and Paul N Jr COSSETTE, 25 Jun 1976 Hudson, NH
MERRILL, Lorraine M and Ernest R LEVESQUE, 31 May 1947 Nashua, NH
MERRILL, Lydia and Asa RICHARDSON, 22 Feb 1798
MERRILL, Mary A and Henry C ROBINSON, 07 Oct 1872 Ayer, MA
MERRILL, Maurice D and Gertrude A COLBURN, 12 Oct 1945 Hudson, NH
MERRILL, Natalie D and Gary H GENDRON, 28 Apr 1973 Hudson, NH
MERRILL, Nathaniel and Olive LUND, 25 Feb 1767
MERRILL, Nathaniel and Olive LUND, 25 Feb 1761
MERRILL, Olive and Isaac MERRILL, 25 Feb 1779
MERRILL, Olive and John H SMITH, 07 Dec 1815
MERRILL, Otis A and Maria J MOORE, 15 Dec 1869
MERRILL, Rachel and Robert DOUGLASS, 22 Nov 1810
MERRILL, Robert B and Terry Lee HUDACEK, 28 Oct 1972 Hudson, NH
MERRILL, Rosamond H and Frank A NUTTING, 05 Oct 1940 Hudson, NH
MERRILL, Ruth and Richard CUTLER, 06 Apr 1789
MERRILL, Ruth and Richard CUTTER, 06 Apr 1789
MERRILL, Sandra L and Roland J LAMOTHE, 05 Sep 1970 Nashua, NH
MERRILL, Sarah B and Charles L SPALDING, 07 Jan 1886 Hudson, NH
  William T Merrill (Hudson, NH) & Lucy A Byam (Hudson, NH)
  Reuben Spalding(Hudson, NH) & Sarah A Lahon (Nashua, NH)
MERRILL, Sarah B and Charles L SPAULDING, 07 Jan 1886 Hudson, NH
MERRILL, Theodore and Mary FLETCHER, 13 Nov 1783
MERRILL, Theodore and Marcy FLETCHER, 13 Nov 1783
MERRILL, William T and Lucy A BYAM, 28 Apr 1856
MERRILL, Winnebel and Joseph O LAMSON, 24 Aug 1922 Salem Depot, NH
MERRY, J Jeannet and Carl P LOVEJOY, 14 Jun 1947 Nashua, NH
MESSENGER, Geraldine&Timothy J Jr McDONALD, 18 Aug 1979 Londonderry
MESSENGER, Susan Jean and Mehrdad LOGHMANI, 11 Jun 1982 Nashua, NH
MESSER, Chandler and Angeline S ROBINSON, 31 Dec 1856
MESSER, Julie A and Michael T MAHER, 01 May 1975 Hollis, NH
MESSER, Orrin and Bell C SANBORN, 01 May 1879 Manchester, NH
  Frederick Messer (New London) & Martha
  Alvin Sanborn & Annie E (Wilmot, NH)
MESSERY, Mary L and John C THOMPSON, 05 Feb 1966 Pelham, NH
MESSIER, Arthur F and Gertrude M McCOY, 27 Jul 1940 Nashua, NH
MESSIER, Diane G and Allan M SANTOS, 06 Aug 1977 Hudson, NH
MESSIER, Paul F and Shirley B CUMMINGS, 22 Jun 1957 Dracut, MA
MESURAY, Frank W and Ruth L REA, 22 Sep 1917 Hudson, NH
METIVIER, Mary Lou and Wilfred A DUBUC, 31 Dec 1974 Nashua, NH
METRANO, Laura M and William R WINTERS, 29 Jun 1980 Pelham, NH
METRANO, Richard R and Carmel P McKEATING, 28 Jul 1974 Hudson, NH
METROS, John G and Phyllis M MORGANTI, 12 Oct 1959 Hudson, NH
METTA, Richard N and Lynn Carol PAQUETTE, 23 Nov 1984 Hudson, NH
METZGER, William F and Michelle McGANDY, 02 Apr 1982 Hudson, NH
MEUNIER, Harvey and Esther I ARVISAIS, 18 Dec 1948 Hudson, NH
MEZIKOFSKY, Rebecca R and Nathan LEBOWITZ, 26 Jul 1933 Nashua, NH
MICARI, Joseph and Mary FESTA, 28 Oct 1950 Hudson, NH
MICHAEL, Margaret J and Thomas Mat RIKKOLA, 23 Jun 1937 Hudson, NH
MICHAUD, Anatole J and Ethelwyn M SIMPSON, 21 Jul 1953 Hudson, NH
MICHAUD, Aurele J and Beatrice BURELLE, 22 Jun 1935 Nashua, NH
MICHAUD, Christine and Shawn E LAROCHE, 14 Aug 1982 Hudson, NH
MICHAUD, Claude I and Linda M PORTER, 11 Oct 1963 Hudson, NH
MICHAUD, Estelle I and Paul LANDRY, 12 Jun 1943 Nashua, NH
MICHAUD, Gilbert W and Mary Jane MORRISON, 26 Nov 1975 Nashua, NH

HUDSON,NH MARRIAGES

MICHAUD, Joseph L and Mabel Gertrude SMITH, 07 Sep 1925 Nashua, NH
MICHAUD, Louis J and Noella T DUMAIS, 06 May 1961 Hudson, NH
MICHAUD, Marie L and Donald F CASSALIA, 19 Aug 1984 Manchester, NH
MICHAUD, Olive B and Robert L DAIGLE, 27 Jun 1981 Hudson, NH
MICHAUD, Paul R and Sally E SANDLER, 31 Aug 1963 Hudson, NH
MICHAUD, Paul R and Nancy L LEVESQUE, 04 Apr 1980 Nashua, NH
MICHAUD, Roland G and Barbara CARROLL, 05 Oct 1957 Hudson, NH
MICHAUD, Shirley A and Daniel A OUELLETTE, 04 Mar 1967 Hudson, NH
MICHAUD, Tamye and Richard E CARON, 02 Jul 1977 Hudson, NH
MICHAUD, Theresa L and John J ALUKONIS, 06 Nov 1954 Nashua, NH
MICHIE, Charles J and Joann LANDRY, 27 Jan 1967 Nashua, NH
MIDDLEMISS, Steven F and Lee Ann RODGERS, 21 Aug 1982 Hudson, NH
MIDDLETON, David F and Mary T SAMPSON, 30 Jul 1983 Hudson, NH
MIELE, Gloria J and William G FOLEY, 26 Sep 1981 Hudson, NH
MIGNEAULT, Elaine L and Richard A BURTON, 10 Oct 1971 Nashua, NH
MIGNEAULT, Henry C and Jean F GAMACHE, 11 Sep 1965 Hudson, NH
MIGNEAULT, Jeanine S and Armand W LEDOUX, 11 Apr 1953 Nashua, NH
MIGNEAULT, Marie A I and William E BARRET, 29 Jun 1922 Nashua, NH
MIGNEAULT, Morris and Helen R MARCLEY, 11 Jun 1923 Nashua, NH
MIHELIA, Charlene J and David A REITAN, 10 Sep 1983 Nashua, NH
MIHELIS, Rose-Ann and Michael P COROSA, 01 Jun 1974 Hudson, NH
MILARDO, Louis R Jr and Diane T CYR, 17 Jul 1976 Nashua, NH
MILES, Aubrey M and Barbara MILES, 22 Nov 1945 Hudson, NH
MILES, Barbara and Aubrey M MILES, 22 Nov 1945 Hudson, NH
MILES, Charles and Nancy DOTY, 01 Feb 1887 Hudson, NH
   William Miles (Maine) & Hannah Scates (Berwick, ME)
   Samuel Shrier(Germany) & Eliza Cota (Canada)
MILES, Louisa D and William E LEONARD, 20 Sep 1846
MILLAR, Milagros and Michael MALIAR, 10 Jan 1981 Hudson, NH
MILLARD, Albert J and Florence A BOUCHER, 20 Nov 1969 Nashua, NH
MILLARD, Coleen A and Michael G MITCHELL, 01 Nov 1968 Nashua, NH
MILLARD, Francis H and Teresa L BURKE, 02 Dec 1949 Hudson, NH
MILLER, Benjamin P and Nancy ROULETTE, 23 Jan 1855
MILLER, Betty M and Geo W Jr SPAULDING, 17 Jan 1949 Hudson, NH
MILLER, David B and Patricia A COOPER, 07 May 1977 Nashua, NH
MILLER, Fred W and Pauline R SHAPIRO, 01 Oct 1978 Nashua, NH
MILLER, George F and Phyllis HANDY, 11 Aug 1938 Hudson, NH
MILLER, Geraldine and Laurent R FOSTER, 03 Mar 1956 Nashua, NH
MILLER, Jennifer J and John G DUBE, 20 Oct 1984 Nashua, NH
MILLER, Joseph R and Betty A BOULERISSE, 13 Nov 1965 Nashua, NH
MILLER, Judy M and Stephen D BERG, 16 Jan 1971 Hudson, NH
MILLER, Karen A and Charles A CAMPBELL, 08 Oct 1982 Amherst, NH
MILLER, Kathleen and Clifford J FLOOD, 06 Nov 1982 Hudson, NH
MILLER, Kathleen A and Lionel C Sr CLOUTIER, 10 Nov 1978 Hudson, NH
MILLER, Lenore A and Albert A NAPLES, 21 Jun 1943 Nashua, NH
MILLER, Leslie J and Stephen J KLEIN, 14 Jun 1979 Nashua, NH
MILLER, Marlene C and Leo P BRIERE, 09 Aug 1952 Hudson, NH
MILLER, Mary D and Donald F SWENSEN, 07 Dec 1980 Nashua, NH
MILLER, Mary J and Edward L CROSS, 05 Oct 1851
MILLER, Michael Ja and Sharon Ann BOULE, 17 Dec 1984 Nashua, NH
MILLER, Neil E and Barbara J CAMPBELL, 11 Nov 1950 Hudson, NH
MILLER, Robert A and Sylvia E COTE, 25 Jun 1955 Hudson, NH
MILLER, Robert J and Nancy E LANDRY, 17 Jul 1960 Nashua, NH
MILLER, Robert L and Josephine GEORGES, 07 Nov 1974 Nashua, NH
MILLER, Royal E III and Kathleen L FERBERT, 07 Jun 1969 Hudson, NH
MILLER, Theresa J and Richard A BENOIT, 27 Jul 1963 Hudson, NH
MILLER, Violet F and Clyde M BAILEY, 29 Nov 1934 Hudson, NH
MILLER, William J and Jennifer L JURKOWSKI, 27 Oct 1979 Hudson, NH
MILLER, William W and Rebecca E PROCTOR, 02 Apr 1848
MILLETT, Diane E and Lewis E III WOODAMAN, 07 Sep 1968 Hudson, NH

HUDSON,NH MARRIAGES

MILLETT, Everett L and Ina E CAMPBELL, 21 Aug 1936 Nashua, NH
MILLETT, Herbert A and Marjorie R COLLINS, 30 Jul 1944 Nashua, NH
MILLETT, Jeremiah and Margaret LINDSAY, 06 Jun 1856
MILLETT, Joan E and Robert V ZELONIS, 14 Aug 1965 Nashua, NH
MILLETT, Joseph C and Sarah L FLETCHER, 25 Oct 1861
MILLETT, Norma H and Nelson E HEROUX, 10 Sep 1960 Nashua, NH
MILLETT, Sherman D Jr and Sylvia R RUSSELL, 05 Oct 1963 Hudson, NH
MILLIGAN, Barbara and Earl L Jr HAUAR, 14 Oct 1946 Hudson, NH
MILLIKEN, Frank S and Gay MONETTE, 16 Mar 1930 Nashua, NH
MILLIKEN, Roy E Jr and Rose Marie BRESCIA, 24 Jun 1953 Nashua, NH
MILLINA, Bennie and Phyllis POLAK, 21 Jan 1944 Nashua, NH
MILLINA, Roberta P and David A COATE, 05 Sep 1981 Nashua, NH
MILLS, Helen E and William C Jr HUNT, 10 Aug 1935 Hudson, NH
MILMAN, Philip and Georgina TREADWELL, 08 May 1941 Nashua, NH
MILNE, Edward and Elizabeth HOLDEN, 18 Aug 1941 Hudson, NH
MILNE, Samuel F and Bonita L MERRILL, 14 Aug 1971 Amherst, NH
MILOSH, Richard J and Donna JoAn LEBLANC, 19 May 1979 Hudson, NH
MILOT, Joseph F and Christine LAMBERT, 15 Jan 1983 Hudson, NH
MIMIS, Marianne and Arthur R PERRY, 22 Aug 1970 Hudson, NH
MINALO, William and Eliza ROCKWELL, 30 Oct 1855
MINER, Edith I and Wilfred J MARTIN, 05 May 1962 Hudson, NH
MINER, Marjorie E and Arthur R BRUNT, 06 Mar 1954 Nashua, NH
MINOT, Diana J and Gary D DIGGINS, 28 Dec 1968 Nashua, NH
MINOT, Harriet T and Hosea C WALLACE, 14 Mar 1877 Hudson, NH
MINOT, Sarah and Abiel Jr COLBURN, 23 Mar 1797
MINTON, Kathleen M and Steven A OUELLETTE, 14 May 1976 Pelham, NH
MIROCHA, Judith M&Jonathan H RICHARDSON, 05 Mar 1983 Peterborough, NH
MIRON, Sheila J and Calvin E THOMPSON, 26 Oct 1973 Hudson, NH
MISH, Harry and Gertrude SANDLER, 20 Jul 1938 Nashua, NH
MISODOULAKIS, Barbara A & Paul R Jr MORIARTY, 10 May 1975 Nashua, NH
MITCHELL, Abbie S and Chas E BUSWELL, 13 Aug 1875 Nashua, NH
MITCHELL, Alfred R and Alice M BARRETT, 01 Nov 1947 Nashua, NH
MITCHELL, Coleen A and Leonard W MARTEL, 04 Feb 1972 Nashua, NH
MITCHELL, Dolores E and Leroy V CALISH, 08 Jan 1949 Hudson, NH
MITCHELL, Dolores T and Edward E JOHNSON, 03 Jun 1950 Hudson, NH
MITCHELL, Donald C and Alyce T POWERS, 04 Sep 1930 Nashua, NH
MITCHELL, Donna M and David P GREENLAW, 24 May 1980 Hudson, NH
MITCHELL, Eileen M and Henry J Jr DECOTEAU, 18 Sep 1971 Nashua, NH
MITCHELL, Emma J and James D MANNING, 23 Sep 1876 Hudson, NH
MITCHELL, Esther and Ernest R LEVESQUE, 11 Aug 1956 Hudson, NH
MITCHELL, George and Jennie COLLINS, 31 Dec 1869 Hudson, NH
MITCHELL, Gladys M and Merrill L CARTER, 22 Jan 1966 Hudson, NH
MITCHELL, Jayne E and James J BROWN, 30 Sep 1982 Londonderry, NH
MITCHELL, Jayne E and James J BROWN, 04 Jun 1983 Hudson, NH
MITCHELL, John J and Rita T NOEL, 23 May 1953 Nashua, NH
MITCHELL, Kim Irene and Bruce Alan BEEDE, 08 Sep 1973 Nashua, NH
MITCHELL, Ludovic and Rita G HAMELIN, 10 Apr 1948 Nashua, NH
MITCHELL, Ludovic L and Winnifred KIMBALL, 03 Sep 1955 Hudson, NH
MITCHELL, Mary E and Horace BUSWELL, 29 Aug 1869 Hudson, NH
MITCHELL, Michael G and Coleen A MILLARD, 01 Nov 1968 Hudson, NH
MITCHELL, Norma J and Leo J BOYLE, 01 Nov 1947 Hudson, NH
MITCHELL, Peter R and Yvonne E LAJOIE, 20 Jun 1953 Nashua, NH
MITCHELL, Rebecca A and Jeffrey J HEATH, 11 Jun 1978 Hudson, NH
MITCHELL, Richard B and Cynthia H DURWIN, 18 Nov 1970 Nashua, NH
MITCHELL, Ricky A and Janet LAW, 01 Jan 1980 Hudson, NH
MITCHELL, Susan Lynn and Gerald K CLOUTIER, 02 Jun 1979 Hudson, NH
MITCHELL, William P and Anne M COOKMAN, 24 Dec 1961 Hudson, NH
MITCHELL, William P and Judith A STONE, 29 Aug 1969 Hudson, NH
MITCHELL, Wm I and Lottie A FARWELL, 13 Aug 1875 Nashua, NH
MITCHESS, Gertrude A and John J BERARDI, 26 Jun 1954 Hudson, NH

HUDSON, NH MARRIAGES

MITCHESS, Gertrude A and Gerard A SIMONEAU, 29 Jan 1949 Nashua, NH
MITE, Dorothy C and Walter J MASTEN, 05 Feb 1972 Merrimack, NH
MITIDES, Anita Ann and Joseph E RACY, 17 Sep 1976 Hudson, NH
MITRA, Mita and Thomas C HOLT, 26 Jun 1983 Hudson, NH
MITTON, Brenda D and Thomas R WALKER, 17 Sep 1966 Hudson, NH
MITTON, Vernon P and Yvette M PAQUETTE, 04 Sep 1971 Hudson, NH
MIXTER, Madaline E and Arthur C LAWSON, 07 May 1936 Hudson, NH
MIZELL, James R and Kathleen M QUIGLEY, 30 Apr 1976 Hudson, NH
MIZO, Earl C and Mary E POWLOWSKY, 31 Aug 1940 Nashua, NH
MLEJ, Marye and William H MORAN, 28 Apr 1934 Manchester, NH
MOARATTY, Harold O and Rose D LOOK, 30 Sep 1950 Hudson, NH
MOBILIA, Charles L and Wendy L KNOWLES, 09 Jun 1985 Nashua, NH
MOBSBY, Jacqueline A and Michael P JONES, 21 Oct 1978 Hudson, NH
MODINI, Joseph and Jean GAUDETTE, 07 Dec 1933 Hudson, NH
MOES, Steven J and Sharmon LEE, 31 Jul 1982 Hudson, NH
MOFFA, Carmela M and Francis H FOURNIER, 15 Jun 1946 Hudson, NH
MOFFA, Eva C and Joseph J DANIELS, 02 Sep 1950 Hudson, NH
MOHLER, Kenneth J and Janetta K COUGLE, 07 Apr 1979 Hudson, NH
MOISAN, Paul A and Carolyn A ALLEN, 28 Aug 1971 Nashua, NH
MOISAN, Paul A III and Jeanne S BARTON, 21 Dec 1980 Hudson, NH
MOISAN, Richard A and Barbara M ROWELL, 20 Aug 1977 Nashua, NH
MOLINARI, Richard and Holly Dawn HARWOOD, 29 Apr 1974 Nashua, NH
MOLIS, William A and Noreen A MARTIN, 04 Oct 1969 Nashua, NH
MOLLOY, Stephen P and Dianna HAND, 20 Jun 1980 Hudson, NH
MOLNAR, David B and Nancy J O'NEAL, 04 Sep 1981 Hudson, NH
MONACO, Doris M and Gene S BEAUDRY, 25 Mar 1977 Nashua, NH
MONACO, Rosemary A and Bruce A CARROLL, 19 May 1979 Hudson, NH
MONDOUX, Raymond E and Sylvia J OUELLETTE, 01 Sep 1952 Hudson, NH
MONETTE, Beatrice and Carl V DODGE, 29 Apr 1936 Nashua, NH
MONETTE, Eva F and John F HARDMAN, 22 Jun 1929 Nashua, NH
MONETTE, Gay and Frank S MILLIKEN, 16 Mar 1930 Nashua, NH
MONETTE, Grace F and Raymond C BERGERON, 30 Sep 1929 Nashua, NH
MONIER, Emelienne and Auguste N GUERRETTE, 18 Oct 1958 Hudson, NH
MONK, Deborah J and Maher A GUIRGUIS, 21 May 1983 Nashua, NH
MONROE, Effie and Damon M KILGORE, 22 Aug 1929 Nashua, NH
MONROE, Kathleen A and Jeffrey L GORNE, 07 Oct 1979 Hudson, NH
MONROE, Kellie P and Dale R DUBOIS, 07 Aug 1982 Hudson, NH
MONROE, Margaret W and Edwin C DAVIS, 29 May 1934 Hudson, NH
MONTANARI, Hilda and Tufanio TARRALLI, 28 Jul 1942 Hudson, NH
MONTESION, Eleanor M and John J PUTIS, 30 Nov 1946 Fitchburg, MA
MONTGOMERY, Barbara and Paul R McLAUGHLIN, 10 Sep 1949 Nashua, NH
MONTGOMERY, F and O B BASSETT, 27 Jun 1916 Lee, NH
   Francis Montgomery (Belfast, Ireland) & Ellen Ellis (Ireland)
   Joseph Bassett(Hudson, NH) & Katie Mulhair (New York)
MONTGOMERY, William and Emily A HUDSON, 15 Aug 1917 Barrington
MONTMINY, Claire A and Robert W SHEAN, 27 Mar 1976 Hudson, NH
MONTMINY, Judith A and David A WILBUR, 31 Dec 1966 Hudson, NH
MONTMINY, Louise M and Eugene D RIVARD, 04 Sep 1967 Hudson, NH
MOODY, Addie B and Fred G STEELE, 28 Jun 1900 Nashua, NH
   Geo W Moody & Addie A Bannister
   Silas T Steele & Elizabeth McDonald
MOODY, Benjamin and Elizabeth GOULD, 13 Sep 1781
MOODY, Carolyn A and Roland E BROOKS, 20 Nov 1965 Hudson, NH
MOODY, James F and Janice H LEBLANC, 02 Dec 1967 Nashua, NH
MOODY, John H and Judith G BRIAND, 31 Jul 1965 Hudson, NH
MOODY, Maurice M Jr and Bettylou DRAKE, 17 Oct 1970 Hudson, NH
MOODY, Orrin P and Cora EAYRS, 06 Feb 1915 Hudson, NH
   Alexander Moody (London, NH) & Betsy Wilson (London, NH)
   Edward Eayrs(Nashua, NH) & Augusta Ford (Hudson, NH)
MOODY, Robert H and Nancy Ann AUDETTE, 01 Jun 1973 Hudson, NH

HUDSON, NH MARRIAGES

MOODY, Stephen M and Lisa J McCARTHY, 27 Oct 1979 Hudson, NH
MOON, Ann D and James W SAVERY, 20 Nov 1976 Nashua, NH
MOON, Melissa W and Joseph FULLER, 18 Dec 1894 Hudson, NH
   Daniel Fuller & Ruth Goodale
MOONEY, Arlene M and Leon E SPAULDING, 06 Oct 1979 Hudson, NH
MOONEY, Margaret M and Joseph W FULLER, 20 Jul 1957 Manchester, NH
MOORE, Alfred L and Ella G HUNTLEY, 24 Feb 1875 Hudson, NH
MOORE, Bernard E and Sarsha M COOLBROTH, 10 Dec 1971 Hudson, NH
MOORE, Betty Ann and Bruce W EINSIDLER, 24 Aug 1974 Windham, NH
MOORE, Brenda A and Russell E GORA, 03 Oct 1970 Hudson, NH
MOORE, Doris I and Morillo E POST, 27 Nov 1943 Nashua, NH
MOORE, Earle B and Vesta I HARRIS, 08 Jul 1916 Hudson, NH
   Stephen Moore (Nova Scotia) & Edith Boynton (Bromfield, ME)
   Robert Harris(Nova Scotia) & Elizabeth McKay (Nova Scotia)
MOORE, Edith W and Ralph DECOTY, 14 Jun 1920 Hudson, NH
MOORE, Edwin R and Agnes D MacINNIS, 20 Aug 1937 Boston, MA
MOORE, George P and C N SARGENT, 25 Aug 1916 Bellows Falls, VT
   Fred Moore (Hollis, NH) & Anna Jackson (Ayer, MA)
   Nathaniel Sargent(Potten, Que) & Ellen Potter (Johnson, VT)
MOORE, Gordon A and Patricia A PATENAUDE, 19 Nov 1955 Hudson, NH
MOORE, Harold L and Vivian S LADNER, 20 Jun 1942 Hudson, NH
MOORE, Herbert E and Agnes J HOLMES, 22 Jun 1907 Hudson, NH
   John Moore & Annie L Littlefield
   George I Holmes & Maria A J Butler
MOORE, James F and Mildred JANSKY, 08 Aug 1950 Hudson, NH
MOORE, James F and Dorothy L AMSDEN, 11 Aug 1962 Alton, NH
MOORE, Janet E and Mark A COUTIER, 01 Oct 1983 Nashua, NH
MOORE, Kristine M and Robert J Jr OTTERSON, 23 Aug 1980 Nashua, NH
MOORE, Lawrence E Jr and Lucille B CORONIS, 02 Nov 1968 Hudson, NH
MOORE, Maria J and Otis A MERRILL, 15 Dec 1869
MOORE, Marlene A and Nicholas HINES, 18 Aug 1979 Hudson, NH
MOORE, Raymond J Jr and Jo Ann M OSMAN, 07 Sep 1973 Hudson, NH
MOORE, Robert A and Denise M HACHEY, 15 Apr 1972 Hudson, NH
MOORE, Robert E and Edna F LINSCOTT, 05 May 1939 New Boston, NH
MOORE, Roselyn Am and Paul A COLBURN, 09 Jun 1973 Hudson, NH
MOORE, Virginia P and Albert E SMITH, 12 Oct 1940 Nashua, NH
MOOREHEAD, Priscilla and Arthur E ELLIS, 24 Jul 1971 Nashua, NH
MOQUIN, Deborah A and Harold A RUSSELL, 25 Oct 1980 Hudson, NH
MOQUIN, Rita E and John GROHOSKY, 28 May 1971 Nashua, NH
MOQUIN, Ronald L and Diana R LONES, 05 May 1962 Hudson, NH
MORAN, Catherine and D M Jr BUCHANAN, 28 Aug 1948 Nashua, NH
MORAN, Eleanor F and Henry MARSDEN, 07 Jun 1947 Hudson, NH
MORAN, Helen I and Victor AKSTEN, 05 Sep 1942 Milford, NH
MORAN, John F Jr and Katherine KEARNS, 19 Nov 1978 Pelham, NH
MORAN, John L and Corinne L MORCERINO, 28 Nov 1948 Hudson, NH
MORAN, John W and Mary E CAST, 12 Sep 1964 Hudson, NH
MORAN, Lorraine R and Elmer H ADAMS, 16 Oct 1948 Nashua, NH
MORAN, Marjorie T and Lestore G RAMSDELL, 14 May 1949 Hudson, NH
MORAN, Myrtle L and Henry J FARNUM, 18 Sep 1948 Hudson, NH
MORAN, Orise D and Richard H DUNCKLEE, 12 Feb 1944 Milford, NH
MORAN, William H and Marye MLEJ, 28 Apr 1934 Manchester, NH
MORASSE, Martin A and Carol A WATTS, 21 Oct 1967 Hudson, NH
MORCERINO, Corinne L and John L MORAN, 28 Nov 1948 Hudson, NH
MOREAU, Beatrice A and Linas B LONES, 07 Jan 1972 Hudson, NH
MOREAU, Blanche R and Forrest F HYDE, 26 May 1946 Nashua, NH
MOREAU, David E and Sheryl A PORTER, 15 Aug 1981 Hudson, NH
MOREAU, Doris B and Edgar E BOUCHER, 09 Jun 1972 Hudson, NH
MOREAU, Edward E and Elizabeth LACASSE, 28 Jun 1969 Hudson, NH
MOREAU, Julienne F and Raymond J CLOUTIER, 25 Apr 1946 Nashua, NH
MOREAU, Katherine and Earle L Jr WHITNEY, 18 Dec 1970 Nashua, NH

HUDSON,NH MARRIAGES

MOREAU, Mary Alice and Arthur VOLGER, 13 Aug 1929 Nashua, NH
MOREAU, Rachel P and Alfred E THERIAULT, 20 Feb 1954 Hudson, NH
MOREAU, Raymond C and Marguerite LUDLAM, 16 Aug 1971 Nashua, NH
MOREAU, Robert R and Cynthia R KANTARGIS, 07 Dec 1957 Nashua, NH
MOREAU, Roseanna B and Richard L CLARK, 14 Feb 1953 Hudson, NH
MORELAND, Amos and Lucinda RICHARDSON, 22 Jun 1823
MORELAND, Sybel and Samuel MARCH, 27 Sep 1842
MORELAND, William and Elizabeth KENNY, 31 Aug 1797
MORELLE, Lucier P and Francois BONNETTE, 27 Nov 1924 Nashua, NH
MORENCY, Elaine C and Alphonse F PALEVICIUS, 28 Sep 1963 Hudson, NH
MORENCY, Lafayette and Madelyn L BUSSIERE, 14 Oct 1960 Hudson, NH
MORENCY, Robert H Jr and Sandra E TATE, 30 Sep 1961 Hudson, NH
MORES, David C and Kathryn L LINNEMANN, 20 Feb 1977 Hudson, NH
MOREY, Alice M and Alexis J MORIN, 11 Jul 1970 Nashua, NH
MOREY, Ernest R and Rosanna LEVESQUE, 30 Apr 1934 Nashua, NH
MOREY, Francis F and Alice M MARQUIS, 11 Oct 1945 Nashua, NH
MOREY, Josephine V and Alonzo A SEARS, 08 Sep 1923 Nashua, NH
MOREY, Martha A and Horace N BURROUGHS, 05 Feb 1868
MOREY, Nancy A and Henry E LAGASSE, 28 Nov 1957 Hudson, NH
MOREY, Noel E and Lucy A ROY, 22 Jun 1936 Nashua, NH
MORGADO, Anthony C and Doris M LEBLANC, 10 Jun 1950 Hudson, NH
MORGAN, Alan A and Pauline R BOURQUE, 12 Aug 1978 Merrimack, NH
MORGAN, Allen B and Alma A LIZOTTE, 24 Jun 1950 Nashua, NH
MORGAN, Annabell and Roy J HONEYWELL, 19 Apr 1922 Hudson, NH
MORGAN, Ethelyn M and Paul E LECLAIR, 04 May 1946 Nashua, NH
MORGAN, Kim E and Bruce Earl YOUNG, 08 Sep 1984 Hudson, NH
MORGAN, Marilyn S & David A ARCHAMBEAULT, 30 Jun 1973 Merrimack, NH
MORGAN, Nancy T and Jon L LAVOIE, 27 Apr 1957 Hudson, NH
MORGAN, Ralph H and Evelyn T WILLIAMS, 02 Jul 1937 Hudson, NH
MORGAN, Ronald P and Gail M BERNARD, 21 Apr 1972 Hudson, NH
MORGANTI, Phyllis M and John G METROS, 12 Oct 1959 Hudson, NH
MORIARTY, Constance & Stephen D DOWNING, 02 Sep 1968 Merrimack, NH
MORIARTY, Helen and Alfred J BARRETT, 14 Apr 1920 Nashua, NH
MORIARTY, Michael J and Debra L WINSLOW, 16 Oct 1981 Nashua, NH
MORIARTY, Paul R Jr&Barbara A MISODOULAKIS, 10 May 1975 Nashua, NH
MORIN, Alexis J and Alice M MOREY, 11 Jul 1970 Nashua, NH
MORIN, Bernice D and Thomas H LYNAH, 28 Jan 1950 Hudson, NH
MORIN, Betty Lou and Daniel J SPEAR, 22 Jun 1968 Nashua, NH
MORIN, Debra L and Kevin C GRAVES, 08 Nov 1980 Nashua, NH
MORIN, Fernand and Helen O BROWN, 17 Jul 1948 Hudson, NH
MORIN, Fleurette and Russell E GAUTHIER, 24 Nov 1956 Nashua, NH
MORIN, Ida B and Charles F HAYES, 05 Aug 1950 Hudson, NH
MORIN, Jeanne H and John P QUIGLEY, 02 Sep 1957 Hudson, NH
MORIN, Jeanne R and David W BROWN, 08 Nov 1958 Hudson, NH
MORIN, Laura J and Daniel L SCOTT, 25 Dec 1982 Hudson, NH
MORIN, Linda B and Dennis A DUBE, 18 Sep 1976 Hudson, NH
MORIN, Marie R and Joseph D A ARCHAMBAULT, 27 Jul 1960 Hudson, NH
MORIN, Mary R and Alfred W GREGORY, 30 Jul 1955 Hudson, NH
MORIN, Robert J and Theresa D TURMEL, 14 Feb 1953 Hudson, NH
MORIN, Roger A and Rita M HILL, 19 Aug 1942 Nashua, NH
MORIN, Ronald J and June S POLAK, 20 Oct 1956 Nashua, NH
MORIN, Roseann and Thomas C BAILEY, 26 Jun 1976 Hudson, NH
MORIN, Seena M and Guy C FLETCHER, 12 May 1928 Nashua, NH
MORISSETTE, Shirley M and Cardin L CORBIT, 02 Oct 1954 Hudson, NH
MORLEY, Christina and Stephen W CURRAN, 20 Dec 1984 Hudson, NH
MORLEY, Nancy E and Lloyd D COX, 01 Jul 1957 Merrimack, NH
MORNEAU, Walter J and Irene J CARIGNAN, 24 Apr 1945 Manchester, NH
MORRELL, Helen E and Frank W CUTTING, 12 Feb 1944 Hudson, NH
MORRILL, Eva G and Harold H MARSHALL, 26 Jun 1922 Hudson, NH
MORRILL, Grover C and Olesia A PETREYKO, 29 Aug 1959 Hudson, NH

HUDSON, NH MARRIAGES

MORRILL, Isabel M and Arthur J GAGNON, 27 Feb 1933 Nashua, NH
MORRILL, Linda L and James C ABBOTT, 23 Nov 1962 Antrim, NH
MORRILL, Nellie E and Henry L SHEPHERD, 05 Feb 1941 Nashua, NH
MORRILL, Robert E and Ruth J GOODWIN, 06 Sep 1941 Hudson, NH
MORRIS, Dennise L and Douglas J HAYES, 31 Oct 1981 Nashua, NH
MORRIS, Henry B and Georgia J SCANTLEBURY, 23 Mar 1940 Hudson, NH
MORRIS, Myrtie A and Harold V SHAW, 12 Aug 1909 Hudson, NH
  William Morris & Annie Burt
  James Shaw & Ernestine Tasker
MORRIS, Roselle E and Austin Win SANBORN, 30 Nov 1935 Hudson, NH
MORRISON, Augustus R and Nettie THOMAS, 06 Dec 1871 Hudson, NH
MORRISON, Charles H and Abbie A FLOYD, 30 Jul 1858
MORRISON, Edwin G and Jane T GROVER, 26 Jun 1912 Hudson, NH
  Byron K Morrison & Hannah Munsey
  John M Thompson & Elizabeth M Marsh
MORRISON, Ester M and Frank E SANBORN, 28 Jul 1877 Hudson, NH
  Mark Morrison
  Sames Sanborn(Lowell, VT)
MORRISON, Mary Jane and Gilbert W MICHAUD, 26 Nov 1975 Nashua, NH
MORRISON, Neil A and Patricia J LEVESQUE, 11 Jun 1983 Hudson, NH
MORRISON, Robert G and Nellie E WOODBURY, 04 Mar 1881 Hudson, NH
MORRISON, Stephen F and Lee-Ann M ROY, 08 Nov 1974 Hudson, NH
MORRISON, Susan M and Nathan P WEBSTER, 17 May 1860
MORRISON, Terri L and Charles N BANAKOS, 22 Jun 1975 Hudson, NH
MORRISSEY, Margaret and Victor A BOCH, 07 Jun 1947 Hudson, NH
MORSE, Betty Ann and Alvin H RODGERS, 20 Jun 1964 Hudson, NH
MORSE, Carol A and Robert E LEIGH, 01 Jul 1958 Hudson, NH
MORSE, Elbridge G and Maude Lucinda KING, 30 Nov 1910 Hudson, NH
  Warren G Morse & Belle Evans
  Wallace E King & Ada Brooks
MORSE, Elizabeth and Thomas G BLACK, 14 May 1983 Hudson, NH
MORSE, Emma M and Charles W BARNES, 29 Jun 1872 Hudson, NH
MORSE, George W and Anne M OSMER, 29 May 1941 Salem, NH
MORSE, Harry F and Viola A BISHOP, 24 Jun 1930 Hudson, NH
MORSE, John H and Helen P GARLAND, 18 Jul 1983 Hudson, NH
MORSE, Kenneth F and Shirley A SMITH, 08 Mar 1952 Manchester, NH
MORSE, Mary and John Jr WILSON, 19 Dec 1816
MORSE, Moody and Susan SPALDING, 22 Feb 1826
MORSE, Nathaniel and Matilda WILSON, 26 Apr 1818
MORSE, Patricia F and Eugene E SIMARD, 25 Sep 1965 Hudson, NH
MORSE, Raymond G and Joan M GRAVELLE, 19 Apr 1969 Hudson, NH
MORSE, Robert L and Linda M GERVAIS, 18 Aug 1981 Bartlett, NH
MORSE, William E and Diane M BROUILLARD, 21 Sep 1984 Hudson, NH
MORTLOCK, Hattie L and Orman S CAMPBELL, 27 Jun 1900 Nashua, NH
  Geo A Mortlock & Eliza Hawes
  Bradford Campbell & Hattie E Putnam
MORTON, Bruce A and Kathleen M KILDUFF, 30 Oct 1983 Hudson, NH
MORTON, Charles A and Josephine CAMP, 28 Apr 1942 Hudson, NH
MORTON, Frances H and Fred B HARDY, 26 Jun 1954 Hudson, NH
MORTON, Hazel and Blakely L CLARKE, 02 Jul 1954 Hampton, NH
MORTON, Henrietta and Harold L AUSTIN, 03 Nov 1946 Hudson, NH
MOSHER, Harry F and Evelyn M SMITH, 22 May 1977 Hudson, NH
MOSKOWITZ, Brenda M and Richard R HELINSKI, 06 Aug 1981 Hudson, NH
MOSQUEDA, Antonio C and Elizabeth ARMSTRONG, 14 May 1948 Hudson, NH
MOSS, Elwin R and Doris I HUSSEY, 23 Dec 1961 Hudson, NH
MOSS, John and Hannah DAVIS, 15 Feb 1810
MOTYLEWSKA, Victoria and Simon M POLAK, 26 Apr 1958 Nashua, NH
MOTZKO, John F and Holly Ann SMALL, 15 Sep 1984 Londonderry, NH
MOULTON, Beatrice M and Joseph R POLAK, 11 Oct 1952 Hudson, NH
MOULTON, Judith A and Richard D PALADINO, 18 May 1979 Salem, NH

HUDSON, NH MARRIAGES

MOULTON, Sarah C and Fred E WINN, 25 Jul 1888 Merrimack, NH
   George W Moulton (Braintree, VT) & Hannah H Spofford (Auburn, NH)
   Wm F Winn(Hudson, NH) & Lucy M Richardson (Wilmington, MA)
MOULTON, William L and Dorothy M WILLIAMSON, 18 Feb 1950 Nashua, NH
MOUSSEAU, George L and Bessie E SOUKAS, 18 Nov 1972 Manchester, NH
MROZEK, Irene M and Robert R MASLANKA, 04 Jul 1963 Hudson, NH
MUELLER, Irma and James Frank HUGHES, 16 Apr 1929 Hudson, NH
MUELLER, Judith M and Donald A CONSTANTINO, 22 Jun 1985 Hudson, NH
MULDOON, Francis B and Pauline P LECUYER, 26 Feb 1945 Hudson, NH
MULHAIR, Katie and Joseph BASSETT, 12 Aug 1890 Nashua, NH
   Michale Mulhair (Ireland) & Bridget McGlynn (Ireland)
   Charles H Bassett(Bangor, ME) & Almeda Pomroy (Bangor, ME)
MULHERN, Thomas P and Pauline Y BERUBE, 21 Sep 1968 Hudson, NH
MULHERN, William J Jr and Marguerite DUPONT, 14 May 1966 Hudson, NH
MULHOLLAND, Markland and Jane STONE, 02 Aug 1941 Hudson, NH
MULLIGAN, Sarah J and James E MARSHALL, 16 Nov 1889 Lowell, MA
   John B Thibodeau (Madanosko, PQ) & Mary Dupont
   Alfred Marshall(Hudson, NH) & Lydia M Hamblett (Hudson, NH)
MULLIN, William D and Dorothy L WELLIVER, 06 Aug 1949 Hudson, NH
MUNCIL, Valena and Charles PUDVAH, 01 Oct 1908 Hudson, NH
   John Muncil & May Doty
   Peter Pudvah & Mary Vivian
MUNDAY, Karl M and Cheryl A RODGERS, 27 Aug 1971 Nashua, NH
MUNDAY, Karl Micha and Carolyn OUELLETTE, 14 Feb 1985 Nashua, NH
MUNDAY, Lake M and Florette D ST JEAN, 30 Aug 1947 Nashua, NH
MUNDAY, Linda D and Earl G BRIAND, 08 Feb 1969 Hudson, NH
MUNDAY, Michelle G and Brian E AHEARN, 25 Jun 1978 Hudson, NH
MUNN, Everett W and Lena May BARBER, 12 Feb 1933 Hudson, NH
MUNRO, Alfred G and Lillian M NICKERSON, 05 Jun 1899 Hudson, NH
   A M Munro & Jessie Gordon
   Walter Nickerson & Clara
MUNROE, Bernice A and Lynwood A PORTER, 04 May 1950 Nashua, NH
MUNROE, Elizabeth and Russell A CHASE, 03 Jul 1938 Hudson, NH
MUNROE, James C and Gertrude P SMITH, 05 Sep 1948 Hudson, NH
MUNROE, Krystal L and David R HAERINCK, 11 Aug 1984 Nashua, NH
MUNROE, Linda M and Cleyon D BARNES, 28 Nov 1970 Hudson, NH
MUNROE, Malvina and Samuel L SHEDD, 03 May 1863
MUNROE, Robert A and Dorothy I McALMAN, 13 Apr 1957 Nashua, NH
MUNROE, Robert F and Brenda G CROOKS, 11 Dec 1976 Nashua, NH
MUNROE, Ruthann and Victor C GIDEON, 31 Mar 1962 Hudson, NH
MUNROE, William J and Donna J ARSENAULT, 05 Feb 1982 Hudson, NH
MUNSON, April S and Richard J LATOUR, 27 Nov 1970 Nashua, NH
MUNSON, Beatrice K and Robert A LOCKE, 09 Oct 1965 Nashua, NH
MUNSON, Earl Jr and Christine STRAUB, 13 May 1977 Hudson, NH
MUNSON, Earl W and Alice E CLARK, 28 Jun 1947 Hudson, NH
MUNSON, Earl W Jr and Barbara L WHEELER, 01 Jan 1971 Manchester, NH
MUNSON, Kenneth L and Theresa G DOUCET, 04 Feb 1961 Hudson, NH
MURDOCK, Helen M and John G WILSON, 31 Jan 1947 Hudson, NH
MURELLI, Michele A and Roy E ELLIOT, 05 Sep 1981 Hudson, NH
MURHEAD, Donald T and Myrtle M CAMPBELL, 16 Oct 1948 Hudson, NH
MURPHY, Andrew A and Ruth A EDGAR, 13 Feb 1934 Nashua, NH
MURPHY, Daniel J and Donna J CONSTANTINEAU, 09 Jul 1983 Salem, NH
MURPHY, Daniel James II and Kim D CHENARD, 18 Jul 1981 Hudson, NH
MURPHY, Edward J and Lorraine B BOWSER, 25 Dec 1949 Hudson, NH
MURPHY, Elaine A and Robert MERCHANT, 14 Dec 1957 Hudson, NH
MURPHY, Evelyn and Charles C WHITE, 19 Jun 1948 Hudson, NH
MURPHY, John T and Helen E DOYLE, 06 Jul 1973 Nashua, NH
MURPHY, Mary A and John M Jr GARVEY, 14 Oct 1950 Hudson, NH
MURPHY, Maureen An and Leo J Jr GAGNON, 02 Jun 1973 Merrimack, NH
MURPHY, Merle D and Alyce M ZENARO, 04 Feb 1950 Hudson, NH

HUDSON,NH MARRIAGES

MURPHY, Mina and Elliot A SMITH, 22 Jun 1940 Lowell, MA
MURPHY, Robert P and Carole L DEE, 03 Oct 1980 Hudson, NH
MURPHY, Rose and Peter MAGUIRE, 22 Oct 1910 Hudson, NH
   John Murphy & Catherine Henry
   Patrick Maguire & Catherine Riley
MURPHY, Sandra A and David C GILBERT, 20 Jun 1970 Nashua, NH
MURPHY, Sheila Ann and Douglas P OUIMET, 29 Sep 1972 Hudson, NH
MURPHY, William M and Deborah G WOLLEN, 20 Sep 1980 Nashua, NH
MURRAY, Alan M and Kathleen E SPRINGER, 28 Mar 1970 Nashua, NH
MURRAY, Judith A and James H FOGG, 15 Dec 1967 Nashua, NH
MURRAY, Mona M and Charles J NOAKES, 13 Oct 1979 Laconia, NH
MURRAY, Terrance M and Merlinda P PRIVEE, 08 Jun 1985 Hudson, NH
MUSGRAVE, Linda E and Gary D RAFFERTY, 29 Nov 1971 Nashua, NH
MUSIKER, Rosamond and Harry GOODMAN, 30 Jun 1940 Hudson, NH
MUTTI, Roberta and Hans KAUFHOLD, 30 Jun 1956 Proctor, VT
MUZZEY, Charles T and Anne M PELLETIER, 29 Oct 1983 Nashua, NH
MYERS, Eric P and Bonnie R LEAOR, 10 Oct 1981 Hudson, NH
MYRICK, Brian J and Robin M STOWELL, 22 Oct 1983 Hudson, NH
MYRICK, Paul B and Barbara J GRACE, 15 Jul 1961 Nashua, NH
NADEAU, Clarie E and Roland S LEFEBVRE, 12 Sep 1960 Nashua, NH
NADEAU, Claudette and Michael N BEAUDRY, 24 May 1975 Hudson, NH
NADEAU, David A and Susan J GRANT, 13 Nov 1982 Hudson, NH
NADEAU, David Emil and Katherine CARDINAL, 04 May 1975 Derry, NH
NADEAU, David P and Katherine PROVENCAL, 20 Jul 1968 Nashua, NH
NADEAU, Denis G and Susan M CARROZZO, 07 Jun 1975 Plaistow, NH
NADEAU, Emery and Marion LAMBERT, 06 Oct 1934 Nashua, NH
NADEAU, Ferdnand R and Sandra V GAMACHE, 25 Aug 1956 Hudson, NH
NADEAU, Hedwidge M and Felix J MAYNARD, 06 Jun 1932 Nashua, NH
NADEAU, Howard B and Claire E COTE, 25 Nov 1954 Hudson, NH
NADEAU, Ida and William J RODONIS, 05 Jul 1941 Nashua, NH
NADEAU, Joyce M and Robert A FINDLEY, 11 Nov 1977 Hudson, NH
NADEAU, Kevin N and Michele E WILLIAMS, 26 Sep 1981 Hudson, NH
NADEAU, Laurette J and Thurlow E WARDWELL, 16 Dec 1967 Hudson, NH
NADEAU, Leon R and Gayle A LEBLANC, 18 Sep 1971 Hudson, NH
NADEAU, Leon R and Virginia L BOULANGER, 09 Jul 1983 Hudson, NH
NADEAU, Lionel W and Theresa M DEMARAIS, 16 May 1968 Hudson, NH
NADEAU, Lori A and Robert A BOUCHER, 29 Sep 1984 Hudson, NH
NADEAU, M Irene and Eldon J CHADBURN, 31 Dec 1966 Hudson, NH
NADEAU, M Irene and Paul E GAUDETTE, 17 Oct 1971 Nashua, NH
NADEAU, Marilyn L & Francis J III O'GARA, 18 Jul 1967 Merrimack, NH
NADEAU, Mark L and Kathryn A PIGNATELLA, 22 Sep 1979 Hudson, NH
NADEAU, Octave and Theotice MARQUIS, 02 Sep 1933 Nashua, NH
NADEAU, Patricia A and Donald R HUOT, 02 Jul 1976 Hudson, NH
NADEAU, Rita T and Eugene J FRENETTE, 14 Feb 1947 Nashua, NH
NADEAU, Rolande G and William F HANDLEY, 29 Dec 1947 Hudson, NH
NADEAU, Ronald N and Lorna M BOULEY, 16 Jul 1966 Hudson, NH
NADEAU, Sandra J and Roland J Jr DEERY, 26 Apr 1969 Nashua, NH
NADEAU, Sandra M and John D Jr GRACE, 21 Feb 1970 Nashua, NH
NADEAU, Suzanne C and George B HIER, 30 Jun 1973 Hudson, NH
NADEAU, Theresa B and Paul M CHASSE, 28 Jun 1947 Nashua, NH
NADEAU, Theresa R & Raymond G BELLEFEUILLE, 18 Sep 1948 Nashua, NH
NADEAU, Thomas Edm and Cheryl Lyn BURTON, 09 Jun 1984 Hudson, NH
NADEAU, Winifred L and Frederick Jr GOWING, 11 Apr 1964 Hudson, NH
NADREAU, Armand T and Rita L LAVALLEE, 28 Aug 1954 Hudson, NH
NAGEL, Arthur E and Elizabeth LEBLANC, 27 Dec 1939 Hudson, NH
NAGLE, Jane M and John F Jr HINES, 25 Mar 1949 Hudson, NH
NAGLE, Patrick B and Madeline I DELESCLUSE, 20 Oct 1972 Hudson, NH
NAGY, Marilyn L and Albert J DUBOIS, 14 Jun 1974 Hudson, NH
NAJARIAN, John O and Helen V PARKER, 10 Sep 1932 Hudson, NH
NALLY, Walter F and Ruth S HARALDSTAD, 21 Jan 1949 Hudson, NH

HUDSON, NH MARRIAGES

NANTEL, Gerard G and Janice A D'AMOUR, 23 Jun 1956 Hudson, NH
NANTEL, Theresa and Adrien A LABRIE, 07 Jun 1947 Nashua, NH
NAPLES, Albert A and Lenore A MILLER, 21 Jun 1943 Nashua, NH
NAPSEY, Charlotte and Edwin A HADRYCH, 16 Dec 1970 Hudson, NH
NARO, Albert A and Rita G LAVOIE, 28 May 1944 Manchester, NH
NARO, Albert A and Martha J TORREY, 21 Jun 1952 Nashua, NH
NARO, Anita Y and Victor L GAGNON, 31 Aug 1946 Nashua, NH
NARO, Carol Ann and William A BERTHOLDT, 19 Mar 1983 Hudson, NH
NARO, Henry L Jr and Nancy I LABEDNICK, 16 May 1959 Nashua, NH
NARO, Jeannette and Ronald A FLANDERS, 27 Oct 1956 Hudson, NH
NARO, Michael A and Charlotte WHITE, 25 Aug 1973 Hollis, NH
NARO, Robert H and Joan T CHAMPAGNE, 03 Jul 1953 Hudson, NH
NARO, Roland C and Shirley M NOLETTE, 18 Nov 1950 Hudson, NH
NARO, Roland C and Shirley M SNELL, 08 Jan 1980 Derry, NH
NASH, Debra Ann and Steven Reg TORRES, 09 Aug 1975 Nashua, NH
NASH, Helen C and Albert C THORN, 09 Nov 1906 Nashua, NH
   John Nash & Ellen Sullivan
   Charles E Thorn & Elyza Esty
NASH, Priscilla and Robert E Jr CLEGG, 24 May 1974 Nashua, NH
NASON, Louisa A and Arthur M ELDRIDGE, 17 Oct 1952 Hudson, NH
NASON, Mary E and Maynard P NASON, 05 Feb 1941 Hudson, NH
NASON, Maynard P and Mary Ella FARLAND, 12 Apr 1935 Dracut, MA
NASON, Maynard P and Mary E NASON, 05 Feb 1941 Hudson, NH
NASOU, Richard C and Shirley A GRANT, 21 Jun 1957 Nashua, NH
NASUTOWICZ, Elizabeth & Rodney R BELLERIVE, 04 Mar 1967 Hudson, NH
NATES, Lila E and Charles F DRISCOLL, 05 Feb 1949 Hudson, NH
NATURALE, Francis and Lorinda J CHAREST, 07 May 1977 Hudson, NH
NAZAKA, June H and Kenneth J KOPKA, 10 May 1980 Nashua, NH
NEAL, Carrie and Frederick SMITH, 06 Oct 1890 Lowell, MA
   Jason Packard (Easton, MA) & Susan Packard (Montpelier, VT)
   John Smith(Germany) & Augusta Alexander (Germany)
NEAULT, Lorraine C and Kenneth Jr GRIFFIN, 10 Oct 1981 Pelham, NH
NEAULT, William F and Shirley T BOISVERT, 02 Jun 1985 Pelham, NH
NEE, George and Alma EVANS, 13 Dec 1934 Hudson, NH
NEE, Kathryn E and Jonathan G RAINE, 04 Jun 1974 Hudson, NH
NEFF, Alonzo D and Maria J LOVEJOY, 08 Apr 1873 Hudson, NH
NEFF, Debra L and Philip M LAVOIE, 09 Oct 1982 Hudson, NH
NEGRI, Ralph and Anna GILLIS, 06 Nov 1938 Hudson, NH
NEGRON, Luis M and Carmen M RODRIGUEZ, 28 May 1966 Derry, NH
NELSON, Alfred P and Zoe M BRADLEY, 26 Oct 1916 Hudson, NH
   Myron H Nelson (Dorchester, NH) & Lillian Applefee (Dover, NH)
   Allen Bradley(Plattsburgh, NY) & Clara Dennison (Cutler, ME)
NELSON, Charlotte and Charles W BARRETT, 11 Nov 1852
NELSON, Donald D and Celeste M ENO, 23 Oct 1982 Hudson, NH
NELSON, Elaine B and Marcel A PROVENCHER, 21 Oct 1966 Hudson, NH
NELSON, John E and Sarah M LOUIS, 03 Dec 1934 Hudson, NH
NELSON, Laurie J & Henry A CHRISTIANSEN, 26 Jan 1953 Manchester, NH
NELSON, Mary Jane and Henry E ROBY, 09 Jun 1844
NELSON, Ralph B and Muriel CONNER, 04 Jul 1872 Hudson, NH
NELSON, Sadie and Alfred V THERRIEN, 09 Feb 1935 Nashua, NH
NELSON, Sally and Ephrium BUTTRICK, 22 Nov 1842
NELSON, Vincent B and Sophie J GEOBOSKY, 08 Apr 1945 Nashua, NH
NELSON, William R and Love S BRINKER, 16 Dec 1967 Nashua, NH
NENNI, Ronald A III and Christine LEBEL, 29 Oct 1982 Hudson, NH
NEPVEU, Vivianne Y and Ronald G BARRETT, 19 Apr 1969 Nashua, NH
NESKEY, Joanne L and Donald W CYR, 26 Oct 1974 Hudson, NH
NESMITH, Walter S and Genevieve CAMPBELL, 28 Jun 1951 Nashua, NH
NESS, Nancy E and Raymond A NOLIN, 11 Nov 1961 Hudson, NH
NESTOR, Cecelia and Melvin B HASKELL, 14 Aug 1948 Hudson, NH
NEUFFER, Carl and Elizabeth WALL, 04 Mar 1946 Milford, NH

HUDSON,NH MARRIAGES

NEUFFER, Carla A and Richard H LAMBERT, 29 Jan 1966 Hudson, NH
NEUMULLER, Emil and Jean C GOTT, 18 Jun 1982 Hudson, NH
NEVEN, Irene and Edward BERNAICHE, 26 Dec 1932 Nashua, NH
NEVENS, James and Betsey JOHNSON, 06 Jun 1799
NEVENS, Mervin R and Pearl R LABOUNTY, 26 Nov 1959 Rye, NH
NEVEUX, Robert A and Mary L INGEROWKSI, 11 Mar 1972 Hudson, NH
NEVILLE, Cynthia D and Charles H DESFOSSES, 30 Aug 1974 Nashua, NH
NEVILLE, Helen F and Bruce K MERRILL, 04 May 1957 Ctr Barnstead, NH
NEVILLE, William F and Jeannine C CHENEVERT, 06 Oct 1984 Hudson, NH
NEVINS, James and Betty JOHNSON, 06 Jun 1799
NEWAL, Thomas and Patience JENKS, 19 Jul 1785
NEWCOMB, Charles H and Rebecca HADLEY, 23 May 1859
NEWCOMB, J Edward and Linda Y ELLIOTT, 19 May 1979 Hudson, NH
NEWCOMBE, Josephine and Charles A HOWARD, 09 Jul 1949 Hudson, NH
NEWEL, Thomas and Patience JENKS, 19 Jul 1785
NEWELL, David Bens and Barbara E DALE, 04 Aug 1981 Hudson, NH
NEWHALL, Otis A and Elizabeth KILDERRY, 11 Apr 1920 Hudson, NH
NEWMAN, Donald and Juliann FORDHAM, 03 Apr 1982 Hudson, NH
NEWMAN, Rosa and William H BAILEY, 09 Feb 1881 Hudson, NH
  Samuel Newman & Julia
  Benjamin Bailey & Sarah Chase
NEWTON, Clara L and Elton E BLANCHARD, 08 Jul 1956 Sandown, NH
NEWTON, Reita A and Robert A JASPER, 15 Mar 1958 Epping, NH
NICHOLS, Alan J and Donna J GUTHRO, 02 Dec 1977 Nashua, NH
NICHOLS, Albert W and R Annette HENSHAW, 17 Mar 1934 Nashua, NH
NICHOLS, Arthur E and Lillian G GRANT, 10 Dec 1943 Nashua, NH
NICHOLS, Barbara and Alfred E NOEL, 24 Aug 1940 Nashua, NH
NICHOLS, Bernice and Edward B Jr HAGGETT, 19 Nov 1944 Hudson, NH
NICHOLS, Beverly G and Walter E KENNEDY, 04 Jul 1966 Nashua, NH
NICHOLS, Carol Lynn and Scott D WILLIAMS, 31 Mar 1983 Hudson, NH
NICHOLS, Chas E Jr and Edith Blan HOAG, 02 Jun 1898 Nashua, NH
  Charles E Nichols & Kate C Frye
  David T Hoag & Charlotte Belknap
NICHOLS, Debra M and Richard BUJNOWSKI, 20 Nov 1982 Nashua, NH
NICHOLS, Elizabeth and Franklin G FOLGER, 01 Dec 1934 Hudson, NH
NICHOLS, Ernest G Jr and Leda-Marie DAMERY, 29 Jun 1953 Hudson, NH
NICHOLS, Evelyn G and Vernon F PEASLEE, 24 May 1941 Hudson, NH
NICHOLS, Frank B and Grace P OSBORNE, 18 Jun 1917 Nashua, NH
NICHOLS, Gertrude E and Harry E ROGERS, 12 Nov 1902 Nashua, NH
  William Nichols & Mae
  Frank P Rogers & Lizzie J Baldwin
NICHOLS, Horace A and Bertha A RICHARDS, 03 Jul 1948 Hudson, NH
NICHOLS, Horace A Jr and Susan A LITTELL, 15 Dec 1973 Nashua, NH
NICHOLS, James M and Helen M DWYER, 26 Jun 1981 Nashua, NH
NICHOLS, Jeffrey W and Loretta Sue YOUNG, 25 Aug 1979 Hudson, NH
NICHOLS, Joseph E and Jossie M BLANCHARD, 10 Aug 1901 Hudson, NH
  L F Nichols (Nashua, NH) & Nettie A Austin (Hollis, NH)
  Charles Marvell(Milford, NH) & May Duscoll (Boston, MA)
NICHOLS, Laura E and Chas K TITCOMB, 19 Mar 1874 Londonderry, NH
NICHOLS, Laura Emil and Charles Ki TITCOMB, 19 Mar 1874
NICHOLS, Lorraine and Walter CORBETT, 04 May 1941 Hudson, NH
NICHOLS, Luther E and Nancy A OUELLETTE, 30 Jun 1984 Hudson, NH
NICHOLS, Maggie and John E GRIFFIN, 07 Jun 1890 Londonderry, NH
  Thomas Fallon (Ireland) & Mary McLeon (Ireland)
  Rufus K Griffin(Manchester, NH) & Susan Merriam (Nashua, NH)
NICHOLS, Mary E and John S HODGMAN, 08 Mar 1873 Hudson, NH
NICHOLS, Michael A and Patricia A WOODS, 26 May 1973 Nashua, NH
NICHOLS, Pauline and John E FORD, 08 Apr 1922 Hudson, NH
NICHOLS, Philip S and Pamela J FOURNIER, 14 Nov 1981 Hudson, NH
NICHOLS, Phineas and Nancy HOBBS, 22 Feb 1823

HUDSON, NH MARRIAGES

NICHOLS, Phinehas and Mary HOBBS, 22 Feb 1822
NICHOLS, Polly and John GREELEY, 08 Jun 1829
NICHOLS, Robert L and Lorette GAGNON, 26 Oct 1946 Nashua, NH
NICHOLS, Roberta A and Bruce D SWEENIE, 11 Sep 1971 Hudson, NH
NICHOLS, Ruth A and Edward R KINVILLE, 16 Nov 1929 Hudson, NH
NICHOLS, Sandra L and Michael Le NOYES, 31 Dec 1981 Nashua, NH
NICHOLS, Shirley A and Donald A WHITING, 13 Apr 1964 Hudson, NH
NICHOLS, Shirley M and Robert O'NEIL, 05 Apr 1944 Nashua, NH
NICHOLS, Susan G and Charles F GOVE, 12 Oct 1968 Hudson, NH
NICHOLS, Walter L and Viola HORTON, 17 Sep 1937 Dunstable, MA
NICHOLS, William A and Sarah MARCH, 25 Dec 1851
NICHOLSON, Estelle F and John W KOZIOL, 02 Sep 1984 Hudson, NH
NICHOLSON, Ruth and Russell R GRANT, 12 Feb 1938 Milford, NH
NICHOLSON, Scott W and June M BELIVEAU, 06 Feb 1971 Nashua, NH
NICHOLSON, Sharen Ann and Alfred S LENTSCH, 27 Jan 1973 Nashua, NH
NICKEL, Barbara I and Robert G Jr LEFAVOR, 30 Mar 1980 Nashua, NH
NICKERSON, Allen P and Blanche H GAGNE, 05 Feb 1936 Hudson, NH
NICKERSON, Ann G and Timothy J CADY, 10 Jun 1978 Pelham, NH
NICKERSON, Lillian M and Alfred G MUNRO, 05 Jun 1899 Hudson, NH
   Walter Nickerson & Clara
   A M Munro & Jessie Gordon
NICKERSON, Ralph A and Ruth A DUNN, 03 Dec 1904 Hudson, NH
   Joseph Nickerson & Rose Dexter
   John H Dunn & Mary A Trickett
NICKLESS, Charles A and Lelie WILSON, 02 Jul 1899 Hudson, NH
   Geo F Nickless & Abbie S Daniels
   Joseph Austin & Charlotte Rogerson
NICOLL, William and Grace V PARKER, 06 Apr 1935 Hudson, NH
NIEMASZYK, Mark J and Monique A LAROSE, 29 Jun 1985 Hudson, NH
NIEMI, Richard O and Barbara J BENSON, 15 Jun 1963 Concord, MA
NIGHTS, Mary and James HARTSHORN, 14 Nov 1819
NIORTH, Anders S and Marjorie Gertru SHAW, 02 May 1938 Nashua, NH
NIQUETTE, Constance and Harvey A ST JEAN, 04 Sep 1950 Nashua, NH
NIQUETTE, Daniel R & Joyce Arline DUBE, 03 Mar 1973 Manchester, NH
NIQUETTE, Edward P and Norma J GAGNON, 03 Jun 1978 Nashua, NH
NIQUETTE, Leonard R and Mary R GUYETTE, 13 Jan 1962 Hudson, NH
NIQUETTE, Leonard R and Elaine F McGRATH, 03 Jul 1965 Hudson, NH
NIQUETTE, Pauline A and Carlton H BROWN, 04 Jun 1983 Hudson, NH
NIQUETTE, Richard J and Kathy J CHAMPIGNY, 18 Aug 1972 Hudson, NH
NIXON, Henry L and Doris V ANDREW, 07 Jul 1951 Hudson, NH
NIXON, Laurie K and Stephen W PARENT, 25 Jun 1977 Nashua, NH
NIXON, Patricia A and Frank A BYRON, 11 Sep 1976 Hudson, NH
NIXON, Richard A and Linda T PELLETIER, 31 Jul 1981 Nashua, NH
NOAKES, Alyce M and Dennis M LAMBERT, 12 Jul 1969 Hudson, NH
NOAKES, Charles J and Mona M MURRAY, 13 Oct 1979 Laconia, NH
NOAKES, Cynthia M and Edward L KINGSLEY, 24 Feb 1968 Milford, NH
NOBLE, Diane L and Ronald K LUONGE, 10 Apr 1976 Londonderry, NH
NOE, Anna L and Elphege J PROVENCHER, 30 Jul 1949 Manchester, NH
NOEL, Alfred E and Barbara NICHOLS, 24 Aug 1940 Nashua, NH
NOEL, Arthur J and Linda A BOULEY, 14 Apr 1971 Hudson, NH
NOEL, Barbara L and James W JOHNSTON, 30 Aug 1963 Hudson, NH
NOEL, Doris A and William T TWARDOSKY, 30 Dec 1961 Nashua, NH
NOEL, James W and Nancy C LINTNER, 10 Jul 1965 Hudson, NH
NOEL, Jeannette and Hazen O JOHNSON, 05 Oct 1974 Nashua, NH
NOEL, Joseph L and Rosette T WHITNEY, 24 Jun 1978 Nashua, NH
NOEL, Judith A and Peter A LACHANCE, 15 Jun 1968 Nashua, NH
NOEL, Maria and Anthony N PERRITANO, 25 Jun 1982 Hudson, NH
NOEL, Mary Yvonne and John B PLANT, 22 Jun 1924 Nashua, NH
NOEL, Oberline and Camille BRODEUR, 30 May 1933 Nashua, NH
NOEL, Rita T and John J MITCHELL, 23 May 1953 Nashua, NH

HUDSON, NH MARRIAGES

NOEL, Spencer H and Betty L CARLSON, 06 Apr 1985 Hudson, NH
NOEL, Stephen W and Cathy Loui LEVESQUE, 26 Jul 1980 Litchfield, NH
NOKES, Frederick and Bertha E CUMMINGS, 12 Mar 1900 Cambridge, MA
   William Nokes & Hannah Rouse
   W P Cummings & Hattie D Lawrence
NOLEN, William D and Ellen A McGRAW, 15 Oct 1977 Hudson, NH
NOLET, Cecile L and Norman J COTE, 04 Nov 1983 Nashua, NH
NOLET, Michael W and June O LACHAPELLE, 20 Nov 1976 Hudson, NH
NOLETTE, Shirley M and Roland C NARO, 18 Nov 1950 Hudson, NH
NOLETTE, Victor and Nola GALIPEAU, 27 Jul 1940 Nashua, NH
NOLIN, Leo E and Linda R JUDKINS, 02 Oct 1966 Milford, NH
NOLIN, Leo Earl and Jolene S FENTON, 06 Jul 1973 Nashua, NH
NOLIN, Raymond A and Nancy E NESS, 11 Nov 1961 Hudson, NH
NOLIN, Raymond A and Betty A FARLAND, 12 Dec 1964 Hudson, NH
NOLIN, Raymond A and Nancy MACOMBER, 03 Jul 1971 Warner, NH
NOLIN, Thomas F and Sandra L NOYES, 07 Jan 1983 Nashua, NH
NONNAN, John J and Georgianna HOULE, 06 May 1895 Nashua, NH
   Lewis Nonnan & Mary Shambeau
   Jestin Houle
NOONEY, Anne M and Richard P TURCOTTE, 23 Nov 1969 Hudson, NH
NORDLING, E Harold and Ruth May G CLAUSON, 23 Nov 1933 Nashua, NH
NORMAN, Rachel A and Donald M SILVA, 20 Apr 1985 Hudson, NH
NORMAN, Rose and Charles BILANGER, 17 Jul 1894 Hudson, NH
   Lewis Norman (Canada) & A Archambeault (Mass)
   Arthemin Dube & Auguste Bilanger
NORMAND, Donna L and Gerard L POLIQUIN, 31 Aug 1972 Nashua, NH
NORMAND, Raymond P and Donna L MARTIN, 02 Jul 1966 Hudson, NH
NORMANDIE, Rita T and Francis G KINVILLE, 29 Nov 1942 Dracut, MA
NORMANDIN, James A and Debra A McHUGH, 20 Oct 1984 Wilton, NH
NORRIS, Eugene and Eva N JAWORSKY, 21 Nov 1942 Hudson, NH
NORRIS, Kitrina and William G SULLIVAN, 27 Aug 1982 Nashua, NH
NORRIS, Mabella L and Charles E MATHEWS, 02 Dec 1936 Nashua, NH
NORTH, Daniel and Hattie A WILSON, 29 Feb 1880 Londonderry, NH
   Daniel North & Goodell
   John Putnam & Abagaill Hart (Temple, NH)
NORTH, Katherine and Albert W VITTUM, 15 Mar 1911 Hudson, NH
   James North & Jane Edwards
   Frank H Vittum & Flora L Merrill
NORTON, Chester W and Dorothea MANAHAN, 24 Dec 1941 Hudson, NH
NORTON, Denise A and Steven M FEBONIO, 28 Aug 1982 Nashua, NH
NORTON, Mary G and Charles K BELMONT, 14 Apr 1945 Hudson, NH
NOTO, Bettina and John T LONG, 08 Jul 1977 Londonderry, NH
NOTTER, Patricia A and Norbert DUVAL, 22 May 1976 Hudson, NH
NOVELLO, Rosario and Catherine HALEY, 19 Jul 1941 Nashua, NH
NOVICK, Marie J and Philip S CHAPMAN, 29 Aug 1931 Nashua, NH
NOWAK, Charles A and Lucille L DAGGETT, 04 Jan 1975 Rochester, NH
NOWAK, Jacalyn E and Robert D Jr ROTH, 04 Nov 1967 Nashua, NH
NOYES, Cathleen J and Donald L LANDRY, 07 Oct 1967 Hudson, NH
NOYES, Edward W and Audrey B COOPER, 17 Jan 1948 Hudson, NH
NOYES, John F and Luceta RICHARDSON, 26 Nov 1908 Hudson, NH
   John L Noyes & Rachael F Freit
   Henry A Richardson & Estelle F Boyd
NOYES, Michael Le and Sandra L NICHOLS, 31 Dec 1981 Nashua, NH
NOYES, Sandra L and Thomas F NOLIN, 07 Jan 1983 Nashua, NH
NUCCI, Richard C and Patricia A BURGESS, 09 Nov 1974 Hudson, NH
NUNES, Anna and Dennis CONNELL, 30 Jun 1942 Hudson, NH
NUTE, Frank L and Melba C KING, 04 Jul 1934 Hudson, NH
NUTE, Frank W and Edith M MARSHALL, 29 May 1912 Hudson, NH
   Frank W Nute & Etta M Gordon
   Eugene J Marshall & Leona Robinson

HUDSON, NH MARRIAGES

NUTE, Georgia E and Cyprian P Jr KVEDAR, 01 Jul 1961 Hudson, NH
NUTE, James A and Mary A KUPCHUNAS, 16 Sep 1961 Nashua, NH
NUTE, Marshall R and Lorraine M QUINN, 03 Jun 1978 Salem, NH
NUTTALL, Albert H and Hope FANNING, 31 Aug 1940 Hudson, NH
NUTTING, Benjamin and Martha J FARRINGTON, 20 Mar 1842
NUTTING, Charles R and Cynthia R CAMPBELL, 21 Jun 1969 Hudson, NH
NUTTING, Frank A and Rosamond H MERRILL, 05 Oct 1940 Hudson, NH
NUTTING, Josephene and Joseph R ROULO, 10 Dec 1877 Hudson, NH
   James Nutting
   Joseph Roulo
NUTTING, Linda R and Mickey L DANNEWITZ, 25 Nov 1967 Hudson, NH
NYE, Kenneth B and Lynn A D'AMBROISE, 28 Sep 1980 Hudson, NH
NYSTROM, Robert E and Joanne L THOMAS, 07 Apr 1973 Nashua, NH
O, Won Suk and Paul W WHITE, 29 Sep 1984 Nashua, NH
O'BEIRNE, Doris C and Donald H WENTWORTH, 16 Jun 1941 Hudson, NH
O'BRIEN, Annie and Jos P GALLAGHER, 30 Nov 1910 Hudson, NH
   John O'Brien & Margaret Tannerhill
   Jos A Gallagher & Margaret Brodie
O'BRIEN, Denise M and Raymond E PELLETIER, 11 Apr 1981 Hudson, NH
O'BRIEN, Frederick & Madeline A CONNELL, 24 Dec 1930 Harrington, ME
O'BRIEN, Howard A and Blanche A ROLLINS, 05 Aug 1938 Hudson, NH
O'BRIEN, Robert P and Dorothea P CADIGAN, 05 Oct 1946 Hudson, NH
O'BRYAN, Francis L and Marion MARSH, 17 Jun 1902 Nashua, NH
   Lafayette O'Bryan & Betty
   Walter H Marsh & Lizzie S Wilder
O'CONNELL, Kevin M and Nancy J DRAKE, 24 Sep 1983 Nashua, NH
O'CONNELL, Michael and Eileen F McNEILL, 01 Nov 1975 Nashua, NH
O'CONNOR, Elaine N and Robert W BENNETT, 19 Feb 1955 Hudson, NH
O'CONNOR, John and Lucy E CLEMENT, 21 Mar 1865
O'CONNOR, Mary A and Roger A BRADLEY, 08 Aug 1969 Jaffrey, NH
O'DONNELL, John P and Mary ZUBEN, 24 May 1934 Nashua, NH
O'DONNELL, Kathleen S and Roger J DOUVILLE, 07 Sep 1979 Nashua, NH
O'DONNELL, William J and Helen G BURRILL, 21 Apr 1943 Hudson, NH
O'GARA, Francis J III & Marilyn L NADEAU, 18 Jul 1967 Merrimack, NH
O'HALLORAN, Barbara A and John L GINNETTY, 31 May 1981 Hudson, NH
O'KEEFE, Sheila A and David A CLEGG, 16 Nov 1973 Salem, NH
O'KEEFE, Sheila A and Dale M PETERS, 27 Nov 1965 Nashua, NH
O'LEARY, Maurine B and David K PURCELL, 15 Jul 1978 Hudson, NH
O'LOUGHLIN, Carol Ann and Gerald R COTE, 30 Mar 1973 Litchfield, NH
O'LOUGHLIN, Frances A & William J SMILIKIS, 21 May 1966 Nashua, NH
O'MALLEY, Marie and Edward J LEBRUN, 21 Aug 1982 Derry, NH
O'NEAL, Nancy J and Joseph H KEUENHOFF, 30 Mar 1974 Nashua, NH
O'NEAL, Nancy J and David B MOLNAR, 04 Sep 1981 Hudson, NH
O'NEIL, Colleen E and Keith A BAKAIAN, 07 Jul 1967 Hudson, NH
O'NEIL, Geraldine and Richard O ANDERSON, 22 Feb 1934 Hudson, NH
O'NEIL, Jerri-Lynn and Anselmo Jr REYNA, 19 Jan 1979 Nashua, NH
O'NEIL, John F E and Valeria T MAGUDER, 03 Sep 1942 Hudson, NH
O'NEIL, Josephine M and Herbert W DANDLEY, 20 Dec 1921 Nashua, NH
O'NEIL, Martin J and Jessie K MALCOLM, 11 Nov 1949 Hudson, NH
O'NEIL, Michael F and Theresa B McGUINNESS, 23 Jun 1984 Hudson, NH
O'NEIL, Robert and Shirley M NICHOLS, 05 Apr 1944 Nashua, NH
O'NEIL, Ruth and Frank VICKERS, 27 Mar 1948 Hudson, NH
O'NEILL, Patti J and George M Jr CANFIELD, 29 May 1971 Nashua, NH
O'ROURKE, Michael J and Linda P STRAUSS, 10 Jul 1982 Milford, NH
OAKES, John F and Marie MANTENUTO, 07 Feb 1942 Hudson, NH
OBAN, Carol A and Donald P LAVOIE, 23 Feb 1963 Hudson, NH
OBAN, Clayton C and Effie M WINN, 24 Jan 1942 Nashua, NH
OBAN, Effie May and Franklin R TORREY, 05 Nov 1977 Hudson, NH
OBELSKY, Freida R and Daniel A BRIENZI, 24 Jan 1931 Nashua, NH
OBORNE, Isabelle and Gunnar ENGSTROM, 17 Dec 1941 Manchester, NH

HUDSON, NH MARRIAGES

OBST, Anneliese and Albert K WEBBER, 02 Aug 1947 Hudson, NH
OGARA, Catherine and Edward A REED, 07 Sep 1910 Hudson, NH
   Domick Ogara & Bridge Ogara
   Philip M Reed & Hannah Reed
OGDON, Ada and E E FORBES, 01 Jul 1876 Hudson, NH
OGILVIE, Clayton P and Janice E BOYNTON, 08 Oct 1971 Hudson, NH
OGINSKY, Vera B and Joseph S KAROS, 27 Nov 1944 Nashua, NH
OHLIN, Peter A and Susan E SHIEBLER, 14 Apr 1979 Hudson, NH
OIKLE, David L and Stacey Ann BIAVA, 20 Apr 1985 Hudson, NH
OIKLE, Harriet Jo and Robert Swa HALGREN, 25 Apr 1981 Nashua, NH
OIKLE, Pamela A and Kevin J KRUPA, 08 Feb 1977 Nashua, NH
OIKLE, Therese M and Charles E BROWN, 30 Apr 1982 Nashua, NH
OLDFIELD, Fred and Grace M ENGLISH, 09 Nov 1946 Hudson, NH
OLENA, Cynthia G and Donald T JEAN, 31 Dec 1964 Salem, NH
OLENA, Raymond W and Charlotte LANE, 29 Jun 1964 Manchester, NH
OLESON, Lloyd A and Dorothy O TUCKER, 09 Jan 1949 Hudson, NH
OLHA, Mary E and Richard J MANNING, 22 May 1983 Hudson, NH
OLIARI, Gloria A and Francis W GODDARD, 17 Feb 1949 Hudson, NH
OLIVER, Bernard L and Florence M BORDEN, 31 Dec 1949 Hudson, NH
OLIVER, Donna M and Floyd L GAWTHORP, 23 Dec 1968 Hudson, NH
OLIVER, George K and Katherine HARWOOD, 21 Aug 1946 Hudson, NH
OLIVER, Pearl B and Harry W BROWN, 20 Jul 1941 Hudson, NH
OLIVIERA, Marie R and Edward J McLAREN, 02 Jan 1949 Hudson, NH
OLIVOLO, Dominic and Leora W WILSON, 25 Feb 1950 Hudson, NH
OLOFSON, Carl E and Margaret SPECK, 13 May 1954 Hudson, NH
OLSON, Lawrence E Jr and Roxanne ROUILLARD, 12 Apr 1980 Hudson, NH
OLSON, Lois M and John R BAKER, 23 Dec 1950 Marlboro, NH
OLSON, Richard E and Nancy L MELANSON, 17 Apr 1965 Seabrook, NH
OPAROWSKI, Hedwig and Stanley KAYROS, 17 May 1941 Manchester, NH
OPSAHL, Jean E and Joseph B HATCH, 04 Jul 1938 Hudson, NH
ORANGE, Raymond V and Dorothy M McCLELLAND, 26 Aug 1950 Hudson, NH
ORDWAY, Frank D and Anna M FOX, 01 Oct 1861
ORDZIE, Edmund A and Christine McKAY, 24 Jun 1972 Pelham, NH
ORLANDO, Madeline R and Albert LAMBERT, 01 Oct 1949 Hudson, NH
ORMES, Ruth M and Hatford O BENT, 15 Dec 1925 Hudson, NH
ORPIK, Mary V and Edward J BOUDROT, 17 Jul 1948 Hudson, NH
ORSER, Betty E and Arthur W Jr CHASE, 30 Nov 1945 Hudson, NH
OSBORN, Norman G and Edna L HENDERSON, 03 Jul 1930 Hudson, NH
OSBORNE, Grace P and Frank B NICHOLS, 18 Jun 1917 Nashua, NH
OSBORNE, Stuart L Sr and Judith A ROUSSEAU, 21 Mar 1981 Hudson, NH
OSGOOD, Ania E and George W Jr MARSHALL, 16 Jun 1878 Tyngsboro, MA
   Josiah Osgood (Milford, NH) & Willminia (Hooksett)
   George W Marshall(Sharon, NH) & Miranda (Hudson, NH)
OSGOOD, Anson and Josephine DICKERMAN, 10 Aug 1905 Hudson, NH
   Robert B Osgood & Susanne Senter
   Jonathan B Foss & Hannah Coombs
OSGOOD, Henry Colb and Betty HAMBLET, 08 Jun 1797
OSGOOD, Josephine and William H THOMAS, 04 Jul 1864
OSGOOD, Mary and Willis Z ACKERMAN, 02 Mar 1891
OSGOOD, Mary P F and Willis D ACKERMAN, 02 May 1891 Hudson, NH
   Anson A Osgood (Lyndeboro, NH) & Hannah M Parker (Boston, MA)
   Wm H Ackerman(Alexandria) & Henrietta Lane (Lee)
OSGOOD, Wilhemina and James CARNES, 09 Sep 1869
OSGOOD, Willemene and James CARNES, 04 Apr 1869
OSMAN, Jo Ann M and Raymond J Jr MOORE, 07 Sep 1973 Hudson, NH
OSMER, Anne M and George W MORSE, 29 May 1941 Salem, NH
OSMER, Frank J Jr and Louise M FARLEY, 08 Sep 1946 Nashua, NH
OSMER, Kelly D and Beverly J DAVIS, 10 Jun 1978 Hudson, NH
OSMER, Lester E and Yolande P HEBERT, 23 Jun 1951 Nashua, NH
OSMER, Marie F O and Gerard E VOYER, 26 Apr 1944 Nashua, NH

HUDSON, NH MARRIAGES

OSMER, Rita M R and Victor A GAGNON, 03 Jan 1944 Hudson, NH
OSMER, Stephen R and Carole A BRETON, 10 Jun 1972 Hudson, NH
OSORIO, Julian D and Laureen KAREM, 22 Jan 1985 Nashua, NH
OTIS, Barbara P and Willard T ELLIS, 24 Dec 1944 Hudson, NH
OTIS, David C and Debra Anne HUGHES, 19 Nov 1976 Windham, NH
OTIS, Eugene W and Joan M GARSIDE, 10 Nov 1956 Hudson, NH
OTIS, Isabelle E and Winthrop E LUND, 21 Sep 1936 Hudson, NH
OTIS, Lloyd E and Dorothy A BOYER, 31 Jul 1965 Hudson, NH
OTIS, Mary Alice and Stanton A Jr HANCOCK, 06 Oct 1962 Hollis, NH
OTIS, Pearl L and Harry C PETERS, 22 Jan 1943 Derry, NH
OTIS, Ruth M and Arthur M DOOLEY, 09 Mar 1935 Hudson, NH
OTIS, Stephen L and Denise R CARON, 30 May 1981 Hudson, NH
OTTE, Frederick and Sharon M DOWLING, 14 May 1983 Nashua, NH
OTTERSON, Robert J Jr and Kristine M MOORE, 23 Aug 1980 Nashua, NH
OUELLET, Arthur J and Alice M BERGERON, 09 May 1959 Nashua, NH
OUELLET, Carole J and Robert P LANDRY, 19 May 1984 Hudson, NH
OUELLET, Raymond A and Gabrielle LACHANCE, 02 Jun 1956 Nashua, NH
OUELLET, Raynald J and Sharon B SZALANSKI, 23 Jun 1979 Hudson, NH
OUELLET, Richard E and Donna M WALTERS, 21 Mar 1981 Hudson, NH
OUELLETTE, Ada V and Hazen O JOHNSON, 18 Nov 1967 Nashua, NH
OUELLETTE, Ann L and Normand A MERCIER, 05 Sep 1970 Nashua, NH
OUELLETTE, August R and Pauline G LAQUERRE, 29 Sep 1947 Nashua, NH
OUELLETTE, Carolyn and Karl Micha MUNDAY, 14 Feb 1985 Nashua, NH
OUELLETTE, Cheryl S and Joseph H KEUENOFF, 11 Jul 1981 Hudson, NH
OUELLETTE, Daniel A and Shirley A MICHAUD, 04 Mar 1967 Hudson, NH
OUELLETTE, Diane E and Robert R PELKEY, 16 Aug 1969 Nashua, NH
OUELLETTE, Donald M and Jean L LEMERISE, 22 Dec 1956 Hudson, NH
OUELLETTE, George J Jr & Marguerite H'T'ISON, 29 Sep 1950 Hudson, NH
OUELLETTE, Gloria L and Herbert O McCARTHY, 12 Jul 1963 Hudson, NH
OUELLETTE, Joey G and Celeste E ROUSSEL, 08 Oct 1976 Hudson, NH
OUELLETTE, John M and Cheryl S HETZER, 22 Jun 1974 Hudson, NH
OUELLETTE, Judith G and Raymond P WHEELER, 16 Mar 1974 Hudson, NH
OUELLETTE, Leonard G and Judith G LAMBERT, 10 Aug 1968 Hudson, NH
OUELLETTE, Mae R and Philip R LANGELIER, 14 Feb 1953 Nashua, NH
OUELLETTE, Michael A and Helen P DANIELS, 06 Jun 1973 Windham, NH
OUELLETTE, Nancy A and Luther E NICHOLS, 30 Jun 1984 Hudson, NH
OUELLETTE, Olive T and Norman L TESSIER, 10 May 1947 Nashua, NH
OUELLETTE, Paul G and Shirley A BEAULIEU, 19 Jan 1979 Hudson, NH
OUELLETTE, Paul R and Louise I PLAMONDON, 19 Jun 1971 Nashua, NH
OUELLETTE, Paula J and Timothy D ENGLISH, 29 Sep 1972 Hudson, NH
OUELLETTE, Phillip E and Alecia Ann ASSELIN, 07 Nov 1981 Hudson, NH
OUELLETTE, Rita M and Lester F GOVE, 28 Jun 1948 Hudson, NH
OUELLETTE, Robert A and Yvonne L GRIGAS, 02 Sep 1967 Hudson, NH
OUELLETTE, Steven A and Kathleen M MINTON, 14 May 1976 Pelham, NH
OUELLETTE, Sylvia J and Raymond E MONDOUX, 01 Sep 1952 Hudson, NH
OUIMET, Douglas P and Sheila Ann MURPHY, 29 Sep 1972 Hudson, NH
OUIMETTE, Patricia L & Edward P MARDEN, 10 Jan 1981 Somersworth, NH
OVERBY, Lori B and Richard M ROZZI, 01 Aug 1981 Hudson, NH
OVERY, Charles E and Linnian A LOVELL, 16 May 1942 Nashua, NH
OWEN, Marian V and Oran E RUMRILL, 24 Sep 1925 Manchester, NH
OWENS, Ralph F and Gail W ABBOTT, 26 Sep 1970 Hudson, NH
PACHECO, Nancy J and Leon J III SNYDER, 16 Apr 1972 Pelham, NH
PACIELLO, Michael G and Kim A WEST, 13 Jun 1981 Nashua, NH
PACKARD, Ina L and Henry D McEWEN, 07 Aug 1938 Hudson, NH
PACKARD, Robert Bur Jr and Wendy B GROSSO, 29 Dec 1984 Hudson, NH
PACKARD, Winthrop H and Marjorie E HILLS, 27 May 1948 Hudson, NH
PACKER, Laurie Ann & David Earl GATES, 24 Dec 1972 Mont Vernon, NH
PACKHURST, Steven H and Cheryl N KELLEY, 13 Nov 1971 Nashua, NH
PACKOR, Joseph and Ruth Anne REYNOLDS, 25 Jun 1938 Nashua, NH
PACKOR, Mary-Ellen and David L JENNEY, 13 Jun 1964 Hudson, NH

HUDSON, NH MARRIAGES

PAGAN, Pedro P and Carol A BISHOP, 02 Aug 1969 Hudson, NH
PAGE, Abraham and Dorothy HADLEY, 04 Dec 1784
PAGE, Betsey and Abel Jr WEBBER, 18 Nov 1819
PAGE, Betsey and Abel Jr WEBBER, 18 May 1819
PAGE, David L and Dierdra L EMERSON, 02 Sep 1984 Nashua, NH
PAGE, Emma A and Edwin E SNOW, 01 Jun 1866
PAGE, Frye and Sarah TENNEY, 24 Oct 1816
PAGE, Hannah and Moody FOSTER, 17 Mar 1830
PAGE, Harriet E and Cyrus ROGERS, 19 Dec 1861
PAGE, James and Carol H MARTEIN, 23 Feb 1974 Hudson, NH
PAGE, James Paul and Sandra Eve EDWARDS, 23 Aug 1980 Hudson, NH
PAGE, Jewel C and Roger O LAVARNWAY, 08 Jun 1974 Nashua, NH
PAGE, John and Rachel SMITH, 18 Aug 1796
PAGE, Lucienne and Lionel GUILBERT, 30 May 1940 Nashua, NH
PAGE, Lucille E and Charles RODONIS, 14 May 1940 Lowell, MA
PAGE, M Frances and George W HASELTON, 25 May 1860
PAGE, Michael L and Sally E MANSFIELD, 02 Sep 1978 Hudson, NH
PAGE, Patti L and Calvin W Jr LOCKE, 27 Oct 1973 Nashua, NH
PAGLIUCA, Michelle J and William G MAINE, 16 May 1981 Hudson, NH
PAIGE, Elaine L and Johnny A GURLEY, 27 Apr 1957 Nashua, NH
PAIGE, George S and Helen B BURNS, 26 Aug 1932 Nashua, NH
PAINE, Carrie I and George W H WEBBER, 01 Feb 1912 Nashua, NH
  Leonard B Paine & Susanna W Beals
  William H Webber & Hattie D Burdett
PAINE, Henry Lee and Olga Marsh ANDREWS, 22 May 1938 Nashua, NH
PAINE, Linda Ann and John M BRIAND, 29 Jul 1972 Hudson, NH
PALADINO, James F and Theresa G HAMELIN, 26 Jan 1957 Hudson, NH
PALADINO, Richard D and Judith A MOULTON, 18 May 1979 Salem, NH
PALANGI, Mary and James J LALLY, 03 Jul 1948 Hudson, NH
PALANSKI, Anne L and John F SOJKA, 20 Jun 1953 Nashua, NH
PALEOSELITI, Vasila and Sotiri BEZA, 10 Jun 1928 Hudson, NH
PALEVICIUS, Alphonse F and Elaine C MORENCY, 28 Sep 1963 Hudson, NH
PALIOCA, Elizabeth and Albert D QUIROZ, 13 Apr 1963 Hudson, NH
PALLEMANS, Walter and Jessie E FROTTON, 12 Oct 1925 Tilton, NH
PALLERIA, Robert A and Lynne S BEAUMONT, 15 Jul 1978 Nashua, NH
PALMER, Benjamin W and Ruby E DUMAS, 02 Jul 1927 Hudson, NH
PALMER, Charles W and Joanne R ALMEIDA, 05 Aug 1961 Hudson, NH
PALMER, Cheryl P and Arthur L MARSHALL, 13 Jun 1981 Hudson, NH
PALMER, Elizabeth and Caleb RICHARDSON, 22 May 1853
PALMER, Ian D and Georgia L SNELL, 15 Jul 1978 Hudson, NH
PALMER, James T and Abigail POLLARD, Apr
PALMER, Janet D and Warren F ELLIS, 07 Nov 1969 Dover, NH
PALMER, Lillian and George A Jr FORRENCE, 14 Feb 1931 Dunstable, MA
PALMER, Lillian L and Donald E CORTELL, 26 Feb 1950 Hudson, NH
PALMER, M Jean and Pasquale DESIMONE, 18 Jul 1964 Hudson, NH
PALMER, Malvina and Dustin RIPLEY, 03 Jan 1847
PALMER, Ralph C Jr and Lauri L BOURGEOIS, 29 May 1982 Nashua, NH
PALMER, Sarah T and Mark H WEBSTER, 06 Mar 1828
PALMER, Sidney H and Mary E GREELEY, 17 May 1862
PALMER, Sidney H and Mary E GREELEY, 14 May 1862
PALMIERI, Mary E and Raymond E BLUNDEN, 11 Jun 1966 Hudson, NH
PALUMBO, William A and Laura J KELLEY, 04 Jul 1982 Hudson, NH
PAMAGOULIS, Peter and Thelma E EDWARDS, 07 Jun 1928 Dunstable, MA
PANAGEOTES, Constance and Dennis J RACINE, 09 Jul 1976 Nashua, NH
PANAGOULIS, Antonia & William ANAGNOST, 11 Sep 1948 Manchester, NH
PANAGOULIS, Euphemia and Constine FOUNDAS, 02 Dec 1934 Nashua, NH
PANAGOULIS, Nicholas G and Lora E McKINNEY, 04 Oct 1952 Hudson, NH
PANARELLI, Theresa M and John P FLANNERY, 01 Oct 1973 Hudson, NH
PANAS, Patricia A and Robert C PANAS, 28 Jan 1984 Hudson, NH
PANAS, Robert C and Patricia A PANAS, 28 Jan 1984 Hudson, NH

HUDSON,NH MARRIAGES

PAPASODORO, Lucy and Franklyn E JACOBSEN, 31 Dec 1949 Hudson, NH
PAPPAS, John N and Rosemarie PICANO, 08 Jul 1971 Nashua, NH
PAPPAS, Martha S and Charles E BROWN, 10 Dec 1977 Pelham, NH
PAQUET, Alice L and Roland A BOSSE, 18 Jul 1954 Dublin, NH
PAQUET, Iris M and Kenneth A MacIVER, 21 Jun 1957 Lakeport, NH
PAQUETTE, Albert J and Rita C BOURGAULT, 04 Jul 1943 Nashua, NH
PAQUETTE, Barden D and Mary Eliza CAMPBELL, 07 Nov 1981 Nashua, NH
PAQUETTE, Brian A and Janet M GOULET, 19 May 1984 Nashua, NH
PAQUETTE, Constance and Gary L WEBSTER, 21 Aug 1971 Hudson, NH
PAQUETTE, Debra J and Stephen J RIESLAND, 12 Sep 1981 Derry, NH
PAQUETTE, Denise T and Thomas G KELLER, 06 Apr 1979 Hudson, NH
PAQUETTE, Diane T and Russell P CROUTEAU, 11 Sep 1976 Hudson, NH
PAQUETTE, Florence M and Louis PELLETIER, 12 Oct 1968 Hudson, NH
PAQUETTE, JoAnn R and Paul T DURAND, 01 Jun 1968 Nashua, NH
PAQUETTE, Joseph A and Alma LEFEBURE, 01 Oct 1923 Nashua, NH
PAQUETTE, Lynn Carol and Richard N METTA, 23 Nov 1984 Hudson, NH
PAQUETTE, Maurice G and Joanne D COTE, 23 Nov 1968 Hudson, NH
PAQUETTE, Robert J&Dorilda I DESBOISBRIAND, 04 Aug 1939 Hudson, NH
PAQUETTE, Victoria T and George C DUPONT, 25 Apr 1959 Hudson, NH
PAQUETTE, Wayne M and Carol J BECKHAM, 06 Nov 1970 Nashua, NH
PAQUETTE, Yvette M and Vernon P MITTON, 04 Sep 1971 Hudson, NH
PAQUIN, Jeffrey A and Connie G LAVOIE, 29 Nov 1980 Hudson, NH
PAQUIN, Real A and Marlene M LEVESQUE, 05 Sep 1970 Hudson, NH
PAQUIN, Rene and Gail S MacGRATH, 23 Jun 1973 Nashua, NH
PARADIS, Armand and Beatrice BERNARD, 29 Jun 1936 Nashua, NH
PARADIS, Conrad and Clarice BERNARD, 25 Oct 1934 Nashua, NH
PARADIS, Debbie M and Daniel SCIRETTA, 19 Sep 1981 Hudson, NH
PARADIS, Irene and Alphonse DUMAIS, 19 Apr 1934 Nashua, NH
PARADIS, Linda A and Daniel E CLOUTIER, 24 Apr 1982 Nashua, NH
PARADIS, Victor and Alice MAILLOUX, 23 Aug 1928 Nashua, NH
PARADIS, Wayne M and Casianna HARTLEN, 15 Feb 1975 Hudson, NH
PARADISE, Claire M and Leo R LATULIPPE, 25 Apr 1964 Hudson, NH
PARADISE, Diane Marie and Robin L PATTEN, 02 May 1981 Hudson, NH
PARADISE, Elaine A and Albert R ANCTIL, 05 Feb 1982 Nashua, NH
PARADISE, Ernest O and Dolores C MAYNARD, 12 Nov 1960 Nashua, NH
PARADISE, Joseph G and Theresa D HART, 28 Feb 1959 Merrimack, NH
PARADISE, Leo P and Lillian O ST ARMAND, 11 Jul 1959 Hudson, NH
PARADISE, Lucille I and Walter E INGRAM, 21 Aug 1981 Hudson, NH
PARADISE, Maurice G and Rita L BERTHIAUME, 20 Jul 1946 Nashua, NH
PARADISE, Nancy P and William J EARLEY, 19 May 1963 Hollis, NH
PARADISE, Normand J and Candace A DEARBORN, 02 May 1970 Hudson, NH
PARADISE, Peter G and Kim T ZIMMERMAN, 16 May 1981 Hudson, NH
PARDY, Mark E and Linda HODGKINS, 16 May 1981 Hudson, NH
PARE, Donald E and Edythe A SNELL, 08 Nov 1974 Nashua, NH
PARE, Gerard R and Claire G PARISEAU, 25 Aug 1951 Hudson, NH
PARE, Marie-Therese and Gerard W LAVOIE, 05 Oct 1953 Nashua, NH
PARE, Michelle I and Brian E TYLER, 08 Oct 1983 Manchester, NH
PARENT, Chester R and Judith M SNYDER, 02 Oct 1971 Manchester, NH
PARENT, Dawn L and Gary A PURINGTON, 05 Jan 1980 Hudson, NH
PARENT, Elaine T and Dennis W RIOUX, 12 May 1973 Nashua, NH
PARENT, Georgette and Robert C PELLERIN, 29 Dec 1956 Nashua, NH
PARENT, Henry L and Bernice E BURTON, 09 Jun 1950 Hudson, NH
PARENT, Richard D and Darlene A BRACCIO, 21 Sep 1974 Hudson, NH
PARENT, Senard B and Alva M GORANSON, 21 Dec 1940 Hudson, NH
PARENT, Stephen W and Laurie K NIXON, 25 Jun 1977 Nashua, NH
PARHAM, Jonathan and Elizabeth POLLARD, 08 May 1777
PARISEAU, Claire G and Gerard R PARE, 25 Aug 1951 Hudson, NH
PARISEAU, Eugene and Germaine LECLERE, 06 Sep 1926 Nashua, NH
PARISEAU, Pauline A and Ronald N LUCAS, 20 Jun 1959 Hudson, NH
PARISEAU, Vita Y and Romeo W LANDRY, 21 Sep 1946 Nashua, NH

HUDSON, NH MARRIAGES

PARK, Frank N and Gladys M THOMPSON, 24 Sep 1921 Nashua, NH
PARKE, Lillian A and Arthur R PHALON, 13 Aug 1940 Hudson, NH
PARKER, Barbara A and Donald L Jr HAES, 28 Jul 1984 Hudson, NH
PARKER, Barbara E and William I DUNN, 04 Nov 1933 Hudson, NH
PARKER, Charles C and Ruth E BLOOD, 09 Apr 1933 Hollis, NH
PARKER, Claudia E and Richard A BOUCHER, 28 Jun 1930 Hudson, NH
PARKER, Donna Ann and Kenneth J KABLIK, 08 Jan 1977 Nashua, NH
PARKER, Edith F and Walter D EATON, 12 Oct 1932 Hudson, NH
PARKER, Edward M and Grace M PHILLIPS, 07 May 1921 Hudson, NH
PARKER, Evelyn E and Romeo F WILLETTE, 01 Sep 1950 Hudson, NH
PARKER, Francis F and Marion N PARKER, 26 Nov 1952 Peterborough, NH
PARKER, George H and Edith F SNOW, 28 Apr 1908 Hudson, NH
   Charles C Parker & Lydia L Batchelder
   Royal G Snow & Ardelle E Walker
PARKER, George H Jr and Lucille SMITH, 24 Oct 1935 Nashua, NH
PARKER, Gerry F and Georgie BOYNTON, 10 Nov 1904 Hudson, NH
   John Parker & Eldora M Dodge
   John E Boynton & Frances Haskell
PARKER, Grace V and William NICOLL, 06 Apr 1935 Hudson, NH
PARKER, Helen V and John O NAJARIAN, 10 Sep 1932 Hudson, NH
PARKER, John E and Grace H CONNELL, 10 Nov 1934 Hudson, NH
PARKER, John E and Virginia G COOLIDGE, 21 Jun 1968 Moultonboro, NH
PARKER, Joseph and Julia WILLOUGHBY, 29 Feb 1848
PARKER, Katherine and Frank H WOODS, 10 Dec 1938 Nashua, NH
PARKER, Lorraine G and Robert M Jr THOMPSON, 20 Apr 1963 Hudson, NH
PARKER, Lydia J and Herbert M SMITH, 19 Mar 1906 Hudson, NH
   Charles C Parker & Lydia F Batchelder
   Isaac N Smith & Roxanna Butler
PARKER, Marilyn H and James H ROLLINS, 22 Aug 1964 Hudson, NH
PARKER, Marion N and Francis F PARKER, 26 Nov 1952 Peterborough, NH
PARKER, Nancy and Werner KAUFHOLD, 27 Dec 1958 Proctor, VT
PARKER, Oscar W and Helen M BROOKS, 19 Feb 1950 Hollis, NH
PARKER, Polly and Solomon DEAN, 25 Feb 1796
PARKER, Raymond E and June BRICKETT, 16 Oct 1955 Hampstead, NH
PARKER, Richard B and Ruby M STODDARD, 24 Nov 1928 Nashua, NH
PARKER, Sarah and John DUSTON, 06 Apr 1743
PARKER, Sarah and Josiah DUTTON, 06 Apr 1743
PARKER, Zebulon and Polly JOHNSON, 18 Mar 1812
PARKES, Jesse and Elizabeth BISSONNETT, 31 Jul 1948 Hudson, NH
PARKHURST, Cheryl J and Donald A KASPER, 09 Mar 1968 Nashua, NH
PARKHURST, Michael P and Darlene E CHARETTE, 22 May 1971 Hudson, NH
PARKHURST, Vicki L and Edward R LAJOIE, 22 Nov 1975 Hudson, NH
PARKINSON, Henry W and Irene M BULDINI, 17 Aug 1940 Hudson, NH
PARMENTER, Marion R and Daniel G WEBSTER, 03 Oct 1931 Nashua, NH
PARON, Marion L and Robert L ROY, 12 Sep 1981 Hudson, NH
PARRIS, Annette and Oscar TOWNES, 26 Feb 1856
PARROTTE, Ethel and Myron DICK, 31 May 1947 Hudson, NH
PARSHLEY, Geraldine and Sanford E KING, 07 Dec 1946 Hudson, NH
PARSLOE, Henry and Alice McDONALD, 19 Mar 1930 Hudson, NH
PARSONS, Elliot W and Bernice M HAGGETT, 03 Aug 1946 Hudson, NH
PARTRIDGE, Joan E and Ivon BOYER, 28 Oct 1960 Nashua, NH
PATENAUDE, Donna E and Paul R BILODEAU, 04 Jul 1959 Hudson, NH
PATENAUDE, Patricia A and Gordon A MOORE, 19 Nov 1955 Hudson, NH
PATRICI, George C and Lillian M SMITH, 14 Aug 1948 Hudson, NH
PATRIDGE, Nancy A and Dennis M BOYKO, 22 Aug 1981 Bedford, NH
PATRIZZI, James and Myrtle A WILSON, 25 May 1933 Nashua, NH
PATRONICK, John J Jr and Kimberly A DONOVAN, 05 Jun 1982 Hudson, NH
PATTEN, Denise G and Francis B JENSEN, 17 Mar 1984 Hudson, NH
PATTEN, Michael A and Mary Jane KUCHINSKI, 15 Mar 1975 Nashua, NH
PATTEN, Raymond E and Elaine A DUPLEASE, 04 Jul 1966 Hudson, NH

HUDSON, NH MARRIAGES

PATTEN, Robin L and Diane Marie PARADISE, 02 May 1981 Hudson, NH
PATTEN, Roger E and Denise G DUPLEASE, 31 May 1971 Hudson, NH
PATTERSON, Marsha K and Charles W III BUSH, 09 Sep 1967 Nashua, NH
PATTERSON, Robert and Esther R SPAULDING, 27 Nov 1809
PATTERSON, Susan H and Clark R WESTNEAT, 24 Mar 1973 Hudson, NH
PATTON, James F and Jeannette LECLERC, 13 Aug 1974 Hudson, NH
PAUL, Armand and Eva JACQUES, 18 Nov 1920 Nashua, NH
PAUL, Catherine and Thomas J BREEN, 11 Sep 1937 Hudson, NH
PAUL, Janet L and Charles M WRIGHT, 13 Oct 1947 Nashua, NH
PAUL, Stanley S and Beatrice L SILVERMAN, 10 May 1947 Hudson, NH
PAVELKA, Thomas S and Jo Ann GREATCHUS, 05 Jul 1969 Hudson, NH
PAVLOSKY, Rena P and Jack P SARNO, 07 Nov 1980 Hudson, NH
PEABODY, Martha L and John A REED, 18 Feb 1964 Nashua, NH
PEACOCK, Phyllis W and Richard M HINCHMAN, 03 Oct 1936 Hudson, NH
PEARCE, Richard A and Donna M LECLER, 01 May 1976 Hudson, NH
PEARL, Harold R and Ina G KIERSTEAD, 12 Aug 1950 Hudson, NH
PEARSON, Ellen J and Thomas J FOLEY, 04 Sep 1939 Manchester, NH
PEARSON, Mark R and Cathy A IRWIN, 19 Jun 1976 Hudson, NH
PEARSON, Mary J and Ashton W BROWN, 27 Sep 1922 Hudson, NH
PEARSONS, Hannah and William FAIRFIELD, 01 Jan 1826
PEARSONS, Helen A and Calvin C MARDEN, 02 Jun 1865
PEARSONS, Kelly and Calvin C MARDEN, 12 Jun 1865
PEARULT, Hazeldel and Leon Josep MANIOU, 31 Dec 1933 Nashua, NH
PEASE, Katie F and John F DODGE, 15 Dec 1864
PEASE, Theresa E and George G GAGE, 13 Dec 1864
PEASE, Thirza and George G GAY, 13 Dec 1864
PEASLEE, Benjamin and Ethel A GAY, 15 Jun 1919 Hudson, NH
PEASLEE, Robyn D and Terrell L ELAM, 14 Jun 1980 Litchfield, NH
PEASLEE, Vernon F and Evelyn G NICHOLS, 24 May 1941 Hudson, NH
PEASLEE, Virginia A and George A FISHER, 18 Jun 1949 Hudson, NH
PEASLEY, Densie Lou and Charles Ot WEBSTER,
PECHECO, Rosemary A and David A TATE, 17 Jun 1972 Pelham, NH
PECK, Barry M and Joanne L BERUBE, 07 Nov 1970 Hudson, NH
PECK, Edwina J and Thomas H CONNELL, 11 Mar 1873 Dracut, MA
PECK, Nickie A and Constance BERUBE, 24 Jan 1970 Hudson, NH
PECKER, Ida and Leo CLINE, 19 Apr 1934 Hudson, NH
PECKHAM, Clarence E and Annie I KIMBALL, 19 Feb 1907 Hudson, NH
   Stepehn C Peckham & Grace I Eldridge
   John R Kimball (Delora Tarbell)
PECKHAM, Viola Y and Alfonse SAULENAS, 04 Jun 1949 Hudson, NH
PEDATO, Frank and Barbara BROWN, 23 Jun 1949 Hudson, NH
PEDRO, Gladys H and Oliver ROBINSON, 03 Apr 1948 Hudson, NH
PELCHAT, Adrian J Jr&Denise B BELLEFEUILLE, 16 Aug 1969 Hudson, NH
PELKEY, Anthony V and Linda L MANSUR, 01 Jul 1968 Hudson, NH
PELKEY, Dean Micha and Claudia Ro LEVESQUE, 03 Feb 1973 Hudson, NH
PELKEY, Juanita R and John D FLAHIVE, 31 Jan 1958 Hudson, NH
PELKEY, Linda I and Thomas C LAWTON, 22 Jul 1967 Hudson, NH
PELKEY, Lizzie and Moses B FORD, 16 Oct 1888 Hudson, NH
   Herbert Pelkey (Houlton, ME) & Virginia Mashiel (Madawaskee, ME)
   Timothy S Ford(W Fairlee, VT) & Sarah G Fuller (Hudson, NH)
PELKEY, Robert R and Diane E OUELLETTE, 16 Aug 1969 Nashua, NH
PELKEY, Robin Mari and Harry R Jr EVERETT, 01 Sep 1984 Nashua, NH
PELKEY, Thomas O and Barbara A GAGNON, 05 Sep 1959 Hudson, NH
PELLAND, Roger W and Claire T BARLOW, 02 Jun 1956 Hudson, NH
PELLEGRINI, Anthony J and Geraldine WITALIS, 15 Feb 1975 Hudson, NH
PELLERIN, Michel L and Laurie A VARNEY, 03 Oct 1981 Hudson, NH
PELLERIN, Robert C and Georgette PARENT, 29 Dec 1956 Nashua, NH
PELLERIN, Roger J and Lucille N SOMERVILLE, 24 Oct 1964 Nashua, NH
PELLERIN, Roger J and Phyliss E CHARRON, 30 Mar 1967 Nashua, NH
PELLETIER, Anita O and Gerald Reed DUNCKLEE, 24 Sep 1938 Nashua, NH

HUDSON, NH MARRIAGES

PELLETIER, Anne M and Charles T MUZZEY, 29 Oct 1983 Nashua, NH
PELLETIER, Carol A and Galen W BILLS, 01 Jul 1967 Londonderry, NH
PELLETIER, Catherine and Paul A LANDRY, 25 Sep 1976 Hudson, NH
PELLETIER, Corrine T and Harold L WILMOT, 22 Sep 1979 Hudson, NH
PELLETIER, Daniel L and Deborah An BROWN, 06 Aug 1977 Pelham, NH
PELLETIER, David L and Wanda L VAYENS, 14 Aug 1982 Hudson, NH
PELLETIER, Dennis L and Pamela M GAY, 31 Jul 1971 Nashua, NH
PELLETIER, Elaine E and Stanley KAZLOUSKAS, 10 May 1946 Nashua, NH
PELLETIER, Ernest J and Ruby E FISH, 18 Aug 1934 Manchester, NH
PELLETIER, Frank and Blanche GIROUARD, 25 Nov 1915 Nashua, NH
    Frank Pelletier (Canada) & Marguerite Peno (Canada)
    Joseph Girouard(Canada) & Calestine Courterie (Canada)
PELLETIER, Gerard L and Deborah L BOULARD, 06 Sep 1980 Hudson, NH
PELLETIER, Gertrude and Henry LORAINE, 19 May 1924 Nashua, NH
PELLETIER, Jacqueline and Paul A LAINE, 01 Sep 1979 Hudson, NH
PELLETIER, Jacqueline & Richard L TREMBLAY, 30 Aug 1958 Hudson, NH
PELLETIER, Jennette and Louis PODODISE, 23 Apr 1917 Jaffrey, NH
PELLETIER, Josephine and Andrew J SOUCY, 24 Nov 1949 Nashua, NH
PELLETIER, Linda T and Richard A NIXON, 31 Jul 1981 Nashua, NH
PELLETIER, Louis and Florence M PAQUETTE, 12 Oct 1968 Hudson, NH
PELLETIER, Louis P and Donna Lee LEVESQUE, 05 Jun 1982 Nashua, NH
PELLETIER, Margaret M and Kenneth E BURTON, 04 Sep 1944 Nashua, NH
PELLETIER, Marie R and Moise MARTIN, 22 Sep 1921 Nashua, NH
PELLETIER, Mary E and Andrew E HOWE, 18 Sep 1924 Hudson, NH
PELLETIER, Michael R and Judith M GAY, 19 Feb 1966 Nashua, NH
PELLETIER, Napoleon L & Mary Delima V GAGNON, 02 Feb 1920 Nashua, NH
PELLETIER, Norman and Constance JARRY, 27 Apr 1985 Nashua, NH
PELLETIER, Norman R and Nadine E DAIGLE, 28 May 1966 Hudson, NH
PELLETIER, Normand A and Phyllis JENKS, 26 Jun 1948 Nashua, NH
PELLETIER, Pamela L and Walter J KOSTYK, 05 Mar 1971 Nashua, NH
PELLETIER, Paul L and Carol A VADNEY, 30 Sep 1967 Hudson, NH
PELLETIER, Paul L and Elaine T KNIGHTS, 14 Feb 1975 Hudson, NH
PELLETIER, Paul N and Sandra M COLLINS, 07 Aug 1983 Hudson, NH
PELLETIER, Pauline J & Michel R DESCOUTEAUX, 28 Jan 1967 Hudson, NH
PELLETIER, Raymond E and Denise M O'BRIEN, 11 Apr 1981 Hudson, NH
PELLETIER, Reginald and Linda M POWELL, 21 Jun 1980 Nashua, NH
PELLETIER, Richard L and Linda M HAYES, 05 Jun 1971 Hudson, NH
PELLETIER, Richard M and Cynthia F CONRAD, 21 Jun 1969 Hudson, NH
PELLETIER, Robert L and Jeanine A LABRANCHE, 31 Aug 1963 Nashua, NH
PELLETIER, Roland H & Sharrel L DAIGLE, 08 Feb 1970 Manchester, NH
PELLETIER, Romeo E and Solange D BIBEAU, 13 May 1950 Hudson, NH
PELLETIER, Ronald E and Lenora M MARRIOTT, 03 Sep 1966 Hudson, NH
PELLETIER, Ronald L and Anne M GUILLOU, 02 Sep 1978 Hudson, NH
PELLETIER, Stella M and Joseph E PLAMONDON, 22 Apr 1961 Hudson, NH
PELLETIER, Susan L and Randy A TURMEL, 16 Nov 1984 Hudson, NH
PELLETIER, Suzanne R and Dennis P LANDRY, 27 Sep 1969 Hudson, NH
PELLETIER, Sylvie Line and James P COLLINS, 09 May 1981 Nashua, NH
PELLETIER, Telepshore and Irene SAVOY, 05 Apr 1926 Nashua, NH
PELLETIER, Theresa M and Conrad C COTE, 03 Jul 1946 Nashua, NH
PELLETIER, Thomas P and Joan V BEDORE, 29 Jul 1967 Hudson, NH
PELLETIER, Yvonne and Emile BOULEY, 04 Jul 1935 Nashua, NH
PELLETIER, Zephirin A and Mary L BENNETT, 24 Jun 1950 Hudson, NH
PELLITIER, Maurice G&Pauline Y JOHNSON, 02 Jul 1983 Londonderry, NH
PELRINE, Charles J and Eleanor M CORDEAU, 28 Mar 1949 Hudson, NH
PELTON, Kimber Lea and Daniel P BASCOM, 14 Aug 1976 Rochester, NH
PEMBERTON, Sarah and Thomas CROSS, 10 Feb 1785
PENDERS, Kenneth W II and Linda Ann LAVOIE, 01 Jun 1985 Hudson, NH
PENDLETON, Edward R Jr and Karen M DEYETT, 11 Jun 1983 Windham, NH
PENDLETON, Harry Jr and Estelle I LANDRY, 17 Jun 1967 Hudson, NH
PENDLEY, Floyd E and Agnes M HAINES, 27 Jul 1946 Hudson, NH

HUDSON, NH MARRIAGES

PENEY, Jo and Olive WINN, 08 Dec 1779
PENNELL, Philip A and Virginia M DUNKLEE, 18 Apr 1964 Hudson, NH
PENNEY, Evelyn and William W LAURENCE, 30 Jul 1930 Hudson, NH
PENNO, Dianna L and James R ARSENAULT, 06 Jun 1980 Nashua, NH
PENNO, Judith C and Harry E HOWE, 08 Sep 1984 Hudson, NH
PENO, Claudette and David K BRIAND, 05 Sep 1959 Hudson, NH
PENO, Kevin Paul and Mary E CAMPBELL, 20 Apr 1974 Hudson, NH
PEPAU, Joanna R and Keith R FOURNIER, 10 Sep 1983 Northumberland
PEPIN, John F and Laura A CLOUTIER, 24 Apr 1971 Hudson, NH
PEPIN, Reginald E and Debra C WOOD, 26 Mar 1982 Hudson, NH
PERANI, Alfred J and Impi I FRYE, 09 Oct 1949 Hudson, NH
PERAULT, Claire L and Simon MARTIN, 04 Jun 1982 Nashua, NH
PERCH, William E and Nancy M FERREURA, 04 Oct 1976 Pelham, NH
PERDUE, Harriet R and George H BESSEY, 28 Mar 1948 Hudson, NH
PEREZ, Pedro B and Elizabeth ANDERSON, 23 Dec 1983 Hudson, NH
PERFITO, Anthony J and Sandra S TALLQUIST, 24 Jul 1975 Milford, NH
PERHAM, Betsey and Elnathan SEARLES, 15 Feb 1812
PERHAM, Charles and Susanna FORD, 07 May 1811
PERHAM, George A and Nellie E BADGER, 22 Dec 1908 Hudson, NH
   William M Perham & Susan H Clark
   Lovejoy & Ellen R Hardy
PERHAM, John and Hannah WYMAN, 09 Mar 1742
PERHAM, John and Hannah WYMAN, 09 Mar 1741
PERHAM, Jonathan and Elizabeth POLLARD, 08 May 1777
PERHAM, Sargent and Mehittabel FOSTER, 29 Jan 1824
PERHAM, Sargent and Mehitable FOSTER, 29 Jan 1824
PERHAM, Willis and Susie Walch BOWEN, 12 Sep 1910 Hudson, NH
   Oliver Perham & Rebecca B Clark
   James E Walch & Susan M Beaman
PERIGNY, Alexander and Jeanette GADOWRY, 25 Jul 1941 Salem, NH
PERKINS, Barbara L and Victor L DOW, 26 Sep 1962 Hudson, NH
PERKINS, Basil N and Blanche D HOLMES, 05 Oct 1912 Lunenburg, MA
   Sumner Perkins & Annie Hayden
   Elmer Holmes & Abbie Merrill
PERKINS, Betsy and Elnathan SEARLES, 15 Feb 1812
PERKINS, Elias A and Mary T F HILL, 29 Oct 1864
PERKINS, Elias A and Mary F HILL, 29 Oct 1863
PERKINS, Ernest E and Flora BRODERICK, 12 Sep 1940 Nashua, NH
PERKINS, Herbert S & Mary E SHERBURN, 21 Feb 1920 New Bedford, MA
PERKINS, John H and Marion H SANDERS, 06 Jul 1911 Nashua, NH
   Sumner N Perkins & Annie Hayden
   James A Sanders & Jennie Hosman
PERKINS, Mary E and H A SHEPHERD, 07 Oct 1916 Nashua, NH
   Sumner Perkins (Albany, NY) & Annie Hayden (Douglastown, N B)
   Herbert F Shepherd(Saltriser, MI) & Delia M Lynch(Dublin, Ireland)
PERKINS, Nelson C and Louise M HARWOOD, 19 Sep 1914 Portsmouth, NH
   Jeremiah Perkins & Dora Hilton
   Henry Harwood & Mary Brennan
PERLAK, Wanda N and Thomas R GLEASON, 20 Dec 1949 Hudson, NH
PERRAULT, John H and Exilia GIROUARD, 09 Aug 1897 Hudson, NH
   Lewis Perrault & Ellen Kelly
   Joseph Girouard & Armini Macy
PERRAULT, Susan Lee and Gregory Al WOOD, 10 Apr 1982 Nashua, NH
PERRITANO, Anthony N and Maria NOEL, 25 Jun 1982 Hudson, NH
PERRON, Daniel R and Candice B JUTRAS, 24 Jul 1971 Hudson, NH
PERRON, Denise Rit and Manuel Ant BRIER, 06 Jul 1974 Nashua, NH
PERRON, Lena and Charles W ALLISON, 07 Apr 1945 Nashua, NH
PERRON, Lisa M and Marcel G LAVOIE, 04 May 1985 Nashua, NH
PERRY, Alice M and William H LEBLANC, 30 Dec 1973 Nashua, NH
PERRY, Arthur R and Marianne MIMIS, 22 Aug 1970 Hudson, NH

HUDSON, NH MARRIAGES

PERRY, Bertha G and Charles F SNOW, 06 Jun 1916 Hudson, NH
  Lewis E Perry (Highgate, VT) & Sarah Lawrence (Bridgewater, MA)
  G Lyman Snow(Newton, MA) & Harriet M Chase (Cambridge, MA)
PERRY, Bruce R and Linda M TESSIER, 05 Sep 1970 Nashua, NH
PERRY, Bruce R and Linda M PERRY, 06 Nov 1982 Nashua, NH
PERRY, Constance and Ronald M ROBERTS, 10 Apr 1982 Hudson, NH
PERRY, Edith L and Clifford H LIBBY, 25 Apr 1912 Hudson, NH
  Lewis E Perry & Sarah L Lawrence
  Henry R Libby & Mary C Libby
PERRY, Emma and Alden J CUDWORTH, 28 Oct 1884 Manchester, NH
  David E Perry (Bangor, NY) & Mary Bell
  John Cudworth(Peterboro, NH) & Sarah Spalding (Haverhill, NH)
PERRY, Fae L and Donald M PRESCOTT, 14 Sep 1946 Hudson, NH
PERRY, Francis K and Patricia S HOUDESHELL, 22 Aug 1980 Hampton, NH
PERRY, Linda M and Bruce R PERRY, 06 Nov 1982 Nashua, NH
PERRY, Margaret A and Andrew TRUMBALL, 18 Jan 1873 Hudson, NH
PERRY, Marguerite and Francis McTIGUE, 26 Dec 1935 Hudson, NH
PERRY, Pamela C and Edward S ATWOOD, 22 Aug 1950 Hudson, NH
PERRY, Patricia L and Glenn J BOULEY, 24 Jul 1982 Brookline, NH
PERUSSE, Ronald J and Sandra J KINVILLE, 09 Mar 1976 Hudson, NH
PETERS, Barbara J and Elwyn E FORD, 17 Apr 1942 Hudson, NH
PETERS, Carol A and James E DANIELS, 20 Oct 1979 Nashua, NH
PETERS, Cynthia J and Michael F HAMMAR, 08 Sep 1973 Hudson, NH
PETERS, Dale M and Sheila A O'KEEFE, 27 Nov 1965 Nashua, NH
PETERS, Erma E and Daniel A DIONNE, 23 Nov 1962 Hudson, NH
PETERS, Frederick and Emily Y USSERY, 07 Oct 1967 Hudson, NH
PETERS, George H and Roberta L LAMPER, 13 Feb 1965 Hudson, NH
PETERS, Harry C and Pearl L OTIS, 22 Jan 1943 Derry, NH
PETERS, Harry C Jr and Drusilla M FORRENCE, 29 Aug 1969 Nashua, NH
PETERS, Larry D and Erma E FOSTER, 08 Jan 1958 Hudson, NH
PETERS, Susan and Roger S BUTLER, 14 Dec 1974 Hudson, NH
PETERS, Wayne S and Gertrude A CURRIER, 05 Jul 1917 Cambridge, MA
PETERS, Wendy and John T GOULET, 11 Feb 1972 Pelham, NH
PETERSEN, George H III&Cynthia P DESFOSSES, 20 Aug 1983 Hudson, NH
PETERSEN, Martin R and Lucy M LEBEL, 29 Jun 1963 Nashua, NH
PETERSON, Arlene and Philip R HOUSE, 24 Sep 1955 Hudson, NH
PETERSON, Carl A Jr and Bernice JA RACINE, 07 Aug 1968 Derry, NH
PETERSON, Carl R and Karin S CATLETT, 10 Jun 1977 Londonderry, NH
PETERSON, Charles E and Victoria M HOLMES, 25 May 1911 Nashua, NH
  Nelse P Peterson & Sarah Johnson
  Victor Holm & Marie Somnersum
PETERSON, Esther J and Mark D CARROLL, 28 Aug 1912 Hudson, NH
  Gustave Peterson & Bessie Anderson
  Frank N Carroll & Anna Dunbar
PETERSON, John L III and Melody A GREENLEAF, 05 Aug 1978 Hudson, NH
PETERSON, Kenneth F and Kathleen A BROWN, 15 May 1976 Hudson, NH
PETERSON, Martin Y and Albina R LAUKASH, 11 Jul 1936 Nashua, NH
PETERSON, Oscar E and Virginia K COURET, 12 Jun 1982 Nashua, NH
PETERSON, Patricia A and Jeffrey A RYAN, 18 May 1985 Amherst, NH
PETERSON, Richard H Jr and Jean L BOUTILIER, 11 Aug 1973 Hudson, NH
PETHIC, Willis E and Nancy E COOKE, 02 Jul 1949 Hudson, NH
PETKEVICH, Anna and Peter Jose CASPER, 26 Oct 1935 Lowell, MA
PETRAIN, Albert W and Joan Z RUSSELL, 26 Oct 1963 Nashua, NH
PETRAIN, Clarice and Raymond A LANDRY, 02 Jun 1956 Nashua, NH
PETRAIN, Linda A and Bradford T BERRY, 28 Dec 1979 Hartford, VT
PETRAIN, Raymond A and Gloria J JOHNSON, 20 Feb 1953 Hudson, NH
PETREAULT, Eugene P and Helen E SMITH, 24 May 1947 Hudson, NH
PETREYKO, Olesia A and Grover C MORRILL, 29 Aug 1959 Hudson, NH
PETRINO, Jaine E and Jeffrey J BIGLEY, 29 Aug 1981 Hudson, NH
PETRONI, Mary G and Richard D FORTIER, 16 Oct 1982 Nashua, NH

HUDSON, NH MARRIAGES

PETRONI, Mary M and James W DERNOGA, 27 Jul 1984 Hudson, NH
PETROVICH, Edward and Muriel J PRUITT, 22 May 1948 Hudson, NH
PETTENGAIL, John and Hannah BURBANK, 16 Nov 1784
PETTINGILL, Melissa and Mark H Jr WEBSTER, Aug 1866
PETTINGILL, Ruth T and Elbridge M CLARK, 30 Nov 1831
PETTS, Doris E and Paul T SMITH, 14 Nov 1973 Hudson, NH
PETTS, Raymond E and Bertha A RAYMOND, 13 Jul 1944 Hudson, NH
PETTS, Raymond E and June A BAILEY, 25 Jun 1949 Nashua, NH
PETTS, Raymond E and Doris E CHARRON, 06 May 1967 Hudson, NH
PHAIR, Terry R and Pamela WALKER, 20 Jun 1970 Dover, NH
PHALON, Arthur R and Lillian A PARKE, 13 Aug 1940 Hudson, NH
PHANEUF, Laurie J and John J McPHERSON, 17 Nov 1979 Hudson, NH
PHANEUF, Lisa A and John Kipli WORRELL, 31 Oct 1981 Hudson, NH
PHANEUF, Raymond L and Irene F BEDARD, 31 Jan 1946 Hudson, NH
PHANEUF, Stephen Roger and Debra Lee HARRIS, 23 Sep 1978 Nashua, NH
PHELAN, Herbert A and Jessie G BROWN, 27 May 1922 Hudson, NH
PHELPS, Bonnie N and Peter D RETKEVICZ, 17 Aug 1968 Goffstown, NH
PHELPS, Robert W and Nina R POMPONIO, 14 Mar 1981 Nashua, NH
PHENEUF, Louise A and Robert D BURNS, 14 Feb 1976 Manchester, NH
PHERIZZI, Alphonse and Mary M ROGATO, 29 Jun 1938 Hudson, NH
PHILBROOK, James E and Kathryn W WHITTEMORE, 22 Sep 1962 Nashua, NH
PHILBROOK, Nathan and Gertrude A WILSON, 17 Jun 1873 Hudson, NH
PHILBROOK, Rachel M and Edward H FLYNN, 09 May 1951 Hudson, NH
PHILBROOK, Sheila I and Norman A COLOMBE, 08 Oct 1965 Hudson, NH
PHILBROOK, Thomas W and Judy J LAROSE, 19 Dec 1976 Hudson, NH
PHILIBERT, Joseph A and Jeannette LAPOINTE, 02 Aug 1958 Hudson, NH
PHILIBOTTE, Pauline F & Walter G TWARDOSKY, 30 Jun 1972 Hudson, NH
PHILIPS, Alice D and Edgar F SMITH, 08 Oct 1878 Hudson, NH
   Philips (Nova Scotia) & Edna J (Nova Scotia)
   Sullivan Smith(Hudson, NH) & Sarah J Sullivan (Hudson, NH)
PHILIPS, Jeremiah and Hannah W CUMMINGS, 12 Feb 1841
   Thomas Cummings
PHILLIPS, Grace M and Edward M PARKER, 07 May 1921 Hudson, NH
PHILLIPS, Ida Alice & Wilber L BLOOD, 28 Jun 1930 Arlington, MA
PHILLIPS, James Angus and Ida Alice FULLER, 25 Aug 1924 Hudson, NH
PHILLIPS, John M and Ruth N BUTLER, 30 Dec 1950 Hudson, NH
PHILLIPS, Kenneth F and Margo A SULLIVAN, 11 Aug 1979 Hudson, NH
PHILLIPS, Mary J and Brian D CROTEAU, 10 Sep 1983 Nashua, NH
PHILLIPS, Maureen Ka and Ronald Rog FORTIN, 19 Jul 1980 Nashua, NH
PHINNEY, Sharon L and Leith L GARLAND, 29 Dec 1984 Nashua, NH
PHINNEY, Walter E and Carolyn L WELLS, 01 May 1954 Nashua, NH
PIANTIDOSI, Augustine&Geneva S YAGIELOWICZ, 14 Jun 1969 Nashua, NH
PIATEK, Betty A and Roger P DESBOISBRIAND, 13 Aug 1955 Hudson, NH
PIATEK, Sandra J and Steven C ALLEN, 21 Jan 1966 Hudson, NH
PICANO, Rosemarie and John N PAPPAS, 08 Jul 1971 Nashua, NH
PICARD, Catherine and David Mich SMITH, 19 Aug 1978 Nashua, NH
PICARD, Claire T and John S MERRILL, 03 Sep 1966 Hudson, NH
PICARD, James E and Constance BOILARD, 23 Oct 1954 Hudson, NH
PICHETTE, Raymond E and Olive E BENN, 25 Apr 1942 Hudson, NH
PICKARD, Herbert T and Fay E LORING, 14 Nov 1942 Hudson, NH
PICKARD, Walter F and Mary M CURRAN, 28 Jun 1934 Nashua, NH
PICKERING, Judith A and Michael V POULIN, 04 Jul 1981 Newington, NH
PIDHORODECKY, Mark A and Jane E ARSENAULT, 20 Jul 1969 Nashua, NH
PIERCE, Caroline P and Benjamin H KIDDER, 13 May 1847
PIERCE, Emma I and Clarence T SALVAIL, 02 Mar 1946 Hudson, NH
PIERCE, J Preble and Martha E CHASE, 24 Oct 1854
PIERCE, Joan E and Francis J Jr BATTLES, 17 Jan 1948 Hudson, NH
PIERCE, Joseph W and Emma L SMITH, 13 Feb 1887 Londonderry, NH
   Henry G Pierce (Chelmsford, MA) & Eliza L Smith (Brandon, VT)
   Sullivan Smith(Hudson, NH) & Sarah Glover (Hudson, NH)

HUDSON, NH MARRIAGES

PIERCE, Kenneth L and Gertrude I SLACK, 18 Dec 1971 Enfield, NH
PIERCE, Lizzie and Edward J SMITH, 10 Oct 1882 Hudson, NH
   John Pierce (Lowell, MA)
   Edward J Smith(Peterboro, NH) & Lydia A (Nashua, NH)
PIERCE, Marion R and Justin J CALLAHAN, 28 Jun 1938 Hudson, NH
PIERCE, Susannah and Reuben Jr SPALDING, 10 Oct 1780
PIGNATELLA, Kathryn A and Mark L NADEAU, 22 Sep 1979 Hudson, NH
PIGNATO, Vincenzo J and Ethel E PIPER, 06 May 1950 Hudson, NH
PIKE, Bernice A and Wilfred A ELLIOTT, 01 Nov 1947 Merimack, NH
PIKE, Clarissa and Parker FARLEY, 20 Oct 1842
PIKE, Forest D and Dorothy J ROCK, 16 Aug 1947 Hudson, NH
PIKE, George M H Jr and Norma G HERRICK, 03 Oct 1943 Nashua, NH
PIMENTAL, Jose E R and Eugenia P AMBAR, 05 Jul 1984 Hudson, NH
PIMM, Barbara W and Kenneth C RICHARDSON, 17 May 1934 Hudson, NH
PINARD, Ann M and James W GROVES, 04 Jul 1975 Hudson, NH
PINET, Alfred G and Helen G HARDY, 06 Sep 1946 Hudson, NH
PINET, Gloria J and Alfred R HAMELIN, 23 Aug 1958 Hudson, NH
PINETTE, Rachel I and Richard J KASHULINES, 01 Sep 1956 Nashua, NH
PINTO, Mary M and Raymond F VINCENT, 08 Jul 1950 Hudson, NH
PINTO, Samuel and Jessie L DELEANHO, 01 Sep 1937 Nashua, NH
PIPER, Charlene A and Peter Jon THOMPSON, 06 Jan 1978 Hudson, NH
PIPER, Darlene B and William J MERCHANT, 04 Sep 1976 Nashua, NH
PIPER, Dean J and Shelley L BLANCHARD, 29 Nov 1975 Contoocook, NH
PIPER, Ethel E and Vincenzo J PIGNATO, 06 May 1950 Hudson, NH
PIPER, Francis S and A Susan FRANCIONE, 03 Mar 1950 Hudson, NH
PIPER, Lawrence L and Janet A WILCOX, 31 Aug 1974 Nashua, NH
PIPER, Luella A and John WEBSTER, 05 Jun 1859
PIPER, Mary R and David CLEMENT, 23 Feb 1870 Hudson, NH
PIPER, Philip R and Annie H RICHARDSON, 05 Sep 1871 Hudson, NH
PIPER, Ward H and Amanda T WHITE, 31 Oct 1970 Auburn, NH
PIRANI, Leo and Mary A DEEGAN, 20 Sep 1947 Hudson, NH
PITCHER, Elizabeth and Charles J WALCH, 08 Apr 1937 Nashua, NH
PITCHER, Ruth E and R Bradley CARLE, 09 May 1935 Hudson, NH
PITTS, Gail M and Brian E LOWE, 24 Jan 1975 Hudson, NH
PLACE, Sue Carol and Andrew J Jr SOUCY, 14 Apr 1973 Enfield, NH
PLAMONDON, Gerard J and Ann Marie BURTON, 23 May 1981 Hudson, NH
PLAMONDON, Joseph E and Stella M PELLETIER, 22 Apr 1961 Hudson, NH
PLAMONDON, Louise I and Paul R OUELLETTE, 19 Jun 1971 Nashua, NH
PLAMONDON, Mary E & Theodore G Jr JEANNOTTE, 21 Aug 1965 Hudson, NH
PLAMONDON, Peter A and Judith A LEDOUX, 28 Jul 1973 Hudson, NH
PLAMONDON, Roger J and Faye WINSTANLEY, 18 Apr 1964 Nashua, NH
PLANK, Sharon L and Frank E McNEIL, 30 Jun 1973 Nashua, NH
PLANT, John B and Mary Yvonne NOEL, 22 Jun 1924 Nashua, NH
PLANTE, Carol L and John W RUSSELL, 25 Apr 1959 Nashua, NH
PLANTE, Gabrielle and Henry Jr BURPEE, 08 Oct 1938 Nashua, NH
PLANTE, Irene A and Roland J CLOUTIER, 26 Jan 1946 Nashua, NH
PLANTE, Kevin Wayn and Karen Ann ANCTIL, 13 Jun 1981 Nashua, NH
PLANTE, Mary Lou and Mark W GUTHRO, 09 Jun 1979 Hudson, NH
PLANTE, Nancy M and Arthur M GAGNON, 04 Feb 1961 Nashua, NH
PLANTE, Robert O Jr and Betty L BEAN, 25 Jun 1962 Nashua, NH
PLANTE, Sylvie M and David P BOUFFARD, 29 Oct 1983 Hudson, NH
PLANTIER, Eugene G and Merilda M KNIGHTS, 02 Mar 1942 Hudson, NH
PLANTIER, Lorraine T and Leonard L HAMBLETT, 11 Oct 1946 Nashua, NH
PLANTIER, Richard T and Constance LAROCHE, 11 May 1953 Nashua, NH
PLATHNER, Hilda E and Walter KRAUCHUK, 29 Jan 1949 Hudson, NH
PLAYLE, Karen S and Robert G ROY, 18 Aug 1984 Hudson, NH
PLOCKETT, Manuel J and Shirley R BULGER, 27 Jul 1946 Hudson, NH
PLONA, Edward J and Pauline R ROY, 24 Nov 1982 Hudson, NH
PLOURDE, Gerard T and Cecilia SIMARD, 21 Nov 1941 Nashua, NH
PLOURDE, Grace M and Berchman T CARVILLE, 21 Dec 1954 Hudson, NH

HUDSON,NH MARRIAGES

PLUMLEY, David J and Jamie L GAGNON, 09 Jan 1983 Hudson, NH
PLUMMER, Alexander and Mary C SULLIVAN, 30 Sep 1972 Hudson, NH
PLUMMER, Edith L and Francis J CALLAHAN, 04 Oct 1941 Hudson, NH
PLUMMER, Nathan and Charlotte BOYD, 10 Apr 1846
PLUMMER, Peter N and Muriel E MARSHALL, 27 Oct 1962 Hudson, NH
PLYNKOFSKY, Adam P and Mildred B JAMESON, 24 Jan 1942 Hudson, NH
PLYNKOFSKY, Cynthia M and Barry G PYNN, 28 Oct 1967 Hudson, NH
PLYNKOFSKY, Patricia L and Edward H VERRY, 28 Sep 1968 Hudson, NH
PODGE, Joanna P and Nathaniel CLARK, 26 Apr 1832
PODODISE, Louis and Jennette PELLETIER, 23 Apr 1917 Jaffrey, NH
POFF, Annie and George H THOMPSON, 24 Apr 1883 Hudson, NH
   John Poff (Ireland) & Eliza Boyd (Ireland)
   Robert Thompson(England) & Mary Hattsley (England)
POFF, Dorothy B and Harry J CHESNULEVICH, 05 Sep 1953 Nashua, NH
POFF, Edward and Eliza CONNELL, 31 Aug 1854 Lowell, MA
POFF, Peter and Betsey BROWN, 08 Apr 1866 Lowell, MA
POINTER, Carol and Gary GREENWOOD, 24 Dec 1977 Hudson, NH
POINTER, Carol A and Richard A BARRETT, 28 Mar 1969 Hudson, NH
POINTER, Dona Mae and Walter L FARRINGTON, 11 Nov 1977 Hudson, NH
POINTER, Laura M and John T CLEMENT, 26 Oct 1975 Hudson, NH
POINTER, Richard M and Dona M TRAFFORD, 08 Nov 1969 Hudson, NH
POINTER, Richard M and Kathleen A COLE, 01 Oct 1976 Nashua, NH
POIRIER, Alfred O and Pearl G WEBB, 07 Dec 1946 Hudson, NH
POIRIER, Cecile G and Walter H PORTER, 12 Jan 1968 Hudson, NH
POIRIER, Leonard J and Constance FRANCOEUR, 26 Jun 1971 Nashua, NH
POIRIER, Patricia A and Gaston R SIMARD, 11 Apr 1959 Hudson, NH
POIRIER, Rose V and Edward T DUFFY, 08 Sep 1962 Hudson, NH
POIRIER, Theresa A and Roland A GENDRON, 20 Oct 1945 Hudson, NH
POIRIER, Vivian E and Richard B WILBORG, 20 Oct 1984 Hudson, NH
POISSON, John J and Karen A GLEASON, 14 Apr 1985 Hudson, NH
POITRAS, James D and Melanie S MADDEN, 28 May 1983 Nashua, NH
POLAK, Cecylia T and John H BOGATY, 23 Nov 1968 Nashua, NH
POLAK, Dorothy A and Lionel R BOUCHER, 08 Oct 1955 Hudson, NH
POLAK, Fredrick S and Bessie KAUFMANN, 13 Nov 1943 Hudson, NH
POLAK, Jennie S and A F CHZANOWSKI, 12 Oct 1940 Nashua, NH
POLAK, Joseph R and Beatrice M MOULTON, 11 Oct 1952 Hudson, NH
POLAK, June S and Ronald J MORIN, 20 Oct 1956 Nashua, NH
POLAK, Phyllis and Bennie MILLINA, 21 Jan 1944 Nashua, NH
POLAK, Simon M and Victoria MOTYLEWSKA, 26 Apr 1958 Nashua, NH
POLIQUIN, Beverly A and Clesson W LEACH, 11 Sep 1948 Hudson, NH
POLIQUIN, Denise G and Robert D D'AMBROISE, 17 Oct 1982 Nashua, NH
POLIQUIN, Gerard L and Donna L NORMAND, 31 Aug 1972 Nashua, NH
POLIQUIN, Mildred H and Russell J MAGNIN, 23 Dec 1950 Hudson, NH
POLIQUIN, Raymond R and Joan SMITH, 14 Oct 1961 Hudson, NH
POLIQUIN, Romeo P and Mary P LEMIEUX, 07 Feb 1958 Hudson, NH
POLKEY, Edward S and Juanita M CURRIER, 27 Aug 1977 Nashua, NH
POLKEY, Katherine and Kevin F IRWIN, 06 Oct 1975 Raymond, NH
POLLARD, Abel and Abigail HILLS, 28 Jun 1796
POLLARD, Abigail and Henry MARSHALL, 04 Sep 1781
POLLARD, Abigail and James T PALMER, Apr
POLLARD, Calvin and Hannah P WADLEIGH, 26 Feb 1861
POLLARD, Calvin and Hannah P WADLEY, 26 Feb 1861
POLLARD, Charlotte and Joseph GREELEY, 17 Dec 1818
POLLARD, Daniel T and Miriam COLBURN, 26 Jun 1817
POLLARD, Dorothy and Solomon A DAVIS, 22 Dec 1852
POLLARD, E Oscar and Elvira O TYRRELL, 07 Nov 1862
POLLARD, E Oscar and Elvira O TYRRELL, 27 Nov 1862
POLLARD, Ebenezer and Dorothy BLODGETT, 21 Feb 1799
POLLARD, Eldesta and Isaac COLBURN, 28 Dec 1826
POLLARD, Elizabeth and Asahal BLODGETT, 13 Dec 1781

HUDSON,NH MARRIAGES

POLLARD, Elizabeth and Jonathan PARHAM, 08 May 1777
POLLARD, Elizabeth and Jonathan PERHAM, 08 May 1777
POLLARD, Frederick and Carolyn JOSEF, 06 Nov 1965 Nashua, NH
POLLARD, George W and Phoebe BENNETT, 17 Dec 1914 Lawrence, MA
  John F Pollard & Janette Macartney
  Hiram Bennett
POLLARD, John and Sarah GOULD, 20 Apr 1778
POLLARD, John Jr and Betsey FORD, 05 Feb 1801
POLLARD, Jon and Sarah GREELEY, 20 Apr 1778
POLLARD, Joseph F and Emily BEMIS, 22 Nov 1869
POLLARD, Lois and Asahel BLODGETT, 11 Oct 1798
POLLARD, Lucinda and Jabez GOLDSMITH, 30 Jun 1814
POLLARD, Lucinda and Jaby GOULDSMITH, 30 Jun 1814
POLLARD, Marjorie J and Walter E JOHNSTON, 11 Apr 1964 Hudson, NH
POLLARD, Raymond J and Cora M HOOPER, 21 Mar 1900 Lowell, MA
  Joseph F Pollard & Emily Bemas
  Charles F Cooper & Leah Barnard
POLLARD, Salley and John QUEEN, 25 Jun 1809
POLLARD, Sally and John QUEEN, 25 Jan 1809
POLLARD, Thomas and Alice INGALLS, 14 Dec 1785
POLLARD, Vernita and Sullivan W BROWN, 14 Jun 1924 Nashua, NH
POLLOCK, Joseph K and Jean F BAKER, 24 Apr 1954 Hudson, NH
POLLOCK, Marion R and Basil K HASKINS, 25 Oct 1933 Hudson, NH
POMERLEAU, Claire B and Roger R TURMEL, 31 Jan 1948 Nashua, NH
POMERLEAU, Joseph H and Marie L LEVESQUE, 17 Nov 1934 Nashua, NH
POMEROY, Linda S and Thomas W POWERS, 16 Sep 1984 Hudson, NH
POMPONIO, Nina R and Robert W PHELPS, 14 Mar 1981 Nashua, NH
PONEY, Lucille I and Lewis F READ, 15 Apr 1950 Nashua, NH
POOLE, Gordon R and Mildred DURIVAGE, 11 Oct 1924 Hudson, NH
POOLE, Linda D and David A REYNOLDS, 23 Mar 1974 Nashua, NH
POOLE, Richard Sr and Aloysia E HICKEY, 15 Oct 1983 Deerfield, NH
POOLE, Roland A and Anna-Maria McCLURE, 03 Jan 1981 Hudson, NH
POOLE, Steven G and Paula J BRIAND, 15 Mar 1980 Nashua, NH
POOLER, Gladys H and Gilbert J SCHUTTE, 11 Dec 1948 Hudson, NH
POOR, Abbie H and Frederick SIMONDS, 20 Jan 1867
POOR, Abby H and Frederick SIMONDS, 20 Jan 1867
POOR, Laura A and George W HASELTON, 14 Jun 1862
POOR, Lora A and George W HASELTON, 18 Feb 1862
POORE, Frederic S III&Elaine S THERRIEN, 18 Apr 1970 Manchester, NH
POORE, Judith E and Donald E HANSON, 26 May 1984 Hudson, NH
POPER, Harry F and Carol I WILLIAMSON, 07 Oct 1978 Nashua, NH
PORCARO, Ann-Marie and Robert O GIGUERE, 05 Feb 1965 Hudson, NH
PORTER, Beverly J and Paul F DION, 26 Nov 1966 Nashua, NH
PORTER, George and Lois A KANE, 23 Jul 1962 Dracut, MA
PORTER, Greta A and Harold M Jr CLIFFORD, 05 Feb 1943 Nashua, NH
PORTER, Irene R and Robert D DION, 05 Jun 1971 Nashua, NH
PORTER, Joseph L and Marion E BAILEY, 09 Feb 1946 Hudson, NH
PORTER, Lawrence B III and Kellie M WINN, 01 Mar 1980 Hudson, NH
PORTER, Linda M and Norman P JALBERT, 05 Oct 1968 Hudson, NH
PORTER, Linda M and Claude I MICHAUD, 11 Oct 1963 Hudson, NH
PORTER, Lynwood A and Bernice A MUNROE, 04 May 1950 Nashua, NH
PORTER, Nancy E and Arthur D DUCHARME, 02 Dec 1967 Hudson, NH
PORTER, Robert L and Debra Ann DUVAL, 25 Aug 1973 Nashua, NH
PORTER, Rose M and Robert L CONSTANT, 20 Jul 1957 Hudson, NH
PORTER, Sandra J and Denis R PRINCE, 14 Nov 1970 Nashua, NH
PORTER, Sheryl A and David E MOREAU, 15 Aug 1981 Hudson, NH
PORTER, Walter H and Cecile G POIRIER, 12 Jan 1968 Hudson, NH
PORTIGUE, Jane E and David L HOWE, 18 May 1968 Hudson, NH
PORTMORE, Harriet H and Stanley L HUNT, 13 Feb 1937 Nashua, NH
POST, Linda A and Joseph R LEVASSEUR, 11 Jun 1977 Londonderry, NH

HUDSON,NH MARRIAGES

POST, Marlyn J and Leroy G SULLIVAN, 29 May 1959 Nashua, NH
POST, Morillo E and Doris I MOORE, 27 Nov 1943 Nashua, NH
POST, Sharon E and Peter J BURGESS, 02 Oct 1965 Hudson, NH
POSTON, Cheryl J and Dennis BEAUDRY, 13 Apr 1974 Hudson, NH
POTTER, Floyd S Jr and Barbara R RODD, 07 Jun 1955 Hudson, NH
POTTER, Francis R and Robin WILLIAMSON, 30 Jun 1979 Hudson, NH
POTTER, Joan L and Charles W FREEMAN, 08 May 1972 Nashua, NH
POTTER, JoAnne L and Paul K BURTON, 26 May 1978 Hudson, NH
POTTER, Julie C and James W Jr SMITH, 06 Nov 1976 Hudson, NH
POTTER, Karlton E and Pierrette COTE, 25 Oct 1969 Hudson, NH
POTTER, Laura E and Peter Jr DOLLOFF, 30 Apr 1983 Hudson, NH
POTTER, Mary Eunic and Rueben GROVES, 24 Jun 1918 Hudson, NH
POTTER, Patrice A & Albert J III MANNIX, 04 Sep 1982 Manchester, NH
POTTER, Patricia A and Stephen R GAGNE, 10 Aug 1980 Hudson, NH
POTTER, Walter A and Mary J REYNOLDS, 24 Jul 1952 Hudson, NH
POTZNER, Roberta Le and Brian E MASTROFINE, 28 May 1983 Hudson, NH
POULIN, Donald L and Eda L WAKER, 07 Nov 1981 Hudson, NH
POULIN, Janet M and Johney M LATHAM, 20 Mar 1971 Hudson, NH
POULIN, Jeanne L and James P MASTERSON, 17 Apr 1971 Nashua, NH
POULIN, John G and Elaine M BOUDLE, 02 Feb 1963 Lancaster, NH
POULIN, Marguerite and Joseph M CHENEY, 17 Sep 1946 Nashua, NH
POULIN, Michael V and Judith A PICKERING, 04 Jul 1981 Newington, NH
POULIN, Monique J and Richard A BARDSLEY, 23 Nov 1974 Hudson, NH
POULIN, Robert J and Evelyn P STEVENS, 18 Aug 1956 Hudson, NH
POULIN, Shirley A and Joseph J Jr KOPKA, 05 Feb 1955 Hudson, NH
POULIN, Susan L and David A GODIN, 24 Jun 1972 Nashua, NH
POULIN, Therese Y and George BOYER, 28 Jun 1958 Nashua, NH
POULIOT, Anne L and Glenn B LETOURNEAU, 26 Sep 1981 Merrimack, NH
POULIOT, Margaret L&Lawrence W Jr ALEXANDER, 14 Feb 1979 Nashua, NH
POVILAN, John and Ann H RUSSELL, 16 Apr 1960 Hudson, NH
POWELCZYK, Linda J and John R JALBERT, 29 May 1978 Hudson, NH
POWELL, John W and Margaret J RIPLEY, 28 Nov 1866
POWELL, John W and Margarett RIPLEY, 28 Nov 1866
POWELL, Leffort M and Martha R SMITH, 13 Nov 1917 Hudson, NH
POWELL, Linda M and Reginald PELLETIER, 21 Jun 1980 Nashua, NH
POWELL, Sandra C and William R ROOD, 18 Dec 1982 Nashua, NH
POWELL, Sandra L and Bruce R McLAVEY, 20 Nov 1971 Nashua, NH
POWELL, Waldo I and Gladys M BYRNES, 11 Sep 1929 Nashua, NH
POWER, Lucille V and Roger F FLOYD, 23 Feb 1985 Hudson, NH
POWERS, Alice and George W FLETCHER, 09 Feb 1924 Nashua, NH
POWERS, Alyce T and Donald C MITCHELL, 04 Sep 1930 Nashua, NH
POWERS, Elizabeth and David D WILSON, 17 Jan 1981 Nashua, NH
POWERS, Henry G and Kathrine COOLBETH, 20 Oct 1964 Hudson, NH
POWERS, James F and Carol Loui KEENAN, 31 Jul 1982 Hudson, NH
POWERS, Joseph H and Lois MacKENZIE, 17 Jul 1932 Nashua, NH
POWERS, Linda J and Francis L Jr BURNS, 31 Dec 1982 Hudson, NH
POWERS, Minerva A and William FLAGG, 04 Jul 1872
    George W Flagg
POWERS, Richard A and Lisa A JARRY, 01 Jun 1985 Hudson, NH
POWERS, Ruth M and Adam M JAMROS, 24 Nov 1945 Nashua, NH
POWERS, Thomas W and Linda S POMEROY, 16 Sep 1984 Hudson, NH
POWLISON, Diane M and Wilfred L HOLDEN, 22 Apr 1972 Burand, MI
POWLOWSKI, Michael H and Sandra E GRAY, 29 Jul 1972 Pelham, NH
POWLOWSKY, Aline M and Rudolph R COUTU, 29 Aug 1981 Hudson, NH
POWLOWSKY, Anthony J and Ann L LAVOIE, 26 Jun 1948 Hudson, NH
POWLOWSKY, Kathryn L and Laurence P TAYLOR, 03 Jun 1972 Hudson, NH
POWLOWSKY, Mary E and Earl C MIZO, 31 Aug 1940 Nashua, NH
POWLOWSKY, Nancy A and Robert R DUQUETTE, 04 Oct 1975 Hudson, NH
POWLOWSKY, Patricia A and Dennis R DROUIN, 26 Jul 1975 Hudson, NH
POWLOWSKY, Peter and Aline M MAURICE, 11 Apr 1953 Nashua, NH

HUDSON, NH MARRIAGES

PRAGER, Abraham and Edith J SABLE, 11 Sep 1948 Hudson, NH
PRATT, Almira S and Robert McQUESTEN, 16 Jul 1854
PRATT, Appolas and Sally WASON, 15 Mar 1804
PRATT, Charles A and Rita BRIAND, 18 Apr 1942 Nashua, NH
PRATT, Glenda E and John SIMO, 11 Jun 1960 Milford, NH
PRATT, Jn and Nepherbeth COOK, 29 Jun 1779
PRATT, Mabel E and Nicholas DEFRONZO, 01 Sep 1946 Nashua, NH
PRATT, Robin T and Robert A ELLIOTT, 02 Sep 1977 Hudson, NH
PRATT, Salley and Andrew TALLANT, 14 Dec 1819
PRATT, Sally and Andrew TALLANT, 14 Dec 1819
PRATT, Sylvia A and Henry F CABANA, 26 Jun 1981 Nashua, NH
PRATT, Sylvia A and Brian CUNNINGHAM, 28 Jul 1970 Hebron, NH
PRATT, Sylvia A and William J DIAZ, 29 Oct 1966 Hudson, NH
PREBLE, Frederick and Mary R STACKNIS, 07 Jun 1941 Nashua, NH
PRENTIS, Myrtle E and Ellery H RUGG, 30 Jun 1948 Hudson, NH
PRESCOTT, Donald M and Fae L PERRY, 14 Sep 1946 Hudson, NH
PREST, Steven R and Donna M BASTILLE, 25 Feb 1978 Hudson, NH
PRESTIPINO, Mary A & Roy E Jr LITTLEFIELD, 09 Jun 1951 Milford, NH
PRETTI, Elizabeth & Thomas L Jr GIAMPIETRO, 17 Jul 1982 Hudson, NH
PREVOST, Fernand J and Myrna A BRALEY, 15 Jun 1957 Hebron, NH
PREVOST, Francis J & Charlotte KIJOWSKI, 11 Feb 1961 Manchester, NH
PREVOST, Hector H and Theresa G TARDIFF, 20 May 1950 Nashua, NH
PREYSNAR, Linda C and Robert M THOMPSON, 20 Nov 1971 Merrimack, NH
PRICE, Martha J and Steven A ROONEY, 28 Apr 1979 Merrimack, NH
PRICKETT, Theodore P and Arlene Edna LAVOIE, 21 Feb 1928 Nashua, NH
PRIEST, Dennis W and Linda N RICHARDSON, 24 Dec 1971 Nashua, NH
PRIEST, Linda N and Robert F CORSON, 19 Jun 1977 Hudson, NH
PRINCE, Alfred J and Juanita P BISHOP, 26 Nov 1947 Nashua, NH
PRINCE, Denis R and Sandra J PORTER, 14 Nov 1970 Nashua, NH
PRISKE, John Moyse & Maude Harmon J HARWOOD, 21 Jun 1911 Hudson, NH
   John Priske & Lylie Pascoe
   Walter J Harwood & Theo Hanson
PRITCHARD, Phyllis E and George F DUKETTE, 20 Nov 1954 Hudson, NH
PRITZ, Catherine and Alphonse E LANDRY, 10 Nov 1956 Hudson, NH
PRIVEE, Merlinda P and Terrance M MURRAY, 08 Jun 1985 Hudson, NH
PROCTOR, Edwin H and Caroline H ALEXANDER, 09 Jan 1949 Hudson, NH
PROCTOR, George F and Evelyn M SMITH, 08 Oct 1950 Hudson, NH
PROCTOR, Rebecca E and William W MILLER, 02 Apr 1848
PROCTOR, Robert L and Brenda L IVES, 15 Aug 1976 Hudson, NH
PROFFITT, A James and Irene G ROY, 14 Aug 1965 Hudson, NH
PROKO, Margaret A and Terre A WEISMAN, 27 Oct 1984 Nashua, NH
PROSPER, Edwin Walter and Rose Y PROSPER, 11 Nov 1978 Hudson, NH
PROSPER, Rose Y and Edwin Walter PROSPER, 11 Nov 1978 Hudson, NH
PROSSER, Albert G and Margaret E FOLEY, 08 Jul 1950 Hudson, NH
PROULX, Jacqueline and Richard O CLOUTIER, 11 Nov 1972 Hudson, NH
PROULX, Paulette A and Paul N LEBLANC, 27 Dec 1965 Hudson, NH
PROULX, Raymond R and Brenda J LING, 01 Jul 1970 Londonderry, NH
PROULX, Rodney A and Susan M GONTHIER, 08 Jun 1985 Hudson, NH
PROVENCAL, Bruce A and Kathryn Le KAGEN, 01 Jul 1972 Nashua, NH
PROVENCAL, Carl J and Donna R GAGNON, 14 Aug 1971 Nashua, NH
PROVENCAL, Carl J and Debra A FOOTE, 04 Aug 1984 Manchester, NH
PROVENCAL, Donald R and Sally E BISBING, 02 Aug 1975 Hudson, NH
PROVENCAL, Ernest A and Janice N CARLETON, 30 Aug 1950 Nashua, NH
PROVENCAL, Ernest A and Marie-Anne ROY, 20 Sep 1958 Hudson, NH
PROVENCAL, Eugene L and Yvette ROBARGE, 29 Jun 1922 Nashua, NH
PROVENCAL, Eugene L and Alice V JERARD, 20 Dec 1924 Claremont, NH
PROVENCAL, Gregory G and Diane M WHITTAKER, 08 Jun 1974 Hudson, NH
PROVENCAL, Janice N and William O LALUMIERE, 31 Jan 1954 Hollis, NH
PROVENCAL, Joseph A and Blanche LUSIGNAN, 03 Nov 1915 Nashua, NH
   Pradent Provencal (Canada) & Delma Gane (Canada)

HUDSON,NH MARRIAGES

Henri Lusignan(E Dublin, MA) & Clista Dupray (Sciotia, NY)
PROVENCAL, Katherine and David P NADEAU, 20 Jul 1968 Nashua, NH
PROVENCAL, Leo W and Beatrice A LASALLE, 19 Feb 1944 Nashua, NH
PROVENCAL, Robert R and Doris LEDOUX, 30 May 1945 Nashua, NH
PROVENCHER, Claude A and Shirley J WALSER, 18 Nov 1967 Hudson, NH
PROVENCHER, Elphege J and Anna L NOE, 30 Jul 1949 Manchester, NH
PROVENCHER, Ernest and Henrietta WILLIAMS, 13 Oct 1918 Hudson, NH
PROVENCHER, Gail A and Mark D SMITH, 23 Jan 1971 Nashua, NH
PROVENCHER, Lucille M and Romeo H THEROUX, 26 Oct 1946 Nashua, NH
PROVENCHER, Marcel A and Elaine B NELSON, 21 Oct 1966 Hudson, NH
PROVINS, Lucille T and Louis P LOCKWOOD, 24 Mar 1973 Nashua, NH
PROVINS, Steve A and Cynthia A LANOIE, 25 Jun 1977 Hudson, NH
PROVOST, Maragaret and David A HAMBLETT, 28 Apr 1979 Nashua, NH
PROVOST, Regina and Joseph RENAUD, 15 Oct 1919 Lowell, MA
PROWKER, Alexander and Cora E HOOKS, 30 Sep 1961 Hudson, NH
PRUITT, Muriel J and Edward PETROVICH, 22 May 1948 Hudson, NH
PRUNIER, David A and Rosemary COSTA, 21 Aug 1982 Windham, NH
PRUTE, Appollos and Sally WASON, 15 Mar 1804
PRYOR, David L and Marion TUTTLE, 30 Jun 1982 Hudson, NH
PUCHEK, Adelle and John J PURCELL, 31 Dec 1948 Hudson, NH
PUCKETT, Theodora P and Maurice R FRENCH, 31 May 1947 Nashua, NH
PUDSEY, Eugene W and Lillian M FARMER, 20 Jun 1948 Hudson, NH
PUDVAH, Charles and Valena MUNCIL, 01 Oct 1908 Hudson, NH
   Peter Pudvah & Mary Vivian
   John Muncil & May Doty
PUFFER, Joseph M Jr and Carol L KNEPPER, 24 Oct 1981 Nashua, NH
PULLEN, Stanley E Jr and Marcia E BALSER, 03 Feb 1974 Hudson, NH
PURCELL, David K and Maurine B O'LEARY, 15 Jul 1978 Hudson, NH
PURCELL, John J and Adelle PUCHEK, 31 Dec 1948 Hudson, NH
PURCELL, William M and Nancy M CURRIE, 24 Jun 1983 Nashua, NH
PURINGTON, Donna J and Gary A RAPANOTTI, 19 Dec 1981 Hudson, NH
PURINGTON, Gary A and Dawn L PARENT, 05 Jan 1980 Hudson, NH
PURINGTON, Ronald G and Ann M SCHIPPERS, 31 May 1980 Hudson, NH
PURINTON, Donna L and Garry E ALLARD, 10 Sep 1966 Nashua, NH
PUSTOLA, Gwendolyn and James H SEVIGNY, 12 Aug 1973 Londonderry, NH
PUTIS, John J and Eleanor M MONTESION, 30 Nov 1946 Fitchburg, MA
PUTIS, Josephine and Leo D GREATCHUS, 07 Jan 1943 Nashua, NH
PUTNAM, Florence E and Frank E AVERY, 27 Aug 1889 Hudson, NH
   M A S Putnam (Danvers, MA) & Lizzie Cross (Litchfield, NH)
   J M Avery(Londonderry, NH) & Julia A Upton (Dunstable, MA)
PUTNAM, Gideon and Sarah BURNS, 19 Sep 1799
PUTNAM, Gideon and Sarah BARNES, 19 Sep 1799
PUTNAM, Hattie L and Bradford CAMPBELL, 04 Jan 1866
PUTNAM, Moses A S and Elizabeth CROSS, 17 Apr 1861
PUTNAM, William J and Jean McHUGH, 31 Oct 1930 Nashua, NH
PUTNEY, Ina H and Harry W SPREADBY, 17 Jul 1926 Hudson, NH
PUTNEY, Mabel F and Aubrey W BOLLIVER, 07 Sep 1927 Hudson, NH
PYE, Erma I and Harold C PYNN, 01 May 1949 Hudson, NH
PYE, William J and Edna M E BARTLETT, 25 Jan 1934 Nashua, NH
PYNE, Eileen F and Dennis V Jr LINEHAN, 30 Jul 1955 Hudson, NH
PYNN, Barry G and Cynthia M PLYNKOFSKY, 28 Oct 1967 Hudson, NH
PYNN, Harold C and Erma I PYE, 01 May 1949 Hudson, NH
QUACKENBUSH, Julia A & Charles F KENISTON, 24 Aug 1938 Penacook, NH
QUEEN, John and Sally POLLARD, 25 Jan 1809
QUEEN, John and Salley POLLARD, 25 Jun 1809
QUEEN, William B and Ruth I SANGER, 18 Jun 1938 Nashua, NH
QUEENEY, G Louise and Warren C WEBB, 02 Sep 1950 Hudson, NH
QUIGG, John and Martha WHITE, 05 May 1857
QUIGLEY, Allan J and Kathleen M HARRON, 26 Feb 1972 Hudson, NH
QUIGLEY, Charles M and Lois J MARTINEAU, 17 Dec 1971 Hudson, NH

HUDSON,NH MARRIAGES

QUIGLEY, Cindy Loui and Robert MARCELLO, 24 Dec 1981 Hudson, NH
QUIGLEY, Colleen A & Joseph A SULLIVAN, 22 Aug 1981 Londonderry, NH
QUIGLEY, Daniel R and Cynthia J CORBITT, 16 May 1981 Salem, NH
QUIGLEY, John P and Jeanne H MORIN, 02 Sep 1957 Hudson, NH
QUIGLEY, John P and Martha B FORBES, 29 Sep 1979 Londonderry, NH
QUIGLEY, Karen A and Kevin M HACKETT, 26 Aug 1983 Hudson, NH
QUIGLEY, Kathleen M and James R MIZELL, 30 Apr 1976 Hudson, NH
QUIGLEY, Kellie J and Thomas D HUDSON, 01 Jul 1983 Hudson, NH
QUIGLEY, Patricia R and Raymond J LaCHANCE, 07 Jul 1967 Nashua, NH
QUIGLEY, Pearl R and Alphonse T D'ANJOU, 03 Jul 1971 Hudson, NH
QUIGLEY, Priscilla and John K ABBOTT, 24 Jul 1965 Hudson, NH
QUIGLEY, Robin B and Leonard J CARTER, 21 Oct 1977 Hudson, NH
QUIGLEY, Ruth E and Robert J BARRIEAU, 19 Aug 1978 Sanbornton, NH
QUIMBY, David S and Mary Jane GRABOSKI, 21 May 1983 Hudson, NH
QUIMBY, Thomas F and Helen M LEARY, 09 Feb 1910 Hudson, NH
   Benjamin F Quimby & Ella Hawkes
   J A Leary & N F Campbell
QUINN, Bernard E and Margaret A COTTING, 05 Nov 1948 Hudson, NH
QUINN, John Denni and Lisa Jane TROMBLY, 20 Jun 1982 Goffstown, NH
QUINN, Karen A and Robert B THEODORE, 12 Apr 1980 Hudson, NH
QUINN, Lawrence and Edna LANE, 05 Sep 1925 Nashua, NH
QUINN, Lori M and Walter N HAYNES, 18 Feb 1978 Hudson, NH
QUINN, Lorraine M and Marshall R NUTE, 03 Jun 1978 Salem, NH
QUINN, Louise and James FARREIRA, 15 Dec 1934 Hudson, NH
QUINN, Richard J and Kim HART, 01 Jan 1981 Hudson, NH
QUINNO, Pauline and Mark W BARGER, 11 Nov 1984 Nashua, NH
QUINT, Helen G and Roland J RODIER, 09 Aug 1950 Hudson, NH
QUINT, Thomas D and Judith M KARLONAS, 06 Dec 1965 Hudson, NH
QUINTON, Anne T and Edward C YOUNG, 16 Nov 1963 Brookline, NH
QUINTON, Catherine and Kittridge SMITH, 08 Feb 1969 Brookline, NH
QUIRK, Mary Marci and Paul W COURNOYER, 04 Jun 1983 Manchester, NH
QUIRK, Patrick F and Edith I CHARTRAIN, 12 Jul 1947 Hudson, NH
QUIROZ, Albert D and Elizabeth PALIOCA, 13 Apr 1963 Hudson, NH
RAAB, Paul J and Rita B BERANGER, 18 Oct 1941 Hudson, NH
RABINOVITZ, Sidney K and Adele F COHEN, 21 Apr 1934 Hudson, NH
RABY, James L and Lorraine W DEWITT, 27 Nov 1975 Hudson, NH
RABY, Janice I and Raymond A LaFOREST, 24 Nov 1966 Hudson, NH
RABY, Maruice G and Gloria M MARQUIS, 12 Aug 1950 Nashua, NH
RABY, Normand R and Pauline G HEBERT, 12 Oct 1946 Nashua, NH
RABY, Priscilla and Paul F DICHARD, 26 Aug 1950 Hudson, NH
RACINE, Bernice JA and Carl A Jr PETERSON, 07 Aug 1968 Derry, NH
RACINE, Danielle M and Robert S Jr WILLEY, 05 Oct 1970 Alton, NH
RACINE, Dennis J and Constance PANAGEOTES, 09 Jul 1976 Nashua, NH
RACKLIFF, Joseph W and Tammy A LEIGH, 16 Jul 1976 Hudson, NH
RACKLIFF, Judith A and John M BRIAND, 10 Jan 1967 Hudson, NH
RACY, Joseph E and Anita Ann MITIDES, 17 Sep 1976 Hudson, NH
RACY, Joseph E and Lois M HIRTLE, 16 Jun 1979 Nashua, NH
RAFFERTY, Daniel J Jr & Barbara M YOUNG, 06 Sep 1947 Manchester, NH
RAFFERTY, Dennis J & Carolyn E MacCANN, 15 Apr 1978 Litchfield, NH
RAFFERTY, Gary D and Linda E MUSGRAVE, 29 Nov 1971 Nashua, NH
RAFFERTY, Kathleen A and Paul R LEBLANC, 17 May 1971 Nashua, NH
RAFFERTY, Leonard and Lillian BELAND, 25 Mar 1944 Nashua, NH
RAGAN, William and Katherine TAYLOR, 18 Dec 1976 Hudson, NH
RAHLAY, Ann Lucill and Thomas L WHITE, 22 Aug 1932 Nashua, NH
RAINE, Jonathan G and Kathryn E NEE, 04 Jun 1974 Hudson, NH
RAISIG, Shirley A and Jacob C HART, 12 Oct 1938 Nashua, NH
RAMASKA, Peter J Jr&Pamela G WILLIAMS, 16 Mar 1974 Londonderry, NH
RAMIREZ, Marguerita and Eric E CORTAGENA, 16 Jul 1981 Hudson, NH
RAMOS, Joseph E and Cecile D MARCOTTE, 03 Dec 1950 Hudson, NH
RAMSAY, Linda L and David W BURKE, 14 Feb 1964 Hudson, NH

HUDSON, NH MARRIAGES

RAMSDELL, Alice J and Francis W BURKETT, 25 Jun 1971 Nashua, NH
RAMSDELL, Lestore G and Marjorie T MORAN, 14 May 1949 Hudson, NH
RAMSEY, Beverly and Frederick GREELEY, 03 Oct 1936 Nashua, NH
RAND, Amanda M and Daniel J ROBBINS, 10 Feb 1859
RAND, Amanda M and Daniel G ROBINSON, 10 Feb 1859
RAND, John W and Alice T MARIA, 01 Apr 1950 Hudson, NH
RAND, Olive A and Walter G RICH, 20 Apr 1914 Nashua, NH
   Joseph Rand & Jennie Craige
   F A Rich & Nellie Caverley
RAND, Pamela S and Brian A AXTELL, 15 Oct 1983 Londonderry, NH
RANDALL, Howard J and Christine JENKINS, 11 Sep 1969 Concord, NH
RANDALL, Stephen F and Carla J BEAUREGARD, 20 Jun 1981 Nashua, NH
RANDALL, Thaddeus S & Maureen E KEENAN, 28 Jul 1984 Manchester, NH
RANDAZZO, Romeo and Esther E BALLEW, 31 Dec 1949 Nashua, NH
RANDOLL, Harold M and Edith L HOPKINS, 26 Jun 1909 Nashua, NH
   Martin Randoll & Ida M Dary
   Charles H Hopkins & Ida S Webster
RANKIN, Richard J and Rita CONSTANT, 05 Feb 1966 Hudson, NH
RANKIN, Stephen and Annie M REDFIELD, 25 Sep 1907 Manchester, NH
   Fred W Rankin & Addie Deugin
   Henry A Redfield & Mary F H Smith
RANKINS, Helene A and Brenton R COLSON, 29 Jan 1977 Merrimack, NH
RANNEY, Frank G and Margaret L HOULEY, 21 Nov 1927 Nashua, NH
RANNEY, Robert W and Carolyn A BROOKS, 01 Aug 1975 Hudson, NH
RANT, Judith and Isaac SPRINGER, 03 Sep 1938 Nashua, NH
RAPANOTTI, Gary A and Donna J PURINGTON, 19 Dec 1981 Hudson, NH
RAPOSA, Manuel P and Brenda E THERNLEY, 15 Apr 1985 Hudson, NH
RAPOZA, Florence M and Peter C FRIES, 11 Dec 1948 Hudson, NH
RAPSIS, Carl Daniel & Danielle P BROUSSEAU, 28 Oct 1978 Hudson, NH
RAPSON, Ralph E and Mary C DOLAN, 02 Sep 1949 Hudson, NH
RASALAS, Douglas P and Cheryl A RUSTON, 12 Nov 1982 Hudson, NH
RATLIFF, Gannon and Charlene R MARTIN, 23 Feb 1965 Nashua, NH
RATTE, Dorothy A and Ludger H GAULIN, 26 Dec 1969 Hudson, NH
RATTE, Peter T and Phebe COTE, 19 Jul 1925 Merrimack, NH
RATTRAY, Flora L and George A STANIELS, 19 Dec 1918 Nashua, NH
RAUDONIS, Raymond J and Anna M USOVICZ, 10 Oct 1964 Hudson, NH
RAVENELLE, Mark Leo and Laura Lee FLANDERS, 26 Jul 1980 Nashua, NH
RAY, Brian K and Deborah L HUSSEY, 18 May 1985 Hudson, NH
RAY, Delbert E and Grethchen RODEN, 06 Sep 1935 Hudson, NH
RAYBOLD, Mary Ann and Roland D CINQ-MARS, 06 Nov 1971 Nashua, NH
RAYMOND, Bertha A and Raymond E PETTS, 13 Jul 1944 Hudson, NH
RAYMOND, Cynthia I and Nelson R BRETON, 23 Oct 1983 Hudson, NH
RAYMOND, Darlene M and Michael G TARDIF, 21 May 1983 Nashua, NH
RAYMOND, Georgette and Sylvio H DION, 21 May 1949 Nashua, NH
RAYMOND, Gilles and Lauria F McGEE, 04 Jul 1981 Hudson, NH
RAYMOND, John G and Amelia THAYER, 16 Oct 1926 Nashua, NH
RAYMOND, Richard D and Carol J GAGNON, 18 Apr 1964 Hudson, NH
RAYMOND, Yvon A and Bonnie D BERG, 08 Feb 1969 Nashua, NH
RAYNO, Arlo T and Judith A DETORO, 07 Mar 1964 Hudson, NH
RAYNO, Heidi J and Kenneth T IVES, 02 Mar 1985 Hudson, NH
REA, Ruth L and Frank W MESURAY, 22 Sep 1917 Hudson, NH
READ, Clayton A and Priscilla CLYDE, 04 Jun 1932 Hudson, NH
READ, Harry A J Jr and Helen F WHITE, 16 Feb 1935 Hollis, NH
READ, Harvey L and Eleanore T LATOUR, 15 Jul 1961 Hudson, NH
READ, Lewis F and Lucille I PONEY, 15 Apr 1950 Nashua, NH
READ, Luther and Martha J FULLER, 23 Mar 1865
READ, Mildred and Wilmer J WILLETTE, 28 Jan 1934 Nashua, NH
READ, Milton D and Ethel M HARVEY, 29 Dec 1942 Nashua, NH
READ, Olive and Samuel GREELEY, 08 Nov 1779
READ, Robert A and Phyllis N DANE, 03 Jul 1948 Nashua, NH

HUDSON,NH MARRIAGES

REAGAN, Thomas and Lorraine C BEAULIEU, 04 Apr 1952 Hudson, NH
REARDON, Elaine D and Oscar L MALETTE, 14 Sep 1944 Nashua, NH
RECORD, Amedee J and Nellie G FORD, 24 Jun 1920 Nashua, NH
RECORD, Earl and Bertha WEIGHTMAN, 13 Jun 1920 Nashua, NH
REDDY, Susan M and Philip D AMATO, 14 Apr 1973 Nashua, NH
REDFIELD, Annie M and Stephen RANKIN, 25 Sep 1907 Manchester, NH
  Henry A Redfield & Mary F H Smith
  Fred W Rankin & Addie Deugin
REDHEAD, Catherine and Alfred A SMITH, 10 Oct 1964 Lowell, MA
REDINGAIL, John and Hannah BURBANK, 16 Nov 1784
REDISKE, Gary D and Elizabeth CUNNINGHAM, 09 May 1982 Hudson, NH
REED, Bobby C and Lorraine J DOYON, 02 Mar 1956 Hudson, NH
REED, Dennis B and Brenda L MERRILL, 10 Apr 1971 Hudson, NH
REED, Donald J and Joan L BROWN, 17 Jul 1971 Hollis, NH
REED, Edward A and Catherine OGARA, 07 Sep 1910 Hudson, NH
  Philip M Reed & Hannah Reed
  Domick Ogara & Bridge Ogara
REED, Flora A and Albert A III BOVYN, 14 Apr 1979 Auburn, NH
REED, Flora A and Andrew M SCHULKIND, 03 Dec 1977 Nashua, NH
REED, George L and Hattie M GERRISH, 14 Nov 1908 Hudson, NH
  Fred H Reed & Seline Libberty
  H Scales & Hattie Allen
REED, Helen and Lyle COVEY, 25 Aug 1934 Nashua, NH
REED, Horace C and Loraine A McVICCAR, 17 Oct 1941 Nashua, NH
REED, John A and Martha L PEABODY, 18 Feb 1964 Nashua, NH
REED, John W Jr and Barbara M CHRISTIANSEN, 25 Apr 1970 Nashua, NH
REED, Laura A and Daniel A STANLEY, 01 Nov 1876 Hudson, NH
REED, Luther and Martha J FULLER, 03 Mar 1865
REED, Rebecca and Abraham LITTLEHALE, 24 Feb 1785
REED, Terri W and Michael E DOERR, 22 Jun 1975 Nashua, NH
REED, Thomas E Jr and Linda S BREWER, 29 Nov 1982 Hudson, NH
REED, William H and Erma L TWISS, 02 Sep 1938 Hudson, NH
REEVES, Frances A and Arthur L ST PIERRE, 07 Aug 1982 Nashua, NH
REEVES, Hilda W and William G CALDER, 20 Jun 1942 Hudson, NH
REEVES, Laura E and Michael L ROBINSON, 02 Jun 1984 Merrimack, NH
REGAN, Bernadette and John L HANNIGAN, 22 Oct 1931 Nashua, NH
REGAN, Francis K and Kathleen M DIONNE, 10 Sep 1983 Hudson, NH
REGAN, Kellie Ann and Kevin Leon SAVAGE, 29 Jul 1978 Pelham, NH
REGAN, Lucy E and Paul W GRILLO, 28 Oct 1984 Nashua, NH
REGAN, Margaret J and David A McNEIL, 26 Nov 1971 Nashua, NH
REGAN, Margaret M and Paul W CHIASSON, 08 Oct 1977 Hudson, NH
REGGIO, Eva M and Cyrus BENJAMIN, 19 Jul 1919 Hudson, NH
REID, David P and Janet E GAMACHE, 10 Sep 1971 Nashua, NH
REID, Russell T and Cheryl L DURANT, 20 Sep 1969 Rochester, NH
REILEY, Maggie and Frank W MARSH, Jan 1861
REILLY, Marisa L and Vincent F II TULLEY, 08 Oct 1983 Nashua, NH
REILLY, Patricia A and Gerard E LEMAY, 07 Jun 1952 Hudson, NH
REILLY, Raymond P Jr and Ramona M WILLETTE, 08 Aug 1953 Hudson, NH
REILLY, Richard R & Phyllis A McQUESTEN, 27 Jun 1959 Litchfield, NH
REILLY, Richard R and Alice M SIMONDS, 04 Sep 1982 Hudson, NH
REITAN, David A and Charlene J MIHELIA, 10 Sep 1983 Nashua, NH
REITAN, Debra J and Craig A LAROUCHE, 05 May 1984 Nashua, NH
REITAN, Donna M and Ronald F GAGNON, 06 May 1978 Hudson, NH
REITAN, Kathryn A and Robert P GAGNON, 24 Sep 1983 Hudson, NH
REIX, Mary L and Samuel A CLAY, 20 Apr 1877
  Samuel J Clay
RELATION, Jessie and Clifford McCOY, 07 Apr 1937 Billerica, MA
RELATION, William F and Judith G WHEELER, 21 Nov 1981 Hudson, NH
RENAUD, Joseph and Regina PROVOST, 15 Oct 1919 Lowell, MA
RENAUD, Paul E and Sandra A KELLEY, 22 Jun 1974 Hudson, NH

HUDSON,NH MARRIAGES

RESNICK, Janis T and Aaron H JOHNSON, 20 Nov 1959 Nashua, NH
RETKEVICZ, Peter D and Bonnie N PHELPS, 17 Aug 1968 Goffstown, NH
REVELL, Constance and Allen T RIZZI, 23 Jun 1949 Hudson, NH
REYNA, Anselmo Jr and Jerri-Lynn O'NEIL, 19 Jan 1979 Nashua, NH
REYNOLDS, David A and Linda D POOLE, 23 Mar 1974 Nashua, NH
REYNOLDS, David A and Catherine McILVEEN, 03 Sep 1977 Hudson, NH
REYNOLDS, George W Jr and Donna M KELLEY, 06 Aug 1966 Nashua, NH
REYNOLDS, Gregory A and Judith C TWOMBLY, 26 Jun 1965 Hudson, NH
REYNOLDS, Hattie A and Charles A STEELE, 27 Dec 1882 Windham, NH
   Hiram S Reynolds (Windham, NH) & Mary A Prescott
   Charles Steele(Hudson, NH) & Martha A Boyd (Londonderry, NH)
REYNOLDS, Hazel E and Paul W BUXTON, 17 Aug 1918 Nashua, NH
REYNOLDS, Helen M and Wheeler ZALANSKAS, 09 Jan 1943 Nashua, NH
REYNOLDS, Joan G and Irving C ALEXANDER, 14 Jun 1958 Hudson, NH
REYNOLDS, Joy E and William A Jr JOHNSON, 23 Jul 1981 Durham, NH
REYNOLDS, Joyce F and Malcolm K BRYANT, 23 May 1964 Nashua, NH
REYNOLDS, Lewis A and Daisy M ELLISON, 07 Jun 1967 Hudson, NH
REYNOLDS, Lois F and Charles L BLANCHARD, 03 Feb 1962 Hudson, NH
REYNOLDS, Mary J and Walter A POTTER, 24 Jul 1952 Hudson, NH
REYNOLDS, Patricia L and Ralph L GILCREAST, 16 Jun 1973 Hudson, NH
REYNOLDS, Phyllis M and Donald J FOSTER, 01 Nov 1961 Nashua, NH
REYNOLDS, Ruth and Joseph J ST MARTIN, 26 May 1945 Nashua, NH
REYNOLDS, Ruth Anne and Joseph PACKOR, 25 Jun 1938 Nashua, NH
REYNOLDS, Sara A and Daniel T DUBE, 25 Jun 1955 Hudson, NH
RHEAULT, Richard R and Mary McCANN, 30 Jul 1977 Nashua, NH
RHEAUME, Lester K and Deanna J BROWN, 11 Aug 1973 Bristol, NH
RHODES, Kelvin F and Lynn A ARSENAULT, 06 Feb 1977 Hudson, NH
RHODES, Randy K and Debra A DUMONT, 19 Feb 1977 Hudson, NH
RHYNER, Cheryl Ann and Alan David BUKOFSKE, 29 Aug 1981 Nashua, NH
RIBEIRO, Joseph A and Karen L CASARANO, 20 Apr 1985 Hudson, NH
RICARD, Clarabelle and William C DOHERTY, 12 May 1934 Nashua, NH
RICARD, Dorothy E and Wilfred J DUGUAY, 21 Aug 1959 Hudson, NH
RICARD, Herve C and Theresa A DUCHARME, 01 Sep 1952 Hudson, NH
RICARD, Jay M and Carol S GRENIER, 13 May 1978 Hudson, NH
RICARD, Lena M and Clarence T JAMESON, 09 Sep 1944 Hudson, NH
RICARD, Lillian A and Gerard J LaFRANCE, 31 Jul 1943 Nashua, NH
RICARD, Linda A and George P BRIAND, 27 Jun 1970 Hudson, NH
RICARD, Norman J and Antoinette BROOKS, 16 Aug 1969 Hudson, NH
RICARD, Normand J and Dorothy E GRENON, 03 Jul 1954 Hudson, NH
RICARD, Paul R and Linda V LEMIRE, 06 Apr 1968 Hudson, NH
RICARD, Ralph M and Lisa E LANDRY, 23 Jan 1981 Hudson, NH
RICARD, Raymond A and Denise A ROBICHEAU, 24 Mar 1979 Nashua, NH
RICARD, Susan T and Geoffrey A BURR, 30 Sep 1977 Hudson, NH
RICARD, Theresa F and Victor F GUILLEMETTE, 10 Feb 1968 Nashua, NH
RICCIO, Anthony R II and Debora M VAYENS, 21 Jan 1978 Hudson, NH
RICE, Abby J and Charles L HOWARD, 01 Aug 1859
RICE, Bruce M and Deborah A JOLIN, 30 Jan 1982 Hudson, NH
RICE, Charles and Anne DORTY, 25 Jun 1879 Hudson, NH
   Michael Rice (Ireland) & Martha (England)
   James Dorty(Ireland) & Ellen (Ireland)
RICE, Mildred H and Donald E ALDRICH, 28 Sep 1957 Hudson, NH
RICE, Raymond A Jr and Marie E BROUILLET, 26 Feb 1968 Nashua, NH
RICELLI, Fred F and Ellena DIDONATO, 03 Sep 1950 Hudson, NH
RICH, Ethel Bern and Natt Head MANNING, 15 Apr 1935 Concord, MA
RICH, Jeannette and Robert S THYLIN, 27 Apr 1957 Hudson, NH
RICH, Katherine and Richard F SWEENEY, 25 Sep 1929 Nashua, NH
RICH, Leon R and Olivette COTE, 28 Aug 1937 Nashua, NH
RICH, Marion E and Clifford M DAVIS, 31 Dec 1955 Hudson, NH
RICH, Nancy and James D HARROLD, 10 Jan 1953 Hudson, NH
RICH, Sarah A and William W TILTON, 17 Sep 1844

HUDSON,NH MARRIAGES

RICH, Susan Lisa and Kenneth A COLLINS, 03 Feb 1979 Hudson, NH
RICH, Walter G & Katherine BRUNESFIELD, 11 Apr 1911 Manchester, NH
   F A Rich & Nellie Caverling
   Patrick Brunsfield & Nora Flinn
RICH, Walter G and Olive A RAND, 20 Apr 1914 Nashua, NH
   F A Rich & Nellie Caverley
   Joseph Rand & Jennie Craige
RICHARD, Adrienne C and Frank E KELLEY, 22 Jun 1946 Nashua, NH
RICHARD, Albert P and Esther J CLYDE, 29 Apr 1933 Hudson, NH
RICHARD, Alfred P and Marie J LALIBERTE, 30 Aug 1947 Nashua, NH
RICHARD, Claire F and Leonard A SMITH, 21 Oct 1942 Hudson, NH
RICHARD, David K and Donna S MAXFIELD, 15 Jul 1983 Hudson, NH
RICHARD, Eva R and George C KNIGHT, 11 Jul 1918 Hudson, NH
RICHARD, George E and Florence E BEAUDIN, 24 Dec 1945 Nashua, NH
RICHARD, Lucille S and Alfred B MANSFIELD, 10 Aug 1946 Hudson, NH
RICHARD, Paula E and Ronald R CLOUTIER, 15 Jun 1968 Nashua, NH
RICHARD, Pauline R and William F RUSTON, 10 Nov 1973 Hudson, NH
RICHARD, Raymond P and Nancy A ANGWIN, 22 Jun 1957 Concord, NH
RICHARDS, Bertha A and Horace A NICHOLS, 03 Jul 1948 Hudson, NH
RICHARDS, Bonnie M and Samuel A LORENTO, 28 Apr 1984 Nashua, NH
RICHARDS, Deborah L and Thomas W CONRAN, 24 Aug 1974 Hudson, NH
RICHARDS, Doris E and Richard L HELIE, 03 Jul 1951 Hudson, NH
RICHARDS, Elizabeth and Joseph BUTTERFIELD, 15 Dec 1741
RICHARDS, Emma C and James McCOY, 22 Dec 1868 Hudson, NH
RICHARDS, Emma C and James II McCOY, 22 Dec 1868
RICHARDS, Estelle M and Frederick LOWE, 07 Oct 1949 Hudson, NH
RICHARDS, Linda J and Glenn T SAKELLAR, 27 Jun 1981 Amherst, NH
RICHARDS, Paula T and Michael W HOGAN, 13 Oct 1973 Hudson, NH
RICHARDS, Robert J and Arlene C KASHULINES, 21 Oct 1950 Hudson, NH
RICHARDSON, Ambrose and Hannah J DAVIDSON, 21 Oct 1869 Hudson, NH
RICHARDSON, Anna and Zadock P WILSON, 12 Apr 1826
RICHARDSON, Annie H and Philip R PIPER, 05 Sep 1871 Hudson, NH
RICHARDSON, Asa and Lydia MERRILL, 22 Feb 1798
RICHARDSON, Caleb and Elizabeth PALMER, 22 May 1853
RICHARDSON, Caleb and Susie J WRIGHT, 11 Apr 1882 Hudson, NH
  Henry Richardson(Corinth, VT) & Charlott Batchelder (Corinth, VT)
  Henry Conant(Harvard, MA) & Harriet Blood (Groton, MA)
RICHARDSON, Cedric A and Edna T SMITH, 11 Oct 1941 Hudson, NH
RICHARDSON, E F and Eliphalet SENTER, 23 May 1890
RICHARDSON, E F and Eliphelet SENTER, 25 May 1890 Tyngsboro, MA
  J F Richardson (Vermont) & Mary Berry (Vermont)
  Oliver Senter(Lyndeboro, NH) & Betsey Mayberry (Lyndeboro, NH)
RICHARDSON, Elizabeth and Jonathan HAMBLETT, 13 Dec 1781
RICHARDSON, Emily A and Frederick JOSE, 11 Mar 1858
RICHARDSON, Emma L and Willard H BEEBE, 14 Mar 1871
RICHARDSON, Ezekiel and Mary DOTY, 19 Sep 1805
RICHARDSON, Gloria J and Raymond W HULS, 19 May 1945 Hudson, NH
RICHARDSON, Hannah G and Richard C STEVENS, 20 Nov 1850
RICHARDSON, Herman P and Hope I TAYLOR, 31 Jul 1937 Nashua, NH
RICHARDSON, James and Abby Ann COOLIDGE, 30 Nov 1871 Hudson, NH
RICHARDSON, John R and Diane L DUCHARME, 13 Apr 1973 Hudson, NH
RICHARDSON, Jonathan H&Judith M MIROCHA, 05 Mar 1983 Peterborough,
RICHARDSON, Joseph L and L Jennie FORD, 09 May 1871
RICHARDSON, Joyce M and William C LILLEY, 19 Apr 1981 Nashua, NH
RICHARDSON, Kenneth C and Barbara W PIMM, 17 May 1934 Hudson, NH
RICHARDSON, Kevin R and Susan E DAIGLE, 16 Dec 1978 Nashua, NH
RICHARDSON, Lidia and Ezra LITTLEHALE, 04 Sep 1777
RICHARDSON, Linda N and Dennis W PRIEST, 24 Dec 1971 Nashua, NH
RICHARDSON, Luceta and John F NOYES, 26 Nov 1908 Hudson, NH
  Henry A Richardson & Estelle F Boyd

HUDSON, NH MARRIAGES

John L Noyes & Rachael F Freit
RICHARDSON, Lucinda and Amos MORELAND, 22 Jun 1823
RICHARDSON, Lucy M and William F WINN, 22 Dec 1862
RICHARDSON, Lydia and Ezra LITTLEHALE, 04 Apr 1777
RICHARDSON, Mercy M and Samuel M BELL, 13 Jan 1861
RICHARDSON, Moses P and Sarah L MARSH, 16 Nov 1865
RICHARDSON, Parker and Avis TARBELL, 25 Feb 1812
RICHARDSON, Paul W and Suezann R DESMARAIS, 28 Dec 1970 Hudson, NH
RICHARDSON, Phebe and Eleazer CUMMINGS, 12 Jul 1764
RICHARDSON, Robert A and Jennie G HANSEN, 23 Nov 1931 Merrimack, NH
RICHARDSON, Samuel and Anna HAMBLETT, 12 Oct 1826
RICHARDSON, Sarah and Peter CUMMINGS, 22 Nov 1763
RICHARDSON, Stephen G and Gail M DOLAN, 14 Jun 1980 Hudson, NH
RICHARDSON, Susan C and Samuel A GREELEY, 15 Mar 1879 Tyngsboro, MA
  Elijah Richardson (Hudson, NH) & Sarah (Hudson, NH)
  Samuel Greeley(Hudson, NH) & Mary Ann (Hudson, NH)
RICKER, Eva Anne and Robert H FRANCOEUR, 12 Aug 1972 Pittsburgh, NH
RIESE, William III and Marcia J ROBERTS, 29 Dec 1967 Hudson, NH
RIESLAND, Stephen J and Debra J PAQUETTE, 12 Sep 1981 Derry, NH
RIESSLE,.Thelma M and Edward L SEARS, 02 Feb 1938 Nashua, NH
RIGG, Peggy J and Raymond R SEUBERT, 29 Nov 1975 Litchfield, NH
RIHINOMA, Mary A and Karl A HILLI, 13 Apr 1941 Hudson, NH
RIKKOLA, Thomas Mat and Margaret J MICHAEL, 23 Jun 1937 Hudson, NH
RILEY, David J and Loretta A RODIER, 01 Jul 1944 Nashua, NH
RILEY, Delores A and Roger M ARNOLD, 06 Dec 1962 Hudson, NH
RILEY, Edward W and Lisa A BOUCHER, 11 Aug 1984 Hudson, NH
RILEY, Girard J and Cecile F HEROUX, 01 Nov 1975 Hudson, NH
RILEY, Helena D and Melville S RILEY, 25 Apr 1942 Hudson, NH
RILEY, James E and Maria T GAGNON, 23 Sep 1972 Nashua, NH
RILEY, Lillian J and Eugene O N TURNBULL, 01 Aug 1936 Hudson, NH
RILEY, Maureen T and Gregory J GEISINGER, 14 Dec 1984 Nashua, NH
RILEY, Melville S and Helena D RILEY, 25 Apr 1942 Hudson, NH
RINGDAHL, Dorothy L and Carl O ECK, 14 Sep 1940 Hudson, NH
RIOUX, Arthur P and Eleanor M WOOLLEY, 29 Jan 1954 Nashua, NH
RIOUX, Dennis W and Elaine T PARENT, 12 May 1973 Nashua, NH
RIOUX, Huguette G and Dustin H SMITH, 07 Oct 1967 Nashua, NH
RIOUX, Lorette H and Reuben J LAFLAMME, 04 May 1946 Nashua, NH
RIOUX, Rachel M and Alfred W GREGORY, 23 Jun 1962 Nashua, NH
RIOUX, Sylvia M and Roy CARROLL, 15 Jul 1961 Nashua, NH
RIPALDI, Carl R and Joyce E GAUDET, 13 Nov 1983 Hudson, NH
RIPLEY, Daniel L and Margaret J WINN, 24 Apr 1845
RIPLEY, Dustin and Malvina PALMER, 03 Jan 1847
RIPLEY, Dustin and BARRETT,
RIPLEY, Edwin and Julia A GRANT, 20 Nov 1858
RIPLEY, Eva A and Daniel G WARE, 05 May 1929 Hudson, NH
RIPLEY, Hannah S and Richard SHEPHARD, 25 Aug 1868
RIPLEY, Margaret J and John W POWELL, 28 Nov 1866
RIPLEY, Margarett and John W POWELL, 28 Nov 1866
RIPLEY, Martha K and George C ATHERTON, 30 Jun 1865
RIPLEY, Mary Ann and Thomas BURSIEL, 24 Feb 1858
RIPLEY, Nathaniel and Mary JEFTS, 20 Apr 1854
RIPLEY, Spencer and Mary CUMMINGS, 31 Dec 1818
RISDON, Carolyn A and Alan R ROBERTSON, 27 Jun 1981 Hudson, NH
RITCHIE, Janice A and John E SMYER, 17 Sep 1958 Hudson, NH
RITCHIE, Lottie A and Edwin L WORTHY, 27 Jul 1873 Hudson, NH
RITSON, Edward I and Ethlyn M FRYE, 21 Oct 1961 Pittsfield, NH
RIVARD, Clement J and Cecile G LEVESQUE, 19 Apr 1947 Nashua, NH
RIVARD, Eugene D and Louise M MONTMINY, 04 Sep 1967 Hudson, NH
RIVARD, Janice A and Keith E SEBEK, 06 Jun 1981 Merrimack, NH
RIVARD, Laurette and Antoine GAGNE, 09 Nov 1925 Nashua, NH

HUDSON, NH MARRIAGES

RIVARD, Ronald E and Shirley E ASHFORD, 02 May 1959 Hudson, NH
RIVARD, Shirley L and John S LAROSE, 15 Oct 1983 Nashua, NH
RIVET, Vernon S and Patricia B HEANEY, 28 Aug 1950 Hudson, NH
RIZZI, Allen T and Constance REVELL, 23 Jun 1949 Hudson, NH
RIZZITANO, Anthony J and Bernice E DROUIN, 11 Nov 1971 Nashua, NH
RIZZO, Charles A and Mary E SHURTLEFF, 01 Jun 1946 Hudson, NH
ROACH, Ella J and Nathaniel ALEXANDER, 16 Jun 1866
ROBARE, Arthur W Jr and Beverly A TITUS, 03 Sep 1949 Hudson, NH
ROBARGE, Yvette and Eugene L PROVENCAL, 29 Jun 1922 Nashua, NH
ROBB, Catherine Mary and William David JERSZYK, 15 Jul 1978 Rye, NH
ROBBINS, Betsy and Thomas R FITZGERALD, 01 Apr 1979 Hudson, NH
ROBBINS, Carl E and Maude A F DOREY, 16 Jun 1923 Tyngsboro, MA
ROBBINS, Daniel J and Amanda M RAND, 10 Feb 1859
ROBBINS, David and Georgiana WHITTIMORE, 13 Jun 1874 Nashua, NH
ROBBINS, Elaine T and Stephen P BROOK, 15 May 1970 Nashua, NH
ROBBINS, Frank E and Emma L BERBAUM, 12 Jan 1951 S Lyndeboro, NH
ROBBINS, John P and Jane M VANVLEET, 31 Dec 1958 Hudson, NH
ROBBINS, Lizzie J and Perley B SMITH, 28 May 1895 Nashua, NH
   D Z Robbins (Dover, NH) & Georgia A Robbins (Nashua, NH)
   Isaac N Smith(Hudson, NH) & Roxanna Bolter (Pelham, NH)
ROBBINS, Marie A and Clayton DAVIS, 28 May 1965 Nashua, NH
ROBBINS, Raymond and Marie A LAJEUNESSE, 05 May 1945 Nashua, NH
ROBBINS, Wilhelmena I & Edward B BLANCHARD, 21 Aug 1889 Nashua, NH
   George W Robbins (Groton, MA) & Alice M Hall (Derry, NH)
   Silas M Blanchard(Windham, NH) & Elener I Bickford(Barnstead, NH)
ROBERGE, Florida and Donat BOULAY, 09 May 1922 Manchester, NH
ROBERGE, Mitchell A and Angela M ROUSSEL, 20 Aug 1983 Hudson, NH
ROBERGE, Muriel D and Lucien L BLAIS, 22 Nov 1973 Berlin, NH
ROBERT, Dianne L and Martin E GEEHAN, 16 Sep 1967 Hudson, NH
ROBERT, Donald Ala and Diane Mari AREL, 14 Jul 1973 Hudson, NH
ROBERT, Linda A and Richard M LAMONTAGNE, 27 Aug 1971 Hudson, NH
ROBERTS, Alan C and Denice M MERRILL, 01 Jul 1972 Hudson, NH
ROBERTS, Alphonse and Martha WARD, 01 Mar 1900 Nashua, NH
   Henry Roberts & Martha Fuller
ROBERTS, Carl E and Marguerite ANCTIL, 30 May 1968 Nashua, NH
ROBERTS, Catherine & Rosaire R Jr GAUTHIER, 27 Dec 1975 Nashua, NH
ROBERTS, Emily and John WEBSTER, 01 Jul 1853
ROBERTS, Joseph A Jr and Gloria J CHAMPIGNY, 29 Jun 1968 Hudson, NH
ROBERTS, Marcia J and William III RIESE, 29 Dec 1967 Hudson, NH
ROBERTS, Mark and Kathleen R BEYER, 12 Oct 1968 Hudson, NH
ROBERTS, Rex A and Caroline D KELLER, 21 Jun 1949 Hudson, NH
ROBERTS, Ronald M and Constance PERRY, 10 Apr 1982 Hudson, NH
ROBERTS, Timothy O and Clara F WEBSTER, 08 Jul 1871
   Simon G Webster
ROBERTS, Tracy A and Philip R BECHARD, 07 Nov 1981 Nashua, NH
ROBERTS, William R Jr & Patricia L BISBING, 15 Jun 1985 Hudson, NH
ROBERTSON, Alan R and Carolyn A RISDON, 27 Jun 1981 Hudson, NH
ROBERTSON, Mary A and Francis J MARTIN, 29 Jan 1977 Litchfield, NH
ROBICHAUD, Marcelle A and Nelson B HOULE, 20 Sep 1957 Hudson, NH
ROBICHEAU, Denise A and Raymond A RICARD, 24 Mar 1979 Nashua, NH
ROBIE, Everett W and Cynthia J ROLLINS, 03 May 1958 Nashua, NH
ROBILLARD, Roland A and Jeanne P TANGUAY, 29 Dec 1973 Hudson, NH
ROBILLARD, Willhelmen and Ronald E FORD, 05 Feb 1972 Nashua, NH
ROBINSON, Alden C and Constance GRIGGS, 28 Aug 1976 Nashua, NH
ROBINSON, Alphonse and Louisa A HASELTON, 23 Dec 1862
ROBINSON, Angeline S and Chandler MESSER, 31 Dec 1856
ROBINSON, Anna D and Elbridge DOW, 24 Jun 1830
ROBINSON, Arintha T and Jonathan F WILLIAMS, 22 Oct 1932 Pelham, NH
ROBINSON, Catherine and Glennon E SHAWCROSS, 06 Sep 1947 Hudson, NH
ROBINSON, Charlotte&Leander C BUTTRICK, 31 Jul 1910 Londonderry, NH

HUDSON,NH MARRIAGES

Frank R Robinson & Alecia A Young
Clifton E Buttrick & Ella F Boynton
ROBINSON, Daniel G and Amanda M RAND, 10 Feb 1859
ROBINSON, Dorothy L and Sigismond SHUMSKY, 26 Jan 1942 Hudson, NH
ROBINSON, Ethel A and John T KIMBALL, 09 Jun 1905 Hudson, NH
  Henry C Robinson & Mary A Merrill
  John R Kimball & Delora Tarbell
ROBINSON, Frank P and Alecia A YOUNG, 08 Sep 1886 Windham, NH
  Simeon Robinson (Hudson, NH) & Charlott Glidden (Jefferson)
  Israel W Young(Londonderry, NH) & Elizabeth (Morse)
ROBINSON, Gary J and Lynne A JOHNSON, 27 May 1984 Hudson, NH
ROBINSON, Harvey H and Myra AVERILL, 08 May 1871 Hudson, NH
ROBINSON, Henry C and Mary A MERRILL, 07 Oct 1872 Ayer, MA
ROBINSON, Henry J and Luvia BLOW, 30 Jun 1934 Nashua, NH
ROBINSON, Henry J and Lucille A LAFRANCE, 15 Dec 1945 Hudson, NH
ROBINSON, John and Sarah J ROLF, 28 Aug 1856
ROBINSON, John A and Julia A WEBSTER, 05 Mar 1890 Nashua, NH
  Alp Robinson (Hudson, NH) & Louisa A Haselton (Hudson, NH)
  Kimball Webster(Pelham, NH) & Abiah Cutter (Pelham, NH)
ROBINSON, John B and Sally BUTTERICK, 24 Apr 1850
ROBINSON, John H and Catherine DRISCOLL, 29 Aug 1935 Hudson, NH
ROBINSON, John P and Sally BUTTRICK, 24 Apr 1850
ROBINSON, Lester W and Anny E WILLWERTH, 05 Sep 1907 Nashua, NH
  George W Robinson & Jennie L Carrington
  Eliott A Morse & Maria M Green
ROBINSON, Linda J and Michael H CARON, 09 Apr 1983 Hudson, NH
ROBINSON, Lorraine P and Norman A LANDRY, 12 Oct 1963 Nashua, NH
ROBINSON, Louisa and James D HERRICK, 17 May 1848
ROBINSON, Lucius F and Clarrisa SMITH, 08 May 1862
ROBINSON, Lucius F and Louisa A SMITH, 24 Apr 1879 Hudson, NH
  Simeon Robinson (Hudson, NH) & Eliza (Hudson, NH)
  James Smith(Hudson, NH) & Margarett Smith (Hudson, NH)
ROBINSON, Mary and George TALBOT, 13 Nov 1825
ROBINSON, Maureen A and John B WELDON, 05 Oct 1968 Hudson, NH
ROBINSON, Mehitable and David HILLS, 08 Sep 1796
ROBINSON, Michael L and Laura E REEVES, 02 Jun 1984 Merrimack, NH
ROBINSON, Oliver and Gladys H PEDRO, 03 Apr 1948 Hudson, NH
ROBINSON, Pathenia and John HAMBLETT, 17 May 1832
ROBINSON, Prentice I and Rosalie VASTA, 27 May 1971 Nashua, NH
ROBINSON, Priscilla and Thomas S COLBY, 11 Sep 1976 Manchester, NH
ROBINSON, Robert S and Margaret E BLAKE, 04 Oct 1941 Hudson, NH
ROBINSON, Robert S and Bernice M ALBERTINI, 17 Jan 1948 Hudson, NH
ROBINSON, Roger and Bertha B ROWELL, 23 Jul 1918 Nashua, NH
ROBINSON, Roger L and Bessie V HARDY, 28 Dec 1957 Hudson, NH
ROBINSON, Simeon and Charlotte GLIDDEN, 14 Dec 1848
ROBINSON, Simeon F and Charlotte STEELE, 01 Nov 1842
ROBINSON, Terry W and Linda L LEMERY, 14 Jun 1969 Hudson, NH
ROBINSON, Vivian I and Stanley BATURA, 16 Aug 1947 Hudson, NH
ROBINSON, William E and Sarah ABBOTT, 30 Nov 1846
ROBITO, Mary C and Anthony J LUONGO, 15 Nov 1948 Hudson, NH
ROBY, Gloria J and Richard W KENNEDY, 16 Dec 1967 Nashua, NH
ROBY, Henry E and Mary Jane NELSON, 09 Jun 1844
ROBY, Silas Jr and Rhoda TARBELL, 14 Mar 1799
ROBY, Silas Jr and Roda TARBELL, 14 Mar 1799
ROCHE, Deborah A and William E SANDALL, 30 Jun 1984 Hudson, NH
ROCHE, Margaret R and Robert B WARDWELL, 19 Dec 1933 Nashua, NH
ROCHE, Stephen P and Mary Louis WASSON, 26 Apr 1969 Hudson, NH
ROCHEVILLE, Tinamarie and Alan J HERRING, 15 Sep 1979 Hudson, NH
ROCK, Barbara Jean and Jeffrey M KEROUAC, 03 Sep 1976 Nashua, NH
ROCK, Carol A and Keith A CHRISTIANSEN, 16 May 1964 Hudson, NH

HUDSON,NH MARRIAGES

ROCK, Clarence D and Barbara A GILLIAM, 05 May 1962 Hudson, NH
ROCK, Dorothy J and Forest D PIKE, 16 Aug 1947 Hudson, NH
ROCK, Rose A and William F BEAUMONT, 14 Mar 1954 Nashua, NH
ROCK, Rose A and Leonard A JACKSON, 06 Sep 1958 Hudson, NH
ROCK, Willard N and Agnes M GREENE, 10 Sep 1945 Hudson, NH
ROCK, William Jr and Ruth ROTHNEY, 23 Sep 1966 Nashua, NH
ROCKE, Barbara A and Jesse L YORK, 06 May 1967 Hudson, NH
ROCKWELL, Bruce A and Linda A GLIDDEN, 11 Jun 1982 Hudson, NH
ROCKWELL, Eliza and William MINALO, 30 Oct 1855
ROCKWELL, Emma A and Wm W COVEY, 21 Jun 1922 Hudson, NH
ROCKWELL, Hazel and Kenneth MANSUR, 09 Jun 1928 Nashua, NH
ROCKWELL, Sandra A and Ronald N SIMONEAU, 16 Nov 1981 Hudson, NH
ROCKWOOD, Rosemarie and Donald E LORAINE, 20 Aug 1955 Nashua, NH
RODD, Barbara R and Floyd S Jr POTTER, 07 Jun 1955 Hudson, NH
RODD, David A and Lorraine M LEFEBVRE, 21 Aug 1965 Hudson, NH
RODEN, Grethchen and Delbert E RAY, 06 Sep 1935 Hudson, NH
RODERICK, Brenda Jea and William J BRANN, 29 Sep 1984 Nashua, NH
RODGERS, Alvin H and Betty Ann MORSE, 20 Jun 1964 Hudson, NH
RODGERS, Brenda A and Kenneth A KLIMAS, 20 Jun 1981 Hudson, NH
RODGERS, Cheryl A and Ralph P BOISVERT, 30 Jun 1973 Hudson, NH
RODGERS, Cheryl A and Karl M MUNDAY, 27 Aug 1971 Nashua, NH
RODGERS, Dana A and Beverly J GRIFFIN, 26 Nov 1977 Hudson, NH
RODGERS, Gary J and Robin A SCOTT, 14 Nov 1981 Hudson, NH
RODGERS, George P and Barbara HAIGHT, 03 Jul 1948 Nashua, NH
RODGERS, Kenneth J and Patricia A DIGGINS, 22 Sep 1956 Nashua, NH
RODGERS, Lee Ann and Steven F MIDDLEMISS, 21 Aug 1982 Hudson, NH
RODGERS, Michael H and Diane C DUCHESNEAU, 13 Nov 1971 Nashua, NH
RODGERS, Roberto A and Maria E CADAVID, 25 Sep 1982 Hudson, NH
RODGERS, Susan L and James D GENDRON, 19 Sep 1970 Hudson, NH
RODIED, Yvonne I and Alfred A JACQUES, 27 Oct 1924 Nashua, NH
RODIER, Albert F and Laurette M JACQUES, 17 Sep 1955 Hudson, NH
RODIER, Cecile B and Leonard A McINTOSH, 12 Jun 1943 Nashua, NH
RODIER, Hormidas D and Marie A BOSSE, 09 Aug 1947 Nashua, NH
RODIER, Joan E and Henry E DESCLOS, 22 Jul 1970 Nashua, NH
RODIER, Loretta A and David J RILEY, 01 Jul 1944 Nashua, NH
RODIER, Maurice H and Doris DIONNE, 27 Apr 1957 Nashua, NH
RODIER, Rachel R and Mahlon P EASTMAN, 30 Aug 1954 Hudson, NH
RODIER, Roland J and Helen G QUINT, 09 Aug 1950 Hudson, NH
RODONIS, Charles and Lucille E PAGE, 14 May 1940 Lowell, MA
RODONIS, Charles J and Josephine LAMB, 10 Nov 1956 Nashua, NH
RODONIS, William J and Ida NADEAU, 05 Jul 1941 Nashua, NH
RODRICK, Anthony and Mary S CALDEIRA, 24 Aug 1968 Nashua, NH
RODRIGUES, Robert R and Frances A LACASSE, 27 Aug 1971 Hudson, NH
RODRIGUEZ, Carmen M and Luis M NEGRON, 28 May 1966 Derry, NH
RODRIGUEZ, Gloria M and Alphonse M BOUCHER, 12 Dec 1944 Nashua, NH
RODRIGUEZ, Gregori M and Luisa M ALAVAREZ, 18 Nov 1967 Nashua, NH
ROGATO, Mary M and Alphonse PHERIZZI, 29 Jun 1938 Hudson, NH
ROGERS, Annie E and Alfred C GLEASON, 11 Sep 1913 Hudson, NH
  Charles O Rogers & Lizzie
  William H Gleason & Augusta Brooks
ROGERS, Avard D and Patricia P FRENCH, 12 Jul 1958 Hudson, NH
ROGERS, Cyrus and Harriet E PAGE, 19 Dec 1861
ROGERS, David R and Hanni E RUDOLPH, 11 Sep 1972 Hudson, NH
ROGERS, Frances G and Vinton Ear DAVIS, 26 Sep 1938 Hudson, NH
ROGERS, George A and Natalie M BURNHAM, 09 Dec 1945 Hudson, NH
ROGERS, Harry E and Gertrude E NICHOLS, 12 Nov 1902 Nashua, NH
  Frank P Rogers & Lizzie J Baldwin
  William Nichols & Mae
ROGERS, Jeffrey A and Claudia L COULOMBE, 28 Sep 1974 Hudson, NH
ROGERS, Lawrence R and Rita D ALMEIDA, 04 Nov 1967 Nashua, NH

HUDSON, NH MARRIAGES

ROGERS, Mary A and Rufus M FLETCHER, 06 Jun 1864
ROGERS, Mary A and Rufus M FLETCHER, 06 Jun 1867
ROGERS, Mary Ellen and Wilfred BERGERON, 16 May 1926 Nashua, NH
ROGERS, Mildred and Myron E WHALEN, 24 Jul 1940 Nashua, NH
ROGERS, Robert C and Margaret R McCAMMOND, 16 Jun 1946 Hudson, NH
ROGERS, Seabury F and Hannah WELLMAN, 01 Nov 1842
ROGERS, William F and Ruth E ANDERSON, 02 Jun 1937 Hudson, NH
ROHAN, George and Olive BROOKS, 07 Feb 1947 Hudson, NH
ROHER, Daniel and Hattie J MERRILL, 06 Sep 1855
ROLF, George and Lucinda P BURNS, 03 Apr 1861
ROLF, Martha M and Albert F SEARLES, 03 Feb 1879 Hudson, NH
   Nathan B Rolf (Maine) & Sarah (Rolf)
   Jana Searles(Pelham, NH) & Mary M
ROLF, Sarah J and John ROBINSON, 28 Aug 1856
ROLFE, Dorothy and Maurice DENNE, 28 Nov 1940 Lowell, MA
ROLFE, George and Lorinda P BURNS, 23 Apr 1862
ROLLINS, Blanche A and Howard A O'BRIEN, 05 Aug 1938 Hudson, NH
ROLLINS, Cynthia J and Everett W ROBIE, 03 May 1958 Nashua, NH
ROLLINS, Jacquelyn and Richard K GOSBEE, 30 Jul 1977 Nashua, NH
ROLLINS, James H and Marilyn H PARKER, 22 Aug 1964 Hudson, NH
ROLLINS, Janet R and Edmond O BRIAND, 01 Apr 1955 Nashua, NH
ROLLINS, Josephine and Nathan P WEBSTER, 22 May 1867
ROLLINS, Lucy A and Norman J A DUFF, 26 Mar 1960 Nashua, NH
ROLLINS, Susan J and Pierre C BERGERON, 15 Apr 1967 Hollis, NH
ROLLS, Frederick and Sarah Louise HARWOOD, 16 Aug 1927 Hudson, NH
ROMANO, Louis V and Jeannette CARON, 03 Sep 1945 Hanover, NH
RONAN, William F and Irene M TOUSSAINT, 29 Jun 1946 Hudson, NH
RONDEAU, Donna-Mari and Steven C DICKEY, 12 Jul 1975 Hudson, NH
ROOD, Agnes Step and William J MARSH, 23 Jan 1982 Nashua, NH
ROOD, William R and Sandra C POWELL, 18 Dec 1982 Nashua, NH
ROONEY, Steven A and Martha J PRICE, 28 Apr 1979 Merrimack, NH
ROOT, Lillian I and Mortimer STEVENS, 26 Jan 1946 Hudson, NH
ROSE, Bertram J and Mary H CHESTNUT, 05 Oct 1897 Hudson, NH
   D P Rose & Laura Kingsbury
   Robert Chestnut & Susan Chestnut
ROSE, Bobby D and Kathleen COOMAS, 05 Aug 1950 Hudson, NH
ROSS, Alex C and Mary T KLUCK, 19 Jun 1982 Hudson, NH
ROSS, Charlotte and William J Jr SAWICKI, 03 Jul 1959 Hudson, NH
ROSS, Debra-Jean and Paul L LAVOIE, 19 Jul 1969 Hudson, NH
ROSS, Elizabeth and Warren F WATERMAN, 29 Jul 1942 Hudson, NH
ROSS, Ernest D III and Gail B KOZLOVSKI, 06 Jun 1981 Hudson, NH
ROSS, Helen M and Peter R BRAGINTON, 30 Jul 1971 Exeter, NH
ROSS, Joseph R and Constance RYAN, 22 Feb 1947 Hudson, NH
ROSS, Kenneth D and Sharon H THOMAS, 10 Jun 1983 Nashua, NH
ROSS, Marie B and Kenneth J BLANCHETTE, 24 Nov 1984 Hudson, NH
ROSS, Rebecca C and Walter E LUFKIN, 16 Sep 1972 Hampton, NH
ROSSI, Mary A and Carmel M LEONE, 25 Sep 1948 Hudson, NH
ROTE, Harry L and Janet HYDE, 17 Dec 1947 Hudson, NH
ROTH, Arline K and William A WATSON, 02 Jul 1963 Nashua, NH
ROTH, Cheryl L and Brian N McLEOD, 04 Jun 1983 Litchfield, NH
ROTH, Michael L and Janet E THIVIERGE, 22 Jan 1982 Nashua, NH
ROTH, Robert D Jr and Jacalyn E NOWAK, 04 Nov 1967 Nashua, NH
ROTHNEY, Ruth and William Jr ROCK, 23 Sep 1966 Nashua, NH
ROUILLARD, David Roger and Claire Ann WHITE, 21 Jul 1973 Pelham, NH
ROUILLARD, Dorothy L and Charles S HANSON, 21 Oct 1966 Hudson, NH
ROUILLARD, Gary W and Roxanne FLETCHER, 11 Aug 1967 Nashua, NH
ROUILLARD, Roxanne and Lawrence E Jr OLSON, 12 Apr 1980 Hudson, NH
ROULETTE, Nancy and Benjamin P MILLER, 23 Jan 1855
ROULO, Joseph R and Josephene NUTTING, 10 Dec 1877 Hudson, NH
   Joseph Roulo

HUDSON,NH MARRIAGES

  James Nutting
ROUNSEVILLE, Helen L and Arthur W ELDRIDGE, 24 Sep 1903 Hudson, NH
  John Rounseville & Cora B Clifford
  A F Eldridge & Anna Britton
ROUSELLE, Doris N and Kenneth E SPENCER, 01 Aug 1971 Pelham, NH
ROUSSEAU, Bart G and Susan I CRONIN, 04 Sep 1971 Deerfield, NH
ROUSSEAU, Judith A and Stuart L Sr OSBORNE, 21 Mar 1981 Hudson, NH
ROUSSEAU, Rose and Gedeon LAQUERRE, 12 Jan 1920 Nashua, NH
ROUSSEAU, Sandra L and John J CURRAN, 20 Mar 1976 Hudson, NH
ROUSSEAU, Thomas E and Paula J STEVENS, 18 Apr 1981 Hudson, NH
ROUSSEL, Angela M and Mitchell A ROBERGE, 20 Aug 1983 Hudson, NH
ROUSSEL, Celeste E and Joey G OUELLETTE, 08 Oct 1976 Hudson, NH
ROUSSEL, Donald J and Joanna C MATHER-LEES, 23 Dec 1983 Nashua, NH
ROUSSEL, Elaine Y & Charles J BOISSONNAULT, 30 Nov 1974 Hudson, NH
ROUSSEL, Jeanne A and James P WAMBOLDT, 12 Oct 1984 Hudson, NH
ROUSSELL, Diana and Charles LOVELY, 29 Sep 1933 Nashua, NH
ROUSSELL, James T and Debra J BROOKS, 14 Nov 1981 Pelham, NH
ROUSSELLE, Jeanne A and James HAMEL, 16 Aug 1941 Nashua, NH
ROUTHIER, Lynn M and Kenneth M CANTARA, 30 Jun 1980 Nashua, NH
ROUTHIER, Sandra A&Donald R Jr FORBES, 23 Apr 1977 Londonderry, NH
ROUX, Reginald L and Roxy P BOURQUE, 19 Nov 1970 Nashua, NH
ROWE, Judith I and Alexander MACIE, 20 Jun 1959 Nashua, NH
ROWE, Raymond R and Marion JARDIN, 15 Dec 1947 Hudson, NH
ROWELL, Barbara M and Alfred J DAVIS, 22 Oct 1955 Hudson, NH
ROWELL, Barbara M and Richard A MOISAN, 20 Aug 1977 Nashua, NH
ROWELL, Bertha B and Roger ROBINSON, 23 Jul 1918 Nashua, NH
ROWELL, Byron A and Elizabeth TYLER, 01 Jun 1918 Barrington
ROWELL, Chester P and Myrtle TAYLOR, 11 Aug 1917 Hudson, NH
ROWELL, Clarence E and Josephine THOMPSON, 29 Mar 1975 Hudson, NH
ROWELL, Clifton H and Mary E KEENAN, 17 Sep 1955 Nashua, NH
ROWELL, Cora L and Gilbert F SEARLES, 26 Oct 1911 Nashua, NH
  Eugene Rowell & Mary Wilson
  Albert F Searles & Sarah T Fletcher
ROWELL, Edwin E and Winnebel LAMSON, 06 Aug 1931 Hudson, NH
ROWELL, Edwin E and Leona M MERRILL, 06 Sep 1938 Lowell, MA
ROWELL, Harold C and Zoula O FERRYALL, 18 Sep 1923 Nashua, NH
ROWELL, Joan E and Raymond W WYNOTT, 17 Oct 1950 Nashua, NH
ROWELL, Lucille and Edward J DEMANCHE, 15 Aug 1959 Hudson, NH
ROWELL, Mehitable and Timothy FORD, 27 Dec 1796
ROWELL, Paula Jean and Donald O DUMAIS, 02 Aug 1980 Nashua, NH
ROWELL, Wallace W and Grace M ATKINS, 14 Jun 1936 Hudson, NH
ROWLETT, Ira A and Dawn K HARDY, 23 Sep 1979 Hudson, NH
ROWLINGS, Edwin A and Vera JOHNSON, 26 Jun 1948 Hudson, NH
ROWMAN, Patricia A and Joseph L CLOUGH, 23 May 1964 Nashua, NH
ROWMAN, Philip J and Patricia A DOUGLAS, 05 Dec 1959 Hudson, NH
ROWMAN, Philip J and Margaret H BEACH, 20 Feb 1965 Amherst, NH
ROY, Barbara J and Robert F SPAULDING, 19 Dec 1981 Hudson, NH
ROY, Gerard A and Lesley N LORING, 20 Feb 1954 Hudson, NH
ROY, Gerard L and Janet R GALLAGHER, 01 Oct 1955 Hudson, NH
ROY, Grace M and Roland J LEVESQUE, 23 Jun 1948 Hudson, NH
ROY, Irene G and A James PROFFITT, 14 Aug 1965 Hudson, NH
ROY, Jeanne A and Aleck BOSKA, 02 Sep 1943 Nashua, NH
ROY, Judith C and Richard N DION, 11 Mar 1967 Hudson, NH
ROY, Kathleen A and Mark S GORDON, 25 May 1985 Nashua, NH
ROY, Lee-Ann M and Stephen F MORRISON, 08 Nov 1974 Hudson, NH
ROY, Linda Lou and John F Jr BALSER, 21 Jul 1972 Nashua, NH
ROY, Lucy A and Noel E MOREY, 22 Jun 1936 Nashua, NH
ROY, Mari G and Joseph A L LAVOIE, 21 Aug 1942 Nashua, NH
ROY, Marie-Anne and Ernest A PROVENCAL, 20 Sep 1958 Hudson, NH
ROY, Michael A and Christine DAWALGA, 26 Jan 1973 Hudson, NH

HUDSON,NH MARRIAGES

ROY, Michael W and Denise A ST CYR, 18 Apr 1980 Hudson, NH
ROY, Michele D and David A BOURRET, 25 Jan 1985 Pelham, NH
ROY, Nancy J and Roger Jr ST LAURENT, 24 Jul 1971 Hudson, NH
ROY, Nancy L and Irving E COOK, 23 Aug 1981 Hudson, NH
ROY, Patricia E and Robert A LEFEBVRE, 19 Sep 1959 Hudson, NH
ROY, Pauline O and Andre L LAVOIE, 05 Jun 1950 Hudson, NH
ROY, Pauline R and Edward J PLONA, 24 Nov 1982 Hudson, NH
ROY, Philip L and Irene N LAMBERT, 23 Jun 1934 Nashua, NH
ROY, Rita I and Romeo J LEVESQUE, 15 Jun 1963 Hudson, NH
ROY, Robert B and Lorraine L LEBLANC, 31 Oct 1974 Nashua, NH
ROY, Robert G and Karen S PLAYLE, 18 Aug 1984 Hudson, NH
ROY, Robert L and Elaine P BERARD, 20 Nov 1954 Hudson, NH
ROY, Robert L and Marion L PARON, 12 Sep 1981 Hudson, NH
ROY, Robert W and Georgina T McGILLIVRAY, 05 Jan 1946 Hudson, NH
ROY, Roland R and Sharon Lee HUGHES, 04 Feb 1967 Nashua, NH
ROY, Ronald L and Margaret A SHAUGHNESSY, 26 Nov 1971 Hudson, NH
ROYCE, Wayne H and Rita L FAUCHER, 21 Oct 1967 Hudson, NH
ROZZI, Richard M and Lori B OVERBY, 01 Aug 1981 Hudson, NH
RUANE, Lyn M and Alan M VIGNOLA, 01 Sep 1979 Hudson, NH
RUBLEE, John H Jr and Margo A MAURER, 29 Jun 1963 Hudson, NH
RUCKMAN, Donald S and Ethel M UPTON, 28 Jun 1975 Litchfield, NH
RUCKMAN, Donald S Jr & Deborah A FALARDEAU, 11 Nov 1983 Hudson, NH
RUDOLPH, Hanni E and David R ROGERS, 11 Sep 1972 Hudson, NH
RUDOLPH, John W and Michelle M GUILL, 18 Jun 1983 Goffstown, NH
RUDOLPH, Sally A and Nicholas DOURIS, 02 Feb 1964 Hudson, NH
RUGG, Ellery H and Myrtle E PRENTIS, 30 Jun 1948 Hudson, NH
RUITER, Esther B and Richard E McGRAW, 03 Sep 1955 Hudson, NH
RUITER, Helen V and James E Jr GIBSON, 15 Nov 1946 Nashua, NH
RUITER, Joan B and John E Jr GONSALVES, 03 Jun 1978 Hudson, NH
RUITER, Katherine and William W TATE, 11 May 1946 Nashua, NH
RUMRILL, Oran E and Marian V OWEN, 24 Sep 1925 Manchester, NH
RUNNELS, Frederick and Hannah CHAMBERLAIN, 20 Aug 1817
RUSH, Gerald L and Anjanette M MAYNARD, 24 Dec 1982 Londonderry, NH
RUSH, Maureen T and Timothy G FOLTZ, 04 Nov 1978 Hudson, NH
RUSS, Miriam and Benjamin FROST, 21 Nov 1743
RUSS, Miriam and Benjamin FROST, 21 Dec 1743
RUSSELL, Abigail and Simeon COLBURN, 27 Sep 1781
RUSSELL, Ann H and John POVILAN, 16 Apr 1960 Hudson, NH
RUSSELL, Carol L and Joseph S Jr TWARDOSKY, 20 Jan 1962 Hudson, NH
RUSSELL, Carolyn E and Gerard F LOCKE, 13 Nov 1971 Hudson, NH
RUSSELL, Harold A and Deborah A MOQUIN, 25 Oct 1980 Hudson, NH
RUSSELL, Harry U and Hellen A CENTER, 09 Oct 1907 Hudson, NH
  Herbert E Russell & Octava E Elliott
  Warren Center & Carrie E Howe
RUSSELL, Helen J and Arthur E FULLER, 30 Aug 1931 Milford, NH
RUSSELL, Joan Z and Albert W PETRAIN, 26 Oct 1963 Nashua, NH
RUSSELL, John W and Carol L PLANTE, 25 Apr 1959 Nashua, NH
RUSSELL, Linda G and Ronald R GAUDETTE, 11 Jan 1974 Hudson, NH
RUSSELL, Marguerite E and Albert N BROWN, 06 Nov 1926 Hudson, NH
RUSSELL, Marie and Raymond L LEFEBVRE, 20 Sep 1958 Hudson, NH
RUSSELL, Michael W and Penny E ADAMS, 14 Oct 1972 Hudson, NH
RUSSELL, Michael W and Nona V AHEARN, 19 Sep 1976 Nashua, NH
RUSSELL, Mildred Smith & Arthur F BROWN, 05 Jul 1928 Worcester, MA
RUSSELL, Raymond T and Eva GINGRAS, 10 Oct 1937 Nashua, NH
RUSSELL, Robert W and Minnie HADDAD, 04 Nov 1934 Hudson, NH
RUSSELL, Shirley N and Raymond BENNETT, 19 Aug 1967 Pelham, NH
RUSSELL, Sylvia R and Sherman D Jr MILLETT, 05 Oct 1963 Hudson, NH
RUSSELL, Toby R and Lorrie A WIECZHALEK, 29 May 1982 Nashua, NH
RUSSELL, Veronica J and Robert R GENEST, 23 Nov 1981 Litchfield, NH
RUSSELL NH, Charles E and E Gladys SHAW, 15 Oct 1907 Hudson, NH

HUDSON, NH MARRIAGES

Joseph E Russell & Lottie Hopkins
John T Shaw & Mary A Nason
RUSSO, Charles J and C R ALESSANDRO, 04 Oct 1947 Hudson, NH
RUSSO, Jennie and Camillo CASCIANO, 13 Jun 1938 Hudson, NH
RUSSO, Joseph T and Winifred E BOLGER, 10 Aug 1947 Hudson, NH
RUSTON, Cheryl A and Douglas P RASALAS, 12 Nov 1982 Hudson, NH
RUSTON, Robert H and Elaine M DEWITT, 20 Apr 1974 Hudson, NH
RUSTON, William F and Pauline R RICHARD, 10 Nov 1973 Hudson, NH
RYAN, Agnes M and Graydon L SHARPE, 09 May 1981 Hudson, NH
RYAN, Constance and Joseph R ROSS, 22 Feb 1947 Hudson, NH
RYAN, James L and Barbara A LAMPRON, 11 Oct 1958 Hudson, NH
RYAN, Jeffrey A and Patricia A PETERSON, 18 May 1985 Amherst, NH
RYAN, Katherine and Allan John ELKE, 08 Apr 1984 Hudson, NH
RYAN, Linda A and Wayne C BEARD, 12 Sep 1970 Hudson, NH
RYAN, Ron K and Peggy Jean LIBBY, 14 Apr 1984 Hollis, NH
SABANSKI, Sophie and Joseph ALLESON, 30 May 1929 Manchester, NH
SABLE, Edith J and Abraham PRAGER, 11 Sep 1948 Hudson, NH
SADAUSKAS, Adolph A and Stacia GALECKI, 03 May 1947 Nashua, NH
SADAUSKIEVE, Mary and Michael BATURA, 11 Feb 1925 Nashua, NH
SADERBERRY, and Roger J COUGHLIN, 24 Oct 1888
SAGER, Sylvanus H and Gladys Clara HARDY, 25 Mar 1925 Hudson, NH
SAJDAK, Joann A and Leonard F McCALLUM, 25 May 1947 Lowell, MA
SAKELLAR, Glenn T and Linda J RICHARDS, 27 Jun 1981 Amherst, NH
SAKELLAR, Jeffrey T and Charlene L LAROCQUE, 23 Nov 1974 Hudson, NH
SAKOVICH, Alice and Frank KUPCHUNAS, 20 Jun 1936 Nashua, NH
SALANITRO, Elena G and James R WOZNICA, 19 Jun 1983 Hudson, NH
SALESKY, James P and Joanne L BOUTILLIER, 06 Nov 1971 Hudson, NH
SALESKY, John D and Nancy E GROSS, 16 Feb 1978 Lincoln, NH
SALIAN, Sarkis and Louise R BYRNE, 25 Jun 1938 Hudson, NH
SALISBURY, Charles H & Earleen M HAWKINS, 16 Nov 1935 Brookline, NH
SALLINGER, Lawrence R & Louise E DESJARDINS, 15 Feb 1969 Nashua, NH
SALOIS, Roland L and Alice L BRUN, 04 May 1976 Nashua, NH
SALTZER, William C & Lorraine G LITTLEFIELD, 07 Nov 1976 Hudson, NH
SALVAIL, Clarence T and Emma I PIERCE, 02 Mar 1946 Hudson, NH
SALVATERRA, Eleanor and Ronald CROSS, 31 May 1947 Hudson, NH
SAMIA, Edward A and Louise C FERRIS, 27 Mar 1935 Hudson, NH
SAMPSON, Arthur P and Stella J INFERRERA, 17 Jul 1948 Hudson, NH
SAMPSON, Mary T and David F MIDDLETON, 30 Jul 1983 Hudson, NH
SAMUEL, George T and Linda A BELANGER, 29 Sep 1982 Nashua, NH
SANBORN, Austin Win and Roselle E MORRIS, 30 Nov 1935 Hudson, NH
SANBORN, Bell C and Orrin MESSER, 01 May 1879 Manchester, NH
 Alvin Sanborn & Annie E (Wilmot, NH)
 Frederick Messer(New London) & Martha
SANBORN, Bertha A and Edwin WENTWORTH, 20 Aug 1901 Hudson, NH
 Frederick Sanborn (Concord) & Jennie H Little (Haverhill, MA)
 Nathaniel Wentworth(Brighton, MA) & Martha E Greeley (Hudson, NH)
SANBORN, Frank E and Ester M MORRISON, 28 Jul 1877 Hudson, NH
 Sames Sanborn (Lowell, VT)
 Mark Morrison
SANBORN, James F and Harriet E HOWE, 28 Apr 1856
SANBORN, Mary M and Charles H FULLER, 09 Oct 1877 Hudson, NH
 James Sanborn
 Joseph Fuller(Hudson, NH) & Balinda Steele (Hudson, NH)
SANBORN, Michael E and Sherry L BOWDEN, 17 Sep 1983 Hudson, NH
SANBORN, Sandra R and Gerard R LACHANCE, 09 Sep 1978 Hudson, NH
SANBORN, Steven N and Barbara J TOWER, 30 May 1982 Hudson, NH
SANBORN, William S and Jennie B SHEPARD, 10 Oct 1931 Hudson, NH
SANDALL, Barbara T and Frederick HALE, 02 Dec 1978 Litchfield, NH
SANDALL, William E and Deborah A ROCHE, 30 Jun 1984 Hudson, NH
SANDERS, Abi A and Palmyra W WHITTEMORE, 08 Jan 1850

HUDSON, NH MARRIAGES

SANDERS, Abraham L and Emma BERNARD, 12 Apr 1896 Hudson, NH
   Thomas Sanders (Whitefield, VT) & Mary Connell
   Daria Bernard & Eliza Connell (Tyngsboro, MA)
SANDERS, Alice J and Joseph J WHITTAKER, 25 Nov 1896 Hudson, NH
   Thomas Sanders (Ireland) & Mary Connell (Ireland)
   John Whittaker(England) & Mary Morris (England)
SANDERS, Annie E and Edward A SPALDING, 27 Oct 1888
SANDERS, Annie E and Edward A SPAULDING, 27 Oct 1888 Hudson, NH
   Thomas Sanders (Ireland) & Mary Connell (Ireland)
   Leander R Spalding(Nashua, NH) & Abbie E Winn (Hudson, NH)
SANDERS, George O and Linda T THOMAS, 30 Nov 1882 Hudson, NH
   Abi Sanders (Hudson, NH) & Palmyra C Whittemore (Hudson, NH)
   Tyler Thomas(Dracut, MA) & Eliza A Sprake (Hudson, NH)
SANDERS, Gladys E and Frank W COLE, 08 Dec 1919 Nashua, NH
SANDERS, Marion H and John H PERKINS, 06 Jul 1911 Nashua, NH
   James A Sanders & Jennie Hosman
   Sumner N Perkins & Annie Hayden
SANDLER, Gertrude and Harry MISH, 20 Jul 1938 Nashua, NH
SANDLER, Sally E and Paul R MICHAUD, 31 Aug 1963 Hudson, NH
SANFORD, Susan J and Charles E CHAGNON, 31 Jul 1982 Nashua, NH
SANGER, Ruth I and William B QUEEN, 18 Jun 1938 Nashua, NH
SANSOM, Theo M and Henry A TRAHAN, 26 May 1945 Nashua, NH
SANTERRE, Paul R and Rita L GAUDETTE, 12 Sep 1942 Nashua, NH
SANTINELLI, Sandra A and Daniel P SOUCY, 14 Nov 1975 Milford, NH
SANTOS, Allan M and Diane G MESSIER, 06 Aug 1977 Hudson, NH
SARASIN, David A and Marcia E HUFF, 21 Jan 1967 Nashua, NH
SARGENT, C N and George P MOORE, 25 Aug 1916 Bellows Falls, VT
   Nathaniel Sargent (Potten, Que) & Ellen Potter (Johnson, VT)
   Fred Moore(Hollis, NH) & Anna Jackson (Ayer, MA)
SARGENT, Dana and Eliza HILLS, 31 Dec 1829
SARGENT, Elaine S and William H BARTER, 06 Oct 1972 Nashua, NH
SARGENT, Eunice K and Thomas MARSH, 02 Jul 1830
SARGENT, Frank N and Dora E HAZELTON, 10 Jul 1912 Londonderry, NH
   Nathiel Sargent & Ellen Potter
   William Hazelton & Bertha Hamblet
SARGENT, George G and Aravinta CLEMENT, 07 Mar 1858
SARGENT, Harley M and Hattie S SMITH, 25 Oct 1909 Nashua, NH
   Nathaniel Sargent & Ellen Potter
   Abel A Smith & Mary F Carter
SARGENT, Helen B and James F DONAHUE, 15 Jul 1934 Hudson, NH
SARGENT, Horace B and Marie L SHEFFIELD, 27 Mar 1915 Newton
   Horace M Sargent (Haverhill, MA) & Ida C Currier (Salem, NH)
   John Sheffield(England) & Francois Currier (England)
SARGENT, Jeffrey T and Marian E ZELONIS, 24 Apr 1976 Hudson, NH
SARGENT, Marion and Joseph H KIMBALL, 28 Sep 1908 Hudson, NH
   Charles H Sargent & Esther H Tenny
   Salon Kimball & Fannie Hoyt
SARGENT, Nellie and Henry McGANN, 16 Jun 1917 Hudson, NH
SARGENT, Virginia F & Kenneth L SHAW, 27 Feb 1938 Hillsborough, NH
SARGENT, William E and Cheryl A BEEDE, 20 May 1972 Hudson, NH
SARKISIAN, Megrdich and Florence DUCHARME, 27 Nov 1947 Nashua, NH
SARNIE, William J and Sarah B ZAPPALA, 24 Jul 1933 Nashua, NH
SARNO, Jack P and Rena P PAVLOSKY, 07 Nov 1980 Hudson, NH
SARNO, Mary A and Kevin J ALMEIDA, 12 Dec 1982 Hudson, NH
SARRIS, John R and Eve V EDELSTEIN, 27 Aug 1975 Dublin, NH
SARVER, David E and Carmen M VIENS, 11 Aug 1984 Hudson, NH
SAUCIER, Russell P and Debra Anne HOLDEN, 20 Nov 1982 Hudson, NH
SAULENAS, Alfonse and Viola Y PECKHAM, 04 Jun 1949 Hudson, NH
SAUNDER, May E and Henry A DAVIS, 16 Jan 1943 Nashua, NH
SAVAGE, Andrea L and Howard R DANIELS, 23 Mar 1946 Nashua, NH

HUDSON,NH MARRIAGES

SAVAGE, Edward T and Gloria M LEMAY, 20 Dec 1974 Hudson, NH
SAVAGE, Evelyn T and Bernard F DAUPHINEE, 18 May 1949 Hudson, NH
SAVAGE, Gregory T and Ellen Mary WARRINGTON, 21 Oct 1972 Nashua, NH
SAVAGE, Kevin Leon and Kellie Ann REGAN, 29 Jul 1978 Pelham, NH
SAVAGE, Larry T and Laurie L SWAIN, 12 Jul 1974 Derry, NH
SAVAGE, Linda I and Eugene M McARTHUR, 08 Aug 1964 Hudson, NH
SAVARD, Donald R and Jacqueline COTE, 02 Jul 1955 Hudson, NH
SAVARY, Emma F and Fred GILBERT, 05 Dec 1936 Hudson, NH
SAVERY, James W and Ann D MOON, 20 Nov 1976 Nashua, NH
SAVOY, Irene and Telepshore PELLETIER, 05 Apr 1926 Nashua, NH
SAVOY, Patricia M and Francis T DOVE, 01 Jul 1950 Hudson, NH
SAWICKI, William J Jr and Charlotte ROSS, 03 Jul 1959 Hudson, NH
SAWICKI, William J Jr and Marjorie E BROWN, 14 Feb 1976 Nashua, NH
SAWYER, Barbara D and Stanley R GILBERT, 26 Jun 1976 Hudson, NH
SAWYER, Beverly J and Vernon E FRANCIS, 11 Jul 1981 Hudson, NH
SAWYER, Sarah E and Hiram CROSS, 12 Dec 1847
SAYERS, Ann E and Ronald L BASTILLE, 23 Jun 1984 Hudson, NH
SAYTANDIES, James E & Jean Elizabeth KEARNS, 09 Sep 1978 Hollis,NH
SBAT, Sue and David C DION, 06 Jan 1976 Derry, NH
SCALERA, Constance and Edward F COX, 18 Oct 1948 Hudson, NH
SCALES, Marjorie T and Arthur DUFOUR, 29 Aug 1959 Hudson, NH
SCALES, Mary B and George H VOSE, 14 Nov 1861
SCAMPORINO, Raymond J and Lillian HERSHEY, 26 Dec 1942 Hudson, NH
SCANNELL, Irenie E and James W McCAFFREY, 20 Nov 1937 Hudson, NH
SCANTLEBURY, Georgia J and Henry B MORRIS, 23 Mar 1940 Hudson, NH
SCARDINA, Andrew F and Diane E TRAVERS, 30 Jan 1976 Hudson, NH
SCARKS, K Michael and Julianne CROCKETT, 01 Jun 1974 Hudson, NH
SCENNA, Leslie and Susan E KOPPENHOFER, 18 Dec 1980 Hudson, NH
SCHACHTER, Matthew W and Sarah A LEWIS, 02 Dec 1967 Concord, NH
SCHARCH, Cherie L and David A SPRAGUE, 14 Feb 1982 Nashua, NH
SCHARCH, Donald P and Lucille Y BOULEY, 22 Aug 1959 Hudson, NH
SCHARCH, Lucille Y and William R LACHANCE, 31 Jul 1971 Hudson, NH
SCHEER, Joan Ellen and Stephen J BONNETTE, 28 Aug 1976 Nashua, NH
SCHIAVI, Joseph C and Ethel P DEMARIA, 09 Oct 1955 Hudson, NH
SCHINDLER, Elizabeth and John P LAVOIE, 05 Jun 1982 Hudson, NH
SCHINDLER, Jane M and Edward R MacLENNAN, 23 Jan 1971 Hudson, NH
SCHINDLER, Walter R and Lillian E WINN, 27 Jun 1942 Hudson, NH
SCHIPPERS, Ann M and Ronald G PURINGTON, 31 May 1980 Hudson, NH
SCHLAGLE, Donald W and Brigitte M GRENIER, 02 Aug 1980 Hudson, NH
SCHLAGLE, Jean M and Bruce A BEEDE, 17 Jun 1978 Hudson, NH
SCHMIDT, Barry N and Jamie M KELLEHER, 30 Mar 1984 Nashua, NH
SCHMITT, Robert Jos Jr and Celeste M LABRIE, 11 Nov 1978 Nashua, NH
SCHNAIR, Richard A and Elizabeth THERIAULT, 02 Sep 1932 Nashua, NH
SCHOFIELD, Harvey E and Irene HUGHES, 23 Jul 1938 Hudson, NH
SCHOFIELD, Henry L and Pauline F HAZELDINE, 12 Nov 1949 Hudson, NH
SCHOFIELD, Mark A and Sally J BARBOUR, 30 Jun 1984 Nashua, NH
SCHOFIELD, Marlene M and Dennis W SURDAM, 14 Mar 1970 Nashua, NH
SCHOFIELD, Richard D and Diana L DEVENS, 08 Jun 1985 Temple, NH
SCHOMMER, Stephen C and Bonnie J STRONG, 23 Jun 1984 Nashua, NH
SCHOOLCRAFT, Mary H and Constant J JOYCE, 30 Aug 1947 Nashua, NH
SCHOR, Henry C and Ruby E SHAWVER, 09 Jan 1947 Hudson, NH
SCHREITERER, Robert R and Gloria R CAMPBELL, 06 Jun 1948 Nashua, NH
SCHULKIND, Andrew M and Flora A REED, 03 Dec 1977 Nashua, NH
SCHULZ, Juergen H and Pauline F SCHULZ, 03 Sep 1983 Nashua, NH
SCHULZ, Pauline F and Juergen H SCHULZ, 03 Sep 1983 Nashua, NH
SCHULZ, Ruth M and Brian S CARON, 04 Jul 1983 Nashua, NH
SCHUMAKER, Eugene J and Katherine GORDON, 25 Jun 1949 Hudson, NH
SCHUPE, William A and Carolyn McDONALD, 31 Oct 1947 Hudson, NH
SCHURMAN, Winford and Grace May WALKER, 18 Mar 1897 Hudson, NH
  Major Schurman & Mary Smith

HUDSON,NH MARRIAGES

James G Walker & Mary Pembleton
SCHUTTE, Gilbert J and Gladys H POOLER, 11 Dec 1948 Hudson, NH
SCHWARTZ, Robert S and Janine A H ANDRE, 06 Sep 1963 Hudson, NH
SCHWELM, Patricia E&Francis L III WURZBURG, 13 Feb 1971 Hudson, NH
SCIABA, Giovanni J and Mildred J GREEN, 10 Jul 1938 Hudson, NH
SCIACCA, William Al and Deborah M BUXTON, 29 Jun 1974 Hudson, NH
SCIRETTA, Daniel and Debbie M PARADIS, 19 Sep 1981 Hudson, NH
SCONTSAS, Peter G and Joan J LEMERISE, 21 Feb 1956 Hudson, NH
SCOTT, Anita L and Craig O DELONG, 06 Aug 1977 Hudson, NH
SCOTT, Charles F and Mildred M GILKES, 16 Dec 1935 Hudson, NH
SCOTT, Claudia J and Ronald G BLEAU, 01 May 1965 Hudson, NH
SCOTT, Daniel L and Lynn J KALIL, 28 Oct 1978 Hudson, NH
SCOTT, Daniel L and Laura J MORIN, 25 Dec 1982 Hudson, NH
SCOTT, Elaine M and David B CHRISTOPHER, 23 Sep 1967 Hudson, NH
SCOTT, Fred W and Florence MacDONALD, 26 Oct 1929 Nashua, NH
SCOTT, Michelle M and Steven W DUBE, 16 Oct 1982 Hudson, NH
SCOTT, Robin A and Gary J RODGERS, 14 Nov 1981 Hudson, NH
SCOTT, Susan L and Donald A LAVOIE, 17 Feb 1973 Hudson, NH
SCOTT, Woodrow F and Ida M LANDRY, 20 May 1943 Nashua, NH
SCRANTON, Harvey A Jr and Alice M DEAU, 24 Aug 1946 Hudson, NH
SCRIBNER, Janet E and William J EATON, 19 Mar 1971 Hudson, NH
SCRIVENER, Diane C and Daniel HODGE, 31 May 1975 Nashua, NH
SCURRAH, Muriel J and Joseph R MARTIN, 20 Nov 1965 Hudson, NH
SEACE, Howard W and Verna CUTLIFFE, 22 Dec 1946 Hudson, NH
SEACE, Meredith B and Dania L BERNARD, 10 Feb 1967 Hudson, NH
SEAGER, John P and Nancy E HUTTON, 01 Jul 1977 Hudson, NH
SEAMAN, Lisa and Thomas P FOLEY, 18 Feb 1980 Derry, NH
SEAMAN, Robin and William J FAULKNER, 30 Aug 1978 Gilmanton, NH
SEAMAN, Sandra A and James M BERTRAND, 05 Sep 1975 Hudson, NH
SEAMAN, William R and Joann GOVE, 24 Jun 1950 Milford, NH
SEAMANS, Charles H and Elaine B HARWOOD, 28 Oct 1937 Nashua, NH
SEARLES, Albert F and Martha M ROLF, 03 Feb 1879 Hudson, NH
  Jana Searles (Pelham, NH) & Mary M
  Nathan B Rolf(Maine) & Sarah (Rolf)
SEARLES, Cynthia A and David W WROCKLAGE, 21 Oct 1978 Nashua, NH
SEARLES, Elnathan and Betsey PERHAM, 15 Feb 1812
SEARLES, Elnathan and Mary FARWELL, 17 Mar 1814
SEARLES, Elnathan and Betsy PERKINS, 15 Feb 1812
SEARLES, Francis and Elizabeth LOVEJOY, 16 Apr 1864
SEARLES, Gilbert F and Cora L ROWELL, 26 Oct 1911 Nashua, NH
  Albert F Searles & Sarah T Fletcher
  Eugene Rowell & Mary Wilson
SEARLES, Kenneth R and Margaret SPECK, 30 Jun 1956 Milford, NH
SEARLES, Lydia and Asa BUTTERICK, 15 Mar 1810
SEARLES, Lydia and Asa BUTTRICK, 15 Mar 1810
SEARLES, Robert P and Amy E CLEVELAND, 14 Jan 1967 Pelham, NH
SEARS, Alonzo A and Josephine V MOREY, 08 Sep 1923 Nashua, NH
SEARS, Edward L and Thelma M RIESSLE, 02 Feb 1938 Nashua, NH
SEAVER, Margaret E and Oswald D BOILARD, 20 Aug 1955 Keene, NH
SEAVEY, Hannah S and Frank E SMART, 20 Oct 1863
SEAVEY, Ida E and George T GOWING, 01 Jan 1884 Pelham, NH
  Augustus Seavey (Pelham, NH) & Louisa A Swan (N Andover, MA)
  Thomas Gowing(Wilmington, MA) & Harriet Greeley (Pelham, NH)
SEAVEY, James and Elizabeth DAVIS, 03 Jun 1784
SEAVEY, Nathaniel and Mary BURNS, 27 Sep 1781
SEAVEY, Sophronia and Andrew A CAMPBELL, 05 Nov 1859
SEAVY, Hannah P and Frank E SMART, 20 Oct 1863
SEBEK, Keith E and Janice A RIVARD, 06 Jun 1981 Merrimack, NH
SEBOR, Cindy S and Jeffrey A HOYT, 18 Aug 1984 Hudson, NH
SECOR, Francis P and Celeste S LAVALLEE, 15 Feb 1942 Hudson, NH

HUDSON, NH MARRIAGES

SEDLEWICZ, Peter A & Judith C ARCHAMBAULT, 02 Sep 1966 Manchester, NH
SEGG, Robert L and Marita M GRANT, 04 Apr 1942 Hudson, NH
SEGGELIN, Lawrence H and Virginia M BABIN, 01 Jun 1934 Nashua, NH
SEGUIN, Marie A and David R BERRY, 01 Jun 1974 Hudson, NH
SEKELLA, Matthew E and Maxine K HOYME, 21 Aug 1980 Nashua, NH
SELFRIDGE, Richard J and Susan M LINCOLN, 23 Mar 1985 Hudson, NH
SELLERS, Doris W and Wilbur L GOUR, 12 Oct 1950 Hudson, NH
SELVIS, Donald R and Patricia L CALLAHAN, 18 Oct 1952 Nashua, NH
SEMONIAN, Ogapan and Barbel KOCHAKIAN, 08 Sep 1906 Boston, MA
   Simon Semonian & H Duredepain
   C Kochakian & V Wolfician
SEMPLE, Alan R III and Suzanne M CRETE, 01 Oct 1980 Hudson, NH
SENECHAL, Gertrude G and Zenon J ST LAURENT, 20 Feb 1954 Nashua, NH
SENNEVILLE, Henri R and Lillian S FORRENCE, 23 Nov 1957 Hudson, NH
SENNEVILLE, Henri R & Lillian S SENNEVILLE, 25 Nov 1966 Hudson, NH
SENNEVILLE, Lillian S & Henri R SENNEVILLE, 25 Nov 1966 Hudson, NH
SENNEVILLE, Pamela A and Charles P HAIGLER, 14 Apr 1978 Hudson, NH
SENNEVILLE, Shirley A and Robert A CHENEY, 29 May 1982 Hudson, NH
SENTER, Eliphalet and E F RICHARDSON, 23 May 1890
SENTER, Eliphelet and E F RICHARDSON, 25 May 1890 Tyngsboro, MA
   Oliver Senter (Lyndeboro, NH) & Betsey Mayberry (Lyndeboro, NH)
   J F Richardson(Vermont) & Mary Berry (Vermont)
SENTER, Eunice R and Joseph P TASKER, May 1855
SENTER, Frances H and William R JONES, 02 May 1855
SENTER, Francis and Elizabeth LOVEJOY, 16 Apr 1864
SENTER, Gans and Sarah A SPALDING, 30 Jan 1844
SENTER, Georgiana and William R JONES, 09 Apr 1874 Hudson, NH
SENTER, Lucy and Alfred GREELEY, 29 Mar 1842
SENTER, Martha R and Henry G GOSS, 26 Mar 1826
SENTER, Mary A and William HARDY, 19 May 1846
SENTER, Richard and Catherine SMITH, 08 Jun 1815
SENTER, Salome V and Charles C GRANT, 19 Jan 1843
SENTER, Susannah and James EAYRES, 25 Jan 1798
SENTER, Thomas and Roxanna CUTLER, 15 Jul 1851
SERINO, Jean S and Peter N TAYLOR, 22 Oct 1983 Nashua, NH
SERVANT, Norman J and Jeanne I DOUCET, 18 Oct 1958 Hudson, NH
SERVANT, Norman J and Ruth L FORRENCE, 15 Nov 1974 Nashua, NH
SESTA, Jeaneen M & Frederick COOLBROTH, 01 Dec 1979 Manchester, NH
SETTLE, John E and Karen L HEALEY, 03 Jul 1976 Nashua, NH
SETTLE, Mary L and Halton B III WOODS, 30 Nov 1968 Nashua, NH
SEUBERT, Raymond R and Peggy J RIGG, 29 Nov 1975 Litchfield, NH
SEVERANCE, Brenda D and James F SMITH, 16 Aug 1969 Hudson, NH
SEVERANCE, Cheryl L and Ernest G Jr STONE, 13 Nov 1971 Hudson, NH
SEVERANCE, Gerogiana and George C FARLEY, 29 Dec 1879 Hudson, NH
   Hezekiah Severance & Sarah J
   James Farley(Hollis, NH) & Lucinda Cadwell (Hollis, NH)
SEVERSON, Norman and Thelma WINSLOW, 05 May 1942 Hudson, NH
SEVIGNY, Arthur L and Dora R SHORT, 18 Aug 1979 Hudson, NH
SEVIGNY, James H and Gwendolyn PUSTOLA, 12 Aug 1973 Londonderry, NH
SEVIGNY, James R and Mary Lou HOLM, 04 Aug 1972 Windham, NH
SEVIGNY, Paul A and Anne Marie LANE, 09 Aug 1980 Hudson, NH
SEYER, Elizabeth and Joseph T MacDONALD, 04 May 1974 Nashua, NH
SEYMOUR, Randy R and Marguerite GINGRAS, 12 May 1984 Manchester, NH
SEYMOUR, Sue Ann and Donald E TROMBLEY, 01 May 1981 Hudson, NH
SHADLE, Robert W and Anne M BEAULIEU, 29 Nov 1982 Hudson, NH
SHAFER, Jonathan E and Deborah HOYT, 24 Oct 1981 Nashua, NH
SHAFNER, Ernest L and Bell J THOMPSON, 15 Jul 1884 Hudson, NH
   Benjamin W Shafner (Granville, N S) & Mary E Hewitt (St John, NB)
   John M Thompson(Kingston, MA) & Elizabeth O Marsh (Hudson, NH)
SHAFNER, G H and Eric N BOLAND, 24 Jun 1916 Hudson, NH

HUDSON,NH MARRIAGES

Ernest Shafner (Nova Scotia) & Belle J Thompson (Hudson, NH)
Elisha S Boland(Canada) & Esther Nichols (Newburyport, MA)
SHALLOW, Robert H and Cheryl A FLOYD, 18 May 1973 Nashua, NH
SHANAHAN, Michael D and Nancy L CHRISICOS, 24 Jul 1981 Nashua, NH
SHANNON, Ada J and Joseph A SHANNON, 31 Dec 1948 Hudson, NH
SHANNON, Joseph A and Ada J SHANNON, 31 Dec 1948 Hudson, NH
SHAPIRO, Alfred E and Diane C FORD, 15 Sep 1979 Hudson, NH
SHAPIRO, Janice M and Richard B WILSON, 18 Mar 1972 Hudson, NH
SHAPIRO, Pauline R and Fred W MILLER, 01 Oct 1978 Nashua, NH
SHAPIRO, Robert K and Patricia A WOLLEN, 20 Apr 1968 Nashua, NH
SHAPLEY, William H and Sarah J HILLS, 27 Sep 1852
SHARP, Margaret and Theophilas BODAMAS, 16 Jan 1866
SHARP, Randall W and Diana M STEINMETZ, 05 May 1978 Hudson, NH
SHARP, Robert R and Rose M CHABOT, 27 Oct 1937 Hudson, NH
SHARP, Terrance R and Katherine BURNEY, 19 Aug 1982 Nashua, NH
SHARPE, Graydon L and Agnes M RYAN, 09 May 1981 Hudson, NH
SHARPE, Margaret J and Theophalin ADAMS, 16 Jan 1866
SHATNEY, Bertha J and Irvin A SMITH, 19 Apr 1915 Manchester, NH
   Joseph J Shatney (Vermont) & Alice Grey (Glover, VT)
   Andrew J Smith(Hudson, NH) & Irene Hunting (Hudson, NH)
SHATTUCK, Flora E and Isaac C HUDSON, 27 Dec 1879 Hudson, NH
   Alfred Shattuck (Mont Vernon, NH) & Rosa Holden
   Silas P Hudson & Eliza A Lemery
SHATTUCK, Frank B and Abbie F BREED, 24 Nov 1880 Hudson, NH
SHAUGHNESSY, James F III&Margaret A GUYETTE, 29 Mar 1969 Nashua, NH
SHAUGHNESSY, Margaret A and Ronald L ROY, 26 Nov 1971 Hudson, NH
SHAUGHNESSY, Richard and Barbara L DOWD, 26 Jan 1976 Hudson, NH
SHAW, E Gladys and Charles E RUSSELL NH, 15 Oct 1907 Hudson, NH
   John T Shaw & Mary A Nason
   Joseph E Russell & Lottie Hopkins
SHAW, George C and Grace MARTIN, 08 Sep 1908 Hudson, NH
   Frank C Shaw & Mabel L Tyler
   Ezra A Martin & Maggie J Clyde
SHAW, Harold V and Myrtie A MORRIS, 12 Aug 1909 Hudson, NH
   James Shaw & Ernestine Tasker
   William Morris & Annie Burt
SHAW, Herbert W and Virginia W LANGFORD, 04 Jul 1981 Hudson, NH
SHAW, James H and Ellen E CUMMINGS, 02 May 1865
SHAW, Kenneth L & Virginia F SARGENT, 27 Feb 1938 Hillsborough, NH
SHAW, Marjorie Gertru and Anders S NIORTH, 02 May 1938 Nashua, NH
SHAW, Sandra D and Ernest E LECLERC, 08 Jan 1966 Nashua, NH
SHAWCROSS, Glennon E and Catherine ROBINSON, 06 Sep 1947 Hudson, NH
SHAWVER, Ruby E and Henry C SCHOR, 09 Jan 1947 Hudson, NH
SHEA, Daniel R and Susan J HILTON, 05 Aug 1977 Hudson, NH
SHEA, Joseph G Jr and Martha MAJOR, 23 Aug 1969 Nashua, NH
SHEA, Rose T and Roy J CARVILLE, 01 Dec 1970 Nashua, NH
SHEAN, Robert W and Claire A MONTMINY, 27 Mar 1976 Hudson, NH
SHECTE, Fanny and Lucius T BAKER, 28 Nov 1861
SHEDD, Samuel L and Malvina MUNROE, 03 May 1863
SHEEHAN, Margaret A and Allen W WELLS, 14 Jul 1936 Manchester, NH
SHEFFIELD, Marie L and Horace B SARGENT, 27 Mar 1915 Newton
   John Sheffield (England) & Francois Currier (England)
   Horace M Sargent(Haverhill, MA) & Ida C Currier (Salem, NH)
SHEFFIELD, Wilbur L and Bertille L SILVA, 21 Feb 1942 Nashua, NH
SHEFFIELD, William J and Marcia E HUFF, 26 Aug 1972 Nashua, NH
SHEIL, Martin C and Carol A BRIAND, 17 Jun 1978 Hudson, NH
SHELDON, Anna M and Charles A DANIELS, 15 Sep 1897 Hudson, NH
   David P Sheldon & Mary A Knight
   John Daniels & Sarah Harris
SHEPARD, Donald C and Sandra A CABRAL, 03 Oct 1982 Nashua, NH

HUDSON, NH MARRIAGES

SHEPARD, Foster F and Ruth G HAMBLETT, 17 Mar 1940 Hudson, NH
SHEPARD, Jennie B and William S SANBORN, 10 Oct 1931 Hudson, NH
SHEPARD, Lauretta A and John E CARROLL, 14 Sep 1936 Nashua, NH
SHEPARD, Lettie V and Eugene W LESLIE, 14 Sep 1905 Hudson, NH
  Charles A Shepard & Addie C Doyle
  Charles C Leslie & Eliza B Leslie
SHEPARD, Robert M and Linda E BERNARD, 15 Aug 1981 Nashua, NH
SHEPHARD, Richard and Hannah S RIPLEY, 25 Aug 1868
SHEPHERD, Arthur H and Beatrice N FULLER, 10 Sep 1934 Hudson, NH
SHEPHERD, Arthur H Jr and Reta M GARSIDE, 29 Jul 1960 Nashua, NH
SHEPHERD, Basil W and Ethel G MERILL, 05 Dec 1917 Barrington
SHEPHERD, Edward C and Dorothy H MAXFIELD, 02 May 1969 Hudson, NH
SHEPHERD, Esther and Gerald HOUSTON, 27 Oct 1926 Hudson, NH
SHEPHERD, Ethel M and Arthur B BORNEMAN, 03 Apr 1929 Nashua, NH
SHEPHERD, H A and Mary E PERKINS, 07 Oct 1916 Nashua, NH
  Herbert F Shepherd(Saltriser, MI)& Delia M Lynch(Dublin, Ireland)
  Sumner Perkins(Albany, NY) & Annie Hayden (Douglastown, N B)
SHEPHERD, Henry L and Nellie E MORRILL, 05 Feb 1941 Nashua, NH
SHEPHERD, Herbert N&Katherine FAIRBANKS, 15 Jul 1961 Manchester, NH
SHEPHERD, LuAnn N and Stephen P JOBIN, 12 Jul 1980 Nashua, NH
SHEPHERD, Marion A and John R BOULEY, 10 Sep 1957 Hudson, NH
SHEPHERD, Miriam A and Stanley E TROMBLY, 01 Jul 1946 Nashua, NH
SHEPHERD, Robert W and Winifred D WARDWELL, 02 May 1964 Hudson, NH
SHEPHERD, Ronald E and Cheryl M KELLEY, 15 Apr 1977 Hudson, NH
SHERBURN, Mary E & Herbert S PERKINS, 21 Feb 1920 New Bedford, MA
SHERMAK, Hedrick P and Alva F MEDEIROS, 22 Feb 1948 Hudson, NH
SHERMAN, Daniel and Almira M MARTIN, 25 May 1880 Hudson, NH
  Telphnah Sherman (Pomfort, CT) & Betsey Allton (Tompson, CT)
  Daniel Eageton(Munson, MA) & Mindwell Fane (Brookfield, MA)
SHERMAN, Florina S and Stephen L GAGNON, 07 Aug 1954 Hudson, NH
SHERMAN, Julia A and Orlando G Jr HILLS, 15 Oct 1945 Hudson, NH
SHERMAN, Stephen S and Harriet A WOODBURY, 05 Feb 1864
SHERRITT, Aline C and David B SMITH, 26 May 1974 Hudson, NH
SHEVENELL, Matthew D & Robin W GILBERT, 08 Jun 1985 Hampton Fls, NH
SHIEBLER, Edward D and Diana E BARDSLEY, 10 Sep 1955 Nashua, NH
SHIEBLER, Judith E and Lloyd D BAUCHMAN, 05 May 1979 Hudson, NH
SHIEBLER, Russell E & Cheryl L CHRISTIANSEN, 20 Feb 1982 Hudson, NH
SHIEBLER, Susan E and Peter A OHLIN, 14 Apr 1979 Hudson, NH
SHINKWIN, John H and Mary P GARRITY, 07 Aug 1948 Hudson, NH
SHINN, Arline M and Harrison E SMITH, 20 Jun 1968 Hudson, NH
SHINN, Susan E and Peter N SMITH, 22 Aug 1971 Merrimack, NH
SHINN, William D III and Arline M MASON, 06 Nov 1954 Hudson, NH
SHIPLEY, Brian W and Rita M A CASPARRO, 09 Jul 1977 Rindge, NH
SHOKAL, Phyllis and Peter J DALEY, 11 May 1946 Nashua, NH
SHOLENBERGER, Herbert and Adele HAYWARD, 06 Jul 1974 Manchester, NH
SHOLKOFF, Edmund A and Nancy L BELANGER, 18 Sep 1983 Hudson, NH
SHORT, Dora R and Arthur L SEVIGNY, 18 Aug 1979 Hudson, NH
SHORT, Thomas D and Margaret McGAFFIHAN, 07 Mar 1937 Hudson, NH
SHULTZ, Glenn D and Lisa M BURTON, 14 Apr 1985 Hudson, NH
SHUMAN, Anella and Lloyd E CROCKETT, 15 May 1945 Hudson, NH
SHUMAN, Gail M and Don WHITNEY, 03 Mar 1984 Nashua, NH
SHUMSKY, Kim E and Paul P LAROSE, 19 Apr 1975 Hudson, NH
SHUMSKY, Michael and Mary Ellen BOURASSA, 22 Aug 1981 Brookline, NH
SHUMSKY, Sigismond and Dorothy L ROBINSON, 26 Jan 1942 Hudson, NH
SHUNAMAN, Mildred and Levi J CHALIFOUX, 23 Jan 1939 Hudson, NH
SHUNAMAN, Stephen L and Harriet A WOODBURY, 25 Feb 1864
SHURTLEFF, Mary E and Charles A RIZZO, 01 Jun 1946 Hudson, NH
SHUTZER, Ethel D and David I KENNEDY, 15 Jun 1931 Nashua, NH
SIANO, Ralph A and Angeline DANDA, 06 Sep 1936 Hudson, NH
SIAS, Etta L and Charles F STEELE, 01 Sep 1880 Boston, MA

HUDSON, NH MARRIAGES

Chauncey Sias & Huldah
Frederick Steele(Hudson, NH) & Caroline E Follett
SICILIANO, Michael P and Sara J CLARENBACH, 05 Jul 1963 Hudson, NH
SIDILEAU, Joyce M & Kourosh Karimi TEHRANI, 02 Sep 1978 Nashua, NH
SIEG, Christopher and Janet E GRAF, 02 Oct 1983 Manchester, NH
SIENKIEWICZ, Joseph S and Deborah A ALLEN, 20 Nov 1970 Nashua, NH
SIGILLO, Fortunato and Ethel E STEVENS, 22 Aug 1951 Hudson, NH
SILES, Pamela S and Joseph F SPADARO, 04 Dec 1982 Hudson, NH
SILK, Elaine A and Richard J LAFORD, 19 Sep 1981 Nashua, NH
SILLANPAA, Lucille A and Romeo A MARQUIS, 15 Aug 1947 Nashua, NH
SILVA, Bertille L and Wilbur L SHEFFIELD, 21 Feb 1942 Nashua, NH
SILVA, Donald M and Rachel A NORMAN, 20 Apr 1985 Hudson, NH
SILVA, Dorothy A and William C Jr McFADDEN, 10 Aug 1963 Hudson, NH
SILVA, Eleanor M and Joseph A Jr CORMIER, 29 Dec 1984 Nashua, NH
SILVA, Frank A and Victoria E LAVALLEY, 18 Mar 1977 Hudson, NH
SILVA, John F and Lorraine M ARRUDA, 08 Jan 1949 Hudson, NH
SILVA, Steven and Wendy J GIAMMARCO, 13 Aug 1975 Hudson, NH
SILVER, Edgar L and Eva HALL, 1875
George W Silver
SILVER, Edmond J Jr and Diane C SLADE, 12 Jul 1980 Hollis, NH
SILVER, George W and Hannah Jan WEBSTER, 1853
SILVER, George W and Ella F BLODGETT, 19 May 1877 Hudson, NH
Daniel Silver (Hudson, NH)
Warren Blodgett & Balinda Barrett (Hudson, NH)
SILVER, Mildred C and Henry C WADLEIGH, 23 Jul 1926 Hudson, NH
SILVERIA, Denise L and Joseph W CANTIN, 23 Nov 1973 Hudson, NH
SILVERIA, Lisa M & Robert E Jr FORTIER, 18 May 1985 Manchester, NH
SILVERMAN, Beatrice L and Stanley S PAUL, 10 May 1947 Hudson, NH
SILVERSTEIN, Anna and Joseph D ARBETTER, 28 Sep 1927 Nashua, NH
SIMARANO, Elaine M and David J AMBROSE, 18 Jan 1969 Hudson, NH
SIMARD, Anita C and Leo E SOUCY, 27 Apr 1968 Nashua, NH
SIMARD, Cecilia and Gerard T PLOURDE, 21 Nov 1941 Nashua, NH
SIMARD, Donald N and Cecile Y BASTILLE, 18 Jun 1955 Nashua, NH
SIMARD, Eugene E and Patricia F MORSE, 25 Sep 1965 Nashua, NH
SIMARD, Gaston R and Patricia A POIRIER, 11 Apr 1959 Hudson, NH
SIMARD, Irene C and George H BERARD, 05 Aug 1950 Nashua, NH
SIMARD, Kim L and Richard S KUCIJ, 12 May 1978 Hudson, NH
SIMARD, Laurette T and Roland H THIBEAULT, 07 Feb 1953 Hudson, NH
SIMARD, Leslie A and Joseph D McDONALD, 06 Apr 1974 Hudson, NH
SIMARD, Pauline L and Edwin C BEDARD, 04 Nov 1961 Hudson, NH
SIMARD, Pauline L and Andre J DANEAULT, 16 Nov 1963 Manchester, NH
SIMARD, Robin and David T GUTOWSKI, 20 Oct 1978 Hudson, NH
SIMARD, Ronald G and Elaine J DIONNE, 21 Mar 1964 Nashua, NH
SIMARD, Ronald G and Micheline GOBEIL, 27 Feb 1970 Nashua, NH
SIMARD, Ronald G and Theresa J BERTHIAUME, 25 Jul 1975 Hudson, NH
SIMARD, Theresa M and Raymond A DESJARDINS, 01 Oct 1949 Nashua, NH
SIMMONS, Harold L and Frances C DOBSON, 30 Nov 1933 Nashua, NH
SIMMONS, Richard M and Denise D BELMORE, 24 Nov 1984 Hudson, NH
SIMO, John and Glenda E PRATT, 11 Jun 1960 Milford, NH
SIMONDS, Alice F and Austin D CORLISS, 21 Mar 1888 Hudson, NH
Amos F Churchill (Solon, ME) & Eleanor Chase (Solon, ME)
James Corliss(Hudson, NH) & Sarah Hamlett (Hudson, NH)
SIMONDS, Alice M and Richard R REILLY, 04 Sep 1982 Hudson, NH
SIMONDS, Frederick and Abby H POOR, 20 Jan 1867
SIMONDS, Frederick and Abbie H POOR, 20 Jan 1867
SIMONDS, Jean C and Robert E SUDSBURY, 28 Oct 1961 Nashua, NH
SIMONDS, Lee Guy and Doris Laighton CRENNER, 24 Jun 1920 Hudson, NH
SIMONEAU, Gerard A and Gertrude A MITCHESS, 29 Jan 1949 Nashua, NH
SIMONEAU, Roger R and Janie P BETTY, 30 Aug 1969 Hudson, NH
SIMONEAU, Ronald N and Sandra A ROCKWELL, 16 Nov 1981 Hudson, NH

HUDSON, NH MARRIAGES

SIMPSON, Albert H and Amanda CARTER, 25 Aug 1975 Hudson, NH
SIMPSON, Betty I and Clarence Jr GIESEKE, 03 Feb 1945 Nashua, NH
SIMPSON, Brenda B and Paul G BREEN, 17 Jun 1961 Nashua, NH
SIMPSON, Edward and Cora B SMITH, 27 May 1939 Hudson, NH
SIMPSON, Ella S and Albert Oli TITCOMB, 05 Jun 1866
SIMPSON, Ethelwyn M and Anatole J MICHAUD, 21 Jul 1953 Hudson, NH
SIMPSON, Hattie and Amos M YOUNG, 26 Jul 1866
SIMPSON, Herbert B and Florence H GRIFFIN, 03 Aug 1973 Nashua, NH
SIMPSON, Leona K and James J LOUGHLIN, 30 Sep 1946 Hudson, NH
SIMPSON, Victoria and Sherwood L FOSTER, 28 Aug 1920 Nashua, NH
SINCLAIR, John and Norma M DEROCHE, 16 Apr 1949 Hudson, NH
SINCLAIR, Sarah and Alonzo JOHNSON, 1850
SING, Margaret A and Philip A SMITH, 17 Jun 1972 Meredith, NH
SINGLETARY, Gloria S and Amos N BAHAM, 03 Jan 1956 Hudson, NH
SINVENIE, Anna and Treffie CHOQUETTE, 21 Feb 1921 Nashua, NH
SIPOLA, Arthur E and Esther P ALBERTA, 15 Jun 1946 Hudson, NH
SIROIS, Andrew D and Nancy C DUFFY, 11 May 1985 Hudson, NH
SIROIS, Dorothy R and James W McLAREN, 19 May 1961 Nashua, NH
SIROIS, Jane D and David J MEADOWS, 08 Feb 1975 Hudson, NH
SIROIS, Linda M and Gary J DOUVILLE, 08 Nov 1969 Hudson, NH
SIROIS, Richard J and Nancy L CARON, 09 Nov 1979 Nashua, NH
SIROIS, Richard J and Elaine Helen EATON, 08 Jul 1978 Nashua, NH
SIROIS, Roger S and Catherine INGRAM, 09 Oct 1971 Nashua, NH
SIRVYDAS, Donna M and Mark W ALLEN, 31 Mar 1984 Nashua, NH
SKALECKI, Catherine and Joseph F Jr WALL, 11 Sep 1948 Hudson, NH
SKAPINSKY, Mary E and Robert W GOULD, 14 Jan 1977 Hudson, NH
SKEAHAN, William J and Georgianna ANASTAS, 04 Oct 1952 Hudson, NH
SKEFFINGTON, Peter J and JoAnn DESILVIO, 08 Nov 1975 Nashua, NH
SKINNER, Friend L and Pauline C HOGAN, 22 Jul 1950 Hudson, NH
SKLINTAS, Anthony J and Bertha AKSTIN, 01 Dec 1945 Nashua, NH
SKONBERG, Theodore A and Ruth E STADIG, 14 Sep 1946 Hudson, NH
SKOVIRA, Anthony H and Pamela J MacKAY, 13 Jun 1964 Nashua, NH
SLACK, Gertrude I and Kenneth L PIERCE, 18 Dec 1971 Enfield, NH
SLADE, Danny K and Diane C WOLCZOK, 26 Sep 1969 Nashua, NH
SLADE, Diane C and Edmond J Jr SILVER, 12 Jul 1980 Hollis, NH
SLAIBY, Linda J and Stephen B HARDIMAN, 27 Nov 1982 Hudson, NH
SLAIBY, William L and Jacalyn A CHOINIERE, 31 Oct 1981 Hudson, NH
SLATE, Betty J and Richard A THERRIEN, 08 Jan 1974 Nashua, NH
SLATE, Charles H and Lizzie F B FORD, 23 Aug 1882 Hudson, NH
  Lyman J Slate (Mass.) & Abby B (Candia)
  Timothy S Ford(Hudson, NH) & Sarah G Fuller (Hudson, NH)
SLATTERY, Gloria M and Claude W BUSHEY, 22 Jan 1950 Hudson, NH
SLATUNAS, Frances and Edmund WOLODZKO, 31 Dec 1949 Nashua, NH
SLATUNAS, William J Jr and Suzanne N VADNEY, 29 Jul 1972 Hudson, NH
SLATUNAS, William J Jr and Margery A KAEFER, 04 Aug 1980 Nashua, NH
SLAVIN, Frances M and Sidney F BAKER, 18 Jun 1928 Dunstable, MA
SLINEY, Bernard L and Frances M DAILY, 08 Nov 1969 Nashua, NH
SLOWIK, Elizabeth and Warren F SMITH, 09 Sep 1967 Nashua, NH
SMALL, Barbara L and Leighton D FOX, 11 Jul 1963 Hudson, NH
SMALL, Brian R and Sharron A SOKOLOWSKI, 17 Sep 1982 Hudson, NH
SMALL, Florence H and Albert E SMITH, 27 Jun 1916 Nashua, NH
  William Small (Stackpole, ME) & Kate Clifford (Searsport, ME)
  Marcell Smith(Charlestown, MA) & Mary E Eaton (Lawrence, MA)
SMALL, Francis E and Patricia C VIGNOLA, 17 Jan 1959 Nashua, NH
SMALL, Francis E Jr and Valerie CRANSTON, 09 May 1981 Nashua, NH
SMALL, Harrison E and Helen A ANDREWS, 16 Oct 1917 Hudson, NH
SMALL, Holly A and Dennis R BOULEY, 13 Sep 1975 Hudson, NH
SMALL, Holly Ann and John F MOTZKO, 15 Sep 1984 Londonderry, NH
SMALL, Margaret K and John E DOHERTY, 26 Apr 1947 Hollis, NH
SMALL, Richard D and Evelynne C STEVENS, 07 Aug 1937 Hudson, NH

HUDSON, NH MARRIAGES

SMALL, Richard M and Christine ERB, 15 Jun 1973 Nashua, NH
SMALLEY, Phillip E Jr and Dorothy A BAILEY, 01 Jun 1985 Nashua, NH
SMART, Frank E and Hannah S SEAVEY, 20 Oct 1863
SMART, Frank E and Hannah P SEAVY, 20 Oct 1863
SMART, Jeffrey A and Michelle M HODGKINS, 09 Jun 1979 Hudson, NH
SMART, Ricky James and Susan Joan BLANCHARD, 15 Jul 1978 Hudson, NH
SMART, Sandra M and Ronald R FOURNIER, 04 Apr 1980 Hudson, NH
SMEAD, Doris E and Arne J LINDAHL, 15 Aug 1937 Hudson, NH
SMILIKIS, Michael J and JoAnn M FAUCHER, 28 Apr 1972 Hudson, NH
SMILIKIS, Peter J and Susan E LISTER, 08 Oct 1960 Concord, NH
SMILIKIS, William J & Frances A O'LOUGHLIN, 21 May 1966 Nashua, NH
SMILLIE, Edward J Jr & Margaret M SULLIVAN, 24 Aug 1946 Nashua, NH
SMITH, Abigail B and John MARLIN, 14 Sep 1826
SMITH, Albert E and Florence H SMALL, 27 Jun 1916 Nashua, NH
   Marcell Smith (Charlestown, MA) & Mary E Eaton (Lawrence, MA)
   William Small(Stackpole, ME) & Kate Clifford (Searsport, ME)
SMITH, Albert E and Virginia P MOORE, 12 Oct 1940 Nashua, NH
SMITH, Alfred A and Catherine REDHEAD, 10 Oct 1964 Lowell, MA
SMITH, Almira and Rufus D ANDREWS, 13 Nov 1853
SMITH, Andrew J and Irene HUNTING, 27 May 1857
SMITH, Annie I and Irving J FOX, 16 Nov 1898 Manchester, NH
   Andrew J Smith & Abby A Davis
   Calvin C Fox & Emme N French
SMITH, Annie M and John H GRANT, 01 Aug 1880 Londonderry, NH
   Norris Smith (Hudson, NH) & Francis M Greeley (Hudson, NH)
   Lynzey W Grant(Berwick, ME) & Martha G Farnham (Rumford, ME)
SMITH, Arthur W and May I SNOW, 16 Sep 1909 Hudson, NH
   Isaac N Smith & Roxanna Butler
   Royal A Snow & Adela E Walker
SMITH, Barbara A and William S CUNNINGHAM, 29 Jul 1961 Hudson, NH
SMITH, Belinda and Henry BUTLER, 24 Apr 1856
SMITH, Bertha M and Walter D EASTON, 01 Aug 1900 Lyme, CT
   Wm H Smith & Eliza M Tuck
   Alfred Eaton & Harriet T Smith
SMITH, Betsey and John MELVIN, 20 Apr 1797
SMITH, Betsy and Abijah ATWOOD, 30 Dec 1819
SMITH, Betty and John MELVIN, 20 Apr 1797
SMITH, Brenda C and Donald A SMITH-WEISS, 02 Aug 1975 Hudson, NH
SMITH, Byron B and Maude LOUPRETTE, 15 Nov 1935 Hudson, NH
SMITH, Carol A and Dana P HOWLAND, 18 Apr 1970 Hudson, NH
SMITH, Catherine and Richard SENTER, 08 Jun 1815
SMITH, Charles and Sarah J GOODWIN, 11 Mar 1869 Hudson, NH
SMITH, Charles A and Juliette S LAVOIE, 28 Apr 1973 Nashua, NH
SMITH, Charles B and Marion DUBOIS, 29 Jul 1927 Nashua, NH
SMITH, Charles D III and Dolores M MARTIN, 27 May 1972 Nashua, NH
SMITH, Clarrisa and Lucius F ROBINSON, 08 May 1862
SMITH, Claudia E and Salvatore MANOLI, 03 Jul 1980 Hudson, NH
SMITH, Clayton A and Joanne CLOUTIER, 12 Jun 1965 Keene, NH
SMITH, Clayton E and Victoria LADNER, 31 Aug 1941 Hudson, NH
SMITH, Cora B and Edward SIMPSON, 27 May 1939 Hudson, NH
SMITH, Curtis R and Deborah A FRENCH, 23 Oct 1971 Nashua, NH
SMITH, Dana and Susan CALDWELL, 12 Oct 1829
SMITH, Dana H and Cynthia H MARQUIS, 07 Sep 1974 Hudson, NH
SMITH, David B and Aline C SHERRITT, 26 May 1974 Hudson, NH
SMITH, David Mich and Catherine PICARD, 19 Aug 1978 Nashua, NH
SMITH, David O and Mary H GREELEY, 30 Aug 1855
SMITH, David P and Hannah SMITH, 27 Sep 1856
SMITH, Deering G and Mary S HAMBLETT, 02 Jul 1921 Nashua, NH
SMITH, Donald A and Kathy A LANGLOIS, 21 May 1982 Windham, NH
SMITH, Donald E Jr and Donna D DUBE, 09 Sep 1984 Nashua, NH

HUDSON,NH MARRIAGES

SMITH, Donna B and Norman T COTE, 12 May 1962 Nashua, NH
SMITH, Doris M and Frederick WIGANDT, 24 Jul 1948 Hudson, NH
SMITH, Doris W and Edmund H WILLIAMS, 27 Oct 1934 Hudson, NH
SMITH, Dorothy E and John H HOLTON, 17 Sep 1938 Londonderry, NH
SMITH, Dorothy T and Donald G BARTON, 06 Sep 1929 Hudson Ctr, NH
SMITH, Dustin H and Huguette G RIOUX, 07 Oct 1967 Nashua, NH
SMITH, Edgar F and Alice D PHILIPS, 08 Oct 1878 Hudson, NH
  Sullivan Smith (Hudson, NH) & Sarah J Sullivan (Hudson, NH)
  Philips(Nova Scotia) & Edna J (Nova Scotia)
SMITH, Edna T and Cedric A RICHARDSON, 11 Oct 1941 Hudson, NH
SMITH, Edward J and Lizzie PIERCE, 10 Oct 1882 Hudson, NH
  Edward J Smith (Peterboro, NH) & Lydia A (Nashua, NH)
  John Pierce (Lowell, MA)
SMITH, Eileen F and Ralph D ENGER, 12 Jul 1947 Windham, NH
SMITH, Elizabeth and George W ALBEE, 22 Feb 1938 Hudson, NH
SMITH, Elizabeth and Troy W Jr ALLARD, 18 Jun 1978 Nashua, NH
SMITH, Elizabeth and William J COYNE, 11 Oct 1947 Hudson, NH
SMITH, Elliot A and Mina MURPHY, 22 Jun 1940 Lowell, MA
SMITH, Elmer F and Ethel M CONNELL, 07 Sep 1910 Londonderry, NH
  Henry F Smith & Elmira Chamberlain
  Robert T Connell & Mary E Marshall
SMITH, Elsie R and Boyd E COOLEY, 19 Jun 1971 Milford, NH
SMITH, Emma L and Joseph W PIERCE, 13 Feb 1887 Londonderry, NH
  Sullivan Smith (Hudson, NH) & Sarah Glover (Hudson, NH)
  Henry G Pierce(Chelmsford, MA) & Eliza L Smith (Brandon, VT)
SMITH, Eric B and Rose M MANNARINI, 02 Oct 1970 Derry, NH
SMITH, Eugene C and Sherron L TOWNSEND, 21 May 1966 Hudson, NH
SMITH, Eugene C and Alice M JEAN, 03 Aug 1974 Hudson, NH
SMITH, Eugene J and Eva D EVIRS, 20 Nov 1946 Hudson, NH
SMITH, Eva R Ober and Lester Alonzo FALL, 29 Jul 1924 Billerica, MA
SMITH, Eveline A and Leo R CARON, 28 Jul 1967 Nashua, NH
SMITH, Evelyn M and Daniel D LYONS, 29 May 1965 Hudson, NH
SMITH, Evelyn M and Harry F MOSHER, 22 May 1977 Hudson, NH
SMITH, Evelyn M and George F PROCTOR, 08 Oct 1950 Hudson, NH
SMITH, F Stanley and Donna L BUTLER, 29 Aug 1975 Nashua, NH
SMITH, Flora M and Hiram J STEARNS, 29 Jun 1946 Hudson, NH
SMITH, Francis T and Marion A VOYMAS, 30 Sep 1938 Hudson, NH
SMITH, Frank C and Eva G M MARSHALL, 09 Feb 1943 Hudson, NH
SMITH, Frank E and Lea D DUVAL, 14 Aug 1970 Hudson, NH
SMITH, Frank L and Mercy F CLARK, 16 Aug 1866
SMITH, Fred E and Addie L CONERY, 16 Nov 1904 Nashua, NH
  Nelson Smith & Caroline M Lee
  S A Conery & Sarah E Hollister
SMITH, Frederick and Carrie NEAL, 06 Oct 1890 Lowell, MA
  John Smith (Germany) & Augusta Alexander (Germany)
  Jason Packard(Easton, MA) & Susan Packard (Montpelier, VT)
SMITH, Frederick and Betty J HEMEON, 09 Jun 1955 Nashua, NH
SMITH, Frederick and Sarah A CORLISS, 19 Oct 1865
SMITH, G P and Susan M GREELEY, 07 Dec 1847
SMITH, Gardner and Ruth Athal HENRY, 11 Jun 1937 Nashua, NH
SMITH, George A and Rosa E CURRIER, 24 Oct 1881 Hudson, NH
  Chas H Smith & Mary Wells
  D S Currier & Clarise T Russ
SMITH, George A and Susan E BUTLER, 27 Feb 1883 Pelham, NH
  Edwin Smith (Hudson, NH) & Sybil Wilson (Dracut, MA)
  James Caldwell(Hudson, NH) & Susan E Senter
SMITH, George S and Jill A CARROLL, 30 Jun 1984 Hudson, NH
SMITH, Gertrude E and Ralph C WALKER, 26 Apr 1955 Hudson, NH
SMITH, Gertrude P and James C MUNROE, 05 Sep 1948 Hudson, NH
SMITH, Gladys A and Paul A ST AMANT, 07 Jul 1970 Nashua, NH

HUDSON, NH MARRIAGES

SMITH, Gloria L and Leslie D BINKS, 22 Nov 1937 Hudson, NH
SMITH, Gordon H and Nathalie J BOILARD, 13 May 1961 Nashua, NH
SMITH, Gordon L and Marion DANSEVICH, 29 Aug 1936 Nashua, NH
SMITH, Granville and Mary J COLBURN, 24 Dec 1874 Hudson, NH
SMITH, Hannah and Amos Jr DAVIS, 24 Nov 1825
SMITH, Hannah and David P SMITH, 27 Sep 1856
SMITH, Hannah and Jesse SMITH, 23 Dec 1819
SMITH, Harold D and Hazel V DETORO, 22 Feb 1948 Hudson, NH
SMITH, Harriet S and Joseph Q FRENCH, 17 Feb 1842
SMITH, Harrison E and Arline M SHINN, 20 Jun 1968 Hudson, NH
SMITH, Harvard P and Mary Jane ANDREWS, 28 Jan 1864
SMITH, Hattie S and Harley M SARGENT, 25 Oct 1909 Nashua, NH
  Abel A Smith & Mary F Carter
  Nathaniel Sargent & Ellen Potter
SMITH, Helen and Kenneth HOLM, 14 Feb 1944 Hudson, NH
SMITH, Helen Beatrice & Wallace Grant BAKER, 22 Jul 1928 Hudson, NH
SMITH, Helen E and Eugene P PETREAULT, 24 May 1947 Hudson, NH
SMITH, Henrietta and David O MARSHALL, 23 Dec 1885 Hudson, NH
  Norris Smith (Hudson, NH) & Fannie M Greeley (Hudson, NH)
  John B Marshall(Hudson, NH) & Ellen A Senter (Hudson, NH)
SMITH, Henry E and Mary F KAYROS, 13 May 1933 Hudson, NH
SMITH, Henry F and Elvira T CHAMBERLAIN, 03 Jan 1882 Hudson, NH
  Dustin B Smith (Hudson, NH) & Sarah J Watts (Peterboro, NH)
  Caleb Chamberlain & Maria Robbins
SMITH, Henry Jr and Clarissa CUMMINGS, 19 Feb 1847
SMITH, Henry O and Marcia A DEARING, 04 Sep 1889 Waterboro, ME
  David O Smith (Hudson, NH) & Mary H Greeley (Hudson, NH)
  Isaac N Dearing(Waterboro, ME) & Almira Guptill (Limerick, ME)
SMITH, Henry O and Marcia A DEERING, 04 Sep 1899
SMITH, Herbert D and Blanche M GREELEY, 13 Nov 1912 Londonderry, NH
  Henry F Smith & Elona Chamberlain
  Charles Greeley & Phebe Clinch
SMITH, Herbert M and Lydia J PARKER, 19 Mar 1906 Hudson, NH
  Isaac N Smith & Roxanna Butler
  Charles C Parker & Lydia F Batchelder
SMITH, Herman K and Ruth I KENNEY, 13 May 1955 Hudson, NH
SMITH, Howard P and Mary Jane ANDREWS, 28 Jan 1864
SMITH, Hugh and Cynthia HOWE, 10 Nov 1842
SMITH, Hugh and Elizabeth CUTLER, 26 Jan 1853
SMITH, Ida E and Vincent DELUCA, 14 Jan 1950 Hudson, NH
SMITH, Irvin A and Bertha J SHATNEY, 19 Apr 1915 Manchester, NH
  Andrew J Smith (Hudson, NH) & Irene Hunting (Hudson, NH)
  Joseph J Shatney(Vermont) & Alice Grey (Glover, VT)
SMITH, Isaac N and Roxanna BUTLER, 06 Apr 1863
SMITH, J H and Frances LOVEJOY, 16 Apr 1864
SMITH, J Parker and Harriet E BUCKMINSTER, 27 Oct 1853
SMITH, J Roy and Gertrude R GUNDERSEN, 29 Aug 1934 Nashua, NH
SMITH, Jacob A and Lydia H SMITH, 12 Apr 1842
SMITH, Jacqueline and Craig M CAREY, 04 Apr 1983 Nashua, NH
SMITH, James and Mary LAWRENCE, 19 Jul 1796
SMITH, James F and Brenda D SEVERANCE, 16 Aug 1969 Hudson, NH
SMITH, James M and Clara A WRIGHT, 27 Dec 1861
SMITH, James M and Clara M WRIGHT, 27 Dec 1861
SMITH, James W B and Ada S CONANT, 25 Feb 1905 Hudson, NH
  John Smith & Mary Ball
  Sam Simpson & Sabina Tibbetts
SMITH, James W Jr and Julie C POTTER, 06 Nov 1976 Hudson, NH
SMITH, James W Jr and Deborah K COLL, 29 Feb 1980 Hudson, NH
SMITH, Jane and Thomas Jr SMITH, 24 Feb 1848
SMITH, Janet A and Joseph E LATOUR, 04 Oct 1957 Hudson, NH

HUDSON,NH MARRIAGES

SMITH, Janet L and Neil O HOVIOUS, 16 Apr 1983 Nashua, NH
SMITH, Janna and Philip MELVIN, 16 Nov 1797
SMITH, Jefferson and Susan SMITH, 07 Dec 1852
SMITH, Jeffrey L and Cynthia L BATCHELDER, 03 Mar 1979 Hudson, NH
SMITH, Jennie and Thomas Jr SMITH, 02 Jun 1801
SMITH, Jennie C and James O McCOY, 16 Aug 1897 Hudson, NH
  George L Smith & Clara O Stevens
  James McCoy
SMITH, Jesse and Hannah SMITH, 23 Dec 1819
SMITH, Jo-Ann and Fred Daniel FRASER, 08 Jul 1978 Goffstown, NH
SMITH, Joan and Raymond R POLIQUIN, 14 Oct 1961 Hudson, NH
SMITH, John H and Olive MERRILL, 07 Dec 1815
SMITH, John K and Marjorie A CARTER, 07 Jul 1951 Hudson, NH
SMITH, Jonathan P and Kathleen A McLLACKY, 27 Dec 1974 Hudson, NH
SMITH, Jonathan Paul & Linda Barbara BEYER, 02 Jul 1978 Hudson, NH
SMITH, Joseph and Sarah WASON, 19 Dec 1816
SMITH, Joyce E and Ronald D CLOUTIER, 25 Mar 1961 Hudson, NH
SMITH, Kathleen E and Richard L LALIBERTE, 27 Dec 1969 Hudson, NH
SMITH, Kenneth B and Margaret M HENDRICKS, 21 Aug 1943 Hudson, NH
SMITH, Kittridge and Catherine QUINTON, 08 Feb 1969 Brookline, NH
SMITH, Larry and Lucy A HUTTON, 07 Jun 1969 Stratham, NH
SMITH, Laura M and Donald E JEWELL, 20 Oct 1959 Concord, NH
SMITH, Lavinia F and Walter A WENTWORTH, 01 May 1871 Hudson, NH
SMITH, Leonard A and Claire F RICHARD, 21 Oct 1942 Hudson, NH
SMITH, Leslie B and Irene A BELAND, 27 Jun 1942 Nashua, NH
SMITH, Lillian F and John A McGILLIVRAY, 11 Feb 1972 Hudson, NH
SMITH, Lillian M and George C PATRICI, 14 Aug 1948 Hudson, NH
SMITH, Linda D and Fred P McQUESTEN, 17 Oct 1981 Nashua, NH
SMITH, Lisa K and Michael W COURTNEY, 28 Oct 1979 Hudson, NH
SMITH, Lizzie H and Brinton M WEBSTER, 29 Aug 1894 Hudson, NH
  Wm H Smith (Guilford, ME) & Elisa M Tuck
  Nathan P Webster & Susan M Morrison
SMITH, Lorraine B and Howard H YOUNG, 03 May 1957 Hudson, NH
SMITH, Louisa A and Lucius F ROBINSON, 24 Apr 1879 Hudson, NH
  James Smith (Hudson, NH) & Margarett Smith (Hudson, NH)
  Simeon Robinson(Hudson, NH) & Eliza (Hudson, NH)
SMITH, Lucille and George H Jr PARKER, 24 Oct 1935 Nashua, NH
SMITH, Lucy T and Isaiah DANDLEY, 22 Sep 1844
SMITH, Lydia and John BOARDMAN, 16 Oct 1814
SMITH, Lydia H and Jacob A SMITH, 12 Apr 1842
SMITH, Mabel Gertrude and Joseph L MICHAUD, 07 Sep 1925 Nashua, NH
SMITH, Marc A and Tammy L DUSSEAULT, 20 Jun 1981 Hudson, NH
SMITH, Marcell H and Mary E EATON, 06 Sep 1890 Wakefield, MA
  Wm H Smith (Guilford, ME) & Eliza M Tuck (Salem, MA)
  Noah M Eaton(Wakefield, MA) & Eliza R Walton (Wakefield, MA)
SMITH, Marguerite and Walter C DUNKLEE, 24 Jul 1945 Hudson, NH
SMITH, Mark D and Gail A PROVENCHER, 23 Jan 1971 Nashua, NH
SMITH, Martha R and Leffort M POWELL, 13 Nov 1917 Hudson, NH
SMITH, Mary and Lee WOODSON, 12 Sep 1942 Nashua, NH
SMITH, Mehitabel and Amos MERRILL, 25 Dec 1800
SMITH, Mehitible and Amos MERRILL, 25 Dec 1800
SMITH, Melaine R and Robert F FAUCHER, 15 Feb 1975 Hudson, NH
SMITH, Morse and Elizabeth HADLEY, 15 Oct 1843
SMITH, Nancy and Willard CUMMINGS, 07 Dec 1815
SMITH, Nancy J and Charles F Jr HAYEK, 21 Jun 1958 Pelham, NH
SMITH, Nancy J and John P KAPIKSY, 19 Feb 1970 Dunbarton, NH
SMITH, Nellie E and Herbert A CROSS, 28 Apr 1887 Hudson, NH
  Daniel B Smith (Hudson, NH) & Hannah Smith (Hudson, NH)
  Hiram Cross(Hudson, NH) & Sarah E Savage (Greenfield, NH)
SMITH, Nelson and Caroline M LEE, 21 Dec 1861

HUDSON, NH MARRIAGES

SMITH, Obediah F and Philena A WASON, 31 May 1865
SMITH, Olive M Harvey & Joseph E LAMBERT, 07 Apr 1928 Chelmsford,MA
SMITH, Orin and Myrtle M CARPENTER, 19 Jan 1924 Hudson, NH
SMITH, Pamela A and Guy F KENDALL, 24 Aug 1966 Hudson, NH
SMITH, Patricia A and Michael M DRUCKMAN, 08 Jan 1977 Hudson, NH
SMITH, Paul F and Patricia B HICKS, 26 Jul 1975 Nashua, NH
SMITH, Paul T and Doris E PETTS, 14 Nov 1973 Hudson, NH
SMITH, Paula L and George R Jr LAROCQUE, 04 Sep 1976 Hudson, NH
SMITH, Pauline M and Amedee R LECLERC, 02 Feb 1952 Nashua, NH
SMITH, Perley B and Lizzie J ROBBINS, 28 May 1895 Nashua, NH
   Isaac N Smith (Hudson, NH) & Roxanna Bolter (Pelham, NH)
   D Z Robbins(Dover, NH) & Georgia A Robbins (Nashua, NH)
SMITH, Peter N and Susan E SHINN, 22 Aug 1971 Merrimack, NH
SMITH, Philip A and Margaret A SING, 17 Jun 1972 Meredith, NH
SMITH, Phyllis M and Paul A VIGNOLA, 07 May 1960 Hudson, NH
SMITH, Polly L and Luther HASELTON, 11 Apr 1826
SMITH, Priscilla and Daniel B LaFLAMME, 10 Sep 1977 Nashua, NH
SMITH, Rachel and John PAGE, 18 Aug 1796
SMITH, Raymond and Helene LEMELIN, 11 Mar 1944 Hudson, NH
SMITH, Raymond Edward & Patricia Jean MASON, 26 Aug 1978 Hudson, NH
SMITH, Raymond F and Virginia P BILLINGSLEY, 16 Dec 1934 Nashua, NH
SMITH, Reed M and Theresa Y WHITE, 27 Nov 1982 Hudson, NH
SMITH, Reuben P and Lydia G CRAIN, 18 Dec 1849
SMITH, Richard E and Teresa M WALLACE, 22 Sep 1984 Hudson, NH
SMITH, Richard P and Virginia MARSHALL, 16 Sep 1942 Hudson, NH
SMITH, Richard P and Edith M CHAPLIN, 24 Jun 1949 Rindge, NH
SMITH, Rita L and John A McCARTY, 04 Apr 1971 Hudson, NH
SMITH, Robert E and Imelda T LEBOEUF, 23 Sep 1950 Hudson, NH
SMITH, Robert M and Rachel E ALDRICH, 06 Jun 1949 Hudson, NH
SMITH, Roger E and Florence L BARRETT, 11 Jun 1960 Claremont, NH
SMITH, Rufus S and Elsie M STEAD, 29 Jun 1916 Everett, MA
   Charles Smith (England) & Mary Richards (Nova Scotia)
   Harry Stead(Mass) & Hannah Johnston (England)
SMITH, Ruth Elizabeth&Everett Marsh HAMBLETT, 24 Feb 1922 Hudson,NH
SMITH, Samuel and Abigail FOSTER, 01 Apr 1824
SMITH, Samuel P and Emma A DAVIS, 05 Dec 1855
SMITH, Sandra D and James W HAYES, 17 May 1967 Hudson, NH
SMITH, Sarah and William WHITNEY, 24 Nov 1825
SMITH, Scott Alan and Karen A SPELLMAN, 17 Jan 1981 Hudson, NH
SMITH, Scott D and Darlene E DAVIS, 29 Jun 1978 Nashua, NH
SMITH, Shirley A and Ernest A BRIAND, 27 Aug 1955 Hudson, NH
SMITH, Shirley A and Kenneth F MORSE, 08 Mar 1952 Manchester, NH
SMITH, Susan and Jefferson SMITH, 07 Dec 1852
SMITH, Thomas E and Katherine VASSILAKOS, 30 Nov 1973 Nashua, NH
SMITH, Thomas Jr and Jennie SMITH, 02 Jun 1801
SMITH, Thomas Jr and Jane SMITH, 24 Feb 1848
SMITH, Victor H and Mable L FOSTER, 29 Aug 1917 Claremont, NH
SMITH, Walter N and Pansy E McWILLIAMS, 14 Sep 1928 Nashua, NH
SMITH, Warren F and Elizabeth SLOWIK, 09 Sep 1967 Nashua, NH
SMITH, Wilford A and Madeline S TUCKER, 27 Feb 1970 Salem, NH
SMITH, Willis P and Martina EATON, 01 Jan 1873 Hudson, NH
SMITH, Wm H and Rosilla ELDRIDGE, 12 Jun 1873 Hudson, NH
SMITH-WEISS, Donald A and Brenda C SMITH, 02 Aug 1975 Hudson, NH
SMURDA, James B and Wilma J COX, 25 May 1957 Hudson, NH
SMYER, John E and Janice A RITCHIE, 17 Sep 1958 Hudson, NH
SMYTHE, Sherry and Wayne GREEN, 27 Dec 1982 Nashua, NH
SNAVELY, Bruce and Grace N MELTON, 02 Jun 1978 Litchfield, NH
SNAY, Francis P and Lois H MARTYN, 20 Feb 1965 Nashua, NH
SNAY, Joseph P and Judith A MERRILL, 18 Jan 1975 Nashua, NH
SNELL, Alton B and Louise J JOHNSON, 09 Nov 1940 Hudson, NH

HUDSON,NH MARRIAGES

SNELL, Dana V S and Robin P BEYER, 19 Mar 1984 Hudson, NH
SNELL, Edythe A and Donald E PARE, 08 Nov 1974 Nashua, NH
SNELL, Ephraim and Lucy E CONNER, 09 Sep 1869 Hudson, NH
SNELL, Georgia L and Ian D PALMER, 15 Jul 1978 Hudson, NH
SNELL, Ja A and Maria L CAMARA, 19 Jul 1980 Pelham, NH
SNELL, Paul F and Deborah S DEXTER, 19 Nov 1971 Pelham, NH
SNELL, Shirley M and Roland C NARO, 08 Jan 1980 Derry, NH
SNOW, Charles F and Bertha G PERRY, 06 Jun 1916 Hudson, NH
   G Lyman Snow (Newton, MA) & Harriet M Chase (Cambridge, MA)
   Lewis E Perry(Highgate, VT) & Sarah Lawrence (Bridgewater, MA)
SNOW, Edith F and George H PARKER, 28 Apr 1908 Hudson, NH
   Royal G Snow & Ardelle E Walker
   Charles C Parker & Lydia L Batchelder
SNOW, Edward G and Isobel DEEVAR, 21 Dec 1947 Hudson, NH
SNOW, Edwin E and Emma A PAGE, 01 Jun 1866
SNOW, Everett M and Irene A HEBERT, 12 May 1930 Hudson, NH
SNOW, Gladys I and Harland S HILLS, 12 Jul 1913 Litchfield, NH
   Royal G Snow & Addie E Walker
   Orlando G Hills & Nettie L Young
SNOW, Lloyd and Grace MacCAUSLAND, 13 Mar 1938 Nashua, NH
SNOW, Maraget E and John F FREEMAN, 19 Dec 1936 Nashua, NH
SNOW, May I and Arthur W SMITH, 16 Sep 1909 Hudson, NH
   Royal A Snow & Adela E Walker
   Isaac N Smith & Roxanna Butler
SNOW, Virginia H and Leo R FAGNANT, 07 Jun 1958 Hudson, NH
SNOWMAN, Linnie E and James G WENTWORTH, 26 Nov 1902 Rangeley, ME
   Geo J Snowman & Cenath J Haley
   Nathaniel Wentworth & Martha E Greeley
SNYDER, Charles W and Marie F BRUNELLE, 12 Jun 1948 Hudson, NH
SNYDER, John M and Kathleen M CASALE, 21 Nov 1980 Nashua, NH
SNYDER, Judith M and Chester R PARENT, 02 Oct 1971 Manchester, NH
SNYDER, Leon J III and Nancy J PACHECO, 16 Apr 1972 Pelham, NH
SNYDER, Phillip C and Lydia N GROHOSKY, 30 Dec 1978 Nashua, NH
SOBEL, Ann-Marie and Clark D Jr GRAVES, 22 Aug 1981 Hudson, NH
SODERBERY, Imogene and Roger J COUGHLIN, 21 Oct 1888 Fishkill, NY
   Robert Soderbery (New York) & Mary Walker (New York)
   Michael Coughlin(Boston, MA) & Ann (Boston, MA)
SOJKA, Chester W and Mary V BOGUSZ, 30 Dec 1944 Nashua, NH
SOJKA, John F and Anne L PALANSKI, 20 Jun 1953 Nashua, NH
SOKOLOWSKI, Sharron A and Brian R SMALL, 17 Sep 1982 Hudson, NH
SOLARI, Leslie G and John Jr GEMIGNANI, 07 Jul 1984 Merrimack, NH
SOLDI, Rose M and Leon R TURMAINE, 17 Jan 1940 Hudson, NH
SOLES, Arthur W and Helen B BURNER, 24 Apr 1974 Nashua, NH
SOLOMON, Sandra F and Burton BARVO, 14 Oct 1950 Hudson, NH
SOMERS, Kittie and William DEWOLFE, 21 Jul 1917 Nashua, NH
SOMERVILL, Eliza J and Harry D BLODGETT, 01 May 1889 Waitsfield, VT
   John Somervill (Waitsfield, VT) & Ann Hoffman (Ireland)
   Augus F Blodgett(Dorchester, MA) & Lucy E Chase (Hudson, NH)
SOMERVILLE, Lucille N and Hector E DUCHARME, 12 Sep 1971 Nashua, NH
SOMERVILLE, Lucille N and Roger J PELLERIN, 24 Oct 1964 Nashua, NH
SOMES, Ralph G and Ruth G FULLER, 20 Feb 1964 Hudson, NH
SOTECK, Stanley J and Victoria VOLSICK, 04 Jul 1947 Hudson, NH
SOUCI, Peter and Alvine LANDRY, 30 May 1916 Nashua, NH
   Andrew Souci (Canada) & Emilia Arsenault (Maine)
   Joseph Landry(Canada) & Aglae Gogne (Canada)
SOUCY, Andrew J and Josephine PELLETIER, 24 Nov 1949 Nashua, NH
SOUCY, Andrew J Jr and Sue Carol PLACE, 14 Apr 1973 Enfield, NH
SOUCY, Armand L and Mary F VIENS, 04 Jul 1942 Nashua, NH
SOUCY, Brenda J and Robert G ANASTASOFF, 09 Aug 1980 Hudson, NH
SOUCY, Cynthia C and Raymond W LANDOLT, 29 Jul 1979 Nashua, NH

HUDSON,NH MARRIAGES

SOUCY, Daniel P and Sandra A SANTINELLI, 14 Nov 1975 Milford, NH
SOUCY, Diane M and Leo D FRANCOEUR, 14 Feb 1982 Hudson, NH
SOUCY, Douglas P and Lisa A LAVALLEE, 19 Jan 1985 Nashua, NH
SOUCY, Jane E and Anthony E FUCCI, 24 Jun 1972 Hudson, NH
SOUCY, Leo E and Anita C SIMARD, 27 Apr 1968 Nashua, NH
SOUCY, Leo W and Carol L CASEY, 08 May 1971 Hudson, NH
SOUCY, Sylvio and Marion LAVOIE, 14 Sep 1925 Nashua, NH
SOUKAS, Bessie E and George L MOUSSEAU, 18 Nov 1972 Manchester, NH
SOULEOTIS, Ardres and Madeline KOTOPOULIS, 18 May 1942 Hudson, NH
SOUTHWICK, Bryan R and Karen L BIRD, 04 Sep 1982 Hudson, NH
SOUTHWICK, Joseph L and Susan I LANPHEAR, 20 Aug 1977 Hudson, NH
SOUZA, Derrick F and Cynthia M COOK, 26 Nov 1983 Hudson, NH
SOWER, Pearl May and Theodore A ANDERSON, 13 Jun 1907 Hudson, NH
   Harvey Lower & Mary Vintener
   Ole Anderson & Tenker Oleson
SPADARO, Joseph F and Pamela S SILES, 04 Dec 1982 Hudson, NH
SPAHN, Mary T and Joseph L JORDAN, 05 Dec 1975 Hudson, NH
SPALDING, Benjamin B and Elizabeth EMERY, 30 Oct 1850
SPALDING, Charles L and Sarah B MERRILL, 07 Jan 1886 Hudson, NH
   Reuben Spalding (Hudson, NH) & Sarah A Lahon (Nashua, NH)
   William T Merrill(Hudson, NH) & Lucy A Byam (Hudson, NH)
SPALDING, Donald H and Dorothy M JOHNSON, 11 Apr 1943 Nashua, NH
SPALDING, Edward A and Annie E SANDERS, 27 Oct 1888
SPALDING, John F and Pat HUTCHINS, 13 Jan 1946 Durham, NH
SPALDING, Leander R and Abbie E WINN, 01 Jan 1866
SPALDING, Martha A and Noah T JOY, 06 Feb 1852
SPALDING, Reuben Jr and Susannah PIERCE, 10 Oct 1780
SPALDING, Sarah A and Gans SENTER, 30 Jan 1844
SPALDING, Sarah M and John C GROVER, 23 Jun 1892
SPALDING, Susan and Moody MORSE, 22 Feb 1826
SPALDING, Willard and Sally MARSH, 24 Apr 1817
SPARKS, Carol A and John F AGRELLA, 25 Nov 1966 Nashua, NH
SPARKS, Gail K and Michael R McGRAW, 21 Jul 1984 Hudson, NH
SPAULDING, Albert M and Theresa R TESSIER, 09 Oct 1948 Nashua, NH
SPAULDING, Benj Brook and Elizabeth EMERY, 30 Oct 1850
SPAULDING, Charles D and Susan A BENNER, 23 Jul 1971 Hudson, NH
SPAULDING, Charles L and Sarah B MERRILL, 07 Jan 1886 Hudson, NH
SPAULDING, Charles W and Mary M FARNUM, 30 Nov 1882 Hudson, NH
   William Spaulding (Hudson, NH) & Sally Marsh (Hudson, NH)
   Charles Steele(Hudson, NH) & Martha Boyd (Londonderry, NH)
SPAULDING, Diane M and Hersey E COOKE, 26 Dec 1962 Nashua, NH
SPAULDING, Donna M and Michael R JARRY, 03 Sep 1977 Nashua, NH
SPAULDING, Edward A and Annie E SANDERS, 27 Oct 1888 Hudson, NH
   Leander R Spalding (Nashua, NH) & Abbie E Winn (Hudson, NH)
   Thomas Sanders(Ireland) & Mary Connell (Ireland)
SPAULDING, Emily and Robert EVANS, 16 Aug 1937 Nashua, NH
SPAULDING, Esther R and Robert PATTERSON, 27 Nov 1809
SPAULDING, Frances A & Clarence W Jr HAIGHT, 28 Jun 1959 Hudson, NH
SPAULDING, Geo W Jr and Betty M MILLER, 17 Jan 1949 Hudson, NH
SPAULDING, Katherine and Kenneth J INGALLS, 10 Oct 1981 Nashua, NH
SPAULDING, Leon E and Donna M LANDRY, 24 Jul 1971 Nashua, NH
SPAULDING, Leon E and Arlene M MOONEY, 06 Oct 1979 Hudson, NH
SPAULDING, Martha A & Arthur J Jr KASHULINES, 03 Jan 1963 Hudson,NH
SPAULDING, Maurice A and Robin J GIGUERE, 26 Aug 1978 Hudson, NH
SPAULDING, Phebe F and Robert LEWISTON, 05 Apr 1864
SPAULDING, Robert E and Katherine KEMPTON, 09 Oct 1971 Hudson, NH
SPAULDING, Robert F and Barbara J ROY, 19 Dec 1981 Hudson, NH
SPAULDING, Sarah M and John C GROVES, 23 Jun 1892 Hudson, NH
   Reuben Spalding (Hudson, NH) & Sarah Laton (Nashua, NH)
   Robert Groves(Ireland) & Lizzie Boyle (Ireland)

HUDSON, NH MARRIAGES

SPEAR, Daniel J and Betty Lou MORIN, 22 Jun 1968 Nashua, NH
SPEAR, Isabelle and Ulfrand LANGLOIS, 25 Jun 1932 Hudson, NH
SPEAR, Joseph and Wanda C LEGARSKY, 28 Nov 1940 Nashua, NH
SPEARS, George D and Alice T BONNETTE, 03 Sep 1960 Hudson, NH
SPECK, Margaret and Carl E OLOFSON, 13 May 1954 Hudson, NH
SPECK, Margaret and Kenneth R SEARLES, 30 Jun 1956 Milford, NH
SPELLMAN, Karen A and Scott Alan SMITH, 17 Jan 1981 Hudson, NH
SPELLMAN, Mary A and Robert N JOHNSON, 30 May 1981 Hudson, NH
SPENCE, Barbara A and Harold S CARTER, 03 Jul 1959 Nashua, NH
SPENCER, Kenneth E and Doris N ROUSELLE, 01 Aug 1971 Pelham, NH
SPENCER, Robert F and Juliette F BOUCHER, 02 Dec 1939 Nashua, NH
SPENCER, William A and Olive R JOHNSON, 01 Nov 1947 Hudson, NH
SPICER, Andria D and George W Jr BRIGHAM, 06 Apr 1970 Hudson, NH
SPINNEY, Forrest H and Roberta L JOHNSON, 18 Jun 1931 Nashua, NH
SPINNEY, Sandra A and David P MARQUIS, 02 Oct 1971 Hudson, NH
SPONGBERG, Steve M and Barbara A LANTAGNE, 21 Aug 1949 Hudson, NH
SPRAGUE, Ada L and William EGLEY, 30 Sep 1919 Nashua, NH
SPRAGUE, Benjamin F and Ellen DENTON, 24 Nov 1860
SPRAGUE, David A and Cherie L SCHARCH, 14 Feb 1982 Nashua, NH
SPRAGUE, Horace and Lucinda A BURBANK, 18 Apr 1847
SPRAGUE, Horace and Rebecca F CHASE, 14 Oct 1856
SPRAGUE, Jacqueline and Michael H ALUKONIS, 30 Jan 1982 Nashua, NH
SPRAGUE, Stanley R and Charlotte BENSON, 08 Aug 1932 Merrimack, NH
SPRAKE, Elizabeth and Tyler THOMAS, 23 Oct 1845
SPRAKE, Oliver and Betsey MARSHALL, 14 Mar 1820
SPRAKE, Samuel and Sarah BARNES, 17 Oct 1830
SPREADBY, Harry W and Ina H PUTNEY, 17 Jul 1926 Hudson, NH
SPRINGER, Isaac and Judith RANT, 03 Sep 1938 Nashua, NH
SPRINGER, Kathleen E and Alan M MURRAY, 28 Mar 1970 Nashua, NH
SQUIRES, Elsie M and Samuel A BATCH, 10 Jan 1876 Nashua, NH
ST AMAND, Lynn A and Charles C KEMPTON, 23 Nov 1974 Hudson, NH
ST AMAND, Mark E and Theresa M FORCIER, 04 Jul 1969 Hudson, NH
ST AMANT, Albert P and June E LaFOREST, 05 Nov 1969 Nashua, NH
ST AMANT, Cathy A and Richard L Jr CLARK, 26 Aug 1978 Hudson, NH
ST AMANT, Michael K and Cathy A CHENARD, 31 Mar 1984 Nashua, NH
ST AMANT, Paul A and Gladys A SMITH, 07 Jul 1970 Nashua, NH
ST ARMAND, Alfred J and Irene C BRICAULT, 19 Feb 1955 Nashua, NH
ST ARMAND, Lillian O and Leo P PARADISE, 11 Jul 1959 Nashua, NH
ST AUBIN, Albert J and Debra Jean MASON, 21 Dec 1980 Hudson, NH
ST CYR, Denise A and Michael W ROY, 18 Apr 1980 Hudson, NH
ST CYR, Robert G and Denise Ann VIENS, 29 Sep 1973 Hudson, NH
ST CYR, William P and Gayle E IVES, 16 Jun 1973 Hudson, NH
ST FRANCOIS, Paul E & Virginia G DESAUTELS, 24 Jan 1962 Hudson, NH
ST FRANCOIS, Veronique and Wilson W CLYDE, 11 Nov 1930 Keene, NH
ST GEORGE, Lucien R and Darlene E WARDWELL, 28 Oct 1967 Nashua, NH
ST HILAIRE, George A and Judith Rae TANGUAY, 25 Aug 1973 Hudson, NH
ST HILAIRE, Linda S and David A BURTON, 03 Mar 1984 Nashua, NH
ST HILAIRE, Patricia E and Robert T WINTER, 30 Oct 1982 Hudson, NH
ST JACQUES, Herbine and Nelson BOUCHER, 13 Nov 1933 Nashua, NH
ST JEAN, Florette D and Lake M MUNDAY, 30 Aug 1947 Nashua, NH
ST JEAN, Harvey A and Constance NIQUETTE, 04 Sep 1950 Nashua, NH
ST JEAN, Simone G and Albert L DESROSIERS, 22 Jun 1946 Nashua, NH
ST JOHN, Sandra M and Kevin P SULLIVAN, 03 Jul 1970 Salem, NH
ST LAURENT, Andre A and Kathleen E GLENN, 04 Mar 1972 Hudson, NH
ST LAURENT, Barbara S and Michael J BRIEN, 20 Aug 1982 Hudson, NH
ST LAURENT, Charles G and Yvonne L BELAND, 30 Jun 1962 Hudson, NH
ST LAURENT, Jeannette and Frank J GRIGAS, 30 Jul 1949 Nashua, NH
ST LAURENT, Laura M and Paul O BOURBEAU, 24 Sep 1966 Hudson, NH
ST LAURENT, Marie Y and Fred S HUGHES, 05 Oct 1963 Nashua, NH
ST LAURENT, Pauline Y and Colin S COLBY, 15 Nov 1980 Hudson, NH

HUDSON,NH MARRIAGES

ST LAURENT, Pauline Y and Charles L JOHNSON, 21 Jun 1980 Hudson, NH
ST LAURENT, Rita and Raymond O WILLIAMSON, 30 Dec 1971 Nashua, NH
ST LAURENT, Roger J and Pearl T BERNIER, 01 Feb 1947 Nashua, NH
ST LAURENT, Roger Jr and Nancy J ROY, 24 Jul 1971 Hudson, NH
ST LAURENT, Roger L and Rita DEMANCHE, 26 Sep 1953 Nashua, NH
ST LAURENT, Roland A and Marion M BURTON, 23 Aug 1947 Nashua, NH
ST LAURENT, Theresa I and Frank H ELLIOTT, 28 May 1955 Hudson, NH
ST LAURENT, Zenon J and Gertrude G SENECHAL, 20 Feb 1954 Nashua, NH
ST LOUIS, Joan A M and Robert O HARNETT, 18 Oct 1980 Hudson, NH
ST MARTIN, Charles V and Carolina BELANGER, 08 May 1924 Nashua, NH
ST MARTIN, Joseph J and Ruth REYNOLDS, 26 May 1945 Nashua, NH
ST ONGE, Normand H and Donna F WATTS, 22 May 1965 Manchester, NH
ST ONGE, William B and Susan B FARLAND, 26 Sep 1969 Nashua, NH
ST PIERRE, Arthur L and Frances A REEVES, 07 Aug 1982 Nashua, NH
ST PIERRE, Russell F and Eva D TETREAULT, 15 Dec 1949 Hudson, NH
STACEY, Frederick and Theresa A KELLEY, 18 Feb 1950 Hudson, NH
STACK, Bridget L and Gordon S HILL, 27 Aug 1948 Hudson, NH
STACK, Mary J and Robert A DISTEFANO, 05 Jul 1969 Salem, NH
STACKHOUSE, Russell C and Lillian C JARVIS, 16 Mar 1974 Hudson, NH
STACKNIS, Helen M and George W CANTY, 19 Jun 1937 Nashua, NH
STACKNIS, Mary R and Frederick PREBLE, 07 Jun 1941 Nashua, NH
STADIG, Ruth E and Theodore A SKONBERG, 14 Sep 1946 Hudson, NH
STAHL, Robin E and Wayne B GENDRON, 11 Sep 1976 Meredith, NH
STANAVICH, Sophie A and Robert W BARNETT, 25 Oct 1947 Hudson, NH
STANDISH, Arnold M and Esther A TROMBLEY, 15 Mar 1975 Nashua, NH
STANDISH, Richard W and Laura A BABINEAU, 02 Sep 1983 Hudson, NH
STANHOPE, Luther E and Marion E HOLTON, 31 Aug 1940 Hudson, NH
STANIELS, George A and Flora L RATTRAY, 19 Dec 1918 Nashua, NH
STANLEY, Beverly A and Brian L MASON, 27 Jun 1975 Nashua, NH
STANLEY, Daniel A and Laura A REED, 01 Nov 1876 Hudson, NH
STANLEY, Mary-Ann and Robert F GILCREAST, 28 Sep 1974 Nashua, NH
STANLEY, Wayne F and E Natalie McGONIGLE, 02 Oct 1982 Hudson, NH
STANTON, Charles P and Lucille C CARRIGAN, 07 Feb 1943 Nashua, NH
STANULONIS, Ellen M and John R Jr FERBERT, 27 Dec 1967 Hudson, NH
STAPANOWICH, David L and Patricia A BROWN, 28 Sep 1963 Hudson, NH
STAPANOWICH, Patricia A & Donald R BEAUCAGE, 25 Mar 1967 Hudson, NH
STAPLES, Minerva and Joseph WILSON, 22 Oct 1826
STARK, Diane S and Eugene F LUZ, 05 Jul 1975 Hudson, NH
STARK, Helen L and Robert H LANFEAR, 25 Apr 1950 Hudson, NH
STARTA, Paul P and Ann F LAHAN, 23 Oct 1947 Hudson, NH
STATTA, Aemil J and Alexandra JAMES, 18 Aug 1950 Hudson, NH
STAWASZ, Thomas P and Mary-Ann WILLIS, 12 Jan 1973 Nashua, NH
STAWSKI, Anthony S and Doris B CONSIGNY, 27 Apr 1943 Hudson, NH
STEAD, Elsie M and Rufus S SMITH, 29 Jun 1916 Everett, MA
   Harry Stead (Mass) & Hannah Johnston (England)
   Charles Smith(England) & Mary Richards (Nova Scotia)
STEARNS, Gloria M and Leon A DIONNE, 30 Aug 1972 Manchester, NH
STEARNS, Hiram J and Flora M SMITH, 29 Jun 1946 Hudson, NH
STECKEVICZ, Chester J and Stephanie KURTA, 09 May 1946 Nashua, NH
STECKEWICZ, Emma A and Andrew S McCAUGNEY, 05 Aug 1940 Nashua, NH
STECKIEWICZ, Helen E&Herbert S BRETTELL, 11 Oct 1947 Manchester, NH
STEEL, Hattie E and John N MARDEN, 01 Sep 1868 Hudson, NH
STEELE, Belinda and Joseph FULLER, 23 Dec 1841
STEELE, Charlene E and Herbert M BROWN, 15 Jun 1932 Nashua, NH
STEELE, Charles A and Ida F GRAY, 12 Jun 1888 Nashua, NH
   Silas T Steele (Hudson, NH) & Elizabeth McDonald (Scotland)
   Charles A Gray(Nashua, NH) & Sarah A P Angier (Amherst, NH)
STEELE, Charles A and Hattie A REYNOLDS, 27 Dec 1882 Windham, NH
   Charles Steele (Hudson, NH) & Martha A Boyd (Londonderry, NH)
   Hiram S Reynolds(Windham, NH) & Mary A Prescott

HUDSON, NH MARRIAGES

STEELE, Charles F and Etta L SIAS, 01 Sep 1880 Boston, MA
  Frederick Steele (Hudson, NH) & Caroline E Follett
  Chauncey Sias & Huldah
STEELE, Charles L and Mina A BOYD, 25 Nov 1913 Newton Ctre, MA
  Charles A Steele & Lottie A Reynolds
  Hirma J Boyd & Sarah L Jameson
STEELE, Charlotte and Simeon F ROBINSON, 01 Nov 1842
STEELE, Clara M and George C WEBBER, Feb 1856
STEELE, Daniel and Rebecca MARSHALL, 18 Nov 1819
STEELE, Fannie and Lucius T BARKER, 28 Nov 1861
STEELE, Fred G and Addie B MOODY, 28 Jun 1900 Nashua, NH
  Silas T Steele & Elizabeth McDonald
  Geo W Moody & Addie A Bannister
STEELE, Frederick and Caroline E FOLLETT, 07 May 1856
STEELE, George S and Edith F COLBURN, 05 Oct 1893 Nashua, NH
  Silas T Steele (Hudson, NH) & Elizabeth McDonald (New York)
  Henry T Colburn(Hudson, NH) & Fanny F Gould (Tyngsboro, MA)
STEELE, Ida N and George T BENSON, 12 Jul 1909 Nashua, NH
  Charles A Steele & Lottie A Reynolds
  Walter E Benson & Laura F Caldwell
STEELE, James A and Rita Y LEVASSEUR, 21 Jun 1975 Nashua, NH
STEELE, Johanna and Mark BATCHELDER, 17 Mar 1842
STEELE, Lydia and Mark BATCHELDER, 13 Dec 1849
STEELE, M Jennie and James M CROWELL, 18 May 1882 Hudson, NH
  Chas Steele (Hudson, NH) & Martha A Boyd (Londonderry, NH)
  Henry C Crowell(Windham, NH) & Mary A Watts (Londonderry, NH)
STEELE, Mary L and Alfred S DAVIS, 15 Jun 1866
STEELE, Mary M and John D FARNHAM, 12 Oct 1866
STEELE, Moody G and Elnora GILBERT, 21 Jun 1941 Nashua, NH
STEELE, Ralph H and Frances A GOODWIN, 12 Jul 1926 Hudson, NH
STEELE, Ralph H and Helen R KARSTOK, 16 Sep 1938 Hudson, NH
STEELE, Samuel and Fanny BLODGETT, 21 Sep 1815
STEELE, Samuel and Fannie BLODGETT, 21 Sep 1815
STEELE, Samuel A and Mary A BUTTRICK, 30 Sep 1862
STEELE, Sarah J and James M BUTLER, 02 Oct 1862
STEELE, Sarah J and James M BUTTER, 20 Oct 1862
STEEVES, Loretta I and Harley A BEAN, 26 Apr 1977 Pelham, NH
STEEVES, Vern Y and Violet BALDWIN, 19 Feb 1931 Nashua, NH
STEFFENS, Madeline N and James W McGUIRE, 19 Jul 1976 Hudson, NH
STEINMETZ, Diana M and Randall W SHARP, 05 May 1978 Hudson, NH
STENGER, Sandra S and Angelo DECICCO, 09 Oct 1977 Amherst, NH
STEPHENS, Darron A & Jessie A CUTHBERTSON, 10 Dec 1983 Atkinson, NH
STEPHENS, James Basil & Maureen E KOBISKY, 13 Oct 1973 Windham, NH
STEPHENS, Laura and William G WRIGHT, 02 Apr 1877 Hudson, NH
    Edward Wright(Oakdale, MA) & Ann Stephens
STEPHENS, Linda A and Roger E GRAY, 14 Mar 1970 Hudson, NH
STEPNEY, Donald A and Karen L LAQUERRE, 11 Sep 1976 Hudson, NH
STERITI, Peter D and Linda A GENEST, 20 Aug 1982 Hudson, NH
STESSENGER, Annette & Lawrence A STOCKDALE, 20 Aug 1932 Chester, NH
STETZLER, Francine E and Dan J KRAMER, 30 Jun 1984 Nashua, NH
STETZLER, Gary L and Susan ANNIS, 27 Aug 1977 Nashua, NH
STETZLER, Glenn Scot and Cathy Dian TRAER, 17 Jul 1982 Hudson, NH
STEVENS, Beatrice J and Raymond F FARIA, 08 Jan 1972 Hudson, NH
STEVENS, Carroll J and Shirley A BONICA, 05 Feb 1964 Hudson, NH
STEVENS, Eleanor S and David S EMMETT, 03 Oct 1969 Hudson, NH
STEVENS, Eliza and John D CLARK, Oct 1840
  John Stevens & Nancy Webster
STEVENS, Ethel E and Fortunato SIGILLO, 22 Aug 1951 Hudson, NH
STEVENS, Evelyn P and Robert J POULIN, 18 Aug 1956 Hudson, NH
STEVENS, Evelynne C and Richard D SMALL, 07 Aug 1937 Hudson, NH

HUDSON,NH MARRIAGES

STEVENS, George E and Martha D HORNE, 30 Dec 1927 Hudson, NH
STEVENS, George L and MA Knight GINGRASS, 29 Oct 1932 Dunstable, MA
STEVENS, John and Nancy WEBSTER, 27 Jan 1811
STEVENS, John J Jr and Ann S DUPREY, 09 Mar 1974 Nashua, NH
STEVENS, Laura and William G WRIGHT, 12 Apr 1877 Hudson, NH
STEVENS, Lucille H and Roland P BOUCHER, 13 Nov 1954 Hudson, NH
STEVENS, Mortimer and Lillian I ROOT, 26 Jan 1946 Hudson, NH
STEVENS, Nancy and Chester CLOUGH, Oct 1849
   John Stevens & Nancy Webster
STEVENS, Paula J and Thomas E ROUSSEAU, 18 Apr 1981 Hudson, NH
STEVENS, Richard A and Marion R BISBING, 12 Feb 1966 Derry, NH
STEVENS, Richard C and Hannah G RICHARDSON, 20 Nov 1850
STEVENS, Richard P and F Joanne SWASEY, 26 Nov 1952 Keene, NH
STEVENS, Samuel H and Mary S INGALLS, 17 Mar 1863
STEVENS, Vinton E and Nora BURNS, 28 Jan 1947 Hudson, NH
STEVENS, William H and Emma E GAGNON, 21 May 1955 Hudson, NH
STEWART, Alida R and Frank B LESLIE, 01 Nov 1924 Hudson, NH
STEWART, Amanda and Albert HARRIS, 28 Nov 1854
STEWART, Angelina M and Charles R JAMESON, 20 Sep 1975 Hudson, NH
STEWART, Benjamin F and Beatrice M LEDOUX, 10 Oct 1942 Nashua, NH
STEWART, Beverly A and Manuel J LOPES, 09 Dec 1976 Pelham, NH
STEWART, Charles T and Barbara E FORD, 20 Aug 1983 Hudson, NH
STEWART, Edith May and C Arthur HAWES, 15 Jun 1934 Hudson, NH
STEWART, Francis and Sarah CUTTER, 27 Jan 1820
STEWART, George F and Laura A CHAPMAN, 18 Oct 1876 Hudson, NH
STICKNEY, Elizabeth and Gary Robert DUBE, 05 Feb 1982 Nashua, NH
STICKNEY, Ronald L and Florence E FORRENCE, 22 Sep 1984 Hudson, NH
STIGLIANI, Patricia A and Stephen R BEASON, 06 Aug 1983 Hudson, NH
STOCKDALE, Lawrence A & Annette STESSENGER, 20 Aug 1932 Chester, NH
STOCKDALE, Lawrence A and Myrtle F WILCOX, 09 Nov 1935 Pembroke, NH
STOCKLEY, Walter J and Rachel L THEROUX, 15 Apr 1950 Nashua, NH
STODDARD, Ruby M and Richard B PARKER, 24 Nov 1928 Nashua, NH
STODDARD, Russell L and Marjorie E DODGE, 23 May 1951 Hudson, NH
STOESSEL, Francis A and Mildred LEES, 30 Sep 1923 Nashua, NH
STOFANAK, Gayle S and Stephen F Jr STOFANAK, 11 Sep 1983 Hudson, NH
STOFANAK, Stephen F Jr and Linda A FORTIER, 01 Aug 1981 Hudson, NH
STOFANAK, Stephen F Jr and Gayle S STOFANAK, 11 Sep 1983 Hudson, NH
STONE, Alfred F and Laura M GRANT, 21 Mar 1969 Hudson, NH
STONE, Donna G and David M CAMPBELL, 15 Aug 1976 Hudson, NH
STONE, Ernest G and Mona J ATKINSON, 13 Jul 1956 Canterbury, NH
STONE, Ernest G Jr and Cheryl L SEVERANCE, 13 Nov 1971 Hudson, NH
STONE, Gail E and Arthur F DOLAN, 22 Nov 1975 Litchfield, NH
STONE, George and Alice G WOOD, 15 May 1943 Newport, NH
STONE, James S and Donna M McILVEEN, 30 Jun 1973 Hudson, NH
STONE, Jane and Markland MULHOLLAND, 02 Aug 1941 Hudson, NH
STONE, Judith A and William P MITCHELL, 29 Aug 1969 Hudson, NH
STONE, Leona M and Arthur E MERRILL, 23 Jan 1932 Peterborough, NH
STONE, Michael W and Elaine C BOULEY, 17 Jun 1978 Hudson, NH
STONE, Norman E and Earlene A DOW, 30 Jul 1955 Nashua, NH
STONE, Philip A and Dorothy M HAITHWAITE, 22 Apr 1962 Nashua, NH
STONE, Robert I and Naomi M MAKI, 11 Mar 1966 New Ipswich, NH
STONE, Robert W and Ellen J WILSON, 17 Sep 1971 Hudson, NH
STONE, Sharon E & William Jr LEFABVRE, 29 Aug 1975 Londonderry, NH
STONE, Timothy W and Elaine M YOUNG, 29 Oct 1983 Hudson, NH
STOODLY, William H and Eva L CRENNER, 23 Dec 1871 Charlestown, MA
STORY, Deborah Lee and Ricky James BRIGHAM, 19 Aug 1978 Hudson, NH
STOUGHTON, Eunice R and Edward F DALTON, 28 Sep 1957 Hudson, NH
STOUT, Elizabeth and David R MAGUE, 23 May 1981 Hudson, NH
STOVER, Miriam L and Thomas A COULIS, 11 Mar 1933 Hudson, NH
STOWELL, Robin M and Brian J MYRICK, 22 Oct 1983 Hudson, NH

HUDSON, NH MARRIAGES

STOWELL, Walter L III & Virginia R AZEVEDO, 25 Apr 1982 Hudson, NH
STR'GSTEIN, Ludmilla L and Fred O CARLSON, 10 Jun 1950 Hudson, NH
STRACCO, Dominic N and Marion L TRUESDALE, 04 Dec 1948 Hudson, NH
STRANGE, Dawn Marie and Edward Paul CLARK, 27 Mar 1982 Hudson, NH
STRATOTI, Diane and David E BURDEN, 22 Jun 1985 Nashua, NH
STRATTON, Mark D and Gloria Jea BOUCHER, 27 Sep 1974 Pelham, NH
STRAUB, Allen N and Susan M ALEXKNOVITCH, 25 May 1984 Hudson, NH
STRAUB, Christine and Earl Jr MUNSON, 13 May 1977 Hudson, NH
STRAUB, Lois M and Stephen KOPISKI, 21 Oct 1961 Hudson, NH
STRAUB, Shirley A and James R WHEELER, 24 Jul 1965 Hudson, NH
STRAUSS, Linda P and Michael J O'ROURKE, 10 Jul 1982 Milford, NH
STRAWBRIDGE, James W and Lois H FAGAN, 22 Nov 1967 Hudson, NH
STREETER, Eliza and James McCOY, 26 Aug 1867
STREETER, Eliza A and James McCOY, 26 Aug 1867
STREIT, William J and Rita M HALE, 22 Mar 1978 Hudson, NH
STRESSENGER, Donald J and Grace M BERNARD, 10 Feb 1940 Hudson, NH
STRESSENGER, John B and Barbara M WALTER, 16 Nov 1929 Hudson, NH
STROMBECK, Royal L and Beulah L CHALIFOUX, 17 Oct 1936 Nashua, NH
STRONG, Bonnie J and Stephen C SCHOMMER, 23 Jun 1984 Nashua, NH
STRUBINGER, Glen J and Lillian J HAWKINS, 12 May 1954 Nashua, NH
STRUTHERS, Clifford W & Jennie B KELSEA, 11 Jan 1941 Goffstown, NH
STUDLEY, Katherine and Jasper D AKERS, 01 Mar 1932 Nashua, NH
STULTZ, Clayton A and Hildreth H MATTHEWS, 17 Nov 1956 Hudson, NH
STULTZ, Isabelle H and Ray A KIMBALL, 04 Mar 1944 Hudson, NH
STULTZ, Kenneth D and Gloria A HOLT, 04 Mar 1950 Hudson, NH
STULTZ, Philip M and Marion E JOY, 22 Jun 1946 Nashua, NH
STURTEVANT, Donald H and Ruth J ADKINS, 01 Oct 1966 Hudson, NH
STYNES, Rita A and Jean-Paul BOULANGER, 30 May 1970 Nashua, NH
SUCLEANTOPOLOS, T and Etta FRECHETTE, 06 Jul 1940 Hudson, NH
SUDSBURY, Leona P and Gordon F MacLATCHEY, 11 Nov 1941 Nashua, NH
SUDSBURY, Phyllis A and Arthur L CROSSAYS, 15 Apr 1939 Hudson, NH
SUDSBURY, Robert E and Patricia WENTWORTH, 28 Sep 1940 Hudson, NH
SUDSBURY, Robert E and Jean C SIMONDS, 28 Oct 1961 Nashua, NH
SUDSBURY, Ruth E and Clarence F BENT, 13 Jun 1936 Hudson, NH
SUKIS, Albert J and M Antoine KASPER, 14 Feb 1955 Nashua, NH
SULHERLAND, Estelle G and Robert J WILSON, 03 Jul 1937 Hudson, NH
SULKIN, Ruth L and Herbert D FREEDMAN, 21 Nov 1937 Hudson, NH
SULLIVAN, Bertha and Morton M WRIGHT, 02 Jul 1950 Hudson, NH
SULLIVAN, Coleen Sue and David L CASSALIA, 01 Sep 1972 Nashua, NH
SULLIVAN, Daniel W & Margaret I McMANUS, 16 Nov 1963 Merrimack, NH
SULLIVAN, Dorothy A and Angelo INGERNI, 28 Jun 1947 Hudson, NH
SULLIVAN, Elizabeth and Frederick BRADLEY, 18 Jun 1918 Nashua, NH
SULLIVAN, Francis M and Sylvia J CALOGERRO, 27 Sep 1947 Hudson, NH
SULLIVAN, John and Mary W WILLOUGHBY, 01 Jan 1853
SULLIVAN, John E and Jean A CADY, 31 Jul 1954 Hudson, NH
SULLIVAN, John J and Clara A GALVIN, 04 Feb 1956 Hudson, NH
SULLIVAN, Joseph A & Colleen A QUIGLEY, 22 Aug 1981 Londonderry, NH
SULLIVAN, Kevin P and Sandra M ST JOHN, 03 Jul 1970 Salem, NH
SULLIVAN, Kevin R and Cynthia A CHARBONNEAU, 27 Dec 1981 Hudson, NH
SULLIVAN, Leroy G and Marlyn J POST, 29 May 1959 Nashua, NH
SULLIVAN, Margaret M and Richard R GAGNON, 28 Aug 1971 Hudson, NH
SULLIVAN, Margaret M & Edward J Jr SMILLIE, 24 Aug 1946 Nashua, NH
SULLIVAN, Margo A and Kenneth F PHILLIPS, 11 Aug 1979 Hudson, NH
SULLIVAN, Marie E and Lloyd H KNUDSEN, 22 May 1948 Hudson, NH
SULLIVAN, Mary Ann and George LIVINGSTON, Aug 1869 Hudson, NH
SULLIVAN, Mary C and Alexander PLUMMER, 30 Sep 1972 Hudson, NH
SULLIVAN, Maureen A and Harry M DAW, 24 Sep 1960 Hudson, NH
SULLIVAN, Michael J and Gloria D BOISCLAIR, 22 Jul 1967 Nashua, NH
SULLIVAN, Michael W and Suzanne T BOUCHARD, 01 Feb 1981 Nashua, NH
SULLIVAN, Minnie S and Smith S JACOBS, 14 Apr 1900 Hudson, NH

HUDSON, NH MARRIAGES

John Mulkey & Katherine Dundon
Lorenzo Jacobs & Amelia Brown
SULLIVAN, Nellie and Henry K LYNCH, 13 Jun 1869 Hudson, NH
SULLIVAN, Therese A and Albert R GETTY, 10 Jan 1970 Hudson, NH
SULLIVAN, William G and Kitrina NORRIS, 27 Aug 1982 Nashua, NH
SUMNER, Crystine A & Michael J MANCINI, 22 Apr 1978 Litchfield, NH
SUMRALL, Carol A and Frank R MENARD, 06 May 1978 Hudson, NH
SUMRALL, Cynthia Lo and David R CHACOS, 02 Aug 1980 Merrimack, NH
SUMRALL, Donna M and Timothy J KINGSLEY, 24 Sep 1978 Hudson, NH
SUND, Sylvia and Raymond HEBERT, 04 Oct 1947 Hudson, NH
SUNDQUIST, Eric L and Janice E DWYER, 08 Aug 1982 Hudson, NH
SUNDQUIST, Marcia J and Thomas A WILA, 14 Nov 1981 Hudson, NH
SURDAM, Dennis W and Marlene M SCHOFIELD, 14 Mar 1970 Nashua, NH
SURPRENANT, Jeannette and Roger J DION, 21 Jan 1967 Pelham, NH
SURPRENANT, Walter J and Lucille P LANGLOIS, 26 Jul 1981 Hudson, NH
SUSALKA, Wanda S and Dwight C ALEXANDER, 23 Nov 1947 Hudson, NH
SUTHERLAND, Alan M III and JoAnn R MELDREM, 04 Apr 1981 Hudson, NH
SUTHERLAND, Edward H and Karen J LOCKE, 26 Jan 1963 Hudson, NH
SUTHERLAND, Walter A and Margaret E CURRIE, 25 Oct 1935 Hudson, NH
SUTTON, Eleanor M and William R DALY, 23 Dec 1950 Hudson, NH
SUYKERBUYK, Guy P and Margaret A CARTER, 31 Jul 1982 Derry, NH
SUZEDELYS, John P and Eva R GAGNON, 12 Jun 1948 Nashua, NH
SWAIN, Howard F and Estella B AUDETTE, 06 Aug 1960 Hudson, NH
SWAIN, Laurie L and Larry T SAVAGE, 12 Jul 1974 Derry, NH
SWALLOW, Sherman J and Nettie MARSHALL, 05 Feb 1923 Nashua, NH
SWALLOW, William A and Nancy J LOVERING, 14 Jan 1873 Hudson, NH
SWANSON, Marc E and Laurie A KLATT, 20 Oct 1984 Hudson, NH
SWASEY, Annie L and Walter S FOGG, 15 Jan 1900 Hudson, NH
  W B Swasey & Fanny Ayre
  W W Fogg & Susan E Lord
SWASEY, F Joanne and Richard P STEVENS, 26 Nov 1952 Keene, NH
SWEATT, Roger R and Bonnie Lee JOHNSON, 06 Oct 1962 Nashua, NH
SWEATT, Safford and Olive LISLE, 03 Nov 1941 Hudson, NH
SWEENEY, Brian L and Shirley A WHEELER, 22 Sep 1978 Nashua, NH
SWEENEY, Clarence L and Marjorie G HOLLAND, 09 Aug 1947 Hudson, NH
SWEENEY, Patricia A and Robert H CLOUTIER, 15 Apr 1961 Nashua, NH
SWEENEY, Richard F and Katherine RICH, 25 Sep 1929 Nashua, NH
SWEENEY, Robert L and Laura C BURKE, 28 Apr 1981 Hudson, NH
SWEENEY, William and Bridget MJ CONSIDINE, 11 Oct 1891 Hudson, NH
  Edward Sweeney & Almira Martin
  Jonas Considine(Ireland)
SWEENIE, Bruce D and Roberta A NICHOLS, 11 Sep 1971 Hudson, NH
SWEET, Henry and Roxie J BARRETT, 10 May 1873 Hudson, NH
SWEET, Roland H and Kathleen M KELLEY, 10 Nov 1970 Nashua, NH
SWENSEN, Donald F and Mary D MILLER, 07 Dec 1980 Nashua, NH
SWIDERSKA, Maryann J and Robert D LOWE, 21 Jul 1955 Nashua, NH
SWINERTON, Berkley E and Thelma I ANNABLE, 23 Mar 1974 Hudson, NH
SWINERTON, Jean L and Dennis F COUTURIER, 21 Nov 1973 Pelham, NH
SWINGLER, Theta R and Michael F ELLIOTT, 30 Aug 1975 Hudson, NH
SWITSER, Jean C and William E ABBOTT, 06 Feb 1957 Hudson, NH
SWORD, Barbara A and Edmund M MARVELLI, 24 Dec 1949 Hudson, NH
SWOYER, Carl E and Christine MacLATCHY, 06 Feb 1982 Nashua, NH
SYLVESTER, Joyce A and Robert C DELONG, 04 Mar 1933 Hudson, NH
SYMONDS, Evan and Francis C III DAWSON, 07 Sep 1971 Hudson, NH
SYRENE, George F and Arlene N JOHNSON, 04 Jun 1957 Nashua, NH
SYRENE, John E and Annette C BLEAU, 05 May 1956 Nashua, NH
SYRENE, Wilfred F and Annette L GENDRON, 08 Oct 1960 Hudson, NH
SZABO, Muriel D and William J III ALLISON, 12 Feb 1966 Hudson, NH
SZALANSKI, Sharon B and Raynald J OUELLET, 23 Jun 1979 Hudson, NH
SZCZECHURA, Ursula M and Patrick J COURCY, 01 Jun 1957 Nashua, NH

HUDSON, NH MARRIAGES

SZEMKOWICZ, Gail J and Thomas R Jr LEMIEUX, 26 Nov 1984 Hudson, NH
SZERLOG, Madeline M & Roger E BOUCHARD, 28 May 1974 Manchester, NH
SZOPA, Richard W and Pamela E BOSKA, 21 Oct 1983 Canterbury, NH
SZOT, Wladyslowa and Stanley GALECKI, 17 Jan 1942 Manchester, NH
SZROM, James J and Pamela K JONES, 10 Jan 1982 Nashua, NH
SZUGDA, Chester F and Judith A KEELER, 18 Apr 1969 Keene, NH
SZUGDA, Leonard W and Margo S TAKACS, 07 Apr 1984 Nashua, NH
SZUKSTA, Walter F Jr & Mary Ellen LAROCQUE, 03 Nov 1984 Hudson, NH
TACEWICZ, Cindy M and Omar P LANPHER, 22 Nov 1984 Nashua, NH
TAFE, Bradley E and Barbara J TURCOTT, 26 Oct 1963 Hudson, NH
TAFFE, Patricia and Alva GALVIN, 18 Apr 1941 Hudson, NH
TAGG, Archie M and Marion B LANE, 07 Oct 1935 Hudson, NH
TAILLEUR, Adele M and John R McLAUGHLIN, 20 Feb 1983 Hudson, NH
TAINTER, David E and Marrietta BARNS, 15 Sep 1876 Nashua, NH
TAKACS, Margo S and Leonard W SZUGDA, 07 Apr 1984 Nashua, NH
TALBOT, George and Mary ROBINSON, 13 Nov 1825
TALBOT, Joseph R and Marianne LEVESQUE, 04 Aug 1934 Nashua, NH
TALBOT, Yvonne and Joseph J JEANNOTTE, 07 Nov 1925 Hudson, NH
TALLANT, Andrew and Sally PRATT, 14 Dec 1819
TALLANT, Andrew and Salley PRATT, 14 Dec 1819
TALLENT, Nita G and Dana L BOUCHER, 25 Apr 1980 Hudson, NH
TALLQUIST, Sandra S and Anthony J PERFITO, 24 Jul 1975 Milford, NH
TALTY, Christopher and Debra D BELLEFEUILLE, 21 Oct 1978 Hudson, NH
TAMERLEVICH, John F and Stella A BUZAREWICZ, 24 Jul 1942 Nashua, NH
TANDY, Helen M and Clayton B ABBOTT, 08 Jun 1935 Amherst, NH
TANEY, Yvette D and David P BIRCH, 04 Dec 1976 Hudson, NH
TANGUAY, Claire A and Turner K BROWN, 31 Aug 1957 Hudson, NH
TANGUAY, Constance and Raymond G LEMERISE, 30 May 1955 Nashua, NH
TANGUAY, Diane T and Lawrence P ARSENAULT, 29 Sep 1973 Hudson, NH
TANGUAY, Jeanne P and Roland A ROBILLARD, 29 Dec 1973 Hudson, NH
TANGUAY, Judith Rae and George A ST HILAIRE, 25 Aug 1973 Hudson, NH
TANGUAY, Patricia A and Terence A BURGESS, 14 Aug 1971 Nashua, NH
TARBELL, Avis and Parker RICHARDSON, 25 Feb 1812
TARBELL, Gertrude E and Lester A JOY, 16 Aug 1924 S Lyndeboro, NH
TARBELL, Rhoda and Silas Jr ROBY, 14 Mar 1799
TARBELL, Roda and Silas Jr ROBY, 14 Mar 1799
TARBOX, Betsey and Elijah HILLS, 12 Mar 1801
TARBOX, Carl C and Pearl I CONRAD, 22 Dec 1934 Hudson, NH
TARBOX, William and Sally WYMAN, 21 Jan 1798
TARBOX, William and Sally WYMAN, 21 Jun 1798
TARDIE, Kimberly A and Thomas P KILDUFF, 22 Jun 1985 Hudson, NH
TARDIF, Michael G and Darlene M RAYMOND, 21 May 1983 Nashua, NH
TARDIF, Rolande A and Joseph H BRESNAHAN, 13 Nov 1946 Salem, NH
TARDIFF, Theresa G and Hector H PREVOST, 20 May 1950 Nashua, NH
TARPINIAN, Zaven A and Helmi AIJALA, 04 Mar 1950 Hudson, NH
TARRALLI, Tufanio and Hilda MONTANARI, 28 Jul 1942 Hudson, NH
TARRANT, Patricia A and Frank J KELLEY, 13 Apr 1985 Hudson, NH
TARTAGLIA, Jean and John F FEROLITO, 13 May 1941 Hudson, NH
TASKER, Joseph P and Eunice R SENTER, May 1855
TATE, David A and Rosemary A PECHECO, 17 Jun 1972 Pelham, NH
TATE, Donna M and Bruce J CHRISTIANSEN, 18 Jul 1971 Hudson, NH
TATE, Geraldine and Ronald K TWARDOSKY, 22 Jun 1968 Hudson, NH
TATE, Gordon B and Dorothy L BEAUBIEN, 29 Apr 1950 Hudson, NH
TATE, June A and Donald J CLOUTIER, 06 Sep 1947 Nashua, NH
TATE, Linda A and Brian K KIERSTEAD, 31 Aug 1978 Nashua, NH
TATE, Millard F and Inez W CHAPPELLE, 28 Sep 1934 Hudson, NH
TATE, Robert A Jr and Diane L LEDOUX, 16 Sep 1967 Hudson, NH
TATE, Rupert E and Alice E BOULEY, 07 Jun 1941 Nashua, NH
TATE, Sandra E and Robert H Jr MORENCY, 30 Sep 1961 Hudson, NH
TATE, William M and Jacqueline McDONALD, 19 Sep 1971 Nashua, NH

HUDSON,NH MARRIAGES

TATE, William W and Katherine RUITER, 11 May 1946 Nashua, NH
TATEM, James M and Julie A LANKHORST, 25 Jun 1983 Hudson, NH
TATRO, Betty C and Roger R TORNSTROM, 29 Dec 1971 Manchester, NH
TATRO, Erlyan O and Ronald O LECLAIR, 06 May 1972 Hudson, NH
TATRO, Peggy D and Richard E DESTEFANO, 21 Aug 1982 Nashua, NH
TAVERNA, Frank J and Dorothy M DUTTON, 18 Mar 1972 Nashua, NH
TAYLOR, Ada E and William E GREEN, 14 Jul 1908 Hudson, NH
  W L Taylor & Ada A Leusotte
  Henry Green & Ida Henchrig
TAYLOR, Alex J and Debra P DOUCETTE, 01 May 1971 Nashua, NH
TAYLOR, Barbara H and Joseph W GRIGAS, 26 Jun 1982 Salem, NH
TAYLOR, Benjamin J and Bernice ELKIND, 26 Sep 1938 Nashua, NH
TAYLOR, Brenda L and Anthony J FERREIRA, 23 Sep 1978 Nashua, NH
TAYLOR, David R and Sandra J CHRISTIAN, 18 Sep 1965 Nashua, NH
TAYLOR, Elmer J and Jayne M BARRETT, 04 Feb 1984 Nashua, NH
TAYLOR, Emma and Jeremiah CARLTON, 20 Jun 1740
TAYLOR, Evalee and Howard C DULEY, 26 Jul 1970 Hudson, NH
TAYLOR, Evelyn and Melvin C ALLEN, 06 Sep 1941 Hudson, NH
TAYLOR, Frederick and Violet E HUNTER, 25 Dec 1936 Hudson, NH
TAYLOR, George and Charlotte FROST, 08 May 1859
TAYLOR, Harland D and Virginia L McLAVEY, 24 Jun 1956 Hudson, NH
TAYLOR, Hope I and Herman P RICHARDSON, 31 Jul 1937 Nashua, NH
TAYLOR, Ida M and Alen S MENTER, 20 Jan 1876 Hudson, NH
TAYLOR, Jacqueline and Vito A CAPRIO, 04 Jul 1959 Nashua, NH
TAYLOR, James E and Lois A MARDEN, 01 Aug 1982 Nashua, NH
TAYLOR, Jenny and Joseph F ANNIS, 15 Feb 1871 Hudson, NH
TAYLOR, Joyce B and Ralph DUDLEY, 05 Apr 1980 Nashua, NH
TAYLOR, Katherine and William RAGAN, 18 Dec 1976 Hudson, NH
TAYLOR, Laura J and Gerald R LALIBERTE, 28 Aug 1965 Nashua, NH
TAYLOR, Laurence P and Kathryn L POWLOWSKY, 03 Jun 1972 Hudson, NH
TAYLOR, Linda S and Raymond E CARROLL, 14 Jun 1969 Nashua, NH
TAYLOR, M Addie and John W FLETCHER, 01 Sep 1864
TAYLOR, Mary and Amos WHITTEMORE, 25 Nov 1766
TAYLOR, May and John H DAVIS, 11 Aug 1915 Nashua, NH
  Sidney T Oldall (England) & Elizabeth Brown (Nova Scotia)
  George W Davis(England) & Mary A Wilson (England)
TAYLOR, Myrtle and Chester P ROWELL, 11 Aug 1917 Hudson, NH
TAYLOR, Peter N and Jean S SERINO, 22 Oct 1983 Nashua, NH
TAYLOR, Richard A and Jean R GALIPEAU, 18 Sep 1981 Hudson, NH
TAYLOR, Richard D and Ellen L LEGASSE, 01 Apr 1970 Nashua, NH
TAYLOR, Robert J and Marion A BOYLE, 21 Aug 1937 Hudson, NH
TAYLOR, Susan and Charles H HOPKINS, 09 Oct 1860
TAYLOR, Suzanne F and Shawn B HOGAN, 01 Apr 1964 Nashua, NH
TAYLOR, Theresa E and Mitchell R FOURNIER, 26 May 1984 Hudson, NH
TAYLOR, Walter and Katherine HEMEON, 31 Oct 1964 Hudson, NH
TAYLOR, Walter T and Beatrice M BROWN, 01 Apr 1950 Hudson, NH
TAYLOR, Willie S and Addie E LEAZOTT, 25 Dec 1876 Hudson, NH
TAYNOR, Kenneth L and Rachel R DELISLE, 10 Jul 1975 Nashua, NH
TEBERAGE, Euserbe and Leah GAGUE, 17 Jul 1915 Nashua, NH
  Peter Teberage (Canada) & Julia Alair (Canada)
  Jules Gague(Canada) & Berube (Canada)
TEHRANI, Kourosh Karimi & Joyce M SIDILEAU, 02 Sep 1978 Nashua, NH
TEICHMANN, William A Jr & Sandra L GOODWIN, 08 Jul 1972 Hudson, NH
TELLIER, Patricia A & Larry D COOLBROTH, 11 Sep 1971 Hollis, NH
TELLIER, Suzanne E and Michael W HEBERT, 14 May 1983 Hudson, NH
TEMBLEY, Doris J and Normand A DUBE, 05 May 1945 Nashua, NH
TENNERINI, Louise and Bernard R LYON, 28 Mar 1948 Hudson, NH
TENNEY, Paul and Sally HILLS, 02 Dec 1819
TENNEY, Sarah and Frye GAGE, 24 Oct 1816
TENNEY, Sarah and Frye PAGE, 24 Oct 1816

HUDSON, NH MARRIAGES

TERRILL, Roger P and Norma L BARDSLEY, 15 Oct 1960 Hudson, NH
TERRIN, Francis E and Marjorie M MacLEOD, 16 Apr 1944 Hudson, NH
TERRY, Alberta and Merton C BENNETT, 15 Jun 1910 Hudson, NH
   Charles A Terry & Lucy M Cushing
   Edward N Bennett & Jennie F Perry
TERRY, Thomas D and Barbara R CROFT, 23 Mar 1949 Hudson, NH
TESSIER, Albert and Jeannette MARQUIS, 08 May 1937 Lowell, MA
TESSIER, Alberta C and Alfred LATULIPPE, 24 Nov 1938 Nashua, NH
TESSIER, Conrad H and Denise G ALLARD, 25 Apr 1969 Nashua, NH
TESSIER, Conrad H and Margaret M CURRAN, 12 Aug 1978 Hudson, NH
TESSIER, Cynthia L and George A Jr WISEMAN, 18 Aug 1974 Nashua, NH
TESSIER, Delaine N and Walter P Jr HOULE, 24 Aug 1968 Hudson, NH
TESSIER, Donald R and Mildred M YORK, 17 Nov 1962 Hudson, NH
TESSIER, Doris L and Ronald J FONTAINE, 17 Sep 1966 Hudson, NH
TESSIER, Henry A and Rose R DUCAS, 12 Nov 1945 Nashua, NH
TESSIER, Henry R and Teresa M GIOE, 12 Apr 1975 Nashua, NH
TESSIER, Jacqueline and Richard G BOILARD, 22 Jun 1957 Hudson, NH
TESSIER, Joseph R and Marie V DUMAIS, 26 Oct 1944 Nashua, NH
TESSIER, Kenneth N and Regina L CLARK, 26 Sep 1981 Hudson, NH
TESSIER, Linda M and Bruce R PERRY, 05 Sep 1970 Nashua, NH
TESSIER, Muriel L and Armand C LAGASSE, 22 Nov 1956 Hudson, NH
TESSIER, Norman L and Olive T OUELLETTE, 10 May 1947 Nashua, NH
TESSIER, Paul A and Rita V LAROUCHE, 25 Apr 1959 Hudson, NH
TESSIER, Raymond J and Linda C CURRAN, 29 Jul 1972 Hudson, NH
TESSIER, Rita P and Lester S GREENWOOD, 26 Feb 1963 Nashua, NH
TESSIER, Suzanne C and Gregory R GEIGER, 26 Aug 1972 Hudson, NH
TESSIER, Theresa R and Albert M SPAULDING, 09 Oct 1948 Nashua, NH
TETLER, Beverly A and Richard W ELLIS, 11 Oct 1952 Hudson, NH
TETLER, George W Jr and Helen C KUPCHUN, 20 Aug 1949 Nashua, NH
TETLOW, George H Jr and Cheryl G TRUDEAU, 09 Mar 1985 Hudson, NH
TETRAULT, Theresa L and Andrew M AUSTIN, 12 Feb 1983 Hudson, NH
TETRAULT, Thomas L and Corinne A GRAVES, 16 May 1976 Hudson, NH
TETREAU, Albert P and Cynthia R AVEDISIAN, 09 Aug 1981 Salem, NH
TETREAULT, Claire and George D KUNGULUS, 26 Nov 1965 Hudson, NH
TETREAULT, Eva D and Russell F ST PIERRE, 15 Dec 1949 Hudson, NH
TETREAULT, Joseph E and Pearl I HODGKINS, 04 Nov 1922 Hudson, NH
TETU, Emile J and Suzanne M CHARRON, 16 Jun 1962 Hudson, NH
THATCHER, Eben A and Angeline P ADAMS, 30 Jun 1903 Plymouth, MA
   Frank Thatcher & Eleanor Knowles
   Prescott Adams & Addie P Hills
THAU, Marcel and Francina KRAMER, 27 Jul 1943 Hudson, NH
THAYER, Amelia and John G RAYMOND, 16 Oct 1926 Nashua, NH
THAYER, Lucy M and Joseph HAMBLETT, 21 Apr 1846
THEBODEAU, Cheryl A and George J Jr BOUCHER, 16 May 1981 Hudson, NH
THEBODEAU, Donna L and Joseph R Jr BRIAND, 31 Oct 1968 Nashua, NH
THEBODEAU, Gloria M and Carl R EDWARDS, 21 Sep 1956 Nashua, NH
THEBODEAU, Louann M and Leonard A BOWDEN, 28 Jul 1984 Plaistow, NH
THEBODEAU, Michael D and Cheryl L LASTOWKA, 23 Apr 1977 Hudson, NH
THEBODEAU, Raymond P & Monique M DESROSIERS, 24 May 1985 Nashua, NH
THEODORE, Catherine and Mark R CHAPERON, 01 Apr 1981 Nashua, NH
THEODORE, Robert B and Karen A QUINN, 12 Apr 1980 Hudson, NH
THEOKAS, Linda G and David E THOMAS, 26 Aug 1984 Hudson, NH
THERIAN, Nettie and Eugene GIROUARD, 21 Jan 1919 Nashua, NH
THERIAULT, Alfred E and Rachel P MOREAU, 20 Feb 1954 Hudson, NH
THERIAULT, Diane and Alden D McGRAW, 15 May 1982 Brookline, NH
THERIAULT, Elizabeth and Richard A SCHNAIR, 02 Sep 1932 Nashua, NH
THERIAULT, Lionel and Yvonne MARTIN, 22 Jun 1935 Nashua, NH
THERIAULT, Lorette M and Edgar R BERARD, 01 Dec 1934 Nashua, NH
THERIAULT, M Claire and Fred T Jr GOODWIN, 27 Feb 1943 Hudson, NH
THERIAULT, Marc R and Patty J WITKOWSKI, 25 May 1985 Hudson, NH

HUDSON, NH MARRIAGES

THERIAULT, Raymond C and Alice FORGET, 14 Oct 1936 Nashua, NH
THERIAULT, William G and Ruthanne WRIGHT, 18 Oct 1969 Hudson, NH
THERNLEY, Brenda E and Manuel P RAPOSA, 15 Apr 1985 Hudson, NH
THEROUX, Lucille M and Leo Chas COUTU, 19 Nov 1976 Hudson, NH
THEROUX, Rachel L and Walter J STOCKLEY, 15 Apr 1950 Nashua, NH
THEROUX, Romeo H and Lucille M PROVENCHER, 26 Oct 1946 Nashua, NH
THEROUX, Therese M and Paul P DUBOWIK, 09 Oct 1976 Nashua, NH
THERRIAULT, Jeanine E & Raymond D LABRECQUE, 03 May 1974 Nashua, NH
THERRIEN, Alfred V and Sadie NELSON, 09 Feb 1935 Nashua, NH
THERRIEN, Alfred V and Claire COURCY, 15 Jul 1942 Nashua, NH
THERRIEN, Elaine S&Frederic S III POORE, 18 Apr 1970 Manchester, NH
THERRIEN, Richard A and Betty J SLATE, 08 Jan 1974 Nashua, NH
THERRIEN, Ronald R and Madeleine JETTE, 24 Nov 1960 Hudson, NH
THIBAULT, Claudette and Arthur A BOUFFARD, 08 Jun 1968 Nashua, NH
THIBAULT, Rose-Alma and Leo R VALLERAND, 04 Jul 1961 Hudson, NH
THIBEAULT, Roland H and Laurette T SIMARD, 07 Feb 1953 Hudson, NH
THIBODEAU, Arline M and Richard S LAWLER, 22 Sep 1979 Hudson, NH
THIBODEAU, Brenda L and Kenneth S DEPERRY, 04 May 1974 Hudson, NH
THIBODEAU, Cecile A and Roland E LATOUR, 20 Jun 1946 Salem, NH
THIBODEAU, Paul L and Dora C BURPEE, 18 Nov 1950 Hudson, NH
THIBODEAU, Robert R and Mildred F LEVESQUE, 15 Mar 1958 Hudson, NH
THIBODEAU, Roderick A and Betty-Jean DROUIN, 05 Mar 1975 Nashua, NH
THIEBAULT, Mary C and Howard R BURR, 01 Nov 1948 Hudson, NH
THIVIERGE, Janet E and Michael L ROTH, 22 Jan 1982 Nashua, NH
THOLANDER, Edith and Joseph R BOULANGER, 06 Jun 1953 Durham, NH
THOMAS, Albert S and Amand J HALL, 06 Oct 1878 Hudson, NH
   Augustus W Thomas (Middleboro, MA) & Sarah C (Middleboro, MA)
   John Hall(Orford, NH)
THOMAS, Annjene and Charles A HALE, 24 Feb 1872
THOMAS, Constantin and Marie VANGOS, 09 Jan 1938 Nashua, NH
THOMAS, David E and Linda G THEOKAS, 26 Aug 1984 Hudson, NH
THOMAS, Doris W and Anthony WALENT, 30 Jun 1949 Dracut, MA
THOMAS, Earl W Sr and Barbara E ESTEY, 06 Jan 1968 Hudson, NH
THOMAS, Ernest R Sr and Florence L DUCAS, 31 Dec 1953 Hudson, NH
THOMAS, Ernestine and George E GRANGER, 17 Oct 1939 Hudson, NH
THOMAS, Fay L and Donald J LITALIEN, 16 Jun 1951 Hudson, NH
THOMAS, Joanne L and Robert E NYSTROM, 07 Apr 1973 Nashua, NH
THOMAS, Linda T and George O SANDERS, 30 Nov 1882 Hudson, NH
   Tyler Thomas (Dracut, MA) & Eliza A Sprake (Hudson, NH)
   Abi Sanders(Hudson, NH) & Palmyra C Whittemore (Hudson, NH)
THOMAS, Marjorie C and John W McCALL, 19 Oct 1947 Hudson, NH
THOMAS, Mary A and Ronald V MEEDEN, 27 Sep 1980 Hudson, NH
THOMAS, Nettie and Augustus R MORRISON, 06 Dec 1871 Hudson, NH
THOMAS, Olive Lest and Albert John LUGIN, 14 Jan 1939 Hudson, NH
THOMAS, Pearl T and Laura E BLAISDELL, 10 Sep 1902 Conway, NH
   Tyler Thomas & Elizabeth A Sprake
   James Blaisdell & Laura Deering
THOMAS, Sharon H and Kenneth D ROSS, 10 Jun 1983 Nashua, NH
THOMAS, Tyler and Elizabeth SPRAKE, 23 Oct 1845
THOMAS, William H and Josephine OSGOOD, 04 Jul 1864
THOMPSON, Bell J and Ernest L SHAFNER, 15 Jul 1884 Hudson, NH
   John M Thompson (Kingston, MA) & Elizabeth O Marsh (Hudson, NH)
   Benjamin W Shafner(Granville, N S) & Mary E Hewitt (St John, N B)
THOMPSON, Blanche M and George M BROCK, 08 Sep 1897 Hudson, NH
   John M Thompson & Elizabeth Marsh
   William S Brock & Helen F Johnson
THOMPSON, Calvin E and Sheila J MIRON, 26 Oct 1973 Hudson, NH
THOMPSON, Dana S and Alice R DESJARDINS, 27 Aug 1937 Nashua, NH
THOMPSON, David G and Cynthia-Ruth HARDY, 19 Nov 1954 Nashua, NH
THOMPSON, Deborah H and Earl A DWIRE, 19 Jun 1971 Hudson, NH

HUDSON,NH MARRIAGES

THOMPSON, George H and Annie POFF, 24 Apr 1883 Hudson, NH
  Robert Thompson (England) & Mary Hattsley (England)
  John Poff(Ireland) & Eliza Boyd (Ireland)
THOMPSON, Gladys M and Frank N PARK, 24 Sep 1921 Nashua, NH
THOMPSON, Hattie E and Charles H CHASE, 09 Aug 1899 Nashua, NH
  M V R Thompson & Eliza E Heath
  Samuel Chase & Harriet E Brown
THOMPSON, Helen L and Rowe W KIMBALL, 20 Oct 1937 Hudson, NH
THOMPSON, Jennie L and Arthur B GROVER, 25 Dec 1893 Hudson, NH
  John M Thompson (Bridgewater) & Elizabeth Marsh (Hudson, NH)
  A H Grover(Berwick, ME) & E K Stoddard (Hingham, MA)
THOMPSON, John C and Mary L MESSERY, 05 Feb 1966 Pelham, NH
THOMPSON, John M and Elizabeth MARSH, 05 Oct 1852
THOMPSON, Josephine and Clarence E ROWELL, 29 Mar 1975 Hudson, NH
THOMPSON, Leslie L and Ruth M WOODWORTH, 24 Aug 1946 Hudson, NH
THOMPSON, Lillian and Hiram P WILSON, 25 Dec 1893 Hudson, NH
  John M Thompson (Bridgewater) & Elizabeth Marsh (Hudson, NH)
  William C Wilson(Concord, NH) & Sarah Tucker (Orange)
THOMPSON, Lydia M and Leland E HOWARD, 11 May 1940 Swanzey, NH
THOMPSON, Marion L and Roger R BOYER, 31 Oct 1959 Hudson, NH
THOMPSON, Nellie M and Paul Anson HEWITT, 28 Apr 1892 Hudson, NH
  John M Thompson (Bridgewater) & Elizabeth Marsh (Hudson, NH)
  Wm Hewett(St John, N B) & Frances Wright (St John, N B)
THOMPSON, Palmer C and Elizabeth GROVES, 05 Dec 1933 Lowell, MA
THOMPSON, Patricia M and Robert B LAWSON, 23 Sep 1978 Hudson, NH
THOMPSON, Peter Jon and Charlene A PIPER, 06 Jan 1978 Hudson, NH
THOMPSON, Peter-Jon and Nancy A WINSLOW, 20 Feb 1981 Hudson, NH
THOMPSON, Randall D & Victoria V VURPILLAT, 01 Jun 1968 Nashua, NH
THOMPSON, Randall D and Mary C MacDONALD, 18 Jun 1978 Nashua, NH
THOMPSON, Robert H and Georgena M MacLEOD, 30 Dec 1941 Hudson, NH
THOMPSON, Robert M and Georgia B HERBERT, 12 Dec 1937 Nashua, NH
THOMPSON, Robert M and Linda C PREYSNAR, 20 Nov 1971 Merrimack, NH
THOMPSON, Robert M Jr and Lorraine G PARKER, 20 Apr 1963 Hudson, NH
THOMPSON, Ruth E and Edward W COLBY, 30 Aug 1938 Hudson, NH
THOMPSON, Wayne L and Claire L LETENDRE, 18 Nov 1961 Nashua, NH
THOMSON, Geraldine and William L BUTMAN, 24 Aug 1969 Nashua, NH
THOMSON, Priscilla & Bartlett M HUTCHINSON, 04 Jun 1967 Nashua, NH
THORN, Albert C and Helen C NASH, 09 Nov 1906 Nashua, NH
  Charles E Thorn & Elyza Esty
  John Nash & Ellen Sullivan
THORNE, Bertha G and Frank H DURIVAGE, 27 May 1903 Hudson, NH
  Chas E Thorne & Eliza Esty
  Ransom Durivage & Genett Goodrich
THORNING, James C and Hattie M DAWSON, 24 Aug 1885 Nashua, NH
  Frederick Thorning (Mass) & Hannah Currier (Wilmington, MA)
  Frederick Dawson(England) & Maria Cook (England)
THORNTON, Deborah L and Richard A KELLEY, 14 Aug 1971 Hudson, NH
THORNTON, Pamela M and David R HOYT, 28 Jan 1970 Hudson, NH
THURLOW, Sylvia A and Edward P DOCKHAM, 08 Jul 1972 Merrimack, NH
THYLIN, Robert S and Jeannette RICH, 27 Apr 1957 Hudson, NH
TIBBETTS, Cecil Jr and Ruth CHAPLIN, 30 Jul 1938 Hudson, NH
TIBBETTS, Larry E and Marian J LEVESQUE, 01 Jun 1974 Hudson, NH
TIEBOR, Roland F Jr and Sharon L MEARS, 02 Apr 1971 Nashua, NH
TIERNEY, Frederick J and Raye A COMAN, 28 Jan 1978 Nashua, NH
TIERNEY, John A and Jacqueline EAVES, 17 Dec 1945 Nashua, NH
TIERNEY, Mary E and Arthur V VIGNOLA, 20 Oct 1942 Hudson, NH
TIERNEY, Vera R and John E BAKER, 05 Nov 1927 Nashua, NH
TIKKANEN, Geraldine and John J DALESSIO, 21 Oct 1983 Hudson, NH
TILTON, Donna L and John C LINDQUIST, 01 Jul 1972 Hudson, NH
TILTON, William W and Sarah A RICH, 17 Sep 1844

HUDSON, NH MARRIAGES

TINGLOF, Patricia G & Dennis J CASSALIA, 09 Oct 1982 Merrimack, NH
TINKER, Elijah and Rebecca H HILL, 12 Oct 1864
TINKER, Janet E and Winston P HEBB, 04 Jul 1941 Nashua, NH
TINKER, Sylvester and Lucinda F BATCHELDER, 30 Dec 1867
TIPPING, Paula E and Richard L KLEINER, 04 Feb 1967 Nashua, NH
TIRRELL, Stephen A and Debra J LAGASSE, 02 May 1981 Hudson, NH
TITCOMB, Albert Oli and Ella S SIMPSON, 05 Jun 1866
TITCOMB, Charles Ki and Laura Emil NICHOLS, 19 Mar 1874
TITCOMB, Chas K and Laura E NICHOLS, 19 Mar 1874 Londonderry, NH
TITCOMB, James Otis and Maria A GOULD, 21 Jul 1880
TITCOMB, Nellie J and Oscar O ARMSTRONG, 14 Mar 1877 Hudson, NH
TITCOMB, Simeon Cha and Sally Hale WEBSTER, 10 Nov 1842
TITELBAUM, Gilbert and Elena CHIARELLA, 15 Nov 1947 Hudson, NH
TITUS, Beverly A and Arthur W Jr ROBARE, 03 Sep 1949 Hudson, NH
TITUS, Orlanda E and Rowena M CUMMINGS, 05 Feb 1863
TOBIN, Stephen J and Linda A LAQUERRE, 27 Aug 1977 Hudson, NH
TODD, Dorothy and Clarence T JAMESON, 12 Oct 1946 Hudson, NH
TODD, Hedwidge L and Adrian G MAGRATH, 30 Nov 1946 Nashua, NH
TOLLE, William J and Alexandria CARRAHER, 01 Aug 1981 Hudson, NH
TOLLES, Henry D and Pauline L BLANCHARD, 06 Jun 1924 Hudson, NH
TOLMAN, Jessie A and Joel P DURANT, 15 Jul 1912 Hudson, NH
  Alexander Walker & Annie M Baker
  George W Durant & Georgianna Lunol
TOLON, Dorothy and Herman E HORNIG, 21 Aug 1934 Hudson, NH
TOMOU, Mary V and Christo C MALONIS, 23 Sep 1956 Nashua, NH
TORCOMIAN, Amy L and Paul F GAUVREAU, 26 Nov 1972 Hudson, NH
TORNSTROM, Roger R and Betty C TATRO, 29 Dec 1971 Manchester, NH
TORRES, John R and Zoe A MacDONALD, 22 Oct 1977 Hudson, NH
TORRES, Steven Reg and Debra Ann NASH, 09 Aug 1975 Nashua, NH
TORREY, David R and Joyce E DEMERS, 16 Jul 1960 Hudson, NH
TORREY, Franklin R and Jeannette GALIPEAULT, 27 Nov 1952 Nashua, NH
TORREY, Franklin R and Effie May OBAN, 05 Nov 1977 Hudson, NH
TORREY, Martha J and Albert A NARO, 21 Jun 1952 Nashua, NH
TORREY, Thomas P and Elaine R LEMIRE, 03 Jun 1972 Hudson, NH
TOTTE, Francis and Carol C McKEE, 16 Mar 1962 Hudson, NH
TOUPLIKIOTIS, Antonios and Karyn E MELOFSKY, 28 Apr 1976 Hudson, NH
TOUSIGNANT, M Cecile and Emery L DUPRES, 04 Oct 1935 Hudson, NH
TOUSSAINT, Irene M and William F RONAN, 29 Jun 1946 Hudson, NH
TOUSSAINT, Richard L and Rita L GAGNON, 08 Feb 1947 Nashua, NH
TOWER, Barbara J and Steven N SANBORN, 30 May 1982 Hudson, NH
TOWER, Kelly Leigh & Peter McGRANAGHAN, 30 Nov 1984 Londonderry, NH
TOWER, Laurie A and Wayne A FORRENCE, 01 Oct 1983 Nashua, NH
TOWLE, Charles H and Lizzie J BALDWIN, 20 Aug 1871
TOWLE, Scott D and Diane E KNIGHT, 14 Jul 1984 Nashua, NH
TOWNE, Georganna and James F BURNETT, 12 Jun 1889 Nashua, NH
  & Lydia E Towne (Nashua, NH)
  James Burnett(Lowell, MA) & Mary L McDonald (Annapolis, NS)
TOWNE, Lucy A and Benjamin C LEAR, 19 Sep 1849
TOWNE, Mary C and George W WOOD, 14 Jan 1862
TOWNE, Mary C and George W WOOD, 14 Jun 1862
TOWNES, Foster and Nancy CROSS, 28 Dec 1826
TOWNES, Mabel A and Daniel A MARTIN, 18 Feb 1894 Londonderry, NH
  Silas Townes & Robinson
  Wm H Martin(Canada) & Pennock
TOWNES, Oscar and Annette PARRIS, 26 Feb 1856
TOWNS, Albert O and Hannah J BURNHAM, 31 Oct 1881 Hudson, NH
  C J Towns (Londonderry, NH) & Clara H Brewster
  Amory Burnham(Hudson, NH) & Martha C Fowler
TOWNSEND, Archie L and Odell M CLAXTON, 05 Jan 1946 Hudson, NH
TOWNSEND, Jacqueline & Dennis J McCARTHY, 26 Nov 1966 Plaistow, NH

HUDSON,NH MARRIAGES

TOWNSEND, Larry W and Catherine LEARY, 16 Aug 1975 Litchfield, NH
TOWNSEND, Lester H and Gail C GOODWIN, 24 Jun 1967 Hudson, NH
TOWNSEND, Sherron L and Eugene C SMITH, 21 May 1966 Hudson, NH
TOZER, Arnold W and Georgina ALGER, 24 Jun 1949 Hudson, NH
TRACEY, Louis C and Madeleine FALZARONE, 18 Jan 1937 Hudson, NH
TRACEY, Maitland M and Donald H HOWES, 01 Jun 1929 Nashua, NH
TRACY, Clayton P and Sally M FAY, 15 Feb 1969 New Ipswich, NH
TRACY, Sadie B and Ezra A MARTIN, 24 Jun 1903 Nashua, NH
   James Wilson & Sarah B Wheeler
   Elisha Martin & Almira M Egerton
TRAER, Cathy Dian and Glenn Scot STETZLER, 17 Jul 1982 Hudson, NH
TRAFFORD, Dona M and Richard M POINTER, 08 Nov 1969 Hudson, NH
TRAFFORD, Doris E and Charles K HOLT, 27 May 1972 Hudson, NH
TRAHAN, Henry A and Theo M SANSOM, 26 May 1945 Nashua, NH
TRANT, John J and Cheryl A GIDLEY, 10 Aug 1981 Hudson, NH
TRASK, Kevin John and Lynne-Ann BURBINE, 08 Jun 1985 Hudson, NH
TRAVERS, Diane E and Andrew F SCARDINA, 30 Jan 1976 Hudson, NH
TRAVIS, Lynda E and Leon A Jr COOK, 24 Nov 1966 Exeter, NH
TREADWELL, Georgina and Philip MILMAN, 08 May 1941 Nashua, NH
TREFRY, Georgette and Nicholas J WHALEN, 31 Aug 1935 Hudson, NH
TREITEL, Robert J and Chong-Cha CLEAVELAND, 30 Sep 1982 Nashua, NH
TREMBLAY, Carmen M and Jay C III CHATMAS, 24 Jul 1981 Hudson, NH
TREMBLAY, Denise B and John M LAW, 15 Jan 1972 Nashua, NH
TREMBLAY, Harvey W and Philomene BLOOD, 14 Sep 1969 Hudson, NH
TREMBLAY, Kathleen A and David A FOLEY, 28 Feb 1970 Nashua, NH
TREMBLAY, Lorraine A and Rollin E BROWN, 21 Jan 1956 Hollis, NH
TREMBLAY, Louis S and Mary M HARRINGTON, 24 Jun 1971 Hudson, NH
TREMBLAY, Richard L & Jacqueline PELLETIER, 30 Aug 1958 Hudson, NH
TREMBLAY, Robert A and Laurette J BERUBE, 15 Nov 1947 Nashua, NH
TREPEN, Pitman N and Mary A FAIRBANKS, 11 Oct 1868 Hudson, NH
TRIPPLETON, Donald W and Lee M MARTIN, 12 Apr 1958 Hudson, NH
TRIPPLETON, Edward H and Gloria T GAGNON, 04 Jul 1973 Nashua, NH
TRIPPLETON, Michael S and Kelly J JUDKINS, 11 Sep 1976 Nashua, NH
TRIPPLETON, Simeon Jr and Vivian A LEMIRE, 19 Nov 1955 Hudson, NH
TRIPPLETON, Vivian A and Edgar G GUERRETTE, 27 May 1959 Hudson, NH
TROAST, Glenna G and Clifton H JOHNSON, 04 Sep 1971 Hudson, NH
TROISI, Phyllis An and Ned GARDNER, 23 Jun 1984 Nashua, NH
TROMBLEY, Clifford A and Constance CLOUTIER, 28 Nov 1959 Hudson, NH
TROMBLEY, Donald E and Sue Ann SEYMOUR, 01 May 1981 Hudson, NH
TROMBLEY, Esther A and Arnold M STANDISH, 15 Mar 1975 Nashua, NH
TROMBLEY, Evelyn R and Armand A Jr DECOTEAU, 30 May 1964 Nashua, NH
TROMBLY, Lisa Jane and John Denni QUINN, 20 Jun 1982 Goffstown, NH
TROMBLY, Stanley E and Miriam A SHEPHERD, 01 Jul 1946 Nashua, NH
TROTT, Melvin R and Shirley L CLARK, 28 Oct 1950 Hudson, NH
TROTTER, Susan M and Gary M BORGMAN, 21 Jan 1984 Hudson, NH
TROW, Arthur A and Laura BENSON, 26 Jun 1912 Londonderry, NH
   George W Trow & Permelia Shattuck
   Levi Cadwell & Abbie Bullard
TRUDEAU, Albert H and Carol P GARANT, 20 Aug 1966 Nashua, NH
TRUDEAU, Cheryl G and George H Jr TETLOW, 09 Mar 1985 Hudson, NH
TRUDEAU, Edgar A and Henrietta LEVESQUE, 30 Aug 1941 Nashua, NH
TRUDEAU, Emile and Margaret BOURDON, 05 Jul 1937 Nashua, NH
TRUDEAU, Lucille R and Gene R GRAVELLE, 12 Feb 1966 Hudson, NH
TRUDEAU, Martha A and Theodore V WATERMAN, 18 Jul 1959 Hudson, NH
TRUDEAU, Mary Jane and Dana E BARNES, 28 Jun 1980 Hudson, NH
TRUDEAU, Phyllis A and Robert C BRODEUR, 11 Jun 1960 Nashua, NH
TRUDEL, Dedier and Fabiana BONNEAU, 21 Dec 1929 Nashua, NH
TRUESDALE, Marion L and Dominic N STRACCO, 04 Dec 1948 Hudson, NH
TRUFANT, Arthur and Gertrude M CAMPBELL, 27 Jun 1923 Hudson, NH
TRUFANT, Frank A and Marion Eth CHASE, 01 Oct 1913 Hudson, NH

HUDSON, NH MARRIAGES

 John M Trufant & Flora E Turner
 DeWitt C Chase & Mabel A Nutt
TRUFANT, Lillian E and John M BREEN, 05 Oct 1920 Nashua, NH
TRUFANT, Ralph S and Annie J McDONALD, 18 Oct 1920 Nashua, NH
TRUFANT, Rena and Kenneth HALL, 25 Dec 1919 Hudson, NH
TRUFENT, Florence M and John MATHEWS, 18 Oct 1909 Nashua, NH
 John M Trufent & Flora Turner
 John Mathews & Isabella Hayes
TRUMBALL, Andrew and Margaret A PERRY, 18 Jan 1873 Hudson, NH
TRUMBULL, Willard I and Alice R ADAMS, 06 Sep 1926 Manchester, NH
TRZOS, Stephen L and Rosemarie LAVOIE, 15 Aug 1953 Hudson, NH
TRZOS, Stephen L and Pauline R ABBOTT, 22 Jan 1971 Hudson, NH
TSOTSIS, Bessie and Gary W ARNOLD, 19 Aug 1972 Manchester, NH
TSVOULEA, Cortena and George G BALUTS, 07 Sep 1921 Manchester, NH
TUBINIS, Thelma T and Jesse W FRANKLIN, 29 Jun 1940 Nashua, NH
TUCKER, Dorothy M and Leon WALKER, 06 Mar 1948 Hudson, NH
TUCKER, Dorothy O and Lloyd A OLESON, 09 Jan 1949 Hudson, NH
TUCKER, Lanora P and William G ACKERMAN, 27 Aug 1914 Nashua, NH
 Samuel Porter & Elenora Brothers
 William Ackerman & Henrietta Lane
TUCKER, Madeline S and Wilford A SMITH, 27 Feb 1970 Salem, NH
TUFTS, Harry J and Dorothy M CARTER, 23 Apr 1949 Hudson, NH
TUFTS, Sophia C and Daniel MARSH, 23 Sep 1849
TUFTS, William V and Anna L HORR, 14 Oct 1939 Nashua, NH
TUFTS, Willis C and Laura J CRESSY, 17 Apr 1912 Hudson, NH
 Joseph W Tufts & Mary S Rowell
 John G Cressy & Alice M Seavey
TULEJA, Joyce R and Jack HURLBERT, 24 Jun 1967 Hudson, NH
TULLEY, Vincent F II and Marisa L REILLY, 08 Oct 1983 Nashua, NH
TULLIS, Sheila A and Maurice R CLOUTIER, 04 Nov 1967 Nashua, NH
TUPPER, Margaret M and Thomas J HIRTH, 27 Feb 1965 Hudson, NH
TUPPER, Theresa A and Richard M Jr YORK, 04 May 1968 Nashua, NH
TURCOTT, Barbara J and Bradley E TAFE, 26 Oct 1963 Hudson, NH
TURCOTT, Robert V and Faith L KIERSTEAD, 21 Aug 1959 Hudson, NH
TURCOTTE, Nancy P & James A MATAROZZO, 25 Aug 1973 Hampton Fls, NH
TURCOTTE, Raymond L and Judith M LANDRY, 04 Oct 1975 Hudson, NH
TURCOTTE, Richard A and Pauline J CASE, 25 Jun 1960 Hudson, NH
TURCOTTE, Richard P and Anne M NOONEY, 23 Nov 1969 Hudson, NH
TURCOTTE, Richard P and Andrea K COPELAND, 21 May 1977 Nashua, NH
TURGEAN, Sylvis and Lawrence BRESNEHAN, 07 Nov 1936 Milford, NH
TURGEON, Carol B and George E HANNIGAN, 22 Feb 1971 Nashua, NH
TURMAINE, Leon R and Rose M SOLDI, 17 Jan 1948 Hudson, NH
TURMEL, Debra T and Eric R ESKELAND, 24 Aug 1979 Nashua, NH
TURMEL, Edgar L and Doris F GIRARD, 27 Sep 1952 Nashua, NH
TURMEL, Gerald J and Rachel P ZERBINOS, 27 Jul 1967 Hudson, NH
TURMEL, Girard J and Diana V BURGESS, 12 Jan 1957 Hudson, NH
TURMEL, Randy A and Susan L PELLETIER, 16 Nov 1984 Hudson, NH
TURMEL, Richard O and Jeanne E COTE, 31 Oct 1959 Nashua, NH
TURMEL, Robert L and Janice L CHERKES, 27 Apr 1957 Nashua, NH
TURMEL, Roger R and Claire B POMERLEAU, 31 Jan 1948 Nashua, NH
TURMEL, Theodore E and Claire E GRAVEL, 12 Jul 1968 Nashua, NH
TURMEL, Theresa D and Robert J MORIN, 14 Feb 1953 Hudson, NH
TURMEL, Virginia P and William R ECKLUND, 21 Nov 1959 Hudson, NH
TURMEL, Yolanda L and Lucien S VAILLANCOURT, 08 Feb 1958 Hudson, NH
TURNBULL, Eugene O N and Lillian J RILEY, 01 Aug 1936 Hudson, NH
TURNER, Janice L and Joseph M DEGULIS, 18 Dec 1971 Nashua, NH
TURNER, Norma N and Norman R APRIL, 05 Aug 1950 Hudson, NH
TURNER, Roderick W and Barbara J BRIGHAM, 26 Mar 1983 Nashua, NH
TURNQUIST, Bruce D and Christine HATFIELD, 21 Apr 1979 Hudson, NH
TURRELL, Barbara A and Joseph A JASPER, 16 Sep 1947 Hudson, NH

HUDSON,NH MARRIAGES

TUTTLE, Lowell and Josephine CLARK, 15 Jan 1894 Nashua, NH
  Francis Tuttle, Jr (Acton, MA) & Lucy Sargent (Stone, MA)
  Silas M Clark(Hillsborough, NH) & Caroline Sargent (Stone, MA)
TUTTLE, Marion and David L PRYOR, 30 Jun 1982 Hudson, NH
TUTTLE, Susan T and James M WAKEFIELD, 04 Jul 1976 Hudson, NH
TWARDOSKY, Carol A and Ernest T DOUCETTE, 27 Jun 1964 Merrimack, NH
TWARDOSKY, Joseph S Jr and Carol L RUSSELL, 20 Jan 1962 Hudson, NH
TWARDOSKY, Lucy A and Leon V Jr LAGASSE, 18 Jan 1964 Hudson, NH
TWARDOSKY, Ronald K and Geraldine TATE, 22 Jun 1968 Hudson, NH
TWARDOSKY, Walter G & Pauline F PHILIBOTTE, 30 Jun 1972 Hudson, NH
TWARDOSKY, William T and Doris A NOEL, 30 Dec 1961 Nashua, NH
TWISS, Darlene and Chris MASTERSON, 25 Mar 1972 Pelham, NH
TWISS, Diamond and Mary JONES, 10 Jul 1817
TWISS, Erma L and William H REED, 02 Sep 1938 Hudson, NH
TWISS, Walter and Ethel May WHEELER, 04 Nov 1918 Nashua, NH
TWITCHELL, Allan L and Jane M FOURNIER, 30 Dec 1972 Nashua, NH
TWOMBLY, James M and Nancy L MacKENZIE, 07 Nov 1981 Nashua, NH
TWOMBLY, Judith C and Gregory A REYNOLDS, 26 Jun 1965 Hudson, NH
TYLER, Brian E and Michelle I PARE, 08 Oct 1983 Manchester, NH
TYLER, Elizabeth and Byron A ROWELL, 01 Jun 1918 Barrington
TYLER, Gerald T and Carol A ALLISON, 05 Sep 1960 Nashua, NH
TYLER, Phoebe and Howard LEGALLEE, 02 Jul 1919 Barrington
TYRRELL, Elvira O and E Oscar POLLARD, 07 Nov 1862
TYRRELL, Elvira O and E Oscar POLLARD, 27 Nov 1862
UMSTEADT, John L and Janis C JAUNBRAL, 21 Apr 1985 Nashua, NH
UNDERCOFLER, Joseph M and Cynthia S MARTEIN, 25 May 1980 Hudson, NH
UNDERWOOD, Jeptha and Sarah CUMMINGS, 05 Aug 1805
UNDERWOOD, Lois and John CHASE, 27 Jun 1864
UNDERWOOD, Louisa and Doliver JOHNSON, Mar 1827
UNDERWOOD, Mary A and Alfred M HILLS, 08 Mar 1865
UNDERWOOD, Mary A and Alphonse HILLS, 28 Mar 1865
UPHAM, Beatrice D and Henry A LECLERC, 05 Oct 1946 Nashua, NH
UPHAM, Timothy W and Linda A JEFFERY, 21 May 1983 Hudson, NH
UPTON, Ethel M and Donald S RUCKMAN, 28 Jun 1975 Litchfield, NH
UPTON, Kathy E and Bernard J MARKS, 09 Jan 1982 Nashua, NH
UPTON, Kenneth E Jr and Kimberly A JONES, 30 Jun 1984 Nashua, NH
UPTON, Nancy E and Joseph KNOWLTON, 26 Nov 1877 Hudson, NH
  & Ina Spaffoni (Sharon, VT)
  Asa Knowlton(Shirley, MA)
URQUHART, Alan B and Rosemary G HORSTKOTTE, 17 Jun 1984 Hudson, NH
URQUHART, Rosamond and Winston L BLAKE, 01 Jan 1940 Lowell, MA
USOVICZ, Anna M and Raymond J RAUDONIS, 10 Oct 1964 Hudson, NH
USOVICZ, Peter M and Mary M DIGGINS, 16 Feb 1968 Nashua, NH
USOVICZ, Sandra M and Roger P COTE, 27 Jan 1962 Nashua, NH
USSERY, Emily Y and Richard C LEACH, 06 Nov 1965 Hudson, NH
USSERY, Emily Y and Frederick PETERS, 07 Oct 1967 Hudson, NH
USSERY, Richard F and Maureen W DAVIS, 18 Mar 1970 Nashua, NH
UZZLE, Molly and Mark D CLARK, 15 Mar 1985 Merrimack, NH
VADNEY, Brian W and Lori A DOW, 21 Jun 1980 Nashua, NH
VADNEY, Carol A and Paul L PELLETIER, 30 Sep 1967 Hudson, NH
VADNEY, Daniel R and France M FAUTEUX, 24 Jul 1976 Nashua, NH
VADNEY, George D and Esther A BORDEN, 07 Apr 1979 Hudson, NH
VADNEY, Suzanne N and William J Jr SLATUNAS, 29 Jul 1972 Hudson, NH
VAILLANCOURT, Catherine & Jackson G FOWLES, 19 May 1979 Hudson, NH
VAILLANCOURT, Corinne A & Robert L Jr BAKER, 15 Sep 1984 Hudson, NH
VAILLANCOURT, Dennis R and Kathleen N GODIN, 13 Sep 1975 Hudson, NH
VAILLANCOURT, Doris G and Robert L MASSEY, 04 Feb 1967 Nashua, NH
VAILLANCOURT, Joseph D and Gail Ann LEAVITT, 04 Jul 1982 Hudson, NH
VAILLANCOURT, Julie L and Roger E JETTE, 07 Jan 1961 Nashua, NH
VAILLANCOURT, Lucien and Lillian MALETTE, 24 Nov 1938 Nashua, NH

HUDSON,NH MARRIAGES

VAILLANCOURT, Lucien S and Yolanda L TURMEL, 08 Feb 1958 Hudson, NH
VALCOURT, Linda S and Michael G BRIAND, 19 Apr 1975 Litchfield, NH
VALCOURT, Therese N and Harold E DOW, 03 Sep 1945 Nashua, NH
VALENTI, Catherine E and Gerald J WALLACE, 18 Aug 1978 Hudson, NH
VALENTINE, Mary and James Unde JOHNSON, 03 Jun 1863
VALEQUET, Adelaide C and Herbert LIVINGSTON, 18 Oct 1903 Nashua, NH
  Manson B Patten & Nellie M Pemson
  Samuel Livingston & Henrietta Newton
VALERAS, Michael C and Leah A BEAULIEU, 23 Jun 1979 Nashua, NH
VALLANCOURT, Kristen G and Ronald E FARROW, 26 Dec 1965 Nashua, NH
VALLERAND, Leo R and Rose-Alma THIBAULT, 04 Jul 1961 Hudson, NH
VANDENBERG, Conrad W and Nancy L VANDERLOSK, 21 Apr 1984 Hudson, NH
VANDER-HEYDEN, Barbara A & Robert E BARNES, 06 Sep 1977 Hudson, NH
VANDERLOSK, Nancy L and Conrad W VANDENBERG, 21 Apr 1984 Hudson, NH
VANGOS, Marie and Constantin THOMAS, 09 Jan 1938 Nashua, NH
VANIER, Alfred Z and Irene I MERCIER, 29 Jan 1925 Hudson, NH
VANIER, Joseph Z and Yvonne LANGEIN, 13 Jun 1925 Hudson, NH
VANIER, Minnie J and Howard Peter MACKEY, 25 Feb 1922 Hudson, NH
VANVLEET, Jane M and John P ROBBINS, 31 Dec 1958 Hudson, NH
VANVLIET, Harold H and Shirley J GARDNER, 26 May 1966 Nashua, NH
VARA, Edward M and Ruth JONES, 26 Jun 1939 Hudson, NH
VARGAN, John G and Blanche E DECOSTA, 22 Feb 1938 Hudson, NH
VARNEY, Cynthia L and Michael E WALSH, 23 Oct 1982 Hudson, NH
VARNEY, Laurie A and Michel L PELLERIN, 03 Oct 1981 Hudson, NH
VARNEY, Mary E and Almon H KELLEY, 28 May 1955 Nashua, NH
VARNEY, Steven Arm and Kathleen A GRIFFIN, 21 Jul 1973 Hudson, NH
VARNUM, Jeremiah and Mehittabel FORD, 05 Mar 1822
VARNUM, Joseph and Ruth Moody JOHNSON, 21 Feb 1800
VARNUM, Joseph and Ruth Moody JOHNSON, 20 Feb 1800
VARNUM, Mary and Eleazer CUMMINGS, 28 Jul 1734
VASHER, Bernice I and Henry J LANDRY, 06 Mar 1965 Nashua, NH
VASSILAKOS, Katherine and Thomas E SMITH, 30 Nov 1973 Nashua, NH
VASSILAKOS, Susan B and James H ABBOTT, 05 Feb 1970 Nashua, NH
VASTA, Rosalie and Prentice I ROBINSON, 27 May 1971 Nashua, NH
VAUGHAN, Nellie R and Leslie H WATERMAN, 10 Oct 1906 Hudson, NH
  Henry E Vaughan & Susan A Ranson
  Herman Waterman & Alocia Ashman
VAYENS, Arthur Jr and Velda V DATU, 12 Jun 1983 Hudson, NH
VAYENS, Debora M and Anthony R II RICCIO, 21 Jan 1978 Hudson, NH
VAYENS, Jane L and Calvin T HAYES, 13 Oct 1962 Hudson, NH
VAYENS, Phyllis E and Edward H KING, 28 Jun 1980 Hudson, NH
VAYENS, Wanda L and David L PELLETIER, 14 Aug 1982 Hudson, NH
VAYO, Joan T and Natale R MARINELLO, 03 Jul 1950 Hudson, NH
VAZAKAS, Dimitrios and Sophie FALCOS, 31 Dec 1981 Hudson, NH
VEILLEUX, Yvan and Judith A DEMANCHE, 12 Jun 1967 Hudson, NH
VEINOT, Robert S and Darlene E JUDKINS, 14 Jun 1975 Nashua, NH
VENNE, Roland and Ruth ANNIS, 15 Nov 1941 Dracut, MA
VENNE, Ruth I and Renie J FRASER, 25 Jun 1955 Hudson, NH
VENNE, Violet and Francis E LOUGEE, 04 Feb 1939 Lowell, MA
VENO, Edith L and Thomas G MARTIN, 14 Oct 1950 Hudson, NH
VENTURA, Walter and Lena R BRIENZA, 14 May 1943 Hudson, NH
VERLEY, Raymond E Jr and Janice R FINNEGAN, 12 Sep 1981 Hudson, NH
VERRIER, Rita M and Walter W JOHNSON, 13 Jan 1949 Hudson, NH
VERRILLI, Anthony J and Maria L BATES, 30 May 1982 Hudson, NH
VERRY, Edward H and Patricia L PLYNKOFSKY, 28 Sep 1968 Hudson, NH
VERSECKES, Val and Josephine LABRIE, 03 Jul 1948 Hudson, NH
VERSECKES, Valdamas and Rita M ANGELO, 04 May 1946 Hudson, NH
VERVILLE, Louise and Francis E WALDORF, 25 Jan 1939 Nashua, NH
VESEY, Helen M and Charles M GUELI, 01 May 1934 Hudson, NH
VICKERS, Frank and Ruth O'NEIL, 27 Mar 1948 Hudson, NH

HUDSON,NH MARRIAGES

VICKERY, William R and Leontine BURELLE, 23 Dec 1961 Nashua, NH
VIENS, Antoine I and Reina I CARON, 26 Nov 1949 Nashua, NH
VIENS, Carmen M and David E SARVER, 11 Aug 1984 Hudson, NH
VIENS, Denise Ann and Robert G ST CYR, 29 Sep 1973 Hudson, NH
VIENS, Diane L and Clyde H MASTERSON, 03 Jul 1970 Bennington, NH
VIENS, Elaine L and Charles D DAVIDSON, 02 May 1981 Hudson, NH
VIENS, Gerard L and Medora LEFEBVRE, 18 May 1946 Allenstown, NH
VIENS, Lorraine G and Leo J Jr GAGNON, 21 May 1966 Hudson, NH
VIENS, Mary F and Armand L SOUCY, 04 Jul 1942 Nashua, NH
VIENS, Reina I and Norman R BOUCHER, 27 Jun 1975 Hudson, NH
VIENS, Ronald A and Susan B FRENCH, 07 Sep 1974 Nashua, NH
VIGDOR, Norma C and Francis D MALTBY, 15 Apr 1947 Hudson, NH
VIGLONE, Anthony C and Catherine BURNS, 12 Dec 1934 Hudson, NH
VIGNEAULT, Edmond and Clara N LAMBERT, 07 Nov 1915 Hudson, NH
   Petrus Vigneault (Canada) & Elenard Gaudette (Canada)
   Albert Langelier(Holbrook, MA) & Phebe Ouilette (Canada)
VIGNEAULT, Joan S and Maurice E LACHANCE, 23 Nov 1967 Nashua, NH
VIGNEAULT, Pauline C and Paul W WHITTEMORE, 12 Aug 1961 Nashua, NH
VIGNEAULT, Victor R & Marion Post HARDMAN, 09 Sep 1978 Nashua, NH
VIGNOLA, Alan M and Lyn M RUANE, 01 Sep 1979 Hudson, NH
VIGNOLA, Arthur V and Mary E TIERNEY, 20 Oct 1942 Hudson, NH
VIGNOLA, Bruce N and Jeanne N BERUBE, 08 Dec 1972 Hudson, NH
VIGNOLA, Mary E and Adrien J CONSTANT, 05 Jul 1952 Hudson, NH
VIGNOLA, Patricia C and Francis E SMALL, 17 Jan 1959 Nashua, NH
VIGNOLA, Paul A and Phyllis M SMITH, 07 May 1960 Hudson, NH
VIGNOLA, Pauline D and Raymond E LUSIGNAN, 08 Jun 1957 Hudson, NH
VIGNOLA, Peggy L and Roger A FRENETTE, 15 Jun 1959 Hudson, NH
VIGNOLA, Philip E and Charlene D GIFFORD, 15 Oct 1966 Nashua, NH
VILLEMAIRE, Grace D and Raymond J MARTIN, 31 Dec 1957 Derry, NH
VILLEMURE, Helene F and Raymond K JOSEF, 29 Sep 1956 Manchester, NH
VINCENT, Jeannine D and Gary P LAMPRON, 11 Apr 1973 Manchester, NH
VINCENT, Raymond F and Mary M PINTO, 08 Jul 1950 Hudson, NH
VIOLETTE, Bertha M and Ralph E DUDLEY, 15 May 1965 Hudson, NH
VIOLETTE, Michael J and Mary E KENNEDY, 15 Jun 1985 Hudson, NH
VISCO, Elizabeth and William H GUTHREAU, 13 Sep 1947 Nashua, NH
VITTUM, Albert W and Katherine NORTH, 15 Mar 1911 Hudson, NH
   Frank H Vittum & Flora L Merrill
   James North & Jane Edwards
VIVIER, Patricia I and Gerald R COBLEIGH, 23 Jan 1982 Hudson, NH
VOGEL, Glenn A and Suh J GOU, 29 Dec 1979 Salem, NH
VOLGER, Arthur and Mary Alice MOREAU, 13 Aug 1929 Nashua, NH
VOLIANITES, Andrea and Bruce L BRIAND, 04 Mar 1979 Pelham, NH
VOLSICK, Victoria and Stanley J SOTECK, 04 Jul 1947 Hudson, NH
VOSE, George H and Mary B SCALES, 14 Nov 1861
VOSE, Lester E and Marion E GOING, 11 Oct 1940 Hudson, NH
VOTSOTIS, Cleopatra and Chris CASTLE, 17 Aug 1948 Hudson, NH
VOYER, Gerard E and Marie F O OSMER, 26 Apr 1944 Nashua, NH
VOYMAS, Marion A and Francis T SMITH, 30 Sep 1938 Hudson, NH
VRABLIC, Walter S and Amanda M CLARKE, 31 Dec 1982 Hudson, NH
VURPILLAT, Victoria V & Randall D THOMPSON, 01 Jun 1968 Nashua, NH
VYDFOL, Sophie and Ernest G GRYGIEL, 01 Feb 1947 Nashua, NH
WADE, Bettie and William L CROSS, 31 Aug 1872 Hudson, NH
WADLEGGER, Robert Jr and Rose-Mari FORSMAN, 25 Oct 1969 Keene, NH
WADLEIGH, Clarence B and Cornelia E FRENCH, 20 Jun 1922 Hudson, NH
WADLEIGH, Hannah P and Calvin POLLARD, 26 Feb 1861
WADLEIGH, Henry C and Mildred C SILVER, 23 Jul 1926 Hudson, NH
WADLEIGH, William H and Rebecca W LADD, 10 Mar 1859
WADLEY, Hannah P and Calvin POLLARD, 26 Feb 1861
WAGNER, Dolores T and John T JACOBS, 31 Mar 1947 Hudson, NH
WAISANEN, Tyler A and Kathy J GIGUERE, 30 Jun 1984 Nashua, NH

HUDSON, NH MARRIAGES

WAISWILOS, Stanley E and Joyce A DELUDE, 27 Nov 1965 Hudson, NH
WAKEFIELD, James M and Susan T TUTTLE, 04 Jul 1976 Hudson, NH
WAKER, Eda L and Donald L POULIN, 07 Nov 1981 Hudson, NH
WALCH, Charles J and Elizabeth PITCHER, 08 Apr 1937 Nashua, NH
WALCH, Frank A and Ella Franc WEBSTER, 11 May 1879
WALCH, Frank A and Ella F WEBSTER, 11 May 1879 Tyngsboro, MA
   James Walch (Barnstead, NH) & Susan (Princeton, MA)
   Kimball Webster(Pelham, NH) & Afiah (Pelham, NH)
WALCH, Marion Jen and Cortes Ear FARNUM, 27 Sep 1909 Hudson, NH
   Clarence E Walch & Delia E Hutchins
   Frank N Farnum & Anna F Curey
WALDORF, Francis E and Louise VERVILLE, 25 Jan 1939 Nashua, NH
WALENT, Anthony and Doris W THOMAS, 30 Jun 1949 Dracut, MA
WALKAWICZ, Agnes S and John E KAPISKY, 04 Sep 1937 Nashua, NH
WALKER, Deborah E and Paul E HOWE, 29 May 1971 Hudson, NH
WALKER, Gerry and Ellen D BUNDY, 04 Jun 1890 Hudson, NH
   James G Walker (New York) & Sarah Bragdon (New York)
   Amasa T Bundy(Walpole, MA) & Ellen F Worcester (Groton, MA)
WALKER, Grace May and Winford SCHURMAN, 18 Mar 1897 Hudson, NH
   James G Walker & Mary Pembleton
   Major Schurman & Mary Smith
WALKER, Leon and Dorothy M TUCKER, 06 Mar 1948 Hudson, NH
WALKER, Louise C & Claude E HAMMOND, 06 Aug 1933 Old Orchard Bch, ME
WALKER, Martha J and Austin BAILEY, 05 Sep 1860
WALKER, Michael C and Betty L McGUIRE, 20 Jun 1981 Hudson, NH
WALKER, Michael W and Joan Marie CRESTA, 03 Aug 1974 Hudson, NH
WALKER, Pamela and Terry R PHAIR, 20 Jun 1970 Dover, NH
WALKER, Phebe and James HUBBARD, 13 Dec 1818
WALKER, Ralph C and Gertrude E SMITH, 26 Apr 1955 Hudson, NH
WALKER, Samuel W and Elizabeth GOODWIN, 11 Jul 1866
WALKER, Thomas R and Brenda D MITTON, 17 Sep 1966 Hudson, NH
WALL, Elizabeth and Carl NEUFFER, 04 Mar 1946 Milford, NH
WALL, Joseph F Jr and Catherine SKALECKI, 11 Sep 1948 Hudson, NH
WALLACE, Bentham A and Adelaide M DENICOLA, 27 Feb 1976 Hudson, NH
WALLACE, Gerald J and Catherine E VALENTI, 18 Aug 1978 Hudson, NH
WALLACE, Geraldine and Peter S EDELMAN, 14 Feb 1970 Nashua, NH
WALLACE, Gregg P and Ev Lynn CAREY, 17 Nov 1981 Nashua, NH
WALLACE, Hosea C and Harriet T MINOT, 14 Mar 1877 Hudson, NH
WALLACE, Mary G and David P GARRIGAN, 22 May 1946 Nashua, NH
WALLACE, Susan J and Gregory A HULL, 30 Aug 1980 Nashua, NH
WALLACE, Teresa M and Richard E SMITH, 22 Sep 1984 Hudson, NH
WALLACE, Valerie and Wayne E YOHE, 05 Jul 1981 Hudson, NH
WALLACE, William C and Gladys McCABE, 06 Dec 1941 Hudson, NH
WALLIS, Harold L and Marilyn P WHITNEY, 30 Jun 1951 Nashua, NH
WALLS, Wilbur L and Gertrude I HINDS, 18 Mar 1949 Hudson, NH
WALSER, Shirley J and Claude A PROVENCHER, 18 Nov 1967 Hudson, NH
WALSH, Arthur E and Mary T WHALEN, 30 Jun 1962 Hudson, NH
WALSH, Debra A and Roy A GREAVES, 19 Sep 1982 Hudson, NH
WALSH, June M and Gary P LAPHAM, 03 Aug 1968 Hudson, NH
WALSH, Michael E and Cynthia L VARNEY, 23 Oct 1982 Hudson, NH
WALSH, Rosemary E and William J GILBRIDE, 19 Aug 1950 Hudson, NH
WALTER, Barbara M and John B STRESSENGER, 16 Nov 1929 Hudson, NH
WALTER, Kenneth I and Sandra E DUDLEY, 08 Jul 1972 Mont Vernon, NH
WALTERS, Betty C and John F Jr KEARNS, 27 Oct 1984 Hudson, NH
WALTERS, Donna M and Richard E OUELLET, 21 Mar 1981 Hudson, NH
WALTON, Addie M and Willard H WEBSTER, 19 Oct 1862
WALTON, Waldo P and Jennie A MARTIN, 19 Feb 1877 Hudson, NH
WALWOOD, George J and Grace A KENEFINK, 13 Aug 1940 Hudson, NH
WAMBOLDT, James P and Jeanne A ROUSSEL, 12 Oct 1984 Hudson, NH
WANDERS, John F and Pamela A GALLANT, 07 Jun 1975 Hudson, NH

HUDSON,NH MARRIAGES

WARD, H Francena and David HASELTON, 28 Nov 1861
WARD, Jonathan P and Kathleen A BOLTON, 27 May 1978 Hudson, NH
WARD, Martha and Alphonse ROBERTS, 01 Mar 1900 Nashua, NH
   Henry Roberts & Martha Fuller
WARDWELL, Darlene E and Lucien R ST GEORGE, 28 Oct 1967 Nashua, NH
WARDWELL, Nancy L and Robert G MEIER, 14 Mar 1964 Hudson, NH
WARDWELL, Robert B and Margaret R ROCHE, 19 Dec 1933 Nashua, NH
WARDWELL, Thurlow E and Laurette J NADEAU, 16 Dec 1967 Hudson, NH
WARDWELL, Winifred D and Robert W SHEPHERD, 02 May 1964 Hudson, NH
WARE, Daniel G and Eva A RIPLEY, 05 May 1929 Hudson, NH
WARLEY, Lillian R and Richard P CARROLL, 27 Jan 1961 Pelham, NH
WARREN, Cyrus and Susanna B WINN, 06 Jun 1826
WARREN, Harriet L and John F MARSH, 22 Jan 1849
WARREN, Philip C and Gloria A LARO, 18 Jun 1983 Hudson, NH
WARRINER, Susan Mari and David Mich JONES, 22 Nov 1980 Hudson, NH
WARRINGTON, Ellen Mary and Gregory T SAVAGE, 21 Oct 1972 Nashua, NH
WARSON, Janna and Jonathan FERGUSON, 23 Oct 1800
WARTELLA, Stephen W and Edi-Lu KENT, 14 Aug 1982 Nashua, NH
WASHBURN, Lola V and John R DONAHUE, 07 Jul 1950 Hudson, NH
WASON, Alcinda and Albon H BAILEY, 01 Sep 1864
WASON, Hannah and Moody HARDY, 21 Jan 1779
WASON, Philena A and Obediah F SMITH, 31 May 1865
WASON, Sally and James BARNET, 02 Mar 1800
WASON, Sally and James BARRETT, 08 Mar 1800
WASON, Sally and Appolas PRATT, 15 Mar 1804
WASON, Sally and Appollos PRUTE, 15 Mar 1804
WASON, Sarah and Joseph SMITH, 19 Dec 1816
WASSON, Marguerite and William C LONGUA, 29 Jan 1972 Nashua, NH
WASSON, Mary Louis and Stephen P ROCHE, 26 Apr 1969 Hudson, NH
WATERMAN, Leslie H and Nellie R VAUGHAN, 10 Oct 1906 Hudson, NH
   Herman Waterman & Alocia Ashman
   Henry E Vaughan & Susan A Ranson
WATERMAN, Theodore V and Martha A TRUDEAU, 18 Jul 1959 Hudson, NH
WATERMAN, Warren F and Elizabeth ROSS, 29 Jul 1942 Hudson, NH
WATKINS, Eileen U & Arthur J Jr KASHULINES, 09 Sep 1950 Nashua, NH
WATKINS, Lellie R and Fred A ANNIS, 24 Jan 1901 Hudson, NH
   John O Clark (Hopkinton) & Arvilla J Runnells (Deering)
   Wm P Annis(Londonderry, NH) & Drusetta S Stearns (Lincolnville)
WATROUSE, Curtis M and Germaine A LAQUERRE, 13 Jun 1970 Nashua, NH
WATSON, Amanda M and Frank W BLAKE, 31 Aug 1893 Hudson, NH
   Joseph H Blake(Alexandria) & Elizabeth Barrett (Charlestown, MA)
WATSON, Angie M and John A FONTAIN, 09 Apr 1894 Londonderry, NH
   Richard S Lund (Conway) & Mary G Maxwell (Madison)
   Joseph Fontain & Loraine Turong (Prov Quebec)
WATSON, James F and Julia BATCHELDER, 20 May 1875
WATSON, Kenneth W and Theresa J COOPER, 22 Jun 1974 Nashua, NH
WATSON, Lilla May and Robert L HAMMOND, 07 Feb 1940 Hudson, NH
WATSON, Owen G and Donna J CAGE, 05 Dec 1983 Nashua, NH
WATSON, Richard A and Priscilla MARSHALL, 25 Apr 1970 Nashua, NH
WATSON, William A and Arline K ROTH, 02 Jul 1963 Nashua, NH
WATTS, Carol A and Martin A MORASSE, 21 Oct 1967 Hudson, NH
WATTS, Cathy L and Albion J Jr CARTER, 15 Feb 1969 Hudson, NH
WATTS, Donna F and Normand H ST ONGE, 22 May 1965 Manchester, NH
WATTS, Ernestine and Ronald G DUPLEASE, 12 Oct 1973 Nashua, NH
WATTS, Linda J and Neil F DESJARDINS, 25 Jul 1969 Hudson, NH
WATTS, Mary E and Frank A CONNELL, 12 Jun 1901 Hudson, NH
   Lorenzo Watts (Chazy, NY) & Alvira Parks (Moores, NY)
   Philip J Connell(Hudson, NH) & Hannah E Hardy (Hudson, NH)
WATTS, Raymond L and Marion I EAGLES, 03 Sep 1932 Hudson, NH
WATTS, Richard R Sr & Marilyn M CHENELLE, 11 May 1985 Merrimack, NH

HUDSON,NH MARRIAGES

WATTS, William H and Ida J WESTON, 17 Sep 1904 Wilton, NH
  Lorenzo Watts & Alvina Parks
  Fred Weston & Ida A Wellman
WEAVER, Clinton M Jr and Lisa M J CLOUTIER, 21 Aug 1982 Hudson, NH
WEAVER, Joseph D and Susan F BOUCHER, 05 Sep 1981 Londonderry, NH
WEBB, Pearl G and Alfred O POIRIER, 07 Dec 1946 Hudson, NH
WEBB, Warren C and G Louise QUEENEY, 02 Sep 1950 Hudson, NH
WEBBER, Abel Jr and Betsey PAGE, 18 Nov 1819
WEBBER, Abel Jr and Betsey PAGE, 18 May 1819
WEBBER, Albert K and Anneliese OBST, 02 Aug 1947 Hudson, NH
WEBBER, George C and Clara M STEELE, Feb 1856
WEBBER, George W H and Carrie I PAINE, 01 Feb 1912 Nashua, NH
  William H Webber & Hattie D Burdett
  Leonard B Paine & Susanna W Beals
WEBER, John F and Louise P DENESKA, 25 Sep 1948 Hudson, NH
WEBSTER, Abigail and Zachariah HARDY, 14 Nov 1822
WEBSTER, Benjamin and Submitte KITTREDGE, 1816
  Jonathan Kittredge
WEBSTER, Brinton M and Lizzie H SMITH, 29 Aug 1894 Hudson, NH
  Nathan P Webster & Susan M Morrison
  Wm H Smith(Guilford, ME) & Elisa M Tuck
WEBSTER, Charles Ot and Laurette HAMBLETT, 17 Apr 1856
  Benjamin Webster
WEBSTER, Charles Ot and Densie Lou PEASLEY,
WEBSTER, Clara F and Timothy O ROBERTS, 08 Jul 1871
  Simon G Webster
WEBSTER, Daniel G and Marion R PARMENTER, 03 Oct 1931 Nashua, NH
WEBSTER, Daniel Haz and Louisa KELLEY, 13 Jan 1847
WEBSTER, Eben W and Ellen WENTWORTH, 03 Jul 1859
WEBSTER, Eliza B and Charles C LESLIE, 16 Dec 1880 Londonderry, NH
  Kimball Webster (Pelham, NH) & Abiah Cutter (Pelham, NH)
  William H Leslie(Cornish, NH) & Betsy McAlpine (Hopkinton, NH)
WEBSTER, Eliza Ball and Charles C LESLIE, 16 Dec 1880
WEBSTER, Elizabeth and Warren BLODGETT, 18 May 1858
WEBSTER, Ella F and Frank A WALCH, 11 May 1879 Tyngsboro, MA
  Kimball Webster (Pelham, NH) & Afiah (Pelham, NH)
  James Walch(Barnstead, NH) & Susan (Princeton, MA)
WEBSTER, Ella Franc and Frank A WALCH, 11 May 1879
WEBSTER, Elmira and Bailey Kim FLAGG, 28 Nov 1847
  Benjamin Webster
WEBSTER, Gary L and Constance PAQUETTE, 21 Aug 1971 Hudson, NH
WEBSTER, Geo K and Emily Ann WOODBURY, 30 Apr 1864
  Benjamin Webster
WEBSTER, George M and Sarah CLATUR, 1855
WEBSTER, Geraldine and Vernon M BUFFUM, 13 Aug 1955 Hudson, NH
WEBSTER, Hannah and Thomas CUMMINGS, Nov 1815
WEBSTER, Hannah Jan and George W SILVER, 1853
WEBSTER, Isaac and Sibbel KELLY, 1812
WEBSTER, James John and Sophia G BLAISDELL, 12 Feb 1833
WEBSTER, John and Emily ROBERTS, 01 Jul 1853
WEBSTER, John and Luella A PIPER, 05 Jun 1859
WEBSTER, John and Sarah HARPER, 17 Nov 1865
WEBSTER, John and Hannah CUMMINGS, 22 Aug 1815
WEBSTER, John C and Addie Lucr CURRIER, 19 Mar 1865
WEBSTER, John E and Hannah C KENNISTON, 13 Nov 1856
WEBSTER, John P and Asenath EMERSON, 10 Sep 1818
WEBSTER, Julia A and John A ROBINSON, 05 Mar 1890 Nashua, NH
  Kimball Webster (Pelham, NH) & Abiah Cutter (Pelham, NH)
  Alp Robinson(Hudson, NH) & Louisa A Haselton (Hudson, NH)
WEBSTER, Kimball and Abiah CUTTER, 29 Jan 1857

HUDSON, NH MARRIAGES

WEBSTER, Lizzie and Horace J MARTIN, 17 Jun 1876 Hudson, NH
WEBSTER, Lizzie Jan and Horace A MARTIN, 18 Jun 1875
WEBSTER, Louisa U and John H BAKER, 09 Dec 1846
WEBSTER, Lucy Ann and Daniel P CLUFF, 29 Dec 1849
WEBSTER, Lydia Fran and Guilford A LEWIS, 15 Apr 1877
WEBSTER, Lyman O and Sarah N BROWN, 07 Sep 1851
WEBSTER, Mark H and Sarah T PALMER, 06 Mar 1828
WEBSTER, Mark H and Sarah HARWOOD, 11 Nov 1835
WEBSTER, Mark H and Sally BAKER, 29 Jan 1837
WEBSTER, Mark H Jr and Melissa PETTINGILL, Aug 1866
WEBSTER, Mary Ann and Samuel J CLAY, 18 Dec 1849
WEBSTER, Mary N and George H ABBOTT, 13 Aug 1896 Hudson, NH
   Kimball Webster (Hudson, NH) & Abiah C Cutter (Pelham, NH)
   Herman Abbott & Elvira Bancroft
WEBSTER, Moses and Lydia M BAKER, 16 Dec 1841
WEBSTER, Nancy and John STEVENS, 27 Jan 1811
WEBSTER, Nathan P and Susan M MORRISON, 17 May 1860
WEBSTER, Nathan P and Josephine ROLLINS, 22 May 1867
WEBSTER, Orrin P and Susan R DAVIS, 10 Apr 1865
WEBSTER, Phyllis M and Paul R DILLAIRE, 15 Jan 1949 Hudson, NH
WEBSTER, Relief Mar and Hiram WOODBURY, 25 Dec 1832
WEBSTER, Ruth Simer and Thomas JOHNSON, 23 Feb 1843
WEBSTER, Sally Hale and Simeon Cha TITCOMB, 10 Nov 1842
WEBSTER, Sarah Ann and Samuel C FLAGG, 29 Nov 1839
   Benjamin Webster
WEBSTER, Simon Brad and Relief JOHNSON, 23 Nov 1811
WEBSTER, Simon G and Maria DOLLOFF, 18 Dec 1849
WEBSTER, Simon Gilm and Relief JONES, 16 Dec 1841
WEBSTER, Stephen and Michelle A ENO, 26 Sep 1981 Hudson, NH
WEBSTER, Stephen and Hannah AYER, 24 Mar 1663
WEBSTER, Susan J and Calvin BOARDMAN,
WEBSTER, Willard H and Addie M WALTON, 19 Oct 1862
WEBSTER, William H and Sophia C FOSTER, 09 Jun 1859
WEDICK, Sandra A and Donald W LAFOREST, 21 Dec 1963 Hudson, NH
WEEKS, Dorothy E and Earl T BROOKS, 09 Jul 1932 Manchester, NH
WEGHORST, George W and Susan B JONES, 17 Jun 1978 Hudson, NH
WEIGHTMAN, Bertha and Earl RECORD, 13 Jun 1920 Nashua, NH
WEILD, Robert M and Diane T MacKINNON, 23 Jun 1984 Hudson, NH
WEISMAN, Terre A and Margaret A PROKO, 27 Oct 1984 Nashua, NH
WELCH, Alice M and Arther A MANNING, 21 Sep 1941 Hudson, NH
WELCH, Dennis W and Katherine ERB, 31 Mar 1976 Nashua, NH
WELCH, Kim P and John R Jr DAUDELIN, 10 May 1981 Hudson, NH
WELCH, Mike Alan and Cris Ann WRENN, 08 Sep 1984 Nashua, NH
WELCH, Rebecca E and Wayne P HODGMAN, 12 Aug 1978 Hudson, NH
WELCOME, Mary-Anne and David K BURTON, 05 Oct 1984 Hudson, NH
WELDON, John B and Maureen A ROBINSON, 05 Oct 1968 Hudson, NH
WELDON, Sharon Ann and Kerry M MANGAN, 21 Oct 1972 Hudson, NH
WELDON, Susan C&Charles J BOISSONNEAULT, 06 Oct 1984 Chichester, NH
WELDON, William C and Leanne M MASSE, 23 Jul 1971 Pelham, NH
WELLIVER, Dorothy L and William D MULLIN, 06 Aug 1949 Hudson, NH
WELLMAN, Anna H and Charles A CHASE, 16 Jun 1841
WELLMAN, Hannah and Seabury F ROGERS, 01 Nov 1842
WELLS, Allen B and Marie E MacDONALD, 08 Apr 1978 Hudson, NH
WELLS, Allen W and Margaret A SHEEHAN, 14 Jul 1936 Manchester, NH
WELLS, Anna Berth and George W CLYDE, 19 Feb 1902 Manchester, NH
   Martin Wells & Ella I Colby
   Samuel W Clyde & Hannah J Boles
WELLS, Burt T and Leslie M BARRETT, 19 Jul 1955 Milton, NH
WELLS, Carolyn L and Walter E PHINNEY, 01 May 1954 Nashua, NH
WELLS, Denise G and Steven P COFFILL, 23 May 1982 Hudson, NH

HUDSON, NH MARRIAGES

WELLS, Harold M and Mildred L McCULLOUGH, 16 Sep 1929 Hudson, NH
WELLS, Hazel E and Edwin A CALHOUN, 18 Oct 1949 Hudson, NH
WELLS, Helen M and Henry F LUND, 29 Mar 1893 Nashua, NH
   George E Wells (Albany, VT) & Sarah Doying (Albany, VT)
   Francis Lund(Hollis, NH) & Marcia E Whiteker (Deering, NH)
WELLS, Maxine G and Irving L DUNCKLEE, 18 Jun 1932 Hudson, NH
WELLS, Oliver B and Mary E BASLEY, 17 Jan 1874 Hudson, NH
WELLS, Susan Paul and Daniel Paul HEROUX, 18 Jul 1980 Nashua, NH
WELLS, Tillie and Leni K CROP, 23 Feb 1875 Nashua, NH
WENERIP, Hilda and William EPSTEIN, 15 Dec 1928 Hudson, NH
WENTWORTH, Christine and David W GARSIDE, 03 Jul 1972 Hudson, NH
WENTWORTH, Daniel G and Mabel F CONNELL, 03 Jun 1903 Nashua, NH
   Nathaniel Wentworth & Martha E Greeley
   Robert T Connell & Lizzie Marshall
WENTWORTH, Donald H and Doris C O'BEIRNE, 16 Jun 1941 Hudson, NH
WENTWORTH, Edwin and Bertha A SANBORN, 20 Aug 1901 Hudson, NH
   Nathaniel Wentworth(Brighton, MA) & Martha E Greeley (Hudson, NH)
   Frederick Sanborn(Concord) & Jennie H Little (Haverhill, MA)
WENTWORTH, Ellen and Eben W WEBSTER, 03 Jul 1859
WENTWORTH, James G and Linnie E SNOWMAN, 26 Nov 1902 Rangeley, ME
   Nathaniel Wentworth & Martha E Greeley
   Geo J Snowman & Cenath J Haley
WENTWORTH, John and Jessie S GILBERT, 21 Sep 1904 Hudson, NH
   Nathaniel Wentworth & Martha E Greeley
   George P Gilbert & Sarah A Rowell
WENTWORTH, June and Donald D MacLEOD, 06 Apr 1942 Milford, NH
WENTWORTH, Nathaniel Jr and Edwina GREELEY, 09 May 1870 Hudson, NH
WENTWORTH, Patricia and Robert E SUDSBURY, 28 Sep 1940 Hudson, NH
WENTWORTH, Sally A and Conrad A MACHIA, 17 Aug 1968 Derry, NH
WENTWORTH, Walter A and Lavinia F SMITH, 01 May 1871 Hudson, NH
WESCOTT, Gail and Michael ALLEN, 14 Feb 1975 Londonderry, NH
WESSON, Bruce E and Marilyn J HOBBS, 09 Jun 1973 Candia, NH
WEST, George A and Laura M MARTIN, 30 May 1942 Hudson, NH
WEST, Kim A and Michael G PACIELLO, 13 Jun 1981 Nashua, NH
WEST, Prudence A and Philip W Jr FOGG, 15 Dec 1967 Nashua, NH
WEST, Valerie F and Francis R GOUDEY, 01 Dec 1934 Nashua, NH
WESTNEAT, Arthur S and Alice B FRENCH, 06 Jul 1920 Hudson, NH
WESTNEAT, Clark R and Susan H PATTERSON, 24 Mar 1973 Hudson, NH
WESTON, Albert E and Vera P BABCOCK, 10 Oct 1936 Hudson, NH
WESTON, Edward E and Christiann WOODWARD, 07 Mar 1882 Lyndeboro, NH
   William S Weston(Waltham, MA) & Sarah M Emerson (Francestown, NH)
   Artemus Woodward(Lyndeboro, NH) & Nancy E Savage (Greenfield, NH)
WESTON, Ida J and William H WATTS, 17 Sep 1904 Wilton, NH
   Fred Weston & Ida A Wellman
   Lorenzo Watts & Alvina Parks
WESTON, Nellie M and Carl A McAFEE, 26 Apr 1916 Nashua, NH
   Alvah K Weston (Portland, ME) & Emma Healey (Chester, NH)
   Charles A McAfee(Bedford, NH) & Susie Druker (Pembroke, NH)
WETHERELL, Louise and Harold HEIGHTON, 04 Oct 1947 Hudson, NH
WHALEN, Eugene M and Lylona D GIRARD, 16 Aug 1941 Hudson, NH
WHALEN, Mary T and Arthur E WALSH, 30 Jun 1962 Hudson, NH
WHALEN, Myron E and Mildred ROGERS, 24 Jul 1940 Nashua, NH
WHALEN, Nicholas J and Georgette TREFRY, 31 Aug 1935 Hudson, NH
WHARTON, John E and Hilda J CLARK, 01 Dec 1960 Merrimack, NH
WHARTON, Richard Ch and Candace S BARINGER, 04 Jul 1981 Nashua, NH
WHEELER, Barbara L and Earl W Jr MUNSON, 01 Jan 1971 Manchester, NH
WHEELER, Charles and Ellen F BRIGHT, 07 Sep 1862
WHEELER, Ethel May and Walter TWISS, 04 Nov 1918 Nashua, NH
WHEELER, James R and Shirley A STRAUB, 24 Jul 1965 Hudson, NH
WHEELER, Jerald E and Daneen G DONNELLY, 29 Jan 1983 Hudson, NH

HUDSON,NH MARRIAGES

WHEELER, Joseph K and Abbie A MARSH, 22 Nov 1849
WHEELER, Josiah K and Abbie A WILSON, 26 Dec 1865
WHEELER, Judith G and William F RELATION, 21 Nov 1981 Hudson, NH
WHEELER, Judson A and Jessie M LOUGEE, 01 Dec 1936 Ayer, MA
WHEELER, Louisa and Fred R MARSHALL, 25 May 1886 Hudson, NH
  Frank C Wheeler & Louisa Gorham
  John B Marshall(Hudson, NH) & Ellen A Senter (Hudson, NH)
WHEELER, Louisa W and Fred R MARSHALL, 25 May 1886 Hudson, NH
WHEELER, Malissa A and George L HOLMES, 22 Nov 1881 Hollis, NH
  Theodore Wheeler
  Luke Holmes(Canada) & Catherine Butler (Hudson, NH)
WHEELER, Mildred A and David R Jr KELLEY, 20 Jun 1970 Nashua, NH
WHEELER, Mildred M and Ernest E McCOY, 30 Apr 1946 Hudson, NH
WHEELER, Norma J and Gene H KINVILLE, 17 Jul 1965 Nashua, NH
WHEELER, Paul A and Doris C HARRISON, 09 Oct 1959 Nashua, NH
WHEELER, Pauline M&Walter A Jr BENNETT, 29 Oct 1960 Harrisville, NH
WHEELER, Raymond P and Judith G OUELLETTE, 16 Mar 1974 Hudson, NH
WHEELER, Richard J and Eleanor R BOYER, 12 May 1945 Hudson, NH
WHEELER, Shirley A and Brian L SWEENEY, 22 Sep 1978 Nashua, NH
WHEELOCK, Viola E and Raymond C BISCHOFF, 06 Oct 1938 Nashua, NH
WHILDEGG, Thomas F and Dorothy C MacDONALD, 22 Oct 1938 Nashua, NH
WHIPPLE, James B and Alice V BOWLES, 27 Aug 1882 Hudson, NH
  John Whipple (New Boston, NH) & Philantha Reed (Berry, VT)
  William Bowles & Mary Greenleaf (Calais, ME)
WHITAKER, Christine and Stephan C GARSIDE, 27 Apr 1985 Hudson, NH
WHITAKER, Dolores C and William P BRIAND, 09 Aug 1968 Nashua, NH
WHITAKER, Michael D and Linda A LITALIEN, 19 Oct 1968 Nashua, NH
WHITAKER, Norman Jr and Mari MAEDA, 17 Dec 1983 Hudson, NH
WHITCHER, Ella B and Clarence T CAMPBELL, 25 Oct 1902 Hudson, NH
  Bert Whitcher & Mary
  Bradford Campbell & Hattie Putnam
WHITCOMB, Lucy and Malichi WOODBURY, 07 Jan 1826
WHITE, Adelbert and Eliza A BURGIN, 30 Mar 1860
WHITE, Amanda T and Ward H PIPER, 31 Oct 1970 Auburn, NH
WHITE, Charles C and Evelyn MURPHY, 19 Jun 1948 Hudson, NH
WHITE, Charles T and Martha C BARRON, 23 Apr 1850
WHITE, Charlotte and Michael A NARO, 25 Aug 1973 Hollis, NH
WHITE, Claire Ann and David Roger ROUILLARD, 21 Jul 1973 Pelham, NH
WHITE, Donald L Jr and Pauline D GAGNON, 16 Feb 1979 Hudson, NH
WHITE, Doris E and Harry J MEAD, 24 Nov 1923 Manchester, NH
WHITE, Eva V and Albert J CHARPENTIER, 26 Oct 1935 Nashua, NH
WHITE, George J and Lois E DROLLETT, 28 Mar 1932 Nashua, NH
WHITE, Helen F and Harry A J Jr READ, 16 Feb 1935 Hollis, NH
WHITE, John J and Ruth V GONSALVES, 04 Nov 1950 Hudson, NH
WHITE, Justin H and June C KOFFINK, 25 Dec 1950 Hudson, NH
WHITE, Lynn C and Christine ZACCAGNINI, 01 Sep 1984 Hudson, NH
WHITE, Marion L and Louis J MARSHALL, 28 Jun 1941 Milford, NH
WHITE, Marjorie L and Kenneth L WINKLEY, 06 Nov 1936 Hudson, NH
WHITE, Martha and John QUIGG, 05 May 1857
WHITE, Marthe G and William MARCHESE, 30 Jun 1984 Nashua, NH
WHITE, Paul A and Angela DELYANI, 14 Jun 1980 Nashua, NH
WHITE, Paul W and Won Suk O, 29 Sep 1984 Nashua, NH
WHITE, Pauline M and Arthur J Jr LAVIOLETTE, 14 Aug 1937 Nashua, NH
WHITE, Rachel L and Everett M HAMBLETT, 05 Feb 1973 Hudson, NH
WHITE, Robert L and Mary E FARRINGTON, 18 Aug 1962 Hudson, NH
WHITE, Theresa Y and Reed M SMITH, 27 Nov 1982 Hudson, NH
WHITE, Thomas L and Ann Lucill RAHLAY, 22 Aug 1932 Nashua, NH
WHITFORD, Fred E and Fannie H MARSH, 09 Jun 1869 Hudson, NH
WHITHAM, Marion Nas and John T GALLAGHER, 23 Jun 1934 Nashua, NH
WHITING, Adrie L and Gerard L GAGNON, 30 Jun 1956 Nashua, NH

HUDSON, NH MARRIAGES

WHITING, Donald A and Shirley A NICHOLS, 13 Apr 1964 Hudson, NH
WHITING, Eva C and Stephen W GIBSON, 28 Aug 1881 Hudson, NH
  Edwiche C Woodbury (Cavendish, VT) & Chestina Baker (Lyme, NH)
  John A Gibson(Sulebury, VT) & Mary S Davis (Dunston, VT)
WHITING, Helen H and William J GUMBRIS, 10 Oct 1942 Hudson, NH
WHITING, Susan E and Stephen W BLAIS, 09 Dec 1967 Hudson, NH
WHITING, Wava M and James E Jr CROWLEY, 04 Nov 1978 Hudson, NH
WHITLOW, Milburn B and Margharita BULZOMI, 01 Feb 1950 Hudson, NH
WHITMORE, Dorothy M and Francis E CREAMER, 04 Jun 1940 Hudson, NH
WHITNEY, Alden W and Charlotte BODGE, 02 Sep 1939 Hudson, NH
WHITNEY, Don and Gail M SHUMAN, 03 Mar 1984 Nashua, NH
WHITNEY, Earle L Jr and Katherine MOREAU, 18 Dec 1970 Nashua, NH
WHITNEY, Hannah and Eleazer Jr CUMMINGS, 26 Nov 1761
WHITNEY, Hannah and Eleazer Jr CUMMINGS, 26 Nov 1763
WHITNEY, James Murray and Helen F BRADLEY, 29 Sep 1923 Hudson, NH
WHITNEY, Joy K and Donald E II GRANT, 11 Jun 1977 Hudson, NH
WHITNEY, Llewellyn and Nancy J CLEMENT, 05 Apr 1952 Nashua, NH
WHITNEY, Lorna D and Myron F BURR, 18 Sep 1931 Hudson, NH
WHITNEY, Louise A and John J Jr HARMON, 07 Mar 1934 Nashua, NH
WHITNEY, Marilyn P and Harold L WALLIS, 30 Jun 1951 Nashua, NH
WHITNEY, Merle L and Jonathan D ZELONIS, 07 Apr 1973 Pelham, NH
WHITNEY, Richard P and Martha E FOX, 19 Oct 1973 Merrimack, NH
WHITNEY, Robert S and Ethel M MARSHALL, 21 Aug 1976 Nashua, NH
WHITNEY, Rosette T and Joseph L NOEL, 24 Jun 1978 Nashua, NH
WHITNEY, William and Sarah SMITH, 24 Nov 1825
WHITNEY, William R and Susan J WHITTEMORE, 10 Nov 1973 Nashua, NH
WHITTAKER, Diane M and Gregory G PROVENCAL, 08 Jun 1974 Hudson, NH
WHITTAKER, Joseph J and Alice J SANDERS, 25 Nov 1896 Hudson, NH
  John Whittaker (England) & Mary Morris (England)
  Thomas Sanders(Ireland) & Mary Connell (Ireland)
WHITTAKER, Ralph J Jr & Helen G BUCKAWICKI, 02 May 1982 Hudson, NH
WHITTEMORE, Alice M and Felix P GURSKA, 28 Jun 1952 Hudson, NH
WHITTEMORE, Amos and Mary TAYLOR, 25 Nov 1766
WHITTEMORE, Carol A and David P FLEWELLING, 22 Aug 1964 Hudson, NH
WHITTEMORE, Charles and Lydia HADLEY, 28 Oct 1813
WHITTEMORE, Charles R and Alice M ANDREW, 28 Nov 1935 Nashua, NH
WHITTEMORE, Charles R and Wanda F KAYROS, 29 Nov 1947 Nashua, NH
WHITTEMORE, Kathryn W and James E PHILBROOK, 22 Sep 1962 Nashua, NH
WHITTEMORE, Palmyra W and Abi A SANDERS, 08 Jan 1850
WHITTEMORE, Paul W and Pauline C VIGNEAULT, 12 Aug 1961 Nashua, NH
WHITTEMORE, Rachel M and Alec A MAHFUZ, 23 Sep 1972 Wilmot Flat, NH
WHITTEMORE, Roy L and Anna May DOHERTY, 22 Feb 1940 Hudson, NH
WHITTEMORE, Susan J and William R WHITNEY, 10 Nov 1973 Nashua, NH
WHITTEN, Lori E and Robert H LAMBERT, 27 Jul 1974 Hudson, NH
WHITTIMORE, Georgiana and David ROBBINS, 13 Jun 1874 Nashua, NH
WHITTLE, James and Hannah BARRETT, 19 Jan 1797
WHYMAN, Doris Mari and Noyes N BARTHOLEMEW, 22 Aug 1937 Hudson, NH
WHYNOT, Sandra A and Richard A WYATT, 18 May 1984 Merrimack, NH
WICOM, Hannah and Moody HARDY, 21 Jan 1779
WIECZHALEK, Diane J and Perry I HAYMANN, 16 Oct 1976 Hudson, NH
WIECZHALEK, Lorrie A and Toby R RUSSELL, 29 May 1982 Nashua, NH
WIEGMANN, Mary E and Paul F McMANUS, 08 Jul 1976 Nashua, NH
WIGANDT, Frederick and Doris M SMITH, 24 Jul 1948 Hudson, NH
WIGGIN, James W Jr and Jewell A AUSTIN, 24 Nov 1955 Hudson, NH
WIGHTMAN, Edwin C and Alice M EATON, 15 Feb 1948 Hudson, NH
WIGMORE, Tami and David W GIBSON, 04 Apr 1981 Hudson, NH
WILA, Thomas A and Marcia J SUNDQUIST, 14 Nov 1981 Hudson, NH
WILBORG, Richard B and Vivian E POIRIER, 20 Oct 1984 Hudson, NH
WILBUR, David A and Judith A MONTMINY, 31 Dec 1966 Hudson, NH
WILCOX, Emily E and Elmer D CLEMENT, 05 Oct 1881 Hudson, NH

HUDSON,NH MARRIAGES

  William Wilcox (England) & Eliza Hewes (England)
  David Clement, Jr(Hudson, NH) & Mariah Hall (Pelham, NH)
WILCOX, Janet A and Lawrence L PIPER, 31 Aug 1974 Nashua, NH
WILCOX, John G and Joyce A FORRENCE, 19 Sep 1976 Hudson, NH
WILCOX, Myrtle F and Lawrence A STOCKDALE, 09 Nov 1935 Pembroke, NH
WILDMAN, Elaine R and Frederick BEDFORD, 14 May 1945 Nashua, NH
WILHELMI, Douglas G and Lisa M GARSIDE, 17 Oct 1981 Hudson, NH
WILKINS, Andrew and Lucy BLANCHARD, 29 Sep 1779
WILKINSON, Brian C and Patricia Ann CLEGG, 01 May 1982 Nashua, NH
WILKINSON, Deborah J and Daniel N AUDETTE, 22 Sep 1979 Raymond, NH
WILLETT, Mary and David C FORD, 31 Mar 1890 Hudson, NH
  Louis Willett (Quebec, P Q) & Hattie Mashiel (Quebec, P Q)
  Timothy S Ford(W Fairlee, VT) & Sarah G Fuller (Hudson, NH)
WILLETTE, Frederick and Maxine V BIRCHALL, 05 Mar 1955 Wilton, NH
WILLETTE, Ramona M and Raymond P Jr REILLY, 08 Aug 1953 Hudson, NH
WILLETTE, Romeo F and Evelyn E PARKER, 01 Sep 1950 Hudson, NH
WILLETTE, Wilmer J and Mildred READ, 28 Jan 1934 Nashua, NH
WILLEY, Robert S Jr and Danielle M RACINE, 05 Oct 1970 Alton, NH
WILLEY, JR, Eriene H and Harold L WILMOT, 09 Feb 1968 Hudson, NH
WILLIAMS, Donald G and Doris E MAXFIELD, 27 Jun 1970 Hudson, NH
WILLIAMS, Earle H and Lorraine G CORMIER, 03 Jun 1967 Hudson, NH
WILLIAMS, Edmund H and Doris W SMITH, 27 Oct 1934 Hudson, NH
WILLIAMS, Elliott C and Virginia M DORRIS, 20 May 1950 Hudson, NH
WILLIAMS, Ernest E and Bertha M HUNT, 12 Jun 1909 Nashua, NH
  John F Williams & Maria Tate
  Riley Smith & Mary Berry
WILLIAMS, Evelyn T and Ralph H MORGAN, 02 Jul 1937 Hudson, NH
WILLIAMS, Henrietta and Ernest PROVENCHER, 13 Oct 1918 Hudson, NH
WILLIAMS, Jack V Jr and Cynthia C JONES, 21 Aug 1982 Nashua, NH
WILLIAMS, James T and Lucille I CORMIER, 04 May 1975 Hudson, NH
WILLIAMS, Jonathan F and Arintha T ROBINSON, 22 Oct 1932 Pelham, NH
WILLIAMS, Josephine and Paul G BEAUREGARDE, 23 Nov 1984 Hudson, NH
WILLIAMS, Lorraine M and Donald R HUDON, 03 May 1980 Hudson, NH
WILLIAMS, M Dean and Sheila M HAINES, 15 Oct 1982 Hudson, NH
WILLIAMS, Michele E and Kevin N NADEAU, 26 Sep 1981 Hudson, NH
WILLIAMS, Myra and Francis N GOODWIN, 07 Dec 1947 Hudson, NH
WILLIAMS, Pamela G&Peter J Jr RAMASKA, 16 Mar 1974 Londonderry, NH
WILLIAMS, Rene K and Peter H ZAGWYN, 15 Jul 1950 Hudson, NH
WILLIAMS, Scott D and Carol Lynn NICHOLS, 31 Mar 1983 Hudson, NH
WILLIAMS, Wendy L and James W ELIA, 16 Aug 1980 Nashua, NH
WILLIAMSON, Archibald Jr & Lucille V FARMER, 21 Apr 1951 Hudson, NH
WILLIAMSON, Carol I and Daniel P DIGGINS, 31 Jul 1971 Nashua, NH
WILLIAMSON, Carol I and Harry F POPER, 07 Oct 1978 Nashua, NH
WILLIAMSON, Dorothy I and Abraham J BRIAND, 13 Oct 1984 Hudson, NH
WILLIAMSON, Dorothy M and William L MOULTON, 18 Feb 1950 Nashua, NH
WILLIAMSON, Raymond O and Rita ST LAURENT, 30 Dec 1971 Nashua, NH
WILLIAMSON, Robin and Francis R POTTER, 30 Jun 1979 Hudson, NH
WILLIAMSON, Thomas C and Dorothy I BARRETT, 07 Aug 1965 Hudson, NH
WILLIAMSTON, Margaret and Philip CONNELL, 20 Nov 1864
WILLIS, Mary-Ann and Thomas P STAWASZ, 12 Jan 1973 Nashua, NH
WILLOCK, Barbara A and Newberry LOCKLEAR, 04 Jul 1947 Hudson, NH
WILLOUGHBY, Edwin and Eliza H MARSH, 30 May 1868
WILLOUGHBY, Edwin and Eliza H MARSH, 13 May 1868
WILLOUGHBY, Ethan and Anna GOULD, 23 Jun 1805
WILLOUGHBY, Frank and Amelia WOOD, 30 Nov 1862
WILLOUGHBY, Julia and Joseph PARKER, 29 Feb 1848
WILLOUGHBY, Mary E and Arden C CROSS, 13 Jun 1893 Nashua, NH
  Nathan Willoughby & Elizabeth Marshall
  Hiram Cross(Litchfield, NH) & Sarah E Savage (Greenfield, NH)
WILLOUGHBY, Mary W and John SULLIVAN, 01 Jan 1853

HUDSON,NH MARRIAGES

WILLOUGHBY, P Frank and Amelia A WOOD, 30 Nov 1862
WILLS, Elsie M and Roger S HILL, 11 Mar 1917 Hudson, NH
WILLWERTH, Anny E and Lester W ROBINSON, 05 Sep 1907 Nashua, NH
   Eliott A Morse & Maria M Green
   George W Robinson & Jennie L Carrington
WILMOT, Harold L and Eriene H WILLEY, JR, 09 Feb 1968 Hudson, NH
WILMOT, Harold L and Corrine T PELLETIER, 22 Sep 1979 Hudson, NH
WILMOT, Herbert L and Rita M GUYETTE, 27 Apr 1935 Nashua, NH
WILMOT, Irene D and Edward L LANDRY, 11 Apr 1969 Nashua, NH
WILMOT, Michele E and David E BOULEY, 17 May 1975 Nashua, NH
WILSHERE, Stephanie and Bill G KEARNS, 02 Oct 1982 Hudson, NH
WILSHIRE, Lilla L and Vernon S BROWN, 15 Jun 1921 Hudson, NH
WILSON, Abbie A and Josiah K WHEELER, 26 Dec 1865
WILSON, Arline M and Walter O LAMBERT, 17 Jul 1946 Hudson, NH
WILSON, Arthur A and Annie L CATE, 05 Jun 1906 Hudson, NH
   James F Wilson & Sarah H Riley
   Byron H Cate & Anna Taylor
WILSON, Clara A and Joseph S BENNETT, 31 Oct 1854
WILSON, Clarissa and Phineas HASELTINE, 17 Dec 1818
WILSON, Clarissa and Phineas HASELTON, 07 Dec 1818
WILSON, Clarissa A and Joseph BENNETT, 02 Nov 1854
WILSON, Cynthia O and Sydney A GARLAND, 27 Oct 1868
WILSON, David D and Elizabeth POWERS, 17 Jan 1981 Nashua, NH
WILSON, Dawn Franc and Raymond Wi ASPREY, 04 Oct 1980 Hudson, NH
WILSON, Donald W and Kathy D McCRADY, 28 Jul 1973 Nashua, NH
WILSON, Donald W and Kathy D WILSON, 10 Apr 1975 Nashua, NH
WILSON, Dorcas and David CLEMENT, 29 Nov 1821
WILSON, Ellen J and Robert W STONE, 17 Sep 1971 Hudson, NH
WILSON, Francis G Jr&Susan D LONSBERRY, 02 Apr 1971 Manchester, NH
WILSON, Frank A and Nettie O COLBY, 21 Jun 1905 Nashua, NH
   James F Wilson & Sarah H Riley
   Luke B Colby & Annie O Cate
WILSON, Franklin and Clarissa GOULD, 07 Feb 1833
WILSON, Geraldine and James R BLAIS, 08 May 1952 Hudson, NH
WILSON, Gertrude A and Nathan PHILBROOK, 17 Jun 1873 Hudson, NH
WILSON, Hattie A and Daniel NORTH, 29 Feb 1880 Londonderry, NH
   John Putnam & Abagaill Hart (Temple, NH)
   Daniel North & Goodell
WILSON, Henry C Jr and Sonja E DAVIDSON, 03 Sep 1960 Nashua, NH
WILSON, Hiram P and Lillian THOMPSON, 25 Dec 1893 Hudson, NH
   William C Wilson (Concord, NH) & Sarah Tucker (Orange)
   John M Thompson(Bridgewater) & Elizabeth Marsh (Hudson, NH)
WILSON, Hudson L and Vera M MARSHALL, 17 Jan 1953 Chester, NH
WILSON, James W and Wanda R BALICKI, 01 Aug 1935 Hudson, NH
WILSON, John G and Helen M MURDOCK, 31 Jan 1947 Hudson, NH
WILSON, John Jr and Mary MORSE, 19 Dec 1816
WILSON, Joseph and Thankful CUMMINGS, 09 Apr 1805
WILSON, Joseph and Minerva STAPLES, 22 Oct 1826
WILSON, Kathy D and Donald W WILSON, 10 Apr 1975 Nashua, NH
WILSON, Lelie and Charles A NICKLESS, 02 Jul 1899 Hudson, NH
   Joseph Austin & Charlotte Rogerson
   Geo F Nickless & Abbie S Daniels
WILSON, Leora W and Dominic OLIVOLO, 25 Feb 1950 Hudson, NH
WILSON, Linda J and Raymond P LABARRE, 29 May 1982 Hudson, NH
WILSON, Lucinda and Jonathan BURBANK, 28 Nov 1822
WILSON, Lucinda and Jonathan BURBANK, 28 Nov 1823
WILSON, Mary Lucin and James Mars COBURN, 04 Sep 1869
WILSON, Matilda and Nathaniel MORSE, 26 Apr 1818
WILSON, Myrtle A and James PATRIZZI, 25 May 1933 Nashua, NH
WILSON, Priscilla and Terry L CLARKSON, 01 Jul 1972 Nashua, NH

HUDSON,NH MARRIAGES

WILSON, Richard B and Janice M SHAPIRO, 18 Mar 1972 Hudson, NH
WILSON, Richard J and Linda M JONES, 25 Jan 1969 Hudson, NH
WILSON, Robert J and Estelle G SULHERLAND, 03 Jul 1937 Hudson, NH
WILSON, Sadie Bell and Milo A DURANT, 05 Feb 1889 Derry, NH
  George W Durant & Anna Lund (Hollis, NH)
WILSON, Steven H and Jeanne M DUGAN, 17 Apr 1982 Merrimack, NH
WILSON, Therese M and Henry E Jr LOWTHER, 03 Jul 1983 Nashua, NH
WILSON, Zadock P and Anna RICHARDSON, 12 Apr 1826
WING, Sandra M and Alfred S JAMES, 17 Sep 1982 Merrimack, NH
WINGATE, Julia M and Frank E ZAMBINO, 28 Jun 1947 Hudson, NH
WINKLER, Joseph N and Gay N BORDEN, 10 Nov 1967 Nashua, NH
WINKLEY, Kenneth L and Marjorie L WHITE, 06 Nov 1936 Hudson, NH
WINN, Abbie E and Leander R SPALDING, 01 Jan 1866
WINN, Abiather and Mary HARRIS, 08 Apr 1824
WINN, Albert N and Augusta M ADAMS, Hudson, NH
WINN, Alonzo N and Lydia M HAMBLETT, 17 Mar 1846
WINN, Effie M and Clayton C OBAN, 24 Jan 1942 Nashua, NH
WINN, Elmer C and Ella A BARKER, 16 Sep 1885 N Chelmsford, MA
  Paul T Winn (Hudson, NH) & Fanny B Parkhurst (Wilton, NH)
  James Barker(Windham, NH) & Agnes L Park (Windham, NH)
WINN, Emily F and Reuben BARNES, 22 Jan 1854
WINN, Emma B and George A MERRILL, 02 Oct 1890 Hudson, NH
  William F Winn (Hudson, NH) & Lucy Richardson (Wilmington)
  James B Merrill(Hudson, NH) & Persis A Winn (Hudson, NH)
WINN, Frances S and Alton L DROWN, 04 Apr 1942 Hudson, NH
WINN, Francis P and Joseph FARMER, 06 Jun 1871
WINN, Frank A and Effie M WYETH, 08 Sep 1915 Nashua, NH
  Franklin A Winn (Hudson, NH) & Lizzie E Stebens (Vermont)
  Willard Wyeth & Marguerite McLennon (New York)
WINN, Frank M and Carrie H WOODBURY, 30 Nov 1869 Hudson, NH
WINN, Fred E and Sarah C MOULTON, 25 Jul 1888 Merrimack, NH
  Wm F Winn (Hudson, NH) & Lucy M Richardson (Wilmington, MA)
  George W Moulton(Braintree, VT) & Hannah H Spofford (Auburn, NH)
WINN, Harriet M and William T CLARK, 13 Dec 1851
WINN, Jennie C and John T MARTIN, 30 Sep 1891 Nashua, NH
  William F Winn (Hudson, NH) & Lucy Richardson (Woburn, MA)
  Silas W Martin(Amy, N B) & Prudence Sage (P E Island)
WINN, Joseph and Althea W GOULD, 04 Jun 1839
WINN, Joseph and Peggy BURNS, 17 Dec 1808
WINN, Joseph Jr and Sarah HILLS, 08 Feb 1753
WINN, Joseph Jr and Mary FRENCH, 05 May 1757
WINN, Joseph Jr and Sarah CHASE, 23 Mar 1786
WINN, Joseph Jr and Peggy BURNS, 17 Dec 1808
WINN, Josiah and Betsey WRIGHT, 17 Nov 1808
WINN, Kellie M and Lawrence B III PORTER, 01 Mar 1980 Hudson, NH
WINN, Leon E and Isabel Woods MAHONEY, 13 Jan 1927 Hudson, NH
WINN, Lillian E and Walter R SCHINDLER, 27 Jun 1942 Hudson, NH
WINN, Margaret J and Daniel L RIPLEY, 24 Apr 1845
WINN, Mary F and Lot EASTY, 30 Mar 1832
WINN, Mary J and Benjamin A MERRILL, 23 Nov 1843
WINN, Nathan and Ruth HADLEY, 18 Mar 1762
WINN, Nathan and Elizabeth KELLEY, 23 Nov 1786
WINN, Olive and Jo PENEY, 08 Dec 1779
WINN, Pamela Ann and Mark R DESMARAIS, 14 Jun 1975 Hudson, NH
WINN, Persis A and James P MERRILL, 21 Jan 1857
WINN, Rufus E and Sarah J FAY, 29 Dec 1903 Hudson, NH
  John Winn & Anna Patch
  Peter Carlin & Eliza Clark
WINN, Rufus E and Ardello CALDWELL, 25 Dec 1877 Hudson, NH
  John Winn (Hudson, NH) & Annah Patch (Groton, MA)

HUDSON, NH MARRIAGES

Thomas Caldwell(Litchfield, NH) & Maria Buttrick (Pelham, NH)
WINN, Susanna B and Cyrus WARREN, 06 Jun 1826
WINN, Willard O and Jennie M CARIE, 01 Jan 1866
WINN, William F and Lucy M RICHARDSON, 22 Dec 1862
WINSLOW, Ada M and Christian CHRISTENSEN, 09 Aug 1921 Derry, NH
WINSLOW, Debra L and Michael J MORIARTY, 16 Oct 1981 Nashua, NH
WINSLOW, Donald R Jr and Susan A ALLEN, 14 Mar 1985 Manchester, NH
WINSLOW, Gerald R and Elizabeth HAMEL, 23 May 1953 Nashua, NH
WINSLOW, Minton A and Martha MacDOUGALL, 29 May 1958 Hudson, NH
WINSLOW, Muriel E and Norman J CROSBY, 20 Sep 1941 Nashua, NH
WINSLOW, Nancy A and Peter-Jon THOMPSON, 20 Feb 1981 Hudson, NH
WINSLOW, Thelma and Norman SEVERSON, 05 May 1942 Hudson, NH
WINSTANLEY, Doreen and Allen R GILSON, 31 Aug 1968 Nashua, NH
WINSTANLEY, Faye and Roger J PLAMONDON, 18 Apr 1964 Nashua, NH
WINTER, Robert T and Patricia E ST HILAIRE, 30 Oct 1982 Hudson, NH
WINTERS, William R and Laura M METRANO, 29 Jun 1980 Pelham, NH
WISELL, Donald and Emily LICCIARDONE, 12 Jul 1941 Nashua, NH
WISEMAN, Douglas C and Bonnie L BERRY, 08 Oct 1960 Hudson, NH
WISEMAN, George A Jr and Cynthia L TESSIER, 18 Aug 1974 Nashua, NH
WISEMAN, Pirley E II and Elaine M BRIER, 12 Sep 1970 Portsmouth, NH
WISNIEWSKI, Mary R and Martin KASPER, 15 Aug 1942 Nashua, NH
WISNOSKY, William W and Karen R GAULIN, 17 Dec 1971 Nashua, NH
WITALIS, Geraldine and Anthony J PELLEGRINI, 15 Feb 1975 Hudson, NH
WITCOMB, Sandra J and Thomas R LAFLEUR, 10 Jun 1978 Durham, NH
WITKOWSKI, Patty J and Marc R THERIAULT, 25 May 1985 Hudson, NH
WITTEMAN, Keith H and Frances M MASTERSON, 15 Jun 1974 Hudson, NH
WITTHUN, Linda M and Sheldon K CUDMORE, 12 Jun 1968 Nashua, NH
WOHLWEND, John H and Judith E BOMENGEN, 27 Jun 1980 Nashua, NH
WOLANGEWICZ, Michael & Caroline ESIELIONIS, 17 Sep 1944 Hudson, NH
WOLCOTT, Leslie R and A Andrew BUSWELL, 20 Aug 1966 Claremont, NH
WOLCZOK, Diane C and Danny K SLADE, 26 Sep 1969 Nashua, NH
WOLCZOK, John S and Cheryl A DUNKLEE, 13 May 1978 Nashua, NH
WOLCZOK, Sophie and Vito P COROSA, 11 Sep 1943 Nashua, NH
WOLFE, Laura E and Robert P CACCIA, 22 Apr 1978 Salem, NH
WOLFENBERGER, Fred M and Linda H M FU, 29 Dec 1971 Hudson, NH
WOLFSON, Linda A and Mark A BARREIRO, 12 Feb 1983 Hudson, NH
WOLLEN, Charles and Nancy V ALUKONIS, 03 Feb 1951 Nashua, NH
WOLLEN, Deborah G and William M MURPHY, 20 Sep 1980 Nashua, NH
WOLLEN, Janice J and Ronald L WOODWARD, 10 Jun 1967 Hudson, NH
WOLLEN, Patricia A and Robert K SHAPIRO, 20 Apr 1968 Nashua, NH
WOLODZKO, Edmund and Frances SLATUNAS, 31 Dec 1949 Nashua, NH
WOO S, Guy H and Hazel B MELVIN, 27 Mar 1918 Nashua, NH
WOOD, Alice G and George STONE, 15 May 1943 Newport, NH
WOOD, Amelia and Frank WILLOUGHBY, 30 Nov 1862
WOOD, Amelia A and P Frank WILLOUGHBY, 30 Nov 1862
WOOD, Benjamin and Sarah KNAPP, 27 Aug 1871 Hudson, NH
WOOD, Charles and Louisa CUMMINGS, 23 Apr 1851
WOOD, David E and June A JORDAN, 16 Aug 1969 Hudson, NH
WOOD, Debra C and Reginald E PEPIN, 26 Mar 1982 Hudson, NH
WOOD, Effie D and Marshall O HUNTER, 13 Aug 1906 Hudson, NH
Wentworth Wood & Ada M Anderson
Henry Hunter & Julia F Gurney
WOOD, Egbert O and Anstris P BALDWIN, 25 Dec 1867
WOOD, Egbert O and Anstris B BALDWIN, 25 Dec 1867
WOOD, Francine L and Charles L HOWE, 11 Mar 1967 Nashua, NH
WOOD, George W and Mary C TOWNE, 14 Jan 1862
WOOD, George W and Mary C TOWNE, 14 Jun 1862
WOOD, Gregory Al and Susan Lee PERRAULT, 10 Apr 1982 Nashua, NH
WOOD, H Francena and David HASELTON, 28 Nov 1861
WOOD, James and Frances A MANNING, 11 Mar 1862

HUDSON,NH MARRIAGES

WOOD, John C and Karen L GOTT, 02 Nov 1963 Hudson, NH
WOOD, Joseph E and Martha L J DURANT, 09 Mar 1885 Nashua, NH
   George S Wood (Chelmsford, MA) & Susan Pierce
   George W Durant & Anna Lund
WOOD, Karen L and Gilbert A KNOX, 08 Oct 1983 Hudson, NH
WOOD, Mary and Dudley DAVIS, 11 Aug 1785
WOOD, Mary and Hadley DAVIS, 11 Aug 1785
WOOD, Robert L and Linda L ABBOTT, 03 Aug 1968 Hudson, NH
WOOD, Sherri M and Kenneth E HOAG, 07 Nov 1981 Merrimack, NH
WOOD, William D and Mari L BLACKSTONE, 23 Jan 1973 Nashua, NH
WOODAMAN, Lewis E III and Diane E MILLETT, 07 Sep 1968 Hudson, NH
WOODBURN, Abbie A and Frank E KIDDER, 04 Apr 1881 Hudson, NH
   John Woodburn (Londonderry, NH) & L A Truell (Nashua, NH)
   Benjamin Kidder(Boston, MA) & Martha C Marshall (Sharon, NH)
WOODBURY, Carrie H and Frank M WINN, 30 Nov 1869 Hudson, NH
WOODBURY, Eben A and Cora M DODGE, 24 Feb 1917 Nashua, NH
WOODBURY, Emily Ann and Geo K WEBSTER, 30 Apr 1864
   Benjamin Webster
WOODBURY, Harriet A and Stephen S SHERMAN, 05 Feb 1864
WOODBURY, Harriet A and Stephen L SHUNAMAN, 25 Feb 1864
WOODBURY, Hiram and Relief Mar WEBSTER, 25 Dec 1832
WOODBURY, Jane and John LAMSON, 31 Oct 1860
WOODBURY, June and John O LAMSON, 31 Oct 1860
WOODBURY, Malichi and Lucy WHITCOMB, 07 Jan 1826
WOODBURY, Nellie E and Robert G MORRISON, 04 Mar 1881 Hudson, NH
WOODMAN, Frances L and Carl J BANNON, 17 Jun 1972 Claremont, NH
WOODMAN, Timothy A and Sharon A HARRIS, 10 Apr 1970 Nashua, NH
WOODS, Clifford S and Pearl MELENDY, 25 Dec 1916 Hudson, NH
   John V Woods (Hollis, NH) & Eliza Clifford (Colebrook, NH)
   Charles Melendy(Brookline, NH) & Eva Hutchinson (Milford, NH)
WOODS, Frances N and Augustus JOHNSON, 26 Aug 1859
WOODS, Frank H and Katherine PARKER, 10 Dec 1938 Nashua, NH
WOODS, Gary G and Collette BULENS, 09 Feb 1980 Hudson, NH
WOODS, Halton B III and Mary L SETTLE, 30 Nov 1968 Nashua, NH
WOODS, Horace and Mary A GREELEY, 09 Jan 1853
WOODS, Leslie B and Roy W LASSITER, 23 Dec 1983 Nashua, NH
WOODS, Patricia A and Michael A NICHOLS, 26 May 1973 Nashua, NH
WOODS, Walter R and Cynthia J JONES, 08 Aug 1969 Merrimack, NH
WOODSON, Lee and Mary SMITH, 12 Sep 1942 Nashua, NH
WOODWARD, Aaron P and Hannah CROSS, 04 May 1847
WOODWARD, Christiann and Edward E WESTON, 07 Mar 1882 Lyndeboro, NH
   Artemus Woodward (Lyndeboro, NH) & Nancy E Savage(Greenfield, NH)
   William S Weston(Waltham, MA) & Sarah M Emerson (Francestown, NH)
WOODWARD, F A and H R McCOY, 04 Oct 1916 Nashua, NH
   Frank A Woodward (Warner, NH) & Carrie Fellows (Newbury, NH)
   James McCoy(Boston, MA) & Emma Richards (Manchester, NH)
WOODWARD, Elizabeth and Benjamin K JONES, 29 Mar 1859
WOODWARD, James A and Lora L HETZER, 04 Jun 1983 Hudson, NH
WOODWARD, Nellie C and D Augustus HOLT, 25 Apr 1858
WOODWARD, Ronald L and Janice J WOLLEN, 10 Jun 1967 Hudson, NH
WOODWORTH, Ruth M and Leslie L THOMPSON, 24 Aug 1946 Hudson, NH
WOOLEY, Milton E and Reby A LADNER, 02 Aug 1952 Hudson, NH
WOOLLEY, Eleanor M and Arthur P RIOUX, 29 Jan 1954 Nashua, NH
WORCESTER, Josephine & Richard J MacMILLAN, 30 Jul 1967 Nashua, NH
WORDEN, Chester A and Nettie L BARRY, 05 Jan 1927 Hudson, NH
WORDEN, Willie M and Mertie J WYMAN, 20 Nov 1892 Hudson, NH
   M B V Worden (New York) & Saphia Currie (New York)
   Jas J Wyman
WORGIOTIS, Charles E and Sharon A FOLEY, 26 Nov 1983 Hudson, NH
WORKMAN, Steven G and Marjean HOLMES, 29 Mar 1985 New Ipswich, NH

HUDSON, NH MARRIAGES

WORMWOOD, Charles A and Rita CHUBADA, 08 Aug 1936 Hudson, NH
WORRELL, John Kipli and Lisa A PHANEUF, 31 Oct 1981 Hudson, NH
WORSTER, Deborah E and David K BRIAND, 11 Feb 1978 Hudson, NH
WORTH, Florence M and Vincent D GAFFORD, 16 Feb 1952 Hudson, NH
WORTH, John W and JoAnn S MARSHALL, 05 Dec 1953 Hudson, NH
WORTH, William A and Ronna C LANGLOIS, 01 Jan 1984 Hudson, NH
WORTHINGTON, Thelma A and John E BRIGGS, 22 Jan 1950 Hudson, NH
WORTHY, Edwin L and Lottie A RITCHIE, 27 Jul 1873 Hudson, NH
WOVORIS, James and Joni LEAVITT, 22 Mar 1980 Hudson, NH
WOZNICA, James R and Elena G SALANITRO, 19 Jun 1983 Hudson, NH
WRENN, Cris Ann and Mike Alan WELCH, 08 Sep 1984 Nashua, NH
WRIGHT, Ann B and Donald F BOWDEN, 12 Nov 1977 Hudson, NH
WRIGHT, Betsey and Josiah WINN, 17 Nov 1808
WRIGHT, Charles M and Janet L PAUL, 13 Oct 1947 Nashua, NH
WRIGHT, Clara A and James M SMITH, 27 Dec 1861
WRIGHT, Clara M and James M SMITH, 27 Dec 1861
WRIGHT, Dorothy M and Aaron L HAMBLETT, 08 Jun 1957 Hudson, NH
WRIGHT, Eunice R and Daniel McQUESTEN, 07 Jun 1882 Hudson, NH
   Lorenzo Wright (Maine) & Nancy Robbins (Nashua, NH)
   Simon McQuesten(Hudson, NH) & Rhoda Glover (Hudson, NH)
WRIGHT, Glenn A and Maureen R MAHONEY, 24 Jul 1981 Hudson, NH
WRIGHT, JoEllen J and Dwight H CARON, 14 Sep 1974 Merrimack, NH
WRIGHT, John G and Cordelia DENSMORE, 04 Apr 1869
WRIGHT, Kenneth N and Myrtle E DROLET, 23 Nov 1933 Nashua, NH
WRIGHT, Morton M and Bertha SULLIVAN, 02 Jul 1950 Hudson, NH
WRIGHT, Ruthanne and William G THERIAULT, 18 Oct 1969 Hudson, NH
WRIGHT, Sharon E and Daryl L KIDD, 06 Apr 1974 Hollis, NH
WRIGHT, Susan A and Alan R CHESNULEVICH, 21 May 1983 Hudson, NH
WRIGHT, Susie J and Caleb RICHARDSON, 11 Apr 1882 Hudson, NH
   Henry Conant (Harvard, MA) & Harriet Blood (Groton, MA)
   Henry Richardson(Corinth, VT) & Charlott Batchelder (Corinth, VT)
WRIGHT, William G and Laura STEPHENS, 02 Apr 1877 Hudson, NH
   Edward Wright (Oakdale, MA) & Ann Stephens
WRIGHT, William G and Laura STEVENS, 12 Apr 1877 Hudson, NH
WROBLEWSKI, Alice and Chester E CUMMINGS, 24 Nov 1943 Hudson, NH
WROBLOWSKI, Thaddeus and Amelia M KOCJARSKI, 22 Jan 1947 Hudson, NH
WROCKLAGE, David W and Cynthia A SEARLES, 21 Oct 1978 Nashua, NH
WULF, Brian A and Gail A GLINES, 27 Sep 1974 Litchfield, NH
WULF, Joan S and Carl T BUSHEE, 16 Dec 1983 Milford, NH
WULF, Vikki L and Wayne L DIONNE, 18 Jun 1977 Hudson, NH
WUNDERLICH, William E and Martha P MERCIER, 29 Aug 1970 Hudson, NH
WURZBURG, Francis L III&Patricia E SCHWELM, 13 Feb 1971 Hudson, NH
WYANT, Tangie F and Stephen E FARIA, 16 Mar 1974 Hudson, NH
WYATT, Richard A and Sandra A WHYNOT, 18 May 1984 Merrimack, NH
WYER, Sidney L and Barbara G GOSSELIN, 25 Jun 1971 Hudson, NH
WYETH, Effie M and Frank A WINN, 08 Sep 1915 Nashua, NH
   Willard Wyeth & Marguerite McLennon (New York)
   Franklin A Winn(Hudson, NH) & Lizzie E Stebens (Vermont)
WYMAN, Betsey and Henry BRADT, 28 Jun 1826
WYMAN, Daniel and Mary FARWELL, 10 May 1826
WYMAN, Donald R and Rosalie S ALLISON, 01 Aug 1959 Hudson, NH
WYMAN, Elbridge and Clarissa H GRIFFIN, 07 Apr 1829
WYMAN, Frances M and Louis R LEAKEAS, 02 Jun 1962 Hudson, NH
WYMAN, George C Jr and Allison F BOWRING, 14 Feb 1983 Hudson, NH
WYMAN, Hannah and John PERHAM, 09 Mar 1742
WYMAN, Hannah and John PERHAM, 09 Mar 1741
WYMAN, Marjorie A and John H HARRIS, 15 Oct 1925 Hudson, NH
WYMAN, Mertie J and Willie M WORDEN, 20 Nov 1892 Hudson, NH
   Jas J Wyman
   M B V Worden(New York) & Saphia Currie (New York)

HUDSON,NH MARRIAGES

WYMAN, Nancy and Moses BARRETT, 21 Feb 1811
WYMAN, Phebe and David Jr CUMMINGS, 24 Dec 1793
WYMAN, Sally and William TARBOX, 21 Jan 1798
WYMAN, Sally and William TARBOX, 21 Jun 1798
WYNOTT, Raymond W and Joan E ROWELL, 17 Oct 1950 Nashua, NH
WYSKIEL, Anna and Joseph GALESKY, 28 Jun 1930 Manchester, NH
YAGIELOWICZ, Geneva S&Augustine PIANTIDOSI, 14 Jun 1969 Nashua, NH
YANUSZEWSKI, Kastanty and Marie C LEVESQUE, 20 Sep 1941 Nashua, NH
YARMOLOVICH, Stacia and Herbert A FONTAINE, 28 Jun 1947 Nashua, NH
YATES, Laura S and David A CASSAVAUGH, 05 Aug 1978 Hudson, NH
YATES, Sharon and Donald R BAKER, 29 May 1976 Hudson, NH
YEATON, Brian L and Kathy A GOULD, 05 Nov 1970 Nashua, NH
YETTAW, Adelia and Willis L FULLER, 19 Jan 1876 Hudson, NH
YLOTRUK, Veronica and John BOISKO, 21 May 1919 Nashua, NH
YOHE, Wayne E and Valerie WALLACE, 05 Jul 1981 Hudson, NH
YORK, Barbara J and William C ANNIS, 29 Jan 1966 Warner, NH
YORK, Jesse L and Barbara A ROCKE, 06 May 1967 Hudson, NH
YORK, Kenneth J and Lisa A CALZINI, 16 Jun 1984 Nashua, NH
YORK, Mildred M and Donald R TESSIER, 17 Nov 1962 Hudson, NH
YORK, Richard M Jr and Theresa A TUPPER, 04 May 1968 Nashua, NH
YORK, Theresa A and Kenneth W LADUE, 16 Sep 1971 Nashua, NH
YOUNG, Albert and Emma Jane ALLEN, 12 Nov 1871 Hudson, NH
YOUNG, Alecia A and Frank P ROBINSON, 08 Sep 1886 Windham, NH
   Israel W Young (Londonderry, NH) & Elizabeth (Morse)
   Simeon Robinson(Hudson, NH) & Charlott Glidden (Jefferson)
YOUNG, Amos M and Hattie SIMPSON, 26 Jul 1866
YOUNG, Arthur E and Ruth May DAVIDSON, 23 Sep 1936 Hudson, NH
YOUNG, Barbara M & Daniel J Jr RAFFERTY, 06 Sep 1947 Manchester, NH
YOUNG, Blanche H and Leon E BROWN, 30 Aug 1930 Hudson, NH
YOUNG, Bruce Earl and Kim E MORGAN, 08 Sep 1984 Hudson, NH
YOUNG, Callie E and J Kendall BANCROFT, 03 Jun 1939 Hudson, NH
YOUNG, Doris and Ernest LAFLAMME, 03 Apr 1937 Nashua, NH
YOUNG, Edward C and Anne T QUINTON, 16 Nov 1963 Brookline, NH
YOUNG, Edward V and Lillian R HENRY, 29 Dec 1970 Hudson, NH
YOUNG, Edward V Jr and Patricia E BOUCHER, 05 Sep 1955 Nashua, NH
YOUNG, Elaine M and Timothy W STONE, 29 Oct 1983 Hudson, NH
YOUNG, Howard H and Lorraine B SMITH, 03 Apr 1957 Hudson, NH
YOUNG, Loretta Sue and Jeffrey W NICHOLS, 25 Aug 1979 Hudson, NH
YOUNG, Marion L and Sean M KRAEMER, 07 Aug 1982 Hudson, NH
YOUNG, Milton and Bertha N JENNINGS, 29 Apr 1895 Hudson, NH
   Israel W Young & E S Morse (Methuen, MA)
   Jennings & Abbie Nichols
YOUNG, Nettie L and Orlando G HILLS, 17 Jun 1889 Hudson, NH
   Israel W Young (Manchester, NH) & Elizabeth S Morse (Methuen, MA)
   Silas Hills(Windham, NH) & Roxanna Farnham (Londonderry, NH)
YOUNG, Nettie L and Orlando G HILLS, 17 Jun 1887
YOUNG, Patricia A and Charles E JONES, 02 Dec 1950 Hudson, NH
YOUNG, Patricia M and Thomas P CAULEY, 07 Jan 1984 Hudson, NH
YOUNG, Sheryl L and Eugene L Jr GAUDREAU, 22 Jul 1967 Hudson, NH
YOUNG, Steven D and Sheila A LUPIEN, 21 Jul 1984 Durham, NH
YOUNG, Susan P and David MERRILL, 28 Mar 1969 Salem, NH
YOUNG, Walter H and Ida W LAMBERT, 30 Sep 1907 Hudson, NH
   Martin J Young & Flora E Thompson
   Edwin Lambert & Lizzie P Aubin
YOUNGHUSBAND, Donna J & Mark Y CHARBONNEAU, 25 Jul 1980 Hudson, NH
YOUNGMAN, Helen and Philip J COUTURE, 19 Jul 1948 Hudson, NH
YUHAS, Barry J and Linda J CATANUSO, 12 Jun 1970 Nashua, NH
YUILL, William P Jr and Barbara R CANFIELD, 20 Jul 1935 Hudson, NH
YUKNEWICZ, William C and Cynthia E GRIFFIN, 14 Dec 1968 Nashua, NH
ZACCAGNINI, Antonette and Bruce P AXTMAN, 21 Mar 1981 Hudson, NH

HUDSON, NH MARRIAGES

ZACCAGNINI, Catherine & Daniel P DESCHENES, 30 Aug 1980 Hudson, NH
ZACCAGNINI, Christine and Lynn C WHITE, 01 Sep 1984 Hudson, NH
ZACCAGNINI, John F Jr and Kathleen M MASON, 06 Nov 1982 Nashua, NH
ZACCARDO, Joseph M Jr & Colleen L MACOMBER, 17 Mar 1982 Nashua, NH
ZAGWYN, Peter H and Rene K WILLIAMS, 15 Jul 1950 Hudson, NH
ZAHOS, Ellen C and Philip J III FRIEL, 25 Oct 1980 Nashua, NH
ZALANSKAS, Helen M and John P LAWRENCE, 27 Jul 1984 Hudson, NH
ZALANSKAS, Wheeler and Helen M REYNOLDS, 09 Jan 1943 Nashua, NH
ZALANSKAS, Wheeler E and Dianne E LATIMER, 24 Apr 1981 Nashua, NH
ZALUSKY, Dennis L and Joanne MacQUEEN, 29 May 1982 Hudson, NH
ZAMBINO, Frank E and Julia M WINGATE, 28 Jun 1947 Hudson, NH
ZANNINI, Nicholas and Irene R CAMPIONE, 01 Oct 1941 Nashua, NH
ZAPPALA, Sarah B and William J SARNIE, 24 Jul 1933 Nashua, NH
ZEDALIS, Adolph J and Anna M HURD, 02 Dec 1939 Nashua, NH
ZEDALIS, Josephine and John T BRESNAHAN, 16 Jan 1928 Nashua, NH
ZELONIS, Charles M and Linda G JOHNSON, 03 May 1969 Hudson, NH
ZELONIS, John H and Anne D HARWOOD, 07 Nov 1948 Hudson, NH
ZELONIS, Jonathan D and Merle L WHITNEY, 07 Apr 1973 Pelham, NH
ZELONIS, Laurie A and Robert S CRETE, 05 Sep 1981 Hudson, NH
ZELONIS, Marian E and Jeffrey T SARGENT, 24 Apr 1976 Hudson, NH
ZELONIS, Robert V and Joan E MILLETT, 14 Aug 1965 Nashua, NH
ZELONIS, Steven J and Judith A CHAMPIGNY, 20 Sep 1974 Nashua, NH
ZELONIS, William J and Susan D JOYAL, 20 Apr 1974 Hudson, NH
ZENARO, Alyce M and Merle D MURPHY, 04 Feb 1950 Hudson, NH
ZERBINOS, Rachel P and Gerald J TURMEL, 27 Jul 1967 Hudson, NH
ZIMMERMAN, Dolores M and Bernard CAMMARATA, 29 Apr 1971 Nashua, NH
ZIMMERMAN, Jeanne M and James R MAIOCCHI, 10 Jul 1971 Hudson, NH
ZIMMERMAN, Kim T and Peter G PARADISE, 16 May 1981 Hudson, NH
ZIMMERMAN, Linda C and Tony J DESROCHES, 07 May 1977 Hudson, NH
ZINK, Ernest and Priscilla BLOOD, 23 Dec 1925 Nashua, NH
ZINKAWICH, Stella N and James E GLISPIN, 15 Jun 1935 Nashua, NH
ZINN, Brenda J and William D JOZAITIS, 31 Aug 1962 Pittsfield, NH
ZINTEL, Bruce R and Eunice A COX, 01 Jan 1949 Merrimack, NH
ZIRPOLO, Sandra M and Wayne P BOUDREAU, 18 May 1985 Derry, NH
ZMITROWICZ, Harriet V & Reginald MATHERSON, 19 Mar 1949 Nashua, NH
ZOLKOS, Mary T and Peter J GALIPEAU, 22 Mar 1969 Pelham, NH
ZUBEN, Mary and John P O'DONNELL, 24 May 1934 Nashua, NH
ZUKOWSKI, Henry R and Dale Ann COMER, 04 Sep 1982 Hudson, NH
ZUORSKI, Andrew G and Linda M HAMILTON, 02 Sep 1983 Nashua, NH
ZWICKER, Jane E and Lawrence S DOLLOFF, 04 Apr 1945 Hudson, NH
[UNKNOWN], Lorraine D & Albert S MATKOWSKY, 25 Aug 1979 Nashua, NH
[UNKNOWN], Nathaniel and Mary BURNS, 27 Sep 1781

HUDSON,NH DEATHS

ABARE,Helen M AGE:41 6 30 Sep 1912 Hudson, NH John Stanion & Louise Knapp
ABBOTT,Ann L AGE:25 18 Jun 1967 Lowell, MA
ABBOTT,Clayton B AGE:42 4 16 01 Dec 1948 Nashua, NH George H Abbott
 & Mary N Webster
ABBOTT,George H AGE:68 5 8 08 May 1929 Hudson, NH Herman Abbott & Bancroft
ABBOTT,James C AGE:29 23 Sep 1967 Nashua, NH
ABBOTT,Kenneth T AGE:74 18 Mar 1979 Nashua, NH
ABBOTT,Mary N AGE:93 05 Mar 1963 Hudson, NH
ABBOTT,Paul A AGE:28 18 Jun 1967 Lowell, MA
ABBOTT,Roland W AGE:67 02 Dec 1964 Nashua, NH
ABBOTT,William H AGE:49 22 Jul 1967 Nashua, NH
ACKERMAN,Edna B AGE:7 01 Jun 1909 Hudson, NH William B Ackerman
 & Mary Hamblett
ACKERMAN,Elizabeth AGE:65 15 Sep 1968 Nashua, NH
ACKERMAN,Joseph AGE:78 07 Jun 1971 Nashua, NH
ACKERMAN,Mary E AGE:45 9 26 23 Nov 1912 Hudson, NH Alvin Hamblet
 & Almira McKean
ACKERMAN,Mary T AGE:71 15 Jun 1972 Nashua, NH
ACKERMAN,Raymond R Sr AGE:69 28 Jan 1967 Nashua, NH
ACKERMAN,William G AGE: 05 Oct 1949 Nashua, NH William Ackerman
ADAMAITIS,Katherine A AGE:92 30 Aug 1974 Nashua, NH
ADAMATIS,John P AGE:69 21 Jul 1952 Hudson, NH
ADAMIAN,Arshavir AGE:84 08 May 1985 Hudson, NH
ADAMS,Addeliza P AGE:59 3 2 27 Oct 1900 Hudson, NH Silas Hills
 & Roxanna Farnum
ADAMS,Frances M AGE:58 27 Oct 1974 Nashua, NH
ADAMS,Percy L AGE:80 03 Nov 1974 Nashua, NH
AHEARN,Vivian M AGE:56 25 Dec 1982 Nashua, NH
AHERN,Mary Evelyn AGE:74 08 Feb 1973 Concord, NH
AIKEN,Ralph E AGE:69 10 Jul 1977 Nashua, NH
AKSTIN,Paul P AGE:58 23 Feb 1954 Hudson, NH
ALEXANDER,Alphonso AGE:71 4 6 03 Oct 1923 Hudson, NH John Alexander
 & Sally Esty
ALEXANDER,Earl AGE:40 10 9 17 Nov 1941 Concord, NH John Alexander
 & Mae J Work
ALEXANDER,Maggie M AGE:27 04 Jul 1895 Hudson, NH William Mountain
ALEXANDER,Shirley Mae AGE:7 15 14 Sep 1923 Hudson, NH Earl E Alexander
 & Lena Hill
ALEXANDER,Walter N AGE:9 17 Aug 1895 Hudson, NH Wm Alexander & M M Mountain
 (England)
ALLBEE,Clara M AGE:78 2 22 11 Nov 1915 Hudson, NH Samuel Steele (Hudson, NH)
 & Fannie Blodgett (Hudson, NH)
ALLEN,Charles E AGE:87 9 14 03 Feb 1942 Hudson, NH Lewis B Allen
 & Annis Bryant
ALLEN,Steven E AGE:56 20 Nov 1967 Nashua, NH
ALLEN,William H AGE:60 9 30 Sep 1888 Hudson, NH
ALLEN,[Unknown] AGE:1 9 18 Jul 1876 Hudson, NH William H Allen
ALLESON,Eva AGE:67 3 15 31 Jul 1947 Hudson, NH Mattia Plokstis
ALLESON,William AGE:63 4 02 Dec 1941 Hudson, NH James Alleson & Rose Alleson
ALLISON,Jaime AGE:5 18 Mar 1983 Boston, MA
ALUKONIS,Alice E AGE:71 29 Sep 1964 Hudson, NH
ALUKONIS,Annie AGE:83 23 Jun 1977 Hudson, NH
ALUKONIS,Emilia AGE:51 1 2 19 Jun 1942 Nashua, NH Martin Stelmak & Mary S
ALUKONIS,John J AGE:41 10 Aug 1966 Nashua, NH
ALUKONIS,Michael P AGE:89 06 Jul 1977 Nashua, NH
ALUKONIS,Steven AGE:89 11 Jun 1969 Nashua, NH
ALUKONIS,Walter A AGE:61 16 Jun 1950 Hudson, NH Steven Alukonis
 & Rose Kazlauskas
ALUKONIS,William A AGE:79 31 Jan 1969 Nashua, NH
AMADON,Leslie J Jr AGE:32 11 Nov 1976 Nashua, NH

HUDSON,NH DEATHS

AMAS,George AGE:68   18 Aug 1932 Hudson, NH Rachel Amas
AMES,Henry G AGE:48   5   16 Mar 1910 Hudson, NH John Ames & Martha Greenwood
AMOS,Annette AGE:81   23 Aug 1950 Nashua, NH Laurent Rocheminor
   & Philomine Lacatelli
ANCTIL,Norman F AGE:78   13 Feb 1980 Hudson, NH
ANDERSON,Alfreda AGE:26   02 Nov 1909 Hudson, NH M O Peterson & Mary Neilson
ANDERSON,Calvin A AGE:11   12 Mar 1949 Hudson, NH Arthur N Anderson
   & Eunice E Mabry
ANDERSON,Sophia Jane AGE:44   23 Jun 1860 Hudson, NH
ANDREW,Arnold G AGE:70 8 15 22 Mar 1944 Hudson, NH Robert Andrew
   & Emma Thorne
ANDREW,Carrie E AGE:86   04 Oct 1968 Nashua, NH
ANDREW,Emma AGE:78 10 13   29 Apr 1923 Hudson, NH John Thorne & Margaret
ANDREW,Robert AGE:50   14 Jun 1895 Hudson, NH Samuel Andrew (England)
   & Susan (England)
ANDREW,Robert A Sr AGE:80   23 Mar 1983 Nashua, NH
ANDREW,Violetta AGE:63   30 May 1967 Nashua, NH
ANDREWS,Albert AGE:21   23 Nov 1825 Hudson, NH James Andrews & Elizabeth
ANDREWS,Allen AGE:58 8   11 Apr 1855 Hudson, NH
ANDREWS,Anna AGE:13   31 Oct 1825 Hudson, NH James Andrews & Elizabeth
ANDREWS,Arthur S AGE:92   19 Jun 1949 Nashua, NH Robert A Andrews
   & Mary M Kenniston
ANDREWS,Asenath AGE: 03 Jul 1878 Hudson, NH
ANDREWS,Asenath A AGE:1 7   29 Aug 1826 Hudson, NH Allen Andrews
ANDREWS,Daniel D AGE:31   29 Nov 1852 Hudson, NH
ANDREWS,Dorothy L AGE:2 17   31 Jan 1916 Hudson, NH Allen Andrews
   & Josephine Gowing
ANDREWS,Enoch AGE:18   04 Oct 1825 Hudson, NH James Andrews & Elizabeth
ANDREWS,Fanny AGE:50   03 Jan 1843 Hudson, NH
ANDREWS,Flora I AGE:2   13 Apr 1869 Hudson, NH Rufus D Andrews
ANDREWS,Flora L AGE:2 8   12 Apr 1868 Hudson, NH Robert D Andrews
ANDREWS,Franklin AGE:11 7   08 Jul 1839 Hudson, NH Levi Andrews
ANDREWS,Franklin P AGE:64   5 12 Jan 1917 Hudson, NH Lylan Andrews
   & Elizabeth Truell
ANDREWS,Gilman AGE:79 5   25 May 1886 Hudson, NH
ANDREWS,Hannah AGE:23   08 Nov 1825 Hudson, NH James Andrews & Elizabeth
ANDREWS,James AGE:57   11 Feb 1826 Hudson, NH
ANDREWS,James AGE:21   08 Nov 1821 Hudson, NH James Andrews & Elizabeth
ANDREWS,Levi AGE:40   14 Sep 1835 Hudson, NH
ANDREWS,Lucinda AGE: Feb 1859 Hudson, NH
ANDREWS,Mary A AGE:36   09 Mar 1873 Hudson, NH
ANDREWS,Mary J AGE:70   02 Nov 1961 Nashua, NH
ANDREWS,Mary M AGE:48   27 Nov 1878 Hudson, NH Wm Keniston & Betsy
ANDREWS,Mary M K AGE:48   27 Nov 1878 Hudson, NH
ANDREWS,Maude S AGE:91   05 Mar 1963 Nashua, NH
ANDREWS,Nathan AGE:59   21 Dec 1853 Hudson, NH
ANDREWS,Rebecca R AGE:36 9   07 Jul 1849 Hudson, NH
ANDREWS,Robert A AGE:90 7 29   01 Feb 1920 Hudson, NH Allen Andrews
   & Asenath Hills
ANDREWS,Sarah H AGE:77 3   03 Jul 1878 Hudson, NH
ANDREWS,Sophia J AGE:44   23 Jun 1860 Hudson, NH
ANDREWS,Thomas AGE:76   04 Apr 1847 Hudson, NH
ANDREWS,Warren S AGE:16   04 Oct 1825 Hudson, NH James Andrews & Elizabeth
ANDREWS,William A AGE:92 2 3   27 Aug 1946 Concord, NH Robert A Andrews
   & Mary Kenniston
ANDREWS,Williette A AGE:83 3   21 Jul 1943 Hudson, NH George W Annis
   & Elvira French
ANDREWS,[Unknown] AGE: 29 Jul 1923 Hudson, NH Allen B Andrews
   & Josie M Gowing
ANGER,Jeannette D AGE:30   27 Jun 1962 Nashua, NH

HUDSON, NH DEATHS

ANNABLE, Charles W AGE:69 18 Oct 1951 Hudson, NH
ANNIS, Andrew J AGE:63 8 19 16 Jul 1945 Hudson, NH Robert Annis & Mary Baland
ANNIS, Anne G AGE:2 07 Oct 1876 Hudson, NH
ANNIS, Sadie A AGE:87 19 Apr 1966 Nashua, NH
APRIL, Teffle G AGE:87 19 Oct 1957 Nashua, NH
ARBOUR, Conrad A AGE:40 31 Jan 1963 Manchester, NH
ARBOUR, Yvonne AGE:74 16 Apr 1971 Hudson, NH
AREL, Leon A AGE:55 06 Jul 1968 Lowell, MA
ARGIROPOULOS, Argris AGE:94 05 May 1954 Hudson, NH
ARMSTRONG, Hattie F AGE:89 22 Dec 1978 Hudson, NH
ARMSTRONG, John E AGE:47 4 29 31 Jan 1890 Hudson, NH James Armstrong
   (Windham, NH) & Alice Kidder (Groton, MA)
ARMSTRONG, Nellie J AGE:58 1 9 22 Jun 1913 Hudson, NH Simeon Titcomb
   & Sally H Webster
ARPIN, Anna B AGE:52 16 Jan 1964 Nashua, NH
ARPIN, Arthur AGE: 12 Feb 1920 Hudson, NH Pierre Arpin & Georgianna Provencal
ARPIN, Ernest AGE:3 10 8 15 May 1942 Nashua, NH Peter Arpin & Anna Levesque
ARPIN, Florence AGE: 30 Nov 1920 Hudson, NH Pierre Arpin
   & Georgianna Provencal
ARPIN, Georgiana AGE:48 18 25 19 Jul 1933 Hudson, NH Prudent Provencal
   & Delcina Gagne
ARPIN, Jeanne AGE: 05 Jun 1922 Hudson, NH Pierre Arpin & Georgiana Provencal
ARPIN, Leo AGE: 21 Mar 1927 Hudson, NH Pierre Arpin & Georg Provencal
ARPIN, Robert AGE: 30 Nov 1920 Hudson, NH Pierre Arpin & Georgianna Provencal
ARRIS, Gerald M AGE:7 28 Jul 1973 Hudson, NH
ASHE, Leo T AGE:13 7 05 Mar 1910 Hudson, NH Thomas Ashe & Bridget Flynn
ASHLAND, Mary L AGE:83 02 Mar 1953 Hudson, NH
ASPIN, Ethel M AGE:81 06 Nov 1969 Hudson, NH
ATKINS, Anthony A AGE:68 16 Jul 1956 Nashua, NH
ATKINS, Bruce E AGE:21 07 May 1985 Nashua, NH
ATKOCAITIS, Stanley AGE:57 11 May 1972 Nashua, NH
ATWOOD, Almira F AGE:51 09 Jun 1900 Hudson, NH
ATWOOD, David AGE:80 2 10 06 Apr 1888 Hudson, NH John Atwood (Hudson, NH)
   & Sarah Hadley (Hudson, NH)
ATWOOD, Electa AGE:82 7 7 27 Jan 1887 Hudson, NH Josiah Haywood (Hudson, NH)
   & Anna Sawins
ATWOOD, Lois B AGE:76 09 Feb 1892 Hudson, NH John Chapman & Lois Brown
ATWOOD, Lois B Chapman AGE:76 09 Feb 1892 Hudson, NH
ATWOOD, Rachel AGE:66 12 Sep 1871 Hudson, NH
ATWOOD, William AGE:49 6 13 01 Mar 1860 Hudson, NH
ATWOOD, William H AGE: 05 Dec 1850 Hudson, NH William H Atwood & Electa
ATWOOD, Willis H AGE:54 8 19 30 Nov 1918 Hudson, NH Daniel Atwood
   & Ella Sleeper
AUDETTE, Wilfred N AGE:61 01 Jul 1953 Manchester, NH
AUDON, William AGE: 1882 Hudson, NH William Audon & Clarisa Fuller
AUGER, Joseph C Jr AGE:44 30 Sep 1972 Nashua, NH
AULT, Albina I AGE:54 23 Aug 1976 Hudson, NH
AUSTIN, David AGE:75 11 Dec 1852 Hudson, NH
AUSTIN, Frank R AGE:74 16 Oct 1972 Columbus, Ohio
AUSTIN, Sarah AGE:69 30 Nov 1847 Hudson, NH
AVERY, James AGE:2 23 Nov 1931 Hudson, NH Edward H Avery & Lola Chapman
AYER, Sarah AGE: 25 May 1770 Hudson, NH Simon Ayer & Abigail
BABB, Anna S AGE:78 3 19 24 Sep 1923 Hudson, NH Solomon Story
   & Sarah Shattuck
BAGLEY, George E AGE:48 3 27 02 Jun 1905 Hudson, NH Ira Bagley
   & Betsey C Angell
BAGLEY, George Fred AGE:64 10 18 27 Aug 1923 Hudson, NH George Bagley
   & Betsey Hanks
BAGLEY, Gerald AGE:76 27 Aug 1957 Goffstown, NH
BAGLEY, Ida AGE:92 16 Feb 1954 Concord, NH

HUDSON,NH DEATHS

BAILEY,Clifford S AGE:58   14 Feb 1967 Nashua, NH
BAILEY,Florette AGE:60   30 May 1974 Nashua, NH
BAILEY,Sarah AGE:91 1 2   16 Apr 1889 Hudson, NH John Chase (Hudson, NH)
    & Elizabeth Gibson (Hudson, NH)
BAKAIAN,Dickran AGE:54   05 Jan 1977 Nashua, NH
BAKER,Alexis AGE:65   14 Oct 1895 Hudson, NH
BAKER,Angelina T AGE:41 3 20   17 Feb 1899 Hudson, NH Elijah Baker
    & Juliette Friend
BAKER,Annie B AGE:63   30 Sep 1972 Nashua, NH
BAKER,Frances S AGE:71   15 Nov 1978 Nashua, NH
BAKER,John E AGE:65   16 Nov 1966 Nashua, NH
BAKER,John H AGE:93 2   06 Jan 1916 Hudson, NH Jesse Baker & Sally Howard
BAKER,John J AGE:85 5 18 12 Feb 1942 Hudson, NH John H Baker & Lavisa Webster
BAKER,Juliette F AGE:67   7   16 Feb 1887 Hudson, NH Simeon Friend (Dracut,
    MA) & Hannah Palmer (Georgetown, MA)
BAKER,Letitia M AGE:87   28 Mar 1955 E Derry, NH
BAKER,Louisa U AGE:76 1 22   22 Mar 1900 Hudson, NH John Webster
    & Hannah Cummings
BAKER,Marie AGE: 09 Dec 1917 Hudson, NH Joseph Baker & Dora Barrette
BAKER,Mittie H AGE:89   18 Jul 1949 Hudson, NH John H Baker & Louisa Webster
BAKER,Oswald P AGE:88 2 9   16 Sep 1948 Hudson, NH Elijah Baker
    & Juliette Friend
BAKER,Richard AGE:88   20 Dec 1860 Hudson, NH
BAKER,Richard AGE:90   15 Jan 1861 Hudson, NH
BAKER,Sarah L AGE:86   25 May 1964 Nashua, NH
BAKER,Wallace G AGE:72   12 Oct 1979 Nashua, NH
BAKER,William H AGE:63   19 Oct 1960 Rutland, MA
BAKER,William W AGE:67 2 19   10 Dec 1932 Hudson, NH John H Baker
    & Lovica U Webster
BAKER,[Unknown] AGE:1   04 Jan 1903 Hudson, NH Oswald Baker & Letitia Church
BALDWIN,Betsey AGE:66   08 Aug 1892 Hudson, NH John Baldwin (Pelham)
    & Elizabeth Blodgett (Hudson, NH)
BALDWIN,Betsey AGE:91 3 11   28 Jan 1881 Hudson, NH Joseph Blodgett
BALDWIN,Capt John AGE:31   21 Jun 1838 Hudson, NH
BALDWIN,Caroline AGE:77 2   25 Nov 1884 Hudson, NH James Baldwin (Woburn, MA)
    & Priscilla Keyes (Westford, MA)
BALDWIN,George M AGE:3   06 Aug 1867 Hudson, NH George Baldwin & Lydia
BALDWIN,John AGE:72   19 Mar 1889 Hudson, NH James Bowers (Woburn, MA)
    & Priscilla Keyes (Chelmsford, MA)
BALDWIN,Mabel E AGE:89   27 Feb 1973 Nashua, NH
BALDWIN,William H AGE:75   26 Jan 1869 Hudson, NH
BALL,Cora B AGE:67 2 8   21 Jun 1946 Hudson, NH Lucius Gilmore
    & Melvina Burnham
BALLOU,Carrie Della B AGE:100   05 Sep 1979 Hudson, NH
BALUKEVICH,Eva M AGE:74   07 Apr 1959 Nashua, NH
BANCROFT,Fred L AGE:69   02 Jan 1952 Nashua, NH
BANCROFT,Ida M AGE:63   17 Jun 1950 Nashua, NH Charles A Fitzgerald
    & Eva Hamblett
BANCROFT,Lester Frank AGE:71   18 Nov 1980 Hudson, NH
BANFIL,W H AGE:41   Hudson, NH
BANISTER,Rose AGE:57 5 21   20 Oct 1918 Hudson, NH John Bisbee & Susan Perkins
BANKER,Justin E AGE:73 6 22   09 Oct 1947 Nashua, NH
BARBOR,Manion AGE:60   27 Aug 1904 Hudson, NH
BARBOUR,Thomas B AGE:74   17 Jul 1961 Nashua, NH
BARDSLEY,James H AGE:58   31 Mar 1966 Nashua, NH
BARETT,Rev Jean A AGE:79   20 Dec 1955 Nashua, NH
BARIL,Ernest AGE:94   14 Sep 1983 Tewksbury, MA
BARINGER,Edward G AGE:76   02 Mar 1985 Nashua, NH
BARKER,Carl E AGE:63   8   06 Mar 1937 Hudson, NH Ebzakhan I Barker
    & Lizzie Wheeler

HUDSON,NH DEATHS

BARKER,Helen M AGE:37 8 3 04 Jun 1911 Hudson, NH Geo K Hutchins
 & Mary Flanders
BARKER,Martha J AGE:74 6 14 01 Dec 1916 Hudson, NH Andrew Park
 & Margaret Morrison
BARKOWSKI,Alexander AGE:81 23 Aug 1980 Nashua, NH
BARNARD,Addie E AGE:45 3 19 14 Dec 1904 Hudson, NH Norman B Taylor
 & Lydia A Potter
BARNES,Eliza AGE:76 06 May 1863 Hudson, NH
BARNES,EllenJ AGE:78 8 26 Aug 1910 Hudson, NH Sumner Morgan & Jane E Pearson
BARNES,Mary AGE:66 4 13 Mar 1895 Hudson, NH
BARNETT,Margaret M AGE:82 07 Nov 1951 Hudson, NH
BARNETT,Mary L AGE:78 11 28 01 Oct 1909 Hudson, NH Edward McDonald
 & Mary Ann Johnson
BARNETT,Mary T AGE:83 18 Dec 1858 Hudson, NH
BARON,Fred AGE:80 8 27 13 Nov 1946 Goffstown, NH Maxime Baron
 & Sylvia Charlottel
BARRETT,Alvarado AGE:53 7 23 06 Dec 1901 Hudson, NH James Barrett (Hudson,
 NH) & Nancy Tarbell (Hudson, NH)
BARRETT,Bessie L AGE:91 23 Jan 1979 Hudson, NH
BARRETT,Bruce AGE:5 01 Dec 1950 Nashua, NH Leslie Barrett
 & Florence Chadwick
BARRETT,Capt Abel AGE:36 17 Aug 1821 Hudson, NH
BARRETT,Dr Dustin AGE:37 01 Jun 1831 Hudson, NH
BARRETT,Evangeline AGE:20 17 Jan 1874 Hudson, NH
BARRETT,Fanny AGE:33 7 09 Nov 1819 Hudson, NH
BARRETT,Florence M AGE:96 18 Mar 1985 Hudson, NH
BARRETT,Florence R AGE:40 09 Oct 1951 Nashua, NH
BARRETT,Gaius H AGE:66 3 05 Oct 1946 Hudson, NH Sidney Barrett & Eva Smith
BARRETT,George F AGE:25 01 May 1862 Hudson, NH
BARRETT,Hannah AGE:21 11 Dec 1812 Hudson, NH Joel Barrett
BARRETT,Hannah Chadwick AGE:50 08 Jan 1845 Hudson, NH
BARRETT,Isaac AGE:75 10 Dec 1826 Hudson, NH
BARRETT,James AGE:73 7 19 12 Nov 1883 Hudson, NH James Barrett & Mary Cole
BARRETT,Joel AGE: 22 Apr 1860 Hudson, NH
BARRETT,Mary AGE:82 30 Jul 1826 Hudson, NH
BARRETT,Mary AGE:88 5 14 Dec 1863 Hudson, NH
BARRETT,Mary AGE:88 16 Dec 1863 Hudson, NH
BARRETT,Michael H AGE:6 29 Jan 1963 Nashua, NH
BARRETT,Moses AGE:42 13 Oct 1829 Hudson, NH
BARRETT,Nancy AGE:30 11 Sep 1825 Hudson, NH
BARRETT,Nancy T AGE:87 11 10 04 May 1898 Hudson, NH David Tarbell
 & Ann Sprague
BARRETT,Polly AGE:16 14 Jul 1811 Hudson, NH Isaac Barrett & Susanna
BARRETT,Sarah A AGE:6 27 Oct 1823 Hudson, NH Abel Barrett & Sarah
BARRETT,Sarah Davis AGE:68 30 Sep 1867 Hudson, NH
BARRETT,Simon AGE:76 5 30 Nov 1821 Hudson, NH
BARRETT,Susanna AGE:82 28 Jan 1838 Hudson, NH
BARRETTE,Joseph V AGE:6 29 Aug 1913 Hudson, NH Joseph Barrette
 & Georgianna Lavoie
BARRETTE,May Eva AGE: 29 Aug 1920 Hudson, NH Joseph Barrette
 Georgianna Lavoie
BARRETTE,Oscar AGE:3 8 07 Mar 1903 Hudson, NH Alfred Barrette
 & Edwidge Boutin
BARRON,Alden H AGE:73 09 Feb 1899 Hudson, NH
BARRON,Elias AGE:68 12 Sep 1861 Hudson, NH
BARRON,Elias AGE:68 11 Sep 1861 Hudson, NH
BARRON,Irwin E AGE:77 14 18 Jul 1939 Hudson, NH Alden Barron
 & Laura Dudley
BARRON,Julia B AGE:71 02 Jun 1950 Hudson, NH George N Ward & Ellen Elliot
BARRON,Laura L AGE:38 Jun 1867 Hudson, NH

HUDSON, NH DEATHS

BARRON, Mary C AGE:79   19 Jul 1867 Hudson, NH
BARRON, Mary C AGE:69   19 Jan 1867 Hudson, NH
BARRON, Sarah A AGE:73   19 Jan 1901 Concord, NH Elias Barron (Massachusetts)
   & Martha Chamberlain (Massachusetts)
BARROW, Elbert AGE:93   01 Jun 1950 Hudson, NH Claiborne Barrow & Betsy M Purdy
BARTLETT, Edwin Ellsworth AGE:68 5 13   04 Jan 1930 Hudson, NH George W
   Bartlett & Elizabeth Harlow
BARTLETT, Horace A AGE:79   29 Nov 1976 Nashua, NH
BARTLETT, Lydia F AGE:75 6 4   22 Aug 1906 Hudson, NH Nathan W Bartlett
   & Fanny Jones
BARTLETT, Sylvina L AGE:74   16 Jun 1905 Hudson, NH Sam Mooers & Sylvina Loock
BARTOSIEWICZ, William AGE:64   18 Jul 1954 Hudson, NH
BASHALANY, Elias AGE:84   07 Jun 1979 Nashua, NH
BASSETT, Almeda M AGE:62 11   30 Mar 1900 Hudson, NH Roland T Pomeroy
   & Cynthia Woodman
BASSETT, Charles H AGE:77   18 May 1913 Hudson, NH
BASSETT, Frank K AGE:14   21 Nov 1911 Hudson, NH Joseph E Bassett
   & Katherine Mulhaur
BASSETT, Katherine A AGE:62 2 22   22 Aug 1932 Hudson, NH Michael Mulhair
   & Bridget McGlynn
BASTELLE, Marie L AGE:78   14 Jan 1973 Nashua, NH
BATCHELDER, Amanda AGE:66   21 Oct 1895 Hudson, NH Messer
BATCHELDER, Andrew T AGE:96   27 Apr 1965 Hudson, NH
BATCHELDER, Belinda AGE:23 6 18   21 Oct 1843 Hudson, NH
BATCHELDER, George W AGE:22   Hudson, NH
BATCHELDER, George W AGE:22   1865 Salisbury, NC
BATCHELDER, Lydia AGE:7 10 11   03 May 1900 Hudson, NH Samuel Steele
   & Fannie Blodgett
BATCHELDER, Mark AGE:80 11 22   23 May 1902 Hudson, NH Jonathan Batchelder
   & Sally Tucker
BATCHELDER, Nira AGE:79 9 3   27 Aug 1904 Hudson, NH Willard Cummings
   & Nancy Smith
BATCHELDER, Reuben AGE:84 1 27   01 Sep 1909 Hudson, NH Jonathan Batchelder
   & Sally Tucker
BATCHELDER, William A AGE:78 2 16   16 Apr 1892 Hudson, NH Nathan Batchelder
   & Hannah Hobbs
BATCHELDER, Wm A AGE:78 2 16   16 Apr 1892 Hudson, NH Nathan Batchelder
   (Beverly, MA) & Hannah Hobbs (Hudson, NH)
BATES, Robert L AGE:39   08 Jul 1963 Nashua, NH
BATURA, Boleslaw F AGE:58 3 4   18 Aug 1944 Nashua, NH
BATURA, Catherine AGE:83   08 Mar 1968 Nashua, NH
BATURA, Helen AGE:53   26 Jul 1979 Laconia, NH
BATURA, Joseph J AGE:54   08 Apr 1976 Nashua, NH
BATURA, Michael AGE:64   14   25 May 1941 Hudson, NH
BAUSHA, Kim M AGE:5   08 Mar 1962 Hudson, NH
BAZINET, Mary L AGE:80   18 Dec 1963 Hudson, NH
BEAN, James M AGE:44   14 Jun 1866 Hudson, NH
BEAN, Jonas M AGE:44   14 Jun 1866 Hudson, NH
BEAN, [Unknown] AGE: Aug 1866 Hudson, NH James M Bean
BEARD, Betsey AGE:80   25 Jun 1850 Hudson, NH
BEAROR, Robert Leroy AGE:1 6 16   16 Sep 1910 Hudson, NH Louis Bearor
   & Isabel Johnson
BEAUCHAINE, Rita AGE:28   28 Feb 1923 Hudson, NH Alfred Beauchaine
   & Clara Desmarais
BEAUDET, Rachel, Sr Marie Ste Monique AGE:78   25 Feb 1954 Hudson, NH
BEAUDETTE, Rodrique AGE:76   07 Sep 1982 Nashua, NH
BEAUDOIN, Josephine AGE:9   7   04 Jan 1932 Hudson, NH Louis Desrochers
   & Marguerite Lessard
BEAUDOIN, Marie L AGE:67   01 May 1968 Hudson, NH
BEAUDOIN, Richard F AGE:78   10 Nov 1983 Hudson, NH

HUDSON,NH DEATHS

BEAUDRY,Joseph AGE:68   04 Apr 1972 Nashua, NH
BEAUDRY,Normand J AGE:54   29 Jun 1983 Hudson, NH
BEAUDRY,Scott AGE:16   20 Apr 1979 Nashua, NH
BEAULIEU,Eileen AGE:58   24 May 1971 Hudson, NH
BEAULIEU,Joseph A T AGE:88   27 Feb 1973 Hudson, NH
BEAULIEU,Kathryn AGE:2   30 Jul 1982 Milford, NH
BEAULIEU,Lawrence P AGE:18   03 Mar 1960 Hudson, NH
BEAULIEU,Maude AGE:81   22 Aug 1972 Hudson, NH
BEAULIEU,Nathan J AGE:5   30 Jul 1982 Milford, NH
BEAUREGARD,Victor R AGE:42   24 Apr 1957 Nashua, NH
BECKHAM,Jane Marie AGE:14   23 Feb 1976 Hudson, NH
BECKHAM,Joseph R AGE:55   19 Oct 1978 Nashua, NH
BEDARD,Albert E AGE:57   07 Nov 1984 Nashua, NH
BEDARD,Clothilda E M AGE:72   03 Nov 1969 Nashua, NH
BEDARD,Olivine AGE:83   08 Dec 1952 Hudson, NH
BEDARD,William AGE:78   18 Sep 1973 Hudson, NH
BEEBE,Emma C AGE:42 10 4   13 Aug 1889 Hudson, NH Elijah Richardson & Sarah
BEEBE,Emma L AGE:42 10 4   13 Aug 1889 Hudson, NH Elijah Richardson (Hudson,
   NH) & Sarah McDonald (Peacham, VT)
BEEBE,Teotis AGE:74   07 Oct 1966 Lowell, MA
BELAND,Edith O AGE:54 4 20   14 Apr 1946 Hudson, NH John O'Donnell
   & Fannie Morre
BELAND,Evangeline AGE:65   18 Sep 1961 Nashua, NH
BELAND,Hormidas AGE:67   27 Jun 1966 Nashua, NH
BELAND,Michelle AGE:75 7 6   24 Mar 1908 Hudson, NH Louis Beland
   & Julie Laforn
BELAND,Peter J AGE:80   04 May 1965 Nashua, NH
BELAND,Roger P AGE:10 3 2   19 Jan 1946 Nashua, NH Rosario Beland
   & Evangeline Anctil
BELAND,Romeo AGE:56   15 Nov 1961 Hudson, NH
BELAND,Rosario J AGE:78   27 Feb 1974 Nashua, NH
BELANGER,Aurore AGE:47   25 Sep 1958 Hudson, NH
BELANGER,Leon AGE:58 11 18   10 May 1947 Hartford, VT
BELANGER,Lucille AGE:56   14 Apr 1982 Hudson, NH
BELANGER,Regina AGE:77   08 Jun 1972 Nashua, NH
BELANGER,Therese L AGE:9   20 Jun 1930 Hudson, NH Albert Belanger
   & Blanche Levesque
BELKNAP,Andrew J AGE:82 3 21   25 Sep 1897 Hudson, NH Moses Belknap
   & Esther Webster
BELKNAP,Sophia S Bennett AGE:72 11 19   29 Dec 1890 Hudson, NH
BELKNAPP,Sophia S AGE:72 11 19   29 Dec 1890 Hudson, NH Abiah Smart
   (Springfield, Vt) & Sophia Bennett (Springfield, Vt)
BELL,Caroline T AGE:70 10 6   11 Oct 1901 Hudson, NH William Campbell
   (Windham) & Margaret Huges (Windham)
BELLAVANCE,Mary Rose L AGE:72   18 Sep 1942 Hudson, NH Alfred Lapierre
   & Exilda Gauthier
BELLEFEUILLE,Joseph H AGE:83   15 Jan 1979 Nashua, NH
BELLEFEUILLE,Raymond G AGE:59   14 Dec 1983 Hudson, NH
BELMORE,Bernadette L AGE:64   29 Jul 1950 Hudson, NH Antoine Lefebvre
   & Philomine Desjardins
BELMORE,Hector P AGE:65   17 Nov 1951 Hudson, NH
BEMIS,Bertha C AGE:83   03 Aug 1953 Hudson, NH
BENJAMIN,Sr Marie Ste Gregoir AGE:50   13 Apr 1949 Hudson, NH Olivier Benjamin
   & Rose Danduranf
BENNETT,Clarissa A AGE: 20 Oct 1858 Hudson, NH
BENNETT,Floyd A Sr AGE:32   12 Oct 1970 Hudson, NH
BENNETT,Marcus F AGE:57   Aug 1874 Hudson, NH
BENNETT,May L AGE:76   20 Nov 1965 Merrimack, NH
BENNETT,[Unknown] AGE:1   23 Apr 1964 Nashua, NH
BENNIS,Monique AGE:60   29 Apr 1969 Nashua, NH

HUDSON,NH DEATHS

BENOIT,Claudia P AGE:88   23 Dec 1978 Hudson, NH
BENOIT,Sr St Peligie AGE:67 9 10   29 Apr 1943 Hudson, NH Didace Benoit
   & Peligie Benoit
BENSON,Charles S AGE:42   04 Jan 1953 Nashua, NH
BENSON,George T AGE:77   26 Jun 1962 Hudson, NH
BENSON,Ida S AGE:74   09 Mar 1959 Nashua, NH
BENSON,John T AGE:72   18 Sep 1943 Nashua, NH Thomas Benson & Sarah M Biscombe
BERARD,Anna SEX: AGE:63   23 Sep 1964 Nashua, NH
BERARD,Leon A AGE:67   14 Mar 1966 Somerville, MA
BERGERON,Wilfred J AGE:73   10 Oct 1978 Nashua, NH
BERGKAMP,Ada AGE:77   24 Nov 1977 Hudson, NH
BERNAICHE,Alice AGE:66   02 Aug 1961 Nashua, NH
BERNAICHE,Wilfred J AGE:79   11 Mar 1979 Nashua, NH
BERNARD,Cora I AGE:20   25   23 Aug 1894 Hudson, NH David Bernard
   & Lize A Cornell
BERNARD,David AGE:48   01 Feb 1893 Hudson, NH John Bernard (Ireland)
   & Eliza Sparing (Ireland)
BERNARD,Frank AGE:86   05 Apr 1963 Hudson, NH
BERNARD,Paul L AGE:47   03 Dec 1967 Hudson, NH
BERNHAM,Amory AGE:81   4   21 Nov 1896 Hudson, NH John Burnham (Bolton, MA)
   & Hannah Blodgett (Hudson, NH)
BERNIER,Gertrude A AGE:67   02 Aug 1978 Nashua, NH
BERNOCHE,Marie AGE: 09 Feb 1902 Hudson, NH Amede Bernoche & Lucie Boutin
BERRY,Andrew J AGE:23   18 Jul 1863 Hudson, NH
BERRY,John W AGE:9   19 Apr 1869 Hudson, NH
BERRY,Julia AGE:23   07 Aug 1873 Hudson, NH
BERRY,Orville AGE:1   Aug 1873 Hudson, NH
BERUBE,Angelina AGE:90   07 May 1964 Concord, NH
BERUBE,Charles E AGE:86   20 Dec 1982 Nashua, NH
BERUBE,Leopoldine M AGE:87   15 Nov 1978 Nashua, NH
BERUBE,Lillian AGE:46   21 Jan 1963 Nashua, NH
BESTON,Lovilla A AGE:79   05 Feb 1954 Nashua, NH
BETE,William A AGE:65 5 26   11 Feb 1941 Nashua, NH Charles Bete
   & Christina Voelker
BETTS,A Radley AGE:69   06 Mar 1981 Nashua, NH
BETTY,Philip Leo A AGE:62   15 Jul 1974 Nashua, NH
BETURNEY,Catherine S AGE:84   23 Jun 1973 Nashua, NH
BETURNEY,John F AGE:60   13 Nov 1949 Hudson, NH Maurice Beturney
   & Regina Daigle
BEYER,Hans P AGE:78   01 Feb 1984 Hudson, NH
BEZA,Sotirios T AGE:50 3 12   16 Aug 1944 Hudson, NH Sterie Beza
BIBEAU,Alice AGE:63   07 Jul 1971 Nashua, NH
BIBEAU,Hector AGE:62   06 Nov 1960 Rochester, NH
BICKFORD,Arthur AGE:20   01 Sep 1896 Hudson, NH Franklin Bickford (Conway)
   & Abbie Jewett (Conway)
BICKFORD,Cora M AGE:94   02 Feb 1968 Hudson, NH
BICKFORD,Ella M AGE:78   15 Apr 1958 Nashua, NH
BICKFORD,Fred AGE:86   22 May 1956 Goffstown, NH
BICKFORD,Lester J AGE:19 1 27   26 Feb 1902 Hudson, NH Edwin D Bickford
   & Harriet Pitman
BICKLEY,Joseph AGE:82   27 Dec 1960 Nashua, NH
BILGER,Alfred A AGE:68   16 Feb 1964 Nashua, NH
BILLS,Wallace A AGE:79   09 Aug 1980 Nashua, NH
BILLY,Ste-Rose Rosanna AGE:91   14 May 1985 Hudson, NH
BILODEAU,Raymond R AGE:15   24 Apr 1977 Nashua, NH
BISHOP,Jeanette AGE:60   05 Jun 1980 Sandown, NH
BISSON,Paulette AGE:1   31 Dec 1967 Nashua, NH
BISSONNETTE,Michael AGE:75   16 Oct 1915 Hudson, NH Michel Bissonnette
   (Canada) & Archangel Theraud (Canada)
BIXBY,Lizzie M AGE:23   15 Feb 1877 Hudson, NH

HUDSON,NH DEATHS

BIXBY,Lizzie M Emery AGE:22 1 15 Feb 1877 Hudson, NH
BIXBY,Nancy G AGE:37 4 27 11 Oct 1925 Hudson, NH Clinton H Bixby
   & Harriet Gardner
BLAIS,Amanda AGE:54 12 Apr 1957 Nashua, NH
BLAISDELL,Arland P AGE:70 25 Jan 1967 Nashua, NH
BLAISDELL,Edith Y AGE:77 26 Apr 1966 Nashua, NH
BLAKE,Beda Amanda AGE: 29 Jul 1907 Hudson, NH Lyman Blake & Nellie M Corey
BLAKE,Elizabeth B AGE:68 2 06 Mar 1892 Hudson, NH Joel Barrett (Concord, MA)
   & Sarah Wyman (Roxbury, MA)
BLAKE,Elizabeth Barrett AGE:68 2 06 Mar 1892 Hudson, NH
BLAKE,Joseph R AGE:58 8 5 17 Jan 1906 Hudson, NH Joseph Blake
   & Elizabeth Barrett
BLANCHARD,Lydia AGE:70 19 Feb 1822 Hudson, NH
BLANCHARD,Silas M AGE:68 9 7 16 Dec 1888 Hudson, NH Benjamin Blanchard
   (Andover, MA) & Sarah M Damdson (Windham)
BLEAU,John AGE:37 11 20 18 Mar 1926 Hudson, NH Napoleon Bleau
   & Marie Chelifoux
BLISS,Acenath M AGE:69 9 19 Aug 1902 Hudson, NH Amos Marsh
BLISS,Orion AGE:31 30 Apr 1860 Hudson, NH
BLISS,Orrin AGE:31 30 Apr 1860 Hudson, NH
BLODGETT,Ann AGE:77 06 Jun 1853 Hudson, NH
BLODGETT,Asa AGE:76 11 Apr 1851 Hudson, NH
BLODGETT,Austin AGE:76 4 11 Aug 1895 Hudson, NH Joseph Blodgett (Hudson, NH)
   & Sarah Spalding (Hudson, NH)
BLODGETT,Austin J AGE:86 1 11 25 Feb 1946 Hudson, NH Austin W Blodgett
   & Susan Davis
BLODGETT,Catherine AGE:34 20 Dec 1795 Hudson, NH
BLODGETT,Catherine AGE:23 10 Dec 1805 Hudson, NH Asahel Blodgett & Catherine
BLODGETT,Clarissa AGE:79 1 18 Apr 1888 Hudson, NH Levi Bales (Methuen, MA)
   & Mary Smith (Methuen, MA)
BLODGETT,Clarissa Boles AGE:79 1 18 Apr 1888 Hudson, NH
BLODGETT,Clementine AGE:75 17 Apr 1863 Hudson, NH
BLODGETT,Clementine H AGE:22 5 17 Apr 1863 Hudson, NH Warren Blodgett
   & Belinda Barrett
BLODGETT,Cora A AGE: 08 Sep 1860 Hudson, NH Warren Blodgett
   & Elizabeth Webster
BLODGETT,Dorcas AGE:34 29 Jun 1763 Hudson, NH
BLODGETT,Dorothy AGE:84 06 Mar 1778 Hudson, NH
BLODGETT,Elizabeth AGE:74 09 Mar 1813 Hudson, NH
BLODGETT,Elizabeth B AGE:93 4 29 Mar 1909 Hudson, NH John Webster
   & Hannah Cummings
BLODGETT,Hannah AGE: 21 Feb 1761 Hudson, NH
BLODGETT,Hannah Davis AGE:86 23 Apr 1842 Hudson, NH
BLODGETT,Harry D AGE:51 5 20 16 May 1915 Hudson, NH Augustus F Blodgett
   (Dorchester, NH) & Lucy E Chase (Hudson, NH)
BLODGETT,Isaac AGE:29 29 Oct 1816 Hudson, NH Asahel Blodgett & Catherine
BLODGETT,Isaac AGE: 21 Jan 1777 Hudson, NH Jeremiah Blodgett
BLODGETT,Jabez AGE:78 19 Jul 1844 Hudson, NH
BLODGETT,Jacob AGE:84 26 Dec 1860 Hudson, NH
BLODGETT,Jacob AGE: 25 Dec 1860 Hudson, NH
BLODGETT,Jonathan AGE:94 02 Nov 1820 Hudson, NH
BLODGETT,Joseph AGE:84 16 Aug 1801 Hudson, NH
BLODGETT,Joseph AGE:87 28 Mar 1847 Hudson, NH
BLODGETT,Joseph AGE:74 03 Dec 1761 Hudson, NH
BLODGETT,Joseph AGE:80 29 Aug 1866 Hudson, NH
BLODGETT,Joseph S AGE:40 11 28 Aug 1854 Hudson, NH
BLODGETT,Lucy Chase AGE:50 8 15 25 Mar 1886 Hudson, NH
BLODGETT,Lucy E AGE:50 8 15 25 Mar 1886 Hudson, NH
BLODGETT,Rachel AGE:82 8 18 May 1850 Hudson, NH
BLODGETT,Sarah AGE: 13 Apr 1756 Hudson, NH

HUDSON,NH DEATHS

BLODGETT,Sarah AGE: 05 Feb 1777 Hudson, NH Jeremiah Blodgett
BLODGETT,Sarah AGE:79 11 26 Apr 1865 Hudson, NH
BLODGETT,Sarah AGE:79   21 Apr 1865 Hudson, NH
BLODGETT,Sarah L AGE:6 6 15 09 Apr 1822 Hudson, NH Joseph Blodgett, Jr
   & Sarah Spalding
BLODGETT,Sarah Spalding AGE:79 26 Apr 1865 Hudson, NH
BLODGETT,Sarah W AGE:76 07 Mar 1808 Hudson, NH
BLODGETT,Susan AGE:77 11 29 02 Mar 1897 Hudson, NH Samuel Davis & Anna Morse
BLODGETT,William AGE:58 03 Jan 1866 Hudson, NH
BLOOD,Arthur V AGE:43 30 Apr 1966 Nashua, NH
BLOOD,Clarence A AGE:9 19 Mar 1908 Hudson, NH Fred C Blood & L Edith Wyman
BLOOD,Dora P AGE:68   19 20 Jun 1934 Hudson, NH Jonathan Day & Hannah Page
BLOOD,Lester A AGE:20 5 20 12 Mar 1917 Hudson, NH George F Blood
   & Dora P Day
BOARDMAN,James AGE:22 7 04 Sep 1854 Hudson, NH
BOARDMAN,John AGE:56 02 Oct 1843 Hudson, NH
BOARDMAN,Lydia AGE:64 12 Dec 1858 Hudson, NH
BOGAN,Daniel AGE:65 17 Jun 1968 Nashua, NH
BOGDEN,Mary E AGE:59 29 Oct 1941 Hudson, NH Charles Kudolis
   & Madeline Savaroski
BOILARD,Leonard F AGE:3   5 27 Mar 1945 Nashua, NH Oswald Boilard
   & Adrienne Marquis
BOISSEAU,Joseph AGE:78 7 7 13 Nov 1943 Hudson, NH Bruno Boisseau
   & Eladie Tetreau
BOISVERT,Yvonne R AGE:74 25 Apr 1974 Nashua, NH
BOLDUC,Gertrude AGE:70 08 Jun 1977 Nashua, NH
BOLDUC,Joseph AGE:69 10 Aug 1956 Hudson, NH
BOLES,Greenleaf AGE:83 08 Mar 1871 Hudson, NH
BOLES,Hannah AGE:78 18 May 1858 Hudson, NH
BOLES,Levi AGE:76 03 Mar 1860 Hudson, NH
BOLES,Mahala AGE: 10 May 1900 Boston, MA
BOLES,Mary AGE:88 12 Dec 1874 Hudson, NH
BOLES,Prescott AGE:68 11 Feb 1892 Hudson, NH John Boles (Methuen, MA)
   & Persis Woodbury (Methuen, MA)
BonCONSEIL,Rev Sr Marie du AGE:75 06 Feb 1956 Hudson, NH
BONIN,Henry AGE:58 1 14 06 Jul 1948 Goffstown, NH Remie Bonin
   & Marie Guertin
BONNETTE,Delia AGE:83 15 May 1974 Nashua, NH
BONNETTE,Frank E AGE:62 20 Aug 1952 Nashua, NH
BONVILLE,John B AGE:70 27 Mar 1974 Nashua, NH
BOOKER,Priscilla AGE:87 11 27 22 Feb 1912 Hudson, NH Abner Barker
   & Priscilla Childs
BORCA,Bronica AGE:1 1 3 09 Aug 1924 Hudson, NH Bromslaw Borca
   & Apolina AcKavich
BORDEN,John J AGE:66 2 3 31 Mar 1946 Nashua, NH
BORTAS,Josephine AGE:81 02 Jul 1966 Concord, NH
BORTHWICK,Raymond P AGE:70 29 Mar 1972 Nashua, NH
BOSKA,Benjamin W AGE:78 27 Oct 1964 Nashua, NH
BOSKA,Gernice AGE:24 02 Jun 1920 Hudson, NH John Boska & Veronica Glatnik
BOSKA,Scott K AGE:2 26 May 1957 Nashua, NH
BOSLEY,Olida M AGE:87 04 Apr 1983 Nashua, NH
BOSS,Marie AGE:79 01 May 1977 Nashua, NH
BOSSE,Joseph A AGE:68 05 Mar 1951 Nashua, NH
BOSSE,Roland A AGE:73 21 Jun 1984 Nashua, NH
BOSSE,Roland A Jr AGE:30 10 Oct 1963 Manchester, NH
BOSSIE,Frederick R AGE:4 08 Jan 1958 Nashua, NH
BOSSIE,John A AGE:1 05 Jan 1958 Nashua, NH
BOSWORTH,Raymond J AGE:46 12 May 1963 Manchester, NH
BOUCHER,Antoine P AGE:77 27 Jun 1953 Nashua, NH
BOUCHER,Armand AGE:65 24 Aug 1962 Hudson, NH

HUDSON,NH DEATHS

BOUCHER,Arthur J AGE: 07 Jul 1946 Nashua, NH Roger L Boucher
  & Esther Daneault
BOUCHER,Arthur J AGE:77 21 Feb 1972 Nashua, NH
BOUCHER,Flora AGE:68 08 Jan 1968 Northampton, MA
BOUCHER,Jean Baptiste AGE:82 11 28 13 Mar 1937 Hudson, NH Jean Bapt Boucher
  & Julie Bertrand
BOUCHER,Leon AGE:57 21 Nov 1937 Hudson, NH George Boucher
  & Felliste Bonenfant
BOUCHER,Marie AGE: 25 Aug 1947 Nashua, NH Roger L Boucher & Esther Daneault
BOUCHER,Peter J AGE:50 3 13   07 Oct 1948 Hudson, NH Joseph Boucher
  & Alphonsine Berube
BOUCHER,Sr Marie St Mederic AGE:76 11 23 27 Dec 1948 Hudson, NH Joseph
  Boucher & Sophie Durand
BOUCHES,Raymond AGE:13 9 28   24 Dec 1923 Hudson, NH Leon Bouches
  & Lodia Ricard
BOULANGER,Joseph AGE:88 16 Jan 1979 Nashua, NH
BOULANGER,Joseph O AGE:85 6 8 23 Mar 1940 Hudson, NH Octave Boulanger
BOULANGER,Virginia B AGE:82 8 2 09 Oct 1944 Hudson, NH Joseph Beaudoin
BOULEY,Eva AGE:56 10 6 08 Jul 1941 Hudson, NH Oliver Ricard & Hermica Dionne
BOULEY,Ferdinand J AGE:96 08 Jul 1956 Hudson, NH
BOULEY,Louise M AGE:90 08 Jun 1981 Hudson, NH
BOULEY,Nicholas L AGE:58 06 Mar 1962 Nashua, NH
BOULEY,Raymond R AGE:62 21 Sep 1970 Hudson, NH
BOURBEAU,Oscar J AGE:72 29 Feb 1984 Nashua, NH
BOURDON,James AGE:20 10 Mar 1969 Nashua, NH
BOURN,Theodore S Jr AGE:28 8 28 27 May 1946 Hudson, NH Theodore S Bourn
  & Mary Doolittle
BOURQUE,Anna T AGE:77 16 Jul 1972 Nashua, NH
BOURQUE,Arthur AGE:66 11 Mar 1965 Hudson, NH
BOURQUE,Ovide AGE:72   25 12 Feb 1948 Goffstown, NH George Bourque
BOURRASSA,Josephine AGE:74 20 Jul 1921 Hudson, NH Joseph Langlois
  & Elizabeth Roy
BOUTAS,Frank AGE:52 13 Mar 1932 Hudson, NH
BOUTIN,Marion AGE:85 10 May 1977 Manchester, NH
BOWDEN,Donald F Sr AGE:66 16 May 1977 Nashua, NH
BOWERS,Elizabeth AGE:31 03 Feb 1794 Hudson, NH Isaac Bowers & Elizabeth
BOWLER,Mary A AGE:76 18 May 1952 Hudson, NH
BOWLES,Mary AGE:87 12 Dec 1874 Hudson, NH
BOWNE,Bernice E AGE:74 01 May 1967 Hudson, NH
BOWNE,Raymond W AGE:66 10 May 1958 Hudson, NH
BOYD,Charles W AGE:74 9 4 27 Feb 1930 Hudson, NH Thomas Boyd & Sarah Chase
BOYD,Emeline T AGE:67 09 Apr 1898 Hudson, NH Willard Spalding & Sally Marsh
BOYER,Albina AGE:71 29 Dec 1969 Nashua, NH
BOYER,Celina AGE:76 22 Dec 1951 Hudson, NH
BOYER,Edgar Jr AGE:3 1 28 Aug 1927 Hudson, NH Edgar Boyer & Mildred Nutting
BOYER,John AGE:13 5 18 Jun 1945 Hudson, NH Joseph E Boyer & Albina Fournier
BOYER,Joseph C Sr AGE:52 25 Oct 1982 Hudson, NH
BOYER,Joseph J AGE:77 24 Aug 1977 Nashua, NH
BOYER,Victory AGE:77 11 Jan 1950 Hudson, NH Constant Boyer
  & Philomine Bouvier
BOYLE,John AGE: 09 Feb 1940 Goffstown, NH
BOYLE,William H AGE:39 2 27 11 Sep 1908 Hudson, NH William Boyle
  & Susan V Brown
BOYNTON,John E AGE:66 9 13 22 Jan 1918 Hudson, NH Jacob Boynton
  & Mehitable Stanley
BRACKETT,Charles Wesley AGE:76 14 Nov 1973 Nashua, NH
BRADLEY,Clara E AGE:79 2 22 01 Dec 1947 Hudson, NH John Dennison
  & Laura Maker
BRADLEY,James R AGE:17 13 Oct 1956 Nashua, NH
BRADLEY,Joseph AGE: 31 Jan 1791 Hudson, NH Joseph Bradley & Mary

HUDSON,NH DEATHS

BRAIN,Lillian AGE:71 7 2 20 Dec 1912 Hudson, NH John Butler
BRAMHALL,Sarah AGE:89 14 Oct 1893 Hudson, NH Jobez Blodgett (Hudson, NH)
 & Rachel Pollard (Hudson, NH)
BRASSE,Andre E AGE:57 30 Sep 1961 Hudson, NH
BREEN,Andrew J AGE:76 27 Jun 1945 Hudson, NH Michael Breen
BREEN,John M AGE:73 11 Aug 1972 Nashua, NH
BREEN,Lillian E AGE:85 24 Mar 1985 Nashua, NH
BRENNAN,Abbie AGE:69 21 Oct 1911 Hudson, NH
BRENNAN,Quentin J AGE:23 27 Feb 1965 Nashua, NH
BRESNAHAN,George M AGE:84 11 12 04 Feb 1947 Nashua, NH Michael Bresnahan
 & Margaret Shea
BRESNAHAN,John J AGE:65 5 7 24 Feb 1941 Nashua, NH John Bresnahan
BRESNAHAN,Robert H AGE:68 03 Nov 1954 Nashua, NH
BRESNAHAN,Zilda L AGE:62 08 Jun 1946 Hudson, NH Raymond Lanoue
 & Aurline Gregoire
BRIAND,Auguste J AGE:85 03 Aug 1973 Manchester, NH
BRIAND,Dorothy AGE:53 31 Oct 1976 Manchester, NH
BRIAND,Edouard AGE:2 22 12 Feb 1933 Hudson, NH Auguste Briand
 & Leonie Pelletier
BRIAND,Esther AGE:61 25 Jul 1975 Nashua, NH
BRIAND,Etienne T SEX: AGE:76 18 Jun 1970 Nashua, NH
BRIAND,Joseph A AGE:7 15 15 Aug 1921 Hudson, NH Auguste Briand
 & Leonie Pelletier
BRIAND,Leonie AGE:53 8 20 29 May 1944 Hudson, NH Alphe Pelletier
BRIAND,Marment AGE:8 18 Jan 1924 Hudson, NH August Briand & Leonie Pelletier
BRIAND,Merrilee G AGE:4 05 Mar 1958 Hudson, NH
BRIAND,Rita AGE:51 19 Jul 1971 Laconia, NH
BRIAND,Violet AGE:60 01 May 1980 Nashua, NH
BRIDGFORD,Ralph A AGE:73 15 Apr 1964 Nashua, NH
BRIEN,Edward L AGE:61   28 27 Feb 1935 Hudson, NH Rev Geo G Brien
 & Lucy Gallop
BRIGHAM,George AGE:54 31 Mar 1977 Nashua, NH
BRINTNALL,William P AGE:83 14 Dec 1960 Nashua, NH
BRISCOE,Edward C AGE:82 21 Apr 1967 Hudson, NH
BRISEBOIS,Paul R Sr AGE:62 01 Oct 1975 Nashua, NH
BRISSETTE, Arthemise,Sr Marie Theodore AGE:75 12 Oct 1952 Hudson, NH
BRITTON,Warren O AGE:9 19 09 Jun 1915 Hudson, NH Joseph A Britton
 (Annondale, VA) & Bertha A Campbell (Nova Scotia
BRODERICK,Thomas M AGE:74 04 Aug 1951 Hudson, NH
BRODEUR,Cecilia AGE:60 21 May 1969 Nashua, NH
BRODEUR,George A AGE:7 29 Dec 1921 Hudson, NH Hormidos Brodeur
 & Bertha Duval
BROOKS,Ann R AGE:86 27 Aug 1907 Hudson, NH Ephraim Cilley
BROOKS,Charles P AGE:86 11 Sep 1965 Nashua, NH
BROSSO,George L AGE:2 2 04 Jun 1899 Hudson, NH Thomas Brosso & Jane Prans
BROTHERS,Malvina AGE:2 20 04 Oct 1941 Nashua, NH Erwin L Brothers
 & Marion Scott
BROUILLET,Omer A AGE:52 13 Jan 1970 Manchester, NH
BROWN,Catherine M AGE:54 04 Nov 1983 Hudson, NH
BROWN,Clara B AGE:88 20 Apr 1949 Hudson, NH George Bryant & Betsey Kidder
BROWN,Eliza W AGE:94 9 07 Apr 1910 Hudson, NH Robert Boyd & Martha Town
BROWN,Frederick A AGE:85 19 Jun 1952 Nashua, NH
BROWN,Harold A AGE:63 07 Jun 1966 Nashua, NH
BROWN,Henry C AGE:81 5 14 08 Aug 1940 Hudson, NH Darwin Woodard
 & Rhoda M Bryant
BROWN,John D AGE:73 7 4 29 Sep 1900 Hudson, NH Deitor Brown & Deborah Smith
BROWN,Kenneth J AGE:63 28 Jul 1973 Nashua, NH
BROWN,Lillian D AGE:45   6 31 Aug 1916 Hudson, NH James W Davis
 & Arabella Foster
BROWN,Lorinda E AGE:67 29 Jan 1888 Hudson, NH Elijah Brown (New Hampshire)

HUDSON,NH DEATHS

BROWN,Russell E Jr AGE:48 01 Oct 1983 Hudson, NH
BROWN,Sarah M AGE:82 10 10 Dec 1898 Hudson, NH
BROWN,Sullivan W AGE:55 11 Oct 1953 Hudson, NH
BROWN,Venita M AGE:47 20 Jan 1950 Nashua, NH Raymond J Pollard & Cora Cooper
BROWN,Walter H AGE:89 2 22 22 Mar 1938 Hudson, NH Willard T Brown
    & Margaret M Brown
BROWN,William M AGE:77 09 Aug 1960 Hudson, NH
BROWNING,Sarah V AGE:73 13 07 Apr 1926 Hudson, NH John Hussey
    & Abbie Hanson
BRUCE,Adelbut F AGE:6 8 23 11 Feb 1893 Hudson, NH Elias Bruce (Nova Scotia)
    & Addie B Farmer (Nashua, NH)
BRUNEAU,Ida AGE:69 18 Mar 1970 Hudson, NH
BRUNELL,Felicia M AGE:79 20 Sep 1951 Nashua, NH
BRUNT,Muriel M AGE:74 08 Nov 1983 Nashua, NH
BRYANT,George W AGE:77 7 2 15 Sep 1932 Hudson, NH George R Bryant
    & Elizabeth Kidder
BRYANT,Warren G AGE:78 26 27 Dec 1927 Hudson, NH George R Bryant
    & Betsey Ann Kidder
BUCHANAN,George H AGE:84 4 11 10 Jul 1942 Hudson, NH George Buchanan
    & Ann Young
BUCKHAM,John D AGE:77 29 Apr 1896 Hudson, NH Buckham (England)
    & Dickerman (England)
BUCKLEY,[Unknown] AGE: Mar 1894 Hudson, NH
BUDRO,Leon A AGE:64 1 8 19 Mar 1944 Nashua, NH David Budro & Clara Ferryall
BUESSING,Vanantius SEX: AGE:86 19 May 1966 Nashua, NH
BUGBEE,Martha R AGE: 08 Dec 1900 W Newton, MA
BUKER,Richard AGE:70 15 Jan 1861 Hudson, NH
BULLARD,John O Jr AGE:24 06 Aug 1960 Nashua, NH
BULLOCK,John J AGE:29 13 Jan 1956 Hudson, NH
BUNDY,Amasa T AGE:70 6 17 Oct 1895 Hudson, NH
BURBANK,Ann Goodspeed AGE:26 26 Oct 1864 Hudson, NH
BURBANK,Cummings AGE:20 5 26 31 Oct 1825 Hudson, NH Jonathan Burbank
    & Elizabeth Cummings
BURBANK,David AGE:18 2 12 14 Jul 1812 Hudson, NH Jonathan Burbank
    & Elizabeth Cummings
BURBANK,Elizabeth AGE:82 2 6 18 Jul 1847 Hudson, NH
BURBANK,Elizabeth AGE:67 10 4 08 Oct 1858 Hudson, NH Jonathan Burbank
    & Elizabeth Cummings
BURBANK,Eunice AGE: 10 Jan 1765 Hudson, NH
BURBANK,Gladys D AGE:72 14 Aug 1981 Nashua, NH
BURBANK,Hannah AGE:27 4 24 07 Feb 1826 Hudson, NH Jonathan Burbank
    & Elizabeth Cummings
BURBANK,John P AGE:26 7 21 29 May 1827 Hudson, NH Jonathan Burbank
    & Elizabeth Cummings
BURBANK,Jonathan AGE:77 04 Mar 1836 Hudson, NH
BURBANK,Jonathan AGE:31 11 Aug 1863 Memphis, TN
BURBANK,Jonathan Jr AGE:34 28 Aug 1830 Hudson, NH
BURBANK,Lizzie Ann AGE:7 22 Mar 1857 Hudson, NH
BURBANK,Lucinda Wilson AGE:22 27 May 1824 Hudson, NH
BURBANK,Ophely AGE:8 09 Jan 1818 Hudson, NH
BURDEN,William A Sr AGE:52 01 Jul 1961 Nashua, NH
BURNELL,Earl F AGE:88 31 Oct 1979 Nashua, NH
BURNER,Eugene AGE:20 23 Jul 1971 Nashua, NH
BURNER,Paul AGE:15 23 Jul 1971 Nashua, NH
BURNES,Milton AGE:65 17 Oct 1976 Nashua, NH
BURNETT,Cleon F AGE:66 19 Apr 1972 Nashua, NH
BURNETT,Helen L AGE:72 05 Mar 1972 Hudson, NH
BURNETT,James AGE:72 2 6 01 Feb 1905 Hudson, NH Samuel Burnett
    & Catherine Moore
BURNHAM,Adaline AGE:39 10 23 Dec 1881 Hudson, NH John Burnham, Jr

HUDSON, NH DEATHS

BURNHAM, Adelaide AGE:39 10 23 Dec 1881 Newton, MA John Burnham
 & Harriet Johnson
BURNHAM, Anna M AGE:18 11 16 Mar 1864 Hudson, NH Amory Burnham & M C
BURNHAM, Daniel AGE:6 3 24 19 Apr 1826 Hudson, NH John Burnham & Hannah
BURNHAM, Hannah AGE:19 03 Apr 1847 Hudson, NH Amory Burnham & M C
BURNHAM, Hannah D AGE:3 4 7 29 Apr 1826 Hudson, NH John Burnham & Hannah
BURNHAM, Hannah P AGE:62 27 Sep 1849 Hudson, NH
BURNHAM, Harriet A AGE:25 16 Aug 1844 Hudson, NH
BURNHAM, Jeremiah P AGE:76 8 15 May 1899 Hudson, NH Joseph Burnham & Esther
BURNHAM, John AGE:85 07 Jan 1869 Hudson, NH
BURNHAM, John Jr SEX: AGE:32 26 Jun 1843 Hudson, NH COND:
BURNHAM, Joseph P AGE:9 13 Jul 1825 Hudson, NH John Burnham & Hannah
BURNHAM, Martha C AGE:76 8 25 Dec 1893 Hudson, NH
BURNHAM, Martha J AGE:7 24 Feb 1851 Hudson, NH Amory Burnham & M C
BURNHAM, Maude M AGE:86 10 Feb 1969 Nashua, NH
BURNHAM, Roxanna M AGE:11 7 16 Mar 1864 Hudson, NH Amory Burnham & M C
BURNS, Abigail E AGE:29 25 May 1848 Hudson, NH David Burns
BURNS, Alvira A AGE:44 05 Sep 1862 Hudson, NH
BURNS, Ann AGE:30 02 Nov 1844 Hudson, NH
BURNS, Capt James AGE:45 25 May 1825 Hudson, NH
BURNS, Capt William AGE:51 01 Oct 1795 Hudson, NH
BURNS, Cathrine D AGE:62 8 09 May 1918 Hudson, NH
BURNS, Charlotte E AGE:67 28 Mar 1956 Nashua, NH
BURNS, Daniel AGE:83 16 Feb 1870 Hudson, NH
BURNS, David AGE:88 7 02 Apr 1876 Hudson, NH
BURNS, David AGE:88 20 Apr 1876 Hudson, NH
BURNS, Eliza AGE:68 19 Jun 1880 Hudson, NH David Burns
BURNS, Eliza A AGE:68 29 Jun 1880 Hudson, NH David Burns & Eliza Childs
BURNS, Eliza C AGE:76 9 06 May 1863 Hudson, NH
BURNS, Eloisa A AGE:44 7 05 Sep 1862 Hudson, NH
BURNS, Fanny AGE:4 15 Jul 1817 Hudson, NH James Burns
BURNS, Frederick AGE:29 01 Apr 1846 Hudson, NH David Burns
BURNS, George AGE:83 1779 Hudson, NH
BURNS, George H AGE:41 28 Oct 1862 Hudson, NH
BURNS, Georgianna AGE:5 22 Feb 1849 Hudson, NH George Burns & Ann
BURNS, Howard K AGE:48 07 Aug 1957 Nashua, NH
BURNS, James E AGE:7 12 29 Mar 1860 Hudson, NH George H Burns & Eloisa A
BURNS, James E AGE:7 12 23 Mar 1861 Hudson, NH
BURNS, John AGE:19 06 Nov 1755 Hudson, NH George Burns & Martha
BURNS, John W AGE:19 11 4 14 Jul 1976 Hudson, NH George H Burns & Eloisa A
BURNS, Luke AGE:66 01 Oct 1881 Hudson, NH Robert Burns & Mary Simonds
BURNS, Lydia AGE:14 17 Sep 1862 Hudson, NH Elias Burns & Hannah
BURNS, Lydia C AGE:65 14 Mar 1880 Hudson, NH David Burns & Eliza Childs
BURNS, Margaret AGE:35 01 Feb 1785 Hudson, NH
BURNS, Martha AGE:98 11 Feb 1811 Hudson, NH
BURNS, Rachel AGE:58 08 Jun 1852 Hudson, NH
BURNS, Richard M AGE:63 08 Aug 1984 Nashua, NH
BURNS, Rita L AGE:56 11 Oct 1973 Hudson, NH
BURNS, Sarah A AGE:15 18 Jul 1835 Hudson, NH James Burns
BURPEE, Maud Fay AGE:28 2 3 16 May 1914 Hudson, NH John H Fay
 & Sarah J Carley
BURROUGHS, Belle G AGE:61 10 25 12 Mar 1941 Hudson, NH Charles McCollough
 & Harriet Lewis
BURSIEL, Mary Ann AGE: 17 May 1893 Litchfield, NH
BURSIEL, Thomas AGE: 01 Jan 1875 Bedford
BURTON, Charles E AGE:70 17 Nov 1979 Nashua, NH
BURTON, Ervin J AGE:78 13 Feb 1978 Nashua, NH
BURTON, Leonard R AGE:52 16 Jun 1985 Nashua, NH
BURTON, Mary A AGE:77 17 Oct 1980 Hudson, NH
BURTON, Mary L AGE:63 08 Jul 1965 Nashua, NH

HUDSON,NH DEATHS

BURTON,Richard P AGE:58 22 Mar 1963 Nashua, NH
BURTON,Steven M AGE:2 22 May 1966 Hanover, NH
BURTT,Annie C AGE:79 08 Dec 1953 Nashua, NH
BURTT,Isabell AGE:87 2 7 09 Apr 1926 Hudson, NH John Carter
BURTT,Verna M AGE:37   9 06 Jul 1929 Hudson, NH Elsworth Mandigs
  & Ella Quigley
BUSWELL,Tencie M AGE:61 02 Aug 1968 Nashua, NH
BUTLER,Belinda AGE:78 4 18 10 Sep 1903 Hudson, NH Henry Smith & Hannah Smith
BUTLER,Charles H AGE:2 9 1864 Hudson, NH
BUTLER,Charles H AGE:2 1863 Hudson, NH
BUTLER,David AGE:88 29 Mar 1873 Hudson, NH
BUTLER,Diana G AGE:64 3 21 Jan 1891 Hudson, NH
BUTLER,Dianna G AGE:64 3 24 Jan 1891 Hudson, NH Enoch Butler (Pelham)
  & Susan Marsh (Hudson, NH)
BUTLER,Henry AGE: 11 Nov 1895 Hudson, NH
BUTLER,Henry AGE:85 5 2 12 Mar 1909 Hudson, NH Jowell Butler & Deborah Gage
BUTLER,James AGE:11 Sep 1869 Hudson, NH Moses Butler
BUTLER,James M AGE:82 3 13 18 May 1906 Hudson, NH Coel Butler & Deborah Daye
BUTLER,Jonathan AGE: 05 Nov 1754 Hudson, NH James Butler & Mary
BUTLER,Jonathan AGE: 03 Nov 1754 Hudson, NH John Butler & Mary
BUTLER,Louisa AGE:80 25 Mar 1950 Hudson, NH Henry A Jones & Abbie Richardson
BUTLER,Moses AGE:59 5 01 Feb 1882 Hudson, NH Joseph Butler & Hannah Butler
BUTLER,Sarah J AGE:79 4 17 29 Mar 1914 Hudson, NH Samuel Steele
  & Fannie Blodgett
BUTLER,Sarah Wyman AGE: 04 Nov 1759 Hudson, NH
BUTLER,Susan AGE:72 20 Mar 1900 Hudson, NH James Caldwell & Susan Center
BUTLER,Thomas AGE:80 25 May 1874 Bedford, NH
BUTMAN,Charles AGE:86 3 5 16 Oct 1900 Hudson, NH Jonathan Butman
  & Annie Lane
BUTMAN,Roxann AGE: 04 Feb 1899 Hudson, NH Luther Lawrence & Eunice Kimball
BUTRICK,Abel AGE:75 06 Jul 1862 Hudson, NH
BUTRICK,Betsy AGE:85 10 22 24 Sep 1884 Hudson, NH James Caldwell
  (Litchfield, NH) & Betsy Marshall (Hudson, NH)
BUTTERFIELD,Annie L AGE:75 31 Dec 1955 Hudson, NH
BUTTERFIELD,Bernard J AGE:72 13 Jan 1954 Hudson, NH
BUTTERFIELD,Walter AGE:61 5 30 03 Sep 1930 Hudson, NH Hiram Butterfield
  & Mary Dobbens
BUTTERICK,Barnett AGE:82 2 25 26 Feb 1912 Hudson, NH
BUTTERICK,Belle AGE:88 17 Jul 1959 Hudson, NH
BUTTERICK,Ellen R AGE:74   7 24 Sep 1912 Hudson, NH Elia Hardy
  & Unice Williams
BUTTRICK,Abel AGE:75 11 06 Jul 1862 Hudson, NH
BUTTRICK,Abel AGE:79 8 15 Feb 1830 Hudson, NH
BUTTRICK,Abia Coburn AGE:64 4 11 Nov 1818 Hudson, NH
BUTTRICK,Anna L AGE:56 8 24 Nov 1897 Hudson, NH
BUTTRICK,Caldwell AGE:76 2 12 26 Jul 1914 Hudson, NH Samuel Buttrick
  & Margaret Caldwell
BUTTRICK,Clifton E AGE:88 9 16 15 May 1935 Hudson, NH Ephraim Buttrick
  & Sarah
BUTTRICK,Ella F AGE:41 11 27 Sep 1897 Hudson, NH Ino W Boyington
  & Melitah S Glidden
BUTTRICK,Ernest C AGE:1 07 Sep 1870 Hudson, NH Clifton C Buttrick
BUTTRICK,Lottie AGE:32 04 Jul 1879 Hudson, NH
BUTTRICK,Mary E AGE:32 28 Jul 1873 Hudson, NH
BUTTRICK,[Unknown] AGE: 26 Sep 1897 Hudson, NH Clifton E Buttrick
  & Ella Boyington
BUXTON,Ella F AGE:97 17 Jun 1962 Hudson, NH
BUXTON,Hazel Elsie AGE:79 05 Nov 1979 Nashua, NH
BUXTON,Jane P AGE:87 4 29 15 Feb 1928 Hudson, NH Sanford Greeley & Phoebe
BUZZELL,Rose M AGE:87 18 Feb 1968 Hudson, NH

HUDSON, NH DEATHS

BYRNE, Thomas AGE:84 09 Aug 1967 Hudson, NH
CADY, Victoria M AGE:36 18 Jul 1980 Nashua, NH
CAGE, Elizabeth M AGE:8 07 Oct 1869 Hudson, NH
CALDWELL, Alexander AGE:67 07 Mar 1849 Hudson, NH
CALDWELL, Alexander AGE:76 05 Jan 1766 Hudson, NH
CALDWELL, Andrew AGE: Sep 1778 Hudson, NH James Caldwell & Jenett
CALDWELL, Betsey AGE:58 22 Jan 1816 Hudson, NH
CALDWELL, Charles F AGE:13 2 14 14 Mar 1856 Hudson, NH William Caldwell & Jane
CALDWELL, Douglass AGE:78 3 4 06 Jan 1899 Hudson, NH
CALDWELL, Edna V AGE:69 13 Feb 1963 Hudson, NH
CALDWELL, Edward AGE:17 28 Jun 1867 Hudson, NH
CALDWELL, Eliza Jane AGE:33 6 16 Jul 1885 Hudson, NH Addison Blanding (Irisburg, VT) & Harriet Dutton (Hudson, NH)
CALDWELL, Henry M AGE:48 11 29 Jun 1901 Pelham, NH William Caldwell (Hudson, NH)
CALDWELL, James AGE:81 30 Dec 1825 Hudson, NH
CALDWELL, James AGE:64 21 May 1808 Hudson, NH
CALDWELL, James AGE:81 30 Oct 1870 Hudson, NH
CALDWELL, Jane AGE:69 16 Jun 1828 Hudson, NH
CALDWELL, Jane M AGE:67 11 04 Jan 1880 Hudson, NH
CALDWELL, Jenett AGE:41 22 Apr 1781 Hudson, NH
CALDWELL, John AGE: Sep 1778 Hudson, NH James Caldwell & Jenett
CALDWELL, John AGE: 25 Feb 1765 Hudson, NH
CALDWELL, Levi M AGE:87 5 21 Nov 1915 Hudson, NH Moses Caldwell (New Boston) & Ann Moore (New Boston)
CALDWELL, Margaret AGE:82 16 Jan 1791 Hudson, NH
CALDWELL, Mary AGE: Sep 1778 Hudson, NH James Caldwell & Jenett
CALDWELL, Mary W AGE:55 25 Oct 1840 Hudson, NH
CALDWELL, Sarah AGE:1   20 25 Dec 1763 Hudson, NH
CALDWELL, Sarah AGE:45 12 Sep 1832 Hudson, NH
CALDWELL, Thomas AGE:86 6 26 Apr 1883 Hudson, NH James Caldwell & Betsey Marshall
CALDWELL, William AGE:58 6 22 09 May 1871 Hudson, NH
CALDWELL, William AGE:15 24 Aug 1808 Hudson, NH James Caldwell & Betsey
CALL, I Mayo AGE:55 28 Jan 1953 Nashua, NH
CALLAN, Peter T AGE:55 11 Dec 1973 Nashua, NH
CALLOWAY, Evan B AGE:43 06 Mar 1980 Nashua, NH
CAMDY, William M AGE: 26 Jan 1900 Hollis, NH
CAMERON, Alice M AGE:87 02 Jan 1985 Nashua, NH
CAMPBELL, Anne M AGE:86 21 Dec 1959 Hudson, NH
CAMPBELL, Erma F AGE:78 18 Dec 1978 Hudson, NH
CAMPBELL, Frank E AGE:82 21 May 1952 Nashua, NH
CAMPBELL, Harriet AGE:73 11 29 17 May 1919 Hudson, NH John Putnam & Edna Saunders
CAMPBELL, Harriet L AGE:57 10 12 15 Feb 1936 Hudson, NH George Mortlock & Eliza Hawes
CAMPBELL, Horace P AGE:66 1 18 07 May 1912 Hudson, NH Robert Campbell & Emiline Parker
CAMPBELL, J Earle AGE:12 6 22 02 Dec 1900 Hudson, NH Horace P Campbell & Lucy Hovey
CAMPBELL, Johanna F AGE:89 16 Feb 1978 Groton, MA
CAMPBELL, Lizzie E AGE:80 10 Apr 1951 Hudson, NH
CAMPBELL, Lucy J AGE:62 2 22 14 Feb 1912 Hudson, NH Joseph Honey & Betsey Colberth
CAMPBELL, Mary F AGE:50 1 1 22 May 1918 Hudson, NH John Vining & Mary Haynes
CAMPBELL, Nellie E AGE:17 9 26 14 Apr 1887 Hudson, NH Bradford Campbell (Bedford) & Harriet E Putnam (Danvers, MA)
CAMPBELL, Orman S AGE:65 1 20 07 Feb 1943 Nashua, NH Bradford Campbell & Hattie Putnam

HUDSON,NH DEATHS

CAMPBELL,Oscar J AGE:76 06 Dec 1970 Manchester, NH
CAMPBELL,Oscar P AGE:70 13 Feb 1973 Nashua, NH
CAMPBELL,Persis H AGE:69 1 21 07 Jan 1891 Hudson, NH George Moore
    (E Lebanon) & Harriet Hawley (Methuen, MA)
CAMPBELL,Ruby M AGE:17 02 Mar 1905 Hudson, NH Chas E Campbell
    & Annie M Knight
CAMPBELL,Ruth AGE:5 15 23 Jul 1905 Hudson, NH Chas E Campbell
    & Anna M Knight
CAMPBELL,Theresa AGE:12 hrs 06 Nov 1957 Nashua, NH
CAMPOLIETO,John A II AGE:2 06 Jul 1966 Nashua, NH
CANFIELD,Addie E AGE:85 14 Dec 1949 Hudson, NH Perley C Giles
    & Clarissa Grant
CANFIELD,Herbert W AGE:82 27 Apr 1977 Nashua, NH
CANFIELD,Rev Edward J AGE:87 21 Aug 1951 Hudson, NH
CANTARA,Jerome C AGE:74 12 Feb 1985 Hudson, NH
CARD,Barbara J AGE:29 30 Aug 1977 Nashua, NH
CARDIN,Adeline J AGE:82 05 May 1972 Nashua, NH
CARDIN,Marie A AGE:86 11 Nov 1969 Nashua, NH
CARKIN,Leonard L AGE:25 10 11 15 Apr 1902 Hudson, NH Albert J Carkin
    & Mary C Avery
CARLETON,Estella AGE:94 03 Jan 1981 Hudson, NH
CARNES,Arthur L AGE:65 07 Jan 1961 Nashua, NH
CARNES,David M AGE:21 4 10 Nov 1865 Hudson, NH James Carnes & Emily Rogers
CARNES,David M AGE:21 Nov 1865 Hudson, NH
CARNES,Emily AGE:49 13 Oct 1868 Hudson, NH
CARNES,James AGE:69 6 29 Nov 1883 Hudson, NH
CARON,Emile E AGE:64 25 May 1966 Nashua, NH
CARR,Charles AGE:78 9 31 Mar 1928 Hudson, NH James Carr
CARR,George AGE: 1862 Hudson, NH
CARROLL,Ellen C AGE:75 09 Jan 1951 Hudson, NH
CARROLL,John J AGE:81 4 20 21 Dec 1940 Hudson, NH
CARROLL,Mark AGE:70 02 Mar 1962 Concord, NH
CARROWE,John AGE:79 29 Jul 1934 Hudson, NH Louis Carrowe & Ellen
CARTER,Annie E AGE:53 4 14 06 Jun 1920 Hudson, NH Henry M Fairfield
    & Saibrina Leach
CARTER,Charles AGE:70 15 Jun 1967 Hudson, NH
CARTER,Eugene AGE: 16 Jul 1918 Hudson, NH
CARTER,Mary AGE:50 1 1 19 Mar 1905 Hudson, NH Charles Mulholland
    & Eliz Feeney
CARTY,Eliza D AGE:82 29 Mar 1979 Hudson, NH
CASE,[Unknown] AGE:4 May 1875 Hudson, NH George Case & Mary
CASEY,Eugene M AGE:73 17 Aug 1979 Nashua, NH
CASSAVAUGH,Carmen M AGE:47 02 Dec 1983 Nashua, NH
CASSIDY,Bernard C AGE:4 01 Mar 1915 Hudson, NH Clifford V Cassidy (Ontario)
    & Ethel M Cummings (Hudson, NH)
CATE,Ann R T AGE:62 2 14 10 Oct 1906 Hudson, NH James Taylor & Upton
CATE,David W AGE:81 1 6 16 Apr 1945 Hudson, NH David C Cate & Emily Gilman
CAVANAUGH,Robert L AGE:7 23 13 Nov 1921 Hudson NH Willis L Hall
    & Hattie Hadley
CENTER,David E AGE:69 7 9 24 Feb 1947 Reading, MA Warren Center
    & Carolyn Howe
CENTER,Elenor AGE:76 17 Jan 1901 Hudson, NH
CENTER,Henderson C AGE:55 24 Jul 1984 Exeter, NH
CENTER,Margaret S AGE:82 16 Nov 1952 Hudson, NH
CHADWICK,Mary P AGE:41 17 Jan 1830 Hudson, NH Joseph Chadwick & Mary
CHALIFOUX,Levi AGE:79 17 Oct 1979 Nashua, NH
CHALIFOUX,Rose D AGE:91 07 Oct 1957 Nashua, NH
CHAMARD,Rita AGE:1 16 14 Jun 1924 Hudson, NH Eustache Chamard
    & Lumina Grulmain
CHAMARD,Therese AGE:4 04 Jun 1927 Hudson, NH Eustache Chamard

HUDSON,NH DEATHS

& Lumina Guilmain
CHAMARD,Viola M AGE:78 29 Sep 1982 Hudson, NH
CHAMPAGNE,Clarence AGE:9 9 13 May 1905 Hudson, NH Frank Champagne
& Edith Leazott
CHAMPIGNY,Calix AGE:66 29 Nov 1984 Nashua, NH
CHAMPIGNY,Charlotte I AGE:41 08 Apr 1954 Nashua, NH
CHAMPIGNY,Edmond AGE:73 2 6 09 Jun 1943 Hudson, NH Calix Champigny
& Marie Beaupre
CHAMPIGNY,Ernest C AGE:54 16 Nov 1957 Nashua, NH
CHANDLER,Mary A AGE:63 7 21 13 Jul 1912 Hudson, NH Oliver W Boynton
& Olive Barker
CHANDONNET,Joseph AGE:81 06 Aug 1982 Derry, NH
CHANDONNET,Leo AGE:45 03 Nov 1982 Nashua, NH
CHAPLIN,Elmer E AGE:59 9 13 19 Dec 1920 Hudson, NH Kimball J Chaplin
& Rhoda Dickson
CHAPLIN,Josephine AGE:86 11 23 30 Oct 1945 Hudson, NH Rodney Fuller
& Martha Farwell
CHAPLIN,Laura J AGE:74 27 Apr 1970 Hudson, NH
CHAPLIN,Leslie A AGE:64 16 Apr 1954 Nashua, NH
CHAPMAN,Amanda M AGE:90 8 17 21 Feb 1926 Hudson, NH Peter Ranger
& Mary Smith
CHAPMAN,Daisy C AGE:2 6 12 31 Dec 1903 Hudson, NH Frank Chapman
& Mederise Lefebvre
CHAPMAN,Dena L AGE:2 8 24 Apr 1895 Hudson, NH Frank M Chapman (Newmarket)
& Medoria Lefebvre (Nashua, NH)
CHAPMAN,Frank W AGE:42 13 Jan 1953 Nashua, NH
CHAPMAN,Guy H AGE:4 2 7 05 Jul 1903 Hudson, NH Frank Chapman & M L Lefebvre
CHAPMAN,Herbert G AGE:50 4 5 16 Mar 1946 Hudson, NH Frank M Chapman
& Mederise Lefebvre
CHAPMAN,James H AGE:82 20 Dec 1960 Hudson, NH
CHAPMAN,John P AGE:46 17 May 1955 Nashua, NH
CHAPMAN,Lilly B AGE:2 1 31 May 1899 Hudson, NH Frank M Chapman
& Mederise Lefelore
CHAPMAN,Mederise L AGE:62 5 26 26 Oct 1931 Hudson, NH Joseph Lefebvre
CHARBONNEAU,Alice AGE:74 13 Apr 1959 Hudson, NH
CHARBONNEAU,Annette AGE:79 22 Jun 1957 Nashua, NH
CHAREST,Marie L AGE:70 06 Mar 1958 Nashua, NH
CHARRON,Joseph H AGE:66 07 Apr 1962 Hudson, NH
CHARRON,Paul L AGE:71 07 Apr 1973 Nashua, NH
CHARTERS,Elias T AGE:64 9 21 05 Dec 1922 Hudson, NH James Charters
& Margaret Miller
CHARTIER,Adelard AGE:84 05 Oct 1967 Hudson, NH
CHASE,Abigail AGE 62 16 May 1863 Hudson, NH
CHASE,Abigail J AGE:62 16 May 1863 Hudson, NH
CHASE,Alice M AGE:22 4 02 Aug 1885 Hudson, NH William F Chase (Hudson, NH)
& Sarah F Greeley (Hudson, NH)
CHASE,Alice Mabel AGE:51 8 17 18 Jul 1909 Hudson, NH Henry Holman
& Mary Wilson
CHASE,Amos P AGE:52 6 12 Jan 1841 Hudson, NH
CHASE,Ann E AGE:17 8 12 25 Nov 1845 Hudson, NH John Chase & Lucy J
CHASE,Arthur E AGE:9 11 Aug 1893 Hudson, NH B F Chase (Vermont)
& Mary J Dobson (England)
CHASE,Benjamin D AGE:90 2 7 14 May 1881 Hudson, NH Joseph Chase & Mary Hardy
CHASE,Benjamin F AGE:64 15 Jun 1872 Hudson, NH
CHASE,Capt Jacob AGE:85 31 Dec 1863 Hudson, NH
CHASE,Capt Solomon AGE:74 30 Jun 1871 Hudson, NH
CHASE,Charles AGE:25 07 Aug 1836 Hudson, NH Jacob Chase
CHASE,Daniel AGE:61 28 Dec 1832 Hudson, NH
CHASE,Dea Joshua AGE:82 7 27 Dec 1822 Hudson, NH
CHASE,Edgar AGE:26 10 11 Jan 1857 Hudson, NH John Chase & Lucy J

HUDSON,NH DEATHS

CHASE,Edwin A AGE: 13 Sep 1833 Hudson, NH John Chase & Lucy J
CHASE,Elizabeth AGE:77   13 Nov 1854 Hudson, NH
CHASE,Elizabeth AGE:46   08 Sep 1838 Hudson, NH John Chase
CHASE,Elizabeth AGE:53   10 Nov 1819 Hudson, NH
CHASE,Enoch AGE: 27 Aug 1753 Hudson, NH
CHASE,Ezekiel Jr AGE:37   12 Jul 1767 Hudson, NH
CHASE,Friend M AGE:60   05 Feb 1861 Hudson, NH
CHASE,Friend Moody AGE:60 11   05 Feb 1861 Hudson, NH
CHASE,Harriet E AGE:87 1 20   08 Apr 1913 Hudson, NH John B Brown
    & Hannah Dustin
CHASE,Henry Jr AGE: 26 Jun 1770 Hudson, NH
CHASE,Jacob AGE:85   31 Dec 1863 Hudson, NH
CHASE,John AGE:76   10 Feb 1837 Hudson, NH
CHASE,John AGE:81 8   22 Nov 1882 Hudson, NH John Chase & Elizabeth
CHASE,Joseph P AGE:30   18   13 Jan 1919 Hudson, NH Moses Chase
    & Charlotte Parks
CHASE,Joshua Jr AGE:19   6   22 Oct 1795 Hudson, NH Joshua Chase
CHASE,Laura A AGE: 06 Sep 1844 Hudson, NH John Chase & Lucy J
CHASE,Lucy A AGE:17 7   07 Feb 1842 Hudson, NH Amos B Chase & Sarah
CHASE,Lucy A AGE: 12 Oct 1833 Hudson, NH John Chase & Lucy J
CHASE,Lucy J AGE:50   22 Aug 1853 Hudson, NH
CHASE,Lydia AGE:89   09 Jan 1872 Hudson, NH
CHASE,Maranda AGE:75   21 Mar 1883 Hudson, NH   Jones
CHASE,Mary AGE:92   27 Mar 1838 Hudson, NH
CHASE,Mary AGE:80 2   17 Sep 1869 Hudson, NH
CHASE,Mary M AGE:83 11 4   09 Jan 1897 Hudson, NH Aaron Warner
    & Rebecca Lawrence
CHASE,Mittie AGE:55   10 Nov 1863 Hudson, NH
CHASE,Mitty AGE:55   10 Nov 1863 Hudson, NH
CHASE,Nathaniel AGE:84   21 Nov 1879 Hudson, NH
CHASE,Phebe AGE:44   12 Dec 1830 Hudson, NH
CHASE,Phebe AGE: 24 Mar 1764 Hudson, NH Stephen Chase & Phebe
CHASE,Priscilla AGE:7   05 Oct 1749 Hudson, NH
CHASE,Priscilla M AGE:59   22 Feb 1768 Hudson, NH
CHASE,Rebecah AGE:97 8 7   16 Apr 1882 Hudson, NH John Barnett
CHASE,Rebecca AGE: 13 Jul 1773 Hudson, NH
CHASE,Rebecca N AGE:39   14 Feb 1877 Hudson, NH John Chase & Martha
CHASE,Sally AGE:79   05 Apr 1860 Hudson, NH
CHASE,Samuel AGE:78 10 24   24 Apr 1911 Hudson, NH Moody Chase
    & Mitty Marshall
CHASE,Samuel AGE:91   07 Feb 1835 Hudson, NH
CHASE,Sarah AGE:85 4   26 Jul 1857 Hudson, NH
CHASE,Sarah AGE: 26 Dec 1755 Hudson, NH
CHASE,Sarah AGE: 23 Oct 1757 Hudson, NH Henry Chase & Rebecca
CHASE,Sarah F AGE:44   14 Jul 1882 Hudson, NH Samuel Greeley & Mary A Buxton
CHASE,Sarah G AGE:13   16 May 1844 Hudson, NH John Chase & Martha
CHASE,Sarah H AGE:48   17 Mar 1855 Hudson, NH
CHASE,Solomon AGE:71   30 Jun 1871 Hudson, NH
CHASE,Stanley J AGE:55   24 May 1975 Nashua, NH
CHASE,Stephen E AGE: 14 Jun 1756 Hudson, NH
CHASE,William F AGE:67 6   15 Mar 1899 Hudson, NH Solomon Chase
    & Miranda Jones
CHASE,William F C AGE: 13 Nov 1844 Hudson, NH John Chase & Martha
CHASE,[Unknown] AGE: Hudson, NH John Chase & Martha
CHAUVIN,Reta AGE:7 2   29 Aug 1915 Hudson, NH Hyacinth Chauvin
    (N Grosven'le, CT) & Emma Michaud (Canada)
CHENEY,Gladys E AGE:71   17 Aug 1970 Nashua, NH
CHESLEY,Emma I AGE:64 3 16   09 Aug 1930 Hudson, NH Sylv Gould & Lizzie Summer
CHEVALIER,Marguerite G AGE:67   17 Aug 1961 Hudson, NH
CHEVALIER,Rev Albert AGE:48 5 24   04 Dec 1948 Hudson, NH Joseph Chevalier

HUDSON, NH DEATHS

& Edna Choquette
CHEVRETTE,Marie L AGE:54 4 5   03 Nov 1946 Hudson, NH Stan Duchesneau
& Antoinette Gendron
CHEZSUM,Benjamin AGE:72 22 Feb 1965 Goffstown, NH
CHICK,Blanche M AGE:85 19 Dec 1984 Hudson, NH
CHICK,Michael AGE:73 20 Oct 1863 Hudson, NH
CHICOINE,Sr Adelaide Z AGE:81 16 Mar 1977 Nashua, NH
CHILCOAT,Gary A AGE:3 03 Jul 1956 Nashua, NH
CHOATE,James Alvin AGE:42 03 Dec 1984 Nashua, NH
CHOATE,Joseph AGE:65 04 May 1880 Hudson, NH
CHOMARD,Eustache AGE:56   3 07 Jun 1943 Nashua, NH Thomas Chomard
& Emelie Bernier
CHOQUETTE, Delphine,Sr Lea de Marie AGE:49 23 Sep 1953 Hudson,NH
CHRISTIANSEN,Donald L AGE:44 01 Jun 1971 Hudson, NH
CHRISTOPHER,Bernard AGE:75 7 29 02 Dec 1940 Rye, NH Francis Christopher
& Emily Troupe
CHRISTOPHER,Elaine M AGE:35 19 Jul 1982 Exeter, NH
CHRISTOPHER,George A AGE:64 25 Jan 1977 Hudson, NH
CHURCH,Mary O AGE:83 8 13 10 Mar 1922 Hudson, NH Timothy Hnderson
& Eliza Henderson
CHURCH,Reuben AGE:86 9 28 04 Nov 1923 Hudson, NH Edward Church
& Letitia Parker
CLARK,Bertha Irene AGE: 06 Mar 1878 Hudson, NH George M Clark & Helen Hill
CLARK,Charles E AGE:72 25 Jun 1976 Nashua, NH
CLARK,Ezekiel B AGE:33 03 Jul 1870 Hudson, NH
CLARK,George A AGE:1 13 Jun 1872 Hudson, NH
CLARK,George H AGE:84 24 Nov 1953 Nashua, NH
CLARK,George H AGE:75 21 Jul 1974 Nashua, NH
CLARK,Harriet AGE:85 9 27 17 Dec 1908 Hudson, NH Michael Clark & Irene Blake
CLARK,Irene AGE:67 15 Oct 1869 Hudson, NH
CLARK,Mary AGE:52 10 14 03 Mar 1905 Hudson, NH James Algeo
CLARK,Michael AGE:73 20 Oct 1863 Hudson, NH
CLARK,Rev Allen Williams AGE:88 10 Dec 1984 Hudson, NH
CLARK,Victor A AGE:64 20 Jan 1949 Nashua, NH John Clark & Augusta Bagley
CLARK,[Unknown] AGE: 05 Aug 1933 Hudson, NH Wallace Clark & Arline Carter
CLARKE,Charles G AGE:90 10 Aug 1965 Hudson, NH
CLAXTON,Elna AGE:68 01 May 1971 Nashua, NH
CLAXTON,Fay B AGE:69 02 Jul 1971 Nashua, NH
CLAXTON,Maxine AGE: 21 Nov 1937 Hudson, NH Fay Claxton & Elna Pulley
CLAY,Ruth S AGE: 14 Apr 1857 Hudson, NH Samuel J Clay
CLAY,Samuel J AGE: 06 Sep 1866 Hudson, NH
CLAY,Vera A AGE:85 28 Mar 1971 Hudson, NH
CLEAVELAND,Leora G AGE:65 13 Jan 1978 Nashua, NH
CLEMENT,Calar Ann AGE:1 06 Oct 1862 Hudson, NH
CLEMENT,Clara A AGE:2 2 7 06 Oct 1862 Hudson, NH David Clement & Maria
CLEMENT,David AGE:91 9 1 20 Oct 1887 Hudson, NH Moses Clement (Dracut, MA)
& Rachel Parham (Tyngsboro, MA)
CLEMENT,David C AGE:83 14 Feb 1911 Hudson, NH David Clement & Dorcas Wilson
CLEMENT,Dorcas AGE:67 19 Sep 1865 Hudson, NH
CLEMENT,Dorcas AGE:67 17 Sep 1865 Hudson, NH
CLEMENT,Elmer D AGE:62 3 21 16 Nov 1925 Hudson, NH David Clement
& Hannah M Hall
CLEMENT,Hannah M AGE:80 08 Jan 1911 Hudson, NH Joseph Hall & Sarah Lund
CLEMENT,Harry E AGE:90 13 Jul 1977 Nashua, NH
CLEMENT,Joseph C AGE:8 3 03 May 1856 Hudson, NH David Clement & Maria
CLEMENT,Nettie E AGE:4 7 31 Aug 1890 Hudson, NH Elmer D Clement (Hudson, NH)
& Emely E Wilcox (Malden, MA)
CLEMENT,Sister Louis AGE:84 14 Jan 1974 Hudson, NH
CLEMENTS,Annie M AGE:84 11 Jul 1962 Nashua, NH
CLEMONS,Frederick M AGE:66 23 Sep 1983 Nashua, NH

HUDSON,NH DEATHS

CLIFFORD,Florentius C AGE:73 09 Aug 1967 Nashua, NH
CLOHESY,Francis Michael AGE:60 18 Jul 1979 Manchester, NH
CLOUGH,Ruth A AGE:40 28 Oct 1861 Hudson, NH
CLOUGH,William H AGE:57 03 Sep 1972 Hudson, NH
CLOUTIER,Claudette Y AGE:2 12 26 Jun 1941 Hudson, NH Joseph Cloutier
 & Ella Levesque
CLOUTIER,Ernest AGE:87 22 Mar 1956 Concord, NH
CLOUTIER,Blanche AGE:70 10 Feb 1967 Nashua, NH
CLOUTIER,Henry J AGE:83 07 May 1979 Nashua, NH COND:
CLOUTIER,Irene AGE:44 27 Oct 1969 Nashua, NH
CLYDE,Anna B AGE:82 25 Mar 1959 Nashua, NH
CLYDE,George W AGE:55 7 29 21 Jun 1921 Hudson, NH Samuel W Clyde
 & Hannah J Boles
CLYDE,Hannah J AGE:89 6 28 10 Apr 1915 Hudson, NH Greenleaf Boles (New
 Hampshire) & Hannah Farnum (New Hampshire)
CLYDE,Samuel W AGE:79 2 15 Oct 1882 Hudson, NH Joseph Clyde
 & Elizabeth Wilson
COBLEIGH,Merlin AGE:53 06 May 1951 Hudson, NH
COBURN,James M AGE:54 17 Sep 1895 Hudson, NH Moses Coburn (Tyngsboro, MA)
 & Hannah Barker (Newry, ME)
COCHRAN,Frank B AGE:64 3 12 05 May 1916 Hudson, NH George Cochran
 & Eliza J Morrill
COCHRAN,George W AGE:80 24 Jun 1907 Hudson, NH John Cochran
COCHRAN,James AGE:52 28 May 1886 Hudson, NH
COCHRAN,James AGE:52 28 May 1885 Hudson, NH
COCHRAN,Joseph N AGE:53 17 Feb 1880 Hudson, NH
COCUR,Sr M Jean-du-Sacre AGE:64 19 Aug 1951 Hudson, NH
CODY,John J AGE:75 12 Dec 1982 Nashua, NH
COGSWELL,John A AGE:72 21 Aug 1960 Hudson, NH
COHEN,Benjamin M AGE:81 09 Jan 1970 Nashua, NH
COHEN,Jennie Kitchener AGE:74 23 Jan 1974 Nashua, NH
COLBURN,Annie T AGE:85 25 May 1956 Hudson, NH
COLBURN,Betsey AGE:10 6 8 26 Nov 1823 Hudson, NH Edward Colburn & Elizabeth
COLBURN,Capt Thomas AGE:64 30 Aug 1765 Hudson, NH
COLBURN,Daniel AGE:87 2 18 14 Apr 1938 Hudson, NH Daniel A Colburn
 & Sarah Colburn
COLBURN,Eldester P AGE:49 6 04 Jan 1853 Hudson, NH
COLBURN,Hannah AGE:53 3 6 26 Mar 1756 Hudson, NH
COLBURN,Hattie T AGE:88 29 Jun 1951 Nashua, NH
COLBURN,Henrietta M AGE:60 11 1 18 Jul 1909 Hudson, NH Henry C Newton
 & Mary Moulten
COLBURN,Josiah C AGE:3 2 08 Apr 1843 Hudson, NH Isaac Colburn & Eldester
COLBURN,Mary F AGE:39 09 Oct 1879 Hudson, NH Cummings Gould & Mary Chase
COLBURN,Mary F G AGE:39 3 29 12 Oct 1879 Hudson, NH
COLBURN,Rachel Hills AGE: 23 Sep 1840 Hudson, NH
COLBURN,S Abbie AGE:2 30 Mar 1840 Hudson, NH Isaac Colburn & Eldester
COLBURN,Sarah AGE:84 02 Jan 1879 Hudson, NH Isaac Colburn & Lydia L
COLBURN,Sarah J AGE:84 4 19 28 Nov 1891 Hudson, NH Obadiah Richardson
 (Dracut, MA) & Rhoda Haselton (Dracut, MA)
COLBURN,Thomas Jr AGE:4 30 Aug 1765 Hudson, NH Thomas Colburn & Mary
COLBURN,Zacheus AGE: 10 Oct 1851 Hudson, NH
COLBY,Alice Blanche AGE:4 28 14 Aug 1911 Hudson, NH John Colby & Ida F Ayers
COLBY,Frank E AGE:9 06 Oct 1909 Hudson, NH John Colby & Ida F Ayer
COLDIRON,Anne D AGE:73 24 Jan 1960 Hudson, NH
COLDWELL,William AGE:65 09 Mar 1871 Hudson, NH
COLE,Jane AGE:83 1 5 24 Sep 1888 Hudson, NH Timothy Lockhart (N B)
 & Elizabeth Tead (N B)
COLE,Percival E AGE:2 02 Mar 1872 Hudson, NH
COLE,Richard AGE:5 11 10 30 Dec 1907 Hudson, NH Fred Cole & Katie F Glubin
COLEMAN,Alice H AGE:82 05 May 1977 Hudson, NH

HUDSON, NH DEATHS

COLEMAN, Eva M AGE:82 29 Jul 1982 Derry, NH
COLLARD, Joseph AGE: 17 Oct 1930 Hudson, NH Leo Collard & Lillian Gendron
COLLARD, Laurette H AGE:5 6 28 05 Dec 1946 Hudson, NH Leo Collard
  & Lillian Gendron
COLLINS, Emma A AGE:90 15 Mar 1957 Concord, NH
COLLINS, Genevieve M AGE:83 01 Jun 1977 Nashua, NH
COLLINS, Hannah O AGE:70 9 19 18 Jan 1913 Hudson, NH Lifelet Blake
  & Martha Hodgson
COLLINS, Harry G AGE:68 11 23 02 May 1941 Nashua, NH Joseph Collins
  & Mary Fowler
COLLINS, James A AGE:52 12 Sep 1979 Nashua, NH
COLLINS, Michael J AGE:38 15 Nov 1965 Nashua, NH
COLLINS, Myra AGE:52 16 Jul 1918 Hudson, NH Thomas Donah & Sloney Forest
COLOMBE, Walter L AGE:57 06 Feb 1969 Nashua, NH
COLSON, Herbert E AGE:61 10 Apr 1976 Nashua, NH
COMBS, Deborah B AGE:8 15 Sep 1828 Hudson, NH Simeon Combs & Hannah
COMBS, Hannah AGE:68 21 Nov 1855 Hudson, NH
COMBS, Lydia M AGE: 09 Mar 1829 Hudson, NH Simeon Combs & Hannah
COMBS, Robert B AGE:36 25 Dec 1852 Hudson, NH
COMBS, Sarah T AGE:82 15 Jan 1903 Hudson, NH Wm Cummings & Betsey Edson
COMBS, Simeon AGE:71 01 Aug 1855 Hudson, NH
COMERFORD, Carol L AGE:73 14 Nov 1980 Nashua, NH
COMFORT, Mary AGE:15 1879 Hudson, NH
CONANT, George C AGE:63 2 26 24 Nov 1910 Hudson, NH Charles O Conant
  & Ann M Crawford
CONDON, Margaret AGE:41 28 Feb 1902 Hudson, NH James Condon & Howard
CONLON, Kimberly S AGE:4 06 Mar 1971 Nashua, NH
CONNELL, Betsey AGE:45 01 Mar 1862 Hudson, NH
CONNELL, Catherine A AGE:1 4 08 May 1866 Hudson, NH
CONNELL, Charles P AGE:3 3 10 Nov 1880 Hudson, NH Philip J Connell
  & Hannah E Hardy
CONNELL, Daisy Evelyn AGE:14 11 9 02 Jul 1922 Hudson, NH Frank A Connell
  & Mary E Watts
CONNELL, Etta M AGE:4 10   Hudson, NH Philip H Connell
CONNELL, Frank A AGE:82 29 May 1961 Nashua, NH
CONNELL, Hannah E AGE:72 5 07 Jan 1910 Hudson, NH Paul Hardy & Mary Gould
CONNELL, Harry J AGE:66 10 18 09 Jul 1947 Nashua, NH Phillip J Connell
  & Hannah Hardy
CONNELL, John W AGE:50 12 Oct 1900 Hudson, NH Philip Connell
  & Betsey Marshall
CONNELL, Mary AGE:71 1 28 13 Jun 1892 Hudson, NH
CONNELL, Mary E AGE:43 8 18 30 Oct 1904 Hudson, NH Henry Marshall
  & Mary E Rogers
CONNELL, Mary E AGE:77 03 Nov 1956 Nashua, NH
CONNELL, Otis R AGE:61 8 8 22 Mar 1942 Nashua, NH Robert T Connell
  & Mary E Marshall
CONNELL, Philip AGE:74 21 Nov 1886 Hudson, NH
CONNELL, Philip C AGE:1 8 23 22 Aug 1904 Hudson, NH Frank A Connell
  & Mary E Watts
CONNELL, Philip J AGE:70 07 May 1980 Nashua, NH
CONNELL, Phillip AGE:74 21 Nov 1886 Hudson, NH
CONNELL, Phillip J AGE:68 11 25 25 Nov 1920 Hudson, NH Tobias Connell
  & Mary Hoffman
CONNELL, Raymond AGE:21 14 Apr 1888 Hudson, NH James E Connell (Hudson, NH)
  & Sadie McEnery (St John, NB)
CONNELL, Robert T AGE:89 2 22 09 Jul 1944 Hudson, NH Tobias Connell
  & Mary Hoffman
CONNELL, Vera B AGE:73 12 May 1954 Nashua, NH
CONNORS, William V AGE:48 02 Jan 1979 Nashua, NH
CONREY, George T AGE:73 6 26 Jan 1894 Hudson, NH

HUDSON,NH DEATHS

CONSIGNY,Agnes E AGE:69   08 Jul 1973 Nashua, NH
CONSIGNY,Jean B AGE:45 9 3   20 Mar 1946 Hudson, NH Joseph Consigny
  & Theotisse Blanchard
CONSIGNY,Joseph AGE:63 8   17 Jul 1921 Hudson, NH Jean B Consigny & Bouselle
CONSTANT,Albert Joseph AGE: 22 Nov 1938 Hudson, NH Leo Constant
  & Jeanette Vignola
CONSTANT,Paul A AGE:2   20 Mar 1952 Nashua, NH
CONSTANT,[Unknown] AGE: 02 Jul 1942 Hudson, NH Leo Constant
  & Jeannette Vignola
CONSTANT,[Unknown] AGE: 07 Dec 1947 Hudson, NH Leo Constant
  & Jeannette Vignola
CONSTANT,[Unknown] AGE: 27 Feb 1938 Hudson, NH Leo Constant
  & Jeanette Vignola
COOK,Leon A AGE:55   27 Feb 1967 Manchester, NH
COOK,Mary E AGE:48 7   10 Nov 1902 Hudson, NH John Miller & Mary White
COOKE,Harold E AGE:59   02 Jun 1962 Nashua, NH
COOKE,Hector R AGE:45   31 Jan 1952 Nashua, NH
COOKE,Hersey Edmund Jr AGE:18   30 Sep 1984 Nashua, NH
COOKE,Hersey F SEX: AGE:68   22 Feb 1973 Nashua, NH COND:
COOKMAN,Harlie E AGE:39 8 16   03 Dec 1948 Nashua, NH Albert Cookman
  & May Lavester
COOLEY,Janet AGE:27   21 Aug 1967 Nashua, NH
COOMBS,Joseph V AGE:76 7 17   24 May 1917 Hudson, NH William Coombs
COOPER,Leah Lucretia AGE:78 9 27   20 Apr 1927 Hudson, NH Josiah Barnard
  & Lucretia Kincard
COPELAND,John S AGE:69   09 Oct 1980 Hudson, NH
CORKINS,Genie R AGE:90   26 Feb 1965 Hudson, NH
CORLISS,Daniel P AGE:82 3   23 Jul 1886 Hudson, NH
CORLISS,James AGE:77 9   16 Oct 1828 Hudson, NH
CORLISS,James AGE:82 8 27   03 Sep 1885 Hudson, NH Jonathan Corliss (Salem)
  & Sally Glover (Hudson, NH)
CORLISS,James N AGE:38 7   04 Aug 1883 Hudson, NH James Corliss
  & Sarah M Hamblett
CORLISS,Sally AGE:84   17 Jun 1866 Hudson, NH
CORLISS,Sarah M AGE:69 10 7   06 Sep 1888 Hudson, NH Amos Hamblett
  (Hudson, NH) & Salley Steele (Hudson, NH)
CORMIER,Joseph L AGE:53   27 Aug 1956 Nashua, NH
CORMIER,Robert F AGE:50   12 Jul 1968 Lowell, MA
COROSA,Charles V AGE:61   30 Aug 1977 Nashua, NH
COROSA,Julius AGE:86   03 Feb 1977 Nashua, NH
COROSA,Victoria AGE:88   21 Aug 1982 Hudson, NH
CORSON,Kelly R AGE: 26 Oct 1977 Nashua, NH
COSSETTE,Blanche AGE:90   13 Apr 1966 Hudson, NH
COSSETTE,Xavier AGE:93   24 Jan 1961 Hudson, NH
COSTELLO,Barrie L AGE:17   14 Dec 1960 Nashua, NH
COTE,Anne Marie AGE:80   31 Dec 1980 Hudson, NH
COTE,Arthur AGE:67   04 Jan 1972 Nashua, NH
COTE,Blanche M AGE:81   07 Feb 1982 Nashua, NH
COTE,Clorinthe AGE:68 8 24   17 Oct 1948 Hudson, NH Octave Cote
  & Odille Marcotte
COTE,Delima AGE:80 8 26   28 Dec 1933 Hudson, NH Felix Parent
  & Adele Boisclair
COTE,Dorothy AGE:77   21 Mar 1976 Nashua, NH
COTE,Leda D AGE:82   31 Mar 1985 Nashua, NH
COTE,Leon P AGE:79   27 Jun 1978 Nashua, NH
COTE,Mervyn E AGE:61   18 Dec 1979 Nashua, NH
COTE,Paul D AGE:63   19 Apr 1978 Nashua, NH
COTE,Velanie AGE:82 7 21   21 Jul 1931 Hudson, NH Cleophas Cote
  & Fannie Laplaire
COTE,Victor A AGE:82   23 Jul 1984 Hudson, NH

HUDSON,NH DEATHS

COTE,William AGE:75 09 Aug 1968 Hudson, NH
COURNOYER,Edward W AGE:85 31 Aug 1974 Nashua, NH
COUTU,Sr Marie St Vincent AGE:35 06 Sep 1949 Hudson, NH Calixte Coutu
  & Elemina Levesque
COX,Edith M AGE:10 10 02 Oct 1897 Hudson, NH David S Cox & Bertha Rolfe
COX,John W AGE:72 08 Jun 1931 Hudson, NH James Cox
CRAWFORD,Janice AGE:3 18 Jan 1974 Manchester, NH
CRENNER,Emma AGE:57 7 20 23 Oct 1918 Hudson, NH John Cheney & Harriet Avery
CROMBIE,Florence A AGE:88 01 Nov 1861 Nashua, NH
CROMPTON,Harry J AGE:74 04 Jun 1970 Nashua, NH
CROMPTON,Margaret D AGE:83 01 Jul 1984 Nashua, NH
CROOKER,Louisa L AGE:84 13 Feb 1971 Hudson, NH
CROSBY,Harry W AGE:72 17 Jun 1964 Nashua, NH
CROSBY,Norman J AGE:58 12 Sep 1975 Nashua, NH
CROSS,Alice A AGE:3 04 Aug 1804 Hudson, NH Levi Cross & Hannah
CROSS,C A AGE: 1778 Hudson, NH
CROSS,C A AGE: 1760 Hudson, NH
CROSS,C E AGE: 1778 Hudson, NH
CROSS,Capt Peter AGE:81 27 Apr 1810 Hudson, NH
CROSS,Col William AGE:56 2 06 Jan 1867 Hudson, NH
CROSS,Elizabeth AGE:85 06 Mar 1820 Hudson, NH
CROSS,Emma L AGE:77 21 Apr 1971 Nashua, NH
CROSS,Ethel M AGE:85 01 Oct 1980 Milford, NH
CROSS,Frances AGE:75 8 10 Nov 1875 Hudson, NH
CROSS,George C AGE:16 24 Dec 1862 Hudson, NH Cyrus Cross & Frances
CROSS,Guy W AGE:82 20 Aug 1980 Nashua, NH
CROSS,Hannah AGE:90 13 Dec 1862 Hudson, NH
CROSS,Henrietta AGE:34 13 Aug 1854 Hudson, NH
CROSS,Hiram AGE:72 3 12 Feb 1892 Hudson, NH Levi Cross & Goodwin
CROSS,Jabez P F AGE:50 02 Aug 1849 Hudson, NH
CROSS,John AGE:81 10 Dec 1816 Hudson, NH
CROSS,Josephine A AGE:45 4 10 02 Jul 1909 Hudson, NH George Howe
  & Mina Morgan
CROSS,Lena M AGE:79 07 Oct 1970 Nashua, NH
CROSS,Levi AGE:71 24 Dec 1838 Hudson, NH
CROSS,Levi AGE:52 01 May 1849 Hudson, NH
CROSS,Lorenzo B AGE:65 25 Aug 1954 Nashua, NH
CROSS,Mary E AGE:68 6 8 22 Aug 1929 Hudson, NH Nathan Willoby
  & Elizabeth Marshall
CROSS,Nathan AGE: 08 Sep 1766 Hudson, NH
CROSS,Peter AGE:75 08 Oct 1841 Hudson, NH
CROSS,Rachel AGE:38 01 Jun 1806 Hudson, NH Peter Cross & Sarah
CROSS,Roy H AGE:70 16 Aug 1959 Hudson, NH
CROSS,Sarah AGE:88 28 Sep 1851 Hudson, NH
CROSS,Sarah AGE:16 02 Sep 1778 Hudson, NH Peter Cross & Sarah
CROSS,Sarah E AGE:74 12 Jan 1964 Nashua, NH
CROSS,Sarah Hale AGE:56 9 7 28 Dec 1789 Hudson, NH
CROSS,William G AGE:86   17 26 Dec 1937 Hudson, NH Hiram Cross
  & Elizabeth Savage
CROSS,William S AGE:17 02 Jun 1797 Hudson, NH Levi Cross & Hannah
CROSS,[Unknonw] AGE: 21 Jul 1799 Hudson, NH Levi Cross & Hannah
CROSSLEY,Margaret E AGE:89 27 Dec 1963 Hudson, NH
CROWELL,Alton W AGE:68 03 Jul 1968 Nashua, NH
CUDWORTH,Alden J AGE:47   2 08 May 1902 Hudson, NH John Cudworth
CUDWORTH,Ernest P AGE:9 6 27 23 Mar 1902 Hudson, NH A J Cudworth
  & Emma Perry
CUDWORTH,Ernestine Mae AGE:1 11 17 15 Dec 1932 Hudson, NH Ivan Cudworth
  & Maude M Sharpe
CUDWORTH,Hildred C AGE:5 4 13 Sep 1891 Hudson, NH Alden J Cudworth
  (Peterborough) & Emma Perry (N Bangor, NY)

HUDSON,NH DEATHS

CUDWORTH,Irene M P AGE:1 4 13   28 Jun 1901 Hudson, NH A J Cudworth
   (Peterborough) & Emma Perry (Banfor, NY)
CUDWORTH,Melvin E AGE:12 9 30 Mar 1902 Hudson, NH A J Cudworth & Emma Perry
CUDWORTH,Milton D AGE:65   24 Nov 1902 Hudson, NH John Cudworth
CULLEN,Mary A AGE:58   30 Jan 1965 Hudson, NH
CULLEN,Mary J AGE:79   09 Oct 1959 Hudson, NH
CUMMINGS,Abby AGE:59 1 13   16 Nov 1889 Hudson, NH Jonathan Clark
   (Lyndeborough, NH) & Sarah Putnam (Lyndeborough, N
CUMMINGS,Abby Clark AGE:59 1 13   16 Nov 1889 Hudson, NH
CUMMINGS,Albert G AGE:13 7   03 Oct 1856 Hudson, NH Hiram Cummings & Abby
CUMMINGS,Aldon E AGE:93   10 Jul 1950 Nashua, NH John Cummings & Emeline Kemp
CUMMINGS,Alfred AGE:58   18 Jul 1862 Hudson, NH
CUMMINGS,Allen AGE:9   29 Apr 1817 Hudson, NH Thomas Cummings & Hannah
CUMMINGS,Angeline W AGE:13 8   02 Mar 1850 Hudson, NH Alfred Cummings
   & Martha C
CUMMINGS,Anna M AGE:90 3 25   31 Dec 1947 Hudson, NH Hiram Cummings
   & Abby Clark
CUMMINGS,Asa AGE: 30 Feb 1794 Hudson, NH David Cummings & Phebe
CUMMINGS,Betsey E AGE:91 6 27   29 Jan 1890 Hudson, NH
CUMMINGS,Calvin AGE: Oct 1845 Hudson, NH Thomas Cummings
CUMMINGS,Capt David AGE: 28 Feb 1803 Hudson, NH
CUMMINGS,Charles E AGE:90   08 Feb 1953 Hudson, NH
CUMMINGS,Charles S AGE:64   02 Apr 1904 Hudson, NH Chas Cummings
CUMMINGS,Eleazer AGE:79 1 18   08 Dec 1780 Hudson, NH
CUMMINGS,Eleazer AGE:78   01 Dec 1843 Hudson, NH
CUMMINGS,Elizabeth AGE:75   23 Oct 1763 Hudson, NH
CUMMINGS,Elizabeth AGE:55   14 Aug 1881 Hudson, NH
CUMMINGS,Elizabeth Butterfield AGE:51   28 Jun 1793 Hudson, NH
CUMMINGS,Elizabeth E AGE:82 7 23   15 Sep 1933 Hudson, NH George W Marshall
   & Marinda Hadley
CUMMINGS,Elizabeth F AGE:67 2   15 Apr 1922 Hudson, NH David Sloan & Simonds
CUMMINGS,Elizabeth W AGE:55   20 14 Aug 1881 Hudson, NH James Conant
   & Sarah Fletcher
CUMMINGS,Enoch AGE:88 4 14   03 Oct 1904 Hudson, NH Willard Cummings
   & Nancy Smith
CUMMINGS,Fannie R AGE:75   03 Sep 1951 Hudson, NH
CUMMINGS,Frances Mary AGE:80 9 5   19 Aug 1938 Hudson, NH David Clement
   & Maria Hall
CUMMINGS,Freddie L AGE: 16 Apr 1878 Hudson, NH W P Cummings
   & Hattie D Lawrence
CUMMINGS,Freddie S AGE:5   16 Apr 1878 Hudson, NH Willis P Cummings
   & Hattie D
CUMMINGS,George W AGE: 1851 Hudson, NH
CUMMINGS,Hannah AGE: 22 Aug 1856 Hudson, NH
CUMMINGS,Hannah AGE:30   26 Feb 1806 Hudson, NH David Cummings
CUMMINGS,Hattie C Lawrence AGE:33   01 Feb 1885 Hudson, NH
CUMMINGS,Hattie D AGE:33 10 10   01 Feb 1885 Hudson, NH Hartwell Lawrence
   (Pepperell, MA) & Sarah M Blood (Londonderry, NH)
CUMMINGS,Helen A AGE:75 3 13   18 Jan 1928 Hudson, NH Hiram Cummings
   & Abby Clark
CUMMINGS,Hiram AGE:88 3 9   07 Jan 1910 Hudson, NH Willard Cummings
   & Nancy Smith
CUMMINGS,James M AGE:66 2 9   12 Dec 1924 Hudson, NH Nathan Cummings
   & Elizabeth Conant
CUMMINGS,Jane S AGE:18   10 Apr 1856 Hudson, NH John Cummings
   & Sophia Lawrence
CUMMINGS,John AGE:67   17 Apr 1873 Hudson, NH
CUMMINGS,John C AGE:4   04 Jul 1839 Hudson, NH John Cummings & Sophia Lawrence
CUMMINGS,Josiah AGE: 08 Feb 1761 Hudson, NH
CUMMINGS,Laura B Blodgett AGE:73 5 16   26 Mar 1935 Hudson, NH Aug F Blodgett

HUDSON,NH DEATHS

& Lucy Chase
CUMMINGS,Leander H AGE: 18 Jul 1863 Hudson, NH
CUMMINGS,Lemuel H AGE:17   Jul 1863 Hudson, NH
CUMMINGS,Lizzie AGE:7   07 May 1876 Hudson, NH
CUMMINGS,Louisa C AGE:66 7   25 May 1883 Hudson, NH Daniel McAlpine
  & Abigail Gould
CUMMINGS,Martha C AGE:70   04 Feb 1877 Hudson, NH
CUMMINGS,Mary Varnum AGE:54   17 Sep 1759 Hudson, NH
CUMMINGS,Nancy AGE:70   03 Feb 1864 Hudson, NH
CUMMINGS,Nancy Smith AGE:70   09 Feb 1865 Hudson, NH
CUMMINGS,Nathan AGE:76   23 Sep 1894 Hudson, NH Willard Cummings (Hudson, NH)
  & Nancy Smith (Hudson, NH)
CUMMINGS,Nellie AGE: 09 Jun 1951 Ontario
CUMMINGS,Nellie AGE:9 1   09 Nov 1863 Hudson, NH Reuben Cummings & Rhoda
CUMMINGS,Nellie AGE:15   09 Nov 1869 Hudson, NH Reuben Cummings
CUMMINGS,Phebe Richardson AGE:61   07 Dec 1788 Hudson, NH
CUMMINGS,Reuben AGE:13   11 Apr 1824 Hudson, NH Willard Cummings & Nancy L
CUMMINGS,Rhoda AGE: 17 Jan 1881 Hudson, NH
CUMMINGS,Samuel AGE: 06 May 1779 Hudson, NH Eben Cummings & Sarah
CUMMINGS,Sarah AGE:47   12 Nov 1772 Hudson, NH
CUMMINGS,Sarah A G AGE:14   28 Apr 1840 Hudson, NH Alfred Cummings & Martha C
CUMMINGS,Sarah Hale AGE:85   07 May 1852 Hudson, NH
CUMMINGS,Sophia Lawrence AGE:36   14 Aug 1843 Hudson, NH
CUMMINGS,Thomas AGE: 23 Jun 1861 Hudson, NH
CUMMINGS,Thomas AGE: Hudson, NH
CUMMINGS,Willard AGE:80   19 Mar 1871 Hudson, NH Eleazer Cummings & Sally
CUMMINGS,William AGE: 29 Aug 1757 Hudson, NH
CUMMINGS,Willis P AGE:89 4 19   15 Jun 1939 Hudson, NH Hiram Cummings
  & Abby Clark
CUMMINGS,[Unknown] AGE:1   04 Aug 1843 Hudson, NH John Cummings
  & Sophia Lawrence
CUMMINS,Emeline M B AGE:92 6 8   28 Sep 1909 Hudson, NH Timothy Kemper
  & Sarah Brown
CUNHA,Frank AGE:67   13 Oct 1972 Nashua, NH
CUNNINGHAM,Carol AGE: 03 Apr 1943 Nashua, NH H Cunningham & Helen Miller
CUNNINGHAM,Edith D AGE:85   08 May 1964 Hudson, NH
CUNNINGHAM,[Unknown] AGE: 08 Jul 1940 Hudson, NH James Cunningham
  & Gladys Miller
CURRAN,Edward A AGE:52   16 Jul 1980 Manchester, NH
CURRAN,Frank AGE:84   12 Sep 1975 Nashua, NH
CURRAN,Keith W AGE:7   05 Aug 1971 Nashua, NH
CURRAN,Michael J AGE:24   21 Feb 1978 Nashua, NH
CURRIER,Mary E AGE:91   13 Dec 1969 Nashua, NH
CURTIS,Sylvina W AGE:83 10 13   18 Sep 1913 Hudson, NH Jesse Jewell
  & Elizabeth Trask
CUTHBERTSON,Angus AGE:84   25 Aug 1962 Hudson, NH
CUTHBERTSON,Clyde A AGE:67   18 Jun 1970 Nashua, NH
CUTHBERTSON,Myrtle AGE:57   19 May 1967 Nashua, NH
CUTLER,Aaron AGE:78 10 30   23 Nov 1917 Hudson, NH Samuel Cutler & Betsy Paul
CUTTER,Charles H AGE:21   17 Jan 1861 Hudson, NH
CUTTER,Elizabeth M AGE:77   31 Dec 1959 Nashua, NH
CUTTER,James AGE:36   27 Apr 1817 Hudson, NH
CUTTER,Jane A AGE:1   11   09 Feb 1811 Hudson, NH
CUTTER,Keziah Pierce AGE:63   19 Dec 1788 Hudson, NH
CUTTER,Richard AGE:70   08 Apr 1795 Hudson, NH
D'AMOUR,Albina AGE:51   16 Apr 1973 Nashua, NH
D'ANJOU,Emelia AGE:85   14 Apr 1976 Goffstown, NH
DAHIMANN,Heinz K AGE:74   06 Mar 1983 Nashua, NH
DAHLMANN,Ella G AGE:74   12 Dec 1983 Hudson, NH
DAKIN,Abigail AGE:94   17 Oct 1844 Hudson, NH

HUDSON,NH DEATHS

DAKIN,Ebenezer AGE: 30 May 1776 Hudson, NH Levi Dakin
DAKIN,Justus AGE:84   09 Nov 1822 Hudson, NH
DALTON,Linda M AGE:5 20   19 Jun 1943 Nashua, NH Roland A Dalton
  & Helen Trumbull
DALZELL,Celeste AGE:3 hrs   31 Jul 1956 Nashua, NH
DAMBROISE,Noemie AGE:83   22 Aug 1984 Hudson, NH
DAME,Helen E AGE:67   13 Sep 1968 Nashua, NH
DAME,Robert D AGE:61   23 Jul 1982 Manchester, NH
DANE,Charles F AGE:66 10 11   28 Jan 1892 Hudson, NH Joseph H Dane
  (Andover, MA) & Rhoda Smith (Hudson, NH)
DANE,Charles G AGE:60 10 11   28 Jun 1892 Hudson, NH Joseph B Dane & Rhoda
DANE,Ellery C AGE:56 8 22   04 Sep 1929 Hudson, NH John P Dane
  & Frances MacLean
DANE,Frances AGE:26 9   24 Feb 1822 Hudson, NH
DANE,Helen M AGE:90   12 Dec 1984 Hudson, NH
DANE,Joseph B AGE:77   11 May 1862 Hudson, NH
DANE,Madeline V AGE:69   22 Jul 1965 Hudson, NH
DANE,Rhoda AGE:78   05 May 1865 Hudson, NH
DANE,Richard C AGE:71   27 Dec 1970 Hudson, NH
DANEAULT,David C AGE:79 11 26   11 May 1944 Hudson, NH Joseph Daneault
DANEAULT,Edward J AGE:70   08 Aug 1965 Manchester, NH
DANEAULT,Regina AGE:61   13 Aug 1959 Concord, NH
DANFORTH,Catherine AGE:71   14 Feb 1891 Hudson, NH David Danforth & Mary
DANFORTH,Nancy H AGE:78 4   06 Oct 1895 Hudson, NH Joshua Pierce
DANFORTH,Willis A AGE:66   08 Apr 1949 Nashua, NH Almon Danforth & Mary Kelly
DANIELEVITCH,Joseph A AGE:87   04 Jul 1973 Nashua, NH
DANIELEVITCH,Mary M AGE:55   04 Nov 1950 Hudson, NH Michael Haleniewski
  & Mary Haleniewski
DANIELS,Carl W AGE:11   23 Apr 1950 Nashua, NH Howard R Daniels
  & Andrea Savage
DANIELS,Charles A AGE:85   27 Dec 1950 Manchester, NH John Daniels
  & Sarah Harris
DANSEREAU,Sister Georgette AGE:73   02 Oct 1984 Nashua, NH
DARRIGO,Anne AGE:70   07 May 1985 Nashua, NH
DAVENPORT,Rebecca H AGE:80   18 Nov 1946 Hudson, NH Anthony Hall
DAVIDSON,Lawrence E AGE:74   17 Jan 1974 Nashua, NH
DAVIDSON,Oscar F AGE:94   04 Dec 1966 Nashua, NH
DAVIS,Abbie E AGE:78 4 13   26 Jan 1929 Hudson, NH Mark Batchelder
  & Lydia Steel
DAVIS,Abigail E AGE:3 10   26 Nov 1833 Hudson, NH Amos Davis & Hannah
DAVIS,Amos AGE:76   22 Aug 1845 Hudson, NH
DAVIS,Anna AGE:93 6   16 Jul 1876 Hudson, NH
DAVIS,Annie Belle AGE: 11 Nov 1902 Hudson, NH Henry C Davis & Grace Heath
DAVIS,Asa AGE:89   27 Mar 1826 Hudson, NH
DAVIS,Blanche E AGE:70   15 Jul 1958 Nashua, NH
DAVIS,Charles A AGE:9 24   14 Nov 1858 Hudson, NH Solomon A Davis
  & Dorothy Pollard
DAVIS,Charles L AGE:57   08 May 1957 Nashua, NH
DAVIS,Clarence L AGE:81   28 Oct 1960 Nashua, NH
DAVIS,Cynthia M AGE:80   03 Apr 1952 Hudson, NH
DAVIS,Daniel T AGE:81   01 Jan 1855 Hudson, NH
DAVIS,Elizabeth AGE:11   26 Aug 1862 Hudson, NH
DAVIS,Elizabeth C AGE:86   11 Nov 1822 Hudson, NH
DAVIS,Elizabeth M AGE:3   27 Feb 1952 Goffstown, NH
DAVIS,Emma C AGE:88 11 8   20 Mar 1918 Hudson, NH Martin Cook
DAVIS,Esther AGE:74   07 Apr 1841 Hudson, NH
DAVIS,Ethel M AGE:90   14 Mar 1970 Nashua, NH
DAVIS,George H AGE:87 7 7   15 Jun 1922 Hudson, NH & Sarah Taylor
DAVIS,George W AGE:66 9 18   12 Mar 1943 Hudson, NH George H Davis
  & Abbie Batchelder

HUDSON,NH DEATHS

DAVIS,Hannah AGE:87 7 30 May 1896 Hudson, NH John H Smith (Hudson, NH)
DAVIS,Henry C AGE:72 11 25 29 Oct 1944 Nashua, NH George W Davis
 & Abbie Batchelder
DAVIS,James M AGE:36 16 Jun 1846 Hudson, NH
DAVIS,John F AGE:72 2 7 10 Oct 1900 Hudson, NH Nathan Davis & Mary Lovejoy
DAVIS,Lizzie AGE:41 26 Aug 1862 Hudson, NH Samuel Davis & Anna
DAVIS,Lucy P AGE:47 4 10 14 Apr 1921 Hudson, NH Neimiah Fuller
 & Maria Fuller
DAVIS,Mabel AGE:75 17 Aug 1959 Hudson, NH
DAVIS,Marguerite L AGE:7 10 15 Feb 1905 Hudson, NH Geo W Davis
 & Lucy P Fuller
DAVIS,Martha Whittier AGE:97 Jul 1825 Hudson, NH
DAVIS,Nancy AGE:85 1 17 Apr 1896 Hudson, NH Samuel Davis (Hudson, NH)
 & Anna Morse (Methuen, MA)
DAVIS,Nathaniel AGE:58 18 Sep 1783 Hudson, NH
DAVIS,Rebecca AGE:73 4 14 27 Jul 1890 Hudson, NH John Baldwin (Pelham)
 & Betsy Blodgett (Hudson, NH)
DAVIS,Samuel AGE:19 26 Jun 1775 Hudson, NH Nathaniel Davis & Martha
DAVIS,Samuel AGE:53 31 Jul 1861 Hudson, NH
DAVIS,Samuel AGE:76 26 Feb 1853 Hudson, NH
DAVIS,Sarah AGE:38 03 Apr 1799 Hudson, NH
DAVIS,Sarah A B AGE:6 27 Mar 1827 Hudson, NH Amos Davis & Hannah
DAVIS,Simeon R AGE:30 08 Oct 1842 Hudson, NH
DAVIS,Susan AGE:82 17 Nov 1866 Hudson, NH
DAVIS,Susan Robinson AGE:81 10 21 Nov 1866 Hudson, NH
DAVOCK,Carolyn L AGE:40 10 Dec 1977 Hudson, NH
DAWALGA,Priscilla AGE:26 14 May 1955 Nashua, NH
DAWSON,Aurille D AGE:62 11 Nov 1905 Hudson, NH Frederick Dawson
 & Marcia Cook
DAY,Maj John E AGE:74 3 12 15 Jan 1930 Hudson, NH John F Day
 & Sybil S Robbins
DAY,Sarah G AGE:87 10 17 05 May 1902 Hudson, NH Jabez Towne & Mary Campbell
DE GRANDPRE, Emilie,Sr St Jeanne-de-Valo AGE:78   12 Nov 1955 Hudson, NH
DEAN,Elizabeth J AGE:71 22 Sep 1984 Nashua, NH
DEAN,John AGE:85 1 1 03 Oct 1906 Hudson, NH J A Dean & Merle Mercier
DEARBORN,Anne M AGE:47 28 Sep 1949 Nashua, NH John J Carroll & Mary Linehan
DEARBORN,Arthur G AGE:73 6 28 30 Jul 1943 Hudson, NH Andrew J Dearborn
 & Anna Delaney
DEARBORN,Melvina AGE:70 14 Feb 1965 Nashua, NH
DEARBORN,Wayne R AGE:65 29 May 1967 Nashua, NH
DECELLE,Alfred AGE:77 21 Sep 1954 Nashua, NH
DeCOLO,Salvatore AGE:75 19 Feb 1984 Nashua, NH
DELACOMBE,Edward AGE:77 12 Jan 1964 Nashua, NH
DELANEY,Catherine AGE:75 05 Dec 1977 Salem, MA
DELISLE,Eva AGE:96 14 Jun 1985 Hudson, NH
DELUDE,Joseph AGE:62 05 Nov 1957 Hudson, NH
DEMANCHE,Elvina AGE:50 22 Jan 1962 Hudson, NH
DEMERS,Arcadi AGE:63 11 18 02 Aug 1915 Hudson, NH Florien Demers (Canada)
 & Julie Mouffette (Canada)
DEMERS,Marie T AGE:46 20 Mar 1970 Nashua, NH
DeNARDI,Tulio AGE:65 11 Jan 1976 Nashua, NH
DENAULT,Joseph F AGE:71 28 Jun 1951 Nashua, NH
DENAULT,Marie A AGE:58 18 Apr 1967 Nashua, NH
DENAULT,Philomene AGE:61 5 13 24 Oct 1924 Hudson, NH Pierre Deschamp
 & Lucie Deneault
DENNEN,Arthur D AGE:47 4 24 10 Sep 1926 Hudson, NH James Dennen
 & Mary A Quinn
DeQUOY,Annie T AGE:G79 08 May 1949 Hudson, NH Jeremiah J Wildes
 & Sarah E Tarleton
DERY,Albert AGE:64 06 Jun 1968 Nashua, NH

HUDSON,NH DEATHS

DESAUTEL,Joseph O AGE:79   04 Jul 1979 Nashua, NH
DESAUTELS,Edmund AGE:57   20 Nov 1969 Nashua, NH
DESCLOS,Wilfred J AGE:73   20 May 1975 Nashua, NH
DESFOSSES,Sr Helen AGE:57   01 Nov 1978 Hudson, NH
DESJADON,Margaret F AGE:77   16 Feb 1979 Nashua, NH
DESJARDINS,Albert AGE:74   18 Nov 1974 Nashua, NH
DESJARDINS,Jean A AGE:44   08 Dec 1966 Nashua, NH
DESJARDINS,Pierre AGE:81   30 May 1974 Nashua, NH
DESJARLAIS,Marie-Jeanne AGE:97   24 Oct 1983 Manchester, NH
DESLAURIERS,Josephine AGE:93   11 May 1979 Nashua, NH
DESMARAIS,Arthur T AGE:70   09 Jun 1970 Nashua, NH
DESMARAIS,Emma AGE:78   01 Oct 1972 Manchester, NH
DESMARAIS,Josephine AGE:57   24   27 Aug 1929 Hudson, NH Ferdina Lucas
   & Lizzie Ouellette
DESMARAIS,Marie AGE:3 1   15 Jul 1913 Hudson, NH Joseph Desmarais
   & Rosanna Simard
DESMARAIS,Rosanna AGE:24 5 6   25 Apr 1919 Hudson, NH Xavier Simard
DESMOND,Lawrence G AGE:41   26 Oct 1968 Hudson, NH
DESNOYERS,Honorine AGE:91   03 Aug 1976 Nashua, NH
DESNOYERS,Sr Marie Ste Brigitt AGE:76   07 Apr 1949 Hudson, NH Jacques
   Desnoyers & Celina Poulin
DESROSIER,Arthur J AGE:83   25 Feb 1977 Tilton, NH
DEVLIN,Rejane O AGE:55   25 Sep 1967 Nashua, NH
DIAMANTOPOULIS,[Unknown] AGE: 06 Dec 1918 Hudson, NH A Diamantopoulis
   & Anastusia Tangalon
DICHARD,Albert L AGE:68   30 Aug 1972 Hudson, NH
DICKERSON,Velda V AGE:82   30 Dec 1979 Nashua, NH
DICKINSON,Grace E Clay AGE:98   21 Oct 1978 Hudson, NH
DINSMORE,Annie M AGE:7 9 2   26 Jan 1892 Hudson, NH Frank W Dinsmore
   (Glendon, ME) & Jennie Douglass (Nova Scotia)
DION,Corrinne AGE:72   04 Jun 1958 Hudson, NH
DION,Frederick W AGE:59   01 Dec 1956 Hudson, NH
DION,Gerard AGE:6 16   21 Feb 1918 Hudson, NH John B Dion & Dora Gauthier
DION,Omer AGE:82   12 Apr 1982 Nashua, NH
DIONNE,Alphonse AGE:83   21 Nov 1977 Nashua, NH
DIONNE,Arthur Joseph AGE:12 1   23 Jul 1933 Hudson, NH Joseph E Dionne
   & Angres St Laurent
DIONNE,Casey A AGE:11   15 Aug 1980 Nashua, NH
DIONNE,Elise Vaillancourt AGE:80   14 Feb 1971 Concord, NH
DIONNE,Joseph E AGE:81   16 Feb 1963 Hudson, NH
DIONNE,Thomas J AGE:57   02 Nov 1953 Hudson, NH
DIONNE,[Unknown] AGE:2 hrs   02 Jan 1966 Nashua, NH
DOBENS,Robert AGE:63   02 Aug 1973 Nashua, NH
DOBROWOLSKI,John AGE:89   16 Nov 1980 Hudson, NH
DOCKHAM,Annie E AGE:60 4 2   27 Jan 1941 Nashua, NH John H Dockham
   & Susan Bradley
DOCKHAM,Therese A AGE:31   10 Mar 1972 Londonderry, NH
DODGE,Albert AGE:56   11 Mar 1962 Concord, NH
DODGE,Emma J AGE:73 9 17   09 Sep 1948 Hudson, NH Andrew Laflamme
   & Mary Hebert
DODGE,William AGE:77 2 26   05 Nov 1948 Nashua, NH Jacob Dodge
   & Malvina Gagnon
DOHERTY,Annie AGE:78   09 Nov 1963 Hudson, NH
DOHERTY,John H AGE:74   2 11 Aug 1933 Hudson, NH Patrick Doherty
   & Cecelia Harkin
DOHERTY,Lorraine A AGE: 04 Jan 1949 Nashua, NH John E Doherty
   & Margaret Small
DOLLIVER,Amos P AGE:97   6   01 Jul 1946 Hudson, NH Amos Dolliver
   & Matilda Anderson
DONAH,Edgar J AGE:71   22 Dec 1983 Nashua, NH

HUDSON,NH DEATHS

DONAH,Eva A AGE:96   24 Mar 1983 Nashua, NH
DONAH,Joseph O AGE:81   11 Dec 1969 Hudson, NH
DONAHUE,Timothy AGE:89   23 Jan 1907 Hudson, NH Patrick Donahue & Abbie Ord
DONLON,Bernard F AGE:81   28 Oct 1968 Manchester, NH
DONNELLY,Eugene AGE:25   02 Oct 1899 Hudson, NH Eugene Donnelly & Mary Buckley
DONNELLY,Johanna AGE:74   23 Nov 1915 Hudson, NH Michael Buckley (Ireland)
 & Ellen Sullivan (Ireland)
DONNELLY,Mary AGE:33   09 Jan 1905 Hudson, NH John Tafe
DONOHOE,Ellen AGE:76   27 Aug 1895 Hudson, NH Patrick Sweeny (Ireland)
 & Julia Rourke (Ireland)
DONOVAN,Cecile Y AGE:48   18 Jan 1964 Nashua, NH
DONOVAN,Timothy H AGE:50 6 27   28 Sep 1944 Nashua, NH Stephen Donovan
 & Catherine Lee
DOOLEY,George N AGE:57 5 22   22 Jun 1928 Hudson, NH James Dooley
 & Martha Goodwin
DORR,Annie J AGE:63 10 5   05 Jul 1940 Concord, NH George D Jaquith
 & Sarah J Fox
DORR,Fred AGE:68   05 Oct 1918 Hudson, NH Alec Dorr
DOUCET,Edward AGE:64   21 Dec 1969 Nashua, NH
DOUCET,Sarah AGE:61 1 2   16 Jun 1912 Hudson, NH Max Martel & Marie Morin
DOUGLASS,Charles AGE:1   20 Mar 1873 Hudson, NH
DOUGLASS,Hannah McCoy AGE:52   22 Apr 1810 Hudson, NH
DOUGLASS,Mary AGE:29   14 Jan 1873 Hudson, NH
DOUGLASS,Rachel AGE:72   08 Nov 1829 Hudson, NH
DOUGLASS,Robert AGE:85   17 Jul 1833 Hudson, NH
DOUGLASS,William J AGE:15   23 Jul 1874 Hudson, NH
DOURIS,Theodore AGE:55   04 Jan 1949 Hudson, NH George Douris & Mary Douris
DOW,Anna D AGE:37 5   12 May 1842 Hudson, NH
DOW,Dora P AGE:18   26 Feb 1863 Hudson, NH
DOW,Drury P AGE:18 10   26 Feb 1862 Hudson, NH
DOW,Jessie F AGE:30   22 Apr 1894 Hudson, NH Thomas B Dow (Woodbury, VT)
 & Frances Hills (Marshfield, VT)
DOWER,Victor H AGE:63   12 May 1976 Manchester, NH
DOYLE,Alice F AGE:72   12 Jan 1975 Milford, NH
DOYLE,James AGE:68   Sep 1865 Hudson, NH
DOYLE,Sarah AGE:56   27 Jan 1894 Hudson, NH James Doyle & Sophia Blodgett
 (Hudson, NH)
DOYLE,Sarah Blodgett AGE:55 7   06 Nov 1878 Hudson, NH
DOYLE,William J AGE:36   27 Sep 1907 Hudson, NH James F Doyle
 & Ellen E Hartegan
DREW,Clara M AGE:12   24 Mar 1891 Hudson, NH George A Drew (Merrimack)
 & F M Clement (Hudson, NH)
DROUIN,Albert AGE:72   23 Jun 1980 Nashua, NH
DROWNS,William P Jr AGE:57   04 Sep 1982 Nashua, NH
DRUCKER,Mary AGE:84 7 13   01 Jun 1905 Hudson, NH Isaac Huffmaster
DUBE,Arthur L AGE:57   17 Mar 1955 Nashua, NH
DUBE,Bertha L AGE:82   07 Mar 1979 Nashua, NH
DUBE,Leda AGE:85   11 Nov 1981 Hudson, NH
DUBE,Odilon AGE:81   07 Nov 1969 Nashua, NH
DuBOIS,Eugene I AGE:83   08 Aug 1979 Hudson, NH
DUBOIS,Marie C AGE:70   05 Sep 1964 Manchester, NH
DUCEY,Daniel R AGE:74   06 Dec 1980 Nashua, NH
DUCHARME,Adelard AGE:75   14 Jun 1969 Hudson, NH
DUCHARME,Bertha AGE:67   30 Mar 1977 Nashua, NH
DUCHARME,Henry AGE:61   14 Jul 1962 Nashua, NH
DUCHARME,Laura AGE:65   20 Apr 1975 Hudson, NH
DUCHARME,Leo AGE:69   12 Feb 1973 Hudson, NH
DUCHARME,Matilda AGE:83 10 27   25 Nov 1944 Nashua, NH Godfroid Deloge
 & Exilda Gauthier
DUCHARME,Rose D AGE:84   04 Jul 1975 Nashua, NH

HUDSON,NH DEATHS

DUCLOS,Louis E AGE:67 29 Dec 1951 Hudson, NH
DUCLOS,Vivian A AGE:39 10 Sep 1976 Goffstown, NH
DUDLEY,Jonathan AGE:43 29 Mar 1864 Hudson, NH
DUDLEY,Jonathan C AGE:43 29 Mar 1865 Hudson, NH
DUDLEY,Louisa J AGE:82 4 14 08 Sep 1900 Hudson, NH K J Emeroy
  & Elizabeth Hurd
DUFFY,Ronda Joan AGE:20 20 Jan 1985 Hanover, NH
DUGAN,John D AGE:31 2 15 15 Feb 1931 Hudson, NH William Dugan & Mary Dugan
DUHAMEL, Brenda L AGE:9 11 Jul 1959 Nashua, NH
DUMAIS,Alphonse AGE:67 30 Nov 1971 Nashua, NH
DUMAIS,Cecile AGE:68 05 May 1979 Nashua, NH
DUMAIS,Debora A AGE:9 25 Nov 1957 Nashua, NH
DUMAIS,Deborah J AGE:20 21 Feb 1985 Nashua, NH
DUMAIS,Irene AGE:61 10 Jan 1973 Hudson, NH
DUMAIS,John B AGE:76 12 Jan 1979 Nashua, NH
DUMONT,Arebille AGE:91 4 25 07 Dec 1934 Hudson, NH Joseph Dumont
DUMOUCHEL,Lillian AGE:43 11 Nov 1953 Hudson, NH
DUNCKLEE,Orise P AGE:51 28 Oct 1954 Nashua, NH
DUNKLEE,Helen T AGE:54 31 Dec 1967 Nashua, NH
DUNKLEE,Walter C AGE:65 24 May 1956 Hudson, NH
DUNTLEY,Charles E AGE:48 20 Mar 1897 Hudson, NH Stephen Duntley
  & Emelia Prescott
DUPONT,Frances AGE:51 21 Apr 1967 Nashua, NH
DUPONT,Lionel AGE:59 10 Aug 1982 Nashua, NH
DUPONT,Marie L AGE:85 01 Mar 1980 Hudson, NH
DURAND,Edward AGE:69 25 Mar 1958 Nashua, NH
DURAND,Ernest J AGE:54 15 Oct 1982 Manchester, NH
DURAND,Jeannine N AGE:29 04 Mar 1966 Hudson, NH
DURAND,Ludivine AGE:68 26 Mar 1958 Nashua, NH
DURANT,Child AGE: Sep 1865 Hudson, NH
DURANT,George O AGE:50 18 Mar 1950 Nashua, NH George Durant & Mary E Anthony
DURANT,Georgianna F AGE:83 6 14 02 Jan 1929 Hudson, NH Plummer Lund
DURANT,Mrs AGE: Sep 1865 Hudson, NH
DURANT,William AGE:70 1865 Hudson, NH
DURIVAGE,George E AGE:73   16 16 Mar 1939 Hudson, NH Ransom Durivage
  & Jeanette Goodrich
DURIVAGE,Halga M AGE:79 28 Jan 1955 Nashua, NH
DURIVAGE,Ida M AGE:89 23 Jan 1960 Nashua, NH
DURIVAGE,Rodney AGE:19 28 Nov 1960 Hudson, NH
DURKIN,Mary J AGE:79 02 Sep 1968 Nashua, NH
DUSSEAULT,Adrien C AGE:49 14 Nov 1971 Lawrence, MA
DUSTIN,Beatrice A AGE:31 10 6 03 Mar 1909 Hudson, NH Luther A Healey
  & Mary Neal
DUSTIN,Etheren E AGE:6   25 21 Jul 1888 Hudson, NH W F Dustin (Antrim, NH)
  & Alfretta Batchelder (Hudson, NH)
DUSTIN,Etherine E AGE:6   25 21 Jul 1888 Hudson, NH W R Dustin & Alfaretta
DUSTIN,Frank AGE:66 1 13 12 Oct 1918 Hudson, NH Jonathan Dustin & Mary Noble
DUTTON,John E AGE:54 3 15 16 Apr 1868 Hudson, NH
DUTTON,John E AGE:54 16 Apr 1878 Hudson, NH John Dutton & Joice Hadley
DUTTON,Joice AGE:72 17 May 1863 Hudson, NH
DUTTON,Joice Hadley AGE:72 1 17 May 1863 Hudson, NH
DUVALL,Arthur H AGE:51 04 Jul 1965 Hudson, NH
DWYER,Augustus L AGE:66 09 Nov 1972 Goffstown, NH
EASTMAN,Eleanor AGE:68 16 Aug 1822 Hudson, NH
EASTMAN,Robert S AGE:50 17 Jul 1970 Enfield, NH
EATON,Albert H AGE:84 14 Mar 1979 Nashua, NH
EATON,Bertha M AGE:39 11 17 09 Jun 1917 Hudson, NH William N Smith
  & Lucy Tuck
EATON,Eva R AGE:76 16 Jan 1974 Nashua, NH
EATON,Harriet S AGE:78 8 6 18 Apr 1905 Hudson, NH James Smith & Sybil Wilson

HUDSON,NH DEATHS

EATON,Helen Julia AGE:1 2 29   22 May 1926 Hudson, NH Albert H Eaton
  & Eva R Smith
EAYRS,Charlotte A AGE:88 5 27   29 Nov 1945 Hudson, NH James Ford
  & Sarah Putnam
EAYRS,Winslow O AGE:74 11 7   06 Aug 1915 Hudson, NH William Eayrs
  (Nashua, NH) & Hannah Fortin (Nashua, NH)
ECONOUPALAS,Demetrius AGE:68   09 Nov 1944 Nashua, NH
EDWARDS,Albert E AGE:61   21 Dec 1962 Nashua, NH
EDWARDS,Albert F AGE:2 15   24 Sep 1901 Hudson, NH Arthur B Edwards
  (New Brunswick) & Lucy M Eayrs (Hudson, NH)
EDWARDS,Carla R AGE:17   28 Mar 1980 Laconia, NH
EDWARDS,Charles AGE:1 3   06 Jun 1906 Hudson, NH Arthur Edwards & Lucy M Eayrs
EGERIS,Joseph A AGE:68   30 Jul 1963 Nashua, NH
ELDRIDGE,Helen Lillian AGE:22 9 14   22 May 1907 Hudson, NH John Rounsavelle
  & Cora Bell Clifford
ELDRIDGE,Louisa S AGE:70   09 Mar 1966 Nashua, NH
ELDRIDGE,Vivian H AGE:4   28 Jan 1907 Hudson, NH Arthur W Eldridge
  & Hellen S Rounsaville
ELKAVICH,[Unknown] AGE: 27 Apr 1943 Nashua, NH Joseph Elkavich
  & Rita Gauthier
ELLIOTT,Elizabeth AGE:69   12 Feb 1951 Manchester, NH
ELLIOTT,Guy M AGE:72   22 Jun 1964 Hudson, NH
ELLIOTT,Rose AGE:65   13 Feb 1943 Hudson, NH
ELLIOTT,Theresa M AGE:46   10 Jul 1973 Nashua, NH
ELLIS,David J AGE:21   17 Sep 1984 Hudson, NH
ELLIS,Susan M AGE:68 4   25 Jul 1913 Hudson, NH Geo E Griffin
  & Susan B Barrett
ELLISON,Delia E AGE:74   11 Feb 1949 Hudson, NH Alfred E Tracy
  & Louisa V Hutchinson
ELLISON,Wellington AGE:79   12 Mar 1949 Hudson, NH Malcolm Ellison
  & Mary Garden
EMERSON,Arthur S AGE:52 2 2   12 Nov 1899 Hudson, NH Steven Emerson
  & Merenda Flanders
EMERSON,Ephraim AGE:16   03 Jul 1860 Hudson, NH
EMERSON,Ephraim F AGE:16   03 Jul 1860 Hudson, NH
EMERSON,Eva D AGE:82 2 30   18 Aug 1934 Hudson, NH Jonathan C Dudley
  & Louisa J Emery
EMERSON,Harry D AGE:80   06 Nov 1952 Nashua, NH
EMERSON,John J AGE:26   03 Sep 1860 Hudson, NH
EMERSON,John J AGE:26   13 Sep 1860 Hudson, NH
EMERSON,Moses W AGE:69 11 18   09 Jul 1892 Hudson, NH Kimball Emerson
  (Haverhill, MA) & Sarah Webster (Salem)
EMERSON,Richard AGE:21   18 Jul 186 Hudson, NH
EMERSON,Richard AGE:21   19 Jul 1860 Hudson, NH
EMERY,Caleb AGE:74   14 Jun 1860 Hudson, NH
EMERY,Charles J AGE:20   05 Aug 1878 Hudson, NH James Emery & Sarah J
EMERY,Elizabeth AGE:91 3   Hudson, NH
EMERY,James AGE:58   30 Sep 1880 Hudson, NH
EMERY,James M D AGE:58 3   30 Sep 1880 Hudson, NH
ENGLISH,Bessie AGE:98   12 Feb 1968 Hudson, NH
ENRIGHT,Juliette S AGE:73   11 Mar 1985 Nashua, NH
ERB,Austin W AGE:84   27 Sep 1968 Nashua, NH
ERB,David A AGE:29   12 Sep 1978 Nashua, NH
ERWIN,Francis K AGE:68   27 Aug 1975 Nashua, NH
ESPEJO,Stasia AGE:76   08 Feb 1985 Hudson, NH
ESPOSITO,Carmen T AGE:34   02 Jan 1953 Nashua, NH
ESTERS,Selina T AGE:74 1 21   12 Dec 1943 Hudson, NH Joseph Tessier
  & Mary Tessier
ESTES,Charles E AGE:79 11 25   19 Dec 1945 Hudson, NH Lew Estes & Mary Estes
ESTEY,George H AGE:72 6   15 Feb 1942 Nashua, NH Edward P Estey

HUDSON,NH DEATHS

   & Lydia Hemphill
ESTEY,Grace E AGE:10 12 29 Oct 1890 Hudson, NH Aaron P Estey (Derry)
   & Mary E Ackerman (Farmington)
ESTY,Aaron P AGE:87 21 Mar 1951 Hudson, NH
ESTY,Della L AGE:65   03 Jan 1971 Hudson, NH
ESTY,Mary J AGE:75 27 Jun 1977 Nashua, NH
EVANS,Anna AGE:89 23 Apr 1965 Nashua, NH
EVANS,Thomas M AGE:45 20 Apr 1912 Hudson, NH
EVERETT,Florence B AGE:91 13 Aug 1954 Nashua, NH
EYARS,Edward F AGE:72 8 15   13 Feb 1913 Hudson, NH John Eyars
   & Lucy H Hartwell
FAGAN,Edmund J AGE:46 23 Apr 1966 Hudson, NH
FAGAN,James M AGE:65 12 Apr 1941 Nashua, NH
FAHEY,Marion J AGE:78 17 Aug 1974 Nashua, NH
FAIRBANKS,Charles AGE:27 19 Jun 1863 Hudson, NH
FAIRBANKS,Clara A AGE:83 2 01 Apr 1917 Hudson, NH Abel B Parker
   & Martha W Evens
FAIRFIELD,Etta M AGE:80 5 5   18 Nov 1947 Hudson, NH Wm H Ackerman
   & Henrietta Loyne
FARLAND,Alice M AGE:73 27 Feb 1963 Nashua, NH
FARLAND,Joseph E AGE:54 15 Jun 1951 Nashua, NH
FARLAND,Robert A AGE:24 18 Sep 1971 Hudson, NH
FARLEY,Ada S AGE:86 24 Aug 1962 Hudson, NH
FARLEY,Donald W AGE:65   14 Feb 1985 Hudson, NH
FARLEY,Eldridge AGE:2 1 23 Aug 1843 Hudson, NH Senter Farley & Louisa
FARLEY,Evelyn E AGE:42 23 Jun 1952 Nashua, NH
FARLEY,George F AGE:78 21 Apr 1960 Hudson, NH
FARLEY,George H AGE:2 2 18 Oct 1851 Hudson, NH George W Farley & Mary A
FARLEY,Martha AGE:8 10 Sep 1814 Hudson, NH Joseph Farley & Susan
FARLEY,Susanna AGE:64 14 Apr 1847 Hudson, NH
FARMER,Charles A AGE:74 06 Sep 1962 Franklin, NH
FARMER,Eugenie B AGE:87 03 Mar 1975 Hudson, NH
FARMER,Hannah AGE:77 5 14 Jul 1905 Hudson, NH Wm Hodgdon
FARMER,Sarah AGE:54 13 Dec 1851 Hudson, NH
FARNHAM,Amos B AGE:72 18 Oct 1896 Hudson, NH
FARNHAM,Ann AGE:77 8 20 29 Dec 1898 Hudson, NH Alex McDonald
   & Catherine White
FARNUM,Dustin P AGE:30 14 Jul 1845 Hudson, NH
FARNUM,Elizabeth W AGE:31 10 17 Jun 1850 Hudson, NH
FARNUM,John P AGE:38 7 02 Oct 1838 Hudson, NH
FARRAR,Susie AGE:77 9 7 18 Jul 1940 Hudson, NH Elizah G Tibbals
   & Rhoda A Holton
FARRELL,Michael AGE:82 01 Jun 1967 Hudson, NH
FARWELL,Hannah E J AGE:58 4 24 Nov 1906 Hudson, NH Benjamen Chesley
   & Mary E Burroughs
FARWELL,Mary AGE:96   18 18 Jun 1887 Hudson, NH Benjamin Parker
(Massachusetts) & Sarah Reed (Massachusetts)
FARWELL,Mary Parker AGE:96   18 18 Jun 1887 Hudson, NH
FASSETTE,Carrie AGE:25 4 31 Dec 1894 Hudson, NH
FAUCHER,Florida AGE:34 2 8 12 Feb 1933 Hudson, NH John Larrivierre
   & M Jane Daigneault
FAUCHER, Alice,Sr Marie Louis-Arthur AGE:51 05 Dec 1958 Hudson, NH
FAYNE,Catherine A AGE:89 14 Aug 1972 Nashua, NH
FELLOWS,Fanny B AGE:84 7 26 31 Oct 1913 Hudson, NH Washington Wheeler
   & Celiah Horton
FELTON,James E AGE:72 16 Apr 1950 Concord, NH William Felton
   & Elizabeth Karr
FERGUSON,Hilda A AGE:67 21 Apr 1965 Nashua, NH
FERGUSON,Winslow W AGE:64 20 May 1964 Nashua, NH
FERRYALL,Fred A AGE:62 7 16 10 Dec 1942 Hudson, NH Abram Ferryall

HUDSON,NH DEATHS

   & Marcelline Trombly
FERUS,John AGE:88 07 Feb 1983 Nashua, NH
FERYALL,Abram AGE:63 8 17 17 Aug 1915 Hudson, NH Alex Feryall (New York)
   & Marcellis Promboro (New York)
FERYALL,Angeline AGE:63 6 8 30 Jan 1943 Hudson, NH Nazaire Salvail
   & Angel Rivard
FERYALL,Marceline T AGE:90   18 05 Nov 1935 Hudson, NH John B Trombly
   & Zoia Trombly
FIELD,Ann AGE:32 15 Jun 1832 Hudson, NH
FIELD,Edward AGE:35 02 Sep 1834 Hudson, NH
FIELD,Elizabeth J AGE:77 10 Dec 1955 Nashua, NH
FIELD,Willabe C AGE:23 8 21 Sep 1852 Hudson, NH
FINLEY,Anna G AGE:76 21 Jan 1978 Hudson, NH
FINNIGAN,Alice K AGE:80 03 Aug 1984 Hudson, NH
FINNIGAN,John F AGE:70 15 Feb 1979 Nashua, NH
FINNING,Anna AGE:82 28 Feb 1957 Hudson, NH
FISH,Annie L AGE:44 6 23 09 Feb 1921 Hudson, NH Henry C Robinson
   & Addie Merrill
FISH,Kendrick R AGE:74 11 9 21 Mar 1916 Hudson, NH Lemuel Fish
   & Polly Rowell
FISHER,E Ethel AGE:41 2 7 05 Jul 1926 Hudson, NH Cyrus Greenwood
   & Amelia Yattaw
FISHER,Elizabeth J AGE:34 08 Jan 1980 Nashua, NH
FISHER,Katherine C AGE:70 28 Aug 1983 Nashua, NH
FISHER,Oliver A AGE:35 5 16 19 Mar 1911 Hudson, NH Fisher & Enna Keach
FISHER,Oliver A AGE:45 10 29 06 Apr 1945 Rut'nd, MA Oliver A Fisher
   & Luloha A Gee
FISHER,Rossiter A AGE:70 28 Feb 1974 Hudson, NH
FISK,Henrietta W AGE:3   05 May 1891 Hudson, NH Ranson Fisk (Nashua, NH)
   & Mary A French (Nashua, NH)
FISKE,Henrietta W AGE:57 05 May 1891 Hudson, NH
FISKE,Mary A AGE:85   12 26 Jul 1886 Hudson, NH
FISKE,Mary Ann AGE:85   12 26 Jul 1886 Hudson, NH
FISSETTE,Frank G AGE:24 26 Dec 1963 Nashua, NH
FITZ,Carl F AGE:67 21 Feb 1982 Nashua, NH
FLANAGAN,Clara E AGE:55 01 Dec 1955 Nashua, NH
FLANDERS,Ernest L AGE:30 6 14 25 Nov 1904 Hudson, NH Dana M Flanders
   & Josephine E Brown
FLEMMING,Alfred P AGE:73 16 Sep 1965 Nashua, NH
FLETCHER,Alice C AGE:79 28 Nov 1961 Hudson, NH
FLETCHER,Dorinda A AGE:70 04 Mar 1883 Hudson, NH
FLETCHER,Mary AGE:65 8 21 24 Jan 1871 Hudson, NH
FLETCHER,Richard D AGE:85 25 Jul 1966 Hudson, NH
FLETCHER,Rufus M AGE:30 10 2 15 Dec 1867 Hudson, NH
FLETCHER,Sarah AGE:18 1 20 20 Mar 1862 Hudson, NH George Fletcher & Mary
FLEURY,Arthur AGE:56 07 Apr 1952 Nashua, NH
FLEURY,Claudette S AGE:33 04 Feb 1977 Nashua, NH
FLEURY,Exilia AGE:82 14 Jun 1975 Nashua, NH
FLEWELLING,Eunice E AGE:61 31 Oct 1969 Hudson, NH
FLIESBACK,Clemmie AGE:3 3 18 Nov 1884 Hudson, NH Otto Fliesback & Nina
FLOYD,Ada B AGE:84 15 Dec 1956 Hudson, NH
FLOYD,Joseph A AGE: 09 Aug 1844 Hudson, NH
FLOYD,Joseph S AGE:46 06 May 1864 Hudson, NH
FLOYD,Lucina W AGE:61 6 4 04 Apr 1888 Hudson, NH Daniel Wyman (Hudson, NH)
   & Mary Farwell (Westford, MA)
FLOYD,Lucinda Wyman AGE:61 6 4 04 Apr 1888 Hudson, NH
FOLEY,Cecelia M AGE:88 13 Jun 1977 Hudson, NH
FOLEY,John F Sr AGE:52 05 May 1969 Nashua, NH
FOLLANSBEE,Ruth Morse AGE:84 5 2 07 Jul 1909 Hudson, NH Amos Morse
   & Sallie Sawyer

HUDSON,NH DEATHS

FONTAINE,Alphonse AGE:40 20 Nov 1933 Hudson, NH Elzear Fontaine
& Camile Gendrean
FONTAINE,Laura M F AGE:42 10 3 13 Jan 1941 Nashua, NH Alphonse Fontaine
FOOTE,Abby V AGE:18 30 Aug 1864 Hudson, NH
FOOTE,Caroline AGE:40 24 Sep 1856 Hudson, NH
FOOTE,Elias C AGE:19 01 Oct 1863 Hudson, NH
FOOTE,Elias L AGE:19 01 Oct 1863 Hudson, NH
FOOTE,George H AGE: 21 Nov 1842 Hudson, NH Thomas Foote
FOOTE,Leander Scott AGE: Hudson, NH
FOOTE,Thomas AGE:77 6 11 Apr 1893 Hudson, NH
FORANCE,John AGE:82 4 14 29 Jan 1938 Hudson, NH John Forance
& Mary Ann Gagnon
FORBUSH,Frances AGE:85   3 03 Apr 1910 Hudson, NH John Starrett & Ann Love
FORD,Abbey J AGE:78   5 14 Aug 1908 Hudson, NH Putnam & Achsah
FORD,David C AGE:59 11 30 03 Jun 1898 Hudson, NH Timothy S Ford
& Sarah G Fuller
FORD,Evelyn E AGE:58 24 Jan 1968 Concord, NH
FORD,Frank W AGE:78 10 May 1963 Nashua, NH
FORD,Fred H Sr AGE:74 13 Oct 1976 Nashua, NH
FORD,George W AGE:4 10 15 05 Dec 1887 Hudson, NH Moses B Ford (Hudson, NH)
& Ella L Demming (E Washington)
FORD,Harriet B AGE:1 15 Mar 1867 Hudson, NH
FORD,Harriet P AGE: 15 Nov 1867 Hudson, NH James C Ford
FORD,James AGE:78 9   Hudson, NH Timothy Ford & Mehitable Rowell
FORD,John E Sr AGE:79 06 Feb 1978 Nashua, NH
FORD,Mary AGE: 11 Aug 1821 Hudson, NH
FORD,Rosabel AGE:79 5 8 13 Aug 1944 Hudson, NH Was'ton Follansbee
& Jane Hardy
FORD,Sarah G AGE:67 3 27 31 May 1882 Hudson, NH Daniel Fuller & Ruth Goodell
FORD,Timothy E AGE:34 06 Dec 1869 Hudson, NH
FORD,Timothy S AGE:75 03 Nov 1885 Hudson, NH Timothy Ford (Hudson, NH)
& Mehitable Rowell (Hudson, NH)
FORD,William R AGE:58 24 Apr 1882 Hudson, NH James Ford & Sally Cutter
FOREST,Marguerite AGE:71 29 Mar 1982 Nashua, NH
FORRENCE,Anna AGE:83 16 Oct 1971 Nashua, NH
FORRENCE,George A AGE:80 18 Sep 1968 Nashua, NH
FORRENCE,Lillian V AGE:66 21 May 1980 Nashua, NH
FORREST,Carrie M AGE:70 26 Feb 1959 Hudson, NH
FORTIN,Jocelyne AGE:30 15 Jul 1964 Nashua, NH
FOSDICK,Capt Alvin AGE:81 07 Jul 1831 Hudson, NH
FOSTER,David AGE:56 13 Dec 1855 Hudson, NH
FOSTER,George A AGE:33 10 15 11 Apr 1914 Hudson, NH C C Foster
& Marinda Flanders
FOSTER,George L AGE:70 20 Jul 1964 Hudson, NH
FOSTER,Horatio L AGE:74 27 Feb 1926 Hudson, NH Leonard Foster
& Sarah Williams
FOSTER,John AGE:6 26 Apr 1818 Hudson, NH John Foster & Lucy
FOSTER,Lelie D AGE:71 17 Mar 1977 Peterborough,NH
FOSTER,Melville G AGE:93 10 Apr 1982 Derry, NH
FOSTER,Sophia AGE:83 4 8 08 Aug 1888 Hudson, NH Joseph Colburn
& Mary Emerson (Haverhill, MA)
FOSTER,Sophia Cochran AGE:83 4 8 08 Aug 1888 Hudson, NH
FOWLER,John AGE: 02 Nov 1850 Hudson, NH
FOX,George W AGE:69 1 7 03 Apr 1900 Hudson, NH Isaac J Fox & Sophia H Wilder
FOX,Gladys J AGE:72 22 Dec 1966 Nashua, NH
FOX,Leighton D AGE:62 28 Mar 1984 Nashua, NH
FOX,Permelia W AGE:79 3 14 18 Jan 1892 Hudson, NH Peter Wilder (New York)
& Sally Joslin
FOX,Permelia Wilder AGE:79 3 14 18 Jan 1892 Hudson, NH
FOX,Phebe AGE: 02 Jul 1838 Hudson, NH

HUDSON, NH DEATHS

FOX,Sophia AGE:74 2 20 17 Mar 1919 Hudson, NH Isaac Fox & Pamelia Wilder
FRASER,Fred M AGE:49 03 Oct 1973 Manchester, NH
FRASER,Raymond J AGE:82 29 Oct 1984 Nashua, NH
FRAZIER,Katherine AGE:80 15 Sep 1972 Nashua, NH
FRAZIER,Maynard O Jr AGE:40 18 Feb 1984 Pittsburg, NH
FREDERICK,Margaret AGE:73 01 Jun 1982 Nashua, NH
FREEMAN,Andrew N AGE:54 1 17 25 Oct 1915 Hudson, NH Patrick Freeman
   (Ireland) & Annie M Nichols (Ireland)
FREEMAN,Annie M AGE:68 21 Apr 1904 Hudson, NH Andrew Nichols & Mary Freeman
FREEMAN,Barbara AGE:47 28 Apr 1977 Goffstown, NH
FREEMAN,Elizabeth AGE:79 10 4 05 Mar 1893 Hudson, NH
FREEMAN,Elmer I AGE:58 5 13 24 Feb 1947 Hudson, NH Elmer D Freeman
   & Bertha Holcomb
FREEMAN,Florence H AGE:70 10 Jun 1978 Nashua, NH
FREEMAN,Lloyd A AGE:43 30 Jan 1972 Lawrence, MA
FREEMAN,William F AGE:76 18 Feb 1983 Nashua, NH
FRENCH,Daniel L AGE:63 20 Jul 1860 Hudson, NH
FRENCH,David S AGE:53 8 19 03 Apr 1941 Hudson, NH William French
   & Celestina George
FRENCH,Esther E AGE:77 11 Oct 1966 Nashua, NH
FRENCH,Ethel A AGE:62 10 19 May 13 1948 Nashua, NH Henry Robinson
FRENCH,George A AGE:77 8 11 06 Jul 1944 Nashua, NH John A French
   & Charlotte L Pierce
FRENCH,Harold Gordon AGE:83 22 Jan 1983 Hudson, NH
FRENCH,Henry AGE:4 1 18 25 May 1875 Hudson, NH Simon French, Jr
FRENCH,John M AGE:72 02 Feb 1953 Nashua, NH
FRENCH,Joseph AGE:75 08 Nov 1969 Hudson, NH
FRENCH,Laura J AGE:90 27 Feb 1983 Hudson, NH
FRENCH,Leonard S AGE:3 9 11 25 Jan 1901 Hudson, NH Menzel S French
   (Templeton, MA) & Jennie P Steavens (Nashua, NH)
FRENCH,Mary AGE:79 21 May 1946 Hudson, NH
FRENCH,Maurice R AGE:63 07 Jun 1984 Nashua, NH
FRENCH,Menzel S AGE:84 4 23 04 Dec 1940 Hudson, NH Abel H French
   & Elizabeth Davis
FRENCH,Rev David L AGE:63 20 Jul 1860 Hudson, NH
FRENETTE,George J AGE:83 04 Mar 1962 Hudson, NH
FRENETTE,Irene M AGE:72 14 Sep 1984 Nashua, NH
FRENETTE,Laura M AGE:71 17 Oct 1957 Nashua, NH
FROST,Ila Leona AGE:80 06 Oct 1981 Hudson, NH
FULLER,Albert Alonzo AGE:74 11 2 13 Apr 1934 Hudson, NH Joseph Fuller
   & Belinda Steele
FULLER,Annette C AGE:62 20 Apr 1975 Nashua, NH
FULLER,Arthur E AGE:66 28 Oct 1961 Manchester, NH
FULLER,Belinda AGE:68 4 3 01 Apr 1891 Hudson, NH Samuel Steele & Blodgett
FULLER,Belinda Steele AGE:68 4 3 01 Apr 1891 Hudson, NH
FULLER,Benjamin AGE:68 7 6 12 Dec 1885 Hudson, NH Daniel Fuller
   & Ruth Goodell
FULLER,Cyrus AGE:60 19 Mar 1890 Hudson, NH Daniel Fuller (Danvers, MA)
   & Ruth Goodell (Middleton, MA)
FULLER,Elizabeth M AGE:85 14 May 1960 Hudson, NH
FULLER,Hazel D AGE:83 08 Feb 1985 Hudson, NH
FULLER,Joseph AGE:77 5 14 Jul 1896 Hudson, NH Daniel Fuller (Danvers, MA)
   & Ruth Goodell (Danvers, MA)
FULLER,Joseph A AGE:58 3 21 13 Feb 1946 Hudson, NH Albert A Fuller
   & Mary C Fuller
FULLER,Joseph W AGE:8 23 21 Feb 1912 Hudson, NH Joseph Fuller
   & Nettie Mortlock
FULLER,Lucy P AGE:2 3 16 Jan 1892 Hudson, NH Albert A Fuller (Hudson, NH)
   & Mary C Fuller (Danvers, MA)
FULLER,Mary A AGE: 29 Jul 1863 Hudson, NH

HUDSON,NH DEATHS

FULLER,Mary A AGE:44 21 Jul 1865 Hudson, NH
FULLER,Mary Caroline AGE:77 4 25 17 Oct 1932 Hudson, NH Joseph J Fuller
  & Mary Ann Glass
FULLER,Melissa J AGE:9 10 30 Mar 1879 Hudson, NH Charles H Fuller & Mary M
FULLER,Mildred M AGE:73 01 Jan 1964 Nashua, NH
FULLER,Myron E AGE:73 12 Jun 1974 Manchester, NH
FULLER,Nettie A AGE:81 11 Aug 1971 Nashua, NH
FULLER,Philip R AGE:79 13 Jun 1961 Nashua, NH
FULLER,Rodney AGE:76 12 9 06 Dec 1900 Hudson, NH Daniel Fuller
  & Ruth Goodell
FULLER,Walter W AGE:65 13 Oct 1974 Nashua, NH
FULLER,William E AGE:47 08 Nov 1964 Nashua, NH
GAFFNEY,Ann I AGE:89 06 Sep 1969 Hudson, NH
GAGE,Daniel T AGE:76 1 5 26 Nov 1890 Hudson, NH Daniel Gage (Pelham)
  & Betsy Tenney (Pelham)
GAGE,Mary Ella AGE:11 11 20 20 Jun 1890 Hudson, NH Daniel Gage
GAGE,Mary Ellen AGE:11 11 20 20 Jun 1890 Hudson, NH Daniel Gage (Hudson, NH)
  & Margetta Marsh (Hudson, NH)
GAGE,Nehemiah H AGE:24 11 Jul 1866 Hudson, NH Daniel T Gage
GAGE,Widow Daniel AGE: 15 Dec 1865 Hudson, NH
GAGE,[Unknown] AGE: 15 Dec 1865 Hudson, NH
GAGEL,Robert A AGE:57 06 Nov 1973 Manchester, NH
GAGNE,Ella C AGE:89 28 Jan 1983 Derry, NH
GAGNE,Eva B AGE:82 29 May 1982 Nashua, NH
GAGNE,Jule AGE:73 24 Dec 1923 Hudson, NH Jule Gagne & Angela Berube
GAGNE,Leda M AGE:80 31 Dec 1979 Nashua, NH
GAGNE,Ovide AGE:76 20 Jun 1969 Nashua, NH
GAGNE,William AGE:89 03 Dec 1959 Nashua, NH
GAGNON,Annette AGE:72 12 May 1982 Nashua, NH
GAGNON,Arthur AGE:8 07 Oct 1900 Hudson, NH Louis Gagnon & Cesain Fournier
GAGNON,Arthur L AGE:62 26 May 1966 Nashua, NH
GAGNON,Brian Ray AGE:10 hrs 07 Jan 1973 Nashua, NH
GAGNON,Catherine G AGE:84 22 Dec 1977 Nashua, NH
GAGNON,Daniel G AGE:4 30 Dec 1962 Nashua, NH
GAGNON,Esther L AGE:38 25 Jan 1956 Nashua, NH
GAGNON,Exillia LaChance AGE:80 07 May 1975 Bedford, NH
GAGNON,Florena S AGE:64 28 Feb 1967 Hudson, NH
GAGNON,Florent A AGE:52 10 Jun 1969 Manchester, NH
GAGNON,Ida M AGE:54 6 18 31 Dec 1938 Hudson, NH James R Poole
  & Orelia Sullivan
GAGNON,Irene AGE:1 1 6 18 Jun 1918 Hudson, NH Eugene Gagnon & Clara Sirois
GAGNON,Isabelle M AGE:68 07 Mar 1975 Nashua, NH
GAGNON,Joseph AGE:9 24 01 Aug 1904 Hudson, NH Eugene Gagnon & Clara Sirois
GAGNON,Joseph C AGE:69 24 Sep 1951 Nashua, NH
GAGNON,Joseph Henri AGE:4 30 Oct 1914 Hudson, NH Joseph Gagnon & Maria Ross
GAGNON,Juliette A AGE:47 16 Mar 1950 Nashua, NH Louis Noel & Melina Rousseau
GAGNON,Leo J Sr AGE:79 27 Jul 1984 Hudson, NH
GAGNON,Lydia AGE:80 12 Mar 1963 Nashua, NH
GAGNON,Marie Alice AGE:2 26 28 Feb 1910 Hudson, NH Eugene Gagnon
  & Clara Sirois
GAGNON,Marie E AGE:1 17 23 Nov 1945 Hudson, NH Andrew Gagnon & Esther Haslam
GAGNON,Marjorie A AGE:72 20 May 1982 Nashua, NH
GAGNON,Ronald Jr AGE:12 29 May 1974 Nashua, NH
GAGNON,Stephen E L AGE:73 06 Jan 1973 Nashua, NH
GAGNON,Xavier AGE:79 29 Jul 1969 Hudson, NH
GALECKI,Amelia AGE:89 05 Nov 1978 Nashua, NH
GALECKI,Anna AGE:73 22 Oct 1957 Hudson, NH
GALECKI,Joseph P AGE:60 21 Apr 1949 Nashua, NH Alexander Galecki
  & Agnes Galecki
GALECKI,William J AGE:75 22 Sep 1962 Nashua, NH

HUDSON,NH DEATHS

GALIPEAU,George J AGE:80 27 Jun 1977 Hudson, NH
GALIPEAU,Paul R AGE:50 03 Apr 1959 Hudson, NH
GALIPEAU,Phelomene AGE:85 11 01 Nov 1923 Hudson, NH Golviel Caregnan
  & Amelie Dehide
GALIPEAULT,Shellie A AGE:6 20 Jun 1975 Pittsfield, NH
GALLISON,Belinda A Pierce AGE:27 14 Jan 1850 Hudson, NH
GALLISON,Edward A AGE:30 20 Oct 1851 Hudson, NH
GALLISON,J Edward AGE:14 17 11 Nov 1847 Hudson, NH
GALLUP,Harry O AGE:73 4 1 23 Sep 1948 Hudson, NH Samuel Gallup
  & Eleanor J Burke
GAMACHE,Doris AGE:3 10 28 Oct 1924 Hudson, NH Joseph Gamache & Mauda Marotte
GAMACHE,Leo A Sr AGE:72 04 Jun 1968 Nashua, NH
GARANT,Joseph P Jr AGE:55 26 Apr 1959 Nashua, NH
GARANT,Victoria B AGE:56 03 Apr 1960 Nashua, NH
GARDNER,Deborah L AGE:4 19 Aug 1957 Nashua, NH
GARDNER,Owen AGE:75 14 Jan 1929 Hudson, NH
GARLAND,Benjamin AGE:62 8 25 07 Mar 1945 Nashua, NH Warren Garland
  & Abbie Nutting
GARRELL,Cora B AGE:49 01 Sep 1908 Hudson, NH John B Bunlett
  & Mary Jane Walker
GARRITY,Michael A AGE:14 03 May 1963 Nashua, NH
GATES,Charles E AGE:81 8 5 25 Sep 1934 Hudson, NH Joseph Gates
  & Susan Lovejoy
GATES,Donald B AGE:4 5 19 26 May 1946 Nashua, NH Joseph E Gates
  & Lillian Haselton
GATES,Martena I AGE:81 06 Jul 1959 Nashua, NH
GATES,Wallace E Jr AGE:54 24 Oct 1982 Hudson, NH
GATINEAU,Marie Anne AGE:79 01 May 1974 Hudson, NH
GATZ,Ernest Arno AGE:62 1 10 25 Sep 1942 Nashua, NH Ernest Gatz
  & Frieda Hempel
GAUDETTE,Elizabeth M AGE:83 05 Sep 1982 Nashua, NH
GAUDETTE,Emma C AGE:72 10 18 Oct 1939 Hudson, NH Victor Corsnier
  & Tharsil Poulier
GAUDETTE,Grace A AGE:58 3 22 22 Jan 1945 Hudson, NH Frank Harris
  & Rosella Boury
GAUDETTE,Joseph AGE:69 11 14 19 Sep 1937 Hudson, NH Eusebe Gaudette
  & Marie Daudelin
GAUDETTE,Lea AGE:29 4 2 28 Mar 1930 Hudson, NH Prudent Gendron
  & Malvina Duchesne
GAULIN,Ludger H AGE:66 15 May 1977 Nashua, NH
GAUTHIER,Emelia M AGE:82 30 Dec 1982 Nashua, NH
GAUTHIER,Gloria AGE:17 31 May 1972 Lowell, MA
GAUTHIER,Joseph AGE:72 1 11 09 Oct 1922 Hudson, NH Gauthier
GAUTHIER,Joseph I AGE:81 14 Oct 1980 Manchester, NH
GAUTHIER,Malvina AGE:67 10 1 27 Sep 1921 Hudson, NH Arnable Chabot
  & Phebe Etier
GAUTHIER,Mary AGE:86 11 Nov 1976 Nashua, NH
GAUTHIER,Raymond C AGE:85 29 Jan 1976 Hudson, NH
GAUTIER,Joseph AGE:77 9 6 22 Apr 1947 Goffstown, NH
GAY,Elbridge L AGE:75 2 6 27 Mar 1910 Hudson, NH Seth Gay & Leafy Barton
GAY,Leonard Allen AGE:77 11 15 14 May 1914 Hudson, NH Timothy Gay
  & Julia Gilson
GAY,Lydia M AGE:70 18 Jul 1914 Hudson, NH Jacob Abbott & Harriet Garnie
GAY,Warren Oliver AGE:47 7 26 27 May 1925 Hudson, NH Elbridge Gay
  & Lydia Abbott
GEAUBARD,Marie R AGE:76 07 Aug 1902 Hudson, NH
GEDDES,Effie A AGE:87 05 Sep 1953 Hudson, NH
GEDDES,Jennie AGE:92 28 Oct 1983 Hudson, NH
GEDDES,Leonard M AGE:94 16 Aug 1956 Hudson, NH
GEHL,Frances E AGE:69 11 Mar 1984 Nashua, NH

HUDSON,NH DEATHS

GELINAS,Maurice R AGE:50   31 Oct 1983 Hudson, NH
GENDRON,Alpheda AGE:88   31 Jan 1985 Nashua, NH
GENDRON,Delia E AGE:65   18 Jun 1960 Nashua, NH
GENDRON,Eugene J AGE:51   21 Dec 1956 Hudson, NH
GENDRON,Joan Houle AGE:11 11   15 Sep 1935 Hudson, NH Joseph Gendron
   & Laura Houle
GENDRON,Leo J AGE:42   22 Jun 1954 Nashua, NH
GENDRON,Malvina D AGE:71 3 16   18 Oct 1944 Hudson, NH Pierre Duchesneau
   & M Duchesneau
GENDRON,Margaret AGE:57   09 Jan 1964 Nashua, NH
GENDRON,Moses J AGE:41   14   11 Oct 1944 Hudson, NH Prudent E Gendron
   & Malvina Gendron
GENDRON,Prudent J AGE:72 1 20   10 Jan 1942 Hudson, NH Prudent J Gendron
   & Hazel Dumont
GENDRON,Rose A AGE:78   29 Jan 1965 Nashua, NH
GENDRON,Rose V AGE:78   11 Sep 1973 Nashua, NH
GENS,Angela C AGE:73   18 May 1976 Nashua, NH
GEROW,Bernice AGE:42 3 7   28 May 1946 Goffstown, NH Charles Gerow
   & Mary Rhodes
GEROW,Charles J AGE:73 3 16   29 Nov 1943 Nashua, NH Michael Gerow & Mary
GEROW,Mary M AGE:73   15 Jan 1952 Hudson, NH
GERVAIS,George F AGE:80   08 Jan 1976 Hudson, NH
GESIN (Gerstein),Anna AGE:81   30 Jan 1984 Hudson, NH
GESTER,Walter T AGE:12 1   03 Mar 1907 Hudson, NH Albert Gester & Rika Napp
GIBSON,James Esq AGE:46   24 Feb 1820 Hudson, NH
GIBSON,Samuel AGE:10   30 Oct 1819 Hudson, NH James Gibson & Dorcas
GIBSON,William S AGE:1   12 Nov 1819 Hudson, NH James Gibson & Dorcas
GIDDINGS,Fred O AGE:59 1 7   18 Mar 1923 Hudson, NH Lorrain Giddings
   & Mary Tiffany
GIDDINGS,Lorrain AGE:77 8 7   21 Dec 1912 Hudson, NH Lorain Giddings
   & Des'mons Cowdry
GIGUERE,Homer AGE:61 2 5   16 Sep 1941 Goffstown, NH Philip Giguere
   & Marion Derochiers
GILBERT,Charles AGE:78   01 Feb 1954 Concord, NH
GILBERT,Florida AGE:81   01 Jan 1985 Hudson, NH
GILBERT,George P AGE:52 3 19   21 Mar 1896 Hudson, NH
GILBERT,James H AGE:61   07 Dec 1979 Nashua, NH
GILBERT,Jessie S AGE:80   04 Dec 1962 Nashua, NH
GILBERT,Mary AGE:84   10 Jun 1985 Hudson, NH
GILBERT,Ralph Wayne AGE:61   12 Apr 1983 Nashua, NH
GILBERT,Sarah G AGE:62   03 Oct 1911 Hudson, NH Hiram Rowell & Ellen Lyman
GILCREAST,Edith L AGE:89   25 Jun 1973 Hudson, NH
GILCREAST,Judith E AGE:2 27   13 Apr 1943 Nashua, NH Francis Gilcreast
   & Bertha Newman
GILCREAST,Keith A AGE:2   28 Sep 1954 Nashua, NH
GILCREAST,Mervyn R AGE:66   19 Oct 1984 Nashua, NH
GILE,Elizabeth M AGE:73   08 Jun 1952 Hudson, NH
GILES,Nettie A AGE:88   06 Mar 1951 Concord, NH
GILLIS,Hannah Georg AGE:77 5 1   22 Jul 1925 Hudson, NH John Gillis
   & Jennie Fulton
GILLIS,Helen Ermina AGE:78 11 1   22 Jul 1925 Hudson, NH John Gillis
   & Jennie Fulton
GILLIS,Jenny F AGE:70   28 Mar 1880 Hudson, NH Fulton
GILLIS,John AGE:83 3   14 May 1891 Hudson, NH John Gillis & Hannah Aikin
GILMAN,John C AGE:43   06 Feb 1974 Nashua, NH
GILSON,Henry E AGE:86   13 Jun 1985 Manchester, NH
GILSON,Mary E AGE:91   20   17 Nov 1920 Hudson, NH John Gilson, Jr
   & Sally Wood
GIRARD,Regina AGE:78   27 Jul 1958 Hudson, NH
GIROUARD,Georgianna AGE:36 1 23   22 Jun 1915 Hudson, NH Napoleon Lamontague

HUDSON,NH DEATHS

(Canada) & Rosalie Gagnon (Canada)
GIROUARD,Joseph A AGE:80 23 Aug 1957 Hudson, NH
GIROUARD,Marie E C AGE:16 29 May 1902 Hudson, NH Joseph Girouard
  & Marie Coutourier
GIROUARD,Marie R A AGE:16 29 May 1902 Hudson, NH Joseph Girouard
  & Marie Coutourier
GIROUARD,Mario AGE:65 3 10 16 Aug 1932 Hudson, NH Louis Couturier
  & Elionard Lehland
GIROUARD, Fabiola,Sr Marie St Louis Ge AGE:59 07 Jan 1954 Hudson, NH
GIROUX,Albert J AGE:72 26 Apr 1979 Nashua, NH
GIROUX,Maude AGE:74 04 Apr 1981 Goffstown, NH
GLAVICKI,John R AGE:85 30 Jul 1977 Nashua, NH
GLOVER,Austin A AGE:28 20 May 1862 Hudson, NH David Glover & Rebecca
GLOVER,Austin A AGE:29 21 Jul 1862 Hudson, NH
GLOVER,David AGE:77 20 Dec 1858 Hudson, NH
GLOVER,David AGE:59 15 Dec 1815 Hudson, NH
GLOVER,George W AGE:72 Apr 1871 Hudson, NH
GLOVER,Hannah AGE:33 22 Feb 1822 Hudson, NH
GLOVER,Rebecah AGE:86 11 14 24 May 1881 Hudson, NH Peter Kelly
  & Sarah Goodwin
GLOVER,Rebecca AGE:86 11 24 May 1881 Hudson, NH
GLOVER,Rebecca A AGE:41 11 05 Jul 1878 Hudson, NH David Glover & Rebecca
GLOVER,Warren AGE:75 17 Apr 1874 Hudson, NH
GODDARD,Charles H AGE:68 7 5 05 Jan 1917 Hudson, NH Chas H Goddard
  & Elizabeth Shepard
GODDU, Irene,S M St J L'Evangelis AGE:62 30 Dec 1951 Hudson, NH
GODIN,Romeo S AGE:71 21 Mar 1963 Nashua, NH
GODING,Albert W AGE:83 09 Jan 1981 Hudson, NH
GODING,Lilla F AGE:84 04 Dec 1962 Nashua, NH
GODING,Theodore H AGE:51 11 19 11 Jun 1929 Hudson, NH William H Goding
  & Emma Hawkins
GOKEY,Henry H AGE:80 11 14 21 Dec 1945 Hudson, NH Frank Gokey
  & Armanda Gokey
GOLDER,Julia A AGE:50 25 Apr 1942 Hudson, NH
GOLDSMITH,Oliver J AGE:76 6 10 02 Sep 1931 Hudson, NH Henry Goldsmith
  & Isabella Hanna
GOODALE,Bertha A AGE:71 15 Sep 1950 Hudson, NH Lucius F Bills & Jane Farley
GOODALE,Ray F AGE:68 15 Jun 1983 Nashua, NH
GOODHUE,Alice G AGE:54 25 Dec 1954 Hudson, NH
GOODSPEED,Donald H AGE:58 14 Dec 1983 Nashua, NH
GOODWIN,Anniemae N AGE:65 29 Nov 1961 Nashua, NH
GOODWIN,Francis N AGE:53 02 Sep 1977 Nashua, NH
GOODWIN,Francis W AGE:82 5 30 15 Nov 1935 Hudson, NH Cyrus T Goodwin
  & Hannah D Colby
GOODWIN,Frederick T AGE:58 24 Dec 1952 Hudson, NH
GOODWIN,Georgianna W AGE:81 8 23 16 Jan 1932 Hudson, NH Daniel Webster
  & Clarice Allen
GOODWIN,Mary E AGE:96 4 14 21 Sep 1946 Hudson, NH Charles Gibson
  & Emma Bateman
GORDON,Celia E AGE:18 10 10 Aug 1897 Hudson, NH
GORDON,Evelyn AGE:86 09 Feb 1985 Hudson, NH
GORDON,Lucy P AGE:75 1 6 05 Jan 1944 Hudson, NH Samuel Faulkner
  & Lydia Woodbury
GORDON,Ralph AGE:40 09 Jan 1976 Nashua, NH
GORMAN,Pamela J AGE:4 19 Jun 1976 Nashua, NH
GOSSELIN,Alfred R AGE:59 21 Dec 1969 Nashua, NH
GOSSELIN,Helen AGE:60 18 May 1970 Nashua, NH
GOUDREAU,Joseph AGE:72 18 Aug 1948 Hudson, NH
GOULD,Angeline AGE:79 10 Jul 1901 Hudson, NH
GOULD,Asa AGE:84 31 Dec 1858 Hudson, NH

HUDSON,NH DEATHS

GOULD,Charles S AGE:72 20 Jul 1961 Nashua, NH
GOULD,Clara E AGE: 17 May 1856 Hudson, NH David C Gould & Mary Cummings
GOULD,Cummings AGE:79 6 29 Mar 1885 Tyngsborough,MA Asa Gould (Hudson, NH)
 & Polly Cummings (Hudson, NH)
GOULD,David Cummings AGE: 29 Mar 1885 Hudson, NH
GOULD,Emma C AGE: 02 Dec 1876 Hudson, NH David C Gould & Mary Cummings
GOULD,Ernest L AGE:92 23 Mar 1951 Hudson, NH
GOULD,Hattie E AGE:70 09 Feb 1954 Nashua, NH
GOULD,John AGE:9 18 May 1766 Hudson, NH Joseph Gould & Mary
GOULD,John AGE: 24 Feb 1757 Hudson, NH Joseph Gould & Mary
GOULD,Joseph Jr AGE: 13 Jan 1776 Hudson, NH
GOULD,Mary Cummings AGE:86 09 Sep 1858 Hudson, NH
GOULD,May J AGE:77 10 11 25 Nov 1893 Hudson, NH Jacob Chase (Hudson, NH)
 & Rebecca Barrett (Windham)
GOULD,Polly AGE: 1795 Hudson, NH Jona Chase & Anna
GOULD,William J AGE:67 28 Nov 1974 Hudson, NH
GOULET,Alice AGE:39 8 19 23 Jan 1945 Hudson, NH Richard Cyr & Flavie Cyr
GOUR,Kelley D AGE:3 26 Sep 1959 Nashua, NH
GOVE,Ethel F AGE:62 08 May 1964 Hudson, NH
GOVE,Louis E AGE:76 20 Apr 1955 Hudson, NH
GOVE,Margaret B AGE:82 21 Nov 1983 Nashua, NH
GOWING,Carrie AGE:21 04 Jun 1860 Hudson, NH
GOWING,Carrie AGE:21 04 Jun 1865 Hudson, NH
GOWING,Carrie Ellen AGE:21 9 10 23 Dec 1907 Hudson, NH George T Gowing
 & Ida Seary
GOWING,Clementine F AGE:81   22 29 Nov 1939 Hudson, NH Rodney Fuller
 & Martha F
GOWING,Edwin E AGE:58 6 5 30 Oct 1940 Hudson, NH Sidney P Gowing
 & Clementine Fuller
GOWING,Frederick L AGE:44 20 Jan 1966 Hudson, NH
GOWING,George Thomas AGE:76 6 3 27 Sep 1922 Hudson, NH Thomas Gowing
 & Harriet Greeley
GOWING,Harriet G AGE:88 29 Mar 1894 Hudson, NH (New Hampshire)
 (Massachusetts)
GOWING,Ida E AGE:93 4 14 23 Apr 1940 Hudson, NH
GOWING,Mabel F AGE:85 19 Jan 1969 Nashua, NH
GOWING,Perley Fuller AGE:1 21 02 Oct 1894 Hudson, NH
GOWING,S Edwin AGE:91 6 6 13 Aug 1933 Hudson, NH Samuel Gowing
 & Sarah Perham
GOWING,Samuel AGE:66 02 Mar 1881 Hudson, NH Thomas Gowing & Rachel
GOWING,Sarah AGE:75 4 25 22 Feb 1888 Hudson, NH Thomas Gowing
 (Wilmington, MA) & Rachel Heaton (Wilmington, MA)
GOWING,Sarah H AGE:58 5 15 30 Jan 1904 Hudson, NH Samuel Gowing
 & Sarah Perham
GOWING,Sarah P AGE:68 6 12 01 Mar 1887 Hudson, NH William Parham
 (Tyngsboro, MA) & Sarah Parham (Tyngsboro, MA)
GOWING,Sarah Perham AGE:68 6 12 01 Mar 1887 Hudson, NH
GOWING,Thomas AGE:69 22 Jan 1874 Hudson, NH
GOWING,Willie J AGE:7 2 2 13 Jun 1893 Hudson, NH Sidney P Gowing
 (Hudson, NH) & Clementine Fuller (Dracut, MA)
GRABOWSKI,John AGE:50 23 Aug 1973 Hanover, NH
GRAFFAM,Effie F AGE:92 08 Aug 1979 Hudson, NH
GRAHAM,Bertha I AGE:82 11 Feb 1954 Nashua, NH
GRAICHEN,[Unknown] AGE:6 hrs 10 Jan 1971 Nashua, NH
GRANDMAISON,Olive May AGE:70 11 Oct 1979 Hudson, NH
GRANT,Averline S AGE:81 31 May 1961 Hudson, NH
GRANT,Bernard M AGE:71 13 May 1958 Mendon, VT
GRANT,David J AGE:17 30 Jun 1980 Derry, NH
GRANT,Gary S AGE:16 09 Nov 1973 Hudson, NH
GRANT,William J AGE:57 01 Feb 1952 Nashua, NH

HUDSON,NH DEATHS

GRANT,William R AGE:37 13 Jul 1973 Nashua, NH
GRASKY,Stanley AGE:50 17 Jan 1928 Hudson, NH
GRAUSLYS,Charles P AGE:60 08 Mar 1979 Nashua, NH
GRAVELLE,Sylvio T AGE:67 24 Mar 1982 Nashua, NH
GRAVELLE,[Unknown] AGE:2 hrs 20 Sep 1971 Nashua, NH
GRAVES,Arthur M AGE:9 13 04 Aug 1890 Hudson, NH Newell Graves (New York)
 & Alma Laforce (Plattsburg, NY)
GRAVES,Beryl V AGE:1 2 9 17 Mar 1918 Hudson, NH Fred H Graves & Cora Newhall
GRAVES,Beverly W AGE:1 2 7 15 Mar 1918 Hudson,NH Fred H Graves & Cora Newhall
GRAY,Elizabeth M AGE:83 28 Apr 1964 Concord, NH
GRAY,James D AGE:72 14 Mar 1949 Hudson, NH Charles Gray & Ann Cruickshank
GRAY,Minnie W AGE:82 29 Oct 1960 Hudson, NH
GRAYENAS,Andrew AGE:28 Apr 1917 Hudson, NH Stohonis Grayenas
 & Anie Pelquirnk
GREELEY,Abigail AGE:14 13 Jun 1763 Hudson, NH Samuel Greeley & Abigail
GREELEY,Abigail AGE:95 29 Mar 1818 Hudson, NH
GREELEY,Anna E AGE:21 18 Jul 1857 Hudson, NH Reuben Greeley
GREELEY,Bridget AGE:25 22 Feb 1789 Hudson, NH Ezekiel Greeley & Esther
GREELEY,Daniel M AGE:94 6 19 01 May 1916 Hudson, NH Reuben Greeley
 & Johanna Merrill
GREELEY,Dastymony AGE:35 6 22 Oct 1825 Hudson, NH
GREELEY,Ezekiel AGE: 21 Jan 1793 Hudson, NH
GREELEY,Frank AGE:82 21 Oct 1949 Concord, NH
GREELEY,Gilbert AGE:7 25 Aug 1752 Hudson, NH Ezekiel Greeley & Esther
GREELEY,Hannah AGE:27 17 Feb 1793 Hudson, NH
GREELEY,Hannah AGE:2 8 07 Jun 1804 Hudson, NH Moses Greeley & Mary
GREELEY,Ida B AGE:38 21 Nov 1897 Hudson, NH Frank Twiss & Lucy Whittier
GREELEY,J Thomas AGE:11 14 Apr 1825 Hudson, NH Reuben Greeley
GREELEY,Jackson E AGE:78 17 Aug 1894 Hudson, NH Moses Greeley
 (Haverhill, MA) & Mary Darby
GREELEY,James C AGE:49 07 Mar 1892 Hudson, NH
GREELEY,James M AGE: 09 Jun 1900 Derry, NH
GREELEY,Jane AGE: 15 Jun 1762 Hudson, NH
GREELEY,Joanna C M AGE:94 4 20 Jan 1890 Hudson, NH Daniel Merrill
 (Georgetown, MA) & Susanna Gale (Salisbury, NH)
GREELEY,Joanne C AGE:94 4 20 Jan 1890 Hudson, NH
GREELEY,John AGE:88 5 16 May 1872 Hudson, NH
GREELEY,John AGE:58 6 13 Aug 1877 Hudson, NH John Greeley
 & Dustimony Eastman
GREELEY,John T AGE:1 4 07 Jun 1830 Hudson, NH Reuben Greeley
GREELEY,Joseph AGE:85 4 10 17 Nov 1882 Hudson, NH
GREELEY,Joseph AGE:95 07 Mar 1845 Hudson, NH
GREELEY,Joseph AGE:2 18 Sep 1749 Hudson, NH Ezekiel Greeley & Esther
GREELEY,Joseph AGE:84 13 May 1840 Hudson, NH
GREELEY,Joseph S AGE:4 02 May 1883 Hudson, NH Samuel A Greeley
 & Susanna C Richardson
GREELEY,Lucy AGE: 13 Feb 1781 Hudson, NH Jos Greeley & Sarah
GREELEY,Lucy A AGE:82 17 Jan 1896 Hudson, NH Ashley Morgan (Wilton)
 & Lucy Barton (Wilton)
GREELEY,Lucy M AGE:29 18 Jul 1849 Hudson, NH
GREELEY,Martha AGE:87 21 Feb 1757 Hudson, NH
GREELEY,Martha J AGE:76 9 19 23 May 1905 Hudson, NH Jonathan Keneston
 & Hannah Seevey
GREELEY,Mary A AGE:67 8 4 08 Sep 1881 Hudson, NH Elijah Buxton
 & Mary A Woods
GREELEY,Mary A Buxton AGE:67 8 4 08 Sep 1881 Hudson, NH
GREELEY,Mary T AGE:83 3 22 Sep 1856 Hudson, NH Moses Greeley
GREELEY,Moses AGE:84 15 Aug 1848 Hudson, NH
GREELEY,Moses R AGE:3 21 Sep 1826 Hudson, NH Reuben Greeley
GREELEY,Moses T D AGE:40 10 08 Oct 1843 Hudson, NH

HUDSON,NH DEATHS

GREELEY,Nancy W AGE:40   18 Jan 1870 Hudson, NH
GREELEY,Phoebe C AGE:85 0 18   13 Jan 1904 Hudson, NH William Glines
   & Naomi Hancock
GREELEY,Rachel AGE:62   19 Sep 1758 Hudson, NH
GREELEY,Reuben AGE:68   30 Mar 1863 Hudson, NH
GREELEY,Samuel AGE:79   5 05 Feb 1919 Hudson, NH Samuel Greeley
   & Mary Buxton
GREELEY,Samuel AGE:76   27 May 1771 Hudson, NH
GREELEY,Samuel AGE:79 10 8   13 Apr 1879 Hudson, NH
GREELEY,Sarah AGE:73   09 Sep 1834 Hudson, NH
GREELEY,Sarah J G AGE:75   04 Jun 1896 Hudson, NH John Gilson (Hudson, NH)
   & Sallie Wood (Hancock)
GREELEY,Stephen D AGE:81 10 12   22 Jul 1892 Hudson, NH Moses Greeley
   (Haverhill, MA) & Mary Derby (Harvard, MA)
GREELEY,Susanna AGE:73   05 Nov 1784 Hudson, NH
GREELEY,Velina AGE:32   22 Aug 1869 Hudson, NH
GREELEY,William C AGE:2   11 Oct 1836 Hudson, NH Reuben Greeley
GREELY,Susannah C AGE:68 8 1   30 Mar 1917 Hudson, NH Elijah Richardson
   & Sarah McDonald
GREEN,Job W AGE:78 11 2   29 Jan 1911 Hudson, NH George Green
GREEN,John W AGE:78 11 2   29 Jan 1910 Hudson, NH George Green
GREENE,Mary V AGE:87   28 Jul 1983 Nashua, NH
GREENE,William Edward AGE:51 6 10   06 Apr 1936 Hudson, NH Henry Greene
   & Ida Humphrey
GREENHALGE,Mary J AGE:72   27 03 Mar 1943 Nashua, NH John Hinde & Mary
GREENWOOD,Cyrus N AGE:74 5 9   31 Jan 1925 Hudson, NH Newell Greenwood
   & Lucinda Scott
GREGAS,Felix AGE:8   01 Aug 1922 Hudson, NH Valentine Gregas & Agnes Wiscavich
GREGOIRE,Eugene C AGE:61   30 Jan 1969 Nashua, NH
GRELE,Joseph AGE:94   07 Mar 1745 Hudson, NH
GRELE,Martha AGE:86   21 Feb 1757 Hudson, NH
GRENEWICZ,Alex AGE:50   25 Dec 1928 Hudson, NH Alex Grenewicz
GRENON,[Unknown] AGE: 20 May 1946 Nashua, NH Joseph E Grenon
   & Albertine Cossett
GRIFFIN,Dolly AGE:82   28 Dec 1869 Hudson, NH
GRIFFIN,Esther M F AGE:11 27   27 Apr 1900 Hudson, NH John E Griffin
   & R A E Cargell
GRIFFIN,Eva M AGE:67   12 Mar 1963 Nashua, NH
GRIFFIN,Gardner F AGE:77   12 Mar 1983 Nashua, NH
GRIFFIN,George E AGE:83   3 01 Apr 1897 Hudson, NH Moses Griffin
   & Dolly Smith
GRIFFIN,Harold W AGE:75   01 Dec 1965 Nashua, NH
GRIFFIN,John W AGE:76 4 8   10 Jan 1926 Hudson, NH Joseph Griffin
   & Jane Crawford
GRIFFIN,Louise A AGE:2   01 Aug 1821 Hudson, NH Moses Griffin
GRIFFIN,Margaret E AGE:31 7   16 Sep 1890 Hudson, NH Thomas Fallon (Ireland)
   & Mary McGlynn (Ireland)
GRIFFIN,Mattie T AGE:78   28 Jul 1970 Nashua, NH
GRIFFIN,Moses AGE:69 10   09 Jul 1858 Hudson, NH
GRIFFIN,Rachel AGE:51   23 Jul 1878 Hudson, NH Moses Griffin
GRIFFIN,Rufus H AGE:71 6 20   24 Jan 1892 Hudson, NH
GRIFFIN,Rufus K AGE:71 6 20   24 Jan 1892 Hudson, NH   & Eliza Quimby
GRIFFIN,Sally AGE:32   10 May 1824 Hudson, NH
GRIFFIN,Susan B AGE:93 2 17   04 Jul 1915 Hudson, NH Ebenezer Burrill
   (Winthrop, MA) & Ann Betcher (Winthrop, MA)
GRIFFIN,Susan M AGE:29   29 Jul 1868 Hudson, NH
GRIGAS,Agatha AGE:70   02 May 1961 Nashua, NH
GRIGAS,Alexander AGE:75   19 May 1954 Goffstown, NH
GRIGAS,John AGE:52   30 Mar 1971 Hudson, NH
GRIGAS,Joseph AGE:38   15 Sep 1964 Nashua, NH

HUDSON,NH DEATHS

GRIGAS,Walantas AGE:78 20 Jan 1971 Nashua, NH
GRIJAVITIS,Arthur AGE:69 13 Jul 1941 Goffstown, NH
GROCHOWSKI,Joseph J AGE:94 17 Nov 1983 Nashua, NH
GROHOSKY,George C AGE:53 07 Aug 1966 Nashua, NH
GROHOSKY,Julia R AGE:68 11 Jan 1979 Nashua, NH
GROHOSKY,Nellie AGE:86 08 Aug 1974 Manchester, NH
GROHOSKY,Victor John AGE:26 01 Mar 1973 Hudson, NH
GROVES,Doris E AGE:33 24 Apr 1957 Nashua, NH
GROVES,Elizabeth AGE:75 05 Jan 1909 Hudson, NH William Boyle
  & Margaret Groves
GROVES,John C AGE:79 15 17 Sep 1941 Hudson, NH Robert Groves
  & Elizabeth Boyle
GROVES,Katherine L AGE:29 5 6 09 Jul 1905 Hudson, NH Robt Groves
  & Elizabeth Boyle
GROVES,Maggie A AGE:19 8 17 30 Dec 1883 Hudson, NH Robert Groves
  & Elizabeth Boyle
GROVES,Mary Eunice AGE:45 5 29 20 Sep 1944 Hudson, NH Daniel Potter
  & Clarice J Locke
GROVES,Reuben S AGE:51 1 28 25 Sep 1944 Hudson, NH John C Groves
  & Sarah M Spaulding
GROVES,Robert AGE:83 14 12 Jan 1917 Hudson, NH & Margaret Vanstan
GROVES,Robert G AGE:65 1 25 28 Nov 1936 Hudson, NH Robert Groves
  & Elizabeth Boyle
GROVES,Robert L AGE:70 14 Oct 1965 Nashua, NH
GROVES,Sarah Marie AGE:85 7 12 Feb 1944 Nashua, NH Reuben Spaulding
  & Sarah Laton
GUAY,Harry A AGE:58 08 Mar 1957 Nashua, NH
GUERETTE,Corene E AGE:2 27 Sep 1970 Nashua, NH
GUERETTE,Roland AGE:64 10 Feb 1979 Nashua, NH
GUERTIN,George AGE:2 7 7 16 Mar 1914 Hudson, NH J B A Guertin
  & Angeline Burque
GUERTIN,Henry J AGE:77 13 Oct 1971 Nashua, NH
GUERTIN,Victor AGE:7 10 18 26 Feb 1914 Hudson, NH J B A Guertin
  & Angeline Burque
GUICHARD,Joseph AGE:64 10 19 21 Mar 1933 Hudson, NH Pascal Guichard
  & Elise Marquis
GUILLAUME,Sr Marie St AGE:79 26 Jul 1952 Hudson, NH
GUILLEMETTE,Lillian AGE:50 16 Sep 1966 Nashua, NH
GUILMETTE,L May AGE:77 15 Nov 1970 Nashua, NH
GUIMOND,Dolores E AGE:80 03 Mar 1982 Nashua, NH
GUIMOND,Emery R AGE:68 23 Mar 1984 Nashua, NH
GURSKI,Patricia AGE:42 30 Aug 1980 Nashua, NH
GUYETTE,Charles E AGE:73 05 Apr 1983 Nashua, NH
GUYETTE,Edward A AGE:63 6 11 07 Jun 1945 Nashua, NH Joseph Guyette
  & Elizabeth Lamoy
GUYETTE,Mabel AGE:81 16 Feb 1968 Concord, NH
HACKETT,Ena AGE:76 05 Dec 1978 Hudson, NH
HACKETT,Robert H AGE:20 12 Dec 1977 Nashua, NH
HADLEY,Francis E AGE:87 17 Oct 1964 Hudson, NH
HADLEY,Isaac AGE: 10 Sep 1777 Hudson, NH Moses Hadley & Lydia
HADLEY,John S AGE:4 22 Oct 1812 Hudson, NH William Hadley & Rachel Blodgett
HADLEY,Lydia AGE: 16 Sep 1778 Hudson, NH Moses Hadley & Rebecca
HADLEY,Moses AGE:79 09 Sep 1829 Hudson, NH
HADLEY,Moses AGE: 24 Oct 1781 Hudson, NH Moses Hadley & Rebecca
HADLEY,Rachel Blodgett AGE:86 4 22 Dec 1874 Hudson, NH
HADLEY,Rebecca AGE:94 7 10 27 Mar 1847 Hudson, NH
HADLEY,Rebecca AGE: 28 Oct 1781 Hudson, NH Moses Hadley & Rebecca
HADLEY,William AGE:69 10 03 Aug 1855 Hudson, NH
HADLEY,William AGE: 25 Jan 1809 Hudson, NH William Hadley & Rachel Blodgett
HADLEY,William F AGE:21 15 Jun 1833 Hudson, NH William Hadley

HUDSON,NH DEATHS

& Rachel Blodgett
HAGMAN,Freddie E AGE:3   21 Mar 1875 Hudson, NH
HAIGHT,Clarence W Sr AGE:78   18 Oct 1970 Nashua, NH
HAIGLER,George F AGE:48   27 Nov 1971 Nashua, NH
HAINES,Mehitable R AGE:42   11 Jun 1882 Hudson, NH Timothy Ford
& Sarah G Fuller
HAINES,Merle H AGE:75   11 Jul 1978 Hudson, NH
HALE,Elizabeth Butler AGE:61   05 Apr 1809 Hudson, NH
HALE,George F AGE:74 6 1   28 Dec 1920 Hudson, NH Abram Hale & Almiva Gilsan
HALE,Henry AGE:63 1 4   23 Jun 1803 Hudson, NH
HALE,Henry AGE:84 9   21 May 1792 Hudson, NH
HALE,June C AGE:75   22 Mar 1964 Nashua, NH
HALE,Margaret AGE:17   15 May 1854 Hudson, NH Henry Hale & Mary
HALE,Mary AGE:78 9 6   08 Dec 1787 Hudson, NH
HALE,Moody AGE: 04 Sep 1778 Hudson, NH John Hale & Sarah
HALE,Thomas AGE:12   03 Jun 1754 Hudson, NH Henry Hale & Mary
HALEY,John R AGE:70   11 May 1975 Derry, NH
HALL,Albert V AGE:43 10 5   29 Jul 1940 Nashua, NH William Hall & Lillian Bull
HALL,Annie E AGE:84   25 Dec 1928 Hudson, NH
HALL,Ida Victoria AGE:58   07 Apr 1928 Hudson, NH George W Blood
& Fidelia Richardson
HALL,John H AGE:74 8   24 Apr 1902 Hudson, NH Jacob Hall & Mary French
HALL,Lillian J AGE:79   08 Sep 1951 Hudson, NH
HAMBLET,Alvin AGE:70 5   27 Jun 1895 Hudson, NH Amos Hamblet (Pelham)
& Sarah Steele (Hudson, NH)
HAMBLET,Amos AGE:76   02 Dec 1866 Hudson, NH
HAMBLET,Edwin Alvan AGE:15   18 Apr 1871 Hudson, NH
HAMBLET,Eli AGE:86 2   05 Aug 1896 Hudson, NH Thomas Hamblet (Dracut, MA)
& Tamar Gilson (Tyngsboro)
HAMBLET,Mabel M AGE:9   18 Mar 1871 Hudson, NH Horace Hamblet & Louisa
HAMBLET,Rebecca AGE:66 10   15 Dec 1885 Hudson, NH Enoch Butler
& Susanna Marsh
HAMBLET,Rebecca Sowina AGE:65 8 9   29 Apr 1911 Hudson, NH Eli Hamblet
& Rebecca Butler
HAMBLETT, AGE: 21 May 1807 Hudson, NH Thomas Hamblett & Tamar
HAMBLETT,Addie M AGE:15 2 27   16 Jan 1881 Hudson, NH Alvin Hamblett
& Almira A McKean
HAMBLETT,Amos AGE:76   02 Dec 1866 Hudson, NH
HAMBLETT,Arvilla AGE:85 6 16   16 Mar 1938 Hudson, NH Eli Hamblet
& Rebecca Butler
HAMBLETT,Dorothy M AGE:62   10 Jan 1967 Nashua, NH
HAMBLETT,Eli AGE: Hudson, NH
HAMBLETT,Ellen L AGE:1   13 Mar 1866 Hudson, NH
HAMBLETT,George W AGE:67 5 5   06 Feb 1906 Hudson, NH James Hamblett & Chapman
HAMBLETT,Grace F AGE:7   06 Feb 1877 Hudson, NH
HAMBLETT,Hattie L AGE:83 2 7   13 Dec 1946 Hudson, NH Augustus Sawyer
& Almira Copeland
HAMBLETT,Ira AGE:3 8 15   13 Mar 1812 Hudson, NH Thomas Hamblett & Tamar
HAMBLETT,Leonard P AGE:20   22 Mar 1969 Nashua, NH
HAMBLETT,Lorina AGE:30   13 Mar 1877 Hudson, NH
HAMBLETT,Margaret L AGE:61   24 Dec 1954 Hudson, NH
HAMBLETT,Martha AGE:25   02 Jul 1767 Hudson, NH
HAMBLETT,Parthena AGE:64   26 Nov 1862 Hudson, NH
HAMBLETT,Rebecca Butler AGE:66   1885 Hudson, NH
HAMBLETT,Ruth S AGE:71   31 May 1967 Nashua, NH
HAMBLETT,Sarah B AGE:65   03 Mar 1866 Hudson, NH
HAMBLETT,Sarah R AGE:65   03 Mar 1866 Hudson, NH
HAMBLETT,Tamar AGE:78   05 Mar 1866 Hudson, NH
HAMBLETT,Thomas AGE:75   09 Nov 1850 Hudson, NH
HAMBLETT,[Unknown] AGE: 04 Jan 1816 Hudson, NH Thomas Hamblett & Tamar

HUDSON, NH DEATHS

HAMBLETT, [Unknown] AGE: 28 Jun 1767 Hudson, NH Thomas Hamblett & Martha
HAMEL, John A AGE:52 10   04 Nov 1941 Hudson, NH John B Hamel & Kate O'Reily
HAMELL, William AGE:2 10 Apr 1863 Hudson, NH
HAMILTON, Maude AGE:73 29 Jul 1949 Concord, NH Andrew Hamilton & Eliza Graham
HAMILTON, Ralph E AGE:80 27 May 1967 Nashua, NH
HAMLETT, Almira A AGE:63 11 7   16 Apr 1896 Hudson, NH
HAMLETT, Willie B AGE:24 1 2   04 Dec 1883 Hudson, NH Alvin Hamlett
    & Elmira McKean
HAMMOND, Lewis F AGE:57 9 17   10 Aug 1948 Hudson, NH John F Hammond
    & Mabel Brown
HANNAFORD, Mabelle E AGE:74   15 Sep 1953 Hudson, NH
HANNAFORD, Orin P AGE:79 01 Jan 1954 Nashua, NH
HANSCOM, Susan AGE:72 4   04 Apr 1889 Hudson, NH
HANSCOMB, Almira AGE:75   08 Dec 1873 Hudson, NH
HANSCOMB, Susan AGE:72 4   04 Apr 1889 Hudson, NH
HANSEN, Einer E AGE:86   28 Dec 1976 Nashua, NH
HANSEN, Ruby J AGE:64   06 Nov 1984 Milford, NH
HANSON, Hans AGE:74   26 Jan 1897 Hudson, NH
HANSON, Roland G Jr AGE:44   08 Feb 1970 Hudson, NH
HANSON, Roland G Sr AGE:67   16 Feb 1966 Nashua, NH
HARDING, Experience AGE:86 5 26   03 Oct 1884 Hudson, NH James Harding
    (Augusta, ME) & Elizabeth White (Augusta, ME)
HARDY, Albert M AGE:74   15 22 Sep 1923 Hudson, NH Benj Hardy & Mary Hardy
HARDY, Asa AGE:41 27 Aug 1821 Hudson, NH
HARDY, Bertha E AGE:87   13 Feb 1984 Hudson, NH
HARDY, David S Jr AGE:17   18 Aug 1969 Hudson, NH
HARDY, Ebenezer AGE:74   11 Mar 1852 Hudson, NH
HARDY, Frances A P AGE:17 26 Feb 1851 Hudson, NH
HARDY, Hannah AGE:45   01 Oct 1821 Hudson, NH
HARDY, Hannah W AGE:1   11 Jun 1837 Hudson, NH
HARDY, John AGE:25   29 May 1767 Hudson, NH Jonas Hardy & Sarah
HARDY, Mary A AGE:26   28 Jul 1855 Hudson, NH Paul Hardy & Mary Smith
HARDY, Mary Gould AGE: 21 Jun 1841 Hudson, NH
HARDY, Mary Kendall AGE: Jul 1877 Hudson, NH
HARDY, Nathaniel AGE:51   26 Feb 1907 Hudson, NH Joseph Hardy
HARDY, Otis AGE: 1836 Hudson, NH Paul Hardy & Mary Smith
HARDY, Paschal E AGE:36 23 Oct 1837 Hudson, NH
HARDY, Paul AGE:77 22 Feb 1869 Hudson, NH
HARDY, Robert H AGE:76 22 Aug 1969 Nashua, NH
HARDY, Sarah E AGE:1 2   28 Mar 1833 Hudson, NH
HARDY, Susanna AGE: 17 Aug 1777 Hudson, NH Daniel Hardy & Esther
HARDY, Zachariah AGE:62 12 Apr 1864 Hudson, NH
HARDY, Zachariah AGE: 19 May 1756 Hudson, NH
HARDY, Zachariah K AGE:39 11 Apr 1846 Hudson, NH
HARMON, Elizabeth E AGE:1 3   18 Feb 1889 Hudson, NH Albion Harmon
HARNETT, Joan AGE:45 27 Nov 1984 Nashua, NH
HARR, Clara F B AGE:70 1 18   28 Feb 1901 Hudson, NH James P Bruce (Mt Vernon)
    & Sarah J Parker (New Boston)
HARRINGTON, Jeremiah AGE:58 26 Nov 1890 Hudson, NH (Ireland) (Ireland)
HARRIS, Amanda M AGE:55   04 Jan 1871 Hudson, NH Albert Harris & Sarah
HARRIS, Ann AGE:90   15 26 Dec 1883 Hudson, NH Ebenezer Harris
    & Rebeckah Hills
HARRIS, Elizabeth M AGE:84 7 21   24 Apr 1938 Hudson, NH Robert McKay
    & Elizabeth McGill
HARRIS, George F AGE:77 16 Feb 1985 Hudson, NH
HARRIS, Hannah C AGE:2 6   30 Oct 1838 Hudson, NH Albert Harris & Sarah
HARRIS, Kristine L AGE:9 31 Jul 1952 Nashua, NH
HARRIS, Lydia AGE:95   24 09 Sep 1882 Hudson, NH Isaac Colburn & Lydia Davis
HARRIS, Rufus AGE:63 29 Jan 1870 Hudson, NH
HARRIS, Rufus AGE:65 30 Jan 1870 Hudson, NH

HUDSON,NH DEATHS

HARRIS,Sarah F AGE:36 20 May 1851 Hudson, NH
HARRON,Mary G AGE:75 17 Apr 1976 Nashua, NH
HARTLEY,Jeanne G AGE:34 23 Dec 1978 Nashua, NH
HARTSHORN,Esther J AGE:82 8 11 24 Jan 1930 Hudson, NH Richard Young
HARTWELL,Alta L AGE:66 22 Jun 1983 Hudson, NH
HARTWELL,Herbert S AGE:64 20 Dec 1971 Nashua, NH
HARVEY,Jeffrey E AGE:1 02 Feb 1955 Nashua, NH
HARVEY,John Franklin AGE:79 2 16 18 Nov 1938 Hudson, NH Samuel Harvey
    & Eliza Harvey
HARVEY,Marion P AGE:2 25 07 Mar 1892 Hudson, NH J Frank Harvey (Freedom)
    & Eva M Parmenter (Nashua, NH)
HARVEY,[Unknown] AGE: 26 Sep 1894 Hudson, NH Frank J Harvey (Freedom)
    & Maud Pannents (Nashua, NH)
HARWOOD,Catherine E AGE:57 2 28 21 Nov 1946 Hudson, NH Alec MacDonald
    & Elizabeth Defoe
HARWOOD,Edward AGE:64 2 16 30 Jan 1915 Hudson, NH Edward Harwood
    (Newport, NH) & Sarah Robinson (Newport, NH)
HARWOOD,Mary Brennan AGE:70 28 Apr 1938 Hudson, NH Cornelius Brennan
    & Abbie Healey
HARWOOD,Ralph Wm AGE:51 4 4 22 Jun 1942 Nashua, NH Walter J Harwood
    & Thea Hanson
HARWOOD,Walter J AGE:80 1 6 18 Oct 1933 Hudson, NH Joseph Harwood
    & Julia Harwood
HARWOOD,Walter T AGE:62 05 Dec 1949 Nashua, NH Walter J Harwood
    & Thea Hanson
HARWOOD,William H AGE:72 27 Dec 1960 Nashua, NH
HARWOOD,William P AGE:72 15 May 1874 Hudson, NH
HASELTON,Alice M AGE:79 10 22 14 Nov 1944 Hudson, NH George W Haselton
    & Lora Poor
HASELTON,Bertha M AGE:63 2 4 13 Mar 1936 Hudson, NH Alvin Hamlett
    & Almira McKean
HASELTON,Capt John AGE:80 25 Jun 1822 Hudson, NH
HASELTON,David AGE:18 01 Jun 1813 Hudson, NH Nathaniel Haselton & Rachel
HASELTON,George W AGE:74 4 6 19 Nov 1906 Hudson, NH Luther Haselton
    & Polly Smith
HASELTON,Lora A AGE:68 6 3 08 Jun 1903 Hudson, NH David Poor & Abigail Hill
HASELTON,Luther AGE:66 07 Feb 1863 Hudson, NH
HASELTON,Mehitabel AGE:35 20 Jul 1782 Hudson, NH
HASELTON,Nathaniel AGE:72 14 Dec 1834 Hudson, NH
HASELTON,Polly AGE:3 26 Oct 1802 Hudson, NH Nathaniel Haselton & Rachel
HASELTON,Polly Ladd AGE:88 4 20 Jul 1886 Hudson, NH
HASELTON,Rachel AGE:71 08 May 1835 Hudson, NH
HASELTON,W S F AGE:1 7 11 21 Aug 1894 Hudson, NH Wm Haselton
    (Townsend, MA) & Bertha M Hamblett (Hudson, NH)
HASELTON,William C AGE:81 28 Apr 1950 Hudson, NH David Haselton
    & Harriett S Wood
HASTINGS,George W AGE:35 10 08 Jun 1873 Hudson, NH
HASTINGS,Louisa H AGE:6 23 04 Aug 1889 Hudson, NH Chas H Hastings
    (Woburn, MA) & Lucy J Glines (Newark NJ)
HATCH,Charles H AGE:76 07 Oct 1950 Hudson, NH Charles W Hatch & Susan Batis
HATCH,Eva L AGE:54 17 Sep 1969 Nashua, NH
HATCH,Frederick J AGE:63 25 May 1980 Hudson, NH
HATCH,Walter T AGE:72 20 Jun 1962 Hudson, NH
HAYDEN,Alice C AGE:86 06 Jun 1953 Hudson, NH
HAYFORD,Jaspar A AGE:48 9 22 22 Sep 1904 Hudson, NH Amos Hayford
HAYWARD,Frederick AGE:86 09 Jan 1974 Nashua, NH
HAYWOOD,Samuel S AGE:68 03 Apr 1801 Hudson, NH
HAYWOOD,Sarah AGE:93 01 Jan 1826 Hudson, NH
HAZARD,George W AGE:66 10 4 08 Jul 1891 Hudson, NH Oliver Hazard
    (Concord, MA) & Chloe Colby (Concord, MA)

HUDSON,NH DEATHS

HAZELTON,Arthur W AGE:79 9 29 21 Feb 1942 Hudson, NH George W Hazelton
& Lora A Poor
HAZELTON,Mary E AGE:46 7 23 28 Jan 1917 Hudson, NH James McCoy
& Emily C Richards
HAZZARD,George W AGE:66 10 4 08 Jul 1891 Hudson, NH
HEALD,Edward G AGE:63 30 Sep 1885 Hudson, NH
HEALEY,Joseph F AGE:74 20 Apr 1985 Nashua, NH
HEALEY,Mabel A AGE:83 18 Dec 1961 Hudson, NH
HEATH,Azalia AGE:62 10 Jul 1967 Hudson, NH
HEATH,Jane AGE:74   4 26 Feb 1899 Hudson, NH Levi Boles & Mary Smith
HEATH,Nellie M AGE:27 3 29 Dec 1883 Hudson, NH Jeremiah Heath & Jane Boles
HEBERT,Charles AGE:76 08 Jul 1963 Hudson, NH
HEBERT,Edith AGE:66 25 Feb 1978 Nashua, NH
HEINO,Lena AGE:93 16 Jan 1983 Hudson, NH
HELLINGS,Michael AGE:68 21 Feb 1952 Hudson, NH
HENDERSON,Elmer D AGE:75 31 Dec 1966 Hudson, NH
HENDERSON,James AGE:55 10 Nov 1968 Hudson, NH
HENDRICK,Josephine M AGE:92 26 Nov 1976 Hudson, NH
HENRY,Robert P AGE:45 04 Sep 1966 Laconia, NH
HERRICK,James D AGE:79 6 20 10 Nov 1889 Hudson, NH Nehemiah Herrick
(Methuen, MA) & Sarah Day (Bradford, MA)
HERRICK,Louisa R AGE:52 10 24 04 Dec 1863 Hudson, NH
HESSE,Adeline AGE:95 12 May 1971 Nashua, NH
HIBBARD,Mary F AGE:64 2 23 01 Jan 1922 Hudson, NH
HICKOX,Thomas S AGE: Jun Hudson, NH
HICOX,Thomas S AGE:6 08 Jun 1865 Hudson, NH
HIGGINS,Elizabeth AGE:77 10 Jan 1899 Hudson, NH John Gerry & Hamale Strange
HIGGINS,William AGE:75 04 Sep 1890 Hudson, NH William Higgins (England)
& Hannah Newton (England)
HIGHAM,Steven F AGE:4 16 Mar 1966 Nashua, NH
HIGSON,Ellen M AGE:2 14 24 Nov 1901 Hudson, NH William Higson
(Fall River, MA) & Margaret Tomlinson (England)
HIGSON,John T AGE:1 4 29 Mar 1899 Hudson, NH William Higson
& Hattie Tomlinson
HILBERT,Louise R AGE:75 17 Feb 1967 Nashua, NH
HILL,Abijah AGE:86 4 22 Sep 1887 Hudson, NH Samuel Hill (Hudson, NH)
& Rhoda Bowers (Nashua, NH)
HILL,Alice M AGE:32 27 Jan 1874 Hudson, NH
HILL,Amelia F AGE:20 17 Aug 1869 Hudson, NH
HILL,Carrie B AGE:31 28 Dec 1880 Hudson, NH William F Bradbury
HILL,Col William AGE:81 03 Sep 1858 Hudson, NH
HILL,Eliza P AGE:49 07 May 1857 Hudson, NH
HILL,Elizabeth J AGE:4 9 05 Jun 1850 Hudson, NH Oliver Hill
HILL,Ella P AGE:79 10 20 31 Jul 1935 Hudson, NH William Carpenter
& Althea Paine
HILL,Emma J AGE:75 8 18 21 Mar 1928 Hudson, NH Dudley
HILL,George E AGE:67 11 10 16 Sep 1904 Hudson, NH Oliver Hill
& Rebecca H Phelps
HILL,Gilbert AGE:8 20 Jul 1806 Hudson, NH Col William Hill
HILL,Granville AGE:68 06 Jun 1877 Hudson, NH
HILL,Hannah AGE:78 6 01 Sep 1875 Hudson, NH
HILL,Hannah AGE:72 20 Oct 1869 Hudson, NH
HILL,Harriet L AGE:38 07 Aug 1873 Hudson, NH
HILL,Harriet S AGE:58 17 Aug 1873 Hudson, NH
HILL,Harry L AGE:52 09 Mar 1964 Hudson, NH
HILL,James AGE:78 10 13 31 Mar 1925 Hudson, NH Thomas Hill & Mary M Hunt
HILL,James C AGE:28 4 6 14 Nov 1897 Hudson, NH James Hill & Emma L Conrey
HILL,John F AGE:1 11 25 Aug 1842 Hudson, NH Abijah Hill & Harriet
HILL,Jonathan AGE:76 2 06 Sep 1874 Hudson, NH
HILL,Loring AGE:61 11 21 14 Feb 1948 Goffstown, NH George Hill & Minnie Hill

HUDSON,NH DEATHS

HILL,Mary AGE:82 9   06 Apr 1896 Hudson, NH Benjamin Chase (Pelham)
HILL,Mary AGE:85   07 Mar 1871 Hudson, NH
HILL,Mary E AGE:54   20 Feb 1869 Hudson, NH
HILL,Mary E Campbell AGE:54   21 Feb 1869 Hudson, NH
HILL,Oliver AGE:56   06 Apr 1863 Hudson, NH
HILL,Osgood AGE:75 2 12   25 Jan 1891 Hudson, NH Moody Hill & Sarah Chase
HILL,Rebecca H AGE:73 5 3   20 Apr 1885 Hudson, NH Simeon Lakin Phelps
   (Hollis, NH) & Rhoda Phelps (Merrimack, NH)
HILL,Robert D AGE:72 6   08 Jun 1886 Hudson, NH
HILL,Roswell F AGE:65   24 Dec 1876 Hudson, NH
HILL,Sarah AGE:86   15 Oct 1868 Hudson, NH
HILL,Silas AGE:82 11   29 Feb 1896 Hudson, NH Jeremiah Hills
   & Margaret Davidson
HILL,Susan M AGE:66   27 Oct 1900 Hudson, NH
HILL,Susanna AGE:89 2 26   13 Sep 1886 Hudson, NH
HILL,Susannah B AGE:89 2 26   13 Sep 1886 Hudson, NH
HILL,Thomas AGE:82 10   14 Feb 1888 Hudson, NH Elijah Hills (Hudson, NH)
   & Betsey Kidder (Hudson, NH)
HILL,Warren AGE:79   20 Jan 1890 Hudson, NH Elijah Hills (Hudson, NH)
   & Betsy Tarbox (Hudson, NH)
HILL,William AGE:9   23 Aug 1825 Hudson, NH Col William Hill & Rachel
HILLS,Alden AGE:83 5 29   09 Sep 1891 Hudson, NH Elijah Hills (Hudson, NH)
   & Betsy Tarbox (Hudson, NH)
HILLS,Amos AGE:68   03 Jun 1850 Hudson, NH
HILLS,Betsey AGE:75   11 Jul 1857 Hudson, NH
HILLS,Edna AGE:18   01 Sep 1753 Hudson, NH James Hills & Abagail
HILLS,Ednah AGE:27   25 Oct 1781 Hudson, NH
HILLS,Elijah AGE:54   10 Mar 1833 Hudson, NH
HILLS,Elijah AGE:90   03 Jan 1828 Hudson, NH
HILLS,Ethel M AGE:8   16 Jul 1893 Hudson, NH Calon W Hills (Hudson, NH)
   & Maud B Degraff (Moors Ic NY)
HILLS,Ezekiel AGE:72   11   14 May 1790 Hudson, NH
HILLS,Franklin Augustus AGE:82   3   10 Nov 1926 Hudson, NH Abjah Hills
   & Harriet Stratton
HILLS,George W AGE:80 6 19   15 Nov 1890 Hudson, NH Samuel Hills (Hudson, NH)
   & Rhoda Bowers (Merrimack)
HILLS,George W AGE:16 9   12 May 1861 Hudson, NH Silas Hills & Roxanna
HILLS,George W AGE:16 5   Hudson, NH
HILLS,H S AGE: Hudson, NH
HILLS,Hannah AGE:97   27 Sep 1816 Hudson, NH
HILLS,Hannah AGE:70   31 Dec 1858 Hudson, NH
HILLS,Hannah AGE:97   25 Jul 1838 Hudson, NH
HILLS,Harland Silas AGE:82   24 Jun 1974 Hudson, NH
HILLS,Helen Marion AGE:16   27 Jun 1898 Hudson, NH Franklin A Hill
   & Luella E Campbell
HILLS,Henry AGE: 20 Aug 1757 Hudson, NH
HILLS,Henry AGE:55   21 Oct 1773 Hudson, NH
HILLS,Jeremiah AGE:83   04 Apr 1810 Hudson, NH
HILLS,John W AGE:3 7   06 Sep 1851 Hudson, NH Silas Hills & Roxanna
HILLS,Jonathan AGE:63   20 Jul 1826 Hudson, NH
HILLS,Kimball AGE:3   20 Nov 1803 Hudson, NH Elijah J Hills & Betsey
HILLS,Mary Colburn AGE:85   09 May 1871 Hudson, NH
HILLS,Mary V AGE:76   24 Aug 1895 Hudson, NH Dr A K Hills (Hudson, NH)
   & Ida V Creutzborg (Philadelphia, PA)
HILLS,Mary W AGE:85   23   03 Jan 1894 Hudson, NH
HILLS,Mirriam AGE:85   14 Aug 1822 Hudson, NH
HILLS,Moody AGE:73   10 Sep 1854 Hudson, NH
HILLS,Nathaniel AGE:24   01 Jun 1823 Hudson, NH
HILLS,Nathaniel AGE: 12 Apr 1748 Hudson, NH
HILLS,Nettie L AGE:77 9 26   07 Jan 1945 Hudson, NH Israel Young

HUDSON,NH DEATHS

   & Elizabeth Morse
HILLS,Parker AGE:35   09 Feb 1837 Hudson, NH
HILLS,Philip AGE:87 4 14 Jul 1841 Hudson, NH
HILLS,Polly AGE:82   23 Feb 1846 Hudson, NH
HILLS,Polly AGE:67   07 May 1839 Hudson, NH
HILLS,Rebecca AGE:53   04 Mar 1871 Hudson, NH Asa Butler
HILLS,Rhoda AGE:66   13 Jul 1842 Hudson, NH
HILLS,Roxanna AGE:84 2 13 Feb 1897 Hudson, NH John N Farnum & Phebe Boles
HILLS,Ruth AGE:75   25 Aug 1826 Hudson, NH
HILLS,Ruth AGE:68   15 Feb 1859 Hudson, NH
HILLS,Samuel AGE:74   25 May 1843 Hudson, NH
HILLS,Sarah AGE:75   29 Jun 1848 Hudson, NH
HILLS,Sarah AGE:27   15 Sep 1791 Hudson, NH
HILLS,Sarah AGE:82   06 Nov 1844 Hudson, NH
HILLS,Thomas AGE:21   14 Apr 1805 Hudson, NH Thomas Hills & Ruth
HILLS,Thomas AGE:82   21 May 1833 Hudson, NH
HOAG,David T AGE:72 10 5   08 Feb 1912 Hudson, NH David Hoag & Almira Tuttle
HOAG,Grace G AGE:3 8 3   Hudson, NH David Hoag & Charlott Belknap
HOBBS,Annie L AGE:89 10 8   14 May 1947 Hudson, NH Joseph O Osborne
   & Lydia Mack
HOBBS,Hannah AGE:27 2   16 Mar 1781 Hudson, NH
HODGE,Edith M AGE:61   29 Jan 1983 Bedford, NH
HODGE,Frederick D AGE:61   29 Sep 1971 Nashua, NH
HODGE,Posie M AGE:78   09 Jan 1980 Hudson, NH
HOEGNER,Mabel Charlotte AGE:54 2 20   09 Jan 1936 Hudson, NH Edwin H Sanborn
   & Helen J Shaw
HOFFMAN,Catherine AGE:100   04 Mar 1886 Hudson, NH
HOFFMAN,Fanny AGE:26   25 May 1873 Hudson, NH
HOFFMAN,Philip AGE:68   24 May 1896 Hudson, NH (Ireland) (Ireland)
HOGAN,John T AGE:75   13 Dec 1980 Hudson, NH
HOITT,Agnes B AGE:83   16 Apr 1970 Nashua, NH
HOITT,William B AGE:69   28 Jul 1950 Nashua, NH Fred P Hoitt & Julia A Pottle
HOLBROOK,Clarence A AGE:84   21 Jul 1963 Hudson, NH
HOLBROOK,David Frederick AGE:2   02 Dec 1931 Hudson, NH Clarence Holbrook
   & Elizabeth Dalcount
HOLBROOK,Elizabeth A AGE:76   07 Nov 1965 Hudson, NH
HOLDEN,Celia L AGE:92   28 Sep 1962 Hudson, NH
HOLDEN,Mary Jane AGE:33   28 Mar 1969 Nashua, NH
HOLMES,Ida J AGE:93   22 Oct 1950 Hudson, NH Rufus Holmes & Mary Howitt
HOLMES,Katherine AGE:82 7 10   28 May 1898 Hudson, NH Joseph Butler
   & Hannah Butler
HOLMES,Levi Jefferson AGE:20   22 Dec 1871 Hudson, NH
HOLMES,Margaret A AGE:88   05 May 1984 Hudson, NH
HOLMES,Mary Ann AGE:96 5 7   01 Apr 1922 Hudson, NH Nathaniel Batchelder
HOLMES,Myra A J AGE:50   1   07 Aug 1904 Hudson, NH William Butler
HOLT,Alice M AGE:87   16 Jun 1969 Concord, NH
HOLT,Edelbert AGE:95   30 Sep 1961 Hudson, NH
HOLT,Eugene AGE:63 7 20   20 May 1919 Hudson, NH Harvey Holt & Lois Cramm
HOLT,George AGE: 28 Sep 1919 Hudson, NH William Holt & Florence Dube
HOLT,Lucy E AGE:72   13 Nov 1900 Hudson, NH John Parker & Elizabeth Rowell
HOLT,Nellie C AGE:82   14 Jul 1975 Nashua, NH
HOLTON,Blanche B AGE:86   15 Aug 1965 Nashua, NH
HOLTON,Charlotte J AGE:5 8 27   28 Sep 1911 Hudson, NH Louis M Holton
   & Blanche Burcham
HOLTON,Jessie M AGE:67   23 Apr 1971 Nashua, NH
HOLTON,Lewis M AGE:76   17 Feb 1951 Hudson, NH
HOLTON,Seth N AGE:14 4   27 Oct 1927 Hudson, NH Louis Holton & Blanche Buckham
HONEYWELL,Sarah A AGE:80 3 27   21 Jan 1930 Hudson, NH Richard Rodgers
   & Ann E Egger
HOOK,Stella AGE:4 5   17 Feb 1923 Hudson, NH Walery Hook & Mary Woolen

HUDSON,NH DEATHS

HOOPER,Edith Florence AGE:96 04 Dec 1984 Hudson, NH
HOOPER,Ralph E AGE:56 1 4 18 Mar 1946 Hudson, NH Samuel Hooper
  & Stella F Kimball
HOPKINS,Charles H AGE:77 8 9 11 Jan 1916 Hudson, NH Samuel Hopkins
  & Betsy Lealand
HOPKINS,Cleaves W AGE:76 10 8 30 Jun 1914 Hudson, NH William Hopkins
  & Nancy Balch
HOPKINS,Ellen M AGE:8 8 24 21 Sep 1903 Hudson, NH Chas H Hopkins
  & Ida Webster
HOPWOOD,Ethel M AGE:69 12 Dec 1960 Nashua, NH
HOPWOOD,James W AGE:68 14 Jun 1959 Nashua, NH
HOPWOOD,William R AGE:79 24 Feb 1972 Manchester, NH
HORN,Marlene AGE:4 04 Apr 1967 Nashua, NH
HOULE,Albert F AGE:73 20 Jun 1968 Manchester, NH
HOULE,Rev Alphonse AGE:68 04 Aug 1971 Nashua, NH
HOULE,Richard C AGE:50 30 Apr 1977 Nashua, NH
HOULE,Rose M AGE:63 01 Aug 1954 Hudson, NH
HOUSE,Alta T AGE:79 8 19 18 Mar 1938 Hudson, NH James Rowe & Ordelia Johnson
HOUSE,Helen M AGE:78 04 Oct 1972 Nashua, NH
HOUSE,Raymond L AGE:80 08 Mar 1967 Nashua, NH
HOWARD,Debra J AGE:10 hrs 05 Nov 1955 Nashua, NH
HOWARD,Jessie AGE:92 04 Jul 1959 Hudson, NH
HOWARD,Leland E AGE:65 26 May 1965 Nashua, NH
HOWARD,William G AGE:51 9 8 28 Dec 1947 Nashua, NH William Howard
  & Florence Whitlock
HOWARD,[Unknown] AGE:7 27 Jun 1861 Hudson, NH
HOWE,Benjamin AGE:76 18 Oct 1883 Hudson, NH Joseph Howe & Mehitble Stickney
HOWE,Cecil P AGE:8 13 Feb 1866 Hudson, NH
HOWE,Daniel F AGE:7 21 Nov 1853 Hudson, NH David R Howe
HOWE,David AGE:3 15 Oct 1828 Hudson, NH John Howe
HOWE,David R AGE:43 31 Dec 1853 Hudson, NH
HOWE,Hannah AGE:42 24 May 1830 Hudson, NH
HOWE,Hannah E AGE:17 9 23 03 Aug 1857 Hudson, NH
HOWE,John Jr AGE:29 1 19 17 Jun 1844 Hudson, NH
HOWE,Lucy M AGE:90 1 13 29 Sep 1900 Hudson, NH Joseph Howe
  & Mahitable Stickney
HOWE,Sarah F AGE:2 4 17 17 Jun 1842 Hudson, NH John Howe
HOWE,Susan AGE:31 7 11 Apr 1851 Hudson, NH
HOWE,Suzanne AGE:76 28 Nov 1968 Nashua, NH
HOYT,Ethel AGE:81 16 May 1979 Nashua, NH
HOYT,Mabel Teele AGE:91 19 Sep 1980 Derry, NH
HOYT,Newell A AGE:78 29 May 1970 Nashua, NH
HOYT,Robert T AGE:57 03 Jul 1982 Nashua, NH
HUBBARD,Mary L AGE:86 1 2 24 Jun 1941 Hudson, NH Lawrence E Wise
  & Mary Rodney
HUBBARD,Mary W AGE:47 4 16 29 Oct 1930 Hudson, NH Waldo F Hubbard
  & Mary L Wise
HUBBARD,Sarah D AGE:86 28 Feb 1978 Nashua, NH
HUBBARD,Waldo Flint AGE:82 7 10 14 Jan 1936 Hudson, NH Richard Hubbard
  & Sarah D Clapp
HUDON,Emile AGE:83 23 Aug 1966 Nashua, NH
HUFF,Lucille B AGE:71 06 Feb 1968 Nashua, NH
HUFF,Roy L AGE:57 07 Apr 1959 Nashua, NH
HUGHES,Anna J AGE:82 11 Jun 1963 Nashua, NH
HUK,Walery AGE:58 21 Aug 1951 Hudson, NH
HULL,Bessie E AGE:91 07 Jan 1985 Nashua, NH
HUNNEWELL,George F AGE:84 30 Nov 1954 Hudson, NH
HUNNEWELL,Mary A AGE:89 06 Jul 1965 Nashua, NH
HUNNEWELL,Ralph E AGE:50 19 Feb 1976 Nashua, NH
HUNT,Jonathan AGE:84 7 26 30 Aug 1881 Hudson, NH Jonathan Hunt

HUDSON,NH DEATHS

    & Rebecah Tucker
HUNT,Philip AGE:53   1861 Hudson, NH
HUNT,Philip AGE:53   Hudson, NH
HUNT,William B AGE:80   23 Apr 1906 Hudson, NH Jonathan Hunt & M R Hunt
HUNTER,Celia E AGE:81 11 10 05 Feb 1931 Hudson, NH   & Sarah Clough
HUNTER,Kenneth M AGE:2 4 18   04 May 1909 Hudson, NH Frank A Hunter
    & Annie Beal
HUNTER,Richard C AGE:76 01 Sep 1983 Nashua, NH
HUNTER,Robert AGE:65 05 Nov 1955 Nashua, NH
HUNTER,Veronica AGE:2 22 26 Sep 1910 Hudson, NH George Hunter
    & Eleanor O'Shea
HUNTING,Jonas AGE:63   04 Apr 1860 Hudson, NH
HUNTLEY,Silas AGE:48   1877 Hudson, NH
HUNTRESS,Everett J AGE:43 8   Hudson, NH Jacob S Huntress & Laura R Smith
HURD,Chester Davis AGE:61 9 4   27 May 1934 Hudson, NH George D Hurd
    & Julia E Davis
HURD,Effie E AGE:70   23 Apr 1950 Derry, NH Sedley A Lowd & Julia M Wilson
HURD,George D AGE:82 5 8   07 May 1922 Hudson, NH
HURD,George E AGE:69   18 Jul 1966 Hudson, NH
HURD,Mary A AGE:70   06 Dec 1977 Nashua, NH
HURD,Mary E AGE:74   25 Nov 1950 Hudson, NH Edward Morin & Clophia Trottier
HUTCHINS,Joseph F AGE:6 6 8 09 Dec 1881 Hudson, NH Alonzo G Hutchins
    & Nancy J Fuller
HUTCHINS,[Unknown] AGE:2 17 Jan 1871 Hudson, NH A G Hutchins & Mary L
HUTCHINSON,Eliza J AGE:70 8   26 Jul 1896 Hudson, NH James Smith
    & Sybil Wilson
HUTCHINSON,William AGE:81 4 28 01 Aug 1912 Hudson, NH Wm Hutchinson
HYDE,Adelaide L AGE:82 6 26 22 Apr 1947 Hudson, NH Abram Watson
    & Hannah Buell
HYDE,Lorenzo F AGE:88 9 15 31 Jan 1944 Hudson, NH Lorenzo O Hyde
    & Mary Thompson
INGALLS,Nancy M AGE:87 6 6   21 Dec 1923 Hudson, NH Eli Blood
    & Elizabeth Blood
INGRAM,Lucile V AGE:48 09 Jun 1978 Hudson, NH
INMAN,Charles H AGE:80 7 2 02 Mar 1921 Hudson, NH James Inman
    & Charlett Collar
IRVINE,Hermaine B AGE:85 30 Mar 1962 Hudson, NH
ISBELL,Brent C AGE:13 19 Mar 1983 Hudson, NH
IVES,Howard F AGE:33 04 Jun 1955 Nashua, NH
IVES,Merrill M AGE:86 19 Feb 1984 Manchester, NH
IVES,Priscilla AGE:8 2 18 07 Aug 1936 Hudson, NH Merrill Ives & Jessie Hill
IVON,Joseph AGE:2 20 Oct 1919 Hudson, NH Arthur Ivon & Rosanna Desmarais
JACKSON,Ella M AGE:69 22 Feb 1968 Nashua, NH
JACKSON,William T AGE:71 23 Dec 1969 Nashua, NH
JACOB,Desire J AGE:86 01 Aug 1962 Nashua, NH
JACOBS,Minnie L AGE:79 7 23 17 Jan 1948 Hudson, NH John Mulcahy
    & Mary Mulcahy
JACOBS,Smith S AGE:72 1 29 14 Jan 1944 Nashua, NH Lorenzo Jacobs
    & Ameila Brown
JACQUES,Blanche A AGE:68 06 Jan 1982 Nashua, NH
JACQUES,Joseph V AGE:53 10 01 Aug 1913 Hudson, NH Pierre Jacques
    & Esther Grenier
JACQUES,Marie A AGE:88 11 4   08 Mar 1948 Hudson, NH Emile Lusignan
    & Julienne Loiselle
JACQUES,Marie J AGE:70 07 Feb 1963 Hudson, NH
JACQUES,Mary E AGE:73 3 19 Feb 1898 Hudson, NH Broadstreet Cross
    & Hannah Chandler
JACQUES,Napoleon AGE:70 11 9 09 Jun 1928 Hudson, NH Joseph Jacques
    & Marie Jacques
JACQUES,Orville B AGE:68 18 Dec 1972 Nashua, NH

HUDSON,NH DEATHS

JACQUITH,Sarah J AGE:82 2 15 20 Feb 1915 Hudson, NH George D Fox
 (Hollis, NH) & Sarah J Jacquith (Jaffrey, NH)
JALBERT,Carole Y AGE:2 08 Aug 1962 Hudson, NH
JALBERT,Doris AGE:57 25 Jan 1975 Nashua, NH
JALBERT,Edward H AGE:62 16 Mar 1976 Nashua, NH
JALBERT,George Ernest AGE:59 18 Mar 1981 Nashua, NH
JALBERT,Walter W AGE:64 23 Jan 1966 Hudson, NH
JAMES,Frank W AGE:66 8 7 30 Apr 1915 Hudson, NH Joseph James (Tamworth, NH)
 & Sarah Sullivan (Tamworth, NH)
JAMESON,David L AGE:21 11 Jun 1970 Hudson, NH
JAMESON,Nellie L AGE:55 2 10 02 May 1924 Hudson, NH Jesse Hamblett
JAMESON,Waldo F AGE:71 13 Nov 1983 Hudson, NH
JANUSYEWCKI,M Ann Zinkovich AGE:72   24 26 Feb 1938 Hudson, NH
 John Zinkovich
JAQUITH,Asa AGE:79 24 Apr 1868 Hudson, NH
JAQUITH,Geo D AGE:55 07 Jan 1892 Hudson, NH Asa Jaquith & Esther Philips
JAQUITH,George D AGE:55 07 Jan 1892 Hudson, NH
JARRY,Ralph H AGE:61 03 May 1984 Nashua, NH
JASPER,Arthur AGE:67 7 11 02 Nov 1925 Hudson, NH Joseph Jasper
JASPER,Bernice L AGE:80 18 Apr 1974 Nashua, NH
JASPER,Grant AGE:65 26 Aug 1956 Hudson, NH
JASPER,Joseph C AGE:77 04 Apr 1964 Nashua, NH
JATKIEWICZ,Walter AGE:61 26 Jan 1961 Concord, NH
JATKWICZ,Stella V AGE:58 08 Jun 1984 Nashua, NH
JAURON,Mary A AGE:62 28 Aug 1953 Nashua, NH
JEAN,Rita K AGE:37 19 Apr 1963 Nashua, NH
JEANNOTTE,Alphonsine AGE:75 7 3 13 Feb 1946 Nashua, NH Ephrem Pepin
 & Loise Presse
JEANNOTTE,Beatrice AGE:74 28 Oct 1975 Nashua, NH
JEANNOTTE,Frederick AGE:94 17 Jul 1965 Hudson, NH
JEANNOTTE,Georgianna AGE:83 09 May 1963 Concord, NH
JEANNOTTE,Joseph J AGE:54 10 Nov 1961 Nashua, NH
JEANNOTTE,M Marg M AGE:6 02 Apr 1927 Hudson, NH Joseph Jeannotte
 & Yvonne Talbot
JEANNOTTE,Valmore J AGE:62 18 Jul 1970 Nashua, NH
JEANOTTE,Aurie A AGE:77 26 Feb 1953 Hudson, NH
JELLISON,Louville M AGE:68 9 6 28 Apr 1930 Hudson, NH Benjaman Jellison
 & M Jane Boothby
JENNETTE,Olivar AGE:72 10 29 20 Feb 1928 Hudson, NH Olivier Jennette
JENNINS,Timothy W AGE:2 30 Apr 1965 Nashua, NH
JETTE,Amerilda AGE:68 10 30 01 Apr 1944 Hudson, NH Ferdinand Gagnon
 & Euphmie Ouellette
JETTE,Arthur AGE:62 3 6 31 Jan 1938 Hudson, NH Desire Jette
 & Elizabeth Farland
JETTE,Arthur V AGE:46 11 10 01 Dec 1946 Hudson, NH Arthur Jette
 & Amerilda Gagnon
JETTE,Delia A AGE:61 05 Jun 1959 Nashua, NH
JETTE,Edmond L AGE:59 09 Sep 1971 Nashua, NH
JETTE,Marie AGE:87 11 30 10 Sep 1940 Hudson, NH Joseph Dupont
 & Florence Paradis
JEWELL,Bertha S AGE:85 09 Jan 1966 Nashua, NH
JEWELL,Burgess D AGE:88 9 26 23 May 1932 Hudson, NH David Jewell
 & Susan Faulkner
JEWELL,Frederick M AGE:1 14 11 Dec 1902 Hudson, NH Albert P Jewell
 & Bertha S Marshall
JEWELL,William A AGE:76 9 28 08 Jan 1909 Hudson, NH Daniel L Jewell
 & Hannah Robbins
JEWETT,Laura G AGE:76 4 15 10 Feb 1947 Hudson, NH Richard Estey
 & Clara Nichols
JEWETT,Nellie F AGE:87 27 Aug 1949 Hudson, NH Benjamin W Jewett

HUDSON, NH DEATHS

    & Emeline F Abbott
JEWETT,William H AGE: 16 Jun 1873 Hudson, NH
JOHANSEN,Ole M AGE:86   10 Feb 1966 Goffstown, NH
JOHNSON,Aaron P AGE:15   13 Mar 1820 Hudson, NH Caleb Johnson
JOHNSON,Anna AGE:75   7 26 Jan 1812 Hudson, NH
JOHNSON,Augustine R AGE:93   28 Dec 1980 Hudson, NH
JOHNSON,Caleb H AGE:5   4 29 Sep 1826 Hudson, NH Caleb Johnson & Hannah
JOHNSON,Charles H AGE:72   28 May 1971 Nashua, NH
JOHNSON,Dustin AGE:7   1814 Hudson, NH Doliver Johnson & Louisa
JOHNSON,Gary AGE:7   10 Jul 1964 Nashua, NH
JOHNSON,Hannah AGE:44   17 Aug 1825 Hudson, NH
JOHNSON,Kimball AGE: 05 Apr 1860 Hudson, NH
JOHNSON,Louisa AGE:29 6 14   20 Apr 1835 Hudson, NH
JOHNSON,Michael C AGE:72   12 Jul 1957 Hudson, NH
JOHNSON,Moses AGE:76 9 17   30 Mar 1814 Hudson, NH
JOHNSON,Phebe AGE:51   22 Jul 1812 Hudson, NH
JOHNSON,Ralph G AGE:37   18 Jun 1982 Manchester, NH
JOHNSON,Samuel AGE:74   04 Jun 1826 Hudson, NH
JOHNSON,Thomas Jr AGE: 29 Apr 1872 Hudson, NH Thomas Johnson & Ruth
JOHNSON,Walter S AGE:52 9 14   01 Aug 1930 Hudson, NH Frank Johnson
    & Jennie Plummer
JOHNSTON,Michael J AGE:3 hrs   16 May 1964 Nashua, NH
JONES,Dennis M AGE:46   26 Feb 1982 Nashua, NH
JONES,Elizabeth M AGE:72 7 12   Hudson, NH
JONES,Marion M AGE:86   15 Apr 1982 Hudson, NH
JONES,Richard Murray AGE:62   06 Mar 1973 Nashua, NH
JORDAN,Ralph L Jr AGE:21   20 Mar 1969 Hudson, NH
JORDAN,Wesley W AGE:17   07 Sep 1979 Nashua, NH
JOSEF,John W AGE:68   21 Oct 1971 Nashua, NH
JOWDERS,David B AGE:53   07 Mar 1967 Hudson, NH
JOY,Arthur L AGE:77 6 29   01 Sep 1941 Concord, NH Lemuel Joy
    & Elizabeth Hadley
JOY,Frank W AGE:25 6   01 Dec 1894 Hudson, NH Lemuel T Joy (Quincy, MA)
    & M E Hadley (Nashua, NH)
JOY,Laura J AGE:73   08 Jan 1969 Nashua, NH
JOY,Lemuel T AGE:73 10   06 Apr 1891 Hudson, NH Caleb Joy (Cohasset, MA)
    & Nancy Woodbury (Bolton, MA)
JOY,Marion I AGE:65   21 May 1959 Nashua, NH
JOY,Mary E AGE:68   22 May 1898 Hudson, NH Ebenezer Hadley & Eliza Hunt
JOYAL,Florida M AGE:90   13 Nov 1982 Nashua, NH
JOYAL,Irene A AGE:80   27 Jan 1978 Nashua, NH
JOYAL,Roland A AGE:69   23 May 1983 Nashua, NH
JOYCE,David A AGE:2   08 Jan 1961 Nashua, NH
JOYCE,Tyler B AGE:68   25 Jul 1978 Nashua, NH
JOZIATIS,William D AGE:44   30 Aug 1983 Nashua, NH
JUBERT,[Unknown] AGE: 01 Jul 1948 Nashua, NH Russell Jubert & Cecile Ledoux
KAMIRNSKA,Bramslaw AGE:35   12 Dec 1924 Hudson, NH Bramslaw Kamirnska
KAPISKY,Agnes S AGE:62   19 Feb 1969 Nashua, NH
KAPISKY,John E AGE:60   09 Aug 1975 Nashua, NH
KAROS,Evelyn C AGE:60   06 Jan 1966 Nashua, NH
KASHULINES,Albert J AGE:61   02 Apr 1966 Nashua, NH
KASHULINES,Arthur J AGE:70   04 Jan 1970 Nashua, NH
KASHULINES,Peter AGE:82   25 Jun 1951 Nashua, NH
KASHULINES,William AGE:4   15 Aug 1962 Boston, MA
KASPER,Amelia AGE:63 11 16   15 May 1941 Nashua, NH Martans Lebnick
    & Agota Tubines
KASPER,Martin AGE:69   15 Mar 1960 Nashua, NH
KASPER,Mary R AGE:94   04 May 1977 Nashua, NH
KASPER,Michael AGE:49   14 Nov 1941 Nashua, NH William Kasper
    & Lenora Vediavich

HUDSON,NH DEATHS

KASPSTYNE,Olive V AGE:2 6   26 Apr 1920 Hudson, NH Florence Belcher
 (Osborn Kaspstyne)
KATSOHIS,Penney B AGE:23   25 Mar 1983 Nashua, NH
KATSOHIS,Vasiliki AGE:70   19 Mar 1972 Nashua, NH
KAUFHOLD,Lina AGE:64   27 Feb 1967 Nashua, NH
KAYRAS,Alice AGE:1 9   06 Apr 1926 Hudson, NH Anthony Kayras
 & Francis Alakonis
KAYRAS,Florence AGE:15   05 Jul 1928 Hudson, NH Anthony Kayras
 & Frances Alkonis
KAYROS,Anthony AGE:67   05 Jan 1952 Hudson, NH
KAYROS,Carol A AGE:3 3   18 Oct 1939 Hudson, NH Peter R Kayros & Wanda Dombek
KAYROS,Frances AGE:80   14 Sep 1971 Hudson, NH
KAZLOUSKAS,Stanley J AGE:44   18 Dec 1967 Nashua, NH
KAZLOUSKAS,Steve AGE:74   10 Oct 1967 Concord, NH
KEEFE,John G AGE:62   12 Jul 1969 Lowell, MA
KEEFE,Michael AGE:17   24 May 1967 Lowell, MA
KEEGAN,Ann AGE:54   16 Dec 1882 Hudson, NH John Keegan & Ann
KEENAN,Paul C AGE:42   30 Oct 1970 Nashua, NH
KEHOE,Helen Nellie AGE:88   10 May 1981 Hudson, NH
KELLEHER,Elizabeth J AGE:75 4   23 Aug 1940 Hudson, NH Ruben Church
 & Mary Church
KELLEY,Annie AGE:91   26 Mar 1967 Hudson, NH
KELLEY,Ellen R AGE:67 11 19   25 Mar 1943 Hudson, NH Felix Galoohly
 & Ellen Galoohly
KELLEY,Jean E AGE:61   19 Mar 1981 Hudson, NH
KELLEY,John AGE:74   26 Nov 1885 Hudson, NH
KELLEY,Margaret H E AGE:45   19 Jun 1891 Hudson, NH
KELLEY,Mary A AGE:85   08 Nov 1972 Nashua, NH
KELLEY,William AGE:76   19 Apr 1890 Hudson, NH Abijah Kelley (Haverhill, MA)
 & Ruth Cluff (Salem)
KELLEY,William J AGE:52   20 Sep 1965 Nashua, NH
KELLOGG,Silas G AGE:68 8 27   21 Dec 1891 Hudson, NH Silas Kellogg
 (Great Barrington) & Sophia Laint (Halifax, VT)
KELLY,Arwilder E AGE:60   04 Apr 1979 Nashua, NH
KELLY,Christopher J AGE:49   08 Jun 1984 Nashua, NH
KELLY,Georgia AGE:2   02 Oct 1877 Hudson, NH
KELLY,Margaret H E AGE:45   19 Jun 1891 Hudson, NH John Cotter (Ireland)
 & Catherine Lovett (Ireland)
KELLY,William AGE:89   28 May 1976 Nashua, NH
KEMP,Florence E AGE:88   06 Sep 1964 Hudson, NH
KEMP,Sally P AGE: 04 Mar 1858 Hudson, NH
KEMPTON,Lena M AGE:81   17 Jan 1978 Nashua, NH
KENDALL,John L AGE:79   15 Jun 1969 Nashua, NH
KENISTON,Albert Leroy AGE:1   11 11 Feb 1925 Hudson, NH Charles F Keniston
 & Mary L Gowing
KENISTON,Charles F AGE:67   06 Mar 1960 Nashua, NH
KENISTON,Ethel L AGE: 04 Sep 1916 Hudson, NH Charles Keniston & Mary Gowing
KENISTON,Evelyn L AGE: 04 Sep 1916 Hudson, NH Charles Keniston & Mary Gowing
KENISTON,Julia A AGE:81   10 Oct 1960 Hudson, NH
KENNEDY,George AGE:72 6 18   05 May 1942 Goffstown, NH John S Kennedy
 & Mary Murrough
KENNEDY,James W AGE:82   12 Sep 1956 Hudson, NH
KENNEDY,John S AGE:74   02 Apr 1952 Hudson, NH
KENNEDY,Sarah F AGE: 24 Aug 1876 Hudson, NH
KENNEY,Thomas AGE: 02 Dec 1762 Hudson, NH
KENRICK,Lena M AGE:83   07 Nov 1958 Nashua, NH
KERPLUCK,Stephen AGE:64 1 14   08 May 1947 Hudson, NH Matthew Kerpluck
 & Katherine Kerpluck
KERR,Robert P AGE:1   04 Dec 1899 Hudson, NH John L Kerr & Mabel M Parker
KERRIGAN,William J AGE:90   25 Aug 1978 Hudson, NH

HUDSON,NH DEATHS

KEYRAS,Gadalga AGE:11   28 Feb 1917 Hudson, NH Anthony Keyras
    & Frances Olukonis
KIAZIM,Henry AGE:33   30 Oct 1960 Hudson, NH
KIDDER,Benjamin AGE:77   16 Feb 1874 Hudson, NH
KIDDER,Benjamin H AGE:65 4 22   20 Oct 1889 Hudson, NH Benjamin Kidder
    (Hudson, NH) & Hannah Peirce (Lincoln, MA)
KIDDER,Capt Jonas AGE:94   01 Nov 1837 Hudson, NH
KIDDER,Caroline Pierce AGE:24   23 Apr 1848 Hudson, NH
KIDDER,Eleazer AGE:10   24 Feb 1759 Hudson, NH Noah Kidder & Eunice
KIDDER,Frank E AGE:45   07 Apr 1905 Hudson, NH Benj H Kidder & Martha Marshall
KIDDER,Hannah AGE:68 7   13 Jun 1863 Hudson, NH
KIDDER,Hannah P AGE:68   13 Jun 1863 Hudson, NH
KIDDER,John AGE:24   18 May 1825 Hudson, NH
KIENIA,Sadie AGE:87   06 Jun 1977 Hudson, NH
KIENIA,Vladimir AGE:63   26 Apr 1955 Hudson, NH
KIMBALL,Anna G AGE:74   24 Jul 1972 Goffstown, NH
KIMBALL,Dorothea I AGE:4 1 2 02 Aug 1899 Hudson, NH John R Kimball
    & Delora Tarbell
KIMBALL,E Eugene AGE:67 6 24   26 Apr 1936 Hudson, NH Wilson Kimball
    & Laura McGilvery
KIMBALL,William Lloyd AGE:6   22 Nov 1911 Hudson, NH Ebner A Kimball
    & Grace G Goodrich
KING,Chandler AGE:73   21 Jul 1950 Nashua, NH Otis King & Annie Park
KING,Dora AGE:83   09 Dec 1970 Nashua, NH
KING,Georgie C AGE:72   27 Jan 1953 Hudson, NH
KING,Isaac J AGE:64 1 13   01 Jan 1945 Hudson, NH Otis King & Annie B Leaghe
KING,Laurel R AGE:85   13 Dec 1984 Nashua, NH
KINGLSEY,Edgar W AGE:54   13 Aug 1968 Nashua, NH
KINVILLE,Antoine AGE:53   6 21 Dec 1922 Hudson, NH Antoine Kinville
    & Sofie Joffrion
KINVILLE,Edward AGE:1   05 Jul 1930 Hudson, NH Edward Kinville
    & Ruth I Nichols
KINVILLE,Emma M AGE:86   25 Jun 1976 Nashua, NH
KINVILLE,Gilbert A AGE:50 5 12   24 Feb 1944 Nashua, NH Antoine Kinville
    & Rose Duprey
KIRBY,William L AGE:73   Hudson, NH
KIRKOS,Agorou AGE:87   27 Apr 1982 Hudson, NH
KIRKPATRICK,William R Sr AGE:82   05 Aug 1968 Hudson, NH
KIRWAN,Joseph AGE:57   06 Apr 1979 Nashua, NH
KLEINER,Harry H AGE:39   30 Nov 1961 Nashua, NH
KLEINER,Margaret A AGE:90   15 Mar 1985 Hudson, NH
KLIMAS,Alexander AGE:59 4 11   28 Jun 1945 Concord, NH Andrew Klimas
KLIMAS,Anna AGE:99   27 May 1983 Hudson, NH
KNIGHT,Alice R AGE:76   26 Jun 1959 Hudson, NH
KNIGHT,George W AGE:68 10 20   12 Jan 1944 Goffstown, NH Gardener Knight
    & Clara Worcester
KNIGHT,Joseph Elwell AGE:88 4 29   26 Jan 1927 Hudson, NH James Knight
    & Mary Riddon
KNIGHT,Mary F AGE:76 6 24   25 Feb 1936 Hudson, NH John Brooks
KNIGHTS,Eva R AGE:66   31 Aug 1964 Nashua, NH
KNIGHTS,Francis R AGE:55   21 Apr 1975 Nashua, NH
KNIGHTS,George C AGE:62   05 Feb 1957 Hudson, NH
KNIGHTS,Marion L AGE:57   14 Mar 1985 Nashua, NH
KOENIG,Claire AGE:73   09 Mar 1974 Nashua, NH
KOPECKO,Mary AGE:3 3   08 Apr 1928 Hudson, NH Albert Kopecko & Mary Murhiski
KOPICKO,Albert AGE:64   31 Dec 1957 Lowell, MA
KOPITSKI,Mary AGE:5 20 15 Jun 1923 Hudson, NH Albert Kopitski & Mary Machuski
KREWSKI,Mary AGE:61   13 Aug 1983 Nashua, NH
KUHN,George W AGE:66 9   13 Jan 1893 Hudson, NH
KULINGOSKI,Debra A AGE:9   23 Jan 1964 Nashua, NH

HUDSON,NH DEATHS

KUPCHUNAS,Frank B AGE:64   06 Jul 1969 Nashua, NH
KUPCHUNAS,Frank J AGE:78   26 Sep 1950 Hudson, NH Peter Kupchunas
   & Josephine Lesonuki
KUPCHUNAS,Mary K AGE:89   15 Mar 1972 Nashua, NH
KWIATKOWSKY,Stanley AGE:89   14 Oct 1960 Goffstown, NH
LABELLE,Joseph F AGE:74   05 Jun 1972 Concord, NH
LaBONVILLE,Elzimire P AGE:83   20 Sep 1956 Hudson, NH
LABOUNTY,Edith L AGE:24 2 5   12 Aug 1909 Hudson, NH Walter B Chase
   & Anna Cross
LaBRECQUE,Raymond J AGE:54   18 Apr 1984 Nashua, NH
LABRIE,Joseph W AGE:75   08 Dec 1971 Nashua, NH
LACHANCE,Joseph AGE:80   04 May 1971 Concord, NH
LACOSHUS,Louise B AGE:71   28 Oct 1968 Nashua, NH
LACOUTURE,Evelyn AGE:85   21 Jun 1977 Manchester, NH
LaFAUCI,Doris AGE:56   12 Jan 1969 Nashua, NH
LAFLAMME,Bonnie A AGE:1 hr   07 Mar 1968 Nashua, NH
LaFLAMME,John B AGE:73   30 Jan 1965 Nashua, NH
LaFLAMME,Julius F AGE:69   15 Jan 1963 Nashua, NH
LAFLAMME,Louise AGE:58   03 May 1930 Hudson, NH Joseph Gaouette
LaFLAMME,Peter J AGE:78   21 Mar 1967 Hudson, NH
LaFLEUR,Richard A AGE:18   01 Oct 1962 Nashua, NH
LAFLOTTE,Adelard J AGE:64   05 Dec 1971 Hudson, NH
LaFONTAINE,Florette AGE:80   15 May 1984 Nashua, NH
LAFONTAINE,Joseph G AGE:87   02 Mar 1982 Hudson, NH
LaFOREST,Albina AGE:81   24 Nov 1968 Nashua, NH
LAFOREST,Lillianne M AGE:59   19 Mar 1978 Nashua, NH
LAFOREST,Wayne D AGE:13   04 Apr 1973 Nashua, NH
LaFRANCE,Ada AGE:87   27 May 1958 Concord, NH
LAGASSE,Alphonse J AGE:46   09 Jun 1964 Nashua, NH
LAGASSE,Gaudias AGE:74   24 Jul 1964 Nashua, NH
LAHTI,Joseph AGE:82   15 May 1954 Hudson, NH
LAJOIE,Normand J AGE:57   22 Mar 1981 Nashua, NH
LAJOIE,Robert A AGE:50   13 Dec 1976 Nashua, NH
LAJOIE,Sedonie AGE:84   28 Nov 1967 Hudson, NH
LAMBERT,Alfred AGE:47 7 18   12 Feb 1937 Hudson, NH Louis Lambert
   & Julienne Lafond
LAMBERT,Joseph AGE:1   21 Aug 1903 Hudson, NH Anthoine Lambert & Marie L Caron
LAMBERT,Joseph A AGE:70   18 Nov 1972 Concord, NH
LAMBERT,Marie B AGE:2 16   25 Jan 1918 Hudson, NH Hilaire Lambert
   & Marie Dubois
LAMBERT,Marie R A AGE:7   18 Jun 1906 Hudson, NH Anthoine Lambert
   & Mamie L Caron
LAMBERT,Phelofile AGE:76 3 10   11 Apr 1917 Hudson, NH Michel Lambert
LAMBERT,Robert AGE:33   23 Dec 1979 Nashua, NH
LAMBERT,Walter H AGE: 01 May 1900 Nashua, NH
LAMON,Jennie E AGE:52 8 13   13 Oct 1921 Hudson, NH Rufus Dube
   & Julia St George
LAMONTE,Alfred L AGE:79   23 Oct 1984 Nashua, NH
LAMOY,Philip C AGE:74 6 14   14 Sep 1929 Hudson, NH Philip C Lamoy
   & Charlotte Sweitzer
LAMPRON,Cora AGE:83   12 Jan 1977 Manchester, NH
LAMSON,Joseph O A AGE:77 2 23   11 Jul 1930 Hudson, NH John Lamson
   & Jane Woodbury
LANCASTER,Dorothy AGE: 12 Aug 1796 Hudson, NH
LANDRY,Aime AGE:79   3   28 Mar 1943 Hudson, NH Francois Landry
   & Helene Gauvin
LANDRY,Bernadette A AGE:70   26 Dec 1968 Nashua, NH
LANDRY,Denis A AGE:86   10 Jul 1980 Hudson, NH
LANDRY,Florida AGE:69   23 Nov 1968 Hudson, NH
LANDRY,J Roland AGE:7 15   14 Aug 1902 Hudson, NH J H Landry & Marie Beaulieu

HUDSON,NH DEATHS

LANDRY,Joseph E AGE:61 04 Dec 1956 Hudson, NH
LANDRY,Paul G AGE:43 22 Jul 1961 Nashua, NH
LANDRY,[Unknown] AGE: 22 Sep 1947 Nashua, NH Jewell Landry & Laura Gingras
LANG,Deborah J AGE:9 12 Apr 1972 Nashua, NH
LANGELIER,Charles M AGE:79 20 Oct 1970 Hudson, NH
LANKHORST,Lawrence AGE:62 28 Mar 1983 Hudson, NH
LANOUE, Rose,Sr Marie St Emma AGE:66 03 Jan 1959 Nashua, NH
LAPIN,Charles AGE:84 10 Mar 1973 Nashua, NH
LaPLANTE,Ernest L AGE:51 18 Aug 1957 Hudson, NH
LAPOINTE,Joseph H AGE:87 04 Feb 1965 Goffstown, NH
LAQUERRE,Arthur P AGE:67 01 Jul 1957 Hudson, NH
LAQUERRE,Georgiana AGE:69 11 20 26 Dec 1920 Hudson, NH Napoleon Beaudette
  & Julie Mayrand
LAQUERRE,Odelie AGE:54 4 7 26 Jun 1947 Nashua, NH Philias Roy & Marie Comeau
LAQUERRE,Telesphore AGE:79 21 Sep 1924 Hudson, NH Pierre Laquerre
  & Adele Spinard
LAREINE,Henry Paul AGE:14 04 Jan 1925 Hudson, NH Henry Lareine
  & Gertrude Pelletier
LARGY,Mary W AGE:77 15 May 1963 Hudson, NH
LARIVIERE,Mary J Daigneault AGE:59 11 1 08 Mar 1932 Hudson, NH Joseph
  Daigneault & Mary Jane Lafoud
LaROCQUE,George R AGE:51 21 Oct 1983 Nashua, NH
LATHAM,Stanley E AGE:77 31 May 1957 Hudson, NH
LATON,Maria A AGE:85 3 8 14 Sep 1915 Hudson, NH Thomas Laton (Virginia)
  & Keziah McKean (Derry, NH)
LATOUR,Roland E AGE:58 23 Nov 1966 Hudson, NH
LATULIPPE,Alfred H AGE:60 08 Jun 1978 Nashua, NH
LAUGHTON,Robert A AGE:48 29 Jun 1982 Nashua, NH
LAVALLEE,Joseph E AGE:75 17 May 1976 Nashua, NH
LAVALLEE,Raymond S AGE:49 09 Jun 1976 Nashua, NH
LAVALLEE,Sister Nellie AGE:88 11 Jun 1979 Hudson, NH
LAVALLEE,Todd M AGE:12 22 Nov 1967 Nashua, NH
LAVALLEY,Charles E AGE:60 02 Sep 1967 Nashua, NH
LAVALLY,Armandine AGE:70 23 Feb 1972 Lowell, MA
LAVALLY,Raymond R AGE:26 12 Oct 1957 Nashua, NH
LAVARNWAY,Gertrude AGE:50 16 Jan 1972 Nashua, NH
LAVERTU,Barthelemy AGE:77 22 Dec 1954 Hudson, NH
LAVOIE,Albert J AGE:62 5 6 12 Sep 1947 Hudson, NH Augustin Lavoie
  & Philomene Michaud
LAVOIE,Augustin N AGE:44 18 Aug 1960 Hudson, NH
LAVOIE,Doris AGE:58 27 Jun 1976 Nashua, NH
LAVOIE,Gerard AGE:26 4 15 14 Nov 1937 Hudson, NH Ludger Lavoie
  & Alma Boucher
LAVOIE,Isabelle AGE:64 18 Feb 1982 Nashua, NH
LAVOIE,Leo P AGE:2 2 19 15 Jan 1921 Hudson, NH Joseph Lavoie
  & Marie A Thibadeau
LAVOIE,Lumena AGE:57 3 3 21 Jul 1918 Hudson, NH Louis Paradis
  & Pauline Landry
LAVOIE,Marie A AGE:75 17 Oct 1963 Nashua, NH
LAVOIE,William J AGE:85 14 Mar 1962 Hudson, NH
LAVRIE,Alphie AGE:26 2 18 17 Jul 1927 Hudson, NH John Lavrie & Larre Saucie
LAWLER,Anna AGE:3 17 16 Dec 1919 Hudson, NH Henry Lawler & Ella Young
LAWRENCE,Amy M AGE:82 06 Nov 1953 Hudson, NH
LAWRENCE,Kirby H AGE:87 26 Dec 1977 Nashua, NH
LAWRENCE,Ruth AGE:73 11 Nov 1979 Nashua, NH
LEAOR,Joseph Carl Jr AGE:5 13 03 Jan 1934 Hudson, NH Joseph C Leaor
  & Lillian Martin
LEARNED,Daniel AGE:66 9 18 Jan 1888 Hudson, NH
LEARY,Emma AGE:10 25 Oct 1862 Hudson, NH
LEAZOTT,Ethel M AGE:4 24 Jun 1894 Hudson, NH Wilbur Leazott (New York)

HUDSON,NH DEATHS

  & Jennie Leazott (New York)
LEBEL,Evelyn AGE:70   31 May 1978 Nashua, NH
LeBLANC,Arthur R AGE:64   20 Feb 1976 Hudson, NH
LeBLANC,Geraldine Mary AGE:52   03 Dec 1984 Hudson, NH
LEBLANC,Louis H AGE:69 5 10   19 Jul 1943 Nashua, NH
LeBLANC,Mary C AGE:54   16 Oct 1961 Nashua, NH
LeBOEUF,Alma A AGE:73   01 Oct 1965 Hudson, NH
LeBOEUF,Hercule AGE:75 4 10   15 Feb 1939 Hudson, NH Alfred LeBoeuf
  & Emilie Fortier
LeBOEUF,Louis A AGE:75   18 Jan 1968 Nashua, NH
LeBOEUF,Lumina AGE:73 6 9   27 Aug 1936 Hudson, NH Joseph Poisson
  & Philomene Poisson
LeBOEUF,Marie A AGE:52   04 May 1956 Nashua, NH
LeBRUN,Eugene P J AGE:64   21 Nov 1974 Manchester, NH
LEBRUN,Leda AGE:84   24 Oct 1971 Hudson, NH
LEBRUN,Theophile J AGE:63   30 May 1958 Nashua, NH
LeCLAIR,Paul E AGE:57   07 Jul 1983 Nashua, NH
LeCLERC,Amedee AGE:51   28 Jul 1979 Nashua, NH
LECLERC,Dorilla R AGE:40 5 18   08 Jul 1939 Hudson, NH Francis LaRoche
  & Exilda Landry
LECLERC,Jean B AGE:56 5 9   17 Feb 1943 Hudson, NH Edmond Leclerc
  & Adelle Chasseur
LEDOUX,Arthur J AGE:56   11 Jan 1978 Manchester, NH
LEDOUX,Blanche M AGE:74   28 Sep 1968 Nashua, NH
LEDOUX,Ernest C AGE:66   13 Jan 1958 Hudson, NH
LEDOUX,George G AGE:76   15 Nov 1969 Nashua, NH
LEDOUX,Joseph AGE:67 9 9   01 Oct 1930 Hudson, NH Marcel Ledoux
  & Angele Jodoni
LEDOUX,Lena E AGE:63   07 Sep 1969 Nashua, NH
LEDOUX,Norbert B AGE:54   21 Mar 1979 Nashua, NH
LEDOUX,Rose A AGE:74   17 Feb 1960 Nashua, NH
LEDOUX,Vera A AGE:53   15 Mar 1983 Nashua, NH
LEE,Barbara E AGE:2 15   30 Aug 1917 Hudson, NH John Lee & Louise Blake
LEE,Joseph AGE:1   03 Aug 1922 Hudson, NH Adelard Lee & Delia Lecompte
LEEMAN,Lillian AGE:98   11 Jun 1984 Hudson, NH
LEFEBRE,Joseph AGE:78 7 7   27 Dec 1921 Hudson, NH Joseph Lefebre
  & Camille Poulin
LEFEBVRE,Napoleon AGE:56   08 Nov 1931 Hudson, NH Philip Lefebvre & Milette
LEFEBVRE,Raymond E AGE:66   07 Nov 1978 Nashua, NH
LEFEBVRE,[Unknown] AGE: 11 Dec 1944 Nashua, NH George T Lefebvre
  & Clara L Martin
LEGALLEE,Eva L AGE:72 6 25   21 Mar 1931 Hudson, NH J Martin Sleeper
  & Louisa Berry
LEGALLEE,Joseph H AGE:79 10 29   11 Aug 1935 Hudson, NH John Legallee
LEGARE,Loretta AGE:80   13 Dec 1965 Hudson, NH
LEGARSKY,Mary AGE:72   04 Mar 1962 Nashua, NH
LEHMAN,Emma A AGE:70   07 Apr 1969 Nashua, NH
LEIES,Helen AGE:50   20 Dec 1969 Nashua, NH
LEMAY,Eugene AGE:68   28 Feb 1964 Hudson, NH
LEMAY,Omer J AGE:76   11 Oct 1971 Nashua, NH
LeMAY,Victor A AGE:20 8   15 Feb 1947 Dracut, MA J Omer LeMay & Yvonne Dionne
LEMERISE,Leo J AGE:59   19 Jan 1965 Nashua, NH
LEMERISE,Rose Alma AGE:81   03 Jun 1982 Nashua, NH
LEMIRE,Alfred W AGE:64   18 Feb 1964 Hudson, NH
LEMOIS, Florina,Sr Marie Laurentia AGE:75   13 Oct 1958 Nashua, NH
LENAHAN,Mary C AGE:31 1 14   29 Feb 1904 Hudson, NH John Lenahan & Mary Glancy
LENAHAN,Rose T AGE:27 10 23   13 Apr 1903 Hudson, NHJohn Lenahan & Mary Clancy
LEONARD,Mary F AGE:70 3   18 May 1895 Hudson, NH
LESLIE,Betsey A AGE:81 7 4   06 Jan 1903 Hudson, NH Daniel McAlpin
  & Abbie Gireld

HUDSON,NH DEATHS

LESLIE,Charles C AGE:93 10 16   13 Apr 1948 Hudson, NH William H Leslie
    & Betsy McAlpin
LESLIE,Eliza W AGE:102   17 Oct 1964 Hudson, NH
LESLIE,Eugene W AGE:90   21 Jun 1972 Nashua, NH
LESLIE,Helen H AGE:98   22 Nov 1978 Hudson, NH
LESLIE,Lucy E AGE:21   Hudson, NH Norris Smith & Frances M Greeley
LESLIE,Michael J AGE:82   21 Oct 1965 Nashua, NH
LESLIE,William H AGE:91 3 29   05 Feb 1924 Hudson, NH George W Leslie
    & Lucy Stearns
LETOURNEAUX,Norman A AGE:55   26 Jul 1969 Nashua, NH
LETOURNEUX,Maria AGE:87   29 Mar 1982 Hudson, NH
LEVESQUE,Bernadette R AGE:53   11 Jan 1968 Nashua, NH
LEVESQUE,Cleance AGE:49 7 9   15 Jul 1942 Nashua, NH Joseph Belanger
    & Marie Dionne
LEVESQUE,Edward J AGE:58   31 Aug 1982 Nashua, NH
LEVESQUE,Etienne AGE:72   11 Sep 1964 Nashua, NH
LEVESQUE,Etienne AGE:76   21 Nov 1968 Hudson, NH
LEVESQUE,Jean B AGE:52 1 4   19 May 1948 Nashua, NH Louis Levesque
    & Lucie Canuelle
LEVESQUE,Lionel E AGE:39   27 Feb 1968 Manchester, NH
LEVESQUE,Madaline AGE:3 6 7   15 Aug 1937 Hudson, NH Etienne Levesque
    & Cleance Belanger
LEVESQUE,Rachel E AGE:55   11 Oct 1984 Nashua, NH
LEVESQUE,Robert A AGE:53   26 Apr 1980 Nashua, NH
LEVESQUE,Robert L AGE:49   21 Jul 1961 Nashua, NH
LEVESQUE,Roland AGE:1 8 24   15 Jun 1925 Hudson, NH Etienne Levesque
    & Cleance Belanger
LEVIS,Jessie May AGE:61 6 29   30 Jan 1937 Hudson, NH   McLeod
LEWIS,Ellen AGE:55 1   12 Apr 1918 Hudson, NH James Condrau & Johanna Howard
LEWIS,Esther AGE:2   11 Dec 1894 Hudson, NH Harvey G Lewis (Hudson, NH)
    & Nellie Condon (Canada)
LEWIS,Grover C AGE:77   13 Apr 1962 Nashua, NH
LEWIS,Lucy F AGE:73   15 Apr 1888 Hudson, NH Abijah Boynton
LEWIS,Lucy F P AGE:73   15 Apr 1888 Hudson, NH
LEWIS,William F AGE:72 4 18   10 Apr 1884 Hudson, NH Joseph Lewis
LEYLAND,Elizabeth G AGE:27 9 2   15 Jul 1903 Hudson, NH James Costello
    & M A Landy
LIAKOS,Helen AGE:58   16 Jul 1974 Nashua, NH
LIGHT,David E AGE:52   27 Sep 1954 Nashua, NH
LINDQUIST,Ethel M AGE:83   27 Mar 1968 Nashua, NH
LINDQUIST,George AGE:94   03 Dec 1977 Concord, NH
LINDQUIST,Oscar M AGE:88   14 Jun 1964 Nashua, NH
LITTLE,Deborah AGE:30   16 Mar 1981 Nashua, NH
LITTLE,Eleanor J AGE:2   19 Oct 1951 Nashua, NH
LITTLEFIELD,Bruce G AGE:47   05 Aug 1974 Nashua, NH
LITTLEFIELD,Kermit E AGE:52   13 Jul 1973 Hudson, NH
LITTLEFIELD,Laura AGE:19   26 Aug 1851 Hudson, NH
LITTLEFIELD,Roy E AGE:72   06 Sep 1958 Hudson, NH
LIVINGSTON,Benjamin AGE:72 8   12 Apr 1862 Hudson, NH
LIVINGSTON,Clarissa AGE:69   16 May 1869 Hudson, NH
LIVINGSTON,Lizzie M AGE:2 10   26 Jan 1861 Hudson, NH
LIVINGSTON,Mary AGE:6 2   13 Feb 1919 Hudson, NH John Barnes & Mary Livingston
LIZOTTE,Albina AGE:73   02 Oct 1956 Goffstown, NH
LOCKE,Barbara AGE:52   29 May 1983 Nashua, NH
LOCKE,Calvin W Sr AGE:69   25 Dec 1982 Nashua, NH
LOCKE,Cyrus AGE:73 11 26   20 Sep 1911 Hudson, NH
LOCKHART,Charles W AGE:60 11 25   12 Jul 1929 Hudson, NH William Lockhart
LOCKHART,Elsie M AGE:72   03 Oct 1977 Nashua, NH
LONGA,William A AGE:73   28 Aug 1952 Hudson, NH
LONGTHORNE,Laurson AGE:59 7 3   13 Dec 1946 Nashua, NH

HUDSON,NH DEATHS

LORAINE,Henry P AGE:68 15 Dec 1970 Nashua, NH
LOUGEE,Arthur L AGE:54 17 Jun 1963 Nashua, NH
LOVEJOY,Charles E AGE:82 22 Mar 1953 Hudson, NH
LUCIEN,Grace S AGE:66 6 13 20 Nov 1947 Nashua, NH Joseph Sakowich
 & Mary Sakowich
LUCIEN,Irene A AGE:75 30 Aug 1983 Nashua, NH
LUCIEN,Joseph AGE:70 25 Jun 1948 Hudson, NH Joseph Lucien
LUCIER,Eugene L AGE:82 17 Jan 1961 Nashua, NH
LUCIER,Grace S AGE:83 09 Apr 1971 Nashua, NH
LUND,Francis AGE:52 12 Mar 1893 Hudson, NH Plummer Lund
LUND,Harry C AGE:71 06 Apr 1971 Hudson, NH
LUSIGNAN,Henry AGE:61 6 9 16 Jul 1933 Hudson, NH William Lusignan
 & Hermine Lariviere
LYNCH,John J AGE:3 05 Apr 1947 Hudson, NH John J Lynch & Judith Lyzette
LYON,Ernest W AGE:72 16 Jul 1966 Nashua, NH
LYONS,Emma AGE:93 20 Jan 1958 Hudson, NH
MacAULEY,Wilfred M AGE:56 18 Sep 1974 Nashua, NH
MacCANN,Constance T AGE:82 16 Jun 1984 Nashua, NH
MacCANN,George W AGE:88 26 Mar 1962 Nashua, NH
MacDONALD,Herbert J AGE:51 15 Oct 1961 Goffstown, NH
MacDONALD,Inez G AGE:62 10 28 08 Feb 1947 Hudson, NH Gray
MacDOWELL,Geo D Sr AGE:47 04 Feb 1958 Nashua, NH
MACE,Sadako AGE:45 17 May 1971 Tokyo, Japan
MACHERAS,Doris R AGE:57 10 Dec 1970 Hudson, NH
MacINTYRE,Velma O AGE:77 20 Jan 1979 Hudson, NH
MACK,Joseph AGE: 25 Nov 1898 Hudson, NH
MacKIRWICZ,Alphoure AGE:55 13 Jun 1926 Hudson, NH Anthony MacKirwicz
MacLEAN,Maude A AGE:83 05 Jun 1949 Hudson, NH
MacLEAN,Sidney H AGE:22 4 17 Mar 1906 Hudson, NH Ross MacLean
 & Annie Backburn
MAGUIRE,[Unknown] AGE:1 hr 22 Sep 1971 Nashua, NH
MAILHOT,Estelle AGE:77 28 Aug 1970 Hudson, NH
MAILHOT,Josephine AGE:95 10 Jun 1980 Nashua, NH
MAIN,Marie L AGE:83 14 Jul 1971 Nashua, NH
MAINES,Walter P AGE:71 9 2 26 Aug 1924 Hudson, NH
MAINVILLE,Laurette Bergeron AGE:53 27 Jul 1978 Nashua, NH
MAJOR,Marion AGE:56 05 Sep 1977 Nashua, NH
MAKARAWICZ,Victor Jr AGE:50 22 Jun 1976 Nashua, NH
MALCOLM,Henry AGE:65 28 Jul 1969 Nashua, NH
MALENFANT,Irene AGE:70 17 Jun 1981 Nashua, NH
MALETTE,Oscar AGE:47 3 15 24 Sep 1945 Goffstown, NH Ira Malette
 & Victoria Malhoit
MALHOIT,Irene F AGE:77 05 Nov 1964 Nashua, NH
MALLON,Catherine AGE:82 07 Mar 1970 Nashua, NH
MALONE,Mattie M AGE:82 9 22 09 Jun 1937 Hudson, NH John Malone
 & Mary Stewart
MALONE,Thomas H AGE:51 21 Dec 1976 Nashua, NH
MANAGAVAS,Nicholas G AGE:34 5 24 13 Apr 1920 Hudson, NH George Managavas
MANDRAVELIS,Paul G AGE:28 25 Jun 1977 Nashua, NH
MANNING,Nellie M AGE:59 11 25 14 Aug 1928 Hudson, NH George H Vase
 & Mary B Ball
MANNING,Rosalie P AGE:74 15 Jul 1984 Nashua, NH
MANOUSOS,Charles J AGE:57 02 Feb 1975 Manchester, NH
MANSFIELD,A Byron AGE:65 30 Jul 1982 Nashua, NH
MANSFIELD,Lavina J AGE:54 8 20 15 Oct 1941 Hudson, NH Alfred Jeannotte
 & Rebecca Jeannotte
MANSFIELD,Walter J AGE:69 23 Jan 1951 Hudson, NH
MANSFIELD,Winfred Victor AGE:62 02 Jan 1974 Nashua, NH
MANSUR,Alfred J AGE:81 24 Jul 1962 Hudson, NH
MANSUR,Kenneth J Sr AGE:69 29 Oct 1978 Nashua, NH

HUDSON,NH DEATHS

MANTEL,Normand AGE:1   7 27 Feb 1932 Hudson, NH Ernest Mantel&Lydia Deneault
MARBLE,Eben M AGE:77   01 Jul 1904 Hudson, NH Daniel C Marble & Henrietta Bray
MARCH,Sybil AGE: 20 Sep 1874 Hudson, NH
MARCHAND,Clarence AGE:53   09 Jan 1980 Nashua, NH
MARCIANO,Virginia AGE:79   30 Jul 1983 Nashua, NH
MARCOTTE,Annie B AGE:75   29 Sep 1953 Hudson, NH
MARION,Lisa A AGE:15   24 Nov 1977 Nashua, NH
MARQUIS,Aline AGE:63   02 Sep 1970 Concord, NH
MARQUIS,Conrad P AGE:53   15 Jan 1982 Nashua, NH
MARQUIS,Isidore AGE:84   16 Aug 1968 Nashua, NH
MARQUIS,Leon H AGE:1   13 22 Aug 1921 Hudson, NH George Marquis & Eva Larose
MARREN,Sybil D AGE:81   24 Oct 1964 Hudson, NH
MARRS,Ann M AGE:83   17 Aug 1978 Nashua, NH
MARSH, AGE:17   04 Oct 1825 Hudson, NH Enoch Marsh & Martha
MARSH,Abby A AGE:38 1 29   12 Jun 1865 Hudson, NH Thomas Marsh & Abigail
MARSH,Abigail AGE:56   06 Nov 1846 Hudson, NH
MARSH,Abigail AGE:57 2 12   21 Sep 1792 Hudson, NH
MARSH,Addie E AGE:78 4 1   21 Feb 1941 Hudson, NH John C Mason & Lucinda True
MARSH,Anna AGE: 19 Apr 1770 Hudson, NH
MARSH,Betsey AGE:87 10   26 Apr 1855 Hudson, NH
MARSH,Betsey AGE:19   01 Oct 1826 Hudson, NH Jonathan Marsh & Betsey
MARSH,Calvin AGE:11 23   21 Sep 1830 Hudson, NH Hiram Marsh & Olivia
MARSH,Capt Jonathan AGE:71   01 Oct 1830 Hudson, NH
MARSH,Dr Nathaniel P AGE:28   17 Dec 1819 Hudson, NH
MARSH,Ebenezer Esq AGE:64   17 Mar 1831 Hudson, NH
MARSH,Ella F AGE:32 3 24   26 May 1898 Hudson, NH Nelson Boyd & Sarah J Melvin
MARSH,Enoch N AGE:2 11   15 Jul 1843 Hudson, NH Enoch Marsh & Martha
MARSH,Enoch S AGE:62   19 Dec 1865 Hudson, NH
MARSH,Esther AGE:79   04 Jul 1831 Hudson, NH
MARSH,Frank E AGE:67   09 May 1900 Hudson, NH Eli C Marsh & R F Sprague
MARSH,George F AGE:56   20 Apr 1917 Hudson, NH
MARSH,Gilman AGE:39   03 Dec 1865 Hudson, NH Enoch Marsh & Martha
MARSH,Hannah AGE:10   03 May 1815 Hudson, NH Ebenezer Marsh & Susanna
MARSH,Hiram AGE:78   25 Jan 1879 Hudson, NH Jonathan Marsh & Betsy Sawyer
MARSH,John AGE:84 2 20   20 Nov 1717 Hudson, NH
MARSH,John AGE:92   21 Dec 1836 Hudson, NH
MARSH,John AGE: 20 May 1756 Hudson, NH Samuel Marsh & Abigail
MARSH,John AGE: 01 Aug 1759 Hudson, NH Samuel Marsh & Abigail
MARSH,John AGE: 23 Nov 1777 Hudson, NH
MARSH,John Jr AGE:77   10 Sep 1861 Hudson, NH
MARSH,Lucinda S AGE:6   02 Jul 1815 Hudson, NH Jonathan Marsh & Betsey
MARSH,Martha W AGE:87 5 21   07 Jul 1892 Hudson, NH Joshua Whittier (Methuen,
   MA) & Abigail Farrington (Andover, MA)
MARSH,Martha Whittier AGE:87 5 21   07 Jul 1892 Hudson, NH
MARSH,Mary E AGE:23   26 May 1848 Hudson, NH Thomas Marsh & Abigail
MARSH,Mary O AGE:87   26 Feb 1959 Nashua, NH
MARSH,Mehittabel AGE:11   15 Oct 1804 Hudson, NH Jonathan Marsh & Betsey
MARSH,Persis R AGE:62   07 Dec 1869 Hudson, NH
MARSH,Rebecca AGE:2   19 Aug 1834 Hudson, NH Thomas Marsh & Abigail
MARSH,Rebecca AGE:35   17 Feb 1829 Hudson, NH
MARSH,Reuben AGE:6   21 Oct 1804 Hudson, NH Jonathan Marsh & Betsey
MARSH,Samuel AGE:87   15 May 1820 Hudson, NH
MARSH,Sarah AGE:6   16 Oct 1804 Hudson, NH Jonathan Marsh & Betsey
MARSH,Sarah AGE:87 1 3   28 Jan 1786 Hudson, NH
MARSH,Sarah AGE: 11 Mar 1762 Hudson, NH Samuel Marsh & Abigail
MARSH,Sarah W AGE:51   12 Mar 1858 Hudson, NH
MARSH,Susanna AGE:77   05 Sep 1843 Hudson, NH
MARSH,Thomas AGE:64   10 Apr 1860 Hudson, NH
MARSH,Thomas F AGE:4   31 Dec 1832 Hudson, NH Thomas Marsh & Abigail
MARSH,Walter H AGE:87 7 16   22 Jul 1940 Hudson, NH Hiram Marsh

HUDSON, NH DEATHS

& Olivia Goodspeed
MARSH,William H AGE:82 16 May 1952 Nashua, NH
MARSHALL,Abigail AGE: 30 Nov 1753 Hudson, NH Daniel Marshall & Rachel
MARSHALL,Alan AGE:18 28 Nov 1960 Hudson, NH
MARSHALL,Ann AGE:73 31 Jul 1829 Hudson, NH
MARSHALL,Annie C AGE:83 03 Sep 1950 Nashua, NH James Doherty & Celia Harkins
MARSHALL,Annie E AGE:36 9 12 Sep 1895 Hudson, NH
MARSHALL,Benjamin S AGE:65 02 Nov 1843 Hudson, NH
MARSHALL,Charlotte W AGE:76 6 04 May 1865 Hudson, NH
MARSHALL,Clara AGE:37 3 9 21 Jul 1893 Hudson, NH
MARSHALL,Dana S AGE:47 08 Jun 1910 Hudson, NH Geo W Marshall
& Marinda Hadley
MARSHALL,David A AGE:34 21 May 1832 Hudson, NH
MARSHALL,David C AGE: Nov 1859 Hudson, NH
MARSHALL,Deborah AGE:78 9 10 01 May 1808 Hudson, NH
MARSHALL,Edward G AGE:67 21 Sep 1969 Nashua, NH
MARSHALL,Elizabeth AGE:33 10 21 03 Dec 1797 Hudson, NH
MARSHALL,Elizabeth E AGE:1 9 02 Feb 1932 Hudson, NH Harold Marshall
& Eva Morrill
MARSHALL,Eugene J AGE:84 25 Oct 1956 Nashua, NH
MARSHALL,George W AGE:67 1 19 16 Jan 1924 Hudson, NH George W Marshall
& Marinda Hadley
MARSHALL,Hannah AGE:6 13 Oct 1754 Hudson, NH John Marshall & Deborah
MARSHALL,Hannah AGE:51 6 02 Sep 1829 Hudson, NH
MARSHALL,Harland Hill AGE:1 3 04 Jul 1920 Hudson, NH Dana C Marshall
& Myrtle Hill
MARSHALL,Herbert W AGE:45 22 14 May 1915 Hudson, NH Geo W Marshall
(Sharron, NH) & Marinda A Hadley (Hudson, NH)
MARSHALL,Jacob AGE:83 10 23 Dec 1871 Hudson, NH
MARSHALL,John AGE:52 2 13 07 Nov 1775 Hudson, NH
MARSHALL,John AGE:74 09 Oct 1827 Hudson, NH
MARSHALL,John AGE:1 8 26 23 Jul 1778 Hudson, NH John Marshall & Susanna
MARSHALL,John AGE: 05 Jan 1756 Hudson, NH
MARSHALL,John AGE: 24 Jun 1870 Hudson, NH
MARSHALL,John Edward AGE:77 11 Apr 1985 Nashua, NH
MARSHALL,John F AGE:18 24 Jul 1870 Hudson, NH John B Marshall & Ellen A
MARSHALL,John N AGE:74 11 22 Jul 1886 Hudson, NH
MARSHALL,Leona AGE:77 04 Oct 1952 Concord, NH
MARSHALL,Leonard AGE:81 2 01 Jul 1890 Hudson, NH Elijah Marshall (Hudson, NH) & Winn (Hudson, NH)
MARSHALL,Lois AGE:2 09 Oct 1754 Hudson, NH John Marshall & Deborah
MARSHALL,Lot AGE:62 16 Oct 1827 Hudson, NH
MARSHALL,Lula A AGE:38 5 16 05 May 1907 Hudson, NH John N Hannon
& Augustas Nutter
MARSHALL,Mahala M AGE:64 8 14 14 Oct 1880 Hudson, NH
MARSHALL,Marinda A AGE:80 26 Dec 1910 Hudson, NH William Hadley
& Rachel Blodgert
MARSHALL,Mary AGE:65 26 May 1827 Hudson, NH
MARSHALL,Mary AGE:44 08 Oct 1851 Hudson, NH
MARSHALL,Mary J AGE:67 06 Dec 1962 Nashua, NH
MARSHALL,Myrtle M AGE:65 25 Aug 1954 Hudson, NH
MARSHALL,Nathan AGE:44 06 Jul 1866 Hudson, NH
MARSHALL,Nathaniel W AGE:85 7 7 27 Feb 1922 Hudson, NH Jacob Marshall
& Eliza Van Valkburg
MARSHALL,Philip AGE:50 09 Sep 1849 Hudson, NH
MARSHALL,Philip AGE:35 Hudson, NH
MARSHALL,Rhoda AGE:40 13 Nov 1810 Hudson, NH
MARSHALL,Roger D AGE:34 13 May 1949 Concord, NH Dana Marshall & Myrtle Hill
MARSHALL,Royal S AGE:4 6 27 Dec 1826 Hudson, NH Stephen C Marshall & Sarah
MARSHALL,Samuel AGE:69 23 Dec 1852 Hudson, NH

HUDSON,NH DEATHS

MARSHALL,Sarah J AGE:45 03 Jul 1891 Hudson, NH John B Thibodeau
 & Mary Dupont (Lowell, MA)
MARSHALL,Susanna AGE:41 11 22 May 1794 Hudson, NH
MARSHALL,Susanna AGE:58 10 Jul 1821 Hudson, NH
MARSHALL,Widow of Elijah AGE: 1862 Hudson, NH
MARSTON,Emily E AGE:45 5 1 10 Feb 1906 Hudson, NH Edward Holton
 & May E Hadley
MARSTON,Mabel P AGE:79 01 Jun 1960 Hudson, NH
MARSTON,Noel P AGE:37 27 Jun 1968 Nashua, NH
MARTEL,Gloria R AGE:49 25 Apr 1971 Nashua, NH
MARTEL,Lomis AGE:58 4 12 02 Jul 1924 Hudson, NH Joseph Martel & Not Known
MARTEL,Marie O AGE:69 29 Jul 1952 Hudson, NH
MARTEL,Wilfred AGE:69 9 9 17 Nov 1948 Hudson, NH August Martel
 & W Brouillard
MARTIN,Almira E AGE:43 4 16 19 Aug 1922 Hudson, NH George Eastman
 & Ida J Cluff
MARTIN,Arthur C AGE:73 01 Jun 1950 Pembroke, NH Wilard H Martin
 & Rose Pennock
MARTIN,Belle AGE:38 5 29 Apr 1886 Hudson, NH
MARTIN,Edna AGE:44 1 11 17 Mar 1918 Hudson, NH Elisha F Martin
 & Susan S Everden
MARTIN,Elisha A AGE:60 7 8 03 Jan 1906 Hudson, NH Elisha Martin
 & Almira M Egerton
MARTIN,Elisha T AGE:71 13 May 1879 Hudson, NH
MARTIN,Elizabeth C AGE:61 7 2 10 Nov 1944 Hudson, NH James Monty
 & Fannie McToff
MARTIN,Ezra A AGE:55 3 23 01 Jan 1910 Hudson, NH Elisha Z Martin
 & Almira M Edgeston
MARTIN,George AGE:2 17 Dec 1921 Hudson, NH Moise Martin & Marie Pelletier
MARTIN,George H AGE:76 3 4 19 Jan 1946 Nashua, NH Jed Martin & Olive Laporte
MARTIN,Gladys M AGE:72 21 Mar 1977 Nashua, NH
MARTIN,Harry A AGE:5 4 1 19 Sep 1882 Hudson, NH Ezra A Martin
 & Maggie J Clyde
MARTIN,Hugh R AGE:69 21 Feb 1978 Nashua, NH
MARTIN,Ida AGE:16 11 12 Jan 1895 Hudson, NH W H Martin (Canada) (Norwich, Vt)
MARTIN,Josephine AGE:81 02 Feb 1958 Hudson, NH
MARTIN,Lillian A AGE:25 4 27 Jan 1896 Hudson, NH Elisha A Martin (Chaplin,
 CT) & Susan S Everdon (Woodstock, CT)
MARTIN,Marie Jeannette AGE:6 22 04 Sep 1926 Hudson, NH Moise Martin
 & Marie Pelletier
MARTIN,Mary A AGE:97 14 Aug 1982 Hudson, NH
MARTIN,Minnie E AGE:28 30 Apr 1898 Hudson, NH James Tobin & Catherine
MARTIN,Remon AGE:1 16 Dec 1921 Hudson, NH Moise Martin & Marie Pelletier
MARTIN,Susan S AGE:91 2 28 02 Feb 1933 Hudson, NH Walter Everden
 & Juliana Hutton
MARTIN,Susie Etta AGE:71 11 7 18 Jun 1935 Hudson, NH Elisha A Martin
 & Susan Everden
MARTINEAU,Ronnie P AGE:10 hrs 19 Aug 1957 Nashua, NH
MARVIN,Beatrice AGE:4 10 17 08 Sep 1901 Hudson, NH Wm J Marvin (Halifax, NS)
 & L Estella Dubia (Cambridge, MA)
MARYHULL,M AGE:80 1862 Hudson, NH
MASON,Barbara A AGE:2 03 Dec 1965 Nashua, NH
MASON,Gertrude E AGE:4 5 10 31 Mar 1893 Hudson, NH Chas Mason (Nashua, NH)
 & Etta M Ackerman (Farmington)
MASSE,Adelard J AGE:58 18 Mar 1973 Nashua, NH
MATHERS,DeForest AGE:85 04 Jun 1985 Nashua, NH
MATHERS,Eileen O AGE:75 07 Oct 1979 Nashua, NH
MATHESON,Cora Louise AGE:84 22 Feb 1982 Hudson, NH
MATTHEWS,George AGE:86 15 Jul 1958 Nashua, NH
MAXFIELD,Millie AGE:76 02 Jul 1949 Nashua, NH Alexander Doty & Mary Laundry

HUDSON,NH DEATHS

MAY,Maria AGE:2 9 26 Feb 1879 Hudson, NH
MAYNARD,Edward E AGE:60 9 15 05 May 1931 Hudson, NH Charles W Maynard
 & Marie E Tarbell
MAYNARD,Felix J AGE:78 03 Nov 1984 Hudson, NH
MAYS,Patrick AGE:13 hrs 07 Aug 1964 Nashua, NH
MAZZEI,Kathleen AGE:24 01 Jul 1978 Nashua, NH
McADOO,Pauline AGE:44 16 01 Feb 1941 Nashua, NH Olin P Lucier
 & Alice L Sargent
McADOO,Samuel AGE:83 30 Aug 1955 Nashua, NH
McAFEE,Alfred Henry AGE:46 8 24 28 Feb 1930 Hudson, NH Charles McAfee
 & Susan Drucker
McAFEE,Charles AGE:63 10 6 13 Feb 1918 Hudson, NH Alfred McAfee
 & Nancy Shepard
McAFEE,Eva E AGE:64 21 Mar 1953 Nashua, NH
McAFEE,Willie E AGE:23 05 Aug 1893 Hudson, NH Chas A McAfee (Bedford, NS)
 & Lucy E Drucker (Pembroke)
McALISTER,Diane AGE:11 14 Jun 1968 Nashua, NH
McALISTER,Franklyn H AGE:50 04 Jul 1949 Nashua, NH Roscoe McAlister
 & Miner Harrington
McANESPIE,Fay AGE:20 09 Nov 1964 Nashua, NH
McAULIFFE,Timothy L AGE:80 07 Jun 1985 Nashua, NH
McAVOY,George AGE:84 06 Dec 1972 Hudson, NH
McAVOY,Jeannette AGE:104 12 Dec 1983 Hudson, NH
McCALLUM,JoAnn E AGE:66 17 Nov 1978 Nashua, NH
McCARTHY,Elizabeth A AGE:62 02 Nov 1983 Nashua, NH
McCARTHY,Richard F AGE:60 12 Dec 1964 Lowell, MA
McCOMMACK,Ida A AGE:75 15 Nov 1972 Nashua, NH
McCOY,Charles AGE:12 5 29 Aug 1865 Hudson, NH Daniel G McCoy & Harriet
McCOY,Charles AGE:12 25 Aug 1865 Hudson, NH
McCOY,Daniel G AGE:84 17 Jul 1965 Nashua, NH
McCOY,Daniel G AGE:41 07 Jan 1856 Hudson, NH
McCOY,Delphine AGE:13 11 19 Aug 1858 Hudson, NH Daniel G McCoy
McCOY,Elgin L AGE:83 07 Mar 1969 Nashua, NH
McCOY,Eliza P AGE:80 1 22 19 Jan 1942 Nashua, NH George Pate & Eliza Hill
McCOY,Emma C AGE:51 8 7 27 Nov 1895 Hudson, NH Richards
McCOY,Ernest E AGE:60 02 Jul 1979 Nashua, NH
McCOY,Flora B AGE:65 16 May 1951 Nashua, NH
McCOY,Harriet AGE:49 25 Aug 1863 Hudson, NH
McCOY,Harriet AGE:49 27 Aug 1863 Hudson, NH
McCOY,Henry H AGE:22 25 Oct 1863 Hudson, NH
McCOY,Henry S AGE:22 9 25 Oct 1863 Hudson, NH Daniel G McCoy
McCOY,Herman R AGE:80 25 Dec 1958 Nashua, NH
McCOY,James AGE:68 5 14 07 Jan 1915 Hudson, NH Daniel G McCoy (Windham, NH)
 & Harriet J Barrett (Hudson, NH)
McCOY,James AGE:85 14 Jul 1873 Hudson, NH
McCOY,Jason W AGE:3 04 Aug 1877 Hudson, NH
McCOY,Jennie C AGE:25 11 14 21 Mar 1903 Hudson, NH George L Smith
 & Clara O Stevens
McCOY,Jessie C AGE:83 26 Nov 1971 Nashua, NH
McCOY,Joseph W AGE:3 01 Aug 1877 Hudson, NH
McCOY,Lena M AGE:76 3 5 19 Feb 1945 Nashua, NH Theodore Clark & June Pike
McCOY,M AGE:70 08 Oct 1865 Hudson, NH
McCOY,Mary AGE:70 08 Oct 1865 Hudson, NH
McCOY,Nancy J AGE:9 14 Sep 1951 Nashua, NH
McCOY,Sylvia M AGE:4 21 07 Apr 1907 Hudson, NH Daniel McCoy
 & Bessie S Rivers
McDONALD,Annabelle AGE:64 13 Mar 1971 Hudson, NH
McGEE,Robert M AGE:1 27 Dec 1949 Nashua, NH Thomas M McGee & Anna Lemay
McGEE,Thomas M AGE:62 15 Jan 1982 Manchester, NH
McGILLIVRAY,Antoinette B AGE:60 18 Feb 1971 Nashua, NH

HUDSON, NH DEATHS

McGUINNES,Agnes AGE:45   14 Nov 1968 Nashua, NH
McGUIRE,Ida AGE:58   08 Dec 1974 Nashua, NH
McGUIRE,James AGE:50   12 May 1866 Hudson, NH
McGUIRE,James AGE:80   19 May 1866 Hudson, NH
McGUIRE,John AGE:2 hrs   11 Nov 1966 Nashua, NH
McINNIS,Margaret AGE:96   24 Nov 1972 Hudson, NH
McINNIS,Walter W AGE:59   19 Jul 1969 Concord, NH
McKAY,Manes F AGE:60   20 Jul 1969 Nashua, NH
McKEAN,Andrew W AGE:69   21 Apr 1953 Nashua, NH
McKEAN,Hannah AGE:52   15 Apr 1834 Hudson, NH
McKEAN,Hugh AGE:53   04 Nov 1835 Hudson, NH
McKENZIE,Anna AGE:71   03 Jul 1971 Hudson, NH
McKENZIE,Edward M AGE:64   05 Aug 1966 Hudson, NH
McLAREN,Elizabeth AGE:66   18 Jun 1979 Goffstown, NH
McLAVEY,Cora M AGE:82   18 Oct 1963 Hudson, NH
McLAVEY,Edward G AGE:55   27 Feb 1967 Nashua, NH
McLELLAN,Mary E AGE:80   19 Jun 1961 Hudson, NH
McLENNAN,Christine AGE:86   24 Jul 1955 Hudson, NH
McMAHON,Martin AGE:65   28 Apr 1965 Nashua, NH
McMAHON,Mary H AGE:78   04 Feb 1978 Nashua, NH
McMILLAN,Donald W AGE:59   08 Jul 1967 Nashua, NH
McMILLAN,John AGE:53   21 Jan 1886 Hudson, NH
McNEIL,Arthur J AGE:71   21 May 1978 Nashua, NH
McNULTY,Francis E AGE:72   12 Nov 1972 Nashua, NH
McNULTY,Paul E AGE:53   20 Jun 1972 Hudson, NH
McSKINSKY,Marguerit AGE:89   14 Mar 1980 Nashua, NH
MEHARG,Mary H AGE:87   19 Mar 1984 Hudson, NH
MELENDY,Adelia Ruth AGE:19   24 Apr 1910 Hudson, NH Charles F Melendy
  & Eva D Hutchinson
MELENDY,Eva D AGE:51   5 30 Jun 1918 Hudson, NH Nathaniel Hutchinson
  & Sally Willowby
MELLOR,Elmer AGE:79   19 Jul 1962 Concord, NH
MELVIN,Allen F AGE:56 1 4   09 Oct 1909 Hudson, NH William Melvin
  & Betsey C Robinson
MELVIN,Benjamin AGE:69   19 Mar 1797 Hudson, NH
MELVIN,Charles G AGE:29   20 01 Mar 1853 Hudson, NH James Melvin & Susan
MELVIN,Charles H AGE:17   Hudson, NH William Melvin & Betsy Robinson
MELVIN,James AGE:83   08 Apr 1860 Hudson, NH
MELVIN,Jerome AGE:6   20 Aug 1825 Hudson, NH James Melvin & Susan
MELVIN,Jerome A AGE:85   17 Apr 1952 Hudson, NH
MELVIN,Jessie M AGE:19 3 16   19 Feb 1885 Hudson, NH William Melvin (Lowell,
  MA) & Betsy C Robinson
MELVIN,Julia G AGE:83 7 12   20 Mar 1917 Hudson, NH Samuel Hopkins
  & Betsy Leland
MELVIN,Mabel S AGE:86   24 Feb 1957 Hudson, NH
MELVIN,Olive L AGE:15 6 28   07 Mar 1902 Hudson, NH Tolford D Melvin
  & Ida Webster
MELVIN,Susan AGE:75 11 7   04 Feb 1855 Hudson, NH
MELVIN,Tolford D AGE:68 7 25 29 Jun 1889 Hudson, NH James Melvin (Hudson, NH)
MELVIN,William AGE:65 6 20   21 Aug 1884 Hudson, NH James Melvin
  & Joanna Melvin
MELZER,Adeline J AGE:46 5   17 Nov 1865 Hudson, NH
MERCHANT,Karl R AGE:33   19 Dec 1958 Hudson, NH
MERCIER,Alfred J AGE:47   21 Feb 1956 Nashua, NH
MERO,Abbie M AGE:89 5 3   06 Oct 1911 Hudson, NH Kenneston & Herd
MERRIFIELD,Kathryn M AGE:62   11 Aug 1980 Manchester, NH
MERRIFIELD,Richard C AGE:35   01 Aug 1975 Hudson, NH
MERRILL,Annie Gertrude AGE:77 5 5   09 Dec 1935 Hudson, NH James B Merrill
  & Persis A Winn
MERRILL,Barsheba Winn AGE:62   12 Sep 1825 Hudson, NH

HUDSON,NH DEATHS

MERRILL,Benjamin AGE: 28 Apr 1756 Hudson, NH Nathaniel Merrill & Elizabeth
MERRILL,Bernice AGE:54   22 16 Feb 1944 Nashua, NH George Swain
    & Ella Clifford
MERRILL,Capt Henry AGE:62 09 Aug 1825 Hudson, NH
MERRILL,Donald K AGE:15 4 6   08 Dec 1918 Hudson, NH James E Merrill
    & Ella S Marble
MERRILL,Elmer L AGE:2 1 12 Jun 1863 Hudson, NH Benjamin A Merrill & Mary J
MERRILL,Emma B AGE:82 8 7 09 Jun 1948 Hudson, NH William F Winn
    & Lucy M Richardson
MERRILL,Etta S AGE:84   14 20 Jan 1942 Hudson, NH Eben B Marble
    & Sarah Jewett
MERRILL,Eva C AGE:83 03 Sep 1961 Hudson, NH
MERRILL,George A AGE:79 2 8 04 Oct 1941 Hudson, NH James B Merrill
    & Persis Winn
MERRILL,George E AGE:53 7 18 13 Oct 1903 Hudson, NH Benj A Merrill
    & Mary J Winn
MERRILL,James B AGE:77 3 09 May 1901 Hudson,NH Benjamin Merrill (Hudson, NH)
MERRILL,James E AGE:76 6 1 28 Dec 1936 Hudson, NH James B Merrill
    & Persis A Merrill
MERRILL,Joseph AGE:66 29 Jun 1872 Hudson, NH
MERRILL,Joseph AGE:66 29 Jan 1873 Hudson, NH
MERRILL,Josie M AGE:87 03 Feb 1977 Nashua, NH
MERRILL,Karl E AGE:53 3 02 Oct 1942 Hudson, NH George A Merrill
    & Sarah E Marble
MERRILL,Lucy A AGE:96 1 21 25 Dec 1932 Hudson, NH Amos A Byam
    & Mary A Bowers
MERRILL,M Louise AGE:62 11 17 09 Nov 1948 Hudson, NH Henry Merrill
MERRILL,Martha J AGE:29 21 Nov 1840 Hudson, NH
MERRILL,Mary AGE:61 16 Jul 1850 Hudson, NH
MERRILL,Mary AGE: 13 Jun 1746 Hudson, NH Nathaniel Merrill & Elizabeth
MERRILL,Mary Jane AGE:49 29 Apr 1874 Hudson, NH
MERRILL,Maurice D AGE:70 06 May 1959 Hudson, NH
MERRILL,Nancy B AGE:87 2 22 Jan 1897 Hudson, NH James Baldwin
    & Priscilla Keyes
MERRILL,Nathan P AGE:21 12 30 Jun 1804 Hudson, NH Capt Henry Merrill
    & Barsheba Winn
MERRILL,Nathaniel AGE:46 16 Oct 1785 Hudson, NH
MERRILL,Olive Lund AGE:79 22 Oct 1820 Hudson, NH
MERRILL,Oliver AGE:47 26 Oct 1826 Hudson, NH
MERRILL,Oliver L AGE:39 25 Sep 1847 Hudson, NH
MERRILL,Persis A AGE:72 6 24 03 Jan 1905 Hudson, NH William Winn
    & Persis G Moore
MERRILL,Samuel AGE:67 14 Mar 1763 Hudson, NH
MERRILL,Samuel Jr AGE: 16 Sep 1758 Hudson, NH
MERRILL,Tamasin AGE: 30 Jan 1755 Hudson, NH
MERRILL,Tamisin AGE:7 28 Oct 1764 Hudson, NH
MERRILL,Thomas AGE:60 9 5 05 Oct 1912 Hudson, NH Richard Merrill
    & Martha J Moses
MERRILL,William G AGE:5 5 11 Aug 1822 Hudson, NH Josiah Merrill & Sally
MERRILL,William T AGE:59 3 21 10 May 1885 Hudson, NH Benjamin Merrill
    (Hudson, NH) & Sarah Plummer (Hudson, NH)
MERRY,Delia AGE:53 3 18 23 Jan 1932 Hudson, NH Oliver Ricard & Arama Dionne
MESSER,Chandler AGE:60 26 Dec 1884 Hudson, NH
MESSIER,Juliet D AGE:87 24 Feb 1982 Hudson, NH
METSIOU,Aneta AGE:3 20 Aug 1921 Hudson, NH Peter Metsiou
    & Panagiota Hatsogio
MEUNIER,Robert E AGE:27 11 18 17 Oct 1931 Hudson, NH Philosime Neunier
    & Eliza Bonnette
MICHAUD,Arsene L AGE:67 15 Sep 1955 Hudson, NH
MICHAUD,Aurele J AGE:38 10 Oct 1949 Nashua, NH Louis Michaud & Marie Meunier

HUDSON,NH DEATHS

MICHAUD,Daniel AGE:6 24 Jul 1970 Hanover, NH
MICHAUD,Marie M AGE:75 19 Apr 1952 Hudson, NH
MICHAUD,Mary A AGE:91 18 May 1973 Hudson, NH
MICHIELS,Eugene P AGE:94 29 Aug 1962 Hudson, NH
MICK,Alexander AGE:86 08 Sep 1976 Hudson, NH
MIESZKINIS,Walter AGE:74 1 20 10 Nov 1947 Nashua, NH Charles Mieszkinis
  & Katherine Badaus
MIGNEAULT,Eugenie AGE:89 06 Nov 1967 Hudson, NH
MIGNEAULT,Maurice Albert AGE:4 15 May 1926 Hudson, NH Maurice Migneault
  & Helen Kinville
MILLER,Ernest J AGE:69 25 Sep 1974 Nashua, NH
MILLER,John F AGE:61   3 31 Dec 1925 Hudson, NH Frank E Miller
  & Angeline Fournier
MILLER,Joseph A AGE:2 4 26 14 Jul 1942 Nashua, NH Joseph Miller
  & Yvonne Provencher
MILLER,Rebecca AGE:60 16 Feb 1872 Hudson, NH
MILLER,William W AGE:81 6 14 Apr 1885 Hudson, NH
MILLETT,Eugene G AGE:78 29 Jan 1962 Hudson, NH
MILLETT,Ina E AGE:28 1 5 16 Dec 1943 Concord, NH Orman S Campbell
  & Harriet Mortlock
MILLETT,Leslie E AGE:5 9 01 Nov 1912 Hudson, NH Eugene Millet
  & Pearl Griswold
MILLETT,Pearl M AGE:66 26 Jun 1951 Nashua, NH
MILLETTE,Alice D AGE:20 16 Apr 1917 Hudson, NH Eugene G Millette
  & Pearl M Griswold
MILLETTE,Evelene S AGE:87 21 Dec 1980 Nashua, NH
MILLS,Arthur W AGE:81 16 Jul 1963 Hudson, NH
MILLS,Winnifred E AGE:84 22 Nov 1978 Hudson, NH
MINER,Louis E AGE:90 03 Jul 1974 Nashua, NH
MINER,Nettie R AGE:79 04 Jul 1959 Hudson, NH
MINER,Peter AGE:43 17 Jan 1961 Haverhill, MA
MINNICK,Edna J AGE:70 30 Jan 1981 Derry, NH
MITCHELL,Minnie L AGE:7 4 3 01 Sep 1917 Hudson, NH Rollins Mitchell
  & Gertrude M Banks
MITCHELL,Peter Roland AGE:53 08 Sep 1984 Hudson, NH
MIZO,[Unknown] AGE: 30 Sep 1943 Hudson, NH Earl C Mizo & Mary Powlowsky
MOISAN,Lillia M AGE:71 2 1 01 Oct 1943 Hudson, NH Flavien Labonte
  & Mary Duclos
MOLKENTINE,[Unknown] AGE:2 hrs 30 Oct 1964 Nashua, NH
MONDOUX,Almanda R AGE:62 06 Apr 1965 Hudson, NH
MONIER,Elizabeth A AGE:72 11 21 21 Jul 1939 Hudson, NH Francois Avard
  & Genevieve Tetrault
MONIER,George AGE:68 20 Nov 1935 Hudson, NH George Monier & Olive Desaurion
MONIER,Julie AGE:59 4 10 03 Nov 1931 Hudson, NH Francos Avard
  & Genevieve Tetreau
MONIER,Theophile AGE:63 18 Jan 1922 Hudson, NH George Monier
  & Olive Bourgouin
MONIER,Thomas F AGE:61 30 Jun 1956 Nashua, NH
MONROE,Eva H L AGE:86 14 Sep 1980 Hudson, NH
MONTGOMERY,Ellen E AGE:77 6 22 25 Dec 1930 Hudson, NH John Ellis
MONTGOMERY,Francis AGE:75 4 17 20 Jan 1929 Hudson, NH John Montgomery
  & Mary Ann Bell
MONTGOMERY,Frank AGE:49 11 08 Jan 1936 Hudson, NH Francis Montgomery
  & Ellen Ellis
MONTGOMERY,Mary A AGE:68 5 4 10 Jan 1948 Hudson, NH Francis Montgomery
  & Ellen Ellis
MOODY,Benjamin F AGE:74 26 Sep 1962 Hudson, NH
MOODY,Elisha AGE:58 12 May 1857 Hudson, NH
MOODY,June AGE:1 12 26 Jul 1909 Hudson, NH John Moody & Minnie Walton
MOODY,Mary E AGE:73 11 May 1962 Manchester, NH

HUDSON,NH DEATHS

MOODY,Orrin P AGE:82   19 Nov 1956 Nashua, NH
MOONEY,Bertha AGE:63   01 Nov 1984 Nashua, NH
MOONEY,James A AGE:58   02 Oct 1978 Nashua, NH
MOONEY,Thomas F AGE:53   07 Dec 1979 Nashua, NH
MOORE,Charles F AGE:86   03 Jul 1984 Hudson, NH
MOORE,Cinderella J AGE:96   06 Aug 1963 Hudson, NH
MOORE,Edwin J AGE:12 11 17   19 May 1911 Hudson, NH Steven Moore
   & Edith Boynton
MOORE,Eugene L AGE:77   09 Oct 1951 Hudson, NH
MOORE,Stephen AGE:49 9 11   14 Jan 1916 Hudson, NH Edward Moore & Laura Tuffs
MOORE,Vesta AGE:86   18 Aug 1979 Milford, NH
MOQUIN,Nellie E AGE:56   21 May 1963 E Derry, NH
MOQUIN,Rose R AGE:71   24 Jun 1968 Nashua, NH
MOREAU,Paul E AGE:49   09 Aug 1967 Nashua, NH
MORENCY,Albina AGE:71   11 Feb 1960 Nashua, NH
MOREY,Adelbart AGE:28 3 16   25 Jul 1915 Hudson, NH Henry Morey (Hudson, NH)
   & J Duchesneau (Canada)
MOREY,Albert J AGE:55 1 3   12 Feb 1944 Hudson, NH Henry Morey
   & Josephine Duchesneau
MOREY,Ernest R AGE:68   24 Mar 1975 Derry, NH
MOREY,Francis F AGE:70   29 Nov 1967 Nashua, NH
MOREY,Josephine AGE:70   30 May 1935 Hudson, NH   Ducharme
MOREY,Roseanna AGE:70   09 Aug 1980 Nashua, NH
MOREY,Samuel S AGE:68   10 Feb 1891 Hudson, NH Samuel Morey (Lowell, MA)
MORGAN,Benton C AGE:82   12 Dec 1972 Nashua, NH
MORGAN,Blanche P AGE:73   12 Jan 1955 Hudson, NH
MORGAN,Mary R AGE:74   25 Dec 1971 Nashua, NH
MORGAN,Newton W AGE:78   01 Apr 1955 Hudson, NH
MORIN,Albert G AGE:53   07 Oct 1954 Hudson, NH
MORIN,Cleophee AGE:83 1 19   01 Sep 1935 Hudson, NH Aug M Trottier
   & Adelaide Ripanit
MORIN,Hattie B AGE:71 2 18   01 Mar 1946 Nashua, NH Charles Henry
   & Eliza J Hoover
MORIN,Marie Anne AGE:92   29 Mar 1982 Hudson, NH
MORIN,Maurice N AGE:29   28 Nov 1961 Hudson, NH
MORIN,Sylvio AGE:61   27 Mar 1964 Hudson, NH
MORIN,William H AGE:3   12 Jan 1951 Hudson, NH
MORISSETTE,Albert J AGE:82   28 Jul 1980 Nashua, NH
MORNEAU,Arthur J AGE:57   21 Mar 1964 Nashua, NH
MORNEAU,Joseph AGE:81   22 Mar 1962 Nashua, NH
MORNEAU,Laura P AGE:82   21 Dec 1964 Hudson, NH
MORRELL,Marguerete AGE:5   15 Mar 1901 Hudson, NH Byron F Morrell
   (Springfield) & Lillian Hunt (Quebec)
MORRILL,Anna A AGE:31   09 Nov 1878 Hudson, NH Solomon Axall & Almira
MORRILL,Arthur E AGE:65   18 Jun 1964 Nashua, NH
MORRILL,Georgia AGE:8   Nov 1878 Hudson, NH George J Morrill & Anna A
MORRILL,Rufus AGE:61   03 Mar 1913 Hudson, NH Not Known & McFadden
MORRIS,Nancy Anna AGE:61 6 24   28 Mar 1928 Hudson, NH   & Isabella Burtt
MORRISON,Achsah A AGE:75 9 2   27 Jun 1893 Hudson, NH Daniel T Davis (Hudson,
   NH) & Susan Robinson (Hudson, NH)
MORRISON,Augustus R AGE:70 7 20   27 Oct 1913 Hudson, NH Samuel Morrison
   & Achsah Davis
MORRISON,Harry A AGE:3   22 Jan 1879 Hudson, NH Augustus R Morrison & Nettie
MORRISON,Helen M AGE:77   09 Sep 1950 Nashua, NH Augustus R Morrison
   & Nettie Thomas
MORRISON,Samuel AGE:80 6 8   13 Sep 1892 Hudson, NH John Morrison (Derry)
   & Jennette Paul (Salem)
MORSE,Hermon AGE:79 11 22   30 Oct 1919 Hudson, NH Nathaniel Morse
   & Matilda Wilson
MORSE,Jennie E AGE:87   01 Aug 1975 Hudson, NH

HUDSON,NH DEATHS

MORSE,Mary E AGE:74   16 May 1917 Hudson, NH John C Caswell & Hannah Caswell
MORSE,Nathaniel M AGE:83   02 Dec 1874 Hudson, NH
MORTLOCK,Walter E AGE:81   11 Mar 1975 Nashua, NH
MORTON,Frank G AGE:37   23 Nov 1951 Nashua, NH
MOTSCHMAN,Alfred F AGE:67   11 Oct 1963 Hudson, NH
MOULTON,Eva L AGE:85   09 Dec 1953 Hudson, NH
MOULTON,Georgia A AGE:59 8   27 Mar 1903 Hudson, NH George E Griffin
  & Susan H Burrill
MOULTON,John R AGE:58 8 16   14 Dec 1902 Hudson, NH Ira Moulton & Mary Griffin
MOVSESIAN,Jannigje AGE:52   23 Mar 1981 Nashua, NH
MUDGETT,Emma J AGE:24 4   23 Oct 1860 Hudson, NH
MUISE,Mary E AGE:38   19 Apr 1984 Nashua, NH
MULHERN,Elsie A AGE:89   26 Mar 1978 Hudson, NH
MULHERN,Harry C AGE:71   29 Aug 1958 Nashua, NH
MUNHALL,Mary AGE:76   21 Aug 1913 Hudson, NH Patrick Caten
MUNROE,David AGE:90 9 3   26 Mar 1941 Hudson, NH John Munroe & Martha
MUNROE,Eliza AGE:84 11 9   10 Aug 1946 Hudson, NH Matthew Robinson
  & Mary Adair
MUNROE,James L AGE:79   13 Aug 1968 Hudson, NH
MUNROE,Mary AGE:71   08 Nov 1964 Nashua, NH
MUNSON,Lynn A AGE:2   05 Nov 1963 Nashua, NH
MUNSON,Willis AGE:49   14 Jun 1949 Nashua, NH Thomas A Munson & Mary Pelletier
MURPHY,Anna J AGE:8   8   1861 Hudson, NH Denis Murphy & Ann
MURPHY,Annie L AGE:8   Hudson, NH
MURPHY,Michael D AGE:68   17 Sep 1954 Hudson, NH
MURRAY,Marguerite F AGE:82   06 May 1974 Nashua, NH
MUSSEY,Abigail AGE:79   19 Feb 1816 Hudson, NH
MYRICK,Cheryl A AGE:7   11 Nov 1971 Nashua, NH
NADEAU,Alcide J AGE:77   22 Mar 1982 Nashua, NH
NADEAU,Andrea A AGE:74   26 Jan 1985 Hudson, NH
NADEAU,Beatrice AGE:68   12 Oct 1974 Nashua, NH
NADEAU,Helen AGE:57   01 Jan 1976 Nashua, NH
NADEAU,Louis AGE:26 1 6   23 Sep 1918 Hudson, NH Louis Nadeau & Olive Lamotte
NADEAU,Lydia Lemieux AGE:79   25 Mar 1979 Nashua, NH
NADEAU,Paul AGE:79   20 May 1978 Nashua, NH
NADEAU,Willard AGE:50   02 Feb 1970 Nashua, NH
NANTEL,Ernest AGE:54   23 Jun 1956 Nashua, NH
NARO,Angeline AGE:69   22 Oct 1969 Nashua, NH
NARO,Henry AGE:70   06 Oct 1964 Hudson, NH
NASH,Jeffrey L AGE:17   03 Aug 1977 Nashua, NH
NEE-BISSETT,Grace King AGE:76   31 Jul 1972 Lowell, MA
NEE-ROY,Blanche Law AGE:80   31 Jul 1972 Lowell, MA
NEEDHAM,Lillian AGE:70   27 Oct 1954 Nashua, NH
NEIER,Charles R AGE:5   08 May 1951 Nashua, NH
NELSON,George Amos AGE:20 11 4   20 Aug 1903 Hudson, NH William Nelson
  & Harriet Batchelder
NELSON,James AGE:48 8 2   19 Jun 1924 Hudson, NH William B Nelson & Not Known
NETTO,Robert W AGE:49   25 Apr 1984 Nashua, NH
NEUFFER,Carl J AGE:67   01 Jun 1969 Manchester, NH
NEUFFER,Elizabeth AGE:52   12 Dec 1972 Nashua, NH
NEWCOMB,Benjamin F AGE:3   21 Feb 1866 Hudson, NH
NEWCOMB,Charles H AGE:85 1 19   14 Nov 1903 Hudson, NH Thomas Newcomb
  & Nancy Hildreth
NEWCOMB,Rebecca AGE:75 6   15 Jul 1891 Hudson, NH William Hadley (Hudson, NH)
  & Rachel Blodgett (Hudson, NH)
NEWCOMB,Rebecca Hadley AGE:75 6   15 Jul 1891 Hudson, NH
NEWELL,Eugene P AGE:67   08 Apr 1980 Nashua, NH
NICHOLLS,Jeanette M AGE:67   10 02 Feb 1929 Hudson, NH
NICHOLS, AGE:3   8   8   27 Sep 1886 Hudson, NH James Nichols
NICHOLS,Anne AGE:47 9 29   24 Apr 1946 Hudson, NH Cyrise Roy & Lydia Cote

HUDSON,NH DEATHS

NICHOLS,Charles L AGE:2 4 9 30 Jan 1888 Hudson, NH Joseph E Nichols (Hollis, NH) & Liona A Griffin (Hudson, NH)
NICHOLS,Charles L AGE:2 4 9 30 Jun 1888 Hudson, NH Joseph Nichols & Lionia A Griffin
NICHOLS,Ensign J AGE:40 17 Jan 1871 Hudson, NH
NICHOLS,Ensign J AGE:46 11 Jan 1871 Hudson, NH
NICHOLS,Etta B AGE:48 7 14 02 Sep 1941 Nashua, NH Andrew J York & Ruth Foss
NICHOLS,Eugene AGE:3 20 Jun 1889 Hudson, NH George Nichols (Hudson, NH) & Maggie E Follen (Nashua, NH)
NICHOLS,Gilman S AGE:73 2 30 26 May 1941 Nashua, NH Edwin Nichols & Elmira Stuart
NICHOLS,Ida L AGE:9 05 May 1869 Hudson, NH W H Nichols
NICHOLS,Julia Anne AGE:1 4 26 05 Jan 1895 Hudson, NH Frank C Nichols (Nashua, NH) & Clara B Smith (Fryeburg, ME)
NICHOLS,Lori E AGE:1 28 Jan 1965 Nashua, NH
NICHOLS,Lucy C AGE:91   1 04 Nov 1922 Hudson, NH John Gilson
NICHOLS,Lydia AGE:3 6 21 13 Nov 1864 Hudson, NH Ensign J Nichols
NICHOLS,Mary AGE:73 07 Jun 1951 Concord, NH
NICHOLS,Philip F AGE:61 4 27 11 Oct 1901 Hudson, NH A Nichols (Lawrence, MA) & Almira W Smith
NICHOLS,Ramon Ernest AGE:53 20 Aug 1980 Nashua, NH
NICHOLS,Walter E AGE:3 8 8 27 Sep 1886 Hudson, NH
NIXON,Lena C AGE:77 20 Apr 1980 Hudson, NH
NOAKES,Esther R AGE:50 31 Jan 1979 Nashua, NH
NOEL,Alfred E AGE:51 28 Apr 1962 Nashua, NH
NOEL,Alice E AGE:49 27 Jun 1967 Nashua, NH
NOEL,Marie AGE:71 17 Aug 1950 Nashua, NH Urbin Pelletier & Arthemise Ouellette
NOEL,Peter AGE:76 19 Sep 1956 Hudson, NH
NOKES,Frederick A AGE:77 01 Jan 1950 Nashua, NH Riley Nokes & Hannah Rouse
NOLAN,Edmund F AGE:7 3 08 Aug 1903 Hudson, NH James J Nolan & Bridget Ward
NOLETTE,Oscar AGE:81 13 Jun 1964 Hudson, NH
NOLIN,Vina E AGE:100 28 Apr 1985 Nashua, NH
NOONAN,Winslow J AGE:65 5 6 09 Apr 1939 Hudson, NH David Noonan & Belinda Joy
NORMAN,George A G AGE:2 3 30 Dec 1893 Hudson, NH Louis P Norman (Canada) & Josephine Miller (S Village, VT)
NORMAND,Joseph AGE:18 Sep 1902 Hudson, NH Paul Normand & Josephine Desnoulin
NORMAND,Marie C A AGE:7 8 20 Mar 1901 Hudson, NH John Normand (Canada) & Angelina Boulette (Canada)
NORMAND,Marie I AGE:5 10 21 Jul 1904 Hudson, NH Paul Normand & Josephine Desnoulin
NORMAND,Rudolph P AGE:40 10 Aug 1950 Hudson, NH Joseph Vignola & Elmira Normand
NORMANDEAU,Mary AGE:81 24 Feb 1958 Hudson, NH
NORRIS,John AGE:1 16 27 Oct 1909 Hudson, NH John Norris
NOURY,Rose A AGE:70 28 Sep 1954 Hudson, NH
NOWAK,Helena AGE:57 22 Dec 1973 Nashua, NH
NOYES,Flora AGE:2 hrs 17 Aug 1916 Hudson, NH Joel Noyes & Anna Morris
NOYES,Harrison H AGE:50 31 Mar 1972 Nashua, NH
NUTE,Frank L AGE:63 30 Apr 1977 Nashua, NH
NUTE,Frank W AGE:24 8 4 06 Dec 1914 Hudson, NH Frank W Nute & Etta M Godon
NUTE,Melba K AGE:68 22 Feb 1983 Nashua, NH
NUTTING,Bernice T AGE:83 11 Mar 1970 Nashua, NH
NUTTING,Florence T AGE:88 15 Apr 1985 Nashua, NH
NUTTING,Frank A AGE:81 15 Oct 1959 Hudson, NH
NUTTING,George F AGE:76 10 Jun 1949 Nashua, NH Charles Nutting & Jennie Manley
NUTTING,John F AGE:88 13 May 1951 Hudson, NH
NUTTING,Kathleen E AGE:92 10 2 27 Jul 1945 Hudson, NH Freeman Elliott & Harriette Scripture

HUDSON, NH DEATHS

NUTTING, Mary AGE:93 03 Dec 1966 Nashua, NH
NUTTON, Cedric AGE:73 16 Dec 1970 West Haven, CT
O'BLENIS, Minnie S AGE:70 4 18 12 Jan 1947 Nashua, NH Charles Fowler
 & Alvina Steve
O'BRIEN, [Unknown] AGE: 24 Sep 1920 Hudson, NH George A O'Brien
 & Mary Abberton
O'CONNELL, Daniel AGE:88 27 Dec 1980 Milford, NH
O'NEAL, James W AGE:3 05 Aug 1956 Nashua, NH
O'NEIL, Alfred AGE:70 18 May 1985 Hudson, NH
O'NEIL, Bessie H AGE:79 15 Jan 1975 Nashua, NH
O'NEIL, James H AGE:45 1 5 15 Jul 1937 Hudson, NH Dennis O'Neil & Mary O'Shea
O'NEIL, Jeremiah AGE:24 26 Jun 1925 Hudson, NH Jeremiah O'Neil
 & Margaret Healey
O'NEIL, Jeremiah J AGE:76 29 Sep 1943 Hudson, NH Timothy O'Neil
 & Margaret Haley
O'NEIL, Lucy A AGE:85 20 Mar 1974 Nashua, NH
O'NEIL, Lucy B AGE:79 5 4 27 Mar 1947 Nashua, NH John Buckley & Lucy Keegan
O'NEIL, Slyvia N AGE:71 10 15 13 Nov 1939 Hudson, NH Sherman A Corney
 & Sarah E Hollister
O'NEIL, Timothy AGE:54 26 Dec 1881 Hudson, NH Jerry O'Neil & Bridgett Shea
O'NEIL, Timothy Joseph AGE:46 11 16 31 Jul 1936 Hudson, NH Jeremiah J O'Neil
 & Lucy Buckley
O'NEILL, Francis C AGE:65 12 May 1985 Nashua, NH
OAKES, Lucille AGE:61 23 Feb 1972 Hudson, NH
OBER, Andrew Morse AGE:81 5 17 29 May 1936 Hudson, NH Phillip Ober
 & Elizabeth Herrick
OBIN, Eva C AGE:85 07 Jun 1984 Hudson, NH
OBIN, Louis AGE:86 2 27 30 Jun 1936 Hudson, NH Benjamin Obin
OGINSKIS, Barbara V AGE:88 19 Dec 1950 Hudson, NH Constantine Martin
 & Ursula Martin
OIKLE, Lawson E AGE:82 09 Nov 1983 Nashua, NH
OLENA, William J AGE:77 31 May 1964 Nashua, NH
OLSON, Albertine AGE:84 25 Feb 1981 Hudson, NH
ORDWAY, Ira J AGE:90 11 Apr 1952 Hudson, NH
ORNE, Thomas J AGE:83 4 8 16 Sep 1920 Hudson, NH
OSGOOD, Hannah M AGE:51 7 19 29 Apr 1894 Hudson, NH Benjamin Parker (Boston)
 & Mary Miller (Boston)
OSGOOD, Josephine B AGE:59 6 10 02 Sep 1905 Hudson, NH Jonathan B Foss
 & Hannah Coombs
OSGOOD, Matilda AGE:75 1 21 26 Dec 1917 Hudson, NH Frederick Danson
 & Eunice Wallace
OTIS, Nettie M AGE:88 13 Oct 1968 Nashua, NH
OTIS, Philip AGE:77 08 Oct 1970 Nashua, NH
OTTMAN, Alvin H AGE:83 21 May 1957 Hudson, NH
OTTMAN, Blanche E AGE:69 20 Feb 1958 Nashua, NH
OUELLETTE, Jane C AGE:44 23 Jun 1978 Nashua, NH
OUELLETTE, Raymonde B AGE:55 05 Aug 1960 Hudson, NH
OUELLETTE, Rose E AGE:64 09 Jan 1975 Nashua, NH
OUTHOUSE, Dutcher W AGE:67 14 Sep 1955 Nashua, NH
OVASKA, Otis G AGE:59 15 Dec 1972 Nashua, NH
OWEN, Minnie J AGE:73 5 13 11 Oct 1938 Hudson, NH William Chase & Sophia Chase
PAGE, Abraham AGE:69 01 Mar 1752 Hudson, NH
PAGE, Capt Abraham AGE:86 11 27 18 Apr 1802 Hudson, NH
PAGE, Elizabeth AGE:68 06 Mar 1782 Hudson, NH
PAGE, Elvina C AGE:79 8 9 13 May 1914 Hudson, NH Timothy Peaslee & Martha Bean
PAGE, Esther AGE:28 30 Jul 1751 Hudson, NH
PAGE, Georgie W AGE:17 15 08 Aug 1894 Hudson, NH W H Page (Manchester)
 & L A Coran (Canada)
PAGE, Judith AGE:75 23 Jul 1759 Hudson, NH
PAIGE, George S AGE:79 18 Nov 1979 Milford, NH

HUDSON,NH DEATHS

PAINE,Franklin T Sr AGE:74 01 Nov 1976 Nashua, NH
PAINE,Hannah AGE:79 9 16 Sep 1884 Hudson, NH
PAINE,Johnson AGE:70 02 Oct 1868 Hudson, NH
PAINE,Mildred I AGE:61 08 Nov 1964 Nashua, NH
PALANSKI,Karolina AGE:85 27 Apr 1983 Nashua, NH
PALEOSELITI,Sofia AGE:64 22 Nov 1953 Nashua, NH
PALLAK,Robert AGE:3 3 23 Oct 1927 Hudson, NH Simon Pallak & Theodora Pasek
PALMER,Abigail Pollard AGE:82 07 Apr 1881 Hudson, NH
PALMER,Abigail W AGE:82 5 7 07 Apr 1882 Hudson, NH Abel Pollard
  & Abigail Hills
PALMER,Freedom Maria AGE:79 6 15 24 Jul 1930 Hudson, NH
PALMER,James T AGE:52 16 Sep 1857 Hudson, NH
PALMER,John M AGE:46 9 11 13 May 1902 Hudson, NH Arthur Palmer& E Herleylight
PALMER,Lizzie AGE:48 17 Aug 1880 Hudson, NH James T Palmer & Abigail
PALMER,Ruby E AGE:29 7 21 28 Jun 1930 Hudson, NH Daniel A Potter& Clara Locke
PANAGEOTES,Alexander K AGE:48 23 Jun 1970 Hudson, NH
PANAGOULIS,George P AGE:90 10 Jan 1962 Nashua, NH
PANAGOULIS,Helen AGE:82 07 Apr 1960 Nashua, NH
PANKO,Walter AGE:66 26 Mar 1980 Manchester, NH
PAPOGIANIS,Christos AGE:68 15 Sep 1957 Hudson, NH
PAPPE,Elsie N AGE:81 16 Feb 1978 Nashua, NH
PAQUETTE,Agnes AGE:87 09 Feb 1980 Nashua, NH
PAQUETTE,William AGE:14 23 Jan 1969 Hudson, NH
PAQUETTE,Wilmer A AGE:78 28 Aug 1981 Nashua, NH
PAQUIN,Edmond E AGE:42 12 Sep 1973 Manchester, NH
PARADIS,Achille E AGE:56 06 Sep 1963 Hudson, NH
PARADIS,Louis AGE:71 19 Aug 1958 Hudson, NH
PARADISE,Armand L AGE:54 19 Feb 1968 Nashua, NH
PARADISE,Jacqueline J AGE:23 26 May 1963 Nashua, NH
PARADISE,Laura M AGE:80 04 Jun 1969 Nashua, NH
PARADISE,Victor AGE:57 04 Mar 1967 Nashua, NH
PARENT,Belanise AGE:84 23 Jul 1959 Nashua, NH
PARENT,Bruno F AGE:78 7 6 27 Nov 1948 Hudson, NH Felix Parent
  & Elide Pelissier
PARENT, Marie-Louise,Sr St Richard AGE:62 10 Oct 1958 Lowell, MA
PARIS,Ella J AGE:89 23 Jan 1972 Nashua, NH
PARISEAU,Germaine L AGE:82 08 Apr 1983 Nashua, NH
PARK,Emma AGE:97 18 Mar 1962 Hudson, NH
PARKER,Alonzo N AGE:62 9   Hudson, NH
PARKER,Charles C AGE:84 5 30 19 Nov 1936 Hudson, NH Rev L W Parker
  & Hannah Wyman
PARKER,Erich L AGE:70 12 Aug 1979 Nashua, NH
PARKER,Ernest J AGE:14 10 28 15 Jul 1898 Hudson, NH C C Parker
  & Lydia L Batchelder
PARKER,Florence L AGE:78 19 Feb 1977 Nashua, NH
PARKER,Frances J AGE:66 1 27 Jul 1898 Hudson, NH Joseph Brackett
  & Eliza W Brackett
PARKER,George H Sr AGE:69   15 16 Nov 1948 Nashua, NH Charles C Parker
  & Lydia Batchelder
PARKER,Georgie AGE:40 6 15 06 Apr 1920 Hudson, NH John Boynton
  & Frances E Haskill
PARKER,Hannah J AGE:88 7 8 26 Jun 1909 Hudson, NH Wyman
PARKER,Harriet L AGE:78 06 Jun 1889 Hudson, NH Obediah Richardson (Dracut,
  MA) & Rhoda Haselton (Dracut, MA)
PARKER,Isabella F AGE:71 06 Dec 1976 Nashua, NH
PARKER,John AGE:60 7 2 23 Jan 1907 Hudson, NH Edward Parker & Mary Kendall
PARKER,Joseph AGE:70 01 Mar 1865 Hudson, NH
PARKER,Julia AGE:92 6 17 04 May 1894 Hudson, NH Chase
PARKER,Laurens AGE:29 05 Aug 1853 Hudson, NH
PARKER,Lydia Low AGE:75   3 10 May 1927 Hudson, NH Mark Batchelder

HUDSON,NH DEATHS

& Lydia Steele
PARKER,Martha A AGE:90 10 18 07 Dec 1920 Hudson, NH Abel B Parker
   & Martha W Evans
PARKER,Retire H AGE:53 7 13 Aug 1893 Hudson, NH Retire H Parker (Greenland,
   MA) & Hannah Chase (Hampton Falls)
PARKER,Ruby Lydia AGE:19   26 07 Jan 1923 Hudson, NH Clarence C Parker
   & Hattie Robinson
PARKER,Susan Helen AGE:71 7 20 27 May 1937 Hudson, NH George W Marshall
   & Merinda Hadley
PARKINSON,Herbert J AGE:6 4 17 Sep 1887 Hudson, NH John Parkinson (Ireland)
   & Amelia Groves (Ireland)
PARMENTER,Lizzie H AGE:80 19 Nov 1909 Hudson, NH Jeremiah P Davis
   & Hannah McCainne
PARR,Michael W AGE:13 hrs 16 Aug 1953 Nashua, NH
PASKALI,Louis AGE:75 20 Apr 1984 Derry, NH
PATCH,Cora W AGE:90 01 Jan 1964 Hudson, NH
PATENAUDE,Beatrice AGE:3 12 02 Mar 1918 Hudson, NH Arthur Patenaude
   & Georgie E Thompson
PATON,Francis A AGE:43 28 Aug 1950 Nashua, NH Frank F Paton & Emma M Paton
PAUL,J Amedee AGE:68 05 Oct 1960 Hudson, NH
PAYNE,Rosetta M AGE:65   26 05 Aug 1917 Hudson, NH William Austin
   & Mary J Anderson
PEACH,Earnest C AGE:10 26 Jul 1887 Hudson, NH William Peach (Salem, MA)
   & Dora B Fuller (Danvers, MA)
PEACH,Ernest C AGE:10 26 Jul 1887 Hudson, NH William Peach
PEARSON,Bertha AGE:84 25 Apr 1973 Hudson, NH
PEASE,Bartlett AGE:84 02 Feb 1874 Hudson, NH
PEASE,Nelson H AGE:75 6 29 12 Aug 1925 Hudson, NH Chauncy O Pease
   & Arvilla Adams
PEASE,William G AGE:2 2 27 May 1835 Hudson, NH Bartlett Pease
PEASLEE,Ivy J AGE:47 3 11 22 Sep 1927 Hudson, NH Robert M Harris
   & Elizabeth McKay
PECK,Joseph AGE: 09 May 1908 Hudson, NH C T Peck & E M Greeley
PELKEY,Alice AGE:92 05 Apr 1981 Hudson, NH
PELKEY,Charles O AGE:76 01 Jul 1970 Nashua, NH
PELLERIN,Camille J AGE:73 09 Mar 1980 Nashua, NH
PELLERIN,Lena Yvonne AGE:73 13 Mar 1980 Nashua, NH
PELLETIER,Blanche A AGE:78 02 Feb 1977 Hudson, NH
PELLETIER,Caroline A AGE:77 21 Dec 1978 Hudson, NH
PELLETIER,Delvina AGE:91 05 Jun 1969 Hudson, NH
PELLETIER,Joseph L AGE:70 17 Sep 1956 Nashua, NH
PELLETIER,Josephine AGE:70 17 Nov 1961 Nashua, NH
PELLETIER,Louis AGE:79 24 Dec 1982 Nashua, NH
PELLETIER,Marguerite AGE:77 26 Oct 1969 Nashua, NH
PELLETIER,Medar AGE:75 4 29 10 Jun 1944 Hudson, NH Joseph Pelletier
   & Blanche Pelletier
PELLETIER,Napoleon AGE:68 22 Jun 1957 Hudson, NH
PELLETIER,Omer J AGE:70 31 Oct 1957 Hudson, NH
PELLETIER,Raymond L AGE:7 08 Aug 1960 Nashua, NH
PELLETIER,Stella V AGE:58 28 Dec 1967 Nashua, NH
PELLETIER,Woodrow J AGE:7 12 09 Apr 1941 Nashua, NH Woodrow Pelletier
   & Anne Jazukevich
PELTIER,John B AGE:65 1 17 12 Apr 1937 Hudson, NH Joseph Peltier
   & Del Sausackagrin
PENNO,Arthur AGE:42 04 Jul 1983 Nashua, NH
PEPIN,Elmire AGE:91 20 Apr 1982 Hudson, NH
PERHAM,Edith B AGE:76 9 1 09 Sep 1947 Hudson, NH Foster Perham
   & Margaret Burbank
PERHAM,George A AGE:70 9 24 17 Apr 1931 Hudson, NH Willard M Perham
   & Susan Clark

HUDSON,NH DEATHS

PERHAM,Lorinda A AGE:49 7 3   17 Aug 1907 Hudson, NH John Boucher & Peltier
PERKINS,Annie Hayden AGE:69   12 Jan 1934 Hudson, NH Thomas Hayden
  & Mary Hayden
PERKINS,Annie Madeline AGE:5 9 9   19 Apr 1923 Hudson, NH John H Perkins
  & Marion Hazel Sanders
PERKINS,Arthur H AGE:5 3 6   01 Nov 1904 Hudson, NH S N Perkins & Annie Hayden
PERKINS,David B AGE:44   10 Apr 1980 Nashua, NH
PERKINS,Ernest E AGE:75 3 13   09 Aug 1941 Nashua, NH James Perkins
  & Levina Murray
PERKINS,Ida C AGE:52 11   08 Mar 1899 Hudson, NH Henry Smith & Mary Barker
PERKINS,John D AGE:84   29 Aug 1972 Nashua, NH
PERKINS,Shirley H AGE:2 2   04 Dec 1922 Hudson, NH Herbert S Perkins
  & Mary E Sherburn
PERKINS,Sumner N AGE:78 7 20   14 May 1939 Hudson, NH John Perkins
PERREAULT,Alphonsine AGE:65 9 14   26 May 1927 Hudson, NH Charles Soucy
  & Vitaline Bernier
PERRON,Daniel R AGE:31   23 Jun 1985 Exeter, NH
PERRY,Flora M AGE:80   04 Nov 1968 Nashua, NH
PERRY,Lurana AGE:59   03 Mar 1843 Hudson, NH
PERRY,Walter C AGE:71   24 Jul 1959 Nashua, NH
PETERS,Dale M AGE:28   28 Nov 1972 Manchester, NH
PETERSON,Albin AGE:62 2 6   27 Dec 1919 Hudson, NH Adolph Peterson
  & Christen Anderson
PETERSON,Gustave AGE:63 6 13   14 Dec 1918 Hudson, NH Olaf Peterson
  & Christine Anderson
PETERSON,Patricia L AGE:33   13 Oct 1976 Nashua, NH
PETRAIN,Donald S AGE:37   30 Sep 1977 Nashua, NH
PETRAIN,Ovide AGE:72 6 5   16 Sep 1940 Hudson, NH Joseph Petrain
  & Olive Perusse
PETTEE,Josie F AGE:98   27 Jul 1962 Hudson, NH
PETTEE,Walter F AGE:84 10 8   06 Apr 1947 Hudson, NH George F Pettee
  & Margianna Hardy
PETTS,Edith G AGE:69   25 Feb 1951 Nashua, NH
PHELAND,Grace J AGE:75   23 27 Jun 1947 Nashua, NH Dwelley Simpson
  & Ida Tabor
PHELPS,Francis H AGE:61 9 17   01 Jul 1926 Hudson, NH Syries Strang
PHELPS,Rhoda H AGE:83   25 Apr 1872 Hudson, NH
PHILBRICK,Roanah E AGE:47 10 4   21 Jun 1902 Hudson, NH D D Hayward
  & Roanah Fisher
PHILIPS,Dolly AGE:86   Oct 1867 Hudson, NH
PHILLIPS,Anna B AGE:52 11 10   01 May 1922 Hudson, NH Lenada Blodget
  & Lydia Holbrook
PHILLIPS,Dolly AGE:86   Oct 1867 Hudson, NH
PHILLIPS,Edna J AGE:79   30 Jan 1985 Hudson, NH
PHILLIPS,James A AGE:62 7 25   19 Apr 1928 Hudson, NH Thomas Phillips
  & Matthenson
PHILLIPS,Lauretta L AGE:91 3 15   08 Oct 1933 Hudson, NH F O Kittredge
  & Mary Ann Kittredge
PHINNEY,Walter E AGE:67   01 Jul 1951 Hudson, NH
PIATEK,Karolina W AGE:87   26 Nov 1971 Nashua, NH
PIERCE,Abraham AGE:5   18 Mar 1801 Hudson, NH Joshua Pierce & Sarah Lund
PIERCE,Belinda AGE:66   15 Mar 1860 Hudson, NH
PIERCE,Belinda Crop AGE:66 8   15 Mar 1861 Hudson, NH
PIERCE,Bernice M AGE:83   12 Sep 1981 Hudson, NH
PIERCE,Charles R AGE:33   10 Nov 1982 Londonderry, NH
PIERCE,Cosmo SEX: AGE:17   28 Feb 1804 Hudson, NH Joshua Pierce & Sarah Lund
PIERCE,Cosmo L AGE:1 1   07 Sep 1834 Hudson, NH James Pierce & Belinda Crop
PIERCE,Dolly AGE:35   25 Sep 1825 Hudson, NH
PIERCE,Esther AGE:92   01 Jun 1819 Hudson, NH
PIERCE,Gertrude AGE:41   02 Aug 1967 Nashua, NH

HUDSON,NH DEATHS

PIERCE,Isaac AGE:18   24 Nov 1798 Hudson, NH Joshua Pierce & Sarah Lund
PIERCE,James AGE:78 11   10 May 1871 Hudson, NH
PIERCE,John AGE:40   11 Nov 1825 Hudson, NH
PIERCE,John P AGE:36   03 Nov 1864 Hudson, NH
PIERCE,John P AGE:35   08 Nov 1864 Hudson, NH
PIERCE,Joshua AGE:49   13 Feb 1771 Hudson, NH
PIERCE,Joshua AGE:101   25 Sep 1857 Hudson, NH
PIERCE,Joshua AGE:1   10 Mar 1785 Hudson, NH Joshua Pierce & Sarah Lund
PIERCE,Joshua AGE:38   16 Sep 1825 Hudson, NH
PIERCE,Martha Chase AGE:27 9   03 Apr 1863 Hudson, NH
PIERCE,Martha E AGE:27   03 Apr 1863 Hudson, NH
PIERCE,Nancy T AGE:17   08 Aug 1847 Hudson, NH James Pierce & Belinda Crop
PIERCE,Sarah Lund AGE:88   20 Oct 1851 Hudson, NH
PIETUCK,Amelia AGE:70   11 Jul 1963 Goffstown, NH
PIKE,Maude L AGE:95   14 Mar 1975 Hudson, NH
PINEAULT,Roseanna R AGE:73   25 Apr 1951 Nashua, NH
PINETTE,Alfred AGE:71   02 Jun 1952 Hudson, NH
PINETTE,Lionel AGE:56   10 Jun 1980 Nashua, NH
PITFIELD,Dorothy E AGE:70   09 May 1980 Nashua, NH
PLATT,Joseph L AGE:9   20 May 1962 Hudson, NH
PLESS,George J AGE:48   11 May 1976 Hudson, NH
PLOURDE,Blanche AGE:68   11 Mar 1963 Nashua, NH
PLOURDE,Gerard N AGE:23 8 28   27 May 1946 Hudson, NH Amedee Plourde
   & Juliette Gagnon
PLOURDE,Horace J AGE:63   13 Nov 1961 Nashua, NH
PLUMLEY,Harold A AGE:47   05 May 1982 Nashua, NH
PLUMLEY,Rebecca A AGE:5   16 Jan 1968 Lowell, MA
PLUMMER,Fred Danford AGE:63 4 26   11 Nov 1935 Hudson, NH Martin B Plummer
   & Ellen Louise Cook
POFF,Francis H AGE:87   05 May 1905 Hudson, NH Francis Poff & Johanna Hoffman
POFF,Jane Kate AGE: 1865 Hudson, NH
POFF,Jane Kate AGE: 1863 Hudson, NH
POFF,Mary Jane AGE:81 9   12 Feb 1909 Hudson, NH Sargent
POFF,Peter AGE:71 2 19   26 Apr 1890 Hudson, NH John Poff (Ireland)
   & Ann Groves (Ireland)
POFF,Sylvester AGE:18   15 Mar 1867 Hudson, NH
POIRIER,Edgar G AGE:58   06 Sep 1964 Hudson, NH
POITRAS,Lilia AGE:92   16 Feb 1952 Hudson, NH
POLAK,Syzmon AGE:79   01 May 1972 Nashua, NH
POLAK,Teodora AGE:60   08 May 1954 Hudson, NH
POLAK,[Unknown] AGE: 06 Nov 1929 Hudson, NH Simon Polak & Theodora Pasek
POLIQUIN,Jane E AGE:67   08 Jun 1972 Nashua, NH
POLKEY,Deborah C AGE:3   17 Mar 1980 Nashua, NH
POLLARD,Abel AGE:80 9   02 Nov 1853 Hudson, NH
POLLARD,Abigail AGE:75   11 Oct 1802 Hudson, NH
POLLARD,Abigail AGE:75   17 Mar 1850 Hudson, NH
POLLARD,Agnes A AGE:4   14 Feb 1871 Hudson, NH
POLLARD,Ann AGE: 19 Jun 1751 Hudson, NH
POLLARD,Asa AGE:37   15 Jul 1805 Hudson, NH
POLLARD,Betsey AGE:42   02 Jun 1822 Hudson, NH
POLLARD,Calvin AGE:66 9 15   21 Apr 1871 Hudson, NH
POLLARD,Calvin AGE:67   24 Apr 1871 Hudson, NH
POLLARD,Cora M AGE:65   22   12 Feb 1941 Concord, NH Charles Cooper
   & Leah Barnard
POLLARD,Daniel T AGE:44   22 Jun 1836 Hudson, NH
POLLARD,Dorcas AGE: 07 Sep 1736 Hudson, NH Thomas Pollard & Mary
POLLARD,Dorkis AGE: 07 Sep 1736 Hudson, NH Thomas Pollard & Mary
POLLARD,Eben AGE:76   20 May 1803 Hudson, NH
POLLARD,Ebenezer AGE:65   14 Mar 1827 Hudson, NH
POLLARD,Ebenezer AGE:66   03 Oct 1866 Hudson, NH

HUDSON,NH DEATHS

POLLARD,Eliza AGE:42 11 12 Jan 1854 Hudson, NH Abel Pollard & Abigail
POLLARD,Elvira O AGE:28 02 Oct 1870 Hudson, NH
POLLARD,Forrest A AGE:18 3 6 05 Apr 1891 Hudson, NH Joseph Pollard (Hudson, NH) & Emily Bemis (Barton, VT)
POLLARD,Hannah AGE:17 20 Dec 1814 Hudson, NH Abel Pollard & Abigail
POLLARD,Hannah D AGE:17 7 20 Dec 1814 Hudson, NH Abel Pollard & Abigail
POLLARD,John AGE:75 17 Dec 1827 Hudson, NH
POLLARD,Joseph AGE:64 03 Feb 1898 Hudson, NH Eben Pollard & Mehitable Davis
POLLARD,Joseph AGE:40 17 Feb 1821 Hudson, NH
POLLARD,Luther AGE:91 9 30 Aug 1898 Hudson, NH Abel Pollard & Abigail Hills
POLLARD,Marian AGE:43 15 Nov 1832 Hudson, NH
POLLARD,Martha AGE:93 8 25 09 Sep 1911 Hudson, NH Abel Pollard & Abigail Hills
POLLARD,Martha E AGE:55 6 29 Mar 1899 Hudson, NH   & Martha Pollard
POLLARD,Mary AGE:81 11 19 Dec 1894 Hudson, NH
POLLARD,Mary AGE: 24 Aug 1753 Hudson, NH Thomas Pollard & Mary
POLLARD,Mehitable AGE:86 11 09 Sep 1891 Hudson, NH Samuel Davis (Salem, MA) & Ann Morse
POLLARD,Mehittabel Davis AGE:86 11 09 Sep 1891 Hudson, NH
POLLARD,Raymond J AGE:93 28 Nov 1971 Nashua, NH
POLLARD,Sarah AGE:80 14 Jan 1836 Hudson, NH
POLLARD,Susan AGE:79 14 Feb 1844 Hudson, NH
POLLARD,Susanna AGE:45 25 Jun 1816 Hudson, NH
POLLARD,Thomas AGE: 23 Jul 1769 Hudson, NH
POLLARD,Thomas Jr AGE: 18 May 1756 Hudson, NH Thomas Pollard & Mary
POLMATIER,Aimee L AGE:85 15 Nov 1967 Nashua, NH
POMBRIO,Anna R AGE:84 29 Apr 1967 Hudson, NH
POMEROY,Cynthia Woodman AGE:75 6 12 05 Dec 1888 Hudson, NH
POMEROY,Roland T AGE:79 2 16 09 Dec 1888 Hudson, NH
POMROY,Cynthia W AGE:75 6 12 05 Dec 1888 Hudson, NH Nathaniel Woodman (Frankfort, ME) & Martha Stevens (N Gloucester)
POMROY,Roland T AGE:79 2 16 09 Dec 1888 Hudson, NH Joseph Pomroy (Hermon, ME) & Susana Luce (Hermon, ME)
POND,Anna M AGE:75 13 Apr 1961 Hudson, NH
POND,Mary E AGE:80 09 Aug 1960 Nashua, NH
POND,Sidney AGE:79 27 Jan 1953 Nashua, NH
POPE,Delia L AGE:83 14 Apr 1949 Nashua, NH Edward La Fay & Mary Vincent
POPE,Eaton H AGE:66 11 22 19 Oct 1940 Hudson, NH Willard Pope & Luvie McCoy
POPER,Jean AGE:37 25 Jan 1977 Nashua, NH
PORTER,Alvin L AGE:74 18 Oct 1968 Nashua, NH
PORTER,Debra L AGE:4 07 Nov 1956 Hudson, NH
PORTER,Edward W Sr AGE:64 18 Mar 1967 Nashua, NH
PORTER,Rosella B AGE:67 11 27 01 Apr 1943 Nashua, NH Joseph Boury & Elizabeth Cummings
POSNER,Max AGE:74 6 17 May 1947 Hudson, NH Charles Posner & Helena Greenberg
POST,Morillo E AGE:48 17 Oct 1961 Nashua, NH
POTTER,Walter A AGE:75 10 Sep 1957 Nashua, NH
POWELL,Dorance AGE:3 10 21 Dec 1840 Hudson, NH Samuel D Powell & Mary A
POWELL,Samuel D AGE:28 03 Apr 1839 Hudson, NH
POWERS,Frances AGE:36 05 Jan 1967 Nashua, NH
POWLOUSKI,Anthony AGE:63 01 Nov 1932 Hudson, NH Natashua Lakaska (Habmel Powlouski)
POWLOWSKY,John AGE:62 04 Aug 1979 Nashua, NH
POWLOWSKY,Nancy AGE:72 04 Apr 1953 Hudson, NH
POWLOWSKY,Peter AGE:51 23 Jun 1973 Nashua, NH
PRATT,Archie AGE:71 03 Aug 1956 Hudson, NH
PRATT,Dana C Jr AGE:3 15 Dec 1949 Hudson, NH Dana C Pratt & Priscilla Luty
PRATT,George Albert AGE:54 2 01 Jan 1927 Hudson, NH
PRATT,Lillian M AGE:67 11 23 05 Nov 1946 Nashua, NH Louis Wade & Augusta Wade

HUDSON,NH DEATHS

PRATT,Robert M AGE:50 1 24 02 Apr 1945 Hudson, NH Fred Pratt & Martha Pratt
PRAY,Emerson D AGE:45 22 Feb 1954 Hudson, NH
PRESTON,Margaret AGE: 28 May 1893 Hudson, NH John Whittie (England)
PRESTON,William H Jr AGE:33 29 Sep 1983 Nashua, NH
PREVOST,Frank J AGE:58 8 9 07 Jul 1946 Hudson, NH Henry Prevost
 & Marguerite Caron
PRIMUS,Robert Jr AGE:1 9 08 Jan 1948 Hudson, NH Robert Primus, Sr
 & Shirley Greenleaf
PRISKE,Maude J AGE:89 20 Jul 1974 Nashua, NH
PROCTOR,[Unknown] AGE: 28 Mar 1815 Hudson, NH James Proctor & Esther
PROCTOR,Elizabeth AGE:48 29 May 1837 Hudson, NH
PROCTOR,Esther AGE:48 17 Feb 1828 Hudson, NH
PROCTOR,Esther W G AGE:4 05 Aug 1825 Hudson, NH James Proctor & Esther
PROCTOR,Eunice AGE:4 08 Jul 1812 Hudson, NH James Proctor & Esther
PROCTOR,Lydia AGE:11 31 Mar 1821 Hudson, NH James Proctor & Esther
PROCTOR,Susan H AGE:7 6 21 Jun 1830 Boston, MA James Proctor & Esther
PROULX,Antoine J AGE:52 07 Mar 1964 Hudson, NH
PROULX, Alma,Sr Marie Louis-Elzea AGE:62 09 Mar 1955 Hudson, NH
PROVENCAL,George J AGE:70 12 Jul 1965 Nashua, NH
PROVENCAL,Margaret AGE:75 06 Dec 1982 Nashua, NH
PROVENCAL,Marie B AGE:53 11 Jul 1951 Hudson, NH
PROVENCAL,Paul E AGE:54 28 Nov 1969 Derry, NH
PROVENCAL,Robert R AGE:63 29 Aug 1984 Wolfeboro, NH
PROVENCAL,Roger AGE:20 16 Apr 1972 Hudson, NH
PUEZ,Jacob AGE:76 27 Apr 1965 Hudson, NH
PURINGTON,Jacquine N AGE:39 19 Jun 1978 Nashua, NH
PUSKUNIGAS,Agate AGE:78 04 Feb 1937 Hudson, NH
PUTIS,Mary AGE:47 04 May 1945 Nashua, NH Thomas Yesicavitch & Anna Kashata
PUTIS,Michael AGE:65 27 May 1953 Hudson, NH
PUTNAM,Edna H AGE:81 24 Jan 1898 Hudson, NH David Saunders & Sophie Greeley
PUTNAM,Elizabeth H AGE:30 18 Sep 1873 Hudson, NH
PUTNAM,John P AGE:82 5 23 31 Jan 1894 Hudson, NH Porter Putnam (Danvers)
 & Sally Tapley (Danvers)
PUTNAM,Sarah F H AGE:9 07 Feb 1861 Hudson, NH
PUTNAM,Sarah T H AGE:9 8 07 Feb 1861 Hudson, NH
PUTRICK,Jerzey AGE:40 13 Jun 1931 Hudson, NH Jerzey Putrick
QUIGLEY,David G AGE:19 03 Dec 1970 Nashua, NH
QUIGLEY,Victoria L AGE:72 30 Nov 1980 Nashua, NH
QUINN,Mildred AGE:3 2 02 Mar 1904 Hudson, NH Peter Quinn & Annie Quinn
RABY,Mildred S AGE:69 14 Jul 1974 Nashua, NH
RABY,Rose Alma AGE:90 18 Feb 1982 Hudson, NH
RABY,Royal W AGE:80 16 Apr 1982 Nashua, NH
RAFFERTY,Lena B AGE:64 5 2 01 Jun 1946 Hudson, NH William Reynolds
 & Annie Lamb
RAGER,Joseph Martin AGE:17 10 Apr 1985 Nashua, NH
RAGONA,Sarah J AGE:88 29 Jan 1984 Nashua, NH
RAMSAY,Louis L AGE:74 20 Aug 1981 Nashua, NH
RANCOURT,Peter A AGE:2   29 Jul 1908 Hudson, NH Henry Rancourt
 & Mary Southerland
RANDALL,Forrest Stanley AGE:1 17 21 Aug 1911 Hudson, NH Harold M Randall
 & Edith L Hopkins
RANDALL,Nathaniel B AGE:85 7 18 Jan 1895 Hudson, NH
RANDALL,Sarah P AGE:57 4 27 Dec 1896 Hudson, NH George W Sargent
 (Haverhill, MA)
RANDOLPH,H M Jr AGE:3 21 23 Jan 1916 Hudson, NH Harold Randall
 & Edith Hopkins
RANNEY,Margaret AGE:70 08 Jan 1976 Nashua, NH
RATTE,Ellen AGE:3 04 Mar 1901 Hudson, NH Peter Ratte (Canada)
 & Nellie Holden (Lowell, MA)
RATTE,Pierre AGE:67 4 15 21 May 1942 Hudson, NH Joseph Ratte & Marie Dubois

HUDSON,NH DEATHS

RAUDONIS,Felix A AGE:83 12 Apr 1964 Nashua, NH
RAUDONIS,Valaria AGE:87 13 Mar 1970 Nashua, NH
RAY,Delbert AGE: 05 Jul 1943 Lowell, MA Delbert Ray & Gretchen Boden
RAYMOND,Marilyn A AGE:6 25 17 Nov 1940 Hudson, NH Ernest Raymond
 & Florence Bernier
READ,Clayton A AGE:50 30 May 1958 Hudson, NH
REBSTAD,Florence R AGE:80 21 Nov 1978 Newton, MA
RECORD,Grace M AGE:89 30 Dec 1964 Hudson, NH
RECORD,Leo L AGE:75 27 Feb 1952 Hudson, NH
REED,D G AGE:55 22 Jun 1894 Hudson, NH
REED,Dora M AGE:39 3 27 16 May 1909 Hudson, NH Clark Mott & Ann Knapp
REED,Stalker Elijah AGE:36 4 24 31 Aug 1926 Hudson, NH Elijah R Reed
 & Mary Stalker
REED,Stella King AGE:37 10 26 17 Dec 1916 Hudson, NH
REGO,Lillie M AGE:52 15 Jun 1963 Nashua, NH
RELATION,Everett L AGE:59 22 Jun 1978 Nashua, NH
REYNOLDS,Charles H AGE:59 5 4 08 Jan 1931 Hudson, NH Ai Reynolds
 & Melvina Leazott
REYNOLDS,Cora AGE:73 13 Jul 1965 Nashua, NH
REYNOLDS,Edna H AGE:75 08 Aug 1975 Nashua, NH
REYNOLDS,Edward F AGE:59 5 21 12 Dec 1943 Hudson, NH W A Reynolds
 & Annie Lamb
REYNOLDS,George W AGE:49 17 Jun 1968 Hudson, NH
REYNOLDS,Kenner E AGE:60 26 Nov 1963 Nashua, NH
REYNOLDS,Mary A AGE:82 8 11 06 Jan 1946 Hudson, NH Robert White
 & Elizabeth Cox
RHEAUME,Charles AGE:23 08 Aug 1974 Hudson, NH
RICARD,Adella AGE:60 8 22 01 Dec 1940 Hudson, NH Luger Labelle
 & Elmire Peron
RICARD,Asarie AGE:67 1 21 08 Jun 1944 Nashua, NH Asarie Ricard & Delima Pare
RICARD,Leo J AGE:86 18 Jan 1981 Hudson, NH
RICARD,Therese A AGE:42 11 Mar 1975 Nashua, NH
RICE,Raymond AGE:73 14 Apr 1979 Nashua, NH
RICH,Emily S AGE:27 8 27 23 Apr 1918 Hudson, NH John Scott & Emily Bryant
RICH,Harry AGE:56 5 25 06 Oct 1945 Concord, NH Forrest A Rich
 & Nellie M Caverly
RICH,Nellie May AGE:76 8 4 27 Jun 1938 Hudson, NH George A Caverly
 & Mary Sanborn
RICHARD,Anna AGE:71 07 Feb 1964 Hudson, NH
RICHARD,Conrad AGE:1 14 Apr 1920 Hudson, NH Alphonse Richard & Mary L'ami
RICHARD,Emerilda AGE:81 14 Aug 1974 Hudson, NH
RICHARD,Esther J AGE:70 25 Oct 1984 Nashua, NH
RICHARD,George E AGE:50 15 Oct 1964 Nashua, NH
RICHARD,Hermance AGE:84 09 Oct 1972 Hudson, NH
RICHARD,Irene AGE:72 23 Nov 1983 Nashua, NH
RICHARD,Joseph AGE: 09 Dec 1915 Hudson, NH Alphonse Richard (Canada)
 & Marie Lamil (Canada)
RICHARD,Joseph AGE:78 1 3 21 Jun 1925 Hudson, NH Godfoi Richard
 & Julie Meraird
RICHARD,Lorette AGE:15 19 May 1921 Hudson, NH Alphonse Richard & Mary Lami
RICHARD,Marie AGE:1 05 Feb 1922 Hudson, NH Alphonse Richard & Marie Lamy
RICHARD,Noe AGE:85 19 Jun 1969 Nashua, NH
RICHARD,Paul A AGE:60 15 Aug 1971 Nashua, NH
RICHARDS,George H AGE:73 3 14 04 Mar 1933 Hudson, NH George Richards
 & Harriet Chesley
RICHARDS,Joseph J AGE:59 04 Aug 1956 Lowell, MA
RICHARDSON,Amos AGE: 15 Jul 1741 Hudson, NH Amos Richardson & Sarah
RICHARDSON,Anna AGE:68 24 Jul 1824 Hudson, NH
RICHARDSON,Benjamin F AGE:38 16 Aug 1880 Hudson, NH B F Richardson & Sally
RICHARDSON,Caroline AGE:94 23 Mar 1980 Hudson, NH

HUDSON,NH DEATHS

RICHARDSON,Elijah AGE:79 4 3 06 Jun 1888 Hudson, NH Jesse Richardson
  (Woburn, MA) & Susanna Richardson (Woburn, MA)
RICHARDSON,Grace B AGE:86 17 Jan 1961 Nashua, NH
RICHARDSON,Henry A AGE:74 9 5 30 Mar 1939 Hudson, NH E C Richardson & Laura
RICHARDSON,Hiram Louis AGE:73 23 Jun 1974 Manchester, NH
RICHARDSON,Karl W AGE:50 06 Feb 1956 Milford, NH
RICHARDSON,Lizzie Palmer AGE:48 07 Aug 1880 Hudson, NH
RICHARDSON,Lydia AGE:21 03 Jul 1807 Hudson, NH
RICHARDSON,Margaret AGE:88 11 Oct 1974 Nashua, NH
RICHARDSON,S Addie AGE:57 03 Feb 1883 Hudson, NH
RICHARDSON,Samuel AGE:81 27 Jun 1844 Hudson, NH
RICHARDSON,Sarah AGE:90 3 27 Apr 1897 Hudson, NH
RICHARDSON,Susanna AGE:5 05 Nov 1760 Hudson, NH Seth Richardson & Sarah
RIDLEY,Mark A AGE:58 3 7 30 Jan 1941 Hartford, VT Eugene Ridley & Mary Clark
RIENDEAU,Joseph AGE:89 4 23 21 Mar 1945 Goffstown, NH Jean B Riendeau
  & Rachel Montier
RIGG,Mary A AGE:83 08 May 1964 Nashua, NH
RIGG,Ruby D AGE:68 24 Mar 1973 Nashua, NH
RIGG,William AGE:68 11 Aug 1971 Nashua, NH
RIOUX, Alice,Sr Ferdinand Marie AGE:53 18 Jul 1958 Hudson, NH
RIPLEY,Celvina AGE: 10 Jan 1858 Hudson, NH
RIPLEY,Daniel T AGE:22 17 Oct 1845 Hudson, NH
RIPLEY,Edwin AGE:50 2 02 Apr 1882 Hudson, NH Spencer Ripley & Mary
RIPLEY,Elizabeth Cummings AGE:2 26 Jun 1826 Hudson, NH Spencer Ripley & Mary
RIPLEY,Louise B AGE: 12 Mar 1900 Lawrence, MA
RIPLEY,Mary Cummings AGE:60 10 Aug 1862 Hudson, NH
RIPLEY,Mary M AGE:38 5 11 Jan 1858 Hudson, NH
RIPLEY,Sarah J AGE:19 3 15 Feb 1846 Hudson, NH Spencer Ripley & Mary
RIPLEY,Spencer AGE:68 21 Jun 1856 Hudson, NH
RIVARD,Delvina AGE:78 02 Jan 1952 Hudson, NH
ROACH,Arthur AGE:79 2 4 23 Apr 1941 Nashua, NH Arthur Roach
  & Margaret Herrin
ROBBINS,Annie R AGE:75 04 Mar 1951 Hudson, NH
ROBBINS,Idell Henrietta AGE:10 17 17 Jun 1924 Hudson, NH Carl E Robbins
  & Maud Dury
ROBBINS,Mary A AGE:80 11 6 26 Aug 1947 Hudson, NH John Robbins & Jenny Smith
ROBBINS,Robert R AGE:62 25 May 1951 Nashua, NH
ROBERGE,Arthur AGE:60 08 Apr 1985 Derry, NH
ROBERT,Gerald R AGE:69 06 May 1984 Nashua, NH
ROBERTS,Ada B AGE:84 12 Apr 1966 Hudson, NH
ROBERTS,Clara Frances Webster AGE: 02 May 1872 Hudson, NH
ROBERTS,Harold F AGE:84 29 Oct 1978 Nashua, NH
ROBERTSON,David O AGE:74 21 Jun 1967 Nashua, NH
ROBILLARD,Jeanne AGE:52 26 Dec 1983 Nashua, NH
ROBINSON,Alecia A AGE:75 4 9 12 Sep 1935 Hudson, NH Israel W Young
  & Elizabeth Morse
ROBINSON,Alphonzo AGE:81 1 19 14 Dec 1918 Hudson, NH John Robinson
  & Marinda Caldwell
ROBINSON,Angelakim AGE:4 3 9 21 Jul 1851 Hudson, NH John Robinson
  & Miranda
ROBINSON,Bessie H AGE:66 25 Jul 1970 Nashua, NH
ROBINSON,Charlotte AGE: 12 Dec 1900 Manchester, NH
ROBINSON,Charlotte G AGE:74 8 26 09 Jan 1892 Hudson, NH Charles Glidden
  (Jefferson, ME) & Prudence Sykes
ROBINSON,Charlotte Glidden AGE:74 8 26 09 Jan 1892 Hudson, NH
ROBINSON,Charlotte P AGE:55 04 Jun 1874 Hudson, NH
ROBINSON,Clarence L AGE:2 05 Sep 1869 Hudson, NH
ROBINSON,Clarissa Smith AGE:70 6 20 Dec 1878 Hudson, NH
ROBINSON,Daniel AGE:68 25 Feb 1840 Hudson, NH
ROBINSON,Daniel AGE:85 Dec 1863 Hudson, NH

HUDSON,NH DEATHS

ROBINSON,Daniel A AGE:49 2 17 30 Jun 1872 Hudson, NH
ROBINSON,David AGE:89 9 12 Dec 1864 Hudson, NH
ROBINSON,Edward AGE:60 30 Oct 1868 Hudson, NH
ROBINSON,Emma J AGE:77 07 May 1965 Nashua, NH
ROBINSON,Emma R AGE:56 9 2 07 Aug 1941 Hudson, NH Joseph Boilard
   & Marie Charette
ROBINSON,Geo W AGE:76 9 7 15 Jun 1920 Hudson, NH John A Robinson
   & Relief Cummings
ROBINSON,Grace T AGE:59 25 Jan 1929 Hudson, NH Roger & Rose
ROBINSON,Henry AGE:71 07 Jul 1981 Derry, NH
ROBINSON,James C AGE:81 03 Jan 1963 Hudson, NH
ROBINSON,Joanna C AGE:80 5 6 01 Mar 1929 Hudson, NH Jacob Corbett
   & Elizabeth MacGeney
ROBINSON,John A AGE:86 04 Dec 1950 Hudson, NH Alphonzo Robinson
   & Louisa Haselton
ROBINSON,John A AGE:62 11 14 Aug 1865 Hudson, NH
ROBINSON,John A AGE:65 Aug 1864 Hudson, NH
ROBINSON,John B AGE:70   Hudson, NH Noah Robinson
ROBINSON,John P AGE:69 9 5 02 Jun 1877 Hudson, NH
ROBINSON,Julia A AGE:93 06 Jun 1961 Nashua, NH
ROBINSON,Louisa AGE:76 7 22 23 Apr 1917 Hudson, NH
ROBINSON,Louisa A AGE:84 4 27 04 Apr 1923 Hudson, NH Luther Haselton
   & Polly Smith
ROBINSON,Lucius F AGE:65 3 17 05 May 1905 Hudson, NH Simeon Robinson
   & Eliza Osgood
ROBINSON,Margaret I AGE:56 1 20 26 Feb 1911 Hudson, NH Andrew Duley
   & Katherine Dryden
ROBINSON,Marinda AGE:86 8 7 23 Jan 1897 Hudson, NH Caldwell & Spalding
ROBINSON,Martha AGE:85 28 Feb 1860 Hudson, NH
ROBINSON,Mary A AGE:54 4 21 20 Dec 1909 Hudson, NH Eben Merrill
   & Letitia Gage
ROBINSON,Noah AGE:79 31 Jan 1863 Hudson, NH
ROBINSON,Noah AGE:71 28 Feb 1863 Hudson, NH
ROBINSON,Rebecca AGE:29 09 Mar 1817 Hudson, NH
ROBINSON,Roger L AGE:73 18 Oct 1966 Nashua, NH
ROBINSON,Sally P AGE:70 15 Jan 1866 Hudson, NH
ROBINSON,Sandra A AGE: 31 Oct 1944 Nashua, NH Roger L Robinson
   & Dorothy Bresnahan
ROBINSON,Sarah AGE:76 10 03 Jul 1887 Hudson, NH Cutler (Nashua, NH)
   & Hannah Lund (Nashua, NH)
ROBINSON,Sarah AGE:11 09 Oct 1862 Hudson, NH
ROBINSON,Sarah Cutter AGE:76 10 03 Jul 1887 Hudson, NH
ROBINSON,Sarah J AGE:6 27 Sep 1825 Hudson, NH Noah Robinson & Sally
ROBINSON,Sarah L AGE:11 8 10 09 Oct 1862 Hudson, NH John B Robinson & Sarah
ROBINSON,Simeon AGE:75 10 08 Jan 1897 Hudson, NH Simeon Robinson
   & Sarah Wyman
ROBINSON,Simeon AGE:76 22 Nov 1820 Hudson, NH
ROBINSON,Susan R AGE:23 09 Mar 1877 Hudson, NH John B Robinson & Sarah
ROBINSON,Susanna AGE:73 13 Apr 1818 Hudson, NH
ROBINSON,Susia AGE:23 07 Mar 1877 Hudson, NH
ROBITAILLE,Josephine M AGE:70 07 May 1984 Nashua, NH
ROBY,Howard H AGE:73 28 Nov 1984 Manchester, NH
ROCK,Ada AGE:82 18 Jul 1973 Nashua, NH
ROCK,Georgianna AGE:77 11 21 07 Feb 1944 Hudson, NH Joseph Wright & Susan
ROCK,Hubert AGE:18 11 Jul 1959 Laconia, NH
ROCK,Julius M AGE:82 25 Mar 1959 Hudson, NH
ROCK,Lea AGE:81 29 Jun 1979 Hudson, NH
ROCK,Lillian D AGE:67 17 May 1984 Nashua, NH
ROCK,Ruth E AGE:75 09 Dec 1982 Nashua, NH
ROCK,Willard N AGE:80 01 Jun 1954 Nashua, NH

HUDSON,NH DEATHS

ROCK,Yvonne F AGE:58   13 Jan 1965 Hudson, NH
RODD,Bertha B AGE:25 4 14   04 Jan 1905 Hudson, NH Charles Balfour
   & Eliz McCullock
RODGERS,Henry F AGE:65 6 26   11 Jul 1929 Hudson, NH
RODGERS,Mary E AGE:31   30 Aug 1962 Nashua, NH
RODGERS,Susan AGE:74   23 Jan 1948 Hudson, NH George Somerville
RODIER,Albert Louis AGE:67   13 Apr 1980 Nashua, NH
RODIER,Hormidas D AGE:56   07 Mar 1980 Nashua, NH
RODIER,Marie AGE: 07 Sep 1917 Hudson, NH Jean B Rodier & Obeline Gagnon
RODIER,Omerine AGE:72   05 Jun 1957 Nashua, NH
RODONIS,Agatha A AGE:64 11 1   08 Dec 1947 Nashua, NH Adam Rodonis
   & Eva Rameika
RODONIS,William AGE:62 2 1   16 Jun 1943 Hudson, NH
RODRIGUES,Marianno A AGE:71   06 Dec 1984 Nashua, NH
ROFF,Nelda R AGE:58   06 Nov 1971 Hudson, NH
ROGERS,Alberta M AGE:71   13 Oct 1957 Hudson, NH
ROGERS,Lisa A AGE:3   31 Jan 1959 Nashua, NH
ROLEAU,[Unknown] AGE:1   13 Oct 1903 Hudson, NH John Roleau & Mary Anderzz
ROLLS,Agnes AGE:62   3   19 Nov 1926 Hudson, NH George Baxter
   & Rachael Henman
ROLLS,Sarah L AGE:73   27 Dec 1955 Lowell, MA
ROLO,Arthur C AGE:78   25 Sep 1970 Nashua, NH
ROLO,Henry F AGE:72   17 Nov 1954 Nashua, NH
ROLO,Susan A AGE:65 8 29   05 Dec 1944 Nashua, NH William E Byrns
   & Margaret Graham
ROMANOWSKI,Clement E AGE:85   28 Feb 1972 Nashua, NH
ROMANOWSKI,Leokada A AGE:70   14 Mar 1963 Nashua, NH
RONDEAU,Joseph A AGE:69   20 Apr 1975 Hudson, NH
ROOT,Charles C AGE:74   30 Mar 1961 Hudson, NH
ROTHNEY,Wilfred J AGE:63   25 Nov 1965 Cambridge, MA
ROULEAU,Louis F AGE:82   22 Oct 1952 Goffstown, NH
ROULEAU,Telesphore AGE:52 3 10   24 Jul 1930 Hudson, NH Napoleon Rouleau
   & Marie Martin
ROUNSAVELLE,John AGE:75 10 2   02 Mar 1929 Hudson, NH John Rounsavelle
   & Mary Wells
ROUNSVELLE,Percy E AGE:41 4 3   22 Jul 1940 Nashua, NH John Rounsvelle
   & Cora B Clifford
ROUSSEL,Vivianne E AGE:54   22 Mar 1985 Nashua, NH
ROWDEN,Henry F AGE:70 9 16   15 Nov 1893 Hudson, NH
ROWE,Clara M AGE:73   14 Feb 1980 Nashua, NH
ROWE,Ethan A AGE:56   22 Jan 1962 Nashua, NH
ROWE,Robert F AGE:54   31 Dec 1983 Manchester, NH
ROWELL,Elizabeth F O AGE:29 11 8   25 Mar 1925 Hudson, NH Francis O Tyler
   & Jennie C Cartland
ROWELL,Eugene E AGE:7   13 Jan 1972 Nashua, NH
ROWELL,Harold C AGE:54   21 Dec 1950 Hudson, NH Clinton Rowell
   & Agnes M Theriault
ROWELL,Mai e le AGE:2   4   16 May 1932 Hudson, NH Harold C Rowell
   & Zoula Ferryall
ROWELL,Sarah A AGE:56   9 5   22 Nov 1892 Hudson, NH
ROWELL,Wallace W AGE:71   09 Aug 1966 Concord, NH
ROWELL,Zoula AGE:75   09 Feb 1978 Nashua, NH
ROY,Cecile AGE:72   03 Feb 1967 Hudson, NH
ROY,Clara AGE: 19 Aug 1933 Hudson, NH Antoine Vanasse & Marie St Martin
ROY,Etudienne AGE:75 11 25   07 Jan 1924 Hudson, NH Paul Chayer
   & Hermine St Cyr
ROY,Hormisdas AGE:62 10 14   16 Nov 1936 Hudson, NH Liborie Roy
ROY,Irene M AGE:70   20 Jul 1982 Nashua, NH
ROY,Joseph L AGE:77   22 Sep 1961 Nashua, NH
ROY,Joyce A AGE:6   24 May 1949 Nashua, NH Robert Roy & Mary Clifford

HUDSON,NH DEATHS

ROY,Lillian AGE:8 15   23 Dec 1923 Hudson, NH Theophile Roy & Elvine Poulin
ROY,Philip L AGE:66   22 Nov 1978 Nashua, NH
ROYS,Fred E AGE:76   12 Oct 1954 Hudson, NH
ROYS,Mary E AGE:86   25 May 1965 Derry, NH
ROZETT,Mildred T AGE:45   22 May 1972 Hudson, NH
RUCH,Martha AGE:89   29 Jun 1977 Hudson, NH
RUITER,Helen S AGE:74   10 Jun 1966 Nashua, NH
RUITER,Miles AGE:62   18 Apr 1955 Hudson, NH
RUNNELLS,Ina M AGE:34 11 24   20 Sep 1921 Hudson, NH Albert F Baxter
   & Ida A Young
RUSHTON,Hannah AGE:85   03 Sep 1969 Nashua, NH
RUSSELL,Ada T AGE:87 8 19   12 Nov 1924 Hudson, NH George Bennett
   & Sarah Allen
RUSSELL,Etta Elva AGE:55 9 29   26 May 1925 Hudson, NH Benjamin E Osgood
   & Matilda Dawson
RUSSELL,Herbert C AGE:79 8 12   09 Nov 1940 Nashua, NH Wellington Russell
   & Sarah Carr
RUSSELL,James E AGE:77   28 Jan 1972 Nashua, NH
RUSSELL,Oscar AGE:81   01 Nov 1969 Manchester, NH
RUSSELL,Sarah M AGE:87 2 22   04 Feb 1910 Hudson, NH Nathan Carr & Betsy Chase
RUTTLE,Elvena F AGE:64   27 Sep 1982 Nashua, NH
RYAN,Ann AGE:58   08 Mar 1884 Hudson, NH Nicholas Cass (Ireland)
   & Catherine Welsh (Ireland)
RYAN,James AGE:65   10 Mar 1894 Hudson, NH John Ryan (Ireland) & Jane Boilard
   (Ireland)
SACKOVICH,Kazmeirka AGE:75   09 Sep 1954 Hudson, NH
SADAUSKAS,Adolph P AGE:63   24 Nov 1977 Nashua, NH
SAKALLAR,Sokrat Naun AGE:88   05 Jan 1973 Nashua, NH
SALLIE,Patricia AGE:8 14   06 Aug 1932 Hudson, NH Frank Sallie
   & Mary Cavanaugh
SALOIS,Roland L AGE:68   03 Nov 1977 Nashua, NH
SALUTA,Dominick AGE:55   21 Mar 1928 Hudson, NH Charles Saluta
   & Agnes Sluibisky
SANBORN,Alice L AGE:74   3 24 Mar 1948 Hudson, NH Jeremiah M Avery
   & Julia A Upton
SANBORN,Braley J AGE:68 2 31 Jul 1891 Hudson, NH Daniel Sanborn (Brentwood)
   & Polly Frye (Deerfield)
SANBORN,[Unknown] AGE:20   03 Apr 1883 Hudson, NH Fred Sanborn
   & Jennie H Little
SANDERS,Emma B AGE:63 8 11   19 Jun 1940 Hudson, NH Daniel Connell
   & Eliza Bernard
SANDERS,James Abern AGE:81 7 12   13 Aug 1934 Hudson, NH Abi A Sanders
   & Pelmira Whitemore
SANDERS,Mabel L AGE:54 10 10   13 Sep 1948 Hudson, NH George O Sanders
   & Linda Thomas
SANDERS,Thoms AGE:83 11 16   04 Sep 1914 Hudson, NH Robert Sanders
SANDERS,[Unknown] AGE: 04 Jul 1897 Hudson, NH Abraham Sanders&Emma M Bernard
SANDERSON,Harold C AGE:53   04 Jun 1958 Hudson, NH
SANDERSON,Nancy J AGE:19   05 Jul 1869 Hudson, NH Arison Sanborn
SANSOM,Charles L AGE:68   23 Jul 1965 Hudson, NH
SARGENT,Adeline D AGE:87   15 Jan 1958 Hudson, NH
SARGENT,Dana AGE:65 11   01 Apr 1866 Hudson, NH
SARGENT,Dana AGE: Hudson, NH
SARGENT,Eliza AGE:66 6   28 Nov 1875 Hudson, NH
SARGENT,Ella AGE:91 1 7   15 Feb 1944 Hudson, NH Daniel Smith & Sarah Whity
SARGENT,Emma S AGE:19 10   07 May 1866 Hudson, NH Dana Sargent & Eliza
SARGENT,Homer E AGE:41 8 20   02 Sep 1911 Hudson, NH Nathaniel Sargent
   & Nellie Potter
SARGENT,Isaac AGE:73   03 Sep 1970 Hudson, NH
SARGENT,Mary E AGE:19   15 Feb 1842 Hudson, NH Dana Sargent & Susan

HUDSON,NH DEATHS

SARGENT,Nathaniel AGE:76 7 20   12 Oct 1914 Hudson, NH Daniel Sargent
& Susan Aikens
SARGENT,Reuben W AGE:11 8   22 Oct 1854 Hudson, NH Dana Sargent & Susan
SARGENT,Ruth A AGE:87 11   18 Jan 1881 Hudson, NH
SARGENT,Susan M AGE:66 6   27 Sep 1890 Hudson, NH William Hadley (Hudson, NH)
& Rachel Blodgett (Hudson, NH)
SARGENT,Susan W Hadley AGE:66 6   27 Sep 1890 Hudson, NH
SARMENTO,Walter C AGE:58   30 Dec 1982 Nashua, NH
SARNO,Sandra J AGE:36   03 May 1980 Nashua, NH
SASSAK,John AGE:48   21 Feb 1982 Nashua, NH
SAUNDERS,Arthur L AGE:80   13 Oct 1966 Nashua, NH
SAUNDERS,Maud E AGE:73 2 2   14 Feb 1944 Nashua, NH George H Nutting
& Clara Sladen
SAUNDERS,[Unknown] AGE: 27 Mar 1944 Nashua, NH Theodore Saunders
& Ella N Rowell
SAWICKI,William J AGE:71   08 Feb 1964 Nashua, NH
SAWYER,Evelyn R AGE:59   17 Nov 1981 Amesbury, MA
SAWYER,Josephine B AGE:91   31 Aug 1960 Hudson, NH
SAWYER,Raymond G AGE:47 8 28   08 Jul 1928 Hudson, NH Frank G Sawyer
& Laura G Morse
SCAMMON,Beth E AGE:1 hr   23 Nov 1959 Nashua, NH
SCANLON,Michael AGE:70   06 Apr 1907 Hudson, NH Michael Scanlon
SCHARCH,Donald P AGE:32   21 Dec 1970 Nashua, NH
SCHINDLER,Richard F AGE:80   04 May 1951 Hudson, NH
SCHREMBS,George G AGE:80   02 Sep 1962 Nashua, NH
SCHUMSKY,Catherine AGE:45   14 Jan 1937 Hudson, NH Joseph Vilkoski
& Marion Tubinos
SCHURMAN,Herbert G AGE:11 19   30 Dec 1902 Hudson, NH W G Schurman
& Grace A Walker
SCOLLEY,Rosana AGE:70 7 5   29 Aug 1892 Hudson, NH
SCOTT,Lilla B AGE:87 9 9   05 Nov 1948 Hudson, NH Isaac Dunn & Christina Snow
SCOTT,Woodrow F AGE:42   14 Apr 1963 Hudson, NH
SCRIBNER,Fred W AGE:48 4 10   25 Aug 1928 Hudson, NH Hiram Scribner & Mary Fly
SCRIBNER,Harold W AGE:65   28 Apr 1966 Hudson, NH
SEAMAN,Blanche M AGE:73   27 Oct 1966 Nashua, NH
SEARLES,Beatrice H AGE:4   21 Oct 1929 Hudson, NH Edwin A Searles
& Beatrice M Patnaud
SEARLES,Elizabeth AGE:70 6 3   15 Jun 1909 Hudson, NH
SEAVEY,Andrew AGE: 01 Jan 1802 Hudson, NH
SEAVEY,Augusta AGE:77 9 13   26 Mar 1888 Hudson, NH Joseph Seavey
& Susanna Chase
SEAVEY,Emma F AGE:8 10 14   25 Oct 1862 Hudson, NH David Seavey
SEAVEY,Howard G AGE: 09 Mar 1858 Hudson, NH John Seavey & Mary
SEAVEY,Mary AGE:93   12 Apr 1825 Hudson, NH
SEIGEL,Joseph AGE:28 5   11 Jun 1899 Hudson, NH Antoine Seigil & Mary Richling
SELVIS,David S AGE:69   18 Oct 1952 Nashua, NH
SELVIS,Helenna AGE:2 6   2 25 Mar 1932 Hudson, NH Sylvio Selvis
& Irene Lafontine
SELVIS,Mary R AGE:81   13 Feb 1967 Nashua, NH
SELVIS,Roland A AGE:71   08 Apr 1978 Nashua, NH
SEMENA,Mikolai AGE:84   29 Apr 1967 Goffstown, NH
SENATO,Anna Theresa AGE:75   23 Apr 1983 Nashua, NH
SENECHAL,Auguste AGE:63   13 Jul 1963 Hudson, NH
SENNEVILLE,Edward E AGE:46 10 28   30 Dec 1943 Nashua, NH Ellas Senneville
& Elexandrine Cote
SENNOTT,Susie M AGE:92   12 May 1962 Hudson, NH
SENTER,Averline AGE:72   14 Oct 1879 Hudson, NH
SENTER,Avinline AGE:72   14 Oct 1879 Hudson, NH Newton Colburn
SENTER,Bridget AGE:16   1793 Hudson, NH Dea Thomas Senter & Esther
SENTER,Cathy AGE:27   1803 Hudson, NH Dea Thomas Senter & Esther

HUDSON,NH DEATHS

SENTER,Charles A AGE:1 9 13 Jan 1860 Hudson, NH Thomas Senter & Esther
SENTER,Charles O AGE:7 1791 Hudson, NH Dea Thomas Senter & Esther
SENTER,Dea Thomas AGE:83 25 Dec 1834 Hudson, NH
SENTER,Eliphalet AGE:87 22 Apr 1914 Hudson, NH Eliphalet Senter
SENTER,Emma J AGE:2 10 13 Jan 1860 Hudson, NH Thomas Senter & Esther
SENTER,Esther AGE:52 1800 Hudson, NH
SENTER,Eunice AGE:88 12 Nov 1842 Hudson, NH
SENTER,Gant AGE:32 8 08 Dec 1842 Hudson, NH
SENTER,Jean AGE:67 10 Jul 1765 Hudson, NH
SENTER,Langdon AGE:56 22 Dec 1862 Hudson, NH
SENTER,Lydia M AGE:48 9 14 Feb 1885 Hudson, NH John R Hamblett (Hudson, NH)
 & Hattie Robinson (Hudson, NH)
SENTER,Mary C AGE:43 24 Mar 1850 Hudson, NH
SENTER,Mary E AGE:11 8 19 23 Jun 1847 Hudson, NH Thomas Senter & Mary
SENTER,Mary E AGE:1 7 05 Aug 1855 Hudson, NH Thomas Senter & Mary
SENTER,Mercy AGE:41 1802 Hudson, NH
SENTER,Roxanna AGE:70 7 5 29 Aug 1892 Hudson, NH
SENTER,Sarah A Spalding AGE:28 10 Sep 1847 Hudson, NH
SENTER,Thomas AGE:78 10 Feb 1863 Hudson, NH
SENTER,Thomas AGE:64 2 28 06 Apr 1873 Hudson, NH
SENTER,Thomas AGE:78 18 Feb 1863 Hudson, NH
SENTER,Thomas AGE:64 16 Apr 1873 Hudson, NH
SENTER,William T AGE:73 20 30 Dec 1920 Hudson, NH Langdon Senter
 & Aveline D Thayer
SETTLE,Lena AGE:86 07 Mar 1963 Hudson, NH
SEVERY,James E AGE:86 3 24 Sep 1920 Hudson, NH James Inman
 & Charlotte Collar
SEVIGNY,Dora Short AGE:71 30 Oct 1979 Nashua, NH
SHATTUCK,Ingalls H AGE:83 4 9 01 Nov 1904 Hudson, NH Noah Shattuck
 & Clarissa Sanders
SHAW,Ellen E AGE:72 4 1 21 Apr 1914 Hudson, NH Enoch Cummings
 & Louisa McAlpine
SHAW,Emma L AGE:24 Feb 1868 Hudson, NH James L Shaw & Nellie E Cummings
SHAW,Emma L AGE: 18 Feb 1867 Hudson, NH Henry Shaw
SHAW,Hermon A AGE:16 4 14 09 Nov 1891 Hudson, NH James L Shaw
 & Nellie E Cummings
SHAW,Hermon O AGE:16 4 14 09 Nov 1891 Hudson, NH Jas H Shaw (Gloucester, MA)
 & Ellen E Cummings (Nashua, NH)
SHAW,James H AGE:44 1 25 01 Oct 1884 Hudson, NH James Shaw (Nova Scotia)
 & Lydia Harrington (Nova Scotia)
SHAY,Daniel AGE:73 17 Jul 1961 Concord, NH
SHAY,Harriet M AGE:68 20 Jun 1955 Nashua, NH
SHELDON,Carrie B AGE:23 7 11 03 Apr 1894 Hudson, NH David P Sheldon
 (Vermont) & Mary A Knight (Massachusetts)
SHELDON,David P AGE:80 9 3 11 Aug 1912 Hudson, NH Unjiel Sheldon
 & Rhoda Parker
SHELDON,Mary A AGE:74 22 01 Apr 1908 Hudson, NH Jason Knight
 & Sarah W Whittemore
SHENK,Marion R AGE:57 16 Jul 1983 Nashua, NH
SHEPARD,Charles Albion AGE:65 3 22 18 Jun 1924 Hudson, NH Benjamin Shepard
 & Lydia Howard
SHEPARD,Hope AGE:1 09 Nov 1965 Nashua, NH
SHEPARD,Lydia A AGE:78 25 24 Apr 1911 Hudson, NH Roswell Howard & Allen
SHEPARD,Margaret H AGE:46 09 Jun 1980 Nashua, NH
SHEPHERD,Ada E AGE:63 3 21 14 Jun 1941 Nashua, NH Oscar Armstrong
 & Nellie Titcomb
SHEPHERD,Arthur H AGE:68 26 Dec 1980 Hudson, NH
SHEPHERD,Estella E AGE:72 4 17 17 Aug 1946 Nashua, NH Ira S McKeen
 & Sarah Hathaway
SHEPHERD,Henry L AGE:76 14 Aug 1983 Nashua, NH

HUDSON,NH DEATHS

SHEPHERD,Herbert A AGE:67 06 Sep 1961 Nashua, NH
SHEPHERD,Lizzie D AGE:90 08 Oct 1959 Hudson, NH
SHERMAN,Almira M AGE:80 9 27 19 Sep 1897 Hudson, NH Daniel Edgerton
 & Mindwell Lane
SHOECRAFT,Alice M AGE:80 6 3 23 Apr 1923 Hudson, NH Dudley E Butler
 & Nancy Robbins
SHORT,Ethel F AGE:10 7 23 Aug 1892 Hudson, NH George Short (Nashua, NH)
 & Rose Gerow (Hodgdon, ME)
SHORT,Ethel F AGE:10 7 20 Aug 1892 Hudson, NH George H Short & Rosean Gerow
SHORT,Percy AGE:8 17 Oct 1890 Hudson, NH George H Short & Rosean Gerow
SHORT,Percy H AGE:8 17 Oct 1890 Hudson, NH George Short & Roseann Gerow
 (Hodgeden, ME)
SHUMSKY,Sigismond AGE:60 26 May 1979 Nashua, NH
SHUNAMAN,Charles G AGE:89 15 Sep 1966 Hudson, NH
SHUNAMAN,Jessie M AGE:72 25 Jan 1958 Hudson, NH
SHUTA,John AGE:31 13 Dec 1904 Hudson, NH Shuta
SIENKIEWICZ,Bonifacy AGE:89 02 May 1979 Nashua, NH
SIENKIEWICZ,Steven M AGE:10 25 Sep 1968 Nashua, NH
SILVER,Everett F AGE:1 4 19 Feb 1913 Hudson, NH Fordie W Silver
 & Eva Furman
SILVER,Hannah J Webster AGE: 16 Oct 1876 Hudson, NH
SIMARD,Alphonse P AGE:63 12 Feb 1974 Nashua, NH
SIMARD,Edward H AGE:65 15 Dec 1978 Hudson, NH
SIMARD,Joseph N AGE:55 03 Dec 1960 Nashua, NH
SIMO,Cornelia AGE:65 01 Nov 1965 Nashua, NH
SIMONDS,Doris L AGE:64 13 Jun 1961 Nashua, NH
SIMONDS,Frank E AGE:38 4 17 07 Aug 1909 Hudson, NH George L Simonds
 & Martha A Griffin
SIMONDS,Lee G AGE:82 23 Jun 1975 Lancaster, NH
SIMONS,Olive AGE:72 14 Feb 1971 Concord, NH
SIMPSON,Alfred L AGE:60 7 8 19 Jan 1921 Hudson, NH Samuel R Simpson
 & Sabrina Tibbetts
SIMPSON,Edward AGE:62 04 Feb 1977 Nashua, NH
SIMPSON,Myrtle L AGE:9 31 Jan 1897 Hudson, NH Alfred L Simpson
 & Abbie L Nichols
SIMPSON,Sabrina W AGE:89 30 Apr 1902 Hudson, NH Tibbitts
SIMPSON,Samuel AGE:81 1 22 02 Aug 1889 Hudson, NH Robert Simpson
SIMPSON,Samuel R AGE:58 8 3 01 Oct 1905 Hudson, NH Samuel Simpson
 & Susanna W Tibbets
SINCLAIR,Grace AGE:5 13 30 Jun 1941 Nashua, NH Leighton Sinclair
 & Edith McKinley
SINCLAIR,Henry AGE:68 1 1 07 Jul 1921 Hudson, NH Wm M Sinclair & Mary Downs
SIRVYDAS,Vytold AGE:82 17 May 1981 Hudson, NH
SIVIGNY,Arthur AGE:82 28 Aug 1981 Derry, NH
SIVIKI,Lavienyia AGE:48 30 Nov 1932 Hudson, NH
SKILANDIS,Agota AGE:60 25 Jan 1946 Hudson, NH Maculaitis
SKINNER,Anna V AGE:81 3 3 19 Jan 1932 Hudson, NH Arthur W Wilson
 & Anna Stinson
SKLAT,Rose K AGE:69 28 Feb 1954 Nashua, NH
SKUZINSKAS,Anna AGE:73 30 Apr 1962 Nashua, NH
SLATE,Annie P AGE:82 3 9 25 Aug 1942 Nashua, NH Edmund Pendergast
 & Charlotte Pickering
SLATE,Clarence A AGE:65 8 1 24 Apr 1921 Hudson, NH Lyman J Slate
 & Abbie B Worthen
SLATE,Florence M AGE:89 09 Jun 1967 Nashua, NH
SLATE,Horace P AGE:71 28 Feb 1958 Hudson, NH
SLATE,Lyman E A AGE:11 10 28 Jul 1880 Hudson, NH Clarance Slate
SLATUNAS,Doris AGE:65 30 Jan 1982 Nashua, NH
SLEEPER,Justin M AGE:74 5 25 29 Aug 1904 Hudson, NH Samuel T W Sleeper
 & Bethana Seavey

HUDSON,NH DEATHS

SLEEPER,Louisa B AGE:74 9 12 14 Nov 1904 Hudson, NH James Berry & Mary Adams
SLOAN,Ralph J AGE:85   12 Dec 1982 Nashua, NH
SMALL,George E AGE:63 9 26 29 Oct 1900 Hudson, NH John Small & Mary Danforth
SMALL,Hannah S AGE:83 11 27 12 Oct 1911 Hudson, NH Aaron Burrows & Stackpole
SMALL,Katie G AGE:58 6 26   04 Sep 1918 Hudson, NH Henry Clifford
  & Henrietta Blanchard
SMALL,Lucy A AGE:50 11 25   07 Apr 1895 Hudson, NH John G Goss (Epson)
  & Lucy A Tear (Allenstown)
SMALL,Marion N AGE:84   19 Oct 1965 Nashua, NH
SMALL,William C AGE:82 29 Dec 1965 Hudson, NH
SMILIKIS,Alphonse Peter AGE:68 24 Jun 1980 Nashua, NH
SMILIKIS,Beatrice H AGE:68   31 Jan 1983 Hudson, NH
SMILIKIS,Peter C AGE:76   21 Feb 1958 Hudson, NH
SMIT,Rev Rudolph AGE:58   16 Dec 1950 Nashua, NH
SMITH,Abbie AGE:84   18 04 Dec 1918 Hudson, NH Amos Davis & Hannah Smith
SMITH,Abigail Foster AGE:79 4 7 09 Jan 1882 Hudson, NH
SMITH,Addie H AGE:10   15 May 1874 Hudson, NH Frederick L Smith
SMITH,Addie L AGE:78 3 27 25 Aug 1940 Nashua, NH Andrew J Smith
  & Irene Hunting
SMITH,Addie L AGE:81   18 May 1954 Nashua, NH
SMITH,Albert E AGE:77 02 Dec 1968 Nashua, NH
SMITH,Alvan AGE:85 11 10 11 Jan 1879 Hudson, NH
SMITH,Alvan AGE:86   Jan 1879 Hudson, NH
SMITH,Andrew J AGE:64 7 4 24 Jan 1898 Hudson, NH Henry Smith & Hannah Smith
SMITH,Andrew J AGE:34   26 Jun 1864
SMITH,Annie M AGE:79   13 Mar 1955 Nashua, NH
SMITH,Arthur M AGE:59   01 Sep 1968 Westport Isl,ME
SMITH,Arthur W AGE:69   27 Apr 1954 Hudson, NH
SMITH,Barbara Ann AGE:1 1 2   15 Jan 1934 Hudson, NH Herbert D Smith
  & Blanche Greeley
SMITH,Benjamin F AGE:23 4   26 Nov 1859 Hudson, NH Samuel Smith
  & Abigail Foster
SMITH,Bertha AGE:36   04 Oct 1918 Hudson, NH Joseph Shotney & Alice Gray
SMITH,Blanche M AGE:63   01 Jun 1958 Nashua, NH
SMITH,Byron B AGE:50   23 Apr 1961 Manchester, NH
SMITH,Carolina M AGE:53 2 27   07 Apr 1890 Hudson, NH
SMITH,Caroline M AGE:53 2 27   07 Apr 1890 Hudson, NH Oliver Lee (Moultonboro)
  & Nancy Hawkins (Centre Harbor)
SMITH,Catherine J AGE:82   25 Nov 1949 Hudson, NH Patrick J Munhall
  & Mary Munhall
SMITH,Catherine Mabel AGE:57 5 20   16 Aug 1934 Hudson, NH Arthur A Bills
  & Mary Ann Bradford
SMITH,Charles AGE:65   17 Oct 1871 Hudson, NH
SMITH,Chloe AGE: Hudson, NH
SMITH,Clara E AGE:79   09 Apr 1953 Hudson, NH
SMITH,Clarissa AGE:22   02 Aug 1873 Hudson, NH
SMITH,Clarissa Cummings AGE:45 02 Aug 1872 Hudson, NH
SMITH,Clayton E AGE:54   08 Nov 1972 Nashua, NH
SMITH,Cloe AGE:84 3 17   06 Oct 1882 Hudson, NH
SMITH,Cora E AGE:63 5 6 26 Mar 1938 Hudson, NH Nelson Smith
  & Caroline M Lee
SMITH,Cunningham F Jr AGE:45   13 Jul 1968 Hudson, NH
SMITH,D Onslow AGE: 12 Nov 1823 Hudson, NH
SMITH,Daniel AGE:79 7 21   20 May 1888 Hudson, NH Thomas Smith (Hudson, NH)
  & Barber Smith (Hudson, NH)
SMITH,Daniel P AGE:1 8   28 Dec 1812 Hudson, NH John H Smith & Rachel
SMITH,David O AGE:82 3 3   15 Feb 1906 Hudson, NH Alvin Smith & Patte Robinson
SMITH,Dea Page AGE:86 8   21 Aug 1838 Hudson, NH
SMITH,Deborah A AGE: 08 Jul 1947 Nashua, NH Clayton Smith & Victoria Ladner
SMITH,Demas AGE:39   23 Mar 1850 Hudson, NH

HUDSON, NH DEATHS

SMITH, Dorcas AGE:18 9 20 Jun 1854 Hudson, NH Jefferson Smith & Sarah
SMITH, Drusilla AGE:59 23 Mar 1874 Hudson, NH
SMITH, Dustin B AGE:75 11 26 Feb 1897 Hudson, NH Henry Smith & Hannah Smith
SMITH, Edgar AGE:48 7 25 Sep 1896 Hudson, NH Samuel Smith (Haverhill, MA)
    & Abigail Foster (Hudson, NH)
SMITH, Edmund AGE:1 5 19 29 Mar 1869 Hudson, NH D Onslow Smith
    & Mary H Greeley
SMITH, Edmund G AGE:11 29 Mar 1869 Hudson, NH Dr H O Smith
SMITH, Effie B AGE:41 06 Jul 1963 Nashua, NH
SMITH, Eliza M AGE:62 1 01 Mar 1900 Hudson, NH James Rue & Margaret Tuck
SMITH, Elizabeth AGE:59 2 8 15 Sep 1802 Hudson, NH
SMITH, Ella D AGE:100 27 Jun 1960 Hudson, NH
SMITH, Ella E AGE:3 3 8 03 Jan 1889 Hudson, NH Henry F Smith (Hudson, NH)
    & Elvira Chamberlin (Nashua, NH)
SMITH, Ella R AGE:77 20 Jan 1985 Nashua, NH
SMITH, Elmer F AGE:85 14 May 1969 Nashua, NH
SMITH, Elvira T AGE:87 5 3 05 Nov 1946 Nashua, NH Caleb Chamberlain
    & Maria Robbins
SMITH, Emma A AGE:54 10 Nov 1874 Hudson, NH
SMITH, Ethelyn A AGE:80 19 Dec 1967 Nashua, NH
SMITH, Fanny AGE:74 8 10 06 Jan 1888 Hudson, NH James Smith (Hudson, NH)
    & Mary Lawrence (Hudson, NH)
SMITH, Frank H AGE:3 18 11 Jan 1941 Hudson, NH Henry E Smith & Mary Kayros
SMITH, Frank Herbert AGE:5 16 Apr 1924 Hudson, NH Herbert D Smith
    & Blanche Greeley
SMITH, Fred A AGE:79 09 Oct 1963 Nashua, NH
SMITH, Fred E AGE:72 3 5 07 Feb 1936 Hudson, NH Nelson Smith & Caroline Lee
SMITH, Fred Lincoln AGE:71 1 23 Apr 1936 Hudson, NH Timothy A Smith
    & Ruth Caldwell
SMITH, Frederick G AGE:81 31 Aug 1967 Nashua, NH
SMITH, Frederick Leroy AGE:30 3 24 17 Mar 1875 Hudson, NH
SMITH, Geo H AGE:69 3 27 31 Jan 1890 Hudson, NH Isaac Smith (N Gloucester)
    & Bethulah Haskell (N Gloucester)
SMITH, George AGE: 23 Feb 1900 Goffstown, NH
SMITH, George AGE:43 05 Mar 1966 Nashua, NH
SMITH, George H AGE:69 3 27 31 Jan 1890 Hudson, NH
SMITH, George L AGE:62 9 12 01 Jan 1914 Hudson, NH Bliss Smith
    & Eliza Johnson
SMITH, Hannah AGE:92 3 1 05 Apr 1801 Hudson, NH
SMITH, Hannah AGE:83 10 Feb 1864 Hudson, NH
SMITH, Hannah P AGE:81 2 15 05 Dec 1916 Hudson, NH Luther Haselton
    & Polly Smith
SMITH, Hannah P Haselton AGE: 20 Sep 1835 Hudson, NH
SMITH, Hannah S AGE:83 08 Feb 1865 Hudson, NH
SMITH, Henry AGE:83 23 Apr 1862 Hudson, NH
SMITH, Henry AGE:56 13 Dec 1874 Hudson, NH
SMITH, Henry Frank AGE:85 1 28 25 Jul 1937 Hudson, NH Dustin D Smith
    & Sarah Jane Watts
SMITH, Henry O AGE:80 4 26 14 May 1945 Londonderry, NH David Smith
    & Mary H Greeley
SMITH, Hiland B AGE:83 16 11 Apr 1925 Hudson, NH Bliss Smith
    & Eliza Johnson
SMITH, Hope B AGE:71   10 16 Jan 1942 Nashua, NH Benjamin Smith
    & Mary McLaughlin
SMITH, Hugh AGE:83 17 Jan 1865 Hudson, NH
SMITH, Ida E AGE:70 7 6 31 Mar 1939 Hudson, NH William H Smith & Eliza R Tuck
SMITH, Irene N AGE:75 2 14 19 Aug 1905 Hudson, NH Jonas Hunting
    & Hannah Smith
SMITH, Irvin A AGE:90 24 Aug 1950 Hudson, NH Andrew J Smith & Irene Huntin
SMITH, Isaac N AGE:71 4 29 18 Dec 1912 Hudson, NH Daniel Smith & Sarah Butler

HUDSON,NH DEATHS

SMITH,Ivan R AGE:69   18 Nov 1966 Hudson, NH
SMITH,James AGE:79 6 15 15 Aug 1849 Hudson, NH
SMITH,James AGE:78   1861 Hudson, NH
SMITH,James AGE:78   Hudson, NH
SMITH,James P AGE:11 6 30 Jan 1839 Hudson, NH Jefferson Smith & Sarah
SMITH,Jane AGE:100 09 Jan 1832 Hudson, NH
SMITH,Jane AGE:70 29 Nov 1874 Hudson, NH
SMITH,Jefferson AGE:81 10 22 09 May 1883 Hudson, NH
SMITH,Jennie AGE:66 27 Jan 1868 Hudson, NH
SMITH,Jeremiah AGE:81 08 Jan 1861 Hudson, NH
SMITH,Jeremiah AGE:81 08 Jun 1862 Hudson, NH
SMITH,Jesse AGE:77 28 Feb 1871 Hudson, NH
SMITH,Jesse AGE:76 27 Feb 1871 Hudson, NH
SMITH,John H AGE:2 8 05 Sep 1778 Hudson, NH Page Smith & Lydia
SMITH,John H AGE: 05 Sep 1878 Hudson, NH Page Smith & Lydia
SMITH,Josephine C AGE:76 28 Feb 1961 Nashua, NH
SMITH,Kimball AGE:77 9 23 Apr 1884 Hudson, NH Henry Smith (Hudson, NH)
   & Hannah Smith (Hudson, NH)
SMITH,Lena A AGE:21 6 22 Mar 1895 Hudson, NH Edgar Smith (Hudson, NH)
   & Addie E Austin (Haverhill, MA)
SMITH,Lieut Hugh AGE:84 19 Jun 1812 Hudson, NH
SMITH,Lizzie J AGE:30 11 28 07 Nov 1905 Hudson, NH David Z Robins
   & C Whittemore
SMITH,Lois Alzira AGE:82 7 11 01 Mar 1926 Hudson, NH Sullivan Smith
   & Sarah Glover
SMITH,Lucinda AGE:76 5 15 Jan 1881 Hudson, NH John Fowler & Martha Stuart
SMITH,Lucy AGE:76 6 6 12 Jan 1900 Hudson, NH Henry Smith & Hannah Smith
SMITH,Lydia AGE:59 11 Dec 1793 Hudson, NH
SMITH,Lydia AGE:64   3 03 Apr 1821 Hudson, NH
SMITH,Lydia AGE:80 07 Apr 1870 Hudson, NH Page Smith & Lydia
SMITH,Lydia G AGE:85 4 5 19 Jun 1907 Hudson, NH James Cram & Betsy Lull
SMITH,Mansfield AGE:73 09 Aug 1873 Hudson, NH
SMITH,Marcia Deering AGE:59 1 9 12 Jul 1926 Hudson, NH Isaac N Deering
   & Almira Guptill
SMITH,Margaret AGE:71 8 27 07 Sep 1886 Hudson, NH
SMITH,Margaret M AGE:67 14 27 Sep 1905 Hudson, NH James Smith
   & Margaret Smith
SMITH,Martha AGE:82 06 Jul 1852 Hudson, NH
SMITH,Mary AGE:88 20 Nov 1861 Hudson, NH
SMITH,Mary AGE:88   1861 Hudson, NH
SMITH,Mary A AGE:90 21 Nov 1979 Nashua, NH
SMITH,Mary E AGE:92 09 Nov 1975 Nashua, NH
SMITH,Mary E E AGE:75 9 3 30 Dec 1939 Hudson, NH N Martin Eaton
   & Eliza R Walton
SMITH,Mary G AGE:26 20 Jun 1859 Hudson, NH Jefferson Smith & Sarah
SMITH,Mary H AGE:74 13 Jan 1980 Nashua, NH
SMITH,Mary H AGE:35 27 Dec 1867 Hudson, NH
SMITH,Mary H Greeley AGE:35 2 Dec 1867 Hudson, NH
SMITH,Nelson AGE:77 2 10 04 Aug 1910 Hudson, NH Samuel Smith
   & Abigail Foster
SMITH,Newton Parker AGE:21 8 21 07 Oct 1928 Hudson, NH Herbert N Smith
   & Lillie Parker
SMITH,Norris AGE:45 19 Jul 1880 Londonderry, NH Samuel Smith
   & Abagail Foster
SMITH,Olivia AGE:73   1861 Hudson, NH
SMITH,Olivia AGE:73   Hudson, NH
SMITH,Otis G AGE:34 30 Jan 1864 Hudson, NH Jefferson Smith & Sarah
SMITH,Parker AGE:45 15 Dec 1849 Hudson, NH
SMITH,Peggy AGE: Dec 1858 Hudson, NH
SMITH,Perley B AGE:90 26 Dec 1961 Hudson, NH

HUDSON,NH DEATHS

SMITH,Polly Robinson AGE:25 1 20 15 Dec 1825 Hudson, NH
SMITH,R Atahlie AGE:60 04 Apr 1977 Nashua, NH
SMITH,Rachel AGE:27 1 26 Oct 1813 Hudson, NH
SMITH,Reuben P AGE:53 10   Hudson, NH Jeremiah Smith
SMITH,Roxanna B AGE:74 11 7 09 Nov 1916 Hudson, NH Darius Butler
 & Laura Whitcher
SMITH,Ruth Ethel AGE:6 2 3 20 Mar 1928 Hudson, NH Herbert D Smith
 & Blanche Greeley
SMITH,Samuel AGE:85   21 02 Jun 1781 Hudson, NH
SMITH,Samuel AGE:82 4 24 04 Apr 1878 Hudson, NH
SMITH,Samuel H AGE:68 07 Oct 1883 Hudson, NH Henry Smith & Hannah Smith
SMITH,Sarah AGE:59 1 7 25 Apr 1857 Hudson, NH James Smith & Mary
SMITH,Sarah AGE:45 20 Apr 1852 Hudson, NH
SMITH,Sarah A AGE:2 9 30 Dec 1855 Hudson, NH Jefferson Smith & Sarah
SMITH,Sarah E AGE:13 8 03 Mar 1864 Hudson, NH Dustin B Smith
SMITH,Sarah E AGE:13 13 Mar 1864 Hudson, NH
SMITH,Sarah J AGE:68 5 19 Nov 1887 Hudson, NH Watts
SMITH,Sarah M AGE:84 31 Aug 1889 Hudson, NH Daniel Butler (Pelham, NH)
 & Tenney (Pelham, NH)
SMITH,Sarah M Butler AGE:84 31 Aug 1889 Hudson, NH
SMITH,Seth AGE:66 10 Dec 1867 Hudson, NH
SMITH,Susan AGE:86 02 Nov 1889 Hudson, NH Jeremiah Smith (Hudson, NH)
 & Susan Spalding (Hudson, NH)
SMITH,Susan AGE:93 1 10 Dec 1901 Hudson, NH Henry Smith (Hudson, NH)
 & Hannah Smith (Hudson, NH)
SMITH,Susan AGE: 14 Feb 1876 Hudson, NH
SMITH,Susan J AGE:28   Hudson, NH James Cunningham & Susan Dutton
SMITH,Susan Spalding AGE:70 2 12 Aug 1853 Hudson, NH
SMITH,Sybil AGE:77   Hudson, NH Daniel Wilson
SMITH,T Emma AGE:22 20 Apr 1866 Hudson, NH Jefferson Smith & Sarah
SMITH,Thomas AGE:67 08 Feb 1872 Hudson, NH
SMITH,Timothy AGE:71 2 19 05 Nov 1802 Hudson, NH
SMITH,Victoria L AGE:60 07 Feb 1982 Nashua, NH
SMITH,W Sherman AGE:87 26 May 1956 Hudson, NH
SMITH,Warren AGE:17 11 28 Aug 1864 Hudson, NH Samuel Smith & Abigail Foster
SMITH,Warren AGE:18 28 Jul 1864
SMITH,Wm Henry AGE:76 8 17 22 May 1908 Hudson, NH Isaac Smith
 & Eliza Mary Tuck
SMITH, [Unknown] AGE: 26 Nov 1908 Hudson, NH Fred E Smith & Addie L Conery
SMITH, [Unknown] AGE:30 min 23 May 1956 Nashua, NH
SMITH Sup'd,Thomas AGE: 19 Oct 1909 Hudson, NH
SNELL,David Kirby AGE:43 20 May 1973 Hudson, NH
SNELL,Lucy E AGE:63 9 20 06 May 1893 Hudson, NH Daniel Clement (Dracut, MA)
 & Dorcas Wilson (Hudson, NH)
SNOW,Adela E AGE:73   1 16 Oct 1941 Hudson, NH George H Walker
 & C Goldthwaite
SNOW,Annabelle G AGE:38 25 May 1942 Nashua, NH George Gilbert
 & Julia Gaucher
SNOW,Annette L AGE:80 14 Feb 1971 Nashua, NH
SNOW,Frederick Donald AGE:75 01 May 1980 Hudson, NH
SNOW,Frederick M AGE:76 02 Dec 1954 Nashua, NH
SNOW,Grace B AGE:77 08 May 1955 Nashua, NH
SNOW,John AGE: 21 Mar 1735 Hudson, NH
SNOW,John AGE:68 4 3 28 Mar 1733 Hudson, NH
SNOW,John T AGE:60 5 22 26 Oct 1913 Hudson, NH John P Snow & Mary E Orn
SNOW,Liet Joseph AGE:51 07 May 1847 Hudson, NH
SNOW,Marcia M AGE:70 31 Mar 1958 Nashua, NH
SNOW,Nathaniel AGE:68 06 Jul 1959 Nashua, NH
SNOW,Philip AGE: 28 Aug 1740 Hudson, NH Jonathan Snow & Sarah
SNOW,Royal G AGE:85 05 May 1951 Hudson, NH

HUDSON,NH DEATHS

SNYDER,Thelma AGE:4 2 03 Oct 1918 Hudson, NH Leon Snyder & Pearl Holbrook
SONEY,Ralph C AGE:78 09 Mar 1978 Nashua, NH
SOUCY,Cathy AGE:3 05 May 1965 Nashua, NH
SOUCY,Sister Edwilda AGE:72 15 Dec 1973 Manchester, NH
SPALDING,Ada L AGE:71 02 Oct 1960 Hudson, NH
SPALDING,Dorothy M AGE:62 05 Nov 1980 Hudson, NH
SPALDING,Elizabeth A P AGE:8 02 Aug 1832 Hudson, NH Reuben Spalding & Hannah
SPALDING,Esther P AGE:23 11 22 21 Jul 1841 Hudson, NH Willard Spalding
  & Sally
SPALDING,Hannah AGE:84 14 Mar 1870 Hudson, NH
SPALDING,Louis L AGE:77 12 May 1968 Nashua, NH
SPALDING,Lucinda M AGE:29   19 01 Aug 1854 Hudson, NH Willard Spalding
  & Sally
SPALDING,Mary M AGE:76 6 19 18 Apr 1922 Hudson, NH Chas Steele & Martha Boyd
SPALDING,Reuben AGE:90 3 3 04 Oct 1901 Hudson, NH Reuben Spalding
  (Hudson, NH) & Hannah Barrett (Hudson, NH)
SPALDING,Reuben AGE:82 10 30 Dec 1863 Hudson, NH
SPALDING,Reuben Jr AGE:37 2 15 20 Nov 1798 Hudson, NH
SPALDING,Sally M AGE:52 19 Nov 1850 Hudson, NH
SPALDING,Sarah A AGE:28 10 Sep 1847 Hudson, NH Willard Spalding & Sally
SPALDING,Sarah L AGE:79 4 21 03 Jun 1898 Hudson, NH Thomas Laton
  & Keziah McKean
SPALDING,Susan AGE:76 11 Apr 1898 Hudson, NH Willard Spalding & Sally Marsh
SPALDING,Willard AGE:74 16 Jan 1868 Hudson, NH
SPALDING,Willard Jr AGE:1 9 25 Apr 1825 Hudson, NH Willard Spalding & Sally
SPARKE,Hannah AGE:86 10 21 18 Jan 1886 Hudson, NH
SPAULDING,Albert M AGE:67 20 May 1965 Nashua, NH
SPAULDING,Anna E AGE:64 6 8 05 Jul 1931 Hudson, NH Thomas Sanders
  & Mary A Connell
SPAULDING,Charles L AGE:88 8 17 22 Dec 1942 Hudson, NH Reuben Spaulding
  & Sarah Laton
SPAULDING,Charles W AGE:82 10 11 14 Aug 1918 Hudson, NH Willard Spaulding
  & Sally Marsh
SPAULDING,Harriet L AGE:81 11 Apr 1965 Hudson, NH
SPAULDING,Helen C AGE:76 27 Sep 1963 Nashua, NH
SPAULDING,Mary E AGE:65 25 Feb 1953 Nashua, NH
SPAULDING,Mary Ellen AGE:61 18 Dec 1984 Hudson, NH
SPAULDING,Maurice E AGE:16 hrs 28 Jan 1952 E Derry, NH
SPAULDING,Ned SEX: AGE:54 05 Jul 1964 Nashua, NH COND:
SPAULDING,Otis M AGE:81   15 07 Sep 1923 Hudson, NH
SPAULDING,Reuben AGE:82 30 Dec 1863 Hudson, NH
SPAULDING,Rupert M AGE:61 18 Aug 1968 Goffstown, NH
SPAULDING,Sarah M AGE:86 21 Jan 1949 Hudson, NH William T Merrill
  & Lucy Byam
SPAULDING,[Unknown] AGE: 07 Jul 1904 Hudson, NH Edw A Spaulding
  & Annie E Sanders
SPEAR,Anton A AGE:91 11 Dec 1974 Nashua, NH
SPEAR,Susan AGE:79 11 19 Jul 1886 Hudson, NH
SPEAR,Susan AGE:79 11 17 Jul 1886 Hudson, NH
SPEAR,Thompson AGE:83 10 07 Nov 1892 Hudson, NH
SPEAR,Wanda C AGE:66 17 Jul 1982 Nashua, NH
SPENCER,Marie L AGE:69 08 Oct 1962 Nashua, NH
SPOFFORD,Mabel AGE:77 19 Sep 1963 Concord, NH
SPRAGUE,April L AGE:1 25 Sep 1967 Nashua, NH
SPRAGUE,C Ellen AGE:41 24 Nov 1873 Hudson, NH
SPRAGUE,Lucinda Burbank AGE:31 28 Mar 1855 Hudson, NH
SPRAGUE,Lucy AGE:84 16 Sep 1863 Hudson, NH
SPRAGUE,Lydia AGE:81 Oct 1866 Hudson, NH
SPRAGUE,P Franklin AGE:56 31 Oct 1870 Hudson, NH
SPRAKE,Anna AGE:86 24 Mar 1830 Hudson, NH

HUDSON,NH DEATHS

SPRAKE,Betsey AGE:55   03 May 1849 Hudson, NH
SPRAKE,Capt Oliver AGE:84   27 Jun 1879 Hudson, NH
SPRAKE,Charles AGE: 24 Jan 1810 Hudson, NH Samuel Sprake
SPRAKE,Hannah AGE:86 10 21   18 Jan 1886 Hudson, NH
SPRAKE,Jonathan AGE:94 10   Hudson, NH Samuel Sprake
SPRAKE,Lucy AGE: 28 Feb 1808 Hudson, NH Samuel Sprake
SPRAKE,Oliver AGE:84   27 Jun 1879 Hudson, NH
SPRAKE,Samuel AGE:86   10 Dec 1836 Hudson, NH
SPRAKE,Thomas AGE:75   1872 Hudson, NH
SPRING,Raymond H Jr AGE:31   14 May 1976 Hudson, NH
ST AMANT,Hermase J AGE:79   30 Jan 1973 Nashua, NH
ST CYR,Rose S AGE:64   16 Oct 1980 Derry, NH
ST JEAN,Almeda AGE:78   13 Dec 1954 Hudson, NH
ST JEAN,Elizabeth AGE:64   02 Nov 1972 Nashua, NH
ST JEAN,Irene AGE:73   02 Jun 1969 Nashua, NH
ST JEAN,Joseph E AGE:74   30 May 1975 Nashua, NH
ST JEAN,Marie Laura AGE:76   30 Nov 1976 Nashua, NH
ST LAURENT,Gertrude G AGE:60   21 Nov 1970 Nashua, NH
ST LAURENT,Roger J AGE:54   23 Mar 1982 Nashua, NH
ST LAURENT,Sadie AGE:49   19 Jun 1953 Nashua, NH
ST LAURENT,Yvonne AGE:74   25 Aug 1974 Nashua, NH
ST MARTIN,Claudia AGE:81   19 Feb 1960 Nashua, NH
ST ONGE,Dora A E AGE:79   28 Mar 1971 Nashua, NH
ST PIERRE,Doris C AGE:54   26 Nov 1982 Nashua, NH
ST PIERRE,Rose H AGE:70   03 Aug 1959 Hudson, NH
STACEY,William AGE:89   02 Oct 1954 Concord, NH
STACKNIS,Mary R AGE:95   18 Feb 1983 Nashua, NH
STACY,Rosabell AGE:43 7 22   01 May 1907 Hudson, NH William H Rhodes
    & Sarah G Frederick
STANAPEDOS,Michael P AGE:74   08 Aug 1965 Nashua, NH
STANAPEDOS,Sophie A AGE:64   07 Apr 1983 Nashua, NH
STANLEY,Alice AGE:1 14   02 Mar 1887 Hudson, NH William Stanley (Boston, MA)
    & Bessie Williams (Boston, MA)
STANLEY,Frances A AGE:75   07 Dec 1980 Nashua, NH
STANLEY,Irving M AGE:79   16 May 1984 Nashua, NH
STANLEY,Lydia O AGE:64 2 4   13 Nov 1908 Hudson, NH David McCoy
    & Lydia Robinson
STAPLES,Elmer F AGE:67   15 Dec 1958 Nashua, NH
STAPLES,Raymond B AGE:81   16 Feb 1977 Nashua, NH
STARK,Fannie A AGE:1 8   04 Jul 1883 Hudson, NH William H Stark & Ella Smith
STAVELEY,Jennie M AGE:70   22 Jan 1965 Nashua, NH
STEARNS,C Helena AGE:83 1 18   22 Feb 1935 Hudson, NH Jones & Clarissa Cooper
STEARNS,George H AGE:33 9 25   14 Apr 1884 Hudson, NH Henry H Stearns
    (Hollis, NH) & Amelia Blake (Hallowell, ME)
STEARNS,Marian E AGE:29 8 4 16 Jan 1883 Hudson, NH Samuel Joy & Mary E Hadley
STEARNS,Mary A AGE:86 2 3   04 Apr 1917 Hudson, NH Warren W Hill
    & Celesta Murdough
STEARNS,Will W AGE:84 9 11 28 Dec 1943 New London, NH Wm Stearns
    & Mary A Hill
STEARNS,William B AGE:64   16 Nov 1893 Hudson, NH
STEELE,Addie M AGE:64 5 20 22 Feb 1940 Hudson, NH George Moody
    & Addie Banister
STEELE,Alice AGE:2 6   01 Jan 1898 Hudson, NH George Steele & Edith F Colburn
STEELE,Alice M AGE:8 10   28 Sep 1878 Hudson, NH Samuel Steele & Mary A
STEELE,Caroline E AGE:79 2 6   28 Dec 1904 Hudson, NH Robert Follett
    & Mary L Walker
STEELE,Charles AGE:68 11   22 Apr 1890 Hudson, NH James Steele (Hudson, NH)
    & Hannah Palmer (Bradford, MA)
STEELE,Charles A AGE:29   24 Jul 1889 Hudson, NH Silas T Steele (Hudson, NH)
    & Elizabeth McDonald (Scotland)

HUDSON,NH DEATHS

STEELE,Charles A AGE:66 3 25   19 Feb 1927 Hudson, NH Charles Steele
& Martha A Boyd
STEELE,Charlotte A AGE:42 8 25   05 Jun 1900 Hudson, NH Hiram Reynolds
& Mary Prescott
STEELE,Everett AGE:7   03 Sep 1912 Hudson, NH George Steel & Edith Colburn
STEELE,Florence E AGE: Jul 1865 Hudson, NH
STEELE,Florence E AGE: Jul Hudson, NH
STEELE,Fred G AGE:83   06 Jun 1955 Nashua, NH
STEELE,Frederick AGE:81 7 23   23 Apr 1909 Hudson, NH Samuel Steele
& Fanny Blodgett
STEELE,George S AGE:85   29 Jul 1951 Hudson, NH
STEELE,George S AGE: 1864 Hudson, NH
STEELE,George S AGE:6   1863 Hudson, NH
STEELE,Hannah AGE:61   01 Jan 1856 Hudson, NH
STEELE,Harold G AGE:72   17 Dec 1973 Hudson, NH
STEELE,James AGE:84   05 Jul 1868 Hudson, NH
STEELE,James E AGE:4 6   14 Sep 1900 Hudson, NH Charles A Steele
& Lottie Reynolds
STEELE,Jesse R AGE:24 4 1   14 Sep 1888 Hudson, NH Silas T Steele (Hudson, NH)
& Elizabeth McDonald (Scotland)
STEELE,Lenia R AGE:66   25 Mar 1984 Nashua, NH
STEELE,Lizzie H AGE:19 8   10 Mar 1873 Hudson, NH Charles Steele & Martha Boyd
STEELE,Martha A AGE:88 6 26   20 Apr 1910 Hudson, NH Jeremiah B Brown
STEELE,Mary AGE:95   9   26 Apr 1849 Hudson, NH
STEELE,Moses AGE:3   10   18 Jan 1792 Hudson, NH William Steele & Polly
STEELE,Samuel AGE:80 10   19 May 1866 Hudson, NH
STEELE,Samuel AGE:80   19 Mar 1866 Hudson, NH
STEELE,Samuel A AGE:52 2   31 Jan 1885 Hudson, NH Samuel Steele (Hudson, NH)
& Fannie Blodgett (Hudson, NH)
STEELE,Sarah AGE:6   13 Jan 1816 Hudson, NH James Steele & Hannah
STEELE,Silas T AGE:84 4 27   19 Nov 1908 Hudson, NH Samuel Steele
& Fannie Blodgett
STEELE,William AGE:68   26 Mar 1816 Hudson, NH
STEELE,[Unknown] AGE:1   12 Nov 1894 Hudson, NH Chas A Steele (Hudson, NH)
& Lottie A Reynolds (Windham)
STEELE,[Unknown] AGE:3   09 Feb 1942 Nashua, NH Ralph H Steele & Lena Karstock
STEREY,Herbert A AGE:80 9   03 Nov 1943 Nashua, NH
STERGION,Athena AGE:89   07 Oct 1984 Nashua, NH
STERGIOU,Peter A AGE:91   14 Dec 1980 Nashua, NH
STEVENS,George L AGE:69   13 Aug 1955 Nashua, NH
STEVENS,Hannah AGE:86   03 Aug 1841 Hudson, NH
STEVENS,Harry H AGE:40 9 7   01 Sep 1906 Hudson, NH Samuel Stevens
& Sophia M Cother
STEVENS,Laura M AGE:80   01 Sep 1955 Hudson, NH
STEVENS,Marion A AGE:54   29 Sep 1951 Nashua, NH
STEVENS,Mary J AGE:67   06 Mar 1909 Hudson, NH John Nutter & Sarah Dudley
STEVENS,William F AGE:82 15 May 1949 Hudson, NH David Stevens & Jane Stevens
STEWART,Albert A AGE:61 2 25   20 Oct 1934 Hudson, NH Robert Stewart & Melvin
STEWART,Augusta A AGE:33   25 Dec 1882 Hudson, NH William Melvin
& Betsy Robinson
STEWART,Robert S AGE:72   12 Nov 1900 Hudson, NH Francis Stewart & Cutter
STICKNEY,John A AGE:77   19 Jan 1984 Nashua, NH
STICKNEY,Sarah Webster AGE: 1857 Hudson, NH
STILWELL,Thomas L AGE:52   23 Aug 1973 Nashua, NH
STRONG,Richard R AGE:68 6   28 Oct 1880 Hudson, NH
STRONG,Sarah A AGE:80 7   20 Oct 1896 Hudson, NH Jonathan Bagley
(Amesbury, MA) & Sarah Smith (Sanbornton)
STULTZ,Edith B AGE:89   23 Apr 1980 Nashua, NH
STULTZ,Harold V AGE:85   18 Mar 1980 Nashua, NH
STULTZ,Pamela J AGE:15   06 Sep 1966 Hudson, NH

HUDSON,NH DEATHS

SULHAM,Martha A AGE: 01 Aug 1900 Hudson, NH Jeremiah Brinkworth
  & Abigail Bailey
SULLIVAN,Bertha I AGE:88 26 Feb 1983 Hudson, NH
SULLIVAN,Bridgett Jane AGE:1 Feb 1872 Hudson, NH
SULLIVAN,Franklin F AGE:58 5 28 Mar 1899 Hudson, NH
SULLIVAN,Isabel L AGE:85 07 Mar 1985 Hudson, NH
SULLIVAN,Jeremiah J AGE:15 26 Aug 1898 Hudson, NH John Sullivan & Jane Shea
SULLIVAN,John M AGE:68 08 Oct 1902 Hudson, NH
SULLIVAN,Matthew C AGE:17 22 Nov 1978 Hudson, NH
SULLIVAN,Scott P AGE:7 23 Mar 1966 Nashua, NH
SULLIVAN,William J AGE:53 8 7 25 Nov 1948 Nashua, NH Jeremiah Sullivan
  & Mary Sughrue
SURETTE,Doris AGE:73 29 Dec 1980 Manchester, NH
SUSKEVICH,John P AGE:69 24 Jun 1962 Hudson, NH
SUTHERLAND,Aurore C AGE:68 31 May 1962 Nashua, NH
SUTHERLAND,James AGE:27 05 Aug 1895 Hudson, NH
SWAIN,Howard F AGE:79 13 Apr 1985 Nashua, NH
SWANSON,John E AGE:89 16 Mar 1985 Nashua, NH
SWEETSER,Laura M AGE:74 23 May 1960 Hudson, NH
SWETT,Daniel S AGE:38 24 Nov 1901 Hudson, NH Benjamin Swett (Perry, ME)
  & Emeyline Rogers (Campton)
SWIFT,M Grace AGE:86 08 Apr 1982 Nashua, NH
SYMONDS,Albert C AGE:34   25 11 Sep 1896 Hudson, NH Thos M Symonds
  (Milltown, NB) & Martha A Hanson (New Brunswick)
SZERLOG,Richard Stanley AGE:29 13 Jan 1974 Nashua, NH
SZOPER,Henryk J AGE:3 18 18 Sep 1913 Hudson, NH Stanley Szoper
  & Henrietta Rzymian
TAFE,William AGE:60 1 5 07 Aug 1940 Goffstown, NH Thomas Tafe & Delia Lynch
TAILLON,Rodrique AGE:19 12 20 21 Jul 1924 Hudson, NH Rodoph Taillon
  & Marie Cote
TALLANT,John AGE:69 21 Jul 1819 Hudson, NH
TAMULEVICH,Gladys P AGE:74 06 Aug 1982 Hudson, NH
TANAR,Harry AGE:68 01 Sep 1975 Hudson, NH
TANAROVICZ,Alice AGE:87 30 Jun 1970 Nashua, NH
TANAROVICZ,Henry AGE:73 21 Sep 1956 Hudson, NH
TANDY,Ethel S AGE:85 17 Dec 1963 Hudson, NH
TANDY,William D AGE:98 27 Aug 1978 Nashua, NH
TANGUAY,Paul P AGE:78 12 Dec 1970 Hudson, NH
TARBELL,Frank W AGE:25 17 Mar 1906 Hudson, NH Charles A Tarbell
  & Mary A Hawlane
TARDIFF,Charles AGE:74 01 Jan 1924 Hudson, NH Joseph Tardiff
  & Arbatine Courterier
TASIAS,James AGE:65 15 Dec 1924 Hudson, NH
TATE,John W AGE:73 1 19 04 Feb 1929 Hudson, NH
TATE,Jonathan Michael AGE:2 hrs 18 May 1974 Nashua, NH
TATE,Nancy AGE:3 29 Aug 1952 Nashua, NH
TATE,Rupert E Sr AGE:69 26 Jun 1971 Derry, NH
TATE,Susie E AGE:89 07 Jul 1964 Nashua, NH
TATRO,Charles E AGE:100 08 Jul 1961 Hudson, NH
TATRO,Oliver H AGE:7 28 Mar 1905 Hudson, NH Charles Tatro & Lizzie McMillen
TATRO,Pearl I AGE:53 17 May 1963 Hudson, NH
TAYLOR,Elizabeth F AGE:78 09 Jun 1954 Hudson, NH
TAYLOR,Henry AGE:20 06 Mar 1862 Hudson, NH Thomas Taylor & Susan
TAYLOR,James AGE:38 27 Jul 1981 Hudson, NH
TAYLOR,Joseph AGE:20 06 May 1860 Hudson, NH Thomas Taylor & Susan
TAYLOR,Martha M AGE:74 3 29 05 Sep 1912 Hudson, NH Wm W Miller & Davis
TAYLOR,Mildred C AGE:4 9 15 Nov 1874 Hudson, NH
TAYLOR,Susan AGE:48 03 May 1860 Hudson, NH
TAYLOR,Thomas AGE:4 23 May 1754 Hudson, NH William Taylor & Sarah
TAYLOR,Thomas AGE:54 20 Dec 1863 Hudson, NH

HUDSON,NH DEATHS

TAYLOR,Thomas AGE: Dec 1863 Hudson, NH
TAYLOR,Walter A AGE:51   31 Jan 1976 Nashua, NH
TAYLOR,William H AGE:78 7 7 23 Dec 1912 Hudson, NH
TAYLOR,William W Jr AGE:55   01 Jan 1982 Nashua, NH
TEELE,George M AGE:71 11 14 08 Jan 1912 Hudson, NH Samuel Teele
 & Elizabeth Carr
TELLIER,Doucite AGE:90 1 6 13 Dec 1947 Hudson, NH Moise Tellier
 & Henriette Baril
TEMPLE,Elizabeth Jane AGE:1 8 17 May 1932 Hudson, NH Joseph E Temple
 & Alenia Burrell
TEMPLE,Joseph AGE:72   08 Jan 1966 Nashua, NH
TEMPLETON,E AGE:3   17 Jan 1865 Hudson, NH
TEMPLETON,E AGE: 31 Jan 1865 Hudson, NH
TENNEY,Dr Paul AGE:58   06 Apr 1821 Hudson, NH
TENNEY,Lucy W Cross AGE: 26 Oct 1822 Hudson, NH
TENNEY,Paul AGE: 09 Dec 1842 Hudson, NH
TENNEY,Sarah AGE:51   25 Oct 1818 Hudson, NH
TENNEY,Sarah Hills AGE:84   22 Nov 1857 Hudson, NH
TERRIS,Hattie R AGE:72   07 Nov 1966 Hudson, NH
TESSIER,Eugene AGE:68   21 Apr 1953 Hudson, NH
TESSIER,Jeannette Cora AGE:66   24 Jun 1979 Nashua, NH
TESSIER,Louis AGE:71 10 07 Sep 1921 Hudson, NH Louis Tessier
 & Theatesle Bourquet
TESSIER,Norman L AGE:59   04 Jun 1985 Nashua, NH
THERIAULT,Marcel AGE:42 6 26 17 Jun 1928 Hudson, NH Adolph Theriault
 & Hermine Theriaut
THERRIEN,Sister Yvonne AGE:81   13 May 1979 Nashua, NH
THIBODEAU,Lottie E AGE:75   24 Jan 1963 Hudson, NH
THIBODEAU,Sophie AGE:80 11 7 22 Oct 1928 Hudson, NH Joseph St Hilaire
 & Marie Poulin
THIBODEAU,Sylvia I AGE:71   31 Dec 1978 Hudson, NH
THOMAS,Eliza A AGE:85 5 26 22 Oct 1907 Hudson, NH Oliver Sprague
 & Betsy Marshall
THOMAS,Ernest R Sr AGE:72   24 Apr 1976 Nashua, NH
THOMAS,Florence AGE:66   23 Nov 1966 Nashua, NH
THOMAS,Hazel M AGE:4 8 16 24 May 1901 Hudson, NH Pearl T Thomas (Hudson,
 NH) & Winnifred M Wells (Vermont)
THOMAS,Helen AGE:8 3 10 22 May 1907 Hudson, NH Pearl J Thomas
 & Winnifred Wells
THOMAS,Kathryne L AGE:21 3 22 17 Jun 1928 Hudson, NH Benjamin Thomas
 & Lucile G Brown
THOMAS,Laura E AGE:85   31 Dec 1954 Nashua, NH
THOMAS,Pearl T AGE:66 3 25 12 Mar 1933 Hudson, NH Tyler Thomas
 & Eliza Sprake
THOMAS,Tyler AGE:66 3 21 24 Nov 1887 Hudson, NH Joseph Thomas (New
 Hampshire) & Betsey Woods (New Hampshire)
THOMAS,Willie AGE:4   15 Oct 1865 Hudson, NH
THOMAS,Winnifred M AGE:24 6 16 06 Oct 1900 Hudson, NH George W Wells
 & Sarah Daving
THOMISSEY,Sarah C AGE:69 21 Aug 1884 Hudson, NH Joshua Cudworth (Greenfield,
 NH) & Whitcomb (Hancock, NH)
THOMPSON,Eliza A AGE: 01 Jan 1900 Nashua, NH
THOMPSON,Elizabeth M AGE:104 10 2 23 Dec 1937 Hudson, NH Hiram Marsh
 & Olivia Goodspeed
THOMPSON,Estella L AGE:59   13 Aug 1967 Nashua, NH
THOMPSON,Fred W AGE:89   02 Feb 1955 Hudson, NH
THOMPSON,George H AGE:40   20 Oct 1884 Hudson, NH Robert Thompson (England)
 & Mary Hattsley (England)
THOMPSON,Henrietta C AGE:81   09 Jan 1962 Nashua, NH
THOMPSON,John M AGE:61 11 27 Jan 1893 Hudson, NH John W Thompson (Gilford)

HUDSON,NH DEATHS

& Mary Eagle (Laconia)
THOMPSON,John W AGE:4   05 Feb 1854 Hudson, NH J H Thompson & Elizabeth Marsh
THOMPSON,Margaret A AGE:60   05 Jul 1942 Hudson, NH
THOMPSON,Palmer Curtis AGE:86 3 16   23 Jun 1942 Nashua, NH Palmer Thompson
 & Abbie Sawyer
THOMPSON,Willie H AGE:1   11 Jun 1862 Hudson, NH J H Thompson
 & Elizabeth Marsh
THOMSON,Stanley AGE:63   20 Nov 1969 Nashua, NH
THORNING,James O AGE:74   22 Nov 1901 Hudson, NH Frederick Thorning
 (Peterborough) & Hannah Carter (Willianton)
THORPE,Rose E AGE:83   31 Mar 1963 Nashua, NH
THYBERG,Albert S AGE:83   09 Feb 1976 Hudson, NH
TILLOTSON,Catherine S AGE:91   09 Jul 1954 Hudson, NH
TITUS,Orlando E AGE: 19 Aug 1891 Hudson, NH
TOLLS,Emily AGE:56   14 Jun 1877 Hudson, NH
TOMOU,George AGE:17   20 Jun 1955 Nashua, NH
TOWNE,Charlotte A AGE:82 4 28   05 Nov 1937 Hudson, NH Wilson Kimball
 & L A McGilverey
TOWNE,Sarah AGE:66   24 Dec 1860 Hudson, NH
TOWNS,Elizabeth Chase AGE:46   08 Sep 1838 Hudson, NH John Chase
TOZIER,George AGE:79 5 24   02 Mar 1919 Hudson, NH Silas Tozier & Martha Tobey
TOZIER,George E AGE:74   08 Mar 1967 Nashua, NH
TRACY,Sarah M AGE:87 11 1   24 May 1923 Hudson, NH Elbridge Gould
 & Sarah Trask
TRAFTON,Georgina D AGE:84   10 Feb 1959 Hudson, NH
TRETTEL,James L Jr AGE:25   17 Aug 1967 Milford, MA
TRIPPLETON,Hildred A AGE:81   12 Oct 1972 Nashua, NH
TROKEM,Helen AGE:44   08 May 1939 Hudson, NH Ukanawicz
TROKIM,Anthony AGE:72   17 Feb 1958 Nashua, NH
TROKIMAS,Helen A AGE:24   22 04 Jun 1942 Concord, NH Anthony Trokimas
 & Helen Yhnere
TROMBLEY,Louis W AGE:57   12 23 May 1946 Hudson, NH Napoleon Trombley
 & Zoie Moran
TROMBLY,Charles N AGE:55   19 Nov 1957 Nashua, NH
TROPEANO,Ester AGE:72   21 Nov 1984 Nashua, NH
TROW,George W AGE:78 6   28 Feb 1903 Hudson, NH Jesse Trow & Nancy Cochran
TROW,Laura F AGE:92   25 Jun 1954 Hudson, NH
TROW,Permelia AGE:82   29 08 Feb 1910 Hudson, NH Noah Shattuck
TROW,Permelia S AGE:82   29 08 Feb 1911 Hudson, NH Noar Shattuck
TROW,Wallace G AGE:71   20 Apr 1940 Hudson, NH George Trow & Pamela Shattuck
TRUDEAU,Leontine AGE:77   12 Feb 1955 Nashua, NH
TRUDEAU,Ulric O AGE:77   02 Mar 1980 Nashua, NH
TRUFANT,Arthur AGE:66   16 Mar 1964 Nashua, NH
TRUFANT,Ernest AGE:71   09 May 1965 Nashua, NH
TRUFANT,Flora E AGE:71 11 27   15 Mar 1942 Nashua, NH Robert Turner, Sr
 & Lacretia Turner
TRUFANT,Gertrude M AGE:59   11 Apr 1964 Nashua, NH
TRUFANT,Mildred Ruth AGE:20 7   22 May 1922 Hudson, NH Albert Trufant
 & Mamie E Ridley
TRUFANT,Rebecca R AGE:78 11 25   21 Jul 1917 Hudson, NH William Mountfort
 & Margaret Campbell
TUBINIS,Andrew AGE:77   15 Nov 1960 Nashua, NH
TULLY,Mary Jane AGE:42   24 Jun 1898 Hudson, NH Thomas Tully
 & Margaret Corniff
TUPPER,Mabel C AGE:83   28 Feb 1949 Hudson, NH Ancil D Holt
 & Catherine Granger
TURCOTT,Jennie J AGE:47   08 Dec 1967 Hudson, NH
TURLA,Ludwik AGE:51   18 Nov 1937 Hudson, NH Michael Turla & Gomecila Kurta
TURMEL,David AGE:74   12 Jan 1968 Nashua, NH
TURNER,Franklin J AGE:10 15   05 Dec 1875 Hudson, NH George R Turner

HUDSON,NH DEATHS

   & Helen V
TUSKI,Clement AGE:63   04 Apr 1950 Hudson, NH Gabrial Tuski & Westa Tuski
TWISS,Ethel M AGE:87   21 Nov 1982 Nashua, NH
TWISS,Howard Alfred AGE:10 8 02 Dec 1922 Hudson, NH Walter F Twiss
   & Ethel M Wheeler
TWISS,Jenny M AGE:85 3 7   04 May 1939 Hudson, NH George W Cochran
   & Eliza M Merrill
TWITCHELL,Raymond AGE:74   18 Apr 1963 Hudson, NH
TWOMBLY,Cora B AGE:87   14 Mar 1977 Nashua, NH
ULOTH,Frederick Lewis AGE:87   29 Oct 1984 Hudson, NH
UNDERWOOD,Dustin AGE: 1814 Malden, MA
UNDERWOOD,Jeptha AGE:67   06 Jan 1851 Hudson, NH
UNDERWOOD,John W AGE:69   23 May 1855 Hudson, NH
UNDERWOOD,Louisa AGE: 20 Apr 1835 Bolton, MA
UNDERWOOD,Phineas AGE:23   04 Dec 1800 Hudson, NH
UNDERWOOD,Phineas AGE:45   09 May 1798 Hudson, NH
UNDERWOOD,Rebecca AGE:66   17 Nov 1815 Hudson, NH
UNDERWOOD,Rebecca AGE:72   19 Sep 1852 Hudson, NH
UNDERWOOD,Sarah Cummings AGE:87   29 Nov 1873 Hudson, NH
USEFORGE,Bernard AGE:17   23 Apr 1976 Pelham, NH
USOVICZ,Peter AGE:51   20 Feb 1963 Nashua, NH
VADNEY,Dennis M AGE:5   25 Oct 1959 Nashua, NH
VAILLANCOURT,Beatrice M AGE:91   27 Jun 1982 Nashua, NH
VAILLANCOURT,Lillian B AGE:36   24 Aug 1956 Nashua, NH
VAILLANCOURT,William AGE:79   05 Aug 1960 Hudson, NH
VALCOURT,Armand AGE:44   19 Apr 1983 Nashua, NH
VALLERAND,Emile F AGE:60   18 Dec 1970 Lowell, MA
Van BUSKIRK,B I AGE:1   06 Oct 1915 Hudson, NH G B Van Buskirk (Algona, Iowa)
   & Mary I Basham (Arcadia, Kansas)
VANASSE,Oscar J AGE:61   08 Jan 1956 Nashua, NH
VANTINE,Bertha Louise AGE:57 11 9   04 Feb 1934 Hudson, NH Marcus W Nye
   & Lettie Stoddard
VENNE,Georgianna AGE:76   27 Apr 1960 Nashua, NH
VERVILLE,Armande AGE:90   03 Jul 1979 Hudson, NH
VICKERS,John D AGE:48 10 17   24 Apr 1933 Hudson, NH
VIENS,Adelard AGE:74   26 Mar 1974 Nashua, NH
VIENS,Evelyn E AGE:50   21 Jun 1978 Nashua, NH
VIENS,Harvey J AGE:80   05 Jun 1974 Nashua, NH
VIENS,Irene AGE:81   01 Aug 1980 Nashua, NH
VIENS,Louise M AGE:2 hrs   03 Oct 1957 Nashua, NH
VIENS,Mary F AGE:66   25 Mar 1958 Hudson, NH
VIGNOLA,Arthur V AGE:4 24   23 Jul 1941 Hudson, NH Arthur Vignola
   & Irene Lavorture
VIGNOLA,Arthur V AGE:30   23 Jul 1951 Nashua, NH
VIGNOLA,Joseph AGE:68 2 21   12 Jun 1948 Nashua, NH
VIGNOLA,Paul AGE:51   13 Jul 1970 Nashua, NH
VIRBALAS,Antonia AGE:87   25 Mar 1980 Nashua, NH
VISKEN,Alec AGE:62   22 Aug 1955 Nashua, NH
VOLTZ,Ella AGE:58 4 5   26 Jun 1944 Nashua, NH Joseph Parent & Phoebe Duhaine
VOSE,George H AGE:80 9 6   22 Jan 1918 Hudson, NH
VOSE,Mary Ball AGE:80 10 23   05 Jul 1912 Hudson, NH Reuel Miller & Sarah Ball
VROUHAS,Christopher AGE:8   09 Aug 1984 Nashua, NH
VURVULIKIS,Gregoreos AGE:10   19 Nov 1924 Hudson, NH James Vurvulikis
   & Annie Morenos
VYDFOL,Albert AGE:73   11 Jan 1960 Hanover, NH
VYDFOL,Matthew AGE:56   18 Jul 1967 Nashua, NH
VYDFOL,Peter AGE:48   04 Oct 1960 Concord, NH
WADDELL,Ellen AGE:89   18 Jul 1959 Hudson, NH
WAISWILOS,Anthony A AGE:75   05 Feb 1984 Nashua, NH
WAISWILOS,Joseph J AGE:62   16 Feb 1968 Hudson, NH

HUDSON,NH DEATHS

WAISWILOS,Stella I AGE:75   02 Jun 1983 Nashua, NH
WALBRIDGE,Edna M AGE:85   06 Feb 1980 Hudson, NH
WALCH,Amy D AGE:18 10 2   31 Jan 1897 Hudson, NH Clarence E Walch
  & Delia C Hutchinson
WALKER,Elbridge AGE:76 4 19   03 Aug 1916 Hudson, NH Townsend Walker
  & Susan Wheeler
WALKER,Gerry AGE:85   10 Jun 1896 Hudson, NH
WALKER,James G AGE:74 1 29   19 Dec 1916 Hudson, NH Gerry Walker
  & Turner Wright
WALKER,Robert Brenton AGE:83   24 Jun 1983 Bedford, NH
WALLACE,Hosea C AGE:46 3   04 Aug 1883 Hudson, NH John Wallace & Lucy Blodgett
WALLACE,Marie E AGE:43   06 Aug 1978 Hanover, NH
WALLACE,Mary F AGE:76 5 29   09 Oct 1929 Hudson, NH Charles Maynard
  & Harriet A Fairbanks
WALLACE, MD,Alonzo S AGE:83 1 23   09 Apr 1930 Hudson, NH David Wallace
  & Margaret Wallace
WALMSLEY,Moses AGE:75   15 Jan 1975 Nashua, NH
WALSH,Joseph AGE:74   08 Dec 1971 Nashua, NH
WALTON,Samuel AGE:75   21 Feb 1892 Hudson, NH Samuel Walton (England)
  & Elizabeth Diggils (England)
WALTON,Samuel AGE:75   02 Feb 1892 Hudson, NH
WARDEN,Charles D AGE:74   20 Apr 1956 Hudson, NH
WARNER,Esther A AGE:83   16 Apr 1903 Hudson, NH Aaron Warner
  & Rebecca Lawrence
WARREN,Adam F AGE:63   01 May 1880 Hudson, NH Labon Warren
WARREN,George Fred AGE:65 7 26   24 Apr 1928 Hudson, NH George H Warren
  & Elizabeth Danforth
WARREN,Mary A AGE:24   26 Oct 1868 Hudson, NH William Warren & Eliza A
WARREN,Sarah D W AGE:70 6 5   16 Apr 1893 Hudson, NH Joel Barrett
  (Concord, MA) & Sarah Wyman (Roxbury, MA)
WARREN,William AGE:43   09 May 1861 Hudson, NH
WASON,Hannah AGE:80   16 Apr 1786 Hudson, NH
WASON,Hannah AGE:1 11 6   18 Oct 1795 Hudson, NH Samuel Wason & Margaret
WASON,James AGE:89   22 Aug 1799 Hudson, NH
WASON,James AGE:70   08 Aug 1851 Hudson, NH
WASON,Lieut Thomas AGE:84   18 Nov 1832 Hudson, NH
WASON,Lucy AGE:52   21 Feb 1843 Hudson, NH
WASON,Margaret AGE:77   10 Aug 1819 Hudson, NH
WASON,Mary AGE:83   20 Oct 1832 Hudson, NH
WASON,Mary AGE:79 5 1   22 May 1873 Hudson, NH
WASON,Mary AGE:80   24 May 1873 Hudson, NH
WASON,Moses AGE:50   17 Feb 1822 Hudson, NH
WASON,Samuel AGE:80   24 Feb 1827 Hudson, NH
WASON,Thomas Boyd AGE:72 7 21   23 Jun 1858 Hudson, NH
WATERS,Henry Otis AGE:86 8   12 Jun 1933 Hudson, NH Joseph F Waters
  & Cynthia E Barrett
WATSON,Louise E AGE:44   06 Jan 1963 Nashua, NH
WATTS,Hugh AGE:54 6   Hudson, NH
WATTS,William H AGE:1 5 26   26 Jan 1912 Hudson, NH Wm Watts & Ida Weston
WEAVER,Nellie A AGE:49   21 Jul 1963 Nashua, NH
WEBSTER,Abiah C AGE:79   1 02 Feb 1916 Hudson, NH Seth Cutter & Deborah Gage
WEBSTER,Benjamin AGE:78 8   16 Jun 1873 Hudson, NH
WEBSTER,Brinton M AGE:57 1 17   23 Nov 1921 Hudson, NH Nathan P Webster
  & Susan Morrison
WEBSTER,Charles AGE: Hudson, NH George Webster & Sarah
WEBSTER,Ebenezer AGE: Oct 1823 Hudson, NH
WEBSTER,Edson T AGE:3   04 Oct 1870 Hudson, NH Mark H Webster, Jr & Melissa
WEBSTER,Eleazer C AGE:2   20 Dec 1823 Hudson, NH John Webster
  & Hannah Cummings
WEBSTER,Emily A Woodbury AGE: 23 Sep 1868 Hudson, NH

HUDSON,NH DEATHS

WEBSTER,Frank K AGE: 27 Oct 1900 Boston, MA
WEBSTER,Freddie AGE: 09 Apr 1863 Hudson, NH
WEBSTER,George Robert AGE: Hudson, NH John Webster
WEBSTER,Hannah AGE:76 03 Feb 1871 Hudson, NH Eleazer Cummings & Sally
WEBSTER,Hannah Cummings AGE:76 5 23 03 Feb 1871 Hudson, NH
WEBSTER,Hannah J AGE:20 05 Sep 1851 Hudson, NH John Webster
    & Hannah Cummings
WEBSTER,Hannah O Kenniston AGE:22 1 5 02 Apr 1858 Hudson, NH
WEBSTER,Henry AGE: Hudson, NH Kimball Webster
WEBSTER,Henry Kimball AGE: 31 Jan 1869 Hudson, NH Moses Webster & Lydia M B
WEBSTER,Isaac AGE:73 28 Nov 1859 Meredith, NH
WEBSTER,John AGE:91 2 4 01 Mar 1883 Hudson, NH Ebenezer Webster
    & Betsy Bradford
WEBSTER,John Baldwin AGE:60 27 Aug 1865 Hudson, NH
WEBSTER,John Johnson AGE: 16 Sep 1866 Hudson, NH
WEBSTER,Kimball AGE:87 7 27 29 Jun 1916 Hudson, NH John Webster
    & Hannah Cummings
WEBSTER,Kimball AGE:26   Hudson, NH
WEBSTER,Laura A AGE: 23 Aug 1848 Hudson, NH Simon G Webster & Relief Jones
WEBSTER,Lauretta Hamblett AGE: 08 Jul 1857 Hudson, NH
WEBSTER,Lettie R AGE:22 3 17 12 Nov 1887 Hudson, NH Kimball Webster
    (Pelham, NH) & Abiah Cutter (Pelham, NH)
WEBSTER,Lettie Ray AGE:22 3 17 12 Nov 1887 Hudson, NH Kimball Webster
    & Abiah Cutter
WEBSTER,Lizette S AGE:72 10 28 25 Jun 1913 Hudson, NH Henry C Fowler
    & Myra Quimby
WEBSTER,Lizzie H AGE:74 4 4 18 Jun 1940 Nashua, NH William H Smith
WEBSTER,Louisa B AGE:2 06 Feb 1851 Hudson, NH Mark H Webster & Sally
WEBSTER,Luelle A Piper AGE:22 24 Jan 1864 Hudson, NH
WEBSTER,Mark H AGE:70 5 25 Apr 1874 Hudson, NH
WEBSTER,Mary Harris AGE: Jun 1809 Hudson, NH
WEBSTER,Mary L AGE:3 22 Apr 1849 Hudson, NH Mark H Webster & Sally
WEBSTER,Melville T AGE:1 4 13 Sep 1867 Hudson, NH Willard H Webster
    & Addie M Walton
WEBSTER,Milton E AGE:8 26 Aug 1847 Hudson, NH John Webster & Hannah Cummings
WEBSTER,Moses AGE:69 2 15 Jan 1887 Vinal Haven, ME
WEBSTER,Nathan P AGE:57 8 28 Jan 1893 Hudson, NH John Webster (Pelham)
    & Hannah Webster (Hudson, NH)
WEBSTER,Nellie T AGE:1 18 Sep 1867 Hudson, NH
WEBSTER,Orin P AGE:23 03 Feb 1867 Hudson, NH
WEBSTER,Orrin P AGE:23 9 24 03 Feb 1867 Hudson, NH John Webster
    & Hannah Cummings
WEBSTER,Relief Johnson AGE:75 9 17 Nov 1867 Hudson, NH
WEBSTER,Relief Jones AGE: Sep 1848 Hudson, NH
WEBSTER,Sarah Harwood AGE: 07 Nov 1836 Hudson, NH
WEBSTER,Sarah T Palmer AGE: 23 Jul 1835 Hudson, NH
WEBSTER,Sarah Woodbury AGE: Oct 1868 Hudson, NH
WEBSTER,Sibbel Kelley AGE:86 30 Apr 1868 Hudson, NH
WEBSTER,Simon B AGE:76 6 08 Oct 1860 Hudson, NH
WEBSTER,Simon Gilman AGE: 30 Mar 1885 Vinal Haven, ME
WEBSTER,Sophia AGE:21 15 Nov 1860 Hudson, NH
WEBSTER,Sophie C Foster AGE:21 4 21 15 Nov 1860 Hudson, NH
WEBSTER,Submitte AGE:79 4 10 May 1876 Hudson, NH
WEBSTER,Susan AGE:25 06 Oct 1864 Boston, MA
WEBSTER,Susan M AGE:25 11 9 06 Oct 1864 Hudson, NH
WEBSTER,Willard H AGE:32 8 1 23 Nov 1869 Hudson, NH
WEBSTER,Willard H AGE:32 25 Nov 1869 Hudson, NH
WEIDMAN,Sheridan H AGE:92 30 Oct 1962 Hudson, NH
WEINER,Louis AGE:74 5 7 21 Sep 1919 Hudson, NH Adam Weiner
    & Marguretta Hellar

HUDSON,NH DEATHS

WELCH,Henry Nelson AGE:83 9 4   16 Jan 1928 Hudson, NH Silas Welch
    & Lucy Keys Gregory
WELDON,Geraldine C AGE:34   22 Jun 1967 Lowell, MA
WELLS,Allen C AGE:47 4 23   21 Jan 1905 Hudson, NH Charles H Wells
    & Elvira Putnam
WELLS,Mary AGE:61 4 11   23 Feb 1889 Hudson, NH John Spalding (Pelham, NH)
    & Sarah Perham (Tyngsboro, MA)
WELLS,Melissa L AGE:73 2 13   14 Apr 1934 Hudson, NH James Wescott
    & Permalia Chase
WENTWORTH,Albert E Jr AGE:31   07 Nov 1971 Dracut, MA
WENTWORTH,Maybell F AGE:21 5 19   17 Apr 1906 Hudson, NH Robert T Connell
    & Mary L Marshall
WENTWORTH,Minnie AGE:15   27 May 1900 Hudson, NH Nathaniel Wentworth
    & Edwina Greeley
WENTWORTH,Nathaniel AGE:79 8 11   19 Aug 1923 Hudson, NH Nathaniel Wentworth
    & Lord
WESTBROOK,Scot J AGE:2   11 Nov 1960 Nashua, NH
WESTNEAT,Rev Arthur S AGE:87   04 Dec 1965 Nashua, NH
WESTON,William S AGE:62 11 13   19 Mar 1885 Hudson, NH Sarson Weston
    (Amherst, NH) & Nancy Weston (Amherst, NH)
WHEELER,Abbie A AGE:76   26   25 Aug 1912 Hudson, NH Matthias Wilson
    & Laura Morgan
WHEELER,Abbie A AGE:38   12 Jun 1865 Hudson, NH Thomas Marsh
WHEELER,Ethel M AGE:50 7 20   26 Jan 1942 Hudson, NH Frank E Smith
    & Mary Carey
WHEELER,Grace F AGE:93   25 May 1966 Nashua, NH
WHEELER,Inez M AGE:72 2 7   09 Apr 1947 Hudson, NH Orcutt A Moffett
    & Estella Converse
WHEELER,Josiah K AGE:88 10 25   10 Jun 1911 Hudson, NH Josiah Wheeler
    & Dollie Shattuck
WHEELER,Norman C AGE:71   26 Aug 1965 Nashua, NH
WHEELER,Olive A AGE:83   01 Jan 1958 Nashua, NH
WHEELER,Richard J Jr AGE:2 1 9   12 Apr 1948 Hudson, NH R J Wheeler, Sr
    & Eleanor Boyer
WHITCOMB,Esther M AGE:83 5 17   13 Sep 1917 Hudson, NH Alanson Miller
    & Hannah Porter
WHITCOMB,Geo W AGE:79   08 Apr 1905 Hudson, NH
WHITE,Annie R AGE:11 17   17 Feb 1896 Hudson, NH William H White (Berwick, ME)
    & Rosalie A Stratton (Wolcott, VT)
WHITE,Lucian AGE:5 17   16 Mar 1885 Hudson, NH Charles White (Haverhill, NH)
    & Marcia Grant (Pawnell, ME)
WHITE,Marcia AGE:49 4 11   02 Jul 1893 Hudson, NH Aran Grant & Mohale Libby
WHITEHEAD,George AGE:82   19 Jun 1961 Hudson, NH
WHITNEY,Carl H AGE:62   01 Jan 1953 Hudson, NH
WHITNEY,Irene F AGE:78   07 Dec 1982 Nashua, NH
WHITNEY,Kevin AGE:1   20 Aug 1966 Hudson, NH
WHITTEMORE,Edward K AGE:58   06 May 1879 Hudson, NH
WHITTEMORE,Rebecca AGE:40   18 Oct 1860 Hudson, NH
WHITTEMORE,Rebecca S AGE:32   18 Oct 1860 Hudson, NH
WHITTEMORE,Wanda AGE:51   13 May 1965 Nashua, NH
WHITTIER,Horatio G AGE:79 10 26   13 Sep 1889 Hudson, NH Reuben Whittier
    (Candia) & Lucy Chaplin (Connecticut)
WHITTIER,Martha AGE:97   Jul 1825 Hudson, NH
WHITTIER,Mary Webster AGE: 1857 Hudson, NH
WHITTIER,Nancy Hill AGE:28   24 Apr 1865 Hudson, NH
WHITTIER,Reuben S AGE: 11 Nov 1901 Hudson, NH Horatio G Whittier
    (Dorchester, MA) & Sarah H Sanderson (Linnfield, MA)
WHITTIER,Sarah H AGE:95 3   26 May 1908 Hudson, NH Benjamin Sanderson
    & Sarah Smith
WHITTLE,Electa A AGE:68 11   10 Jul 1887 Hudson, NH

HUDSON,NH DEATHS

WHITTLE,Frank L AGE:23 2 10 Feb 1868 Hudson, NH
WHITTLE,Ralph L AGE:73 03 May 1881 Hudson, NH
WHYTE,John T AGE:71 23 Aug 1967 Manchester, NH
WIGGIN,Charles E AGE:60 02 May 1952 Nashua, NH
WIGGIN,Charles E Jr AGE:50 12 Oct 1964 Nashua, NH
WIGGIN,Georgia A AGE:100 09 Jan 1958 Hudson, NH
WIGGIN,May AGE:59 20 Apr 1951 Concord, NH
WILBUR,Hollis W AGE:59 08 Aug 1970 Hudson, NH
WILCOX,Bernice M AGE:74 06 Jul 1968 Nashua, NH
WILCOX,Clyde E AGE:80 23 Oct 1965 Hudson, NH
WILCOX,Elmer E AGE:4 3 10 Sep 1882 Hudson, NH William Wilcox & Eliza Hughs
WILDER,Rev Robt H AGE:75 2 24 29 Sep 1905 Hudson, NH Willis Wilder
  & Laura Houston
WILKINS,Hazel G AGE:81 16 Mar 1981 Nashua, NH
WILLARD,Elliot K AGE:8 21 05 Sep 1912 Hudson, NH Francis Willard
  & Ina Kilbourn
WILLETT,Mary B AGE:71   20 20 Jan 1948 Hudson, NH Michael Collins
  & Mary O'Neil
WILLETTE,Alfred P AGE:80   16 10 Sep 1947 Hudson, NH
WILLETTE,Laurent AGE:76 5 16 01 Oct 1930 Hudson, NH Louis Willette
  & Philam Michaud
WILLEY,Mary M AGE:81 27 Feb 1976 Derry, NH
WILLIAMS,Claude J AGE:43 26 Dec 1971 Nashua, NH
WILLIAMS,Earl F AGE:81 15 Aug 1973 Nashua, NH
WILLIAMS,Eliza AGE:81 25 May 1973 Nashua, NH
WILLIAMS,Gertrude L AGE:89 26 Dec 1962 Hudson, NH
WILLIAMSON,Kendall AGE:74 6 24 24 Dec 1916 Hudson, NH Harry Williamson
  & Welthea Willey
WILLIAMSON,Maybelle R AGE:59 20 Sep 1960 Nashua, NH
WILLOBY,Harvey M AGE:80 10 14 27 Nov 1913 Hudson, NH Oliver Willoughby
  & Martha Hardy
WILLOBY,Helen W AGE:68 10 13 05 Apr 1914 Hudson, NH Daniel Willoby
WILLOUGHBY,Benjamin F AGE:72 7 23 25 Jul 1913 Hudson, NH Mark Willoughby
  & Susan Blodgett
WILLOUGHBY,Edwin AGE:33 22 Jan 1879 Hudson, NH Mark Willoughby & Susan
WILLOUGHBY,Eliza M AGE:43 13 Aug 1878 Hudson, NH Samuel Marsh & Fanny
WILLOUGHBY,Ethan AGE:48 5 11 25 Sep 1855
WILLOUGHBY,Ethan V B AGE:18 3 18 07 Jul 1855 Hudson, NH Ethan Willoughby
  & Alice
WILLOUGHBY,Mark AGE:77 5 21 Apr 1886 Hudson, NH
WILLOUGHBY,Mary F AGE:4 13 Oct 1868 Hudson, NH
WILLOUGHBY,Susan AGE:75 7 17 Dec 1887 Hudson, NH Jabez Blodgett (Hudson, NH)
  & Rachel Pollard (Hudson, NH)
WILLOUGHBY,Susan Blodgett AGE:75 7 17 Dec 1887 Hudson, NH
WILLOUGHBY,Susan F AGE:2 13 Nov 1839 Hudson, NH Ethan Willoughby & Alice
WILLS,Myrant AGE:57 11 24 21 May 1925 Hudson, NH Bliss Wills
  & Marshia Wallbridge
WILMOT,Gertrude A AGE:47 17 Aug 1950 Nashua, NH John Ferguson
  & Fannie Ellsworth
WILMOT,Helen AGE:58 6 21 Feb 1886 Groton, MA
WILMOT,Lillian A AGE:77 1 10 24 Apr 1944 Nashua, NH
WILSON,Clarissa AGE:80 9 16 21 Jan 1890 Hudson, NH Asa Gould (Hudson, NH)
  & Mary Cummings (Hudson, NH)
WILSON,Clarissa Gould AGE:80 9 16 21 Jan 1890 Hudson, NH Asa Gould
WILSON,Elizabeth M AGE:91 13 Jan 1949 Hudson, NH Edward Berry
  & Letitia Smithwick
WILSON,Franklin AGE:76 8 05 Apr 1883 Hudson, NH James Wilson & Lucinda Page
WILSON,Henry C AGE:57 23 Aug 1970 E Meadow, NY
WILSON,James F AGE:74 6 4 12 Apr 1912 Hudson, NH Franklin Wilson
  & Clarrisa Gould

HUDSON,NH DEATHS

WILSON,Joseph P AGE:80   18 Jun 1842 Hudson, NH
WILSON,Julianna AGE:21   08 Nov 1828 Hudson, NH
WILSON,Lillian T AGE:94   16 Oct 1961 Hudson, NH
WILSON,Lucinda AGE:38   05 Apr 1831 Hudson, NH
WILSON,Marie A AGE:54   07 Jan 1972 Nashua, NH
WILSON,Marie W AGE:60   02 Nov 1967 Nashua, NH
WILSON,Orin AGE:47 3 8   22 Apr 1931 Hudson, NH Frank Wilson & Abbie Walker
WILSON,Phebe AGE:73   17 Sep 1837 Hudson, NH
WILSON,Sarah H AGE:72 3 27   28 Nov 1912 Hudson, NH Edward Riley
    & Martha Colburn
WILSON,Seneca AGE:25 8   08 Sep 1823 Hudson, NH
WILSON,Willis H AGE:80   11 Nov 1950 Hudson, NH Charles H Wilson
    & Eliza Chamberlain
WINEY,Cloyd L AGE:90   07 Sep 1965 Hudson, NH
WINN,Abiathar AGE:67   16 Feb 1868 Hudson, NH Reuben Winn
WINN,Abiathar AGE:5 3   18 Dec 1831 Hudson, NH Abiathar Winn & Mary
WINN,Abiathar AGE: Hudson, NH
WINN,Abiather AGE:38   24 Aug 1783 Hudson, NH
WINN,Abiather AGE:67   16 Feb 1868 Hudson, NH
WINN,Alice M AGE:30 9   10 Nov 1905 Hudson, NH George Mocklock & Eliza Hawes
WINN,Alvah AGE:25   26 Sep 1821 Hudson, NH
WINN,Amos AGE:74   1   15 Aug 1892 Hudson, NH Reuben Winn (Hudson, NH)
    & Mary Bowman (Milton, MA)
WINN,Anna P AGE:61 1 3   18 Nov 1876 Hudson, NH
WINN,Ardelia C AGE:45   13 Sep 1900 Hudson, NH Thomas Caldwell & Mary Butrick
WINN,Benjamin AGE:4 6   25 Jul 1780 Hudson, NH   Abiather Winn & Abigail
WINN,Benjamin AGE:38   30 Apr 1766 Hudson, NH
WINN,Charles P AGE:16   28 Nov 1823 Hudson, NH
WINN,Clara G AGE:21   29 May 1872 Hudson, NH
WINN,Clarinda A AGE:2   1 17   14 Mar 1854 Hudson, NH John Winn & Anna P
WINN,Cyrus AGE:26 6 18   03 Jul 1819 Hudson, NH Joseph Winn & Sarah
WINN,Elizabeth AGE:74   17 Sep 1778 Hudson, NH
WINN,Elizabeth AGE:89   26 Jun 1860 Hudson, NH
WINN,Elizabeth Chase AGE:4 4   16 Aug 1825 Hudson, NH Joseph Winn & Margaret
WINN,Ellen M AGE:17 6   12 Nov 1867 Hudson, NH John Winn & Anna P
WINN,Elmer C AGE:72 8 25   07 May 1926 Hudson, NH Paul T Winn
    & Fannie Parkhurst
WINN,Emeline AGE:16   17 Aug 1818 Hudson, NH Reuben Winn & Mary
WINN,Fanny B AGE:55   Hudson, NH John Parkhurst & Betsy Edwards
WINN,Franklin M AGE:76 2 22   05 Jun 1915 Hudson, NH William Winn (Hudson, NH)
    & Persis G Moore (Goffs Falls, NH)
WINN,Hannah AGE:68   18 Nov 1876 Hudson, NH
WINN,Hannah Roxanna AGE:2   16 Aug 1825 Hudson, NH Joseph Winn & Margaret
WINN,Isaac AGE:51 3 14   03 Sep 1854 Hudson, NH
WINN,J Sylvanus AGE:65 5 4   01 Jun 1903 Hudson, NH John Winn & Anna Patch
WINN,Jacob AGE:1   1 16   28 Aug 1848 Hudson, NH John Winn & Anna P
WINN,John AGE:76   02 Sep 1876 Hudson, NH
WINN,Joseph AGE:83   01 Dec 1805 Hudson, NH
WINN,Joseph AGE:73   06 Sep 1833 Hudson, NH
WINN,Joseph AGE:87   29 Jun 1874 Hudson, NH
WINN,Joseph A AGE:29   06 Oct 1873 Hudson, NH
WINN,Joseph G AGE:34   18 Sep 1862 Virginia
WINN,Joseph Sylvanus AGE:7 5   03 Sep 1825 Hudson, NH Joseph Winn & Margaret
WINN,Judith AGE:72   17 Feb 1792 Hudson, NH
WINN,Lieut Joseph AGE:84   25 Aug 1781 Hudson, NH
WINN,Lucy M AGE:73 5 5   05 Dec 1915 Hudson, NH Elijah Richardson (Woburn, MA)
    & Lorain Butters
WINN,Margaret B AGE:83   25 Jan 1873 Hudson, NH
WINN,Margaret Burns AGE:88 10   25 Jan 1873 Hudson, NH
WINN,Marietta AGE:45 8 9   24 Sep 1854 Hudson, NH

HUDSON,NH DEATHS

WINN,Marietta A AGE:10 10   19 May 1838 Hudson, NH Isaac Winn & Marietta E
WINN,Mary AGE:77   16 Aug 1858 Hudson, NH
WINN,Mary AGE:60 6   13 Jul 1862 Hudson, NH
WINN,Mary AGE:60   18 Jul 1862 Hudson, NH
WINN,Mary A AGE:43 1 9   03 Jun 1884 Hudson, NH John Winn (Hudson, NH)
    & Anna Patch (Groton, MA)
WINN,Mary French AGE:86   02 Mar 1807 Hudson, NH
WINN,Mary L AGE:21   23 Oct 1870 Hudson, NH Paul L Winn
WINN,Micahajah AGE:19   25 Jul 1790 Hudson, NH Abiather Winn & Abigail
WINN,Mifs Sary AGE:22   04 Mar 1763 Hudson, NH Lieut Joseph Winn & Elizabeth
WINN,Nathan AGE:26   05 Feb 1765 Hudson, NH
WINN,Nathan AGE:44   25 Sep 1809 Hudson, NH
WINN,Nathan AGE:23   07 Dec 1813 Hudson, NH
WINN,Paul T AGE:93   29 29 Aug 1898 Hudson, NH Joseph Winn & Sarah Chase
WINN,Persis G Moore AGE: 29 Nov 1843 Hudson, NH
WINN,Phebe AGE:72   May 1863 Hudson, NH
WINN,Phebe C AGE:67   10 May 1863 Hudson, NH
WINN,Reuben AGE:56   01 Oct 1835 Hudson, NH
WINN,Rosilla AGE:31   30 Apr 1830 Hudson, NH
WINN,Rufus E AGE:87 8 6   27 Mar 1933 Hudson, NH John Winn & Anna Patch
WINN,Sarah AGE:3   17 Dec 1776 Hudson, NH Abiather Winn & Abigail
WINN,Sarah AGE:19   24 Aug 1753 Hudson, NH James Winn & Abigail Hills
WINN,Sarah AGE:58   16 Feb 1824 Hudson, NH
WINN,Sarah AGE:45   16 Sep 1834 Hudson, NH Joseph Winn & Sarah
WINN,Sarah J AGE:78 5 7   08 Jun 1928 Hudson, NH Peter Carley & Louisa Clark
WINN,Statira AGE:12   14 Nov 1813 Hudson, NH
WINN,Susanna AGE: 04 Mar 1763 Hudson, NH Joseph Winn & Elizabeth
WINN,William AGE: 20 Jun 1879 Hudson, NH
WINN,William F AGE:72 1 27   21 May 1911 Hudson, NH Abitha Winn & Mary Harris
WINN,Wyzeman C AGE:37   24 Sep 1832 Hudson, NH
WINN,Wyzeman C AGE:2   16 Sep 1796 Hudson, NH
WINSLOW,Emily Veronica AGE:64   05 Jul 1984 Nashua, NH
WINSLOW,Minnie AGE:87 1 16   17 May 1947 Hudson, NH Samuel Russell
    & Ada Bennett
WINSLOW,Violet J AGE:60   16 Mar 1957 Nashua, NH
WINTHER,Samuel AGE:82   15 Apr 1965 Nashua, NH
WISNOSKY,William A AGE:40   14 Jul 1983 Nashua, NH
WITHAM,Velma E AGE:61 2 22   08 Feb 1944 Hudson, NH Eulicid Williams
    & Jennie Sanborn
WITHERELL,Rose AGE:96   03 Apr 1969 Hudson, NH
WITKOWSKI,Mary B AGE:65   30 Dec 1958 Hudson, NH
WITKOWSKI,John AGE:77   23 Jan 1968 Hudson, NH
WODGE,Jacob AGE:83 7   09 May 1924 Hudson, NH James Wodge & Angele Vasseur
WOLCZOK,John S AGE:53   12 Jul 1970 Alton, NH
WOLCZOK,Mary AGE:80   12 Jan 1975 Nashua, NH
WOLCZOK,Peter AGE:39   06 Oct 1929 Hudson, NH Peter Wolczok
WOLLEN,David A AGE:11   17 Nov 1961 Hudson, NH
WOLLEN,Elizabeth V AGE:90   06 Jan 1980 Hudson, NH
WOLLEN,Mary AGE:83   23 Apr 1977 Goffstown, NH
WOLLEN,Michael Sr AGE:78   04 Feb 1969 Nashua, NH
WOOD,Alfred AGE:52   10 Jan 1950 Nashua, NH Sam Wood & Lucy Wood
WOOD,Charles AGE:71 4 26   06 Sep 1886 Hudson, NH
WOOD,Ebenezer AGE:78   09 Jun 1829 Hudson, NH
WOOD,Ella AGE: 21 Jun 1873 Hudson, NH Charles Wood & Louisa
WOOD,Ella F AGE: 21 Jun 1873 Hudson, NH
WOOD,Emma E AGE:40 9   12 Aug 1894 Hudson, NH Charles Wood (Andover, MA)
    & Louisa Cummings (Hudson, NH)
WOOD,George W AGE:72   25   13 Sep 1902 Hudson, NH Phineau Wood
    & Rebecca Wichester
WOOD,Louisa AGE:88   13 22 May 1916 Hudson, NH Willard Cummings

HUDSON,NH DEATHS

 & Nancy Smith
WOOD,Lulu B AGE:64 08 Jun 1950 Nashua, NH Clarence C Morgan & Clara B Clough
WOOD,Mary C AGE:65 11 Jul 1891 Hudson, NH Jabez Towne (Topsfield, MA)
 & Mary Kendall (Londonderry)
WOOD,Mary Ella AGE:82 07 Sep 1957 Hudson, NH
WOOD,Molly AGE:77 31 Aug 1830 Hudson, NH
WOOD,Phineas AGE:85 10 19 Nov 1868 Hudson, NH
WOOD,Phineas AGE:85 19 Dec 1868 Hudson, NH
WOOD,Rebecca AGE:80 7 05 Apr 1877 Hudson, NH
WOOD,William W AGE:56 06 Jun 1892 Hudson, NH
WOODBURY,Abram AGE:71 6 30 Jan 1894 Hudson, NH Benj Woodbury & Hannah Smith
WOODBURY,Juliana A AGE:85 06 May 1963 Nashua, NH
WOODBURY,Martha J AGE:71 6 23 07 Jan 1915 Hudson, NH Charles Clyde (Windham,
 NH) & Abbie Winkley (Strafford, NH)
WOODBURY,Mary J AGE:81 1 29 21 Aug 1903 Hudson, NH Ezra Drown & Sarah Young
WOODIN,Leo D AGE:65 27 Dec 1966 Hudson, NH
WOODMAN,Caroline AGE:2 01 Nov 1909 Hudson, NH Ernest Woodman
 & Caroline Graves
WOODS,Charles AGE:71 4 26 06 Sep 1886 Hudson, NH
WOODS,Grace M AGE:11 8 10 Nov 1892 Hudson, NH Jos E Woods (Chelmsford, MA)
 & Martha L Durant (Hudson, NH)
WOODS,Guy H AGE:58 05 Mar 1952 Hudson, NH
WOODS,Hazel M AGE:67 13 Oct 1962 Nashua, NH
WOODS,John L AGE:83 5 6 05 Oct 1922 Hudson, NH Stephen Woods
WOODS,Nathaniel H AGE: 15 Sep 1871 Hudson, NH
WOODS,Pearl E AGE:69 15 Feb 1966 Hudson, NH
WOODS,Ruth S AGE:84 18 Aug 1959 Hudson, NH
WOODS,Susan P AGE:53 11 Apr 1875 Hudson, NH
WOODS,Wm W AGE:56 06 Jun 1892 Hudson, NH Phineas Woods (Andover, MA)
 & Rebecca Winchester (Methuen, MA)
WOODWARD,Hannah AGE:82 6 12 Jan 1894 Hudson, NH
WOODWARD,Jesse H AGE:76 6 19 Jan 1894 Hudson, NH Daniel Woodward
 (Lyndeborough) & Hannah Hardy (Lyndeborough)
WOODWARD,Lila J AGE:79 8 4 04 Aug 1939 Hudson, NH Herman A Peabody
 & Mildred Gutterson
WORMWOOD,Frank W AGE:62 20 Jan 1964 Hudson, NH
WORTHEN,Phebe AGE:80 4 13 Feb 1882 Hudson, NH
WORTHLEY,Linnie A AGE:89   7 16 Apr 1941 Nashua, NH Andrew J Smith
 & Abbie Davis
WORTHLEY,William P AGE:67 5 05 Feb 1886 Hudson, NH
WOZNIAK,Lucille A AGE:47 12 Mar 1972 Nashua, NH
WRIGHT,Emmie P AGE:47 11 27 07 Nov 1925 Hudson, NH A Prescott Wright
 & Lorraine H Patrick
WRIGHT,Sarah T AGE:84 15 Jan 1966 Hudson, NH
WYETH,Margaret AGE:76 2 16 16 Jun 1943 Hudson, NH A McLennan
 & Mary Finlayson
WYETH,Willard B AGE:80 10 16 25 Mar 1942 Hudson, NH Hiram Wyeth
 & Abigail Burgess
WYLES,William AGE:43 11 7 07 Feb 1893 Hudson, NH William Wyles (Ireland)
 & Catherine Connell (Ireland)
WYMAN,Abigail AGE: 04 Nov 1774 Hudson, NH Seth Wyman
WYMAN,Abigail M AGE:60 4 06 Feb 1894 Hudson, NH Samuel Collis
WYMAN,Angeline AGE:20 15 Aug 1866 Hudson, NH
WYMAN,Betsey AGE: 27 Feb 1804 Hudson, NH
WYMAN,Daniel AGE:63 14 Mar 1860 Hudson, NH
WYMAN,Mary AGE:52 18 Aug 1852 Hudson, NH
WYMAN,Millie O AGE:15 3 23 Jun 1887 Hudson, NH James I Wyman
WYMAN,Seth AGE: 17 Nov 1795 Hudson, NH
WYMAN,Thomas AGE: 29 Mar 1775 Hudson, NH Seth Wyman
WYNOTT,Elsie AGE:75 02 Jul 1955 Nashua, NH

HUDSON,NH DEATHS

WYNOTT,Peter S AGE:76 10 17   13 Aug 1947 Nashua, NH Solomon Wynott
   & Emma Wynott
YAGIELOWICZ,Bronislaw J AGE:73   01 Nov 1960 Nashua, NH
YAGIELOWICZ,Petronelia A AGE:79   05 Jan 1985 Nashua, NH
YANIS,Stanley AGE:62   03 Nov 1970 Nashua, NH
YESICOVITCH,Anie AGE:77   10 Sep 1946 Hudson, NH Kasheta
YEZCKEUIC,Thoms AGE:59   21 May 1930 Hudson, NH
YORK,Craig R AGE:18   02 Jun 1984 Nashua, NH
YOUNG,Bertha M AGE:20 1 16   30 Aug 1896 Hudson, NH George Jennings
   & Abbie Nichols (Dracut, MA)
YOUNG,Elizabeth S AGE: 27 Dec 1900 Hudson, NH Amos Morse & Sarah Sawyer
YOUNG,Emma J AGE:24 2   30 Jun 1876 Hudson, NH William H Allen
YOUNG,Emma M AGE:82   19 Apr 1983 Nashua, NH
YOUNG,Hannah K AGE:89 9 21   03 May 1908 Hudson, NH Daniel Jewell
   & Hannah R Robins
YOUNG,Ida W AGE:64 2 22   27 Aug 1948 Nashua, NH Eben M Lambert
YOUNG,Israel W AGE:71   24 Jul 1894 Hudson, NH
YOUNG,John F AGE:58   03 Apr 1868 Hudson, NH
YOUNG,Kenneth AGE:2 1 17   11 Feb 1944 Nashua, NH Kenneth Young
   & Alice Laflamme
YOUNG,Lillian AGE:66   27 Feb 1974 Nashua, NH
YOUNG,Martin J AGE:55   17 Jun 1907 Hudson, NH Steven Young & Mary Jane Brown
YOUNG,Moses C AGE:76 1 8   22 Dec 1924 Hudson, NH Moses Young & Mary Tebbets
YOUNG,Rose E AGE:56   20 Sep 1966 Nashua, NH
YOUNG,Sina AGE:24 1 17   14 Oct 1918 Hudson, NH John Matson
YOUNG,Walter H AGE:68   02 Feb 1950 Nashua, NH Martin J Young
   & Flora E Thompson
ZALANSKAS,Wheeler AGE:63   14 Jun 1979 Nashua, NH
ZALL,William N AGE:50   14 Oct 1969 Nashua, NH
ZELONIS,Antonia AGE:95   28 Jun 1985 Nashua, NH
ZINK,Chas W AGE:19   19 Feb 1926 Hudson, NH Ernest Zink & Priscilla R Blood
ZINKAWICH,Anna G AGE:77   19 May 1969 Hudson, NH
ZINKAWICH,Frank G AGE:66   25 May 1950 Nashua, NH John Zinkawich & Anna
ZUPUKA,James AGE:60   29 Jun 1949 Hudson, NH
[UNKNOWN],[Unknown] AGE: 06 Jun 1897 Hudson, NH

www.ingramcontent.com/pod-product-compliance
Lightning Source LLC
Chambersburg PA
CBHW071429300426
44114CB00013B/1370